WEST'S

FLORIDA DIGEST 2d

Volume 28A

SALES — SEARCHES AND SEIZURES  35

THOMSON REUTERS®

Mat # 41766094

CLOSING WITH CASES REPORTED IN

COPYRIGHT © 2017 Thomson Reuters

PREFACE

West's Florida Key Number Digest 2d covers State and Federal cases decided since 1935.

The original Florida Digest should be consulted for cases prior to 1935.

This Digest is compiled and arranged under the West Key Number plan. All Topics of the American Digest System are represented and each Topic carries a complete analysis of the scope of all its Key Numbers.

New and revised topics and greatly expanded Key Numbers have been provided for many areas of law, including those covered by the topics ARREST, COMMON INTEREST COMMUNITIES, CONSTITUTIONAL LAW, CONVERSION AND CIVIL THEFT, CONVICTS, CORPORATIONS AND BUSINESS ORGANIZATIONS, CRIMINAL LAW, CURRENCY REGULATION, DISORDERLY CONDUCT, DIVORCE, EDUCATION, ELECTION LAW, EQUITABLE CONVERSION, EXTORTION, FEDERAL COURTS, FORFEITURES, GAMING AND LOTTERIES, INDIANS, JOINT VENTURES, LANDLORD AND TENANT, LOBBYING, MARRIAGE AND COHABITATION, MORTGAGES AND DEEDS OF TRUST, OBSCENITY, OBSTRUCTING JUSTICE, PARENT AND CHILD, PARTNERSHIP, PATENTS, PRISONS, PRIVILEGED COMMUNICATIONS AND CONFIDENTIALITY, PRODUCTS LIABILITY, PROTECTION OF ENDANGERED PERSONS, PUBLIC ASSISTANCE, PUBLIC CONTRACTS, PUBLIC EMPLOYMENT, SALES, SEX OFFENSES, SOCIAL SECURITY, STATUTES, THREATS, STALKING, AND HARASSMENT, UNITED STATES, UNITED STATES MAGISTRATE JUDGES, UNITED STATES MARSHALS, WAR AND NATIONAL EMERGENCY, WATER LAW, WEAPONS, WORKERS' COMPENSATION, and ZONING AND PLANNING. Refer to the Outline of the Law to assist in locating specific areas of interest.

The TABLE OF CASES lists alphabetically the title of each case, by both the Plaintiff's and Defendant's names, the volume and page of the Reports in which each is published, the subsequent case history, and the digest Topic and Key Number under which each point of law is digested. A guide to title arrangement is also included in this volume.

The WORDS AND PHRASES section lists alphabetically words or phrases that have been judicially defined in the cases indexed by the Digest, and sets out the headnotes, titles and citations of the cases in which such definitions appear.

PREFACE

A comprehensive DESCRIPTIVE–WORD INDEX has been specially prepared, providing immediate and convenient access to the case law within the scope of the Digest.

UPDATING WITH WESTLAW

WESTLAW provides easy and quick access to those cases reported after the latest available digest supplementation.

The WESTLAW query is entered in any appropriate case law data base of interest. The query format used substitutes a numerical equivalent for the digest topic name and adds the key number through the use of "K" as illustrated in the search for later Contracts ⬗ 155 cases published after December 31, 2016.

ad(after 12-31-16) & 95K155.

A list of topics and their numerical equivalents may be found in the DIGEST TOPICS section of this volume, in the WESTLAW Reference Manual or in the WESTLAW Directory.

THE PUBLISHER

August, 2017

ABBREVIATIONS OF COURTS

***

Florida Courts

Federal Courts

Other

ABBREVIATIONS

OF

PUBLICATIONS CITED

A.L.R.	American Law Reports
A.L.R.2d	American Law Reports, Second Series
A.L.R.3d	American Law Reports, Third Series
A.L.R.4th	American Law Reports, Fourth Series
B.R.	Bankruptcy Reporter
F.	Federal Reporter
F.2d	Federal Reporter, Second Series
F.3d	Federal Reporter, Third Series
Fed.Appx.	Federal Appendix
Fed.Cas.No.	Federal Cases
F.R.D.	Federal Rules Decisions
F.Supp.	Federal Supplement
F.Supp.2d	Federal Supplement, Second Series
F.Supp.3d	Federal Supplement, Third Series
Fla.	Florida Reports
Fla. B.J.	Florida Bar Journal
Fla. L. Rev.	Florida Law Review
Fla. St. U. L. Rev.	Florida State University Law Review
F.S.A.	Florida Statutes Annotated
L.Ed.	U.S. Reports, Lawyers' Edition
L.Ed.2d	U.S. Reports, Lawyers' Edition, Second Series
Nova L. Rev.	Nova Law Review
S.Ct.	Supreme Court Reporter
So.	Southern Reporter
So.2d	Southern Reporter, Second Series
So.3d	Southern Reporter, Third Series
Stetson L. Rev.	Stetson Law Review
St. Thomas L. Rev.	St. Thomas Law Review
U.S.	United States Reports
U.S.C.A.	United States Code Annotated
U. Miami L. Rev.	University of Miami Law Review

OUTLINE OF THE LAW

Digest Topics are arranged for your convenience by Seven Main Divisions of Law. Complete alphabetical list of Digest Topics with topic numbers follows this section.

---

1. **PERSONS**
2. **PROPERTY**
3. **CONTRACTS**
4. **TORTS**
5. **CRIMES**
6. **REMEDIES**
7. **GOVERNMENT**

1. PERSONS

RELATING TO NATURAL PERSONS IN GENERAL

Civil Rights
Dead Bodies
Death
Domicile
Food
Health
Holidays
Intoxicating Liquors
Names
Seals
Signatures
Sunday
Time
Weapons

PARTICULAR CLASSES OF NATURAL PERSONS

Absentees
Aliens, Immigration, and Citizenship
Chemical Dependents
Convicts
Indians
Infants
Mental Health
Protection of Endangered Persons
Slaves
Spendthrifts

PERSONAL RELATIONS

Adoption
Attorney and Client
Child Custody
Child Support
Executors and Administrators
Guardian and Ward
Labor and Employment
Marriage and Cohabitation
Parent and Child
Principal and Agent
Workers' Compensation

ASSOCIATED AND ARTIFICIAL PERSONS

Associations
Beneficial Associations
Building and Loan Associations
Clubs
Corporations and Business Organizations
Exchanges
Partnership
Religious Societies

PARTICULAR OCCUPATIONS

Accountants
Agriculture
Antitrust and Trade Regulation
Auctions and Auctioneers
Aviation
Banks and Banking
Bridges

DIGEST TOPICS AND ABBREVIATIONS

See, also, Outline of the Law by Seven Main Divisions of Law
preceding this section.

The topic numbers shown below may be used in WESTLAW searches for cases
within the topic and within specified key numbers.

1	Abandoned and Lost Property	Aband L P	36	Arson	Arson
2	Abatement and Revival	Abate & R	37	Assault and Battery	Assault
4	Abortion and Birth Control	Abort	38	Assignments	Assign
5	Absentees	Absentees	40	Assistance, Writ of	Assist
6	Abstracts of Title	Abstr of T	41	Associations	Assoc
7	Accession	Accession	42	Assumpsit, Action of	Assumpsit
8	Accord and Satisfaction	Accord	43	Asylums and Assisted Living Facilities	Asylums
9	Account	Acct	44	Attachment	Attach
10	Account, Action on	Acct Action on	45	Attorney and Client	Atty & C
11	Account Stated	Acct St	46	Attorney General	Atty Gen
11A	Accountants	Accnts	47	Auctions and Auctioneers	Auctions
12	Acknowledgment	Ack	48	Audita Querela	Aud Quer
13	Action	Action	48A	Automobiles	Autos
14	Action on the Case	Action on Case	48B	Aviation	Aviation
15	Adjoining Landowners	Adj Land	49	Bail	Bail
15A	Administrative Law and Procedure	Admin Law	50	Bailment	Bailm
16	Admiralty	Adm	51	Bankruptcy	Bankr
17	Adoption	Adop	52	Banks and Banking	Banks
18	Adulteration	Adulteration	54	Beneficial Associations	Ben Assoc
20	Adverse Possession	Adv Poss	56	Bills and Notes	Bills & N
21	Affidavits	Afft	58	Bonds	Bonds
23	Agriculture	Agric	59	Boundaries	Bound
24	Aliens, Immigration, and Citizenship	Aliens	60	Bounties	Bounties
25	Alteration of Instruments	Alt of Inst	63	Bribery	Brib
25T	Alternative Dispute Resolution	Alt Disp Res	64	Bridges	Bridges
26	Ambassadors and Consuls	Amb & C	65	Brokers	Brok
27	Amicus Curiae	Am Cur	66	Building and Loan Associations	B & L Assoc
28	Animals	Anim	67	Burglary	Burg
29	Annuities	Annuities	69	Cancellation of Instruments	Can of Inst
29T	Antitrust and Trade Regulation	Antitrust	70	Carriers	Carr
30	Appeal and Error	App & E	71	Cemeteries	Cem
31	Appearance	Appear	72	Census	Census
34	Armed Services	Armed S	73	Certiorari	Cert
35	Arrest	Arrest	74	Champerty and Maintenance	Champ
			75	Charities	Char
			76	Chattel Mortgages	Chat Mtg
			76A	Chemical Dependents	Chem Dep
			76D	Child Custody	Child C
			76E	Child Support	Child S

DIGEST TOPICS AND ABBREVIATIONS

DIGEST TOPICS AND ABBREVIATIONS

DIGEST TOPICS AND ABBREVIATIONS

DIGEST TOPICS AND ABBREVIATIONS

TOPICS IN THIS VOLUME

SALES

SUBJECTS INCLUDED

Transfers, whether absolute or conditional, of ownership of personal property for a price, especially where transaction is within the scope of Article 2 of the Uniform Commercial Code

Contracts for such transfers, and the rights, obligations, and liabilities of the parties thereto

Warranties, whether express or implied, attendant to such transfers

Remedies relating to such transfers, contracts, and warranties, and actions thereon

Rights and liabilities of parties as to third persons, and actions thereon

SUBJECTS EXCLUDED AND COVERED BY OTHER TOPICS

Arbitration of disputes under sales contracts, see ALTERNATIVE DISPUTE RESOLUTION

Assignees for benefit of creditors, receivers, etc., sales, see BANKRUPTCY, DEBTOR AND CREDITOR, RECEIVERS, and other specific topics

Auctions, regulation and conduct of sales by, see AUCTIONS AND AUCTIONEERS

Bailment, see BAILMENT

Barter or exchange, transfers by, see EXCHANGE OF PROPERTY

Bills of sale as security for debt, see CHATTEL MORTGAGES

Champertous contracts, sales as, see CHAMPERTY AND MAINTENANCE ☞4(4)

Chattel mortgages, sales to enforce, see CHATTEL MORTGAGES

Consignment, bailment for sale, and factorage, see FACTORS

Fiduciary or representative relations, sales by persons in, see BROKERS, GUARDIAN AND WARD, and other specific topics

Frauds, statute of, affecting validity of sale, see FRAUDS, STATUTE OF

Judgments, decrees, and orders of courts, sales under, see JUDICIAL SALES and other specific topics

Judicial process, sales under, see ATTACHMENT, EXECUTION, GARNISHMENT, and other specific topics

Leases of personal property, see BAILMENT

Particular classes of persons, sales by or to, see ALIENS, IMMIGRATION, AND CITIZENSHIP, HUSBAND AND WIFE, INFANTS, MENTAL HEALTH, and other specific topics

Particular kinds of property, sales of, especially as to questions not governed by Article 2 of the Uniform Commercial Code—

Aircraft, see AVIATION ☞14

Automobiles, see AUTOMOBILES ☞19

Bonds, see BONDS ☞84, 87

Businesses and business assets, see CORPORATIONS AND BUSI-NESS ORGANIZATIONS, PARTNERSHIP

Commercial paper, see BILLS AND NOTES ☞216, VIII(C)

Copyrights, see COPYRIGHTS AND INTELLECTUAL PROPERTY ☞43

Corporate stock and securities, see CORPORATIONS AND BUSI-NESS ORGANIZATIONS, SECURITIES REGULATION

Electricity, see ELECTRICITY ☞11(3)

Gas, see GAS ☞13(1), 14(2)

Good will, see GOOD WILL ☞4

Impounded animals, see ANIMALS ☞106

Log or lumber sales, see LOGS AND LOGGING ☞34

Minerals, see MINES AND MINERALS ☞92.66, 93.5

Patents, see PATENTS VI(C)

Real property, see VENDOR AND PURCHASER

Rights of action, see ASSIGNMENTS

Software, see COPYRIGHTS AND INTELLECTUAL PROPERTY ☞107

Tickets, see CARRIERS IV(B), PUBLIC AMUSEMENT AND EN-TERTAINMENT ☞68

Trademarks, see TRADEMARKS ☞1197

Vessels, see SHIPPING ☞23

Water, see WATER LAW

Pledges, sales to enforce, see PLEDGES

Powers, sales in execution of, see POWERS

Regulation of sales, see ANTITRUST AND TRADE REGULATION, FOOD, INTOXICATING LIQUORS, and other specific topics

Secured transactions, see SECURED TRANSACTIONS

Speculative transactions and dealings, sales as, see GAMING AND LOT-TERIES ☞227

Storage of goods, see BAILMENT, WAREHOUSEMEN

Tax sales, see INTERNAL REVENUE, TAXATION

Tort liability for injuries from defects in goods sold, see PRODUCTS LIABILITY

Transfer of possession of personal property without transfer of ownership, see BAILMENT

Transportation of goods, see CARRIERS

Uniform Commercial Code generally, see STATUTES ⚷1320

Uniform Commercial Code, other articles—

>   Article 2A, see BAILMENT

>   Article 3, see BILLS AND NOTES

>   Articles 4, 4A, and 5, see BANKS AND BANKING

>   Article 6, see FRAUDULENT CONVEYANCES

>   Article 7, see PROPERTY and other specific topics

>   Article 8, see CORPORATIONS AND BUSINESS ORGANIZA-
>   TIONS V

>   Article 9, see SECURED TRANSACTIONS

War, effect of on preexisting contracts of sale, see WAR AND NATIONAL
EMERGENCY ⚷1022

For detailed references to other topics, see Descriptive-Word Index

---

Analysis

II. PARTIES TO TRANSACTION OR CONTRACT.—Continued.

III. NATURE AND FORMATION OF CONTRACT.

V. TERMS OF CONTRACT; RIGHTS AND OBLIGATIONS OF PARTIES.
—Continued.

(C) DELIVERY AND ACCEPTANCE OF GOODS.—Continued.

V. TERMS OF CONTRACT; RIGHTS AND OBLIGATIONS OF PARTIES. —Continued.

IX. WARRANTIES.

(A) IN GENERAL.

(B) EXPRESS WARRANTIES.

IX. WARRANTIES.—Continued.

(B) EXPRESS WARRANTIES.—Continued.

2. OPERATION AND EFFECT.—Continued.

1650. —— Food and beverages.
1651. —— Motor vehicles.
1652. —— Mobile homes or structures.
1653. —— Drugs and medical devices.
1654. —— Computers and software.
1655. Design defects.
1656. Duration of warranty.
1657. —— In general.
1658. —— Future defects and events; future performance.
1659. Used or second-hand goods.
1660. Causation.

(C) WARRANTIES IMPOSED BY LAW; IMPLIED WARRANTIES.

1. IN GENERAL.

☞1671. In general.
1672. Breach and elements thereof in general.
1673. Particular cases and goods in general.

2. PARTICULAR WARRANTIES.

☞1681. In general.
1682. Identity or genuineness.
1683. Quantity.
1684. Quality, fitness, or condition.
1685. —— In general.
1686. —— Knowledge of defects.
1687. —— Obvious, latent, or hidden defects.
1688. —— Doctrine of caveat emptor.
1689. —— Examination or inspection.
1690. —— Sale by sample.
1691. —— Fitness for intended purpose or use.
1692. Redhibitory defects or vices.
1693. —— In general.
1694. —— Breach and elements thereof in general.
1695. —— Particular cases and goods.
1696. Title.
1697. —— In general.
1698. —— Breach and elements thereof in general.
1699. —— Particular cases and goods.

3. FITNESS FOR ORDINARY PURPOSE OR USE; MERCHANTABILITY.

☞1711. In general.
1712. Reliance.
1713. Buyer's knowledge.
1714. Seller's knowledge.

IX. WARRANTIES.—Continued.

(C) WARRANTIES IMPOSED BY LAW; IMPLIED WARRANTIES.—Continued.

IX. WARRANTIES.—Continued.

X. REMEDIES.—Continued.

(B) PARTICULAR REMEDIES OF SELLER.—Continued.

X. REMEDIES.—Continued.

(B) PARTICULAR REMEDIES OF SELLER.—Continued.

5. MONETARY REMEDIES OF SELLER.—Continued.

2005. —— Expenses connected with delivery, transportation, care, and custody of goods.

2006. Special, indirect, or consequential damages.

2007. Mitigation or reduction of loss.

2008. —— In general.

2009. —— Expenses saved and costs avoided.

2010. Punitive or exemplary damages.

(C) PARTICULAR REMEDIES OF BUYER.

1. LIEN OR SECURITY INTEREST OF BUYER.

☜2111. In general.

2112. Particular cases and goods.

2. RECOVERY OF GOODS BY BUYER.

☜2121. In general.

2122. Nature and form of remedy.

2123. Right to remedy; grounds and defenses.

2124. —— In general.

2125. —— Insolvency of seller.

2126. —— Ability of buyer to effect cover.

2127. —— Payment or tender of price.

2128. Right to follow proceeds.

2129. Demand or notice.

3. RESALE OF GOODS BY BUYER.

☜2131. In general.

2132. Particular cases and goods.

2133. Right to proceeds.

4. MONETARY REMEDIES OF BUYER IN GENERAL.

☜2141. In general.

2142. Damages in general.

2143. —— In general.

2144. —— Nondelivery or repudiation by seller.

2145. —— Nonconforming goods.

2146. Particular cases and goods in general.

2147. —— In general.

2148. —— Buildings, structures, and construction.

2149. —— Plants, crops, and agriculture.

2150. —— Animals and livestock.

2151. —— Machinery and equipment.

2152. —— Food and beverages.

2153. —— Motor vehicles.

2154. —— Mobile homes or structures.

2155. —— Drugs and medical devices.

X. REMEDIES.—Continued.

(C) PARTICULAR REMEDIES OF BUYER.—Continued.

X. REMEDIES.—Continued.

(C) PARTICULAR REMEDIES OF BUYER.—Continued.

5. MONETARY REMEDIES OF BUYER FOR BREACH OF WARRANTY.—Continued.

2218. —— Particular cases and goods.
    (1). In general.
    (2). Buildings, structures, and construction.
    (3). Plants, crops, and agriculture.
    (4). Animals and livestock.
    (5). Machinery and equipment.
    (6). Food and beverages.
    (7). Motor vehicles.
    (8). Mobile homes or structures.
    (9). Drugs and medical devices.
    (10). Computers and software.
2219. Lost, destroyed, or worthless goods.
2220. Injuries to other property.
2221. Personal injuries.
2222. Mitigation or reduction of loss.
2223. —— In general.
2224. —— Expenses saved and costs avoided.
2225. —— Use or resale of defective goods.
2226. Punitive or exemplary damages.
2227. Monetary remedies for breach of warranty of title.
2228. —— In general.
2229. —— Particular cases and goods.
2230. Interest.

(D) RESCISSION.

⚷2241. In general.
2242. Status of doctrine under Uniform Commercial Code.
2243. Right to rescind; grounds.
2244. —— In general.
2245. —— Invalidity of contract.
2246. —— Breach of contract or condition in general.
2247. —— Nonpayment of price.
2248. —— Insolvency.
2249. —— Failure of consideration.
2250. —— Failure to deliver.
2251. —— Defect in title.
2252. —— Defect in quantity or quality of goods.
2253. —— Breach of warranty.
2254. —— Redhibitory defects or vices.
2255. Persons against whom rescission may be had.
2256. —— In general.
2257. —— Privity in general.
2258. —— Manufacturers.
2259. Waiver or estoppel.

X. REMEDIES.—Continued.

XI. ACTIONS.—Continued.

(A) IN GENERAL.—Continued.

(B) ACTIONS ON WARRANTIES.

1. IN GENERAL.

XI. ACTIONS.—Continued.

    (B) ACTIONS ON WARRANTIES.—Continued.

      1. IN GENERAL.—Continued.

    (C) PRESUMPTIONS, INFERENCES, AND BURDEN OF PROOF.

XI. ACTIONS.—Continued.

(D) ADMISSIBILITY OF EVIDENCE.—Continued.

XI. **ACTIONS.**—Continued.

XI. ACTIONS.—Continued.

  (F) QUESTIONS OF LAW OR FACT.—Continued.

XII. RIGHTS AND LIABILITIES AS TO THIRD PERSONS.—Continued.

XIII. CONDITIONAL SALES.

For detailed references to other topics, see Descriptive-Word Index

TABLE 1

KEY NUMBER TRANSLATION TABLE

FORMER KEY NUMBER TO PRESENT KEY NUMBER

The topic SALES has been extensively revised to reflect current developments in the law.

This table lists the former Key Numbers with their corresponding present Key Numbers.

In many instances there is no one-to-one relation between the Key Numbers, new and old. This table recognizes only significant correspondence. For the present classification of a particular case, see the Table of Cases.

The absence of a Key Number indicates that there is no useful parallel.

Former SALES Key Number	Present SALES Key Number	Former SALES Key Number	Present SALES Key Number
1(1)	516, 701, 710, 711, 818, 819	30	738(5)
		31	739
1(2)	536	32	740
1(3)	707	33	744
1(4)	705, 706	34	Implied and Constructive Contracts 2.1, 31
1.5	503–506		
2	509–511	35	801, 810
3.1	528	36	803, 804
4(1–3)	517(1, 2)	38(1)	807(1, 2)
4(4)	519	38(2)	807(2)
4(5)	520	38(3)	807(3)
5	517(1, 2)	38(4)	807(4)
6	521	38(5)	807(5)
7	522	38(6)	807(6)
8	523	38(7)	807(7)
9.1	526	38(8)	807(8)
10	532(1–26)	38(9)	809
11, 12	529	39	807(9)
13	530	40	807(10)
14	531	41	807(11)
15.1	601–604	43(1)	808(1)
16	606	43(2)	808(2)
17	607	43(3)	808(3)
19	729	43(4)	808(4)
21	730	43(5)	808(5)
22(.5)	720(1)	43(6)	809
22(1)	720(1, 2)	44	808(6)
22(2)	723(2)	45	808(7)
22(3)	720(3)	46	808(8)
22(4)	725(1–4)	47	808(9)
22(5)	722	48	813
23(.5, 1)	721(1, 2)	48.5	Antitrust and Trade Regulation 455, 466, 472; Consumer Credit 4
23(2)	723(3)		
23(3)	721(2, 3)		
23(4)	725(1, 3, 4)	49	820
23(5)	722	50	821
24	732, 733	51	822
25	732, 734	52(.5)	2665, 2725
26	743(1, 2)	52(1)	2601–2610
27.1	738(1)	52(2.1)	2661, 2665, 2666
28	738(2)	52(3)	2663
29	738(3, 4)	52(4)	2669

Former SALES Key Number	Present SALES Key Number	Former SALES Key Number	Present SALES Key Number
52(5.1)	2721, 2722, 2725, 2726, 2728	87(1)	2612, 2614(2, 3), 2615–2617
52(6)	2723	87(2)	2672, 2674(1–3), 2675, 2677
52(7)	2729	87(3)	2732, 2733, 2734(2, 3), 2735, 2736
53(1)	2782, 2783, 2785, 2788	88	2792, 2793, 2794(2, 3), 2795, 2796
53(2)	2786	89	1502, 1504, 1507–1510
53(3)	2789	90	1509, 1510
54	903, 904, 906(2), 913	91	1307
54.5	503–507	92	2271
55	509–511	93	1309, 2271
56	745	94	1510, 2272
57	743(2)	96	1304, 2244–2246
58	911	97	2245
59	905(1, 2)	98	1304, 2246
60	906(1, 2)	99	1304, 2247
61	917	100	2248
62	918	101	1243, 2259
63, 64	919	103	2261, 2293
65	911	104	2262
66	601–608	105	1304, 2264
67.1	911, 931	106	2266, 2267
68	932	107	1306, 2293
69	933	108	2269, 2293
70	934	109	2270
71(1)	1001–1003	110(1)	2293, 2407
71(2)	1004	110(2)	2431(5)
71(3)	1002, 1003	110(3)	2516, 2517
71(4)	1006–1008	110(4)	2518
71(5)	1001, 1004	111	2272
72(1)	981–983	113	2244
72(2)	981, 982, 990	114	2245
72(3)	981–983	115	2249
72(4)	989, 991	116	2246
72(5)	989–991, 1052	117	2250
73	992	118	2251
74.1	1073, 1074(2), 1079, 1081	119	1032, 2252, 2254
75	1074(1, 2)	120	2253
76	1075	121	2259
77(1)	1074(2)	123	2261
77(2)	1081, 1091–1093	124	2263
78	1075–1077	125	2264
79	965	126(1)	1039, 2268(1)
80	1104	126(2)	2268(1, 2)
81(1)	967, 968, 970	126(3)	1039, 2268(3)
81(2)	970	126(4)	2794(5), 2819
81(3)	969	127	1038, 2294
81(4)	967, 970	128	2269
81(5)	955	129	2270
81(6)	967	130(.5)	2462, 2507
81(7)	962, 967	130(1)	2407, 2502
82(1)	1106	130(2)	2431(5), 2512
82(2)	1107	130(3)	2639, 2751, 2759
82(3)	1108	130(3.5)	2794(5), 2819
82(4)	1109	130(4)	2192, 2518, 2519
82(5)	1110	131	1041, 2272
83	958, 963	133	2274
84	1301–1306, 1308	134	2275
85(1)	746, 914	135–139	935
85(2)	1221		
85(3)	989–991		
86	1401–1403		

Former SALES Key Number	Present SALES Key Number
140	1155
141	1156
143	1157(1)
144	1157(2)
145	1158
146	1159
147	1160
148	1161
149	1162
150(1)	953
150(2)	987
150(3)	967–970
151	954, 1212, 1216
152	955
153	956
154	934
156	958
157	959
158	960
159	961
160	962
161	963
162	964
163	977
164	1001, 1003
166(1)	981–983
166(2)	984
166(3)	984, 1249(4)
166(4)	985
166(5)	992
166(6)	986
167	993
168(1)	989
168(2)	990
168(3)	991
168(4)	1012–1015
168(5)	992
168(6)	2172
168.5(.5)	1051
168.5(1)	1052
168.5(2)	1053
168.5(3)	1054
168.5(4.1)	1056
168.5(5)	1057
168.5(6)	1058
168.5(7)	1059
168.5(8)	1060
168.5(9)	1061
168.5(10)	1062
169	951
170	967, 968
172	1221–1226
173	1228–1230
174	1229
175	1230
176(1)	1241, 1243, 1247, 1248, 1249(1), 1255
176(2)	1249(1)
176(3)	1247, 1248, 1249(1), 1250, 1255
176(4)	1249(2)

Former SALES Key Number	Present SALES Key Number
176(5)	1249(3, 4)
176(6)	1249(5), 1255
177	971
178(1)	973
178(2)	975, 1020
178(3)	974, 1015
178(4)	976, 1012
178(5)	973, 976, 981
179(1)	973, 1247
179(2)	1247, 1249(2), 1250
179(3)	1248
179(4)	1249(1–5)
179(5)	1250
179(6)	973, 974, 1014, 1015
180(1)	977, 1013
180(2)	1013
180(3)	1248
180(4)	1013
181(.5)	2614(2), 2734(2, 4)
181(1)	2614(1–6)
181(2.1)	2674(1, 2, 4)
181(3)	2674(1)
181(4)	2674(3)
181(5)	2674(2, 4)
181(6, 7)	2674(2)
181(8)	2674(2, 4, 6)
181(9)	2674(1), 2681
181(10)	2674(4)
181(11.1)	2734(1, 3), 2741
181(12)	2734(2)
181(13)	2734(1–6)
182(1)	2794(1–6)
182(2)	2794(1)
182(3)	2802
182(4)	2794(1–6)
183	1101
184	1102, 1193, 1195, 1196
185	1103
186	1115
187	1080
188	1079
190	1112, 1113
191	1114
192	1116
193	1101
194	1101, 1213
195	1233
196	1243
197, 199	1121, 1122
200(1)	1123
200(2)	1124
200(3)	1139
200(4)	1141
201(.5)	1133
201(1)	1133, 1174
201(2)	1134, 1174
201(3)	1135, 1174
201(4)	1136, 1175
201(5)	1137
201(6)	1138, 1174
201(7)	1140, 1174

Former SALES Key Number	Present SALES Key Number	Former SALES Key Number	Present SALES Key Number
202(.5, 1)	1143	233(2)	2987
202(2)	1144	233(3)	2963, 2989–2991
202(4)	1145	233(4)	2993–2995
202(5)	1146	234(1)	2921, 2923, 2974
202(6)	1147	234(2)	2922
202(7)	1148	234(3)	2925–2927
202(8)	1245	234(4)	2925, 2927, 2974
203	1149	234(5)	2928
204	1150	234(6)	2961–2965
205	1151	234(7)	2951–2956
206	Factors 18, 53	234(8)	2925, 2927, 2928, 2929(3)
208	1126	234(9)	2940
209	1127	235(1)	2931
210	1128	235(2)	2932
211	1129	235(3)	2933
212	1130	235(4)	2934
213	1131	237	2936
214	1152	238	2937
215	1155, 1159, 1162	239	2938
216	1163	240	2942
217	1164	241	2939
218	1165	242	2941
218.5	2618, 2738, 2798	243	2987
219(.5)	2912	244(1)	2990
219(1)	2916, 2973	244(2)	2989
219(2, 3)	2902, 2916, 2973	244(3)	2991
219(4)	2902, 2914, 2973	245	2994
220	2914–2916	245.5	2995, 2996
221	2916	246	1601
222	Factors 65; Sales 2973	248	1603–1605
223	2901, 2902, 2916	249	1604
224	2961, 2963	250	1601, 1611, 1613
225(.5)	2986	251	1606
225(1)	2982	253	1601, 1613, 1687
225(2)	2983	254	1658
225(3)	2986, 2987	255	1811–1843
225(4)	2989–2991	257	1608
225(5)	2994	258	1609
225(6)	2995	260	1623, 1791, 1792
225(7)	2997	261(1)	1624(2, 4, 7), 1628
226(.5, 1)	2901, 2912, 2927	261(2)	1624(3)
226(2.1)	2912, 2927	261(3)	1624(4)
226(3)	2901, 2902, 2912, 2927	261(4)	1624(5)
226(4)	2912, 2927	261(5)	1624(6)
226(5, 6)	2902, 2912, 2927	261(6)	1624(7)
226(7, 8)	2927	261(7)	1624(8), 1625
226(9)	2901, 2912, 2927	262	1626
226(10)	Factors 53, 65	262.5	1671, 1673
226(11, 12)	2902, 2912, 2927	263	1697, 1699
226(13)	2912, 2927	264	1682
226(14)	2912	266	1685
226(15)	2901, 2912, 2927	267	1771–1788
227	2911, 2972	268(1)	1686, 1687
228, 229	2915	268(2)	1687
230	2972	269	1688
231	Corporations and Business Organizations 2724(2); Sales 2902	270	1689
		271	1690
		272	1711, 1718
232	2961, 2963	273(1, 2)	1741, 1747, 1751
233(1)	2915, 2961, 2963	273(3)	1744, 1751
233(1.5)	2983	273(4)	1749

Former SALES Key Number	Present SALES Key Number	Former SALES Key Number	Present SALES Key Number
273(5)	1741, 1742, 1747, 1751	322	2427, 2428
274	1752	323	2431(2), 2432(1)
275	1683	324(1)	1956, 2609, 2638
277	1642, 1649	324(2)	2669, 2674(1), 2677
278	1813, 1816(1), 1817, 1818, 1822, 1824	324(3)	2729, 2737, 2758
		326	2436
279	1649, 1658	327	2789, 2794(2), 2798, 2818
280	1792	328	2849, 2878
282	1612, 1643	329	2436
283	1698, 1699	330	1983, 1987(1), 2437
284(1)	1716, 1718	332	1971
284(3)	1689	333	1974
284(4)	1745, 1747	334	1975
285(.5)	1851, 1855	335	1976
285(1)	1854, 1855	336	1977
285(2)	1858–1860	337	1971, 1989
285(3)	1862–1865	338	1978
285(4)	1856	339	1990, 1991(1)
286	1866, 2308	340	1981, 1986, 1987(1), 2283
287(.5–2)	1868	342, 343	1986, 1987(1–7)
287(3–5)	1020, 1868	345	2410
287(6)	1869	347(1–6)	1987(1), 2414(1)
288(1)	1881, 1882	348(.5)	2417, 2418(1)
288(2)	1882	348(1–3)	2418(1)
288(3)	1882, 1883	349	2420
288(4)	1884	350	2422, 2423
288(5)	1885	351	2427
288(6)	1886, 1887	353(.5–8)	2431(2)
288.5	2640	354(1–10)	2432(1)
289	1911	355(.5–4)	2433
290	1912	357(1)	2614(1, 2), 2615
291	1913	357(2)	2617
292	1914	358(1)	2674(1, 2), 2700
294	1916	358(2)	2687, 2699
295	1917	358(3)	2662
296	1918	358(4)	2674(2), 2701, 2704
297	1919	358(5)	2677
298	1920	358(6)	2674(1–3), 2701, 2705
299	1921	359(1)	2721, 2723, 2734(1, 2), 2760, 2761
300	1931	359(2)	2760, 2761
301	1932	359(3)	2737
302	1933	360(1, 2)	1983, 1985, 1987(1)
303	1934	360(3)	1982, 1983, 1985, 1987(1)
304	1935	362	2435
305	1936	363	2794(1, 2), 2795, 2797
306	1937	364(1)	2857, 2880
307	1938	364(2)	2854(2)
308	1939	364(3)	2854(1, 2), 2857
309	1940	364(4)	2845, 2849
311	1942	364(5)	2865, 2867
312	1943	364(6)	2852
313	1944	364(7)	2854(1, 2)
314	1945	364(8)	2854(2)
315	1946	364(9)	2854(6)
316(1)	1954–1957	364(10)	2854(1)
316(2)	1952, 1955	365	2436
317	1959	366	2437
318	1958	367	Appeal and Error 1050.1(5), 1135
319	1960, 2410		
320	2414(1)	368	2438
321	1957, 1960		

Former SALES Key Number	Present SALES Key Number	Former SALES Key Number	Present SALES Key Number
369, 370	2404	418(2)	2168, 2169(1, 3)
371	2410	418(3)	2168, 2169(1)
372	2414(1)	418(4)	2167, 2168, 2169(1)
373	2420	418(5)	2169(1)
374	2422, 2423	418(6)	2301–2303, 2308
376.1	2430	418(7)	2162, 2165(1)
377	2431(2)	418(8)	2174, 2175, 2177
378	2432(1)	418(9)	2181
379	2433	418(10)	2175, 2177
380.1	2700	418(11.1)	2178
381	2612, 2642, 2644	418(12)	2179
382	2672, 2674(1, 2), 2700, 2701, 2704	418(13)	2178
		418(14.1)	2174, 2175
383	2721, 2732, 2734(1), 2760, 2762, 2764	418(15)	2175, 2179
		418(16.1)	2176
384(1)	1982, 1983, 1997	418(17)	2176, 2179
384(2)	1994, 1995(1)	418(18)	2176
384(3)	1983, 1994, 1997	418(19)	2177
384(4)	2004, 2005	419.1	2435
384(5)	1983, 1994, 1995(1), 1997	420	2792, 2820, 2823, 2826, 2827, 2831
384(6)	1983, 1997	421	2852, 2854(1, 2), 2861, 2880, 2884
384(7)	1990		
386	2435	422	2436
387	2820	423	2437
388	2852, 2880	425	1905
389	2436	426	2305–2308
390	1904	427	514, 2452
391(1)	2158, 2159, 2405	428	2414(2), 2418(2)
391(2, 3)	2158, 2160	429	2453
391(3.5–7)	2158	430	2455–2458
391(8)	2204	431	2461
391(9)	2158, 2159	432	2462
391.5	2111, 2112	433.1, 434	2465, 2466
392	2411	435(1–5)	2432(2)
393	2415	436	2467
394	2424	437(.5, 1)	2468
395	2427	437(2)	2433, 2468
396	2431(3), 2432(1)	437(3)	2468, 2631
397	2640	437(4)	2468
398	2437	439	2629–2631
399, 400	2124	440(1–3)	2689–2691
401	2127, 2411	440(4)	2700, 2701, 2704–2707
402	2415	441(1)	2749–2756
403	2436, 2437	441(2, 3)	2749–2751
404	909, 2286	441(4)	2760, 2761, 2767
405	909, 2143–2145	442(1)	2192, 2217
406	2411	442(2)	2210, 2212(5)
407	2415	442(3)	2211, 2212(1, 5, 7)
409	2422, 2424	442(4)	2210
409.5	2427	442(5)	2217, 2218(1, 5)
410.1	2430	442(6)	2214, 2215
411	2431(3)	442(8)	2220
412	2432(1)	442(9)	2221
413	2433	442(10)	2230
415	2614(1, 2), 2617, 2621, 2640, 2643	442(11)	2196, 2212(3), 2218(3)
416(1)	2672, 2674(1–3)	442(12)	2228, 2229
416(2)	2700, 2703, 2704, 2707	442(13, 14)	2225
417	2732, 2734(2), 2760, 2763, 2764, 2767	442(15)	2192, 2214, 2215
		442(16)	2219
418(1)	2147, 2169(1)	444	2470, 2689

Former SALES Key Number	Present SALES Key Number	Former SALES Key Number	Present SALES Key Number
445(1)	2810–2812	474(2)	3029(2)
445(2)	2810	475	3030
445(3)	2810–2812	476	3031
445(4)	2809–2811	477(1)	3033
445(5)	2815	477(2)	3034
445(6)	1882, 2816	477(3)	3035
446(1–3)	2869–2871	477(4)	3036
446(4)	2870	477(5)	3037
446(5)	2871	477(6)	3038
446(6)	2870, 2871	477(7)	3039
446(7)	2869–2871	479	3041
446(8)	2875	479.1	3042
446(9)	2880, 2881, 2885	479.2(1)	3043(1)
447	2471	479.2(2)	3043(2)
448	2472	479.2(3)	3043(3)
450	3001	479.2(4)	3043(4)
451	3002	479.2(5)	3043(5)
452	3003	479.2(6)	3043(6)
454	3005	479.2(7)	3043(7)
455	3006	479.2(8)	3043(8)
456	3007	479.2(9)	3043(9)
457	3008	479.2(10)	3043(10)
458	3009	479.2(11)	3043(11)
459	3010	479.2(12)	3043(12)
460	3011	479.2(13)	3043(13)
461	3012	479.3	3044
462	3013	479.4	3045
463	3014	479.5	3046
464	3015	479.6	3047
465	3016	480(.5)	3048(1)
467	3018	480(1.1)	3048(3)
468	3019	480(2)	3048(4)
469	3020	480(3)	3048(5)
470	3021	480(3.5)	3048(6)
472(1)	3023	480(4)	3048(7)
472(2)	3024	480(4.5)	3048(8)
472(3)	3025	480(5)	3048(9)
472(4)	3026	480(6)	3048(10)
472(5)	3027	481	3049
473(1)	3028(1)	482	3050
473(2)	3028(2)	483	3051
474(1)	3029(1)	484	3052

TABLE 2
KEY NUMBER TRANSLATION TABLE
PRESENT KEY NUMBER TO FORMER KEY NUMBER

The topic SALES has been extensively revised to reflect current developments in the law.

This table lists the present Key Numbers with their corresponding former Key Numbers.

In many instances there is no one-to-one relation between the Key Numbers, new and old. This table recognizes only significant correspondence.

The absence of a Key Number indicates that there is no useful parallel.

Present SALES Key Number	Former SALES Key Number	Present SALES Key Number	Former SALES Key Number
501	1(1)	721(3)	23(3)
503–507	1.5, 54.5	722	22(5), 23(5)
509–511	2, 55	723(1)	22(2), 23(2)
513, 514	427	723(2)	22(2)
516	1(1), 3.1	723(3)	23(2)
517(1, 2)	4(1–3), 5	725(1)	22(4), 23(4)
518, 519	4(4)	725(2)	22(4)
520	4(5)	725(3)	23(4)
521	6	725(4), 726	22(4), 23(4)
522	7	729	19
523	8	730	21
525	9.1, 10	732	24, 25
526	12	733	24
527, 528	3.1	734	25
529	11, 12	735	24
530	13	738(1)	27.1
531	14	738(2)	28
532(1)	3.1, 10	738(3, 4)	29
532(2–26)	10	738(5)	30
533, 535	1(1)	739	31
536	1(2)	740	32
601	66	743(1, 2)	26
602	15.1, 66	744	33
603	66	745	56
604	15.1, 66	746	85(1)
605	66	801	1(1), 35
606	16, 66	803, 804	36
607	17	806	38(1), 43(1)
608	66	807(1)	38(1)
701, 702	1(1)	807(2)	38(1, 2)
704–706	1(1, 4)	807(3)	38(3)
707	1(3, 4)	807(4)	38(4)
708	1(1, 3, 4)	807(5)	38(5)
710, 711	1(1)	807(6)	38(6)
712	Contracts 10(4)	807(7)	38(7)
714	1(1)	807(8)	38(8)
715	1(1), 56	807(9)	39
716, 717	1(1)	807(10)	40
719	1(1), 22(.5, 1, 3), 23(1)	807(11)	41
720(1, 2)	22(1)	808(1)	43(1)
720(3)	22(3)	808(2)	43(2)
721(1)	23(.5, 1)	808(3)	43(3)
721(2)	23(1, 3)	808(4)	43(4)

SALES

Present SALES Key Number	Former SALES Key Number
808(5)	43(5)
808(6)	44
808(7)	45
808(8)	46
808(9)	47
809	38(9), 43(6)
810, 811	35
813, 814	48
816–819	1(1)
820	49
821	50
822	51
901, 903, 904	54
905(1)	59
905(2)	54, 59
906(1, 2)	54, 60
908, 909	404, 405
911	58, 65
912, 913	54
914	85(1)
915	179(6)
916	58
917	61, 197
918	62
919	64
931	67.1, 71(1)
932	68
933	69
934	70, 154
935	135–139
951	81(7), 169, 170, 177
953	150(1)
954	151
955	81(5), 152
956	153
958	83, 156
959	157
960	156, 158
961	159
962	81(7), 160
963	83, 161
964	162
965	79
967	81(1, 4, 6), 150(3)
968	81(1), 170
969	81(3), 150(3)
970	81(1, 2), 150(3)
971	177
973	178(1), 179(1, 6)
974	178(3), 179(6)
975	178(1, 2), 179(1)
976	178(1, 4)
977	163, 180(1)
981–983	72(1), 166(1)
984	166(2)
985	166(1, 4)
986	166(6)
987	150(2)
989	72(4, 5), 168(1)
990	168(2)
991	72(5), 85(3), 168(3)

Present SALES Key Number	Former SALES Key Number
992	73, 166(5), 168(5)
993	167
1001	71(1, 5), 164
1002	71(1, 3)
1003	71(1), 164
1004	71(2, 5)
1006–1008	71(4)
1011	168(4), 177, 178(1, 4), 179(6)
1012	168(4), 177, 178(1, 4)
1013	180(1, 2, 4)
1014	166(1), 168(4), 179(6)
1015	168(4), 178(3), 179(6)
1017	168(4), 177, 179(6)
1018	179(6)
1020	168(4), 178(4), 179(6), 287(1, 3)
1021	179(6)
1022	168(4), 178(4)
1031	113, 119, 124
1032	119
1034	113, 120
1035	113
1036	113, 120
1037	129
1038	127
1039	126(1, 3)
1040	125, 126(1)
1041	131
1042	121
1051	168.5(.5), 204, 205
1052	72(5), 168.5(1)
1053	168.5(2)
1054	168.5(3)
1056	168.5(4.1)
1057	168.5(5)
1058	168.5(6)
1059	168.5(7)
1060	168.5(8)
1061	168.5(9)
1062	168.5(10)
1071, 1073	74.1
1074(1)	75
1074(2)	75, 77(1)
1075	76, 77(1), 78
1076, 1077	78
1078	77(2), 187
1079	77(1), 188
1080	187
1081	74.1, 77(2)
1091–1093	77(2)
1101	183, 194
1102	184, 194
1103	185
1104	80
1106	82(1)
1107	82(2)
1108	82(3)
1109	82(4)
1110	82(5)
1112, 1113	190

Present SALES Key Number	Former SALES Key Number	Present SALES Key Number	Former SALES Key Number
1114	191	1215	151, 170, 194
1115	186	1216	151
1116	192	1217	177, 194
1121, 1122	197, 199	1218	151, 177, 194, 195
1123	200(1)	1221	85(2), 172
1124	200(2)	1222	172, 195
1126	208	1223–1226	172
1127	209	1228	172, 173
1128	210	1229	173, 174
1129	211	1230	173, 175
1130	212	1231	172
1131	213	1233	195
1133	201(1)	1234	172, 195
1134	201(1, 2)	1235	172, 176(3), 179(6), 195
1135	201(1, 3)	1241	176(1)
1136	201(4)	1243	176(1), 196
1137	201(4, 5)	1244	176(1)
1138	201(.5, 1, 5, 6)	1245	202(8)
1139	200(3, 4)	1247	176(1, 3), 179(1)
1140	201(1, 7)	1248	176(1, 3), 179(3)
1141	200(4)	1249(1)	176(1), 179(4, 6)
1143	202(1)	1249(2)	176(4), 179(4)
1144	202(2)	1249(3)	176(5), 179(4)
1145	202(4)	1249(4)	121, 176(5), 179(4)
1146	202(5)	1249(5)	176(6)
1147	202(6)	1250	176(1, 3), 179(5)
1148	202(7)	1251	101, 176(1)
1149	203	1253, 1254	176(1)
1150	204	1255	176(1, 3), 179(4)
1151	205	1301, 1303	84
1152	214	1304	84, 98, 99
1154, 1155	140, 215	1305	84
1156	141, 215	1306	84, 107
1157(1)	143, 215	1307	91
1157(2)	144, 215	1308	84
1158	145, 215	1309	93
1159	146, 215	1401–1403	86
1160	147, 215	1501–1508	89
1161	148, 215	1509	89, 90
1162	149, 215	1510	89, 90, 94
1163	216	1511	89, 94
1164	217	1601	246
1165	218	1603	246, 248
1171	197, 199, 200(2)	1604	246, 248, 249
1172	197, 201(1)	1605	246, 248
1174	201(1–7)	1606	251
1175	201(4)	1608	257, 258
1176	200(2)	1609	258
1178	204	1611	246, 277, 279, 427
1180	214	1612	282, 284(1), 427
1181	197, 199	1613	246, 279, 427
1191	184	1621	246, 260
1193, 1194	152, 184	1623	260
1195	184	1624(1, 2)	260, 261(1)
1196	152, 184	1624(3)	260, 261(2)
1198	151, 152, 184	1624(4)	261(1, 3)
1199	152, 184	1624(5)	261(4)
1200	184	1624(6)	261(5)
1211	151, 177, 194	1624(7)	261(1, 6)
1212	151, 170	1624(8)	261(7)
1213	177, 194	1625	260, 261(7)

Present SALES Key Number	Former SALES Key Number	Present SALES Key Number	Former SALES Key Number
1626	262	1754	273(1, 2, 5)
1627	260, 261(1), 262	1755	273(1, 5), 274, 284(4)
1628, 1629	260, 261(1)	1756	273(1, 3, 5)
1630	260, 280	1757	273(5), 284(4)
1641, 1642	277, 279	1759	279
1643	282, 284(1), 427	1760	277, 279
1645–1649	279, 284(1)	1761	273(1, 3)
1650	277, 279, 284(1)	1762	284(4), 427
1651–1653	279, 284(1)	1771–1775	267
1654	277, 279, 284(1)	1776, 1777	267, 280
1655	279, 282, 284(1)	1779–1783	267
1657	277, 279, 280	1785, 1786	267, 283
1658	279	1787	260, 267
1659	279, 284(1)	1788	267
1660	282, 284(1), 427	1791, 1792	260, 267, 280
1671	262.5, 266	1801	267
1672	284(1), 427	1802	260
1673	262.5, 266, 427	1803	279
1681	279	1804	267
1682	264	1811–1816(2)	255
1683	275	1817, 1818	255, 278
1685	266	1820, 1821	255
1686	268(1)	1822	255, 278
1687	266, 268(2)	1823, 1824	255
1688	269	1826	255, 278
1689	270, 284(3)	1827	255
1690	271	1828	255, 278
1691	266, 279	1830–1833	255
1693	113, 266, 279	1835	255, 278, 425
1694	113, 123, 268(2)	1836–1843	255
1695	113, 279	1851	123, 286
1697	263	1853	285(1), 286, 429
1698, 1699	263, 283	1854, 1855	285(1)
1711	272, 279	1856	285(4)
1712	272	1858–1860	285(2)
1713	268(1), 272	1862, 1863	285(3)
1714	279, 284(1), 427	1864	285(3), 286
1715	272	1865	285(3)
1716	284(1), 427	1866	286
1718–1722	272, 284(1)	1868	287(.5–5)
1723	272, 284(1, 4), 427	1869	287(6)
1724	272, 279, 284(1)	1881	288(1)
1725	272, 273(1), 284(1)	1882	288(2)
1726	284(1), 427	1883	288(3)
1727, 1728	284(1)	1884	288(4)
1730	277, 279, 280	1885	288(5)
1731	279, 284(1)	1886	288(1, 6)
1732	272, 284(1)	1887	288(1, 2, 6)
1733	284(1), 427	1901	404, 418(1)
1741	273(1, 2, 5)	1902	340
1742	273(1, 5)	1904	390, 404, 405, 425
1743	273(1, 2), 284(4)	1905	425
1744	273(3, 5)	1906	130(4), 390, 425
1745	273(1, 5), 284(4), 427	1911	289
1747	273(1–3, 5), 284(4)	1912	290
1748	273(1–3, 5)	1913	291
1749	273(1, 3, 4)	1914	292
1750	273(1, 3), 274	1916	294
1751	273(1–3, 5)	1917	295
1752	274	1918	296
1753	273(1, 3, 5), 284(4)	1919	297

Present SALES Key Number	Former SALES Key Number	Present SALES Key Number	Former SALES Key Number
1920	298	1995(3)	384(2, 7)
1921	299	1995(4)	384(1–3)
1931	300	1995(5)	384(1, 2)
1932	301	1995(6)	384(1, 2, 7)
1933	302	1995(7)	384(1, 2)
1934	303	1995(9)	384(2)
1935	304	1997	384(1, 6)
1936	305	1998	384(1, 7)
1937	306	1999	384(1)
1938	307	2001	340, 384(1, 6, 7)
1939	308	2002	384(6, 7)
1940	309	2004	384(1, 4, 7)
1942	311	2005	384(4)
1943	312	2006	384(1)
1944	313	2008	384(1, 7)
1945	314	2009	384(1, 6, 7)
1946	315	2010	384(1, 6)
1947	300, 304, 311, 313	2111, 2112	391.5
1951	316(1), 360(2), 479.3	2121	400
1952	316(1, 2)	2122	399
1954	316(1)	2124, 2125	399, 400
1955	316(1, 2)	2126	400, 404
1956, 1957	316(1)	2127	399, 400, 404
1958	318	2129	392, 401
1959	317	2133	418(1)
1960	316(1), 318, 319	2141	130(4)
1971	332	2143	130(4), 404, 405, 418(1)
1972	332, 339, 384(7)	2144	405, 418(1)
1973	332	2145	404, 405, 418(1)
1974	333	2147	418(1, 2)
1975	334, 384(7)	2148	418(1)
1976	335	2149	418(1, 2)
1977	336, 384(7)	2150, 2151	130(4), 418(1)
1978	338, 384(7)	2152	397, 418(1, 2)
1981	340, 384(1)	2153	130(4), 418(1)
1982	384(1, 6, 7)	2154	130(4), 418(1, 3)
1983	384(1, 6)	2156	130(4), 391(7), 418(1, 19)
1985	340, 360(1), 384(1)	2158	391(1, 5, 7)
1986	340–343	2159	391(1, 7, 9)
1987(1)	340–343, 347(1)	2160	391(2), 397
1987(2)	342, 343, 347(1), 360(1), 370	2162–2165(10)	418(7)
1987(3)	340–343, 360(1), 370	2167	418(2–4)
1987(4)	340, 342, 360(1)	2168	418(1–4)
1987(5)	340–343	2169(1)	418(1–3)
1987(6)	342, 347(1), 370	2169(2)	418(1, 3)
1987(7)	342, 347(1, 2), 360(1), 370	2169(3)	418(2, 3)
		2169(4)	418(1–3)
1987(8)	360(2)	2169(5)	418(1, 3, 19)
1987(9)	343, 360(1)	2169(6)	418(2, 3)
1987(10)	360(1), 384(1)	2169(7)	130(4), 397, 418(1–3)
1989	337, 384(7)	2169(8)	130(4), 418(1, 3)
1990, 1991(1)	339, 384(7)	2169(9)	418(1)
1991(2)	384(6, 7)	2171	130(4), 418(1, 19)
1991(3, 4)	339, 384(7)	2172	168(6), 418(1, 19)
1991(5)	384(7)	2174	418(1, 8, 14.1, 15, 19)
1991(6–8)	339, 384(7)	2175	418(14.1, 15)
1991(10)	384(7)	2176	418(16.1, 17)
1993	384(1, 2, 7)	2177	418(19)
1994, 1995(1)	384(1, 2)	2178	418(11.1, 13)
1995(2)	384(1, 2, 6)	2179	418(12, 15)
		2181	130(4), 418(1, 7)

Present SALES Key Number	Former SALES Key Number	Present SALES Key Number	Former SALES Key Number
2182	418(1), 442(6)	2261	103, 123
2183	418(1)	2262	104, 124
2191	425, 442(1)	2263	124
2192	130(4), 442(1)	2264	125
2194	442(1)	2266	106, 126(1)
2195	418(1), 442(1)	2267	106
2196	442(1, 11)	2268(1)	126(1)
2197–2199	442(1)	2268(2)	126(2)
2200, 2201	418(1), 442(1)	2268(3)	126(3)
2202	442(1)	2269	108, 128
2203	130(4), 391(7), 418(1), 442(1)	2270	92, 109, 129
		2271	92
2204	391(8)	2272	94, 111, 131
2205	130(4), 391(7), 397, 398	2274	133
2206	130(4), 442(1)	2275	134
2208	442(1, 2, 4)	2281	340, 404
2209	442(1–4)	2283	340
2210	442(2)	2284	316(2), 340, 479.2(11)
2211	442(3)	2286	390, 404
2212(1)	442(1–3)	2287	130(1), 131, 391(5), 404
2212(2)	442(1, 2, 4)	2288	418(7)
2212(3)	442(11)	2289	390, 404, 425
2212(4)	442(1, 2)	2290	425, 427
2212(5–7)	442(1–3)	2292	130(.5)
2212(8)	442(1, 2)	2293	103, 107, 108, 340
2212(9)	442(2)	2294	127
2212(10)	442(1, 2)	2295	127, 390
2214	442(1, 6)	2296	131
2215	442(6)	2301–2303	418(6), 426
2217, 2218(1, 2)	442(1, 5, 6)	2305–2307	426
2218(3)	442(5, 6, 11)	2308	286, 418(6), 426
2218(4–6)	442(1, 5, 6)	2310, 2311	Damages 74–86
2218(7)	418(19), 442(5, 6)	2403	369, 370, 404
2218(8)	418(19), 442(6, 10)	2404	369, 370
2218(9)	442(6)	2405	391(1, 5)
2218(10)	442(1, 6)	2406	370, 391(4), 405
2219	442(16)	2407	130(1), 391(5)
2220	442(8)	2409	85(1, 2), 406
2221	442(9)	2410	319, 345, 371
2223, 2224	442(1, 6)	2411	392, 406
2225	442(13, 14)	2413	407
2226	442(1)	2414(1)	347(1–6), 372
2228, 2229	442(12)	2414(2)	428
2230	442(10)	2415	393, 407
2241	96, 99, 113	2417	348(.5, 1), 428
2242	113, 119	2418(1)	348(1)
2244	96, 113	2418(2)	348(1), 428
2245	96, 97, 114	2419	348(1), 407
2246	98, 116	2420	349
2247	99	2422	350, 374, 409
2248	100	2423	350, 374
2249	115	2424	394, 409
2250	117	2425	409
2251	118	2426	126(1), 130(.5)
2252	119	2427	351, 395, 409.5
2253	120, 425	2428	255, 405, 409.5
2254	119	2430	411
2256	96, 113, 120	2431(1)	377, 411
2257	113, 119, 255	2431(2)	353(.5–8), 377
2258	113, 119, 120	2431(3)	396, 411
2259	101, 121	2431(4)	411

Present SALES Key Number	Former SALES Key Number	Present SALES Key Number	Former SALES Key Number
2431(5)	110(2), 130(2)	2621	181(1), 415
2432(1)	354(.5–10)	2622	87(1), 179(4), 181(1), 415
2432(2)	435(1–5)	2624	87(1), 397
2433	355(.5–4), 379, 413	2625	52(1), 87(1), 92, 130(3)
2435	362, 363, 386	2626	87(1), 381
2436	365, 389, 422	2627	89
2437	130(4), 366, 398	2629, 2630	439
2438	Costs 194.36; Sales 130(4), 368	2631	130(3), 439
2451	391(1, 3.5), 427	2632, 2633	439
2452	427	2634	437(3), 439
2453	429	2635	439
2455–2459	430	2636	130(3), 439
2460	425	2638	324(1), 415
2461	431	2639	130(3)
2462	130(.5), 427, 432	2640	357(1), 381, 397, 415, 439
2463	255, 427, 432	2641	357(1), 415, 439
2465	427, 434	2642	339, 357(1), 381
2466	434	2643	415
2467	434, 436	2644, 2645	381, 415
2468	437(.5–4)	2646	381, 415, 418(14.1), 439
2470	426, 444	2647, 2648	381, 415, 439
2471	447	2650	381, 415
2472	398, 448	2651	418(6)
2473	Costs 194.36	2661	52(2.1), 358(1), 382, 416(1)
2501	130(.5), 391(5, 7, 8)	2662	358(3)
2502	130(1), 390, 427	2663	52(3), 358(1)
2503	85(1, 2), 123, 392	2665	52(2.1), 416(1)
2504	125, 130(.5), 393	2666	52(2.1)
2506	130(.5)	2668	52(2.1), 416(1)
2507	126(1), 130(.5), 394, 431	2669	52(4)
2508	130(.5, 4)	2670	52(2.1), 416(2)
2511	130(2, 3), 434	2672	87(2), 358(1), 382, 416(1)
2512	130(2), 434	2673	87(2), 181(2.1), 358(1), 416(1)
2513	130(2), 396, 436	2674(1)	87(2), 181(2.1, 3, 9), 358(1), 382
2514	130(2), 437(3, 4)	2674(2)	181(5), 358(1, 4), 416(1)
2516	110(3)	2674(3)	87(2), 181(4), 358(1), 416(1)
2517	110(3), 130(3.5), 357(1), 422, 447	2674(4)	181(2.1, 5, 10)
2518	110(4), 130(4), 398	2674(5)	128, 130(3), 181(2.1), 358(1, 2)
2519	Costs 194.36; Sales 130(4)	2674(6)	52(2.1), 87(2), 181(5, 8)
2601	52(1), 357(1), 415	2675	87(2), 358(1)
2602, 2603	52(1), 357(1)	2676	87(2), 181(2.1), 416(1)
2605	52(1)	2677	87(2), 358(1, 5), 416(1)
2606	22(4), 23(4), 52(1)	2678	87(2), 218.5, 382
2608–2610	52(1)	2679	181(2.1), 397
2612	87(1), 181(1), 357(1), 381, 415	2680	181(2.1), 382, 416(1, 2)
2613	87(1), 181(1), 381, 415	2681	181(2.1, 9), 416(1)
2614(1, 2)	181(1), 357(1)	2682	181(2.1)
2614(3)	87(1), 181(1), 357(1)	2684	87(2)
2614(4)	181(1)	2685	52(2.1), 130(3), 181(2.1), 416(1, 2)
2614(5)	130(3), 181(1), 357(1)	2687	358(2), 416(1)
2614(6)	181(1)	2689–2692	440(1–3)
2615	87(1), 357(1)	2693	440(2)
2616	87(1), 181(1), 415	2694	440(1)
2617	87(1), 357(2), 415	2695, 2696	440(1, 3)
2618	218.5	2698	324(2), 416(1, 2)
2619	181(1), 357(1)		
2620	181(1), 381, 415		

Present SALES Key Number	Former SALES Key Number	Present SALES Key Number	Former SALES Key Number
2699	130(3)	2768	130(4), 383, 417, 441(4)
2700	358(1), 382, 416(2), 440(4)	2769	359(1), 417, 441(4)
		2771	359(1), 418(6), 441(2, 3)
2701	358(1, 4, 6), 382, 440(1, 4)	2781	53(1), 363, 387
		2782	53(1)
2702	339, 382, 416(2)	2783	53(1), 88, 363
2703	416(1, 2)	2785	53(1), 363
2704	358(4), 382, 416(2)	2786	53(1, 2)
2705	358(6), 382, 416(2), 440(4)	2788	53(1)
		2789	53(3)
2706	358(1), 416(2), 440(4)	2790	1(1), 53(1), 363
2707	416(2), 440(4)	2792	88, 420
2708	382, 416(1, 2), 440(4)	2793	88, 363
2709	382, 416(2), 440(4)	2794(1)	182(1, 4), 363
2711	382, 416(2)	2794(2)	182(1), 363
2721	52(5.1), 359(1), 383	2794(3)	88, 182(1), 363, 420
2722	52(5.1), 359(1)	2794(4)	182(1, 4), 363
2723	52(6), 359(1)	2794(5)	126(4), 130(3.5), 182(4)
2725, 2726, 2728	52(5.1)	2794(6)	88, 182(1, 4), 363
2729	52(7)	2795	88, 363
2730	52(5.1)	2796	88
2732	87(3), 181(11.1), 359(1), 383, 417	2797	88, 363
		2798	218.5
2733	87(3), 181(11.1), 359(1), 383	2799	182(1), 420
		2800	182(1), 363, 387, 420
2734(1)	181(11.1, 13), 359(1)	2801	88, 182(1), 387, 420
2734(2)	181(12), 359(1), 417	2802	182(3)
2734(3)	87(3), 181(11.1), 359(1), 417	2804	88, 363
		2805	88, 130(3.5), 363, 420
2734(4)	181(11.1–13)	2806	88, 420
2734(5)	130(3), 181(11.1, 12)	2807	89, 363
2734(6)	87(3), 181(11.1–13)	2809	445(1, 4)
2735	87(3), 417	2810	445(1–4)
2736	87(3), 181(11.1), 417	2811	445(1, 4)
2737	87(3), 359(3), 417	2812	445(1, 2)
2738	218.5	2813	445(3)
2739	181(11.1)	2814	445(1, 2)
2740	181(11.1), 383, 417	2815	445(5)
2741	181(11.1), 417	2816	445(6)
2742	87(3), 181(11.1)	2818	387
2744	87(3), 359(1), 383, 417	2819	126(4), 130(3.5)
2745	87(3), 130(3), 359(1), 383, 417	2820	387, 420, 445(1)
		2821	363, 387, 445(1)
2746	87(3)	2822	339, 387
2747	359(1), 383, 417	2823	420
2749, 2750	441(1–3)	2824	387, 420
2751	130(3), 441(1–3)	2825	387, 420, 445(1)
2752	441(1, 2)	2826	420, 445(1)
2753	441(1, 3)	2827, 2828	387, 420, 445(1)
2754	441(1, 2)	2829	420, 445(1)
2755	441(1, 3)	2830	445(1)
2756	288(2), 441(1)	2831	Damages 83; Sales 387, 420
2758	359(1)		
2759	130(3)	2841	388, 421
2760	359(1), 383, 417, 441(4)	2842	328, 364(1, 3)
2761	359(1, 2), 441(4)	2843	364(1, 2, 4), 421
2762	339, 383, 417, 441(4)	2845	364(4), 421
2763	417, 418(7)	2846	364(2), 388, 421
2764, 2765	383, 417, 441(4)	2848	388, 421
2766	417, 418(14.1), 441(4)	2849	328, 364(4)
2767	383, 417, 441(4)	2850	364(1)

SALES

Present SALES Key Number	Former SALES Key Number	Present SALES Key Number	Former SALES Key Number
2852	364(6), 388, 421	2936	237
2853	364(5, 6), 421	2937	238
2854(1)	364(7), 388, 421	2938	239
2854(2)	364(7, 8), 421	2939	241, 316(1)
2854(3)	364(1), 388, 421	2940	234(9)
2854(4)	364(7), 388, 398, 421	2941	242
2854(5)	130(3.5)	2942	240
2854(6)	364(9)	2951–2956	234(7)
2855	364(1, 2)	2961, 2963	224, 232, 234(6)
2856	364(1, 10)	2964	234(6)
2857	364(1, 3), 421	2965	233(3), 234(3, 6)
2858	218.5, 364(1, 2, 7), 398, 421	2971	219(2), 234(1)
2859	364(1, 2, 4, 6), 421	2972	219(2), 230
2860	364(1, 2, 4), 388, 421	2973	219(1, 2), 222
2861	364(10), 421	2974	234(1, 4)
2862	388, 421	2982	225(1)
2864	364(1, 5), 388	2983	225(2), 233(1.5)
2865	130(3.5), 364(5), 421	2984	225(1), 234(1, 3)
2866	421	2986	225(.5, 1, 3)
2867	364(5), 421	2987	225(3), 233(2), 243
2869	446(1, 2, 7)	2989	225(4), 233(3), 244(2)
2870	446(1, 2, 4, 6, 7)	2990	225(4), 233(3), 244(1)
2871	446(1, 2, 5, 7)	2991	225(4), 233(3), 244(3)
2872	446(1, 2, 5, 6)	2993	233(4)
2873	446(1, 7)	2994	225(5), 233(4), 245
2874	255, 446(1, 6)	2995	225(6), 233(4), 245.5
2875	446(8)	2996	233(4), 245.5
2876	446(1, 2, 8)	2997	225(7)
2878	328, 364(1), 388, 421	3001	450
2879	130(3.5), 398, 421	3002	451
2880	388, 421, 446(9)	3003	452
2881	364(1), 398, 446(9)	3005	454
2882	339, 388, 421	3006	455
2883	418(7), 421, 446(9)	3007	456
2884	364(1), 388, 421, 446(9)	3008	457
2885	388, 421, 446(9)	3009	458
2886	421, 446(9)	3010	459
2887–2889	388, 421, 446(9)	3011	460
2890	364(1)	3012	461
2891	418(6), 421, 446(9)	3013	462
2901	226(.5, 1, 3)	3014	463
2902	219(2), 226(3)	3015	464
2911	219(1), 227, 233(1, 3)	3016	465
2912	226(1, 2.1, 14)	3018	467
2914	219(1), 220, 226(1)	3019	468
2915	220, 228	3020	469
2916	219(2), 220, 221	3021	470
2921	234(1)	3023	472(1)
2922	234(2)	3024	472(2)
2923	234(1, 8)	3025	472(3)
2925	234(3–5, 8)	3026	472(4)
2926	234(3, 5)	3027	472(5)
2927	226(2.1, 3), 234(3, 8)	3028(1)	473(1)
2928	234(5)	3028(2)	473(2)
2929(1)	234(1, 5, 8)	3029(1)	474(1)
2929(2, 3)	234(1, 3, 5, 8)	3029(2)	474(2)
2931	235(1)	3030	475
2932	235(2)	3031	476
2933	235(3)	3033	477(1)
2934	235(4)	3034	477(2)
		3035	477(3)
		3036	477(4)
		3037	477(5)

Present SALES Key Number	Former SALES Key Number	Present SALES Key Number	Former SALES Key Number
3038	477(6)	3044	479.3
3039	477(7)	3045	479.4
3041	479	3046	479.5
3042	479.1	3047	479.6
3043(1)	479.2(1)	3048(1)	480(.5)
3043(2)	479.2(2)	3048(3)	480(1.1)
3043(3)	479.2(3)	3048(4)	480(2)
3043(4)	479.2(4)	3048(5)	480(3)
3043(5)	479.2(5)	3048(6)	480(3.5)
3043(6)	479.2(6)	3048(7)	480(4)
3043(7)	479.2(7)	3048(8)	480(4.5)
3043(8)	479.2(8)	3048(9)	480(5)
3043(9)	479.2(9)	3048(10)	480(6)
3043(10)	479.2(10)	3049	481
3043(11)	479.2(11)	3050	482
3043(12)	479.2(12)	3051	483
3043(13)	479.2(13)	3052	484

🗝1–484.

SALES Key Numbers 1 to 484 are no longer valid and have been replaced by new Key Numbers. See topic analysis and translation tables.

I. IN GENERAL.

🗝501–504. *For other cases see earlier editions of this digest, the Decennial Digests, and WESTLAW.*

🗝502. Statutory provisions.

🗝505. —— Operation and effect.

C.A.11 (Fla.) 2003. Parties may, by agreement, vary the provisions of the Florida Uniform Commercial Code (UCC). West's F.S.A. § 671.102(3).

SCADIF, S.A. v. First Union Nat., 344 F.3d 1123.

Fla.App. 3 Dist. 1977. Material date in determining applicability of statute providing that implied warranties of fitness and merchantability shall not be applicable to use of blood for injection into the human body as to a defect that cannot be detected or removed by reasonable use of scientific procedures or techniques is the time the cause of action arose rather than time of commission of tortious act. West's F.S.A. § 672.316(5).

Lewis v. Associated Medical Institutions, Inc., 345 So.2d 852, certiorari denied 353 So.2d 676.

🗝506. —— Validity.

For other cases see earlier editions of this digest, the Decennial Digests, and WESTLAW.

🗝507. —— Retroactive or prospective operation.

Fla.App. 3 Dist. 1972. Where blood which was supplied by hospital for transfusion prior to enactment of statute providing that implied warranty of fitness for particular purpose is not applicable to distribution of blood for transfusion purposes and which allegedly resulted in injury to recipient came from blood bank created and maintained by hospital, hospital warranted fitness of such blood. F.S.A. § 672.316(5).

Mercy Hospital, Inc. v. Benitez, 257 So.2d 51.

🗝508. What law governs.

🗝509. —— In general.

C.A.11 (Fla.) 1993. To extent implied warranty claim against pesticide manufacturer depends upon inadequacies in labeling or packaging, it is expressly preempted by Federal Insecticide, Fungicide, and Rodenticide Act. Federal Insecticide, Fungicide, and Rodenticide Act, § 24(b), as amended, 7 U.S.C.A. § 136v(b).

Papas v. Upjohn Co., 985 F.2d 516, certiorari denied 114 S.Ct. 300, 510 U.S. 913, 126 L.Ed.2d 248.

C.A.5 (Fla.) 1980. Uniform Commercial Code as adopted and interpreted in lex loci governed questions of contract formation, while remedy questions, such as damage award, prejudgment interest and counterclaim for warranty breach were governed by Uniform Commercial Code as adopted and interpreted in forum state, considered together with other pertinent rules of forum state. U.C.C. §§ 2–201, 2–314, 2–314(2)(c), 2–315, 2–606, 2–608, 2–610(c), 2–703, 2–704, 2–706, 2–708; West's F.S.A. § 687.01.

Automated Medical Laboratories, Inc. v. Armour Pharmaceutical Co., 629 F.2d 1118.

C.A.5 (Fla.) 1978. Where buyers of tire resided in Florida and sale, service and vast majority of use of tire occurred in Florida, cause of action for death of one of buyers resulting from automobile accident in Texas allegedly caused by defect in tire, arose in Florida and right of action was guaranteed by Florida Wrongful Death Act, with theory of recovery on warranty claims governed by Florida's interpretation of Uniform Commercial Code's actions for breach of expressed and implied warranties. West's F.S.A. §§ 671.105(1), 768.19.

Westerman v. Sears, Roebuck & Co., 577 F.2d 873.

C.A.5 (Fla.) 1975. Where both carpet manufacturer and its dealer knew that carpet sold to dealer was to be installed in Florida, and where alleged injury to dealer because of lost sales due to defects in carpeting occurred solely in Florida, Florida law governed dealer's claims against manufacturer for breach of warranty and negligence in manufacture of carpeting.

West's F.S.A. §§ 671.105(1), 672.103, 672.714(2, 3), 672.715.

> Aldon Industries, Inc. v. Don Myers & Associates, Inc., 517 F.2d 188, appeal after remand 547 F.2d 924.

C.A.5 (Fla.) 1968. Where requirements contract specifically provided that seller's products were to be re-sold at retail by buyer exclusively within Florida over 20-year period from 1957 and buyer breached its duty to perform the contract appropriate law for determining recoverable elements of damage was substantive law of Florida where contract was to be performed.

> Center Chemical Co. v. Avril, Inc., 392 F.2d 289.

C.A.5 (Fla.) 1964. Tenet of conflict of laws in claim on breach of implied warranty was that which governed sales rather than general rule applicable in contract situations.

> Sperry Rand Corp. v. Industrial Supply Corp., 337 F.2d 363.

Whether applicable substantive law was that of situs, place of performance or center of gravity, law of state where buyer's business was located and computer and related equipment for business records system were delivered and used would govern on claim for breach of implied warranty on equipment which was first leased under agreement containing clause providing that it would be construed in accordance with law of another state, no clause like which was incorporated into sales agreement.

> Sperry Rand Corp. v. Industrial Supply Corp., 337 F.2d 363.

M.D.Fla. 1992. Under Florida choice-of-law rules, substantive law of state in which townhomes were located applied to builder's warranty claims founded in contract against manufacturers and sellers of allegedly defective plywood used in the townhomes, even if contracts to purchase plywood were entered into in other states. West's F.S.A. §§ 95.11, 671.105.

> Pulte Home Corp., Inc. v. Ply Gem Industries, Inc., 804 F.Supp. 1471.

S.D.Fla. 2001. Action for breach of warranty brought by Florida buyer against Georgia seller, incorporated under Delaware law, alleging that chemical company produced defective chemical used by buyer to produce exterior coating for swimming pools which became discolored was governed by Florida law, even though invoices sent by seller purported to adopt Delaware law; all injuries caused by allegedly defective chemical occurred in pools located in Florida, chemical was delivered in Florida, and negotiations for purchase of chemical took place in Florida. U.C.C. § 1–105; West's F.S.A. § 671.105(1).

> Premix-Marbletite Mfg. Corp. v. SKW Chemicals, Inc., 145 F.Supp.2d 1348.

Bkrtcy.S.D.Fla. 1987. State law is dispositive in deciding whether title to goods passed to bankruptcy debtor under consignment contract.

> In re Denmark Co., Inc., 73 B.R. 325.

Fla. 1940. In Florida action for reimbursement for meat shipped by Florida seller to Maryland buyer under Maryland contract, which was spoiled when received, and for cost of salvaging other meat which was required to be pickled, the contract was governed by Maryland law and Florida law governed case in regard to procedure.

> Farris & Co. v. William Schluderberg, T. J. Kurdle Co., 193 So. 429, 141 Fla. 462, rehearing denied 196 So. 184, 142 Fla. 765.

Fla.App. 1 Dist. 2007. In interpreting asset purchase agreements providing for transfer of ownership of air filtration and purification system and supporting patents, the District Court of Appeal would apply the law of the states where the contracts were made and performed.

> Goswami v. Lennox Industries, Inc., 947 So.2d 1221.

Fla.App. 1 Dist. 1994. FIFRA did not preempt farmers' breach of express warranty claim against manufacturer of fungicide that allegedly burned their watermelon crop; claim arose from facts showing that manufacturer had informed its sales representatives that he could assure farmers that fungicide would not burn their watermelons, and was distinct from any representation made on the fungicide label. Federal Insecticide, Fungicide, and Rodenticide Act, §§ 2–31, as amended, 7

U.S.C.A. §§ 136–136y; West's F.S.A. § 672.313(1).

ISK Biotech Corp. v. Douberly, 640 So.2d 85, review denied 651 So.2d 1194.

Fla.App. 4 Dist. 1993. Federal Insecticide, Fungicide, and Rodenticide Act (FIFRA) did not preempt plaintiff's breach of warranty claim against manufacturer of methyl bromide; manufacturer's liability for such breach arises out of terms of warranty itself, a voluntarily undertaken contractual commitment. Federal Insecticide, Fungicide, and Rodenticide Act, § 24, as amended, 7 U.S.C.A. § 136v.

Brennan v. Dow Chemical Co., 613 So.2d 131.

Fla.App. 4 Dist. 1978. Where both place of making and place of performance of contract were located in Wisconsin, Wisconsin law was applicable to action in Florida court between Wisconsin manufacturer of marine goods and Florida dealer on contract for sale of goods.

Boat Town U.S. A., Inc. v. Mercury Marine Division Of Brunswick Corp., 364 So.2d 15.

Fla.App. 5 Dist. 1984. Florida trial court, in replevin action to recover possession of stolen earthmover which was resold in Louisiana, should have declined to apply Louisiana law, which allows one who acquires possession of property by theft to confer good title, as such contravenes contrary Florida law.

Brown & Root, Inc. v. Ring Power Corp., 450 So.2d 1245.

⌬510. —— **Common law.**

S.D.Fla. 2004. Dispute regarding insurer's obligations under contract with reinsurer regarding administration of group life insurance policies was governed by common law, not the Uniform Commercial Code, under Florida law, since the dispute did not involve contract for sale of goods. West's F.S.A. § 672.102.

Excess Risk Underwriters, Inc. v. Lafayette Life Ins. Co., 328 F.Supp.2d 1319.

Bkrtcy.M.D.Fla. 1981. Provision of the Uniform Commercial Code dealing with reclamation rights of a seller cuts off any common-law fraud claims of the seller. West's F.S.A. § 672.702(2).

Matter of Eli Witt Co., 12 B.R. 757.

Fla.App. 4 Dist. 1968. Common-law rules governing the sale of automobiles may apply in lieu of compliance with statutory provisions.

Smith v. Baker, 206 So.2d 409.

⌬511. —— **International issues.**

S.D.Fla. 2002. Oral contract to distribute goods in Latin America was not governed by United Nations Convention on Contracts for the International Sale of Goods where, at time "proposal for concluding" contract was made, between proposed distributors, which were Spanish and Argentine corporations, and product developers, which were British corporations, the United Kingdom was not signatory to treaty. United Nations Convention on Contracts for the International Sale of Goods, Art. 100(1), 15 U.S.C.A.App.

Impuls I.D. Intern., S.L. v. Psion-Teklogix, Inc., 234 F.Supp.2d 1267.

In determining whether oral contract to distribute goods in Latin American was governed by United Nations Convention on Contracts for the International Sale of Goods, which was dependent on whether parties had their places of business in signatory states at time of contract formation, fact that Canadian corporation was later acquired by British corporations and assumed contract obligations in their stead was to be disregarded, because what parties knew at time of contract formation was that United Kingdom was not signatory to treaty. United Nations Convention on Contracts for the International Sale of Goods, Arts. 1(2), 100, 15 U.S.C.A.App.

Impuls I.D. Intern., S.L. v. Psion-Teklogix, Inc., 234 F.Supp.2d 1267.

Court may look to history of negotiation and practice under United Nations Convention on Contracts for the International Sale of Goods to determine whether it governs contract. United Nations Convention on Contracts for the International Sale of Goods, Art. 1 et seq., 15 U.S.C.A.App.

Impuls I.D. Intern., S.L. v. Psion-Teklogix, Inc., 234 F.Supp.2d 1267.

United Nations Convention on Contracts for the International Sale of Goods could not be applied when all parties to contracting state were not from contracting states, where United States ratified CISG with declaration that it would not be bound by section which allowed for its application when party to contract was not from contracting state. United Nations Convention on Contracts for the International Sale of Goods, Arts. 1(1)(b), 95, 15 U.S.C.A.App.

> Impuls I.D. Intern., S.L. v. Psion-Teklogix, Inc., 234 F.Supp.2d 1267.

☞512. Federal preemption.

☞513. —— In general.

Fla.App. 1 Dist. 1978. Florida statute recognizing total federal preemption of recordation of interests in aircraft and the rights derived therefrom is not inconsistent with provisions of the Uniform Commercial Code dealing with buyers in the ordinary course of business and is not repealed by it. West's F.S.A. §§ 329.01, 679.302(3)(a), 680.103.

> O'Neill v. Barnett Bank of Jacksonville, N. A., 360 So.2d 150.

☞514. —— Warranties and redhibition.

C.A.11 (Fla.) 1994. Medical Device Amendments of 1976 to the Food, Drug and Cosmetic Act preempted cataract patient's state law claims against manufacturers of intraocular lenses for eye injuries allegedly caused by manufacturers' negligence, strict liability in tort, and breach of implied warranty. Federal Food, Drug, and Cosmetic Act, § 521(a), as amended, 21 U.S.C.A. § 360k(a).

> Duncan v. Iolab Corp., 12 F.3d 194.

M.D.Fla. 2015. Federal government established requirements applicable to bone graft device used in patient's surgery, as required for Medical Device Amendments (MDA) to the Federal Food, Drug, and Cosmetic Act (FDCA) to preempt patient's state-law fraud, negligence, products liability, and warranty claims arising from off-label use of the device, where device was approved through pre-market approval process. Medical Device Amendments of 1976, § 2(a), 21 U.S.C.A. § 360k(a).

> Byrnes v. Small, 60 F.Supp.3d 1289.

Medical Device Amendments (MDA) to the Federal Food, Drug, and Cosmetic

Act (FDCA) did not expressly preempt patient's breach of express warranty claim under Florida law against manufacturer of bone graft device, premised on alleged voluntary, affirmative, but false, warranty statements made by manufacturer, aside from any Food and Drug Administration (FDA) approved label or warning, to promote off-label use of device, since federal law required manufacturer to ensure that any voluntary warranty statements were truthful, accurate, and not misleading, such that state law requirement holding manufacturer to voluntary express warranties made during off-label promotion would not impose requirements different from, or in addition to, federal requirements. Federal Food, Drug, and Cosmetic Act, § 301(b), 21 U.S.C.A. § 331(b); Medical Device Amendments of 1976, § 2(a), 21 U.S.C.A. § 360k(a).

> Byrnes v. Small, 60 F.Supp.3d 1289.

Federal Food, Drug, and Cosmetic Act (FDCA) did not impliedly preempt patient's breach of express warranty claim against manufacturer of bone graft device, premised on alleged voluntary, affirmative, but false, warranty statements made by manufacturer, aside from any Food and Drug Administration (FDA) approved label or warning, to promote off-label use of device, since claim stood independently under Florida law and did not seek simply to enforce requirements of the FDCA. Federal Food, Drug, and Cosmetic Act, § 310(a), 21 U.S.C.A. § 337(a).

> Byrnes v. Small, 60 F.Supp.3d 1289.

M.D.Fla. 2012. Consumers' implied warranty claim under Florida law against generic manufacturer of drug metoclopramide stemming from manufacturer's failure to provide additional warnings relating to risks associated with long-term metoclopramide use or manufacturer's failure to stop manufacturing and marketing generic version of metoclopramide was preempted by Federal Food, Drug and Cosmetic Act (FDCA) duty to keep label the same. Federal Food, Drug, and Cosmetic Act, § 1, 21 U.S.C.A. § 301.

> Metz v. Wyeth LLC, 872 F.Supp.2d 1335, affirmed 525 Fed.Appx. 893.

N.D.Fla. 2014. Consumers' claims, alleging violations of Florida Deceptive and Unfair Trade Practices Act (DUTPA), Florida's false advertising statute, breach of express and implied warranties, negligence, and unjust enrichment as result of fact that labels on two of company's fruit-and-vegetable juices were allegedly misleading, were preempted by Food, Drug and Cosmetic Act (FDCA), as company's labels complied with FDCA and related regulations. Federal Food, Drug, and Cosmetic Act, § 403(i), 21 U.S.C.A. § 343(i); 21 C.F.R. § 101.30, West's F.S.A. §§ 501.201 et seq., 817.44.

Bell v. Campbell Soup Co., 65 F.Supp.3d 1328.

S.D.Fla. 2015. Medical Device Amendments to Food, Drug and Cosmetic Act (FDCA) preempted Florida state law claims against manufacturer of hip joint replacement system for breach of express warranty and implied warranty of merchantability based on patient's development of unsafe levels of metal toxicity allegedly caused by system; patient failed to state parallel state law claim because, as provided by preemption clause, state law warranty claim could not allege a device was unsafe and ineffective when FDA made express finding in contravention of that claim, and patient's consent to participate in clinical study that provided safety monitoring was inconsistent with allegations that manufacturer warranted that system would not release metal ions into his blood. Federal Food, Drug, and Cosmetic Act § 510, 21 U.S.C.A. § 360(k).

Mink v. Smith & Nephew, Inc., 145 F.Supp.3d 1208.

S.D.Fla. 2014. Consumers' claims in class action complaint against manufacturers of cereal and snack food products, for violations of Florida's Deceptive and Unfair Trade Practices Act (FDUTPA), negligent misrepresentation, breach of implied warranty of fitness for purpose, breach of express warranty, declaratory judgment, money had and received, and violations of California's Business and Professions Code, based on contention that "all natural" representation on manufacturers' packaging misled reasonable consumers, were not preempted by Food and Drug Administration's (FDA) rejection of requirement that bioengineered foods be labeled differently, since consumers did not seek to impose disclosure requirement on manufacturers' products. West's F.S.A. § 501.201 et seq.; West's Ann.Cal.Civ.Code

§ 1750; West's Ann.Cal.Bus. & Prof.Code §§ 17200, 17500.

Garcia v. Kashi Co., 43 F.Supp.3d 1359.

Consumers' allegations in complaint asserting claims for violations of Florida's Deceptive and Unfair Trade Practices Act (FDUTPA), negligent misrepresentation, breach of implied warranty of fitness for purpose, breach of express warranty, declaratory judgment, money had and received, and violations of California's Business and Professions Code, based on contention that use of Genetically Modified Organisms (GMOs) and other allegedly synthetic ingredients in cereal and snack products precluded manufacturers' products from being characterized as "all natural," were not expressly preempted by section of Nutrition Labeling and Education Act's (NLEA) governing misbranded food containing artificial flavoring, artificial coloring, or chemical preservative, since consumers did not allege that products contained artificial flavoring, coloring, or chemical preservatives. Federal Food, Drug, and Cosmetic Act, § 403A(a)(3), 21 U.S.C.A. § 343–1(a)(3); West's F.S.A. § 501.201 et seq.; West's Ann.Cal.Civ.Code § 1750; West's Ann.Cal. Bus. & Prof.Code §§ 17200, 17500.

Garcia v. Kashi Co., 43 F.Supp.3d 1359.

Food and Drug Administration (FDA) did not have policy permitting food containing Genetically Modified Organisms (GMOs) to be described as "natural," and had not regulated term "all natural," and thus consumers' state law claims for violations of Florida's Deceptive and Unfair Trade Practices Act (FDUTPA), negligent misrepresentation, breach of implied warranty of fitness for purpose, breach of express warranty, declaratory judgment, money had and received, and violations of California's Business and Professions Code, as brought in class action complaint against manufacturers of cereal and snack food products asserting that GMOs and other allegedly synthetic ingredients precluded manufacturers' products from being characterized as "all natural," were not impliedly preempted by FDA policy or regulations. West's F.S.A. § 501.201 et seq.; West's Ann.Cal.Civ.Code § 1750;

† This Case was not selected for publication in the National Reporter System
For legislative history of cited statutes, see Florida Statutes Annotated

West's Ann.Cal.Bus. & Prof.Code §§ 17200, 17500.

> Garcia v. Kashi Co., 43 F.Supp.3d 1359.

Consumers' claims in putative class action complaint against manufacturers of cereal and snacks, alleging violations of Florida's Deceptive and Unfair Trade Practices Act (FDUTPA), negligent misrepresentation, breach of implied warranty of fitness for purpose, breach of express warranty, declaratory judgment, money had and received, and violations of California's Business and Professions Code, that a reasonable consumer would not expect Pyridoxine Hydrochloride, Alpha–Tocopherol Acetate, Hexane–Processed Soy ingredients and Calcium Pantothenate in "all natural" labeled food, were not preempted by Food and Drug Administration (FDA) regulations and policy allegedly permitting "natural" foods to contain synthetic ingredients and processing aids as long as they are normally expected in the food, since consumers alleged that reasonable consumers did not expect fake vitamins and processing aids to be in foods labeled "all natural." West's F.S.A. § 501.201 et seq.; West's Ann.Cal.Civ.Code § 1750; West's Ann.Cal.Bus. & Prof.Code §§ 17200, 17500.

> Garcia v. Kashi Co., 43 F.Supp.3d 1359.

S.D.Fla. 2010. Patient's breach of warranty products liability claim under Florida law against manufacturer of artificial discs that were implanted in the patient's spine was preempted by the Medical Device Amendments (MDA) to the Federal Food, Drug, and Cosmetic Act (FDCA), since the disc was given premarket approval by the Food and Drug Administration (FDA), and patient's claim was not premised on a violation of FDA regulations. Medical Device Amendments of 1976, § 2(a), 21 U.S.C.A. § 360k(a).

> Wheeler v. DePuy Spine, Inc., 706 F.Supp.2d 1264.

Fla.App. 2 Dist. 2005. Magnuson-Moss Act does not supersede state law privity requirements for implied warranty claims. Magnuson-Moss Warranty—Fed-

eral Trade Commission Improvement Act, § 101 et seq., 15 U.S.C.A. § 2301 et seq.

> Cerasani v. American Honda Motor Co., 916 So.2d 843, review granted 925 So.2d 1029.

Fla.App. 3 Dist. 2005. With regard to warranties on consumer products, the Magnuson–Moss Warranty Act (MMWA) modifies the applicability and operation of the Uniform Commercial Code (UCC) and, to the extent applicable, supersedes inconsistent provisions of the UCC. Magnuson–Moss Warranty—Federal Trade Commission Improvement Act, § 110(d)(1), 15 U.S.C.A. § 2310(d)(1).

> Mesa v. BMW of North America, LLC, 904 So.2d 450, rehearing denied.

Magnuson–Moss Warranty Act (MMWA) does not supplant state law privity requirements for implied warranty claims. Magnuson–Moss Warranty—Federal Trade Commission Improvement Act, § 101(7), 15 U.S.C.A. § 2301(7).

> Mesa v. BMW of North America, LLC, 904 So.2d 450, rehearing denied.

☞**515. Nature and definition of sale; other transactions distinguished.**

Conditional sales, see ☞3004. Chattel mortgages, see CHATTEL MORTGAGES ☞6. Secured transactions, see SECURED TRANSACTIONS ☞10. Gifts, see GIFTS ☞5(2).

☞**516. —— In general.**

Fla.App. 4 Dist. 2007. A "sale" is a transfer of goods for consideration, and the seller is generally the party that receives the consideration and effects the transfer.

> Magner Intern. Corp. v. Brett, 960 So.2d 841, rehearing denied.

Fla.App. 4 Dist. 1971. Word "sale" indicates a transfer of title even though, under statute, sale or transfer of title may be to an uncertain or undeterminate estate or interest. F.S.A. § 672.106(1).

> Martyn v. First Federal Sav. & Loan Ass'n of West Palm Beach, 257 So.2d 576, certiorari denied First Federal Savings and Loan Association of West Palm Beach v. Martyn, 262 So.2d 446.

Fla.App. 4 Dist. 1968. A "sale" requires that there be two parties who stand to each other in the relationship of seller and buyer.

Smith v. Baker, 206 So.2d 409.

⚷517. —— **Bailments and leases.**

⚷517(1). In general.

Fla.App. 4 Dist. 1984. Term "transaction," used in statute providing that sales article of Uniform Commercial Code applies to "transactions" in goods, encompasses leasing agreements. West's F.S.A. § 672.102.

Capital Associates, Inc. v. Hudgens, 455 So.2d 651.

⚷517(2). Particular transactions.

C.A.5 (Fla.) 1980. Without evidence relating to the anticipated economic value of equipment over the term of the lease, court could not characterize transaction in which computer manufacturer sold computer to a second party who immediately leased it to a third party as either a sale or a financing arrangement.

Earman Oil Co., Inc. v. Burroughs Corp., 625 F.2d 1291.

M.D.Fla. 1991. Under Florida law, evidence did not support computer lessee's contention that its lease agreement was in fact disguised sales transaction between itself and supplier, with financing to be provided by purported lessor; thus, lessee could not maintain claim against supplier for breach of implied warranty of fitness for particular purpose. West's F.S.A. § 672.315.

Interfase Marketing, Inc. v. Pioneer Technologies Group, Inc., 774 F.Supp. 1351.

Fla.App. 1 Dist. 1988. Closed-end lease of motor vehicle was not "transaction in goods" for purposes of Uniform Commercial Code, and lessee thus could not revoke acceptance or recover for breach of implied warranties due to defects in vehicle, even though rental payments were sufficient to amortize most of vehicle's value; written agreement stated that transaction was lease and not sale, lessee did not have option to purchase at end of lease, and there was no provision for passage of title. West's F.S.A. §§ 672.302, 672.608.

Sellers v. Frank Griffin AMC Jeep, Inc., 526 So.2d 147.

Fla.App. 1 Dist. 1961. Franchised Michigan automobile dealer's delivery of automobile to nonfranchised Tennessee dealer in reliance upon promise that Tennessee dealer's agent would deliver purchase check upon returning to Detroit did not modify essential cash character of transaction but operated to constitute Tennessee dealer bailee with implied duty to return automobile if check was not delivered and paid in due course.

Trumbull Chevrolet Sales Co. v. Seawright, 134 So.2d 829, certiorari denied 143 So.2d 491.

Fla.App. 3 Dist. 2012. Creditor who purchased silver from a company that was running a Ponzi scheme was the victim of a fraud, not an owner or bailor of the silver purportedly sold to her by debtor, and, thus, assignee for the benefit of creditors could sell precious metals that were turned over by debtor, where there was no evidence that silver was set aside for creditor or that 1,000 ounces of silver were purchased with her funds or segregated as her separate property.

O'Brien v. Stermer, 98 So.3d 1245, rehearing denied.

Fla.App. 4 Dist. 1988. Machinery lease memorandum, which contained provision that there were no agreements or representations outside of memorandum, and that machinery lessee agreed to return equipment to lessor's storage yard, demonstrated that lease agreement was what it purported to be: a lease, and not a sale.

Barber Greene Co. v. Urbantes, 517 So.2d 768.

Fla.App. 4 Dist. 1984. Equipment lease for video game, pool table, and jukebox was subject to the sales article of the Uniform Commercial Code; thus, Code section governing unconscionable contracts or clauses was applicable to the lease. West's F.S.A. §§ 672.102, 672.105(1), 672.302.

Capital Associates, Inc. v. Hudgens, 455 So.2d 651.

Fla.App. 4 Dist. 1971. Where agreement involving truck designated one party as owner and the other party as lessee and stated that first party leased to second party certain "leased equipment," thereafter describing the truck, and where such agreement was for definite period of 34 months and did not give second party the option to purchase but rather provided that upon termination the "leased equipment" was to be returned to first party in as good condition as when received by second party, parties intended such agreement to be equipment lease and not to pass ownership of the truck.

> Leaseco, Inc. v. Bartlett, 257 So.2d 629, certiorari denied 262 So.2d 447.

⛛**518–522.**   *For other cases see earlier editions of this digest, the Decennial Digests, and WESTLAW.*

⛛**523.** —— **Consignment.**

Fla. 1940. An agreement providing that fertilizers, consigned by manufacturer to storekeeper, and proceeds of consignee's sales thereof should be consignor's exclusive property and held by consignee in trust for consignor, did not pass title in fertilizers to consignee, but at most made him consignor's agent.

> Lee v. Smith, 198 So. 197, 144 Fla. 557.

⛛**524–525.**   *For other cases see earlier editions of this digest, the Decennial Digests, and WESTLAW.*

⛛**524. Subject matter of sale.**

⛛**526.** —— **Goods in general.**

S.D.Fla. 1978. Aircraft constituted a "good" within meaning of sale of goods provision of Florida Uniform Commercial Code. West's F.S.A. §§ 672.102, 672.105, 672.201.

> McCollum Aviation, Inc. v. CIM Associates, Inc., 446 F.Supp. 511.

Fla.App. 3 Dist. 2015. Article 2 of the Uniform Commercial Code (UCC) applies only to transactions in goods; it does not apply to contracts for services, which are governed by the common law. West's F.S.A. § 672.102.

> Allied Shelving & Equipment, Inc. v. National Deli, LLC, 154 So.3d 482.

⛛**527.** —— **Services in general.**

Fla.App. 3 Dist. 2015. Article 2 of the Uniform Commercial Code (UCC) applies only to transactions in goods; it does not apply to contracts for services, which are governed by the common law. West's F.S.A. § 672.102.

> Allied Shelving & Equipment, Inc. v. National Deli, LLC, 154 So.3d 482.

For purposes of determining the applicability of Article 2 of the Uniform Commercial Code (UCC), the term "services," unlike the term "goods," is not defined in the UCC, but generally refers to some sort of manual labor or personal utility rather than a physical object that has been sold or purchased. West's F.S.A. § 672.102.

> Allied Shelving & Equipment, Inc. v. National Deli, LLC, 154 So.3d 482.

⛛**528.** —— **Mixed or hybrid transactions.**

C.A.11 (Fla.) 1998. Under predominant factor test for determining whether contracts involving both goods and services are covered or excluded from coverage under Uniform Commercial Code (UCC), court determines whether their predominant factor, their thrust, their purpose, reasonably stated, is the rendition of service, with goods incidentally involved, or is transaction of sale, with labor incidentally involved. West's F.S.A. § 672.105(1).

> BMC Industries, Inc. v. Barth Industries, Inc., 160 F.3d 1322, certiorari denied 119 S.Ct. 1807, 526 U.S. 1132, 143 L.Ed.2d 1010.

Language in "hybrid" contract involving both goods and services that refers to transaction as a "purchase," or identifies parties as the "buyer" and "seller," indicates that transaction is for goods, rather than services, for purposes of determining whether contract is governed by Uniform Commercial Code (UCC). West's F.S.A. § 672.105(1).

> BMC Industries, Inc. v. Barth Industries, Inc., 160 F.3d 1322, certiorari denied 119 S.Ct. 1807, 526 U.S. 1132, 143 L.Ed.2d 1010.

When price of "hybrid" contract involving both goods and services does not include the cost of services, or the charge for goods exceeds that for services, the contract is more likely to be for goods, for purposes of determining whether contract is governed by Uniform Commercial Code (UCC). West's F.S.A. § 672.105(1).

> BMC Industries, Inc. v. Barth Industries, Inc., 160 F.3d 1322, certiorari denied 119 S.Ct. 1807, 526 U.S. 1132, 143 L.Ed.2d 1010.

Bkrtcy.S.D.Fla. 2013. When faced with a "hybrid contract," Florida courts use the predominant factor test to determine whether the contract is for goods or services.

> In re All American Semiconductor, Inc., 490 B.R. 418.

Fla.App. 3 Dist. 2015. Determining whether a contract is for goods or services, for purposes of applicability of Article 2 of the Uniform Commercial Code (UCC), is not a completely binary choice; many contracts, commonly referred to as hybrids, involve transactions for both goods and services. West's F.S.A. § 672.102.

> Allied Shelving & Equipment, Inc. v. National Deli, LLC, 154 So.3d 482.

Whether Article 2 of the Uniform Commercial Code (UCC) or the common law applies to a particular hybrid contract depends on whether the predominant factor, the thrust, the purpose of the contract, reasonably stated, is the rendition of service, with goods incidentally involved, such as a contract with an artist for a painting, or is a transaction of sale, with labor incidentally involved, such as a contract for installation of a water heater in a bathroom. West's F.S.A. § 672.102.

> Allied Shelving & Equipment, Inc. v. National Deli, LLC, 154 So.3d 482.

Fla.App. 4 Dist. 2011. In determining whether to apply the Uniform Commercial Code's Article 2, regarding sale of goods, the court must look to the predominant nature of the transaction. West's F.S.A. § 672.201(1).

> Ge Lin v. Ecclestone Signature Homes of Palm Beach, LLC, 59 So.3d 267, rehearing denied.

⟨ला529. —— **Existence of subject matter; future goods.**

For other cases see earlier editions of this digest, the Decennial Digests, and WEST-LAW.

⟨ला530. —— **Ownership or interest of seller.**

Fla.App. 5 Dist. 1988. Fact that seller has neither possession nor title to goods at time he enters into contract to sell them does not void contract. West's F.S.A. § 672.105(2).

> Equico Lessors, Inc. v. Maruka Machinery Corp. of America, 523 So.2d 665.

⟨ला531–532. *For other cases see earlier editions of this digest, the Decennial Digests, and WESTLAW.*

⟨ला532. —— **Particular cases and subjects.**

⟨ला532(1). **In general.**

Fla.App. 2 Dist. 1975. Uniform Commercial Code was inapplicable in determining any liability of contractor to independent subcontractor, which had been engaged by contractor to install carpeting and which was to receive sum of $1 per yard for installation, 35 cents per foot for metal and 75 cents per yard for padding, with the contractor to furnish the carpeting, since the subject agreement was a service contract and not one regarding goods. West's F.S.A. § 672.101 et seq.

> Dionne v. Columbus Mills, Inc., 311 So.2d 681.

Fla.App. 5 Dist. 1986. Contract to repair, sealcoat and restripe private roadway was not a transaction in goods within meaning of West's F.S.A. § 672.314, despite use of sealer in resurfacing, and defective resurfacing was not actionable as a breach of implied warranty of merchantability for goods sold by a merchant.

> Jackson v. L.A.W. Contracting Corp., 481 So.2d 1290, review denied 492 So.2d 1333, review denied Stromberg-Carlson v. L.A.W. Contracting Corp., 492 So.2d 1335.

⟨ला532(2). **Personal property and chattels in general.**

Fla.App. 2 Dist. 1977. Definition of "goods" under Uniform Commercial Code is sufficiently broad to include books. West's F.S.A. § 672.105.

> Cardozo v. True, 342 So.2d 1053, certiorari denied 353 So.2d 674.

Fla.App. 4 Dist. 1984. Video game, pool table, and jukebox were movable things and, thus, met the definition of "goods" set forth in the sales article of the Uniform Commercial Code. West's F.S.A. § 672.105(1).

Capital Associates, Inc. v. Hudgens, 455 So.2d 651.

⚷532(3)–532(4). *For other cases see earlier editions of this digest, the Decennial Digests, and WESTLAW.*

⚷532(5). **Buildings, structures, and construction.**

Fla.App. 2 Dist. 1998. Renovation contractor made no express warranty to homeowners that windows, which leaked after being installed, were free from defect and suitable for their intended purposes and no warranty as to condition of windows was implied by law. West's F.S.A. §§ 672.104, 672.314.

Lonnie D. Adams Bldg. Contractor, Inc. v. O'Connor, 714 So.2d 1178.

Fla.App. 2 Dist. 1976. Where predominant nature of transaction wherein materialman contracted to furnish, fabricate and deliver certain steel piping systems for construction project was furnishing of a product rather than services, fabricated pipe could properly be characterized as "goods" within meaning of Uniform Commercial Code provisions pertaining to sales and to rejection of goods by buyer. West's F.S.A. §§ 672.105, 672.606(1)(b).

U.S. Fidelity & Guaranty Co. v. North Am. Steel Corp., 335 So.2d 18.

⚷532(6). **Plants, crops, and agriculture.**

Fla.App. 1 Dist. 1986. Timber may now be classified as "goods" under Uniform Commercial Code. West's F.S.A. §§ 672.107(2), 679.105(1)(h).

Konas v. Coastal Lumber Co., 496 So.2d 868, review denied 506 So.2d 1040.

⚷532(7). **Animals and livestock.**

For other cases see earlier editions of this digest, the Decennial Digests, and WESTLAW.

⚷532(8). **Machinery and equipment.**

C.A.11 (Fla.) 1998. Equipment or materials that were movable, but were installed and became immobile fixtures as part of the contract, are still "movable" within the Uniform Commercial Code's (UCC) meaning, for purposes of determining whether "hybrid" contract involving both goods and services is contract for goods. West's F.S.A. § 672.105(1).

BMC Industries, Inc. v. Barth Industries, Inc., 160 F.3d 1322, certiorari denied 119 S.Ct. 1807, 526 U.S. 1132, 143 L.Ed.2d 1010.

Contract for design, manufacture, and installation of equipment to automate eyeglass lense manufacturer's production line was predominantly a "transaction in goods" covered by Uniform Commercial Code (UCC), where contract was titled "PURCHASE ORDER," contract referred to parties as "Buyer" and "Seller," automated equipment to be purchased was "movable" at time it was identified to contract, and contract's payment schedule called for delivery and acceptance of each equipment line to be met with payment. West's F.S.A. § 672.105(1).

BMC Industries, Inc. v. Barth Industries, Inc., 160 F.3d 1322, certiorari denied 119 S.Ct. 1807, 526 U.S. 1132, 143 L.Ed.2d 1010.

Bkrtcy.M.D.Fla. 1999. Contract between owner of convenience store and contractor for removal of old gasoline tanks from store, installation of new tanks, and construction of self service islands and canopy was in nature of contract for performance of services, which was governed by Florida common law, and not for sale of goods, though materials and equipment allegedly made up more than half of contract price.

In re Sunshine-Jr. Stores, Inc., 240 B.R. 788.

Fla.App. 3 Dist. 1985. Local distributor, as seller of engines and distributor of industrial engines was both "seller" and "merchant," within West's F.S.A. §§ 672.103(1)(d), 672.104(1) setting forth definitions for sales article of state's version of uniform commercial code.

R.A. Jones & Sons, Inc. v. Holman, 470 So.2d 60, review dismissed Ford Motor Co. v. R.A. Jones & Sons, Inc., 482 So.2d 348.

⚷532(9)–532(10). *For other cases see earlier editions of this digest, the Decennial Digests, and WESTLAW.*

⚷532(11). Food and beverages.

Fla. 1937. A bill of sale of fruit crop in part payment of an existing obligation without present consideration, executed by vendor after final foreclosure of mortgage on the real estate had been entered against the vendor, and after vendor had surrendered possession of the entire property to foreclosure plaintiff, was not effective to convey the fruit crop to vendee.

  E. C. Fitz & Co. v. Eldridge, 176 So. 539, 129 Fla. 647.

⚷532(12). Motor vehicles.

For other cases see earlier editions of this digest, the Decennial Digests, and WESTLAW.

⚷532(13). Mobile homes or structures.

Bkrtcy.M.D.Fla. 1995. Proposal and agreement of sale between buyer and seller was contract for sale of goods, within meaning of Florida's Uniform Commercial Code (UCC), where seller agreed to sell and buyer agreed to buy mobile office unit for price and on terms set forth, which included $8,768.89 in cash on delivery. West's F.S.A. §§ 672.105(1), 672.106.

  In re Edgerton, 186 B.R. 143.

⚷532(14). Aircraft and aviation.

For other cases see earlier editions of this digest, the Decennial Digests, and WESTLAW.

⚷532(15). Vessels and shipping.

† C.A.11 (Fla.) 2016. New York's Uniform Commercial Code (UCC) did not apply to service contract between customer and marine repair service provider, which limited provider's liability to 20% of the purchase order that gave rise to the claim. N.Y.McKinney's Uniform Commercial Code § 2–101 et seq.

  Mount Sage, Ltd. v. Rolls-Royce Commercial Marine Inc., 635 Fed.Appx. 833, on remand 2016 WL 7507887.

⚷532(16). Tangible or intangible property.

For other cases see earlier editions of this digest, the Decennial Digests, and WESTLAW.

⚷532(17). Intellectual property.

† C.A.11 (Fla.) 2007. Sale of intellectual property was not a "transaction in goods" under California law, so as to be subject to the Uniform Commercial Code (UCC). West's Ann.Cal.Com.Code § 2102.

  Systems Unlimited, Inc. v. Cisco Systems, Inc., 228 Fed.Appx. 854, certiorari denied 128 S.Ct. 209, 552 U.S. 943, 169 L.Ed.2d 247.

⚷532(18)–532(21). *For other cases see earlier editions of this digest, the Decennial Digests, and WESTLAW.*

⚷532(22). Health care.

Fla.App. 2 Dist. 1968. Transfer of blood by a hospital to a patient is not a "sale" but a service and there was no implied warranty of fitness or merchantability.

  White v. Sarasota County Public Hospital Bd., 206 So.2d 19, certiorari denied 211 So.2d 215.

Fla.App. 2 Dist. 1966. Even though a hospital supplying whole blood to a patient may be merely performing a service incident to the overall medical attention being furnished, such a "service" characterization is not extended to a blood bank which originally collects and distributes the commodity.

  Russell v. Community Blood Bank, Inc., 185 So.2d 749, reversed 196 So.2d 115.

  Supplying of blood by blood bank to a patient for a consideration is a sale, and law of implied warranties applies to transaction.

  Russell v. Community Blood Bank, Inc., 185 So.2d 749, reversed 196 So.2d 115.

Fla.App. 3 Dist. 1967. Transfer of blood by hospital to a patient is generally considered a "service" as opposed to a "sale," and allegation of a breach of an implied warranty in such transferring of blood does not state a cause of action against the hospital.

Hoder v. Sayet, 196 So.2d 205.

A blood bank which supplies blood to a patient for a consideration makes a "sale" so that there may be a cause of action stated against a breach of an implied warranty.

Hoder v. Sayet, 196 So.2d 205.

Complaint seeking recovery for death of blood donee from homologous serum hepatitis allegedly contracted from blood received by transfusion on ground of breach of implied warranty that blood was fit for human use did not state cause of action against hospital which administered the transfusion using blood obtained from commercial blood bank.

Hoder v. Sayet, 196 So.2d 205.

⊶532(23). **Power and electricity.**

For other cases see earlier editions of this digest, the Decennial Digests, and WESTLAW.

⊶532(24). **Telecommunications.**

C.A.11 (Fla.) 1998. Contract for construction of cable television system was contract for services, and not contract for sale of goods subject to Florida Uniform Commercial Code's (UCC) duty of good faith. West's F.S.A. § 671.203.

Johnson Enterprises of Jacksonville, Inc. v. FPL Group, Inc., 162 F.3d 1290.

⊶532(25)–536. *For other cases see earlier editions of this digest, the Decennial Digests, and WESTLAW.*

II. PARTIES TO TRANSACTION OR CONTRACT.

⊶601. **In general.**

For other cases see earlier editions of this digest, the Decennial Digests, and WESTLAW.

⊶602. **Buyer.**

Bkrtcy.S.D.Fla. 1980. Where invoice and written security agreement provided that seller sold and delivered restaurant equipment jointly to debtor and debtor's

tenant, seller could not be heard to contend otherwise.

Matter of Outrigger Club, Inc., 6 B.R. 78.

Fla.App. 3 Dist. 1959. Ordinarily where two persons promise to make payment for goods ordered and delivered, contract is joint obligation, unless wording requires contrary construction.

Edward Corp. of Miami v. David M. Woolin & Son, Inc., 113 So.2d 252.

⊶603–605. *For other cases see earlier editions of this digest, the Decennial Digests, and WESTLAW.*

⊶606. **Capacity and right to buy or sell.**

Bkrtcy.M.D.Fla. 1983. There was no evidence that son of debtor's president, who accepted check in payment for materials furnished to general contractor and filed lien waiver, was authorized to sign lien waiver or waiver intended to waive all lien rights including those which might have been based on material previously furnished to defaulting general contractor, and therefore, because there was an understanding of parties that unless general contractor agreed to pay all outstanding bills incurred in connection with furnishing material to subject president, they would not have agreed to furnish additional material to general contractor in order to enable it to complete project; therefore, general contractor impliedly assumed obligation to pay for bills including bills incurred by defaulting general contractor.

Matter of American Pre-Cast Corp., 30 B.R. 316.

Fla.App. 2 Dist. 1977. Where prospective seller's president did not participate in sale of airplane to buyer nor did he sign sales contract in any capacity, and no allegations were made nor was it shown at trial that seller was formed or used for fraudulent purposes or was alter ego of president, president could not be held personally liable for breach of contract.

Charter Air Center, Inc. v. Miller, 348 So.2d 614, certiorari denied 354 So.2d 983.

† This Case was not selected for publication in the National Reporter System
For legislative history of cited statutes, see Florida Statutes Annotated

⚷607. Participation in and relation to transaction.

C.A.11 (Fla.) 1985. Water ski school, whose day-to-day operator purchased the materials and made tow handle and rope which student was using when he was injured, was not the manufacturer or assembler of the allegedly defective tow handle and rope under Florida law.

Hurley v. Larry's Water Ski School, 762 F.2d 925.

S.D.Fla. 2016. There was no evidence that a direct oral contract existed between commercial airline and distributor of commercial paint products under Florida law, thus precluding airline's breach of contract claims against distributor after repainted aircraft sustained accelerated filiform corrosion, even though distributor made representations to commercial airline about the quality and performance of its paint products and provided a technical service representative at the facility that painted airline's aircraft, upon request and free of charge, where distributor never agreed or contracted to provide anything to airline, no consideration was provided, and no officer of airline who had the authority to enter into a contract was at any meeting with distributor.

Hawaiian Airlines, Inc. v. AAR Aircraft Services, Inc., 167 F.Supp.3d 1311, appeal dismissed (11th cir. 16-11536).

Fla.App. 2 Dist. 1991. Individual buyer of ophthalmology practice could be held liable for installment payments in sale agreement, but that debt could not be accelerated pursuant to note, where buyer signed sale agreement in corporate and individual capacities, but signed note only in corporate capacity as president of professional association buyer.

J. McHenry Nielsen, M.D., P.A. v. Stephen N. Schindler, M.D., P.A., 587 So.2d 498.

⚷608. Privity in general.

N.D.Fla. 1995. Plaintiff who purchases product but does not buy it directly from defendant is not in privity with that defendant for purposes of Article 2 of the Uniform Commercial Code.

T.W.M. v. American Medical Systems, Inc., 886 F.Supp. 842.

Fla. 1967. Action may be brought against manufacturer by ultimate purchaser notwithstanding want of privity.

Manheim v. Ford Motor Co., 201 So.2d 440, opinion conformed to 201 So.2d 909.

Fla. 1953. General rule that ultimate purchaser may not sue wholesaler is not absolute.

Hoskins v. Jackson Grain Co., 63 So.2d 514.

Fla.App. 3 Dist. 1966. Although plaintiff manufacturer of outboard powered watercraft was not in direct privity of contract with defendant who supplied substance used to fill skis sold to plaintiff by another, plaintiff was entitled to sue defendant when substance used to fill skis allegedly expanded on exposure to warm sunlight causing pontoon to burst apart with result that customers returned the watercraft.

Power Ski of Florida, Inc. v. Allied Chemical Corp., 188 So.2d 13.

Fla.App. 3 Dist. 1958. The general rule that an ultimate purchaser may not sue the wholesaler is not absolute.

Continental Copper & Steel Industries, Inc. v. E. C. 'Red' Cornelius, Inc., 104 So.2d 40.

III. NATURE AND FORMATION OF CONTRACT.

⚷701–703. *For other cases see earlier editions of this digest, the Decennial Digests, and WESTLAW.*

⚷703. Certainty and definiteness.

⚷704. —— In general.

M.D.Fla. 2002. Where a sales contract contains several open terms, the contract does not necessarily fail for indefiniteness, because such open terms may be supplemented by the UCC's "gap-filler" provisions.

Lockheed Martin Corp. v. Galaxis USA, Ltd., 222 F.Supp.2d 1315, affirmed 88 Fed.Appx. 389.

⚷705. —— As to subject matter.

C.A.5 (Fla.) 1977. In action by plaintiff, the purchaser, against defendant, the seller, for failure to complete alleged oral contract for the sale of ammonia, fact that date of effectiveness of contract was unclear or that certain contract details had remained unresolved did not require a directed verdict as long as sufficient evidence existed of the agreement and of the basis for granting a remedy. West's F.S.A. §§ 672.204, 672.204(1–3).

> Transammonia Export Corp. v. Conserv, Inc., 554 F.2d 719.

M.D.Fla. 2007. Contract for sale of aircraft was sufficiently definite to be enforceable under Florida law, where contract described subject of sale as "Diamond Single Engine Jet Aircraft (D–JET), aircraft was to include IFR avionics, including Auto pilot / HSI," "[g]lass cockpit," and "premium interior," contract stated that seller would seek Federal Aviation Administration (FAA) IFR-certification and JAA certification, and remaining gaps could be filled in through exercise of good faith and commercial reasonableness under Uniform Commercial Code (UCC). West's F.S.A. § 672.204(3).

> Horowitch v. Diamond Aircraft Industries, Inc., 526 F.Supp.2d 1236, certificate of appealability granted by 2007 WL 2904135, vacated, appeal dismissed 299 Fed.Appx. 951, on remand 2009 WL 1537896, order vacated in part on reconsideration 2009 WL 1537896.

Fla.App. 2 Dist. 1972. "Bird dogging" agreement to sell at fixed price for future delivery specific quantity of oranges which seller did not own was not void under statute relating to identification of specific goods before interest in goods passes. F.S.A. § 851.01.

> Quality Fruit Buyers, Inc. v. Killarney Fruit Co., 269 So.2d 424.

☞706. —— **As to quantity; requirements contracts.**

C.A.5 (Fla.) 1977. Where the quantity term in sales contract is clearly established, a binding contract may be found to exist despite the absence of precise price terms.

> Transammonia Export Corp. v. Conserv, Inc., 554 F.2d 719.

Fla.App. 2 Dist. 1972. Statute relating to identification of specific goods before an interest in the goods passes does

not forbid the sale of fungible goods without specific identification. F.S.A. § 672.105(2).

> Quality Fruit Buyers, Inc. v. Killarney Fruit Co., 269 So.2d 424.

Fla.App. 5 Dist. 2005. Motorcycle dealer satisfied its contractual obligations with motorcycle manufacturer by purchasing three motorcycles, given that dealer never agreed to purchase a specific number of motorcycles beyond the two required in the contract and there was no meeting of the minds on purchasing a set number beyond the first two motorcycles.

> Beach Street Bikes, Inc. v. Bourgett's Bike Works, Inc., 900 So.2d 697.

☞707. —— **As to price.**

Fla.App. 3 Dist. 1986. Agreement for sale was not valid contract where it did not state purchase price, and parties did not provide objective method of determining price.

> Bee Line Air Transport, Inc. v. Dodd, 496 So.2d 874, review denied 506 So.2d 1040.

☞708–709. *For other cases see earlier editions of this digest, the Decennial Digests, and WESTLAW.*

☞709. Intent of parties; assent.

☞710. —— **In general.**

M.D.Fla. 2009. Under Florida law, actions of parties following their creation of letter of intent (LOI) for contemplated asset purchase did not transform LOI into enforceable contract despite parties' unambiguous expression of their intent, in LOI, not to be bound in the absence of formal written agreement where sellers partially performed under LOI by terminating their lease rights for quarry, thereby facilitating negotiation of lease in buyers' names, buyers accepted sellers' performance by executing lease for quarry, buyers repeatedly promised to go forward with purchase transaction once one seller's criminal proceedings were resolved, buyers represented to owners of other quarries that sellers had agreed to sell their assets to them, buyers prepared agreements and instruments contemplated by LOI, and LOI barred one seller from negotiating assets sale with third parties.

White Const. Co., Inc. v. Martin Marietta Materials, Inc., 633 F.Supp.2d 1302.

⚷711. —— Meeting of the minds.

S.D.Fla. 2016. There was no evidence that a direct oral contract existed between commercial airline and distributor of commercial paint products under Florida law, thus precluding airline's breach of contract claims against distributor after repainted aircraft sustained accelerated filiform corrosion, even though distributor made representations to commercial airline about the quality and performance of its paint products and provided a technical service representative at the facility that painted airline's aircraft, upon request and free of charge, where distributor never agreed or contracted to provide anything to airline, no consideration was provided, and no officer of airline who had the authority to enter into a contract was at any meeting with distributor.

Hawaiian Airlines, Inc. v. AAR Aircraft Services, Inc., 167 F.Supp.3d 1311, appeal dismissed (11th cir. 16-11536).

Fla.App. 1 Dist. 1971. Where machine was delivered by seller to prospective buyer for demonstration purposes only, where neither buyer nor seller considered it to be a sale at that time and where prospective buyer attempted to have machine returned to seller for eight months after it had become stuck on prospective buyer's property, there was never a meeting of minds necessary to constitute a valid contract of sale.

First Am. Farms, Inc. v. Marden Mfg. Co., 255 So.2d 536, certiorari denied 261 So.2d 845.

⚷712. Mutuality of obligation.

C.A.11 (Fla.) 1983. In contract under which plaintiff sold stock in his former businesses to defendant corporation in exchange for stock in, and employment with, defendant, provision that, inter alia, defendant agreed to provide additional working capital for expansion of plaintiff's former business was not unenforceable under New York law as illusory or vague and indefinite, notwithstanding that defendant's obligation under that provision was subject to condition that it be done with and subject to normal operating financial policies of defendant, because defendant was still obligated to exercise good faith, and notwithstanding that parties did not state a precise amount of working capital to be provided.

Gregg v. U.S. Industries, Inc., 715 F.2d 1522, decision clarified on rehearing 721 F.2d 345, certiorari denied 104 S.Ct. 2173, 466 U.S. 960, 80 L.Ed.2d 556, appeal after remand 887 F.2d 1462, certiorari denied 104 S.Ct. 2173, 466 U.S. 960, 80 L.Ed.2d 556.

M.D.Fla. 2006. When there is nothing in a writing which requires a party to take, or limits its demand to, any ascertainable quantity, a contract is not enforceable for lack of consideration and mutuality under California law; such a contract is referred to as an "indefinite quantities contract."

In re Anchor Glass Container Corp., 345 B.R. 765.

S.D.Fla. 1975. Under the Uniform Commercial Code, requirements contracts are enforceable. West's F.S.A. § 672.306.

Eastern Air Lines, Inc. v. Gulf Oil Corp., 415 F.Supp. 429.

Where airline and its fuel supplier had consistently over the years relied upon each other to act in good faith in the purchase and sale of required quantities of aviation fuel, where various estimates had been exchanged from time to time during the course of the contract, and where discussion of estimated requirements had been on a monthly or more frequent basis since advent of petroleum allocation programs, contract which called for oil company to supply the airline with its requirements for aviation fuel was enforceable. West's F.S.A. § 672.306.

Eastern Air Lines, Inc. v. Gulf Oil Corp., 415 F.Supp. 429.

Fla.App. 1 Dist. 1998. Where a contract is for a specified time and obligates the purchaser to buy all that he or she needs from the vendor, purchaser's obligation to buy to the extent of his or her requirements supplies mutuality; it is immaterial to the issue of mutuality of obligation that the right to buy is at the purchaser's option or discretion. West's F.S.A. § 672.306(2).

Pullam v. Hercules Inc., 711 So.2d 72, rehearing denied, review denied 728 So.2d 202.

Fla.App. 3 Dist. 1985. Damages of prospective purchasers of time-share condominiums should not be limited to damages stipulated in contract which were return of purchaser's deposit, as that damage provision rendered vendor's obligation wholly illusory and would permit him to breach contract for conveyance of condominiums with impunity.

Port Largo Club, Inc. v. Warren, 476 So.2d 1330.

Fla.App. 4 Dist. 1987. Absence of mutuality of remedies did not destroy validity of contract for sale of assets of corporation; thus, after seller sought declaratory relief due to buyer's accusation that seller misrepresented financial condition of business, buyer was entitled to arbitration pursuant to contract terms.

LaBonte Precision, Inc. v. LPI Industries Corp., 507 So.2d 1202.

☞713–715. *For other cases see earlier editions of this digest, the Decennial Digests, and WESTLAW.*

☞713. **Finality and completeness.**

☞716. —— **Negotiations and preliminary agreements.**

M.D.Fla. 2009. Mining facilities operators and mining company did not intend to be bound by letter of intent (LOI) for company's contemplated purchase of operators' assets, and therefore LOI was not enforceable agreement under Florida law; LOI merely set forth agreement to agree in the future pending outcome of various negotiations, due diligence investigations, and other conditions precedent, LOI allowed for either party to terminate it via written notice, and LOI expressly disavowed any intent of parties to be bound or to create legal obligation to conclude transaction under any terms or conditions short of execution of legally binding agreement.

White Const. Co., Inc. v. Martin Marietta Materials, Inc., 633 F.Supp.2d 1302.

☞717–720. *For other cases see earlier editions of this digest, the Decennial Digests, and WESTLAW.*

☞718. **Offer and acceptance.**

☞720. —— **Offer to sell.**

☞720(1). **In general.**

M.D.Fla. 2005. Seller of radios did not make contractually binding commitment, under Florida law, to provide buyer with "trunking" receivers, capable of searching for available frequencies, when it wrote letter to buyer saying that feature would not be available until following year, without stating price or availability terms.

Business Radio, Inc. v. Relm Wireless Corp., 373 F.Supp.2d 1317, affirmed 209 Fed.Appx. 899.

Fla.App. 3 Dist. 1982. Document specifically conditioning contractual effectiveness of proposal by projected seller upon seller's own subsequent approval constitutes no more than solicitation to prospective buyer to make an offer.

Meekins-Bamman Prestress, Inc. v. Better Const., Inc., 408 So.2d 1071.

☞720(2)–721(1). *For other cases see earlier editions of this digest, the Decennial Digests, and WESTLAW.*

☞721. —— **Offer to buy.**

☞721(2). **Orders for goods.**

M.D.Fla. 2005. There was no contract, under Florida law, requiring seller to providing radios with "trunking feature," allowing for searches for available frequencies, created through buyer's issuance of purchase order, which covered only standard radios not having feature, and which made no reference to seller's letter predicting availability of feature in following year.

Business Radio, Inc. v. Relm Wireless Corp., 373 F.Supp.2d 1317, affirmed 209 Fed.Appx. 899.

☞721(3). **Acceptance of offer to buy.**

Fla. 1972. To constitute valid acceptance of buyer's offer, it was necessary that sellers do more than indicate their acceptance by signing deposit receipt; they were required to set in motion some means by which knowledge of that acceptance would come to buyer before any enforceable contract could arise.

Kendel v. Pontious, 261 So.2d 167.

Fla.App. 3 Dist. 1984. Communication required in order to effect acceptance of offer to buy is not satisfied where document which constitutes sole means of acceptance is still in hands of sellers' agent after time for acceptance has expired.

Weiner v. Tenenbaum, 452 So.2d 986, petition for review dismissed 458 So.2d 274.

Fla.App. 3 Dist. 1982. Location of words indicating approval by corporate seller directly under line on which seller's representative signed document did not imply that he had given the required approval, where from language of proposal it was obvious that representative's name and signature appeared only in his capacity as employee and that document later must be approved by officer of seller to be binding.

Meekins-Bamman Prestress, Inc. v. Better Const., Inc., 408 So.2d 1071.

☞722–723(2). *For other cases see earlier editions of this digest, the Decennial Digests, and WESTLAW.*

☞723. —— **Withdrawal or revocation of offer.**

☞723(3). Offer to buy.

Fla. 1972. Where offer to purchase was transmitted to sellers by mail and was silent as to method of acceptance and buyer's letter revoking offer to purchase was postmarked prior to posting of notice of execution of contract, letter of revocation was effective, notwithstanding that sellers had signed contract prior to posting of letter of revocation.

Kendel v. Pontious, 261 So.2d 167.

Fla.App. 3 Dist. 1971. Where offer to purchase was transmitted to seller by mail and offer was silent as to method of acceptance and purchaser's letter revoking offer to purchase was postmarked prior to posting of notice of execution of contract, letter of revocation was effective, notwithstanding that sellers had signed contract prior to posting of letter of revocation.

Kendel v. Pontious, 244 So.2d 543, writ discharged 261 So.2d 167.

☞724–725. *For other cases see earlier editions of this digest, the Decennial Digests, and WESTLAW.*

☞725. —— **Variance from offer; additional terms in acceptance or confirmation.**

☞725(1). In general.

S.D.Fla. 2008. Under Georgia law, contract is materially altered by terms accompanying merchant's acceptance of offer, and thus constitutes counteroffer, rather than valid acceptance, when additional terms result in surprise or hardship if incorporated without express awareness by other party. West's Ga.Code Ann. § 11–2–207.

Pycsa Panama, S.A. v. Tensar Earth Technologies, Inc., 625 F.Supp.2d 1198, affirmed 329 Fed.Appx. 257.

S.D.Fla. 2001. When the parties' conduct establishes a contract, but the parties have failed to adopt expressly a particular writing as their agreement, and writings exchanged by the parties do not agree, the contract provision of the Uniform Commercial Code determines the terms of the contract. U.C.C. § 2–207.

Premix-Marbletite Mfg. Corp. v. SKW Chemicals, Inc., 145 F.Supp.2d 1348.

Fla.App. 2 Dist. 2007. "Battle of the forms" provision of Uniform Commercial Code (UCC) allows the formation of a contract where an acceptance contains additional or different terms than the original offer; while such an acceptance ordinarily would not meet the strict requirements of the common law mirror image rule, the UCC provides a more flexible approach. West's F.S.A. § 672.207(1, 2).

Paul Gottlieb & Co., Inc. v. Alps South Corp., 985 So.2d 1, rehearing denied.

Additional terms included in an acceptance are construed as proposals for addition to the contract, and, between merchants, the terms become part of the contract unless they fall into an exception. West's F.S.A. § 672.207(2).

Paul Gottlieb & Co., Inc. v. Alps South Corp., 985 So.2d 1, rehearing denied.

Fla.App. 3 Dist. 2001. Uniform Commercial Code (UCC) section governing additional terms in an acceptance or confirmation for the sale of goods permits an acceptance to be operative as an acceptance even though it introduces additional or different terms. West's F.S.A. § 672.207.

> General Tool Industries, Inc. v. Premier Machinery, Inc., 790 So.2d 449, rehearing en banc denied, review denied 805 So.2d 806.

☞725(2). **Offer to sell.**

Fla.App. 4 Dist. 1992. Denial of warranty in seller's offer and requirement of express warranty in buyer's acceptance cancelled each other out, and implied warranties of merchantability and fitness were read into the contract to supply the missing terms, allowing the buyer to recover both incidental and consequential damages. West's F.S.A. §§ 672.104(1), 672.314, 672.315, 672.715.

> Eastern Cement v. Halliburton Co., 600 So.2d 469, review denied 613 So.2d 4, appeal after remand 672 So.2d 844, modified on clarification, review denied 683 So.2d 483.

☞725(3). **Offer to buy.**

S.D.Fla. 2008. Under Georgia law, contract is materially altered by terms accompanying merchant's acceptance of offer, and thus constitutes counteroffer, rather than valid acceptance, when additional terms result in surprise or hardship if incorporated without express awareness by other party. West's Ga.Code Ann. § 11–2–207.

> Pycsa Panama, S.A. v. Tensar Earth Technologies, Inc., 625 F.Supp.2d 1198, affirmed 329 Fed.Appx. 257.

Under Georgia law, additional terms become part of agreement where buyer repeatedly receives seller's conditions of sale, and consistently fails to object. West's Ga.Code Ann. § 11–2–207.

> Pycsa Panama, S.A. v. Tensar Earth Technologies, Inc., 625 F.Supp.2d 1198, affirmed 329 Fed.Appx. 257.

Under Georgia law, conditions of sale printed on back of seller's invoices, which limited seller's liability for damages to third parties, excluded consequential or incidental damages, and limited buyer's remedies to repayment of purchase price or, at seller's option, replacement of nonconforming goods, applied to sale of its product to buyer, where purchase orders did not limit acceptance to terms of offer, and buyer received fourteen invoices containing conditions of sale, but never objected to additional terms. West's Ga. Code Ann. § 11–2–207.

> Pycsa Panama, S.A. v. Tensar Earth Technologies, Inc., 625 F.Supp.2d 1198, affirmed 329 Fed.Appx. 257.

S.D.Fla. 2001. Disclaimer of warranties, and limitation of liability provisions contained in invoice sent by seller to buyer following sale of chemical was not part of contract for sale under Florida's version of Uniform Commercial Code, and thus provisions did not apply in buyer's action against seller alleging that chemical was defective; those provisions were contained only in seller's invoices, and not in buyer's documents. U.C.C. § 2–207; West's F.S.A. § 672.207(3).

> Premix-Marbletite Mfg. Corp. v. SKW Chemicals, Inc., 145 F.Supp.2d 1348.

Fla.App. 2 Dist. 2007. Limitation of consequential damages clause on back of seller's finished goods form, as an additional contractual term, was not material alteration of contract, within meaning of material alteration exception of "battle of the forms" provision of Uniform Commercial Code (UCC), and, as such, clause was enforceable against buyer with respect to buyer's counterclaim for breach of warranty; clause was not an unreasonable surprise to buyer, in that contract was the sixth in a series between parties and each contract included limitation of liability clause, and, because buyer failed to inform seller of the larger consequences of breach, seller could not foresee greater extent of its potential liability, such that incorporation of clause in contract would not result in severe economic hardship to buyer. West's F.S.A. § 672.207(2).

> Paul Gottlieb & Co., Inc. v. Alps South Corp., 985 So.2d 1, rehearing denied.

Fla.App. 2 Dist. 1995. Term in seller's invoices stating that buyer was responsible for all sales taxes was material alteration of buyer's offer to purchase roofing materials, and therefore unenforceable under Uniform Commercial Code (UCC) despite buyer's failure to reject invoices, where buyer presented testimony that it understood price that seller quoted for goods to be all inclusive, and seller failed to present any evidence that buyer consented explicitly or implicitly, through course of dealings, to pay sales tax on goods from seller. West's F.S.A. § 627.207(2)(b).

> Advanced Mobilehome Systems of Tampa, Inc. v. Alumax Fabricated Products, Inc., 666 So.2d 166.

Term of invoices stating that buyer would be responsible for all sales taxes for roofing material it purchased from seller was additional term in acceptance or confirmation, which would become part of contract under Uniform Commercial Code (UCC) unless offer expressly limited acceptance to terms of offer, term materially altered offer, or notification of objection was already given or given within reasonable time, in light of buyer's and seller's failure to specifically discuss issue of who would pay sales tax. West's F.S.A. § 672.207(2).

> Advanced Mobilehome Systems of Tampa, Inc. v. Alumax Fabricated Products, Inc., 666 So.2d 166.

Fla.App. 3 Dist. 2001. Proposals made by manufacturer and installer of milling machine and lathe and purchase orders submitted by buyer formed part of contract between parties, and thus limitation of remedies provisions contained in proposals were applicable, even though purchase orders contained terms that were additional to or different from those contained in proposals, where those terms did not address limitation of remedies provisions, proposals did not expressly limit acceptance to terms of proposals, additional terms did no materially alter proposals, and manufacturer and installer did not object to additional terms. West's F.S.A. § 672.207.

> General Tool Industries, Inc. v. Premier Machinery, Inc., 790 So.2d 449, rehearing en banc denied, review denied 805 So.2d 806.

Uniform Commercial Code (UCC) section governing additional terms in an acceptance or confirmation for the sale of goods permits an acceptance to be operative as an acceptance even though it introduces additional or different terms. West's F.S.A. § 672.207.

> General Tool Industries, Inc. v. Premier Machinery, Inc., 790 So.2d 449, rehearing en banc denied, review denied 805 So.2d 806.

Fla.App. 4 Dist. 2000. Buyer's failure to object to venue provision in seller's invoice in prior sales transactions was not implied acquiescence to provision, as buyer's continued use of same purchase order, which was silent as to venue, and thus proposed to rely on venue fixed by statute, evinced renewed unwillingness to be bound by any previous unilateral writings routinely sent by seller with its shipment of goods, and thus sellers's venue provision was not enforceable. West's F.S.A. § 672.207(2).

> Dependable Component Supply, Inc. v. Pace Electronics Inc., 772 So.2d 582.

⚷**725(4). Qualified or conditional acceptance.**

N.D.Fla. 2001. Seller did not accept in writing buyer's purchase orders so as to form contract, but rather made counteroffer, by including with shipment invoices stating that its acceptance of orders was "subject to and expressly conditioned" on buyer's assent to liability-limiting terms printed on reverse of invoices, even though invoices also provided that "buyer shall be deemed to have assented to the provisions hereof in all respects by its acceptance of any goods"; buyer's express acceptance of counteroffer would be required. N.Y.McKinney's Uniform Commercial Code § 2–207(1).

> Coastal & Native Plant Specialties, Inc. v. Engineered Textile Products, Inc., 139 F.Supp.2d 1326.

Fla.App. 3 Dist. 1982. Document which specifically conditioned contractual effectiveness of proposal to sell product upon seller's own subsequent approval was not, in the words of the document, "approved" by the seller when its sales representative signed it, and no binding agreement was formed, even though prospective buyer also signed.

> Meekins-Bamman Prestress, Inc. v. Better Const., Inc., 408 So.2d 1071.

⚖️**726. —— Rejection of offer.**

For other cases see earlier editions of this digest, the Decennial Digests, and WESTLAW.

⚖️**727. —— "Shrinkwrap" agreements.**

See also COPYRIGHTS AND INTELLECTUAL PROPERTY ⚖️107.

⚖️**728. Consideration.**

⚖️**729. —— In general.**

† **C.A.11 (Fla.) 2008.** Agreement to sell goods at cost was supported by consideration.

    Gedimex, S.A. v. Nidera, Inc., 290 Fed.Appx. 311.

M.D.Fla. 2006. Under California law, a promise to buy all that the promisor requires or needs in its business from the promisee constitutes a valid consideration for the promise to furnish the goods or merchandise which the promisor may need.

    In re Anchor Glass Container Corp., 345 B.R. 765.

Fla.App. 1 Dist. 2015. Homeowner's forbearance from hiring lawyer or suing window manufacturer was adequate consideration for parties' oral agreement that, in exchange for that forbearance, manufacturer would replace all defective windows in home and issue a new ten-year warranty; homeowner refrained from enforcing legal right by not suing under initial warranty, it was at manufacturer's insistence that homeowner not engage legal counsel or sue, despite upcoming end to initial warranty, and, thus, forbearance was fundamental basis of agreement, and forbearance was not limitless or without boundary, as it was limited by cutoff date of initial warranty.

    Loper v. Weather Shield Mfg., Inc., 203 So.3d 898.

Fla.App. 4 Dist. 2003. Benefit distributor purportedly received from wholesaler's ongoing marketing of office chairs was not consideration for wholesaler's contract with distributor to supply chairs.

    Office Pavilion South Florida, Inc. v. ASAL Products, Inc., 849 So.2d 367, rehearing denied, review denied 861 So.2d 428.

⚖️**730. —— Want or failure of consideration.**

C.A.11 (Fla.) 1983. Under Florida law, want of consideration means total lack of any valid consideration for contract; substantial impairment to buyer of goods by reason of defects therein is not sufficient to raise defense of failure of consideration. West's F.S.A. § 673.408.

    Royal Typewriter Co., a Div. of Litton Business Systems, Inc. v. Xerographic Supplies Corp., 719 F.2d 1092.

S.D.Fla. 2016. There was no evidence that a direct oral contract existed between commercial airline and distributor of commercial paint products under Florida law, thus precluding airline's breach of contract claims against distributor after repainted aircraft sustained accelerated filiform corrosion, even though distributor made representations to commercial airline about the quality and performance of its paint products and provided a technical service representative at the facility that painted airline's aircraft, upon request and free of charge, where distributor never agreed or contracted to provide anything to airline, no consideration was provided, and no officer of airline who had the authority to enter into a contract was at any meeting with distributor.

    Hawaiian Airlines, Inc. v. AAR Aircraft Services, Inc., 167 F.Supp.3d 1311, appeal dismissed (11th cir. 16-11536).

Fla.App. 3 Dist. 1970. Even though buyer failed to avail itself of opportunity to determine condition of aircraft, including its equipment, prior to buying it, it was reasonable to assume that aircraft would contain customary and necessary equipment, and, to extent that such were missing, there was partial failure of consideration, but, since items were replaceable, their absence was not basis for rescission and was compensable in money damages.

    Pinellas Central Bank & Trust Co. v. International Aerodyne, Inc., 233 So.2d 872, certiorari denied 239 So.2d 829.

⚖️**731. Options.**

⚖️**732. —— In general.**

Fla.App. 2 Dist. 1961. Unless a statute or option contract itself requires a written acceptance or exercise, option may be exercised or accepted orally.

Rank v. Sullivan, 132 So.2d 32.

🔑733. —— Options to buy.

Bkrtcy.S.D.Fla. 1983. In determining whether consideration paid for the exercise of a prepaid option to purchase is nominal, court should examine the relationship of the option price to the original purchase price or the list price and if the option price is less than 25 percent of the original purchase price or the list price then the consideration is regarded as nominal.

In re AAA Mach. Co., Inc., 30 B.R. 323.

Fla. 1948. An "option" is a continuing offer by optionor to sell and, if limited to a certain time, must be accepted within that time, so that it is an executory unilateral contract and not an executed one, until converted into an executed contract by compliance with its terms.

Baker v. Coleman, 34 So.2d 538, 160 Fla. 297.

Options to purchase are strictly construed and can be satisfied only by positive and unequivocal declaration to accept.

Baker v. Coleman, 34 So.2d 538, 160 Fla. 297.

Fla.App. 2 Dist. 1961. Whether payment of purchase money is required as condition precedent to exercise of an option is a matter of intent of parties to be gleaned from the instrument.

Rank v. Sullivan, 132 So.2d 32.

🔑734. —— Options to sell.

For other cases see earlier editions of this digest, the Decennial Digests, and WESTLAW.

🔑735. —— Rights of first refusal.

Fla.App. 5 Dist. 1992. Holder of conditional right of first refusal to purchase certain new car dealerships and related assets was entitled to right of first refusal with regard to any contract offered by prospective purchaser sellers had entered into agreement with one month before right of first refusal was given that was not substantially in accordance with agree-

ment; term "third parties" as used in option included that purchaser.

Bryan v. Braun Cadillac, Inc., 599 So.2d 1050.

🔑736–740. *For other cases see earlier editions of this digest, the Decennial Digests, and WESTLAW.*

🔑736. **Manner and requisites of expression of agreement.**

🔑741. —— Invoices.

Fla.App. 1 Dist. 1971. Where there was no agreement for sale of machine prior to time seller sent prospective buyer an invoice following attempt over course of eight months to remove machine from prospective buyer's property, where it had gotten stuck after being sent for demonstration purposes, seller's unilateral act of sending invoice did not constitute contract of sale.

First Am. Farms, Inc. v. Marden Mfg. Co., 255 So.2d 536, certiorari denied 261 So.2d 845.

🔑742. —— Electronic media.

S.D.Fla. 2012. Florida statute providing that a "contract for sale of goods may be made in any manner sufficient to show agreement, including conduct by both parties which recognizes the existence of such a contract," includes "shrinkwrap contracts," in which an agreement becomes effective as soon as a customer opens the product. West's F.S.A. § 672.204(1).

TracFone Wireless, Inc. v. Pak China Group Co. Ltd., 843 F.Supp.2d 1284.

S.D.Fla. 2010. Florida statute providing that a contract for sale of goods may be made in any manner sufficient to show agreement, including conduct by both parties which recognizes the existence of such a contract, includes "shrinkwrap contracts," where an agreement becomes effective as soon as a customer opens the product. West's F.S.A. § 672.204(1).

TracFone Wireless, Inc. v. SND Cellular, Inc., 715 F.Supp.2d 1246.

⟳743–743(2). *For other cases see earlier editions of this digest, the Decennial Digests, and WESTLAW.*

⟳744. —— **Conduct of parties; implied agreements.**

N.D.Fla. 2001. Though buyer's purchase order and seller's counteroffer did not in themselves create contract, performance by both parties, including delivery of and payment for goods, constituted "conduct which recognize[d] the existence of a contract," and thus established contract under Uniform Commercial Code. N.Y.McKinney's Uniform Commercial Code § 2–207(3).

Coastal & Native Plant Specialties, Inc. v. Engineered Textile Products, Inc., 139 F.Supp.2d 1326.

Where purchase order contained no provision as to limitation of seller's liability or exclusion of warranties and seller's counteroffer contained such provisions, and contract arose only through parties' performance, liability-limiting and warranty provisions in counteroffer were not terms of such contract; parties had not agreed to terms, and they could not be considered "supplementary terms" incorporated under some other provision of Uniform Commercial Code. N.Y.McKinney's Uniform Commercial Code § 2–207(2, 3).

Coastal & Native Plant Specialties, Inc. v. Engineered Textile Products, Inc., 139 F.Supp.2d 1326.

Disputed additional terms in buyer's and seller's writings, which under Uniform Commercial Code (UCC) are excluded by virtue of parties' disagreement from contract subsequently formed through parties' conduct, cannot be brought back into such contract under guise of "supplementary terms"; "supplementary terms," under UCC provision governing performance-based contract, are limited to those supplied by standard "gap-filler" provisions of UCC, plus those relating to course of performance and usage of trade. N.Y.McKinney's Uniform Commercial Code §§ 1–205, 2–207(2, 3), 2–208, 2–301 et seq.

Coastal & Native Plant Specialties, Inc. v. Engineered Textile Products, Inc., 139 F.Supp.2d 1326.

S.D.Fla. 2001. When the parties' conduct establishes a contract, but the parties have failed to adopt expressly a particular writing as their agreement, and writings exchanged by the parties do not agree, the contract provision of the Uniform Commercial Code determines the terms of the contract. U.C.C. § 2–207.

Premix-Marbletite Mfg. Corp. v. SKW Chemicals, Inc., 145 F.Supp.2d 1348.

⟳745–746. *For other cases see earlier editions of this digest, the Decennial Digests, and WESTLAW.*

IV. VALIDITY AND ENFORCEABILITY OF CONTRACT.

⟳801–802. *For other cases see earlier editions of this digest, the Decennial Digests, and WESTLAW.*

⟳802. **Mistake.**

⟳803. —— **In general.**

Fla. 1957. Where defendant had abundant opportunity to ascertain precisely what type and size of awning he was to receive under a contract, for the sale and installation thereof, and knew or should have known what he was purchasing and causing to be installed, as a mature and experienced business man, he could not escape liability for purchase price on theory of mutual mistake as to specifications for awning installed.

Jaffe v. Endure-A-Life Time Awning Sales, Inc., 98 So.2d 77.

Where a mistake complained of by buyer results from want of that degree of care and diligence which would be exercised by persons of reasonable prudence under the same circumstances, equity will not relieve against it.

Jaffe v. Endure-A-Life Time Awning Sales, Inc., 98 So.2d 77.

Fla.App. 3 Dist. 1984. Purchasers of restaurant were entitled to rescission where parties to the sale labored under mutual mistake concerning availability and transferability of full-scale liquor license for the premises which was material, indeed vital, to the transaction.

Mar-Char Enterprises, Inc. v. Charlie's The Lakes Restaurant, Inc., 451 So.2d 930, petition for review denied 461 So.2d 113.

⚷804. ——— Signing in ignorance of contents.

C.A.11 (Fla.) 1998. Fact that written order form memorializing agreement between purchaser and foreign seller of ceramic tiles was entirely in Italian and that individual who signed contract on purchaser's behalf neither spoke nor read Italian did not preclude finding that purchaser was bound by terms of that agreement.

MCC-Marble Ceramic Center, Inc., v. Ceramica Nuova d'Agostino, S.p.A., 144 F.3d 1384, rehearing denied, certiorari denied 119 S.Ct. 1496, 526 U.S. 1087, 143 L.Ed.2d 650.

⚷805–807. *For other cases see earlier editions of this digest, the Decennial Digests, and WESTLAW.*

⚷805. Misrepresentation and fraud.

⚷807. ——— By seller.

⚷807(1). In general.

C.A.5 (Fla.) 1970. If seller makes statement as to what he proposes to do at time when he knows he cannot do so, there is a misrepresentation of a material fact to buyer.

Entron, Inc. v. General Cablevision of Palatka, 435 F.2d 995.

If seller represents to buyer what he proposes to do at time when he is either without knowledge as to his ability to perform or if he represents what he proposes to do under circumstances in which he should have known, but may not have known, of his inability to carry out his promise, there is a misrepresentation of material fact.

Entron, Inc. v. General Cablevision of Palatka, 435 F.2d 995.

S.D.Fla. 2001. Under Florida law, buyer established prima facie claim for rescission based upon coin dealer's alleged fraudulent conduct in procuring ten purchases of bullion coins at grossly inflated prices, so long as it was possible for par-

ties to be returned to their precontractual positions through claim.

Wilson v. De Angelis, 156 F.Supp.2d 1335.

Fla.App. 1 Dist. 1984. Vendor should not be allowed to profit from transaction induced by fraud and misrepresentation, and it is within discretion of trial court to formulate equitable remedies, including rescission of transaction and restoration of parties to their original positions.

Yost v. Rieve Enterprises, Inc., 461 So.2d 178, review denied 469 So.2d 750.

Trial court did not abuse its discretion in denying vendor damages caused by purchaser's breach of the contract which was later rescinded on the ground of vendor's fraud.

Yost v. Rieve Enterprises, Inc., 461 So.2d 178, review denied 469 So.2d 750.

⚷807(2)–807(6). *For other cases see earlier editions of this digest, the Decennial Digests, and WESTLAW.*

⚷807(7). Reliance on representations.

Bkrtcy.M.D.Fla. 1987. Seller of heavy construction equipment neither falsely represented condition of equipment at time of purchase, nor warranted condition of equipment, where buyer had ample opportunity to inspect equipment and did, in fact, use equipment extensively prior to purchase.

Matter of Trah Enterprises, Inc., 71 B.R. 44.

Fla. 1950. Where purchasers of wheel alignment business were experienced businessmen, inspected vendor's place of business and equipment at length before signing contract to purchase and making deposit thereunder, and their accountant examined vendor's books, purchasers could not rescind contract upon ground that vendor falsely represented annual profits.

Fote v. Reitano, 46 So.2d 891.

Fla.App. 3 Dist. 1975. In order to rely upon representation of a seller, every person must use reasonable diligence for his own protection.

Morton v. Young, 311 So.2d 755.

🔑**807(8). Fraudulent procurement of signature.**

For other cases see earlier editions of this digest, the Decennial Digests, and WESTLAW.

🔑**807(9). Title or interest.**

C.A.11 (Fla.) 2005. Although computer software was not licensed or authorized by manufacturer, contracts to purchase software that was already licensed and authorized by manufacturer did not violate Texas public policy, and were therefore enforceable by buyer against seller, which knew its software kits did not include royalty payments to manufacturer, and that buyer was purchasing the software kits with the understanding that it had no obligations to pay royalties, but mislead buyer by treating it as an approved customer and failing to correct the belief that the software was royalty-free. V.T.C.A., Bus. & C. § 2.312(c).

 HGI Associates, Inc. v. Wetmore Printing Co., 427 F.3d 867, appeal after remand 236 Fed.Appx. 563.

🔑**807(10). Quality or value.**

For other cases see earlier editions of this digest, the Decennial Digests, and WESTLAW.

🔑**807(11). Doctrine of caveat emptor.**

C.A.5 (Fla.) 1954. The maxim caveat emptor applies whenever buyer in the particular circumstances has full opportunity to inspect what he is buying but fails to do so and relies on seller's mere statements amounting to no more than puffing, boosting, or expression of opinion.

 Weil Clothing Co. v. Glasser, 213 F.2d 296.

Where fraud is knowingly and willfully committed by seller, under circumstances where there is no reasonable opportunity for buyer to discover the fraud, buyer in good faith, acting and relying on such representations, is not barred from recovery under the maxim caveat emptor.

 Weil Clothing Co. v. Glasser, 213 F.2d 296.

🔑**808. —— By buyer.**

🔑**808(1). In general.**

C.A.5 (Fla.) 1957. Where buyer of three thoroughbred brood mares agreed, under written contract of purchase, to give sellers third foal dropped by each of the mares after execution of contract, buyer, who purchased one of the foals from sellers by means of a dummy, had only duty not to deceive buyers as to value of foal, either by direct statements or by omitting pertinent information, and fiduciary relationship did not exist between buyer and sellers.

 Feinberg v. Leach, 243 F.2d 64.

🔑**808(2)–809.** *For other cases see earlier editions of this digest, the Decennial Digests, and WESTLAW.*

🔑**810. Duress.**

S.D.Fla. 2016. Buyer failed to plausibly allege that it had no reasonable alternative course of action but to sign purchase invoice that showed buyer's $2 million payment reducing its outstanding balance owed to seller for equipment and machinery purchases, which was allegedly inconsistent with parties' oral agreement, as required to support buyer's claim in its breach of contract action that invoice was executed under duress and therefore void under Florida law; after seller allegedly violated parties' agreement, buyer could have elected to not execute the invoice or could have filed suit for breach of contract at that juncture.

 Leader Global Solutions, LLC v. Tradeco Infraestructura, S.A. DE C.V., 155 F.Supp.3d 1310.

🔑**811–812.** *For other cases see earlier editions of this digest, the Decennial Digests, and WESTLAW.*

🔑**812. Illegality.**

🔑**813. —— In general.**

Fla.App. 3 Dist. 1983. Where employee and third parties entered into a commercial bribery scheme involving kickbacks to employee of half of the profits realized from transactions he secretly effected between employer and third parties, and the kickback arrangement by which employee was to benefit was the sole reason and inducement for employer's agreement to purchase products from third parties, the scheme which gave rise to the contract constituted a complete defense to third parties' claim for the product which had been received by employer.

Phillips Chemical Co. v. Morgan, 440 So.2d 1292, petition for review denied Gamble v. Phillips Chemical Co., 450 So.2d 486.

☞814–816. **For other cases see earlier editions of this digest, the Decennial Digests, and WESTLAW.**

☞815. **Unreasonable or oppressive contracts.**

☞817. —— **Adhesion contracts in general.**

Fla.App. 1 Dist. 1999. "Adhesion contract" is a standardized contract form offered to consumers of goods and services on essentially a "take it or leave it" basis without affording the consumer a realistic opportunity to bargain and under such conditions that the consumer cannot obtain the desired product or services except by acquiescing in the form contract.

Powertel, Inc. v. Bexley, 743 So.2d 570, rehearing denied, review denied 763 So.2d 1044.

Fla.App. 4 Dist. 2005. "Adhesion contract" is a standardized contract form offered to consumers of goods and services on essentially a "take it or leave it" basis without affording the consumer a realistic opportunity to bargain and under such conditions that the consumer cannot obtain the desired product or services except by acquiescing in the form contract.

Fonte v. AT&T Wireless Services, Inc., 903 So.2d 1019, review denied 918 So.2d 292.

☞818. —— **Unconscionability in general.**

Fla.App. 4 Dist. 1984. Under section of Uniform Commercial Code governing unconscionable contracts or clauses, trial court has authority to declare any provision of a contract void on its own initiative if it finds the clause unconscionable after holding the requisite hearing. West's F.S.A. § 672.302.

Capital Associates, Inc. v. Hudgens, 455 So.2d 651.

☞819. —— **Particular contracts and provisions.**

Fla.App. 2 Dist. 1975. Installment sales contract on mobile home which called for annual interest rate of 11.75% was not so unconscionable as to be unenforcible. West's F.S.A. § 672.302; U.C.C. § 2–302.

Mobile America Corp. v. Howard, 307 So.2d 507.

Fla.App. 3 Dist. 1987. Contracts for lease of modem and purchase of computer system were not demonstrated to be unenforceable due to unconscionability, absent evidence that parties were of unequal bargaining power.

Meeting Makers, Inc. v. American Airlines, Inc., 513 So.2d 700.

☞820. **Partial invalidity.**

For other cases see earlier editions of this digest, the Decennial Digests, and WESTLAW.

☞821. **Estoppel or waiver as to defects or objections.**

Fla.App. 3 Dist. 1988. Seller's delivery of copier machine and bringing of action to enforce sales agreement effected a waiver of the contract term allegedly requiring formal acceptance by the seller of contract signed by salesman in order for agreement to be binding.

Copy Service, Inc. v. Florida Copy Corp., 527 So.2d 247.

☞822. **Ratification of contract.**

Fla.App. 4 Dist. 2005. By seeking damages rather than rescission concerning claim against sellers for fraudulent inducement, buyers were bound by terms of contract governing sale of equipment to commence laundromat; suing for damages affirmed contract and its terms.

Mac-Gray Services, Inc. v. DeGeorge, 913 So.2d 630.

V. TERMS OF CONTRACT; RIGHTS AND OBLIGATIONS OF PARTIES.

(A) IN GENERAL.

☞901–902. **For other cases see earlier editions of this digest, the Decennial Digests, and WESTLAW.**

☞902. **General rules of construction.**

☞903. —— **In general.**

Fla.App. 5 Dist. 2005. Trial court lacked authority to rewrite contract for sale of motorcycles from motorcycle manufacturer to motorcycle dealer where contract's provisions were clear and unambiguous.

> Beach Street Bikes, Inc. v. Bourgett's Bike Works, Inc., 900 So.2d 697.

⚷904. —— **Construction against drafter.**

Fla.App. 2 Dist. 2004. Any ambiguity in documents for selling corporation's assets had to be construed against seller who created the documents modeling them after outdated forms that had been used when he purchased the business years earlier.

> Carr v. Lammie, 868 So.2d 636.

⚷905. —— **Construing documents together.**

⚷905(1). **In general.**

† **C.A.11 (Fla.) 2007.** California canons of contract construction, including principle that several contracts relating to the same matters between the same parties as part of one transaction are to be taken together, did not apply to unambiguous bill of sale. West's Ann.Cal.Civ.Code § 1642.

> Systems Unlimited, Inc. v. Cisco Systems, Inc., 228 Fed.Appx. 854, certiorari denied 128 S.Ct. 209, 552 U.S. 943, 169 L.Ed.2d 247.

C.A.5 (Fla.) 1980. Principle that, where two or more documents are executed by the same parties at or near the same time in the course of the same transaction and concern the same subject matter, they will be read and construed together applied to equipment sales contract, purchase order, and lease agreement executed in the course of a single transaction even though they were executed days or weeks apart.

> Earman Oil Co., Inc. v. Burroughs Corp., 625 F.2d 1291.

If arrangement whereby computer was sold by manufacturer to lessor and then leased to lessee was merely a financing arrangement, the real economic affect of the transaction was a sale directly from the manufacturer to the lessee and, under the contemporaneous transaction principle, effect would be given to unambiguous statements of lessee's rights against the manufacturer contained in an earlier

equipment sales contract executed by the two.

> Earman Oil Co., Inc. v. Burroughs Corp., 625 F.2d 1291.

Fla.App. 2 Dist. 1997. Conditional sales contract, as contract that required return of vehicle upon dealership's failure to find financing for buyers, had to be read together with other documents that were executed together as part of one transaction, including security agreement/retail installment contract that named specific outside lender, and thus, read in that manner, it was clear that buyers agreed to return vehicle to dealership if dealership could not find financing with outside lender.

> Dodge City, Inc. v. Byrne, 693 So.2d 1033.

⚷905(2). **Incorporation by reference.**

C.A.5 (Fla.) 1980. Dealings between lessee, lessor, and manufacturer of computer indicated that purchase order between the manufacturer and the lessor was intended to refer to equipment sales contract initially negotiated between the manufacturer and the lessee, thereby incorporating it by reference.

> Earman Oil Co., Inc. v. Burroughs Corp., 625 F.2d 1291.

S.D.Fla. 2008. Under New York law, terms of separate, independent purchase order used by one party were not incorporated by reference into contract through reference to generic term "purchase orders" in one schedule to contract; language did not employ proper noun, so as to alert reader that reference was being made to party's particular purchase orders, and nothing in schedule indicated with any semblance of clarity that language referring to purchase orders was intended to incorporate an unattached document by reference.

> Grandis Family Partnership, Ltd. v. Hess Corp., 588 F.Supp.2d 1319.

Fla. 1941. A statement, in request for quotation of price for conveyor belt, that "You have the complete information as to the installation and operation of this belt", was not sufficient as a description of or reference to data sheet accompanying prior request for quotation, so as to include such data sheet as part of the contract, as affecting extent of warranty of the belt.

U.S. Rubber Products v. Clark, 200 So. 385, 145 Fla. 631.

⬤➡**906–906(1).** *For other cases see earlier editions of this digest, the Decennial Digests, and WESTLAW.*

⬤➡**906.** —— **Extrinsic circumstances; construction by parties.**

⬤➡**906(2). Course of dealing; course of performance.**

C.A.11 (Fla.) 2003. Under Florida law, court may consider course of dealing, usage of trade, and course of performance in deciding whether parties to transaction governed by the Uniform Commercial Code (UCC) entered into agreement to vary UCC provisions. West's F.S.A. §§ 671.102(3), 671.201(3).

SCADIF, S.A. v. First Union Nat., 344 F.3d 1123.

S.D.Fla. 2001. Although a course of dealing may become part of an agreement, via a type of estoppel, when one party fails to object to the manner in which other party performs under the agreement, terms and conditions contained in a form continually sent by one party do not constitute "performance" and cannot becoming binding as a course of dealing, under Florida's version of Uniform Commercial Code. U.C.C. § 2–208; West's F.S.A. § 672.208(1).

Premix-Marbletite Mfg. Corp. v. SKW Chemicals, Inc., 145 F.Supp.2d 1348.

⬤➡**907–908.** *For other cases see earlier editions of this digest, the Decennial Digests, and WESTLAW.*

⬤➡**907. Performance and breach in general.**

⬤➡**909.** —— **By seller.**

S.D.Fla. 1975. Where seller had never attempted to follow proscribed remedy set forth in contract provisions dealing with a particular eventuality, it could not, when buyer brought action against seller based on breach of contract, assert that the rights of the parties should be governed by the particular provision.

Eastern Air Lines, Inc. v. Gulf Oil Corp., 415 F.Supp. 429.

Fla.App. 3 Dist. 1981. Purchaser of automobile from dealer was not entitled to recover on theory of breach of contract because of dealer's failure to give another automobile to purchaser pursuant to dealer's advertisement to effect that it would give a free small car with each purchase of a new luxury car or demonstrator.

Rhita B. Behrman Interiors, Inc. v. Braman Cadillac, Inc., 407 So.2d 282.

Fla.App. 3 Dist. 1969. In suit by general contractor and subcontractor against supplier, in which contract existed between supplier and subcontractor but was breached by supplier, causing subcontractor to use other material, where record showed that upon purchasing material elsewhere general contractor made it available to subcontractor, who then proceeded to apply it on the project, general contractor rather than subcontractor sustained the loss, so that subcontractor could not recover since it was put to no extra cost for the material.

Flintkote Co. v. Brewer Co. of Fla., 221 So.2d 784, certiorari denied 225 So.2d 920.

⬤➡**910.** —— **By buyer.**

For other cases see earlier editions of this digest, the Decennial Digests, and WESTLAW.

⬤➡**911. Particular terms and obligations in general.**

† **C.A.11 (Fla.) 2006.** Seller of robotic surgical device to private university did not breach its obligation, in sales contract, to collaborate with university to establish university as a robotic surgical training center; university never requested such collaboration, and contract did not give seller the responsibility to initiate collaboration.

University of Miami v. Intuitive Surgical, Inc., 166 Fed.Appx. 450.

S.D.Fla. 1999. Oil company's good faith obligation in sales agreements could be explained or supplemented by evidence of course of dealing, usage of trade, or course of performance, as well as by other evidence which explained company's good faith obligation; such evidence did not modify or contradict express terms of sales agreements and was not inconsistent with express terms of any agreement, within meaning of parol evidence rule, since each sales agreement expressly included "good faith" obligation. U.C.C. § 2–202.

> Allapattah Services, Inc. v. Exxon Corp., 61 F.Supp.2d 1300, affirmed 333 F.3d 1248, rehearing en banc denied 362 F.3d 739, certiorari granted in part 125 S.Ct. 317, 543 U.S. 924, 160 L.Ed.2d 221, affirmed 125 S.Ct. 2611, 545 U.S. 546, 162 L.Ed.2d 502.

Evidence of course of dealing, usage of trade, and course of performance was admissible, not only to explain sales agreements and oil company's good faith obligations to its dealers, but to determine whether good faith obligation had been breached, and to show that offset arrangement that oil company implemented with its dealers was common in the trade.

> Allapattah Services, Inc. v. Exxon Corp., 61 F.Supp.2d 1300, affirmed 333 F.3d 1248, rehearing en banc denied 362 F.3d 739, certiorari granted in part 125 S.Ct. 317, 543 U.S. 924, 160 L.Ed.2d 221, affirmed 125 S.Ct. 2611, 545 U.S. 546, 162 L.Ed.2d 502.

☞912. Implied terms and obligations in general.

For other cases see earlier editions of this digest, the Decennial Digests, and WEST-LAW.

☞913. Good faith and fair dealing in general.

M.D.Fla. 2005. Failure of buyer of radios, to state claim that seller was required to provide units capable of "trunking," searching out available frequencies, precluded under Florida law any claim that seller breached any implied covenant of good faith.

> Business Radio, Inc. v. Relm Wireless Corp., 373 F.Supp.2d 1317, affirmed 209 Fed.Appx. 899.

M.D.Fla. 1991. Texas law adopts section of Uniform Commercial Code pertaining to breach of duty of good faith. U.C.C. § 1–203.

> Rentclub, Inc. v. Transamerica Rental Finance Corp., 775 F.Supp. 1460.

S.D.Fla. 2007. Under Florida's version of Uniform Commercial Code (UCC), a party may unilaterally alter key terms in a contract if the party uses "good faith" in supplying the term based on honesty in fact and the observance of reasonable commercial standards of fair dealing in the trade; a party's decision will not violate the implied covenant of good faith and fair dealing unless no reasonable party would have made the same discretionary decision. West's F.S.A. § 672.305.

> Barnes v. Diamond Aircraft Industries, Inc., 499 F.Supp.2d 1311.

Under Florida law, aircraft manufacturer did not violate implied covenant of good faith and fair dealing in the reservation agreement by requiring that buyer pay over $1.3 million for an aircraft that it had agreed to sell for $850,000 where manufacturer had the express right under the reservation agreement to change the price and specifications of the aircraft without notice for the reasons stated in agreement and the evidence demonstrated that manufacturer set the firm price for its jet in good faith. West's F.S.A. § 672.305.

> Barnes v. Diamond Aircraft Industries, Inc., 499 F.Supp.2d 1311.

S.D.Fla. 1999. Policy considerations underlying Uniform Commercial Code's (UCC) good faith doctrine are generally to effectuate the intentions of the parties or to honor their reasonable expectations; satisfaction of those considerations requires performance of contractual obligations faithfully as to an agreed common purpose and consistent with the justified expectations of the other party. U.C.C. §§ 1–203, 2–103(1)(b).

> Allapattah Services, Inc. v. Exxon Corp., 61 F.Supp.2d 1308.

Under Uniform Commercial Code (UCC), bad faith occurs when a party acts to exploit changing economic conditions to secure gains that exceed those reasonably expected at the time of contracting. U.C.C. §§ 1–203, 2–103(1)(b).

> Allapattah Services, Inc. v. Exxon Corp., 61 F.Supp.2d 1308.

Obligation to act in good faith exists under Uniform Commercial Code (UCC) when determining terms to be implied in a contract where the terms are not expressly provided therein; moreover, duty to act in good faith is directly correlative to the amount of discretionary authority delegated by the contract. U.C.C. §§ 1–203, 2–103(1)(b).

> Allapattah Services, Inc. v. Exxon Corp., 61 F.Supp.2d 1308.

Fla.App. 1 Dist. 1991. Duty of good faith under the Uniform Commercial Code may not be imposed to override express terms of a contract. West's F.S.A. § 671.203.

> Riedel v. NCNB Nat. Bank of Florida, Inc., 591 So.2d 1038.

Fla.App. 3 Dist. 1961. If purchaser of a business promises to pay therefor out of profits to be made, there is an implied promise to keep the business going in good faith.

> Coast Cities Coaches, Inc. v. Whyte, 130 So.2d 121.

Fla.App. 5 Dist. 2005. Because there was no meeting of the minds on the number of motorcycles that motorcycle dealer was obligated to purchase beyond the initial two mentioned in the contract with motorcycle manufacturer, implied covenant of good faith should not have been invoked to impose upon dealer the obligation to purchase 15 motorcycles, which was never negotiated by the parties.

> Beach Street Bikes, Inc. v. Bourgett's Bike Works, Inc., 900 So.2d 697.

⚷**914. Conditions and provisos in general.**

Fla.App. 4 Dist. 1982. In action by buyers against seller to recover earnest money deposit paid toward purchase of mobile home, circuit court's finding that sale of buyers' house was not necessary condition precedent to closing on sale of mobile home was not erroneous.

> Honsberg v. Lystra, 410 So.2d 661.

⚷**915–917.** *For other cases see earlier editions of this digest, the Decennial Digests, and WESTLAW.*

⚷**918. Entire or severable contracts.**

† **C.A.11 (Fla.) 2013.** Under Florida law, yacht manufacturer's letter to dealer, which referred to the warranty clause of the selling contract for the yacht, was simply providing one clause of a preexisting contract and not creating a separate and divisible contract.

> Marlborough Holdings Group, Ltd. v. Azimut-Benetti, Spa, Platinum Yacht Collection No. Two, Inc., 505 Fed.Appx. 899, certiorari denied 134 S.Ct. 152, 187 L.Ed.2d 39.

Fla. 1935. Contract for sale of all merchantable fruit of various kinds then growing in seller's fields to be taken in installments, price being arrived at by consideration of all fruit rather than separate kinds, and first payment being applied to purchase price of crop as a whole held not divisible, so as to permit buyer who failed to gather less valuable fruit to maintain action against seller who thereafter sold more valuable fruit to another.

> Metcalf v. R. D. Keene & Co., 164 So. 704, 122 Fla. 27.

⚷**919. Options; rights of first refusal.**

Fla. 1948. Options to purchase are strictly construed and can be satisfied only by positive and unequivocal declaration to accept.

> Baker v. Coleman, 34 So.2d 538, 160 Fla. 297.

Fla.App. 1 Dist. 1980. Even if manufacturer of pipe was obligated to supply pipe in event contractor became successful bidder on public contract, that did not create a corresponding obligation on part of contractor to order pipe from manufacturer.

> Wolf Ridge Plastics, Inc. v. Jacksonville Elec. Authority, 388 So.2d 1298, review denied 397 So.2d 780.

(B) GOODS SUBJECT TO CONTRACT IN GENERAL.

⚷**931. In general.**

† **C.A.11 (Fla.) 2006.** Contract for sale of robotic surgical devices to private university, stating that university was entitled to all product software upgrades at no charge during warranty, service, and support term, and to any additional requested hardware upgrades at 75 percent of current list price, did not require seller to

continue producing the devices or technological upgrades.

> University of Miami v. Intuitive Surgical, Inc., 166 Fed.Appx. 450.

🔑932. Description in general.

For other cases see earlier editions of this digest, the Decennial Digests, and WESTLAW.

🔑933. Specific articles or goods.

† C.A.11 (Fla.) 2013. Under Florida law, provisions in initial contract for purchase and sale of coal, some of which provided greater detail on pricing, risk, and transfer regarding particular sources of coal but which made no provision for or reference to alternative sources of coal, did not render contract a single source agreement which would allow seller to justify its breach, under force majeure argument, when one coal source became unavailable.

> Gulf Power Co. v. Coalsales II, LLC, 522 Fed.Appx. 699.

† C.A.11 (Fla.) 2006. Failure of seller of robotic surgical devices to private university, to deliver cutting-edge devices, was not breach of sales contract; contract identified specific devices that seller would deliver to university, and seller delivered those devices.

> University of Miami v. Intuitive Surgical, Inc., 166 Fed.Appx. 450.

M.D.Fla. 1982. Five automobiles, which were subject of action by bank to recover certain sums advanced to an authorized dealer in connection with floorplan financing, were delivered to dealer by manufacturer on a C.O.D. basis and therefore were beyond scope of contractual agreements under which dealer was authorized to order automobiles under line of credit, and under which manufacturer was required to repurchase unsold automobiles upon which bank held loan paper.

> Key Bank of Tampa v. Saab-Scania of America, Inc., 549 F.Supp. 96.

N.D.Fla. 2009. Provisions in parties' initial contract for purchase and sale of coal, some of which provided greater detail on pricing, risk, and transfer regarding particular sources of coal but which made no provision for or reference to alternative sources of coal, did not render contract a

single source agreement and preclude alternative sources under Florida law; because parties anticipated that coal would be supplied primarily from two sources, it was reasonable to expect that the agreement would provide the most detail regarding those sources, including pricing, risk of loss, transfer of title, and shipping instructions.

> Gulf Power Co. v. Coalsales II, L.L.C., 661 F.Supp.2d 1270, motion for relief from judgment granted 2011 WL 3269412, on reconsideration 2011 WL 4552185, affirmed 522 Fed.Appx. 699, affirmed 522 Fed. Appx. 699.

Sections of contract for purchase and sale of coal which indicated that parties "anticipated" that seller, a coal company, would supply to buyer, a power company, a blend of coal from two primary sources, did not reflect the parties' intent to limit seller's obligation to supply coal to only those two sources under Florida law; sections explicitly referred to other approved sources of coal.

> Gulf Power Co. v. Coalsales II, L.L.C., 661 F.Supp.2d 1270, motion for relief from judgment granted 2011 WL 3269412, on reconsideration 2011 WL 4552185, affirmed 522 Fed.Appx. 699, affirmed 522 Fed. Appx. 699.

Under Florida law, coal seller's right, under initial contract for sale and purchase of coal to power plant, to choose between approved sources of coal and to determine specifics of performance, did not also give seller the right to refuse to supply coal at all when only one of the approved sources became unavailable.

> Gulf Power Co. v. Coalsales II, L.L.C., 661 F.Supp.2d 1270, motion for relief from judgment granted 2011 WL 3269412, on reconsideration 2011 WL 4552185, affirmed 522 Fed.Appx. 699, affirmed 522 Fed. Appx. 699.

Market reopener amendments between coal seller, a coal company, and buyer, a power company, which designated one mine as a primary source of coal provided under contract, did not have the effect of rendering parties' initial coal sales contract a sole source agreement under Florida law; "primary" did not mean "sole," particularly in light of seller's supply of coal from multiple sources other than the primary mine, and there was no express limiting language in the contract, having identified three sources and having made provisions for other approved sources of coal as well.

Gulf Power Co. v. Coalsales II, L.L.C., 661 F.Supp.2d 1270, motion for relief from judgment granted 2011 WL 3269412, on reconsideration 2011 WL 4552185, affirmed 522 Fed.Appx. 699, affirmed 522 Fed. Appx. 699.

⚷934. Identification, selection, and appropriation.

M.D.Fla. 2006. Under California law, agreement between bottle supplier and customer restricted production of bottles to be sold to customer to specific facility, given that agreement specifically stated that the product "shall be manufactured" at named facility, that such facility was only plant owned by supplier, its parent company, or affiliate which was approved to meet customer's product requirements, and that neither supplier nor its parent company built or acquired facility capable of producing products closer to customer's corporate location, so as to trigger exception to provision designating production facility.

In re Anchor Glass Container Corp., 345 B.R. 765.

⚷935. Title or possession of seller.

Transfer of title, see V(G). Warranties, see IX.

Fla.App. 4 Dist. 1991. In context of motor vehicle buyer's claim for breach of warranty of title, seller did not convey "good title" where there was discrepancy between year of vehicle's manufacture and number of digits in vehicle identification number on certificate of title, where representative of Department of Motor Vehicles indicated that title was subject to cancellation, and where there were other documents in existence identifying another vehicle with same VIN number. West's F.S.A. § 672.312.

Maroone Chevrolet, Inc. v. Nordstrom, 587 So.2d 514.

⚷936. Property interest of buyer.

For other cases see earlier editions of this digest, the Decennial Digests, and WESTLAW.

(C) DELIVERY AND ACCEPTANCE OF GOODS.

1. IN GENERAL.

⚷951–952. *For other cases see earlier editions of this digest, the Decennial Digests, and WESTLAW.*

⚷952. Delivery in general.

⚷953. —— In general.

Bkrtcy.S.D.Fla. 1993. Chapter 11 debtor that had been selling automobile parts breached agreement with manufacturer that manufacturer would buy back parts under certain conditions precedent where debtor failed to meet many of the conditions, including failing to ship parts to manufacturer within designated time period and failing to submit acceptable inventory of parts.

In re South Motor Co. of Dade County, 161 B.R. 532.

Fla.App. 5 Dist. 1989. Contractual duty of one who delivers product or manual services is to conform to quality or quantity specified in express contract, if any; or, in absence of such specification or when duty and level of performance is implied by law, to deliver product reasonably suited for purposes for which product was intended; or to deliver services performed in good and workmanlike manner.

Lochrane Engineering, Inc. v. Willingham Realgrowth Inv. Fund, Ltd., 552 So.2d 228, review denied Anderson v. Willingham Realgrowth Inv. Fund, Ltd., 563 So.2d 631.

⚷954. —— Ability and readiness of seller to deliver.

Fla.App. 2 Dist. 1973. Impossibility of performance of agricultural contracts varies according to whether seller contracts to sell his own produce, in which case individual crop failure constitutes "legal impossibility," or whether an obligation is assumed to furnish produce regardless of source; but in the latter case there is still a concept of legal impossibility.

Holly Hill Fruit Products Co., Inc. v. Bob Staton, Inc., 275 So.2d 583.

Where defendant contracted to deliver oranges from various groves located in two specified counties, his obligation upon occurrence of freeze was not to buy fruit wherever he could find it to fulfill the contract but to find fruit, if possible, even at greater expense than anticipated, in the two specified counties.

Holly Hill Fruit Products Co., Inc. v. Bob Staton, Inc., 275 So.2d 583.

☞955. —— Demand or notice by buyer.

C.A.11 (Fla.) 1998. When a delivery date passes without the seller's delivery, the buyer must object within a reasonable time and warn the seller that it is in breach.

BMC Industries, Inc. v. Barth Industries, Inc., 160 F.3d 1322, certiorari denied 119 S.Ct. 1807, 526 U.S. 1132, 143 L.Ed.2d 1010.

☞956–958. *For other cases see earlier editions of this digest, the Decennial Digests, and WESTLAW.*

☞957. Manner or mode of delivery; acts constituting delivery.

☞959. —— Property left in possession of seller.

Bkrtcy.M.D.Fla. 2005. Final sea trial for boat that seller had agreed to construct for buyer, at which buyer was present, and after which it was normal practice, according to seller's representative, for him to collect final payment and for buyers to take possession of watercraft, qualified as "delivery" of boat under Florida's Uniform Commercial Code (UCC), of kind triggering buyer's obligation, if he decided to reject boat as nonconforming, to do so within reasonable time. West's F.S.A. § 672.602.

In re Dorado Marine, Inc., 321 B.R. 581.

☞960. —— Property in possession of buyer.

For other cases see earlier editions of this digest, the Decennial Digests, and WESTLAW.

☞961. —— Property left in possession of third person.

Fla.App. 3 Dist. 1970. Delivery required for sale of aircraft in custody of bailee in Luxemburg was sufficiently accomplished by notice from Florida seller to its bailee to surrender possession to Florida buyer.

Pinellas Central Bank & Trust Co. v. International Aerodyne, Inc., 233 So.2d 872, certiorari denied 239 So.2d 829.

☞962. —— Access of and removal by buyer.

C.C.A.5 (Fla.) 1941. Where contract for sale of citrus fruit crop gave buyer access to grove up to and including December 31, 1937, to remove fruit and provided that, in case buyer was prevented from shipping fruit prior to that time by act of God or other matter beyond the buyer's control, time for removal should be extended, and crop was damaged by frost in December, 1937, and the Florida Citrus Commission prohibited issuance of grade certificates until January 1, 1938, the buyer was entitled to delay beyond December 31 in which to pick and remove the fruit, and denial of such right by the seller constituted breach of the contract.

Eustis Packing Co. v. Martin, 122 F.2d 648.

Fla. 1935. Contract for sale of growing fruit which stated that buyer should take merchantable fruit when he was "ready" within time specified held not to require buyer to take fruit until end of specified period as against contention that "ready" meant when buyer was physically able to remove fruit after it was ready for picking and that it implied reasonable time.

Metcalf v. R. D. Keene & Co., 164 So. 704, 122 Fla. 27.

☞963. —— Delivery to or through carrier or other intermediary.

Fla.App. 3 Dist. 1985. A "C.I.F. contract" is not a contract that the goods shall arrive but, rather, a contract to ship goods complying with the contract of sale, to obtain the ordinary contract of carriage to the place of destination unless the contract otherwise provides, to obtain the ordinary contract of insurance of the goods on that voyage, and to tender the documents against payment of the contract price.

Kumar Corp. v. Nopal Lines, Ltd., 462 So.2d 1178, petition for review denied S.E.L. Maduro (Florida), Inc. v. Kumar Corp., 476 So.2d 675.

Fla.App. 3 Dist. 1979. A "shipment contract" is considered the normal contract in which seller is required to send subject goods by carrier to the buyer but is not required to guarantee delivery thereof at a particular destination and, under a "shipment contract," the seller, unless otherwise agreed, must put the goods sold in possession of a carrier and make a contract for their transportation, obtain and promptly deliver or tender in due form any document necessary to enable buyer to obtain possession of goods and notify buyer of shipment. F.S.1977, §§ 672.503 comment, 672.504, 672.509(1).

Pestana v. Karinol Corp., 367 So.2d 1096.

Parties must explicitly agree to a destination contract; otherwise contract will be considered a shipment contract. F.S. 1977, §§ 672.319(1)(b), 672.503 comment, 672.509(1).

Pestana v. Karinol Corp., 367 So.2d 1096.

☞964. —— Symbolical or constructive delivery.

Fla. 1941. A contract for sale of fruit, providing that damaged fruit of specified types was not included in the contract, contemplated that risk of damage from frost should fall on seller and not on buyer, and buyer was not obliged to gather frost-damaged fruit.

Givens v. Vaughn-Griffin Packing Co., 1 So.2d 714, 146 Fla. 575.

☞965. Place of delivery.

Fla.App. 4 Dist. 1984. Contract for sale of plastic parts and molding expressed by forms incorporated uncontradicted provisions contained in one form stating that contract was for shipment of parts FOB Clearwater, and thus, seller's delivery point was in Clearwater, and there the risk of loss passed to buyer. West's F.S.A. § 672.207.

A & M Engineering Plastics, Inc. v. Energy Saving Technology Co., 455 So.2d 1124.

☞966. Time of delivery.

☞967. —— In general.

C.A.5 (Fla.) 1976. Government's "jawboning" policy in effect during period of nation's heavy involvement in Vietnam war, under which aircraft manufacturing industry was informally forced to grant priority to military aircraft production, came within terms of excusable delay clause in aircraft manufacturer's contract with airline to supply 99 civilian aircraft, contrary to airline's contention that only priorities imposed under Defense Production Act would qualify to excuse delay under such contract clause. Defense Production Act of 1950, §§ 2, 101 et seq., 101(a), 103, 703, 704 as amended 50 U.S.C.A. App. §§ 2062, 2071 et seq., 2071(a), 2073, 2153, 2154; Executive Order Nos. 10161, 10480, 50 U.S.C.A. App. §§ 2071 note, 2153 note; Federal Rules of Evidence, rule 803(8) 28 U.S.C.A.; West's Ann.Cal.Com.Code, §§ 2615, 2616, 2616(2).

Eastern Air Lines, Inc. v. McDonnell Douglas Corp., 532 F.2d 957.

Where contract for manufacture and sale of 99 jet aircraft to airline provided that excusable delay must be result of "one or more of the listed events" in the excusable delay clause of the contracts, doctrine of ejusdem generis did not limit aircraft manufacturer's affirmative defense to delays caused by events similar to those specifically listed when, in fact, contract excused all delays which were not manufacturer's fault; contract provisions therefore did not result in waiver of applicability of doctrine of commercial impracticability. West's Ann.Cal.Com.Code, §§ 2615, 2616, 2616(2).

Eastern Air Lines, Inc. v. McDonnell Douglas Corp., 532 F.2d 957.

C.C.A.5 (Fla.) 1947. The written orders proposed by buyers and acted on by seller control as respects time for performance of contracts of sale.

Morris v. Prefabrication Engineering Co., 160 F.2d 779.

Bkrtcy.S.D.Fla. 1993. Chapter 11 debtor that had been selling automobile parts breached agreement with manufacturer that manufacturer would buy back parts under certain conditions precedent where debtor failed to meet many of the conditions, including failing to ship parts to manufacturer within designated time period and failing to submit acceptable inventory of parts.

> In re South Motor Co. of Dade County, 161 B.R. 532.

Fla. 1941. A contract for sale of fruit to be removed by specified date, subject to right to extension of time under certain circumstances, which specifically excluded damaged fruit, could reasonably be taken as excluding any fruit damaged between time of execution of contract and date for removal of fruit.

> Givens v. Vaughn-Griffin Packing Co., 1 So.2d 714, 146 Fla. 575.

Under contract for sale of fruit requiring buyer to remove fruit within specified time, but giving buyer right to extension of time if removal were prevented by act of God, buyer's request for extension of time because of freeze and consequent frost damage need not be for any stated length of time, but buyer was entitled to such time as it was actually delayed in picking and shipping the fruit because of the freeze.

> Givens v. Vaughn-Griffin Packing Co., 1 So.2d 714, 146 Fla. 575.

Fla.App. 3 Dist. 1989. Agreement requiring seller to deliver landfill material within 90 days of request from buyer, for period of five years after implementation date of agreement, did not obligate seller when request was made within, but 90–day period expired after, the five-year period.

> Williams Island Associates, Ltd. v. Cohen, 547 So.2d 954, review denied 558 So.2d 17.

☞968. —— **Time as being "of the essence".**

C.C.A.5 (Fla.) 1947. Where time was of the essence of two separate contracts covering wedge bolts and each contract provided that shipment must begin by "June 7th to 10th and be completed by _____" shipments were required to begin by June 10, and where no bolts had been shipped by late June and notice of cancellation was given but small shipment of bolts was later received and used and notice of cancellation was given on July 29th, the latter notice of cancellation controlled.

> Morris v. Prefabrication Engineering Co., 160 F.2d 779.

S.D.Fla. 1989. Under Florida law, delivery time was not of the essence under contract for sale of chemicals even though contract originally called for delivery to take place within 45 days of seller's receipt of letter of credit and even though, approximately one month after letter of credit was amended to extend its validity, seller told buyer that its supplier was requesting certain time-frame for delivery and that it could not afford to change time-frame again; amendment of letter of credit resulted in amendment of time for shipment, and seller's communication with buyer about supplier was more expression of desire than explicit notice of requirement that shipment had to take place on certain date or contract was cancelled.

> Fertilizer Corp. of America v. P.S. Intern., Inc., 729 F.Supp. 837.

☞969. —— **Immediate delivery or as soon as possible.**

For other cases see earlier editions of this digest, the Decennial Digests, and WESTLAW.

☞970. —— **Reasonable time.**

C.A.11 (Fla.) 1998. Seller was required to deliver machines within reasonable time period after buyer waived contractual delivery date. West's F.S.A. § 672.209.

> BMC Industries, Inc. v. Barth Industries, Inc., 160 F.3d 1322, certiorari denied 119 S.Ct. 1807, 526 U.S. 1132, 143 L.Ed.2d 1010.

S.D.Fla. 1989. Under Florida contract for a sale of chemicals, reasonable date of delivery was either by January 25 or February 2 after original contract, which stated that delivery was to be within 45 days of receipt of letter of credit or January 15, was amended by amending letter of credit to permit delivery by February 2. West's F.S.A. §§ 672.309, 672.309 comment.

> Fertilizer Corp. of America v. P.S. Intern., Inc., 729 F.Supp. 837.

⟐971. Acceptance in general.

C.A.5 (Fla.) 1971. Contract to purchase certain aircraft and all spare parts for such aircraft was clear and unambiguous and buyer's failure to take delivery of the aircraft and parts for which it had contracted wrongfully breached contract.

Eastern Air Lines, Inc. v. Hartford Acc. & Indem. Co., 437 F.2d 449, certiorari denied Hartford Accident and Indemnity Co. v. Eastern Airlines Inc., 91 S.Ct. 2191, 402 U.S. 1009, 29 L.Ed.2d 431.

Fla. 1943. A corporation, contracting to purchase grapefruit crop from one assuming risk of freeze damage by clause also providing that corporation should not be required to pick or pay for fruit so damaged, was obligated to endeavor to merchandise fruit, notwithstanding freeze which damaged more than percentage of fruit fixed by law as tolerance limit for shipping, and remained bound by contract, in absence of reasonable effort to grade out damaged fruit. F.S.A. § 594.01 et seq.

Stanford Fruit Growers v. Singer, 12 So.2d 464, 152 Fla. 588.

⟐972. Manner or mode of acceptance; acts constituting acceptance.

⟐973. —— In general.

N.D.Fla. 2010. Acceptance of goods occurs under Florida law when the buyer, after a reasonable opportunity to inspect them, signifies that the goods are conforming or will be accepted despite a nonconformity, or if the buyer fails to make an effective rejection after having a reasonable opportunity to inspect the goods; an acceptance with knowledge of a nonconformity cannot be revoked because of that nonconformity. West's F.S.A. §§ 672.606, 672.607.

JDI Holdings, LLC v. Jet Management, Inc., 732 F.Supp.2d 1205.

⟐974. —— Timeliness; effect of buyer's delay.

For other cases see earlier editions of this digest, the Decennial Digests, and WESTLAW.

⟐975. —— Failure or refusal to return goods.

Bkrtcy.S.D.Fla. 1993. Doctrine of laches did not apply to preclude creditor from refusing to repurchase automobile parts from Chapter 11 debtor as required under contract where debtor failed to substantially perform conditions precedent under agreement in timely fashion, thus excusing creditor from performing its repurchase obligation.

In re South Motor Co. of Dade County, 161 B.R. 532.

⟐976–977. *For other cases see earlier editions of this digest, the Decennial Digests, and WESTLAW.*

2. QUALITY, VALUE, FITNESS, AND CONDITION OF GOODS.

Warranties, see IX.

⟐981. In general.

Fla. 1940. Where contract is made for purchase of certain goods, they must be of the quantity as well as the quality stipulated.

Vaughn-Griffin Packing Co. v. Fisher, 193 So. 553, 141 Fla. 428.

Fla.App. 3 Dist. 1972. Every buyer has the right to assume his new car, with the exception of minor adjustments, will be mechanically new and factory furnished, operate perfectly, and be free of substantial defects.

Orange Motors of Coral Gables, Inc. v. Dade County Dairies, Inc., 258 So.2d 319, certiorari denied 263 So.2d 831.

⟐982. Particular cases and goods in general.

M.D.Fla. 2015. A drum kit distributer sufficiently alleged that drum kits provided by manufacturer were not suitable for retail sale due to their defective nature as well as high volume of customer complaints to retailers, and also sufficiently alleged that the drum kits did not match the quality of representative samples provided to distributor, as required to state claim for breach of contract of specially manufactured goods under Florida's Uniform Commercial Code (UCC). Fla. Stat. Ann. §§ 672.102, 672.105(1).

> Armadillo Distribution Enterprises, Inc. v. Hai Yun Musical Instruments Manufacture Co. Ltd., 142 F.Supp.3d 1245.

N.D.Fla. 2002. Importer-exporter breached terms of its contract with beef packing company under Florida law as determined by usage of trade, where, in meat product trade, when purchase order specified particular country of destination, before diverting the product to destination other than that specified, recipient was required to determine whether ordered product met requirements of new destination country, and importer-exporter did not determine whether Egypt would accept products prepared "for Russia." West's F.S.A. § 672.208(2).

> IBP, Inc. v. Hady Enterprises, Inc., 267 F.Supp.2d 1148, affirmed 52 Fed.Appx. 487.

Fla.App. 3 Dist. 1988. Inability of seller of computer and software to conform computer system to buyer's dated needs, despite 18 months of performing modifications, demonstrated its breach of contract and warranty obligations.

> Money Mortg. and Inv. Corp. v. CPT of South Florida, Inc., 537 So.2d 1015.

Fla.App. 3 Dist. 1962. "Completion", within contract providing for payment of purchase price in specified amount on delivery and remainder on completion, required air conditioner seller to provide working machines.

> Herman v. Dade Linen & Furniture Co., 143 So.2d 878.

☞**983. Conformity to contract; perfect tender.**

N.D.Fla. 2002. Importer-exporter breached its duty of good faith under Florida law in its contract with beef packing company, where importer-exporter purchased product for Russia intending to send it to Egypt, behavior that was dishonest in fact, and which was in violation of reasonable commercial standards of fair

dealing in its trade. West's F.S.A. §§ 671.203, 672.103(1)(b).

> IBP, Inc. v. Hady Enterprises, Inc., 267 F.Supp.2d 1148, affirmed 52 Fed.Appx. 487.

Fla.App. 2 Dist. 2000. A seller ordinarily tenders conforming goods to the buyer when the goods are in accordance with the terms of a contract.

> Gulfwind South, Inc. v. Jones, 775 So.2d 311.

Fla.App. 3 Dist. 2006. A purchaser of goods is entitled to receive what he wanted to buy and pay for, and the seller is not free to supply any non-conforming item she wishes just so long as the deviant goods are worth just as much. West's F.S.A. §§ 672.106(2), 672.601, 672.608.

> Jauregui v. Bobb's Piano Sales & Service, Inc., 922 So.2d 303.

☞**984. Fitness for purpose intended.**

Fla.App. 1 Dist. 1970. In determining whether gravity feed fuel system of front end loader was a design defect, question was not whether designer used best possible judgment but whether or not front end loader was rendered not reasonably fit for use by reason of the design adopted.

> Fletcher Co. v. Melroe Mfg. Co., 238 So.2d 142, certiorari denied 242 So.2d 463, appeal after remand 261 So.2d 191.

☞**985–986.** *For other cases see earlier editions of this digest, the Decennial Digests, and WESTLAW.*

☞**987. Loss of or injury to goods.**

Fla.App. 3 Dist. 1979. Where risk of loss falls on seller at time goods sold are lost or destroyed, seller is liable in damages to buyer for nondelivery unless seller tenders a performance in replacement for lost or destroyed goods and, on the other hand, where risk of loss falls on buyer at time the goods sold are lost or destroyed, buyer is liable to seller for purchase price of goods sold.

> Pestana v. Karinol Corp., 367 So.2d 1096.

⟐**988. Inspection and testing.**

⟐**989. —— In general.**

Fla.App. 3 Dist. 1959. Where subcontract contained a provision that subcontractor was to fulfill contract to supply products designed and manufactured by subcontractor and approved and accepted by owner, architect and contractor, and owner and architect failed to approve subcontractor's product, subcontractor was not liable for alleged breach of contract to general contractor for failure to furnish the materials and services.

> Windowmaster Corp. v. Jefferson Const. Co., 114 So.2d 626.

Where a subcontractor is to fulfill the subcontract only by furnishing its own products and only if its products are approved and accepted by third parties, such an agreement is subject to consent of third party and therefore is a conditional agreement, and liability will arise under such contract only when condition has been met.

> Windowmaster Corp. v. Jefferson Const. Co., 114 So.2d 626.

⟐**990. —— Time and place.**

S.D.Fla. 1984. Generally, buyer must make payment against tender of required documents to entitle and enable him to receive goods under CIF shipment, but where contract indicates that payment is to await arrival of goods, goods are "available for inspection" and inspection before payment is proper. West's F.S.A. §§ 672.320 comment, 672.512, 672.513 comment.

> William D. Branson, Ltd. v. Tropical Shipping & Const. Co., Ltd., 598 F.Supp. 680.

⟐**991. —— Mode, extent, and reasonableness.**

For other cases see earlier editions of this digest, the Decennial Digests, and WEST-LAW.

⟐**992. Sale by sample.**

M.D.Fla. 2015. Drum kit distributor sufficiently alleged that drum kit manufacturer knowingly failed to discharge its specific contractual obligations to provide drum kits of a certain quality represented in samples given to distributor, and that

such failure caused damage in the form of lost profits and lost goodwill associated with distributor's drum brands, as required to state claim for breach of implied covenant of good faith and fair dealing under Florida's Uniform Commercial Code (UCC). Fla. Stat. Ann. § 671.203.

> Armadillo Distribution Enterprises, Inc. v. Hai Yun Musical Instruments Manufacture Co. Ltd., 142 F.Supp.3d 1245.

⟐**993. Doctrine of caveat emptor.**

For other cases see earlier editions of this digest, the Decennial Digests, and WEST-LAW.

3. QUANTITY OF GOODS.

Warranties, see IX.

⟐**1001. In general.**

For other cases see earlier editions of this digest, the Decennial Digests, and WEST-LAW.

⟐**1002. Definite, indefinite, or unknown quantity in general.**

M.D.Fla. 2006. Generally, a contract for sale must be definite and certain as to the quantity of the goods or articles sold, or provide means, by some fixed conditions or circumstances, by which the quantities involved in the contract can be determined.

> In re Anchor Glass Container Corp., 345 B.R. 765.

When there is nothing in a writing which requires a party to take, or limits its demand to, any ascertainable quantity, a contract is not enforceable for lack of consideration and mutuality under California law; such a contract is referred to as an "indefinite quantities contract."

> In re Anchor Glass Container Corp., 345 B.R. 765.

Bkrtcy.M.D.Fla. 2003. Supply contract may fall into one of three categories, a definite quantity, indefinite quantity, or requirements contract, and when supply contract is ambiguous as to type, court should examine extrinsic evidence to determine what type of supply contract the parties intended.

> In re Anchor Glass Container Corp., 297 B.R. 887, affirmed 345 B.R. 765.

Courts should look to course of dealing between parties and to trade norms to determine what type of supply contract was intended.

> In re Anchor Glass Container Corp., 297 B.R. 887, affirmed 345 B.R. 765.

For supply contract to be enforceable as "definite quantity supply contract," it must obligate buyer to buy specific amount of product for specific amount of money.

> In re Anchor Glass Container Corp., 297 B.R. 887, affirmed 345 B.R. 765.

To be enforceable, indefinite quantity supply contract, which does not obligate buyer to buy exclusively from seller or to satisfy all of its requirements for goods of particular kind from seller, must state a minimum quantity term; absent a minimum quantity term, indefinite quantity supply contact is illusory and unenforceable.

> In re Anchor Glass Container Corp., 297 B.R. 887, affirmed 345 B.R. 765.

Indefinite quantity supply contract, under which buyer was not obligated to buy glass bottles for use in wine industry exclusively from seller or to satisfy all of its requirements for bottles from seller, and pursuant to which buyer first had to place purchase order which was then accepted by seller before any obligations arose, was illusory and unenforceable, and would not support proof of claim against seller's bankruptcy estate for not performing under contract, where there was no language in contract that required buyer to purchase minimum quantity of bottles from seller.

> In re Anchor Glass Container Corp., 297 B.R. 887, affirmed 345 B.R. 765.

Fla. 1940. Where contract is made for purchase of certain goods, they must be of the quantity as well as the quality stipulated.

> Vaughn-Griffin Packing Co. v. Fisher, 193 So. 553, 141 Fla. 428.

Fla.App. 3 Dist. 1966. Contract between seller of fill and landowner for purchase of sufficient fill to bring properties to certain specification of grade level could not be implied to have required landowner to purchase sufficient fill to anticipate subsidence to a definite time in future, and where landowner established that filled area was dredged in excess of elevation required under contract so that any deficiency in grade was due to settlement over intervening years, seller failed to prove his entitlement to recover any money from landowner.

> Tropic-South, Inc. v. Key Broadcasting, Inc., 184 So.2d 920.

☞**1003. Particular cases and goods in general.**

C.A.11 (Fla.) 1985. Fact that automobile dealers were allegedly taking steps to subvert exclusive importer and distributor of foreign automobiles' allocation system for automobiles in periods of shortages did not render such system unreasonable so as to breach distributor's agreement with nonexclusive dealership, where distributor was taking reasonable steps to detect such subversion by intensifying its auditing of dealerships in certain regions to discover any false reporting of sales.

> Cabriolet Porsche Audi, Inc. v. American Honda Motor Co., Inc., 773 F.2d 1193, certiorari denied 106 S.Ct. 1641, 475 U.S. 1122, 90 L.Ed.2d 186, rehearing denied 106 S.Ct. 2929, 476 U.S. 1189, 91 L.Ed.2d 557.

Allocation system established by exclusive importer and distributor of foreign automobiles for allocation of automobiles in periods of shortages was not unreasonable so as to breach distributor's contract with nonexclusive dealership, where allocations were based essentially on dealers' sales record and where a certain number of cars were reserved to replace damaged cars, to help new dealerships, and to encourage dealers to establish exclusive facilities.

> Cabriolet Porsche Audi, Inc. v. American Honda Motor Co., Inc., 773 F.2d 1193, certiorari denied 106 S.Ct. 1641, 475 U.S. 1122, 90 L.Ed.2d 186, rehearing denied 106 S.Ct. 2929, 476 U.S. 1189, 91 L.Ed.2d 557.

Refusal of exclusive importer and distributor of foreign automobiles to execute

---

written agreement with nonexclusive dealership guaranteeing a specific number of additional cars if dealership expanded was not a lack of good faith in violation of dealership agreement, where distributor had no control over number of cars sent by its Japanese parent corporation and could not guarantee in advance how many cars it would have at any given time.

> Cabriolet Porsche Audi, Inc. v. American Honda Motor Co., Inc., 773 F.2d 1193, certiorari denied 106 S.Ct. 1641, 475 U.S. 1122, 90 L.Ed.2d 186, rehearing denied 106 S.Ct. 2929, 476 U.S. 1189, 91 L.Ed.2d 557.

Even if agreement between exclusive importer and distributor of foreign automobiles and nonexclusive dealership contained implied condition of cooperation, such condition was not breached by distributor's refusal to give dealership more cars than were allocated to it from 15% holdback pool established by distributor unless dealership established exclusive facility, where dealership received every car to which it was entitled under allocation system, and where dealership was not in financial trouble.

> Cabriolet Porsche Audi, Inc. v. American Honda Motor Co., Inc., 773 F.2d 1193, certiorari denied 106 S.Ct. 1641, 475 U.S. 1122, 90 L.Ed.2d 186, rehearing denied 106 S.Ct. 2929, 476 U.S. 1189, 91 L.Ed.2d 557.

Fla. 1940. Contract to purchase citrus fruit was construable as executory contract under which the buyer had duty to gather merchantable fruit and discard fruit which was damaged by frost, regardless of whether there was as much merchantable fruit harvested as estimated in the purchase contract.

> Vaughn-Griffin Packing Co. v. Fisher, 193 So. 553, 141 Fla. 428.

Fla.App. 5 Dist. 2005. Motorcycle dealer satisfied its contractual obligations with motorcycle manufacturer by purchasing three motorcycles, given that dealer never agreed to purchase a specific number of motorcycles beyond the two required in the contract and there was no meeting of the minds on purchasing a set number beyond the first two motorcycles.

> Beach Street Bikes, Inc. v. Bourgett's Bike Works, Inc., 900 So.2d 697.

🔑**1004–1005.** *For other cases see earlier editions of this digest, the Decennial Digests, and WESTLAW.*

🔑**1005. Output contracts, requirements contracts, and exclusive dealings.**

🔑**1006. —— In general.**

C.A.11 (Fla.) 1985. Dealership agreement between exclusive importer and distributor of foreign automobiles and nonexclusive dealership, which expressly authorized adoption of allocation system in times of shortage or restricted supply, did not prohibit distributor from adopting and implementing allocation system for automobiles to be distributed to dealership in times of surplus or unrestricted supply, where agreement expressly granted distributor discretion as to allocation of cars by providing that dealership's orders could be accepted by distributor in whole or as to any part thereof.

> Cabriolet Porsche Audi, Inc. v. American Honda Motor Co., Inc., 773 F.2d 1193, certiorari denied 106 S.Ct. 1641, 475 U.S. 1122, 90 L.Ed.2d 186, rehearing denied 106 S.Ct. 2929, 476 U.S. 1189, 91 L.Ed.2d 557.

Exclusive importer and distributor of foreign automobiles' system for allocating automobiles to dealerships in periods of automobile shortages, which was based on sales and travel rates established by dealerships during periods of nonshortages, did not breach reasonableness requirement of agreement with nonexclusive dealership, where dealership had been told that its failure to sell aggressively during nonshortage periods would affect its allocation in future, and where dealership was not at any time in financial trouble.

> Cabriolet Porsche Audi, Inc. v. American Honda Motor Co., Inc., 773 F.2d 1193, certiorari denied 106 S.Ct. 1641, 475 U.S. 1122, 90 L.Ed.2d 186, rehearing denied 106 S.Ct. 2929, 476 U.S. 1189, 91 L.Ed.2d 557.

Alleged failure of exclusive importer and distributor of foreign automobiles to inform nonexclusive dealership of its 15% holdback policy in periods of automobile shortages did not render distributor's allocation system unreasonable, so as to breach dealership agreement, where dealership was told that it could obtain additional cars, under such policy, if it provided exclusive facility.

Cabriolet Porsche Audi, Inc. v. American Honda Motor Co., Inc., 773 F.2d 1193, certiorari denied 106 S.Ct. 1641, 475 U.S. 1122, 90 L.Ed.2d 186, rehearing denied 106 S.Ct. 2929, 476 U.S. 1189, 91 L.Ed.2d 557.

M.D.Fla. 2006. Agreement between bottle supplier and customer was unenforceable indefinite quantity supply contract, rather than valid requirements contract, under California law, given that agreement merely provided that customer would buy product as it might desire, without any definite minimum purchase amount and without any obligation to buy from supplier or its parent company, and that neither supplier nor its parent company were obligated to produce a specific volume for customer. West's Ann.Cal. Com.Code § 2306.

In re Anchor Glass Container Corp., 345 B.R. 765.

Under California law, a true "requirements contract" exists when the seller agrees to supply all of the buyer's requirements.

In re Anchor Glass Container Corp., 345 B.R. 765.

Bkrtcy.M.D.Fla. 2003. Supply contract may fall into one of three categories, a definite quantity, indefinite quantity, or requirements contract, and when supply contract is ambiguous as to type, court should examine extrinsic evidence to determine what type of supply contract the parties intended.

In re Anchor Glass Container Corp., 297 B.R. 887, affirmed 345 B.R. 765.

For supply contract to be enforceable as "requirements contract," certain conditions must be satisfied: (1) contract must obligate buyer to buy goods; (2) it must obligate buyer to buy exclusively from sell-

er; and (3) it must obligate buyer to buy all of its requirements for goods of particular kind from seller.

In re Anchor Glass Container Corp., 297 B.R. 887, affirmed 345 B.R. 765.

Fla.App. 5 Dist. 2000. For a contract to constitute an exclusive agreement to purchase or sell, it is not necessary that such terms be express.

Danforth Orthopedic Brace & Limb, Inc. v. Florida Health Care Plan, Inc., 750 So.2d 774.

⚷**1007. —— Buyer's obligations, performance, and breach.**

Fla.App. 4 Dist. 1989. Construction company was not required to pay for fill, provided under contract which required it to pay only if it "used" the fill, where some unknown third party spread fill upon land long after construction company had departed from work site; furthermore, there was no benefit conferred upon construction company by spreading of fill since construction company did not own land. (Per Walden, J., with one Judge concurring specially with opinion).

L.J. Clark Const. Co. v. Hardrives Co., Inc., 547 So.2d 963.

⚷**1008. —— Seller's obligations, performance, and breach.**

S.D.Fla. 1975. If a buyer's demands under a requirements contract become excessive, the seller may, in an appropriate case, refuse to deliver the unreasonable amounts demanded, although seller's basic contract obligation is not eliminated; if a customer repeatedly makes no requirements at all, seller may be excused from performance if the buyer suddenly and without warning should descend upon him and demand his entire inventory.

Eastern Air Lines, Inc. v. Gulf Oil Corp., 415 F.Supp. 429.

4. ACCEPTANCE OR REJECTION OF NONCONFORMING GOODS.

⚷**1011. In general.**

N.D.Fla. 2010. Acceptance of goods occurs under Florida law when the buyer, after a reasonable opportunity to inspect them, signifies that the goods are conforming or will be accepted despite a nonconformity, or if the buyer fails to make an effective rejection after having a reasonable opportunity to inspect the goods; an acceptance with knowledge of a nonconformity cannot be revoked because of that nonconformity. West's F.S.A. §§ 672.606, 672.607.

> JDI Holdings, LLC v. Jet Management, Inc., 732 F.Supp.2d 1205.

Fla.App. 3 Dist. 1997. Buyer accepted allegedly nonconforming merchandise when it resold, or attempted to resell, merchandise, and thus buyer was obligated to pay seller contract rate for the same. West's F.S.A. §§ 672.606(1)(c), 672.607(1).

> Hawke Distributing, Inc. v. Nuevo Sol Partners, Inc., 689 So.2d 1202.

⚷1012. Particular cases and goods in general.

† C.A.11 (Fla.) 2013. Venezuelan state-owned purchasing company accepted shipments of powdered milk from China from Florida-based import company before it arrived in port in Venezuela, and thus without discovery of nonconformity for purposes of breach of contract analysis under Florida law, where purchasing company had bargained for a contractual right to inspect the milk before its shipment from China, it paid for the goods while they were in transit, and it also notified import company that the shipment was "received, reviewed, confirmed and accepted." West's F.S.A. § 672.606.

> Exim Brickell LLC v. PDVSA Services Inc., 516 Fed.Appx. 742.

Fla.App. 5 Dist. 1989. Buyer which operated shopping mall accepted Christmas tree decorations within meaning of U.C.C. by keeping delivered goods and using them as mall's Christmas decorations, even though it attempted to negotiate lower price because of perceived unsuitable quality. West's F.S.A. § 672.606.

> B.P. Development and Management Corp. v. P. Lafer Enterprises, Inc., 538 So.2d 1379.

⚷1013. Partial delivery and acceptance; installments.

For other cases see earlier editions of this digest, the Decennial Digests, and WESTLAW.

⚷1014. Notice and opportunity to cure.

† C.A.11 (Fla.) 2013. Venezuelan state-owned purchasing company accepted shipments of powdered milk from China from Florida-based import company before it arrived in port in Venezuela, and thus without discovery of nonconformity for purposes of breach of contract analysis under Florida law, where purchasing company had bargained for a contractual right to inspect the milk before its shipment from China, it paid for the goods while they were in transit, and it also notified import company that the shipment was "received, reviewed, confirmed and accepted." West's F.S.A. § 672.606.

> Exim Brickell LLC v. PDVSA Services Inc., 516 Fed.Appx. 742.

S.D.Fla. 2008. Under Georgia law, conditions of sale incorporated into agreement for sale of concrete modular blocks to construction company barred company's assignee's claims against seller, where agreement required company to give notice of any defects within two days of receipt, but company failed to give notice of any defects in product, and failed to inform seller that wrong component parts were shipped. West's Ga.Code Ann. § 11–2–207.

> Pycsa Panama, S.A. v. Tensar Earth Technologies, Inc., 625 F.Supp.2d 1198, affirmed 329 Fed.Appx. 257.

Fla.App. 1 Dist. 1981. Purchaser of continuous belt conveyor system for use by bakery in its pizza freezing business did not waive his right to cover, when, upon discovering that the system could not be modified to meet specifications in the purchase contract, he notified the seller that the contract would be cancelled and no other damages would be claimed if his deposit money was returned. West's F.S.A. §§ 672.711, 672.712.

> Goodell v. K. T. Enterprises, Ltd., 394 So.2d 1087.

Fla.App. 4 Dist. 1969. Finding that purchaser of crane knew that it was insufficient but nonetheless retained it and allowed damages to accumulate for nearly three years was sufficient to bar an action for rescission, and would also bar an action for damages if no notice of defects was given the seller.

> Ferncrest Mining Co. v. H. F. Mason Equipment Corp., 225 So.2d 354.

⚷**1015. Time for acceptance, rejection, or notice.**

S.D.Fla. 2008. Under Georgia law, conditions of sale incorporated into agreement for sale of concrete modular blocks to construction company barred company's assignee's claims against seller, where agreement required company to give notice of any defects within two days of receipt, but company failed to give notice of any defects in product, and failed to inform seller that wrong component parts were shipped. West's Ga.Code Ann. § 11–2–207.

> Pycsa Panama, S.A. v. Tensar Earth Technologies, Inc., 625 F.Supp.2d 1198, affirmed 329 Fed.Appx. 257.

Bkrtcy.S.D.Fla. 1983. Under Florida law, debtor accepted goods shipped by creditor where evidence established that goods were delivered, debtor had opportunity to inspect and debtor failed to notify creditor of any defect within reasonable time. West's F.S.A. §§ 672.602, 672.606, 672.607(4).

> In re Holistic Services Corp., 29 B.R. 509.

Purpose and effect of Florida Commercial Code provision requiring buyer's notice to seller within reasonable time of breach is to require that parties act in commercially reasonable manner and to make it possible for seller to exercise his rights to cure defect and thereby mitigate damages. West's F.S.A. §§ 672.508, 672.607(3)(a).

> In re Holistic Services Corp., 29 B.R. 509.

Fla.App. 3 Dist. 1988. Buyer of computer and software did not delay unreasonably in asserting that seller breached its contract, but promptly notified seller of defects in the software and gave seller ample time to remedy the matter, and, when those efforts failed, buyer revoked its acceptance.

> Money Mortg. and Inv. Corp. v. CPT of South Florida, Inc., 537 So.2d 1015.

⚷**1016–1022.** *For other cases see earlier editions of this digest, the Decennial Digests, and WESTLAW.*

5. REVOCATION OF ACCEPTANCE.

Repudiation, see V(J). Cancellation and termination, see VI. Rescission, see X(D).

⚷**1031. In general.**

C.A.11 (Fla.) 1983. For purpose of revocation of acceptance, nonconformity of goods must be present at time of sale and delivery. West's F.S.A. § 672.608(1, 2).

> Royal Typewriter Co., a Div. of Litton Business Systems, Inc. v. Xerographic Supplies Corp., 719 F.2d 1092.

Fla.App. 1 Dist. 1988. There must be some warranty or provision in contract to which goods must conform in order for goods to be nonconforming, for purposes of doctrine of revocation of acceptance. West's F.S.A. §§ 672.106, 672.314 comment.

> McCormick Machinery, Inc. v. Julian E. Johnson & Sons, Inc., 523 So.2d 651.

⚷**1032. Grounds; substantial impairment.**

† **C.A.11 (Fla.) 2013.** Communication from Venezuelan state-owned purchasing company to Florida-based import company asking for an "urgent meeting" due to test results showing that powdered milk from China was toxic, and further demanding that import company reply within 48 hours or purchasing company reserved the right to take legal action, constituted a revocation of acceptance, for purposes of breach of contract analysis under Florida law. West's F.S.A. § 672.608(2).

> Exim Brickell LLC v. PDVSA Services Inc., 516 Fed.Appx. 742.

† **C.A.11 (Fla.) 2013.** Venezuelan buyer's revocation of contract with seller of contaminated powdered milk from China was made in good faith, under Florida law, although revocation of all shipments of milk occurred upon buyer's discovery of melamine contamination in third shipment out of 20 shipments, where value of milk

purchased because of extensive food shortages in Venezuela was impaired as potentially lethal, and buyer's discovery of contamination in third shipment critically called into question safety of all other shipments and provided basis to infer that other shipments were also contaminated. West's F.S.A. § 672.608.

Absolute Trading Corp. v. Bariven S.A., 503 Fed.Appx. 694.

M.D.Fla. 2002. Allegations by purchasers of motor home that defects were numerous and continuous, that purchasers sought repair of motor home on numerous occasions, and that repairs became impossible, were sufficient to state claim against manufacturer for revocation of acceptance under Florida law. West's F.S.A. § 672.608.

Bland v. Freightliner LLC, 206 F.Supp.2d 1202.

N.D.Fla. 2010. Acceptance of goods occurs under Florida law when the buyer, after a reasonable opportunity to inspect them, signifies that the goods are conforming or will be accepted despite a nonconformity, or if the buyer fails to make an effective rejection after having a reasonable opportunity to inspect the goods; an acceptance with knowledge of a nonconformity cannot be revoked because of that nonconformity. West's F.S.A. §§ 672.606, 672.607.

JDI Holdings, LLC v. Jet Management, Inc., 732 F.Supp.2d 1205.

Fla.App. 1 Dist. 1992. Violation of unfair trade practices chapter is not a sufficient basis for revocation of acceptance. West's F.S.A. § 501.001 et seq.

Frank Griffin Volkswagen, Inc. v. Smith, 610 So.2d 597, review denied 620 So.2d 762, appeal after remand 645 So.2d 585, cause dismissed Volkswagen of America, Inc. v. Smith, 654 So.2d 132, rehearing denied, appeal after remand 690 So.2d 1328, rehearing denied.

Fla.App. 1 Dist. 1983. Value of automobile, which required frequent trips back to the shop, which had problems with radio, air conditioning, windshield washers, cruise control, tires, and paint, and on which repairs had not been successful, was substantially impaired so as to permit revocation of acceptance in view of buy-

er's testimony and long list of relatively minor problems.

Tom Bush Volkswagen, Inc. v. Kuntz, 429 So.2d 398.

Fla.App. 2 Dist. 2000. Before a buyer can legally revoke acceptance, the buyer must show that the goods were nonconforming, that the nonconformity substantially impaired the goods' value, that the seller had the opportunity to cure the defects, but failed to do so seasonably, and that the buyer revoked her acceptance within a reasonable time. West's F.S.A. § 672.608.

Gulfwind South, Inc. v. Jones, 775 So.2d 311.

Before a buyer can elect to revoke acceptance, he or she must demonstrate a nonconformity to some provision in the contract, or nonconformity to a warranty, to which the goods must conform.

Gulfwind South, Inc. v. Jones, 775 So.2d 311.

Fla.App. 2 Dist. 1975. Within statute providing buyer with right to revoke acceptance of goods, whose nonconformity substantially impairs its value to him, "impairment" is that suffered by purchaser himself which must be subjectively measured from standpoint of purchaser; it has nothing to do with purchaser's financial ability or inability. West's F.S.A. §§ 672.106, 672.608.

Barrington Homes of Florida, Inc. v. Kelley, 320 So.2d 841.

Within statute providing buyer with right to revoke acceptance of goods, whose nonconformity substantially impairs its value to him, "value" to purchaser is to be measured by essential purposes to be served by buyer's purchase of goods in first place and if such purpose is substantially frustrated or interfered with by "non-conformities", then "value" of goods has been "substantially impaired" as to him. West's F.S.A. §§ 672.106, 672.608.

Barrington Homes of Florida, Inc. v. Kelley, 320 So.2d 841.

Fla.App. 3 Dist. 1972. One test for rescission or revocation of sales contract is whether there has been a substantial impairment of value to the buyer. F.S.A. § 672.608.

> Orange Motors of Coral Gables, Inc. v. Dade County Dairies, Inc., 258 So.2d 319, certiorari denied 263 So.2d 831.

☞1033. Persons against whom revocation may be had.

☞1034. —— In general.

Fla.App. 1 Dist. 1992. Where automobile dealer properly disclaimed all warranties, delivering, presenting, or explaining of manufacturer's warranty, without more, did not render dealer a cowarrantor by adoption and did not create contractual obligation which could serve as basis for buyer's later revocation of acceptance. West's F.S.A. §§ 672.106(2), 672.608(1).

> Frank Griffin Volkswagen, Inc. v. Smith, 610 So.2d 597, review denied 620 So.2d 762, appeal after remand 645 So.2d 585, cause dismissed Volkswagen of America, Inc. v. Smith, 654 So.2d 132, rehearing denied, appeal after remand 690 So.2d 1328, rehearing denied.

When limited remedy provided by automobile manufacturer failed of its essential purpose, that did not render the goods nonconforming under buyer's contract with dealer and did not entitle buyer to pursue any available remedy under UCC, including revocation of acceptance, where dealer disclaimed all warranties. West's F.S.A. §§ 672.608, 672.719.

> Frank Griffin Volkswagen, Inc. v. Smith, 610 So.2d 597, review denied 620 So.2d 762, appeal after remand 645 So.2d 585, cause dismissed Volkswagen of America, Inc. v. Smith, 654 So.2d 132, rehearing denied, appeal after remand 690 So.2d 1328, rehearing denied.

Fla.App. 2 Dist. 2000. Before a buyer can elect to revoke acceptance, he or she must demonstrate a nonconformity to some provision in the contract, or nonconformity to a warranty, to which the goods must conform.

> Gulfwind South, Inc. v. Jones, 775 So.2d 311.

☞1035–1037. *For other cases see earlier editions of this digest, the Decennial Digests, and WESTLAW.*

☞1038. Notice and opportunity to cure.

† C.A.11 (Fla.) 2013. Communication from Venezuelan state-owned purchasing company to Florida-based import company asking for an "urgent meeting" due to test results showing that powdered milk from China was toxic and further demanding that import company reply within 48 hours or purchasing company reserved the right to take legal action constituted sufficient notice of revocation of acceptance of all existing shipments, for purposes of breach of contract analysis under Florida law, since it put import company on notice that the goods were non-conforming in a specific way and purchasing company was not required to have proof that each shipment was substantially nonconforming. West's F.S.A. § 672.608.

> Exim Brickell LLC v. PDVSA Services Inc., 516 Fed.Appx. 742.

Fla.App. 5 Dist. 1989. Delay in giving notice of revocation of contract to purchase Christmas tree decorations, which had been delivered shortly before Thanksgiving, until following June was unreasonable in view of seasonal nature of decorations; moreover, even if notice of revocation had been given earlier, buyer's actions in displaying and using decorations for its own benefit during Christmas season was inconsistent with claimed revocation. West's F.S.A. § 672.608.

> B.P. Development and Management Corp. v. P. Lafer Enterprises, Inc., 538 So.2d 1379.

☞1039. Timeliness.

† C.A.11 (Fla.) 2013. Notice of revocation of acceptance of shipments of powdered milk from China communicated from Venezuelan state-owned purchasing company to Florida-based import company was timely, for purposes of breach of contract analysis under Florida law, given difficulties in testing milk shipments and previous lack of awareness in industry of the possibility of melamine contamination. West's F.S.A. § 672.608.

> Exim Brickell LLC v. PDVSA Services Inc., 516 Fed.Appx. 742.

† **C.A.11 (Fla.) 2013.** Venezuelan buyer's delayed revocation of contract with seller of contaminated powdered milk from China was reasonable, under Florida law, although revocation occurred seven months after buyer received notice that milk could be contaminated with melamine, where buyer unsuccessfully searched for laboratory in Venezuela with capacity to test for melamine, then sent samples to customs agency for transport to United States, but later discovered that agency lacked required licenses, so buyer conducted further search to locate customs agent with required licenses, agent sent samples to buyer's subsidiary in United States, subsidiary sent samples to testing laboratory, and buyer revoked contract less than one week after receiving test results that all milk samples were contaminated. West's F.S.A. §§ 671.204(1), 672.608.

Absolute Trading Corp. v. Bariven S.A., 503 Fed.Appx. 694.

Fla.App. 5 Dist. 1987. By failing to seek rescission of contract for purchase of television satellite system until buyer had been in possession of system for one and one-half years, buyer did not act "within a reasonable time" within meaning of statute authorizing revocation of acceptance. West's F.S.A. § 672.608.

Central Florida Antenna Service, Inc. v. Crabtree, 503 So.2d 1351.

⚷**1040. Substantial change in condition of goods.**

C.A.11 (Fla.) 1983. Purported revocation of acceptance by dealer of copier machines was not effective, inasmuch as it was made after substantial changes in condition of the goods had taken place, such changed condition not resulting from any alleged defects in the machines. West's F.S.A. § 672.608(1, 2).

Royal Typewriter Co., a Div. of Litton Business Systems, Inc. v. Xerographic Supplies Corp., 719 F.2d 1092.

⚷**1041. Rights and duties after rightful revocation.**

M.D.Fla. 2015. Under Florida law, where the buyer rightfully revokes acceptance of non-conforming goods, the buyer is entitled to the return of the purchase price that has been paid.

Armadillo Distribution Enterprises, Inc. v. Hai Yun Musical Instruments Manufacture Co. Ltd., 142 F.Supp.3d 1245.

⚷**1042. Acceptance after revocation; reacceptance.**

For other cases see earlier editions of this digest, the Decennial Digests, and WESTLAW.

6. SALE ON TRIAL OR APPROVAL; CONTRACTS FOR SALE OR RETURN.

⚷**1051. In general.**

Bkrtcy.S.D.Fla. 2003. Motor vehicle owners "delivered" these vehicles to used car dealership for resale, such that parties' transactions were governed by "consignment" provision of the Florida Uniform Commercial Code (UCC), even though owners retained possession of certificates of title; owners' retention of certificates did not prevent "delivery" from occurring, as that term is used in the Florida UCC. West's F.S.A. § 672.326.

In re Corvette Collection of Boston, Inc., 294 B.R. 409.

Fla.App. 3 Dist. 1988. Copier machine buyer had agreed to purchase the merchandise and was liable for the purchase price under agreement sued upon by seller, unambiguously denominated as "equipment and supplies contract," which provided that the buyer both entered an order for the equipment in question and agreed to pay for it in cash and which was thus wholly inconsistent with a "sale on approval" transaction.

Copy Service, Inc. v. Florida Copy Corp., 527 So.2d 247.

Clause in an equipment and supplies contract which provided that, if the particular unit being used by the buyer were not satisfactory, it would be replaced by another, did not alter the buyer's obligation to pay the seller for the copier machine, and did not render the transaction a "sale on approval."

Copy Service, Inc. v. Florida Copy Corp., 527 So.2d 247.

For references to other topics, see Descriptive-Word Index

⚷1052–1055. *For other cases see earlier editions of this digest, the Decennial Digests, and WESTLAW.*

⚷1055. Exercise of right to return or reject goods.

⚷1056. —— In general.

Bkrtcy.M.D.Fla. 1990. Under Florida law, broker did not properly reject tomatoes, and thus broker was liable for agreed price of tomatoes, where broker did not obtain Department of Agriculture inspection within 24 hours after arrival, as required by seller's shipping orders, even though broker alleged that it was enticed into accepting more shipments on promise of better shipments to come. West's F.S.A. § 672.602.

Matter of East Coast Brokers and Packers, Inc., 120 B.R. 221, affirmed 134 B.R. 41, reversed 961 F.2d 1543.

⚷1057. —— Time and place of return or rejection.

Bkrtcy.M.D.Fla. 2005. Under Florida law, buyer clearly and unambiguously rejected boat that it had paid seller to construct on its behalf, which failed to achieve top speed promised by seller at time contract was signed during three different sea trials, when, within three days of final sea trial, buyer indicated that he did not want boat but instead wanted his money back. West's F.S.A. §§ 672.601, 672.602.

In re Dorado Marine, Inc., 321 B.R. 581.

⚷1058–1061. *For other cases see earlier editions of this digest, the Decennial Digests, and WESTLAW.*

⚷1062. Effect of failure to return goods.

Fla. 1941. Contract for sale of garment bag machinery constructed for buyer was, in view of prior correspondence between the parties, construable as constituting a "sale on approval" so that in view of fact that machinery was not acceptable to the buyer, the seller could effect its return by way of replevin.

Jacksonville Paper Co. v. Smith & Winchester Mfg. Co., 2 So.2d 890, 147 Fla. 311.

(D) AMOUNTS PAYABLE.

⚷1071–1074. *For other cases see earlier editions of this digest, the Decennial Digests, and WESTLAW.*

⚷1072. Price.

⚷1074. —— Amount agreed on; contract price.

⚷1074(1). In general.

Fla. 1939. Where $1,500 paid by buyer to seller of citrus fruit was forfeited under contract of sale for nonperformance of contract, and buyer subsequently paid $1,500 to seller under new contract for purchase of same fruit not referring to original $1,500, buyer could not deduct the $1,500 forfeited under old contract from purchase price provided in new contract.

Lee & Edwards Corp. v. Carlton, 191 So. 453, 140 Fla. 242.

Fla.App. 2 Dist. 1969. Contract provision that buyer would purchase one hundred thousand boxes of fruit with a floor of 60 cents per lb. constituted a guarantee of a minimum price and subsequent general provision of contract regarding "participation plan" did not allow buyer to deduct a 10 cents per box "retain" from the guaranteed minimum price. F.S.A. § 618.01 et seq.

Cypress Gardens Citrus Products, Inc. v. Bowen Bros., Inc., 223 So.2d 776.

Fla.App. 3 Dist. 1997. Buyer accepted allegedly nonconforming merchandise when it resold, or attempted to resell, merchandise, and thus buyer was obligated to pay seller contract rate for the same. West's F.S.A. §§ 672.606(1)(c), 672.607(1).

Hawke Distributing, Inc. v. Nuevo Sol Partners, Inc., 689 So.2d 1202.

⚷1074(2). Ascertainment.

S.D.Fla. 1999. Because dealers' dispute with gasoline supplier was not over the actual amount of the price supplier charged for its wholesale gasoline to its dealers, but rather, over the manner in which the wholesale price was calculated without considering the doubled charge for credit card processing, dealers' breach of contract action was not the "normal" case such that supplier's "price in effect" was, by definition, a price set in good faith. U.C.C. §§ 1–203, 2–103(1)(b), 2–311.

> Allapattah Services, Inc. v. Exxon Corp., 61 F.Supp.2d 1308.

S.D.Fla. 1975. Where provision, contained in contract for sale of aviation fuel, covering contingency of suspension of publication of industry newsletter which contained price postings which were used to determine price to be paid under the contract referred to a complete cessation of publishing of the newsletter or at least of the specified postings, that provision was not made applicable by fact that the newsletter, during government price control program, published only the lower, controlled, price applicable to "old oil" and not the price applicable to "new" oil.

> Eastern Air Lines, Inc. v. Gulf Oil Corp., 415 F.Supp. 429.

Fla.App. 3 Dist. 1971. Under franchise agreement which provided that where food offered by licensee was purchased from licensor the cost should not exceed licensor's costs of raw materials plus 13 percent, licensee was not entitled to restrict licensor on a 13 percent price on an item per item basis, and licensor was entitled to have cost of necessary processing of food products included in price thereof when purchased from licensor.

> Trail Burger King, Inc. v. Burger King of Miami, Inc., 249 So.2d 483.

⚷**1075. —— Market price.**

For other cases see earlier editions of this digest, the Decennial Digests, and WESTLAW.

⚷**1076. —— Reasonable price.**

M.D.Fla. 1999. Under Florida law, in a "complete gap" case, in which contacting parties have said nothing as to the price term of a sale contract, the court may look to several factors to ascertain reasonable price, including evidence of the (1) course of performance, (2) usage of trade, and (3) the fair market value at the time and place of delivery.

> Offices Togolais Des Phosphates v. Mulberry Phosphates, Inc., 62 F.Supp.2d 1316, affirmed 228 F.3d 414.

District court's use of a "bone phosphate of lime" (BPL) value of 80 in calculating the reasonable price for phosphate rock sold to buyer in a suit for breach of a sales contract which had left the price to be determined by agreement at a later date was not manifestly erroneous, and thus, the use of that value did not warrant granting of buyer's motion to alter or amend judgment; buyer itself considered the phosphate to have a BPL value of 80 one month following the arrival of the shipment. Fed.Rules Civ.Proc.Rule 59(e), 28 U.S.C.A.

> Offices Togolais Des Phosphates v. Mulberry Phosphates, Inc., 62 F.Supp.2d 1316, affirmed 228 F.3d 414.

⚷**1077. —— Open price.**

M.D.Fla. 1999. Under Florida law, a reasonable price for a shipment of phosphate rock was the market price for a shipment of phosphate rock in the buyer's locale, adjusted for the enhanced "bone phosphate of lime" (BPL) content of the delivered rock and converting the metric tons to short tons; the parties operated in different markets with little overlap, and had contracted for the sale with the price to be agreed to at a later date. West's F.S.A. §§ 672.204(3), 672.305.

> Offices Togolais Des Phosphates v. Mulberry Phosphates, Inc., 62 F.Supp.2d 1316, affirmed 228 F.3d 414.

S.D.Fla. 2005. Under Florida law, fuel supplier did not breach its obligation under the Uniform Commercial Code (UCC) to set its price for motor fuel in good faith, despite claim by operators of gasoline service stations that supplier charged them a higher price than it charged other dealers, where supplier's price was commercially reasonable in that it fell within range of prices that other suppliers in the relevant geographic market charged, and it was non-discriminatory in that it was applied uniformly among supplier's similarly-situated dealers. West's F.S.A. §§ 671.203, 672.305(2).

> United Food Mart, Inc. v. Motiva Enterprises, LLC, 457 F.Supp.2d 1329.

Under Florida law, a commercially reasonable price for motor fuel, that is, one within the range of prices charged for motor fuel by other refiners in the market, is a good faith price under the Uniform Commercial Code's (UCC) open price term requirement of good faith in price fixing, absent some evidence that the refiner used pricing to discriminate among its purchasers. West's F.S.A. § 672.305(2).

> United Food Mart, Inc. v. Motiva Enterprises, LLC, 457 F.Supp.2d 1329.

S.D.Fla. 1999. Duty of good faith under Uniform Commercial Code (UCC) is especially applicable in situations when the contract confers one party with the discretion to determine certain terms of a contract, such as an open price term agreed to be unilaterally set; duty acts to preserve and to control opportunistic behavior, by requiring that the price be reasonable and set pursuant to reasonable commercial standards of fair dealing in the trade. U.C.C. §§ 1–203, 2–103(1)(b).

> Allapattah Services, Inc. v. Exxon Corp., 61 F.Supp.2d 1308.

Gasoline supplier had an implied duty to each of its dealers to set its open price term in good faith and within the limits set by commercial reasonableness; that duty was part of each sales agreement and was independent of any subsequent amendment or modification. U.C.C. §§ 1–203, 2–103(1)(b), 2–311.

> Allapattah Services, Inc. v. Exxon Corp., 61 F.Supp.2d 1308.

🗝**1078. Expenses in general.**

M.D.Fla. 1999. Excluding consideration of the full value of phosphate rock buyer's storage and shipping expenses when calculating a reasonable price in a breach of contract suit was not manifest error, so as to warrant granting of buyer's motion to alter or amend judgment; buyer incurred the cost of storing the rock at the facility in question because it apparently did not have the capability or the proper storage facilities, and transportation expenses were considered in determining the reasonable price of the rock. Fed.Rules Civ.Proc.Rule 59(e), 28 U.S.C.A.

> Offices Togolais Des Phosphates v. Mulberry Phosphates, Inc., 62 F.Supp.2d 1316, affirmed 228 F.3d 414.

🗝**1079. Credits and deductions; abatement.**

Fla.App. 2 Dist. 1969. Contract provision that buyer would purchase one hundred thousand boxes of fruit with a floor of 60 cents per lb. constituted a guarantee of a minimum price and subsequent general provision of contract regarding "participation plan" did not allow buyer to deduct a 10 cents per box "retain" from the guaranteed minimum price. F.S.A. § 618.01 et seq.

> Cypress Gardens Citrus Products, Inc. v. Bowen Bros., Inc., 223 So.2d 776.

🗝**1080. Interest and service charges.**

For other cases see earlier editions of this digest, the Decennial Digests, and WEST-LAW.

🗝**1081. Taxes.**

Fla.App. 5 Dist. 2002. Handwritten language contained in "other provisions" section of contract for sale of modular diner unit, which language listed sales tax as an item which was to be priced after plans for unit were approved, was clear and did not create conflict with an article of contract stating that any taxes imposed on unit were responsibility of buyer, and thus, buyer was responsible for sales tax subsequently assessed by Department of Revenue on sale of unit, where buyer did not delete or modify article of the contract or refer to article in writing in any way, and to allow seller to absorb all or any part of sales tax under contract would have rendered contract illegal. West's F.S.A. § 212.07(4).

> Starlite Diners, Inc. v. Oswalt, 823 So.2d 312.

(E) DUTIES AND EXPENSES OF TRANSPORTATION.

🗝**1091. In general.**

M.D.Fla. 1999. Excluding consideration of the full value of phosphate rock buyer's storage and shipping expenses when calculating a reasonable price in a breach of contract suit was not manifest error, so as to warrant granting of buyer's motion to alter or amend judgment; buyer incurred the cost of storing the rock at the facility in question because it apparently did not have the capability or the proper storage facilities, and transportation expenses were considered in determining the reasonable price of the rock. Fed.Rules Civ.Proc.Rule 59(e), 28 U.S.C.A.

Offices Togolais Des Phosphates v. Mulberry Phosphates, Inc., 62 F.Supp.2d 1316, affirmed 228 F.3d 414.

S.D.Fla. 2016. Consumers who had paid invoices from building materials supply company that contained "fuel surcharges" and "environmental charges" stated putative class action claims against the company for breach of contract under Florida law by alleging that although sales contract indicated company would compute these fees according to particular formula, it charged the same fuel surcharge and environmental charge no matter how many gallons of fuel it used and without any indication of its actual or increased environmental costs, simply to make additional profit.

Deere Construction, LLC v. Cemex Construction Materials Florida, LLC, 198 F.Supp.3d 1332.

⟜1092. Free on board (F.O.B.) contracts.

Fla.App. 4 Dist. 1988. The words "F.O.B." the destination for delivery of a yacht under a sales contract placed responsibility on the seller to pay for the ocean freight delivery charge incurred prior to the boat's reaching its destination as a matter of law, and thus it would be erroneous leave determination of payment of the ocean freight delivery charge to jury. West's F.S.A. § 672.319.

Boyman v. Stuart Hatteras, Inc., 527 So.2d 853.

⟜1093. Cost, insurance, and freight (C.I.F.) contracts.

For other cases see earlier editions of this digest, the Decennial Digests, and WESTLAW.

(F) PAYMENT.

⟜1101. In general.

C.A.5 (Fla.) 1971. Provision requiring trading stamp company which bought another trading stamp business to supply seller with monthly report of number of seller's trading stamps redeemed by buyer was not an agreement independent of contract requiring seller to reimburse buyer

for stamps redeemed, where it did not appear that sales agreement would have been entered into if reporting provision had not been included, but in view of fact that seller conceded that its injury from failing to receive reports could not be measured in dollars, the breach of buyer was not material and did not relieve seller of its obligation to pay for the stamps redeemed by buyer.

Gold Bond Stamp Co. of Ga. v. Gilt-Edge Stamps, Inc., 437 F.2d 27.

C.A.5 (Fla.) 1967. Inasmuch as parties to conditional sales contract treated buyer's default in payment as only partial breach of contract, all of rest of buyer's obligations under contract continued.

Brunswick Corp. v. Vineberg, 370 F.2d 605.

S.D.Fla. 2009. Under Florida law, buyers' failure to pay full price agreed upon in contract for purchase and delivery of food commodities constituted a "material breach of contract," where seller delivered food commodities, which were accepted by buyers. West's F.S.A. § 672.601(1).

Validsa, Inc. v. PDVSA Services Inc., 632 F.Supp.2d 1219, affirmed in part, reversed in part 424 Fed.Appx. 862.

Fla.App. 1 Dist. 1961. Temporary postponement of delivery purchase check executed by nonfranchised Tennessee automobile dealer which had ordered automobiles from franchised Michigan dealer did not result in sale by Michigan dealer of automobile on credit where order was made when Tennessee dealer's agent was out of town, and agent was to deliver check immediately upon return to town.

Trumbull Chevrolet Sales Co. v. Seawright, 134 So.2d 829, certiorari denied 143 So.2d 491.

Fla.App. 3 Dist. 1979. Where risk of loss falls on seller at time goods sold are lost or destroyed, seller is liable in damages to buyer for nondelivery unless seller tenders a performance in replacement for lost or destroyed goods and, on the other hand, where risk of loss falls on buyer at time the goods sold are lost or destroyed, buyer is liable to seller for purchase price of goods sold.

> Pestana v. Karinol Corp., 367 So.2d 1096.

Fla.App. 5 Dist. 1987. Sellers of business were entitled to collect escrow deposit paid as part of purchase price notwithstanding partial failure of consideration after transaction was closed, absent proof of damage or contract provision indicating disposition of deposit in event of partial breach after closing.

> Dube v. Puente De La Vega, 505 So.2d 697.

☞1102–1105. *For other cases see earlier editions of this digest, the Decennial Digests, and WESTLAW.*

☞1105. **Time of payment and terms of credit.**

☞1106. —— **In general.**

† **C.A.11 (Fla.) 2013.** District court's finding, following bench trial, that contract documents established that payment by buyer's customer was condition precedent to buyer's payment to manufacturer for high-powered radio amplifiers was not clearly erroneous; one document stated that payment was due either after "delivery to customer" or "customer acceptance," whichever occurred first, and parties used term "customer" to refer to buyer's customer, and another document also conditioned payment to manufacturer upon receipt of funds from buyer's customer.

> Delta RF Technology, Inc. v. RIIMIC, LLC, 533 Fed.Appx. 872.

Fla. 1939. Where fruit grower contracted for sale to company of grower's entire crop of oranges, grapefruit, and tangerines at certain price per box, and contract stipulated that grower had received $2,000 to apply on purchase price of fruit to be deducted as fruit was picked under contract, and that, should fruit not be taken by company, the $2,000 should be forfeited to grower as his sole liquidated damage, the $2,000 would be applied to purchase price of fruit as it was taken from grove, and would not be deemed to have been intended to apply pro rata on each box of fruit as picked.

> Squires v. Citrus Fruit Products, 191 So. 455, 140 Fla. 253.

Fla.App. 2 Dist. 1994. Reasonable interpretation of agreement for sale of assets providing that letter of intent's provisions would merge into agreement and in the next sentence stating "However, the terms of this Agreement shall supercede [sic] any provisions of the Letter of Intent which are inconsistent with the provisions herein" was that all provisions of letter of intent not inconsistent with agreement were incorporated into agreement; accordingly, time of the essence clause in letter of intent was incorporated into sales agreement, and seller did not breach implied duty of good faith by requiring buyer to close in time contract provided for while buyer breached agreement by not timely closing transaction.

> Seabreeze Restaurant, Inc. v. Paumgardhen, 639 So.2d 69.

Fla.App. 4 Dist. 1968. A reasonable time for performance of a citrus sales agreement is not necessarily synonymous in all cases with the length of time dictated by condition of fruit and what would produce maximum yield.

> Tyner v. Woodruff, 206 So.2d 684.

☞1107–1113. *For other cases see earlier editions of this digest, the Decennial Digests, and WESTLAW.*

☞1111. **Mode and sufficiency of payment.**

☞1114. —— **Notes or other obligations, and payment thereof.**

Fla.App. 1 Dist. 1961. Contemplated sale of automobile on cash basis was never consummated where check was not honored upon presentment for payment.

> Trumbull Chevrolet Sales Co. v. Seawright, 134 So.2d 829, certiorari denied 143 So.2d 491.

Fla.App. 2 Dist. 1994. Cancellation of promissory note given by buyer of medical beds to seller, upon buyer's resale of beds to third party and third party's execution of promissory note to seller, did not alter efficacy of repurchase agreement in letter agreement between buyer and seller, pursuant to which seller agreed to repurchase beds if, after 12 months, buyer was not completely satisfied.

Pinnacle Holding, Inc. v. Biologics, Inc., 643 So.2d 642.

⚷1115. Payment in full.

For other cases see earlier editions of this digest, the Decennial Digests, and WEST-LAW.

⚷1116. Installments and deferred payments.

Retail installment sales statutes, see CONSUMER CREDIT.

Fla.App. 4 Dist. 2001. Buyers order was not a binding contract that allowed automobile dealer to dispose of buyers' trade in vehicle immediately upon tender, in proceeding for breach of vehicle sale contract and for the return of trade-in vehicle, where buyers order stated that it was not a binding contract unless a manager of dealer signed the order within five days, the order was assigned and acceptable for financing, and both parties signed an installment contract, and those contingencies did not occur.

Samuels v. King Motor Co. of Fort Lauderdale, 782 So.2d 489.

Fla.App. 5 Dist. 1992. Present sale can be based on deferred payment.

Ferran Engineering Group, Inc. v. Reid, 600 So.2d 1307.

Fla.App. 5 Dist. 1984. Purchasers of accounting practice were entitled to offset against installment payments amount due the firm from a client, part of which seller had personally accepted, making collection of remainder impossible, and thus purchasers were not in default when seller attempted to accelerate sums due on a promissory note.

Wells v. Cobb, 455 So.2d 1069.

(G) TRANSFER OF TITLE.

Title or possession of seller, see ⚷935.

⚷1121. In general.

Bkrtcy.M.D.Fla. 1985. Under V.T.C.A., Bus. & C. § 2.401(c), parties to sale may explicitly agree to time of passage of title.

In re Charter Co., 49 B.R. 513.

Fla.App. 4 Dist. 1968. Under the common law, passing of title between seller and buyer depends largely on intention of parties.

Smith v. Baker, 206 So.2d 409.

⚷1122. Specific articles or goods in general.

Fla. 1937. Under contract of sale of citrus fruit stipulating that seller "has this day sold" marketable fruit in grove described, "said fruit to be purchased at 75 cents per standard field box, on trees," title to marketable fruit passed to buyer though he did not take possession, and buyer was liable for unpicked marketable fruit.

Gregg Maxcy, Inc. v. Bateman, 171 So. 811, 126 Fla. 747.

Fla.App. 1 Dist. 2005. Beneficial ownership of an automobile is determined by the overt acts of the buyer and seller at the time of the sale agreement and thereafter.

State Farm Mut. Auto. Ins. Co. v. Hartzog, 917 So.2d 363.

Fla.App. 1 Dist. 1959. Whether beneficial ownership of automobile has actually passed depends upon a determination of legal rights under agreement to purchase between buyer and seller.

Cox Motor Co. v. Faber, 113 So.2d 771.

⚷1123. Acts to be done before passage of title in general.

C.A.5 (Fla.) 1951. Under Florida law, in sales of personal property, as between parties, to contract, title does not pass so long as anything remains to be done either by seller or buyer to make sale complete.

Greenwood Products Co. v. U.S., 188 F.2d 401.

Bkrtcy.M.D.Fla. 1985. Under Uniform Commercial Code, passage of title to sold goods is not dependent on consummation of sale. V.T.C.A., Bus. & C. §§ 2.106(a), 2.401.

In re Charter Co., 49 B.R. 513.

Fla.App. 2 Dist. 2004. A person acquiring a motor vehicle from the owner thereof, whether or not the owner is a licensed dealer, shall not acquire marketable title until he has had issued to him a certificate of title to the motor vehicle; the purchaser's failure to obtain the title certificate at the time of sale does not, however, prevent the passage of title from the seller to the buyer.

> In re Forfeiture of $7464 + 2002 Cadillac Escalade, Identification No. 3GYEK63N02G222802, 872 So.2d 1017.

🗝**1124–1125.** *For other cases see earlier editions of this digest, the Decennial Digests, and WESTLAW.*

🗝**1125. Identification of goods.**

🗝**1126. —— In general.**

Bkrtcy.S.D.Fla. 1984. At time ice vending machines were identified by number and location, they were sufficiently identified and delivered for title to pass to the buyer, defendant, and since trustee's proof on his claim that title did not and could not pass to defendant because debtor did not have title to sell, having sold same machines many times previously, was insufficient, defendant had title.

> Matter of Polar Chips Intern., Inc., 40 B.R. 586.

Fla. 1937. A contract for sale of growing citrus fruit which vested title in buyer was an "executed contract," though it provided that buyer was to take from the trees only that fruit which was merchantable during time provided for removal of fruit, so as to entitle seller, as damages for merchantable fruit not removed, to the difference between contract price and resale price, provided that seller in good faith used all reasonable effort to resell fruit not removed by buyer to best possible advantage.

> Winter Haven Fruit Sales Corp. v. C. L. Bundy & Sons, 174 So. 726, 128 Fla. 324.

Fla.App. 5 Dist. 1993. Goods need not be in deliverable state in order for identification to contract to occur. West's F.S.A. § 672.501.

> Kit Car World, Inc. v. Skolnick, 616 So.2d 1051.

🗝**1127–1132.** *For other cases see earlier editions of this digest, the Decennial Digests, and WESTLAW.*

🗝**1132. Delivery and acceptance.**

🗝**1133. —— In general; necessity and effect.**

Bkrtcy.M.D.Fla. 1985. Any retention or reservation by seller of title in goods shipped or delivered to buyer is limited in effect to reservation of security interest. V.T.C.A., Bus. & C. §§ 1.201(37), 2.401(c).

> In re Charter Co., 49 B.R. 513.

Fla.App. 1 Dist. 2005. Exclusive possession and control, taken by the buyer at the time of the agreement to buy a vehicle, is a key factor in determining beneficial ownership of the vehicle, regardless of whether legal title remains in the seller's name.

> State Farm Mut. Auto. Ins. Co. v. Hartzog, 917 So.2d 363.

🗝**1134. —— Provisions of contract.**

Bkrtcy.M.D.Fla. 1985. Seller's retention of title was limited in effect to retention of security interest where buyer and seller agreed that delivery of oil in buyer's possession would be by in-tank transfer but did not agree when delivery would take place. V.T.C.A., Bus. & C. §§ 1.201(37), 2.106(a), 2.401, 2.401(c), (c)(2).

> In re Charter Co., 49 B.R. 513.

Fla.App. 2 Dist. 1963. Title to oranges did not pass from sellers to buyer under contract which in its printed form contemplated passing of title of fruit to buyer but which included inconsistent typewritten provisions, one of which provided for delivery beginning not before a certain date by sellers rather than removal of fruit by buyer.

> McDonald v. Connell, 158 So.2d 780.

Fla.App. 3 Dist. 1979. A "destination contract" is considered the variant contract in which seller specifically agrees to deliver the goods sold to buyer at particular destination and to bear the risk of loss of goods until tender of delivery; this can be accomplished by express provision in sales contract to that effect or by use of delivery terms such as F.O.B. F.S.1977,

§§ 672.319(1)(b), 672.503 comment, 672.509(1).

> Pestana v. Karinol Corp., 367 So.2d 1096.

⚷1135. —— Character, location, and possession of property.

C.A.11 (Fla.) 1983. A security may be delivered without the purchaser taking physical possession. N.Y.McKinney's Uniform Commercial Code § 8–313 comment.

> Louisiana State School Lunch Employees Retirement System v. Legel, Braswell Government Securities Corp., 699 F.2d 512.

Bkrtcy.S.D.Fla. 1995. Under Florida law, pool company which had contracted to install heater on buyer's pool did not "deliver" heater to buyer merely by dropping heater off on buyer's driveway; "delivery" did not occur until heater was actually installed, so that where heater disappeared before installation had been completed, risk of loss remained with pool company. West's F.S.A. § 672.510(1).

> In re Thomas, 182 B.R. 347.

⚷1136. —— Delivery to or through carrier or other intermediary.

C.A.5 (Fla.) 1967. When terms of contract provide for inspection of goods sold at a point other than place of shipment, title passes only conditionally on delivery to the carrier and, under Florida law, is subject to purchaser's rights to reject the goods if they do not conform to contract's requirements.

> Exhibition Display Service Co. v. Liberty Mut. Ins. Co., 378 F.2d 903.

S.D.Fla. 1996. Korean manufacturer of computer equipment, which claimed that buyer had not paid for equipment, had no possessory right to containers of computer equipment being held by buyer's ocean carrier, and therefore was not entitled to replevin equipment under Florida law; although equipment had not yet been delivered to buyer, title and risk of loss had passed to buyer by virtue of terms of sale F.O.B. Korea, and nothing in record established that items in containers were items of computer equipment for which buyer had not paid. West's F.S.A. §§ 78.01, 78.055.

> Future Tech Intern., Inc. v. Tae Il Media, Ltd., 944 F.Supp. 1538.

S.D.Fla. 1984. Title and risk of loss under CIF shipment contract passes to buyer on shipment if seller has properly performed all his obligations with respect to goods. West's F.S.A. § 672.320 comment.

> William D. Branson, Ltd. v. Tropical Shipping & Const. Co., Ltd., 598 F.Supp. 680.

Fla.App. 3 Dist. 1985. Parties to contract for sale and delivery of goods must specifically agree to destination contract, otherwise contract will be considered a shipment contract. U.C.C. § 2–503 comment.

> Ladex Corp. v. Transportes Aereos Nacionales, S.A., 476 So.2d 763.

Fla.App. 3 Dist. 1985. Parties may vary the terms of a C.I.F. contract to meet their own requirements but, if the agreed upon variation is such that it removes a vital ingredient of a C.I.F. contract, the contract ceases be to be a C.I.F. contract.

> Kumar Corp. v. Nopal Lines, Ltd., 462 So.2d 1178, petition for review denied S.E.L. Maduro (Florida), Inc. v. Kumar Corp., 476 So.2d 675.

If, according to the intention of the parties, the actual delivery of the goods to the buyer is an essential condition or performance, the contract is not a C.I.F. contract.

> Kumar Corp. v. Nopal Lines, Ltd., 462 So.2d 1178, petition for review denied S.E.L. Maduro (Florida), Inc. v. Kumar Corp., 476 So.2d 675.

Fla.App. 4 Dist. 1984. Contract for sale of plastic parts and molding expressed by forms incorporated uncontradicted provisions contained in one form stating that contract was for shipment of parts FOB Clearwater, and thus, seller's delivery point was in Clearwater, and there the risk of loss passed to buyer. West's F.S.A. § 672.207.

> A & M Engineering Plastics, Inc. v. Energy Saving Technology Co., 455 So.2d 1124.

⚷1137–1138. *For other cases see earlier editions of this digest, the Decennial Digests, and WESTLAW.*

⚷1139. —— Inspection, trial, or test.

Fla. 1955. Where buyer reserves right of inspection at point other than place of shipment, from which goods sold are to be shipped f.o.b., title to the goods passes to buyer only conditionally on delivery to carrier and subject to buyer's right to check the goods upon failure of goods to conform to contract requirements.

McNeill v. Jack, 83 So.2d 704.

Where wholesale lumber dealer ordered cars of lumber from lumber supplier "F.O.B. Cars Mill", and order also provided that the lumber was being shipped under certain rules which provided for inspection and rejection upon receipt of the lumber, dealer took title to the lumber when it was placed on the freight cars at the mill, but such title was accepted conditionally upon condition that the lumber would be up to the quantity stipulated by the contract when received at ultimate destination.

McNeill v. Jack, 83 So.2d 704.

☞1140–1142. *For other cases see earlier editions of this digest, the Decennial Digests, and WESTLAW.*

☞1142. Payment of price.

☞1143. —— In general; necessity and effect.

Fla. 1952. Where personalty is sold for cash, payment is generally a condition of the passing of title.

Ragg v. Hurd, 60 So.2d 673.

Fla.App. 1 Dist. 2005. The mere fact that the seller of a vehicle retains title until after the full purchase price is paid is not enough to prove that the seller and purchaser did not intend to transfer beneficial ownership of the vehicle immediately upon reaching agreement for the sale.

State Farm Mut. Auto. Ins. Co. v. Hartzog, 917 So.2d 363.

Fla.App. 1 Dist. 1987. Title and possession merged in buyer, and seller therefore had no enforceable security interest in medical equipment delivered to buyer, where sales agreement contained no explicit provision or term reserving title to seller until payment had actually been accomplished. West's F.S.A. §§ 672.401(2), 672.606(1, 2).

St. Paul Fire and Marine Ins. Co. v. Pensacola Diagnostic Center and Breast Clinic, 505 So.2d 513.

Fla.App. 1 Dist. 1966. As a general rule title to goods sold does not pass until payment is made.

General Finance Corp. v. East Lake Auto Sales Co., 190 So.2d 399, certiorari denied 201 So.2d 460.

☞1144. —— Payment by note, check, or acceptance.

C.A.11 (Fla.) 1999. Under British Columbia law, buyer who obtains title to property via worthless check has "voidable title" to the property, and seller can avoid that title as against buyer upon discovery of the fraud.

B.R.L. Equipment Rentals Ltd. v. Seabring Marine Industries, Inc., 168 F.3d 413.

Under British Columbia law, seller of luxury boats, which obtained possession of boats from supplier via worthless check, had "voidable title" to boats, and thus supplier could avoid that title as against seller upon discovery of fraud.

B.R.L. Equipment Rentals Ltd. v. Seabring Marine Industries, Inc., 168 F.3d 413.

Bkrtcy.M.D.Fla. 1988. Under Florida law, title to property never passed to purchaser, where purchaser attempted to pay for property by dishonored check.

In re Harlequin Dinner Theater, 89 B.R. 944.

☞1145. —— Effect of delivery of goods in general.

For other cases see earlier editions of this digest, the Decennial Digests, and WESTLAW.

☞1146. —— Delivery to or through carrier in general.

C.A.5 (Fla.) 1973. Where cargo was shipped CIF port of destination, title to boiler passed to consignee when it was shipped from Miami in accordance with the terms of the contract and shipper had no property rights in boiler at time it was damaged and therefore had no insurable interest and lacked standing to bring cargo insurance suit.

York-Shipley, Inc. v. Atlantic Mut. Ins. Co., 474 F.2d 8.

Fla. 1940. Generally when goods are shipped under "C.A.F. contract", meaning cost and freight allowed to point of destination, being the equivalent of shipment F.O.B. from point of origin, the responsibility of the shipper ceases when the goods are delivered to the carrier, but if issue is raised as to whether the goods moved from point of shipment promptly or when loaded were up to contract requirements, evidence on such issues may be taken and if proven, judgment rendered accordingly.

Farris & Co. v. William Schluderberg, T. J. Kurdle Co., 196 So. 184, 142 Fla. 765.

A C.A.F. contract may not operate before time for the goods to move, but thereafter the consignor is not responsible for delicts.

Farris & Co. v. William Schluderberg, T. J. Kurdle Co., 196 So. 184, 142 Fla. 765.

Fla.App. 3 Dist. 1959. Where contract for sale of baskets provided that the baskets would be shipped f. o. b. Hamburg or Bremen, title to the baskets passed to buyer when they were delivered to carrier at point of shipment in Hamburg, and risk of loss in course of journey from Hamburg to Miami was on buyer, notwithstanding provision in invoice, forwarded at time of shipment, to effect that title would remain in seller until goods were paid for.

Jacobson v. Neuensorger Korbwaren-Industrie Friedrich Kretz, K.-G., 109 So.2d 612.

Where contract for sale of baskets provided that baskets would be shipped f. o. b. Hamburg or Bremen, provision in invoice, forwarded at time of shipment, to effect that title would remain in seller until goods were paid for, operated to retain title in seller for security purposes only, and beneficial interest in property was transferred to buyer at the f. o. b. shipment point with the result that risk of loss thereafter would be on the buyer.

Jacobson v. Neuensorger Korbwaren-Industrie Friedrich Kretz, K.-G., 109 So.2d 612.

⚷1147. —— **Bill of lading, shipping receipt, and order for collection of price.**

For other cases see earlier editions of this digest, the Decennial Digests, and WESTLAW.

⚷1148. —— **Effect of partial payment.**

Fla. 1976. Anything short of full payment will not have effect of making sale absolute so as to vest title in buyer.

Encore, Inc. v. Olivetti Corp. of America, 326 So.2d 161.

Fla.App. 5 Dist. 1992. Jury could consider whether satisfactory deferred payment agreement had been reached between owner of record and buyer of vehicle in determining beneficial ownership of vehicle involved in accident which gave rise to suit.

Ferran Engineering Group, Inc. v. Reid, 600 So.2d 1307.

⚷1149–1154. *For other cases see earlier editions of this digest, the Decennial Digests, and WESTLAW.*

⚷1153. **Bill of sale or other instrument of conveyance.**

⚷1155. —— **Necessity and duty to make.**

Fla.App. 1 Dist. 1966. The transfer of ownership of automobiles in Alabama is normally evidenced by seller's notarized bill of sale.

General Finance Corp. v. East Lake Auto Sales Co., 190 So.2d 399, certiorari denied 201 So.2d 460.

⚷1156–1158. *For other cases see earlier editions of this digest, the Decennial Digests, and WESTLAW.*

⚷1159. —— **Delivery.**

Fla. 1971. Title to automobile passed from seller to buyer at time buyer received bill of sale and took possession of automobile even though automobile was subject to bank lien. F.S.A. § 672.2–401(2).

Grimm v. Prudence Mut. Cas. Co., 243 So.2d 140.

⚷1160–1162. *For other cases see earlier editions of this digest, the Decennial Digests, and WESTLAW.*

⚷1163. **Place of transfer of title.**

C.A.5 (Fla.) 1967. Term "delivery point", as used in guarantee clause of contract between corporation and government agency, did not refer to original point of delivery where goods were initially transferred from corporation to the agency but meant the point at which some latent defect was discovered and where goods were thereupon delivered for a return shipment to corporation for repair, so that, under Florida law, risk of loss did not remain on corporation until delivery to government's facility in Virginia.

> Exhibition Display Service Co. v. Liberty Mut. Ins. Co., 378 F.2d 903.

⚭1164–1165. *For other cases see earlier editions of this digest, the Decennial Digests, and WESTLAW.*

(H) RISK OF LOSS.

⚭1171. In general.

C.A.5 (Fla.) 1967. Guarantee clause in contract between corporation and government agency, which provided, inter alia, that models sold to agency would be free from defects in material and workmanship and would conform to contract's requirements at time of delivery, was an express warranty against faulty materials, faulty workmanship and latent defects rather than an expression of parties' intention to switch risk of loss from its normal placement on the purchaser, having nothing to do with externally caused damage which was only type of damage covered by corporation's insurance policy, so that ordinary Florida risk of loss rule applied, risk of loss in transit was on government agency, and thus there was no coverage under corporation's policy.

> Exhibition Display Service Co. v. Liberty Mut. Ins. Co., 378 F.2d 903.

C.A.5 (Fla.) 1951. There is exception to general rule under Florida law that risk of loss is upon seller of personal property until title passes in instances where, though legal title is retained by seller as security, buyer is given complete possession of personal property with right to use it as his own, and risk of loss incident to complete ownership is upon buyer in absence of contractual provision to contrary.

> Greenwood Products Co. v. U.S., 188 F.2d 401.

Bkrtcy.S.D.Fla. 1995. Under Florida law, seller cannot shift risk of loss to buyer unless seller's actions conform with all of the conditions resting on seller under sales agreement. West's F.S.A. § 672.510(1).

> In re Thomas, 182 B.R. 347.

⚭1172. Relation to title in general.

C.A.5 (Fla.) 1967. Under Florida law, risk of loss ordinarily accompanies the passing of title.

> Exhibition Display Service Co. v. Liberty Mut. Ins. Co., 378 F.2d 903.

C.A.5 (Fla.) 1951. Under Florida law it is general rule, in sale of personal property, that risk of loss is upon seller until title passes.

> Greenwood Products Co. v. U.S., 188 F.2d 401.

⚭1173. Delivery and acceptance.

⚭1174. —— In general.

Bkrtcy.S.D.Fla. 1995. Under Florida law, pool company which had contracted to install heater on buyer's pool did not "deliver" heater to buyer merely by dropping heater off on buyer's driveway; "delivery" did not occur until heater was actually installed, so that where heater disappeared before installation had been completed, risk of loss remained with pool company. West's F.S.A. § 672.510(1).

> In re Thomas, 182 B.R. 347.

Fla.App. 3 Dist. 1979. A "destination contract" is considered the variant contract in which seller specifically agrees to deliver the goods sold to buyer at particular destination and to bear the risk of loss of goods until tender of delivery; this can be accomplished by express provision in sales contract to that effect or by use of delivery terms such as F.O.B. F.S.1977, §§ 672.319(1)(b), 672.503 comment, 672.509(1).

> Pestana v. Karinol Corp., 367 So.2d 1096.

⚭1175. —— Delivery to or through carrier or other intermediary.

C.A.5 (Fla.) 1980. If contract were shipment contract, as is ordinary contract without specific contrary terms, shipper retains risk of loss until he delivers goods to carrier, but shipper carries risk of loss until carrier tenders goods to buyer if contract is destination contract. West's

F.S.A. §§ 672.320, 672.501(2), 672.503, 672.503 comment, 672.509(1).

> Sig M. Glukstad, Inc. v. Lineas Aereas Paraguayas, 619 F.2d 457.

Ordinary CIF contract is shipment contract, upon which shipper retains risk of loss until he delivers goods to carrier. West's F.S.A. § 672.320.

> Sig M. Glukstad, Inc. v. Lineas Aereas Paraguayas, 619 F.2d 457.

S.D.Fla. 1984. Title and risk of loss under CIF shipment contract passes to buyer on shipment if seller has properly performed all his obligations with respect to goods. West's F.S.A. § 672.320 comment.

> William D. Branson, Ltd. v. Tropical Shipping & Const. Co., Ltd., 598 F.Supp. 680.

Fla.App. 3 Dist. 1979. Contract for sale of goods which stipulates place where goods sold are to be sent by carrier but contains no explicit provisions allocating risk of loss while the goods are in possession of carrier and no delivery terms such as "F.O.B." place of destination, without more, constitutes a "shipment contract" wherein risk of loss passes to buyer when seller duly delivers the goods to the carrier under a reasonable contract of carriage for shipment to the buyer. F.S.1977, §§ 672.319(1)(b), 672.503 comment, 672.504, 672.509(1).

> Pestana v. Karinol Corp., 367 So.2d 1096.

Fla.App. 4 Dist. 2005. Risk of loss passed to buyer upon seller's delivery to city free on board (FOB).

> Rad Source Technologies, Inc. v. Colony Nat. Ins. Co., 914 So.2d 1006, rehearing denied.

Fla.App. 4 Dist. 1984. Contract for sale of plastic parts and molding expressed by forms incorporated uncontradicted provisions contained in one form stating that contract was for shipment of parts FOB Clearwater, and thus, seller's delivery point was in Clearwater, and there the risk of loss passed to buyer. West's F.S.A. § 672.207.

> A & M Engineering Plastics, Inc. v. Energy Saving Technology Co., 455 So.2d 1124.

⊷1176–1181. *For other cases see earlier editions of this digest, the Decennial Digests, and WESTLAW.*

(I) ASSURANCE OF PERFORMANCE.

⊷1191–1192. *For other cases see earlier editions of this digest, the Decennial Digests, and WESTLAW.*

⊷**1192. Grounds for request or demand.**

⊷**1193. —— In general.**

C.A.11 (Fla.) 2010. Under Georgia law, a party already in breach is not entitled to invoke statute permitting, in certain situations, a party to demand in writing adequate assurance of due performance and suspend any performance until receiving such assurance. West's Ga.Code Ann. § 11–2–609(1).

> Advanced Bodycare Solutions, LLC v. Thione Intern., Inc., 615 F.3d 1352.

⊷**1194. —— By buyer to seller.**

For other cases see earlier editions of this digest, the Decennial Digests, and WESTLAW.

⊷**1195. —— By seller to buyer.**

† **C.A.11 (Fla.) 2011.** Under Florida law, international food commodities seller had reasonable grounds for insecurity and made written demand from Venezuelan buyer and its U.S. purchasing agent for adequate assurances of performance of contracts for sale and delivery of sugar and beef. West's F.S.A. § 672.609(1).

> Validsa, Inc. v. PDVSA Services, Inc., 424 Fed.Appx. 862.

S.D.Fla. 2009. Seller of food commodities under contracts for sale and delivery of food commodities had more than reasonable grounds for insecurity to request adequate assurances with respect to buyers' performance under Florida law, where e-mail mistakenly sent to seller by buyers contained string of e-mail messages between buyers' employees relaying instructions to cancel contracts with seller and to suspend all payments, at time seller requested assurances buyers had fallen behind on payments, and seller was not in breach of contract at time it requested assurances. West's F.S.A. § 672.609(1, 2).

> Validsa, Inc. v. PDVSA Services Inc., 632 F.Supp.2d 1219, affirmed in part, reversed in part 424 Fed.Appx. 862.

☜**1196. Adequacy of request or demand.**

C.A.11 (Fla.) 2010. A reasonable jury could have concluded that purchaser's e-mail to supplier inquiring whether pink ampoules meant that there was "a production issue" did not constitute a writing that demanded adequate assurance of due performance, so as to support purchaser's suspension of its performance under the parties' installment contract under Georgia law. West's Ga.Code Ann. § 11–2–609(1).

> Advanced Bodycare Solutions, LLC v. Thione Intern., Inc., 615 F.3d 1352.

S.D.Fla. 2009. Letter written by principal for seller of food commodities under contract for sale and delivery of commodities, which requested an immediate written explanation of buyers' intent to cancel contract as stated in e-mail mistakenly sent to seller, constituted a request for adequate assurances under Florida law, despite letter's failure to track statutory language for such requests. West's F.S.A. § 672.609.

> Validsa, Inc. v. PDVSA Services Inc., 632 F.Supp.2d 1219, affirmed in part, reversed in part 424 Fed.Appx. 862.

☜**1197. Adequacy of assurance offered or provided.**

☜**1198. —— In general.**

S.D.Fla. 2009. Proposed modifications to existing terms of a contract cannot qualify as adequate assurance under Florida law. West's F.S.A. § 672.610.

> Validsa, Inc. v. PDVSA Services Inc., 632 F.Supp.2d 1219, affirmed in part, reversed in part 424 Fed.Appx. 862.

☜**1199–1200.** *For other cases see earlier editions of this digest, the Decennial Digests, and WESTLAW.*

(J) REPUDIATION.

Revocation of acceptance, see V(C)5.
Cancellation and termination, see VI.
Rescission, see X(D).

☜**1211. In general.**

Fla.App. 1 Dist. 1988. Under UCC provision authorizing demand for assurance of performance when grounds for insecurity arise, if demand is made and adequate assurance is not forthcoming, aggrieved party may then treat contract as breached by repudiation. West's F.S.A. § 672.609.

> Ford Motor Credit Co. v. Alachua Trading Co., Inc., 531 So.2d 982.

☜**1212. By seller.**

For other cases see earlier editions of this digest, the Decennial Digests, and WEST-LAW.

☜**1213. By buyer.**

† C.A.11 (Fla.) 2013. Although Florida-based import company waited less than statutory maximum time of 30 days after its demand for assurances from Venezuelan state-owned purchasing company regarding installment contract for powdered milk from China before initiating breach of contract suit, this period of time was sufficient to trigger repudiation of shipment under Florida law because requests for inspections and payment had begun earlier and purchasing company had communicated its inability to perform inspections. West's F.S.A. § 672.609.

> Exim Brickell LLC v. PDVSA Services Inc., 516 Fed.Appx. 742.

Venezuelan state-owned purchasing company's response to Florida-based import company's demand for adequate assurances regarding installment contract did not give rise to immediate repudiation, under Florida law, even though it threatened litigation and claimed possible breach based on past shipments. West's F.S.A. § 672.609.

> Exim Brickell LLC v. PDVSA Services Inc., 516 Fed.Appx. 742.

Venezuelan state-owned purchasing company did not clearly repudiate future shipments of powdered milk from China under installment contract with Florida-based import company, under Florida law, when it communicated to import company that it was unable at the time to send inspectors for latest shipment. West's F.S.A. § 672.610.

Exim Brickell LLC v. PDVSA Services Inc., 516 Fed.Appx. 742.

S.D.Fla. 2009. Under Florida law, buyers' failure to immediately provide seller with requested assurances relating to contracts for sale and delivery of food commodities within a period of less than thirty days constituted a repudiation of the contracts, where seller was insecure as to status of contracts and whether seller would continue to receive payments from sellers. West's F.S.A. § 672.609(4).

Validsa, Inc. v. PDVSA Services Inc., 632 F.Supp.2d 1219, affirmed in part, reversed in part 424 Fed.Appx. 862.

Under Florida law, buyer under contract for sale and delivery of food commodities could not maintain express breach of contract claims against seller for contracts buyer repudiated, and thus buyer could also not maintain a claim for breach of implied covenant of good faith and fair dealing.

Validsa, Inc. v. PDVSA Services Inc., 632 F.Supp.2d 1219, affirmed in part, reversed in part 424 Fed.Appx. 862.

⚷1214–1216. *For other cases see earlier editions of this digest, the Decennial Digests, and WESTLAW.*

⚷1214. **Anticipatory repudiation.**

⚷1217. —— **By buyer.**

† **C.A.11 (Fla.) 2013.** Florida-based import company that shipped toxic powdered milk from China to Venezuelan state-owned purchasing company was permitted to demand adequate assurances from purchasing company, for purposes of analyzing anticipatory repudiation of installment contract under Florida law, since neither party knew of purchasing company's breach at time of demand letter and thus its demands were not made in bad faith. West's F.S.A. § 672.609.

Exim Brickell LLC v. PDVSA Services Inc., 516 Fed.Appx. 742.

Response of Venezuelan state-owned purchasing company to Florida-based import company's request for adequate as-surances regarding installment contract for powdered milk from China, which called for a meeting to discuss nationalization of the milk powder, was inadequate under Florida law governing anticipatory repudiation of a contract, since purchasing company had refused to pay for several shipments and blocked payment under the letter of credit, causing immediate harm to import company. West's F.S.A. § 672.609.

Exim Brickell LLC v. PDVSA Services Inc., 516 Fed.Appx. 742.

Response of Venezuelan state-owned purchasing company to Florida-based import company's request for adequate assurances regarding installment contract for powdered milk from China, which called for a meeting to discuss positive toxicity results and a response within 48 hours or purchasing company reserved the right to take legal action, was inadequate under Florida law governing anticipatory repudiation of a contract, given import company's repeated demands to perform. West's F.S.A. § 672.609.

Exim Brickell LLC v. PDVSA Services Inc., 516 Fed.Appx. 742.

Thirty-day statutory maximum waiting period following Florida-based import company's demand for adequate assurances from Venezuelan state-owned purchasing company was reasonable as to future shipments of powdered milk from China, under Florida law governing anticipatory repudiation of a contract, since performance had not been requested previously. West's F.S.A. § 672.609.

Exim Brickell LLC v. PDVSA Services Inc., 516 Fed.Appx. 742.

C.A.11 (Fla.) 1987. Buyer's letters indicating inability to consume any more than 45% of quantity of phosphate rock previously budgeted constituted anticipatory breach of contract under New Jersey law. N.J.S.A. 12A:2–610 comment.

American Cyanamid Co. v. Mississippi Chemical Corp., 817 F.2d 91.

Buyer's anticipatory breach permitted seller to sue immediately under New Jersey law. N.J.S.A. 12A:2–610.

American Cyanamid Co. v. Mississippi Chemical Corp., 817 F.2d 91.

---

† **This Case was not selected for publication in the National Reporter System**
For legislative history of cited statutes, see Florida Statutes Annotated

☞1218. Retraction of repudiation.

For other cases see earlier editions of this digest, the Decennial Digests, and WEST-LAW.

(K) EXCUSES FOR NONPERFORMANCE OR BREACH.

☞1221. In general.

For other cases see earlier editions of this digest, the Decennial Digests, and WEST-LAW.

☞1222. Frustration.

S.D.Fla. 1975. Where contract for sale of aviation fuel did not require interpretation and did not require an excursion into the subjective intention of the parties but clearly called for the price to be based on postings in an industry newsletter, there was no failure of a presupposed condition, such as would excuse seller, based on fact that price controls which had been put into effect created a two-tier pricing structure and the industry newsletter was posting only the lower, controlled price, applicable to "old" oil. West's F.S.A. § 672.615.

     Eastern Air Lines, Inc. v. Gulf Oil Corp., 415 F.Supp. 429.

Oil company which had entered into requirements contract for aviation fuel with airline could not, following advent of energy crisis and imposition of certain government controls, avoid its obligation on the theory that agreed means or manner of payment had failed because of domestic or foreign governmental regulation. West's F.S.A. § 672.614.

     Eastern Air Lines, Inc. v. Gulf Oil Corp., 415 F.Supp. 429.

☞1223. Impossibility.

Bkrtcy.M.D.Fla. 2003. Where supply agreement specified that bottles that seller agreed to produce upon buyer's behalf would be produced at particular plant owned by seller's corporate parent, and where this plant was sold to third party in connection with parent's Canadian bankruptcy proceedings, seller was excused from performing under doctrine of impossibility.

     In re Anchor Glass Container Corp., 297 B.R. 887, affirmed 345 B.R. 765.

☞1224. Impracticability.

C.A.5 (Fla.) 1976. Where excusable delay clause in contracts for manufacture and sale of commercial jet aircraft was phrased in general terms, court could not, in absence of evidence to contrary, hold that aircraft manufacturer was exempt from all liability for any delay, regardless of foreseeability, due to causes beyond its control. West's Ann.Cal.Com.Code, § 2615.

     Eastern Air Lines, Inc. v. McDonnell Douglas Corp., 532 F.2d 957.

Where, under contract for sale of commercial jet airliners to airline, manufacturer was exonerated only for delays which were not attributable to its fault, it was not excused by delays caused by fault of subcontractors.

     Eastern Air Lines, Inc. v. McDonnell Douglas Corp., 532 F.2d 957.

Where, under terms of excusable delay clause in contract for sale of commercial jet airplanes to airline, delay was excusable if caused by "act of government," such phrase encompassed informal demands by government that manufacturer accorded priority to military contracts, and it was not necessary that government obtain precedence for its orders by means of formal, published regulations and orders under Defense Production Act. Defense Production Act of 1950, §§ 101(a), 704, 707 as amended 50 U.S.C.A. App. §§ 2071(a), 2154, 2157; National Defense Act, § 120, 39 Stat. 166; Second War Powers Act, 1942, § 301, 56 Stat. 176; 5 U.S.C.A. §§ 551 et seq., 552(a)(1).

     Eastern Air Lines, Inc. v. McDonnell Douglas Corp., 532 F.2d 957.

Even assuming that government's informal method of obtaining defense priorities with aircraft manufacturers during Vietnam hostilities had to have been published in manner prescribed by Administrative Procedure Act in order for such policy to be relied on by aircraft manufacturer in excusing delay in fulfillment of nongovernment contract, airline could not, in its suit for damages for delay in delivery of commercial jet aircraft, rely on lack of such publication when it was, by its own admission, well aware of government's policy. 5 U.S.C.A. §§ 551 et seq., 552(a)(1).

Eastern Air Lines, Inc. v. McDonnell Douglas Corp., 532 F.2d 957.

S.D.Fla. 1975. If a buyer's demands under a requirements contract become excessive, the seller may, in an appropriate case, refuse to deliver the unreasonable amounts demanded, although seller's basic contract obligation is not eliminated; if a customer repeatedly makes no requirements at all, seller may be excused from performance if the buyer suddenly and without warning should descend upon him and demand his entire inventory.

Eastern Air Lines, Inc. v. Gulf Oil Corp., 415 F.Supp. 429.

In order for seller to avoid obligation to deliver on basis of asserted failure of a presupposed condition, there must be a failure of such a presupposed condition which was an underlying assumption of the contract, the failure must have been unforeseeable, and the risk of failure must not have been specifically allocated to the seller; burden of proving each element of the claimed commercial impracticability is on the party claiming the defense. West's F.S.A. § 672.615.

Eastern Air Lines, Inc. v. Gulf Oil Corp., 415 F.Supp. 429.

Since events associated with the so-called energy crisis were reasonably foreseeable at the time that requirements contract for sale of aviation fuel was executed, seller could not avoid obligations under the contract on grounds of commercial impracticability. West's F.S.A. § 672.615.

Eastern Air Lines, Inc. v. Gulf Oil Corp., 415 F.Supp. 429.

Fla.App. 4 Dist. 1997. Negligence of third person is not legal excuse for non-performance where contract was simply to provide certain quantity and quality of product.

Ciba-Geigy Ltd. v. Fish Peddler, Inc., 691 So.2d 1111, rehearing and rehearing denied, review denied 699 So.2d 1372.

☞1225. **Force majeure.**

† **C.A.11 (Fla.) 2013.** Under Florida law, provisions in initial contract for purchase and sale of coal, some of which provided greater detail on pricing, risk,

and transfer regarding particular sources of coal but which made no provision for or reference to alternative sources of coal, did not render contract a single source agreement which would allow seller to justify its breach, under force majeure argument, when one coal source became unavailable.

Gulf Power Co. v. Coalsales II, LLC, 522 Fed.Appx. 699.

N.D.Fla. 2009. Under Florida law, coal seller's nonperformance was not excused by force majeure clause within contract with buyer for sale and purchase of coal, despite closure of mine that provided primary source of coal under contract, where other mines were approved and available to seller.

Gulf Power Co. v. Coalsales II, L.L.C., 661 F.Supp.2d 1270, motion for relief from judgment granted 2011 WL 3269412, on reconsideration 2011 WL 4552185, affirmed 522 Fed.Appx. 699, affirmed 522 Fed. Appx. 699.

☞1226–1227. *For other cases see earlier editions of this digest, the Decennial Digests, and WESTLAW.*

☞1227. **Acts of buyer as excuse.**

☞1228. —— **In general.**

Fla.App. 4 Dist. 1986. Buyer cannot unilaterally change contract to create default by seller midway through seller's installation.

Solitron Devices, Inc. v. Veeco Instruments, Inc., 492 So.2d 1357.

☞1229–1235. *For other cases see earlier editions of this digest, the Decennial Digests, and WESTLAW.*

(L) WAIVER AND ESTOPPEL.

☞1241. **In general.**

C.A.11 (Fla.) 1998. Conduct may constitute waiver of a contract term under Uniform Commercial Code (UCC), but such an implied waiver must be demonstrated by clear evidence. West's F.S.A. § 672.209.

> BMC Industries, Inc. v. Barth Industries, Inc., 160 F.3d 1322, certiorari denied 119 S.Ct. 1807, 526 U.S. 1132, 143 L.Ed.2d 1010.

Waiver of contract term under Uniform Commercial Code (UCC) may be implied when a party's actions are inconsistent with continued retention of the right. West's F.S.A. § 672.209.

> BMC Industries, Inc. v. Barth Industries, Inc., 160 F.3d 1322, certiorari denied 119 S.Ct. 1807, 526 U.S. 1132, 143 L.Ed.2d 1010.

Uniform Commercial Code (UCC) does not require consideration or detrimental reliance for waiver of contract term. West's F.S.A. § 672.209.

> BMC Industries, Inc. v. Barth Industries, Inc., 160 F.3d 1322, certiorari denied 119 S.Ct. 1807, 526 U.S. 1132, 143 L.Ed.2d 1010.

🗝**1242. Waiver of seller's rights.**

🗝**1243. —— In general.**

C.A.11 (Fla.) 1989. Under Florida law, ethane gas producer did not waive its right to be paid at higher substitute price index called for under contract with purchaser by its inaction in calculating and demanding substitute price index for over five years, as there was no indication that producer intentionally or voluntarily waived its right to retroactive application of substitute price index; for majority of five-year period, inflation escalation price provided higher price for ethane due to economic conditions so there was no reason for producer to insist upon substitute price index.

> Air Products and Chemicals, Inc. v. Louisiana Land and Exploration Co., 867 F.2d 1376.

🗝**1244–1247.** *For other cases see earlier editions of this digest, the Decennial Digests, and WESTLAW.*

🗝**1246. Waiver of buyer's rights.**

🗝**1248. —— As to time, place, and manner of delivery.**

C.A.11 (Fla.) 1998. Eyeglass lense manufacturer waived delivery date of contract for design, manufacture, and installation of equipment to automate its production line through its conduct after delivery date had passed, where, after delivery date had passed, manufacturer accepted contractor's parent company's oral promise to ensure that equipment was "timely" completed and delivered, and manufacturer agreed to increase purchase price and continued to work with contractor. West's F.S.A. § 672.209.

> BMC Industries, Inc. v. Barth Industries, Inc., 160 F.3d 1322, certiorari denied 119 S.Ct. 1807, 526 U.S. 1132, 143 L.Ed.2d 1010.

Fla.App. 1 Dist. 1976. In action by supplier against general contractor to recover for steel furnished building project, trial court properly gave effect to contractual provisions specifying that acceptance of deliveries would constitute waiver of claims for delay in delivery notwithstanding supplier's stated "anticipation" of meeting a more rapid delivery schedule.

> Southeastern Builders, Inc. of Alabama v. Joe Brashears Steel, Inc., 336 So.2d 1228.

🗝**1249. —— As to quality, value, fitness, and condition of goods.**

🗝**1249(1). In general.**

Bkrtcy.S.D.Fla. 1983. Under Florida law, where debtor to whom creditor delivered merchandise accepted goods, had sufficient time to discover breach with respect to goods, and to extent that there were any defects, failed to notify creditor within reasonable time of any alleged defect, debtor was barred from any remedy. West's F.S.A. § 672.607(3)(a).

> In re Holistic Services Corp., 29 B.R. 509.

Fla.App. 1 Dist. 1976. Contractual provision that general contractor's acceptance of materials on delivery would constitute a waiver of any claims for damages on account of delay did not foreclose contractor's claim against supplier for damages caused by delivery of defective and nonconforming materials.

> Southeastern Builders, Inc. of Alabama v. Joe Brashears Steel, Inc., 336 So.2d 1228.

⚷1249(2). Inspection or opportunity to inspect.

Bkrtcy.S.D.Fla. 1993. Agreement by creditor of Chapter 11 debtor to reinspect automobile parts and perhaps to seek resolution of dispute about whether creditor had to repurchase parts did not actually or constructively waive creditor's rights under original agreement to insist upon substantial performance by debtor in timely fashion of those conditions precedent to creditor's obligation to repurchase parts from debtor where original agreement contained express reservation of any defenses in event of subsequent litigation, and original agreement also contained nonwaiver provision.

In re South Motor Co. of Dade County, 161 B.R. 532.

Bkrtcy.S.D.Fla. 1983. Under Florida law, where debtor to whom creditor delivered merchandise accepted goods, had sufficient time to discover breach with respect to goods, and to extent that there were any defects, failed to notify creditor within reasonable time of any alleged defect, debtor was barred from any remedy. West's F.S.A. § 672.607(3)(a).

In re Holistic Services Corp., 29 B.R. 509.

Fla.App. 1 Dist. 1986. Recovery for defective plastic bobbin sleeves would not be precluded due to failure to discover defective sleeves when buyer "could and should have inspected" items before use absent such a condition in contract for purchase of sleeves.

Aetna Cas. & Sur. Co. v. Monsanto Co., 487 So.2d 398.

⚷1249(3)–1249(4). *For other cases see earlier editions of this digest, the Decennial Digests, and WESTLAW.*

⚷1249(5). Payment.

C.C.A.5 (Fla.) 1939. Where buyer entered into agreement with full understanding of its conditions and accepted equipment, used it for a long time and paid major portion of purchase price in numerous installments, buyer could not escape conditions of its agreement, in absence of failure of consideration or fraud.

Miami Lime & Chemical Co. v. York Ice Machinery Corp., 104 F.2d 312.

⚷1250–1254. *For other cases see earlier editions of this digest, the Decennial Digests, and WESTLAW.*

⚷1252. Estoppel.

⚷1255. —— Estoppel of buyer.

Bkrtcy.S.D.Fla. 1993. Creditor who agreed to repurchase automobiles from Chapter 11 debtor was not equitably estopped from refusing to repurchase automobile parts on ground that debtor failed to substantially comply with conditions precedent to creditor's repurchase of parts, even though debtor asserted that it took similar steps with regard to repurchase of automobiles, where there was not sufficient evidence that creditor willfully or negligently acted under contract to debtor's detriment, and debtor fully complied with contract's procedures on the automobiles, but not with the parts.

In re South Motor Co. of Dade County, 161 B.R. 532.

Fla. 1957. Buyer of bedspreads failing to meet specifications would not be estopped from denying obligation to pay full purchase price thereof merely because of temporary use thereof necessitated by urgent need, but buyer would be liable for fair value of use.

Sax Enterprises, Inc. v. David & Dash, Inc., 92 So.2d 421.

VI. DURATION OF CONTRACT.

⚷1301. In general.

C.A.5 (Fla.) 1970. Contract which provided that seller of aircraft engines would furnish buyer with all logs, papers, technical data and descriptive material available to it with respect to such engines did not create continuing obligation.

General Dynamics Corp. v. Miami Aviation Corp., 421 F.2d 416.

⚷1302. Cancellation or termination.

Revocation of acceptance, see V(C)5. Repudiation, see V(J). Rescission, see X(D).

🗝1303. —— In general.

For other cases see earlier editions of this digest, the Decennial Digests, and WEST-LAW.

🗝1304. —— By seller.

Fla.App. 4 Dist. 1998.   Without an agreement in writing specifying a term and then an attempted unjustified termination before that term has elapsed, distributor had no valid claim against a manufacturer for future damages in lost profits under an oral contract terminable at will.

Centro Nautico Representacoes Nauticas, LDA. v. International Marine Co-op, Ltd., 719 So.2d 967, rehearing denied, prohibition denied International Marine Co-op., Ltd. v. Caravelle Boats, Inc., 727 So.2d 906, review granted 743 So.2d 509, opinion quashed 761 So.2d 279.

🗝1305. —— By buyer.

For other cases see earlier editions of this digest, the Decennial Digests, and WEST-LAW.

🗝1306. —— Notice and timeliness.

C.A.11 (Fla.) 2002.   Under Florida's Uniform Commercial Code (UCC), when party is not given reasonable notice prior to termination of terminable-at-will contract, it is entitled to recover profits it would have made from contract during notice period.   West's F.S.A. § 672.309(3).

Maytronics, Ltd. v. Aqua Vac Systems, Inc., 277 F.3d 1317.

🗝1307. —— Options to cancel or terminate.

C.C.A.5 (Fla.) 1939.   As respects option to cancel, the trial court properly permitted lines to be drawn through notations, "Balance cancelled," on margins of sales contracts in evidence, where they contained no provisions as to how buyer's option to cancel them should be exercised and uncontradicted testimony showed absence of intention to cancel them.

Southern Tallow Co. v. David J. Joseph & Co., 101 F.2d 862.

Time held not of essence of sales contracts providing that buyer might cancel them or charge seller's account with difference between contract prices and market prices of material sold on delivery date, in view of prior dealings between parties.

Southern Tallow Co. v. David J. Joseph & Co., 101 F.2d 862.

Fla.App. 3 Dist. 1975.   Contract providing, in part, that seller agreed that transaction could be cancelled in event buyer was unable to make satisfactory arrangements with automobile manufacturer's credit division and automobile manufacturing division for continuation of the business and operations of the corporation, was unambiguous as to whether buyer alone had option of cancelling.

Dolphin Truck Leasing, Inc. v. Perry, 317 So.2d 122.

🗝1308–1309.   *For other cases see earlier editions of this digest, the Decennial Digests, and WESTLAW.*

VII. ASSIGNMENT OF CONTRACT.

🗝1401. In general.

Fla.App. 3 Dist. 1971.   Where assignee of purchase and sale contract took the assignment based upon representation that he would get a return of 7% on his investment but property failed to produce the return, there was misrepresentation as to material fact which was relied on by assignee and assignee was entitled to rescind the transaction.

Cohen v. Landow, 242 So.2d 801.

Where assignor of purchase and sale agreement was the purchaser of the agreement and assigned contract prior to closing date and after it was assigned assignee closed the transaction but there was a misrepresentation as to material fact which was relied on, by returning the property to assignor she was placed in identical position that she would have been in if she had performed the contract of purchase and sale which she assigned and there was no impossibility of return to status quo that would prevent rescission.

Cohen v. Landow, 242 So.2d 801.

🗝1402. Consent.

For other cases see earlier editions of this digest, the Decennial Digests, and WEST-LAW.

⚷1403. Delegation.

Fla.App. 3 Dist. 1974. Although the Uniform Commercial Code makes an assignment of a contract or all rights under a contract an assignment of rights and a delegation of duties, as well as an implied promise to perform the duties by the act of acceptance of the assignment, the Code does not make one liable on an obligation where he merely purchases a chattel without assumption of the obligation. West's F.S.A. § 672.210.

De La Rosa v. Tropical Sandwiches, Inc., 298 So.2d 471, certiorari denied 312 So.2d 760.

VIII. MODIFICATION OF CONTRACT.

⚷1501. In general.

S.D.Fla. 2016. Under Florida law, to overcome the clauses in the master sales agreement that limited amendments to signed writings, the party seeking to enforce amendment was required to show: (1) mutual assent; (2) that both parties, or at least the party seeking to enforce the amendment, performed consistent with the terms of the alleged oral modification, not merely consistent with their obligations under the original contract; and, (3) that due to party's performance under the contract as amended the other party received and accepted a benefit that it otherwise was not entitled to under the original contract, i.e., independent consideration.

Leader Global Solutions, LLC v. Tradeco Infraestructura, S.A. DE C.V., 155 F.Supp.3d 1310.

⚷1502–1503. *For other cases see earlier editions of this digest, the Decennial Digests, and WESTLAW.*

⚷1504. Consideration.

Fla.App. 4 Dist. 2003. Wholesaler's acceptance of contract to purchase chairs involved no promised performance, and therefore did not constitute consideration to support contract modification, where, under contract, distributor agreed to sell to wholesaler any chairs it chose to order at price set forth in price list.

Office Pavilion South Florida, Inc. v. ASAL Products, Inc., 849 So.2d 367, rehearing denied, review denied 861 So.2d 428.

⚷1505–1506. *For other cases see earlier editions of this digest, the Decennial Digests, and WESTLAW.*

⚷1505. Manner and requisites of expression.

⚷1507. —— Modification by conduct, course of performance, or course of dealing.

S.D.Fla. 1999. Modifications to contracts under Uniform Commercial Code (UCC) must meet the test of good faith. U.C.C. § 2–209(2).

Allapattah Services, Inc. v. Exxon Corp., 61 F.Supp.2d 1308.

Bkrtcy.M.D.Fla. 1988. Contract price for crude oil was not changed midquarter by prior conduct of parties or by telexes sent between parties, where contract was governed by Mexican law, and, under Mexican law, contract could only be modified by following exactly same formalities by which original contract was created, not by conduct between parties.

In re Charter Co., 93 B.R. 286.

Fla. 1937. A buyer, introducing in evidence seller's instruction book on methods of selling products, purchased under written contract for resale, and testifying as to his receipt of, but failing to produce, seller's letters supporting buyer's special pleas, alleging modified contract whereby he became seller's agent, failed to prove such modification of written contract and hence could not set off price of goods sold by him on credit against balance due seller under latter contract.

W. T. Rawleigh Co. v. Langford, 175 So. 339, 128 Fla. 663.

⚷1508. —— Oral or written.

S.D.Fla. 2016. Invoice and acceptance order expressly contradicted buyer's allegations that seller breached amended master sales agreement, under which seller purchased equipment and machinery for buyer's resale to its customers, by applying $2 million payment to buyer's outstanding debt, and thus buyer failed to plausibly allege oral modification to agreement as required to support its breach of contract claim under Florida law; although buyer alleged that seller agreed to disburse the $2 million to buyer's suppliers, the invoice reflected purchases, pur-

---

† **This Case was not selected for publication in the National Reporter System**
For legislative history of cited statutes, see Florida Statutes Annotated

chase fee, and showed the $2 million reducing buyer's outstanding balance, and invoice stated that all purchases were subject to master sales agreement.

Leader Global Solutions, LLC v. Tradeco Infraestructura, S.A. DE C.V., 155 F.Supp.3d 1310.

🔑**1509. Validity and enforceability.**

Fla.App. 1 Dist. 2011. Retail buyer's order that was signed by vehicle buyers on same day they executed a retail installment sale contract for purchase of vehicle was not part of "this contract" as that phrase was used in retail installment sale contract's merger clause, which provided that "this contract" contained the entire agreement between the parties, and thus merger clause and parol evidence rule precluded consideration of the retail buyer's order and its arbitration clause in resolving dispute between the parties under the retail installment sale contract; the retail installment sale contract did not refer to any other document as part of the contract and purported, by its title, to represent the parties' contract.

Duval Motors Co. v. Rogers, 73 So.3d 261, rehearing denied.

Retail buyer's order which identified vehicle being purchased and listed vehicle's price and fees associated with purchase and which contained arbitration agreement was not a valid "change" to retail installment sale contract, within meaning of retail installment sale contract's merger clause stating that any change to the contract needed to be in writing and signed, where nothing in order indicated that it was intended as a modification of a pre-existing contract, and order indicated that it was signed before the retail installment sale contract.

Duval Motors Co. v. Rogers, 73 So.3d 261, rehearing denied.

Fla.App. 1 Dist. 1982. In breach of contract action concerning written purchase order for electronic security devices, evidence as to the parties' conduct was sufficient to support finding both of a waiver of the written requirement that subsequent modifications be in writing and signed by both parties, and that subsequent modification occurred such that seller agreed to repurchase the units at full wholesale purchase price upon request by purchaser. West's F.S.A. § 672.209(2, 4).

Linear Corp. v. Standard Hardware Co., 423 So.2d 966.

🔑**1510. Operation and effect.**

C.A.5 (Fla.) 1968. Since purchaser orders executed by manufacturer of heaters as seller and corporate buyer thereof after production had been started constituted a complete integration of prior negotiations and agreements between seller, corporate buyer and buyer's president who seller sought to hold individually liable, in absence of fraud, mistake, or duress, the identity of the corporation as buyer in orders laid to rest earlier oral dealings relating to such identity.

Carolina Metal Products Corp. v. Larson, 389 F.2d 490.

M.D.Fla. 2009. Parties' conduct in entering into comprehensive, detailed, and enforceable written agreement that expressly covered mining company's operation of sellers' mining facilities at three quarries and company's purchase of sellers' mining assets, which were same transactions contemplated under parties' earlier letter of intent (LOI), discharged sellers' claims for breach of LOI under Florida law, particularly given written agreement's merger and integration clause, which specifically provided that all prior agreements and understandings regarding agreement's subject matter were superseded by agreement.

White Const. Co., Inc. v. Martin Marietta Materials, Inc., 633 F.Supp.2d 1302.

Mining services agreement between mining facilities operators and mining company, which expressly contradicted company's alleged oral promise to buy operators' assets at price certain and contained merger and integration clause providing that any prior agreements and understandings between the parties were superseded by agreement, precluded operators' claim against company for breach of alleged oral contract under Florida law.

White Const. Co., Inc. v. Martin Marietta Materials, Inc., 633 F.Supp.2d 1302.

N.D.Fla. 2009. Market reopener amendments between coal seller, a coal company, and buyer, a power company, which designated one mine as a primary source of coal provided under contract, did not have the effect of rendering parties' initial coal sales contract a sole source agreement under Florida law; "primary" did not mean "sole," particularly in light of seller's supply of coal from multiple sources other than the primary mine, and there was no express limiting language in the contract, having identified three sources and having made provisions for other approved sources of coal as well.

Gulf Power Co. v. Coalsales II, L.L.C., 661 F.Supp.2d 1270, motion for relief from judgment granted 2011 WL 3269412, on reconsideration 2011 WL 4552185, affirmed 522 Fed.Appx. 699, affirmed 522 Fed. Appx. 699.

⚷**1511. Retraction.**

For other cases see earlier editions of this digest, the Decennial Digests, and WESTLAW.

IX. WARRANTIES.

Tort liability for injuries from defects in goods sold, see PRODUCTS LIABILITY.

(A) IN GENERAL.

⚷**1601. In general.**

M.D.Fla. 2002. Under Florida law, a warranty, whether express or implied, is fundamentally a contract.

Bland v. Freightliner LLC, 206 F.Supp.2d 1202.

S.D.Fla. 2016. Under Florida law, purchaser of writing instrument for tablet computer did not agree to seller's warranty, and thus purchaser was not bound by warranty's terms, including arbitration provision; warranty stated that purchaser agreed to warranty by "using" instrument, and purchaser never used instrument or even opened its packaging, as he bought it for someone else and gave it to that person.

Guarisma v. Microsoft Corporation, 209 F.Supp.3d 1261.

Fla.App. 1 Dist. 1975. Warranty is an incident to a contract of sale, and assumes or necessarily implies the existence thereof; a warranty is not an essential element of a sale, which can exist without it, but there can be no warranty without a sale.

Marini v. Town & Country Plaza Merchants Ass'n, Inc., 314 So.2d 180.

⚷**1602–1603.** *For other cases see earlier editions of this digest, the Decennial Digests, and WESTLAW.*

⚷**1602. Warranty distinguished from other grounds of liability.**

⚷**1604.** —— **Other contractual terms or obligations.**

Bkrtcy.S.D.Fla. 1987. Debtor's contract with owner of wastewater treatment plant, pursuant to which debtor agreed to design and supervise construction of wastewater treatment system, constituted "contract to provide services," in connection with which no claim for breach of warranty would lie.

In re VTN, Inc., 69 B.R. 1005.

⚷**1605–1610.** *For other cases see earlier editions of this digest, the Decennial Digests, and WESTLAW.*

⚷**1610. Construction, operation, and effect in general.**

⚷**1611.** —— **In general.**

Fla.App. 2 Dist. 1969. Warranties, as relates to sales, are strictly contractual in nature and this is so whether warranty is expressed or implied.

Brown v. Hall, 221 So.2d 454.

Fla.App. 4 Dist. 2009. To the extent the terms of a warranty are not clear, the contract will be construed against the party who drafted the language.

Detroit Diesel Corp. v. Atlantic Mut. Ins. Co., 18 So.3d 618.

⚷**1612.** —— **Breach and elements thereof in general.**

C.A.11 (Fla.) 1983. Breach of warranty occurs only if goods are defective upon delivery, not if buyer's abuse and neglect results in goods becoming defective. West's F.S.A. §§ 672.313(1)(a),

672.314, 672.314(2), 672.315; U.C.C. § 2–315 comment.

> Royal Typewriter Co., a Div. of Litton Business Systems, Inc. v. Xerographic Supplies Corp., 719 F.2d 1092.

C.A.5 (Fla.) 1972. Showing that product was defective when it left manufacturer's control was essential element of plaintiff's case against manufacturer for negligence and breach of warranty in the manufacture.

> Porter v. Eckert, 465 F.2d 1307.

M.D.Fla. 2009. A warranty itself is not breached simply because a defect occurs.

> Brisson v. Ford Motor Co., 602 F.Supp.2d 1227, affirmed in part, vacated in part, remanded 349 Fed. Appx. 433.

S.D.Fla. 1981. Workman, seeking to recover against manufacturer for negligence, breach of warranty and strict liability, was asserting a right protected by the Florida Constitution at time the "access to courts" provision was readopted. West's F.S.A.Const. Art. 1, § 21.

> Ellison v. Northwest Engineering Co., 521 F.Supp. 199.

Fla.App. 1 Dist. 1978. Breach of warranty is a species of liability which may or may not involve actual fault or active negligence on the part of the manufacturer.

> Home Indem. Co. v. Edwards, 360 So.2d 1112, quashed Houdaille Industries, Inc. v. Edwards, 374 So.2d 490.

Fla.App. 3 Dist. 2003. A plaintiff cannot prevail on claims for negligence, breach of warranty or strict liability unless the plaintiff establishes that the product which allegedly caused the plaintiff's injury was manufactured or sold by the defendant.

> Liggett Group Inc. v. Engle, 853 So.2d 434, rehearing and rehearing denied, review granted 873 So.2d 1222, decision approved in part, quashed in part 945 So.2d 1246, certiorari denied R.J. Reynolds To-

bacco Co. v. Engle, 128 S.Ct. 96, 552 U.S. 941, 169 L.Ed.2d 244, rehearing denied 128 S.Ct. 694, 552 U.S. 1056, 169 L.Ed.2d 541.

⚷**1613. —— Particular cases and goods.**

C.A.11 (Fla.) 1986. Under Florida law, customer, who injured her wrist while examining cookie jar in store, had no breach of warranty action against store; that cause of action required "sale" of product, and customer had not purchased cookie jar or even formed any intent to purchase it. West's F.S.A. §§ 672.106, 672.314.

> McQuiston v. K-Mart Corp., 796 F.2d 1346.

Fla.App. 2 Dist. 1968. Transfer of blood by a hospital to a patient is not a "sale" but a service and there was no implied warranty of fitness or merchantability.

> White v. Sarasota County Public Hospital Bd., 206 So.2d 19, certiorari denied 211 So.2d 215.

Fla.App. 2 Dist. 1964. The only obligation imposed on manufacturer of underground lawn sprinkling system installed by purchasers relying on manufacturer's trade name was to provide pipe which was reasonably fit for use in residential lawn sprinkling systems.

> Wisner v. Goodyear Tire & Rubber Co., 167 So.2d 254.

Fla.App. 4 Dist. 1997. Statute governing warranty actions rising from procurement, processing, storage, distribution, or use of blood and blood products was clearly an effort by legislature to limit implied warranty actions against blood suppliers. West's F.S.A. § 672.316(5).

> Raskin v. Community Blood Centers of South Florida, Inc., 699 So.2d 1014, rehearing denied, review denied 707 So.2d 1124.

Fla.App. 4 Dist. 1975. Delivery of new truck to tire store to have tires changed was not a "sale" within Uniform Commercial Code warranty section, but a "bailment for mutual benefit"; thus tire store employees injured when rim on truck pulled apart and exploded were not entitled to recover under that section from truck owner for their injuries. West's F.S.A. § 672.314; U.C.C. § 2–101 et seq.

Favors v. Firestone Tire & Rubber Co., 309 So.2d 69, appeal after remand Sansing v. Firestone Tire & Rubber Co., 354 So.2d 895, certiorari denied 360 So.2d 1250.

(B) EXPRESS WARRANTIES.

1. IN GENERAL.

⬳1621–1622. *For other cases see earlier editions of this digest, the Decennial Digests, and WESTLAW.*

⬳1622. Making and requisites.

⬳1623. —— In general.

M.D.Fla. 2001. Under Florida law, as predicted by the district court, express warranties are bargained-for terms of a contractual agreement, any breach of which is actionable notwithstanding proof of non-reliance at the time of closing on the contract.

Southern Broadcast Group, LLC v. Gem Broadcasting, Inc., 145 F.Supp.2d 1316, affirmed 49 Fed. Appx. 288.

S.D.Fla. 2013. Under California law, an "express warranty" is a contractual promise from the seller that the goods conform to the promise; if they do not, the buyer is entitled to recover the difference between the value of the goods accepted by the buyer and the value of the goods had they been as warranted.

In re Horizon Organic Milk Plus DHA Omega-3 Marketing and Sales Practice Litigation, 955 F.Supp.2d 1311.

Fla.App. 2 Dist. 1969. Express warranty of fitness for particular purpose arises by written contract or oral affirmation.

Brown v. Hall, 221 So.2d 454.

⬳1624. —— Statements or representations constituting warranty.

⬳1624(1). In general.

M.D.Fla. 2015. Under Florida's Uniform Commercial Code (UCC), an express warranty may arise by words or conduct. Fla. Stat. Ann. § 672.313(c).

Armadillo Distribution Enterprises, Inc. v. Hai Yun Musical Instruments Manufacture Co. Ltd., 142 F.Supp.3d 1245.

⬳1624(2). Affirmations and promises in general.

M.D.Fla. 2001. Under Florida law, an express warranty arises where the seller asserts a fact of which the buyer is ignorant prior to the beginning of the transaction, and on which the buyer justifiably relies as part of the basis of the bargain.

Southern Broadcast Group, LLC v. Gem Broadcasting, Inc., 145 F.Supp.2d 1316, affirmed 49 Fed. Appx. 288.

S.D.Fla. 2010. Even if patient's breach of express warranty claim against manufacturer of artificial discs that were implanted in patient's spine was not preempted by the Medical Device Amendments (MDA) to the Food, Drug, and Cosmetic Act (FDCA), statements and photographic images upon which patient allegedly relied in deciding to proceed with surgery to implant artificial discs were not an "affirmation of fact or promise" which became "part of the basis of the bargain," as required to state claim for breach of express warranty under Florida law. Federal Food, Drug, and Cosmetic Act, § 1 et seq., 21 U.S.C.A. § 301 et seq.; Medical Device Amendments of 1976, § 2 et seq., 21 U.S.C.A. § 360c et seq.; West's F.S.A. § 672.313.

Wheeler v. DePuy Spine, Inc., 740 F.Supp.2d 1332.

Bkrtcy.M.D.Fla. 1987. Seller can create express warranty by making affirmation of fact or promise which relates to goods and becomes part of basis of bargain. West's F.S.A. § 672.313(1)(a).

Matter of Trah Enterprises, Inc., 71 B.R. 44.

Fla.App. 1 Dist. 1984. Express warranty generally arises only when seller asserts fact of which buyer is ignorant prior to beginning of transaction and on which buyer justifiably relies as part of the basis of the bargain. West's F.S.A. § 672.313; U.C.C. § 2–313.

> Thursby v. Reynolds Metals Co., 466 So.2d 245, petition for review denied 476 So.2d 676.

🔑1624(3). Intention of parties.

Fla.App. 3 Dist. 1979. The intent of the seller is not controlling as to whether a warranty arises. West's F.S.A. § 672.313.

> Carter Hawley Hale Stores, Inc. v. Conley, 372 So.2d 965.

🔑1624(4). Specific words or language.

C.A.11 (Fla.) 1983. Manufacturer's statement that rental or lease of certain copier machines would produce profit did not create express warranty; however, statements that copiers had useful life of ten years calculated at rate of 8,000 copies per month and that maintenance factor for each copier would be one-half cent per copy did constitute type of affirmations giving rise to express warranties. West's F.S.A. § 672.313(1)(a).

> Royal Typewriter Co., a Div. of Litton Business Systems, Inc. v. Xerographic Supplies Corp., 719 F.2d 1092.

Bkrtcy.S.D.Fla. 1982. Bankruptcy trustee's advertisement and his bill of sale representing, without qualification, sale of "4,200 pairs of pants" created express warranty of quantity. West's F.S.A. § 672.313(1).

> In re Duty Free Shops Corp., 17 B.R. 274.

Fla.App. 3 Dist. 1990. It is not necessary for creation of "express warranty" that seller use formal words such as "warrant" or "guarantee" or that he have specific intention to make warranty.

> State Farm Ins. Co. v. Nu Prime Roll-A-Way of Miami, 557 So.2d 107.

Seller's representation in newspaper, advertisements, catalogues, circulars, etc., may become part of contract of sale and constitute express warranty.

> State Farm Ins. Co. v. Nu Prime Roll-A-Way of Miami, 557 So.2d 107.

🔑1624(5). Descriptions.

Fla.App. 3 Dist. 1979. Where a description of the goods is included in all phases of the sale, such description is part of the basis of the bargain, especially when the buyer justifiably relies on the description. West's F.S.A. § 672.313.

> Carter Hawley Hale Stores, Inc. v. Conley, 372 So.2d 965.

Fla.App. 3 Dist. 1977. Express warranty need not be made by words, but can be by conduct as well, such as by showing blueprint or other description of goods sold to buyer.

> Miles v. Kavanaugh, 350 So.2d 1090.

🔑1624(6). Matters of opinion or commendation.

S.D.Fla. 2013. Under Florida law, mere puffery or sales talk is not sufficient to create an express warranty.

> Aprigliano v. American Honda Motor Co., Inc., 979 F.Supp.2d 1331.

Under Florida law, motorcycle manufacturer's representations that motorcycle was "the world's ultimate touring motorcycle," and "unbelievably vibration-free," were mere puffery that did not create an express warranty between motorcycle purchasers and manufacturer.

> Aprigliano v. American Honda Motor Co., Inc., 979 F.Supp.2d 1331.

Fla. 1952. Statements by retail salesman in inducing purchase of stepladder that stepladder would last a lifetime and that buyer would never break it were merely trade talk, rather than such representations as would afford basis for suit by buyer for injuries sustained when stepladder broke.

> Lambert v. Sistrunk, 58 So.2d 434.

Fla.App. 2 Dist. 1967. Affirmations which merely express seller's opinion, belief or judgment, do not constitute a warranty, and seller may indulge in puffing or praising of goods without becoming liable under warranty.

> Keating v. DeArment, 193 So.2d 694, certiorari denied 201 So.2d 549.

Fla.App. 3 Dist. 1979. Where opinion, contained in report describing ten carat diamond as color grade "D," was not the opinion of the seller but, rather, the opinion of the third party who made the report, the report was capable of creating an express warranty. West's F.S.A. § 672.313(2).

> Carter Hawley Hale Stores, Inc. v. Conley, 372 So.2d 965.

Under the Uniform Commercial Code, the category of statements that are "merely the seller's opinion or commendation" includes statements on which a buyer has no right to rely, as when the buyer and the author of the "seller's opinion or commendation" are equally knowledgeable. West's F.S.A. §§ 672.313(2), 672.313 comment.

> Carter Hawley Hale Stores, Inc. v. Conley, 372 So.2d 965.

Fla.App. 4 Dist. 1990. Salesmen's talk comprised of affirmation of value of goods or opinion or commendation of goods is "puffing" and does not create warranty. West's F.S.A. § 672.313(2).

> Lou Bachrodt Chevrolet, Inc. v. Savage, 570 So.2d 306, review denied 581 So.2d 165.

©⚏**1624(7). Statements as to kind, quality, condition, or value.**

C.A.11 (Fla.) 1983. Manufacturer of copier machines did not warrant machines' "profitability" by using several "assumptions" regarding maintenance costs in computing certain tax advantages of renting the machines. West's F.S.A. § 672.313(1)(a).

> Royal Typewriter Co., a Div. of Litton Business Systems, Inc. v. Xerographic Supplies Corp., 719 F.2d 1092.

Fla. 1952. Statement of retail salesman that stepladder was strong was not such warranty or fraudulent representation as would afford basis for suit by buyer of stepladder for injuries sustained when stepladder broke, in view of facts that such comment was not unethical business practice, salesman did not represent manufacturer, and did not withhold any information, and that buyer could know as much as the salesman about the stepladder by simply looking at it.

> Lambert v. Sistrunk, 58 So.2d 434.

Fla.App. 3 Dist. 1977. Private party, who sold his used airplane to buyer and to induce sale showed buyer engine and propeller logbook setting forth repair history of airplane, expressly warranted accuracy of information contained in logbook where that information formed part of basis of bargain between parties. West's F.S.A. § 672.313.

> Miles v. Kavanaugh, 350 So.2d 1090.

Fla.App. 4 Dist. 1986. Seller warranted that ion implanter would be fit for purpose of processing thin silicon wafers where seller was aware that such was intended use, and where warranty clause provided that "and if selected or specified for buyer's purposes shall be fit for such purposes."

> Solitron Devices, Inc. v. Veeco Instruments, Inc., 492 So.2d 1357.

©⚏**1624(8). Comparisons.**

Fla.App. 3 Dist. 1979. Certain affirmations of a seller amount only to "puffing" and do not give rise to warranties, for example, describing a car as the "nicest car in town." West's F.S.A. §§ 672.313, 672.313 comment.

> Carter Hawley Hale Stores, Inc. v. Conley, 372 So.2d 965.

©⚏**1625. —— Samples or models.**

For other cases see earlier editions of this digest, the Decennial Digests, and WESTLAW.

©⚏**1626. —— Reliance.**

C.A.11 (Fla.) 1983. Buyer's knowledge or absence of reliance will negate existence of express warranty. West's F.S.A. § 672.313(1)(a).

> Royal Typewriter Co., a Div. of Litton Business Systems, Inc. v. Xerographic Supplies Corp., 719 F.2d 1092.

C.A.5 (Fla.) 1972. Buyer is entitled to rely upon express warranty of seller, especially where warranty is descriptive and defects are not readily apparent, and buyer's failure to inspect constitutes no defense for seller.

> U.S. v. Aerodex, Inc., 469 F.2d 1003.

M.D.Fla. 2001. Under Florida law, an express warranty arises where the seller asserts a fact of which the buyer is ignorant prior to the beginning of the transaction, and on which the buyer justifiably relies as part of the basis of the bargain.

> Southern Broadcast Group, LLC v. Gem Broadcasting, Inc., 145 F.Supp.2d 1316, affirmed 49 Fed. Appx. 288.

Under Florida law, as predicted by the district court, express warranties are bargained-for terms of a contractual agreement, any breach of which is actionable notwithstanding proof of non-reliance at the time of closing on the contract.

> Southern Broadcast Group, LLC v. Gem Broadcasting, Inc., 145 F.Supp.2d 1316, affirmed 49 Fed. Appx. 288.

Under Florida law, as predicted by district court, fact that buyer of radio station assets discovered seller's breach of express warranties after entering purchase agreement but prior to closing did not preclude buyer from suing seller for breach of warranty, where buyer relied on warranties and representations when it decided to purchase assets at time it entered into agreement and did not get what it bargained for when seller breached those warranties.

> Southern Broadcast Group, LLC v. Gem Broadcasting, Inc., 145 F.Supp.2d 1316, affirmed 49 Fed. Appx. 288.

S.D.Fla. 2013. Under Florida law, an express warranty is generally considered to arise only where the seller asserts a fact of which the buyer is ignorant prior to the beginning of the transaction and on which the buyer justifiably relies as part of the basis of the bargain. West's F.S.A. § 672.313(1)(a).

> Nature's Products, Inc. v. Natrol, Inc., 990 F.Supp.2d 1307, appeal dismissed (11th cir. 14-10907), and appeal dismissed (11th cir. 15-11180).

S.D.Fla. 2013. Under Florida law, statements made in promotional materials, advertisements, and brochures may be sufficient to create an express warranty if the buyer relies on those statements in making his purchase. West's F.S.A. § 672.313(1)(a).

> Aprigliano v. American Honda Motor Co., Inc., 979 F.Supp.2d 1331.

S.D.Fla. 2013. Under Arkansas law, reliance is an essential element of an express warranty claim. West's A.C.A. § 4–2–313.

> In re Horizon Organic Milk Plus DHA Omega-3 Marketing and Sales Practice Litigation, 955 F.Supp.2d 1311.

Bkrtcy.M.D.Fla. 1987. Seller of heavy construction equipment neither falsely represented condition of equipment at time of purchase, nor warranted condition of equipment, where buyer had ample opportunity to inspect equipment and did, in fact, use equipment extensively prior to purchase.

> Matter of Trah Enterprises, Inc., 71 B.R. 44.

Bkrtcy.M.D.Fla. 1986. Even if representative of manufacturer stated that hammerheads on portable rock crusher would have useful life without maintenance of at least six months or more, buyer, which was informed that hammerheads had relatively short life span and were high maintenance item, was not entitled to rely on any statement made by representative regarding useful life, and thus, such absence of reliance precluded existence of express warranty as to useful life, under Florida law. West's F.S.A. § 672.313.

> Matter of Bob Rigby, Inc., 62 B.R. 900.

Fla. 1952. Statement of retail salesman that stepladder was strong was not such warranty or fraudulent representation as would afford basis for suit by buyer of stepladder for injuries sustained when stepladder broke, in view of facts that such comment was not unethical business practice, salesman did not represent manufacturer, and did not withhold any information, and that buyer could know as much as the salesman about the stepladder by simply looking at it.

> Lambert v. Sistrunk, 58 So.2d 434.

Fla.App. 1 Dist. 1984. Express warranty generally arises only when seller asserts fact of which buyer is ignorant prior to beginning of transaction and on which buyer justifiably relies as part of the basis of the bargain. West's F.S.A. § 672.313; U.C.C. § 2–313.

> Thursby v. Reynolds Metals Co., 466 So.2d 245, petition for review denied 476 So.2d 676.

Manufacturer of aluminum can manufacturing machine was not liable on basis of express warranty for injury to employee using machine where there was no reliance by buyer on any affirmations of particular facts on the part of manufacturer regarding safety features. West's F.S.A. § 672.313; U.C.C. § 2–313.

> Thursby v. Reynolds Metals Co., 466 So.2d 245, petition for review denied 476 So.2d 676.

Fla.App. 2 Dist. 1969. To support liability upon contractual warranty, purchaser must have relied thereon.

> Adair v. The Island Club, 225 So.2d 541.

Fla.App. 2 Dist. 1967. To support liability on basis of contractual warranty, buyer must have relied thereon and in addition his reliance must have been justified under the circumstances.

> Keating v. DeArment, 193 So.2d 694, certiorari denied 201 So.2d 549.

Fla.App. 4 Dist. 1991. Automobile buyer could not rely on written express warranty of title contained in application submitted to state Department of Motor Vehicles to argue that seller breached warranty of title; buyer never saw, never signed, and was never given copy of application for certificate of title. West's F.S.A. § 672.312.

> Maroone Chevrolet, Inc. v. Nordstrom, 587 So.2d 514.

⟜1627. —— **Basis of bargain.**

M.D.Fla. 2001. Under Florida law, an express warranty arises where the seller asserts a fact of which the buyer is ignorant prior to the beginning of the transaction, and on which the buyer justifiably relies as part of the basis of the bargain.

> Southern Broadcast Group, LLC v. Gem Broadcasting, Inc., 145 F.Supp.2d 1316, affirmed 49 Fed. Appx. 288.

S.D.Fla. 2013. Under Florida law, an express warranty is generally considered to arise only where the seller asserts a fact of which the buyer is ignorant prior to the beginning of the transaction and on which the buyer justifiably relies as part of the basis of the bargain. West's F.S.A. § 672.313(1)(a).

> Nature's Products, Inc. v. Natrol, Inc., 990 F.Supp.2d 1307, appeal dismissed (11th cir. 14-10907), and appeal dismissed (11th cir. 15-11180).

S.D.Fla. 2013. Under Arizona law, to create an express warranty, a seller must provide an affirmation of fact or promise, a description of the goods, or a sample or model that becomes part of the basis of the bargain. A.R.S. § 47–2313(A).

> In re Horizon Organic Milk Plus DHA Omega-3 Marketing and Sales Practice Litigation, 955 F.Supp.2d 1311.

Under Arkansas law, an affirmation of fact must be part of the basis of the parties bargain to be an express warranty. West's A.C.A. § 4–2–313.

> In re Horizon Organic Milk Plus DHA Omega-3 Marketing and Sales Practice Litigation, 955 F.Supp.2d 1311.

S.D.Fla. 2010. Even if patient's breach of express warranty claim against manufacturer of artificial discs that were implanted in patient's spine was not preempted by the Medical Device Amendments (MDA) to the Food, Drug, and Cosmetic Act (FDCA), statements and photographic images upon which patient allegedly relied in deciding to proceed with surgery to implant artificial discs were not an "affirmation of fact or promise" which became "part of the basis of the bargain," as required to state claim for breach of express warranty under Florida law. Federal Food, Drug, and Cosmetic Act, § 1 et seq., 21 U.S.C.A. § 301 et seq.; Medical Device Amendments of 1976, § 2 et seq., 21 U.S.C.A. § 360c et seq.; West's F.S.A. § 672.313.

> Wheeler v. DePuy Spine, Inc., 740 F.Supp.2d 1332.

S.D.Fla. 2010. To claim breach of express warranty under Florida law, each plaintiff in putative class action would be required to show that yogurt manufacturer's claim that eating its specially-formulated yogurt promoted digestive health in ways that eating normal yogurt did not was part of the basis in plaintiff's decision to buy the product.

> Fitzpatrick v. General Mills, Inc., 263 F.R.D. 687, vacated 635 F.3d 1279.

Bkrtcy.M.D.Fla. 1987. Seller can create express warranty by making affirmation of fact or promise which relates to goods and becomes part of basis of bargain. West's F.S.A. § 672.313(1)(a).

Matter of Trah Enterprises, Inc., 71 B.R. 44.

Fla.App. 1 Dist. 1984. Express warranty generally arises only when seller asserts fact of which buyer is ignorant prior to beginning of transaction and on which buyer justifiably relies as part of the basis of the bargain. West's F.S.A. § 672.313; U.C.C. § 2–313.

Thursby v. Reynolds Metals Co., 466 So.2d 245, petition for review denied 476 So.2d 676.

Fla.App. 3 Dist. 1977. Fraud is not essential ingredient of action for breach of express warranty and indeed it is not even necessary that seller have specific intention to make express warranty, but it is sufficient that warranty was made which formed part of basis of bargain.

Miles v. Kavanaugh, 350 So.2d 1090.

☞**1628. —— Advertising and promotion.**

S.D.Fla. 2013. Under Florida law, statements made in promotional materials, advertisements, and brochures may be sufficient to create an express warranty if the buyer relies on those statements in making his purchase. West's F.S.A. § 672.313(1)(a).

Aprigliano v. American Honda Motor Co., Inc., 979 F.Supp.2d 1331.

☞**1629. —— Warranty subsequent to contract of sale.**

For other cases see earlier editions of this digest, the Decennial Digests, and WEST-LAW.

☞**1630. Validity and enforceability.**

Fla. 1983. In proceeding on contractor's claim against seller of hardening agent to recover amount contractor paid property owner when hardening agent contaminated property owner's foodstuffs, in which case went to jury on negligence theory and there was no count in strict liability, seller of hardening agent was entitled to present to jury the warranty clause which was contained in document received by contractor from the seller prior or to purchase of the hardening agent and

which provided that the only obligation of seller and its distributor would be to replace any of the product which proved to be defective; the limitations of remedy provision was not prima facie unconscionable and should have been given effect absent a showing of unconscionability.

Radiation Technology, Inc. v. Ware Const. Co., 445 So.2d 329.

2. OPERATION AND EFFECT.

☞**1641. In general.**

For other cases see earlier editions of this digest, the Decennial Digests, and WEST-LAW.

☞**1642. Construction in general.**

S.D.Fla. 2013. Under Florida law, a written warranty is treated like a contract between the seller and the buyer; as such, the terms of an express warranty may limit or foreclose the remedies available to the buyer.

Aprigliano v. American Honda Motor Co., Inc., 979 F.Supp.2d 1331.

Fla.App. 3 Dist. 1977. Most prominent principle in construction of warranties in sale of consumer goods is ascertainment of intentions of parties in light of surrounding circumstances.

Knipp v. Weinbaum, 351 So.2d 1081, certiorari denied 357 So.2d 188.

Fla.App. 4 Dist. 1986. Seller's warranty of fitness for buyer's purpose necessarily included representation that breakage would be within reasonable limits.

Solitron Devices, Inc. v. Veeco Instruments, Inc., 492 So.2d 1357.

☞**1643. Breach and elements thereof in general.**

M.D.Fla. 2015. To state a cause of action for breach of an express warranty under Florida's Uniform Commercial Code (UCC), the plaintiff must allege: (1) the sale of goods; (2) the express warranty; (3) breach of the warranty; (4) notice to seller of the breach; and (5) the injuries sustained by the buyer as a result of the breach of the express warranty. Fla. Stat. Ann. § 672.313(c).

Armadillo Distribution Enterprises, Inc. v. Hai Yun Musical Instruments Manufacture Co. Ltd., 142 F.Supp.3d 1245.

M.D.Fla. 1992. In breach of express warranty, test of defectiveness of product is whether product performs in accordance with express warranty given.

Pulte Home Corp., Inc. v. Ply Gem Industries, Inc., 804 F.Supp. 1471.

S.D.Fla. 2014. Under Florida law, there can be no cause of action for breach of an express limited warranty unless the consumer can allege and prove that the manufacturer did not comply with the limited express warranty's terms. West's F.S.A. § 672.313.

Sanchez-Knutson v. Ford Motor Co., 52 F.Supp.3d 1223.

S.D.Fla. 2013. Under Florida law, a manufacturer's liability for breach of an express warranty derives from, and is measured by, the terms of that warranty.

Aprigliano v. American Honda Motor Co., Inc., 979 F.Supp.2d 1331.

S.D.Fla. 2013. Under California law, in order to prevail on a breach of express warranty, plaintiff must prove that seller: (1) made an affirmation of fact or promise or provided a description of its goods; (2) the promise or description formed the basis of the bargain; (3) the express warranty was breached; and (4) the breach caused injury to plaintiff.

In re Horizon Organic Milk Plus DHA Omega-3 Marketing and Sales Practice Litigation, 955 F.Supp.2d 1311.

Fla.App. 3 Dist. 2008. Under Florida law, there can be no cause of action for breach of an express limited warranty unless the consumer can allege and prove that the manufacturer did not comply with the limited express warranty's terms. West's F.S.A. § 672.313.

Ocana v. Ford Motor Co., 992 So.2d 319, rehearing denied.

Fla.App. 3 Dist. 1990. Liability for breach of warranty exists where persons or property are damaged because of a product's failure to live up to an express or implied representation by a manufacturer or supplier.

State Farm Ins. Co. v. Nu Prime Roll-A-Way of Miami, 557 So.2d 107.

Fla.App. 3 Dist. 1977. Fraud is not essential ingredient of action for breach of express warranty and indeed it is not even necessary that seller have specific intention to make express warranty, but it is sufficient that warranty was made which formed part of basis of bargain.

Miles v. Kavanaugh, 350 So.2d 1090.

☞1644. Particular cases and goods.

☞1645. —— In general.

† **C.A.11 (Fla.) 2013.** Manufacturer's high-powered radio amplifiers did not meet designated performance specifications, and therefore manufacturer breached its warranty that amplifiers would meet or exceed those specifications.

Delta RF Technology, Inc. v. RIIMIC, LLC, 533 Fed.Appx. 872.

M.D.Fla. 2015. Drum kit distributor sufficiently alleged that drum kit manufacturer failed to provide drum kits of a quality represented in samples provided to distributor, and failed to take any steps to cure defects in the non-conforming drum kits, as required to state a claim for breach of express warranty under Florida's Uniform Commercial Code (UCC). Fla. Stat. Ann. § 672.313(c).

Armadillo Distribution Enterprises, Inc. v. Hai Yun Musical Instruments Manufacture Co. Ltd., 142 F.Supp.3d 1245.

N.D.Fla. 2010. Evidence established that aircraft was delivered by seller in an airworthy condition, fulfilling the express warranty of airworthiness required in the aircraft purchase agreement, and that seller did not breach a duty of fair dealing under Florida law; the only evidence of a possible airworthy defect in the aircraft at the time of delivery was a bald nose tire, which buyer, which accepted the aircraft at closing after a reasonable opportunity to inspect it, had full knowledge of and agreed to accept. West's F.S.A. § 672.313(1)(a).

JDI Holdings, LLC v. Jet Management, Inc., 732 F.Supp.2d 1205.

Fla.App. 3 Dist. 1979. Where ten carat diamond which was warranted to be color grade "D" was on the date of sale and always was color grade "E," warranty was breached and breach entitled buyer to recover the difference between the value of the diamond as warranted and what the diamond was actually worth. West's F.S.A. § 672.714.

　Carter Hawley Hale Stores, Inc. v. Conley, 372 So.2d 965.

Fla.App. 4 Dist. 1999. Paint manufacturer representative's oral statement relating to replacement paint job on vessel, that manufacturer would warranty its product after sand sweeping of vessel bottom, as opposed to sandblasting down to steel hull as called for in warranty preparation instructions, acted to modify and expand manufacturers' written express warranty, and extended written express warranty on initial job to second paint job, even though hull was also not sandblasted on initial job.

　New Nautical Coatings, Inc. v. Scoggin, 731 So.2d 145.

🗝**1646. —— Buildings, structures, and construction.**

Fla.App. 2 Dist. 1998. Renovation contractor made no express warranty to homeowners that windows, which leaked after being installed, were free from defect and suitable for their intended purposes and no warranty as to condition of windows was implied by law. West's F.S.A. §§ 672.104, 672.314.

　Lonnie D. Adams Bldg. Contractor, Inc. v. O'Connor, 714 So.2d 1178.

Fla.App. 3 Dist. 1982. Subcontractor breached its express warranty as well as its implied warranties of fitness and merchantability so as to be liable to condominium association for damages which resulted from subcontractor's substitution of roof materials without authorization.

　Biscayne Roofing Co. v. Palmetto Fairway Condominium Ass'n, Inc., 418 So.2d 1109.

🗝**1647–1648.** *For other cases see earlier editions of this digest, the Decennial Digests, and WESTLAW.*

🗝**1649. —— Machinery and equipment.**

Fla. 1941. A warranty made in sale of conveyor belt, that belt would "earn its cost against the average of the last six belts used on this installation", such average being shown by performance record attached, and that belt would earn its cost when credited with the average cost per ton of the last six belts, when operated under the "same" conditions, meant conditions under which former belts operated and not those described in a data sheet attached to prior request for quotation, which was not sufficiently described or referred to.

　U.S. Rubber Products v. Clark, 200 So. 385, 145 Fla. 631.

🗝**1650. —— Food and beverages.**

S.D.Fla. 2014. Consumers' allegations in class action complaint against manufacturers of cereal and snack food products, that consumers were induced to buy products by the words "all natural" on packaging and manufacturers' representations that products had "nothing artificial," stated claim for breach of express warranty under Florida law. West's F.S.A. § 672.313(1)(a).

　Garcia v. Kashi Co., 43 F.Supp.3d 1359.

🗝**1651. —— Motor vehicles.**

M.D.Fla. 2002. Allegations by purchasers of motor home that manufacturer provided express warranty at time of purchase, that motor home contained several defects, that manufacturer was given multiple chances to cure defects, that defects could not be cured, and that purchasers suffered damages in form of sleeping and lodging expenses and costs of repairs, were sufficient to state claim against manufacturer for breach of warranty under Florida law.

　Bland v. Freightliner LLC, 206 F.Supp.2d 1202.

🗝**1652–1653.** *For other cases see earlier editions of this digest, the Decennial Digests, and WESTLAW.*

🗝**1654. —— Computers and software.**

　See also COPYRIGHTS AND INTELLECTUAL PROPERTY 🗝107.

🗝**1655. Design defects.**

S.D.Fla. 2014. Under Florida law, design defects, in addition to manufacturing defects, were covered by automobile manufacturer's express warranty, where warranty contained no express exclusion for coverage for design defect claims, and design defects were not included in warranty's "what is not covered" section. West's F.S.A. § 672.313.

Sanchez-Knutson v. Ford Motor Co., 52 F.Supp.3d 1223.

⟶1656–1657. *For other cases see earlier editions of this digest, the Decennial Digests, and WESTLAW.*

⟶1656. Duration of warranty.

⟶1658. ⸺ Future defects and events; future performance.

C.A.5 (Fla.) 1967. Guarantee clause in contract between corporation and government agency, which provided, inter alia, that models sold to agency would be free from defects in material and workmanship and would conform to contract's requirements at time of delivery, was an express warranty against faulty materials, faulty workmanship and latent defects rather than an expression of parties' intention to switch risk of loss from its normal placement on the purchaser, having nothing to do with externally caused damage which was only type of damage covered by corporation's insurance policy, so that ordinary Florida risk of loss rule applied, risk of loss in transit was on government agency, and thus there was no coverage under corporation's policy.

Exhibition Display Service Co. v. Liberty Mut. Ins. Co., 378 F.2d 903.

M.D.Fla. 2005. Alleged express warranty of radio seller, that future models would have "trunking" capability allowing for search of available frequencies did not apply under Florida law to current models being sold under contract that was subject of suit. West's F.S.A. § 672.313(1)(a).

Business Radio, Inc. v. Relm Wireless Corp., 373 F.Supp.2d 1317, affirmed 209 Fed.Appx. 899.

⟶1659–1660. *For other cases see earlier editions of this digest, the Decennial Digests, and WESTLAW.*

(C) WARRANTIES IMPOSED BY LAW; IMPLIED WARRANTIES.

1. IN GENERAL.

⟶1671. In general.

C.A.11 (Fla.) 1985. In Florida, a manufacturer, assembler or seller may be sued, subject to certain limitations, under breach of implied warranty and strict liability theories whenever personal injury or property damage results from use of a product it has manufactured, assembled or sold.

Hurley v. Larry's Water Ski School, 762 F.2d 925.

C.A.5 (Fla.) 1964. Implied warranty is incident of sale, arising apart from and independent of contract of sale from nature of transaction and situation of parties, though it is a contractual right.

Sperry Rand Corp. v. Industrial Supply Corp., 337 F.2d 363.

C.A.5 (Fla.) 1959. It is immaterial whether liability of manufacturer for defective goods be considered as arising by implied warranty or under concepts of tort law, because in any event, in absence of any contract or cases establishing any higher standard of care, duty on party to be charged remains one of due care.

Clarkson v. Hertz Corp., 266 F.2d 948.

C.A.5 (Fla.) 1950. An express warranty as to any particular matter excludes any implied warranty with reference to the same matter or matters.

Cohen v. Frima Products Co., 181 F.2d 324.

Fla.App. 1 Dist. 1975. An implied warranty arises from a sale of goods or property though it has on some occasions been extended to a lease.

Marini v. Town & Country Plaza Merchants Ass'n, Inc., 314 So.2d 180.

A shopping center which had engaged a retired fire department captain to operate a fireworks display was not liable on theory of implied warranty for injuries sustained by the captain as result of explosion of a pyrotechnic device, where the captain was familiar with the manufacturer of the fireworks, he made no objection to the use of the fireworks, the captain did not rely on the shopping center's selection of the fireworks, and there was no sale or lease of the fireworks between the center and the captain.

Marini v. Town & Country Plaza Merchants Ass'n, Inc., 314 So.2d 180.

Fla.App. 2 Dist. 1998. Implied warranties in the Uniform Commercial Code

(UCC) do not generally pass from a contractor to an owner, because a contractor is viewed as a provider of services, not a merchant. West's F.S.A. §§ 672.104, 672.314.

>Lonnie D. Adams Bldg. Contractor, Inc. v. O'Connor, 714 So.2d 1178.

Fla.App. 3 Dist. 1984. In modern products liability suit, recovery is generally predicated upon a trireme of negligence, implied warranty and strict liability.

>Copeland v. Celotex Corp., 447 So.2d 908, quashed 471 So.2d 533.

Fla.App. 4 Dist. 1975. Implied warranty doctrine developed prior to adoption of Uniform Commercial Code is still viable.

>Favors v. Firestone Tire & Rubber Co., 309 So.2d 69, appeal after remand Sansing v. Firestone Tire & Rubber Co., 354 So.2d 895, certiorari denied 360 So.2d 1250.

⟶**1672. Breach and elements thereof in general.**

C.A.5 (Fla.) 1969. Under Florida law, doctrine of implied warranty is clearly one of which there has to first be actual adulteration in product before there can be liability from harm resulting from its use.

>Green v. American Tobacco Co., 409 F.2d 1166, certiorari denied 90 S.Ct. 912, 397 U.S. 911, 25 L.Ed.2d 93.

C.A.5 (Fla.) 1968. Under Florida law, breach of implied warranty protection against defect in machine manufactured extends not only to mechanical defect but also to defect in design.

>Vandercook & Son, Inc. v. Thorpe, 395 F.2d 104.

Under Florida law, plaintiff seeking to recover from manufacturer of machine for breach of implied warranty must show that defect existed in the machine before it left the manufacturer, and that such defect caused the injury, and that plaintiff was a person who was reasonably intended to use the machine, and that the machine was being used in the intended manner.

>Vandercook & Son, Inc. v. Thorpe, 395 F.2d 104.

S.D.Fla. 1975. Under Florida law, plaintiff suing for breach of implied warranty must show that a defect existed in the product before it left manufacturer, that the defect caused the injury, that the plaintiff was the person who was reasonably intended to use the product, and that the product was being used in the intended manner.

>Serksnas v. Engine Support, Inc., 392 F.Supp. 392.

Fla. 1979. For there to be recovery in action for implied warranty or strict liability, it must be shown that plaintiff's injury was proximately caused by some defect in product.

>Houdaille Industries, Inc. v. Edwards, 374 So.2d 490.

Fla.App. 3 Dist. 1990. Liability for breach of warranty exists where persons or property are damaged because of a product's failure to live up to an express or implied representation by a manufacturer or supplier.

>State Farm Ins. Co. v. Nu Prime Roll-A-Way of Miami, 557 So.2d 107.

Fla.App. 4 Dist. 1992. Elements to prove liability under implied warranty theory are that plaintiff was foreseeable user of product, that product was being used in intended manner at time of injury, that product was defective when transferred from warrantor, and that defect caused injury.

>Amoroso v. Samuel Friedland Family Enterprises, 604 So.2d 827, rehearing denied, review granted 618 So.2d 1369, decision approved 630 So.2d 1067.

Fla.App. 4 Dist. 1978. Liability is imposed under theory of implied warranty when it has been proved that plaintiff was a foreseeable user of the product, the product was being used in the intended manner at the time of the injury, the product was defective when transferred from the warrantor and the defect caused the injury.

>Sansing v. Firestone Tire & Rubber Co., 354 So.2d 895, certiorari denied 360 So.2d 1250.

☞1673. Particular cases and goods in general.

C.A.5 (Fla.) 1977. Florida doctrine of implied warranty extends to embrace some concept of "crashworthiness."

Smith v. Fiat-Roosevelt Motors, Inc., 556 F.2d 728.

C.A.5 (Fla.) 1970. Where contract for construction of cable television system designated defendant for whom system was constructed as the "buyer" and provided that title and all incidents of title and ownership should remain with plaintiff contractor until completion of work and that it was intention of parties that all equipment and material used should remain personal property at least until such time as acceptance of and final payment for entire system was made, contract was sufficiently sale of goods so as to bring it within contemplation of Uniform Commercial Code with respect to warranties. F.S.A. §§ 672.2–102, 672.2–316.

Entron, Inc. v. General Cablevision of Palatka, 435 F.2d 995.

C.A.5 (Fla.) 1962. Cigarette manufacturer, under theory of implied warranty, was not liable as an absolute insurer for death of cigarette smoker who had died from lung cancer caused by smoking manufacturer's cigarettes, in view of jury's finding that there was no developed human skill or foresight which could afford the manufacturer a knowledge of the harmful effects. Federal Food, Drug, and Cosmetic Act, § 1 et seq., 21 U.S.C.A. § 301 et seq.; Federal Trade Commission Act, § 1 et seq., 15 U.S.C.A. § 41 et seq.; F.S.A. §§ 500.01 et seq., 768.01, 768.02; Fed.Rules Civ.Proc. rules 25(a), 49(b), 28 U.S.C.A.; 28 U.S.C.A. § 1821; 69 P.S.Pa. §§ 1–339.

Green v. American Tobacco Co., 304 F.2d 70, certified question answered 154 So.2d 169, answer to certified question conformed to 325 F.2d 673, certiorari denied 84 S.Ct. 1349, 377 U.S. 943, 12 L.Ed.2d 306, certiorari denied 84 S.Ct. 1351, 377 U.S. 943, 12 L.Ed.2d 306.

Fla. 1965. Retail druggists were not liable to patient-purchaser on theory of implied warranty for injuries resulting from taking drug where prescription was filled precisely in accordance with its directions, and even then, in manufacturer's packets and there was no adulteration of drug which was available only to a limited segment of public on a medical doctor's prescription therefor.

McLeod v. W. S. Merrell Co., Division of Richardson-Merrell, Inc., 174 So.2d 736.

Fla. 1956. An implied warranty does not protect against hazards apparent to the plaintiff, but protects against an usual or apparent use, and does not protect against injury imposed while carelessly using a dangerous mechanism.

Matthews v. Lawnlite Co., 88 So.2d 299.

Fla.App. 1 Dist. 1979. Where sale involved only gasoline and did not include empty plastic milk carton container, which purchaser supplied, self-service gasoline station did not breach implied warranty, despite contention that statute, which requires attendant to prevent dispensing of gasoline into portable containers not bearing seal of approval of nationally recognized testing agency, had to be read in pari materia with Uniform Commercial Code section governing implied warranties, so that breach of implied warranty occurred, and that even in absence of first statute, second statute was susceptible to interpretation that breach of implied warranty occurred. West's F.S.A. §§ 526.141, 672.314, 672.314 comment.

Hurd v. Munford, Inc., 378 So.2d 86, certiorari denied 389 So.2d 1111.

Fla.App. 1 Dist. 1975. Hospital and physicians could be held responsible on theory of implied warranty for serum hepatitis which patient contracted and which was allegedly caused by blood administered to her only upon showing that defect in the blood was detectable or removable through the reasonable use of scientific procedures or techniques; under statute there would be no liability without fault. West's F.S.A. § 672.316(5); 32 West's F.S.A. Florida Appellate Rules, rule 4.6.

Williamson v. Memorial Hospital of Bay County, 307 So.2d 199.

Fla.App. 1 Dist. 1971. Under Florida law, doctrine of implied warranty requires that there be shown actual adulteration in product before there can be liability for harm resulting from its use.

> E. R. Squibb & Sons, Inc. v. Jordan, 254 So.2d 17.

Fla.App. 2 Dist. 1977. Book merchant impliedly warranted the tangible, physical properties; i. e., printing and binding, of books sold. West's F.S.A. §§ 672.105, 672.314(1), (2)(c).

> Cardozo v. True, 342 So.2d 1053, certiorari denied 353 So.2d 674.

The Uniform Commercial Code, in codifying the law of sales, did nothing to restrict common-law doctrine of implied warranty under state law. West's F.S.A. § 672.314.

> Cardozo v. True, 342 So.2d 1053, certiorari denied 353 So.2d 674.

Fla.App. 2 Dist. 1972. Consumer, who, while attempting to get contents of soft drink bottle out by sucking upon it, discovered foreign substance that resembled a rat with hair sucked off, and who then became nauseated and went outside and vomited, was entitled to recover on theory of implied warranty and negligence.

> Way v. Tampa Coca Cola Bottling Co., 260 So.2d 288.

Fla.App. 2 Dist. 1966. Supplying of blood by blood bank to a patient for a consideration is a sale, and law of implied warranties applies to transaction.

> Russell v. Community Blood Bank, Inc., 185 So.2d 749, reversed 196 So.2d 115.

A plaintiff can state a cause of action against a blood bank for breach of implied warranty, but can only recover for injuries if they were caused by failure to detect or remove a deleterious substance capable of detection or removal.

> Russell v. Community Blood Bank, Inc., 185 So.2d 749, reversed 196 So.2d 115.

Fla.App. 3 Dist. 1986. Manufacturer of drywall products was not liable on basis of negligent manufacture, breach of implied warranty, or strict liability for injuries suffered by employee of company to which manufacturer sold its entire operation, including ribbon blender, as a result of alleged defect in ribbon blender, as manufacturer was not in business of manufacturing and distributing ribbon blenders.

> Johnson v. Supro Corp., 498 So.2d 528.

Fla.App. 4 Dist. 1997. Statute allowing recipient of tainted blood to bring implied warranty action if defect could have been detected or removed by reasonable use of scientific procedures or techniques does not require that recipient allege and prove negligence on part of blood supplier in performing scientific procedures or techniques. West's F.S.A. § 672.316(5).

> Raskin v. Community Blood Centers of South Florida, Inc., 699 So.2d 1014, rehearing denied, review denied 707 So.2d 1124.

Fla.App. 4 Dist. 1983. Recovery on basis of strict liability and implied warranty was not justified on ground that automobile manufactured by defendant was defective, notwithstanding that automatic brake release failed to work, where designers of automobile anticipated that very contingency by providing for alternate manual release, and proximate cause of injuries sustained by plaintiff when vehicle began to roll was not failure of automatic brake release, but plaintiff's use of properly functioning manual brake release.

> Cohen v. General Motors Corp., Cadillac Div., 427 So.2d 389, appeal after remand 444 So.2d 1170.

Fla.App. 4 Dist. 1980. In view of evidence that developer retook condominium office voluntarily and not under any legal compulsion when problems arose with the wood paneling, it could not recover on a theory of breach of implied warranty from the manufacturer of the paneling for the loss which it allegedly suffered following its retaking of the unit and its eventual resale.

> Georgia-Pacific Corp. v. Squires Development Corp., 387 So.2d 986.

2. PARTICULAR WARRANTIES.

🗝**1681. In general.**

Fla. 1965. Retailer's implied-warranty liability as to food does not extend to containers of the food.

> Foley v. Weaver Drugs, Inc., 177 So.2d 221.

---

† This Case was not selected for publication in the National Reporter System
For legislative history of cited statutes, see Florida Statutes Annotated

Fla. 1965. A druggist who sells a prescription warrants that he has compounded the drug prescribed, that he has used due and proper care in filling the prescription, that proper methods were used in compounding process and that drug has not been infected with some adulterating foreign substance.

McLeod v. W. S. Merrell Co., Division of Richardson-Merrell, Inc., 174 So.2d 736.

⚸1682. Identity or genuineness.

Fla. 1939. A sale of seed by name raises an implied warranty that seed is true to name, and fact that buyer inspected before purchasing is immaterial, when its character cannot ordinarily be ascertained by reasonable inspection.

West Coast Lumber Co. v. Wernicke, 188 So. 357, 137 Fla. 363.

⚸1683. Quantity.

For other cases see earlier editions of this digest, the Decennial Digests, and WEST-LAW.

⚸1684. Quality, fitness, or condition.

Fitness for ordinary purpose or use, see IX(C)3. Merchantability, see IX(C)3. Fitness for particular purpose or use, see IX(C)4.

⚸1685. —— In general.

C.A.5 (Fla.) 1977. Under Florida law, the merchant vendor of an automobile impliedly warrants its "crashworthiness" in some degree.

Smith v. Fiat-Roosevelt Motors, Inc., 556 F.2d 728.

C.A.5 (Fla.) 1969. While Uniform Commercial Code has strengthened rights of the buyer, it did not change the common-law rule that in order for there to be an implied warranty of sufficiency of a design the seller must be responsible for the design, either by initiation or adoption.

School Supply Service Co. v. J. H. Keeney & Co., 410 F.2d 481.

C.A.5 (Fla.) 1963. Under Florida law, the manufacturer's or seller's actual knowledge or opportunity for knowledge of a defective or unwholesome condition

in his product is irrelevant to his liability for breach of implied warranty of fitness.

Green v. American Tobacco Co., 325 F.2d 673, certiorari denied 84 S.Ct. 1349, 377 U.S. 943, 12 L.Ed.2d 306, certiorari denied 84 S.Ct. 1351, 377 U.S. 943, 12 L.Ed.2d 306.

M.D.Fla. 1975. Importer of vehicles for purpose of resale did not impliedly warrant vehicle to have been equipped with "crashworthy seat backs." West's F.S.A. § 672.314(2)(c).

Smith v. Fiat-Roosevelt Motors, Inc., 402 F.Supp. 116, reversed 556 F.2d 728.

Fla. 1953. Seller of seed may not escape liability for varietal difference between seed represented for sale and seed actually purchased by buyer.

Hoskins v. Jackson Grain Co., 63 So.2d 514.

Fla.App. 1 Dist. 1980. A contract for the sale of second–hand goods involves only such obligation as is appropriate to such goods for that is their contract description. West's F.S.A. § 672.314 comment.

Fuquay v. Revels Motors, Inc., 389 So.2d 1238.

Fla.App. 2 Dist. 1967. Generally, there is no implied warranty as to the condition, fitness or quality of secondhand articles of personal property.

Keating v. DeArment, 193 So.2d 694, certiorari denied 201 So.2d 549.

Fla.App. 2 Dist. 1966. The basis of liability on a breach of implied warranty of fitness is the agreement, imposed by law, to be responsible in the event the thing sold is not in fact fit for the use and purpose for which it is intended.

Enix v. Diamond T. Sales & Service Co., 188 So.2d 48, certiorari denied 195 So.2d 566.

Fla.App. 2 Dist. 1964. Basis of liability on breach of implied warranty of fitness is undertaking or agreement, attributed by law, to be responsible in event thing sold is not in fact fit for use and purposes intended.

Arcade Steam Laundry v. Bass, 159 So.2d 915.

Fla.App. 3 Dist. 1967. Rationale that imposes warranty upon retail druggists filling prescriptions that drug prescribed has been compounded, that due and proper care in filling prescription has been used, that proper methods were used in the compounding process and that drug has not been infected with some adulterating foreign substance should be applied to processors of blood which is to be used by purchasers for transfusions into human beings.

Hoder v. Sayet, 196 So.2d 205.

⌐**1686. —— Knowledge of defects.**

M.D.Fla. 2005. Seller did not breach implied warranty of fitness for particular purpose, under Florida law, by not providing radios that had "trunking" feature, allowing for utilization of available frequencies; buyer knew radios did not have that feature.

Business Radio, Inc. v. Relm Wireless Corp., 373 F.Supp.2d 1317, affirmed 209 Fed.Appx. 899.

Fla. 1963. Manufacturer's or seller's actual knowledge or opportunity for knowledge of defective or unwholesome condition is irrelevant to his liability on theory of implied warranty.

Green v. American Tobacco Co., 154 So.2d 169, answer to certified question conformed to 325 F.2d 673, certiorari denied 84 S.Ct. 1349, 377 U.S. 943, 12 L.Ed.2d 306, certiorari denied 84 S.Ct. 1351, 377 U.S. 943, 12 L.Ed.2d 306.

Although cigarette user's fatal lung cancer had developed before manufacturer and distributor thereof could have, by reason of reasonable application of human skill and foresight, known that users of cigarettes would be in danger of contracting cancer of lung, Florida law imposed on manufacturer and distributor absolute liability, as for breach of implied warranty of fitness, for death caused by use of cigarettes. F.S.A. § 25.031; 31 F.S.A. Florida Appellate Rules, rule 4.61.

Green v. American Tobacco Co., 154 So.2d 169, answer to certified question conformed to 325 F.2d 673, certiorari denied 84 S.Ct. 1349, 377 U.S. 943, 12 L.Ed.2d 306, certiorari denied 84 S.Ct. 1351, 377 U.S. 943, 12 L.Ed.2d 306.

Proof of actual or implied knowledge of defect is not essential to liability on implied warranty.

Green v. American Tobacco Co., 154 So.2d 169, answer to certified question conformed to 325 F.2d 673, certiorari denied 84 S.Ct. 1349, 377 U.S. 943, 12 L.Ed.2d 306, certiorari denied 84 S.Ct. 1351, 377 U.S. 943, 12 L.Ed.2d 306.

⌐**1687. —— Obvious, latent, or hidden defects.**

Fla. 1963. If defect in article is discoverable by simple observation then law will imply no warranty against its existence.

Green v. American Tobacco Co., 154 So.2d 169, answer to certified question conformed to 325 F.2d 673, certiorari denied 84 S.Ct. 1349, 377 U.S. 943, 12 L.Ed.2d 306, certiorari denied 84 S.Ct. 1351, 377 U.S. 943, 12 L.Ed.2d 306.

Fla.App. 1 Dist. 1970. Where buyer of front end loader had a number of employees familiar with mechanized equipment, including a full time mechanic, it could not assert implied warranty against alleged defects in obvious gravity feed fuel system against seller and manufacturer.

Fletcher Co. v. Melroe Mfg. Co., 238 So.2d 142, certiorari denied 242 So.2d 463, appeal after remand 261 So.2d 191.

⌐**1688. —— Doctrine of caveat emptor.**

C.A.5 (Fla.) 1954. At common law, the doctrine of caveat emptor applies to all sales unless the seller expressly warrants against defects or a warranty is implied by operation of law.

Valdosta Milling Co. v. Garretson, 217 F.2d 625.

⌐**1689. —— Examination or inspection.**

N.D.Fla. 2010. Under Florida law, when a buyer has examined goods before entering into the contract or has refused to examine the goods, there is no implied warranty with respect to defects that the examination should have revealed. West's F.S.A. § 672.316(3)(b).

JDI Holdings, LLC v. Jet Management, Inc., 732 F.Supp.2d 1205.

Fla.App. 1 Dist. 1970. When a buyer examines goods, or samples of goods, before buying, there is no implied warranty against defects which an examination ought to reveal.

> Fletcher Co. v. Melroe Mfg. Co., 238 So.2d 142, certiorari denied 242 So.2d 463, appeal after remand 261 So.2d 191.

Fla.App. 3 Dist. 1964. Retail druggists did not impliedly warrant products they dispensed pursuant to doctor's prescription, where there was no opportunity for inspection and no foreign material in product and purchaser was not entitled to recover from druggists, for injuries allegedly resulting from nature of product.

> McLeod v. W. S. Merrell Co., Division of Richardson-Merrell, Inc., 167 So.2d 901, certiorari discharged 174 So.2d 736.

Fla.App. 3 Dist. 1960. Where supplier of sulky attachment for lawn mowers was not the manufacturer thereof, machine was purchased from supplier by trade name, and purchaser had opportunity for inspection or rejection equal to that of the supplier, and where there was no proof that supplier knew or should have known that article he offered to sell contained a defect in design, supplier did not impliedly warrant that the article was free of such defect, and was not liable to employee of purchaser for personal injuries received when frame of sulky broke while employee was using it.

> Hector Supply Co. v. Carter, 122 So.2d 22, certiorari discharged 128 So.2d 390.

Fla.App. 5 Dist. 2000. Only implied warranties are potentially waived when a buyer makes or is given an opportunity to complete a pre-purchase inspection of the goods. West's F.S.A. § 672.316(3)(b).

> Doug Connor, Inc. v. Proto-Grind, Inc., 761 So.2d 426, rehearing denied.

⚷1690. —— **Sale by sample.**

Fla.App. 1 Dist. 1970. When a buyer examines goods, or samples of goods, before buying, there is no implied warranty against defects which an examination ought to reveal.

> Fletcher Co. v. Melroe Mfg. Co., 238 So.2d 142, certiorari denied 242 So.2d 463, appeal after remand 261 So.2d 191.

⚷1691. —— **Fitness for intended purpose or use.**

Fitness for ordinary purpose or use, see IX(C)3. Merchantability, see IX(C)3. Fitness for particular purpose or use, see IX(C)4.

Fla.App. 2 Dist. 1980. Implied warranty of fitness does not extend beyond obligation to supply an article reasonably fit for purpose intended, and does not impose a duty to furnish the best article of its kind or an article equal to any other similar or competing article.

> Borrell-Bigby Elec. Co., Inc. v. United Nations, Inc., 385 So.2d 713.

Fla.App. 2 Dist. 1969. Basis of liability on breach of implied warranty of fitness is agreement, imposed by law, to be responsible in event thing sold is not in fact fit for use and purpose for which it is intended.

> Brown v. Hall, 221 So.2d 454.

Fla.App. 2 Dist. 1964. An implied warranty of fitness does not extend beyond the obligation to supply an article reasonably fit for the purpose intended, and does not impose a duty to furnish the best article of its kind or an article equal to any other similar or competing article.

> Wisner v. Goodyear Tire & Rubber Co., 167 So.2d 254.

⚷1692–1696. *For other cases see earlier editions of this digest, the Decennial Digests, and WESTLAW.*

⚷1696. **Title.**

⚷1697. —— **In general.**

Fla.App. 4 Dist. 1991. Under warranty of title provision of Florida Uniform Commercial Code, where there is writing concerning sale that is silent on issue of exclusion of warranty, existence of circumstances that would exclude or modify warranty is not precluded. West's F.S.A. § 672.312.

> Maroone Chevrolet, Inc. v. Nordstrom, 587 So.2d 514.

⚷**1698. —— Breach and elements thereof in general.**

For other cases see earlier editions of this digest, the Decennial Digests, and WESTLAW.

⚷**1699. —— Particular cases and goods.**

Fla.App. 1 Dist. 1981. There was an implied warranty of title by sellers of truck. West's F.S.A. § 672.312.

> Lawson v. Turner, 404 So.2d 424.

In order to exclude the implied warranty of title, seller of vehicle must do so in very precise and unambiguous language. West's F.S.A. § 672.312.

> Lawson v. Turner, 404 So.2d 424.

Statement made by seller to buyer that he did not have title but that he would guaranty that the buyer would get it as soon as the seller received it from another person was insufficient to exclude the implied warranty of title. West's F.S.A. § 672.312.

> Lawson v. Turner, 404 So.2d 424.

Fla.App. 2 Dist. 1987. Title to restaurant equipment vested in buyer when it acquired possession of it, and thus third party's subsequent payment of remaining purchase price to seller, in order to lease equipment to buyer, did not constitute sale of equipment to third-party which resulted in seller's warranting title to equipment. West's F.S.A. §§ 672.312, 672.401(2).

> Hayes Leasing Systems, Inc. v. Ice House, Inc., 506 So.2d 1073.

Fla.App. 3 Dist. 1968. In view of fact that Michigan proceeding by lienor against party holding possession of automobile for buyer resulted in a declaratory judgment ruling that there was outstanding lien for an amount in excess of price paid for automobile by buyer, and in the enforcement of lien by an award of possession of automobile to lien claimant, breach of warranty of title to automobile was established, and buyer was entitled to judgment against sellers as a matter of law.

> Steingold v. L & L Motors, Inc., 207 So.2d 19.

Fla.App. 4 Dist. 1991. Under sales section of Florida Uniform Commercial Code, buyer can recover for breach of warranty of title when he demonstrates existence of substantial cloud or shadow on title, regardless of whether it eventually develops that third party's title is superior. West's F.S.A. § 672.312.

> Maroone Chevrolet, Inc. v. Nordstrom, 587 So.2d 514.

3. FITNESS FOR ORDINARY PURPOSE OR USE; MERCHANTABILITY.

⚷**1711. In general.**

C.A.11 (Fla.) 1983. Under Florida law, tests of merchantability of goods are standards of minimal quality measured in accordance with standards of the trade. West's F.S.A. §§ 672.314, 672.314(2).

> Royal Typewriter Co., a Div. of Litton Business Systems, Inc. v. Xerographic Supplies Corp., 719 F.2d 1092.

C.A.5 (Fla.) 1963. An implied warranty encompasses only the ordinary use or purposes for which the article is sold.

> Green v. American Tobacco Co., 325 F.2d 673, certiorari denied 84 S.Ct. 1349, 377 U.S. 943, 12 L.Ed.2d 306, certiorari denied 84 S.Ct. 1351, 377 U.S. 943, 12 L.Ed.2d 306.

M.D.Fla. 2015. Under Florida's Uniform Commercial Code (UCC), there are two distinct implied warranties: an implied warranty of merchantability and an implied warranty of fitness for a particular purpose. Fla. Stat. Ann. §§ 672.314(1), 672.314(2)(c), 672.315.

> Armadillo Distribution Enterprises, Inc. v. Hai Yun Musical Instruments Manufacture Co. Ltd., 142 F.Supp.3d 1245.

M.D.Fla. 2007. Florida has a liberal policy of allowing litigants their day in court on suits involving breaches of implied warranty of fitness and merchantability.

> McGuire v. Ryland Group, Inc., 497 F.Supp.2d 1347, on reconsideration in part 497 F.Supp.2d 1356.

Fla. 2013. Statute that attempted to retroactively limit the scope of the implied warranties of fitness and merchantability violated state constitutional provision that provided for right of access to the courts, where statute attempted to abolish the common law cause of action for breach of the implied warranties for certain injuries to property. West's F.S.A. Const. Art. 1, § 21; West's F.S.A. § 553.835.

> Maronda Homes, Inc. of Florida v. Lakeview Reserve Homeowners Ass'n, Inc., 127 So.3d 1258.

Fla. 1965. Warranty of merchantability applies when goods are offered for consumption by public generally.

> McLeod v. W. S. Merrell Co., Division of Richardson-Merrell, Inc., 174 So.2d 736.

In order for goods to be merchantable, the goods must be fit for ordinary uses for which such goods are sold.

> McLeod v. W. S. Merrell Co., Division of Richardson-Merrell, Inc., 174 So.2d 736.

⟜**1712–1713.** *For other cases see earlier editions of this digest, the Decennial Digests, and WESTLAW.*

⟜**1714. Seller's knowledge.**

Fla. 1963. Basis of implied warranty is the undertaking or agreement, attributed by law, to be responsible in event thing sold is not in fact merchantable or fit for its ordinary use or purpose, and assumption of responsibility is not necessarily co-equivalent with skill and knowledge.

> Green v. American Tobacco Co., 154 So.2d 169, answer to certified question conformed to 325 F.2d 673, certiorari denied 84 S.Ct. 1349, 377 U.S. 943, 12 L.Ed.2d 306, certiorari denied 84 S.Ct. 1351, 377 U.S. 943, 12 L.Ed.2d 306.

⟜**1715. Seller as merchant.**

For other cases see earlier editions of this digest, the Decennial Digests, and WESTLAW.

⟜**1716. Breach and elements thereof in general.**

M.D.Fla. 2009. To sustain a claim of defective product under Florida law, whether alleging strict products liability, breach of implied warranty of merchantability of goods, or products liability based on negligence, a plaintiff must demonstrate that: (1) a defect existed in the product; (2) the defect caused the injury; and (3) the defect in the product existed at the time the product left the possession of the manufacturer.

> Cooper v. Old Williamsburg Candle Corp., 653 F.Supp.2d 1220.

M.D.Fla. 1992. In breach of implied warranty, product is defective if it is not reasonably fit for intended use or reasonably foreseeable use at time it left possession of manufacturer.

> Pulte Home Corp., Inc. v. Ply Gem Industries, Inc., 804 F.Supp. 1471.

S.D.Fla. 2013. Under Florida law, a cause of action for breach of implied warranty of merchantability requires allegations that: (1) the plaintiff was a foreseeable user of the product, (2) the product was used in the intended manner at the time of the injury, (3) the product was defective when transferred from the warrantor, and (4) the defect caused the injury. West's F.S.A. § 672.314.

> Nature's Products, Inc. v. Natrol, Inc., 990 F.Supp.2d 1307, appeal dismissed (11th cir. 14-10907), and appeal dismissed (11th cir. 15-11180).

S.D.Fla. 2011. Under Florida law, a cause of action for breach of implied warranty of merchantability requires allegations that (1) the plaintiff was a foreseeable user of the product, (2) the product was used in the intended manner at the time of the injury, (3) the product was defective when transferred from the warrantor, and (4) the defect caused the injury. West's F.S.A. § 672.314.

> Jovine v. Abbott Laboratories, Inc., 795 F.Supp.2d 1331.

Fla.App. 3 Dist. 1984. In products liability action, theories of negligence, implied warranty and strict liability center upon alleged inferiority in product, an inferiority referred to as a "defect"; this defect is the cause of the alleged injury, and in a very general sense its existence must constitute under respective theories of recovery a breach of duty, a breach of warranty and, under strict liability, the presence of an "unreasonably dangerous condition" in product.

> Copeland v. Celotex Corp., 447 So.2d 908, quashed 471 So.2d 533.

Fla.App. 4 Dist. 1973. Whether product is adequately contained and packaged within requirements of statutory warranty of merchantability depends on whether, at time of purchase, container and packaging were reasonably suited for their ordinarily intended function. F.S.A. §§ 671.1–101 et seq., 672.2–314.

> Schuessler v. Coca-Cola Bottling Co. of Miami, 279 So.2d 901.

☞1717. **Particular cases and goods.**

☞1718. —— **In general.**

C.A.5 (Fla.) 1980. Seller's implied warranty of merchantability as well as implied warranty of fitness for purpose were breached by sale of blood plasma without suitable screening for hepatitis, as result of which buyer's tests of some units yielded positive results. U.C.C. §§ 2–314, 2–314(2)(c), 2–315, 2–606, 2–608.

> Automated Medical Laboratories, Inc. v. Armour Pharmaceutical Co., 629 F.2d 1118.

M.D.Fla. 2015. Drum kit distributor sufficiently alleged that drum kit manufacturer was a merchant with respect to the sale of musical instruments, that manufacturer impliedly warranted that the drum kits were merchantable, that the drum kits were not of average or fair quality, that manufacturer failed to take any steps to cure the non-conforming drum kits, and that distributor suffered lost profits and a loss of goodwill, as required to state a claim for breach of the implied warranted of merchantability under Florida's Uniform Commercial Code (UCC). Fla. Stat. Ann. § 672.314(1).

> Armadillo Distribution Enterprises, Inc. v. Hai Yun Musical Instruments Manufacture Co. Ltd., 142 F.Supp.3d 1245.

S.D.Fla. 1989. Yacht seller was not "merchant" for purposes of imposing liability for breach of implied warranty of merchantability either by virtue of fact that he may have sold five boats during one-year period or that he hired broker to facilitate sale of yacht. West's F.S.A. § 672.314(1); U.C.C. § 1–101 et seq.

> Czarnecki v. Roller, 726 F.Supp. 832.

Bkrtcy.M.D.Fla. 1981. Drapery and carpeting could not be said to have been not of merchantable quality within meaning of Florida law of implied warranty of merchantability where only thing buyers established was that the carpeting was soiled and matted and that some of the strands were untwisted and there was no evidence that it was a manufacturing defect and was caused by any inherent defect in the carpeting and as to draperies there was no evidence except that there were vertical streaks on the drapes but no evidence to establish that it was caused by inherent defect in manufacturing or below standard quality of the fabric. West's F.S.A. § 672.314.

> Matter of Vincent, 10 B.R. 549.

Fla.App. 2 Dist. 1980. Where fire alarm system installed in warehouse, which was designed to telephone alarm to a local fire station in case of fire, satisfied minimum military requirements for storage of items belonging to military personnel, as desired by warehouse owner and contained two indicator lights on its control panel designed to warn of a power loss or malfunction, and evidence indicated that nothing would have prevented system from transmitting a signal after fire started had system been energized, company that designed and installed system did not breach any implied warranty of merchantability by failing to include external or emergency power source and supervisory circuit to warn of power loss.

> Borrell-Bigby Elec. Co., Inc. v. United Nations, Inc., 385 So.2d 713.

Fla.App. 2 Dist. 1977. Retail book dealer was not liable under Uniform Commercial Code to purchaser of cookbook for injuries and damages caused by improper instructions or lack of adequate warnings as to poisonous ingredients used in recipe. West's F.S.A. §§ 672.105, 672.314(1), (2)(c).

> Cardozo v. True, 342 So.2d 1053, certiorari denied 353 So.2d 674.

Absent allegations that book seller knew that there was reason to warn public as to contents of book, implied warranty in respect to sale of books by merchant who regularly sells them is limited to warranty of physical properties of such book and does not extend to material communicated by book's author or publisher. West's F.S.A. § 672.314.

> Cardozo v. True, 342 So.2d 1053, certiorari denied 353 So.2d 674.

⚷1719. —— Buildings, structures, and construction.

Fla.App. 3 Dist. 1982. Subcontractor breached its express warranty as well as its implied warranties of fitness and merchantability so as to be liable to condominium association for damages which resulted from subcontractor's substitution of roof materials without authorization.

> Biscayne Roofing Co. v. Palmetto Fairway Condominium Ass'n, Inc., 418 So.2d 1109.

Fla.App. 4 Dist. 1980. Purchaser of condominium unit could maintain action against developer for breach of implied warranty of merchantability with respect to paneling in the unit, even though the developer was not a merchant dealing in paneling. West's F.S.A. § 672.104(1).

> Georgia-Pacific Corp. v. Squires Development Corp., 387 So.2d 986.

Fla.App. 4 Dist. 1972. Condominiums' seller who was not dealing in goods and consequently was not merchant did not come under Uniform Commercial Code whose provisions concerning implied warranties of merchantability and fitness were therefore not applicable with respect to condominiums' defective air-conditioning system. F.S.A. §§ 672.104, 672.105, 672.314, 672.315.

> Gable v. Silver, 258 So.2d 11, 50 A.L.R.3d 1062, certiorari discharged, opinion adopted 264 So.2d 418.

Fla.App. 5 Dist. 1988. Stucco sold by supplier to subcontractor which applied stucco to apartment building contained implied warranty of merchantability; supplier was "merchant" within meaning of statute as party dealing in goods of that kind, regardless of whether supplier held himself out as having knowledge or skill peculiar to practices or goods involved in transaction. West's F.S.A. §§ 672.104(1), 672.314.

> Ashley Square, Ltd. v. Contractors Supply of Orlando, Inc., 532 So.2d 710.

⚷1720. —— Plants, crops, and agriculture.

M.D.Fla. 1985. Fact that certain wheat seed was late maturity variety of seed not recommended for planting in Florida did not support conclusion that seed was not fit for ordinary purpose of raising wheat; thus, seed purchased by farmer was merchantable under Florida law. West's F.S.A. § 672.314(2)(a, c).

> Crawford v. Gold Kist, Inc., 614 F.Supp. 682.

Even if seed merchant had duty to sell only seed which could be expected to produce commercially reasonable and harvestable crop given climatological conditions prevalent in sales area, seed sold to farmer could reasonably be expected to produce commercially reasonable and harvestable crop in Florida; therefore, duty was not breached.

> Crawford v. Gold Kist, Inc., 614 F.Supp. 682.

Fla.App. 1 Dist. 1982. Soybean seeds incapable of producing healthy plants were not fit for their intended use, and seed distributor who sold such seeds breached implied warranty of merchantability and fitness.

> Pennington Grain and Seed, Inc. v. Tuten, 422 So.2d 948.

⚷1721–1722. *For other cases see earlier editions of this digest, the Decennial Digests, and WESTLAW.*

⚷1723. —— Food and beverages.

Fla.App. 1 Dist. 1988. In a breach of implied warranty action based on the presence of harmful substance in food, test of whether the presence of a harmful substance constitutes a breach of the implied warranty is whether the consumer can reasonably expect to find the substance in the food as served.

> Coulter v. American Bakeries Co., 530 So.2d 1009.

Fla.App. 1 Dist. 1972. If a bottler or manufacturer of a product intended for human consumption packages its product in a glass container and product is such that it cannot be ordinarily consumed without at the same time handling and using the container itself, manufacturer or bottler impliedly warrants that container is reasonably fit for the purpose for which it is intended and if, under such circumstances, a defect is shown to be the cause of the container breaking or exploding, liability for any damages suffered by purchaser of product may be imposed upon manufacturer or bottler.

Reese v. Florida Coca-Cola Bottling Co., 256 So.2d 392.

Fla.App. 2 Dist. 1976. In products liability action against soft drink manufacturer and retailer which sold carton of soft drink to consumer, it was error for trial court to direct verdict in favor of retailer, but where jury, by its verdict, found that bug which was discovered in soft drink bottle got into bottle after it had been opened in plaintiffs' home, retailer was not liable to plaintiffs, either on theory of implied warranty or on theory of negligence, and error was harmless.

Tarwacki v. Royal Crown Bottling Co. of Tampa, Inc., 330 So.2d 253.

Fla.App. 2 Dist. 1972. Consumer, who, while attempting to get contents of soft drink bottle out by sucking upon it, discovered foreign substance that resembled a rat with hair sucked off, and who then became nauseated and went outside and vomited, was entitled to recover on theory of implied warranty and negligence.

Way v. Tampa Coca Cola Bottling Co., 260 So.2d 288.

Fla.App. 2 Dist. 1960. It is universally known that when one purchases a bottle of soda it will be opened preparatory to use, so that the implied warranty of fitness for use extends to the bottle as well as the soda contained in the bottle.

Canada Dry Bottling Co. of Fla. v. Shaw, 118 So.2d 840.

Fla.App. 4 Dist. 1973. Uniform Commercial Code imposes on retailer a warranty of merchantability covering not only product but adequacy of container and packaging, including paper carton for carrying soft drinks. F.S.A. §§ 671.1–101 et seq., 672.2–314.

Schuessler v. Coca-Cola Bottling Co. of Miami, 279 So.2d 901.

Fla.App. 4 Dist. 1967. Test of whether presence of harmful substance in food is result of negligence or constitutes breach of implied warranty of reasonable fitness of such food is not whether the substance is foreign or natural to the food, although that may have some importance in determining degree of negligence of food pro-

cessor, but whether consumer reasonably expects to find it in the food as served.

Zabner v. Howard Johnson's, Inc., 201 So.2d 824.

⚷**1724. —— Motor vehicles.**

Fla.App. 5 Dist. 1981. In sale of repossessed automobile, bank was not "merchant" and sale did not carry with it implied warranty of merchantability, notwithstanding bank's sale of four other repossessed vehicles in the same year. West's F.S.A. § 672–314(1).

Joyce v. Combank/Longwood, 405 So.2d 1358.

⚷**1725. —— Mobile homes or structures.**

For other cases see earlier editions of this digest, the Decennial Digests, and WEST-LAW.

⚷**1726. —— Drugs and medical devices.**

Fla.App. 4 Dist. 1997. Recipient of tainted blood may maintain action against blood supplier for damages on ground of breach of implied warranty of fitness or merchantability only if he alleges and proves that defect of which he complains is detectable or removable by use of reasonable scientific procedures or techniques. West's F.S.A. § 672.316(5).

Raskin v. Community Blood Centers of South Florida, Inc., 699 So.2d 1014, rehearing denied, review denied 707 So.2d 1124.

⚷**1727. —— Computers and software.**

See also COPYRIGHTS AND INTELLECTUAL PROPERTY ⚷107.

⚷**1728. Design defects.**

S.D.Fla. 1984. Manufacturer's design of aircraft in which plaintiff's decedent was killed constituted a breach of warranty of merchantability, fitness, and freedom from defects so as to proximately cause death of decedent, a navy pilot who was entitled to rely upon such warranties.

Shaw v. Grumman Aerospace Corp., 593 F.Supp. 1066, affirmed 778 F.2d 736, certiorari denied 108 S.Ct. 2896, 487 U.S. 1233, 101 L.Ed.2d 930, rehearing denied 109 S.Ct. 10, 487 U.S. 1250, 101 L.Ed.2d 961.

☞**1729–1731.** *For other cases see earlier editions of this digest, the Decennial Digests, and WESTLAW.*

☞**1732. Used or second-hand goods.**

Fla.App. 1 Dist. 1988. Standard that must be met for used goods to meet requirement of merchantability is necessarily different from that required of new goods. West's F.S.A. § 672.314(1).

McCormick Machinery, Inc. v. Julian E. Johnson & Sons, Inc., 523 So.2d 651.

Fla.App. 1 Dist. 1980. Florida statutory provisions for implied warranties of merchantability and fitness are applicable to used motor vehicles. West's F.S.A. §§ 672.314, 672.315.

Fuquay v. Revels Motors, Inc., 389 So.2d 1238.

Fla.App. 2 Dist. 1981. Implied warranties of merchantability and fitness accompany sale of a used car. West's F.S.A. §§ 672.314, 672.315.

Bert Smith Oldsmobile, Inc. v. Franklin, 400 So.2d 1235.

☞**1733. Causation.**

For other cases see earlier editions of this digest, the Decennial Digests, and WESTLAW.

4. FITNESS FOR PARTICULAR PURPOSE OR USE.

☞**1741. In general.**

C.A.11 (Fla.) 1983. With respect to implied warranty of fitness for particular purpose, particular purpose differs from ordinary purpose in that it envisages specific use by buyer which is peculiar to nature of his business. West's F.S.A. § 672.315; U.C.C. § 2–315.

Royal Typewriter Co., a Div. of Litton Business Systems, Inc. v. Xerographic Supplies Corp., 719 F.2d 1092.

M.D.Fla. 2015. Under Florida's Uniform Commercial Code (UCC), there are two distinct implied warranties: an implied warranty of merchantability and an implied warranty of fitness for a particular purpose. Fla. Stat. Ann. §§ 672.314(1), 672.314(2)(c), 672.315.

Armadillo Distribution Enterprises, Inc. v. Hai Yun Musical Instruments Manufacture Co. Ltd., 142 F.Supp.3d 1245.

For purposes of a claim for breach of the implied warranty of fitness for a particular purpose, Florida's Uniform Commercial Code (UCC) distinguishes a particular purpose from a use to which the goods are ordinarily put; a particular purpose envisages a specific use by the buyer which is peculiar to the nature of his business. Fla. Stat. Ann. § 672.315.

Armadillo Distribution Enterprises, Inc. v. Hai Yun Musical Instruments Manufacture Co. Ltd., 142 F.Supp.3d 1245.

Fla. 2013. Statute that attempted to retroactively limit the scope of the implied warranties of fitness and merchantability violated state constitutional provision that provided for right of access to the courts, where statute attempted to abolish the common law cause of action for breach of the implied warranties for certain injuries to property. West's F.S.A. Const. Art. 1, § 21; West's F.S.A. § 553.835.

Maronda Homes, Inc. of Florida v. Lakeview Reserve Homeowners Ass'n, Inc., 127 So.3d 1258.

Fla.App. 3 Dist. 1983. There is an implied warranty that a product will be suitable for the purpose for which it is sold, and when the evidence discloses that this is not the case, the buyer has a right to recover his damages occasioned by the use of the product. West's F.S.A. § 672.315.

Beede Elec. Instrument, Co. v. K.E.S., Inc., 433 So.2d 59.

☞**1742. Reliance.**

C.A.11 (Fla.) 1983. Under Florida law, implied warranty of fitness for particular purpose arises where seller has reason to know particular purpose for which goods are required and buyer relies on seller's skill or judgment to select or furnish suitable goods. West's F.S.A. § 672.315; U.C.C. § 2–315 comment.

Royal Typewriter Co., a Div. of Litton Business Systems, Inc. v. Xerographic Supplies Corp., 719 F.2d 1092.

C.A.5 (Fla.) 1964. It is only where an inspection would have revealed to purchaser that subject of purchase was not fit or suitable for intended purpose that implied warranty may not be relied upon.

Sperry Rand Corp. v. Industrial Supply Corp., 337 F.2d 363.

Fla. 1965. An implied warranty of fitness for particular purpose is conditioned upon buyer's reliance on skill and judgment of seller to supply a commodity suitable for intended purpose.

McLeod v. W. S. Merrell Co., Division of Richardson-Merrell, Inc., 174 So.2d 736.

Fla. 1940. Where a buyer makes known to the seller the purpose for which he buys an article and relies upon the seller's skill and judgment, an implied warranty of fitness for which the article is purchased as a matter of law arises.

Smith v. Burdine's, Inc., 198 So. 223, 144 Fla. 500, 131 A.L.R. 115.

Fla.App. 2 Dist. 1964. Where buyer makes known to seller purpose for which he buys article and relies upon seller's skill and judgment, implied warranty of fitness for which article is purchased arises as matter of law.

Wagner v. Mars, Inc., 166 So.2d 673.

Fla.App. 3 Dist. 1962. An implied warranty of fitness for which an article is purchased arises where buyer makes known to seller purpose for which he buys an article and relies upon seller's skill and judgment.

Atlantic Distributors, Inc. v. Alson Mfg. Co., 141 So.2d 305.

☞**1743. Buyer's knowledge.**

M.D.Fla. 2015. Under Florida's Uniform Commercial Code (UCC), the implied warranty of fitness for a particular purpose arises only when a seller has reason to know a particular purpose for which the goods are required and the buyer relies on the seller's skill or judgment to select or furnish suitable goods. Fla. Stat. Ann. § 672.315.

Armadillo Distribution Enterprises, Inc. v. Hai Yun Musical Instruments Manufacture Co. Ltd., 142 F.Supp.3d 1245.

☞**1744. Seller's knowledge.**

C.A.11 (Fla.) 1983. Under Florida law, implied warranty of fitness for particular purpose arises where seller has reason to know particular purpose for which goods are required and buyer relies on seller's skill or judgment to select or furnish suitable goods. West's F.S.A. § 672.315; U.C.C. § 2–315 comment.

Royal Typewriter Co., a Div. of Litton Business Systems, Inc. v. Xerographic Supplies Corp., 719 F.2d 1092.

C.A.5 (Fla.) 1962. Doctrine of implied warranty by a manufacturer and seller of the quality and fitness of thing sold for purpose for which it was intended or desired if founded upon his superior opportunity to gain knowledge of the product and to form a judgment of its fitness.

Green v. American Tobacco Co., 304 F.2d 70, certified question answered 154 So.2d 169, answer to certified question conformed to 325 F.2d 673, certiorari denied 84 S.Ct. 1349, 377 U.S. 943, 12 L.Ed.2d 306, certiorari denied 84 S.Ct. 1351, 377 U.S. 943, 12 L.Ed.2d 306.

Fla. 1940. Where a buyer makes known to the seller the purpose for which he buys an article and relies upon the seller's skill and judgment, an implied warranty of fitness for which the article is purchased as a matter of law arises.

Smith v. Burdine's, Inc., 198 So. 223, 144 Fla. 500, 131 A.L.R. 115.

Fla.App. 2 Dist. 1964. Where buyer makes known to seller purpose for which he buys article and relies upon seller's skill and judgment, implied warranty of fitness for which article is purchased arises as matter of law.

Wagner v. Mars, Inc., 166 So.2d 673.

Fla.App. 3 Dist. 1962. An implied warranty of fitness for which an article is purchased arises where buyer makes known to seller purpose for which he buys an article and relies upon seller's skill and judgment.

Atlantic Distributors, Inc. v. Alson Mfg. Co., 141 So.2d 305.

† This Case was not selected for publication in the National Reporter System
For legislative history of cited statutes, see Florida Statutes Annotated

🗝**1745. Breach and elements thereof in general.**

S.D.Fla. 2013. Under Florida law, to prevail on a claim for breach of warranty of fitness for a particular purpose, a plaintiff must prove that the defendant, at the time the sale was made, knew of a particular purpose for which the goods were going to be used and that the plaintiff relied upon the defendant's skill and judgment when purchasing said product.

Nature's Products, Inc. v. Natrol, Inc., 990 F.Supp.2d 1307, appeal dismissed (11th cir. 14-10907), and appeal dismissed (11th cir. 15-11180).

🗝**1746. Particular cases and goods.**

🗝**1747. —— In general.**

C.A.5 (Fla.) 1980. Seller's implied warranty of merchantability as well as implied warranty of fitness for purpose were breached by sale of blood plasma without suitable screening for hepatitis, as result of which buyer's tests of some units yielded positive results. U.C.C. §§ 2–314, 2–314(2)(c), 2–315, 2–606, 2–608.

Automated Medical Laboratories, Inc. v. Armour Pharmaceutical Co., 629 F.2d 1118.

S.D.Fla. 1989. Yacht buyer did not have viable claim against seller under Florida warranty for fitness for particular purpose; even if buyer intended to use yacht for particular purpose, he failed to adduce evidence that seller knew of such purpose or that he relied on seller's skill or judgment. West's F.S.A. §§ 672.314, 672.315.

Czarnecki v. Roller, 726 F.Supp. 832.

S.D.Fla. 1984. Given Navy's determination as to capabilities aircraft purchased from manufacturer should have had, as embodied in the performance specifications it submitted to manufacturer, aircraft in which plaintiff's decedent was killed was not fit for its intended use.

Shaw v. Grumman Aerospace Corp., 593 F.Supp. 1066, affirmed 778 F.2d 736, certiorari denied 108 S.Ct. 2896, 487 U.S. 1233, 101 L.Ed.2d 930, rehearing denied 109 S.Ct. 10, 487 U.S. 1250, 101 L.Ed.2d 961.

Fla.App. 5 Dist. 1990. Designer of safety glasses did not breach warranty for particular purpose where no allegations were made by seller that glasses would not slip and slippage was cause of user's injuries; designer represented strength of glasses if struck by projectile and user admitted knowledge of proclivity of glasses to slip. West's F.S.A. §§ 45.061, 57.041, 672.316(3)(b).

Light v. Weldarc Co., Inc., 569 So.2d 1302.

🗝**1748. —— Buildings, structures, and construction.**

Fla.App. 2 Dist. 1998. Renovation contractor made no express warranty to homeowners that windows, which leaked after being installed, were free from defect and suitable for their intended purposes and no warranty as to condition of windows was implied by law. West's F.S.A. §§ 672.104, 672.314.

Lonnie D. Adams Bldg. Contractor, Inc. v. O'Connor, 714 So.2d 1178.

Fla.App. 3 Dist. 1983. In the absence of evidence that seller had been asked to supply a paint which would render an outside surface skid-proof or rain-resistant, seller of concrete paint could not be held liable for breach of implied warranty of fitness for particular purpose when plaintiff slipped and fell on slippery concrete surface following painting.

Halpryn v. Highland Ins. Co., 426 So.2d 1050.

🗝**1749. —— Plants, crops, and agriculture.**

C.A.5 (Fla.) 1954. Under Florida law, the doctrine of implied warranty of fitness is extended to foods for animals by statute making it a misdemeanor for any manufacturer to place in commerce any feed containing a substance injurious to the health of livestock or poultry. F.S.A. §§ 578.13, 580.22.

Valdosta Milling Co. v. Garretson, 217 F.2d 625.

M.D.Fla. 1985. While it would have been preferable for seed merchant to discuss wheat seed's limited zone of adaptation with farmer-buyer, there was no such duty under Florida law, and farmer, who purchased allegedly defective wheat seed, thus could not maintain action against merchant for breach of implied warranty of fitness for a particular purpose. West's

† **This Case was not selected for publication in the National Reporter System**
For legislative history of cited statutes, see Florida Statutes Annotated

F.S.A. §§ 672.101 et seq., 672.105(1), 672.315.

> Crawford v. Gold Kist, Inc., 614 F.Supp. 682.

☞1750. —— Animals and livestock.

For other cases see earlier editions of this digest, the Decennial Digests, and WEST-LAW.

☞1751. —— Machinery and equipment.

C.A.11 (Fla.) 1983. Leasing of copier machines for use as copiers, as opposed to selling them, was not a "particular purpose" to which protections of section relating to implied warranty of fitness for particular purpose attach. West's F.S.A. § 672.315; U.C.C. § 2–315 comment.

> Royal Typewriter Co., a Div. of Litton Business Systems, Inc. v. Xerographic Supplies Corp., 719 F.2d 1092.

C.A.5 (Fla.) 1964. Termination of lease of computer and related equipment forming business records system and purchase of equipment did not operate as rejection of opportunity by lessee-buyer of continuing inspection, and rights of parties with respect to implied warranty of fitness for disclosed purpose were the same as if there had been no intervening lease.

> Sperry Rand Corp. v. Industrial Supply Corp., 337 F.2d 363.

Sale of group of specifically described machines which have been combined into an integrated system specially arranged for purchaser is not exempted from otherwise applicable operation of doctrine of implied warranty on ground that machines comprising system are patented and have been designated by trade names.

> Sperry Rand Corp. v. Industrial Supply Corp., 337 F.2d 363.

M.D.Fla. 1991. Even if lease of computer equipment was a disguised sales transaction between lessee and equipment supplier, with financing by lessor, absent any reference in lease agreement to supplier as being party thereto, lessee had no contractual remedy against supplier for breach of implied warranty of fitness for particular purpose, and in absence of contractual remedy, lessee could maintain action for misrepresentation against supplier

as exception to the "economic loss rule." West's F.S.A. §§ 671.101 et seq., 672.315.

> Interfase Marketing, Inc. v. Pioneer Technologies Group, Inc., 774 F.Supp. 1355.

Bkrtcy.M.D.Fla. 1986. Even if implied warranty of fitness for intended purpose ran to manufacturer under Florida law, fact that portable rock crushing machine did not function as well when used to crush materials of high moisture and clay content was not breach of such warranty, where machine was designed to process dry, free-flowing material. West's F.S.A. § 672.314.

> Matter of Bob Rigby, Inc., 62 B.R. 900.

Fla.App. 3 Dist. 1975. Where boat owner replaced engines and outdrives with engine and outdrives recommended by engine manufacturer, and where the manufacturer knew of the problems which owner had had with the original engines and outdrives, there was an implied warranty of fitness for particular purpose on the second engines and outdrives and, when the second power system did not perform adequately and boat owner was required to install a third system, owner was entitled to recover for breach of the warranty. West's F.S.A. § 672.315.

> Chrysler Corp. v. Miller, 310 So.2d 356.

☞1752. —— Food and beverages.

C.A.5 (Fla.) 1963. Under Florida law, as to products intended for human consumption the use of which may cause injury or death, the jury may properly apply a very strict standard of reasonableness.

> Green v. American Tobacco Co., 325 F.2d 673, certiorari denied 84 S.Ct. 1349, 377 U.S. 943, 12 L.Ed.2d 306, certiorari denied 84 S.Ct. 1351, 377 U.S. 943, 12 L.Ed.2d 306.

C.A.5 (Fla.) 1954. It is generally recognized that there is an implied warranty of fitness where food is sold for human consumption.

> Valdosta Milling Co. v. Garretson, 217 F.2d 625.

Fla. 1958. Bottlers of cold drinks are under the same rule of absolute liability of implied warranty as are canners of food.

Miami Coca Cola Bottling Co. v. Todd, 101 So.2d 34.

Fla. 1953. Person who purchases items of food or other products in original package, which items are offered for sale for human consumption or use, generally purchases such items in reliance upon express or implied condition that they are wholesome and fit for uses or purposes for which they are advertised or sold, and person who is injured as result of unwholesome or deleterious substances therein which are unknown to buyer, may hold either manufacturer or retailer liable regardless of privity of contract.

Hoskins v. Jackson Grain Co., 63 So.2d 514.

Fla. 1950. A retail dealer in food products sold in sealed packages or cans to consuming public is liable on theory of implied warranty for injuries sustained by a purchasing consumer because of deleterious, unwholesome or unfit substance for human consumption contained in package or can.

Sencer v. Carl's Markets, 45 So.2d 671.

Fla. 1949. A purveyor of foods for valuable consideration to immediate consumers in public restaurant or dining room is absolutely liable for damages proximately resulting from impurities therein, deleterious to health, on theory of implied warranty of food's fitness for human consumption, regardless of negligence.

Cliett v. Lauderdale Biltmore Corp., 39 So.2d 476.

A restaurant keeper cannot escape liability to paying guest for damages resulting from service of unwholesome or poisonous food to him on ground that only a service, not sale of meal purchased, is involved, though not shown to be guilty of specific acts of negligence in care or preparation of food.

Cliett v. Lauderdale Biltmore Corp., 39 So.2d 476.

The basis of implied warranty of food's fitness for human consumption is justifiable reliance by consumer on warrantor's judgment or skill.

Cliett v. Lauderdale Biltmore Corp., 39 So.2d 476.

The proprietor of hotel dining room or restaurant is held to same degree of duty regarding wholesomeness of food ordered, received, eaten, and paid for by guest therein as law imposes on retailer of food for consumption away from retailer's premises.

Cliett v. Lauderdale Biltmore Corp., 39 So.2d 476.

Fla. 1944. A manufacturer or packer of food products is liable for injuries sustained by ultimate consumer purchasing from middleman or retailer food products which are unwholesome, unhealthful, and unfit for human consumption.

Blanton v. Cudahy Packing Co., 19 So.2d 313, 154 Fla. 872.

A manufacturer or canner of food product sold to retailer in sealed packages or cans is liable for breach of implied warranty that such product is wholesome and fit for human consumption, where consumer purchasing product from retailer is injured because of deleterious, unhealthy, or poisonous substances therein.

Blanton v. Cudahy Packing Co., 19 So.2d 313, 154 Fla. 872.

Fla.App. 1 Dist. 1972. If a bottler or manufacturer of a product intended for human consumption packages its product in a glass container and product is such that it cannot be ordinarily consumed without at the same time handling and using the container itself, manufacturer or bottler impliedly warrants that container is reasonably fit for the purpose for which it is intended and if, under such circumstances, a defect is shown to be the cause of the container breaking or exploding, liability for any damages suffered by purchaser of product may be imposed upon manufacturer or bottler.

Reese v. Florida Coca-Cola Bottling Co., 256 So.2d 392.

Fla.App. 2 Dist. 1964. As to items of food in original package, there is implied warranty of fitness for use and purposes for which they are offered for sale and sold and one injured as result of injurious substances which are unknown to him may hold either manufacturer or retailer liable for breach of implied warranty.

> Wagner v. Mars, Inc., 166 So.2d 673.

Theory of implied warranty of fitness for use extended to candy bar in sealed paper wrapper.

> Wagner v. Mars, Inc., 166 So.2d 673.

Under Uniform Sales Act, purchase of food is sufficient to make known to seller use for which it is intended by buyer.

> Wagner v. Mars, Inc., 166 So.2d 673.

Fla.App. 3 Dist. 1965. Purchaser of bottle of milk is entitled to rely on bottler to extent that container in which product is packaged will be reasonably fit for purpose for which it was intended.

> Renninger v. Foremost Dairies, Inc., 171 So.2d 602, certiorari denied 177 So.2d 480.

Fla.App. 4 Dist. 1973. Bottler of beverage intended for human consumption impliedly warrants to ultimate consumer that beverage is reasonably fit for purpose, and likewise warrants, as of time it leaves bottler's possession, soundness of bottle containing beverage. F.S.A. §§ 671.1–101 et seq., 672.2–314, 672.2–318.

> Schuessler v. Coca-Cola Bottling Co. of Miami, 279 So.2d 901.

Where bottled soft drink carton was readily subject to examination, for soundness, by customer of store, there was no warranty of merchantability by bottler in favor of store customer as to the carton. F.S.A. §§ 671.1–101 et seq., 672.2–314, 672.2–318.

> Schuessler v. Coca-Cola Bottling Co. of Miami, 279 So.2d 901.

Fla.App. 4 Dist. 1967. When patron orders and pays for food at public restaurant, there is sale of such food, and there exists an implied warranty that food sold is reasonably fit for human consumption.

> Zabner v. Howard Johnson's, Inc., 201 So.2d 824.

Fla.App. 5 Dist. 1990. Implied covenant exists in every restaurant-patron transaction that restaurant is only entitled to be paid, or retain payment, if food served by restaurant is edible.

> Lashley v. Bowman, 561 So.2d 406.

⚷**1753–1754.** *For other cases see earlier editions of this digest, the Decennial Digests, and WESTLAW.*

⚷**1755. —— Drugs and medical devices.**

Fla.App. 1 Dist. 1991. Florida statute providing that blood bank can be liable, on breach of implied warranty theory, for supplying contaminated blood for use in medical procedure only if defect could have been detected or removed by reasonable scientific procedures or techniques applied only to warranty actions, and did not apply to suit sounding in negligence; plaintiff seeking to recover for blood bank's negligently providing her with HIV-positive blood did not have to demonstrate that defect was detectable or removable by reasonable scientific procedures or techniques. West's F.S.A. § 672.316(5).

> Sicuranza v. Northwest Florida Blood Center, Inc., 582 So.2d 54.

Fla.App. 3 Dist. 1972. Where woman obtained wrinkle cream by purchasing a certain amount of cosmetics produced by same manufacturer, transaction was not a gift but a "sale" subject to the implied warranties of merchantability or of ordinary use. F.S.A. §§ 671.201(11), (44)(d), 672.106(1), 672.304, 672.313, 672.314.

> Sheppard v. Revlon, Inc., 267 So.2d 662.

⚷**1756. —— Computers and software.**

See also COPYRIGHTS AND INTELLECTUAL PROPERTY ⚷107.

C.A.5 (Fla.) 1964. Rule that there is no implied warranty of fitness where known, described and definite article is purchased by its trade name could have no application to purchase of 10 items including a computer to be incorporated into a system intended to be tailored by a manufacturer-seller to needs of buyer.

> Sperry Rand Corp. v. Industrial Supply Corp., 337 F.2d 363.

⚷**1757. Design defects.**

Fla.App. 1 Dist. 1970. A defect in design which does not render a machine not reasonably fit for its intended use is not a breach of warranty.

> Fletcher Co. v. Melroe Mfg. Co., 238 So.2d 142, certiorari denied 242 So.2d 463, appeal after remand 261 So.2d 191.

⚷1758–1760. *For other cases see earlier editions of this digest, the Decennial Digests, and WESTLAW.*

⚷1761. Used or second-hand goods.

Fla.App. 1 Dist. 1980. Florida statutory provisions for implied warranties of merchantability and fitness are applicable to used motor vehicles. West's F.S.A. §§ 672.314, 672.315.

> Fuquay v. Revels Motors, Inc., 389 So.2d 1238.

Fla.App. 2 Dist. 1981. Implied warranties of merchantability and fitness accompany sale of a used car. West's F.S.A. §§ 672.314, 672.315.

> Bert Smith Oldsmobile, Inc. v. Franklin, 400 So.2d 1235.

Fla.App. 2 Dist. 1969. When seller knows purpose for which buyer buys article and that he is relying on seller's skill and judgment, implied warranty of fitness for which article is purchased arises as a matter of law; rule applies to secondhand articles sold prior to effective date of Uniform Commercial Code; overruling anything to contrary in Keating v. De Arment, Fla.App.1967, 193 So.2d 694.

> Brown v. Hall, 221 So.2d 454.

If seller of used dump truck, which was sold prior to effective date of Uniform Commercial Code, knew purpose for which buyer was acquiring truck and that buyer was relying on seller's skill and judgment in selection of particular truck, implied warranty arose as matter of law that truck, wheel rim of which subsequently proved defective and caused rear tandem wheel to fly off and strike service station attendant as he was attempting to change inside wheel, was in fact fit and in condition for purpose intended.

> Brown v. Hall, 221 So.2d 454.

Fla.App. 2 Dist. 1966. When the seller knows the purpose for which the buyer buys article and that he is relying upon seller's skill and judgment, an implied warranty of fitness for which the article is purchased arises as a matter of law, and this rule applies to second hand articles.

> Enix v. Diamond T. Sales & Service Co., 188 So.2d 48, certiorari denied 195 So.2d 566.

⚷1762. Causation.

Fla. 1950. A retail dealer in food products sold in sealed packages or cans to consuming public is liable on theory of implied warranty for injuries sustained by a purchasing consumer because of deleterious, unwholesome or unfit substance for human consumption contained in package or can.

> Sencer v. Carl's Markets, 45 So.2d 671.

Fla. 1944. A manufacturer or canner of food product sold to retailer in sealed packages or cans is liable for breach of implied warranty that such product is wholesome and fit for human consumption, where consumer purchasing product from retailer is injured because of deleterious, unhealthy, or poisonous substances therein.

> Blanton v. Cudahy Packing Co., 19 So.2d 313, 154 Fla. 872.

Fla.App. 1 Dist. 1972. If a bottler or manufacturer of a product intended for human consumption packages its product in a glass container and product is such that it cannot be ordinarily consumed without at the same time handling and using the container itself, manufacturer or bottler impliedly warrants that container is reasonably fit for the purpose for which it is intended and if, under such circumstances, a defect is shown to be the cause of the container breaking or exploding, liability for any damages suffered by purchaser of product may be imposed upon manufacturer or bottler.

> Reese v. Florida Coca-Cola Bottling Co., 256 So.2d 392.

(D) EXCLUSION, MODIFICATION, OR LIMITATION OF WARRANTIES.

1. IN GENERAL.

⚷1771. In general.

C.A.11 (Fla.) 2017. Under Florida law, a collateral document, such as a limited warranty, is deemed to be incorporated by reference into a contract if the contract specifically provides that it is subject to the incorporated collateral document, and the collateral document to be incorporated must be sufficiently described or referred to in the incorporating agreement so that the intent of the parties may be ascertained.

> Global Quest, LLC v. Horizon Yachts, Inc., 849 F.3d 1022.

Fla.App. 1 Dist. 2008. The Uniform Commercial Code (UCC) contemplates that a seller may disclaim warranties as long as the buyer reasonably understands this is being done. West's F.S.A. § 672.316(2).

> Rose v. ADT Sec. Services, Inc., 989 So.2d 1244.

Fla.App. 3 Dist. 1977. Uniform Commercial Code contemplates that seller may disclaim warranties as long as buyer reasonably understands that is being done. West's F.S.A. § 671.101 et seq.

> Knipp v. Weinbaum, 351 So.2d 1081, certiorari denied 357 So.2d 188.

To be effective, seller's disclaimer of warranties in sale of consumer goods must be part of basis of bargain between parties.

> Knipp v. Weinbaum, 351 So.2d 1081, certiorari denied 357 So.2d 188.

Fla.App. 3 Dist. 1962. There can be no express or implied warranty contrary to written warranty which provides that it is in lieu of all other warranties.

> Rozen v. Chrysler Corp., 142 So.2d 735.

Fla.App. 5 Dist. 1982. To be effective, seller's disclaimer of warranties in sale of consumer goods must be part of basis of bargain between parties. West's F.S.A. §§ 672.316(3)(a), 679.109(1).

> First New England Financial Corp. v. Woffard, 421 So.2d 590.

Fla.App. 5 Dist. 1980. To be effective, a warranty disclaimer must be part of the sales bargain between the parties.

> McNamara Pontiac, Inc. v. Sanchez, 388 So.2d 620.

☞**1772. Particular cases, goods, and warranties in general.**

C.A.5 (Fla.) 1980. Fact of the relatively short period between signing of computer equipment sales contract and lease, fact that there were only two or three meetings between the manufacturer and the lessee prior to the signing, and fact that the lessee was in the business of selling oil and oil products and was thus presumably unfamiliar with computers did not show that limitations of liability and disclaimers of warranty were unconscionable. West's F.S.A. § 672.302.

> Earman Oil Co., Inc. v. Burroughs Corp., 625 F.2d 1291.

S.D.Fla. 2001. Florida's express and implied breach of warranty statutes applied to buyer's action against seller for breach of express warranty and breach of implied warranty arising out sale of allegedly defective chemical, since warranty and limitation of liability provisions of seller's standard invoice were not incorporated by the parties' agreement for chemical sale and did not give rise to a binding course of conduct, and parties' agreement was otherwise silent on those issues. U.C.C. §§ 2–314, 2–315; West's F.S.A. §§ 672.314, 672.315.

> Premix-Marbletite Mfg. Corp. v. SKW Chemicals, Inc., 145 F.Supp.2d 1348.

S.D.Fla. 1982. Express, conspicuous disclaimers of liability for breach of warranty contained in agreement for service of reverse osmosis water treatment system, under which agreement parts were installed in system, were effective and barred owner from recovering for breach of warranty when components failed.

> Ocean Reef Club, Inc. v. UOP, Inc., 554 F.Supp. 123.

Fla.App. 1 Dist. 1985. Motor home manufacturer's limited warranty of repair or replacement was not the sole remedy exclusive of any other remedy which might be available against manufacturer or seller under Uniform Commercial Code, notwithstanding that warranty notice was conspicuous as warranty notice did not specify that the limited remedies provided were the exclusive or sole remedies. West's F.S.A. §§ 672.719, 672.719(1)(b), 672.719 comment; U.C.C. § 2–719(1)(b).

> Parsons v. Motor Homes of America, Inc., 465 So.2d 1285.

Fla.App. 1 Dist. 1982. Herbicide manufacturer's statement of warranty was

---

† This Case was not selected for publication in the National Reporter System
For legislative history of cited statutes, see Florida Statutes Annotated

"conspicuous" where it appeared on each can of its herbicide as well as in directions for use of product, was captioned as limit of warranty and liability, mentioned merchantability and expressly excluded other express or implied warranties, and was printed in capital letters.

Monsanto Agr. Products Co. v. Edenfield, 426 So.2d 574.

Limitation of warranty and liability in use of herbicide was made part of bargain between manufacturer and farmer where reference to limit of warranty and liability appeared on face of booklet of directions for use and included express invitation to purchasers to return product if terms of warranty were unacceptable, and where farmer read directions before using product and did not return it.

Monsanto Agr. Products Co. v. Edenfield, 426 So.2d 574.

Even if buyer of herbicide had not read label containing limit of warranty and liability, he would be charged with knowledge of limitation where limitation was conspicuous. West's F.S.A. § 671.201(10).

Monsanto Agr. Products Co. v. Edenfield, 426 So.2d 574.

Fla.App. 1 Dist. 1982. Warranty printed on each bag of seeds delivered to farmer by seed distributor purporting to disclaim any implied warranty and limiting recoverable damages to value of seeds was postcontract, unbargained-for unilateral attempt to limit distributor's obligations under prior contract, and was, as such, ineffective, where farmers neither directly nor indirectly knew of such nonwarranty at time of sale, nor subsequently assented to it. West's F.S.A. §§ 672.316, 672.316(3)(d), 672.714, 672.715, 672.719, 672.719(1)(b).

Pennington Grain and Seed, Inc. v. Tuten, 422 So.2d 948.

Fla.App. 2 Dist. 1972. Fact that purchaser of automobile had read retail installment contract, including the disclaimer clause, did not render effective the disclaimer which did not comply with statute requiring disclaimer to be conspicuous. F.S.A. § 672.316(2).

Rehurek v. Chrysler Credit Corp., 262 So.2d 452, 54 A.L.R.3d 1210, certiorari denied 267 So.2d 833.

Fla.App. 3 Dist. 1972. Where warranty provision excluding all express or implied warranties except as provided in contract was in the same color and size of type used for other provisions of automobile sales contract, the disclaimer was not "conspicuous" and was ineffective and did not bar remedy of rescission, despite contention that contract provided for a remedy by agreement in providing only for replacement or repair. F.S.A. §§ 672.316(2), 672.719.

Orange Motors of Coral Gables, Inc. v. Dade County Dairies, Inc., 258 So.2d 319, certiorari denied 263 So.2d 831.

⬤1773. Implied warranties in general.

C.A.11 (Fla.) 1987. Purchaser's acceptance of spray rig and instruction manual which contained disclaimer of implied warranties was insufficient to show that purchaser assented to modification of original bargain; disclaimer did not offer purchaser opportunity to return product if purchaser did not wish to accept the disclaimer.

Bowdoin v. Showell Growers, Inc., 817 F.2d 1543.

N.D.Fla. 2010. In Florida, a seller may exclude implied warranties by an express and conspicuous provision referring to either the implied warranty of merchantability or implied warranty of fitness. West's F.S.A. § 672.316(2).

JDI Holdings, LLC v. Jet Management, Inc., 732 F.Supp.2d 1205.

Fla. 1953. Where watermelon seeds purchased from seller produced a different variety of watermelon from variety produced by seeds purportedly sold to buyer, and variety of watermelon produced would not be affected by conditions entirely outside seller's control, seller was liable for breach of implied warranty, notwithstanding seller's disclaimer or non-warranty clause inserted in invoice and attached to bags of seeds.

Corneli Seed Co. v. Ferguson, 64 So.2d 162.

Fla.App. 1 Dist. 1992. Term "service contract," for purposes of Magnuson-Moss Act section prohibiting supplier from disclaiming or modifying implied warrant if supplier enters into service contract with consumer, did not encompass situation where automobile dealer merely guaranteed repair work on isolated post-sale repair job. Magnuson-Moss Warranty-Federal Trade Commission Improvement Act, § 101(8), 15 U.S.C.A. § 2301(8).

> Frank Griffin Volkswagen, Inc. v. Smith, 610 So.2d 597, review denied 620 So.2d 762, appeal after remand 645 So.2d 585, cause dismissed Volkswagen of America, Inc. v. Smith, 654 So.2d 132, rehearing denied, appeal after remand 690 So.2d 1328, rehearing denied.

Fla.App. 3 Dist. 1977. Implied warranties may be imposed on sale of used goods in limited circumstances, despite ostensible disclaimers. West's F.S.A. §§ 672.314, 672.315.

> Knipp v. Weinbaum, 351 So.2d 1081, certiorari denied 357 So.2d 188.

Fla.App. 3 Dist. 1968. Notwithstanding new automobile warranty provision that there was no warranty, express or implied, made by either manufacturer or selling dealer except direct company vehicle warranty, action in implied warranty could be maintained by buyer against both manufacturer and selling dealer.

> Crown v. Cecil Holland Ford, Inc., 207 So.2d 67.

☞**1774. Warranties of quality, fitness, or condition.**

☞**1775. —— In general.**

C.A.11 (Fla.) 1987. Manufacturers of high pressure spray rig that caused injuries to users did not effectively disclaim implied warranties of fitness and merchantability by including disclaimer with instruction manual that accompanied spray rig when it was delivered to purchaser; even assuming disclaimer was otherwise conspicuous, it was delivered to purchaser after sale, and so did not form part of basis of bargain between the parties to the sale.

> Bowdoin v. Showell Growers, Inc., 817 F.2d 1543.

C.A.5 (Fla.) 1950. Where buyer of tomatoes refused to pay therefor on ground of alleged express warranty as to freedom from blight, and it was known to experienced produce sellers and buyers that such blight was not discoverable by inspection immediately after picking or packing and that, if it did exist, it rendered the merchandise unmarketable, express warranty excluded any possibility of an implied warranty with respect to freedom from blight.

> Cohen v. Frima Products Co., 181 F.2d 324.

Fla. 1967. Neither absence of privity between automobile manufacturer and purchaser, nor the execution of written warranty agreement between manufacturer and its dealer disclaiming any implied warranty of merchantability or fitness or any other obligation except as assumed by manufacturer operated to preclude recovery by purchaser from manufacturer on basis of implied warranty due to automobile's alleged defects and lack of fitness and suitability.

> Manheim v. Ford Motor Co., 201 So.2d 440, opinion conformed to 201 So.2d 909.

Fla.App. 1 Dist. 2008. Seller of home security services disclaimed implied warranties of merchantability and fitness arising from contract with buyers, where disclaimer provision of contract specifically mentioned both warranties and was conspicuous, having been printed in bold, capital letters in section of contract entitled "General Terms and Conditions." West's F.S.A. § 672.316(2).

> Rose v. ADT Sec. Services, Inc., 989 So.2d 1244.

Fla.App. 1 Dist. 1969. Where the Secretary of manufacturer of automobile admitted that manufacturer neither sold nor serviced vehicles to the ultimate retail purchaser but sold vehicles to authorized dealerships which in turn sold vehicles to, and serviced them for, retail purchasers, the manufacturer was not the seller of the automobile within the Uniform Commercial Code and could not, pursuant to Code, disclaim implied warranty of merchantability and fitness. F.S.A. §§ 672.2–103, 672.2–106(1), 672.2–201, 672.2–316.

> Ford Motor Co. v. Pittman, 227 So.2d 246, certiorari denied 237 So.2d 177.

In order for manufacturer to be entitled under Uniform Commercial Code to disclaim implied warranties of merchantability and fitness, manufacturer must show that it is seller within the terms of the

Code, that there was contract of type required by the Code, and that disclaimer expressly negating implied warranties was part of contract rather than of other materials handed to buyer at time of purchase. F.S.A. §§ 672.2–103, 672.2–106(1), 672.2–201, 672.2–202, 672.2–316.

> Ford Motor Co. v. Pittman, 227 So.2d 246, certiorari denied 237 So.2d 177.

Fla.App. 2 Dist. 1981. Disclaimers of implied warranties contained in used car dealer's retail order were ineffective where one of the alleged disclaimers referred only to new vehicles, second disclaimer was inconspicuous, having been printed in same size, style and type and included among myriad of other provisions on face of retail order form, and third disclaimer, although in bold type and all capitals, stating that any implied warranty of fitness or merchantability was limited to the duration of express limited warranty, only limited duration of the implied warranty and the breach of implied warranty occurred within limitation period. West's F.S.A. § 672.316.

> Bert Smith Oldsmobile, Inc. v. Franklin, 400 So.2d 1235.

Fla.App. 2 Dist. 1972. Disclaimer clause appearing in small print on back page of automobile retail installment contract failed for lack of conspicuousness to exclude warranties of merchantability and fitness. F.S.A. § 672.316(2).

> Rehurek v. Chrysler Credit Corp., 262 So.2d 452, 54 A.L.R.3d 1210, certiorari denied 267 So.2d 833.

Where disclaimer clause in automobile warranty booklet was not incorporated into the contract and was not the basis for the bargain, the disclaimer was ineffective to exclude implied warranties of merchantability and fitness. F.S.A. § 672.316(2).

> Rehurek v. Chrysler Credit Corp., 262 So.2d 452, 54 A.L.R.3d 1210, certiorari denied 267 So.2d 833.

Automobile manufacturer, not being the "seller" to the ultimate consumer, may not disclaim warranties of merchantability and fitness. F.S.A. §§ 672.316, 672.316(2).

> Rehurek v. Chrysler Credit Corp., 262 So.2d 452, 54 A.L.R.3d 1210, certiorari denied 267 So.2d 833.

Fla.App. 3 Dist. 1981. Disclaimer of warranty was conspicuous, as required to exclude or modify implied warranty of fitness, where contract, which was printed on single sheet of paper, stated in bold type at bottom of front side "The Terms and Conditions are to be found on the reverse hereof and constitute a part of this contract," and last paragraph on reverse side was titled "Disclaimer of Warranties" and stated "LESSOR MAKES NO EXPRESS OR IMPLIED WARRANTY WHATSOEVER WITH RESPECT TO THE EQUIPMENT, INCLUDING BUT NOT LIMITED TO THE IMPLIED WARRANTIES OF MERCHANTABILITY AND FITNESS." West's F.S.A. §§ 671.201(10), 672.316.

> Rudy's Glass Const. Co. v. E. F. Johnson Co., 404 So.2d 1087.

Fla.App. 3 Dist. 1962. Automobile buyer was not entitled to recover on theory that dealer and manufactuer breached warranty that automobile was well constructed without defective parts and suitable as passenger automobile for private use, where manufacturer's standard warranty of freedom from defects in material and workmanship was expressly in lieu of all other warranties, express or implied, and manufacturer complied with standard warranty.

> Rozen v. Chrysler Corp., 142 So.2d 735.

Fla.App. 4 Dist. 1968. Disclaimer in written contract between seller of bulldozer and buyer that seller warranted the machine to be free from defects in materials or workmanship and that the warranty was in lieu of all other warranties, express or implied, was valid and precluded an implied warranty of fitness or merchantability. F.S.A. § 672.2–316; F.S.A.Const. Declaration of Rights, § 1.

> Desandolo v. F & C Tractor & Equipment Co., 211 So.2d 576, certiorari denied 221 So.2d 746.

⚷1776. —— **Obvious, latent, or hidden defects.**

Fla.App. 3 Dist. 1980. Where contract for sale of copier contained a conspicuous disclaimer of all express or implied warranties, the seller could not have been held liable to the buyer when copier proved defective and, hence, corporation with which buyer had entered into lease application whereby the corporation financed the purchase and leased the copier back to the buyer, had no claims against seller based on breach of warranty when buyer sought to be relieved of its lease obligations. West's F.S.A. §§ 671.201(10), 672.316(2).

> Xerographic Supplies Corp. v. Hertz Commercial Leasing Corp., 386 So.2d 299.

―**1777–1778.** *For other cases see earlier editions of this digest, the Decennial Digests, and WESTLAW.*

―**1778. Warranties of fitness for ordinary purpose or use; merchantability.**

―**1779. —— In general.**

Fla.App. 1 Dist. 1969. In order for manufacturer to be entitled under Uniform Commercial Code to disclaim implied warranties of merchantability and fitness, manufacturer must show that it is seller within the terms of the Code, that there was contract of type required by the Code, and that disclaimer expressly negating implied warranties was part of contract rather than of other materials handed to buyer at time of purchase. F.S.A. §§ 672.2–103, 672.2–106(1), 672.2–201, 672.2–202, 672.2–316.

> Ford Motor Co. v. Pittman, 227 So.2d 246, certiorari denied 237 So.2d 177.

Fla.App. 5 Dist. 1982. Under Florida law and Uniform Commercial Code, all implied warranties, whether of merchantability or fitness for a purpose, are excluded, unless circumstances indicate otherwise, by any language making it plain that there is no implied warranty. West's F.S.A. § 672.316(3)(a).

> First New England Financial Corp. v. Wofford, 421 So.2d 590.

―**1780. —— Particular cases and goods.**

C.A.11 (Fla.) 1987. Manufacturers of high pressure spray rig that caused injuries to users did not effectively disclaim implied warranties of fitness and merchantability by including disclaimer with instruction manual that accompanied spray rig when it was delivered to purchaser; even assuming disclaimer was

otherwise conspicuous, it was delivered to purchaser after sale, and so did not form part of basis of bargain between the parties to the sale.

> Bowdoin v. Showell Growers, Inc., 817 F.2d 1543.

C.A.5 (Fla.) 1980. Where language disclaiming warranties and limiting liability was in type larger than the surrounding terms and included the word "merchantability," the implied warranties disclaimer fully complied with the requirements of the UCC and were effective. West's F.S.A. § 672.316(2).

> Earman Oil Co., Inc. v. Burroughs Corp., 625 F.2d 1291.

C.A.5 (Fla.) 1970. Disclaimer of warranties in sales contract was not "conspicuous" within Florida statute, requiring that written exclusion of implied warranty of merchantability must be conspicuous, where disclaimer was in same color and size of other type used for other provisions of contract. F.S.A. §§ 672.2–102, 672.2–316.

> Entron, Inc. v. General Cablevision of Palatka, 435 F.2d 995.

M.D.Fla. 2005. There was no breach of implied merchantability, under Florida law, when seller sold radios lacking "trunking" capability, of searching for available frequencies; it was clear that the feature was not part of radios that were bargained for.

> Business Radio, Inc. v. Relm Wireless Corp., 373 F.Supp.2d 1317, affirmed 209 Fed.Appx. 899.

Fla.App. 1 Dist. 2008. Seller of home security services disclaimed implied warranties of merchantability and fitness arising from contract with buyers, where disclaimer provision of contract specifically mentioned both warranties and was conspicuous, having been printed in bold, capital letters in section of contract entitled "General Terms and Conditions." West's F.S.A. § 672.316(2).

> Rose v. ADT Sec. Services, Inc., 989 So.2d 1244.

Fla.App. 1 Dist. 1988. Disclaimer of warranties in contract for sale of bulldozer was insufficient to disclaim implied warranty of merchantability under the Uniform Commercial Code, where disclaimer failed to specifically mention "merchantability." West's F.S.A. §§ 672.314(1), 672.316(2), (3)(a).

> McCormick Machinery, Inc. v. Julian E. Johnson & Sons, Inc., 523 So.2d 651.

Fla.App. 1 Dist. 1969. Where the Secretary of manufacturer of automobile admitted that manufacturer neither sold nor serviced vehicles to the ultimate retail purchaser but sold vehicles to authorized dealerships which in turn sold vehicles to, and serviced them for, retail purchasers, the manufacturer was not the seller of the automobile within the Uniform Commercial Code and could not, pursuant to Code, disclaim implied warranty of merchantability and fitness. F.S.A. §§ 672.2–103, 672.2–106(1), 672.2–201, 672.2–316.

> Ford Motor Co. v. Pittman, 227 So.2d 246, certiorari denied 237 So.2d 177.

Fla.App. 2 Dist. 2000. Boat buyer could not establish claims against seller for breach of contract and breach of implied warranties stemming from buyer's dissatisfaction with the paint applied to the pontoons on the boat, as purchase contract explicitly disclaimed any express warranty from the seller, including any implied warranties of merchantability and fitness for a particular purpose. West's F.S.A. § 672.316.

> Family Boating & Marine Centers of Florida, Inc. v. Bell, 779 So.2d 402, rehearing denied.

Fla.App. 2 Dist. 1981. Where buyer employed services of expert for inspection of grader, expert had ample opportunity to inspect grader, and could have tested its only function, of leveling and pushing earth, on premises before sale, defect was functionally basic to operation of grader in that grader did not push earth, and buyer knew that grader was not new machine and that seller had obtained it only few days before sale, defect ought to have been revealed by examination and buyer's failure to adequately examine grader negated any implied warranty of merchantability. West's F.S.A. §§ 672.314, 672.316(3)(b).

> Hall Truck Sales, Inc. v. Wilder Mobile Homes, Inc., 402 So.2d 1299, review denied 412 So.2d 471.

Fla.App. 2 Dist. 1981. Disclaimers of implied warranties contained in used car dealer's retail order were ineffective where one of the alleged disclaimers referred only to new vehicles, second disclaimer was inconspicuous, having been printed in same size, style and type and included among myriad of other provisions on face of retail order form, and third disclaimer, although in bold type and all capitals, stating that any implied warranty of fitness or merchantability was limited to the duration of express limited warranty, only limited duration of the implied warranty and the breach of implied warranty occurred within limitation period. West's F.S.A. § 672.316.

> Bert Smith Oldsmobile, Inc. v. Franklin, 400 So.2d 1235.

Fla.App. 2 Dist. 1972. Disclaimer clause appearing in small print on back page of automobile retail installment contract failed for lack of conspicuousness to exclude warranties of merchantability and fitness. F.S.A. § 672.316(2).

> Rehurek v. Chrysler Credit Corp., 262 So.2d 452, 54 A.L.R.3d 1210, certiorari denied 267 So.2d 833.

Where disclaimer clause in automobile warranty booklet was not incorporated into the contract and was not the basis for the bargain, the disclaimer was ineffective to exclude implied warranties of merchantability and fitness. F.S.A. § 672.316(2).

> Rehurek v. Chrysler Credit Corp., 262 So.2d 452, 54 A.L.R.3d 1210, certiorari denied 267 So.2d 833.

Automobile manufacturer, not being the "seller" to the ultimate consumer, may not disclaim warranties of merchantability and fitness. F.S.A. §§ 672.316, 672.316(2).

> Rehurek v. Chrysler Credit Corp., 262 So.2d 452, 54 A.L.R.3d 1210, certiorari denied 267 So.2d 833.

Fla.App. 3 Dist. 1987. Disclaimers of all warranties of merchantability or fitness for particular purpose, contained in written contracts for lease of modem and purchase of computer system, complied with statutory requirements. West's F.S.A. §§ 672.302, 672.316(2).

> Meeting Makers, Inc. v. American Airlines, Inc., 513 So.2d 700.

Fla.App. 3 Dist. 1975. Air-conditioning system which is attached and immovable carries implied warranty of fitness and merchantability even when it is sold with express warranty which purports to limit guarantee to one year.

> Forte Towers South, Inc. v. Hill York Sales Corp., 312 So.2d 512.

Fla.App. 4 Dist. 1968. Disclaimer in written contract between seller of bulldozer and buyer that seller warranted the machine to be free from defects in materials or workmanship and that the warranty was in lieu of all other warranties, express or implied, was valid and precluded an implied warranty of fitness or merchantability. F.S.A. § 672.2–316; F.S.A.Const. Declaration of Rights, § 1.

> Desandolo v. F & C Tractor & Equipment Co., 211 So.2d 576, certiorari denied 221 So.2d 746.

🔑**1781. Warranties of fitness for particular purpose or use.**

🔑**1782. —— In general.**

Fla.App. 2 Dist. 2000. To exclude a warranty of fitness for a particular purpose, the language must express that there are no warranties which extend beyond the description on the face of the agreement. West's F.S.A. § 672.316(2).

> Family Boating & Marine Centers of Florida, Inc. v. Bell, 779 So.2d 402, rehearing denied.

Fla.App. 5 Dist. 1982. Under Florida law and Uniform Commercial Code, all implied warranties, whether of merchantability or fitness for a purpose, are excluded, unless circumstances indicate otherwise, by any language making it plain that there is no implied warranty. West's F.S.A. § 672.316(3)(a).

> First New England Financial Corp. v. Woffard, 421 So.2d 590.

🔑**1783. —— Particular cases and goods.**

C.A.5 (Fla.) 1964. So-called integration clause of sales contract not providing that there were no implied warranties could not preclude recovery for breach of implied warranty of fitness for disclosed purpose.

> Sperry Rand Corp. v. Industrial Supply Corp., 337 F.2d 363.

Fla.App. 2 Dist. 2000. Boat buyer could not establish claims against seller for breach of contract and breach of implied warranties stemming from buyer's dissatisfaction with the paint applied to the pontoons on the boat, as purchase contract explicitly disclaimed any express warranty from the seller, including any implied warranties of merchantability and fitness for a particular purpose. West's F.S.A. § 672.316.

> Family Boating & Marine Centers of Florida, Inc. v. Bell, 779 So.2d 402, rehearing denied.

Fla.App. 3 Dist. 1987. Disclaimers of all warranties of merchantability or fitness for particular purpose, contained in written contracts for lease of modem and purchase of computer system, complied with statutory requirements. West's F.S.A. §§ 672.302, 672.316(2).

> Meeting Makers, Inc. v. American Airlines, Inc., 513 So.2d 700.

🔑**1784–1786.** *For other cases see earlier editions of this digest, the Decennial Digests, and WESTLAW.*

🔑**1787. "As is" provisions.**

C.A.11 (Fla.) 2017. "As is" clause in purchase agreement for yacht, which disclaimed all warranties as to condition of yacht, did not preclude buyer's claim against seller for fraudulent inducement under Florida law, which precluded a party from contracting against liability for its own fraud, absent a disclaimer of liability for fraud.

> Global Quest, LLC v. Horizon Yachts, Inc., 849 F.3d 1022.

Fla.App. 2 Dist. 1974. The "conspicuous" requirements of second subdivision were applicable to an "as is" disclaimer under third subdivision, it being intent of drafters of Uniform Commercial Code that disclaimer, however written, be set forth in conspicuous manner, and disclaimer provision written in same size and color type as balance of contract was ineffective to exclude implied warranties in connection with sale of mobile home. F.S.A. §§ 671.201(10), 672.316(2), (3)(a).

> Osborne v. Genevie, 289 So.2d 21.

Fla.App. 3 Dist. 1995. Absent evidence that seller made any fraudulent misrepresentations to buyer to induce him to buy used car, written warranties established parameters of seller's responsibilities, and thus seller was not responsible for cost of repairs made to car which were not covered by extremely limited written warranty; car was sold "as is," and separate written 30–day limited warranty covered certain enumerated items.

David v. Davenport, 656 So.2d 952.

Fla.App. 3 Dist. 1977. Automatic absolution is not achieved in sale of used consumer goods merely by inclusion in a bill of sale of words "as is"; this, however, is not to say that seller of used goods may not absolve himself from responsibility for defects in goods sold where both he and buyer understand this to be intended meaning of phrase "as is." West's F.S.A. §§ 672.316(3), 672.719(3), comment 3.

Knipp v. Weinbaum, 351 So.2d 1081, certiorari denied 357 So.2d 188.

Fla.App. 4 Dist. 1990. " 'As is' warranty", which defines rights and presupposes repairs are needed, that contains written disclaimer of oral representations made by seller with respect to condition of car, while usually effective in negating seller's liability for fraud in the inducement, may in some cases be ineffective in negating seller's liability.

Lou Bachrodt Chevrolet, Inc. v. Savage, 570 So.2d 306, review denied 581 So.2d 165.

Fla.App. 5 Dist. 1981. Used car dealer was not liable for breach of warranty because of brake failure of used car purchased "as is," in absence of anything being offered to challenge effectiveness of "as is" provision. West's F.S.A. § 672–316(3)(a).

Masker v. Smith, 405 So.2d 432.

⌐1788. Course of dealing or course of performance.

S.D.Fla. 2001. Seller's repeated sending of its standard invoice following sales of chemicals to buyer did not establish disclaimer of warranties and limitation of liability provisions contained in invoice as binding course of dealing under Florida law, for purposes of buyer's action against seller alleging that chemical sold

was defective. U.C.C. § 2–208; West's F.S.A. § 672.208(1).

Premix-Marbletite Mfg. Corp. v. SKW Chemicals, Inc., 145 F.Supp.2d 1348.

Florida's express and implied breach of warranty statutes applied to buyer's action against seller for breach of express warranty and breach of implied warranty arising out sale of allegedly defective chemical, since warranty and limitation of liability provisions of seller's standard invoice were not incorporated by the parties' agreement for chemical sale and did not give rise to a binding course of conduct, and parties' agreement was otherwise silent on those issues. U.C.C. §§ 2–314, 2–315; West's F.S.A. §§ 672.314, 672.315.

Premix-Marbletite Mfg. Corp. v. SKW Chemicals, Inc., 145 F.Supp.2d 1348.

2. EXPRESS WARRANTIES.

⌐1791. In general.

N.D.Fla. 1980. Florida allows contracts to limit damages recoverable for breach of warranty and breach of contract. West's F.S.A. §§ 672.316(4), 672.719.

Hi Neighbor Enterprises, Inc. v. Burroughs Corp., 492 F.Supp. 823.

⌐1792. Particular cases and goods.

C.A.5 (Fla.) 1965. Warranty and limitation of liability contained in contract between can company and bread company, which purchased cans from can company and then had cans shipped to bakery corporation for use by it, was binding on bakery corporation which had entered into contract with bread company, pursuant to which former agreed to sell to latter its entire canned product, and such limitation of liability should have been received in evidence and damages, if any, calculated in accordance with its provisions.

American Can Co. v. Horlamus Corp., 341 F.2d 730.

N.D.Fla. 1980. Limitations on warranty contained in contract for sale of computer software and hardware met requirements of the Uniform Commercial Code and, thus, were enforceable under

Florida law. West's F.S.A. §§ 672.314, 672.315, 672.316(2).

> Hi Neighbor Enterprises, Inc. v. Burroughs Corp., 492 F.Supp. 823.

Provisions in contract for sale of computer software and hardware limiting damages recoverable for breach of warranty and breach of contract were enforceable under Florida law. West's F.S.A. §§ 672.316(4), 672.719.

> Hi Neighbor Enterprises, Inc. v. Burroughs Corp., 492 F.Supp. 823.

S.D.Fla. 2014. Under Florida law, design defects, in addition to manufacturing defects, were covered by automobile manufacturer's express warranty, where warranty contained no express exclusion for coverage for design defect claims, and design defects were not included in warranty's "what is not covered" section. West's F.S.A. § 672.313.

> Sanchez-Knutson v. Ford Motor Co., 52 F.Supp.3d 1223.

S.D.Fla. 2013. Under Florida law, motorcycle purchasers who purchased their motorcycles after expiration of the manufacturer's factory warranties, which limited remedies available to owners to the reparation or replacement of defective parts for a three-year period, did not have an ownership interest in their motorcycles during the motorcycles' warranty periods, could not state a claim for breach of express warranty in their putative class action against manufacturer.

> Aprigliano v. American Honda Motor Co., Inc., 979 F.Supp.2d 1331.

(E) CUMULATION AND CONFLICT OF WARRANTIES.

☞1801–1803. *For other cases see earlier editions of this digest, the Decennial Digests, and WESTLAW.*

☞1804. **Consistency of express and implied warranties.**

C.A.5 (Fla.) 1964. Express warranty in sales contract could not exclude implied warranties where they were not of same kind as implied warranty or inconsistent with it.

> Sperry Rand Corp. v. Industrial Supply Corp., 337 F.2d 363.

There was no inconsistency between express warranty of making adjustments and replacement of broken and defective parts in computer and related equipment forming business records system and asserted implied warranty of fitness for use for disclosed purpose, and, accordingly, the implied warranty was unaffected by the express warranty.

> Sperry Rand Corp. v. Industrial Supply Corp., 337 F.2d 363.

Although there may be a valid express disclaimer of implied warranty, right to assert such a warranty is not precluded by express warranties which are not inconsistent, and implied warranty is not rejected by integration clause.

> Sperry Rand Corp. v. Industrial Supply Corp., 337 F.2d 363.

Fla.App. 1 Dist. 1962. Implied warranty of merchantability is not excluded by express warranty against defective parts and workmanship, which is not inconsistent with implied warranty.

> Posey v. Pensacola Tractor & Equipment Co., 138 So.2d 777.

Implied warranty obligations are unaffected by what is undertaken as means of express warranties not inconsistent with implied warranty obligations.

> Posey v. Pensacola Tractor & Equipment Co., 138 So.2d 777.

Fla.App. 4 Dist. 1996. In contract between distributor of resin and boat builder, contractual exclusion of warranties provision was not inconsistent with limitation of remedies provision in same contract, and thus, even if distributor could be found liable, measure of damages was limited to cost of goods sold.

> Jarmco, Inc. v. Polygard, Inc., 668 So.2d 300, review granted 678 So.2d 339, decision approved 684 So.2d 732.

(F) PARTIES TO WARRANTIES, PRIVITY, AND THIRD-PARTY BENEFICIARIES.

☞1811. **In general.**

M.D.Fla. 2010. To recover under Florida products liability law for a breach of warranty, either express or implied, the plaintiff must be in privity of contract with the defendant.

> Levine v. Wyeth Inc., 684 F.Supp.2d 1338.

N.D.Fla. 2007. Privity of contract is required for actions premised on express warranties under Florida Uniform Commercial Code. West's F.S.A. § 672.101 et seq.

> Yvon v. Baja Marine Corp., 495 F.Supp.2d 1179.

S.D.Fla. 2009. The privity requirement in Florida breach of warranty claims is a moving target which depends on factors including whether the warranty is express or implied and the type of injury alleged.

> Smith v. Wm. Wrigley Jr. Co., 663 F.Supp.2d 1336.

Fla. 1961. Injured user of commodity which is not a foodstuff or a dangerous instrumentality, is not in privity with retailer and to recover for injuries he must bring an action for negligence which requires allegation and proof of fault.

> Carter v. Hector Supply Co., 128 So.2d 390.

Fla.App. 2 Dist. 1979. There is no inconsistency in allowing maintenance of an action for negligence in performance of a contractual duty absent privity, yet disallowing maintenance of an action for breach of warranty absent privity.

> Navajo Circle, Inc. v. Development Concepts Corp., 373 So.2d 689.

⚷1812. Express warranties in general.

M.D.Fla. 2013. Under Florida law, warranty-based claims, including breach of express warranty, require privity of contract between parties.

> Kaiser v. Depuy Spine, Inc., 944 F.Supp.2d 1187.

N.D.Fla. 2012. The law of Florida is that to recover for the breach of a warranty, either express or implied, the plaintiff must be in privity of contract with the defendant. West's F.S.A. § 672.313.

> Hill v. Hoover Co., 899 F.Supp.2d 1259.

N.D.Fla. 2009. Under Florida law, a plaintiff must be in privity of contract to

recover under theories of breach of express or implied warranties.

> Fields v. Mylan Pharmaceuticals, Inc., 751 F.Supp.2d 1257.

N.D.Fla. 1995. Under Florida law, plaintiff must be in privity of contract with defendant in order to recover for breach of warranty, either express or implied.

> T.W.M. v. American Medical Systems, Inc., 886 F.Supp. 842.

S.D.Fla. 2016. Under Florida law, express- and implied warranty-based claims require privity of contract between the parties.

> Hawaiian Airlines, Inc. v. AAR Aircraft Services, Inc., 167 F.Supp.3d 1311, appeal dismissed (11th cir. 16-11536).

S.D.Fla. 2013. Under Florida law, a claim for breach of an express warranty generally requires the parties to have contractual privity.

> Aprigliano v. American Honda Motor Co., Inc., 979 F.Supp.2d 1331.

⚷1813. Implied warranties in general.

M.D.Fla. 2009. To sustain a claim under Florida law for breach of implied warranty of merchantability of goods, the plaintiff must demonstrate that he is in privity with the defendant.

> Cooper v. Old Williamsburg Candle Corp., 653 F.Supp.2d 1220.

M.D.Fla. 2009. Under Florida law, privity of contract is required in order to recover under a breach of implied warranty claim.

> Brisson v. Ford Motor Co., 602 F.Supp.2d 1227, affirmed in part, vacated in part, remanded 349 Fed. Appx. 433.

N.D.Fla. 2012. The law of Florida is that to recover for the breach of a warranty, either express or implied, the plaintiff must be in privity of contract with the defendant. West's F.S.A. § 672.313.

> Hill v. Hoover Co., 899 F.Supp.2d 1259.

N.D.Fla. 2009. Under Florida law, a plaintiff must be in privity of contract to recover under theories of breach of express or implied warranties.

> Fields v. Mylan Pharmaceuticals, Inc., 751 F.Supp.2d 1257.

N.D.Fla. 2007. Under Florida law, an implied warranty cannot exist where there is no privity of contract.

Yvon v. Baja Marine Corp., 495 F.Supp.2d 1179.

N.D.Fla. 1995. Under Florida law, plaintiff must be in privity of contract with defendant in order to recover for breach of warranty, either express or implied.

T.W.M. v. American Medical Systems, Inc., 886 F.Supp. 842.

S.D.Fla. 2014. Florida law requires privity of contract to sustain a breach of implied warranty claim.

Garcia v. Kashi Co., 43 F.Supp.3d 1359.

S.D.Fla. 2009. Florida law requires privity of contract to sustain a breach of implied warranty claim.

David v. American Suzuki Motor Corp., 629 F.Supp.2d 1309.

S.D.Fla. 1992. Privity of contract between plaintiff and defendant is essential element of breach of implied warranty cause of action.

Airport Rent-A-Car, Inc. v. Prevost Car, Inc., 788 F.Supp. 1203, question certified 18 F.3d 1555, certified question answered 660 So.2d 628, rehearing denied, answer to certified question conformed to 67 F.3d 901, affirmed 67 F.3d 901.

Florida law does not recognize exception to privity requirement for breach of implied warranty actions in cases in which plaintiff cannot recover from manufacturer of faulty goods under strict liability or negligence.

Airport Rent-A-Car, Inc. v. Prevost Car, Inc., 788 F.Supp. 1203, question certified 18 F.3d 1555, certified question answered 660 So.2d 628, rehearing denied, answer to certified question conformed to 67 F.3d 901, affirmed 67 F.3d 901.

Fla. 1988. Doctrine of strict liability in tort supplants all no-privity, breach of implied warranty cases, but contract action for breach of implied warranty remains where privity of contract is shown. West's F.S.A. § 672.318.

Kramer v. Piper Aircraft Corp., 520 So.2d 37, answer to certified question conformed to 868 F.2d 1538.

Fla. 1976. If user is injured by defective product, but circumstances do not create contractual relationship with manufacturer, then vehicle for recovery could be strict liability in tort, but if there is a contractual relationship with the manufacturer, the vehicle of implied warranty remains.

West v. Caterpillar Tractor Co., Inc., 336 So.2d 80, answer to certified question conformed to 547 F.2d 885.

Fla. 1961. Implication of warranty of fitness arises out of contractual relationship.

Carter v. Hector Supply Co., 128 So.2d 390.

Fla.App. 1 Dist. 2008. The doctrine of strict liability evolved as a vehicle for recovery for personal injury or property damage resulting from use of a product, when, due to lack of privity with the manufacturer, the injured user has no recourse under traditional warranty theory grounded in contract; however, if there is a contractual relationship with the manufacturer, the vehicle of implied warranty remains.

Rose v. ADT Sec. Services, Inc., 989 So.2d 1244.

Fla.App. 2 Dist. 1974. Doctrine of privity no longer obtains in Florida in an implied warranty suit by a consumer against a manufacturer.

McCarthy v. Florida Ladder Co., 295 So.2d 707.

Fla.App. 2 Dist. 1969. Test of extent of implied warranty of fitness for particular purpose is one of privity of contract.

Brown v. Hall, 221 So.2d 454.

Fla.App. 2 Dist. 1967. In most instances, privity of contract is unnecessary for recovery on theory of breach of implied warranty.

Barfield v. Atlantic Coast Line R. Co., 197 So.2d 545.

Fla.App. 3 Dist. 2008. Under Florida law, privity of contract is required to maintain an action for breach of an implied warranty.

Ocana v. Ford Motor Co., 992 So.2d 319, rehearing denied.

† **This Case was not selected for publication in the National Reporter System**
For legislative history of cited statutes, see Florida Statutes Annotated

Fla.App. 3 Dist. 1987. Privity of contract between consumer and computer manufacturer was necessary to maintain action for breach of implied warranty causing defects in computer.

Affiliates for Evaluation and Therapy, Inc. v. Viasyn Corp., 500 So.2d 688.

Fla.App. 3 Dist. 1966. Direct privity with manufacturer is no longer a necessary prerequisite to breach of implied warranty case.

Power Ski of Florida, Inc. v. Allied Chemical Corp., 188 So.2d 13.

Fla.App. 3 Dist. 1960. Lack of privity of contract between seller and ultimate user of article sold does not prevent the existence of an implied warranty that the article is fit for the purpose for which it is sold, and does not prevent recovery by the user for damages for breach of such warranty.

Hector Supply Co. v. Carter, 122 So.2d 22, certiorari discharged 128 So.2d 390.

Fla.App. 4 Dist. 1973. Provision of Uniform Commercial Code for implied warranty arising from sale by merchant does not govern rights and duties as between retail buyer and remote seller with whom buyer has no privity of contract. F.S.A. §§ 671.1–101 et seq., 672.2–314, 672.2–318.

Schuessler v. Coca-Cola Bottling Co. of Miami, 279 So.2d 901.

⚷1814. Seller and parties related thereto; vertical privity.

⚷1815. —— In general.

C.A.5 (Fla.) 1977. Implied warranty under the Uniform Commercial Code runs in Florida as a theory of recovery against manufacturers, and also against merchants. West's F.S.A. § 672.314.

Smith v. Fiat-Roosevelt Motors, Inc., 556 F.2d 728.

Fla.App. 4 Dist. 1983. Delivering, presenting, or explaining manufacturer's warranty, without more, does not render dealer a cowarrantor by adoption.

Motor Homes of America, Inc. v. O'Donnell, 440 So.2d 422, petition for review denied 451 So.2d 849.

⚷1816. —— Manufacturers and others in distribution chain.

⚷1816(1). In general.

N.D.Fla. 2012. Consumer was not in contractual privity with vacuum manufacturer, as required to maintain breach of express warranty and breach of implied warranty claims, under Florida law, and thus, consumer's Magnuson–Moss Warranty Act (MMWA) claim against manufacturer was also barred, where consumer purchased the vacuum from a third-party retailer, and not directly from the manufacturer. Magnuson–Moss Warranty—Federal Trade Commission Improvement Act, § 101, 15 U.S.C.A. § 2301; West's F.S.A. § 672.313.

Hill v. Hoover Co., 899 F.Supp.2d 1259.

N.D.Fla. 2009. Under Florida law, a plaintiff who purchases a product but does not buy it directly from the defendant, is not in privity with that defendant, for purposes of the rule that a plaintiff must be in privity of contract to recover under theories of breach of express or implied warranties.

Fields v. Mylan Pharmaceuticals, Inc., 751 F.Supp.2d 1257.

N.D.Fla. 1998. Under Florida law, privity between manufacturer and consumer of product is required in order for consumer to assert breach of implied warranty claim.

Baker v. Danek Medical, 35 F.Supp.2d 875.

S.D.Fla. 2013. Under Arizona law, a plaintiff may not proceed with a breach of warranty action under the Uniform Commercial Code (UCC) against a manufacturer not in privity with the plaintiff. A.R.S. § 47–2313(A).

In re Horizon Organic Milk Plus DHA Omega-3 Marketing and Sales Practice Litigation, 955 F.Supp.2d 1311.

Under Arizona law a lack of privity between a manufacturer and retail purchaser does not preclude a claim outside the Uniform Commercial Code (UCC) for breach of express warranty. A.R.S. § 47–2313(A).

In re Horizon Organic Milk Plus DHA Omega-3 Marketing and Sales Practice Litigation, 955 F.Supp.2d 1311.

S.D.Fla. 2012. Environmental products company did not owe duty of care to ground worker for vegetation management company in design or manufacturing of wood chipper that severed substantial portion of worker's hand, as required to support worker's claims for negligence, breach of warranty, and strict products liability under Florida law, where products company did not design, manufacture, or distribute subject wood chipper, and products company was distinct legal entity from wood chipper manufacturer.

> Hernandez v. Altec Environmental Products, LLC, 903 F.Supp.2d 1350, reconsideration denied 2013 WL 836870, appeal denied 2013 WL 3448212.

S.D.Fla. 1981. Abrogation of the privity requirement by the Florida Uniform Commercial Code did not apply, and injured workman's claim against manufacturer for breach of implied warranty was barred for lack of privity, where underlying transaction occurred prior to effective date of Code. West's F.S.A. §§ 672.318, 680.101(2).

> Ellison v. Northwest Engineering Co., 521 F.Supp. 199.

Bkrtcy.M.D.Fla. 1986. Under Florida uniform commercial code, fact that manufacturer of portable rock crusher was not actual seller of machine did not preclude buyer from establishing express warranty by manufacturer if, in fact, express warranty arose by virtue of means described in code. West's F.S.A. § 672.313.

> Matter of Bob Rigby, Inc., 62 B.R. 900.

Fla.App. 3 Dist. 1988. Contract action for breach of implied warranty did not lie against escalator manufacturer where there was no privity of contract between manufacturer of escalator and four-year-old child whose hand was lacerated by escalator.

> Westinghouse Corp. v. Ruiz, 537 So.2d 596.

Fla.App. 3 Dist. 1958. Purchaser of cable from a wholesale dealer for burial in the ground and transmission of high voltage current was entitled to sue the manufacturer of electrical cable for breach of implied warranty as against claim that privity of contract was necessary.

> Continental Copper & Steel Industries, Inc. v. E. C. 'Red' Cornelius, Inc., 104 So.2d 40.

Fla.App. 5 Dist. 1994. Manufacturer of floor paint could not be held liable to general contractor for breach of express warranties, breach of implied warranties of merchantability, or breach of implied warranties of fitness, where there was no sale from manufacturer to contractor, no privity between them, no contract between them, no reliance by contractor on any warranty, and no warranty was given to contractor.

> Spolski General Contractor, Inc. v. Jett-Aire Corp. Aviation Management of Cent. Florida, Inc., 637 So.2d 968.

🗝**1816(2). Motor vehicles.**

M.D.Fla. 2009. Generally, under Florida law, when a vehicle is purchased directly from a dealer, as opposed to the manufacturer, no privity exists between the two for purposes of warranty.

> Brisson v. Ford Motor Co., 602 F.Supp.2d 1227, affirmed in part, vacated in part, remanded 349 Fed. Appx. 433.

S.D.Fla. 2016. Consumer lacked privity with vehicle manufacturer, and thus could not maintain claim for breach of implied warranty under Florida law and, as a result, a claim under the Magnuson Moss Warranty Act (MMWA), where manufacturer was an automotive distributor, not a dealer, such that consumer could not have purchased his vehicle from manufacturer. Magnuson-Moss Warranty—Federal Trade Commission Improvement Act, § 101 et seq., 15 U.S.C.A. § 2301 et seq.

> In re Takata Airbag Products Liability Litigation, 193 F.Supp.3d 1324.

S.D.Fla. 2009. Lack of privity between motorcycle buyer and motorcycle manufacturer precluded buyers' claim for breach of implied warranty under Florida law and federal Magnuson-Moss Warranty Act (MMWA); implied warranty under MMWA referred to implied warranty arising under state law, and Florida law required privity for claim for breach of implied warranty. Magnuson-Moss Warranty-Federal Trade Commission Improvement Act, § 101 et seq., 15 U.S.C.A. § 2301 et seq.

> David v. American Suzuki Motor Corp., 629 F.Supp.2d 1309.

Fla. 1967. Neither absence of privity between automobile manufacturer and purchaser, nor the execution of written warranty agreement between manufacturer and its dealer disclaiming any implied warranty of merchantability or fitness or any other obligation except as assumed by manufacturer operated to preclude recovery by purchaser from manufacturer on basis of implied warranty due to automobile's alleged defects and lack of fitness and suitability.

> Manheim v. Ford Motor Co., 201 So.2d 440, opinion conformed to 201 So.2d 909.

Fla.App. 1 Dist. 1992. Dealer agreement which obligated automobile dealer to make text of manufacturer's warranties part of its contracts for sale of authorized products and comply with provisions of manufacturer's dealer warranty manual did not make dealer a cowarrantor by adoption along with manufacturer where retail buyer's order and installment contract signed by buyer contained no language from which it could be inferred that dealer intended to incorporate by reference provisions of manufacturer's warranty and there was no indication that buyer was made aware of provisions of dealer agreement.

> Frank Griffin Volkswagen, Inc. v. Smith, 610 So.2d 597, review denied 620 So.2d 762, appeal after remand 645 So.2d 585, cause dismissed Volkswagen of America, Inc. v. Smith, 654 So.2d 132, rehearing denied, appeal after remand 690 So.2d 1328, rehearing denied.

Fla.App. 1 Dist. 1981. Individual who guaranteed note given by one person to purchase truck was not a seller of that truck when the purchaser subsequently sold it to a third party and thus was not liable for any breach of implied warranty of title. West's F.S.A. § 672.312.

> Lawson v. Turner, 404 So.2d 424.

Individual who had purchased dump truck and another person to whom he gave the truck for use were both sellers of the truck to a third person where that third person paid the user for the equity in the truck and assumed the payments and both were thus liable for breach of warranty of title. West's F.S.A. § 672.312.

> Lawson v. Turner, 404 So.2d 424.

Fla.App. 1 Dist. 1963. Complaint of automobile buyer against dealer for breach of implied warranty of fitness of automobile was inherently defective since dealer could not be held liable for alleged breach of implied warranty of fitness resulting from defects in manufacture, and final judgment of dismissal of complaint for failure to state a cause of action operated as an adjudication on merits and action was properly dismissed with prejudice. 30 F.S.A. Rules of Civil Procedure, rule 1.35(b).

> Hardee v. Gordon Thompson Chevrolet, Inc., 154 So.2d 174.

Fla.App. 2 Dist. 2005. Absence of privity of contract between lessee of new automobile and manufacturer of automobile precluded lessee from maintaining action against manufacturer for breach of implied warranty under Magnuson-Moss Act. Magnuson-Moss Warranty—Federal Trade Commission Improvement Act, § 101 et seq., 15 U.S.C.A. § 2301 et seq.

> Cerasani v. American Honda Motor Co., 916 So.2d 843, review granted 925 So.2d 1029.

Fla.App. 2 Dist. 1972. Purchaser of new automobile is not prohibited from asserting breach of implied warranty of merchantability and fitness against a manufacturer notwithstanding want of privity.

> Rehurek v. Chrysler Credit Corp., 262 So.2d 452, 54 A.L.R.3d 1210, certiorari denied 267 So.2d 833.

Automobile manufacturer, not being the "seller" to the ultimate consumer, may not disclaim warranties of merchantability and fitness. F.S.A. §§ 672.316, 672.316(2).

> Rehurek v. Chrysler Credit Corp., 262 So.2d 452, 54 A.L.R.3d 1210, certiorari denied 267 So.2d 833.

Fla.App. 4 Dist. 2006. Privity between buyers of used car and car manufacturer was not required for buyers to state claim for breach of express warranty under federal Magnuson–Moss Warranty

Act (MMWA). Magnuson–Moss Warranty–Federal Trade Commission Improvement Act, § 101(6), 15 U.S.C.A. § 2301(6).

> Rentas v. DaimlerChrysler Corp., 936 So.2d 747.

Lack of privity between buyers of used car and car manufacturer precluded buyers' claim for breach of implied warranty under federal Magnuson–Moss Warranty Act (MMWA); implied warranty under MMWA referred to implied warranty arising under state law, and Florida law required privity for claim for breach of implied warranty. Magnuson–Moss Warranty–Federal Trade Commission Improvement Act, § 101(7), 15 U.S.C.A. § 2301(7).

> Rentas v. DaimlerChrysler Corp., 936 So.2d 747.

🗝1817–1819. *For other cases see earlier editions of this digest, the Decennial Digests, and WESTLAW.*

🗝1819. **Buyer and parties related thereto; horizontal privity.**

🗝1820. —— **In general.**

N.D.Fla. 1961. One who was not purchaser of tire was not entitled to any warranties to which purchaser might have been entitled.

> Odum v. Gulf Tire & Supply Co., 196 F.Supp. 35.

Fla. 1961. Subject to limited exceptions retailer is liable only to his customer for strict and absolute liability implicit in warranty of fitness.

> Carter v. Hector Supply Co., 128 So.2d 390.

Fla.App. 2 Dist. 1990. Corporation could not recover warranty damages in connection with sale of computer system to individual buyer in absence of privity between corporation and seller.

> Intergraph Corp. v. Stearman, 555 So.2d 1282.

Fla.App. 2 Dist. 1971. Although lessors had purchased dining room table from defendant, plaintiff husband and wife, as lessees of residence containing table, surface of which became detached from foundation and fell upon wife, causing her injury, were not "third-party beneficiaries" within statute extending seller's warranty, whether express or implied, to third-party beneficiaries; thus, privity requirement which would otherwise be encountered in common-law actions on implied warranties was not circumvented, and cause of action brought under statute was properly dismissed for lack of privity. F.S.A. § 672.318.

> Barry v. Ivarson Inc., 249 So.2d 44.

Fla.App. 3 Dist. 1967. Clients could not recover for alleged breach of implied warranty of fitness of book purchased by their attorneys and not used by clients.

> Engel v. Lawyers Co-op. Pub. Co., 198 So.2d 93, certiorari denied 201 So.2d 894.

Fla.App. 3 Dist. 1963. Liability of manufacturer on implied warranty of fitness does not extend to one who merely rents or bails to another personalty purchased from manufacturer.

> Brookshire v. Florida Bendix Co., 153 So.2d 55, certiorari dismissed 163 So.2d 881.

🗝1821. —— **Users and consumers.**

C.A.5 (Fla.) 1965. Under Florida law, manufacturer, as distinguished from retailer of product, may be held liable to person injured by product for breach of implied warranty that product manufactured is reasonably fit for purposes intended without regard to whether injured person is in privity of contract, if injured person is one of those reasonably intended to use product, and if at time of injury the product was being used generally in manner intended. F.S.A. § 25.031.

> Vandercook & Son, Inc. v. Thorpe, 344 F.2d 930, appeal after remand 395 F.2d 104.

Fla.App. 2 Dist. 2005. Definition of "consumer" under Magnuson-Moss Warranty Act (MMWA) as any person to whom product was transferred during warranty's duration, or any person who was entitled by terms of warranty to enforce warranty, is not limited only to buyers and MMWA does not require sale to ultimate consumer. Magnuson–Moss Warranty—Federal Trade Commission Improvement Act, § 101(3), 15 U.S.C.A. § 2301(3).

> O'Connor v. BMW of North America, LLC, 905 So.2d 235.

Lessee of new car qualified as "consumer" under second prong of Magnuson-Moss Warranty Act (MMWA), which defined "consumer" as any person to whom product was transferred during warranty's duration, and thus lessee could bring breach of warranty action under MMWA against car manufacturer; car was in service and warranty had begun when vehicle was transferred to lessee, and written warranty was made in connection with sale of car by automobile dealer to leasing company that leased car to lessee. Magnuson-Moss Warranty—Federal Trade Commission Improvement Act, § 101(3), 15 U.S.C.A. § 2301(3).

> O'Connor v. BMW of North America, LLC, 905 So.2d 235.

Lessee of new car qualified as "consumer" under third prong of Magnuson-Moss Warranty Act (MMWA) that defined "consumer" as any person who was entitled by terms of warranty to enforce warranty, and thus lessee could bring breach of warranty action under MMWA against car manufacturer; repair and service records of car showed that lessee had enforced terms of warranty. Magnuson-Moss Warranty—Federal Trade Commission Improvement Act, § 101(3), 15 U.S.C.A. § 2301(3).

> O'Connor v. BMW of North America, LLC, 905 So.2d 235.

Fla.App. 3 Dist. 1972. Even if woman's obtaining of wrinkle cream as a result of purchasing a certain amount of manufacturer's cosmetics was not a sale, warranty liability for injury caused to woman by use of cream could be imposed on cosmetic manufacturer; warranty liability is not limited to a sales contract or to direct parties. F.S.A. §§ 671.201(11), (44)(d), 672.106(1), 672.304, 672.313, 672.314.

> Sheppard v. Revlon, Inc., 267 So.2d 662.

Fla.App. 4 Dist. 1975. Privity is not required in action by foreseeable user of product against manufacturer charging breach of implied warranty.

> Favors v. Firestone Tire & Rubber Co., 309 So.2d 69, appeal after remand Sansing v. Firestone Tire & Rubber Co., 354 So.2d 895, certiorari denied 360 So.2d 1250.

Sales warranty provisions of Uniform Commercial Code do not govern rights and duties between user of goods and remote manufacturer with whom user has no privity of contract. West's F.S.A. §§ 672.314, 672.318.

> Favors v. Firestone Tire & Rubber Co., 309 So.2d 69, appeal after remand Sansing v. Firestone Tire & Rubber Co., 354 So.2d 895, certiorari denied 360 So.2d 1250.

⚷1822. —— **Family, household, and guests.**

Fla. 1962. Minor for whom father bought playground equipment upon which minor was injured was naturally intended and reasonably contemplated beneficiary of warranty of fitness for use or merchantability implied by law, and stood in shoes of purchaser in enforcing warranty.

> McBurnette v. Playground Equipment Corp., 137 So.2d 563, on remand 138 So.2d 372.

Fla.App. 3 Dist. 1963. Wives and representatives of passengers killed as the result of crash of a commercial aircraft assembled by defendant could maintain a cause of action against defendant for breach of implied warranty that the equipment was of merchantable quality and reasonably fit for the use intended, based on allegations that an engine used on the aircraft, although manufactured by a codefendant, was defective, and facts that the engine had been transferred from another aircraft and had been safely used for 3,000 hours did not foreclose liability but were for jury consideration.

> King v. Douglas Aircraft Co., 159 So.2d 108.

⚷1823. —— **Employees.**

S.D.Fla. 1993. Employee of company hired by purchaser of fire extinguisher to replace it could not maintain action against manufacturer of extinguisher for breach of implied warranty for injuries which occurred during dismantling of extinguisher. West's F.S.A. § 672.314.

> Boscarino v. Convenience Marine Products, Inc., 817 F.Supp. 116.

Fla. 1961. Injured employee of purchaser of riding sulky, not an inherently dangerous instrumentality, could not impose liability upon retailer for breach of implied warranty of fitness because of lack of privity.

> Carter v. Hector Supply Co., 128 So.2d 390.

Fla.App. 2 Dist. 1969. Service station attendant, who was called by purchaser of used truck to change inside rear tandem wheel and tire and who was injured when wheel and tire suddenly and without warning flew against him allegedly as result of a bent or defective rim and snap or lock rim, could not recover from seller, with whom attendant was not in privity of contract and who had impliedly warranted to purchaser that truck was fit and in condition for purpose intended, for breach of warranty.

> Brown v. Hall, 221 So.2d 454.

Fla.App. 2 Dist. 1967. Oil company's employees who were using lightweight oil discharge hose, which had been purchased by oil company, in the manner intended when gasoline escaped from eight-inch slit in the hose and fumes therefrom exploded were entitled to bring suit in implied warranty against manufacturer for their injuries though no privity of contract existed.

> Barfield v. Atlantic Coast Line R. Co., 197 So.2d 545.

⚷**1824. —— Remote or subsequent purchasers.**

† **C.A.11 (Fla.) 2013.** Second owner of yacht could not enforce manufacturer's express ten-year warranty, under Florida law, since agreement between manufacturer and dealer did not extend coverage to the first retail purchaser, dealer did not assign its rights to the ten-year warranty under the agreement, and second owner was at most an incidental beneficiary of the agreement. West's F.S.A. § 672.313(1)(a).

> Marlborough Holdings Group, Ltd. v. Azimut-Benetti, Spa, Platinum Yacht Collection No. Two, Inc., 505 Fed.Appx. 899, certiorari denied 134 S.Ct. 152, 187 L.Ed.2d 39.

C.A.5 (Fla.) 1965. Under Florida law, a manufacturer's limitation of liability clause is valid and enforceable against the ultimate consumer.

> American Can Co. v. Horlamus Corp., 341 F.2d 730.

S.D.Fla. 2014. Allegation that purchaser of allegedly defective automobile, rather than dealer that sold automobile to purchaser, was intended consumer of manufacturer's automobile, alleged that purchaser was third-party beneficiary of contract between dealer and manufacturer, as required to state claim for breach of implied warranty against manufacturer, despite lack of vertical privity between purchaser and manufacturer, under Florida law. West's F.S.A. § 672.313.

> Sanchez-Knutson v. Ford Motor Co., 52 F.Supp.3d 1223.

Fla.App. 4 Dist. 2005. Buyers of allegedly defective new automobile could assert claims against manufacturer for breach of express warranty and violation of Magnuson-Moss Warranty Act, even if buyers were not in contractual privity with manufacturer; warranty expressly applied to original retail purchaser and all subsequent owners within the warranty period. Magnuson–Moss Warranty—Federal Trade Commission Improvement Act, § 101 et seq., 15 U.S.C.A. § 2301 et seq.

> Fischetti v. American Isuzu Motors, Inc., 918 So.2d 974, rehearing denied.

⚷**1825–1826.** *For other cases see earlier editions of this digest, the Decennial Digests, and WESTLAW.*

⚷**1825. Other parties.**

⚷**1827. —— Bystanders.**

C.A.5 (Fla.) 1977. Under Florida law, strict liability, but not implied warranty, lies in bystanders' actions and want of ordinary due care, in its comparative negligence form, is a defense to both, except for the sort consisting of failure to discover a defect in the article or guard against the possibility of its existence.

> West v. Caterpillar Tractor Co., Inc., 547 F.2d 885.

Fla.App. 3 Dist. 1962. Plaintiff who was injured when recently purchased rubber disc disintegrated into three parts, one of which flew into his eye, could not recover on implied warranty from retailer who had sold the disc to another, where plaintiff was not using the disc at the time of injury, but was a mere bystander.

> Rodriguez v. Shell's City, Inc., 141 So.2d 590, certiorari denied 148 So.2d 279.

⚷1828–1830. *For other cases see earlier editions of this digest, the Decennial Digests, and WESTLAW.*

⚷1829. **Nature of injury, damage, or loss.**

⚷1831. —— **Personal injuries.**

C.A.5 (Fla.) 1968. Under Florida law, manufacturer may be held liable for breach of implied warranty that product or machine manufactured is reasonably fit for purposes intended without regard to whether the plaintiff is in privity of contract, and it is enough that injured person be one of those reasonably intended to use product or machine and that when injury occurred product or machine was being used generally in manner intended.

> Vandercook & Son, Inc. v. Thorpe, 395 F.2d 104.

M.D.Fla. 2009. Manufacturer of citronella candle for warding off insects was not liable to consumer under Florida law for breach of implied warranty of merchantability of goods, relating to consumer being burned when she used water in an attempt to extinguish the candle's flame, in absence of evidence of privity between manufacturer and consumer.

> Cooper v. Old Williamsburg Candle Corp., 653 F.Supp.2d 1220.

Fla.App. 3 Dist. 1965. Manufacturer will be held liable in implied warranty without privity to consumer injured by defective product manufactured for human consumption or other intimate bodily use.

> Bernstein v. Lily-Tulip Cup Corp., 177 So.2d 362, certiorari discharged 181 So.2d 641.

⚷1832. —— **Property damage.**

For other cases see earlier editions of this digest, the Decennial Digests, and WESTLAW.

⚷1833. —— **Economic loss.**

S.D.Fla. 2011. Under Florida law, a plaintiff cannot recover economic losses for breach of implied warranty in the absence of privity.

> Jovine v. Abbott Laboratories, Inc., 795 F.Supp.2d 1331.

S.D.Fla. 2009. Barring certain exceptions, under Florida law, a plaintiff cannot recover economic losses for breach of implied warranty in the absence of privity.

> Smith v. Wm. Wrigley Jr. Co., 663 F.Supp.2d 1336.

Fla.App. 2 Dist. 2005. Plaintiff cannot recover economic losses for breach of implied warranty in absence of privity.

> Cerasani v. American Honda Motor Co., 916 So.2d 843, review granted 925 So.2d 1029.

Fla.App. 3 Dist. 1984. Roofing contractor had no breach-of-warranty cause of action against manufacturer of defective roofing, even though contractor had been sued by reason of the defective roofing and judgments had been rendered against it, absent contractual privity between contractor and manufacturer; contractor's sole remedy, if any, for economic losses sustained would be action for breach of implied warranty of merchantability or related breach of contract action against party which sold the defective roofing materials. West's F.S.A. § 672.314.

> GAF Corp. v. Zack Co., 445 So.2d 350, petition for review denied 453 So.2d 45.

⚷1834–1835. *For other cases see earlier editions of this digest, the Decennial Digests, and WESTLAW.*

⚷1834. **Nature of good or product.**

⚷1836. —— **Dangerous instrumentalities in general.**

S.D.Fla. 1987. Under Florida law, painter's allegation, that manufacturer sold paint containing asbestos to his employer, with knowledge that others like plaintiff would use product, was sufficient to meet privity requirement for implied warranty of merchantability under state commercial code. West's F.S.A. §§ 672.314, 672.318.

> Carlson v. Armstrong World Industries, Inc., 693 F.Supp. 1073.

S.D.Fla. 1987. Under Florida law, asbestos plaintiff's suit for breach of implied warranty against asbestos manufacturers was not barred by lack of privity of contract.

> In re Asbestos Litigation, 679 F.Supp. 1096, reconsideration denied 679 F.Supp. 1094.

Fla. 1966. Privity of contract is not required to support action by consumer against manufacturer for breach of implied warranty of product that is neither dangerous instrumentality nor foodstuff.

> Lily-Tulip Cup Corp. v. Bernstein, 181 So.2d 641.

Fla.App. 2 Dist. 1975. One need not be in privity with the retailer in order to have an action against him for breach of an implied warranty if the plaintiff can prove that the product in question is inherently dangerous.

> Dudley v. Mae's Discount Fabrics, 323 So.2d 279.

Fla.App. 2 Dist. 1969. Supplier and transporter of chlorine gas were not liable to officer, who inhaled gas while removing tank from under water on theory of breach of implied warranty, where officer did not rely on implied warranty and officer was aware of dangerous condition of chlorine containers.

> Adair v. The Island Club, 225 So.2d 541.

Gas mask is not "inherently dangerous commodity" within rule that one who is not in privity with retailer has no action against him for breach of implied warranty, except in situations involving foodstuffs or dangerous instrumentalities.

> Adair v. The Island Club, 225 So.2d 541.

Officer allegedly injured by reason of defective gas mask, not an inherently dangerous commodity, could not maintain action against owner and supplier of mask for breach of implied warranty.

> Adair v. The Island Club, 225 So.2d 541.

Fla.App. 2 Dist. 1969. For purpose of determining whether one not in privity of contract with seller is entitled to recover for seller's alleged breach of warranty of fitness for particular purpose, an automobile is a dangerous instrumentality only while it is being operated on public ways.

> Brown v. Hall, 221 So.2d 454.

☞1837. —— **Food and beverages.**

S.D.Fla. 2014. Privity of contract between consumers and manufacturers of cereal and snack foods was not required for consumers' claim for breach of express warranty under Florida law against manufacturers. West's F.S.A. § 672.313(1)(a).

> Garcia v. Kashi Co., 43 F.Supp.3d 1359.

Fla. 1966. Privity of contract is not required to support action by consumer against manufacturer for breach of implied warranty of product that is neither dangerous instrumentality nor foodstuff.

> Lily-Tulip Cup Corp. v. Bernstein, 181 So.2d 641.

Fla. 1965. Both retail seller and manufacturer of food stuff sold in sealed container are liable to consumer, upon implied warranty of fitness and wholesomeness, for injuries caused by unwholesome or deleterious substances therein.

> Foley v. Weaver Drugs, Inc., 177 So.2d 221.

Fla. 1953. Person who purchases items of food or other products in original package, which items are offered for sale for human consumption or use, generally purchases such items in reliance upon express or implied condition that they are wholesome and fit for uses or purposes for which they are advertised or sold, and person who is injured as result of unwholesome or deleterious substances therein which are unknown to buyer, may hold either manufacturer or retailer liable regardless of privity of contract.

> Hoskins v. Jackson Grain Co., 63 So.2d 514.

Fla. 1953. An ultimate consumer who purchased a bottle of soft beverage from a retailer and who was allegedly injured by swallowing of broken glass contained therein, could maintain an action directly against the bottler upon the theory of implied warranty.

> Florida Coca-Cola Bottling Co. v. Jordan, 62 So.2d 910.

Fla.App. 2 Dist. 1967. Professional food caterer who was member of church and assisted in preparation of food served at church fund-raising dinner was not liable, on theory of breach of warranty of fitness, to those who suffered food poisoning where there was no contract between caterer and plaintiffs and at no time was caterer acting as vendor.

Wentzel v. Berliner, 204 So.2d 905, certiorari denied 212 So.2d 871.

There need be no contractual privity between plaintiff and defendant in a suit based upon breach of implied warranty of fitness of foodstuffs, but before the doctrine of implied warranty of fitness is applicable there must be something more than mere voluntary activity on the part of the defendant.

Wentzel v. Berliner, 204 So.2d 905, certiorari denied 212 So.2d 871.

Fla.App. 2 Dist. 1964. As to items of food in original package, there is implied warranty of fitness for use and purposes for which they are offered for sale and sold and one injured as result of injurious substances which are unknown to him may hold either manufacturer or retailer liable for breach of implied warranty.

Wagner v. Mars, Inc., 166 So.2d 673.

Fla.App. 2 Dist. 1960. Although "multi-trip" beverage bottle had been damaged before buyer purchased it and bottle broke and injured buyer as she attempted to open it, implied warranty of fitness of bottle existed as to both the retailer and the bottler.

Canada Dry Bottling Co. of Fla. v. Shaw, 118 So.2d 840.

⋘1838–1839. *For other cases see earlier editions of this digest, the Decennial Digests, and WESTLAW.*

⋘1839. —— **Drugs and medical devices.**

⋘1839(1). **In general.**

M.D.Fla. 2013. Under Florida law, patient lacked privity with medical device manufacturer, and thus could not assert claim against manufacturer for breach of express warranty, where device was available to patient only through prescription use from licensed physician or healthcare provider, and patient did not allege that he purchased device directly from manufacturer.

Kaiser v. Depuy Spine, Inc., 944 F.Supp.2d 1187.

M.D.Fla. 2010. Under Florida products liability law, pharmaceutical corporations that manufactured name-brand drug metoclopramide could not be held liable for breach of warranty to plaintiff who allegedly developed drug-induced neurological movement disorder as a result of his ingestion of generic metoclopramide, since the generic metoclopramide ingested by the plaintiff was not manufactured by the corporations.

Levine v. Wyeth Inc., 684 F.Supp.2d 1338.

M.D.Fla. 1992. Under Florida law, absence of privity between user of contraceptive sponge and manufacturer necessitated dismissal of implied warranty claims pled in conjunction with strict product liability claims.

Mitchell v. VLI Corp., 786 F.Supp. 966, also published at 1992 WL 12501030.

N.D.Fla. 2009. Plaintiff who alleged that after taking drug prescribed for the treatment of epilepsy and seizure disorders, he developed a rash and was ultimately diagnosed with Stevens–Johnson Syndrome and/or toxic epidermal necrolysis, failed to state a claim against drug manufacturer upon which relief could be granted under Florida law for breach of express or implied warranties, since the complaint did not allege privity of contract.

Fields v. Mylan Pharmaceuticals, Inc., 751 F.Supp.2d 1257.

N.D.Fla. 1998. Under Florida law, patient in whom pedicle bone screws were implanted at hospital after being sold to hospital by manufacturer was not in privity with manufacturer, as required to assert claim against manufacturer for breach of implied warranty.

Baker v. Danek Medical, 35 F.Supp.2d 875.

Under Florida law, recipient of medical implant is not in privity with manufacturer, and thus may not sue manufacturer for breach of implied warranty, when im-

SALES ☞1854

plant is purchased by recipient's medical provider.

Baker v. Danek Medical, 35 F.Supp.2d 875.

S.D.Fla. 2008. Since professional corporation, rather than its principal, was buyer of permanent endosseous dental implant, corporation was in privity with seller, and thus had standing to assert claim against seller, under Florida law, for breach of implied warranty.

Cohen v. Implant Innovations, Inc., 259 F.R.D. 617.

Fla.App. 3 Dist. 1984. Privity existed between manufacturer of x-ray equipment and hospital which purchased such x-ray equipment from dealer, where manufacturer's sales representative allegedly called upon hospital, and made representations that such equipment was very advanced, high quality, and capable of handling hospital's high volume of work; thus, hospital could maintain action against manufacturer for breach of express warranty and implied warranty of fitness for particular purpose, despite fact that only damage hospital suffered was to x-ray equipment itself. West's F.S.A. §§ 672.313, 672.315, 672.714, 672.715.

Cedars of Lebanon Hosp. Corp. v. European X-Ray Distributors of America, Inc., 444 So.2d 1068.

☞1839(2). **Learned-intermediary doctrine.**

M.D.Fla. 2015. Florida's learned intermediary doctrine, which provides that prescription drug manufacturer's duty to warn of risks associated with drug is directed to physicians rather than patients, did not bar prescription drugs user's breach of express warranty claim against drug manufacturer and distributor, where user did not allege that defendants made affirmation or promise as to adequacy of drug's warnings.

Small v. Amgen, Inc., 134 F.Supp.3d 1358.

☞1840–1841. *For other cases see earlier editions of this digest, the Decennial Digests, and WESTLAW.*

☞1840. **Representations.**

☞1842. —— **Advertising, marketing, and labeling.**

Fla.App. 4 Dist. 1983. Adoption of written affirmation of fact, promise, or undertaking of another person or business in regard to consumer products may only render supplier of that product liable where affirmation, promise, or undertaking adopted is written warranty under Magnuson-Moss Warranty Act. Magnuson-Moss Warranty-Federal Trade Commission Improvement Act, § 110, 15 U.S.C.A. § 2310.

Motor Homes of America, Inc. v. O'Donnell, 440 So.2d 422, petition for review denied 451 So.2d 849.

☞1843. **Assignment or other transfer of warranty.**

Fla.App. 5 Dist. 1988. For implied warranty purposes, owner of building on which allegedly defective stucco was applied was in privity with supplier of stucco through written assignment from subcontractor, which applied stucco purchased from supplier, to building owner.

Ashley Square, Ltd. v. Contractors Supply of Orlando, Inc., 532 So.2d 710.

(G) NOTICE AND OPPORTUNITY TO CURE.

☞1851–1852. *For other cases see earlier editions of this digest, the Decennial Digests, and WESTLAW.*

☞1852. **Necessity and effect.**

☞1853. —— **In general.**

M.D.Fla. 2015. For purposes of claims for breach of the implied warranty of merchantability and the implied warranty of fitness for a particular purpose under Florida's Uniform Commercial Code (UCC), the buyer must provide notice to the seller of the breach of warranty. Fla. Stat. Ann. §§ 672.314(1), 672.315.

Armadillo Distribution Enterprises, Inc. v. Hai Yun Musical Instruments Manufacture Co. Ltd., 142 F.Supp.3d 1245.

☞1854. —— **Notice as condition precedent.**

C.A.5 (Fla.) 1976. Provision of Uniform Commercial Code to effect that where tender has been accepted by buyer, buyer must notify seller within reasonable time after he discovers breach or be barred from any remedy, is applicable to delivery delays as well as other breaches; trial court therefore erred in not applying such section to delivery delays at issue in airline's action against aircraft manufacturer for alleged delays in delivery of jet airplanes. West's Ann.Cal.Com.Code, §§ 2607, 2607(3)(a).

> Eastern Air Lines, Inc. v. McDonnell Douglas Corp., 532 F.2d 957.

Buyer's good faith is governing criterion under section of Uniform Commercial Code requiring buyer to give notice to seller of any breach of contract asserted after acceptance of tender by buyer; even though adequate notice may have been given at one point in transaction, subsequent actions by buyer may have dissipated its effect and buyer's conduct, then, taken as whole, must constitute timely notification that transaction is claimed to involve breach. West's Ann.Cal.Com. Code, §§ 1201(26), 2607.

> Eastern Air Lines, Inc. v. McDonnell Douglas Corp., 532 F.2d 957.

Bkrtcy.M.D.Fla. 1986. Even if implied warranty of fitness for a particular purpose had arisen as to portable rock crushing machine, buyer was barred from any remedy for that breach under Florida law on basis of its failure to notify manufacturer within a reasonable time of its claim of breach on ground that machinery did not conform with specifications for use provided to manufacturer. West's F.S.A. §§ 672.607(2), 672.315.

> Matter of Bob Rigby, Inc., 62 B.R. 900.

Fla.App. 2 Dist. 1980. Although finding of state department of agriculture that canned grapefruit sections should not be sold for human consumption was entitled to great weight, finding was not conclusive and distributor of the goods was entitled to opportunity to verify it; thus food broker's failure to notify distributor of breach before destruction of goods by retailer barred broker from any remedy against distributor for the breach. West's F.S.A. § 672.607(3)(a).

> General Matters, Inc. v. Paramount Canning Co., 382 So.2d 1262.

⚓1855. —— **Parties entitled to notice.**

S.D.Fla. 1987. Under Florida law, Uniform Commercial Code notice require-

ment to manufacturers of defective product did not bar products liability suit for asbestos-related injuries, where plaintiff was merely warranty beneficiary rather than buyer. West's F.S.A. § 672.607(3)(a).

> In re Asbestos Litigation, 679 F.Supp. 1096, reconsideration denied 679 F.Supp. 1094.

⚓1856–1857. *For other cases see earlier editions of this digest, the Decennial Digests, and WESTLAW.*

⚓1857. **Time for giving notice.**

⚓1858. —— **In general.**

C.A.11 (Fla.) 1983. Under Florida law, buyer's notice of breach of warranty must be both timely and sufficient under the circumstances and is governed by buyer's obligation to act in good faith. West's F.S.A. §§ 671.203, 672.103, 672.607.

> Royal Typewriter Co., a Div. of Litton Business Systems, Inc. v. Xerographic Supplies Corp., 719 F.2d 1092.

Fla. 1983. By failing to file complaint with Florida Department of Agriculture within ten days after defect in seed became apparent, farmer was barred from maintaining legal action for damages against seller based on theories of negligence or breach of warranty. West's F.S.A. §§ 578.09, 578.26, 578.26(1).

> Ferry-Morse Seed Co. v. Hitchcock, 426 So.2d 958.

Seller's actual knowledge of defects in seed not acquired within ten days of discovery of defect by farmer did not estop seller from raising farmer's failure to file complaint with Florida Department of Agriculture as defense to farmer's action against seller for negligence and breach of warranty. West's F.S.A. §§ 578.09, 578.26, 578.26(1).

> Ferry-Morse Seed Co. v. Hitchcock, 426 So.2d 958.

Fla.App. 2 Dist. 1976. Pursuant to contract wherein materialman guaranteed workmanship and material on any defective item provided claims were made within one year from date of shipment, the parties thereby determined length of time within which buyer, principal on surety bond, would have to notify materialman of breach, and since buyer made its claims against materialman well within one-year period, claim was timely made and trial court should have considered question of whether pipe was defective. West's F.S.A. §§ 672.105, 672.606(1)(b), 672.608, 672.714.

　　U.S. Fidelity & Guaranty Co. v. North Am. Steel Corp., 335 So.2d 18.

Fla.App. 3 Dist. 1991. Buyer of stevedoring equipment, who was aware of defective wiring in engine but continued to use equipment without giving seller notice of claim that express warranty had been breached until after wiring had caused explosion in engine, failed to give seller timely notice of breach, thereby barring recovery. West's F.S.A. § 672.607(3)(a).

　　Hapag-Lloyd, A.G. v. Marine Indem. Ins. Co. of America, 576 So.2d 1330.

🗝**1859. —— Reasonable time.**

S.D.Fla. 2013. Under California law, in order to prevail on a breach of express warranty, plaintiff must allege that notice of alleged breach was provided to the seller within a reasonable time after discovery of the breach.

　　In re Horizon Organic Milk Plus DHA Omega-3 Marketing and Sales Practice Litigation, 955 F.Supp.2d 1311.

S.D.Fla. 1987. Under Florida law, painter, who was a warranty beneficiary, not a buyer of paint manufacturer's products, was not required to give notice of alleged breach of implied warranty of merchantability leading to suit within reasonable time. West's F.S.A. §§ 672.607(3)(a), 672.318.

　　Carlson v. Armstrong World Industries, Inc., 693 F.Supp. 1073.

Bkrtcy.M.D.Fla. 1981. Under Florida law, buyers of carpeting and draperies allegedly not of merchantable quality failed to notify seller within reasonable time where no complaint concerning quality was lodged until a year and one-half after purchase. West's F.S.A. § 672.607(3)(a).

　　Matter of Vincent, 10 B.R. 549.

Fla.App. 2 Dist. 1976. Following acceptance of tender, buyer is required to notify seller of breach within reasonable time after he discovers or should have

discovered it; however, whenever the Uniform Commercial Code requires action within "reasonable time," any time which is not manifestly unreasonable may be fixed by agreement. West's F.S.A. §§ 671.204, 672.607(3)(a).

　　U.S. Fidelity & Guaranty Co. v. North Am. Steel Corp., 335 So.2d 18.

🗝**1860–1861.** *For other cases see earlier editions of this digest, the Decennial Digests, and WESTLAW.*

🗝**1861. Mode and sufficiency of notice.**

🗝**1862. —— In general.**

C.A.11 (Fla.) 1983. Under Florida law, buyer's notice of breach of warranty must be both timely and sufficient under the circumstances and is governed by buyer's obligation to act in good faith. West's F.S.A. §§ 671.203, 672.103, 672.607.

　　Royal Typewriter Co., a Div. of Litton Business Systems, Inc. v. Xerographic Supplies Corp., 719 F.2d 1092.

C.A.5 (Fla.) 1976. Notice of breach of contract given by buyer after it accepts tender from seller need not be specific claim for damages or assertion of legal rights, but not every expression of discontent by buyer always satisfies requirement for such notice; thus, while buyer must inform seller that transaction is "still troublesome," notification must be such as to inform seller that transaction is claimed to involve breach, and thus open way for normal settlements through negotiation. West's Ann.Cal.Com.Code, § 2607.

　　Eastern Air Lines, Inc. v. McDonnell Douglas Corp., 532 F.2d 957.

Merchants will be held to higher standard than ordinary buyers in manner in which, after delivery is accepted, seller is informed that buyer asserts claim for breach of contract; unlike ordinary purchaser, merchant's good faith in serving such notice will be measured by reasonable commercial standards of fair dealing in trade. West's Ann.Cal.Com.Code, §§ 2103(1)(b), 2104, 2104(1), 2607.

　　Eastern Air Lines, Inc. v. McDonnell Douglas Corp., 532 F.2d 957.

S.D.Fla. 2013. Under California law, "notice" of breach of express warranty to a defendant, as required for plaintiff to prevail on claim, means pre-suit notice.

> In re Horizon Organic Milk Plus DHA Omega-3 Marketing and Sales Practice Litigation, 955 F.Supp.2d 1311.

Bkrtcy.M.D.Fla. 1986. Rejection letter sent by buyer of portable rock crushing machine to distributor almost one year after delivery of machine was not reasonable notice of breach, and thus, buyer never effectively revoked its acceptance of machine so that buyer could not recover from manufacturer for breach of express warranties, under Florida law. West's F.S.A. §§ 672.607, 672.607(2).

> Matter of Bob Rigby, Inc., 62 B.R. 900.

☞1863–1869. *For other cases see earlier editions of this digest, the Decennial Digests, and WESTLAW.*

(H) WAIVER OF BREACH.

☞1881. **In general.**

M.D.Fla. 2001. Under Florida law, buyer did not waive its right to sue seller for breach of warranty as to structural and financial condition of radio station assets buyer sought to purchase, despite buyer's learning of seller's breach after entering asset purchase agreement but prior to closing, where asset purchase agreement contained non-waiver clause, which provided that neither buyer nor seller could waive any covenant or provision without written consent, and warranty survival clause, which provided that all warranties and representations in agreement remained operative and survived in full force for one year.

> Southern Broadcast Group, LLC v. Gem Broadcasting, Inc., 145 F.Supp.2d 1316, affirmed 49 Fed. Appx. 288.

☞1882. **Acceptance, use, or failure to return or object.**

Bkrtcy.M.D.Fla. 1986. Buyer of portable rock crushing machine, which was offered option either to refuse to purchase machine, return machine and recover down payment and cancel entire transaction or proceed and complete transaction and purchase machine, and which elected to accept machine, could not recover on claim that machine did not perform as warranted by manufacturer, under Florida law. West's F.S.A. §§ 672.607, 672.607(2).

> Matter of Bob Rigby, Inc., 62 B.R. 900.

Fla.App. 2 Dist. 1976. Under Uniform Commercial Code, while failure to reject goods may affect amount of damages buyer can recover, it does not preclude him from making claim for breach of warranty. West's F.S.A. §§ 672.105, 672.606(1)(b), 672.608, 672.714.

> U.S. Fidelity & Guaranty Co. v. North Am. Steel Corp., 335 So.2d 18.

Contractual provision permitting buyer to have 30 days within which to inspect and reject delivery of materials could not be construed as terms foreclosing buyer's suit for breach of warranty upon acceptance of goods. West's F.S.A. §§ 672.105, 672.606(1)(b), 672.608, 672.714.

> U.S. Fidelity & Guaranty Co. v. North Am. Steel Corp., 335 So.2d 18.

Fla.App. 5 Dist. 1989. Under Uniform Commercial Code, failure to reject goods or revoke acceptance will affect buyer's remedies, but does not necessarily preclude him from making claim for breach of warranty.

> B.P. Development and Management Corp. v. P. Lafer Enterprises, Inc., 538 So.2d 1379.

Buyer was not precluded from claiming that delivered Christmas tree decorations were nonconforming by its failure to either reject or revoke acceptance of decorations, and thus entry of summary judgment on seller's breach of contract claim against company did not preclude company from asserting breach of warranty.

> B.P. Development and Management Corp. v. P. Lafer Enterprises, Inc., 538 So.2d 1379.

Fla.App. 5 Dist. 1987. While failure to properly reject goods may affect amount of damages buyer can recover, it does not preclude him from making claim for breach of warranty.

> Central Florida Antenna Service, Inc. v. Crabtree, 503 So.2d 1351.

† This Case was not selected for publication in the National Reporter System
For legislative history of cited statutes, see Florida Statutes Annotated

☞**1883. Retention induced by promise or assurance by seller.**

For other cases see earlier editions of this digest, the Decennial Digests, and WEST-LAW.

☞**1884. Failure or delay as to notice of defects.**

† **C.A.11 (Fla.) 2012.** Under Florida Uniform Commercial Code (FL-UCC), buyers of defective recreational vehicle failed to give written notice to manufacturer that vehicle was defective and that seller was unable to satisfactorily repair vehicle, as required under manufacturer's limited warranty, and thus, manufacturer never had opportunity to remedy defects, which was benefit of bargain that manufacturer had contracted for under warranty. West's F.S.A. § 672.607(3)(a).

Burns v. Winnebago Industries, Inc., 492 Fed.Appx. 44.

☞**1885–1886.** *For other cases see earlier editions of this digest, the Decennial Digests, and WESTLAW.*

☞**1887. Estoppel.**

Bkrtcy.M.D.Fla. 1993. Buyer of assets of wholesale distributor of frozen fruits and vegetables relied on seller's warranty that, since specified date, it had not received any written or oral notice of or citation for noncompliance with any law, and buyer was not estopped from enforcing breach of warranty, which was based on seller's failure to disclose adversary proceedings commenced by vendors in seller's Chapter 11 case, which were based on alleged violations of Perishable Agricultural Commodities Act (PACA), even though buyer's officers, who were former officers of seller, knew that vendors were not paid by seller and knew that they notified seller of their intention to preserve trust benefits pursuant to PACA; warranty was specifically limited to time after former officers left seller, and former officers did not know of adversary proceedings, which were filed after they left seller.

In re Finevest Foods, Inc., 159 B.R. 972.

X. REMEDIES.

Actions to obtain remedies, see XI.

(A) IN GENERAL.

☞**1901–1903.** *For other cases see earlier editions of this digest, the Decennial Digests, and WESTLAW.*

☞**1903. Buyer's remedies in general.**

☞**1904. —— In general.**

M.D.Fla. 1977. Where evidence disclosed that loss of portion of cargo of urea being shipped CIF by vessel was due to negligent spillage during loading, improper stowage, negligent failure to provide sweat battens, and negligent flooding of lower hold of vessel, all of which were covered by "all risk" policy procured by seller, buyer's recourse and remedy was against insurer, and seller was not liable to buyer.

Morrison Grain Co., Inc. v. Utica Mut. Ins. Co., 446 F.Supp. 415, affirmed in part, remanded in part 632 F.2d 424.

When goods are sold on CIF basis, if loss occurs, buyer's recourse is to make claim under insurance policy.

Morrison Grain Co., Inc. v. Utica Mut. Ins. Co., 446 F.Supp. 415, affirmed in part, remanded in part 632 F.2d 424.

☞**1905. —— Breach of warranty.**

C.A.11 (Fla.) 1989. Injured airplane passengers had no cause of action in implied warranty separate and distinct from strict liability action under Florida law.

Kramer v. Piper Aircraft Corp., 868 F.2d 1538.

M.D.Fla. 1982. Under Florida law, where breach of implied warranty action has been brought against a seller standing in relation of privity with consumer, provisions of Uniform Commercial Code are applied. West's F.S.A. § 672.314 et seq.

Taylor v. American Honda Motor Co., Inc., 555 F.Supp. 59.

S.D.Fla. 2008. Under Georgia law, absent personal injury or damage to property other than to allegedly defective product itself, action in negligence does not lie and any such cause of action may be brought only as contract warranty action.

Pycsa Panama, S.A. v. Tensar Earth Technologies, Inc., 625 F.Supp.2d 1198, affirmed 329 Fed.Appx. 257.

Fla. 1988. Injured airplane passengers had no cause of action against manufacturer in implied warranty separate and distinct from strict liability action. West's F.S.A. § 672.318.

Kramer v. Piper Aircraft Corp., 520 So.2d 37, answer to certified question conformed to 868 F.2d 1538.

Fla.App. 1 Dist. 2008. In Florida there are two parallel but independent bodies of products liability law: one, strict liability, is an action in tort; the other, implied warranty, is an action in contract.

Rose v. ADT Sec. Services, Inc., 989 So.2d 1244.

Fla.App. 2 Dist. 1979. A given set of facts can support alternative theories of recovery in a products liability case, in tort for negligence or strict liability and in contract for breach of implied warranty; there is nothing in conceptual foundation of crashworthiness doctrine which prevents these theories of recovery from being as available in a crashworthiness case as in any other products liability case.

Nicolodi v. Harley-Davidson Motor Co., Inc., 370 So.2d 68.

Fla.App. 2 Dist. 1968. An "implied warranty" action is one founded on a contract not in writing.

Creviston v. General Motors Corp., 210 So.2d 755, quashed 225 So.2d 331.

Fla.App. 3 Dist. 1988. Doctrine of strict liability in torts supplants all no-privity breach of implied warranty cases.

Westinghouse Corp. v. Ruiz, 537 So.2d 596.

Fla.App. 3 Dist. 1979. Under the Uniform Commercial Code, when nonconforming tender is delivered, it is the buyer's choice whether to reject the goods and cause a recission of the contract and bring suit for their purchase price or to accept the goods and receive as damages for breach of warranty the difference at the time and place of acceptance between the value of the goods accepted and the value they would have had if they had been as warranted. West's F.S.A. § 672.714.

Carter Hawley Hale Stores, Inc. v. Conley, 372 So.2d 965.

Fla.App. 5 Dist. 1989. Remedy for breach of implied warranty of fitness for particular purpose is recovery of money damages.

Storchwerke, GMBH v. Mr. Thiessen's Wallpapering Supplies, Inc., 538 So.2d 1382.

☞1906. —— Redhibitory defects or vices.

For other cases see earlier editions of this digest, the Decennial Digests, and WESTLAW.

(B) PARTICULAR REMEDIES OF SELLER.

1. STOPPING, WITHHOLDING, OR REFUSING DELIVERY.

☞1911–1916. *For other cases see earlier editions of this digest, the Decennial Digests, and WESTLAW.*

☞1915. Persons against whom right may be exercised.

☞1917. —— Subsequent purchasers.

Bkrtcy.M.D.Fla. 1992. Under Florida law, statutory right of seller to reclaim ice cream bars sold to Chapter 11 debtor was limited by existence of lien holder with preexisting, perfected floating lien on debtor's inventory; lien holder was good-faith purchaser with rights superior to those of reclaiming seller. West's F.S.A. § 672.702(2, 3); Bankr.Code, 11 U.S.C.A. § 546(c).

Matter of Sunstate Dairy & Food Products Co., 145 B.R. 341.

Lien holder with preexisting, perfected floating lien on inventory is good-faith purchaser with rights superior to those of reclaiming seller absent showing of bad faith. Bankr.Code, 11 U.S.C.A. § 546(c).

Matter of Sunstate Dairy & Food Products Co., 145 B.R. 341.

Under Florida law, existence of intervening good-faith purchaser did not extinguish seller of goods' right of reclamation against Chapter 11 debtor but merely made right subject to good-faith purchaser's perfected preexisting lien; seller was still entitled to reclaim ice cream bars but seller took ice cream bars subject to preexisting lien. West's F.S.A. § 672.702(3); U.C.C. § 2–702(3).

Matter of Sunstate Dairy & Food Products Co., 145 B.R. 341.

† This Case was not selected for publication in the National Reporter System
For legislative history of cited statutes, see Florida Statutes Annotated

🗝**1918–1921.** *For other cases see earlier editions of this digest, the Decennial Digests, and WESTLAW.*

2. LIEN OR SECURITY INTEREST OF SELLER.

Equitable liens, see LIENS 🗝7.

🗝**1931–1937.** *For other cases see earlier editions of this digest, the Decennial Digests, and WESTLAW.*

🗝**1938. Property or interest subject to lien.**

S.D.Fla. 1987. Citrus fruits and other citrus products were not "other material" under Florida statute, providing lien in favor of any person who furnished logs, timber, clay, sand, stone, or other material whatsoever, and thus supplier of citrus fruits had no lien in citrus fruits provided to fruit products manufacturer as a result of manufacturer's failure to pay full amount due under sales contract. West's F.S.A. § 713.62.

> Lloyd Citrus Trucking, Inc. v. Treesweet Products, Inc., 655 F.Supp. 385.

🗝**1939–1943.** *For other cases see earlier editions of this digest, the Decennial Digests, and WESTLAW.*

🗝**1944. Waiver, loss, or discharge.**

Fla. 1957. Seller of truck did not have a lien on it for purchase price, in view of fact that, upon entry of judgment in a replevin action brought by seller, the truck became seller's property, and even if any lien existed, it was extinguished by its merger with the title, and such judgment fixed the status both of the truck and money recoverable from seller by buyer, and such lien, if it had existed, could not be revived against money which seller was adjudicated to owe buyer.

> Luby Chevrolet Co. v. King, 98 So.2d 784.

Fla.App. 2 Dist. 1966. Evidence in suit by plaintiffs to assert lien on assets transferred by seller corporation to buyer corporation disclosed nothing which would show that plaintiffs had led buyer to believe that they would not assert rights to lien under sales contract or that buyer after taking possession of assets did anything more with respect thereto than it was obligated to do under contract or would have done normally.

> Blumin v. Ellis, 186 So.2d 286, certiorari denied 189 So.2d 634.

Fla.App. 3 Dist. 1960. Where defendants manufactured automatic die pursuant to written contract and delivered same to plaintiff who thereupon redelivered the die to defendants for corrections but defendants then refused to make corrections and stated they would hold die until contract price had been paid in full, assuming that defendants may originally have had a right to a lien for unpaid balance of purchase price, such lien rights as they may have had were lost upon first delivery of die to plaintiff and redelivery of die for express purpose of making alterations did not revive defendants' lien rights for unpaid balance of purchase price, but at most constituted a basis of lien for alterations made. F.S.A. § 85.12.

> Huckleberry v. Davis Double Seal Jalousies, Inc., 117 So.2d 519, certiorari denied 120 So.2d 616.

🗝**1945. Payment or satisfaction.**

For other cases see earlier editions of this digest, the Decennial Digests, and WESTLAW.

🗝**1946. Enforcement.**

Fla.App. 2 Dist. 1966. Evidence in suit by plaintiffs to assert lien on assets transferred by seller corporation to buyer corporation disclosed nothing which would show that plaintiffs had led buyer to believe that they would not assert rights to lien under sales contract or that buyer after taking possession of assets did anything more with respect thereto than it was obligated to do under contract or would have done normally.

> Blumin v. Ellis, 186 So.2d 286, certiorari denied 189 So.2d 634.

🗝**1947. Security interest.**

> Security interests under Article 9 of the Uniform Commercial Code, see SECURED TRANSACTIONS.

3. RECOVERY OF GOODS BY SELLER; RECLAMATION.

🗝**1951–1953.** *For other cases see earlier editions of this digest, the Decennial Digests, and WESTLAW.*

🗝**1953. Right to remedy; grounds and defenses.**

🗝**1954. —— In general.**

Bkrtcy.M.D.Fla. 2005. Under Florida law, although a seller's right of reclamation is subordinate to any prior perfected liens on the property sold to buyer, the right of reclamation continues to exist as a seller's remedy. West's F.S.A. § 672.702.

In re Nitram, Inc., 323 B.R. 792.

Where bank's prior perfected lien on Chapter 11 debtor's inventory, equipment, receivables, instruments, fixtures, general intangibles, and proceeds thereof exceeded the value of its collateral, including certain equipment sold to debtor the day before it sought bankruptcy relief, seller's right of reclamation was rendered valueless under Florida law, and seller was not entitled to an administrative claim pursuant to the Bankruptcy Code. Bankr.Code, 11 U.S.C.A. § 546(c)(2); West's F.S.A. § 672.702.

In re Nitram, Inc., 323 B.R. 792.

Bkrtcy.M.D.Fla. 1985. Fungible crude oil can be the subject of reclamation. Bankr.Code, 11 U.S.C.A. § 546; U.C.C. § 2–702; Texas V.T.C.A., Bus. & C. § 2.105(a, d); W.S.1977, § 34–21–205(a, d).

In re Charter Co., 54 B.R. 91.

Bkrtcy.M.D.Fla. 1985. Nonpossession of goods by defaulting buyer at time of reclamation demand is not invariably a bar to reclamation by seller. Bankr.Code, 11 U.S.C.A. § 546(c); U.C.C. § 2–702.

In re Charter Co., 52 B.R. 263.

Bkrtcy.M.D.Fla. 1981. Intervening lien creditor cuts off the rights of a reclaiming seller of goods. West's F.S.A. § 672.702.

Matter of Eli Witt Co., 12 B.R. 757.

⚷1955. —— **Misrepresentation or fraud in general.**

Bkrtcy.S.D.Fla. 1994. To establish its entitlement to reclamation from insolvent buyer under the Uniform Commercial Code (UCC) and bankruptcy reclamation statute, seller must establish that buyer was insolvent at time goods were delivered by seller, that written demand was made on buyer within ten days after delivery of goods, that goods were identifiable at time demand was made, and that goods were in possession and control of debtor at time demand was made. Bankr.Code, 11

U.S.C.A. § 546(c); West's F.S.A. § 672.702(2).

In re Graphic Productions Corp., 176 B.R. 65.

⚷1956. —— **Insolvency of buyer.**

C.A.5 (Fla.) 1975. Without showing that buyer was insolvent when it received shipment of goods and without showing that seller demanded reclamation within ten days of buyer's receipt of goods, seller had no claim under Florida statute permitting, under certain circumstances, seller's reclamation on buyer's receipt of goods on credit while insolvent. West's F.S.A. § 672.702(2).

National Ropes, Inc. v. National Diving Service, Inc., 513 F.2d 53.

Under Florida statute which permits seller to reclaim goods upon demand made within ten days after receipt of goods if seller discovers that buyer received goods on credit while insolvent, and which provides that ten-day limitation does not apply if misrepresentation of solvency was made to seller in writing within three months before delivery, seller whose officer testified that an officer of buyer admitted, between shipments, that written financial statement furnished was not true financial picture of buyer could not reclaim after expiration of ten-day limitation. West's F.S.A. § 672.702(2).

National Ropes, Inc. v. National Diving Service, Inc., 513 F.2d 53.

Conversation in which officer of buyer purportedly admitted, between shipments of goods, that written financial statement furnished was not true financial picture of buyer did not establish insolvency of buyer when misrepresentation was made and was not written "misrepresentation of solvency" within Florida statute allowing seller to reclaim goods without ten-day limitation where misrepresentation of solvency was made to seller in writing within three months before delivery of goods on credit to insolvent buyer. West's F.S.A. § 672.702(2).

National Ropes, Inc. v. National Diving Service, Inc., 513 F.2d 53.

Bkrtcy.M.D.Fla. 1985. Oil seller's demand of reclamation was made while the subject crude oil was identifiable and in the possession of Chapter 11 debtor, even though the oil had been commingled with other oil of like kind and grade in storage tanks and pipeline within hours after it came into debtor's possession, as the subject oil could be traced into an identifiable mass that was subject to debtor's control on day of demand; thus seller would have right to reclaim the oil or to receive priority if it could prove debtor's insolvency as of the day it sent the debtor its notice of reclamation. Bankr.Code, 11 U.S.C.A. §§ 546, 546(c)(2)(A); U.C.C. § 2–702.

In re Charter Co., 54 B.R. 91.

⚷1957. —— Cash or credit sale.

Bkrtcy.M.D.Fla. 1995. In determining whether buyer has right to retain goods following dishonor of check delivered to seller by buyer, court should look to any claims that delay by seller in reclaiming goods caused prejudice to buyer, to any claims of waiver, estoppel or ratification of buyer's right to retain possession, and to common-law rules and precedents governing those principles. West's F.S.A. § 672.507.

In re Edgerton, 186 B.R. 143.

Under Florida's Uniform Commercial Code (UCC), Chapter 13 debtor did not have right to retain mobile office unit following dishonor of check delivered to seller by debtor, but instead seller had right to reclaim goods, and, thus, automatic stay would be lifted to allow creditor to proceed with its replevin action, where there was no assertion that seller's delay in reclaiming goods had been prejudicial, and there had been no assertion of waiver, estoppel or ratification of debtor's right to retain possession. West's F.S.A. § 672.507.

In re Edgerton, 186 B.R. 143.

Fla. 1948. Where defendant and companion purchased a new automobile from plaintiff and defendant traded in her used automobile, plaintiff was entitled to replevin the automobile from defendant when companion gave a worthless check for the balance, subject to defendant's right to interpose a counterclaim for net value of automobile traded in and subject to plaintiff's damages for any depreciation

of the new automobile. F.S.A. §§ 52.11, 78.18 to 78.21.

Thompson v. Guntner, 36 So.2d 826, 160 Fla. 856.

⚷1958. —— Waiver or loss of right.

Bkrtcy.M.D.Fla. 1995. In determining whether buyer has right to retain goods following dishonor of check delivered to seller by buyer, court should look to any claims that delay by seller in reclaiming goods caused prejudice to buyer, to any claims of waiver, estoppel or ratification of buyer's right to retain possession, and to common-law rules and precedents governing those principles. West's F.S.A. § 672.507.

In re Edgerton, 186 B.R. 143.

⚷1959. Right to follow proceeds.

For other cases see earlier editions of this digest, the Decennial Digests, and WEST-LAW.

⚷1960. Demand or notice.

C.A.5 (Fla.) 1975. Without showing that buyer was insolvent when it received shipment of goods and without showing that seller demanded reclamation within ten days of buyer's receipt of goods, seller had no claim under Florida statute permitting, under certain circumstances, seller's reclamation on buyer's receipt of goods on credit while insolvent. West's F.S.A. § 672.702(2).

National Ropes, Inc. v. National Diving Service, Inc., 513 F.2d 53.

Under Florida statute which permits seller to reclaim goods upon demand made within ten days after receipt of goods if seller discovers that buyer received goods on credit while insolvent, and which provides that ten-day limitation does not apply if misrepresentation of solvency was made to seller in writing within three months before delivery, seller whose officer testified that an officer of buyer admitted, between shipments, that written financial statement furnished was not true financial picture of buyer could not reclaim after expiration of ten-day limitation. West's F.S.A. § 672.702(2).

National Ropes, Inc. v. National Diving Service, Inc., 513 F.2d 53.

Bkrtcy.M.D.Fla. 1985. Failure of seller of crude oil to make timely reclamation demand cut off seller's rights in the oil delivered more than ten days before demand was made, and thus seller was not entitled to reclaim that oil sold to Chapter 11 debtor. Bankr.Code, 11 U.S.C.A. § 546(c); U.C.C. § 2–702.

In re Charter Co., 52 B.R. 263.

Bkrtcy.S.D.Fla. 1994. To establish its entitlement to reclamation from insolvent buyer under the Uniform Commercial Code (UCC) and bankruptcy reclamation statute, seller must establish that buyer was insolvent at time goods were delivered by seller, that written demand was made on buyer within ten days after delivery of goods, that goods were identifiable at time demand was made, and that goods were in possession and control of debtor at time demand was made. Bankr.Code, 11 U.S.C.A. § 546(c); West's F.S.A. § 672.702(2).

In re Graphic Productions Corp., 176 B.R. 65.

Letter from paper supplier offering to pay shipping charges and asking that paper be returned qualified as written demand for return of paper, such as was required to establish supplier's entitlement to reclamation under Florida Uniform Commercial Code (UCC) and bankruptcy reclamation statute, though supplier's letter did not contain the word "reclamation" or refer to bankruptcy statute or to relevant section of Florida UCC. Bankr. Code, 11 U.S.C.A. § 546(c); West's F.S.A. § 672.702(2).

In re Graphic Productions Corp., 176 B.R. 65.

Obligation imposed on seller to make timely written demand for return of goods, as prerequisite to exercising right of reclamation under bankruptcy statute and Florida Uniform Commercial Code (UCC), requires seller to take such steps as might reasonably be required to inform buyer that it is exercising its reclamation rights; notice is sufficient if it reflects intention on part of seller to rescind sale. Bankr.Code, 11 U.S.C.A. § 546(c); West's F.S.A. § 672.702(2).

In re Graphic Productions Corp., 176 B.R. 65.

Bkrtcy.S.D.Fla. 1984. Seller who did not make written demand for reclamation of goods sold to debtor within ten days after debtor received goods and at a time while debtor was insolvent was not entitled to reclamation under either Bankruptcy Code or Florida law. Bankr.Code, 11 U.S.C.A. § 546(c), West's F.S.A. § 672.702.

In re United Precious Metals, Inc., 39 B.R. 14.

4. RESALE OF GOODS BY SELLER.

⚷1971–1978. *For other cases see earlier editions of this digest, the Decennial Digests, and WESTLAW.*

5. MONETARY REMEDIES OF SELLER.

⚷1981. **In general.**

For other cases see earlier editions of this digest, the Decennial Digests, and WESTLAW.

⚷1982. **Damages in general.**

Fla.App. 3 Dist. 1978. Seller is entitled to his full measure of damages from buyer who breaches contract for sale of goods. West's F.S.A. § 672.101 et seq.

Vagabond Container, Inc. v. City of Miami Beach, 356 So.2d 1266, certiorari denied 364 So.2d 882.

Fla.App. 3 Dist. 1964. Where contract for sale of business was totally breached, seller must elect either the method of damages which seeks to treat contract as void or the method whereby he affirms contract and seeks to recover loss of profits; he could pursue only one method, and he could not introduce evidence as to both methods.

Sundie v. Lindsay, 166 So.2d 152.

⚷1983. **Particular cases and goods in general.**

Fla.App. 3 Dist. 1973. Evidence supported findings that buyer of airplane and airplane parts had defaulted under terms of contract, that seller had sustained damages and was entitled to retain buyer's deposit and that buyer was indebted to seller for the services of its attorneys.

Jovanovich v. Aero-Tech, Inc., 277 So.2d 555.

Fla.App. 4 Dist. 1982. Provision of mobile home sales agreement that earnest money deposit constituted funds securing to seller the actual amount of damages he sustained by reason of buyers' failure or refusal to complete purchase entitled seller only to actual amount of damages provable upon buyers' default and theory of equitable distribution could not be applied to divide remaining amount of deposit.

Honsberg v. Lystra, 410 So.2d 661.

⚷**1984. Price or value.**

⚷**1985. —— In general.**

Bkrtcy.N.D.Fla. 2005. Uniform Commercial Code (UCC) allows a seller to recover from a buyer the price of goods identified in a contract if the seller is unable to resell them at a reasonable price or if any effort to sell them would be unavailing. U.C.C. § 2-709.

In re Moltech Power Systems, Inc., 326 B.R. 179.

⚷**1986–1987.** *For other cases see earlier editions of this digest, the Decennial Digests, and WESTLAW.*

⚷**1987. —— Particular cases and goods.**

⚷**1987(1). In general.**

Bkrtcy.S.D.Fla. 1982. Where buyer made no objection to goods delivered by debtor until time of trial and goods sent to buyer were currently being shipped to other customers without objection, goods sold and delivered by debtor were not obsolete and unfit for their intended use; thus, buyer was liable for amount due based upon account stated and goods sold and delivered.

In re Nailite Weather Shield Products, Inc., 18 B.R. 905.

Fla.App. 2 Dist. 1987. Seller cannot recover deposit not actually made, when sales contract provides that if sale is not closed because of fault of buyer, deposit paid under contract is to be retained by seller.

Alvis v. Investment I, Inc., 504 So.2d 508.

Deposit had been "paid" into escrow within meaning of default clause in contract for sale of business, and sellers could sue buyer to retain those funds, where

escrow agent advised sellers that deposit check had been received, and deposit check was subsequently returned for insufficient funds.

Alvis v. Investment I, Inc., 504 So.2d 508.

Fla.App. 3 Dist. 1989. Wholesale aircraft part supplier could not recover for second turbine supplied corporation after first one failed within 30 days of delivery in action for purchase price based solely on failure of corporation to answer demand letter for payment of invoice. West's F.S.A. § 672.709.

Page Avjet Corp. v. Cosgrove Aircraft Service, Inc., 546 So.2d 16.

Fla.App. 3 Dist. 1966. Contract between seller of fill and landowner for purchase of sufficient fill to bring properties to certain specification of grade level could not be implied to have required landowner to purchase sufficient fill to anticipate subsidence to a definite time in future, and where landowner established that filled area was dredged in excess of elevation required under contract so that any deficiency in grade was due to settlement over intervening years, seller failed to prove his entitlement to recover any money from landowner.

Tropic-South, Inc. v. Key Broadcasting, Inc., 184 So.2d 920.

Fla.App. 3 Dist. 1965. Requiring buyer which had admitted receipt of goods, reasonableness of value and dominion of goods, to extent that it had placed a lien on them, to pay for the chattels was supportable under count for goods bargained and sold and not on breach of contract count in absence of completion of documents as to terms relative to mode of payment.

Wingreen Co. v. Montgomery Ward & Co., 171 So.2d 408, certiorari denied 177 So.2d 477.

⚷**1987(2). Buildings, structures, and construction.**

Fla. 1955. Where, upon receipt of carload of lumber, wholesale lumber dealer had sold all the salable lumber for $1,330.32 and kept the balance intact, lumber supplier, who brought action against dealer for invoice price of the lumber, was properly allowed to recover the proceeds of the salvage-sale.

McNeill v. Jack, 83 So.2d 704.

Fla.App. 1 Dist. 1990. Manufacturer which sued buyer for price of three steel-rendering tanks could hold the tanks for the buyer's credit until manufacturer received payment of the judgment, without receiving an impermissible double recovery.

Royal Jones & Associates, Inc. v. First Thermal Systems, Inc., 566 So.2d 853.

⟜**1987(3). Plants, crops, and agriculture.**

Fla.App. 2 Dist. 1982. In suit in which recovery was sought on promissory note given in payment of dairy's antecedent obligation to pay for silage and in which defendants counterclaimed on theory that 172 tons of the silage were defective, testimony that defective silage was worth $14 less per ton than the agreed price of $22 per ton did not support an award of $3,409.75 on counterclaim, but, rather, would have supported award of only $2,408.

Lea v. Suhl, 417 So.2d 1179.

⟜**1987(4). Animals and livestock.**

For other cases see earlier editions of this digest, the Decennial Digests, and WEST-LAW.

⟜**1987(5). Machinery and equipment.**

Fla.App. 3 Dist. 1989. Permitting aircraft part supplier both to retain turbine returned to it after it failed within 30 days of delivery and to recover for purchase price for new turbine constituted impermissible double recovery. West's F.S.A. § 672.709.

Page Avjet Corp. v. Cosgrove Aircraft Service, Inc., 546 So.2d 16.

⟜**1987(6)–1987(9).** *For other cases see earlier editions of this digest, the Decennial Digests, and WESTLAW.*

⟜**1987(10). Computers and software.**

See also COPYRIGHTS AND INTELLECTUAL PROPERTY ⟜107.

⟜**1988–1989.** *For other cases see earlier editions of this digest, the Decennial Digests, and WESTLAW.*

⟜**1988. Resale price.**

⟜**1990. —— Difference from contract price.**

C.A.5 (Fla.) 1980. In making calculations mandated by Uniform Commercial Code section concerning resale of goods by seller after buyer's breach, district court was to use, as contract price, price as modified by agreement of the parties. U.C.C. §§ 2–706, 2–706 comment.

Automated Medical Laboratories, Inc. v. Armour Pharmaceutical Co., 629 F.2d 1118.

⟜**1991. —— Particular cases and goods.**

⟜**1991(1). In general.**

C.A.5 (Fla.) 1950. Where buyer had become entitled to rescind contract for purchase of wedges and bolts but did not make a reasonable return, or effort to return, bolts and wedges already shipped, buyer was not in position to claim that seller was entitled to credit for only negligible salvage value of such bolts and wedges, rather than to credit predicated upon full unit price of bolts and wedges delivered.

Morris v. Prefabrication Engineering Co., 181 F.2d 23.

⟜**1991(2)–1991(9).** *For other cases see earlier editions of this digest, the Decennial Digests, and WESTLAW.*

⟜**1991(10). Computers and software.**

See also COPYRIGHTS AND INTELLECTUAL PROPERTY ⟜107.

⟜**1992–1995(9).** *For other cases see earlier editions of this digest, the Decennial Digests, and WESTLAW.*

⟜**1992. Market price or value.**

⟜**1995. —— Particular cases and goods.**

⟜**1995(10). Computers and software.**

See also COPYRIGHTS AND INTELLECTUAL PROPERTY ⟜107.

☞**1996. Lost profits.**

☞**1997. —— In general.**

C.A.5 (Fla.) 1980. "Net profits" for purposes of determining damages for breach of sale contract are equal to contract price minus "direct costs," i. e., costs specifically tied to volume of output under particular contract and minus "overhead costs," such as rent, static utility costs and other costs incurred regardless of volume of output, while to calculate "gross profits," it was only necessary to subtract direct costs from contract price, in which event aggrieved seller would be recovering overhead costs in addition to net profits. U.C.C. §§ 2–708, 2–708(2).

　　Automated Medical Laboratories, Inc. v. Armour Pharmaceutical Co., 629 F.2d 1118.

Under Florida law, seller's lost profits recoverable for buyer's breach included reasonable overhead, in light of agreement of parties to such effect. U.C.C. §§ 2–708, 2–708(2).

　　Automated Medical Laboratories, Inc. v. Armour Pharmaceutical Co., 629 F.2d 1118.

Where because of posture of parties reasonable overhead was includable in lost profits to be recovered by seller on buyer's breach of contract to purchase blood plasma, seller's overhead costs were not recoverable to extent they were incurred in servicing current client, and court was to take into account various considerations, though mathematical certainty in proof of damages was not required. U.C.C. §§ 2–708, 2–708(2).

　　Automated Medical Laboratories, Inc. v. Armour Pharmaceutical Co., 629 F.2d 1118.

Fla.App. 2 Dist. 2003. A seller is entitled to the full measure of its damages from a breaching buyer under contract for sale of goods, including lost profits and incidental damages. West's F.S.A. §§ 672.708(2), 672.710.

　　Florida Recycling Services, Inc. v. Petersen Industries, Inc., 858 So.2d 1114, also published at 2003 WL 24313043.

Fla.App. 2 Dist. 1989. Buyer of goods may recover consequential damages for a seller's breach of contract, while a seller is limited to recovering lost profits and incidental damages as its remedy for a breach of contract. West's F.S.A. §§ 672.708, 672.713–672.715.

　　Florida Min. & Materials Corp. v. Standard Gypsum Corp., 550 So.2d 47.

Fla.App. 3 Dist. 1966. It was error for court, in action by seller against purchaser for breach of contract, to base amount of damages on theory that seller customarily realized 40% profit on such transactions.

　　Aerospace Electronics, Inc. v. Control Parts Corp., 183 So.2d 875.

Where a purchase contract calls for manufacture and delivery of certain articles for a stated contract sale price, the loss of profit recoverable is that which relates to the particular contract transaction, that is, the difference between the contract sale price and the cost or expense to the seller.

　　Aerospace Electronics, Inc. v. Control Parts Corp., 183 So.2d 875.

Fla.App. 3 Dist. 1964. Where contract for sale of business was totally breached, seller must elect either the method of damages which seeks to treat contract as void or the method whereby he affirms contract and seeks to recover loss of profits; he could pursue only one method, and he could not introduce evidence as to both methods.

　　Sundie v. Lindsay, 166 So.2d 152.

☞**1998–2000.** *For other cases see earlier editions of this digest, the Decennial Digests, and WESTLAW.*

☞**2000. Unique or specialty goods.**

☞**2001. —— In general.**

Fla.App. 1 Dist. 1990. Evidence was sufficient to show that any efforts by manufacturer of steel-rendering tanks to resell tanks following buyer's breach would have been unavailing, so as to entitle manufacturer to full contract price as damages, in light of uncontroverted testimony that these were the only rendering tanks manufacturer had ever made, that the tanks were made to the buyer's specifications, that the manufacturer had no other customers to which it could resell the tanks and that manufacturer did not know how to market the tanks for resale. West's F.S.A. § 672.709.

> Royal Jones & Associates, Inc. v. First Thermal Systems, Inc., 566 So.2d 853.

⚷2002–2003. *For other cases see earlier editions of this digest, the Decennial Digests, and WESTLAW.*

⚷2003. Additional or incidental damages.

⚷2004. —— In general.

Fla.App. 2 Dist. 2003. Seller of truck-borne loader device used to pick up and transport large items was entitled to award of incidental damages, in addition to award of lost profits, as result of buyer's breach of contract, which incidentals represented cost of modification of loader and truck required to fit loader on buyer's truck, although seller managed to resell loader to another, and that second sale price also included cost of modification, where seller established that it incurred modification costs with every sale, and second buyer did not compensate seller for initial modification. West's F.S.A. §§ 672.708(2), 672.710.

> Florida Recycling Services, Inc. v. Petersen Industries, Inc., 858 So.2d 1114, also published at 2003 WL 24313043.

Fla.App. 2 Dist. 1989. Buyer of goods may recover consequential damages for a seller's breach of contract, while a seller is limited to recovering lost profits and incidental damages as its remedy for a breach of contract. West's F.S.A. §§ 672.708, 672.713–672.715.

> Florida Min. & Materials Corp. v. Standard Gypsum Corp., 550 So.2d 47.

Fla.App. 3 Dist. 1973. Evidence supported findings that buyer of airplane and airplane parts had defaulted under terms of contract, that seller had sustained damages and was entitled to retain buyer's deposit and that buyer was indebted to seller for the services of its attorneys.

> Jovanovich v. Aero-Tech, Inc., 277 So.2d 555.

⚷2005. —— Expenses connected with delivery, transportation, care, and custody of goods.

Fla.App. 1 Dist. 1976. Section of the Uniform Commercial Code providing that incidental damages to an aggrieved seller include any commercially reasonable charges, expenses or commissions resulting from buyer's breach could not serve as basis for awarding attorney fees to plaintiff in damage action against issuer of irrevocable letter of credit which was dishonored upon presentation and which did not provide for attorney fees. West's F.S.A. § 672.710.

> Florida Nat. Bank at Gainesville v. Alfred & Ann Goldstein Foundation, Inc., 327 So.2d 110.

⚷2006. Special, indirect, or consequential damages.

† C.A.11 (Fla.) 2011. Florida law does not allow for recovery of seller's consequential damages.

> Validsa, Inc. v. PDVSA Services, Inc., 424 Fed.Appx. 862.

S.D.Fla. 1987. Consequential damages are not recoverable by aggrieved seller from buyer in action for breach of contract for sale of goods. U.C.C. § 2–101 et seq.

> Tew v. Arizona State Retirement System, 69 B.R. 608, reversed 873 F.2d 1400.

Fla.App. 2 Dist. 1989. The mere written recitation in a gypsum requirements contract that a breach by the buyer would cause the seller to "suffer substantial and irreversible financial damages" and that seller's equitable remedies for buyer's breach should be in addition to other remedies, including "appropriate damages," did not give the seller the clear and express right to recover consequential damages for the alleged loss of business, sufficient to overcome the UCC prohibition of recovery of such damages by a seller. West's F.S.A. § 672.708.

> Florida Min. & Materials Corp. v. Standard Gypsum Corp., 550 So.2d 47.

☞2007–2010. *For other cases see earlier editions of this digest, the Decennial Digests, and WESTLAW.*

(C) PARTICULAR REMEDIES OF BUYER.

1. LIEN OR SECURITY INTEREST OF BUYER.

Equitable liens, see LIENS ☞7.

☞2111–2112. *For other cases see earlier editions of this digest, the Decennial Digests, and WESTLAW.*

2. RECOVERY OF GOODS BY BUYER.

☞2121–2124. *For other cases see earlier editions of this digest, the Decennial Digests, and WESTLAW.*

☞2123. **Right to remedy; grounds and defenses.**

☞2125. —— **Insolvency of seller.**

Bkrtcy.M.D.Fla. 1984. For buyer to recover goods in seller's possession after seller has become insolvent, buyer must have special property interest in goods, have paid part or all of purchase price, and kept good a tender of any unpaid portion of purchase price, and additionally, seller must become insolvent within ten days following receipt of first installment of purchase price. West's F.S.A. §§ 672.501, 672.502.

Matter of CSY Yacht Corp., 42 B.R. 619.

☞2126–2129. *For other cases see earlier editions of this digest, the Decennial Digests, and WESTLAW.*

3. RESALE OF GOODS BY BUYER.

☞2131–2133. *For other cases see earlier editions of this digest, the Decennial Digests, and WESTLAW.*

4. MONETARY REMEDIES OF BUYER IN GENERAL.

☞2141–2142. *For other cases see earlier editions of this digest, the Decennial Digests, and WESTLAW.*

☞2142. **Damages in general.**

☞2143. —— **In general.**

Fla.App. 4 Dist. 1995. General rule is that proper measure of damages for breach of contract resulting from defective performance is reasonable cost of remedying breach by making article furnished or work performed conform to contract. West's F.S.A. §§ 672.714(3), 672.715(2).

Koplowitz v. Girard, 658 So.2d 1183.

☞2144. —— **Nondelivery or repudiation by seller.**

For other cases see earlier editions of this digest, the Decennial Digests, and WESTLAW.

☞2145. —— **Nonconforming goods.**

Fla.App. 4 Dist. 1996. Ordinarily, where buyer has accepted nonconforming goods and sued for breach, buyer is entitled to general, incidental and consequential damages, which in proper case may be an amalgam of some or all three. West's F.S.A. §§ 672.714, 672.715.

Halliburton Co. v. Eastern Cement Corp., 672 So.2d 844, modified on clarification, review denied 683 So.2d 483.

☞2146. **Particular cases and goods in general.**

☞2147. —— **In general.**

M.D.Fla. 2015. Under Florida's Uniform Commercial Code (UCC), drum kit distributor was entitled to direct damages award of $41,384 for container full of drum kits that did not conform to samples provided to distributor by manufacturer; drum kits were not salvageable and had no value. Fla. Stat. Ann. § 672.714.

Armadillo Distribution Enterprises, Inc. v. Hai Yun Musical Instruments Manufacture Co. Ltd., 142 F.Supp.3d 1245.

Fla.App. 4 Dist. 1996. In contract between distributor of resin and boat builder, contractual exclusion of warranties provision was not inconsistent with limitation of remedies provision in same contract, and thus, even if distributor could be found liable, measure of damages was limited to cost of goods sold.

Jarmco, Inc. v. Polygard, Inc., 668 So.2d 300, review granted 678 So.2d 339, decision approved 684 So.2d 732.

Fla.App. 4 Dist. 1993. Seller was entitled to credit with respect to damages in buyer's breach of contract claim, alleging that seller wrongfully stopped supplying buyer with parts used in manufacture of buyer's products, in amount of three percent price increase provided in contract.

ACR Electronics, Inc. v. Switlik Parachute Co., Inc., 624 So.2d 1144.

⊸2148. —— Buildings, structures, and construction.

Fla. 1955. Where, at time wholesale lumber dealer ordered one car of lumber, he did not intend to pay for it, dealer was not entitled to recover from lumber supplier for expenses incident to handling of such car or any loss in anticipated profits on lumber in such car.

McNeill v. Jack, 83 So.2d 704.

Fla.App. 2 Dist. 1983. Where seller of concrete structures was without authority to waive requirement that Navy give it six months' notice of its intent to exercise option to purchase concrete structures Navy had been leasing from seller, and value of six months rent was $19,500, purchasers of structures who also received assignment of seller's rights in Navy contract had right to receive six months' notice and rental for those six months; thus, purchasers were entitled to $19,500 damages for lost rent.

Dolphus Newman, Inc. v. Barber Industries, Inc., 437 So.2d 228.

⊸2149–2151. *For other cases see earlier editions of this digest, the Decennial Digests, and WESTLAW.*

⊸2152. —— Food and beverages.

Fla. 1940. In action for reimbursement for meat which was shipped under "C.A.F. contract," under which consideration paid covered cost and freight to destination, on ground that part of the meat was spoiled when it was received and part of it was required to be pickled in order to salvage, evidence relating to date of shipment, and precooling of car when packed, and relating to whether car contained "old cuts" contrary to contract, and whether plain words of contract rather than custom of trade governed, sustained judgment for buyer.

Farris & Co. v. William Schluderberg, T. J. Kurdle Co., 193 So. 429, 141 Fla. 462, rehearing denied 196 So. 184, 142 Fla. 765.

⊸2153. —— Motor vehicles.

For other cases see earlier editions of this digest, the Decennial Digests, and WESTLAW.

⊸2154. —— Mobile homes or structures.

Fla.App. 2 Dist. 1982. Trial court abused its discretion, in fashioning an equitable remedy for fraud and misrepresentation of seller in inducing buyers to purchase two mobile home lots and five new mobile homes, in leaving parties where it found them, and thus, in effect, giving buyers possession of lots and mobile homes for which they made only a $21,706 down payment and forgiving mortgage payments with accrued interest amounting to approximately $165,000 while permitting buyers to retain benefit of all rentals earned, an amount in excess of $9,000.

Florando Inv. Corp. v. Fried, 412 So.2d 14.

⊸2155. —— Drugs and medical devices.

For other cases see earlier editions of this digest, the Decennial Digests, and WESTLAW.

⊸2156. —— Computers and software.

See also COPYRIGHTS AND INTELLECTUAL PROPERTY ⊸107.

Fla.App. 3 Dist. 1974. Jury acted properly in awarding purchaser of computer $20,000 in damages on its evidence that seller had breached contract to internally program the equipment, despite seller's showing that contract price for equipment was only $18,240.58. West's F.S.A. §§ 672.302, 672.714, 672.719(3).

Burroughs Corp. v. Joseph Uram Jewelers, Inc., 305 So.2d 215.

Fla.App. 5 Dist. 1982. Under statute, plaintiff who alleged that software computer package which she purchased from defendant did not perform as represented was entitled, with or without cancellation, to refund in full of purchase price paid and reasonable expenses, if any incurred as result of breach, if plaintiff was found by jury to be entitled to damages, and assuming return of undamaged equipment, and refusal so to instruct was harmful error. West's F.S.A. § 672.711(1).

> Jones, Morrison, Stalnaker, P.A. v. Contemporary Computer Services, Inc., 414 So.2d 637.

☞**2157. Recovery of amounts paid.**

☞**2158. ——— In general.**

C.C.A.5 (Fla.) 1947. On a justified rescission, buyers were entitled to reclaim what they had paid but as a condition of doing so they must have announced and adhered to the rescission and must also restore, as far as possible, the status quo.

> Morris v. Prefabrication Engineering Co., 160 F.2d 779.

Fla. 1941. In action by buyer of fruit to recover money paid under sales contract allegedly rescinded by seller, seller could not invoke rule that there could be no rescission unless both parties could have been restored to the condition they were in before contract was made, where seller did not deny that he had been paid for all fruit picked before the alleged rescission and never offered to return such payments, and did not charge buyer's prior failure to live up to the contract.

> Givens v. Vaughn-Griffin Packing Co., 1 So.2d 714, 146 Fla. 575.

Fla.App. 1 Dist. 2004. Buyer of computer system for retail outlet stores was entitled to the purchase price after rightfully revoking acceptance under the Uniform Commercial Code (UCC). West's F.S.A. § 672.711(1).

> Fryatt v. Lantana One, Ltd., 866 So.2d 158.

Fla.App. 3 Dist. 1972. Where original purchase price of automobile was $7,675 and buyer had use of the automobile for approximately 45 days and during the remainder of three-month period, while the automobile was in seller's shop for repairs, seller provided buyer with another automobile for transportation, buyer was not entitled to amount of purchase price upon entry of judgment of rescission and cancellation for breach of warranties of merchantability or fitness and was

properly awarded the sum of $6,500. F.S.A. §§ 672.608, 672.719.

> Orange Motors of Coral Gables, Inc. v. Dade County Dairies, Inc., 258 So.2d 319, certiorari denied 263 So.2d 831.

☞**2159. ——— Deposits, earnest money, and down payments.**

C.C.A.5 (Fla.) 1947. Where buyers canceled contract for purchase of wedge bolts because of failure to make timely shipment but retained bills of lading covering bolts shipped before and after cancellation and did not return or offer to return such bolts, buyers were not entitled to recover full amount of down payment less only the purchase price of small amount of bolts used.

> Morris v. Prefabrication Engineering Co., 160 F.2d 779.

Fla. 1951. Where buyers refused to carry out contract for purchase of wheel alignment business and filed suit to rescind contract but failed to establish ground for rescission, and seller meantime sold business to another, buyers were not entitled to recover back deposit made under contract on purchase price.

> Reitano v. Fote, 50 So.2d 873.

Fla. 1940. Where contract for sale of crop of citrus fruit estimated the quantity of fruit but did not obligate seller to deliver any particular quantity and frost-damaged fruit was excluded, a damage by frost to only part of the crop did not relieve buyer of his obligation to accept undamaged fruit so as to warrant his recovery of entire amount paid as deposit.

> Vaughn-Griffin Packing Co. v. Fisher, 193 So. 553, 141 Fla. 428.

Fla.App. 4 Dist. 1995. Trial court erred in breach of contract action by awarding buyer return of all sums paid under contract in addition to cost of remedying seller's breach; such award placed buyer in better position than it would have been had contract been fully performed. West's F.S.A. §§ 672.714(3), 672.715(2).

> Koplowitz v. Girard, 658 So.2d 1183.

Fla.App. 4 Dist. 1981. Where airline furnished refundable security deposit pending its inspection and determination to buy jet aircraft, if airline bought aircraft, refundable deposit was to be carried over and applied to second aircraft, and airline bought neither aircraft, airline was entitled to return of security deposit.

World Jet-Aircraft Industries, Inc. v. Allred Intern. Ltd., 397 So.2d 1192.

⚷2160–2162. For other cases see earlier editions of this digest, the Decennial Digests, and WESTLAW.

⚷2161. Procurement and price of substitute goods; "cover".

⚷2163. —— Difference from contract price.

Fla.App. 3 Dist. 1982. Under statutory section allowing a buyer to "cover" a breach by purchasing, within a reasonable time and in good faith, substitute goods for those due from seller, measure of damages is the difference between cost of cover and the contract price along with any incidental damages less expenses saved. West's F.S.A. § 672.712.

Shreve Land Co., Inc. v. J & D Financial Corp., 421 So.2d 722.

⚷2164–2165. For other cases see earlier editions of this digest, the Decennial Digests, and WESTLAW.

⚷2165. —— Particular cases and goods.

⚷2165(1). In general.

† **C.A.11 (Fla.) 2013.** Under Florida law, market remedy provision of Uniform Commercial Code (UCC), rather than UCC's cover provision, governed coal buyer's damages resulting from breach of coal supply agreement where buyer failed to cover coal supply it needed with a reasonable like kind replacement; although contract provided for sale of coal not exceeding 1.7 pounds of sulfur dioxide per MMBtu, buyer purchased coal which contained sulfur amounts above contractual cap. West's F.S.A. §§ 672.712, 672.713.

Gulf Power Co. v. Coalsales II, LLC, 522 Fed.Appx. 699.

Under Florida law, coal buyer's purchase of replacement coal following seller's breach of coal supply contract was a reasonable like kind replacement, so as to allow calculation of damages under cover provision of Uniform Commercial Code (UCC), even though some of the coal purchased as cover for one year contained

sulfur dioxide levels at a higher rate than that allowed for in contract, since buyer then blended the higher-sulfur coal with a similar quantity of lower-sulfur coal to produce a blend of coal with a sulfur content identical to that called for under the contract. West's F.S.A. § 672.712.

Gulf Power Co. v. Coalsales II, LLC, 522 Fed.Appx. 699.

Fla. 1974. Consideration should have been given at trial of contract action as to whether business owner reasonably could have mitigated its losses by obtaining equipment from another supplier.

Baring Industries, Inc. v. Rayglo, Inc., 303 So.2d 625, opinion adopted 306 So.2d 549.

Fla.App. 4 Dist. 1990. Buyer who contracted to purchase airplane failed to establish that it had made reasonable efforts to "cover" by purchasing substitute when seller subsequently refused to release plane, and thus buyer had no right of replevin under the UCC. U.C.C. § 2–101 et seq.; West's F.S.A. §§ 672.101 et seq., 672.716(3).

T and T Air Charter, Inc. v. Duncan Aircraft Sales, 566 So.2d 361.

⚷2165(2). Buildings, structures, and construction.

Fla.App. 4 Dist. 1986. After contractor installed particle board shelves in shoe store rather than plywood or wood shelves as required by contract, proper measure of damages was replacement cost of the shelves, without crediting contractor for value of particle board shelves.

Vanater v. Tom Lilly Const., 483 So.2d 506.

⚷2165(3). Plants, crops, and agriculture.

For other cases see earlier editions of this digest, the Decennial Digests, and WEST-LAW.

⚷2165(4). Animals and livestock.

C.A.11 (Fla.) 1987. Difference in economic value of original and revised leases were "consequential damages," under Florida law, triggering obligation, on part of buyers of cattle for lease to dairy farmer, to cover or otherwise mitigate their losses sustained when lease was revised after veterinarians had determined that cattle were substantially older than

---

† **This Case was not selected for publication in the National Reporter System**
For legislative history of cited statutes, see Florida Statutes Annotated

represented by seller. West's F.S.A. § 672.715(2)(a).

Nyquist v. Randall, 819 F.2d 1014.

Buyers of cattle for lease to dairy farmer were not required to procure more cattle to lease to replace defective ones, in order to be entitled to consequential damages from seller under Florida law, where buyers lacked wherewithal to purchase additional cattle, and did attempt to mitigate their loss by entering revised lease with farmer. West's F.S.A. § 672.715.

Nyquist v. Randall, 819 F.2d 1014.

🗝**2165(5). Machinery and equipment.**

Fla.App. 1 Dist. 1981. Purchaser of continuous belt conveyor system for use by bakery in its pizza freezing business was entitled to recover not only his deposit money but also the cost of cover, when the seller failed to timely deliver and furnish the conveyor in compliance with specifications. West's F.S.A. § 672.712.

Goodell v. K. T. Enterprises, Ltd., 394 So.2d 1087.

Fla.App. 3 Dist. 1980. In action for breach of contract for sale of oven by seller, damages were to be determined in accordance with statute providing that buyer may recover from seller as damages difference between cost of cover and contract price together with any incidental or consequential damages but less expenses saved in consequence of seller's breach. West's F.S.A. § 672.712.

A & P Bakery Supply & Equipment Co. v. Hawatmeh, 388 So.2d 1071.

🗝**2165(6)–2165(8).** *For other cases see earlier editions of this digest, the Decennial Digests, and WESTLAW.*

🗝**2165(9). Drugs and medical devices.**

Fla.App. 3 Dist. 1986. Forty-two day period, whose end coincided with industry-wide price increase, was reasonable time to make cover purchases following anticipatory breach of contract to supply vitamins in light of volatile market. West's F.S.A. § 672.712(1).

Mason Distributors, Inc. v. Encapsulations, Inc., 484 So.2d 1275.

🗝**2165(10). Computers and software.**

See also COPYRIGHTS AND INTELLECTUAL PROPERTY 🗝107.

C.A.11 (Fla.) 2005. Under Florida law, buyer could recover its lost profits from the resale of computer software it contracted for when seller repudiated the contracts, however, seller could limit the award of lost profits if it could present sufficient evidence to show that buyer's failure to cover was inexcusable given the circumstances; there was sufficient evidence to show that seller's repudiation of the software contracts directly caused buyer's loss of future profits from its resale of that software, buyer's loss was not too speculative and conjectural to be determined, and seller had reason to know when it formed the contracts that buyer was a reseller. West's F.S.A. § 672.715(2).

HGI Associates, Inc. v. Wetmore Printing Co., 427 F.3d 867, appeal after remand 236 Fed.Appx. 563.

🗝**2166–2169.** *For other cases see earlier editions of this digest, the Decennial Digests, and WESTLAW.*

🗝**2166. Market price or value.**

🗝**2169. —— Particular cases and goods.**

🗝**2169(1). In general.**

C.C.A.5 (Fla.) 1944. The proper measure of damages for breach of contract to sell to plaintiff a landlord's claim against corporation in reorganization proceedings is difference between price plaintiff agreed to pay for claim and value on market of such claim at date of breach where there was a market for such claims. Bankr.Act § 77B, 11 U.S.C.A. § 207.

Roth v. Hyer, 142 F.2d 227, certiorari denied 65 S.Ct. 38, 323 U.S. 712, 89 L.Ed. 573.

Fla.App. 3 Dist. 1988. Remedy for breach of contract resulting from seller's failure to deliver chairs bought on sale was award of full market price, rather than sale price. West's F.S.A. § 672.713(1).

Kneale v. Jay Ben Inc., 527 So.2d 917.

⟜2169(2)–2169(9). *For other cases see earlier editions of this digest, the Decennial Digests, and WESTLAW.*

⟜2169(10). Computers and software.

See also COPYRIGHTS AND INTELLECTUAL PROPERTY ⟜107.

⟜2170. Additional or incidental damages; expenses.

⟜2171. —— In general.

† **C.A.11 (Fla.) 2013.** Under Florida law, storage costs of toxic powdered milk from China could be claimed as damages by Venezuelan state-owned purchasing company in breach of contract suit with Florida-based import company, even though its sister-company incurred the costs, given nuances of a state-owned conglomerate. West's F.S.A. §§ 672.714, 672.715.

Exim Brickell LLC v. PDVSA Services Inc., 516 Fed.Appx. 742.

M.D.Fla. 2015. Under Florida's Uniform Commercial Code (UCC), a buyer's expenses incurred before discovering a defect are recoverable as incidental damages. Fla. Stat. Ann. § 672.715(1).

Armadillo Distribution Enterprises, Inc. v. Hai Yun Musical Instruments Manufacture Co. Ltd., 142 F.Supp.3d 1245.

Fla.App. 2 Dist. 1988. Damages recoverable from seller of machinery which failed to deliver the machinery on time could not include expenses incurred by the buyer in its operations prior to entry into the contract for the purchase of the machine, including expenses incurred in operations to which the machines did not relate.

John Brown Automation, Inc. v. Nobles, 537 So.2d 614, review denied 547 So.2d 1210.

Fla.App. 4 Dist. 1996. Ordinarily, where buyer has accepted nonconforming goods and sued for breach, buyer is entitled to general, incidental and consequential damages, which in proper case may be an amalgam of some or all three. West's F.S.A. §§ 672.714, 672.715.

Halliburton Co. v. Eastern Cement Corp., 672 So.2d 844, modified on clarification, review denied 683 So.2d 483.

⟜2172. —— Inspection, receipt, transportation, care, and custody of goods.

† **C.A.11 (Fla.) 2013.** Florida's version of the Uniform Commercial Code (UCC) did not impose a numerical limitation on damages recoverable by Venezuelan state-owned purchasing company in breach of contract suit with Florida-based import company resulting from installment contract for powdered milk and rice from China, where purchasing company produced uncontested invoices for all of its storage costs and import company did not claim that the rates were unreasonable. West's F.S.A. §§ 672.714(1), 672.715(1).

Exim Brickell LLC v. PDVSA Services Inc., 516 Fed.Appx. 742.

M.D.Fla. 2015. Under Florida's Uniform Commercial Code (UCC) drum kit distributor was entitled to documented incidental damages stemming from drum kit manufacturer's delivery of defective drum kits that did not conform to samples for provided to distributor, including incoming freight charges, off-site storage, and disposal costs. Fla. Stat. Ann. § 672.715(1).

Armadillo Distribution Enterprises, Inc. v. Hai Yun Musical Instruments Manufacture Co. Ltd., 142 F.Supp.3d 1245.

⟜2173. Special, indirect, or consequential damages; lost profits.

⟜2174. —— In general.

Fla.App. 2 Dist. 2007. Seller's undisputed breach of contract entitled buyer to seek certain benefit-of-the-bargain damages that flowed directly and incidentally from seller's breach, pursuant to Uniform Commercial Code (UCC), even though buyer was not entitled to consequential damages as result of enforcement of limitation of consequential damages clause on back of seller's finished goods form.

† **This Case was not selected for publication in the National Reporter System**
For legislative history of cited statutes, see Florida Statutes Annotated

West's F.S.A. §§ 671.106, 672.714, 672.715, 672.719.

> Paul Gottlieb & Co., Inc. v. Alps South Corp., 985 So.2d 1, rehearing denied.

Buyer was not entitled to damages in form of lost profits due to seller's breach of contract, as buyer failed to prove lost profits with reasonable certainty, in that lost profits were not based on relevant marketplace considerations including, but not limited to, data on open orders that could not be immediately filled.

> Paul Gottlieb & Co., Inc. v. Alps South Corp., 985 So.2d 1, rehearing denied.

Fla.App. 2 Dist. 1989. Buyer of goods may recover consequential damages for a seller's breach of contract, while a seller is limited to recovering lost profits and incidental damages as its remedy for a breach of contract. West's F.S.A. §§ 672.708, 672.713–672.715.

> Florida Min. & Materials Corp. v. Standard Gypsum Corp., 550 So.2d 47.

☞2175. —— Due to nondelivery or repudiation by seller.

C.A.11 (Fla.) 2005. Under Florida law, buyer could recover its lost profits from the resale of computer software it contracted for when seller repudiated the contracts, however, seller could limit the award of lost profits if it could present sufficient evidence to show that buyer's failure to cover was inexcusable given the circumstances; there was sufficient evidence to show that seller's repudiation of the software contracts directly caused buyer's loss of future profits from its resale of that software, buyer's loss was not too speculative and conjectural to be determined, and seller had reason to know when it formed the contracts that buyer was a reseller. West's F.S.A. § 672.715(2).

> HGI Associates, Inc. v. Wetmore Printing Co., 427 F.3d 867, appeal after remand 236 Fed.Appx. 563.

C.A.5 (Fla.) 1981. Agreement, made between canned citrus juice buyer and one not party to buyer's suit against seller for breach of contract, concerning disposition of buyer's profits from all of its sales

contracts had no bearing on amount of profit buyer would have realized if seller had fully performed contract and thus reducing lost-profits damages awarded to buyer in accordance with division of profits in such other agreement was error.

> General Matters, Inc. v. Penny Products, Inc., 651 F.2d 1017.

Fla.App. 2 Dist. 1988. Where investor decided to invest in manufacturing company prior to time that it entered into contract for purchase of machines, he could not recover, as compensatory damages from manufacturer which failed to timely deliver the machines, the amount of his investment.

> John Brown Automation, Inc. v. Nobles, 537 So.2d 614, review denied 547 So.2d 1210.

Fla.App. 3 Dist. 1980. Buyer was not entitled to damages for lost profits as a result of seller's breaching a contract for sale of oven where buyer's business venture for which oven was purchased was in its inception at time of seller's breach.

> A & P Bakery Supply & Equipment Co. v. Hawatmeh, 388 So.2d 1071.

☞2176. —— Due to delay in delivery.

For other cases see earlier editions of this digest, the Decennial Digests, and WEST-LAW.

☞2177. —— Due to nonconforming goods.

C.A.5 (Fla.) 1975. Where, in trial of carpet dealer's counterclaim against carpet manufacturer for damages for alleged loss of prospective sales because of defects in carpet, dealer admitted knowingly installing defective carpet, such conduct by dealer interrupted chain of causation and was independent intervening cause for dealer's removal from school boards' bidding lists which prevented recovery of damages for resulting loss of prospective sales to school boards. West's F.S.A. § 672.715.

> Aldon Industries, Inc. v. Don Myers & Associates, Inc., 517 F.2d 188, appeal after remand 547 F.2d 924.

M.D.Fla. 2015. Under Florida's Uniform Commercial Code (UCC) drum kit distributor that received non-conforming drum kits from manufacturer was not entitled to consequential damages for credit extended to a third-party distributor as a refund for defective drum kits, where there was no documentation illustrating purchase of drum kits by the third party, and no evidence of complaints from the third-party regarding the drum kits. Fla. Stat. Ann. § 672.715(2).

> Armadillo Distribution Enterprises, Inc. v. Hai Yun Musical Instruments Manufacture Co. Ltd., 142 F.Supp.3d 1245.

Drum kit distributor was not entitled to alleged lost profits as consequential damages for defective drum kits in breach of contract claim against manufacturer, representing the difference between the price at which it would have sold the drum kits and the price it paid the manufacturer for the drums; distributor failed to prove to a reasonable degree of certainty that sale of the drum kits would have occurred. Fla. Stat. Ann. § 672.715(2).

> Armadillo Distribution Enterprises, Inc. v. Hai Yun Musical Instruments Manufacture Co. Ltd., 142 F.Supp.3d 1245.

M.D.Fla. 1973. When manufacturer agreed to sell turbine generator to electric company, it must have foreseen that company would enter into contracts to sell the electrical power to be generated and that, if manufacturer were negligent, resulting in damage to generators, loss of such contracts would be natural and proximate result; thus electric company was entitled to claim loss of capacity charges as element of its damages in action against manufacturer arising out of fire allegedly resulting from defect in generator.

> Tampa Elec. Co. v. Stone & Webster Engineering Corp., 367 F.Supp. 27.

Fla.App. 1 Dist. 2004. Work of buyer's salaried employee in attempting to get computer system operating properly in buyer's retail stores did not entitle buyer to $10,000 from seller after revocation of acceptance; the buyer did not incur additional cost for the labor, and although the employee testified that productivity was affected, she did not explain how it was affected and whether the buyer incurred a loss as a result. West's F.S.A. § 672.715(1, 2).

> Fryatt v. Lantana One, Ltd., 866 So.2d 158.

Fla.App. 4 Dist. 1996. Ordinarily, where buyer has accepted nonconforming goods and sued for breach, buyer is entitled to general, incidental and consequential damages, which in proper case may be an amalgam of some or all three. West's F.S.A. §§ 672.714, 672.715.

> Halliburton Co. v. Eastern Cement Corp., 672 So.2d 844, modified on clarification, review denied 683 So.2d 483.

⚷2178. —— Goods intended for particular purpose.

For other cases see earlier editions of this digest, the Decennial Digests, and WEST-LAW.

⚷2179. —— Goods intended for resale.

C.A.5 (Fla.) 1975. Dealer cannot recover for loss of prospective profits simply as result of customer dissatisfaction with manufacturer's product; rather, dealer, to recover, must have become so identified with defective product that in eyes of third parties it and not manufacturer is held responsible for defects, and its business is thereby damaged.

> Aldon Industries, Inc. v. Don Myers & Associates, Inc., 517 F.2d 188, appeal after remand 547 F.2d 924.

⚷2180. Mitigation or reduction of loss.

⚷2181. —— In general.

† C.A.11 (Fla.) 2013. For purposes of mitigating damages from breach of contract under Florida law, Venezuelan state-owned purchase company that received powdered milk and rice from China pursuant to an installment contract with a Florida-based import company did not have to attempt to nationalize the goods by means of a letter of commitment. West's F.S.A. §§ 672.714(1), 672.715(1).

> Exim Brickell LLC v. PDVSA Services Inc., 516 Fed.Appx. 742.

C.A.11 (Fla.) 1987. Difference in economic value of original and revised leases were "consequential damages," under Florida law, triggering obligation, on part of buyers of cattle for lease to dairy farmer, to cover or otherwise mitigate their losses sustained when lease was revised after veterinarians had determined that cattle were substantially older than represented by seller. West's F.S.A. § 672.715(2)(a).

Nyquist v. Randall, 819 F.2d 1014.

Fla.App. 1 Dist. 1983. Seller was entitled to set-off for buyer's use of automobile before buyer's revocation of acceptance under Uniform Commercial Code.

Tom Bush Volkswagen, Inc. v. Kuntz, 429 So.2d 398.

Set-off to which seller was entitled for buyer's use of automobile before revocation of acceptance under Uniform Commercial Code was value to buyer of use of defective automobile.

Tom Bush Volkswagen, Inc. v. Kuntz, 429 So.2d 398.

Fla.App. 1 Dist. 1980. Failure of buyer of nonconforming shrimp to make a salvage sale to seafood merchant who allegedly made an offer was not at buyer's "peril," in that question was whether there was a good–faith exercise of reasonable business judgment by buyer in an effort to mitigate damages, and there was no showing of a lack of good faith by buyer. West's F.S.A. §§ 672.2–601, 672.2–603, 672.2–603(1, 3).

Sullivans Island Seafood Co. v. Island Seafood Co., 390 So.2d 113.

Fla.App. 2 Dist. 1983. In action brought by purchasers of concrete structures against seller for its alleged wrongful sale of same structures to third party which had been leasing structures with option to buy, purchasers were entitled to $55,000 in compensatory damages rather than award of full value of $151,000, where difference involved was paid by third party to Small Business Administration pursuant to bankruptcy proceedings of seller, and purchasers were notified of bankruptcy proceedings, but chose not to become involved.

Dolphus Newman, Inc. v. Barber Industries, Inc., 437 So.2d 228.

☞2182. —— **Expenses saved and costs avoided.**

For other cases see earlier editions of this digest, the Decennial Digests, and WEST-LAW.

☞2183. **Punitive or exemplary damages.**

S.D.Fla. 1999. Dealers could not recover punitive damages for oil company's

alleged breach of implied obligation of good faith and fair dealing under its sales agreements with dealers, in failing to offset wholesale price of its gasoline to its dealers by amount which was, on average, equal to three percent credit card processing fee; oil company's alleged misconduct did not rise to level of any independent tort.

Allapattah Services, Inc. v. Exxon Corp., 61 F.Supp.2d 1326.

Fla.App. 2 Dist. 1980. Automobile buyer's testimony that he went to automobile dealer's place of business and made a deal with named individual to buy an automobile to be delivered to his residence and that such vehicle was delivered by named individual but that buyer could not obtain title papers because vehicle had been reported stolen did not constitute a tort but gave rise to breach of sales contract and, hence, buyer was not entitled to punitive damages. West's F.S.A. §§ 672.312, 672.714(2.3).

Bill Branch Chevrolet, Inc. v. Redmond, 378 So.2d 319.

Fla.App. 3 Dist. 1982. Based on wrongful conduct of a franchiser's employee in accepting a deposit from individual seeking to acquire franchise and in selling next available franchise to another broker, trial court properly awarded nominal and punitive damages in action on alleged contract to sell franchise.

Greater Coral Springs Realty, Inc. v. Century 21 Real Estate of Southern Florida, Inc., 412 So.2d 940.

Fla.App. 3 Dist. 1979. In action for breach of an oral contract to sell racehorse, wherein buyer neither pled nor proved an independent tort for fraud or deceit, buyer was not entitled to recover punitive damages.

Greer v. Williams, 375 So.2d 333, certiorari denied 385 So.2d 762.

5. MONETARY REMEDIES OF BUYER
FOR BREACH OF WARRANTY.

☞2191–2193. *For other cases see earlier editions of this digest, the Decennial Digests, and WESTLAW.*

☞2193. **Particular cases and goods in general.**

☞2194. —— **In general.**

N.D.Fla. 2007. Relief sought by consumers who brought claims against manufacturers of allegedly faulty sportfishing boat under Magnuson–Moss Warranty Act and Florida's Deceptive and Unfair Trade Practices Act, and breach of warranty under Florida Uniform Commercial Code did not exceed that authorized by statute or otherwise; consumers sought full purchase price of boat, collateral charges, finance charges, incidental and consequential damages, as well as costs and fees. Magnuson–Moss Warranty–Federal Trade Commission Improvement Act, § 110(d)(1, 2), 15 U.S.C.A. § 2310(d)(1, 2); West's F.S.A. §§ 501.211(2), 671.101 et seq., 672.101 et seq.

> Yvon v. Baja Marine Corp., 495 F.Supp.2d 1179.

Fla.App. 4 Dist. 2017. Compensatory damages awards of $7.5 million to wife's minor daughter and $4 million to wife's minor son were not excessive in action by husband of deceased wife, who was heavy smoker before she died of lung cancer, against tobacco company for strict liability, fraud by concealment, conspiracy to commit fraud by concealment, negligence, breach of express warranty, and breach of implied warranty; daughter was only nine years old when wife was diagnosed with lung cancer and son was infant, wife's illness and death had devastating effect on children, as daughter retained vivid memories of illness and decline and testified that she felt robbed by wife's death and often thought about relationship they would have had and what wife's role would have been in her life, and son testified that his only true memory of wife was watching paramedics take her dead body out of their home in body bag and that not having more time with wife negatively affected him for rest of his life.

> R.J. Reynolds Tobacco Company v. Grossman, 211 So.3d 221.

⚷2195. —— **Buildings, structures, and construction.**

For other cases see earlier editions of this digest, the Decennial Digests, and WEST-LAW.

⚷2196. —— **Plants, crops, and agriculture.**

Fla. 1940. Judgment for damages from failure of warranty as to variety and quality of certain bean seed would be affirmed on writ of error.

> Phillips v. Beamer, 198 So. 695, 144 Fla. 769.

⚷2197. —— **Animals and livestock.**

For other cases see earlier editions of this digest, the Decennial Digests, and WEST-LAW.

⚷2198. —— **Machinery and equipment.**

C.A.5 (Fla.) 1979. Where only three of eight late shipments occurred after scheduled delivery date of filling machine, to extent that trial court, in breach of warranty action, awarded food processor damages against the manufacturer on basis of earlier shipments the award was clearly erroneous. West's F.S.A. §§ 672.714, 672.715; Fed.Rules Civ.Proc. rule 52(a), 28 U.S.C.A.

> National Papaya Co. v. Domain Industries, Inc., 592 F.2d 813.

Fla.App. 3 Dist. 1977. Measure of damages in breach of warranty action in sale of defective airplane could include expense of transporting airplane for repairs, expense of overhauling airplane and damages due to loss of use of airplane during repairs.

> Miles v. Kavanaugh, 350 So.2d 1090.

In action by buyer for breach of express warranty and misrepresentation in sale of airplane, evidence of expense of transporting airplane for repairs, expense of overhauling airplane and damages due to loss of use of airplane during repairs was sufficient to support award of damages in amount of $5,800.

> Miles v. Kavanaugh, 350 So.2d 1090.

⚷2199–2202. *For other cases see earlier editions of this digest, the Decennial Digests, and WESTLAW.*

⚷2203. —— **Computers and software.**

See also COPYRIGHTS AND INTELLECTUAL PROPERTY ⚷107.

⚷2204–2207. *For other cases see earlier editions of this digest, the Decennial Digests, and WESTLAW.*

⚷2207. **Value of goods.**

⚷2208. —— **In general.**

Fla.App. 5 Dist. 1989. Amount purchaser is entitled to recover from seller as damages on counterclaim for breach of implied warranty of fitness for particular purpose is set off against amount seller would otherwise be entitled to as purchase money; seller is entitled to judgment against purchaser for difference if amount purchaser is entitled to recover from seller as damages for breach of warranty is less than amount seller is entitled to recover as purchase money, and purchaser is entitled to judgment against seller for difference if purchaser's damages for breach of warranty exceed amount due seller for purchase money.

> Storchwerke, GMBH v. Mr. Thiessen's Wallpapering Supplies, Inc., 538 So.2d 1382.

⌖2209. —— **Market value or price in general.**

For other cases see earlier editions of this digest, the Decennial Digests, and WEST-LAW.

⌖2210. —— **Difference from value as warranted.**

S.D.Fla. 2013. Under California law, an "express warranty" is a contractual promise from the seller that the goods conform to the promise; if they do not, the buyer is entitled to recover the difference between the value of the goods accepted by the buyer and the value of the goods had they been as warranted.

> In re Horizon Organic Milk Plus DHA Omega-3 Marketing and Sales Practice Litigation, 955 F.Supp.2d 1311.

Bkrtcy.M.D.Fla. 1981. Damages which a buyer may recover under Florida law for breach of implied warranty are equal to the difference at the time and place of acceptance between actual value of the goods accepted and the value they would have had if they had been as warranted, less any proper deductions and recovery is not permitted where the difference in value is not shown. West's F.S.A. §§ 672.314, 672.607.

> Matter of Vincent, 10 B.R. 549.

⌖2211–2212. *For other cases see earlier editions of this digest, the Decennial Digests, and WESTLAW.*

⌖2212. —— **Particular cases and goods.**

⌖2212(1). **In general.**

Fla.App. 2 Dist. 1980. Since court gave supplier of nonconforming aluminum sheeting right to retrieve unused portion of the shipment, supplier could not claim that manufacturer even had benefit of scrap value of such portion of the shipment, and thus manufacturer was entitled to damages of corresponding percentage of contract price. West's F.S.A. §§ 672.607(1), (3)(a), 672.714, 612.717.

> Adam Metal Supply, Inc. v. Electrodex, Inc., 386 So.2d 1316.

In determining damages sustained by manufacturer due to acceptance of nonconforming shipment of aluminum sheeting, use of value of the aluminum after it was sheared by manufacturer rather than value of aluminum at time of its acceptance was proper where it was necessary to shear the aluminum in order to determine that it was nonconforming. West's F.S.A. § 672.714(2).

> Adam Metal Supply, Inc. v. Electrodex, Inc., 386 So.2d 1316.

Fla.App. 3 Dist. 1979. Where ten carat diamond which was warranted to be color grade "D" was on the date of sale and always was color grade "E," warranty was breached and breach entitled buyer to recover the difference between the value of the diamond as warranted and what the diamond was actually worth. West's F.S.A. § 672.714.

> Carter Hawley Hale Stores, Inc. v. Conley, 372 So.2d 965.

⌖2212(2). **Buildings, structures, and construction.**

For other cases see earlier editions of this digest, the Decennial Digests, and WEST-LAW.

⌖2212(3). **Plants, crops, and agriculture.**

Fla. 1953. In action for breach of implied warranty that watermelon seeds purchased from seller were of a certain variety when, in fact, they produced a different variety, amount of damages would be net difference between market value of crop raised and crop estimated from seed ordered.

> Corneli Seed Co. v. Ferguson, 64 So.2d 162.

Fla. 1939. The measure of damages for breach of implied warranty that seed sold by name is true to the name is difference between market value of crop raised and the crop which would have been raised from the seed ordered.

West Coast Lumber Co. v. Wernicke, 188 So. 357, 137 Fla. 363.

⚷2212(4)–2212(9). *For other cases see earlier editions of this digest, the Decennial Digests, and WESTLAW.*

⚷2212(10). **Computers and software.**

See also COPYRIGHTS AND INTELLECTUAL PROPERTY ⚷107.

⚷2213. **Additional or incidental damages; expenses.**

⚷2214. —— **In general.**

Fla.App. 2 Dist. 1980. Evidence of lost work and monetary inconvenience resulting from inability to use unregistered car and buyer's attempts to obtain title supported award of $2,500 against automobile dealer as incidental damages for breach of implied warranty of good title. West's F.S.A. §§ 672.312, 672.715(1).

Bill Branch Chevrolet, Inc. v. Redmond, 378 So.2d 319.

Fla.App. 4 Dist. 1986. Buyer suing for breach of implied warranty is entitled to both incidental and consequential damages that are proximately caused by breach.

Marcus v. Anderson/Gore Homes, Inc., 498 So.2d 1051.

Fla.App. 4 Dist. 1970. Defendant who manufactured and installed sliding glass doors in plaintiff's building, and who guaranteed water tightness of installation, was liable for water damage resulting from entry of water during hurricane and for costs of altering doors to make them immobile.

Window Master Corp. v. Home Federal Sav. & Loan Ass'n of Hollywood, 244 So.2d 524.

⚷2215. —— **Expenses connected with repair, recall, or return.**

Fla.App. 1 Dist. 1980. Damages recoverable by buyers of air conditioning system were to be limited to repairs necessary to place existing system in working condition, not in such condition as would be necessary to guarantee its working life for any specific period of time, no such guarantee being in agreement between parties that systems were in working order at time of closing, and it was error to award damages measured by cost of installation of two new systems.

Campbell v. Rawls, 381 So.2d 744.

Fla.App. 2 Dist. 1980. Manufacturer, which incurred expense in shearing aluminum sheets before it realized that the sheets were nonconforming, was entitled to percentage of such expense applicable to unusable portion of the shipment where it was necessary to shear the aluminum in order to determine that it was nonconforming. West's F.S.A. § 672.714(3).

Adam Metal Supply, Inc. v. Electrodex, Inc., 386 So.2d 1316.

Fla.App. 3 Dist. 1977. Measure of damages in breach of warranty action in sale of defective airplane could include expense of transporting airplane for repairs, expense of overhauling airplane and damages due to loss of use of airplane during repairs.

Miles v. Kavanaugh, 350 So.2d 1090.

⚷2216. **Special, indirect, or consequential damages; lost profits.**

⚷2217. —— **In general.**

C.A.5 (Fla.) 1979. In a proper case, Florida law provides for recovery of profits lost because of breach of warranty. West's F.S.A. §§ 672.714, 672.715.

National Papaya Co. v. Domain Industries, Inc., 592 F.2d 813.

Despite element of conjecture inherent in any proof of anticipated profits, an inability to establish the amount of damages with absolute exactness will not defeat recovery, under Florida law, for breach of warranty. West's F.S.A. §§ 672.714, 672.715.

National Papaya Co. v. Domain Industries, Inc., 592 F.2d 813.

Fla.App. 3 Dist. 1977. Measure of damages in breach of warranty action where goods have been accepted by buyer includes any consequential damage proximately caused by breach of warranty. West's F.S.A. §§ 672.714(3), 672.715(2).

Miles v. Kavanaugh, 350 So.2d 1090.

Fla.App. 4 Dist. 1999. Evidence of lost profits were relevant to establish value of business on date of sale but were not proper measure of damages in breach of contract case claiming that express warranty in contract was not true.

> Teca, Inc. v. WM-TAB, Inc., 726 So.2d 828, rehearing denied, review denied 743 So.2d 511.

Fla.App. 4 Dist. 1995. Under Florida's Uniform Commercial Code (UCC), measure of damages in breach of warranty action where goods have been accepted includes any consequential damages proximately caused by breach of warranty. West's F.S.A. §§ 672.714(3), 672.715(2).

> Koplowitz v. Girard, 658 So.2d 1183.

Fla.App. 4 Dist. 1986. Buyer suing for breach of implied warranty is entitled to both incidental and consequential damages that are proximately caused by breach.

> Marcus v. Anderson/Gore Homes, Inc., 498 So.2d 1051.

2218. ——— Particular cases and goods.

2218(1). In general.

Fla.App. 3 Dist. 1963. Special damages for loss of manufacturer's reputation were too speculative to be allowed in a suit for breach of warranty as to product used in the manufacture.

> Allied Chemical Corp. v. Eubanks Industries, Inc., 155 So.2d 740.

2218(2). Buildings, structures, and construction.

Fla.App. 4 Dist. 1980. Even if purchase of a comparable new condominium unit was required because of defects in paneling, there was no connection between the defects in the paneling and the condominium owner's purchase of a new unit twice as large as the original unit, with one half of the unit being rented out, so that purchaser of the condominium unit could not recover from the paneling manufacturer the increased closing cost attributable to the increase in the cost of the second unit.

> Georgia-Pacific Corp. v. Squires Development Corp., 387 So.2d 986.

Where owner of condominium unit recovered $7,500 for loss of income to its business as result of defective paneling, it could not also recover from the paneling manufacturer additional amounts for time and trouble which its staff incurred in trying to solve the paneling problem as the latter was not a compensable item of damages in a claim for breach of warranty.

> Georgia-Pacific Corp. v. Squires Development Corp., 387 So.2d 986.

2218(3)–2218(4). *For other cases see earlier editions of this digest, the Decennial Digests, and WESTLAW.*

2218(5). Machinery and equipment.

C.A.5 (Fla.) 1979. Fact of limited capacity levels for pasteurizer and cooling tunnel did not establish that factors other than substandard performance of defendant manufacturer's filling machine may have been responsible for food processor's business woes, in view of evidence that pasteurizer and cooling tunnel could easily have been increased to match the warranted capacity of defendant's machines, had they performed as warranted. West's F.S.A. §§ 672.714, 672.715.

> National Papaya Co. v. Domain Industries, Inc., 592 F.2d 813.

Although deficient performance of defendant's filling machine caused serious production problems for food processor, which in turn caused it to lose business, recovery could not be had under Florida law for entire amount of profits allegedly lost because of breach of warranty where many late or unfilled orders could not be attributed to defendant's machine with the reasonable certainty required under Florida law for recovery of lost profits. West's F.S.A. §§ 672.714, 672.715.

> National Papaya Co. v. Domain Industries, Inc., 592 F.2d 813.

Where certain sales would have been lost even if manufacturer had delivered filling machine on time and had machine performed as warranted, the award of damages to food processor, suing for breach of warranty, was clearly erroneous insofar as it included amount for profits lost on such sales. West's F.S.A. §§ 672.714, 672.715; Fed.Rules Civ.Proc. rule 52(a), 28 U.S.C.A.

> National Papaya Co. v. Domain Industries, Inc., 592 F.2d 813.

Fla. 1947. In seller's replevin action for recovery of machine, wherein defendant buyer filed plea in recoupment for damages on ground that machine did not perform as represented by contract, denial of items claimed by defendant as consequential damages which had to do primarily with wages of employees while machine was in possession of buyer but not in operation was not error, where there was a definite agreement that seller would make repairs and additions to the machine and that it would not run until these additions were made.

> Jacksonville Paper Co. v. Smith & Winchester Mfg. Co., 32 So.2d 326, 159 Fla. 532.

Fla.App. 3 Dist. 1985. Jury verdict of $260,000 in favor of commercial buyer of industrial engines against manufacturer did not shock conscience of court where engines were incorporated into irrigation systems and malfunctioned, causing losses to users of irrigation systems, which assigned their claims to buyer, and to buyer, through loss of customers, and because excessiveness of verdict was neither apparent nor ascertainable from record, trial court's order of remittitur constituted abuse of discretion.

> R.A. Jones & Sons, Inc. v. Holman, 470 So.2d 60, review dismissed Ford Motor Co. v. R.A. Jones & Sons, Inc., 482 So.2d 348.

Fla.App. 4 Dist. 1996. Award of profits lost from proposed containerized cargo business which buyer alleged it would have entered had single pneumatic cement pumping system it brought from defendant been as warranted was too speculative; buyer alleged it would have purchased four additional systems had the one system sold under the contract performed as warranted, but there was not even a proposed contract for the future purchase of these four additional systems, and no discussion between buyer and seller as to possible terms. West's F.S.A. § 672.715(1), (2)(b).

> Halliburton Co. v. Eastern Cement Corp., 672 So.2d 844, modified on clarification, review denied 683 So.2d 483.

⟜**2218(6)–2218(9).** *For other cases see earlier editions of this Decennial Digests, and WESTLAW.*

⟜**2218(10). Computers and software.**

See also COPYRIGHTS AND INTELLECTUAL PROPERTY ⟜107.

C.A.5 (Fla.) 1964. Trial court in breach of implied warranty case in which it granted rescission, upon finding that computer and related equipment forming business records system did not function as impliedly warranted, properly denied damages for supplies some of which were consumed in use and for expenses of employees who rendered some service to buyer where evidence did not show extent of admitted benefits to buyer.

> Sperry Rand Corp. v. Industrial Supply Corp., 337 F.2d 363.

Whether buyer of computer and related equipment forming business records system, entitled to rescind because of breach of warranty of fitness, was entitled to damages for cost of construction of special room, court could not be held in error for refusing to grant damages therefor where there was no certainty of proof of amount of loss and no salvage credit given.

> Sperry Rand Corp. v. Industrial Supply Corp., 337 F.2d 363.

⟜**2219. Lost, destroyed, or worthless goods.**

For other cases see earlier editions of this digest, the Decennial Digests, and WESTLAW.

⟜**2220. Injuries to other property.**

Fla.App. 4 Dist. 1970. Defendant who manufactured and installed sliding glass doors in plaintiff's building, and who guaranteed water tightness of installation, was liable for water damage resulting from entry of water during hurricane and for costs of altering doors to make them immobile.

> Window Master Corp. v. Home Federal Sav. & Loan Ass'n of Hollywood, 244 So.2d 524.

⟜**2221. Personal injuries.**

Fla.App. 2 Dist. 1977. Retail book dealer was not liable under Uniform Commercial Code to purchaser of cookbook for injuries and damages caused by improper instructions or lack of adequate warnings as to poisonous ingredients used in recipe. West's F.S.A. §§ 672.105, 672.314(1), (2)(c).

> Cardozo v. True, 342 So.2d 1053, certiorari denied 353 So.2d 674.

🗝**2222. Mitigation or reduction of loss.**

🗝**2223. —— In general.**

Fla.App. 4 Dist. 2017. Trial court was required to reduce jury's compensatory damages award by its finding that deceased wife, who was heavy smoker before she died of lung cancer, was 25 percent at fault in husband's action against tobacco company for strict liability, fraud by concealment, negligence, breach of express warranty, and breach of implied warranty; application of comparative negligence to fraud-based claims by plaintiff in tobacco case was always required.

    R.J. Reynolds Tobacco Company v. Grossman, 211 So.3d 221.

🗝**2224. —— Expenses saved and costs avoided.**

For other cases see earlier editions of this digest, the Decennial Digests, and WEST-LAW.

🗝**2225. —— Use or resale of defective goods.**

Fla.App. 1 Dist. 1973. Where buyer contracted with seller for purchase of new automobile but received automobile which had been substantially wrecked prior to sale and buyer was not able to enjoy use of the automobile and sought to have seller remedy defects and exerted every reasonable effort to procure new automobile from seller, seller was not entitled to have fair rental value of the automobile, the use of which buyer had for approximately one year, offset against buyer's award of damages for breach of contract.

    Cowart v. Claude Nolan, Inc., 281 So.2d 907.

🗝**2226. Punitive or exemplary damages.**

C.A.11 (Fla.) 1983. Under Florida law, punitive damage awards are not allowed for breach of warranty claims under the Uniform Commercial Code. West's F.S.A. §§ 671.101 et seq., 672.314, 672.314(2), 672.315; U.C.C. § 2–315 comment.

    Royal Typewriter Co., a Div. of Litton Business Systems, Inc. v. Xerographic Supplies Corp., 719 F.2d 1092.

Under Florida law, plaintiffs may recover punitive damages based upon breach of warranty claims only when acts of contractual breach also amount to separate and independent tort which was willfully and wantonly committed or attended by abuse, malice, or gross negligence. West's F.S.A. §§ 671.101 et seq., 672.313(1)(a), 672.314, 672.314(2), 672.315; U.C.C. § 2–315 comment.

    Royal Typewriter Co., a Div. of Litton Business Systems, Inc. v. Xerographic Supplies Corp., 719 F.2d 1092.

Under Florida law, dealer's claims for damages predicated on allegations that manufacturer misrepresented features of copier machines were not distinct from breach of warranty claims and could not support award of punitive damages.

    Royal Typewriter Co., a Div. of Litton Business Systems, Inc. v. Xerographic Supplies Corp., 719 F.2d 1092.

M.D.Fla. 1996. Plaintiff provided reasonable basis for punitive damages claim under Florida law in negligence, strict liability, breach of express warranty, breach of implied warranty, and misrepresentation action against acetaminophen manufacturer; plaintiff alleged that defendant had actual knowledge of alcohol/acetaminophen problem, that defendant's intent was to "muddy the waters" in event of publicity, that defendant sent letter to pharmacists and hospitals stating that there was no link between liver damage and casual alcohol consumption combined with acetaminophen, and that defendant did not convey to consumers risk of liver damage arising from alcohol/acetaminophen interaction. West's F.S.A. § 768.72.

    Domke v. McNeil-P.P.C., Inc., 939 F.Supp. 849.

Fla.App. 1 Dist. 1983. Plaintiff was not entitled to award of punitive damages in action against insecticide manufacturer for breach of warranty where plaintiff did not plead and prove independent tort against manufacturer in that representations which allegedly created warranty were precisely same representations as those which plaintiff chose to characterize as tortious.

    Mobil Chemical Co., a Div. of Mobil Corp. v. Hawkins, 440 So.2d 378, petition for review denied 449 So.2d 264.

Fla.App. 3 Dist. 1968. Failure to show an independent tort, separate and apart from breach of contract, precluded award of punitive damages in action for breach of implied or oral warranty of fitness for particular purpose and for breach of oral agreement to forbear.

Maco Supply Corp. v. Masciarelli, 213 So.2d 265, affirmed in part, quashed in part 224 So.2d 329, on remand 223 So.2d 790, opinion vac in part 223 So.2d 790.

Fla.App. 4 Dist. 2017. Punitive damages award of $22.5 million against tobacco company, in light of $13.5 million compensatory damages award, was not excessive in action by husband of deceased wife, who was heavy smoker before she died of lung cancer, for strict liability, fraud by concealment, conspiracy to commit fraud by concealment, negligence, breach of express warranty, and breach of implied warranty; award fell under constitutionally acceptable range as established by other cases against tobacco companies.

R.J. Reynolds Tobacco Company v. Grossman, 211 So.3d 221.

⚷2227–2228. *For other cases see earlier editions of this digest, the Decennial Digests, and WESTLAW.*

⚷2227. Monetary remedies for breach of warranty of title.

⚷2229. —— Particular cases and goods.

Fla.App. 1 Dist. 1976. Recovery by buyer of tractor in contract action brought against seller for breach of warranty of title after tractor which was stolen was claimed by its rightful owner could not be reduced by amount of insurance proceeds received by buyer for damage sustained by tractor before it was claimed by owner.

Walker v. Hilliard, 329 So.2d 44.

Fla.App. 2 Dist. 1980. Evidence of lost work and monetary inconvenience resulting from inability to use unregistered car and buyer's attempts to obtain title supported award of $2,500 against automobile dealer as incidental damages for breach of implied warranty of good title. West's F.S.A. §§ 672.312, 672.715(1).

Bill Branch Chevrolet, Inc. v. Redmond, 378 So.2d 319.

Fla.App. 4 Dist. 1981. Purchaser, which was told that fixtures were free and clear of all encumbrances while it turned out that they were owned by other parties, was entitled to recover $6,000 for auto dealership seller's breach of warranty in sale of certain fixtures.

AMC/Jeep of Vero Beach, Inc. v. Funston, 403 So.2d 602.

⚷2230. Interest.

For other cases see earlier editions of this digest, the Decennial Digests, and WESTLAW.

(D) RESCISSION.

Revocation of acceptance, see V(C)5. Repudiation, see V(J). Cancellation and termination, see VI.

⚷2241. In general.

Fla.App. 3 Dist. 1982. Remedies of cancellation and revocation of acceptance under the Uniform Commercial Code are equitable in nature so as to invoke the jurisdiction of the circuit court. West's F.S.A. §§ 672.608, 672.711.

Peppler v. Kasual Kreations, Inc., 416 So.2d 864.

⚷2242. Status of doctrine under Uniform Commercial Code.

Fla.App. 4 Dist. 2003. Aircraft buyers did not have the right, under the Uniform Commercial Code (UCC), to revoke their acceptance of the aircraft based on a reasonable assumption that its nonconformity would be cured, where the sales agreement expressly provided the aircraft was being sold "as is." West's F.S.A. § 672.608.

Giallo v. New Piper Aircraft, Inc., 855 So.2d 1273, cause dismissed 869 So.2d 539, rehearing denied.

⚷2243. Right to rescind; grounds.

⚷2244. —— In general.

Fla.App. 2 Dist. 1965. Contract for sale of "snow ice" manufactured by defendant for plaintiff in ice making machinery maintained by defendant in plaintiff's fresh vegetable packing house was properly rescinded on basis of impossibility of performance or frustration of purpose, where plaintiff had been induced to enter into contract through misrepresentation that defendant could and would furnish all ice required by plaintiff as needed and machinery installed by defendant was not capable of fulfilling these needs.

> Crown Ice Mach. Leasing Co. v. Sam Senter Farms, Inc., 174 So.2d 614, certiorari denied 180 So.2d 656.

Fla.App. 3 Dist. 1987. Contract and security agreement regarding purchase of automobile were properly rescinded, based on finding that they did not accurately reflect agreement reached by parties.

> Braman Dodge, Inc. v. Smith, 515 So.2d 1053.

Fla.App. 3 Dist. 1970. Buyer of airplane was not entitled to rescind contract of purchase on basis of temporary unavailability of records of aircraft, where it resulted at most in some inconvenience.

> Pinellas Central Bank & Trust Co. v. International Aerodyne, Inc., 233 So.2d 872, certiorari denied 239 So.2d 829.

👈**2245. —— Invalidity of contract.**

For other cases see earlier editions of this digest, the Decennial Digests, and WEST-LAW.

👈**2246. —— Breach of contract or condition in general.**

Fla. 1941. Under contract for sale of fruit, requiring buyer to pick and pay for all merchantable fruit by specified date unless he was entitled to extension of time for picking under specified circumstances, seller's insistence that buyer pick first the fruit from most badly damaged grove, after freeze, and refusal to grant extension of time for such picking, was sufficiently material if unwarranted, to entitle buyer to treat the contract as rescinded.

> Givens v. Vaughn-Griffin Packing Co., 1 So.2d 714, 146 Fla. 575.

Fla.App. 2 Dist. 1963. Citrus fruit buyer was not entitled to rescission and cancellation of contract providing for delivery of fruit from specified groves although sellers sold and removed almost half the oranges from those groves, leaving less than half the amount of fruit to be delivered in the groves, where oranges in those groves had no particular or peculiar value, the alleged injuries were compensa-

ble in damages, and sellers were not claimed to be insolvent.

> McDonald v. Connell, 158 So.2d 780.

Fla.App. 3 Dist. 1980. Fact that seller's employees made $597.08 in direct sales of wallpaper, in violation of exclusive distribution provision of parties' agreement, did not justify purchaser's recission of entire contract by refusing to honor its undertaking to purchase well over $100,000 of material from seller, since seller's breach was not material or substantial one.

> Gittlin Companies, Inc. v. David & Dash, Inc., 390 So.2d 86.

Fla.App. 4 Dist. 1986. Buyer could not terminate contract based on seller's failure to timely complete installation where buyer's request for installation completion could reasonably be interpreted as request and not ultimatum, and where buyer had caused previous installation delay.

> Solitron Devices, Inc. v. Veeco Instruments, Inc., 492 So.2d 1357.

👈**2247–2248.** *For other cases see earlier editions of this digest, the Decennial Digests, and WESTLAW.*

👈**2249. —— Failure of consideration.**

Fla.App. 3 Dist. 1970. Buyer of personalty may not rescind sale for partial failure of consideration, if it is compensable by damages and is not so substantial and fundamental as to tend to defeat object of parties in making the contract.

> Pinellas Central Bank & Trust Co. v. International Aerodyne, Inc., 233 So.2d 872, certiorari denied 239 So.2d 829.

👈**2250. —— Failure to deliver.**

C.A.11 (Fla.) 1983. Under Florida law, any breach which may have occurred by delay in delivery of securities was not material to performance of option contract and purchaser's attempt, without notice to seller, to terminate contract unilaterally was without legal justification entitling seller to damages for breach of contract, even though contract stated that delivery had to occur on a certain date, as there was no language in contract suggesting that time of delivery was an essential element of seller's performance and purchaser failed to establish any damages resulting from delay in delivery.

Westcap Government Securities, Inc. v. Homestead Air Force Base Federal Credit Union, 697 F.2d 911.

Fla. 1957. Where orders for propeller assemblies were executed on identical forms and were signed by both plaintiff and defendant, but they bore different dates, described varying quantities of goods and different prices, and no dates of delivery appeared in first order but dates of delivery were specified in second order, orders constituted separate contracts and defendant-purchaser was justified in cancelling second contract for failure of plaintiff-seller to deliver on specified dates even though buyer had delayed acceptance of some of propellers delivered under first order.

Riley Aircraft Mfg. Inc. v. Koppers Co., 99 So.2d 227.

⌇2251. —— Defect in title.

Fla.App. 3 Dist. 1970. Bailee's charge for maintenance and storage, the only outstanding lien against aircraft, was not ground for rescission of contract to purchase aircraft, where parties had agreed that existence of outstanding lien would be basis for buyer to renounce sale only if neither of parties was willing to discharge it by payment and, when advised of charge, seller readily recognized his obligation to pay it and subsequently did so.

Pinellas Central Bank & Trust Co. v. International Aerodyne, Inc., 233 So.2d 872, certiorari denied 239 So.2d 829.

⌇2252. —— Defect in quantity or quality of goods.

M.D.Fla. 2002. Allegations by purchasers of motor home that dealership that sold motor home was agent for manufacturer, and thus purchasers were in contractual privity with manufacturer, that valid contract existed when they bought motor home, that benefits for which purchasers bargained were frustrated due to defects in motor home which dealership had been unable to repair, that purchasers gave manufacturer notice of their intention to rescind, and that purchasers had

attempted to restore parties to their original positions, were sufficient to state claim against manufacturer for rescission of contract under Florida law.

Bland v. Freightliner LLC, 206 F.Supp.2d 1202.

Fla.App. 3 Dist. 2006. Buyer of new piano that was not in new condition when delivered was entitled to cancel the sale, return the piano to buyer, and recover the entire purchase price, even if piano as delivered was worth at least as much as buyer paid; buyer of non-conforming goods such as the piano retained the option either to claim the difference in value or to cancel the sale. West's F.S.A. §§ 672.711, 672.714.

Jauregui v. Bobb's Piano Sales & Service, Inc., 922 So.2d 303.

Fla.App. 5 Dist. 1983. Even if seller's breach of sales contract, in failing to provide mobile home with beamed living room ceiling, with ceramic tile in bathrooms and with a 36-inch wide door, was curable by damage award, buyers were entitled to cancel the contract. West's F.S.A. §§ 672.711, 672.711(1).

Royco, Inc. v. Cottengim, 427 So.2d 759, petition for review denied 431 So.2d 989.

⌇2253. —— Breach of warranty.

Fla.App. 3 Dist. 1979. Under the Uniform Commercial Code, when nonconforming tender is delivered, it is the buyer's choice whether to reject the goods and cause a recission of the contract and bring suit for their purchase price or to accept the goods and receive as damages for breach of warranty the difference at the time and place of acceptance between the value of the goods accepted and the value they would have had if they had been as warranted. West's F.S.A. § 672.714.

Carter Hawley Hale Stores, Inc. v. Conley, 372 So.2d 965.

Fla.App. 3 Dist. 1972. Where warranty provision excluding all express or implied warranties except as provided in contract was in the same color and size of type used for other provisions of automobile sales contract, the disclaimer was not "conspicuous" and was ineffective and did not bar remedy of rescission, despite contention that contract provided for a remedy by agreement in providing only for replacement or repair. F.S.A. §§ 672.316(2), 672.719.

> Orange Motors of Coral Gables, Inc. v. Dade County Dairies, Inc., 258 So.2d 319, certiorari denied 263 So.2d 831.

2254. —— Redhibitory defects or vices.

Fla.App. 5 Dist. 1986. Buyers of computer hardware and software which were purchased as a package to solve a business problem could rescind purchase of both hardware and software based on finding that the software did not perform satisfactorily, although some of the hardware performed as expected. West's F.S.A. § 672.608(1).

> Winterbotham v. Computer Corps, Inc., 490 So.2d 1282.

2255–2258. *For other cases see earlier editions of this digest, the Decennial Digests, and WESTLAW.*

2259. Waiver or estoppel.

Fla.App. 2 Dist. 1967. Where buyer admitted contract to buy toys and delivery and receipt of toys and failure to pay for them and alleged that under contract he was to have exclusive right to sell toys but that seller had prior to consummation of contract sold goods to another retailer, and buyer had since disposed of all toys, parties could not be placed in status quo and buyer's ratification of contract precluded rescission.

> Watson v. Knox Instruments, Inc., 193 So.2d 697.

2260. Conditions precedent.

2261. —— In general.

C.A.5 (Fla.) 1973. Under Florida law, since it is inequitable to allow one party to sales contract to retain both the subject matter of the transaction and the benefit conferred upon him by the other party, the interests of both parties must be recognized and enforced.

> Gentry v. Smith, 487 F.2d 571, appeal after remand Smith v. American Motor Inns of Florida, Inc., 538 F.2d 1090, on rehearing 544 F.2d 900.

Fla.App. 5 Dist. 1987. Before granting rescission of sales contract, compliance with applicable Uniform Commercial Code provisions must be shown.

> Central Florida Antenna Service, Inc. v. Crabtree, 503 So.2d 1351.

Fla.App. 5 Dist. 1986. Rescission was available remedy, whether or not sellers could be restored to condition preceding contract, where sellers fraudulently misrepresented income of business and refused buyer's offer to restore businesses to sellers at time restoration was possible.

> Mulle v. Scheiler, 484 So.2d 47, review denied 492 So.2d 1334.

2262. —— Restoration of consideration.

For other cases see earlier editions of this digest, the Decennial Digests, and WESTLAW.

2263. —— Restoration of goods.

C.A.5 (Fla.) 1973. Under Florida law, since it is inequitable to allow one party to sales contract to retain both the subject matter of the transaction and benefit conferred upon him by the other party, the interests of both parties must be recognized and enforced.

> Gentry v. Smith, 487 F.2d 571, appeal after remand Smith v. American Motor Inns of Florida, Inc., 538 F.2d 1090, on rehearing 544 F.2d 900.

C.A.5 (Fla.) 1956. Where there has been total or partial payment of purchase price by buyer, buyer may not be required to show an unconditional return of property as prerequisite to rescission of purchase, where seller has refused to accept buyer's offer to return.

> Alegre v. Marine Motor Sales Corp., 228 F.2d 713.

Fla. 1941. A contract for sale of fruit, providing that fruit which had been damaged in specified manner was not included, was "severable" and under it buyer's duty was to pick only good merchantable fruit, discarding the frost-damaged fruit which he was under no obligation to pick or pay for, and hence buyer was not obliged to restore executed portion of the contract before treating arbitrary and unjustifiable demand of seller as an offer to rescind.

>Givens v. Vaughn-Griffin Packing Co., 1 So.2d 714, 146 Fla. 575.

Fla.App. 4 Dist. 1992. Remedy of rescission was not available to buyer of automobile who had established fraud in connection with nondisclosure of accident in which vehicle had been involved; restoration of parties to situation prior to contract was required for rescission to be available, and trial court had expressly found that restoration was not possible due to depreciation of car.

>Bush v. Palm Beach Imports, Inc., 610 So.2d 68.

Fla.App. 5 Dist. 1986. Remedy of rescission, generally not available unless condition of parties as it existed prior to execution of contract can be restored, is subject to an exception where inability of buyer to restore is caused by the very fraud perpetrated by the sellers.

>Mulle v. Scheiler, 484 So.2d 47, review denied 492 So.2d 1334.

⚷**2264–2268.** *For other cases see earlier editions of this digest, the Decennial Digests, and WESTLAW.*

⚷**2265. Time for rescission, and laches.**

⚷**2268. —— Rescission by buyer.**

⚷**2268(1). In general.**

Fla. 1953. Party claiming fraud, misrepresentation, or deceit cannot sit idly by and wait until conditions suit him to put other party on notice or to take action with reference to rescission of sales contract, or to claim damages because of claimed inaccurate financial statement.

>Street v. Bartow Growers Processing Corp., 67 So.2d 228.

Fla.App. 3 Dist. 1974. One asserting that he has been victim of fraud and is entitled to rescission of sales agreement should assert his rights promptly and without delay.

>Gladding Corp. v. Register, 293 So.2d 729, certiorari discharged 322 So.2d 911.

Although buyers of business accused seller of various prevarications and intentional falsehoods regarding financial status

of business and ability to manufacture certain goods, buyer which made no effort to rescind until 15 months after closing date of sale waived a right to rescind sale.

>Gladding Corp. v. Register, 293 So.2d 729, certiorari discharged 322 So.2d 911.

Fla.App. 4 Dist. 1969. Finding that purchaser of crane knew that it was insufficient but nonetheless retained it and allowed damages to accumulate for nearly three years was sufficient to bar an action for rescission, and would also bar an action for damages if no notice of defects was given the seller.

>Ferncrest Mining Co. v. H. F. Mason Equipment Corp., 225 So.2d 354.

Delay in instituting suit, keeping equipment purchased and having repairs and adjustments made, may bar an action for rescission since the parties cannot be placed in the same position, but it does not preclude an action for damages.

>Ferncrest Mining Co. v. H. F. Mason Equipment Corp., 225 So.2d 354.

⚷**2268(2)–2269.** *For other cases see earlier editions of this digest, the Decennial Digests, and WESTLAW.*

⚷**2270. Partial rescission.**

Fla. 1941. Where seller of fruit improperly refused to permit buyer an extension of time in which to gather fruit, so that buyer might determine what fruit had been damaged by frost, buyer could treat such attitude as an offer to rescind and act thereon without restoring the executed portion of the contract, consisting of merchantable fruit which buyer had already picked, shipped and paid for in accordance with the contract, where seller did not offer to return the payments.

>Givens v. Vaughn-Griffin Packing Co., 1 So.2d 714, 146 Fla. 575.

⚷**2271. Agreements to rescind; mutual rescission.**

C.A.5 (Fla.) 1980. Under Florida law, Uniform Commercial Code did not preclude mutual rescission under circumstances in which no breach had occurred. West's F.S.A. §§ 671.103, 672.711.

> USA for Use and Benefit of Vulcan Materials v. Volpe Const., 622 F.2d 880.

Fla. 1951. Mere repossession by seller of goods sold that had been returned to him or abandoned by buyer does not of itself necessarily effect or evidence a mutual rescission of sale.

> Collier v. Fox, 49 So.2d 801.

🔑**2272. Operation and effect.**

Fla.App. 2 Dist. 2003. Voluntary rescission of asset sale by veterinary practice did not resurrect practice's ability to enforce former employee's covenant not to compete which was extinguished by sale; employee was not party to rescinded contract, contract did not convey any rights to his services, and termination of covenant could not be unilaterally undone. F.S. 1991, § 542.33(2)(a).

> Wolf v. James G. Barrie, P.A., 858 So.2d 1083, rehearing denied.

🔑**2273–2275.** *For other cases see earlier editions of this digest, the Decennial Digests, and WESTLAW.*

(E) EXCLUSIVE, CONCURRENT, AND CONFLICTING REMEDIES; ELECTION.

🔑**2281–2282.** *For other cases see earlier editions of this digest, the Decennial Digests, and WESTLAW.*

🔑**2282. Seller's remedies.**

🔑**2283. —— In general.**

Fla. 1943. Where property is sold on a credit and title reserved by vendor, upon breach of conditions of sale, vendor may treat the sale as absolute and sue for the price thereof or treat the sale as canceled and recover the property, but he cannot pursue both courses.

> Kauffman v. International Harvester Co., 14 So.2d 387, 153 Fla. 188.

🔑**2284. —— Recovery of goods; reclamation.**

Fla. 1976. Upon default, seller of goods under conditional sales contract may elect to sue on debt or to maintain action in replevin for property, but once having sought recovery of sale price seller cannot thereafter retake possession in replevin, under election of remedies doctrine.

> Encore, Inc. v. Olivetti Corp. of America, 326 So.2d 161.

Action for recovery of entire purchase price of property sold under conditional sales contract is irrevocable election to treat transaction as sale which passes title to buyer, and such vesting of absolute title in buyer is inconsistent with any subsequent action for repossession of property, which is considered to be based on rescission of contract.

> Encore, Inc. v. Olivetti Corp. of America, 326 So.2d 161.

🔑**2285–2289.** *For other cases see earlier editions of this digest, the Decennial Digests, and WESTLAW.*

🔑**2285. Buyer's remedies.**

🔑**2290. —— Economic loss doctrine.**

Fla. 1987. Product value and quality is covered by express and implied warranties, and warranty law, not tort law, should control a claim for purely economic losses resulting from damage to product itself.

> Florida Power & Light Co. v. Westinghouse Elec. Corp., 510 So.2d 899, answer to certified question conformed to 835 F.2d 817.

Contract principles are more appropriate than tort principles for resolving economic loss, resulting from product defect, without accompanying physical injury or property damage.

> Florida Power & Light Co. v. Westinghouse Elec. Corp., 510 So.2d 899, answer to certified question conformed to 835 F.2d 817.

🔑**2291–2293.** *For other cases see earlier editions of this digest, the Decennial Digests, and WESTLAW.*

🔑**2291. Relation of rescission to other remedies.**

🔑**2294. —— Rescission by buyer.**

C.A.5 (Fla.) 1976. Where both parties to contracts for manufacture and sale of commercial jet airliners continued to perform under contracts as though they remained in force, without ever making reference to procedures proscribed by Uniform Commercial Code for termination of contract on showing of commercial impracticability, contracts were not automatically terminated under such procedures. West's Ann.Cal.Com.Code, §§ 2615, 2616, 2616(2).

> Eastern Air Lines, Inc. v. McDonnell Douglas Corp., 532 F.2d 957.

C.C.A.5 (Fla.) 1947. Where time was of the essence of two separate contracts covering wedge bolts and each contract provided that shipment must begin by "June 7th to 10th and be completed by _____" shipments were required to begin by June 10, and where no bolts had been shipped by late June and notice of cancellation was given but small shipment of bolts was later received and used and notice of cancellation was given on July 29th, the latter notice of cancellation controlled.

> Morris v. Prefabrication Engineering Co., 160 F.2d 779.

⚷2295–2296. *For other cases see earlier editions of this digest, the Decennial Digests, and WESTLAW.*

(F) CONTRACTUAL MODIFICATION OR LIMITATION OF REMEDY.

⚷2301. In general.

† C.A.11 (Fla.) 2007. Under Florida law, prospective buyer of jet aircraft was not entitled to recover additional damages against seller for alleged breach of contract, in connection with seller's unilateral termination of agreement, where the parties' agreement specified that the sole remedy in the event of non-delivery of the jet was the return of the deposit and repayment of inspection costs, and seller returned the deposit and repaid the inspection costs. West's F.S.A. § 672.719(1)(b).

> Jet Sales of Stuart, LLC v. Jet Connection Travel, GmbH, 240 Fed.Appx. 839.

M.D.Fla. 2007. Where the seller breaches a contract, the buyer's remedies under Florida law are not necessarily lim-

ited under a limitation clause to a return of the initial deposit.

> Horowitch v. Diamond Aircraft Industries, Inc., 526 F.Supp.2d 1236, certificate of appealability granted by 2007 WL 2904135, vacated, appeal dismissed 299 Fed.Appx. 951, on remand 2009 WL 1537896, order vacated in part on reconsideration 2009 WL 1537896.

⚷2302. Validity and enforceability in general.

N.D.Fla. 1980. Provisions in contract for sale of computer software and hardware limiting damages recoverable for breach of warranty and breach of contract were enforceable under Florida law. West's F.S.A. §§ 672.316(4), 672.719.

> Hi Neighbor Enterprises, Inc. v. Burroughs Corp., 492 F.Supp. 823.

⚷2303. Incidental, consequential, indirect, or special damages.

C.A.11 (Fla.) 2009. To extent that contract for construction of ship was treated as being for sale of goods and not for performance of services, clause in contract purporting to relieve ship builder of liability for consequential damages was enforceable under the Florida Uniform Commercial Code (UCC), and served to relieve ship builder of any liability to ship owner on third-party indemnity and contribution claims for sums which ship owner had paid in settlement of maritime tort claims asserted by vessel's captain based on alleged defect in design, construction or installation of food lift on ship; application of this contractual prohibition on consequential damages was not unconscionable. West's F.S.A. § 672.719.

> Cooper v. Meridian Yachts, Ltd., 575 F.3d 1151, rehearing denied.

⚷2304. Warranties.

⚷2305. —— In general.

S.D.Fla. 2013. Under Florida law, a written warranty is treated like a contract between the seller and the buyer; as such, the terms of an express warranty may limit or foreclose the remedies available to the buyer.

> Aprigliano v. American Honda Motor Co., Inc., 979 F.Supp.2d 1331.

S.D.Fla. 2009. Under Florida law, a written warranty is treated as a contract between buyer and seller, and therefore may, by its terms, limit the remedies available. West's F.S.A. §§ 672.316, 672.719.

David v. American Suzuki Motor Corp., 629 F.Supp.2d 1309.

Fla.App. 3 Dist. 1990. Complaint of greenhouse owner alleging that negligent manufacturer of fiberglass panels for greenhouse caused them to fail during rainstorm, resulting in damage to owner's plants, stated cause of action despite claim that owner's remedy was limited to manufacturer's express warranty; warranty purported only to limit breach of warranty contractual damages and did not expressly absolve manufacturer of any liability for manufacturer's own negligence.

Kerry's Bromeliad Nursery, Inc. v. Reiling, 561 So.2d 1305.

☞**2306.** —— **Validity and enforceability in general.**

C.A.5 (Fla.) 1980. Fact of the relatively short period between signing of computer equipment sales contract and lease, fact that there were only two or three meetings between the manufacturer and the lessee prior to the signing, and fact that the lessee was in the business of selling oil and oil products and was thus presumably unfamiliar with computers did not show that limitations of liability and disclaimers of warranty were unconscionable. West's F.S.A. § 672.302.

Earman Oil Co., Inc. v. Burroughs Corp., 625 F.2d 1291.

C.A.5 (Fla.) 1973. Florida Uniform Commercial Code creates a presumption that clauses prescribing remedies are cumulative rather than exclusive, and, if parties intend for a written warranty to prescribe an exclusive remedy, this must be clearly expressed. F.S.A. § 672.719.

Council Bros., Inc. v. Ray Burner Co., 473 F.2d 400.

Fla. 1983. In proceeding on contractor's claim against seller of hardening agent to recover amount contractor paid property owner when hardening agent contaminated property owner's foodstuffs, in which case went to jury on negligence theory and there was no count in strict liability, seller of hardening agent was en-

titled to present to jury the warranty clause which was contained in document received by contractor from the seller prior to purchase of the hardening agent and which provided that the only obligation of seller and its distributor would be to replace any of the product which proved to be defective; the limitations of remedy provision was not prima facie unconscionable and should have been given effect absent a showing of unconscionability.

Radiation Technology, Inc. v. Ware Const. Co., 445 So.2d 329.

Fla.App. 2 Dist. 1979. Plaintiff's reliance upon crashworthiness doctrine in suit against motorcycle manufacturer did not preclude plaintiff from asserting claims for breach of implied warranty and strict liability.

Nicolodi v. Harley-Davidson Motor Co., Inc., 370 So.2d 68.

Fla.App. 3 Dist. 1990. Clause in contract for sale of goods, stating that all agreements were contained in written contract, did not operate to bar recovery under warranty theory.

State Farm Ins. Co. v. Nu Prime Roll-A-Way of Miami, 557 So.2d 107.

☞**2307.** —— **Incidental, consequential, indirect, or special damages.**

C.A.11 (Fla.) 1983. Where no defective material or workmanship was alleged in action for breach of contract and warranty in regard to sale of typesetter, trial court properly applied provision of contract limiting remedy to "the repair or replacement of defective or non-conforming parts or units resulting from defective material or poor workmanship" to proscribe award of consequential damages. West's F.S.A. § 672.719.

Typographical Service, Inc. v. Itek Corp., 721 F.2d 1317.

S.D.Fla. 2008. Under Georgia law, conditions of sale incorporated into agreement for sale of concrete modular blocks to construction company barred company's assignee's claims against seller for consequential or incidental damages, where agreement's exclusive remedy for breach of limited warranty was repayment of purchase price or, at seller's option, replacement of non-conforming goods.

> Pycsa Panama, S.A. v. Tensar Earth Technologies, Inc., 625 F.Supp.2d 1198, affirmed 329 Fed.Appx. 257.

⚷2308. —— Repair or replacement.

† **C.A.11 (Fla.) 2014.** Under Florida law, aircraft was subject to limited warranty in purchase agreement between purchaser and dealer, and thus limited warranty effectively limited purchaser's remedy to repair or replacement at manufacturer's option; purchase agreement stated that all new aircraft were covered by the limited warranty, and purchaser executed limited warranty when he took possession of the aircraft.

> HTC Leleu Family Trust v. Piper Aircraft, Inc., 571 Fed.Appx. 772.

C.A.11 (Fla.) 1983. Under Florida law, limitation to repair or replace in contract for sale of goods fails of its essential purpose if seller does not provide goods that conform to contract within reasonable time. U.C.C. § 2–719; West's F.S.A. § 672.719.

> Typographical Service, Inc. v. Itek Corp., 721 F.2d 1317.

Where no defective material or workmanship was alleged in action for breach of contract and warranty in regard to sale of typesetter, trial court properly applied provision of contract limiting remedy to "the repair or replacement of defective or non-conforming parts or units resulting from defective material or poor workmanship" to proscribe award of consequential damages. West's F.S.A. § 672.719.

> Typographical Service, Inc. v. Itek Corp., 721 F.2d 1317.

M.D.Fla. 2009. Under Florida law, a repair-or-replace warranty is breached only if the warrantor does not remedy the covered defects within a reasonable time.

> Brisson v. Ford Motor Co., 602 F.Supp.2d 1227, affirmed in part, vacated in part, remanded 349 Fed. Appx. 433.

S.D.Fla. 2013. Under Florida law, motorcycle purchasers who purchased their motorcycles after expiration of the manufacturer's factory warranties, which limited remedies available to owners to the reparation or replacement of defective parts for a three-year period, did not have an ownership interest in their motorcycles during the motorcycles' warranty periods, could not state a claim for breach of express warranty in their putative class action against manufacturer.

> Aprigliano v. American Honda Motor Co., Inc., 979 F.Supp.2d 1331.

Fla.App. 1 Dist. 1985. Even if motor home sellers' disclaimer of any warranties other than repair or replacement had created an exclusive remedy, that remedy had failed of its essential purpose where motor home had been bought for family trips and on each trip the buyers encountered difficulties of a degree that went beyond simple inconvenience and efforts to repair the defects were unsuccessful. West's F.S.A. §§ 672.719, 672.719(1)(b), 672.719 comment; U.C.C. § 2–719(1)(b).

> Parsons v. Motor Homes of America, Inc., 465 So.2d 1285.

Even if motor home manufacturer's warranty notice effectively limited buyers' remedy to stated remedy of repair or replacement, that limitation was not effective to preclude other U.C.C. remedies, in view of the Magnuson-Moss Warranty—Federal Trade Commission Improvement Act, in that in addition to receiving their written limited warranty the buyers also purchased a service contract. West's F.S.A. §§ 672.714, 672.719, 672.719(1)(b), 672.719 comment; U.C.C. § 2–719(1)(b).

> Parsons v. Motor Homes of America, Inc., 465 So.2d 1285.

Fla.App. 3 Dist. 1972. After the purchase of an automobile, the same should be put in good running condition and the seller does not have an unlimited time for the performance of the obligation to replace and repair parts or to tinker with the automobile in the hope that it may ultimately be made to comply with the warranty.

> Orange Motors of Coral Gables, Inc. v. Dade County Dairies, Inc., 258 So.2d 319, certiorari denied 263 So.2d 831.

Fla.App. 5 Dist. 1985. There was no procedural unconscionability when customer signed contract with film processor, which limited liability for any loss or damage to film to replacement cost of nonexposed roll of film, as evidence showed that customer, who was well-educated and experienced in business transactions, saw and read limitation of liability clause, even though customer was given no opportunity to negotiate terms of agreement. West's F.S.A. § 672.302.

Fotomat Corp. of Florida v. Chanda, 464 So.2d 626.

⚷2309. Liquidated damages.

⚷2310. —— In general.

M.D.Fla. 1991. Under Florida law, contract may limit damages recoverable for breach and, if such provision is made, greater compensatory damages may not be awarded. West's F.S.A. §§ 672.718, 672.719.

Action Orthopedics, Inc. v. Techmedica, Inc., 759 F.Supp. 1566.

Bkrtcy.M.D.Fla. 1990. Grocery store chain, which had obtained damages from supplier for lost profits due to supplier's failure to maintain inventory, was not additionally allowed to keep unamortized portion of prepaid rent as form of liquidated damages; allowing chain to retain both rent and lost damages payment would constitute unlawful penalty.

In re Sav-A-Stop Inc., 119 B.R. 317.

Fla. 1952. Provision in a sales agreement for "liquidated damages" or "penalty" in event agreement is breached is not conclusive, but question of damages is one of law to be determined by the court, depending on terms of the instrument, its real character, circumstances surrounding its execution, and conditions attending its breach.

Paradis v. Second Ave. Used Car Co., 61 So.2d 919.

Fla.App. 2 Dist. 1979. Under contract in which buyer agreed to pick and buy all of the fruit of merchantable quality from grower's grove, grower would be entitled to further recovery if he could prove that damages limited to figure in liquidated damages clause would be unconscionably small. West's F.S.A. §§ 672.101 et seq., 672.102, 672.105(1), 672.107(2), 672.302(1), 672.718(1), 672.718 comment.

Varner v. B. L. Lanier Fruit Co., Inc., 370 So.2d 61.

Complaint alleging that plaintiff grower entered into contract with defendant buyer whereby latter was to pick and buy all fruit of merchantable qualities from grower's grove and to pay for the same at a specified rate per box, and that buyer picked 12,000 boxes but left some 9500 boxes of merchantable fruit on the trees, which grower was unable to sell elsewhere, stated cause of action despite contract provision that buyer's advance payment of $11,000 would be retained by grower in full payment of liquidated damages on buyer's breach, and fact that buyer had already paid over $16,000 on account of the agreement. West's F.S.A. §§ 672.302(1), 672.718(1), 672.719(2).

Varner v. B. L. Lanier Fruit Co., Inc., 370 So.2d 61.

⚷2311. —— Deposits, forfeitures, and restitution.

Fla.App. 2 Dist. 1979. Absent finding of unconscionability of liquidated damages clause in contract whereby buyer agreed to pick and buy all of the fruit of merchantable quality from grower's grove and parties agreed that advance payment by buyer would, in event of buyer's breach, be retained by grower in full payment of liquidated damages, buyer could recover additional damages if liquidated damages provision were found to have failed of its essential purpose, in situation where buyer had already picked enough fruit to use up the deposit but left approximately 9500 boxes of merchantable fruit on the trees, which grower was unable to sell elsewhere. West's F.S.A. §§ 672.703–672.710, 672.719(2).

Varner v. B. L. Lanier Fruit Co., Inc., 370 So.2d 61.

Fla.App. 4 Dist. 2004. Forfeiture of $50,000 deposit was an appropriate amount of liquidated damages for breach of a contract for sale of an airplane, where price of airplane was $1.7 million, and actual damages were not readily ascertainable at time contract was executed.

Atlanta Jet v. Liberty Aircraft Services, LLC, 866 So.2d 148.

Fla.App. 5 Dist. 1988. Under sales contract providing that default in payment would, at option of seller, render price at once due and payable and/or entitle seller to immediate possession and title of goods and any money retained by seller as liqui-dated damages was mutual, unequivocal and reasonable, so that upon seller's elec-tion to keep machine and deposit, as liqui-dated damages, after purchaser refused to accept delivery, seller could not recover as damages any amount more than deposit.

Design Time, Inc. v. Monco of Orlan-do, Inc., 518 So.2d 454, review de-nied 525 So.2d 879.

XI. ACTIONS.

(A) IN GENERAL.

⚷2401–2403. *For other cases see earlier editions of this digest, the Decennial Digests, and WESTLAW.*

⚷2402. Existence, nature, and form of action.

⚷2404. —— Action by seller.

C.A.11 (Fla.) 2010. Under Georgia law, provision of installment contract stat-ing that if purchaser "fail[ed] to order and pay for at least the minimum dollar amount of Products during any applicable period of time," supplier could, "at [its] sole and absolute discretion," terminate or renegotiate the agreement, or revoke its exclusivity, did not effectively limit suppli-er's remedies to the listed remedies; con-tract did not clearly express that the listed remedies were the exclusive remedies available to supplier. West's Ga.Code Ann. § 11–2–719(1).

Advanced Bodycare Solutions, LLC v. Thione Intern., Inc., 615 F.3d 1352.

Fla.App. 3 Dist. 1989. Distributor which purchased pearl necklaces from supplier and resold them to buyer at a profit had standing to sue buyer for breach of contract.

Ivens Corp. v. Hobe Cie Ltd., 555 So.2d 425, review denied 564 So.2d 1086.

Fla.App. 3 Dist. 1964. Where con-tract for sale of business was totally breached, seller must elect either the method of damages which seeks to treat contract as void or the method whereby he affirms contract and seeks to recover loss of profits; he could pursue only one meth-od, and he could not introduce evidence as to both methods.

Sundie v. Lindsay, 166 So.2d 152.

⚷2405. —— Action by buyer.

For other cases see earlier editions of this digest, the Decennial Digests, and WEST-LAW.

⚷2406. —— Good faith and fair dealing.

S.D.Fla. 2009. Under Florida law, buyer under contract for sale and delivery of food commodities could not maintain express breach of contract claims against seller for contracts buyer repudiated, and thus buyer could also not maintain a claim for breach of implied covenant of good faith and fair dealing.

Validsa, Inc. v. PDVSA Services Inc., 632 F.Supp.2d 1219, affirmed in part, reversed in part 424 Fed.Appx. 862.

⚷2407. —— Rescission.

C.C.A.5 (Fla.) 1947. On a justified rescission, buyers were entitled to reclaim what they had paid but as a condition of doing so they must have announced and adhered to the rescission and must also restore, as far as possible, the status quo.

Morris v. Prefabrication Engineering Co., 160 F.2d 779.

Fla. 1941. In action by buyer of fruit to recover money paid under sales con-tract allegedly rescinded by seller, seller could not invoke rule that there could be no rescission unless both parties could have been restored to the condition they were in before contract was made, where seller did not deny that he had been paid for all fruit picked before the alleged re-scission and never offered to return such payments, and did not charge buyer's pri-or failure to live up to the contract.

Givens v. Vaughn-Griffin Packing Co., 1 So.2d 714, 146 Fla. 575.

Fla.App. 3 Dist. 1977. Although ac-tion by buyer to recover purchase price paid ordinarily rests on rescission of con-tract of sale, such action may be based on breach of contract where goods have not been delivered.

Freund v. Gross, 345 So.2d 1097.

⚷2408–2410. *For other cases see earlier editions of this digest, the Decennial Digests, and WESTLAW.*

⚷2408. **Conditions precedent.**

⚷2411. —— **Action by buyer.**

C.A.5 (Fla.) 1976. Notification of seller by buyer of breach after buyer has accepted tender of goods is integral part of buyer's cause of action and is not affirmative defense of seller; therefore, buyer must both plead and prove that notice requirement has been complied with. West's Ann.Cal.Com.Code, §§ 2607, 2607(3)(a).

Eastern Air Lines, Inc. v. McDonnell Douglas Corp., 532 F.2d 957.

M.D.Fla. 2006. Under California law, bottle supplier's inability to manufacture product for customer at facility designated by contract, due to sale of such facility during bankruptcy proceedings of supplier's parent company, rendered performance under parties' supply contract impossible, excusing supplier's performance.

In re Anchor Glass Container Corp., 345 B.R. 765.

Fla.App. 2 Dist. 1980. Under statute providing that buyer must, within reasonable time after he discovers or should have discovered any breach, notify seller of breach or be barred from any remedy, the notice requirement is valid precondition of imposing liability on seller. West's F.S.A. § 672.607(3)(a).

General Matters, Inc. v. Paramount Canning Co., 382 So.2d 1262.

Fla.App. 4 Dist. 1982. In action by buyers against seller to recover earnest money deposit paid toward purchase of mobile home, circuit court's finding that sale of buyers' house was not necessary condition precedent to closing on sale of mobile home was not erroneous.

Honsberg v. Lystra, 410 So.2d 661.

⚷2412–2414. *For other cases see earlier editions of this digest, the Decennial Digests, and WESTLAW.*

⚷2412. **Defenses.**

⚷2414. —— **Action by seller; buyer's defenses.**

⚷2414(1). **In general.**

C.A.5 (Fla.) 1980. Commercial bribery would be recognized under Florida law as defense to payment for goods received.

Excel Handbag Co., Inc. v. Edison Bros. Stores, Inc., 630 F.2d 379.

Defense of commercial bribery, under Florida law, requires some evidence of a causal relationship between giving of the bribe and purchasing of goods by the bribed agent.

Excel Handbag Co., Inc. v. Edison Bros. Stores, Inc., 630 F.2d 379.

Bkrtcy.S.D.Fla. 1981. Fact that there may have been minor problems in installation of carpet and defects in the carpet itself was a matter of setoff, not an absolute defense, to an action to recover the sales price, where the carpet was installed in a commercial establishment and the purchasers had had the use and benefit of the carpet for more than one year.

Matter of Gamy & Levy Associates, Inc., 11 B.R. 588.

Fla. 1983. Farmer's failure to file complaint with Florida Department of Agriculture within ten days after defect in seed became apparent did not bar farmer from pleading lack of consideration as defense to action by seller for payment for allegedly defective seed. West's F.S.A. §§ 578.09, 578.26, 578.26(1).

Ferry-Morse Seed Co. v. Hitchcock, 426 So.2d 958.

Fla. 1941. In seller's replevin action to recover garment bag machinery which was constructed for buyer and sold on approval, and which was not acceptable to buyer, expenditures made by buyer in attempting to improve the machinery were so interwoven with the efforts of the seller for the same purpose that buyer's claim for such expenditures could be litigated by way of recoupment in replevin action. Acts 1931, c. 14823.

Jacksonville Paper Co. v. Smith & Winchester Mfg. Co., 2 So.2d 890, 147 Fla. 311.

⚷2414(2). **Breach of warranty as defense.**

C.C.A.5 (Fla.) 1938. Although a contract has not been rescinded but affirmed, a suit for money due thereunder may be defended by a recoupment of damages arising either from breach of warranty or fraudulent misrepresentation touching that contract.

> Seward v. South Florida Securities, 96 F.2d 964.

Fla.App. 5 Dist. 1989. Purchaser's assertion against seller of goods that goods were defective and breached implied warranty of fitness was not affirmative defense barring or voiding seller's action to recover purchase money, but rather was counterclaim. West's F.S.A. RCP Rule 1.110(b, d).

> Storchwerke, GMBH v. Mr. Thiessen's Wallpapering Supplies, Inc., 538 So.2d 1382.

⚷2415–2416. For other cases see earlier editions of this digest, the Decennial Digests, and WESTLAW.

⚷2416. Set-off and counterclaim.

⚷2417. —— In general.

Fla.App. 2 Dist. 1980. Manufacturer, which accepted shipment of aluminum sheeting and thus was liable for contract price, was entitled to damages for nonconforming use which he could subtract from contract price where it notified supplier of the nonconforming use within reasonable time after discovery. West's F.S.A. §§ 672.607(1), (3)(a), 672.714, 672.717.

> Adam Metal Supply, Inc. v. Electrodex, Inc., 386 So.2d 1316.

⚷2418. —— Buyer's set-off and counterclaim against seller.

⚷2418(1). In general.

Fla.App. 2 Dist. 1963. Defendants, who were sued on notes and for merchandise allegedly sold on open account, could assert by way of setoff that, of amount allegedly due plaintiff, part was for merchandise held by defendants as memorandum merchandise and hence was not due and payable.

> Skaf's Jewelers, Inc. v. Antwerp Import Corp., 150 So.2d 260.

Fla.App. 3 Dist. 1991. Wine seller's claim against buyer for purchase price was not subject to setoff on ground of alleged defects in wine, in that claim of defects was not supported by substantial competent evidence; claim was raised for first time at trial, and seller presented expert testimony regarding quality of wine.

> Jean Claude Boisset Wine, USA, Inc. v. Sambor, 574 So.2d 1221.

Fla.App. 4 Dist. 1980. Where seller was guilty of fraud and misrepresentation in sale of business, but rescission was not available because seller could not be returned to status quo, buyer was entitled to award of damages by way of judgment therefor against seller or buyer was entitled to setoff against note and mortgage held by seller for amount of damages sustained as a result of seller's tortious conduct.

> Vinyl Repair Service, Inc. v. Menzel, 385 So.2d 1055, dismissed 392 So.2d 1377.

⚷2418(2). Breach of warranty.

C.C.A.5 (Fla.) 1938. Although a contract has not been rescinded but affirmed, a suit for money due thereunder may be defended by a recoupment of damages arising either from breach of warranty or fraudulent misrepresentation touching that contract.

> Seward v. South Florida Securities, 96 F.2d 964.

⚷2419–2421. For other cases see earlier editions of this digest, the Decennial Digests, and WESTLAW.

⚷2421. Time to sue; limitations and laches.

⚷2422. —— In general.

Fla.App. 2 Dist. 1976. Uniform Commercial Code limitation period generally prevails over that contained in a general statute of limitations. West's F.S.A. § 672.725.

> Lake Wales Pub. Co., Inc. v. Florida Visitor, Inc., 335 So.2d 335.

⚷2423. —— Action by seller.

Fla.App. 1 Dist. 1959. Where shoe retailer owed manufacturer on open account and agreement was made between manufacturer and retailer that if retailer would pay a certain lump sum manufacturer would then ship another order and balance due could be paid at the rate of $50 per week, agreement was without consideration, and even though retailer had paid the lump sum and had made the weekly installments manufacturer's suit for balance due was not prematurely brought.

> International Shoe Co. v. Carmichael, 114 So.2d 436.

Fla.App. 2 Dist. 1976. Plaintiff's production of printed pamphlets and related materials for defendants was the production of "goods" within the meaning of the Uniform Commercial Code, and plaintiff's action was therefore governed by the four-year statute of limitations under the UCC, not by the three-year statute governing unwritten contracts. West's F.S.A. §§ 95.11(3)(k), (5)(e), 672.725.

> Lake Wales Pub. Co., Inc. v. Florida Visitor, Inc., 335 So.2d 335.

🔑**2424. —— Action by buyer.**

C.A.11 (Fla.) 1987. Florida's four-year statute of limitations applicable to action for breach of contract for sale that was in effect at time bus buyer's cause of action accrued, when buyer learned of rust problems on both series of purchased buses, applied, although that statute of limitations was repealed before action was brought by bus buyer. F.S.1973, § 672.725.

> Dade County v. Rohr Industries, Inc., 826 F.2d 983.

🔑**2425–2426.** *For other cases see earlier editions of this digest, the Decennial Digests, and WESTLAW.*

🔑**2427. Parties.**

Fla.App. 3 Dist. 1989. Supplier of pearl necklaces was not an indispensable party in distributor's action for breach of contract against buyer to whom it resold necklaces at a profit. West's F.S.A. RCP Rule 1.210(a).

> Ivens Corp. v. Hobe Cie Ltd., 555 So.2d 425, review denied 564 So.2d 1086.

🔑**2428–2431.** *For other cases see earlier editions of this digest, the Decennial Digests, and WESTLAW.*

🔑**2429. Pleading.**

🔑**2431. —— Particular actions and claims.**

🔑**2431(1). In general.**

C.A.5 (Fla.) 1980. Where complaint alleged that defendant had contracted with plaintiff, an electronics company, to purchase a security camera system, that defendant requested that the sale be made through plaintiff's local agent and that, after the sale was made as requested through the local agent, defendant cancelled the order, the complaint stated a claim for relief under Florida law. Fed. Rules Civ.Proc. Rule 12(b)(6), 28 U.S.C.A.

> Impossible Electronic Techniques, Inc. v. Wackenhut Protective Systems, Inc., 610 F.2d 371, appeal after remand 669 F.2d 1026.

🔑**2431(2). Action by seller.**

Fla. 1951. Vendors' allegation that, after purchaser stopped payment on their check given vendors as binder on purchase of vendors' business vendors accepted a redelivery of business with consent of defendants, was not sufficient to show that parties mutually agreed to rescind the contract.

> Collier v. Fox, 49 So.2d 801.

Where vendors alleged in their declaration that at time of repudiation of contract of purchase by purchasers, vendors had performed and were able and in a position to carry out and perform each and every covenant and agreement which had been made and agreed to be performed and carried out by them, a fact which was always well known to defendants, allegations showed sufficient performance of conditions.

> Collier v. Fox, 49 So.2d 801.

Where buyer of personalty, under terms of written contract of purchase, must necessarily perform certain obligations before seller can be required to carry out a particular obligation under contract, it is not necessary for seller, in action against buyer for failure to carry out such obligations, to allege performance of such particular obligation on his part.

> Collier v. Fox, 49 So.2d 801.

Declaration alleging that purchasers stopped payment on check given vendors as binder on purchase and in part payment of purchase price of vendors' business and thereby breached and failed to perform their agreement with vendor without cause or provocation and that vendors with consent of defendants took and accepted a redelivery to them by purchasers of business, stated cause of action for damages for breach of contract.

Collier v. Fox, 49 So.2d 801.

Fla.App. 1 Dist. 1962. A complaint for goods sold and delivered and for account stated was sufficient to state a cause of action where complaint followed official forms approved under Rules of Civil Procedure. 30 F.S.A. Rules of Civil Procedure, rule 1.8.

Edgewater Drugs, Inc. v. Jax Drugs, Inc., 138 So.2d 525.

⚷**2431(3). Action by buyer.**

M.D.Fla. 1996. Soft drink manufacturer properly alleged breach of contract claim against supplier of apple juice concentrate where manufacturer pled terms of contract upon which liability rested, and that supplier commenced performance of contract by delivering juice.

Coca-Cola Foods v. Empresa Comercial Internacional De Frutas S.A., 941 F.Supp. 1182.

S.D.Fla. 2011. Consumer failed to sufficiently allege that he entered into valid and enforceable contract with manufacturer to purchase infant formula, as required to state breach of contract claim under Florida law against manufacturer based on recall of infant formula products contaminated with insect parts and larvae; consumer failed to allege that he made any offer to manufacturer, and never alleged that manufacturer made offer to consumer.

Jovine v. Abbott Laboratories, Inc., 795 F.Supp.2d 1331.

Fla.App. 3 Dist. 1989. Complaint of motor vehicle buyer denied $3,000 allowance on trade-in stated claim for breach of contract on ground that, objectively considered, car dealer's advertisement offered $3,000 toward purchase of truck for any vehicle buyer would produce; under rule that allegedly binding offer must be viewed as whole, with due emphasis placed upon each of what may be inconsistent or conflicting provisions, there was potential for disregarding both superfine print and apparent qualification as to value of trade-in, as contradictory to far more prominent thrust of advertising to effect that $3,000 would be allowed for any trade-in.

Izadi v. Machado (Gus) Ford, Inc., 550 So.2d 1135.

Motor vehicle buyer's complaint stated cause of action for breach of contract on ground that car dealer, through carefully chosen language and arrangement of advertisement, wrongly sought to make public believe that $3,000 would be allowed for any trade-in on purchase of any dealer's automobiles, while never intending to adhere to representation; offer was to be used as "bait" to be followed by "switch" to another deal when acceptance of offer was refused.

Izadi v. Machado (Gus) Ford, Inc., 550 So.2d 1135.

Fla.App. 3 Dist. 1984. Although buyer's complaint against automobile dealer, which sold subject automobile to another, did not assert cause of action based on breach of contract but improperly relied on conversion theory, buyer was entitled to return of their deposit because the seller failed to perform.

Douglas v. Braman Porsche Audi, Inc., 451 So.2d 1038.

Fla.App. 3 Dist. 1965.   Amended complaint which asked the return of a sum deposited for uncompleted purchase of an automobile stated a cause of action in nature of general assumpsit for money had and received.

Lytell v. McGahey Chrysler-Plymouth, Inc., 180 So.2d 354.

⚷**2431(4). Good faith and fair dealing.**

For other cases see earlier editions of this digest, the Decennial Digests, and WESTLAW.

⚷**2431(5). Rescission.**

C.A.5 (Fla.) 1957.   Complaint by which sellers of thoroughbred brood mares sought rescission of written contract of sale on ground that buyer had failed to live up to contemporaneous oral understanding that he would personally care for the mares, that nothing would be done without one seller's consent, and that buyer would assume responsibility for death, disability, or destruction of the mares or of third foal of each, which according to written contract was to go to sellers failed to state claim showing that sellers were entitled to relief. Fed.Rules Civ.Proc. rules 8(a)(2), (f), 12(b), 28 U.S.C.A.

Feinberg v. Leach, 243 F.2d 64.

Fla.App. 2 Dist. 1965. Complaint sufficiently alleged impossibility of performance or frustration of purpose as grounds for rescission of contract for sale of 'snow ice' manufactured by defendant for plaintiff in ice making machinery maintained by defendant in plaintiff's fresh vegetable packing house, because machinery was not capable of fulfilling plaintiff's needs.

Crown Ice Mach. Leasing Co. v. Sam Senter Farms, Inc., 174 So.2d 614, certiorari denied 180 So.2d 656.

Complaint for rescission of contract for sale of "snow ice" manufactured by defendant for plaintiff in ice making machinery maintained by defendant in plaintiff's fresh vegetable packing house was not required to allege offer by plaintiff to restore benefits, where defendant had removed machinery and leased it to another and had been compensated for all ice delivered to plaintiff.

Crown Ice Mach. Leasing Co. v. Sam Senter Farms, Inc., 174 So.2d 614, certiorari denied 180 So.2d 656.

☞2432. —— Answer and subsequent pleadings.

☞2432(1). In general.

Fla. 1949. In action for goods bought and sold, payment is an affirmative defense which must be specially pleaded.

Parker v. Priestley, 39 So.2d 210.

Fla. 1948. In suit to replevin automobile purchased by defendant and companion who gave a worthless check for balance of price after acceptance of defendant's traded-in automobile, plea that actual value of automobile purchased was substantially in excess of that described in declaration did not state a defense. F.S.A. §§ 52.11, 78.18 to 78.21.

Thompson v. Guntner, 36 So.2d 826, 160 Fla. 856.

Fla. 1937. In action on note given for balance of price of newspaper and executed two years or more after defendant had taken over business, pleas of fraudulent inducement and failure of con-

sideration disclosing such fact were not available to defendant as defense to note and were subject to demurrer, since pleas disclosed that transaction had been affirmed by defendant's actions.

Storrs v. Storrs, 178 So. 841, 130 Fla. 711.

Fla.App. 1 Dist. 1976. General contractor's setoff against supplier for damages resulting from delays in furnishing supplies which were defective or did not conform to specifications should have been pleaded as a counterclaim in supplier's action to recover contract price.

Southeastern Builders, Inc. of Alabama v. Joe Brashears Steel, Inc., 336 So.2d 1228.

General contractor was not entitled to setoff against supplier of structural steel for damages arising from absence of sequential delivery to which supplier did not assent in the exchange of contract documents.

Southeastern Builders, Inc. of Alabama v. Joe Brashears Steel, Inc., 336 So.2d 1228.

Fla.App. 4 Dist. 1992. Failure to mitigate damages was affirmative defense that should have been pled specifically by airplane buyer in seller's action to recover difference between contract price and price ultimately received from third party.

Maxfly Aviation, Inc. v. Gill, 605 So.2d 1297.

☞2432(2). Buyer's assertion of breach of warranty.

C.A.5 (Fla.) 1967. Defense of breach of warranty should be pleaded as affirmative defense to an action to collect on contract for sale of goods.

Atlantic Elec., Inc. v. Allis-Chalmers Mfg. Co., 375 F.2d 726.

S.D.Fla. 1981. Assertion that injury to workman was caused by a third party over whom manufacturer had no control or by an intervening and unforeseeable cause was a proper affirmative defense under law of Florida in action for negligence, breach of warranty, and strict liability.

Ellison v. Northwest Engineering Co., 521 F.Supp. 199.

⚷2433. —— Variance between pleadings and proof.

C.A.5 (Fla.) 1976. Notification of seller by buyer of breach after buyer has accepted tender of goods is integral part of buyer's cause of action and is not affirmative defense of seller; therefore, buyer must both plead and prove that notice requirement has been complied with. West's Ann.Cal.Com.Code, §§ 2607, 2607(3)(a).

Eastern Air Lines, Inc. v. McDonnell Douglas Corp., 532 F.2d 957.

S.D.Fla. 1975. Airline had specific notice of oil company's intention to rely on claim of commercial impossibility of fulfilling requirements contract for aviation fuel when the oil company filed a memorandum of law in opposition to the airline's motion for summary judgment in action centering around the contract so that airline had sufficient notice to permit the oil company to rely on asserted failure of presupposed conditions as a defense to claim that it had breached the contract. West's F.S.A. § 672.615.

Eastern Air Lines, Inc. v. Gulf Oil Corp., 415 F.Supp. 429.

Fla. 1974. Where complaint alleged breaches of contract for sale and installation of equipment but did not contain specific allegations that breach resulted in foreseeable loss of investment over period of months, i. e., loss of accounts, loss of profits, and loss of business during the period, damages should have been restricted to losses commensurate with use or rental value of contract equipment over period during which it was not delivered and installed; loss of investment, etc., should not have been implied from general language of complaint.

Baring Industries, Inc. v. Rayglo, Inc., 303 So.2d 625, opinion adopted 306 So.2d 549.

Fla. 1949. In action for goods bargained and sold, burden of proof under defense of payment is upon defendant.

Parker v. Priestley, 39 So.2d 210.

Fla.App. 3 Dist. 1964. Defendant, which was sued for goods sold, which pleaded general denial that it was indebted, and which filed no pleading raising issue of setoff for inferior goods, was not entitled to introduce evidence as to quality of goods delivered by plaintiff. 30 F.S.A. Rules of Civil Procedure, rule 1.11(b).

Clutter Const. Co. v. Naples Builders Supply Co., 166 So.2d 813.

Fla.App. 4 Dist. 1968. In action for breach of citrus sales contract which specified no time limit for performance by dealer who was to pick the fruit, whether a reasonable time for performance had expired was a material issue.

Tyner v. Woodruff, 206 So.2d 684.

⚷2434. Trial or hearing.

For other cases see earlier editions of this digest, the Decennial Digests, and WEST-LAW.

⚷2435. —— In general.

Evidence, see XI(C), XI(D), XI(E). Questions of law or fact, see XI(F). Instructions, see XI(G).

⚷2436. —— Verdict and findings.

Fla.App. 2 Dist. 1975. In action by buyers of mobile home to recover purchase price and interest after revoking their acceptance of mobile home, court erred in failing to make subjective analysis of buyers' purposes to be served by purchase, in failing to consider extent to which such purposes would be impaired or frustrated by specific defects or nonconformities complained of, in considering complained of defects per se to be equivalent of required impairment and in considering as viable test of "substantial impairment" financial ability of purchasers. West's F.S.A. §§ 672.106, 672.608.

Barrington Homes of Florida, Inc. v. Kelley, 320 So.2d 841.

⚷2437. Judgment, order, or decree.

Remedies, see X.

Fla.App. 3 Dist. 1983. In suit by alleged owner of thoroughbred race horse to invalidate bill of sale of one-half interest in horse to alleged buyer and to compel reconveyance, and in which alleged buyer counter and cross-claimed for affirmance of bill of sale and for partition of animal, trial court correctly confirmed claimed interest of buyer and ordered horse partitioned.

Occhuizzo v. Perlmutter, 426 So.2d 1060.

Fla.App. 3 Dist. 1974. Where buyers of goods, which were sold on credit, had not paid for goods at time they were replevied prior to the expiration of the credit period, buyers, which elected to take money judgment, were not entitled to recover value of goods but only any special equity they might have had. West's F.S.A. §§ 78.19(1), 78.21.

> Modine Mfg. Co. v. Israel, 294 So.2d 369, certiorari denied 303 So.2d 644, appeal after remand 367 So.2d 232, certiorari denied ABC Radiator, Inc. v. Modine Manufacturing Co., 378 So.2d 342.

Fla.App. 3 Dist. 1960. Where automatic die, manufactured by defendants under written contract with plaintiff, was delivered to plaintiff who redelivered the same in order that corrections might be made, but defendants announced they would make no additional corrections but hold the same until balance of contract price had been paid in full and plaintiffs then instituted replevin action and property replevied was not returned under forthcoming bond to defendants, only triable issue before court was a determination of who was entitled to possession, and statutory right for determination of special interest never existed because judgment of possession was in favor of plaintiff. F.S.A. §§ 46.08, 78.18, 78.19, 78.21.

> Huckleberry v. Davis Double Seal Jalousies, Inc., 117 So.2d 519, certiorari denied 120 So.2d 616.

⚷2438. Costs and fees.

† C.A.11 (Fla.) 2007. Under Florida law, seller of jet was not "defaulting party" under purchase agreement, based on non-completion of the sale, as would entitle prospective buyer to attorney fees; although seller failed to deliver the jet as promised, it adhered to its obligations under the agreement in the event of a breach, by returning buyer's downpayment and inspection costs.

> Jet Sales of Stuart, LLC v. Jet Connection Travel, GmbH, 240 Fed.Appx. 839.

Under Florida law, seller of jet was not entitled to recover attorney fees as prevailing party, in action brought by prospective buyer for breach of contract based upon non-delivery of the jet; although buyer did not recover additional damages it sought, the agreement did not provide for prevailing party to recover attorney fees.

> Jet Sales of Stuart, LLC v. Jet Connection Travel, GmbH, 240 Fed.Appx. 839.

Fla. 1942. In action on common counts by assignee of corporate seller against corporate buyer owing a balance for the goods purchased, allowance of attorneys' fees was not error, where invoice approved by buyer provided for reasonable attorney's fee, and claim therefor was supported by proof and amount allowed was not unreasonable.

> Producers Supply v. Harz, 6 So.2d 375, 149 Fla. 594.

Fla.App. 1 Dist. 1980. Under purchase and sale agreement providing for reasonable attorney fees to prevailing party, attorney fees were properly awarded, except that reasonableness should be redetermined, with court considering all relevant factors appearing in resolution of case, in which amount of award of damages had been adjusted on appeal. West's F.S.A. § 59.46.

> Campbell v. Rawls, 381 So.2d 744.

Fla.App. 2 Dist. 1985. Two letters written by seller to buyer dealing with prior purchase and dispute over excess loading charges which resulted in instant litigation did not establish seller's right to attorney fees or prejudgment interest above statutory rate, as one of the letters which contained quoted terms of sale had nothing to do with transaction in question and other letter was not written until after product had been delivered and dispute had ensued, so that there was no evidence that quoted terms of sale were part of contract for purchase of rock, which was subject of lawsuit. West's F.S.A. § 687.01.

> Wilkinson & Jenkins Const. Co., Inc. v. Florida Rock Industries, Inc., 475 So.2d 743.

Fla.App. 3 Dist. 2012. Automobile buyers who prevailed on automobile dealership's breach of contract claim, in which dealership alleged that buyers never paid the $4,000 cash down payment reflected in the retail order contract, could not recover prevailing party attorney fees, even though buyers pled entitlement to such fees pursuant to statute providing for mutuality of attorney fee provisions in contract cases; retail order contract did not contain an attorney fee provision, retail installment sale contract, which did contain an attorney fee provision, was not relied on by dealership or admitted as an exhibit at trial, and buyers did not plead any other statutory basis for recovering attorney fees. West's F.S.A. § 57.105(7).

Tylinski v. Klein Automotive, Inc., 90 So.3d 870, rehearing denied.

Fla.App. 4 Dist. 1992. Seller was entitled to attorney fees to the extent that it prevailed on its claim that it was entitled to retain deposit as liquidated damages.

Curtis v. Sargent Const., Inc., 595 So.2d 258.

Fla.App. 5 Dist. 1988. Although purchaser breached its agreement to purchase laminator manufactured by seller, seller sued for damages to which it was not entitled, and therefore seller could not recover attorney fees.

Design Time, Inc. v. Monco of Orlando, Inc., 518 So.2d 454, review denied 525 So.2d 879.

Fla.App. 5 Dist. 1986. Under meat delivery contract on account which provided that customer agreed to pay all costs including reasonable attorney fees if legal action were "necessary" for collection on account, seller who filed law action to recover balance due on account and who obtained judgment and order for legal costs and prejudgment interest was also entitled to court reporting costs and reasonable attorney fees; that seller could have collected balance due by nonlegal efforts did not render the legal action not "necessary" within the contract provision. West's F.S.A. § 57.071(2).

Golden Cleaver Packing, Inc. v. G & M Hughes Corp., 490 So.2d 1381.

(B) ACTIONS ON WARRANTIES.

1. IN GENERAL.

⚷2451. In general.

Fla.App. 4 Dist. 1978. Judgment for defendant was affirmed in case in which it was alleged that defendant negligently designed or manufactured short leg brace and breached its warranties in connection with failure of brace to support user when calf band failed to hold after fastener which had been replaced by someone other than defendant, broke.

Douglas v. Winkley Co., 363 So.2d 849, certiorari denied 372 So.2d 468.

⚷2452. Existence, nature, and form of action.

M.D.Fla. 1999. With adoption of doctrine of strict liability, Florida abolished no-privity, breach of implied warranty cause of action for personal injury. West's F.S.A. § 672.318.

Blinn v. Smith & Nephew Richards, Inc., 55 F.Supp.2d 1353.

M.D.Fla. 1982. Under Florida law, action for breach of implied warranty of merchantability may embrace notion of "crashworthiness."

Taylor v. American Honda Motor Co., Inc., 555 F.Supp. 59.

S.D.Fla. 1981. Causes of action for negligence and breach of warranty were within the "access to courts" provision of the Florida Constitution at time it was readopted. West's F.S.A.Const. Art. 1, § 21.

Ellison v. Northwest Engineering Co., 521 F.Supp. 199.

S.D.Fla. 1975. Although doctrine of strict liability in tort has not been adopted in Florida, and although count of complaint was entitled strict liability in tort, count did allege a claim for breach of implied warranty under Florida law, a tort which closely resembles the doctrine of strict liability.

Serksnas v. Engine Support, Inc., 392 F.Supp. 392.

Florida's breach of implied warranty action does not apply to the retailer.

Serksnas v. Engine Support, Inc., 392 F.Supp. 392.

Fla.App. 2 Dist. 1972. Automobile purchaser who answers the inducements made in the advertising campaign carried on by the automobile industry has the right to expect the automobile to perform properly and as represented, and if it does not, through no fault of his, he should be allowed to seek redress.

> Rehurek v. Chrysler Credit Corp., 262 So.2d 452, 54 A.L.R.3d 1210, certiorari denied 267 So.2d 833.

Fla.App. 2 Dist. 1966. A plaintiff can state a cause of action against a blood bank for breach of implied warranty, but can only recover for injuries if they were caused by failure to detect or remove a deleterious substance capable of detection or removal.

> Russell v. Community Blood Bank, Inc., 185 So.2d 749, reversed 196 So.2d 115.

Fla.App. 3 Dist. 1983. There is an implied warranty that a product will be suitable for the purpose for which it is sold, and when the evidence discloses that this is not the case, the buyer has a right to recover his damages occasioned by the use of the product. West's F.S.A. § 672.315.

> Beede Elec. Instrument, Co. v. K.E.S., Inc., 433 So.2d 59.

Fla.App. 3 Dist. 1974. Automobile manufacturer may be liable in negligence and for breach of an implied warranty where a defect in manufacture causes injury to a user as a result of a collision even though the defect was not a cause of the collision.

> Evancho v. Thiel, 297 So.2d 40.

Fla.App. 4 Dist. 1983. Manufacturer of diesel engine for boat was not liable to secondhand purchaser under theory of breach of implied warranty of merchantability for cost of repairing water leak and for profits lost during time it took to repair engine where break in bearing cap and bolt caused no injury whatever either to persons or property.

> Continental Ins. Co. v. Montella, 427 So.2d 796.

☞**2453. Conditions precedent.**

N.D.Fla. 2013. Under Florida law, as predicted by the district court, heading of statute purportedly indicating that farmer had to complete an administrative process with the Florida Department of Agriculture before bringing a legal action against seed seller for allegedly defective seeds, rather than merely file a sworn complaint to start the process as required by the statute's text, did not make the statute ambiguous; the statute itself was not ambiguous, the heading was not part of the statutory text, and the heading did not indicate legislative intent, since it was subject to modification by Florida Division of Statutory Revisions. West's F.S.A. §§ 11.242, 578.26.

> TRA Farms, Inc. v. Syngenta Seeds, Inc., 932 F.Supp.2d 1251.

Under Florida law, as predicted by the district court, statute provision requiring that farmer file a sworn complaint with the Florida Department of Agriculture to start an administrative process before bringing action against seed seller for allegedly defective seeds was not ambiguous when read in context with the rest of the statute providing for a continuation of the administrative process, and did not render the rest of the statute meaningless; complaint merely started administrative process as a permissive, rather than mandatory, remedy, and was designed to put potential defendants on notice of whether the action against them would be in a legal, or non-legal setting. West's F.S.A. § 578.26.

> TRA Farms, Inc. v. Syngenta Seeds, Inc., 932 F.Supp.2d 1251.

Fla. 1983. By failing to file complaint with Florida Department of Agriculture within ten days after defect in seed became apparent, farmer was barred from maintaining legal action for damages against seller based on theories of negligence or breach of warranty. West's F.S.A. §§ 578.09, 578.26, 578.26(1).

> Ferry-Morse Seed Co. v. Hitchcock, 426 So.2d 958.

Seller's actual knowledge of defects in seed not acquired within ten days of discovery of defect by farmer did not estop seller from raising farmer's failure to file complaint with Florida Department of Agriculture as defense to farmer's action against seller for negligence and breach of warranty. West's F.S.A. §§ 578.09, 578.26, 578.26(1).

> Ferry-Morse Seed Co. v. Hitchcock, 426 So.2d 958.

Fla.App. 3 Dist. 1995. Seed buyer's breach of warranty action against seller and supplier of allegedly defective melon seeds, brought before supplier filed administrative complaint with Florida Department of Agriculture, was premature, requiring abatement of proceeding until administrative filing requirements are met. West's F.S.A. § 578.26.

> Interlatin Supply, Inc. v. S & M Farm Supply, Inc., 654 So.2d 254, review denied 659 So.2d 1088.

⚷2454. Defenses.

⚷2455. —— In general.

C.A.5 (Fla.) 1972. Buyer is entitled to rely upon express warranty of seller, especially where warranty is descriptive and defects are not readily apparent, and buyer's failure to inspect constitutes no defense for seller.

> U.S. v. Aerodex, Inc., 469 F.2d 1003.

⚷2456. —— **Misuse or unreasonable use.**

C.A.5 (Fla.) 1978. Misuse is properly defense to both strict liability and breach of warranty.

> Westerman v. Sears, Roebuck & Co., 577 F.2d 873.

Fla.App. 3 Dist. 1966. Manufacturer should not be liable for product which failed because it was improperly compounded in accordance with directions by another, mishandled or misused.

> Power Ski of Florida, Inc. v. Allied Chemical Corp., 188 So.2d 13.

⚷2457. —— **Negligence or fault.**

C.A.5 (Fla.) 1978. Under law of Florida, contributory negligence is available defense to action for breach of warranty. West's F.S.A. §§ 672.313, 672.314.

> Westerman v. Sears, Roebuck & Co., 577 F.2d 873.

C.A.5 (Fla.) 1974. Under Florida law, any contributory negligence was an absolute bar to recovery in breach of warranty action prior to July 10, 1973.

> Florida Power & Light Co. v. R. O. Products, Inc., 489 F.2d 549.

M.D.Fla. 1973. Under Florida law, evidence of plaintiff's negligence will be allowed to diminish amount of his recovery on claim of breach of implied warranty.

> Tampa Elec. Co. v. Stone & Webster Engineering Corp., 367 F.Supp. 27.

Fla.App. 1 Dist. 1988. Comparative negligence is a defense in an implied warranty action.

> Coulter v. American Bakeries Co., 530 So.2d 1009.

When asserting the defense of comparative negligence in an implied warranty action, issue pertains to the misuse of the product as opposed to the failure to discover or guard against defect.

> Coulter v. American Bakeries Co., 530 So.2d 1009.

Purchaser of doughnut was not comparatively negligent in not chewing doughnut with her teeth and using milk to dissolve it, which would reduce her recovery in an implied warranty action, even though her use of milk resulted in her failure to discover small piece of wire in doughnut which lodged in her throat; purchaser's lack of expectation to find wire in doughnut, lack of evidence that purchaser used doughnut in an abnormal, unintended or unforeseen way, and purchaser's use of milk to dissolve doughnut because she had an abscessed tooth foreclosed doughnut manufacturer's comparative negligence claim.

> Coulter v. American Bakeries Co., 530 So.2d 1009.

Fla.App. 1 Dist. 1972. Contributory negligence is available as a defense in action for breach of implied warranty.

> Coleman v. American Universal of Fla., Inc., 264 So.2d 451.

⚷2458. —— **Assumption of risk.**

Fla. 1976. Unreasonable exposure to a known and appreciated risk should bar recovery in action based upon implied warranty.

> West v. Caterpillar Tractor Co., Inc., 336 So.2d 80, answer to certified question conformed to 547 F.2d 885.

Fla.App. 3 Dist. 1981. In action based on implied warranty as well as in action for negligence, unreasonable exposure to known and appreciated risk bars recovery.

> Clark v. Boeing Co., 395 So.2d 1226.

🗝**2459. Set-off and counterclaim.**

For other cases see earlier editions of this digest, the Decennial Digests, and WEST-LAW.

🗝**2460. Jurisdiction and venue.**

S.D.Fla. 2014. Doctrine of primary jurisdiction did not require referral of claims alleging violations of Florida's Deceptive and Unfair Trade Practices Act (FDUTPA), negligent misrepresentation, breach of implied warranty of fitness for purpose, breach of express warranty, declaratory judgment, money had and received, and violations of California's Business and Professions Code, in consumers' class action complaint against manufacturers of cereal and snack food products, that Genetically Modified Organisms (GMOs) and other allegedly synthetic ingredients precluded manufacturers' products from being characterized as "all natural" to Food and Drug Administration (FDA); determination of whether manufacturer's "all natural" and "nothing artificial" representations on products' labeling were misleading and whether customers purchased products in reliance upon representations was not technical area in which FDA had greater technical expertise than courts, and FDA had not promulgated comprehensive regulatory scheme regarding assertions of "all natural" or "nothing artificial" on food labeling. West's F.S.A. § 501.201 et seq.; West's Ann.Cal.Civ.Code § 1750; West's Ann.Cal.Bus. & Prof.Code §§ 17200, 17500.

　　Garcia v. Kashi Co., 43 F.Supp.3d 1359.

🗝**2461. Time to sue; limitations and laches.**

　† C.A.11 (Fla.) 2014. Florida two-year statute of limitations for professional malpractice, rather than four-year statute for product liability claims, applied to customer's claims of breach of warranty arising out of pharmacist's alleged negligence in filling a prescription. West's F.S.A. § 95.11(3), (4)(a).

　　Kasterowicz v. Walgreen Co., 597 Fed.Appx. 560.

　M.D.Fla. 1993. Florida's "blood-shield" statute limited claims for breach of implied warranty of fitness or merchantability, but did not limit failure-to-warn products liability claim against seller of blood and, thus, products liability statute of limitation rather than negligence statute of limitation applied to personal injury action filed on behalf of hemophiliac patient who allegedly contracted acquired immune deficiency syndrome (AIDS) from plasma product.

　　Walls v. Armour Pharmaceutical Co., 832 F.Supp. 1467, affirmed Christopher v. Cutter Laboratories, 53 F.3d 1184, rehearing and suggestion for rehearing denied 65 F.3d 185.

　Fla.App. 4 Dist. 1969. Finding that purchaser of crane knew that it was insufficient but nonetheless retained it and allowed damages to accumulate for nearly three years was sufficient to bar an action for rescission, and would also bar an action for damages if no notice of defects was given the seller.

　　Ferncrest Mining Co. v. H. F. Mason Equipment Corp., 225 So.2d 354.

Delay in instituting suit, keeping equipment purchased and having repairs and adjustments made, may bar an action for rescission since the parties cannot be placed in the same position, but it does not preclude an action for damages.

　　Ferncrest Mining Co. v. H. F. Mason Equipment Corp., 225 So.2d 354.

🗝**2462. Parties.**

　Fla.App. 1 Dist. 1992. Claims with respect to revocation of acceptance, breach of warranty, and violation of Magnuson-Moss Act may be pursued against automobile manufacturer rather than dealer. Magnuson-Moss Warranty—Federal Trade Commission Improvement Act, § 101 et seq., 15 U.S.C.A. § 2301 et seq.

　　Claude Nolan Cadillac, Inc. v. Griffin, 610 So.2d 725, review denied 621 So.2d 432.

🗝**2463. Standing.**

　S.D.Fla. 2014. Consumers' standing to bring claims for violations of Florida's Deceptive and Unfair Trade Practices Act (FDUTPA), negligent misrepresentation, breach of implied warranty of fitness for purpose, breach of express warranty, declaratory judgment, money had and received, and violations of California's Business and Professions Code on behalf of class of consumers against manufacturers of cereal and snack food products challenging manufacturers' use of term "all natural" on product packaging was limited to products actually purchased by consumers. West's F.S.A. § 501.201 et seq.; West's Ann.Cal.Civ.Code § 1750; West's Ann.Cal.Bus. & Prof.Code §§ 17200, 17500.

> Garcia v. Kashi Co., 43 F.Supp.3d 1359.

⚷2464. Pleading.

⚷2465. —— In general.

M.D.Fla. 2009. To assert a cause of action for breach of express warranty, under Florida law, a consumer must allege that the manufacturer did not comply with the limited express warranty's terms, that is, the consumer must allege that the manufacturer refused or failed to adequately repair a covered item.

> Brisson v. Ford Motor Co., 602 F.Supp.2d 1227, affirmed in part, vacated in part, remanded 349 Fed. Appx. 433.

S.D.Fla. 2011. To plead a cause of action for breach of express warranties under the Florida Uniform Commercial Code (UCC), a complaint must allege: (1) the sale of goods, (2) the express warranty, (3) breach of the warranty, (4) notice to seller of the breach, and (5) the injuries sustained by the buyer as a result of the breach of the express warranty. West's F.S.A. §§ 672.313, 672.607(3).

> Jovine v. Abbott Laboratories, Inc., 795 F.Supp.2d 1331.

S.D.Fla. 2011. To plead a cause of action for breach of express warranties under the Florida Uniform Commercial Code, a complaint must allege: (1) the sale of goods; (2) the express warranty; (3) breach of the warranty; (4) notice to seller of the breach; and (5) the injuries sustained by the buyer as a result of the breach of the express warranty. West's F.S.A. § 672.313.

> Moss v. Walgreen Co., 765 F.Supp.2d 1363.

Bkrtcy.S.D.Fla. 2013. In order to sustain an action for breach of warranty in Florida, the complaint must allege the facts in respect to sale of goods, the type of warranty created, the facts giving rise to

the creation of the warranty, notice of breach, and injury.

> In re All American Semiconductor, Inc., 490 B.R. 418.

Fla.App. 4 Dist. 1977. To properly plead a cause of action for breach of warranty under Uniform Commercial Code, complaint should at least contain allegations in regard to the facts in respect to sale of the goods, identification of the types of warranties created, facts in respect to creation of the particular warranty, facts in respect to breach of the warranty, notice to seller of breach, and the injuries sustained by buyer as a result of the breach of warranty. West's F.S.A. §§ 672.313, 672.314, 672.315, 672.607(3)(a).

> Dunham-Bush, Inc. v. Thermo-Air Service, Inc., 351 So.2d 351.

To plead a cause of action for breach of implied warranty of fitness for a particular purpose, complaint should allege that seller had reason to know the particular purpose for which the goods were purchased by the buyer and that buyer relied on seller's judgment in providing suitable goods. West's F.S.A. § 672.315.

> Dunham-Bush, Inc. v. Thermo-Air Service, Inc., 351 So.2d 351.

Fla.App. 4 Dist. 1969. Pleader seeking to allege cause of action based on warranty must expressly set forth facts in respect to sale of product or other circumstances giving rise to warranty, express or implied, identifying types of warranties accompanying pertinent transactions involved, reliance upon representations by seller or skill and judgment of seller if action is based upon express warranty or warranty of fitness for particular purpose, circumstances of injury as caused by breach of warranty, notice of breach of warranty, and injuries sustained and damages. F.S.A. § 672.2–313.

> Weimar v. Yacht Club Point Estates, Inc., 223 So.2d 100.

⚷2466. —— Particular actions and claims.

† **C.A.11 (Fla.) 2015.** Prisoner's claims against pharmaceutical company for fraud, negligence, failure to warn, defective design, breach of express and implied warranties, wrongful death, and

unjust enrichment which were based on allegation that prisoner committed murders while "in a manic and psychotic state" after taking two of company's drugs, were barred by Florida's wrongful conduct doctrine, where claims were explicitly based on harms to prisoner resulting from his own criminal conduct.

> Jacobson v. Pfizer, Inc., 618 Fed. Appx. 509.

† **C.A.11 (Fla.) 2011.** Health and welfare fund did not sufficiently allege that drug produced by pharmaceutical company was not reasonably fit for the purpose intended, that any of its members had suffered side effects from the drug, or that defects in drug proximately caused members to suffer economic damages, as required to state claim against company for breach of implied warranty under New Jersey law; although fund alleged that it suffered economic harm by paying excess money for the drug, such harm was not caused by any condition which rendered the drug unmerchantable or unsafe.

> Southeast Laborers Health and Welfare Fund v. Bayer Corp., 444 Fed. Appx. 401.

† **C.A.11 (Fla.) 2008.** Personal representative's amended complaint satisfied district court's instruction against commingling claims for breach of implied warranty of merchantability and breach of warranty of fitness for a particular purpose on part of drug store chain, although representative referred to drug as not being fit for a particular purpose when pleading merchantability claim, where complaint did not alleged other elements of fitness claim, and thus court would ignore reference as surplusage, claim was only pleaded against chain, and allegations only stated factual basis to state claim for breach of merchantability. West's F.S.A. § 672.315.

> Bailey v. Janssen Pharmaceutica, Inc., 288 Fed.Appx. 597.

C.A.5 (Fla.) 1965. Fifth count of amended complaint of publishing company's employee, who sued manufacturer of printing press sold to publishing company for injuries sustained by employee when press malfunctioned, alleging that manufacturer impliedly warranted that press was safe for operation and was properly and correctly designed, constructed, and installed and was safe for operation by employee in manner in which he was operating and using press at time of injury sufficiently alleged a cause of action against manufacturer under Florida law for breach of implied warranty. F.S.A. § 25.031.

> Vandercook & Son, Inc. v. Thorpe, 344 F.2d 930, appeal after remand 395 F.2d 104.

M.D.Fla. 2015. Patient who suffered injuries resulting from off-label use of a bone graft device in her spinal fusion surgery did not sufficiently allege claim against device manufacturer for breach of express warranty; although patient alleged in sufficient detail the affirmations of fact that were made by manufacturer to patient's surgeon, patient failed to allege facts that would support her allegations that surgeon justifiably relied upon any of the express warranties, making only vague and conclusory allegations that surgeon relied on manufacturer's express warranty representations regarding the safety and efficacy of off-label use of device, and that such off-label uses were not effective, safe, and proper for the use as warranted.

> Byrnes v. Small, 142 F.Supp.3d 1262.

M.D.Fla. 2015. Drum kit distributor failed to allege that drum kits provided by manufacturer were to be used for a particular purpose, and thus failed to state a claim for breach of the implied warranty of fitness for a particular purpose under Florida's Uniform Commercial Code (UCC). Fla. Stat. Ann. § 672.315.

> Armadillo Distribution Enterprises, Inc. v. Hai Yun Musical Instruments Manufacture Co. Ltd., 142 F.Supp.3d 1245.

M.D.Fla. 2015. Patient failed to state claim against bone graft device manufacturer for breach of express warranty under Florida law, based on alleged affirmative warranty statements made by manufacturer to promote off-label use of device, absent allegations regarding what affirmations of fact were made by manufacturer to patient's doctor or how those express warranties proximately caused patient's injury. West's F.S.A. § 672.313(1)(a).

> Byrnes v. Small, 60 F.Supp.3d 1289.

M.D.Fla. 2014. Prescription drug user stated claim under Florida law for breach of express warranty by alleging that drug manufacturer expressly warranted in package inserts and other documents that drug was of merchantible quality, fit, safe, and otherwise not injurious to health of user, that such representations were material to user's decision to use drug, that drug did not conform to representations, and that user was injured as result of drug's nonconformity. West's F.S.A. § 672.313(1)(a).

Small v. Amgen, Inc., 2 F.Supp.3d 1292.

M.D.Fla. 1982. Under Florida law, motorcyclist's complaint against motorcycle seller alleging breach of implied warranty of merchantability was deficient in that complaint failed to allege either that motorcyclist purchased motorcycle from seller or that he was otherwise within class of persons to whom such a warranty extended. West's F.S.A. § 672.318.

Taylor v. American Honda Motor Co., Inc., 555 F.Supp. 59.

If motorcyclist or parents were "buyers" of motorcycle within meaning of Uniform Commercial Code, then complaint against motorcycle seller must allege compliance with UCC section requiring that seller be given notice of defective goods if it is to state cause of action for breach of implied warranty of merchantability. West's F.S.A. §§ 672.103(1)(a), 672.607(3)(a).

Taylor v. American Honda Motor Co., Inc., 555 F.Supp. 59.

If motorcyclist or parents were merely warranty beneficiaries with respect to sale of motorcycle, motorcyclist and parents would not be considered "buyers" under Uniform Commercial Code, so that complaint against motorcycle seller need not allege compliance with UCC section providing that seller be notified within reasonable time of defective goods in order to state cause of action for breach of implied warranty of merchantability. West's F.S.A. §§ 672.103(1)(a), 672.607(3)(a).

Taylor v. American Honda Motor Co., Inc., 555 F.Supp. 59.

N.D.Fla. 1995. Under Florida version of Article 2 of Uniform Commercial Code, recipient of allegedly defective penile implant did not state claim for breach of express warranty or breach of implied

warranties of merchantability and fitness for particular purpose absent any allegation that he purchased implant directly from manufacturer or contracted with manufacturer. West's F.S.A. § 672.101 et seq.

T.W.M. v. American Medical Systems, Inc., 886 F.Supp. 842.

S.D.Fla. 2014. Consumers alleged sufficient factual content in class action complaint against manufacturers of cereal and snack food products to show that it was more than "conceivable" that manufacturers' products actually contained bioengineered or artificial ingredients, as required to plead claims for violations of Florida's Deceptive and Unfair Trade Practices Act, negligent misrepresentation, breach of implied warranty of fitness for purpose, breach of express warranty, declaratory judgment, money had and received, and violations of California's Business and Professions Code with particularity; complaint alleged which consumers purchased which specific food items that were manufactured, marketed, advertised, distributed, and sold by manufacturers, where consumers purchased items and when, and provided extensive list of manufacturers' products that were labeled as "All Natural" and a separate list of the products that were labeled as "Nothing Artificial." Fed.Rules Civ.Proc.Rule 9(b), 28 U.S.C.A.; West's F.S.A. § 501.201 et seq.; West's Ann.Cal.Civ.Code § 1750 et seq.; West's Ann.Cal.Bus. & Prof.Code § 17200 et seq.

Garcia v. Kashi Co., 43 F.Supp.3d 1359.

Consumers' class action complaint against manufacturers of cereal and snack foods failed to allege privity of contract between consumers and manufacturers, as required for breach of implied warranty claim under Florida law.

Garcia v. Kashi Co., 43 F.Supp.3d 1359.

S.D.Fla. 2013. Consumers stated claim against milk product manufacturer for breach of express warranty under Arizona common law, and under Arkansas statute, by alleging that they had a contract with manufacturer to purchase milk, that the manufacturer's "brain health" representation based on DHA-fortification of its milk became part of the basis for their bargain, which consumers had accepted by purchasing the milk products, and that consumers had been damaged by manufacturer's breach in not providing products that would support brain health, as represented. West's A.C.A. § 4–2–313.

> In re Horizon Organic Milk Plus DHA Omega-3 Marketing and Sales Practice Litigation, 955 F.Supp.2d 1311.

Consumers failed to state claim against milk product manufacturer for breach of express warranty, under California law, based on advertising and product labels claiming a "brain health" benefit from its milk's DHA-fortification, since there were no allegations that consumers had provided manufacturer with any notice of alleged breach within a reasonable time after discovering it.

> In re Horizon Organic Milk Plus DHA Omega-3 Marketing and Sales Practice Litigation, 955 F.Supp.2d 1311.

S.D.Fla. 2011. Consumer failed to state a claim for breach of express warranty under Florida Uniform Commercial Code (UCC) against manufacturer of infant formula products, which had been recalled due to contamination with inset parts and larvae, where consumer did not allege that he ever notified manufacturer of the alleged breach of warranty. West's F.S.A. §§ 672.313, 672.607(3).

> Jovine v. Abbott Laboratories, Inc., 795 F.Supp.2d 1331.

Consumer failed to allege that he was in privity with infant formula manufacturer, as required to state claim for breach of implied warranty of merchantability under Florida law against manufacturer based on recall of infant formula products contaminated with insect parts and larvae. West's F.S.A. § 672.314.

> Jovine v. Abbott Laboratories, Inc., 795 F.Supp.2d 1331.

S.D.Fla. 2011. Consumer's allegations that mouthwash developer claimed mouthwash helped "fight visible plaque above the gum line" in labeling and advertising, that consumer purchased mouthwash based on these claims, that mouthwash did not provide the benefits it described, and that consumer provided notice to developer of the failure were sufficient to state a claim for breach of express warranty under Florida law, as

required for consumer's putative class action. West's F.S.A. § 672.313.

> Moss v. Walgreen Co., 765 F.Supp.2d 1363.

S.D.Fla. 2009. Consumer's allegations that chewing gum company advertised brand of gum as "scientifically proven to help kill the germs that cause bad breath," that there was no scientific proof to substantiate company's advertisement, and that consumer purchased gum in reliance on such advertising, adequately stated claim under Florida law for breach of express warranty. West's F.S.A. § 672.714.

> Smith v. Wm. Wrigley Jr. Co., 663 F.Supp.2d 1336.

S.D.Fla. 1992. Where owner of passenger buses which had caught fire did not unambiguously state that manufacturer was seller of ill-fated buses, breach of implied warranty count would fail for absence of allegation of privity theory.

> Airport Rent-A-Car, Inc. v. Prevost Car, Inc., 788 F.Supp. 1203, question certified 18 F.3d 1555, certified question answered 660 So.2d 628, rehearing denied, answer to certified question conformed to 67 F.3d 901, affirmed 67 F.3d 901.

S.D.Fla. 1987. Under Florida law, allegations by asbestos plaintiff that manufacturers of asbestos product possessed superior knowledge of product's dangerous propensities, and that plaintiff relied on defendants' skill, superior knowledge and judgment to furnish a safe product to him, and that plaintiff was injured as result of defective asbestos products, sufficiently stated cause of action for breach of implied warranty under Uniform Commercial Code. West's F.S.A. § 672.318.

> In re Asbestos Litigation, 679 F.Supp. 1096, reconsideration denied 679 F.Supp. 1094.

Bkrtcy.S.D.Fla. 2013. Complaint, which, in defining contractual relationship between company and consultant, described the relationship solely in terms of services, failed to allege what, if any, goods were to be provided under the contract, as required to state a claim for breach of implied warranty under Florida law.

    In re All American Semiconductor, Inc., 490 B.R. 418.

Complaint, which described company's contract with consultant as one that primarily, if not exclusively, provided for services, failed to allege what goods were to be provided under the contract, as required to state a claim for breach of warranty under Florida law.

    In re All American Semiconductor, Inc., 490 B.R. 418.

Fla. 1967. Complaint which alleged, inter alia, that blood bank sold certain blood to plaintiff which was impure and unfit for use intended as it contained certain virus commonly known as serum hepatitis, and that an implied warranty arose between the blood bank, as seller, and plaintiff, as buyer, of the blood, stated a cause of action.

    Community Blood Bank, Inc. v. Russell, 196 So.2d 115.

Fla. 1965. Complaint failed to state cause of action against retailer for breach of implied warranty based on sale of reducing pills in glass bottle which broke and lacerated wrist of consumer attempting to open bottle.

    Foley v. Weaver Drugs, Inc., 177 So.2d 221.

Fla. 1962. Complaint by father, who purchased playground equipment which caused injury to minor, for damages because of injury to minor son, sufficiently showed privity to support father's claim against retailer on theory of implied warranty.

    McBurnette v. Playground Equipment Corp., 137 So.2d 563, on remand 138 So.2d 372.

Fla.App. 1 Dist. 1979. Counts in complaint of children and personal representative of deceased in action against funeral home that funeral home breached implied warranty of merchantability and implied warranty of fitness by providing casket which allegedly fell apart as body of deceased was being carried from hearse to grave and which required supreme effort of pallbearers and staff of funeral director to transport body to grave sufficiently stated cause of action. West's F.S.A. §§ 672.314, 672.315, 672.714, 672.715.

    Estate of Harper v. Orlando Funeral Home, Inc., 366 So.2d 126, certiorari denied 386 So.2d 637.

Fla.App. 1 Dist. 1967. It was not necessary for consumer injured when bottle containing soft drink fell through bottom of six-pack carton and struck her foot to allege that privity of contract existed between her and manufacturer of six-pack carton to state cause of action for breach of implied warranty against manufacturer.

    Gay v. Kelly, 200 So.2d 568.

Complaint of consumer injured when bottle containing soft drink fell through bottom of six-pack carton and struck her foot against alleged manufacturer of carton sufficiently stated cause of action against manufacturer on theory of implied warranty.

    Gay v. Kelly, 200 So.2d 568.

Fla.App. 1 Dist. 1967. Complaint against snap-tie manufacturer for injuries sustained when scaffold, attached to snap-tie during wall construction, fell, stated cause of action for negligent design and manufacture and breach of implied warranty. 30 F.S.A. Rules of Civil Procedure, rule 1.110(b)(2).

    Gates & Sons, Inc. v. Brock, 199 So.2d 291, certiorari denied 204 So.2d 328.

Fla.App. 1 Dist. 1962. Complaint stated cause of action against automobile manufacturer for breach of implied warranty that automobile was useful for travel with reasonable minimum of inconvenience, but failed to state cause of action against local authorized agent of manufacturer.

    Smith v. Platt Motors, Inc., 137 So.2d 239.

Fla.App. 1 Dist. 1961. Complaint of tractor buyer that manufacturer and dealer each represented that tractor was well constructed, was suitable for use as a general farm tractor, that buyer was thereby induced to purchase it, and that such warranties were breached to injury of buyer, did state a cause of action.

    Posey v. Ford Motor Co., 128 So.2d 149.

† This Case was not selected for publication in the National Reporter System
For legislative history of cited statutes, see Florida Statutes Annotated

Fla.App. 2 Dist. 1981. Used car buyer properly alleged breach of implied warranties of merchantability and fitness against used car dealer where buyer alleged that dealer had violated various rules proposed by State Department of Legal Affairs and approved by the Governor and Cabinet, including rule that it shall be an unfair or deceptive act or practice for a motor vehicle dealer to fail to honor his express warranty agreement or any warranties implied by law. West's F.S.A. §§ 501.202, 501.203(1, 5), 501.205, 501.211(2), 672.314, 672.315.

Bert Smith Oldsmobile, Inc. v. Franklin, 400 So.2d 1235.

Fla.App. 2 Dist. 1979. Where plaintiff, who was riding as passenger when it collided with truck and who suffered serious injuries and lost one leg, brought action against motorcycle manufacturer and where breach of implied warranty count alleged existence of implied warranty by manufacturer that its motorcycles were reasonably fit for ordinary use as motorcycles upon which passengers could be transported with reasonable degree of safety and that breach of warranty occurred when manufacturer failed to provide any safety device on its motorcycle to protect passengers' legs during collisions, breach of implied warranty count stated cause of action.

Nicolodi v. Harley-Davidson Motor Co., Inc., 370 So.2d 68.

Fla.App. 2 Dist. 1975. Complaint alleging that dangerous product was a certain piece of fabric which was used as a kitchen drapery and further alleging that, when minor child was attempting to put some hot paraffin wax in sink, drapery exploded and burst into flames, severely injuring minor, was at least adequate to state a cause of action for breach of implied warranty and for negligence on part of retailer in spite of a lack of privity between parties.

Dudley v. Mae's Discount Fabrics, 323 So.2d 279.

Fla.App. 2 Dist. 1973. Complaint by boat passenger, who allegedly was injured when he was thrown from boat when steering cable broke, stated a cause of action for breach of implied warranty against manufacturer, where the plaintiff alleged, inter alia, that there was an implied warranty that the steering mechanism was merchantable and reasonably fit for its intended use, that at time of occurrence the mechanism was being used for its intended purpose, and that unknown to passenger the mechanism was not merchantable or reasonably fit for its intended use, as a result of which the cable broke and caused passenger's injuries.

Marrillia v. Lyn Craft Boat Co., 271 So.2d 204.

Fla.App. 2 Dist. 1966. Complaint which alleged that blood sold to plaintiff by blood bank and administered to plaintiff in the form of a transfusion was impure and unfit for the use intended and that, as a direct result of the use and administration of the blood, the plaintiff contracted the disease known as serum hepatitis was sufficient to state a cause of action for breach of implied warranty in the sale of blood.

Russell v. Community Blood Bank, Inc., 185 So.2d 749, reversed 196 So.2d 115.

Fla.App. 2 Dist. 1964. Complaint filed by purchaser of candy bar which had been in completely sealed paper wrapper stated cause of action against candy bar manufacturer and retailer for injuries allegedly sustained when plaintiff's tongue was pierced by nail or pin allegedly concealed in candy bar on theory of breach of implied warranty of fitness for use.

Wagner v. Mars, Inc., 166 So.2d 673.

Fla.App. 2 Dist. 1964. Buyer's complaint against seller alleging that hot water tank was impliedly warranted as fit for use in buyer's business and that after a short time tank proved unfit stated a cause of action for breach of implied warranty of fitness. 30 F.S.A. Rules of Civil Procedure, rule 1.11(b).

Arcade Steam Laundry v. Bass, 159 So.2d 915.

Complaint by laundry operator against hot water storage tank seller for breach of implied warranty of fitness with resulting loss of business profits was sufficient to support an award of damages.

Arcade Steam Laundry v. Bass, 159 So.2d 915.

Fla.App. 3 Dist. 1981. Complaint by flight attendant who allegedly contracted multiple sclerosis by exposure to noise and jet fuel emission when ordered to open aft door during engine operation against aircraft and aircraft engine manufacturers failed to plead cause of action for breach of warranty where complaint did not allege that aircraft failed to carry passengers safely, that manufacturers warranted noise-free engines, or that engine manufacturer placed engines on aircraft.

Clark v. Boeing Co., 395 So.2d 1226.

Fla.App. 3 Dist. 1974. Complaint was sufficient to state cause of action against automobile manufacturer for breach of an implied warranty because of the defect in design and manufacture of front seat track and rail mechanism on the automobile which allegedly caused injury to passenger as a result of a collision even though the defect was not a cause of the collision.

Evancho v. Thiel, 297 So.2d 40.

Fla.App. 3 Dist. 1974. Complaint alleging that, if motel swimming pool had not been painted with paint manufactured by defendant so as to camouflage plaintiff's decedent, other tenants would have observed decedent's difficulty and removed her from pool prior to her drowning was insufficient to state a cause of action for implied breach of warranty absent an allegation that paint was inherently defective or dangerous or not suited for purpose for which it was manufactured.

Kelly v. Koppers Co., Inc., 293 So.2d 763, certiorari denied 302 So.2d 415.

Fla.App. 3 Dist. 1968. Allegation in complaint that manufacturer had furnished two metal tanks to be used for installation in aircraft as supplemental fuel tanks, which were of poor workmanship and quality and were in dangerous and defective condition when sold and delivered, was not sufficient to state cause of action against manufacturer for breach of implied warranty.

Starkey v. Miami Aviation Corp., 214 So.2d 738.

Fla.App. 3 Dist. 1967. Complaint seeking recovery for death of blood donee who died from homologous serum hepatitis allegedly contracted from blood received by transfusion on ground that commercial blood bank had breached implied warranty that blood was fit for human use stated cause of action against the blood bank.

Hoder v. Sayet, 196 So.2d 205.

Fla.App. 3 Dist. 1964. That count of building supplier's complaint against manufacturer of allegedly defective snap-ties stating that snap-ties were purchased from distributor who purchased them from manufacturer and that they were not fit for purpose for which they were manufactured was insufficient in absence of allegation that supplier paid for ties and had used them.

Advance Scaffolds-Southeast, Inc. v. Universal Scaffolding Co., 164 So.2d 835.

Allegation of building supplier that it had been required to give credit in specified sum to construction company for selling improper snap-ties to construction company and that it had suffered loss in that amount did not set forth recoverable damage, and allegation did not show injury or loss to sufficiently set forth a cause of action.

Advance Scaffolds-Southeast, Inc. v. Universal Scaffolding Co., 164 So.2d 835.

Fla.App. 3 Dist. 1962. Complaint alleging that child's finger was cut off when caught between sharp edges of bars on "slide gym" manufactured by defendant stated a cause of action against manufacturer on the theory of breach of warranty as well as on the basis of negligence.

McBurnette v. Playground Equipment Corp., 138 So.2d 372.

Fla.App. 3 Dist. 1961. Complaint alleging that child's finger was cut off when caught between sharp edge of vertical bar and horizontal bar on "slide gym," and that defect in manufacture was patent and was known or should have been known by retailer which sold the equipment, stated a cause of action against manufacturer and against retailer on theory of negligence but not under claim of warranty.

McBurnette v. Playground Equipment Corp., 130 So.2d 117, quashed in part 137 So.2d 563, on remand 138 So.2d 372.

Fla.App. 4 Dist. 1976. Complaint failed to state cause of action for breach of implied warranty of fitness for particular purpose, in view of failure to allege a particular or unusual use different from purpose for which item sold was ordinarily used.

> Fred's Excavating & Crane Service, Inc. v. Continental Ins. Co., 340 So.2d 1220.

Fla.App. 4 Dist. 1975. Complaint filed against manufacturer of truck wheel and rim and against manufacturer of truck by tire store employees, who were injured when, after tire was mounted, rim pulled apart, exploded and came off the wheel with great force, stated claim for relief for breach of implied warranty on theory that, by reason of improper design or manufacture by defendants, the wheel and rim assembly was not safe for its intended use and was inherently dangerous to persons in vicinity of its probable use.

> Favors v. Firestone Tire & Rubber Co., 309 So.2d 69, appeal after remand Sansing v. Firestone Tire & Rubber Co., 354 So.2d 895, certiorari denied 360 So.2d 1250.

Complaint filed by tire store employees injured, after mounting tire on new truck, when rim exploded failed to state claim for relief against manufacturer of wheel assembly and truck manufacturer for breach of contractual warranty of merchantability of goods on theory that tire store employees were employees of agent of truck purchaser and, as such were employed by purchaser to mount tires on wheel assembly, in absence of alleging facts to establish any agency relationship between truck owner and tire store owner or any employer-employee relationship between truck owner and tire store employees. West's F.S.A. §§ 672.314, 672.318.

> Favors v. Firestone Tire & Rubber Co., 309 So.2d 69, appeal after remand Sansing v. Firestone Tire & Rubber Co., 354 So.2d 895, certiorari denied 360 So.2d 1250.

Fla.App. 4 Dist. 1971. Complaint against retailer by injured person not in privity based on claim that injury from exploding patio torch was caused by a dangerous instrumentality was adequate to state a cause of action in breach of warranty.

> Keller v. Eagle Army-Navy Dept. Stores, Inc., 256 So.2d 248, certiorari denied 264 So.2d 426, appeal after remand 291 So.2d 58.

Fla.App. 4 Dist. 1969. Complaint, which asserted that flooring laid in plaintiff's home by flooring subcontractor became badly discolored and that individual squares of flooring became loose, thus rendering entire floor unfit for purpose for which it was intended, failed to set forth cause of action against subcontractor based on breach of express warranty of merchantable quality.

> Weimar v. Yacht Club Point Estates, Inc., 223 So.2d 100.

Fla.App. 5 Dist. 2007. Complaint brought against manufacturer of prescription nutrient solution by personal representative of estate of patient who allegedly died from contaminated solution adequately alleged a breach of a pharmacist's implied warranties, where representative specifically alleged that manufacturer's pharmacist had compounded and delivered to patient a solution that was contaminated with E–Coli and other bacteria and was improperly laced with insulin.

> Fontanez v. Parenteral Therapy Associates, Inc., 974 So.2d 1101, rehearing denied.

Fla.App. 5 Dist. 1980. Where plaintiff, who was injured when he fell from leased tractor while performing inspection of refrigeration unit, alleged that the tractor was unreasonably dangerous because of the absence of devices for safe footing in light of lessor's knowledge of the specific use to which the tractor would be put, and that it was defective, complaint sounding in strict liability, general negligence and breach of warranty stated cause of action and should have been sustained.

> Futch v. Ryder Truck Rental, Inc., 391 So.2d 808.

👈**2467. —— Answer and subsequent pleadings.**

C.A.5 (Fla.) 1963. A plea of contributory negligence is inapposite to a claim based on breach of implied warranty.

> Green v. American Tobacco Co., 325 F.2d 673, certiorari denied 84 S.Ct. 1349, 377 U.S. 943, 12 L.Ed.2d 306, certiorari denied 84 S.Ct. 1351, 377 U.S. 943, 12 L.Ed.2d 306.

**† This Case was not selected for publication in the National Reporter System
For legislative history of cited statutes, see Florida Statutes Annotated**

☜2468. —— Variance between pleadings and proof.

Bkrtcy.M.D.Fla. 1981. Under Florida law, buyers of property and draperies, which allegedly were not of merchantable quality, were entitled to no recovery against seller where they failed to present any evidence of damage suffered as result of the alleged breach of warranty. West's F.S.A. §§ 672.314, 672.607.
Matter of Vincent, 10 B.R. 549.

Fla.App. 3 Dist. 1965. Plaintiff who was injured when body of paper cup came apart from handle and caused hot contents to spill on her resulting in her being scalded was not required to prove that privity of contract existed between parties in order to recover against manufacturer on theory of implied warranty.
Bernstein v. Lily-Tulip Cup Corp., 177 So.2d 362, certiorari discharged 181 So.2d 641.

☜2469. Trial or hearing.

For other cases see earlier editions of this digest, the Decennial Digests, and WESTLAW.

☜2470. —— In general.
Evidence, see XI(C), XI(D), XI(E).
Questions of law or fact, see XI(F).
Instructions, see XI(G).

☜2471. —— Verdict and findings.

For other cases see earlier editions of this digest, the Decennial Digests, and WESTLAW.

☜2472. Judgment, order, or decree.
Remedies, see X.

☜2473. Costs and fees.

Fla.App. 4 Dist. 1983. Even if various defects in recreational vehicle were covered by written warranty issued by manufacturer, recreational vehicle dealer did not adopt warranty as matter of state law by referring to sales and specification literature of manufacturer in making certain representations about vehicle sold to buyers so as to entitle buyers to attorney fees under Magnuson-Moss Warranty Act. Magnuson-Moss Warranty-Federal Trade Commission Improvement Act, § 110, 15 U.S.C.A. § 2310; West's F.S.A. § 672.316.
Motor Homes of America, Inc. v. O'Donnell, 440 So.2d 422, petition for review denied 451 So.2d 849.

2. ACTIONS FOR RESCISSION OR REDHIBITION.

☜2501–2506. *For other cases see earlier editions of this digest, the Decennial Digests, and WESTLAW.*

☜2507. Time to sue; limitations and laches.

C.A.5 (Fla.) 1968. Since Florida helicopter pilot was not owner of helicopter which crashed in Louisiana and had not purchased helicopter from defendant manufacturer, under applicable Louisiana law, implied warranty action was classified as ex delictual and was barred where brought more than one year after crash. LSA-C.C. art. 3544; F.S.A. § 95.10.
Beasley v. Fairchild Hiller Corp., 401 F.2d 593.

☜2508. Parties.

Fla.App. 1 Dist. 1992. Claims with respect to revocation of acceptance, breach of warranty, and violation of Magnuson-Moss Act may be pursued against automobile manufacturer rather than dealer. Magnuson-Moss Warranty—Federal Trade Commission Improvement Act, § 101 et seq., 15 U.S.C.A. § 2301 et seq.
Claude Nolan Cadillac, Inc. v. Griffin, 610 So.2d 725, review denied 621 So.2d 432.

☜2509–2515. *For other cases see earlier editions of this digest, the Decennial Digests, and WESTLAW.*

☜2515. Trial or hearing.

☜2516. —— In general.
Evidence, see XI(C), XI(D), XI(E).
Questions of law or fact, see XI(F).
Instructions, see XI(G).

☜2517. —— Verdict and findings.

For other cases see earlier editions of this digest, the Decennial Digests, and WESTLAW.

† This Case was not selected for publication in the National Reporter System
For legislative history of cited statutes, see Florida Statutes Annotated

☞**2518. Judgment, order, or decree.**

Remedies, see X.

☞**2519. Costs and fees.**

For other cases see earlier editions of this digest, the Decennial Digests, and WEST-LAW.

(C) PRESUMPTIONS, INFERENCES, AND BURDEN OF PROOF.

☞**2601–2604.** *For other cases see earlier editions of this digest, the Decennial Digests, and WESTLAW.*

☞**2604. Nature and formation of contract.**

☞**2605. —— In general.**

C.A.5 (Fla.) 1977. In action by plaintiff, the purchaser, against defendant, the seller, for failure to complete alleged oral contract for the sale of ammonia, court properly instructed that, under Florida law, plaintiff bore only the burden to prove the existence of an oral contract by a preponderance of the evidence. West's F.S.A. § 671.201(8).

Transammonia Export Corp. v. Conserv, Inc., 554 F.2d 719.

Fla. 1954. To recover in action for breach of contract to sell, deliver and install in plaintiff's yacht two marine engines, plaintiff must prove a contract, that is, a meeting of parties' minds, or conduct of defendant establishing estoppel to deny existence of contract.

National Airlines v. Florida Equipment Co. of Miami, 71 So.2d 741.

☞**2606. —— Offer, acceptance, and consideration.**

Fla.App. 2 Dist. 2007. A party seeking the exclusion of a contractual term or provision as constituting a material alteration of contract, pursuant to the Uniform Commercial Code (UCC), has the burden of proof. West's F.S.A. § 672.207(2).

Paul Gottlieb & Co., Inc. v. Alps South Corp., 985 So.2d 1, rehearing denied.

To carry burden of showing surprise, within meaning of material alteration exception of "battle of the forms" provision of Uniform Commercial Code (UCC), party must establish that, under the circumstances, it cannot be presumed that a rea-sonable merchant would have consented to the additional term. West's F.S.A. § 672.207(2).

Paul Gottlieb & Co., Inc. v. Alps South Corp., 985 So.2d 1, rehearing denied.

☞**2607. Validity and enforceability of contract.**

☞**2608. —— In general.**

Fla.App. 2 Dist. 1960. Where deceased's widow and executrix of his estate sought to set aside bill of sale on ground of fraud and undue influence, it was incumbent upon widow and executrix to prove allegations of fraud and undue influence.

Courington v. Courington, 120 So.2d 64.

☞**2609. —— Misrepresentation and fraud.**

Fla.App. 2 Dist. 1960. Where deceased's widow and executrix of his estate sought to set aside bill of sale on ground of fraud and undue influence, it was incumbent upon widow and executrix to prove allegations of fraud and undue influence.

Courington v. Courington, 120 So.2d 64.

☞**2610–2611.** *For other cases see earlier editions of this digest, the Decennial Digests, and WESTLAW.*

☞**2611. Terms of contract; rights and obligations of parties.**

☞**2612. —— In general.**

Fla.App. 2 Dist. 1980. Burden is on plaintiff buyer to show that within reasonable time he gave seller notice of breach as required by statute. West's F.S.A. § 672.607(3)(a).

General Matters, Inc. v. Paramount Canning Co., 382 So.2d 1262.

☞**2613–2614.** *For other cases see earlier editions of this digest, the Decennial Digests, and WESTLAW.*

☞**2614. —— Delivery and acceptance.**

☞**2614(1). In general.**

Fla. 1940. Generally when goods are shipped under "C.A.F. contract", meaning cost and freight allowed to point of destination, being the equivalent of shipment F.O.B. from point of origin, the responsibility of the shipper ceases when the goods are delivered to the carrier, but if issue is raised as to whether the goods moved from point of shipment promptly or when loaded were up to contract requirements, evidence on such issues may be taken and if proven, judgment rendered accordingly.

Farris & Co. v. William Schluderberg, T. J. Kurdle Co., 196 So. 184, 142 Fla. 765.

⚷2614(2). Quality, value, fitness, and condition of goods.

C.A.11 (Fla.) 1987. Buyers seeking damages for nonconformity, rather than revocation of acceptance, were not required, under Florida law, to prove substantial nonconformity. West's F.S.A. § 672.714.

Nyquist v. Randall, 819 F.2d 1014.

Fla.App. 3 Dist. 1970. Although agreement between Florida seller and Florida buyer of aircraft in custody of seller's bailee in Luxemburg did not specify that sale was "as is" and did not expressly provide with reference to condition of the aircraft, parties must be presumed to have understood that aircraft would reflect wear and tear and depreciation which reasonably could be expected to have occurred thereto as result of use to which it had been put since prior sale thereof.

Pinellas Central Bank & Trust Co. v. International Aerodyne, Inc., 233 So.2d 872, certiorari denied 239 So.2d 829.

⚷2614(3)–2617. *For other cases see earlier editions of this digest, the Decennial Digests, and WESTLAW.*

⚷2618. —— Transfer of title; risk of loss.

Fla.App. 3 Dist. 1985. If buyer and seller adopt a C.I.F. contract, they will be presumed, in the absence of any express term to the contrary, to have adopted all the normal incidents of that type of contract, one of which is that buyer, not the seller, bears the risk of loss when the goods are delivered to the carrier and the seller's other contractual obligations are fulfilled.

Kumar Corp. v. Nopal Lines, Ltd., 462 So.2d 1178, petition for review denied S.E.L. Maduro (Florida), Inc. v. Kumar Corp., 476 So.2d 675.

Fla.App. 4 Dist. 1968. Delivery of automobile before title had been placed in name of minor buyer's mother created rebuttable presumption that sale condition, that title to the automobile be placed in name of mother, had been waived and that title had passed.

Smith v. Baker, 206 So.2d 409.

⚷2619–2620. *For other cases see earlier editions of this digest, the Decennial Digests, and WESTLAW.*

⚷2621. —— Excuses for nonperformance or breach.

C.A.5 (Fla.) 1976. Trial court in action for breach of contract to manufacture and deliver commercial jet aircraft did not err in instructing jury that manufacturer had burden of proving excusable delay.

Eastern Air Lines, Inc. v. McDonnell Douglas Corp., 532 F.2d 957.

S.D.Fla. 1975. In order for seller to avoid obligation to deliver on basis of asserted failure of a presupposed condition, there must be a failure of such a presupposed condition which was an underlying assumption of the contract, the failure must have been unforeseeable, and the risk of failure must not have been specifically allocated to the seller; burden of proving each element of the claimed commercial impracticability is on the party claiming the defense. West's F.S.A. § 672.615.

Eastern Air Lines, Inc. v. Gulf Oil Corp., 415 F.Supp. 429.

⚷2622. —— Waiver and estoppel.

Fla. 1954. To recover in action for breach of contract to sell, deliver and install in plaintiff's yacht two marine engines, plaintiff must prove a contract, that is, a meeting of parties' minds, or conduct of defendant establishing estoppel to deny existence of contract.

National Airlines v. Florida Equipment Co. of Miami, 71 So.2d 741.

🗝**2623–2628.** *For other cases see earlier editions of this digest, the Decennial Digests, and WESTLAW.*

🗝**2628. Warranties.**

🗝**2629. —— In general.**

Bkrtcy.M.D.Fla. 1981. Under Florida law, burden is on a buyer to establish any breach of warranty with respect to goods accepted. West's F.S.A. § 672.607(4).

Matter of Vincent, 10 B.R. 549.

Fla.App. 1 Dist. 1985. Even if manufacturer could be held strictly liable, plaintiff would have to prove proximate causation to recover for breach of warranty, negligence, or strict liability.

Vaughn v. Edward M. Chadbourne, Inc., 462 So.2d 512, quashed 491 So.2d 551, 62 A.L.R.4th 1055.

Fla.App. 3 Dist. 1975. Workman's widow, who sought to recover for breach of warranty, was not under a duty to pinpoint any exact mechanical deficiency for or by reason of which the device proved defective and failed.

Armor Elevator Co. v. Wood, 312 So.2d 514, certiorari denied 330 So.2d 14.

🗝**2630. —— Express warranties.**

C.A.11 (Fla.) 1983. Allegation of breach of express warranty does not require proof of intent. West's F.S.A. § 672.313(1)(a).

Royal Typewriter Co., a Div. of Litton Business Systems, Inc. v. Xerographic Supplies Corp., 719 F.2d 1092.

🗝**2631. —— Warranties imposed by law; implied warranties.**

C.A.5 (Fla.) 1971. In absence of proof of defect in article on date of delivery, the manufacturer thereof may not be held liable on theory of implied warranty.

Holcomb v. Cessna Aircraft Co., 439 F.2d 1150, certiorari denied 92 S.Ct. 62, 404 U.S. 827, 30 L.Ed.2d 56.

C.A.5 (Fla.) 1963. Under the circumstances, it would be assumed, in action for wrongful death of plaintiff's decedent allegedly due to smoking cigarettes manufactured by defendant, that decedent purchased manufacturer's cigarettes in reliance upon manufacturer's implied warranty of fitness.

Green v. American Tobacco Co., 325 F.2d 673, certiorari denied 84 S.Ct. 1349, 377 U.S. 943, 12 L.Ed.2d 306, certiorari denied 84 S.Ct. 1351, 377 U.S. 943, 12 L.Ed.2d 306.

M.D.Fla. 1985. Plaintiff bringing action for breach of implied warranty of fitness for a particular purpose must prove under Florida law that defendant, at time sale was made, knew of particular purpose for which goods were going to be used and that plaintiff relied upon defendant's skill and judgment when purchasing product. West's F.S.A. § 672.315.

Crawford v. Gold Kist, Inc., 614 F.Supp. 682.

In the absence of evidence that seed merchant had been asked to supply wheat seed which would satisfy a particular purpose, farmer, who purchased allegedly defective wheat seed from merchant, could not maintain action under Florida law for breach of implied warranty of fitness for particular purpose. West's F.S.A. §§ 672.101 et seq., 672.105(1), 672.315.

Crawford v. Gold Kist, Inc., 614 F.Supp. 682.

Bkrtcy.M.D.Fla. 1981. Under Florida law, to assert cause of action for breach of implied warranty the buyer must prove that there is an implied warranty, a breach thereof and damage resulting as a proximate cause of the breach. West's F.S.A. §§ 672.314, 672.314(2).

Matter of Vincent, 10 B.R. 549.

Fla.App. 1 Dist. 1971. In case for damages for breach of implied warranty, plaintiff must show that product was transferred from manufacturer's defendant while in defective state and as result of defect plaintiff was injured.

E. R. Squibb & Sons, Inc. v. Jordan, 254 So.2d 17.

Fla.App. 1 Dist. 1962. Buyer, who seeks to recover damages in reliance on breach of implied warranty of fitness or merchantability, must establish both nature of breach and fact that his own acts did not produce result on which breach is predicated, where article involved is of such nature that proper performance of purpose for which it is manufactured and purchased to be used depends substantially on type of care and method of operation given to it by buyer.

Posey v. Pensacola Tractor & Equipment Co., 138 So.2d 777.

Fla.App. 2 Dist. 1974. In order to recover from manufacturer on theory of implied warranty, consumer must prove that he was foreseeable user of product, that product was being used in intended manner at time of injury, that product was defective when transferred from manufacturer, and that defect caused his injury.

McCarthy v. Florida Ladder Co., 295 So.2d 707.

Fla.App. 3 Dist. 1990. The burden of proof is on buyer to show facts giving rise to express or implied warranty but ultimate issue is determined by jury.

State Farm Ins. Co. v. Nu Prime Roll-A-Way of Miami, 557 So.2d 107.

Fla.App. 4 Dist. 1983. Under either strict liability or breach of implied warranty of merchantability theory there must be proof of defect.

Husky Industries, Inc. v. Black, 434 So.2d 988.

⚷2632. —— Exclusion, modification, or limitation of warranties.

C.A.5 (Fla.) 1980. Burden of proof on affirmative defense that limitations of warranty and liability were unconscionable as matter of law rested on party asserting it. West's F.S.A. § 672.302.

Earman Oil Co., Inc. v. Burroughs Corp., 625 F.2d 1291.

⚷2633. —— Cumulation and conflict of warranties.

For other cases see earlier editions of this digest, the Decennial Digests, and WEST-LAW.

⚷2634. —— Parties to warranties, privity, and third-party beneficiaries.

Fla. 1962. Presumption of intended benefit of implied warranties attaching to sales of household goods should be governed by principles controlling contracts for third-party beneficiaries under which test is not privity between them, or consid-

eration moving from third person, but intent of parties to contract that third person should benefit by it.

McBurnette v. Playground Equipment Corp., 137 So.2d 563, on remand 138 So.2d 372.

Fla.App. 3 Dist. 1965. Proof of privity is not required in implied warranty suit by consumer against manufacturer.

Bernstein v. Lily-Tulip Cup Corp., 177 So.2d 362, certiorari discharged 181 So.2d 641.

⚷2635. —— Notice and opportunity to cure.

C.A.11 (Fla.) 1983. Under Florida law, buyer bears burden of showing that he gave required notice of breach of warranty within reasonable time. West's F.S.A. § 672.607.

Royal Typewriter Co., a Div. of Litton Business Systems, Inc. v. Xerographic Supplies Corp., 719 F.2d 1092.

⚷2636–2639. *For other cases see earlier editions of this digest, the Decennial Digests, and WESTLAW.*

⚷2637. Remedies.

⚷2640. —— Monetary remedies and damages in general.

C.A.5 (Fla.) 1975. Where carpet dealer, in counterclaim against carpet manufacturer for breach of warranty and negligence, sought recovery of damages resulting from statewide loss of sales, dealer was required to prove statewide rather than localized injury; statewide injury to dealer's reputation and consequent loss of sales could not be inferred from dealer's removal from bidding lists of two out of a total of 67 county school boards.

Aldon Industries, Inc. v. Don Myers & Associates, Inc., 517 F.2d 188, appeal after remand 547 F.2d 924.

C.A.5 (Fla.) 1964. To recover for an asserted loss, buyer had burden of proving fact, cause and extent of such loss.

Sperry Rand Corp. v. Industrial Supply Corp., 337 F.2d 363.

☞2641. —— **Price or value of goods in general.**

For other cases see earlier editions of this digest, the Decennial Digests, and WEST-LAW.

☞2642. —— **Resale of goods and price thereof.**

Fla. 1955. Wholesale lumber dealer, who was entitled to new trial on counterclaim for loss of profits due to alleged shortage of quantity and defective quality of lumber in certain car, would have burden of proving that, at time of the shipment, lumber supplier, from whom dealer sought recovery, had been informed of the proposed resale of the carload or was chargeable with such knowledge.

McNeill v. Jack, 83 So.2d 704.

☞2643–2651. *For other cases see earlier editions of this digest, the Decennial Digests, and WESTLAW.*

(D) ADMISSIBILITY OF EVIDENCE.

☞2661–2667. *For other cases see earlier editions of this digest, the Decennial Digests, and WESTLAW.*

☞2667. **Validity and enforceability of contract.**

☞2668. —— **In general.**

C.A.11 (Fla.) 1985. Where parties never executed proposed contract for sale of metric mold, trial court, in suit against manufacturer and seller by buyer alleging, inter alia, fraud and breach of contract and warranties, did not abuse its discretion in refusing to admit the proposed contract as irrelevant.

Pesaplastic, C.A. v. Cincinnati Milacron Co., 750 F.2d 1516.

☞2669–2671. *For other cases see earlier editions of this digest, the Decennial Digests, and WESTLAW.*

☞2671. **Terms of contract; rights and obligations of parties.**

☞2672. —— **In general.**

† **C.A.11 (Fla.) 2005.** Decision to admit evidence of rebates that retailer had secured from other manufacturers that had previously produced certain products

on its behalf, as evidence of alleged "wink and nod" agreements between retailer and these other manufacturers at time when plaintiff-manufacturer had contract to be retailer's exclusive supplier of such products, and as relevant to rebut explanations offered by retailer for failing to purchase products from plaintiff-manufacturer, was not abuse of district court's discretion.

SEB S.A. v. Sunbeam Corp., 148 Fed. Appx. 774, appeal after remand 476 F.3d 1317, appeal after remand 302 Fed.Appx. 870.

☞2673–2674(1). *For other cases see earlier editions of this digest, the Decennial Digests, and WESTLAW.*

☞2674. —— **Delivery and acceptance.**

☞2674(2). **Quality, value, fitness, and condition of goods.**

S.D.Fla. 1981. In contract action in which defendant raised a counterclaim seeking lost profits resulting from allegedly defective condition of display racks manufactured by plaintiff, evidence of lost profits with respect to such racks was properly excluded, in that defendant failed to prove a causal connection between termination of a contract with retailer and the allegedly defective racks.

Diane Mfg. Co. v. Sheffield Industries, Inc., 514 F.Supp. 185, affirmed Diane Manufacturing Co. v. Sheffield Ind., 685 F.2d 1387.

Fla. 1940. In action to recover amount paid by buyer to seller on contract to purchase citrus fruit, evidence of condition of fruit as late as April 13, 1938, approximately four months after fruit was damaged by frost, was admissible in view of provision of contract that fruit could be removed as late as April 1.

Vaughn-Griffin Packing Co. v. Fisher, 193 So. 553, 141 Fla. 428.

Fla.App. 1 Dist. 2016. Evidence of failures of carpet manufacturer's other products, which did not use resin manufacturer's resin, was irrelevant to the issue of liability in carpet manufacturer's action against manufacturer of resin used in the carpet's backing system, alleging breach of contract, breach of express warranty, and breach of implied warranty of fitness for a particular purpose; carpet manufacturer

† This Case was not selected for publication in the National Reporter System
For legislative history of cited statutes, see Florida Statutes Annotated

did not argue that the claims rate alone established causation, but pointed to evidence of actual resin degradation, carpet manufacturer's claims-spike analysis was specific to the product at issue and was argued only in conjunction with other points, there was no evidence connecting the failure of the carpet at issue with the failures of the other products, and the evidence showed causation only to the extent that it showed a propensity to produce bad carpet, which was an improper purpose for introduction of the evidence. West's F.S.A. § 90.404(2)(a).

   Arizona Chemical Co., LLC v. Mohawk Industries, Inc., 193 So.3d 95, rehearing denied, review dismissed 2016 WL 5395580.

⚖2674(3)–2674(5). *For other cases see earlier editions of this digest, the Decennial Digests, and WESTLAW.*

⚖2674(6). **Sale on trial or approval; contracts for sale or return.**

Fla. 1941. Where contract for sale of garment bag machinery constructed for buyer contained no provisions from which the court could determine whether sale was a 'sale or return' or "sale on approval", the correspondence between the parties prior to execution of the contract was admissible to determine whether the buyer had the option to purchase if he was satisfied with the property or the option to return if dissatisfied.

   Jacksonville Paper Co. v. Smith & Winchester Mfg. Co., 2 So.2d 890, 147 Fla. 311.

⚖2675. —— **Amounts payable; price.**

Fla.App. 1 Dist. 1988. Market report showing average value for sales of watermelons and another watermelon buyer's testimony as to prices she paid for watermelons were properly excluded as irrelevant in administrative hearing on watermelon farmer's claim that buyer underpaid him because he had agreed to pay fixed price rather than price based on fair market value; farmer testified that buyer's offer was only offer he received, and there was no evidence suggesting that farmer could have sold his watermelons to anyone else.

   J.R. Sales, Inc. v. Dicks, 521 So.2d 366.

⚖2676. —— **Duties and expenses of transportation.**

C.A.11 (Fla.) 1982. In breach of contract action, trial court did not err in permitting buyer to introduce evidence of load capacity of ship in which goods were to be transported while prohibiting seller from showing why ship was not loaded in view of fact that load capacity of ship was highly relevant to buyer's damages while, in contrast, reason ship was not loaded was irrelevant to lawsuit since breach occurred beforehand.

   Fabrica Italiana Lavorazione Materie Organiche, S.A.S. v. Kaiser Aluminum & Chemical Corp., 684 F.2d 776.

⚖2677–2688. *For other cases see earlier editions of this digest, the Decennial Digests, and WESTLAW.*

⚖2688. **Warranties.**

⚖2689. —— **In general.**

C.A.11 (Fla.) 1985. Where parties never executed proposed contract for sale of metric mold, trial court, in suit against manufacturer and seller by buyer alleging, inter alia, fraud and breach of contract and warranties, did not abuse its discretion in refusing to admit the proposed contract as irrelevant.

   Pesaplastic, C.A. v. Cincinnati Milacron Co., 750 F.2d 1516.

Fla.App. 1 Dist. 2016. Evidence of failures of carpet manufacturer's other products, which did not use resin manufacturer's resin, was irrelevant to the issue of liability in carpet manufacturer's action against manufacturer of resin used in the carpet's backing system, alleging breach of contract, breach of express warranty, and breach of implied warranty of fitness for a particular purpose; carpet manufacturer did not argue that the claims rate alone established causation, but pointed to evidence of actual resin degradation, carpet manufacturer's claims-spike analysis was specific to the product at issue and was argued only in conjunction with other points, there was no evidence connecting the failure of the carpet at issue with the failures of the other products, and the evidence showed causation only to the extent that it showed a propensity to produce bad carpet, which was an improper purpose for introduction of the evidence. West's F.S.A. § 90.404(2)(a).

> Arizona Chemical Co., LLC v. Mohawk Industries, Inc., 193 So.3d 95, rehearing denied, review dismissed 2016 WL 5395580.

Fla.App. 1 Dist. 1979. In suit for negligence, breach of warranty and strict liability in the manufacture of a punch press on which plaintiff injured her hand, the trial court correctly allowed defendant's argument to the jury as to the negligence of plaintiff's employer, the owner of the press on which there was no guard device, and the introduction into evidence of 1971 industry safety standards and government regulations.

> Clement v. Rousselle Corp., 372 So.2d 1156, certiorari denied 383 So.2d 1191.

In suit for negligence, breach of warranty and strict liability in the manufacture of a punch press on which plaintiff injured her hand the trial court properly allowed into evidence ANSI (American National Standards Institute) and OSHA (Occupational Safety and Health Act) standards, which were promulgated after the manufacture and sale of the press in question, but prior to the accident; the standards were admissible to refute plaintiff's claim of a continuing duty on the part of defendant to track down and locate the owner of a press sold 11 years before so as to warn of the danger of operating the machine without a point of operation guard, and the standards were also properly used in cross-examination of plaintiff's expert witness, a safety specialist.

> Clement v. Rousselle Corp., 372 So.2d 1156, certiorari denied 383 So.2d 1191.

☞2690–2691. *For other cases see earlier editions of this digest, the Decennial Digests, and WESTLAW.*

☞2692. —— **Exclusion, modification, or limitation of warranties.**

C.A.5 (Fla.) 1965. Warranty and limitation of liability contained in contract between can company and bread company, which purchased cans from can company and then had cans shipped to bakery corporation for use by it, was binding on bakery corporation which had entered into contract with bread company, pursuant to which former agreed to sell to latter its entire canned product, and such limitation of liability should have been received in evidence and damages, if any, calculated in accordance with its provisions.

> American Can Co. v. Horlamus Corp., 341 F.2d 730.

☞2693–2699. *For other cases see earlier editions of this digest, the Decennial Digests, and WESTLAW.*

☞2697. **Remedies.**

☞2700. —— **Monetary remedies and damages in general.**

Fla.App. 3 Dist. 1972. Where there was evidence that $13,000 deposit was agreed upon in negotiations between buyer and seller and trial court determined that $13,000 was not liquidated damages, trial court did not err in refusing testimony regarding reasonableness of the $13,000 deposit as down payment.

> Carol Management Co. v. Baring Industries, 257 So.2d 270.

☞2701–2702. *For other cases see earlier editions of this digest, the Decennial Digests, and WESTLAW.*

☞2703. —— **Procurement and price of substitute goods; "cover".**

C.A.11 (Fla.) 1982. Where, at moment of seller's breach, buyer was entitled to suspend performance of contract and cover and buyer did exactly that, at such moment buyer's damages for covering were fixed and subsequent boycott by longshoremen's union of Soviet vessel nominated by buyer was legally irrelevant to damages arising from cover. U.C.C. §§ 2–610, 2–712.

> Fabrica Italiana Lavorazione Materie Organiche, S.A.S. v. Kaiser Aluminum & Chemical Corp., 684 F.2d 776.

⚷2704–2706. *For other cases see earlier editions of this digest, the Decennial Digests, and WESTLAW.*

⚷2707. —— Lost profits.

C.A.11 (Fla.) 1983. In action for breach of contract and warranty in regard to sale of typesetter, trial court did not abuse its discretion in excluding oral testimony of lost profits that lacked specificity to tie those lost profits to seller's alleged breach.

Typographical Service, Inc. v. Itek Corp., 721 F.2d 1317.

⚷2708–2711. *For other cases see earlier editions of this digest, the Decennial Digests, and WESTLAW.*

(E) WEIGHT AND SUFFICIENCY OF EVIDENCE.

⚷2721. In general.

Fla. 1949. In action by grower of citrus fruit for defendant's failure to perform a written contract to purchase a crop growing on the trees, evidence justified judgment in favor of plaintiff.

Purpura Bros. v. Oxner, 40 So.2d 890.

Fla. 1937. Evidence held to support finding that vendee had neither possession nor right of possession of crop of fruit at time he transmitted purported bill of sale thereto to vendor, as respects alleged conversion of crop by assignee of real estate mortgage who had foreclosed on the premises and acquired possession and control of the entire property prior to execution of the bill of sale.

E. C. Fitz & Co. v. Eldridge, 176 So. 539, 129 Fla. 647.

Fla.App. 2 Dist. 1961. Evidence warranted trial court finding for citrus canning company maintaining action on contract involving sale and delivery of citrus fruit.

Hudson Co. v. Holly Hill Citrus Canning Co., 133 So.2d 758.

⚷2722. Nature and subject matter of sale.

For other cases see earlier editions of this digest, the Decennial Digests, and WESTLAW.

⚷2723. Parties to transaction or contract.

C.A.5 (Fla.) 1968. Weight of evidence supported finding of trial court that the purchase orders executed between manufacturer as seller and corporate buyer after all negotiations and commencement of production were intended to be an integration of prior negotiations and agreements between seller and corporate buyer and its president who seller sought to hold individually liable.

Carolina Metal Products Corp. v. Larson, 389 F.2d 490.

Fla.App. 2 Dist. 1960. In action on open account for materials furnished for residential development project, evidence sustained finding that one who had purchased land for project, taking title in his own name but later transferring title to a corporation, was not liable as an individual for such materials.

Tampa Sand & Material Co. v. Davis, 125 So.2d 126.

Fla.App. 3 Dist. 1965. Evidence supported finding that sale of furniture used to furnish apartment building manager's apartment was made to owner of apartment building and not to manager.

Lake Towers, Inc. v. A. T. Euster Furniture Co., 174 So.2d 448.

⚷2724. Nature and formation of contract.

⚷2725. —— In general.

C.A.5 (Fla.) 1974. Failure of seller to respond to "Confirmations" sent by buyer did not relieve buyer, in its action for breach of alleged oral contract for sale of 10,000 tons of citrus pulp, of burden of convincing jury by a preponderance of the evidence that an oral contract was made, and the essential terms thereof. F.S.A. § 672.201.

I. S. Joseph Co., Inc. v. Citrus Feed Co., Inc., 490 F.2d 185, rehearing denied 492 F.2d 1242.

C.A.5 (Fla.) 1955. In action for unpaid portion of price of rewinding machine sold by plaintiff to defendant paper company, testimony of defendant's president as to his telephone conversations with plaintiff company's vice-president in charge of sales, when considered with parties' subsequent correspondence, showed that prices mentioned in conversations were only estimates not intended to be firm offer, and trial judge was correct in interpreting conversations as mere preliminary negotiations and concluding that sale contract consisted of resulting correspondence.

　　Calcasieu Paper Co. v. Cameron Mach. Co., 220 F.2d 876.

Bkrtcy.M.D.Fla. 1983. Although agreement existed between wholesaler and retailer concerning sale of floor covering, evidence in wholesaler's action on account receivable supported finding of a second oral agreement whereby wholesaler would retrieve unsold carpeting and credit retailer's account.

　　Matter of Fashion Mills of Florida, Inc., 27 B.R. 112.

Fla. 1938. Where seller and buyer's agent contracted for purchase and sale of potatoes at fixed prices for different kinds, but potatoes were already loaded in freight car so that quantity of each kind was to be determined at destination, and contract stated nothing about price depending on amount realized by buyer on resale, evidence did not sustain finding that there was no meeting of the minds.

　　Lyng v. Bugbee Distributing Co., 182 So. 801, 133 Fla. 419.

Fla.App. 3 Dist. 1969. In dispute between contractor, subcontractor and supplier, evidence was sufficient to show existence of contract between subcontractor and supplier, and to show that there was no contract between contractor and supplier for purchase of material.

　　Flintkote Co. v. Brewer Co. of Fla., 221 So.2d 784, certiorari denied 225 So.2d 920.

　　Substantial competent evidence existed in dispute between general contractor, subcontractor and supplier to show that supplier, who contracted with subcontractor to supply material, was aware of the required specification, which its product could not meet.

　　Flintkote Co. v. Brewer Co. of Fla., 221 So.2d 784, certiorari denied 225 So.2d 920.

Fla.App. 3 Dist. 1966. Evidence sustained finding, in action by seller against purchaser for breach of contract, that after

the placing of an order by the purchaser and a counteroffer made by the vendor, the parties reached an agreement as to the items to be manufactured and sold and as to their prices, and that a purchase contract was made between the seller and purchaser.

　　Aerospace Electronics, Inc. v. Control Parts Corp., 183 So.2d 875.

☞2726–2727. *For other cases see earlier editions of this digest, the Decennial Digests, and WESTLAW.*

☞2727. **Validity and enforceability of contract.**

☞2728. —— **In general.**

Fla.App. 2 Dist. 1960. In action by widow and executrix of deceased's estate to set aside deceased's bill of sale to his brother representing deceased's interest in bar and tavern, there was substantial evidence to sustain findings of trial court that bill of sale was not a fraud and not made as a result of deceased's brother's undue influence.

　　Courington v. Courington, 120 So.2d 64.

☞2729. —— **Misrepresentation and fraud.**

C.A.11 (Fla.) 1983. In action for breach of contract and warranty in regard to sale of typesetter, finding of no fraud in procurement of purchase agreement was not clearly erroneous, in light of knowledge and sophistication of parties, contents of agreement, and lack of any evidence of intent to deceive.

　　Typographical Service, Inc. v. Itek Corp., 721 F.2d 1317.

Fla. 1957. Evidence justified cancellation of conditional sales contract of house trailer on ground that contract was obtained under circumstances of misinformation and overreaching, if not actual duress, such as to relieve buyer of any liability.

　　Motor Credit Corp. v. Woolverton, 99 So.2d 286, 72 A.L.R.2d 334.

Fla. 1954. In suit to rescind the sale of a used automobile on the ground that the defendant had fraudulently misrepresented the condition of the automobile to the plaintiff, evidence was insufficient to establish fraudulent representations.

Faulk v. Weller K-F Cars, Inc., 70 So.2d 578.

Fla. 1953. In action to rescind, cancel, and set aside alleged bill of sale and purchase agreement on ground of fraud, evidence was sufficient to sustain master's finding that there was no fraud in the inducement of the contract.

Yarnelle v. Kollar, 62 So.2d 915.

Fla. 1950. In purchasers' action to rescind contract for purchase of wheel alignment business, on ground that seller misrepresented net profit of business, evidence did not sustain purchasers' burden of proving exact occasion and circumstances under which alleged misrepresentation occurred, or that purchasers were justified in relying upon misrepresentation or that they did in fact rely upon it.

Fote v. Reitano, 46 So.2d 891.

Where purchasers signed contract to purchase wheel alignment business, and contract provided that purchasers had inspected property, verified and investigated all oral representations made and all details set forth therein, to their entire satisfaction, such recital was evidence, in purchasers' action to rescind contract, that purchasers did not, in fact, rely upon alleged misrepresentation of profits of business.

Fote v. Reitano, 46 So.2d 891.

Fla.App. 2 Dist. 1960. In action by widow and executrix of deceased's estate to set aside deceased's bill of sale to his brother representing deceased's interest in bar and tavern, there was substantial evidence to sustain findings of trial court that bill of sale was not a fraud and not made as a result of deceased's brother's undue influence.

Courington v. Courington, 120 So.2d 64.

Fla.App. 3 Dist. 2005. Evidence in breach of contract and fraudulent misrepresentation action by buyers of business against seller was sufficient to establish that seller's wrongdoing caused buyers' damage; conflicting evidence as to causation was introduced at trial, and it was jury's role to resolve the conflict.

Gonzalez v. Garcia, 913 So.2d 735.

⌖**2730–2731.** *For other cases see earlier editions of this digest, the Decennial Digests, and WESTLAW.*

⌖**2731. Terms of contract; rights and obligations of parties.**

⌖**2732.** —— **In general.**

Fla.App. 3 Dist. 1989. Wholesale aircraft parts supplier could not recover against corporation for price of turbine engine supplied after first supplied turbine failed within 30 days under action to recover price of goods where record failed to demonstrate additional sale. West's F.S.A. § 672.709.

Page Avjet Corp. v. Cosgrove Aircraft Service, Inc., 546 So.2d 16.

Fla.App. 3 Dist. 1966. Evidence supported finding that collateral agreement allegedly entered into between seller and buyer of goods, under which representative of seller would assist buyer in resale of the goods, was not a part of the purchase order and was not a condition precedent to sale of merchandise to the buyer.

Francine Co. v. Haber, 189 So.2d 211.

Fla.App. 4 Dist. 1981. Purchaser, which failed to demonstrate that conduct of corporate seller of auto dealership had caused it any damage in connection with failure to provide written assignment of its rights under leases to purchaser, was not entitled to recover $30,000 for failure to provide written assignment.

AMC/Jeep of Vero Beach, Inc. v. Funston, 403 So.2d 602.

⌖**2733–2734.** *For other cases see earlier editions of this digest, the Decennial Digests, and WESTLAW.*

⌖**2734.** —— **Delivery and acceptance.**

⌖**2734(1). In general.**

C.A.5 (Fla.) 1975. In action by carpet manufacturer to recover price of carpeting sold to its dealer, computer printout of manufacturer's accounts receivable, together with testimony that accounts receivable information was not entered into manufacturer's computer until delivery was made, was evidence sufficient to show that carpeting was actually delivered to dealer. West's F.S.A. § 672.709(1)(a).

> Aldon Industries, Inc. v. Don Myers & Associates, Inc., 517 F.2d 188, appeal after remand 547 F.2d 924.

Fla.App. 3 Dist. 1980. In action brought by materialman for balance due for materials delivered to certain construction project, record contained substantial competent evidence to sustain trial court's finding that materialman had in fact delivered all of materials alleged in its complaint. West's F.S.A. § 255.05.

> Mikanto Const. Corp. v. Dade County for Use and Benefit of Gory Associated Industries, Inc., 379 So.2d 138, certiorari denied 388 So.2d 1111.

Fla.App. 3 Dist. 1977. Based upon testimony heard by trial court and exhibits entered into evidence in action based upon goods sold and delivered, plaintiff failed to prove that it delivered certain paper products to defendant's various hotels and, as such, no prima facie case for goods sold and delivered was established.

> Bosem v. A.R.A. Corp., 350 So.2d 526.

⚷2734(2). **Quality, value, fitness, and condition of goods.**

C.A.11 (Fla.) 2010. Under Georgia law, sufficient evidence supported jury's finding, in entering judgment in favor of supplier, that one order in which less than 20 percent of the goods were impaired did not breach supplier and purchaser's installment contract as a whole, especially when the order in question covered only $41,250 of the nearly $9 million contract. West's Ga.Code Ann. § 11–2–612.

> Advanced Bodycare Solutions, LLC v. Thione Intern., Inc., 615 F.3d 1352.

C.A.5 (Fla.) 1955. In action for balance due on price of rewinding machine sold by plaintiff to defendant paper company, trial judge's findings for plaintiff on conflicting evidence as to whether defects in latches caused rewind shafts to be thrown to floor when machine was operating at high speed, as defendant contended, or shafts became damaged and unusable because of improper handling by defendant's employees, as plaintiff contended, was not clearly erroneous.

> Calcasieu Paper Co. v. Cameron Mach. Co., 220 F.2d 876.

M.D.Fla. 1985. Evidence failed to establish that there was a lack of good faith on part of seed merchant or failure to deal fairly with farmer, who purchased seed which was not adaptable for use in his area. West's F.S.A. § 671.203.

> Crawford v. Gold Kist, Inc., 614 F.Supp. 682.

Fla.App. 1 Dist. 1986. Evidence supported finding that plastic yarn bobbin sleeves were defective; evidence included testimony that sleeve microgrooves were shallower than required, that shallow grooves caused entrapment of yarn and that other possible causes of yarn breaks had been investigated and excluded.

> Aetna Cas. & Sur. Co. v. Monsanto Co., 487 So.2d 398.

Fla.App. 3 Dist. 1972. Evidence, in action by buyers of cold storage warehouse against sellers for damages, reformation of contract, specific performance and declaratory relief as a result of alleged nonfunction and malfunction of blast freezing unit, was sufficient to sustain finding that the warehouse and blast freezing facility were not complete and fully functioning on date set forth in agreement between the parties.

> Itvenus, Inc. v. Poultry, Inc., 258 So.2d 478.

Fla.App. 4 Dist. 2005. Competent substantial evidence supported trial court's finding of fact that gap between doors and floor was result of installation, rather than lumber company's failure to order the correct doors, in lumber company's action to recover unpaid invoices; there was testimony that workers' installation of the flooring contributed to the gap, and gap could have been eliminated by cutting down frames or jambs or lowering the door.

> Bellino v. W & W Lumber and Bldg. Supplies, Inc., 902 So.2d 829, rehearing denied.

⚷2734(3). **Quantity of goods.**

C.A.11 (Fla.) 1985. District court's finding that exclusive importer and distributor of foreign automobiles breached contract with nonexclusive dealership by establishing allocation rate at time when there was not a shortage or a restricted supply of automobiles was clearly erroneous, in light of evidence that importer could obtain only those cars foreign automobile company chose to send and that its supply of automobiles was not unlimited.

Cabriolet Porsche Audi, Inc. v. American Honda Motor Co., Inc., 773 F.2d 1193, certiorari denied 106 S.Ct. 1641, 475 U.S. 1122, 90 L.Ed.2d 186, rehearing denied 106 S.Ct. 2929, 476 U.S. 1189, 91 L.Ed.2d 557.

District court's finding that exclusive importer and distributor of foreign automobiles never disclosed manner in which automobiles were allocated to dealers, and thus, that allocation system was unreasonable and breached dealership agreement, was clearly erroneous, in light of testimony of representatives of other dealerships that they were aware of allocation system and knew that, under system, the more cars a dealer sold and the faster cars were sold, the more cars the dealer would receive.

Cabriolet Porsche Audi, Inc. v. American Honda Motor Co., Inc., 773 F.2d 1193, certiorari denied 106 S.Ct. 1641, 475 U.S. 1122, 90 L.Ed.2d 186, rehearing denied 106 S.Ct. 2929, 476 U.S. 1189, 91 L.Ed.2d 557.

District court's determination that exclusive importer and distributor of foreign automobiles' allocation system for automobiles in periods of shortages was unreasonable, and in breach of agreement with unexclusive dealership, on basis of finding that system was incapable of being fully described in same manner by any two witnesses, was a mischaracterization of evidence, which varied as to some details regarding system, but which indicated that thrust of system was that the more automobiles a dealer sold and the faster a dealer sold automobiles, the more automobiles the dealer would receive.

Cabriolet Porsche Audi, Inc. v. American Honda Motor Co., Inc., 773 F.2d 1193, certiorari denied 106 S.Ct. 1641, 475 U.S. 1122, 90 L.Ed.2d 186, rehearing denied 106 S.Ct. 2929, 476 U.S. 1189, 91 L.Ed.2d 557.

District court's finding that 15% holdback of automobiles under exclusive importer and distributor of foreign automo-

biles' allocation system was left to whim and caprice of distributor's lower management personnel, and thus, that system was unreasonable and breach of distributor's contract with nonexclusive dealership, was clearly erroneous, in light of evidence that 15% holdback pool of automobiles was used to replace cars damaged on trips from Japan, to establish inventory for new dealerships, and to provide extra cars to dealers that established exclusive facilities.

Cabriolet Porsche Audi, Inc. v. American Honda Motor Co., Inc., 773 F.2d 1193, certiorari denied 106 S.Ct. 1641, 475 U.S. 1122, 90 L.Ed.2d 186, rehearing denied 106 S.Ct. 2929, 476 U.S. 1189, 91 L.Ed.2d 557.

District court's finding that exclusive importer and distributor of foreign automobiles' allocation system was not uniformly applied so as to be unreasonable and in breach of distributor's agreement with nonexclusive dealership was not supported by evidence, which indicated that allocations were based on number of cars other dealers in zone sold during relevant period and how quickly they sold cars, number of cars that were sent from Japan during relevant period, whether dealer provided exclusive facility, and whether dealership was new.

Cabriolet Porsche Audi, Inc. v. American Honda Motor Co., Inc., 773 F.2d 1193, certiorari denied 106 S.Ct. 1641, 475 U.S. 1122, 90 L.Ed.2d 186, rehearing denied 106 S.Ct. 2929, 476 U.S. 1189, 91 L.Ed.2d 557.

District court's finding that exclusive importer and distributor of foreign automobiles used its 15% holdback pool of automobiles pursuant to its allocation system to coerce dealers into making extra-contractual concessions, thus rendering allocation system unreasonable and in breach of distributor's agreement with nonexclusive dealership, was not supported by record, which indicated that distributor responded to dealership's request for more cars by suggesting that dealership could obtain extra cars if it established exclusive facility, and which indicated that another dealer who allegedly was coerced into establishing exclusive dealership established such dealership because his dealership in another line of automobiles was not profitable.

> Cabriolet Porsche Audi, Inc. v. American Honda Motor Co., Inc., 773 F.2d 1193, certiorari denied 106 S.Ct. 1641, 475 U.S. 1122, 90 L.Ed.2d 186, rehearing denied 106 S.Ct. 2929, 476 U.S. 1189, 91 L.Ed.2d 557.

District court's finding that "Minimum Planning Volume" document attached to dealership agreement indicating that nonexclusive dealership's minimum planning volume was 264 cars per year was the agreed minimum number of cars dealership was to receive per year from exclusive importer and distributor of foreign automobiles was not supported by evidence, which indicated that "planning volume" was only reflection of sales market expectation in a particular area for a particular dealer, and was used for planning purposes only, and thus, district court's finding that distributor breached written contract by providing dealership with less than 264 cars per year was clearly erroneous.

> Cabriolet Porsche Audi, Inc. v. American Honda Motor Co., Inc., 773 F.2d 1193, certiorari denied 106 S.Ct. 1641, 475 U.S. 1122, 90 L.Ed.2d 186, rehearing denied 106 S.Ct. 2929, 476 U.S. 1189, 91 L.Ed.2d 557.

S.D.Fla. 1975. Evidence that airline's "lifting" of fuel had been subject to substantial variations through history, that the factors involved were known to oil companies and taken into account by them when entering into fuel contracts, and evidence that oil company which was supplying aviation fuel to one particular airline had not challenged the airline's practice of "freighting" or "tankering" over a series of years demonstrated that the airline was not violating contract for sale of aviation fuel by manipulating its requirements through "fuel freighting."

> Eastern Air Lines, Inc. v. Gulf Oil Corp., 415 F.Supp. 429.

Fla.App. 1 Dist. 1984. Evidence sustained finding that general contractor re-

ceived amount of concrete from supplier for which it was billed.

> Hobbs Const. & Development, Inc. v. Colonial Concrete Co., 461 So.2d 255.

🗝️**2734(4). Acceptance or rejection of nonconforming goods.**

Fla.App. 1 Dist. 1980. In action by buyer of shrimp for damages resulting from a nonconforming tender of the shrimp, evidence was insufficient to sustain findings that a seafood merchant made a good–faith offer to buy the tendered lot from buyer, and that buyer was entitled to recover the difference between the price offered by merchant and the purchase price. West's F.S.A. § 672.2–601.

> Sullivans Island Seafood Co. v. Island Seafood Co., 390 So.2d 113.

Fla.App. 3 Dist. 1979. In action for breach of an oral contract to sell a racehorse, evidence sustained finding that defendants breached contract by refusing to accept return of racehorse after delivery thereof and to refund purchase price after defendants' veterinarian had examined racehorse and found bone chips in horse's knee.

> Greer v. Williams, 375 So.2d 333, certiorari denied 385 So.2d 762.

🗝️**2734(5). Revocation of acceptance.**

C.A.11 (Fla.) 1983. In action for breach of contract and warranty in regard to sale of typesetter, finding that nonconformity did not substantially impair typesetter's value sufficient to allow buyer to revoke acceptance was not clearly erroneous. West's F.S.A. § 672.608; U.C.C. § 2–608.

> Typographical Service, Inc. v. Itek Corp., 721 F.2d 1317.

Fla.App. 1 Dist. 1985. Although on each family trip the buyers of motor home encountered difficulties with the unit of a degree that went beyond simple inconvenience and although sellers efforts to repair were unsuccessful, the trial court's finding of lack of impairment of value sufficient to warrant revocation of acceptance was not with out evidentiary support. West's F.S.A. § 672.608.

> Parsons v. Motor Homes of America, Inc., 465 So.2d 1285.

---

† **This Case was not selected for publication in the National Reporter System**
For legislative history of cited statutes, see Florida Statutes Annotated

⟲2734(6). Sale on trial or approval; contracts for sale or return.

Fla.App. 3 Dist. 1984. In action brought by plaintiff against defendant seeking to collect on account receivable, defendant was not entitled to recover on its counterclaim alleging an agreement to repurchase merchandise, since evidence failed to establish a clear undertaking on part of plaintiff of responsibilities and obligations of previous supplier of merchandise to defendant.

    N.A.P. Consumer Electronics Corp. v. Electron Tubes Intern., Inc., 458 So.2d 831.

⟲2735. —— Amounts payable; price.

Fla.App. 1 Dist. 1988. Competent substantial evidence supported finding that, pursuant to parties' oral agreement, watermelon farmer was to receive fair market value for his watermelons based on markets available to buyer and prices buyer paid to other farmers in relevant time period, notwithstanding farmer's contention that buyer had agreed to pay fixed price.

    J.R. Sales, Inc. v. Dicks, 521 So.2d 366.

⟲2736. —— Duties and expenses of transportation.

For other cases see earlier editions of this digest, the Decennial Digests, and WEST-LAW.

⟲2737. —— Payment.

C.A.5 (Fla.) 1968. Evidence established that subcontractor was obligated to supplier to pay for materials supplied and used by subcontractor on jobsite and that subcontractor had produced no evidence at trial in support of contention that it was not legally obligated for payment of materials ordered and received from supplier.

    Continental Cas. Co. v. Westinghouse Elec. Supply Co., 403 F.2d 761.

Fla. 1955. In action by lumber supplier against wholesale lumber dealer for invoice price of one car of lumber, wherein dealer counterclaimed for loss of profits due to alleged shortage of quantity and defective quality of lumber in such car and two others, evidence was sufficient to sustain trial judge's conclusion that, when dealer ordered the one car, he did not intend to pay for it.

    McNeill v. Jack, 83 So.2d 704.

Fla.App. 2 Dist. 1962. Evidence was sufficient to support finding of oral contract for sale of business providing for down payment which had been made and definite monthly payments of which only a portion had been made.

    Cramer v. Pringle, 136 So.2d 653.

Fla.App. 3 Dist. 1980. Where, although, in action brought by materialman for balance due for materials delivered to certain construction project, valued at $22,134.34, materialman claimed it had received payment of $11,187.13 for these materials, defendants had shown, by unrebutted evidence, that they had in fact paid $19,359.16 of materialman's claim, it was error for trial court not to apply that amount as a credit against said claim. West's F.S.A. § 255.05.

    Mikanto Const. Corp. v. Dade County for Use and Benefit of Gory Associated Industries, Inc., 379 So.2d 138, certiorari denied 388 So.2d 1111.

Fla.App. 3 Dist. 1974. Evidence in replevin action supported finding that although seller, seeking replevin, had security interest in goods the defendant buyers were entitled to possession at time suit was instituted, in that agreed period for payment of goods had not expired, and seller had merely become worried about the deal.

    Modine Mfg. Co. v. Israel, 294 So.2d 369, certiorari denied 303 So.2d 644, appeal after remand 367 So.2d 232, certiorari denied ABC Radiator, Inc. v. Modine Manufacturing Co., 378 So.2d 342.

Fla.App. 4 Dist. 1978. In action by buyer against seller for conversion of trailer and unlawfully terminating purchase agreement without proper notice, evidence on issue whether written purchase agreement, which provided that buyer would pay $500 down and pay a minimum of $400 per month until total was paid, meant that payments in excess of minimum in one month could be applied to future months when minimum was not paid was sufficient for jury.

    Matthews v. Page, 354 So.2d 458.

SALES ⚷2749

⚷2738–2739. *For other cases see earlier editions of this digest, the Decennial Digests, and WESTLAW.*

⚷2740. —— **Repudiation.**

Fla.App. 3 Dist. 1971. In action for breach of contract to furnish carpeting for plaintiff's new condominium, evidence supported finding that defendant repudiated its contract and award of damages to plaintiff.

Dade Linen & Furniture Co. v. Buckley Development Co., 244 So.2d 562.

⚷2741. —— **Excuses for nonperformance or breach.**

S.D.Fla. 1975. Evidence was insufficient to show that, because of increase in market price of foreign crude oil and certain domestic crude oils, requirements contract covering sale of aviation fuel had become commercially impracticable. West's F.S.A. § 672.615.

Eastern Air Lines, Inc. v. Gulf Oil Corp., 415 F.Supp. 429.

⚷2742. —— **Waiver and estoppel.**

C.A.11 (Fla.) 1998. Conduct may constitute waiver of a contract term under Uniform Commercial Code (UCC), but such an implied waiver must be demonstrated by clear evidence. West's F.S.A. § 672.209.

BMC Industries, Inc. v. Barth Industries, Inc., 160 F.3d 1322, certiorari denied 119 S.Ct. 1807, 526 U.S. 1132, 143 L.Ed.2d 1010.

⚷2743–2748. *For other cases see earlier editions of this digest, the Decennial Digests, and WESTLAW.*

⚷2748. **Warranties.**

⚷2749. —— **In general.**

† **C.A.11 (Fla.) 2016.** Evidence overwhelmingly supported jury's verdict in favor of manufacturer of biliary stent, in surviving son's action individually and as personal representative of patient's estate against manufacturer, alleging negligence, products liability, failure to warn, and breach of warranty, arising out of patient's implantation with biliary stent to clear renal artery; manufacturer introduced compelling testimony indicating it did not promote off-label uses of its biliary stent, was unaware of any risk of stroke associated with its use in renal arteries at the time of mother's procedure, and did not violate any alleged duty to warn.

Horrillo v. Cook Incorporated, 664 Fed.Appx. 874.

C.A.11 (Fla.) 1983. In action alleging odometer violation of Motor Vehicle Information and Cost Savings Act, breach of warranties, and willful fraud with regard to sale of truck tractor, evidence was sufficient to support finding that no warranty existed. Motor Vehicle Information and Cost Savings Act, § 401 et seq., 15 U.S.C.A. § 1981 et seq.

Witkowski v. Mack Trucks, Inc., 712 F.2d 1352.

C.A.5 (Fla.) 1968. Diversity action under Florida law by employee of publishing company against manufacturer of printing press for injuries sustained by employee because of malfunction of printing press sold by manufacturer to publishing company was properly submitted to jury.

Vandercook & Son, Inc. v. Thorpe, 395 F.2d 104.

Bkrtcy.M.D.Fla. 1995. Buyer of steam distribution coils from Chapter 11 debtor failed to satisfy its burden of proof regarding alleged breach of warranty and failed to establish that any manufacturing defect was proximate cause of damage, and, thus, buyer's claim had to be disallowed, where each witness simply offered his own theory or theories of how leaks might have been caused based on review of second-hand information obtained after-the-fact, and no basis existed to determine that any particular theory was more credible than any of the others or that it was more likely than not that leaks resulted from one of the specific causes described rather than any from other cause.

In re Bicoastal Corp., 178 B.R. 875.

Fla.App. 1 Dist. 1979. In suit for negligence, breach of warranty and strict liability in the manufacture of a punch press on which plaintiff injured her hand, the jury was entitled to find on the evidence presented that defendant's negligence, if any, in failing to attach a point of operation guard to the press it sold in

1962 was not the proximate cause of plaintiff's injury in 1973.

> Clement v. Rousselle Corp., 372 So.2d 1156, certiorari denied 383 So.2d 1191.

Fla.App. 2 Dist. 1966. Evidence did not support conclusion that there was no warranty on used truck-tractor.

> Enix v. Diamond T. Sales & Service Co., 188 So.2d 48, certiorari denied 195 So.2d 566.

Fla.App. 3 Dist. 1977. In products liability action to recover for injuries sustained by plaintiff while using winch manufactured by defendant, evidence supported jury's findings that defendant manufacturer and defendant distributor were guilty of negligence and of breaching their warranties, causing plaintiff's injury, and that plaintiff was 15% negligent, manufacturer 60% negligent and distributor 25% negligent.

> Warn Industries v. Geist, 343 So.2d 44, certiorari denied 353 So.2d 680.

⚷2750. —— **Express warranties.**

C.A.11 (Fla.) 1983. In action alleging odometer violation of Motor Vehicle Information and Cost Savings Act, breach of warranties, and willful fraud with regard to sale of truck tractor, district court did not clearly err in finding that, although buyers had established a discrepancy between mileage actually showing on odometers and that recorded on title certificate by previous owners, there was no evidence to suggest discrepancy arose from previous owners' intent to defraud. Motor Vehicle Information and Cost Savings Act, § 401 et seq., 15 U.S.C.A. § 1981 et seq.

> Witkowski v. Mack Trucks, Inc., 712 F.2d 1352.

C.A.5 (Fla.) 1950. In action to recover purchase price of certain tomatoes, evidence supported a finding that seller did not expressly warrant the merchandise to be free from blight.

> Cohen v. Frima Products Co., 181 F.2d 324.

S.D.Fla. 1952. In action by corporation against chemical company for damages caused to interior walls of buildings constructed by contractor for corporation when wood preservative manufactured by chemical company bled through lath and plaster, evidence was insufficient to show that corporation relied on an implied warranty of fitness in purchasing and using the preservative, or that corporation relied upon any express warranty of lumber company which sold preservative, or that chemical company had issued express warranty of fitness by advertisement or that preservative was unfit to be used for the purpose for which it was manufactured.

> International Const. Corp. v. Chapman Chemical Co., 103 F.Supp. 679.

In action by corporation against chemical company for damages caused to interior walls of buildings constructed by contractor for corporation when wood preservative manufactured by chemical company bled through lath and plaster, evidence was insufficient to show that chemical company, after preservative had bled through plaster on first three houses, had made express warranty that the remaining eight houses should be plastered at the end of three weeks and that preservative would not bleed through walls.

> International Const. Corp. v. Chapman Chemical Co., 103 F.Supp. 679.

Bkrtcy.M.D.Fla. 1986. Evidence that debtor intended to purchase portable rock crushing machine capable of processing mined materials suitable to be used in road construction and stated its desire to seller, but that manufacturer made it clear that, without benefit of "run of mine" sample material, it would be unable to guarantee specific rate of production was insufficient to establish that manufacturer expressly warranted capacity of machine, under Florida law. West's F.S.A. § 672.313.

> Matter of Bob Rigby, Inc., 62 B.R. 900.

Fla.App. 2 Dist. 1977. Where building owners entered into contract with installer for installation of furnace and air conditioner and duct work and received from manufacturer of furnace and air conditioner express warranty against defects in material and workmanship of its products, since there was no evidence of defect in either furnace or air conditioner there could be no recovery for breach of express warranties by manufacturer in view of evidence tending to show that the problems which occurred were caused by installation of equipment and design of duct system.

Chrysler Airtemp v. Stevens, 346 So.2d 1236.

Fla.App. 4 Dist. 1986. Finding of seller's breach of express warranty of fitness for particular purpose was supported by expert testimony that seller's equipment was not appropriate for use intended by buyer, seller's vice-president's testimony that equipment should not be sold for use intended by buyer, and seller's expert testimony that breakage rate caused by equipment exceeded reasonable limits.

Solitron Devices, Inc. v. Veeco Instruments, Inc., 492 So.2d 1357.

🔑**2751.** —— **Warranties imposed by law; implied warranties.**

C.A.11 (Fla.) 1983. Evidence failed to show that copier machines failed to conform to existing standards of the trade at time of sale, for merchantability warranty purposes, despite postsale incidents regarding fire hazards and spare parts problems. West's F.S.A. §§ 672.314, 672.314(2).

Royal Typewriter Co., a Div. of Litton Business Systems, Inc. v. Xerographic Supplies Corp., 719 F.2d 1092.

C.A.5 (Fla.) 1972. In diversity suit, predicated on the breach of an implied warranty, to recover damages arising out of an accident allegedly caused by a defective tire manufactured by defendant, plaintiff motorist was not required to establish by expert testimony, as distinguished from other proof, that the tire was defective.

Lucas v. Firestone Tire & Rubber Co., 458 F.2d 495.

C.A.5 (Fla.) 1964. Evidence established knowledge of manufacturer-seller as to particular purpose for which buyer desired to purchase computer and related equipment for business records system and reliance by buyer upon judgment of seller, and reviewing court would accept determination that equipment was not fit and suitable for intended purpose and that

it did not perform required functions in accordance with known purpose.

Sperry Rand Corp. v. Industrial Supply Corp., 337 F.2d 363.

Evidence supported finding that, notwithstanding any and all reasonable efforts which buyer made and might be expected to have made, computer and related equipment sold by defendant as business records system would not function as previously represented by defendant or as needed by buyer in its business. Fed. Rules Civ.Proc. rule 52(a), 28 U.S.C.A.

Sperry Rand Corp. v. Industrial Supply Corp., 337 F.2d 363.

S.D.Fla. 1952. In action by corporation against chemical company for damages caused to interior walls of buildings constructed by contractor for corporation when wood preservative manufactured by chemical company bled through lath and plaster, evidence was insufficient to show that corporation relied on an implied warranty of fitness in purchasing and using the preservative, or that corporation relied upon any express warranty of lumber company which sold preservative, or that chemical company had issued express warranty of fitness by advertisement or that preservative was unfit to be used for the purpose for which it was manufactured.

International Const. Corp. v. Chapman Chemical Co., 103 F.Supp. 679.

Bkrtcy.M.D.Fla. 1986. Evidence that manufacturer's representative was shown dry, free-flowing stockpiled materials buyer intended to crush with portable rock crushing machine, but that manufacturer was never informed that machine would be taken to a different site and fed materials high in moisture and clay content established that, under Florida law, implied warranty did not arise that machine was fit for a particular purpose. West's F.S.A. § 672.315.

Matter of Bob Rigby, Inc., 62 B.R. 900.

Bkrtcy.M.D.Fla. 1981. While under Florida law a buyer of goods may recover on a claim for breach of implied warrant by proving the breach through direct or circumstantial evidence and it is not necessary to produce evidence by a qualified expert, the buyer has the burden to show that there are existing circumstances which tend to exclude all reasonable inferences except defectiveness. West's F.S.A. §§ 672.314, 672.607.

Matter of Vincent, 10 B.R. 549.

Fla. 1953. In action for breach of implied warranty that watermelon seeds purchased from seller were of a certain variety, evidence established that seeds produced a different variety of watermelon from variety produced by seeds purportedly sold to buyer.

Corneli Seed Co. v. Ferguson, 64 So.2d 162.

Fla.App. 1 Dist. 1974. For injured purchaser to recover from bottler as result of injuries resulting from exploded bottle, either on theory of negligence, including res ipsa loquitur, or on theory of implied warranty of product or container, where product was purchased from intermediate retailer, there must be proof that bottle was not handled improperly from time it left possession of bottler up to the time of its explosion.

Coca-Cola Bottling Co. v. Clark, 299 So.2d 78, certiorari dismissed 301 So.2d 100.

Fla.App. 1 Dist. 1969. Evidence that automobile dealer did not completely check electrical system of automobile, as specified in manufacturer's predelivery check list, and that fire which damaged automobile after it had been driven less than 400 miles by purchaser was caused by malfunction in electrical system, was sufficient to support findings that automobile was not fit for purpose intended or was either negligently manufactured or negligently inspected by manufacturer's agent-dealer, though no particular defective part of the electrical system was identified.

Ford Motor Co. v. Pittman, 227 So.2d 246, certiorari denied 237 So.2d 177.

Fla.App. 2 Dist. 1980. In action by warehouse tenant against company that designed and installed fire alarm system in warehouse for losses suffered in fire in which alarm did not work, evidence was not sufficient to establish that alleged breach of warranty of merchantability of the system by company was most probable

cause of tenant's loss, in that unrebutted inference was raised that an arsonist had sabotaged the system.

Borrell-Bigby Elec. Co., Inc. v. United Nations, Inc., 385 So.2d 713.

Fla.App. 2 Dist. 1974. Absence of ladder would not preclude suit by person who was injured when upright of ladder broke against manufacturer for breach of implied warranty.

McCarthy v. Florida Ladder Co., 295 So.2d 707.

Fla.App. 3 Dist. 1983. Jury verdict that automobile manufacturer was strictly liable and breached an implied warrant of merchantability which resulted in damages to plaintiff was amply supported by evidence and was not against its manifest weight.

Honda Motor Co., Ltd. v. Marcus, 440 So.2d 373, petition for review dismissed 447 So.2d 886.

Fla.App. 3 Dist. 1979. Evidence failed to establish that aircraft had a defect sufficient to sustain a cause of action for breach of implied warranty or negligence where, though evidence was presented that accident was caused by an antisymmetrical flutter, no evidence was presented that flutter was caused by a structural or design defect in aircraft.

C & B Airways Co. v. Ashurst, 369 So.2d 631, certiorari denied 378 So.2d 342, certiorari denied C & B Airways, Inc. v. Ashurst, 378 So.2d 343.

Fla.App. 3 Dist. 1975. Evidence that, in course of installation of elevator on construction project, it became necessary to lock the elevator into position, after it had been hoisted part way up in its well, for purpose of affixing another cable with which to continue the lifting, that the locking device supplied for such purpose was set, that it failed, that the elevator fell, and that workman, who was standing on the elevator, was killed sustained finding that implied warranty of fitness of locking device was breached.

Armor Elevator Co. v. Wood, 312 So.2d 514, certiorari denied 330 So.2d 14.

Fla.App. 4 Dist. 1974. In action for injuries, evidence which failed to show which bottle actually caused injury to plaintiff or that injury was caused by defective bottle or that bottle was dangerous instrumentality so as to enable plaintiff, who was a bystander rather than a purchaser or user, to overcome privity requirement in warranty was insufficient to sustain allegations and claim under theory of implied warranty.

> Mattes v. Coca Cola Bottling Co. of Miami, 311 So.2d 417, certiorari dismissed 328 So.2d 843.

⚷2752–2757. *For other cases see earlier editions of this digest, the Decennial Digests, and WESTLAW.*

⚷2757. Remedies.

⚷2758. —— In general.

Fla.App. 2 Dist. 1973. Judgment for buyer in seller's action to recover for goods allegedly sold and delivered to buyer based upon finding that seller failed to establish a prima facie case showing that buyer was indebted to seller in any sum would be affirmed. 31 F.S.A. Rules of Civil Procedure, Forms 1.932, 1.933, 1.935.

> Pillsbury Co. v. Chernin & Pila Dairy & Livestock Co., Inc., 280 So.2d 49, certiorari denied 285 So.2d 22.

Fla.App. 2 Dist. 1964. Evidence in action for asphalt products sold to defendant supported findings for defendant as to one item and for plaintiff with respect to other items.

> Hardrives Co. v. East Coast Asphalt Corp., 166 So.2d 810.

⚷2759. —— Rescission in general.

Fla. 1951. Evidence of an agreement to rescind a contract must be clear, positive, unequivocal, and inconsistent with existence of contract, and it is not enough to merely recognize that purchaser has broken contract and refused to proceed further with it.

> Collier v. Fox, 49 So.2d 801.

Fla.App. 2 Dist. 1965. The evidence, in suit for rescission of contract for sale of "snow ice" manufactured by defendant for plaintiff in ice making machinery maintained by defendant in plaintiff's fresh vegetable packing house, supported chancellor's finding that defendant as-

sured plaintiff that the machinery would furnish all of ice needed by plaintiff when needed and that machinery installed was incapable of filling plaintiff's needs.

> Crown Ice Mach. Leasing Co. v. Sam Senter Farms, Inc., 174 So.2d 614, certiorari denied 180 So.2d 656.

Fla.App. 3 Dist. 1974. Evidence in action by seller to recover purchase price supported order of revocation of acceptance of carpeting because of breach of warranty of merchantability because carpet was wet and seams split, despite seller's contention that moisture seeped up into carpeting from concrete slab on which seller installed it. West's F.S.A. § 672.608.

> Federated Dept. Stores, Inc. v. Planes, 305 So.2d 248.

⚷2760. —— Monetary remedies and damages in general.

C.A.5 (Fla.) 1977. Where occupant of automobile sued importer distributor for breach of implied warranty, claiming back injury when driver's seat-back broke backward in rear-end collision, inability of plaintiff's physician to apportion plaintiff's injuries between those caused by the initial rear-end impact and those caused by the seat's reclining did not preclude recovery on theory that plaintiff lacked competent evidence linking the alleged defect and his damages.

> Smith v. Fiat-Roosevelt Motors, Inc., 556 F.2d 728.

C.A.5 (Fla.) 1964. Absence of evidence to prove damages to buyer of computer and related equipment forming business records system was not supplied by conjectural assertions regarding loss of business, customer dissatisfaction, and personnel problems.

> Sperry Rand Corp. v. Industrial Supply Corp., 337 F.2d 363.

Fla. 1957. In breach of implied warranty action against food vendor for illness allegedly sustained by plaintiffs from eating canned spinach which was crawling with worms and segments thereof, evidence on issues of whether plaintiffs' vomiting, stomach pains and diarrhea were mere psychological reactions or whether they actually resulted from eating the worms supported verdict for plaintiffs.

Food Fair Stores of Fla., Inc. v. Macurda, 93 So.2d 860.

Fla.App. 1 Dist. 1980. In action by buyer of shrimp for damages resulting from a nonconforming tender of the shrimp, evidence was insufficient to sustain findings that a seafood merchant made a good–faith offer to buy the tendered lot from buyer, and that buyer was entitled to recover the difference between the price offered by merchant and the purchase price. West's F.S.A. § 672.2–601.

Sullivans Island Seafood Co. v. Island Seafood Co., 390 So.2d 113.

Fla.App. 2 Dist. 1998. Trial court erred by awarding buyer of used aluminum fabricating equipment total damages claimed on two counts of breach of warranty, when count for breach of warranty for particular purpose was not supported by evidence.

Buss Aluminum Products, Inc. v. Alumflo, Inc., 722 So.2d 269.

Fla.App. 2 Dist. 1981. In action for damages for breach of implied warranties in sale of used car, there was substantial competent evidence of breach of the warranties to support jury's award of compensatory damages and sufficient evidence of fraud to sustain award of punitive damages. West's F.S.A. § 501.201 et seq.

Bert Smith Oldsmobile, Inc. v. Franklin, 400 So.2d 1235.

Fla.App. 3 Dist. 1971. In action for goods sold and delivered, wherein buyer counterclaimed for damages for breach of contract, evidence sustained findings against seller on its claim and in favor of buyer on its counterclaim.

Max Bauer Meat Packer, Inc. v. S-M Vacu-Freeze Corp., 245 So.2d 132.

Fla.App. 4 Dist. 1981. Auto dealership purchaser was not entitled to recover $30,000 for corporate seller's allegedly improper refusal to terminate lien on dealership's address where alleged injury to purchaser, which claimed that refusal irreparably impaired its financial standing and forced it to close its doors, was not borne out by the record, which indicated that irrespective of filed security interest,

bank would not have provided additional financing.

AMC/Jeep of Vero Beach, Inc. v. Funston, 403 So.2d 602.

Fla.App. 4 Dist. 1978. In suit by painting contractor to recover from paint supplier for breach of implied warranty, on ground that paint did not adhere, wherein supplier counterclaimed for value of paint purchased, evidence supported findings on basis of which contractor was determined to be entitled to sum to be set off against amount of summary judgment entered on counterclaim.

Royal Painting Co., Inc. v. Eagle-Picher Industries, Inc., 358 So.2d 99.

⚷2761. —— **Price or value of goods in general.**

Fla. 1958. In action by seed company against four joint adventurers, who engaged in planting, cultivating, and marketing of 100 acres of tomatoes, to recover purchase price of seeds, fertilizers, spray, and other agricultural commodities, evidence that each item was sold to one of the joint adventurers, that amount due for each purchase was exhibited to him on charge slip in connection with each transaction, that charge slip showed that amount due was delivered to him with each delivery of goods, that there was no question raised by him or any one else as to amount of each charge, and that goods were accepted under such circumstances on each delivery, was sufficient to justify jury in concluding that price of goods was agreed on.

Kilgore Seed Co. v. Pearce, 103 So.2d 112.

Fla.App. 1 Dist. 1991. Finding that food buyer, who was contractually obligated to pay seller only for salvage value as determined by buyer, was not liable for any payment was supported by evidence that food product was totally infested by saw-toothed grain beetles and had no salvage value.

Chitty & Co. v. Riceland Foods, Inc., 589 So.2d 996.

Fla.App. 2 Dist. 1980. Manufacturer, which was able to use 40 percent of nonconforming shipment of aluminum sheeting, did not demonstrate that value of such portion of the shipment was less than the contract price, and thus failed to prove damages for breach of warranty as to 40 percent of the shipment. West's F.S.A. §§ 672.607(1), (3)(a), 672.714, 672.717.

    Adam Metal Supply, Inc. v. Electrodex, Inc., 386 So.2d 1316.

Fla.App. 3 Dist. 1971. In action for goods sold and delivered, wherein buyer counterclaimed for damages for breach of contract, evidence sustained findings against seller on its claim and in favor of buyer on its counterclaim.

    Max Bauer Meat Packer, Inc. v. S-M Vacu-Freeze Corp., 245 So.2d 132.

Fla.App. 3 Dist. 1968. Record in action by seller to recover balance of purchase price from buyer who claimed that goods delivered were not as represented failed to disclose any evidence upon which jury could have determined value of goods as received and trial court properly granted judgment n. o. v. in favor of seller for full amount of purchase price.

    W. P. Simpson Co. v. Crompton-Richmond Co., 210 So.2d 467.

Fla.App. 4 Dist. 1999. Purchaser of gas station/convenience store business could not recover on breach of contract count against vendor on claim that an express warranty in purchase contract was not true, in absence of evidence fixing actual value of business on date of sale, even though expert had testified as to lost profits.

    Teca, Inc. v. WM-TAB, Inc., 726 So.2d 828, rehearing denied, review denied 743 So.2d 511.

Fla.App. 4 Dist. 1992. Evidence supported award to airplane seller of $23,800 for buyer's failure to close on transaction, even though there was evidence that difference between price seller would have received from buyer and price ultimately received from third party had been $35,000; there was conflicting evidence about expenditures that could have affected price seller ultimately received.

    Maxfly Aviation, Inc. v. Gill, 605 So.2d 1297.

🗝**2762. —— Resale of goods and price thereof.**

C.A.5 (Fla.) 1980. In view of testimony of sales of blood plasma made by seller after buyer's breach and in view of testi-

mony that three centers of seller remained open, district court's findings of fact that seller made repeated but unsuccessful attempts to sell after breach and ceased collecting plasma at each of its six centers were clearly erroneous. U.C.C. §§ 2–706, 2–706 comment.

    Automated Medical Laboratories, Inc. v. Armour Pharmaceutical Co., 629 F.2d 1118.

🗝**2763. —— Procurement and price of substitute goods; "cover".**

For other cases see earlier editions of this digest, the Decennial Digests, and WESTLAW.

🗝**2764. —— Market price or value.**

Fla.App. 1 Dist. 1973. In absence of evidence as to value of automobile at time it was destroyed by fire allegedly resulting from dealer's breach of warranty, trial court in suit against dealer for breach of warranty properly directed verdict in favor of dealer.

    McCraney v. Ford Motor Co., 282 So.2d 878, certiorari dismissed 285 So.2d 618.

🗝**2765–2766.** *For other cases see earlier editions of this digest, the Decennial Digests, and WESTLAW.*

🗝**2767. —— Lost profits.**

C.A.11 (Fla.) 1983. Copier machine dealer failed to establish with requisite certainty alleged lost profits caused by having to operate their business with defective copiers.

    Royal Typewriter Co., a Div. of Litton Business Systems, Inc. v. Xerographic Supplies Corp., 719 F.2d 1092.

C.A.5 (Fla.) 1979. Evidence that food processor had problems with late deliveries prior to installation of defendant's filling machine and that its production was not significantly greater while using machine subsequently acquired from another did not preclude recovery of lost profits on ground that substandard performance of defendant's machine was not cause of processor's business woes, since prior delivery problems were caused by production equipment inadequacies which processor hoped to rectify by purchasing defendant's equipment and after defendant's equipment was replaced increased production was no longer necessary because of business lost by using defendant's machine. West's F.S.A. §§ 672.714, 672.715.

> National Papaya Co. v. Domain Industries, Inc., 592 F.2d 813.

Proof was insufficient to support award of amount claimed by food processor as profits lost because of breach of warranties in connection with sale of filling machine where there were serious deficiencies in method used to calculate damages, in that evidence did not warrant assumption that delay in filling and shipping orders was caused by defendant's fillers or that shipment was a "late delivery" because made within two weeks after the customer placed the order or that processor incurred lost sales equal to amount by which the order remained unfilled within the requisite time period. West's F.S.A. §§ 672.714, 672.715.

> National Papaya Co. v. Domain Industries, Inc., 592 F.2d 813.

C.A.5 (Fla.) 1975. In cross-action by carpet dealer against carpet manufacturer to recover for loss of prospective sales allegedly caused by defects in carpet shipped by manufacturer, dealer's unsubstantiated allegations of statewide sub rosa blacklisting of dealer by school boards were insufficient basis for recovery of such damages; dealer's contention that he could not bid on school carpet installation because he could not obtain bonding, and that inability to claim bonding was result of claims on defective carpet, were likewise insufficient to show substantial damage. West's F.S.A. §§ 235.31, 235.32.

> Aldon Industries, Inc. v. Don Myers & Associates, Inc., 517 F.2d 188, appeal after remand 547 F.2d 924.

Evidence in proceeding on carpet dealer's counterclaim against carpet manufacturer for loss of prospective profits allegedly due to defects in carpet furnished by manufacturer was insufficient to prove amount of damages to reasonable certainty where it did not permit conclusion as to what part, if any, of dealer's lost market share resulted from manufacturer's wrongdoing.

> Aldon Industries, Inc. v. Don Myers & Associates, Inc., 517 F.2d 188, appeal after remand 547 F.2d 924.

Fla. 1953. In action for breach of implied warranty that watermelon seeds purchased from seller were of a certain variety when, in fact, they produced a different variety, evidence failed to sustain finding that had variety of seeds sold by seller been of variety purportedly sold, buyer could have anticipated production of more than 18 or 20 carloads of variety of watermelon produced by seeds purportedly sold.

> Corneli Seed Co. v. Ferguson, 64 So.2d 162.

Fla. 1939. In buyers' action for breach of warranty brought on ground that 60 per cent. of seed purchased as Texas Seed Ribbon Cane Seed was Kaffir Corn seed, and that the crop harvested was unfit for ensilage for which it was intended, evidence sustained judgment for buyers for $1,750 for loss sustained as direct result of breach of warranty by seller.

> West Coast Lumber Co. v. Wernicke, 188 So. 357, 137 Fla. 363.

Fla.App. 3 Dist. 1985. Commercial buyer's claim for lost profits to be derived from unconsummated sale of two irrigation systems to two committed and long-standing customers was capable of being proved by competent evidence to reasonable certainty and therefore was not speculative; evidence showed that lost profits alleged were directly caused by manufacturer's breach of warranty in connection with sale of its engines, and established that manufacturer's breach caused loss of some reasonably definite amounts of profits.

> R.A. Jones & Sons, Inc. v. Holman, 470 So.2d 60, review dismissed Ford Motor Co. v. R.A. Jones & Sons, Inc., 482 So.2d 348.

Evidence demonstrated requisite causal connection between poor irrigation and reduced crop yields, lost profits owing to reduced yields were capable of proof to a reasonable degree of certainty, and manufacturer had burden to prove amount of damage attributable to freeze, and any failure to apportion damages attributable to 1977 freeze was owing to manufacturer's failure to carry its burden; thus, claims for lost profits from lost crops were not "speculative," and evidence relating to such claims was properly considered

† This Case was not selected for publication in the National Reporter System
For legislative history of cited statutes, see Florida Statutes Annotated

against manufacturer of engines employed to power irrigation systems and could be considered at new trial against manufacturer and its dealer.

> R.A. Jones & Sons, Inc. v. Holman, 470 So.2d 60, review dismissed Ford Motor Co. v. R.A. Jones & Sons, Inc., 482 So.2d 348.

Fla.App. 3 Dist. 1972. Even if buyers of cold storage warehouse were entitled to sue and recover for loss of anticipated profits for new business when blast freezing unit allegedly malfunctioned, they were not entitled to recover for such loss where record failed to show any substantial competent evidence of overhead, costs, or operating expenses which would have had to have been charged against the anticipated profits or gross revenues.

> Itvenus, Inc. v. Poultry, Inc., 258 So.2d 478.

⌕2768. —— Mitigation or reduction of loss.

For other cases see earlier editions of this digest, the Decennial Digests, and WEST-LAW.

⌕2769. —— Punitive or exemplary damages.

Fla.App. 2 Dist. 1981. In action for damages for breach of implied warranties in sale of used car, there was substantial competent evidence of breach of the warranties to support jury's award of compensatory damages and sufficient evidence of fraud to sustain award of punitive damages. West's F.S.A. § 501.201 et seq.

> Bert Smith Oldsmobile, Inc. v. Franklin, 400 So.2d 1235.

⌕2770–2771. *For other cases see earlier editions of this digest, the Decennial Digests, and WESTLAW.*

(F) QUESTIONS OF LAW OR FACT.

⌕2781. In general.

For other cases see earlier editions of this digest, the Decennial Digests, and WEST-LAW.

⌕2782. Nature and subject matter of sale.

C.A.11 (Fla.) 1998. Question whether a "hybrid" contract involving both

goods and services is predominantly for goods or services is generally one of fact; however, when there is no genuine issue of material fact concerning the contract's provisions, a court may determine the issue as a matter of law. West's F.S.A. § 672.105(1).

> BMC Industries, Inc. v. Barth Industries, Inc., 160 F.3d 1322, certiorari denied 119 S.Ct. 1807, 526 U.S. 1132, 143 L.Ed.2d 1010.

Bkrtcy.S.D.Fla. 2013. Under Florida law, whether a contract is predominantly for goods or services is generally a question of fact, but when there is no genuine issue of material fact concerning a contract's provisions, court may determine the issue as a matter of law.

> In re All American Semiconductor, Inc., 490 B.R. 418.

Fla.App. 3 Dist. 2015. In cases where a court must determine whether Article 2 of the Uniform Commercial Code (UCC) or the common law applies to a hybrid contract, the determination whether the predominant factor in the contract is for goods or for services is a factual inquiry unless the court can determine that the contract is exclusively for goods or services as a matter of law. West's F.S.A. § 672.102.

> Allied Shelving & Equipment, Inc. v. National Deli, LLC, 154 So.3d 482.

Fla.App. 3 Dist. 2001. Question of whether a contract is predominantly for goods or services is generally one of fact, which court can only decide, as a question of law, if there are no genuine issues of material fact concerning the contract's provisions.

> Birwelco-Montenay, Inc. v. Infilco Degremont, Inc., 827 So.2d 255, rehearing en banc denied, review denied 842 So.2d 844.

⌕2783. Parties to transaction or contract.

C.A.5 (Fla.) 1968. Court was empowered to determine as a matter of law whether parties after all negotiations and commencement of production by manufacturer intended that subsequently executed purchase orders between manufacturer as seller and corporation as buyer were such an integration of negotiations and agreements between seller and corporate buyer and corporate buyer's president that individual corporate president had no contract with seller which claimed that individual was personally liable for order.

> Carolina Metal Products Corp. v. Larson, 389 F.2d 490.

Fla. 1957. In action by hatchery to recover sale price of shipment of baby chicks received by transshipping agent, who allegedly entered into oral agreement assuming responsibility of paying hatchery for chicks, question of whether agent directly assumed liability or only agreed to operate as paying agent for ultimate purchaser was one of fact for determination by jury.

> Hilkmeyer v. Latin Am. Air Cargo Expediters, Inc., 94 So.2d 821.

⚷2784. Nature and formation of contract.

⚷2785. —— In general.

C.A.5 (Fla.) 1977. In action by plaintiff, the purchaser, against defendant, the seller, for failure to complete alleged oral contract for the sale of ammonia, evidence was sufficient for jury on issue of existence of agreement and its modification, despite defendant's claim that first transaction constituted negotiations and second transaction constituted a one-time spot sale, since evidence also included more than enough terms of agreements to provide a remedy, that is, product, quantity, price, due dates, and FOB delivery terms.

> Transammonia Export Corp. v. Conserv, Inc., 554 F.2d 719.

Fla.App. 1 Dist. 2005. Whether a sale of a vehicle was actually consummated is a question of law to be determined by the facts in evidence.

> State Farm Mut. Auto. Ins. Co. v. Hartzog, 917 So.2d 363.

⚷2786–2787. *For other cases see earlier editions of this digest, the Decennial Digests, and WESTLAW.*

⚷2787. Validity and enforceability of contract.

⚷2788. —— In general.

C.A.11 (Fla.) 1991. Under Florida law, there was sufficient evidence for jury

to conclude that corporation entered into contract with seller for sale of yacht and that corporation breached that contract, where $50,000 and $200,000 checks were drawn on corporation's account for partial payment and payment was stopped on $200,000 check at request of corporation's representative.

> Palm Beach Atlantic College, Inc. v. First United Fund, Ltd., 928 F.2d 1538.

⚷2789. —— Misrepresentation and fraud.

C.A.5 (Fla.) 1975. Evidence in proceeding on counterclaim by carpet dealer against carpet manufacturer for loss of prospective profits allegedly caused by defective carpet furnished by manufacturer was insufficient to create jury issues as to fraud and punitive damages.

> Aldon Industries, Inc. v. Don Myers & Associates, Inc., 517 F.2d 188, appeal after remand 547 F.2d 924.

Fla.App. 2 Dist. 1977. Whether acts of fraud and misrepresentation on part of defendant and consequent reliance thereon by plaintiff occurred in respect to sale of a ready-to-wear business and, if so, whether plaintiff was entitled to recoup paid portion of purchase price paid to defendant at closing and be relieved of his obligation on note were questions of fact for jury.

> Poneleit v. Reksmad, 346 So.2d 615.

Fla.App. 5 Dist. 1986. Whether sellers fraudulently represented gross income, expenses and profits of two stores they were negotiating to sell and, if so, whether buyer justifiably relied thereon were questions for jury.

> Mulle v. Scheiler, 484 So.2d 47, review denied 492 So.2d 1334.

⚷2790. —— Unreasonable, oppressive, or unconscionable contract.

C.A.5 (Fla.) 1980. In breach of contract action brought by handbag manufacturer against retailer arising from retailer's alleged failure to pay for certain goods, there was no evidence from which a reasonable jury could draw inference that a bribe allegedly made by manufacturer to retailer's former buyer bore any relation to purchase of the goods in question and thus, under Florida law, evidence presented was insufficient to raise defense of commercial bribery.

Excel Handbag Co., Inc. v. Edison Bros. Stores, Inc., 630 F.2d 379.

⟊**2791. Terms of contract; rights and obligations of parties.**

⟊**2792. —— In general.**

C.A.5 (Fla.) 1968. Where issue was whether parties intended writings to be an integration of prior negotiations, trial judge followed appropriate procedure to present questions for appeal while preserving benefits of jury determination after lengthy trial by submitting to jury seller's contentions of liability on oral contract but reserving for determination by court after verdict question of law of whether writings were an integration.

Carolina Metal Products Corp. v. Larson, 389 F.2d 490.

Fla.App. 1 Dist. 1959. Interpretation of an ordinary automobile contract to purchase subject to conditions delineating rights of the respective parties was a question of law for the court when there were no apparent ambiguities in the contract.

Cox Motor Co. v. Faber, 113 So.2d 771.

Fla.App. 3 Dist. 1959. Construction of written contract for purchase of automobile was for the court.

Berman v. Gables Lincoln-Mercury, Inc., 108 So.2d 53.

⟊**2793. —— Goods subject to contract in general.**

C.A.11 (Fla.) 1987. Issue as to whether invoices representing parts ordered by Argentina prior to date of credit memo, but shipped after that date were "future purchases," as that term was used in credit memo, or whether transactions were past purchases to which Argentina was required to pay remaining outstanding balance, was for jury in action brought by corporation against Argentina for failure to pay for parts.

Hercaire Intern., Inc. v. Argentina, 821 F.2d 559.

C.A.5 (Fla.) 1970. Construction to be placed upon words "available to it" within contract for sale of aircraft engines whereby seller promised to furnish all logs, papers, technical data and descriptive material available to it with respect to such engines was for court rather than jury.

General Dynamics Corp. v. Miami Aviation Corp., 421 F.2d 416.

⟊**2794. —— Delivery and acceptance.**

⟊**2794(1). In general.**

C.A.11 (Fla.) 1991. Under Florida law, there was sufficient evidence for jury to conclude that corporation entered into contract with seller for sale of yacht and that corporation breached that contract, where $50,000 and $200,000 checks were drawn on corporation's account for partial payment and payment was stopped on $200,000 check at request of corporation's representative.

Palm Beach Atlantic College, Inc. v. First United Fund, Ltd., 928 F.2d 1538.

Fla.App. 3 Dist. 1959. In action to recover agreed price and reasonable value of steel shelving allegedly sold by plaintiff to corporate defendant, evidence raised question for jury as to whether there had been a delivery of the shelving to the corporate defendant.

United Steel Warehouse Corp. v. Metal Products Co., 109 So.2d 793.

⟊**2794(2). Quality, value, fitness, and condition of goods.**

C.C.A.5 (Fla.) 1941. In action for breach of contract for sale of citrus fruit crop wherein there was substantial conflict in the material evidence concerning extent of frost damage to the crop, a jury question was presented, and the trial court erred in directing verdict for sellers on assumption that fruit was worth contract price.

Eustis Packing Co. v. Martin, 122 F.2d 648.

Fla. 1943. In action for breach of contract to purchase grapefruit crop, whether defendant made reasonable effort to grade out fruit damaged by cold, so as to enable remainder to pass legal shipping test, was fact question for jury on conflicting evidence. F.S.A. § 594.01 et seq.

Stanford Fruit Growers v. Singer, 12 So.2d 464, 152 Fla. 588.

Fla. 1941. In action by buyer of fruit to recover money paid under sale contract, evidence held to make jury question whether seller had rescinded the contract by refusing to permit buyer an extension of time in which to pick fruit, so that buyer might determine what fruit had been damaged by frost.

> Givens v. Vaughn-Griffin Packing Co., 1 So.2d 714, 146 Fla. 575.

Fla. 1940. In action by consignee of meat shipment to be reimbursed for spoiled meat and for cost of salvaging other meat which was required to be pickled, whether car in which meat was shipped was prechilled properly, and whether it contained "old cuts" contrary to contract, was properly submitted to jury, notwithstanding the meat was shipped under C. A. F. contract.

> Farris & Co. v. William Schluderberg, T. J. Kurdle Co., 196 So. 184, 142 Fla. 765.

Fla.App. 3 Dist. 1962. Evidence raised jury question whether contract calling for 208 volt air conditioners could be performed by installation by seller, suing for price of the machines, of air conditioners with 230-volt fan motors.

> Herman v. Dade Linen & Furniture Co., 143 So.2d 878.

🔑2794(3). Quantity of goods.

C.A.5 (Fla.) 1974. In buyer's action for breach of alleged oral contract to unconditionally deliver 10,000 tons of citrus pulp, jury question was presented as to whether seller was excused from performance of such contract, if it was made, after delivery of 2,500 tons by reason of buyer's delay in payments and failure to pay at all as to certain shipments.

> I. S. Joseph Co., Inc. v. Citrus Feed Co., Inc., 490 F.2d 185, rehearing denied 492 F.2d 1242.

Fla.App. 1 Dist. 1966. In action by seller to recover on account for chicken feed and other supplies furnished to defendant, conflicting evidence was sufficient to take case to jury on defense of general denial based on (1) alleged agreement that defendant would not be required to pay for chicken feed delivered to him unless egg production of his flock increased and (2) alleged decrease in egg production.

> Cosby-Hodges Mill. Co. v. Sheffield, 183 So.2d 749.

🔑2794(4). Acceptance or rejection of nonconforming goods.

C.A.5 (Fla.) 1976. In action by airline against aircraft manufacturer for damages for delay in delivery of jet aircraft, evidence made jury issue as to whether airline gave adequate and timely notice to manufacturer, after accepting delivery of planes, that late delivery was regarded as breach of contract; such notice was not, as matter of law, inadequate or untimely. West's Ann.Cal.Com.Code, §§ 1201(26), 2103(1)(b), 2104, 2104(1), 2607; West's Ann.Cal.Civ.Code, § 1721 et seq.

> Eastern Air Lines, Inc. v. McDonnell Douglas Corp., 532 F.2d 957.

🔑2794(5)–2794(6). *For other cases see earlier editions of this digest, the Decennial Digests, and WESTLAW.*

🔑2795. —— Amounts payable; price.

S.D.Fla. 1999. Question of fact is raised when ascertaining parties' intentions as to open price term in their contract.

> Allapattah Services, Inc. v. Exxon Corp., 61 F.Supp.2d 1300, affirmed 333 F.3d 1248, rehearing en banc denied 362 F.3d 739, certiorari granted in part 125 S.Ct. 317, 543 U.S. 924, 160 L.Ed.2d 221, affirmed 125 S.Ct. 2611, 545 U.S. 546, 162 L.Ed.2d 502.

🔑2796. —— Duties and expenses of transportation.

Fla. 1941. Under contract for sale of fruit, giving buyer right to an extension of time for picking fruit if act of God prevented removing and shipping of fruit within time specified, freeze and consequent frost damage was an "act of God" such that buyer's right to extension of time was for jury.

> Givens v. Vaughn-Griffin Packing Co., 1 So.2d 714, 146 Fla. 575.

Fla.App. 4 Dist. 1988. The words "F.O.B." the destination for delivery of a yacht under a sales contract placed responsibility on the seller to pay for the ocean freight delivery charge incurred prior to the boat's reaching its destination as a matter of law, and thus it would be erroneous leave determination of payment of the ocean freight delivery charge to jury. West's F.S.A. § 672.319.

 Boyman v. Stuart Hatteras, Inc., 527 So.2d 853.

⚷2797. —— Payment.

 Fla.App. 1 Dist. 1978. Whether extension of credit was made by feed company for specific amount of credit in return for specific package of finance agreements in addition to anticipated feed purchases by poultry raiser was question for jury in action by feed company to recover amount due on account and counterclaim by poultry raiser for breach of contract.

 C. Q. Farms, Inc. v. Cargill Inc., 363 So.2d 379.

⚷2798. —— Transfer of title; risk of loss.

 Fla. 1956. In replevin action by automobile distributor against dealer, which had given insufficient fund checks to distributor for automobiles, and finance company, which had loaned money to dealer, and which had received notes and trust receipts describing the automobiles from dealer, and which had taken possession of automobiles under trust receipts on default by dealer on loans from finance company, evidence was sufficient to raise a material issue of fact with respect to whether dealer acquired title, which inured to benefit of finance company, to the automobiles from distributor. F.S.A. §§ 673.01 et seq., 673.02(1)(c), 673.08.

 Volusia Discount Co. v. Alexander K-F Motors, 88 So.2d 302.

⚷2799–2806. *For other cases see earlier editions of this digest, the Decennial Digests, and WESTLAW.*

⚷2807. Modification of contract.

 C.A.5 (Fla.) 1977. In action by plaintiff, the purchaser, against defendant, the seller, for failure to complete alleged oral contract for the sale of ammonia, evidence was sufficient for jury on issue of existence of agreement and its modification, despite defendant's claim that first transaction constituted negotiations and second transaction constituted a one-time spot sale, since evidence also included more than enough terms of agreements to provide a remedy, that is, product, quantity, price, due dates, and FOB delivery terms.

 Transammonia Export Corp. v. Conserv, Inc., 554 F.2d 719.

⚷2808. Warranties.

⚷2809. —— In general.

 Fla.App. 4 Dist. 1981. In buyer's action under Magnuson-Moss Warranty Act against automobile manufacturer, there was more than slight evidence of breach of warranty, and thus, sufficient evidence to go to jury on question of whether there had been breach of warranty which had not been remedied although warrantor had been given reasonable opportunity to cure breach. Magnuson-Moss Warranty Federal Trade Commission Improvement Act, § 104(a)(1), 15 U.S.C.A. § 2304(a)(1).

 Gates v. Chrysler Corp., 397 So.2d 1187.

 Fla.App. 5 Dist. 2000. Relative knowledge of grinder manufacturer and buyer was a jury issue, not a complete bar to recovery by buyer, in buyer's breach of warranty action, even if buyer was more savvy than he acknowledged.

 Doug Connor, Inc. v. Proto-Grind, Inc., 761 So.2d 426, rehearing denied.

 Fla.App. 5 Dist. 1997. Whether vehicle contained defect or malfunction was question for trier of fact in vehicle owner's warranty action brought under Magnuson-Moss Warranty Act; expert testimony that shudder in vehicle was abnormal and unacceptable and testimony as to what he believed to be cause of shudder was competent evidence that vehicle contained defect or malfunction. Magnuson–Moss Warranty–Federal Trade Commission Improvement Act, §§ 104(a)(4), 110(d)(1)(A), 15 U.S.C.A. §§ 2304(a)(4), 2310(d)(1)(A).

 Mason v. Porsche Cars of North America, Inc., 688 So.2d 361, rehearing denied.

⚷2810. —— Express warranties.

 M.D.Fla. 2014. Under Florida law, the existence of an express warranty is a factual issue for the jury to decide.

 Small v. Amgen, Inc., 2 F.Supp.3d 1292.

 Fla.App. 1 Dist. 1962. Fact that plaintiff in deposition testified to certain specific representations, which were allegedly made by defendants, and on which plaintiff relied, did not raise such representations to level of comprehensive express warranty taking place of implied warranty of merchantability and fitness as matter of law.

Posey v. Pensacola Tractor & Equipment Co., 138 So.2d 777.

Fla.App. 1 Dist. 1960. In action against gas company, which sold, installed, and undertook to repair gas range, for injuries sustained by buyer in explosion which occurred when she thereafter attempted to light oven, plaintiffs' evidence was insufficient to take case to jury on question of alleged breach of express warranty.

Russell v. Jacksonville Gas Corp., 117 So.2d 29.

Fla.App. 2 Dist. 1977. Where evidence was legally insufficient to support a verdict for building owners suing furnace and air-conditioning manufacturer for breach of express warranty as to products, a directed verdict should have been granted to manufacturer.

Chrysler Airtemp v. Stevens, 346 So.2d 1236.

Fla.App. 3 Dist. 1990. Whether advertising flyer for shutters stating "when fully closed, [the] shutters automatically lock to prevent break-ins" created express warranty, whether goods were defective when they left seller's possession, and, if so, whether such defect was legal cause of buyer's losses from break-in, were questions for jury.

State Farm Ins. Co. v. Nu Prime Roll-A-Way of Miami, 557 So.2d 107.

Fla.App. 3 Dist. 1970. In view of direct testimony as to existence of defect in .22 calibre rifle which allegedly fired with the safety on some five months after purchase, resulting in injury to plaintiff, submission of case to jury was not improper on theory that jury was permitted to pile inference upon inference.

Sears, Roebuck & Co. v. Davis, 234 So.2d 695.

Fla.App. 4 Dist. 1991. Whether circumstances gave buyer reason to know that seller was not warranting validity of motor vehicle's title was question of fact to be resolved by trier of fact in buyer's action for breach of warranty of title. West's F.S.A. § 672.312.

Maroone Chevrolet, Inc. v. Nordstrom, 587 So.2d 514.

Whether substantial cloud or shadow exists in relation to buyer's title is mixed question of law and fact and must be determined on case-by-case basis; however, cloud must be predicated on some objective factor, and baseless anxiety of hypersensitive buyer regarding validity of title will not result in breach of warranty of title. West's F.S.A. § 672.312.

Maroone Chevrolet, Inc. v. Nordstrom, 587 So.2d 514.

Fla.App. 4 Dist. 1977. In suit alleging breach of warranty, fraud and negligence on the part of defendants in advertising, manufacturing and applying a fiberglass and asbestos material advertised to be an end to painting problems on house exteriors, the trial court erred in directing a verdict for defendants, since plaintiffs proved, for example, that they relied upon allegedly untrue statements in a brochure one defendant distributed by or through the other defendants, and plaintiffs established that their reliance thereon was to their detriment and otherwise established a prima facie case against defendants.

Garesche v. Textured Coatings of America, Inc., 352 So.2d 1207.

Fla.App. 5 Dist. 2000. Whether manufacturer made the express warranty that griding machine could reduce palmettos and palm trees to mulch on a regular basis or whether sales agents' statements were merely non-actionable puffing was issue for jury in buyer's breach of warranty claim.

Doug Connor, Inc. v. Proto-Grind, Inc., 761 So.2d 426, rehearing denied.

⚖2811. —— **Warranties imposed by law; implied warranties.**

C.A.11 (Fla.) 1983. Question was for jury whether certain modifications to copier machines by dealer were unauthorized in view of manufacturer's notice that such modifications would remove warranty protection and as to whether improper maintenance by dealer precluded any breach of warranty claim. West's F.S.A. §§ 672.313(1)(a), 672.314, 672.314(2), 672.315; U.C.C. § 2–315 comment.

　Royal Typewriter Co., a Div. of Litton Business Systems, Inc. v. Xerographic Supplies Corp., 719 F.2d 1092.

Question was for jury whether copier machines had been fully tested and were free from design and operational defects prior to delivery to dealer for leasing.

　Royal Typewriter Co., a Div. of Litton Business Systems, Inc. v. Xerographic Supplies Corp., 719 F.2d 1092.

C.A.5 (Fla.) 1971. Evidence in suit by purchaser of airplane against airplane and airplane engine manufacturers, on theory of implied warranty, was insufficient on issue of existence of defect on date of delivery to make submissible case.

　Holcomb v. Cessna Aircraft Co., 439 F.2d 1150, certiorari denied 92 S.Ct. 62, 404 U.S. 827, 30 L.Ed.2d 56.

Evidence of difficulty in similar engines in aircraft used for rigorous military training did not make submissible case on theory of breach of implied warranty against airplane and airplane engine manufacturer.

　Holcomb v. Cessna Aircraft Co., 439 F.2d 1150, certiorari denied 92 S.Ct. 62, 404 U.S. 827, 30 L.Ed.2d 56.

C.A.5 (Fla.) 1970. Jury question was presented as to damage resulting from existence of implied warranty of fitness for use in contract for construction of cable television system, in action for amount due under contract wherein defendant filed counterclaim based upon implied warranty that system would be well constructed, of workmanlike quality and suitable for purposes for which it was intended.

　Entron, Inc. v. General Cablevision of Palatka, 435 F.2d 995.

C.A.5 (Fla.) 1963. Evidence, in action for wrongful death of plaintiff's decedent who allegedly developed fatal lung cancer due to smoking defendant's cigarettes, was sufficient to present question for jury as to whether manufacturer's ciga-

rettes were not reasonably fit and wholesome for human consumption.

　Green v. American Tobacco Co., 325 F.2d 673, certiorari denied 84 S.Ct. 1349, 377 U.S. 943, 12 L.Ed.2d 306, certiorari denied 84 S.Ct. 1351, 377 U.S. 943, 12 L.Ed.2d 306.

Fla. 1940. Existence or nonexistence of an implied warranty of fitness for particular purpose is question of fact, depending upon whether the buyer relied upon his own judgment at the time of the purchase or relied on the skill or judgment of the seller.

　Smith v. Burdine's, Inc., 198 So. 223, 144 Fla. 500, 131 A.L.R. 115.

Where buyer requested of saleslady at cosmetic counter a good lipstick and saleslady not only selected a certain lipstick but recommended it for intended use, and lipstick was not sold by trade-name and was shown to have contained poisonous substance which allegedly injured health of buyer, whether buyer relied on judgment of saleslady and whether there was a breach of implied warranty of fitness were for jury.

　Smith v. Burdine's, Inc., 198 So. 223, 144 Fla. 500, 131 A.L.R. 115.

Fla.App. 1 Dist. 1984. Evidence as to whether restaurant's egg rolls were cause of eight-year-old child's illness was sufficient for jury in personal injury action alleging that restaurant breached its implied warranty that egg rolls would be free from impurities likely to cause injury.

　Gant v. Lucy Ho's Bamboo Garden, Inc., 460 So.2d 499.

Fla.App. 1 Dist. 1971. Whether beef bone processed and sold by defendant pharmaceutical house was defective was for jury in action for breach of implied warranty and negligence arising from alleged ill effects of use of beef bone in surgery upon plaintiff.

　E. R. Squibb & Sons, Inc. v. Jordan, 254 So.2d 17.

Fla.App. 1 Dist. 1970. Where there was no undisputed direct and conclusive evidence that power booster unit of plaintiff's automobile was proximate cause of accident following loss of brakes, and uncontroverted evidence that tailstock within sealed booster unit was broken was accompanied by testimony from manufacturer's expert witnesses that even if tailstock was broken, only effect would be loss of power assist so that nonpower brake system would still be operative, plaintiff was not entitled to directed verdict against manufacturer as matter of law either on basis of negligence or breach of implied warranty.

> Holman v. Ford Motor Co., 239 So.2d 40, appeal after remand Arenson v. Ford Motor Co., 254 So.2d 812, certiorari denied 262 So.2d 444.

Fla.App. 1 Dist. 1967. Evidence in action against snap-tie manufacturer for injuries sustained when scaffold attached to snap-tie fell presented jury question on issue of proximate cause and breach of implied warranty.

> Gates & Sons, Inc. v. Brock, 199 So.2d 291, certiorari denied 204 So.2d 328.

Fla.App. 1 Dist. 1962. Fact that plaintiff in deposition testified to certain specific representations, which were allegedly made by defendants, and on which plaintiff relied, did not raise such representations to level of comprehensive express warranty taking place of implied warranty of merchantability and fitness as matter of law.

> Posey v. Pensacola Tractor & Equipment Co., 138 So.2d 777.

Fla.App. 3 Dist. 1990. Whether shutters, which were forced open by an intruder into buyers' home, were not reasonably fit for uses intended or reasonably foreseeable by seller; in breach of implied warranty, was for jury.

> State Farm Ins. Co. v. Nu Prime Roll-A-Way of Miami, 557 So.2d 107.

Fla.App. 3 Dist. 1985. In buyer's action against seller for breach of implied warranty of merchantability, whether engines sold were merchantable was question for jury. West's F.S.A. § 672.314.

> R.A. Jones & Sons, Inc. v. Holman, 470 So.2d 60, review dismissed Ford Motor Co. v. R.A. Jones & Sons, Inc., 482 So.2d 348.

In action by buyer of industrial engines against seller for breach of implied warranty of fitness for a particular purpose, whether buyer relied upon its own judgment at time of purchase, or upon skill or judgment of seller, was question for jury.

> R.A. Jones & Sons, Inc. v. Holman, 470 So.2d 60, review dismissed Ford Motor Co. v. R.A. Jones & Sons, Inc., 482 So.2d 348.

Fla.App. 3 Dist. 1975. Evidence indicating that, in negotiating for sale of boat to plaintiff, individual defendant represented that he had purchased boat two years previously and that, after plaintiff purchased boat, discovery was made that boat had been stolen some months earlier, sold to a third party, and thereafter transferred to corporate defendant was sufficient on which to present a presentable case to jury in action for breach of warranty and for fraud and misrepresentation.

> Lloyd v. DeFerrari, 314 So.2d 224, certiorari denied 330 So.2d 19.

Fla.App. 3 Dist. 1975. In action by building owner against subcontractor for faulty design and installation of air-conditioning system, evidence on issues of negligence and breach of implied warranty was sufficient for jury.

> Forte Towers South, Inc. v. Hill York Sales Corp., 312 So.2d 512.

Fla.App. 3 Dist. 1970. Evidence was sufficient for jury, in action for breach of warranty of fitness of .22 calibre rifle which allegedly fired with safety on, some five months after purchase resulting in injury to plaintiff.

> Sears, Roebuck & Co. v. Davis, 234 So.2d 695.

Whether plaintiff suing for injuries sustained when rifle purchased from defendant fired with safety on was guilty of contributory negligence was for jury, in action for breach of warranty of fitness of rifle.

> Sears, Roebuck & Co. v. Davis, 234 So.2d 695.

Fla.App. 3 Dist. 1963. Wives and representatives of passengers killed as the result of crash of a commercial aircraft assembled by defendant could maintain a cause of action against defendant for breach of implied warranty that the equipment was of merchantable quality and reasonably fit for the use intended, based on allegations that an engine used on the aircraft, although manufactured by a codefendant, was defective, and facts that the engine had been transferred from another aircraft and had been safely used for 3,000 hours did not foreclose liability but were for jury consideration.

> King v. Douglas Aircraft Co., 159 So.2d 108.

Fla.App. 3 Dist. 1962. Evidence presented questions for trier of fact as to existence and breach of an implied warranty in the sale of certain personalty.

> Atlantic Distributors, Inc. v. Alson Mfg. Co., 141 So.2d 305.

Fla.App. 4 Dist. 1973. Whether product is adequately contained and packaged within requirements of statutory warranty of merchantability is fact question for jury, where legally sufficient evidence is presented. F.S.A. §§ 671.1–101 et seq., 672.2–314.

> Schuessler v. Coca-Cola Bottling Co. of Miami, 279 So.2d 901.

Fla.App. 4 Dist. 1967. Whether restaurant patron who, while consuming maple walnut ice cream in restaurant, suffered punctured upper gums and fracture of teeth as result of presence of piece of walnut shell concealed in ice cream might have reasonably expected to find piece of shell in food as served was jury question, in action for breach of implied warranty and negligence.

> Zabner v. Howard Johnson's, Inc., 201 So.2d 824.

☞2812. —— **Exclusion, modification, or limitation of warranties.**

C.A.5 (Fla.) 1971. Although airplane manufacturer's warranty excluding any implied warranty of merchantability or fitness for a particular purpose did not meet requirement of conspicuosity in that warranty form was printed in the same size type throughout, issues of fact existed as to whether purchaser who had owned four airplanes with similar warranties could have been surprised by the exclusion of the implied warranties. K.S.A. 84–2–316(2).

> Holcomb v. Cessna Aircraft Co., 439 F.2d 1150, certiorari denied 92 S.Ct. 62, 404 U.S. 827, 30 L.Ed.2d 56.

Fla.App. 1 Dist. 1982. Whether limitation of warranty and liability is conspic-

uous is decision for court, not jury. West's F.S.A. § 671.201(10).

> Monsanto Agr. Products Co. v. Edenfield, 426 So.2d 574.

Fla.App. 4 Dist. 1986. Question of conspicuousness of disclaimer of warranties was one of law where there was no dispute as to what contract said or as to size and color of print. West's F.S.A. § 672.101 et seq.

> Food Associates, Inc. v. Capital Associates, Inc., 491 So.2d 345.

☞2813–2814. *For other cases see earlier editions of this digest, the Decennial Digests, and WESTLAW.*

☞2815. —— **Notice and opportunity to cure.**

C.A.11 (Fla.) 1983. Where buyer gives some notice of breach of warranty, issues of timeliness and sufficiency are questions of fact. West's F.S.A. §§ 671.203, 672.103, 672.607.

> Royal Typewriter Co., a Div. of Litton Business Systems, Inc. v. Xerographic Supplies Corp., 719 F.2d 1092.

Question was for jury whether buyer's notice of alleged breaches of warranties was both sufficient and timely. West's F.S.A. §§ 671.203, 672.103, 672.607.

> Royal Typewriter Co., a Div. of Litton Business Systems, Inc. v. Xerographic Supplies Corp., 719 F.2d 1092.

☞2816–2818. *For other cases see earlier editions of this digest, the Decennial Digests, and WESTLAW.*

☞2817. **Remedies.**

☞2819. —— **Rescission in general.**

† C.A.11 (Fla.) 2005. Whether foreign manufacturer, by sending memorandum to retailer that notified it of its alleged failure to fulfill its obligations under product supply agreement, and by issuing debit note to retailer for return of rebate payment that manufacturer had previously made, had clearly indicated its intent to rescind contract and waive its right to assert damages claim was question for jury, and district court did not err in

---

† This Case was not selected for publication in the National Reporter System
For legislative history of cited statutes, see Florida Statutes Annotated

denying retailer's motion for judgment as matter of law on waiver issue.

> SEB S.A. v. Sunbeam Corp., 148 Fed. Appx. 774, appeal after remand 476 F.3d 1317, appeal after remand 302 Fed.Appx. 870.

☞2820. —— Monetary remedies and damages in general.

C.A.5 (Fla.) 1970. Jury question was presented as to damage resulting from existence of implied warranty of fitness for use in contract for construction of cable television system, in action for amount due under contract wherein defendant filed counterclaim based upon implied warranty that system would be well constructed, of workmanlike quality and suitable for purposes for which it was intended.

> Entron, Inc. v. General Cablevision of Palatka, 435 F.2d 995.

Fla.App. 1 Dist. 1978. Whether extension of credit was made by feed company for specific amount of credit in return for specific package of finance agreements in addition to anticipated feed purchases by poultry raiser was question for jury in action by feed company to recover amount due on account and counterclaim by poultry raiser for breach of contract.

> C. Q. Farms, Inc. v. Cargill Inc., 363 So.2d 379.

☞2821–2822. *For other cases see earlier editions of this digest, the Decennial Digests, and WESTLAW.*

☞2823. —— Procurement and price of substitute goods; "cover".

C.A.5 (Fla.) 1977. In action by plaintiff, the purchaser, against defendant, the seller, for failure to complete alleged oral contract for the sale of ammonia, since reasonable men could differ over when breach occurred, the right to cover and therefore to collect cover damages depended on a factual issue that court correctly submitted to jury. West's F.S.A. §§ 672.711, 672.712, 672.712(1, 2).

> Transammonia Export Corp. v. Conserv, Inc., 554 F.2d 719.

In action by plaintiff, the purchaser, against defendant, the seller, for failure to complete alleged oral contract for the sale of ammonia, whether plaintiff had made his cover purchases in a reasonable manner, as required under Florida Uniform Commercial Code, presented a jury issue. West's F.S.A. § 672.712(1).

> Transammonia Export Corp. v. Conserv, Inc., 554 F.2d 719.

Fla.App. 3 Dist. 1986. Whether purchaser made reasonable efforts to cover following an anticipatory breach of sales contract and whether cover purchases occurred within reasonable period of time are questions of fact which will not be set aside unless clearly erroneous. West's F.S.A. § 672.712(1).

> Mason Distributors, Inc. v. Encapsulations, Inc., 484 So.2d 1275.

☞2824–2828. *For other cases see earlier editions of this digest, the Decennial Digests, and WESTLAW.*

☞2829. —— Punitive or exemplary damages.

C.A.5 (Fla.) 1975. Evidence in proceeding on counterclaim by carpet dealer against carpet manufacturer for loss of prospective profits allegedly caused by defective carpet furnished by manufacturer was insufficient to create jury issues as to fraud and punitive damages.

> Aldon Industries, Inc. v. Don Myers & Associates, Inc., 517 F.2d 188, appeal after remand 547 F.2d 924.

☞2830. —— Exclusive, concurrent, and conflicting remedies; election.

For other cases see earlier editions of this digest, the Decennial Digests, and WESTLAW.

☞2831. —— Contractual modification or limitation of remedy.

Fla. 1952. Provision in a sales agreement for "liquidated damages" or "penalty" in event agreement is breached is not conclusive, but question of damages is one of law to be determined by the court, depending on terms of the instrument, its real character, circumstances surrounding its execution, and conditions attending its breach.

> Paradis v. Second Ave. Used Car Co., 61 So.2d 919.

(G) INSTRUCTIONS.

⨁2841. In general.

Fla. 1941. In action by buyer of fruit to recover money paid under sale contract allegedly rescinded by seller, instruction that mere "breaching" of contract is not necessarily a "rescinding" of the contract, and that when contract is "rescinded" it is done away with and ceases to be a contract, but when it is "breached" it continues to live and parties have right to damages for the breach instead of on theory of rescission, was not erroneous.

Givens v. Vaughn-Griffin Packing Co., 1 So.2d 714, 146 Fla. 575.

⨁2842–2844. *For other cases see earlier editions of this digest, the Decennial Digests, and WESTLAW.*

⨁2844. Nature and formation of contract.

⨁2845. —— In general.

C.A.5 (Fla.) 1977. In action by plaintiff, the purchaser, against defendant, the seller, for failure to complete alleged oral contract for the sale of ammonia, court properly instructed that, under Florida law, plaintiff bore only the burden to prove the existence of an oral contract by a preponderance of the evidence. West's F.S.A. § 671.201(8).

Transammonia Export Corp. v. Conserv, Inc., 554 F.2d 719.

⨁2846–2854(1). *For other cases see earlier editions of this digest, the Decennial Digests, and WESTLAW.*

⨁2851. Terms of contract; rights and obligations of parties.

⨁2854. —— Delivery and acceptance.

⨁2854(2). Quality, value, fitness, and condition of goods.

Fla. 1941. In action by buyer of fruit to recover money paid under sale contract allegedly rescinded by seller, instruction that "frost damaged" fruit meant individual oranges showing any perceptible amount of damage resulting from climatic temperatures of 32 degrees Fahrenheit or less was not erroneous.

Givens v. Vaughn-Griffin Packing Co., 1 So.2d 714, 146 Fla. 575.

⨁2854(3)–2860. *For other cases see earlier editions of this digest, the Decennial Digests, and WESTLAW.*

⨁2861. —— Excuses for nonperformance or breach.

C.A.5 (Fla.) 1976. In action for breach of contract to manufacture and sell commercial jet airplane to airline, trial court erred in instructing jury on foreseeability so as to imply that events specifically listed in excusable delay clause in contract must have been unforeseeable at time agreement was executed. West's Ann.Cal. Com.Code, § 2615.

Eastern Air Lines, Inc. v. McDonnell Douglas Corp., 532 F.2d 957.

⨁2862–2868. *For other cases see earlier editions of this digest, the Decennial Digests, and WESTLAW.*

⨁2868. Warranties.

⨁2869. —— In general.

C.A.5 (Fla.) 1978. Evidence, in products liability action arising under Texas and Florida Wrongful Death Acts, did not warrant instructions on strict liability defense of assumption of risk or warranty defenses of contributory negligence and assumption of risk. West's F.S.A. 768.16 et seq.; Vernon's Ann.Tex.Civ.St. art. 4671.

Westerman v. Sears, Roebuck & Co., 577 F.2d 873.

C.A.5 (Fla.) 1974. Charge on contributory negligence in breach of warranty action which refers to "misuse" of the product need not incorporate "sole proximate cause" language, under Florida law prior to July 10, 1973.

Florida Power & Light Co. v. R. O. Products, Inc., 489 F.2d 549.

Charge on contributory negligence of power company, bringing breach of warranty action against seller of hydraulic outrigger devices which extended unexpectedly from power company truck and struck vehicle and injured occupants of vehicle whose claims were settled by power company, was sufficient in incorporating, in effect, a "misuse" charge and "a proximate cause" charge without a "sole proximate cause" charge, under Florida law prior to July 10, 1973.

> Florida Power & Light Co. v. R. O. Products, Inc., 489 F.2d 549.

Fla.App. 1 Dist. 1967. Instructions in action against snap-tie manufacturer for injuries sustained when scaffold attached to snap-tie fell adequately covered applicable law.

> Gates & Sons, Inc. v. Brock, 199 So.2d 291, certiorari denied 204 So.2d 328.

Fla.App. 4 Dist. 1981. Failure to instruct on restaurant's comparative negligence in breach of warranty count against manufacturer of air conditioning system installed in restaurant's building constituted reversible error, which required a new trial rather than reduction of award by amount equal to restaurant's contributory negligence found under negligence count, where finding of comparative negligence might well have been different if jury had considered it within warranty count or if jury had considered it under proper instructions in negligence count and thus complex procedural setting precluded such a clear cut solution.

> ITT-Nesbitt, Inc. v. Valle's Steak House of Fort Lauderdale, Inc., 395 So.2d 217, petition for review dismissed 408 So.2d 1096.

☞2870. —— Express warranties.

For other cases see earlier editions of this digest, the Decennial Digests, and WESTLAW.

☞2871. —— Warranties imposed by law; implied warranties.

C.A.5 (Fla.) 1963. Giving instruction, in action for wrongful death of plaintiff's decedent who allegedly developed fatal lung cancer due to smoking defendant's cigarettes, that implied warranty of fitness did not cover substances in the manufacturer's product the harmful effects of which developed human skill or foresight could afford knowledge was prejudicial error.

> Green v. American Tobacco Co., 325 F.2d 673, certiorari denied 84 S.Ct. 1349, 377 U.S. 943, 12 L.Ed.2d 306, certiorari denied 84 S.Ct. 1351, 377 U.S. 943, 12 L.Ed.2d 306.

Fla.App. 1 Dist. 1971. Defendant pharmaceutical house, sued for breach of implied warranty and for negligence following spinal surgery on plaintiff in which beef bone processed and sold by defendant was employed, was entitled to instruction that to find defendant liable in damages on either theory defect in beef bone actually used on plaintiff had to be found, and failure to give such instruction was reversible error.

> E. R. Squibb & Sons, Inc. v. Jordan, 254 So.2d 17.

☞2872–2874. *For other cases see earlier editions of this digest, the Decennial Digests, and WESTLAW.*

☞2875. —— Notice and opportunity to cure.

C.A.11 (Fla.) 1986. District court's refusal to instruct jury as to effect of manufacturer's continued assurances that it would conform product to its warranties upon timeliness of buyer's notice of breach of warranties was not reversible error, where buyer argued to jury in closing arguments its case regarding continued assurances and fact that such assurances excused buyer from giving timely notice of breach.

> Dancey Co., Inc. v. Borg-Warner Corp., 799 F.2d 717.

☞2876–2877. *For other cases see earlier editions of this digest, the Decennial Digests, and WESTLAW.*

☞2877. Remedies.

☞2878. —— In general.

Fla. 1941. In action by buyer of fruit to recover money paid under sale contract allegedly rescinded by seller, instruction that if jury found that substantial percentage of the fruit covered by contract was frost damaged, and that seller insisted upon removal of damaged fruit and payment therefor at contractual rate, buyer was excused from performing with respect to any part of remaining crop and could recover deposit, was not erroneous.

> Givens v. Vaughn-Griffin Packing Co., 1 So.2d 714, 146 Fla. 575.

For references to other topics, see Descriptive-Word Index

⚷2879. —— Rescission in general.

Fla. 1941. In action by buyer of fruit to recover money paid under sale contract allegedly rescinded by seller, instruction that contract provision excluded particular classes of damaged fruit and that buyer was not required to pick fruit which was within any of such classes on or before the date of performance was not erroneous.
Givens v. Vaughn-Griffin Packing Co., 1 So.2d 714, 146 Fla. 575.

In action by buyer of fruit to recover money paid under sale contract allegedly rescinded by seller, instruction that seller's sale or disposition of the fruit involved after time for performance had arrived, or after buyer's failure to perform, would not rescind the contract, was not erroneous.
Givens v. Vaughn-Griffin Packing Co., 1 So.2d 714, 146 Fla. 575.

In action by buyer of fruit to recover money paid under sale contract allegedly rescinded by seller, instruction that generally a contract of sale may be rescinded only in its entirety, and cannot be affirmed in part and disaffirmed, repudiated or rescinded in part by either seller or buyer, was not erroneous.
Givens v. Vaughn-Griffin Packing Co., 1 So.2d 714, 146 Fla. 575.

In action by buyer of fruit to recover money paid under sale contract allegedly rescinded by seller, instruction that in sale contracts time is usually a material and essential element of the contract, and if a period is fixed during which contract is to continue, the time will be strictly limited to that fixed by the contract, especially where subject of contract is of fluctuating value, was not erroneous.
Givens v. Vaughn-Griffin Packing Co., 1 So.2d 714, 146 Fla. 575.

Fla.App. 2 Dist. 1976. In action involving alleged fraud in sale of employment agency, instruction given pertaining to actionable fraudulent inducement was fatally defective since it failed to include any language placing duty upon buyer, who was not in confidential relationship with sellers, to investigate beyond representations made by sellers, i. e., it omitted any reference to law appertaining to buyer's "right of reliance" and instruction thus effectively removed any burden from buyer in transaction and improperly led jury to believe that mere misrepresentations by sellers would constitute sufficient grounds for rescission.
Folz v. Beard, 332 So.2d 129.

⚷2880. —— Monetary remedies and damages in general.

Fla.App. 3 Dist. 1978. In determining full measure of damages to be awarded seller for breach of contract for sale of goods by buyer, jury should have been instructed in following areas: lost profits, incidental damages, and recovery of contract price of any goods "accepted" by buyer. West's F.S.A. §§ 672.101 et seq., 672.708(2), 672.709, 672.710.
Vagabond Container, Inc. v. City of Miami Beach, 356 So.2d 1266, certiorari denied 364 So.2d 882.

Fla.App. 5 Dist. 1982. Under statute, plaintiff who alleged that software computer package which she purchased from defendant did not perform as represented was entitled, with or without cancellation, to refund in full of purchase price paid and reasonable expenses, if any incurred as result of breach, if plaintiff was found by jury to be entitled to damages, and assuming return of undamaged equipment, and refusal so to instruct was harmful error. West's F.S.A. § 672.711(1).
Jones, Morrison, Stalnaker, P.A. v. Contemporary Computer Services, Inc., 414 So.2d 637.

⚷2881. —— Price or value of goods in general.

Fla. 1941. In action by buyer of fruit to recover money paid under sale contract allegedly rescinded by seller, instruction that court would instruct jury as to meaning of "frost damaged" fruit as used in contract, but jury should determine whether substantial part of the fruit was frost damaged, was not erroneous.
Givens v. Vaughn-Griffin Packing Co., 1 So.2d 714, 146 Fla. 575.

Fla. 1939. An instruction that measure of damage for breach of warranty in sale of seed would be difference between crop actually raised and value of crop had the seed been true to name, after taking into consideration whether proper care was shown by buyers in growing and harvesting the crop, was proper.

West Coast Lumber Co. v. Wernicke, 188 So. 357, 137 Fla. 363.

⟳2882–2886. *For other cases see earlier editions of this digest, the Decennial Digests, and WESTLAW.*

⟳2887. —— Lost profits.

Fla.App. 3 Dist. 1978. Trial court erred in failing to charge jury on damages attributable to lost profits, in seller's suit against buyer for breach of contract for sale of goods, and, in light of applicable law and recovery received, it was presumed that such error harmfully influenced jury's verdict, requiring new trial on damages issue. West's F.S.A. § 672.708(2).

Vagabond Container, Inc. v. City of Miami Beach, 356 So.2d 1266, certiorari denied 364 So.2d 882.

⟳2888–2891. *For other cases see earlier editions of this digest, the Decennial Digests, and WESTLAW.*

XII. RIGHTS AND LIABILITIES AS TO THIRD PERSONS.

(A) IN GENERAL.

⟳2901. In general.

For other cases see earlier editions of this digest, the Decennial Digests, and WESTLAW.

⟳2902. Particular cases and contexts in general.

S.D.Fla. 2016. Neither the purchase documents between distributor of commercial paint products and aircraft maintenance company nor the dealings between distributor and maintenance company expressed a clear intent by both parties for their contract to primarily and directly benefit a commercial airline, whose aircraft were painted at the maintenance company with distributor's paint, thus precluding airline's breach of third-party beneficiary contract claims against distributor under Florida law, even if both parties were aware that purchased paint would be used on airline's aircraft, where the terms and conditions

of distributor's order confirmations did not mention airline, and maintenance company's purchase orders only incidentally referenced airline.

Hawaiian Airlines, Inc. v. AAR Aircraft Services, Inc., 167 F.Supp.3d 1311, appeal dismissed (11th cir. 16-11536).

Fla.App. 1 Dist. 1991. Agreement for purchase of water utility system did not obligate seller to deliver title to water system free of county's lien for water supplied, but rather, simply released purchaser from his obligation to accept title subject to county's lien unless "pass through" rate increase was not approved by Public Service Commission; thus, in county's action foreclosing on lien, purchaser was not entitled to recover from seller the value of utility.

McEnally v. Pioneer Woodlawn Utilities, Inc. By and Through Bd. of County Com'rs, 587 So.2d 623.

Fla.App. 4 Dist. 1980. With adoption of Uniform Commercial Code, the location of title is no longer significant and, hence, it was error to permit retention of title in contract for sale of air-conditioning equipment to induce reliance on statute voiding fraudulent loan so as to give priority to the seller, notwithstanding that it had failed to perfect its security interest while prior holder of construction mortgage on buyer's property had perfected its interest. West's F.S.A. §§ 679.101 et seq., 679.203(1), 726.09.

Suburbia Federal Sav. and Loan Ass'n v. Bel-Air Conditioning Co., Inc., 385 So.2d 1151.

As they apply to retain title contracts which meet Uniform Commercial Code requirements of the "security interest," the provisions of the UCC supersede statute voiding certain loans of goods and chattels and including reservations or limitations by way of reversion, remainder or otherwise; however, there are factual situations where the latter can apply without conflicting with the Code. West's F.S.A. §§ 679.101 et seq., 679.203(1), 726.09.

Suburbia Federal Sav. and Loan Ass'n v. Bel-Air Conditioning Co., Inc., 385 So.2d 1151.

(B) TRANSFEREES AND PURCHASERS IN GENERAL.

☜2911. In general.

For other cases see earlier editions of this digest, the Decennial Digests, and WESTLAW.

☜2912. Extent of title or interest acquired from transferor in general.

Fla. 1992. Person who acquires possession of property by theft cannot convey good title to another person, even to bona fide purchaser.

Battles v. State, 602 So.2d 1287.

Fla.App. 2 Dist. 1993. Purchaser of goods acquires all title which his transferor had or had power to transfer. West's F.S.A. § 672.403(1).

Green Tree Acceptance, Inc. v. Zimerman, 611 So.2d 608.

Fla.App. 3 Dist. 1993. Thief cannot pass good title.

Alamo Rent-a-Car, Inc. v. Williamson Cadillac Co., 613 So.2d 517.

☜2913–2916. *For other cases see earlier editions of this digest, the Decennial Digests, and WESTLAW.*

(C) GOOD-FAITH PURCHASERS.

☜2921. In general.

Fla. 1979. The bona fide purchaser for value without notice does not lose his interests because of wrongdoing by seller. F.S.1977, § 672.403(1).

Everglades Marina, Inc. v. American Eastern Development Corp., 374 So.2d 517, answer to certified question conformed to 608 F.2d 123.

Fla.App. 1 Dist. 1982. Sale of fire truck to Department of Corrections was made out of dealer's "inventory" notwithstanding that truck was special order and was not present at dealer's place of business at time of sale. West's F.S.A. § 679.109(4); U.C.C. § 9–109 comment.

Florida Dept. of Corrections v. Blount Pontiac-GMC, Inc., 411 So.2d 930.

☜2922. Application of doctrine of market overt or caveat emptor.

Fla.App. 2 Dist. 1961. English common-law principle of title acquired by purchase in market overt does not obtain in this country.

R. S. Evans Motors of Jacksonville, Inc. v. Hanson, 130 So.2d 297.

☜2923. "Ordinary course of business" in general.

Bkrtcy.M.D.Fla. 2005. Under Florida law, only a buyer who takes possession of goods or has a right to recover the goods from the seller pursuant to the Uniform Commercial Code may be a buyer in the ordinary course of business. West's F.S.A. §§ 671.201(9), 672.101 et seq.

In re Aquamarine USA, Inc., 330 B.R. 280.

Fla.App. 5 Dist. 1992. If breeding right or stallion service certificate were a farm product for purposes of Food Security Act or goods for purposes of Uniform Commercial Code, owner of mare could be a buyer in the ordinary course, despite claim that the right to breed the stallion to his mare was gratuitously transferred by the manager of the stallion syndicate or was a transfer for total or partial satisfaction of preexisting debt, where owner of mare had paid $15,000 to either the manager of the syndicate or to the owner of the share used for breeding. Food Security Act of 1985, § 1324, 7 U.S.C.A. § 1631; West's F.S.A. § 679.306(2).

Shields v. Equine Capital Corp., 607 So.2d 468.

☜2924. Factors affecting whether transferor may pass good title.

☜2925. —— In general.

Bkrtcy.M.D.Fla. 1998. Basic tenet of the law governing sales of personalty is that a seller cannot transfer better title to a chattel than it possesses.

In re Celotex Corp., 224 B.R. 853.

Fla. 1956. In absence of some intervening principle of estoppel, no one can convey better title than he has, and, conversely, in absence of some such intervening right, one cannot claim a better title than he, in fact, receives.

Dicks v. Colonial Finance Corp., 85 So.2d 874.

Fla.App. 1 Dist. 1962. In absence of intervening principle of estoppel, no one can convey better title than he has.

　Joel Strickland Enterprises, Inc. v. Atlantic Discount Co., 137 So.2d 627.

Fla.App. 1 Dist. 1961. In absence of estoppel or waiver, no one can convey better title than he has, and one cannot claim better title than he in fact receives.

　Trumbull Chevrolet Sales Co. v. Seawright, 134 So.2d 829, certiorari denied 143 So.2d 491.

Where consignment occurs or property is delivered with indicia of ownership or authority to sell, buyer who pays value therefor and takes possession without notice of terms or conditions of delivery, consignment, or sale obtains good title as against original owner, and such title in general prevails against original owner's reserved title.

　Trumbull Chevrolet Sales Co. v. Seawright, 134 So.2d 829, certiorari denied 143 So.2d 491.

Fla.App. 2 Dist. 1963. No one can transfer or confer better title to chattel than he himself has.

　Avis Rent-A-Car System, Inc. v. Harrison Motor Co., 151 So.2d 855.

Fla.App. 2 Dist. 1961. One cannot transfer or confer better title to personalty than he has, unless claim under otherwise better title is barred by estoppel.

　R. S. Evans Motors of Jacksonville, Inc. v. Hanson, 130 So.2d 297.

◌➤**2926. —— Transferor with voidable title.**

M.D.Fla. 2001. As a general rule, a buyer acquires no better title than that of the seller; however, a person with voidable title has power to transfer a good title to a buyer who is good faith purchaser for value.

　U.S. v. McCorkle, 143 F.Supp.2d 1311.

Fla.App. 4 Dist. 1980. Owner of automobile dealership who acquired possession of automobile lawfully by virtue of lease agreement could convey voidable title which could be protected upon sale to buyer in ordinary course of business. West's F.S.A. § 672.403.

　Carlsen v. Rivera, 382 So.2d 825.

◌➤**2927. —— Goods delivered to or in possession of transferor.**

For other cases see earlier editions of this digest, the Decennial Digests, and WESTLAW.

◌➤**2928. —— Goods procured by transferor through fraud or deceit.**

Fla.App. 3 Dist. 1967. Where owner has voluntarily parted with possession of his chattel, though induced to do so by means of criminal act, bona fide purchaser, by his purchase, acquires title good against true owner.

　Southeast Foods, Inc. v. Penguin Frozen Foods, 203 So.2d 39, certiorari denied 210 So.2d 226.

◌➤**2929–2929(2).** *For other cases see earlier editions of this digest, the Decennial Digests, and WESTLAW.*

◌➤**2929. —— Method by which transferor paid for goods.**

◌➤**2929(3). Bad or dishonored checks.**

C.A.11 (Fla.) 1999. Under British Columbia law, supplier of luxury boats had not avoided the voidable title held by seller at time of sale to buyers, where seller which obtained possession of boats via worthless check informed supplier that it had no intention of returning the boats, supplier did not bring legal action against seller, and supplier did not repossess boats until after they had been sold.

　B.R.L. Equipment Rentals Ltd. v. Seabring Marine Industries, Inc., 168 F.3d 413.

◌➤**2930. Notice to purchaser.**

◌➤**2931. —— In general.**

Fla.App. 3 Dist. 1966. If notice of outstanding equity or unrecorded interest is given before purchaser has paid purchase price or has become irrevocably bound for its payment, he is not protected as bona fide purchaser even though he may have received an instrument purporting to convey to him the whole title, both legal and equitable.

　Fraser v. Lewis, 187 So.2d 684.

🔑**2932. —— Actual or constructive notice.**

For other cases see earlier editions of this digest, the Decennial Digests, and WESTLAW.

🔑**2933. —— Duty to make investigation, and facts putting purchaser on inquiry.**

Fla.App. 1 Dist. 1961. Sticker which reflected delivery of new automobile to franchised Michigan dealer and was attached to automobile window as required by federal law constituted clear notice to nonfranchised Florida dealer and its buyer that Michigan dealer was former owner, and such ownership could be ignored only at peril of buyer, where buyer failed to obtain from Florida dealer sworn statement required by statute. F.S.A. § 319.27(f); Automobile Information Disclosure Act, § 1 et seq., 15 U.S.C.A. § 1231 et seq.

  Trumbull Chevrolet Sales Co. v. Seawright, 134 So.2d 829, certiorari denied 143 So.2d 491.

Fla.App. 2 Dist. 1965. If innocent purchaser of automobile does not make inquiry in state of prior registration concerning existence of any liens against vehicle, then duly recorded foreign lien is enforceable against vehicle under rule of comity, even against interest of an innocent purchaser for value and without notice. F.S.A. § 319.01 et seq.

  City of Cars, Inc. v. General Motors Acceptance Corp., 175 So.2d 63.

If innocent purchaser of automobile makes diligent inquiry in state of prior registration concerning existence of any liens against vehicle and such inquiry fails to disclose existence of encumbrance or claim sought to be enforced, then innocent purchaser will be protected against enforcement of duly recorded foreign lien. F.S.A. § 319.01 et seq.

  City of Cars, Inc. v. General Motors Acceptance Corp., 175 So.2d 63.

Where innocent purchaser of automobile for value and without notice of recorded foreign lien upon vehicle failed to make diligent inquiry in state of prior registration to ascertain existence of any such encumbrance, purchaser was not protected from enforcement of such foreign lien

under rule of comity. F.S.A. § 319.01 et seq.

  City of Cars, Inc. v. General Motors Acceptance Corp., 175 So.2d 63.

Fla.App. 4 Dist. 1968. If innocent purchaser of automobile does not make inquiry into state of prior registration concerning existence of any liens against vehicle, duly recorded lien is enforceable against vehicle under rule of comity, even against interest of innocent purchaser for value and without notice.

  Brinkley v. Freedom Nat. Bank of New York, 210 So.2d 465.

🔑**2934. —— Filing, recording, and registration.**

Fla.App. 2 Dist. 1963. A horse is within "livestock" classification under statute that instruments relating to sale or mortgage of livestock must be recorded in order to constitute notice. F.S.A. § 699.07.

  Austin v. Harden, 152 So.2d 751.

Fla.App. 2 Dist. 1960. Records in office of motor vehicle commissioner constitute notice to prospective buyers of any defect in title to motor vehicle or encumbrance thereon and timely inquiry as to condition of title as recorded with commissioner is a prerequisite to obtaining status of "bona fide purchaser". F.S.A. §§ 319.21, 319.22(1).

  Castner v. Ziemer, 125 So.2d 134.

Buyer of used motor vehicle assumes the burden of existing defects and liens on title thereto, as shown on records in office of motor vehicle commissioner, and one who purchases such vehicle in reliance upon representation of seller, without making timely inquiry as to condition of title as shown by such records, cannot escape the result of his own carelessness. F.S.A. §§ 319.21, 319.22(1).

  Castner v. Ziemer, 125 So.2d 134.

Fla.App. 4 Dist. 1968. If innocent purchaser of automobile makes diligent inquiry in state of prior registration concerning existence of any liens against vehicle and such inquiry fails to disclose existence of encumbrance or claim sought to be enforced, then innocent purchaser will be protected against enforcement of duly recorded foreign lien.

>Brinkley v. Freedom Nat. Bank of New York, 210 So.2d 465.

⚏2935–2938. *For other cases see earlier editions of this digest, the Decennial Digests, and WESTLAW.*

⚏2939. **Title and rights acquired by good-faith purchasers.**

Bkrtcy.M.D.Fla. 2005. Under Florida's version of the Uniform Commercial Code (UCC), a seller's right of reclamation is subject to the rights of a good faith purchaser under Florida law. West's F.S.A. §§ 672.403, 672.702.

>In re Nitram, Inc., 323 B.R. 792.

Bkrtcy.M.D.Fla. 1998. Under Florida law, seller's right, upon discovering that buyer is insolvent, to reclaim goods sold on credit is subject to rights of good faith purchaser. West's F.S.A. § 672.403.

>In re Affiliated of Florida, Inc., 237 B.R. 495.

Bkrtcy.M.D.Fla. 1985. No reclamation remedy can lie for seller if goods sought to be reclaimed are not in hands of buyer and are in hands of good faith purchaser. Bankr.Code, 11 U.S.C.A. § 546(c); U.C.C. § 2–702.

>In re Charter Co., 52 B.R. 263.

Oil corporation which purchased oil from Chapter 11 debtor who had purchased oil from seller was good faith purchaser of oil, and its good faith purchaser status cut off reclamation rights which seller would otherwise have had to oil delivered within ten days before reclamation demand. Bankr.Code, 11 U.S.C.A. § 546(c); U.C.C. § 2–702.

>In re Charter Co., 52 B.R. 263.

Fla.App. 2 Dist. 1961. Possession of personalty in good faith by purchaser for value is only prima facie evidence of title.

>R. S. Evans Motors of Jacksonville, Inc. v. Hanson, 130 So.2d 297.

Fla.App. 4 Dist. 1980. Buyer who bought automobile for valid consideration and without notice of defect in title was buyer in ordinary course of business and was entitled to prevail against interests of original owner who leased automobile to

owner of automobile dealership who sold automobile. West's F.S.A. § 672.403.

>Carlsen v. Rivera, 382 So.2d 825.

⚏2940–2942. *For other cases see earlier editions of this digest, the Decennial Digests, and WESTLAW.*

(D) ENTRUSTED GOODS.

⚏2951. **In general.**

Fla.App. 5 Dist. 1984. A voidable title may be successfully perfected by the ultimate buyer who purchases for a valid consideration and without notice of title defect where the rightful owner lost possession through conversion following entrustment. West's F.S.A. § 672.403.

>Brown & Root, Inc. v. Ring Power Corp., 450 So.2d 1245.

⚏2952. **Entrustment to merchant.**

Bkrtcy.M.D.Fla. 2004. Florida statute governing good faith purchasers of goods entrusted to merchants in goods of that kind promotes the free flow of commerce by transferring superior rights to buyers in the ordinary course. West's F.S.A. § 672.403(2).

>In re Aquamarine USA Inc., 319 B.R. 270.

Fla.App. 3 Dist. 1993. Purpose of section of Uniform Commercial Code providing that any entrusting of goods to merchant who deals in goods of that kind gives him power to transfer all rights of entrustor to buyer in ordinary course of business is to place on owner burden of losing his property if he knowingly takes chance of delivering it to a person in the business of dealing with goods of that kind. West's F.S.A. § 672.403(2).

>Alamo Rent-a-Car, Inc. v. Williamson Cadillac Co., 613 So.2d 517.

Fla.App. 4 Dist. 2005. Purpose of statute stating that any "entrusting of possession of goods to a merchant who deals in goods of that kind gives the merchant power to transfer all rights of the entruster to a buyer in ordinary course of business" is to place on the owner the burden of losing his property if he knowingly takes the chance of delivering it to a person in the business of dealing with goods of that kind. West's F.S.A. § 672.403(2).

> Maroone Chevrolet, L.L.C. v. SunTrust Bank, 904 So.2d 618.

⚏**2953. Particular goods.**

⚏**2954. —— In general.**

Fla. 1948. The mere possession of personalty is only prima facie evidence of title, but where owner consigns personalty to dealer in such personalty, with authority to sell, or delivers or consigns to another, personalty with indicia of ownership, or of authority to sell, but with title reserved in owner until payment of purchase price, a purchaser, who pays value for personalty and gets possession without notice of terms of original delivery, consignment, or sale, obtains good title as against the original owner, which will in general prevail against the original owner's reserved title.

> Nash Miami Motors v. Bandel, 37 So.2d 366, 160 Fla. 925.

⚏**2955. —— Motor vehicles.**

Bkrtcy.M.D.Fla. 2004. Under Florida law, if the owner of a motor vehicle entrusts it with a dealer who deals in the sale of motor vehicles, that dealer has the power to pass on valid title to a buyer in the ordinary course of business, even though a title certificate is retained by the original owner. West's F.S.A. § 672.403(2).

> In re Aquamarine USA Inc., 319 B.R. 270.

Fla. 1948. Where owner, without transferring title, placed automobiles on lot of defendant, and there was no evidence of a lien having been given by defendant to owner, purchaser of automobiles from defendant for a valuable consideration without notice of terms of original delivery to defendant would have good title as against original owner, but corporation which loaned money to defendant and secured a lien represented by floor plan chattel mortgages, without investigating authority of defendant to encumber the automobiles, had no lien as against owner.

> Nash Miami Motors v. Bandel, 37 So.2d 366, 160 Fla. 925.

Fla.App. 1 Dist. 1982. Having created situation whereby valid although not "marketable" title was passed to ultimate purchaser of fire truck, by entrusting cab and chassis to dealer and its agent distributor while retaining manufacturer's statement of origin pending payment, seller of chassis and cab was required to bear onus of dealer's bankruptcy and could not prevail in suit for replevin against ultimate purchaser. West's F.S.A. § 319.22(1).

> Florida Dept. of Corrections v. Blount Pontiac-GMC, Inc., 411 So.2d 930.

Fla.App. 1 Dist. 1972. Where defendants purchased in good faith a mobile home from dealer with nothing to put them on notice of dealings between the dealer and manufacturer, defendants were bona fide purchasers for value and were entitled to rely upon the representations and apparent authority to sell by the dealer precluding the manufacturer which never delivered a title to the dealer and never received payment from replevying the mobile home from the purchasers.

> Harmony Homes, Inc. v. Zeit, 260 So.2d 218.

Fla.App. 2 Dist. 1963. A bailee of a rental automobile who never obtained title thereto but who illegally forged a title certificate into his name could not convey title which he himself did not have.

> Avis Rent-A-Car System, Inc. v. Harrison Motor Co., 151 So.2d 855.

Fla.App. 3 Dist. 1993. Section of Uniform Commercial Code providing that any entrusting of goods to a merchant who deals in goods of that kind gives him power to transfer all rights of entrustor to buyer in ordinary course of business was not applicable to pass good title to automobile dealer which purchased automobile from seller who had leased car from car rental company and sold car on basis of fraudulently obtained duplicate title; rental company did not "entrust" vehicle to a "merchant who deals in goods of that kind"; moreover, vehicle could not have been "entrusted," a term which connotes knowledge and volition, in absence of any indication that rental company was aware of lessee's unlawful intent. West's F.S.A. § 672.403(2).

> Alamo Rent-a-Car, Inc. v. Williamson Cadillac Co., 613 So.2d 517.

⚷2956. —— Art and jewelry.

S.D.Fla. 1987. Original possessor rather than subsequent purchaser of ring was entitled to possession, though original possessor entrusted the ring to merchant who dealt in similar goods, in that, under Florida law, subsequent sale of ring was not in ordinary course of business; purchaser did not know merchant, and paid for ring with nine separate checks made out to unknown individual named by merchant. West's F.S.A. § 672.403(2).

Richter v. U.S., 663 F.Supp. 68, affirmed 844 F.2d 795.

(E) LOST, STOLEN, OR DAMAGED GOODS.

⚷2961. In general.

Fla.App. 1 Dist. 1984. Where an owner has voluntarily parted with possession of his chattel, even though induced by a criminal act, a bona fide purchaser can acquire good title, under the theory that where one or two innocent parties must suffer because of wrongdoing of a third person, loss must fall on party who by his conduct created the circumstances which enabled the third party to perpetuate the wrong.

Anderson Contracting Co., Inc. v. Zurich Ins. Co., 448 So.2d 37.

One in possession of stolen property, even if he has innocently purchased it from a "dealer," has no possessory or ownership right to the property as against the rightful owner from whom the property was stolen, since the dealer could convey no better title than he received from the thief.

Anderson Contracting Co., Inc. v. Zurich Ins. Co., 448 So.2d 37.

Fla.App. 5 Dist. 1984. Florida follows a general rule that one who acquires possession of property by theft cannot confer good title by its sale, even to a bona fide purchaser and, at best, a purchaser in good faith has the title and right to possession of the properties against all except the rightful owner.

Brown & Root, Inc. v. Ring Power Corp., 450 So.2d 1245.

⚷2962. Particular goods.

⚷2963. —— In general.

Fla.App. 1 Dist. 1984. Insurer of tractor, which had been stolen and sold by a heavy equipment dealer to purchaser, was entitled to immediate possession of the tractor from purchaser.

Anderson Contracting Co., Inc. v. Zurich Ins. Co., 448 So.2d 37.

In action brought in Florida to determine rights of two insurers and the purchaser of a stolen tractor, which tractor was stolen in Texas, sold to a Louisiana heavy equipment dealer, and then sold to a tractor equipment company which transported it to Florida where it was sold to purchaser, comity did not require application of Louisiana law, in light of Florida public policy.

Anderson Contracting Co., Inc. v. Zurich Ins. Co., 448 So.2d 37.

⚷2964–2965. *For other cases see earlier editions of this digest, the Decennial Digests, and WESTLAW.*

(F) CREDITORS' RIGHTS AND LIABILITIES.

⚷2971–2974. *For other cases see earlier editions of this digest, the Decennial Digests, and WESTLAW.*

(G) ACTIONS.

⚷2981–2990. *For other cases see earlier editions of this digest, the Decennial Digests, and WESTLAW.*

⚷2988. Evidence.

⚷2991. —— Weight and sufficiency.

Fla.App. 3 Dist. 1966. Evidence was sufficient to support finding that purchaser of automobile from individual to whom it had been transferred by purchaser's sister, a judgment debtor, in fraud or hindrance of judgment creditor, was not a bona fide purchaser for value. F.S.A. §§ 55.52–55.61.

Licata v. Acolite Sign Co., 183 So.2d 865.

---

† This Case was not selected for publication in the National Reporter System
For legislative history of cited statutes, see Florida Statutes Annotated

🔑**2992–2998.** *For other cases see earlier editions of this digest, the Decennial Digests, and WESTLAW.*

XIII. CONDITIONAL SALES.

Secured transactions, particularly those within the scope of Article 9 of the Uniform Commercial Code, see SECURED TRANSACTIONS. Chattel mortgages, see CHATTEL MORTGAGES.

🔑**3001. In general; nature of sales on condition.**

Fla.App. 1 Dist. 1959. An agreement to sell is generally held to be a sale on condition or a conditional sale.

Cox Motor Co. v. Faber, 113 So.2d 771.

🔑**3002. What law governs.**

Fla.App. 2 Dist. 1960. Under Florida law, although original buyer of automobile was resident of Alabama, where sale of automobile, which was located in Georgia, took place in Georgia, and buyer executed, in Georgia, conditional bill of sale to bank which financed balance on price, recording law of Georgia, not recording law of Alabama, was applicable to determine whether buyer who purchased automobile in Florida received automobile free from bank's rights. Code Ga. § 67–1305; Code Ala.1940, Tit. 47, §§ 110, 111; F.S.A. § 319.27(3) (f).

Greer v. Commercial and Exchange Bank, 118 So.2d 566.

🔑**3003–3006.** *For other cases see earlier editions of this digest, the Decennial Digests, and WESTLAW.*

🔑**3004. Conditional sales distinguished from other transactions.**

🔑**3007. —— Lease or contract of hiring.**

Fla. 1990. "Lease" is different from "conditional sales contract"; sale has been consummated under conditional sales contract even though vendor holds legal title as security for payment of purchase price, whereas lease is agreement of delivery of property to another under certain limitations for specified period of time

after which property is to be returned to owner.

Kraemer v. General Motors Acceptance Corp., 572 So.2d 1363, appeal after remand 613 So.2d 483, review denied 624 So.2d 266.

Fla.App. 1 Dist. 1994. For purposes of characterizing transfer of personal property, a "sale" will be deemed to have been consummated if a conditional sales contract is involved, even though seller holds legal title as security for payment of purchase price, and "lease" will be deemed to have occurred if there is delivery of property to another person under certain limitations for specified period of time after which property is to be returned to an owner.

Bush Leasing, Inc. v. Gallo, 634 So.2d 737, review denied 645 So.2d 450.

In determining whether document is lease or conditional sales contract, court is to look at level of beneficial ownership maintained by putative lessor.

Bush Leasing, Inc. v. Gallo, 634 So.2d 737, review denied 645 So.2d 450.

Fla.App. 2 Dist. 1968. A lease which provided that in event of cancellation of agreement lessee agreed to purchase all of motor vehicles leased thereunder was conditional sale contract and under law in effect prior to adoption of commercial code, repossession of leased motor vehicles constituted a binding election which precluded recovery of unpaid rental charges from defaulting lessee.

National City Truck Rental Co. v. Southern Mill Creek Products Co., 213 So.2d 261.

🔑**3008–3009.** *For other cases see earlier editions of this digest, the Decennial Digests, and WESTLAW.*

🔑**3010. Contracts creating conditions on transfer of title in general.**

Fla.App. 1 Dist. 1959. Under automobile contract to purchase providing that purchaser acquired no right, title or interest in or to property until it was delivered to him and either full purchase price was paid in cash or a satisfactory deferred payment agreement was executed by the parties, performance of conditions was a condition precedent to vesting of legal title

---

† This Case was not selected for publication in the National Reporter System
For legislative history of cited statutes, see Florida Statutes Annotated

in purchaser but not to vesting of certain contractual rights, and contract was a conditional sales contract even though it contemplated execution of another contract to secure purchase price.

> Cox Motor Co. v. Faber, 113 So.2d 771.

Fla.App. 4 Dist. 2005. Car dealership was authorized to sell car pursuant to a conditional sales agreement, which was contingent on the assignment of the car loan to a third party. West's F.S.A. §§ 319.001(8), 320.60(1), 520.02(14).

> King v. King Motor Co. of Fort Lauderdale, Inc., 900 So.2d 619, rehearing denied, review denied 917 So.2d 194.

⚷**3011–3015.** *For other cases see earlier editions of this digest, the Decennial Digests, and WESTLAW.*

⚷**3016. Filing, recording, and registration.**

Fla.App. 3 Dist. 1964. Enactment of Florida statutes dealing with validity of liens for purchase money or security for debt in form of retain title contract does not affect respective legal rights of buyer and seller between whom retain title agreement is valid even in absence of filing of notice. F.S.A. § 319.15.

> Crawford v. Commercial Credit Corp., 167 So.2d 28.

Unfiled retain title agreement between assignor of agreement and automobile buyer, who subsequently became bankrupt after failing to pay installments due, was valid between the parties entitling assignee to possession of automobiles upon default, and since rights of parties to possession were to be determined as of date replevin complaint was filed, the subsequent filing of petition for bankruptcy by buyer did not make contract unenforceable ab initio and did not defeat assignee's right to writ of replevin.

> Crawford v. Commercial Credit Corp., 167 So.2d 28.

⚷**3017. Construction and operation of conditions as between parties.**

⚷**3018. —— In general.**

C.A.5 (Fla.) 1967. Seller of bowling equipment had right to insist upon nonre-

moval of equipment as provided by contract and was under no duty to remove on order of defaulting buyer.

> Brunswick Corp. v. Vineberg, 370 F.2d 605.

N.D.Fla. 1950. Where buyer takes possession, even though title is reserved in seller to secure purchase price, the risk of loss is in purchaser under Florida Law.

> U.S. v. Greenwood Products Co., 87 F.Supp. 785, affirmed 188 F.2d 401.

Fla.App. 1 Dist. 1959. Where a party contracts to purchase an automobile, makes a payment thereon, and receives delivery, control and authority of use, he is considered beneficial owner even though transfer of title is to be later perfected.

> Cox Motor Co. v. Faber, 113 So.2d 771.

Fla.App. 2 Dist. 1997. Conditional sales contract, as contract that required return of vehicle upon dealership's failure to find financing for buyers, had to be read together with other documents that were executed together as part of one transaction, including security agreement/retail installment contract that named specific outside lender, and thus, read in that manner, it was clear that buyers agreed to return vehicle to dealership if dealership could not find financing with outside lender.

> Dodge City, Inc. v. Byrne, 693 So.2d 1033.

⚷**3019. —— Conditions precedent in general.**

For other cases see earlier editions of this digest, the Decennial Digests, and WESTLAW.

⚷**3020. —— Payment of price.**

Fla. 1936. Ordinarily, contract of conditional sale is not changed to one of absolute sale by fact that buyer gives note whereby he promises unconditionally to pay purchase price.

> Lakeland Silex Brick Co. v. Jackson & Church Co., 168 So. 411, 124 Fla. 347.

Where there is express agreement between parties to conditional sale that title is not to pass until payment of purchase-money notes or payment in cash, sale remains conditional until payment is made.

> Lakeland Silex Brick Co. v. Jackson & Church Co., 168 So. 411, 124 Fla. 347.

☞**3021–3023.** *For other cases see earlier editions of this digest, the Decennial Digests, and WESTLAW.*

☞**3022. Operation and effect of conditions as to third persons.**

☞**3024. —— Filing, recording, and registration.**

Fla.App. 2 Dist. 1963. At common law and in absence of statute requiring it, recording of conditional sale contract is not essential to its validity against third persons.

> Richardson Tractor Co. v. Square Deal Machinery & Supply Co., 149 So.2d 388.

Fla.App. 3 Dist. 1966. It is not necessary for a seller of personal property who reserves title to prove or record the instrument by which title is reserved in order to protect seller's interest as against third persons obtaining a lien or interest via buyer within two years after the date that buyer is placed in possession, and whether or not such third party so gaining an interest or lien within such period of time had notice, actual or constructive, of the reserved title in the seller is immaterial. F.S.A. § 726.09.

> Rood v. Miami Air Conditioning Co., 193 So.2d 216.

☞**3025. —— Purchasers from buyer in general.**

C.C.A.5 (Fla.) 1942. In Florida, a conditional sales contract retains the title and protects seller in payment of his money even though articles covered by the contract are exposed for sale, notwithstanding that a different rule applies to a chattel mortgage.

> McKaig v. Commercial Credit Corp., 126 F.2d 68.

Fla.App. 2 Dist. 1966. Where dragline owner had acquired properties from original purchaser and had made monthly payments, under original purchase contract, to assignee, dragline owner and assignee of purchase contract stood in con-tractual relationship each with the other, so that refinancing agreement, involving other contracts, between original purchaser and assignee wherein current indebtedness under original purchase contract was added to defaulted indebtedness under other contracts, amounted to a complete modification of contract and impairment of dragline owner's property right without its breach, knowledge or consent, precluding inclusion of dragline in foreclosure of mortgage securing refinancing agreement.

> United Contractors, Inc. v. United Const. Corp., 187 So.2d 695.

Fla.App. 2 Dist. 1963. Conditional sale contract is valid against conditional buyer's creditors and subsequent buyers even though contract is not recorded, if conditional buyer's possession is for less than statutory two-year period after which recording is required. F.S.A. § 726.09.

> Richardson Tractor Co. v. Square Deal Machinery & Supply Co., 149 So.2d 388.

☞**3026–3028.** *For other cases see earlier editions of this digest, the Decennial Digests, and WESTLAW.*

☞**3028. —— Bona fide purchasers from buyer.**

☞**3028(1). In general.**

Fla. 1962. Florida dealer purchasing used automobile originally sold in Massachusetts failed to make inquiry in Massachusetts to extent required under rule of comity to acquire title as against original Massachusetts seller under retain title contract where application for Florida certificate of title, tax receipt and Florida title certificate revealed sources of information from which Florida dealer could have informed itself as to liens. F.S.A. §§ 319.01 et seq., 319.27(3) (f).

> Municipal Auto Sales, Inc. v. Ferry Street Motor Sales, Inc., 143 So.2d 323.

Fla. 1948. The mere possession of personalty is only prima facie evidence of title, but where owner consigns personalty to dealer in such personalty, with authority to sell, or delivers or consigns to another, personalty with indicia of ownership, or of authority to sell, but with title reserved in owner until payment of purchase price, a purchaser, who pays value for personalty and gets possession without notice of terms of original delivery, consignment, or sale, obtains good title as against the original owner, which will in general prevail against the original owner's reserved title.

> Nash Miami Motors v. Bandel, 37 So.2d 366, 160 Fla. 925.

Fla. 1939. Where owner consigns personalty to dealer with express or implied authority to sell, or delivers to another personalty with indicia of ownership or of authority to sell, but with title reserved in owner until payment of price, purchaser, who pays value for goods and gets possession without notice of terms of original delivery, obtains good title as against original owner.

> Marriott v. Meadows, 189 So. 415, 138 Fla. 436.

The purchaser of an automobile from automobile agency to which owner had delivered it with authority to sell, but reserving title until payment of price, without knowledge of such title retention, obtained good title as against original owner.

> Marriott v. Meadows, 189 So. 415, 138 Fla. 436.

Fla.App. 2 Dist. 1965. The rule to effect that anyone who purchased personal property from a conditional vendee acquires no interest against the prior conditional vendor even though the purchaser pays value and takes without notice is subject to an exception when there is a failure to record the conditional sales contract within two years; the rule is subject to another exception where conditional vendee is in business of selling personal property which he received under title retention contract and conditional vendor is estopped from asserting his retained title contract against an innocent purchaser for value from such dealer. F.S.A. § 726.09.

> Maas Bros., Inc. v. Guaranty Federal Sav. & Loan Ass'n, 180 So.2d 195.

Fla.App. 2 Dist. 1962. Original sellers were not entitled to foreclosure of conditional sales agreements against subsequent purchasers, where intermediate purchasers under the conditional sales agreements although not maintaining showrooms or holding themselves out to the general public as dealers in the machines, were permitted by nature of their dealings with original sellers to assume position of owners and dealers in the handling, disposition and sales of the vending machines to subsequent purchasers who were without notice of original seller's liens.

> Hal Rivers Standard Service Station v. Continental Industries, Inc., 140 So.2d 617.

Fla.App. 2 Dist. 1961. Conditional seller and holder of lien reflected on 1956 title certificate were not estopped from asserting title and right to possession of house trailer under chain of title from manufacturer as against one claiming under chain of title from dealer and title certificate first issued in 1957, even if dealer's transferee was bona fide purchaser for value without notice of defect or infirmity of title, in absence of showing that conditional seller or lienholder caused dealer to have possession or indicia of ownership or had reason to know of possession by dealer or anyone claiming under dealer until after default by conditional buyer.

> R. S. Evans Motors of Jacksonville, Inc. v. Hanson, 130 So.2d 297.

⚷3028(2). Filing, recording, and registration.

Fla.App. 2 Dist. 1965. The rule to effect that anyone who purchased personal property from a conditional vendee acquires no interest against the prior conditional vendor even though the purchaser pays value and takes without notice is subject to an exception when there is a failure to record the conditional sales contract within two years; the rule is subject to another exception where conditional vendee is in business of selling personal property which he received under title retention contract and conditional vendor is estopped from asserting his retained title contract against an innocent purchaser for value from such dealer. F.S.A. § 726.09.

> Maas Bros., Inc. v. Guaranty Federal Sav. & Loan Ass'n, 180 So.2d 195.

Fla.App. 2 Dist. 1960. Where an automobile was sold by a Georgia dealer in Georgia under a conditional sales contract which was assigned to a finance company, and under a Georgia statute, a conditional bill of sale filed for record within 30 days from its date has priority from the date of its execution, and finance company recorded the contract within 30 days from its execution, defendants, who purchased the automobile, were charged with knowledge of such Georgia statute under the law of comity, which was applicable, and defendants could not escape liability on theory that because the contract was not of record on the date of the purchase, they had no actual notice thereof and were not chargeable with notice of the contract. Code Ga. § 67–1403.

> Strickland v. Motors Acceptance, Inc., 126 So.2d 156, certiorari denied 127 So.2d 679.

Fla.App. 2 Dist. 1960. Where sale of automobile which was located in Georgia, to original buyer who was Alabama resident took place in Georgia, and bank, which financed balance on price, recorded in county of original buyer's residence in Alabama conditional bill of sale executed in Georgia by original buyer but did not record such bill in county of conveyance in Georgia as required by Georgia recording statute, and original buyer then sold automobile in Florida, and Florida buyer sold automobile in Georgia to innocent purchaser for value without notice, innocent purchaser in Georgia obtained good title, and bank could not replevy automobile from buyer who subsequently purchased the automobile in Florida. Code Ga. § 67–1305; Code Ala.1940, Tit. 47, §§ 110, 111; F.S.A. § 319.27(3) (f).

> Greer v. Commercial and Exchange Bank, 118 So.2d 566.

Fla.App. 2 Dist. 1958. Although conditional sales contract covering sale of tractor was recorded by the vendor, bona fide purchaser for value of tractor from conditional vendee was not bound by constructive notice of vendor's interest afforded by recording of conditional sales contract, and vendor could not recover such tractor upon default of the vendee.

> Llewellyn Machinery Corp. v. Miller, 108 So.2d 916.

🗝3029. —— **Creditors of buyer.**

🗝3029(1). **In general.**

C.C.A.5 (Fla.) 1942. Even if a bald attempt by seller to retain title in face of provisions in sales agreement and conduct inconsistent therewith would be ineffective against creditors of buyer under Florida law, it would not avail creditors of an automobile dealer who purchased automobiles under conditional sales contracts, where provisions of contracts were consistent only with theory of retention of title to, and dominion over the property by seller, and were wholly inconsistent with passage of title by absolute sale and complete delivery of possession with a bare mortgage back.

> McKaig v. Commercial Credit Corp., 126 F.2d 68.

🗝3029(2). **Filing, recording, and registration.**

Fla.App. 2 Dist. 1963. Conditional sale contract is valid against conditional buyer's creditors and subsequent buyers even though contract is not recorded, if conditional buyer's possession is for less than statutory two-year period after which recording is required. F.S.A. § 726.09.

> Richardson Tractor Co. v. Square Deal Machinery & Supply Co., 149 So.2d 388.

🗝3030. **Effect of assignment of contract.**

Fla. 1957. Where dealer has parted with possession of property conditionally sold but has regained possession of it, as upon retaking after default of purchaser, without authorization of assignee and without his knowledge or consent, a subsequent purchaser from dealer does not obtain title as against assignee, but if assignee expressly or impliedly consents to resale after repossession, purchaser from conditional seller secures good title.

> Motor Credit Corp. v. Woolverton, 99 So.2d 286, 72 A.L.R.2d 334.

Fla. 1953. Where used car dealer, who never had possession of or title to automobile, assigned contract for conditional sale thereof in blank and assignee knew or could have obtained actual knowledge of details by exercise of ordinary diligence, assignee had no right to automobile as against new car dealer who had obtained possession of automobile from buyer and relinquishment of his rights therein when checks received in payment therefor were dishonored.

Commercial Credit Corp. v. McGriff, 66 So.2d 52.

Fla. 1939. Where assignment of conditional sales contract contained express guaranty that assignors would pay any deficiency arising upon repossession and resale, assignors were liable for such deficiency notwithstanding general rule that conditional vendor may not enforce debt for purchase price after retaking possession.

White Motor Co. v. Briles, 188 So. 222, 137 Fla. 268.

Fla.App. 1 Dist. 1969. Where purchasers did not comply with statutory duty to investigate as to outstanding liens before purchasing a used trailer which seller had repossessed from original purchaser for failure to make payments and against which prior purchaser's conditional sales contract had been recorded, subsequent purchasers were not innocent purchasers for value without notice and did not attain a title free of claim of assignee who was entitled to possession. F.S.A. § 319.22(1).

James Talcott, Inc. v. Eckert, 220 So.2d 17.

Fla.App. 2 Dist. 1962. Where defendant sold time payment agreements to plaintiff and there was oral agreement that plaintiff would retain ten percent as a reserve account to cover any default on any of the agreements, which were guaranteed by defendant, court did not err in holding that plaintiff was entitled to 21 percent of reserve accounts in absence of evidence that a fixed percentage of reserve account should be applied to any defaulted agreement.

Pulsnation Enterprises, Inc. v. Appliance Plan Co., 141 So.2d 814.

Fla.App. 2 Dist. 1961. Company which purchased conditional sales contract, on used automobile, from dealer, was under duty to take notice of duly recorded lien of bank against automobile. F.S.A. §§ 319.21, 319.22, 319.27(2), 319.27(3) (b), 320.272(1).

American Discount Co. v. Central Bank of Tampa, 135 So.2d 264.

Fla.App. 3 Dist. 1966. Where purchaser informed conditional seller-assign-

or that hotel had been sold and that seller should pick up all television sets, receipt taken by purchaser, which stated that seller was storing the sets as an accommodation to the buyer, was consistent with buyer's continued ownership of the sets.

National State Bank of Newark v. Robert Richter Hotel, Inc., 186 So.2d 321.

Purchaser recognized assignment of conditional sales contract where after receiving notice of assignment it made payments to the assignee.

National State Bank of Newark v. Robert Richter Hotel, Inc., 186 So.2d 321.

In absence of evidence to the contrary, the seller-assignor has no authority to act for the assignee of a conditional sales contract.

National State Bank of Newark v. Robert Richter Hotel, Inc., 186 So.2d 321.

Evidence was susceptible to a reasonable interpretation which would support a jury verdict for plaintiff bank, assignee of conditional sales contract, against purchaser for balance due for television sets which had been picked up and receipted for by dealer assignor which subsequently had sold the sets and had accounted to no one for the proceeds.

National State Bank of Newark v. Robert Richter Hotel, Inc., 186 So.2d 321.

Fla.App. 3 Dist. 1965. Where plaintiff, which acquired bill of sale to motor vehicle purchased by it, failed to acquire from seller a manufacturer's statement of origin, as required by statute, and made no inquiry concerning certificate of title which seller was to procure for it until after firm which had acquired statement of origin and certificate of title executed purported conditional sales agreement and such instrument was assigned to defendant, which had no knowledge of any interest of plaintiff until after issuance of new certificate of title naming defendant as first lienholder, defendant's lien was prior, superior and paramount to rights, claims and interest of plaintiff.

Lowry of Fla., Inc. v. Coconut Grove Bank, 179 So.2d 861, certiorari denied 188 So.2d 317.

Fla.App. 3 Dist. 1965. Finance company assignee of conditional sales contract and installment note which had knowledge that only about one-half of equipment covered by contract had been delivered to buyer at time of execution of extension agreement was not holder in due course, and conditional buyer could properly raise defense of failure of consideration in assignee's action for breach of contract.

Industrial Credit Co. v. Mike Bradford & Co., 177 So.2d 878, certiorari denied 183 So.2d 835.

Fla.App. 3 Dist. 1959. Conditional sales contracts for automobiles are assignable and upon default in payment the assignee may regain possession in a replevin action.

Colonial Finance, Inc. v. All Miami Ford, Inc., 112 So.2d 857.

⊸3031. Performance or breach of conditions.

Fla.App. 1 Dist. 1963. Provision of retail installment contract requiring automobile owner to keep vehicle free of liens did not prohibit delivery of possession of automobile to a garage to have it repaired and contract provision was not breached until garage asserted its lien.

General Finance Corp. of Jacksonville v. Sexton, 155 So.2d 159.

⊸3032. Waiver of condition or of forfeiture for breach.

⊸3033. —— In general.

C.A.5 (Fla.) 1967. Since upon partial breach of installment sales contract by buyer, seller was not obligated to do anything to keep its rights alive, it could not be estopped by its failure to act at that time.

Brunswick Corp. v. Vineberg, 370 F.2d 605.

⊸3034–3035. *For other cases see earlier editions of this digest, the Decennial Digests, and WESTLAW.*

⊸3036. —— Enforcing or attempting to enforce payment of price.

Fla. 1937. Where seller delivered furniture to buyer on agreement that title should not pass until payment was made, took notes for indebtedness, and subsequently sued on notes, seller could not claim priority over mortgagee under prior mortgage deed of buyer's property containing after-acquired property provision, since seller's action on notes constituted election to treat transaction with buyer as a debt and operated to pass title to buyer, whereupon furniture became subject to lien provided for by mortgage deed eo instante.

Central Farmers' Trust Co. v. McCampbell Furniture Stores, 174 So. 748, 127 Fla. 721, 128 Fla. 60.

Fla.App. 2 Dist. 1963. Institution of suit by assignee of conditional sales contract against the defaulting buyer of the automobile covered by the contract constituted an election of the assignee's remedies which buyer could have interposed as a defense in the assignee's subsequent repossession of the automobile, but buyer could not interpose the repossession as a bar when, after allowing the buyer the value of the repossessed automobile, the assignee proceeded to final judgment in the action on the contract.

First Bank & Trust Co. v. Mellay, 156 So.2d 518.

Fla.App. 2 Dist. 1962. Owner of kitchen cabinets under a retain title contract when it filed its claim of lien elected to treat the title as having passed to the vendee.

Coronet Kitchens, Inc. v. Mortgage Mart, Inc., of St. Petersburg, 146 So.2d 768.

In action to foreclose mortgages, owner of kitchen cabinets on the property under a retain title contract by filing its claim of lien pursuant to the statute, vested title in its vendee and having done so, it had no title in or right of possession of the cabinets and was barred from recovering them. F.S.A. §§ 84.01 et seq., 84.32.

Coronet Kitchens, Inc. v. Mortgage Mart, Inc., of St. Petersburg, 146 So.2d 768.

Fla.App. 3 Dist. 1961. Automobile seller under retain title contract, by first seeking recovery of sales price by suing therefor, treated sale as absolute and was not thereafter entitled to possession. F.S.A. §§ 78.19 to 78.21.

Cecil Holland Ford, Inc. v. Jameson, 132 So.2d 621.

☞3037. —— Extension of time for payment.

For other cases see earlier editions of this digest, the Decennial Digests, and WESTLAW.

☞3038. —— Acceptance of payment after default.

Fla. 1940. Where conditional sales contract provided that in case of default seller could declare whole amount due and repossess automobile without legal process and that, if seller failed to promptly exercise any remedy in his favor, he should not in the future be precluded from doing so, seller's acceptance of one payment which was late did not preclude seller from repossessing automobile after second payment was tendered late and refused.

Kent v. Tallahassee Motor Co., 193 So. 821, 141 Fla. 789.

☞3039–3041. *For other cases see earlier editions of this digest, the Decennial Digests, and WESTLAW.*

☞3040. Remedies of seller.

☞3042. —— Nature, form and election of remedy.

C.A.5 (Fla.) 1967. Failure of buyer of bowling equipment to pay installments on conditional sales contract did not put seller to election of remedies of removing equipment or suing for installments and seller's failure to remove did not preclude it from suing for damages for removal by buyer and those in control of buyer, inasmuch as contract precluded removal of equipment by anyone other than seller upon default.

Brunswick Corp. v. Vineberg, 370 F.2d 605.

Inasmuch as seller of bowling equipment under installment contract was not under any prior obligation to act upon buyer's default in making installment payments, inaction was not an election of remedies and seller was not precluded from suing for damages for removal of equipment on basis that it was an inconsistent remedy.

Brunswick Corp. v. Vineberg, 370 F.2d 605.

Fla.App. 2 Dist. 1964. Where chattels purchased under contract of conditional sale were returned by buyers for resale upon default in payment of purchase price and were resold by seller and proceeds of resale after deducting expenses thereof were insufficient to pay balance due under conditional sales contract, seller could not thereafter recover such deficiency from buyers, notwithstanding contract provision for repossession and sale of chattels and payment of any deficiency by buyers.

Bill Smith, Inc. v. Cox, 166 So.2d 497.

Fla.App. 2 Dist. 1963. Institution of suit by assignee of conditional sales contract against the defaulting buyer of the automobile covered by the contract constituted an election of the assignee's remedies which buyer could have interposed as a defense in the assignee's subsequent repossession of the automobile, but buyer could not interpose the repossession as a bar when, after allowing the buyer the value of the repossessed automobile, the assignee proceeded to final judgment in the action on the contract.

First Bank & Trust Co. v. Mellay, 156 So.2d 518.

Fla.App. 3 Dist. 1959. A conditional vendor may treat the sale as absolute and seek the purchase price or he may treat the sale as rescinded and recover the property. F.S.A. § 520.11.

Colonial Finance, Inc. v. All Miami Ford, Inc., 112 So.2d 857.

☞3043. —— Recovery of goods or proceeds thereof; actions for conversion.

☞3043(1). In general.

Fla.App. 1 Dist. 1959. Provision in a conditional sales contract that if seller deems himself insecure or the property in danger of misuse, of which seller shall be the sole judge, seller may retake possession of the property, purports to invest the seller with arbitrary power to repossess on the basis of his state of mind, and veers close to affording the seller power to work a forfeiture of the buyer's rights, and such arbitrary power is abhorred in the law and contrary to public policy.

Jacksonville Tractor Co. v. Nasworthy, 114 So.2d 463.

Under provision in a sales contract that if seller deems himself insecure or the property in danger or misuse of confiscation (of which seller shall be the sole judge), seller may retake possession, test of seller's right to repossess was whether under all the facts and circumstances an ordinarily careful and prudent person would have "deemed himself insecure" in the premises.

Jacksonville Tractor Co. v. Nasworthy, 114 So.2d 463.

Fla.App. 1 Dist. 1957. Assignee of contract for conditional sale of automobile was entitled to take possession of automobile in a lawful manner where purchaser was delinquent in his payments.

Lewis v. Atlantic Discount Co., 99 So.2d 241.

Fla.App. 3 Dist. 1969. Where document entitled "retail installment contract" contained no reservation of title and provided that in event of default of buyer any surplus resulting from repossession and sale should be paid to buyer, seller was not entitled to immediate possession of property described in contract.

Miami Air Conditioning Co. v. Rood, 223 So.2d 78.

Fla.App. 3 Dist. 1964. Where by terms of assigned retail installment contract covering purchase of three automobiles entire amount of loan was due on failure to make particular payment, assignee of contract was entitled to possession of vehicles on default, and since under agreement assignee could have resorted to self help in order to reduce vehicles to its possession, assignee would not be penalized for resorting to judicial remedy of replevin against bankrupt purchaser.

Crawford v. Commercial Credit Corp., 167 So.2d 28.

🗝**3043(2)–3043(3).** *For other cases see earlier editions of this digest, the Decennial Digests, and WESTLAW.*

🗝**3043(4). Demand or tender.**

Fla. 1937. Where conditional seller was entitled to possession of conditionally sold property because of default and demanded property before institution of replevin suit, conditional buyer was guilty of unlawful detention of property at least

from date suit was instituted and was answerable in damages therefor.

Pavlis v. Atlas-Imperial Diesel Engine Co., 172 So. 57, 126 Fla. 808.

🗝**3043(5). Defenses.**

Fla.App. 3 Dist. 1958. Where conditional seller of automobile brought action for replevin of same the conditional buyer urged in answer that trial court construe conditional sales agreement as lien for purchase price, relieve him against forfeiture under contract and permit payment of balance of purchase price and decree title to be vested in buyer, while such grounds might be proper subjects of affirmative relief in equity, they did not constitute defense upon equitable grounds in action of replevin at law. F.S.A. §§ 33.02, 52.20.

Klein v. G. F. C. Corp., 103 So.2d 120.

🗝**3043(6). Parties.**

For other cases see earlier editions of this digest, the Decennial Digests, and WESTLAW.

🗝**3043(7). Pleading and evidence.**

Fla. 1955. In action for repossession of bulldozer, being purchased under oral retain title arrangement whereby buyer was entitled to "work out" part of purchase price, by seller, who contended that buyer quit and refused to work, against buyer, who contended that seller refused to give him any more work and pay him a reasonable wage, evidence sustained verdict for buyer.

Wood v. Weeks, 81 So.2d 498.

In action in replevin by seller for repossession of bulldozer being purchased by buyer under oral retain title arrangement, the value of bulldozer fixed by jury verdict should have been special value to buyer, based on competent evidence and appropriate instructions and in order to support the jury award for detention damages, some appropriate evidence should have been offered. F.S.A. § 78.21.

Wood v. Weeks, 81 So.2d 498.

Fla. 1943. In replevin for automobile sold under retention of title contract, defendant had burden of proving defense of payment.

Hooper v. Atkinson, 12 So.2d 898, 152 Fla. 726.

In replevin for automobile sold under retention of title contract, evidence was admissible to show that defendant's original note was paid pursuant to new financing agreement made several months after sale.

Hooper v. Atkinson, 12 So.2d 898, 152 Fla. 726.

Fla.App. 1 Dist. 1965. Evidence in replevin action was sufficient to support finding of invalidity of conditional sales contract and its assignment, which were bases of plaintiff's alleged right of possession of subject automobile.

Southside Atlantic Bank v. Lewis, 174 So.2d 470.

Fla.App. 3 Dist. 1969. Evidence in support of seller's claim for damages for wrongful detention of merchandise described in retain title contract was insufficient to prove that merchandise had usable value.

Miami Air Conditioning Co. v. Rood, 223 So.2d 78.

⚷3043(8). Trial.

Fla. 1955. Where verdict in replevin action by seller for repossession of bulldozer had the effect of allowing buyer, who had not made complete payment under oral retain title arrangement, to retain possession of bulldozer or elect to receive $7,500, the value of bulldozer at time of replevin, plus $1,700 detention damages, there was reversible error on questions of value of property, or buyer's interest therein, and damages for detention. F.S.A. § 78.21.

Wood v. Weeks, 81 So.2d 498.

Fla. 1943. In replevin for automobile sold under retention of title contract, whether defendant's original note was paid pursuant to new financing agreement made several months after sale was for jury.

Hooper v. Atkinson, 12 So.2d 898, 152 Fla. 726.

⚷3043(9). Damages, judgment or execution.

Fla. 1955. In action in replevin by seller for repossession of bulldozer being purchased by buyer under oral retain title arrangement, the value of bulldozer fixed by jury verdict should have been special

value to buyer, based on competent evidence and appropriate instructions and in order to support the jury award for detention damages, some appropriate evidence should have been offered. F.S.A. § 78.21.

Wood v. Weeks, 81 So.2d 498.

Fla.App. 3 Dist. 1969. Seller which failed to prove by preponderance of evidence that merchandise described in retain title contract had usable value could recover only the interest on the value of the merchandise wrongfully detained.

Miami Air Conditioning Co. v. Rood, 223 So.2d 78.

Fla.App. 3 Dist. 1965. Where defendant defaulted in payments for merchandise sold under retain title contract, and plaintiff brought replevin action for repossession, damages for wrongful detention, and attorney fees, measure of damages was not price of merchandise or expense of plaintiff in connection with sale.

Harbour Tower Development Corp. v. Seaboard Equipment Co., 179 So.2d 405.

Plaintiff, which brought replevin action for repossession of merchandise sold under retain title contract on default in payments by defendant, was entitled to attorney fees, where sale contract contained sufficient provision for attorney fees.

Harbour Tower Development Corp. v. Seaboard Equipment Co., 179 So.2d 405.

Fla.App. 3 Dist. 1959. In replevin action based on purported conditional sales contract, which was in fact a security device by which personalty of defendant was subjected to pre-existing indebtedness to plaintiff on open account, plaintiff's claim for damages for full value of such personalty was limited by plaintiff's special interest therein.

Spencer v. Florida-Georgia Tractor Co., 114 So.2d 466.

In replevin action based on conditional sales contract, which was in fact a security device by which property of defendant was made subject to pre-existing indebtedness to plaintiff on an open account, plaintiff was entitled to judgment for unpaid balance owing on the account.

    Spencer v. Florida-Georgia Tractor Co., 114 So.2d 466.

⚷3043(10). Effect of recovery of property in general.

Fla.App. 2 Dist. 1968. A lease which provided that in event of cancellation of agreement lessee agreed to purchase all of motor vehicles leased thereunder was conditional sale contract and under law in effect prior to adoption of commercial code, repossession of leased motor vehicles constituted a binding election which precluded recovery of unpaid rental charges from defaulting lessee.

    National City Truck Rental Co. v. Southern Mill Creek Products Co., 213 So.2d 261.

Inasmuch as amounts expended by vendor for operation, as opposed to maintenance, of motor vehicles used by vendee benefited vendee, vendor could recover those expenditures on theory of unjust enrichment even though motor vehicles had been repossessed.

    National City Truck Rental Co. v. Southern Mill Creek Products Co., 213 So.2d 261.

⚷3043(11)–3043(13). *For other cases see earlier editions of this digest, the Decennial Digests, and WESTLAW.*

⚷3044. —— Resale.

Fla.App. 3 Dist. 1959. A repairman having a lien on conditional buyer's interest in the car can be protected to the extent that the buyer would be, by requiring resale of the car after repossession by the seller or the seller's assignee and application upon the repairman's lien of the excess proceeds of the sale over defined costs and expenses and amount due the repossession-plaintiff. F.S.A. § 520.11.

    Colonial Finance, Inc. v. All Miami Ford, Inc., 112 So.2d 857.

⚷3045. —— Recovery of price or value.

S.D.Fla. 1945. Defense to note given by conditional buyer that there had been no tender of title to the goods to buyer and that such transfer was a prerequisite to suit on note was insufficient, since holder of note could not be called on to execute a bill of sale to goods before agreed consideration was paid.

    U.S. v. Bryant, 58 F.Supp. 663, affirmed 157 F.2d 767.

Fla. 1943. Where buyer executed conditional sales note for purchase price of personalty and defaulted in payment of first two installments, assignee of note could declare remaining installments due and sue for the full purchase price.

    Kauffman v. International Harvester Co., 14 So.2d 387, 153 Fla. 188.

⚷3046. —— Breach of contract by buyer.

C.A.5 (Fla.) 1967. Failure of buyer of bowling equipment to pay installments on conditional sales contract did not put seller to election of remedies of removing equipment or suing for installments and seller's failure to remove did not preclude it from suing for damages for removal by buyer and those in control of buyer, inasmuch as contract precluded removal of equipment by anyone other than seller upon default.

    Brunswick Corp. v. Vineberg, 370 F.2d 605.

⚷3047. —— Lien and foreclosure thereof.

Fla. 1936. In suit to foreclose mortgage on realty and conditional sales contract embracing personalty, given to secure single debt, after default in payment of first installment due, decree requiring real estate to be sold first and personalty to be sold only in case of necessity to make up total amount of decree held proper.

    Reichert v. Nelson, 169 So. 726, 125 Fla. 347.

⚷3048–3048(2). *For other cases see earlier editions of this digest, the Decennial Digests, and WESTLAW.*

⚷3048. —— Against third persons.

⚷3048(2). Recovery of goods or proceeds thereof.

⚷3048(3). —— In general.

Fla. 1956. Where seller sold automobile to dealer who resold it, subject to conditional sales contract, and automobile was returned to seller, unknown to contract assignee, which had filed papers for certificate of title with first lien to it with tag agency, and seller then sold automobile to second dealer who conveyed it to ultimate buyer, and after that Commissioner received title application from tag agency and issued certificate showing lien and subsequently received ultimate buyer's application for title, sales contract assignee had lien, subject to being recorded, prior in dignity to rights of ultimate buyer and could replevy automobile upon default under contract. F.S.A. §§ 319.15, 319.23(5), 319.27(2).

> Dicks v. Colonial Finance Corp., 85 So.2d 874.

Fla. 1939. In replevin by owner of automobile against purchaser who bought automobile from automobile agency to which owner had delivered it with authority to sell, but reserving title until payment of price, judgment in favor of purchaser was not limited to value of his special interest as established and costs, as provided by statute where right of possession is based on claim of lien or special interest, since plaintiff was not a general owner but was a stranger to purchaser's title. F.S.A. §§ 78.19, 78.21.

> Marriott v. Meadows, 189 So. 415, 138 Fla. 436.

Fla.App. 3 Dist. 1962. Massachusetts conditional seller of automobile which had been removed from Massachusetts without seller's permission by defaulting buyer after seller had exercised option of acceleration could recover from defendant purchasing automobile in Florida from buyer who had procured Florida title certificate, where defendant failed to make adequate inquiry in Massachusetts as required by rule of comity. F.S.A. §§ 319.01 et seq., 319.27(3) (f).

> Ferry St. Motor Sales, Inc. v. Municipal Auto Sales, Inc., 137 So.2d 842, affirmed 143 So.2d 323.

⟜**3048(4).** —— **Conditions   precedent and defenses.**

For other cases see earlier editions of this digest, the Decennial Digests, and WESTLAW.

⟜**3048(5).** —— **Time for proceeding, and laches.**

Fla. 1936. Replevin action for brick presses and material hoppers sold under title retention contract dated July 15, 1925, which was commenced in June, 1934, held not barred by laches, where intermittently from July 8, 1927, to January 22, 1934, buyer had acknowledged seller's right to repossess property and within two months from date of commencement of action, purchaser of property from buyer had recognized seller's title.

> Lakeland Silex Brick Co. v. Jackson & Church Co., 168 So. 411, 124 Fla. 347.

⟜**3048(6)–3048(7).** *For other cases see earlier editions of this digest, the Decennial Digests, and WESTLAW.*

⟜**3048(8).** —— **Trial.**

Fla. 1936. In replevin action by conditional seller of brick presses and material hoppers against purchaser taking from buyer, question whether buyer's note executed subsequent to contract of sale was given and received in payment and satisfaction of seller's title retention contract, or as evidence of debt, held for jury under proper instructions.

> Lakeland Silex Brick Co. v. Jackson & Church Co., 168 So. 411, 124 Fla. 347.

⟜**3048(9)–3048(10).** *For other cases see earlier editions of this digest, the Decennial Digests, and WESTLAW.*

⟜**3049. Remedies of buyer.**

Fla. 1969. Where petitioner in action arising out of conditional sales contract failed to allege willful, independent tort separate and apart from breach of contract, he was not entitled to punitive damages.

> Masciarelli v. Maco Supply Corp., 224 So.2d 329, on remand 223 So.2d 790.

Fla. 1949. Allegation that plaintiff purchased automobile under conditional sale contract providing that if automobile were repossessed and resold surplus received would be paid plaintiff, and defendant later repossessed automobile and retained proceeds obtained upon resale, in excess of amount owed by plaintiff, was sufficient as against demurrer.

Pardo v. R. S. Evans-Lakeland, Inc., 38 So.2d 307.

Fla. 1936. Judgment for conditional buyer against seller's assignee for repossessing and converting automobile held proper under evidence of waiver of right to retake automobile without prior notice or demand, in view of acceptance of payments after default on contract installments.

Commercial Credit Co. v. Willis, 171 So. 304, 126 Fla. 444.

Fla.App. 1 Dist. 1962. Evidence established that finance company received from collision insurer only amount necessary to liquidate unpaid balance due it from purchaser under contract, after automobile was damaged in accident.

Stoudt v. Securities Inv. Co., 140 So.2d 122.

Fla.App. 1 Dist. 1959. In view of fact there is no ready means for one adversely affected to explore or contradict the bona fides of one who has the arbitrary right under a conditional sales contract, to repossess the property, when he deems himself insecure, one who exercises such contractual prerogative has the burden of presenting facts justifying its exercise.

Jacksonville Tractor Co. v. Nasworthy, 114 So.2d 463.

⬯3050–3051. *For other cases see earlier editions of this digest, the Decennial Digests, and WESTLAW.*

⬯3052. **Criminal responsibility for removal or transfer of property.**

Fla. 1941. A suit of clothes was "personal property" within statute defining offense of disposing of personal property under lien, and hence warrant charging that relator purchased suit under a retain title contract and did unlawfully hide and

conceal and transfer suit with intent to defeat, hinder and delay recovery of such property by sellers thereof, charged an offense. F.S.A. § 818.01.

Hayes v. Jones, 2 So.2d 588, 147 Fla. 238.

Proof that personal wearing apparel purchased under a retain title contract had been completely worn out by purchaser in ordinary usage of articles would constitute a defense to prosecution under statute defining offense of disposing of personal property under lien. F.S.A. § 818.01.

Hayes v. Jones, 2 So.2d 588, 147 Fla. 238.

In determining whether disposing of property obtained under retain title contract constitutes an offense within statute defining offense of disposing of personal property under lien, character of property, aside from its being personal property, has no controlling effect. F.S.A. § 818.01.

Hayes v. Jones, 2 So.2d 588, 147 Fla. 238.

Fla. 1939. As respects criminal liability, under contract for conditional sale of automobile providing that buyer should not remove automobile from county and state, removal of automobile not only from county but from the county and state was required to breach the contract.

Herring v. State, 191 So. 290, 140 Fla. 170.

Under contract for conditional sale of automobile providing that buyer should not remove automobile from county and state, buyer had written consent of seller to remove property outside county so long as he did not remove it from county and state, and hence could not be convicted of violation of statute penalizing removal of property subject to conditional sales contract from county without consent of seller in absence of showing that automobile was removed from state or of fraud in removal of automobile from county. F.S.A. § 818.01.

Herring v. State, 191 So. 290, 140 Fla. 170.

For Cross-References or Descriptive Words
see
DESCRIPTIVE–WORD INDEX

SALVAGE

SUBJECTS INCLUDED

Allowances made by law out of the value or proceeds of vessels or cargoes saved in whole or in part from danger or loss, to persons by whose assistance they were so saved, whether made by way of compensation or otherwise

Nature of the services for which, and grounds upon which, such allowances may be made

What property may be subject thereto

Who may be entitled to salvage and waiver or forfeiture thereof

Amount to be awarded and apportionment thereof

Lien for salvage and waiver, discharge, or extinguishment thereof

Priorities of liens

Proceedings for recovery of salvage

SUBJECTS EXCLUDED AND COVERED BY OTHER TOPICS

Admiralty jurisdiction and procedure in general, see ADMIRALTY

For detailed references to other topics, see Descriptive-Word Index

---

Analysis

For detailed references to other topics, see Descriptive-Word Index

I. RIGHT TO COMPENSATION.

Research Notes

See West's Florida Legal Forms, Specialized Forms.

☞1. **Nature and grounds in general.**

C.A.11 (Fla.) 2016. A "salvage award" is the compensation allowed to persons by whose voluntary assistance a ship at sea or her cargo or both have been saved in whole or in part from impending sea peril.

Girard v. M/V 'Blacksheep', 840 F.3d 1351.

In order to obtain a salvage award for assisting a ship at sea, a salvor must prove three elements: (1) a marine peril; (2) service voluntarily rendered when not required as an existing duty or from a special contract; and (3) success in whole or in part, or that service rendered contributed to such success.

Girard v. M/V 'Blacksheep', 840 F.3d 1351.

The law of salvage is rooted in a public policy to encourage mariners to come to the aid of a ship in distress; it aims to induce all to render aid in the face of marine peril, and to do so before it is a do-or-die wager with high risks.

Girard v. M/V 'Blacksheep', 840 F.3d 1351.

C.A.11 (Fla.) 2000. Law of salvage generally governs efforts to save vessels in distress, but vessel without owner is subject to the law of finds, summed up succinctly as "finders keepers."

International Aircraft Recovery, L.L.C. v. Unidentified, Wrecked and Abandoned Aircraft, 218 F.3d 1255, certiorari denied International Aircraft Recovery, LLC v. U.S., 121 S.Ct. 1079, 531 U.S. 1144, 148 L.Ed.2d 956, appeal after remand 373 F.3d 1147.

Law of salvage is intended to encourage rescue.

International Aircraft Recovery, L.L.C. v. Unidentified, Wrecked and Abandoned Aircraft, 218 F.3d 1255, certiorari denied International Aircraft

Recovery, LLC v. U.S., 121 S.Ct. 1079, 531 U.S. 1144, 148 L.Ed.2d 956, appeal after remand 373 F.3d 1147.

C.A.11 (Fla.) 1985. Claim for salvage award requires maritime peril from which ship or other property could not have been rescued without assistance by the salvor, a voluntary act by salvor who is under no official or legal duty to render assistance, and success in saving or at least in helping to save part of the endangered property.

Klein v. Unidentified Wrecked and Abandoned Sailing Vessel, 758 F.2d 1511.

C.A.5 (Fla.) 1974. Maritime laws encourage all efforts to salve ship, cargo and persons.

U.S. v. Raven, 500 F.2d 728, certiorari denied 95 S.Ct. 809, 419 U.S. 1124, 42 L.Ed.2d 824.

C.A.5 (Fla.) 1974. Elements which must be shown for a valid salvage claim are a marine peril, service voluntarily rendered when not required as an existing duty or from a special contract, and success in whole or in part, or that the service rendered contributed to such success.

Legnos v. M/V Olga Jacob, 498 F.2d 666, 26 A.L.R. Fed. 848, rehearing denied 503 F.2d 567, rehearing denied Eller and Company, Inc. v. Legnos, 503 F.2d 567, rehearing denied 503 F.2d 567, rehearing denied Schiffahrtsgesellschaft Jacob & Co. v. Eller and Company, Inc., 503 F.2d 568, affirmed 535 F.2d 857, rehearing denied 540 F.2d 1085.

C.C.A.5 (Fla.) 1938. To give a right to salvage, it is not enough that the property be saved, but it must be saved by the instrumentality of the asserted salvors, or their services must contribute in some degree to the result.

The No. 105, 97 F.2d 425.

M.D.Fla. 2010. Under the law of salvage, rescuers take possession of, but not title to, a distressed vessel and its contents and realize a compensatory salvage award.

Odyssey Marine Exploration, Inc. v. Unidentified, Wrecked and Abandoned Sailing Vessel, 727 F.Supp.2d 1341.

The law of salvage and the law of finds serve different purposes and promote different behaviors, and a claimant cannot "have its cake and eat it too" by invoking both during a single recovery.

> Odyssey Marine Exploration, Inc. v. Unidentified, Wrecked and Abandoned Sailing Vessel, 727 F.Supp.2d 1341.

The law of salvage functions as a trust on behalf of the true owner and imposes duties of good faith, honesty, and diligence in protecting the property in the salvors' care.

> Odyssey Marine Exploration, Inc. v. Unidentified, Wrecked and Abandoned Sailing Vessel, 727 F.Supp.2d 1341.

Under the law of salvages, a salvor removes property from a wreck in trust for the owner; exploitation of the salvaged property terminates the right to a salvage award.

> Odyssey Marine Exploration, Inc. v. Unidentified, Wrecked and Abandoned Sailing Vessel, 727 F.Supp.2d 1341.

M.D.Fla. 2009. The "law of salvage" and the "law of finds" are mutually exclusive: under the "law of salvage," a rescuer takes possession, but not title to, the distressed vessel and its contents, and can obtain an award for services rendered; the "law of finds" takes a more direct approach to ownership, "finders keepers."

> Odyssey Marine Exploration, Inc. v. Unidentified, Shipwrecked Vessel, 675 F.Supp.2d 1126, affirmed 657 F.3d 1159, certiorari denied 132 S.Ct. 2379, 182 L.Ed.2d 1051, certiorari denied Republic of Peru v. Unidentified Shipwrecked Vessel, 132 S.Ct. 2380, certiorari denied De Aliaga v. Kingdom of Spain, 132 S.Ct. 2380, 182 L.Ed.2d 1051.

M.D.Fla. 1997. Elements of valid salvage claim are: maritime peril from which ship could not have been rescued without salvor's assistance; voluntary act by salvor under no pre-existing official or contractual duty to the owner; and success in saving, or in helping to save at least part of property at risk.

> Sands v. One Unnamed 23' Seacraft, Pleasure Vessel, 959 F.Supp. 1488, affirmed 144 F.3d 55.

M.D.Fla. 1993. Law of maritime salvage is concerned not with title to property, but with successful recovery of possession of lost property from oceans and waterways; "salvage" involves right to possess another's property and save it from destruction, danger or loss.

> Lathrop v. Unidentified, Wrecked & Abandoned Vessel, 817 F.Supp. 953.

Once salvor is in possession of salvaged property, no other person can lawfully intrude on possession, including vessel's master or owner.

> Lathrop v. Unidentified, Wrecked & Abandoned Vessel, 817 F.Supp. 953.

To establish claim for salvage, plaintiff must prove marine peril, service voluntarily rendered, and success, either whole or partial, in recovering imperiled property.

> Lathrop v. Unidentified, Wrecked & Abandoned Vessel, 817 F.Supp. 953.

Rivers and Harbors Act, Antiquities Act, and United States Park Service Regulations restrict manner in which potential salvor can excavate abandoned shipwrecks located on federal lands, and, enactments restricting manner of salvaging do not conflict with underlying principles of salvage. U.S.C.A. Const. Art. 3, § 2, cl. 1; 28 U.S.C.A. § 1333; Abandoned Shipwreck Act of 1987, §§ 3(a), 6(a)(1), 43 U.S.C.A. §§ 2102(a), 2105(a)(1).

> Lathrop v. Unidentified, Wrecked & Abandoned Vessel, 817 F.Supp. 953.

Congressional enactments restricting manner in which potential salvor excavates property located on federally owned or managed lands does not offend constitutional limitations on congressional power to supplement or alter admiralty law. U.S.C.A. Const. Art. 3, § 2, cl. 1; 28 U.S.C.A. § 1333; Abandoned Shipwreck Act of 1987, §§ 3(a), 6(a)(1), 43 U.S.C.A. §§ 2102(a), 2105(a)(1).

> Lathrop v. Unidentified, Wrecked & Abandoned Vessel, 817 F.Supp. 953.

Laws prohibiting appropriation of historic artifacts or excavation on federal lands without first obtaining permit from corps of engineers did not deprive federal court of admiralty jurisdiction and did not necessarily prohibit salvage activities, but rather statute supplemented admiralty law by providing substantive rules for lawful salvage operations on federally owned or managed lands. 16 U.S.C.A. §§ 433, 459j–2(b); 33 U.S.C.A. § 403.

> Lathrop v. Unidentified, Wrecked & Abandoned Vessel, 817 F.Supp. 953.

Possession of abandoned property is not sufficient to establish salvage claim; salvor must acquire possession lawfully before valid claim can be established.

> Lathrop v. Unidentified, Wrecked & Abandoned Vessel, 817 F.Supp. 953.

Restrictions on salvage activities which were necessary to ensure safety of both salvors and public were within Congress' broad powers over all public lands; legislation supplementing admiralty jurisdiction by imposing necessary restrictions on salvage activities was important legislative function properly reserved to Congress. 16 U.S.C.A. §§ 433, 459j–2(b); 33 U.S.C.A. § 403.

> Lathrop v. Unidentified, Wrecked & Abandoned Vessel, 817 F.Supp. 953.

Potential salvors do not have inherent right to save distressed vessels, but rather salvage award may be denied if salvor forces its services on vessel despite rejection by owner or by person with authority.

> Lathrop v. Unidentified, Wrecked & Abandoned Vessel, 817 F.Supp. 953.

S.D.Fla. 2014. The law of salvage rewards the voluntary salvor for the successful rescue of life or property imperiled at sea.

> Girard v. The M/Y Quality Time, 4 F.Supp.3d 1352, affirmed in part, remanded in part 596 Fed.Appx. 846, certiorari denied 136 S.Ct. 153, 193 L.Ed.2d 43.

S.D.Fla. 2007. Power to regulate salvaging on the coast of Florida is not a power properly vested in the judiciary pursuant to Vesting Clause of Article III. U.S.C.A. Const. Art. 3, § 1; 46 U.S.C.A. § 80102.

> In re Beck, 526 F.Supp.2d 1291.

S.D.Fla. 2007. Salvage is the reward or compensation allowed by the maritime law for service rendered in saving maritime property, at risk or in distress, by those under no legal obligation to render it, which results in benefit to the property.

> Atlantis Marine Towing, Inc. v. THE M/V PRISCILLA, 491 F.Supp.2d 1096.

To prove entitlement to a salvage award, a plaintiff must demonstrate three elements: (1) that a maritime peril existed from the which the ship or other property could not have been rescued without the salvor's assistance; (2) that the salvor acted voluntarily, i.e., he or she was under no official or legal obligation to render the assistance; and (3) that the salvor was successful in saving or helping to save at least part of the property at risk.

> Atlantis Marine Towing, Inc. v. THE M/V PRISCILLA, 491 F.Supp.2d 1096.

S.D.Fla. 2004. To succeed on claim for salvage, plaintiff has burden of proving: (1) maritime peril from which ship or other property could not have been rescued without salvor's assistance; (2) voluntary act by salvor without pre-existing contractual, official, or legal duty to render assistance; and (3) success in saving, or helping to save, in whole or in part, property at risk.

> Atlantis Marine Towing, Inc. v. M/V/ELZABETH, 346 F.Supp.2d 1266.

S.D.Fla. 2003. Three elements of a salvage claim are: (1) that marine peril exists; (2) that the service was voluntarily rendered; and (3) that the effort was successful in whole or in part.

> Southernmost Marine Services, Inc. v. One (1) 2000 Fifty Four Foot (54') Sea Ray named M/V POTENTIAL, 250 F.Supp.2d 1367, affirmed Southernmost Marine Svcs. v. M/V POTENTIAL, 91 Fed.Appx. 655.

S.D.Fla. 1995. Law of salvage rewards voluntary salvor for successful rescue of life and property from maritime peril.

> Fine v. Rockwood, 895 F.Supp. 306.

As long as requirements for salvage claim are met, salvor's pecuniary motivations are irrelevant to his entitlement to salvage award.

> Fine v. Rockwood, 895 F.Supp. 306.

To be entitled to salvage award, plaintiff has burden of proving: maritime peril from which ship or other property could not have been rescued without salvor's assistance, voluntary act by salvor under no preexisting official or contractual duty to owner, and success in saving, or in helping to save, at least part of property at risk.

Fine v. Rockwood, 895 F.Supp. 306.

S.D.Fla. 1993. Admiralty and maritime law of salvage rewards voluntary salvor for his or her successful rescue of life or property imperiled at sea.

Ocean Services Towing and Salvage, Inc. v. Brown, 810 F.Supp. 1258.

Award on action for salvage, unknown for land activities, is not one of quantum meruit as compensation for work performed, but is bounty historically given in interests of public policy, to encourage humanitarian rescue of life and property at sea, and to promote maritime commerce.

Ocean Services Towing and Salvage, Inc. v. Brown, 810 F.Supp. 1258.

Fact that salvor's efforts have pecuniary motivations is immaterial to his or her entitlement to salvage award, as long as prerequisites for salvage claim have been proven.

Ocean Services Towing and Salvage, Inc. v. Brown, 810 F.Supp. 1258.

Three elements for valid salvage claim must be found: maritime peril from which ship or other property could not have been rescued without salvor's assistance; voluntary act by salvor under no preexisting official or contractual duties to owner; and success in saving, or in helping to save at least part of property at risk.

Ocean Services Towing and Salvage, Inc. v. Brown, 810 F.Supp. 1258.

S.D.Fla. 1988. The rights of potential salvors are inchoate until an abandoned vessel is actually found and a salvage action commenced and, even at that point the owner is not divested of its interest in the vessel, as it retains title to the res subject only to the maritime lien for the salvage services and the right to refuse salvage services.

Jupiter Wreck, Inc. v. Unidentified, Wrecked and Abandoned Sailing Vessel, 691 F.Supp. 1377.

S.D.Fla. 1988. A "salvage" occurs when there is marine peril, voluntary services rendered, and success in whole or part.

Hernandez v. Roberts, 675 F.Supp. 1329.

S.D.Fla. 1986. Distinguished from the law of finds, law of salvage primarily is concerned with successful recovery and possession of lost property from oceans and waterways, rather than title; salvage contemplates right to possess property for purpose of saving it from destruction, damage or loss, and to retain it until proper compensation has been paid.

MDM Salvage, Inc. v. Unidentified, Wrecked and Abandoned Sailing Vessel, 631 F.Supp. 308.

Salvage claim requires proof of three elements: marine peril, service voluntarily rendered and not required as preexisting duty and success, wholly or partly, in recovering imperiled property.

MDM Salvage, Inc. v. Unidentified, Wrecked and Abandoned Sailing Vessel, 631 F.Supp. 308.

S.D.Fla. 1984. On the high seas a voluntary salvor is entitled to a reward, but only if there is a marine peril from which ship or property could not have escaped without the salvor's assistance, salvor's aid must have been voluntarily rendered, and not required as a preexisting duty, and the salvor must have been successful, in whole or in part, of recovery of the imperilled ship or property.

Sea Lift, Inc. v. Refinadora Costarricense De Petroleo, S.A., 601 F.Supp. 457, reversed 792 F.2d 989.

S.D.Fla. 1983. Three elements of salvage claim are that marine peril exists, that service was voluntarily rendered, and that effort was successful in whole or in part.

Treasure Salvors, Inc. v. Unidentified, Wrecked and Abandoned Sailing Vessel, 556 F.Supp. 1319.

S.D.Fla. 1982. The three elements of a salvage claim are that a marine peril exists, that the service was voluntarily rendered, and that the effort was successful in whole or in part.

> Cobb Coin Co., Inc. v. Unidentified, Wrecked and Abandoned Sailing Vessel, 549 F.Supp. 540.

S.D.Fla. 1981. A person presenting a salvage claim must establish a marine peril, a service voluntarily rendered when not required as a preexisting duty, and a success, in whole or in part, of recovery of imperiled property.

> Treasure Salvors, Inc. v. Unidentified Wrecked and Abandoned Sailing Vessel, 546 F.Supp. 919.

S.D.Fla. 1981. The right of potential salvors to search and explore the open waters for salvageable goods is a fundamental adjunct to the principle that the high seas be freely navigable to all seafaring persons to navigate for pleasure or commerce or otherwise to ply their trades.

> Cobb Coin Co., Inc. v. Unidentified, Wrecked and Abandoned Sailing Vessel, 525 F.Supp. 186.

Under traditional salvage rules, salvor receives a lien against the salved property and is usually entitled to his expenses plus a salvage award.

> Cobb Coin Co., Inc. v. Unidentified, Wrecked and Abandoned Sailing Vessel, 525 F.Supp. 186.

S.D.Fla. 1971. Requisites for salvage award are that there must have been a maritime peril from which ship could not have been rescued without salvor's assistance, salvor's act must have been voluntary, meaning that salvor must have been under no official or legal duty to render assistance, and efforts of salvor must have been successful in saving or helping to save at least a part of property at risk.

> Crawford v. West India Carriers, Inc., 337 F.Supp. 262, reversed Twenty Grand Offshore, Inc. v. West India Carriers, Inc., 492 F.2d 679, certiorari denied 95 S.Ct. 63, 419 U.S. 836, 42 L.Ed.2d 63.

⚷2. What law governs.

C.A.5 (Fla.) 1978. Abandoned Property Act was not legislative enactment of sovereign prerogative and did not apply to suit brought by corporations for possession and confirmation of title to unidenti-

fied wrecked and abandoned vessel thought to be Spanish vessel which sank in 1622. 40 U.S.C.A. § 310.

> Treasure Salvors, Inc. v. Unidentified Wrecked and Abandoned Sailing Vessel, 569 F.2d 330.

⚷3. Vessels and other property subject to salvage.

C.A.11 (Fla.) 2000. Admiralty law presumes that owners do not give up title to ships and cargo in marine peril, even if cargo is swept overboard or a crew has to leave its vessel on the open water, but the law does recognize that owners can "abandon" all interests in their vessels.

> International Aircraft Recovery, L.L.C. v. Unidentified, Wrecked and Abandoned Aircraft, 218 F.3d 1255, certiorari denied International Aircraft Recovery, LLC v. U.S., 121 S.Ct. 1079, 531 U.S. 1144, 148 L.Ed.2d 956, appeal after remand 373 F.3d 1147.

United States Navy did not abandon all interests in Navy torpedo bomber, so as to warrant application of the law of finds rather than the law of salvage, when Navy struck the bomber from its inventory of active planes after the bomber crashed in international waters during World War II. U.S.C.A. Const. Art. 4, § 3, cl. 2.

> International Aircraft Recovery, L.L.C. v. Unidentified, Wrecked and Abandoned Aircraft, 218 F.3d 1255, certiorari denied International Aircraft Recovery, LLC v. U.S., 121 S.Ct. 1079, 531 U.S. 1144, 148 L.Ed.2d 956, appeal after remand 373 F.3d 1147.

M.D.Fla. 2010. The law of salvage presumes that property lost at sea is not abandoned, and thus the true owner retains title to the lost property, whereas the law of finds traditionally applies only to objects, such as flora and fauna, never owned.

> Odyssey Marine Exploration, Inc. v. Unidentified, Wrecked and Abandoned Sailing Vessel, 727 F.Supp.2d 1341.

S.D.Fla. 2013. The law of salvage calls for a "marine peril," and that ele-

---

† This Case was not selected for publication in the National Reporter System
For legislative history of cited statutes, see Florida Statutes Annotated

ment may be satisfied by an ancient, abandoned shipwreck.

> JTR Enterprises, LLC v. An Unknown Quantity of Colombian Emeralds, Amethysts and Quartz Crystals, 922 F.Supp.2d 1326, appeal dismissed (11th cir. 13-10870).

S.D.Fla. 1984. Vessel from which crew departed upon approach of salvor's boat, but to which certain individuals later returned to board and attempt to offload its illegal cargo, was at no time either "derelict" or "abandoned," so that salvors could not establish ownership of vessel on such grounds.

> Unnamed But Identifiable Master and Crew of That Certain U.S. Documented Vessel Bearing Documentation No. 567135 v. Certain Unnamed Motor Vessel Bearing Florida Registration No. FL5607 EM, 592 F.Supp. 1191.

S.D.Fla. 1981. Process of natural history which eroded vessel's structure and scattered the contents of the vessel did not diminish the federal rights and remedies available to the salvor who successfully returned to the mainstream of commerce goods otherwise bearing beneath the sea; the absence of a hull does not affect the traditional maritime right of a salvor to uninterrupted salvage operation where the salvor, in conducting his operations on an identifiable wreck site, does so in a manner demonstrating the degree of dominion and control which is appropriate under the circumstances.

> Cobb Coin Co., Inc. v. Unidentified, Wrecked and Abandoned Sailing Vessel, 525 F.Supp. 186.

⚷4. **Derelict.**

C.A.11 (Fla.) 2000. When ship is in distress and has been deserted by its crew, anyone can attempt salvage without prior assent of the ship's owner or master; in other words, when salvor comes upon a vessel in distress, he can assume the owner would want assistance.

> International Aircraft Recovery, L.L.C. v. Unidentified, Wrecked and Abandoned Aircraft, 218 F.3d 1255, certiorari denied International Aircraft

Recovery, LLC v. U.S., 121 S.Ct. 1079, 531 U.S. 1144, 148 L.Ed.2d 956, appeal after remand 373 F.3d 1147.

Owner of derelict vessel cannot contest salvor's right to attempt a rescue by claiming after the fact that the assistance was unwanted.

> International Aircraft Recovery, L.L.C. v. Unidentified, Wrecked and Abandoned Aircraft, 218 F.3d 1255, certiorari denied International Aircraft Recovery, LLC v. U.S., 121 S.Ct. 1079, 531 U.S. 1144, 148 L.Ed.2d 956, appeal after remand 373 F.3d 1147.

C.A.5 (Fla.) 1981. Salvage of vessel or goods at sea, even when goods have been abandoned, does not divest original owner of title or grant ownership rights to salvor, except in extraordinary cases as where property has been lost or abandoned for very long time; under these unusual circumstances, maritime law of finds supplements the possessory interest normally granted to salvor and vests title by occupancy in one who discovers such abandoned property and reduces it to possession.

> Treasure Salvors, Inc. v. Unidentified Wrecked & Abandoned Sailing Vessel, 640 F.2d 560, on remand 546 F.Supp. 919.

C.A.5 (Fla.) 1978. In corporations' suit for possession of and confirmation of title to unidentified wrecked and abandoned vessel thought to be Spanish vessel which sank in 1622, district court correctly applied law of finds, in view of fact that disposition of wrecked vessel whose very location had been lost for centuries as though its owner was still in existence would be stretching fiction to absurd lengths.

> Treasure Salvors, Inc. v. Unidentified Wrecked and Abandoned Sailing Vessel, 569 F.2d 330.

Primary difference between law of finds and "salvage law" is that under "salvage law" claim of finder of abandoned property is satisfied by proceeds from sale of property paid into court.

> Treasure Salvors, Inc. v. Unidentified Wrecked and Abandoned Sailing Vessel, 569 F.2d 330.

---

† This Case was not selected for publication in the National Reporter System
For legislative history of cited statutes, see Florida Statutes Annotated

C.C.A.5 (Fla.) 1938. "Dereliction" or "renunciation" of property at sea as well as on land requires both the intention to abandon and external action.

The No. 105, 97 F.2d 425.

In libel against a steel barge on a claim for salvage for rescuing barge from impending perils of the sea, the District Court erroneously held that barge had become a "derelict" and erroneously awarded its full value to salvors as compensation for their services, where barge was severed from tug in a storm, owner immediately undertook to recover it, and there was no evidence indicating a voluntary intention to abandon barge.

The No. 105, 97 F.2d 425.

S.D.Fla. 1984. Vessel from which crew departed upon approach of salvor's boat, but to which certain individuals later returned to board and attempt to offload its illegal cargo, was at no time either "derelict" or "abandoned," so that salvors could not establish ownership of vessel on such grounds.

Unnamed But Identifiable Master and Crew of That Certain U.S. Documented Vessel Bearing Documentation No. 567135 v. Certain Unnamed Motor Vessel Bearing Florida Registration No. FL5607 EM, 592 F.Supp. 1191.

S.D.Fla. 1981. Under the prevailing American rule regarding ownership of lost or abandoned property, in the absence of an express statutory claim by the sovereign, abandoned goods successfully recovered become the property of the salvor.

Cobb Coin Co., Inc. v. Unidentified, Wrecked and Abandoned Sailing Vessel, 525 F.Supp. 186.

S.D.Fla. 1976. Under general principles of maritime and international law, an abandonment constitutes a repudiation of ownership, and party which takes possession under salvage operations may be considered a finder under the doctrine that the owner has no intention of returning.

Treasure Salvors, Inc. v. Abandoned Sailing Vessel Believed to Be Nuestra Senora De Atocha, 408 F.Supp. 907, affirmed and modified 569 F.2d 330.

Under American rule relating to sovereign prerogative, the legislature must manifest a specific intent to appropriate derelict property.

Treasure Salvors, Inc. v. Abandoned Sailing Vessel Believed to Be Nuestra Senora De Atocha, 408 F.Supp. 907, affirmed and modified 569 F.2d 330.

Phrase "ought to come to the United States" in Abandoned Property Act refers to abandoned or derelict property strewn about country during Civil War and did not encompass ship wreck discovered on outer continental shelf. 40 U.S.C.A. § 310.

Treasure Salvors, Inc. v. Abandoned Sailing Vessel Believed to Be Nuestra Senora De Atocha, 408 F.Supp. 907, affirmed and modified 569 F.2d 330.

Ship wreck discovered on continental shelf outside territorial waters of the United States was neither within the jurisdiction of the United States for purposes of the Abandoned Property Act nor owned or controlled by the United States government for purposes of the Antiquities Act. 16 U.S.C.A. §§ 432, 433; 40 U.S.C.A. § 310; Outer Continental Shelf Lands Act, §§ 3 et seq., 3(b), 43 U.S.C.A. §§ 1332 et seq., 1332(b).

Treasure Salvors, Inc. v. Abandoned Sailing Vessel Believed to Be Nuestra Senora De Atocha, 408 F.Supp. 907, affirmed and modified 569 F.2d 330.

Statutory provision which declares that policy of United States is that subsoil and seabed of outer continental shelf are subject to jurisdiction and control of United States merely asserts jurisdiction over minerals in and under continental shelf and did not bring abandoned vessel found on outer continental shelf within jurisdiction of United States and thus within purview of Antiquities Act and Abandoned Property Act. 16 U.S.C.A. §§ 432, 433; 40 U.S.C.A. § 310; Outer Continental Shelf Lands Act, §§ 3 et seq., 3(b), 43 U.S.C.A. §§ 1332 et seq., 2332(b).

Treasure Salvors, Inc. v. Abandoned Sailing Vessel Believed to Be Nuestra Senora De Atocha, 408 F.Supp. 907, affirmed and modified 569 F.2d 330.

---

† This Case was not selected for publication in the National Reporter System
For legislative history of cited statutes, see Florida Statutes Annotated

⚷5. Existence and extent of peril.

C.A.11 (Fla.) 2016. To meet the "marine peril" element of a claim for a salvage award, salvor need not show that the vessel he assisted could not have been rescued without the salvor's assistance.

Girard v. M/V 'Blacksheep', 840 F.3d 1351.

Professional marine salvor who undertook rescue mission for yacht that was taking on water sufficiently demonstrated that the vessel was in "marine peril," as required to obtain salvage award for assisting the ship at sea; salvor heard yacht's captain radio a distress call to the United States Coast Guard saying there was an emergency, in that the vessel's prop shaft had come out and that the yacht was taking on water, and captain requested assistance from anyone nearby who could help with the vessel's pumps.

Girard v. M/V 'Blacksheep', 840 F.3d 1351.

† **C.A.11 (Fla.) 2008.** District court did not clearly err in its determination that vessel was not in situation in which there was reasonable apprehension of maritime peril, thereby precluding towing company from entitlement to salvage award for recovery and towing services, in light of evidence that weather had dramatically improved from earlier hurricane conditions, vessel was located in marina, afloat, and secured by rope to another boat, and concrete pilings did not damage or pose further risk of damage to vessel's hull.

Cape Ann Towing v. M/Y "Universal Lady", 268 Fed.Appx. 901.

C.A.11 (Fla.) 1992. In order to make out claim for pure salvage, as opposed to contract salvage, salvor must establish three elements: marine peril; service voluntarily rendered when not required as existing duty or from special contracts; and success in whole or in part, or service contributing to such success.

Flagship Marine Services, Inc. v. Belcher Towing Co., 966 F.2d 602, opinion vacated, appeal dismissed, opinion reinstated 23 F.3d 341.

C.A.5 (Fla.) 1978. "Marine peril" includes more than threat of storm, fire, or piracy to vessel in navigation.

Treasure Salvors, Inc. v. Unidentified Wrecked and Abandoned Sailing Vessel, 569 F.2d 330.

C.A.5 (Fla.) 1974. Showing of necessity for claiming salvors' services is not required to establish existence of marine peril, and thus asserted fact that employees of stevedore, who helped to extinquish fire on board vessel, had not done anything the other fire fighters would not have done did not preclude a salvage award.

Legnos v. M/V Olga Jacob, 498 F.2d 666, 26 A.L.R. Fed. 848, rehearing denied 503 F.2d 567, rehearing denied Eller and Company, Inc. v. Legnos, 503 F.2d 567, rehearing denied 503 F.2d 567, rehearing denied Schiffahrtsgesellschaft Jacob & Co. v. Eller and Company, Inc., 503 F.2d 568, affirmed 535 F.2d 857, rehearing denied 540 F.2d 1085.

To establish marine peril, one of elements of a valid salvage claim, salvors need not prove that their actions were necessary to eliminate or alleviate such condition.

Legnos v. M/V Olga Jacob, 498 F.2d 666, 26 A.L.R. Fed. 848, rehearing denied 503 F.2d 567, rehearing denied Eller and Company, Inc. v. Legnos, 503 F.2d 567, rehearing denied 503 F.2d 567, rehearing denied Schiffahrtsgesellschaft Jacob & Co. v. Eller and Company, Inc., 503 F.2d 568, affirmed 535 F.2d 857, rehearing denied 540 F.2d 1085.

Fact that vessel's crew and local fire fighter groups acted promptly and efficiently to extinguish fire and that there were more than adequate numbers of competent fire personnel on scene bore on contribution made by stevedore's employees, if any, and the relative value toward successful extinguishment of fire, but did not warrant denial of salvage award on ground that there was no peril, where bottom of lower hold where fire started and burned contained highly combustible materials, and had fire not been extinguished it was just a question of time until the fire would have spread throughout the hold.

Legnos v. M/V Olga Jacob, 498 F.2d 666, 26 A.L.R. Fed. 848, rehearing denied 503 F.2d 567, rehearing denied Eller and Company, Inc. v. Legnos, 503 F.2d 567, rehearing denied 503 F.2d 567, rehearing denied

Schiffahrtsgesellschaft Jacob & Co. v. Eller and Company, Inc., 503 F.2d 568, affirmed 535 F.2d 857, rehearing denied 540 F.2d 1085.

C.A.5 (Fla.) 1968. The test of "marine peril" as basis for recovery for salvage is not whether the peril is imminent, but whether it is reasonably to be apprehended, and vessel stranded so that it is subject to potential danger of damage or destruction may be a subject of salvage services.

> Fort Myers Shell & Dredging Co. v. Barge NBC 512, 404 F.2d 137.

S.D.Fla. 2013. A marine peril exists in an ancient, abandoned shipwreck, as element of a valid salvage claim.

> JTR Enterprises, LLC v. An Unknown Quantity of Colombian Emeralds, Amethysts and Quartz Crystals, 922 F.Supp.2d 1326, appeal dismissed (11th cir. 13-10870).

The law of salvage calls for a "marine peril," and that element may be satisfied by an ancient, abandoned shipwreck.

> JTR Enterprises, LLC v. An Unknown Quantity of Colombian Emeralds, Amethysts and Quartz Crystals, 922 F.Supp.2d 1326, appeal dismissed (11th cir. 13-10870).

Treasure hunters failed to establish existence of a marine peril, as required to recover a salvage award in connection with gems they discovered on the floor of the Gulf of Mexico, where there was no shipwreck, and no other proof that the gems were ever lost in the first place.

> JTR Enterprises, LLC v. An Unknown Quantity of Colombian Emeralds, Amethysts and Quartz Crystals, 922 F.Supp.2d 1326, appeal dismissed (11th cir. 13-10870).

S.D.Fla. 2007. For purposes of a salvage claim, "maritime peril" (or "marine peril") exists where a ship is in a situation that might expose her to loss or destruction; no peril exists where there is no reasonable apprehension for her safety in the future if left to her own unaided efforts.

> Atlantis Marine Towing, Inc. v. THE M/V PRISCILLA, 491 F.Supp.2d 1096.

S.D.Fla. 2004. For purposes of assessing claim for salvage, fire aboard vessel is classic "marine peril."

> Atlantis Marine Towing, Inc. v. M/V/ELZABETH, 346 F.Supp.2d 1266.

S.D.Fla. 2003. A "marine peril" exists, for purposes of salvage claim, where a vessel is in danger of being partially or totally lost through the action of the elements and where it is not being successfully salved when the plaintiff voluntarily undertakes its salvage operation.

> Southernmost Marine Services, Inc. v. One (1) 2000 Fifty Four Foot (54') Sea Ray named M/V POTENTIAL, 250 F.Supp.2d 1367, affirmed Southernmost Marine Svcs. v. M/V POTENTIAL, 91 Fed.Appx. 655.

Because vessel was in peril of sinking and breaking apart if it had been simply pulled off its impaled position on massive rock jetty, without the prior affixing of substantial floatation gear, it was subject to "marine peril" for purposes of salvage claim.

> Southernmost Marine Services, Inc. v. One (1) 2000 Fifty Four Foot (54') Sea Ray named M/V POTENTIAL, 250 F.Supp.2d 1367, affirmed Southernmost Marine Svcs. v. M/V POTENTIAL, 91 Fed.Appx. 655.

S.D.Fla. 1995. To determine whether maritime peril existed, as required to establish claim for salvage award, court examines whether, at time that assistance was rendered, ship was in situation that might expose her to loss or destruction, however, danger need not be immediate or actual, but rather, all that is necessary is reasonable apprehension of peril.

> Fine v. Rockwood, 895 F.Supp. 306.

If vessel has situation under control such that there is no reasonable apprehension for safety in future if left to her own unaided efforts, then there is absence of maritime peril, precluding recovery on claim of salvage award.

> Fine v. Rockwood, 895 F.Supp. 306.

Submerged boat was not in maritime peril as required for scuba divers to have been entitled to salvage award for their aid in salvage operation, since weather was clear, sea was calm, boat was secured to dock and settled on channel bottom, and boat was not exposed to loss or destruction, or reasonable apprehension for her future safety, despite hole in hull.

Fine v. Rockwood, 895 F.Supp. 306.

S.D.Fla. 1984. In determining whether a would-be salvor is entitled to an award under admiralty law salvage doctrine, court must determine that there was maritime peril, that claimant's service was voluntarily rendered and not required by duty or contract, that there was success in whole or part, with service rendered having contributed to success, and that claimant was not responsible for causing condition putting vessel in peril.

Unnamed But Identifiable Master and Crew of That Certain U.S. Documented Vessel Bearing Documentation No. 567135 v. Certain Unnamed Motor Vessel Bearing Florida Registration No. FL5607 EM, 592 F.Supp. 1191.

Where claimants did not in any way force crew out of vessel as claimants approached, even though crew may have left vessel out of belief that claimants were some type of governmental or police officials, where vessel was in peril following departure of crew, since it was taking on water and in danger of sinking, and where service rendered voluntarily by claimants did in fact prevent vessel from possibly sinking or being apprehended by individuals who later approached in small motorboat and attempted to board and offload illegal cargo from vessel, claimants were entitled to award of salvage from United States, which had obtained forfeiture of vessel.

Unnamed But Identifiable Master and Crew of That Certain U.S. Documented Vessel Bearing Documentation No. 567135 v. Certain Unnamed Motor Vessel Bearing Florida Registration No. FL5607 EM, 592 F.Supp. 1191.

S.D.Fla. 1982. Marine peril exists in an ancient, abandoned shipwreck for purposes of meeting the requirements of a valid salvage action, even where the general location of the wreck is known.

Cobb Coin Co., Inc. v. Unidentified, Wrecked and Abandoned Sailing Vessel, 549 F.Supp. 540.

Wrecked Spanish treasure galleon was subject to a "marine peril" for purposes of plaintiff's salvage claim, even though its site was known and it was subject to prior salvage efforts, where it still was in peril of being lost through the action of the elements or of pirates and was not being successfully salved when plaintiff undertook its salvage operation.

Cobb Coin Co., Inc. v. Unidentified, Wrecked and Abandoned Sailing Vessel, 549 F.Supp. 540.

S.D.Fla. 1981. A "marine peril" includes more than threat of storm, fire or piracy to a vessel in navigation and includes a vessel which is discovered after being lost but is still in peril of being lost through actions of the elements.

Treasure Salvors, Inc. v. Unidentified Wrecked and Abandoned Sailing Vessel, 546 F.Supp. 919.

Activities of plaintiffs with respect to their search of ancient shipwreck as salvors and/or treasure hunters satisfied all elements for establishing a "marine peril" and, hence, constituted a salvage operation within the meaning of the law.

Treasure Salvors, Inc. v. Unidentified Wrecked and Abandoned Sailing Vessel, 546 F.Supp. 919.

⚷6. **Nature of service.**

⚷7. —— **In general.**

S.D.Fla. 1995. Salvage service includes towage, stranding, fire fighting, recovery of cargo, life salvage, supplying men and stores, standing by or securing aid, giving advice, pilotage, preventing collision, recapture from enemies, pirates and privateers, and raising sunken craft and property.

Fine v. Rockwood, 895 F.Supp. 306.

Averting environmental pollution by itself is insufficient basis for salvage claim.

Fine v. Rockwood, 895 F.Supp. 306.

S.D.Fla. 1993. Salvor that rescued distressed vessel had valid salvage claim against vessel owners, where vessel would have sunk without salvor's efforts, salvor was not under prior obligation to vessel or its owners but responded voluntarily pursuant to its business practice of monitoring emergency radio channel and responding to distress calls, and entered into oral "no cure, no pay" agreement with owner.

Ocean Services Towing and Salvage, Inc. v. Brown, 810 F.Supp. 1258.

S.D.Fla. 1991. That salvor is motivated by opportunity for material gain does not prevent him from receiving award in salvage, so long as salvor can establish conditions of salvage.

Flagship Marine Services, Inc. v. Belcher Towing Co., 761 F.Supp. 792, reversed 966 F.2d 602, opinion vacated, appeal dismissed, opinion reinstated 23 F.3d 341.

S.D.Fla. 1988. Efforts by pleasure boater in attempting to tow, drive, and anchor unmanned vessel was a "salvage"; pleasure boater was under no duty to salvage vessel, vessel was in minimal apprehension of danger, even though not in an immediate or absolute danger, and boater's action of calling Coast Guard and staying with vessel until Coast Guard arrived contributed to success of salvage operation.

Hernandez v. Roberts, 675 F.Supp. 1329.

S.D.Fla. 1984. Fact that would-be salvors may have been motivated by opportunity for material gain does not prevent them from receiving an award in salvage where existence of salvage conditions of peril, voluntary service, and success is proven.

Unnamed But Identifiable Master and Crew of That Certain U.S. Documented Vessel Bearing Documentation No. 567135 v. Certain Unnamed Motor Vessel Bearing Florida Registration No. FL5607 EM, 592 F.Supp. 1191.

S.D.Fla. 1981. Federal admiralty procedures did not sanction salvaging methods which fail to safeguard items and invaluable archeological information associated with the artifacts salved.

Cobb Coin Co., Inc. v. Unidentified, Wrecked and Abandoned Sailing Vessel, 525 F.Supp. 186.

⚲8. —— **Peril at sea.**

C.A.11 (Fla.) 2000. Party states valid claim for a salvage award if it renders

voluntary assistance that contributes to the rescue of a vessel in marine peril.

International Aircraft Recovery, L.L.C. v. Unidentified, Wrecked and Abandoned Aircraft, 218 F.3d 1255, certiorari denied International Aircraft Recovery, LLC v. U.S., 121 S.Ct. 1079, 531 U.S. 1144, 148 L.Ed.2d 956, appeal after remand 373 F.3d 1147.

S.D.Fla. 1991. In order for valid salvage claim to exist, there must be maritime peril from which ship or other property could not have been rescued without salvor's assistance; voluntary act by salvor under no legal or contractual duty to owner; and success in saving, or in helping to save at least part of property at risk.

Flagship Marine Services, Inc. v. Belcher Towing Co., 761 F.Supp. 792, reversed 966 F.2d 602, opinion vacated, appeal dismissed, opinion reinstated 23 F.3d 341.

S.D.Fla. 1984. Action of the United States Navy, despite court's finding that Navy should have called Coast Guard sooner, would support award of salvor's lien to the Navy, plaintiff's unmanned sailboat having been in sinking condition at time of its being sighted by submarine, and needing to be pumped out, and Navy having made considerable efforts to salvage the sailboat. 14 U.S.C.A. § 88.

Port Tack Sailboats, Inc. v. U.S., 593 F.Supp. 597.

⚲9. —— **Stranding.**

S.D.Fla. 1980. Because vessel was hard aground when pilot came aboard, and thus not capable of being piloted, pilot was under no preexisting duty to render assistance as would preclude award for salvage services performed.

Jackson v. Costa Lines, Inc., 490 F.Supp. 393, affirmed 667 F.2d 97.

⚲10. —— **Fire.**

For other cases see earlier editions of this digest, the Decennial Digests, and WEST-LAW.

⚲11. —— **Sunken vessel or cargo.**

C.A.5 (Fla.) 1978. Where unidentified wrecked and abandoned vessel was thought to be Spanish vessel which sank in

---

† This Case was not selected for publication in the National Reporter System
For legislative history of cited statutes, see Florida Statutes Annotated

1622 and whose location was unknown for over 300 years, "marine peril" existed, even after discovery of vessel's location, since vessel was still in peril of being lost through actions of the elements.

> Treasure Salvors, Inc. v. Unidentified Wrecked and Abandoned Sailing Vessel, 569 F.2d 330.

⚷12. —— Recapture.

For other cases see earlier editions of this digest, the Decennial Digests, and WEST-LAW.

⚷13. —— Towage.

S.D.Fla. 1980. A pilot, while acting in strict line of his duty, cannot be entitled to claim salvage.

> Jackson v. Costa Lines, Inc., 490 F.Supp. 393, affirmed 667 F.2d 97.

When pilot performs salvage services beyond line of his appropriate duties, or under circumstances to which those duties do not justly attach, he stands in relation to the property as any other salvor.

> Jackson v. Costa Lines, Inc., 490 F.Supp. 393, affirmed 667 F.2d 97.

S.D.Fla. 1951. Where motor vessel was adrift on high seas with perishable cargo of green bananas, without means of propulsion or communication, and was in distress at time it was taken in tow by another vessel, but weather was good, sea was calm and wind was gentle, assistance which was rendered to adrift vessel was salvage service, but of low order.

> Higgins, Inc. v. The Tri-State, 99 F.Supp. 694.

⚷14. —— Saving life.

For other cases see earlier editions of this digest, the Decennial Digests, and WEST-LAW.

⚷15. Request for or acceptance of services.

C.A.11 (Fla.) 2004. Letter written by the director of the National Museum of Naval Aviation, as assignee of whatever rights the Navy had in sunken torpedo bomber, to would-be salvor, advising the latter that any attempt at salvaging this torpedo bomber, without express written permission of the Navy, would result in whatever action was appropriate to pre-vent unauthorized taking, operated as effective rejection of salvage services, so that would-be salvor was not entitled to be compensated for any salvage services which it provided, after receiving this letter, without a written agreement with the Navy.

> International Aircraft Recovery, L.L.C. v. Unidentified, Wrecked and Abandoned Aircraft, 373 F.3d 1147.

C.A.11 (Fla.) 2000. United States, as owner of Navy torpedo bomber that had crashed in international waters during World War II, could prohibit salvage efforts, and salvage company had no right to continue salvage operations over the express objections of the plane's owner, even if rejecting salvage services would not be prudent, even if government had not made alternative plans to recover the aircraft, and even if bomber, which was submerged in a corrosive environment and slowly disintegrating, was in a state of marine peril.

> International Aircraft Recovery, L.L.C. v. Unidentified, Wrecked and Abandoned Aircraft, 218 F.3d 1255, certiorari denied International Aircraft Recovery, LLC v. U.S., 121 S.Ct. 1079, 531 U.S. 1144, 148 L.Ed.2d 956, appeal after remand 373 F.3d 1147.

Though salvor can attempt salvage of vessel in distress without the prior assent of the ship's owner or master, this does not mean that an owner cannot reject salvage assistance in a timely manner.

> International Aircraft Recovery, L.L.C. v. Unidentified, Wrecked and Abandoned Aircraft, 218 F.3d 1255, certiorari denied International Aircraft Recovery, LLC v. U.S., 121 S.Ct. 1079, 531 U.S. 1144, 148 L.Ed.2d 956, appeal after remand 373 F.3d 1147.

The law of salvage permits the owner of a vessel in marine peril to decline the assistance of others so long as only the owner's property interests are at stake.

> International Aircraft Recovery, L.L.C. v. Unidentified, Wrecked and Abandoned Aircraft, 218 F.3d 1255, certiorari denied International Aircraft

Recovery, LLC v. U.S., 121 S.Ct. 1079, 531 U.S. 1144, 148 L.Ed.2d 956, appeal after remand 373 F.3d 1147.

Although salvage company had no right to continue salvage operations with respect to military aircraft that crashed in international waters in 1943, over the express objection of the United States which owned the plane, the company could potentially be eligible for salvage award for past salvage efforts, depending on when the United States rejected salvage efforts, where plane had been in state of marine peril since company's owner learned of its location, company owner's efforts to recover the plane were not based on a legal duty or contractual obligation, and he had taken constructive steps toward the ultimate preservation of the aircraft.

International Aircraft Recovery, L.L.C. v. Unidentified, Wrecked and Abandoned Aircraft, 218 F.3d 1255, certiorari denied International Aircraft Recovery, LLC v. U.S., 121 S.Ct. 1079, 531 U.S. 1144, 148 L.Ed.2d 956, appeal after remand 373 F.3d 1147.

C.A.11 (Fla.) 1985. Where it was possible that the United States as owner of submerged 18th century English vessel in public park might not even have desired for the property to be "rescued" and where plaintiff in moving articles from the shipwreck site did not mark or identify them so as to preserve their archeological provenience, salvage award was properly denied. 16 U.S.C.A. §§ 1, 431; Archeological Resources Protection Act of 1979, § 2 et seq., 16 U.S.C.A. § 470aa et seq.

Klein v. Unidentified Wrecked and Abandoned Sailing Vessel, 758 F.2d 1511.

C.A.5 (Fla.) 1974. Whether actions of individuals seeking salvage award were sought by ship's master or other fire fighters or persons superintending the operations was not determinative of validity of salvage claim.

Legnos v. M/V Olga Jacob, 498 F.2d 666, 26 A.L.R. Fed. 848, rehearing denied 503 F.2d 567, rehearing denied Eller and Company, Inc. v. Legnos, 503 F.2d 567, rehearing denied 503 F.2d 567, rehearing denied

Schiffahrtsgesellschaft Jacob & Co. v. Eller and Company, Inc., 503 F.2d 568, affirmed 535 F.2d 857, rehearing denied 540 F.2d 1085.

So long as services are voluntary and are not rejected by those in authority, a bystander or interloper is eligible for salvage award in proportion to value of his contributory efforts.

Legnos v. M/V Olga Jacob, 498 F.2d 666, 26 A.L.R. Fed. 848, rehearing denied 503 F.2d 567, rehearing denied Eller and Company, Inc. v. Legnos, 503 F.2d 567, rehearing denied 503 F.2d 567, rehearing denied Schiffahrtsgesellschaft Jacob & Co. v. Eller and Company, Inc., 503 F.2d 568, affirmed 535 F.2d 857, rehearing denied 540 F.2d 1085.

M.D.Fla. 1993. Potential salvors do not have inherent right to save distressed vessels, but rather salvage award may be denied if salvor forces its services on vessel despite rejection by owner or by person with authority.

Lathrop v. Unidentified, Wrecked & Abandoned Vessel, 817 F.Supp. 953.

Doctrine of rejection normally applies when master of distressed vessel directly and unequivocally rejects salvor's services; salvor who continues efforts to rescue vessel after master has communicated rejection will not be entitled to salvage award.

Lathrop v. Unidentified, Wrecked & Abandoned Vessel, 817 F.Supp. 953.

Constructive rejection of salvage services bars award if rejection was reasonably understood by salvor.

Lathrop v. Unidentified, Wrecked & Abandoned Vessel, 817 F.Supp. 953.

Salvor, who typically acts as agent for vessel's owner, acquires right to possess abandoned shipwreck but does not acquire title; title remains with owner as does right to refuse salvage.

Lathrop v. Unidentified, Wrecked & Abandoned Vessel, 817 F.Supp. 953.

Salvor should have known that Florida, as presumed owner of submerged lands and any property embedded in soil, might refuse offer to excavate alleged vessel where state had dedicated its land to government to establish national park and government had authority to manage and protect land, marine life, and historic arti-facts from damage caused by dredging or excavating; even without decision as to ownership, salvor must reasonably have known that state rejected offer of salvage services.

> Lathrop v. Unidentified, Wrecked & Abandoned Vessel, 817 F.Supp. 953.

S.D.Fla. 2003. Actions of salvors and vessel owner's insurance company, the exchange of confirming letter detailing the negotiations between the parties and the mailing of the check in full payment of the salvage services rendered met all the requirements of Florida law for the for-mation of a valid binding contract; accep-tance of settlement agreement was effec-tive upon the salvors' issuance transmittal of faxed letter, or as of the time insurance company sent out the settlement check to salvors via overnight mail.

> Southernmost Marine Services, Inc. v. One (1) 2000 Fifty Four Foot (54') Sea Ray named M/V POTENTIAL, 250 F.Supp.2d 1367, affirmed Southernmost Marine Svcs. v. M/V POTENTIAL, 91 Fed.Appx. 655.

S.D.Fla. 1999. Owner may not refuse services of a voluntary salvor if a prudent man would have accepted.

> International Aircraft Recovery, L.L.C. v. Unidentified, Wrecked and Aban-doned Aircraft, 54 F.Supp.2d 1172, reversed 218 F.3d 1255, certiorari denied International Aircraft Recov-ery, LLC v. U.S., 121 S.Ct. 1079, 531 U.S. 1144, 148 L.Ed.2d 956, appeal after remand 373 F.3d 1147.

S.D.Fla. 1995. Scuba divers were en-titled to quantum meruit compensation for their aid and assistance to submerged boat and its crew, to encourage assistance of vessels in distress, even though they did not qualify for salvage award.

> Fine v. Rockwood, 895 F.Supp. 306.

S.D.Fla. 1983. So long as owner or his agent remains in possession, he is entitled to refuse unwelcome offers of sal-vage.

> Klein v. Unidentified, Wrecked and Abandoned Sailing Vessel, 568 F.Supp. 1562, affirmed 758 F.2d 1511.

☞16. Services rendered under contract.

C.A.11 (Fla.) 1992. In order to make out claim for pure salvage, as opposed to contract salvage, salvor must establish three elements: marine peril; service vol-untarily rendered when not required as existing duty or from special contracts; and success in whole or in part, or service contributing to such success.

> Flagship Marine Services, Inc. v. Bel-cher Towing Co., 966 F.2d 602, opinion vacated, appeal dismissed, opinion reinstated 23 F.3d 341.

Verbal exchange between captain of damaged tug and captain of salvor vessel created valid oral agreement which barred salvor from recovering award on basis of pure voluntary salvage; although there was no contract to pay given sum for services rendered, following verbal ex-change salvor was no longer assuming "no cure, no pay" risks associated with pure voluntary salvage and was entitled to com-pensation from damaged vessel at reason-able price and rate to be determined later.

> Flagship Marine Services, Inc. v. Bel-cher Towing Co., 966 F.2d 602, opinion vacated, appeal dismissed, opinion reinstated 23 F.3d 341.

C.A.5 (Fla.) 1968. Fact that shipown-er requests salvage service and that salvors in response furnish it, standing alone, does not create an implied contract so as to defeat salvage claim.

> Fort Myers Shell & Dredging Co. v. Barge NBC 512, 404 F.2d 137.

S.D.Fla. 1984. In righting, refloating and transporting barge ultimately to jetty at Port Moin, plaintiff salvage company satisfied and fulfilled obligations which it undertook in executing marine salvage contract, despite defendant's contention that since barge turned out to be worth-less, and since it was left on a nearby jetty unable even to be scrapped, there was no "cure," and salvage operation was not successful in whole or in part, in that engine might have been taken from barge before capsizing, barge was rusted, barge was clearly a marine peril, and plaintiff attempted to obtain permission to leave barge at several locations other than on jetty and, moreover, parties in using the term "cure" clearly did not intend refurbishing or restoration of the vessel.

Sea Lift, Inc. v. Refinadora Costarricense De Petroleo, S.A., 601 F.Supp. 457, reversed 792 F.2d 989.

S.D.Fla. 1983. Where salvage company and vessel captain had contracted before concerning same type of exploration and salvaging contract, where parties met during period of precontract negotiations to discuss location of lost Spanish galleon and marked their "best guesses" as to location of galleon on map of area in which it was reported to have gone down, and where captain's course of performance under contract was to explore for location of galleon, parties' intention in entering into contract of employment was to allow captain as salvage company's employee to locate remains of galleon and begin salvage operations, not solely to begin salvage operations.

Treasure Salvors, Inc. v. Unidentified, Wrecked and Abandoned Sailing Vessel, 556 F.Supp. 1319.

Contract employing vessel captain to explore and begin salvage operations on Spanish galleon was not voidable on ground of material misrepresentation of fact concerning status of ownership or location of galleon wrecksite where purpose of contract was to pinpoint location of wrecked galleon and where captain knew purpose of his employment was to ripen employer's ownership in wrecksite and where, even if there was a material misrepresentation, captain had affirmed contract by accepting its benefits.

Treasure Salvors, Inc. v. Unidentified, Wrecked and Abandoned Sailing Vessel, 556 F.Supp. 1319.

Vessel captain breached fiduciary duty owed to salvage company which had hired him to search for location of sunken Spanish galleon and also breached contract of employment with salvage company by failing to deliver salvaged treasures and artifacts to salvage company as lawful custodian and by attempting to establish claim to galleon while under salvage company's salaried employ and while using company's information, fuel, food, crew, and equipment; accordingly, captain forfeited any right to equitable consideration under

theory of quantum meruit for services rendered after date of breach.

Treasure Salvors, Inc. v. Unidentified, Wrecked and Abandoned Sailing Vessel, 556 F.Supp. 1319.

S.D.Fla. 1982. Whether it was working under a contract for salvage or voluntarily, salvor and its assignors waived federal rights to salvage award, with respect to artifacts salved prior to institution of the instant lawsuit, by operating expressly under a contract with state in whose territorial waters the wreck was located.

Cobb Coin Co., Inc. v. Unidentified, Wrecked and Abandoned Sailing Vessel, 549 F.Supp. 540.

S.D.Fla. 1951. Where motor vessel was adrift on high seas with perishable cargo of green bananas, without means of propulsion or communication, and captain of salvaging vessel would only tow distressed vessel to his port of destination, required execution of salvage agreement stating that such tow had to be made and required signing of statement which exaggerated conditions of wind, sea and dangers to vessels and their cargoes before surrendering towed vessel, salvage agreement and statement were procured by master of salvaging vessel under circumstances of moral compulsion and were invalid and unenforceable.

Higgins, Inc. v. The Tri-State, 99 F.Supp. 694.

Fla.App. 2 Dist. 1988. Contract, which contained provision in which company agreed to pursue search and salvage operations "until January 1, 1975 or until operations are no longer profitable" and which contained second provision which stated that "agreement expires January 1, 1975, unless mutually extended by written agreement at that time," was not ambiguous, and was to remain in force until January 1, 1975 unless salvage operations became unprofitable prior to that date.

Treasure Salvors, Inc. v. Tilley, 534 So.2d 834.

☞17. Beneficial result of services.

† **C.A.11 (Fla.) 2012.** Salvor's efforts to rescue capsized, mostly submerged yacht were successful, entitling salvor to a salvage award; salvor's efforts in towing the boat to a harbor led to a professional

salvage company's righting and pumping of the yacht a few days later, and but for salvor's voluntary actions, yacht would have likely sunk in 6,000 feet of water, drifted further into open sea, been struck by another vessel, or would have run aground in nearby reefs.

> Esoteric, LLC v. One (1) 2000 Eighty-Five Foot Azimut Motor Yacht Named M/V STAR ONE, 478 Fed. Appx. 639.

C.A.11 (Fla.) 1992. In order to make out claim for pure salvage, as opposed to contract salvage, salvor must establish three elements: marine peril; service voluntarily rendered when not required as existing duty or from special contracts; and success in whole or in part, or service contributing to such success.

> Flagship Marine Services, Inc. v. Belcher Towing Co., 966 F.2d 602, opinion vacated, appeal dismissed, opinion reinstated 23 F.3d 341.

C.A.11 (Fla.) 1985. Where it was possible that the United States as owner of submerged 18th century English vessel in public park might not even have desired for the property to be "rescued" and where plaintiff in moving articles from the shipwreck site did not mark or identify them so as to preserve their archeological provenience, salvage award was properly denied. 16 U.S.C.A. §§ 1, 431; Archeological Resources Protection Act of 1979, § 2 et seq., 16 U.S.C.A. § 470aa et seq.

> Klein v. Unidentified Wrecked and Abandoned Sailing Vessel, 758 F.2d 1511.

S.D.Fla. 1991. In order for valid salvage claim to exist, there must be maritime peril from which ship or other property could not have been rescued without salvor's assistance; voluntary act by salvor under no legal or contractual duty to owner; and success in saving, or in helping to save at least part of property at risk.

> Flagship Marine Services, Inc. v. Belcher Towing Co., 761 F.Supp. 792, reversed 966 F.2d 602, opinion vacated, appeal dismissed, opinion reinstated 23 F.3d 341.

S.D.Fla. 1984. In determining whether a would-be salvor is entitled to an award under admiralty law salvage doctrine, court must determine that there was

maritime peril, that claimant's service was voluntarily rendered and not required by duty or contract, that there was success in whole or part, with service rendered having contributed to success, and that claimant was not responsible for causing condition putting vessel in peril.

> Unnamed But Identifiable Master and Crew of That Certain U.S. Documented Vessel Bearing Documentation No. 567135 v. Certain Unnamed Motor Vessel Bearing Florida Registration No. FL5607 EM, 592 F.Supp. 1191.

S.D.Fla. 1971. Where barge was not ballasted by pumping operations initiated by resident engineer of hotel and reporter for local newspaper who had boarded barge in front of hotel property and dropping of anchor with anchor line vertically extended from barge to water was ineffectual and marine surveyor testified unequivocally that salvage efforts of resident engineer of hotel and reporter did not prevent barge from going ashore, resident engineer of hotel and reporter were not entitled to salvage award because their efforts did not deliver barge from peril nor preserve it from damage, even partially.

> Crawford v. West India Carriers, Inc., 337 F.Supp. 262, reversed Twenty Grand Offshore, Inc. v. West India Carriers, Inc., 492 F.2d 679, certiorari denied 95 S.Ct. 63, 419 U.S. 836, 42 L.Ed.2d 63.

🔑**18. Vessels and persons entitled to compensation.**

C.A.11 (Fla.) 2000. Although salvage company had no right to continue salvage operations with respect to military aircraft that crashed in international waters in 1943, over the express objection of the United States which owned the plane, the company could potentially be eligible for salvage award for past salvage efforts, depending on when the United States rejected salvage efforts, where plane had been in state of marine peril since company's owner learned of its location, company owner's efforts to recover the plane were not based on a legal duty or contractual obligation, and he had taken constructive steps toward the ultimate preservation of the aircraft.

International Aircraft Recovery, L.L.C. v. Unidentified, Wrecked and Abandoned Aircraft, 218 F.3d 1255, certiorari denied International Aircraft Recovery, LLC v. U.S., 121 S.Ct. 1079, 531 U.S. 1144, 148 L.Ed.2d 956, appeal after remand 373 F.3d 1147.

S.D.Fla. 2007. Statute vesting power in district court judges of Florida to issue licenses to salvage on the coast of Florida directed the district court judges of Florida to act in the capacity of commissioners who were officers of the United States. 46 U.S.C.A. § 80102.

In re Beck, 526 F.Supp.2d 1291.

S.D.Fla. 2004. Salvor was successful in saving, or helping to save, in whole or in part, yacht, and thus salvor was entitled to salvage award, despite witness's testimony that city fire department extinguished fire by itself, where evidence from other witnesses demonstrated that salvor arrived at marina several minutes before fire trucks and commenced spraying yacht with water, smoke emanating from yacht changed from black to gray prior to fire department's arrival, and salvor's actions minimized ultimate damage to yacht and prevented potential explosion.

Atlantis Marine Towing, Inc. v. M/V/ELIZABETH, 346 F.Supp.2d 1266.

S.D.Fla. 1999. In order to state a claim for a salvage award on a historic aircraft, it is an essential element that the salvors document to admiralty court's satisfaction that they have made adequate provision, and have the funding necessary, to recover the aircraft in such a way as to minimize further damage to the in rem defendant because of the recovery operation; further, salvor must make adequate provisions for the stabilization and preservation of the remains of the historic aircraft after recovery.

International Aircraft Recovery, L.L.C. v. Unidentified, Wrecked and Abandoned Aircraft, 54 F.Supp.2d 1172, reversed 218 F.3d 1255, certiorari denied International Aircraft Recovery, LLC v. U.S., 121 S.Ct. 1079, 531 U.S. 1144, 148 L.Ed.2d 956, appeal after remand 373 F.3d 1147.

S.D.Fla. 1983. Once in possession and control of identifiable wrecksite, exclusive right to recover on continuing basis depends upon intent of salvor to do so and his proven capacity to continue recovery.

Treasure Salvors, Inc. v. Unidentified, Wrecked and Abandoned Sailing Vessel, 556 F.Supp. 1319.

Rights of salvor who continues uninterrupted operations on identifiable wrecksite are dependent upon its demonstration of that degree of dominion and control which is appropriate under the circumstances.

Treasure Salvors, Inc. v. Unidentified, Wrecked and Abandoned Sailing Vessel, 556 F.Supp. 1319.

Salvor whose employees first discovered wrecksite containing scattered remains of Spanish galleon during their employment for that purpose was entitled to all rights of first finder since, through its agents and employees, it had been in continuous possession and control of wrecksite, had brought discovered artifacts and treasure into custody of federal district court, and had preserved archeological provenance of shipwreck and demonstrated its competence to satisfactorily salvage remains of vessel.

Treasure Salvors, Inc. v. Unidentified, Wrecked and Abandoned Sailing Vessel, 556 F.Supp. 1319.

Salvage company was entitled to salvage award for articles retrieved from Spanish galleon wrecksite where company voluntarily rendered salvage service and successfully saved property of considerable historic, archeological, and monetary value.

Treasure Salvors, Inc. v. Unidentified, Wrecked and Abandoned Sailing Vessel, 556 F.Supp. 1319.

S.D.Fla. 1982. Under the maritime law of salvage, salvor has the right to search and explore navigable waters for salvageable sites and upon "finding" a site which is not being actively and successfully worked by another salvor, may undertake to rescue the imperiled cargo and bring it before admiralty court for determination of salvage award, and salvor is entitled to protection of the court to continue working wreck as long as he exercis-

es such complete and continuous possession as the circumstances dictate and
demonstrates reasonable success in saving
the valuables from their peril.

> Cobb Coin Co., Inc. v. Unidentified,
> Wrecked and Abandoned Sailing
> Vessel, 549 F.Supp. 540.

⊶19. Different sets of salvors, and successive salvors.

C.A.5 (Fla.) 1981.   Original salvor
has right to exclude others from participating in salvage operations, so long as
original salvor appears ready, willing and
able to complete salvage project, and has
right to possession of salved property, a
right exclusive even of owner, until such
time as salvage lien on property is extinguished or adequate security for this obligation is given.

> Treasure Salvors, Inc. v. Unidentified
> Wrecked & Abandoned Sailing Ves-
> sel, 640 F.2d 560, on remand 546
> F.Supp. 919.

M.D.Fla. 2010.   Enforcement of an
exclusive right to salvage in international
water depends on the eventual arrival of
the person or property at issue within the
territorial jurisdiction.

> Odyssey Marine Exploration, Inc. v.
> Unidentified, Wrecked and Aban-
> doned   Sailing   Vessel,   727
> F.Supp.2d 1341.

Under the law of finds, a finder cannot exclude others from their attempts to
obtain first possession of artifacts recovered from an abandoned wreck; in contrast, the law of salvage grants exclusive
possession to ensure that the salvor recovers the owner's property intact, and this
need supports the exercise of extra-territorial jurisdiction.

> Odyssey Marine Exploration, Inc. v.
> Unidentified, Wrecked and Aban-
> doned   Sailing   Vessel,   727
> F.Supp.2d 1341.

S.D.Fla. 1986.   If a first finder maintains appropriate possession and control
of an identifiable abandoned wreck site, he
may acquire exclusive right to continue
recoveries.

> MDM Salvage, Inc. v. Unidentified,
> Wrecked and Abandoned Sailing
> Vessel, 631 F.Supp. 308.

In a first finder situation, law of finds
and salvage merge to give first finder/sal-
vor sole possession of property.

> MDM Salvage, Inc. v. Unidentified,
> Wrecked and Abandoned Sailing
> Vessel, 631 F.Supp. 308.

If wreck site and recoveries are
brought within jurisdiction of federal
court, salvor's exclusive right to possess
can be protected by enjoining subsequent
rival salvors from interfering with current
salvor's efforts; to enjoy continued right to
exclusive possession and protection, salvor
must exercise due diligence and must be
capable of actually saving property, intending to reduce it to physical possession
by dealing with entire wreck site in such
manner as to warn other potential salvors
of claimed area.

> MDM Salvage, Inc. v. Unidentified,
> Wrecked and Abandoned Sailing
> Vessel, 631 F.Supp. 308.

One who discovers, but does not assiduously undertake to rescue abandoned
property, may lose right to uninterrupted
salvage operations; notorious possession
is prerequisite to creation and maintenance of salvor's privilege.

> MDM Salvage, Inc. v. Unidentified,
> Wrecked and Abandoned Sailing
> Vessel, 631 F.Supp. 308.

Neither of two salvors was entitled to
exclusive salvage rights to search various
areas of ocean for vessel or vessels, possible existence of which in the area had
been common knowledge for 25 years,
when parties had not been actively salvaging the sites for sufficient number of days,
had not invested sufficient capital in respective projects and had not sought to
reserve archaeological integrity of area or
exercise dominion or control over areas
claimed.

> MDM Salvage, Inc. v. Unidentified,
> Wrecked and Abandoned Sailing
> Vessel, 631 F.Supp. 308.

S.D.Fla. 1982.   Salvor's presence on
site prior to filing of its in rem suit to
determine its salvage rights and its participation in state leases on site prior to that
date were irrelevant to determination of its
rights in the admiralty action where all

previous "finders" or "salvors" of the wreck had abandoned it.

> Cobb Coin Co., Inc. v. Unidentified, Wrecked and Abandoned Sailing Vessel, 549 F.Supp. 540.

Prior salvor of wrecked Spanish treasure galleon abandoned salvage, not by relinquishment of state lease, but by cessation of active searching and salvaging efforts, and subsequent salvor did not exercise requisite diligence or success necessary to obtain right to continue salvaging under the protection of the admiralty court.

> Cobb Coin Co., Inc. v. Unidentified, Wrecked and Abandoned Sailing Vessel, 549 F.Supp. 540.

S.D.Fla. 1981. Defendants, who neither possessed capability to, nor historically cultivated information to, direct them to the site of ancient shipwreck, and who relied solely on information divulged to them by plaintiffs and learned from on-site salvage operations for plaintiffs, could not be permitted to indiscriminately compete with plaintiffs without affording protection to first finder since to do so would constitute unjust enrichment.

> Treasure Salvors, Inc. v. Unidentified Wrecked and Abandoned Sailing Vessel, 546 F.Supp. 919.

S.D.Fla. 1981. Salvage law permits one whose salvage efforts are continuous and reasonably diligent to work a wreck site to the exclusion of others but, until discovery and subsequent dominion of the site occurs, no one may be restricted from exploring the navigable waters for salvageable sites.

> Cobb Coin Co., Inc. v. Unidentified, Wrecked and Abandoned Sailing Vessel, 525 F.Supp. 186.

Action of potential salvor in recovering 16 silver coins from wreck site in two years of salvage operations and working for 49 days in those two years were insufficient to give it the right to exclude competing salvors.

> Cobb Coin Co., Inc. v. Unidentified, Wrecked and Abandoned Sailing Vessel, 525 F.Supp. 186.

In order for a salvor to enjoy continued right to exclusive possession, it must exercise due diligence and be reasonably successful in its attempt to save the subject property.

> Cobb Coin Co., Inc. v. Unidentified, Wrecked and Abandoned Sailing Vessel, 525 F.Supp. 186.

In order for a salvor to receive exclusive right to salve a wreck site, there must be an intent to reduce the property in question to physical possession by dealing with the wreck, when taken as a whole, in such a manner to at least warn, if not exclude, any other salvors.

> Cobb Coin Co., Inc. v. Unidentified, Wrecked and Abandoned Sailing Vessel, 525 F.Supp. 186.

One who discovers but does not assiduously undertake to rescue abandoned property may lose his right to uninterrupted salvage operations.

> Cobb Coin Co., Inc. v. Unidentified, Wrecked and Abandoned Sailing Vessel, 525 F.Supp. 186.

The rights of a first finder who abandons his claim inure to the benefit of any finder who diligently undertakes the salvaging operations.

> Cobb Coin Co., Inc. v. Unidentified, Wrecked and Abandoned Sailing Vessel, 525 F.Supp. 186.

Notorious possession, with the avowal of the object of that possession, are cardinal requisites to the creation or maintenance of the privileges of a salvor; where they do not exist, any person may take the property with all the advantages of first finder.

> Cobb Coin Co., Inc. v. Unidentified, Wrecked and Abandoned Sailing Vessel, 525 F.Supp. 186.

If a salvor vacates a site for any legitimate reason with an intention to return with reasonable diligence, that absence will not result in the forfeiture of finder's rights.

> Cobb Coin Co., Inc. v. Unidentified, Wrecked and Abandoned Sailing Vessel, 525 F.Supp. 186.

In order to claim an exclusive right to conduct salvage operations on a particular site, it is a requisite under federal maritime law that salvor be able to render effective assistance to the distressed property; in order to maintain exclusive possession, salvor must be not only willing and diligent, but also capable of actually saving the goods.

> Cobb Coin Co., Inc. v. Unidentified, Wrecked and Abandoned Sailing Vessel, 525 F.Supp. 186.

☞20. Vessels or persons contributing to peril.

For other cases see earlier editions of this digest, the Decennial Digests, and WESTLAW.

☞21. Forfeiture by negligence or misconduct.

C.A.5 (Fla.) 1968. Claim for salvage would be barred by salvor's negligence in failing to provide adequate safeguards to hold barges in tow.

> Fort Myers Shell & Dredging Co. v. Barge NBC 512, 404 F.2d 137.

C.A.5 (Fla.) 1963. Where salvaged vessel was damaged by negligent performance of salvage operation, under the doctrine of avoidable consequence a substantial burden was heavy on the salvor to establish that the resulting damage to the salvaged vessel would have been substantially different if the salvaged vessel had exercised prudence after the negligence of the salvor.

> Oil Screw Noah's Ark v. Bentley & Felton Corp., 322 F.2d 3.

District court had sufficient basis for concluding that as to a number of items the salvor had carried the burden of showing distinguishable damages due solely to salvaged vessel's failure to take steps to minimize the damage after the salvor negligently cast off the vessel without warning and that as to other items a division of damages was in order.

> Oil Screw Noah's Ark v. Bentley & Felton Corp., 322 F.2d 3.

The expense which salvaged vessel would have incurred in minimizing danger after salvor negligently cast off derelict without warning should be considered in determining the extent to which the amount of the salvage award should be diminished.

> Oil Screw Noah's Ark v. Bentley & Felton Corp., 322 F.2d 3.

The fact that repair period was extended because of marshal's seizure under salvor's libel for salvage was no extenuation, as respects allowance for detention losses.

> Oil Screw Noah's Ark v. Bentley & Felton Corp., 322 F.2d 3.

Even though vessel required salvage because of engine breakdown, from the moment the time required for the engine repairs expired, down to the completion of the repairs for the grounding (not subsequent sinking) damage occasioned after the salvor negligently cast off the vessel without warning, the vessel owner could recover in full for detention losses from the salvor even though during such time distinguishable "sinking" damages were being repaired.

> Oil Screw Noah's Ark v. Bentley & Felton Corp., 322 F.2d 3.

M.D.Fla. 2010. The law of salvage functions as a trust on behalf of the true owner and imposes duties of good faith, honesty, and diligence in protecting the property in the salvors' care.

> Odyssey Marine Exploration, Inc. v. Unidentified, Wrecked and Abandoned Sailing Vessel, 727 F.Supp.2d 1341.

Under the law of salvages, a salvor removes property from a wreck in trust for the owner; exploitation of the salvaged property terminates the right to a salvage award.

> Odyssey Marine Exploration, Inc. v. Unidentified, Wrecked and Abandoned Sailing Vessel, 727 F.Supp.2d 1341.

S.D.Fla. 2013. Treasure hunters forfeited their rights to salvage in connection with gems they discovered on the floor of the Gulf of Mexico, where they removed property from the res for their own use, by providing hundreds of gems to jeweler to make pieces of finished jewelry from them, and by giving their investors three gems, one of which was made into a necklace for investor's wife.

> JTR Enterprises, LLC v. An Unknown Quantity of Colombian Emeralds, Amethysts and Quartz Crystals, 922 F.Supp.2d 1326, appeal dismissed (11th cir. 13-10870).

S.D.Fla. 1978. Maritime law allows forfeiture of all salvage claims for acts of extreme bad faith.

> Treasure Salvors, Inc. v. Unidentified Wrecked and Abandoned Sailing Vessel, 459 F.Supp. 507, affirmed State of Fla., Dept. of State v. Treasure Salvors, Inc., 621 F.2d 1340, rehearing denied 629 F.2d 1350, certiorari granted Florida Dept. of State v. Treasure Salvors Inc., 101 S.Ct. 2312, 451 U.S. 982, 68 L.Ed.2d 838, affirmed in part, reversed in part 102 S.Ct. 3304, 458 U.S. 670, 73 L.Ed.2d 1057, on remand 689 F.2d 1254.

S.D.Fla. 1951. Any right to compensation for salvage will generally be forfeited or reduced in amount in cases where salvors have taken advantage or attempted to take advantage of distressed party by embezzlement of salved property, gross exaggerations of values and dangers, false representations of material matters, or other acts of misconduct.

> Higgins, Inc. v. The Tri-State, 99 F.Supp. 694.

Where motor vessel was adrift on high seas with perishable cargo of green bananas, without means of propulsion or communication, and was in distress, though weather was good, sea was calm and wind was gentle, but master of salvaging vessel compelled execution of purported salvage agreement and statement concerning conditions of weather, sea and wind, which misrepresented such conditions, and owner, officers and crew of salvaging vessel exaggerated value of salvaged ship, cargo and dangers, action of owner and crew of salvaging vessel was not such as to warrant forfeiture of their right to salvage award.

> Higgins, Inc. v. The Tri-State, 99 F.Supp. 694.

⚷**22. Liabilities of salvors for negligence or wrongful acts.**

C.A.5 (Fla.) 1963. Even though a professional salvor was available and capable of pulling salvaged derelict away from dock against which it fetched up after the successful salvor had negligently cast derelict off without warning, the successful salvor was responsible for substantial damages sustained by derelict during the time the derelict was smashing against dock waiting for the professional salvor to commence operations.

> Oil Screw Noah's Ark v. Bentley & Felton Corp., 322 F.2d 3.

C.A.5 (Fla.) 1961. Salvor had not acted with ordinary prudence in casting off towline before derelict was secure in heavy weather.

> The Noah's Ark v. Bentley & Felton Corp., 292 F.2d 437, on remand BENTLEY & FELTON CORPORATION AS OWNERS OF THE OIL SCREW CUDJOE, AND ON BEHALF OF HER MASTER· AND CREW, Libellants and Cross-Respondents. vs. OIL SCREW NOAH'S ARK, ETC., AND CHARLES E. GRAHAM, Respondents and Cross-Libellant., 1962 WL 115668, reversed and remanded Oil Screw Noah's Ark v. Bentley & Felton Corp., 322 F.2d 3.

Derelict vessel, after salvor had cast it adrift in heavy weather, had been free from fault while drifting and until it fetched up along sea wall.

> The Noah's Ark v. Bentley & Felton Corp., 292 F.2d 437, on remand BENTLEY & FELTON CORPORATION AS OWNERS OF THE OIL SCREW CUDJOE, AND ON BEHALF OF HER MASTER AND CREW, Libellants and Cross-Respondents. vs. OIL SCREW NOAH'S ARK, ETC., AND CHARLES E. GRAHAM, Respondents and Cross-Libellant., 1962 WL 115668, reversed and remanded Oil Screw Noah's Ark v. Bentley & Felton Corp., 322 F.2d 3.

For distinguishable independent damage done by salvor, salvor is held to usual standard of ordinary prudence.

> The Noah's Ark v. Bentley & Felton Corp., 292 F.2d 437, on remand BENTLEY & FELTON CORPORATION AS OWNERS OF THE OIL SCREW CUDJOE, AND ON BEHALF OF HER MASTER AND CREW, Libellants and Cross-Respondents. vs. OIL SCREW NOAH'S ARK, ETC., AND CHARLES E. GRAHAM, Respon-

dents and Cross-Libellant., 1962 WL 115668, reversed and remanded Oil Screw Noah's Ark v. Bentley & Felton Corp., 322 F.2d 3.

Requirement for willful or gross negligence as element of salvor liability relates to injury of nondistinguishable, nonindependent kind, broadly covering errors that made salvage ineffectual.

The Noah's Ark v. Bentley & Felton Corp., 292 F.2d 437, on remand BENTLEY & FELTON CORPORATION AS OWNERS OF THE OIL SCREW CUDJOE, AND ON BEHALF OF HER MASTER AND CREW, Libellants and Cross-Respondents. vs. OIL SCREW NOAH'S ARK, ETC., AND CHARLES E. GRAHAM, Respondents and Cross-Libellant., 1962 WL 115668, reversed and remanded Oil Screw Noah's Ark v. Bentley & Felton Corp., 322 F.2d 3.

A "distinguishable injury" for which salvor is held to ordinary prudence is some type of damage sustained by salved vessel other than that which she would have suffered had not salvage efforts been undertaken; it is harm distinct from that from which vessel is being saved.

The Noah's Ark v. Bentley & Felton Corp., 292 F.2d 437, on remand BENTLEY & FELTON CORPORATION AS OWNERS OF THE OIL SCREW CUDJOE, AND ON BEHALF OF HER MASTER AND CREW, Libellants and Cross-Respondents. vs. OIL SCREW NOAH'S ARK, ETC., AND CHARLES E. GRAHAM, Respondents and Cross-Libellant., 1962 WL 115668, reversed and remanded Oil Screw Noah's Ark v. Bentley & Felton Corp., 322 F.2d 3.

Damage suffered by derelict after salvor, which had successfully towed derelict to harbor, cast off towline on false assumption that derelict was secure, was distinguishable injury for which salvor could be held liable for simple negligence.

The Noah's Ark v. Bentley & Felton Corp., 292 F.2d 437, on remand BENTLEY & FELTON CORPORATION AS OWNERS OF THE OIL SCREW CUDJOE, AND ON BEHALF OF HER MASTER AND

CREW, Libellants and Cross-Respondents. vs. OIL SCREW NOAH'S ARK, ETC., AND CHARLES E. GRAHAM, Respondents and Cross-Libellant., 1962 WL 115668, reversed and remanded Oil Screw Noah's Ark v. Bentley & Felton Corp., 322 F.2d 3.

M.D.Fla. 1997. Liability of salvor for damages sustained by vessel in course of salvage operations is dependent on type of damage sustained; where the injury is a "distinguishable injury," i.e., some type of damage sustained by the salved vessel other than that which she would have suffered had not salvage efforts been undertaken, salvor's duty is measured under a duty of reasonable care under the circumstances; where the injury is not distinguishable from that which the vessel would have suffered had salvage not been undertaken, salvor is not liable in absence of gross negligence or willful misconduct.

Sands v. One Unnamed 23' Seacraft, Pleasure Vessel, 959 F.Supp. 1488, affirmed 144 F.3d 55.

Salvors were not liable for loss of center console and T-Tower on recreational vessel which occurred during salvage of vessel which capsized in shoal waters; evidence that gross negligence or willful misconduct; loss of console and T-Tower would have occurred without salvage efforts, and thus injury was not distinguishable from that which vessel would have suffered had salvage not been undertaken, rendering salvors' liable only for gross negligence and willful misconduct, of which there was no evidence.

Sands v. One Unnamed 23' Seacraft, Pleasure Vessel, 959 F.Supp. 1488, affirmed 144 F.3d 55.

M.D.Fla. 1993. Requirement that salvor act lawfully while salvaging vessel was consistent with general admiralty law.

Lathrop v. Unidentified, Wrecked & Abandoned Vessel, 817 F.Supp. 953.

S.D.Fla. 1987. Coast Guard does not have mandatory duty to provide rescue or salvage services and owes no duty to render fire fighting services to any ship, but is held to same standard of care as private person for any voluntary undertaking it assumes. 14 U.S.C.A. § 88.

DFDS Seacruises (Bahamas) Ltd. v. U.S., 676 F.Supp. 1193.

When distressed vessel is damaged by original peril to which it was exposed, such as fire, salvor is liable for damages arising only from its gross negligence or wilful misconduct.

DFDS Seacruises (Bahamas) Ltd. v. U.S., 676 F.Supp. 1193.

Under "good samaritan doctrine," liability will not be imposed on would-be rescuer of vessel unless that party was negligent under circumstances and its conduct worsened position of vessel in distress.

DFDS Seacruises (Bahamas) Ltd. v. U.S., 676 F.Supp. 1193.

Coast Guard's efforts in fighting fire aboard cruise ship, including failure to take any action to cease volunteer fire department's nonnegligent ventilation efforts, were not grossly negligent or reckless, if negligent at all, and Coast Guard's supervision of fire fighting efforts by local, regional, and federal agencies also was not negligent; tremendous resources obtained, numerous fire fighters flown in, and multi-organizational efforts procured demonstrated massive, well-organized, and orchestrated fire fighting effort.

DFDS Seacruises (Bahamas) Ltd. v. U.S., 676 F.Supp. 1193.

S.D.Fla. 1984. Salvage, when assumed, may not be performed with impunity, if performed negligently. 14 U.S.C.A. § 88.

Port Tack Sailboats, Inc. v. U.S., 593 F.Supp. 597.

Decision of captain of United States submarine to continue pumping in efforts to "de-water" plaintiff's sailboat in view of fact that it had been observed settling by the bow as well to preserve possible crime scene could not be held to be matter of negligence, considering all circumstances, but, rather, salvage effort by submarine was good-faith effort and performed at considerable risk and inconvenience to its personnel so that it could turn over

pumped-out buoyant sailboat to Coast Guard upon its arrival. 14 U.S.C.A. § 88.

Port Tack Sailboats, Inc. v. U.S., 593 F.Supp. 597.

Although ballistic missile submarine might be most ill-suited and least-equipped vessel to perform any kind of salvage operation, command decision of submarine skipper to send over raft to find out what was wrong with plaintiff's sailboat and to render whatever rescue assistance was necessary or possible was not negligence nor was there negligence on part of submarine for its action during pumping-out process in utilizing best method available in effort to achieve "de-watering," and there was no negligence in failing to call Coast Guard at time of initial sighting of sailboat or at time of decision to sail sailboat back to submarine for pumping out. 14 U.S.C.A. § 88.

Port Tack Sailboats, Inc. v. U.S., 593 F.Supp. 597.

Although it would not be negligence for United States submarine to fail to call Coast Guard at time of initial sighting of plaintiff's sailboat or at time of decision to sail sailboat back to submarine for pumping out, it was negligence in salvage effort to fail to call Coast Guard at time of beginning the pumping-out process or at least within a few minutes after it could be seen what the pumping-out process was going to entail in terms of repeated grinding effort of the submarine's pressure hull against the sailboat. 14 U.S.C.A. § 88.

Port Tack Sailboats, Inc. v. U.S., 593 F.Supp. 597.

Evidence as to postsalvage damage fell far short of establishing either that there was "second sinking" of plaintiff's sailboat, after Navy submarine arrived on scene or that it was responsibility of the Coast Guard, and sailboat owner could not recover from the United States on such theory. 14 U.S.C.A. § 88.

Port Tack Sailboats, Inc. v. U.S., 593 F.Supp. 597.

Although Navy was negligent in that submarine failed to summon Coast Guard to assist in effort to salvage plaintiff's sailboat, evidence militated against any award of damages, there being failure to show that any damage was result of negligence of the Navy in failing to call the Coast

Guard sooner than they did. 14 U.S.C.A. § 88.

Port Tack Sailboats, Inc. v. U.S., 593 F.Supp. 597.

S.D.Fla. 1961. Evidence in cross libel established that vessels were damaged in being removed from beach by salvor which used little skill in operation.

Beach Salvage Corp. of Fla. v. The Cap't. Tom, 201 F.Supp. 479.

Salvor which was not licensed as a wrecker on Florida coast and which did not have experienced mariners or experienced salvage persons, was not charged with same duty as if it were professional salvor or salvor licensed by court under law.

Beach Salvage Corp. of Fla. v. The Cap't. Tom, 201 F.Supp. 479.

Salvor is charged with duty to take reasonable care of property it undertakes to save.

Beach Salvage Corp. of Fla. v. The Cap't. Tom, 201 F.Supp. 479.

⟛23. Persons and property liable.

C.A.5 (Fla.) 1976. In suit for salvage award, based on services rendered by employees of stevedore in helping to extinguish fire on vessel containing military equipment destined for the Federal Republic of Germany (FRG), brought against the United States and FRG, the lower court, properly giving controlling weight to the intention of the contracting nations, was both legally and factually correct in finding that the sovereigns involved were not dealing in ordinary commerce, that both nations consistently acted as if title passed to FRG well before the salvage effort, and that FRG had assumed the risk for the damaged property. West's F.S.A. § 672.319.

Legnos v. U.S., 535 F.2d 857, rehearing denied 540 F.2d 1085.

S.D.Fla. 1981. Even if state were to be considered the nominal owner of sunken treasures on the ocean bottom, maritime precedent would provide for a salvage award to one saving property owned by the sovereign by virtue of its expressed sovereign prerogative.

Cobb Coin Co., Inc. v. Unidentified, Wrecked and Abandoned Sailing Vessel, 525 F.Supp. 186.

II. AMOUNT AND APPORTIONMENT.

⟛24. Theory and purpose of remuneration.

S.D.Fla. 2007. Salvage award, which is unique to maritime and admiralty law, is not one of quantum meruit as compensation for work performed, but is a bounty given on grounds of public policy to encourage the rescue of life and property imperiled at sea and to foster maritime commerce.

Atlantis Marine Towing, Inc. v. THE M/V PRISCILLA, 491 F.Supp.2d 1096.

S.D.Fla. 1995. Salvage award, which is unique to maritime and admiralty law, is not one of quantum meruit as compensation for work performed, but rather, is bounty given on grounds of public policy to encourage rescue of life and property imperiled at sea and to foster maritime commerce.

Fine v. Rockwood, 895 F.Supp. 306.

S.D.Fla. 1981. More than a quantum meruit is involved in a salvage award; salvors are to be paid a bonus according to the merit of their services; awards will vary according to the judge's conclusion that salvage service was of high order, medium order, or low order; in the case of abandoned property, the entire value of the salved property may be awarded to the salvor; the consistent policy underlying admiralty's salvage awards is that salvors will be liberally rewarded.

Cobb Coin Co., Inc. v. Unidentified, Wrecked and Abandoned Sailing Vessel, 525 F.Supp. 186.

⟛25. Discretion of court as to amount.

For other cases see earlier editions of this digest, the Decennial Digests, and WESTLAW.

⟛26. Elements in determination of amount.

C.A.5 (Fla.) 1981. Awards for performance of salvage services are not limited to strict quantum meruit measure of value of services performed; rather, award is calculated to include bounty or premi-

---

† This Case was not selected for publication in the National Reporter System
For legislative history of cited statutes, see Florida Statutes Annotated

um based upon risk involved in operation and skill with which it was performed.

> Treasure Salvors, Inc. v. Unidentified Wrecked & Abandoned Sailing Vessel, 640 F.2d 560, on remand 546 F.Supp. 919.

M.D.Fla. 2010. After recovering lost property, under the law of salvage, a salvor obtains a maritime lien that allows the salvor to proceed in rem to secure a salvage award and gains exclusive "possession" over the salvaged property to allow for the uninterrupted delivery of the property to the court-appointed custodian; the value of the recovered property governs the salvage award, and, if the salvage award exceeds the value of the salvaged property, the salvor receives title to the property.

> Odyssey Marine Exploration, Inc. v. Unidentified, Wrecked and Abandoned Sailing Vessel, 727 F.Supp.2d 1341.

S.D.Fla. 2014. There is no precise formula to determine a salvage award; rather, salvage awards are determined on a fact specific basis.

> Girard v. The M/Y Quality Time, 4 F.Supp.3d 1352, affirmed in part, remanded in part 596 Fed.Appx. 846, certiorari denied 136 S.Ct. 153, 193 L.Ed.2d 43.

The factors to be considered when determining a salvage award amount are: (1) the degree of danger from which the vessel was rescued; (2) the post-casualty value of the vessel; (3) the risk incurred in saving the vessel from the impending peril; (4) the promptitude and skill displayed by the salvors; (5) the value of the property employed by the salvors; and (6) the time and labor expended in rendering the salvage service.

> Girard v. The M/Y Quality Time, 4 F.Supp.3d 1352, affirmed in part, remanded in part 596 Fed.Appx. 846, certiorari denied 136 S.Ct. 153, 193 L.Ed.2d 43.

S.D.Fla. 2004. In determining amount of salvage award, court should consider: (1) labor expended by salvors in rendering salvage service; (2) promptitude, skill, and energy displayed in rendering service and saving property; (3) value of property employed by salvors in rendering

service and danger to which such property was exposed; (4) risk incurred by salvors in securing property from impending peril; (5) value of property saved; and (6) degree of danger from which property was rescued.

> Atlantis Marine Towing, Inc. v. M/V/ELIZABETH, 346 F.Supp.2d 1266.

S.D.Fla. 2003. Public policy underlying salvage awards in the admiralty court is to hold out a continuing incentive to undertake the physical and financial risk entailed in salvage operations and to bring the property thus recovered into court for a salvage determination.

> Southernmost Marine Services, Inc. v. One (1) 2000 Fifty Four Foot (54') Sea Ray named M/V POTENTIAL, 250 F.Supp.2d 1367, affirmed Southernmost Marine Svcs. v. M/V POTENTIAL, 91 Fed.Appx. 655.

Elements considered by an admiralty court in determining a salvage award are: (1) the labor expended by the salvors in rendering the salvage service; (2) the promptitude, skill and energy displayed in rendering the service and saving the property; (3) the value of the property employed by the salvors in rendering the service and the danger to which such property was exposed; (4) the risk incurred by the salvors in securing the property from the impending peril; (5) the value of the property saved; and (6) the degree of danger from which the property was rescued.

> Southernmost Marine Services, Inc. v. One (1) 2000 Fifty Four Foot (54') Sea Ray named M/V POTENTIAL, 250 F.Supp.2d 1367, affirmed Southernmost Marine Svcs. v. M/V POTENTIAL, 91 Fed.Appx. 655.

S.D.Fla. 1993. Six factors to be considered in determining amount of salvage award, in descending order of importance, are: degree of danger from which ship was rescued; postcasualty value of property saved; risk incurred in saving property from impending peril; promptitude, skill and energy displayed in rendering service in salving property; value of property employed by salvor and danger to which it was exposed; costs in terms of labor and materials expended by salvors in rendering salvage service.

> Ocean Services Towing and Salvage, Inc. v. Brown, 810 F.Supp. 1258.

Value of salved boat is only one of the factors to be considered in fixing salvage award; it should not be principal guide for determining award, but should be merely factor to be considered along with the others.

> Ocean Services Towing and Salvage, Inc. v. Brown, 810 F.Supp. 1258.

S.D.Fla. 1991. When determining salvage award, admiralty court considers labor expended by salvors in rendering salvage service; promptitude, skill and energy displayed in rendering service and saving property; value of equipment employed by salvors in rendering service and saving property; risk incurred by salvors in securing property from impending peril; value of property saved; and degree of danger from which property was rescued.

> Flagship Marine Services, Inc. v. Belcher Towing Co., 761 F.Supp. 792, reversed 966 F.2d 602, opinion vacated, appeal dismissed, opinion reinstated 23 F.3d 341.

S.D.Fla. 1984. In computing salvage award, court reviews labor expended by salvors in rendering salvage service, promptitude, skill and energy displayed in rendering service and saving property, value of property employed by salvors in rendering service and saving property, risk incurred by salvors in securing property from impending peril, value of property saved, and degree of danger from which property was rescued.

> Unnamed But Identifiable Master and Crew of That Certain U.S. Documented Vessel Bearing Documentation No. 567135 v. Certain Unnamed Motor Vessel Bearing Florida Registration No. FL5607 EM, 592 F.Supp. 1191.

S.D.Fla. 1983. Elements considered by admiralty court in determining salvage award are labor expended by salvors in rendering salvage service, promptitude, skill and energy displayed in rendering service and saving property, value of property employed by salvors in rendering service and danger to which such property was exposed, risk incurred by salvors in

securing property from impending peril, value of property saved, and degree of danger from which property was rescued.

> Treasure Salvors, Inc. v. Unidentified, Wrecked and Abandoned Sailing Vessel, 556 F.Supp. 1319.

S.D.Fla. 1982. Elements considered by admiralty court in determining salvage award are: labor expended by salvors; promptitude, skill and energy displayed; value of property employed by salvors in rendering the service and danger to which such property was exposed; risk incurred by salvors; value of property saved; and degree of danger from which the property was rescued.

> Cobb Coin Co., Inc. v. Unidentified, Wrecked and Abandoned Sailing Vessel, 549 F.Supp. 540.

In order to state a claim for salvage award on an ancient vessel of historical and archeological significance, it is an essential element that the salvors document to the admiralty court's satisfaction that they have preserved the archeological provenance of shipwreck, but by meeting this threshold requirement, salvor simultaneously "enhances" the value of his recovery in such a way as will be explicitly recognized by the court in the determination of the salvage award.

> Cobb Coin Co., Inc. v. Unidentified, Wrecked and Abandoned Sailing Vessel, 549 F.Supp. 540.

S.D.Fla. 1981. More than a quantum meruit is involved in a salvage award; salvors are to be paid a bonus according to the merit of their services; awards will vary according to the judge's conclusion that salvage service was of high order, medium order, or low order; in the case of abandoned property, the entire value of the salved property may be awarded to the salvor; the consistent policy underlying admiralty's salvage awards is that salvors will be liberally rewarded.

> Cobb Coin Co., Inc. v. Unidentified, Wrecked and Abandoned Sailing Vessel, 525 F.Supp. 186.

S.D.Fla. 1961. In considering compensation to be awarded for successful removal of stranded boat court is to consider degree of danger from which lives and property were rescued, value of property saved, risk incurred by salvors in securing property from impending peril, promptitude, skill and energy displayed by salvors in rendering service and saving property, value of property employed by salvors in rendering their services and danger to which property was exposed, and time and labor spent by salvors.

> Beach Salvage Corp. of Fla. v. The Cap't. Tom, 201 F.Supp. 479.

Damage to vessels caused by lack of skill in salvage operations would be considered in making any award for salvage.

> Beach Salvage Corp. of Fla. v. The Cap't. Tom, 201 F.Supp. 479.

In considering amount to be awarded for entire salvage operation of stranded shrimp boats, court would consider not only efforts of salvor but those of Coast Guard and actual and necessary expenses incurred by salvor.

> Beach Salvage Corp. of Fla. v. The Cap't. Tom, 201 F.Supp. 479.

Cost of appraisals made after salvor brought libel to recover for salvage operations would be deducted from award of salvor which failed to comply with court rule setting forth appraisals in original libel.

> Beach Salvage Corp. of Fla. v. The Cap't. Tom, 201 F.Supp. 479.

⌖**27. Amount awarded and computation in general.**

† **C.A.11 (Fla.) 2015.** Salvage of yacht that had run aground was low-level salvage, and salvor's efforts, while commendable and worthy of compensation, were limited to routine salvage services typical of any professional salvor, and thus awarding salvor 12% of yacht's value, or $16,796.06, was appropriate, where salvor pumped or de-watered yacht, patched her hull, and towed her to boatyard, seas were moderate and weather was relatively calm during operation, and United States Coast Guard, which arrived on scene prior to salvor and departed only after yacht was stabilized, had already removed passengers from yacht.

> Girard v. M/Y Quality Time, 596 Fed. Appx. 846, certiorari denied 136 S.Ct. 153, 193 L.Ed.2d 43.

Salvor did not face any risks out of ordinary for typical professional salvor, and thus he was not entitled to liberal award for salvaging yacht that had run aground.

> Girard v. M/Y Quality Time, 596 Fed. Appx. 846, certiorari denied 136 S.Ct. 153, 193 L.Ed.2d 43.

Awarding professional salvor 12% of yacht's value was appropriate, rather than salvor's requested minimum of 33% of yacht's value, which he based on selected past cases, since awards should be based on facts and circumstances of each case, rather than applying fixed percentages of value and comparing percentages from previous awards.

> Girard v. M/Y Quality Time, 596 Fed. Appx. 846, certiorari denied 136 S.Ct. 153, 193 L.Ed.2d 43.

† **C.A.11 (Fla.) 2012.** Weight of evidence supported conclusion of salvor's expert witness that post-salvage value of yacht salvor rescued was worth $565,000 in salvor's action against yacht owner for salvage award; salvor's expert used methodology of valuation including in person inspection, and national appraisal standards, whereas yacht owner's expert never established that he inspected the yacht, or explained how he reached his valuation of only $150,000.

> Esoteric, LLC v. One (1) 2000 Eighty-Five Foot Azimut Motor Yacht Named M/V STAR ONE, 478 Fed. Appx. 639.

C.A.11 (Fla.) 2000. Under the law of salvage, rescuers take possession of, but not title to, the distressed vessel and its contents, and court then fashions appropriate award for salvors' services.

> International Aircraft Recovery, L.L.C. v. Unidentified, Wrecked and Abandoned Aircraft, 218 F.3d 1255, certiorari denied International Aircraft Recovery, LLC v. U.S., 121 S.Ct. 1079, 531 U.S. 1144, 148 L.Ed.2d 956, appeal after remand 373 F.3d 1147.

S.D.Fla. 2014. Salvors were entitled to salvage award of 12% of yacht's post-casualty value, or $16,796.06, in connection with rescuing yacht after it ran aground near Key West, Florida; although salvage was low level, as there were no special salvage skills or significant amount of danger involved, salvage was at nighttime, diver incurred risk of being cut by the propeller, and salvors, who were professionals entitled to uplift of two percent of value of yacht, were prompt and efficient.

> Girard v. The M/Y Quality Time, 4 F.Supp.3d 1352, affirmed in part, remanded in part 596 Fed.Appx. 846, certiorari denied 136 S.Ct. 153, 193 L.Ed.2d 43.

A salvage involving no special skills or equipment or significant amount of danger is considered a low level salvage and is equivalent to a salvage award of 5–10% of the vessel's post-casualty value.

> Girard v. The M/Y Quality Time, 4 F.Supp.3d 1352, affirmed in part, remanded in part 596 Fed.Appx. 846, certiorari denied 136 S.Ct. 153, 193 L.Ed.2d 43.

Salvage awards are calculated as a percentage of the value of the salvaged vessel, which is obtained by subtracting the repair costs from the vessel's precasualty value.

> Girard v. The M/Y Quality Time, 4 F.Supp.3d 1352, affirmed in part, remanded in part 596 Fed.Appx. 846, certiorari denied 136 S.Ct. 153, 193 L.Ed.2d 43.

There is no precise formula to determine a salvage award; rather, salvage awards are determined on a fact specific basis.

> Girard v. The M/Y Quality Time, 4 F.Supp.3d 1352, affirmed in part, remanded in part 596 Fed.Appx. 846, certiorari denied 136 S.Ct. 153, 193 L.Ed.2d 43.

S.D.Fla. 2004. In calculating salvage award, salved value would normally be fair market value of property.

> Atlantis Marine Towing, Inc. v. M/V/ELZABETH, 346 F.Supp.2d 1266.

S.D.Fla. 2003. Settlement dollar amount to which the parties agreed was the fair value of the salvage award for the exemplary salvage service rendered; property was fully preserved and protected and the salvors demonstrated promptitude, skill and energy at great personal risk to

themselves where there was substantial risk of total loss of the vessel.

> Southernmost Marine Services, Inc. v. One (1) 2000 Fifty Four Foot (54') Sea Ray named M/V POTENTIAL, 250 F.Supp.2d 1367, affirmed Southernmost Marine Svcs. v. M/V POTENTIAL, 91 Fed.Appx. 655.

S.D.Fla. 1993. Salved value of boat is postcasualty value of property, in her damaged state, at time of salvage or after vessel is brought into safe harbor.

> Ocean Services Towing and Salvage, Inc. v. Brown, 810 F.Supp. 1258.

Ordinarily, fair market value of salved property determines property value.

> Ocean Services Towing and Salvage, Inc. v. Brown, 810 F.Supp. 1258.

Use of precasualty book value for salved boat and subtracting estimated repair cost is permissible method for determining value of salved property, where there is no established market value for vessel.

> Ocean Services Towing and Salvage, Inc. v. Brown, 810 F.Supp. 1258.

Where book value of salved boat is available, or market price has been fixed for boat by actual sale, use of insured value of boat would be improper.

> Ocean Services Towing and Salvage, Inc. v. Brown, 810 F.Supp. 1258.

Where actual sale of salved vessel has occurred after salvage, and sale was conducted in commercially reasonable manner, actual selling price is best manifestation of fair market value of boat.

> Ocean Services Towing and Salvage, Inc. v. Brown, 810 F.Supp. 1258.

Salved boat was sold by salvor in commercially reasonable manner, making sales price boat's fair market value in determining amount of salvage award; sale was negotiated at arm's length, and salvor had boat properly cleaned and engine flushed and maintained in order to attract higher bids.

> Ocean Services Towing and Salvage, Inc. v. Brown, 810 F.Supp. 1258.

S.D.Fla. 1988. Pleasure boater was entitled to $500 for his efforts to salvage unmanned vessel; vessel was only in "minimal" apprehension of danger and was in no immediate or absolute threat of harm, pleasure boater's risk was minimal, boater and his family were already heading out toward their fishing destination when they happened upon vessel, and the time pleasure boater spent waiting for Coast Guard to tow vessel did not preclude him or his family from doing what they came to the ocean to do.

> Hernandez v. Roberts, 675 F.Supp. 1329.

S.D.Fla. 1984. Salvors of vessel with a value of approximately $130,000 were entitled to award of $5,000 as fair recompense for salvage services rendered in view of little maritime risk or difficulty incurred in securing vessel.

> Unnamed But Identifiable Master and Crew of That Certain U.S. Documented Vessel Bearing Documentation No. 567135 v. Certain Unnamed Motor Vessel Bearing Florida Registration No. FL5607 EM, 592 F.Supp. 1191.

S.D.Fla. 1983. Salvage company was entitled to salvage award of all artifacts recovered from Spanish galleon as compensation for its expenses and award for superlative salvage services.

> Treasure Salvors, Inc. v. Unidentified, Wrecked and Abandoned Sailing Vessel, 556 F.Supp. 1319.

S.D.Fla. 1982. Considering the large expenses incurred by salvor, its high degree of skill and energy, value of the property utilized, risks incurred including risks of arrest by state claiming right to wreck, value of property saved, and degree of danger from which it was rescued, salvor of wrecked Spanish treasure galleon would be awarded all artifacts that it recovered since inception of the lawsuit as compensation for its expenses and award for superlative salvage services.

> Cobb Coin Co., Inc. v. Unidentified, Wrecked and Abandoned Sailing Vessel, 549 F.Supp. 540.

State's possession of representative cross section of recovered artifacts from wreck of 1715 Spanish treasure fleet made it presently inappropriate to award state further artifacts out of salvage award, but this was without prejudice to right of state to intervene in future salvage award determinations.

> Cobb Coin Co., Inc. v. Unidentified, Wrecked and Abandoned Sailing Vessel, 549 F.Supp. 540.

S.D.Fla. 1961. Evidence warranted finding that value of salvage services rendered in removal of two stranded shrimp boats by both Coast Guard and salvor was $2,000 of which $1,000 was apportioned to work of Coast Guard and $1,000 to salvor which in addition was entitled to be reimbursed for $150 expenses for tug boat which towed shrimp boat to shipyard, $50 for lost anchor and for $25 damage to dukw. 14 U.S.C.A. § 88.

> Beach Salvage Corp. of Fla. v. The Cap't. Tom, 201 F.Supp. 479.

⊂⇁**28. Derelict.**

C.A.5 (Fla.) 1978. Salvage awards may include entire derelict property.

> Treasure Salvors, Inc. v. Unidentified Wrecked and Abandoned Sailing Vessel, 569 F.2d 330.

United States was not entitled to possession and title of remains of sunken Spanish vessel discovered by American citizens off coast of Florida as successor to prerogative rights of English Crown.

> Treasure Salvors, Inc. v. Unidentified Wrecked and Abandoned Sailing Vessel, 569 F.2d 330.

S.D.Fla. 1978. Florida statute which purports to vest title in state over lost and abandoned sea vessel located off coast of Florida would not apply as property was not on "sovereignty lands of the state." West's F.S.A. § 267.011 et seq.

> Treasure Salvors, Inc. v. Unidentified Wrecked and Abandoned Sailing Vessel, 459 F.Supp. 507, affirmed State of Fla., Dept. of State v. Treasure Salvors, Inc., 621 F.2d 1340, rehearing denied 629 F.2d 1350, certiorari granted Florida Dept. of State v. Treasure Salvors Inc., 101 S.Ct. 2312, 451 U.S. 982, 68 L.Ed.2d 838, affirmed in part, reversed in part 102 S.Ct. 3304, 458 U.S. 670, 73 L.Ed.2d 1057, on remand 689 F.2d 1254.

🗝29. Peril at sea.

C.C.A.5 (Fla.) 1938.　$1,200 to libelants as compensation for their services in rescuing a steel barge from the impending perils of the sea was excessive by $600, in view of value of property restored to owner.

The No. 105, 97 F.2d 425.

S.D.Fla. 1991.　Marine service company that saved tug from sinking and secured barges tug was pushing was entitled to $125,000 salvage award; award was fair and equitable considering, among other things, hazards and risk involved, service rendered and prompt action taken.

Flagship Marine Services, Inc. v. Belcher Towing Co., 761 F.Supp. 792, reversed 966 F.2d 602, opinion vacated, appeal dismissed, opinion reinstated 23 F.3d 341.

🗝30. Stranding.

† C.A.11 (Fla.) 2015.　Salvage of yacht that had run aground was low-level salvage, and salvor's efforts, while commendable and worthy of compensation, were limited to routine salvage services typical of any professional salvor, and thus awarding salvor 12% of yacht's value, or $16,796.06, was appropriate, where salvor pumped or de-watered yacht, patched her hull, and towed her to boatyard, seas were moderate and weather was relatively calm during operation, and United States Coast Guard, which arrived on scene prior to salvor and departed only after yacht was stabilized, had already removed passengers from yacht.

Girard v. M/Y Quality Time, 596 Fed. Appx. 846, certiorari denied 136 S.Ct. 153, 193 L.Ed.2d 43.

S.D.Fla. 1980.　Where contract for unlimited lifetime worldwide cruising privileges claimed by pilot in return for his services was unenforceable, salvage services rendered by pilot entitled him to $55,000, representing $100,000 value of low to moderate order salvage services he rendered, less $11,400 for value of cruises already taken and less other adjustments.

Jackson v. Costa Lines, Inc., 490 F.Supp. 393, affirmed 667 F.2d 97.

🗝31. Fire.

S.D.Fla. 2004.　Salvor was entitled to salvage award in amount of $150,000 for its efforts in extinguishing fire aboard yacht, even though city fire department arrived on scene five or ten minutes after salvor's arrival, where salvor assisted fire department, salvor was exceptionally energetic in fighting fire and securing yacht's safety, value of salvor's vessel was about $100,000, salvor was exposed to dangers inherent in fighting fires, yacht's pre-fire value was $2.5 million and its salved value was roughly $1.22 million, and damage to yacht could have been catastrophic.

Atlantis Marine Towing, Inc. v. M/V/ELIZABETH, 346 F.Supp.2d 1266.

🗝32. Sunken vessel or cargo.

C.A.5 (Fla.) 1978.　Title to abandoned sunken vessel vests in finder and not sovereign.

Treasure Salvors, Inc. v. Unidentified Wrecked and Abandoned Sailing Vessel, 569 F.2d 330.

S.D.Fla. 1986.　Salvors of artifacts from 18th century Spanish fleet were entitled to liberal salvage award consisting of all artifacts recovered by them, other than artifacts recovered in state waters, conditioned upon compliance with customs regulations.

MDM Salvage, Inc. v. Unidentified, Wrecked and Abandoned Sailing Vessel, 631 F.Supp. 308.

S.D.Fla. 1978.　Where wreck site of abandoned sailing vessel was outside territorial boundaries of the United States and Florida, under provisions of applicable treaties, which are supreme law of the land, no claim could be made to ship and treasure it carried on basis of sovereign ownership.

Treasure Salvors, Inc. v. Unidentified Wrecked and Abandoned Sailing Vessel, 459 F.Supp. 507, affirmed State of Fla., Dept. of State v. Treasure Salvors, Inc., 621 F.2d 1340, rehearing denied 629 F.2d 1350, certiorari granted Florida Dept. of State v. Treasure Salvors Inc., 101 S.Ct. 2312, 451 U.S. 982, 68

L.Ed.2d 838, affirmed in part, reversed in part 102 S.Ct. 3304, 458 U.S. 670, 73 L.Ed.2d 1057, on remand 689 F.2d 1254.

Treasure-hunting company, which had located ship and treasure in waters outside territory of Florida or the United States, under the judgment of federal district court, as affirmed by the Fifth Circuit, was the owner of unidentified wrecked and abandoned vessel and property contained therein and was entitled to possession.

> Treasure Salvors, Inc. v. Unidentified Wrecked and Abandoned Sailing Vessel, 459 F.Supp. 507, affirmed State of Fla., Dept. of State v. Treasure Salvors, Inc., 621 F.2d 1340, rehearing denied 629 F.2d 1350, certiorari granted Florida Dept. of State v. Treasure Salvors Inc., 101 S.Ct. 2312, 451 U.S. 982, 68 L.Ed.2d 838, affirmed in part, reversed in part 102 S.Ct. 3304, 458 U.S. 670, 73 L.Ed.2d 1057, on remand 689 F.2d 1254.

⚷⇒33. Recapture.

For other cases see earlier editions of this digest, the Decennial Digests, and WEST-LAW.

⚷⇒34. Towage.

C.A.5 (Fla.) 1975. Tug owner was entitled to recover from barge owner salvage for towing capsized barge, which had been improperly loaded by shipper, back to port and barge owner was entitled to recover from shipper the amount due tug owner less 50% because of unseaworthiness of barge.

> Nat G. Harrison Overseas Corp. v. American Tug Titan, 520 F.2d 1104.

S.D.Fla. 1951. Where there was misconduct on part of owner and crew of salvaging vessel, but salvaged vessel was towed for period of approximately two days, and salvaging ship was delayed 13 hours in arrival, award of double towage rate plus value of time lost was full and sufficient compensation for salvage rendered to distressed vessel.

> Higgins, Inc. v. The Tri-State, 99 F.Supp. 694.

⚷⇒35. Services and expenses exceeding value of property saved.

S.D.Fla. 1993. Value of salved boat is only one of the factors to be considered in fixing salvage award; it should not be principal guide for determining award, but should be merely factor to be considered along with the others.

> Ocean Services Towing and Salvage, Inc. v. Brown, 810 F.Supp. 1258.

Salved value of vessel generally serves as ceiling for maximum allowable total salvage award.

> Ocean Services Towing and Salvage, Inc. v. Brown, 810 F.Supp. 1258.

⚷⇒36. Contracts as to compensation.

† C.A.11 (Fla.) 2013. Florida law did not recognize mutual mistake as claim for which party to contract could obtain relief, but only as avoidance pleaded by party sued on contract, and so shipwreck researcher's claim of mutual mistake asserted against underwater salvage corporation did not state a claim; corporation allegedly offered researcher cash payment in lieu of previous oral agreement for share of shipwreck if it were salvaged, researcher accepted that payment, but after corporation announced discovery of unidentified, wrecked ship, researcher believed he was induced to give up his share of salvage for cash buyout worth far less.

> Odyssey Marine Exploration, Inc. v. Unidentified, Shipwrecked Vessel or Vessels, 512 Fed.Appx. 890.

C.A.5 (Fla.) 1980. Contract between treasure hunters in State of Florida, which entitled state to 25% of artifacts found in shipwreck off Florida coast, was void for failure of consideration and for mutual mistake where agreement was entered into under belief that vessel was resting on land owned by Florida, but Supreme Court subsequently held that Florida did not and never had owned seabed upon which vessel rested.

> State of Fla., Dept. of State v. Treasure Salvors, Inc., 621 F.2d 1340, rehearing denied 629 F.2d 1350, certiorari granted Florida Dept. of State v. Treasure Salvors Inc., 101 S.Ct. 2312, 451 U.S. 982, 68

---

† This Case was not selected for publication in the National Reporter System
For legislative history of cited statutes, see Florida Statutes Annotated

L.Ed.2d 838, affirmed in part, reversed in part 102 S.Ct. 3304, 458 U.S. 670, 73 L.Ed.2d 1057, on remand 689 F.2d 1254.

C.A.5 (Fla.) 1978. A salvage settlement between the salvor shipowner and the owners of the salved vessel and cargo cannot bind the salvor crew without their consent.

> Compania Galeana, S.A. v. Motor Vessel Caribbean Mara, 565 F.2d 358.

Where master of vessel was aware of settlement between owner of his vessel and other vessel and its cargo, which had been towed to port after having been found abandoned and burning on the high seas, but where master neither filed objection to settlement nor appeared at hearing to oppose it, there was passive approval of settlement by master which prevented master from attacking order approving settlement on ground that he had not consented to it.

> Compania Galeana, S.A. v. Motor Vessel Caribbean Mara, 565 F.2d 358.

C.A.5 (Fla.) 1971. Where salvor entered into no cure-no pay salvage agreement with vessel owner whereby salvor would receive $85,000 for salvaging leaking and stranded ship of warranted value of $620,000, and salvor did in fact deliver vessel to port, judgment was properly rendered in favor of salvor on its salvage claim of $85,000.

> Fredelos v. Merritt-Chapman & Scott Corp., 447 F.2d 435, on rehearing 1971 WL 217579.

S.D.Fla. 2003. Fact that vessel owner only signed in one place on the document and did not sign in other blank spaces for his signature did not establish Florida law that he signed salvage contract in ignorance of an agreement to be responsible for the salvage of his vessel.

> Southernmost Marine Services, Inc. v. One (1) 2000 Fifty Four Foot (54') Sea Ray named M/V POTENTIAL, 250 F.Supp.2d 1367, affirmed Southernmost Marine Svcs. v. M/V POTENTIAL, 91 Fed.Appx. 655.

S.D.Fla. 1989. Provision of contract calling for investment in salvage operations which gave the investor a four-fifths of one percent interest in treasure recovered prior to the agreement and an additional four-fifths of one percent interest in all treasure recovered from the site gave investor an interest only in treasure recovered from the site during the contract period and not in any treasure recovered thereafter.

> DiLucia v. Treasure Salvors, Inc., 713 F.Supp. 1425.

S.D.Fla. 1984. It is not within discretion of a court of admiralty to set aside salvage contracts in cases where, after service is performed, stipulated compensation may appear to be unreasonable.

> Sea Lift, Inc. v. Refinadora Costarricense De Petroleo, S.A., 601 F.Supp. 457, reversed 792 F.2d 989.

Court could not modify the $265,000 figure contained in marine salvage contract to take into account plaintiff salvage company's actual costs, or the actual ultimate value of the salved barge, because, when contract was executed, the price agreed to be paid appeared to be just and reasonable, in view of the value of the property at stake, the danger from which it was to be rescued, and risk to salvors and salving property.

> Sea Lift, Inc. v. Refinadora Costarricense De Petroleo, S.A., 601 F.Supp. 457, reversed 792 F.2d 989.

S.D.Fla. 1978. Where property was never actually located on Florida sovereignty submerged lands, property did not belong to the state and, as a result, the state Division of Archives lacked all authority to enter a contract conveying salvage rights. West's F.S.A. §§ 267.031(5), 267.061(1)(b).

> Treasure Salvors, Inc. v. Unidentified Wrecked and Abandoned Sailing Vessel, 459 F.Supp. 507, affirmed State of Fla., Dept. of State v. Treasure Salvors, Inc., 621 F.2d 1340, rehearing denied 629 F.2d 1350, certiorari granted Florida Dept. of State v. Treasure Salvors Inc., 101 S.Ct. 2312, 451 U.S. 982, 68 L.Ed.2d 838, affirmed in part, reversed in part 102 S.Ct. 3304, 458 U.S. 670, 73 L.Ed.2d 1057, on remand 689 F.2d 1254.

Contract does not vest title in and of itself and under maritime law the most any contract for salvage vests in parties to salvage contract is a maritime lien. West's F.S.A.Const. art. 10, § 13.

> Treasure Salvors, Inc. v. Unidentified Wrecked and Abandoned Sailing Vessel, 459 F.Supp. 507, affirmed State of Fla., Dept. of State v. Treasure Salvors, Inc., 621 F.2d 1340, rehearing denied 629 F.2d 1350, certiorari granted Florida Dept. of State v. Treasure Salvors Inc., 101 S.Ct. 2312, 451 U.S. 982, 68 L.Ed.2d 838, affirmed in part, reversed in part 102 S.Ct. 3304, 458 U.S. 670, 73 L.Ed.2d 1057, on remand 689 F.2d 1254.

☞37. Apportionment among persons and property liable.

For other cases see earlier editions of this digest, the Decennial Digests, and WEST-LAW.

☞38. Apportionment among salvors.

† C.A.11 (Fla.) 2011. Shares of salvage award attributable to voluntary co-salvors of yachts who did not file claims against yacht owner should have inured to the benefit of owner of the salvaged vessels, rather than to co-salvors who filed claim.

> O'Hagan v. M & T Marine Group, LLC, 424 Fed.Appx. 811.

Individual's voluntary participation in untying lines that bound yachts to dock, which was essential to saving them, required apportionment of some part of salvage award to that individual, and because he did not make a claim for his share, credit for his share of the award should have inured to the benefit of owner of the salvaged vessels, rather than to benefit of salvors who filed claim for salvage award.

> O'Hagan v. M & T Marine Group, LLC, 424 Fed.Appx. 811.

C.A.5 (Fla.) 1978. Proportional distribution based on wages of each crew member is a generally accepted means of distributing a salvage award fairly.

> Compania Galeana, S.A. v. Motor Vessel Caribbean Mara, 565 F.2d 358.

C.A.5 (Fla.) 1974. Making of contribution, and not performance of actions or the furnishing of services supplied by no one else, is what is required to share in salvage award.

> Legnos v. M/V Olga Jacob, 498 F.2d 666, 26 A.L.R. Fed. 848, rehearing denied 503 F.2d 567, rehearing denied Eller and Company, Inc. v. Legnos, 503 F.2d 567, rehearing denied 503 F.2d 567, rehearing denied Schiffahrtsgesellschaft Jacob & Co. v. Eller and Company, Inc., 503 F.2d 568, affirmed 535 F.2d 857, rehearing denied 540 F.2d 1085.

Stevedore's employees, who performed some acts which bore directly on successful efforts to extinguish fire on vessel, were entitled to have these services properly evaluated in light of interests at risk and contributions of all others whether claiming or eligible to claim a salvage award in their own right.

> Legnos v. M/V Olga Jacob, 498 F.2d 666, 26 A.L.R. Fed. 848, rehearing denied 503 F.2d 567, rehearing denied Eller and Company, Inc. v. Legnos, 503 F.2d 567, rehearing denied 503 F.2d 567, rehearing denied Schiffahrtsgesellschaft Jacob & Co. v. Eller and Company, Inc., 503 F.2d 568, affirmed 535 F.2d 857, rehearing denied 540 F.2d 1085.

III. LIEN AND RECOVERY.

Research Notes

Salvage; liens; libels in admiralty, see West's Federal Forms.

☞39. Nature and incidents of lien.

C.A.5 (Fla.) 1981. Performance of salvage services, like furnishing of other services to a ship, gives rise to maritime lien; thus, salvor may assert his right to salvage award either in an in rem proceeding against salved vessel or cargo or in an in personam proceeding against owner of salved property.

> Treasure Salvors, Inc. v. Unidentified Wrecked & Abandoned Sailing Vessel, 640 F.2d 560, on remand 546 F.Supp. 919.

Original salvor has right to exclude others from participating in salvage operations, so long as original salvor appears ready, willing and able to complete salvage project, and has right to possession of salved property, a right exclusive even of owner, until such time as salvage lien on property is extinguished or adequate security for this obligation is given.

> Treasure Salvors, Inc. v. Unidentified Wrecked & Abandoned Sailing Vessel, 640 F.2d 560, on remand 546 F.Supp. 919.

M.D.Fla. 2010. After recovering lost property, under the law of salvage, a salvor obtains a maritime lien that allows the salvor to proceed in rem to secure a salvage award and gains exclusive "possession" over the salvaged property to allow for the uninterrupted delivery of the property to the court-appointed custodian; the value of the recovered property governs the salvage award, and, if the salvage award exceeds the value of the salvaged property, the salvor receives title to the property.

> Odyssey Marine Exploration, Inc. v. Unidentified, Wrecked and Abandoned Sailing Vessel, 727 F.Supp.2d 1341.

S.D.Fla. 1999. Salvage services advanced by plaintiff, and its predecessors in interest, constituted a valid maritime lien against *in rem* defendant, a rare and historic United States military aircraft that crashed in waters beyond the territorial limits of the United States in 1943.

> International Aircraft Recovery, L.L.C. v. Unidentified, Wrecked and Abandoned Aircraft, 54 F.Supp.2d 1172, reversed 218 F.3d 1255, certiorari denied International Aircraft Recovery, LLC v. U.S., 121 S.Ct. 1079, 531 U.S. 1144, 148 L.Ed.2d 956, appeal after remand 373 F.3d 1147.

S.D.Fla. 1981. Under traditional salvage rules, salvor receives a lien against the salved property and is usually entitled to his expenses plus a salvage award.

> Cobb Coin Co., Inc. v. Unidentified, Wrecked and Abandoned Sailing Vessel, 525 F.Supp. 186.

⚷40. Priority of lien.

S.D.Fla. 1959. Where owner of yacht authorized libelants to salvage his yacht, then lying stranded in the Bahamas, and libelants performed the salvage operations as authorized, and owner authorized intervenor to repair the yacht and intervenor performed repairs on yacht subsequent to the time it was salved, claim of libelants against yacht and owner was superior to and had priority over claim of intervenor.

> Hempstead v. The Escapade, 173 F.Supp. 833.

⚷41–42.1. *For other cases see earlier editions of this digest, the Decennial Digests, and WESTLAW.*

⚷42. Suits for salvage.

⚷43. —— Nature and form of remedy.

C.A.5 (Fla.) 1981. Performance of salvage services, like furnishing of other services to a ship, gives rise to maritime lien; thus, salvor may assert his right to salvage award either in an in rem proceeding against salved vessel or cargo or in an in personam proceeding against owner of salved property.

> Treasure Salvors, Inc. v. Unidentified Wrecked & Abandoned Sailing Vessel, 640 F.2d 560, on remand 546 F.Supp. 919.

S.D.Fla. 1982. In rem action for salvage award against artifacts recovered from the remains of a centuries-old shipwreck states a claim within federal district court's admiralty jurisdiction, governed by the judicial law of finds or doctrine of maritime salvage.

> Cobb Coin Co., Inc. v. Unidentified, Wrecked and Abandoned Sailing Vessel, 549 F.Supp. 540.

⚷44. —— Right of action and defenses.

S.D.Fla. 1976. Assertion that finder in possession is owner of an abandoned vessel is properly within scope of a salvage action.

> Treasure Salvors, Inc. v. Abandoned Sailing Vessel Believed to Be Nuestra Senora De Atocha, 408 F.Supp. 907, affirmed and modified 569 F.2d 330.

⚷45. —— Jurisdiction.

† C.A.11 (Fla.) 2014. Bronze rod and chests were not part of undivided res so as to allow district court to exercise constructive in rem jurisdiction over chests based on explorer's salvage of rod that was presented to court, as required to issue warrant of arrest as to chests under law of salvage, where explorer located three "large metallic objects" that he believed were piratical cargo consisting of copper chests containing gold, silver, and jewelry, but chests were "isolated [from the rod] and not in geographical association with any shipwreck."

Martin v. One Bronze Rod, 581 Fed. Appx. 744.

C.A.11 (Fla.) 2011. Salvor is able to bring a shipwreck found in international waters constructively within a court's territorial jurisdiction by having a portion of the shipwreck within the jurisdiction.

Odyssey Marine Exploration, Inc. v. Unidentified Shipwrecked Vessel, 657 F.3d 1159, certiorari denied 132 S.Ct. 2379, 182 L.Ed.2d 1051, certiorari denied Republic of Peru v. Unidentified Shipwrecked Vessel, 132 S.Ct. 2380, certiorari denied De Aliaga v. Kingdom of Spain, 132 S.Ct. 2380, 182 L.Ed.2d 1051.

C.A.5 (Fla.) 1978. District court was authorized to declare title to that portion of wrecked vessel within its territorial jurisdiction.

Treasure Salvors, Inc. v. Unidentified Wrecked and Abandoned Sailing Vessel, 569 F.2d 330.

Even assuming lack of in rem jurisdiction of that part of wrecked vessel lying outside territorial waters of United States, district court was not deprived of jurisdiction over government's counterclaim in corporations' suit for possession of and confirmation of title to wrecked and abandoned vessel, in view of fact that government based its claim to rights in sunken vessel on Antiquities Act and Abandoned Property Act, so that district court had jurisdiction to determine applicability of statutes to that portion of vessel situated in international waters. 16 U.S.C.A. § 431 et seq.; 28 U.S.C.A. § 1331; 40 U.S.C.A. § 310.

Treasure Salvors, Inc. v. Unidentified Wrecked and Abandoned Sailing Vessel, 569 F.2d 330.

M.D.Fla. 2010. To avoid "rigid legalism," the law of salvage permits the exercise of in rem jurisdiction by constructive possession, even if the court possesses only a portion of the total res.

Odyssey Marine Exploration, Inc. v. Unidentified, Wrecked and Abandoned Sailing Vessel, 727 F.Supp.2d 1341.

Constructive in rem jurisdiction allows the enforcement of an exclusive right to salvage a wreck in international water by expanding the traditional notion of in rem jurisdiction by constructive possession.

Odyssey Marine Exploration, Inc. v. Unidentified, Wrecked and Abandoned Sailing Vessel, 727 F.Supp.2d 1341.

Under the law of finds, a finder cannot exclude others from their attempts to obtain first possession of artifacts recovered from an abandoned wreck; in contrast, the law of salvage grants exclusive possession to ensure that the salvor recovers the owner's property intact, and this need supports the exercise of extra-territorial jurisdiction.

Odyssey Marine Exploration, Inc. v. Unidentified, Wrecked and Abandoned Sailing Vessel, 727 F.Supp.2d 1341.

S.D.Fla. 1999. Salvage of items from navigable waters, both within and without the United States, constitutes the core of the exclusive admiralty and maritime jurisdiction of United States District Courts. U.S.C.A. Const. Art. 3, § 2, cl. 1.

International Aircraft Recovery, L.L.C. v. Unidentified, Wrecked and Abandoned Aircraft, 54 F.Supp.2d 1172, reversed 218 F.3d 1255, certiorari denied International Aircraft Recovery, LLC v. U.S., 121 S.Ct. 1079, 531 U.S. 1144, 148 L.Ed.2d 956, appeal after remand 373 F.3d 1147.

S.D.Fla. 1983. Federal district court had in rem jurisdiction over wreck and wrecksite of Spanish galleon where artifacts from wrecksite had been brought into physical possession of court, court had physical presence and control of wrecksite by vessels, divers, equipment and otherwise of its substitute custodian, and wrecksite lay wholly and exclusively within waters of contiguous zone of United States in Atlantic Ocean.

> Treasure Salvors, Inc. v. Unidentified, Wrecked and Abandoned Sailing Vessel, 556 F.Supp. 1319.

In rem action for salvage award against artifacts recovered from remains of centuries-old shipwreck states claim within federal district court's admiralty jurisdiction, governed by judicial doctrine of finds and principles of maritime salvage.

> Treasure Salvors, Inc. v. Unidentified, Wrecked and Abandoned Sailing Vessel, 556 F.Supp. 1319.

S.D.Fla. 1982. Following salvor's filing of complaint for declaration of rights in a wrecked Spanish treasure vessel, district court had jurisdiction in rem over artifacts which had actually been brought up and turned over to United States marshal, had maritime jurisdiction based on in personam principles to adjudicate disputes between competing salvors or claimants who had answered the admiralty complaint, and had in rem jurisdiction, coupled with in personam jurisdiction over the claimants, to dispose of all articles brought up from the site of the wreck from the inception of the lawsuit. 28 U.S.C.A. § 1333.

> Cobb Coin Co., Inc. v. Unidentified, Wrecked and Abandoned Sailing Vessel, 549 F.Supp. 540.

S.D.Fla. 1981. Subject matter as well as in personam jurisdiction was vested in district court with respect to action wherein plaintiffs sought to enjoin opposing salvors and/or treasure hunters from interfering with search and salvage operations of an ancient shipwreck and from searching for or salvaging within an area extending 2500 yards to either side of a line drawn between two points were anchors were found. U.S.C.A.Const. Art. 3, § 2, cl. 1; 28 U.S.C.A. § 1333; Fed.Rules Civ.Proc. Rule 9(h), 28 U.S.C.A.

> Treasure Salvors, Inc. v. Unidentified, Wrecked and Abandoned Sailing Vessel, 546 F.Supp. 919.

District court had jurisdiction over that portion of an ancient shipwreck which was within its territorial jurisdiction, and since a reasonable likelihood existed that other portions constituting a significant additional salvaging result would be within court's territorial jurisdiction, district court had, at least, qualified jurisdiction in rem which was likely to ripen into full in rem jurisdiction in action wherein plaintiffs sought to enjoin opposing salvors and/or treasure hunters from interfering with search and salvage operation of wreck and from searching for or salvaging within area.

> Treasure Salvors, Inc. v. Unidentified, Wrecked and Abandoned Sailing Vessel, 546 F.Supp. 919.

S.D.Fla. 1981. Once a salvor who discovers and brings up an artifact from an identifiable wreck site initiates suit by taking that object into federal court, the court acquires jurisdiction not only to adjudicate the disposition of the article already within its territorial jurisdiction but maritime jurisdiction, based on in personam principles, to adjudicate disputes between competing salvors and in rem jurisdiction to dispose of all articles thereafter brought up from that site.

> Cobb Coin Co., Inc. v. Unidentified, Wrecked and Abandoned Sailing Vessel, 525 F.Supp. 186.

In rem action for salvage award against artifacts recovered from the remains of a centuries-old shipwreck states a claim within the federal district court's admiralty jurisdiction.

> Cobb Coin Co., Inc. v. Unidentified, Wrecked and Abandoned Sailing Vessel, 525 F.Supp. 186.

⊕⊸**45.5. —— Time to sue and limitations.**

For other cases see earlier editions of this digest, the Decennial Digests, and WEST-LAW.

⊕⊸**46. —— Parties.**

C.A.5 (Fla.) 1978. In corporations' suit for possession of and confirmation of title to unidentified wrecked and abandoned vessel thought to be Spanish vessel which sank in 1622, district court did not have power to hold that corporations had exclusive title to, and right to immediate and sole possession of, vessel and cargo as to other claimants, if any, who were not parties or privies to litigation.

> Treasure Salvors, Inc. v. Unidentified, Wrecked and Abandoned Sailing Vessel, 569 F.2d 330.

S.D.Fla. 1999. United States was permitted to intervene in in rem admiralty action and request that salvaged rare and historic military aircraft be awarded to the National Museum of Naval Aviation.

International Aircraft Recovery, L.L.C. v. Unidentified, Wrecked and Abandoned Aircraft, 54 F.Supp.2d 1172, reversed 218 F.3d 1255, certiorari denied International Aircraft Recovery, LLC v. U.S., 121 S.Ct. 1079, 531 U.S. 1144, 148 L.Ed.2d 956, appeal after remand 373 F.3d 1147.

⚷47. —— **Pleading.**

† **C.A.11 (Fla.) 2013.** Under Florida law, shipwreck researcher who sought rescission of contract with underwater salvage corporation upon restoration of funds paid by corporation to researcher in excess of funds owed by corporation to researcher failed to state a claim, where researcher did not plead that restoration of the full amount he received from corporation was impossible; Florida law on rescission required that plaintiff plead offer to restore benefits furnished under contract by defendant if restoration was possible.

Odyssey Marine Exploration, Inc. v. Unidentified, Shipwrecked Vessel or Vessels, 512 Fed.Appx. 890.

⚷48. —— **Evidence.**

† **C.A.11 (Fla.) 2012.** Salvor was entitled to present expert witness at trial regarding post-salvage value of capsized yacht that it had towed to a harbor in its action to recover a salvage award from yacht owner, despite salvor's untimely witness disclosure; yacht owner's motion to strike salvor's witness was untimely, neither party disclosed its expert witness properly, and yacht owner had access to survey report and appraisal of yacht's value made by salvor's expert witness several months before trial.

Esoteric, LLC v. One (1) 2000 Eighty-Five Foot Azimut Motor Yacht Named M/V STAR ONE, 478 Fed. Appx. 639.

† **C.A.11 (Fla.) 2011.** District court did not clearly err by accepting salvor's competent testimony about the sticker prices of yachts in determining fair market value of yachts, where such testimony was unrebutted.

O'Hagan v. M & T Marine Group, LLC, 424 Fed.Appx. 811.

C.A.5 (Fla.) 1968. Evidence did not support denial of claim for salvage on ground that salvor was contractually obligated to unbeach barges.

Fort Myers Shell & Dredging Co. v. Barge NBC 512, 404 F.2d 137.

Evidence did not warrant denial of salvage recovery on theory that salvor was negligent.

Fort Myers Shell & Dredging Co. v. Barge NBC 512, 404 F.2d 137.

Facts did not warrant denial of claim for salvage on theory that it would be grossly inequitable to pay for services forced upon vessels.

Fort Myers Shell & Dredging Co. v. Barge NBC 512, 404 F.2d 137.

S.D.Fla. 2013. As the plaintiff in an rem action for salvage award has the burden to prove marine peril, the plaintiff must show that the subject material was lost.

JTR Enterprises, LLC v. An Unknown Quantity of Colombian Emeralds, Amethysts and Quartz Crystals, 922 F.Supp.2d 1326, appeal dismissed (11th cir. 13-10870).

S.D.Fla. 1984. Although action of Navy with respect to sailboat in sinking condition would support award of salvor's lien to the Navy, there could be no recovery for salvage in view of Navy's failure to prove damage suffered by it other than loss of rubber raft which was used, unintentionally, as fender between sailboat and hull of submarine, and there being no competent evidence as to value of the raft. 14 U.S.C.A. § 88.

Port Tack Sailboats, Inc. v. U.S., 593 F.Supp. 597.

S.D.Fla. 1982. In order to state a claim for salvage award on an ancient vessel of historical and archeological significance, it is an essential element that the salvors document to the admiralty court's satisfaction that they have preserved the archeological provenance of shipwreck, but by meeting this threshold requirement, salvor simultaneously "enhances" the value of his recovery in such a way as will be explicitly recognized by the court in the determination of the salvage award.

> Cobb Coin Co., Inc. v. Unidentified, Wrecked and Abandoned Sailing Vessel, 549 F.Supp. 540.

S.D.Fla. 1961. Evidence in libel by salvor disclosed, that neither of stranded shrimp vessels was in imminent danger of being broken up, that both vessels were together worth $23,000 at time of stranding, that any peril could have been avoided, that salvor was prompt but used minimal skill, that salvor used $2,000 to $5,000 worth of property in salvage operation, and that salvor spent slightly more than twenty-four hours in all. 14 U.S.C.A. § 88; 46 U.S.C.A. § 724.

> Beach Salvage Corp. of Fla. v. The Cap't. Tom, 201 F.Supp. 479.

⚷49. —— **Trial or hearing.**

† **C.A.11 (Fla.) 2012.** District court clearly erred when it stated in its findings of fact and conclusions of law that yacht owner failed to proffer testimony as to post-salvage value of yacht and that salvor's expert witness testimony as to a $565,000 value of yacht was uncontradicted, where court had expressly stated that it would consider testimony of yacht owner's expert witness that the yacht's post-salvage value was $150,000 as some evidence.

> Esoteric, LLC v. One (1) 2000 Eighty-Five Foot Azimut Motor Yacht Named M/V STAR ONE, 478 Fed. Appx. 639.

† **C.A.11 (Fla.) 2011.** Yacht owner sued for salvage award was not entitled to continuance on grounds that salvors' expert disclosure was not timely, where salvors had produced a detailed expert report and answers to expert interrogatories several months before the motion, and thus owner had notice of the expert and had plenty of time before trial to get its own expert.

> O'Hagan v. M & T Marine Group, LLC, 424 Fed.Appx. 811.

C.A.5 (Fla.) 1968. Where barges were stranded with pilings nearby in Gulf of Mexico where sudden storms arise, it could not be said as matter of law, as

defense against claim for salvage that peril was not reasonably to be apprehended.

> Fort Myers Shell & Dredging Co. v. Barge NBC 512, 404 F.2d 137.

⚷50. —— **Decree and enforcement thereof.**

For other cases see earlier editions of this digest, the Decennial Digests, and WEST-LAW.

⚷51. —— **Appeal.**

C.A.5 (Fla.) 1981. Statute authorizing interlocutory appeals in admiralty from orders "determining the rights and liabilities of the parties to admiralty cases * * *" did not authorize appeal of district court order issuing preliminary injunction prohibiting defendant salvors from interfering with plaintiff salvor's search and salvage operations, since order did not have effect of ultimately determining rights and obligations of the parties. 28 U.S.C.A. § 1292(a)(3).

> Treasure Salvors, Inc. v. Unidentified Wrecked & Abandoned Sailing Vessel, 640 F.2d 560, on remand 546 F.Supp. 919.

C.A.5 (Fla.) 1978. Appellate courts will not disturb salvage award unless it is based on erroneous principles or a misapprehension of the facts or is so grossly excessive or inadequate as to be deemed an abuse of discretion.

> Compania Galeana, S.A. v. Motor Vessel Caribbean Mara, 565 F.2d 358.

C.A.5 (Fla.) 1963. Where salvage case had been tried and appealed twice and parties were desirous of winding up case and another trial would produce more, not less, contention, Court of Appeals would not remand with an indication of the guidelines to be followed for recomputation of damages but would remand with directions to enter a decree allowing the amounts fixed by the Court of Appeals.

> Oil Screw Noah's Ark v. Bentley & Felton Corp., 322 F.2d 3.

C.A.5 (Fla.) 1960. In action by yacht owner against insurer on hull policy for damage to vessel, which was stranded while being operated in breach of private pleasure use, warranty of policy which also contained a sue and labor clause, wherein owner asserted insurer was estopped to assert defense of breach of warranty, findings of trial court that actions of insurer, which knew of breach but required owner to look after and protect yacht and to authorize contract of salvage by salvor of insurer's choice, were inconsistent with nonliability because of known breach of warranty and that owner had been induced by this conduct to take action to his detriment, were not clearly erroneous. Fed.Rules Civ.Proc. rule 52(a), 28 U.S.C.A.

    Reliance Ins. Co. v. The Escapade, 280 F.2d 482, 86 A.L.R.2d 1236.

C.C.A.5 (Fla.) 1938. In libel against a steel barge on a claim for salvage, whether with the aid of veering winds libelants contributed in some material degree to the rescue or preservation of the barge, which had been severed from tug in a storm, or whether they simply pulled on barge a considerable time before favorable wind and wave cast it on the beach, was a fact question for District Judge.

    The No. 105, 97 F.2d 425.

⊶**52. —— Costs.**

    † **C.A.11 (Fla.) 2012.** Yacht owner's dispute of salvor's entitlement to a salvage award for towing his capsized, mostly submerged yacht to a harbor was not done in bad faith, as required to merit an award of attorney's fees to salvor under admiralty law; district court's post hoc reasoning that yacht owner had no cognizable defense at law ignored yacht owner's trial testimony that, in effect, all the salvor did was tow the yacht to anchor, and that the yacht was still submerged and capsized after salvor's efforts.

    Esoteric, LLC v. One (1) 2000 Eighty-Five Foot Azimut Motor Yacht Named M/V STAR ONE, 478 Fed. Appx. 639.

    † **C.A.11 (Fla.) 2012.** District court did not abuse its discretion in awarding attorney fees and costs to maritime service company on grounds that vessel owner's defense of company's salvage claim was frivolous and in bad faith; mere fact that owner had valid defense to company's contract theory did not mean that his defense to company's pure salvage claim could not be found to be frivolous, owner's argument in defending the pure salvage

claim, namely, that his vessel was not in peril because it was not taking on water and there was no inclement weather, was not well-founded given the weather conditions the vessel would have faced for several days had it not been assisted by company, owner conceded that company was owed a salvage fee for it services, owner failed to pay company when his insurer denied the claim, and owner never argued that the sum billed by company was excessive.

    Reliable Salvage and Towing, Inc. v. Bivona, 476 Fed.Appx. 852.

C.A.11 (Fla.) 2005. Attorney fees could not be awarded in an *in rem* action to enforce a salvage lien, since attorney fees incurred in the litigation and arbitration were not part of the value of the salvage lien against the vessel; attorney fees were not a measure of the labor expended by the salvor, the skill of the salvor, the value of salving property, or the risk to the salvor or the property. 46 U.S.C.A. § 31301(5)(F).

    Offshore Marine Towing, Inc. v. MR23, 412 F.3d 1254.

C.A.5 (Fla.) 1978. Where counsel for master of vessel filed no pleading and did not participate in trial of salvage case, trial court, which approved settlement between parties, did not abuse its discretion in failing to award attorney fees to counsel for master of vessel.

    Compania Galeana, S.A. v. Motor Vessel Caribbean Mara, 565 F.2d 358.

C.A.5 (Fla.) 1963. Both trial and appellate costs in salvage case would be divided equally in view of adjustment of damages and the fact of substantial injury sustained by salvaged vessel after it was negligently cast off by salvor.

    Oil Screw Noah's Ark v. Bentley & Felton Corp., 322 F.2d 3.

C.C.A.5 (Fla.) 1938. Where respondents appealing from a final decree for libelants on a claim for salvage lost appeal on question of liability but won a reduction of amount recovered, costs of appeal were divided between respondents and libelants.

    The No. 105, 97 F.2d 425.

S.D.Fla. 2004. Salvor was not entitled to recover attorney fees and costs in connection with litigation regarding its entitlement to salvage award, where vessel owner did not act in bad faith.

Atlantis Marine Towing, Inc. v. M/V/ELIZABETH, 346 F.Supp.2d 1266.

S.D.Fla. 2003. Award of attorney fees in admiralty actions is discretionary and is specifically permitted in salvage cases.

Southernmost Marine Services, Inc. v. One (1) 2000 Fifty Four Foot (54') Sea Ray named M/V POTENTIAL, 250 F.Supp.2d 1367, affirmed Southernmost Marine Svcs. v. M/V POTENTIAL, 91 Fed.Appx. 655.

In determining whether to exercise court's broad discretion under admiralty salvage law to award attorney's fees and costs, consideration is given to the necessity for the litigation and the trial upon the issues raised.

Southernmost Marine Services, Inc. v. One (1) 2000 Fifty Four Foot (54') Sea Ray named M/V POTENTIAL, 250 F.Supp.2d 1367, affirmed Southernmost Marine Svcs. v. M/V POTENTIAL, 91 Fed.Appx. 655.

There was a sufficient legal basis to award salvors its attorney fees and costs where vessel owner's insurer had very little, if any, basis in fact for disputing the salvage award it had agreed to, contracted for, and paid.

Southernmost Marine Services, Inc. v. One (1) 2000 Fifty Four Foot (54') Sea Ray named M/V POTENTIAL, 250 F.Supp.2d 1367, affirmed Southernmost Marine Svcs. v. M/V POTENTIAL, 91 Fed.Appx. 655.

S.D.Fla. 1983. Award of attorney fees and costs in admiralty is discretionary and specifically permitted in salvage cases.

Treasure Salvors, Inc. v. Unidentified, Wrecked and Abandoned Sailing Vessel, 556 F.Supp. 1319.

Salvage company, which was successful in pursuing its claim and entitlement to salvage award for recovering treasure from wrecked Spanish galleon as against claim of captain it had hired to conduct search, was entitled to award of attorney fees and costs from captain.

Treasure Salvors, Inc. v. Unidentified, Wrecked and Abandoned Sailing Vessel, 556 F.Supp. 1319.

S.D.Fla. 1982. Award of attorney fees against state of Florida was appropriate in admiralty salvage action where most of the massive litigation would have been unnecessary if state had not intervened and filed its claims and defenses and where 11-day injunction hearing was necessitated by bad-faith harassment conducted by state officers and attorneys attempting to enforce Florida laws in derogation of federal court's jurisdiction.

Cobb Coin Co., Inc. v. Unidentified, Wrecked and Abandoned Sailing Vessel, 549 F.Supp. 540.

SCHOOLS

See EDUCATION

For Cross-References or Descriptive Words
see
DESCRIPTIVE–WORD INDEX

SCIRE FACIAS

SUBJECTS INCLUDED

Writs of scire facias for enforcement of obligations of record

Nature and scope of the remedy in general

Grounds of such writs and defenses thereto

To and against whom and on what matters of record they are allowed

Jurisdiction to grant and proceedings to obtain the writ

Issuance, requisites and validity of writs, service thereof, return thereto and proceedings thereon

SUBJECTS EXCLUDED AND COVERED BY OTHER TOPICS

Writs of scire facias and proceedings by motion, etc., or by action, to—

Continue or revive actions, see ABATEMENT AND REVIVAL

Enforce forfeited bail bonds and recognizances, see BAIL, RECOGNIZANCES

Foreclose mortgages or mechanics' liens, see MORTGAGES AND DEEDS OF TRUST, MECHANICS' LIENS

Revive judgments or executions, see JUDGMENT, EXECUTION

For detailed references to other topics, see Descriptive-Word Index

---

Analysis

⚷1. **Nature and scope of remedy.**

Fla.App. 2 Dist. 1963. Purpose of the writ of scire facias is to give the party against whom execution is about to issue notice so that he may urge defenses which have arisen after creation of the original record. 31 F.S.A. Rules of Civil Procedure, rule 2.12; F.S.A. § 77.01 et seq. Seven-Up Bottling Co. of Miami v. J. N. Rawleigh Co., 156 So.2d 180.

⚷2–15. *For other cases see earlier editions of this digest, the Decennial Digests, and WESTLAW.*

For Cross-References or Descriptive Words
see
DESCRIPTIVE–WORD INDEX

SEALS

SUBJECTS INCLUDED

Signs and devices, representing parties to instruments in writing, attached or affixed to such instruments to attest their genuineness or their formal execution

Necessity, attaching or affixing, and sufficiency thereof in general

SUBJECTS EXCLUDED AND COVERED BY OTHER TOPICS

Particular classes of instruments, seals affixed to, see DEEDS and other specific topics

Particular classes of persons, officers, or bodies corporate or politic, seals of, see CORPORATIONS AND BUSINESS ORGANIZATIONS and other specific topics

For detailed references to other topics, see Descriptive-Word Index

---

Analysis

⚷1. Necessity and use in general.

Fla. 1942. "Seals" serve as an authentication of an instrument and also as the badge of a specialty.

Caruthers v. Peninsular Life Ins. Co., 7 So.2d 841, 150 Fla. 467.

⚷2. Statutory provisions.

For other cases see earlier editions of this digest, the Decennial Digests, and WEST-LAW.

⚷3. Requisites and mode of impressing or affixing.

Fla.App. 4 Dist. 1967. Letters "L.S." are abbreviation for "locus sigilli" meaning place where seal or that which stands instead of seal is to be affixed.

Pitts v. Pitchford, 201 So.2d 563, certiorari denied 207 So.2d 452.

⚷4. Adopting seal previously affixed.

For other cases see earlier editions of this digest, the Decennial Digests, and WEST-LAW.

⚷5. Recital or other recognition in instrument.

Fla.App. 3 Dist. 1966. Where broker's real estate sale contract recited that "the parties hereto have hereunto set their hands and seals" and all signatures, except broker's, were followed by word "seal", contract was "sealed instrument" and broker would be presumed to have adopted seals which appeared on contract.

Megdell v. Bailey, 194 So.2d 13.

⚷6. Evidence as to seals.

Fla.App. 3 Dist. 1966. Where broker's real estate sale contract recited that "the parties hereto have hereunto set their hands and seals" and all signatures, except broker's, were followed by word "seal", contract was "sealed instrument" and broker would be presumed to have adopted seals which appeared on contract.

Megdell v. Bailey, 194 So.2d 13.

⚷6.5. Questions for jury.

For other cases see earlier editions of this digest, the Decennial Digests, and WEST-LAW.

⚷7. Loss of seal.

For other cases see earlier editions of this digest, the Decennial Digests, and WEST-LAW.

For Cross-References or Descriptive Words
see
DESCRIPTIVE–WORD INDEX

SEAMEN

SUBJECTS INCLUDED

Employment, regulation, and protection of seamen

Mutual rights, duties, and liabilities of seamen and of owners, charterers, and masters of vessels on which they are employed

Liabilities to seamen of vessels, their cargoes and freight

SUBJECTS EXCLUDED AND COVERED BY OTHER TOPICS

Labor relations involving seamen, see LABOR AND EMPLOYMENT

Longshoremen and similar workers, see SHIPPING, WORKERS' COMPENSATION

Masters of vessels, see SHIPPING

Pilots, see PILOTS

Salvage by seamen, see SALVAGE

For detailed references to other topics, see Descriptive-Word Index

---

Analysis

For detailed references to other topics, see Descriptive-Word Index

Research Notes

Seamen; carelessness; Jones Act; libels in admiralty, see West's Federal Forms.

See Wright & Miller, Federal Practice and Procedure: Civil.

☞1. Power to regulate and protect.

C.A.11 (Fla.) 1996. Seamen are wards of admiralty whose rights federal courts are duty-bound to jealously protect.

Isbrandtsen Marine Services, Inc. v. M/V Inagua Tania, 93 F.3d 728.

M.D.Fla. 1977. Seamen are a class of persons whom the law especially favors.

Matter of Jama, 436 F.Supp. 963.

S.D.Fla. 1995. Twin aims of maritime law are achieving uniformity in the exercise of admiralty jurisdiction and providing special solicitude to seamen.

Williams v. Carnival Cruise Lines, Inc., 907 F.Supp. 403.

S.D.Fla. 1957. Injured libellant, who was a seaman, was a ward of admiralty and as such entitled to the jealous protection of his rights by the admiralty court and neither his employer nor insurance carrier could abrogate those rights by voluntary payment of workmen's compensation benefits.

Chesser v. General Dredging Co., 150 F.Supp. 592.

☞2. Who are seamen.

C.A.11 (Fla.) 1993. Biologist who was on Japanese driftnet fishing vessel plying international waters was not "seaman" for purposes of Jones Act and, therefore, could not recover for slip and fall injuries on vessel as borrowed servant employee of the United States under Jones Act, general maritime law, or as employee under Federal Employees Compensation Act (FECA); biologist was aboard vessel solely because treaty provided for placement of American observers on Japanese driftnet fishing vessels in international waters, biologist's mission was to collect data and conduct scientific studies and not to catch fish or to have anything to do with vessel, and biologist was simply employee of company which contracted with government to provide scientific observers, aboard vessel as business invitee. 5 U.S.C.A. §§ 8101–8193; United States-Japan Fishery Agreement Approval Act of 1987, § 4001 et seq., 16 U.S.C.A. § 1822 note; Jones Act, 46 App.U.S.C.A. § 688.

O'Boyle v. U.S., 993 F.2d 211.

C.A.11 (Fla.) 1990. To qualify for seaman status under Jones Act, worker must have more or less permanent connection with vessel in navigation, and capacity in which he is employed or duties which he performs must contribute to function of vessel, accomplishment of its mission, or its operation or welfare in terms of its maintenance during its movement or during anchorage for its future trips. Jones Act, 46 U.S.C.A.App. § 688.

Hurst v. Pilings & Structures, Inc., 896 F.2d 504, rehearing denied 912 F.2d 1470.

C.A.11 (Fla.) 1988. Cruise ship's assistant pantryman, attained "seaman" status at time he checked in at office of ship's food and beverage concessionaire, which had hired him, and was "in the service of the ship" at time he was injured in automobile accident while on personal pleasure trip prior to departure of ship, where pantryman's reporting to concessionaire's office prior to scheduled departure was a prerequisite both to commencing work aboard ship and to his entry into United States.

Archer v. Trans/American Services, Ltd., 834 F.2d 1570.

Cruise ship assistant pantryman was a "blue water seaman" on shore leave at time of his injury in automobile accident prior to departure of ship, where pantryman lived on ship for most of the two-year period preceding accident, and would have boarded ship for duration of his 12–month employment contract had he not been injured, and where purpose for his presence at location of accident was solely to serve interest of ship concessionaire, which had hired him, in marshaling personnel prior to departure of ship.

Archer v. Trans/American Services, Ltd., 834 F.2d 1570.

C.A.11 (Fla.) 1987. To be "in navigation" for purposes of the "Jones Act" definition of seaman, a vessel must be "engaged as an instrument of commerce and

transportation on navigable waters."
Jones Act, 46 U.S.C.A. § 688.

> Caruso v. Sterling Yacht and Ship-builders, Inc., 828 F.2d 14, rehearing denied 833 F.2d 1021.

A newly constructed ship was not a vessel "in navigation" as required in order for injured employee to recover damages for negligence under Jones Act where vessel was not licensed for navigation at time of injury and, although launched and afloat, had not been tested in sea trials. Jones Act, 46 U.S.C.A. § 688.

> Caruso v. Sterling Yacht and Ship-builders, Inc., 828 F.2d 14, rehearing denied 833 F.2d 1021.

C.A.5 (Fla.) 1973. To prove seaman status, for purpose of recovery under Jones Act, person is required to prove that vessel on which alleged injury occurred was in navigation at time of such injury, that he was aboard vessel primarily as an aid to navigation and that his connection with vessel was more or less permanent. Jones Act, 46 U.S.C.A. § 688.

> Garcia v. Queen, Ltd., 487 F.2d 625.

C.A.5 (Fla.) 1968. The same test is to be applied to ascertaining whether a person is a "seaman" for purposes of Jones Act jurisdiction, or is "a member of a crew of a vessel" for purpose of Longshoremen's Act jurisdiction. Longshoremen's and Harbor Workers' Compensation Act, § 1 et seq., 33 U.S.C.A. § 901 et seq.; Jones Act, 46 U.S.C.A. § 688.

> Hardaway Contracting Co. v. O'Keeffe, 414 F.2d 657, 20 A.L.R. Fed. 593.

C.A.5 (Fla.) 1968. For purposes of maritime relationships under Admiralty Jurisdiction Extension Act, bridge workers injured when outboard rigger of shrimp boat struck leaf of bridge on which they were working were treated as crew of bridge which, in turn, was treated as vessel, and thus workers could not be treated as vessels for divided damages purposes. Admiralty Jurisdiction Extension Act, 46 U.S.C.A. § 740.

> Empire Seafoods, Inc. v. Anderson, 398 F.2d 204, certiorari denied 89 S.Ct. 449, 393 U.S. 983, 21 L.Ed.2d 444.

C.A.5 (Fla.) 1966. Essential elements of term "seaman", as used in Jones Act, are that vessel must be in navigation, that there must be more or less permanent connection with vessel, and that worker be aboard primarily to aid in navigation. Jones Act, 46 U.S.C.A. § 688.

> Bodden v. Coordinated Caribbean Transport, Inc., 369 F.2d 273, 5 A.L.R. Fed. 668.

Question whether vessel is in navigation, as element in determining whether worker aboard vessel is "seaman" within preview of Jones Act, is to be resolved by consideration of totality of circumstances. Jones Act, 46 U.S.C.A. § 688.

> Bodden v. Coordinated Caribbean Transport, Inc., 369 F.2d 273, 5 A.L.R. Fed. 668.

Whether person is "seaman" within purview of Jones Act depends largely on facts of particular case. Jones Act, 46 U.S.C.A. § 688.

> Bodden v. Coordinated Caribbean Transport, Inc., 369 F.2d 273, 5 A.L.R. Fed. 668.

If vessel is temporarily in dry dock for repairs, it remains in navigation for purpose of determining whether injured worker is "seaman" within purview of Jones Act. Jones Act, 46 U.S.C.A. § 688.

> Bodden v. Coordinated Caribbean Transport, Inc., 369 F.2d 273, 5 A.L.R. Fed. 668.

Where vessel is laid up for winter, crew has been discharged, and boat is being secured by workmen paid an hourly rate and living ashore, ship is no longer in navigation for purpose of determining whether injured workman is "seaman" within purview of Jones Act. Jones Act, 46 U.S.C.A. § 688.

> Bodden v. Coordinated Caribbean Transport, Inc., 369 F.2d 273, 5 A.L.R. Fed. 668.

Where vessel is tied up for winter with only maintenance crew, and crew member during season is retained as laborer on hourly basis and is not required to live aboard vessel, vessel is no longer in navigation for purpose of determining whether laborer is "seaman" within purview of Jones Act. Jones Act, 46 U.S.C.A. § 688.

Bodden v. Coordinated Caribbean Transport, Inc., 369 F.2d 273, 5 A.L.R. Fed. 668.

C.A.5 (Fla.) 1960. Where corporation purchased inboard cruiser, which was originally for pleasure of corporation's president and for entertainment of customers, and subsequently corporation's construction engineer was permitted to use cruiser, and while cruiser was in boatyard engineer and friend went to boatyard to remove defective bilge pump from cruiser and engineer decided to pump water out of cruiser before removing pump, and, while engineer, with help of friend, was attempting to start motor, electric spark caused explosion of gas, and friend was fatally injured, Jones Act and Death on the High Seas Act were not available to deceased friend's widow, who sought to recover for deceased friend's death, and she was not entitled to death benefits under Longshoremen's and Harbor Workers' Compensation Act. Jones Act, 46 U.S.C.A. § 688; Death on the High Seas Act, § 1 et seq., 46 U.S.C.A. § 761 et seq.; Longshoremen's and Harbor Workers' Compensation Act, § 1 et seq., 33 U.S.C.A. § 901 et seq.

Emerson v. Holloway Concrete Products Co., 282 F.2d 271, certiorari denied 81 S.Ct. 459, 364 U.S. 941, 5 L.Ed.2d 372.

C.A.5 (Fla.) 1954. A plaintiff who was employed by defendant operator of resort hotel as a cabana boy, and who went fishing for pleasure with speed boat owner not operating boat as agent, servant or employee of defendant, and who was injured from contacting propeller when holding boat at beach to prevent boat from scraping, was not under record a seaman, did not sustain injuries in course of employment as seaman, was not master or member of crew, and showed no negligence on part of defendant, nor was defendant owner pro hac vice of boat at time of injury, and plaintiff was not entitled to recover under Jones Act. Jones Act, 46 U.S.C.A. § 688.

Kanischer v. Irwin Operating Co., 215 F.2d 300, certiorari denied 75 S.Ct. 363, 348 U.S. 942, 99 L.Ed. 737, rehearing denied 75 S.Ct. 529, 348 U.S. 977, 99 L.Ed. 761.

M.D.Fla. 2004. In determining claimant's seaman status for Jones Act purposes, courts should examine the claimant's overall job assignments as they existed at the time of the injury to determine whether there is sufficient connection to a vessel in navigation, without focusing solely on the specific activity in which the employee was engaged at the time of his injury. Jones Act, 46 App. U.S.C.A. § 688.

In re Williams Marine Const. and Services, Inc., 350 F.Supp.2d 975.

S.D.Fla. 1973. Test of whether one employed on vessel is "seaman" and entitled to maintenance and cure is that vessel must be in navigation, that there be more or less permanent connection with vessel or substantial part of duties be performed aboard vessel, and that worker be aboard primarily to aid in navigation or his duties contribute directly to mission or purpose of vessel.

Steuer v. N.V. Nederl-Amerik Stoomvaart Maatschappf (Holand-Ameriklijn), 362 F.Supp. 600.

Definition of "seaman" is same for both maintenance and cure doctrine and Jones Act. Jones Act, 46 U.S.C.A. § 688.

Steuer v. N.V. Nederl-Amerik Stoomvaart Maatschappf (Holand-Ameriklijn), 362 F.Supp. 600.

Clergyman who was aboard cruise ship to conduct certain services during cruise and who ate with passengers, slept in passenger accommodations, had shipboard privileges of passenger and carried a passenger ticket was not a "seaman" so as to be entitled to assert claim for cure.

Steuer v. N.V. Nederl-Amerik Stoomvaart Maatschappf (Holand-Ameriklijn), 362 F.Supp. 600.

S.D.Fla. 1972. Plaintiff who had served on crew of commercial fishing vessel, who had been paid off and had no further duties to perform on or for vessel, and who had no assurance that he would be on vessel when it next sailed, was not "seaman" entitled to warranty of seaworthiness or to maintenance and cure in connection with injury sustained when he was attacked aboard vessel by another former crew member, even though both had been allowed to remain aboard by owner and captain.

> Rainville v. F/V "Gem", 351 F.Supp. 369.

Seaman status in each case depends upon facts of particular case, and analysis of duties performed for employer in aid of ship is crucial to determination.

> Rainville v. F/V "Gem", 351 F.Supp. 369.

S.D.Fla. 1965. Jones Act concept of "seaman" since passage of Longshoremen's and Harbor Workers' Compensation Act has been narrowed to include only one who is member of crew of vessel plying in navigable waters. Jones Act, 46 U.S.C.A. § 688; Longshoremen's and Harbor Workers' Compensation Act, § 1 et seq., 33 U.S.C.A. § 901 et seq.

> Bodden v. Coordinated Caribbean Transport, Inc., 249 F.Supp. 561, reversed 369 F.2d 273, 5 A.L.R. Fed. 668.

Essential and decisive elements of definition of "member of crew" for Jones Act purposes are that ship be in navigation, that there be more or less permanent connection with ship, and that worker be aboard primarily to aid in navigation. Jones Act, 46 U.S.C.A. § 688.

> Bodden v. Coordinated Caribbean Transport, Inc., 249 F.Supp. 561, reversed 369 F.2d 273, 5 A.L.R. Fed. 668.

Person who sustains injuries aboard vessel which is withdrawn from navigation is not a "seaman" within intendment of Jones Act. Jones Act, 46 U.S.C.A. § 688.

> Bodden v. Coordinated Caribbean Transport, Inc., 249 F.Supp. 561, reversed 369 F.2d 273, 5 A.L.R. Fed. 668.

Though he had signed shipping articles for service as second engineer on vessel, plaintiff was not a "seaman" entitled to protection of Jones Act when he was engaged in assisting in removal of piston from engine of ship at least four days prior to time when it was put in navigation. Jones Act, 46 U.S.C.A. § 688.

> Bodden v. Coordinated Caribbean Transport, Inc., 249 F.Supp. 561, reversed 369 F.2d 273, 5 A.L.R. Fed. 668.

S.D.Fla. 1963. Lack of long continued attachment to vessel does not serve to deny seaman's status under Jones Act to person injured while assigned to and performing normal crew service. Jones Act, 46 U.S.C.A. § 688.

> Petition of Read, 224 F.Supp. 241.

Claimant, who came to port where yacht was moored seeking to participate in yacht race for personal pleasure, who was not promised wage or salary , but who was actually performing normal crew service when injured was "seaman" within Jones Act. Jones Act, 46 U.S.C.A. § 688.

> Petition of Read, 224 F.Supp. 241.

S.D.Fla. 1957. Where libellant at time of injury was working as a mate aboard dredge employed in navigable waters, dredge was a vessel under maritime law notwithstanding fact that it had no motive power of its own, and libellant was a seaman.

> Chesser v. General Dredging Co., 150 F.Supp. 592.

A seaman need not eat or sleep aboard the vessel on which he works or hold a seaman's papers or sign ship's articles in order to be classified as a seaman over which the admiralty court has jurisdiction, so long as his primary duties are concerned with furthering the main purpose of the vessel upon which he is employed.

> Chesser v. General Dredging Co., 150 F.Supp. 592.

Fla. 1976. Under Jones Act, master of a vessel, no less than the crew he commands, may be a "seaman." Jones Act, 46 U.S.C.A. § 688.

> City of Plantation v. Roberts, 342 So.2d 69.

In order to qualify as a "seaman" under Jones Act, person must be more or less permanently attached to the vessel. Jones Act, 46 U.S.C.A. § 688.

> City of Plantation v. Roberts, 342 So.2d 69.

Fla. 1952. A member of crew of dredge which was engaged in filling land for a public park, and which was not concerned with navigation when such member was injured, was not entitled to maintain action for injuries under Jones Act which covers members of crew of vessel who are on board aiding in her navigation. Jones Act, 46 U.S.C.A. § 688.

Covington v. Standard Dredging Corp., 61 So.2d 644.

Fla.App. 2 Dist. 1993. In determining whether worker is entitled to seaman status for purposes of Jones Act, courts consider whether he was assigned permanently to, or performed substantial part of his work on vessel in navigation and whether capacity in which he was employed, or duty which he performed, contributed to function of vessel or accomplishment of its mission. Jones Act, 46 App.U.S.C.A. § 688.

Juneau Tanker Corp. v. Sims, 627 So.2d 1230.

Maintenance worker satisfied requirement for Jones Act coverage in connection with injury, that he be assigned to vessel, even though he was part of labor pool hired to perform shipboard maintenance, rather than being member of regular crew; worker had functioned for several days prior to injury as performer of maintenance traditionally done by seamen, and had lived aboard ship. Jones Act, 46 App. U.S.C.A. § 688.

Juneau Tanker Corp. v. Sims, 627 So.2d 1230.

Injured worker satisfied requirement, for Jones Act coverage, that vessel on which he was injured was "in navigation," even though at time he sustained injury ship was in dry dock undergoing repair; repairs were preparatory to voyages worker would have made but for his injuries. Jones Act, 46 App.U.S.C.A. § 688.

Juneau Tanker Corp. v. Sims, 627 So.2d 1230.

Fla.App. 3 Dist. 1982. Where great bulk of employee's work consisting of working on pontoons, pipes and other appurtenances of dredge took place on shore and he was assigned to work on vessel at sea only sporadically, perhaps once or twice during seven-day work week, and then for only a few hours at a time, and while on board dredge itself, he assisted welder who was exclusively and permanently employed on vessel, employee was a "shore-based worker" who was neither assigned permanently to nor performed substantial part of his work on vessel as required to satisfy definitive test of one's

status as a Jones Act "seaman." Jones Act, 46 U.S.C.A. § 688.

Ruiz v. Great Lakes Dredge and Dock Co., 414 So.2d 30.

Fla.App. 4 Dist. 1972. Before a maritime worker may properly be considered a seaman it must be shown that the worker was on board a vessel, that the vessel was in navigation or plying navigable waters, that the worker had a more or less permanent connection with the vessel and that the worker was aboard primarily to aid in navigation.

Potashnick-Badgett Dredging Inc. v. Whitfield, 269 So.2d 36, certiorari denied Potashnick-Badgett Dredging, Incorporated v. Trans-State Dredging Company, 272 So.2d 819, certiorari denied 272 So.2d 820.

A dredge may, in appropriate circumstances, be found to be a vessel, for purpose of determining whether worker employed aboard dredge is a seaman.

Potashnick-Badgett Dredging Inc. v. Whitfield, 269 So.2d 36, certiorari denied Potashnick-Badgett Dredging, Incorporated v. Trans-State Dredging Company, 272 So.2d 819, certiorari denied 272 So.2d 820.

In order to be considered to be in navigation, for purpose of determining whether a worker on board the vessel is a seaman, the vessel need not be in motion at the time in question, as long as it is performing its particular function in waters that are navigable.

Potashnick-Badgett Dredging Inc. v. Whitfield, 269 So.2d 36, certiorari denied Potashnick-Badgett Dredging, Incorporated v. Trans-State Dredging Company, 272 So.2d 819, certiorari denied 272 So.2d 820.

Being hired as a regular mate is sufficient to establish that a worker has a more or less permanent connection with a vessel, for purpose of determining whether he is a seaman.

Potashnick-Badgett Dredging Inc. v. Whitfield, 269 So.2d 36, certiorari denied Potashnick-Badgett Dredging, Incorporated v. Trans-State Dredging Company, 272 So.2d 819, certiorari denied 272 So.2d 820.

† This Case was not selected for publication in the National Reporter System
For legislative history of cited statutes, see Florida Statutes Annotated

Requirement that to be considered a seaman a worker must have been aboard a vessel primarily to aid in navigation is satisfied it can be shown that the capacity in which the worker was employed or the duties which he performed contributed to function of the vessel or accomplishment of its mission, or contributed to operation or welfare of vessel in terms of its maintenance during its movement or during anchorage for its future trips.

> Potashnick-Badgett Dredging Inc. v. Whitfield, 269 So.2d 36, certiorari denied Potashnick-Badgett Dredging, Incorporated v. Trans-State Dredging Company, 272 So.2d 819, certiorari denied 272 So.2d 820.

Test of whether a given individual is or is not a seaman is characterized as whether he is employed on a vessel and is performing duties traditionally performed by seamen.

> Potashnick-Badgett Dredging Inc. v. Whitfield, 269 So.2d 36, certiorari denied Potashnick-Badgett Dredging, Incorporated v. Trans-State Dredging Company, 272 So.2d 819, certiorari denied 272 So.2d 820.

Where experienced barge worker hired as mate aboard dredge had been working some 13 days before he was injured when cable holding plugged discharge pipe parted while nonselfpropelled dredge was digging channel several miles from shore in Gulf of Mexico to provide barge channel power plant, his duties included overseeing operations of two smaller derrick barges, moving anchors when necessary, checking shore lines and shifting spill pontoons and, apparently, helping to unstop clogged pipes, worker was a seaman within meaning of federal maritime law; recovery for injuries was not limited to adjacent state's Workmen's Compensation Law. Jones Act, 46 U.S.C.A. § 688; F.S.A. § 440.01 et seq.

> Potashnick-Badgett Dredging Inc. v. Whitfield, 269 So.2d 36, certiorari denied Potashnick-Badgett Dredging, Incorporated v. Trans-State Dredging Company, 272 So.2d 819, certiorari denied 272 So.2d 820.

⊙⇌**3. What law governs.**

† **C.A.11 (Fla.) 2014.** Maritime law of United States did not apply, and thus district court did not abuse its discretion in its forum non conveniens dismissal of seaman's complaint against shipping company, alleging violations of Jones Act and federal maritime law of unseaworthiness, failure to provide maintenance and cure, and failure to treat him for injuries he suffered; seaman suffered his alleged injury in Bahamas, vessel flew under Honduran flag and was domiciled in Dominican Republic, shipowner was incorporated in Bahamas and had its principal place of business in Nassau, seaman signed operative shipping articles in Bahamas, Bahamas provided accessible forum, and shipowner resisted defending suit in United States.

> Vasquez v. YII Shipping Co., Ltd., 559 Fed.Appx. 841.

C.A.11 (Fla.) 2009. To resolve choice of law question presented in indemnity/contribution action arising out of earlier maritime tort claims, the Court of Appeals would not simply apply same law that governed underlying maritime tort claims, but would apply the eight-factor *Lauritzen* test, in recognition of different parties, interests and policies involved in maritime tort and indemnity/contribution actions, and of international interests implicated by the latter, which involved claims against Dutch builder and designer of vessel on which captain was serving at time of his injuries.

> Cooper v. Meridian Yachts, Ltd., 575 F.3d 1151, rehearing denied.

Indemnity and contribution claims asserted by vessel itself, by vessel's manager, and by maritime employer of captain who was injured due to purported defect in design, construction and installation of food lift on ship, seeking to recover from ship's builder and designer on strict liability theory for sums that they had paid in settlement of captain's maritime tort claims, were governed by law of the Netherlands, as place where vessel was constructed and alleged wrongful act occurred and where both the builder and designer of ship had their principal place of business, notwithstanding that alleged defect did not manifest itself until vessel was on the high seas, and that ship builder was part of venture that also operated in the United States, where none of parties seeking indemnity/contribution presented sufficient evidence establishing that they had United States base of operations; accordingly, indemnity/contribution claims were barred by Dutch ten year statute of repose, given that action was not filed until more than ten years after vessel was constructed.

> Cooper v. Meridian Yachts, Ltd., 575 F.3d 1151, rehearing denied.

Among factors that court considers when confronted with making a choice between applying federal maritime law or law of foreign country in suit arising out of maritime tort are: (1) place of the wrongful act; (2) flag under which ship sailed; (3) allegiance or domicile of the injured party; (4) allegiance or domicile of shipowner defendants; (5) place of contract between injured party and shipowner; (6) accessibility of foreign forum; (7) law of forum; and (8) shipowner's base of operations; however, these factors are not exhaustive nor are they meant to be mechanically applied.

> Cooper v. Meridian Yachts, Ltd., 575 F.3d 1151, rehearing denied.

Significance of one or more the *Lauritzen* factors bearing on choice of law questions in maritime tort actions must be considered in light of national interest served by assertion of federal maritime jurisdiction.

> Cooper v. Meridian Yachts, Ltd., 575 F.3d 1151, rehearing denied.

Controlling considerations for court, when confronted with making a choice between applying federal maritime law or law of foreign country in suit arising out of maritime tort, are interacting interests of the United States and of foreign countries, and in assessing them, court must move with the circumspection appropriate when adjudicating issues inevitably entangled in conduct of international relations.

> Cooper v. Meridian Yachts, Ltd., 575 F.3d 1151, rehearing denied.

Choice of law analysis in suit arising out of maritime tort requires court to look beyond corporate formalities and examine parties' operational contacts with the United States; in deciding whether a party has "base of operations" in the United States, important question is whether party's U.S. contacts, irrespective of party's contacts with other countries, amount to a substantial relation to the United States.

> Cooper v. Meridian Yachts, Ltd., 575 F.3d 1151, rehearing denied.

Complete choice of law analysis in suit arising out of maritime tort requires court to examine the base of operations of all parties.

> Cooper v. Meridian Yachts, Ltd., 575 F.3d 1151, rehearing denied.

Beneficial ownership by United States citizen, by itself, is not sufficient to establish a United States base of operations, for purpose of choice of law analysis in suit arising out of maritime tort, where the U.S. citizen has used advantages offered by foreign jurisdiction's law by incorporating in that jurisdiction.

> Cooper v. Meridian Yachts, Ltd., 575 F.3d 1151, rehearing denied.

To determine whether the United States has substantial interest in lawsuit arising out of maritime tort, for purpose of deciding whether suit is governed by federal maritime law or by law of foreign country, court must do more than engage in a contact counting exercise; rather, it must review the substance of those contacts by analyzing both the policies underlying the issues on which dispute centers and the factual contexts under which dispute arose.

> Cooper v. Meridian Yachts, Ltd., 575 F.3d 1151, rehearing denied.

Fla.App. 2 Dist. 1960. In determining whether vessel was making coasting voyages within meaning of federal statute prescribing penalties for failure of master of owner of any such vessel to pay seaman's wages in the manner therein provided or was engaged in coastwise trade within meaning of statute exempting vessels engaged in such trade from prescribed penalties, state court must look to related decisions of federal courts in attempt to construe federal statute in a manner that will best effectuate its purpose. 46 U.S.C.A. §§ 544, 596.

> Carson v. Gulf Oil Corp., 123 So.2d 35.

🗝**4. Statutory provisions.**

C.A.11 (Fla.) 2013. The provisions of the Seaman's Wage Act must be liberally construed in favor of seamen. 46 U.S.C.A. § 10313 et seq.

> Wallace v. NCL (Bahamas) Ltd., 733 F.3d 1093, certiorari denied 134 S.Ct. 1520, 188 L.Ed.2d 450.

M.D.Fla. 1977. Special legislative solicitude to seamen should be interpreted liberally to achieve remedies intended to benefit seamen, the members of the favored class.

> Matter of Jama, 436 F.Supp. 963.

S.D.Fla. 2012. Congressional legislation in aid of seamen is largely remedial and calls for liberal interpretation in favor of seamen. 46 U.S.C.A. § 10313(f).

> Wallace v. NCL (Bahamas) Ltd., 891 F.Supp.2d 1343, affirmed 733 F.3d 1093, certiorari denied 134 S.Ct. 1520, 188 L.Ed.2d 450.

☞**5. Shipping commissioners.**

For other cases see earlier editions of this digest, the Decennial Digests, and WEST-LAW.

☞**6. Employment in general.**

C.A.5 (Fla.) 1951. Where no articles were signed by persons hired by person purporting to be captain of vessel as members of crew thereof, any contract of hire between them and vessel was merely verbal and without definite term and hence terminable at will by either party, even if such person had authority to hire crew.

> Findley v. Red Top Super Markets, 188 F.2d 834, certiorari denied 72 S.Ct. 112, 342 U.S. 870, 96 L.Ed. 654.

C.C.A.5 (Fla.) 1939. A letter written by motorboat owner offering employment did not constitute any part of maritime contract of employment where offer was never accepted.

> Swift v. Knowles, 100 F.2d 977.

S.D.Fla. 2013. District court could not excise choice of law provision without invalidating entire employment agreement between seaman and vessel owner, where that agreement appeared to contain no severability clause, and unless entire agreement was void the choice of law provision had to remain.

> Ballesteros v. NCL (Bahamas) Ltd., 925 F.Supp.2d 1303.

S.D.Fla. 2012. Under Florida law, senior stateroom attendants did not modify their employment contracts with cruise line employer by continuing to reenlist with cruise line, despite their knowledge that they would be unable to complete their assigned duties on embarkation day and have to hire and pay helpers, where attendants complained repeatedly about having to pay for helpers and never consented.

> Wallace v. NCL (Bahamas) Ltd., 891 F.Supp.2d 1343, affirmed 733 F.3d 1093, certiorari denied 134 S.Ct. 1520, 188 L.Ed.2d 450.

S.D.Fla. 2010. Health, accident, and death benefits provision of agreement governing vessel owner's employment of seaman, stating that seaman "shall be eligible for compensation," indicated that $50,000 payment and required release were optional, not mandatory, and therefore provision did not cap seaman's damages for injuries at $50,000.

> Krstic v. Princess Cruise Lines, Ltd. (Corp), 706 F.Supp.2d 1271.

S.D.Fla. 2003. Acts of the Philippine Overseas Employment Administration (POEA), when it approved standard form employment contracts between Philippine seamen and cruise line, had to be deemed valid, and it was not court's role to second-guess that decision when assessing seamen's challenges to hiring process and to manner in which they entered into employment contracts.

> Bautista v. Star Cruises, 286 F.Supp.2d 1352, affirmed 396 F.3d 1289, certiorari dismissed 125 S.Ct. 2954, 545 U.S. 1136, 162 L.Ed.2d 884.

S.D.Fla. 1995. Statute prohibiting person from demanding or receiving employment fee for providing seaman with employment does not apply to payment of employment fee by seamen in foreign ports, for service on foreign vessels, but applies to payments made in American ports. 46 U.S.C.A. § 10314(b).

> Gary v. D. Agustini & Asociados, S.A., 898 F.Supp. 901.

S.D.Fla. 1963. Whether or not employee-employer relationship existed between yacht owners and person who came aboard for purpose of aiding in navigation of vessel was to be determined by common law tests, and relationship was same as that of master and servant.

Petition of Read, 224 F.Supp. 241.

⊙7. Shipping articles.

For other cases see earlier editions of this digest, the Decennial Digests, and WEST-LAW.

⊙8. Lists, certificates, and return of crew.

S.D.Fla. 1982. A master should exercise extreme caution so as not to cause a seaman to be imprisoned in a foreign jail.

Murray v. Hunt, 552 F.Supp. 234.

Since acts of Greek police, who discovered hashish locked in safe in owner's cabin, would not have resulted in yacht captain's being incarcerated absent owner's conduct and since captain's incarceration in Greek jail was not due to any action of the captain, the doctrine of abandonment applied, entitling captain to recovery from the owner.

Murray v. Hunt, 552 F.Supp. 234.

⊙9. Seaworthiness of vessel.

C.A.5 (Fla.) 1970. Vessel owner is under absolute duty to furnish seaworthy ship but such duty is to furnish vessel and appurtenances reasonably fit for their intended use. Jones Act, 46 U.S.C.A. § 688.

Little v. Green, 428 F.2d 1061, certiorari denied 91 S.Ct. 366, 400 U.S. 964, 27 L.Ed.2d 384.

S.D.Fla. 2008. Warranty of seaworthiness only protects cargo and seamen, and does not apply to passengers.

Smith v. Carnival Corp., 584 F.Supp.2d 1343.

S.D.Fla. 2005. Ship's passengers are not covered by the warranty of seaworthiness, which imposes absolute liability on a sea vessel for the carriage of cargo and seamen's injuries.

Doonan v. Carnival Corp., 404 F.Supp.2d 1367.

Fla.App. 3 Dist. 2011. The warranty of seaworthiness extends only to seamen; a shipowner owes no duty of seaworthiness to passengers or to others on board for a purpose other than to perform the ship's work.

Flueras v. Royal Caribbean Cruises, Ltd., 69 So.3d 1101.

Liability under the doctrine of unseaworthiness is not dependent upon the shipowner's actual or constructive knowledge of an unseaworthy condition, nor does liability depend upon fault.

Flueras v. Royal Caribbean Cruises, Ltd., 69 So.3d 1101.

The duty to provide a seaworthy vessel is not mitigated or discharged by the exercise of reasonable care or due diligence.

Flueras v. Royal Caribbean Cruises, Ltd., 69 So.3d 1101.

Only a condition renders a ship unseaworthy, and isolated, personal negligent acts are categorically excluded as a basis for liability on the part of the shipowner.

Flueras v. Royal Caribbean Cruises, Ltd., 69 So.3d 1101.

The warranty of seaworthiness a shipowner owes to its seamen is absolute, nondelegable, and cannot be disclaimed.

Flueras v. Royal Caribbean Cruises, Ltd., 69 So.3d 1101.

Fla.App. 3 Dist. 2001. A shipowner may be liable for a temporary unseaworthy condition.

Lane v. Tripp, 788 So.2d 351.

Fla.App. 5 Dist. 2001. Encompassed within the ambit of maritime law is the doctrine of unseaworthiness which has evolved into a rule of strict liability.

Doles v. Koden Intern., Inc., 779 So.2d 609.

A vessel is not seaworthy if it lacks the proper equipment or devices to allow it to engage safely in the trade for which it was intended.

Doles v. Koden Intern., Inc., 779 So.2d 609.

⊙10–11. *For other cases see earlier editions of this digest, the Decennial Digests, and WESTLAW.*

⊙11. Medical treatment and maintenance of disabled seamen.

⊙11(1). In general.

† **C.A.11 (Fla.) 2013.** Crewmember's claims against vessel owner fell within

scope of arbitration clause contained in agreement amounting to seaman's employment agreement, despite crewmember's argument that claims arose under Jones Act, which protects injured seamen, rather than under agreement; crewmembers claims alleging Jones Act negligence, unseaworthiness, and maintenance and cure would not have been viable except for crewmember's service on vessel, and so dispute arose out of service on vessel. 46 U.S.C.A. § 30104 et seq.

> Montero v. Carnival Corp., 523 Fed. Appx. 623.

† **C.A.11 (Fla.) 2012.** Cruise line did not violate its "maintenance and cure" obligations to employees who were not injured.

> Rankin v. Celebrity Cruises, Ltd., 489 Fed.Appx. 362.

C.A.11 (Fla.) 2001. Under general maritime law, seamen are entitled to bring an action for "maintenance and cure," a remedy available to compensate seamen who fall ill or become injured during the term of their employment.

> Cabrera Espinal v. Royal Caribbean Cruises, Ltd., 253 F.3d 629.

Remedies of maintenance and cure provided for in maritime law may be altered although not abrogated by collective bargaining agreements.

> Cabrera Espinal v. Royal Caribbean Cruises, Ltd., 253 F.3d 629.

General maritime law guarantees seamen: (1) "maintenance," which is a living allowance; (2) "cure," which covers nursing and medical expenses; and (3) wages.

> Cabrera Espinal v. Royal Caribbean Cruises, Ltd., 253 F.3d 629.

C.A.11 (Fla.) 2000. The duty of a vessel owner to pay an injured seaman "maintenance," which consists of payments sufficient to provide a seaman with food and lodging comparable to the kind received aboard ship, is imposed by general maritime law and attaches once the seaman enters the service of a ship.

> Frederick v. Kirby Tankships, Inc., 205 F.3d 1277, certiorari denied 121 S.Ct. 46, 531 U.S. 813, 148 L.Ed.2d 16.

No private agreement is competent to abrogate the shipowner's duty to pay maintenance to an injured seaman.

> Frederick v. Kirby Tankships, Inc., 205 F.3d 1277, certiorari denied 121 S.Ct. 46, 531 U.S. 813, 148 L.Ed.2d 16.

C.A.11 (Fla.) 1996. When seaman is injured or becomes ill while employed aboard vessel, he is entitled to daily subsistence and medical treatment until maximum cure has been reached.

> Kasprik v. U.S., 87 F.3d 462.

Seaman's right to maintenance and cure is implicit in contractual relationship between seaman and his employer, and is designed to ensure recovery of seaman upon injury or sickness sustained in service of ship; maintenance and cure are due without regard to negligence of employer or unseaworthiness of ship.

> Kasprik v. U.S., 87 F.3d 462.

C.A.11 (Fla.) 1995. If seaman whose income consists mainly of tips becomes ill or injured and is unable to work, he can recover those tips under remedy for wages provided by admiralty law as component of maintenance and cure; average tip income seaman was earning prior to his incapacitation is includable in measure of wages he is due if he becomes unable to work.

> Flores v. Carnival Cruise Lines, 47 F.3d 1120.

C.A.11 (Fla.) 1990. Seaman who is injured during pursuit of recreational activities should receive maintenance and cure, whether injury was suffered ashore or aboard.

> Garay v. Carnival Cruise Line, Inc., 904 F.2d 1527, rehearing denied 915 F.2d 698, certiorari denied 111 S.Ct. 1072, 498 U.S. 1119, 112 L.Ed.2d 1178, certiorari denied 111 S.Ct. 1072, 112 L.Ed.2d 1178.

Shipowner's failure to pay maintenance and cure may support cause of action under Jones Act for breach of duty to provide maintenance and cure. Jones Act, 46 U.S.C.A.App. § 688.

> Garay v. Carnival Cruise Line, Inc., 904 F.2d 1527, rehearing denied 915 F.2d 698, certiorari denied 111 S.Ct. 1072, 498 U.S. 1119, 112 L.Ed.2d 1178, certiorari denied 111 S.Ct. 1072, 112 L.Ed.2d 1178.

C.A.11 (Fla.) 1988. Cruise ship pantryman, who was a blue water seaman on shore leave at time of his injury in automobile accident, was entitled to maintenance and cure for injuries suffered in the accident, even though accident occurred in course of pleasure trip, prior to departure of ship.

Archer v. Trans/American Services, Ltd., 834 F.2d 1570.

Cruise ship pantryman who was a blue water seaman on shore leave in foreign port at time of his injury, was entitled to maintenance and cure under principles of maritime law and thus was also entitled to lost wages for one year, the full term of his contract.

Archer v. Trans/American Services, Ltd., 834 F.2d 1570.

C.A.5 (Fla.) 1963. Expressed intention of seaman who spent several months convalescing at home of cousin to make payment therefor from whatever money seaman would obtain and expectation on part of cousin to receive it, absent intention on part of either that seaman be object of charity, sustained award for maintenance and cure, irrespective of whether there was a legally enforceable obligation.

McCormick Shipping Corp. v. Duvalier, 311 F.2d 933.

C.A.5 (Fla.) 1958. A seaman has a claim in the nature of a tort claim if, after his right to maintenance and cure attaches, further medical treatment, care and attention is needed, the shipowner knows of the need but unreasonably failed to supply it, the seaman has no facilities by which to procure it, and as a consequence the medical condition is made worse.

Murphy v. Light, 257 F.2d 323.

C.A.5 (Fla.) 1957. The District Court, in denying relief, sought by former seaman filing libel against owner and operator of fishing vessel for maintenance and cure because of tuberculosis contracted as result of extended exposure to wind and stormy weather, on ground that disability came from ship's service, erred in applying notions of assumed risk, which are not permissible in action for either damages or maintenance and cure. Jones Act, 46 U.S.C.A. § 688.

Couts v. Erickson, 241 F.2d 499.

Liability of vessel and her owners for maintenance and cure of sick or injured seamen is implied provision of marine employment contracts and not predicated on fault or negligence of shipowner, who is liable for expense of curing seaman's injury or sickness as incident of marine employer-employee relationship, regardless of whether owner is responsible for injury or sickness.

Couts v. Erickson, 241 F.2d 499.

Conceptions of contributory negligence, fellow servant doctrine and assumption of risk have no place in shipowner's liability or defense against liability for maintenance and cure of sick or injured seaman, but only some wilful misbehavior or deliberate act of indiscretion by seaman suffices to deprive him of such protection.

Couts v. Erickson, 241 F.2d 499.

M.D.Fla. 1987. There is strong federal policy in favor of maintenance and cure benefits for seaman who becomes ill or suffers injury while in service of vessel. Jones Act, 46 U.S.C.A. § 688.

Shields v. U.S., 662 F.Supp. 187.

S.D.Fla. 2012. Maintenance and cure is designed to provide seaman with food and lodging when he becomes sick or injured in ship's service, and it extends during period when he is incapacitated to do seaman's work and continues until he reaches maximum medical recovery.

Kostoski v. Steiner Transocean, Ltd., 278 F.R.D. 695.

Maintenance and cure are due without regard to employer's negligence or ship's unseaworthiness.

Kostoski v. Steiner Transocean, Ltd., 278 F.R.D. 695.

"Maintenance" is per diem living allowance, paid so long as seaman is outside hospital and has not reached point of maximum cure.

Kostoski v. Steiner Transocean, Ltd., 278 F.R.D. 695.

"Cure" involves payment of therapeutic, medical, and hospital expenses not otherwise furnished to seaman, until point of maximum cure.

Kostoski v. Steiner Transocean, Ltd., 278 F.R.D. 695.

† **This Case was not selected for publication in the National Reporter System**
For legislative history of cited statutes, see Florida Statutes Annotated

Employer's allegations that seaman concealed his prior treatment for right leg pain, that it paid seaman maintenance and cure for right leg injury, and that preexisting injury was directly related to "new" injury were sufficient to state claim against seaman for recoupment of maintenance payments under theory of unjust enrichment.

> Kostoski v. Steiner Transocean, Ltd., 278 F.R.D. 695.

S.D.Fla. 2004. Cargo agent, which was not injured seaman's employer, was not liable for maintenance and cure.

> Wai v. Rainbow Holdings, 350 F.Supp.2d 1019.

A shipowner has a duty to promptly provide adequate emergency medical care, as is reasonable under the circumstances, for an injured seaman.

> Wai v. Rainbow Holdings, 350 F.Supp.2d 1019.

S.D.Fla. 2002. Maintenance and cure is not available when seaman's injury results from either voluntary intoxication or venereal disease.

> Thomas v. New Commodore Cruise Lines Ltd., Inc., 202 F.Supp.2d 1356.

Venereal disease exception applied to bar seaman, who tested positive for HIV, from recovering maintenance and cure from shipowner; there was no basis for distinguishing HIV from other venereal diseases for purposes of maintenance and cure, as it had same impact as other venereal diseases and ADA did not require it to be distinguished, although HIV could qualify as disability under ADA. Americans with Disabilities Act of 1990, § 2 et seq., 42 U.S.C.A. § 12101 et seq.

> Thomas v. New Commodore Cruise Lines Ltd., Inc., 202 F.Supp.2d 1356.

S.D.Fla. 2000. Employer cannot abrogate duty to pay maintenance, but amount of maintenance may be established in contractual relationship between seaman and employer.

> Gheorghita v. Royal Caribbean Cruises, Ltd., 93 F.Supp.2d 1237.

S.D.Fla. 1996. Ambiguities or doubts in application of law of maintenance and cure are resolved in favor of seamen; if

leeway is to be given in either direction, all considerations which brought doctrine of maintenance and cure into being dictate that it should be applied on sailor's behalf.

> Costa Crociere, S.p.A. v. Rose, 939 F.Supp. 1538.

"Maintenance" is a per diem subsistence allowance designed to provide seaman with compensation sufficient to cover his food and lodging until the time of maximum medical improvement; it is designed to encompass the reasonable cost of food and lodging comparable to that received aboard the vessel; "cure" represents the cost of medical and nursing care during the seaman's affliction, again until the point of maximum improvement.

> Costa Crociere, S.p.A. v. Rose, 939 F.Supp. 1538.

Right to maintenance and cure springs from seaman's dependence on his ship, and does not turn on fault of shipowner or seaworthiness of the vessel.

> Costa Crociere, S.p.A. v. Rose, 939 F.Supp. 1538.

Cause of seaman's ailment is irrelevant to right to maintenance and cure, so long as ailment manifests itself while seaman is in service of his vessel.

> Costa Crociere, S.p.A. v. Rose, 939 F.Supp. 1538.

S.D.Fla. 1986. Seaman's right to maintenance and cure is implicit in contractual relationship between seaman and employer.

> Belcher Towing Co. v. Howard, 638 F.Supp. 242.

S.D.Fla. 1973. Liability to seaman for maintenance and cure is not contingent on fault or negligence of ship or shipowners and injury need not be causally related to his shipboard duties.

> Steuer v. N.V. Nederl-Amerik Stoomvaart Maatschappf (Holand-Ameriklijn), 362 F.Supp. 600.

Bkrtcy.S.D.Fla. 1997. "Maintenance and cure" entitles seaman who suffers illness or injury while in service of vessel the right to payment for medical expenses, living expenses and certain unpaid wages.

> In re Coltellaro, 204 B.R. 640.

"Maintenance" is right of seaman to food and lodging if he falls ill or becomes

injured on ship, while "cure" is right to necessary medical services.
In re Coltellaro, 204 B.R. 640.

Entire expense of maintenance and cure is borne by shipowner.
In re Coltellaro, 204 B.R. 640.

Right to maintenance and cure does not turn upon fault of shipowner, and cause of ailment is irrelevant; only eligibility requirement is that seaman be injured while in service of vessel.
In re Coltellaro, 204 B.R. 640.

Seaman cannot waive right to maintenance and cure, by contract or otherwise.
In re Coltellaro, 204 B.R. 640.

Fla.App. 1 Dist. 1993. Recovery for maintenance, cure and unearned wages is a no-fault concept arising out of relationship between injured seaman and vessel, neither subject to comparative negligence nor dependent upon shipowner's negligence.
Moran Towing of Florida, Inc. v. Mays, 620 So.2d 1088, on subsequent appeal 623 So.2d 850.

"Maintenance" seeks to provide ill or injured seaman with compensation sufficient to pay for care, including lodging expenses; it is in the nature of a per diem living allowance, which extends until the seaman reaches the point of maximum cure.
Moran Towing of Florida, Inc. v. Mays, 620 So.2d 1088, on subsequent appeal 623 So.2d 850.

Fla.App. 3 Dist. 2008. As a matter of general maritime law, Jones Act employers are required to provide maintenance and cure benefits to their employees who are injured within the course of their employment, and accompanying this duty is the shipowner's right to monitor the seaman's treatment to determine when maximum medical improvement (MMI) is reached and maintenance and cure is no longer required. Jones Act, 46 App.U.S.C.(2000 Ed.) § 688.
Royal Caribbean Cruises, Ltd. v. Cox, 974 So.2d 462.

Fla.App. 3 Dist. 2003. An action for maintenance and cure under the Jones Act is a maritime remedy designed to provide a seaman with food and lodging when he becomes sick or injured in the ship's service; and it extends during the period when he is incapacitated to do a seaman's work. Jones Act, 46 App.U.S.C.A. § 688.
Barahona v. Kloster Cruise Ltd., 851 So.2d 235.

Fla.App. 3 Dist. 2000. "Maintenance and cure" is an ancient duty under the law of admiralty that arises against a shipowner in favor of a seaman who becomes ill, injured, or incapacitated, or whose condition becomes aggravated or enhanced for any reason, at least until the time that the seaman has achieved maximum medical recovery.
Duarte v. Royal Caribbean Cruises, Ltd., 761 So.2d 367, rehearing denied, review denied 804 So.2d 330, certiorari denied 122 S.Ct. 196, 534 U.S. 886, 151 L.Ed.2d 138.

Fla.App. 3 Dist. 1992. "Maintenance and cure" is right of seaman to receive compensation for illnesses or injuries suffered while working aboard ship.
Langmead v. Admiral Cruises, Inc., 610 So.2d 565, appeal after remand 696 So.2d 1189, rehearing denied.

Fla.App. 3 Dist. 1989. Trial court erroneously instructed jury that seaman suing shipowner must establish that his injury was suffered as a result of shipowner's failure to provide maintenance and cure before award for maintenance and cure could be made; when seaman became injured while in service of his ship, shipowner was required to pay for maintenance and cure whether or not shipowner was at fault.
Porto v. Carnival Cruise Lines, Inc., 555 So.2d 394.

Fla.App. 3 Dist. 1958. Under general maritime law, a shipowner is responsible to seaman for maintenance and cure for injuries sustained while in service of ship.
Corella v. McCormick Shipping Corp., 101 So.2d 903.

Right of seaman to maintenance and cure arises out of contract of employment and by reason of relationship of seaman and shipowner.
Corella v. McCormick Shipping Corp., 101 So.2d 903.

Obligation of maintenance and cure is imposed on a shipowner without regard to manner in which injury of seaman may have occurred, or whether injury was with or without fault of shipowner.

> Corella v. McCormick Shipping Corp., 101 So.2d 903.

Right of seaman to damages from shipowner for alleged aggravation of injury because of alleged failure of shipowner to provide proper medical care and treatment, must of necessity have had its origin in seaman's alleged right of maintenance and cure.

> Corella v. McCormick Shipping Corp., 101 So.2d 903.

Where seaman did not come within provisions of the Jones Act, the only remedy left to seaman for aggravation of his injury because of alleged failure of shipowner to provide proper medical care and treatment would be under general maritime law based on seaman's contractual relationship with shipowner. Jones Act, 46 U.S.C.A. § 688.

> Corella v. McCormick Shipping Corp., 101 So.2d 903.

Where seaman did not come within provisions of the Jones Act, seaman was not entitled to recover from shipowner under count of complaint charging negligent or tortious failure of shipowner to provide proper medical care and treatment so as to cause aggravation of seaman's injuries. Jones Act, 46 U.S.C.A. § 688.

> Corella v. McCormick Shipping Corp., 101 So.2d 903.

Fla.App. 4 Dist. 2002. A captain or shipowner is required by law to insure the well being of a crew member whether or not the crew member requests such aid.

> Van Mill v. Bay Data, Inc., 819 So.2d 963.

Fla.App. 4 Dist. 2002. "Maintenance" is a per diem living allowance, which extends until a seaman reaches the point of maximum cure.

> Bouchard Transp. Co., Inc. v. Connors, 811 So.2d 787, on remand 2002 WL 34192825.

The duty to pay maintenance is imposed by general maritime law.

> Bouchard Transp. Co., Inc. v. Connors, 811 So.2d 787, on remand 2002 WL 34192825.

Fla.App. 4 Dist. 1972. "Maintenance and cure" is a maritime remedy whereby an injured seaman's employer pays the seaman's medical expenses and a specified daily amount until the seaman is able to resume work or his disability has been declared permanent.

> Potashnick-Badgett Dredging Inc. v. Whitfield, 269 So.2d 36, certiorari denied Potashnick-Badgett Dredging, Incorporated v. Trans-State Dredging Company, 272 So.2d 819, certiorari denied 272 So.2d 820.

Fla.App. 5 Dist. 2012. Under general maritime law, a seaman has the right to receive compensation for food, lodging, and medical services resulting from illnesses or injuries suffered while working aboard a ship; the duty to provide said compensation, that is, "maintenance and cure," continues during a seaman's recuperative period until maximum medical recovery, or maximum medical improvement (MMI), is reached.

> Gabriel v. Disney Cruise Line, 93 So.3d 1121, rehearing denied.

Under the Jones Act, a shipowner is required to provide prompt and adequate medical care to a sick or injured crew member as is reasonable under the circumstances; there is no duty to provide such care to the limits of maximum medical improvement (MMI). 46 U.S.C.A. § 30104.

> Gabriel v. Disney Cruise Line, 93 So.3d 1121, rehearing denied.

☞11(2)–11(3). *For other cases see earlier editions of this digest, the Decennial Digests, and WESTLAW.*

☞11(4). **Persons entitled.**

Fla.App. 3 Dist. 1979. Employee, who was in course of his employment and "in the service of the ship" while on his way at his employer's instructions to make repairs at crew's living quarters when he was injured while riding motorcycle, if in fact a "seaman" when accident occurred, would be entitled to recovery of "maintenance and cure," i. e., his medical expenses and daily stipend until maximum medical improvement, from his employer.

> Brown v. Stanwick Intern., Inc., 367 So.2d 241.

⚷11(5). Fault or negligence of seaman or fellow servants.

C.A.11 (Fla.) 1990. Seaman will not lose his right to maintenance and cure unless he engages in positively vicious conduct, such as gross negligence or willful disobedience of orders.

> Garay v. Carnival Cruise Line, Inc., 904 F.2d 1527, rehearing denied 915 F.2d 698, certiorari denied 111 S.Ct. 1072, 498 U.S. 1119, 112 L.Ed.2d 1178, certiorari denied 111 S.Ct. 1072, 112 L.Ed.2d 1178.

If seaman is injured through his willful misconduct, shipowner is relieved of his duty of providing maintenance and cure.

> Garay v. Carnival Cruise Line, Inc., 904 F.2d 1527, rehearing denied 915 F.2d 698, certiorari denied 111 S.Ct. 1072, 498 U.S. 1119, 112 L.Ed.2d 1178, certiorari denied 111 S.Ct. 1072, 112 L.Ed.2d 1178.

Defense of willful misconduct was not available to shipowner upon injured seaman's claim for maintenance and cure, notwithstanding evidence that seaman had been drinking when he fell down stairs, given ship's tacit policy of permitting drinking and even drunkenness on board.

> Garay v. Carnival Cruise Line, Inc., 904 F.2d 1527, rehearing denied 915 F.2d 698, certiorari denied 111 S.Ct. 1072, 498 U.S. 1119, 112 L.Ed.2d 1178, certiorari denied 111 S.Ct. 1072, 112 L.Ed.2d 1178.

C.A.5 (Fla.) 1963. Seaman was entitled to no maintenance and cure for injuries caused by his own affirmative misconduct in affray.

> McConville v. Florida Towing Corp., 321 F.2d 162.

C.A.5 (Fla.) 1957. Negligence of, or acts short of culpable misconduct by, sick or injured seaman will not relieve shipowner of responsibility for seaman's maintenance and cure.

> Couts v. Erickson, 241 F.2d 499.

Conceptions of contributory negligence, fellow servant doctrine and assumption of risk have no place in shipowner's liability or defense against liability for maintenance and cure of sick or injured seaman, but only some wilful misbehavior

or deliberate act of indiscretion by seaman suffices to deprive him of such protection.

> Couts v. Erickson, 241 F.2d 499.

A seaman contracting tuberculosis as result of extended exposure to wind and stormy weather on open deck of fishing vessel did not lose right to maintenance and cure because of concealment of his prior history of tuberculosis, in absence of evidence of any purpose, plan or attempt by him to mislead, conceal or misrepresent such history or state of his health, where he thought himself fit, as did vessel's master, who engaged him after seeing him, and vessel owner, on another ship of which seaman had served without untoward effects.

> Couts v. Erickson, 241 F.2d 499.

A seaman, contracting tuberculosis as result of extended exposure to wind and stormy weather on fishing vessel did not lose right to maintenance and cure on ground that he should have known, because of his medical history of extended treatments for such disease, that he was unfit for service on fishing vessels, when master of such vessel engaged him, in view of uncontradicted medical evidence that seaman was discharged from sanitarium as fit for duty five months before such time and undisputed evidence that wet rigors of his two weeks' service on vessel were sufficient to reactivate tuberculosis then in quiescent, inactive, recovered state.

> Couts v. Erickson, 241 F.2d 499.

C.A.5 (Fla.) 1955. Fault of seaman sufficient to forfeit right to maintenance and cure must be some positively vicious conduct such as gross negligence or wilful disobedience of orders.

> Murphy v. Light, 224 F.2d 944, certiorari denied 76 S.Ct. 348, 350 U.S. 960, 100 L.Ed. 834.

Conceptions of contributory negligence, assumption of risk and fellow servant doctrine are not defenses to action for maintenance and cure, but only some wilful misbehavior or deliberate act of indiscretion suffices to deprive seaman of his protection.

> Murphy v. Light, 224 F.2d 944, certiorari denied 76 S.Ct. 348, 350 U.S. 960, 100 L.Ed. 834.

M.D.Fla. 2002. When determining whether an individual is entitled to maintenance and cure, the doctrines of contributory negligence, assumption of risk, and the fellow-servant rule of the common law are not applicable, and even if the seaman is injured through his own negligence, he does not forfeit his right to maintenance and cure.

Bloom v. Weeks Marine, Inc., 225 F.Supp.2d 1334.

S.D.Fla. 2009. A seaman's maintenance and cure claim cannot be reduced even if he is shown to be contributorily negligent; therefore, it may be important under certain circumstances to ascertain the amount that a damages award in a Jones Act case is reduced because of contributory negligence to accurately determine the amount awarded in the maintenance and cure claim that may be duplicative. 46 U.S.C.A. § 30104.

Royal Caribbean Cruises, Ltd. v. Whitefield ex rel. Martinez, 664 F.Supp.2d 1270.

S.D.Fla. 1989. Where seaman's drunkenness was cause of his injury, seaman was not entitled to maintenance and cure.

Garay v. Carnival Cruise Lines, Inc., 716 F.Supp. 1421, reversed 904 F.2d 1527, rehearing denied 915 F.2d 698, certiorari denied 111 S.Ct. 1072, 498 U.S. 1119, 112 L.Ed.2d 1178, certiorari denied 111 S.Ct. 1072, 112 L.Ed.2d 1178.

⚷11(6). Extent and duration of liability.

C.A.11 (Fla.) 2001. Rule that sick wages for incapacitated tip-earning seamen should be measured based on their average tip income was not applicable where collective bargaining agreement (CBA) expressly modified maritime law to limit sick wages to seaman's basic monthly wage.

Cabrera Espinal v. Royal Caribbean Cruises, Ltd., 253 F.3d 629.

Under collective bargaining agreement (CBA) and general maritime law, seaman was owed no further duty at time he was recuperating from eye injury after he signed off the ship, where employer paid sick wages for 63 days, and repatriated him at company expense; moreover,

seaman's final voyage was completed and only two days were left on his employment contract when he signed off the ship.

Cabrera Espinal v. Royal Caribbean Cruises, Ltd., 253 F.3d 629.

C.A.11 (Fla.) 2000. If a maintenance rate is fixed in a collective bargaining agreement (CBA), the court should accept the specified rate as reasonable, even if the seaman spent substantially more for maintenance; the changed circumstance of unionization undercuts the rationale supporting the traditional right to maintenance and cure, and policies undergirding federal labor law require adherence to the CBA.

Frederick v. Kirby Tankships, Inc., 205 F.3d 1277, certiorari denied 121 S.Ct. 46, 531 U.S. 813, 148 L.Ed.2d 16.

Vessel owner acted equitably in paying maintenance and cure to seaman in lump sum five months after seaman was injured, where seaman was staying at his sick mother's home so that vessel owner had trouble locating him, and, once vessel owner located seaman, he said he would advise owner at later date regarding proper time and location to send money.

Frederick v. Kirby Tankships, Inc., 205 F.3d 1277, certiorari denied 121 S.Ct. 46, 531 U.S. 813, 148 L.Ed.2d 16.

C.A.11 (Fla.) 1986. Injured seaman who had not paid own expenses, but relied on parents to feed and care for him, could not recover on maintenance claim.

Nichols v. Barwick, 792 F.2d 1520.

Seaman under contract for year can collect year's lost wages as part of maintenance claim.

Nichols v. Barwick, 792 F.2d 1520.

Seaman under contract for less than year is entitled to wages only to end of voyage as part of maintenance claim.

Nichols v. Barwick, 792 F.2d 1520.

C.A.5 (Fla.) 1973. Trial judge was neither clearly erroneous in his fact findings nor mistaken in his application of law in determining that seaman was entitled to maintenance until date which was the last day prior to achieving maximum cure possible.

Price v. Mosler, 483 F.2d 275.

C.A.5 (Fla.) 1958. A shipowner's obligation for maintenance and cure continues until such time as the medical condition has become static, even though this may be long after the seaman has left vessel.

Murphy v. Light, 257 F.2d 323.

C.A.5 (Fla.) 1957. A vessel and her owners are liable for maintenance and cure of seaman falling sick or injured in service of vessel, at least so long as voyage is continued, whether injuries were received by negligence or accident.

Couts v. Erickson, 241 F.2d 499.

C.A.5 (Fla.) 1955. Where seaman suffers from incurable disease, he is entitled to maintenance and cure only for fair time, after voyage, in which to effect such improvements in seaman's condition as reasonably may be expected to result from nursing, care and medical treatment.

Rofer v. Head & Head, Inc., 226 F.2d 927.

N.D.Fla. 1956. Where seaman was suffering from rash of hands and feet when he went on board fishing vessel, and during voyage his condition became worse and he was taken to a hospital in Brownsville, Texas, and after treatment he was discharged from hospital and directed to report back for final examination at expiration of two weeks, and after five days he suffered a heart attack, for which he returned to hospital, and when his heart condition was cleared up his rash was also cleared up, and he returned to his home port of Pensacola, Florida, he was entitled to maintenance of $5 a day for five days he was out of the hospital and for the two days he spent on bus while returning home, and $16 for transportation home.

Bass v. Warren Fish Co., 146 F.Supp. 742.

N.D.Fla. 1955. Fact that seaman becomes incapacitated for work does not place burden upon employer the seaman was working for at time of becoming incapacitated to furnish maintenance and cure for seaman for the rest of his life.

Knight v. E. E. Saunders & Co., 134 F.Supp. 7, affirmed 231 F.2d 448.

S.D.Fla. 2012. Maintenance and cure is designed to provide seaman with food and lodging when he becomes sick or injured in ship's service, and it extends during period when he is incapacitated to do seaman's work and continues until he reaches maximum medical recovery.

Kostoski v. Steiner Transocean, Ltd., 278 F.R.D. 695.

"Maintenance" is per diem living allowance, paid so long as seaman is outside hospital and has not reached point of maximum cure.

Kostoski v. Steiner Transocean, Ltd., 278 F.R.D. 695.

"Cure" involves payment of therapeutic, medical, and hospital expenses not otherwise furnished to seaman, until point of maximum cure.

Kostoski v. Steiner Transocean, Ltd., 278 F.R.D. 695.

S.D.Fla. 2004. Under general maritime law, a vessel and her owners are liable, in case a seaman falls sick, or is wounded, in the service of the ship, to the extent of his maintenance and cure, and to his wages, at least so long as the voyage is continued; the duty, which arises from the contract of employment, does not rest upon negligence or culpability on the part of the owner or master, nor is it restricted to those cases where the seaman's employment is the cause of the injury or illness.

Wai v. Rainbow Holdings, 350 F.Supp.2d 1019.

S.D.Fla. 2000. Employer cannot abrogate duty to pay maintenance, but amount of maintenance may be established in contractual relationship between seaman and employer.

Gheorghita v. Royal Caribbean Cruises, Ltd., 93 F.Supp.2d 1237.

Cabin stewardess who worked for two days as bell desk attendant while recuperating from illness was entitled to receive as maintenance estimated actual earnings of her usual position for those days.

Gheorghita v. Royal Caribbean Cruises, Ltd., 93 F.Supp.2d 1237.

S.D.Fla. 1996. "Maintenance" is a per diem subsistence allowance designed to provide seaman with compensation sufficient to cover his food and lodging until the time of maximum medical improvement; it is designed to encompass the reasonable cost of food and lodging comparable to that received aboard the vessel;

"cure" represents the cost of medical and nursing care during the seaman's affliction, again until the point of maximum improvement.

> Costa Crociere, S.p.A. v. Rose, 939 F.Supp. 1538.

Seaman's entitlement to maintenance and cure continues to the point of "maximum medical improvement," when there is no possibility of betterment in the seaman's physical "condition"; point of maximum medical improvement is not reached when seaman's underlying disease is established to be incurable, when further improvement in seaman's "condition" is possible.

> Costa Crociere, S.p.A. v. Rose, 939 F.Supp. 1538.

When available treatment leaves seaman feeling better without enhancing his bodily function and moving him to an improved state of health, then point of "maximum medical improvement" has been reached, and shipowner's liability for maintenance and cure may be extinguished.

> Costa Crociere, S.p.A. v. Rose, 939 F.Supp. 1538.

Seaman diagnosed with incurable kidney disease had not reached point of maximum medical improvement, where record established that appropriate treatment, in form of dialysis or kidney transplant would result in betterment of seaman's medical condition, and thus shipowner's obligation to pay maintenance and cure was not extinguished.

> Costa Crociere, S.p.A. v. Rose, 939 F.Supp. 1538.

Probability of betterment in seaman's condition as a result of kidney transplant was sufficient to bring such treatment within maintenance and cure obligation.

> Costa Crociere, S.p.A. v. Rose, 939 F.Supp. 1538.

Shipowner's obligation to provide maintenance and cure is not extinguished due to financial burden of the undertaking or length of time it is needed to effect a betterment of seaman's condition.

> Costa Crociere, S.p.A. v. Rose, 939 F.Supp. 1538.

S.D.Fla. 1993. Injured or sick seaman under contract for year may collect year's wages as part of maintenance, otherwise he is entitled to wages only until end of voyage.

> Joaquim v. Royal Caribbean Cruises, Ltd., 899 F.Supp. 600, reversed in part, vacated in part 52 F.3d 1071.

S.D.Fla. 1989. Shipowner's duty to provide prompt medical care did not require that it treat injured seaman until he reached maximum medical improvement and thus, seaman had no claim for failure to treat where shipowner's initial treatment of seaman was prompt and adequate and continued for three weeks after accident.

> Garay v. Carnival Cruise Lines, Inc., 716 F.Supp. 1421, reversed 904 F.2d 1527, rehearing denied 915 F.2d 698, certiorari denied 111 S.Ct. 1072, 498 U.S. 1119, 112 L.Ed.2d 1178, certiorari denied 111 S.Ct. 1072, 112 L.Ed.2d 1178.

S.D.Fla. 1986. Employer's obligation to provide maintenance and cure to injured seaman ends at point of maximum cure.

> Belcher Towing Co. v. Howard, 638 F.Supp. 242.

Shipowner's obligation to furnish maintenance and cure is not discharged until earliest time that those caring for seaman can make reasonable and good-faith determination that maximum, reasonably possible cure has been obtained.

> Belcher Towing Co. v. Howard, 638 F.Supp. 242.

Further treatment of seaman who was injured more than five years ago and who continued to suffer aches and injuries provided no reasonable medical possibility of curing seaman or effecting permanent improvement of alleged chronic and static condition and, therefore, was not required by employer pursuant to duty to provide maintenance and cure. Jones Act, 46 U.S.C.A. § 688.

> Belcher Towing Co. v. Howard, 638 F.Supp. 242.

S.D.Fla. 1957. Where seaman was injured aboard vessel while in employ of respondent which made voluntary payments of workmen's compensation benefits, respondent was entitled to a set-off of the amounts paid by its insurance carrier against amount ultimately found to be due in seaman's action for maintenance and cure. F.S.A. § 440.01 et seq.

> Chesser v. General Dredging Co., 150 F.Supp. 592.

In a seaman's action for maintenance and cure, seaman's recovery must be measured in each case by the reasonable cost of maintenance and cure to which he is entitled at the time of trial, and in the discretion of the court such an amount as may be needful in the immediate future for maintenance and cure of a kind and for a period which can be definitely ascertained.

> Chesser v. General Dredging Co., 150 F.Supp. 592.

Under doctrine that admiralty courts are empowered in seaman's action for maintenance and cure to award a decree for such reasonable sums as circumstances of case indicate to cover future treatment for a foreseeable period of time, the "foreseeable period" contemplates such time as evidenced by the testimony of competent medical witnesses.

> Chesser v. General Dredging Co., 150 F.Supp. 592.

Bkrtcy.S.D.Fla. 1997. Shipowner is responsible for maintenance and cure until maximum cure is reached.

> In re Coltellaro, 204 B.R. 640.

Fla.App. 1 Dist. 1993. "Maintenance" seeks to provide ill or injured seaman with compensation sufficient to pay for care, including lodging expenses; it is in the nature of a per diem living allowance, which extends until the seaman reaches the point of maximum cure.

> Moran Towing of Florida, Inc. v. Mays, 620 So.2d 1088, on subsequent appeal 623 So.2d 850.

"Cure" is medical care necessitated by a seaman's illness or injury which is borne by the employer or by the ship until the point of "maximum cure."

> Moran Towing of Florida, Inc. v. Mays, 620 So.2d 1088, on subsequent appeal 623 So.2d 850.

Fla.App. 3 Dist. 2008. As a matter of general maritime law, Jones Act employers are required to provide maintenance and cure benefits to their employees who are injured within the course of their employment, and accompanying this duty is the shipowner's right to monitor the seaman's treatment to determine when maximum medical improvement (MMI) is reached and maintenance and cure is no longer required. Jones Act, 46 App.U.S.C.(2000 Ed.) § 688.

> Royal Caribbean Cruises, Ltd. v. Cox, 974 So.2d 462.

Fla.App. 3 Dist. 2003. An action for maintenance and cure under the Jones Act is a maritime remedy designed to provide a seaman with food and lodging when he becomes sick or injured in the ship's service; and it extends during the period when he is incapacitated to do a seaman's work. Jones Act, 46 App.U.S.C.A. § 688.

> Barahona v. Kloster Cruise Ltd., 851 So.2d 235.

A ship owner's duty to pay maintenance and cure under Jones Act terminates as soon as the seaman reaches the point of maximum cure, or maximum medical improvement. Jones Act, 46 App. U.S.C.A. § 688.

> Barahona v. Kloster Cruise Ltd., 851 So.2d 235.

Former seaman who was previously employed by cruise line reached maximum medical improvement with respect to his guttate and plaque psoriasis, and thus, cruise line's duty to pay maintenance and cure under Jones Act terminated; both seaman's expert dermatologist and his treating physician testified that guttate and plaque psoriasis were chronic conditions for which seaman would have to undergo treatment for the rest of his life, and that when seaman left his position with cruise line, he controlled his psoriasis with ointment and was sunbathing as recommended by physicians. Jones Act, 46 App. U.S.C.A. § 688.

> Barahona v. Kloster Cruise Ltd., 851 So.2d 235.

Fla.App. 3 Dist. 2000. "Maintenance and cure" is an ancient duty under the law of admiralty that arises against a shipowner in favor of a seaman who becomes ill, injured, or incapacitated, or whose condition becomes aggravated or enhanced for any reason, at least until the time that the seaman has achieved maximum medical recovery.

> Duarte v. Royal Caribbean Cruises, Ltd., 761 So.2d 367, rehearing denied, review denied 804 So.2d 330, certiorari denied 122 S.Ct. 196, 534 U.S. 886, 151 L.Ed.2d 138.

Admiralty courts have traditionally been liberal in interpreting the scope of the shipowner's duty to pay maintenance and cure to a seaman who becomes ill, injured, or incapacitated, or whose condition becomes aggravated or enhanced for any reason.

> Duarte v. Royal Caribbean Cruises, Ltd., 761 So.2d 367, rehearing denied, review denied 804 So.2d 330, certiorari denied 122 S.Ct. 196, 534 U.S. 886, 151 L.Ed.2d 138.

Injured seamen are wards of the court, and maintenance and cure should be afforded as long as there is any ambiguity or uncertainty about the continuation of that status.

> Duarte v. Royal Caribbean Cruises, Ltd., 761 So.2d 367, rehearing denied, review denied 804 So.2d 330, certiorari denied 122 S.Ct. 196, 534 U.S. 886, 151 L.Ed.2d 138.

The nature and foundations of the shipowner's duty to pay maintenance and cure to a seaman who becomes ill, injured, or incapacitated, or whose condition becomes aggravated or enhanced for any reason, require that this duty be not narrowly confined or whittled down by restrictive and artificial distinctions defeating its broad and beneficial purposes.

> Duarte v. Royal Caribbean Cruises, Ltd., 761 So.2d 367, rehearing denied, review denied 804 So.2d 330, certiorari denied 122 S.Ct. 196, 534 U.S. 886, 151 L.Ed.2d 138.

Seaman who had been receiving maintenance and cure for several months when she was seriously injured in automobile accident was entitled to maintenance and cure from ship owner for expenses arising from that accident; seaman had yet to obtain maximum medical recovery at time of accident, and thus, she was still in service of ship.

> Duarte v. Royal Caribbean Cruises, Ltd., 761 So.2d 367, rehearing denied, review denied 804 So.2d 330, certiorari denied 122 S.Ct. 196, 534 U.S. 886, 151 L.Ed.2d 138.

Fla.App. 3 Dist. 1992. Right of maintenance and cure continues during seaman's recuperative period until he reaches maximum medical recovery.

> Langmead v. Admiral Cruises, Inc., 610 So.2d 565, appeal after remand 696 So.2d 1189, rehearing denied.

Fla.App. 4 Dist. 2002. "Maintenance" is a per diem living allowance, which extends until a seaman reaches the point of maximum cure.

> Bouchard Transp. Co., Inc. v. Connors, 811 So.2d 787, on remand 2002 WL 34192825.

The right of maintenance consists of the right to payments sufficient to provide a seaman with food and lodging comparable to the kind received aboard ship.

> Bouchard Transp. Co., Inc. v. Connors, 811 So.2d 787, on remand 2002 WL 34192825.

Where a daily maintenance rate is fixed under the terms of a collective bargaining agreement, it should be accepted by reviewing courts as reasonable, absent evidence that the collective bargaining contract as a whole is unfair or that the union did not adequately represent the claimant.

> Bouchard Transp. Co., Inc. v. Connors, 811 So.2d 787, on remand 2002 WL 34192825.

Although injured seaman was not a member of union, he was part of bargaining unit represented by the union, and thus, he was not entitled to maintenance damages in excess of daily living expenses provided for under the terms of collective bargaining agreement between union and vessel owner.

> Bouchard Transp. Co., Inc. v. Connors, 811 So.2d 787, on remand 2002 WL 34192825.

Fla.App. 5 Dist. 2012. Under general maritime law, a seaman has the right to receive compensation for food, lodging, and medical services resulting from illnesses or injuries suffered while working aboard a ship; the duty to provide said compensation, that is, "maintenance and cure," continues during a seaman's recuperative period until maximum medical recovery, or maximum medical improvement (MMI), is reached.

> Gabriel v. Disney Cruise Line, 93 So.3d 1121, rehearing denied.

Musician who was injured while working on cruise ship could not maintain Jones Act claim that cruise line was negligent for failing to provide prompt and adequate medical care after date orthopedic surgeon reported that musician had reached maximum medical improvement (MMI) absent evidence of negligence concerning the medical care musician received from the date of his injury to the date of the surgeon's report. 46 U.S.C.A. § 30104.

> Gabriel v. Disney Cruise Line, 93 So.3d 1121, rehearing denied.

Under the Jones Act, a shipowner is required to provide prompt and adequate medical care to a sick or injured crew member as is reasonable under the circumstances; there is no duty to provide such care to the limits of maximum medical improvement (MMI). 46 U.S.C.A. § 30104.

> Gabriel v. Disney Cruise Line, 93 So.3d 1121, rehearing denied.

⊂⇒11(7). **Subsequent conduct or conditions affecting liability.**

N.D.Fla. 1956. Where injured assistant port engineer refused to enter marine hospital, recommended by public health physician to whom employer sent him but instead, went to his own personal physician who put him in a private hospital, refusal of the maritime hospital care barred any claim by the engineer for maintenance and cure. Jones Act, 46 U.S.C.A. § 688.

> Ouzts v. A. P. Ward & Son, Inc., 146 F.Supp. 733.

⊂⇒11(8). **Mistaken diagnosis, neglect, or improper treatment.**

For other cases see earlier editions of this digest, the Decennial Digests, and WESTLAW.

⊂⇒11(9). **Actions.**

U.S.Fla. 1959. In action by seaman against shipowner for damages and maintenance and cure based on claim that injuries sustained by seaman when he was pitched into the air and fell back to the deck activated or aggravated a previously latent tubercular condition, evidence sustained conclusion that accident caused the seaman's subsequent illness. Jones Act, 46 U.S.C.A. § 688.

> Sentilles v. Inter-Caribbean Shipping Corp., 80 S.Ct. 173, 361 U.S. 107, 4 L.Ed.2d 142.

In action by seaman against shipowner for damages and maintenance and cure based on claim that injuries sustained by seaman when he was pitched into the air and fell back to the deck activated or aggravated a previously latent tubercular condition, the jury's power to draw inference that aggravation of seaman's tubercular condition was in fact caused by the accident, was not impaired by failure of any medical witness to testify that it was in fact the cause, or by lack of medical unanimity as to respective likelihood of potential causes of aggravation, or by fact that other potential causes of aggravation existed and were not conclusively negated by the proofs. Jones Act, 46 U.S.C.A. § 688.

> Sentilles v. Inter-Caribbean Shipping Corp., 80 S.Ct. 173, 361 U.S. 107, 4 L.Ed.2d 142.

In action by seaman against shipowner for damages and maintenance and cure based on claim that injuries sustained by seaman when he was pitched into the air and fell back to the deck activated or aggravated a previously latent tubercular condition, members of jury were entitled to take all the circumstances, including medical testimony, into consideration. Jones Act, 46 U.S.C.A. § 688.

> Sentilles v. Inter-Caribbean Shipping Corp., 80 S.Ct. 173, 361 U.S. 107, 4 L.Ed.2d 142.

† **C.A.11 (Fla.) 2013.** Seaman's complaint against owner of cruise ship failed to plead sufficient facts to invoke diversity jurisdiction over his negligence claim, under Jones Act, and maritime law claims for unseaworthiness of ship, failure to provide maintenance and cure, and failure to treat his injuries incurred while serving as first pastryman on board ship in navigable waters, where complaint did not allege citizenship of seaman or owner. 28 U.S.C.A. § 1332(a)(2); 46 U.S.C.A. § 30104 et seq.

> Quiroz v. MSC Mediterranean Shipping Co. S.A., 522 Fed.Appx. 655.

---

† **This Case was not selected for publication in the National Reporter System**
For legislative history of cited statutes, see Florida Statutes Annotated

C.A.11 (Fla.) 2007. In action for maintenance and cure, both reasonable attorney fees and punitive damages may be legally awarded upon showing of shipowner's willful and arbitrary refusal to pay maintenance and cure.

> Atlantic Sounding Co., Inc. v. Townsend, 496 F.3d 1282, rehearing and rehearing denied 284 Fed.Appx. 805, certiorari granted 129 S.Ct. 490, 555 U.S. 993, 172 L.Ed.2d 355, affirmed and remanded 129 S.Ct. 2561, 557 U.S. 404, 174 L.Ed.2d 382, on remand 579 F.3d 1340.

C.A.11 (Fla.) 2000. Captain's report stating that seaman suffered injuries to "leg, knee to hip" in slip and fall, testimony from orthopedic surgeon that fall probably wrenched seaman's hips and accelerated deterioration of his hips, and treating physician's testimony that seaman had used his knees and back to compensate for his degenerative hip condition and that he could have continued working if not for his fall was sufficient to support finding that fall aggravated pre-existing hip condition, precluding judgment as matter of law in favor of vessel owner on maintenance and cure claim. Fed.Rules Civ.Proc.Rule 50, 28 U.S.C.A.

> Frederick v. Kirby Tankships, Inc., 205 F.3d 1277, certiorari denied 121 S.Ct. 46, 531 U.S. 813, 148 L.Ed.2d 16.

C.A.11 (Fla.) 1996. SAA does not authorize award of attorney fees for refusal to provide maintenance and cure in bad faith, callously, or unreasonably. Suits in Admiralty Act, § 1 et seq., 46 App.U.S.C.A. § 741 et seq.

> Kasprik v. U.S., 87 F.3d 462.

C.A.11 (Fla.) 1995. Punitive damage award against employer that refused to pay seaman his average tip income as part of unearned wage component of maintenance and cure was not warranted; because case was one of first impression, employer did not abrogate any established legal duty towards seaman, and thus did not exhibit willful and wanton misconduct.

> Flores v. Carnival Cruise Lines, 47 F.3d 1120.

Seaman who prevailed on appeal on claim that he was entitled to average tip income as part of wage component of maintenance and cure was not entitled to award of attorney fees against employer; given that case was one of first impression, and that seaman did not object to sums he was receiving as unearned wages prior to expiration of second employment contract and initiation of suit, employer did not act in bad faith, callously, or unreasonably.

> Flores v. Carnival Cruise Lines, 47 F.3d 1120.

C.A.11 (Fla.) 1990. Jury could find that injured seaman was intoxicated at time of fall, for purposes of seaman's claim for maintenance and cure, even though testimony of persons who examined seaman after his fall downstairs and while he was unconscious that seaman's breath smelled of alcohol was extremely weak evidence of intoxication; seaman had been ashore drinking in the afternoon, imbibing four to six beers in course of no more than two hours.

> Garay v. Carnival Cruise Line, Inc., 904 F.2d 1527, rehearing denied 915 F.2d 698, certiorari denied 111 S.Ct. 1072, 498 U.S. 1119, 112 L.Ed.2d 1178, certiorari denied 111 S.Ct. 1072, 112 L.Ed.2d 1178.

C.A.11 (Fla.) 1990. In order for district court to determine whether seamen had actual notice of Icelandic admiralty proceeding, such that they unduly delayed in asserting their rights, supporting vessel purchaser's affirmative defense of laches, court was required to determine whether seamen's employer knew of seamen's claims when suit in Iceland was filed and, if so, whether employer had obligation to inform either Icelandic court or vessel purchaser at auction of claims made to employer, as well as when purchaser first learned of claims and whether purchaser would be prejudiced by enforcement of claims.

> Thorsteinsson v. M/V Drangur, 891 F.2d 1547.

C.A.11 (Fla.) 1987. Cook for newly constructed vessel failed to show vessel, which had not been licensed for navigation or tested in sea trials, was "in navigation" at time of her injury as required for claim of maintenance and cure under general maritime law. Jones Act, 46 U.S.C.A. § 688.

> Caruso v. Sterling Yacht and Shipbuilders, Inc., 828 F.2d 14, rehearing denied 833 F.2d 1021.

C.A.5 (Fla.) 1967. Instruction that injured seaman was entitled to maintenance and cure from date of injury to date of maximum medical cure, less all days he was confined in hospital and less any further days for which he had already been paid by shipowner was proper.

> Gibbs v. Kiesel, 382 F.2d 917.

Any allowance of maintenance and cure for injured seaman based on aggravation of a pre-existing schizophrenic condition was matter which was properly left to jury in view of conflicting medical testimony.

> Gibbs v. Kiesel, 382 F.2d 917.

C.A.5 (Fla.) 1958. In action against owner of vessel for maintenance and cure claimed to have been necessitated by assault on libelant, evidence sustained finding that libelant received injuries requiring care and attention for the period for which the award was made.

> Light v. Murphy, 257 F.2d 322.

C.A.5 (Fla.) 1958. In action by chief engineer against shipowner for damages and for maintenance and cure for pulmonary tuberculosis which became evident after accident on shipboard, evidence was insufficient to take to jury question whether tubercular condition was probably caused by the incident on shipboard.

> Inter-Caribbean Shipping Corp. v. Sentilles, 256 F.2d 156, certiorari granted 79 S.Ct. 604, 359 U.S. 923, 3 L.Ed.2d 627, reversed 80 S.Ct. 173, 361 U.S. 107, 4 L.Ed.2d 142.

C.A.5 (Fla.) 1957. Evidence showed that seaman contracting tuberculosis as result of extended exposure to wind and stormy weather on fishing vessel neither had nor should have had conscious awareness of his basic unfitness for service on such vessel before being engaged by master of vessel and hence did not lose his right to maintenance and cure.

> Couts v. Erickson, 241 F.2d 499.

C.A.5 (Fla.) 1955. In action for wages, maintenance and cure by seaman who was suffering from emotional immaturity and who had paranoid tendencies and who had not complied with public health service's suggestion that he receive further psychiatric treatment at his own expense, evidence supported trial court's findings that owners of vessel could not be required to furnish him with maintenance and cure for such disorders.

> Rofer v. Head & Head, Inc., 226 F.2d 927.

In seaman's action for wages, maintenance and cure based on various ailments including back sprain and cold, evidence sustained trial court's findings as to dates on which maximum cures for back sprain and cold were achieved.

> Rofer v. Head & Head, Inc., 226 F.2d 927.

C.A.5 (Fla.) 1955. In action in personam, against owner of vessel, to recover maintenance and cure claimed to have been necessary by assault or beating administered to libelant by seaman from other vessel which libelant's vessel was towing, evidence compelled conclusion that insulting and inflammatory language used by libelant to other seaman was not such wilful misconduct as to forfeit his right to maintenance and cure.

> Murphy v. Light, 224 F.2d 944, certiorari denied 76 S.Ct. 348, 350 U.S. 960, 100 L.Ed. 834.

C.A.5 (Fla.) 1954. A finding, in libel in personam against shipowner for maintenance and cure made necessary by an assault or beating administered to libelant, that libelant received his injuries by reason of an assault and battery committed by third party not employed by respondent or on respondent's vessel, did not support summary judgment for respondent. Admiralty Rule 44, 28 U.S.C.A.

> Murphy v. Light, 211 F.2d 824.

In libel in personam against owner of vessel to recover maintenance and cure claimed to have been necessary by assault or beating administered to the libelant, wherein both libelant and respondent sought summary judgment, and respondent asserted that injuries were due to an assault and battery committed by third party not employed by respondent or on its vessel, evidence presented issues of fact requiring a trial on the merits. Admiralty Rule 44, 28 U.S.C.A.

> Murphy v. Light, 211 F.2d 824.

C.C.A.5 (Fla.) 1939. A seaman's failure to prove his allegation that captain required him to continue his services after he became ill was not a fatal variance but was merely a failure of proof as to such allegation and did not affect seaman's right to recover maintenance and cure sued for.

> Erotokritos v. Velousios, 104 F.2d 761.

Evidence warranted seaman's recovery for maintenance and cure while ill on ground that seaman became ill after he entered upon voyage.

> Erotokritos v. Velousios, 104 F.2d 761.

In seaman's suit for maintenance and care while ill, recovery for actually incurred expenses for hospitalization and cure and for maintenance limited to a reasonable time and for operation which was reasonable on its face and resulting in effecting a cure much sooner than mere hospitalization and medication would have done was proper.

> Erotokritos v. Velousios, 104 F.2d 761.

M.D.Fla. 2002. Maritime employer, being sued by injured seaman, could not require seaman to submit to "maintenance and cure" medical examination which was in addition to or separate from its rights under procedural rule allowing for medical examinations under certain conditions. Fed.Rules Civ.Proc.Rule 35(a), 28 U.S.C.A.

> Bloom v. Weeks Marine, Inc., 227 F.Supp.2d 1273.

M.D.Fla. 2002. Pretrial adjudication of merits of maintenance and cure claim could not be awarded prior to adjudication of claims; seaman failed to cite any authority establishing that merits of maintenance and cure claim could be adjudicated based merely on a motion for maintenance and cure, seaman did not move for summary judgment, he did not address whether there was a dispute of material fact.

> Bloom v. Weeks Marine, Inc., 225 F.Supp.2d 1334.

N.D.Fla. 1955. Where seaman's instant claims for maintenance and cure were substantially the same as the claims that had been denied in prior action, the denial was res judicata.

> Knight v. E. E. Saunders & Co., 134 F.Supp. 7, affirmed 231 F.2d 448.

S.D.Fla. 2014. Personal injury claimants in actions brought under general maritime law have no claim for non-pecuniary damages, including punitive damages, except in exceptional circumstances such as willful failure to furnish maintenance and cure to a seaman, intentional denial of a vessel owner to furnish a seaworthy vessel to a seaman, and in those very rare situations of intentional wrongdoing.

> Terry v. Carnival Corp., 3 F.Supp.3d 1363, appeal dismissed (11th circ. 15-13280).

S.D.Fla. 2009. A seaman with a maintenance and cure claim typically has the option to choose a federal or state forum if the maintenance and cure claim is combined with other related claims.

> Royal Caribbean Cruises, Ltd. v. Whitefield ex rel. Martinez, 664 F.Supp.2d 1270.

S.D.Fla. 2002. The ADA did not displace the venereal disease exception, which barred seaman from recovering maintenance and cure when his injuries resulted from venereal disease; nothing in the ADA suggested that Congress intended to have any effect on doctrine of maintenance and cure or specifically venereal disease defense. Americans with Disabilities Act of 1990, § 2 et seq., 42 U.S.C.A. § 12101 et seq.

> Thomas v. New Commodore Cruise Lines Ltd., Inc., 202 F.Supp.2d 1356.

S.D.Fla. 1996. Burden of proving right to maintenance and cure rests with seaman.

> Costa Crociere, S.p.A. v. Rose, 939 F.Supp. 1538.

Once seaman establishes his right to maintenance and cure, burden of persuasion shifts to shipowner to prove that seaman has reached point of maximum medical improvement, precluding further obligation to provide maintenance and cure.

> Costa Crociere, S.p.A. v. Rose, 939 F.Supp. 1538.

In some if not all contexts, it is shipowner's burden to establish that a particular treatment is overly expensive or unnecessary, relieving shipowner of maintenance and cure obligation with respect to that treatment.

Costa Crociere, S.p.A. v. Rose, 939 F.Supp. 1538.

S.D.Fla. 1989. On "failure to treat" claim, seaman's recovery is limited to punitive damages and damages for aggravation in seaman's condition caused by defendant's failure to treat.

Garay v. Carnival Cruise Lines, Inc., 716 F.Supp. 1421, reversed 904 F.2d 1527, rehearing denied 915 F.2d 698, certiorari denied 111 S.Ct. 1072, 498 U.S. 1119, 112 L.Ed.2d 1178, certiorari denied 111 S.Ct. 1072, 112 L.Ed.2d 1178.

Bkrtcy.S.D.Fla. 1997. Shipowner bears burden of proving that seaman receiving maintenance and cure has reached maximum cure.

In re Coltellaro, 204 B.R. 640.

Fla.App. 3 Dist. 2014. Seaman could not recover attorney fees, based on state's offer of judgment statute, in an action to recover Jones Act and other damages under maritime law, as the award conflicted with general rule of maritime law that parties pay their own fees absent an exception; receding from *Royal Caribbean Corp. v. Modesto*, 614 So.2d 517. 46 App. U.S.C.(2000 Ed.) § 688; West's F.S.A. § 768.79.

Royal Caribbean Cruises, Ltd. v. Cox, 137 So.3d 1157, review dismissed 145 So.3d 822, on remand 2014 WL 10295978.

Fla.App. 3 Dist. 2012. Evidentiary hearing was required to determine if seaman had achieved maximum medical improvement (MMI), even if a pre-trial order summarily adjudicated the merits of seaman's maintenance and cure claim and vessel owner was paying maintenance and cure pending the hearing, where the pre-trial order was not appealed.

Royal Caribbean Cruises, Ltd. v. Rigby, 96 So.3d 1146.

Fla.App. 3 Dist. 2007. Sufficient evidence supported trial court's factual determination that cruise ship operator was unreasonable in failing to provide back surgery to injured seaman and in terminating his maintenance and cure.

Carnival Corp. v. Mendoza, 949 So.2d 1154.

Evidence at trial of injured seaman's maintenance and cure claim was insufficient to support trial court's award of compensatory damages to seaman for future pain and suffering.

Carnival Corp. v. Mendoza, 949 So.2d 1154.

Fla.App. 3 Dist. 2006. In some circumstances, advice of counsel can be considered as a defense to an attorney fees claim for failure to provide maintenance and cure.

Paradise Divers, Inc. v. Upmal, 943 So.2d 812.

Fla.App. 3 Dist. 1998. Federal maritime law does not provide plaintiffs with absolute right to bring substantive claim for punitive damages, with respect to denial of maintenance and cure payments, but, rather, to award punitive damages in maintenance and cure case, plaintiff must show substantive evidence of willful, callous, or egregious conduct on part of shipowner.

Norwegian Cruise Lines, Ltd. v. Zareno, 712 So.2d 791.

Seaman's punitive damages claim would be stricken in his action alleging breach of employer's maintenance and cure obligations, given seaman's failure to proffer evidentiary basis for his punitive damages claim as required by state law. West's F.S.A. § 768.72.

Norwegian Cruise Lines, Ltd. v. Zareno, 712 So.2d 791.

Fla.App. 3 Dist. 1997. Punitive damages award of $3.5 million against cruise line for willful failure to provide cure for injured employee was so grossly excessive as to violate substantive due process, considering that cruise line behaved in good faith and was not guilty of misconduct in refusing to pay two doctor's bills totaling $235 on ground that doctor had been retained for purposes of litigation, and that ratio of punitive damages to actual harm was 3,626 to 1. U.S.C.A. Const. Amend. 14.

> Langmead v. Admiral Cruises, Inc., 696 So.2d 1189, rehearing denied.

Fla.App. 3 Dist. 1996. Punitive damages remain available for shipowner's willful refusal to pay maintenance and cure.

> Kloster Cruise Ltd. v. Segui, 679 So.2d 10, rehearing denied.

Fla.App. 3 Dist. 1996. Recovery of attorney fees in seaman's action for willful and arbitrary failure to provide maintenance and cure is nonseverable part of cause of action and, as such, in addition to proof of entitlement to fees, seaman must present evidence relating to appropriate amount of fees to jury, unless right is waived, so that jury may determine amount of award if seaman is found entitled to attorney fees.

> Kloster Cruise Ltd. v. De Sousa, 677 So.2d 50, rehearing denied.

Absent stipulation to handle issue otherwise, seaman's attorney fee claim based on willful and arbitrary failure to provide maintenance and cure must be decided by jury, as to both entitlement and amount.

> Kloster Cruise Ltd. v. De Sousa, 677 So.2d 50, rehearing denied.

Award of attorney fees to seaman who prevailed on claim of willful and arbitrary failure to provide maintenance and cure would be reversed and case remanded for jury determination of amount of fees recoverable by seaman, where seaman presented no evidence before jury in support of amount claimed, and over defense objection and without obtaining formal stipulation from parties, trial court took it upon itself to determine issue of amount of reasonable fee in posttrial proceedings.

> Kloster Cruise Ltd. v. De Sousa, 677 So.2d 50, rehearing denied.

Fla.App. 3 Dist. 1995. Trial court properly entered directed verdict in favor of maritime defendants on issue of punitive damages and attorney fees in connection with seaman's claim for maintenance and cure, where seaman did not present any evidence of willful or arbitrary failure

to provide him with maintenance and cure.

> Natoel v. Royal Caribbean Cruise, Ltd., 657 So.2d 26, rehearing denied.

Fla.App. 3 Dist. 1994. Jury's finding that defendant willfully or arbitrarily failed to provide maintenance and cure was supported by substantial evidence, and thus seaman was entitled to punitive damages.

> International Ships Services, Ltd. v. Canales, 639 So.2d 74.

Jury's finding that defendant willfully or arbitrarily failed to provide maintenance and cure was supported by substantial evidence, and thus, seaman was entitled to attorney's fees.

> International Ships Services, Ltd. v. Canales, 639 So.2d 74.

Fla.App. 3 Dist. 1992. Maintenance and cure issue was question for jury where evidence was presented that cruise line employee's condition due to injuries suffered while aboard ship had not yet reached maximum medical improvement, even though evidence was not uncontradicted.

> Langmead v. Admiral Cruises, Inc., 610 So.2d 565, appeal after remand 696 So.2d 1189, rehearing denied.

Fla.App. 3 Dist. 1990. In regard to claim against shipowner for maintenance and cure, seaman was entitled to jury instructions that referred to seaman's entitlement to maintenance and cure regardless of any negligence on part of seaman, and to duration of shipowner's duty.

> Canales v. Compania De Vapores Realma, S.A., 564 So.2d 1212.

Fla.App. 3 Dist. 1988. Ship owner's and personnel suppliers' refusal to furnish maintenance and cure at a time when seaman needed at least another month of convalescence, and the fact that prior to trial no physician had expressed an opinion that seaman had reached maximum medical improvement, constituted sufficient evidence to create jury question as to whether owner and suppliers arbitrarily and capriciously failed to provide seaman with maintenance and cure, as would support claim for punitive damages.

> Dos Santos v. Ajax Nav. Corp., 531 So.2d 231, certiorari dismissed 109 S.Ct. 1304, 489 U.S. 1048, 103 L.Ed.2d 574.

Fla.App. 3 Dist. 1986. Issue of whether seaman's absence from ship was justified was question for jury in action by injured seaman who had signed engagement articles with vessel and was under obligation to vessel at time he left, and desertion instruction was proper.

> Conde v. Marlu Nav. Co., Ltd., 495 So.2d 847.

Fla.App. 4 Dist. 2010. In action by chief engineer on a yacht against the owner and operator of the yacht for unseaworthiness, maintenance and cure, and negligence arising out of back, neck, and shoulder injuries allegedly sustained while working on yacht, trial court could not exclude evidence of workers' compensation case involving back and neck injuries that engineer failed to disclose during discovery, despite engineer's contention that the injuries were unrelated; injuries were to the same area of engineer's body, evidence was relevant to engineer's credibility, and engineer's position that the injuries were unrelated was a matter of argument for trial, rather than exclusion from evidence.

> JVA Enterprises, I, LLC v. Prentice, 48 So.3d 109.

Fla.App. 4 Dist. 2000. Punitive damages are not recoverable in a maintenance and cure case.

> Nurkiewicz v. Vacation Break U.S.A., Inc., 771 So.2d 1271.

⚿12. Discharge.

C.C.A.5 (Fla.) 1939. An employment contract under which employee was to service motorboat during winter and was to be caretaker of premises on land during summer did not include washing motorboat owner's automobile in February, and discharge of employee for not washing it was unjustified.

> Swift v. Knowles, 100 F.2d 977.

Fla.App. 3 Dist. 1998. To prevail on claim for retaliatory discharge, seaman must first establish that employer's decision to discharge him was motivated, in substantial part, by knowledge that seaman intends to, or has, filed personal injury action against employer.

> Kloster Cruise Lines v. Taay, 712 So.2d 1233.

Retaliatory discharge claim by seaman against cruise ship employer failed where seaman was not discharged but instead as result of his shipboard injury was determined not fit for duty aboard ship by his doctor; seaman's original physician released him for work, seaman saw another physician and seaman's attorney sent letter to employer stating seaman was not fit for duty and employer acquiesced to requests of seaman's attorney and treating physician to continue physical therapy and employer was never notified that seaman was ready to return to work.

> Kloster Cruise Lines v. Taay, 712 So.2d 1233.

Fla.App. 3 Dist. 1995. Employer may not retaliate against at-will employee for filing Jones Act personal injury claim. Jones Act, 46 App.U.S.C.A. § 688.

> Baiton v. Carnival Cruise Lines, Inc., 661 So.2d 313, rehearing denied.

Employee had cause of action for retaliatory discharge that was motivated in substantial part by employee's giving, or agreeing to give, truthful testimony in personal injury action against maritime employer, or his refusal to give false statement in proceeding.

> Baiton v. Carnival Cruise Lines, Inc., 661 So.2d 313, rehearing denied.

Employee's allegations that he was discharged for refusing to give false statement in fellow employee's personal injury action against maritime employer were sufficient to state cause of action under state whistle-blower statute. West's F.S.A. §§ 448.101–448.105.

> Baiton v. Carnival Cruise Lines, Inc., 661 So.2d 313, rehearing denied.

Written presuit notice was not condition precedent to recovery under whistle-blower statute for retaliatory discharge of employee who refused to give false statement in connection with fellow employee's personal injury suit against maritime employer. West's F.S.A. § 448.102(3).

> Baiton v. Carnival Cruise Lines, Inc., 661 So.2d 313, rehearing denied.

⌖13. Expenses of return to port of shipment.

For other cases see earlier editions of this digest, the Decennial Digests, and WEST-LAW.

⌖14. Performance of services.

C.A.5 (Fla.) 1981. Duty of a seaman is to do the work assigned, not to find the safest method for doing that work. Jones Act, 46 U.S.C.A. § 688.

Bobb v. Modern Products, Inc., 648 F.2d 1051.

⌖15. Wages.

⌖15.1. —— In general.

M.D.Fla. 1991. Seamen's wages statute did not apply to persons serving as port relief officers, who did not sign articles of employment or go to sea with a vessel, inasmuch as port relief officers were not exposed to dangers against which statute protected. 46 U.S.C.A. § 10313(f, g).

Marine Transport Lines, Inc. v. International Organization of Masters, Mates and Pilots, 766 F.Supp. 1564, affirmed 963 F.2d 385.

S.D.Fla. 2000. Unearned wages are those that seagoing employee would have earned had she been able to complete terms of employment, include reasonably anticipated tips when employment agreement incorporates receipt of such gratuities by employee.

Gheorghita v. Royal Caribbean Cruises, Ltd., 93 F.Supp.2d 1237.

⌖16. —— Right in general.

C.A.11 (Fla.) 2001. General maritime law guarantees seamen: (1) "maintenance," which is a living allowance; (2) "cure," which covers nursing and medical expenses; and (3) wages.

Cabrera Espinal v. Royal Caribbean Cruises, Ltd., 253 F.3d 629.

C.A.11 (Fla.) 1988. Cruise ship pantryman who was a blue water seaman on shore leave in foreign port at time of his injury, was entitled to maintenance and cure under principles of maritime law and thus was also entitled to lost wages for one year, the full term of his contract.

Archer v. Trans/American Services, Ltd., 834 F.2d 1570.

C.A.5 (Fla.) 1955. Where seaman was engaged on month-to-month basis for coastwise yacht voyage and signed no articles on coming aboard, there was assumption that he was obligated to serve for fixed period of a month, and upon his becoming incapacitated while on board, he was entitled to wages for such period only, and where seaman left yacht 27th day of month and was cured 31st day, he was entitled to wages until 31st day of month, in addition to maintenance and cure.

Rofer v. Head & Head, Inc., 226 F.2d 927.

C.A.5 (Fla.) 1951. Members of vessel's crew, who were paid for their services until date of their discharge on being advised that one falsely purporting to act as vessel's captain at time of hiring them had no authority to do so, were not entitled to further payments for wages and subsistence after such date.

Findley v. Red Top Super Markets, 188 F.2d 834, certiorari denied 72 S.Ct. 112, 342 U.S. 870, 96 L.Ed. 654.

C.A.5 (Fla.) 1951. Where members of crew of vessel were signed on to work during fishing trip for share in proceeds of catch of fish, and vessel sailed on fishing voyage off coast of New York state, but returned because of bad weather, and vessel subsequently sailed for Florida coastal waters, where weather and fish were expected to be better, to continue fishing venture, the run to Florida was not an ordinary coasting voyage for which crew members would be entitled to wages as merchant seamen, but was simply a move from one fishing ground to another in furtherance of fishing enterprise. 46 U.S.C.A. § 594.

Sigurjonsson v. Trans-American Traders, 188 F.2d 760, certiorari denied 72 S.Ct. 46, 342 U.S. 831, 96 L.Ed. 629, rehearing denied 72 S.Ct. 105, 342 U.S. 874, 96 L.Ed. 657.

S.D.Fla. 2000. Right to recover unearned wages, which is separate component of right to maintenance and cure, cannot be eliminated in employment contract.

Gheorghita v. Royal Caribbean Cruises, Ltd., 93 F.Supp.2d 1237.

† This Case was not selected for publication in the National Reporter System
For legislative history of cited statutes, see Florida Statutes Annotated

S.D.Fla. 1993. Unearned wages to sick or injured seaman under general maritime law are payable as part of maintenance and cure.

Joaquim v. Royal Caribbean Cruises, Ltd., 899 F.Supp. 600, reversed in part, vacated in part 52 F.3d 1071.

Fla.App. 1 Dist. 1993. Recovery for maintenance, cure and unearned wages is a no-fault concept arising out of relationship between injured seaman and vessel, neither subject to comparative negligence nor dependent upon shipowner's negligence.

Moran Towing of Florida, Inc. v. Mays, 620 So.2d 1088, on subsequent appeal 623 So.2d 850.

☞17. —— Amount.

C.A.11 (Fla.) 1998. Unearned wages in maintenance and cure action would be based on assistant wine steward's average weekly tips actually earned rather than tips guaranteed under his employment contract, where contract neither estimated tips nor purported to place ceiling on unearned wages to which he was entitled; expectation of parties was that tip income would constitute substantial portion of his compensation.

Aksoy v. Apollo Ship Chandlers, Inc., 137 F.3d 1304.

S.D.Fla. 2000. Unearned wages are those that seagoing employee would have earned had she been able to complete terms of employment, include reasonably anticipated tips when employment agreement incorporates receipt of such gratuities by employee.

Gheorghita v. Royal Caribbean Cruises, Ltd., 93 F.Supp.2d 1237.

When seagoing employee has no contract or has contract with no enforceable term of duration, she only is entitled to unearned wages from time she becomes unfit for duty to end of that voyage.

Gheorghita v. Royal Caribbean Cruises, Ltd., 93 F.Supp.2d 1237.

Cabin stewardess was entitled to unearned wages only until end of voyage during which she became ill, and not until end of six month period for which she was engaged, where collective bargaining agreement specified that employment agreement would be "regarded as being terminated from the date the Employee signs off the vessel" and that employees could be terminated without cause or notice.

Gheorghita v. Royal Caribbean Cruises, Ltd., 93 F.Supp.2d 1237.

Unearned wages in cabin stewardess's maintenance and cure action included amount of estimated actual tips and proportionate amount of monthly actual pay, rather than monthly guaranteed pay in employment contract.

Gheorghita v. Royal Caribbean Cruises, Ltd., 93 F.Supp.2d 1237.

Cabin stewardess seeking maintenance and cure was not entitled to recover actual tips for days on which she was declared fit for duty, but did not perform her duties or notify someone of her decision not to do so.

Gheorghita v. Royal Caribbean Cruises, Ltd., 93 F.Supp.2d 1237.

S.D.Fla. 1993. Employment contract under which seaman was to serve as busboy/waiter aboard vessel for one year was terminable at will, so that seaman was not entitled to recover unearned wages in excess of monthly payment, where contract provided that agreement may be terminated without particular reason, and seaman failed to allege either date on which voyage ended or total amount that he received from his employer.

Joaquim v. Royal Caribbean Cruises, Ltd., 899 F.Supp. 600, reversed in part, vacated in part 52 F.3d 1071.

Injured or sick seaman under contract for year may collect year's wages as part of maintenance, otherwise he is entitled to wages only until end of voyage.

Joaquim v. Royal Caribbean Cruises, Ltd., 899 F.Supp. 600, reversed in part, vacated in part 52 F.3d 1071.

Fla.App. 1 Dist. 1993. Injured seaman was not due any unearned wages beyond the end of the voyage on which he was injured; collective bargaining agreement was not an employment contract between seaman and vessel owner, and no evidence indicated that seaman had continuing obligation to present himself for work with vessel owner until expiration of agreement.

> Moran Towing of Florida, Inc. v. Mays, 620 So.2d 1088, on subsequent appeal 623 So.2d 850.

⬤⟶18. —— Extra wages.

C.A.11 (Fla.) 2013. District court, sitting as trier of fact in action brought by senior stateroom stewards against cruise line under Seamen's Wage Act, was not clearly erroneous in finding that stewards were not entitled to penalty wages by crediting testimony of two senior stewards who testified that they told cruise line that they were able to finish their work without paying helpers; although those stewards may have been "outliers," that designation was not determinative, and although other witnesses testified that completing the work without aid of helpers was impossible, court could adopt one permissible view of trial evidence over other. 46 U.S.C.A. § 10313(f, g); Fed.Rules Civ.Proc. Rule 52(a), 28 U.S.C.A.

> Wallace v. NCL (Bahamas) Ltd., 733 F.3d 1093, certiorari denied 134 S.Ct. 1520, 188 L.Ed.2d 450.

District court's conclusion that employer violated its duty of good faith and fair dealing under Florida law with regard to how it compensated senior stateroom stewards did not require court to award of penalty wages under Seaman's Wage Act, since Seaman's Wage Act applied subjective test to wages claim and state law claim applied objective test. 46 U.S.C.A. § 10313(f, g).

> Wallace v. NCL (Bahamas) Ltd., 733 F.3d 1093, certiorari denied 134 S.Ct. 1520, 188 L.Ed.2d 450.

Cruise line did not engage in willful, arbitrary, or willful misconduct, as required for award of penalty wages under Seaman's Wage Act; although cruise line created situation where it was nearly impossible for stewards to clean their assigned cabins without helpers and knew of need for helpers to be utilized to complete most of the work, some stewards were able to finish their work without paying helpers. 46 U.S.C.A. § 10313(g).

> Wallace v. NCL (Bahamas) Ltd., 733 F.3d 1093, certiorari denied 134 S.Ct. 1520, 188 L.Ed.2d 450.

C.A.11 (Fla.) 2000. Oil tanker, which was carrying heating oil from port in Mississippi to port in Connecticut when seaman was injured in slip and fall, was engaged in "coastwise commerce," precluding seaman from collecting under penalty wage statute. 46 U.S.C.A. §§ 10301(a), 10501(a), 10504(d)(1).

> Frederick v. Kirby Tankships, Inc., 205 F.3d 1277, certiorari denied 121 S.Ct. 46, 531 U.S. 813, 148 L.Ed.2d 16.

C.A.5 (Fla.) 1951. Members of crew of vessel, who worked under contract providing that they were not guaranteed salaries or disbursements for their time and labor, and under which their compensation was to be specified percentage of proceeds from fish caught on fishing trip for which they signed, were not merchant "seamen" entitled to recover penalties imposed by statute imposing penalties for delay in payment of wages of seamen, or by statute providing penalties for reduction of allowance of provisions to which seaman is entitled under statute. 46 U.S.C.A. §§ 596, 665.

> Sigurjonsson v. Trans-American Traders, 188 F.2d 760, certiorari denied 72 S.Ct. 46, 342 U.S. 831, 96 L.Ed. 629, rehearing denied 72 S.Ct. 105, 342 U.S. 874, 96 L.Ed. 657.

M.D.Fla. 1991. Retroactive seamen's wage payments were not required to be made within time period specified in statute governing seamen's wages and mandating penalties for failure to pay wages without sufficient cause, inasmuch as wages remained negotiable at will of seamen's labor organization and were thus not vested "wages" as term was used in statute. 46 U.S.C.A. § 10313(f, g).

> Marine Transport Lines, Inc. v. International Organization of Masters, Mates and Pilots, 766 F.Supp. 1564, affirmed 963 F.2d 385.

Even if seamen's wages statute applied to retroactive wage payments, statutory penalty for nonpayment of wages without sufficient cause was not appropriate because there was legitimate dispute between employer and seamen's labor organization as to date retroactive payments were required and as to amount of cost of living adjustment required by contract, thus precluding any finding that delay in payment was without sufficient cause. 46 U.S.C.A. § 10313(f, g).

> Marine Transport Lines, Inc. v. International Organization of Masters, Mates and Pilots, 766 F.Supp. 1564, affirmed 963 F.2d 385.

In order for seaman to recover statutory double wage penalties, master or owner must have refused to pay seaman his wages within period specified, and failure must be without sufficient cause. 46 U.S.C.A. § 10313(f, g).

> Marine Transport Lines, Inc. v. International Organization of Masters, Mates and Pilots, 766 F.Supp. 1564, affirmed 963 F.2d 385.

Statutory penalty for nonpayment of seaman's wages is mandatory if shipowner withholds payment of wages without sufficient cause. 46 U.S.C.A. § 10313(f, g).

> Marine Transport Lines, Inc. v. International Organization of Masters, Mates and Pilots, 766 F.Supp. 1564, affirmed 963 F.2d 385.

That shipowner wrongfully withholds payment of seaman's wages does not by itself establish absence of sufficient cause for withholding within meaning of statute mandating penalty for withholding wages without sufficient cause. 46 U.S.C.A. § 10313(f, g).

> Marine Transport Lines, Inc. v. International Organization of Masters, Mates and Pilots, 766 F.Supp. 1564, affirmed 963 F.2d 385.

That seamen's retroactive wage payments were delayed in processing did not give rise to imposition of penalties against shipowner pursuant to seamen's wages statute where delays were not arbitrary or unreasonable; actions taken by shipowner in response to demands of seamen's labor organization were performed in good faith, and any computational errors in issuing checks arose as result of shipowner's attempt to meet wage demands of labor organization while comptroller responsible for that function was unavailable. 46 U.S.C.A. § 10313(f, g).

> Marine Transport Lines, Inc. v. International Organization of Masters, Mates and Pilots, 766 F.Supp. 1564, affirmed 963 F.2d 385.

S.D.Fla. 2012. Cruise line employer created a situation where it was nearly impossible for its senior stateroom attendants to clean all their assigned cabins within the allotted time period on embarkation day, which forced the attendants to hire and pay helpers, so that the attendants did not receive their full wages, in violation of the Seamen's Wage Act; cruise line allowed disembarking passengers to leave the cruise ship late in the morning and permitted the embarking passengers to board in the early afternoon, and each attendant had to clean approximately 30 to 35 cabins in about 4.5 hours. 46 U.S.C.A. § 10313(f, g).

> Wallace v. NCL (Bahamas) Ltd., 891 F.Supp.2d 1343, affirmed 733 F.3d 1093, certiorari denied 134 S.Ct. 1520, 188 L.Ed.2d 450.

A wrongful withholding of seamen's wages alone does not establish the absence of sufficient cause, as required to support an award of penalties under the Seamen's Wage Act. 46 U.S.C.A. § 10313(f, g).

> Wallace v. NCL (Bahamas) Ltd., 891 F.Supp.2d 1343, affirmed 733 F.3d 1093, certiorari denied 134 S.Ct. 1520, 188 L.Ed.2d 450.

A shipowner withholds seamen's wages without sufficient cause, as will support an award of penalties under the Seamen's Wage Act, if it is not only contrary to law but also arbitrary, wilful, or unreasonable. 46 U.S.C.A. § 10313(f, g).

> Wallace v. NCL (Bahamas) Ltd., 891 F.Supp.2d 1343, affirmed 733 F.3d 1093, certiorari denied 134 S.Ct. 1520, 188 L.Ed.2d 450.

Penalty wages do not apply, under the Seamen's Wage Act, where the shipowner had a reasonable belief that the wages were not due, where the shipowner committed an error of judgment, or where there was a dispute as to the wages owed. 46 U.S.C.A. § 10313(f, g).

> Wallace v. NCL (Bahamas) Ltd., 891 F.Supp.2d 1343, affirmed 733 F.3d 1093, certiorari denied 134 S.Ct. 1520, 188 L.Ed.2d 450.

Cruise line employer was not liable for penalties under the Seamen's Wage Act for its conduct in creating a situation that forced senior stateroom attendants to hire and pay helpers so that attendants could complete their work in the time allotted; there was a dispute about whether the employer owed the attendants the wages that the attendants paid to their helpers, and the employer had a reasonable belief that the wages were not withheld, within the meaning of the Act. 46 U.S.C.A. § 10313(f, g).

> Wallace v. NCL (Bahamas) Ltd., 891 F.Supp.2d 1343, affirmed 733 F.3d 1093, certiorari denied 134 S.Ct. 1520, 188 L.Ed.2d 450.

S.D.Fla. 1964. Statute excepting application of the double wage penalty to steam vessels engaged in certain trade had to be read so that the exemption applied to coastwise trade, to lake-going trade, and trade between the United States and British North American possessions, but not to coastwise trade between the Atlantic and Pacific coast, and therefore double wage penalty did not apply to a ship engaged in trade between the Port of Miami, Florida, and British North American possessions of Nassau and New Providence, Bahama Islands. 46 U.S.C.A. §§ 544, 596.

> Watler v. M/V Sea Lane, 232 F.Supp. 387.

Absence of sufficient cause is required to entitle a seaman to benefit of double wage penalty statute. 46 U.S.C.A. §§ 544, 596.

> Watler v. M/V Sea Lane, 232 F.Supp. 387.

Fla.App. 2 Dist. 1960. The word "voyage" may have different meanings under different circumstances, depending upon the subject to which it relates or the context of the particular contract or statute in which the term is employed.

> Carson v. Gulf Oil Corp., 123 So.2d 35.

Federal statute prescribing penalties for failure of master or owner of any vessel making coasting voyages to pay seaman's wages in the manner therein provided deals with voyages as differentiated from maritime activity confined to a harbor or port, or which does not require going to sea. 46 U.S.C.A. § 596.

> Carson v. Gulf Oil Corp., 123 So.2d 35.

A tanker engaged in transporting oil between Texas and Florida ports was mak-

ing "coasting voyages" within meaning of federal statute prescribing penalties for failure of master or owner of any vessel making such voyages to pay seaman's wages in the manner therein provided, and statute exempting vessels engaged in "coastwise trade" from statutory penalties was not applicable. 46 U.S.C.A. §§ 544, 596.

> Carson v. Gulf Oil Corp., 123 So.2d 35.

⚷19. —— Wages on discharge.

C.A.11 (Fla.) 1985. To constitute cognizable claim under statute [46 U.S.C. (1982 Ed.) § 596] providing that seaman is to be paid within two days of his discharge or termination from employment, that claim must be advanced in "good faith," and whether such claim is bona fide is factual question entrusted to discretion of trial court and subject to reversal only if clearly erroneous.

> Sigalas v. Lido Maritime, Inc., 776 F.2d 1512.

Under statute [46 U.S.C. (1982 Ed.) § 596] providing that seaman is to be paid within two days of his discharge or termination from employment, claims are due and payable upon discharge; death is not a discharge for purposes of such statute.

> Sigalas v. Lido Maritime, Inc., 776 F.2d 1512.

C.A.5 (Fla.) 1951. Members of crew of vessel, who worked under contract providing that they were not guaranteed salaries or disbursements for their time and labor, and under which their compensation was to be specified percentage of proceeds from fish caught on fishing trip for which they signed, were not merchant "seamen" entitled to seamen's wages under statute authorizing a seaman discharged without his fault before commencement of voyage or before one month's wages are earned to recover compensation therein specified. 46 U.S.C.A. 594.

> Sigurjonsson v. Trans-American Traders, 188 F.2d 760, certiorari denied 72 S.Ct. 46, 342 U.S. 831, 96 L.Ed. 629, rehearing denied 72 S.Ct. 105, 342 U.S. 874, 96 L.Ed. 657.

S.D.Fla. 1995. Statute stating that, when master or seaman applies to consular officer for discharge of seaman, consular officer shall require master to pay seaman's wages if it appears that seaman has carried out the agreement required by statute governing shipping articles agreements or otherwise is entitled to be discharged was inapplicable to seaman and charter vessels upon which he worked; seaman did not allege or present evidence demonstrating that he entered into shipping agreement required by statute or that he was otherwise entitled to be discharged. 46 U.S.C.A. § 10318.

Fowler v. Towse, 900 F.Supp. 454.

🗝20–21(4). *For other cases see earlier editions of this digest, the Decennial Digests, and WESTLAW.*

🗝21. —— Forfeiture and fines.

🗝21(4). Desertion.

🗝21(4.1). —— In general.

Fla.App. 2 Dist. 1960. As used in federal statute providing for forfeiture of all wages for "desertion," quoted word means abandonment of duty by quitting ship before termination of engagement, without justification and with intention of not returning. 46 U.S.C.A. § 701.

Carson v. Gulf Oil Corp., 123 So.2d 35.

🗝21(5)–21(7). *For other cases see earlier editions of this digest, the Decennial Digests, and WESTLAW.*

🗝22. —— Persons liable.

S.D.Fla. 2004. Under general maritime law, a vessel and her owners are liable, in case a seaman falls sick, or is wounded, in the service of the ship, to the extent of his maintenance and cure, and to his wages, at least so long as the voyage is continued; the duty, which arises from the contract of employment, does not rest upon negligence or culpability on the part of the owner or master, nor is it restricted to those cases where the seaman's employment is the cause of the injury or illness.

Wai v. Rainbow Holdings, 350 F.Supp.2d 1019.

🗝23. —— Advances.

C.C.A.5 (Fla.) 1942. Sponge boats are "fishing boats" within statute excepting fishing boats from prohibition against advances of a seaman's wages, and hence advances may be made to crew members of such boats. 46 U.S.C.A. §§ 598, 599; Act Dec. 21, 1898, § 26, 30 Stat. 764.

Pavlis v. Jackson, 131 F.2d 362, certiorari denied 63 S.Ct. 761, 318 U.S. 769, 87 L.Ed. 1140.

Where sponge boat obtained a crew by promising to pay an agreed share in each catch, and it was customary to pay crew members in advance, some money to be repaid out of share of catch, and if share did not equal the advance, the vessel lost the difference, advances made to master or to crew members directly constituted "wages" and not mere anticipations of profit on a "joint enterprise" within statute excepting sponge boats from prohibition against advances of seaman's wages. 46 U.S.C.A. 598, 599; Act Dec. 21, 1898, Sec. 26, 30 Stat. 764.

Pavlis v. Jackson, 131 F.2d 362, certiorari denied 63 S.Ct. 761, 318 U.S. 769, 87 L.Ed. 1140.

S.D.Fla. 1995. Statute prohibiting advance wage payments to seamen does not apply to advances made to seamen in foreign ports, for service on foreign vessels, but applies to advances made in American ports. 46 U.S.C.A. § 10314(a).

Gary v. D. Agustini & Asociados, S.A., 898 F.Supp. 901.

🗝24. —— Payment.

C.A.11 (Fla.) 2013. On a claim under the Seaman's Wage Act, the phrase "without sufficient cause" must be taken to mean something more than merely valid defenses to a wage claim; its meaning, in effect, is a willful, unreasonable and arbitrary attitude upon the part of the master or shipowner in refusing to pay earned wages to the seamen. 46 U.S.C.A. § 10313(f, g).

Wallace v. NCL (Bahamas) Ltd., 733 F.3d 1093, certiorari denied 134 S.Ct. 1520, 188 L.Ed.2d 450.

Where the master or owner has acted in a reasonable manner throughout and without any showing of arbitrariness or unjustness, where he had an honest doubt as to the justification of the demand, and where the facts and circumstances surrounding the wage demand are susceptible to an honest doubt as to the justness of the seaman's demand, it cannot be said that the refusal is without sufficient cause on a claim under the Seaman's Wage Act. 46 U.S.C.A. § 10313(f, g).

> Wallace v. NCL (Bahamas) Ltd., 733 F.3d 1093, certiorari denied 134 S.Ct. 1520, 188 L.Ed.2d 450.

⚷═25. —— **Release.**

S.D.Fla. 2006. Seaman's settlement and release must be carefully scrutinized.

> Borcea v. Carnival Corp., 238 F.R.D. 664.

Seaman's settlement or release is considered valid if it was executed freely, without deception or coercion, and if it was made by seaman with full understanding of his rights.

> Borcea v. Carnival Corp., 238 F.R.D. 664.

Factors in appraising seaman's understanding of his rights before signing release include: (1) nature of legal advice available to seaman at time of signing; (2) adequacy of consideration; (3) whether parties negotiated at arm's length and in good faith; and (4) whether there was appearance of fraud or coercion.

> Borcea v. Carnival Corp., 238 F.R.D. 664.

⚷═26. —— **Actions.**

C.A.11 (Fla.) 2013. On a claim under the Seaman's Wage Act, once a seaman establishes his wages were wrongfully withheld, the burden of proof shifted to the employer to show that the delay in payment was justified, i.e., it was not without sufficient cause. 46 U.S.C.A. § 10313(f, g).

> Wallace v. NCL (Bahamas) Ltd., 733 F.3d 1093, certiorari denied 134 S.Ct. 1520, 188 L.Ed.2d 450.

† **C.A.11 (Fla.) 2012.** Cruise line employees who failed to allege that they were not paid after being discharged from foreign or intercoastal voyage were precluded from asserting claims under Seaman's Wage Act. 46 U.S.C.A. § 10313.

> Rankin v. Celebrity Cruises, Ltd., 489 Fed.Appx. 362.

C.A.11 (Fla.) 1990. In order for district court to determine whether seamen had actual notice of Icelandic admiralty proceeding, such that they unduly delayed in asserting their rights, supporting vessel purchaser's affirmative defense of laches, court was required to determine whether seamen's employer knew of seamen's claims when suit in Iceland was filed and, if so, whether employer had obligation to inform either Icelandic court or vessel purchaser at auction of claims made to employer, as well as when purchaser first learned of claims and whether purchaser would be prejudiced by enforcement of claims.

> Thorsteinsson v. M/V Drangur, 891 F.2d 1547.

C.A.11 (Fla.) 1985. Suit cannot be maintained on wage claim under statute [46 U.S.C. (1982 Ed.) § 596] providing that seaman is to be paid within two days of his discharge or termination from employment, unless prior to suit there has been demand for payment and denial or disregard of that demand. 46 U.S.C. (1982 Ed.) § 597.

> Sigalas v. Lido Maritime, Inc., 776 F.2d 1512.

Suit could not be maintained for unpaid wages due deceased seaman, where no demand for payment had been made prior to suit. 46 U.S.C. (1982 Ed.) §§ 596, 597.

> Sigalas v. Lido Maritime, Inc., 776 F.2d 1512.

C.A.5 (Fla.) 1963. Imperfect or lacking in factual particularity as they might have been, seaman's allegations were enough to satisfy liberal standards of admiralty pleadings to permit amendment to assert statutory penalties for nonpayment or improper payment of wages. 46 U.S.C.A. § 597, 600, 601; F.S.A. §§ 95.11(7) (b).

> McConville v. Florida Towing Corp., 321 F.2d 162.

Libelant seaman failed to make minimum showing required, to defeat laches defense, of any justification for delay of as much as 8 years on claim under statutes for wage payments on complaint of illegal advances and improper deductions of advances, and as respondent shipowner was exposed to substantial prejudice, laches defense was properly sustained. 46 U.S.C.A. §§ 597, 600, 601.

> McConville v. Florida Towing Corp., 321 F.2d 162.

Court improperly sustained laches exception to count of seaman's amended libel seeking statutory penalties for failure to pay earned wages due at time of discharge from vessel, though laches exception was properly sustained with respect to claim for alleged illegal advances and improper deductions. 46 U.S.C.A. § 596.

> McConville v. Florida Towing Corp., 321 F.2d 162.

There was legal-factual question, requiring hearing to determine merits, presented on discharged seaman's pleadings for statutory penalties for nonpayment of wages at time of discharge following affray, as to whether nonpayment constituted case of master or owner refusing or neglecting to make payment on discharge without sufficient cause within statute entitling seaman, in such event, to two days pay for each day during which payment was delayed. 46 U.S.C.A. §§ 544, 596.

> McConville v. Florida Towing Corp., 321 F.2d 162.

C.A.5 (Fla.) 1955. In action for wages, maintenance and cure by seaman employed in coastwise voyage on month-to-month basis, evidence compelled conclusion that seaman, when he disembarked during a month, informing captain to procure replacement for him, was not discharged for own misconduct but was ill, and that vessel did not have adequate medical facilities to care for him.

> Rofer v. Head & Head, Inc., 226 F.2d 927.

C.A.5 (Fla.) 1951. In action brought against vessel owner by libellant who had signed on board vessel for a fishing trip, judgment for libellants was not justified under evidence on ground that vessel's owner wrongfully abandoned fishing enterprise, so as to entitle libellants to recover either quantum meruit as at common law, or within admiralty rule that a contract of employment will be enforced in behalf of seamen, notwithstanding failure of voyage, when failure is occasioned by wrongful act of master or owner.

> Sigurjonsson v. Trans-American Traders, 188 F.2d 760, certiorari denied 72 S.Ct. 46, 342 U.S. 831, 96 L.Ed. 629, rehearing denied 72 S.Ct. 105, 342 U.S. 874, 96 L.Ed. 657.

S.D.Fla. 1964. Evidence, in libel by seaman for double wage penalties, established that seaman did not perform his duties as a mate of the vessel on dates for which he was allegedly not paid, and evidence also established that, even if wages were due and penalty statute were applicable to respondent vessel, failure to pay the wages was not without sufficient cause. 46 U.S.C.A. §§ 544, 596.

> Watler v. M/V Sea Lane, 232 F.Supp. 387.

Fla.App. 1 Dist. 1993. Third item of recovery in a maintenance and cure action is for unearned wages.

> Moran Towing of Florida, Inc. v. Mays, 620 So.2d 1088, on subsequent appeal 623 So.2d 850.

Fla.App. 2 Dist. 1960. In action by seaman for back wages and expenses incurred as a result of captain's refusal to reinstate plaintiff to position of oiler aboard defendant's vessel, evidence was sufficient to take case to jury on questions of whether refusal of plaintiff to surrender written unconditional temporary leave of absence or consider himself to be quitting the job constituted sufficient cause for refusal to pay wages then due plaintiff within meaning of federal statute prescribing penalties for such refusal and whether plaintiff had forfeited such wages by leaving vessel after captain retracted leave of absence previously granted. 46 U.S.C.A. §§ 596, 701.

> Carson v. Gulf Oil Corp., 123 So.2d 35.

⚷27–27(.5). *For other cases see earlier editions of this digest, the Decennial Digests, and WESTLAW.*

⚷27. —— Lien.

⚷27(1). **Creation and existence in general.**

C.C.A.5 (Fla.) 1937. If a seaman performs services on a vessel of a nature that would usually entitle him to a lien under the general admiralty law for wages, that he is improperly designated as a master or captain will not deprive him of the lien. 46 U.S.C.A. § 596.

Burdine v. Walden, 91 F.2d 321.

State statute creating a lien in favor of any person performing labor on, to, or for benefit of a vessel, including masters, mates, and members of crew, grants a lien only for amount earned for labor actually performed or services actually rendered, and does not cover wages for future services, although claimant might be entitled to recover them in a suit in personam. F.S.A. § 85.11.

Burdine v. Walden, 91 F.2d 321.

M.D.Fla. 1985. Claims for unpaid contribution to marine engineers' union's money purchase benefit plan were not wages for purpose of determining priority as between plan and holder of preferred ship mortgage. Ship Mortgage Act, 1920, § 30, subsec. M, 46 U.S.C.A. § 953.

Puerto Rico Maritime Shipping Authority v. Point Vigilance Corp., 643 F.Supp. 661, affirmed 803 F.2d 1183.

⊙═27(2). Persons entitled.

C.A.5 (Fla.) 1967. Fact that a person is described or describes himself or signs ship's papers as "master" is not conclusive as to his status as a seaman entitled to lien for wages. Ship Mortgage Act of 1920, § 30, subsecs. P, Q, 46 U.S.C.A. §§ 971, 972.

Barber v. Motor Vessel 'Blue Cat', 372 F.2d 626.

C.C.A.5 (Fla.) 1939. Although a true master has no maritime lien for wages, a person who was employed to service motorboat and who constituted both captain and crew was entitled to claim lien.

Swift v. Knowles, 100 F.2d 977.

S.D.Fla. 1948. Neither master of vessel nor first mate who were also stockholders, directors and officers of corporation owning vessel, were entitled to a maritime lien for their wages as master and mate respectively.

The Odysseus III, 77 F.Supp. 297.

S.D.Fla. 1942. Where owner of vessel of foreign registry resided in State of Florida, the captain of the vessel was entitled to a lien in the nature of a maritime lien on vessel by virtue of Florida statute for wages. F.S.A. §§ 85.01, 85.11.

The Diane, 45 F.Supp. 510.

⊙═27(3). Services in port.

C.C.A.5 (Fla.) 1939. An employment contract requiring employee to service motorboat during winter and to be caretaker of premises on land during summer constituted a maritime contract only during winter, and therefore employee who was wrongfully discharged was not entitled to maritime lien upon boat for wages accruing after boat was to go into storage.

Swift v. Knowles, 100 F.2d 977.

⊙═27(4). Services rendered on vessel in custody of law.

S.D.Fla. 2007. The general rule in admiralty law that no lien can attach to a vessel while she is in judicial custody trumps a seaman's sacred claim for wages, with the sole exception that post-judicial custody claims for necessaries can be paid as expenses of justice if equity and good conscience so require.

Admiral Cruise Services, Inc. v. M/V ST. TROPEZ, 524 F.Supp.2d 1378.

Cruise vessel under management of bankruptcy trustee was not in "judicial custody," and therefore crew members had valid maritime lien on proceeds of vessel's sale for tips collected during time vessel was under control of trustee and before its arrest for benefit of bankruptcy estate, since trustee stepped into shoes of vessel's owner and retained crew members to serve vessel's passengers as owner had in past, and so lien for wages attached to vessel as if still under owner's control.

Admiral Cruise Services, Inc. v. M/V ST. TROPEZ, 524 F.Supp.2d 1378.

⊙═27(5)–27(6). *For other cases see earlier editions of this digest, the Decennial Digests, and WESTLAW.*

⊙═27(5). Property subject.

⊙═27(7). —— Vessels.

M.D.Fla. 1991. Seaman's lien for unpaid wages is common law lien against vessel.

Ramirez v. U.S., 767 F.Supp. 1563.

Maritime lien for unpaid seaman's wages is property right in vessel, arising in favor of seaman.

Ramirez v. U.S., 767 F.Supp. 1563.

⚷27(8). Amount and extent.

C.C.A.5 (Fla.) 1939. A contract of employment requiring employee to service motorboat during winter and to be caretaker of premises on land during summer was enforceable against boat as a contract for maritime employment for period during which boat was used.

Swift v. Knowles, 100 F.2d 977.

M.D.Fla. 1991. Captain and crew of vessel which was seized for importing cocaine into United States were entitled to lien for wages, to be valued under breach of contract theory, in light of evidence that they neither knew nor participated in illegal importation of cocaine; captain and crew members were each entitled to maritime liens equal to amounts owed for wages earned before seizure and for wages and vacation pay which seizure prevented them from earning. Tariff Act of 1930, §§ 608, 615, as amended, 19 U.S.C.A. §§ 1608, 1615.

Ramirez v. U.S., 767 F.Supp. 1563.

⚷27(9). Priority.

C.A.11 (Fla.) 1996. By statute, superpriority is afforded seamen's liens for wages, since such liens are "sacred and indelible" and are entitled to be paid as long as a plank of the ship remains. 46 U.S.C.A. § 10313.

Isbrandtsen Marine Services, Inc. v. M/V Inagua Tania, 93 F.3d 728.

C.A.5 (Fla.) 1971. Salvage claims had priority upon fund from sale of vessel, after wages, maintenance and cure.

Fredelos v. Merritt-Chapman & Scott Corp., 447 F.2d 435, on rehearing 1971 WL 217579.

Wages, maintenance and cure were entitled to priority of first category, of rank ahead of salvage claim, against salvaged vessel.

Fredelos v. Merritt-Chapman & Scott Corp., 447 F.2d 435, on rehearing 1971 WL 217579.

S.D.Fla. 2007. Claims for wages by seamen occupy a preferential place in the echelon of maritime liens, and indeed, a bedrock of maritime law is that seamen's wages are sacred liens, so that as long as a plank of the ship remains, the sailor is entitled, against all other persons, to the proceeds as a security for his wages.

Admiral Cruise Services, Inc. v. M/V ST. TROPEZ, 524 F.Supp.2d 1378.

Crew members' claims for unpaid tips are the quintessential example of an expense of justice for which district court has equitable power to give priority, arising out of the administration of a vessel in judicial custody.

Admiral Cruise Services, Inc. v. M/V ST. TROPEZ, 524 F.Supp.2d 1378.

S.D.Fla. 1942. In libels against vessels by lien claimants and others, claimants were entitled to have liens or claims satisfied in the following order: maritime lien for seaman's wages; general maritime liens for repairs and supplies; state statutory lien by captain for wages and advances; mortgages on vessel where statutory provisions were not complied with. 46 U.S.C.A. § 971; F.S.A. §§ 85.01, 85.11.

The Diane, 45 F.Supp. 510.

⚷27(10). Assignment of claim or lien.

For other cases see earlier editions of this digest, the Decennial Digests, and WEST-LAW.

⚷27(11). Waiver, loss, or discharge.

C.C.A.5 (Fla.) 1937. State statute creating a lien in favor of any person performing labor on, to, or for benefit of a vessel, including masters, mates, and members of crew, does not require that the lienor retain possession to preserve his lien. F.S.A. § 85.11.

Burdine v. Walden, 91 F.2d 321.

⚷27(12). Enforcement.

For other cases see earlier editions of this digest, the Decennial Digests, and WEST-LAW.

⚷28. Share in earnings.

N.D.Fla. 1956. Seaman was entitled to recover his share of catch on voyage, even though he was taken ill and was forced to leave fishing vessel before it returned from fishing trip.

> Bass v. Warren Fish Co., 146 F.Supp. 742.

⊷**29. Personal injuries.**

⊷**29(1). In general.**

U.S.Fla. 1955. Purpose of the Jones Act was to benefit and protect seamen who are peculiarly the wards of admiralty. Jones Act, 46 U.S.C.A. § 688.

> Cox v. Roth, 75 S.Ct. 242, 348 U.S. 207, 99 L.Ed. 260.

Jones Act as welfare legislation is entitled to liberal construction to accomplish its beneficent purposes. Jones Act, 46 U.S.C.A. § 688.

> Cox v. Roth, 75 S.Ct. 242, 348 U.S. 207, 99 L.Ed. 260.

C.A.11 (Fla.) 2014. The Jones Act provides a cause of action in negligence for "a seaman" personally injured "in the course of employment," in the same way that the Federal Employers' Liability Act provides a cause of action in negligence for injured railroad employees against their employers. Federal Employers' Liability Act, § 1 et seq., 45 U.S.C.A. § 51 et seq.; 46 U.S.C.A. § 30104.

> Skye v. Maersk Line, Ltd. Corp., 751 F.3d 1262, certiorari denied 135 S.Ct. 2048, 191 L.Ed.2d 955.

Not all work-related injuries are cognizable under the Federal Employers' Liability Act and, by extension, the Jones Act; for employers to be liable, the employees' injuries must be caused by the negligent conduct of their employers that threatens them imminently with physical impact. Federal Employers' Liability Act, § 1 et seq., 45 U.S.C.A. § 51 et seq.; 46 U.S.C.A. § 30104.

> Skye v. Maersk Line, Ltd. Corp., 751 F.3d 1262, certiorari denied 135 S.Ct. 2048, 191 L.Ed.2d 955.

Excessive work hours and erratic sleep schedule that resulted in physical injury to seaman in the form of left ventricular hypertrophy was not cognizable under Jones Act, since cause of seaman's injury was work-related stress, not physical perils. Federal Employers' Liability Act, § 1 et seq., 45 U.S.C.A. § 51 et seq.; 46 U.S.C.A. § 30104.

> Skye v. Maersk Line, Ltd. Corp., 751 F.3d 1262, certiorari denied 135 S.Ct. 2048, 191 L.Ed.2d 955.

The Jones Act does not allow seaman to recover for injuries caused by work-related stress because work-related stress is not a "physical peril." Federal Employers' Liability Act, § 1 et seq., 45 U.S.C.A. § 51 et seq.; 46 U.S.C.A. § 30104.

> Skye v. Maersk Line, Ltd. Corp., 751 F.3d 1262, certiorari denied 135 S.Ct. 2048, 191 L.Ed.2d 955.

† **C.A.11 (Fla.) 2013.** Crewmember's claims against vessel owner fell within scope of arbitration clause contained in agreement amounting to seaman's employment agreement, despite crewmember's argument that claims arose under Jones Act, which protects injured seamen, rather than under agreement; crewmembers claims alleging Jones Act negligence, unseaworthiness, and maintenance and cure would not have been viable except for crewmember's service on vessel, and so dispute arose out of service on vessel. 46 U.S.C.A. § 30104 et seq.

> Montero v. Carnival Corp., 523 Fed. Appx. 623.

C.A.11 (Fla.) 1996. Difference between general admiralty law claim and Jones Act claim is not mere semantic difference between suit in admiralty and suit at law; difference is substantive and may determine whether there is right to recover at all. Jones Act, 46 App.U.S.C.A. § 688.

> Larue v. Joann M., 73 F.3d 325, as modified on denial of rehearing.

C.A.11 (Fla.) 1993. To recover damages under Jones Act, plaintiff must have status of seaman. Jones Act, 46 App. U.S.C.A. § 688.

> O'Boyle v. U.S., 993 F.2d 211.

C.A.11 (Fla.) 1986. Causation was necessary element of seaman's cause of action under Jones Act for negligence, products liability, and alleged unseaworthiness of vessel on which he was employed. Jones Act, 46 U.S.C.A. § 688.

> Nichols v. Barwick, 792 F.2d 1520.

C.A.5 (Fla.) 1972. Duty to furnish seaworthy vessel, that is, a vessel and appurtenances reasonably fit for their intended use, is absolute, and results in a kind of liability without fault that may be incurred without negligence.

> Weeks v. Alonzo Cothron, Inc., 466 F.2d 578, appeal after remand 493 F.2d 538.

Doctrine of seaworthiness does not require vessel to be equipped with latest developments in maritime safety.

> Weeks v. Alonzo Cothron, Inc., 466 F.2d 578, appeal after remand 493 F.2d 538.

Barge owners' practice of permitting single diver to work alone under barge without visual or physical connection to another member of the crew and without any safety precautions amounted to unseaworthiness and owners were liable for death of seaman who drowned while applying underside patches to leaks.

> Weeks v. Alonzo Cothron, Inc., 466 F.2d 578, appeal after remand 493 F.2d 538.

Barge owners' practice of permitting a single diver to work alone under barge without visual or physical connection to another member of the crew and without any safety precautions was not a seaworthy practice merely because divers in the area traditionally dove without life lines.

> Weeks v. Alonzo Cothron, Inc., 466 F.2d 578, appeal after remand 493 F.2d 538.

Unseaworthy practice does not become seaworthy on basis that it is ratified by custom and usage.

> Weeks v. Alonzo Cothron, Inc., 466 F.2d 578, appeal after remand 493 F.2d 538.

C.A.5 (Fla.) 1970. Rationale behind doctrine of unseaworthiness is to protect seamen from dangerous conditions beyond their control.

> Little v. Green, 428 F.2d 1061, certiorari denied 91 S.Ct. 366, 400 U.S. 964, 27 L.Ed.2d 384.

C.A.5 (Fla.) 1967. "Seaworthiness" is a relative concept, depending in each instance on the particular circumstances.

> Gibbs v. Kiesel, 382 F.2d 917.

Shipowner owes an absolute duty to provide a seaworthy vessel; however, the absolute duty is only to furnish a vessel and equipment reasonably fit for their intended use.

> Gibbs v. Kiesel, 382 F.2d 917.

C.A.5 (Fla.) 1966. Longshoremen's and Harbor Workers' Compensation Act and Jones Act are mutually exclusive, with Jones Act being limited to master or member of crew of vessel. Longshoremen's and Harbor Workers' Compensation Act, § 1 et seq., 33 U.S.C.A. § 901 et seq.; Jones Act, 46 U.S.C.A. § 688.

> Bodden v. Coordinated Caribbean Transport, Inc., 369 F.2d 273, 5 A.L.R. Fed. 668.

C.A.5 (Fla.) 1966. Fact that heavy equipment that caused death and injury to seamen aboard vessel on high seas did not belong to shipowner and was not part of ship's own equipment does not alter fact that vessel had become unseaworthy because improperly spliced cable was used to move heavy equipment. Death on the High Seas Act, §§ 1–8, 46 U.S.C.A. §§ 761–768; Jones Act, 46 U.S.C.A. § 688.

> Symonette Shipyards, Limited v. Clark, 365 F.2d 464, certiorari denied 87 S.Ct. 1690, 387 U.S. 908, 18 L.Ed.2d 625.

C.A.5 (Fla.) 1965. The Jones Act is remedial legislation which is to be considered liberally in favor of enlarging remedies of injured seamen. Jones Act, 46 U.S.C.A. § 688; 28 U.S.C.A. §§ 1391(c), 1400(b); F.S.A. §§ 47.34, 47.36, 47.43.

> Pure Oil Co. v. Suarez, 346 F.2d 890, certiorari granted 86 S.Ct. 549, 382 U.S. 972, 15 L.Ed.2d 464, affirmed 86 S.Ct. 1394, 384 U.S. 202, 16 L.Ed.2d 474.

C.A.5 (Fla.) 1963. Seamen who sustained injuries by reason of unseaworthiness of ship or her tackle may recover compensatory damages, termed an indemnity, from owner.

> Daniels v. Florida Power & Light Co., 317 F.2d 41, certiorari denied 84 S.Ct. 78, 375 U.S. 832, 11 L.Ed.2d 63.

C.A.5 (Fla.) 1962. That deceased dredge employee's nautical career had begun only 10 days before it ended in his death and that his training was in agricultural science to fit him for life of farmer

---

† This Case was not selected for publication in the National Reporter System
For legislative history of cited statutes, see Florida Statutes Annotated

was important not alone on damages question but more so from standpoint of duty owed by ship to such untutored inexperienced, green-hand. Jones Act, 46 U.S.C.A. § 688.

> Davis v. Parkhill-Goodloe Co., 302 F.2d 489.

Shipowner could not absolve itself of prevailing obligation to furnish seaworthy vessel and exercise prudent care for seamen by leaving important decision of whether or not to wear life vest up to inexperienced, untrained farm boy who had not yet begun to get his sea legs. Jones Act, 46 U.S.C.A. § 688.

> Davis v. Parkhill-Goodloe Co., 302 F.2d 489.

There is a duty to warn in an effective way of dangers not reasonably known and duty to take effective action in light of particular condition of particular seaman.

> Davis v. Parkhill-Goodloe Co., 302 F.2d 489.

Shipowner was negligent as matter of law in not giving adequate instructions with respect to perils of not wearing life vest to inexperienced seaman whose body was found in water after he had last been seen traversing 10-inch plank running from dredge over discharge line. Jones Act, 46 U.S.C.A. § 688.

> Davis v. Parkhill-Goodloe Co., 302 F.2d 489.

C.A.5 (Fla.) 1961. Seaman's widow had no cause of action under general maritime law, apart from Jones Act, for death of seaman who, through shipowner's alleged negligence, was stabbed by shipmate with switchblade knife. Jones Act, 46 U.S.C.A. § 688.

> Fall v. Esso Standard Oil Co., 297 F.2d 411, certiorari denied 83 S.Ct. 24, 371 U.S. 814, 9 L.Ed.2d 55.

Jones Act applies to injuries resulting from unseaworthiness due to shipowner's negligent failure to comply with absolute duty to furnish seaworthy vessel. Jones Act, 46 U.S.C.A. § 688.

> Fall v. Esso Standard Oil Co., 297 F.2d 411, certiorari denied 83 S.Ct. 24, 371 U.S. 814, 9 L.Ed.2d 55.

C.A.5 (Fla.) 1961. To be inadequately or improperly manned is a classic case of an unseaworthy vessel.

> June T., Inc. v. King, 290 F.2d 404.

C.A.5 (Fla.) 1954. A plaintiff who was employed by defendant operator of resort hotel as a cabana boy, and who went fishing for pleasure with speed boat owner not operating boat as agent, servant or employee of defendant, and who was injured from contacting propeller when holding boat at beach to prevent boat from scraping, was not under record a seaman, did not sustain injuries in course of employment as seaman, was not master or member of crew, and showed no negligence on part of defendant, nor was defendant owner pro hac vice of boat at time of injury, and plaintiff was not entitled to recover under Jones Act. Jones Act, 46 U.S.C.A. § 688.

> Kanischer v. Irwin Operating Co., 215 F.2d 300, certiorari denied 75 S.Ct. 363, 348 U.S. 942, 99 L.Ed. 737, rehearing denied 75 S.Ct. 529, 348 U.S. 977, 99 L.Ed. 761.

C.A.5 (Fla.) 1953. Barge owners had absolute and nondelegable duty to furnish seamen in their employ with safe and seaworthy appliances and a safe place in which to work.

> Sanford v. Caswell, 200 F.2d 830, certiorari denied 73 S.Ct. 831, 345 U.S. 940, 97 L.Ed. 1366.

M.D.Fla. 1990. General principles of negligence are utilized to analyze maritime tort case; standard of care is duty of ordinary care.

> Russell v. AT & T Technologies, Inc., 750 F.Supp. 1099.

M.D.Fla. 1985. Causative element in Jones Act cases is less than common-law standard of proximate cause; question of proximate cause thereunder focuses upon whether actions of defendant contributed to injury even in the slightest degree. Jones Act, 46 U.S.C.A. § 688.

> Complaint of Chevron Transport Corp., 613 F.Supp. 1428, affirmed in part, reversed in part Self v. Great Lakes Dredge & Dock Co., 832 F.2d 1540, rehearing denied 837 F.2d 1095, rehearing denied 837 F.2d 1095, rehearing denied Great Lakes Dredge & Dock Co. v.

Chevron Shipping Co., 837 F.2d 1095, certiorari denied Great Lakes Dredge and Dock Co. v. Chevron Transport Corp., 108 S.Ct. 2017, 486 U.S. 1033, 100 L.Ed.2d 604.

Employer's negligence need not be sole proximate cause of an injury to result in liability under the Jones Act but need merely be a contributing cause of the accident. Jones Act, 46 U.S.C.A. § 688.

> Complaint of Chevron Transport Corp., 613 F.Supp. 1428, affirmed in part, reversed in part Self v. Great Lakes Dredge & Dock Co., 832 F.2d 1540, rehearing denied 837 F.2d 1095, rehearing denied 837 F.2d 1095, rehearing denied Great Lakes Dredge & Dock Co. v. Chevron Shipping Co., 837 F.2d 1095, certiorari denied Great Lakes Dredge and Dock Co. v. Chevron Transport Corp., 108 S.Ct. 2017, 486 U.S. 1033, 100 L.Ed.2d 604.

Negligent acts of owner of tanker and operator of dredge flotilla were contributing causes in collision between tanker and barge which was part of dredge flotilla, and thus they were liable under the Jones Act for death of member of crew of dredge who drowned after collision. Jones Act, 46 U.S.C.A. § 688.

> Complaint of Chevron Transport Corp., 613 F.Supp. 1428, affirmed in part, reversed in part Self v. Great Lakes Dredge & Dock Co., 832 F.2d 1540, rehearing denied 837 F.2d 1095, rehearing denied 837 F.2d 1095, rehearing denied Great Lakes Dredge & Dock Co. v. Chevron Shipping Co., 837 F.2d 1095, certiorari denied Great Lakes Dredge and Dock Co. v. Chevron Transport Corp., 108 S.Ct. 2017, 486 U.S. 1033, 100 L.Ed.2d 604.

N.D.Fla. 1974. Hatch of barge was unseaworthy where it was not capable of being opened by use of hand winch and cable, and unseaworthiness was proximate cause of fall and injuries of worker engaged in unloading barge.

> Henderson v. S. C. Loveland Co., Inc., 381 F.Supp. 1102, opinion supplemented 390 F.Supp. 347, amended 396 F.Supp. 658.

N.D.Fla. 1956. An owner of a tug did not owe its assistant port engineer engaged in lifting a dead battery out of a tug, the duty to supervise his work and see that he would perform the work safely. Jones Act, 46 U.S.C.A. § 688.

> Ouzts v. A. P. Ward & Son, Inc., 146 F.Supp. 733.

S.D.Fla. 2009. A Jones Act claim is an in personam action for a seaman who suffers injury in the course of employment due to negligence of his employer, the vessel owner, or crew members. 46 U.S.C.A. § 30104.

> Royal Caribbean Cruises, Ltd. v. Whitefield ex rel. Martinez, 664 F.Supp.2d 1270.

S.D.Fla. 2004. Under the general maritime law, a vessel and its owner may be liable for injuries received by seamen in consequence of the unseaworthiness of the ship, or a failure to supply and keep in order the proper appliances appurtenant to the ship.

> Wai v. Rainbow Holdings, 350 F.Supp.2d 1019.

Cargo agent, which was neither the owner nor the bareboat charterer of the vessel, could not be held liable injuries to seaman due to alleged unseaworthiness of the vessel; furthermore, cargo agent was under no duty to provide emergency medical care to seaman.

> Wai v. Rainbow Holdings, 350 F.Supp.2d 1019.

S.D.Fla. 1995. General maritime law, when applied to seamen, must conform to the Jones Act. Jones Act, 46 App.U.S.C.A. § 688.

> Williams v. Carnival Cruise Lines, Inc., 907 F.Supp. 403.

S.D.Fla. 1994. Jones Act creates wrongful death action grounded in negligence for personal representative of seaman who died in course of employment; it does not create cause of action for deaths of nonseamen or for suits brought under theories other than negligence. Jones Act, 46 App.U.S.C.A. § 688.

> Complaint of American Dredging Co., 873 F.Supp. 1539, affirmed American Dredging Co. v. Lambert, 81 F.3d 127.

S.D.Fla. 1972. Warranty of seaworthiness does not extend to invitees, licensees, or other persons on board vessel who are not doing seaman's work and incurring seaman's hazards.

Rainville v. F/V "Gem", 351 F.Supp. 369.

S.D.Fla. 1965. Jones Act does not cover probable or expectant seamen but seamen in being, and fact that he expected in the future to be seaman does not bring one within meaning of Act. Jones Act, 46 U.S.C.A. § 688.

Bodden v. Coordinated Caribbean Transport, Inc., 249 F.Supp. 561, reversed 369 F.2d 273, 5 A.L.R. Fed. 668.

S.D.Fla. 1963. Yacht aboard which seaman was injured when handle of pedestal winch spun suddenly was unseaworthy.

Petition of Read, 224 F.Supp. 241.

Fla. 1968. "Unseaworthiness" as basis for liability under maritime law has to do with the absolute nondelegable duty of shipowner to provide members of the vessel's crew, including longshoremen when engaged in loading, unloading, or stowing the cargo, with a vessel sufficient in all respects for the trade in which it is employed and to prevent their injury by any part of vessel or equipment used in ordinary course of their employment.

Moragne v. State Marine Lines, Inc., 211 So.2d 161, answer to certified question conformed to 409 F.2d 32, certiorari granted 90 S.Ct. 212, 396 U.S. 900, 24 L.Ed.2d 176, reversed 90 S.Ct. 1772, 398 U.S. 375, 26 L.Ed.2d 339, on remand 446 F.2d 906.

Death of longshoreman within territorial waters of State of Florida was not covered by either the Death on the High Seas Act or the Jones Act. Death on the High Seas Act, § 1, 46 U.S.C.A. § 761; Jones Act, 46 U.S.C.A. § 688; Longshoremen's and Harbor Workers' Compensation Act, § 1 et seq., 33 U.S.C.A. § 901 et seq.

Moragne v. State Marine Lines, Inc., 211 So.2d 161, answer to certified question conformed to 409 F.2d 32, certiorari granted 90 S.Ct. 212, 396

U.S. 900, 24 L.Ed.2d 176, reversed 90 S.Ct. 1772, 398 U.S. 375, 26 L.Ed.2d 339, on remand 446 F.2d 906.

Fla.App. 1 Dist. 1959. The Jones Act, like workmen's compensation laws, should be liberally construed in aid of its beneficent purpose to give protection to seamen and to those dependent upon their earnings. Jones Act, 46 U.S.C.A. § 688.

Gaymon v. Quinn Menhaden Fisheries of Tex., Inc., 108 So.2d 641.

Fla.App. 2 Dist. 1974. Equality of the sexes is the rule in actions governed by maritime law.

Davidson v. Schlussel Reederei Kg, 295 So.2d 700.

Fla.App. 2 Dist. 1966. The doctrine of seaworthiness is based upon the admiralty doctrine of breach of warranty, not on negligence.

Farrington v. McConnell, 183 So.2d 585.

"Doctrine of seaworthiness" requires vessel and its owners to indemnify seaman for injuries caused by unseaworthiness of vessel or its appurtenant appliances and equipment.

Farrington v. McConnell, 183 So.2d 585.

Shipowner must, under doctrine of seaworthiness, provide vessel that is reasonably adequate in materials, construction, equipment, stores, officers, men, and outfit for the trade or service in which the vessel is employed.

Farrington v. McConnell, 183 So.2d 585.

The Jones Act must be read in conjunction with Federal Employers' Liability Act provision making common rail carriers liable for injury or death resulting in whole or part from negligence of their officers, agents, or employees or by reason of defect or insufficiency due to negligence in carrier's appliances, machinery, or other equipment. Jones Act, 46 U.S.C.A. § 688; Federal Employers' Liability Act, § 1, 45 U.S.C.A. § 51.

Farrington v. McConnell, 183 So.2d 585.

Fla.App. 3 Dist. 2011. If the unseaworthy condition is the proximate cause of a seaman's injury, the shipowner will incur liability to the seaman in an action for unseaworthiness under the general maritime law.

> Flueras v. Royal Caribbean Cruises, Ltd., 69 So.3d 1101.

The shipowner's duty to furnish a seaworthy vessel is completely independent of his duty to exercise reasonable care under the Jones Act. 46 U.S.C.A. § 30104 et seq.

> Flueras v. Royal Caribbean Cruises, Ltd., 69 So.3d 1101.

The fact that the ship's physician errs in his treatment does not prove that he was incompetent so as to render the ship unseaworthy, but the error tends to make an inference of incompetence more probable.

> Flueras v. Royal Caribbean Cruises, Ltd., 69 So.3d 1101.

Cruise ship owner did not have an affirmative duty to promulgate policies and procedures to govern medical care and emergency evacuations on board its vessel for ship personnel, and the failure to promulgate such procedures did not render the vessel unseaworthy.

> Flueras v. Royal Caribbean Cruises, Ltd., 69 So.3d 1101.

The shipowner's duty to furnish a seaworthy vessel extends to the procedures crew members are instructed to use for assigned tasks.

> Flueras v. Royal Caribbean Cruises, Ltd., 69 So.3d 1101.

Where the shipowner has established a policy or procedure to govern one or more functions of the vessel's crew, failure to comply with the policy may result in liability, particularly if the crew instead engaged in an improper or unsafe method of work.

> Flueras v. Royal Caribbean Cruises, Ltd., 69 So.3d 1101.

While an isolated, personal act of negligence is neither necessary nor sufficient to establish the unseaworthiness of the vessel, a series of negligent acts may combine to give rise to an unseaworthy condition.

> Flueras v. Royal Caribbean Cruises, Ltd., 69 So.3d 1101.

Where the facts indicate that negligence was pervasive or repetitive, such that it would constitute an unsafe or improper work method, courts are more likely to find an unseaworthy condition instead of an isolated act of negligence.

> Flueras v. Royal Caribbean Cruises, Ltd., 69 So.3d 1101.

Fla.App. 3 Dist. 1996. Seaman, who was injured while working as cabin steward aboard cruise ship, could maintain unseaworthiness claim based on his allegation that vessel owner breached its duty to provide seaworthy vessel when it failed to properly train its cabin stewards how to carry heavy objects on stairs, even without any evidence that ship itself was defective.

> Waggon-Dixon v. Royal Caribbean Cruises, Ltd., 679 So.2d 811, rehearing denied.

Fla.App. 3 Dist. 1995. Absence of evidence that helmsman on cruise ship had said or done anything which indicated likelihood or even possibility that he would harm himself in any way was fatal to claim made by helmsman's widow that shipowner was under a duty to take some precautions to prevent helmsman from committing suicide by jumping overboard; helmsman was a formerly happy person with no history of mental difficulty and had become depressed presumably because of death of close relative and his inability to be with his family on shore.

> Rafferman v. Carnival Cruise Lines, Inc., 659 So.2d 1271.

In order for shipowner to have obligation to protect crewman from himself, there must be evidence of serious medical problem so as to put shipowner's personnel on notice that crewman requires protective precautions to ensure his safety or that he has taken actions which indicate that he may do harm to others or to himself.

> Rafferman v. Carnival Cruise Lines, Inc., 659 So.2d 1271.

Fla.App. 3 Dist. 1992. Cruise ship hairdresser's employer was, as matter of law, not guilty of any negligence in accident which occurred when hairdresser slipped and fell on slippery deck while en route to ship hospital for examination, and therefore employer could not be held liable under Jones Act, where deck was controlled and maintained entirely by cruise ship, and employer had no duty to maintain deck. Jones Act, 46 App.U.S.C.A. § 688.

> Thornton v. Steiner Products, Ltd., 608 So.2d 508.

Fla.App. 3 Dist. 1983. Under general maritime law, seaman has no common-law right of recovery for negligence of vessel owners or crew members.

> Rigdon v. Belcher Towing Co., 435 So.2d 939.

Fla.App. 3 Dist. 1979. Unlike maintenance and cure, which is general maritime law's equivalent of workmen's compensation, recovery under the Jones Act requires a showing of employer negligence, while recovery for unseaworthiness requires demonstration of breach of warranty of vessel's seaworthiness; both require legally adequate causal link between negligence or unseaworthy condition and accident and injuries. Jones Act, 46 U.S.C.A. § 688.

> Brown v. Stanwick Intern., Inc., 367 So.2d 241.

Where only relationship between alleged uninhabitability of living facilities on vessel and motorcycle accident was suggestion that if proper living quarters had been available on board, employee would not have had to go to crew's living quarters to fix boiler, employee was precluded from recovery for Jones Act negligence and unseaworthiness by his failure to show legal relationship between employer's alleged wrongdoing in failing to properly maintain ship's living facilities and his injuries sustained while riding motorcycle. Jones Act, 46 U.S.C.A. § 688.

> Brown v. Stanwick Intern., Inc., 367 So.2d 241.

Fla.App. 3 Dist. 1958. Until the Jones Act, a seaman was never accorded right to a recovery against shipowner for negligent acts, and it is only by reason of the Jones Act that seaman is entitled to recovery today. Jones Act, 46 U.S.C.A. § 688.

> Corella v. McCormick Shipping Corp., 101 So.2d 903.

Fla.App. 4 Dist. 2002. A captain or shipowner is required by law to insure the

well being of a crew member whether or not the crew member requests such aid.

> Van Mill v. Bay Data, Inc., 819 So.2d 963.

⊙⇒**29(2). Tools, machinery, appliances, and places for work.**

C.A.5 (Fla.) 1981. Providing good equipment in addition to poor equipment does not excuse an owner's failure to provide safe equipment to a seaman. Jones Act, 46 U.S.C.A. § 688.

> Bobb v. Modern Products, Inc., 648 F.2d 1051.

C.A.5 (Fla.) 1972. Unseaworthiness does not extend to negligent use of seaworthy appliances.

> Weeks v. Alonzo Cothron, Inc., 466 F.2d 578, appeal after remand 493 F.2d 538.

C.A.5 (Fla.) 1970. Vessel is not unseaworthy because it fails to carry equipment not shown to exist or if thought to exist, was not shown by some competent proof to be safer or superior to method being used.

> Little v. Green, 428 F.2d 1061, certiorari denied 91 S.Ct. 366, 400 U.S. 964, 27 L.Ed.2d 384.

C.A.5 (Fla.) 1967. Fact that wooden doors to shrimp net fell and struck seaman indicated existence of a defective condition rendering the vessel unseaworthy so that seaman was entitled to recover in libel for unseaworthiness whether doors fell because a cable broke or because they were improperly tied down.

> Gibbs v. Kiesel, 382 F.2d 917.

C.A.5 (Fla.) 1953. In action under Jones Act by employee of defendant barge owners for injury which resulted when employee attempted to descend ladder which led from dock to vessel, and which had been furnished by employees of molasses company, and slackness in wire by which ladder was fastened to dock by employees of molasses company allowed ladder to slip, resulting in disconnection of sections of ladder causing employee to fall and strike arm on barge which employee had been instructed to assist in loading with molasses, barge owners were guilty of negligence under evidence in not providing employee with a safe ladder. Jones Act, 46 U.S.C.A. § 688.

> Sanford v. Caswell, 200 F.2d 830, certiorari denied 73 S.Ct. 831, 345 U.S. 940, 97 L.Ed. 1366.

Where employee was injured when he attempted to descend ladder which led from dock to vessel and which had been furnished by employees of molasses company, and slackness in wire by which ladder was fastened to dock by employees of molasses company allowed ladder to slip, resulting in disconnection of sections of ladder causing employee to fall and strike arm on barge which employee had been instructed to assist in loading with molasses, and barge owners were negligent in failing to provide employee with a safe ladder, barge owners were liable to employee for injuries under Jones Act even if molasses company was a volunteer in furnishing ladder rather than barge owners' agent. Jones Act, 46 U.S.C.A. § 688.

> Sanford v. Caswell, 200 F.2d 830, certiorari denied 73 S.Ct. 831, 345 U.S. 940, 97 L.Ed. 1366.

M.D.Fla. 1976. Deaths and personal injuries suffered by fish meal plant workers and seamen aboard fishing vessel docked at fish meal reduction plant, which were caused by inhalation of lethal quantities of hydrogen sulphide gas which had formed in recirculation equipment used at plant, resulted from unseaworthy condition of hold of vessel caused by activation of unseaworthy equipment, and vessel owner, by virtue of absolute and nondelegable duty to furnish seaworthy vessel, was liable for unseaworthy condition which caused deaths and injuries.

> Consolidated Mach., Inc. v. Protein Products Corp., 428 F.Supp. 209.

S.D.Fla. 2004. Under the general maritime law, a vessel and its owner may be liable for injuries received by seamen in consequence of the unseaworthiness of the ship, or a failure to supply and keep in order the proper appliances appurtenant to the ship.

> Wai v. Rainbow Holdings, 350 F.Supp.2d 1019.

S.D.Fla. 1982. A seaman claiming that a vessel was unseaworthy must prove that an unseaworthiness condition proximately caused his injuries.

> Murray v. Hunt, 552 F.Supp. 234.

Bkrtcy.S.D.Fla. 1997. For Chapter 7 debtor-seaman to recover against employer cruise line under Jones Act or on theory of unseaworthiness for injuries sustained while working aboard cruise ship, seaman was required to prove negligence or other tortious conduct on part of employer, and thus any recovery under those theories would not be exempt property of debtor's bankruptcy estate. Bankr.Code, 11 U.S.C.A. § 522(d)(10); Jones Act, 46 App. U.S.C.A. § 688.

> In re Coltellaro, 204 B.R. 640.

Fla.App. 2 Dist. 1966. "Doctrine of seaworthiness" requires vessel and its owners to indemnify seaman for injuries caused by unseaworthiness of vessel or its appurtenant appliances and equipment.

> Farrington v. McConnell, 183 So.2d 585.

Ladder which had been borrowed from boat yard by yacht owner and had been used by yacht crewman to ascend to deck of yacht, undergoing repairs out of water, when sides of the ladder suddenly broke causing crewman to fall and sustain injury had not been adopted as part of vessel's gear, and crewman could not recover from yacht owner under doctrine of seaworthiness.

> Farrington v. McConnell, 183 So.2d 585.

Yacht owner who had borrowed from boat yard at which yacht was undergoing repairs out of water a ladder not shown to have patent defect of which owner knew or in exercise of reasonable care should have known was not liable under Jones Act to yacht crewman who was ascending the ladder to board the vessel when sides of the ladder suddenly broke. Jones Act, 46 U.S.C.A. § 688; Federal Employers' Liability Act, § 1, 45 U.S.C.A. § 51.

> Farrington v. McConnell, 183 So.2d 585.

Yacht owner was not liable at common law on theory of failure to supply safe place to work to yacht crewman who was attempting to board yacht, undergoing repairs out of water at boat yard, by ascending ladder which had been borrowed by yacht owner from boat yard and sides of which broke, causing crewman to fall.

> Farrington v. McConnell, 183 So.2d 585.

Fla.App. 3 Dist. 1996. Duty to provide seaworthy vessel obliges owner of vessel to provide its seamen with proper equipment to carry out their respective jobs.

> Waggon-Dixon v. Royal Caribbean Cruises, Ltd., 679 So.2d 811, rehearing denied.

Unsafe working environment aboard vessel may lead to finding of unseaworthiness.

> Waggon-Dixon v. Royal Caribbean Cruises, Ltd., 679 So.2d 811, rehearing denied.

Fla.App. 3 Dist. 1992. Employer's duty to maintain safe workplace for hairdresser aboard cruise ship did not extend to ship's deck, and thus cruise line's negligence in maintaining deck could not be imputed to employer in Jones Act action brought by hairdresser who slipped and fell on slippery deck. Jones Act, 46 App. U.S.C.A. § 688.

> Thornton v. Steiner Products, Ltd., 608 So.2d 508.

Fla.App. 3 Dist. 1988. Cause of action for negligence arises under the Jones Act if a ship owner fails to provide a reasonably safe place to work for its crew. Jones Act, 46 U.S.C.App. § 688.

> Dos Santos v. Ajax Nav. Corp., 531 So.2d 231, certiorari dismissed 109 S.Ct. 1304, 489 U.S. 1048, 103 L.Ed.2d 574.

Transitory nature of the alleged unseaworthy condition, butter on floor of ship's kitchen, and concepts of negligence were irrelevant to unseaworthiness determination.

> Dos Santos v. Ajax Nav. Corp., 531 So.2d 231, certiorari dismissed 109 S.Ct. 1304, 489 U.S. 1048, 103 L.Ed.2d 574.

Fla.App. 3 Dist. 1970. Existence of an open hatch under particular circumstances can result in a vessel being unseaworthy or the shipowner being negligent.

> Bowen v. Seaward Dredging Corp., 242 So.2d 151.

Breakage of ship's equipment under normal use may give rise to logical inference that equipment was defective, rendering the vessel unseaworthy.

> Bowen v. Seaward Dredging Corp., 242 So.2d 151.

⊶29(3). Fellow servants.

C.A.5 (Fla.) 1963. Seaworthiness warranty requires crew members equal in disposition and seamanship to ordinary men in calling.

> McConville v. Florida Towing Corp., 321 F.2d 162.

S.D.Fla. 2009. A Jones Act claim is an in personam action for a seaman who suffers injury in the course of employment due to negligence of his employer, the vessel owner, or crew members. 46 U.S.C.A. § 30104.

> Royal Caribbean Cruises, Ltd. v. Whitefield ex rel. Martinez, 664 F.Supp.2d 1270.

Fla.App. 3 Dist. 2011. The shipowner's warranty of seaworthiness extends to the vessel's crew; the shipowner breaches the duty of seaworthiness by manning the vessel with an unfit, incompetent, inadequate, defective, or improperly trained or supervised crew.

> Flueras v. Royal Caribbean Cruises, Ltd., 69 So.3d 1101.

The ship's crew need not be competent to meet all contingencies, and the crew's incompetence or unfitness must rise to the level of a hazard of the vessel to produce the requisite unseaworthy condition.

> Flueras v. Royal Caribbean Cruises, Ltd., 69 So.3d 1101.

A condition of a crew member rendering him not fit for his ordinary duties or not up to the ordinary standards of his profession is an unseaworthy condition sufficient to warrant the imposition of liability on the shipowner.

> Flueras v. Royal Caribbean Cruises, Ltd., 69 So.3d 1101.

An isolated, negligent act performed by an otherwise competent crew member is not a condition of the vessel and does not render the ship unseaworthy.

> Flueras v. Royal Caribbean Cruises, Ltd., 69 So.3d 1101.

If incompetence results in a navigational error which causes the collision, it is crew incompetence, and therefore the unseaworthiness of the vessel, which has caused the damage.

Flueras v. Royal Caribbean Cruises, Ltd., 69 So.3d 1101.

Cruise ship was not unseaworthy based on allegation that ship's doctor was negligent in diagnosing and treating patient's ectopic pregnancy in the absence of any allegation that doctor was not fit for his ordinary duties or not up to the ordinary standards of his profession.

Flueras v. Royal Caribbean Cruises, Ltd., 69 So.3d 1101.

When a doctor is employed for the purpose of treating the ship's seamen, the Jones Act makes the shipowner liable to seamen for the doctor's negligent treatment. 46 U.S.C.A. § 30104 et seq.

Flueras v. Royal Caribbean Cruises, Ltd., 69 So.3d 1101.

Fla.App. 3 Dist. 1999. Whether blue water seamen were acting within scope of employment for purposes of rental car company's third-party suit against employer arising out of seamen's accident in rental car was not determined by fact that employer paid seamen maintenance and cure benefits under the Jones Act; there was no special relationship between employer and rental car company that would allow car company to be able to stand in seamen's shoes so as to reap benefits of special relationship between seamen and employer. Jones Act, 46 App.U.S.C.A. § 688.

Carnival Corp. v. Hertz Corp., 748 So.2d 323.

Fellow servant doctrine was not a viable defense for seamen's employer in rental car company's third-party action against employer arising out of accident involving rental car in which seamen were injured, as policy of having employees be more careful for their own safety in absence of remedy when injured by co-worker would not be furthered by allowing employer to raise defense against rental car company.

Carnival Corp. v. Hertz Corp., 748 So.2d 323.

Fla.App. 3 Dist. 1996. Unprovoked, sudden, and unusually savage assault by one seaman against another constitutes breach of vessel owner's duty to provide seaworthy vessel.

Waggon-Dixon v. Royal Caribbean Cruises, Ltd., 679 So.2d 811, rehearing denied.

Failure to properly train or supervise crew of vessel may lead to finding of unseaworthiness.

Waggon-Dixon v. Royal Caribbean Cruises, Ltd., 679 So.2d 811, rehearing denied.

Fla.App. 3 Dist. 1983. Under general maritime law, seaman has no common-law right of recovery for negligence of vessel owners or crew members.

Rigdon v. Belcher Towing Co., 435 So.2d 939.

⚷29(4). Assumption of risk, contributory negligence, and division of damages.

C.A.11 (Fla.) 1987. Assumption of risk and contributory negligence are not defenses to claim of "unseaworthiness," but may only be proven in mitigation of damages.

Villers Seafood Co., Inc. v. Vest, 813 F.2d 339.

Officer's failure to discover and correct defects in ship's ladder did not prevent him from recovering from owner for injuries he sustained as result of ladder's "unseaworthiness," even though it was duty of officer to keep vessel in repair; declining to extend *Walker v. Lykes Bros. S.S.Co.*, 193 F.2d 772 (2d Cir.); *Dixon v. United States*, 219 F.2d 10 (2d Cir.); *Reinhart v. United States*, 457 F.2d 151 (9th Cir.); and *Peymann v. Perini Corp.*, 507 F.2d 1318 (1st Cir.).

Villers Seafood Co., Inc. v. Vest, 813 F.2d 339.

C.A.11 (Fla.) 1983. Musician employed aboard vessel was neither negligent in failing to self-diagnose his heart attack, nor in failing to stop work even though ship's doctor did not disclose musician's illness or instruct him not to work. Jones Act, 46 U.S.C.A. § 688.

Szumlicz v. Norwegian America Line, Inc., 698 F.2d 1192.

C.A.5 (Fla.) 1981. Contributory negligence will not defeat a seaman's claim

---

† This Case was not selected for publication in the National Reporter System
For legislative history of cited statutes, see Florida Statutes Annotated

under Jones Act, but may be considered as comparative negligence to mitigate damages in proportion to degree of plaintiff's negligence; however, for contributory negligence to exist the seaman must have had a duty to act or refrain from acting. Jones Act, 46 U.S.C.A. § 688.

> Bobb v. Modern Products, Inc., 648 F.2d 1051.

Whereas the employer's duty to provide a safe place for a seaman to work is a broad one, the seaman's duty to protect himself is slight. Jones Act, 46 U.S.C.A. § 688.

> Bobb v. Modern Products, Inc., 648 F.2d 1051.

A seaman has some duty to use reasonable care, even though that duty is slight and, for example, the seaman must in some circumstances exercise reasonable care to prudently choose the proper equipment for the work to be done, if that equipment is available. Jones Act, 46 U.S.C.A. § 688.

> Bobb v. Modern Products, Inc., 648 F.2d 1051.

If plaintiff seaman, who was injured while attempting to attach a second whip line to shrimp bags when the first line, obviously frayed and worn, did not appear strong enough to withstand strain of load was subject to orders of a coequal fellow seaman, who was manning the winch and who suggested that second line be attached, the plaintiff, injured when the first line snapped, could not have been contributorily negligent. Jones Act, 46 U.S.C.A. § 688.

> Bobb v. Modern Products, Inc., 648 F.2d 1051.

Suggestion by a fellow seaman, not amounting to an order, does not relieve the seaman from exercising his slight duty of care. Jones Act, 46 U.S.C.A. § 688.

> Bobb v. Modern Products, Inc., 648 F.2d 1051.

Assumption of risk is not a defense under the Jones Act. Jones Act, 46 U.S.C.A. § 688.

> Bobb v. Modern Products, Inc., 648 F.2d 1051.

C.A.5 (Fla.) 1981. Under 1972 amendments to Longshoremen's and Harbor Workers' Compensation Act, seamen and longshoremen are to be treated alike for purposes of impermissibility of assumption of risk defense. Longshoremen's and Harbor Workers' Compensation Act, § 1 et seq. as amended 33 U.S.C.A. § 901 et seq.

> Byrd v. Reederei, 638 F.2d 1300, rehearing granted 650 F.2d 1324, on rehearing 688 F.2d 324, on rehearing Culver v. Slater Boat Co., 722 F.2d 114, certiorari denied 104 S.Ct. 3537, 467 U.S. 1252, 82 L.Ed.2d 842, certiorari denied St. Paul Fire & Marine Ins. Co. v. Culver, 105 S.Ct. 90, 469 U.S. 819, 83 L.Ed.2d 37.

C.A.5 (Fla.) 1973. Neither contributory negligence nor assumption of risk is an absolute maritime defense and these defenses are applicable only in conjunction with maritime rule of comparative fault.

> Price v. Mosler, 483 F.2d 275.

Where person was hired to captain a yacht and in performing duties undertook some routine maintenance functions during which he was injured, rule that person who is injured while repairing the very defect which he was employed to repair may not recover damages was inapplicable.

> Price v. Mosler, 483 F.2d 275.

C.A.5 (Fla.) 1972. A seaman does not assume risk of unseaworthy vessel.

> In re Double D Dredging Co., 467 F.2d 468.

C.A.5 (Fla.) 1972. Where barge owners' employee's refusal of life line before patching underside of barge was not in disregard of long observed, safe practice of using life lines, but conformed with practice of not using a life line, owners could not avoid liability for death of employee by drowning on finding of unseaworthiness on theory that employee's failure to use proffered life line was sole proximate cause of his death.

> Weeks v. Alonzo Cothron, Inc., 466 F.2d 578, appeal after remand 493 F.2d 538.

C.A.5 (Fla.) 1968. For purposes of maritime relationships under Admiralty Jurisdiction Extension Act, bridge workers injured when outboard rigger of shrimp boat struck leaf of bridge on which they were working were treated as crew of bridge which, in turn, was treated as vessel, and thus workers could not be treated as vessels for divided damages purposes. Admiralty Jurisdiction Extension Act, 46 U.S.C.A. § 740.

> Empire Seafoods, Inc. v. Anderson, 398 F.2d 204, certiorari denied 89 S.Ct. 449, 393 U.S. 983, 21 L.Ed.2d 444.

Where each of personally injured claimants is guilty of negligence contributing to his own injury to degree of 20%, his damages are reduced by that amount and divided damages rule in mutual fault collisions is then applied.

> Empire Seafoods, Inc. v. Anderson, 398 F.2d 204, certiorari denied 89 S.Ct. 449, 393 U.S. 983, 21 L.Ed.2d 444.

C.A.5 (Fla.) 1967. Shipowner's contention that seaman who was struck by doors to shrimp net was contributorily negligent in that he participated to some degree in lashing down the doors and in consciously electing to expose himself to the risk that the doors might fall could be considered in mitigation of damages on unseaworthiness claim, although not as an absolute bar to recovery nor as assumption of risk.

> Gibbs v. Kiesel, 382 F.2d 917.

C.A.5 (Fla.) 1966. Where negligence of one seaman contributed 50% to his death and other seaman's negligence contributed 25% to his injury, trial court properly reduced damages rather than denying recovery in actions for death and injury caused by unseaworthiness of vessel. Death on the High Seas Act, §§ 1–8, 46 U.S.C.A. §§ 761–768; Jones Act, 46 U.S.C.A. § 688.

> Symonette Shipyards, Limited v. Clark, 365 F.2d 464, certiorari denied 87 S.Ct. 1690, 387 U.S. 908, 18 L.Ed.2d 625.

C.A.5 (Fla.) 1961. Seaman's contributory negligence, if any, would merely reduce the damage award.

> June T., Inc. v. King, 290 F.2d 404.

C.A.5 (Fla.) 1957. A seaman does not assume risk of illness or injuries created or brought about by vessel's unseaworthiness

or her owner's negligence, even if known to him.

> Couts v. Erickson, 241 F.2d 499.

C.A.5 (Fla.) 1953. A seaman in performance of his duties is not deemed to assume risk of unseaworthy appliances. Jones Act, 46 U.S.C.A. § 688.

> Sanford v. Caswell, 200 F.2d 830, certiorari denied 73 S.Ct. 831, 345 U.S. 940, 97 L.Ed. 1366.

An employee of barge owners who was injured when he attempted to descend ladder which led from dock to vessel, and which had been furnished by employees of molasses company, and slackness in wire by which ladder was fastened to dock by employees of molasses company allowed ladder to slip, resulting in disconnection of sections of ladder causing employee to fall and strike arm on barge which employee had been instructed to assist in loading with molasses, would not be deemed to have assumed risk of inherent defects of ladder. Jones Act, 46 U.S.C.A. § 688.

> Sanford v. Caswell, 200 F.2d 830, certiorari denied 73 S.Ct. 831, 345 U.S. 940, 97 L.Ed. 1366.

N.D.Fla. 1974. Where evidence disclosed that worker who was engaged in emptying barge had never before worked on barge equipped with roller hatch covers and had received no instructions as to how they could be opened or how workmen should conduct themselves for safety's sake in course of opening such hatch covers, worker's action in standing on nearby hatch cover, from which he fell when hatch cover being opened began moving and struck another intervening hatch cover, did not constitute contributory negligence.

> Henderson v. S. C. Loveland Co., Inc., 381 F.Supp. 1102, opinion supplemented 390 F.Supp. 347, amended 396 F.Supp. 658.

Fla.App. 3 Dist. 1992. Seaman was not comparatively negligent with respect to injury which occurred when, while waiting with a number of other workers for a locked fire door to be opened following a drill, the crew members in front of him suddenly stepped backwards, knocking him off balance; because the fire door was to slide into a wall rather than swinging towards the crowd when opened, a reasonably prudent person would not have anticipated that the crowd might surge backward to him.

> Cuadros v. Carnival Cruise Lines, Inc., 604 So.2d 861.

Fla.App. 4 Dist. 2002. Employer was not relieved of its responsibility to provide adequate medical care to injured stewardess, even though stewardess declined the captain's offers for assistance; law placed a greater obligation on captain to provide for a crew member's welfare than it did on the crew members themselves.

> Van Mill v. Bay Data, Inc., 819 So.2d 963.

Fla.App. 4 Dist. 2000. Captain of vessel made decision to purchase 24-can cartons of soda, rather than 12-can packs, to store them in hatch of vessel, and to load them two at a time, and thus, defendants who provided fishing vessel were not liable to captain for back injury sustained in unloading soda on basis of negligence or unseaworthiness claims under Jones Act. Jones Act, 46 App.U.S.C.A. § 688.

> Nurkiewicz v. Vacation Break U.S.A., Inc., 771 So.2d 1271.

⚷29(5). Action for damages in general.

U.S.Fla. 1955. Provision of Jones Act that a seaman should have same right of action as would railroad employee does not mean that words of Federal Employers' Liability Act must be lifted bodily from context and applied mechanically to specific facts of maritime events, but that those contingencies against which Congress has provided to insure recovery to railroad employees should also be met in the admiralty setting. Jones Act, 46 U.S.C.A. § 688; Federal Employers' Liability Act, §§ 1 et seq., 7, 45 U.S.C.A. §§ 51 et seq., 57.

> Cox v. Roth, 75 S.Ct. 242, 348 U.S. 207, 99 L.Ed. 260.

S.D.Fla. 1982. Yacht owner's leaving store of hashish in his locked cabin safe, with the unknowing captain incarcerated in Greek jail when the drug was discovered by Greek authorities, created an unseaworthy condition entitling the captain to recover punitive and compensatory damages from the owner.

> Murray v. Hunt, 552 F.Supp. 234.

Fla.App. 3 Dist. 1999. Cruise line was not entitled to striking of captain's testimony nor a continuance to retain expert to rebut captain's testimony, a day before start of trial, that changes had been made to stairs after seaman's accident, which had gone undetected on his previous inspections of stairway; cruise line could not claim surprise or prejudice given that condition of stairs was at issue throughout litigation, and stairwell was within cruise line's exclusive control.

> Dolphin Cruise Line, Inc. v. Stassinopoulos, 731 So.2d 708, rehearing denied.

⚷29(5.1). Nature and form of remedy.

U.S.Fla. 1970. Seaman's right of recovery under Jones Act against his employer for negligence follows from the seaman's employment status and is not limited to the injury or death occurring on the high seas. Jones Act, 46 U.S.C.A. § 688.

> Moragne v. States Marine Lines, Inc., 90 S.Ct. 1772, 398 U.S. 375, 26 L.Ed.2d 339, on remand 446 F.2d 906.

Jones Act is intended to achieve uniformity in the exercise of admiralty jurisdiction by giving seamen a federal right to recover from their employers for negligence regardless of location of the injury or death. Jones Act, 46 U.S.C.A. § 688.

> Moragne v. States Marine Lines, Inc., 90 S.Ct. 1772, 398 U.S. 375, 26 L.Ed.2d 339, on remand 446 F.2d 906.

Fla.App. 3 Dist. 1983. Jones Act provided sole remedy available to seaman for alleged negligence of his employer during course of seaman's employment on one of employer's tugs, but claim was barred by statute of limitations. Jones Act, 46 U.S.C.A. § 688.

> Rigdon v. Belcher Towing Co., 435 So.2d 939.

Fla.App. 3 Dist. 1979. Injuries employee sustained when motorcycle he was riding swerved to avoid colliding with a truck on his way to crew's living quarters to repair boiler were not such as would naturally result from breach of employer's obligation to provide living quarters aboard ship and thus his breach of contract claim was barred under rule of *Hadley v. Baxendale.*

> Brown v. Stanwick Intern., Inc., 367 So.2d 241.

29(5.2). What law governs.

† **C.A.11 (Fla.) 2014.** Maritime law of United States did not apply, and thus district court did not abuse its discretion in its forum non conveniens dismissal of seaman's complaint against shipping company, alleging violations of Jones Act and federal maritime law of unseaworthiness, failure to provide maintenance and cure, and failure to treat him for injuries he suffered; seaman suffered his alleged injury in Bahamas, vessel flew under Honduran flag and was domiciled in Dominican Republic, shipowner was incorporated in Bahamas and had its principal place of business in Nassau, seaman signed operative shipping articles in Bahamas, Bahamas provided accessible forum, and shipowner resisted defending suit in United States.

> Vasquez v. YII Shipping Co., Ltd., 559 Fed.Appx. 841.

C.A.11 (Fla.) 2005. In determining whether the Jones Act or general maritime law of United States applies to cause of action arising out of injuries sustained by seaman, court should consider: (1) place of wrongful act; (2) flag under which ship sails; (3) allegiance or domicile of injured party; (4) allegiance of defendant shipowner; (5) place of contract between injured party and shipowner; (6) inaccessibility of foreign forum; (7) law of forum; and (8) shipowner's base of operations. Jones Act, 46 App.U.S.C.A. § 688.

> Membreno v. Costa Crociere S.p.A., 425 F.3d 932.

Mere fact that Italian company that owned ship on which seaman was injured, through an intermediary Italian holding company, was wholly owned subsidiary of corporation that maintained its principal place of business in the United States was insufficient to establish that shipowner had substantial base of operations in the United States, or to support application of the Jones Act or general maritime law of United States in personal injury action brought by seaman, where United States parent did not exercise day-to-day control over shipowner's operations and observed

all corporate formalities, and where seaman was Honduran national whose injuries occurred in international waters, while he was working on Italian flag ship under employment agreement executed outside the United States. Jones Act, 46 App.U.S.C.A. § 688.

> Membreno v. Costa Crociere S.p.A., 425 F.3d 932.

Fact that shipowner has substantial base of operations in the United States may alone justify application of United States law to cause of action arising out of injuries sustained by seaman.

> Membreno v. Costa Crociere S.p.A., 425 F.3d 932.

C.A.11 (Fla.) 1983. Where foreign employee sought personal injury damages from foreign shipowner under Jones Act, application of Act involved question of choice of law, requiring decision, under choice of law principles, whether law of United States should be applied, and, if so, whether case should be dismissed for forum non conveniens. Jones Act, 46 U.S.C.A. § 688.

> Szumlicz v. Norwegian America Line, Inc., 698 F.2d 1192.

Substantial use of United States base of operations for shipping and revenues of vessel and its owner, together with many United States contacts justified choice of Jones Act and of general maritime law though place of wrongful act occurred aboard vessel between Puerto Rico and Florida where plaintiff went ashore and was hospitalized, though law of flag was Norwegian, plaintiff was domiciled in Poland, shipowner was Norwegian, place of contract was Norway and Germany, forum was accessible in Norway and law of forum was Norway. Jones Act, 46 U.S.C.A. § 688.

> Szumlicz v. Norwegian America Line, Inc., 698 F.2d 1192.

C.A.5 (Fla.) 1966. Most significant factor in determination of choice of law applicable in consolidated actions for death and injury of United States seamen aboard vessel of Bahamas registry was the nationality of the injured seamen. Death on the High Seas Act, §§ 1–8, 46 U.S.C.A. §§ 761–768; Jones Act, 46 U.S.C.A. § 688.

> Symonette Shipyards, Limited v. Clark, 365 F.2d 464, certiorari denied 87 S.Ct. 1690, 387 U.S. 908, 18 L.Ed.2d 625.

United States law rather than the law of the Bahamas was applicable in consolidated death and injury actions arising out of accident aboard Bahamian vessel where injured and deceased seamen were United States citizens who were part of crew assembled by American businessman to help transfer equipment to an enterprise in Haiti, the ship's articles were signed in the United States and the contract between the businessman and shipowner to transport the equipment was made in the United States. Death on the High Seas Act, §§ 1–8, 46 U.S.C.A. §§ 761–768; Jones Act, 46 U.S.C.A. § 688.

> Symonette Shipyards, Limited v. Clark, 365 F.2d 464, certiorari denied 87 S.Ct. 1690, 387 U.S. 908, 18 L.Ed.2d 625.

Where evidence of law in the Bahamas was vague and indefinite in consolidated actions for death and injury of United States seamen arising out of accident aboard Bahamian vessel and law of United States was established and easily determinable, the law of the forum would be significant in choice of applicable law. Death on the High Seas Act, §§ 1–8, 46 U.S.C.A. §§ 761–768; Jones Act, 46 U.S.C.A. § 688.

> Symonette Shipyards, Limited v. Clark, 365 F.2d 464, certiorari denied 87 S.Ct. 1690, 387 U.S. 908, 18 L.Ed.2d 625.

Bahamian shipowner who sought application of law of the Bahamas in consolidated actions for death and injury to United States seamen had burden to present clear proof of relevant legal principles because no body of reported decisions of Bahamian cases existed and only source of Bahamian case law was found in knowledge and memory of Bahamian practitioners. Death on the High Seas Act, §§ 1–8, 46 U.S.C.A. §§ 761–768; Jones Act, 46 U.S.C.A. § 688.

> Symonette Shipyards, Limited v. Clark, 365 F.2d 464, certiorari denied 87 S.Ct. 1690, 387 U.S. 908, 18 L.Ed.2d 625.

M.D.Fla. 1976. General maritime law governed actions brought for wrongful deaths of seamen and fish meal plant workers who died in hold of fishing vessel as result of inhalation of lethal quantities of hydrogen sulphide gas injected into hold by recirculation equipment utilized by fish meal reduction plant at which vessel was docked.

> Consolidated Mach., Inc. v. Protein Products Corp., 428 F.Supp. 209.

S.D.Fla. 2016. In determining whether Jones Act and United States general maritime law should be applied, court should consider: (1) place of wrongful act; (2) flag of ship; (3) injured party's allegiance or domicile; (4) defendant shipowner's allegiance; (5) place of contract between injured party and shipowner; (6) accessibility of foreign forum; (7) law of forum; and (8) shipowner's base of operations. 46 U.S.C.A. § 30104.

> Navarette v. Silversea Cruises Ltd., 169 F.Supp.3d 1314.

S.D.Fla. 2004. In determining whether Jones Act or general maritime law of United States applies to particular set of facts, court should consider: (1) place of wrongful act, (2) law of flag, (3) allegiance or domicile of injured, (4) allegiance of defendant shipowner, (5) place of contract, (6) inaccessibility of foreign forum, (7) law of forum, and (8) actual operational contacts that ship and owner have with United States. Jones Act, 46 App.U.S.C.A. § 688.

> Membreno v. Costa Crociere, S.p.A., 347 F.Supp.2d 1289, affirmed 425 F.3d 932.

S.D.Fla. 2004. United States had insufficient contacts with case to make application of American law reasonable in wrongful death action brought under the Jones Act; accident occurred in Nicaragua, vessel was registered in Antigua, victim was a domiciliary of Nicaragua and his representative and children were citizens there, vessel's owner did not owe its allegiance to the U.S., place of contract was Nicaragua, Nicaragua was an available and adequate forum, fact that jurisdiction had been perfected in American court was entitled to little deference, and vessel's owners did not have a substantial base of operations in the U.S. Jones Act, 46 App. U.S.C.A. § 688.

> Callasso v. Morton & Co., 324 F.Supp.2d 1320.

Relevant factors to be considered in a choice of law determination for a case brought under the Jones Act include (1) the place of the wrongful act, (2) the law of the flag, (3) the allegiance or domicile of the injured, (4) the allegiance of the defendant shipowner, (5) the place of the contract, (6) inaccessibility of the foreign forum, and (7) the law of the forum. Jones Act, 46 App.U.S.C.A. § 688.

> Callasso v. Morton & Co., 324 F.Supp.2d 1320.

In making a choice of law determination in a case brought under the Jones Act, court must view the case as a whole in order to determine which law can be most fairly applied to govern the contractual relationship. Jones Act, 46 App.U.S.C.A. § 688.

> Callasso v. Morton & Co., 324 F.Supp.2d 1320.

S.D.Fla. 2004. Ownership of cruise ship owner's stock was proper consideration in applying base of operations factor for determining whether Jones Act applied to injured employee's claim against cruise ship owner. Jones Act, 46 App.U.S.C.A. § 688.

> Williams v. Cruise Ships Catering and Service International, N.V., 320 F.Supp.2d 1347.

In applying base of operations factor for determining whether Jones Act applied to injured employee's claim against cruise ship owner, note in securities filing regarding accounting policies of owner's principal shareholder was properly considered as tending to show that principal shareholder used ship owner to conduct business in forum. Jones Act, 46 App. U.S.C.A. § 688.

> Williams v. Cruise Ships Catering and Service International, N.V., 320 F.Supp.2d 1347.

Facts that chief executive officer (CEO) of principal shareholder of cruise ship owner resided in and conducted business in Florida, and that shareholder's principal place of business was in Florida supported determination, justifying application of Jones Act to claim of injured cruise ship employee, that ship owner's base of operations was in United States. Jones Act, 46 App.U.S.C.A. § 688.

> Williams v. Cruise Ships Catering and Service International, N.V., 320 F.Supp.2d 1347.

S.D.Fla. 2003. Whether United States law is applicable in a seaman's action to recover for injuries sustained aboard vessel depends on eight choice of law factors including: (1) the place of the wrongful act; (2) the law of the ship's flag; (3) the allegiance or domicile of the injured seamen; (4) the allegiance of the shipowner; (5) the place where the shipping articles were signed; (6) the accessibility of the foreign forum; (7) the law of the forum; and (8) the base of operations.

> Bautista v. Cruise Ships Catering and Service Intern., N.V., 350 F.Supp.2d 987, reconsideration denied, affirmed 120 Fed.Appx. 786.

The factors for determining whether United States law is applicable in a seaman's action to recover for injuries sustained aboard vessel are not to be applied "mechanically," but they must be viewed in the totality of the circumstances.

> Bautista v. Cruise Ships Catering and Service Intern., N.V., 350 F.Supp.2d 987, reconsideration denied, affirmed 120 Fed.Appx. 786.

Application of United States law was not appropriate in seaman's action against his employer and vessel owner, alleging claims under the Jones Act to recover for injuries sustained while he was working for caterer aboard vessel, for purposes of defendants' motion to dismiss on forum non conveniens grounds; alleged wrongful act occurred in Italy, law of vessel's flag was Italian law, seaman was a citizen of Colombia, vessel was owned by either an Italian or Netherlands Antilles corporation, and disputed degree of vessel's base of operations in the United States was insufficient basis for a decision to use United States law. Jones Act, 46 App. U.S.C.A. § 688.

> Bautista v. Cruise Ships Catering and Service Intern., N.V., 350 F.Supp.2d 987, reconsideration denied, affirmed 120 Fed.Appx. 786.

For purposes of determining whether United States law is applicable in a seaman's action to recover for injuries sustained aboard vessel, while the fact that a plaintiff chose to file suit in the United States normally weighs in favor of applying United States law, a weaker presumption applies when the case is brought by a foreign plaintiff.

> Bautista v. Cruise Ships Catering and Service Intern., N.V., 350 F.Supp.2d 987, reconsideration denied, affirmed 120 Fed.Appx. 786.

For purposes of determining whether United States law is applicable in a seaman's action to recover for injuries sustained aboard vessel, in examining the base of operations factor, the court must look for a substantial relation that would justify the application of United States law.

> Bautista v. Cruise Ships Catering and Service Intern., N.V., 350 F.Supp.2d 987, reconsideration denied, affirmed 120 Fed.Appx. 786.

Under the base of operations factor for determining whether United States law is applicable in a seaman's action to recover for injuries sustained aboard vessel, the mere fact that the bulk of a company's profits comes from United States pockets is insufficient alone to warrant the application of United States law.

> Bautista v. Cruise Ships Catering and Service Intern., N.V., 350 F.Supp.2d 987, reconsideration denied, affirmed 120 Fed.Appx. 786.

S.D.Fla. 2003. The factors for determining whether the Jones Act is applicable to a claim include the place of the wrongful act, the law of the ship's flag, the allegiance or domicile of the injured seaman, the allegiance of the shipowner, the place where the shipping articles were signed, the accessibility of the foreign forum, the law of the forum, and the shipowner's base of operations. Jones Act, 46 App.U.S.C.A. § 688.

> Williams v. Cruise Ships Catering, 299 F.Supp.2d 1273, reconsideration denied 320 F.Supp.2d 1347.

Jones Act applied to employee's action against cruise ship owner, even though place of alleged injury was on high seas, law of ship's flag was Italian, and employee was domiciled in Costa Rica, where

United States was owner's base of operations, as indicated by facts that it conducted substantial business in United States ports generating revenues for owner, that employee was treated for his medical condition in United States, and that important decisions relating to employee's care and maintenance were made by owner's subsidiary in United States. Jones Act, 46 App.U.S.C.A. § 688.

> Williams v. Cruise Ships Catering, 299 F.Supp.2d 1273, reconsideration denied 320 F.Supp.2d 1347.

In determining whether a defendant's base of operations is in the United States, for purposes of deciding whether the Jones Act applies, it is necessary to look beyond corporate formalities to examine both the ship's and shipowner's operational contacts with the United States. Jones Act, 46 App.U.S.C.A. § 688.

> Williams v. Cruise Ships Catering, 299 F.Supp.2d 1273, reconsideration denied 320 F.Supp.2d 1347.

Percentages and relative comparisons of United States versus non-United States business are not primary factors in deciding the base of operations factor for deciding whether the Jones Act applies; rather, the important question is whether the contacts, irrespective of the defendant's contacts in other countries, amount to a substantial relation to the United States. Jones Act, 46 App.U.S.C.A. § 688.

> Williams v. Cruise Ships Catering, 299 F.Supp.2d 1273, reconsideration denied 320 F.Supp.2d 1347.

S.D.Fla. 2002. United States law did not govern suit by family members of foreign crewmen who perished in international or Honduran waters while aboard foreign-flagged vessel, which was owned by Panamanian corporation controlled by U.S. shareholders, as result of a hurricane; while shipowners maintained close operational ties with the United States, vessel did not operate between the United States and foreign ports. Jones Act, 46 App. U.S.C.A. § 688; Death on the High Seas Act, § 1 et seq., 46 App.U.S.C.A. § 761 et seq.

> In re Complaint of Fantome, S.A., 232 F.Supp.2d 1298, reversed in part, vacated in part Fantome v. Frederick, 58 Fed.Appx. 835.

Fla. 1976. Unlike Longshoremen's and Harbor Workers' Compensation Act, Jones Act has no provision rendering inoperative state laws which create parallel remedies such as workmen's compensation statutes. Longshoremen's and Harbor Workers' Compensation Act, § 5 as amended 33 U.S.C.A. § 905; Jones Act, 46 U.S.C.A. § 688; West's F.S.A. § 440.01 et seq.

City of Plantation v. Roberts, 342 So.2d 69.

Fla.App. 1 Dist. 1960. In action in Florida state court under the Jones Act by administratrix of estate of deceased seaman against employer for wrongful death of seaman, who allegedly fell from fishing boat docked at employer's plant and drowned, question of quantum of proof necessary to constitute a jury question was governed by decisions of United States Supreme Court construing the Jones Act, and not by Florida general rules concerning quantum of proof in wrongful death actions. Jones Act, 46 U.S.C.A. § 688.

Gaymon v. Quinn Menhaden Fisheries of Tex., Inc., 118 So.2d 42, 81 A.L.R.2d 1165.

General rules, which govern quantum of proof in wrongful death actions in Florida, do not apply and have no bearing on cases brought under the Jones Act or the Federal Employers' Liability Act. Jones Act, 46 U.S.C.A. § 688; Federal Employers' Liability Act, § 1 et seq., 45 U.S.C.A. § 51 et seq.

Gaymon v. Quinn Menhaden Fisheries of Tex., Inc., 118 So.2d 42, 81 A.L.R.2d 1165.

Fla.App. 3 Dist. 2004. Because both venue and forum non conveniens are procedural issues, rather than substantive, they can be left to the states to govern in Jones Act actions brought before state courts. Jones Act, 46 App.U.S.C.A. § 688(a).

Tananta v. Cruise Ships Catering and Services Int'l., N.V., 909 So.2d 874, rehearing denied, review denied 917 So.2d 195, review denied Chamo v. Costa Crociere, S.P.A., 917 So.2d 192, review denied Simpson v. Costa Crociere, S.P.A., 917 So.2d 195.

Fla.App. 3 Dist. 2003. Cruise ship's base of operations was in United States,

for purpose of determining whether Jones Act applied to injured crew member's claim against shipowner, cruise-ship company, and company's operating agent, even though cruise ship never entered a United States port; United States was where operations of cruise ship's fleet were based, where advertising, reservations, and sales of cruises took place, and where repairs, inspections, and supervision were coordinated, and record did not suggest that these activities were carried out in any foreign country. Jones Act, 46 App.U.S.C.A. § 688.

Henry v. Windjammer Barefoot Cruises, 851 So.2d 731, rehearing and rehearing denied.

Where the owner of a vessel has substantial contacts with the United States, the fact that the vessel never enters the navigable waters of the United States does not militate against a finding that either the ship or the shipowner has a base of operations in the United States, for purpose of determining whether Jones Act applies to an action arising from seaman's injury or death. Jones Act, 46 App. U.S.C.A. § 688.

Henry v. Windjammer Barefoot Cruises, 851 So.2d 731, rehearing and rehearing denied.

Jones Act applied to injured crew member's claim against cruise-ship owner, cruise-ship company, and company's operating agent, even though ship never entered a United States port, and crew member was a Guyana national, where shipowner's allegiance was to United States, and cruise ship's base of operations was in United States. Jones Act, 46 App.U.S.C.A. § 688.

Henry v. Windjammer Barefoot Cruises, 851 So.2d 731, rehearing and rehearing denied.

In determining whether Jones Act applies to an action arising from seaman's injury or death, court's task is not to weigh or balance present against absent contacts between shipowner and United States, but merely to determine whether the contacts which are present are substantial. Jones Act, 46 App.U.S.C.A. § 688.

Henry v. Windjammer Barefoot Cruises, 851 So.2d 731, rehearing and rehearing denied.

† This Case was not selected for publication in the National Reporter System
For legislative history of cited statutes, see Florida Statutes Annotated

Court's responsibility in conducting a *Lauritzen-Rhoditis* choice-of-law analysis in action brought by injured seaman is to examine the substance of the connections between shipowner and United States for the purpose of determining the reasonableness of applying Jones Act under the circumstances. Jones Act, 46 App.U.S.C.A. § 688.

> Henry v. Windjammer Barefoot Cruises, 851 So.2d 731, rehearing and rehearing denied.

Fla.App. 3 Dist. 1992. Jones Act claim brought in state court is governed by federal substantive law. Jones Act, 46 App.U.S.C.A. § 688.

> Royal Caribbean Corp. v. Modesto, 614 So.2d 517, review denied 626 So.2d 207.

Jones Act does not preempt procedural scheme designed by Florida legislature to mediate claims as an alternative to judicial action. Jones Act, 46 App. U.S.C.A. § 688; West's F.S.A. § 768.79; F.S.1987, § 44.302.

> Royal Caribbean Corp. v. Modesto, 614 So.2d 517, review denied 626 So.2d 207.

Fla.App. 4 Dist. 1972. State courts can exercise jurisdiction over actions arising under the Jones Act and general maritime law, but federal principles of law control such actions and must be applied by both trial and appellate courts. Jones Act, 46 U.S.C.A. § 688; F.S.A. § 440.01 et seq.

> Potashnick-Badgett Dredging Inc. v. Whitfield, 269 So.2d 36, certiorari denied Potashnick-Badgett Dredging, Incorporated v. Trans-State Dredging Company, 272 So.2d 819, certiorari denied 272 So.2d 820.

The "doctrine of local concern" did not bar application of federal maritime law, rather than merely state Workmen's Compensation Law, in action seeking recovery for injuries sustained by mate aboard barge dredging channel in Gulf of Mexico to be used in interstate commerce to barge coal and other materials to land based power plant. Jones Act, 46 U.S.C.A. § 688; F.S.A. § 440.01 et seq.

> Potashnick-Badgett Dredging Inc. v. Whitfield, 269 So.2d 36, certiorari denied Potashnick-Badgett Dredging, Incorporated v. Trans-State Dredging Company, 272 So.2d 819, certiorari denied 272 So.2d 820.

Where experienced barge worker hired as mate aboard dredge had been working some 13 days before he was injured when cable holding plugged discharge pipe parted while nonselfpropelled dredge was digging channel several miles from shore in Gulf of Mexico to provide barge channel power plant, his duties included overseeing operations of two smaller derrick barges, moving anchors when necessary, checking shore lines and shifting spill pontoons and, apparently, helping to unstop clogged pipes, worker was a seaman within meaning of federal maritime law; recovery for injuries was not limited to adjacent state's Workmen's Compensation Law. Jones Act, 46 U.S.C.A. § 688; F.S.A. § 440.01 et seq.

> Potashnick-Badgett Dredging Inc. v. Whitfield, 269 So.2d 36, certiorari denied Potashnick-Badgett Dredging, Incorporated v. Trans-State Dredging Company, 272 So.2d 819, certiorari denied 272 So.2d 820.

⚷**29(5.3). Persons entitled to sue.**

C.A.5 (Fla.) 1953. An employee of barge owners who was injured when he attempted to descend ladder which led from dock to vessel and which had been furnished by employees of molasses company, and slackness in wire by which ladder was fastened to dock by employees of molasses company allowed ladder to slip, resulting in disconnection of sections of ladder causing employee to fall and strike arm on barge which employee had been instructed to assist in loading with molasses, could bring suit at law against his employers for injuries under Jones Act regardless of whether such employee was in command of barge. Jones Act, 46 U.S.C.A. § 688.

> Sanford v. Caswell, 200 F.2d 830, certiorari denied 73 S.Ct. 831, 345 U.S. 940, 97 L.Ed. 1366.

S.D.Fla. 2016. Filipino seaman was not Jones Act seaman, even though shipowner maintained office in United States, where injury occurred while seaman was working on Bahamian vessel during mooring operations in St. Maarten, shipowner was organized under Bahamian laws and headquartered in Monaco, employment contract was entered into in Philippines and called for application of Philippine law, Philippine forum was accessible, and shipowner's American office only handled marketing and sales activities for Americas. 46 U.S.C.A. § 30104.

Navarette v. Silversea Cruises Ltd., 169 F.Supp.3d 1314.

S.D.Fla. 2002. In order to recover damages under the Jones Act, a plaintiff must have the status of a seaman. Jones Act, 46 App.U.S.C.A. § 688.

Eckert v. U.S., 232 F.Supp.2d 1312.

S.D.Fla. 1965. Benefits of Jones Act are available only to either a "seaman" injured in course of employment or personal representative of seaman in event injuries received resulted in seaman's death. Jones Act, 46 U.S.C.A. § 688.

Bodden v. Coordinated Caribbean Transport, Inc., 249 F.Supp. 561, reversed 369 F.2d 273, 5 A.L.R. Fed. 668.

Fla.App. 3 Dist. 1958. Where seaman was a Cuban national, he was injured in foreign waters, shipowner, which employed seaman, was a Panamanian corporation, ship flew flag of Panama and was also registered there, and contract of employment of seaman provided for application of Panamanian law, the Jones Act was not applicable in action by seaman against shipowner in Florida circuit court for injury, on ground that shipowner was negligent, though employment contract was signed by seaman in Florida. Jones Act, 46 U.S.C.A. § 688.

Corella v. McCormick Shipping Corp., 101 So.2d 903.

↔29(5.4). Persons against whom suit may be brought.

C.A.5 (Fla.) 1954. The Jones Act does not grant to seamen a right to bring an action against any one except his employer and does not in turn provide for the survival of actions against the estate of the deceased tort-feasor. Jones Act, 46 U.S.C.A. § 688.

Roth v. Cox, 210 F.2d 76, certiorari granted 74 S.Ct. 864, 347 U.S. 1009, 98 L.Ed. 1133, affirmed 75 S.Ct. 242, 348 U.S. 207, 99 L.Ed. 260.

M.D.Fla. 1976. Owner of fishing vessel would be jointly and severally liable with corporation engaged in production of fish meal for damages resulting from death of one crewman on vessel and personal injuries sustained by another crewman as result of inhalation of hydrogen sulphide gas injected into hold of vessel by recirculation hose utilized at reduction plant.

Consolidated Mach., Inc. v. Protein Products Corp., 428 F.Supp. 209.

S.D.Fla. 2004. A seaman has the advantages of Jones Act only against his employer. Jones Act, 46 App.U.S.C.A. § 688(a).

Wai v. Rainbow Holdings, 350 F.Supp.2d 1019.

When a seaman contends that one who did not sign his payroll checks is in fact his employer under the Jones Act, he must prove the employment relationship. Jones Act, 46 App.U.S.C.A. § 688(a).

Wai v. Rainbow Holdings, 350 F.Supp.2d 1019.

Chemical tanker's cargo agent could not be considered seaman's employer under borrowed servant doctrine and therefore was not liable under the Jones Act or the general maritime law for seaman's injuries; seaman failed to describe any communication from cargo agent, or provide any other evidence indicating that cargo agent controlled the vessel's operations, furnished equipment or tools, controlled the details of seaman's work, hired him, paid him, or had the authority to fire him, and did not submit evidence indicating that cargo agent, which had overlapping officers and shared a common address with owner of seaman's direct employer, dominated or controlled direct employer or owner so as to warrant disregard of their existence as separate legal entities. Jones Act, 46 App.U.S.C.A. § 688(a).

Wai v. Rainbow Holdings, 350 F.Supp.2d 1019.

If a seaman is injured by a vessel's unseaworthiness, he may sue its owner or bareboat charterer; allocation of ultimate liability should be the responsibility of the owner and charterer, who can sort out which between them will bear the final cost of recovery.

Wai v. Rainbow Holdings, 350 F.Supp.2d 1019.

Cargo agent, which was neither the owner nor the bareboat charterer of the vessel, could not be held liable injuries to seaman due to alleged unseaworthiness of the vessel; furthermore, cargo agent was under no duty to provide emergency medical care to seaman.

> Wai v. Rainbow Holdings, 350 F.Supp.2d 1019.

S.D.Fla. 2002. In determining whether a plaintiff and defendant in a Jones Act case have the requisite employee-employer relationship, one must look at the venture as a whole. Jones Act, 46 App.U.S.C.A. § 688.

> Eckert v. U.S., 232 F.Supp.2d 1312.

S.D.Fla. 1954. An action could not be maintained under Jones Act against plaintiff's employer for injuries sustained by plaintiff while on fishing trip aboard another's boat because of such owner's alleged negligence, in absence of showing of connection between employer and operation of boat or owner's operation thereof as employer's agent, servant or employee; there being no showing that employer was either owner or owner pro hac vice of boat at time of accident. Jones Act, 46 U.S.C.A. § 688.

> Kanischer v. Kaplan, 118 F.Supp. 847, affirmed 215 F.2d 300, certiorari denied 75 S.Ct. 363, 348 U.S. 942, 99 L.Ed. 737, rehearing denied Kanisher v. Irwin Operating Co., 75 S.Ct. 529, 348 U.S. 977, 99 L.Ed. 761.

Fla.App. 4 Dist. 1972. The bare boat or demise charterer, as owner, is the warrantor of seaworthiness of the vessel to seaman working aboard her and, in consequence, may be held liable for personal injury suffered as result of breach of absolute duty to provide a safe place to work and safe implements with which to work; he is also the "employer" for purposes of personal injury liabilities to seamen under the Jones Act. Jones Act, 46 U.S.C.A. § 688; F.S.A. § 440.01 et seq.

> Potashnick-Badgett Dredging Inc. v. Whitfield, 269 So.2d 36, certiorari denied Potashnick-Badgett Dredging, Incorporated v. Trans-State Dredging Company, 272 So.2d 819, certiorari denied 272 So.2d 820.

Where agreement covering rental of floating dredge referred to arrangement as being on a "bare boat rental basis," party

renting vessel paid captain and crew and hired mate and was to pay for all repairs, except that major repairs to major equipment was to be responsibility of owner, and there was no evidence that owner exercised any control over operation of dredge in any way, rental arrangement was a bare boat charter, for purpose of determining liability of owner and/or renter for injuries mate sustained because of unseaworthiness and negligence.

> Potashnick-Badgett Dredging Inc. v. Whitfield, 269 So.2d 36, certiorari denied Potashnick-Badgett Dredging, Incorporated v. Trans-State Dredging Company, 272 So.2d 819, certiorari denied 272 So.2d 820.

⚷29(5.5). Jurisdiction and venue.

U.S.Fla. 1966. General venue statute definition of residence of corporation as "any judicial district in which it is incorporated or licensed to do business or is doing business" is applicable to Jones Act venue provision. 28 U.S.C.A. § 1391(c); Jones Act, 46 U.S.C.A. § 688.

> Pure Oil Co. v. Suarez, 86 S.Ct. 1394, 384 U.S. 202, 16 L.Ed.2d 474.

Where defendant corporation in Jones Act action was transacting business in Southern District of Florida, venue was properly laid there, even though principal office of defendant was maintained in Illinois. 28 U.S.C.A. § 1391(c); Jones Act, 46 U.S.C.A. § 688.

> Pure Oil Co. v. Suarez, 86 S.Ct. 1394, 384 U.S. 202, 16 L.Ed.2d 474.

Thrust of Jones Act was not primarily directed at venue but rather at giving seamen substantive rights and federal forum for their vindication. Jones Act, 46 U.S.C.A. § 688.

> Pure Oil Co. v. Suarez, 86 S.Ct. 1394, 384 U.S. 202, 16 L.Ed.2d 474.

† C.A.11 (Fla.) 2013. Seaman's complaint against owner of cruise ship failed to plead sufficient facts to invoke diversity jurisdiction over his negligence claim, under Jones Act, and maritime law claims for unseaworthiness of ship, failure to provide maintenance and cure, and failure to treat his injuries incurred while serving as first pastryman on board ship in navigable waters, where complaint did not allege citi-

zenship of seaman or owner. 28 U.S.C.A.
§ 1332(a)(2); 46 U.S.C.A. § 30104 et seq.

> Quiroz v. MSC Mediterranean Ship-
> ping Co. S.A., 522 Fed.Appx. 655.

† C.A.11 (Fla.) 2012. Venue provision of FELA did not apply to Jones Act
claim. Federal Employer's Liability Act,
§ 1 et seq., 45 U.S.C.A. § 51 et seq.; 46
App.U.S.C.A. § 688.

> Escobal v. Celebration Cruise Opera-
> tor, Inc., 482 Fed.Appx. 475, certio-
> rari denied 133 S.Ct. 1998, 185
> L.Ed.2d 866.

† C.A.11 (Fla.) 2010. Injured seaman
had no right to discovery, prior to dismissal on forum non conveniens grounds of his
action against his employer catering company and cruise ship owner, to determine
whether there was evidence to support his
claim that owner had base of operations in
United States, where seaman failed to
make timely request for jurisdictional discovery in district court, and, even assuming that owner had some ties to United
States, it would not be enough to overcome all other factors weighing against
jurisdiction.

> Vesuna v. CSCS Intern. N.V., 405 Fed.
> Appx. 371.

† C.A.11 (Fla.) 2008. Denial of Colombian seaman's motion to reinstate his
action for alleged violations of Jones Act,
which had been dismissed on basis of
forum non conveniens, was not abuse of
discretion, given that seaman's financial
inability to file suit in alternative fora or
unavailability of contingency fee arrangements in alternative fora did not, standing
alone, render those fora unavailable, and
district court considered appropriate forum non conveniens factors and found
that, as a whole, they supported dismissal
in favor of another forum. 46
U.S.C.App.(2000 Ed.) § 688.

> Vega v. Cruise Ship Catering and Ser-
> vice Intern., N.V., 279 Fed.Appx.
> 946.

C.A.5 (Fla.) 1965. Provision of Jones
Act that jurisdiction shall be under court
of the district in which the defendant employer resides or in which his principal
office is located refers only to proper venue, and therefore such provision need not

be given effect unless defendant insists
upon it. Jones Act, 46 U.S.C.A. § 688.

> Pure Oil Co. v. Suarez, 346 F.2d 890,
> certiorari granted 86 S.Ct. 549, 382
> U.S. 972, 15 L.Ed.2d 464, affirmed
> 86 S.Ct. 1394, 384 U.S. 202, 16
> L.Ed.2d 474.

Special venue provisions of the Federal Employers' Liability Act are not applicable in determining proper venue in Jones
Act cases. Jones Act, 46 U.S.C.A. § 688.

> Pure Oil Co. v. Suarez, 346 F.2d 890,
> certiorari granted 86 S.Ct. 549, 382
> U.S. 972, 15 L.Ed.2d 464, affirmed
> 86 S.Ct. 1394, 384 U.S. 202, 16
> L.Ed.2d 474.

The Jones Act venue provision was
meant to provide a convenient federal
form for satisfaction of the seaman's personal injury claims against his employer,
and it is consonant with such purpose to
give the term "residence" as used in venue
provision of the Jones Act an expansive
interpretation. Jones Act, 46 U.S.C.A.
§ 688; 28 U.S.C.A. § 1391(c).

> Pure Oil Co. v. Suarez, 346 F.2d 890,
> certiorari granted 86 S.Ct. 549, 382
> U.S. 972, 15 L.Ed.2d 464, affirmed
> 86 S.Ct. 1394, 384 U.S. 202, 16
> L.Ed.2d 474.

Venue of a Jones Act case against a
corporate defendant was properly laid in
the Southern District of Florida in which
defendant was transacting business, even
though defendant maintained its principal
office in Illinois. Jones Act, 46 U.S.C.A.
§ 688; 28 U.S.C.A. §§ 1292(b), 1391(c).

> Pure Oil Co. v. Suarez, 346 F.2d 890,
> certiorari granted 86 S.Ct. 549, 382
> U.S. 972, 15 L.Ed.2d 464, affirmed
> 86 S.Ct. 1394, 384 U.S. 202, 16
> L.Ed.2d 474.

S.D.Fla. 2004. Dismissal on forum
non conveniens grounds was warranted in
seaman's action to recover for personal
injuries sustained while working on cruise
ship, even though cruise during which
injury occurred began and ended in United States, shipowner marketed cruises to
United States customers, owner's parent
company had principal place of business
in United States, and surgery to repair
seaman's wrist occurred in United States,
where injury occurred at sea, vessels involved in action were Italian flagged ships,

seaman lived in and was citizen of Honduras, owner was Italian corporation, parent did not control owner's day-to-day operations, corporate distinctions were maintained, control over owner's operations resided in its Italian corporate headquarters, only about 7% of owner's passengers and 4% of its worldwide net revenues came from sale of cruises in United States, place of contract was apparently not United States, alternative fora were available in Italy, Honduras, or Netherlands Antilles, comparison of law of available fora was not significant issue, and employer did not arrange to have operation in United States.

> Membreno v. Costa Crociere, S.p.A., 347 F.Supp.2d 1289, affirmed 425 F.3d 932.

S.D.Fla. 2004. Nicaragua was an available and adequate forum for wrongful death action arising out of seaman's death aboard a vessel in a Nicaraguan port; defendants had consented to jurisdiction of the Nicaraguan courts, and remedies available to the plaintiff in Nicaragua were not clearly unsatisfactory.

> Callasso v. Morton & Co., 324 F.Supp.2d 1320.

Private factors weighed in favor of dismissal, on forum non conveniens grounds, of wrongful death action under Jones Act arising out of seaman's death aboard a vessel in a Nicaraguan port, even though American court was plaintiff's choice of forum; virtually all witnesses were in Nicaragua, the accident took place there, the plaintiffs were residents and citizens of Nicaragua, all of the documentation and testimony would likely be in Spanish, access to evidence and sites would be in Nicaragua, and the practicalities and expenses of the litigation favored Nicaragua. Jones Act, 46 App.U.S.C.A. § 688.

> Callasso v. Morton & Co., 324 F.Supp.2d 1320.

Public factors weighed in favor of dismissal, on forum non conveniens grounds, of wrongful death action under Jones Act arising out of seaman's death aboard a vessel in a Nicaraguan port; Nicaragua's interest in deciding the dispute was greater than the United States' interest, there was a strong possibility that Nicaraguan law would have to be applied to decide the case, and fact that two of the defendants were Florida corporations did not provide a sufficient connection to the U.S. to warrant bringing the case in a federal court. Jones Act, 46 App.U.S.C.A. § 688.

> Callasso v. Morton & Co., 324 F.Supp.2d 1320.

Plaintiff would not be inconvenienced or prejudiced by dismissal, on forum non conveniens grounds, of her Jones Act action arising out of a seaman's death aboard a vessel in a Nicaraguan port, requiring her to reinstate her action in Nicaragua, where defendants stipulated to personal jurisdiction before a competent tribunal in that country and waived any time limitation defenses; plaintiff was a Nicaraguan citizen and resident, virtually all witnesses were in Nicaragua, the accident took place there, and access to other evidence and sites would be there. Jones Act, 46 App.U.S.C.A. § 688.

> Callasso v. Morton & Co., 324 F.Supp.2d 1320.

S.D.Fla. 2003. For purposes of forum non conveniens analysis, private interests did not favor a trial in the United States in seaman's action against his employer and vessel owner, alleging claims under the Jones Act to recover for injuries sustained in Italy while he was working for caterer aboard vessel, where defendants consented to jurisdiction in foreign fora, there was no indication that foreign fora would afford seaman no remedy at all, and bulk of evidence and witnesses were overseas. Jones Act, 46 App. U.S.C.A. § 688.

> Bautista v. Cruise Ships Catering and Service Intern., N.V., 350 F.Supp.2d 987, reconsideration denied, affirmed 120 Fed.Appx. 786.

For purposes of forum non conveniens analysis, public interests did not favor a trial in the United States in seaman's action against his employer and vessel owner, alleging claims under the Jones Act to recover for injuries sustained in Italy while he was working for caterer aboard vessel, where only major connection to the United States was law practice of seaman's attorneys. Jones Act, 46 App.U.S.C.A. § 688.

> Bautista v. Cruise Ships Catering and Service Intern., N.V., 350 F.Supp.2d 987, reconsideration denied, affirmed 120 Fed.Appx. 786.

S.D.Fla. 2003. In determining whether to dismiss Jones Act action on forum non conveniens ground, District Court first would decide, under choice of law principles, whether law of United States applied, and, if it did, Court would not dismiss case on such grounds, and if it did not, Court would examine traditional considerations of forum non conveniens to determine whether it should exercise its discretion and decline to assert jurisdiction over case. Jones Act, 46 App.U.S.C.A. § 688.

> Williams v. Cruise Ships Catering, 299 F.Supp.2d 1273, reconsideration denied 320 F.Supp.2d 1347.

S.D.Fla. 2002. The United States was not acoustic engineer's employer for purposes of claims brought pursuant to the Jones Act arising from injuries sustained when engineer fell from testing platform while performing repairs to weather equipment located at a testing tower associated with a Navy testing center, where engineer unequivocally stated that he was employed by the non-government contract operator of the testing center and not the United States government. Jones Act, 46 App.U.S.C.A. § 688.

> Eckert v. U.S., 232 F.Supp.2d 1312.

S.D.Fla. 1999. Relevant factors in determining whether a federal court can exercise jurisdiction over a Jones Act claim are: (1) the place of the wrongful act; (2) the law of the flag; (3) the allegiance or domicile of the injured seaman; (4) allegiance of the defendant shipowner; (5) the place where the contract of employment was made; (6) the inaccessibility of a foreign forum; (7) the law of the forum; and (8) substantial use of a United States base of operations for the shipping and revenues of the vessel and its owner, together with the other United States contacts. Jones Act, 46 App.U.S.C.A. § 688.

> Baydar v. Renaissance Cruises, Inc., 35 F.Supp.2d 916.

Mere existence of a United States base of operations does not, without more, create federal jurisdiction in Jones Act action. Jones Act, 46 App.U.S.C.A. § 688.

> Baydar v. Renaissance Cruises, Inc., 35 F.Supp.2d 916.

District court lacked subject matter jurisdiction over Jones Act claim brought by Turkish national, who resided in the United Kingdom and who was a seaman aboard Liberian-flagged vessel, against Italian vessel owner incorporated under the laws of Antigua arising from injury sustained while the vessel was in Argentina; there were no contacts between owner and the United States, other than the fact that owner's office was located in Florida and that its officers lived in Florida. Jones Act, 46 App.U.S.C.A. § 688.

> Baydar v. Renaissance Cruises, Inc., 35 F.Supp.2d 916.

Fla.App. 3 Dist. 2004. Even if catering service employing seamen serving on ships in foreign cruise line was doing business in Florida, such would not be controlling or dispositive on issue of whether seamen's personal injury actions brought under the Jones Act should be dismissed due to forum non conveniens, as it would only weigh in favor of exercising jurisdiction, and would be but one factor to consider in whether the cases could be fairly and more conveniently litigated elsewhere so that the ends of justice were better served. Jones Act, 46 App.U.S.C.A. § 688(a).

> Tananta v. Cruise Ships Catering and Services Int'l., N.V., 909 So.2d 874, rehearing denied, review denied 917 So.2d 195, review denied Chamo v. Costa Crociere, S.P.A., 917 So.2d 192, review denied Simpson v. Costa Crociere, S.P.A., 917 So.2d 195.

There were adequate alternative forums to Miami, Florida courts for personal injury actions that foreign seamen brought against foreign cruise line and its affiliates under the Jones Act, for purposes of determining whether such actions should be dismissed under the doctrine of forum non conveniens, where seamen's homelands had been found in other actions to be a satisfactory venue for personal injury causes of action, seamen's cases were dismissed on a conditional basis to assure alternative forums did accept jurisdiction over the whole case, and defendants through affidavit waived time limitation and jurisdictional defenses to seamen refiling actions in their respective homelands, in country in which cruise line defendant conducted its day to day business, or country in which affiliated defendants had their registered office. Jones Act, 46 App.U.S.C.A. § 688(a).

> Tananta v. Cruise Ships Catering and Services Int'l., N.V., 909 So.2d 874, rehearing denied, review denied 917 So.2d 195, review denied Chamo v. Costa Crociere, S.P.A., 917 So.2d 192, review denied Simpson v. Costa Crociere, S.P.A., 917 So.2d 195.

Private interests did not favor Miami, Florida as forum for litigating personal injury actions that foreign seamen brought against foreign cruise line and its affiliates under the Jones Act, for purposes of determining whether such actions should be dismissed under the doctrine of forum non conveniens, though marketing affiliate of cruise line had an office in Miami, company that processed seamen's medical claims was in Miami, and seamen signed employment contracts in Miami, where seamen were injured far from Florida's shores, vessels seamen were injured on did not call on United States ports, seamen had few if any ties to Florida, and no relevant evidence could be found in Miami regarding their respective injuries. Jones Act, 46 App.U.S.C.A. § 688(a).

> Tananta v. Cruise Ships Catering and Services Int'l., N.V., 909 So.2d 874, rehearing denied, review denied 917 So.2d 195, review denied Chamo v. Costa Crociere, S.P.A., 917 So.2d 192, review denied Simpson v. Costa Crociere, S.P.A., 917 So.2d 195.

Public interests did not favor Miami, Florida as forum for litigating personal injury actions that foreign seamen brought against foreign cruise line and its affiliates under the Jones Act, for purposes of determining whether such actions should be dismissed under the doctrine of forum non conveniens, where seamen were injured on the high seas aboard non-U.S. vessels, were treated by foreign doctors, and had foreign witnesses of their incident to proffer. Jones Act, 46 App.U.S.C.A. § 688(a).

> Tananta v. Cruise Ships Catering and Services Int'l., N.V., 909 So.2d 874, rehearing denied, review denied 917 So.2d 195, review denied Chamo v. Costa Crociere, S.P.A., 917 So.2d 192, review denied Simpson v. Costa Crociere, S.P.A., 917 So.2d 195.

Foreign seaman would suffer no undue inconvenience or prejudice as a result of re-filing their personal injury actions originally brought in Miami, Florida against foreign cruise line and its affiliates under the Jones Act, for purposes of determining whether such actions should be dismissed under the doctrine of forum non conveniens, where defendants stipulated that they waived any statute of limitations defenses if seamen re-filed actions in their respective homelands, in country in which cruise line defendant conducted its day to day business, or country in which affiliated defendants had their registered office. Jones Act, 46 App.U.S.C.A. § 688(a).

> Tananta v. Cruise Ships Catering and Services Int'l., N.V., 909 So.2d 874, rehearing denied, review denied 917 So.2d 195, review denied Chamo v. Costa Crociere, S.P.A., 917 So.2d 192, review denied Simpson v. Costa Crociere, S.P.A., 917 So.2d 195.

Fla.App. 3 Dist. 2002. Defendants, an Italian corporation which owned the ship on which plaintiff was injured, the catering service by which he was employed, and the Netherlands Antilles corporation which had chartered the ship, were entitled to dismissal of plaintiff's Jones Act claims on forum non conveniens grounds; plaintiff was from Peru and had there signed his employment contract, the Netherlands Antilles and Peru could each provide an adequate alternate forum, given that defendants were amenable to process in either jurisdiction and plaintiff could recover damages in either jurisdiction, the public and private factors weighed in favor of the alternate fora, as most of the witnesses resided in one place or the other and Florida had no interest in plaintiff's accident, and plaintiff would suffer neither undue inconvenience nor prejudice in reinstating his claim. Jones Act, 46 App.U.S.C.A. § 688; West's F.S.A. RCP Rule 1.061.

> Cruise Ships Catering and Services International, N.V. v. Tananta, 823 So.2d 258, on subsequent appeal Tananta v. Cruise Ships Catering and Services Int'l., N.V., 909 So.2d 874, rehearing denied, review denied 917 So.2d 195, review denied Chamo v. Costa Crociere, S.P.A., 917 So.2d 192, review denied Simpson v. Costa Crociere, S.P.A., 917 So.2d 195.

Fla.App. 3 Dist. 1998. Venue was not proper in county in which seaman sued vessel owner to recover for injuries suffered at sea while working in Alaska, even though vessel owner sold tickets through travel agents in that county, and even if owner advertised in local newspapers that tickets could be purchased through travel agents there; none of owner's vessels operated out of that county, owner did not have office there, and there was insufficient evidence to show per se agency relationship or any other agency relationship between owner and travel agents in question. West's F.S.A. § 47.051.

New Commodore Cruise Lines, Ltd. v. Sabio, 724 So.2d 149, rehearing denied.

Fla.App. 3 Dist. 1994. Trial court had jurisdiction over Delaware owner of vessel in action brought by seaperson injured while the vessel was in the Virgin Islands where the owner took delivery of the vessel in Florida, used it to provide pleasure voyages for guests of its parent corporation, operated all cruises from Miami, and had the vessel refitted and repaired for three months annually in Miami. West's F.S.A. § 48.193(2).

Morley v. Lady Allison, Inc., 633 So.2d 1173.

Fla.App. 3 Dist. 1993. Court's determination as to whether sufficient nexus exists with United States, to impose federal court jurisdiction on Jones Act cases, is guided by place of wrongful act, law of flag, allegiance or domicile of injured seaman, allegiance of defendant shipowner, place where contract of employment was made, inaccessibility of foreign forum, law of forum, and ship builder's base of operation. Jones Act, 46 App.U.S.C.A. § 688.

Haave v. Tor Husfjord Shipping A/S, 630 So.2d 623.

Federal district court in Florida had jurisdiction over Jones Act case, even though place of wrongful act was Costa Rica, vessel flew Norwegian flag, allegiance of shipowner was Norwegian, employment contract was executed in Norway, seaman had access to Norwegian courts and principal base of operations was in Norway; shipper had registered agent and office in Florida and made extensive use of United States seaports, and

injured seaman was domiciled in Florida. Jones Act, 46 App.U.S.C.A. § 688.

Haave v. Tor Husfjord Shipping A/S, 630 So.2d 623.

Fla.App. 3 Dist. 1992. A Filipino seaman's action for Jones Act negligence and unseaworthiness under United States Maritime law was not barred by improper venue, forum non conveniens, or lack of subject matter jurisdiction, even though the seaman slipped and fell aboard vessel while in Bahamas; vessel owner's principal place of business and base of operations was in Florida. Jones Act, 46 App. U.S.C.A. § 688.

Royal Caribbean Cruises, Ltd. v. Payumo, 608 So.2d 862.

Fla.App. 3 Dist. 1990. Defendants' vessel's sporadic visits and other contacts with State of Florida did not constitute "continuous and systematic" activity necessary to sustain claim of personal jurisdiction against them under statute requiring "substantial and not isolated activity" within state in seaman's personal injury action, which arose at sea and had no "connexity" to state. West's F.S.A. § 48.193(2).

Spanier v. Suisse-Outremer Reederei A.G., 557 So.2d 83.

Fla.App. 3 Dist. 1989. Owner of cruise ship, a Norwegian corporation, was a Jones Act "employer" and was subject to United States jurisdiction with respect to injuries suffered by crew member, a Chilean national, while vessel was docked in the Bahamas, where vessel was operated exclusively out of the Port of Miami. Jones Act, 46 U.S.C.App. § 688.

Rojas v. Kloster Cruise, A/S, 550 So.2d 59, review denied Kloster Cruise v. Francisco Sergio Quiroga Rojas, 562 So.2d 346.

Fla.App. 3 Dist. 1974. Circuit court lacked jurisdiction over subject matter of complaint for damages under the Jones Act where, inter alia, plaintiff was a citizen and domiciliary of Spain, contract of employment was signed in Spain, said contract provided that plaintiff's rights and obligations were those under Norwegian law, defendant was a Norwegian corporation, accident occurred on high seas off the coast of the Bahamas, and plaintiff's only contact with this country was upon

† This Case was not selected for publication in the National Reporter System
For legislative history of cited statutes, see Florida Statutes Annotated

the ship's arrival in port to pick up passengers and supplies. Jones Act, 46 U.S.C.A. § 688.

> Valverde v. Klosters Rederi A/S, 294 So.2d 101.

Fla.App. 4 Dist. 2002. A court's determination as to whether a sufficient nexus exists between the matter being litigated and the United States, for purposes of determining whether a court has subject matter jurisdiction to hear Jones Act claims, is decided by considering the totality of the circumstances. Jones Act, 46 App.U.S.C.A. § 688.

> Amanquiton v. Peterson, 813 So.2d 112, rehearing denied, review denied 832 So.2d 103.

German ship owner which employed seaman did not have sufficient nexus with Florida or United States to confer subject matter jurisdiction to hear seaman's Jones Act claim, although ship was subject of time share relationship with Miami corporation and ship had stopped twice in Fort Lauderdale, where seaman was injured while ship was off Jamaica, ship was of German registry, seaman was domiciliary and citizen of Philippines, seaman's employment contract was made in Philippines and pursuant to Philippine law, and seaman had received compensation from Philippine courts. Jones Act, 46 App. U.S.C.A. § 688.

> Amanquiton v. Peterson, 813 So.2d 112, rehearing denied, review denied 832 So.2d 103.

Mere existence of a United States base of operations does not, without more, create jurisdiction for the court over a Jones Act claim. Jones Act, 46 App.U.S.C.A. § 688.

> Amanquiton v. Peterson, 813 So.2d 112, rehearing denied, review denied 832 So.2d 103.

☞29(5.6). **Limitations and laches.**

See also LIMITATION OF ACTIONS.

C.A.11 (Fla.) 2009. While ten-year statute of repose applicable under Dutch law to strict products liability claims prevented owner of vessel, which had previously settled maritime tort claims asserted by captain of vessel for injuries that he sustained as result of purported defect in design, construction or installation of food lift on ship, from seeking to recover in indemnity or contribution from ship builder to extent that these third-party claims were based on strict liability theory, statute of repose did not apply to claims sounding in negligence, and vessel owner could pursue its third-party claims, despite fact that more than ten years had passed since vessel was constructed and parties had agreed that their relationship would be governed by Dutch law, as long as claims were based on ship builder's alleged negligence.

> Cooper v. Meridian Yachts, Ltd., 575 F.3d 1151, rehearing denied.

C.A.5 (Fla.) 1967. Claims against shipowner based on unseaworthiness of vessel are barred only if delay in filing of the libel beyond the three-year Jones Act limitation period is inexcusable and if the delay has prejudiced the defense of the suit. Jones Act, 46 U.S.C.A. § 688 et seq.

> Crews v. Arundel Corp., 386 F.2d 528.

C.A.5 (Fla.) 1967. Where libel of seaman, who sought recovery from owner of vessel for injuries, alleged that owner's employees knew of accidents and injuries, that seaman was sent to doctor, that owner received full medical report, that witnesses were available for interrogation and production as witnesses as needed, and that vessel was under control of owner and was in active use by owner so that it and its equipment were subject to inspection, federal District Court could not permit presumption that delay in bringing libel was detrimental and erred in dismissing libel on ground that laches were reflected on face of libel because intervals between times of injuries and filing time ranged from three years and two months to four years and six months. Jones Act, 46 U.S.C.A. § 688; Admiralty Rules, rule 58, 28 U.S.C.A.

> Molnar v. Gulfcoast Transit Co., 371 F.2d 639.

If owner of vessel knew of accidents of seaman, made detailed investigations, and still had facts concerning injuries and disabling consequences in form of evidence, live or documentary, and from witnesses whose recollections were still fresh, equitable principles of laches ought not to become absolute obstacle to determination of intrinsic merits of seaman's claims for injuries. Jones Act, 46 U.S.C.A. § 688.

> Molnar v. Gulfcoast Transit Co., 371 F.2d 639.

C.A.5 (Fla.) 1954. The three year limitation provision of the Employers' Liability Act which was incorporated by adoption in the Jones Act is one of substantive right, setting a limit to the existence of the obligation which the Jones Act creates and necessarily implies that the action is maintainable as a substantive right if commenced within three years. Jones Act, 46 U.S.C.A. § 688; Federal Employers' Liability Act, § 6, 45 U.S.C.A. § 56.

> Roth v. Cox, 210 F.2d 76, certiorari granted 74 S.Ct. 864, 347 U.S. 1009, 98 L.Ed. 1133, affirmed 75 S.Ct. 242, 348 U.S. 207, 99 L.Ed. 260.

Provision of the Employers' Liability Act establishing a three year limitation period thereunder and incorporated by adoption in the Jones Act is one of substantive right setting a limit to the existence of the obligation which the Jones Act creates and it may not be impaired by the Florida nonclaim statute. Federal Employers' Liability Act, § 6, 45 U.S.C.A. § 56; Jones Act, 46 U.S.C.A. § 688; F.S.A. § 733.16(1).

> Roth v. Cox, 210 F.2d 76, certiorari granted 74 S.Ct. 864, 347 U.S. 1009, 98 L.Ed. 1133, affirmed 75 S.Ct. 242, 348 U.S. 207, 99 L.Ed. 260.

Fla.App. 3 Dist. 1983. Jones Act provided sole remedy available to seaman for alleged negligence of his employer during course of seaman's employment on one of employer's tugs, but claim was barred by statute of limitations. Jones Act, 46 U.S.C.A. § 688.

> Rigdon v. Belcher Towing Co., 435 So.2d 939.

⟜29(5.7). Parties.

For other cases see earlier editions of this digest, the Decennial Digests, and WESTLAW.

⟜29(5.8). Process.

Fla. 1962. Where tug owned by Louisiana resident had been moored within state in harbor area as directed by tug owner pending further orders after tug had towed barges on navigable waters from Texas to Florida, statute relating to service of process on nonresident vessel owners was applicable to Jones Act action brought against tug owner for death of employee from drowning at mooring area. F.S.A. § 47.162; Jones Act, 46 U.S.C.A. § 688.

> Edmundson v. Hamilton, 148 So.2d 262, 99 A.L.R.2d 279.

⟜29(5.9). Pleading in general.

C.A.5 (Fla.) 1977. City policeman's complaint under Jones Act claiming that he was injured by a fusillade of coconuts launched by young hooligans while he was patrolling canal in city vessel and that vessel offered inadequate protection from such assault stated cause of action sufficient to withstand motion to dismiss. Jones Act, 46 U.S.C.A. § 688.

> Roberts v. City of Plantation, 558 F.2d 750.

Fla.App. 2 Dist. 1966. For purpose of recovering against yacht owner for injuries received by crewman because sides of ladder borrowed by yacht owner from boat yard broke while crewman was attempting to board yacht, undergoing repairs out of water, it was essential for crewman to plead that yacht owner had knowledge of the defective condition of the ladder.

> Farrington v. McConnell, 183 So.2d 585.

⟜29(5.10)–29(5.11). *For other cases see earlier editions of this digest, the Decennial Digests, and WESTLAW.*

⟜29(5.12). Presumptions and burden of proof.

C.A.11 (Fla.) 1987. Presumption of "unseaworthiness" arose, where hook and eye fastener had been removed from top of ship's ladder, and ladder had subsequently given way while seaman was using it in normal manner.

> Villers Seafood Co., Inc. v. Vest, 813 F.2d 339.

C.A.5 (Fla.) 1967. Doctrine of res ipsa loquitur is applicable to an action for unseaworthiness.

> Gibbs v. Kiesel, 382 F.2d 917.

C.A.5 (Fla.) 1963. Seaman seeking recovery on unseaworthiness theory for

---

injuries sustained in affray with fellow crew member had burden to make crew member out to be seaman with wicked disposition, a propensity to evil conduct, a savage and vicious nature.

> McConville v. Florida Towing Corp., 321 F.2d 162.

S.D.Fla. 2015. The mere happening of an accident does not give rise to a res ipsa inference of negligence or breach of duty under the Jones Act or general maritime law. Jones Act, 46 U.S.C.A. § 30104 et seq.

> Millan v. Celebration Cruise Operator, Inc., 212 F.Supp.3d 1301.

Fla.App. 1 Dist. 1959. Doctrine of res ipsa loquitur was inapplicable to action for death of seaman whose body, clad only in an undershirt, was discovered in water about a half mile from mooring place of boat unequipped with toilet facilities; and in absence of showing that employer's negligence had had anything to do with seaman's death, there could be no recovery. Jones Act, 46 U.S.C.A. § 688.

> Gaymon v. Quinn Menhaden Fisheries of Tex., Inc., 108 So.2d 641.

Fla.App. 2 Dist. 1966. Yacht owner who borrowed ladder from boat yard which had exclusively used the ladder until yacht crewman began to ascend the ladder for purpose of boarding the yacht, which was undergoing repairs out of water, at the boat yard, was not liable on theory of res ipsa loquitur for injuries sustained by the crewman when sides of the ladder broke causing him to fall. Jones Act, 46 U.S.C.A. § 688; Federal Employers' Liability Act, § 1, 45 U.S.C.A. § 51.

> Farrington v. McConnell, 183 So.2d 585.

☞**29(5.13). Admissibility of evidence.**

U.S.Fla. 1959. In action by seaman against shipowner for damages and maintenance and cure based on claim that injuries sustained by seaman when he was pitched into the air and fell back to the deck activated or aggravated a previously latent tubercular condition, members of jury were entitled to take all the circumstances, including medical testimony, into consideration. Jones Act, 46 U.S.C.A. § 688.

> Sentilles v. Inter-Caribbean Shipping Corp., 80 S.Ct. 173, 361 U.S. 107, 4 L.Ed.2d 142.

C.A.5 (Fla.) 1962. Provisions of Corps of Engineers' manual with respect to requirements for life preservers were receivable as proof of industry-wide acceptance of need for extraordinary care in protecting against hazards prevailing.

> Davis v. Parkhill-Goodloe Co., 302 F.2d 489.

Fla.App. 3 Dist. 1999. Probative value of evidence of fight between seaman and his wife, also a crew member, as a reason for seaman's termination from cruise line was outweighed by its prejudicial effect in seaman's Jones Act and unseaworthiness action to recover damages for injuries sustained when he fell down a flight of stairs. Jones Act, 46 App.U.S.C.A. § 688.

> Dolphin Cruise Line, Inc. v. Stassinopoulos, 731 So.2d 708, rehearing denied.

☞**29(5.14). Weight and sufficiency of evidence.**

U.S.Fla. 1959. In action by seaman against shipowner for damages and maintenance and cure based on claim that injuries sustained by seaman when he was pitched into the air and fell back to the deck activated or aggravated a previously latent tubercular condition, the jury's power to draw inference that aggravation of seaman's tubercular condition was in fact caused by the accident, was not impaired by failure of any medical witness to testify that it was in fact the cause, or by lack of medical unanimity as to respective likelihood of potential causes of aggravation, or by fact that other potential causes of aggravation existed and were not conclusively negated by the proofs. Jones Act, 46 U.S.C.A. § 688.

> Sentilles v. Inter-Caribbean Shipping Corp., 80 S.Ct. 173, 361 U.S. 107, 4 L.Ed.2d 142.

C.A.11 (Fla.) 1986. Seaman injured when boot he was wearing became entangled on rotating spool of shrimp boat winch failed to satisfy burden of showing, for purpose of Jones Act claims, that placement of winch upon boat was proximate cause of injuries, where placement of winch was typical for boat of that size and type, and where turned-down hip boots that seaman was wearing substantially contributed to injury. Jones Act, 46 U.S.C.A. § 688.

> Nichols v. Barwick, 792 F.2d 1520.

C.A.5 (Fla.) 1973. There was ample evidence to support jury's verdict that seaman, who was hired to captain yacht and who injured his back when he slipped and fell on oil and grease, was not contributorily negligent in neglecting to clean up the oil and grease which precipitated his fall.

> Price v. Mosler, 483 F.2d 275.

C.A.5 (Fla.) 1972. Plaintiff suing for death of barge owners' employee, who was found dead in water under barge where he had been repairing leaks, proved the death had been caused by unseaworthiness, in case in which owners suggested that employee may have died of a heart attack.

> Weeks v. Alonzo Cothron, Inc., 466 F.2d 578, appeal after remand 493 F.2d 538.

C.A.5 (Fla.) 1970. In view of evidence that winch overrides were neither dangerous nor condition that demanded correction to permit completion of shrimp trawler's mission, evidence sustained finding that shrimp trawler was not unseaworthy by virtue of fact that override occurred while winches were being operated to bring in nets. Jones Act, 46 U.S.C.A. § 688.

> Little v. Green, 428 F.2d 1061, certiorari denied 91 S.Ct. 366, 400 U.S. 964, 27 L.Ed.2d 384.

Evidence that shrimp trawler's winches were customary in trade did not establish that vessel was seaworthy. Jones Act, 46 U.S.C.A. § 688.

> Little v. Green, 428 F.2d 1061, certiorari denied 91 S.Ct. 366, 400 U.S. 964, 27 L.Ed.2d 384.

Evidence in action under Jones Act sustained finding that captain who was in wheelhouse at time seaman was injured while winching in net was in proper location. Jones Act, 46 U.S.C.A. § 688.

> Little v. Green, 428 F.2d 1061, certiorari denied 91 S.Ct. 366, 400 U.S. 964, 27 L.Ed.2d 384.

Evidence in action by seaman to recover for injuries sustained while winching in nets failed to establish that shrimp trawler and appurtenances were not reasonably fit for their intended use. Jones Act, 46 U.S.C.A. § 688.

> Little v. Green, 428 F.2d 1061, certiorari denied 91 S.Ct. 366, 400 U.S. 964, 27 L.Ed.2d 384.

Evidence in action by seaman to recover for injury sustained when leg was caught in winch established that injury was attributable to contrivance brought aboard ship by seaman and used by him at time of injury. Jones Act, 46 U.S.C.A. § 688.

> Little v. Green, 428 F.2d 1061, certiorari denied 91 S.Ct. 366, 400 U.S. 964, 27 L.Ed.2d 384.

C.A.5 (Fla.) 1966. Evidence supported trial court's finding in consolidated actions for death and injury to seamen that shipowner breached the duty to furnish a seaworthy vessel when master allowed inexperienced seamen to use heavy equipment to move cargo about the vessel on the high seas in anticipation of unloading and allowed an improper and dangerous splice to be made in the cable and that such unseaworthy condition was proximate cause of the injuries and death when the cable split and dropped heavy machinery on seamen. Death on the High Seas Act, §§ 1–8, 46 U.S.C.A. §§ 761–768; Jones Act, 46 U.S.C.A. § 688.

> Symonette Shipyards, Limited v. Clark, 365 F.2d 464, certiorari denied 87 S.Ct. 1690, 387 U.S. 908, 18 L.Ed.2d 625.

Evidence in consolidated actions for death and injuries to seamen caused by unseaworthy vessel supported finding that deceased seaman's negligence in making defective cable splice contributed 50% to his death and other seaman's negligence in walking under trailer suspended by defective cable contributed 25% to his injury. Death on the High Seas Act, §§ 1–8, 46

U.S.C.A. §§ 761–768; Jones Act, 46 U.S.C.A. § 688.

Symonette Shipyards, Limited v. Clark, 365 F.2d 464, certiorari denied 87 S.Ct. 1690, 387 U.S. 908, 18 L.Ed.2d 625.

C.A.5 (Fla.) 1965. Evidence sustained finding that yacht in port had not been undermanned and hence not unseaworthy at time seaman, who had suffered slight sprain to his left arm requiring him to carry his arm in a sling, had been injured when he slipped on gangway while carrying garbage pail causing serious aggravation to original sprain, and that there had been no negligence in requiring him to perform housekeeping duties.

Carver v. Partlow Corp., 344 F.2d 932.

C.A.5 (Fla.) 1963. Evidence supported finding that libellant did not receive injuries while aboard ship and therefore failed to prove injury due to unseaworthiness.

Todd v. Peninsular & Occidental S. S. Co., 326 F.2d 196.

C.A.5 (Fla.) 1963. Findings that seaman suing shipowner for injuries sustained in affray with fellow crew member was himself the aggressor whose own gross and willful misconduct in form of drunkenness was sole and proximate cause of injuries and that there was no negligence on part of shipowner or unseaworthiness were warranted.

McConville v. Florida Towing Corp., 321 F.2d 162.

C.A.5 (Fla.) 1963. Evidence in libel in rem and in personam for injuries sustained when libelant fell in shower on a Panamanian vessel in foreign port sustained trial court's finding that injuries had been proximately caused by employer's failure to exercise due care and finding as to nature and extent of injuries and damages.

McCormick Shipping Corp. v. Tomacen, 316 F.2d 730.

C.A.5 (Fla.) 1962. Circumstantial evidence warranted inference of negligent breach of duty by dredge owner proximately causing death by drowning of 24-year-old farm boy whose nautical career had begun only 10 days earlier and whose

body was found floating in water after he had been last seen walking toward shore on 10-inch plank walkway over discharge line without life vest on.

Davis v. Parkhill-Goodloe Co., 302 F.2d 489.

C.A.5 (Fla.) 1961. In action for injuries sustained by crew member of shrimper when his fingers were pinched off by net towing cable, master's testimony that a two-man crew was customary did not preclude finding that vessel with two-man crew was unseaworthy because of insufficient crew.

June T., Inc. v. King, 290 F.2d 404.

In weighing testimony of master who testified for owner in seaman's personal injury action, master was in a position similar to that of a "managing agent" within Civil Procedure Rule permitting interrogation of managing agent of an adverse party. Fed.Rules Civ.Proc. rule 43(b), 28 U.S.C.A.

June T., Inc. v. King, 290 F.2d 404.

In action for loss of crew member's fingers crushed by net towing cable, evidence that third crew member had been removed because of intoxication and that hence there was no one available to stop winches in case of trouble with the cables sustained finding that vessel was unseaworthy because of insufficient crew.

June T., Inc. v. King, 290 F.2d 404.

C.A.5 (Fla.) 1961. Evidence in Jones Act action for death of seaman who disappeared from vessel supported finding that plaintiff had failed to establish that defendant was guilty of any negligence proximately causing death. Jones Act, 46 U.S.C.A. § 688.

Barrios v. Waterman S. S. Corp., 290 F.2d 310.

N.D.Fla. 1956. In action to recover under the Jones Act for injuries sustained by an assistant port engineer for defendant when changing a battery on a tug on the ground that services of two men were needed and that the employer failed to furnish the additional help necessary, evidence established that plaintiff was negligent and that such was proximate cause of his own injury when he placed his foot on a a pipe and slipped when he was aware that he was going to lift a battery to move it out of position. Jones Act, 46 U.S.C.A. § 688.

> Ouzts v. A. P. Ward & Son, Inc., 146 F.Supp. 733.

N.D.Fla. 1955. In action under Jones Act for damages for injuries to seaman's health wherein seaman alleged the unseaworthiness of vessel he was working on at time health was impaired, seaman failed to carry burden of establishing unseaworthy condition of vessel. Jones Act, 46 U.S.C.A. § 688.

> Knight v. E. E. Saunders & Co., 134 F.Supp. 7, affirmed 231 F.2d 448.

S.D.Fla. 1963. Evidence failed to establish negligence on part of yacht owners in failing to warn person performing normal crew service or to give him instructions concerning pedestal winch which caused injury.

> Petition of Read, 224 F.Supp. 241.

Fla. 1962. In action under Jones Act against tug owner for death of employee, there was evidence of record from which, with reason, the conclusion could have been drawn that the tug owner had failed to furnish the employee a safe means to board and leave the tug and that this negligence had a part in the employee's death from drowning. Jones Act, 46 U.S.C.A. § 688.

> Edmundson v. Hamilton, 148 So.2d 262, 99 A.L.R.2d 279.

Fla.App. 1 Dist. 1960. Evidence was sufficient to sustain finding that operator of fishing boat was negligent in putting out with a shorthanded crew and that injury to seaman was a result of operator's negligence. Jones Act, 46 U.S.C.A. § 688.

> Fribley v. Bebe, Inc., 121 So.2d 446.

Fla.App. 3 Dist. 2011. Although a single incident of negligence is certainly not conclusive evidence of crew incompetence for purposes of finding a ship unseaworthy, such evidence is probative.

> Flueras v. Royal Caribbean Cruises, Ltd., 69 So.3d 1101.

Demonstrated compliance with relevant policies, procedures, regulations, statutes, and/or industry practices is not prima facie evidence of seaworthiness.

> Flueras v. Royal Caribbean Cruises, Ltd., 69 So.3d 1101.

Fla.App. 3 Dist. 2001. The plaintiff has a featherweight burden of proof in establishing a claim for Jones Act negligence. Jones Act, 46 App.U.S.C.A. § 688.

> Lane v. Tripp, 788 So.2d 351.

Fla.App. 3 Dist. 1986. Uncontradicted testimony of witness that fumes which emanated from oil-based paint while he was painting ship's generator room without ventilation caused him to become dizzy, resulting in his subsequent slip and fall, established prima facie case in Jones Act/unseaworthiness proceeding; no expert testimony was required. 46 U.S.C.A. § 688.

> Solano v. Carnival Cruise Lines, Inc., 491 So.2d 325.

⌐29(5.15). **Trial in general.**

For other cases see earlier editions of this digest, the Decennial Digests, and WESTLAW.

⌐29(5.16). **Questions for jury.**

C.A.11 (Fla.) 1990. Whether worker qualifies for seaman status under Jones Act is ordinarily question for trier of fact; question of seaman status should only be removed from trier of fact (by summary judgment or directed verdict) in rare circumstances, and even marginal Jones Act claims should be submitted to jury. Jones Act, 46 U.S.C.A.App. § 688.

> Hurst v. Pilings & Structures, Inc., 896 F.2d 504, rehearing denied 912 F.2d 1470.

C.A.5 (Fla.) 1970. Whether vessel owner supplied sufficient crew to accomplish task of bringing in trawl nets was question of fact for jury in action by seaman under Jones Act. Jones Act, 46 U.S.C.A. § 688.

> Little v. Green, 428 F.2d 1061, certiorari denied 91 S.Ct. 366, 400 U.S. 964, 27 L.Ed.2d 384.

C.A.5 (Fla.) 1962. Evidence on whether negligence of dredge owner, in not giving inexperienced seaman adequate instructions with respect to wearing of life vest proximately caused death of seaman whose body was found in water after he had last been seen traversing 10-inch plank over discharge line and on damages sustained by parents presented questions for trier of fact. Jones Act, 46 U.S.C.A. § 688.

> Davis v. Parkhill-Goodloe Co., 302 F.2d 489.

C.A.5 (Fla.) 1961. Evidence in widow's action for death of seaman who was stabbed by shipmate with switchblade knife was sufficient to take to jury questions whether switchblade knife was dangerous weapon and whether shipowner should have known that shipmate had knife and should have taken prudent action to protect crew, but was insufficient to take to jury question of seaman's negligence. Act July 27, 1866, §§ 1, 2, 46 U.S.C.A. § 710; 15 U.S.C.A. §§ 1241(b), 1242, 1243; 18 U.S.C.A. § 2277; Jones Act, 46 U.S.C.A. § 688; 46 U.S.C.A. §§ 563–568, 713.

> Fall v. Esso Standard Oil Co., 297 F.2d 411, certiorari denied 83 S.Ct. 24, 371 U.S. 814, 9 L.Ed.2d 55.

C.A.5 (Fla.) 1961. Seaman, who was only crew member other than master, and who lost three fingers while seeking to prevent net towing cable from piling up on winch drums, was not contributorily negligent as a matter of law in seeking to fix cable with his hand.

> June T., Inc. v. King, 290 F.2d 404.

C.A.5 (Fla.) 1958. In action by chief engineer against shipowner for damages and for maintenance and cure for pulmonary tuberculosis which became evident after accident on shipboard, evidence was insufficient to take to jury question whether tubercular condition was probably caused by the incident on shipboard.

> Inter-Caribbean Shipping Corp. v. Sentilles, 256 F.2d 156, certiorari granted 79 S.Ct. 604, 359 U.S. 923, 3 L.Ed.2d 627, reversed 80 S.Ct. 173, 361 U.S. 107, 4 L.Ed.2d 142.

C.A.5 (Fla.) 1956. In action under the Jones Act for death of seamen as result of alleged negligent loading causing unseaworthiness of a vessel presumably lost at sea, evidence was sufficient to make out a case for the jury on the ground that the jury could have inferred from all of the plaintiffs' testimony that loss of vessel and deaths of the decedents were due to the unseaworthiness caused by the negligent loading of the vessel. Jones Act, 46 U.S.C.A. § 688.

> Roth v. Bird, 239 F.2d 257.

M.D.Fla. 2005. Where plaintiff joins Jones Act claim with admiralty or maritime claims that arise out of one set of facts, all claims must be submitted to jury. Jones Act, 46 App.U.S.C.A. § 688.

> Marmac, LLC v. Reed, 232 F.R.D. 409.

M.D.Fla. 1993. There can only be a determination, as a matter of law, that a plaintiff does not qualify as a seaman where there is no evidentiary basis for a different finding; however, when conflicting inferences may be drawn from undisputed underlying facts, determination of whether individual is a seaman must be made by fact finder.

> Antoniou v. Thiokol Corp. Group Long Term Disability Plan (Plan No. 503), 829 F.Supp. 1323.

S.D.Fla. 2004. Whether a borrowed servant relationship exists between a seaman and a defendant against whom recovery is sought is a question of law.

> Wai v. Rainbow Holdings, 350 F.Supp.2d 1019.

S.D.Fla. 1965. Where question of whether person was seaman within meaning of Jones Act is question of law it should be determined by court. Jones Act, 46 U.S.C.A. § 688.

> Bodden v. Coordinated Caribbean Transport, Inc., 249 F.Supp. 561, reversed 369 F.2d 273, 5 A.L.R. Fed. 668.

Fla. 1962. In action brought under the Jones Act against tug owner for failure to provide safe place of work which allegedly resulted in death of employee, the amount of proof necessary to raise a jury question was of a different degree from that necessary to support an action based on common law negligence, and the test of a jury case was simply whether the proof justified with reason the conclusion that the employer's negligence played any part, even the slightest, in producing the death. Jones Act, 46 U.S.C.A. § 688.

> Edmundson v. Hamilton, 148 So.2d 262, 99 A.L.R.2d 279.

Evidence as to authority of relief captain who was in command to move the tug if it was moored in an unsafe place was sufficient for jury in action under Jones Act against tug owner for death of relief captain who was discovered drowned where theory of action was that tug owner had failed to furnish relief captain a safe means to board and leave the tug. Jones Act, 46 U.S.C.A. § 688.

>   Edmundson v. Hamilton, 148 So.2d 262, 99 A.L.R.2d 279.

Fla.App. 1 Dist. 1960. Under the Jones Act and the Federal Employers' Liability Act it is not necessary to show that employer's negligence was the proximate cause of the injury or death complained of, but it is sufficient to establish a jury question by simply showing some negligence on part of employer, coupled by direct or circumstantial evidence to injury or death of employee. Jones Act, 46 U.S.C.A. § 688; Federal Employers' Liability Act, § 1 et seq., 45 U.S.C.A. § 51 et seq.

>   Gaymon v. Quinn Menhaden Fisheries of Tex., Inc., 118 So.2d 42, 81 A.L.R.2d 1165.

In action under the Jones Act by administratrix of estate of deceased seaman against employer for wrongful death of seaman, who allegedly fell from fishing boat docked at employer's plant and drowned, question whether employer was guilty of negligence which was the proximate cause of the seaman's death was for jury. Jones Act, 46 U.S.C.A. § 688.

>   Gaymon v. Quinn Menhaden Fisheries of Tex., Inc., 118 So.2d 42, 81 A.L.R.2d 1165.

Fla.App. 3 Dist. 2011. Whether a vessel is unseaworthy is a factual question to be decided on a case-by-case basis.

>   Flueras v. Royal Caribbean Cruises, Ltd., 69 So.3d 1101.

Unseaworthiness is generally a question of fact reserved for the jury.

>   Flueras v. Royal Caribbean Cruises, Ltd., 69 So.3d 1101.

Fla.App. 3 Dist. 1996. Motion for a directed verdict on unseaworthiness claim may be granted only where reasonable minds could not differ on question of whether unseaworthy condition of vessel caused plaintiff's injury.

>   Waggon-Dixon v. Royal Caribbean Cruises, Ltd., 679 So.2d 811, rehearing denied.

Whether vessel owner failed to properly train its cabin stewards how to carry heavy objects on stairs, thereby breaching its duty to provide seaworthy vessel, was for jury in injured steward's unseaworthiness action.

>   Waggon-Dixon v. Royal Caribbean Cruises, Ltd., 679 So.2d 811, rehearing denied.

Injured seaman's uncontradicted testimony regarding wet, slippery condition of stairs on which he allegedly fell was sufficient to establish prima facie case of unseaworthiness, and thus issue of defective condition of ship was for jury.

>   Waggon-Dixon v. Royal Caribbean Cruises, Ltd., 679 So.2d 811, rehearing denied.

Fla.App. 3 Dist. 1992. Question of seaman's comparative negligence creates jury question only when there is some evidence to support it.

>   Cuadros v. Carnival Cruise Lines, Inc., 604 So.2d 861.

Fla.App. 3 Dist. 1988. In a Jones Act case, a simple showing of some negligence on part of employer coupled by direct or circumstantial evidence to the injury sustained by employee creates a jury question. Jones Act, 46 U.S.C.App. § 688.

>   Dos Santos v. Ajax Nav. Corp., 531 So.2d 231, certiorari dismissed 109 S.Ct. 1304, 489 U.S. 1048, 103 L.Ed.2d 574.

Question of fact for jury regarding employer's negligence was created by evidence showing that seaman was injured when he slipped on butter in crowded area of ship's kitchen, and that area was restricted to ship's personnel. Jones Act, 46 U.S.C.App. § 688.

>   Dos Santos v. Ajax Nav. Corp., 531 So.2d 231, certiorari dismissed 109 S.Ct. 1304, 489 U.S. 1048, 103 L.Ed.2d 574.

Whether seaman, who slipped on butter in crowded area of ship's kitchen was guilty of comparative negligence, was for jury. Jones Act, 46 U.S.C.App. § 688.

> Dos Santos v. Ajax Nav. Corp., 531 So.2d 231, certiorari dismissed 109 S.Ct. 1304, 489 U.S. 1048, 103 L.Ed.2d 574.

Seaman's claim of unseaworthiness should have gone to jury against ship owner only, and not against suppliers of food and beverage personnel.

> Dos Santos v. Ajax Nav. Corp., 531 So.2d 231, certiorari dismissed 109 S.Ct. 1304, 489 U.S. 1048, 103 L.Ed.2d 574.

Fla.App. 3 Dist. 1986. Issue of whether seaman's absence from ship was justified was question for jury in action by injured seaman who had signed engagement articles with vessel and was under obligation to vessel at time he left, and desertion instruction was proper.

> Conde v. Marlu Nav. Co., Ltd., 495 So.2d 847.

Fla.App. 3 Dist. 1986. Evidence in Jones Act/unseaworthiness proceeding, including plaintiff's testimony that fumes which emanated from oil-based paint while he was painting ship's generator room without ventilation caused him to become dizzy, resulting in his subsequent slip and fall, was for jury. 46 U.S.C.A. § 688.

> Solano v. Carnival Cruise Lines, Inc., 491 So.2d 325.

Fla.App. 3 Dist. 1977. Under Jones Act, it is not necessary to show employer's negligence was proximate cause of injury, but it is sufficient to establish jury question by simply showing some negligence on the part of the employer coupled by direct or circumstantial evidence to the injury of the employee. Jones Act, 46 U.S.C.A. § 688.

> Trochez v. Holland-American Cruise Lines, 353 So.2d 864.

Fla.App. 3 Dist. 1970. Evidence, in action for injuries suffered by rodman when he fell through a hatch on board dredge on which he was working, was for jury on issue of shipowner's negligence or unseaworthiness of his vessel.

> Bowen v. Seaward Dredging Corp., 242 So.2d 151.

Fla.App. 4 Dist. 1972. Where undisputed facts in federal maritime action con-clusively demonstrate that the individual concerned is or is not a seaman, the trial court may properly remove the issue from the jury's consideration by directing a verdict as to the individual's status.

> Potashnick-Badgett Dredging Inc. v. Whitfield, 269 So.2d 36, certiorari denied Potashnick-Badgett Dredging, Incorporated v. Trans-State Dredging Company, 272 So.2d 819, certiorari denied 272 So.2d 820.

⌧29(5.17). Instructions.

C.A.11 (Fla.) 1982. Since Jones Act employee in negligence action against employer was entitled to recover against either of several tort-feasors without regard to percentage of fault, it was error for trial court to distract jurors' attention by requiring allocation of degree of fault between employer and nonparty. Jones Act, 46 U.S.C.A. § 688.

> Ebanks v. Great Lakes Dredge & Dock Co., 688 F.2d 716, rehearing denied 693 F.2d 135, certiorari denied 103 S.Ct. 1774, 460 U.S. 1083, 76 L.Ed.2d 346, on remand Complaint of Chevron Transport Corp., 613 F.Supp. 1428, affirmed in part, reversed in part Self v. Great Lakes Dredge & Dock Co., 832 F.2d 1540, rehearing denied 837 F.2d 1095, rehearing denied 837 F.2d 1095, rehearing denied Great Lakes Dredge & Dock Co. v. Chevron Shipping Co., 837 F.2d 1095, certiorari denied Great Lakes Dredge and Dock Co. v. Chevron Transport Corp., 108 S.Ct. 2017, 486 U.S. 1033, 100 L.Ed.2d 604.

Fla.App. 1 Dist. 1983. Where seaman was simply ordered by his superior to use the capstan, not to use it improperly, he was not "carrying out orders given to him by his superior" and thus trial court properly refused to instruct in seaman's personal injury action that a seaman may not be negligent for carrying out orders given to him by his superior that result in his own injury, even if he recognizes possible danger.

> Fernandez v. Sea-Land Service, Inc., 426 So.2d 1249.

Fla.App. 3 Dist. 1999. Since "scope of employment" issue was properly submitted to the jury in rental car company's third-party action against shipowner arising out of automobile accident involving rental car driven by shipowner's employee, confusing instruction on respondeat superior liability, unsupported by the facts in evidence, was not harmless error.

Carnival Corp. v. Hertz Corp., 748 So.2d 323.

Fla.App. 3 Dist. 1986.   Issue of whether seaman's absence from ship was justified was question for jury in action by injured seaman who had signed engagement articles with vessel and was under obligation to vessel at time he left, and desertion instruction was proper.

Conde v. Marlu Nav. Co., Ltd., 495 So.2d 847.

🔑29(5.18). Verdict and findings.

C.A.5 (Fla.) 1961.   In seaman's personal injury action, where pretrial order in specifying particulars of unseaworthiness contained catchall charge that "vessel was otherwise unseaworthy", and testimony on issue of size of crew was received early in the trial and both sides utilized opportunity of offering evidence pro and con on the matter, finding of unseaworthiness because of insufficient crew was not subject to objection that finding was on issue not in the case.

June T., Inc. v. King, 290 F.2d 404.

M.D.Fla. 1985.   A claim under the Jones Act, 46 U.S.C.A. § 688, requires a finding of both negligent breach of duty and proximate cause.

Complaint of Chevron Transport Corp., 613 F.Supp. 1428, affirmed in part, reversed in part Self v. Great Lakes Dredge & Dock Co., 832 F.2d 1540, rehearing denied 837 F.2d 1095, rehearing denied 837 F.2d 1095, rehearing denied Great Lakes Dredge & Dock Co. v. Chevron Shipping Co., 837 F.2d 1095, certiorari denied Great Lakes Dredge and Dock Co. v. Chevron Transport Corp., 108 S.Ct. 2017, 486 U.S. 1033, 100 L.Ed.2d 604.

S.D.Fla. 1982.   Jury verdict on counts of unseaworthiness and abandonment were not treated as advisory and district court would not determine damages to yacht captain who sued owner charging liability under Jones Act, unsea-

worthiness and abandonment when captain was imprisoned by Greek authorities after the authorities found the owner's hashish locked in the owner's cabin safe. Jones Act, 46 U.S.C.A. § 688.

Murray v. Hunt, 552 F.Supp. 234.

🔑29(5.19)–31. *For other cases see earlier editions of this digest, the Decennial Digests, and WESTLAW.*

🔑32. **Wages and effects of deceased seamen.**

M.D.Fla. 1977.   Statute enacted to provide expedient, informal, and inexpensive method for protecting the disposing of deceased's seaman's money and personal effects was to be construed liberally to effectuate its purpose and to benefit its intended objects, and court had wide discretion to do so.   46 U.S.C.A. §§ 621–628.

Matter of Jama, 436 F.Supp. 963.

Under statute providing that when wages and personal effects of deceased seaman exceed $1,500, wages and personal effects must be delivered to the "legal personal representatives" of the deceased, the term "legal personal representatives" should be understood in the flexible context of general admiralty legislation, not in the technical common-law sense that has developed in estate and property law.   46 U.S.C.A. § 627.

Matter of Jama, 436 F.Supp. 963.

Where deceased seaman's widow and children were all citizens and domiciliaries of Kenya, where wages, valuables, and personal effects of deceased seaman greatly exceeded $1,500, and where widow was unable to acquire appointment of herself as administratrix of decedent's estate under Kenya law, court would adopt and adapt law of Florida in order to comply with federal statute's command to deliver deceased seaman's assets to "legal personal representatives of the deceased," and thus Florida personal legal representative would be appointed and would be ordered to distribute decedent's assets to beneficiaries under Florida law.   46 U.S.C.A. §§ 621–628, 627; West's F.S.A. §§ 733.302, 733.602.

Matter of Jama, 436 F.Supp. 963.

☞33. Penalties and forfeitures for violations of regulations.

S.D.Fla. 1994.   Statute prohibiting persons from receiving remuneration for providing seamen with employment did not create private right of action for seaman who allegedly paid illegal fee; neither statutory language nor legislative history indicated congressional intent to provide such right, and review of chapter containing statute indicated that where Congress intended to provide seamen with private right of action it did so explicitly.   46 U.S.C.A. §§ 10301, 10314.

Gary v. D. Agustini & Asociados, S.A., 865 F.Supp. 818.

☞34. Offenses.

For other cases see earlier editions of this digest, the Decennial Digests, and WESTLAW.

For later cases
see
Same Topic and Key Number
in Pocket Part

SEARCHES AND SEIZURES

SUBJECTS INCLUDED

Examination of persons or places for discovery of property stolen or otherwise unlawfully obtained or held, or of evidence of the commission of an offense

Taking into legal custody such property or proofs, or property forfeited for violation of law

Nature and scope of such remedies in general

Constitutional and statutory provisions relating to such searches and seizures

In what cases and to and against whom and in respect of what property they are allowed

Jurisdiction over and proceedings to obtain searches or seizures

Issuance, requisites and validity of search warrants and warrants for seizure, etc.

Execution of warrants, making searches and seizures, proceedings to enforce seizures, and disposition of property seized

Liabilities for wrongfully procuring or making searches or seizures

SUBJECTS EXCLUDED AND COVERED BY OTHER TOPICS

[Note exceptions indicated below, as at ☞13]

Arrest, searches incidental to, see ARREST

Due process violations, see CONSTITUTIONAL LAW XXVII(G)23

Environmental protection of plants and wildlife, see ENVIRONMENTAL LAW ☞546

Evidence wrongfully obtained, see CRIMINAL LAW ☞392.1 et seq. and EVIDENCE ☞154

Forfeiture for crime, grounds, see FORFEITURES and specific topics involving forfeitures

International law, operation as to seizures, see INTERNATIONAL LAW

Military cases decided by military courts, see MILITARY JUSTICE in the Federal Practice Digests

Particular objects, subjects, or purposes at search or seizure:

Automobile traffic offenses, search after stop or arrest, see AUTOMOBILES ☞349

Coast Guard searches of vessels, see SHIPPING ☞9

Customs or border searches, see CUSTOMS DUTIES ☞126

Electronic surveillance, see TELECOMMUNICATIONS ☞491 et seq

Fires, see FIRES ☞9

For detailed references to other topics, see Descriptive-Word Index

---

Analysis

For detailed references to other topics, see Descriptive-Word Index

TABLE 1

KEY NUMBER TRANSLATION TABLE

SEARCHES AND SEIZURES TO
SEARCHES AND SEIZURES (REVISED)

The topic SEARCHES AND SEIZURES has been extensively revised. This table lists key numbers in the original topic along with the key numbers in the revised topic at which cases are presently digested. The absence of a key number indicates that there is no useful parallel.

For the present classification of a particular case, see the Table of Cases.

Searches and Seizures Key Number	Searches and Seizures (Revised) Key Number	Searches and Seizures Key Number	Searches and Seizures (Revised) Key Number
1	11, 13.1–22, 30, 31.1	7(1)	11, 12, 23–25.1, 30–32, 35, 47.1–51, 53.1, 54, 57, 58, 78–80.1, 82
2	12	7(2)	31.1, 32
3.1	30, 80.1, 101, 102	7(3)	31.1
3.2	24, 42.1, 43, 45, 58, 59, 79, 101	7(4)	31.1, 33, 34
3.3	11, 24, 43, 53–55, 57, 58, 79, 101	7(5)	24, 101, 108, 112, 113.1
3.3(1)	11, 24, 25.1, 28, 36.1–39, 42.1–45, 53–55, 57, 58, 67.1, 72, 73, 78, 79, 101	7(6)	81, 103.1, 104, 109, 110, 113.1
		7(7)	107, 108, 111, 112, 113.1–121.1
3.3(2)	40.1, 41, 43, 44, 72, 79, 101	7(8)	123–127
3.3(3)	40.1, 43, 72, 73, 78, 101	7(9)	141–143, 147.1–149
3.3(4)	43, 47.1–51, 63, 69, 101, 149	7(10)	11, 24–30, 47.1–51, 53, 54, 56, 59, 60.1–63, 65–67.1, 72, 75, 78–80.1, 82, and other topics (see scope note, above).
3.3(5)	43, 44, 46, 67.1, 70, 71, 101		
3.3(6)	59, 62–66, 68, 69, 80.1, 101		
3.3(7)	62, 64–66, 69, 101	7(11)	73
3.3(8)	53, 54, 56, 58, 73, 80.1–82, 101	7(12)	52, 55, 58, 60.1, 62, 70, 71, 78; Arrest ⭖63.5(8); Automobiles ⭖349
3.3(9)	101, 192, 195, 201		
3.4	81, 101, 103.1, 104, 110, 112, 120, 122–127, 129, 142, 144	7(14)	Prisons ⭖4(7)
		7(15)	76
3.5	101, 103.1, 104, 106, 107–110, 121.1, 128, 129	7(17)	Game ⭖10
		7(18)	74
3.6	101, 108, 109, 111, 112, 120, 121.1	7(19)	Intoxicating Liquors ⭖244–249
3.6(1)	105.1–109, 111, 112, 117, 120, 121.1	7(20)	Drugs and Narcotics ⭖181–189, 198
3.6(2)	105.1, 108, 112–114, 117, 120–122	7(22)	77
3.6(3, 4)	111–121.1	7(24)	67.1–72
3.6(5)	111–122	7(25)	75
3.7	123–129	7(26)	161–165
3.8(1)	121.1, 141–147.1, 150	7(27)	171–178, 179.1–185, 186, 191, 194, 197, 198, 201
3.8(2)	147.1–149		
3.9	191, 192.1, 195.1, 196, 199, 200–202	7(28)	179.1–185, 194, 198, 201
4	83	7(29)	192.1–194
5	84	8	85
7	13.1–22	9	191 et seq.

TABLE 2

KEY NUMBER TRANSLATION TABLE

SEARCHES AND SEIZURES (REVISED) TO SEARCHES AND SEIZURES

Listing the key numbers in the revised topic SEARCHES AND SEIZURES with the key numbers in the original topic, or other topics, where similar cases were digested.

Searches and Seizures (Revised) Key Number	Searches and Seizures Key Number	Searches and Seizures (Revised) Key Number	Searches and Seizures Key Number
11	1, 3.3, 3.3(1), 7(1, 10)	82	3.3(8), 7(1, 10)
12	2, 7(1)	83	4
13.1–22	1, 7	84	5
23	7(1, 10)	85	8
24	3.2, 3.3, 3.3(1), 7(1, 5, 10)	101	3.1–3.6, 7(5)
25.1	3.3(1), 7(1, 10)	102	3.1 et seq.
26, 27	7(10)	103.1, 104	3.4, 3.5, 7(6)
28	3.3(1), 7(10)	105.1	3.6(1, 2)
29	7(10)	106	3.5, 3.6(1)
30	1, 3.1, 7(1, 10)	107	3.5, 3.6(1), 7(7)
31.1	1, 7(1–4)	108	3.5, 3.6–3.6(2), 7(5, 7)
32	7(1, 2)	109	3.5–3.6(1), 7(6)
33, 34	7(4)	110	3.4, 3.5, 7(6)
35	7(1)	111	3.6–3.6(5), 7(7)
36.1–39	3.3(1)	112	3.4, 3.6–3.6(5), 7(5, 7)
40.1	3.3(2, 3)	113.1	3.6(2–5), 7(5–7)
41	3.3(2)	114	3.6(2–5)
42.1	3.2, 3.3(1)	115.1	3.6(3–5), 7(7)
43	3.2–3.3(5)	116	3.6(3–5)
44	3.3(1, 2, 5)	117	3.6(1–5), 7(7)
45	3.2, 3.3(1)	118, 119	3.6(3–5)
46	3.3(5)	120	3.4, 3.6–3.6(5)
47.1–51	3.3(4), 7(1, 10)	121.1	3.5, 3.6–3.6(5), 3.8(1), 7(7)
52	7(12)	122	3.4, 3.6(2, 5)
53.1, 54	3.3, 3.3(1, 8), 7(1, 10)	123.1–127	3.4, 3.7, 7(8)
55	3.3, 3.3(1), 7(10, 12)	128	3.5, 3.7
56	3.3(8), 7(10)	129	3.4 et seq.;
57	3.3, 3.3(1), 7(1)		Inspection 1, 5
58	3.2–3.3(1), 3.3(8), 7(1, 12)	141	3.8(1), 7(9)
59	3.2, 3.3(6), 7(10)	142	3.4, 3.8(1), 7(9)
60.1	3.3(6), 7(10, 12)	143.1	3.8(1), 7(9)
61	7(10)	144	3.4, 3.8(1)
62	3.3(6, 7), 7(10, 12)	145.1, 146	3.8(1)
63	3.3(4, 6), 7(10)	147.1	3.8(1, 2), 7(9)
64	3.3(6, 7)	148	3.8(2), 7(9)
65, 66	3.3(6, 7), 7(10)	149	3.3(4), 3.8(2), 7(9)
67.1	3.3(1, 5), 7(24)	150	3.8(1)
68	3.3(6), 7(10, 24)	161–165	7(26)
69	3.3(4, 6, 7), 7(24)	171–178	7(27)
70, 71	3.3(5), 7(12, 24)	179.1–185	7(27, 28)
72	3.3(1–3), 7(10, 24)	186	7(27)
73	3.3(1, 3, 8), 7(11)	191	3.9, 7(27), 9
74	7(18)	192.1	3.3(9), 3.9, 7(29), 9
75	7(10, 25)	193	3.9, 7(29), 9
76	7(15)	194	7(27–29), 9
77	7(22)	195.1	3.3(9), 3.9, 9
78	3.3(1, 3), 7(1, 10, 12)	196	3.9, 9
79	3.2–3.3(2), 7(1, 10);	197	7(27), 9
	Inspection 1, 3, 5	198	7(27, 28), 9
		199, 200	3.9, 9
80.1	3.1, 3.3(6, 8), 7(1, 10)	201	3.3(9), 3.9, 7(27, 28), 9
81	3.3(8), 3.4, 7(6)	202	3.9, 9

⟐1–9.

SEARCHES AND SEIZURES Key Numbers 1 to 9 are no longer valid and have been replaced by new Key Numbers. See topic analysis and translation tables.

I. IN GENERAL.

Research Notes

Search and seizures; warrants, see West's Federal Forms.

See Wright & Miller, Federal Practice and Procedure: Civil.

See Wright, Federal Practice and Procedure: Criminal.

⟐11. In general.

C.A.5 (Fla.) 1978. Greater the intrusion, the greater must be the reason for conducting a search that results in such invasion. U.S.C.A.Const. Amend. 4.

U.S. v. Afanador, 567 F.2d 1325.

S.D.Fla. 1949. Where plaintiffs in conducting their business of selling at retail jewelry, rugs, etc., adopted method of effecting sales which embraced some of the feature of public auction sales but differed in that plaintiffs permitted patrons who submitted bids to return merchandise within one year period and procure refund of full amount paid, application of ordinance of defendant municipality prohibiting auction sales of certain goods after six p.m. to plaintiffs and their methods of doing business would be violative of rights guaranteed to plaintiffs by Federal Constitution. U.S.C.A.Const. Amends. 4, 5, 14.

Zaconick v. City of Hollywood, 85 F.Supp. 52.

Fla. 2006. Essentially, an "impoundment" is the temporary taking of tangible, personal property; a "forfeiture" is the permanent taking of real or personal property (tangible or intangible).

City of Hollywood v. Mulligan, 934 So.2d 1238, on remand 4 So.3d 1258, rehearing granted.

Fla. 1976. If Florida law enforcement officers engage in violations of fundamental rights of Floridians, Supreme Court will not hesitate to override their acts in favor of rights conferred in Florida Constitution. West's F.S.A.Const. art. 1, § 12.

Sheff v. State, 329 So.2d 270.

Fla. 1953. The Fourth Amendment to the Federal Constitution is part of the history of the guarantees imbedded in the State Constitution for protection of the rights of the people. F.S.A.Const. Declaration of Rights, § 22; U.S.C.A.Const. Amend. 4.

Boynton v. State, 64 So.2d 536.

Fla. 1952. An illegal search cannot be made legal by the fruits it produces. F.S.A.Const.Declaration of Rights, § 22; U.S.C.A.Const. Amend. 4.

Brown v. State, 62 So.2d 348.

Fla. 1952. A search must be lawful in toto and one which is unlawful ab initio is not made lawful by what is found in consequence thereof. F.S.A.Const. Declaration of Rights, § 22; U.S.C.A.Const. Amend. 4.

Kraemer v. State, 60 So.2d 615.

Fla.App. 1 Dist. 1976. Where there is no search, constitutional guarantee against unlawful searches and seizures is not applicable.

Smith v. State, 333 So.2d 91.

Fla.App. 2 Dist. 1967. Right of person to be secure from illegal search and seizure and to be insulated from giving evidence against himself is inalienable and must be protected at risk that individual criminal may go without punishment.

Carter v. State, 199 So.2d 324.

Oath of officer to support, protect and defend Constitution precludes his seizing property in violation of provision of Declaration of Rights governing searches and seizures. F.S.A.Const. Declaration of Rights, § 22.

Carter v. State, 199 So.2d 324.

Fla.App. 2 Dist. 1962. Right of a person to be secure from illegal search and seizure and to be free from necessity of giving evidence against himself is inalienable and must be protected at risk that an individual criminal may go without punishment. F.S.A.Const.Declaration of Rights, §§ 12, 22; U.S.C.A.Const.Amends. 4, 5.

Collins v. State, 143 So.2d 700, certiorari denied 148 So.2d 280.

Fla.App. 4 Dist. 1967. Constitutional provision regulating searches and seizures is intended to protect persons against oppression and not to bring into being numerous minute technical obstructions against enforcement of criminal law. U.S.C.A.Const. Amend. 4; F.S.A.Const. Declaration of Rights, § 22.

Webster v. State, 201 So.2d 789.

Fla.App. 5 Dist. 1991. Statutes and rules authorizing search and seizure must be strictly construed and affidavits and warrants issued pursuant to such authority must meticulously conform to statutory and constitutional provisions. West's F.S.A. § 933.18.

Bonilla v. State, 579 So.2d 802.

☞12. Constitutional and statutory provisions.

C.A.11 (Fla.) 2013. Party is entitled to facial invalidation of law on Fourth Amendment grounds only if party can demonstrate that there are no constitutional applications of that law. U.S.C.A. Const.Amend. 4.

American Federation of State, County and Mun. Employees Council 79 v. Scott, 717 F.3d 851, certiorari denied 134 S.Ct. 1877, 188 L.Ed.2d 912.

District court's grant of relief to union representing state employees, in union's action challenging governor's executive order (EO) mandating suspicionless drug testing of state employees on Fourth Amendment grounds, was facial, rather than as-applied, in nature; despite explicitly stating that it was granting only as-applied relief, court granted what effectively amounted to facial relief by declaring EO unconstitutional and enjoining its application to all 85,000 current state employees, and court's relief was not limited in any way by concession union itself made that Fourth Amendment did not bar random drug testing of government employees in high-risk, safety-sensitive jobs. U.S.C.A. Const.Amend. 4.

American Federation of State, County and Mun. Employees Council 79 v. Scott, 717 F.3d 851, certiorari denied 134 S.Ct. 1877, 188 L.Ed.2d 912.

C.A.11 (Fla.) 2008. The Florida Constitution affords the same protections against unreasonable searches and seizures as the Fourth Amendment, and Florida courts follow opinions of the United States Supreme Court in interpreting the Florida Constitution's search and seizure protections. U.S.C.A. Const.Amend. 4; West's F.S.A. Const. Art. 1, § 12.

Johnston v. Tampa Sports Authority, 530 F.3d 1320, rehearing and rehearing denied 285 Fed.Appx. 745, certiorari denied 129 S.Ct. 1013, 555 U.S. 1138, 173 L.Ed.2d 295.

C.A.11 (Fla.) 2007. Statute authorizing administrative inspections of a closely regulated business is constitutional if the state has a substantial interest in regulating the particular business, the inspection is necessary to further the regulatory scheme, and the statute's inspection program, in view of the certainty and regularity of its application, provides a constitutionally adequate substitute for a warrant. U.S.C.A. Const.Amend. 4.

Bruce v. Beary, 498 F.3d 1232.

† C.A.11 (Fla.) 2005. Under totality of circumstances, government's legitimate interest in creating permanent identification record of convicted felons for law enforcement purposes outweighed minor intrusion involved in collecting DNA samples from prisoners, given prisoners' reduced expectation of privacy in their identities, and thus, statute requiring collection of DNA samples from convicted felons did not violate Fourth Amendment rights of defendant convicted of illegal reentry following deportation. U.S.C.A. Const. Amend. 4; DNA Analysis Backlog Elimination Act of 2000, § 3, 42 U.S.C.A. § 14135a.

U.S. v. Rodriguez-Benavides, 148 Fed. Appx. 813, certiorari denied 126 S.Ct. 1107, 546 U.S. 1125, 163 L.Ed.2d 917.

C.A.11 (Fla.) 1985. Statute which, prior to its 1984 amendment, required a warrant showing probable cause to search for possible violations of the currency reporting provisions applied equally to searches of people, places and objects, and there was no basis in the statute or in the *Chemaly* decision for treating searches of objects differently than searches of people. 31 U.S.C.A. § 5317(a).

U.S. v. Arends, 776 F.2d 262.

C.A.11 (Fla.) 1985. County pawnbroker ordinance, permitting warrantless inspection by law enforcement officers of transaction registers which ordinance required dealers in secondhand goods to maintain as to description of persons from whom articles were bought and description of property acquired, did not violate Fourth Amendment, since ordinance's requirements were of central importance to county's efforts to impede the sale of stolen goods. U.S.C.A. Const.Amend. 4.

Peterman v. Coleman, 764 F.2d 1416.

C.C.A.5 (Fla.) 1936. Search and seizure provisions of Espionage Act furnish cumulative remedy, in addition to existing search warrant provisions (Espionage Act, tit. 11, 18 U.S.C.A. 611 et seq.)

Hysler v. U.S., 86 F.2d 918.

S.D.Fla. 2008. While a statute governing administrative inspections of businesses may not permit unbridled discretion, where it is tailored to address specific concerns and provides sufficient predictability such that a business is on notice that it is subject to periodic inspection undertaken for specific purposes, the assurance of regularity provided by a warrant may be unnecessary. U.S.C.A. Const. Amend. 4.

Sosa v. Hames, 581 F.Supp.2d 1254.

S.D.Fla. 1994. Florida statute authorizing law enforcement officers to use necessary force to make unconsented entry into third party's residence to execute arrest warrant was unconstitutional as applied to resident; officer's belief that suspect was inside did not justify search in absence of search warrant or exigent circumstances. West's F.S.A. § 901.19(1); U.S.C.A. Const.Amend. 4.

McClain v. Crowder, 840 F.Supp. 897.

Fla. 1997. With conformity clause amendment, Supreme Court is bound to follow interpretations of United States Supreme Court with respect to Fourth Amendment and provide to Florida citizens no greater protection than those interpretations; amendment applies to both past and future United States Supreme Court decisions. U.S.C.A. Const.Amend. 4; West's F.S.A. Const. Art. 1, § 12.

Rolling v. State, 695 So.2d 278, rehearing denied, certiorari denied 118 S.Ct. 448, 522 U.S. 984, 139 L.Ed.2d 383, denial of post-conviction relief affirmed 825 So.2d 293, rehearing denied, denial of habeas corpus affirmed 438 F.3d 1296, certiorari denied 126 S.Ct. 2943, 548 U.S. 913, 165 L.Ed.2d 966, denial of post-conviction relief affirmed 944 So.2d 176, certiorari denied 127 S.Ct. 466, 549 U.S. 990, 166 L.Ed.2d 332.

Fla. 1996. With amendment to conformity clause of State Constitution, state courts are bound to follow interpretations of United States Supreme Court with respect to Fourth Amendment and provide to state citizens no greater protection than those interpretations. U.S.C.A. Const. Amend. 4; West's F.S.A. Const. Art. 1, § 12.

Soca v. State, 673 So.2d 24, certiorari denied 117 S.Ct. 273, 519 U.S. 910, 136 L.Ed.2d 196.

Fla. 1994. Protection afforded by section of State Constitution protecting people from unreasonable searches and seizures is expressly limited to that afforded under Fourth Amendment as interpreted by United States Supreme Court. U.S.C.A. Const.Amend. 4; West's F.S.A. Const. Art. 1, § 12.

Jones v. State, 648 So.2d 669, rehearing denied, certiorari denied 115 S.Ct. 2588, 515 U.S. 1147, 132 L.Ed.2d 836, post-conviction relief denied 2005 WL 6932251, affirmed 998 So.2d 573, revised on rehearing, post-conviction relief denied 2005 WL 6932252, affirmed 998 So.2d 573, revised on rehearing, and revised on rehearing, habeas corpus denied 998 So.2d 573, revised on rehearing, and revised on rehearing, and revised on rehearing, post-conviction relief denied 2009 WL 9047495, affirmed 53 So.3d 230, rehearing denied, post-conviction relief denied 2011 WL 10483396, affirmed 141 So.3d 132, rehearing denied, certiorari denied 133 S.Ct. 661, 184 L.Ed.2d 471, habeas corpus denied 2013 WL 5504371, affirmed 834 F.3d 1299.

Fla. 1988. Amendment of provision of Florida Constitution relating to search and seizure brought Florida's search and seizure laws into conformity with all decisions of the United States Supreme Court rendered both before and subsequent to the adoption of the amendment. West's

F.S.A. Const. Art. 1, § 12; U.S.C.A. Const. Amend. 4.

Bernie v. State, 524 So.2d 988.

Fla. 1987. Right of privacy provision of the Florida Constitution does not modify applicability of search and seizure provision of the Constitution which is required to be interpreted in conformity with United States Supreme Court decisions interpreting the Fourth Amendment. U.S.C.A. Const.Amend. 4; West's F.S.A. Const. Art. 1, §§ 12, 23.

State v. Hume, 512 So.2d 185.

Fla. 1985. Statute providing for regulatory searches of places of business and of vehicles in connection with inspections for particular diseased, defective, or unlicensed agricultural products does not unconstitutionally permit random searches and is not deficient in neutral criteria to guide officers charged with inspection duty in identifying members of the delineated class; hence, search of defendant's van at agricultural inspection station pursuant to regulatory search warrant was proper and marijuana discovered in course of the search was admissible in drug-trafficking case. West's F.S.A. Const. Art. 1, § 12; West's F.S.A. § 570.15.

Roche v. State, 462 So.2d 1096.

Fla. 1983. Statute allowing warrantless administrative searches of junkyards, scrap metal processing plants, motor vehicle salvage yards, licensed motor vehicle dealers' lots and other establishments dealing with salvaged motor vehicle parts is constitutional, as it is limited to business establishments that easily could be involved in theft and unlawful disposition of vehicles, and is restricted to normal business hours. West's F.S.A. § 812.055; U.S.C.A. Const.Amend. 4; West's F.S.A. Const. Art. 1, § 12.

Moore v. State, 442 So.2d 215.

Fla. 1980. The "reason to believe" standard found in the statute which provides that law enforcement officers of the Department of Natural Resources have the authority, based on reasonable belief, to conduct warrantless searches and inspections is the equivalent of probable cause and, therefore, the section is not unconsti-

tutional. West's F.S.A. §§ 370.021, 370.021(5), 370.14(3)(c).

Tingley v. Brown, 380 So.2d 1289.

Fla. 1953. Statutes authorizing search of premises licensed for liquor business without search warrant are constitutional. F.S.A. §§ 561.07, 562.03; F.S.A.Const. Declaration of Rights, §§ 12, 22.

Boynton v. State, 64 So.2d 536.

Fla. 1946. The provisions of second paragraph of F.S.A. § 933.18 relating to issuance of warrant for search of private dwelling, being consistent with other sections of same chapter and provisions of state constitution, prevail over provisions of first paragraph of the section insofar as they conflict therewith. F.S.A. §§ 933.02(2)(b), 933.07, 933.18; F.S.A.Const. Declaration of Rights, § 22.

Johnson v. State, 27 So.2d 276, 157 Fla. 685, certiorari denied 67 S.Ct. 491, 329 U.S. 799, 91 L.Ed. 683.

Fla. 1945. The act authorizing judge of municipal court of Tampa to issue search warrants in aid of enforcement of ordinances of that city is not violative of constitutional provision relating to unreasonable searches and seizures. Sp.Acts 1923, c. 9922; F.S.A.Const. Declaration of Rights, § 22.

Farragut v. City of Tampa, 22 So.2d 645, 156 Fla. 107.

The act authorizing judge of municipal court of Tampa to issue search warrants in aid of enforcement of ordinances of that city is not violative of constitutional provision prohibiting passage of special or local laws regulating the jurisdiction and duties of any class of officers except municipal officers or regulating the practice of courts of justice except municipal courts. Sp.Acts 1923, c. 9922; F.S.A.Const. art. 3, § 20; art. 5, § 34; art. 8, § 8.

Farragut v. City of Tampa, 22 So.2d 645, 156 Fla. 107.

Fla. 1944. Statutes authorizing searches and seizures must be strictly construed, and affidavits made and search warrants issued thereunder must strictly conform to the constitutional and statutory provisions. F.S.A. §§ 933.01, 933.02, 933.07.

> State ex rel. Wilson v. Quigg, 17 So.2d 697, 154 Fla. 348.

Fla.App. 1 Dist. 2010. Florida courts are required to interpret search and seizure issues in conformity with the Fourth Amendment as interpreted by the United States Supreme Court. U.S.C.A. Const. Amend. 4; West's F.S.A. Const. Art. 1, § 12.

> Higerd v. State, 54 So.3d 513, rehearing denied, review denied 64 So.3d 1260, certiorari denied 132 S.Ct. 521, 565 U.S. 979, 181 L.Ed.2d 350.

Fla.App. 1 Dist. 2007. In search-and-seizure cases, Florida courts are required to follow the United States Supreme Court's interpretation of the Fourth Amendment. U.S.C.A. Const.Amend. 4.

> Kimball v. State, 951 So.2d 35, review denied 959 So.2d 716.

Fla.App. 1 Dist. 1996. In codifying the knock-and-announce requirement, prohibiting unannounced intrusion by police, established exceptions to the common law rule applied; exceptions justifying unannounced entry are where person within already knows of officer's authority and purpose; where officers are justified in belief that persons within are in imminent peril of bodily harm; where officer's peril would have been increased by announcement; or where officers are justified in belief that escape or destruction of evidence is being attempted. West's F.S.A. §§ 901.19, 933.09.

> Wilson v. State, 673 So.2d 505, rehearing denied, review denied 682 So.2d 1101.

Fla.App. 1 Dist. 1995. Conformity amendment to state constitutional provision against unreasonable searches and seizures requires state court to look to United States Supreme Court for guidance in determining whether police roadblocks are constitutional. U.S.C.A. Const.Amend. 4; West's F.S.A. Const. Art. 1, § 12.

> Campbell v. State, 667 So.2d 279, review granted 668 So.2d 602, quashed 679 So.2d 1168.

Fla.App. 1 Dist. 1985. Amendment to searches and seizures provision of State Constitution, providing that the provision

is to be construed in conformity with Fourth Amendment of the United States Constitution, applied to question of admissibility of electronic surveillance which occurred after the amendment's effective date. West's F.S.A. Const. Art. 1, § 12; U.S.C.A. Const.Amend. 4.

> State v. Hume, 463 So.2d 499, approved in part, quashed in part 512 So.2d 185.

Fla.App. 1 Dist. 1982. Statute permitting issuance of agricultural search warrant is not unconstitutional. West's F.S.A. § 570.15(1)(b); West's F.S.A. Const. Art. 1, § 12.

> Roche v. State, 447 So.2d 890, decision approved 462 So.2d 1096.

Fla.App. 1 Dist. 1982. Statute authorizing searches of motor vehicle repair shops, junk yards, and similar businesses during normal business hours for the purpose of locating stolen motor vehicles is not unconstitutional. West's F.S.A. § 812.055.

> State v. Moore, 424 So.2d 882, decision approved 442 So.2d 215.

Fla.App. 1 Dist. 1975. Absence of efficient administrative machinery on part of sovereign does not repeal constitutional guarantee to citizen to be secure in his bedroom during nighttime. U.S.C.A.Const. Amend. 4; West's F.S.A.Const. art. 1, § 12.

> Shepard v. State, 319 So.2d 127, certiorari denied 328 So.2d 845.

Fla.App. 1 Dist. 1975. Presumption arose that framers of present constitution intended to effect some change in meaning when they changed language of former constitution, which provided that no search warrant will issue "but upon probable cause, supported by oath or affirmation * * *," to read that no warrant shall be issued except upon "probable cause supported by affidavit * * *." F.S.A.Const.1885, Declaration of Rights, § 22; West's F.S.A.Const. art. 1, § 12.

> Swartz v. State, 316 So.2d 618, certiorari denied 333 So.2d 465.

Insofar as statute might be construed to permit issuance of search warrant for search of things or premises other than a private dwelling based upon an affidavit which does not in and of itself demon-

---

† This Case was not selected for publication in the National Reporter System
For legislative history of cited statutes, see Florida Statutes Annotated

strate probable cause for issuance of the warrant the statute is unconstitutional as violating constitutional section providing, inter alia, that no warrant shall be issued except upon "probable cause, supported by affidavit * * *." West's F.S.A.Const. art. 1, § 12; West's F.S.A. § 933.06.

> Swartz v. State, 316 So.2d 618, certiorari denied 333 So.2d 465.

Fla.App. 2 Dist. 1985. Criminal statutes authorizing searches and seizures must be strictly construed.

> State v. Bernie, 472 So.2d 1243, decision approved 524 So.2d 988.

Fla.App. 2 Dist. 1967. Constitutional and statutory provisions regulating use of search warrants must be strictly construed. F.S.A.Const. Declaration of Rights, § 22; F.S.A. §§ 933.01–933.08, 933.09–933.15.

> Carter v. State, 199 So.2d 324.

Fla.App. 2 Dist. 1960. The statute expressly setting forth who may issue search warrants and the limitation of their authority must be strictly construed; affidavits made and search warrants issued thereunder must strictly conform to constitutional and statutory provisions. F.S.A. § 933.01.

> Robinson v. State, 124 So.2d 714, modified 132 So.2d 156, certiorari dismissed 132 So.2d 159.

Fla.App. 3 Dist. 2011. Florida courts are required to interpret Florida's constitutional search and seizure provision in conformity with the Fourth Amendment to the United States Constitution, as interpreted by the United States Supreme Court, and in the absence of controlling precedent from the United States Supreme Court, Florida appellate courts may look to other state and federal court decisions for guidance. U.S.C.A. Const.Amend. 4; West's F.S.A. Const. Art. 1, § 12.

> D.P. v. State, 65 So.3d 123, rehearing denied, review denied 90 So.3d 270.

Fla.App. 3 Dist. 1995. State constitutional article governing searches and seizures is to be interpreted in conformity with the Fourth Amendment and may not be read to provide any greater protections.

U.S.C.A. Const.Amend. 4; West's F.S.A. Const. Art. 1, § 12.

> Soca v. State, 656 So.2d 536, review granted 663 So.2d 631, quashed 673 So.2d 24, certiorari denied 117 S.Ct. 273, 519 U.S. 910, 136 L.Ed.2d 196.

Fla.App. 3 Dist. 1995. States are privileged under their state law to adopt higher, but not lower, standards for police conduct than those required by the Fourth Amendment; in Florida, such higher standards may not as a matter of state law, be imposed under state constitutional guarantee against unreasonable searches and seizures, but may be imposed by other provisions of Florida law, including state statute. U.S.C.A. Const.Amend. 4; West's F.S.A. Const. Art. 1, § 12.

> State v. Slaney, 653 So.2d 422, rehearing denied.

Fla.App. 3 Dist. 1962. Statutes authorizing seizures and search warrants should be strictly construed.

> Leveson v. State, 138 So.2d 361, remanded 147 So.2d 524, on remand 149 So.2d 80, transferred to 151 So.2d 283.

Fla.App. 4 Dist. 2009. City ordinance that failed to require notice of seized vehicle to owner who was not on the scene at the time of arrest was constitutionally deficient for its lack of due process. U.S.C.A. Const.Amend. 14; West's F.S.A. Const. Art. 1, § 9.

> Mulligan v. City of Hollywood, 4 So.3d 1258, rehearing granted.

Fla.App. 4 Dist. 2008. Statutes authorizing searches and seizures should be strictly construed and searches must strictly conform to such statutory provisions. U.S.C.A. Const.Amend. 4.

> State v. Hill, 980 So.2d 1181, rehearing denied.

Fla.App. 4 Dist. 2006. Search and seizure provision of State Constitution does not prevent District Court of Appeal from granting more protection than that provided in Fourth Amendment, in the absence of United States Supreme Court precedent directly on point to the con-

---

† **This Case was not selected for publication in the National Reporter System**
For legislative history of cited statutes, see Florida Statutes Annotated

trary. U.S.C.A. Const.Amend. 4; West's F.S.A. Const. Art. 1, § 12.

State v. Rabb, 920 So.2d 1175, review denied 933 So.2d 522, certiorari denied 127 S.Ct. 665, 549 U.S. 1052, 166 L.Ed.2d 513.

Fla.App. 4 Dist. 1995. Florida's constitutional right to be free from unreasonable searches and seizures requires Court of Appeals to interpret that right in conformity with Fourth Amendment to United States Constitution, as interpreted by United States Supreme Court. U.S.C.A. Const. Amend. 4; West's F.S.A. Const. Art. 1, § 12.

Daniels v. Cochran, 654 So.2d 609.

Fla.App. 4 Dist. 1982. Statute which authorizes the police, during normal business hours and for the purpose of locating stolen vehicles, investigating the titling and registration of vehicles, inspecting vehicles wrecked or dismantled, or inspecting records, to make a warrantless physical inspection of any junkyard, scrap metal processing plant, motor vehicle salvage yard, licensed motor vehicle dealer's lot, motor vehicle repair shop, parking lot, public garage, or other establishment dealing with salvaged motor vehicle parts is constitutional. U.S.C.A.Const.Amend. 4; West's F.S.A.Const.Art. 1, § 12; West's F.S.A. § 812.055.

Bludworth v. Arcuri, 416 So.2d 882.

Fla.App. 4 Dist. 1975. District Court of Appeal was required to strictly construe statute governing issuance of search warrant for private dwelling. West's F.S.A. § 933.18.

Gerardi v. State, 307 So.2d 853.

Fla.App. 5 Dist. 2005. Statutes and rules authorizing searches and seizures are strictly construed and affidavits and warrants issued pursuant to such authority must, absent a valid exception, meticulously conform to statutory and constitutional provisions. U.S.C.A. Const.Amend. 4; Fed.Rules Cr.Proc.Rule 3, 18 U.S.C.A.; West's F.S.A. Const. Art. 1, § 12; West's F.S.A. § 948.06; West's F.S.A. RCrP Rule 3.120.

Crain v. State, 914 So.2d 1015, review denied 940 So.2d 427.

Fla.App. 5 Dist. 1999. Statute providing that issuance of notice to appear

did not affect law enforcement officer's authority to conduct an otherwise lawful search was unconstitutional, to extent it authorized officers to search vehicle as incident to issuing criminal citation in lieu of making an arrest of driver. U.S.C.A. Const.Amend. 4; West's F.S.A. Const. Art. 1, § 12; West's F.S.A. § 901.28.

Welch v. State, 741 So.2d 1268.

⊸13. What constitutes search or seizure.

Includes all cases, whatever the nature or purpose of the activity.

⊸13.1. —— In general.

U.S.Fla. 2013. When the Government obtains information by physically intruding on persons, houses, papers, or effects, a "search" within the original meaning of the Fourth Amendment has undoubtedly occurred. U.S.C.A. Const. Amend. 4.

Florida v. Jardines, 133 S.Ct. 1409, 185 L.Ed.2d 495.

† C.A.11 (Fla.) 2016. Voluntary request by property owners, who were cited for failing to obtain permits for accessory buildings on their property as required by zoning ordinance, for a determination from zoning manager regarding the interpretation of ordinance, subsequent fees paid to appeal that decision, and potential application for a special exception did not amount to an illegal seizure under the Fourth Amendment. U.S.C.A. Const. Amend. 4.

Foley v. Orange County, 638 Fed. Appx. 941, certiorari denied 137 S.Ct. 378, 196 L.Ed.2d 294.

C.A.11 (Fla.) 2015. Where governmental authorities exert dominion and control over an effect for their own purposes, a "seizure" has occurred, though not necessarily an unreasonable one; property need not be seized from the immediate custody and control of the owner to qualify as a "seizure." U.S.C.A. Const. Amend. 4.

U.S. v. Sparks, 806 F.3d 1323, certiorari denied Johnson v. U.S., 137 S.Ct. 34, 196 L.Ed.2d 46.

C.A.11 (Fla.) 2015. A party may establish a Fourth Amendment search by showing that the government engaged in conduct that would have constituted a search within the original meaning of the

Fourth Amendment. U.S.C.A. Const. Amend. 4.

U.S. v. Davis, 785 F.3d 498, certiorari denied 136 S.Ct. 479, 193 L.Ed.2d 349.

To determine whether a search occurred under the reasonable-expectation-of-privacy test requires a two-part inquiry: (1) has an individual manifested a subjective expectation of privacy in the object of the challenged search; and (2) is society willing to recognize that expectation as reasonable. U.S.C.A. Const.Amend. 4.

U.S. v. Davis, 785 F.3d 498, certiorari denied 136 S.Ct. 479, 193 L.Ed.2d 349.

C.A.11 (Fla.) 2015. A "seizure" of property occurs, within the meaning of the Fourth Amendment, when there is some meaningful interference with an individual's possessory interests in that property. U.S.C.A. Const.Amend. 4.

U.S. v. Odoni, 782 F.3d 1226, certiorari denied Gunter v. U.S., 135 S.Ct. 2335, 191 L.Ed.2d 981, certiorari denied 135 S.Ct. 2339, 191 L.Ed.2d 981.

Agents of the government do not violate the Fourth Amendment when they replicate a prior search without a warrant. U.S.C.A. Const.Amend. 4.

U.S. v. Odoni, 782 F.3d 1226, certiorari denied Gunter v. U.S., 135 S.Ct. 2335, 191 L.Ed.2d 981, certiorari denied 135 S.Ct. 2339, 191 L.Ed.2d 981.

C.A.11 (Fla.) 2014. Fourth Amendment "search" occurs when the government violates a subjective expectation of privacy that society recognizes as reasonable. U.S.C.A. Const.Amend. 4.

Gennusa v. Canova, 748 F.3d 1103.

Officer's returning to interview room after suspect's attorney refused to give suspect's written statement to officer and forcibly taking statement from underneath attorney's hand constituted seizure of statement within meaning of Fourth Amendment, regardless of whether or not attorney was physically touched or restrained. U.S.C.A. Const.Amend. 4.

Gennusa v. Canova, 748 F.3d 1103.

† **C.A.11 (Fla.) 2012.** There was no meaningful interference with tenant's pos-

sessory interests and no "seizure" of property, within the meaning of the Fourth Amendment, when officer banged on and kicked tenant's apartment door several times, unprovoked, cracking the doorframe and damaging the deadbolt, for purposes of tenant's § 1983 claims against officer, police chief, and city; officer did not kick the door down or permanently destroy the door, and thus, at most, the damage was only a temporary deprivation of tenant's possessory interests, and because this damage was relatively minor and was able to be repaired within an hour, the damage was de minimis. U.S.C.A. Const.Amend. 4; 42 U.S.C.A. § 1983.

Porter v. Jewell, 453 Fed.Appx. 934.

† **C.A.11 (Fla.) 2007.** Attempt by Florida Department of Health (DOH) and municipal officials to inspect property where church operated school and issuing pastor a notice to appear for his refusal to allow inspection was neither a search nor a seizure under Fourth Amendment; officials and inspectors did not search or seize anything, and notice to appear merely required pastor to appear in court at a later date. U.S.C.A. Const.Amend. 4.

Youngblood v. Florida Dept. of Health, 224 Fed.Appx. 909.

C.A.11 (Fla.) 2004. Probation officer's mere entry into closed medical office to locate and apprehend individual suspected of violating his probation was sufficient to constitute "search" for Fourth Amendment purposes, given its intrusion on medical office manager's reasonable expectation of privacy. U.S.C.A. Const. Amend. 4.

O'Rourke v. Hayes, 378 F.3d 1201.

C.A.11 (Fla.) 1999. Even assuming Fifth Amendment would require pretrial probable cause hearing where government had seized or restrained property in anticipation of forfeiture, government's filing of notices of lis pendens regarding defendant's property was not pretrial "seizure" that would entitle defendant to hearing on legitimacy of government's claim to his property under criminal forfeiture statute. U.S.C.A. Const.Amend. 5; Comprehensive Drug Abuse Prevention and Control Act of

1970, § 413, as amended, 21 U.S.C.A. § 853; West's F.S.A. § 48.23(1).

> U.S. v. Register, 182 F.3d 820, rehearing and rehearing denied 196 F.3d 1263, certiorari denied 120 S.Ct. 2703, 530 U.S. 1250, 147 L.Ed.2d 973, certiorari denied 121 S.Ct. 123, 531 U.S. 849, 148 L.Ed.2d 78.

C.A.11 (Fla.) 1985. Communication between police and citizens involving no coercion or detention are outside scope of Fourth Amendment. U.S.C.A. Const. Amend. 4.

> U.S. v. Alvarez-Sanchez, 774 F.2d 1036.

C.A.5 (Fla.) 1978. Examination of two United States Treasury checks contained in an open envelope that was in proper custody of police authorities was not a "search" within the proscriptions of the Fourth Amendment. U.S.C.A.Const. Amend. 4.

> U.S. v. Duckett, 583 F.2d 1309.

C.A.5 (Fla.) 1971. Under circumstances of case, a "search" would be defined as an examination of one's premises with a view to discovery of contraband or evidence to be used in prosecution of a criminal action; the term implied an exploratory investigation or quest. U.S.C.A.Const. Amend. 4.

> U.S. v. Clarke, 451 F.2d 584.

C.A.5 (Fla.) 1969. Whether government's activity is considered a "search" depends upon whether individual's reasonable expectations of privacy are disturbed. U.S.C.A.Const. Amend. 4.

> Davis v. U.S., 413 F.2d 1226.

C.C.A.5 (Fla.) 1945. Where federal officer possessing information regarding manufacture and transportation of illicit liquor, but acting without warrant, stopped truck and announced that he was a federal officer, but defendant using a shotgun drove officer away and prevented search, constitutional rights of defendant against unreasonable search had not been violated and motion to suppress evidence was properly denied, in prosecution for knowingly resisting federal officer in attempted performance of duty.

> Palmquist v. U.S., 149 F.2d 352, certiorari denied 66 S.Ct. 33, 326 U.S. 727, 90 L.Ed. 431.

M.D.Fla. 2012. A "seizure" of property occurs when there is some meaningful interference with an individual's possessory interests in that property. U.S.C.A. Const.Amend. 4.

> Gennusa v. Shoar, 879 F.Supp.2d 1337, affirmed 748 F.3d 1103.

Officer's actions in seizing arrestee's written statement from arrestee's attorney's hand without a warrant or exception to the warrant requirement constituted an unreasonable "seizure" under the Fourth Amendment. U.S.C.A. Const.Amend. 4.

> Gennusa v. Shoar, 879 F.Supp.2d 1337, affirmed 748 F.3d 1103.

M.D.Fla. 1996. "Seizure" of property occurs when there is some meaningful interference with individual's possessory interests in that property.

> U.S. v. St. Pierre, 950 F.Supp. 334.

M.D.Fla. 1996. Warrant of arrest in rem accompanying forfeiture order against real property did not allow or require unconstitutional "seizure" of real property at issue; warrant ordered release of property immediately after arrest, preserved right to predeprivation notice and hearing essential to due process, preserved owners' rights to maintain control over their home, to be free from governmental interference and to ownership of property, permitted owners to obtain expedited hearing within 30 days of property's arrest, and did not permit government to evict occupants, modify property, condition occupancy, receive rents, or supersede owner in other rights pertaining to use, possession and enjoyment of property. U.S.C.A. Const.Amends. 5, 14.

> U.S. v. Real Property Located at 3284 Brewster Drive, Kissimmee, Fla., Including any Buildings, Appurtenances, and Improvements Thereon, 949 F.Supp. 832.

M.D.Fla. 1980. For constitutional purposes, "search" may be defined as visual examination or use of some other means of gathering evidence, which infringes upon person's reasonable expectation of privacy. U.S.C.A.Const. Amend. 4.

> U.S. v. Hartley, 486 F.Supp. 1348, affirmed 678 F.2d 961, rehearing denied 688 F.2d 852, certiorari denied 103 S.Ct. 815, 459 U.S. 1170,

74 L.Ed.2d 1014, certiorari denied Treasure Isle, Inc., v. U.S., 103 S.Ct. 834, 459 U.S. 1183, 74 L.Ed.2d 1027.

In view of relationship between corporation and government inspectors allowed in areas which were closed to general public, duties and responsibilities of inspectors being well known to corporate employees, corporate expectation of privacy could not be justified as to items and conduct assertedly protected by Fourth Amendment, and thus, as to corporate defendant, as well as to its employees, there was no "search," for constitutional purposes. U.S.C.A.Const. Amend. 4.

U.S. v. Hartley, 486 F.Supp. 1348, affirmed 678 F.2d 961, rehearing denied 688 F.2d 852, certiorari denied 103 S.Ct. 815, 459 U.S. 1170, 74 L.Ed.2d 1014, certiorari denied Treasure Isle, Inc., v. U.S., 103 S.Ct. 834, 459 U.S. 1183, 74 L.Ed.2d 1027.

S.D.Fla. 2015. City employee's access of driver's information from database of driver's license information, even for an impermissible purpose, was not a "search" within meaning of Fourth Amendment, nor did such an action impinge on a reasonable expectation of privacy. U.S. Const.Amend. 4.

Watts v. City of Hollywood, Florida, 146 F.Supp.3d 1254.

S.D.Fla. 2011. Fourth Amendment violation requires intentional acquisition of physical control. U.S.C.A. Const. Amend. 4.

Abella v. Simon, 831 F.Supp.2d 1316, vacated in part 482 Fed.Appx. 522.

S.D.Fla. 2008. A "seizure" of property occurs when there is some meaningful interference with an individual's possessory interests in that property. U.S.C.A. Const.Amend. 4.

Sosa v. Hames, 581 F.Supp.2d 1254.

Fla. 2014. Defendant had subjective expectation of privacy in real time cell site location information (CSLI) regarding location of defendant's cellular telephone, as would support finding that police officers' use of CSLI to track defendant was a search falling under purview of Fourth Amendment, even if defendant knew or

should have know that telephone gave off signals to enable service provider to detect telephone's location; simply knowing that telephone gave off locating signals to service provider did not mean that defendant consented to use of that location information by third parties for unrelated purposes. U.S.C.A. Const.Amend. 4.

Tracey v. State, 152 So.3d 504, on remand 162 So.3d 217.

Expectation of privacy in real time cell site location information (CSLI) regarding location of cellular telephone was objectively reasonable, as would support finding that police officers' use of CSLI to track defendant was a search falling under purview of Fourth Amendment; significant portion of population relied on cellular telephones for email and other communications, electronic monitoring of a citizen's location could generate a comprehensive record of a person's public movements, and police officers' ability to accomplish such monitoring at relatively low cost could alter relationship between citizen and government in way that was inimical to democratic society. U.S.C.A. Const.Amend. 4.

Tracey v. State, 152 So.3d 504, on remand 162 So.3d 217.

The touchstone of Fourth Amendment analysis of a search is whether a person has a constitutionally-protected reasonable expectation of privacy, and in applying the test, the court examines whether the individual manifested a subjective expectation of privacy and whether society is willing to recognize that expectation as reasonable. U.S.C.A. Const.Amend. 4.

Tracey v. State, 152 So.3d 504, on remand 162 So.3d 217.

Fla. 2010. A Fourth Amendment "search" occurs when the government violates a subjective expectation of privacy that society recognizes as reasonable. U.S.C.A. Const.Amend. 4.

Twilegar v. State, 42 So.3d 177, rehearing denied, certiorari denied 131 S.Ct. 1476, 562 U.S. 1225, 179 L.Ed.2d 315, denial of post-conviction relief affirmed 175 So.3d 242, rehearing denied.

Fla. 2009. In Fourth Amendment analyses of whether a seizure has occurred, the totality of all the circumstances surrounding the specific encounter must be considered. U.S.C.A. Const.Amend. 4.

G.M. v. State, 19 So.3d 973.

Fla. 1989. Setting in which challenged police conduct occurs may provide strong evidence of "seizure."

Bostick v. State, 554 So.2d 1153, certiorari granted 111 S.Ct. 241, 498 U.S. 894, 112 L.Ed.2d 201, reversed 111 S.Ct. 2382, 501 U.S. 429, 115 L.Ed.2d 389, on remand 593 So.2d 494.

Fla. 1976. Fourth Amendment governs all intrusions on personal security by agents of public; if there is intrusion upon personal security by officer, there is search. U.S.C.A.Const. Amend. 4.

Elson v. State, 337 So.2d 959.

Fla. 1971. "Search" is inspection of examination of places closed from public or general view, and requires some measure of force or intrusion.

State v. Ashby, 245 So.2d 225.

"Seizure" is act of taking custody of evidence or contraband.

State v. Ashby, 245 So.2d 225.

Amount of intrusion or force required to constitute a "search" may be slight, but some minimum action is required.

State v. Ashby, 245 So.2d 225.

Fla.App. 1 Dist. 2005. Securing a dwelling, on the basis of probable cause, to prevent the destruction or removal of evidence while a search warrant is being sought is not itself an unreasonable seizure of either the dwelling or its contents. U.S.C.A. Const.Amend. 4.

Smith v. State, 904 So.2d 534, rehearing denied.

Fla.App. 1 Dist. 1997. Law enforcement's warrantless examination of contents of briefcase was not "search" within Fourth Amendment after briefcase was delivered to police by repossession company upon its determination, in inventorying contents of repossessed car and opening briefcase, that its contents were suspicious. U.S.C.A. Const.Amend. 4; West's F.S.A. Const. Art. 1, § 12.

Warren v. State, 701 So.2d 404.

Fla.App. 1 Dist. 1997. Police officer's demand that suspect disclose or produce concealed object constitutes a "search."

K.L. v. State, 699 So.2d 819.

Officer's actions of touching suspect's pocket and asking suspect to remove items from pocket was an illegal warrantless "search."

K.L. v. State, 699 So.2d 819.

Fla.App. 1 Dist. 1990. Detective's command to stand and plain viewing of crack cocaine in chair did not amount to "search" after valid investigatory stop and detention. U.S.C.A. Const.Amend. 4.

State v. Neely, 560 So.2d 1230.

Fla.App. 1 Dist. 1985. Where initial search of envelope containing cocaine was performed by employee of private carrier which contacted police, package remained unsealed until officer arrived, and officer's examination of envelope and its contents did not significantly exceed the scope of the private search in that removal of plastic bag from envelope and officer's visual inspection of contents enabled him to learn nothing that had not previously been learned during the private search, officer's examination infringed no legitimate expectation of privacy and was not a "search" within meaning of the Fourth Amendment; moreover, subsequent field testing of powder found in plastic bag did not compromise any legitimate privacy interest. U.S.C.A. Const.Amend. 4.

State v. Palmer, 474 So.2d 1250.

Fla.App. 1 Dist. 1985. Defendant had no legitimate expectation of privacy which society would recognize as reasonable, under either the Fourth Amendment or Florida Constitution [West's F.S.A. Const. Art. 1, § 12], with regard to numbers dialed into commercial telephone system; hence, use of pen register to ascertain numbers dialed from defendant's telephone did not constitute a "search" or require a warrant. U.S.C.A. Const.Amend. 4.

Yarbrough v. State, 473 So.2d 766.

Fla.App. 1 Dist. 1981. Demand to disclose or produce a concealed object is treated as a "search."

M. J. v. State, 399 So.2d 996.

Where there was a demand that student produce cannabis before actual production of cannabis cigarette, there was a "search."

M. J. v. State, 399 So.2d 996.

Fla.App. 1 Dist. 1973. To "seize" means to take possession of forcibly, to grasp, to snatch or to put in possession.

State v. Dees, 280 So.2d 51, writ discharged 291 So.2d 195.

Fla.App. 1 Dist. 1973. Where officers, investigating the burglary of a seafood market, saw some shrimp in the trunk of defendant's car and placed him under arrest, but defendant struggled with officers and a matchbox containing 14 decks of heroin fell from defendant's clothing, seizure of heroin was not illegal as no personal search of defendant was necessary.

Jones v. State, 276 So.2d 550, certiorari denied 280 So.2d 689, certiorari denied 94 S.Ct. 1409, 415 U.S. 914, 39 L.Ed.2d 468.

Fla.App. 2 Dist. 2011. Officers' warrantless entry into fenced curtilage through an unlocked gate without "no trespassing" sign or similar warning, for a "knock and talk" was not a "search," even though officers' entry may have been a statutory trespass; defendant's reasonable expectation of privacy in his house did not include an expectation that persons would not occasionally enter through the unlocked gate and approach the front door. U.S.C.A. Const. Amend. 4; West's F.S.A. § 810.09.

Nieminski v. State, 60 So.3d 521.

Fla.App. 2 Dist. 2007. A person's home is accorded the full range of Fourth Amendment protections because there is an expectation of privacy in one's dwelling; thus, a nonconsensual entry into a home, a motel room, or other residence constitutes a search. U.S.C.A. Const. Amend. 4.

Holloman v. State, 959 So.2d 403.

Fla.App. 2 Dist. 1999. Police officer conducted a "seizure," rather than a "strip search," by pulling top of defendant's pants toward officer and seizing plastic bag of crack cocaine from inside defendant's pants. West's F.S.A. § 901.211(1).

State v. Days, 751 So.2d 87, rehearing denied.

A "search" is generally accepted to be an inspection or examination of places closed from public or general view, and requires some measure of force or intrusion. U.S.C.A. Const.Amend. 4.

State v. Days, 751 So.2d 87, rehearing denied.

A "seizure" is the act of taking custody of evidence or contraband. U.S.C.A. Const.Amend. 4.

State v. Days, 751 So.2d 87, rehearing denied.

Fla.App. 2 Dist. 1998. Officer effected a "seizure" of fishing rods possessed by defendant by taking them without consent and placing them in officer's vehicle. U.S.C.A. Const.Amend. 4.

Cliett v. State, 722 So.2d 916.

Fla.App. 2 Dist. 1997. Photocopying of lease agreement found in passenger's wallet during search following passenger's detention for failing to report to custom's officials that he was carrying more than $10,000 cash did not constitute seizure in violation of Fourth Amendment, though state received lease from federal agent who interrogated passenger during detention; initial search of wallet was permissible routine border search that did not violate Fourth Amendment. U.S.C.A. Const.Amend. 4; 31 U.S.C.A. §§ 5316, 5317(b).

State v. Codner, 696 So.2d 806.

Fla.App. 2 Dist. 1993. Illegal search resulted from officer's order to defendant to "spit it out" after defendant attempted to conceal something in his mouth when defendant was startled by officer's appearance as defendant was standing on porch of house under surveillance for drug activity. U.S.C.A. Const.Amend. 4.

M.J.S. v. State, 620 So.2d 1080.

Fla.App. 2 Dist. 1990. Officer's conduct in demanding that passenger in vehicle which had been stopped for speeding pull cocaine out of her pants constituted a search for which probable cause was required.

Blair v. State, 563 So.2d 824.

Fla.App. 2 Dist. 1984. "Search" occurs within meaning of the Fourth Amendment when government action invades an individual's justifiable or reasonable expectation of privacy. U.S.C.A. Const. Amend. 4.

Randall v. State, 458 So.2d 822.

Fla.App. 2 Dist. 1983. Police officer's warrantless entry and occupancy of house constituted Fourth Amendment search and seizure. U.S.C.A. Const.Amend. 4.

Alderton v. State, 438 So.2d 1000.

Fla.App. 2 Dist. 1982. Where it was defendant himself who went beyond officer's initial inquiry as to what was in defendant's pants and spontaneously extracted marijuana from his shorts into plain view, there was no search and, thus, no illegal search and seizure and marijuana was subject to proper seizure.

State v. Hicks, 415 So.2d 878.

Fla.App. 2 Dist. 1981. Where defendant went beyond police officers' inquiry about what caused bulge in his pocket and spontaneously pulled methaqualone tablets out of his pockets, no search took place and, therefore, methaqualone was properly seized as contraband when defendant brought it into plain view. West's F.S.A. § 901.151.

Neely v. State, 402 So.2d 477.

Fla.App. 2 Dist. 1976. An inventory is a search within the Fourth Amendment prohibition against unreasonable searches and seizures. U.S.C.A.Const. Amend. 4.

G. B. v. State, 339 So.2d 696.

Fla.App. 2 Dist. 1974. Without an intrusion, there can be no search.

State v. Flores, 305 So.2d 292, certiorari denied 315 So.2d 189.

Fla.App. 2 Dist. 1974. Where police officer, relying upon information gained from an informer, went to defendant's dwelling and reached into a small vent beneath the house and found a pistol, which could not be seen before it was pulled out of the vent, there was a search and, as it occurred on a Monday afternoon with no attempt being made to obtain a search warrant, it was unreasonable.

Dinkens v. State, 291 So.2d 122.

Fla.App. 3 Dist. 2009. Asking a question of a person not in custody is neither a search nor a seizure.

D.A. v. State, 10 So.3d 674, review denied 20 So.3d 848, vacated 49 So.3d 746, review denied 49 So.3d 746.

Fla.App. 3 Dist. 2008. Official conduct that does not compromise any legitimate interest in privacy is not a search subject to the Fourth Amendment. U.S.C.A. Const.Amend. 4.

State v. Jardines, 9 So.3d 1, review granted 3 So.3d 1246, quashed 73 So.3d 34, rehearing denied, certiorari granted in part 132 S.Ct. 995, 565 U.S. 1104, 181 L.Ed.2d 726, affirmed 133 S.Ct. 1409, 185 L.Ed.2d 495.

Fla.App. 3 Dist. 1985. "Seizure" of property under Fourth Amendment occurs when there is some meaningful interference with individual's possessory interest in that property. U.S.C.A. Const.Amend. 4.

State v. Gonzalez, 467 So.2d 723, petition for review denied 476 So.2d 675.

Detective's nonconsensual retention of medical records of minor after defendant-doctor's attorney requested their return constituted "meaningful interference" with defendant-doctor's possessory interest in records and was police "seizure" within meaning of Fourth Amendment. U.S.C.A. Const.Amend. 4.

State v. Gonzalez, 467 So.2d 723, petition for review denied 476 So.2d 675.

Fla.App. 3 Dist. 1981. Entry and occupancy of defendant's home while officers awaited a search warrant constituted a search and seizure for purposes of the Fourth Amendment. U.S.C.A.Const. Amend. 4.

State v. Ramos, 405 So.2d 1001.

Fla.App. 3 Dist. 1981. For constitutional purposes, "seizure" of a tangible object cannot involve anything less than an act of taking actual and physical control.

State v. Steffani, 398 So.2d 475, decision approved 419 So.2d 323.

Fla.App. 3 Dist. 1981. Police officer's placing of key, which had been lawfully seized from duffel bag containing marijuana, in trunk lock of defendant's lawfully stopped vehicle did not violate any constitutional right of defendant and police officer's testimony that the key fit the lock was admissible in prosecution of defendant for possession of marijuana.

State v. Dunlap, 392 So.2d 1366.

Fla.App. 3 Dist. 1981. Detective's moving suitcase from baggage cart to floor at airport, so as to facilitate sniff by dog, was de minimis intrusion not amounting to Fourth Amendment's "seizure." U.S.C.A.Const. Amend. 4.

State v. Mosier, 392 So.2d 602, appeal after remand 415 So.2d 771.

Fla.App. 3 Dist. 1980. A "seizure" is defined as the act of taking custody of evidence or contraband. U.S.C.A.Const. Amend. 4.

Mata v. State, 380 So.2d 1157, petition for review denied 389 So.2d 1112.

Broadly speaking, a search and seizure under the Fourth Amendment covers any official invasion of the person's expectation of privacy as to his person, house, papers or effects. U.S.C.A.Const. Amend. 4.

Mata v. State, 380 So.2d 1157, petition for review denied 389 So.2d 1112.

Fla.App. 3 Dist. 1979. A "search and seizure" covers any official invasion of a person's reasonable expectations of privacy as to his person, house, papers or effects. West's F.S.A.Const. art. 1, § 12; U.S.C.A.Const. Amends. 4, 14.

State v. Oliver, 368 So.2d 1331, certiorari dismissed 383 So.2d 1200.

Searches of the person include any physical touching of an individual's body or clothing that causes hidden objects or matters to be revealed, such as rummaging through one's pockets or clothing, patting down one's outer clothing without going into the pockets or other inner recesses, knocking property loose from an individual by tackling him, extracting an individual's blood by means of a hypodermic needle, or taking scrapings from beneath his fingernails. West's F.S.A.Const. art. 1, § 12; U.S.C.A.Const. Amends. 4, 14.

State v. Oliver, 368 So.2d 1331, certiorari dismissed 383 So.2d 1200.

Police demand that an individual disclose or hand over a concealed object is treated as a search as is a police demand that individual open drawers and physical-ly move the contents therein from side to side for police viewing. West's F.S.A.Const. art. 1, § 12; U.S.C.A.Const. Amends. 4, 14.

State v. Oliver, 368 So.2d 1331, certiorari dismissed 383 So.2d 1200.

Fla.App. 3 Dist. 1977. Within rule concerning what constitutes search, areas which are outside of hotel room, such as hallways, which are open to use by others may not be reasonably considered as private, and officer had legal right to be there.

Brant v. State, 349 So.2d 674.

Fla.App. 3 Dist. 1972. Where there was no search of premises nor any evidence presented as result of use of key to open motel room door other than that the key found in automobile abandoned near site of the offense belonged to motel room occupied by defendant, use by police of motel key to open door of motel room did not amount to an illegal search.

Greenwood v. State, 270 So.2d 427.

Fla.App. 3 Dist. 1968. Inventory taken by police of contents of automobile was a "search".

Gagnon v. State, 212 So.2d 337.

Fla.App. 3 Dist. 1967. There may be a search without a seizure and there may be a seizure without a search.

Boim v. State, 194 So.2d 313.

Fla.App. 3 Dist. 1967. Items of evidence which are easily found in a person's dwelling are as much the fruit of a search as those which can be found only by ransacking the dwelling.

O'Neil v. State, 194 So.2d 40.

Fla.App. 4 Dist. 2008. For Fourth Amendment purposes, a "search" occurs when an expectation of privacy that society is prepared to consider reasonable is infringed. U.S.C.A. Const.Amend. 4.

Lindo v. State, 983 So.2d 672.

For Fourth Amendment purposes, a "seizure" of property occurs when there is some meaningful interference with an individual's possessory interests in that property. U.S.C.A. Const.Amend. 4.

Lindo v. State, 983 So.2d 672.

The temporary detention of two packages at mailing facility was not so unreasonable as to interfere, in any meaningful way, with the defendant's packages, and therefore, the temporary detention was not a "seizure" within the meaning of the Fourth Amendment, and because there was no seizure, there was no need for the State to establish reasonable suspicion, and considering that the dog sniff of the packages was also not a search, the defendant's Fourth Amendment rights were not implicated. U.S.C.A. Const.Amend. 4.

Lindo v. State, 983 So.2d 672.

Fla.App. 4 Dist. 2006. In order to be classified as a "search," law enforcement conduct must violate a constitutionally protected reasonable expectation of privacy. U.S.C.A. Const.Amend. 4.

State v. Rabb, 920 So.2d 1175, review denied 933 So.2d 522, certiorari denied 127 S.Ct. 665, 549 U.S. 1052, 166 L.Ed.2d 513.

Fla.App. 4 Dist. 2004. In order to be classified as a search, law enforcement conduct must violate a constitutionally protected reasonable expectation of privacy. U.S.C.A. Const.Amend. 4; West's F.S.A. Const. Art. 1, § 12.

State v. Rabb, 881 So.2d 587, rehearing denied, certiorari granted, vacated 125 S.Ct. 2246, 544 U.S. 1028, 161 L.Ed.2d 1051, on remand 920 So.2d 1175, review denied 933 So.2d 522, certiorari denied 127 S.Ct. 665, 549 U.S. 1052, 166 L.Ed.2d 513.

Fla.App. 4 Dist. 2002.   Fourth Amendment search occurs when the government violates a subjective expectation of privacy that society recognizes as reasonable. U.S.C.A. Const.Amend. 4.

State v. Lampley, 817 So.2d 989.

Fla.App. 4 Dist. 2000. Officer's conduct in grabbing defendant's hand as defendant removed it from his pocket constituted a "search." U.S.C.A. Const.Amend. 4.

Cenieus v. State, 758 So.2d 1250.

Fla.App. 4 Dist. 1997. Officers' action of securing residence while seeking search warrant did not amount to unreasonable "seizure" of contents of safe in residence. U.S.C.A. Const.Amend. 4.

Conner v. State, 701 So.2d 441.

Fla.App. 4 Dist. 1993. Search and seizure provision of State Constitution does not apply to seizure of private papers pursuant to execution. West's F.S.A. Const. Art. 1, § 12.

Luskin v. Luskin, 616 So.2d 556, review denied 629 So.2d 134.

Fla.App. 4 Dist. 1993. Defendant was not entitled to *Miranda* warnings before undercover officer ordered defendant to produce drugs which detective observed defendant using; order to disclose concealed drugs was search rather than an arrest. U.S.C.A. Const.Amends. 4, 5.

State v. Meyer, 615 So.2d 205.

Fla.App. 4 Dist. 1991. Having dial of safe cobalt tested after safe was seized from unoccupied apartment for safekeeping after shooting did not constitute search but merely enhanced police's plain view of safe. U.S.C.A. Const.Amend. 4.

State v. Heiser, 583 So.2d 389, review denied 593 So.2d 1052.

Search within meaning of Fourth Amendment did not occur when white powder fell from strongbox after it was seized by police officers from unoccupied apartment of shooting victim for safekeeping. U.S.C.A. Const.Amend. 4.

State v. Heiser, 583 So.2d 389, review denied 593 So.2d 1052.

Fla.App. 4 Dist. 1978. "Search" is an inspection or examination of places closed from public or general view, and requires some measure of force or intrusion, while "seizure" is the act of taking custody of evidence or contraband.

Lightfoot v. State, 356 So.2d 331, certiorari denied 361 So.2d 833.

Fla.App. 4 Dist. 1977. Inventory is search. West's F.S.A.Const. art. 1, § 12; U.S.C.A.Const. Amend. 4.

Jones v. State, 345 So.2d 809.

Fla.App. 4 Dist. 1976. Inventory search is a search within the contemplation of the Fourth Amendment and reasonableness or unreasonableness of such a search depends upon the particular facts and circumstances of each case. U.S.C.A.Const. Amend. 4.

Chuze v. State, 330 So.2d 166.

Fla.App. 4 Dist. 1975. An "inventory" search is a "search" within the Fourth Amendment prohibitions against unreasonable searches and seizures. U.S.C.A.Const. Amend. 4.

State v. Jenkins, 319 So.2d 91.

☞14. —— Taking samples of blood, or other physical specimens; handwriting exemplars.

C.A.11 (Fla.) 2016. Transvaginal ultrasounds to which state college required sonography students to submit for pedagogical purposes constituted "searches" under Fourth Amendment, even though transvaginal ultrasounds were not conducted to discover violations of law. U.S. Const. Amend. 4.

Jane Doe I v. Valencia College Board of Trustees, 838 F.3d 1207.

C.A.11 (Fla.) 2016. While the administration of a breath test for blood alcohol concentration is a search, such a test is unlikely to cause embarrassment and does not implicate significant privacy concerns under the Fourth Amendment, since the physical intrusion involved, consisting of blowing into a straw-like mouthpiece that is connected by a tube to the test machine, is almost negligible and entails a minimum of inconvenience. U.S. Const. Amend. 4.

Ziegler v. Martin County School District, 831 F.3d 1309.

Breath and urine tests implicate the Fourth Amendment's protection against unreasonable searches and seizures. U.S. Const. Amend. 4.

Ziegler v. Martin County School District, 831 F.3d 1309.

C.A.11 (Fla.) 2013. Testing urine sample, which can reveal host of private medical facts about government employee, and which entails process that itself implicates privacy interests, is search within meaning of Fourth Amendment. U.S.C.A. Const.Amend. 4.

American Federation of State, County and Mun. Employees Council 79 v. Scott, 717 F.3d 851, certiorari denied 134 S.Ct. 1877, 188 L.Ed.2d 912.

C.A.11 (Fla.) 2013. Government-mandated drug testing is a "search" within the meaning of the Fourth Amendment. U.S.C.A. Const.Amend. 4.

Lebron v. Secretary, Florida Dept. of Children and Families, 710 F.3d 1202.

M.D.Fla. 2013. Mandatory drug testing by the government is a "search" under the Fourth Amendment and is subject to the Fourth Amendment's reasonableness requirement. U.S.C.A. Const.Amend. 4.

Lebron v. Wilkins, 990 F.Supp.2d 1280.

M.D.Fla. 2011. Drug tests are considered searches under the Fourth Amendment. U.S.C.A. Const.Amend. 4.

Lebron v. Wilkins, 820 F.Supp.2d 1273, affirmed 710 F.3d 1202.

Suspicionless drug tests required by Florida statute in order to be eligible for benefits under federal Temporary Assistance for Needy Families (TANF) program constituted searches under Fourth Amendment, where tests involved collection of individual's urine, subsequent urinalysis could reveal private medical facts, positive drug tests were not kept confidential, as they were shared with third-parties, including Florida Department of Children and Families (DCF), medical reviewers, and counselors for Florida Abuse Hotline, and those positive test results were also memorialized in database that was accessible to state's law enforcement officers. U.S.C.A. Const.Amends. 4, 14; West's F.S.A. § 414.0652.

Lebron v. Wilkins, 820 F.Supp.2d 1273, affirmed 710 F.3d 1202.

S.D.Fla. 2014. It is well-settled that drug testing which utilizes urinalysis is a "search" that falls within the ambit of the Fourth and Fourteenth Amendments. U.S.C.A. Const.Amends. 4, 14.

Voss v. City of Key West, 24 F.Supp.3d 1219.

Fla. 1994. Breathalyzer test is "search" within meaning of Rule of Appellate Procedure authorizing state to appeal order suppressing before trial confessions, admissions or evidence obtained by search and seizure. West's F.S.A. R.App.P.Rule 9.140(c)(1)(B).

Blore v. Fierro, 636 So.2d 1329.

Fla.App. 2 Dist. 1988. Withdrawal of blood to determine alcohol content constitutes "search" within meaning of Fourth Amendment. U.S.C.A. Const.Amend. 4.

State v. Quartararo, 522 So.2d 42, review denied 531 So.2d 1354.

Fla.App. 3 Dist. 1995. It is not an unreasonable search within meaning of the Fourth Amendment to the United States Constitution for police to obtain a warrantless involuntary blood sample from a defendant who was under arrest for driving under the influence (DUI) provided there is probable cause to arrest defendant for that offense, and blood is extracted in a reasonable manner by medical personnel pursuant to medically approved procedures. U.S.C.A. Const.Amend. 4.

State v. Slaney, 653 So.2d 422, rehearing denied.

Fla.App. 4 Dist. 1995. Blood test is "search" to which Fourth Amendment applies. U.S.C.A. Const.Amend. 4.

Fosman v. State, 664 So.2d 1163.

Fla.App. 5 Dist. 2016. A blood draw conducted at the direction of the police is a search and seizure under the Fourth Amendment. U.S.C.A. Const.Amend. 4.

State v. Liles, 191 So.3d 484, rehearing and rehearing denied, review denied 2016 WL 4245500, review denied Willis v. State, 2016 WL 4247056, certiorari denied 137 S.Ct. 688, 196 L.Ed.2d 528.

To comply with the Fourth Amendment, law enforcement officers must obtain a warrant or consent for a blood draw, or there must be some other exception to the warrant requirement; when no warrant is obtained, the state has the burden to prove that an exception to the warrant requirement applies. U.S.C.A. Const.Amend. 4.

State v. Liles, 191 So.3d 484, rehearing and rehearing denied, review denied 2016 WL 4245500, review denied Willis v. State, 2016 WL 4247056, certiorari denied 137 S.Ct. 688, 196 L.Ed.2d 528.

Fla.App. 5 Dist. 2015. The drawing of blood for the testing of intoxicants constitutes a search under the Fourth Amendment. U.S.C.A. Const.Amend. 4; West's F.S.A. § 316.1933.

State v. Kleiber, 175 So.3d 319, rehearing denied.

Fla.App. 5 Dist. 2015. A breath-alcohol test is a search subject to Fourth Amendment protections. U.S.C.A. Const. Amend. 4; West's F.S.A. § 316.1939.

Williams v. State, 167 So.3d 483, rehearing denied, opinion vacated 2016 WL 6637817, on remand 210 So.3d 774.

⚷**15. ——— Taking items abandoned, voluntarily surrendered, or sold.**

C.A.11 (Fla.) 1989. Officer's inspection of debris discarded on public street during daylight hours after observing pieces of brown paper dropped to ground as defendant passed front of pickup truck in area of large amount of drug-related activity was not "search" under the Fourth Amendment. U.S.C.A. Const.Amend. 4.

U.S. v. Eubanks, 876 F.2d 1514.

Fla. 1977. Where allegedly obscene magazines were voluntarily bought and sold in ordinary course of business, there was no seizure nor confiscation to which objection could reasonably be made. West's F.S.A. § 847.011.

Johnson v. State, 351 So.2d 10.

Fla.App. 1 Dist. 1990. Where police seize abandoned contraband as a result of an unlawful stop, question becomes whether contraband seized was abandoned voluntarily or whether abandonment was an involuntary act directly attributable to unlawful stop; if abandonment was voluntary, no search of the person occurred. U.S.C.A. Const. Amend. 4.

State v. Bartee, 568 So.2d 523, quashed 623 So.2d 458.

Fla.App. 1 Dist. 1990. Although justification for detention of probationer whose driver's license had been revoked may have disappeared when it was determined that he was not driving his vehicle, no "search" for which voluntary consent was necessary arose when probationer, of his own volition, removed large wad of money and contraband from his pocket in response to police officer's suggestion that bulge in his pocket might be wallet containing proper identification. U.S.C.A. Const.Amend. 4.

Mitchell v. State, 559 So.2d 243.

Fla.App. 1 Dist. 1985. Where initial search of envelope containing cocaine was performed by employee of private carrier which contacted police, package remained unsealed until officer arrived, and officer's examination of envelope and its contents did not significantly exceed the scope of the private search in that removal of plastic bag from envelope and officer's visual inspection of contents enabled him to learn nothing that had not previously been learned during the private search, officer's examination infringed no legitimate expectation of privacy and was not a "search" within meaning of the Fourth Amendment; moreover, subsequent field testing of powder found in plastic bag did not compromise any legitimate privacy interest. U.S.C.A. Const.Amend. 4.

State v. Palmer, 474 So.2d 1250.

Fla.App. 1 Dist. 1976. Requirement of statute that all trucks and trailers stop at inspection stations of Department of Agriculture and Consumer Services for agricultural inspection is entirely reasonable and valid exercise of police power of state; stopping of vehicle for such purpose is not a "search" and is not an "unreasonable seizure" and does not violate right of owners of truck to due process of law or equal protection of the law. West's F.S.A. §§ 570.15, 570.15(1, 2), 570.44(3); U.S.C.A.Const. Amend. 4.

Stephenson v. Department of Agr. and Consumer Services, 329 So.2d 373, affirmed 342 So.2d 60, appeal dismissed 98 S.Ct. 32, 434 U.S. 803, 54 L.Ed.2d 61, rehearing denied 98 S.Ct. 493, 434 U.S. 960, 54 L.Ed.2d 321.

Fla.App. 2 Dist. 2000. Police do not conduct a "search" within the meaning of the Fourth Amendment when they retrieve property which a defendant has voluntarily abandoned in an area where he has no reasonable expectation of privacy, as where a person discards property in a hotel room or shack which has been vacated. U.S.C.A. Const.Amend. 4.

State v. Williams, 751 So.2d 170.

Fla.App. 2 Dist. 1995. Police officer's inquiry regarding whether defendant had any weapons in hip bag that officer observed during traffic stop was not a search for Fourth Amendment purposes, and officer could properly seize marijuana contained in bag when defendant voluntarily opened it, revealing marijuana sitting on top of other items. U.S.C.A. Const.Amend. 4.

State v. Bernard, 650 So.2d 100.

Fla.App. 2 Dist. 1980. No search occurs when police retrieve property which a suspect has voluntarily abandoned in an area where he has no reasonable expectation of privacy. West's F.S.A. § 901.151; U.S.C.A.Const. Amend. 4.

Patmore v. State, 383 So.2d 309.

Fla.App. 3 Dist. 1990. Even if officer lacked founded suspicion to support stop, juvenile voluntarily abandoned bag containing cocaine when he threw it to ground and fled after officer shouted "police," for purpose of determining whether bag was admissible in action on petition for delinquency. U.S.C.A. Const.Amend. 4.

A.G. v. State, 562 So.2d 400.

Fla.App. 3 Dist. 1989. Defendant's admission of police officers into his place of business, and his voluntary production of identification, did not give rise to illegal search and seizure. U.S.C.A. Const. Amend. 4.

Oliva v. State, 553 So.2d 1284.

Fla.App. 3 Dist. 1985. Initial production of medical records of minor upon whom abortion had been performed was made freely and voluntarily where there were no indicia of coercion when detective initially requested to see records and defendant-doctor produced them for police inspection; thus, initial production was not "search" within meaning of Fourth Amendment. U.S.C.A. Const.Amend. 4.

State v. Gonzalez, 467 So.2d 723, petition for review denied 476 So.2d 675.

Fla.App. 3 Dist. 1979. Police retrieval of evidence discarded in a public street by a defendant after being illegally ordered to stop by the police but before the police have begun a physical search of defendant's person or property does not constitute a "search of defendant's person" within meaning of search and seizure provisions of the State and Federal Constitutions. West's F.S.A.Const. art. 1, § 12; U.S.C.A.Const. Amends. 4, 14.

State v. Oliver, 368 So.2d 1331, certiorari dismissed 383 So.2d 1200.

It is not a search for the police to retrieve property which a defendant has voluntarily abandoned in an area where he has no reasonable expectation of privacy, as where a person discards property in the open fields while being pursued by the police or in the public street either prior to an attempted police stop, or after such a stop has been attempted or completed, or in a hotel room or shack which has been vacated; central to such rule is such a seizure does not invade a reasonable expectation of privacy. West's F.S.A.Const. art. 1, § 12; U.S.C.A.Const. Amends. 4, 14.

State v. Oliver, 368 So.2d 1331, certiorari dismissed 383 So.2d 1200.

Fla.App. 3 Dist. 1975. When prisoner informed jail authorities that she had gun in her purse and turned weapon over to them, there was no search of prisoner's person; but even if there was, prisoner would be deemed to have voluntarily consented thereto.

Jones v. State, 313 So.2d 105.

Fla.App. 3 Dist. 1965. Where defendant on being requested to produce driver's license voluntarily offered to show further identification and, in attempting to show same, accidentally dropped marijuana debris, search did not thereby transpire, and ensuing arrest and search were valid.

Beacham v. State, 175 So.2d 796.

Fla.App. 4 Dist. 2016. No "search" occurs when police retrieve property voluntarily abandoned by a suspect in an area where the latter has no reasonable expectation of privacy. U.S. Const. Amend. 4.

State v. K.C., 207 So.3d 951.

Fla.App. 4 Dist. 1982. No search occurs when police retrieve property voluntarily abandoned by a suspect in area in which he has no reasonable expectation of privacy. U.S.C.A.Const.Amend. 4.

State v. Milligan, 411 So.2d 946.

Fla.App. 4 Dist. 1975. A search is generally accepted to be an inspection or examination of places closed from public or general view and requires some measure of force or intrusion.

State v. Daniel, 319 So.2d 582.

Fla.App. 5 Dist. 2015. It is not a search for the police to retrieve property which a defendant has voluntarily abandoned in an area where he has no reasonable expectation of privacy; in such cases, the person has made a voluntary decision to avoid a police search by discarding evidence in an area where he has no Fourth Amendment protection. U.S.C.A. Const.Amend. 4.

K.W. v. State, 183 So.3d 1123.

Fla.App. 5 Dist. 1995. Juvenile defendant's relinquishment of cocaine was consensual, where police officers approached defendant in parking lot after she left motel room, officer told defendant that, if she had any controlled substance, he would like for her to give him the controlled substance, and defendant then relinquished cocaine.

S.L.R. v. State, 652 So.2d 978.

⚷16. —— **Observation; items in plain view.**

† **C.A.11 (Fla.) 2010.** Homeowners' allegations that police officers looked over their fence erected to prevent people from seeing into their yard were insufficient to plead an unreasonable search, for purposes of their § 1983 action alleging violations of the Fourth Amendment, absent allegations that officers were looking from a vantage point where they did not have the right to be. U.S.C.A. Const.Amend. 4; 42 U.S.C.A. § 1983.

Manseau v. City of Miramar, 395 Fed. Appx. 642, rehearing and rehearing denied 410 Fed.Appx. 297, certiorari denied 131 S.Ct. 2450, 563 U.S. 993, 179 L.Ed.2d 1218, rehearing denied 132 S.Ct. 49, 564 U.S. 1055, 180 L.Ed.2d 917.

C.A.11 (Fla.) 1989. Under the Fourth Amendment, no governmental "search" occurs if place or object examined is publicly exposed such that no person can reasonably have expectation of privacy. U.S.C.A. Const.Amend. 4.

U.S. v. Eubanks, 876 F.2d 1514.

C.A.5 (Fla.) 1978. Police view subsequent to search conducted by private citizens does not constitute "search" within meaning of Fourth Amendment so long as view is confined to scope and product of initial search. U.S.C.A.Const. Amend. 4.

U.S. v. Bomengo, 580 F.2d 173, certiorari denied 99 S.Ct. 1022, 439 U.S. 1117, 59 L.Ed.2d 75.

Where chief engineer and security director of apartment complex, after unsuccessfully attempting to locate occupants of apartment from which water was observed leaking, and after obtaining entry to apartment in order to locate source of leak, inadvertently noted that doors of den closet were ajar and that two handguns with attached silencers, in plain view, were inside closet, where police were then called, and where, upon arrival, detective was led directly to closet where handguns with silencers were located, and merely looked at silencers through open closet door, but then left to procure search warrant, there was no "search" within ambit of Fourth Amendment; police view was confined strictly to scope of initial discovery. U.S.C.A.Const. Amend. 4.

U.S. v. Bomengo, 580 F.2d 173, certiorari denied 99 S.Ct. 1022, 439 U.S. 1117, 59 L.Ed.2d 75.

C.A.5 (Fla.) 1969. Where, when postal inspectors approached defendant and deprived him of his liberty while he was picking up airplane tickets which he had ordered under fictitious name and for which he was signing receipt using fictitious name, they had every reason to believe that envelopes in full view in defendant's hands contained airplane tickets feloniously acquired, there was no search involved and seizure of tickets was lawful.

U.S. v. Chapman, 420 F.2d 925.

C.A.5 (Fla.) 1969. Items in plain view of law enforcement officers are not discovered as a result of search.

Agius v. U.S., 413 F.2d 915, rehearing denied 417 F.2d 635, certiorari denied 90 S.Ct. 1116, 397 U.S. 992, 25 L.Ed.2d 399.

S.D.Fla. 2011. Name which appeared on caller ID screen of defendant's cell phone when the phone rang after it was seized incident to his arrest was within plain view, such that its warrantless observation by agents did not constitute a "search" within meaning of the Fourth Amendment. U.S.C.A. Const.Amend. 4.

U.S. v. Gomez, 807 F.Supp.2d 1134.

Fla. 1971. It is not "search" for officer to see what may be observed from where he has legal right to be.

State v. Ashby, 245 So.2d 225.

Fla. 1967. In murder prosecution, permitting over objection testimony of ballistics analyst of laboratory of sheriff's bureau to testify that bullet recovered from body of victim was fired from pistol found on front seat of vehicle in which defendants were riding was not error, where arresting trooper could see portion of pistol lying under raincoat when defendants were stopped because of defective lights on vehicle, and no search of vehicle was necessary to its production.

Schneble v. State, 201 So.2d 881, vacated 88 S.Ct. 2067, 392 U.S. 298, on remand 215 So.2d 611, certiorari granted 91 S.Ct. 2279, 403 U.S. 952, 29 L.Ed.2d 863, affirmed 92 S.Ct. 1056, 405 U.S. 427, 31 L.Ed.2d 340.

Fla.App. 1 Dist. 1990. Detective's command to stand and plain viewing of crack cocaine in chair did not amount to "search" after valid investigatory stop and detention. U.S.C.A. Const.Amend. 4.

State v. Neely, 560 So.2d 1230.

Fla.App. 1 Dist. 1985. Observations made from place where officers have legal right to be do not rise to level of impermissible search.

Clark v. State, 469 So.2d 167.

Fla.App. 1 Dist. 1976. When officer, engaged in performing his duties, sees goods that he has probable cause to believe were stolen, he may seize goods without warrant and goods are admissible in evidence; it is not search to observe and to seize goods placed where they may be seen by officer where he has the equal right to be. U.S.C.A.Const. Amend. 4.

Atland v. State, 330 So.2d 85, certiorari denied 339 So.2d 1167.

Fla.App. 2 Dist. 1981. Although deputy who first spotted marijuana plants in backyard may have had no legal right to be in backyard, where other deputy was invited into home and observed plants in plain view, deputy not only had a right but a duty to seize marijuana plants. U.S.C.A.Const. Amend. 4.

Hall v. State, 395 So.2d 1258.

Fla.App. 3 Dist. 1979. It is not a search to observe and seize what is so placed where it may be seen by an officer who is where he has a legal right to be.

State v. Hughes, 375 So.2d 615.

Fla.App. 3 Dist. 1979. It is not a search to observe what is so placed where it may be seen by an officer who is where he has a legal right to be.

State v. Garcia, 374 So.2d 601.

Fla.App. 3 Dist. 1977. Search is inspection or examination of places closed from public or general view and requires some measure of force or intrusion, however slight, and it is not search to observe and to seize what is so placed that it may be seen by officer who is where he has legal right to be.

Brant v. State, 349 So.2d 674.

Officer's observation of defendant when he was pulling gun from under his shirt in hallway outside hotel room does not constitute search. West's F.S.A. § 901.21.

Brant v. State, 349 So.2d 674.

Fla.App. 3 Dist. 1976. It is not search to observe and to seize what is so placed that it may be seen by police officer who is where he has legal right to be.

Jester v. State, 339 So.2d 242, certiorari denied 348 So.2d 948.

Observation by police officer of object in plain view when officer has legal right to be in position to have that view is not search and such object may be properly seized by officer and introduced into evidence in criminal proceeding.

Jester v. State, 339 So.2d 242, certiorari denied 348 So.2d 948.

Fla.App. 3 Dist. 1967. Detectives' seizure of heroin lying in plain sight on dresser in defendant's room constituted a search.

O'Neil v. State, 194 So.2d 40.

Discovery of evidence by looking around in a room or dwelling constitutes a search.

O'Neil v. State, 194 So.2d 40.

Fla.App. 4 Dist. 1993. Unfenced front yard was equivalent of open field for which police officers passed to get to threshold front door and was not within scope of Fourth Amendment; therefore, officers' approach to front door and knocking on door was not an illegal entry

upon property merely because of display of "No Trespassing" sign. U.S.C.A. Const. Amend. 4.

Wysong v. State, 614 So.2d 670, review denied 632 So.2d 1029.

Fla.App. 4 Dist. 1978. Where police officer could see copper wire in plain view from place where officer had a legal right to be, there was no search and, therefore, tangible evidence thus observed by officer should not have been suppressed.

State v. Stevens, 354 So.2d 1244.

Fla.App. 4 Dist. 1977. It is not a "search" for a police officer to see what may be observed from where he has a legal right to be; objects which fall within plain view of the officers are subject to seizure and may be introduced into evidence.

Lovely v. State, 351 So.2d 1114.

Fla.App. 4 Dist. 1976. Contraband seized in plain view is not search and evidence thus obtained is clearly admissible.

Shiver v. State, 327 So.2d 251.

Fla.App. 4 Dist. 1975. Observation by police officer of object in plain view when officer has legal right to be in position to have that view is not a search and said object may be properly seized by officer and introduced into evidence in criminal proceeding.

State v. Daniel, 319 So.2d 582.

Fla.App. 4 Dist. 1974. Under plain view doctrine, no search occurs and evidence is deemed to have been properly seized where it is so placed that it may be seen by an officer who is where he has a right to be.

Bailey v. State, 295 So.2d 133, quashed 319 So.2d 22.

Fla.App. 4 Dist. 1972. Where patrolling officer had stopped defendant in early morning hours as defendant was walking on street in fashionable hotel and residential area, officer's inquiry concerning bulge in watchpocket of defendant's trousers did not amount to a search and defendant's conduct in producing a vial from his watchpocket and throwing vial, into adjacent waterway was an abandonment of possession; thus, vial, which was found to contain marijuana, was admissible, notwithstanding that officer had no valid ba-

† This Case was not selected for publication in the National Reporter System
For legislative history of cited statutes, see Florida Statutes Annotated

sis to stop defendant and interrogate him. F.S.A. § 901.151.

Riley v. State, 266 So.2d 173.

Fla.App. 4 Dist. 1970. To observe that which is open to view is not generally considered a search, and objects which fall within plain view of police officer who has right to be in position to have such view are subject to seizure and may be introduced into evidence.

State v. Clarke, 242 So.2d 791, certiorari denied 246 So.2d 112.

⌐17. —— Interior of premises, view from outside.

C.A.5 (Fla.) 1955. Standing on man's premises and looking in his bedroom window is violation of his "right to be left alone" as guaranteed by Fourth Amendment. U.S.C.A.Const. Amend. 4.

Brock v. U.S., 223 F.2d 681.

⌐18. —— Vehicles.

C.A.11 (Fla.) 1986. Opening a locked car trunk and removing the contents is a "search."

Jasinski v. Adams, 781 F.2d 843, rehearing denied 788 F.2d 694.

C.A.5 (Fla.) 1980. Examination of a vehicle for the purpose of identifying the VIN plates or identification number inscriptions is not a "search" for purposes of the Fourth Amendment. West's F.S.A. § 320.33; U.S.C.A.Const. Amend. 4.

U.S. v. Forrest, 620 F.2d 446, appeal after remand 649 F.2d 355.

An inspection by police officers is not a search merely because the police must open the door of the vehicle in order to examine the VIN plate. West's F.S.A. § 320.33; U.S.C.A.Const. Amend. 4.

U.S. v. Forrest, 620 F.2d 446, appeal after remand 649 F.2d 355.

C.A.5 (Fla.) 1978. Where a legitimate reason exists to do so, mere checking by a police officer of a vehicle identification number in order more positively to identify the vehicle is not a "search" within the meaning of the Fourth Amendment and, even if it were a "search," it would be a reasonable search. U.S.C.A.Const. Amend. 4.

U.S. v. Duckett, 583 F.2d 1309.

M.D.Fla. 1974. Whether a "search" occurred when officer looked through window of automobile and saw a box and some bills covering the part of floorboard on driver's side turned on officer's intent to conduct a "probing, exploratory quest for evidence of a crime"; whether a protected interest was involved turned on existence of reasonable expectation of privacy with respect to the vehicle's exposed interior. U.S.C.A.Const. Amend. 4.

U. S. ex rel. McDougald v. Hassfurder, 372 F.Supp. 395.

Fla. 1991. Stopping motor vehicle and detaining occupant constitutes "seizure" within meaning of Fourth and Fourteenth Amendments, even though stop is limited and resulting detention is quite brief; as such, stop must comport with objective standards of reasonableness, whether that amounts to probable cause or less stringent test. U.S.C.A. Const. Amends. 4, 14.

Nelson v. State, 578 So.2d 694.

Fla.App. 1 Dist. 2008. Use of a narcotics dog to sniff a vehicle does not constitute a search or seizure, and may be conducted during a consensual encounter or traffic stop; accordingly, when an officer is still writing a citation during a traffic stop when a backup officer or canine unit arrives, the lapse of time is generally not unreasonable. U.S.C.A. Const.Amend. 4.

Napoleon v. State, 985 So.2d 1170.

Fla.App. 1 Dist. 1990. Law enforcement official's act of looking into interior of automobile did not constitute "search" under Fourth Amendment. U.S.C.A. Const.Amend. 4.

State v. Starkey, 559 So.2d 335.

If automobile is located in area where police have right to be, police may lawfully look through automobile's windows and view objects which can be seen within, as such observation is not "search" under Fourth Amendment and involves no legally recognized intrusion. U.S.C.A. Const. Amend. 4.

State v. Starkey, 559 So.2d 335.

Fla.App. 3 Dist. 1979. Where officer properly stopped defendant's vehicle for routine traffic offense, defendant was placed under arrest for driving with suspended license, and defendant signed release relieving police of any responsibility for vehicle while it was left on the scene and where, in the process of securing defendant's vehicle, officer observed clear plastic bag, which appeared to contain marijuana, protruding from black plastic garbage bag which was on right rear floorboard and on which briefcase was lying, officer was not permitted to open briefcase without first securing warrant authorizing that action, even assuming that officer had probable cause to believe that briefcase contained contraband. U.S.C.A.Const. Amend. 4.

Cobb v. State, 378 So.2d 82, certiorari denied 388 So.2d 1111.

Fla.App. 3 Dist. 1973. Where there was legitimate reason to do so, the mere checking of a serial number on a parked automobile in order to more positively identify it was not a "search" within the prohibitions of the Fourth Amendment or, if it was a search, it was reasonable and no warrant was necessary. U.S.C.A.Const. Amend. 4.

State v. Cohn, 284 So.2d 426.

Fla.App. 4 Dist. 1974. Officer who stopped automobile for weaving, who did not make an arrest for any traffic violation, who, when male passenger got out of automobile in order to get his driver's license identification, observed a plastic bag sticking out from under leg of defendant, sitting in middle on front seat, and who reached in and got the bag, opened it up and found ashes which had a strong odor of marijuana, conducted a search which was not made as an incident to lawful arrest; thus plastic bag was result of unlawful search and seizure and should have been suppressed.

Bailey v. State, 295 So.2d 133, quashed 319 So.2d 22.

Fla.App. 4 Dist. 1972. Where officers who had observed unmarked truck enter and leave motel construction site at 9:30 p. m. upon stopping vehicle, observed carpet in plain view in truck, there was no "search" even though one officer subsequently opened the rear door of truck to ascertain color of the carpet.

State v. Miller, 267 So.2d 352, cause dismissed 273 So.2d 80.

Fla.App. 5 Dist. 2016. Police officer's act of pressing button on key fob seized from defendant, which activated alarm sounding from nearby vehicle, did not constitute a "search"; defendant had no reasonable expectation of privacy in the only information that could be obtained when officer touched button on fob lawfully in defendant's hand, i.e., presence of defendant's vehicle in public lot. U.S.C.A. Const.Amend. 4.

State v. Maye, 199 So.3d 357.

⊙═**19. —— Use of artificial light or visual aids.**

Fla.App. 1 Dist. 2005. Without a search warrant, using a thermal-imaging device to scan a home to determine whether heat emanating from the home is consistent with an indoor marijuana-growing operation is an illegal search in violation of the Fourth Amendment. U.S.C.A. Const.Amend. 4.

Smith v. State, 904 So.2d 534, rehearing denied.

Fla.App. 2 Dist. 2006. Police officer's act of shining flashlight into defendant's vehicle after defendant was arrested for gambling was not a "search" and thus did not implicate Fourth Amendment protections. U.S.C.A. Const.Amend. 4.

State v. Green, 943 So.2d 1004.

Fla.App. 2 Dist. 1994. Use of flashlight to illuminate area where officer has right to be does not constitute search or violate constitutional principles; flashlight merely enhances officer's plain view. U.S.C.A. Const.Amend. 4.

State v. Hite, 642 So.2d 55.

Fla.App. 4 Dist. 2006. Initial approach by police officer to vehicle in which defendant was sitting was a consensual encounter, even though officer approached vehicle with a flashlight and shined it inside vehicle. U.S.C.A. Const. Amend. 4.

State v. Echevarria, 937 So.2d 1276.

Fla.App. 4 Dist. 1982. Use of nightscope, under conditions in case, did not constitute a "search" within intent of those cases that require warrant before a "search" using electronic or other artificial devices may be constitutionally permissible. U.S.C.A.Const.Amend. 4.

> Newberry v. State, 421 So.2d 546, dismissed 426 So.2d 27.

Fla.App. 5 Dist. 1982. Police detective's use of binoculars to confirm his suspicions that green foliage protruding through open door and top of defendant's greenhouse was marijuana did not constitute "search." U.S.C.A.Const.Amend. 4.

> Bernstiel v. State, 416 So.2d 827.

20. —— Aerial surveillance.

U.S.Fla. 1989. Officer's observation, with his naked eye, of interior of partially covered greenhouse in residential backyard from vantage point of helicopter circling 400 feet above did not constitute a "search" for which a warrant was required. (Per Justice White with the Chief Justice and two Justices concurring, and one Justice concurring in the judgment.) U.S.C.A. Const.Amend. 4.

> Florida v. Riley, 109 S.Ct. 693, 488 U.S. 445, 102 L.Ed.2d 835, rehearing denied 109 S.Ct. 1659, 490 U.S. 1014, 104 L.Ed.2d 172, on remand Riley v. State, 549 So.2d 673.

S.D.Fla. 1992. Aerial inspection of land suspected to be used for marijuana growing did not constitute "search," for Fourth Amendment purposes. U.S.C.A. Const.Amend. 4.

> U.S. v. Seidel, 794 F.Supp. 1098.

Fla.App. 2 Dist. 1994. Viewing property from aircraft does not constitute a search requiring a warrant. U.S.C.A. Const.Amend. 4.

> State v. Lewinson, 644 So.2d 137.

21. —— Use of electronic devices; tracking devices or "beepers.".

† **C.A.11 (Fla.) 2016.** Government did not conduct "search" in violation of alleged conspirators' Fourth Amendment rights when, acting without warrant issued on showing of probable cause, it obtained cell phone records and cell tower records from telecommunications provider to establish general location of conspirators at time of charged robberies. U.S.C.A. Const.Amend. 4.

> U.S. v. Johnson, 645 Fed.Appx. 954, certiorari denied 137 S.Ct. 234, 196 L.Ed.2d 181.

C.A.11 (Fla.) 2015. Government obtaining court order under Stored Communications Act (SCA) for production of cell phone carrier's business records containing historical cell tower location information as to defendant was not a search under the Fourth Amendment; records were created by carrier and stored on its own premises, defendant exercised no control over the records, defendant knew that his cell phone transmitted information to cell towers and registered his phone under fictitious alias, and no law required collection of information in records. U.S.C.A. Const.Amend. 4; 18 U.S.C.A. § 2703(d).

> U.S. v. Davis, 785 F.3d 498, certiorari denied 136 S.Ct. 479, 193 L.Ed.2d 349.

C.A.11 (Fla.) 2013. Attachment of a Global—Positioning—System (GPS) tracking device to an individual's vehicle, and subsequent use of that device to monitor the vehicle's movements on public streets, constitutes a search or seizure within the meaning of the Fourth Amendment. U.S.C.A. Const.Amend. 4.

> U.S. v. Curbelo, 726 F.3d 1260, certiorari denied 134 S.Ct. 962, 187 L.Ed.2d 822, post-conviction relief denied 2017 WL 1134977.

C.A.11 (Fla.) 2013. Government's installation of a global positioning system (GPS) tracking device on a target's vehicle, and its use of that device to monitor the vehicle's movements, constitutes a search within the meaning of the Fourth Amendment. U.S.C.A. Const.Amend. 4.

> U.S. v. Gibson, 708 F.3d 1256, certiorari denied 134 S.Ct. 342, 187 L.Ed.2d 238.

C.A.11 (Fla.) 2003. The use of an x-ray device to project electronic emanations through an object and reveal, in picture form, the shape of the objects within the package constitutes a search within the meaning of the Fourth Amendment. U.S.C.A. Const.Amend. 4.

> U.S. v. Young, 350 F.3d 1302, rehearing and rehearing denied 97 Fed. Appx. 909.

C.A.5 (Fla.) 1979. *Holmes* decision that installation of a beeper on an automobile is a search within meaning of Fourth Amendment because it defeats expectation of privacy of automobile's occupant and is therefore prohibited unless a warrant is obtained or there is sufficient basis for failure to obtain a warrant to render act reasonable cannot be restricted to automobiles, because there is at least as great an expectation of privacy in vessels. U.S.C.A.Const. Amend. 4.

> U.S. v. Conroy, 589 F.2d 1258, rehearing denied U.S. v. Walker, 594 F.2d 241, rehearing denied 594 F.2d 241, certiorari denied 100 S.Ct. 60, 444 U.S. 831, 62 L.Ed.2d 40.

C.A.5 (Fla.) 1976. Use of battery-operated beacon or "beeper" attached to criminal suspect's van was illegal "search" because of failure to obtain warrant for beacon installation, and evidence obtained through use of such device was properly suppressed as "fruit" of initial illegal search (Per Curiam opinion with eight Circuit Judges dissenting).

> U.S. v. Holmes, 537 F.2d 227.

C.A.5 (Fla.) 1975. Installation of electronic tracking device on motor vehicle was "search" within meaning of Fourth Amendment and probable cause was required to justify issuance of warrant authorizing such installation. U.S.C.A.Const. Amend. 4.

> U.S. v. Holmes, 521 F.2d 859, rehearing granted 525 F.2d 1364, on rehearing 537 F.2d 227.

C.A.5 (Fla.) 1969. Recording of defendant's telephone conversation with informer did not violate defendant's reasonable expectations of privacy, hence no "search" occurred and no warrant was necessary. U.S.C.A.Const. Amend. 4.

> Davis v. U.S., 413 F.2d 1226.

C.A.5 (Fla.) 1967. Use of electronic devices to capture telephone conversation is a "search" within Fourth Amendment. U.S.C.A.Const. Amend. 4.

> Fountain v. U.S., 384 F.2d 624, certiorari denied Marshall v. U S, 88 S.Ct. 1246, 390 U.S. 1005, 20 L.Ed.2d 105.

M.D.Fla. 1972. Use of a pen register does not constitute a general search in violation of the Fourth Amendment. U.S.C.A.Const. Amend. 4.

> U.S. v. Lanza, 341 F.Supp. 405, supplemented 349 F.Supp. 929.

N.D.Fla. 2010. Use of a global positioning system (GPS) tracking device on the defendant's vehicle to trace the his movements as part of drug investigation did not violate his Fourth Amendment rights, since defendant had no legitimate expectation of privacy in the movements of his automobile on public roads, and the intrusion caused by affixing the magnetic tracking device to the vehicle was minimal, given that it was placed on the vehicle's undercarriage from a public sidewalk, and the vehicle was not fenced in, kept inside a garage, or otherwise shielded from contact with any member of the public. U.S.C.A. Const.Amend. 4.

> U.S. v. Burton, 698 F.Supp.2d 1303.

There is no Fourth Amendment violation for using a tracking device as a substitute for visual surveillance where the substitute is for an activity, namely following a car on a public street, that is unequivocally not a search within the meaning of the amendment. U.S.C.A. Const.Amend. 4.

> U.S. v. Burton, 698 F.Supp.2d 1303.

Fla.App. 1 Dist. 1985. Defendant had no legitimate expectation of privacy which society would recognize as reasonable, under either the Fourth Amendment or Florida Constitution [West's F.S.A. Const. Art. 1, § 12], with regard to numbers dialed into commercial telephone system; hence, use of pen register to ascertain numbers dialed from defendant's telephone did not constitute a "search" or require a warrant. U.S.C.A. Const.Amend. 4.

> Yarbrough v. State, 473 So.2d 766.

Fla.App. 3 Dist. 1965. Mechanical recording of defendant's conversation with person on whose person microphone was secreted did not constitute illegal search and seizure or entrapment.

> Gomien v. State, 172 So.2d 511.

⊶**22.   —— Scent; use of dogs.**

U.S.Fla. 2013. Law enforcement officers' use of drug-sniffing dog on front porch of home, to investigate an unverified tip that marijuana was being grown in the home, was a trespassory invasion of the curtilage which constituted a "search" for

---

† This Case was not selected for publication in the National Reporter System
For legislative history of cited statutes, see Florida Statutes Annotated

Fourth Amendment purposes. U.S.C.A. Const.Amend. 4.

Florida v. Jardines, 133 S.Ct. 1409, 185 L.Ed.2d 495.

† C.A.11 (Fla.) 2016. Officer's decision to conduct a dog sniff did not unreasonably prolong traffic stop of defendant's vehicle, and thus was not a search subject to the Fourth Amendment. U.S. Const. Amend. 4.

United States v. Wilson, 662 Fed. Appx. 693.

C.A.11 (Fla.) 1998. A canine sniff is not considered a "search" for Fourth Amendment purposes. U.S.C.A. Const. Amend. 4.

U.S. v. Glinton, 154 F.3d 1245, certiorari denied Hatten v. U.S., 119 S.Ct. 1281, 526 U.S. 1032, 143 L.Ed.2d 374, certiorari denied Heath v. U.S., 119 S.Ct. 1587, 526 U.S. 1104, 143 L.Ed.2d 681, certiorari denied Davis v. U.S., 119 S.Ct. 1587, 526 U.S. 1104, 143 L.Ed.2d 681, habeas corpus dismissed by 2012 WL 3028044, reconsideration denied 2012 WL 3757482, reconsideration denied 2012 WL 4718631, affirmed 522 Fed.Appx. 161, affirmed 522 Fed. Appx. 161, affirmed 522 Fed.Appx. 161.

C.A.11 (Fla.) 1997. Canine sniff of exterior of vehicle which resulted in alert for presence of drugs was not a "search" for Fourth Amendment purposes. U.S.C.A. Const.Amend. 4.

U.S. v. Holloman, 113 F.3d 192.

C.A.11 (Fla.) 1995. Use of dogs to sniff exterior of cars at roadblock checkpoint without individualized suspicion of drug-related criminal activity was not unconstitutional search, where sniffs occurred while motorists were lawfully stopped in public place during license check, and they were not delayed to conduct sniffs. U.S.C.A. Const.Amend. 4.

Merrett v. Moore, 58 F.3d 1547, suggestion for rehearing denied 77 F.3d 1304, certiorari denied 117 S.Ct. 58, 519 U.S. 812, 136 L.Ed.2d 21.

C.A.5 (Fla.) 1981. Use of dogs to sniff exteriors of suitcases did not constitute search within meaning of Fourth Amendment, and light press of the hands

along outside of case was not sufficiently intrusive to require different result. U.S.C.A.Const. Amend. 4.

U.S. v. Viera, 644 F.2d 509, certiorari denied Alonso v. U.S., 102 S.Ct. 332, 454 U.S. 867, 70 L.Ed.2d 169, certiorari denied 102 S.Ct. 332, 454 U.S. 867, 70 L.Ed.2d 169.

C.A.5 (Fla.) 1981. Drug agents' use of a dog's trained olfactory sense did not convert the dog sniffing of the exterior of the suitcases into a search.

U.S. v. Goldstein, 635 F.2d 356, rehearing denied 640 F.2d 385, certiorari denied 101 S.Ct. 3111, 452 U.S. 962, 69 L.Ed.2d 972.

Fla. 2011. A "sniff test" by a drug detection dog conducted at the front door of a private residence is a substantial government intrusion into the sanctity of the home and constitutes a "search" within the meaning of the Fourth Amendment, such that it must be preceded by an evidentiary showing of wrongdoing. U.S.C.A. Const.Amend. 4.

Jardines v. State, 73 So.3d 34, rehearing denied, certiorari granted in part 132 S.Ct. 995, 565 U.S. 1104, 181 L.Ed.2d 726, affirmed 133 S.Ct. 1409, 185 L.Ed.2d 495.

Fla.App. 1 Dist. 2008. Dog sniff at front door of apartment did not constitute Fourth Amendment search as it did not violate legitimate privacy interest; binary nature of dog sniff rendered it unique in that it was distinguishable from traditional search methods, and dog was located on common walkway within apartment complex when sniff occurred. U.S.C.A. Const. Amend. 4.

Stabler v. State, 990 So.2d 1258, review granted, quashed 90 So.3d 267.

Fla.App. 1 Dist. 1990. Use of narcotics dog during valid traffic stop is not "search" or "seizure.".

Blackmon v. State, 570 So.2d 1074.

Fla.App. 1 Dist. 1978. It is not a search for a police officer to observe contraband in plain view or to detect odor of marijuana from a place where he has a right to be.

St. John v. State, 356 So.2d 32.

Fla.App. 2 Dist. 1991. Use of "sniff" dog during normal course of traffic stop does not constitute search or seizure. U.S.C.A. Const.Amend. 4.

Joseph v. State, 588 So.2d 1014.

Fla.App. 3 Dist. 2008. The use of a drug detector dog at defendant's house door did not constitute a search, for purposes of determining whether probable cause existed for subsequent warrant to search defendant's home for live marijuana plants and the equipment used to grow them; a dog's nose was not a device nor was it improved by technology, and detection of contraband by a dog while standing on a front porch open to the public was not search which compromised a legitimate privacy interest for Fourth Amendment purposes. U.S.C.A. Const.Amend. 4.

State v. Jardines, 9 So.3d 1, review granted 3 So.3d 1246, quashed 73 So.3d 34, rehearing denied, certiorari granted in part 132 S.Ct. 995, 565 U.S. 1104, 181 L.Ed.2d 726, affirmed 133 S.Ct. 1409, 185 L.Ed.2d 495.

The fact that a dog, as odor detector, is more skilled than a human does not render the dog's sniff illegal under the Fourth Amendment. U.S.C.A. Const. Amend. 4.

State v. Jardines, 9 So.3d 1, review granted 3 So.3d 1246, quashed 73 So.3d 34, rehearing denied, certiorari granted in part 132 S.Ct. 995, 565 U.S. 1104, 181 L.Ed.2d 726, affirmed 133 S.Ct. 1409, 185 L.Ed.2d 495.

A canine sniff is not a search within the meaning of the Fourth Amendment as long as the sniffing canine is legally present at its vantage point when its sense is aroused. U.S.C.A. Const.Amend. 4.

State v. Jardines, 9 So.3d 1, review granted 3 So.3d 1246, quashed 73 So.3d 34, rehearing denied, certiorari granted in part 132 S.Ct. 995, 565 U.S. 1104, 181 L.Ed.2d 726, affirmed 133 S.Ct. 1409, 185 L.Ed.2d 495.

Fla.App. 3 Dist. 1983. Ventilation or "prepping" of defendant's luggage, i.e., forcing air from within to be expelled, so as to enhance ability of trained dog to detect any contraband was such a de minimis intrusion as not to constitute a "search and seizure" within prohibitions of Federal and State Constitutions. West's F.S.A. Const. Art. 1, § 12; U.S.C.A. Const. Amend. 4.

Sprowls v. State, 433 So.2d 1271.

Fla.App. 3 Dist. 1980. Where defendant approached police officer, engaged him in conversation about officer's dog, and commented on beauty of dog as officer, dog, defendant, and codefendant walked along, where officer identified himself, showed his badge, asked defendants for identification, and defendants handed officers their drivers' licenses, and where, within seconds, dog gave positive alert to presence of narcotics within suitcase defendant had set down, dog sniff itself was not a search requiring showing of probable cause.

Harpold v. State, 389 So.2d 279, review denied 397 So.2d 777.

Fla.App. 3 Dist. 1980. Slight movement of defendant's unopened luggage from cart to airport floor did not amount to a Fourth Amendment seizure, much less a "search" of defendant's luggage so as to require existence of probable cause and "narcotics" dog's sniffing of exterior of defendant's bag, which was in custody of airline, did not invade legitimate expectation of privacy held by defendant. U.S.C.A.Const. Amend. 4.

State v. Goodley, 381 So.2d 1180.

Fla.App. 3 Dist. 1980. Where, after narcotics dog alerted on subject luggage, officer removed the luggage and placed them some distance away amongst other baggage, there was no seizure. U.S.C.A.Const. Amend. 4.

Mata v. State, 380 So.2d 1157, petition for review denied 389 So.2d 1112.

Fla.App. 4 Dist. 1999. A dog alert to the outside of a vehicle does not constitute a search within the meaning of the Fourth Amendment. U.S.C.A. Const.Amend. 4.

Castro v. State, 755 So.2d 657.

Fla.App. 4 Dist. 1995. Canine sniff by narcotics detection dog, which discloses presence or absence of narcotics, is regarded as constitutionally proper because its limited scope and method of investigation do not constitute search, however, canine sniff that alerts to package does not eliminate requirement that, absent exigent circumstances, consent or other recognized exceptions, search warrant must be obtained before search of contents of package passes constitutional muster. U.S.C.A. Const.Amend. 4.

Daniels v. Cochran, 654 So.2d 609.

Fla.App. 5 Dist. 2010. The use of a narcotics dog to sniff a vehicle does not constitute a search and may be conducted during a consensual encounter or traffic stop; however, the canine search of the exterior of the vehicle must be completed within the time required to issue a citation. U.S.C.A. Const.Amend. 4.

Whitfield v. State, 33 So.3d 787.

⚷23. Fourth Amendment and reasonableness in general.

U.S.Fla. 1999. In deciding whether a challenged governmental action violates Fourth Amendment, court inquires whether the action was regarded as an unlawful search and seizure when the Amendment was framed. U.S.C.A. Const.Amend. 4.

Florida v. White, 119 S.Ct. 1555, 526 U.S. 559, 143 L.Ed.2d 748, on remand White v. State, 753 So.2d 548.

U.S.Fla. 1991. Touchstone of Fourth Amendment is reasonableness. U.S.C.A. Const.Amend. 4.

Florida v. Jimeno, 111 S.Ct. 1801, 500 U.S. 248, 114 L.Ed.2d 297, on remand State v. Jimeno, 588 So.2d 233.

Fourth Amendment does not proscribe all state-initiated searches and seizures; it merely proscribes those which are unreasonable. U.S.C.A. Const.Amend. 4.

Florida v. Jimeno, 111 S.Ct. 1801, 500 U.S. 248, 114 L.Ed.2d 297, on remand State v. Jimeno, 588 So.2d 233.

C.A.11 (Fla.) 2017. Under the Fourth Amendment, an individual has a right to be free from unreasonable searches and seizures; an arrest is a seizure of the person. U.S. Const. Amend. 4.

Stephens v. DeGiovanni, 852 F.3d 1298.

C.A.11 (Fla.) 2016. Touchstone of the constitutionality of a governmental

search is reasonableness. U.S. Const. Amend. 4.

Ziegler v. Martin County School District, 831 F.3d 1309.

C.A.11 (Fla.) 2016. Under the general Fourth Amendment approach, a court examines the totality of the circumstances to determine whether a search is reasonable. U.S.C.A. Const.Amend. 6.

Castillo v. U.S., 816 F.3d 1300.

Whether a search is reasonable is determined by assessing, on the one hand, the degree to which it intrudes upon an individual's privacy and, on the other, the degree to which it is needed for the promotion of legitimate governmental interests. U.S.C.A. Const.Amend. 6.

Castillo v. U.S., 816 F.3d 1300.

C.A.11 (Fla.) 2015. The Fourth Amendment prohibits unreasonable searches, not warrantless searches; the ultimate measure of the constitutionality of a governmental search is reasonableness. U.S.C.A. Const.Amend. 4.

U.S. v. Davis, 785 F.3d 498, certiorari denied 136 S.Ct. 479, 193 L.Ed.2d 349.

The reasonableness of a search or seizure is evaluated under traditional standards of reasonableness by assessing, on the one hand, the degree to which it intrudes upon an individual's privacy and, on the other, the degree to which it is needed for the promotion of legitimate governmental interests. U.S.C.A. Const. Amend. 4.

U.S. v. Davis, 785 F.3d 498, certiorari denied 136 S.Ct. 479, 193 L.Ed.2d 349.

C.A.11 (Fla.) 2014. In Fourth Amendment context, the greatest dangers to liberty lurk in insidious encroachment by men of zeal, well-meaning but without understanding. U.S.C.A. Const.Amend. 4.

Gennusa v. Canova, 748 F.3d 1103.

C.A.11 (Fla.) 2013. A law enforcement officer's subjective motivation for conducting a search is irrelevant in the Fourth Amendment context. U.S.C.A. Const.Amend. 4.

U.S. v. Timmann, 741 F.3d 1170.

C.A.11 (Fla.) 2013. Fourth Amendment protects right of people to be secure in their persons, houses, papers, and effects, against unreasonable searches and seizures, and applies to states through Due Process Clause of Fourteenth Amendment. U.S.C.A. Const.Amends. 4, 14.

American Federation of State, County and Mun. Employees Council 79 v. Scott, 717 F.3d 851, certiorari denied 134 S.Ct. 1877, 188 L.Ed.2d 912.

To be reasonable under Fourth Amendment, search ordinarily must be based on individualized suspicion of wrongdoing. U.S.C.A. Const.Amend. 4.

American Federation of State, County and Mun. Employees Council 79 v. Scott, 717 F.3d 851, certiorari denied 134 S.Ct. 1877, 188 L.Ed.2d 912.

In limited circumstances, where privacy interests implicated by search are minimal, and where important governmental interest furthered by intrusion would be placed in jeopardy by requirement of individualized suspicion, search may be reasonable despite absence of such suspicion. U.S.C.A. Const.Amend. 4.

American Federation of State, County and Mun. Employees Council 79 v. Scott, 717 F.3d 851, certiorari denied 134 S.Ct. 1877, 188 L.Ed.2d 912.

"Compelling interest" is one important enough to justify particular search at hand, for Fourth Amendment purposes, in light of other factors that show search to be relatively intrusive upon genuine expectation of privacy. U.S.C.A. Const.Amend. 4.

American Federation of State, County and Mun. Employees Council 79 v. Scott, 717 F.3d 851, certiorari denied 134 S.Ct. 1877, 188 L.Ed.2d 912.

C.A.11 (Fla.) 2013. Ordinarily, to be reasonable, a search must be based on individualized suspicion of wrongdoing; in most cases, this standard is met only when a search is accomplished pursuant to a judicial warrant issued upon a finding of probable cause. U.S.C.A. Const.Amend. 4.

Lebron v. Secretary, Florida Dept. of Children and Families, 710 F.3d 1202.

C.A.11 (Fla.) 2012. A court must examine the totality of the circumstances in order to determine whether a search or seizure is reasonable under the Fourth Amendment. U.S.C.A. Const.Amend. 4.

U.S. v. Lewis, 674 F.3d 1298.

The touchstone of the Fourth Amendment is reasonableness, not individualized suspicion. U.S.C.A. Const.Amend. 4.

U.S. v. Lewis, 674 F.3d 1298.

C.A.11 (Fla.) 2011. When dealing with limited seizures not subject to the probable-cause requirement, a seizure that is reasonable at its inception may quickly become unreasonable if it extends beyond its unique justification. U.S.C.A. Const. Amend. 4.

Croom v. Balkwill, 645 F.3d 1240.

C.A.11 (Fla.) 2010. To determine the reasonableness of a border search, or of any search for that matter, courts weigh its intrusion on an individual's Fourth Amendment interests against its promotion of legitimate governmental interests. U.S.C.A. Const.Amend. 4.

U.S. v. Alfaro-Moncada, 607 F.3d 720, rehearing and rehearing denied 408 Fed.Appx. 347, certiorari denied 131 S.Ct. 1604, 562 U.S. 1273, 179 L.Ed.2d 505.

C.A.11 (Fla.) 2009. Whether search or seizure is unreasonable in violation of the Fourth Amendment is judged by balancing its intrusion on individual's Fourth Amendment interests against its promotion of legitimate governmental interests. U.S.C.A. Const.Amend. 4.

Denson v. U.S., 574 F.3d 1318, rehearing and rehearing denied 400 Fed.Appx. 551, certiorari denied 130 S.Ct. 3384, 560 U.S. 952, 177 L.Ed.2d 302.

C.A.11 (Fla.) 2009. The Fourth Amendment does not apply to actions against foreign citizens on foreign soil. U.S.C.A. Const.Amend. 4.

U.S. v. Valencia-Trujillo, 573 F.3d 1171, rehearing and rehearing denied 373 Fed.Appx. 43, certiorari denied 130 S.Ct. 1726, 559 U.S. 987, 176 L.Ed.2d 205.

C.A.11 (Fla.) 2009. Fourth Amendment's "reasonableness" standard requires balancing the nature of the Fourth Amendment violation against the government's interests, which include protecting the safety of the police officers involved as well as the public at large. U.S.C.A. Const.Amend. 4.

> Garczynski v. Bradshaw, 573 F.3d 1158.

C.A.11 (Fla.) 2009. Governments may not prevent protests, punish the exercise of the right under the First Amendment free speech clause to protest peacefully by arresting the demonstrators, nor unduly burden the right by forcing demonstrators to undergo excessive searches that violate the Fourth Amendment. U.S.C.A. Const.Amends. 1, 4.

> Amnesty Intern., USA v. Battle, 559 F.3d 1170, rehearing and rehearing denied 347 Fed.Appx. 555.

C.A.11 (Fla.) 2009. Under the Fourth Amendment, an individual has a right to be free from unreasonable searches and seizures. U.S.C.A. Const.Amend. 4.

> Case v. Eslinger, 555 F.3d 1317.

"Reasonableness" of a seizure or arrest under the Fourth Amendment turns on the presence or absence of probable cause. U.S.C.A. Const.Amend. 4.

> Case v. Eslinger, 555 F.3d 1317.

† C.A.11 (Fla.) 2007. The constitutional prohibition against unreasonable searches and seizures by the government is not implicated by entry upon private land to knock on a citizen's door for legitimate police purposes unconnected with a search of the premises; accordingly, officers are allowed to approach a residence intending to speak with the inhabitants. U.S.C.A. Const.Amend. 4.

> U.S. v. Del Val, 223 Fed.Appx. 963.

C.A.11 (Fla.) 2006. The Fourth Amendment, which prohibits unreasonable searches and seizures by the government, is not implicated by entry upon private land to knock on a citizen's door for legitimate police purposes unconnected with a search of the premises. U.S.C.A. Const. Amend. 4.

> U.S. v. Taylor, 458 F.3d 1201.

C.A.11 (Fla.) 2004. While constitutional reasonableness of police investigation does not depend on officer's subjective intent or ulterior motive in conducting investigation, officer may not choose to ignore information that has been offered to him, nor conduct investigation in biased fashion, nor elect not to obtain easily discoverable facts. U.S.C.A. Const.Amend. 4.

> Kingsland v. City of Miami, 382 F.3d 1220, rehearing and rehearing denied 124 Fed.Appx. 644.

C.A.11 (Fla.) 2000. Fourth Amendment is not a guarantee against all searches and seizures, but only against unreasonable searches and seizures. U.S.C.A. Const.Amend. 4.

> U.S. v. Smith, 201 F.3d 1317, postconviction relief dismissed by 2016 WL 3194980, motion denied 2016 WL 5933396.

C.A.11 (Fla.) 1997. To establish Fourth Amendment violation, federal civil rights plaintiff must demonstrate that seizure occurred and that it was unreasonable. U.S.C.A. Const.Amend. 4; 42 U.S.C.A. § 1983.

> Evans v. Hightower, 117 F.3d 1318.

C.A.11 (Fla.) 1995. Fourth Amendment prohibits only unreasonable searches, and unreasonableness is determined by case-by-case balancing of state's interests against individual's. U.S.C.A. Const.Amend. 4.

> Lenz v. Winburn, 51 F.3d 1540.

C.A.11 (Fla.) 1993. Test for determining whether person has reasonable or justifiable expectation of privacy, for purposes of Title III of the Omnibus Crime Control and Safe Streets Act and the Fourth Amendment, has two prongs: first, whether person's conduct exhibits subjective expectation of privacy, and second, whether person's subjective expectation of privacy is one that society is willing to recognize as reasonable. 18 U.S.C.A. §§ 2510(2), 2511; U.S.C.A. Const.Amend. 4.

> U.S. v. McKinnon, 985 F.2d 525, certiorari denied 114 S.Ct. 130, 510 U.S. 843, 126 L.Ed.2d 94.

C.A.11 (Fla.) 1989. Fourth Amendment protects individuals from unreasonable searches and seizures by law enforcement authorities of the United States Government. U.S.C.A. Const.Amend. 4.

> U.S. v. Garcia, 890 F.2d 355.

C.A.11 (Fla.) 1989. Police-citizen communications involving no coercion or detention do not implicate the Fourth Amendment. U.S.C.A. Const.Amend. 4.

U.S. v. Hastamorir, 881 F.2d 1551.

C.A.11 (Fla.) 1989. Warrantless seizure that is fundamentally fair in due process sense is also reasonable under Fourth Amendment; interests protected by both due process and Fourth Amendment are parallel as both due process and Fourth Amendment analyses balance governmental interest against owner's rights in property. U.S.C.A. Const.Amends. 4, 5, 14.

U.S. v. Valdes, 876 F.2d 1554.

C.A.11 (Fla.) 1987. Permissibility of particular law enforcement practice relating to searches is judged by balancing its intrusion on individual's Fourth Amendment interest against its promotion of legitimate governmental interest. U.S.C.A. Const.Amend. 4.

U.S. v. Hernandez-Salazar, 813 F.2d 1126.

C.A.11 (Fla.) 1986. Reasonableness of search depends upon complexity of crime being investigated and difficulty involved in determining whether certain documents evidence the crime.

U.S. v. Sawyer, 799 F.2d 1494, certiorari denied Leavitt v. U.S., 107 S.Ct. 961, 479 U.S. 1069, 93 L.Ed.2d 1009.

C.A.11 (Fla.) 1986. Objectively reasonable stop or other seizure is not invalid solely because the officer acted out of improper motivation. U.S.C.A. Const. Amend. 4.

U.S. v. Smith, 799 F.2d 704.

C.A.11 (Fla.) 1985. Reasonableness of an official invasion of citizen's privacy must be appraised on basis of the facts as they existed at the time that invasion occurred.

U.S. v. O'Bryant, 775 F.2d 1528.

C.A.11 (Fla.) 1983. Two requirements must be met before a person may successfully prevail on Fourth Amendment claim: first, there must be a search and seizure of that individual's person, house, papers, or effects, conducted by an agent of the government; second, challenged search and seizure must be unreasonable. U.S.C.A. Const.Amend. 4.

U.S. v. Bachner, 706 F.2d 1121, certiorari denied 104 S.Ct. 247, 464 U.S. 896, 78 L.Ed.2d 235.

C.A.11 (Fla.) 1983. Objective of Fourth Amendment is to protect liberty and privacy from arbitrary and oppressive interference by government officials, and achieving such objective requires striking correct balance between government's interest and the individual's interest in dignity and privacy. U.S.C.A. Const.Amend. 4.

U.S. v. Hidalgo-Gato, 703 F.2d 1267.

C.A.11 (Fla.) 1982. Magnitude of a search is insufficient, by itself, to establish a constitutional violation; rather, relevant inquiry is whether the search and seizure were reasonable under all the circumstances. U.S.C.A.Const.Amend. 4.

U.S. v. Wuagneux, 683 F.2d 1343, certiorari denied 104 S.Ct. 69, 464 U.S. 814, 78 L.Ed.2d 83.

C.A.11 (Fla.) 1982. Where Fourth Amendment issues are involved, fundamental inquiry is whether search or seizure was reasonable under all the circumstances. U.S.C.A.Const.Amend. 4.

U.S. v. Wilson, 671 F.2d 1291, certiorari denied 103 S.Ct. 98, 459 U.S. 844, 74 L.Ed.2d 89.

C.A.5 (Fla.) 1981. Because Fourth Amendment expressly prohibits only unreasonable warrantless searches, it patently incorporates a balancing test, weighing level of intrusion into individual privacy against public interest to be served. U.S.C.A.Const. Amend. 4.

U.S. v. Richards, 638 F.2d 765, rehearing denied 646 F.2d 962, certiorari denied 102 S.Ct. 669, 454 U.S. 1097, 70 L.Ed.2d 638.

C.A.5 (Fla.) 1979. In any Fourth Amendment case, court must consider not only the reasons for initiating the search but also how the search was conducted. U.S.C.A.Const. Amend. 4.

U.S. v. Klein, 592 F.2d 909.

C.A.5 (Fla.) 1979. Where cartons were sent by bus with fictitious name given for addressee, where employees of corporation whose name was similar to that of fictitious addressee took cartons from bus terminal after being notified of shipment, opened cartons, examined individual film boxes and ascertained nature of films, and then called FBI, and where activities of corporation's employees constituted a private search, FBI's acceptance of films from corporation's employees was not a "seizure" within meaning of Fourth Amendment. U.S.C.A.Const. Amend. 4.

> U.S. v. Sanders, 592 F.2d 788, rehearing denied 597 F.2d 63, certiorari granted Walter v. U.S., 100 S.Ct. 227, 444 U.S. 914, 62 L.Ed.2d 168, reversed 100 S.Ct. 2395, 447 U.S. 649, 65 L.Ed.2d 410, on remand 625 F.2d 1311.

C.A.5 (Fla.) 1979. Mere existence of statutory authority to make a search does not obviate need for Fourth Amendment compliance. U.S.C.A.Const. Amend. 4.

> U.S. v. Conroy, 589 F.2d 1258, rehearing denied U.S. v. Walker, 594 F.2d 241, rehearing denied 594 F.2d 241, certiorari denied 100 S.Ct. 60, 444 U.S. 831, 62 L.Ed.2d 40.

C.A.5 (Fla.) 1978. The ultimate standard for measuring the validity of searches under the Fourth Amendment is reasonableness. U.S.C.A.Const. Amend. 4.

> U.S. v. Sink, 586 F.2d 1041, certiorari denied 99 S.Ct. 3102, 443 U.S. 912, 61 L.Ed.2d 876, certiorari denied Grim v. U.S., 99 S.Ct. 3102, 443 U.S. 912, 61 L.Ed.2d 876.

C.A.5 (Fla.) 1978. Fourth Amendment imposes general reasonableness standard upon all searches and seizures. U.S.C.A.Const. Amend. 4.

> U.S. v. Freeman, 579 F.2d 942.

What is "reasonable" within meaning of Fourth Amendment depends upon circumstances of each case. U.S.C.A.Const. Amend. 4.

> U.S. v. Freeman, 579 F.2d 942.

C.A.5 (Fla.) 1977. The Fourth Amendment protects the citizen against invasion of privacy, and once that interest is invaded legally by an official of the state, the citizen has lost his reasonable expectation of privacy to the extent of the invasion. U.S.C.A.Const. Amend. 4.

> U.S. v. Brand, 556 F.2d 1312, rehearing denied 561 F.2d 831, certiorari denied 98 S.Ct. 1237, 434 U.S. 1063, 55 L.Ed.2d 763, rehearing denied 98 S.Ct. 1593, 435 U.S. 961, 55 L.Ed.2d 811.

C.A.5 (Fla.) 1977. "Reasonableness" in the Fourth Amendment sense always depends on a balance which must be struck between, on the one hand, the level of official intrusion into individual privacy and, on the other hand, the public interest to be served by such an intrusion. U.S.C.A.Const. Amend. 4.

> U.S. v. Himmelwright, 551 F.2d 991, certiorari denied 98 S.Ct. 298, 434 U.S. 902, 54 L.Ed.2d 189.

C.A.5 (Fla.) 1977. Fourth Amendment embodies the comprehensive right of privacy against unwarranted governmental intrusions. U.S.C.A.Const. Amend. 4.

> Nordskog v. Wainwright, 546 F.2d 69.

C.A.5 (Fla.) 1976. Arbitrary invasion of the privacy of the home or dwelling is the "chief evil" to which the Fourth Amendment is directed. 42 U.S.C.A. § 1983; U.S.C.A.Const. Amend. 4.

> U.S. v. Cravero, 545 F.2d 406, certiorari denied Miller v. U.S., 97 S.Ct. 1123, 429 U.S. 1100, 51 L.Ed.2d 549, certiorari denied Cook v. U.S., 97 S.Ct. 1679, 430 U.S. 983, 52 L.Ed.2d 377, rehearing denied 97 S.Ct. 2689, 431 U.S. 960, 53 L.Ed.2d 279, certiorari denied 97 S.Ct. 1679, 430 U.S. 983, 52 L.Ed.2d 377, rehearing denied 97 S.Ct. 2990, 433 U.S. 915, 53 L.Ed.2d 1102.

C.A.5 (Fla.) 1976. Fourth Amendment does not require adoption of every proposal that might deter police misconduct. U.S.C.A.Const. Amend. 4.

> U.S. v. Turk, 526 F.2d 654, rehearing denied 529 F.2d 523, certiorari denied 97 S.Ct. 74, 429 U.S. 823, 50 L.Ed.2d 84.

C.A.5 (Fla.) 1975. Fourth Amendment is given generous interpretation in order to insure that its safeguards are not evaded by circuities. U.S.C.A.Const. Amend. 4.

> U.S. v. Mekjian, 505 F.2d 1320.

C.A.5 (Fla.) 1974. Fourth Amendment prohibits equally unreasonable searches and unreasonable seizures. U.S.C.A.Const. Amend. 4.

> U.S. v. Soriano, 497 F.2d 147.

C.A.5 (Fla.) 1973. Reach of Fourth Amendment cannot turn upon presence or absence of a physical intrusion into any given enclosure. U.S.C.A.Const. Amend. 4.

U.S. v. Cyzewski, 484 F.2d 509, certiorari denied 94 S.Ct. 936, 415 U.S. 902, 39 L.Ed.2d 459.

C.A.5 (Fla.) 1973. Fourth Amendment proscribes only unreasonable searches. U.S.C.A.Const. Amend. 4.

U.S. v. Gravitt, 484 F.2d 375, certiorari denied 94 S.Ct. 879, 414 U.S. 1135, 38 L.Ed.2d 761.

C.A.5 (Fla.) 1972. Scope of the Fourth Amendment is not determined by the subjective conclusion of a law enforcement officer. U.S.C.A.Const. Amend. 4.

U.S. v. Resnick, 455 F.2d 1127, rehearing denied 459 F.2d 1390, certiorari denied Carlton v. U.S., 93 S.Ct. 121, 409 U.S. 875, 34 L.Ed.2d 127, appeal after remand 483 F.2d 354, certiorari denied 94 S.Ct. 370, 414 U.S. 1008, 38 L.Ed.2d 246.

C.A.5 (Fla.) 1959. The Fourth Amendment of the Federal Constitution applies directly to proceedings in the federal courts. U.S.C.A.Const. Amend. 4.

Field v. U.S., 263 F.2d 758, certiorari denied 79 S.Ct. 1436, 360 U.S. 918, 3 L.Ed.2d 1534.

C.A.5 (Fla.) 1953. Not all searches, but only unreasonable ones, are proscribed by amendment to federal Constitution prohibiting unreasonable searches and seizures. U.S.C.A.Const. Amend. 4.

Drayton v. U.S., 205 F.2d 35.

There is no precise formula for determining whether a search is an unreasonable one prohibited by the Fourth Amendment to the federal Constitution, and each case must turn on its own facts. U.S.C.A.Const. Amend. 4.

Drayton v. U.S., 205 F.2d 35.

Where a dwelling is searched, stricter requirements in determining reasonableness of search may apply. U.S.C.A.Const. Amend. 4.

Drayton v. U.S., 205 F.2d 35.

Fact that search may have been necessary and expedient will not validate an unreasonable search. U.S.C.A.Const. Amend. 4.

Drayton v. U.S., 205 F.2d 35.

C.A.5 (Fla.) 1952. Whether a search or seizure is unreasonable is a judicial question, determinable from a consideration of the circumstances involved. U.S.C.A.Const. Amend. 4.

Kelly v. U.S., 197 F.2d 162.

What is a reasonable search is not to be determined by any fixed formula, but is to be resolved according to the facts in each case. U.S.C.A.Const. Amend. 4.

Kelly v. U.S., 197 F.2d 162.

C.C.A.5 (Fla.) 1946. The amendment securing the people against unreasonable searches and seizures secures the people against not all, but only unreasonable searches and seizures of their persons, houses, papers, and effects. U.S.C.A.Const. Amend. 4.

Martin v. U.S., 155 F.2d 503.

M.D.Fla. 2014. Court must examine the totality of the circumstances in order to determine whether a search or seizure is reasonable under the Fourth Amendment. U.S.C.A. Const.Amend. 4.

U.S. v. Davis, 65 F.Supp.3d 1352.

M.D.Fla. 2013. The Fourth Amendment, as applicable to the states through the Fourteenth Amendment, does not prohibit all searches; only unreasonable searches are unconstitutional. U.S.C.A. Const.Amends. 4, 14.

Lebron v. Wilkins, 990 F.Supp.2d 1280.

To be reasonable under the Fourth Amendment, a search ordinarily must be based on individualized suspicion of wrongdoing. U.S.C.A. Const.Amend. 4.

Lebron v. Wilkins, 990 F.Supp.2d 1280.

M.D.Fla. 2012. The Fourth Amendment proscribes all unreasonable searches and seizures. U.S.C.A. Const.Amend. 4.

Gennusa v. Shoar, 879 F.Supp.2d 1337, affirmed 748 F.3d 1103.

M.D.Fla. 2011. Fourth Amendment, as applicable to the states through the Fourteenth Amendment, does not prohibit all searches; only unreasonable searches are unconstitutional. U.S.C.A. Const. Amends. 4, 14.

Lebron v. Wilkins, 820 F.Supp.2d 1273, affirmed 710 F.3d 1202.

To be "reasonable" under the Fourth Amendment, a search ordinarily must be based on an individualized suspicion of wrongdoing. U.S.C.A. Const.Amend. 4.

Lebron v. Wilkins, 820 F.Supp.2d 1273, affirmed 710 F.3d 1202.

Right to be free from unreasonable searches and seizures under the Fourth Amendment is a fundamental constitutional right, the violation of which is enough to demonstrate irreparable harm for purposes of a motion for preliminary injunctive relief. U.S.C.A. Const.Amend. 4.

Lebron v. Wilkins, 820 F.Supp.2d 1273, affirmed 710 F.3d 1202.

M.D.Fla. 2011. Fourth Amendment protects an individual's right to be free from unreasonable searches and seizures. U.S.C.A. Const.Amend. 4.

U.S. v. Hill, 795 F.Supp.2d 1304.

M.D.Fla. 2010. The ultimate touchstone of the Fourth Amendment is reasonableness. U.S.C.A. Const.Amend. 4.

U.S. v. Bergin, 732 F.Supp.2d 1235, affirmed 455 Fed.Appx. 908, certiorari denied 132 S.Ct. 1948, 566 U.S. 954, 182 L.Ed.2d 802, post-conviction relief denied in part, dismissed in part 2014 WL 5093853, affirmed U.S. v. Powner, 481 Fed.Appx. 529, post-conviction relief denied 2016 WL 5239831.

M.D.Fla. 2010. Ultimate touchstone of the Fourth Amendment is reasonableness, and the warrant requirement is subject to certain exceptions. U.S.C.A. Const. Amend. 4.

U.S. v. Franklin, 721 F.Supp.2d 1229, affirmed 694 F.3d 1.

M.D.Fla. 2009. Fourth Amendment protects individuals from unreasonable governmental intrusion into their persons, houses, papers, and effects. U.S.C.A. Const.Amend. 4.

Swofford v. Eslinger, 671 F.Supp.2d 1289, affirmed 395 Fed.Appx. 559, rehearing and rehearing denied 409 Fed.Appx. 316, certiorari denied Morris v. Swofford, 131 S.Ct. 1053, 562 U.S. 1201, 178 L.Ed.2d 866.

Fourth Amendment protects individuals from "unreasonable" seizures. U.S.C.A. Const.Amend. 4.

Swofford v. Eslinger, 671 F.Supp.2d 1289, affirmed 395 Fed.Appx. 559, rehearing and rehearing denied 409 Fed.Appx. 316, certiorari denied Morris v. Swofford, 131 S.Ct. 1053, 562 U.S. 1201, 178 L.Ed.2d 866.

M.D.Fla. 2009. While reasonable suspicion does not alone justify a warrantless search of a residence, it permits law enforcement to approach a residence to ask questions; thus, absent express orders from the person in possession, an officer may walk up the steps and knock on the front door of any man's castle, with the honest intent of asking questions of the occupant thereof. U.S.C.A. Const.Amend. 4.

U.S. v. Quintana, 594 F.Supp.2d 1291.

M.D.Fla. 1990. Fourth Amendment is implicated whenever governmental entity conducts an unreasonable search, even when government is acting as an employer. U.S.C.A. Const.Amend. 4.

Beattie v. City of St. Petersburg Beach, 733 F.Supp. 1455.

To determine whether particular governmental activity violates Fourth Amendment, court must decide whether activity constitutes search, and, if it does, whether search is unreasonable. U.S.C.A. Const. Amend. 4.

Beattie v. City of St. Petersburg Beach, 733 F.Supp. 1455.

Lack of probable cause or individualized suspicion does not make a search per se unreasonable.

Beattie v. City of St. Petersburg Beach, 733 F.Supp. 1455.

N.D.Fla. 2010. The Fourth Amendment protects against invasions of one's legitimate expectation of privacy. U.S.C.A. Const.Amend. 4.

U.S. v. Burton, 698 F.Supp.2d 1303.

N.D.Fla. 2008. Fourth Amendment prohibits unreasonable searches and seizures, and its proper invocation depends on the nature of the search or seizure as well as the factual circumstances surrounding it. U.S.C.A. Const.Amend. 4.

Kilpatrick v. U.S., 578 F.Supp.2d 1339.

S.D.Fla. 2014. Fourth Amendment is not implicated by entry upon private land to knock on a citizen's door for legitimate police purposes unconnected with a search of the premises. U.S. Const. Amend. 4.

United States v. Jackson, 155 F.Supp.3d 1320, affirmed 618 Fed. Appx. 472, certiorari denied 136 S.Ct. 376, 193 L.Ed.2d 303.

S.D.Fla. 2014. To be reasonable under the Fourth Amendment, a search ordinarily must be based on individualized suspicion of wrongdoing. U.S.C.A. Const. Amend. 4.

Voss v. City of Key West, 24 F.Supp.3d 1219.

S.D.Fla. 2013. Fourth Amendment's protection extends beyond the sphere of criminal investigations, without regard to whether the government actor is investigating crime or performing another function; thus, the Fourth Amendment applies even when the government acts as an employer. U.S.C.A. Const.Amend. 4.

Hudson v. City of Riviera Beach, 982 F.Supp.2d 1318.

S.D.Fla. 2012. To be reasonable under the Fourth Amendment, search ordinarily must be based on individualized suspicion of wrongdoing. U.S.C.A. Const. Amend. 4.

American Federation of State County and Mun. Employees (AFSCME) Council 79 v. Scott, 857 F.Supp.2d 1322, vacated 717 F.3d 851, certiorari denied 134 S.Ct. 1877, 188 L.Ed.2d 912.

S.D.Fla. 2011. Fourth Amendment protects individuals from unreasonable searches and seizures. U.S.C.A. Const. Amend. 4.

U.S. v. Gomez, 807 F.Supp.2d 1134.

S.D.Fla. 2008. Warrantless searches and seizures are presumptively unreasonable under Fourth Amendment. U.S.C.A. Const.Amend. 4.

U.S. v. Smalls, 617 F.Supp.2d 1240, affirmed 342 Fed.Appx. 505, certiorari denied 130 S.Ct. 1094, 558 U.S. 1128, 175 L.Ed.2d 912.

S.D.Fla. 2008. Fourth Amendment protects individuals' possessory interests in property as well as their expectation of privacy. U.S.C.A. Const.Amend. 4.

Sosa v. Hames, 581 F.Supp.2d 1254.

S.D.Fla. 1992. Seizure that is initially lawful may nevertheless violate Fourth Amendment if there is some meaningful interference with individual's possessory interests in that property. West's F.S.A. Const. Art. 1, § 12; U.S.C.A. Const. Amend. 4.

Pottinger v. City of Miami, 810 F.Supp. 1551.

S.D.Fla. 1991. Entry into a home to conduct a search or make an arrest is unreasonable under the Fourth Amendment unless done pursuant to a warrant, and search or seizure carried out on a suspect's premises without a warrant is per se unreasonable unless police can show exigent circumstances. U.S.C.A. Const.Amend. 4.

U.S. v. Mazuera, 756 F.Supp. 564.

S.D.Fla. 1980. The reasonableness of search will depend on the nature of the intrusion into the privacy interest affected as balanced against the public interest to be served by that intrusion. U.S.C.A.Const. Amend. 4.

U.S. v. Burgos, 484 F.Supp. 605, affirmed U.S. v. Vargas, 643 F.2d 296.

S.D.Fla. 1968. Insofar as constitutional protection of individual's right of privacy is concerned, there is no distinction between civil seizure and criminal seizure. U.S.C.A.Const. Amend. 4.

U.S. v. Undetermined Quantities of Depressant or Stimulant Drugs, 282 F.Supp. 543.

Fla. 2013. Conformity clause in Florida constitution's search-and-seizure provision does not apply to decisions construing the Fourth Amendment of federal constitution by federal courts other than the United States Supreme Court. U.S.C.A. Const.Amend. 4; West's F.S.A. Const. Art. 1, § 12.

Smallwood v. State, 113 So.3d 724.

Fla. 2010. The Fourth Amendment to the United States Constitution protects against unlawful searches and seizures and is made applicable to the states by the Fourteenth Amendment to the United

States Constitution. U.S.C.A. Const. Amends. 4, 14.

Caraballo v. State, 39 So.3d 1234.

Fla. 2002. The Florida Supreme Court is required to follow the United States Supreme Court's interpretations of the Fourth Amendment. U.S.C.A. Const. Amend. 4; West's F.S.A. Const. Art. 1, § 12.

State v. Betz, 815 So.2d 627.

Fla. 1997. Where United States Supreme Court has not previously addressed particular search and seizure issue which comes before Florida Supreme Court for review, Florida Supreme Court is free under conformity clause to look to its own precedent for guidance. U.S.C.A. Const. Amend. 4; West's F.S.A. Const. Art. 1, § 12.

Rolling v. State, 695 So.2d 278, rehearing denied, certiorari denied 118 S.Ct. 448, 522 U.S. 984, 139 L.Ed.2d 383, denial of post-conviction relief affirmed 825 So.2d 293, rehearing denied, denial of habeas corpus affirmed 438 F.3d 1296, certiorari denied 126 S.Ct. 2943, 548 U.S. 913, 165 L.Ed.2d 966, denial of post-conviction relief affirmed 944 So.2d 176, certiorari denied 127 S.Ct. 466, 549 U.S. 990, 166 L.Ed.2d 332.

Fla. 1991. Right of privacy provision of State Constitution does not modify applicability of provision requiring that Fourth Amendment issues be construed in conformity with rulings of United States Supreme Court. U.S.C.A. Const.Amend. 4; West's F.S.A. Const. Art. 1, §§ 12, 23.

State v. Jimeno, 588 So.2d 233.

Fla. 1980. Fourth Amendment provides that people are entitled to be secure from unreasonable searches and seizures. U.S.C.A.Const. Amend. 4.

Shapiro v. State, 390 So.2d 344, certiorari denied 101 S.Ct. 1519, 450 U.S. 982, 67 L.Ed.2d 818.

Fla. 1979. Seizure of any material arguably protected by the First Amendment must sustain a particularly high hurdle in evaluation of reasonableness under the Fourth Amendment. U.S.C.A.Const. Amends. 1, 4.

Roberts v. State, 373 So.2d 672.

Fla. 1978. The Fourth Amendment protects persons against unreasonable searches and seizures, but prior restraint of right of expression under the First Amendment calls for higher hurdle in the evaluation of reasonableness. U.S.C.A.Const. Amends. 1, 4.

First Amendment Foundation of Florida, Inc. v. State, 364 So.2d 450.

Fla. 1957. Question of "reasonableness" or "unreasonableness" of a search is to be resolved on basis of factual situation presented in each case, and every situation is to be tested by traditional requirements of judicial precedents as well as by legislative enactments established to implement the requirements of the Constitution. U.S.C.A.Const. Amend. 4; F.S.A.Const. Declaration of Rights, §§ 12, 22; F.S.A. § 933.19.

Chacon v. State, 102 So.2d 578.

Fla. 1956. Only unreasonable searches are condemned by the Constitution. F.S.A.Const. Declaration of Rights, § 22.

Brown v. State, 91 So.2d 175.

Fla. 1956. Only unreasonable searches and seizures are condemned by the Constitution.

Gaskins v. State, 89 So.2d 867.

Fla. 1956. Test of whether a search was reasonable must be determined upon due consideration of circumstances and manner under which search was made. F.S.A.Const. Declaration of Rights, § 22.

State v. Simmons, 85 So.2d 879.

Fla. 1955. Constitutional inhibition against unlawful searches and seizures secures to every citizen in his person, property, papers and effects, freedom from unreasonable search and seizure.

Weiner v. Kelly, 82 So.2d 155.

Fla. 1946. Only unreasonable searches without a warrant are prohibited by constitution.

Joyner v. State, 27 So.2d 349, 157 Fla. 874.

Fla. 1946. What is a reasonable or valid search, and therefore lawful, must be determined by the court upon due consideration of circumstances and manner under which the search is made.

Longo v. State, 26 So.2d 818, 157 Fla. 668.

Fla. 1942. The Fourth Amendment, prohibiting unreasonable searches and seizures, stems from the principle of the common law securing to every citizen in his home and office immunity from interference by the state and the protection of his person, property, and papers from legal process, and its primary purpose is to protect personal liberty and private property. U.S.C.A.Const. Amend. 4.

Church v. State, 9 So.2d 164, 151 Fla. 24.

The Fourth Amendment prohibiting unreasonable searches and seizures cannot be invoked to protect one in the commission of a crime, and cannot be invoked to inhibit a search to ascertain whether the law is being violated. U.S.C.A.Const. Amend. 4.

Church v. State, 9 So.2d 164, 151 Fla. 24.

Fla.App. 1 Dist. 2017. The ultimate standard set forth in the Fourth Amendment is reasonableness. U.S. Const. Amend. 4.

State v. Johnson, 208 So.3d 843.

Fla.App. 1 Dist. 2011. Facts learned only in hindsight should not enter into the evaluation of the reasonableness of a search or seizure. U.S.C.A. Const.Amend. 4.

Majors v. State, 70 So.3d 655, rehearing denied, review denied 79 So.3d 745.

Fla.App. 1 Dist. 2008. Evaluating the legality of a law enforcement officer's actions under the Fourth Amendment involves an objective examination of the totality of the circumstances. U.S.C.A. Const.Amend. 4.

Cox v. State, 975 So.2d 1163.

Fla.App. 1 Dist. 2002. The Florida constitutional right of the people to be secure in their persons, houses, papers and effects against unreasonable searches and seizures shall be construed in conformity with the Fourth Amendment to the United States Constitution, as interpreted by the United States Supreme Court.

U.S.C.A. Const.Amend. 4; West's F.S.A. Const. Art. 1, § 12.

Green v. State, 824 So.2d 311.

Fla.App. 1 Dist. 2001. In evaluating search and seizure issues, Florida courts are bound by the Fourth Amendment precedents of the United States Supreme Court. U.S.C.A. Const.Amend. 4; West's F.S.A. Const. Art. 1, § 12.

State v. Shaw, 784 So.2d 529.

Fla.App. 1 Dist. 2001. Witnesses for the state are protected by provisions of State Constitution relating to searches and seizures and to the right of privacy. West's F.S.A. Const. Art. 1, §§ 12, 23.

Reed v. State, 783 So.2d 1192, review granted, review granted 797 So.2d 587, quashed 837 So.2d 366.

Fla.App. 1 Dist. 1983. Fourth Amendment condemns unreasonable warrantless searches and seizures. U.S.C.A. Const.Amend. 4.

Rosell v. State, 433 So.2d 1260, petition for review denied 446 So.2d 100.

Fla.App. 1 Dist. 1981. Where there is evidence before trial judge that object sought to be removed from accused's body is relevant and surgical procedure required to remove it will entail only minor intrusion into body with negligible risk of harm or injury to accused, intrusion neither violates right of privacy nor prohibition against unreasonable intrusion into body. West's F.S.A. Rules Crim.Proc., Rule 3.220(b)(1)(vii).

Doe v. State, 409 So.2d 25, review denied McCaskill v. State, 418 So.2d 1280.

Trial court's order permitting removal of bullet from accused's leg did not violate accused's right to privacy nor prohibition against unreasonable intrusion into body where there was evidence that bullet sought to be removed was approximately one-half inch below surface of skin and could be removed by minor surgery involving use of local anesthetic, pain involved would be minimal and surgery was not type that would result in permanent injury to accused, and bullet itself was relevant to prosecution since its physical examination would provide positive confirmation as to its caliber and as to whether victim, before expiring, might have discharged bullet into accused. West's F.S.A. Rules Crim.Proc., Rule 3.220(b)(1)(vii).

> Doe v. State, 409 So.2d 25, review denied McCaskill v. State, 418 So.2d 1280.

Fla.App. 1 Dist. 1980. Under Fourth and Fourteenth Amendments, individual's reasonable expectation of privacy is protected from arbitrary invasions solely at unfettered discretion of police officers in field. U.S.C.A.Const. Amends. 4, 14.

> Robinson v. State, 388 So.2d 286.

Fla.App. 1 Dist. 1978. Fundamental aspect of personhood's integrity is the power to control what we shall reveal about our intimate self, to whom, and for what purpose; that is implication of both Fourth and Fifth Amendments. U.S.C.A.Const. Amends. 4, 5, 14.

> Byron, Harless, Schaffer, Reid and Associates, Inc. v. State ex rel. Schellenberg, 360 So.2d 83, quashed Shevin v. Byron, Harless, Schaffer, Reid and Associates, Inc., 379 So.2d 633.

Fla.App. 1 Dist. 1976. Absent a judicial warrant, exigency or other exceptional circumstances, Fourth Amendment protects and makes effective a citizen's reasonable expectation of privacy. U.S.C.A.Const. Amend. 4.

> Britton v. State, 336 So.2d 663, certiorari denied 344 So.2d 326.

Fla.App. 1 Dist. 1974. Whether a particular warrantless search is reasonable must be determined by the circumstances and facts surrounding that particular search and the manner in which it is conducted.

> Gilbert v. State, 289 So.2d 475, certiorari denied 294 So.2d 660.

Fact that a reasonable search happens to yield evidence of a crime even though not so intended is irrelevant to its reasonableness.

> Gilbert v. State, 289 So.2d 475, certiorari denied 294 So.2d 660.

Fla.App. 2 Dist. 2010. It is the nature of the search, not the label the officer places upon it, that controls. U.S.C.A. Const.Amend. 4.

> State v. Townsend, 40 So.3d 103.

Fla.App. 2 Dist. 2009. Reasonableness of an entry by police officers onto private property without a warrant depends on the totality of the circumstances. U.S.C.A. Const.Amend. 4.

> Wright v. State, 1 So.3d 409.

Fla.App. 2 Dist. 2007. Reasonableness of an entry by police officers upon private property is measured by the totality of existing circumstances. U.S.C.A. Const.Amend. 4.

> P.B.P. v. State, 955 So.2d 618, review denied 966 So.2d 967.

Fla.App. 2 Dist. 2006. An action is "reasonable" under the Fourth Amendment, regardless of the individual police officer's state of mind, as long as the circumstances, viewed objectively, justify the action. U.S.C.A. Const.Amend. 4.

> Vanslyke v. State, 936 So.2d 1218.

Fla.App. 2 Dist. 2006. The essential purpose of the proscription in the Fourth Amendment is to impose a standard of reasonableness upon the exercise of discretion by a government official in order to safeguard the privacy and security of individuals against arbitrary invasions. U.S.C.A. Const.Amend. 4.

> Ellis v. State, 935 So.2d 29, rehearing denied, review denied 949 So.2d 197.

The permissibility of a particular law enforcement practice is judged by balancing its intrusion on the individual's Fourth Amendment interests against its promotion of legitimate governmental interests; implemented in this manner, reasonableness standard usually requires that the facts upon which an intrusion is based be capable of measurement against an objective standard such as probable cause or a less stringent test such as reasonable suspicion. U.S.C.A. Const.Amend. 4.

> Ellis v. State, 935 So.2d 29, rehearing denied, review denied 949 So.2d 197.

Fla.App. 2 Dist. 2005. Generally, warrantless searches or seizures are per se unreasonable unless the search or seizure falls within an exception to the warrant requirement, one of which is consent. U.S.C.A. Const.Amend. 4.

> V.H. v. State, 903 So.2d 321.

Fla.App. 2 Dist. 2000. Searches conducted outside the judicial process, without prior approval by judge or magistrate, are per se unreasonable under the Fourth Amendment. (Per Casanueva, J., with one Judge concurring specially). U.S.C.A. Const.Amend. 4.

    Smith v. State, 753 So.2d 713.

Fla.App. 2 Dist. 1992. Searches and seizures article of State Constitution should be construed in conformity with Fourth Amendment to United States Constitution. West's F.S.A. Const. Art. 1, § 12; U.S.C.A. Const.Amend. 4.

    State v. Sarantopoulos, 604 So.2d 551, review granted 618 So.2d 210, decision approved 629 So.2d 121.

Fla.App. 2 Dist. 1984. Constitutionality of a particular seizure is judged by balancing the degree of its intrusion on the individual's Fourth Amendment interest in privacy and personal security against a seizure's promotion of legitimate governmental interests. U.S.C.A. Const.Amends. 4, 14.

    Jones v. State, 459 So.2d 1068, order approved 483 So.2d 433.

Fla.App. 2 Dist. 1983. Strictures of Fourth Amendment apply during investigatory as well as accusatory or arrest stage of criminal process. U.S.C.A. Const. Amend. 4.

    Hayes v. State, 439 So.2d 896, petition for review denied 447 So.2d 886, certiorari granted 105 S.Ct. 82, 469 U.S. 816, 83 L.Ed.2d 30, reversed 105 S.Ct. 1643, 470 U.S. 811, 84 L.Ed.2d 705, on remand 488 So.2d 77, certiorari denied 107 S.Ct. 119, 479 U.S. 831, 93 L.Ed.2d 65.

When probable cause requirement of Fourth Amendment is not implicated in facts of particular case, courts must examine all attendant facts and circumstances involved to determine whether governmental intrusion was reasonable for Fourth Amendment purposes; in undertaking examination, court must compare and then balance competing interests involved. U.S.C.A. Const.Amend. 4.

    Hayes v. State, 439 So.2d 896, petition for review denied 447 So.2d 886, certiorari granted 105 S.Ct. 82, 469 U.S. 816, 83 L.Ed.2d 30, re-

versed 105 S.Ct. 1643, 470 U.S. 811, 84 L.Ed.2d 705, on remand 488 So.2d 77, certiorari denied 107 S.Ct. 119, 479 U.S. 831, 93 L.Ed.2d 65.

In balancing legitimate public interest in detection and prevention of crime against individual's interest in being free from physical intrusions under Fourth Amendment, analysis must proceed at two different levels: first, there must be seizure of individual by law enforcement officials, and second, there must be search for and seizure of evidence. U.S.C.A. Const. Amend. 4.

    Hayes v. State, 439 So.2d 896, petition for review denied 447 So.2d 886, certiorari granted 105 S.Ct. 82, 469 U.S. 816, 83 L.Ed.2d 30, reversed 105 S.Ct. 1643, 470 U.S. 811, 84 L.Ed.2d 705, on remand 488 So.2d 77, certiorari denied 107 S.Ct. 119, 479 U.S. 831, 93 L.Ed.2d 65.

Fla.App. 2 Dist. 1979. Search and seizure provision of the Florida Constitution imposes no higher standard than that of Fourth Amendment. West's F.S.A. § 901.151; U.S.C.A.Const. Amend. 4; West's F.S.A.Const. art. 1, § 12.

    State v. Hetland, 366 So.2d 831, decision approved 387 So.2d 963.

Fla.App. 2 Dist. 1975. A man's home should not be subjected to unreasonable governmental intrusion.

    Lawton v. State, 320 So.2d 463.

Fla.App. 2 Dist. 1975. In loco parentis doctrine is so compelling in light of public necessity and as social concept antedating Fourth Amendment that any action, including search, taken thereunder upon reasonable suspicion should be accepted as necessary and reasonable. U.S.C.A.Const. Amend. 4.

    Nelson v. State, 319 So.2d 154.

Fla.App. 2 Dist. 1975. Whenever an individual harbors a reasonable expectation of privacy, he is entitled to be free from unreasonable governmental intrusion. U.S.C.A.Const. Amend. 4.

    Olivera v. State, 315 So.2d 487, certiorari denied 330 So.2d 21.

Fla.App. 2 Dist. 1966. In determining whether a reasonable and valid search

was made, court will be guided by circumstances surrounding the search and manner in which it was carried out. F.S.A.Const. Declaration of Rights, § 22.
> State v. Coyle, 181 So.2d 671.

Fla.App. 2 Dist. 1966. Generally, search is reasonable if made on authority of search warrant.
> Beck v. State, 181 So.2d 659, certiorari denied 188 So.2d 814, certiorari denied 87 S.Ct. 394, 385 U.S. 958, 17 L.Ed.2d 304.

Fla.App. 2 Dist. 1963. Not every search without warrant is unlawful, but only search which is unreasonable.
> Range v. State, 156 So.2d 534.

In determining whether reasonable and valid search was made, circumstances surrounding search and manner in which it was conducted will be considered.
> Range v. State, 156 So.2d 534.

Fla.App. 2 Dist. 1963. Only search that is unreasonable, and not every search without warrant, is unlawful, and what constitutes reasonable and valid search is to be determined by court through due consideration of circumstances and manner in which search was made.
> McCain v. State, 151 So.2d 841, certiorari denied 157 So.2d 817.

Immunity to unreasonable search and seizure cannot be invoked to protect one in commission of crime but serves only as a constitutional guaranty against unreasonable search and seizure.
> McCain v. State, 151 So.2d 841, certiorari denied 157 So.2d 817.

Fla.App. 2 Dist. 1962. Where constitutional safeguards are involved, and doubt exists as to whether officer was reasonable in concluding that search was justified, doubt must be resolved in favor of defendant whose property was searched. F.S.A.Const. Declaration of Rights, § 22; U.S.C.A.Const. Amend. 4.
> Miller v. State, 137 So.2d 21.

Fla.App. 2 Dist. 1961. Section of declaration of rights as to searches and seizures was designed to safeguard people against unreasonable searches and seizures, whether pursuant to warrant or

incident to arrest without warrant. F.S.A.Const. Declaration of Rights, § 22.
> Urso v. State, 134 So.2d 810.

Fla.App. 2 Dist. 1959. It is not every search without a warrant that is unlawful but only the search that is unreasonable, and what is reasonable and valid search must be determined upon a due consideration of the circumstances and manner in which the search is made.
> Starks v. State, 108 So.2d 788.

Fla.App. 2 Dist. 1958. Immunity against unreasonable searches and seizures cannot be invoked to protect one in commission of crime but serves only as a guarantee against unreasonable searches and seizures. F.S.A.Const. Declaration of Rights, § 22; U.S.C.A.Const. Amend. 4.
> Tribue v. State, 106 So.2d 630.

Fla.App. 3 Dist. 2013. Because the central inquiry under the Fourth Amendment is reasonableness in all the circumstances, no single level of reliability applies in every situation; neither a warrant nor probable cause, nor, indeed, any measure of individualized suspicion, is an indispensable component of reasonableness in every circumstance. U.S.C.A. Const.Amend. 4.
> K.P. v. State, 129 So.3d 1121, review denied 157 So.3d 1045.

When judging the reasonableness of a search, courts must consider the severity of the need and determine whether the government's legitimate interest appears important enough to justify the particular search at hand. U.S.C.A. Const.Amend. 4.
> K.P. v. State, 129 So.3d 1121, review denied 157 So.3d 1045.

Fla.App. 3 Dist. 1987. Police officers, who had lawful custody of cotenant, did not violate his Fourth Amendment rights when they accompanied him into his apartment so that he could retrieve documents showing his immigration status. U.S.C.A. Const.Amend. 4.
> State v. Monge, 508 So.2d 450, review denied 518 So.2d 1276.

Fla.App. 3 Dist. 1981. Two requirements must necessarily be met before any person may successfully claim that his rights guaranteed by Fourth Amendment to United States Constitution or similar section of State Constitution have been violated; first, there must be a search and seizure of that individual's person, house, papers or effects conducted by an agent of the government; second, the search and seizure in question must be unreasonable, as not all searches and seizures are proscribed by the above constitutional provisions, but only those which are "unreasonable." U.S.C.A.Const.Amend. 4; West's F.S.A.Const.Art. 1, § 12.

> Morales v. State, 407 So.2d 321.

Fla.App. 3 Dist. 1980. Search and seizure provision of Florida Constitution generally imposes no higher standard than the Fourth Amendment to the United States Constitution. U.S.C.A.Const. Amend. 4.

> Mata v. State, 380 So.2d 1157, petition for review denied 389 So.2d 1112.

Just exactly what is reasonable in the Fourth Amendment sense always depends on a balance which must be struck between, on the one hand, the level of official intrusion into individual privacy and, on the other hand, the public interest to be served by such intrusion. U.S.C.A.Const. Amend. 4.

> Mata v. State, 380 So.2d 1157, petition for review denied 389 So.2d 1112.

Fla.App. 3 Dist. 1979. Central to invoking constitutional guarantees against unreasonable searches and seizures is a threshold showing that a government officer has seized and searched a person. West's F.S.A.Const. art. 1, § 12; U.S.C.A.Const. Amends. 4, 14.

> State v. Oliver, 368 So.2d 1331, certiorari dismissed 383 So.2d 1200.

Fla.App. 3 Dist. 1978. State and federal constitutional guarantees against unreasonable searches should receive a liberal construction to safeguard the right of privacy. West's F.S.A.Const. art. 1, § 12; U.S.C.A.Const. Amend. 4.

> Taylor v. State, 355 So.2d 180, certiorari denied 361 So.2d 835.

Fla.App. 3 Dist. 1970. Fourth Amendment does not proscribe all searches, but only those which are unreasonable. U.S.C.A.Const. Amend. 4.

> Adams v. State, 240 So.2d 529.

Fla.App. 3 Dist. 1967. Relevant test is not whether it is reasonable to procure a search warrant but whether the search was reasonable.

> Fountain v. State, 199 So.2d 738.

Fla.App. 3 Dist. 1967. Where no search is required, constitutional provision against unlawful searches and seizures is not applicable.

> Boim v. State, 194 So.2d 313.

Federal constitution does not forbid all searches and seizures but only unreasonable searches and seizures.

> Boim v. State, 194 So.2d 313.

Fla.App. 4 Dist. 2016. The touchstone of the Fourth Amendment protection against unreasonable searches and seizures is reasonableness. U.S.C.A. Const. Amend. 4.

> Colas v. State, 196 So.3d 565.

Fla.App. 4 Dist. 2012. The touchstone of Fourth Amendment analysis is the reasonableness in all the circumstances of the governmental invasion of a citizen's personal security. U.S.C.A. Const.Amend. 4.

> K.S. v. State, 85 So.3d 566.

Fla.App. 4 Dist. 2008. Fourth Amendment protects two types of expectations, one involving "searches" the other "seizures." U.S.C.A. Const.Amend. 4.

> Lindo v. State, 983 So.2d 672.

Fla.App. 4 Dist. 2005. In order for reasonable suspicion justifying a search to exist, the action must be justified at its inception, and the search must be reasonably related in scope to the reason for the search. U.S.C.A. Const.Amend 4.

> State v. Bullard, 891 So.2d 1158.

Fla.App. 4 Dist. 2004. Right of privacy provision of State Constitution does not modify applicability of provision requiring that search and seizure issues be construed in conformity with rulings of United States Supreme Court. U.S.C.A. Const. Amend. 4; West's F.S.A. Const. Art. 1, §§ 12, 23.

> Limbaugh v. State, 887 So.2d 387, rehearing denied, and question certified, review denied 903 So.2d 189.

Fla.App. 4 Dist. 1995. Fourth Amendment does not prohibit all searches, but rather, prohibits only unreasonable searches. U.S.C.A. Const.Amend. 4.

Fosman v. State, 664 So.2d 1163.

Whether search is "reasonable" under Fourth Amendment is determined by balancing need to search against invasion which search entails. U.S.C.A. Const. Amend. 4.

Fosman v. State, 664 So.2d 1163.

Fla.App. 4 Dist. 1994. Random interdiction programs are not per se offensive to principles embodied in Fourth Amendment, but rather trial court must conduct factual inquiry into whether defendant consented to search to determine whether particular encounter pursuant to random interdiction program violates Fourth Amendment. U.S.C.A. Const.Amend. 4.

State v. Dean, 639 So.2d 1009.

Fla.App. 4 Dist. 1981. In any Fourth Amendment case, fundamental inquiry is whether search or seizure was reasonable under all circumstances. U.S.C.A.Const. Amend. 4.

State v. Melendez, 392 So.2d 587.

Fla.App. 4 Dist. 1975. Only unreasonable searches are condemned by Federal and State Constitutions.

State v. White, 312 So.2d 475.

Fla.App. 4 Dist. 1975. Absent knowledge of contents of search warrant, search of accused's residence was unreasonable.

Swinford v. State, 311 So.2d 727.

Fla.App. 4 Dist. 1974. The Fourth Amendment puts a restraint on the arm of the government and prevents it from invading the sanctity of a man's home or his private quarters except under safeguards calculated to prevent oppression and abuse of authority. U.S.C.A.Const. Amend. 4.

State v. Gansz, 297 So.2d 614, certiorari denied 303 So.2d 645.

Fla.App. 4 Dist. 1973. Balance must be maintained between the recognition of the liberty of a citizen to be free from unreasonable searches and seizures and the recognition of the common-sense performance of law enforcement activities; it is court's duty to seek a reconciliation of these principles whenever circumstances suggest a collision course, and such reconciliation is not determined by a pro-

nouncement of general principles of recognition but rather by an evaluation of the facts of the particular situation and an application of those principles to those facts. U.S.C.A.Const. Amend. 4.

State v. Hetzko, 283 So.2d 49.

Fla.App. 4 Dist. 1969. Provisions of State and Federal Constitutions relating to searches and seizures protect private persons from invasion of their premises by governments. U.S.C.A.Const. Amend. 4; F.S.A.Const.1968, art. 1, § 12.

State v. Williams, 227 So.2d 331.

Fla.App. 4 Dist. 1967. Only unreasonable searches are prohibited, not all searches. U.S.C.A.Const. Amend. 4; F.S.A.Const. Declaration of Rights, § 22.

Webster v. State, 201 So.2d 789.

The reasonableness of a search is largely determined by the facts of the particular case regarding the circumstances surrounding the search and the manner in which it was conducted. U.S.C.A.Const. Amend. 4; F.S.A.Const. Declaration of Rights, § 22.

Webster v. State, 201 So.2d 789.

Fla.App. 5 Dist. 2016. The touchstone of analysis under the Fourth Amendment is always the reasonableness in all circumstances of the particular governmental invasion of a citizen's personal security; that reasonableness, in turn, depends on a balance between the public interest and the individual's right to personal security free from arbitrary interference by law enforcement officers. U.S.C.A. Const.Amend. 4.

Aguiar v. State, 199 So.3d 920, review denied 2016 WL 3459769.

Fla.App. 5 Dist. 2009. The Fourth Amendment protects people, not places, and only under circumstances where the person enjoys a reasonable expectation of privacy. U.S.C.A. Const.Amend. 4.

Brown v. State, 24 So.3d 671, review denied 39 So.3d 1264, certiorari denied 134 S.Ct. 2730, 189 L.Ed.2d 771.

Fla.App. 5 Dist. 2009. Because the keystone of a Fourth Amendment analysis is reasonableness, the search warrant requirement is subject to certain important exceptions, including when a law enforcement officer is confronted with exigent circumstances. U.S.C.A. Const.Amend. 4.

Ortiz v. State, 24 So.3d 596, review denied 37 So.3d 848.

Fla.App. 5 Dist. 2004. The touchstone of Fourth Amendment analysis is the reasonableness in all the circumstances of the governmental invasion of a citizen's personal security. U.S.C.A. Const.Amend. 4.

Brown v. State, 863 So.2d 459.

Fla.App. 5 Dist. 2003. Extent to which the Fourth Amendment offers protection may well depend on the status and location of the defendant at the time of the search. U.S.C.A. Const.Amend. 4.

Hicks v. State, 852 So.2d 954.

Fla.App. 5 Dist. 2001. Gist of the Fourth Amendment protection against unreasonable searches and seizures is that the disclosure sought shall not be unreasonable. U.S.C.A. Const.Amend. 4.

Check 'n Go of Florida, Inc. v. State, 790 So.2d 454, rehearing denied, review denied 817 So.2d 845.

Fla.App. 5 Dist. 1995. Physical entry of home is chief evil against which wording of Fourth Amendment is directed. U.S.C.A. Const.Amend. 4.

Anderson v. State, 665 So.2d 281, rehearing denied.

Fla.App. 5 Dist. 1985. Only unreasonable searches and seizures are unconstitutional.

Lang v. State, 475 So.2d 1354.

Fla.App. 5 Dist. 1984. Constitutional right to be free from unreasonable searches and seizures is paramount over drug laws. U.S.C.A. Const.Amend. 4; West's F.S.A. Const. Art. 1, § 12.

Dilyerd v. State, 444 So.2d 577, quashed 467 So.2d 301.

⚷**24. Necessity of and preference for warrant, and exceptions in general.**

U.S.Fla. 1983. Fourth Amendment protection is not diluted in situations where it has been determined that legitimate law enforcement interests justify warrantless search, but rather search must be limited in scope to that which is justified by particular purposes served by exception e.g., warrantless search is permissible incident to lawful arrest because of legitimate concerns for safety of officer and to prevent destruction of evidence by arrestee, but such search is limited to person of arrestee and area immediately within his control. U.S.C.A. Const.Amend. 4.

Florida v. Royer, 103 S.Ct. 1319, 460 U.S. 491, 75 L.Ed.2d 229.

U.S.Fla. 1980. Fact that packages and one or more of the boxes therein had been opened by a private party before they were acquired by the FBI did not excuse the FBI agents' failure to obtain a search warrant. (Per Mr. Justice Stevens, with one Justice joining, two Justices concurring in part and in the judgment, and the one Justice concurring in the judgment.)

Walter v. U.S., 100 S.Ct. 2395, 447 U.S. 649, 65 L.Ed.2d 410, on remand U.S. v. Sanders, 625 F.2d 1311.

U.S.Fla. 1972. Warrant represents independent assurance that a search and arrest will not proceed without probable cause to believe that a crime has been committed and that the person or place named in warrant is involved in the crime. U.S.C.A.Const. Amend. 4.

Shadwick v. City of Tampa, 92 S.Ct. 2119, 407 U.S. 345, 32 L.Ed.2d 783.

C.A.11 (Fla.) 2016. Without a warrant, a search is reasonable only if it falls within a specific exception to the warrant requirement; one exception is that a warrantless search is lawful when a person with actual or apparent authority voluntarily consents to law enforcement officers conducting a search. U.S. Const. Amend. 4.

Fish v. Brown, 838 F.3d 1153.

C.A.11 (Fla.) 2016. Without a warrant, a search is reasonable only if it falls within a specific exception to the warrant requirement. U.S.C.A. Const.Amend. 4.

U.S. v. Thomas, 818 F.3d 1230, certiorari denied 137 S.Ct. 171, 196 L.Ed.2d 142.

C.A.11 (Fla.) 2015. A warrant is not required to establish the reasonableness of all government searches, and when a warrant is not required, probable cause is not invariably required either. U.S.C.A. Const.Amend. 4.

U.S. v. Davis, 785 F.3d 498, certiorari denied 136 S.Ct. 479, 193 L.Ed.2d 349.

C.A.11 (Fla.) 2015. The fact that police have lawfully come into possession of an item does not necessarily mean they are entitled to search that item without a warrant. U.S.C.A. Const.Amend. 4.

U.S. v. Odoni, 782 F.3d 1226, certiorari denied Gunter v. U.S., 135 S.Ct. 2335, 191 L.Ed.2d 981, certiorari denied 135 S.Ct. 2339, 191 L.Ed.2d 981.

C.A.11 (Fla.) 2014. In general, the Fourth Amendment requires a warrant supported by probable cause to effectuate a search. U.S.C.A. Const.Amend. 4.

Berry v. Leslie, 767 F.3d 1144, opinion vacated on rehearing en banc 771 F.3d 1316.

The basic premise of search and seizure doctrine is that searches undertaken without a warrant issued upon probable cause are per se unreasonable under the Fourth Amendment, subject only to a few specifically established and well-delineated exceptions. U.S.C.A. Const.Amend. 4.

Berry v. Leslie, 767 F.3d 1144, opinion vacated on rehearing en banc 771 F.3d 1316.

C.A.11 (Fla.) 2014. In absence of warrant, search is reasonable only if it falls within a specific exception to the warrant requirement. U.S.C.A. Const. Amend. 4.

U.S. v. Watkins, 760 F.3d 1271.

C.A.11 (Fla.) 2014. Searches and seizures without a warrant are presumptively unreasonable. U.S.C.A. Const.Amend. 4.

U.S. v. Davis, 754 F.3d 1205, rehearing granted, opinion vacated 573 Fed.Appx. 925, on rehearing en banc in part 785 F.3d 498, certiorari denied 136 S.Ct. 479, 193 L.Ed.2d 349.

C.A.11 (Fla.) 2014. In the ordinary case, seizures of personal property are unreasonable within the meaning of the Fourth Amendment, without more, unless accomplished pursuant to a judicial warrant, issued by a neutral magistrate after

finding probable cause. U.S.C.A. Const. Amend. 4.

Gennusa v. Canova, 748 F.3d 1103.

There are limited exceptions to the Fourth Amendment's warrant requirement. U.S.C.A. Const.Amend. 4.

Gennusa v. Canova, 748 F.3d 1103.

C.A.11 (Fla.) 2013. Ordinarily, to be reasonable, a search must be based on individualized suspicion of wrongdoing; in most cases, this standard is met only when a search is accomplished pursuant to a judicial warrant issued upon a finding of probable cause. U.S.C.A. Const.Amend. 4.

Lebron v. Secretary, Florida Dept. of Children and Families, 710 F.3d 1202.

C.A.11 (Fla.) 2013. A warrantless and nonconsensual entry into a person's home, and any resulting search or seizure, violates the Fourth Amendment unless it is supported by both probable cause and exigent circumstances. U.S.C.A. Const. Amend. 4.

Feliciano v. City of Miami Beach, 707 F.3d 1244.

C.A.11 (Fla.) 2008. Among the exceptions to the Fourth Amendment's general warrant requirement are exceptions to address the special needs of the government beyond the normal need for law enforcement. U.S.C.A. Const.Amend. 4.

Johnston v. Tampa Sports Authority, 530 F.3d 1320, rehearing and rehearing denied 285 Fed.Appx. 745, certiorari denied 129 S.Ct. 1013, 555 U.S. 1138, 173 L.Ed.2d 295.

In evaluating whether to create a special needs exception to the Fourth Amendment's general warrant requirement, courts undertake a context-specific inquiry examining the competing public or governmental interests advanced by the searches with the private interests invaded by it. U.S.C.A. Const.Amend. 4.

Johnston v. Tampa Sports Authority, 530 F.3d 1320, rehearing and rehearing denied 285 Fed.Appx. 745, certiorari denied 129 S.Ct. 1013, 555 U.S. 1138, 173 L.Ed.2d 295.

C.A.11 (Fla.) 2006. Officers are allowed to knock on a residence's door or otherwise approach the residence seeking to speak to the inhabitants just as any private citizen may, without probable cause, a warrant, or exigent circumstances. U.S.C.A. Const.Amend. 4.

U.S. v. Taylor, 458 F.3d 1201.

C.A.11 (Fla.) 2005. In most circumstances, for a search that is not based on consent to comply with the Fourth Amendment, law enforcement must obtain a warrant supported by probable cause. U.S.C.A. Const.Amend. 4.

U.S. v. Magluta, 418 F.3d 1166, rehearing and rehearing denied 163 Fed.Appx. 852, certiorari denied 126 S.Ct. 2966, 548 U.S. 903, 165 L.Ed.2d 949, appeal after new sentencing hearing 313 Fed.Appx. 201, rehearing and rehearing denied 285 Fed.Appx. 744, certiorari denied 129 S.Ct. 2050, 556 U.S. 1207, 173 L.Ed.2d 1132, habeas corpus denied in part 2012 WL 488078, affirmed 660 Fed.Appx. 803.

C.A.11 (Fla.) 2003. Child welfare worker's warrantless entry into parents' home to investigate suspected child abuse did not violate the Fourth Amendment, since parents consented to worker's entry. U.S.C.A. Const.Amend. 4.

Doe v. Kearney, 329 F.3d 1286, certiorari denied 124 S.Ct. 389, 540 U.S. 947, 157 L.Ed.2d 277.

C.A.11 (Fla.) 2000. Under Fourth Amendment, searches and seizures inside home without warrant are presumptively unreasonable. U.S.C.A. Const.Amend. 4.

U.S. v. Santa, 236 F.3d 662.

Where law enforcement agents have ample time and information to secure anticipatory search warrant, lack of time to obtain warrant after delivery of contraband is insufficient to justify warrantless search. U.S.C.A. Const.Amend. 4.

U.S. v. Santa, 236 F.3d 662.

C.A.11 (Fla.) 1994. Warrantless search is presumptively unreasonable. U.S.C.A. Const.Amend. 4.

U.S. v. McGregor, 31 F.3d 1067, certiorari denied 116 S.Ct. 328, 516 U.S. 926, 133 L.Ed.2d 228.

C.A.11 (Fla.) 1991. Warrantless search of home is presumptively unreasonable; however, warrantless search is allowed where both probable cause and exi-

gent circumstances exist. U.S.C.A. Const. Amend. 4.

U.S. v. Tobin, 923 F.2d 1506, rehearing denied 935 F.2d 1297, certiorari denied 112 S.Ct. 299, 502 U.S. 907, 116 L.Ed.2d 243.

C.A.11 (Fla.) 1989. Individual's residence enjoys special protection under Fourth Amendment; thus, officer must have probable cause before searching someone's house, and even then officer may proceed only with warrant or under exigent circumstances. U.S.C.A. Const. Amend. 4.

U.S. v. Tobin, 890 F.2d 319, rehearing granted, vacated 902 F.2d 821, on rehearing 923 F.2d 1506, rehearing denied 935 F.2d 1297, certiorari denied 112 S.Ct. 299, 502 U.S. 907, 116 L.Ed.2d 243.

C.A.11 (Fla.) 1987. Outside limited confines of statutory provision allowing customs officers to search vehicle, container, or person departing from United States, general rule requiring probable cause and search warrant for treasury agent to search for violations of currency reporting requirements applies; reasonable suspicion will not be sufficient in all cases to render search lawful. 31 U.S.C.A. §§ 5316, 5317(a, b).

U.S. v. Hernandez-Salazar, 813 F.2d 1126.

C.A.11 (Fla.) 1985. Search of private commercial property without proper consent is unreasonable under Fourth Amendment unless search is authorized by valid search warrant. U.S.C.A. Const.Amend. 4.

Peterman v. Coleman, 764 F.2d 1416.

C.A.11 (Fla.) 1984. Congress intended to require search warrants for searches for currency violations by outgoing travelers. 31 U.S.C. (1976 Ed.) § 1105.

U.S. v. Chemaly, 741 F.2d 1346, opinion reinstated on rehearing U.S. v. Bacca-Beltran, 764 F.2d 747.

C.A.11 (Fla.) 1984. Fourth Amendment protection contemplates that a neutral and detached magistrate issue warrant, supported by probable cause, before law enforcement officers may enter premises, and only in the face of "exigent circumstances," where obtaining warrant would greatly compromise important law enforcement objectives, does warrant requirement yield. U.S.C.A. Const.Amend. 4.

U.S. v. Pantoja-Soto, 739 F.2d 1520, rehearing denied 749 F.2d 733, certiorari denied 105 S.Ct. 1369, 470 U.S. 1008, 84 L.Ed.2d 389.

C.A.11 (Fla.) 1983. Relevant exceptions to requirement of search warrant are searches in exigent circumstances, border searches and administrative searches. Immigration and Nationality Act, §§ 274, 274(a), 275, 8 U.S.C.A. §§ 1324, 1324(a), 1325; U.S.C.A. Const.Amend. 4.

U.S. v. Hidalgo-Gato, 703 F.2d 1267.

C.A.5 (Fla.) 1981. There must be something more than reasonableness to justify an exception to search warrant requirement. U.S.C.A.Const. Amend. 4.

U.S. v. Kreimes, 649 F.2d 1185.

C.A.5 (Fla.) 1981. Under the Fourth Amendment, all warrantless searches and seizures are unreasonable except those conducted in a few narrowly defined situations where circumstances justifying the search outweigh privacy rights. U.S.C.A.Const. Amend. 4.

U.S. v. Richards, 638 F.2d 765, rehearing denied 646 F.2d 962, certiorari denied 102 S.Ct. 669, 454 U.S. 1097, 70 L.Ed.2d 638.

A warrantless search is justified when it is incident to a lawful arrest, when it is conducted with probable cause under exigent circumstances, when it involves a vehicle, or when it is made for administrative purposes to satisfy a special governmental need and necessity outweighs the invasion entailed. U.S.C.A.Const. Amend. 4.

U.S. v. Richards, 638 F.2d 765, rehearing denied 646 F.2d 962, certiorari denied 102 S.Ct. 669, 454 U.S. 1097, 70 L.Ed.2d 638.

C.A.5 (Fla.) 1980. Generally, a search of private property is unconstitutional unless it is conducted pursuant to a properly issued search warrant; however, in a limited number of situations, warrantless searches have been upheld as "reasonable" under the Fourth Amendment. U.S.C.A.Const. Amend. 4.

U.S. v. Staller, 616 F.2d 1284, certiorari denied 101 S.Ct. 207, 449 U.S. 869, 66 L.Ed.2d 89.

C.A.5 (Fla.) 1978. Though warrantless searches are per se unreasonable, the Government may show that the facts fall within one of the narrow, judicially defined exemptions to the warrant requirement. U.S.C.A.Const. Amend. 4.

U.S. v. Sink, 586 F.2d 1041, certiorari denied 99 S.Ct. 3102, 443 U.S. 912, 61 L.Ed.2d 876, certiorari denied Grim v. U.S., 99 S.Ct. 3102, 443 U.S. 912, 61 L.Ed.2d 876.

C.A.5 (Fla.) 1978. Warrantless search of one defendant's apartment and codefendant's suitcase, which was discovered in apartment, was unconstitutional where neither defendant, who had been arrested at another location, freely and voluntarily consented to the search. U.S.C.A.Const. Amend. 4.

U.S. v. Fredericks, 586 F.2d 470, certiorari denied 99 S.Ct. 1507, 440 U.S. 962, 59 L.Ed.2d 776.

C.A.5 (Fla.) 1977. Reasonableness of search under exigent circumstances exception to warrant requirement is not foreclosed by failure to obtain warrant at earliest practicable moment.

U.S. v. Gardner, 553 F.2d 946, rehearing denied 559 F.2d 29, certiorari denied 98 S.Ct. 722, 434 U.S. 1011, 54 L.Ed.2d 753.

C.A.5 (Fla.) 1975. Where government agent trespassed upon defendants' rural property and peered into hole in shed on property for sole purpose of securing evidence of crime which would support later issuance of search warrant, agent's action was unlawful search and seizure which did not fall within "open fields" exception to warrant requirement. U.S.C.A.Const. Amend. 4.

U.S. v. Holmes, 521 F.2d 859, rehearing granted 525 F.2d 1364, on rehearing 537 F.2d 227.

C.A.5 (Fla.) 1973. Warrant requirement of the Fourth Amendment is operative only when there is a need to determine probable cause. U.S.C.A.Const. Amend. 4.

U.S. v. Gravitt, 484 F.2d 375, certiorari denied 94 S.Ct. 879, 414 U.S. 1135, 38 L.Ed.2d 761.

C.A.5 (Fla.) 1973. Searches conducted outside judicial process without prior approval by judge or magistrate, as matter of law, are not reasonable, unless government can show that search falls within one of few well-delineated exceptions. U.S.C.A.Const. Amend. 4.

U.S. v. Soriano, 482 F.2d 469, on rehearing 497 F.2d 147.

The Fourth Amendment does not deny law enforcement the support of usual inferences which reasonable men draw from evidence, but its protection consists in requiring that those inferences be drawn by neutral and detached magistrate instead of being judged by government enforcement agents. U.S.C.A.Const. Amend. 4.

U.S. v. Soriano, 482 F.2d 469, on rehearing 497 F.2d 147.

C.A.5 (Fla.) 1971. A search conducted outside judicial process, that is, without a warrant, is per se unreasonable in violation of Fourth Amendment. U.S.C.A.Const. Amend. 4.

U.S. v. Sokolow, 450 F.2d 324.

While rule that search conducted without a warrant is per se unreasonable is subject to limited and well-defined exceptions that may justify a warrantless search and seizure, exceptions are jealously and carefully drawn and there must be showing by those who seek exemption that exigencies of situation made that course imperative. U.S.C.A.Const. Amend. 4.

U.S. v. Sokolow, 450 F.2d 324.

C.A.5 (Fla.) 1971. Record-making of police agent's conversations with defendant and subsequent testimony concerning them, without warrant authorizing encounters with defendant, did not violate defendant's Fourth Amendment rights. U.S.C.A.Const. Amend. 4.

U.S. v. Castillo, 449 F.2d 1300.

C.A.5 (Fla.) 1953. Fact that premises bore an unsavory reputation did not, of itself, authorize an exploratory search without a warrant, nor did it place the occupants of the premises beyond protection of constitutional amendment prohibiting unreasonable searches and seizures. U.S.C.A.Const. Amend. 4.

Drayton v. U.S., 205 F.2d 35.

C.C.A.5 (Fla.) 1942. If the securing of a search warrant is reasonably practicable, it must be used and when properly supported by affidavit and issued after judicial approval it protects the seizing officer against actions for damages.

Walker v. U.S., 125 F.2d 395.

M.D.Fla. 2012. Searches conducted outside the judicial process, without prior approval by a judge or magistrate, are per se unreasonable under the Fourth Amendment, subject only to a few specifically established and well-delineated exceptions. U.S.C.A. Const.Amend. 4.

U.S. v. Hernandez-Penaloza, 899 F.Supp.2d 1269, appeal dismissed (11th circ. 12-14867).

M.D.Fla. 2012. Searches conducted outside the judicial process, without prior approval by judge or magistrate, are per se unreasonable under the Fourth Amendment, subject only to a few specifically established and well-delineated exceptions. U.S.C.A. Const.Amend. 4.

Gennusa v. Shoar, 879 F.Supp.2d 1337, affirmed 748 F.3d 1103.

M.D.Fla. 2010. Ultimate touchstone of the Fourth Amendment is reasonableness, and the warrant requirement is subject to certain exceptions. U.S.C.A. Const. Amend. 4.

U.S. v. Franklin, 721 F.Supp.2d 1229, affirmed 694 F.3d 1.

M.D.Fla. 2009. Unless consent is given, law enforcement officers generally must obtain warrant supported by probable cause to justify search pursuant to Fourth Amendment. U.S.C.A. Const. Amend. 4.

Bryant v. Mostert, 636 F.Supp.2d 1303.

M.D.Fla. 2006. Under "special needs" exception, to general principle that warrantless searches of person must be based on individualized suspicion of criminal activity, requires showing of risk to public safety that is substantial, real, and concrete, and not simply hypothetical. U.S.C.A. Const.Amend. 4.

> Johnston v. Tampa Sports Authority, 442 F.Supp.2d 1257, reversed and remanded 490 F.3d 820, opinion vacated and superseded on rehearing 530 F.3d 1320, rehearing and rehearing denied 285 Fed.Appx. 745, certiorari denied 129 S.Ct. 1013, 555 U.S. 1138, 173 L.Ed.2d 295, reversed and remanded 530 F.3d 1320, rehearing and rehearing denied 285 Fed.Appx. 745, certiorari denied 129 S.Ct. 1013, 555 U.S. 1138, 173 L.Ed.2d 295.

M.D.Fla. 2001. A warrantless search is per se unreasonable even if there is probable cause, unless the search falls within a recognized exception to the warrant requirement. U.S.C.A. Const.Amend. 4.

> U.S. v. Davis, 170 F.Supp.2d 1234.

M.D.Fla. 1994. Generally, warrantless search based on probable cause is per se illegal, unless government shows that it falls into one of the few limited and well-defined exceptions recognized by law. U.S.C.A. Const.Amend. 4.

> U.S. v. Adams, 845 F.Supp. 1531.

M.D.Fla. 1981. Except under certain narrowly defined circumstances, search of private property without proper consent is unreasonable unless it has been authorized by a valid search warrant. U.S.C.A.Const. Amend. 4.

> Mid-Fla Coin Exchange, Inc. v. Griffin, 529 F.Supp. 1006.

M.D.Fla. 1978. The Fourth Amendment protects against involuntary intrusions by government, whether administrative or criminal; therefore, a valid search warrant is necessary absent consent or a showing of exigent circumstances that justify one of the carefully defined exceptions to the warrant requirement. U.S.C.A.Const. Amend. 4.

> U.S. v. Roux Laboratories, Inc., 456 F.Supp. 973.

M.D.Fla. 1976. Searches and seizures are to be conducted pursuant to search warrants of current and particularized specificity.

> U.S. v. Cooper, 409 F.Supp. 364, affirmed 542 F.2d 1171.

Congress has power to authorize by statute warrantless searches of federally licensed or regulated businesses, if the searches are specifically and reasonably restricted to comply with Fourth Amendment standards. U.S.C.A.Const. Amend. 4.

> U.S. v. Cooper, 409 F.Supp. 364, affirmed 542 F.2d 1171.

In situations where search of federally licensed or regulated business is conducted pursuant to statutory authority, statutory authority is equivalent of valid search warrant and neither question of valid consent, nor issue of valid warrant, arise.

> U.S. v. Cooper, 409 F.Supp. 364, affirmed 542 F.2d 1171.

Treasury agent searching logbook of firearms dealer pursuant to statutory authority rightfully seized evidence discovered thereupon of illegal sales or recordkeeping.

> U.S. v. Cooper, 409 F.Supp. 364, affirmed 542 F.2d 1171.

M.D.Fla. 1975. Seizure of material such as an allegedly obscene film must be made pursuant to a warrant, issued by the proper judicial officer, after determination by that officer that probable cause exists to believe that the seized material is offensive to the law.

> Ellwest Stereo Theatres, Inc. v. Nichols, 403 F.Supp. 857.

M.D.Fla. 1972. Search and seizure carried out on suspect's premises without a warrant is per se unreasonable, unless it falls within one of carefully defined exceptions. U.S.C.A.Const. Amends. 4, 14.

> Shuler v. Wainwright, 341 F.Supp. 1061, vacated 491 F.2d 1213.

M.D.Fla. 1971. General requirement that a search warrant be obtained is not lightly to be disregarded, and burden is on those seeking an exemption from such requirement to show the need for it.

> U.S. v. Tranquillo, 330 F.Supp. 871.

S.D.Fla. 2012. Under the Fourth Amendment, searches conducted without a warrant issued upon probable cause are per se unreasonable, subject only to a few

---

† This Case was not selected for publication in the National Reporter System
For legislative history of cited statutes, see Florida Statutes Annotated

specifically established and well-delineated exceptions. U.S.C.A. Const.Amend. 4.

> Corbett v. Transportation Sec. Admin., 968 F.Supp.2d 1171, affirmed 568 Fed.Appx. 690, certiorari denied 135 S.Ct. 1559, 191 L.Ed.2d 639.

S.D.Fla. 2011. Searches conducted outside the judicial process, without prior approval by judge or magistrate, are per se unreasonable under the Fourth Amendment, subject only to a few specifically established and well-delineated exceptions. U.S.C.A. Const.Amend. 4.

> U.S. v. Gomez, 807 F.Supp.2d 1134.

S.D.Fla. 2010. With respect to a person's Fourth Amendment rights, law enforcement officials must obtain a warrant supported by probable cause in most circumstances, unless there is consent, to justify a search. U.S.C.A. Const.Amend. 4.

> Lippman v. City of Miami, 724 F.Supp.2d 1240.

S.D.Fla. 2008. Ordinarily, a seizure of personal property is per se unreasonable within the meaning of the Fourth Amendment unless accomplished pursuant to a warrant. U.S.C.A. Const.Amend. 4.

> Sosa v. Hames, 581 F.Supp.2d 1254.

S.D.Fla. 1991. Principal protection against intrusions into the dwellings of individuals is the warrant requirement imposed upon agents of the government who seek to enter a home for the purpose of a search or arrest. U.S.C.A. Const.Amend. 4.

> U.S. v. Mazuera, 756 F.Supp. 564.

Entry into a home to conduct a search or make an arrest is unreasonable under the Fourth Amendment unless done pursuant to a warrant, and search or seizure carried out on a suspect's premises without a warrant is per se unreasonable unless police can show exigent circumstances. U.S.C.A. Const.Amend. 4.

> U.S. v. Mazuera, 756 F.Supp. 564.

S.D.Fla. 1981. An exception to probable cause requirement of Fourth Amendment for searches cannot be made on basis of complexity of indictment returned by a grand jury supervised by government. U.S.C.A.Const. Amend. 4.

> U.S. v. Defalco, 509 F.Supp. 127.

S.D.Fla. 1978. As a fundamental rule, searches conducted without prior approval of a judge or magistrate are unreasonable per se under the Fourth Amendment, subject only to a few well-delineated exceptions. U.S.C.A.Const. Amend. 4.

> U.S. v. Marshall, 452 F.Supp. 1282, reversed 609 F.2d 152, appeal after remand 672 F.2d 425, rehearing denied 680 F.2d 1392.

S.D.Fla. 1976. As a general rule, any search which is initiated without a warrant is per se unreasonable unless it falls within one of the narrowly defined exceptions to the warrant requirement.

> U.S. v. Bowdach, 414 F.Supp. 1346, affirmed 561 F.2d 1160, rehearing denied 565 F.2d 163.

S.D.Fla. 1974. Absent exigent circumstances, a search conducted outside the judicial process is per se unreasonable. U.S.C.A.Const. Amend. 4.

> U.S. v. Chapman, 384 F.Supp. 1232, affirmed 523 F.2d 1054.

S.D.Fla. 1967. Police officers were not trespassers in searching ground and shrubbery outside of and directly below motel room occupied by suspect who fled from police.

> U. S. ex rel. Fletcher v. Wainwright, 269 F.Supp. 276, rehearing denied 280 F.Supp. 905, reversed 399 F.2d 62.

Fla. 2017. Warrantless searches are presumed unreasonable with a few carefully tailored exceptions. U.S. Const. Amend. 4; Fla. Const. art. 1, § 12.

> State v. Markus, 211 So.3d 894, rehearing denied 2017 WL 944231.

Fla. 2015. Searches or seizures executed without prior approval by a judge or magistrate are per se unreasonable. U.S.C.A. Const.Amend. 4.

> Rodriguez v. State, 187 So.3d 841, rehearing denied, certiorari denied 137 S.Ct. 124, 196 L.Ed.2d 199.

The warrant requirement is an important working part of the machinery of government, not merely an inconvenience to be somehow weighed against the claims of police efficiency. U.S.C.A. Const. Amend. 4.

Rodriguez v. State, 187 So.3d 841, rehearing denied, certiorari denied 137 S.Ct. 124, 196 L.Ed.2d 199.

Fla. 2014. Subject only to a few well-delineated exceptions, searches conducted without prior judicial approval are per se unreasonable under the Fourth Amendment. U.S.C.A. Const.Amend. 4.

Lebron v. State, 135 So.3d 1040, rehearing denied.

Fla. 2012. A search conducted without a warrant issued upon probable cause is per se unreasonable, subject only to a few specifically established and well-delineated exceptions. U.S.C.A. Const.Amends. 4, 14.

Delhall v. State, 95 So.3d 134.

Fla. 2011. Searches conducted outside the judicial process, without prior approval by judge or magistrate, are per se unreasonable under the Fourth Amendment—subject only to a few specifically established and well-delineated exceptions. U.S.C.A. Const.Amend. 4.

Harris v. State, 71 So.3d 756, revised on rehearing, certiorari granted 132 S.Ct. 1796, 566 U.S. 904, 182 L.Ed.2d 615, reversed 133 S.Ct. 1050, 568 U.S. 237, 185 L.Ed.2d 61, on remand 123 So.3d 1144, opinion withdrawn 123 So.3d 1144.

Fla. 1998. A warrantless search is per se unreasonable under the Fourth Amendment; however, a search will be considered lawful if conducted pursuant to consent which was given freely and voluntarily. U.S.C.A. Const.Amend. 4.

Jorgenson v. State, 714 So.2d 423.

Fla. 1994. Generally, warrantless search or seizure is per se unreasonable, unless search or seizure falls within one of well-established exceptions to warrant requirement. U.S.C.A. Const.Amend. 4; West's F.S.A. Const. Art. 1, § 12.

Jones v. State, 648 So.2d 669, rehearing denied, certiorari denied 115 S.Ct. 2588, 515 U.S. 1147, 132 L.Ed.2d 836, post-conviction relief denied 2005 WL 6932251, affirmed 998 So.2d 573, revised on rehearing, post-conviction relief denied 2005 WL 6932252, affirmed 998 So.2d 573, revised on rehearing, and revised on rehearing, habeas corpus denied 998 So.2d 573, revised on rehearing, and revised on rehearing, and revised on rehearing, post-conviction relief denied 2009 WL 9047495, affirmed 53 So.3d 230, rehearing denied, post-conviction relief denied 2011 WL 10483396, affirmed 141 So.3d 132, rehearing denied, certiorari denied 133 S.Ct. 661, 184 L.Ed.2d 471, habeas corpus denied 2013 WL 5504371, affirmed 834 F.3d 1299.

Fla. 1981. When there is no legal right to observe an article of contraband, it is illegal to seize the article. U.S.C.A.Const. Amend. 4.

State v. Morsman, 394 So.2d 408, certiorari denied 101 S.Ct. 3066, 452 U.S. 930, 69 L.Ed.2d 431.

Fla. 1978. Searches without warrants are unreasonable under Fourth Amendment unless justified by one of exceptions to rule. U.S.C.A.Const. Amend. 4.

Martin v. State, 360 So.2d 396, appeal after remand 377 So.2d 706.

Fla. 1977. Unless consent to search is given by owner or rightful possessor of property, a warrant must be obtained; the only exception to such requirement occurs where consent by a joint owner has been obtained in absence of the person whose property is the object of the search.

Silva v. State, 344 So.2d 559.

Fla. 1952. An officer without a search warrant or warrant of arrest has no right to stop one on the public highway, particularly in the nighttime, and demand that he surrender what he has in his possession.

Kersey v. State, 58 So.2d 155.

Fla. 1950. Search without search warrant although it is practical to secure one, does not necessarily constitute violation of constitutional provision against unreasonable searches and seizures. U.S.C.A.Const. Amend. 4.

Brown v. State, 46 So.2d 479.

Fla. 1950. Court's paramount concern is for guarantee in the organic law against unreasonable searches irrespective of whether guilty persons may go free where convincing evidence against them is held inadmissible because obtained by defective search warrants. F.S.A.Const. Declaration of Rights, § 22; U.S.C.A.Const. Amend. 4.

De Lancy v. City of Miami, 43 So.2d 856, 14 A.L.R.2d 602.

Fla.App. 1 Dist. 2016. Warrants are generally required to search a person's home or his person unless the exigencies of the situation make the needs of law enforcement so compelling that the warrantless search is objectively reasonable under the Fourth Amendment. U.S.C.A. Const.Amend. 4.

State v. McRae, 194 So.3d 524.

Fla.App. 1 Dist. 2015. Warrantless searches conducted in a constitutionally protected area are per se unreasonable unless they fall within one of the five established exceptions to the search warrant requirement: (1) with the occupant's consent, (2) incident to lawful arrest, (3) with probable cause to search but with exigent circumstances, (4) in hot pursuit, or (5) pursuant to a stop and frisk. U.S.C.A. Const.Amend. 4.

State v. Smith, 172 So.3d 993.

Fla.App. 1 Dist. 2015. Warrantless searches and seizures are per se unreasonable under the Fourth Amendment subject to only a few exceptions. U.S.C.A. Const. Amend. 4.

Herring v. State, 168 So.3d 240, rehearing denied, review dismissed 173 So.3d 966.

Fla.App. 1 Dist. 2013. Searches conducted outside the judicial process, without prior approval by judge or magistrate, are per se unreasonable under the Fourth Amendment, subject only to a few specifically established and well-delineated exceptions. U.S.C.A. Const.Amend. 4.

Thomas v. State, 127 So.3d 658, appeal after new trial 207 So.3d 928.

Fla.App. 1 Dist. 2011. A warrantless search is per se unreasonable under the Fourth Amendment, subject to a few well-defined exceptions. U.S.C.A. Const. Amend. 4.

Kilburn v. State, 54 So.3d 625.

Fla.App. 1 Dist. 2010. In general, a warrantless search is per se unreasonable unless the search or seizure falls into one of the well established exceptions to the warrant requirement. U.S.C.A. Const. Amend. 4.

Higerd v. State, 54 So.3d 513, rehearing denied, review denied 64 So.3d 1260, certiorari denied 132 S.Ct. 521, 565 U.S. 979, 181 L.Ed.2d 350.

Fla.App. 1 Dist. 2008. Warrantless searches are per se unreasonable under both the federal and state constitutional prohibitions against reasonable searches and seizures subject to a few specifically established and well-delineated exceptions, and one of these is the emergency or exigency doctrine. U.S.C.A. Const.Amend. 4; West's F.S.A. Const. Art. 1, § 12.

Watson v. State, 979 So.2d 1148.

Fla.App. 1 Dist. 2008. To validate a warrantless search, the state must show that the search falls within a constitutional exception, one of which is voluntary consent. U.S.C.A. Const.Amend. 4.

Cox v. State, 975 So.2d 1163.

Fla.App. 1 Dist. 2003. A warrantless search is presumptively unreasonable but, when probable cause exists, if exigent circumstances make it impossible or impracticable to obtain a warrant, a warrantless search will be excused. U.S.C.A. Const. Amend. 4; West's F.S.A. Const. Art. 1, § 12.

Hendrix v. State, 843 So.2d 1003, review denied 851 So.2d 729.

Fla.App. 1 Dist. 1996. Warrantless search or seizure is per se unreasonable unless it falls within one of well-established exceptions to warrant requirement. U.S.C.A. Const.Amend. 4; West's F.S.A. Const. Art. 1, § 12.

Stalling v. State, 678 So.2d 843, rehearing denied.

Fla.App. 1 Dist. 1989. Warrantless searches and seizures inside home are considered presumptively unreasonable. U.S.C.A. Const.Amend. 4.

Eason v. State, 546 So.2d 57.

Even when felony has been committed and officers have probable cause to believe that incriminating evidence will be found within home, warrantless entry into home to search for weapons or contraband is unconstitutional in absence of exigent circumstances. U.S.C.A. Const.Amend. 4.

Eason v. State, 546 So.2d 57.

† This Case was not selected for publication in the National Reporter System
For legislative history of cited statutes, see Florida Statutes Annotated

Fla.App. 1 Dist. 1981. Florida does not recognize a good-faith exception to the search warrant requirement.

Lovett v. State, 403 So.2d 1079.

Fla.App. 1 Dist. 1980. When there are no exigent circumstances, where consent is not voluntarily given, and where there is no probable cause to suspect contraband, warrantless search may not be conducted. U.S.C.A.Const. Amend. 4.

Loftis v. State, 391 So.2d 219, review denied 399 So.2d 1146.

Fla.App. 1 Dist. 1979. A search warrant must be obtained in accordance with statutory provisions to conduct agricultural inspection search where there are no exigent circumstances, consent is not offered voluntarily, there is no probable cause to suspect that vehicle contains contraband. West's F.S.A. § 570.15(1)(b).

Rose v. State, 369 So.2d 447.

Fla.App. 1 Dist. 1976. All searches without a valid warrant are unreasonable unless established by the state to fall within one of the exception categories.

Parsons v. State, 334 So.2d 308, decision approved 351 So.2d 723.

Fla.App. 1 Dist. 1976. All searches without warrant are unreasonable, unless shown to be within one of exceptions to rule that search must rest upon a valid warrant.

Raffield v. State, 333 So.2d 534, quashed in part 351 So.2d 945, on remand 362 So.2d 138.

Fla.App. 1 Dist. 1976. Warrantless searches are per se unreasonable subject only to a few specifically established and well-delineated exceptions.

Benton v. State, 329 So.2d 385.

Fla.App. 1 Dist. 1974. In the absence of exigent circumstances, a search or seizure carried out on a suspect's premises without a warrant is per se unreasonable.

Mahoney v. State, 300 So.2d 743.

Fla.App. 1 Dist. 1974. It is only "unreasonable" warrantless searches that are prohibited, not all warrantless searches.

Gilbert v. State, 289 So.2d 475, certiorari denied 294 So.2d 660.

Fla.App. 1 Dist. 1970. Every search without a warrant is not an unlawful or unreasonable search condemned by provisions of State and Federal Constitutions.

Donar v. State, 236 So.2d 145.

Fla.App. 2 Dist. 2017. Without a warrant or an exception to the warrant requirement, a law enforcement officer has no right to physically intrude into the curtilage of a house. U.S. Const. Amend. 4; Fla. Const. art. 1, § 12.

Daniels v. State, 208 So.3d 1223.

Fla.App. 2 Dist. 2016. A warrantless search of a home is per se unreasonable under the Fourth Amendment, subject to a few specifically established and well-delineated exceptions. U.S.C.A. Const.Amend. 4; West's F.S.A. Const. Art. 1, § 12.

State v. Fultz, 189 So.3d 155, rehearing denied.

The exceptions to the warrant requirement are based on a police officer's ability to articulate objective facts which make the procuring of a warrant impractical. U.S.C.A. Const.Amend. 4; West's F.S.A. Const. Art. 1, § 12.

State v. Fultz, 189 So.3d 155, rehearing denied.

Police may not approach a dwelling, armed only with their own subjective suspicion that illegal activity was afoot, and wait for some justification to break down the door and burst into the dwelling without a warrant. U.S.C.A. Const.Amend. 4; West's F.S.A. Const. Art. 1, § 12.

State v. Fultz, 189 So.3d 155, rehearing denied.

Fla.App. 2 Dist. 2015. The Fourth Amendment to the U.S. Constitution prohibits warrantless searches; however, a warrantless search may be validated if the State proves that the search falls into an established constitutional exception to the warrant requirement, such as consent. U.S.C.A. Const.Amend. 4.

Thompson v. State, 170 So.3d 856.

Fla.App. 2 Dist. 2012. Searches conducted without a warrant are per se unreasonable under the Fourth and Fourteenth Amendments unless they are conducted within one of the recognized exceptions to the warrant requirement. U.S.C.A. Const.Amends. 4, 14.

Ferrer v. State, 113 So.3d 860.

Fla.App. 2 Dist. 2010. Warrantless searches are per se unreasonable under the Fourth Amendment, subject only to a few specifically established and well-delineated exceptions. U.S.C.A. Const.Amend. 4.

State v. K.S., 28 So.3d 985.

Fla.App. 2 Dist. 2006. A warrantless search of a home is presumptively unreasonable and a violation of the Fourth Amendment, unless the search falls within certain recognized constitutional exceptions. U.S.C.A. Const.Amend. 4.

Barth v. State, 955 So.2d 1115.

Fla.App. 2 Dist. 2006. Because the ultimate touchstone of the Fourth Amendment is reasonableness, the search warrant requirement is subject to certain exceptions. U.S.C.A. Const.Amend. 4.

Vanslyke v. State, 936 So.2d 1218.

Fla.App. 2 Dist. 2005. Generally, warrantless searches or seizures are per se unreasonable unless the search or seizure falls within an exception to the warrant requirement, one of which is consent. U.S.C.A. Const.Amend. 4.

V.H. v. State, 903 So.2d 321.

Fla.App. 2 Dist. 2004. To validate a warrantless search, the State must prove that the search falls into an established constitutional exception to the warrant requirement, such as consent. U.S.C.A. Const.Amend. 4.

Alamo v. State, 891 So.2d 1059.

Fla.App. 2 Dist. 2004. To validate a warrantless search, State must prove that it falls into one of the recognized exceptions to the warrant requirement, one of which is consent. U.S.C.A. Const.Amend. 4.

E.B. v. State, 866 So.2d 200.

Fla.App. 2 Dist. 2003. In the absence of exigent circumstances or permission, the police clearly may not enter a home without a search warrant simply because they think they have probable cause to believe evidence of a crime may be found therein. U.S.C.A. Const.Amend. 4.

McDuffy v. State, 837 So.2d 590.

Fla.App. 2 Dist. 2002. Warrantless entry of a person's home to search for objects of a crime is generally barred by the Fourth Amendment. U.S.C.A. Const. Amend. 4.

Moore v. State, 830 So.2d 883, rehearing denied.

Fla.App. 2 Dist. 2000. Warrantless searches conducted by instruments of the state are per se unreasonable unless the searches fall within one of a few specifically-established and well-delineated exceptions. U.S.C.A. Const.Amend. 4; West's F.S.A. Const. Art. 1, § 12.

State v. Iaccarino, 767 So.2d 470.

Fla.App. 2 Dist. 2000. To validate a warrantless search, the government must prove that the search falls into one of the recognized constitutional exceptions, one of which is consent. (Per Casanueva, J., with one Judge concurring specially). U.S.C.A. Const.Amend. 4.

Smith v. State, 753 So.2d 713.

Fla.App. 2 Dist. 1999. Absent consent or exigent circumstances, law enforcement may not cross the threshold of a residence without a warrant. U.S.C.A. Const.Amend. 4.

Davis v. State, 744 So.2d 586.

Fla.App. 2 Dist. 1995. Searches conducted without a warrant are per se unreasonable unless conducted within framework of a few specifically established and well delineated exceptions. U.S.C.A. Const.Amend. 4.

Gnann v. State, 662 So.2d 406.

Fla.App. 2 Dist. 1991. Warrantless seizures are per se unreasonable unless they fall within certain well-defined and established exceptions to warrant requirement.

Mercier v. State, 579 So.2d 308.

Fla.App. 2 Dist. 1985. Warrantless searches are per se unreasonable under the Fourth Amendment to the United States Constitution and Article I, section 12 of the Florida Constitution, subject to a few specifically established and well-delineated exceptions. West's F.S.A. Const. Art. 1, § 12; U.S.C.A. Const.Amend. 4.

Cross v. State, 469 So.2d 226, decision approved 487 So.2d 1056, certiorari dismissed 107 S.Ct. 248, 479 U.S. 805, 93 L.Ed.2d 172.

Fla.App. 2 Dist. 1983. To be valid under Fourth Amendment, search and seizure should be made only pursuant to warrant that is based upon probable cause, and warrantless search is per se invalid unless it falls within one of carefully defined exceptions to warrant requirement. U.S.C.A. Const.Amend. 4.

> Hayes v. State, 439 So.2d 896, petition for review denied 447 So.2d 886, certiorari granted 105 S.Ct. 82, 469 U.S. 816, 83 L.Ed.2d 30, reversed 105 S.Ct. 1643, 470 U.S. 811, 84 L.Ed.2d 705, on remand 488 So.2d 77, certiorari denied 107 S.Ct. 119, 479 U.S. 831, 93 L.Ed.2d 65.

Fla.App. 2 Dist. 1980. Any admission by defendant or search of her purse occurring prior to her arrest were unaffected by the questioned legality of her subsequent arrest.

> State v. Cahill, 388 So.2d 354.

Fla.App. 2 Dist. 1980. Search without warrant is prima facie unreasonable.

> State v. Sanders, 387 So.2d 391, decision disapproved 403 So.2d 973.

Fla.App. 2 Dist. 1980. Unless a warrantless search falls within one of delineated exceptions to Fourth Amendment warrant requirement, it is unreasonable and violative of Fourth Amendment. U.S.C.A.Const. Amend. 4.

> State v. Tsavaris, 382 So.2d 56, certified question answered 394 So.2d 418, appeal after remand 414 So.2d 1087, review denied 424 So.2d 763.

Fla.App. 2 Dist. 1974. Not all warrantless searches are unreasonable. U.S.C.A.Const. Amend. 4.

> Giannetta v. State, 296 So.2d 654.

Fla.App. 2 Dist. 1969. Reasonableness of any search without a warrant is measured from standpoint of the conduct of the searchers and if their conduct is in some way reprehensible, or if they precipitate a search and are motivated therein solely by desire to hunt for incriminating evidence, or if they do so without any plausible explanation or justification, the invasion is an unreasonable one.

> Godbee v. State, 224 So.2d 441.

Fla.App. 2 Dist. 1967. Officer, without search warrant or warrant of arrest, has no right to stop any one on public highway, particularly at night, and demand that he surrender what he has in his possession or take it from him without his consent. F.S.A. §§ 933.01–933.08, 933.09–933.15.

> Carter v. State, 199 So.2d 324.

It is required procedure for police officer to comply with constitutional and statutory provisions and court decisions construing them before making search, provided he has reasonable opportunity, both in point of time and circumstances, to do so. F.S.A.Const. Declaration of Rights, § 22; F.S.A. §§ 933.01–933.08, 933.09–933.15.

> Carter v. State, 199 So.2d 324.

Police officer should be armed with arrest or search warrant where reasonably possible.

> Carter v. State, 199 So.2d 324.

Fourth Amendment proscription against unreasonable search and seizure does not deny law enforcement support of usual inferences which reasonable men draw from evidence, and its protection consists in requiring that those inferences be drawn by neutral and detached magistrate instead of being judged by officer engaged in competitive enterprise of ferreting out crime. U.S.C.A.Const. Amend. 4.

> Carter v. State, 199 So.2d 324.

When right of privacy must reasonably yield to right of search is, as a rule, to be decided by judicial officer, not by policeman or government enforcement agent. U.S.C.A.Const. Amend. 4.

> Carter v. State, 199 So.2d 324.

Fla.App. 3 Dist. 2015. To validate a search without a warrant, the State must demonstrate that the search falls within a constitutional exception, one of which is voluntary consent. U.S.C.A. Const. Amend. 4.

> State v. Hall, 201 So.3d 66.

Fla.App. 3 Dist. 2010. Warrantless searches or arrests in constitutionally protected areas, particularly one's home, are per se unreasonable unless they fall within one of the established exceptions to the warrant requirement. U.S.C.A. Const. Amend. 4.

> State v. Brown, 36 So.3d 770, review denied 63 So.3d 748.

---

† This Case was not selected for publication in the National Reporter System
For legislative history of cited statutes, see Florida Statutes Annotated

Fla.App. 3 Dist. 2008. Searches conducted outside the judicial process, without prior approval by judge or magistrate, are per se unreasonable under the Fourth Amendment, subject only to a few specifically established and well-delineated exceptions. U.S.C.A. Const.Amend. 4; West's F.S.A. Const. Art. 1, § 12.

State v. Hollingshead, 974 So.2d 1123, rehearing denied.

Fla.App. 3 Dist. 1995. All searches must be authorized by valid search warrant or fall within certain limited exceptions to warrant requirement including consent, lawful arrest, hot pursuit, stop and frisk, and probable cause with exigent circumstances. West's F.S.A. Const. Art. 1, § 12.

Potts v. Johnson, 654 So.2d 596.

Fla.App. 3 Dist. 1991. Searches conducted without a warrant are per se unreasonable under the Fourth and Fourteenth Amendments unless conducted within one of the recognized exceptions to the warrant requirement, which are consent, search incident to lawful arrest, probable cause to search with exigent circumstances, hot pursuit, and stop and frisk. U.S.C.A. Const.Amends. 4, 14.

Alvarez v. State, 573 So.2d 400.

Fla.App. 3 Dist. 1985. General rule is that warrantless searches are per se unreasonable.

State v. Fuksman, 468 So.2d 1067.

Fla.App. 3 Dist. 1981. All searches without warrant are per se unreasonable unless conducted within framework of a few established exceptions. U.S.C.A.Const.Amend. 4.

Graham v. State, 406 So.2d 503.

Fla.App. 3 Dist. 1981. Warrantless searches are per se unreasonable under the Fourth Amendment, subject only to a few specifically established and well-delineated exception which are jealously and carefully drawn, and burden is on State to demonstrate that procurement of warrant was not feasible because of exigencies of situation which made particular course of action imperative. U.S.C.A.Const. Amend. 4.

State v. Parker, 399 So.2d 24, review denied 408 So.2d 1095.

Fla.App. 3 Dist. 1981. Mere existence or prior fruitless unlawful search does not taint subsequent lawful one.

State v. Jacobson, 398 So.2d 857, approved in part, disapproved in part 476 So.2d 1282.

Fla.App. 3 Dist. 1980. In determining whether search and seizure were permissible, courts must consider scope of particular intrusion, manner in which it was conducted, justification for initiating it and place in which it is conducted. U.S.C.A.Const. Amend. 4.

Mata v. State, 380 So.2d 1157, petition for review denied 389 So.2d 1112.

Fla.App. 3 Dist. 1979. Unlike the search of private premises, there is no general constitutional requirement that a police officer obtain a search or arrest warrant before he may seize and search a person. West's F.S.A.Const. art. 1, § 12; U.S.C.A.Const. Amend. 4.

State v. Ramos, 378 So.2d 1294.

Fla.App. 3 Dist. 1979. A search of private property conducted by state or federal agents without a duly issued search warrant is per se "unreasonable" within meaning of applicable constitutional provisions, subject only to a few specifically established and well-delineated exceptions justified by absolute necessity. West's F.S.A.Const. art. 1, § 12; U.S.C.A.Const. Amend. 4.

Haugland v. State, 374 So.2d 1026, certiorari denied 390 So.2d 360.

Fla.App. 3 Dist. 1979. Reasonableness of any search without a warrant is measured from standpoint of conduct of searchers and if their conduct is in some way reprehensible, or if they precipitate a search and are motivated therein solely by desire to hunt for incriminating evidence, or if they do so without any plausible explanation or justification, the invasion is an unreasonable one.

Gordon v. State, 368 So.2d 59, certiorari denied 378 So.2d 345.

Fla.App. 3 Dist. 1978. Search of private property conducted by state or federal agents without duly issued search warrant is per se "unreasonable" under Federal and State Constitutions, subject only to a few specifically established and well-delineated exceptions justified by absolute necessity. West's F.S.A.Const. art. 1, § 12; U.S.C.A.Const. Amends. 4, 14, 14, § 1.

> Miranda v. State, 354 So.2d 411, certiorari denied 364 So.2d 888.

Fla.App. 3 Dist. 1967. A search is permissible only if it is made on a proper warrant duly issued or as incident to a lawful arrest.

> Parnell v. State, 204 So.2d 910, quashed 221 So.2d 129, on remand 233 So.2d 437.

Fla.App. 4 Dist. 2016. A warrantless search is per se unreasonable under the Fourth Amendment subject to a few well-defined exceptions; the state has the burden to prove that an exception to the warrant requirement applies. U.S.C.A. Const.Amend. 4.

> Tyler v. State, 185 So.3d 659, rehearing denied.

Fla.App. 4 Dist. 2014. A warrantless search is per se unreasonable under the Fourth Amendment; however, a search will be considered lawful if conducted pursuant to consent which was given freely and voluntarily. U.S.C.A. Const.Amend. 4.

> Henderson v. State, 149 So.3d 61, rehearing denied, denial of post-conviction relief reversed 199 So.3d 553.

Fla.App. 4 Dist. 2012. Warrantless searches are per se unreasonable under the Fourth Amendment, subject only to a few specifically established and delineated exceptions. U.S.C.A. Const.Amend. 4.

> Nshaka v. State, 92 So.3d 843, rehearing denied, on remand 2013 WL 10546069.

Fla.App. 4 Dist. 2012. Even when police officers have probable cause, they may not enter a dwelling without a warrant absent a recognized exception to the warrant requirement, such as consent or exigent circumstances. U.S.C.A. Const. Amend. 4.

> Rowell v. State, 83 So.3d 990.

Fla.App. 4 Dist. 2012. Warrantless searches are per se unreasonable under the Fourth Amendment—subject only to a few specifically established and well-delineated exceptions. U.S.C.A. Const.Amend. 4.

> Nshaka v. State, 82 So.3d 174.

Fla.App. 4 Dist. 2012. A warrantless search is per se unreasonable under the Fourth Amendment. U.S.C.A. Const. Amend. 4.

> Hernandez v. State, 80 So.3d 416, post-conviction relief dismissed by 2013 WL 10858940.

Fla.App. 4 Dist. 2011. Warrantless searches are per se unreasonable under the Fourth Amendment, subject only to a few specifically established and well-delineated exceptions. U.S.C.A. Const.Amend. 4.

> Ferguson v. State, 58 So.3d 360, post-conviction relief denied 2013 WL 10858907, affirmed 140 So.3d 595, review dismissed 139 So.3d 297.

Fla.App. 4 Dist. 2010. Warrantless searches are considered, under the Fourth Amendment, per se unreasonable, subject to certain exceptions. U.S.C.A. Const. Amend. 4.

> Diaz v. State, 34 So.3d 797.

Fla.App. 4 Dist. 2006. Warrantless searches of homes and motel rooms are not unreasonable within the framework of a few specifically established and well delineated exceptions to the warrant requirement. U.S.C.A. Const.Amend. 4.

> Reed v. State, 944 So.2d 1054.

Fla.App. 4 Dist. 2001. Where the contraband is seen in a constitutionally protected area, such as a dwelling, the open view of the contraband furnishes the officer probable cause to seize the item, but the officer must still obtain a warrant or qualify under an exception to the warrant requirement to enter the dwelling and seize the contraband. U.S.C.A. Const. Amend. 4.

> Gilbert v. State, 789 So.2d 426.

Fla.App. 4 Dist. 1996. Even when they have probable cause, police officers may not enter a dwelling without warrant, absent consent or exigent circumstances. U.S.C.A. Const.Amend. 4.

> Levine v. State, 684 So.2d 903.

Fla.App. 4 Dist. 1982. Law is better served by requiring strict compliance with statute requiring issuance of search warrant. West's F.S.A. § 933.06.

> State v. Tolmie, 421 So.2d 1087.

Fla.App. 4 Dist. 1980. Subjective intent cannot change what would otherwise be a valid stop and entry into an illegal one. U.S.C.A.Const. Amend. 4.

State v. Richards, 388 So.2d 573, certiorari denied 102 S.Ct. 359, 454 U.S. 879, 70 L.Ed.2d 188.

Fla.App. 4 Dist. 1980. The statute which permits a law enforcement officer to temporarily detain a person for the purpose of ascertaining his or her identity and the circumstances which led the officer to believe that he had committed or was about to commit a criminal offense neither contemplates nor approves the seizure of goods without probable cause. West's F.S.A. § 901.151(2).

In Interest of G. A. R., 387 So.2d 404.

Fla.App. 4 Dist. 1975. Generally, a warrantless search is illegal.

State v. Jenkins, 319 So.2d 91.

Fla.App. 4 Dist. 1972. Search without warrant may be valid in certain instances.

State v. Miller, 267 So.2d 352, cause dismissed 273 So.2d 80.

Fla.App. 5 Dist. 2016. A search conducted without a warrant issued upon probable cause is per se unreasonable under the Fourth Amendment, subject only to a few well-established exceptions; one of the well-established exceptions to the requirements of both a warrant and probable cause is a search conducted pursuant to consent. U.S.C.A. Const.Amend. 4.

State v. Liles, 191 So.3d 484, rehearing and rehearing denied, review denied 2016 WL 4245500, review denied Willis v. State, 2016 WL 4247056, certiorari denied 137 S.Ct. 688, 196 L.Ed.2d 528.

Fla.App. 5 Dist. 2015. Warrantless searches are per se unreasonable unless the search falls within an exception to the warrant requirement; the State has the burden to show that the defendant freely and voluntarily gave the necessary consent. U.S.C.A. Const.Amend. 4.

K.W. v. State, 183 So.3d 1123.

Fla.App. 5 Dist. 2015. To validate a warrantless search, the State must show that the search falls within a constitutional exception, one of which is voluntary consent. U.S.C.A. Const.Amend. 4.

State v. Toussaint, 168 So.3d 308.

Fla.App. 5 Dist. 2015. Generally, warrantless searches are presumptively unreasonable unless they fall within a recognized exception to the warrant requirement. U.S.C.A. Const.Amend. 4.

Williams v. State, 167 So.3d 483, rehearing denied, opinion vacated 2016 WL 6637817, on remand 210 So.3d 774.

The search warrant requirement ensures that inferences to support the search are drawn by a neutral and detached magistrate instead of being judged by the officer engaged in the often competitive enterprise of ferreting out crime. U.S.C.A. Const.Amend. 4.

Williams v. State, 167 So.3d 483, rehearing denied, opinion vacated 2016 WL 6637817, on remand 210 So.3d 774.

Fla.App. 5 Dist. 2010. Warrantless searches are per se unreasonable, subject only to a few specifically established and well-delineated exceptions. U.S.C.A. Const.Amend. 4.

Grant v. State, 43 So.3d 864, cause dismissed 48 So.3d 836, reinstatement denied, denial of post-conviction relief affirmed 135 So.3d 295, denial of post-conviction relief affirmed 212 So.3d 375.

Fla.App. 5 Dist. 2005. Absent exigent circumstances, warrantless searches and seizures from a constitutionally protected place are per se unreasonable and the state has the burden to establish any exception to the requirement of obtaining a warrant prior to a search or seizure in a protected place. U.S.C.A. Const.Amend. 4.

Murphy v. State, 898 So.2d 1031, rehearing denied, review denied 910 So.2d 262.

Fla.App. 5 Dist. 2003. The seizure of items from a person's home without a warrant based on probable cause violates the person's right to be secure in their homes against unreasonable searches and seizures, rendering the items inadmissible in evidence. U.S.C.A. Const.Amend. 4; West's F.S.A. Const. Art. 1, § 12.

Davis v. State, 834 So.2d 322.

A warrantless search of a home is presumed illegal. U.S.C.A. Const.Amend. 4; West's F.S.A. Const. Art. 1, § 12.

Davis v. State, 834 So.2d 322.

Fla.App. 5 Dist. 2000. Searches conducted outside the judicial process, without prior approval by judge or magistrate, are per se unreasonable under the Fourth Amendment, subject only to a few specifically established and well-delineated exceptions. U.S.C.A. Const.Amend. 4.

Bryant v. State, 765 So.2d 903.

Fla.App. 5 Dist. 1999. Warrantless searches are at least suspect and often unreasonable and violative of constitutional requirements. U.S.C.A. Const.Amend. 4.

State v. Williams, 739 So.2d 717.

When no other course of action is available, warrantless search and seizure is permissible. U.S.C.A. Const.Amend. 4.

State v. Williams, 739 So.2d 717.

Fla.App. 5 Dist. 1995. Searches and seizures inside a home without a warrant are presumptively unreasonable. U.S.C.A. Const.Amend. 4.

Anderson v. State, 665 So.2d 281, rehearing denied.

Fla.App. 5 Dist. 1980. All searches conducted without a warrant are per se unreasonable unless conducted within the framework of a few specifically established and well–delineated exceptions, and burden is upon the state to show that a warrantless search comes within one of the recognized exceptions, which are: consent; incident to a lawful arrest; probable cause to search but with exigent circumstances; hot pursuit; and stop and frisk. U.S.C.A.Const. Amend. 4.

Engle v. State, 391 So.2d 245.

Fla.App. 5 Dist. 1980. Warrantless searches are per se unreasonable, subject only to a few specifically established and well-defined exceptions, including emergency situation, sometimes called the "exigency rule."

Johnson v. State, 386 So.2d 302.

Fla.App. 5 Dist. 1979. General rule is that a search conducted without a warrant and without consent is per se unreasonable, subject only to a limited number of well-defined exceptions. U.S.C.A.Const. Amend. 4; West's F.S.A.Const. art. 1, § 12.

Ulesky v. State, 379 So.2d 121.

Warrantless search will not be upheld unless it clearly falls within one of the delineated exceptions to the warrant requirement. U.S.C.A.Const. Amend. 4; West's F.S.A.Const. art. 1, § 12.

Ulesky v. State, 379 So.2d 121.

In addition to a search based on consent and a seizure of evidence under the "plain view" doctrine, there are five generally accepted exceptions to the warrant requirement; first, a search incident to lawful arrest; second, a search based on probable cause coupled with exigent circumstances; third, a search in connection with seizure of an automobile for purpose of a forfeiture proceeding; fourth, a bona fide inventory search; and fifth, a protective search for weapons known as a "frisk," incident to a valid "stop." U.S.C.A.Const. Amend. 4; West's F.S.A.Const. art. 1, § 12.

Ulesky v. State, 379 So.2d 121.

⚷**25. Persons, places and things protected.**

⚷**25.1. —— In general.**

U.S.Fla. 2013. The Fourth Amendment indicates with some precision the places and things encompassed by its protections: persons, houses, papers, and effects. U.S.C.A. Const.Amend. 4.

Florida v. Jardines, 133 S.Ct. 1409, 185 L.Ed.2d 495.

At the Fourth Amendment's very core stands the right of a man to retreat into his own home and there be free from unreasonable governmental intrusion. U.S.C.A. Const.Amend. 4.

Florida v. Jardines, 133 S.Ct. 1409, 185 L.Ed.2d 495.

While law enforcement officers need not shield their eyes when passing by a home on public thoroughfares, an officer's leave to gather information is sharply circumscribed when he steps off those thoroughfares and enters the Fourth Amendment's protected areas. U.S.C.A. Const. Amend. 4.

Florida v. Jardines, 133 S.Ct. 1409, 185 L.Ed.2d 495.

† C.A.11 (Fla.) 2016. Police chief did not unlawfully seize court order from activist who sought to videotape inside of town hall; there was no more than a de minimis intrusion on activist's property rights, as he voluntarily relinquished the order for the specific purpose of an official inspection by the chief, the substance of the order was a matter of public record, and chief only briefly retained the order to make a photocopy, and any intrusion was outweighed by the town's interest in conducting searches of individuals entering public buildings. U.S.C.A. Const.Amend. 4.

O'Boyle v. Thrasher, 638 Fed.Appx. 873.

C.A.11 (Fla.) 2015. Under Fourth Amendment, home is sacrosanct place that enjoys special protection from government intrusion. U.S.C.A. Const.Amend. 4.

Moore v. Pederson, 806 F.3d 1036, certiorari denied 136 S.Ct. 2014, 195 L.Ed.2d 216.

C.A.11 (Fla.) 2014. Fourth Amendment protections against unreasonable searches and seizures apply to commercial premises, as well as to private homes. U.S.C.A. Const.Amend. 4.

Berry v. Leslie, 767 F.3d 1144, opinion vacated on rehearing en banc 771 F.3d 1316.

C.A.11 (Fla.) 2014. Searches and seizures inside a home without a warrant are presumptively unreasonable under the Fourth Amendment, and that presumption is subject only to a few jealously and carefully drawn exceptions. U.S.C.A. Const.Amend. 4.

U.S. v. Yeary, 740 F.3d 569, motion for relief from judgment denied 135 S.Ct. 1153, 190 L.Ed.2d 915.

C.A.11 (Fla.) 2013. Central to the protections provided by the Fourth Amendment is the right of a man to retreat into his own home and there be free from unreasonable governmental intrusion. U.S.C.A. Const.Amend. 4.

U.S. v. Timmann, 741 F.3d 1170.

Searches and seizures inside a home without a warrant are presumptively unreasonable under the Fourth Amendment. U.S.C.A. Const.Amend. 4.

U.S. v. Timmann, 741 F.3d 1170.

C.A.11 (Fla.) 2013. Fourth Amendment is not implicated by entry upon private land to knock on a citizen's door for legitimate police purposes unconnected with a search of the premises. U.S.C.A. Const.Amend. 4.

U.S. v. Williams, 731 F.3d 1222, certiorari denied 134 S.Ct. 1564, 188 L.Ed.2d 575.

C.A.11 (Fla.) 2013. The chief evil against which the Fourth Amendment is directed is a government agent's warrantless entry into a person's home. U.S.C.A. Const.Amend. 4.

Feliciano v. City of Miami Beach, 707 F.3d 1244.

C.A.11 (Fla.) 2012. Searches and seizures inside a home without a warrant are presumptively unreasonable. U.S.C.A. Const.Amend. 4.

U.S. v. Franklin, 694 F.3d 1.

C.A.11 (Fla.) 2011. Physical entry of home is the chief evil against which the Fourth Amendment is directed, and never is the Fourth Amendment zone of privacy more clearly defined than when bounded by unambiguous physical dimensions of individual's home. U.S.C.A. Const. Amend. 4.

Coffin v. Brandau, 642 F.3d 999.

Police officers can enter onto residential property, including portions that would be considered part of the curtilage for Fourth Amendment purposes, in order to carry out legitimate police business. U.S.C.A. Const.Amend. 4.

Coffin v. Brandau, 642 F.3d 999.

C.A.11 (Fla.) 2010. Physical entry of the home is the chief evil against which the wording of the Fourth Amendment is directed. U.S.C.A. Const.Amend. 4.

Coffin v. Brandau, 609 F.3d 1204, rehearing granted, opinion vacated 614 F.3d 1240, on rehearing 642 F.3d 999.

C.A.11 (Fla.) 2009. While Fourth Amendment protections apply irrespective of a person's location, those protections do wane in some limited contexts, especially in airports or at international borders, where government's interest in preventing persons and effects from entering the nation rises to its zenith. U.S.C.A. Const. Amend. 4.

> Denson v. U.S., 574 F.3d 1318, rehearing and rehearing denied 400 Fed.Appx. 551, certiorari denied 130 S.Ct. 3384, 560 U.S. 952, 177 L.Ed.2d 302.

Not only is expectation of privacy less at the border than in the interior, but the Fourth Amendment balance between interests of government and privacy rights of individual is also struck much more favorably to government at border. U.S.C.A. Const.Amend. 4.

> Denson v. U.S., 574 F.3d 1318, rehearing and rehearing denied 400 Fed.Appx. 551, certiorari denied 130 S.Ct. 3384, 560 U.S. 952, 177 L.Ed.2d 302.

C.A.11 (Fla.) 2006. While public servants are not relegated to watered-down version of constitutional rights, nothing in the Fourth Amendment endows public employees with greater workplace rights than those enjoyed by their counterparts in private sector. U.S.C.A. Const.Amend. 4.

> Reyes v. Maschmeier, 446 F.3d 1199, rehearing and rehearing denied 186 Fed.Appx. 987.

C.A.11 (Fla.) 2002. A warrantless entry into a suspect's home to search the premises is presumed to be unreasonable. U.S.C.A. Const.Amend. 4.

> U.S. v. Ramirez-Chilel, 289 F.3d 744, rehearing and rehearing denied 45 Fed.Appx. 881, certiorari denied 123 S.Ct. 850, 537 U.S. 1114, 154 L.Ed.2d 789.

C.A.11 (Fla.) 1999. Government's ability to conduct searches of a warehouse is far broader than its ability to search a residence. U.S.C.A. Const.Amend. 4.

> U.S. v. Chaves, 169 F.3d 687, rehearing denied, certiorari denied Garcia v. U.S., 120 S.Ct. 534, 528 U.S. 1022, 145 L.Ed.2d 414, certiorari denied 120 S.Ct. 585, 528 U.S. 1048, 145 L.Ed.2d 486.

C.A.11 (Fla.) 1989. Individual's residence enjoys special protection under Fourth Amendment; thus, officer must have probable cause before searching someone's house, and even then officer may proceed only with warrant or under

exigent circumstances. U.S.C.A. Const. Amend. 4.

> U.S. v. Tobin, 890 F.2d 319, rehearing granted, vacated 902 F.2d 821, on rehearing 923 F.2d 1506, rehearing denied 935 F.2d 1297, certiorari denied 112 S.Ct. 299, 502 U.S. 907, 116 L.Ed.2d 243.

C.A.11 (Fla.) 1988. Fourth Amendment's prohibition against unreasonable searches and seizures extends to commercial businesses. U.S.C.A. Const.Amend. 4.

> McLaughlin v. Elsberry, Inc., 868 F.2d 1525.

C.A.11 (Fla.) 1984. Extent that there might be different Fourth Amendment standards for a home and a business would not depend upon whether the business was in a building that looked like a home; the difference in standard would be based on reduced expectation of privacy in a business. U.S.C.A. Const.Amend. 4.

> U.S. v. Holland, 740 F.2d 878, rehearing denied 748 F.2d 690, certiorari denied 105 S.Ct. 2654, 471 U.S. 1124, 86 L.Ed.2d 271.

C.A.11 (Fla.) 1984. Fourth Amendment protection extends to business premises. U.S.C.A. Const.Amend. 4.

> U.S. v. Pantoja-Soto, 739 F.2d 1520, rehearing denied 749 F.2d 733, certiorari denied 105 S.Ct. 1369, 470 U.S. 1008, 84 L.Ed.2d 389.

C.A.11 (Fla.) 1983. Fourth Amendment protects people, not places. U.S.C.A. Const.Amend. 4.

> U.S. v. Yonn, 702 F.2d 1341, certiorari denied Weeks v. U.S., 104 S.Ct. 283, 464 U.S. 917, 78 L.Ed.2d 261.

C.A.11 (Fla.) 1982. For Fourth Amendment purposes, person writing the president or president-elect should expect that letter will be screened by one other than the addressee. 18 U.S.C.A. § 871.

> U.S. v. Wilson, 671 F.2d 1291, certiorari denied 103 S.Ct. 98, 459 U.S. 844, 74 L.Ed.2d 89.

C.A.11 (Fla.) 1982. Where under circumstances of case, motel room was, however temporarily, equivalent to defendant's home, warrantless invasion of motel room by law enforcement officials for purpose of arresting him violated his Fourth Amendment rights, there being no showing of exigent circumstances which would excuse obtaining arrest warrant. U.S.C.A.Const. Amend. 4.

> U.S. v. Bulman, 667 F.2d 1374, rehearing denied 673 F.2d 1342, certiorari denied Howard v. U.S., 102 S.Ct. 2305, 456 U.S. 1010, 73 L.Ed.2d 1307.

C.A.5 (Fla.) 1979. Fourth Amendment not only protects all within bounds of the United States; it also shelters citizens wherever they may be in the world from unreasonable searches by the United States Government. U.S.C.A.Const. Amend. 4.

> U.S. v. Conroy, 589 F.2d 1258, rehearing denied U.S. v. Walker, 594 F.2d 241, rehearing denied 594 F.2d 241, certiorari denied 100 S.Ct. 60, 444 U.S. 831, 62 L.Ed.2d 40.

C.A.5 (Fla.) 1975. Once defendant knew that general control over entry to warehouse premises where he had rented space reposed in others unknown to him, both in number and identity, whose right of access was general, not limited, and was in no sense derivative from his, such persons were the functional equivalent of the public, and defendant had no Fourth Amendment protection in the area, whether one of such others admitted officers by informed consent, or as a result of a ruse, or even as a result of bribery or coercion. U.S.C.A.Const. Amend. 4.

> U.S. v. Novello, 519 F.2d 1078, certiorari denied 96 S.Ct. 797, 423 U.S. 1060, 46 L.Ed.2d 651.

What a person knowingly exposes to the public, even in his own home or office, is not a subject of Fourth Amendment protection. U.S.C.A.Const. Amend. 4.

> U.S. v. Novello, 519 F.2d 1078, certiorari denied 96 S.Ct. 797, 423 U.S. 1060, 46 L.Ed.2d 651.

C.A.5 (Fla.) 1971. Those lawfully entitled to use the public highways have a right to free passage without being subjected to unreasonable searches and seizures. U.S.C.A.Const. Amend. 4.

> U.S. v. Pennington, 441 F.2d 249, certiorari denied 92 S.Ct. 97, 404 U.S. 854, 30 L.Ed.2d 94.

C.A.5 (Fla.) 1964. Top of brick pillar supporting motel cabin was not place protected by Fourth Amendment from unreasonable search, and reasonableness of search was not relevant constitutional consideration in determining admissibility of evidence there seized. U.S.C.A.Const. Amend. 4.

> Marullo v. U.S., 330 F.2d 609.

C.A.5 (Fla.) 1964. From standpoint of searches and seizures, home owner or tenant has exclusive enjoyment of his home, his garage, his barn or other buildings, and also area around his home, but transient occupant of motel must share corridors, sidewalks, yards and trees with other occupants. U.S.C.A.Const. Amend. 4.

> Marullo v. U.S., 328 F.2d 361, rehearing denied 330 F.2d 609, certiorari denied 85 S.Ct. 93, 379 U.S. 850, 13 L.Ed.2d 53.

C.C.A.5 (Fla.) 1946. The examination by officers, without a search warrant, of five-gallon jug left on the ground under the automobile of accused did not violate the constitutional amendment securing the people against unreasonable searches and seizures. U.S.C.A.Const. Amend. 4.

> Martin v. U.S., 155 F.2d 503.

C.C.A.5 (Fla.) 1945. Search of business premises occupied by subject of Japan on day following Japanese attack on Pearl Harbor, although made by Treasury agents without a warrant, was not "unreasonable" within constitutional prohibition against unreasonable searches and seizures. U.S.C.A.Const. Amend. 4.

> Shinyu Noro v. U.S., 148 F.2d 696, certiorari denied 66 S.Ct. 25, 326 U.S. 720, 90 L.Ed. 426.

The ratification by Congress of searches by Treasury agents on day following Japanese attack on Pearl Harbor of premises occupied by citizens of Japan and seizure of their books and papers made searches and seizures good from beginning. Trading with the Enemy Act § 5(b), as amended by Joint Resolution May 7, 1940, § 1, 54 Stat. 179, 50 U.S.C.A.Appendix § 5(b) and § 2 of Joint Resolution, 12 U.S.C.A. § 95 note; U.S.C.A.Const. Amend. 4.

> Shinyu Noro v. U.S., 148 F.2d 696, certiorari denied 66 S.Ct. 25, 326 U.S. 720, 90 L.Ed. 426.

C.C.A.5 (Fla.) 1938. A search without a warrant of a building occupied by defendant and codefendant after officers broke in door following arrest of codefendant who had been observed carrying whisky in a sack toward automobile which was parked outside building and in which whisky was found was violative of defendant's constitutional rights, in absence of showing that defendant owned or controlled automobile or was connected with codefendant in possession of liquor.

Kauz v. U.S., 95 F.2d 473.

M.D.Fla. 2015. A person's home is at the core of the Fourth Amendment's protection against unreasonable searches and seizures; this protection extends to the curtilage or area immediately surrounding and associated with the house. U.S. Const. Amend. 4.

United States v. Holmes, 143 F.Supp.3d 1252.

Nowhere is the Fourth Amendment's protection of the individual's zone of privacy more clearly defined than when bounded by the unambiguous physical dimensions of an individual's home; for this reason, the Fourth Amendment has drawn a firm line at the entrance of the house. U.S. Const. Amend. 4.

United States v. Holmes, 143 F.Supp.3d 1252.

Absent exigent circumstances, the threshold of a person's house may not reasonably be crossed without a warrant. U.S. Const. Amend. 4.

United States v. Holmes, 143 F.Supp.3d 1252.

M.D.Fla. 2014. Under the Fourth Amendment, warrantless searches inside a home are presumptively unreasonable. U.S.C.A. Const.Amend. 4.

Montanez v. Celaya, 49 F.Supp.3d 1010.

M.D.Fla. 2011. Searches and seizures inside home without warrant are presumptively unreasonable. U.S.C.A. Const.Amend. 4.

U.S. v. Garcia, 853 F.Supp.2d 1177, remanded 2013 WL 10509665, appeal after remand 556 Fed.Appx. 924, affirmed 556 Fed.Appx. 924.

M.D.Fla. 2011. A warrantless search of a person's home is presumptively unreasonable. U.S.C.A. Const.Amend. 4.

Frias v. Demings, 823 F.Supp.2d 1279.

M.D.Fla. 2011. Screened-in lanai area in back of defendant's residence was either part of residence itself or included in curtilage of residence, and in either case was within protections provided by Fourth Amendment. U.S.C.A. Const. Amend. 4.

U.S. v. Hill, 795 F.Supp.2d 1304.

Officer's initial warrantless entry into screened-in lanai area in back of defendant's residence violated Fourth Amendment, absent exigent circumstances; nothing indicated that public would be expected to go to lanai at rear of house. U.S.C.A. Const.Amend. 4.

U.S. v. Hill, 795 F.Supp.2d 1304.

Law enforcement officer in carrying out his or her duties is free to go where public would be expected to go without violating Fourth Amendment; this includes knocking on front door, and in some circumstances back door. U.S.C.A. Const. Amend. 4.

U.S. v. Hill, 795 F.Supp.2d 1304.

In terms that apply equally to seizures of property and to seizures of persons, Fourth Amendment has drawn firm line at entrance to the house; absent exigent circumstances, that threshold may not reasonably be crossed without warrant. U.S.C.A. Const.Amend. 4.

U.S. v. Hill, 795 F.Supp.2d 1304.

Fourth Amendment is not implicated when officer enters upon private land to knock on citizen's door for legitimate police purposes unconnected with search of premises. U.S.C.A. Const.Amend. 4.

U.S. v. Hill, 795 F.Supp.2d 1304.

Absent express orders from person in possession, an officer may walk up steps and knock on front door of any man's castle, with honest intent of asking questions of occupant thereof. U.S.C.A. Const. Amend. 4.

U.S. v. Hill, 795 F.Supp.2d 1304.

Under Fourth Amendment, an officer may approach residence just as private citizen is permitted to approach residence's door. U.S.C.A. Const.Amend. 4.

U.S. v. Hill, 795 F.Supp.2d 1304.

Officer may enter property and go to front door and knock in order to investigate suspicious activity; this "knock and talk" initial entry onto property is not prohibited by Fourth Amendment. U.S.C.A. Const.Amend. 4.

U.S. v. Hill, 795 F.Supp.2d 1304.

Officers are generally permitted under Fourth Amendment to approach back door of residence but only after officers attempted to contact someone at front door, and contact at front door was fruitless. U.S.C.A. Const.Amend. 4.

U.S. v. Hill, 795 F.Supp.2d 1304.

Under Fourth Amendment, an officer may initiate contact somewhere other than an individual's front door, however, officer needs some reason to initiate contact in area other than front door such as seeing vehicle elsewhere on property. U.S.C.A. Const.Amend. 4.

U.S. v. Hill, 795 F.Supp.2d 1304.

M.D.Fla. 2010. While a search or seizure inside a home without a warrant is presumptively unreasonable, that presumption can be overcome. U.S.C.A. Const.Amend. 4.

U.S. v. Bergin, 732 F.Supp.2d 1235, affirmed 455 Fed.Appx. 908, certiorari denied 132 S.Ct. 1948, 566 U.S. 954, 182 L.Ed.2d 802, post-conviction relief denied in part, dismissed in part 2014 WL 5093853, affirmed U.S. v. Powner, 481 Fed.Appx. 529, post-conviction relief denied 2016 WL 5239831.

An entry into a residence cannot be justified on the basis that there was nothing physically seized and therefore no violation of the Fourth Amendment; the Fourth Amendment can be violated even if there are no physical product of an unlawful entry. U.S.C.A. Const.Amend. 4.

U.S. v. Bergin, 732 F.Supp.2d 1235, affirmed 455 Fed.Appx. 908, certiorari denied 132 S.Ct. 1948, 566 U.S. 954, 182 L.Ed.2d 802, post-conviction relief denied in part, dismissed

in part 2014 WL 5093853, affirmed U.S. v. Powner, 481 Fed.Appx. 529, post-conviction relief denied 2016 WL 5239831.

M.D.Fla. 2009. Fourth Amendment protects individuals from unreasonable governmental intrusion into their persons, houses, papers, and effects. U.S.C.A. Const.Amend. 4.

Swofford v. Eslinger, 671 F.Supp.2d 1289, affirmed 395 Fed.Appx. 559, rehearing and rehearing denied 409 Fed.Appx. 316, certiorari denied Morris v. Swofford, 131 S.Ct. 1053, 562 U.S. 1201, 178 L.Ed.2d 866.

What person knowingly exposes to public, even in his own house or office, is not subject of Fourth Amendment protection. U.S.C.A. Const.Amend. 4.

Swofford v. Eslinger, 671 F.Supp.2d 1289, affirmed 395 Fed.Appx. 559, rehearing and rehearing denied 409 Fed.Appx. 316, certiorari denied Morris v. Swofford, 131 S.Ct. 1053, 562 U.S. 1201, 178 L.Ed.2d 866.

M.D.Fla. 2008. Warrantless entry into person's home is presumed to be an unreasonable violation of one's Fourth Amendment rights. U.S.C.A. Const. Amend. 4.

U.S. v. Stiner, 551 F.Supp.2d 1350.

Warrantless search of residence is presumed to be unreasonable under Fourth Amendment. U.S.C.A. Const. Amend. 4.

U.S. v. Stiner, 551 F.Supp.2d 1350.

M.D.Fla. 1994. Warrantless search of home is presumptively unreasonable, unless probable cause and exigent circumstances exist. U.S.C.A. Const.Amend. 4.

U.S. v. Adams, 845 F.Supp. 1531.

M.D.Fla. 1980. Corporation may possess legitimate expectation of privacy through its employees or as separate entity. U.S.C.A.Const. Amend. 4.

U.S. v. Hartley, 486 F.Supp. 1348, affirmed 678 F.2d 961, rehearing denied 688 F.2d 852, certiorari denied 103 S.Ct. 815, 459 U.S. 1170, 74 L.Ed.2d 1014, certiorari denied Treasure Isle, Inc., v. U.S., 103 S.Ct. 834, 459 U.S. 1183, 74 L.Ed.2d 1027.

M.D.Fla. 1972. Paying tenant in house, boarding house or hotel is entitled to protection, constitutionally guaranteed, against unreasonable searches and seizures. U.S.C.A.Const. Amends. 4, 14.

Shuler v. Wainwright, 341 F.Supp. 1061, vacated 491 F.2d 1213.

S.D.Fla. 2015. Fourth Amendment's prohibition on unreasonable searches and seizures applies not only to private residences, but also to property used for commercial purposes. U.S. Const. Amend. 4.

United States v. Medina, 158 F.Supp.3d 1303.

S.D.Fla. 2014. A warrantless search and seizure in a home is presumptively unreasonable. U.S. Const.Amend. 4.

United States v. Jackson, 155 F.Supp.3d 1320, affirmed 618 Fed. Appx. 472, certiorari denied 136 S.Ct. 376, 193 L.Ed.2d 303.

S.D.Fla. 2008. Warrantless inspections of commercial property may be constitutionally objectionable if their occurrence is so random, infrequent, or unpredictable that the owner, for all practical purposes, has no real expectation that his property will from time to time be inspected by government officials. U.S.C.A. Const.Amend. 4.

Sosa v. Hames, 581 F.Supp.2d 1254.

Interest of the owner of commercial property is not one in being free from any inspections. U.S.C.A. Const.Amend. 4.

Sosa v. Hames, 581 F.Supp.2d 1254.

S.D.Fla. 1967. Before habeas corpus petitioner can claim that his Fourth Amendment rights have been violated by unreasonable search and seizure, it must be shown that area searched was one that is constitutionally protected by the Fourth Amendment. 28 U.S.C.A. § 2254; U.S.C.A.Const. Amend. 4.

U. S. ex rel. Fletcher v. Wainwright, 269 F.Supp. 276, rehearing denied 280 F.Supp. 905, reversed 399 F.2d 62.

Corridors and yards about a motel are shared or public property, and therefore are not protected by Fourth Amendment against unreasonable searches. U.S.C.A.Const. Amend. 4.

U. S. ex rel. Fletcher v. Wainwright, 269 F.Supp. 276, rehearing denied 280 F.Supp. 905, reversed 399 F.2d 62.

S.D.Fla. 1967. Before party can complain that his constitutional rights had been violated by an unreasonable search and seizure, it must be shown that area searched was one that was constitutionally protected by Fourth Amendment. U.S.C.A.Const. Amend. 4.

U. S. ex rel. Fletcher v. Wainwright, 269 F.Supp. 224, reversed 399 F.2d 62.

S.D.Fla. 1966. Fourth Amendment requirements were not designed to apply only to urban areas; people in rural areas have an equal right to be secure against unreasonable searches and seizures. U.S.C.A.Const. Amend. 4.

U.S. v. Melvin, 258 F.Supp. 252.

Fla. 2015. When it comes to the Fourth Amendment, the home is first among equals; at the Amendment's very core stands the right of a person to retreat into his or her own home and there be free from unreasonable governmental intrusion. U.S.C.A. Const.Amend. 4.

Rodriguez v. State, 187 So.3d 841, rehearing denied, certiorari denied 137 S.Ct. 124, 196 L.Ed.2d 199.

Fla. 2014. A cellular telephone is an "effect" protected by the Fourth Amendment from unreasonable search and seizure. U.S.C.A. Const.Amend. 4.

Tracey v. State, 152 So.3d 504, on remand 162 So.3d 217.

A vehicle is an "effect" protected by the Fourth Amendment from unreasonable search and seizure. U.S.C.A. Const. Amend. 4.

Tracey v. State, 152 So.3d 504, on remand 162 So.3d 217.

Letters and other sealed packages are in the general class of an "effect" protected by the Fourth Amendment from unreasonable search and seizure. U.S.C.A. Const.Amend. 4.

Tracey v. State, 152 So.3d 504, on remand 162 So.3d 217.

Personal luggage is an "effect" protected by the Fourth Amendment from unreasonable search and seizure. U.S.C.A. Const.Amend. 4.

> Tracey v. State, 152 So.3d 504, on remand 162 So.3d 217.

The Fourth Amendment protects people, not places. U.S.C.A. Const.Amend. 4.

> Tracey v. State, 152 So.3d 504, on remand 162 So.3d 217.

Fla. 2009. For purposes of a search-and-seizure analysis, privacy expectations associated with a motel room are similar to those afforded in the home, although the transient nature of the occupancy may diminish the extent of the privacy a person is entitled to reasonably expect. U.S.C.A. Const.Amend. 4.

> Jackson v. State, 18 So.3d 1016, certiorari denied 130 S.Ct. 1144, 558 U.S. 1151, 175 L.Ed.2d 979, post-conviction relief denied 2012 WL 10716486, affirmed 127 So.3d 447, habeas corpus denied 127 So.3d 447.

During occupancy, motel rooms are legally imbued with the sanctity of private dwellings, ordinarily afforded the most stringent Fourth Amendment protection. U.S.C.A. Const.Amend. 4.

> Jackson v. State, 18 So.3d 1016, certiorari denied 130 S.Ct. 1144, 558 U.S. 1151, 175 L.Ed.2d 979, post-conviction relief denied 2012 WL 10716486, affirmed 127 So.3d 447, habeas corpus denied 127 So.3d 447.

Fla. 2006. A warrantless search of a home is per se unreasonable and thus unconstitutional under the Fourth Amendment. U.S.C.A. Const.Amend. 4.

> Seibert v. State, 923 So.2d 460, rehearing denied, certiorari denied 127 S.Ct. 198, 549 U.S. 893, 166 L.Ed.2d 162, denial of post-conviction relief affirmed 64 So.3d 67, revised on rehearing, and rehearing denied.

Fla. 1998. Common living areas within rooming houses are accorded same Fourth Amendment protection extended to interior of private homes, and presence of visitors in kitchen does not change character of building from residence into public

building, nor does absence of locks or even doors on entrances change character. U.S.C.A. Const.Amend. 4.

> State v. Titus, 707 So.2d 706.

Fourth Amendment protection does not extend to common hallways in unlocked apartment buildings, which generally serve only to connect separate, self-contained living units typically complete with traditional living areas, such as bathrooms, dining rooms, living rooms, kitchens. U.S.C.A. Const.Amend. 4.

> State v. Titus, 707 So.2d 706.

Fla. 1994. Even if privacy interests of defendant while he was in hospital were in no way compromised, there was meaningful interference with his constitutionally protected possessory rights when his personal effects were seized without warrant from hospital room. U.S.C.A. Const. Amend. 4; West's F.S.A. Const. Art. 1, § 12.

> Jones v. State, 648 So.2d 669, rehearing denied, certiorari denied 115 S.Ct. 2588, 515 U.S. 1147, 132 L.Ed.2d 836, post-conviction relief denied 2005 WL 6932251, affirmed 998 So.2d 573, revised on rehearing, post-conviction relief denied 2005 WL 6932252, affirmed 998 So.2d 573, revised on rehearing, and revised on rehearing, habeas corpus denied 998 So.2d 573, revised on rehearing, and revised on rehearing, and revised on rehearing, post-conviction relief denied 2009 WL 9047495, affirmed 53 So.3d 230, rehearing denied, post-conviction relief denied 2011 WL 10483396, affirmed 141 So.3d 132, rehearing denied, certiorari denied 133 S.Ct. 661, 184 L.Ed.2d 471, habeas corpus denied 2013 WL 5504371, affirmed 834 F.3d 1299.

Fla. 1994. Motel room is considered private dwelling if occupant is there legally, has paid or arranged to pay, and has not been asked to leave, and so constitutional rights and privileges that apply to occupants of private permanent dwellings also apply to motel guests.

> Turner v. State, 645 So.2d 444.

Fla. 1986. Defendant who has been taken into custody is entitled to Fourth Amendment protection against warrantless

---

† This Case was not selected for publication in the National Reporter System
For legislative history of cited statutes, see Florida Statutes Annotated

search of premises in which he was residing at time of arrest absent some lawful exception to warrant requirement. U.S.C.A. Const.Amend. 4.

> Cooper v. State, 492 So.2d 1059, certiorari denied 107 S.Ct. 1330, 479 U.S. 1101, 94 L.Ed.2d 181, denial of post-conviction relief affirmed 856 So.2d 969, rehearing denied, certiorari denied 124 S.Ct. 1512, 540 U.S. 1222, 158 L.Ed.2d 159, habeas corpus denied 2008 WL 5252267, certificate of appealability granted in part, denied in part 2009 WL 1809854, affirmed in part, reversed in part 646 F.3d 1328.

Fla. 1985. Warrantless open-field searches are proper and evidence received as a result thereof should not be suppressed.

> DeMontmorency v. State, 464 So.2d 1201.

Fla. 1981. Fourth Amendment protects people, not places. U.S.C.A.Const. Amend. 4.

> State v. Brady, 406 So.2d 1093, certiorari granted 102 S.Ct. 2266, 456 U.S. 988, 73 L.Ed.2d 1282, vacated in part, certiorari dismissed in part 104 S.Ct. 2380, 467 U.S. 1201, 81 L.Ed.2d 339, on remand 466 So.2d 1064, on remand Eckard v. Trowbridge, 483 So.2d 450.

What person knowingly exposes to public, even in his own home or office, is not subject of Fourth Amendment protection. U.S.C.A.Const. Amend. 4.

> State v. Brady, 406 So.2d 1093, certiorari granted 102 S.Ct. 2266, 456 U.S. 988, 73 L.Ed.2d 1282, vacated in part, certiorari dismissed in part 104 S.Ct. 2380, 467 U.S. 1201, 81 L.Ed.2d 339, on remand 466 So.2d 1064, on remand Eckard v. Trowbridge, 483 So.2d 450.

What person seeks to preserve as private, even in area accessible to public, may be constitutionally protected from unreasonable searches and seizures. U.S.C.A.Const. Amend. 4.

> State v. Brady, 406 So.2d 1093, certiorari granted 102 S.Ct. 2266, 456 U.S. 988, 73 L.Ed.2d 1282, vacated in part, certiorari dismissed in part

104 S.Ct. 2380, 467 U.S. 1201, 81 L.Ed.2d 339, on remand 466 So.2d 1064, on remand Eckard v. Trowbridge, 483 So.2d 450.

Fences and locked gates are evidence of owner's or possessor's expectation of privacy within purview of Fourth Amendment guarantee of freedom from unreasonable searches and seizures. U.S.C.A.Const. Amend. 4.

> State v. Brady, 406 So.2d 1093, certiorari granted 102 S.Ct. 2266, 456 U.S. 988, 73 L.Ed.2d 1282, vacated in part, certiorari dismissed in part 104 S.Ct. 2380, 467 U.S. 1201, 81 L.Ed.2d 339, on remand 466 So.2d 1064, on remand Eckard v. Trowbridge, 483 So.2d 450.

Fla. 1981. Fourth Amendment does not protect a person from the possibility that one in whom he confides will violate the confidence. U.S.C.A.Const. Amend. 4.

> Odom v. State, 403 So.2d 936, certiorari denied 102 S.Ct. 1970, 456 U.S. 925, 72 L.Ed.2d 440.

Fla. 1980. Tobacco barn on premises leased by defendant in which defendant had cognizable property right by virtue of his rental agreement was an integral part of defendant's farming business and enjoyed same Fourth Amendment protection as do other business premises. U.S.C.A.Const. Amends. 4, 14, 14, § 1; West's F.S.A.Const. art. 1, § 12.

> Norman v. State, 379 So.2d 643.

Fla.App. 1 Dist. 2016. A private home, including a motel room, is an area where a person enjoys the highest reasonable expectation of privacy under the Fourth Amendment; even so, police, like any other citizen, may approach a residence and knock, hoping that the occupant will open the door. U.S.C.A. Const. Amend. 4.

> State v. McRae, 194 So.3d 524.

Fla.App. 1 Dist. 2011. While the Fourth Amendment usually prohibits law enforcement officers from entering an individual's home without a warrant, a search conducted pursuant to a valid consent is constitutionally permissible. U.S.C.A. Const.Amend. 4.

> Kohn v. State, 69 So.3d 388, review denied 130 So.3d 692.

Fla.App. 1 Dist. 2008. The Fourth Amendment protects people, not places. U.S.C.A. Const.Amend. 4.

State v. Butler, 1 So.3d 242, rehearing denied.

Fla.App. 1 Dist. 2008. A person's home is entitled to the highest degree of protection under the Fourth Amendment. U.S.C.A. Const.Amend. 4.

McDonnell v. State, 981 So.2d 585, review denied 993 So.2d 513, certiorari denied 129 S.Ct. 1585, 556 U.S. 1107, 173 L.Ed.2d 680.

Fla.App. 1 Dist. 2003. Law enforcement officers may not enter a legally occupied motel room without a warrant. U.S.C.A. Const.Amend. 4.

Lee v. State, 856 So.2d 1133.

For Fourth Amendment purposes, a motel room is considered a private dwelling where the occupant is legally there, has paid for the room, and has not been asked to leave. U.S.C.A. Const.Amend. 4.

Lee v. State, 856 So.2d 1133.

Fla.App. 1 Dist. 2002. As homes to the peripatetic, hotel and motel rooms are legally imbued with the sanctity of private dwellings, ordinarily afforded the most stringent Fourth Amendment protection against unreasonable searches and seizures; however, the room's protected status does not outlast the guest's right to occupy the room. U.S.C.A. Const.Amend. 4.

Green v. State, 824 So.2d 311.

Fla.App. 1 Dist. 1998. Unauthorized police entry into guest room at hotel violates Fourth Amendment. U.S.C.A. Const. Amend. 4.

Dempsey v. State, 717 So.2d 1071.

Fla.App. 1 Dist. 1996. Fourth Amendment protects people, not places; what person knowingly exposes to public, even in his home or office, is not subject of Fourth Amendment protection, but what he seeks to preserve as private, even in area accessible to public, may be constitutionally protected. U.S.C.A. Const.Amend. 4.

Brandin v. State, 669 So.2d 280, rehearing denied.

Fla.App. 1 Dist. 1985. Defendant's interest in remaining in barn undiscovered and preventing others from entering and seizing marijuana was not interest that Fourth Amendment was intended to protect; even though his guard duty spanned three days and therefore included sleeping and eating, character of defendant's occupation of barn was not equivalent to tenancy based on right to control and exclude others where agreement was merely that he would not open barn to anyone except owner and his only alleged proprietary interest in marijuana was that from anticipated potential proceeds, he would be paid back unrelated debt by third confederate involved in drug transaction. U.S.C.A. Const.Amend. 4.

Rodriguez v. State, 468 So.2d 312, review denied 480 So.2d 1295.

Fla.App. 1 Dist. 1983. Fourth Amendment does not protect a person from possibility that one in whom he confides will violate that confidence. U.S.C.A. Const.Amend. 4.

Powe v. State, 443 So.2d 154.

Fla.App. 1 Dist. 1980. What a person knowingly exposes to public is not subject of Fourth Amendment protections. U.S.C.A.Const. Amend. 4.

State v. Barnes, 390 So.2d 1243, review denied 399 So.2d 1145.

"Public" to whom something is knowingly exposed, in order for that object to be exempt from Fourth Amendment protections must be ordinary run of people, not those who happen to possess powerful and sophisticated devices and curiosity to use them to spy on their fellows. U.S.C.A.Const. Amend. 4.

State v. Barnes, 390 So.2d 1243, review denied 399 So.2d 1145.

Fla.App. 1 Dist. 1978. Child is entitled to protection of Fourth Amendment and corresponding state constitutional provision, but does not have constitutional right of immunity from searches and seizures by its parents. U.S.C.A.Const. Amend. 4; West's F.S.A. Const. art. 1, § 12.

State v. F. W. E., 360 So.2d 148.

Fla.App. 1 Dist. 1977. Individual's personal effects are as fully protected from unreasonable searches when individual is not suspected of criminal behavior as

† **This Case was not selected for publication in the National Reporter System**
For legislative history of cited statutes, see Florida Statutes Annotated

when individual is suspected of criminal behavior.

Shepherd v. State, 343 So.2d 1349, certiorari denied 352 So.2d 175.

Fla.App. 1 Dist. 1974. Hotel room or motel room is private dwelling of occupant so long as he is legally there, has paid or arranged to pay rent and has not been requested by management to leave for any valid or legal reason and rights and privileges guaranteed by Constitution to occupants of private permanent dwellings must be accorded with equal vigor to transient hotel or motel guests.

Sheff v. State, 301 So.2d 13, affirmed 329 So.2d 270.

Fla.App. 1 Dist. 1970. Protected premises under terms of Fourth Amendment guarantee against unreasonable searches and seizures include places of business. U.S.C.A.Const. Amend. 4.

Carter v. State, 238 So.2d 681.

Fla.App. 2 Dist. 2017. A warrantless search of a home is per se unreasonable under the Fourth Amendment and the state constitution, subject to a few specifically established and well-delineated exceptions. U.S. Const. Amend. 4; Fla. Const. art. 1, § 12.

Daniels v. State, 208 So.3d 1223.

Fla.App. 2 Dist. 2015. Ordinarily, a law enforcement officer must obtain a warrant prior to seizing the personal effects of an individual. U.S.C.A. Const. Amend. 4.

Hanifan v. State, 177 So.3d 277.

Fla.App. 2 Dist. 2007. A person's home is accorded the full range of Fourth Amendment protections because there is an expectation of privacy in one's dwelling; thus, a nonconsensual entry into a home, a motel room, or other residence constitutes a search. U.S.C.A. Const. Amend. 4.

Holloman v. State, 959 So.2d 403.

Searches and seizures inside a home without a warrant are presumptively unreasonable. U.S.C.A. Const.Amend. 4.

Holloman v. State, 959 So.2d 403.

Fla.App. 2 Dist. 2007. A warrantless search of a home is per se unreasonable and thus unconstitutional under the Fourth Amendment. U.S.C.A. Const. Amend. 4.

Wheeler v. State, 956 So.2d 517, rehearing denied.

With few exceptions, the question whether a warrantless search of a home is reasonable and hence constitutional must be answered no. U.S.C.A. Const.Amend. 4.

Wheeler v. State, 956 So.2d 517, rehearing denied.

Fla.App. 2 Dist. 2006. Searches and seizures inside a home without a warrant are presumptively unreasonable. U.S.C.A. Const.Amend. 4.

Nolin v. State, 946 So.2d 52, on remand 2007 WL 7010152.

Fla.App. 2 Dist. 2006. Searches and seizures inside a home without a warrant are presumptively unreasonable for Fourth Amendment purposes. U.S.C.A. Const. Amend. 4.

Vanslyke v. State, 936 So.2d 1218.

Fla.App. 2 Dist. 2003. A private home is an area where a person enjoys the highest reasonable expectation of privacy under the Fourth Amendment. U.S.C.A. Const.Amend. 4.

Vasquez v. State, 870 So.2d 26.

A search of a private home without a duly issued search warrant is per se unreasonable under the Fourth Amendment, subject only to a few specifically established and narrowly drawn exceptions. U.S.C.A. Const.Amend. 4.

Vasquez v. State, 870 So.2d 26.

Constitutional rights and privileges afforded to occupants of private permanent dwellings against unreasonable searches also apply to motel guests legally occupying the premises. U.S.C.A. Const.Amend. 4.

Vasquez v. State, 870 So.2d 26.

Fla.App. 2 Dist. 1999. College dormitory suite is comparable to motel room or room in boarding house, for purposes of determining Fourth Amendment expectation of privacy. U.S.C.A. Const.Amend. 4.

Beauchamp v. State, 742 So.2d 431.

Campus police officers did not have right to enter defendant's dormitory suite without permission or a warrant in order to conduct safety sweep, since defendant had expectation of privacy in suite. U.S.C.A. Const.Amend. 4.

Beauchamp v. State, 742 So.2d 431.

Fla.App. 2 Dist. 1998. Occupants of a motel room enjoy Fourth Amendment protection which includes the proscription against police making a warrantless entry for purposes of search or arrest, unless police are acting under exigent circumstances or proceeding with a valid consent. U.S.C.A. Const.Amend. 4.

Cooper v. State, 706 So.2d 369.

Fla.App. 2 Dist. 1995. Motel room is considered "private dwelling," for Fourth Amendment purposes, where occupant is there legally, has paid or arranged to pay, and has not been asked to leave. U.S.C.A. Const.Amend. 4.

Gnann v. State, 662 So.2d 406.

Constitutional rights and privileges that apply to occupants of private permanent dwellings also apply to motel guests. U.S.C.A. Const.Amend. 4.

Gnann v. State, 662 So.2d 406.

Absent showing of exigent circumstances, warrantless search of motel room and warrantless arrest of motel guest were invalid. U.S.C.A. Const.Amend. 4.

Gnann v. State, 662 So.2d 406.

Fla.App. 2 Dist. 1991. Hotel room or motel room is the private dwelling of the occupant and the constitutional protections of the Fourth Amendment apply to transient guests. U.S.C.A. Const.Amend. 4.

Sturdivant v. State, 578 So.2d 869.

Fla.App. 2 Dist. 1983. Tennis shoes seen on defendant's front porch during discussion about obtaining fingerprints were not in constitutionally protected area and so were subject to seizure.

Hayes v. State, 439 So.2d 896, petition for review denied 447 So.2d 886, certiorari granted 105 S.Ct. 82, 469 U.S. 816, 83 L.Ed.2d 30, reversed 105 S.Ct. 1643, 470 U.S. 811, 84 L.Ed.2d 705, on remand 488 So.2d 77, certiorari denied 107 S.Ct. 119, 479 U.S. 831, 93 L.Ed.2d 65.

Fla.App. 2 Dist. 1974. Where dwelling which was subject of search was characterized as an apartment which consisted of an upstairs and a downstairs, both of which were occupied by defendant, area beneath the building was within the constitutional protection against unreasonable search and seizure.

Dinkens v. State, 291 So.2d 122.

Fla.App. 2 Dist. 1969. While the ground surrounding a building may not be protected by the constitutional mandate against unreasonable searches and seizures, the building itself is protected. F.S.A.Const.1968, art. 1, § 12; U.S.C.A.Const. Amend. 4.

Ashby v. State, 228 So.2d 400, affirmed in part, quashed in part 245 So.2d 225.

Fla.App. 2 Dist. 1968. Right against unreasonable searches and seizures does not extend to grounds of the property even though searching authority is trespasser. F.S.A.Const. Declaration of Rights, § 22; U.S.C.A.Const. Amend. 4.

Cobb v. State, 213 So.2d 492, certiorari dismissed 224 So.2d 259.

Fla.App. 3 Dist. 2015. As a general rule, a warrantless search of a home is per se unreasonable and thus unconstitutional. U.S.C.A. Const.Amend. 4; West's F.S.A. Const. Art. 1, § 12.

State v. Yee, 177 So.3d 72, review granted 2016 WL 1082745, review dismissed as improvidently granted by 214 So.3d 540.

Fla.App. 3 Dist. 2014. At the Fourth Amendment's very core stands the right of a man to retreat into his own home and there be free from unreasonable governmental intrusion. U.S.C.A. Const. Amend. 4.

Brown v. State, 152 So.3d 619, rehearing denied, review denied 168 So.3d 228, appeal after remand 210 So.3d 61.

Fla.App. 3 Dist. 2013. An invasion of privacy results, for purposes of the Fourth Amendment, from a search of a child's person or of a closed purse or other bag carried on her person, no less than a similar search carried out on an adult. U.S.C.A. Const.Amend. 4.

K.P. v. State, 129 So.3d 1121, review denied 157 So.3d 1045.

Fla.App. 3 Dist. 2012. A warrantless entry of the home is one of the primary evils which the Fourth Amendment was designed to protect. U.S.C.A. Const. Amend. 4.

State v. Williams, 128 So.3d 30.

The home generally may not be entered without a warrant. U.S.C.A. Const. Amend. 4.

State v. Williams, 128 So.3d 30.

Fla.App. 3 Dist. 2010. Warrantless searches or arrests in constitutionally protected areas, particularly one's home, are per se unreasonable unless they fall within one of the established exceptions to the warrant requirement. U.S.C.A. Const. Amend. 4.

State v. Brown, 36 So.3d 770, review denied 63 So.3d 748.

Fla.App. 3 Dist. 2009. The Fourth Amendment has drawn a firm line at the entrance to the house. U.S.C.A. Const. Amend. 4.

Mestral v. State, 16 So.3d 1015.

Fla.App. 3 Dist. 2008. Though the Fourth Amendment protects the right of the people to be secure in their persons, houses, papers, and effects, from unreasonable government intrusions into their legitimate expectations of privacy, it does not necessarily protect areas of a home which are open and exposed to public view. U.S.C.A. Const.Amend. 4.

State v. Jardines, 9 So.3d 1, review granted 3 So.3d 1246, quashed 73 So.3d 34, rehearing denied, certiorari granted in part 132 S.Ct. 995, 565 U.S. 1104, 181 L.Ed.2d 726, affirmed 133 S.Ct. 1409, 185 L.Ed.2d 495.

Fla.App. 3 Dist. 1981. What person seeks to preserve as private may be constitutionally protected despite fact that it is in area accessible to the public. U.S.C.A.Const. Amend. 4.

State v. Parker, 399 So.2d 24, review denied 408 So.2d 1095.

Fla.App. 3 Dist. 1979. The Fourth Amendment does not protect a wrongdoer's misplaced belief that a person to whom he voluntarily confides his wrongdoing will not reveal it. U.S.C.A.Const. Amend. 4.

Franco v. State, 376 So.2d 1168, certiorari denied 386 So.2d 636.

Fla.App. 4 Dist. 2011. A private home is an area where a person enjoys the highest reasonable expectation of privacy under the Fourth Amendment. U.S.C.A. Const.Amend. 4.

Rozzo v. State, 75 So.3d 409, on remand 2012 WL 12144986.

Physical entry of the home is the chief evil against which the wording of the Fourth Amendment is directed. U.S.C.A. Const.Amend. 4.

Rozzo v. State, 75 So.3d 409, on remand 2012 WL 12144986.

Absent consent or exigent circumstances, police officers may not enter a dwelling without a warrant. U.S.C.A. Const.Amend. 4.

Rozzo v. State, 75 So.3d 409, on remand 2012 WL 12144986.

Fla.App. 4 Dist. 2011. Entry into a home is permissible only by a warrant, consent, or exigent circumstances. U.S.C.A. Const.Amend. 4.

Gonzalez v. State, 59 So.3d 182.

Fla.App. 4 Dist. 2011. Police officers may not enter a dwelling without a warrant absent consent or exigent circumstances. U.S.C.A. Const.Amend. 4.

Ferguson v. State, 58 So.3d 360, postconviction relief denied 2013 WL 10858907, affirmed 140 So.3d 595, review dismissed 139 So.3d 297.

Fla.App. 4 Dist. 2011. A private home is an area where a person enjoys the highest reasonable expectation of privacy under the Fourth Amendment; therefore, the factors bearing on the voluntariness of a consent to search a home must be scrutinized with special care. U.S.C.A. Const. Amend. 4.

Ruiz v. State, 50 So.3d 1229.

Fla.App. 4 Dist. 2010. The highest level of Fourth Amendment protection lies at the entrance of one's home or apartment. U.S.C.A. Const.Amend. 4.

Dixon v. State, 36 So.3d 920.

A warrantless search of a home is per se unreasonable and in violation of the Fourth Amendment. U.S.C.A. Const. Amend. 4.

Dixon v. State, 36 So.3d 920.

Fla.App. 4 Dist. 2010. The threshold to the entrance of a house may not reasonably be crossed without a search warrant absent exigent circumstances. U.S.C.A. Const.Amend. 4.

Diaz v. State, 34 So.3d 797.

Even if they have probable cause, police officers may not enter a dwelling without a search warrant, absent consent or exigent circumstances; the measure of reasonableness is totality of the circumstances. U.S.C.A. Const.Amend. 4.

Diaz v. State, 34 So.3d 797.

Fla.App. 4 Dist. 2009. Highest level of Fourth Amendment protection lies at the entrance of one's home or apartment. U.S.C.A. Const.Amend. 4.

Cote v. State, 14 So.3d 1137, rehearing denied.

Fla.App. 4 Dist. 2008. A private home is an area where a person enjoys the highest reasonable expectation of privacy under the Fourth Amendment, and accordingly, the factors bearing on the voluntariness of a consent to search a home must be scrutinized with special care. U.S.C.A. Const.Amend. 4.

State v. Bartling, 989 So.2d 757.

Fla.App. 4 Dist. 2006. For Fourth Amendment purposes, a motel room is considered a private dwelling when the occupant is legally there, has paid for the room, and has not been asked to leave. U.S.C.A. Const.Amend. 4.

Reed v. State, 944 So.2d 1054.

Fla.App. 4 Dist. 2006. At the center of the search and seizure provision of the Fourth Amendment stands the right of a man to retreat into his own home and there be free from unreasonable governmental intrusion. U.S.C.A. Const.Amend. 4.

State v. Rabb, 920 So.2d 1175, review denied 933 So.2d 522, certiorari denied 127 S.Ct. 665, 549 U.S. 1052, 166 L.Ed.2d 513.

The physical entry of the home is the chief evil against which the wording of the search and seizure provision of the Fourth Amendment is directed. U.S.C.A. Const. Amend. 4.

State v. Rabb, 920 So.2d 1175, review denied 933 So.2d 522, certiorari denied 127 S.Ct. 665, 549 U.S. 1052, 166 L.Ed.2d 513.

Search and seizure provision of Fourth Amendment operates to draw a firm line at the entrance to the house. U.S.C.A. Const.Amend. 4.

State v. Rabb, 920 So.2d 1175, review denied 933 So.2d 522, certiorari denied 127 S.Ct. 665, 549 U.S. 1052, 166 L.Ed.2d 513.

Occupant of a hotel room is entitled to the protection of the search and seizure provision of the Fourth Amendment to much the same degree as occupants of a house, but the extent of the privacy he is entitled to reasonably expect may very well diminish; a hotel room may be nearly identical to house for Fourth Amendment purposes, but it is not a house. U.S.C.A. Const.Amend. 4.

State v. Rabb, 920 So.2d 1175, review denied 933 So.2d 522, certiorari denied 127 S.Ct. 665, 549 U.S. 1052, 166 L.Ed.2d 513.

Search and seizure provision of Fourth Amendment protects conversations that cannot be heard except by means of artificial enhancement. U.S.C.A. Const. Amend. 4.

State v. Rabb, 920 So.2d 1175, review denied 933 So.2d 522, certiorari denied 127 S.Ct. 665, 549 U.S. 1052, 166 L.Ed.2d 513.

Fla.App. 4 Dist. 2004. Fourth Amendment protects conversations that cannot be heard except by means of artificial enhancement. U.S.C.A. Const.Amend. 4.

State v. Rabb, 881 So.2d 587, rehearing denied, certiorari granted, vacated 125 S.Ct. 2246, 544 U.S. 1028, 161 L.Ed.2d 1051, on remand 920 So.2d 1175, review denied 933 So.2d 522, certiorari denied 127 S.Ct. 665, 549 U.S. 1052, 166 L.Ed.2d 513.

Fla.App. 4 Dist. 2002. Core of the Fourth Amendment is the right of an individual to be free from unreasonable intrusion into his or her home. U.S.C.A. Const. Amend. 4.

V.P.S. v. State, 816 So.2d 801.

Fla.App. 4 Dist. 2002. Although it is well settled that one has an expectation of privacy in his home or its curtilage, the Fourth Amendment is not necessarily a protection in areas of the home, which are open and exposed to public view. U.S.C.A. Const.Amend. 4.

State v. Duhart, 810 So.2d 972, re-hearing denied.

Fla.App. 4 Dist. 2001. For Fourth Amendment purposes, a motel room is considered a private dwelling where the occupant is legally there, has paid for the room, and has not been asked to leave. U.S.C.A. Const.Amend. 4.

Gilbert v. State, 789 So.2d 426.

Defendant was entitled to the constitutional protections afforded to a private dwelling since he occupied the motel room and no evidence was presented that he did not pay for it or had been asked to leave. U.S.C.A. Const.Amend. 4.

Gilbert v. State, 789 So.2d 426.

Fla.App. 4 Dist. 2000. Hotel or motel room is considered a private dwelling in which police may not conduct warrantless search absent probable cause and exigent circumstances or consent, if occupant is there legally, has paid or arranged to pay, and has not been asked to leave. U.S.C.A. Const.Amend. 4.

Rebello v. State, 773 So.2d 579.

Fla.App. 4 Dist. 1997. There is no exception to warrant requirement of Fourth Amendment where police enter and search common areas of rooming house. U.S.C.A. Const.Amend. 4.

Titus v. State, 696 So.2d 1257, review granted 700 So.2d 687, decision approved 707 So.2d 706.

Home is accorded full range of Fourth Amendment protections against unreasonable searches and seizures. U.S.C.A. Const.Amend. 4.

Titus v. State, 696 So.2d 1257, review granted 700 So.2d 687, decision approved 707 So.2d 706.

Unless case involves recognized exception to warrant requirement, Fourth Amendment bars a police officer from simply walking into a home and searching for evidence of criminal conduct by its inhabitants. U.S.C.A. Const.Amend. 4.

Titus v. State, 696 So.2d 1257, review granted 700 So.2d 687, decision approved 707 So.2d 706.

Fla.App. 4 Dist. 1993. Secret and unauthorized tape recording of defendant's conversation in back seat of police car while defendant was not in custody, but was sitting in car for his own safety, was invasion of privacy and statutory violation. West's F.S.A. § 934.03; U.S.C.A. Const. Amend. 1.

Nelson v. State, 616 So.2d 84, cause dismissed 621 So.2d 1066.

Fla.App. 4 Dist. 1986. A business may, by its special nature and voluntary existence, open itself to intrusions that would not be permissible in a purely private context. U.S.C.A. Const.Amend. 4.

State v. Showcase Products, Inc., 501 So.2d 11.

A businessman, like an occupant of a residence, has a constitutional right to go about his business free from unreasonable official entries upon his private commercial property. U.S.C.A. Const.Amend. 4.

State v. Showcase Products, Inc., 501 So.2d 11.

Fla.App. 4 Dist. 1982. Person who conducts illegal activity or possesses contraband that is completely open to view from adjacent property will not generally be deemed to have reasonable expectation of privacy.

State v. Bell, 417 So.2d 822.

Fla.App. 4 Dist. 1970. Person has right to have his own home or residence, depending on character of residence, reasonably secure from invasion, visual or otherwise, by police or anyone else.

State v. Clarke, 242 So.2d 791, certiorari denied 246 So.2d 112.

Fla.App. 4 Dist. 1967. Ordinarily a house may not be searched without a search warrant except as incidental to an arrest which takes place on the premises. U.S.C.A.Const. Amend. 4; F.S.A.Const. Declaration of Rights, § 22.

Webster v. State, 201 So.2d 789.

Fla.App. 5 Dist. 2016. Police generally must obtain a warrant before searching a suspect's cell phone and may not, as a matter of course, search a phone incident to a lawful arrest. U.S.C.A. Const. Amend. 4.

Burton v. State, 191 So.3d 543.

Fla.App. 5 Dist. 2015. Absent consent, a search warrant, or an arrest warrant, a police officer may enter a private home only when there are exigent circumstances for the entry. U.S.C.A. Const. Amend. 4.

Durham v. State, 174 So.3d 1074.

Fla.App. 5 Dist. 2013. Person's dwelling, whether in a hotel or in a private home, is protected by the Fourth Amendment. U.S.C.A. Const.Amend. 4.

McBride v. State, 158 So.3d 608, rehearing denied, review denied 145 So.3d 826.

Fla.App. 5 Dist. 2009. The Fourth Amendment protects people, not places. U.S.C.A. Const.Amend. 4.

State v. Halpin, 13 So.3d 75.

Fla.App. 5 Dist. 2007. A private home is the area where a person enjoys the highest expectation of privacy under the Fourth Amendment, and therefore, the warrantless entry of a person's home by law enforcement officers to search for objects of a crime is generally barred by the Fourth Amendment, subject only to a few carefully drawn exceptions. U.S.C.A. Const.Amend. 4.

State v. Clavette, 969 So.2d 463.

Fla.App. 5 Dist. 2004. Areas outside of a hotel room, such as hallways, which are open to use by others may not be reasonably considered as private.

Nelson v. State, 867 So.2d 534, review denied 115 So.3d 1001.

Defendant did not have reasonable expectation of privacy for Fourth Amendment purposes in hotel hallway; hallway was on premises controlled by hotel management and was common walkway for use of hotel guests, visitors, employees and probably by general public. U.S.C.A. Const.Amend. 4.

Nelson v. State, 867 So.2d 534, review denied 115 So.3d 1001.

Fla.App. 5 Dist. 2000. Occupants of a motel room enjoy the protection of the Fourth Amendment. U.S.C.A. Const. Amend. 4.

State v. Wesley, 749 So.2d 592.

Fla.App. 5 Dist. 1985. Gratuitous protection of trespasser from prospective liability against third party is not legitimate governmental interest sufficient to justify search or seizure, particularly when third party's constitutional rights are infringed by such actions.

Lang v. State, 475 So.2d 1354.

Fla.App. 5 Dist. 1980. Guest in motel room is entitled to constitutional protection against unreasonable searches and seizures, and thus warrantless search of guest's person in his motel room was unreasonable absent exigent circumstances. U.S.C.A.Const. Amend. 4.

Engle v. State, 391 So.2d 245.

⟐26. ⸺ **Expectation of privacy.**

U.S.Fla. 2013. Property rights are not the sole measure of Fourth Amendment violations, but though the *Katz* "reasonable expectation of privacy" test may add to the baseline, it does not subtract anything from the Amendment's protections when the Government does engage in a physical intrusion of a constitutionally protected area. U.S.C.A. Const.Amend. 4.

Florida v. Jardines, 133 S.Ct. 1409, 185 L.Ed.2d 495.

C.A.11 (Fla.) 2016. Students did not have any actual or reasonable expectation of privacy in party bus, which they had abandoned once they exited to go into prom, precluding their § 1983 claim against, inter alia, school officials and resource officer employed by sheriff's office, alleging violations of Fourth Amendment with respect to search of bus for alcohol, where students did not expect additional transportation on party bus once they arrived at prom location, and they had all exited bus when officer told them to stand together away from bus and that bus would be searched, and none of them had left any personal belongings on bus to indicate they intended to return to bus at any point after exiting. U.S. Const. Amend. 4; 42 U.S.C.A. § 1983.

Ziegler v. Martin County School District, 831 F.3d 1309.

To assert a Fourth Amendment violation, an individual must establish he or she had a legitimate expectation of privacy in the place searched, which is a two-fold requirement, first that a person have exhibited an actual, subjective expectation of privacy, and second that the expectation be one that society is prepared to recognize as reasonable. U.S. Const. Amend. 4.

Ziegler v. Martin County School District, 831 F.3d 1309.

C.A.11 (Fla.) 2016. The expectations of privacy of an individual taken into police custody necessarily are of a diminished scope. U.S.C.A. Const.Amend. 4.

Castillo v. U.S., 816 F.3d 1300.

C.A.11 (Fla.) 2015. A party alleging an unconstitutional search under the Fourth Amendment must establish both a subjective and an objective expectation of privacy to succeed. U.S.C.A. Const. Amend. 4.

U.S. v. Davis, 785 F.3d 498, certiorari denied 136 S.Ct. 479, 193 L.Ed.2d 349.

C.A.11 (Fla.) 2015. District court did not err in denying defendant's motion to suppress electronic evidence, and fruits thereof, which U.S. received directly from United Kingdom's Serious Fraud Office (SFO) in connection with ongoing international investigation into fraud schemes; Fourth Amendment did not apply to searches and seizures made by foreign authorities enforcing foreign laws in their own country, and defendant did not have an objectively reasonable expectation of privacy in the data files when U.S. agents examined them, to extent British officials searched those files before sending them. U.S.C.A. Const.Amend. 4.

U.S. v. Odoni, 782 F.3d 1226, certiorari denied Gunter v. U.S., 135 S.Ct. 2335, 191 L.Ed.2d 981, certiorari denied 135 S.Ct. 2339, 191 L.Ed.2d 981.

A "search" occurs, within the meaning of the Fourth Amendment, when an expectation of privacy that society is prepared to consider reasonable is infringed. U.S.C.A. Const.Amend. 4.

U.S. v. Odoni, 782 F.3d 1226, certiorari denied Gunter v. U.S., 135 S.Ct. 2335, 191 L.Ed.2d 981, certiorari denied 135 S.Ct. 2339, 191 L.Ed.2d 981.

An objectively reasonable expectation of privacy, protected by the Fourth Amendment, is one that society is prepared to recognize as reasonable. U.S.C.A. Const.Amend. 4.

U.S. v. Odoni, 782 F.3d 1226, certiorari denied Gunter v. U.S., 135 S.Ct. 2335, 191 L.Ed.2d 981, certiorari denied 135 S.Ct. 2339, 191 L.Ed.2d 981.

An individual does not have a reasonable expectation of privacy in an object to the extent the object has been searched by a private party. U.S.C.A. Const.Amend. 4.

U.S. v. Odoni, 782 F.3d 1226, certiorari denied Gunter v. U.S., 135 S.Ct. 2335, 191 L.Ed.2d 981, certiorari denied 135 S.Ct. 2339, 191 L.Ed.2d 981.

C.A.11 (Fla.) 2014. Citizens do not abandon all hope of privacy by applying for government assistance. U.S.C.A. Const.Amend. 4.

Lebron v. Secretary of Florida Dept. of Children and Families, 772 F.3d 1352.

C.A.11 (Fla.) 2014. Because society recognizes as reasonable an expectation of privacy under the Fourth Amendment for confidential conversations between individuals, the government needs a warrant to intercept or record such conversations. U.S.C.A. Const.Amend. 4.

Gennusa v. Canova, 748 F.3d 1103.

Suspect and his attorney had a reasonable expectation of privacy for their privileged attorney-client conversations in interview room at county sheriff's office, and thus officers' surreptitious recording and monitoring of those conversations, without notice to suspect or attorney, and without a warrant, was an unlawful search under the Fourth Amendment. U.S.C.A. Const.Amend. 4.

Gennusa v. Canova, 748 F.3d 1103.

Expectations of privacy of an individual taken into police custody necessarily are of a diminished scope for Fourth Amendment purposes. U.S.C.A. Const.Amend. 4.

Gennusa v. Canova, 748 F.3d 1103.

† C.A.11 (Fla.) 2013. For Fourth Amendment purposes, defendant extinguished any reasonable expectation of privacy she had in her computers by allowing her daughter to retrieve the machines from her hotel room to sell them. U.S.C.A. Const.Amend. 4.

> U.S. v. Kannell, 545 Fed.Appx. 881, certiorari denied 134 S.Ct. 1569, 188 L.Ed.2d 578, certiorari denied Harvey v. U.S., 134 S.Ct. 1916, 188 L.Ed.2d 941.

† C.A.11 (Fla.) 2013. Defendant did not have reasonable expectation of privacy in conversation conducted through a cellphone's speaker system, therefore, a video recording of the conversation, taken on computer web camera, did not violate Title III of the Omnibus Crime Control and Safe Streets Act or his Fourth Amendment right to privacy. U.S.C.A. Const.Amend. 4; 18 U.S.C.A. § 2511.

> U.S. v. Curtis, 513 Fed.Appx. 823, certiorari denied 134 S.Ct. 536, 187 L.Ed.2d 384.

† C.A.11 (Fla.) 2011. Defendant did not suffer any invasion of his right to privacy under the Fourth Amendment when hotel's director of security knocked on the door of defendant's room to evict its occupants and the women who were inside opened the door; officers were permitted to question the women they observed through the open door, and to follow the director of security into the hotel room. U.S.C.A. Const.Amend. 4.

> U.S. v. Collins, 437 Fed.Appx. 760, certiorari denied 132 S.Ct. 430, 565 U.S. 954, 181 L.Ed.2d 279, postconviction relief denied 2013 WL 6259114, appeal dismissed (11th circ. 14-10063).

† C.A.11 (Fla.) 2010. Defendant did not have reasonable expectation of privacy in subscriber identification information given to internet services providers (ISP) and telephone companies, within scope of Fourth Amendment; investigators did not recover any information related to content, but instead, received identifying information transmitted during internet usage and telephone calls necessary for ISPs and telephone company to perform their services. U.S.C.A. Const.Amend. 4.

> U.S. v. Beckett, 369 Fed.Appx. 52.

C.A.11 (Fla.) 2010. Touchstone of the analysis used in determining whether an instance of officer trespass amounts to a Fourth Amendment violation is whether a person enjoyed a reasonable expectation

of privacy associated with the intruded area. U.S.C.A. Const.Amend. 4.

> Coffin v. Brandau, 609 F.3d 1204, rehearing granted, opinion vacated 614 F.3d 1240, on rehearing 642 F.3d 999.

Individual enjoys a reasonable expectation of privacy in his home, for purposes of determining whether an instance of officer trespass amounts to a Fourth Amendment violation. U.S.C.A. Const.Amend. 4.

> Coffin v. Brandau, 609 F.3d 1204, rehearing granted, opinion vacated 614 F.3d 1240, on rehearing 642 F.3d 999.

For purposes of determining whether an instance of officer trespass amounts to a Fourth Amendment violation, the zone of privacy is most clearly defined when bounded by the unambiguous physical dimensions of an individual's home. U.S.C.A. Const.Amend. 4.

> Coffin v. Brandau, 609 F.3d 1204, rehearing granted, opinion vacated 614 F.3d 1240, on rehearing 642 F.3d 999.

† C.A.11 (Fla.) 2008. Defendant did not have an objectively reasonable expectation of privacy in his hunting stand, as required for Fourth Amendment protection, where stand was a wooden box located in the woods with windows on three sides and a door on the fourth, other hunters and non-invitees often entered the area, defendant did not use the stand for anything other than hunting-related activities and drinking coffee, and defendant did not attempt to restrict access to the stand. U.S.C.A. Const.Amend. 4.

> U.S. v. Siau, 281 Fed.Appx. 949, certiorari denied 129 S.Ct. 901, 555 U.S. 1104, 173 L.Ed.2d 119.

Defendant did not have an objectively reasonable expectation of privacy in a wrapped but unlocked container holding grenades, as required for Fourth Amendment protection, where box was located in unlocked deer stand in the open outdoors, box was unsecured and did not include any writing identifying the owner of the property or warning third parties to keep out, trespassers and children came onto the property, and things went missing quite often. U.S.C.A. Const.Amend. 4.

U.S. v. Siau, 281 Fed.Appx. 949, certiorari denied 129 S.Ct. 901, 555 U.S. 1104, 173 L.Ed.2d 119.

† **C.A.11 (Fla.) 2005.** Alleged conspirators did not have reasonable expectation of privacy in text messages received or sent by alleged co-conspirator using text message pager, so that this co-conspirator could testify for government regarding content of those messages in drug conspiracy prosecution.

U.S. v. Jones, 149 Fed.Appx. 954, certiorari denied 126 S.Ct. 1373, 546 U.S. 1189, 164 L.Ed.2d 80, certiorari denied Lofton v. U.S., 126 S.Ct. 1373, 546 U.S. 1189, 164 L.Ed.2d 80, certiorari denied Ford v. U.S., 126 S.Ct. 2019, 547 U.S. 1132, 164 L.Ed.2d 785, post-conviction relief denied Cobb v. U.S., 2006 WL 1360924, post-conviction relief denied 2006 WL 1406584, motion for relief from judgment denied 2013 WL 12201089, post-conviction relief denied Langdon v. U.S., 2007 WL 656460, post-conviction relief denied 2007 WL 1789117, dismissal of habeas corpus affirmed Jones v. Warden, FCC Coleman-Medium, 520 Fed.Appx. 942, certiorari denied 134 S.Ct. 711, 187 L.Ed.2d 571.

C.A.11 (Fla.) 2004. Though physical entry of home is chief evil against which wording of Fourth Amendment is directed, its protection extends to any area in which individual has reasonable expectation of privacy. U.S.C.A. Const.Amend. 4.

O'Rourke v. Hayes, 378 F.3d 1201.

C.A.11 (Fla.) 2003. The test of *Katz v. United States*, for determining whether a defendant has an expectation of privacy for purposes of the Fourth Amendment, requires a court to ask whether defendants' actions exhibited an actual, that is, subjective, expectation of privacy, and to question whether this subjective expectation is one that society is prepared to recognize as reasonable. U.S.C.A. Const. Amend. 4.

U.S. v. Young, 350 F.3d 1302, rehearing and rehearing denied 97 Fed. Appx. 909.

C.A.11 (Fla.) 2003. Expectations of privacy in area to be searched must be reasonable in order to be honored by the law. U.S.C.A. Const.Amend. 4.

U.S. v. Backus, 349 F.3d 1298, certiorari denied 124 S.Ct. 1690, 541 U.S. 951, 158 L.Ed.2d 381.

C.A.11 (Fla.) 2002. A person has an expectation of privacy protected by the Fourth Amendment if he has a subjective expectation of privacy, and if society is prepared to recognize that expectation as objectively reasonable. U.S.C.A. Const. Amend. 4.

U.S. v. Miravalles, 280 F.3d 1328.

Where the lock on entrance to large, multiple-unit apartment building is not functioning, so that anyone may enter building, tenants of such a building do not have a reasonable expectation of privacy for purposes of Fourth Amendment in common areas of building. U.S.C.A. Const.Amend. 4.

U.S. v. Miravalles, 280 F.3d 1328.

Tenants of large, high-rise apartment building lacked a reasonable expectation of privacy, for purposes of Fourth Amendment, in common areas of building, including lobby, hallways, and other areas, where building's front door had an undependable lock that was inoperable on day in question, so that common areas were open not only to tenants and their visitors, landlord and its employees, and other workers and delivery people, but also to the public at large, and there was nothing to prevent anyone and everyone who wanted to do so from walking in unlocked door and moving freely about premises. U.S.C.A. Const.Amend. 4.

U.S. v. Miravalles, 280 F.3d 1328.

C.A.11 (Fla.) 2000. The Fourth Amendment's guarantee of freedom from warrantless searches and seizures is not premised on arcane concepts of property and possessory interests; instead, the Fourth Amendment protects an individual in those places where he or she can demonstrate a reasonable expectation of privacy against government intrusion. U.S.C.A. Const.Amend. 4.

U.S. v. Cooper, 203 F.3d 1279.

A hotel room can be included among places where an individual has a reasonable expectation of privacy against government intrusion and thus is protected by the Fourth Amendment. U.S.C.A. Const. Amend. 4.

U.S. v. Cooper, 203 F.3d 1279.

C.A.11 (Fla.) 1999. Under the Fourth Amendment, an individual is not limited to one place of business; the Fourth Amendment protects the reasonable expectation of privacy he or she has in multiple places. U.S.C.A. Const.Amend. 4.

U.S. v. Chaves, 169 F.3d 687, rehearing denied, certiorari denied Garcia v. U.S., 120 S.Ct. 534, 528 U.S. 1022, 145 L.Ed.2d 414, certiorari denied 120 S.Ct. 585, 528 U.S. 1048, 145 L.Ed.2d 486.

C.A.11 (Fla.) 1996.   Warrantless search of home is presumptively unreasonable, but is allowed when both probable cause and exigent circumstances exist; "probable cause" exists when, under totality of circumstances, there is fair probability that contraband or evidence of crime will be discovered in particular place, and "exigent circumstances" exist when authorities have reason to believe that evidence is in danger of being destroyed or removed. U.S.C.A. Const.Amend. 4.

U.S. v. Mikell, 102 F.3d 470, certiorari denied Young v. U.S., 117 S.Ct. 1459, 520 U.S. 1181, 137 L.Ed.2d 563.

C.A.11 (Fla.) 1995. Warrantless entry of person's home is presumptively unreasonable;   however,   warrantless searches and seizures of evidence in residences are permitted when both probable cause and exigent circumstances exist. U.S.C.A. Const.Amend. 4.

U.S. v. Tovar-Rico, 61 F.3d 1529.

C.A.11 (Fla.) 1995. Child's grandparents did not have reasonable expectation of privacy in child's closet and bedroom and, thus, could not maintain Fourth Amendment claim against child's guardian ad litem for searching those areas, while guardian ad litem accompanied social worker to residence to retrieve belongings of child, who was being removed from custody of her father.   U.S.C.A. Const. Amend. 4; 42 U.S.C.A. § 1983.

Lenz v. Winburn, 51 F.3d 1540.

C.A.11 (Fla.) 1995. Whether Fourth Amendment's protections are invoked to protect sanctity of home or of commercial property, touchstone of inquiry into objective reasonableness of expectation of privacy is whether governmental intrusion infringes upon personal and societal values Fourth Amendment protects.   U.S.C.A. Const.Amend. 4.

U.S. v. Hall, 47 F.3d 1091, certiorari denied 116 S.Ct. 71, 516 U.S. 816, 133 L.Ed.2d 31.

Expectation of privacy that owner of commercial property enjoys in such property differs significantly from protection afforded individual's home; thus, for persons to preserve Fourth Amendment protection in area immediately surrounding their residence, they must not conduct activity or leave object in plain view of those outside area, while occupant of commercial building must take additional precaution of affirmatively barring public from area. U.S.C.A. Const.Amend. 4.

U.S. v. Hall, 47 F.3d 1091, certiorari denied 116 S.Ct. 71, 516 U.S. 816, 133 L.Ed.2d 31.

C.A.11 (Fla.) 1993.   Defendant did not have reasonable expectation of privacy while in backseat of police car and, therefore, tape recording of his prearrest conversations did not violate Title III of the Omnibus Crime Control and Safe Streets Act or his Fourth Amendment right to privacy.   18 U.S.C.A. §§ 2510(2), 2511; U.S.C.A. Const.Amend. 4.

U.S. v. McKinnon, 985 F.2d 525, certiorari denied 114 S.Ct. 130, 510 U.S. 843, 126 L.Ed.2d 94.

C.A.11 (Fla.) 1993. "Reasonable expectation of privacy" requires subjective expectation of privacy that society is prepared   to   recognize   as   reasonable. U.S.C.A. Const.Amend. 4.

U.S. v. Diaz-Lizaraza, 981 F.2d 1216.

C.A.11 (Fla.) 1990. A dwelling, together with its surrounding curtilage, is not always a sanctuary from law enforcement activity, even if police act without a warrant. U.S.C.A. Const.Amend. 4.

U.S. v. Emmens, 893 F.2d 1292, certiorari denied 111 S.Ct. 48, 498 U.S. 812, 112 L.Ed.2d 24.

C.A.11 (Fla.) 1989. Legitimate expectation of privacy for Fourth Amendment purposes is expectation actually and subjectively held by defendant and one which society is prepared to recognize as reasonable. U.S.C.A. Const.Amend. 4.

> U.S. v. Tobin, 890 F.2d 319, rehearing granted, vacated 902 F.2d 821, on rehearing 923 F.2d 1506, rehearing denied 935 F.2d 1297, certiorari denied 112 S.Ct. 299, 502 U.S. 907, 116 L.Ed.2d 243.

C.A.11 (Fla.) 1989. Determining whether individual has legitimate expectation of privacy requires inquiry into whether the individual has manifested a subjective expectation of privacy and whether society is willing to recognize the individual's expectation of privacy as legitimate; the former is a factual determination which is reviewed under the clearly erroneous standard, whereas the latter is a legal question which is reviewed plenarily. U.S.C.A. Const.Amend. 4.

> U.S. v. Hastamorir, 881 F.2d 1551.

C.A.11 (Fla.) 1986. The less intrusive the search or seizure, and the less the expectation of privacy involved, the broader the scope of what is reasonable.

> U.S. v. Reeh, 780 F.2d 1541.

C.A.11 (Fla.) 1986. A "reasonable expectation of privacy" means more than a subjective expectation of not being discovered. U.S.C.A. Const.Amend. 4.

> U.S. v. Whaley, 779 F.2d 585, rehearing denied 784 F.2d 404, certiorari denied 107 S.Ct. 931, 479 U.S. 1055, 93 L.Ed.2d 982.

Reasonableness of an expectation of privacy is logically dependent principally on degree to which locale is viewable by member of public without visual aids. U.S.C.A. Const.Amend. 4.

> U.S. v. Whaley, 779 F.2d 585, rehearing denied 784 F.2d 404, certiorari denied 107 S.Ct. 931, 479 U.S. 1055, 93 L.Ed.2d 982.

Mere fact that person may be engaging in criminal conduct within his home does not necessarily destroy his expectation of privacy; however, reasonableness of that person's expectation of privacy is affected, where it appears that he has engaged in suspicious activity outside home that would tend to attract attention of the police. U.S.C.A. Const.Amend. 4.

> U.S. v. Whaley, 779 F.2d 585, rehearing denied 784 F.2d 404, certiorari denied 107 S.Ct. 931, 479 U.S. 1055, 93 L.Ed.2d 982.

Use of vision-enhancing devices can taint an otherwise valid surveillance of interior of home, where devices allow observer to view not only activities homeowner should realize might be seen by unenhanced viewing but also details of activities homeowner legitimately expects will not be observed. U.S.C.A. Const. Amend. 4.

> U.S. v. Whaley, 779 F.2d 585, rehearing denied 784 F.2d 404, certiorari denied 107 S.Ct. 931, 479 U.S. 1055, 93 L.Ed.2d 982.

C.A.11 (Fla.) 1985. Fourth Amendment does not protect subjective expectations of privacy that are unreasonable or otherwise illegitimate. U.S.C.A. Const. Amend. 4.

> U.S. v. Lopez, 761 F.2d 632.

To receive protection of the Fourth Amendment, expectation of privacy must be one society is prepared to recognize as legitimate. U.S.C.A. Const.Amend. 4.

> U.S. v. Lopez, 761 F.2d 632.

Requirement for a justifiable expectation of privacy in order to receive protection of the Fourth Amendment is twofold, namely, defendant must show an actual or subjective expectation of privacy in area searched and expectation must be one that society is prepared to recognize as reasonable. U.S.C.A. Const.Amend. 4.

> U.S. v. Lopez, 761 F.2d 632.

It is not sufficient that a sailor have the right to exclude others from his ship in order to have legitimate expectation of privacy for Fourth Amendment purposes, because a coast guard officer may without permission conduct a safety and document search and gain access to all common areas of boat. U.S.C.A. Const.Amend. 4.

> U.S. v. Lopez, 761 F.2d 632.

C.A.11 (Fla.) 1984. Legitimacy of a defendant's privacy claim as to areas searched is determined by totality of circumstances.

> U.S. v. Baron-Mantilla, 743 F.2d 868.

Although defendant did not own premises searched, nor did he rent them, and telephone in premises was not listed in his name, defendant could have nonetheless established legitimate expectation of privacy in premises by demonstrating an unrestricted right of occupancy or custody and control of premises as distinguished from occasional presence on premises as a mere guest or invitee.

U.S. v. Baron-Mantilla, 743 F.2d 868.

Defendant who did not own or rent premises searched, did not have telephone in premises listed in his name, and failed to produce any neighbor or building employee who could have established his residency there had no claim of privacy to premises which would require that a warrant be obtained prior to search. U.S.C.A. Const.Amend. 4.

U.S. v. Baron-Mantilla, 743 F.2d 868.

More evidence than possession of a key to apartment was necessary to satisfy defendant's burden of establishing legitimate expectation of privacy on premises.

U.S. v. Baron-Mantilla, 743 F.2d 868.

C.A.11 (Fla.) 1984. No expectation of privacy was established by mere presence on searched premises belonging to a brother. U.S.C.A. Const.Amend. 4.

U.S. v. Ard, 731 F.2d 718.

C.A.11 (Fla.) 1983. Although mere ownership is not talisman for Fourth Amendment jurisprudence, it is, nevertheless, bright star by which courts are guided when place invaded enjoys universal acceptance as haven of privacy, such as a home. U.S.C.A. Const.Amend. 4.

U.S. v. Freire, 710 F.2d 1515, rehearing denied 717 F.2d 1401, certiorari denied 104 S.Ct. 1277, 465 U.S. 1023, 79 L.Ed.2d 681.

C.A.11 (Fla.) 1983. Evidence as to guilt or innocence of the substantive offense charged has no bearing on whether a defendant enjoys legitimate expectation of privacy in the place searched. U.S.C.A. Const.Amend. 4.

U.S. v. Torres, 705 F.2d 1287, opinion vacated 718 F.2d 998, on remand 720 F.2d 1506, appeal after remand 741 F.2d 1323.

C.A.11 (Fla.) 1983. Constitutionally protected expectation of privacy does not attach to wrongdoer's misplaced belief that person to whom he voluntarily confides his wrongdoing will not reveal it. U.S.C.A. Const.Amend. 4.

U.S. v. Yonn, 702 F.2d 1341, certiorari denied Weeks v. U.S., 104 S.Ct. 283, 464 U.S. 917, 78 L.Ed.2d 261.

C.A.5 (Fla.) 1981. Threshold inquiry in a Fourth Amendment challenge is whether challenger had a legitimate expectation of privacy in invaded place. U.S.C.A.Const. Amend. 4.

U.S. v. Glasgow, 658 F.2d 1036.

C.A.5 (Fla.) 1981. Whether defendant's Fourth Amendment rights have been violated by an unlawful search turns on his legitimate expectation of privacy in the area searched. U.S.C.A.Const. Amend. 4.

U.S. v. Meyer, 656 F.2d 979, appeal after remand U.S. v. McMahon, 715 F.2d 498, rehearing denied 715 F.2d 580, certiorari denied 104 S.Ct. 507, 464 U.S. 1001, 78 L.Ed.2d 697, certiorari denied 104 S.Ct. 1413, 465 U.S. 1065, 79 L.Ed.2d 739.

C.A.5 (Fla.) 1981. Fourth Amendment protection is accorded only to person who has a privacy interest in area searched. U.S.C.A.Const. Amend. 4.

U.S. v. Richards, 638 F.2d 765, rehearing denied 646 F.2d 962, certiorari denied 102 S.Ct. 669, 454 U.S. 1097, 70 L.Ed.2d 638.

C.A.5 (Fla.) 1980. For purposes of Fourth Amendment, one may have protected expectation of privacy in absence of property interest; on other hand, one may have fee simple title to property upon which one has no expectation of privacy. U.S.C.A.Const. Amend. 4.

U.S. v. DeWeese, 632 F.2d 1267, rehearing denied 641 F.2d 879, certiorari denied 102 S.Ct. 358, 454 U.S. 878, 70 L.Ed.2d 188.

C.A.5 (Fla.) 1980. Legitimate expectations of privacy protected by the Fourth Amendment must have a source outside the Fourth Amendment, either by reference to concepts of real or personal property law or to understandings that are recognized and permitted by society. U.S.C.A.Const. Amend. 4.

> U.S. v. Vicknair, 610 F.2d 372, certiorari denied 101 S.Ct. 83, 449 U.S. 823, 66 L.Ed.2d 25.

C.A.5 (Fla.) 1975. Where defendant knew that rental agent at warehouse, and others doing work or storing matter in area, had joint access to warehouse area in which defendant was storing his truck containing more than half a ton of marijuana, he took his chance that other persons might enter at inconvenient time or grant permission for law enforcement officials to come upon the premises, and thus had no reasonable expectation of privacy, and there was no violation of defendant's Fourth Amendment rights when officers, by ruse, induced one of the other persons having right of access to admit them to the premises, which they searched and thereby obtained probable cause for warrant to search truck. U.S.C.A.Const. Amend. 4.

> U.S. v. Novello, 519 F.2d 1078, certiorari denied 96 S.Ct. 797, 423 U.S. 1060, 46 L.Ed.2d 651.

C.A.5 (Fla.) 1974. Sacredness of person's home and his right of personal privacy and individuality are paramount considerations which are specifically protected by the Fourth Amendment which extends farther than the walls of the physical structure of building itself to include the area immediately surrounding and closely relating to the dwelling. U.S.C.A.Const. Amend. 4.

> Fixel v. Wainwright, 492 F.2d 480.

C.A.5 (Fla.) 1964. Fourth Amendment was designed to safeguard individual's right of privacy in his home and in his personal effects against arbitrary intrusion by government officials. U.S.C.A.Const. Amend. 4.

> Marullo v. U.S., 328 F.2d 361, rehearing denied 330 F.2d 609, certiorari denied 85 S.Ct. 93, 379 U.S. 850, 13 L.Ed.2d 53.

Motel occupants did not have right to privacy in top of brick pillar supporting motel cabin, and evidence seized by officers from top of such pillar without warrant was not excludable in criminal prosecution on ground that it had been obtained by unreasonable search and seizure. Fed. Rules Crim.Proc. rule 41(e), 18 U.S.C.A.;

18 U.S.C.A. § 371; U.S.C.A.Const. Amend. 4.

> Marullo v. U.S., 328 F.2d 361, rehearing denied 330 F.2d 609, certiorari denied 85 S.Ct. 93, 379 U.S. 850, 13 L.Ed.2d 53.

M.D.Fla. 2012. Both arrestee and his attorney had a possessory interest in arrestee's written statement which was entitled to the protections of the Fourth Amendment, where arrestee created the statement and placed it in the care of his attorney. U.S.C.A. Const.Amend. 4.

> Gennusa v. Shoar, 879 F.Supp.2d 1337, affirmed 748 F.3d 1103.

The Fourth Amendment governs not only the seizure of tangible items, but extends as well to the recording of oral statements; the constitutional question is whether the person invoking its Fourth Amendment protection can claim a justifiable, a reasonable, or a legitimate expectation of privacy that has been invaded by government action. U.S.C.A. Const. Amend. 4.

> Gennusa v. Shoar, 879 F.Supp.2d 1337, affirmed 748 F.3d 1103.

To prove a Fourth Amendment violation, a plaintiff therefore must show both that he had a subjective expectation of privacy and that his subjective expectation of privacy is one that society is willing to recognize as reasonable. U.S.C.A. Const. Amend. 4.

> Gennusa v. Shoar, 879 F.Supp.2d 1337, affirmed 748 F.3d 1103.

When the police take actions during an interview or interrogation which suggest that a suspect's conversations will be private, an expectation of privacy is more reasonable. U.S.C.A. Const.Amend. 4.

> Gennusa v. Shoar, 879 F.Supp.2d 1337, affirmed 748 F.3d 1103.

Arrestee and his attorney had a reasonable expectation of privacy in attorney-client conversations held in police interview room in county sheriff's office, and thus the surreptitious recording of those conversations violated the Fourth Amendment and constituted an actionable interception of "oral communication" under the Federal Wiretapping Act; officer's actions in closing door to interview room when exiting and allowing arrestee and officer to speak alone fostered an expectation of privacy, attorney clearly conveyed to arrestee that she believed their conversations were private by providing legal advice, discussing legal strategy, and asking questions regarding the subject of her representations, and attorney testified that, in the past, when police interviews with her clients had been recorded, she had been informed of that fact so she could arrange for private communications, and that, as a member of the local defense bar, she had been told that the sheriff's office recorded only confessions and statements from suspects rather than the full contents of all interviews. U.S.C.A. Const.Amend. 4; 18 U.S.C.A. §§ 2510(2), 2511(1)(a), 2520(a).

Gennusa v. Shoar, 879 F.Supp.2d 1337, affirmed 748 F.3d 1103.

M.D.Fla. 2011. Fourth Amendment is violated when government conducts an unreasonable search in an area where a person has a reasonable expectation of privacy. U.S.C.A. Const.Amend. 4.

Kastritis v. City of Daytona Beach Shores, 835 F.Supp.2d 1200.

M.D.Fla. 2009. Focus of Fourth Amendment analysis is whether society is prepared to recognize an expectation of privacy as reasonable. U.S.C.A. Const. Amend. 4.

Swofford v. Eslinger, 671 F.Supp.2d 1289, affirmed 395 Fed.Appx. 559, rehearing and rehearing denied 409 Fed.Appx. 316, certiorari denied Morris v. Swofford, 131 S.Ct. 1053, 562 U.S. 1201, 178 L.Ed.2d 866.

M.D.Fla. 2006. There was no diminished right of privacy, for spectators at professional football game, for purposes of determining whether mandatory pat-down search of every spectator entering stadium violated Fourth Amendment. U.S.C.A. Const.Amend. 4.

Johnston v. Tampa Sports Authority, 442 F.Supp.2d 1257, reversed and remanded 490 F.3d 820, opinion vacated and superseded on rehearing 530 F.3d 1320, rehearing and rehearing denied 285 Fed.Appx. 745, certiorari denied 129 S.Ct. 1013, 555 U.S. 1138, 173 L.Ed.2d 295, reversed and remanded 530

F.3d 1320, rehearing and rehearing denied 285 Fed.Appx. 745, certiorari denied 129 S.Ct. 1013, 555 U.S. 1138, 173 L.Ed.2d 295.

M.D.Fla. 2002. While the Fourth Amendment's prohibition on unreasonable searches applies to commercial premises, the expectation of privacy in commercial premises is different from and less than the expectation of privacy within the home. U.S.C.A. Const.Amend. 4.

Alexis, Inc. v. Pinellas County, Florida, 194 F.Supp.2d 1336.

For Fourth Amendment purposes, the expectation of privacy is further reduced in the context of a closely regulated industry, such as the liquor industry. U.S.C.A. Const.Amend. 4.

Alexis, Inc. v. Pinellas County, Florida, 194 F.Supp.2d 1336.

M.D.Fla. 1999. Question of whether an employee has a reasonable expectation of privacy in the workplace must be addressed on a case-by-case basis, and relevant factors include whether the person shared the area with anyone else, whether others could be expected to enter the area or disturb papers in it without permission, and whether the person has a key. U.S.C.A. Const.Amend. 4.

U.S. v. Evaschuck, 65 F.Supp.2d 1360.

M.D.Fla. 1980. On challenge to search or seizure, court must ask whether individual has shown by his conduct that he seeks to preserve something as private, and court must then determine whether individual's subjective expectation of privacy was one which society is prepared to recognize as reasonable, and, to answer second question, court must look to all circumstances surrounding intrusion complained of. U.S.C.A.Const. Amend. 4.

U.S. v. Hartley, 486 F.Supp. 1348, affirmed 678 F.2d 961, rehearing denied 688 F.2d 852, certiorari denied 103 S.Ct. 815, 459 U.S. 1170, 74 L.Ed.2d 1014, certiorari denied Treasure Isle, Inc., v. U.S., 103 S.Ct. 834, 459 U.S. 1183, 74 L.Ed.2d 1027.

Fourth Amendment prohibitions apply in civil as well as criminal investigations, and protect commercial premises as well as homes, but Fourth Amendment protects legitimate expectations of privacy of persons, not places, and defendant must establish that his own Fourth Amendment rights were violated by conduct upon which he wishes to base exclusion. U.S.C.A.Const. Amend. 4.

U.S. v. Hartley, 486 F.Supp. 1348, affirmed 678 F.2d 961, rehearing denied 688 F.2d 852, certiorari denied 103 S.Ct. 815, 459 U.S. 1170, 74 L.Ed.2d 1014, certiorari denied Treasure Isle, Inc., v. U.S., 103 S.Ct. 834, 459 U.S. 1183, 74 L.Ed.2d 1027.

S.D.Fla. 2015. To establish reasonable expectation of privacy, defendant challenging legality of search or seizure must manifest subjective expectation of privacy in items searched or seized, and society must be prepared to recognize that expectation as legitimate or objectively reasonable. U.S. Const. Amend. 4.

United States v. Medina, 158 F.Supp.3d 1303.

Owner of commercial property has reasonable expectation of privacy in those areas immediately surrounding property only if affirmative steps have been taken to exclude public. U.S. Const. Amend. 4.

United States v. Medina, 158 F.Supp.3d 1303.

In evaluating defendant's expectation of privacy in business premises for Fourth Amendment purposes, court may consider whether documents seized were prepared by defendant, whether area searched was storage area and not defendant's personal working area, whether defendant was on premises at time of search, and whether search was directed at corporate activity generally and not at corporate officer personally. U.S. Const. Amend. 4.

United States v. Medina, 158 F.Supp.3d 1303.

S.D.Fla. 2014. Two requirements must be met before a person may successfully prevail on a Fourth Amendment claim; first, the claimant's legitimate expectation of privacy must be invaded by the search and seizure, and, second, the

search and seizure must be unreasonable. U.S. Const.Amend. 4.

United States v. Jackson, 155 F.Supp.3d 1320, affirmed 618 Fed. Appx. 472, certiorari denied 136 S.Ct. 376, 193 L.Ed.2d 303.

Once a privacy interest is invaded legally by an official of the State, the citizen has lost his reasonable expectation of privacy to the extent of the invasion. U.S. Const.Amend. 4.

United States v. Jackson, 155 F.Supp.3d 1320, affirmed 618 Fed. Appx. 472, certiorari denied 136 S.Ct. 376, 193 L.Ed.2d 303.

S.D.Fla. 2011. Defendant had standing to challenge, on Fourth Amendment grounds, the warrantless search of his cell phone as a whole; defendant had a reasonable expectation of privacy in his phone's call and text message folder. U.S.C.A. Const.Amend. 4.

U.S. v. Gomez, 807 F.Supp.2d 1134.

S.D.Fla. 2008. Fourth Amendment protects individuals' possessory interests in property as well as their expectation of privacy. U.S.C.A. Const.Amend. 4.

Sosa v. Hames, 581 F.Supp.2d 1254.

S.D.Fla. 1994. Generally, occupant of hotel room has legitimate expectation of privacy no less than tenant of house, or occupant of room in boarding house. U.S.C.A. Const.Amend. 4.

U.S. v. Wai-Keung, 845 F.Supp. 1548, affirmed 115 F.3d 874, rehearing and suggestion for rehearing denied U.S. v. Chi-Cheong, 127 F.3d 42, certiorari denied Li v. U.S., 118 S.Ct. 1095, 522 U.S. 1135, 140 L.Ed.2d 150.

Defendants had no legitimate expectation of privacy in hotel rooms; defendants could be considered merely guests of person who rented rooms, they had no reasonable expectation of privacy in rooms obtained fraudulently through improper use of credit card, and possession of rooms had reverted to hotel after checkout time. U.S.C.A. Const.Amend. 4; West's F.S.A. § 509.402.

U.S. v. Wai-Keung, 845 F.Supp. 1548, affirmed 115 F.3d 874, rehearing and suggestion for rehearing denied U.S. v. Chi-Cheong, 127 F.3d 42, certiorari denied Li v. U.S., 118 S.Ct. 1095, 522 U.S. 1135, 140 L.Ed.2d 150.

Mere presence in hotel room registered to another does not establish expectation of privacy. U.S.C.A. Const.Amend. 4.

> U.S. v. Wai-Keung, 845 F.Supp. 1548, affirmed 115 F.3d 874, rehearing and suggestion for rehearing denied U.S. v. Chi-Cheong, 127 F.3d 42, certiorari denied Li v. U.S., 118 S.Ct. 1095, 522 U.S. 1135, 140 L.Ed.2d 150.

Where defendant has neither registered nor paid for room himself, and has left no personal belongings in room, he has not established legitimate expectation of privacy in the room. U.S.C.A. Const. Amend. 4.

> U.S. v. Wai-Keung, 845 F.Supp. 1548, affirmed 115 F.3d 874, rehearing and suggestion for rehearing denied U.S. v. Chi-Cheong, 127 F.3d 42, certiorari denied Li v. U.S., 118 S.Ct. 1095, 522 U.S. 1135, 140 L.Ed.2d 150.

S.D.Fla. 1992. For Fourth Amendment purposes, determining nature of any legitimate expectation of privacy that individuals have in their personal property involves two inquiries: first, whether individual has subjective expectation of privacy in belongings; and second, whether that expectation is one that society is prepared to recognize as reasonable. West's F.S.A. Const. Art. 1, § 12; U.S.C.A. Const. Amend. 4.

> Pottinger v. City of Miami, 810 F.Supp. 1551.

For Fourth Amendment purposes, homeless persons had legitimate expectation of privacy in their personal belongings that were seized in public areas. West's F.S.A. Const. Art. 1, § 12; U.S.C.A. Const. Amend. 4.

> Pottinger v. City of Miami, 810 F.Supp. 1551.

City's seizures of personal belongings of homeless persons in public areas violated Fourth Amendment. 42 U.S.C.A. § 1983; West's F.S.A. Const. Art. 1, § 12; U.S.C.A. Const.Amend. 4.

> Pottinger v. City of Miami, 810 F.Supp. 1551.

S.D.Fla. 1992. Defendant had reasonable expectation of privacy in building in which he lived, even though officers claimed structure looked like barn rather than house. U.S.C.A. Const.Amend. 4.

> U.S. v. Seidel, 794 F.Supp. 1098.

S.D.Fla. 1987. In determining whether claim to privacy from Government intrusion is reasonable in light of all surrounding circumstances, no single factor invariably will be determinative, but variety of elements must be considered, including whether movant has asserted interest in premises searched or property seized, whether movant was legitimately on premises at time of intrusion, whether movant has right or power to exclude others from place, whether movant has evinced subjective expectation that premises would remain free from governmental intrusion and whether movant has taken normal precautions to maintain his privacy. U.S.C.A. Const.Amend. 4.

> U.S. v. Puliese, 671 F.Supp. 1353.

Where interest in privacy from governmental intrusion is claimed by invited guest at home, factors that should be considered in determining whether claim to privacy is reasonable include who has invited guest into home, for what purpose and for how long has guest been invited into home, has owner or lessee given guest key or other means of entry to home, what use has guest made of home and what use has been made of intruded area, does guest have power and authority to exclude others from home and with how many other people has use of area been shared. U.S.C.A. Const.Amend. 4.

> U.S. v. Puliese, 671 F.Supp. 1353.

Invited guest who slept in home for one night and who brought small amount of clothing and toilet articles into bedroom had no legitimate expectation of privacy in areas searched deserving of protections of Fourth Amendment, and thus had no standing to contest search of premises which revealed cocaine and items used in manufacture of cocaine; there was no indication that person who invited guest onto premises was lawful owner of home, guest was not given key to home to facilitate reentry, guest had no right or power to exclude others from place, and use of premises to manufacture cocaine was neither hidden nor unclear to anyone who occupied premises. U.S.C.A. Const. Amend. 4.

U.S. v. Puliese, 671 F.Supp. 1353.

S.D.Fla. 1986. Sailor's right to exclude others from ship does not establish legitimate expectation of privacy, in that coast guard officer may board ship without permission to conduct safety and document search and gain access to all common areas of boat. U.S.C.A. Const. Amend. 4.

U.S. v. Marrero, 644 F.Supp. 570.

Neither captain nor crew member has legitimate expectation of privacy in area on boat subject to common access of those legally aboard vessel, including cargo holds, ice holds, and engine rooms. U.S.C.A. Const.Amend. 4.

U.S. v. Marrero, 644 F.Supp. 570.

S.D.Fla. 1984. Since passports remain government property, a defendant has no reasonable expectation of privacy in them. U.S.C.A. Const.Amend. 4.

U.S. v. Segall, 589 F.Supp. 856.

Defendants did not have legitimate expectation of privacy in their passports and therefore did not standing to contest admissibility of their passports on basis of the exclusionary rule. U.S.C.A. Const. Amend. 4.

U.S. v. Segall, 589 F.Supp. 856.

Fla. 2017. The reasonable expectation of privacy under the Fourth Amendment not only applies to the inside of a person's home, but to the curtilage of the home as well. U.S. Const. Amend. 4.

State v. Markus, 211 So.3d 894, rehearing denied 2017 WL 944231.

Fla. 2014. Defendant had subjective expectation of privacy in real time cell site location information (CSLI) regarding location of defendant's cellular telephone, as would support finding that police officers' use of CSLI to track defendant was a search falling under purview of Fourth Amendment, even if defendant knew or should have know that telephone gave off signals to enable service provider to detect telephone's location; simply knowing that telephone gave off locating signals to service provider did not mean that defendant consented to use of that location informa-

tion by third parties for unrelated purposes. U.S.C.A. Const.Amend. 4.

Tracey v. State, 152 So.3d 504, on remand 162 So.3d 217.

Expectation of privacy in real time cell site location information (CSLI) regarding location of cellular telephone was objectively reasonable, as would support finding that police officers' use of CSLI to track defendant was a search falling under purview of Fourth Amendment; significant portion of population relied on cellular telephones for email and other communications, electronic monitoring of a citizen's location could generate a comprehensive record of a person's public movements, and police officers' ability to accomplish such monitoring at relatively low cost could alter relationship between citizen and government in way that was inimical to democratic society. U.S.C.A. Const.Amend. 4.

Tracey v. State, 152 So.3d 504, on remand 162 So.3d 217.

The touchstone of Fourth Amendment analysis of a search is whether a person has a constitutionally-protected reasonable expectation of privacy, and in applying the test, the court examines whether the individual manifested a subjective expectation of privacy and whether society is willing to recognize that expectation as reasonable. U.S.C.A. Const.Amend. 4.

Tracey v. State, 152 So.3d 504, on remand 162 So.3d 217.

Fla. 2013. Under normal circumstances, individuals do not have any expectation of privacy for Fourth Amendment purposes while within police custody. U.S.C.A. Const.Amend. 4.

Davis v. State, 121 So.3d 462.

A citizen's right to privacy under the Fourth Amendment is determined by a two prong test: (1) whether the citizen had a subjective expectation of privacy; and (2) whether that expectation was one that society recognizes as reasonable. U.S.C.A. Const.Amend. 4.

Davis v. State, 121 So.3d 462.

Fla. 2013. Officer's seizure of suicide note from capital murder defendant's jail cell after defendant attempted suicide did not violate Fourth Amendment; defendant had been placed in a one-man cell with constant monitoring after he threatened family members of investigators, his cell was routinely searched, and he had no reasonable expectation of privacy within his cell. U.S.C.A. Const.Amend. 4.

> Bolin v. State, 117 So.3d 728, certiorari denied 134 S.Ct. 695, 187 L.Ed.2d 561.

To establish a Fourth Amendment violation, an individual must have a subjective expectation of privacy that society recognizes is reasonable. U.S.C.A. Const. Amend. 4.

> Bolin v. State, 117 So.3d 728, certiorari denied 134 S.Ct. 695, 187 L.Ed.2d 561.

Fla. 2011. Wherever an individual may harbor a reasonable expectation of privacy he is entitled to be free from unreasonable governmental intrusion. U.S.C.A. Const.Amend. 4.

> Jardines v. State, 73 So.3d 34, rehearing denied, certiorari granted in part 132 S.Ct. 995, 565 U.S. 1104, 181 L.Ed.2d 726, affirmed 133 S.Ct. 1409, 185 L.Ed.2d 495.

Fla. 2010. A person who claims the protection of the Fourth Amendment must have a legitimate expectation of privacy in the invaded place. U.S.C.A. Const.Amend. 4.

> Caraballo v. State, 39 So.3d 1234.

Fla. 2009. In evaluating conduct pursuant to a valid search warrant, the fact that a container is locked does not create any greater expectation of privacy in its contents than the limited privacy expectation that exists in the rest of the premises. U.S.C.A. Const.Amend. 5.

> Jackson v. State, 18 So.3d 1016, certiorari denied 130 S.Ct. 1144, 558 U.S. 1151, 175 L.Ed.2d 979, postconviction relief denied 2012 WL 10716486, affirmed 127 So.3d 447, habeas corpus denied 127 So.3d 447.

There is no reasonable expectation of privacy in a police vehicle or in a telephone communication from jail during which warnings are issued; therefore, any interception of conversations that occur there would not be prohibited by the Flori-

da wiretapping act. U.S.C.A. Const. Amend. 4; West's F.S.A. § 943.01 et seq.

> Jackson v. State, 18 So.3d 1016, certiorari denied 130 S.Ct. 1144, 558 U.S. 1151, 175 L.Ed.2d 979, postconviction relief denied 2012 WL 10716486, affirmed 127 So.3d 447, habeas corpus denied 127 So.3d 447.

Fla. 1996. Person in custody in back of police car has no right of privacy.

> Farina v. State, 679 So.2d 1151, rehearing denied, appeal after remand 801 So.2d 44, rehearing denied, certiorari denied 122 S.Ct. 2369, 536 U.S. 910, 153 L.Ed.2d 189, denial of post-conviction relief affirmed 992 So.2d 819, rehearing denied, habeas corpus denied 2012 WL 1016723, denial of post-conviction relief affirmed 937 So.2d 612, rehearing denied, certiorari denied 127 S.Ct. 1153, 549 U.S. 1183, 166 L.Ed.2d 999, habeas corpus denied 2012 WL 1016723.

Fla. 1994. In order to challenge search, defendant must demonstrate that he or she had reasonable expectation of privacy in premises or property searched. U.S.C.A. Const.Amend. 4; West's F.S.A. Const. Art. 1, § 12.

> Jones v. State, 648 So.2d 669, rehearing denied, certiorari denied 115 S.Ct. 2588, 515 U.S. 1147, 132 L.Ed.2d 836, post-conviction relief denied 2005 WL 6932251, affirmed 998 So.2d 573, revised on rehearing, post-conviction relief denied 2005 WL 6932252, affirmed 998 So.2d 573, revised on rehearing, and revised on rehearing, habeas corpus denied 998 So.2d 573, revised on rehearing, and revised on rehearing, and revised on rehearing, post-conviction relief denied 2009 WL 9047495, affirmed 53 So.3d 230, rehearing denied, post-conviction relief denied 2011 WL 10483396, affirmed 141 So.3d 132, rehearing denied, certiorari denied 133 S.Ct. 661, 184 L.Ed.2d 471, habeas corpus denied 2013 WL 5504371, affirmed 834 F.3d 1299.

Fla. 1994. Fourth Amendment right to privacy is measured by two-part test: person must have subjective expectation of

---

† This Case was not selected for publication in the National Reporter System
For legislative history of cited statutes, see Florida Statutes Annotated

privacy; and expectation must be one that society recognizes as reasonable. U.S.C.A. Const.Amend. 4.

State v. Smith, 641 So.2d 849.

Motorist in rear of police vehicle for safety and comfort reasons while consensual search of motorist's automobile was conducted had no reasonable expectation of privacy under State Constitution, even though motorist was neither under arrest nor under an articulable suspicion, and, thus, tape recorded conversation between motorist and companion was admissible. West's F.S.A. Const. Art. 1, § 12.

State v. Smith, 641 So.2d 849.

Statute making it a crime to willfully intercept oral communications was not violated when conversation between motorist and companion sitting in rear of police vehicle for safety and comfort reasons during consensual search of automobile were recorded; motorist had no reasonable expectation of privacy in police car. West's F.S.A. § 934.03.

State v. Smith, 641 So.2d 849.

For oral conversation to be protected under statute making it a crime to willfully intercept oral communications, speaker must have actual subjective expectation of privacy, along with societal recognition that expectation is reasonable. West's F.S.A. § 934.02(2).

State v. Smith, 641 So.2d 849.

Fla. 1993. Defendant had no reasonable expectation of privacy in garage, so that search of garage, which revealed bottle of poison in work bench drawer, was not unlawful, even though defendant commented about returning to garage for cleaning after he moved from house; defendant personally supervised movers, specifically identifying items to be left behind, bottle was one of items left behind, undercover agent entered into oral rental agreement with defendant, rental agreement contained no reservations concerning agent's occupancy, defendant and agent discussed use of garage for woodworking purposes, agent was shown interior of garage, defendant never returned to property, and defendant told movers that what was left behind in garage was trash.

Trepal v. State, 621 So.2d 1361, certiorari denied 114 S.Ct. 892, 510 U.S. 1077, 127 L.Ed.2d 85, habeas corpus denied 846 So.2d 405, re-

hearing denied, certiorari denied 124 S.Ct. 412, 540 U.S. 958, 157 L.Ed.2d 295, motion to reopen denied 898 So.2d 83, rehearing denied, habeas corpus denied 898 So.2d 83, rehearing denied, and rehearing denied, denial of habeas corpus affirmed 684 F.3d 1088, rehearing and rehearing denied 485 Fed.Appx. 428, certiorari denied 133 S.Ct. 1598, 185 L.Ed.2d 592.

Fla. 1989. There is well-established privacy interest in luggage one carries during travels, for purposes of state and federal protections against searches and seizures. U.S.C.A. Const.Amend. 4; West's F.S.A. Const. Art. 1, § 12.

Bostick v. State, 554 So.2d 1153, certiorari granted 111 S.Ct. 241, 498 U.S. 894, 112 L.Ed.2d 201, reversed 111 S.Ct. 2382, 501 U.S. 429, 115 L.Ed.2d 389, on remand 593 So.2d 494.

Fla. 1984. Common authority of third person over premises to be searched or effects sought to be inspected to justify consent to search by third party is determined by suspect's reasonable expectation of privacy in area, whether others generally had access to area, or whether objects searched were personal effects of suspect not subject to consent. U.S.C.A. Const. Amend. 4.

Preston v. State, 444 So.2d 939, vacated 564 So.2d 120, appeal after remand 607 So.2d 404, certiorari denied 113 S.Ct. 1619, 507 U.S. 999, 123 L.Ed.2d 178, denial of post-conviction relief affirmed 970 So.2d 789, rehearing denied, habeas corpus denied 2012 WL 1549529, affirmed 785 F.3d 449.

Defendant had no reasonable expectation of privacy in items seized from his room pursuant to his mother's alleged consent to search, where defendant took no precaution to lock door of his room before search, nor instruct his mother not to let anyone enter room, nor otherwise exhibit expectation of privacy, and defendant was obviously aware of his mother's access to particular items seized as well as anything within regular scope of her cleaning activities. U.S.C.A. Const. Amend. 4.

> Preston v. State, 444 So.2d 939, vacated 564 So.2d 120, appeal after remand 607 So.2d 404, certiorari denied 113 S.Ct. 1619, 507 U.S. 999, 123 L.Ed.2d 178, denial of post-conviction relief affirmed 970 So.2d 789, rehearing denied, habeas corpus denied 2012 WL 1549529, affirmed 785 F.3d 449.

Fla. 1983. After person allows his personal effects to be taken into custody by police and inventoried, any privacy interest previously attached thereto is dissipated.

> Lightbourne v. State, 438 So.2d 380, certiorari denied 104 S.Ct. 1330, 465 U.S. 1051, 79 L.Ed.2d 725, denial of post-conviction relief reversed in part 549 So.2d 1364, certiorari denied 110 S.Ct. 1505, 494 U.S. 1039, 108 L.Ed.2d 640, denial of post-conviction relief affirmed 644 So.2d 54, rehearing denied, certiorari denied 115 S.Ct. 1406, 514 U.S. 1038, 131 L.Ed.2d 292, denial of post-conviction relief remanded 742 So.2d 238, appeal after remand 841 So.2d 431, rehearing denied, certiorari denied 124 S.Ct. 533, 540 U.S. 1006, 157 L.Ed.2d 412, habeas corpus denied 889 So.2d 71, rehearing denied, certiorari denied 125 S.Ct. 2917, 545 U.S. 1120, 162 L.Ed.2d 305, denial of post-conviction relief affirmed 956 So.2d 456, denial of post-conviction relief affirmed 969 So.2d 326, rehearing denied, certiorari denied 128 S.Ct. 2485, 553 U.S. 1059, 171 L.Ed.2d 777.

Fla. 1982. Citizen's expectation of privacy is diminished when participating in specific types of regulated activity.

> State v. Casal, 410 So.2d 152, on remand 411 So.2d 1040, certiorari granted 103 S.Ct. 50, 459 U.S. 821, 74 L.Ed.2d 56, certiorari dismissed 103 S.Ct. 3100, 462 U.S. 637, 77 L.Ed.2d 277.

Fla. 1981. Fact that property was not only fenced and locked, but was also surrounded by dike and was posted evidenced expectation of privacy within purview of Fourth Amendment guarantee of freedom from unreasonable searches and seizures. U.S.C.A.Const. Amend. 4.

> State v. Brady, 406 So.2d 1093, certiorari granted 102 S.Ct. 2266, 456 U.S. 988, 73 L.Ed.2d 1282, vacated in part, certiorari dismissed in part 104 S.Ct. 2380, 467 U.S. 1201, 81 L.Ed.2d 339, on remand 466 So.2d 1064, on remand Eckard v. Trowbridge, 483 So.2d 450.

Landowner's expectation of privacy was reasonable in light of fact that land was fenced, locked, surrounded by a dike and posted and that arresting authorities, after crossing dike and fences, had to traverse several hundred yards of field in order to reach vantage point from which they could observe activity. U.S.C.A.Const. Amend. 4.

> State v. Brady, 406 So.2d 1093, certiorari granted 102 S.Ct. 2266, 456 U.S. 988, 73 L.Ed.2d 1282, vacated in part, certiorari dismissed in part 104 S.Ct. 2380, 467 U.S. 1201, 81 L.Ed.2d 339, on remand 466 So.2d 1064, on remand Eckard v. Trowbridge, 483 So.2d 450.

Fla. 1981. To establish Fourth Amendment violation, defendant was required to establish reasonable expectation of privacy to be free from particular intrusion involved, and standard of reasonableness was an objective one. U.S.C.A.Const. Amend. 4; West's F.S.A.Const. art. 1, § 12.

> Wells v. State, 402 So.2d 402.

Fla. 1981. One can only expect to be free from intrusion where there is reasonable expectation of privacy.

> Clark v. State, 395 So.2d 525.

Fla. 1980. In order for defendant to claim that his Fourth Amendment rights were violated, he must first establish that he had a reasonable expectation of privacy to be free from this particular intrusion by the detective. U.S.C.A.Const. Amend. 4.

> Shapiro v. State, 390 So.2d 344, certiorari denied 101 S.Ct. 1519, 450 U.S. 982, 67 L.Ed.2d 818.

A reasonable expectation of privacy under a given set of circumstances depends not only upon one's actual subjective expectation of privacy but also upon whether society is prepared to recognize this expectation as reasonable. U.S.C.A.Const. Amend. 4.

> Shapiro v. State, 390 So.2d 344, certiorari denied 101 S.Ct. 1519, 450 U.S. 982, 67 L.Ed.2d 818.

Fla. 1980. Person's expectations of privacy in area searched will be recognized as legitimate if that person has exhibited actual, subjective expectation of privacy, and such expectation is one that society is prepared to recognize as reasonable. U.S.C.A.Const. Amends. 4, 14, 14, § 1; West's F.S.A.Const. art. 1, § 12.

> Norman v. State, 379 So.2d 643.

Fla.App. 1 Dist. 2016. A legitimate expectation of privacy in the area searched or the item seized consists of both a subjective expectation and an objectively reasonable expectation, as determined by societal standards. U.S.C.A. Const.Amend. 4.

> State v. Williams, 184 So.3d 1205, rehearing denied.

A legitimate expectation of privacy in the area searched or the item seized is not created by a mere ownership or financial interest in the item seized. U.S.C.A. Const.Amend. 4.

> State v. Williams, 184 So.3d 1205, rehearing denied.

Whether an individual possesses a constitutionally protected privacy interest in the area searched or the item seized depends upon the totality of circumstances. U.S.C.A. Const.Amend. 4.

> State v. Williams, 184 So.3d 1205, rehearing denied.

Fla.App. 1 Dist. 2015. Defendant had reasonable expectation to privacy in his real-time cell phone location data. U.S.C.A. Const.Amend. 4.

> Herring v. State, 168 So.3d 240, rehearing denied, review dismissed 173 So.3d 966.

Fla.App. 1 Dist. 2014. In order to claim that Fourth Amendment rights were violated, one must first establish a reasonable expectation of privacy to be free from a particular intrusion by the police. U.S.C.A. Const.Amend. 4.

> Cooper v. State, 162 So.3d 15, rehearing denied.

A reasonable expectation of privacy under a given set of circumstances depends not only upon one's actual subjective expectation of privacy but also upon whether society is prepared to recognize this expectation as reasonable. U.S.C.A. Const.Amend. 4.

> Cooper v. State, 162 So.3d 15, rehearing denied.

Fla.App. 1 Dist. 2013. Under the Fourth Amendment, overnight houseguests have a legitimate expectation of privacy even in temporary quarters. U.S.C.A. Const.Amend. 4.

> Thomas v. State, 127 So.3d 658, appeal after new trial 207 So.3d 928.

Fla.App. 1 Dist. 2013. People have an expectation of privacy in their homes that society recognizes as reasonable, for Fourth Amendment purposes; indeed, this expectation exists even for overnight guests in a home. U.S.C.A. Const.Amend. 4.

> Powell v. State, 120 So.3d 577, on rehearing.

The Fourth Amendment grants explicit protection to people to be secure in their houses so they may retreat therein and exclude others. U.S.C.A. Const.Amend. 4.

> Powell v. State, 120 So.3d 577, on rehearing.

Fla.App. 1 Dist. 2010. Defendant had a reasonable expectation of privacy, for Fourth Amendment purposes, in package that listed his last name and address, but was mistakenly delivered to another individual's residence. U.S.C.A. Const. Amend. 4.

> Armstrong v. State, 46 So.3d 589, review denied 44 So.3d 581.

Fla.App. 1 Dist. 2008. The application of the Fourth Amendment depends on whether the person invoking its protection can claim a justifiable, a reasonable, or a legitimate expectation of privacy that has been invaded by government action. U.S.C.A. Const.Amend. 4.

> State v. Butler, 1 So.3d 242, rehearing denied.

Defendant, who allegedly suffered from Munchausen syndrome by proxy which was disorder whereby defendant factitiously induced illness in child to draw attention to herself, did not have reasonable expectation of privacy when she was in her child's hospital room, and thus, the state action, namely court's broad delegation to hospital staff of the power to conduct video surveillance, together with court's authorization for the State to take immediate custody of child if surveillance showed he was in danger, did not amount to a search for Fourth Amendment purposes; even though defendant did not know about surveillance, she would have expected that efforts to interrupt child's breathing would have triggered medical response, and she could not have reasonably expected privacy in her actions affecting the health and well-being of a heavily monitored patient. U.S.C.A. Const. Amend. 4.

State v. Butler, 1 So.3d 242, rehearing denied.

Analysis of whether the individual's expectation of privacy is legally sufficient, for Fourth Amendment purposes, involves two discrete questions: (1) the first is whether the individual, by his conduct, has exhibited an actual subjective expectation of privacy; and (2) the second question is whether the individual's subjective expectation of privacy is one that society is prepared to recognize as reasonable. U.S.C.A. Const.Amend. 4.

State v. Butler, 1 So.3d 242, rehearing denied.

For Fourth Amendment purposes, patients admitted to private hospital rooms may reasonably expect that law enforcement will not search their belongings; the more private the treatment space, the more reasonable the patient's expectation of privacy with respect to official activity. U.S.C.A. Const.Amend. 4.

State v. Butler, 1 So.3d 242, rehearing denied.

Fla.App. 1 Dist. 2008. A legitimate expectation of privacy in the area searched or the item seized consists of both a subjective expectation and an objectively reasonable expectation, as determined by societal standards. U.S.C.A. Const.Amend. 4.

State v. Young, 974 So.2d 601, rehearing denied, review denied 988 So.2d 623, certiorari denied 129 S.Ct. 1002, 555 U.S. 1137, 173 L.Ed.2d 293.

The reasonableness of an expectation of privacy in a particular place or item to be searched or seized depends on context. U.S.C.A. Const.Amend. 4.

State v. Young, 974 So.2d 601, rehearing denied, review denied 988 So.2d 623, certiorari denied 129 S.Ct. 1002, 555 U.S. 1137, 173 L.Ed.2d 293.

Under the Fourth Amendment, the reasonableness of an employee's expectation of privacy in his or her office or the items contained therein depends on the operational realities of the workplace, not on legal possession or ownership. U.S.C.A. Const.Amend. 4.

State v. Young, 974 So.2d 601, rehearing denied, review denied 988 So.2d 623, certiorari denied 129 S.Ct. 1002, 555 U.S. 1137, 173 L.Ed.2d 293.

The likelihood that a person has an objectively reasonable expectation of privacy in an office setting is increased where the area or item searched is reserved for the defendant's exclusive personal use. U.S.C.A. Const.Amend. 4.

State v. Young, 974 So.2d 601, rehearing denied, review denied 988 So.2d 623, certiorari denied 129 S.Ct. 1002, 555 U.S. 1137, 173 L.Ed.2d 293.

Under the Fourth Amendment, many times an employee may have a legitimate expectation of privacy in his or her personal office and in personal items stored in a desk or file cabinet. U.S.C.A. Const. Amend. 4.

State v. Young, 974 So.2d 601, rehearing denied, review denied 988 So.2d 623, certiorari denied 129 S.Ct. 1002, 555 U.S. 1137, 173 L.Ed.2d 293.

Under the Fourth Amendment, evaluation of an expectation of privacy in a workplace computer involves unique considerations, but as with any other item in the workplace, the evaluation should focus on the operational realities of the workplace; relevant factors include whether the office has a policy regarding the employer's ability to inspect the computer, whether the computer is networked to other computers, and whether the employer, or a department within the agency, regularly

† This Case was not selected for publication in the National Reporter System
For legislative history of cited statutes, see Florida Statutes Annotated

monitors computer use. U.S.C.A. Const. Amend. 4.

> State v. Young, 974 So.2d 601, rehearing denied, review denied 988 So.2d 623, certiorari denied 129 S.Ct. 1002, 555 U.S. 1137, 173 L.Ed.2d 293.

Where an employer has a clear policy allowing others to monitor a workplace computer, an employee who uses the computer has no reasonable expectation of privacy in it under the Fourth Amendment; in the absence of such a policy, the legitimacy of an expectation of privacy depends on the other circumstances of the workplace. U.S.C.A. Const.Amend. 4.

> State v. Young, 974 So.2d 601, rehearing denied, review denied 988 So.2d 623, certiorari denied 129 S.Ct. 1002, 555 U.S. 1137, 173 L.Ed.2d 293.

If the circumstances of the workplace indicate that the employee has a legitimate expectation of privacy in the place searched or items seized in the workplace, and the employee has invoked the protection of the Fourth Amendment, the state must prove that the search and seizure was reasonable in order to use the evidence secured in the search and seizure at trial. U.S.C.A. Const.Amend. 4.

> State v. Young, 974 So.2d 601, rehearing denied, review denied 988 So.2d 623, certiorari denied 129 S.Ct. 1002, 555 U.S. 1137, 173 L.Ed.2d 293.

Under Fourth Amendment, pastor had legitimate expectation of privacy in his office and workplace computer, and thus police could not search office and computer without obtaining search warrant or valid consent to search, although church owned computer; pastor kept office locked when he was away, use of pastor's office by others was for limited purposes, pastor was sole regular user of computer, and computer was not networked to other computers. U.S.C.A. Const.Amend. 4.

> State v. Young, 974 So.2d 601, rehearing denied, review denied 988 So.2d 623, certiorari denied 129 S.Ct. 1002, 555 U.S. 1137, 173 L.Ed.2d 293.

Fla.App. 1 Dist. 2001. The Fourth Amendment protects only searches that intrude upon an expectation of privacy that society is prepared to recognize as reasonable. U.S.C.A. Const.Amend. 4.

> State v. Shaw, 784 So.2d 529.

Fla.App. 1 Dist. 1997. Defendant had no reasonable expectation of privacy in contents of briefcase that had been previously unlocked and opened by repossession company in inventorying contents of repossessed auto, and thus police did not violate defendant's Fourth Amendment rights in conducting warrantless examination of contents in same manner after repossession company delivered briefcase to police. U.S.C.A. Const.Amend. 4; West's F.S.A. Const. Art. 1, § 12.

> Warren v. State, 701 So.2d 404.

Fla.App. 1 Dist. 1992. Person's expectation of privacy in motorboat is less than same expectation of privacy in automobile. U.S.C.A. Const.Amend. 4.

> State v. Starkey, 605 So.2d 963.

Fla.App. 1 Dist. 1990. Court must evaluate totality of circumstances in determining whether defendant has a legitimate expectation of privacy in area searched; ownership of seized property is a factor to be considered.

> Roberson v. State, 566 So.2d 561, review denied 576 So.2d 291.

Fla.App. 1 Dist. 1985. Defendant had no legitimate expectation of privacy which society would recognize as reasonable, under either the Fourth Amendment or Florida Constitution [West's F.S.A. Const. Art. 1, § 12], with regard to numbers dialed into commercial telephone system; hence, use of pen register to ascertain numbers dialed from defendant's telephone did not constitute a "search" or require a warrant. U.S.C.A. Const.Amend. 4.

> Yarbrough v. State, 473 So.2d 766.

Fla.App. 1 Dist. 1983. Defendant had no reasonable expectation of privacy in the area underneath a mattress in a hospital emergency room bed, since medical personnel were constantly walking in and out of the emergency room and defendant could have expected to remain only a few hours in the room at most.

> Buchanan v. State, 432 So.2d 147.

Fla.App. 1 Dist. 1981. Question of whether defendant exhibited a reasonable expectation of privacy in a particular

---

† This Case was not selected for publication in the National Reporter System
For legislative history of cited statutes, see Florida Statutes Annotated

place, so that open view theory can justify search by one standing outside the area looking into it, involves the question of whether the defendant manifested an actual subjective expectation of privacy to personal effects within the area and whether his expectation was one which society is prepared to recognize as reasonable.

Raettig v. State, 406 So.2d 1273.

Fla.App. 1 Dist. 1981. Where defendant did not have a reasonable expectation of privacy as to jeans that were hanging on a clothesline in plain view from the street, he was not entitled to suppression of jeans at trial.

Shade v. State, 400 So.2d 850.

Fla.App. 1 Dist. 1976. Defendant did not have reasonable expectation of privacy in front porch of his home where delivery men and others were free to observe plants thereon.

State v. Detlefson, 335 So.2d 371.

Fla.App. 2 Dist. 2016. In determining whether the speaker's expectation of privacy in a recorded statement is reasonable, courts should examine the location of the conversation, the type of communication at issue, and the manner in which the communication was made. West's F.S.A. § 934.06.

State v. Caraballo, 198 So.3d 819.

Fla.App. 2 Dist. 2015. Defendant had reasonable expectation of privacy in his real property, such that police officers were required to obtain warrant or consent for search of property, where property was a semirural homestead, property was surrounded by a chain-link fence, property had a closed gate with a "no trespassing-violators will be prosecuted" sign and a "beware of dog" sign, and property had a mailbox accessible from outside the fence. U.S.C.A. Const.Amend. 4.

Robinson v. State, 164 So.3d 742.

Fla.App. 2 Dist. 2013. Defendant seeking to suppress evidence in prosecution for drug conspiracy and trafficking offenses had no reasonable expectation of privacy in fraudulent prescriptions. U.S.C.A. Const.Amend. 4.

State v. Mitchell, 124 So.3d 1046.

Fla.App. 2 Dist. 2011. A search violates a defendant's Fourth Amendment rights only if (1) a defendant demonstrates that he or she had an actual, subjective expectation of privacy in the property searched and (2) a defendant establishes that society would recognize that subjective expectation as objectively reasonable. U.S.C.A. Const. Amend. 4.

Nieminski v. State, 60 So.3d 521.

Defendant had a reasonable expectation of privacy, for Fourth Amendment purposes, in a house he had lived in for a month with his girlfriend and pets, and in which he was growing marijuana. U.S.C.A. Const. Amend. 4.

Nieminski v. State, 60 So.3d 521.

Fla.App. 2 Dist. 2011. The Fourth Amendment does not protect a defendant from a warrantless search of property that he stole, because regardless of whether he expects to maintain privacy in the contents of the stolen property, such an expectation is not one that society is prepared to accept as reasonable. U.S.C.A. Const. Amend. 4.

Hendley v. State, 58 So.3d 296, review denied 65 So.3d 515.

Fla.App. 2 Dist. 2007. Defendant had reasonable expectation of privacy in his hotel room for purposes of search; defendant testified without contradiction that he was guest at motel and had not been asked to leave. U.S.C.A. Const.Amend. 4.

Holloman v. State, 959 So.2d 403.

Fla.App. 2 Dist. 2006. Defendant did not have reasonable expectation of privacy in contents of computer that he did not lawfully possess and to which he asserted no property or possessory interest; defendant did not contest initial traffic stop and failed to establish reasonable expectation of privacy in stolen computer, although defendant stated at scene of traffic stop that his uncle gave him computer, defendant never introduced any evidence at suppression hearing, for example, how long he had used computer or whether he had any programs on it, and only officers testified at suppression hearing. U.S.C.A. Const.Amend. 4.

Hicks v. State, 929 So.2d 13.

Whether a defendant has a reasonable expectation of privacy is a threshold inquiry. U.S.C.A. Const.Amend. 4.

Hicks v. State, 929 So.2d 13.

A search violates a defendant's Fourth Amendment rights only if (1) a defendant demonstrates that he or she had an actual, subjective expectation of privacy in the property searched and (2) a defendant establishes that society would recognize that subjective expectation as objectively reasonable. U.S.C.A. Const.Amend. 4.

Hicks v. State, 929 So.2d 13.

Fla.App. 2 Dist. 2005. The home is where a person enjoys the highest expectation of privacy, for Fourth Amendment purposes. U.S.C.A. Const. Amend. 4.

Kutzorik v. State, 891 So.2d 645.

Fla.App. 2 Dist. 2004. To successfully claim the protection afforded by the Fourth Amendment, a defendant must demonstrate that he personally has an expectation of privacy in the place searched and that this expectation is reasonable; the expectation of privacy must originate from a source outside the Fourth Amendment, either by reference to concepts of real or personal property law or to understandings that are recognized and permitted by society. U.S.C.A. Const.Amend. 4.

State v. Washington, 884 So.2d 97.

Fla.App. 2 Dist. 2002. For Fourth Amendment purposes, a room in a boarding house is no different from a room in a motel, which is considered a private dwelling if the occupant is there legally, has paid or arranged to pay, and has not been asked to leave. U.S.C.A. Const.Amend. 4.

Burt v. State, 821 So.2d 437.

Fla.App. 2 Dist. 2000. Officer who knocked on defendant's motel room door to advise defendant that management had requested him to leave, and thereafter was invited in by defendant, acted lawfully and did not force defendant to abandon his property, and thus defendant had no legitimate expectation of privacy in vacated motel room and relinquished his interest in any property left there; after officer advised defendant that he was to leave motel, defendant packed his belongings, turned in his key, and left in his truck. U.S.C.A. Const.Amend. 4.

State v. Williams, 751 So.2d 170.

Fla.App. 2 Dist. 1999. While a resident does not have a reasonable expectation of privacy in the front door or front porch area of his or her residence because salesmen or visitors frequently appear there, a resident does have a reasonable expectation of privacy in his or her back yard because it is more private, and passers-by generally cannot see into the back yard. U.S.C.A. Const.Amend. 4.

Glass v. State, 736 So.2d 788.

Fla.App. 2 Dist. 1993. Person does not have reasonable expectation of privacy in his oral communications while in police vehicle when law enforcement authorities have founded suspicion that person is committing, has committed, or is about to commit crime. U.S.C.A. Const.Amend. 4.

State v. Fedorchenko, 630 So.2d 213.

Fla.App. 2 Dist. 1992. In determining whether person has constitutionally protected reasonable expectation of privacy, court will consider whether person manifested subjective expectation of privacy in object of challenged search, and whether society is prepared to recognize that expectation as reasonable. U.S.C.A. Const.Amend. 4.

State v. Sarantopoulos, 604 So.2d 551, review granted 618 So.2d 210, decision approved 629 So.2d 121.

Fla.App. 2 Dist. 1987. Neither actual practices nor legitimate regulation reduced hospital employee's expectation of privacy in pill bottle in his desk on premises of hospital operated by Department of Health and Rehabilitative Services, where he had not shared office or desk with anyone else during his 19–year tenure at hospital, and where hospital regulations specified standard of reasonable cause and outlined search procedures which were not observed in search by government investigator and security guard.

Bateman v. State, 513 So.2d 1101.

Fla.App. 2 Dist. 1986. Defendant had reasonable expectation to privacy in second floor balcony surrounded by masonry walls.

Hartwell v. State, 500 So.2d 640.

Fla.App. 2 Dist. 1984. For purposes of the Fourth Amendment, a "reasonable expectation of privacy" exists if individual had exhibited an actual, subjective expectation of privacy which society is prepared to recognize as reasonable. U.S.C.A. Const.Amend. 4.

Randall v. State, 458 So.2d 822.

Fla.App. 2 Dist. 1978. Standard by which applicability of Fourth Amendment is determined is whether evidence at issue was seized from a zone clothed by a reasonable expectation of privacy into which government could not reasonably intrude to conduct a search or seizure. U.S.C.A.Const. Amend. 4.

Morsman v. State, 360 So.2d 137, writ dismissed 394 So.2d 408, certiorari denied 101 S.Ct. 3066, 452 U.S. 930, 69 L.Ed.2d 431.

Fla.App. 2 Dist. 1975. Defendants who were sitting on couch on porch of residence and who were observed by police officer on the street to be handling jewelry had no reasonable expectation of privacy, and officers by walking to the porch to investigate did not violate defendants' Fourth Amendment rights. U.S.C.A.Const. Amend. 4.

State v. Belcher, 317 So.2d 842.

Fla.App. 3 Dist. 2016. In determining whether a defendant's expectation of privacy is reasonable under the Fourth Amendment, courts employ an objective standard. U.S.C.A. Const.Amend. 4.

Strawder v. State, 185 So.3d 543, rehearing denied, review denied 2016 WL 4440970.

Fla.App. 3 Dist. 2014. A search violates an individual's Fourth Amendment rights only if: (1) a defendant demonstrates that he or she had an actual, subjective expectation of privacy in the property searched; and (2) a defendant establishes that society would recognize that subjective expectation as objectively reasonable. U.S.C.A. Const. Amend. 4.

Brown v. State, 152 So.3d 619, rehearing denied, review denied 168 So.3d 228, appeal after remand 210 So.3d 61.

Fla.App. 3 Dist. 2014. One does not harbor an expectation of privacy where salesmen or visitors may appear. U.S.C.A. Const.Amend. 4.

State v. Ojeda, 147 So.3d 53.

Fla.App. 3 Dist. 2007. The Fourth Amendment does not protect a defendant from a warrantless search of property that he stole, because regardless of whether he expects to maintain privacy in the contents of the stolen property, such an expectation is not one that society is prepared to accept as reasonable. U.S.C.A. Const. Amend. 4.

State v. Lennon, 963 So.2d 765, rehearing and rehearing denied, review denied 978 So.2d 160.

Fla.App. 3 Dist. 2001. Defendant did not have reasonable expectation of privacy in police interview room where his statement was videotaped without his knowledge.

Bell v. State, 802 So.2d 485, cause dismissed 828 So.2d 384, rehearing denied.

Fla.App. 3 Dist. 1986. An invited guest has reasonable expectation of privacy in home while physically on premises at invitation of home dweller. U.S.C.A. Const. Amend. 4.

State v. Suco, 502 So.2d 446, decision approved 521 So.2d 1100.

Fla.App. 3 Dist. 1982. An individual who lawfully possesses or controls premises searched has an expectation of privacy in the premises even though he is absent from the premises when the search occurs; this legitimate expectation of privacy in the premises does not evaporate merely because the right to exclude others, the very heart of any legitimate expectation of privacy in premises, is a shared right.

State v. Barrowclough, 416 So.2d 47.

Fla.App. 3 Dist. 1981. In order to establish zone of privacy upon which government may not intrude without first obtaining search warrant, person must show actual expectation of privacy in area in question and that such expectation is in area that society is prepared to recognize as reasonable. U.S.C.A.Const. Amend. 4.

State v. Parker, 399 So.2d 24, review denied 408 So.2d 1095.

Fla.App. 3 Dist. 1979. For purposes of state constitutional provision that right to be secure against the unreasonable interception of private communications shall not be violated, it is per se "unreasonable" for government agents to intercept private communications by electronic means without first obtaining a valid intercept warrant if under the circumstances it would have been practicable for the agents to

† This Case was not selected for publication in the National Reporter System
For legislative history of cited statutes, see Florida Statutes Annotated

have obtained such a warrant. West's F.S.A.Const. art. 1, § 12.

   Sarmiento v. State, 371 So.2d 1047, decision approved 397 So.2d 643.

Fla.App. 3 Dist. 1977. Defendant had no right of possession or occupation of room adjacent to his hotel room, and no expectation of privacy therein, and officers by occupying such adjacent vacant room did not invade his privacy.

   Brant v. State, 349 So.2d 674.

Fla.App. 4 Dist. 2016. For the purpose of the Fourth Amendment, a legitimate expectation of privacy consists of both a subjective expectation and an objectively reasonable expectation, as determined by societal standards. U.S.C.A. Const.Amend. 4.

   Strachan v. State, 199 So.3d 1022.

Fla.App. 4 Dist. 2014. Defendant had no expectation of privacy when in custody at the police station, and thus he could not challenge admission of recording of a telephone conversation between himself and his mother at the police station; police detectives never made any assurances to defendant that his calls would be made in private and he knew he was being recorded, and defendant never requested privacy during the conversation and allowed a detective to be present in the room for at least portions of the conversation.

   Davis v. State, 151 So.3d 4.

Individuals do not have an expectation of privacy while within police custody, unless police officers deliberately foster an expectation of privacy in the inmate's conversation especially where the obvious purpose was to circumvent a defendant's assertion of the right to remain silent. U.S.C.A. Const.Amend. 5.

   Davis v. State, 151 So.3d 4.

Fla.App. 4 Dist. 2013. Historical cell phone site information was not content-based, and because defendant had no expectation of privacy in those records, they were admissible at his trial for three charged robberies, even though the records were obtained without a warrant in violation of statutory provision that required notice of disclosure of customer communications or records; the historical records disclosed only the defendant's past locations and did not pinpoint his current

location in a private area, as required to implicate Fourth Amendment protections. U.S.C.A. Const.Amend. 4; West's F.S.A. § 934.23.

   Johnson v. State, 110 So.3d 954, review denied 163 So.3d 510, review denied 173 So.3d 963.

Fla.App. 4 Dist. 2012. For Fourth Amendment analysis, it is the expectation of privacy that is controlling. U.S.C.A. Const.Amend. 4.

   B.L. v. State, 127 So.3d 552.

Fla.App. 4 Dist. 2012. A private home is an area where a person enjoys the highest reasonable expectation of privacy under the Fourth Amendment. U.S.C.A. Const.Amend. 4.

   Rowell v. State, 83 So.3d 990.

Fla.App. 4 Dist. 2012. For Fourth Amendment purposes, a legitimate expectation of privacy consists of both a subjective expectation and an objectively reasonable expectation, as determined by societal standards. U.S.C.A. Const.Amend. 4.

   Kelly v. State, 77 So.3d 818, rehearing denied, review denied 97 So.3d 823, denial of post-conviction relief affirmed 199 So.3d 277.

For Fourth Amendment purposes, the reasonableness of an expectation of privacy in a particular place or item depends on context. U.S.C.A. Const.Amend. 4.

   Kelly v. State, 77 So.3d 818, rehearing denied, review denied 97 So.3d 823, denial of post-conviction relief affirmed 199 So.3d 277.

For Fourth Amendment purposes, the reasonableness of an employee's expectation of privacy in his or her office or the items contained therein depends on the operational realities of the workplace, not on legal possession or ownership. U.S.C.A. Const.Amend. 4.

   Kelly v. State, 77 So.3d 818, rehearing denied, review denied 97 So.3d 823, denial of post-conviction relief affirmed 199 So.3d 277.

For Fourth Amendment purposes, the likelihood that a person has an objectively reasonable expectation of privacy in an office setting is increased where the area or item searched is reserved for the defendant's exclusive personal use. U.S.C.A. Const.Amend. 4.

> Kelly v. State, 77 So.3d 818, rehearing denied, review denied 97 So.3d 823, denial of post-conviction relief affirmed 199 So.3d 277.

Under the Fourth Amendment, many times an employee may have a legitimate expectation of privacy in his or her personal office and in personal items stored in a desk or file cabinet. U.S.C.A. Const. Amend. 4.

> Kelly v. State, 77 So.3d 818, rehearing denied, review denied 97 So.3d 823, denial of post-conviction relief affirmed 199 So.3d 277.

Employee had no legitimate expectation of privacy regarding his desk at work, and thus warrantless search of desk did not violate Fourth Amendment; employee shared office with another employee, other employees had full access to office, no locks were on desk, desk drawers were accessible to others who, upon at least some occasions, did look through desk, and employee's permission was not always sought in going through his desk. U.S.C.A. Const.Amend. 4.

> Kelly v. State, 77 So.3d 818, rehearing denied, review denied 97 So.3d 823, denial of post-conviction relief affirmed 199 So.3d 277.

Fla.App. 4 Dist. 2011. To invoke the Fourth Amendment, a criminal defendant must establish standing by demonstrating a legitimate expectation of privacy in the area searched or the item seized, and a legitimate expectation of privacy consists of both a subjective expectation and an objectively reasonable expectation, as determined by societal standards. U.S.C.A. Const.Amend. 4.

> Peraza v. State, 69 So.3d 338.

Fla.App. 4 Dist. 2010. A citizen's right to privacy is determined by a two prong test: 1) whether the citizen had a subjective expectation of privacy; and 2) whether that expectation was one that society recognizes as reasonable.

> Cox v. State, 26 So.3d 666, appeal after new trial 127 So.3d 561, review granted, quashed 133 So.3d 525, on remand 132 So.3d 956, appeal after remand 192 So.3d 581.

Fla.App. 4 Dist. 2008. A person in a closed stall in a public restroom is entitled to be free from unwarranted intrusion; however, this expectation gives way where two persons enter a stall together under circumstances reasonably indicating that they are doing drugs. U.S.C.A. Const. Amend. 4.

> State v. Powers, 991 So.2d 1040.

Fla.App. 4 Dist. 2008. Law enforcement officers did not violate defendant's Fourth Amendment right to privacy by recording him in interview room; when officers attempted an interview, defendant invoked his right to counsel and interview was terminated, defendant did not ask for privacy, and there was no suggestion that defendant had any privacy. U.S.C.A. Const.Amend. 4.

> Williams v. State, 982 So.2d 1190.

A citizen's right to privacy under the Fourth Amendment is determined by a two-prong test, which asks (1) whether the citizen had a subjective expectation of privacy and (2) whether that expectation was one that society recognizes as reasonable. U.S.C.A. Const.Amend. 4.

> Williams v. State, 982 So.2d 1190.

Fla.App. 4 Dist. 2006. Answers to questions of legality of searches under Fourth Amendment are highly situation-sensitive, because the situation provides the context necessary to determine whether an individual has a constitutionally protected reasonable expectation of privacy. U.S.C.A. Const.Amend. 4.

> State v. Rabb, 920 So.2d 1175, review denied 933 So.2d 522, certiorari denied 127 S.Ct. 665, 549 U.S. 1052, 166 L.Ed.2d 513.

Fla.App. 4 Dist. 2002. In considering whether one's Fourth Amendment rights have been violated, the analysis is whether that person has a constitutionally protected reasonable expectation of privacy. U.S.C.A. Const.Amend. 4.

> State v. Duhart, 810 So.2d 972, rehearing denied.

Fla.App. 4 Dist. 2000. Defendant had no reasonable expectation of privacy from observations of his roof from the adjoining property. U.S.C.A. Const.Amend. 4.

> State v. Havel, 756 So.2d 1067, on remand 2001 WL 36125689.

Fla.App. 4 Dist. 1999. Test for measurement of the Fourth Amendment right of privacy requires a determination of whether the individual had a subjective expectation of privacy and whether society recognizes that expectation as reasonable. U.S.C.A. Const.Amend. 4.

> Boyer v. State, 736 So.2d 64, rehearing denied.

Fla.App. 4 Dist. 1997. People may allow neighbors into kitchens within their homes without connoting thereby any general invitation to police. U.S.C.A. Const. Amend. 4.

> Titus v. State, 696 So.2d 1257, review granted 700 So.2d 687, decision approved 707 So.2d 706.

Absence of locks on entrances to residences does not erode constitutional protection against unreasonable searches and seizures. U.S.C.A. Const.Amend. 4.

> Titus v. State, 696 So.2d 1257, review granted 700 So.2d 687, decision approved 707 So.2d 706.

Fla.App. 4 Dist. 1996. Motel room was "dwelling," for Fourth Amendment purposes, where defendant lived in room. U.S.C.A. Const.Amend. 4.

> Levine v. State, 684 So.2d 903.

Fla.App. 4 Dist. 1993. Recording of defendant's conversation with friends as they sat in patrol car while police officer searched their vehicle constituted invasion of privacy, and thus, tape was inadmissible in trial on charges of possession of cocaine, where police officer asked defendant and friends to sit in patrol car for what appeared to be safety and comfort reasons, defendant was neither under arrest nor articulable suspicion at that time, and defendant did not request or authorize tape recording. West's F.S.A. §§ 934.03, 934.06.

> Barrett v. State, 618 So.2d 269, cause dismissed 623 So.2d 495.

Fla.App. 4 Dist. 1993. Tape recording of defendant's conversation while he sat in rear of police vehicle at time when he was neither under arrest nor under articulable suspicion was invasion of right of privacy. West's F.S.A. §§ 934.03, 934.06; U.S.C.A. Const.Amend. 4.

> Smith v. State, 616 So.2d 509, quashed 641 So.2d 849.

Fla.App. 4 Dist. 1993. Normally there is no expectation of privacy regarding defendants' oral communications in a police car.

> Springle v. State, 613 So.2d 65, review dismissed 626 So.2d 208.

Secretly recording defendants' conversation in backseat of police car violated defendants' reasonable expectation of privacy, where defendants were not under arrest and officers deliberately led them to believe that their conversation would be private. West's F.S.A. §§ 934.03, 934.06; West's F.S.A. Const. Art. 1, §§ 12, 23.

> Springle v. State, 613 So.2d 65, review dismissed 626 So.2d 208.

Fla.App. 4 Dist. 1990. Passenger lacked reasonable expectation of privacy in car and lacked standing to contest search and seizure of baggie on floor on passenger's side. U.S.C.A. Const.Amend. 4.

> State v. Fontana, 566 So.2d 937, jurisdiction accepted 576 So.2d 286, opinion approved 581 So.2d 585.

Fla.App. 4 Dist. 1990. The issue of a "reasonable" or "justified" expectation of privacy within protection against unreasonable searches and seizures turns on two requirements: subjective expectation of privacy and whether the expectation is one that society has prepared to recognize as reasonable. U.S.C.A. Const.Amend. 4.

> Cleveland v. State, 557 So.2d 959.

Fla.App. 4 Dist. 1982. In applying the Fourth Amendment, critical inquiry is whether a defendant had an expectation of privacy in area searched, and fact that one may be legitimately on the premises, while relevant to one's expectation of privacy, is not determinative of the issue. U.S.C.A. Const.Amend. 4.

> Sims v. State, 425 So.2d 563, petition for review denied 436 So.2d 100.

Fla.App. 4 Dist. 1980. For purposes of determining whether individual has legitimate expectation of privacy in area where search occurred, some locations give rise to greater and more reasonable expectation of privacy than others. U.S.C.A.Const. Amend. 4.

> State v. Schultz, 388 So.2d 1326.

Fla.App. 5 Dist. 2009. The Fourth Amendment protects people, not places,

---

† This Case was not selected for publication in the National Reporter System
For legislative history of cited statutes, see Florida Statutes Annotated

and only under circumstances where the person enjoys a reasonable expectation of privacy. U.S.C.A. Const.Amend. 4.

> Brown v. State, 24 So.3d 671, review denied 39 So.3d 1264, certiorari denied 134 S.Ct. 2730, 189 L.Ed.2d 771.

Fla.App. 5 Dist. 2009. Defendant did not exhibit a reasonable expectation of privacy in public restroom stall, and thus evidence of police officer's observations of defendant in stall were admissible in prosecution for lewd conduct, where defendant affirmatively invited officer's intrusion through his non-verbal invitations to engage in lewd conduct. U.S.C.A. Const. Amend. 4.

> State v. Halpin, 13 So.3d 75.

Fla.App. 5 Dist. 2008. Legal ownership is not a prerequisite for a legitimate expectation of privacy; even when a defendant does not own the property searched, he or she may nonetheless have a reasonable expectation of privacy by virtue of his or her relationship with that place. U.S.C.A. Const.Amend. 4.

> Evans v. State, 989 So.2d 1219.

Fla.App. 5 Dist. 2007. Fourth Amendment protects areas where a person has a constitutionally protected reasonable expectation of privacy. U.S.C.A. Const. Amend. 4.

> State v. E.D.R., 959 So.2d 1225.

Fla.App. 5 Dist. 2004. Persons convicted of crimes, or ones who have been arrested on probable cause, lose many rights to personal privacy under the Fourth Amendment, as well as probationers. U.S.C.A. Const.Amend. 4.

> Smalley v. State, 889 So.2d 100.

Fla.App. 5 Dist. 2003. While there are occasions where an overnight guest might have a legitimate expectation of privacy in someone else's home, one who is merely present with the consent of a homeowner generally may not claim that expectation. U.S.C.A. Const.Amend. 4.

> Hicks v. State, 852 So.2d 954.

Temporary visitors or short-term invitees are generally unable to advance a position that they had a reasonable expectation of privacy in someone else's home with success. U.S.C.A. Const.Amend. 4.

> Hicks v. State, 852 So.2d 954.

Whether a temporary visitor or short-term invitee had a legitimate expectation of privacy in someone else's home for Fourth Amendment purposes, is, in the final analysis, dependent on the totality of the circumstances. U.S.C.A. Const. Amend. 4.

> Hicks v. State, 852 So.2d 954.

Defendant had reasonable expectation of privacy in closed part of his backpack, located in home in which police officers conducted warrantless search, even though defendant was merely short-term invitee of resident of home. U.S.C.A. Const.Amend. 4.

> Hicks v. State, 852 So.2d 954.

Fla.App. 5 Dist. 2001. In order for the Fourth Amendment right to privacy to exist, the person must have a subjective expectation of privacy, and that expectation must be one that society recognizes as reasonable. U.S.C.A. Const.Amend. 4.

> Bedoya v. State, 779 So.2d 574, rehearing denied, review denied 797 So.2d 584.

A defendant does not have a reasonable expectation of privacy in a police interview room. U.S.C.A. Const.Amend. 4.

> Bedoya v. State, 779 So.2d 574, rehearing denied, review denied 797 So.2d 584.

Fla.App. 5 Dist. 1999. A government search which is prompted by a preceding private search and does not exceed the scope of the private search does not violate the Fourth Amendment because at that point the party's expectation of privacy has already been frustrated. U.S.C.A. Const. Amend. 4.

> State v. Olsen, 745 So.2d 454.

Fla.App. 5 Dist. 1999. Defendant and wife did not have reasonable expectation of privacy in conversation in police interview room, and thus, police officers' secret taping of conversation did not violate Fourth Amendment prohibition on unreasonable searches and seizures. U.S.C.A. Const.Amend. 4.

> Johnson v. State, 730 So.2d 368.

Listening to secret audiotape of conversation between defendant and wife in police interview room was permissible way of discovering location of firearm, and thus, suppression of firearm was not required. U.S.C.A. Const.Amend. 4.

Johnson v. State, 730 So.2d 368.

Fla.App. 5 Dist. 1995. Defendant had no expectation of privacy in friend's residence and friend had authority to consent to search of room in his residence that contained boxes that defendant had left there. U.S.C.A. Const.Amend. 4.

Velazquez v. State, 648 So.2d 302.

Fla.App. 5 Dist. 1994. Police officer did not have probable cause to believe crime was being committed or about to be committed, sufficient to sustain his warrantless peeking into toilet stall in public bathroom, and evidence that he observed defendant masturbating was required to be suppressed in criminal case charging display of sexual organs in public place in vulgar and indecent manner. U.S.C.A. Const.Amend. 4; West's F.S.A. § 800.03.

Ward v. State, 636 So.2d 68.

Fla.App. 5 Dist. 1984. Once person is taken into custody by law enforcement authorities, his right to privacy has been effectively diminished, and he has no reasonable expectation that his conversation will be private. U.S.C.A. Const.Amends. 4, 5.

DiGuilio v. State, 451 So.2d 487, approved and remanded 491 So.2d 1129.

No reasonable expectation of privacy exists while one is detained in rear seat of police vehicle, and communications therein are neither constitutionally nor statutorily protected. U.S.C.A. Const.Amends. 4, 5; West's F.S.A. §§ 943.01 et seq., 934.02(1).

DiGuilio v. State, 451 So.2d 487, approved and remanded 491 So.2d 1129.

☞27. —— **Curtilage or open fields; yards and outbuildings.**

U.S.Fla. 2013. The Fourth Amendment does not prevent all investigations conducted on private property, and an officer may, subject to the *Katz* "reasonable expectation of privacy" test, gather information in open fields, even if those fields are privately owned, because such fields are not enumerated in the Amendment's text. U.S.C.A. Const.Amend. 4.

Florida v. Jardines, 133 S.Ct. 1409, 185 L.Ed.2d 495.

The "curtilage" of a home, which is the area immediately surrounding and associated with the home, is part of the home itself for Fourth Amendment purposes. U.S.C.A. Const.Amend. 4.

Florida v. Jardines, 133 S.Ct. 1409, 185 L.Ed.2d 495.

The curtilage of a home is intimately linked to the home, both physically and psychologically, and is where privacy expectations are most heightened, for Fourth Amendment purposes. U.S.C.A. Const. Amend. 4.

Florida v. Jardines, 133 S.Ct. 1409, 185 L.Ed.2d 495.

A police officer not armed with a warrant may approach a home and knock, precisely because that is no more than any private citizen might do. U.S.C.A. Const. Amend. 4.

Florida v. Jardines, 133 S.Ct. 1409, 185 L.Ed.2d 495.

C.A.11 (Fla.) 2011. Police officers can enter onto residential property, including portions that would be considered part of the curtilage for Fourth Amendment purposes, in order to carry out legitimate police business. U.S.C.A. Const.Amend. 4.

Coffin v. Brandau, 642 F.3d 999.

C.A.11 (Fla.) 2010. For Fourth Amendment purposes, a garage is not included within the unambiguous physical dimensions of an individual's home; rather, a garage enjoys the protections of the home only if it constitutes curtilage. U.S.C.A. Const.Amend. 4.

Coffin v. Brandau, 609 F.3d 1204, rehearing granted, opinion vacated 614 F.3d 1240, on rehearing 642 F.3d 999.

For Fourth Amendment purposes, "curtilage" is defined by reference to the factors that determine whether an individual reasonably may expect that an area immediately adjacent to the home will remain private. U.S.C.A. Const.Amend. 4.

Coffin v. Brandau, 609 F.3d 1204, rehearing granted, opinion vacated 614 F.3d 1240, on rehearing 642 F.3d 999.

Dunn factors used to assist in the task of defining the extent of a home's curtilage, for Fourth Amendment purposes, are: the proximity of the area claimed to be curtilage to the home, whether the area is included within an enclosure surrounding the home, the nature of the uses to which the area is put, and the steps taken by the resident to protect the area from observation by people passing by. U.S.C.A. Const.Amend. 4.

> Coffin v. Brandau, 609 F.3d 1204, rehearing granted, opinion vacated 614 F.3d 1240, on rehearing 642 F.3d 999.

C.A.11 (Fla.) 2006. The private property immediately adjacent to a home is entitled to the same protection against unreasonable search and seizure as the home itself. U.S.C.A. Const.Amend. 4.

> U.S. v. Taylor, 458 F.3d 1201.

Curtilage questions in search and seizure context should be resolved by considering the following factors: (1) the proximity of the area claimed to be curtilage to the home; (2) the nature of the uses to which the area is put; (3) whether the area is included within an enclosure surrounding the home; and (4) the steps the resident takes to protect the area from observation. U.S.C.A. Const.Amend. 4.

> U.S. v. Taylor, 458 F.3d 1201.

Pond on defendant's property, located approximately sixty yards away from the house and separated by a barn and another structure, was not within the curtilage of defendant's home, such that defendant had a reasonable expectation of privacy in the pond area for purposes of Fourth Amendment protection; pond was not being used in connection with any intimate activity of the home, there was no fencing around the house and pond, and the pond area was an unoccupied and undeveloped area outside of the immediate domestic establishment. U.S.C.A. Const.Amend. 4.

> U.S. v. Taylor, 458 F.3d 1201.

There is no reasonable expectation of privacy, for Fourth Amendment purposes, for activities conducted out of doors or in open fields, except in the areas shielded from view and immediately surrounding the home. U.S.C.A. Const.Amend. 4.

> U.S. v. Taylor, 458 F.3d 1201.

The Fourth Amendment does not extend protection to open fields, which includes any unoccupied or undeveloped area beyond the immediate domestic establishment of the home. U.S.C.A. Const. Amend. 4.

> U.S. v. Taylor, 458 F.3d 1201.

A perimeter fence around property does not create a constitutionally protected interest in all the open fields on the property under the Fourth Amendment. U.S.C.A. Const.Amend. 4.

> U.S. v. Taylor, 458 F.3d 1201.

† C.A.11 (Fla.) 2005. Even if area at back of dwelling in which law enforcement agent saw items in plain view was part of curtilage of dwelling, agent did not violate defendant's reasonable expectation of privacy by approaching front door of dwelling in an attempt to speak with defendant, and once there, proceeding around to back door as sign on front door directed visitors to do. U.S.C.A. Const. Amend. 4.

> U.S. v. Carroll, 144 Fed.Appx. 3, rehearing and rehearing denied 159 Fed.Appx. 986, certiorari denied 126 S.Ct. 782, 546 U.S. 1052, 163 L.Ed.2d 606, post-conviction relief denied 2007 WL 1299334, motion to reopen denied 2012 WL 1142515.

C.A.11 (Fla.) 1995. Whether Fourth Amendment protects privacy interests within curtilage of dwelling house depends on proximity of area claimed to be curtilage to home, nature of uses to which area is put, whether area is included within enclosure surrounding home, and steps resident takes to protect area from observation. U.S.C.A. Const.Amend. 4.

> U.S. v. Hall, 47 F.3d 1091, certiorari denied 116 S.Ct. 71, 516 U.S. 816, 133 L.Ed.2d 31.

C.A.11 (Fla.) 1991. What is curtilage, and thus within realm of legitimate privacy expectations, is question of fact. U.S.C.A. Const.Amend. 4.

> U.S. v. Hatch, 931 F.2d 1478, certiorari denied 112 S.Ct. 235, 502 U.S. 883, 116 L.Ed.2d 191.

Fact that defendant had erected perimeter fence surrounding his 300–acre tract of land did not create constitutionally protected privacy interest in open fields on his property. U.S.C.A. Const.Amend. 4.

> U.S. v. Hatch, 931 F.2d 1478, certiorari denied 112 S.Ct. 235, 502 U.S. 883, 116 L.Ed.2d 191.

C.A.11 (Fla.) 1990. A dwelling, together with its surrounding curtilage, is not always a sanctuary from law enforcement activity, even if police act without a warrant. U.S.C.A. Const.Amend. 4.

> U.S. v. Emmens, 893 F.2d 1292, certiorari denied 111 S.Ct. 48, 498 U.S. 812, 112 L.Ed.2d 24.

C.A.5 (Fla.) 1975. Where government agent trespassed upon defendants' rural property and peered into hole in shed on property for sole purpose of securing evidence of crime which would support later issuance of search warrant, agent's action was unlawful search and seizure which did not fall within "open fields" exception to warrant requirement. U.S.C.A.Const. Amend. 4.

> U.S. v. Holmes, 521 F.2d 859, rehearing granted 525 F.2d 1364, on rehearing 537 F.2d 227.

C.A.5 (Fla.) 1974. When officers physically invade the yard, courtyard or other piece of ground included within the fence surrounding dwelling house, either to seize evidence or to obtain a view of illegal activities, such invasion is violation of the Fourth Amendment. U.S.C.A.Const. Amend. 4.

> Fixel v. Wainwright, 492 F.2d 480.

Whether police officer was physically encroaching on enclosed yard behind four-unit apartment building in which defendant lived when officer made his initial observations of suspicious activity of defendant who was frequently traveling from his apartment to a shaving kit concealed in back yard, officer unlawfully encroached on constitutionally protected area when he entered back yard without a warrant and seized the shaving kit and searched it as defendant was being arrested by another officer in his apartment. U.S.C.A.Const. Amend. 4.

> Fixel v. Wainwright, 492 F.2d 480.

Where enclosed back yard of property containing four-unit apartment building in which defendant lived was not a common passageway normally used by building's tenants for gaining access to apartments or an area open as a corridor to salesmen or other businessmen who might approach tenants in course of trade, the back yard, which was completely removed from the street and surrounded by a chain link fence, was entitled to protection of Fourth Amendment. U.S.C.A.Const. Amend. 4.

> Fixel v. Wainwright, 492 F.2d 480.

C.A.5 (Fla.) 1972. No application of the "open field doctrine" could sustain the search of the interior of a locked, windowless building, in the nighttime, by federal agents climbing a ladder, thrusting their heads into a hole in the eaves, and scrutinizing the interior with the aid of a flashlight.

> U.S. v. Resnick, 455 F.2d 1127, rehearing denied 459 F.2d 1390, certiorari denied Carlton v. U.S., 93 S.Ct. 121, 409 U.S. 875, 34 L.Ed.2d 127, appeal after remand 483 F.2d 354, certiorari denied 94 S.Ct. 370, 414 U.S. 1008, 38 L.Ed.2d 246.

C.A.5 (Fla.) 1962. Trespass upon ground surrounding building does not constitute illegal search as protection of Fourth Amendment does not extend to grounds. U.S.C.A.Const. Amend. 4.

> Monnette v. U.S., 299 F.2d 847.

C.A.5 (Fla.) 1958. Outbuilding which was approximately 150 to 180 feet from nearest residence, separated by a fence and a gate, was not a part of or located within the curtilage of the residence, even if the residence were occupied, and search of the outbuilding was not a search of a dwelling.

> Brock v. U.S., 256 F.2d 55.

C.A.5 (Fla.) 1957. Where chicken house containing still was about 150 feet from house and separated from it by two fences, chicken house, enclosed area in which it is situated, and large pasture area still further removed from house, were not part of owner's curtilage and were not within constitutional protection against unreasonable search and seizure and search warrant based upon information obtained by use of binoculars by agent, who was stationed in pasture area, was legal. U.S.C.A.Const. Amend. 4.

> Hodges v. U.S., 243 F.2d 281.

Special protection accorded by Fourth Amendment to people in their persons, houses, papers and effects does not extend to open fields. U.S.C.A.Const. Amend. 4.

Hodges v. U.S., 243 F.2d 281.

C.C.A.5 (Fla.) 1946. The amendment securing the people against unreasonable searches and seizures does not apply to inclosed or uninclosed grounds or open fields around their houses. U.S.C.A.Const. Amend. 4.

Martin v. U.S., 155 F.2d 503.

M.D.Fla. 2015. A person's home is at the core of the Fourth Amendment's protection against unreasonable searches and seizures; this protection extends to the curtilage or area immediately surrounding and associated with the house. U.S. Const. Amend. 4.

United States v. Holmes, 143 F.Supp.3d 1252.

Where officers without a warrant gather information in the curtilage of the house, they engage in an unreasonable search unless their conduct is explicitly or implicitly permitted by the homeowner. U.S. Const. Amend. 4.

United States v. Holmes, 143 F.Supp.3d 1252.

Law enforcement officers lacking a warrant may, like any other citizen, take advantage of the implied license to approach a home and knock. U.S. Const. Amend. 4.

United States v. Holmes, 143 F.Supp.3d 1252.

While officers need not avert their eyes in the course of conducting a lawful knock and talk, they may not exceed the scope of the implied license to approach a home's front door by conducting a search. U.S. Const. Amend. 4.

United States v. Holmes, 143 F.Supp.3d 1252.

The license granted to enter property to knock on a person's door is not unlimited; rather, it extends unless and until the homeowner provides express orders to the contrary. U.S. Const. Amend. 4.

United States v. Holmes, 143 F.Supp.3d 1252.

In determining the scope of the implied license to knock and talk, and there-fore whether a police officer's approach to the front door was permissible under the Fourth Amendment, courts ask whether a reasonable person could do as the police did; factors that may aid in the analysis include the appearance of the property, whether entry might cause a resident alarm, what ordinary visitors would be expected to do, and what a reasonably respectful citizen would be expected to do. U.S. Const. Amend. 4.

United States v. Holmes, 143 F.Supp.3d 1252.

A porch is typically considered part of the curtilage and, barring revocation of the implied license to enter, a porch may be entered to approach the front door to conduct a knock and talk. U.S. Const. Amend. 4.

United States v. Holmes, 143 F.Supp.3d 1252.

Defendant's porch was functionally and structurally different and distinct from his house, and thus officers could enter porch without warrant to conduct knock and talk, although porch shared roof with main house, where porch was entered through unlocked screen door, walls of porch were half screen and half lattice, porch was empty of furnishings, porch had porch light near main locked door into house, and house door had burglar-bars on it. U.S. Const. Amend. 4.

United States v. Holmes, 143 F.Supp.3d 1252.

A proper knock and talk does not violate a defendant's reasonable expectation of privacy because it is limited to areas impliedly open to the public. U.S. Const. Amend. 4.

United States v. Holmes, 143 F.Supp.3d 1252.

In the absence of another barrier, such as a fence and gate, "No Trespassing" signs do not, in and of themselves, withdraw the implied consent to conduct a knock and talk. U.S. Const. Amend. 4.

United States v. Holmes, 143 F.Supp.3d 1252.

Defendant, in placing "No Trespassing" sign on fence surrounding his property, did not do enough to revoke implied license for visitors to approach his front door, and thus police officers' warrantless knock and talk did not violate defendant's Fourth Amendment rights, where fence's gate was partially open. U.S. Const. Amend. 4.

> United States v. Holmes, 143 F.Supp.3d 1252.

M.D.Fla. 2014. In determining what constitutes curtilage in the search and seizure context, courts consider the proximity of the area claimed to be curtilage to the home, whether the area is included within an enclosure surrounding the home, the nature of the uses to which the area is put, and the steps taken by the resident to protect the area from observation by people passing by. U.S.C.A. Const.Amend. 4.

> Montanez v. Celaya, 49 F.Supp.3d 1010.

Police officers can enter private property, even the curtilage, to conduct legitimate police business or to go where the public would be expected to go; this includes walkways, driveways, and porches. U.S.C.A. Const.Amend. 4.

> Montanez v. Celaya, 49 F.Supp.3d 1010.

M.D.Fla. 2011. Barn was not within protected curtilage of defendant's home, for Fourth Amendment purposes, even though it was possible to exit front of house and arrive at barn's garage-style doors without crossing over or through continuous fence, where barn was approximately 20 yards from house, barn was largely surrounded by third fence such that area surrounding barn stood as distinct portion of defendant's property apart from house, individual exiting rear of house, or individual in immediate back yard of house, would not be able to access barn without crossing over or through that fence, and barn was used for housing horses. U.S.C.A. Const.Amend. 4.

> U.S. v. Garcia, 853 F.Supp.2d 1177, remanded 2013 WL 10509665, appeal after remand 556 Fed.Appx. 924, affirmed 556 Fed.Appx. 924.

Fourth Amendment protects house's curtilage from intrusion by law enforcement. U.S.C.A. Const.Amend. 4.

> U.S. v. Garcia, 853 F.Supp.2d 1177, remanded 2013 WL 10509665, appeal after remand 556 Fed.Appx. 924, affirmed 556 Fed.Appx. 924.

In defining extent of home's curtilage, for Fourth Amendment purposes, courts should consider: proximity of area claimed to be curtilage to home, whether area is included within enclosure surrounding home, nature of uses to which area is put, and steps taken by resident to protect area from observation by people passing by. U.S.C.A. Const.Amend. 4.

> U.S. v. Garcia, 853 F.Supp.2d 1177, remanded 2013 WL 10509665, appeal after remand 556 Fed.Appx. 924, affirmed 556 Fed.Appx. 924.

M.D.Fla. 2011. Screened-in lanai area in back of defendant's residence was either part of residence itself or included in curtilage of residence, and in either case was within protections provided by Fourth Amendment. U.S.C.A. Const. Amend. 4.

> U.S. v. Hill, 795 F.Supp.2d 1304.

Fourth Amendment protection extends to curtilage but not to open fields. U.S.C.A. Const.Amend. 4.

> U.S. v. Hill, 795 F.Supp.2d 1304.

To determine if an area is curtilage, and thus protected by Fourth Amendment, district court must determine whether an individual reasonably may expect that area in question should be treated as home itself. U.S.C.A. Const.Amend. 4.

> U.S. v. Hill, 795 F.Supp.2d 1304.

M.D.Fla. 2009. In addition to protecting privacy within house itself, Fourth Amendment also protects "curtilage" of house, that is, area immediately surrounding dwelling house. U.S.C.A. Const. Amend. 4.

> Swofford v. Eslinger, 671 F.Supp.2d 1289, affirmed 395 Fed.Appx. 559, rehearing and rehearing denied 409 Fed.Appx. 316, certiorari denied Morris v. Swofford, 131 S.Ct. 1053, 562 U.S. 1201, 178 L.Ed.2d 866.

An individual may not legitimately demand privacy for activities conducted out of doors in fields, except in area immediately surrounding the home. U.S.C.A. Const.Amend. 4.

> Swofford v. Eslinger, 671 F.Supp.2d 1289, affirmed 395 Fed.Appx. 559, rehearing and rehearing denied 409 Fed.Appx. 316, certiorari denied Morris v. Swofford, 131 S.Ct. 1053, 562 U.S. 1201, 178 L.Ed.2d 866.

Open fields surrounding a house are not protected under Fourth Amendment, and search of them need not be accompanied by warrant issued upon probable cause. U.S.C.A. Const.Amend. 4.

> Swofford v. Eslinger, 671 F.Supp.2d 1289, affirmed 395 Fed.Appx. 559, rehearing and rehearing denied 409 Fed.Appx. 316, certiorari denied Morris v. Swofford, 131 S.Ct. 1053, 562 U.S. 1201, 178 L.Ed.2d 866.

Perimeter fence around property does not create constitutionally protected interest in all open fields on property. U.S.C.A. Const.Amend. 4.

> Swofford v. Eslinger, 671 F.Supp.2d 1289, affirmed 395 Fed.Appx. 559, rehearing and rehearing denied 409 Fed.Appx. 316, certiorari denied Morris v. Swofford, 131 S.Ct. 1053, 562 U.S. 1201, 178 L.Ed.2d 866.

To distinguish whether property is curtilage versus open field, a district court must consider four factors: proximity of area claimed to be curtilage to home, whether area is included within an enclosure surrounding home, nature of uses to which area is put, and steps taken by resident to protect area from observation by people passing by. U.S.C.A. Const. Amend. 4.

> Swofford v. Eslinger, 671 F.Supp.2d 1289, affirmed 395 Fed.Appx. 559, rehearing and rehearing denied 409 Fed.Appx. 316, certiorari denied Morris v. Swofford, 131 S.Ct. 1053, 562 U.S. 1201, 178 L.Ed.2d 866.

M.D.Fla. 2009. The paved driveway area near the front of defendant's residence, which state troopers accessed by jumping over a fence and then unlocking a locked, electronic driveway gate, was within the curtilage of the residence for Fourth Amendment purposes; the paved area was in close proximity to the home, but was approximately 50 yards from the fenced enclosure, and the troopers were unable to view the residence or the paved area from the driveway gate because of a wooded area. U.S.C.A. Const.Amend. 4.

> U.S. v. Quintana, 594 F.Supp.2d 1291.

Like the home itself, the private property immediately adjacent to a home is entitled to protection against unreasonable search and seizure. U.S.C.A. Const. Amend. 4.

> U.S. v. Quintana, 594 F.Supp.2d 1291.

The extent of the area of private property immediately adjacent to a home that is entitled to protection against unreasonable search and seizure, known as the curtilage, is determined by factors that bear upon whether an individual reasonably may expect that the area in question should be treated as the home itself. U.S.C.A. Const.Amend. 4.

> U.S. v. Quintana, 594 F.Supp.2d 1291.

There are four factors that must be examined to determine the boundaries of the curtilage of a home, for Fourth Amendment purposes: the proximity of the area claimed to be curtilage to the home, whether the area is included within an enclosure surrounding the home, the nature of the uses to which the area is put, and the steps taken by the resident to protect the area from observation by people passing by. U.S.C.A. Const.Amend. 4.

> U.S. v. Quintana, 594 F.Supp.2d 1291.

M.D.Fla. 1997. Deputies entered petitioner's curtilage when they crossed through his back yard to knock on his back screen door, and thus infringed on petitioner's Fourth Amendment rights, as yard was immediately adjacent to petitioner's house and was enclosed by fence which partially obstructed view of house to passers-by. U.S.C.A. Const.Amend. 4.

> U.S. v. Searle, 974 F.Supp. 1433.

Courts determine whether area is considered to be curtilage of home, and thus subject to same Fourth Amendment protections as home itself, by considering proximity of area to home, whether area is enclosed, nature of uses to which area is put, and whether any steps had been taken by resident to protect area from passers-by. U.S.C.A. Const.Amend. 4.

> U.S. v. Searle, 974 F.Supp. 1433.

S.D.Fla. 2014. "Curtilage," which is the land immediately surrounding and associated with the home to which extends the intimate activity associated with the sanctity of a man's home and the privacies of life, receives the same Fourth Amendment protections that attach to the home. U.S. Const.Amend. 4.

> United States v. Jackson, 155 F.Supp.3d 1320, affirmed 618 Fed. Appx. 472, certiorari denied 136 S.Ct. 376, 193 L.Ed.2d 303.

A police officer not armed with a warrant may approach a home and knock, precisely because that is no more than any private citizen might do. U.S. Const. Amend. 4.

> United States v. Jackson, 155 F.Supp.3d 1320, affirmed 618 Fed. Appx. 472, certiorari denied 136 S.Ct. 376, 193 L.Ed.2d 303.

S.D.Fla. 2011. Police may enter person's curtilage for legitimate purposes. U.S.C.A. Const.Amend. 4.

> Abella v. Simon, 831 F.Supp.2d 1316, vacated in part 482 Fed.Appx. 522.

Fourth Amendment is not violated when police simply enter a porch. U.S.C.A. Const.Amend. 4.

> Abella v. Simon, 831 F.Supp.2d 1316, vacated in part 482 Fed.Appx. 522.

Fla. 2017. The reasonable expectation of privacy under the Fourth Amendment not only applies to the inside of a person's home, but to the curtilage of the home as well. U.S. Const. Amend. 4.

> State v. Markus, 211 So.3d 894, rehearing denied 2017 WL 944231.

Fla. 2006. Zone of protection under the Fourth Amendment extends to the curtilage of a home, which includes a fenced or enclosed area encompassing the dwelling. U.S.C.A. Const.Amend. 4.

> Tillman v. State, 934 So.2d 1263.

Fla. 1993. Defendant failed to create reasonable zone of privacy in his backyard by surrounding it with six-foot fence that one could not see through, for purposes of determining whether Fourth Amendment protection applied, as the backyard was protected from view only as to those who remained on the ground and were unable to see over six-foot fence unaided. U.S.C.A. Const.Amend. 4.

> Sarantopoulos v. State, 629 So.2d 121.

Purported civil trespass of officers in entering neighbor's yard without permission in order to peer over defendant's fence did not make search illegal under Fourth Amendment or State Constitution since entry into neighbor's yard did not violate defendant's right to privacy. U.S.C.A. Const.Amend. 4; West's F.S.A. Const. Art. 1, § 12.

> Sarantopoulos v. State, 629 So.2d 121.

Fla. 1987. Defendant had clearly exhibited subjective expectation of privacy in greenhouse and its contents, located on his residential property within curtilage, in light of opacity of greenhouse, fence surrounding it, "Do Not Enter" sign posted in front of mobile home located 10 to 20 feet from greenhouse, notwithstanding that two panels were missing from roof of greenhouse, exposing approximately one-tenth of roof area. U.S.C.A. Const.Amend. 4.

> Riley v. State, 511 So.2d 282, certiorari granted 108 S.Ct. 1011, 484 U.S. 1058, 98 L.Ed.2d 977, reversed 109 S.Ct. 693, 488 U.S. 445, 102 L.Ed.2d 835, rehearing denied 109 S.Ct. 1659, 490 U.S. 1014, 104 L.Ed.2d 172, on remand 549 So.2d 673.

Defendant had a reasonable expectation of privacy in greenhouse, and its contents located within curtilage of his mobile home, from aerial observations by police officer flying in helicopter 400 feet above greenhouse, notwithstanding that two panels were missing from roof of greenhouse exposing approximately one-tenth of roof area. U.S.C.A. Const.Amend. 4; West's F.S.A. Const. Art. 1, § 12.

> Riley v. State, 511 So.2d 282, certiorari granted 108 S.Ct. 1011, 484 U.S. 1058, 98 L.Ed.2d 977, reversed 109 S.Ct. 693, 488 U.S. 445, 102 L.Ed.2d 835, rehearing denied 109 S.Ct. 1659, 490 U.S. 1014, 104 L.Ed.2d 172, on remand 549 So.2d 673.

Right to be let alone includes not only right to be free from surveillance within confines of four walls and roof of home but also the right to enjoy outdoor activities in private in one's own backyard. U.S.C.A. Const.Amend. 4.

> Riley v. State, 511 So.2d 282, certiorari granted 108 S.Ct. 1011, 484 U.S. 1058, 98 L.Ed.2d 977, reversed 109 S.Ct. 693, 488 U.S. 445, 102

L.Ed.2d 835, rehearing denied 109 S.Ct. 1659, 490 U.S. 1014, 104 L.Ed.2d 172, on remand 549 So.2d 673.

Fla. 1985. Warrantless "open field" searches are proper, and evidence received as a result thereof should not be suppressed. U.S.C.A. Const.Amend. 4.

> State v. Brady, 466 So.2d 1064, on remand Eckard v. Trowbridge, 483 So.2d 450.

Fla. 1981. Open fields doctrine cannot be used as carte blanche for warrantless search simply because location searched is not part of dwelling or adjacent curtilage. U.S.C.A.Const. Amend. 4.

> State v. Brady, 406 So.2d 1093, certiorari granted 102 S.Ct. 2266, 456 U.S. 988, 73 L.Ed.2d 1282, vacated in part, certiorari dismissed in part 104 S.Ct. 2380, 467 U.S. 1201, 81 L.Ed.2d 339, on remand 466 So.2d 1064, on remand Eckard v. Trowbridge, 483 So.2d 450.

If owner or occupier of field seeks to keep it private and demonstrates actual intention to do so and if his expectation is one that society is willing to recognize as reasonable, then Fourth Amendment protections extend to activities in such field. U.S.C.A.Const. Amend. 4.

> State v. Brady, 406 So.2d 1093, certiorari granted 102 S.Ct. 2266, 456 U.S. 988, 73 L.Ed.2d 1282, vacated in part, certiorari dismissed in part 104 S.Ct. 2380, 467 U.S. 1201, 81 L.Ed.2d 339, on remand 466 So.2d 1064, on remand Eckard v. Trowbridge, 483 So.2d 450.

Activities carried on in truly open field or in any area which one knowingly exposes to public are not subject to Fourth Amendment protections; there can be no reasonable expectation of privacy in field open, visible and easily accessible to others. U.S.C.A.Const. Amend. 4.

> State v. Brady, 406 So.2d 1093, certiorari granted 102 S.Ct. 2266, 456 U.S. 988, 73 L.Ed.2d 1282, vacated in part, certiorari dismissed in part 104 S.Ct. 2380, 467 U.S. 1201, 81 L.Ed.2d 339, on remand 466 So.2d 1064, on remand Eckard v. Trowbridge, 483 So.2d 450.

Fla. 1980. Where defendant took overt steps to designate his farm and barn as place not open to the public, contraband was found covered and wrapped in tobacco sheets within closed tobacco barn, and farm itself was fenced and gate to fence was kept locked, defendant exhibited subjective expectation of privacy in tobacco barn and its contents. U.S.C.A.Const. Amends. 4, 14, 14, § 1; West's F.S.A.Const. art. 1, § 12.

> Norman v. State, 379 So.2d 643.

"Open fields doctrine," which stands for proposition that Fourth Amendment's protection of one's person, house, papers, and effects does not extend to the open fields, does not extend to warrantless search of closed structure on fenced property. U.S.C.A.Const. Amends. 4, 14, 14, § 1; West's F.S.A.Const. art. 1, § 12.

> Norman v. State, 379 So.2d 643.

Fla.App. 1 Dist. 2013. Because it is appurtenant to the home, the curtilage, which is the area closely surrounding the home, is entitled to the same Fourth Amendment protection as the area within the home; this is so because the curtilage is an area intimately linked to the home, both physically and psychologically, thereby entitling it to protection from unreasonable searches. U.S.C.A. Const.Amend. 4.

> Powell v. State, 120 So.3d 577, on rehearing.

That the area is within a home's curtilage does not itself bar all police observation; the Fourth Amendment protection of the home has never been extended to require law enforcement officers to shield their eyes when passing by a home on public thoroughfares, nor does the mere fact that an individual has taken measures to restrict some views of his activities preclude an officer's observations from a public vantage point where he has a right to be and which renders the activities clearly visible. U.S.C.A. Const.Amend. 4.

> Powell v. State, 120 So.3d 577, on rehearing.

Police officers may use ordinary means from a public position outside a home's curtilage to view activities occurring within the curtilage. U.S.C.A. Const. Amend. 4.

> Powell v. State, 120 So.3d 577, on rehearing.

† This Case was not selected for publication in the National Reporter System
For legislative history of cited statutes, see Florida Statutes Annotated

The existence and extent of a license that would permit a police "knock and talk" encounter with a resident of a home depends on the circumstances; home-owners who post "No Trespassing" or "No Soliciting" signs effectively negate a license to enter the posted property, and where no signs forbid entry, and there is a recognizable pathway to a front door, a limited license to enter the property on the pathway and knock on the door exists, and where such a license is established, the resident does not have a reasonable expectation of privacy in what is plainly viewed from the vantage point of a temporary visitor who walks along the pathway or stands at the doorway. U.S.C.A. Const. Amend. 4; West's F.S.A. § 810.09.

> Powell v. State, 120 So.3d 577, on rehearing.

Fla.App. 1 Dist. 2009. Officer's warrantless entry into defendant's backyard area was unlawful search; defendant had constitutionally protected privacy interest in side and backyard area of his home. U.S.C.A. Const.Amend. 4.

> Lollie v. State, 14 So.3d 1078.

Fla.App. 1 Dist. 2008. While defendant lacked privacy rights, with respect to Fourth Amendment protection against unreasonable searches, as to officers going to front door of defendant's home, which was a place where visitors might be expected, defendant had right of privacy as to officers' uninvited and warrantless entry into side-yard and back-yard areas of home, which were more private. U.S.C.A. Const. Amend. 4.

> Waldo v. State, 975 So.2d 542, rehearing denied.

Fla.App. 1 Dist. 2007. Defendant's Fourth Amendment rights were not violated when law enforcement personnel crossed unenclosed front yard to reach front door of defendant's house, regardless of whether property was posted with "no trespassing" signs. U.S.C.A. Const. Amend. 4.

> State v. Kennedy, 953 So.2d 655.

Fla.App. 1 Dist. 1988. Car parked in motel parking lot was within "curtilage" of motel room for purposes of warrant authorizing search of motel room and persons or vehicles located on the curtilage, where suspect drove car into motel park-ing lot and was seen entering the motel from the car.

> Menendez v. State, 521 So.2d 210, denial of post-conviction relief affirmed in part, reversed in part 562 So.2d 858.

Fla.App. 1 Dist. 1981. Defendant is entitled to protection of Fourth Amendment to extent of curtilage of her dwelling. U.S.C.A.Const. Amend. 4.

> DeMontmorency v. State, 401 So.2d 858, decision approved 464 So.2d 1201.

Open fields doctrine may be applicable to fenced as well as unfenced property. U.S.C.A.Const. Amend. 4.

> DeMontmorency v. State, 401 So.2d 858, decision approved 464 So.2d 1201.

Fla.App. 1 Dist. 1976. Behind the door of his home a citizen has an expectation of privacy far surpassing his similar interest in his driveway, front porch or other parts of the curtilage.

> Britton v. State, 336 So.2d 663, certiorari denied 344 So.2d 326.

Fla.App. 1 Dist. 1976. Where sheriff's deputies on routine patrol found stolen goods located in open field or clearing exposed to and accessible to public, such goods could lawfully be seized without search warrant and were admissible in evidence. U.S.C.A.Const. Amend. 4.

> Atland v. State, 330 So.2d 85, certiorari denied 339 So.2d 1167.

Fla.App. 2 Dist. 2017. Without a warrant or an exception to the warrant requirement, a law enforcement officer has no right to physically intrude into the curtilage of a house. U.S. Const. Amend. 4; Fla. Const. art. 1, § 12.

> Daniels v. State, 208 So.3d 1223.

Fla.App. 2 Dist. 2008. The zone of protection under the Fourth Amendment extends to the curtilage of a home, which includes a fenced or enclosed area encompassing the dwelling. U.S.C.A. Const. Amend. 4.

> Oliver v. State, 989 So.2d 16, rehearing denied, review denied 4 So.3d 677.

Fla.App. 2 Dist. 2007. A reasonable expectation of privacy exists in the backyard of a residence that is not generally viewed by the public, but that expectation gives way in an emergency situation. U.S.C.A. Const.Amend. 4.

P.B.P. v. State, 955 So.2d 618, review denied 966 So.2d 967.

Fla.App. 2 Dist. 1999. While a resident does not have a reasonable expectation of privacy in the front door or front porch area of his or her residence because salesmen or visitors frequently appear there, a resident does have a reasonable expectation of privacy in his or her back yard because it is more private, and passers-by generally cannot see into the back yard. U.S.C.A. Const.Amend. 4.

Glass v. State, 736 So.2d 788.

Fla.App. 2 Dist. 1999. Deputy sheriff's entry into defendant's backyard, warrantless search of defendant's barbecue, and seizure of burned financial documents not belonging to defendant or her family members was illegal search, where backyard was fenced-in and not plainly visible. U.S.C.A. Const.Amend. 4.

Maggard v. State, 736 So.2d 763.

Fla.App. 2 Dist. 1996. Fourth Amendment protects curtilage of a house and law enforcement officers must obtain warrant, or some exception to warrant requirement must exist, before they can enter protected area and seize contraband. U.S.C.A. Const.Amend. 4.

Abel v. State, 668 So.2d 1121.

In determining whether an area falls within "curtilage" of house for search and seizure purposes, test includes distance between home and area, whether area is within enclosure surrounding house, how area is used, and how owner protect area from observation of others.

Abel v. State, 668 So.2d 1121.

Fla.App. 2 Dist. 1994. "Curtilage" for Fourth Amendment purposes encompasses enclosed area around dwelling. U.S.C.A. Const.Amend. 4.

Hamilton v. State, 645 So.2d 555, review granted 654 So.2d 920, affirmed in part, quashed in part 660 So.2d 1038.

Fla.App. 2 Dist. 1992. Area of defendant's fenced backyard was clearly within "curtilage" of his home and warranted

Fourth Amendment protection. U.S.C.A. Const.Amend. 4.

State v. Sarantopoulos, 604 So.2d 551, review granted 618 So.2d 210, decision approved 629 So.2d 121.

Defendant established element for finding constitutionally protected reasonable expectation of privacy, that defendant had manifested subjective expectation of privacy, where defendant had erected solid six-foot fence around his backyard. West's F.S.A. Const. Art. 1, § 12; U.S.C.A. Const.Amend. 4.

State v. Sarantopoulos, 604 So.2d 551, review granted 618 So.2d 210, decision approved 629 So.2d 121.

Defendant's expectation of privacy in his fenced backyard, viewed objectively, was unreasonable, and therefore police officer's entry into neighbor's yard, without permission, to look over fence into defendant's backyard did not violate defendant's constitutionally protected right to privacy, and search warrant based on officer's observations was not invalid. West's F.S.A. Const. Art. 1, § 12; U.S.C.A. Const. Amend. 4.

State v. Sarantopoulos, 604 So.2d 551, review granted 618 So.2d 210, decision approved 629 So.2d 121.

Defendant, by building a solid six-foot fence, created zone of privacy from persons in adjoining yards attempting to peer into his yard from six feet or lower, but did not create zone of privacy from neighbor's observations over that fence if that neighbor was seven feet tall, or from observations of person in adjoining yard standing on a ladder trimming trees or repairing a roof, for purpose of determining validity of search following police officer's peering over fence. West's F.S.A. Const. Art. 1, § 12; U.S.C.A. Const. Amend. 4.

State v. Sarantopoulos, 604 So.2d 551, review granted 618 So.2d 210, decision approved 629 So.2d 121.

Police officers may stand upon adjoining land and look for contraband or fruits of crime within curtilage of defendant's residence.

State v. Sarantopoulos, 604 So.2d 551, review granted 618 So.2d 210, decision approved 629 So.2d 121.

Defendant had no legitimate expectation of privacy in his neighbor's property, and his Fourth Amendment rights were not violated by police detective's presence on that property without permission. U.S.C.A. Const.Amend. 4.

State v. Sarantopoulos, 604 So.2d 551, review granted 618 So.2d 210, decision approved 629 So.2d 121.

Fla.App. 2 Dist. 1991. Warrantless search of treehouse in which defendant was staying was illegal. U.S.C.A. Const. Amend. 4.

Talley v. State, 581 So.2d 635.

Fla.App. 2 Dist. 1985. Protection afforded "houses" in Fourth Amendment to Federal Constitution and declaration of rights of Florida Constitution also includes "curtilage," i.e., ground and buildings immediately surrounding dwelling and customarily used in connection with it. U.S.C.A. Const.Amend. 4, West's F.S.A. Const.Art. 1, § 12.

A.E.R. v. State, 464 So.2d 152, petition for review denied 472 So.2d 1180, certiorari denied 106 S.Ct. 541, 474 U.S. 1011, 88 L.Ed.2d 471.

Fla.App. 2 Dist. 1984. Defendant who installed a reed fence around perimeter of his property and thus obstructed area from view by adjacent neighbors and other passersby exhibited a "reasonable expectation of privacy" in the backyard of his duplex apartment. U.S.C.A. Const. Amend. 4.

Randall v. State, 458 So.2d 822.

Individual need not construct "an opaque bubble" over his backyard in order to have a reasonable expectation of privacy regarding his activities. U.S.C.A. Const.Amend. 4.

Randall v. State, 458 So.2d 822.

Fla.App. 2 Dist. 1978. As general rule, yard adjacent to a residential dwelling, particularly part of backyard blocked from view from front yard or street by dwelling, is clothed with a reasonable expectation of privacy from unreasonable government intrusion but, since test is necessarily subjective, such rule is not necessarily always true. U.S.C.A.Const. Amend. 4.

Morsman v. State, 360 So.2d 137, writ dismissed 394 So.2d 408, certiorari denied 101 S.Ct. 3066, 452 U.S. 930, 69 L.Ed.2d 431.

Fla.App. 3 Dist. 2014. There are four factors that determine the boundaries of a curtilage in a search and seizure context: the proximity of the area claimed to be curtilage to the home, whether the area is included within an enclosure surrounding the home, the nature of the uses to which the area is put, and the steps taken by the resident to protect the area from observation by people passing by. U.S.C.A. Const. Amend. 4.

Brown v. State, 152 So.3d 619, rehearing denied, review denied 168 So.3d 228, appeal after remand 210 So.3d 61.

Front and side yards of defendant's home were part of the curtilage of the home and therefore a constitutionally protected area under the Fourth Amendment; yards were enclosed by two layers of fencing, and several "No Trespassing" signs were posted on the outside fence. U.S.C.A. Const. Amend. 4.

Brown v. State, 152 So.3d 619, rehearing denied, review denied 168 So.3d 228, appeal after remand 210 So.3d 61.

Defendant exhibited his subjective expectation of privacy in curtilage of his home, as required for it to have Fourth Amendment protection; curtilage was enclosed by two layers of fencing and could not be seen from outside the fences, defendant posted three "No Trespassing" signs on the first fence, and his mailbox was located on the outside of that fence. U.S.C.A. Const. Amend. 4.

Brown v. State, 152 So.3d 619, rehearing denied, review denied 168 So.3d 228, appeal after remand 210 So.3d 61.

Police officers' warrantless entry into curtilage of defendant's home during robbery investigation was not a valid "knock and talk," and therefore violated the Fourth Amendment; no visitor or salesman would have gone through the two layers of fencing surrounding the curtilage without an invitation, and officers knew that the car that defendant was accused of stealing was reported returned before they entered defendant's property. U.S.C.A. Const. Amend. 4.

> Brown v. State, 152 So.3d 619, rehearing denied, review denied 168 So.3d 228, appeal after remand 210 So.3d 61.

Fla.App. 3 Dist. 2011. Warrantless entry by police officers onto defendant's property when entry gate opened to allow defendant to leave violated defendant's Fourth Amendment rights; defendant manifested his subjective expectation of privacy in the curtilage of his home by erecting barriers obstructing a view of the property, and officers did not enter in the manner that a salesman or visitor might, but rather effectively committed a trespass by taking advantage of the momentary opening of the gate, which was not an open invitation to the public, or the police, to enter. U.S.C.A. Const.Amend. 4; West's F.S.A. §§ 810.08(1), 810.011(1).

> Fernandez v. State, 63 So.3d 881.

A yard adjacent to a residential dwelling, particularly one blocked from view from the street, is clothed with a reasonable expectation of privacy from unreasonable governmental intrusion. U.S.C.A. Const.Amend. 4.

> Fernandez v. State, 63 So.3d 881.

Putting up fences, and affirmatively taking express steps to exclude the public or other persons from using an area, seeing into it, or gaining access to the area are ways to establish a subjective expectation of privacy potentially entitled to constitutional protection from unreasonable government intrusion. U.S.C.A. Const. Amend. 4.

> Fernandez v. State, 63 So.3d 881.

Fla.App. 3 Dist. 2007. Defendant had no reasonable expectation of privacy at entrance to his property which was open to the public, which included his front porch, for Fourth Amendment purposes. U.S.C.A. Const.Amend. 4.

> State v. Pereira, 967 So.2d 312, rehearing denied.

Fla.App. 3 Dist. 1995. Police officer's right to approach suspect's front door is tempered by general rule that curtilage surrounding home is entitled to the same

search and seizure protection as home. West's F.S.A. Const. Art. 1, § 12.

> Potts v. Johnson, 654 So.2d 596.

A person's back yard falls within area protected by reasonable expectation of privacy into which government cannot reasonably intrude to conduct search. West's F.S.A. Const. Art. 1, § 12.

> Potts v. Johnson, 654 So.2d 596.

Typically, yard adjacent to residential dwelling, particularly part of backyard blocked from view from street by dwelling, is clothed with a reasonable expectation of privacy from unreasonable governmental intrusion. West's F.S.A. Const. Art. 1, § 12.

> Potts v. Johnson, 654 So.2d 596.

Fla.App. 3 Dist. 1981. Generally, backyard is considered more private than front because passers by cannot view such area. U.S.C.A.Const. Amend. 4.

> State v. Parker, 399 So.2d 24, review denied 408 So.2d 1095.

Although defendant's backyard was visible to his neighbors, he had reasonable expectation of privacy there as to public in general, especially as to the location of revolver secreted in stairwell crevice not readily visible to the untrained eye. U.S.C.A.Const. Amend. 4.

> State v. Parker, 399 So.2d 24, review denied 408 So.2d 1095.

Fla.App. 4 Dist. 2012. Zone of protection under the Fourth Amendment extends to the curtilage of a home, which includes a fenced or enclosed area encompassing the dwelling. U.S.C.A. Const. Amend. 4.

> Bethel v. State, 93 So.3d 410.

Fla.App. 4 Dist. 2008. If a law enforcement officer does not have consent, a search warrant, or an arrest warrant, he may not enter a private home or its curtilage except when it is justified by exigent circumstances. U.S.C.A. Const.Amend. 4.

> Herrera-Fernandez v. State, 984 So.2d 644.

Fla.App. 4 Dist. 2003. Where an inspection is in the curtilage, that area is given the same Fourth Amendment protection as one within the walls of the home. U.S.C.A. Const.Amend. 4.

> Florida Dept. of Agriculture and Consumer Services v. Haire, 836 So.2d 1040, rehearing denied, review granted Haire v. Florida Dept. of Agr. and Consumer Services, 842 So.2d 844, review granted Brooks Tropical, Inc. v. Florida Dept. of Agr. and Consumer Services, 842 So.2d 842, on subsequent appeal 865 So.2d 610, rehearing denied, decision approved 870 So.2d 774, rehearing denied.

Fla.App. 4 Dist. 2002. Defendant charged with grand theft of a motorcycle lacked a reasonable expectation of privacy, for purposes of Fourth Amendment, in "garage" area that law enforcement officer entered to retrieve vehicle identification number of motorcycle; although area where defendant was working was referred to as a garage, police officer described it as covered open area that was attached to house, more like a carport, and law enforcement officer was lawfully on premises and vehicle identification number was in plain view. U.S.C.A. Const.Amend. 4.

> State v. Duhart, 810 So.2d 972, rehearing denied.

Fla.App. 4 Dist. 1999. Defendant's parked vehicle, from which shots were fired on interstate highway injuring driver of another vehicle, was in open view and was not part of curtilage of house, and thus, vehicle was not in area protected under search and seizure provision of Fourth Amendment, where police officer, who was lawfully on premises by invitation, saw vehicle, vehicle was clearly visible from public alley, and area was not covered, fenced, or enclosed. U.S.C.A. Const.Amend. 4.

> Ruiz v. State, 743 So.2d 581.

Fla.App. 4 Dist. 1997. Search of fenced lot in well-populated urban area fell within "open field" exception to Fourth Amendment: lot was not residence or curtilage of residence, or legitimate business property, and gate to fence was closed but not locked. U.S.C.A. Const. Amend. 4.

> O'Neal v. State, 689 So.2d 1135, rehearing denied.

Fla.App. 4 Dist. 1993. Unfenced front yard was equivalent of open field for which police officers passed to get to threshold front door and was not within scope of Fourth Amendment; therefore, officers' approach to front door and knocking on door was not an illegal entry upon property merely because of display of "No Trespassing" sign. U.S.C.A. Const. Amend. 4.

> Wysong v. State, 614 So.2d 670, review denied 632 So.2d 1029.

Fla.App. 4 Dist. 1980. Reasonable expectation of privacy extended to 1,800-acre tract of land which was fenced, locked, occupied, and posted, and evidence seized as result of a forced entry by deputies without a search warrant onto such tract was required to be suppressed, in view of fact that there was plenty of time to apply for a search warrant. U.S.C.A.Const. Amend. 4.

> State v. Brady, 379 So.2d 1294, decision approved 406 So.2d 1093, certiorari granted 102 S.Ct. 2266, 456 U.S. 988, 73 L.Ed.2d 1282, vacated in part, certiorari dismissed in part 104 S.Ct. 2380, 467 U.S. 1201, 81 L.Ed.2d 339, on remand 466 So.2d 1064, on remand Eckard v. Trowbridge, 483 So.2d 450.

Fla.App. 4 Dist. 1974. Building located 30 feet from building occupied as a residence, although not itself occupied as a residence, was part of the curtilage included within the protection of the Fourth Amendment. U.S.C.A.Const. Amend. 4.

> Kishel v. State, 287 So.2d 414.

Fla.App. 5 Dist. 2011. Defendant's parked vehicle, located on city right-of-way in front of residence and partially in residence's driveway, was not within the "curtilage" of residence, and thus police authorization to search residence and its curtilage for drugs did not extend to vehicle; vehicle was outside chain-link fence that surrounded the residence, and homeowner manifested no attempt to protect against observation by people passing by. U.S.C.A. Const.Amend. 4.

> Wheeler v. State, 62 So.3d 1218.

The term "curtilage" in the Fourth Amendment context describes the area around a home that is intimately tied to the home itself; the extent of the curtilage is determined by factors that bear upon whether an individual reasonably may expect that the area in question should be treated as the home itself. U.S.C.A. Const. Amend. 4.

Wheeler v. State, 62 So.3d 1218.

The legal boundaries of a given piece of property do not necessarily define its "curtilage" for Fourth Amendment purposes. U.S.C.A. Const.Amend. 4.

Wheeler v. State, 62 So.3d 1218.

To determine the scope of the "curtilage" to a particular residence, for Fourth Amendment purposes, the court must consider: (1) the proximity of the area claimed to be curtilage to the home, (2) whether the area is included within an enclosure surrounding the home, (3) the nature of the uses to which the area is put, and (4) the steps taken by the resident to protect the area from observation by people passing by. U.S.C.A. Const.Amend. 4.

Wheeler v. State, 62 So.3d 1218.

Although not conclusive, fencing configurations are important factors in defining the "curtilage" in the Fourth Amendment context. U.S.C.A. Const.Amend. 4.

Wheeler v. State, 62 So.3d 1218.

In the context of the Fourth Amendment, for most homes, the boundaries of the "curtilage" will be clearly marked; and the conception defining the curtilage, as the area around the home to which the activity of home life extends, is a familiar one easily understood from daily experience. U.S.C.A. Const.Amend. 4.

Wheeler v. State, 62 So.3d 1218.

Fla.App. 5 Dist. 2007.   Fourth Amendment does not protect areas of the home that are open and exposed to public view. U.S.C.A. Const.Amend. 4.

State v. E.D.R., 959 So.2d 1225.

One does not harbor an expectation of privacy on a front porch where salesmen or visitors may appear at any time. U.S.C.A. Const.Amend. 4.

State v. E.D.R., 959 So.2d 1225.

Fla.App. 5 Dist. 2007. First *Dunn* factor to consider in determining whether an area is protected curtilage of a home is

the distance between the home and the area. U.S.C.A. Const.Amend. 4.

Wilson v. State, 952 So.2d 564, rehearing denied.

Second *Dunn* factor to consider in determining whether an area is protected curtilage of a home is whether the area is included within an enclosure surrounding the home. U.S.C.A. Const.Amend. 4.

Wilson v. State, 952 So.2d 564, rehearing denied.

Third *Dunn* factor to consider in determining whether an area is protected curtilage of a home requires that a court analyze the use to which the area is put to determine if it was so associated with the activities and privacies of domestic life that it should be deemed a part of the residence. U.S.C.A. Const.Amend. 4.

Wilson v. State, 952 So.2d 564, rehearing denied.

Fourth *Dunn* factor to consider in determining whether an area is protected curtilage of a home involves an examination of the steps taken by the homeowner to protect the area from observation by people passing by. U.S.C.A. Const.Amend. 4.

Wilson v. State, 952 So.2d 564, rehearing denied.

Fla.App. 5 Dist. 2001. Curtilage area outside commercial business was not entitled to constitutional protection against warrantless search where owner made no effort to exclude access by public or others to area at issue. U.S.C.A. Const.Amend. 4.

Ratcliff v. State, 783 So.2d 1099.

In questioning whether owner of commercial property is entitled to Fourth Amendment protection against warrantless searches, court must ask if owner demonstrates subjective manifestation of claimed privacy in the area at issue, and if such claim is recognized by society; this is a legal determination, requiring no deference on review, provided facts and circumstances are not in dispute. U.S.C.A. Const.Amend. 4.

Ratcliff v. State, 783 So.2d 1099.

To preserve or establish Fourth Amendment protection in area surrounding commercial business, owner must make subjective manifestation of claimed privacy in the area, taking precautions to not leave objects in plain view of those outside area, and must affirmatively bar public from area. U.S.C.A. Const.Amend. 4.

    Ratcliff v. State, 783 So.2d 1099.

Fla.App. 5 Dist. 1997. Warrantless search of screened-in back porch violated legitimate privacy expectation of home's owner, despite fact that yard was not fenced and owner could be seen through screen, and despite contention that it was reasonable for deputy to go to rear of house to find its owner; porch was not visible without entering back yard, and deputy was on property only to investigate misdemeanor boating violation, did not plan to make arrest, and was subject to no other exception to warrant requirement. U.S.C.A. Const.Amend. 4.

    State v. Witherington, 702 So.2d 263.

Back yard of house is within zone clothed by reasonable expectation of privacy into which government may not reasonably intrude to conduct warrantless search. U.S.C.A. Const.Amend. 4.

    State v. Witherington, 702 So.2d 263.

⚷28. —— Abandoned, surrendered, or disclaimed items.

† C.A.11 (Fla.) 2016. Defendant abandoned his backpack, and thus he retained no reasonable expectation of privacy with regard to backpack at time of search; while fleeing from officers, defendant hid his backpack under porch of another person's house, and defendant subsequently attempted to deceive officers by implying that backpack was located at his house. U.S.C.A. Const.Amend. 4.

    U.S. v. Witten, 649 Fed.Appx. 880, certiorari denied 137 S.Ct. 696, 196 L.Ed.2d 572.

Defendant abandoned his backpack by hiding it under house prior to being detained by officers, and thus, even if detention was unconstitutional, officers' search of backpack could not be fruit of poisonous tree; officers' action of setting up perimeter to locate defendant did not amount to detention. U.S.C.A. Const. Amend. 4.

    U.S. v. Witten, 649 Fed.Appx. 880, certiorari denied 137 S.Ct. 696, 196 L.Ed.2d 572.

C.A.11 (Fla.) 2016. Reasonable expectation of privacy, as a requirement of a claimed Fourth Amendment violation, can be abandoned, and abandonment is primarily a question of intent and may be inferred from words spoken, acts done, and objective facts. U.S. Const. Amend. 4.

    Ziegler v. Martin County School District, 831 F.3d 1309.

C.A.11 (Fla.) 2015. Fourth Amendment claims do not lie when the defendant has abandoned the searched property. U.S.C.A. Const.Amend. 4.

    U.S. v. Sparks, 806 F.3d 1323, certiorari denied Johnson v. U.S., 137 S.Ct. 34, 196 L.Ed.2d 46.

A court assesses objectively whether abandonment of searched property has occurred, based primarily on the prior possessor's intent, as discerned from statements, acts, and other facts. U.S.C.A. Const.Amend. 4.

    U.S. v. Sparks, 806 F.3d 1323, certiorari denied Johnson v. U.S., 137 S.Ct. 34, 196 L.Ed.2d 46.

A court uses a common sense approach in evaluating abandonment of searched property; the critical inquiry when determining whether an abandonment has occurred is whether the person prejudiced voluntarily discarded, left behind, or otherwise relinquished his interest in the property in question. U.S.C.A. Const.Amend. 4.

    U.S. v. Sparks, 806 F.3d 1323, certiorari denied Johnson v. U.S., 137 S.Ct. 34, 196 L.Ed.2d 46.

Loss alone cannot support a finding of abandonment of a possessory interest in searched property, and the filing of a claim for a lost item and the replacement of that item with the resulting insurance money, in and of itself, does not demonstrate an intent to abandon; instead, a court must view all of the facts and consider the totality of the circumstances to determine whether an intent to abandon may objectively be discerned. U.S.C.A. Const.Amend. 4.

    U.S. v. Sparks, 806 F.3d 1323, certiorari denied Johnson v. U.S., 137 S.Ct. 34, 196 L.Ed.2d 46.

† C.A.11 (Fla.) 2014. Firearm defendant discarded during flight from police

---

† This Case was not selected for publication in the National Reporter System
For legislative history of cited statutes, see Florida Statutes Annotated

officers was not fruit of unlawful seizure, and thus was admissible at trial for being a felon in possession of a firearm; defendant was not actually seized, despite officers' earlier attempt to contain defendant's vehicle at traffic light, until after he had discarded the firearm. U.S.C.A. Const. Amend. 4.

U.S. v. Dolomon, 569 Fed.Appx. 889.

C.A.11 (Fla.) 2014. Although locale can matter in determining whether individual has reasonable expectation of privacy in conversation, it is not dispositive in evaluating Fourth Amendment unlawful search claim. U.S.C.A. Const.Amend. 4.

Gennusa v. Canova, 748 F.3d 1103.

† **C.A.11 (Fla.) 2007.** For purposes of a Fourth Amendment analysis, defendant did not have a reasonable expectation of privacy in a briefcase after he abandoned it partially unlocked and unattended on the trunk of a third party's car in an apartment complex parking lot. U.S.C.A. Const.Amend. 4.

Chrispen v. Secretary, Florida Dept. of Corrections, 246 Fed.Appx. 599.

For purposes of a Fourth Amendment analysis, police officer's search of a briefcase abandoned partially unlocked and unattended on the trunk of a car in an apartment complex parking lot was a reasonable inventory-like administrative search conducted for the purpose of identifying the seemingly abandoned briefcase's owner. U.S.C.A. Const.Amend. 4.

Chrispen v. Secretary, Florida Dept. of Corrections, 246 Fed.Appx. 599.

C.A.11 (Fla.) 2006. Defendant charged with murdering his wife and children had abandoned his house, where murders were committed, thus making any expectation of privacy unreasonable and discovery of dead bodies inevitable, where, when deputy searched house four days after the murders, in response to information that defendant could not be located, defendant had already fled to Hawaii, where he remained for four months before turning himself in, and had no plans to return to the house or to provide for its upkeep. U.S.C.A. Const.Amend. 4.

Zakrzewski v. McDonough, 455 F.3d 1254, rehearing and rehearing denied 218 Fed.Appx. 981, certiorari denied 127 S.Ct. 2051, 549 U.S. 1349, 167 L.Ed.2d 782.

C.A.11 (Fla.) 1997. While landlord generally lacks common authority to consent to search of tenant's apartment, tenant who abandons property loses any reasonable expectation of privacy he once had. U.S.C.A. Const.Amend. 4.

U.S. v. Brazel, 102 F.3d 1120, certiorari denied Jefferson v. U.S., 118 S.Ct. 78, 522 U.S. 822, 139 L.Ed.2d 37, certiorari denied Archer v. U.S., 118 S.Ct. 78, 522 U.S. 822, 139 L.Ed.2d 37, certiorari denied McNealy v. U.S., 118 S.Ct. 78, 522 U.S. 822, 139 L.Ed.2d 37, certiorari denied 118 S.Ct. 79, 522 U.S. 822, 139 L.Ed.2d 37, certiorari denied Burgess v. U.S., 118 S.Ct. 720, 522 U.S. 1060, 139 L.Ed.2d 659, postconviction relief denied U.S. v. McKinnon, 27 F.Supp.2d 1369.

C.A.11 (Fla.) 1995. Business did not have "reasonable expectation of privacy" in documents it shredded, then placed inside green garbage bag, which was in turn placed in garbage dumpster on its own premises that could only be accessed by traveling 40 yards on private road and, thus, federal agent did not violate business' Fourth Amendment rights by seizing those documents; business did not take affirmative steps to exclude public from its premises, and fact that private, rather than government, collector handled business' garbage did not diminish fact that garbage was conveyed to third party. U.S.C.A. Const.Amend. 4.

U.S. v. Hall, 47 F.3d 1091, certiorari denied 116 S.Ct. 71, 516 U.S. 816, 133 L.Ed.2d 31.

Fact that business conveys its garbage to private garbage collector does not increase objective reasonableness of business' expectation of privacy in that garbage. U.S.C.A. Const.Amend. 4.

U.S. v. Hall, 47 F.3d 1091, certiorari denied 116 S.Ct. 71, 516 U.S. 816, 133 L.Ed.2d 31.

C.A.11 (Fla.) 1992. District court properly determined that defendant abandoned suitcase that he had left with acquaintance and, therefore, lacked standing to challenge its search, where defendant and his purported representatives promised but failed to retrieve suitcase from acquaintance for over one year. U.S.C.A. Const.Amend. 4.

> U.S. v. Lehder-Rivas, 955 F.2d 1510, certiorari denied Reed v. U.S., 113 S.Ct. 347, 506 U.S. 924, 121 L.Ed.2d 262.

C.A.11 (Fla.) 1990. Under Fourth Amendment, in determining whether there has been abandonment, critical inquiry is whether person prejudiced by search voluntarily discarded, left behind, or otherwise relinquished his interest in property in question so that he could no longer retain reasonable expectation of privacy with regard to it at time of search. U.S.C.A. Const.Amend. 4.

> U.S. v. Winchester, 916 F.2d 601.

C.A.11 (Fla.) 1990. By relinquishing possession to another, owner or lessee of vehicle evidences abandonment of privacy interest in vehicle; thus, it is reasonable to conclude that third party to whom possession was surrendered was also given authority to consent to search of all areas of vehicle.

> U.S. v. Dunkley, 911 F.2d 522, certiorari denied Brown v. U.S., 111 S.Ct. 765, 498 U.S. 1052, 112 L.Ed.2d 785, certiorari denied Baker v. U.S., 111 S.Ct. 766, 498 U.S. 1052, 112 L.Ed.2d 785, certiorari denied 111 S.Ct. 987, 498 U.S. 1096, 112 L.Ed.2d 1071.

C.A.11 (Fla.) 1986. Search of extortion defendant's apartment did not violate his Fourth Amendment rights against unreasonable search and seizure where defendant told roommate he was leaving town and not coming back, and thus property was abandoned; though defendant left town to avoid capture, lawful police investigation did not constitute such coercion that abandonment should be considered involuntary. U.S.C.A. Const.Amend. 4.

> U.S. v. De Parias, 805 F.2d 1447, certiorari denied Ramirez v. United States, 107 S.Ct. 3189, 482 U.S. 916, 96 L.Ed.2d 678.

C.A.5 (Fla.) 1981. Defendant has no right to protest warrantless search of property which he has abandoned, and test of whether he has abandoned is whether he voluntarily discarded, left behind or otherwise relinquished his interest in property in question so that he could no longer retain reasonable expectation of privacy with regard to it at time of search. U.S.C.A.Const. Amend. 4.

> U.S. v. Edwards, 644 F.2d 1, certiorari denied 102 S.Ct. 302, 454 U.S. 855, 70 L.Ed.2d 148.

C.A.5 (Fla.) 1981. A defendant cannot challenge search or seizure of abandoned property.

> U.S. v. Richards, 638 F.2d 765, rehearing denied 646 F.2d 962, certiorari denied 102 S.Ct. 669, 454 U.S. 1097, 70 L.Ed.2d 638.

M.D.Fla. 2008. Police officer had reasonable suspicion for investigatory stop of defendant, and, thus, defendant's alleged abandonment of firearm while fleeing from police officer was not involuntary pursuant to an unlawful stop, where defendant was in a high crime area conversing with a known prostitute, and he engaged in evasive and erratic driving when he noticed officer. U.S.C.A. Const.Amend. 4.

> U.S. v. Muhammad, 554 F.Supp.2d 1314, affirmed 340 Fed.Appx. 548.

S.D.Fla. 2000. In determining whether there has been an abandonment of property, for search and seizure purposes, the critical inquiry is whether the person prejudiced by the search in question voluntarily discarded, left behind, or otherwise relinquished his interest in the property in question so that he could no longer retain a reasonable expectation of privacy with regard to it at the time of the search. U.S.C.A. Const.Amend. 4.

> U.S. v. Cofield, 108 F.Supp.2d 1374, vacated 272 F.3d 1303, on remand 242 F.Supp.2d 1260.

Whether abandonment of property occurred, for search and seizure purposes, is a question of intent which court may infer from words, acts, and other objective criteria. U.S.C.A. Const.Amend. 4.

> U.S. v. Cofield, 108 F.Supp.2d 1374, vacated 272 F.3d 1303, on remand 242 F.Supp.2d 1260.

One who abandons personal property may not contest the constitutionality of its subsequent acquisition by the police. U.S.C.A. Const.Amend. 4.

> U.S. v. Cofield, 108 F.Supp.2d 1374, vacated 272 F.3d 1303, on remand 242 F.Supp.2d 1260.

A suspect who asserts a privacy interest in luggage by refusing consent to search and attempts to leave the area does not abandon the property after being detained. U.S.C.A. Const.Amend. 4.

> U.S. v. Cofield, 108 F.Supp.2d 1374, vacated 272 F.3d 1303, on remand 242 F.Supp.2d 1260.

S.D.Fla. 1994. If arrest is lawfully made, abandonment in police car of items belonging to defendants is voluntary. U.S.C.A. Const.Amend. 4.

> U.S. v. Wai-Keung, 845 F.Supp. 1548, affirmed 115 F.3d 874, rehearing and suggestion for rehearing denied U.S. v. Chi-Cheong, 127 F.3d 42, certiorari denied Li v. U.S., 118 S.Ct. 1095, 522 U.S. 1135, 140 L.Ed.2d 150.

Leaving hotel room without intending to return, leaving indicia of that intent, or paying for room, is abandonment of that room and any right to privacy in it. U.S.C.A. Const.Amend. 4.

> U.S. v. Wai-Keung, 845 F.Supp. 1548, affirmed 115 F.3d 874, rehearing and suggestion for rehearing denied U.S. v. Chi-Cheong, 127 F.3d 42, certiorari denied Li v. U.S., 118 S.Ct. 1095, 522 U.S. 1135, 140 L.Ed.2d 150.

S.D.Fla. 1992. Test for abandonment is whether defendant voluntarily discarded, left behind, or otherwise relinquished his interest in the property in question so that he could no longer retain a reasonable expectation of privacy with regard to it at the time of the search. U.S.C.A. Const. Amend. 4.

> U.S. v. Rojas, 801 F.Supp. 644, affirmed 53 F.3d 1212, certiorari denied 116 S.Ct. 478, 516 U.S. 976, 133 L.Ed.2d 407.

Abandonment, for Fourth Amendment purposes, is primarily a question of intent, and intent may be inferred from words,

acts, and other objective facts. U.S.C.A. Const.Amend. 4.

> U.S. v. Rojas, 801 F.Supp. 644, affirmed 53 F.3d 1212, certiorari denied 116 S.Ct. 478, 516 U.S. 976, 133 L.Ed.2d 407.

Fla. 2017. The test for abandonment is whether a defendant voluntarily discarded, left behind, or otherwise relinquished his interest in the property in question so that he could no longer retain a reasonable expectation of privacy with regard to it at the time of the search. U.S. Const. Amend. 4.

> Heyne v. State, 214 So.3d 640.

Fla. 2010. The test for abandonment, for purposes of search and seizure law, is whether a defendant voluntarily discarded, left behind, or otherwise relinquished his interest in the property in question so that he could no longer retain a reasonable expectation of privacy with regard to it at the time of the search. U.S.C.A. Const. Amend. 4.

> Twilegar v. State, 42 So.3d 177, rehearing denied, certiorari denied 131 S.Ct. 1476, 562 U.S. 1225, 179 L.Ed.2d 315, denial of post-conviction relief affirmed 175 So.3d 242, rehearing denied.

No search occurs when police retrieve property voluntarily abandoned by a suspect in an area where the suspect has no reasonable expectation of privacy. U.S.C.A. Const.Amend. 4.

> Twilegar v. State, 42 So.3d 177, rehearing denied, certiorari denied 131 S.Ct. 1476, 562 U.S. 1225, 179 L.Ed.2d 315, denial of post-conviction relief affirmed 175 So.3d 242, rehearing denied.

Defendant, who had no intention of retrieving property he left at camp site lot, due to an outstanding warrant for his arrest, abandoned the property, and thus, there was no illegal seizure of the property, to the extent that the police ultimately retained possession of the property, i.e., campground hosts and officer believed the lot had been burglarized and ransacked or vandalized, officer suggested that perhaps the prudent thing to do was to remove the remaining items for safekeeping purposes because otherwise the person who burglarized the lot might return and take the remaining items, and since hosts had no room at their residence for the property, the officer took the property to the police station. U.S.C.A. Const.Amend. 4.

> Twilegar v. State, 42 So.3d 177, rehearing denied, certiorari denied 131 S.Ct. 1476, 562 U.S. 1225, 179 L.Ed.2d 315, denial of post-conviction relief affirmed 175 So.3d 242, rehearing denied.

Fla. 2010. Defendant had abandoned his interest in apartment where he barricaded himself following victim's murder, and thus did not have a reasonable expectation of privacy as required to challenge warrantless search of apartment by police; although defendant had rented apartment and eviction proceedings were not yet final, eviction notice had been posted on apartment door, apartment maintenance supervisor had conducted a walk-through of the apartment and determined that it had been abandoned, and weeks later, and shortly before the murder, defendant returned and asked for a key so that he could pick up some final items. U.S.C.A. Const.Amend. 4; West's F.S.A. Const. Art. 1, § 12.

> Caraballo v. State, 39 So.3d 1234.

Although warrantless searches and seizures are generally prohibited, police may conduct a search without a warrant if consent is given or if the individual has abandoned his or her interest in the property in question. U.S.C.A. Const.Amend. 4; West's F.S.A. Const. Art. 1, § 12.

> Caraballo v. State, 39 So.3d 1234.

The test for abandonment of an interest in property for purposes of challenging a warrantless search or seizure is whether a defendant voluntarily discarded, left behind, or otherwise relinquished his interest in the property in question so that he could no longer retain a reasonable expectation of privacy with regard to it at the time of the search. U.S.C.A. Const. Amend. 4; West's F.S.A. Const. Art. 1, § 12.

> Caraballo v. State, 39 So.3d 1234.

Fla. 2004. Police may conduct a search without a warrant if consent is given or if the individual has abandoned his or her interest in the property in ques-

tion. U.S.C.A. Const.Amend. 4; West's F.S.A. Const. Art. 1, § 12.

> Peterka v. State, 890 So.2d 219, rehearing denied, certiorari denied 125 S.Ct. 2911, 545 U.S. 1118, 162 L.Ed.2d 301.

Fla. 1993. Police call for defendant to halt and subsequent chase did not constitute a seizure until defendant was caught; therefore, firearm which defendant dropped during chase was abandoned and recovery of firearm was not an illegal seizure. U.S.C.A. Const.Amend. 4; West's F.S.A. Const. Art. 1, § 12.

> Perez v. State, 620 So.2d 1256.

Fla. 1992. Abandonment which is product of illegal stop is involuntary, and abandoned property must be suppressed. U.S.C.A. Const.Amend. 4.

> State v. Anderson, 591 So.2d 611.

Fla.App. 1 Dist. 2013. Defendant abandoned medicine bottle that fell out of his pocket following pat down search of defendant by police officer during investigatory stop, such that defendant had no reasonable expectation of privacy in the bottle, for purposes of Fourth Amendment analysis, as defendant stated that the bottle was not his, such that he ceded his interest in it. U.S.C.A. Const.Amend. 4.

> State v. Williams, 119 So.3d 544.

In determining whether property was abandoned for purposes of search and seizure analyses, the test is whether a defendant voluntarily discarded, left behind, or otherwise relinquished his interest in the property in question so that he could no longer retain a reasonable expectation of privacy with regard to it at the time of the search. U.S.C.A. Const. Amend. 4.

> State v. Williams, 119 So.3d 544.

In deciding whether property was abandoned for purposes of search and seizure analyses, in determining whether a defendant voluntarily discarded, left behind, or otherwise relinquished his interest in the property, the primary question concerns the individual's intent, to be inferred from the words and actions of the parties and other circumstances surrounding the purported abandonment. U.S.C.A. Const. Amend. 4.

> State v. Williams, 119 So.3d 544.

† This Case was not selected for publication in the National Reporter System
For legislative history of cited statutes, see Florida Statutes Annotated

Fla.App. 1 Dist. 1996. Trial court did not err in making factual determination that there was no reasonable expectation of privacy as to contents of garbage can left outside privacy fence.

Craft v. State, 670 So.2d 112, rehearing denied, review granted 678 So.2d 339, quashed 685 So.2d 1292.

Fla.App. 1 Dist. 1992. Warrantless searches are per se unreasonable unless conducted within an established exception such as personal consent, abandonment, or consent by a third party with common authority over the premises. U.S.C.A. Const.Amend. 4.

Morse v. State, 604 So.2d 496.

Warrantless search of defendant's motel room could not be justified on the basis of abandonment where defendant left personal items such as clothing and furnishings in the room, defendant was not evicted in accordance with applicable statutes, and there was no other evidence of intent on defendant's part to relinquish control over the room. U.S.C.A. Const.Amend. 4.

Morse v. State, 604 So.2d 496.

Fla.App. 1 Dist. 1992. Gun which defendant dropped to the ground while he was being pursued by officer was lawfully recovered by the police and should have been admitted; assuming that pursuit constituted show of authority enjoining defendant to halt, he did not comply and was not seized until he was caught; thus, defendant voluntarily abandoned the gun.

State v. Wilson, 595 So.2d 1106.

Fla.App. 1 Dist. 1988. Defendant had not abandoned his bicycle and attached backpack as would justify police officer's search of backpack; defendant was present with bicycle and had left in automobile only five-ten minutes before officer searched it, there was no evidence to suggest that defendant did not intend to return soon, and bicycle was left near group of people, at least one of whom knew defendant. U.S.C.A. Const.Amend. 4.

Kelly v. State, 536 So.2d 1113.

Fla.App. 1 Dist. 1981. Defendant had no reasonable expectation of privacy in items placed for collection in opaque trash container just inside his property, where items had been abandoned by defendant as

trash. U.S.C.A.Const. Amend. 4; West's F.S.A.Const. Art. 1, § 12.

Stone v. State, 402 So.2d 1330.

Fla.App. 2 Dist. 2007. A suspect who abandons or discards property as a result of an illegal stop or arrest does so involuntarily, and the abandoned or discarded property must be suppressed. U.S.C.A. Const.Amend. 4.

Bravo v. State, 963 So.2d 370.

Fla.App. 2 Dist. 2006. There is no unlawful seizure when the person drops contraband, then stops, even where the drop occurs after an order to stop. U.S.C.A. Const.Amend. 4; West's F.S.A. Const. Art. 1, § 12.

State v. Battis, 926 So.2d 427, rehearing denied.

Fla.App. 2 Dist. 2004. Drug suspect abandoned his jacket by continuing to run after jacket came off in officer's hands, and retained no protectable Fourth Amendment privacy interest therein; suspect's actions permitted inference that he did not intend to return to retrieve jacket. U.S.C.A. Const.Amend. 4.

State v. Collins, 874 So.2d 724.

Fla.App. 2 Dist. 2003. An unconstitutional seizure or arrest which prompts a disclaimer of property vitiates the disclaimer. U.S.C.A. Const.Amend. 4.

Baggett v. State, 849 So.2d 1154.

To determine whether a disclaimer of property is voluntary, courts must look to whether there is a causal nexus between the unlawful police conduct and the defendant's disclaimer of the property.

Baggett v. State, 849 So.2d 1154.

Fla.App. 2 Dist. 2001. Automobile passenger did not abandon her fanny pack merely by placing it on the floorboard as she left the vehicle, and thus, officer was compelled to get passenger's consent to open the zippered pack and look inside it, where passenger's action in leaving pack behind was in response to officer's show of authority in ordering her out of car and officer was presented with sufficient evidence that passenger owned the pack. U.S.C.A. Const.Amend. 4.

Brown v. State, 789 So.2d 1021, rehearing denied, review dismissed 796 So.2d 537.

Fla.App. 2 Dist. 2000. Where a defendant abandons property as a direct result of unlawful police conduct, he does not relinquish his reasonable expectation of privacy in his property, and retains standing to challenge the introduction of the abandoned items into evidence. U.S.C.A. Const.Amend. 4.

State v. Williams, 751 So.2d 170.

Fla.App. 2 Dist. 1998. Defendant did not abandon fishing rods when he stepped five to ten feet away from them during brief encounter with police officer; officer confiscated rods before defendant demonstrated any intention to part with them forever. U.S.C.A. Const.Amend. 4.

Cliett v. State, 722 So.2d 916.

Fla.App. 2 Dist. 1996. Contraband abandoned during defendant's flight from police was not subject to suppression.

Washington v. State, 685 So.2d 858.

Fla.App. 2 Dist. 1995. Defendant abandoned her interest in cigarette pouch by hiding it under wheel of vehicle in public area and walking away. U.S.C.A. Const.Amend. 4.

State v. Kennon, 652 So.2d 396, rehearing denied.

Whether property has been abandoned is different under the Fourth Amendment than under property law. U.S.C.A. Const.Amend. 4.

State v. Kennon, 652 So.2d 396, rehearing denied.

Fla.App. 2 Dist. 1993. Police officer's search of truck was permissible because defendant voluntarily abandoned truck, which was unlocked and illegally parked, by walking away from truck without saying anything to officer, and therefore giving up any expectation of privacy defendant had in the vehicle. U.S.C.A. Const. Amend. 4.

State v. Wynn, 623 So.2d 848.

Fla.App. 2 Dist. 1980. Defendant, who had left his luggage at motel and informed motel owner that he would return to pay his bill, did not "abandon" his luggage by his failure to return by the following afternoon in that he had at all times exhibited an intention to return for his luggage as soon as he had obtained funds to pay his outstanding bill and had in effect left luggage as collateral, and

thus, warrantless search of luggage by police was not justified. U.S.C.A.Const. Amends. 4, 14; West's F.S.A.Const. Art. 1, § 12.

Hackett v. State, 386 So.2d 35, review denied 392 So.2d 1379.

Fla.App. 3 Dist. 2016. Abandoned property is not subject to Fourth Amendment protection against unreasonable searches and seizures. U.S.C.A. Const. Amend. 4.

State v. Milewski, 194 So.3d 376, rehearing denied, review denied 2016 WL 6722865.

There is a distinction between abandonment in the context of property law and the law of search and seizure. U.S.C.A. Const.Amend. 4.

State v. Milewski, 194 So.3d 376, rehearing denied, review denied 2016 WL 6722865.

The test to determine whether an expectation of privacy in property has been abandoned is whether a defendant voluntarily discarded, left behind, or otherwise relinquished his interest in the property in question so that he could no longer retain a reasonable expectation of privacy with regard to it at the time of the search. U.S.C.A. Const.Amend. 4.

State v. Milewski, 194 So.3d 376, rehearing denied, review denied 2016 WL 6722865.

Whether the expectation of privacy in property has been abandoned is an issue that is viewed primarily as a question of intent, which is to be inferred from the words and actions of the parties and other circumstances surrounding the purported abandonment. U.S.C.A. Const.Amend. 4.

State v. Milewski, 194 So.3d 376, rehearing denied, review denied 2016 WL 6722865.

Defendant abandoned his expectation of privacy in puppy's remains, and thus his Fourth Amendment rights were not violated when animal services seized puppy's remains from animal hospital without warrant to investigate charge of animal cruelty; even though defendant initially stated he wanted puppy's ashes to be returned following cremation, defendant changed his mind, consciously choosing and tendering payment for group cremation over private cremation, which showed lack of desire to preserve his possessory and privacy interests. U.S.C.A. Const. Amends. 4, 14.

> State v. Milewski, 194 So.3d 376, re-hearing denied, review denied 2016 WL 6722865.

Fla.App. 3 Dist. 2016.   Defendant abandoned any reasonable expectation of privacy in black box when he placed it in garbage can, and thus warrantless search of box, in which a gun and cocaine were found, was justified; contents of garbage can might have been collected by trash hauler, rummaged by animals, or box might have been taken by scavengers, children, or owner of the garbage can. U.S.C.A. Const.Amend. 4.

> Strawder v. State, 185 So.3d 543, re-hearing denied, review denied 2016 WL 4440970.

Courts examine two components of an abandonment in a Fourth Amendment context: (1) whether the defendant voluntarily relinquished or discarded the property; and (2) whether the property was relinquished or discarded in an area where the defendant had no claim to privacy. U.S.C.A. Const.Amend. 4.

> Strawder v. State, 185 So.3d 543, re-hearing denied, review denied 2016 WL 4440970.

Fla.App. 3 Dist. 2012. In the law of search and seizure, the question of abandonment of property is whether the defendant has, in discarding the property, relinquished his reasonable expectation of privacy so that its seizure and search is reasonable within the limits of the Fourth Amendment; in essence, what is abandoned is not necessarily the defendant's property, but his reasonable expectation of privacy. U.S.C.A. Const.Amend. 4.

> J.W. v. State, 95 So.3d 372.

Fla.App. 3 Dist. 2002. A search of curbside garbage requires no warrant. U.S.C.A. Const.Amend. 4.

> State v. Gross, 833 So.2d 777.

Fla.App. 3 Dist. 2000. Defendant was illegally seized when he was approached by officers with guns drawn, ordered to lie on ground, and handcuffed, and thus paper bag containing marijuana he threw to ground was not abandoned and could not

be admitted into evidence. U.S.C.A. Const.Amend. 4.

> Bryan v. State, 760 So.2d 246.

Fla.App. 3 Dist. 1992. Gun which defendant abandoned could not be suppressed as fruit of unlawful seizure as defendant, who was fleeing from officer, had not been seized when he abandoned gun.

> State v. Green, 601 So.2d 617.

Fla.App. 3 Dist. 1989.   Defendant's flight from car, leaving it unattended and running in middle of street, was effectively abandonment, thus relinquishing any reasonable expectation of privacy in property abandoned in private street.

> Diaz v. State, 548 So.2d 843.

Fla.App. 3 Dist. 1988. Record was legally insufficient to establish that defendant abandoned credit cards which apparently fell to ground during struggle with police officer, so as to render seizure of credit cards legal, and thus denial of defendant's motion to suppress was error. U.S.C.A. Const.Amend. 4.

> Gilbert v. State, 534 So.2d 882.

Fla.App. 3 Dist. 1987. In delinquency proceeding, evidence contained in paper bag which juvenile had discarded was properly admitted; juvenile relinquished any legitimate expectation of privacy in property at time he abandoned bag, and thus, search of bag did not violate his Fourth Amendment rights. U.S.C.A. Const.Amend. 4.

> M.S. v. State, 513 So.2d 231.

Fla.App. 3 Dist. 1984. Disclaiming of ownership or knowledge of item ends any legitimate expectation of privacy in such item. U.S.C.A. Const.Amend. 4.

> State v. Jones, 454 So.2d 774.

Defendant's disavowal of any knowledge of boxes at issue and subsequent statement that he was merely keeping an eye on them for someone else refuted any legitimate expectation of privacy he may have had in such boxes. U.S.C.A. Const. Amend. 4.

> State v. Jones, 454 So.2d 774.

Fla.App. 3 Dist. 1983. Person has no expectations of privacy in trash which he has bagged and placed on his property adjacent to alley so that it may be picked up by local trash collectors.

State v. Slatko, 432 So.2d 635.

Fla.App. 3 Dist. 1982. Defendant, by removing his jacket, placing it on hedge a few feet from him and commencing to walk away in front of officer, did not renounce his justified expectation of privacy in jacket or its contents; indeed, officer's act of picking up jacket to return it to defendant alone belied any belief on officer's part that jacket was abandoned.

O'Shaughnessy v. State, 420 So.2d 377.

Fla.App. 3 Dist. 1981. To constitute "abandonment" so as to justify seizure of property, property must be discovered in place where person has no reasonable expectation of privacy, such as open field or public street. U.S.C.A.Const. Amend. 4.

State v. Parker, 399 So.2d 24, review denied 408 So.2d 1095.

Fla.App. 3 Dist. 1979. Where defendant, totally without reference to any police activity which was either threatened or actually undertaken, voluntarily abandoned allegedly stolen property under bush about ten feet from street, defendant had voluntarily abandoned the property in place in which he had no reasonable expectation of privacy, and thus discovery and retrieval by police did not amount to Fourth Amendment search or seizure and any impropriety involved in investigating officer's detention of defendant did not render seizure of the property invalid. U.S.C.A.Const. Amend. 4.

State v. Washington, 376 So.2d 1216.

Fla.App. 3 Dist. 1979. Although officers investigating residential burglaries had received reports that some burglaries may have been committed by young black teen-agers on bicycles, the officers, who observed two black teen-agers riding bicycles in vicinity on a pleasant day, who had never seen the pair before and who followed them for a few blocks during which nothing untoward or suspicious occurred, engaged in an unconstitutional seizure when they stopped the pair for temporary questioning; however, paper bag which one youth threw onto the street after being ordered to stop was properly seized since it had been voluntarily abandoned in an area where the youth had no reasonable

expectation of privacy and such abandonment was not prompted or tainted by the illegal stop. West's F.S.A.Const. art. 1, § 12; U.S.C.A.Const. Amends. 4, 14; West's F.S.A. §§ 893.03(1)(c), 893.13(1)(e, f).

State v. Oliver, 368 So.2d 1331, certiorari dismissed 383 So.2d 1200.

A person's otherwise voluntary abandonment of property cannot be tainted or made involuntary by prior illegal police stop; only when the police begin to conduct an illegal search can a subsequent abandonment of property be held involuntary as being tainted by the prior illegal search. West's F.S.A.Const. art. 1, § 12; U.S.C.A.Const. Amends. 4, 14.

State v. Oliver, 368 So.2d 1331, certiorari dismissed 383 So.2d 1200.

No one can have a reasonable expectation of privacy, which is at the core of Fourth Amendment protection, with respect to property which he has decided to discard in the public streets in hope of avoiding a police search. West's F.S.A.Const. art. 1, § 12; U.S.C.A.Const. Amends. 4, 14.

State v. Oliver, 368 So.2d 1331, certiorari dismissed 383 So.2d 1200.

The abandonment or plain sight doctrine should not be cynically employed by the State as a way around the Fourth Amendment. West's F.S.A.Const. art. 1, § 12; U.S.C.A.Const. Amends. 4, 14.

State v. Oliver, 368 So.2d 1331, certiorari dismissed 383 So.2d 1200.

Fla.App. 4 Dist. 2016. A warrant was required to search defendant's password-protected cell phone that was left in a stolen car and that was not claimed by anyone at the police station; the quantitative and qualitative nature of the information contained on a cell phone set it apart from other physical objects, even locked containers. U.S. Const. Amend. 4.

State v. K.C., 207 So.3d 951.

A categorical rule permitting warrantless searches of abandoned cell phones, the contents of which are password protected, violates the Fourth Amendment. U.S. Const. Amend. 4.

State v. K.C., 207 So.3d 951.

Fla.App. 4 Dist. 2002. The test for abandonment, in the context of search and seizure law, is whether a defendant voluntarily discarded, left behind, or otherwise relinquished his interest in the property in question so that he could no longer retain a reasonable expectation of privacy with regard to it at the time of the search. U.S.C.A. Const.Amend. 4.

State v. Lampley, 817 So.2d 989.

No search occurs when police retrieve property voluntarily abandoned by a suspect in an area where the latter has no reasonable expectation of privacy. U.S.C.A. Const.Amend. 4.

State v. Lampley, 817 So.2d 989.

Fla.App. 4 Dist. 1997. Even if defendant had submitted to police officers' initial investigatory stop, he was not "seized" at time he discarded handgun while fleeing from officers, and therefore handgun was admissible evidence. U.S.C.A. Const. Amend. 4.

Johnson v. State, 689 So.2d 376, rehearing denied, review denied 698 So.2d 543.

Fla.App. 4 Dist. 1991. Unconstitutional seizure or arrest which prompts disclaimer of property vitiates disclaimer. U.S.C.A. Const.Amend. 4.

State v. Daniels, 576 So.2d 819.

"Abandonment," as applied to illegal seizures, does not refer to traditional meaning of that term in context of property law. U.S.C.A. Const.Amend. 4.

State v. Daniels, 576 So.2d 819.

To determine for Fourth Amendment purposes whether abandonment of property is voluntary and not product of police misconduct, court must determine if there is causal nexus between unlawful conduct and defendant's abandonment. U.S.C.A. Const.Amend. 4.

State v. Daniels, 576 So.2d 819.

If officers have illegally seized defendant or had begun to conduct illegal search of property before defendant has abandoned it, abandonment may be involuntary, depending on facts of case. U.S.C.A. Const.Amend. 4.

State v. Daniels, 576 So.2d 819.

Defendant, if illegally stopped, did not necessarily lose reasonable expectation of privacy in luggage by denying that she owned it. U.S.C.A. Const.Amend. 4.

State v. Daniels, 576 So.2d 819.

Defendant's abandonment of suitcase was voluntary, and therefore defendant lacked standing to challenge either search of suitcase or seizure of its contents, where encounter between deputies and defendant was not a legal seizure of her person, and defendant abandoned suitcase in train station in which she had no Fourth Amendment protection. U.S.C.A. Const.Amend. 4.

State v. Daniels, 576 So.2d 819.

Fla.App. 4 Dist. 1990. Where defendant, when complying with police officer's order to expose his hands, threw manila envelope to ground, defendant freely and voluntarily abandoned envelope and could not object to its search and seizure. U.S.C.A. Const.Amend. 4.

State v. Louis, 571 So.2d 1358.

Fla.App. 4 Dist. 1982. There was no reasonable expectation of privacy in trash deposited for collection. U.S.C.A. Const. Amend. 4.

Sims v. State, 425 So.2d 563, petition for review denied 436 So.2d 100.

Fla.App. 4 Dist. 1981. An otherwise voluntary abandonment of property cannot be tainted or made involuntary by a prior illegal police stop.

State v. Lawson, 394 So.2d 1139.

Fla.App. 4 Dist. 1980. While individual may demonstrate intention to forever part with his trash by placing it in container at rear of his home or in garage or carport, he may still harbor reasonable expectation of privacy in it in sense that it is retrievable. U.S.C.A.Const. Amend. 4.

State v. Schultz, 388 So.2d 1326.

Once trash is deposited on swale for collection it is unreasonable to expect that its security will remain inviolate until it is commingled with all other trash, and, therefore, defendant cannot have reasonable expectation of privacy concerning contents of his trash bags once he places the trash in swale area in front of his home. U.S.C.A.Const. Amend. 4.

State v. Schultz, 388 So.2d 1326.

Fla.App. 5 Dist. 2015. It is not a search for the police to retrieve property

† This Case was not selected for publication in the National Reporter System
For legislative history of cited statutes, see Florida Statutes Annotated

which a defendant has voluntarily abandoned in an area where he has no reasonable expectation of privacy; in such cases, the person has made a voluntary decision to avoid a police search by discarding evidence in an area where he has no Fourth Amendment protection. U.S.C.A. Const.Amend. 4.

K.W. v. State, 183 So.3d 1123.

Courts consider the defendant's intent, inferred from words and actions and other circumstances when determining if property has been abandoned for search and seizure purposes. U.S.C.A. Const.Amend. 4.

K.W. v. State, 183 So.3d 1123.

The reasonable expectation of privacy carries significant weight in the consideration of abandonment for search and seizure purposes. U.S.C.A. Const.Amend. 4.
K.W. v. State, 183 So.3d 1123.

Fla.App. 5 Dist. 2001. Although a suspect's voluntary abandonment of evidence can remove the taint of illegal conduct, the abandonment must be truly voluntary and not merely the product of police conduct. U.S.C.A. Const.Amend. 4.

Clinton v. State, 780 So.2d 960.

Fla.App. 5 Dist. 1990. Drugs or other evidence thrown by a defendant after being ordered by police to "stop" or "freeze" are voluntarily abandoned and thus need not be suppressed even though police lacked founded suspicion sufficient to allow investigative stop. U.S.C.A. Const. Amend. 4; West's F.S.A. § 901.151.

Curry v. State, 570 So.2d 1071.

Fla.App. 5 Dist. 1980. There is no reasonable expectation of privacy in regard to articles thrown into garbage or abandoned.

State v. Preston, 387 So.2d 495, appeal after remand 444 So.2d 939, vacated 564 So.2d 120, appeal after remand 607 So.2d 404, certiorari denied 113 S.Ct. 1619, 507 U.S. 999, 123 L.Ed.2d 178, denial of post-conviction relief affirmed 970 So.2d 789, rehearing denied, habeas corpus denied Preston v. Secretary, Dept. of Corrections, 2012 WL 1549529, affirmed 785 F.3d 449.

⌾29. —— Containers.

U.S.Fla. 1980. Fact that FBI agents were lawfully in possession of boxes of film did not give them authority to search their contents. (Per Mr. Justice Stevens, with one Justice joining, two Justices concurring in part and in the judgment, and the one Justice concurring in the judgment.)

Walter v. U.S., 100 S.Ct. 2395, 447 U.S. 649, 65 L.Ed.2d 410, on remand U.S. v. Sanders, 625 F.2d 1311.

Fact that cartons of film boxes, which cartons were securely wrapped and had no markings indicating the character of their contents, were unexpectedly opened by a third party before the shipment was delivered to its intended consignee, thus uncovering the descriptive labels on the film boxes, did not alter the consignor's legitimate expectation of privacy in the films; the private search merely frustrated that expectation in part and did not strip the remaining unfrustrated portion of that expectation of all Fourth Amendment protection. (Per Mr. Justice Stevens, with one Justice joining, two Justices concurring in part and in the judgment, and the one Justice concurring in the judgment.) U.S.C.A.Const. Amend. 4.

Walter v. U.S., 100 S.Ct. 2395, 447 U.S. 649, 65 L.Ed.2d 410, on remand U.S. v. Sanders, 625 F.2d 1311.

Consignor's expectation of privacy in the contents of a carton delivered to a private carrier must be measured by the condition of the package at the time it was shipped unless there is reason to assume that it would be opened before it arrived at its destination. (Per Mr. Justice Stevens, with one Justice joining, two Justices concurring in part and in the judgment, and the one Justice concurring in the judgment.)

Walter v. U.S., 100 S.Ct. 2395, 447 U.S. 649, 65 L.Ed.2d 410, on remand U.S. v. Sanders, 625 F.2d 1311.

† C.A.11 (Fla.) 2008. Defendant, a government postal worker, did not have a reasonable expectation of privacy in her purse, given posted regulation informing individuals entering postal property that purses were subject to inspection, and office rules requiring employees to read all posted regulations. U.S.C.A. Const. Amend. 4.

> U.S. v. Esser, 284 Fed.Appx. 757.

C.A.11 (Fla.) 2003. Packages sent through carrier were "effects" in context of Fourth Amendment, and senders therefore presumptively possessed legitimate expectation of privacy in their contents. U.S.C.A. Const.Amend. 4.

> U.S. v. Young, 350 F.3d 1302, rehearing and rehearing denied 97 Fed. Appx. 909.

Defendant had no legitimate expectation of privacy in packages of cash he sent through private carrier, and, thus, warrantless government search, consisting of x-raying of packages by IRS agents after they had initiated contact with carrier, did not violate defendant's Fourth Amendment rights, where airbill stated that carrier had right to open and inspect packages, and packages plainly stated "DO NOT SEND CASH." U.S.C.A. Const.Amend. 4.

> U.S. v. Young, 350 F.3d 1302, rehearing and rehearing denied 97 Fed. Appx. 909.

C.A.11 (Fla.) 1985. Defendant did not have a reasonable expectation of privacy in a briefcase which had been in a vehicle that was stolen and which was found by a police officer next to an overflowing trash dumpster on a busy city street; furthermore, failure to compile a complete written inventory of the briefcase's contents or notify the defendant that his briefcase had been recovered did not invalidate the search.

> U.S. v. O'Bryant, 775 F.2d 1528.

C.A.11 (Fla.) 1983. Briefcase is often repository for more than business documents and is extension of person's clothing in that it serves as larger "pocket" in which such items as wallet and credit cards, address books, personal calendar/diaries, correspondence, and reading glasses are often carried; therefore, few places outside one's home justify greater expectation of privacy than does briefcase.

> U.S. v. Freire, 710 F.2d 1515, rehearing denied 717 F.2d 1401, certiorari denied 104 S.Ct. 1277, 465 U.S. 1023, 79 L.Ed.2d 681.

C.A.5 (Fla.) 1973. Defendants' suitcases were "effects," within Fourth Amendment's protection of right of people to be secure in their persons, houses, papers and effects. U.S.C.A.Const. Amend. 4.

> U.S. v. Soriano, 482 F.2d 469, on rehearing 497 F.2d 147.

S.D.Fla. 2000. In determining whether luggage search violates Fourth Amendment, an individual will be deemed to enjoy a reasonable expectation of privacy in personal luggage. U.S.C.A. Const. Amend. 4.

> U.S. v. Cofield, 108 F.Supp.2d 1374, vacated 272 F.3d 1303, on remand 242 F.Supp.2d 1260.

S.D.Fla. 1986. Crew members aboard small fishing boat which they did not own did not have legitimate expectation of privacy in 12 large aluminum containers containing cocaine that were stored in lavatory of boat and storage compartments and that were unmarked, unidentified, interchangeable, and heavy. U.S.C.A. Const.Amend. 4.

> U.S. v. Marrero, 644 F.Supp. 570.

Fla. 1983. Warrantless search of suitcase taken from bus did not violate defendant's right to be free from unreasonable searches and seizures, where defendant and companion each claimed one suitcase when they were detained for questioning but left third suitcase on bus, as they thus abandoned all possessory interests and expectations of privacy in that suitcase. U.S.C.A. Const.Amend. 4.

> Maxwell v. State, 443 So.2d 967, denial of post-conviction relief reversed 603 So.2d 490, appeal after remand 647 So.2d 871, opinion withdrawn on grant of rehearing, review granted 659 So.2d 1087, decision approved 657 So.2d 1157.

Fla.App. 1 Dist. 2016. When determining whether a defendant has a legitimate privacy interest in a package sent through the mail or container shipped via a transportation company that was subject to a warrantless search, courts have generally considered the following factors: (1) whether the defendant is listed as the sender or addressee of the package, (2) if there is a fictitious name listed on the package, whether there is a connection between the defendant and the fictitious name, and (3) whether the defendant can demonstrate a legitimate expectation of privacy in the location where the package was delivered. U.S.C.A. Const.Amend. 4.

State v. Williams, 184 So.3d 1205, rehearing denied.

Fla.App. 1 Dist. 2002. An officer must have probable cause that a container contains contraband in order to conduct a search of the container. U.S.C.A. Const. Amend. 4.

Graham v. State, 822 So.2d 576.

Fla.App. 1 Dist. 1981. Courts may permit search of container if container announces that its likely contents are not personal possessions in which one would have reasonable privacy interest. West's F.S.A.Const. Art. 1, § 12; U.S.C.A.Const. Amend. 4.

Knight v. State, 398 So.2d 908.

Fla.App. 1 Dist. 1980. Absent consent or some other exception to the warrant requirement, a search warrant was needed before the lockers located in the trucks driven by defendants could be searched; however, a general search of the trucks and a seizure of their contents was authorized without a warrant since the odor of marijuana gave agricultural inspector cause to believe the trucks contained contraband.

Sower v. State, 382 So.2d 1257, dismissed 386 So.2d 642.

Fla.App. 3 Dist. 1990. Defendant relinquished his privacy rights in gym bag's contents when he displayed weapon taken from bag in public, permitting undercover police officer who observed defendant display weapon to conduct warrantless search of bag without violating defendant's privacy rights. U.S.C.A. Const.Amend. 4.

State v. V.M., 564 So.2d 610, review denied 576 So.2d 294.

Accessible container may be seized without warrant based on probable cause and it may then be searched without warrant when contents of container were in plain view or otherwise inferable to a virtual certainty. U.S.C.A. Const.Amend. 4.

State v. V.M., 564 So.2d 610, review denied 576 So.2d 294.

Fla.App. 3 Dist. 1989. Search of metal cigarette case found in juvenile suspect's back pants pocket was illegal; although bulge in pocket initially may have given rise to reasonable suspicion that suspect was armed, that suspicion disappeared once officer determined that object in pocket was a cigarette case and not a weapon; there was no evidence that officer had a reasonable suspicion that case contained any kind of weapon, and search could not be justified on ground that razor blade was found inside case. U.S.C.A. Const.Amend. 4.

C.H. v. State, 548 So.2d 895.

Fla.App. 3 Dist. 1984. When defendant turned his purse over to manager of hotel he had reasonable expectation of privacy therein which would render warrantless search by government agents unreasonable and violation of Fourth Amendment, but where initial invasion of defendant's purse was occasioned by private action, of hotel manager, invasion did not violate Fourth Amendment. U.S.C.A. Const.Amend. 4.

State v. Weiss, 449 So.2d 915.

Fla.App. 3 Dist. 1981. Defendant had no expectation of privacy in duffel bags or keys, which were left on the side of the road when police helicopter approached, and, therefore, police officers' seizure of the duffel bags and keys did not implicate any right of defendant under the Fourth Amendment, and the duffel bag, and the marijuana found therein, and the keys were admissible in evidence in prosecution of defendant for possession of marijuana.

State v. Dunlap, 392 So.2d 1366.

Fla.App. 3 Dist. 1980. One's legitimate privacy interest in his personal luggage concerns its contents, not its exterior. U.S.C.A.Const. Amend. 4.

State v. Goodley, 381 So.2d 1180.

Fla.App. 3 Dist. 1979. The Fourth Amendment and applicable Florida Constitution section guarantees to people right to be secure in their effects against unreasonable searches and seizures, and personal luggage such as footlockers or suitcases constitute "effects" within meaning of these constitutional provisions and may not be subjected to an "unreasonable" search and seizure thereof; moreover, there is a strong expectation of privacy which people reasonably entertain with respect to private contents of their personal luggage, and thus such luggage enjoys independent constitutional protection. West's F.S.A.Const. art. 1, § 12; U.S.C.A.Const. Amend. 4.

Haugland v. State, 374 So.2d 1026, certiorari denied 390 So.2d 360.

Fla.App. 4 Dist. 1995. Fourth Amendment, in protecting persons from unreasonable government intrusion into their legitimate expectations of privacy, extends to contents of personal packages. U.S.C.A. Const.Amend. 4.

Daniels v. Cochran, 654 So.2d 609.

Fla.App. 4 Dist. 1991. Search of defendant's bag on bus was not impermissibly coercive, absent evidence that any intimidation was exerted on defendant. U.S.C.A. Const.Amend. 4.

State v. Florius, 587 So.2d 1160, review denied 599 So.2d 655.

Fla.App. 5 Dist. 1984. Owner of locked box found in undesignated parking space in condominium parking lot that was unenclosed and unrestricted to traverse by the public did not have a reasonable expectation of privacy in the parking space.

State v. McLaughlin, 454 So.2d 617.

🔑**30. Items subject to seizure in general; nexus.**

C.A.11 (Fla.) 1983. Documents seized from defendant's law office were not obtained illegally on grounds that papers were "mere evidence" of crime, rather than instrumentalities of crime, fruits, or contraband.

U.S. v. Haimowitz, 706 F.2d 1549, 71 A.L.R. Fed. 78, rehearing denied 712 F.2d 457, certiorari denied 104 S.Ct. 974, 464 U.S. 1069, 79 L.Ed.2d 212.

C.A.5 (Fla.) 1980. Ordinarily, Fourth Amendment does not apply to arrests and searches made by foreign authorities in their own country and in enforcement of foreign law. U.S.C.A.Const. Amend. 4.

U.S. v. Heller, 625 F.2d 594.

M.D.Fla. 1994. Exceptions to general rule, that warrantless search based on probable cause is per se illegal, include vehicle exception, search incident to lawful arrest, and seizure as evidence of crime. U.S.C.A. Const.Amend. 4.

U.S. v. Adams, 845 F.Supp. 1531.

Warrantless inventory search of motor home was not justified by probable cause to seize motor home as evidence of crime, where motor home was being used as residence and was located on private property in rural setting. U.S.C.A. Const. Amend. 4.

U.S. v. Adams, 845 F.Supp. 1531.

Inventory search of motor home being used as residence is not valid as search as evidence of crime. U.S.C.A. Const.Amend. 4.

U.S. v. Adams, 845 F.Supp. 1531.

S.D.Fla. 1971. Testimonial evidence is subject to seizure. 18 U.S.C.A. § 2518(6); U.S.C.A.Const. Amend. 4.

U.S. v. Sklaroff, 323 F.Supp. 296.

Fla. 1975. Seizure of so-called "mere evidence" of crime is not proscribed by Fourth Amendment. U.S.C.A.Const. Amend. 4.

Alford v. State, 307 So.2d 433, certiorari denied 96 S.Ct. 3227, 428 U.S. 912, 49 L.Ed.2d 1221, rehearing denied 97 S.Ct. 191, 429 U.S. 873, 50 L.Ed.2d 155.

Fla. 1969. Search for rape victim's pocketbook at backyard of defendant's father's house by defendant's sister and other children at request of sheriff did not intrude into that sphere of privacy safeguarded by constitutional prohibitions against unreasonable searches and seizures. U.S.C.A.Const. Amend. 4.

Perkins v. State, 228 So.2d 382.

Fla.App. 1 Dist. 1981. Where a law enforcement officer accompanies hotel manager and participates in search of hotel room occupied by a guest, all constitutional restrictions on warrantless searches apply. U.S.C.A.Const. Amend. 4; West's F.S.A.Const. Art. 1, § 12.

McGibiany v. State, 399 So.2d 125.

Warrantless search of defendant's hotel room by off-duty police officer, who had accompanied assistant hotel manager in investigation of suspected fraudulent occupancy, and who saw nothing from doorway which gave him probable cause to believe a felony had been or was being committed, or that room contained illegal drugs, was unreasonable by constitutional standards. U.S.C.A.Const. Amend. 4; West's F.S.A.Const. Art. 1, § 12.

McGibiany v. State, 399 So.2d 125.

Fla.App. 1 Dist. 1981. Not only fruits or implements of crime, weapons and property, the possession of which is itself a crime, may be seized, but also mere evidence can be seized provided there is probable cause to believe that evidence will aid in a particular apprehension or conviction.

Wooten v. State, 398 So.2d 963, petition for review dismissed 407 So.2d 1107.

Fla.App. 2 Dist. 2001. Possession of "contraband," which is subject to seizure as evidence of a civil or criminal infraction, means possessing any property, object, or thing that is against any law or regulation.

B.W. v. State, 784 So.2d 1219.

Definition of contraband is not limited to only those items which are described in statute as being contraband subject to forfeiture; forfeiture statute itself does not change illicit nature of an item from being contraband which is subject to seizure as evidence of a civil or criminal infraction. West's F.S.A. § 932.701(2)(a).

B.W. v. State, 784 So.2d 1219.

Fla.App. 2 Dist. 1971. "Contraband" is any substance, article or thing the making, possession or trafficking of which is unlawful.

State v. Bryant, 250 So.2d 344.

Fla.App. 3 Dist. 1968. Inasmuch as officers were conducting an authorized search of premises for alleged stolen property they were entitled to seize contraband items found therein.

Diaz v. State, 206 So.2d 37.

Fla.App. 4 Dist. 1991. Safe and strongbox discovered in apartment of shooting victim were evidence of identity and motive, and police officer acted reasonably when he chose to take safe and strongbox from unoccupied apartment to police station for safekeeping rather than choosing impracticable alternative of posting around-the-clock guard.

State v. Heiser, 583 So.2d 389, review denied 593 So.2d 1052.

🗝**31. Persons subject to limitations; governmental involvement.**

Includes all cases, whatever the nature or purpose of the activity, excepting school searches, for which see EDUCATION 🗝742–745, and communication company interception, TELECOMMUNICATIONS 🗝1440.

🗝**31.1. —— In general.**

C.A.11 (Fla.) 2015. The protection the Fourth Amendment affords extends to governmental action only; it is wholly inapplicable to a search or seizure, even an unreasonable one, effected by a private individual not acting as an agent of the government or with the participation or knowledge of any governmental official. U.S.C.A. Const.Amend. 4.

U.S. v. Sparks, 806 F.3d 1323, certiorari denied Johnson v. U.S., 137 S.Ct. 34, 196 L.Ed.2d 46.

C.A.11 (Fla.) 2015. The Fourth Amendment exclusionary rule does not apply to searches and seizures conducted by foreign officials on foreign soil; the exclusionary rule does, however, apply to searches and seizures conducted by state and federal officials of the United States. U.S.C.A. Const.Amend. 4.

U.S. v. Odoni, 782 F.3d 1226, certiorari denied Gunter v. U.S., 135 S.Ct. 2335, 191 L.Ed.2d 981, certiorari denied 135 S.Ct. 2339, 191 L.Ed.2d 981.

C.A.11 (Fla.) 2009. The Fourth Amendment does not apply to actions against foreign citizens on foreign soil. U.S.C.A. Const.Amend. 4.

U.S. v. Valencia-Trujillo, 573 F.3d 1171, rehearing and rehearing denied 373 Fed.Appx. 43, certiorari denied 130 S.Ct. 1726, 559 U.S. 987, 176 L.Ed.2d 205.

C.A.11 (Fla.) 2006. Fourth Amendment regulates supervisor conduct in government workplace, at least to some extent and in some manner. U.S.C.A. Const. Amend. 4.

Reyes v. Maschmeier, 446 F.3d 1199, rehearing and rehearing denied 186 Fed.Appx. 987.

S.D.Fla. 2013. Fourth Amendment's protection extends beyond the sphere of criminal investigations, without regard to whether the government actor is investigating crime or performing another function; thus, the Fourth Amendment applies even when the government acts as an employer. U.S.C.A. Const.Amend. 4.

> Hudson v. City of Riviera Beach, 982 F.Supp.2d 1318.

S.D.Fla. 1985. Constitutional guarantees of the Fourth Amendment apply when United States enforcement officers act against United States citizens on another nation's sovereign territory, e.g., another nation's sovereign flag ship on the high seas. U.S.C.A. Const.Amend. 4.

> U.S. v. Crews, 605 F.Supp. 730, affirmed U.S. v. McGill, 800 F.2d 265.

Fla.App. 2 Dist. 1974. Uniformed city policeman hired by management of dance hall to work during off-duty hours acted as officer of city in seizing weapon from handbag of customer, for purposes of determining whether there was any Fourth Amendment violation in the seizure. U.S.C.A.Const. Amend. 4.

> State v. Williams, 297 So.2d 52.

Fla.App. 3 Dist. 2013. Generally, the Fourth Amendment prohibits state actors from making searches or seizures of the person in the absence of probable cause. U.S.C.A. Const.Amend. 4.

> State v. T.S., 114 So.3d 343, review granted 143 So.3d 922, review dismissed as improvidently granted by 158 So.3d 556.

Fla.App. 4 Dist. 1974. Fourth Amendment exempts no branch of government from the commandment that "The right of the people to be secure in their persons, houses, papers, and effects, against unreasonable searches and seizures, shall not be violated." U.S.C.A.Const. Amend. 4.

> State v. Gansz, 297 So.2d 614, certiorari denied 303 So.2d 645.

⊜**32. —— Application of federal standards to states and territories.**

C.A.5 (Fla.) 1955. Limitations of Fourth Amendment, giving protection against unlawful searches and seizures, and of exclusionary rule in sanction thereof, reach Federal Government and its agencies, but are not directed to misconduct of state or municipal officials or other persons not acting in collusion with or under direction of federal officers. U.S.C.A.Const. Amend. 4.

> Watson v. U.S., 224 F.2d 910.

Fla. 1956. The Fourth and Fifth Amendments to the Federal Constitution offer direct protection to the citizens only against unlawful search and seizure by agents of the federal government, and such amendments safeguard the citizen from unlawful invasions by agents of the state only indirectly, through the medium of the due process clause of the Fourteenth Amendment. U.S.C.A.Const. Amends. 4, 5, 14.

> Vann v. State, 85 So.2d 133.

Fla. 1953. The Fourth Amendment to the Federal Constitution was not applicable to state criminal proceeding. U.S.C.A.Const. Amend. 4; F.S.A.Const. Declaration of Rights, § 22; F.S.A. §§ 561.07, 562.03.

> Boynton v. State, 64 So.2d 536.

The Fourth Amendment to the Federal Constitution is a limitation upon powers of Federal Government, not upon powers of states or their officers or agents. U.S.C.A.Const. Amend. 4; F.S.A.Const. Declaration of Rights, § 22; F.S.A. §§ 561.07, 562.03.

> Boynton v. State, 64 So.2d 536.

Fla.App. 1 Dist. 1997. Florida courts are constitutionally required to interpret search and seizure issues in conformity with Fourth Amendment of United States Constitution as interpreted by United States Supreme Court. U.S.C.A. Const. Amend. 4; West's F.S.A. Const. Art. 1, § 12.

> Warren v. State, 701 So.2d 404.

Fla.App. 1 Dist. 1990. Florida citizens are extended no greater right under Florida Constitution to freedom from governmental intrusion into contents of their personal automobiles than they are afforded under United States Constitution. West's F.S.A. Const. Art. 1, § 12; U.S.C.A. Const.Amend. 4.

> State v. Starkey, 559 So.2d 335.

Fla.App. 2 Dist. 1990. Fourth Amendment issues are interpreted in accordance with decisions of United States

Supreme Court. West's F.S.A. Const. Art. 1, § 12; U.S.C.A. Const.Amend. 4.

> Brown v. State, 561 So.2d 1248.

⚷33. —— Private persons.

† **C.A.11 (Fla.) 2015.** Employees of computer repair store where defendant brought his inoperable laptop computer to have data from the computer's hard drive transferred onto a new computer were private actors when they initially viewed defendant's data during the data transfer from his laptop to the store's system, and thus, the government was free to use the information provided by the store, that defendant had child pornography on his computer, to seize his laptop and obtain a search warrant. U.S.C.A. Const.Amend. 4.

> U.S. v. Meister, 596 Fed.Appx. 790.

C.A.11 (Fla.) 2015. The protection the Fourth Amendment affords extends to governmental action only; it is wholly inapplicable to a search or seizure, even an unreasonable one, effected by a private individual not acting as an agent of the government or with the participation or knowledge of any governmental official. U.S.C.A. Const.Amend. 4.

> U.S. v. Sparks, 806 F.3d 1323, certiorari denied Johnson v. U.S., 137 S.Ct. 34, 196 L.Ed.2d 46.

Once an individual's expectation of privacy in particular information has been frustrated by a private individual, the Fourth Amendment does not prohibit law enforcement's subsequent use of that information, even if obtained without a warrant; as a result, a warrantless law-enforcement search conducted after a private search violates the Fourth Amendment only to the extent to which it is broader than the scope of the previously occurring private search. U.S.C.A. Const.Amend. 4.

> U.S. v. Sparks, 806 F.3d 1323, certiorari denied Johnson v. U.S., 137 S.Ct. 34, 196 L.Ed.2d 46.

District court did not clearly err when it determined, as matter of fact, on defendants' motion to suppress that scope of private search included all images contained within one digital photograph album stored in photo application of cellular telephone and when it found that police officer viewed content stored only within that same album, in prosecution of defendants on charges of possession of child pornography and production of child pornography, since district court's factual findings were amply supported by the record. U.S.C.A. Const.Amend. 4; 18 U.S.C.A. §§ 2251(a, e), 2252(a)(4)(B), (b)(2).

> U.S. v. Sparks, 806 F.3d 1323, certiorari denied Johnson v. U.S., 137 S.Ct. 34, 196 L.Ed.2d 46.

Police officer's warrantless search of cellular telephone for child pornography that exceeded scope of private search by employee of retail store who found that telephone at store violated Fourth Amendment rights of person who owned that phone. U.S.C.A. Const.Amend. 4; 18 U.S.C.A. §§ 2251(a, e), 2252(a)(4)(B), (b)(2).

> U.S. v. Sparks, 806 F.3d 1323, certiorari denied Johnson v. U.S., 137 S.Ct. 34, 196 L.Ed.2d 46.

C.A.11 (Fla.) 2014. The Fourth Amendment does not prohibit the obtaining of information revealed to a third party and conveyed by him to government authorities. U.S.C.A. Const.Amend. 4.

> U.S. v. Davis, 754 F.3d 1205, rehearing granted, opinion vacated 573 Fed.Appx. 925, on rehearing en banc in part 785 F.3d 498, certiorari denied 136 S.Ct. 479, 193 L.Ed.2d 349.

† **C.A.11 (Fla.) 2013.** No Fourth Amendment violation occurred when items recovered from defendant's storage unit at a storage facility without a warrant, because the manager for the storage facility, a private individual, delivered the items to a law enforcement agent. U.S.C.A. Const.Amend. 4.

> U.S. v. Kannell, 545 Fed.Appx. 881, certiorari denied 134 S.Ct. 1569, 188 L.Ed.2d 578, certiorari denied Harvey v. U.S., 134 S.Ct. 1916, 188 L.Ed.2d 941.

† **C.A.11 (Fla.) 2010.** Electric company employee acted as a private individual, rather than state agent, when he entered property to inspect an electrical installation on property, and thus search did not violate Fourth Amendment, although sheriff's detectives knew of and acquiesced in employee's inspection of installation; employee entered property for private and

legitimate purpose of investigating whether electricity was being stolen. U.S.C.A. Const.Amend. 4; Comprehensive Drug Abuse Prevention and Control Act of 1970, § 401(a)(1), (b)(1)(D), 21 U.S.C.A. § 841(a)(1), (b)(1)(D).

> U.S. v. Sanchez-Paz, 402 Fed.Appx. 498, post-conviction relief denied 2012 WL 1344905.

† C.A.11 (Fla.) 2009. Defendant's Fourth Amendment rights were not violated by two entries by a leasing company employee into an apartment in which drugs, drug paraphernalia, and firearms were found; employee was not working as an agent of the Government and her entry, made after she received written notice from the person who had leased the apartment that it would be vacated, was for the purpose of determining its status before re-renting, and in any case the leasing agreement was irrelevant, since defendant was a non-resident. U.S.C.A. Const. Amend. 4.

> U.S. v. Garcon, 349 Fed.Appx. 377, post-conviction relief dismissed by Garcon v. Florida, 2013 WL 12086685, habeas corpus dismissed by 2014 WL 819467, affirmed 581 Fed.Appx. 193, certiorari dismissed 135 S.Ct. 2851, 192 L.Ed.2d 873, habeas corpus dismissed by 2015 WL 4557146.

C.A.11 (Fla.) 2009. Police search following unsolicited private search does not constitute "search" under Fourth Amendment as long as search is confined to same scope as initial private search. U.S.C.A. Const.Amend. 4.

> U.S. v. Garcia-Bercovich, 582 F.3d 1234, certiorari denied 130 S.Ct. 1562, 559 U.S. 960, 176 L.Ed.2d 148.

C.A.11 (Fla.) 1985. Fourth Amendment proscribes only governmental action and, therefore, search by a private individual does not raise Fourth Amendment implications; however, it is applicable when private citizen acts as an instrument or agent of the state. U.S.C.A. Const.Amend. 4.

> U.S. v. Ford, 765 F.2d 1088.

Defendant's brother, with whom defendant was living, was not acting as an instrument or agent of the Government when he broke lock on defendant's bedroom door and searched bedroom for cocaine; rather, brother, having had benefit of counsel, conducted his own search two days after agents visited his home and, while he may have been motivated in part by fear of prosecution, he was concerned for safety of his wife and child due to suspicious attempted break-in which he attributed to the cocaine allegedly in the bedroom; thus, the search did not implicate the Fourth Amendment. U.S.C.A. Const.Amend. 4.

> U.S. v. Ford, 765 F.2d 1088.

C.A.5 (Fla.) 1979. The Fourth Amendment's warrant requirement is intended solely as a restraint upon sovereign authority, and a search conducted by a private individual for purely private reasons does not fall within protective ambit of Fourth Amendment; however, if, under circumstances of case, private party acted as an instrument or agent of the Government, the ostensibly private search must meet Fourth Amendment's standards. U.S.C.A.Const. Amend. 4.

> U.S. v. Sanders, 592 F.2d 788, rehearing denied 597 F.2d 63, certiorari granted Walter v. U.S., 100 S.Ct. 227, 444 U.S. 914, 62 L.Ed.2d 168, reversed 100 S.Ct. 2395, 447 U.S. 649, 65 L.Ed.2d 410, on remand 625 F.2d 1311.

C.A.5 (Fla.) 1978. Fourth Amendment proscribes only governmental actions; search by private individual for purely private reasons does not raise Fourth Amendment implications. U.S.C.A.Const. Amend. 4.

> U.S. v. Bomengo, 580 F.2d 173, certiorari denied 99 S.Ct. 1022, 439 U.S. 1117, 59 L.Ed.2d 75.

That security director of apartment complex had formerly been employed as police officer and had previously supplied detectives with reliable information regarding criminal activity did not mean that there was "state action" in his and engineer's obtaining entrance to defendant's apartment in attempt to locate source of water leakage after attempts to locate occupants of apartment were unsuccessful; entry into apartment was effected by private persons for nonofficial purposes

---

† This Case was not selected for publication in the National Reporter System
For legislative history of cited statutes, see Florida Statutes Annotated

and was outside bounds of Fourth Amendment. U.S.C.A.Const. Amend. 4.

> U.S. v. Bomengo, 580 F.2d 173, certiorari denied 99 S.Ct. 1022, 439 U.S. 1117, 59 L.Ed.2d 75.

C.A.5 (Fla.) 1977. Actions of security personnel at privately operated amusement park in detaining defendants and asking them to empty their pockets did not fall within the protection of the Fourth Amendment and did not give rise to application of the exclusionary rule. U.S.C.A.Const. Amend. 4.

> U.S. v. Francoeur, 547 F.2d 891, certiorari denied Pacheco v. U.S., 97 S.Ct. 2182, 431 U.S. 918, 53 L.Ed.2d 228, certiorari denied Pizio v. U.S., 97 S.Ct. 2197, 431 U.S. 923, 53 L.Ed.2d 238, certiorari denied 97 S.Ct. 2640, 431 U.S. 932, 53 L.Ed.2d 249.

C.A.5 (Fla.) 1975. Fourth Amendment was intended as restraint on activities of Government and its agents and is not addressed to actions, legal or illegal, of private parties; where no official of federal Government has any connection with wrongful seizure, or any knowledge of it until after the fact, evidence is admissible. U.S.C.A.Const. Amend. 4.

> U.S. v. Mekjian, 505 F.2d 1320.

Where federal officials actively participate in search being conducted by private parties or stand by watching with approval as search continues, federal authorities are clearly implicated in search and it must comport with Fourth Amendment requirements. U.S.C.A.Const. Amend. 4.

> U.S. v. Mekjian, 505 F.2d 1320.

C.A.5 (Fla.) 1972. Where stolen money order was not seized but was turned over to police by store manager, a private citizen, Fourth Amendment did not apply. U.S.C.A.Const. Amend. 4.

> U.S. v. Jones, 457 F.2d 697.

C.A.5 (Fla.) 1971. Defendant's son-in-law, who was a deputy sheriff and was requested by defendant's stepmother to enter unoccupied home of defendant for purpose of obtaining and forwarding certain stock certificates owned by defendant's father, and who, while he was within home, undertook a side venture of looking behind a mirror and there discov-

ered certificates which were shown to have been stolen with certain bonds, was acting in his capacity as a law enforcement officer, rather than exclusively as a son-in-law on a family mission, and, absent a search warrant, search and seizure was violative of Fourth Amendment, and admission of testimony concerning certificates to establish scienter on charge of aiding and abetting the forging and passing of bonds was prejudicial error. 18 U.S.C.A. §§ 2, 495; U.S.C.A.Const. Amend. 4.

> U.S. v. Clarke, 451 F.2d 584.

C.A.5 (Fla.) 1968. Under circumstances, including conceded right of motel operator to enter room for housekeeping purposes, no Fourth Amendment rights of defendants were invaded, and subsequent arrest, at a time officers knew defendants were in possession of marijuana, was fully warranted.

> Leibman v. U.S., 404 F.2d 348.

C.A.5 (Fla.) 1967. Where defendant left motel room leaving behind travel case and motel owner searched case on his own initiative and discovered forged checks and became suspicious and called local police and informed them of case's contents and made it available to authorities, there was no illegal search within meaning of Fourth Amendment. U.S.C.A.Const. Amend. 4.

> Barnes v. U.S., 373 F.2d 517.

M.D.Fla. 2006. Stadium authority was "state actor," capable of being sued by professional football team season ticket holder claiming that being subjected to pat-down search before being allowed entry to stadium violated his rights under Fourth Amendment and Florida Constitution, despite claim that in implementing searches authority was acting as agent for team, and actual searches were conducted by private firm; authority was instrumentality of state, created to manage sports facilities, and could not avoid responsibility to operate in conformity with law by entering into purported agency agreements or by otherwise delegating its commitments. U.S.C.A. Const.Amend. 4; West's F.S.A. Const. Art. 1, § 12.

> Johnston v. Tampa Sports Authority, 442 F.Supp.2d 1257, reversed and remanded 490 F.3d 820, opinion vacated and superseded on rehear-

ing 530 F.3d 1320, rehearing and rehearing denied 285 Fed.Appx. 745, certiorari denied 129 S.Ct. 1013, 555 U.S. 1138, 173 L.Ed.2d 295, reversed and remanded 530 F.3d 1320, rehearing and rehearing denied 285 Fed.Appx. 745, certiorari denied 129 S.Ct. 1013, 555 U.S. 1138, 173 L.Ed.2d 295.

S.D.Fla. 1980. In light of public purpose to thwart air piracy and protect passengers, and fact that private security guard acted in concert with government agents at airport in advancing such interests, search of defendant's bag by private security guard involved sufficient governmental participation to constitute a "search" within the meaning of the Fourth Amendment. U.S.C.A.Const. Amend. 4.

U.S. v. Gorman, 484 F.Supp. 529.

S.D.Fla. 1970. Assuming arguendo that search and seizure provisions of Fourth Amendment apply to issuance of summary process to satisfy a debt, where essence of conditional sales contract was to allow seller to enter premises of buyer (whether alone or through an officer who was executing a writ of replevin) in order to repossess property in which seller had a security interest, seller's peaceable repossession of goods under authority of contract at a time when buyer was admittedly delinquent in payments (termed a "default" under terms of contract) did not constitute an unlawful search and seizure. F.S.A. §§ 78.01, 78.04, 78.07, 78.08, 78.10, 78.12; U.S.C.A.Const. Amend. 14.

> Fuentes v. Faircloth, 317 F.Supp. 954, probable jurisdiction noted 91 S.Ct. 893, 401 U.S. 906, 27 L.Ed.2d 804, vacated 92 S.Ct. 1983, 407 U.S. 67, 32 L.Ed.2d 556, rehearing denied 93 S.Ct. 177, 409 U.S. 902, 34 L.Ed.2d 165, rehearing denied Parham v. Cortese, 93 S.Ct. 180, 409 U.S. 902, 34 L.Ed.2d 165.

Absent an authorization to break down the door or otherwise enter forcibly, Fourth Amendment does not prohibit parties to a conditional sales contract from contracting for peaceable repossession. F.S.A. §§ 78.01, 78.04, 78.07, 78.08, 78.10, 78.12; U.S.C.A.Const. Amend. 14.

> Fuentes v. Faircloth, 317 F.Supp. 954, probable jurisdiction noted 91 S.Ct. 893, 401 U.S. 906, 27 L.Ed.2d 804, vacated 92 S.Ct. 1983, 407 U.S. 67,

32 L.Ed.2d 556, rehearing denied 93 S.Ct. 177, 409 U.S. 902, 34 L.Ed.2d 165, rehearing denied Parham v. Cortese, 93 S.Ct. 180, 409 U.S. 902, 34 L.Ed.2d 165.

Fla. 1976. Since Fourth Amendment protects only against governmental intrusions on the privacy of the individual, no constitutional rights were violated by fact that motel cleaning maid entered room from which defendant was temporarily absent, nor by fact that maid summoned motel manager and owner after she noticed what she thought was marijuana in the room. U.S.C.A.Const. Amend. 4; West's F.S.A.Const. art. 1, § 12.

Sheff v. State, 329 So.2d 270.

Fla. 1973. Protection against unreasonable searches and seizures applies in cases involving governmental action only and does not apply to searches and seizures made by private individuals. U.S.C.A.Const. Amend. 4.

Bernovich v. State, 272 So.2d 505.

Fla.App. 1 Dist. 2010. Individual, to whom postal service mistakenly delivered package addressed to defendant, was acting in his private capacity, rather than in his capacity as a F.B.I. agent, when searching the package, even though he wrote down the tag numbers of the vehicles in front of the listed address and took the package to the nearest F.B.I. office, where it was scanned and opened in the presence of a law enforcement officer, and thus individual's actions did not infringe on defendant's Fourth Amendment rights, where, due to the nature of his work, individual became concerned, upon opening the outer package, that it might contain a dangerous substance; it was undisputed that individual was acting in his private capacity when he received the package at his home, and individual's actions after receiving the package had a legitimate private purpose. U.S.C.A. Const.Amend. 4.

Armstrong v. State, 46 So.3d 589, review denied 44 So.3d 581.

The protection against unreasonable searches and seizures applies only to cases involving governmental action; it does not apply when the search or seizure was conducted by a private individual. U.S.C.A. Const.Amend. 4.

>Armstrong v. State, 46 So.3d 589, review denied 44 So.3d 581.

A two-pronged analysis applies in deciding whether an off-duty law enforcement officer is acting in his official capacity or as a private citizen at the time of a search and seizure: first, court must examine the capacity in which the off-duty police officer was functioning when the officer initially confronted the situation, and second, court must examine the manner in which the off-duty police officer conducted himself or herself from that point forward. U.S.C.A. Const.Amend. 4.

>Armstrong v. State, 46 So.3d 589, review denied 44 So.3d 581.

When considering the second prong of the analysis for determining whether an off-duty law enforcement officer is acting in his official capacity or as a private citizen at the time of a search, i.e. the manner in which the off-duty officer conducted himself, a court must determine whether the off-duty officer's actions fell outside the sphere of legitimate private action; crucial to this consideration is the purpose behind the off-duty officer's decision to conduct the search. U.S.C.A. Const.Amend. 4.

>Armstrong v. State, 46 So.3d 589, review denied 44 So.3d 581.

If a search conducted by an off-duty officer is motivated by a legitimate private purpose, it retains its private character; if it is motivated solely by a governmental purpose, it becomes state action. U.S.C.A. Const.Amend. 4.

>Armstrong v. State, 46 So.3d 589, review denied 44 So.3d 581.

So long as there is a reasonable private purpose for search conducted by off-duty officer, the search will not violate the Fourth Amendment. U.S.C.A. Const. Amend. 4.

>Armstrong v. State, 46 So.3d 589, review denied 44 So.3d 581.

To show that individual, to whom postal service mistakenly delivered package addressed to defendant, was acting in his capacity as a F.B.I. agent when searching the package, defendant had to establish by a preponderance of the evidence that either individual was acting in his official capacity when he received the package or individual's actions after receiving the package demonstrated a solely official purpose. U.S.C.A. Const.Amend. 4.

>Armstrong v. State, 46 So.3d 589, review denied 44 So.3d 581.

Actions taken by F.B.I. agent after marijuana was discovered in package addressed to defendant, but mistakenly delivered to agent, were irrelevant as to whether agent was acting as a law enforcement officer at the time the package was opened. U.S.C.A. Const.Amend. 4.

>Armstrong v. State, 46 So.3d 589, review denied 44 So.3d 581.

Participation of sheriff's deputy in search of package addressed to defendant, but mistakenly delivered to F.B.I. agent's residence, did not change the private nature of the search, even though deputy used his pen knife to open the inner wrappings of the package, where F.B.I. agent's decision to involve authorities was to ensure it was safe to open the package, and deputy became involved simply because he was the closest individual with a pen knife; safety was a legitimate private purpose separate and apart from any benefit to the government, and deputy's involvement in the search was minimal. U.S.C.A. Const. Amend. 4.

>Armstrong v. State, 46 So.3d 589, review denied 44 So.3d 581.

A search by a private person becomes a government search if the government coerces, dominates, or directs the actions of a private person conducting the search. U.S.C.A. Const.Amend. 4.

>Armstrong v. State, 46 So.3d 589, review denied 44 So.3d 581.

A private search becomes a governmental act if, due to government participation, the private actor becomes an instrumentality or agent of the state. U.S.C.A. Const.Amend. 4.

>Armstrong v. State, 46 So.3d 589, review denied 44 So.3d 581.

The test for determining whether a private actor conducting a search has become a state agent is two-fold: (1) whether the government was aware of and/or acquiesced in the search; and (2) whether the individual's purpose in conducting the search was solely to assist the police. U.S.C.A. Const.Amend. 4.

> Armstrong v. State, 46 So.3d 589, review denied 44 So.3d 581.

When a dual purpose for a search exists such that a private actor is not just furthering a government interest, but also pursuing his own ends, the search generally retains its private character. U.S.C.A. Const.Amend. 4.

> Armstrong v. State, 46 So.3d 589, review denied 44 So.3d 581.

Minimal involvement by a law enforcement officer does not transform a private search into a governmental action, particularly when there is a private purpose for the search. U.S.C.A. Const. Amend. 4.

> Armstrong v. State, 46 So.3d 589, review denied 44 So.3d 581.

Fla.App. 1 Dist. 2008. State action is present, for Fourth Amendment purposes, when (1) a private party acts as an instrument or agent of the state in effecting a search and seizure, and the government knows of and acquiesces to the conduct, and (2) the search is conducted solely in pursuit of a governmental interest, rather than the private actor's self-interest. U.S.C.A. Const.Amend. 4.

> State v. Butler, 1 So.3d 242, rehearing denied.

West Virginia court's broad delegation to hospital staff of the power to conduct video surveillance in hospital room of child of defendant, who allegedly suffered from Munchausen syndrome by proxy which was disorder whereby defendant factitiously induced illness in child to draw attention to herself, together with court's authorization for the State of West Virginia to take immediate custody of child if the surveillance showed he was in danger, indicated that the surveillance was undertaken pursuant to state action, and though the state's involvement was minimal, it was sufficient to trigger a further Fourth Amendment analysis. U.S.C.A. Const. Amend. 4.

> State v. Butler, 1 So.3d 242, rehearing denied.

Fla.App. 1 Dist. 2002. While the Fourth Amendment protects against un-

reasonable searches conducted under the aegis of governmental authority, it does not protect against unlawful searches by private individuals. U.S.C.A. Const. Amend. 4.

> Green v. State, 824 So.2d 311.

Fla.App. 1 Dist. 1981. When a law enforcement officer directs, participates, or acquiesces in a search conducted by private parties, that search must comport with the usual constitutional standards.

> M. J. v. State, 399 So.2d 996.

Purely private searches are not subject to any Fourth Amendment considerations. U.S.C.A.Const. Amend. 4.

> M. J. v. State, 399 So.2d 996.

Fla.App. 2 Dist. 2011. Electric company investigator's entry into defendant's backyard to investigate electricity theft did not implicate Fourth Amendment, even though police officer who suspected indoor marijuana cultivation had arranged for investigator to inspect the property; investigator's motivation to conduct search to further electric company's own ends was not negated by dual motive to detect or prevent crime or assist police. U.S.C.A. Const.Amend. 4.

> State v. Delrio, 56 So.3d 848, rehearing denied, review denied Delguy v. State, 67 So.3d 198, review denied 67 So.3d 199.

Fla.App. 2 Dist. 2010. Driver of car stopped by police was not acting as agent of police for Fourth Amendment purposes when driver asked passenger to give him the marijuana that was in passenger's possession, after police officer asked driver, who had exited the car, to get marijuana out of the car, as officer testified that when he asked driver to get marijuana from the car, he had no idea where marijuana was located and he was not attempting to gather evidence against passenger, and fact that driver testified that he felt obligated to cooperate with officer did not transform driver into an agent of police. U.S.C.A. Const.Amend. 4.

> State v. C.D.M., 50 So.3d 659, rehearing denied.

While a certain degree of governmental participation is necessary before a private citizen is transformed into an agent of the state, de minimis or incidental contacts between the citizen and law enforcement agents prior to or during the course of a search or seizure will not subject the search to Fourth Amendment scrutiny. U.S.C.A. Const.Amend. 4.

    State v. C.D.M., 50 So.3d 659, rehearing denied.

The government must be involved either directly as a participant or indirectly as an encourager of the private citizen's actions before the citizen will be deemed to be an agent of the state for Fourth Amendment purposes. U.S.C.A. Const. Amend. 4.

    State v. C.D.M., 50 So.3d 659, rehearing denied.

Fla.App. 2 Dist. 2007. Minor victim who had talked to law enforcement officers was acting as an instrument or agent of the state when she entered residence of defendant, who was her father, and retrieved two condoms, for purpose of determining whether retrieval of condoms violated defendant's Fourth Amendment right against unreasonable searches and seizures; victim's retrieval of condoms was precipitated by one officer's suggestions and encouragement, interest being fulfilled by retrieval was law enforcement interest in obtaining evidence to support a criminal prosecution, and nothing suggested that victim, of her own motivation, considered taking condoms for any private purpose. U.S.C.A. Const.Amend. 4.

    State v. Moninger, 957 So.2d 2, rehearing denied, review granted 968 So.2d 558, review dismissed as improvidently granted 982 So.2d 682.

Fourth Amendment is implicated if the sole purpose of a private search is to further a government interest. U.S.C.A. Const.Amend. 4.

    State v. Moninger, 957 So.2d 2, rehearing denied, review granted 968 So.2d 558, review dismissed as improvidently granted 982 So.2d 682.

Fla.App. 2 Dist. 2000. Implicit in the constitutional guarantee of the right to be free from unreasonable searches and seizures is the requirement that an agent of the government perform those searches and seizures. U.S.C.A. Const.Amend. 4; West's F.S.A. Const. Art. 1, § 12.

    State v. Iaccarino, 767 So.2d 470.

The test for determining whether private individuals are agents of the government, in analysis of whether a search or seizure by those private individuals offends constitutional protections, is whether, in consideration of the circumstances, the individuals acted as instruments of the state. U.S.C.A. Const.Amend. 4; West's F.S.A. Const. Art. 1, § 12.

    State v. Iaccarino, 767 So.2d 470.

To determine whether a private individual acts as an instrument of the state, for purposes of deciding whether searches or seizures by those private individuals violates constitutional protections, courts look to: (1) whether the government was aware of and acquiesced in the conduct, and (2) whether the individual intended to assist the police or further his own ends. U.S.C.A. Const.Amend. 4; West's F.S.A. Const. Art. 1, § 12.

    State v. Iaccarino, 767 So.2d 470.

The standard used to determine whether a private individual acts as an instrument of the state, so as to decide whether a search or seizure by that private individual offends constitutional protections, also applies to the actions of an off-duty police officer. U.S.C.A. Const. Amend. 4; West's F.S.A. Const. Art. 1, § 12.

    State v. Iaccarino, 767 So.2d 470.

Off-duty police officers were acting as instruments of the state, for purposes of determining whether searches of patrons at entry gate of music festival and seizures of drug contraband violated constitutional protections; government acquiesced in off-duty police officer's conduct, in that it coordinated the extra-duty assignment and placed a paddy wagon in front of the patron entrance, and the off-duty officers' priority was to the sheriff's office, rather than to furthering their own needs. U.S.C.A. Const.Amend. 4; West's F.S.A. Const. Art. 1, § 12.

    State v. Iaccarino, 767 So.2d 470.

Fla.App. 2 Dist. 1996. Although police officer was accompanied by electric company employee when he initially went onto defendant's property, search was not private search devoid of Fourth Amendment protection, where officer solicited employee to go onto property as subterfuge so that officer could search property before he had probable cause. U.S.C.A. Const.Amend. 4.

> State v. Gibson, 670 So.2d 1006, rehearing denied.

Fla.App. 3 Dist. 2015. No state actor was involved when one of defendant's treating physicians called the police to report that he believed defendant was doctor shopping for the purpose of obtaining a prescription for a controlled substance, as required to implicate defendant's Fourth Amendment rights and to exclude physician as a witness; as defendant conceded, it was the physician that initiated contact with the police, not the other way around, and the information provided by physician was merely investigatory material that probably never would have been admissible at trial. U.S.C.A. Const.Amend. 4; Health Insurance Portability and Accountability Act of 1996, § 262(a), 42 U.S.C.A. § 1320d; 45 C.F.R. §§ 160.103, 164.512(f)(2); West's F.S.A. § 456.057(7)(a).

> State v. Strickling, 164 So.3d 727.

Fla.App. 3 Dist. 1994. Police did not coerce defendant's wife into letting them borrow photograph from which defendant was identified, even though owner of apartment building in which defendant and wife lived threatened to evict them unless wife acceded to police officers' request for photograph; police did not accompany or force building owner to take action they sought, but rather, owner, armed with independent, legitimate, and private business interest, had motive to prevail upon wife which was separate apart from interest of police.

> Gillis v. State, 634 So.2d 725, review denied 651 So.2d 1193.

Fla.App. 3 Dist. 1984. When defendant turned his purse over to manager of hotel he had reasonable expectation of privacy therein which would render warrantless search by government agents unreasonable and violation of Fourth Amendment, but where initial invasion of defendant's purse was occasioned by private action, of hotel manager, invasion did not violate Fourth Amendment. U.S.C.A. Const.Amend. 4.

> State v. Weiss, 449 So.2d 915.

Where initial invasion of defendant's purse was occasioned by private action of hotel manager, and police officers who examined contents of partially open purse found exactly what they were told they would find by manager, police officers' actions did not constitute "search" within meaning in Fourth Amendment. U.S.C.A. Const.Amend. 4.

> State v. Weiss, 449 So.2d 915.

Fla.App. 3 Dist. 1979. Neither Florida nor federal Constitution proscription against unreasonable searches and seizures affords any protection against purely private searches and seizures no matter how unreasonable. U.S.C.A.Const. Amends. 4, 14; West's F.S.A.Const. art. 1, § 12.

> Pomerantz v. State, 372 So.2d 104, appeal dismissed, certiorari denied 386 So.2d 642.

Fla.App. 4 Dist. 2016. When determining whether private citizen confidential informants have acted in a manner that makes them agents of the government, the court must apply a similar test when asking whether the informant, in light of all the circumstances of the case, must be regarded as having acted as an instrument or agent of the state; this includes examining the purpose of the conduct in which the actor engaged. West's F.S.A. § 914.28(2)(a) (2011).

> Osorio v. State, 186 So.3d 601, rehearing denied, review denied 2016 WL 1749455.

Under certain situations, informants can be considered agents of the State, especially when acting in accordance with agreements made with authorities; in other words, the government must be involved either directly as a participant or indirectly as an encourager of the private citizen's actions before a court deems the citizen to be an instrument of the state. West's F.S.A. § 914.28(2)(a) (2011).

> Osorio v. State, 186 So.3d 601, rehearing denied, review denied 2016 WL 1749455.

The test for determining whether private individuals are agents of the government, for purposes of the hearsay exception for statements of a party-opponent, is whether, in consideration of the circumstances, the individuals acted as instruments of the state; to determine whether a private individual acts as an instrument of the state, courts look to (1) whether the government was aware of and acquiesced in the conduct; and (2) whether the individual intended to assist the police or further his own ends. West's F.S.A. § 90.803(18).

> Osorio v. State, 186 So.3d 601, rehearing denied, review denied 2016 WL 1749455.

Fla.App. 4 Dist. 1999. While certain degree of governmental participation is necessary before private citizen is transformed into agent of state, de minimis or incidental contacts between citizen and law enforcement agents prior to or during course of citizen's search or seizure will not subject search to Fourth Amendment scrutiny. U.S.C.A. Const.Amend. 4.

> Glasser v. State, 737 So.2d 597.

Government must be involved either directly as participant or indirectly as encourager of private citizen's actions in searching and seizing property before courts deem citizen to be instrument of state subject to Fourth Amendment scrutiny; requisite degree of governmental participation involves some degree of knowledge and acquiescence in the search. U.S.C.A. Const.Amend. 4.

> Glasser v. State, 737 So.2d 597.

Removal of vehicle identification number (VIN) sticker from defendant's car by private citizen, who was acting solely at direction of police officer, was an illegal seizure in violation of defendant's Fourth Amendment rights. U.S.C.A. Const.Amend. 4.

> Glasser v. State, 737 So.2d 597.

Fla.App. 4 Dist. 1980. The Fourth Amendment protects individuals from unreasonable searches or seizures by agents of government, not from intrusion by neighbors or others. U.S.C.A.Const. Amend. 4.

> State v. Schultz, 388 So.2d 1326.

Fla.App. 5 Dist. 2011. The protection against unreasonable searches and seizures applies only to cases involving governmental action; it does not apply when the search or seizure was conducted by a private individual. U.S.C.A. Const.Amend. 4.

> State v. Oliveras, 65 So.3d 1162.

Statute that conditioned the requirement by law enforcement for a provider of electronic communication service of the contents of an electronic communication that had been in electronic storage in an electronic communications system for 180 days or less on a warrant did not apply to private tracking software company that tracked alleged theft victim's computer to defendant's home; police never required company to do anything, and to the contrary, the victim consented and, in fact, requested company to provide information to the police, and company complied. West's F.S.A. § 934.23.

> State v. Oliveras, 65 So.3d 1162.

Fla.App. 5 Dist. 1999. Employer's search of employee's desk after his arrest and police search when employer opened the desk and showed them a gun did not violate the Fourth Amendment; the police search did not exceed the scope of the private search. U.S.C.A. Const.Amend. 4.

> State v. Olsen, 745 So.2d 454.

The Fourth Amendment protects only against illegal searches conducted by government officials. U.S.C.A. Const.Amend. 4.

> State v. Olsen, 745 So.2d 454.

A search by a private citizen will not be considered private if it was instigated by law enforcement or conducted by the citizen acting as an agent of law enforcement. U.S.C.A. Const.Amend. 4.

> State v. Olsen, 745 So.2d 454.

Fla.App. 5 Dist. 1984. Defendant's Fourth Amendment rights were not violated as a result of removal by hospital employee of sealed envelope from defendant's pants pockets when he was being treated at hospital emergency room while in a semiconscious state or when employee gave police officer the envelope and officer opened it and observed a white powder or when officer tested the white powder without obtaining a search warrant. U.S.C.A. Const.Amend. 4.

> State v. Gans, 454 So.2d 655.

☞34. —— **Carriers and communication companies.**

† C.A.11 (Fla.) 2015. Manager at store for package delivery service acted as private citizen, rather than as agent for government, in opening two packages at store, and therefore, search of packages did not implicate the Fourth Amendment; packages were heavily taped and had chemical odor, sender refused to consolidate packages to reduce shipping charges, manager contacted police, officer stated that carriers had right to inspect a package if it was suspected to contain hazardous materials, and officer did not take part in search. U.S.C.A. Const.Amend. 4.

U.S. v. Emile, 618 Fed.Appx. 953.

C.A.11 (Fla.) 2003. Packages sent through carrier were "effects" in context of Fourth Amendment, and senders therefore presumptively possessed legitimate expectation of privacy in their contents. U.S.C.A. Const.Amend. 4.

U.S. v. Young, 350 F.3d 1302, rehearing and rehearing denied 97 Fed. Appx. 909.

C.A.5 (Fla.) 1979. Where cartons containing films were shipped by bus with fictitious name given for addressee, where corporation whose name was similar to that of fictitious addressee was notified of shipment, where corporation's employees took shipment of films from bus terminal on their own initiative, opened cartons, examined individual film boxes, ascertained nature of films, and then notified FBI, and where there was no indication that employees acted at the behest or suggestion, with the aid, advice or encouragement, or under the direction or influence of the FBI, activities of corporation's employees constituted private search and search was therefore beyond scope of Fourth Amendment. U.S.C.A.Const. Amend. 4.

U.S. v. Sanders, 592 F.2d 788, rehearing denied 597 F.2d 63, certiorari granted Walter v. U.S., 100 S.Ct. 227, 444 U.S. 914, 62 L.Ed.2d 168, reversed 100 S.Ct. 2395, 447 U.S. 649, 65 L.Ed.2d 410, on remand 625 F.2d 1311.

Fla.App. 3 Dist. 1988. Airport security personnel involved in search of person were acting under federal aviation law and regulations such that their actions constituted "governmental action" implicating search and seizure guarantee of Fourth Amendment. U.S.C.A. Const.Amend. 4.

State v. Baez, 530 So.2d 405.

Fla.App. 3 Dist. 1979. Where officers, observed two black plastic trash bags laying in open suitcase when they arrived in airline baggage area, the officers opened the bags, examined the contents and seized suspected marijuana, and one officer, following opening by airline employee of other suitcases, opened black plastic trash bags contained in second suitcase discovering more suspected marijuana and looked through clothing and other articles in third suitcase discovering other incriminating identification evidence, fact that private party, the airline employee, had hand in search did not make it any less a governmentally conducted search as it was enough, for purpose of invoking protection of Fourth Amendment and provision of Florida Constitution, that police actively participated in the search. U.S.C.A.Const. Amends. 4, 14; West's F.S.A.Const. art. 1, § 12.

Pomerantz v. State, 372 So.2d 104, appeal dismissed, certiorari denied 386 So.2d 642.

Fla.App. 4 Dist. 1973. Where baggage service manager's opening of unlocked suitcase, which had arrived on airplane flight as personal luggage with no name or identification tag on outside and remained unclaimed for more than an hour, was done in accordance with airlines' policy to promptly ascertain owner of luggage which was apparently lost or abandoned, such opening involved a search by private individual for legitimate and proper purpose; and thus, Fourth Amendment protection was not applicable to search. U.S.C.A.Const. Amend. 4.

State v. Bookout, 281 So.2d 215.

⊙━35. —— **Foreign states or officers.**

C.A.11 (Fla.) 2015. District court did not err in denying defendant's motion to suppress electronic evidence, and fruits thereof, which U.S. received directly from United Kingdom's Serious Fraud Office (SFO) in connection with ongoing international investigation into fraud schemes; Fourth Amendment did not apply to searches and seizures made by foreign authorities enforcing foreign laws in their own country, and defendant did not have an objectively reasonable expectation of privacy in the data files when U.S. agents examined them, to extent British officials

---

† This Case was not selected for publication in the National Reporter System
For legislative history of cited statutes, see Florida Statutes Annotated

searched those files before sending them. U.S.C.A. Const.Amend. 4.

> U.S. v. Odoni, 782 F.3d 1226, certiorari denied Gunter v. U.S., 135 S.Ct. 2335, 191 L.Ed.2d 981, certiorari denied 135 S.Ct. 2339, 191 L.Ed.2d 981.

The Fourth Amendment exclusionary rule does not apply to searches and seizures conducted by foreign officials on foreign soil; the exclusionary rule does, however, apply to searches and seizures conducted by state and federal officials of the United States. U.S.C.A. Const.Amend. 4.

> U.S. v. Odoni, 782 F.3d 1226, certiorari denied Gunter v. U.S., 135 S.Ct. 2335, 191 L.Ed.2d 981, certiorari denied 135 S.Ct. 2339, 191 L.Ed.2d 981.

C.A.11 (Fla.) 2009. Fourth Amendment does not apply to search and seizure by United States agents of property that is owned by nonresident alien and located in foreign country. U.S.C.A. Const.Amend. 4.

> U.S. v. Emmanuel, 565 F.3d 1324, certiorari denied 130 S.Ct. 1032, 558 U.S. 1099, 175 L.Ed.2d 632.

C.A.11 (Fla.) 1994. Fourth Amendment is generally inapplicable to actions carried out by foreign officials in their own countries enforcing their own laws, even if American officials are present and cooperate in some degree. U.S.C.A. Const.Amend. 4.

> U.S. v. Behety, 32 F.3d 503, certiorari denied 115 S.Ct. 2568, 515 U.S. 1137, 132 L.Ed.2d 820.

C.A.5 (Fla.) 1980. Exceptions to general rule that neither Fourth Amendment nor *Miranda* requirements apply to foreign officers' conduct in their own nations exists where: (1) conduct of foreign officers shocks conscience of American court or (2) American officials participated in foreign search or interrogation or the foreign authorities were acting as agents for their American counterparts. U.S.C.A.Const. Amends. 4, 5.

> U.S. v. Heller, 625 F.2d 594.

Arresting and interrogating British officers were not acting as agents of American officers where defendant was detained and counterfeit treasury bills seized before any American agents arrived, defendant was charged initially with violating British law, American agent interviewed defendant only after first obtaining permission from British authorities and then only for limited time allowed by British authorities, and American agent and British officers did not exchange information regarding their separate interrogations of defendant, and thus defendant could not invoke protection of Fourth and Fifth Amendments. U.S.C.A.Const. Amends. 4, 5.

> U.S. v. Heller, 625 F.2d 594.

C.A.5 (Fla.) 1976. Fourth Amendment exclusionary rule does not apply to arrests and searches made by foreign authorities on their home territory and in the enforcement of foreign law, even if the persons arrested and from whom evidence is seized are American citizens, but exceptions apply if the circumstances of the foreign search and seizure are so extreme that they "shock the judicial conscience," or if American law enforcement officials participated in the foreign search or the foreign authorities were acting as agents for their American counterparts. U.S.C.A.Const. Amend. 4.

> U.S. v. Morrow, 537 F.2d 120, rehearing denied 541 F.2d 282, certiorari denied Martin v. U.S., 97 S.Ct. 1602, 430 U.S. 956, 51 L.Ed.2d 806, certiorari denied Brennan v. U.S., 97 S.Ct. 1602, 430 U.S. 956, 51 L.Ed.2d 806.

Conduct of FBI agent in alerting Canadian authorities to possession of information by an American informant living in Canada was not such participation by American law enforcement officials in warrantless search and seizure in Canada by Canadian officials as to invoke for the benefit of defendant, who was arrested during the warrantless search and against whom evidence was uncovered, the protections of the Fourth Amendment, as there was no unlawful or unreasonable conduct on the part of the American officers. U.S.C.A.Const. Amend. 4.

> U.S. v. Morrow, 537 F.2d 120, rehearing denied 541 F.2d 282, certiorari denied Martin v. U.S., 97 S.Ct. 1602, 430 U.S. 956, 51 L.Ed.2d 806, certiorari denied Brennan v. U.S., 97 S.Ct. 1602, 430 U.S. 956, 51 L.Ed.2d 806.

---

† This Case was not selected for publication in the National Reporter System
For legislative history of cited statutes, see Florida Statutes Annotated

M.D.Fla. 1979. Jurisprudence of the Fourth Amendment and the exclusionary rule designed for its enforcement does not apply to searches made by foreign authorities on their own territory even if persons from whom evidence is seized are citizens of the United States; on the other hand, if it is shown that American agents are in privity with the search to direct partic- ipation or procurement, rule of exclusion may be invoked and subject to that exception, standard to be applied in deciding the admissibility of fruits of foreign search is whether circumstances surrounding seizure are so extreme as to shock the judicial conscience. U.S.C.A.Const. Amend. 4.

U.S. v. Phillips, 479 F.Supp. 423.

Key Numbers 36 et seq. in Next Volume

For Cross-References or Descriptive Words
see
DESCRIPTIVE–WORD INDEX

.

West's
FLORIDA DIGEST 2d

Vol. 28A

Sales — Searches and Seizures ⚷ 35
(Now Sales — Search, Seizure, and Arrest ⚷ 900)

2024
Cumulative Annual Pocket Part
Covering opinions 2017 to date

THE WEST DIGEST TOPIC NUMBERS WHICH CAN BE
USED FOR WESTLAW® SEARCHES ARE LISTED ON
PAGE III OF THIS POCKET PART.

**Up-Dated Weekly by West's
Reporter Advance Sheets
or WESTLAW**

**For Florida Cases Prior to 1935
Consult Florida Digest First Series**

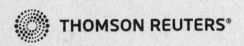

THOMSON REUTERS®

Closing with Cases Reported in

Southern Reporter, Third Series 376 So.3d 431
Supreme Court Reporter .... 144 S.Ct. 535
Federal Reporter, Fourth Series 91 F.4th 1172
Federal Appendix .... 861 Fed.Appx.
Federal Supplement, Third Series 668 F.Supp.3d
Federal Rules Decisions .... 344 F.R.D.
Bankruptcy Reporter .... 656 B.R. 482

DIGEST TOPICS AND ABBREVIATIONS

WESTLAW provides easy and quick access to those cases reported after the latest available digest supplementation.

The WESTLAW query is entered in any appropriate case law data base of interest. The query format used substitutes a numerical equivalent for the digest topic name and adds the key number through the use of "K" as illustrated in the search for later Contracts ⚬ 155 cases published after December 31, 2023.

ad(after 12-31-23) & 95K155.

1	Abandoned and Lost Property .... Aband L P	29	Annuities .... Annuities
2	Abatement and Revival .... Abate & R	29T	Antitrust and Trade Regulation .... Antitrust
4	Abortion and Birth Control .... Abort	30	Appeal and Error .... App & E
5	Absentees .... Absentees	31	Appearance .... Appear
8	Accord and Satisfaction .... Accord	34	Armed Services .... Armed S
9	Account .... Acct	36	Arson .... Arson
10	Account, Action on .... Acct Action on	37	Assault and Battery ..... Assault
11	Account Stated .... Acct St	38	Assignments .... Assign
11A	Accountants .... Accnts	40	Assistance, Writ of .... Assist
12	Acknowledgment .... Ack	41	Associations .... Assoc
13	Action .... Action	42	Assumpsit, Action of .... Assumpsit
14	Action on the Case .... Action on Case	43	Asylums and Assisted Living Facilities .... Asylums
15	Adjoining Landowners ... Adj Land	46	Attorney General .... Atty Gen
15A	Administrative Law and Procedure .... Admin Law	46H	Attorneys and Legal Services .... Attys & Leg S
16	Admiralty .... Adm	47	Auctions and Auctioneers .... Auctions
17	Adoption .... Adop	48	Audita Querela .... Aud Quer
18	Adulteration .... Adulteration	48A	Automobiles .... Autos
20	Adverse Possession ...... Adv Poss	48B	Aviation .... Aviation
21	Affidavits .... Afft	49	Bail .... Bail
23	Agriculture .... Agric	50	Bailment .... Bailm
23H	Alcoholic Beverages ..... Alco Bev	51	Bankruptcy .... Bankr
24	Aliens, Immigration, and Citizenship .... Aliens	58	Bonds .... Bonds
25	Alteration of Instruments .... Alt of Inst	59	Boundaries .... Bound
		63	Bribery .... Brib
25T	Alternative Dispute Resolution .... Alt Disp Res	64	Bridges .... Bridges
		65	Brokers .... Brok
27	Amicus Curiae .... Am Cur	67	Burglary .... Burg
28	Animals .... Anim	69	Cancellation of Instruments .... Can of Inst
		70	Carriers .... Carr
		71	Cemeteries .... Cem

III

DIGEST TOPICS AND ABBREVIATIONS

DIGEST TOPICS AND ABBREVIATIONS

DIGEST TOPICS AND ABBREVIATIONS

DIGEST TOPICS AND ABBREVIATIONS

DIGEST TOPICS AND ABBREVIATIONS

SALES

☞1–484.
SALES Key Numbers 1 to 484 are no longer valid and have been replaced by new Key Numbers. See topic analysis and translation tables.

I. IN GENERAL.

☞509. —— In general.
S.D.Fla. 2022. Florida law governed breach of contract claim brought by buyer of two cargo loads of frozen shrimp, which was a New York company with its principal place of business in Florida, against Ecuadorian frozen shrimp seller arising from purported breach of letter of warranty guaranteeing that seller would reimburse buyer for any unforeseen setback with the shrimp at its destination port in China because of customs clearance; buyer stated that contract at issue was negotiated and invoiced out of Florida, letters of warranty were provided to buyer at its Florida headquarters, and reimbursement under letters of warranty was supposedly to be paid to buyer in Florida.—Seven Seas International, LLC v. Frigopesca, C.A., 616 F.Supp.3d 1323.
S.D.Fla. 2021. Under Florida's choice-of-law rules, consumers' various claims against automobile manufacturer for false advertising, breach of warranty, and unjust enrichment, based on allegations that manufacturer knew lack of transmission and differential coolers in automobile model would be fatal to track performance consumers expected, were governed by laws of states where vehicles were purchased, not where consumers resided.—Tershakovec v. Ford Motor Company, 546 F.Supp.3d 1348, amended in part 2021 WL 3711444, affirmed in part, vacated in part, reversed in part 79 F.4th 1299.

☞511. —— International issues.
S.D.Fla. 2022. District Court would assume, for purpose of choice of law analysis at default judgment stage of action brought by buyer of frozen shrimp, which was a New York company with its principal place of business in Florida, against Ecuadorian shrimp seller, that buyer's breach of contract and conversion claims arising from alleged breach of letter of warranty guaranteeing that seller would reimburse buyer for any unforeseen setback with shrimp at destination port in China because of customs clearance, were asserted as Florida state law causes of action, and that buyer did not intend to invoke United Nations Convention on Contracts for International Sale of Goods, to which United States, Ecuador, and China were signatories, where buyer invoked Court's diversity jurisdiction and erroneously referenced Florida civil procedure rules. Fed. R. Civ. P. 55(b).—Seven Seas International, LLC v. Frigopesca, C.A., 616 F.Supp.3d 1323.
S.D.Fla. 2002. Universalist approach which sought to apply the rules of the 1964 Hague Convention to international sales regardless of whether the parties had contact with a contracting state had no application in interpreting scope of United Nations Convention on Contracts for the International Sale of Goods, where negotiations leading up to CISG specifically rejected universalist approach to its application. United Nations Convention on Contracts for the International Sale of Goods. Art. 1 et seq., 15 U.S.C.A.App.—Impuls I.D. Intern., S.L. v. Psion-Teklogix, Inc., 234 F.Supp.2d 1267.

☞513. —— In general.
C.A.11 (Fla.) 2023. Restaurants' putative class action against food distributor for breach of contract concerned voluntary commitments rather than state-imposed obligations, and thus Poultry Products Inspection Act (PPIA) did not preempt restaurants' claim that food distributor breached its contracts with them providing for pricing to be based on fee per pound when it regularly delivered underweight boxes of poultry. 21 U.S.C.A. § 467e.—A1A Burrito Works, Inc. v. Sysco Jacksonville, Inc., 87 F.4th 1280.

☞514. —— Warranties and redhibition.
C.A.11 (Fla.) 2018. Husband's fraudulent misrepresentation, negligent misrepresentation, fraudulent marketing and promotion, and breach of express warranty claims under Florida law against manufacturer, in connection with wife's death after suffering cardiac arrest while wearing external defibrillator that did not administer shock to her, were not expressly or impliedly preempted under Medical Device Amendments (MDA) to FDCA, since such claims were based on alleged misrepresentations made by manufacturer, including that external defibrillator had 98% first treatment shock success rate for resuscitating patients and that external defibrillator would administer shock whenever one was needed, that stated higher standard than that required by Food and Drug Administration (FDA) or imposed by the State. Federal Food, Drug, and Cosmetic Act §§ 331, 521, 21 U.S.C.A. §§ 337(a), 360k(a); Fla. Stat. Ann. §§ 817.40(5), 817.41(1).—Godelia v. Doe 1, 881 F.3d 1309, on remand 2019 WL 3821211.
M.D.Fla. 2022. Breach of implied warranty of merchantability claim brought by estate of consumer who went into respiratory shock and died after ingesting generic blood pressure drug against drug's manufacturer was preempted by federal law requiring generic drugs to have same active ingredients, route of administration, dosage form, strength, and labeling as brand-name drug upon which they are based; increasing the drug's usefulness or reducing its alleged risk of danger would have required redesigning the drug, as both usefulness and risk of danger were direct results of drug's chemical design and active ingredients. Federal Food, Drug, and Cosmetic Act § 505, 21 U.S.C.A. § 355(j); 21 C.F.R. § 314.70(b)(2)(i).—Hernandez v. Aurobindo Pharma USA, Inc., 582 F.Supp.3d 1192.
S.D.Fla. 2020. Drug consumers' state-law claims against drug retailers and distributors, including for negligent and strict-liability failure to warn of risks that drug could degrade into carcinogen, strict-liability design defect, breach of express and implied warranties, and deceptive acts, were based on allegations that drug had defective design and inadequate labels and warnings, and, thus, were pre-empted by impossibility, under federal statutory and regulatory framework for drug design and labeling; other than by ceasing to sell drug altogether, retailers and distributors could not cure any design defect in drug, make changes to drug label, or issue warnings without FDA approval in order to comply with state-law duties. Federal Food, Drug, and Cosmetic Act § 505, 21 U.S.C.A. § 355; 21 C.F.R. § 314.94(a)(8)(iii), (iv).—In re Zantac (Ranitidine) Products Liability Litigation, 510 F.Supp.3d 1234.
S.D.Fla. 2015. Medical Device Amendments to Food, Drug and Cosmetic Act (FDCA) preempted Florida state law claims against man-

ufacturer of hip joint replacement system for breach of express warranty and implied warranty of merchantability based on patient's development of unsafe levels of metal toxicity allegedly caused by system; patient failed to state parallel state law claim because, as provided by preemption clause, state law warranty claim could not allege a device was unsafe and ineffective when FDA made express finding in contravention of that claim, and patient's consent to participate in clinical study that provided safety monitoring was inconsistent with allegations that manufacturer warranted that system would not release metal ions into his blood. Federal Food, Drug, and Cosmetic Act § 510, 21 U.S.C.A. § 360(k).—Mink v. Smith & Nephew, Inc., 145 F.Supp.3d 1208, affirmed in part, reversed in part and remanded 860 F.3d 1319.

⚙️515. Nature and definition of sale; other transactions distinguished.
Conditional sales, see ⚙️3004. Chattel mortgages, see CHATTEL MORTGAGES ⚙️6. Secured transactions, see SECURED TRANSACTIONS ⚙️10. Gifts, see GIFTS ⚙️5(2).

⚙️516. —— In general.
Fla.App. 4 Dist. 2018. A "sale" is the transfer of property or title for a price.—Morris v. MGZ Properties, LLC, 251 So.3d 929.

⚙️517(2). Particular transactions.
Fla.App. 3 Dist. 2012. Creditor who purchased silver from a company that was running a Ponzi scheme was the victim of a fraud, not an owner or bailor of the silver purportedly sold to her by debtor, and, thus, assignee for the benefit of creditors could sell precious metals that were turned over by debtor, where there was no evidence that silver was set aside for creditor or that 1,000 ounces of silver were purchased with her funds or segregated as her separate property.—O'Brien v. Stermer, 98 So.3d 1245, rehearing denied.

⚙️528. —— Mixed or hybrid transactions.
M.D.Fla. 2021. Under Michigan law, application of Uniform Commercial Code (UCC) turns on whether the predominant factor, the thrust, the purpose, reasonably stated, is the rendition of service, with goods incidentally involve or is transaction of sale, with labor incidentally involved; if the thrust of the transaction is a sale of goods, then the UCC governs. Mich. Comp. Laws Ann. § 440.1101 et seq.—Knudsen v. Ethicon, Inc., 535 F.Supp.3d 1231.

⚙️532(8). Machinery and equipment.
S.D.Fla. 2020. HVAC units constituted "goods" under Florida's adoption of Article 2 of the Uniform Commercial Code (UCC), and thus UCC, not common law of contracts, governed action brought by units' buyer against manufacturers and distributor, alleging breach of express warranty and implied warranty of merchantability and violations of Magnuson-Moss Warranty Act (MMWA) based on defective heater components, where units were movable. Federal Trade Commission Improvement Act §§ 101-112, 15 U.S.C.A. §§ 2301-2312; Fla. Stat. Ann. §§ 672.102, 672.105(1).—Toca v. Tutco, LLC, 430 F.Supp.3d 1313.

⚙️532(14). Aircraft and aviation.
† C.A.11 (Fla.) 2017. Under Kansas law, breach-of-contract claim by purchaser of private aircraft against seller was governed by Uniform Commercial Code (UCC), rather than by common law, even though purchase agreement involved both sale of goods and of services, since purpose of purchase agreement was to obtain aircraft, which was a good, and enrollment in management program, which was a service whereby seller's subsidiary would manage and rent out aircraft on behalf of purchaser for five years, was secondary to purchase of aircraft. Kan. Stat. Ann. § 84-1-103(b).—Sack v. Cessna Aircraft Company, 676 Fed.Appx. 887.

S.D.Fla. 2007. Under Florida law, reservation agreement, which expressly provided that additional options were "to be determined," was not an enforceable contract for the purchase of a specific aircraft, but rather, was an agreement to reserve an order position for an aircraft to be defined later at a price that was subject to change pending the aircraft's development; projected price was placed on the reservation agreement as a placeholder, but it did not and could not bind the parties to the purchase and sale of an aircraft that did not yet exist.—Barnes v. Diamond Aircraft Industries, Inc., 499 F.Supp.2d 1311.

⚙️532(21). Insurance.
† C.A.11 (Fla.) 2018. Buyer's purchase of insurance agency, pursuant to franchise agreement and asset-purchase agreement in which buyer was required to transfer all title to agency assets to seller's financing entity as security for his loans, was one in which acquisition and use of services predominated over purchase of goods, precluding buyer from invoking protections of sales article of Uniform Commercial Code; predominate purpose of agreement was to establish franchise relationship as joint endeavor between seller and buyer. U.C.C. Article 2; Kan. Stat. Ann. §§ 84-2-105(1), 84-2-105(2).—DZ Bank AG Deutche Zentral-Genossenschaftsbank v. McCranie, 720 Fed.Appx. 576.

⚙️532(22). Health care.
M.D.Fla. 2021. The Uniform Commercial Code (UCC), as adopted in Michigan, applied to a patient's claim for breach of implied warranty in the patient's product liability action against the manufacturers of a medical mesh; the manufacturers did not provide a service, the patient was not suing the medical provider who implanted the mesh, and the thrust of the patient's case was that there was an alleged defect in the mesh, which was a good. Mich. Comp. Laws Ann. § 440.1101 et seq.—Knudsen v. Ethicon, Inc., 535 F.Supp.3d 1231.

II. PARTIES TO TRANSACTION OR CONTRACT.

⚙️607. Participation in and relation to transaction.
† C.A.11 (Fla.) 2014. Purchaser that bought aircraft from a dealer, pursuant to purchase agreement, did not enter into oral contract with aircraft's manufacturer during visit to manufacturer's facility, as required to establish breach of contract claim against manufacturer under Florida law; essential terms of sale were negotiated and finalized between purchaser and dealer, the only changes made to the terms of the agreement were the serial number and expected delivery date, which occurred prior to purchaser's visit to manufacturer's facility, purchaser made all the payments before visiting facility, and no conduct occurred during purchaser's visit that would support a finding of mutual assent between purchaser and manufacturer.—HTC Leleu Family Trust v. Piper Aircraft, Inc., 571 Fed.Appx. 772.

† This Case was not selected for publication in the National Reporter System

☞608. Privity in general.
M.D.Fla. 2020. Under Michigan law, no privity of contract exists between a consumer who buys from a retailer and the manufacturer who has not sold a product directly to the consumer. Mich. Comp. Laws Ann. § 440.2313.—Yachera v. Westminster Pharmaceuticals, LLC, 477 F.Supp.3d 1251.

III. NATURE AND FORMATION OF CONTRACT.

☞705. —— As to subject matter.
N.D.Fla. 2023. Revised purchase order which buyer's principal sent to seller's contractor reflected agreement on all material terms for sale of ilmenite, as required to form contract under Article 2 of the Uniform Commercial Code (UCC), as adopted in Florida, even though purchase order did not contain a term as to quality; contractor had previously sent email to buyer's principal containing a list of terms and asked him to send purchase order if he agreed to those terms, principal responded that terms "will work" and sent purchase order containing those terms and agreeing to pay certain sum for the ilmenite, and quality could be inferred from price agreed upon in the purchase order. Fla. Stat. Ann. § 672.204(3).—US Iron FLA, LLC v. GMA Garnett (USA) Corp., 660 F.Supp.3d 1212.

☞710. —— In general.
† C.A.11 (Fla.) 2014. Purchaser that bought aircraft from a dealer, pursuant to purchase agreement, did not enter into oral contract with aircraft's manufacturer during visit to manufacturer's facility, as required to establish breach of contract claim against manufacturer under Florida law; essential terms of sale were negotiated and finalized between purchaser and dealer, the only changes made to the terms of the agreement were the serial number and expected delivery date, which occurred prior to purchaser's visit to manufacturer's facility, purchaser made all the payments before visiting facility, and no conduct occurred during purchaser's visit that would support a finding of mutual assent between purchaser and manufacturer.—HTC Leleu Family Trust v. Piper Aircraft, Inc., 571 Fed.Appx. 772.

☞717. —— Agreements to agree.
† C.A.11 (Fla.) 2017. Memorandum of understanding between glass manufacturer and operator of commercial glass fabrication plants, in which operator agreed to sell manufacturer its glass fabrication equipment conditioned on parties working out acceptable lease transition agreement, was not legally binding contract imposing specific obligations on parties, and thus operator was not bound by implied covenant of good faith and fair dealing under Florida law, although agreement indicated parties intended document to be legally binding; terms of agreement were indefinite, at best constituting mere agreement to agree in future, and parties did not discuss terms of potentially acceptable lease arrangements or define criteria for such arrangements in agreement itself.—Aldora Aluminum & Glass Products, Inc. v. Poma Glass & Specialty Windows, Inc., 683 Fed.Appx. 764.

☞720(3). Acceptance of offer to sell.
N.D.Fla. 2017. Vessel owner entered into a contract with fuel provider when vessel's engineer accepted provider's fuel and signed provider's bunkering certificate under Florida law, even though provider had a preexisting duty pursuant to a contract with an intermediary to deliver the fuel and the certificate did not specify the cost of the fuel, where the bunkering certificate set out in clear terms that the ship bore ultimate liability for the debt arising out from the delivery of fuel, and the amount of the debt could be readily determined by reference to provider's contract with the intermediary.—Martin Energy Services, LLC v. M/V Bravante IX, 233 F.Supp.3d 1269, affirmed 733 Fed.Appx. 503.

☞727. —— "Shrinkwrap" agreements.
See also COPYRIGHTS AND INTELLECTUAL PROPERTY ☞107.

IV. VALIDITY AND ENFORCEABILITY OF CONTRACT.

☞803. —— In general.
Fla.App. 3 Dist. 2018. Diamond buyer's alleged omission of information regarding actual value of diamond could not constitute an inducement of store's mistake in selling diamond to buyer for ½₀ of its retail value and, thus, did not provide basis to rescind purchase contract based on unilateral mistake; inducement required some type of action, not mere knowledge, and thus buyer had to act in some way to induce store into making a mistake.—DePrince v. Starboard Cruise Services, Inc., 347 So.3d 31, superseded on rehearing 271 So.3d 11.
To satisfy the negligence prong of test for defense of unilateral mistake, operator of cruise ship jewelry store, which sought to rescind purchase contract for diamond on basis of unilateral mistake, was required to show that there was no negligence or want of due care on its part in selling the diamond to buyer for ½₀ of its retail value; it was not sufficient for store to show that there was no inexcusable lack of due care under the circumstances.—Id.

V. TERMS OF CONTRACT; RIGHTS AND OBLIGATIONS OF PARTIES.

(A) IN GENERAL.

☞913. Good faith and fair dealing in general.
S.D.Fla. 2020. Commercial reasonableness acts as a guide for courts to determine whether a party acted in good faith within the meaning of the Uniform Commercial Code (UCC). Fla. Stat. Ann. § 672.103(1)(b).—ConSeal International Incorporated v. Neogen Corporation, 488 F.Supp.3d 1257.
Because there is no precise definition of the term commercial reasonableness, the facts of the case will be determinative of whether conduct is commercially reasonable under the Uniform Commercial Code (UCC). Fla. Stat. Ann. § 672.103(1)(b).—Id.

☞915. Notice requirements in general.
S.D.Fla. 2020. Pre-suit notice requirement established in provision of Florida's Uniform Commercial Code (UCC) requiring buyer, after having accepted tender, to notify seller of any breach within reasonable time after he or she discovers or should have discovered breach in order to obtain remedy is a precondition of imposing liability. Fla. Stat. Ann. § 672.607(3)(a).—Toca v. Tutco, LLC, 430 F.Supp.3d 1313.

† This Case was not selected for publication in the National Reporter System

(B) GOODS SUBJECT TO CONTRACT IN GENERAL.

⟨⇒**935. Title or possession of seller.**
Transfer of title, see V(G). Warranties, see IX.

(C) DELIVERY AND ACCEPTANCE OF GOODS.

1. IN GENERAL.

⟨⇒**967. —— In general.**
Fla.App. 2 Dist. 2021. Buyer's cancellation of contract for purchase of citrus trees several months after anticipated delivery date and several months before trees could be delivered by nursery did not violate contract's section requiring buyer to accept delivery of trees within 60-day delivery period; delivery period began to run when nursery provided notice that trees were ready for transplanting, and nursery never provided notice. —Charlotte 650, LLC v. Phillip Rucks Citrus Nursery, Inc., 320 So.3d 863.

⟨⇒**968. —— Time as being "of the essence".**
Fla.App. 4 Dist. 2004. Time was not of the essence in contract for the sale of an airplane, and thus seller's failure to have plane ready by original closing date, or by second closing date suggested by seller after first closing date had passed, did not entitle buyer to terminate contract and receive refund of nonrefundable deposit; contract did not specify that time was of the essence, buyer did not suffer any undue hardship from the delay, and buyer did not send seller express notice requesting that the contract be performed within a reasonable time.—Atlanta Jet v. Liberty Aircraft Services, LLC, 866 So.2d 148.

2. QUALITY, VALUE, FITNESS, AND CONDITION OF GOODS.

Warranties, see IX.

⟨⇒**983. Conformity to contract; perfect tender.**
S.D.Fla. 2017. There was no evidence that seller of fuel failed to provide to buyer the agreed upon quantity and type of fuel, or that seller made insufficient fuel deliveries, as required, under Florida law, to support buyer's claim that seller was first to breach the parties' fixed price forward contract for the sale of ultra-low sulfur diesel, as would excuse buyer's further performance.—World Fuel Services, Inc. v. John E. Retzner Oil Company, Inc., 234 F.Supp.3d 1234.

3. QUANTITY OF GOODS.

Warranties, see IX.

⟨⇒**1006. —— In general.**
S.D.Fla. 2017. The general purpose of a take or pay clause in a contract for the sale of fuel is to apportion the risks of fuel production and sales between the buyer and seller, in that seller bears risk of production or supply, and buyer bears risk of market demand; such clause insures that if demand for gas goes down, seller will still receive the price for the contract quantity delivered each year.—World Fuel Services, Inc. v. John E. Retzner Oil Company, Inc., 234 F.Supp.3d 1234.

Under Florida law, contract between buyer and seller of ultra-low sulfur diesel, which required buyer to purchase from seller 630,000 gallons per month for a one-year period, was a "take or pay contract," entitling seller to the full contract price upon buyer's breach, rather than damages based on seller's actual losses in accordance with Florida's Uniform Commercial Code (UCC); contract indicated that buyer agreed that in order for seller to offer fuel at fixed price over one-year period, seller has entered into hedging transactions with third parties, and in the event that buyer purchases less than full contracted quantity for any reason, buyer shall be liable for all damages incurred. Fla. Stat. Ann. § 672.709.—Id.

⟨⇒**1007. —— Buyer's obligations, performance, and breach.**
S.D.Fla. 2017. Under Florida law, fixed price forward contract for the sale of ultra-low sulfur diesel required buyer to pay for 630,000 gallons of fuel each month, regardless of whether buyer took the full amount, therefore, buyer's refusal to pay for remaining fuel under the one-year contract went to the essence of the contract, so as to constitute a material breach.—World Fuel Services, Inc. v. John E. Retzner Oil Company, Inc., 234 F.Supp.3d 1234.

Under Florida law, a "take or pay contract" for fuel obligates a buyer to purchase a specified amount of a fuel at a specified price and, if it is unable to do so, to pay for that amount.—Id.

Take or pay agreements, which obligate buyers to purchase a specific amount of a product, whether or not they actually take it, are standard in the oil industry.—Id.

Under Florida law, "take or pay agreements" for fuel are alternative performance contracts, whereby buyer has the option to take or not to take the fuel, but it must pay the contracted amount regardless.—Id.

Under Florida law, a take or pay contract for fuel requires buyer to compensate seller for his efforts and promise to supply the fuel rather than the fuel itself.—Id.

Under Florida law, court interpreting take or pay agreement, which obligates buyer to purchase a specific amount of product, whether or not it actually takes it, views a buyer's payment as its promise in the agreement rather than a measure of damages.—Id.

Under Florida law, mere lack of a make up clause, whereby buyer of fuel could recoup the fuel paid for but not taken within a certain amount of time, did not negate unambiguous "take or pay" language in the parties' one year fixed price forward contract for the sale of ultra-low sulfur diesel.—Id.

⟨⇒**1008. —— Seller's obligations, performance, and breach.**
S.D.Fla. 2017. Under Florida law, fixed price forward contract for the sale of ultra-low sulfur diesel required seller to deliver enough fuel at sufficient intervals to allow buyer to take 630,00 gallons ratably; contract did not specify a particular amount of fuel to be delivered each day, but rather required buyer to take fuel in approximately equal amounts prorated over each month.—World Fuel Services, Inc. v. John E. Retzner Oil Company, Inc., 234 F.Supp.3d 1234.

There was no evidence that seller of fuel failed to provide to buyer the agreed upon quantity and type of fuel, or that seller made insufficient fuel deliveries, as required, under Florida law, to support buyer's claim that seller was first to breach the parties' fixed price forward contract for the sale of ultra-low sulfur diesel, as would excuse buyer's further performance.—Id.

† **This Case was not selected for publication in the National Reporter System**

5. REVOCATION OF ACCEPTANCE.

Repudiation, see V(J). Cancellation and termination, see VI. Rescission, see X(D).

⊗**1039. Timeliness.**

S.D.Fla. 2021. Buyer of allegedly defective card-reading systems for its entertainment and gaming centers did not properly revoke acceptance of the systems and thus buyer, even if it could demonstrate that systems' manufacturer breached an express warranty or implied warranty of merchantability under Florida law, would not be entitled to the full purchase price of the systems or the full purchase price of a replacement system as damages; buyer used the allegedly defective system for three years even though buyer might have known about the defects shortly after delivery, buyer then resold some of the systems' hardware components, and buyer's purported attempt to revoke acceptance did not occur until almost five years had passed since delivery and until 28 months had passed since the latest date at which the evidence indicated that buyer knew about the defects. Fla. Stat. Ann. §§ 672.608(1)(a), 672.608(2), 672.711, 672.714.— A&E Adventures LLC v. Intercard, Inc., 529 F.Supp.3d 1333.

⊗**1040. Substantial change in condition of goods.**

S.D.Fla. 2021. Buyer of allegedly defective card-reading systems for its entertainment and gaming centers did not properly revoke acceptance of the systems and thus buyer, even if it could demonstrate that systems' manufacturer breached an express warranty or implied warranty of merchantability under Florida law, would not be entitled to the full purchase price of the systems or the full purchase price of a replacement system as damages; buyer used the allegedly defective system for three years even though buyer might have known about the defects shortly after delivery, buyer then resold some of the systems' hardware components, and buyer's purported attempt to revoke acceptance did not occur until almost five years had passed since delivery and until 28 months had passed since the latest date at which the evidence indicated that buyer knew about the defects. Fla. Stat. Ann. §§ 672.608(1)(a), 672.608(2), 672.711, 672.714.— A&E Adventures LLC v. Intercard, Inc., 529 F.Supp.3d 1333.

(F) PAYMENT.

⊗**1101. In general.**

S.D.Fla. 2017. Under Florida law, fixed price forward contract for the sale of ultra-low sulfur diesel required buyer to pay for 630,000 gallons of fuel each month, regardless of whether buyer took the full amount, therefore, buyer's refusal to pay for remaining fuel under the one-year contract went to the essence of the contract, so as to constitute a material breach.—World Fuel Services, Inc. v. John E. Retzner Oil Company, Inc., 234 F.Supp.3d 1234.

Under Florida law, a "take or pay contract" for fuel obligates a buyer to purchase a specified amount of a fuel at a specified price and, if it is unable to do so, to pay for that amount.—Id.

Take or pay agreements, which obligate buyers to purchase a specific amount of a product, whether or not they actually take it, are standard in the oil industry.—Id.

Under Florida law, "take or pay agreements" for fuel are alternative performance contracts,

whereby buyer has the option to take or not to take the fuel, but it must pay the contracted amount regardless.—Id.

Under Florida law, a take or pay contract for fuel requires buyer to compensate seller for his efforts and promise to supply the fuel rather than the fuel itself.—Id.

⊗**1116. Installments and deferred payments.**

Retail installment sales statutes, see FINANCE, BANKING, AND CREDIT III.

(G) TRANSFER OF TITLE.

Title or possession of seller, see ⊗935.

⊗**1155. —— Necessity and duty to make.**

Bkrtcy.S.D.Fla. 1984. Under master lease of aircraft requiring lessee to promptly notify lessor in writing that aircraft engine had been destroyed and to replace the engine by duly conveying title to replacement engine free and clear of all liens to owner of the destroyed engine, formal written bill of sale was not required to transfer title to replacement engine to the owner where lessee breached prompt notice requirement by not giving any notice, retained insurance proceeds for destroyed engine which it had no right to retain without transferring title to replacement engine, and had removed the original engine from the leased aircraft almost two years before it was destroyed after being placed in another plane. 13 Pa.C.S.A. § 2401.—In re Air Florida, Inc., 44 B.R. 798.

(J) REPUDIATION.

Revocation of acceptance, see V(C)5. Cancellation and termination, see VI. Rescission, see X(D).

⊗**1216. —— By seller.**

C.A.11 (Fla.) 2022. There was no evidence tying buyer's inability to secure financing for its coal gasification plant that never opened to the alleged breach of the parties' contract by seller of coal gasification burners and other equipment, and, thus, there was no evidence of a causal relationship between seller's alleged anticipatory repudiation of its contract with buyer by leaving the coal gasification market and the damages buyer sought, as was required for buyer to establish claim for anticipatory breach of contract under New York law, where buyer's discussion with financiers that were troubled by the performance of seller's gasifiers occurred more than three years before seller's alleged repudiation.— MidAmerica C2L Incorporated v. Siemens Energy Inc., 25 F.4th 1312, vacated and superseded on rehearing 2023 WL 2733512, on remand 2024 WL 414620.

Buyer was not ready, willing, and able to perform its obligations under contract with seller to purchase coal gasification burners and other equipment to be used in buyer's coal gasification plant, which never opened, at the time seller allegedly repudiated the contract by leaving the coal gasification market, and thus, buyer could not maintain claim for anticipatory breach of contract under New York law, where buyer was in financial ruin and had missed multiple payments on the contract before the alleged repudiation by seller.—Id.

(K) EXCUSES FOR NONPERFORMANCE OR BREACH.

➡1225. Force majeure.
Fla.App. 2 Dist. 2021. Nursery's delay in delivering citrus trees to buyer due to damage that occurred to trees when ventilation system was turned off overnight in one of nursery's greenhouses was not excused by sale contract's force majeure provision, which allowed nursery to reduce quantity of trees to be delivered if damage to trees occurred from cause that was not within nursery's reasonable control; ventilator system switch was in locked box to which only nursery's managers had keys, switch was in off position when ventilator shut-off problem was discovered, system was reactivated when switch was turned back on, and there was no indication that there were electrical problems or that power had gone out.—Charlotte 650, LLC v. Phillip Rucks Citrus Nursery, Inc., 320 So.3d 863.

(L) WAIVER AND ESTOPPEL.

➡1247. —— In general.
Fla.App. 3 Dist. 2020. Buyer was not entitled to repudiate entire agreement with seller, in which seller agreed to ship goods to buyer and install those goods on a vessel belonging to buyer's client, based on seller's alleged failure to perform the installation work, where buyer affirmed the agreement, elected to keep the goods that seller shipped and perform the installation work itself, and profited by charging the client for the installation services at a markup.—Cuomo Trading, Inc. v. World Contract S.R.L., 314 So.3d 309, review denied 2021 WL 98719.

VI. DURATION OF CONTRACT.

➡1302. Cancellation or termination.
Revocation of acceptance, see V(C)5. Repudiation, see V(J). Rescission, see X(D).

➡1304. —— By seller.
† C.A.11 (Fla.) 2017. Purchaser of private aircraft sufficiently alleged that seller had obligation under purchase agreement to maintain purchaser's enrollment in management program, in which seller's subsidiary managed aircraft and rented it out on behalf of purchaser, for five years, as required to state breach of contract claim under Kansas Uniform Commercial Code (UCC) against seller, since five-year management program provision in purchase agreement expressly permitted purchaser to remove aircraft from management program, but it contained no provision permitting seller to end enrollment in program, and purchaser alleged that seller ended enrollment. Kan. Stat. Ann. § 84-1-304.—Sack v. Cessna Aircraft Company, 676 Fed.Appx. 887.

VIII. MODIFICATION OF CONTRACT.

➡1504. Consideration.
S.D.Fla. 2016. Under Florida law, to overcome the clauses in the master sales agreement that limited amendments to signed writings, the party seeking to enforce amendment was required to show: (1) mutual assent; (2) that both parties, or at least the party seeking to enforce the amendment, performed consistent with the terms of the alleged oral modification, not merely consistent with their obligations under the original contract; and, (3) that due to party's performance under the contract as amended the other party received and accepted a benefit that it otherwise was not entitled to under the original contract, i.e., independent consideration.—Leader Global Solutions, LLC v. Tradeco Infraestructura, S.A. DE C.V., 155 F.Supp.3d 1310.
Fla.App. 2 Dist. 2021. Purported modification of sales contract so that nursery could deliver citrus trees at later date was not supported by additional consideration and thus was not enforceable, though nursery undertook to rehabilitate damaged trees and invested time and resources in so doing; nursery would have rehabilitated damaged trees regardless of any modification of sales contract.—Charlotte 650, LLC v. Phillip Rucks Citrus Nursery, Inc., 320 So.3d 863.

IX. WARRANTIES.

Tort liability for injuries from defects in goods sold, see PRODUCTS LIABILITY.

(A) IN GENERAL.

➡1601. In general.
M.D.Fla. 2023. Under Florida and California law, procedural unconscionability of a warranty may arise from unequal bargaining power, but more than mere knowledge of a defect at the time of sale is required.—Riley v. General Motors, LLC, 664 F.Supp.3d 1336.
S.D.Fla. 2019. Under Florida law, a written warranty is treated as a contract between buyer and seller.—Weiss v. General Motors LLC, 418 F.Supp.3d 1173.

➡1605. —— Negligence, products liability, and torts in general.
M.D.Fla. 2021. In Michigan, the elements of proof for a breach of implied warranty claim in a products liability case are the same as those required in a negligence claim.—Knudsen v. Ethicon, Inc., 535 F.Supp.3d 1231.

➡1613. —— Particular cases and goods.
N.D.Fla. 2021. Under "bulk supplier doctrine," bulk suppliers of products to manufacturers, who are sophisticated users, have no duty, under Washington law, in negligence, strict liability, or breach of warranty to warn ultimate purchasers of manufacturer's product.—In re 3M Combat Arms Earplug Products Liability Litigation, 545 F.Supp.3d 1239.

(B) EXPRESS WARRANTIES.

1. IN GENERAL.

➡1623. —— In general.
S.D.Fla. 2020. Under Florida law, an express warranty is generally considered to arise only where the seller asserts a fact of which the buyer is ignorant prior to the beginning of the transaction, and on which the buyer justifiably relies as part of the basis of the bargain. Fla. Stat. Ann. § 672.313.—Toca v. Tutco, LLC, 430 F.Supp.3d 1313.

➡1624(2). Affirmations and promises in general.
S.D.Fla. 2010. Even if patient's breach of express warranty claim against manufacturer of artificial discs that were implanted in patient's spine was not preempted by the Medical Device Amendments (MDA) to the Food, Drug, and Cosmetic Act (FDCA), statements and photographic images upon which patient allegedly relied in

deciding to proceed with surgery to implant artificial discs were not an "affirmation of fact or promise" which became "part of the basis of the bargain," as required to state claim for breach of express warranty under Florida law. Federal Food, Drug, and Cosmetic Act, § 1 et seq., 21 U.S.C.A. § 301 et seq.; Medical Device Amendments of 1976, § 2 et seq., 21 U.S.C.A. § 360c et seq.; West's F.S.A. § 672.313.—Wheeler v. DePuy Spine, Inc., 740 F.Supp.2d 1332.

⚓**1624(4). Specific words or language.**
S.D.Fla. 2021. It is not necessary to the creation of an express warranty that the seller use formal words such as warrant or guarantee to make a warranty. Fla. Stat. Ann. § 672.313(a)-(b).—Merino v. Ethicon Inc., 536 F.Supp.3d 1271.

⚓**1624(6). Matters of opinion or commendation.**
M.D.Fla. 2020. Under Pennsylvania law, puffery does not create a cause of action for breach of express warranty. 13 Pa. Cons. Stat. Ann. § 2313(a)(1).—Yachera v. Westminster Pharmaceuticals, LLC, 477 F.Supp.3d 1251.

Under Pennsylvania law, "puffery" consists of exaggeration or overstatement expressed in broad, vague, and commendatory language. 13 Pa. Cons. Stat. Ann. § 2313(a)(1).—Id.

Under Pennsylvania law, although an assertion of absolute safety may be actionable, a claim that a product is safe generally is puffery because it conveys only the seller's judgment that the risk is low enough to be called safe. 13 Pa. Cons. Stat. Ann. § 2313(a)(1).—Id.

Under Pennsylvania law, bald assertions of superior quality are puffery if they lack detailed claims that could be measured or tested. 13 Pa. Cons. Stat. Ann. § 2313(a)(1).—Id.

Purchasers who bought pharmaceutical company's medication at retail pharmacy failed to allege company's representations that medication would be superior and safe were specific enough to be falsifiable, as required to state claim for breach of express warranty under Pennsylvania law against company alleging medication did not contain amount of active ingredients stated on label, where representations conveyed only company's opinion that its product was superior. 13 Pa. Cons. Stat. Ann. § 2313(a)(1).—Id.

S.D.Fla. 2013. Under Florida law, mere puffery or sales talk is not sufficient to create an express warranty.—Aprigliano v. American Honda Motor Co., Inc., 979 F.Supp.2d 1331.

Under Florida law, motorcycle manufacturer's representations that motorcycle was "the world's ultimate touring motorcycle," and "unbelievably vibration-free," were mere puffery that did not create an express warranty between motorcycle purchasers and manufacturer.—Id.

⚓**1626. —— Reliance.**
S.D.Fla. 2013. Under Florida law, statements made in promotional materials, advertisements, and brochures may be sufficient to create an express warranty if the buyer relies on those statements in making his purchase. West's F.S.A. § 672.313(1)(a).—Aprigliano v. American Honda Motor Co., Inc., 979 F.Supp.2d 1331.

⚓**1627. —— Basis of bargain.**
S.D.Fla. 2010. Even if patient's breach of express warranty claim against manufacturer of artificial discs that were implanted in patient's spine was not preempted by the Medical Device Amendments (MDA) to the Food, Drug, and Cosmetic Act (FDCA), statements and photographic

images upon which patient allegedly relied in deciding to proceed with surgery to implant artificial discs were not an "affirmation of fact or promise" which became "part of the basis of the bargain," as required to state claim for breach of express warranty under Florida law. Federal Food, Drug, and Cosmetic Act, § 1 et seq., 21 U.S.C.A. § 301 et seq.; Medical Device Amendments of 1976, § 2 et seq., 21 U.S.C.A. § 360c et seq.; West's F.S.A. § 672.313.—Wheeler v. DePuy Spine, Inc., 740 F.Supp.2d 1332.

⚓**1628. —— Advertising and promotion.**
S.D.Fla. 2021. A patient, who had medical device manufacturers' pelvic mesh product implanted in her during her surgery and subsequently developed complications from the implanted device, sufficiently alleged that the manufacturers made express and implied warranties, as required for the patient's claims for breach of those warranties under Article 2 of the Uniform Commercial Code (UCC), as adopted in Florida, where the manufacturers made express and implied assurance to physicians that the pelvic mesh products were safe and fit for their intended use by circulating brochures and information online offering exaggerated and misleading expectations as to the safety and utility of the products, misrepresenting, downplaying and omitting the known risks, dangers, defects, and disadvantages of the products, and promoting the products as an innovative and minimally invasive procedure with minimal local tissue reactions. Fla. Stat. Ann. §§ 672.313(a)-(b), 672.314.—Merino v. Ethicon Inc., 536 F.Supp.3d 1271.

S.D.Fla. 2013. Under Florida law, statements made in promotional materials, advertisements, and brochures may be sufficient to create an express warranty if the buyer relies on those statements in making his purchase. West's F.S.A. § 672.313(1)(a).—Aprigliano v. American Honda Motor Co., Inc., 979 F.Supp.2d 1331.

2. OPERATION AND EFFECT.

⚓**1642. Construction in general.**
S.D.Fla. 2013. Under Florida law, a written warranty is treated like a contract between the seller and the buyer; as such, the terms of an express warranty may limit or foreclose the remedies available to the buyer.—Aprigliano v. American Honda Motor Co., Inc., 979 F.Supp.2d 1331.

⚓**1643. Breach and elements thereof in general.**
M.D.Fla. 2022. To state a claim for breach of express warranties under the Florida Uniform Commercial Code (UCC), a plaintiff must allege: (1) the sale of goods; (2) the express warranty; (3) breach of the warranty; (4) notice to seller of the breach; and (5) the injuries sustained by the buyer as a result of the breach of express warranty. Fla. Stat. Ann. § 672.313.—Trophia v. Camping World, Inc., 616 F.Supp.3d 1305.

M.D.Fla. 2020. Under Pennsylvania law, to prevail on a breach of express warranty claim, a plaintiff must establish that a breach of warranty occurred and that the breach was the proximate cause of the specific damages sustained. 13 Pa. Cons. Stat. Ann. § 2313(a)(1).—Yachera v. Westminster Pharmaceuticals, LLC, 477 F.Supp.3d 1251.

M.D.Fla. 2017. Under Florida law, to recover for breach of express warranty, plaintiff must establish (1) a sale of goods; (2) an express warranty; (3) a breach of the warranty; (4) notice

† This Case was not selected for publication in the National Reporter System

to seller of the breach; and (5) the injuries sustained by the buyer as a result of the breach.—Hummel v. Tamko Building Products, Inc., 303 F.Supp.3d 1288.

S.D.Fla. 2021. The elements of a claim for breach of express warranty under Florida law are: (1) a sale of goods; (2) an express warranty relating to those goods; (3) a breach of that express warranty; (4) notice to the seller of the alleged breach; and (5) damages sustained by the buyer as a result of the breach.—A&E Adventures LLC v. Intercard, Inc., 529 F.Supp.3d 1333.

S.D.Fla. 2020. To establish a claim for breach of express warranty under Ohio law, a plaintiff must show that: (1) a warranty existed; (2) the product failed to perform as warranted; (3) plaintiff provided the defendant with reasonable notice of the defect; and (4) plaintiff suffered injury as a result of the defect.—Ohio State Troopers Association, Inc. v. Point Blank Enterprises, Inc., 481 F.Supp.3d 1258.

S.D.Fla. 2013. Under Florida law, a manufacturer's liability for breach of an express warranty derives from, and is measured by, the terms of that warranty.—Aprigliano v. American Honda Motor Co., Inc., 979 F.Supp.2d 1331.

⬥**1645. —— In general.**
M.D.Fla. 2022. Consumer stated claims for breach of express warranty and breach of implied warranty of merchantability under Florida law in action against retailer from which consumer purchased recreational vehicle mat, on which consumer slipped and fell; consumer provided color copy of informational insert for mat to complaint and alleged that it showed retailer's mat being used as recreational vehicle entrance mat, and retailer's arguments to the contrary, such as that language in insert obviously pertained to mat's life-expectancy, not its suitability for use as an entrance mat, and that insert's representations that mat was weather resistant and would dry quickly could not reasonable by understood to mean that mat would dry within approximately 30 minutes, were conclusory and speculative.—Trophia v. Camping World, Inc., 616 F.Supp.3d 1305.

⬥**1649. —— Machinery and equipment.**
S.D.Fla. 2022. Purchasers of purportedly defective pressure cookers alleged that they or their family members purchased pressure cookers, that express limited warranty was provided by manufacturer on product packaging and in owner's manual, that manufacturer represented that pressure cookers had "locking, air-tight lid[,]" that manufacturer breached warranties by providing products that were not free of defects and by failing to repair or replace defective pressure cookers, that purchasers notified manufacturer of breach of express warranty, and that purchasers all suffered damages as result of defects, as required to state claim for breach of express warranty under Florida law. Fla. Stat. Ann. §§ 672.313(1), 672.313(2).—Rife v. Newell Brands, Inc., 632 F.Supp.3d 1276.

⬥**1651. —— Motor vehicles.**
S.D.Fla. 2021. Consumers' allegations that automobile manufacturer failed to replace headrests with defective active head restraint (AHR) system were sufficient to state claims for breach of express warranty under Florida and New York law, where consumers' complaint identified express warranty terms covering "cost of all parts and labor needed to repair any item on your vehicle when it left the manufacturing plant that

is defective in material, workmanship, or factory preparation," and alleged that manufacturer took position that because AHR was not defective, costs for repairing or replacing it were to be borne entirely by consumers.—Nuwer v. FCA US LLC, 552 F.Supp.3d 1344.

S.D.Fla. 2021. Consumers who alleged that automobile model's "limp mode," in which automobile would rapidly decelerate when engine temperature got too high, was design defect but failed to present their vehicles to manufacturer for repair did not comply with terms of limited warranty, as required for consumers to prevail on their breach-of-warranty claims under various state laws, notwithstanding consumers' argument that manufacturer waived presentment requirement by instructing its dealers to let consumers know limp mode was normal and to refer them to owner's guide for instructions on aftermarket coolers, where manufacturer's instructions to dealers did not make it impossible for manufacturer to perform its obligation, and, in fact, instructed dealers on exactly how to perform obligation.—Tershakovec v. Ford Motor Company, 546 F.Supp.3d 1348, amended in part 2021 WL 3711444, affirmed in part, vacated in part, reversed in part 79 F.4th 1299.

⬥**1653. —— Drugs and medical devices.**
M.D.Fla. 2020. Purchasers who bought pharmaceutical company's medication at retail pharmacy plausibly alleged company's representations and express warranties regarding dosage of medication listed on label were directed at consumers and made to induce purchase of company's medication, as required to state claim for breach of express warranty under Pennsylvania law against company alleging medication did not contain amount of active ingredients stated on label. 13 Pa. Cons. Stat. Ann. § 2313(a)(1).—Yachera v. Westminster Pharmaceuticals, LLC, 477 F.Supp.3d 1251.

⬥**1654. —— Computers and software.**
See also COPYRIGHTS AND INTELLECTUAL PROPERTY ⬥107.

⬥**1655. Design defects.**
S.D.Fla. 2019. Named plaintiff for class of vehicle owners stated a claim for breach of express warranty under Florida law against vehicle manufacturer based on allegedly defective drive shafts in vehicles purchased by class members; manufacturer's warranty covered any vehicle defect except for normal characteristics of the vehicle related to materials or workmanship, and plaintiff alleged that drive shaft was a design defect inherent in each of the class vehicles.—Weiss v. General Motors LLC, 418 F.Supp.3d 1173.

⬥**1660. Causation.**
M.D.Fla. 2020. Under Pennsylvania law, to prevail on a breach of express warranty claim, a plaintiff must establish that a breach of warranty occurred and that the breach was the proximate cause of the specific damages sustained. 13 Pa. Cons. Stat. Ann. § 2313(a)(1).—Yachera v. Westminster Pharmaceuticals, LLC, 477 F.Supp.3d 1251.

(C) WARRANTIES IMPOSED BY LAW;
IMPLIED WARRANTIES.

1. IN GENERAL.

⬥**1672. Breach and elements thereof in general.**
S.D.Fla. 2020. To prevail on an implied warranty in tort claim under Ohio law, a plaintiff

must prove: (1) a defect existed in a defendant's product which made it unfit for its ordinary, intended use; (2) the defect existed at the time the product left the defendant's possession; and (3) the defect was the proximate cause of the plaintiff's injuries.—Ohio State Troopers Association, Inc. v. Point Blank Enterprises, Inc., 481 F.Supp.3d 1258.

2. PARTICULAR WARRANTIES.

⟲**1684. Quality, fitness, or condition.**
Fitness for ordinary purpose or use, see IX(C)3.
   Merchantability, see IX(C)3. Fitness for particular purpose or use, see IX(C)4.

⟲**1687. —— Obvious, latent, or hidden defects.**
S.D.Fla. 2020. Consumers stated breach of implied warranty claims under laws of Arkansas, California, Indiana, Louisiana, Massachusetts, Michigan, Mississippi, New Jersey, New York, Pennsylvania, Rhode Island, Texas, and Virginia, against vehicle manufacturers that installed purportedly defective airbags that contained ammonium nitrate as a propellant in their vehicles, even if vehicles purchased by consumers did not manifest the defect.—In re Takata Airbag Products Liability Litigation, 462 F.Supp.3d 1304.

⟲**1691. —— Fitness for intended purpose or use.**
Fitness for ordinary purpose or use, see IX(C)3.
   Merchantability, see IX(C)3. Fitness for particular purpose or use, see IX(C)4.

3. FITNESS FOR ORDINARY PURPOSE OR USE; MERCHANTABILITY.

⟲**1711. In general.**
M.D.Fla. 2020. Under Pennsylvania law, the implied warranty of merchantability arises by operation of law and serves to protect buyers from loss where the goods purchased are below commercial standards or are unfit for the buyer's purpose. 13 Pa. Cons. Stat. Ann. § 2314(b)(3).— Yachera v. Westminster Pharmaceuticals, LLC, 477 F.Supp.3d 1251.

Under Pennsylvania law, to be merchantable, goods must be fit for the ordinary purposes for which such goods are used. 13 Pa. Cons. Stat. Ann. § 2314(b)(3).—Id.

Under Pennsylvania law, implied warranty of merchantability is designed to protect the purchaser by allowing it to obtain the benefit of the bargain, thereby placing it in the same position it would have been in if the product had functioned properly. 13 Pa. Cons. Stat. Ann. § 2314.—Id.

Fla.App. 3 Dist. 2022. The implied warranty of merchantability applies when goods are offered for consumption by the public generally; therefore, in order to be merchantable the goods must be fit for ordinary uses for which such goods are sold.—D-I Davit International-Hische GMBH v. Carpio, 346 So.3d 197.

⟲**1716. Breach and elements thereof in general.**
M.D.Fla. 2022. Under Florida law, cause of action for breach of implied warranty of merchantability requires allegations that plaintiff was foreseeable user of product, product was used in intended manner at time of injury, product was defective when transferred from warrantor, and defect caused injury.—Trophia v. Camping World, Inc., 616 F.Supp.3d 1305.

M.D.Fla. 2022. A cause of action for breach of implied warranty of merchantability under Florida law requires allegations that (1) the plaintiff was a foreseeable user of the product, (2) the product was used in the intended manner at the time of the injury, (3) the product was defective when transferred from the warrantor, and (4) the defect caused the injury.—Hernandez v. Aurobindo Pharma USA, Inc., 582 F.Supp.3d 1192.

M.D.Fla. 2020. Under Pennsylvania law, a plaintiff establishes a breach of the implied warranty of merchantability by showing that the product purchased was defective. 13 Pa. Cons. Stat. Ann. § 2314(b)(3).—Yachera v. Westminster Pharmaceuticals, LLC, 477 F.Supp.3d 1251.

Under Pennsylvania law, a product's defectiveness can be proven, as required to establish breach of the implied warranty of merchantability, by pointing to some specific dereliction by the manufacturer in constructing or designing the product, or by demonstrating that the product functioned improperly in the absence of abnormal use and reasonable secondary causes. 13 Pa. Cons. Stat. Ann. § 2314(b)(3).—Id.

Under Michigan law, in a claim of breach of the implied warranty of merchantability, the product's lack of fitness for its intended use amounts to an actionable defect.—Id.

S.D.Fla. 2021. A claim for breach of the implied warranty of merchantability requires proof that: (1) the plaintiff was a foreseeable user of the product; (2) the plaintiff used the product in the intended manner at the time of injury; (3) the product was defective when the warrantor transferred it to the plaintiff; and (4) the defect caused the plaintiff's injuries.—A&E Adventures LLC v. Intercard, Inc., 529 F.Supp.3d 1333.

S.D.Fla. 2011. Under Florida law, a cause of action for breach of implied warranty of merchantability requires allegations that (1) the plaintiff was a foreseeable user of the product, (2) the product was used in the intended manner at the time of the injury, (3) the product was defective when transferred from the warrantor, and (4) the defect caused the injury. West's F.S.A. § 672.314.—Jovine v. Abbott Laboratories, Inc., 795 F.Supp.2d 1331.

⟲**1718. —— In general.**
M.D.Fla. 2022. Consumer stated claims for breach of express warranty and breach of implied warranty of merchantability under Florida law in action against retailer from which consumer purchased recreational vehicle mat, on which consumer slipped and fell; consumer provided color copy of informational insert for mat to complaint and alleged that it showed retailer's mat being used as recreational vehicle entrance mat, and retailer's arguments to the contrary, such as that language in insert obviously pertained to mat's life-expectancy, not its suitability for use as an entrance mat, and that insert's representations that mat was weather resistant and would dry quickly could not reasonable by understood to mean that mat would dry within approximately 30 minutes, were conclusory and speculative.—Trophia v. Camping World, Inc., 616 F.Supp.3d 1305.

⟲**1724. —— Motor vehicles.**
S.D.Fla. 2020. Consumers stated breach of implied warranty of merchantability claim under Virginia law against tire dealer and its parent company by alleging that defendants sold them tires that they impliedly warranted were of merchantable quality when they were, in fact, not of merchantable quality because of defendants' fail-

ure to register the tires with tire manufacturers, since federal regulation required independent tire dealers to register tires they sell to consumers with tire manufacturers, and unregistered tires would not pass without objection in the trade under the contract description. Va. Code Ann. § 8.2-314(1)(a); 49 C.F.R. § 574.8.—Exum v. National Tire and Battery, 437 F.Supp.3d 1141.

S.D.Fla. 2019. Vehicle owner, who asserted breach of implied warranty claims against vehicle manufacturer, plausibly alleged that defect in vehicle's drive shaft affected drivability and safety of the vehicle, such that vehicle was unmerchantable under Florida law, where owner alleged that defect caused vehicle to shake violently when it reached certain interstate cruising speeds, which made it feel unstable and could cause loss of control, and, if left unaddressed, drive shaft defect could cause the part to deteriorate, culminating in failure as the shaft dropped to the ground and rendered vehicle underivable. Fla. Stat. Ann. § 672.314(2)(c).—Weiss v. General Motors LLC, 418 F.Supp.3d 1173.

👈1726. —— Drugs and medical devices.
M.D.Fla. 2020. Purchasers who bought pharmaceutical company's medication at retail pharmacy plausibly alleged they suffered economic injury from medication that had manufacturing defect, as required to state claim for breach of the implied warranty of merchantability under Pennsylvania law against company, where purchasers alleged company sold adulterated tablets that contained inconsistent amount of active pharmaceutical ingredient, and that they would not have purchased medication on same terms if they knew that medication contained adulterations. 13 Pa. Cons. Stat. Ann. § 2314(b)(3).—Yachera v. Westminster Pharmaceuticals, LLC, 477 F.Supp.3d 1251.

Under Pennsylvania law, because strict-liability claims based on a manufacturing defect are not precluded, there is no basis for declining to recognize a claim against a drug manufacturer for breach of the implied warranty of merchantability where it is based on a manufacturing defect. 13 Pa. Cons. Stat. Ann. § 2314.—Id.

Purchasers who bought pharmaceutical company's medication at retail pharmacy plausibly alleged they suffered economic injury from defective medication, as required to state claim for breach of the implied warranty of merchantability under Michigan law against company, where purchasers alleged they were denied the benefit of the bargain when they purchased medication that did not contain therapeutic dose specified on medication label.—Id.

S.D.Fla. 2021. A patient, who had medical device manufacturers' pelvic mesh product implanted in her during her surgery and subsequently developed complications from the implanted device, sufficiently alleged that the manufacturers made express and implied warranties, as required for the patient's claims for breach of those warranties under Article 2 of the Uniform Commercial Code (UCC), as adopted in Florida, where the manufacturers made express and implied assurance to physicians that the pelvic mesh products were safe and fit for their intended use by circulating brochures and information online offering exaggerated and misleading expectations as to the safety and utility of the products, misrepresenting, downplaying and omitting the known risks, dangers, defects, and disadvantages of the products, and promoting the products as an innovative and minimally invasive procedure with minimal local tissue reactions. Fla. Stat. Ann. §§ 672.313(a)-(b), 672.314.—Merino v. Ethicon Inc., 536 F.Supp.3d 1271.

👈1727. —— Computers and software.
See also COPYRIGHTS AND INTELLECTUAL PROPERTY 👈107.

👈1733. Causation.
M.D.Fla. 2020. Under Michigan law, to establish breach of the implied warranty of merchantability the plaintiff must show that a defect in the product, attributable to the manufacturer, caused the harm.—Yachera v. Westminster Pharmaceuticals, LLC, 477 F.Supp.3d 1251.

4. FITNESS FOR PARTICULAR PURPOSE OR USE.

👈1741. In general.
S.D.Fla. 2022. Under Florida law regarding warranties, a "particular purpose" for a product differs from an ordinary purpose in that it envisages a specific use by the buyer which is peculiar to the nature of his business. Fla. Stat. Ann. § 672.315.—PR Overseas Boating, Ltd. v. Talaria Company, LLC, 601 F.Supp.3d 1285, affirmed in part, vacated in part, remanded Martin v. Quick SpA, 2023 WL 5321037.

Fla.App. 3 Dist. 2022. A cause of action for breach of an implied warranty of fitness for a particular purpose focuses on the relationship between the buyer and the seller.—D-I Davit International-Hische GMBH v. Carpio, 346 So.3d 197.

👈1742. Reliance.
S.D.Fla. 2022. Under Florida law, a warranty arises where the seller has reason to know a particular purpose for which the goods are required and the buyer relies on the seller's skill or judgment to select or furnish the suitable goods. Fla. Stat. Ann. § 672.315.—PR Overseas Boating, Ltd. v. Talaria Company, LLC, 601 F.Supp.3d 1285, affirmed in part, vacated in part, remanded Martin v. Quick SpA, 2023 WL 5321037.

Fla.App. 3 Dist. 2022. An implied warranty of fitness for a particular purpose is conditioned upon the buyer's reliance on the skill and judgment of the seller to supply a commodity suitable for the intended purpose.—D-I Davit International-Hische GMBH v. Carpio, 346 So.3d 197.

👈1744. Seller's knowledge.
M.D.Fla. 2015. Under Florida's Uniform Commercial Code (UCC), the implied warranty of fitness for a particular purpose arises only when a seller has reason to know a particular purpose for which the goods are required and the buyer relies on the seller's skill or judgment to select or furnish suitable goods. Fla. Stat. Ann. § 672.315.—Armadillo Distribution Enterprises, Inc. v. Hai Yun Musical Instruments Manufacture Co. Ltd., 142 F.Supp.3d 1245.

S.D.Fla. 2022. Under Florida law, a warranty arises where the seller has reason to know a particular purpose for which the goods are required and the buyer relies on the seller's skill or judgment to select or furnish the suitable goods. Fla. Stat. Ann. § 672.315.—PR Overseas Boating, Ltd. v. Talaria Company, LLC, 601 F.Supp.3d 1285, affirmed in part, vacated in part, remanded Martin v. Quick SpA, 2023 WL 5321037.

👈1751. —— Machinery and equipment.
S.D.Fla. 2022. Buyer of purportedly defective gyroscope stabilizers intended for stabilizers to be used for their ordinary purpose of providing

† **This Case was not selected for publication in the National Reporter System**

stabilization to buyer's yacht, and thus buyer could not maintain claim against seller, which was a boat repair facility, for breach of implied warranty of fitness for particular purpose under Article 2 of the Uniform Commercial Code (UCC), as adopted in Florida. Fla. Stat. Ann. § 672.315. —PR Overseas Boating, Ltd. v. Talaria Company, LLC, 601 F.Supp.3d 1285, affirmed in part, vacated in part, remanded Martin v. Quick SpA, 2023 WL 5321037.

☞**1756. —— Computers and software.**
See also COPYRIGHTS AND INTELLECTUAL PROPERTY ☞107.

(D) EXCLUSION, MODIFICATION, OR LIMITATION OF WARRANTIES.

1. IN GENERAL.

☞**1773. Implied warranties in general.**
C.A.11 (Fla.) 2022. Under New York law, contract may explicitly disclaim any implied warranties. N.Y. Uniform Commercial Code § 2-316.— MidAmerica C2L Incorporated v. Siemens Energy Inc., 25 F.4th 1312, vacated and superseded on rehearing 2023 WL 2733512, on remand 2024 WL 414620.

Under New York law, if written disclaimer of any implied warranties is agreed-upon, a party cannot justifiably rely on a representation that is specifically disclaimed in the agreement. N.Y. Uniform Commercial Code § 2-316.—Id.

Under New York law, buyer of coal gasification equipment could not assert claim against seller for breach of implied warranty, where the parties' contracts disclaimed, in all capital letters, that all other warranties and guarantees, whether statutory, expressed or implied, including all implied warranties of merchantability and fitness for purpose, and all warranties arising from course of dealing or usage of trade. N.Y. Uniform Commercial Code § 2-316(2).—Id.

2. EXPRESS WARRANTIES.

☞**1792. Particular cases and goods.**
† **C.A.11 (Fla.) 2020.** Under Florida law, recreational vehicle manufacturer did not breach its one-year limited warranty to buyer, where buyer declared on her pre-delivery inspection form that her vehicle was in good condition when she purchased it, dealership and others repaired problems with her slide-out panels and windshield without charge, even beyond her first year of ownership, slide-out panels on vehicle operated normally and were defect-free, and allegedly defective windshield was an "after-market" item that required adhesive to affix it to the molding. Fla. Stat. Ann. § 672.607(3)(a).—Kelly v. Lee County RV Sales Company, 819 Fed.Appx. 713.

S.D.Fla. 2013. Under Florida law, motorcycle purchasers who purchased their motorcycles after expiration of the manufacturer's factory warranties, which limited remedies available to owners to the reparation or replacement of defective parts for a three-year period, did not have an ownership interest in their motorcycles during the motorcycles' warranty periods, could not state a claim for breach of express warranty in their putative class action against manufacturer. —Aprigliano v. American Honda Motor Co., Inc., 979 F.Supp.2d 1331.

(F) PARTIES TO WARRANTIES, PRIVITY, AND THIRD-PARTY BENEFICIARIES.

☞**1812. Express warranties in general.**
M.D.Fla. 2020. Under Pennsylvania law, privity of contract between the party issuing a warranty and the party seeking to enforce the warranty is not required for a breach of express warranty claim. Mich. Comp. Laws Ann. § 440.2313.—Yachera v. Westminster Pharmaceuticals, LLC, 477 F.Supp.3d 1251.

Under Michigan law, a plaintiff is required to allege that she was in privity with the defendant in order to properly plead a breach-of-express-warranty claim. Mich. Comp. Laws Ann. § 440.2313.—Id.

Under Michigan law, an intended third-party beneficiary is in privity of contact with the original parties for purposes of an express warranty. Mich. Comp. Laws Ann. § 440.2313.—Id.

Under Michigan law, to plead third-party beneficiary status, for purposes of a breach of express warranty claim, a plaintiff must allege that the contracting parties intended the plaintiff to benefit from their agreement. Mich. Comp. Laws Ann. § 440.2313.—Id.

M.D.Fla. 2018. Under Florida law, privity is required in order to recover damages from the seller of a product for breach of express or implied warranties.—Douse v. Boston Scientific Corporation, 314 F.Supp.3d 1251.

S.D.Fla. 2021. Under Florida law, privity is required in order to recover damages from the seller of a product for breach of express or implied warranties. Fla. Stat. Ann. §§ 672.313(a)-(b), 672.314.—Merino v. Ethicon Inc., 536 F.Supp.3d 1271.

S.D.Fla. 2013. Under Florida law, a claim for breach of an express warranty generally requires the parties to have contractual privity.—Aprigliano v. American Honda Motor Co., Inc., 979 F.Supp.2d 1331.

☞**1813. Implied warranties in general.**
M.D.Fla. 2020. Under Michigan law, plaintiffs are not required to allege privity to successfully state a claim for breach of the implied warranty of merchantability.—Yachera v. Westminster Pharmaceuticals, LLC, 477 F.Supp.3d 1251.

M.D.Fla. 2018. Under Florida law, privity is required in order to recover damages from the seller of a product for breach of express or implied warranties.—Douse v. Boston Scientific Corporation, 314 F.Supp.3d 1251.

M.D.Fla. 2018. Under Florida law, a plaintiff cannot recover economic losses for breach of implied warranty in the absence of privity.— Rowe v. Mentor Worldwide, LLC, 297 F.Supp.3d 1288.

S.D.Fla. 2021. Under Florida law, privity is required in order to recover damages from the seller of a product for breach of express or implied warranties. Fla. Stat. Ann. §§ 672.313(a)-(b), 672.314.—Merino v. Ethicon Inc., 536 F.Supp.3d 1271.

S.D.Fla. 2020. Under Florida law, privity of contract is required to maintain an action for breach of an implied warranty of merchantability.—Toca v. Tutco, LLC, 430 F.Supp.3d 1313.

S.D.Fla. 2017. Florida, Arizona and Illinois require privity for implied warranty claims.— Melton v. Century Arms, Inc., 243 F.Supp.3d 1290.

S.D.Fla. 2016. Under Florida law, express- and implied warranty-based claims require privity of contract between the parties.—Hawaiian Airlines, Inc. v. AAR Aircraft Services, Inc., 167 F.Supp.3d 1311, appeal dismissed (11th cir. 16-11536).

⚖1816(1). In general.

C.A.11 (Fla.) 2018. Husband, whose wife died after suffering cardiac arrest while wearing external defibrillator that did not administer shock to her, sufficiently alleged that his wife had been in privity of contract, and, thus, stated breach of express warranty claim under Florida law against manufacturer, where husband alleged that, after wife was prescribed external defibrillator by her physician, she contracted directly with manufacturer to purchaser her external defibrillator.—Godelia v. Doe 1, 881 F.3d 1309, on remand 2019 WL 3821211.

M.D.Fla. 2022. Under Florida law, consumer's allegations that manufacturer had represented neurostimulator's battery had five-year lifespan, but consumer underwent two surgeries within three years to replace battery, failed to state claims for breach of implied warranty and breach of express warranty, absent allegations that consumer purchased neurostimulator directly from manufacturer so as to establish privity.—Holland v. Abbott Laboratories, Inc., 626 F.Supp.3d 1256.

M.D.Fla. 2020. Purchasers who bought pharmaceutical company's medication at retail pharmacy failed to allege third-party beneficiary status, as required to state claim for breach of express warranty under Michigan law against company alleging medication did not contain amount of active ingredients stated on label, where purchaser failed to allege that pharmacy and company intended end-users to benefit from any agreement they entered regarding the sale of medication, and that purchaser was intended beneficiary of any contract between pharmacy and company. Mich. Comp. Laws Ann. § 440.2313.—Yachera v. Westminster Pharmaceuticals, LLC, 477 F.Supp.3d 1251.

M.D.Fla. 2018. The interests of privity, in order to recover damages from the seller of a product for breach of express or implied warranties under Florida law, are satisfied by direct contact, but only in the sense of personal contact between the consumer and the manufacturer.—Douse v. Boston Scientific Corporation, 314 F.Supp.3d 1251.

Patient did not allege sufficient contacts in order to establish privity, as was required to support claims against medical device manufacturer for breach of express warranty, breach of implied warranty of merchantability, and breach of the implied warranty of fitness, under Florida law, arising from complications patient purportedly sustained from a permanent inferior vena cava filter; the only contacts alleged between manufacturer and patient, or her doctor, took place through manufacturer's product brochure, website, and advertisements.—Id.

S.D.Fla. 2022. Purchasers of purportedly defective pressure cookers failed to allege that they were in privity of contract with manufacturer or that they qualified for statutory exceptions for third-party beneficiaries, and thus failed to state claim for breach of implied warranty of merchantability under Florida law. Fla. Stat. Ann. § 672.318.—Rife v. Newell Brands, Inc., 632 F.Supp.3d 1276.

S.D.Fla. 2020. Buyer of HVAC units failed to satisfy third-party-beneficiary and direct-contact exceptions to the privity requirement for claims

for breach of implied warranty of merchantability under Article 2 of the Uniform Commercial Code (UCC), as adopted in Florida, and breach of implied warranty under the Magnuson-Moss Warranty Act (MMWA) asserted against units' manufacturers and distributor, which did not sell the units directly to buyer, based on allegedly defective heater components; buyer's complaint contained no allegation satisfying exception for third-party beneficiaries, and fact that the manufacturers provided warranty certificates "directly" to buyer was insufficient to satisfy the direct-contact exception, which required one-on-one communication between a buyer and manufacturer. Fla. Stat. Ann. § 672.314.—Toca v. Tutco, LLC, 430 F.Supp.3d 1313.

S.D.Fla. 2019. Although a consumer who purchases a product from a dealer is in privity with the dealer, the consumer is not in privity with the manufacturer for purposes of enforcing an implied warranty of merchantability under Florida law.—Weiss v. General Motors LLC, 418 F.Supp.3d 1173.

S.D.Fla. 2017. Under Florida, Arizona, and Illinois law, rifle owners failed to establish privity required to sustain breach of implied warranty claims and Magnuson-Moss Warranty Act claims against rifle manufacturer, alleging that safety mechanism in certain rifle models was defectively designed and allowed rifles to fire when safety lever was moved above safety position; four owners purchased their rifles from non-party sellers and fifth owner purchased rifle from his father. Federal Trade Commission Improvement Act § 101, 15 U.S.C.A. § 2301(7).—Melton v. Century Arms, Inc., 243 F.Supp.3d 1290.

S.D.Fla. 2012. Environmental products company did not owe duty of care to ground worker for vegetation management company in design or manufacturing of wood chipper that severed substantial portion of worker's hand, as required to support worker's claims for negligence, breach of warranty, and strict products liability under Florida law, where products company did not design, manufacture, or distribute subject wood chipper, and products company was distinct legal entity from wood chipper manufacturer.—Hernandez v. Altec Environmental Products, LLC, 903 F.Supp.2d 1350, reconsideration denied 2013 WL 836870, appeal denied 2013 WL 3448212.

⚖1816(2). Motor vehicles.

† C.A.11 (Fla.) 2020. Recreational vehicle buyer lacked contractual privity with manufacturer required to be consumer entitled to recover from manufacturer for breach of implied warranty under the Magnuson-Moss Warranty Act or Florida law, where buyer purchased her vehicle from and entered into a contract with dealership, her complaint identified dealership as the "seller," she acknowledged in purchase contract that dealership was "in no respect the agent of the manufacturer," and buyer admitted she had no contact with manufacturer prior to the sale. Federal Trade Commission Improvement Act § 102, 15 U.S.C.A. § 2302; Fla. Stat. Ann. § 320.835.—Kelly v. Lee County RV Sales Company, 819 Fed.Appx. 713.

S.D.Fla. 2019. Car owners lacked contractual privity with car manufacturer necessary to state a breach of implied warranty claim under Florida law arising from safety defect in cooling system of certain car models, where manufacturer did not directly sell, or negotiate the sale of the cars, but instead, owners purchased their cars from

---

† This Case was not selected for publication in the National Reporter System

used car dealerships.—Padilla v. Porsche Cars North America, Inc., 391 F.Supp.3d 1108.

⌬1817. —— Agents and other representatives.

S.D.Fla. 2021. Consumers adequately alleged that authorized dealerships from which they purchased or leased automobiles were in privity with automobile manufacturer, as necessary to state claims against manufacturer for breach of implied warranty under Florida, New York, and Arizona law, where consumers alleged that dealerships were authorized to operate as manufacturer's agents, and specifically, that employees of dealerships received training from manufacturer at training facilities, that technicians followed manufacturer's instructions when diagnosing and repairing automobiles, that service managers reported to manufacturer all faults detected in automobiles brought in for service or repair, and that manufacturer approved or denied payment for services and repairs provided under warranty. —Nuwer v. FCA US LLC, 552 F.Supp.3d 1344.

⌬1821. —— Users and consumers.

S.D.Fla. 2019. Vehicle owner's allegations that he purchased allegedly defective vehicle from authorized dealer who was an agent of manufacturer, that he, rather than the dealer, was the intended consumer of manufacturer's vehicle, and that manufacturer's warranty was intended to benefit the consumer, not the dealership, were sufficient to show that he was third-party beneficiary of contract between dealer and manufacturer, as required to state a claim against manufacturer for breach of implied warranty under Florida law. Fla. Stat. Ann. § 672.314(2)(c).—Weiss v. General Motors LLC, 418 F.Supp.3d 1173.

S.D.Fla. 2017. Class of consumers who purchased vehicles with allegedly defective airbags that contained ammonium nitrate as a propellant did not have to demonstrate privity between themselves and vehicle manufacture in order to assert claims for violations of Michigan's implied warranty of merchantability, and their derivative claims under the Magnuson–Moss Warranty Act. Magnuson-Moss Warranty—Federal Trade Commission Improvement Act, § 101 et seq., 15 U.S.C.A. § 2301 et seq.—In re Takata Airbag Products Liability Litigation, 255 F.Supp.3d 1241.

⌬1824. —— Remote or subsequent purchasers.

S.D.Fla. 2017. Under Florida, Arizona, and Illinois law, rifle owners failed to establish privity required to sustain breach of implied warranty claims and Magnuson-Moss Warranty Act claims against rifle manufacturer, alleging that safety mechanism in certain rifle models was defectively designed and allowed rifles to fire when safety lever was moved above safety position; four owners purchased their rifles from non-party sellers and fifth owner purchased rifle from his father. Federal Trade Commission Improvement Act § 101, 15 U.S.C.A. § 2301(7).—Melton v. Century Arms, Inc., 243 F.Supp.3d 1290.

⌬1833. —— Economic loss.

S.D.Fla. 2019. Under Florida law, a plaintiff cannot recover economic losses for breach of implied warranty in the absence of privity.— Padilla v. Porsche Cars North America, Inc., 391 F.Supp.3d 1108.

S.D.Fla. 2011. Under Florida law, a plaintiff cannot recover economic losses for breach of implied warranty in the absence of privity.—

Jovine v. Abbott Laboratories, Inc., 795 F.Supp.2d 1331.

⌬1839(1). In general.

M.D.Fla. 2018. Consumer failed to allege that she had privity with manufacturer of implants used for breast augmentation surgeries and, thus, failed to state claim for breach of implied warranty of merchantability under Florida law; implant was prescription medical device unavailable for purchase directly by consumers.—Rowe v. Mentor Worldwide, LLC, 297 F.Supp.3d 1288.

⌬1839(2). Learned-intermediary doctrine.

S.D.Fla. 2021. A patient, who had medical device manufacturers' pelvic mesh product implanted in her during her surgery and subsequently developed complications from the implanted device, alleged privity with the manufacturers as a third-party beneficiary of the manufacturers' warranties, as required to state claims for breach of express and implied warranties under Article 2 of the Uniform Commercial Code (UCC), as adopted in Florida; the patient alleged she chose the manufacturers' product based on their warranties to her or her physician and relied on those warranties in consenting to an implant procedure, and the patient alleged the warranties were made to benefit her as a patient and therefore that she was the intended consumer of the product. Fla. Stat. Ann. §§ 672.313(a)-(b), 672.314.—Merino v. Ethicon Inc., 536 F.Supp.3d 1271.

(G) NOTICE AND OPPORTUNITY TO CURE.

⌬1854. —— Notice as condition precedent.

M.D.Fla. 2021. Patient failed to provide requisite pre-suit notice to manufacturers of a medical mesh implanted in the patient during two hernia surgeries, as required to assert claim for breach of implied warranty under Article 2 of the Uniform Commercial Code (UCC), as adopted in Michigan. Mich. Comp. Laws Ann. § 440.2607(3)(a).—Knudsen v. Ethicon, Inc., 535 F.Supp.3d 1231.

M.D.Fla. 2017. Under Florida law, notice requirement, which provides that the buyer must within a reasonable time after he or she discovers or should have discovered any breach notify the seller of breach or be barred from any remedy, is a valid precondition of imposing liability on a seller of goods for breach of warranty. Fla. Stat. Ann. § 672.607(3)(a).—Hummel v. Tamko Building Products, Inc., 303 F.Supp.3d 1288.

⌬1855. —— Parties entitled to notice.

S.D.Fla. 2021. Florida statute requiring buyers of goods to provide pre-suit notice to sellers did not require consumers to provide pre-suit notice to automobile manufacturer prior to asserting claim against it for breach of express warranty; manufacturer was not seller of automobiles, which consumers bought or leased from dealership. Fla. Stat. Ann. § 672.607(3)(a).— Nuwer v. FCA US LLC, 552 F.Supp.3d 1344.

S.D.Fla. 2020. Failure of buyer of HVAC units to give pre-suit notice to units' manufacturers and distributor did not preclude buyer's claims for breach of express and implied warranties under Article 2 of the Uniform Commercial Code (UCC) based on allegedly defective heater components; buyer was only required to notify the "seller" of a breach, manufacturers and distributor were not sellers, and there was no indication or allegation that the parties had agreed to additional pre-suit notice beyond the requirements of Article 2. Federal Trade Commission Improvement Act, § 101 et seq., 15 U.S.C.A. § 2301 et seq.; Fla. Stat. Ann. § 672.607(3)(a).—Toca v. Tutco, LLC, 430 F.Supp.3d 1313.

⊫1862. —— In general.
S.D.Fla. 2022. Truck purchaser plausibly alleged that he provided sufficient pre-suit notice of purported breach of express warranties to owner of fleet vehicles by providing notice to individual who brokered sale of truck, as required to proceed with claims against owner for breach of express warranties governed by Article 2 of the Uniform Commercial Code (UCC), as adopted in Florida, arising from owner purportedly selling, through the individual as the owner's agent, a truck that had its odometer altered; existence of agency relationship could be inferred from purchaser's allegation claiming that individual brokered and effectuated sale of truck lawfully owned by and registered to owner, and purchaser further alleged that, upon discovering the fraud, he contacted individual and demanded a refund, but individual failed to refund the money. Fla. Stat. Ann. § 672.607(3)(a).—Aguila v. Ripa & Associates, LLC, 587 F.Supp.3d 1159.

⊫1863. —— Actual or constructive notice.
S.D.Fla. 2021. Consumer who alleged that automobile model's "limp mode," in which automobile would rapidly decelerate when engine temperature got too high, was design defect failed to provide manufacturer with pre-suit notice, as required for consumer to prevail on claims of breach of express and implied warranties under Illinois law, although manufacturer had actual knowledge that limp mode occurred in that model of automobile because manufacturer designed model that way, where under Illinois law, manufacturer had to be on notice that consumer's particular automobile was troublesome rather than merely knowing that automobile model in general had limp mode issues, and manufacturer did not know that consumer wanted his car remedied. 810 Ill. Comp. Stat. Ann. 5/2-607.—Tershakovec v. Ford Motor Company, 546 F.Supp.3d 1348, amended in part 2021 WL 3711444, affirmed in part, vacated in part, reversed in part 79 F.4th 1299.
Illinois law provides two exceptions to the requirement that a plaintiff alleging a breach of warranty provide pre-suit notice to the defendant: when (1) the seller has actual knowledge of the defect of the particular product or (2) the seller is deemed to have been reasonably notified by the filing of the buyer's complaint alleging breach of warranty. 810 Ill. Comp. Stat. Ann. 5/2-607.—Id.
Under Illinois law, a seller's generalized knowledge about the safety concerns of third parties is insufficient to fulfill the requirement that a plaintiff alleging a breach of warranty provide pre-suit notice to the seller. 810 Ill. Comp. Stat. Ann. 5/2-607.—Id.
S.D.Fla. 2020. Prior lawsuits against manufacturers and distributor of HVAC units did not satisfy the pre-suit notice requirement under Article 2 of the of the Uniform Commercial Code (UCC) for a buyer's breach of express and implied warranty claims based on allegedly defective heater components; buyer provided no case law supporting his position that the pre-suit notice requirement could be satisfied by pointing to prior lawsuits, and Article 2 specifically placed the burden on "the buyer" to provide notice, but the prior lawsuits were filed by other plaintiffs

with no connection to buyer's action. Fla. Stat. Ann. § 672.607(3)(a).—Toca v. Tutco, LLC, 430 F.Supp.3d 1313.

⊫1865. —— Commencement of litigation as notice.
S.D.Fla. 2021. New York statute requiring notice of claims of breach to be provided to sellers of goods within a reasonable time did not require dismissal of consumers' claim against automobile manufacturer for breach of express warranty under New York law; filing of complaint containing such claim could constitute sufficient notice under statute, and issue of whether consumers in fact provided reasonable notice by filing complaint was question of fact that was proper for resolution at summary judgment rather than on motion to dismiss complaint. N.Y. Uniform Commercial Code § 2-607(3).—Nuwer v. FCA US LLC, 552 F.Supp.3d 1344.
S.D.Fla. 2021. Illinois law provides two exceptions to the requirement that a plaintiff alleging a breach of warranty provide pre-suit notice to the defendant: when (1) the seller has actual knowledge of the defect of the particular product or (2) the seller is deemed to have been reasonably notified by the filing of the buyer's complaint alleging breach of warranty. 810 Ill. Comp. Stat. Ann. 5/2-607.—Tershakovec v. Ford Motor Company, 546 F.Supp.3d 1348, amended in part 2021 WL 3711444, affirmed in part, vacated in part, reversed in part 79 F.4th 1299.

X. REMEDIES.

Actions to obtain remedies, see XI.

(A) IN GENERAL.

⊫1905. —— Breach of warranty.
M.D.Fla. 2020. Under Pennsylvania law, economic harms are properly recoverable under contract theories of breach of implied warranty. 13 Pa. Cons. Stat. Ann. § 2314.—Yachera v. Westminster Pharmaceuticals, LLC, 477 F.Supp.3d 1251.

(B) PARTICULAR REMEDIES OF SELLER.

2. LIEN OR SECURITY INTEREST OF SELLER.

Equitable liens, see LIENS ⊫7.

⊫1947. Security interest.
Security interests under Article 9 of the Uniform Commercial Code, see SECURED TRANSACTIONS.

5. MONETARY REMEDIES OF SELLER.

⊫1985. —— In general.
S.D.Fla. 2017. Under Florida law, court interpreting take or pay agreement, which obligates buyer to purchase a specific amount of product, whether or not it actually takes it, views a buyer's payment as its promise in the agreement rather than a measure of damages.—World Fuel Services, Inc. v. John E. Retzner Oil Company, Inc., 234 F.Supp.3d 1234.

⊫1987(1). In general.
S.D.Fla. 2017. Under Florida law, contract between buyer and seller of ultra-low sulfur diesel, which required buyer to purchase from seller 630,000 gallons per month for a one-year period, was a "take or pay contract," entitling seller to the full contract price upon buyer's breach, rather than damages based on seller's actual losses in

accordance with Florida's Uniform Commercial Code (UCC); contract indicated that buyer agreed that in order for seller to offer fuel at fixed price over one-year period, seller has entered into hedging transactions with third parties, and in the event that buyer purchases less than full contracted quantity for any reason, buyer shall be liable for all damages incurred. Fla. Stat. Ann. § 672.709.—World Fuel Services, Inc. v. John E. Retzner Oil Company, Inc., 234 F.Supp.3d 1234.

Under Florida law, breach of a take or pay agreement, which obligates buyer to purchase a specific amount of a product, whether or not he actually takes it, entitles non-breaching party to payments it would have received under the contract with no duty to mitigate damages.—Id.

Fla.App. 4 Dist. 2019. Pre-negotiated residual values of aviation products that had been returned to seller at end of lease prior to sale to buyer could be used to determine award of damages to seller for buyer's breach of sales contract, though sales contract allowed for adjustment of pre-negotiated values; contract required buyer to remit purchase price for each item within 30 days of receiving invoice or equipment, and buyer did not challenge residual price upon receiving any invoices or equipment.—Volvo Aero Leasing, LLC v. VAS Aero Services, LLC, 268 So.3d 785, review denied 2019 WL 6320164.

☞1987(10). Computers and software.
See also COPYRIGHTS AND INTELLECTUAL PROPERTY ☞107.

☞1991(10). Computers and software.
See also COPYRIGHTS AND INTELLECTUAL PROPERTY ☞107.

☞1995(10). Computers and software.
See also COPYRIGHTS AND INTELLECTUAL PROPERTY ☞107.

☞2006. Special, indirect, or consequential damages.
Fla.App. 1 Dist. 2019. "Consequential damages" do not arise within the scope of the immediate buyer-seller transaction, but rather stem from losses incurred by the non-breaching party in its dealings, often with third parties, which were a proximate result of the breach, and which were reasonably foreseeable by the breaching party at the time of contracting.—Keystone Airpark Authority v. Pipeline Contractors, Inc., 266 So.3d 1219, review denied 2019 WL 1371949.

☞2008. —— In general.
S.D.Fla. 2017. Under Florida law, breach of a take or pay agreement, which obligates buyer to purchase a specific amount of a product, whether or not he actually takes it, entitles non-breaching party to payments it would have received under the contract with no duty to mitigate damages.—World Fuel Services, Inc. v. John E. Retzner Oil Company, Inc., 234 F.Supp.3d 1234.

(C) PARTICULAR REMEDIES OF BUYER.

1. LIEN OR SECURITY INTEREST OF BUYER.

Equitable liens, see LIENS ☞7.

4. MONETARY REMEDIES OF BUYER IN GENERAL.

☞2156. —— Computers and software.
See also COPYRIGHTS AND INTELLECTUAL PROPERTY ☞107.

☞2158. —— In general.
S.D.Fla. 2022. District Court would award buyer of frozen shrimp, which was New York company with principal place of business in Florida, default final judgment against Ecuadorian frozen shrimp seller for damages in principal amount of $103,921.60, plus post-judgment interest, for seller's breach of contract via failure to compensate buyer per letters of warranty under which seller assumed responsibility for reimbursing buyer upon unforeseen setbacks with seller's product at destination port in China due to customs clearance; Court accepted buyer's representations in its affidavit in support of its motion for entry of default judgment that the principal balance owned under the letter of warranty was $103,921.60, consisting of $102,121.60 for shipment of frozen shrimp plus $1,800.00 in freight costs. Fed. R. Civ. P. 55(b).—Seven Seas International, LLC v. Frigopesca, C.A., 616 F.Supp.3d 1323.

S.D.Fla. 2021. Under Florida law, a buyer must properly reject nonconforming goods—or timely revoke acceptance—before it can rescind the contract and obtain a full refund. Fla. Stat. Ann. § 672.711.—A&E Adventures LLC v. Intercard, Inc., 529 F.Supp.3d 1333.

☞2165(10). Computers and software.
See also COPYRIGHTS AND INTELLECTUAL PROPERTY ☞107.

☞2169(10). Computers and software.
See also COPYRIGHTS AND INTELLECTUAL PROPERTY ☞107.

5. MONETARY REMEDIES OF BUYER
FOR BREACH OF WARRANTY.

☞2192. Damages in general.
Fla.App. 2 Dist. 2018. A claimant in an action for breach of warranty may recover damages for the diminished value of the warranted goods as well as incidental and consequential damages resulting from the breach. Fla. Stat. Ann. §§ 672.714(2), 672.714(3).—Kia Motors America, Inc. v. Doughty, 242 So.3d 1172.

☞2198. —— Machinery and equipment.
S.D.Fla. 2021. Buyer of allegedly faulty card-reading systems for its entertainment and gaming centers waived on its claims that manufacturer, from which it had purchased the systems, breached an express warranty, breached an implied warranty, was liable for promissory estoppel, and violated the Florida Deceptive and Unfair Trade Practices Act (FDUTPA) all damages that were not based on what it had paid manufacturer; despite buyer's contention that it had only waived damages based on lost profits, buyer, by confirming in an e-mail to manufacturer that it would be seeking only the money that it had paid manufacturer, unambiguously disavowed any other damages claim that it might have had for payments that it made to third parties, and that meant that manufacturer did not have a chance to take discovery on buyer's third-party transactions.—A&E Adventures LLC v. Intercard, Inc., 529 F.Supp.3d 1333.

☞2203. —— Computers and software.
See also COPYRIGHTS AND INTELLECTUAL PROPERTY ☞107.

☞2210. —— Difference from value as warranted.
M.D.Fla. 2020. Under Michigan law, the implied warranty of merchantability allows the purchaser of defective goods to recover the benefit of the bargain, which is the difference between the value of the goods as delivered and the value the

goods would have had they complied with the warranty.—Yachera v. Westminster Pharmaceuticals, LLC, 477 F.Supp.3d 1251.

⟟2212(10). **Computers and software.**
See also COPYRIGHTS AND INTELLECTUAL PROPERTY ⟟107.

⟟2214. —— **In general.**
S.D.Fla. 2021. A party asserting a breach-of-warranty claim under Florida law may pursue incidental and consequential damages. Fla. Stat. Ann. § 672.714.—A&E Adventures LLC v. Intercard, Inc., 529 F.Supp.3d 1333.

⟟2217. —— **In general.**
S.D.Fla. 2021. A party asserting a breach-of-warranty claim under Florida law may pursue incidental and consequential damages. Fla. Stat. Ann. § 672.714.—A&E Adventures LLC v. Intercard, Inc., 529 F.Supp.3d 1333.
Fla.App. 1 Dist. 2019. "Consequential damages" do not arise within the scope of the immediate buyer-seller transaction, but rather stem from losses incurred by the non-breaching party in its dealings, often with third parties, which were a proximate result of the breach, and which were reasonably foreseeable by the breaching party at the time of contracting.—Keystone Airpark Authority v. Pipeline Contractors, Inc., 266 So.3d 1219, review denied 2019 WL 1371949.

⟟2218(10). **Computers and software.**
See also COPYRIGHTS AND INTELLECTUAL PROPERTY ⟟107.

(D) RESCISSION.

Revocation of acceptance, see V(C)5. Repudiation, see V(J). Cancellation and termination, see VI.

⟟2249. —— **Failure of consideration.**
Fla.App. 3 Dist. 1970. Even though buyer failed to avail itself of opportunity to determine condition of aircraft, including its equipment, prior to buying it, it was reasonable to assume that aircraft would contain customary and necessary equipment, and, to extent that such were missing, there was partial failure of consideration, but, since items were replaceable, their absence was not basis for rescission and was compensable in money damages.—Pinellas Central Bank & Trust Co. v. International Aerodyne, Inc., 233 So.2d 872, certiorari denied 239 So.2d 829.

(E) EXCLUSIVE, CONCURRENT, AND CONFLICTING REMEDIES; ELECTION.

⟟2283. —— **In general.**
Fla.App. 3 Dist. 1989. Permitting aircraft part supplier both to retain turbine returned to it after it failed within 30 days of delivery and to recover for purchase price for new turbine constituted impermissible double recovery. West's F.S.A. § 672.709.—Page Avjet Corp. v. Cosgrove Aircraft Service, Inc., 546 So.2d 16.

⟟2289. —— **Warranties.**
M.D.Fla. 2020. Under Pennsylvania law, the theories of strict liability and breach of the implied warranty of merchantability are parallel theories of recovery, one in contract and the other in tort. 13 Pa. Cons. Stat. Ann. § 2314.—Yachera v. Westminster Pharmaceuticals, LLC, 477 F.Supp.3d 1251.

Under Pennsylvania law, because strict-liability claims based on a manufacturing defect are not precluded, there is no basis for declining to recognize a claim against a drug manufacturer for breach of the implied warranty of merchantability where it is based on a manufacturing defect. 13 Pa. Cons. Stat. Ann. § 2314.—Id.
S.D.Fla. 2014. Doctrine of primary jurisdiction did not require referral of claims alleging violations of Florida's Deceptive and Unfair Trade Practices Act (FDUTPA), negligent misrepresentation, breach of implied warranty of fitness for purpose, breach of express warranty, declaratory judgment, money had and received, and violations of California's Business and Professions Code, in consumers' class action complaint against manufacturers of cereal and snack food products, that Genetically Modified Organisms (GMOs) and other allegedly synthetic ingredients precluded manufacturers' products from being characterized as "all natural" to Food and Drug Administration (FDA); determination of whether manufacturer's "all natural" and "nothing artificial" representations on products' labeling were misleading and whether customers purchased products in reliance upon representations was not technical area in which FDA had greater technical expertise than courts, and FDA had not promulgated comprehensive regulatory scheme regarding assertions of "all natural" or "nothing artificial" on food labeling. West's F.S.A. § 501.201 et seq.; West's Ann.Cal.Civ.Code § 1750; West's Ann.Cal.Bus. & Prof.Code §§ 17200, 17500.—Garcia v. Kashi Co., 43 F.Supp.3d 1359.

⟟2290. —— **Economic loss doctrine.**
S.D.Fla. 2022. Under Florida law, fact that a party does not assert a breach of express warranty claim does not preclude application of the economic loss doctrine.—PR Overseas Boating, Ltd. v. Talaria Company, LLC, 601 F.Supp.3d 1285, affirmed in part, vacated in part, remanded Martin v. Quick SpA, 2023 WL 5321037.

(F) CONTRACTUAL MODIFICATION OR LIMITATION OF REMEDY.

⟟2301. **In general.**
S.D.Fla. 2007. Under Florida law, prospective buyer waived and released her breach of contract claims against aircraft manufacturer pursuant to the limitation of liability provisions in the reservation agreement, which reserved her order position for an aircraft to be defined later at a price that was subject to change pending the aircraft's development; by signing the agreement, buyer agreed that manufacturer could retain her deposit in the event she breached the agreement, and similarly, if manufacturer breached, she could demand the return of her deposit.—Barnes v. Diamond Aircraft Industries, Inc., 499 F.Supp.2d 1311.

⟟2302. **Validity and enforceability in general.**
M.D.Fla. 2007. Contractual provision in agreement to sell aircraft limiting buyer's remedies to return of his deposit was invalid under Florida law as unreasonable and lacking mutuality, where seller drafted contract, there was no similar provision exclusively defining seller's remedies, and return of deposit as damages was inadequate.—Horowitch v. Diamond Aircraft Industries, Inc., 526 F.Supp.2d 1236, certificate of appealability granted by 2007 WL 2904135, va-

---

† **This Case was not selected for publication in the National Reporter System**

cated, appeal dismissed 299 Fed.Appx. 951, on remand 2009 WL 1537896, order vacated in part on reconsideration 2009 WL 1537896.

⟜**2305. —— In general.**

M.D.Fla. 2023. Under Florida and California law, a warranty may limit the remedies available to a buyer, and such limitations may include a time requirement for making a warranty claim for repair. Cal. Com. Code § 2719(1)(a); Fla. Stat. Ann. § 672.316(4).—Riley v. General Motors, LLC, 664 F.Supp.3d 1336.

S.D.Fla. 2013. Under Florida law, a written warranty is treated like a contract between the seller and the buyer; as such, the terms of an express warranty may limit or foreclose the remedies available to the buyer.—Aprigliano v. American Honda Motor Co., Inc., 979 F.Supp.2d 1331.

⟜**2308. —— Repair or replacement.**

S.D.Fla. 2022. Purchasers of purportedly defective pressure cookers alleged that they or their family members purchased pressure cookers, that express limited warranty was provided by manufacturer on product packaging and in owner's manual, that manufacturer represented that pressure cookers had "locking, air-tight lid[,]" that manufacturer breached warranties by providing products that were not free of defects and by failing to repair or replace defective pressure cookers, that purchasers notified manufacturer of breach of express warranty, and that purchasers all suffered damages as result of defects, as required to state claim for breach of express warranty under Florida law. Fla. Stat. Ann. §§ 672.313(1), 672.313(2).—Rife v. Newell Brands, Inc., 632 F.Supp.3d 1276.

S.D.Fla. 2021. Consumers who alleged that automobile model's "limp mode," in which automobile would rapidly decelerate when engine temperature got too high, was design defect but failed to present their vehicles to manufacturer for repair did not comply with terms of limited warranty, as required for consumers to prevail on their breach-of-warranty claims under various state laws, notwithstanding consumers' argument that manufacturer waived presentment requirement by instructing its dealers to let consumers know limp mode was normal and to refer them to owner's guide for instructions on aftermarket coolers, where manufacturer's instructions to dealers did not make it impossible for manufacturer to perform its obligation, and, in fact, instructed dealers on exactly how to perform obligation.—Tershakovec v. Ford Motor Company, 546 F.Supp.3d 1348, amended in part 2021 WL 3711444, affirmed in part, vacated in part, reversed in part 79 F.4th 1299.

S.D.Fla. 2013. Under Florida law, motorcycle purchasers who purchased their motorcycles after expiration of the manufacturer's factory warranties, which limited remedies available to owners to the reparation or replacement of defective parts for a three-year period, did not have an ownership interest in their motorcycles during the motorcycles' warranty periods, could not state a claim for breach of express warranty in their putative class action against manufacturer. —Aprigliano v. American Honda Motor Co., Inc., 979 F.Supp.2d 1331.

XI. ACTIONS.

(A) IN GENERAL.

⟜**2428. Standing.**

S.D.Fla. 2020. Consumers' allegations, in putative class action, that they were exposed to harm by not being reachable by manufacturers of their tires was sufficiently concrete injury for consumers to have standing to sue tire dealer and its parent company for claims, including consumer protection, negligence, and breach of warranty, related to their failure to comply with federal regulation requiring independent tire dealers to register tires they sell to consumers with tire manufacturers; regulation created expectation that tires would be registered with tire manufacturers so that consumers could be contacted by tire manufacturers in event of recall, and driving on unregistered tires placed consumers in dangerous zone of harm in event that such tires were defective and recalled. U.S. Const. art. 3, § 2, cl. 1; 49 C.F.R. § 574.8.—Exum v. National Tire and Battery, 437 F.Supp.3d 1141.

Consumers' allegations that they were deprived of full benefit of tires they purchased because tires were unregistered was sufficiently concrete injury for consumers to have standing to sue tire dealer and its parent company for claims, including consumer protection, negligence, and breach of warranty, asserted in putative class action, related to their failure to comply with federal regulation requiring independent tire dealers to register tires they sell to consumers with tire manufacturers; by purchasing unregistered tires, consumers arguably purchased a less valuable product than properly registered tires. U.S. Const. art. 3, § 2, cl. 1; 49 C.F.R. § 574.8.—Id.

⟜**2431(3). Action by buyer.**

C.A.11 (Fla.) 2017. Under Florida law, patient failed to state claim against manufacturer of hip joint replacement system for breach of contract; although patient had conceded any claim based on oral contract with manufacturer and had limited claim solely to the written consent agreement, patient alleged only that manufacturer breached oral contract, and failed to allege that manufacturer breached any promises in written consent agreement.—Mink v. Smith & Nephew, Inc., 860 F.3d 1319.

S.D.Fla. 2022. Buyer of frozen shrimp, which was a New York company with its principal place of business in Florida, established breach of contract under Florida law by its well-pled allegations for purposes of default judgment in action against Ecuadorian frozen shrimp seller; buyer alleged that it and seller entered into an agreement for the delivery of frozen shrimp from Ecuador to China, seller issued letter of warranty in which it assumed responsibility for reimbursing buyer upon unforeseen setbacks with seller's product at the destination port in China because of customs clearance, customs officials in China rejected shipment of frozen shrimp, notified seller of that rejection, and seller issued a second letter of warranty, and seller nonetheless failed to reimburse buyer. Fed. R. Civ. P. 55(b).—Seven Seas International, LLC v. Frigopesca, C.A., 616 F.Supp.3d 1323.

S.D.Fla. 2011. Consumer failed to sufficiently allege that he entered into valid and enforceable contract with manufacturer to purchase infant formula, as required to state breach of contract claim under Florida law against manufacturer based on recall of infant formula products contaminated with insect parts and larvae; consumer failed to allege that he made any offer to manufacturer, and never alleged that manufacturer made offer to consumer.—Jovine v. Abbott Laboratories, Inc., 795 F.Supp.2d 1331.

⚖2435. —— In general.
Evidence, see XI(C), XI(D), XI(E). Questions of law or fact, see XI(F). Instructions, see XI(G).

⚖2437. Judgment, order, or decree.
Remedies, see X.

(B) ACTIONS ON WARRANTIES.

1. IN GENERAL.

⚖2452. Existence, nature, and form of action.
S.D.Fla. 2020. Fact that neither the National Traffic and Motor Vehicle Safety Act nor regulation promulgated thereunder, requiring independent tire dealers to register tires they sell to consumers with tire manufacturers, provided for a private cause of action did not preclude consumers' federal and state consumer protection, negligence, and breach of warranty claims against tire dealer and its parent company, which arose from defendants' failure to register tires sold in compliance with the Safety Act and regulation; consumers were relying on regulation that created defendants' duty to register tires with manufacturers and as evidence of their claims, and they were not asserting a cause of action under either the Safety Act or the regulation. 49 U.S.C.A. § 30101 et seq.; 49 C.F.R. § 574.8.—Exum v. National Tire and Battery, 437 F.Supp.3d 1141.

⚖2455. —— In general.
N.D.Fla. 2021. Under Washington law, the bulk-supplier doctrine, under which bulk suppliers of products to manufacturers, who are sophisticated users, have no duty in negligence, strict liability, or breach of warranty to warn ultimate purchasers of manufacturer's product, is an affirmative defense.—In re 3M Combat Arms Earplug Products Liability Litigation, 545 F.Supp.3d 1239.

⚖2463. Standing.
† C.A.11 (Fla.) 2020. Consumer lacked concrete injury, as required to have standing to bring putative class action claim against cereal manufacturer for violation of Florida's Deceptive and Unfair Trade Practices Act (FDUTPA) and breach of warranty, based on its failure to disclose cereal contained glyphosate, since consumer failed to allege that she purchased any boxes of the cereal that contained any glyphosate, much less a level that was so harmful as to render the purchase worthless. U.S. Const. Art. 3, § 1; Fla. Stat. Ann. § 501.201 et seq.—Doss v. General Mills, Inc., 816 Fed.Appx. 312.
M.D.Fla. 2023. Buyers who were named plaintiffs lacked Article III standing to bring state law claims on behalf of putative nationwide class against automobile manufacturer arising from failure to fully pay to repair paint deterioration under warranty, where named plaintiffs bought their cars in Florida and California, and named plaintiffs could not bring claims on behalf of consumers who bought their cars in other states. U.S. Const. art. 3, § 2, cl. 1; Fed. R. Civ. P. 23.—Riley v. General Motors, LLC, 664 F.Supp.3d 1336.

M.D.Fla. 2020. Purchasers who bought pharmaceutical company's medication at retail pharmacy plausibly alleged that they would not have purchased medication had they known it was defective, as required to establish injury-in-fact element of standing in putative class action against company alleging company sold adulterated medication and asserting various claims including breach of warranty, strict liability, and deceptive trade practices, where purchasers alleged that medication did not contain amount of active pharmaceutical ingredients stated on label, and that they would not have purchased medication had they known it did not contain amount of ingredients purchasers thought they were receiving. U.S. Const. art. 3, § 2, cl. 1.—Yachera v. Westminster Pharmaceuticals, LLC, 477 F.Supp.3d 1251.
S.D.Fla. 2021. Dog owner failed to allege sufficient details of his independent analysis of dog-food manufacturer's grain-free food, and therefore owner failed to establish injury-in-fact and, thus, failed to establish Article III standing to assert claims under Florida law for breach of express warranty, breach of implied warranty of merchantability, unjust enrichment, and violation of Florida Deceptive and Unfair Trade Practices Act (FDUTPA), arising out of his purchase of manufacturer's grain-free food that allegedly included wheat that caused adverse reactions in his dogs; owner's complaint did not specify on which product his analysis was performed, methodology of his analysis, or results of analysis, other than to state that it revealed amount of wheat above 1% cross-contamination threshold amount. U.S. Const. art. 3, § 2, cl. 1; Fla. Stat. Ann. § 501.201 et seq.—Sabater v. American Journey (PET), LLC, 570 F.Supp.3d 1160.
S.D.Fla. 2020. Police officer lacked standing to represent his proposed classes of all individuals and entities in California that purchased a new concealable self-suspending ballistic system vest from manufacturer, in action alleging that manufacturer of vests violated various consumer protection statutes and breached express and implied warranties by selling vests with allegedly defective straps; officer only purchased one model of manufacturer's self-suspending ballistic system vest.—Ohio State Troopers Association, Inc. v. Point Blank Enterprises, Inc., 481 F.Supp.3d 1258.
S.D.Fla. 2020. Buyer of HVAC units did not sufficiently allege malfunction of units or overpayment for units and, thus, failed to satisfy the injury-in-fact requirement for Article III standing to bring action, on behalf of himself and others similarly situated, against manufacturers and distributor of units for breach of express warranty and implied warranty of merchantability and violations of Magnuson-Moss Warranty Act (MMWA) for breach of written warranty and breach of implied warranty; only mention of malfunction in complaint was that others had units overheat or catch fire, which was preceded by "upon information and belief," and buyer did not plead allegations of what he paid for units or of diminished value, and instead only allegations were general references to damages. U.S. Const. art. 3, § 2, cl. 1; Federal Trade Commission Improvement Act §§ 101-112, 15 U.S.C.A. §§ 2301-2312.—Toca v. Tutco, LLC, 430 F.Supp.3d 1313.
S.D.Fla. 2019. Vehicle owner had Article III standing to assert Deceptive and Unfair Trade Practices Act (FDUTPA) and breach of express and implied warranties claims against vehicle manufacturer on behalf of putative class mem-

---

† This Case was not selected for publication in the National Reporter System

bers who purchased vehicles with allegedly defective drive shafts in the state of Florida, even if he purchased a different model year and type than some of the class members, where owner alleged that the defect existed in range of model types and model years, and discovery would reveal whether manufacturer used same drive shaft in those vehicles over different model years and types. U.S. Const. art. 3, § 2, cl. 1; Fla. Stat. Ann. § 501.201 et seq.—Weiss v. General Motors LLC, 418 F.Supp.3d 1173.

S.D.Fla. 2018. Law enforcement officers, as named plaintiffs in putative class action against manufacturer of ballistic vests, failed to establish Article III standing for each class subclaim, and thus, their breach of warranty class could not be certified; officers only purchased and used two different models of manufacturer's vests, but sought to bring claims on behalf of all individuals and entities in several states that purchased and/or used new self-suspending ballistic system (SSBS) vests from manufacturer, which included hundreds of different models of vests, and even if such vests all contained identical SSBS systems with the same defect, similarity between products did not confer standing. U.S. Const. art. 3, § 2, cl. 1; Fed. R. Civ. P. 23.—Ohio State Troopers Association, Inc. v. Point Blank Enterprises, Inc., 347 F.Supp.3d 1207.

Law enforcement officers had standing to bring individual breach of warranty claims against manufacturer of ballistic vests, with respect to the two models of manufacturer's vests that officers purchased; injury in fact suffered by officers was the purchase price of the defective vests, the harm was fairly traceable to manufacturer, as manufacturer of the vests, and damages would remedy the harm by making officers whole.—Id.

S.D.Fla. 2017. Consumers' allegations that they overpaid for electric unitary heaters and heating, ventilation and air conditioning (HVAC) equipment products were sufficient to establish standing, on motion to dismiss consumers' products liability class action against manufacturers of heaters and HVAC equipment, asserting claims for breach of warranty and violations of Florida Deceptive and Unfair Trade Practices Act (FDUTPA); although none of the consumers alleged that they experienced a problem with their HVAC systems and heaters due to defect, allegations of overpayment were sufficient to establish standing at motion to dismiss stage in breach of warranty and FDUTPA cases. Fla. Stat. Ann. § 501.201 et seq.—Koski v. Carrier Corporation, 347 F.Supp.3d 1185.

⟨⟩**2465. —— In general.**
S.D.Fla. 2022. In order to properly plead a cause of action for breach of warranties under the Florida Uniform Commercial Code, a complaint should contain at least the following allegations: (1) facts in respect to the sale of the goods; (2) identification of the types of warranties created; (3) facts in respect to the creation of the particular warranty; (4) facts in respect to the breach of the warranty; (5) notice to seller of the breach; and· (6) the injuries sustained by the buyer as a result of the breach of warranty. Fla. Stat. Ann. § 672.301 et seq.—Rife v. Newell Brands, Inc., 632 F.Supp.3d 1276.

S.D.Fla. 2020. To state a claim for breach of implied warranty of merchantability under Virginia state law, it is not necessary for the complaining party to plead with specificity the trade or industry standard for merchantability; instead, this is an inquiry best left for summary judgment

stage when the court has the benefit of considering all the evidence.—Exum v. National Tire and Battery, 437 F.Supp.3d 1141.

S.D.Fla. 2020. To state a claim for breach of an express warranty under Florida law, the plaintiff must first identify the express warranty that the defendant allegedly breached. Fla. Stat. Ann. § 672.313.—Toca v. Tutco, LLC, 430 F.Supp.3d 1313.

S.D.Fla. 2011. To plead a cause of action for breach of express warranties under the Florida Uniform Commercial Code (UCC), a complaint must allege: (1) the sale of goods, (2) the express warranty, (3) breach of the warranty, (4) notice to seller of the breach, and (5) the injuries sustained by the buyer as a result of the breach of the express warranty. West's F.S.A. §§ 672.313, 672.607(3).—Jovine v. Abbott Laboratories, Inc., 795 F.Supp.2d 1331.

S.D.Fla. 2011. To plead a cause of action for breach of express warranties under the Florida Uniform Commercial Code, a complaint must allege: (1) the sale of goods; (2) the express warranty; (3) breach of the warranty; (4) notice to seller of the breach; and (5) the injuries sustained by the buyer as a result of the breach of the express warranty. West's F.S.A. § 672.313.—Moss v. Walgreen Co., 765 F.Supp.2d 1363.

⟨⟩**2466. —— Particular actions and claims.**
M.D.Fla. 2023. Buyers who were named plaintiffs failed to allege that they sought repairs to their vehicles within warranty period, and thus failed to state individual claims or claims on behalf of putative Florida and California classes against automobile manufacturer for breach of Magnuson-Morris Warranty Act (MMWA) and breach of express warranty under Florida and California law, arising from manufacturer's refusal to fully pay to repair paint deterioration under warranty. Cal. Com. Code § 2719(1)(a); Fla. Stat. Ann. § 672.316(4).—Riley v. General Motors, LLC, 664 F.Supp.3d 1336.

Though buyers alleged in briefing on motion to dismiss that warranties covering their vehicles were unconscionable, their complaint was silent on any allegations that warranty was unconscionable, and thus buyers failed to state individual claims or claims on behalf of putative Florida and California classes against automobile manufacturer for breach of Magnuson-Morris Warranty Act (MMWA) and breach of express warranty under Florida and California law, arising from manufacturer's refusal to fully pay to repair paint deterioration under warranty. Magnuson-Moss Warranty-Federal Trade Commission Improvement Act § 101 et seq., 15 U.S.C.A. § 2301 et seq.; Cal. Com. Code § 2719(1)(a); Fla. Stat. Ann. § 672.316(4).—Id.

M.D.Fla. 2021. A patient, who had medical mesh implanted in two hernia surgeries, failed to identify any safer alternative design for the medical mesh that would have prevented his injury, as required to state a claim for breach of implied warranty under Michigan law, in the patient's products liability action against the manufacturers of the medical mesh, where the patient asserted that the mesh's design was defective due to the use of polypropylene, but the patient did not identify any alternative or allege any facts beyond a speculative level that the manufacturer caused the alleged injury. Mich. Comp. Laws Ann. § 600.2946(2).—Knudsen v. Ethicon, Inc., 535 F.Supp.3d 1231.

S.D.Fla. 2020. Buyer of HVAC units failed to state claims for breach of express warranty under

Article 2 of the Uniform Commercial Code (UCC) and breach of written warranty under the Magnuson-Moss Warranty Act (MMWA) against the units' manufacturers and distributor based on allegedly defective heater components; buyer's complaint did not allege creation of an express warranty in any of the three ways specified under Article 2, speculation on what the terms of the warranty might have been was insufficient, and, even if manufacturers and distributor made affirmative promises of fact and created express warranties on which the buyer could have stated a claim, buyer's complaint pointed to no promise that the units would include a fail-safe mechanism absent from the heater components. Federal Trade Commission Improvement Act §§ 101-112, 15 U.S.C.A. §§ 2301-2312; Fla. Stat. Ann. § 672.313.—Toca v. Tutco, LLC, 430 F.Supp.3d 1313.

S.D.Fla. 2019. Automobile purchaser from Florida failed to allege contractual privity with automobile company entities, and thus failed to state implied warranty of merchantability claim under Florida law in class action alleging entities defrauded purchasers and engaged in unfair trade practices by concealing defect in heating, ventilation, and air conditioning systems installed in certain automobiles, where purchaser failed to allege he purchased automobile directly from any entity.—Cardenas v. Toyota Motor Corporation, 418 F.Supp.3d 1090.

S.D.Fla. 2011. Consumer failed to state a claim for breach of express warranty under Florida Uniform Commercial Code (UCC) against manufacturer of infant formula products, which had been recalled due to contamination with inset parts and larvae, where consumer did not allege that he ever notified manufacturer of the alleged breach of warranty. West's F.S.A. §§ 672.313, 672.607(3).—Jovine v. Abbott Laboratories, Inc., 795 F.Supp.2d 1331.

Consumer failed to allege that he was in privity with infant formula manufacturer, as required to state claim for breach of implied warranty of merchantability under Florida law against manufacturer based on recall of infant formula products contaminated with insect parts and larvae. West's F.S.A. § 672.314.—Id.

S.D.Fla. 2011. Consumer's allegations that mouthwash developer claimed mouthwash helped "fight visible plaque above the gum line" in labeling and advertising, that consumer purchased mouthwash based on these claims, that mouthwash did not provide the benefits it described, and that consumer provided notice to developer of the failure were sufficient to state a claim for breach of express warranty under Florida law, as required for consumer's putative class action. West's F.S.A. § 672.313.—Moss v. Walgreen Co., 765 F.Supp.2d 1363.

⟠2470. ⸺ In general.
Evidence, see XI(C), XI(D), XI(E). Questions of law or fact, see XI(F). Instructions, see XI(G).

⟠2472. Judgment, order, or decree.
Remedies, see X.

2. ACTIONS FOR RESCISSION OR REDHIBITION.

⟠2516. ⸺ In general.
Evidence, see XI(C), XI(D), XI(E). Questions of law or fact, see XI(F). Instructions, see XI(G).

⟠2518. Judgment, order, or decree.
Remedies, see X.

(C) PRESUMPTIONS, INFERENCES, AND BURDEN OF PROOF.

⟠2612. ⸺ In general.
S.D.Fla. 2020. In order to fulfill pre-suit notice requirement, as established in Florida's Uniform Commercial Code (UCC), which requires buyer, after having accepted tender, to notify seller of any breach within reasonable time after he or she discovers or should have discovered breach in order to obtain remedy, the burden is on the buyer to show that he gave the required notice within a reasonable time. Fla. Stat. Ann. § 672.607(3)(a).—Toca v. Tutco, LLC, 430 F.Supp.3d 1313.

⟠2631. ⸺ Warranties imposed by law; implied warranties.
M.D.Fla. 2020. Under Michigan law, for purposes of a breach of implied warranty of merchantability claim, it is reasonable to infer that medication that does not contain the listed amount of active pharmaceutical ingredient is not fit for its intended use and thus contains an actionable defect.—Yachera v. Westminster Pharmaceuticals, LLC, 477 F.Supp.3d 1251.

(E) WEIGHT AND SUFFICIENCY OF EVIDENCE.

⟠2728. ⸺ In general.
Fla.App. 3 Dist. 2018. Sufficient evidence supported jury's finding that all required elements for rescission of a contract on the basis of unilateral mistake had been met in diamond buyer's breach of contract action against operator of a cruise ship jewelry store arising out of store operator's mistaken agreement to sell a 20-carat diamond to buyer for millions of dollars less than its actual value; store received incorrect information from its home office, which caused it to quote a price that was a fraction of its cost to purchase diamond wholesale, and jury was entitled to find that the mistake was not inexcusable, and that buyer did not detrimentally rely on the mistake such that it would be unconscionable to rescind the sales contract.—DePrince v. Starboard Cruise Services, Inc., 271 So.3d 11.

⟠2729. ⸺ Misrepresentation and fraud.
Fla.App. 4 Dist. 1992. Evidence supported judgment awarding airplane seller damages for breach of contract, despite buyer's claim that seller fraudulently misrepresented frequency of necessary aircraft inspections which allegedly gave buyer grounds to rescind and cancel contract.—Maxfly Aviation, Inc. v. Gill, 605 So.2d 1297.

⟠2751. ⸺ Warranties imposed by law; implied warranties.
C.A.11 (Fla.) 2022. Florida law does not require plaintiffs in contract cases alleging breach of an implied warranty to prove the defective nature of the product at issue with expert testimony.—MidAmerica C2L Incorporated v. Siemens Energy Inc., 25 F.4th 1312, vacated and superseded on rehearing 2023 WL 2733512, on remand 2024 WL 414620.

⟠2760. ⸺ Monetary remedies and damages in general.
Fla.App. 4 Dist. 1992. Evidence supported judgment awarding airplane seller damages for

---

† **This Case was not selected for publication in the National Reporter System**

breach of contract, despite buyer's claim that seller fraudulently misrepresented frequency of necessary aircraft inspections which allegedly gave buyer grounds to rescind and cancel contract.—Maxfly Aviation, Inc. v. Gill, 605 So.2d 1297.

(F) QUESTIONS OF LAW OR FACT.

⟲2781. In general.

† **C.A.11 (Fla.) 2012.** District court did not improperly award aircraft manufacturer liquidated damages, without manufacturer having filed any claim for such award, on manufacturer's motion for summary judgment in purchaser's action alleging fraudulent and negligent inducement to enter into purchase contract; instead, court simply held that manufacturer's retention of $2,250,000 deposit did not constitute unjust enrichment, because purchase agreement governed parties' rights and duties and allowed for such retention of deposit after purchaser's failure to pay remaining sums due.—Extreme Crafts VII, LLC v. Cessna Aircraft Co., 479 Fed.Appx. 247.

C.A.11 (Fla.) 1983. Mere allegation that seller of securities entered into option contract with reason to believe that it would not be able to deliver securities promptly was insufficient to prevent entry of summary judgment in favor of seller under Florida law in an action for breach of option contract when purchaser unilaterally terminated contract after delay in delivery of securities.—Westcap Government Securities, Inc. v. Homestead Air Force Base Federal Credit Union, 697 F.2d 911.

C.A.5 (Fla.) 1982. Where first amended complaint against buyer and complaint in separate action against alleged agent were not sworn, the plaintiff seller could not rely on such documents to resist buyer's summary judgment motion in action for breach of contract; however, since the complaints were sufficient to raise a legal issue, i.e., agency, they thereby imposed on buyer the burden to show that the facts underlying such issue were not disputed. Fed.Rules Civ.Proc. Rule 56(c), 28 U.S.C.A.—Impossible Electronic Techniques, Inc. v. Wackenhut Protective Systems, Inc., 669 F.2d 1026.

Where defendant buyer moved for summary judgment on ground of failure to satisfy statute of frauds for sales contracts the defendant buyer had burden of overcoming plaintiff seller's assertion that statute was not applicable because the goods were specially manufactured for the buyer. Fed.Rules Civ.Proc. Rule 56(c), 28 U.S.C.A.; West's F.S.A. § 672.201(1), (3)(a).—Id.

C.A.5 (Fla.) 1952. In action to recover money for meat which plaintiff sold to a defendant which resold meat and assigned to another defendant its rights to receive payment, wherein plaintiff contended that title to meat had not passed to defendant which bought from plaintiff because of alleged fraud in that check given by such defendant was fraudulently issued when such defendant did not have sufficient funds on deposit to cover check, and such defendant sought to have witness subpoenaed to prove plaintiff had agreed to accept an open check, in which case such defendant contended title would have passed and that such defendant would be entitled to the money, plaintiff was not entitled to summary judgment in view of unresolved counter-contentions of law and fact.—Gruber v. Wm. Coady & Co., 199 F.2d 554.

M.D.Fla. 2007. Issue of whether aircraft manufacturer breached implied covenants of good faith and fair dealing under Florida law with prospective customer with regard to sale of aircraft could not be resolved on summary judgment where there was genuine issue of material fact on breach of contract claim as to terms of contract and that issue was intrinsically entwined with implied covenants issue. Fed.Rules Civ.Proc. Rule 56, 28 U.S.C.A.—Horowitch v. Diamond Aircraft Industries, Inc., 526 F.Supp.2d 1236, certificate of appealability granted by 2007 WL 2904135, vacated, appeal dismissed 299 Fed. Appx. 951, on remand 2009 WL 1537896, order vacated in part on reconsideration 2009 WL 1537896.

M.D.Fla. 1992. Fact issue as to whether allegedly defective plywood used by builder created clear danger of death or personal injury precluded summary judgment on builder's negligence claim against manufacturers and sellers of the plywood, on grounds builder only suffered economic loss. Fed.Rules Civ.Proc.Rule 56, 28 U.S.C.A.—Pulte Home Corp., Inc. v. Ply Gem Industries, Inc., 804 F.Supp. 1471.

Fact issue as to whether corporation aided and abetted fraudulent conduct of two manufacturers of allegedly defective plywood precluded summary judgment in builder's action against corporation based on sales of such plywood. Fed. Rules Civ.Proc.Rule 56(e), 28 U.S.C.A.—Id.

S.D.Fla. 1999. Fact issues existed as to whether gasoline supplier modified its sales agreement with its dealers or whether the sales agreement constituted a final expression of the parties' intentions and justifiable expectations, precluding summary judgment in favor of supplier on dealers' breach of contract claim based on supplier's methodology in setting wholesale motor fuel prices.—Allapattah Services, Inc. v. Exxon Corp., 61 F.Supp.2d 1308.

Fact issues existed underlying determination as to whether gasoline supplier acted in good faith in setting its wholesale price when it allegedly refused to offset the wholesale price of its fuel by an amount comparable to its 3% credit card recovery charge, precluding summary judgment in favor of supplier on dealers' breach of contract claim based on supplier's methodology in setting wholesale motor fuel prices.—Id.

S.D.Fla. 1981. In action by airline to recover alleged overcharges for jet fuel, issue of material fact existed as to whether fuel supplier complied with regulations governing correct computation of "posted prices," precluding summary judgment.—Eastern Airlines, Inc. v. Mobil Oil Corp., 512 F.Supp. 1231, reversed 677 F.2d 879, on remand 564 F.Supp. 1131, affirmed 735 F.2d 1379.

⟲2783. Parties to transaction or contract.

N.D.Fla. 2023. Genuine issues of material fact existed as to whether seller's consulting contractor, who cold-called buyer to ask if it was interested in buying ilmenite, had authority to enter into contracts on seller's behalf, precluding grant of summary judgment as to the existence of a contract, for purposes of buyer's breach of contract claim against seller under Florida law.—US Iron FLA, LLC v. GMA Garnett (USA) Corp., 660 F.Supp.3d 1212.

⟲2785. —— In general.

Fla.App. 4 Dist. 2018. Genuine issues of material fact existed as to whether buyer received terms and conditions and whether terms and conditions were part of parties' agreement, precluding summary judgment in action brought by seller against buyer for non-payment of goods.—Twin Rivers Engineering, Inc. v. Pacer USA, LLC, 257 So.3d 140.

⚷2788. —— In general.
Fla.App. 5 Dist. 1995. Fact question regarding whether purchaser knew that residence he had contracted to purchase was a modular home precluded summary judgment on vendors' suit for specific performance and breach of contract.—Watson v. Hahn, 664 So.2d 1083.

⚷2789. —— Misrepresentation and fraud.
Fla.App. 3 Dist. 1982. In purchasers' fraud action against automobile dealership and against automobile manufacturer, genuine issues of material fact existed as to whether conduct of dealer and manufacturer of partially repairing purchased automobile without revealing that the automobile had been damaged constituted fraudulent concealment, thus precluding summary judgment.—Heider v. Cooper Brown Oldsmobile, Inc., 424 So.2d 46.

⚷2792. —— In general.
C.A.11 (Fla.) 1998. Material issues of fact as to whether parties to international sales contract intended not to be bound by certain terms in their original sales agreement, and as to interpretation of other agreements between parties, precluded summary judgment for foreign seller of ceramic tiles in breach of contract action brought by purchaser of tiles under United Nations Convention on Contracts for the International Sale of Goods. United Nations Convention on Contracts for the International Sale of Goods, Art. 1 et seq., 15 U.S.C.A.App.—MCC-Marble Ceramic Center, Inc., v. Ceramica Nuova d'Agostino, S.p.A., 144 F.3d 1384, rehearing denied, certiorari denied 119 S.Ct. 1496, 526 U.S. 1087, 143 L.Ed.2d 650.
M.D.Fla. 2002. Genuine issues of material fact existed as to various issues including whether certain of defective scanners were accepted, whether seller failed to comply with the ninety-day notice-of-termination provision in the memorandum of agreement and the effect of that provision on the claimed breaches of the production contract, and the meaning of the production contract in light of the parties' conduct and course of performance, precluding summary judgment in favor of seller on issue of whether buyer breached production contract by failing to pay for scanners.—Lockheed Martin Corp. v. Galaxis USA, Ltd., 222 F.Supp.2d 1315, affirmed 88 Fed.Appx. 389.
S.D.Fla. 2013. Under Florida law, genuine issue of material fact as to the rights and duties of the contractual relationship between buyer and seller of healthcare products who did not have a thorough written contract memorializing their arrangement precluded summary judgment on breach of contract claim brought by seller alleging buyer failed to pay invoices.—Nature's Products, Inc. v. Natrol, 990 F.Supp.2d 1307, appeal dismissed (11th cir. 14-10907), and appeal dismissed (11th cir. 15-11180).
Fla.App. 1 Dist. 1980. In action brought by buyers of farm equipment against seller to recover damages for seller's delivery of equipment allegedly differing from that ordered by buyers, substantial fact issue existed as to whether instrument signed by buyer was a blank form with no writing describing the farm equipment, precluding summary judgment.—Deal Farms, Inc. v. Farm & Ranch Supply, Inc., 382 So.2d 888.

Fla.App. 2 Dist. 1980. In contract action, disputed issue of material fact existed as to identity of term "seller" in contract clause at issue, precluding summary judgment.—Criterion Corp. v. Hunt Properties, Inc., 382 So.2d 438.
Fla.App. 2 Dist. 1978. In seller's action against buyer for alleged wrongful cancellation of contracts for sale of corn, material issues of fact existed as to whether remedies provided by Grain and Feed Dealers National Association rules incorporated in contracts by parties, limiting buyer's remedy for nonconforming shipments to those contained in rules and specifically providing that buyer could not rescind entire contract because of nonconforming shipments, failed of their "essential purpose," so as to permit resort to remedies provided by Uniform Commercial Code, including cancellation, precluding summary judgment. West's F.S.A. § 672.719(1)(a), (2).—Tampa Farm Service, Inc. v. Cargill, Inc., 356 So.2d 347.
Fla.App. 2 Dist. 1962. In action to recover purchase price for heat pump, fact questions, precluding summary judgment for plaintiff, were presented as to whether buyer, seller, or carrier was responsible for damage.—Forston v. Atlantic Engineering & Mfg. Corp., 143 So.2d 364.
Fla.App. 3 Dist. 2015. Genuine issue of material fact existed as to whether cruise ship jewelry store made a reasonable and understandable mistake, or acted negligently, in selling cruise passenger a loose diamond at an excessive low price, an element required to establish the defense of unilateral mistake of fact, precluding summary judgment in passenger's action for breach of sales contract against store in which store sought to rescind the contract based on unilateral mistake of fact.—DePrince v. Starboard Cruise Services, Inc., 163 So.3d 586, abrogated in later appeal 271 So.3d 11.
Fla.App. 3 Dist. 2003. Genuine issues of material fact as to whether buyer had contract with seller at time of purchase of analog telecommunications equipment, which would be rendered obsolete by seller's discontinuance of analog service, precluded summary judgment for seller on breach of contract claim.—H & J Paving of Florida, Inc. v. Nextel, Inc., 849 So.2d 1099, rehearing denied.
Fla.App. 3 Dist. 1983. In action against seller of computer system for alleged fraudulent misrepresentations as to compatibility of particular software package with system, material issues of fact existed as to all elements of cause of action, including false representations of material fact, intention to induce representation thereon, and resulting injury to buyer acting in justifiable reliance on representation, thus precluding summary judgment.—Suntogs of Miami, Inc. v. Burroughs Corp., 433 So.2d 581, quashed 472 So.2d 1166, on remand 482 So.2d 391.
Fla.App. 4 Dist. 1988. Genuine issues of material fact existed as to whether supplier was dealing directly with hospital and whether subcontractor was liable for unpaid balance of supplies and labor furnished to hospital, precluding summary judgment in action brought by supplier.—Hawthorne Elec. Corp. v. Executone Systems, Inc., 531 So.2d 1064.
Fla.App. 4 Dist. 1982. In seller's action for shipping costs against buyers, material issue of fact existed as to whether buyers' responsibility for shipping costs was part of overall agreement between seller and buyer for purchase and sale of certain steel products, thus, precluding summary

† This Case was not selected for publication in the National Reporter System

judgment.—Devcon (Panama) Intern. Corp. v. Sheffield Steel Products, Inc., 409 So.2d 214.

☞**2794(2). Quality, value, fitness, and condition of goods.**

Fla.App. 1 Dist. 1966. Issues as to nature and extent of alleged defects in steel products purchased by defendant from plaintiff, whether defects were acknowledged by plaintiff's agent, authority of plaintiff's agent to authorize correction of defects at plaintiff's expense, and reasonable costs incurred by defendant in correcting defects were presented precluding summary judgment for plaintiff suing for judgment on account stated and for goods sold to defendant.—Strode v. Southern Steel Const. Co., 188 So.2d 690.

Fla.App. 2 Dist. 1964. In action by purchasers to recover from manufacturer expenses incurred by purchasers in repairing old underground lawn sprinkling system and cost of installing new one, issue existed as to whether sprinkling system should have lasted for a longer period than six years, precluding summary judgment.—Wisner v. Goodyear Tire & Rubber Co., 167 So.2d 254.

Fla.App. 3 Dist. 1980. In action to recover for alleged fraud and deceit arising out of sale of yacht, substantial fact issue existed as to whether corporation employed by owner for the purpose of selling yacht was acting within the course and scope of its employment, whether plaintiff buyer had a right to rely upon corporation's representations, and whether buyer had opportunity to inspect and learn of alleged defect, precluding summary judgment.—Nessim v. DeLoache, 384 So.2d 1341.

☞**2794(4). Acceptance or rejection of nonconforming goods.**

Fla.App. 3 Dist. 2003. Genuine issues of material fact existed as to the existence and cause of defects in plastic tubes made by manufacturer, whether distributor provided timely and sufficient notice of the defects to manufacturer, and the nature of manufacturer's response, precluding summary judgment on manufacturer's claims against distributor for unpaid invoices, and distributor's counterclaims for nonconforming goods.—Nomo Research, Inc. v. CCL Plastic Packaging, Inc., 862 So.2d 785, rehearing denied.

Fla.App. 4 Dist. 2018. Whether a buyer's rejection of goods was within a reasonable time pursuant to the Uniform Commercial Code (UCC) is a factual issue to be decided by a jury and cannot be resolved on summary judgment.—Twin Rivers Engineering, Inc. v. Pacer USA, LLC, 257 So.3d 140.

☞**2794(5). Revocation of acceptance.**

Fla.App. 2 Dist. 1989. Material issue of fact as to whether buyer of Christmas trees had rejected defective trees or revoked acceptance and whether the rejection or revocation of acceptance was within a reasonable time precluded summary judgment in favor or seller in an action brought by buyer for recision or breach of contract.—Ballas v. Spolyar, 548 So.2d 1168.

☞**2795. —— Amounts payable; price.**

S.D.Fla. 2020. Genuine issues of material fact existed as to whether the manufacturer of a chemical used in livestock facilities for sanitizing and disinfecting acted in good faith under Article 2 of the Uniform Commercial Code (UCC), as adopted in Florida, in setting a price for the chemical, which the manufacturer sold to a buyer pursuant to a license agreement that contained an open price term, including the parties' inten-

tions in setting an open price term and the reasonableness of the open price term, precluding summary judgment for a company that acquired the buyer, in the manufacturer's action against the company for breach of contract. Fla. Stat. Ann. §§ 672.103(1)(b), 672.305(2); Fed. R. Civ. P. 56(a).—ConSeal International Incorporated v. Neogen Corporation, 488 F.Supp.3d 1257.

☞**2797. —— Payment.**

Fla.App. 1 Dist. 2011. Genuine issue of material fact as to whether buyer made payment for materials and construction equipment purchased on credit for which seller asserted that buyer was responsible precluded summary judgment in seller's action to recover a debt.—Grant Builders Group, Inc. v. South Bay Ace Hardware Lumber and Paint Co., 58 So.3d 348.

Fla.App. 3 Dist. 1985. In action by seller against buyer for money allegedly due for merchandise sold and delivered, genuine issue of fact existed as to whether buyer authorized seller to strike payment in full language on buyer's check, precluding summary judgment for buyer.—D & E Trading Co. v. Southern Synthetics, Inc., 466 So.2d 394.

☞**2799. —— Assurance of performance.**

† **C.A.11 (Fla.) 2011.** Genuine issue of material fact, as to whether Venezuelan buyer and its U.S. purchasing agent provided adequate assurances of performance of contracts for delivery of sugar and beef, precluded summary judgment for international food commodities seller on its claims of anticipatory repudiation of those contracts under Florida law. West's F.S.A. § 672.609.—Validsa, Inc. v. PDVSA Services, Inc., 424 Fed.Appx. 862.

☞**2800. —— Repudiation.**

N.D.Fla. 2023. Genuine issue of material fact existed as to whether buyer's principal agreed to modify agreement for sale of ilmenite so as to include additional term providing that buyer would not resell ilmenite to Chinese buyers, due to competition with seller's own supply to the region, precluding grant of summary judgment on question of whether buyer breached contract through anticipatory repudiation when it stated it would not continue with sale absent confirmation that buyer agreed to resale limitation.—US Iron FLA, LLC v. GMA Garnett (USA) Corp., 660 F.Supp.3d 1212.

☞**2805. —— Cancellation or termination of contract.**

S.D.Fla. 2020. Genuine issues of material fact existed as to whether a manufacturer of a chemical used in livestock facilities for sanitizing and disinfecting and a company that acquired a buyer of the chemical agreed to the termination of the manufacturer's license agreement with the buyer, precluding summary judgment for the company on its request that damages be limited to the minimum purchase requirements for the year leading up to the purported termination, in the manufacturer's action against the company for breach of contract under Florida law. Fed. R. Civ. P. 56(a).—ConSeal International Incorporated v. Neogen Corporation, 488 F.Supp.3d 1257.

☞**2809. —— In general.**

Fla.App. 1 Dist. 2012. Genuine issues of material fact as to whether garbage truck's tarping unit was "safety device," for purposes of statute prohibiting vehicles from being wider than 102 inches, exclusive of safety devices, and as to whether garbage hauler substantially altered tarping unit precluded summary judgment in favor of truck's manufacturer and installer of tarping unit in hauler's action asserting claims for strict liability, breach of implied warranty of merchantability, and contribution toward bicyclist's personal-injury settlement. West's F.S.A. § 316.515.—Sunbelt Environmental, Inc. v. Gulf Coast Truck & Equipment Co., Inc., 82 So.3d 1196, on remand Smith v. Sunbelt Environmental, Inc., 2013 WL 5526011.

Fla.App. 1 Dist. 1991. Genuine issue of material fact, as to whether recreational vehicle seller was manufacturer's agent for purposes of receiving notice under contract of alleged defects in subject vehicle, precluded summary judgment for manufacturer on buyer's third-party claim against manufacturer for breach of warranty.—Foote v. Green Tree Acceptance, Inc., 597 So.2d 803, modified on clarification.

Fla.App. 1 Dist. 1986. Issues of material fact concerning number of opportunities afforded sellers to effect repairs of automobile during warranty period precluded summary judgment in action for breach of warranty under Magnuson-Moss Warranty Act. Magnuson-Moss Warranty—Federal Trade Commission Improvement Act, § 101 et seq., 15 U.S.C.A. § 2301 et seq.—Gilbert v. Astro Lincoln Mercury, Inc., 496 So.2d 987.

Fla.App. 2 Dist. 1983. In seller's action on two promissory notes given in sale of business, failure of affidavit supporting seller's motion for summary judgment to contravene buyers' affirmative defenses or allegations in counterclaim concerning breach of warranties and failure to disclose material evidence raised substantial fact issue precluding summary judgment. West's F.S.A. §§ 817.15, 817.41.—Foxfire Inn of Stuart, Florida, Inc. v. Neff, 433 So.2d 1304.

Fla.App. 2 Dist. 1966. Where buyer of second hand truck-tractor averred that seller represented and warranted truck-tractor to be in good operating condition and where letter from seller referred to a warranty, an issue of existence of warranty was raised precluding summary judgment.—Enix v. Diamond T. Sales & Service Co., 188 So.2d 48, certiorari denied 195 So.2d 566.

Fla.App. 3 Dist. 1984. In automobile buyer's breach of warranty, negligence, and strict liability action against seller of automobile, evidence that steering mechanism of automobile locked, causing car to veer off road into bridge embankment, and that seller had not performed any repairs or service of car for which it was responsible raised substantial fact issue as to whether there was defect in automobile which precluded summary judgment under strict liability and breach of warranty theories; summary judgment was proper, however, on issue of negligence. West's F.S.A. § 672.314.—Perry v. Luby Chevrolet, Inc., 446 So.2d 1150.

Fla.App. 3 Dist. 1962. Summary judgment was improperly granted plaintiff in an action for breach of warranty that wire sold would meet certain specifications where genuine issues of fact were presented, whether wire did meet specifications and whether rusting and pitting were due to defendant's failure properly to package it or to plaintiff's negligence in storing outdoors for a protracted period. 30 F.S.A. Rules of Civil Procedure, rule 1.36(c).—C. M. Whitney Co. v. Mid-State Prestressed Concrete Co., 140 So.2d 641, certiorari denied 146 So.2d 376.

Fla.App. 4 Dist. 1997. Genuine issue of material fact as to whether reasonable use of scientific procedures and techniques could have detected viral hepatitis in blood which recipient received

in transfusion, as required to allow recovery on recipient's implied warranty claim against blood supplier, precluded summary judgment. West's F.S.A. § 672.316(5).—Raskin v. Community Blood Centers of South Florida, Inc., 699 So.2d 1014, rehearing denied, review denied 707 So.2d 1124.

Fla.App. 4 Dist. 1986. Material question of fact as to whether hot water heater installed in buyer's home was defective at time of sale precluded entry of summary judgment for either party in buyer's breach of warranty action.—Marcus v. Anderson/Gore Homes, Inc., 498 So.2d 1051.

Fla.App. 4 Dist. 1975. Fact issues were presented as to whether automobile manufacturer through its regional service representative warranted or fraudulently represented to plaintiff the new and unused condition of automobile purchased by plaintiff and whether manufacturer was vicariously liable for claimed warranties and fraudulent representations made by dealer, through its employees, precluding summary judgment in action for damages for fraud, misrepresentation and breach of warranty. 31 West's F.S.A. Rules of Civil Procedure, rule 1.510(c).—Chrysler Motor Corp. v. Nail, 317 So.2d 147.

☞2810. —— **Express warranties.**

Fla.App. 1 Dist. 1962. Corporate defendant was not entitled to summary judgment in action for alleged breach of alleged seller's warranty of fitness in sale of farm tractor, where there existed genuine issue of fact as to whether there was breach of warranty, express or implied, on part of corporate defendant.—Posey v. Ford Motor Co., 138 So.2d 781.

☞2811. —— **Warranties imposed by law; implied warranties.**

† C.A.11 (Fla.) 2019. Inconsistencies in expert's declaration and deposition did not create a material factual dispute on summary judgment in breach of implied warranty of merchantability action about whether pressure switch installed by marine chiller unit manufacturer caused its unit's evaporator heat exchanger to freeze; undisputed evidence established that water hoses were improperly plumbed in reverse, and while expert stated in initial declaration that, had properly-sized low pressure switch been installed, evaporator would not have frozen even with reversed connections, during deposition expert abandoned that theory and stated that the reversed connections resulted in outflowing cold water bypassing the freeze protection switch and causing heat exchanger to freeze.—Tri-Lady Marine, Ltd. v. Aqua-Air Manufacturing, 760 Fed.Appx. 969.

N.D.Fla. 2001. Issues of fact as to terms of sales contract which was formed through parties' performance, rather than through exchange of forms, precluded summary judgment in buyer's action against seller for breach of implied warranty of fitness for particular purpose.—Coastal & Native Plant Specialties, Inc. v. Engineered Textile Products, Inc., 139 F.Supp.2d 1326.

S.D.Fla. 2013. Under Florida law, genuine issue of material fact as to amount of healthcare product buyer/reseller's lost profits and whether buyer failed to mitigate, as a result of manufacturer/seller's inaccurate representations that the products were wheat and gluten free, precluded summary judgment on issue of damages stemming from buyer's claims against seller for breach of indemnity agreement and breach of implied warranty of merchantability.—Nature's Products, Inc. v. Natrol, Inc., 990 F.Supp.2d

† This Case was not selected for publication in the National Reporter System

1307, appeal dismissed (11th cir. 14-10907), and appeal dismissed (11th cir. 15-11180).

Fla.App. 1 Dist. 1998. Genuine issues of material fact existed relating to intent and scope of release between homeowners and construction company, precluding summary judgment in homeowners' action against company for negligent construction, breach of implied warranty, and breach of contract.—Floyd v. Homes Beautiful Const. Co., 710 So.2d 177.

Fla.App. 1 Dist. 1962. Corporate defendant was not entitled to summary judgment in action for alleged breach of alleged seller's warranty of fitness in sale of farm tractor, where there existed genuine issue of fact as to whether there was breach of warranty, express or implied, on part of corporate defendant.—Posey v. Ford Motor Co., 138 So.2d 781.

☞**2814. —— Parties to warranties, privity, and third-party beneficiaries.**
Fla.App. 1 Dist. 1962. Individual defendant was not entitled to summary judgment in action for alleged breach of alleged seller's warranty of fitness in sale of farm tractor, where there existed genuine issue of fact whether individual defendant, acting in individual capacity and independent of any connection he may have had with corporate defendant, was bound by any warranty, express or implied, on his part.—Posey v. Ford Motor Co., 138 So.2d 781.

☞**2815. —— Notice and opportunity to cure.**
Fla.App. 2 Dist. 2022. Issue of material fact existed as to whether car manufacturer was furnished sufficient opportunity to cure its alleged breach of warranty under Magnuson-Moss Warranty Act with respect to car that required numerous repairs, precluding summary judgment in car purchaser's lawsuit against manufacturer for breach of warranty under Act. Federal Trade Commission Improvement Act § 110, 15 U.S.C.A. § 2310.—Mack v. Hyundai Motor America Corporation, 346 So.3d 661, review dismissed 2022 WL 17246322.

☞**2819. —— Rescission in general.**
Fla.App. 3 Dist. 2015. Genuine issue of material fact existed as to whether cruise ship passenger knew price quoted by cruise ship jewelry store for a loose diamond was in error, an element required to establish defense of unilateral mistake of fact, precluding summary judgment in breach of sales contract action where store sought rescission of the sales contract based on unilateral mistake of fact.—DePrince v. Starboard Cruise Services, Inc., 163 So.3d 586, abrogated in later appeal 271 So.3d 11.

☞**2820. —— Monetary remedies and damages in general.**
S.D.Fla. 2004. Factual issues as to whether assets seller suffered damages as a result of buyer's allegedly delinquent installment payment precluded summary judgment for seller on claim alleging that late payment breached parties' contract.—Centurion Air Cargo, Inc. v. United Parcel Service Co., 300 F.Supp.2d 1281, affirmed 420 F.3d 1146.

(G) INSTRUCTIONS.

☞**2848. —— In general.**
Fla.App. 3 Dist. 2018. Jury instruction on unilateral mistake as a defense to enforcement of a contract adequately instructed the jury on the elements of the defense in diamond buyer's ac-

tion to enforce his contract with the operator of a cruise ship jewelry store for the sale of a 20-carat diamond for millions of dollars less than its actual value, even though instruction included extra language on inducement, which was not an element of the defense; jury was instructed that store operator was required to show "that there was no inexcusable lack of due care under the circumstance on its part," that "denial of release from the agreement would be inequitable," and that the buyer "did not change his position in any way and that granting relief would not be unjust."—DePrince v. Starboard Cruise Services, Inc., 271 So.3d 11.

XII. RIGHTS AND LIABILITIES AS TO THIRD PERSONS.

(C) GOOD-FAITH PURCHASERS.

☞**2921. In general.**
Fla.App. 4 Dist. 2022. Purpose of Uniform Commercial Code section providing protection for a good faith purchase of goods is to protect the buyer in the ordinary course of business and thus to eliminate impediments to the free flow of commerce. Fla. Stat. Ann. § 672.403(2).—Santana Equestrian Private Financial, LLC v. Richtmyer, 349 So.3d 441.

☞**2939. Title and rights acquired by good-faith purchasers.**
Fla.App. 4 Dist. 2022. Buyer in the ordinary course of business obtains good title by virtue of Uniform Commercial Code section providing protection for a good faith purchase of goods. Fla. Stat. Ann. § 672.403(2).—Santana Equestrian Private Financial, LLC v. Richtmyer, 349 So.3d 441.

(D) ENTRUSTED GOODS.

☞**2952. Entrustment to merchant.**
Fla.App. 4 Dist. 2022. If goods are entrusted to merchant who deals in goods of that kind and ultimately goods are sold to good-faith buyer in ordinary course of business, then entruster's intent, intervening sales, and merchant's fraudulent actions are irrelevant. Fla. Stat. Ann. §§ 671.201(9), 672.403.—Santana Equestrian Private Financial, LLC v. Richtmyer, 349 So.3d 441.

(G) ACTIONS.

☞**2991. —— Weight and sufficiency.**
Fla.App. 4 Dist. 2022. Testimony of equestrian expert was sufficient to establish that buyer of competitive jumping horse was a good faith purchaser in ordinary course of business, and thus that its purchase of horse from seller, a party allegedly entrusted to sell the horse by a third-party entrusted with horse by horse's owner, was protected under Article 2 of the Uniform Commercial Code (UCC), as adopted in Florida; expert witness testified that seller was an established company in business of buying and selling jumping horses, buyer considered horse's athletic ability and equestrian records, including viewing horses' performance on jump and opinion of a professional rider, and expert testified that the sales price and negotiations were typical in the industry and not out of the ordinary. Fla. Stat. Ann. §§ 671.201(9), 672.403.—Santana Equestrian Private Financial, LLC v. Richtmyer, 349 So.3d 441.

† This Case was not selected for publication in the National Reporter System

XIII. CONDITIONAL SALES.

Secured transactions, particularly those within the scope of Article 9 of the Uniform Commercial Code, see SECURED TRANSACTIONS. Chattel mortgages, see CHATTEL MORTGAGES.

SALVAGE

I. RIGHT TO COMPENSATION.

Research Notes

See West's Florida Legal Forms, Specialized Forms.

⊶**1. Nature and grounds in general.**
M.D.Fla. 2021. General maritime law embraces policies that promote rescue and salvage. —Jolly v. Hoegh Autoliners Shipping AS, 546 F.Supp.3d 1105.

The "law of salvage" is a uniquely maritime construct that rewards those who voluntarily engage in rescuing persons or property in distress. —Id.

S.D.Fla. 2020. Under maritime salvage law, a vessel owner benefiting from a salvor's rescue must pay a price for the recovery of his vessel.— Offshore Marine Towing, Inc. v. Gismondi, 504 F.Supp.3d 1349.

To determine whether a salvage occurred, which is a service that is voluntarily rendered to a vessel needing assistance and is designed to relieve her from some distress or danger either present or to be reasonably apprehended, a court must find three elements: (1) marine peril; (2) voluntary services rendered; and (3) success in whole or part.—Id.

⊶**5. Existence and extent of peril.**
S.D.Fla. 2020. To determine whether a maritime peril existed, which is a necessary element for a valid salvage claim, a court examines whether, at the time the assistance was rendered, the vessel was in a situation that might expose her to loss or destruction.—Offshore Marine Towing, Inc. v. Gismondi, 504 F.Supp.3d 1349.

The danger need not be immediate or actual for a maritime peril to exist, which is a necessary element for a valid salvage claim; all that is necessary is reasonable apprehension of injury or destruction if the salvage services are not rendered.—Id.

Reasonable grounds existed to believe that vessel at least was in minimal apprehension of danger, as required for salvage claim; although vessel was not in immediate or absolute marine peril, vessel ran aground near rock and coral, grounding occurred during high tide shortly before falling tide, and it was left at mercy of wind and water which could have pushed it in such way as to damage it further.—Id.

The peril necessary to give rise to a claim for salvage need not be immediate or absolute; only the potential for danger is required.—Id.

⊶**7. —— In general.**
S.D.Fla. 2020. Voluntary service, as required for a salvage claim, is rendered in the absence of a legal duty or obligation.—Offshore Marine Towing, Inc. v. Gismondi, 504 F.Supp.3d 1349.

Whatever may be the motive impelling the true volunteer in undertaking the enterprise, whether for reasons of monetary gain, whether to aid in his own rescue, or even where his services have been offered through error, it cannot detract from the voluntary status which the law accords to him, when determining whether a salvage occurred; thus, professional salvors, who perform their services for monetary gain, may claim salvage awards.—Id.

Maritime salvage company did not have legal duty to salvage vessel, and therefore it acted voluntarily, as required for salvage claim, since company was not governmental entity and was not under any other legal obligation to act as it did.—Id.

Maritime law distinguishes between pure salvage and contract salvage; in a pure salvage situation, the salvor is a volunteer and the compensation is dependent on success.—Id.

Efforts of maritime salvage company likely constituted salvage, and therefore arrest could not be vacated, where company voluntarily conducted salvage operation and ultimately succeeded in removing vessel from peril.—Id.

⊶**16. Services rendered under contract.**
S.D.Fla. 2020. Where a contract does not contain either an agreement to pay a given sum or to pay without regard to success, but provides only that the salvor will be entitled to an award in the event of success on a "no cure-no pay" basis, the services do not become contract salvage but retain their status as pure salvage services.—Offshore Marine Towing, Inc. v. Gismondi, 504 F.Supp.3d 1349.

S.D.Fla. 2020. Vessel owner's judicial admission that maritime salvage company performed salvage work voluntarily had no effect on the validity of salvage contract.—Offshore Marine Towing, Inc. v. Gismondi, 473 F.Supp.3d 1353, reconsideration denied 2020 WL 5742646.

⊶**17. Beneficial result of services.**
S.D.Fla. 2020. Maritime law distinguishes between pure salvage and contract salvage; in a pure salvage situation, the salvor is a volunteer and the compensation is dependent on success.— Offshore Marine Towing, Inc. v. Gismondi, 504 F.Supp.3d 1349.

Lack of success, no matter how great the effort, will preclude a salvage award.—Id.

The salvor is precluded from obtaining a salvage reward when no benefit is conferred because the purpose of engaging in a salvage operation is to render a beneficial service to the owner or vessel.—Id.

Efforts of maritime salvage company likely constituted salvage, and therefore arrest could not be vacated, where company voluntarily conducted salvage operation and ultimately succeeded in removing vessel from peril.—Id.

II. AMOUNT AND APPORTIONMENT.

⊶**25. Discretion of court as to amount.**
S.D.Fla. 2020. The value of a salvage award is largely a matter of fact and discretion, which cannot be reduced to precise rules, but depends upon a consideration of all the circumstances of each case.—Offshore Marine Towing, Inc. v. Gismondi, 504 F.Supp.3d 1349.

⊶**26. Elements in determination of amount.**
S.D.Fla. 2020. The value of a salvage award is largely a matter of fact and discretion, which cannot be reduced to precise rules, but depends upon a consideration of all the circumstances of each case.—Offshore Marine Towing, Inc. v. Gismondi, 504 F.Supp.3d 1349.

† This Case was not selected for publication in the National Reporter System

⚖27. Amount awarded and computation in general.

S.D.Fla. 2020. Promptitude, skill, and energy displayed in rendering service and saving vessel weighed in favor of salvor on claim for salvage award, since salvor with 30 years of experience promptly arrived on scene within minutes and it was exceptionally energetic in pulling vessel away from jetty and securing safety of vessel in under 15 minutes.—Offshore Marine Towing, Inc. v. Gismondi, 504 F.Supp.3d 1349.

⚖29. Peril at sea.

S.D.Fla. 2020. A situation of little peril to the grounded vessel or to the towing vessel results in a low order salvage award.—Offshore Marine Towing, Inc. v. Gismondi, 504 F.Supp.3d 1349.

Vessel was in minimal apprehension of danger, weighing in favor of low order salvage award, where salvage operation occurred in broad daylight, while seas were relatively calm, weather clear and sunny, and few feet from beach in water so shallow that person could walk across it to reach vessel.—Id.

Risk by salvor of walking across rocks in waves was not extraordinary in nature and potential for injury was augmented by salvor's own poor judgment, weighing in favor of low order salvor award, since there was no visibly imminent threat to vessel, everyone on vessel was wearing a life jacket and no one was injured, and salvor could have minimized his risk.—Id.

⚖30. Stranding.

S.D.Fla. 2020. Time and labor expended by professional salvage team in ungrounding vessel were minimal, weighing in favor of low order salvor award, since vessel readily came off ground, special equipment was not required or used, and ungrounding could be regarded as routine and simple.—Offshore Marine Towing, Inc. v. Gismondi, 504 F.Supp.3d 1349.

⚖34. Towage.

S.D.Fla. 2020. Value of property employed by salvor in rendering service and danger to which property was exposed weighed in favor of low order salvor award, since only one towboat was needed to pull vessel off jetty and it was able to do so within relatively short amount of time.— Offshore Marine Towing, Inc. v. Gismondi, 504 F.Supp.3d 1349.

⚖36. Contracts as to compensation.

S.D.Fla. 2020. Salvage contract for beached vessel was not ambiguous, even though it provided both for arbitration and resolution of claims in federal court, where the contract contemplated arbitration to resolve any dispute regarding salvage or concerning reasonableness of fees while resolution of claims by federal courts under the contract was only for purposes of securing a maritime lien and resolving issues concerning the arrest of the vessel and the posted security.— Offshore Marine Towing, Inc. v. Gismondi, 473 F.Supp.3d 1353, reconsideration denied 2020 WL 5742646.

III. LIEN AND RECOVERY.

Research Notes

Salvage; liens; libels in admiralty, see West's Federal Forms.

⚖39. Nature and incidents of lien.

C.A.11 (Fla.) 2017. Performance of salvage services, like furnishing of other services to ship, gives rise to maritime lien.—Salvors, Inc. v. Unidentified Wrecked & Abandoned Vessel, 861 F.3d 1278.

Maritime liens arising from salvage services presume that claimant participated in salvage of property at issue, but claimant need not actually salvage property in order to be entitled to maritime lien based on salvage services.—Id.

⚖42. Suits for salvage.

See ⚖42.1.

⚖42.1. —— In general.

C.A.11 (Fla.) 2017. Salvor's in rem proceeding to obtain exclusive salvaging rights to shipwreck was proper forum for salvor's former subcontractor to assert maritime lien based on salvor's purported use of its proprietary maps, software, and data to locate artifacts from shipwreck after subcontract's termination.—Salvors, Inc. v. Unidentified Wrecked & Abandoned Vessel, 861 F.3d 1278.

⚖45. —— Jurisdiction.

C.A.11 (Fla.) 2017. Salvor had constructive possession of shipwreck, and thus district court had admiralty jurisdiction over salvor's in rem action to obtain exclusive salvaging rights to shipwreck, even though wreck had occurred nearly 300 years earlier, and had been scattered along 41 miles of coastline, where salvor presented cannon from wreck to court.—Salvors, Inc. v. Unidentified Wrecked & Abandoned Vessel, 861 F.3d 1278.

So long as court constructively possesses part of scattered wreck, it may exercise constructive in rem jurisdiction over entirety of that wreck just as court would exercise constructive in rem jurisdiction over entirety of intact vessel.—Id.

Abandoned Shipwreck Act (ASA) did not denude district court of constructive in rem jurisdiction over shipwreck and return both title to res and jurisdiction over dispute to state, even though parties to initial litigation were no longer in existence, where salvor had commenced proceeding before ASA's effective date, original salvor's successor-in-interest annually sought adjudication of title to each year's salvaged artifacts, and state continued to consent to district court's arrangement of matter. Abandoned Shipwreck Act of 1987 §§ 2, 6, 7, 43 U.S.C.A. §§ 2101, 2105, 2106.—Id.

M.D.Fla. 2018. Republic of France showed by preponderance of evidence that unidentified shipwrecked vessel was French sovereign ship, and thus vessel possessed sovereign immunity from salvor's in rem action, depriving District Court of subject matter jurisdiction; shipwreck site was in vicinity where French sovereign ship sank, shipwreck site included French cannons consistent with those listed in French sovereign ship's records, salvor found stone monument bearing French king's coat of arms at shipwreck site, and contemporaneous record suggested that French sovereign ship was carrying multiple such monuments when it sank, whereas salvor merely speculated that vessel was some other unnamed non-French ship that somehow gained items recorded as having been on French sovereign ship when it sank.—Global Marine Exploration, Inc. v. Unidentified , Wrecked and (for Finders-Right Purposes) Abandoned Sailing Vessel, 348 F.Supp.3d 1221.

⚖46. —— Parties.

† **C.A.11 (Fla.) 2019.** Florida, a non-party, was not required to have standing in order to respond to salvor's motion for distribution of five

gold coins recovered from abandoned vessel that sunk off Florida coast and salvor's motion for status conference, where Florida's filings were court-ordered responses to salvor's request for a status conference and salvor's objections to magistrate's Report and Recommendation, Florida argued in responses that district court should not relitigate previously decided issues, and Florida did not attempt to make a claim and instead argued that all operative issues had been resolved either by agreements or previous district court orders.—Jupiter Wreck, Inc. v. Unidentified Wrecked and Abandoned Sailing Vessel, 762 Fed. Appx. 852.

Florida, a non-party, was not required to consent to suit in order to respond to salvor's motion for distribution of five gold coins recovered from abandoned vessel that sunk off Florida coast, salvor's motion for status conference, or salvor's objection to magistrate's Report and Recommendation; Florida's filings were court-ordered responses, nothing in Florida's responses suggested that it was attempting to seek relief, in the form of title adjudication or otherwise, from the federal courts, and Florida argued that status conference was unnecessary because all operative issues had been resolved either by its agreements with salvor or by district court.—Id.

C.A.11 (Fla.) 2017. Salvor's former subcontractor alleged sufficient injury to establish standing to intervene in salvor's in rem action to enforce its salvage rights by claiming that salvor unlawfully retained exclusive salvaging rights to forty-one-mile stretch of Florida coastline, thereby preventing it from conducting profitable salvage operations and causing it to suffer substantial loss of livelihood, that salvor damaged or destroyed artifacts, thereby forfeiting its salvage rights, and that it had maritime lien over recovered artifacts. U.S. Const. art. 3, § 2, cl. 1; Fed. R. Civ. P. 24(a)(2).—Salvors, Inc. v. Unidentified Wrecked & Abandoned Vessel, 861 F.3d 1278.

Salvor's former subcontractor was entitled to intervene as of right in salvor's in rem action to enforce its salvage rights in order to assert maritime lien based on salvor's purported use of its proprietary maps, software, and data to discover artifacts from shipwreck after subcontract's termination, even though state was party to suit, and district court had scheduled hearing on distribution of artifacts, where any disposition of action without allowing intervention would deprive subcontractor of opportunity to be heard on those in rem claims, there was no reason for state to advance subcontractor's interests, and no sale of artifacts was pending. Fed. R. Civ. P. 24(a).—Id.

⬾49. —— **Trial or hearing.**

† **C.A.11 (Fla.) 2015.** Genuine issues of material fact existed as to vessel's ability to move itself out of harm's way, and whether maritime peril existed, precluding summary judgment on maritime claim for salvage. Fed.Rules Civ.Proc.Rule 56, 28 U.S.C.A.—Biscayne Towing & Salvage, Inc. v. M/Y Backstage, 615 Fed.Appx. 608.

S.D.Fla. 2007. Genuine issues of material fact as to whether the benefit, if any, conferred upon a vessel by an alleged salvor's employees, who extinguished a fire on an inflatable tender tied up at the stern of a yacht, directly forward of the vessel's bow pulpit, was incidental to services rendered to the yacht and/or the tender, or was rendered directly to the vessel precluded summary judgment for the vessel on the salvor's claim for a salvage award.—Atlantis Marine Towing, Inc. v. THE M/V PRISCILLA, 491 F.Supp.2d 1096.

Genuine issues of material fact as to whether a vessel was exposed to marine peril as a result of a fire aboard an inflatable tender tied up at the stern of a yacht, directly forward of the vessel's bow pulpit, precluded summary judgment for the vessel in an action by the employer of workers who extinguished the fire, seeking a salvage award.—Id.

⬾51. —— **Appeal.**

† **C.A.11 (Fla.) 2019.** Salvor's motion for distribution of five gold coins recovered from abandoned vessel that sunk off Florida coast, motion for status conference, and, later, motion to strike Florida's response to its objections to magistrate's Report and Recommendation, were properly considered post-judgment motions that were fully resolved, and thus, Court of Appeals had jurisdiction to review district court orders denying motion for status conference and motion to strike, even though there was no final judgment in the docket, where prior district court opinion held that salvor, which had moved for a preliminary injunction seeking to prevent Florida and all others from interfering with its salvaging, was entitled to relief against any party except Florida, district court dismissed case and closed it for statistical purposes after salvor and Florida reached an agreement, and orders fully resolved motions that sparked it. 28 U.S.C.A. §§ 1291, 1292.—Jupiter Wreck, Inc. v. Unidentified Wrecked and Abandoned Sailing Vessel, 762 Fed. Appx. 852.

SCHOOLS

See EDUCATION

SCIRE FACIAS

⬾1. **Nature and scope of remedy.**

Fla.App. 4 Dist. 2023. A "scire facias," at common law, is defined as a judicial writ, founded on some matter of record, such as a judgment or a recognizance.—Marchisio v. Gurley, 376 So.3d 55.

SEAMEN

Research Notes

Seamen; carelessness; Jones Act; libels in admiralty, see West's Federal Forms.
See Wright & Miller, Federal Practice and Procedure: Civil.

⬾1. **Power to regulate and protect.**

S.D.Fla. 2021. Seamen are wards of admiralty whose rights federal courts are duty-bound to jealously protect.—Rybovich Boat Company, LLC v. M/Y BLUE STAR, 546 F.Supp.3d 1270.

S.D.Fla. 2006. Seaman's settlement and release must be carefully scrutinized.—Borcea v. Carnival Corp., 238 F.R.D. 664.

⬾2. **Who are seamen.**

S.D.Fla. 2021. There is a two-part test to establish seaman status under the Jones Act: first, the employee's duties must contribute to the function of the vessel or to the accomplishment of its mission, and, second, a seaman must have a connection to a vessel in navigation that is sub-

---

† **This Case was not selected for publication in the National Reporter System**

stantial both in terms of its duration and its nature. 46 U.S.C.A. § 30104 et seq.—Butts v. ALN Group, LLC, 512 F.Supp.3d 1301.

The fundamental purpose of only conferring seaman status on an employee who has a connection to a vessel in navigation that is substantial both in duration and nature is to separate the sea-based maritime employees who are entitled to Jones Act protection from those land-based workers who only have a transitory or sporadic connection to a vessel in navigation, and therefore whose employment does not regularly expose them to the perils of the sea. 46 U.S.C.A. § 30104 et seq.—Id.

Yacht chef sufficiently pled her status as a seaman under the Jones Act in action against yacht owners for negligence, failure to pay maintenance and cure, unseaworthiness, and false imprisonment, weighing against grant of owners' motion to dismiss for failure to state a claim; chef alleged that owners hired her with the assistance of a crew-placing agency, that her duties consisted of cooking for the vessel's crew, and that she assisted yacht owner with provisioning the vessel and hiring additional crew for the anticipated charter. 46 U.S.C.A. § 30104 et seq.—Id.

S.D.Fla. 2019. The Jones Act does not define the term "seaman" and therefore leaves to the courts the determination of exactly which maritime workers are entitled to admiralty's special protection. 46 U.S.C.A. § 30104.—NCL (Bahamas) Ltd. v. Kaczkowski, 396 F.Supp.3d 1185.

"Substantial connection" criterion, as part of determination whether a maritime worker is a seaman under the Jones Act, does not mechanically require the worker have a connection to one single vessel, as an identifiable fleet or a finite group of vessels subject to common ownership or control will qualify. 46 U.S.C.A. § 30104.—Id.

The fundamental purpose of substantial connection requirement for a maritime worker to qualify as seaman under Jones Act is to give full effect to the remedial scheme created by Congress and to separate the sea-based maritime employees who are entitled to Jones Act protection from those land-based workers who have only a transitory or sporadic connection to a vessel in navigation, and therefore whose employment does not regularly expose them to the perils of the sea. 46 U.S.C.A. § 30104.—Id.

The duration of a worker's connection to a vessel and the nature of a worker's activities, taken together, determine whether a maritime employee is a seaman under Jones Act. 46 U.S.C.A. § 30104.—Id.

A worker who spends less than about 30 percent of his time in the service of a vessel in navigation generally should not qualify as a seaman under the Jones Act. 46 U.S.C.A. § 30104.—Id.

The inquiry into the nature of the employee's connection to a vessel to determine whether the employee qualifies as a seaman under the Jones Act must concentrate on whether the employee's duties take him to sea. 46 U.S.C.A. § 30104.—Id.

Thirty-percent rule, which provides that a worker who spends less than about 30 percent of his time in the service of a vessel in navigation generally should not qualify as a seaman under the Jones Act, was relevant and thus applicable when deciding whether welder had substantial connection to vessel in navigation and thus was a seaman under Jones Act. 46 U.S.C.A. § 30104.—Id.

Thirty-percent rule, which provides that a worker who spends less than about 30 percent of

his time in the service of a vessel in navigation generally should not qualify as a seaman under the Jones Act, aims to distinguish sea-based maritime employees entitled to Jones Act protection from land-based workers who have only a transitory or sporadic connection to a vessel in navigation. 46 U.S.C.A. § 30104.—Id.

In evaluating the employment-related connection of a maritime worker to a vessel in navigation, courts should not employ a snapshot test for seaman status under the Jones Act, inspecting only the situation as it exists at the instant of the injury; a more enduring relationship is contemplated in the jurisprudence. 46 U.S.C.A. § 30104.—Id.

Borrowed servant status alone does not confer seaman status under the Jones Act. 46 U.S.C.A. § 30104.—Id.

Relevant time period under 30% percent rule, which considers time spent in service of a vessel in navigation to qualify as a seaman under the Jones Act, included both welder's employment with operator of passenger vessel and employment with independent contractor. 46 U.S.C.A. § 30104.—Id.

Courts determining whether a maritime worker qualifies as a seaman under the Jones Act may look outside the worker's time with a borrowing employer if he has been reassigned to a new position such that his essential duties or work location is permanently changed, rather than simply serving on a boat sporadically. 46 U.S.C.A. § 30104.—Id.

Specific facts of each case, especially one where the allegations involve a borrowing employer, must guide courts to determine whether an employee's entire employment is relevant or not to determination whether the employee qualifies as a seaman under the Jones Act. 46 U.S.C.A. § 30104.—Id.

Welder, who was employed by independent contractor and who was provided to work on operator's passenger vessel, failed to establish substantial connection to vessel in navigation and thus failed to qualify as "seaman" under the Jones Act; welder spent, at best, roughly 12% of work hours at sea working on operator's vessel in navigation. 46 U.S.C.A. § 30104.—Id.

Thirty percent figure, which considers time spent in service of a vessel in navigation to qualify as a seaman under the Jones Act, serves as a guideline, and departure from it may be justified in appropriate cases. 46 U.S.C.A. § 30104.—Id.

⚷**3. What law governs.**

Fla.App. 3 Dist. 2017. Jones Act does not per se prohibit a seaman who is a foreign national residing outside the United States from being bound by a contract provision mandating a specific foreign forum for disputes under the contract. 46 U.S.C.A. § 30104.—Durkovic v. Park West Galleries, Inc., 217 So.3d 159.

⚷**9. Seaworthiness of vessel.**

M.D.Fla. 2023. Vessel owners have an absolute duty to furnish a seaworthy vessel.—Sprengle v. Smith Maritime Inc., 660 F.Supp.3d 1337.

Vessel owner breaches its absolute duty to furnish seaworthy vessel when it provides vessel that is not reasonably fit for its intended purpose. —Id.

Absolute duty of vessel owners to furnish a seaworthy vessel extends not only to the vessel itself, but also to equipment appurtenant to the ship.—Id.

Duty of seaworthiness extends to equipment temporarily brought aboard by others.—Id.

A vessel can be rendered seaworthy by equipment of others.—Id.

Vessel is unseaworthy when its equipment is defective.—Id.

Equipment is defective, rendering a vessel unseaworthy, when it is not reasonably fit for its intended purpose.—Id.

To determine whether a vessel's equipment is reasonably fit, for purposes of determining whether that equipment renders the vessel unseaworthy, court should consider equipment's purpose, hazards, perils, and forces equipment will likely face, and ability of equipment to withstand those anticipated forces.—Id.

If vessel owner can reasonably anticipate that equipment will be used in certain manner, owner warrants that equipment is fit to meet all foreseeable hazards that accompany such use, for purposes of assessing whether equipment renders vessel unseaworthy.—Id.

If a vessel's equipment fails during anticipated use, it is unseaworthy.—Id.

A vessel owner's absolute duty to furnish a seaworthy ship exists independent from the duty to exercise reasonable care.—Id.

Liability of a vessel owner for unseaworthiness does not rest upon concepts of fault or negligence.—Id.

If an unseaworthy condition exists, no amount of care, prudence, or diligence will absolve the vessel owner.—Id.

In determining the threshold question of whether an unseaworthy condition exists, courts look to whether the equipment is reasonably fit for its intended purpose; this threshold inquiry concerns foreseeability, and it necessarily requires the language of negligence.—Id.

Unseaworthy condition arises when crew members dangerously misuse equipment that is otherwise seaworthy.—Id.

An unseaworthy condition can arise when crew members utilize an unsafe method of work.—Id.

⚖**11(1). In general.**

M.D.Fla. 2023. Shipowners must pay maintenance and cure to seamen who fall ill or are injured while in service of ship.—Sprengle v. Smith Maritime Inc., 660 F.Supp.3d 1337.

"Maintenance" is the right of a seaman to a daily stipend for living expenses.—Id.

"Cure" is a seaman's right to necessary medical expenses.—Id.

The right to maintenance and cure springs from the seaman's dependence on the ship; it does not turn on principles of negligence, causation, or seaworthiness.—Id.

M.D.Fla. 2021. "Maintenance and cure" involves a shipowner's duty to provide food, lodging, and medical services to a seaman injured while serving the ship.—Jolly v. Hoegh Autoliners Shipping AS, 546 F.Supp.3d 1105.

S.D.Fla. 2021. Maintenance and cure is a legal duty that obligates a vessel owner to provide for a seaman who becomes ill or injured in service of the ship; maintenance is a living allowance, while cure is intended to cover medical expenses.—Butts v. ALN Group, LLC, 512 F.Supp.3d 1301.

All a seaman must prove in order to establish a right to maintenance and cure is that the injury or illness arose during his employment; no causal connection to his duties need be shown.—Id.

S.D.Fla. 2019. "Maintenance and cure" is a common-law maritime remedy for seamen who

are injured while in the service of a vessel.—Hurtado v. Balerno International Ltd., 408 F.Supp.3d 1315.

The shipowner's obligation to pay maintenance and cure to a seaman who is injured while working on the ship is deep-rooted in maritime law and is an incident or implied term of a contract for maritime employment.—Id.

Courts are generally liberal in interpreting the duty of a vessel owner to pay maintenance and cure for workers injured while working aboard the vessel for the benefit and protection of seamen who are wards of the owner.—Id.

A shipowner's liability for maintenance and cure is among the most pervasive of all, and is not to be defeated by restrictive distinctions nor narrowly confined.—Id.

Ambiguities or doubts in the application of the law of maintenance and cure are resolved in favor of the seaman.—Id.

Maintenance and cure may be awarded to a seaman even where the seaman has suffered from an illness pre-existing his employment aboard the vessel, but there is a general principle that it will be denied where he knowingly or fraudulently conceals his illness from the shipowner.—Id.

To establish that the seaman knowingly or fraudulently concealed a preexisting condition from the vessel owner, as an affirmative defense to the owner's liability for maintenance and cure, the owner must show that: (1) the seaman intentionally misrepresented or concealed medical facts; (2) the nondisclosed facts were material to the owner's decision to hire him; and (3) a connection exists between the withheld medical information and the injury or illness forming the basis of the seaman's claim for maintenance and cure.—Id.

"Concealment" by a seaman of a preexisting condition, which provides defense to vessel owner's liability for maintenance and cure, occurs when the shipowner requires a seaman to submit to a pre-hiring medical examination or interview and the seaman intentionally misrepresents or conceals material medical facts.—Id.

"Nondisclosure," as may provide defense to vessel owner's liability for maintenance and cure, occurs when the shipowner does not require a pre-employment medical examination or interview; in that event, the rule is that a seaman must disclose a past illness or injury only when in his own opinion the shipowner would consider it a matter of importance.—Id.

When a seaman fails to disclose a preexisting medical condition which forms the basis of his claim for maintenance and cure, without the shipowner requiring a preemployment medical examination, the shipowner will be liable for maintenance and cure only if it is found that there existed reasonable grounds for the seaman's good-faith belief that he was fit for duty.—Id.

Yacht owner had obligation to pay maintenance and cure to seaman who suffered strangulated umbilical hernia while working aboard yacht for which he required surgery, notwithstanding owner's claim that seaman failed to disclose his alleged preexisting condition, where seaman's primary care doctor examined him two months before voyage and found no signs of umbilical hernia, and although seaman had asymptomatic inguinal hernia, that did not render him unfit to work on yacht, and seaman experienced no hernia symptoms prior to working on vessel, so that seaman had reasonable good-faith belief that he was fit for duty and his preexisting inguinal hernia diagnosis was not material to owner's decision to hire him, and the preexisting inguinal hernia condition was entirely unrelated to the disability seaman claimed resulting from his umbilical hernia.—Id.

In the context of a seaman's nondisclosure of a prior illness or injury, as may provide defense to vessel owner's liability for maintenance and cure, the materiality requirement and the nondisclosure requirement necessarily overlap; if the court finds that the seaman had a reasonable, good-faith belief that he was fit for duty, the court will necessarily find that he had reasonable grounds to believe that his preexisting condition was immaterial to the vessel owner.—Id.

The defense to a vessel owner's obligation to pay maintenance and cure that a seaman knowingly concealed material medical information will not prevail unless there is a causal link between the preexisting condition that was concealed and the seaman's disability incurred during the voyage.—Id.

The cause of action for maintenance and cure includes three specific items of recovery: (1) maintenance, which is a living allowance; (2) cure, which covers nursing and medical expenses; and (3) lost wages.—Id.

S.D.Fla. 2019. Unlike indemnity and negligence claims such as those governed by the Death on the High Seas Act or the Jones Act, a maintenance and cure claim does not rest upon negligence or culpability on the part of the owner or master, nor is it restricted to those cases where the seaman's employment is the cause of the injury or illness. Jones Act, 46 U.S.C.A. § 30104 et seq.; Death on the High Seas Act, 46 App.U.S.C.A. § 761 et seq.—Kennedy v. Carnival Corporation, 385 F.Supp.3d 1302, report and recommendation adopted 2019 WL 2254962.

A cause of action for maintenance and cure does not provide an award of compensation for any disability suffered by a seaman.—Id.

The right to "maintenance and cure" is an obligation of support running from the vessel owner or becomes ill, whenever the mariner is hurt or becomes ill, whatever its cause.—Id.

Fla.App. 3 Dist. 2022. "Maintenance and cure" is an ancient duty under law of admiralty that arises against a shipowner in favor of a seaman who becomes ill, injured, or incapacitated, or whose condition becomes aggravated or enhanced for any reason, at least until time that the seaman has achieved maximum medical recovery.—God's Blessing Ltd v. Salas, 339 So.3d 1086, appeal after remand 352 So.3d 405.

"Maintenance and cure" includes food, lodging, and medical services that a shipowner has legal responsibility to provide to a crew member injured in its service.—Id.

When there are ambiguities or doubts concerning a seaman's right to maintenance and cure, they are resolved in favor of the seaman.—Id.

Fla.App. 5 Dist. 2021. "Maintenance and cure," for purposes of maritime law, is a shipowner's legal responsibility to provide food, lodging, and medical services to a crew member injured in its service.—Magical Cruise Company Limited v. Martins, 330 So.3d 993, rehearing denied.

Fla.App. 5 Dist. 2019. Under general maritime law, a seaman has the right to receive compensation for food, lodging, and medical services resulting from illnesses or injuries suffered while working aboard a ship.—Grazette v. Magical Cruise Company Limited, 280 So.3d 1120.

☞11(4). Persons entitled.

S.D.Fla. 2021. Yacht chef stated a claim against yacht owners for maintenance and cure, where employee alleged that she was a seaman under the Jones Act, that she suffered injuries during employment on yacht when one owner recklessly navigated yacht's tender in an apparent attempt to sink nearby vessels, that owners refused to pay her maintenance and cure, and that she was experiencing continuing losses from her injury. 46 U.S.C.A. § 30104 et seq.—Butts v. ALN Group, LLC, 512 F.Supp.3d 1301.

Maintenance and cure are due to a seaman who becomes ill or injured in service of the ship, regardless of the fault of the employer or unseaworthiness of the ship.—Id.

Dismissal for failure to state a claim was not warranted as to yacht chef's claim against yacht owners for unseaworthiness, where owners' motion to dismiss was based solely on their argument that chef was not a seaman, but chef adequately pled her seaman status under the Jones Act. 46 U.S.C.A. § 30104 et seq.—Id.

S.D.Fla. 2019. Only seamen are entitled to assert claims under the Jones Act, claims for maintenance and cure, and claims for unseaworthiness of a vessel. 46 U.S.C.A. § 30104.—NCL (Bahamas) Ltd. v. Kaczkowski, 396 F.Supp.3d 1185.

☞11(5). Fault or negligence of seaman or fellow servants.

† C.A.11 (Fla.) 2018. Cruise ship contract worker's undisclosed back pain from degenerative disk issues was not sufficiently connected to herniated disks associated with slip and fall on onion peel in cruise ship corridor, so as to allow shipowner to invoke affirmative defense to worker's cure claim under the Jones Act, even though both affected the same location on the body. Jones Act, 46 U.S.C.A. § 30104 et seq.—Jackson v. NCL America, LLC, 730 Fed.Appx. 786.

S.D.Fla. 2021. Maintenance and cure are due to a seaman who becomes ill or injured in service of the ship, regardless of the fault of the employer or unseaworthiness of the ship.—Butts v. ALN Group, LLC, 512 F.Supp.3d 1301.

☞11(6). Extent and duration of liability.

C.A.11 (Fla.) 2019. When a seaman falls ill or suffers an injury in the service of the ship, maritime law requires her employer or the shipowner to provide maintenance and cure of the seaman for illness or injury during the period of the voyage, and in some cases for a period thereafter.—Cvoro v. Carnival Corporation, 941 F.3d 487.

† C.A.11 (Fla.) 2018. Cruise ship contract worker's cure claim under the Jones Act was properly limited to shipowner's network rates, where worker who was injured in slip and fall was directed to contact employee from shipowner's medical department for care, worker ignored this and instead hired a local doctor based on her attorney's advice, and shipowner sent letter to attorney informing him that his client would only be reimbursed up to its network rate. Jones Act, 46 U.S.C.A. § 30104 et seq.—Jackson v. NCL America, LLC, 730 Fed.Appx. 786.

M.D.Fla. 2023. A seaman's right to maintenance and cure is not open ended, and a shipowner's obligation to provide maintenance and cure ends at point of maximum medical improvement (MMI).—Sprengle v. Smith Maritime Inc., 660 F.Supp.3d 1337.

A seaman reaches maximum medical improvement (MMI), ending the shipowner's obligation to provide maintenance and cure, when it is not reasonably possible that future medical treatment will result in the betterment of the seaman's condition.—Id.

M.D.Fla. 2021. "Maintenance and cure" involves a shipowner's duty to provide food, lodging, and medical services to a seaman injured while serving the ship.—Jolly v. Hoegh Autoliners Shipping AS, 546 F.Supp.3d 1105.

S.D.Fla. 2021. Yacht chef stated a claim against yacht owners for maintenance and cure, where employee alleged that she was a seaman under the Jones Act, that she suffered injuries during employment on yacht when one owner recklessly navigated yacht's tender in an apparent attempt to sink nearby vessels, that owners refused to pay her maintenance and cure, and that she was experiencing continuing losses from her injury. 46 U.S.C.A. § 30104 et seq.—Butts v. ALN Group, LLC, 512 F.Supp.3d 1301.

S.D.Fla. 2019. A shipowner's obligation to pay maintenance and cure continues until the seaman has reached maximum cure.—Hurtado v. Balerno International Ltd., 408 F.Supp.3d 1315.

Maximum cure is the date on which further treatment will result in no betterment of the seaman's condition, so that the shipowner's maintenance and cure obligation terminates.—Id.

Seaman who suffered from strangulated umbilical hernia while working aboard vessel, which required surgery that was performed in Cuba, had not yet reached maximum medical improvement, and thus, vessel owner's obligation to pay maintenance and cure continued, in light of treating physician's expert opinion that hernia was improperly repaired in Cuba, causing it to reoccur, causing post-surgical scar to heal incorrectly, resulting in seaman's ongoing abdominal pain, and requiring additional surgery.—Id.

A seaman is entitled to recover the reasonable cost of food and lodging, in an action for maintenance and cure, provided he has incurred such expenses.—Id.

If the seaman presents evidence of his food and lodging expenses, in an action for maintenance and cure, the court must then estimate both the seaman's actual costs of food and lodging and the reasonable cost of food and lodging in the seaman's locality.—Id.

In determining reasonable food and lodging costs, in a maintenance and cure action, the court may consider maintenance rates awarded in other cases.—Id.

Seamen have a claim for compensation for the suffering and physical injury which follow when the vessel owner's failure to provide maintenance and cure aggravates the illness.—Id.

A shipowner who is in fact liable for maintenance and cure, but who has been reasonable in denying liability, may be held liable only for the amount of maintenance and cure, and not for pain and suffering resulting from the delay in providing maintenance and cure.—Id.

If the shipowner has refused to pay maintenance and cure without a reasonable defense, he becomes liable in addition for compensatory pain and suffering damages resulting from the failure to pay maintenance and cure.—Id.

Fla.App. 3 Dist. 2022. "Maintenance and cure" is an ancient duty under law of admiralty that arises against a shipowner in favor of a seaman who becomes ill, injured, or incapacitated, or whose condition becomes aggravated or enhanced for any reason, at least until time that the seaman has achieved maximum medical recovery.—God's Blessing Ltd v. Salas, 339 So.3d 1086, appeal after remand 352 So.3d 405.

Fla.App. 5 Dist. 2021. "Maintenance and cure," for purposes of maritime law, is a shipowner's legal responsibility to provide food, lodging, and medical services to a crew member injured in its service.—Magical Cruise Company Limited v. Martins, 330 So.3d 993, rehearing denied.

Obligation of a shipowner to provide maintenance and cure under maritime law to a crew member injured in its service concludes when a seaman reaches maximum medical improvement (MMI).—Id.

Under maritime law, once a seaman's incapacity is declared to be permanent, the shipowner's obligation to provide maintenance and cure ends; thus, maintenance and cure must only be provided until it appears that future treatment will merely relieve pain and suffering but not otherwise improve the seaman's physical condition.—Id.

Fla.App. 5 Dist. 2019. The duty to provide compensation to a seaman, that is, maintenance and cure, continues during a seaman's recuperative period until maximum medical recovery, or maximum medical improvement (MMI), is reached.—Grazette v. Magical Cruise Company Limited, 280 So.3d 1120.

Claims for maintenance and cure are deemed to have accrued when the seaman becomes incapacitated to do a seaman's work, and continue until the seaman reaches maximum medical improvement (MMI).—Id.

⨀11(7). Subsequent conduct or conditions affecting liability.

S.D.Fla. 2019. A seaman is not barred from recovering maintenance and cure when he is forced by financial necessity to return to his regular employment.—Hurtado v. Balerno International Ltd., 408 F.Supp.3d 1315.

⨀11(9). Actions.

S.D.Fla. 2019. Once the seaman establishes his right to maintenance and cure, the burden of persuasion shifts to the shipowner to prove that the seaman has reached the point of maximum medical improvement.—Hurtado v. Balerno International Ltd., 408 F.Supp.3d 1315.

The seaman's burden of producing evidence of food and lodging expenses is feather light, in an action to recover maintenance and cure, and a court may award reasonable expenses, even if the precise amount of actual expenses is not conclusively proved.—Id.

To support a claim for recovery of lodging and food costs, in a maintenance and cure action, a seaman need not present evidence of the reasonable rate; a court may take judicial notice of the prevailing rate for such costs in the seaman's locality.—Id.

Seaman who suffered from strangulated umbilical hernia while working aboard vessel, for which he underwent surgery in Cuba, was entitled to recover $56,486.16 for reasonable food and lodging expenses, in maintenance and cure action; seaman provided itemized list of food and lodging expenses he incurred while in Cuba for three weeks after surgery totaling $4,166.16, and his estimated food and lodging expenses after he returned to the United States, as based on rates awarded in other cases, were $60 per day for 872 days.—Id.

Seaman who suffered from strangulated umbilical hernia while working aboard vessel, for which he underwent surgery in Cuba, was entitled to recover $7,000 for cost of future additional surgery, in maintenance and cure action, based

† This Case was not selected for publication in the National Reporter System

on undisputed testimony from seaman's treating physician that seaman required another surgery because his hernia was improperly repaired in Cuba, causing it to reoccur.—Id.

If the vessel owner not only lacks a reasonable defense for his refusal to pay seaman maintenance and cure, but has also exhibited callousness and indifference to the seaman's plight, he becomes liable for punitive damages and attorney fees.—Id.

Awards of pain and suffering, based on vessel owner's failure to pay maintenance and cure, are fact-specific and depend to a great extent on the factfinder's observation of the seaman and its subjective determination of the amount needed to achieve full compensation.—Id.

In estimating an award for pain and suffering, based on a vessel owner's failure to pay maintenance and cure, the court may derive rough guidance from past awards to seamen in other cases.—Id.

Seaman who suffered from strangulated umbilical hernia while working aboard vessel, for which he underwent surgery in Cuba, was entitled to recover pain and suffering damages based on vessel owner's refusal to pay seaman maintenance and cure without a reasonable defense; owner refused to provide seaman with $1,000 deposit so that he could receive hernia repair surgery at initial hospital seaman presented at in Cuba, which forced seaman to wait in pain for two days until he was transfered to public hospital, which was significantly inferior to initial hospital, where he was eligible for free surgery, public hospital botched the surgery, resulting in reoccurrence of hernia and requiring additional surgery, and seaman was unable to obtain additional surgery and continued to suffer pain and discomfort because of owner's failure to pay maintenance and cure for more than two years.—Id.

Seaman who suffered from strangulated umbilical hernia while working aboard vessel, for which he underwent surgery in Cuba, was entitled to recover $300,000 in damages for pain and suffering based on vessel owner's refusal to pay seaman maintenance and cure without a reasonable defense; owner refused to provide seaman with $1,000 deposit so that he could receive hernia repair surgery at initial hospital seaman presented at in Cuba, which forced seaman to wait in pain for two days until he was transfered to public hospital, which was significantly inferior to initial hospital, where he was eligible for free surgery, public hospital botched the surgery, resulting in reoccurrence of hernia and requiring additional surgery, seaman has been unable to obtain additional surgery and has continued to suffer pain and discomfort because of owner's failure to pay maintenance and cure for more than two years, and award was in line with other similar cases of prolonged suffering caused by owner's denial of seaman's basic medical needs.—Id.

Punitive damages and attorney fees may be awarded to a seaman under general maritime law for the willful and wanton disregard of the maintenance and cure obligation.—Id.

Seaman who suffered from strangulated umbilical hernia while working aboard vessel, for which he underwent surgery in Cuba, was entitled to recover punitive damages based on vessel owner's shocking disregard for seaman's well-being and indifference to seaman's suffering, as demonstrated by owner's conduct in refusing to pay for seaman's emergency surgery, firing sea-man and cutting off his wages shortly after he left for hospital, refusing to bring food or medical supplies to seaman while he was stranded in Cuba and recovering from his surgery, not allowing seaman to travel home on vessel, refusing to allow seaman to retrieve his personal belongings from vessel, and continuing to refuse to pay maintenance and cure, without a reasonable defense, for period of more than two years.—Id.

S.D.Fla. 2019. Punitive damages are available for a vessel owner's breach of its maintenance and cure obligation to seamen.—Kennedy v. Carnival Corporation, 385 F.Supp.3d 1302, report and recommendation adopted 2019 WL 2254962.

Fla.App. 3 Dist. 2022. Party seeking maintenance and cure against a shipowner on an interim, pretrial basis in a Florida court must utilize the processes and procedures adopted by Florida Supreme Court.—God's Blessing Ltd v. Salas, 339 So.3d 1086, appeal after remand 352 So.3d 405.

Fla.App. 3 Dist. 2019. Trial court could not dismiss seaman's complaint against cruise company, which alleged that seaman was entitled to maintenance and cure from cruise company after being injured while in service of cruise company's vessel, on grounds that cruise company was not seaman's employer, although seaman was actually employed by cruise company's subcontractor; seaman's complaint alleged that she was acting within course and scope of her employment as a seaman aboard cruise company's vessel when she was injured, and trial court was limited to four corners of complaint and required to assume truth of all allegations in complaint when ruling on cruise company's motion to dismiss.—Florescu v. Royal Caribbean Cruises, LTD., 274 So.3d 502.

Fla.App. 3 Dist. 2003. Genuine issue of material fact existed as to whether administration of oral steroids by cruise ship physician to seaman who worked for cruise line exacerbated seaman's psoriasis, precluding summary judgment for cruise line on issue of failure to treat, in seaman's Jones Act action. Jones Act, 46 App.U.S.C.A. § 688.—Barahona v. Kloster Cruise Ltd., 851 So.2d 235.

Fla.App. 4 Dist. 2000. Material issues of fact existed on issue of whether injured seaman reached maximum medical cure, and thus was entitled to medical benefits, irrespective of whether claimed medical expense was for palliative rather than curative care, precluding summary judgment for defendants, who provided vessel, on seaman's claim for maintenance and cure.—Nurkiewicz v. Vacation Break U.S.A., Inc., 771 So.2d 1271.

Fla.App. 5 Dist. 2021. Vessel owner did not act with requisite callousness or bad faith in refusing to reinstate crew member's maintenance and cure, as would support punitive damages in crew member's action against vessel owner; vessel owner was entitled to rely on two maximum medical improvements (MMIs) from crew member's treating physicians to terminate maintenance and cure, and, when crew member initiated her request for reinstatement of maintenance and cure, vessel owner's refusal, which was based upon recommendations of vessel owner's marine claims representative and independent neurologist who reviewed crew member's submitted medical records, concluding that medical records did not prescribe curative treatment or contradict second MMI, was unreasonable at worst, but not callous.—Magical Cruise Compa-

---

ny Limited v. Martins, 330 So.3d 993, rehearing denied.

Much more than unreasonable denial of reinstatement of maintenance and cure under maritime law is required for award of punitive damages; there must be evidence that shipowner acted with level of callousness, recalcitrance, and bad faith.—Id.

Attorneys' fees are available for maintenance and cure claims under maritime law where the defendant was found to have willfully and arbitrarily withheld maintenance and cure.—Id.

Generally, in a case for maintenance and cure under maritime law, a jury rather than the judge determines entitlement to attorneys' fees, and, if the jury finds entitlement, the judge then determines the amount of attorneys' fees post-judgment.—Id.

Fla.App. 5 Dist. 2019. Genuine issue of material fact existed as to when cruise ship employee became incapacitated to do seaman's work, precluding summary judgment for cruise line on employee's claim for maintenance and cure damages.—Grazette v. Magical Cruise Company Limited, 280 So.3d 1120.

Fla.App. 5 Dist. 2012. Genuine issue of material fact as to when musician who was injured while working on a cruise ship reached maximum medical improvement (MMI) precluded summary judgment on musician's claim against cruise line for maintenance and cure.—Gabriel v. Disney Cruise Line, 93 So.3d 1121, rehearing denied.

⚿**12. Discharge.**
M.D.Fla. 2023. Claim for retaliatory discharge lies when seaman is fired by his employer in retaliation for seaman bringing personal injury action against employer.—Sprengle v. Smith Maritime Inc., 660 F.Supp.3d 1337.

To prove retaliatory discharge, seaman must affirmatively establish that employer's discharge decision was substantially motivated by knowledge that seaman either intends to, or already has, filed personal injury action against employer.—Id.

Seaman stated claim for retaliatory discharge against tugboat company arising from accident wherein pickup line broke in lifting pennant chain as part of process of connecting tugboat to barge, striking seaman across the face, where seaman alleged that he was terminated by tugboat company after accident, seaman quoted a letter predating his termination where tugboat's former counsel wrote that seaman's ability to return to work was directly conditioned on him abandoning his personal injury claim against tugboat company, seaman did not drop his personal injury suit, and he was accordingly terminated nearly two months later, plausibly showing that his termination was substantially motivated by his personal injury suit.—Id.

⚿**13. Expenses of return to port of shipment.**
S.D.Fla. 2021. Captain of yacht abandoned by its owners was entitled to maritime lien in amount of $3,163.50 to reimburse captain for funds he spent repatriating two of yacht's crewmembers to their home country; crewmembers' employment agreements explicitly provided that they would be governed and construed in accordance with laws of Gibraltar, which required that a seaman's last employer make provision for seaman's return to Gibraltar if seaman were left behind in any country outside Gibraltar, as yacht's two crewmembers were.—Rybovich Boat

Company, LLC v. M/Y BLUE STAR, 546 F.Supp.3d 1270.

Boat owners bear general obligation to repatriate seamen who find themselves adrift without passage home.—Id.

When assessing claims for repatriation expenses, courts look to terms of seamen's contracts.—Id.

⚿**16. ——— Right in general.**
S.D.Fla. 2019. The cause of action for maintenance and cure includes three specific items of recovery: (1) maintenance, which is a living allowance; (2) cure, which covers nursing and medical expenses; and (3) lost wages.—Hurtado v. Balerno International Ltd., 408 F.Supp.3d 1315.

For purposes of a maintenance and cure award, a seaman's unearned wages are measured from the time of the seaman's incapacity until the end of his employment contract with vessel owner.—Id.

⚿**27(9). Priority.**
S.D.Fla. 2021. Seamen's wages are sacred liens, and, as long as a plank of ship remains, sailor is entitled, against all other persons, to proceeds as security for his wages.—Rybovich Boat Company, LLC v. M/Y BLUE STAR, 546 F.Supp.3d 1270.

⚿**29(1). In general.**
† **C.A.11 (Fla.) 2018.** Fact that crewmember of cruise ship dropped onion peel in corridor that contract worker slipped on did not establish that shipowner had actual notice of the dangerous condition, as required for a negligence claim under the Jones Act. Jones Act, 46 U.S.C.A. § 30104 et seq.—Jackson v. NCL America, LLC, 730 Fed.Appx. 786.

M.D.Fla. 2021. Under Florida law and general maritime law, if the duty of a party, such as a vessel owner, to act reasonably and in consideration for the safety of others is breached by negligently starting a fire that requires rescue personnel to respond, the negligent party will be responsible for the injuries to all who are affected by it, whether they be seamen protected by the Jones Act or firefighters who knowingly enter a blaze to rescue life and property. 46 U.S.C.A. § 30104.—Jolly v. Hoegh Autoliners Shipping AS, 546 F.Supp.3d 1105.

S.D.Fla. 2021. A Jones Act negligence claim has four elements: (1) plaintiff is a seaman, (2) plaintiff suffered an injury in the course of employment, (3) plaintiff's employer was negligent, and (4) employer's negligence caused the employee's injury, at least in part. 46 U.S.C.A. § 30104(a).—Butts v. ALN Group, LLC, 512 F.Supp.3d 1301.

⚿**29(2). Tools, machinery, appliances, and places for work.**
M.D.Fla. 2023. Equipment is appurtenant to vessel, falling under vessel owner's absolute duty to furnish a seaworthy vessel, when equipment is physically and firmly attached to vessel, equipment is fundamentally related to vessel's maritime activities, and injury occurs aboard ship.—Sprengle v. Smith Maritime Inc., 660 F.Supp.3d 1337.

Physical attachment of equipment need not be permanent or substantial for equipment to be appurtenant to a vessel, for purposes of determining whether equipment falls under vessel owner's absolute duty to furnish a seaworthy vessel; when injury occurs aboard ship, temporary minimal attachment is enough to give rise to duty.—Id.

† This Case was not selected for publication in the National Reporter System

Seaman adequately alleged that pickup line that broke while lifting pennant chain in process of connecting tugboat to barge, injuring seaman, was equipment appurtenant to tugboat, for purposes of seaman's unseaworthiness claim against tugboat company; although tugboat company asserted that it had no duty to provide a seaworthy pickup line because barge owner supplied line at issue, pickup line was physically and firmly attached to tugboat, given that it was wrapped around tugboat's cathead with enough tension to lift pennant chain, pickup line was fundamentally related to tugboat's maritime mission of transporting barge because it was necessary to attach tugboat to barge, and seaman's injury occurred aboard tugboat because he was spooling pickup line around cathead when line parted.—Id.

Seaman plausibly alleged that tugboat company could foresee pickup line being used to pull pennant and bridle chains during connection of tugboat to barge, for purposes of seaman's unseaworthiness claim against tugboat company arising from accident wherein pickup line broke, striking seaman; tugboat company asserted that pickup line was only meant to pull chain pigtail, not pennant and bridle chains, which was communicated to tugboat captain by barge's crew members the day before the incident when he raised concerns about pickup line's size, but tugboat crew's initial rejection of pickup line as too weak for the job suggested that they knew it would be used to pull the heavier pennant bridle chains, and it was customary for crews to use a pickup line to lift pennant and bridle chains.—Id.

☞29(3). Fellow servants.

M.D.Fla. 2023. Seaman plausibly alleged that tugboat crew created a dangerous condition independent from pickup line's inherent fitness by misusing pickup line in an unsafe manner, for purposes of his unseaworthiness claim against tugboat company arising from accident where pickup line broke while lifting pennant chain towards tugboat's deck, striking seaman across the face; seaman alleged that tugboat crewmembers taxed pickup line beyond its load limit, with tugboat's first mate acknowledging that pickup line was too worn, frayed, and thin for job of lifting pennant chain.—Sprengle v. Smith Maritime Inc., 660 F.Supp.3d 1337.

☞29(5.3). Persons entitled to sue.

† **C.A.11 (Fla.) 2017.** Borrowed servant doctrine did not apply to allow seaman to bring a Jones Act claim against owner and manager of limited liability company (LLC) that owned fishing vessel; seaman was not under the direct control of the LLC's owner and manager at the time he slipped and fell on a slippery floor on the vessel, breaking his leg, but rather, was under the control of the vessel's captain, and was on the payroll of the LLC. 46 U.S.C.A. § 30104.— Daughtry v. Jenny G. LLC, 703 Fed.Appx. 883.

S.D.Fla. 2019. Only seamen are entitled to assert claims under the Jones Act, claims for maintenance and cure, and claims for unseaworthiness of a vessel. 46 U.S.C.A. § 30104.—NCL (Bahamas) Ltd. v. Kaczkowski, 396 F.Supp.3d 1185.

☞29(5.4). Persons against whom suit may be brought.

S.D.Fla. 2019. Under the "borrowed servant theory," as related to determination whether a maritime worker qualifies as a seaman under the Jones Act, an employee may recover from an entity which, although not his technical employer, exercises de facto control over him. 46 U.S.C.A. § 30104.—NCL (Bahamas) Ltd. v. Kaczkowski, 396 F.Supp.3d 1185.

☞29(5.5). Jurisdiction and venue.

S.D.Fla. 2022. Under Florida law, alleged failure by management company, which was vessel owner's agent, to adequately perform its contractual duties from its Florida office gave rise to worker's estate's cause of action, such that there was sufficient connexity between company's forum-related activities and estate's cause of action against owner to establish specific personal jurisdiction over vessel owner under Florida's long-arm statute; company's contractual obligations included hiring and training doctor that was aboard vessel when worker died from illness, company also fulfilled shipboard medical facility's equipment and promulgated and enforced vessel's medical policies, and estate alleged that vessel owner failed to properly provide medical care to worker, resulting in his death from toxic shock. Fla. Stat. Ann. § 48.193.—Sarmiento Lopez v. CMI Leisure Management, Inc., 591 F.Supp.3d 1232.

☞29(5.6). Limitations and laches.

See also LIMITATION OF ACTIONS.

☞29(5.16). Questions for jury.

† **C.A.11 (Fla.) 2019.** Genuine issue of material fact existed as to whether employee, and her co-worker, who were members of charter yacht crew, were acting within scope of their employment while conducting sea trial of smaller, tender vessel when employee was injured, precluding summary judgment for employer on employee's Jones Act claim that co-worker was negligent and employer was vicariously liable. 46 U.S.C.A. § 30104.—Herrera v. 7R Charter Limited, 789 Fed.Appx. 820.

C.A.5 (Fla.) 1973. Genuine issue of material fact existed as to whether counsel who represented seaman who executed release for shipboard injury were in a position to advise seaman as to the adequacy of the proposed settlement and whether either counsel was aware of any potential dual Liberian-American claim or took it into account in arriving at their evaluation, precluding summary judgment.—Blanco v. Moran Shipping Co., 483 F.2d 63, rehearing denied 485 F.2d 687, certiorari denied 94 S.Ct. 1608, 416 U.S. 904, 40 L.Ed.2d 108.

C.A.5 (Fla.) 1966. In action for injuries allegedly sustained by plaintiff in course of his employment as seaman aboard defendant's vessel, evidence that plaintiff had been employed to aid in putting vessel into operating condition after having been taken out of service, had signed shipping articles for forthcoming voyage, was living on vessel when injured, and was subject to ship discipline raised substantial fact issue as to whether vessel was in navigation and thus as to whether plaintiff was "seaman" within Jones Act precluding summary judgment. Jones Act, 46 U.S.C.A. § 688; 46 U.S.C.A. §§ 564, 567.—Bodden v. Coordinated Caribbean Transport, Inc., 369 F.2d 273, 5 A.L.R. Fed. 668.

C.A.5 (Fla.) 1958. In action by seaman against shipowner for damages for shipowner's failure to furnish continued maintenance and cure, papers incorporated in defendant's motion for summary judgment disclosed existence of genuine issues of fact, precluding summary judgment.—Murphy v. Light, 257 F.2d 323.

M.D.Fla. 2004. In barge owner's limitation action, genuine issue of material fact existed as to

---

† This Case was not selected for publication in the National Reporter System

whether claimant was a seaman or alternatively covered by the Longshoremen's and Harbor Workers' Compensation Act (LHWCA), and whether barge and crane were unseaworthy, precluding summary judgment in favor of claimant on claims arising from his injury while on board the barge. 46 App.U.S.C.A. § 183; Longshoremen's and Harbor Workers' Compensation Act, § 5, 33 U.S.C.A. § 905.—In re Williams Marine Const. and Services, Inc., 350 F.Supp.2d 975.

Genuine issue of material fact existed as to whether claimant had sufficient connection to a "vessel in navigation" in order to make him a "seaman" under the Jones Act, even though his injury actually occurred on a floating barge, precluding summary judgment in favor of barge owner in its action for exoneration from liability under the Jones Act. Jones Act, 46 App.U.S.C.A. § 688; 46 App.U.S.C.A. § 183.—Id.

M.D.Fla. 1990. Questions of fact regarding engineering company's duty to civil service seaman employed by Navy's Military Sealift Command during cable-laying operations precluded summary judgment in seaman's action to recover for injury when link connecting two lines parted under tension.—Russell v. AT & T Technologies, Inc., 750 F.Supp. 1099.

S.D.Fla. 2019. Where undisputed facts reveal that a maritime worker has a clearly inadequate temporal connection to vessels in navigation, a court may grant summary judgment as to issue of whether the worker qualifies as a seaman under the Jones Act. 46 U.S.C.A. § 30104.—NCL (Bahamas) Ltd. v. Kaczkowski, 396 F.Supp.3d 1185.

S.D.Fla. 2002. Genuine issue of material fact existed as to whether acoustic engineer was a "seaman" for purposes of Jones Act claim, precluding summary judgment for employer in Jones Act claim brought by engineer who sustained

injuries when he fell from tower while performing repairs to weather equipment. Jones Act, 46 App.U.S.C.A. § 688.—Eckert v. U.S., 232 F.Supp.2d 1312.

S.D.Fla. 1991. Evidence that vehicle rental paperwork was prepared in Coast Guard seaman's name and that another crewman picked up truck from lessor raised genuine issue of material fact precluding summary judgment on issue of lessor's consent and authorization to seaman's use of truck and on issue of lessor's liability on United States claim to recover indemnification for accident caused by seaman.—Ashworth v. U.S., 772 F.Supp. 1268.

Fla.App. 2 Dist. 2002. Genuine issue of material fact existed as to whether claimant was a land-based or sea-based employee, precluding summary judgment on claimant's status for purposes of determining whether Jones Act or the Longshore and Harbor Workers' Compensation Act (LHWCA) applied. Jones Act, 46 App. U.S.C.A. § 688; Longshore and Harbor Workers' Compensation Act., § 1 et seq., 33 U.S.C.A. § 901 et seq.—Gulfcoast Transit Co. v. Burns, 817 So.2d 889, rehearing denied.

©—29(5.20). Lien.

M.D.Fla. 2019. Viable claim existed as to maritime lien against fishing vessel as part of fisherman's in rem action stemming from his slip and fall while employed on the vessel, and thus probable cause existed to arrest vessel, where fisherman was on vessel approximately 40 days prior to two visits to hospital emergency room, and fisherman immediately sought medical care at hospital each time vessel arrived at certain port. Supplemental Admiralty and Maritime Claims Rule E(4)(f), 28 U.S.C.A.—Borge v. F/V Double E, 420 F.Supp.3d 1296.

SEARCH, SEIZURE, AND ARREST

SUBJECTS INCLUDED

Examination of persons or places for discovery of property stolen or otherwise unlawfully obtained or held, or of evidence of the commission of an offense

Taking and keeping persons in legal custody to answer charges of crime, or to prevent commission of crime

Investigatory stop or stop and frisk

Searches incident to arrests, stops, and other seizures of persons

Interception or disclosure of electronic communications

Grounds for, and scope and conduct of, such searches, seizures, and arrests

Issuance, requisites, validity, and execution of warrants to search, seize, or arrest

Custody and disposition of property seized and persons arrested

Judicial review or determination of propriety of such searches, seizures, and arrests

Liabilities for wrongfully procuring or making searches, seizures, and arrests

Arrests in civil actions

SUBJECTS EXCLUDED AND COVERED BY OTHER TOPICS

Actions for violations of constitutional rights, see CIVIL RIGHTS

Appellate review, see APPEAL AND ERROR, CRIMINAL LAW XXIV; and FEDERAL COURTS XVII

Bail, admission to, and rights and liabilities of bail, see BAIL

Commencing civil actions, arrest as a means of, see PROCESS

Contempt proceedings, arrests involving, see CONTEMPT ⚖56

Debt, constitutional prohibitions of imprisonment for, see CONSTITUTIONAL LAW ⚖1106

Due process, see CONSTITUTIONAL LAW XXVII

Detainers, see EXTRADITION AND DETAINERS

Evidence wrongfully obtained, see CRIMINAL LAW ⚖392.1 et seq. and EVIDENCE XVII

Extradition, see EXTRADITION AND DETAINERS

False arrest or imprisonment, see FALSE IMPRISONMENT and CIVIL RIGHTS

Forfeitures, see FORFEITURES and specific topics involving forfeitures

Habeas corpus, writs of, see HABEAS CORPUS

International law, operation as to seizures, see INTERNATIONAL LAW

Judgment, motions in arrest of, see CRIMINAL LAW and JUDGMENT

Military cases decided by military courts, see MILITARY JUSTICE in the Federal Practice Digests

Ne exeat, writs of, see NE EXEAT

Offenses committed in making or resisting arrest or delivering prisoner from custody, see ASSAULT AND BATTERY, HOMICIDE, OBSTRUCTING JUSTICE, ESCAPE, RESCUE

Officers' duties and liabilities in respect of arrests, care and custody of prisoners, escapes, etc., see CLERKS OF COURTS, SHERIFFS AND CONSTABLES, PRISONS, and other specific topics

Parole violators, arrest of, see PARDON AND PAROLE ⚖80

Particular classes of persons, liability of to arrest, see INFANTS and other specific topics

Particular objects, subjects, or purposes at search or seizure:

Alcoholic beverages, see ALCOHOLIC BEVERAGES IV

Coast Guard searches of vessels, see SHIPPING ⚖9

Customs or border searches, see CUSTOMS DUTIES ⚖126

Gambling and lotteries, see GAMING AND LOTTERIES V

Internal Revenue searches, see INTERNAL REVENUE XXIX

Medicinal drugs and devices, cosmetics, and animal drugs, seizure of, see HEALTH ⬥330

Parolees, see PARDON AND PAROLE ⬥68

Postal searches, see POSTAL SERVICE ⬥47

Prison inmates, staff, and visitors, see PRISONS ⬥134, 359, 385, 391

Probationers, see SENTENCING AND PUNISHMENT IX(H)

School searches, see EDUCATION ⬥742-745

Workplace safety searches and inspections, see LABOR AND EMPLOYMENT ⬥2600, 2661

Probation violators, arrest of, see SENTENCING AND PUNISHMENT ⬥2012

Vessels, arrest of, see ADMIRALTY

For detailed references to other topics, see Descriptive-Word Index

---

Analysis

XIII. LIABILITY FOR WRONGFUL SEIZURE OF PROPERTY, ☞1941–1950.

XIV. ARRESTS IN CIVIL ACTIONS, ☞1951–1975.

II. SEARCHES AND SEIZURES IN GENERAL.—Cont'd

II. SEARCHES AND SEIZURES IN GENERAL.—Cont'd

II. SEARCHES AND SEIZURES IN GENERAL.—Cont'd

(E) GROUNDS AND SCOPE.—Cont'd

2. PARTICULAR CASES AND CONTEXTS.—Cont'd

⟐674. —— Particular items in general.
⟐675. —— Luggage, bags, and other containers.
⟐676. —— Vehicles.
⟐677. —— Garbage, trash, and other discarded items.
⟐678. Temporary investigative detention of property.
⟐679. Forfeitures, seizure of property subject to.
⟐680. Private search; subsequent government search.

3. EMERGENCIES AND EXIGENT CIRCUMSTANCES; OPPORTUNITY TO OBTAIN WARRANT.

⟐691. In general.
⟐692. Presence of probable cause in general.
⟐693. What constitutes exigent circumstances or emergency in general.
⟐694. Particular cases in general.
⟐695. Community caretaking.
⟐696. Providing medical aid.
⟐697. Preventing injury or harm.
⟐698. —— In general.
⟐699. —— Injury or harm to officer; officer safety.
⟐700. Risk of escape or destruction of evidence.
⟐701. —— In general.
⟐702. —— Particular cases in general.
⟐703. —— Vehicles.
⟐703(1). In general.
⟐703(2). Particular cases.
⟐704. Pursuit.

⟐705. —— In general.
⟐706. —— Particular cases in general.
⟐707. —— Vehicles.
⟐707(1). In general.
⟐707(2). Particular cases.
⟐708. Other particular emergencies or exigent circumstances.

4. PLAIN VIEW.

⟐711. In general.
⟐712. Elements of plain view exception in general.
⟐713. Inadvertency.
⟐714. Lawful presence or vantage point.
⟐715. Incriminating nature of item; nexus.
⟐716. Vehicles in general.
⟐717. Particular items.
⟐718. —— In general.
⟐719. —— Stolen property in general.
⟐720. —— Weapons.
⟐720(1). In general.
⟐720(2). Particular cases.
⟐721. —— Controlled substances and related items.
⟐722. —— Documents.
⟐723. —— Clothing, shoes, and hats.
⟐724. —— Electronic devices.
⟐725. —— Luggage, bags, and other containers.
⟐726. Artificial light or visual aids.

(F) EFFECT OF ILLEGAL CONDUCT.

⟐731. In general.
⟐732. Particular cases.

III. SEARCH WARRANTS.

(A) IN GENERAL.

⟐741. In general.
⟐742. Nature and purpose.
⟐743. Permissible subjects of warrants.
⟐744. Requirements in general.

(B) AUTHORITY TO ISSUE.

⟐751. In general.
⟐752. Particular courts, judges, or magistrates.
⟐753. Impartiality; neutral and detached magistrate.
⟐754. —— In general.
⟐755. —— Particular cases.

(C) PROCEEDINGS FOR ISSUANCE.

⟐761. In general.
⟐762. Application or affidavit.

⟐763. —— In general.
⟐764. —— Persons who may apply or sign affidavit.
⟐765. —— Necessity for writing.
⟐765(1). In general.
⟐765(2). Matters appearing on the face of affidavit; four corners.
⟐766. —— Formal requirements.
⟐767. —— Construction in general.
⟐768. —— Sufficiency in general.
⟐769. —— Specificity or particularity; bare bones.
⟐770. Presumptions, inferences, and burden of proof.
⟐771. Conduct of proceedings.
⟐772. —— In general.
⟐773. —— Recording testimony or oral statements.
⟐774. Electronic warrants.

III. SEARCH WARRANTS.—Cont'd

III. SEARCH WARRANTS.—Cont'd

IV. CONSENT TO SEARCH; WAIVER OF RIGHTS.

IV. CONSENT TO SEARCH; WAIVER OF RIGHTS.—Cont'd

V. SEIZURES OF PERSONS IN GENERAL.

VI. INVESTIGATORY STOPS.

(A) IN GENERAL.

VI. INVESTIGATORY STOPS.—Cont'd

VI. INVESTIGATORY STOPS.—Cont'd

VII. ARRESTS.

VII. ARRESTS.—Cont'd

VII. ARRESTS.—Cont'd

VII. ARRESTS.—Cont'd

VIII. SEARCHES INCIDENT TO SEIZURES OF PERSONS.

VIII. SEARCHES INCIDENT TO SEIZURES OF PERSONS.—Cont'd

IX. USE OF FORCE.

IX. USE OF FORCE.—Cont'd

(B) USE OF FORCE DURING SEARCHES.

(C) USE OF FORCE DURING INVESTIGATORY STOPS.

(D) USE OF FORCE DURING ARRESTS.

X. INTERCEPTION OR DISCLOSURE OF ELECTRONIC COMMUNICATIONS.

(A) IN GENERAL.

(B) AUTHORIZATION BY COURTS OR PUBLIC OFFICERS.

X. INTERCEPTION OR DISCLOSURE OF ELECTRONIC COMMUNICATIONS.—Cont'd

XI. JUDICIAL REVIEW OR DETERMINATION.—Cont'd

XI. JUDICIAL REVIEW OR DETERMINATION.—Cont'd

XII. CUSTODY AND DISPOSITION OF PROPERTY SEIZED.

XIII. LIABILITY FOR WRONGFUL SEIZURE OF PROPERTY.

XIV. ARRESTS IN CIVIL ACTIONS.

XIV. ARRESTS IN CIVIL ACTIONS.—Cont'd

☞1971. Proceedings to support or enforce arrest.

☞1972. Quashing or vacating.

☞1973. Discharge.

☞1974. Rearrest; subsequent arrests.

☞1975. Liability on bonds or undertakings.

For detailed references to other topics, see Descriptive-Word Index

TABLE 1
KEY NUMBER TRANSLATION TABLE
FORMER KEY NUMBER TO PRESENT KEY NUMBER

The topic SEARCHES AND SEIZURES has been revised, supplemented, and retitled SEARCH, SEIZURE, AND ARREST to reflect current developments in the law. The revised topic comprises paragraphs from the former SEARCHES AND SEIZURES Key Numbers, the former topic ARREST, paragraphs formerly classified to AUTOMOBILES ⬤349–349.5(12), CONTROLLED SUBSTANCES ⬤101–159 and OBSCENITY ⬤270–299, and other relevant lines.

This table lists the former Key Numbers with their corresponding present Key Numbers.

In many instances there is no one-to-one relation between the Key Numbers, new and old. This table recognizes only significant correspondence. For the present classification of a particular case, see the Table of Cases.

The absence of a Key Number indicates that there is no useful parallel.

Former ARREST Key Number	Present SEARCH, SEIZURE, AND ARREST Key Number	Former ARREST Key Number	Present SEARCH, SEIZURE, AND ARREST Key Number
1	1952	60	1186
3	406(3)	60.1(1)	1029, 1032
4	1953	60.1(2)	1027–1030(3), 1030(9, 10)
5	1954	60.1(3)	1030(2, 3, 10)
6	1955	60.1(4)	1030(5–10), 1049
8	1957	60.2(1)	1042–1044
9	1958	60.2(3)	1043, 1046–1048
10.1–17	1959	60.2(4)	1049, 1050
18	1960	60.2(5)	1062, 1075–1080, 1115, 1129, 1134
19	1961		
20	1962	60.2(7)	1061, 1065–1068, 1115, 1119, 1130, 1132
22–32	1963		
33	1964	60.2(8)	1135
34	1965	60.2(9)	1133
35	1966	60.2(10)	1063–1069
36	1967	60.2(11)	1136
37	1968	60.2(12)	1122
38	1969	60.2(13)	1075–1080, 1122, 1126, 1134
39	1970		
40	1971	60.2(14)	1204, 1591–1594, 1601(2), 1606
42–45	1972		
47–53	1973	60.2(15)	1154
54, 55	1974	60.2(17)	1199–1201, 1204, 1205
56	1975	60.2(18)	1199, 1202–1205
57.1	1012, 1013, 1028, 1029	60.2(19)	1490(1–9)
57.3	1191, 1193, 1196	60.2(20)	1152, 1153, 1162, 1167, 1491(1–3), 1606
57.4	1194–1197		
57.6	1191, 1193	60.3(1)	1085–1088, 1090(1)
57.7	1194, 1196	60.3(2)	1089, 1091, 1117, 1129–1134
57.8	Federal Courts 3088(2); Search, Seizure, and Arrest 402, 408	60.3(3)	1157, 1158, 1164, 1490(9), 1498, 1499
58	1012, 1027, 1181, 1187, 1226	60.4(1)	1015–1017(1), 1018, 1022, 1025(1)
58.1	1183	60.4(2)	1021, 1022, 1025(2)
59.1	1185	62	408, 1211, 1223

SEARCH, SEIZURE, & ARREST

Former ARREST Key Number	Present SEARCH, SEIZURE, AND ARREST Key Number
63.1	1222, 1223, 1228, 1249
63.2	1211, 1212, 1393
63.3	1245, 1249, 1256, 1267, 1309
63.4(.5)	1232, 1294
63.4(1)	1224, 1231–1236, 1249
63.4(2)	1234–1236, 1239, 1241
63.4(3)	1242
63.4(4)	1315–1317
63.4(5)	1248, 1249, 1256
63.4(6)	1243, 1251, 1254, 1256, 1263, 1271
63.4(7.1)	1297–1299(2), 1301(2), 1303(2)
63.4(8)	1299(1, 2), 1303(2)
63.4(9)	1256, 1300(1, 2), 1301(2)
63.4(10)	1301(1, 2)
63.4(11)	1302(1, 2), 1303(2)
63.4(12)	1271, 1303(1, 2)
63.4(13)	1244, 1245, 1254, 1256
63.4(14)	1305
63.4(15)	1251, 1256, 1258, 1270
63.4(16)	1309, 1312
63.4(17)	1307, 1308
63.4(18)	1789, 1839
64	1215, 1218
65	1391, 1399, 1401, 1408
66(1)	1404
66(2)	1054, 1217, 1394, 1395
66(3)	1396
67	1406, 1407(1, 4, 5), 1788
68.1(1)	1410, 1412
68.1(2)	1412
68.1(3)	1458
68.1(4)	1563, 1565, 1613
68.1(5)	1576, 1625, 1626
68.2(1)	1421–1424, 1427
68.2(2)	1295, 1421
68.2(4)	1423, 1425, 1432
68.2(5)	1430–1432, 1435
68.2(6)	1426, 1432
68.2(7)	1436
68.2(8)	1432, 1435
68.2(9)	1427
68.2(10)	1438–1440, 1444
68.2(11)	1443, 1444
68.2(12)	1446, 1448
69	1413
70(1)	1452–1458
70(2)	1460–1462(2)
71	1464, 1548, 1922
71.1(1)	1511, 1512, 1515–1518
71.1(2.1)	1522, 1523
71.1(3)	1524
71.1(4.1)	1527–1532, 1534(1), 1536, 1538
71.1(5)	1538, 1548, 1551(2)
71.1(6)	1530–1532, 1534(1, 2), 1545
71.1(7)	1227, 1520, 1523

Former ARREST Key Number	Present SEARCH, SEIZURE, AND ARREST Key Number
71.1(8)	1513, 1518
71.1(9)	1527
71.1(10)	1525
71.1(12)	1526
72, 73	1465

Former AUTOMOBILES Key Number	Present SEARCH, SEIZURE, AND ARREST Key Number
349(1)	1025(1), 1043, 1050, 1098, 1171, 1750
349(2.1)	1095, 1096, 1098, 1111(1, 9, 11)
349(4)	1111(2), 1279
349(5)	1111(4), 1281
349(5.1)	1111(3, 5), 1280
349(5.2)	1111(5)
349(5.3)	1111(6), 1283
349(6)	1112(1, 2), 1134, 1293(1, 2)
349(8)	1248, 1256, 1270, 1274
349(9)	1113(1–3)
349(10)	1025(1, 2), 1050, 1195
349(11)	1053, 1211, 1212, 1219
349(12)	1054, 1212, 1295
349(14.1)	1157, 1506
349(15)	1171, 1278, 1279
349(16)	1158, 1160
349(17)	1157, 1164–1167, 1170, 1171, 1506
349(18)	1165–1171
349(19)	Bail 42, 49(5); Search, Seizure, and Arrest 1458–1461, 1462(2)
349.5(1)	1481, 1498, 1532, 1548, 1551(2)
349.5(3)	1106(1, 2), 1135, 1227
349.5(4)	1483, 1498, 1548
349.5(5.1)	1498, 1501(1, 2), 1548, 1551(2)
349.5(6)	1498, 1548
349.5(7)	1498, 1500, 1506, 1548
349.5(8)	1500, 1502, 1503, 1550
349.5(9)	1489, 1491(2), 1506, 1532
349.5(10)	1490(9), 1491(2), 1499, 1500, 1501(2), 1533(2)
349.5(11)	1501(3), 1503, 1551(2, 3), 1552, 1553
349.5(12)	661(1, 2, 4)

Former CONTROLLED SUBSTANCES Key Number	Present SEARCH, SEIZURE, AND ARREST Key Number
101	532, 595
102	406(1), 595
103, 104	595
105	694, 702, 708
106	721

Former CONTROLLED SUBSTANCES Key Number	Present SEARCH, SEIZURE, AND ARREST Key Number
108	595
109	1711
111	657, 658(4), 660, 679
112	657, 658(2), 660
113	657
114	657, 694, 703(2)
115	721
116	658(2–4)
117	658(2), 661(2, 4)
118	666, 702, 721, 968
119	663, 702, 721
121	600, 601, 721, 1490(5), 1491(3)
122	595, 600, 1490(9), 1524
123	694, 699, 702
124	600, 601
125	617, 618, 721, 725
126	634
128	499, 602–606
129	602–606
130	694, 695, 699, 702, 708
131	721
132	602–606
133	605, 721, 1538
134	611–613, 721
135	607, 694, 702, 721
136	608, 721
137	595, 605, 617, 660
138	674–677
142	752, 862, 882, 890(1)
143	882, 890(1, 2)
145	800, 825(2), 839(2)
146	800, 815, 825(2), 835(2)
147	848, 852
148(1)	800, 825(2)
148(2)	800, 815, 825(2), 830(2), 835(2)
148(3)	815, 825(2), 830(2), 835(2)
148(4)	835(2)
149	867
151	937, 938, 940, 945
152	800, 925, 926, 927(1)
153	919, 921–923
154	945
155	800, 825(2), 945
156	1921, 1922

Former OBSCENITY Key Number	Present SEARCH, SEIZURE, AND ARREST Key Number
274(2)	516
275(1)	597, 614
275(2)	614, 647
276	694, 702
277	718, 724
278	614, 680
280	782, 803
281	772

Former OBSCENITY Key Number	Present SEARCH, SEIZURE, AND ARREST Key Number
282(1)	796
282(2)	796, 797, 803, 815
283(1)	796, 797, 803, 839(3)
283(2)	815, 825(3), 835(3)
284	848, 852
285(2)	868
286(2)	878
286(3)	885
286(4)	889, 890(1), 891
286(5)	895
287(1)	929, 948
287(2)	926
287(3)	938, 939, 948
289	1851
290	1853, 1855
291	1856
292	1801, 1851, 1856
293	1871, 1911
294	1922

Former SEARCHES AND SEIZURES Key Number	Present SEARCH, SEIZURE, AND ARREST Key Number
11	402, 423, 551
12	402, 405(1), 406(1), 423
13.1	431, 436, 441, 442
14	467, 469
15	446(1, 2)
16	438–442
17	453
18	445
19	455
20	454
21	457, 458, 460, 461
22	452
23	402, 411, 423, 555
24	553, 554, 1767
25.1	482, 499–503
26	484–487, 500–503, 509
27	506–508
28	527–531
29	511–514
30	557
31.1	541, 542
32	408
33	541, 545, 548
34	547
35	543
36.1	555, 577
37	564, 575
38	566–569, 571
39	605, 606
40.1	413, 559–564
41	567, 569, 571
42.1	691, 693–698
43	705, 706
44	691, 692
45	701, 702
46	565

Former SEARCHES AND SEIZURES Key Number	Present SEARCH, SEIZURE, AND ARREST Key Number
201	1871, 1876, 1877
202	1911
211	1631
213	404
214	405(2)
215	406(2)
216	407(2)
217	408
218	409
219	1632
220	1633
222	518
223	519
225	1635
226	1636
227	1637
228	1638
231	1641
233	1643
234	1644
236	1646
237	1647
238	1648
240	1650
241	1651
242	1652
244	1654
245	1655
246	1656
247	1657
249	1659
250	1660
252	1662
253	1663
254	1664
255	1665
256	1666
257	1667
258	1668
260	1670
261	1671
262	1672
264	1674
265	1675
266	1676
267	1677

Former SEARCHES AND SEIZURES Key Number	Present SEARCH, SEIZURE, AND ARREST Key Number
268	1678
269	1679
271	1681
273	1683
274	1684
275	1685
276	1686
277	1687
278	1688
280	1690
281	1691
282	1692
283	1693
284	1694
286	1696
287	1697
288	1698
289	1699
290	1700
291	1701
292	1702
301	1711
302	1712
303	1713
304	1714
305	1715
306	1716
307	1717
308	1718
309	1719
311	1721
313	1757
314	1758
315	1792
316	1842
317	1864
318	1906
319	1882
320	1912

Former WAR AND NATIONAL EMERGENCY Key Number	Present SEARCH, SEIZURE, AND ARREST Key Number
1332	591, 663

TABLE 2
KEY NUMBER TRANSLATION TABLE
PRESENT KEY NUMBER TO FORMER KEY NUMBER

The topic SEARCHES AND SEIZURES has been revised, supplemented, and retitled SEARCH, SEIZURE, AND ARREST to reflect current developments in the law. The revised topic comprises paragraphs from the former SEARCHES AND SEIZURES Key Numbers, the former topic ARREST, paragraphs formerly classified to AUTOMOBILES ⬅349–349.5(12), CONTROLLED SUBSTANCES ⬅101–159 and OBSCENITY ⬅270–299, and other relevant lines.

This table lists the present Key Numbers with their corresponding former Key Numbers.

In many instances there is no one-to-one relation between the Key Numbers, new and old. This table recognizes only significant correspondence.

The absence of a Key Number indicates that there is no useful parallel.

Present SEARCH, SEIZURE, AND ARREST Key Number	Former SEARCHES AND SEIZURES Key Number	Present SEARCH, SEIZURE, AND ARREST Key Number	Former SEARCHES AND SEIZURES Key Number
402	12, 23	465	14, 78
405(1)	12, 23, 26	466	14
405(2)	214	467–469	14, 78
406(1)	12	470	13.1, 33
406(2)	215	481–484	25.1, 26
406(3)	Arrest 3	485	26
407(1)	12	486	25.1, 26
407(2)	216	487	13.1, 25.1, 26
408	Arrest 62; Searches and Seizures 32, 101	489	25.1, 26
		490	26
409	218	492	25.1, 26
410	23–25.1, 101	493	26
411, 412	23	494	25.1, 26
413	Arrest 63.4(2); Searches and Seizures 40.1	495	25.1, 76
		496	26, 78
414	23	497	25.1, 26
415	42.1	499, 500	24–26
422	11, 23, 24	501–504	25.1, 26
423	12, 13.1, 23	505	26
431–536	13.1	506, 507	26, 27
438–442	13.1, 16	508	27
443	13.1	509	25.1, 26, 76
444	13.1, 16	511	26, 29
445	13.1, 16, 18	512, 513	29
446(1, 2)	15	514, 515	26, 29
447–449	13.1	516	Obscenity 274(2); Searches and Seizures 25.1, 26
451, 452	22		
453	17		
454	20, 27	518	26, 222
455	19	519	26, 223
457	13.1, 19, 21	521	25.1, 26
458	13.1, 21	522	26, 60.1, 61
459	13.1	523	26
460	21	524	23, 25.1
461	13.1, 21	525	25.1, 26
462	13.1	527	26, 28
464	13.1, 14	528	28

Present SEARCH, SEIZURE, AND ARREST Key Number	Former SEARCHES AND SEIZURES Key Number
851, 852	Controlled Substances 147; Searches and Seizures 112
861	113.1, 121.1
862	122
864–866	121.1
867	Controlled Substances 149
868	Obscenity 285(2); Searches and Seizures 121.1
869	101, 113.1
871, 872	123.1
873	101, 123.1, 124, 200
875	123.1, 124, 126
876, 877	124
878	123.1–126
880	124, 125
881	124, 125, 148
882	142, 143
883, 884	124, 125
885	Obscenity 286(3); Searches and Seizures 125
886	125
888	124, 126
889	126
890(1, 2)	Controlled Substances 143; Searches and Seizures 126
891	125, 126
892	Controlled Substances 143; Searches and Seizures 125, 126
894	101, 123.1, 124, 127
896(1, 2)	127
897	101, 123.1–125
898	128
900, 901	129
911, 912	141
914, 915	141, 142
916	142
918	143.1
919	Controlled Substances 153; Searches and Seizures 143.1
921	Controlled Substances 153; Searches and Seizures 143.1, 144
922	Controlled Substances 153; Searches and Seizures 143.1
923	Controlled Substances 153; Searches and Seizures 143.1, 144
925	Controlled Substances 152; Searches and Seizures 121.1, 145.1, 146

Present SEARCH, SEIZURE, AND ARREST Key Number	Former SEARCHES AND SEIZURES Key Number
926	Controlled Substances 152; Searches and Seizures 145.1
927(1)	Controlled Substances 152; Searches and Seizures 146
927(2)	146
928, 929	Controlled Substances 151; Searches and Seizures 141
931, 932	147.1, 148
933	Controlled Substances 151; Searches and Seizures 141, 147.1, 148
936	Controlled Substances 151; Searches and Seizures 148
937	Controlled Substances 151; Searches and Seizures 141, 147.1, 148
938	Controlled Substances 151; Searches and Seizures 148
939	Obscenity 287(3); Searches and Seizures 142, 148
940	Controlled Substances 151; Searches and Seizures 148
942	147.1, 148
943	47.1, 149
944	148, 149
945	Controlled Substances 151, 154
946, 947	148, 149
948	Obscenity 287(3); Searches and Seizures 148, 149
949	148, 149
950	141
951	Controlled Substances 151; Searches and Seizures 141, 145.1
952, 953	150
961, 962	171
963	171, 179.1
964	171, 197
966	171
967(1)	172
967(2)	171, 172
967(3)	172
967(4)	171, 172
968	185
970	173.1
971, 172	173.1, 177
973	173.1
974, 175	173.1, 174
976	175
977	173.1
978	176, 177

Present SEARCH, SEIZURE, AND ARREST Key Number	Former SEARCHES AND SEIZURES Key Number	Present SEARCH, SEIZURE, AND ARREST Key Number	Former SEARCHES AND SEIZURES Key Number
1117	Arrest 60.2(5, 13), 60.3(1, 2)	1171	Automobiles 349(15, 17, 18)
1119	Arrest 60.2(5, 7); Searches and Seizures 141	1172	Arrest 60.3(2); Automobiles 349(17, 18)
1120	Arrest 60.2(5, 13, 20); Searches and Seizures 141	1181	Arrest 58, 63.1
		1182	Arrest 58
		1183	Arrest 58, 58.1
1122	Arrest 60.2(5, 10, 12, 13	1185	Arrest 59.1
1123	Arrest 60.2(5), 60.3(2); Automobiles 349(2.1)	1186	Arrest 60
		1187	Arrest 57.1, 58, 62, 63.1; Searches and Seizures 23
1125	Arrest 60.2(7, 10)		
1126	Arrest 60.2(5, 13)		
1127	Arrest 60.3(2)	1188	Arrest 58, 62, 63.1; Searches and Seizures 23
1129	Arrest 60.2(5, 7, 10, 13), 60.3(2); Automobiles 349(6)	1191	Arrest 57.3, 57.6
		1192	Arrest 57.3
1130	Arrest 60.2(5, 7, 10), 60.3(2); Automobiles 349(6)	1193	Arrest 57.3, 57.6
		1194	Arrest 57.4, 57.7
1131	Arrest 60.2(5, 10), 60.3(2); Automobiles 349(6)	1195	Arrest 57.4; Automobiles 349(10)
		1196, 1197	Arrest 57.3, 57.4, 57.7
1132	Arrest 60.2(5, 7, 10), 60.3(2); Automobiles 349(6)	1199	Arrest 60.2(10, 17, 18)
		1200	Arrest 60.2(17)
1133	Arrest 60.2(5, 9, 10), 60.3(1, 2)	1201	Arrest 60.2(17, 20)
		1202	Arrest 60.2(18)
1134	Arrest 60.2(5, 13), 60.3(2); Automobiles 349(6)	1203	Arrest 60.2(18), 60.3(2); Automobiles 349(10)
1135	Arrest 60.2(5, 8), 60.3(2); Automobiles 349(2.1), 349.5(3)	1204	Arrest 60.2(14, 17, 18, 20); Automobiles 349(10)
		1205	Arrest 60.2(17, 18, 20)
1136	Arrest 60.2(10, 11)	1206	Arrest 60.2(17, 18)
1151	Arrest 60.2(10, 20), 60.3(3)	1211	Arrest 62, 63.1, 63.2, 64; Automobiles 349(11)
1152, 1153	Arrest 60.2(10, 20)	1212	Arrest 63.2; Automobiles 349(11, 12)
1154	Arrest 60.2(15)	1213	Automobiles 349(12)
1155	Arrest 60.2(20), 60.3(3)	1215	Arrest 64
1156	Arrest 60.2(20)	1216	Arrest 63.2, 64
1157	Arrest 60.3(3); Automobiles 349(14.1, 17)	1217	Arrest 63.2, 64, 66(2)
		1218	Arrest 64
1158	Arrest 60.3(3); Automobiles 349(16)	1219	Arrest 64; Automobiles 349(11)
1159	Arrest 60.3(2, 3)	1221, 1222	Arrest 63.1, 63.4(1)
1160	Arrest 60.2(20), 60.3(3); Automobiles 349(16–18)	1223	Arrest 62, 63.1, 63.4(1); Criminal Law 216
1162	Arrest 60.2(20)	1224	Arrest 63.1, 63.4(1)
1163	Arrest 60.2(20), 60.3(3)	1226	Arrest 58, 63.1, 63.4(1); Automobiles 349.5(3)
1164	Arrest 60.3(3); Automobiles 349(14.1, 17, 18)	1227	Arrest 63.1, 71.1(1, 7); Automobiles 349.5(3)
1165	Automobiles 349(17, 18)	1228	Arrest 63.1, 63.4(15)
1167	Arrest 60.2(20); Automobiles 349(18)	1229	Arrest 58, 63.1, 63.4(1)
		1231	Arrest 63.4(1, 2)
1168	Arrest 60.2(20), 60.3(3); Automobiles 349(18)	1232	Arrest 63.4(1)
		1233	Arrest 63.4(.5, 1, 2)
1169	Arrest 60.2(20); Automobiles 349(18)	1234–1236	Arrest 63.4(1, 2)
		1237–1241	Arrest 63.4(2)
		1242	Arrest 63.4(2, 3)
1170	Automobiles 349(17, 18)	1243	Arrest 63.4(2, 6)

Present SEARCH, SEIZURE, AND ARREST Key Number	Former SEARCHES AND SEIZURES Key Number
1244	Arrest 63.4(2, 13)
1245	Arrest 63.3, 63.4(13)
1246	Arrest 63.4(2, 15)
1248	Arrest 63.4(1, 2, 5); Automobiles 349(8)
1249	Arrest 63.1, 63.3, 63.4(1, 2, 5)
1251	Arrest 63.1, 63.4(6, 15)
1252	Arrest 63.4(6, 13, 15)
1253	Arrest 63.3, 63.4(5, 13, 15)
1254	Arrest 63.4(6, 13, 15, 17)
1255	Arrest 63.4(6, 15)
1256	Arrest 63.3, 63.4(6, 13, 15); Automobiles 349(8)
1257	Arrest 63.4(5, 13, 15)
1258	Arrest 63.3, 63.4(5, 15)
1260	Arrest 63.4(5, 15)
1261	Arrest 63.4(13, 15)
1262	Arrest 63.3, 63.4(13, 15)
1263	Arrest 63.4(6, 13, 15)
1264	Arrest 63.4(1, 15)
1265	Arrest 63.4(13, 15)
1266	Arrest 63.4(6, 13, 15)
1267	Arrest 63.3, 63.4(5, 13, 15)
1268	Arrest 63.4(6, 13, 15)
1269	Arrest 63.1, 63.3, 63.4(13, 15)
1270	Arrest 63.4(5, 15); Automobiles 349(8)
1271	Arrest 63.4(6, 12, 13, 15)
1272	Arrest 63.3, 63.4(6, 12, 13, 15)
1274	Arrest 63.3, 63.4(13, 15); Automobiles 349(8)
1275	Arrest 63.3, 63.4(5, 13, 15)
1278	Arrest 63.4(13); Automobiles 349(2.1, 8, 15)
1279	Automobiles 349(4)
1280	Automobiles 349(5.1)
1281	Automobiles 349(5)
1282	Automobiles 349(5.1)
1283	Automobiles 349(5.3)
1284	Automobiles 349(2.1)
1285	Automobiles 349(2.1, 15)
1286	Arrest 63.3; Automobiles 349(2.1, 15)
1288	Automobiles 349(2.1)
1293(1, 2)	Automobiles 349(6)
1294	Arrest 63.4(.5, 1, 2, 13)
1295	Arrest 63.1, 63.4(1, 2, 6); Automobiles 349(12)
1297	Arrest 63.4(7.1)
1298	Arrest 63.4(6–8); Automobiles 349(6)
1299(1, 2)	Arrest 63.4(7.1, 8)
1300(1)	Arrest 63.4(8, 9)

Present SEARCH, SEIZURE, AND ARREST Key Number	Former SEARCHES AND SEIZURES Key Number
1300(2)	Arrest 63.4(7.1–9); Automobiles 349(6)
1301(1)	Arrest 63.4(10)
1301(2)	Arrest 63.4(7.1, 9, 10)
1302(1)	Arrest 63.4(11)
1302(2)	Arrest 63.4(11); Automobiles 349(6)
1303(1)	Arrest 63.4(8, 12)
1303(2)	Arrest 63.4(8, 11, 12)
1304	Arrest 63.4(6)
1305	Arrest 63.4(14)
1307, 1308	Arrest 63.4(17)
1309	Arrest 63.3, 63.4(16)
1311, 1312	Arrest 63.4(16)
1313	Arrest 63.4(6, 16)
1315	Arrest 63.4(2, 4)
1316, 1317	Arrest 63.4(4); Automobiles 349(6)
1318	Arrest 63.1
1321	Criminal Law 215.1, 217, 218(1)
1322	Criminal Law 216
1324, 1325	Criminal Law 217
1326	Criminal Law 212, 217
1328	Criminal Law 214
1329	Criminal Law 209, 217
1330	Criminal Law 210
1331	Criminal Law 211(1, 3)
1332	Criminal Law 211(1, 2), 217
1333	Criminal Law 211(1); Searches and Seizures 191
1335, 1336	Criminal Law 211(1, 3), 217
1337	Criminal Law 211(1, 3), 212, 217
1338–1341	Criminal Law 211(1, 3), 217
1342	Criminal Law 211(3)
1343	Criminal Law 211(1, 3)
1345	Criminal Law 211(3), 218
1346	Criminal Law 211(1, 3), 218
1349	Criminal Law 211(3, 4), 218
1354	Criminal Law 211(3, 4)
1361	Criminal Law 211(3, 4), 218
1364	Criminal Law 211(1, 3, 4)
1365	Criminal Law 211(4)
1366	Criminal Law 218
1370	Criminal Law 211(1, 3, 4)
1371	Criminal Law 211(3, 4), 218, 217
1374	Criminal Law 211(4)

Present SEARCH, SEIZURE, AND ARREST Key Number	Former SEARCHES AND SEIZURES Key Number
1377	Arrest 65; Criminal Law 217, 218(1), 219
1378	Criminal Law 218(3)
1379	Criminal Law 218(4)
1380	Criminal Law 218(1, 5)
1381	Criminal Law 213, 219
1391	Arrest 65; Automobiles 349(14.1)
1393	Arrest 63.2, 65
1394	Arrest 66(2)
1395	Arrest 64, 65, 66(2)
1396	Arrest 66(3)
1397	Arrest 65; Automobiles 349(8)
1399–1401	Arrest 65
1403	Arrest 63.1, 65
1404	Arrest 65, 66(1)
1406	Arrest 63.4(4), 67
1407(1)	Arrest 67
1407(2)	Arrest 63.4(4), 67
1407(3–5)	Arrest 67
1408	Arrest 65
1410, 1411	Arrest 68.1(1)
1412	Arrest 68.1(1, 2)
1413	Arrest 69
1414	Criminal Law 218(2), 220
1421	Arrest 68.2(1, 2)
1423, 1424	Arrest 68.2(1, 4)
1425	Arrest 68.2(4)
1426	Arrest 68.2(6)
1427	Arrest 68.2(1, 6, 9)
1428	Arrest 68.2(1)
1430, 1431	Arrest 68.2(5)
1432	Arrest 68.2(4–6, 8)
1433	Arrest 68.2(5)
1435	Arrest 68.2(5, 8)
1436	Arrest 68.2(5, 7)
1438–1440	Arrest 68.2(10)
1442, 1443	Arrest 68.2(11)
1444	Arrest 68.2(10, 11)
1446–1448	Arrest 68.2(12)
1452	Arrest 70(1, 2)
1453–1457	Arrest 70(1)
1458	Arrest 70(1, 2); Automobiles 349(19)
1460	Arrest 70(1, 2)
1461–1463	Arrest 70(2)
1464	Arrest 71
1465	Arrest 72, 73
1481	Arrest 60.2(20); Automobiles 349.5(1)
1482	201
1483	Automobiles 349.5(1, 4, 7)
1484	Arrest 60.2(10, 19, 20)
1485	Arrest 60.2(20); Automobiles 349.5(10); Searches and Seizures 70

Present SEARCH, SEIZURE, AND ARREST Key Number	Former SEARCHES AND SEIZURES Key Number
1489	Arrest 60.3(3), 71.1(6); Automobiles 349.5(7, 9)
1490(1–3)	Arrest 60.2(19)
1490(4)	Arrest 60.2(10, 19)
1490(5)	Arrest 60.2(19), 63.3(3)
1490(6–8)	Arrest 60.2(19)
1490(9)	Arrest 60.2(19), 60.3(3); Automobiles 349.5(10)
1491(1)	Arrest 60.2(20)
1491(2)	Arrest 60.2(20); Automobiles 349.5(10)
1491(3)	Arrest 60.2(20); Controlled Substances 121; Searches and Seizures 47.1
1493, 1494	Arrest 60.2(20)
1498	Arrest 60.3(3); Automobiles 349.5(1, 4–7); Searches and Seizures 62
1499	Arrest 60.3(3); Automobiles 349.5(10)
1500	Automobiles 349.5(7, 8, 10)
1501(1)	Arrest 60.3(3); Automobiles 349.5(5.1, 7, 10); Searches and Seizures 65
1501(2)	Arrest 60.3(3); Automobiles 349.5(10); Searches and Seizures 63
1501(3)	Automobiles 349.5(7, 10, 11)
1502	Automobiles 349.5(7, 8)
1503	Automobiles 349.5(7, 8, 10, 11)
1506	Automobiles 349(14.1, 17), 349.5(7)
1511	Arrest 71.1(1)
1512	Arrest 71.1(1); Searches and Seizures 24
1513	Arrest 71.1(8)
1514, 1515	Arrest 71.1(1)
1516, 1517	Arrest 71.1(1, 4.1)
1518	Arrest 71.1(1, 7, 8)
1519	Arrest 71.1(7)
1520	Arrest 71.1(1, 7)
1522	Arrest 71.1(1, 2.1, 7)
1523	Arrest 71.1(2.1, 7)
1524	Arrest 71.1(3)
1525	Arrest 71.1(10)
1526	Arrest 71.1(12)
1527	Arrest 71.1(4.1, 6, 9)
1528	Arrest 71.1(4.1, 5)
1529	Arrest 71.1(4.1, 5); Searches and Seizures 49
1530	Arrest 71.1(4.1–6)
1532	Arrest 71.1(4.1–6); Automobiles 349.5(9)

Present SEARCH, SEIZURE, AND ARREST Key Number	Former SEARCHES AND SEIZURES Key Number
1697	287
1698	288
1699	289
1700	290
1701	291
1711	Controlled Substances 109; Searches and Seizures 301
1712	302
1713	303
1714	304
1716	306
1717	307
1718	308
1719	309
1721	191, 311
1722–1724, 1726	191
1731	161
1732–1734	161, 162
1735	163
1737–1743	164
1744(1)	Arrest 60.3(1); Searches and Seizures 165
1744(2)	164, 165
1745	161, 162, 164, 165
1750	Arrest 60.3(2), 63.1; Automobiles 349(1)
1752, 1753	Arrest 63.1
1757	313
1758	314
1761	192.1
1762	161, 165, 192.1
1763	162, 192.1
1764, 1766	192.1
1767	24, 192.1
1768	47.1, 192.1
1769, 1770	192.1
1772	193
1773(1)	191, 193, 200
1773(2)	191, 193
1774	193
1775	191, 193
1776, 1777	193
1779	194
1780	173.1, 194
1781	194
1782	Arrest 60.4(1), 63.1
1784	Arrest 60.2(7, 10, 20)
1786	Arrest 60.3(1); Automobiles 349(2.1, 17)
1788	Arrest 63.4(18), 67, 70(2)
1789	Arrest 63.1, 63.4(18), 68.2(5)
1790	Arrest 65, 67; Criminal Law 213
1792	315
1803	191
1807	Arrest 63.4(18)
1812–1817	195.1
1818	42.1, 195.1

Present SEARCH, SEIZURE, AND ARREST Key Number	Former SEARCHES AND SEIZURES Key Number
1819	Automobiles 349.5(12); Searches and Seizures 195.1
1821	143.1, 195.1, 196
1823	193, 196
1824	113.1, 196
1825	196
1826	141, 196
1828	194, 197
1830	194, 197, 198
1831	197, 198
1834	Arrest 60.2(10)
1836	Automobiles 349(2.1)
1838	Arrest 63.4(18); 68.1(4)
1839	Arrest 63.4(18)
1841	Arrest 71.1(2.1); Automobiles 349.5(7)
1842	316
1851	Obscenity 289; Searches and Seizures 199
1853	Obscenity 290; Searches and Seizures 199
1854	199
1855	Obscenity 290; Searches and Seizures 199
1856	199
1861	199, 200
1864	317
1871	201
1872	161, 201
1873	27, 201
1874	33, 201
1875	42.1, 60.1, 201
1876	201
1877	180, 201
1878	Arrest 60.4(1)
1879	Arrest 60.2(10), 60.3(1); Automobiles 349(2.1)
1880	Arrest 63.4(1, 2)
1882	319
1891	200
1892	191, 200
1894, 1896	200
1899	143.1, 191, 200
1900–1901(3)	191, 200
1903	Arrest 60.2(7, 10)
1904	Criminal Law 211(1, 3), 213, 219; Searches and Seizures 200
1906	318
1911	191, 202
1912	320
1921	Controlled Substances 156; Searches and Seizures 84
1922–1927	84
1928	84, 85
1929–1933	84
1941	85
1942	Controlled Substances 156; Searches and Seizures 85
1952	Arrest 1

Present SEARCH, SEIZURE, AND ARREST Key Number	Former SEARCHES AND SEIZURES Key Number	Present SEARCH, SEIZURE, AND ARREST Key Number	Former SEARCHES AND SEIZURES Key Number
1953	Arrest 4	1965	Arrest 34
1954	Arrest 5	1966	Arrest 35
1955	Arrest 6	1967	Arrest 36
1957	Arrest 8	1968	Arrest 37
1958	Arrest 9	1969	Arrest 38
1959	Arrest 12–16	1970	Arrest 39
1960	Arrest 18	1971	Arrest 40
1961	Arrest 19	1972	Arrest 42–44
1962	Arrest 20	1973	Arrest 47–53
1963	Arrest 22, 27–29	1974	Arrest 54, 55
1964	Arrest 33	1975	Arrest 56

SEARCH, SEIZURE, AND ARREST

⌐1–320.

SEARCHES AND SEIZURES Key Numbers 1 to 320 are no longer valid and have been replaced by new Key Numbers. See topic analysis and translation tables.

I. IN GENERAL.

⌐**402. Application of Fourth Amendment and state equivalents in general.**

C.A.11 (Fla.) 2021. The Fourth Amendment, incorporated to apply to the States through the Fourteenth Amendment, protects individuals against unreasonable seizures. U.S. Const. Amends. 4, 14.—Sosa v. Martin County, Florida, 13 F.4th 1254, rehearing granted, vacated 21 F.4th 1362, on rehearing en banc 57 F.4th 1297, on remand 2023 WL 1776253, certiorari denied 144 S.Ct. 88, 217 L.Ed.2d 19.

C.A.11 (Fla.) 2012. The purpose of the Fourth Amendment is not to eliminate all contact between the police and the citizenry, but to prevent arbitrary and oppressive interference by enforcement officials with the privacy and personal security of individuals. U.S.C.A. Const.Amend. 4.— Chandler v. Secretary of Florida Dept. of Transp., 695 F.3d 1194.

S.D.Fla. 2022. Fourth Amendment's protection against unreasonable searches and seizures does not apply to searches and seizures (arrests) by the United States of a non-citizen/non-resident alien arrested in international waters or a foreign country. U.S. Const. Amend. 4; Fed. R. Crim. P. 5(b).—United States v. Santana, 640 F.Supp.3d 1293.

S.D.Fla. 2018. Claims under provision of Florida constitution governing searches and seizure is analyzed consistent with the corresponding provisions of the Fourth Amendment to the United States Constitution. U.S. Const. Amend. 4; Fla. Const. art. 1, § 12.—C.F.C. v. Miami-Dade County, 349 F.Supp.3d 1236.

Fla. 2002. The Florida Supreme Court is required to follow the United States Supreme Court's interpretations of the Fourth Amendment. U.S.C.A. Const.Amend. 4; West's F.S.A. Const. Art. 1, § 12.—State v. Betz, 815 So.2d 627.

Fla.App. 1 Dist. 2021. A person's right to be let alone by other people is left largely to the law of the individual states and is not contained in the Fourth Amendment of the U.S. Constitution. Fla. Const. art. 1, § 23; U.S. Const. Amend. 4.—Green v. Alachua County, 323 So.3d 246, rehearing denied.

Fla.App. 1 Dist. 2020. There must be a "search" or a "seizure" to trigger the Fourth Amendment's protections. U.S. Const. Amend. 4. —Bailey v. State, 311 So.3d 303, rehearing denied, review denied 2021 WL 2408431, certiorari denied 142 S.Ct. 568, 211 L.Ed.2d 354.

Fla.App. 2 Dist. 2023. The Fourth Amendment applies where officers are engaged in a noncriminal function, such as where they are conducting welfare checks. U.S. Const. Amend. 4.—K.M. v. State, 359 So.3d 414.

Fla.App. 2 Dist. 2022. The inestimable Fourth Amendment right of personal security belongs as much to the citizen on the streets of cities as to the homeowner closeted in his study to dispose of his secret affairs. U.S. Const. Amend. 4.—S.P. v. State, 331 So.3d 883.

Fourth Amendment's right of personal security most frequently arises in the context of criminal investigations, but it also applies when the state's law enforcement officers are engaged in a noncriminal function. U.S. Const. Amend. 4.—Id.

Fla.App. 3 Dist. 2019. Although interpretation of section of the state constitution governing search and seizure is circumscribed to jurisprudence from the United States Supreme Court, the limiting language in that section does not prohibit the legislature from passing statutes that give citizens of the state greater protections than the Fourth Amendment. U.S. Const. Amend. 4; Fla. Const. art. 1, § 12.—State v. Quintanilla, 276 So.3d 941, rehearing denied, review denied 2020 WL 633783.

Fla.App. 4 Dist. 2019. Florida Constitution provision which mirrors the Fourth Amendment's protection against unlawful searches and seizures is construed in conformity with the Fourth Amendment as interpreted by the Supreme Court of the United States. U.S. Const. Amend. 4; Fla. Const. art. 1, § 12.—State v. Martin, 287 So.3d 645.

Fla.App. 4 Dist. 2018. The search and seizure provision of the Florida Constitution imposes no higher standard than that of the Fourth Amendment. U.S. Const. Amend. 4; Fla. Const. art. 1, § 12.—McGraw v. State, 245 So.3d 760, rehearing granted 2018 WL 3342880, vacated 289 So.3d 836, rehearing granted in part 2020 WL 838040, on remand 299 So.3d 12.

⌐**404. —— In general.**

C.A.5 (Fla.) 1979. Mere existence of statutory authority to make a search does not obviate need for Fourth Amendment compliance. U.S.C.A.Const. Amend. 4.—U.S. v. Conroy, 589 F.2d 1258, rehearing denied U.S. v. Walker, 594 F.2d 241, rehearing denied 594 F.2d 241, certiorari denied 100 S.Ct. 60, 444 U.S. 831, 62 L.Ed.2d 40.

⌐**405(1). In general.**

Fla.App. 1 Dist. 2020. In the context of historical understandings of what was deemed an unreasonable search and seizure when the Fourth Amendment was adopted, the Fourth Amendment's primary goal is the prevention of activity which would lead to arbitrary and too-permeating police surveillance and power. U.S. Const. Amend. 4.—Bailey v. State, 311 So.3d 303, rehearing denied, review denied 2021 WL 2408431, certiorari denied 142 S.Ct. 568, 211 L.Ed.2d 354.

⌐**405(2). Interception or disclosure of electronic communications.**

C.A.5 (Fla.) 1976. While Congress in enacting proscriptions against the unauthorized interception of oral communications was clearly concerned with protection of individual's privacy interest against unjustifiable intrusions, it did not attempt to deal with all such intrusions; its specific focus was on problem of wiretapping and electronic surveillance. 18 U.S.C.A. § 2510.— U.S. v. Turk, 526 F.2d 654, rehearing denied 529 F.2d 523, certiorari denied 97 S.Ct. 74, 429 U.S. 823, 50 L.Ed.2d 84.

Fla. 2014. In construing statute governing security of communications, the Supreme Court must give the statutory language its plain and ordinary meaning, and is not at liberty to add words that were not placed there by the Legislature. West's F.S.A. § 934.06.—McDade v. State, 154 So.3d 292.

Fla. 1981. Chapter governing security of communications was intended to afford broad protec-

---

† This Case was not selected for publication in the National Reporter System

tion to private communications, evincing greater concern for protection of one's privacy interests in conversation than does federal act. West's F.S.A. § 934.03(2)(d); 18 U.S.C.A. § 2510 et seq.; U.S.C.A.Const. Amend. 1.—State v. Tsavaris, 394 So.2d 418, appeal after remand 414 So.2d 1087, review denied 424 So.2d 763.

Fla. 1980. Congress intended electronic surveillance provisions of Omnibus Crime Control and Safe Streets Act of 1968 to be uniform model to be followed by all states. 18 U.S.C.A. § 2516. —State v. Daniels, 389 So.2d 631.

Fla. 1973. Portion of security of communications statute authorizing interception of wire or oral communications is a statutory exception to constitutional (federal and state) right to privacy and, therefore, must be strictly construed and narrowly limited in application to uses delineated by legislature. F.S.A. § 934.07.—In re Grand Jury Investigation, 287 So.2d 43.

Fla.App. 2 Dist. 1994. Wiretap statutes are exceptions to federal and state constitutional rights to privacy and must be strictly construed. West's F.S.A. §§ 934.07, 934.09.—Jackson v. State, 636 So.2d 1372, review granted 645 So.2d 455, decision approved 650 So.2d 24.

Fla.App. 2 Dist. 1983. Portions of the Security of Communications Act authorizing interception of wire or oral communications are statutory exceptions to federal and state constitutional right of privacy, and as such, must be strictly construed. West's F.S.A. §§ 934.01 et seq., 934.07, 934.09(1)(c), (3)(c), (4)(e); U.S.C.A. Const.Amends. 1, 4.—Copeland v. State, 435 So.2d 842, petition for review denied 443 So.2d 980.

Fla.App. 4 Dist. 1994. State Security of Communications Act was intended to flesh out constitutional protections afforded private communications, while at same time giving guidance to law enforcement as to legitimate circumstances under which they may use interception of communications as investigative tool. West's F.S.A. §§ 934.01 et seq., 934.02(1, 2), 934.03(1)(a-d); West's F.S.A. Const. Art. 1, § 12.—Mozo v. State, 632 So.2d 623, review granted 640 So.2d 1108, decision approved 655 So.2d 1115, rehearing denied.

Although state Security of Communications Act evinces greater concern for protection of privacy interests in conversation than does federal Omnibus Crime Control and Safe Streets Act, legislative history of federal act may be consulted for guidance on interpreting state statute. West's F.S.A. § 934.01 et seq.; 18 U.S.C.A. §§ 2510-2520.—Id.

Fla.App. 5 Dist. 2021. Florida "wiretap" statute must be strictly construed and narrowly limited in its application by the specific provisions set out by the legislature. Fla. Stat. Ann. § 934.07(1).—State v. Wright, 327 So.3d 366, rehearing denied.

Fla.App. 5 Dist. 2002. Since wiretap statutes are exceptions to the federal and state constitutional rights to privacy, they must be strictly construed and narrowly applied.—State v. Fratello, 835 So.2d 312, rehearing denied, reversed State v. Otte, 887 So.2d 1186.

Fla.App. 5 Dist. 1981. As an exception to constitutional right to privacy, statute authorizing interception of wire or oral communications of persons must be strictly construed. West's F.S.A. §§ 934.01 et seq., 934.09(1), (1)(a–f); 18 U.S.C.A. § 2518(1); U.S.C.A.Const. Amend. 1.—Bagley v. State, 397 So.2d 1036.

⬤~406(1). In general.
† C.A.11 (Fla.) 2017. City ordinance permitting city to obtain warrant to conduct minimum housing quality standards and community appearance inspection of rental properties did not, on its face, violate landlord's or tenant's Fourth Amendment rights, even though ordinance stated that refusal to permit inspection or to reschedule inspection within ten days was sufficient to issue inspection warrant, where state statutes required that warrant be issued only upon showing of probable cause, that supporting affidavit state that consent was sought and refused or explain why consent was not sought, and that reasonable legislative or administrative standards for conducting routine or area inspection be satisfied. U.S. Const. Amend. 4; Fla. Stat. Ann. §§ 933.21, 933.22.—2051 Lush Apartments, LLC v. City of Lauderhill, 711 Fed.Appx. 522.

Fla. 1980. Statute which authorizes warrantless arrest if officers have reason to believe that one has committed battery upon his or her spouse and officers either find evidence of bodily harm or reasonably believe that victimized spouse would be placed in further danger if assailant were not arrested without delay satisfies rationality test for equal protection purposes; statute need not apply to all parties who might be involved with or affected by domestic violence. West's F.S.A. § 901.15(6); U.S.C.A.Const. Amend. 14.—LeBlanc v. State, 382 So.2d 299.

Fla.App. 2 Dist. 2022. The Baker Act does not, and could not, categorically preclude the protections of the Fourth Amendment. U.S. Const. Amend. 4; Fla. Stat. Ann. § 394.451, et seq.—S.P. v. State, 331 So.3d 883.

Fla.App. 2 Dist. 1979. To extent that seafood quality control code rule purports to permit warrantless search without any requirement of probable cause, it is contrary to controlling statute, and thus it is invalid as beyond quasi-legislative rule-making authority conferred upon Department of Natural Resources. West's F.S.A. § 370.021(5).—Roth v. State, 378 So.2d 794, certiorari denied 386 So.2d 641, certiorari denied Rich v. Florida, 101 S.Ct. 919, 449 U.S. 1111, 66 L.Ed.2d 839.

⬤~406(2). Interception or disclosure of electronic communications.
C.A.11 (Fla.) 2014. Provision of the Stored Communications Act (SCA) which allowed the government to obtain cell site location information from cell phone service providers on a showing that there were reasonable grounds to believe that the records or other information sought, were relevant and material to an ongoing criminal investigation violated a defendant's Fourth Amendment rights; the defendant had a reasonable expectation of privacy in his location, as it was unlikely that a cell phone customer was aware that their cell phone providers collected and stored historical location information. U.S.C.A. Const.Amend. 4; 18 U.S.C.A. § 2703(c, d).—U.S. v. Davis, 754 F.3d 1205, rehearing granted, vacated 573 Fed.Appx. 925, on rehearing en banc in part 785 F.3d 498, certiorari denied 136 S.Ct. 479, 577 U.S. 975, 193 L.Ed.2d 349, appeal after new sentencing hearing 711 Fed.Appx. 605, certiorari denied 138 S.Ct. 1548, 584 U.S. 935, 200 L.Ed.2d 749, denial of post-conviction relief affirmed 2022 WL 402915, certiorari denied 143 S.Ct. 647, 215 L.Ed.2d 88.

C.A.5 (Fla.) 1975. Provisions of the Omnibus Crime Control and Safe Streets Act of 1968 which authorize the interception of wire communications are constitutional. 18 U.S.C.A. §§ 2510–2520; U.S.C.A.Const. Amends. 1, 4, 5.— U.S. v. Sklaroff, 506 F.2d 837, certiorari denied 96 S.Ct. 142, 423 U.S. 874, 46 L.Ed.2d 105.

S.D.Fla. 1982. Federal electronic surveillance statute is constitutional. 18 U.S.C.A. § 2510 et seq.—U.S. v. Harvey, 560 F.Supp. 1040, affirmed U.S. v. Van Horn, 789 F.2d 1492, certiorari denied 107 S.Ct. 190, 479 U.S. 854, 93 L.Ed.2d 123, certiorari denied 107 S.Ct. 192, 479 U.S. 855, 93 L.Ed.2d 124, certiorari denied Sikes v. U.S., 107 S.Ct. 279, 479 U.S. 886, 93 L.Ed.2d 255.

S.D.Fla. 1971. Provisions of Omnibus Crime Control and Safe Streets Act of 1968 which provide for wire tap and electronic interception of telephone conversations are constitutional. 18 U.S.C.A §§ 2517–2519; U.S.C.A.Const. Amend. 4. —U.S. v. Sklaroff, 323 F.Supp. 296.

S.D.Fla. 1970. Federal statute providing limited system of wire surveillance and electronic eavesdropping for law enforcement use satisfies demands of Fourth Amendment and controlling United States Supreme Court decisions though statute allows seizure and use of communications not otherwise subject to seizure and though both ends of communication are overheard. 18 U.S.C.A. §§ 2510 et seq., 2518, 2518(1) (b, d), (2– 4), (4) (e), (5, 6), (8) (a, d), (10) (a); U.S.C.A.Const. Amend. 4.—U.S. v. Escandar, 319 F.Supp. 295.

Federal statute providing limited system of wire surveillance and electronic eavesdropping for law enforcement use was not violative of constitutional right of free speech. U.S.C.A.Const. Amends. 1, 4; 18 U.S.C.A. § 2510 et seq.—Id.

Fla. 1995. States are free to adopt legislation that is more restrictive than federal wiretap statute, or they may pass no legislation at all, but they may not pass less restrictive legislation. 18 U.S.C.A. §§ 2510–2520.—State v. Rivers, 660 So.2d 1360, rehearing denied, certiorari denied 116 S.Ct. 1019, 516 U.S. 1147, 134 L.Ed.2d 98.

Fla. 1982. Section of State Constitution providing that right of people to be secure in their persons, houses, papers and effects against unreasonable searches and seizures and against unreasonable interception of private communications by any means, shall not be violated, is not violated by statute making it lawful for law enforcement officer or person acting under direction of law enforcement officer to intercept wire or oral communication when such person is party to communication or one party to communication has given prior consent to interception and purpose of interception is to obtain evidence of criminal act. West's F.S.A. Const. Art. 1, § 12; Art. 5, § 3(b)(4); West's F.S.A. § 934.03(2)(c).— Morningstar v. State, 428 So.2d 220, certiorari denied 104 S.Ct. 86, 464 U.S. 821, 78 L.Ed.2d 95.

Fla. 1981. Statute which authorizes law enforcement officer to intercept an oral communication when such person is a party to the conversation or where one of the parties to the communication has given prior consent to the interception is unconstitutional insofar as it authorizes the warrantless interception of a private conversation conducted in the home. West's F.S.A.Const. Art. 1, § 12; West's F.S.A. § 934.03(2)(c).—State v. Sarmiento, 397 So.2d 643.

Fla. 1980. With regard to telephone communications, Congress enacted legislation regulating practice of interception of wire and oral communications under commerce clause.

U.S.C.A.Const. Art. 1, § 8, cl. 3; 18 U.S.C.A. § 2516(2).—State v. Daniels, 389 So.2d 631.

Fla. 1978. Statutes relating to security of communications were constitutional as applied to case in which prosecution was precluded from introducing electronic recording to corroborate extortion victim's testimony as to oral threats. West's F.S.A. §§ 934.02(2), 934.03, 934.06.—State v. Walls, 356 So.2d 294.

Fla. 1955. Statute providing that public utilities should not be expected to violate Federal Communications Act in meeting responsibilities placed on them by state law is not an adoption of Federal Communications Act provisions and does not render a violation of federal Act a violation of state law. Communications Act of 1934, § 605, 47 U.S.C.A. § 605; F.S.A. § 364.31.—Perez v. State, 81 So.2d 201.

Fla.App. 5 Dist. 2021. Federal statute governing authorization for wiretaps represents the minimum requirements for obtaining a wiretap, leaving States with the option to pass more restrictive measures. 18 U.S.C.A. § 2516(2).—State v. Wright, 327 So.3d 366, rehearing denied.

Fla.App. 5 Dist. 1982. Rule that Florida statute, insofar as it authorized warrantless interception of private conversation conducted in home, was unconstitutional would not be extended to warrantless interception in home of a defendant's friend or to defendant's truck. West's F.S.A. Const. Art. 1, § 12; West's F.S.A. § 934.03, subd. 2(c).—Zacke v. State, 418 So.2d 1118, petition for review denied 426 So.2d 29.

Fla.App. 5 Dist. 1982. Where conversations took place in parking lot, and not in enclosed or secluded area and where it was not shown that defendant took any measures to ensure his privacy, statute under which agent with electronic listening device transmitted conversations to other officers stationed nearby who monitored and recorded entire marijuana sale transaction was not shown to be unconstitutional. West's F.S.A.Const.Art. 1, § 12; West's F.S.A. § 934.02(2)(c); U.S.C.A.Const.Amend. 4.—Ruiz v. State, 416 So.2d 32.

⚮407(2). Interception or disclosure of electronic communications.

Fla. 1983. Where operative events took place prior to effective date of 1982 constitutional amendment, provisions of 1968 Constitution governed validity of warrantless recordings of telephone conversations emanating from defendant's home and interception and taping were not in contravention of that version. West's F.S.A. Const. Art. 1, § 12.—State v. Williams, 443 So.2d 952.

⚮408. What law governs.

C.A.5 (Fla.) 1978. When an arrest is made by state officers acting pursuant to state authority, the requisite standard of probable cause for lawful arrest is determined by state law, provided that that law meets federal constitutional standards.—U.S. v. Ullrich, 580 F.2d 765, rehearing denied 589 F.2d 1114.

M.D.Fla. 1996. Validity of warrantless arrest in a misdemeanor case is usually governed by state law.—U.S. v. Svaib, 924 F.Supp. 137.

M.D.Fla. 1991. Subject to constitutional constraints, lawfulness of arrest by state officers is determined by reference to law of state where arrest occurs. U.S.C.A. Const.Amend. 4.—U.S. v. Williams, 784 F.Supp. 1553.

S.D.Fla. 2001. United States Government had no duty to comply with the International Covenant on Civil and Political Rights (ICCPR) when

---

† **This Case was not selected for publication in the National Reporter System**

it was outside the United States and within the boundaries of another country; even if the operation to capture defendant was under the direction of the United States Drug Enforcement Administration (DEA), the other country's government was still in charge and was a sovereign nation responsible for its own actions regarding the defendant.—U.S. v. Duarte-Acero, 132 F.Supp.2d 1036, affirmed 296 F.3d 1277, certiorari denied 123 S.Ct. 573, 537 U.S. 1038, 154 L.Ed.2d 459, habeas corpus dismissed by Duarte-Acero v. Haynes, 2012 WL 289885.

Fla. 1964. Lawfulness of arrest by state officer for offense against state is to be determined by state law.—Benefield v. State, 160 So.2d 706.

⟜409. Federal preemption.

Fla. 2004. Violations of Florida's Racketeer Influenced and Corrupt Organization (RICO) statute, based on predicate acts related to prostitution, constitute crimes "dangerous to life, limb, or property," within meaning of federal wiretap statute, and thus, the federal wiretap statute does not preempt Florida's wiretap statute, which authorizes wiretaps to investigate any Florida RICO offense. U.S.C.A. Const. Art. 6, cl. 2; 18 U.S.C.A. § 2516(2); West's F.S.A. §§ 895.03, 934.07.—State v. Otte, 887 So.2d 1186.

The federal wiretap statute preempts the field of wiretapping and electronic surveillance and limits a state's authority to legislate in this area; thus, states are allowed to adopt procedures for intercepting communications in a criminal investigation that are similar to the federal statute, and states are free to adopt more restrictive statutes, but they cannot adopt less restrictive ones. U.S.C.A. Const. Art. 6, cl. 2; 18 U.S.C.A. § 2516(2).—Id.

Fla. 1995. Congress has preempted field of interception of wire communications under its power to regulate interstate communications by passing wiretap statute. U.S.C.A. Const. Art. 1, § 8, cl. 3; 18 U.S.C.A. §§ 2510–2520.—State v. Rivers, 660 So.2d 1360, rehearing denied, certiorari denied 116 S.Ct. 1019, 516 U.S. 1147, 134 L.Ed.2d 98.

Federal wiretap statute did not authorize wiretaps to investigate nonviolent prostitution-related offenses, and thus preempted Florida's authority to permit such wiretaps; spread of virus causing acquired immune deficiency syndrome (AIDS) did not make prostitution intrinsically "dangerous to life." 18 U.S.C.A. § 2516(2); West's F.S.A. § 934.07.—Id.

Fla.App. 1 Dist. 1979. Notwithstanding that under state statute governing interception of wire or oral communications assistant state attorney would be authorized to make application for authority to intercept communications, federal statute governing such interception was preemptive and assistant state attorney was not "principal prosecuting attorney" for purposes of federal statute which provided that only the "principal prosecuting attorney" was authorized to make application for order authorizing or approving interception of oral or wire communications. West's F.S.A. § 934.09; 18 U.S.C.A. §§ 2516(2), 2518(1)(c).—Daniels v. State, 381 So.2d 707, affirmed 389 So.2d 631.

Fla.App. 2 Dist. 1977. In passing Title III of Omnibus Crime Control and Safe Streets Act, Congress preempted field of interception of wire communications under its power to regulate interstate communications. 18 U.S.C.A. § 2516 et seq.—State v. McGillicuddy, 342 So.2d 567.

Fla.App. 4 Dist. 2011. Federal electronic surveillance law preempts the field of interception of wire communications under Congress' power to regulate interstate communications. 18 U.S.C.A. §§ 2510–2520.—Tracey v. State, 69 So.3d 992, rehearing denied, review granted 116 So.3d 1264, quashed 152 So.3d 504, rehearing denied, on remand 162 So.3d 217.

Fla.App. 4 Dist. 1981. Federal law has preempted the ability of certain state officials to authorize an application for the interception of oral communications; federal law reference to the "principal prosecuting attorney" refers to the appropriate state attorney and precludes the exercise of that power by general class of prosecutors known as assistant state attorneys. 18 U.S.C.A. § 2516(2); West's F.S.A. § 934.07.—State v. Birs, 394 So.2d 1054.

Fla.App. 4 Dist. 1978. Federal law has preempted field of wiretaps, and any state regulated interception of wire communication must provide safeguards at least as stringent as those set out in the federal statute. 18 U.S.C.A. §§ 2510–2520; West's F.S.A. § 934.01 et seq.—State v. Aurilio, 366 So.2d 71, certiorari denied 376 So.2d 76.

Fla.App. 5 Dist. 2002. By enacting legislation authorizing the interception of private wire and oral communications in circumstances where federal or state law enforcement officials are investigating certain specified crimes provided that they receive prior judicial authorization, Congress specifically preempted the field of interception of wire communications under its power to regulate interstate communications, yet at the same time authorized the individual states to adopt their own wiretap statutes so long as they were not less restrictive than the federal legislation. U.S.C.A. Const. Art. 1, §8, cl. 3; 18 U.S.C.A. §§ 2510–2520.—State v. Fratello, 835 So.2d 312, rehearing denied, reversed State v. Otte, 887 So.2d 1186.

Fla.App. 5 Dist. 1994. Florida's wiretap statute must be read in conjunction with federal equivalent, and if portion of Florida law is broader than federal law, that part of statute is invalid. 18 U.S.C.A. § 2516(2); West's F.S.A. § 934.07.—State v. Rivers, 643 So.2d 3, rehearing denied, review granted 651 So.2d 1196, decision approved 660 So.2d 1360, rehearing denied, certiorari denied 116 S.Ct. 1019, 516 U.S. 1147, 134 L.Ed.2d 98.

Federal legislature preempted authority of state of Florida to include crime of prostitution in its wiretap statute; crime of prostitution was not punishable by more than one year in prison and crime of deriving support from proceeds of prostitution was not dangerous to life, limb or property. West's F.S.A. §§ 796.07(5), 934.07; 18 U.S.C.A. § 2516(2).—Id.

⟜410. Necessity of and preference for warrant in general; exceptions in general.

C.A.11 (Fla.) 2014. Searches and seizures inside a home without a warrant are presumptively unreasonable under the Fourth Amendment, and that presumption is subject only to a few jealously and carefully drawn exceptions. U.S.C.A. Const. Amend. 4.—U.S. v. Yeary, 740 F.3d 569, postconviction relief denied 2018 WL 10647239.

Fla.App. 2 Dist. 2003. A search of a private home without a duly issued search warrant is per se unreasonable under the Fourth Amendment, subject only to a few specifically established and narrowly drawn exceptions. U.S.C.A. Const. Amend. 4.—Vasquez v. State, 870 So.2d 26.

Fla.App. 6 Dist. 2023. Exceptions to the search warrant requirement are jealously and carefully drawn, and there must be a showing by those who seek exemption that the exigencies of the situation made that course imperative; the burden is on those seeking the exemption to show the need for it. U.S. Const. Amend. 4; Fla. Const. art. 1, § 12.—Jean v. State, 369 So.3d 1235.

☞411. Reasonableness in general.

C.A.11 (Fla.) 2024. Ultimate touchstone of Fourth Amendment is reasonableness. U.S. Const. Amend. 4.—Bailey v. Swindell, 89 F.4th 1324.

C.A.11 (Fla.) 2022. A court must examine the totality of the circumstances in order to determine whether a search or seizure is reasonable under the Fourth Amendment. U.S. Const. Amend. 4.—Club Madonna Inc. v. City of Miami Beach, 42 F.4th 1231.

C.A.11 (Fla.) 2022. Whether a search and seizure is unreasonable within the meaning of the Fourth Amendment depends upon the facts and circumstances of each case. U.S. Const. Amend. 4.—United States v. Cohen, 38 F.4th 1364.

C.A.11 (Fla.) 2019. Reasonableness is always the touchstone of Fourth Amendment analysis, because what the Constitution forbids is not all searches and seizures, but unreasonable searches and seizures. U.S. Const. Amend. 4.—United States v. Johnson, 921 F.3d 991, certiorari denied 140 S.Ct. 376, 205 L.Ed.2d 215.

C.A.11 (Fla.) 2018. First factor court considers in balancing competing private and public interests at stake, for purposes of determining the reasonableness of a suspicionless search, is the nature of the privacy interest at issue. U.S. Const. Amend. 4.—Friedenberg v. School Board of Palm Beach County, 911 F.3d 1084.

C.A.11 (Fla.) 2018. The Fourth Amendment protects the people against unreasonable searches and seizures. U.S. Const. Amend. 4.—United States v. Plasencia, 886 F.3d 1336, certiorari denied 139 S.Ct. 837, 202 L.Ed.2d 608.

C.A.11 (Fla.) 2009. "Reasonableness" of a seizure or arrest under the Fourth Amendment turns on the presence or absence of probable cause. U.S.C.A. Const.Amend. 4.—Case v. Eslinger, 555 F.3d 1317.

C.A.11 (Fla.) 2004. While constitutional reasonableness of police investigation does not depend on officer's subjective intent or ulterior motive in conducting investigation, officer may not choose to ignore information that has been offered to him, nor conduct investigation in biased fashion, nor elect not to obtain easily discoverable facts. U.S.C.A. Const.Amend. 4.—Kingsland v. City of Miami, 382 F.3d 1220, rehearing and rehearing denied 124 Fed.Appx. 644.

C.A.5 (Fla.) 1973. Necessity alone, whether produced by danger or otherwise, does not in itself make all nonprobable cause searches reasonable; reasonableness requires that the courts weigh more than the necessity of an airport security search in terms of possible harm to the public; the equation must also take into account the likelihood that the search procedure will be effective in averting the potential harm and, on the opposite balance, the court must evaluate the degree and nature of intrusion into the privacy of the person and effects of the citizen which the search entails.—U.S. v. Skipwith, 482 F.2d 1272.

M.D.Fla. 2018. The determination of whether a seizure is reasonable requires a careful balancing of the nature and quality of the intrusion on the individual's Fourth Amendment interests against the countervailing governmental interests at stake; it turns on the facts and circumstances of each particular case, which includes whether an immediate threat to the safety of the law enforcement officer is posed. U.S. Const. Amend. 4.—Chastang v. Levy, 319 F.Supp.3d 1244.

M.D.Fla. 2016. The Fourth Amendment prohibits unreasonable seizures by police, and its protections extend to brief investigatory stops of persons that fall short of traditional arrest. U.S. Const. Amend. 4.—Montanez v. Carvajal, 224 F.Supp.3d 1274, reversed 889 F.3d 1202, affirmed Rivera v. Carvajal, 777 Fed.Appx. 434.

M.D.Fla. 1997. Test of reasonableness of seizure under Fourth Amendment is not capable of precise definition or mechanical application, and requires careful attention to facts and circumstances of each particular case. U.S.C.A. Const. Amend. 4.—Ogletree v. Columbia County, 34 F.Supp.2d 1349, affirmed 146 F.3d 871.

S.D.Fla. 2019. The ultimate touchstone of the Fourth Amendment is reasonableness. U.S. Const. Amend. 4.—United States v. Javat, 549 F.Supp.3d 1344, report and recommendation adopted 2019 WL 3729060.

S.D.Fla. 2018. Although Fourth Amendment claims typically arise in criminal proceedings, its protections against unreasonable searches and seizures extend to civil matters as well. U.S. Const. Amend. 4.—Federal Trade Commission v. PointBreak Media, LLC, 343 F.Supp.3d 1282.

Although still measured against the standards of probable cause, in the civil context, Fourth Amendment's reasonableness requirement for search and seizure is assessed less stringently than in a criminal context. U.S. Const. Amend. 4.—Id.

S.D.Fla. 2001. Fourth Amendment permits seizures that are reasonable. U.S.C.A. Const. Amend. 4.—U.S. v. Ozuna, 129 F.Supp.2d 1345, affirmed 48 Fed.Appx. 739.

Fla. 2017. The touchstone of an analysis under the Fourth Amendment is always the reasonableness in all the circumstances of the particular governmental invasion of a citizen's personal security; "reasonableness" depends on a balance between the public interest and the individual's right to personal security free from arbitrary interference by law officers. U.S. Const. Amend. 4.—Presley v. State, 227 So.3d 95, certiorari denied 138 S.Ct. 1007, 583 U.S. 1130, 200 L.Ed.2d 274.

Fla. 2017. Both the federal and state constitutions prohibit the government from conducting unreasonable searches. U.S. Const. Amend. 4; Fla. Const. art. 1, § 12.—Davis v. State, 217 So.3d 1006.

Fla. 2006. In justifying particular intrusion, police officer must be able to point to specific and articulable facts which, taken together with rational inferences from those facts, reasonably warrant that intrusion. U.S.C.A. Const.Amend. 4.—Tillman v. State, 934 So.2d 1263.

Fla.App. 1 Dist. 2021. The touchstone of any Fourth Amendment analysis, including one involving a welfare check, is reasonableness, which is measured by the totality of existing circumstances. U.S. Const. Amend. 4.—Taylor v. State, 326 So.3d 115.

Fla.App. 1 Dist. 2020. The ultimate standard set forth in the Fourth Amendment is reasonableness. U.S. Const. Amend. 4.—Calhoun v. State, 308 So.3d 1110.

† This Case was not selected for publication in the National Reporter System

An action is reasonable under the Fourth Amendment, regardless of the individual officer's state of mind, as long as the circumstances, viewed objectively, justify the action. U.S. Const. Amend. 4.—Id.

Fla.App. 1 Dist. 2019. The ultimate standard set forth in the Fourth Amendment is reasonableness of a search and seizure. U.S. Const. Amend. 4.—Hilliard v. State, 285 So.3d 1022.

Determining reasonableness of a search and seizure requires balancing the need for the particular search against the invasion of personal rights that the search entails. U.S. Const. Amend. 4.—Id.

Fla.App. 2 Dist. 2019. A police officer's action is "reasonable" under the Fourth Amendment, regardless of the individual officer's state of mind, as long as the circumstances, viewed objectively, justify the action. U.S. Const. Amend. 4.—State v. M.B.W., 276 So.3d 501.

Fla.App. 3 Dist. 2023. The touchstone of any Fourth Amendment analysis, including one involving a welfare check, is reasonableness, which is measured by the totality of existing circumstances. U.S. Const. Amend. 4.—R.A. v. State, 355 So.3d 1028.

Fla.App. 3 Dist. 2019. In order to satisfy the reasonableness requirement of the Fourth Amendment, what is generally demanded of the many factual determinations that must regularly be made by agents of the government is not that they always be correct, but that they always be reasonable. U.S. Const. Amend. 4.—Alvarez-Mena v. Miami-Dade County, 305 So.3d 63.

Because many situations which confront police officers in the course of executing their duties are more or less ambiguous, room must be allowed for some mistakes on their part, but, under Fourth Amendment, the mistakes must be those of reasonable people, acting on facts leading sensibly to their conclusions of probability. U.S. Const.Amend. 4.—Id.

Fla.App. 3 Dist. 2019. The touchstone of the Fourth Amendment is reasonableness. U.S. Const. Amend. 4.—State v. Quintanilla, 276 So.3d 941, rehearing denied, review denied 2020 WL 633783.

Fla.App. 4 Dist. 2022. Both the federal and state constitutions prohibit the government from conducting unreasonable searches. U.S. Const. Amend. 4; Fla. Const. art. 1, § 12.—Bowman v. State, 335 So.3d 135.

Fla.App. 4 Dist. 2017. Fourth Amendment prohibits unreasonable searches and seizures by the government, and its protections extend to brief investigatory stops of persons or vehicles that fall short of traditional arrest. U.S. Const. Amend. 4.—N.S. v. State, 227 So.3d 132.

Fla.App. 5 Dist. 2019. As its text makes clear, the ultimate touchstone of the Fourth Amendment is reasonableness. U.S. Const. Amend. 4.—State v. Phillips, 266 So.3d 873, review denied 2019 WL 2265037.

Courts generally employ a balancing test to determine the reasonableness of a warrantless search by assessing, on the one hand, the degree to which it intrudes upon an individual's privacy and, on the other, the degree to which it is needed for the promotion of legitimate governmental interests. U.S. Const. Amend. 4; Fla. Const. art. 1, § 12.—Id.

⟜**413. Probable cause in general.**

M.D.Fla. 2018. Officer conducting investigation to establish probable cause may not conduct investigation in a biased fashion. U.S. Const.

Amend. 4.—Davis v. City of Apopka, 356 F.Supp.3d 1366, affirmed 78 F.4th 1326.

N.D.Fla. 2023. "Probable cause" exists when the facts, considering the totality of the circumstances and viewed from the perspective of a reasonable officer, establish a probability or substantial chance of criminal activity; the issue thus is what a reasonable officer could conclude. U.S. Const. Amend. 4.—Warren v. DeSantis, 653 F.Supp.3d 1118, vacated and remanded 2024 WL 105340, vacated and superseded 90 F.4th 1115, vacated and remanded 90 F.4th 1115.

A deficient inquiry and willful ignorance do not establish probable cause. U.S. Const. Amend. 4.—Id.

Fla.App. 1 Dist. 2019. The probable cause standard is a practical and common-sensical standard, and it is enough if there is the kind of fair probability on which reasonable and prudent people, not legal technicians, act.—Johnson v. State, 275 So.3d 800.

Fla.App. 2 Dist. 2004. "Probable cause" is a fluid concept—turning on the assessment of probabilities in particular factual contexts—not readily, or even usefully, reduced to a neat set of legal rules. U.S.C.A. Const.Amend. 4.—State v. Gonzalez, 884 So.2d 330.

Fla.App. 3 Dist. 2020. Probable cause requires only a probability or substantial chance of criminal activity, not an actual showing of such activity; it is not a high bar. U.S. Const. Amend. 4.—J.J. v. State, 312 So.3d 116.

The standard for probable cause does not rely on one factor and does not consider the various factors in isolation; instead, it depends on the totality of the circumstances. U.S. Const. Amend. 4.—Id.

While probable cause must be particularized to a defendant, the Fourth Amendment does not dictate any particular investigative procedure whereby certain specific questions must be asked of the suspect or about the suspect before probable cause is established. U.S. Const. Amend. 4.—Id.

The probable cause analysis is intended to be a practical, nontechnical conception that deals with the factual and practical considerations of everyday life on which reasonable and prudent men, not legal technicians, act. U.S. Const. Amend. 4.—Id.

The probable cause standard is based on the reality that many situations which confront officers in the course of executing their duties are more or less ambiguous. U.S. Const. Amend. 4.—Id.

Fla.App. 3 Dist. 2012. Probable cause is a fluid concept, turning on the assessment of probabilities in particular factual contexts, not readily, or even usefully, reduced to a neat set of legal rules. U.S.C.A. Const.Amend. 4.—State v. M.R., 100 So.3d 272.

Fla.App. 4 Dist. 2002. Probable cause deals with probabilities, which are not technical; they are the factual and practical considerations of everyday life on which reasonable and prudent men, not legal technicians, act. U.S.C.A. Const. Amend. 4.—State v. McDonald, 826 So.2d 1081.

Fla.App. 5 Dist. 2023. Probable cause requires only a probability or substantial chance of criminal activity, not an actual showing of such activity; it is not a high bar. U.S. Const. Amend. 4.—N.H. v. State, 358 So.3d 477.

† This Case was not selected for publication in the National Reporter System

⚿414. Subjective or objective test in general; motive, intent, and pretext in general.

Fla.App. 4 Dist. 1980. Subjective intent cannot change what would otherwise be a valid stop and entry into an illegal one. U.S.C.A.Const. Amend. 4.—State v. Richards, 388 So.2d 573, certiorari denied 102 S.Ct. 359, 454 U.S. 879, 70 L.Ed.2d 188.

⚿415. Special needs in general.

C.A.11 (Fla.) 2018. When a special need is claimed to justify suspicionless search, courts are obliged to undertake a context-specific inquiry, examining closely the competing private and public interests advanced by the parties. U.S. Const. Amend. 4.—Friedenberg v. School Board of Palm Beach County, 911 F.3d 1084.

II. SEARCHES AND SEIZURES IN GENERAL.

(A) IN GENERAL.

⚿423. Application of Fourth Amendment and state equivalents in general.

C.A.11 (Fla.) 2018. A compelling state interest, in the Fourth Amendment context, does not describe a fixed, minimum quantum of governmental concern. U.S. Const. Amend. 4.—Friedenberg v. School Board of Palm Beach County, 911 F.3d 1084.

C.A.11 (Fla.) 2017. Fourth Amendment requires that those searches deemed necessary should be as limited as possible. U.S. Const. Amend. 4.—United States v. Blake, 868 F.3d 960, certiorari denied 138 S.Ct. 1580, 584 U.S. 944, 200 L.Ed.2d 767.

Specific evil targeted by limitation that Fourth Amendment searches be as limited as possible is not that of intrusion per se, but of a general, exploratory rummaging in a person's belongings. U.S. Const. Amend. 4.—Id.

C.A.5 (Fla.) 1973. Warrant requirement of the Fourth Amendment is operative only when there is a need to determine probable cause. U.S.C.A.Const. Amend. 4.—U.S. v. Gravitt, 484 F.2d 375, certiorari denied 94 S.Ct. 879, 414 U.S. 1135, 38 L.Ed.2d 761.

M.D.Fla. 2021. When addressing facial challenge to statute authorizing warrantless searches, proper focus of constitutional inquiry is searches that law actually authorizes, not those for which it is irrelevant; if exigency or warrant justifies officer's search, subject of search must permit it to proceed irrespective of whether it is authorized by statute. U.S. Const. Amend. 4.—Barnett v. MacArthur, 548 F.Supp.3d 1203, motion for relief from judgment denied 2021 WL 4281328, reversed and remanded 2023 WL 4635893.

Fla. 2003. The Fourth Amendment mandates that citizens remain free from unlawful searches and seizures by law enforcement officers. U.S.C.A. Const.Amend. 4.—State v. Diaz, 850 So.2d 435, rehearing denied, certiorari denied 124 S.Ct. 936, 540 U.S. 1075, 157 L.Ed.2d 745.

Fla.App. 1 Dist. 2017. Protection against unreasonable searches and seizures afforded by state constitution is limited to that afforded under Fourth Amendment as interpreted by United States Supreme Court. U.S. Const. Amend. 4; Fla. Const. art. 1, § 12.—Purifoy v. State, 225 So.3d 867, review denied 2017 WL 5508743.

Fla.App. 2 Dist. 2023. Local law enforcement agency policies may be indicative of whether a search occasioned by a noncriminal seizure is reasonable, but they do not dictate ipso facto the parameters of the Fourth Amendment. U.S. Const. Amend. 4.—K.M. v. State, 359 So.3d 414.

Fla.App. 2 Dist. 2007. Reasonableness of an entry by police officers upon private property is measured by the totality of existing circumstances. U.S.C.A. Const.Amend. 4.—P.B.P. v. State, 955 So.2d 618, review denied 966 So.2d 967.

Fla.App. 5 Dist. 2009. The Fourth Amendment protects people, not places, and only under circumstances where the person enjoys a reasonable expectation of privacy. U.S.C.A. Const. Amend. 4.—Brown v. State, 24 So.3d 671, review denied 39 So.3d 1264, certiorari denied 134 S.Ct. 2730, 573 U.S. 908, 189 L.Ed.2d 771.

(B) WHAT CONSTITUTES SEARCH OR SEIZURE.

⚿431. In general.

C.A.11 (Fla.) 2020. "Search" occurs, for purposes of the Fourth Amendment, when government violates subjective expectation of privacy that society recognizes as reasonable. U.S. Const. Amend. 4.—United States v. Trader, 981 F.3d 961, certiorari denied 142 S.Ct. 296, 211 L.Ed.2d 139.

C.A.11 (Fla.) 2015. To determine whether a search occurred under the reasonable-expectation-of-privacy test requires a two-part inquiry: (1) has an individual manifested a subjective expectation of privacy in the object of the challenged search; and (2) is society willing to recognize that expectation as reasonable. U.S.C.A. Const.Amend. 4.—U.S. v. Davis, 785 F.3d 498, certiorari denied 136 S.Ct. 479, 577 U.S. 975, 193 L.Ed.2d 349, appeal after new sentencing hearing 711 Fed.Appx. 605, certiorari denied 138 S.Ct. 1548, 584 U.S. 935, 200 L.Ed.2d 749, denial of post-conviction relief affirmed 2022 WL 402915, certiorari denied 143 S.Ct. 647, 215 L.Ed.2d 88.

M.D.Fla. 2018. A "search," in the context of the Fourth Amendment, occurs when an expectation of privacy that society is prepared to consider reasonable is infringed. U.S. Const. Amend. 4.—Chastang v. Levy, 319 F.Supp.3d 1244.

Fla.App. 1 Dist. 2021. A "search" under the Fourth Amendment occurs when an expectation of privacy that society is prepared to consider reasonable is infringed. U.S. Const. Amend. 4.—Robinson v. State, 327 So.3d 1276.

Fla.App. 1 Dist. 2020. Fourth Amendment searches now fall into two general hemispheres: trespassory searches in which the government physically intrudes onto the person or property of an individual, and intrusion into an area in which a person possesses a reasonable expectation of privacy. U.S. Const. Amend. 4.—Bailey v. State, 311 So.3d 303, rehearing denied, review denied 2021 WL 2408431, certiorari denied 142 S.Ct. 568, 211 L.Ed.2d 354.

In order to claim protection from unreasonable search under the privacy-based approach to the Fourth Amendment, a defendant's conduct must exhibit an actual, subjective expectation of privacy and that subjective expectation must be one which society recognizes as objectively reasonable; where these two requirements are met, official intrusion into that private sphere generally qualifies as a search and requires a warrant supported by probable cause. U.S. Const. Amend. 4.—Id.

The "mosaic theory" applies a cumulative understanding of data collection by police and analyzes searches as a collective sequence of steps rather than individual ones; it considers police action to be viewed over time as a collective "mosaic" of surveillance and allows the whole picture to qualify as a protected Fourth Amendment search, even if the individual steps that contribute to the full picture do not, in isolation, reach that constitutional threshold. U.S. Const. Amend. 4.—Id.

Fla.App. 1 Dist. 2019. Under the Fourth Amendment, a "search" occurs when an individual's reasonable expectation of privacy is infringed by an agent of the government. U.S. Const. Amend. 4.—Bryant v. State, 265 So.3d 726.

Fla.App. 1 Dist. 2017. "Search" occurs when expectation of privacy that society is prepared to consider reasonable is infringed. U.S. Const. Amend. 4; Fla. Const. art. 1, § 12.—Purifoy v. State, 225 So.3d 867, review denied 2017 WL 5508743.

Fla.App. 2 Dist. 2022. For purposes of the Fourth Amendment, a "search" occurs only when an individual's reasonable expectation of privacy is infringed by an agent of the government. U.S. Const. Amend. 4.—Youngman v. State, 342 So.3d 770.

A Fourth Amendment "search" does not occur unless the individual manifested a subjective expectation of privacy in the object of the challenged search, and society is willing to recognize that expectation as reasonable. U.S. Const. Amend. 4.—Id.

Fla.App. 2 Dist. 2018. A Fourth Amendment "search" does not occur unless the individual manifested a subjective expectation of privacy in the object of the challenged search and society is willing to recognize that expectation as reasonable. U.S. Const. Amend. 4.—McClelland v. State, 255 So.3d 929.

Fla.App. 4 Dist. 2018. A "search" occurs within the meaning of the Fourth Amendment when government action invades an individual's justifiable or reasonable expectation of privacy. U.S. Const. Amend. 4.—Osorio v. State, 244 So.3d 1115.

Fla.App. 4 Dist. 2017. A Fourth Amendment search occurs when the government violates a subjective expectation of privacy that society recognizes as reasonable. U.S. Const. Amend. 4.—State v. Worsham, 227 So.3d 602, certiorari denied 138 S.Ct. 264, 583 U.S. 873, 199 L.Ed.2d 125.

Fla.App. 4 Dist. 2004. In order to be classified as a search, law enforcement conduct must violate a constitutionally protected reasonable expectation of privacy. U.S.C.A. Const.Amend. 4; West's F.S.A. Const. Art. 1, § 12.—State v. Rabb, 881 So.2d 587, rehearing denied, certiorari granted, vacated 125 S.Ct. 2246, 544 U.S. 1028, 161 L.Ed.2d 1051, on remand 920 So.2d 1175, review denied 933 So.2d 522, certiorari denied 127 S.Ct. 665, 549 U.S. 1052, 166 L.Ed.2d 513.

Fla.App. 4 Dist. 1978. "Search" is an inspection or examination of places closed from public or general view, and requires some measure of force or intrusion, while "seizure" is the act of taking custody of evidence or contraband.—Lightfoot v. State, 356 So.2d 331, certiorari denied 361 So.2d 833.

⟶**433. —— In general.**

C.A.11 (Fla.) 2005. To assert a Fourth Amendment claim based on the use of excessive force, the plaintiffs must allege (1) that a seizure occurred and (2) that the force used to effect the seizure was unreasonable. U.S.C.A. Const. Amend. 4.—Troupe v. Sarasota County, Fla., 419 F.3d 1160, certiorari denied 126 S.Ct. 1914, 547 U.S. 1112, 164 L.Ed.2d 664.

Fla.App. 4 Dist. 2012. Per se rules are inappropriate in the context of Fourth Amendment seizure analyses. U.S.C.A. Const.Amend. 4.—R.J.C. v. State, 84 So.3d 1250.

⟶**435. Physical intrusion in general.**

Fla.App. 1 Dist. 2020. Fourth Amendment searches now fall into two general hemispheres: trespassory searches in which the government physically intrudes onto the person or property of an individual, and intrusion into an area in which a person possesses a reasonable expectation of privacy. U.S. Const. Amend. 4.—Bailey v. State, 311 So.3d 303, rehearing denied, review denied 2021 WL 2408431, certiorari denied 142 S.Ct. 568, 211 L.Ed.2d 354.

⟶**436. Interference with property interests in general.**

C.A.11 (Fla.) 2022. Under Fourth Amendment, a "seizure" of property occurs when there is some meaningful interference with individual's possessory interests in that property. U.S. Const. Amend. 4.—Public Risk Management of Florida v. Munich Reinsurance America, Inc., 38 F.4th 1298.

C.A.11 (Fla.) 2019. A person suffers a "seizure" of his property within the meaning of the Fourth Amendment when there is a meaningful interference with his possessory interest in it. U.S. Const. Amend. 4.—United States v. Babcock, 924 F.3d 1180, appeal from denial of post-conviction relief dismissed 2023 WL 4117503.

C.A.11 (Fla.) 2018. A seizure of property within meaning of the Fourth Amendment occurs when there is a meaningful interference with a person's possessory interest in it. U.S. Const. Amend. 4.—Crocker v. Beatty, 886 F.3d 1132.

M.D.Fla. 2018. A "seizure of property," in the context of the Fourth Amendment, occurs when there is some meaningful interference with an individual's possessory interests in that property. U.S. Const. Amend. 4.—Chastang v. Levy, 319 F.Supp.3d 1244.

Fla.App. 1 Dist. 2017. "Seizure" of property occurs when there is some meaningful interference with individual's possessory interests in that property. U.S. Const. Amend. 4; Fla. Const. art. 1, § 12.—Purifoy v. State, 225 So.3d 867, review denied 2017 WL 5508743.

Fla.App. 2 Dist. 2019. A "seizure" in the Fourth Amendment context occurs when there is some meaningful interference with an individual's possessory interests in that property. U.S. Const. Amend. 4.—State v. Miller, 281 So.3d 583.

⟶**439. —— Items in plain view.**

Fla.App. 2 Dist. 2020. When a suspect empties his pockets in response to an officer's directive that he do so, the legal effect is the same as if the officer had himself searched the suspect's pockets; in contrast, when an officer simply asks a question and the suspect goes beyond the officer's initial inquiry and spontaneously empties his pockets, no search occurs. U.S. Const. Amend. 4.—State v. J.C., 292 So.3d 30.

Fla.App. 4 Dist. 2018. The rationale of the plain-view doctrine is that if contraband is left in open view and is observed by a police officer from a lawful vantage point, there has been no invasion of a legitimate expectation of privacy and thus no "search" within the meaning of the

† This Case was not selected for publication in the National Reporter System

Fourth Amendment—or at least no search independent of the initial intrusion that gave the officers their vantage point. U.S. Const. Amend. 4.—T.T. v. State, 253 So.3d 15.

⚷=**441. —— In general.**

† **C.A.11 (Fla.) 2018.** Detective's inquiry into firearm's serial number was not a "search" under the Fourth Amendment, since detective's possession of firearm was lawful; detective came across firearm while conducting a lawful search of defendant's garage, detective did not take any unauthorized action that brought into view any concealed portion of the firearm, and detective's call to run the serial number did not result in any additional invasion into defendant's privacy interests. U.S. Const. Amend. 4.—United States v. Kendricks, 758 Fed.Appx. 687, certiorari denied 139 S.Ct. 2038, 204 L.Ed.2d 236.

† **C.A.11 (Fla.) 2007.** Attempt by Florida Department of Health (DOH) and municipal officials to inspect property where church operated school and issuing pastor a notice to appear for his refusal to allow inspection was neither a search nor a seizure under Fourth Amendment; officials and inspectors did not search or seize anything, and notice to appear merely required pastor to appear in court at a later date. U.S.C.A. Const.Amend. 4.—Youngblood v. Florida Dept. of Health, 224 Fed.Appx. 909.

Fla.App. 1 Dist. 2018. Law enforcement officers do not engage in a search by merely asking questions. U.S. Const. Amend. 4.—Tripp v. State, 251 So.3d 982.

Asking a question of a person not in custody is neither a search nor a seizure. U.S. Const. Amend. 4.—Id.

Fla.App. 2 Dist. 2020. When a suspect empties his pockets in response to an officer's directive that he do so, the legal effect is the same as if the officer had himself searched the suspect's pockets; in contrast, when an officer simply asks a question and the suspect goes beyond the officer's initial inquiry and spontaneously empties his pockets, no search occurs. U.S. Const. Amend. 4.—State v. J.C., 292 So.3d 30.

Fla.App. 2 Dist. 1999. Police officer conducted a "seizure," rather than a "strip search," by pulling top of defendant's pants toward officer and seizing plastic bag of crack cocaine from inside defendant's pants. West's F.S.A. § 901.211(1).—State v. Days, 751 So.2d 87, rehearing denied.

Fla.App. 3 Dist. 2009. Asking a question of a person not in custody is neither a search nor a seizure.—D.A. v. State, 10 So.3d 674, review denied 20 So.3d 848, vacated 49 So.3d 746, review denied 49 So.3d 746.

Fla.App. 4 Dist. 1993. Defendant was not entitled to *Miranda* warnings before undercover officer ordered defendant to produce drugs which detective observed defendant using; order to disclose concealed drugs was search rather than an arrest. U.S.C.A. Const.Amends. 4, 5.—State v. Meyer, 615 So.2d 205.

Fla.App. 4 Dist. 1972. Where patrolling officer had stopped defendant in early morning hours as defendant was walking on street in fashionable hotel and residential area, officer's inquiry concerning bulge in watchpocket of defendant's trousers did not amount to a search and defendant's conduct in producing a vial from his watchpocket and throwing vial, into adjacent waterway was an abandonment of possession; thus, vial, which was found to contain marijuana, was admissible, notwithstanding that officer had

no valid basis to stop defendant and interrogate him. F.S.A. § 901.151.—Riley v. State, 266 So.2d 173.

⚷=**442. —— Dwellings and residences in general.**

† **C.A.11 (Fla.) 2018.** Detective's inquiry into firearm's serial number was not a "search" under the Fourth Amendment, since detective's possession of firearm was lawful; detective came across firearm while conducting a lawful search of defendant's garage, detective did not take any unauthorized action that brought into view any concealed portion of the firearm, and detective's call to run the serial number did not result in any additional invasion into defendant's privacy interests. U.S. Const. Amend. 4.—United States v. Kendricks, 758 Fed.Appx. 687, certiorari denied 139 S.Ct. 2038, 204 L.Ed.2d 236.

Fla.App. 1 Dist. 2021. A person's private residence is accorded a special status under the Fourth Amendment, and a substantial government intrusion into the sanctity of the home constitutes a search within the Fourth Amendment. U.S. Const. Amend. 4.—Robinson v. State, 327 So.3d 1276.

Fla.App. 3 Dist. 1980. Broadly speaking, a search and seizure under the Fourth Amendment covers any official invasion of the person's expectation of privacy as to his person, house, papers or effects. U.S.C.A.Const. Amend. 4.—Mata v. State, 380 So.2d 1157, petition for review denied 389 So.2d 1112.

⚷=**443. —— Occasional or temporary dwellings; hotels and motels.**

Fla.App. 2 Dist. 2007. A person's home is accorded the full range of Fourth Amendment protections because there is an expectation of privacy in one's dwelling; thus, a nonconsensual entry into a home, a motel room, or other residence constitutes a search. U.S.C.A. Const.Amend. 4.—Holloman v. State, 959 So.2d 403.

⚷=**444. —— Luggage, bags, and other containers.**

C.A.5 (Fla.) 1981. Use of dogs to sniff exteriors of suitcases did not constitute search within meaning of Fourth Amendment, and light press of the hands along outside of case was not sufficiently intrusive to require different result. U.S.C.A.Const. Amend. 4.—U.S. v. Viera, 644 F.2d 509, certiorari denied Alonso v. U.S., 102 S.Ct. 332, 454 U.S. 867, 70 L.Ed.2d 169, certiorari denied 102 S.Ct. 332, 454 U.S. 867, 70 L.Ed.2d 169.

C.A.5 (Fla.) 1981. Warrantless search of package after addressee had picked it up at post office and after a prior search at foreign mail center had revealed the package to contain heroin was not unreasonable. U.S.C.A.Const. Amend. 4.—U.S. v. Richards, 638 F.2d 765, rehearing denied 646 F.2d 962, certiorari denied 102 S.Ct. 669, 454 U.S. 1097, 70 L.Ed.2d 638.

Fla.App. 3 Dist. 1984. Temporary seizure of defendant's luggage for narcotics "dog sniff" was reasonable, where defendant was traveling under assumed name, denied luggage in question was his, although he had been previously observed by police arriving at station in possession of the luggage, claimed that someone else present nearby owned the luggage, although no one else was in lobby area of station, and defendant was extremely nervous. U.S.C.A. Const.Amend. 4.—State v. Bullock, 460 So.2d 517.

Fla.App. 3 Dist. 1983. Evidence did not show that delay in airplane's departure was brought

---

† **This Case was not selected for publication in the National Reporter System**

about by state action so as to convert removal of defendant's suitcase from baggage cart, otherwise de minimis intrusion, either into detention without founded suspicion or seizure without probable cause.—Baston v. State, 436 So.2d 1092.

Fla.App. 4 Dist. 2008. The temporary detention of two packages at mailing facility was not so unreasonable as to interfere, in any meaningful way, with the defendant's packages, and therefore, the temporary detention was not a "seizure" within the meaning of the Fourth Amendment, and because there was no seizure, there was no need for the State to establish reasonable suspicion, and considering that the dog sniff of the packages was also not a search, the defendant's Fourth Amendment rights were not implicated. U.S.C.A. Const.Amend. 4.—Lindo v. State, 983 So.2d 672.

⟜**445. —— Vehicles.**
† **C.A.11 (Fla.) 2020.** Defendant had no reasonable expectation of privacy in a vehicle's license tag, and thus police officer running the tag information through a law enforcement database without warrant was not a search under the Fourth Amendment, even though defendant was parked at a privately owned gas station rather than driving on a public road, where license tags were required by law to be displayed in plain view and the gas station was open to the public. U.S. Const. Amend. 4.—United States v. Johnson, 811 Fed.Appx. 564.

Fla. 1991. Stopping motor vehicle and detaining occupant constitutes "seizure" within meaning of Fourth and Fourteenth Amendments, even though stop is limited and resulting detention is quite brief; as such, stop must comport with objective standards of reasonableness, whether that amounts to probable cause or less stringent test. U.S.C.A. Const.Amends. 4, 14.—Nelson v. State, 578 So.2d 694.

⟜**447. —— Damage to or destruction of property.**
M.D.Fla. 2018. Destroying property may constitute a seizure under the Fourth Amendment if the destruction was unreasonable under the circumstances. U.S. Const. Amend. 4.—Chastang v. Levy, 319 F.Supp.3d 1244.

⟜**448. —— Killing or injuring animals.**
M.D.Fla. 2018. A police officer's shooting of a pet dog may constitute a seizure under the Fourth Amendment if it was objectively unreasonable in light of the facts and circumstances. U.S. Const. Amend. 4.—Chastang v. Levy, 319 F.Supp.3d 1244.

⟜**452. —— Use of dogs.**
U.S.Fla. 2013. Law enforcement officers' use of drug-sniffing dog on front porch of home, to investigate an unverified tip that marijuana was being grown in the home, was a trespassory invasion of the curtilage which constituted a "search" for Fourth Amendment purposes. U.S.C.A. Const.Amend. 4.—Florida v. Jardines, 133 S.Ct. 1409, 569 U.S. 1, 185 L.Ed.2d 495.

Fla.App. 1 Dist. 2021. Dog sniff conducted on common external walkway in front of defendant's motel room did not constitute search under Fourth Amendment; walkway was open to use by others, including other motel guests, visitors, and employees, walkway was in nature of public, not private, area, police could walk down motel walkway without warrant, walkway in front of motel room was not curtilage, and defendant did not take steps to protect walkway from observation by people passing by. U.S. Const. Amend. 4.—Robinson v. State, 327 So.3d 1276.

Fla.App. 1 Dist. 2018. A warrantless canine sniff test on a residence or its curtilage violates the Fourth Amendment. U.S. Const. Amend. 4.—Davis v. State, 257 So.3d 1159.

Fla.App. 1 Dist. 2008. Use of a narcotics dog to sniff a vehicle does not constitute a search or seizure, and may be conducted during a consensual encounter or traffic stop; accordingly, when an officer is still writing a citation during a traffic stop when a backup officer or canine unit arrives, the lapse of time is generally not unreasonable. U.S.C.A. Const.Amend. 4.—Napoleon v. State, 985 So.2d 1170.

Fla.App. 3 Dist. 1984. Temporary seizure of defendant's luggage for narcotics "dog sniff" was reasonable, where defendant was traveling under assumed name, denied luggage in question was his, although he had been previously observed by police arriving at station in possession of the luggage, claimed that someone else present nearby owned the luggage, although no one else was in lobby area of station, and defendant was extremely nervous. U.S.C.A. Const.Amend. 4.—State v. Bullock, 460 So.2d 517.

Fla.App. 3 Dist. 1981. There was reasonable expectation of privacy as to contents of airline passenger's suitcase, but dog sniff was not Fourth Amendment "search." U.S.C.A.Const. Amend. 4.—State v. Mosier, 392 So.2d 602, appeal after remand 415 So.2d 771.

Fla.App. 3 Dist. 1980. Where police had founded suspicion that individuals were engaged in criminal activity and observed such individuals check baggage at airline, use of narcotics dog to sniff baggage in baggage area was reasonable and did not violate search and seizure provisions of State or Federal Constitution. U.S.C.A.Const. Amend. 4.—Mata v. State, 380 So.2d 1157, petition for review denied 389 So.2d 1112.

Fla.App. 4 Dist. 1995. Canine sniff by narcotics detection dog, which discloses presence or absence of narcotics, is regarded as constitutionally proper because its limited scope and method of investigation do not constitute search, however, canine sniff that alerts to package does not eliminate requirement that, absent exigent circumstances, consent or other recognized exceptions, search warrant must be obtained before search of contents of package passes constitutional muster. U.S.C.A. Const.Amend. 4.—Daniels v. Cochran, 654 So.2d 609.

Fla.App. 5 Dist. 2010. The use of a narcotics dog to sniff a vehicle does not constitute a search and may be conducted during a consensual encounter or traffic stop; however, the canine search of the exterior of the vehicle must be completed within the time required to issue a citation. U.S.C.A. Const.Amend. 4.—Whitfield v. State, 33 So.3d 787.

⟜**454. Aerial surveillance.**
Fla. 1987. Defendant had a reasonable expectation of privacy in greenhouse, and its contents located within curtilage of his mobile home, from aerial observations by police officer flying in helicopter 400 feet above greenhouse, notwithstanding that two panels were missing from roof of greenhouse exposing approximately one-tenth of roof area. U.S.C.A. Const.Amend. 4; West's F.S.A. Const. Art. 1, § 12.—Riley v. State, 511 So.2d 282, certiorari granted 108 S.Ct. 1011, 484 U.S. 1058, 98 L.Ed.2d 977, reversed 109 S.Ct. 693, 488 U.S. 445, 102 L.Ed.2d 835, rehearing

denied 109 S.Ct. 1659, 490 U.S. 1014, 104 L.Ed.2d 172, on remand 549 So.2d 673.

⟜457. —— In general.

Fla.App. 2 Dist. 2018. Detectives' use of a Yagi antenna from outside residence with open Wi-Fi network to determine where device that was accessing the network without authorization and downloading and sharing child pornography was physically located did not constitute a "search" within meaning of Fourth Amendment; defendant could not assert a subjective expectation of privacy that society would consider as reasonable or legitimate where defendant did not confine his activities to the interior of his motorhome but instead extended an invisible, virtual arm outside the motorhome in order to illegally access the Wi-Fi network. U.S. Const. Amend. 4. —McClelland v. State, 255 So.3d 929.

⟜460. —— Global positioning system; trackers.

C.A.11 (Fla.) 2020. Acquisition of historical cell-site records is a "search" under the Fourth Amendment, so the government must obtain a warrant to access such records. U.S. Const. Amend. 4.—United States v. Green, 981 F.3d 945, certiorari denied 141 S.Ct. 2690, 210 L.Ed.2d 845.

C.A.11 (Fla.) 2020. Acquisition of historical cell-site records is a "search" under the Fourth Amendment, so the government must obtain a warrant to access such records. U.S. Const. Amend. 4.—United States v. Green, 969 F.3d 1194, vacated and superseded 981 F.3d 945, certiorari denied 141 S.Ct. 2690, 210 L.Ed.2d 845.

⟜461. Accessing electronic devices or information.

S.D.Fla. 2011. Name which appeared on caller ID screen of defendant's cell phone when the phone rang after it was seized incident to his arrest was within plain view, such that its warrantless observation by agents did not constitute a "search" within meaning of the Fourth Amendment. U.S.C.A. Const.Amend. 4.—U.S. v. Gomez, 807 F.Supp.2d 1134.

⟜464. —— In general.

Fla.App. 3 Dist. 1979. Searches of the person include any physical touching of an individual's body or clothing that causes hidden objects or matters to be revealed, such as rummaging through one's pockets or clothing, patting down one's outer clothing without going into the pockets or other inner recesses, knocking property loose from an individual by tackling him, extracting an individual's blood by means of a hypodermic needle, or taking scrapings from beneath his fingernails. West's F.S.A.Const. art. 1, § 12; U.S.C.A.Const. Amends. 4, 14.—State v. Oliver, 368 So.2d 1331, certiorari dismissed 383 So.2d 1200.

⟜467. —— Blood, breath, urine, saliva, or hair samples in general.

Fla.App. 3 Dist. 2019. A blood draw conducted at the direction of the police constitutes a search and seizure under the Fourth Amendment. U.S. Const. Amend. 4.—State v. Quintanilla, 276 So.3d 941, rehearing denied, review denied 2020 WL 633783.

Fla.App. 4 Dist. 2018. Compulsory administration of a blood test involves the broadly conceived reach of a search and seizure under the Fourth Amendment. U.S. Const. Amend. 4; Fla. Const. art. 1, § 12.—McGraw v. State, 245 So.3d

760, review granted 2018 WL 3342880, vacated 289 So.3d 836, rehearing granted in part 2020 WL 838040, on remand 299 So.3d 12.

Fla.App. 4 Dist. 2017. A blood draw conducted under police direction is considered a search and seizure under the Fourth Amendment. U.S. Const. Amend. 4.—Goodman v. State, 229 So.3d 366, review denied 2018 WL 1256499, certiorari denied 139 S.Ct. 274, 202 L.Ed.2d 135.

⟜468. —— DNA testing.

Fla.App. 1 Dist. 2020. The retention of a lawfully obtained DNA record on the Combined DNA Index System (CODIS) for future use does not constitute a separate search or implicate the Fourth Amendment. U.S. Const. Amend. 4.— Porter v. State, 298 So.3d 140, review denied 2020 WL 6336032.

⟜469. —— Drug testing.

S.D.Fla. 2017. A government-mandated drug test is a search within the meaning of the Fourth Amendment. U.S. Const. Amend. 4.—Friedenberg v. School Board of Palm Beach County, 257 F.Supp.3d 1295, affirmed 911 F.3d 1084.

Fla. 2019. A blood alcohol test is a "search," for purposes of the Fourth Amendment's protection of the right to be free of unreasonable searches and seizures. U.S. Const. Amend. 4.— McGraw v. State, 289 So.3d 836, rehearing granted in part 2020 WL 838040, on remand 299 So.3d 12.

⟜470. Private search, government intrusions within scope of.

Fla.App. 1 Dist. 2018. Police officers did not conduct search when they opened one of several Universal Serial Bus (USB) drives and viewed video file depicting what appeared to be a sexual battery by man later identified as defendant; officers initially viewed one file on one USB drive after being informed by private individual in possession of USB drives that video on the drive contained "some sick shit," individual's description of the video was consistent with what officers described seeing prior to turning over drives to Sex Crimes Unit, and because individual only viewed one video, it was reasonable to infer that he directed officers to the specific USB drive that contained the video that he reviewed. U.S. Const. Amend. 4.—Duke v. State, 255 So.3d 478, rehearing denied, habeas corpus denied 312 So.3d 857, rehearing denied.

(C) PERSONS, PLACES, AND THINGS PROTECTED.

⟜481. In general.

S.D.Fla. 2021. Probable cause to arrest alone is not enough justify entry into a home's curtilage to conduct a warrantless search or seizure, and so the government must also show an applicable exception to the warrant requirement to justify the search. U.S. Const. Amend. 4.—United States v. Howard, 557 F.Supp.3d 1262.

⟜482. Protection of people or places in general.

C.A.11 (Fla.) 2020. Fourth Amendment protects people, not places. U.S. Const. Amend. 4.— United States v. Gayden, 977 F.3d 1146, certiorari denied 142 S.Ct. 128, 211 L.Ed.2d 42.

M.D.Fla. 1980. Fourth Amendment prohibitions apply in civil as well as criminal investigations, and protect commercial premises as well as homes, but Fourth Amendment protects legitimate expectations of privacy of persons, not

---

† **This Case was not selected for publication in the National Reporter System**

places, and defendant must establish that his own Fourth Amendment rights were violated by conduct upon which he wishes to base exclusion. U.S.C.A.Const. Amend. 4.—U.S. v. Hartley, 486 F.Supp. 1348, affirmed 678 F.2d 961, rehearing denied 688 F.2d 852, certiorari denied 103 S.Ct. 815, 459 U.S. 1170, 74 L.Ed.2d 1014, certiorari denied Treasure Isle, Inc., v. U.S., 103 S.Ct. 834, 459 U.S. 1183, 74 L.Ed.2d 1027.

Fla.App. 1 Dist. 2021. The Fourth Amendment protects people, not places, and whether it affords protection depends on (1) whether the person has exhibited an actual, subjective expectation of privacy in the object of the search, and (2) whether society is prepared to recognize that expectation as reasonable. U.S. Const. Amend. 4.—Robinson v. State, 327 So.3d 1276.

Fla.App. 4 Dist. 2020. The Fourth Amendment protects people from unreasonable searches, not places. U.S. Const. Amend. 4.—State v. Kraft, 301 So.3d 981.

Fla.App. 5 Dist. 2009. The Fourth Amendment protects people, not places. U.S.C.A. Const.Amend. 4.—State v. Halpin, 13 So.3d 75.

←484. —— In general.

C.A.11 (Fla.) 2020. What person knowingly exposes to public, even in his home or office, is not subject of Fourth Amendment protection. U.S. Const. Amend. 4.—United States v. Gayden, 977 F.3d 1146, certiorari denied 142 S.Ct. 128, 211 L.Ed.2d 42.

Fourth Amendment's application depends on whether person invoking its protection can claim justifiable, reasonable, or legitimate expectation of privacy that has been invaded by government action. U.S. Const. Amend. 4.—Id.

C.A.11 (Fla.) 2018. The Fourth Amendment exists to protect the citizen against invasion of privacy. U.S. Const. Amend. 4.—Montanez v. Carvajal, 889 F.3d 1202.

Fla.App. 1 Dist. 2020. Generally, information that a person knowingly exposes to the public is not subject of Fourth Amendment protection. U.S. Const. Amend. 4.—Bailey v. State, 311 So.3d 303, rehearing denied, review denied 2021 WL 2408431, certiorari denied 142 S.Ct. 568, 211 L.Ed.2d 354.

Fla.App. 1 Dist. 2018. A "search" occurs only when an individual's reasonable expectation of privacy is infringed by an agent of the government. U.S. Const. Amend. 4.—Duke v. State, 255 So.3d 478, rehearing denied, habeas corpus denied 312 So.3d 857, rehearing denied.

Fla.App. 2 Dist. 2019. The capacity to claim constitutional protection of privacy depends upon the person and not merely upon a property right in the invaded place. U.S. Const. Amend. 4.—State v. Pettis, 266 So.3d 238, on remand 2019 WL 8195122.

Fla.App. 3 Dist. 1980. Broadly speaking, a search and seizure under the Fourth Amendment covers any official invasion of the person's expectation of privacy as to his person, house, papers or effects. U.S.C.A.Const. Amend. 4.—Mata v. State, 380 So.2d 1157, petition for review denied 389 So.2d 1112.

Fla.App. 4 Dist. 2017. Information someone seeks to preserve as private, even where that information is accessible to the public, may be constitutionally protected under the Fourth Amendment. U.S. Const. Amend. 4.—State v. Worsham, 227 So.3d 602, certiorari denied 138 S.Ct. 264, 583 U.S. 873, 199 L.Ed.2d 125.

←485. —— Legitimacy of interest or expectation in general; factors considered.

M.D.Fla. 2018. The protections afforded to individuals under the Fourth Amendment depend upon whether the individual had a legitimate expectation of privacy in the invaded place. U.S. Const. Amend. 4.—United States v. Valdarnini, 314 F.Supp.3d 1312.

Fla.App. 1 Dist. 2008. The application of the Fourth Amendment depends on whether the person invoking its protection can claim a justifiable, a reasonable, or a legitimate expectation of privacy that has been invaded by government action. U.S.C.A. Const.Amend. 4.—State v. Butler, 1 So.3d 242, rehearing denied.

Fla.App. 4 Dist. 2011. To invoke the Fourth Amendment, a criminal defendant must establish standing by demonstrating a legitimate expectation of privacy in the area searched or the item seized, and a legitimate expectation of privacy consists of both a subjective expectation and an objectively reasonable expectation, as determined by societal standards. U.S.C.A. Const.Amend. 4. —Peraza v. State, 69 So.3d 338.

←486. —— Subjective or objective expectation.

Fla. 2014. The touchstone of Fourth Amendment analysis of a search is whether a person has a constitutionally-protected reasonable expectation of privacy, and in applying the test, the court examines whether the individual manifested a subjective expectation of privacy and whether society is willing to recognize that expectation as reasonable. U.S.C.A. Const.Amend. 4.—Tracey v. State, 152 So.3d 504, rehearing denied, on remand 162 So.3d 217.

Fla.App. 1 Dist. 2020. In order to claim protection from unreasonable search under the privacy-based approach to the Fourth Amendment, a defendant's conduct must exhibit an actual, subjective expectation of privacy and that subjective expectation must be one which society recognizes as objectively reasonable; where these two requirements are met, official intrusion into that private sphere generally qualifies as a search and requires a warrant supported by probable cause. U.S. Const. Amend. 4.—Bailey v. State, 311 So.3d 303, rehearing denied, review denied 2021 WL 2408431, certiorari denied 142 S.Ct. 568, 211 L.Ed.2d 354.

The mere fact that an individual has on some level allowed information to be conveyed to a third party is not an end-all point of consideration preventing such individual from showing a subjective expectation of privacy in regards to a putative privacy interest, as required to bring such information within the protections of the Fourth Amendment. U.S. Const. Amend. 4.—Id.

←487. —— Reasonableness; reasonable expectation of privacy.

C.A.11 (Fla.) 2020. Individual's Fourth Amendment rights are not infringed, or even implicated, by a search of a thing or place in which he has no reasonable expectation of privacy. U.S. Const. Amend. 4.—United States v. Ross, 964 F.3d 1034, certiorari denied 141 S.Ct. 1394, 209 L.Ed.2d 132.

C.A.11 (Fla.) 2020. An individual's Fourth Amendment rights are not infringed, or even implicated, by a search of a thing or place in which he has no reasonable expectation of privacy. U.S. Const. Amend. 4.—United States v. Ross, 963 F.3d 1056, on remand 964 F.3d 1034,

---

† This Case was not selected for publication in the National Reporter System

certiorari denied 141 S.Ct. 1394, 209 L.Ed.2d 132.

C.A.11 (Fla.) 2019. An individual's Fourth Amendment rights are not infringed, or even implicated, by a search of a thing or place in which he has no reasonable expectation of privacy. U.S. Const. Amend. 4.—United States v. Ross, 941 F.3d 1058, rehearing granted, vacated 953 F.3d 744, on rehearing 963 F.3d 1056, on remand 964 F.3d 1034, certiorari denied 141 S.Ct. 1394, 209 L.Ed.2d 132.

C.A.11 (Fla.) 2018. Under the Fourth Amendment, once the privacy interest is invaded legally by an official of the state, the citizen has lost his reasonable expectation of privacy to the extent of the invasion. U.S. Const. Amend. 4.—Montanez v. Carvajal, 889 F.3d 1202.

C.A.11 (Fla.) 2015. To determine whether a search occurred under the reasonable-expectation-of-privacy test requires a two-part inquiry: (1) has an individual manifested a subjective expectation of privacy in the object of the challenged search; and (2) is society willing to recognize that expectation as reasonable. U.S.C.A. Const.Amend. 4.—U.S. v. Davis, 785 F.3d 498, certiorari denied 136 S.Ct. 479, 577 U.S. 975, 193 L.Ed.2d 349, appeal after new sentencing hearing 711 Fed.Appx. 605, certiorari denied 138 S.Ct. 1548, 584 U.S. 935, 200 L.Ed.2d 749, denial of post-conviction relief affirmed 2022 WL 402915, certiorari denied 143 S.Ct. 647, 215 L.Ed.2d 88.

C.A.11 (Fla.) 2014. Because society recognizes as reasonable an expectation of privacy under the Fourth Amendment for confidential conversations between individuals, the government needs a warrant to intercept or record such conversations. U.S.C.A. Const.Amend. 4.—Gennusa v. Canova, 748 F.3d 1103.

M.D.Fla. 2018. A subjective expectation of privacy is legitimate if it is one that society is prepared to recognize as reasonable. U.S. Const. Amend. 4.—United States v. Valdarnini, 314 F.Supp.3d 1312.

S.D.Fla. 2019. Under privacy-based Fourth Amendment limitation on governmental action, the government cannot invade a location where a person (1) has a subjective expectation of privacy and (2) that privacy expectation is objectively one that society will recognize as reasonable. U.S. Const. Amend. 4.—United States v. Sigouin, 494 F.Supp.3d 1252.

S.D.Fla. 2018. To establish a reasonable expectation of privacy, the defendant must manifest a subjective expectation of privacy in the items searched or seized, and society must be prepared to recognize that expectation as legitimate or objectively reasonable. U.S. Const. Amend. 4.—Federal Trade Commission v. PointBreak Media, LLC, 343 F.Supp.3d 1282.

Fla. 1981. To establish Fourth Amendment violation, defendant was required to establish reasonable expectation of privacy to be free from particular intrusion involved, and standard of reasonableness was an objective one. U.S.C.A.Const. Amend. 4; West's F.S.A.Const. art. 1, § 12.—Wells v. State, 402 So.2d 402.

Fla.App. 1 Dist. 2021. The Fourth Amendment protects people, not places, and whether it affords protection depends on (1) whether the person has exhibited an actual, subjective expectation of privacy in the object of the search, and (2) whether society is prepared to recognize that expectation as reasonable. U.S. Const. Amend. 4.—Robinson v. State, 327 So.3d 1276.

Fla.App. 1 Dist. 2020. In order to claim protection from unreasonable search under the privacy-based approach to the Fourth Amendment, a defendant's conduct must exhibit an actual, subjective expectation of privacy and that subjective expectation must be one which society recognizes as objectively reasonable; where these two requirements are met, official intrusion into that private sphere generally qualifies as a search and requires a warrant supported by probable cause. U.S. Const. Amend. 4.—Bailey v. State, 311 So.3d 303, rehearing denied, review denied 2021 WL 2408431, certiorari denied 142 S.Ct. 568, 211 L.Ed.2d 354.

The nature of particular documents sought must be considered in determining whether there is a legitimate expectation of privacy concerning their contents, such that law enforcement's acquisition of them is a "search" to which the protections of the Fourth Amendment apply. U.S. Const. Amend. 4.—Id.

The question of whether a privacy interest is one which society is prepared to recognize, as required for it to come within the protections of the Fourth Amendment, is informed by historical understandings of what was deemed an unreasonable search and seizure when the Fourth Amendment was adopted. U.S. Const. Amend. 4. —Id.

Fla.App. 1 Dist. 2020. For an individual's expectation of privacy to be reasonable and warrant Fourth Amendment protection, the individual must show both a subjective and objective expectation of privacy in the area searched. U.S. Const. Amend. 4.—State v. Ware, 292 So.3d 863, review denied 2020 WL 5588673.

Fla.App. 1 Dist. 2019. To support suppression of a communication under the wiretap law, the person who made the statement must show more than a subjective expectation of privacy; they must show that they have a reasonable expectation of privacy under the circumstances, which depends on one's actual subjective expectation of privacy as well as whether society is prepared to recognize that expectation as reasonable. Fla. Stat. Ann. § 934.02(2).—Smiley v. State, 279 So.3d 262, rehearing denied.

Fla.App. 1 Dist. 2019. For purposes of the Fourth Amendment, a search occurs only when an individual's reasonable expectation of privacy is infringed by an agent of the government. U.S. Const. Amend. 4.—Morales v. State, 274 So.3d 1213.

A Fourth Amendment search does not occur unless the individual manifested a subjective expectation of privacy in the object of the challenged search, and society is willing to recognize that expectation as reasonable. U.S. Const. Amend. 4.—Id.

Fla.App. 1 Dist. 2019. When a citizen has a reasonable expectation of privacy, police officers may not enter a property without a warrant, absent consent or exigent circumstances. U.S. Const. Amend. 4.—Bryant v. State, 265 So.3d 726.

Fla.App. 2 Dist. 2022. The touchstone of any Fourth Amendment analysis is whether the defendant had a reasonable expectation of privacy in the place searched. U.S. Const. Amend. 4.—Youngman v. State, 342 So.3d 770.

For purposes of the Fourth Amendment, a "search" occurs only when an individual's reasonable expectation of privacy is infringed by an agent of the government. U.S. Const. Amend. 4. —Id.

† **This Case was not selected for publication in the National Reporter System**

Fla.App. 2 Dist. 2019. The touchstone of any Fourth Amendment analysis is whether the defendant had a reasonable expectation of privacy in the place searched. U.S. Const. Amend. 4.—State v. M.B.W., 276 So.3d 501.

Fla.App. 2 Dist. 2019. To invoke Fourth Amendment protections, a defendant must demonstrate a reasonable expectation of privacy in the place searched. U.S. Const. Amend. 4.—State v. Pettis, 266 So.3d 238, on remand 2019 WL 8195122.

Defendant's expectation of privacy must originate from a source outside of the Fourth Amendment, either by reference to concepts of real or personal property law or to understandings that are recognized and permitted by society. U.S. Const. Amend. 4.—Id.

A search violates a defendant's Fourth Amendment rights only if: (1) a defendant demonstrates that he or she had an actual, subjective expectation of privacy in the property searched and (2) a defendant establishes that society would recognize that subjective expectation as objectively reasonable. U.S. Const. Amend. 4.—Id.

Fla.App. 2 Dist. 2011. A search violates a defendant's Fourth Amendment rights only if (1) a defendant demonstrates that he or she had an actual, subjective expectation of privacy in the property searched and (2) a defendant establishes that society would recognize that subjective expectation as objectively reasonable. U.S.C.A. Const. Amend. 4.—Nieminski v. State, 60 So.3d 521.

Fla.App. 3 Dist. 2019. Generally, a person's Fourth Amendment rights are implicated only if the search or seizure infringes on an expectation of privacy that society is prepared to consider reasonable. U.S. Const. Amend. 4.—Edwards v. State, 274 So.3d 1222.

A legitimate expectation of privacy under the Fourth Amendment consists of both a subjective expectation and an objectively reasonable expectation, as determined by societal standards. U.S. Const. Amend. 4.—Id.

The reasonableness of an expectation of privacy in a particular place or item under the Fourth Amendment depends on context. U.S. Const. Amend. 4.—Id.

In assessing the reasonableness under the Fourth Amendment of a search or seizure involving a work computer, relevant factors include whether the office has a policy regarding the employer's ability to inspect the computer, whether the computer is networked to other computers, and whether the employer (or a department within the agency) regularly monitors computer use. U.S. Const. Amend. 4.—Id.

Fla.App. 4 Dist. 2021. For an oral conversation to be protected under statute governing the interception of electronic communications, the speaker must have an actual subjective expectation of privacy, along with a societal recognition that the expectation is reasonable. Fla. Stat. Ann. § 934.03.—Silversmith v. State Farm Insurance Company, 324 So.3d 517.

Fla.App. 4 Dist. 2020. The inquiry into whether a defendant has a legitimate expectation of privacy under the Fourth Amendment in an area searched or an item seized involves two distinct questions: (1) whether the individual has exhibited an actual (subjective) expectation of privacy – i.e., whether the individual has shown that he or she seeks to preserve something as private, and (2) whether the subjective expectation of privacy is one that society recognizes as reasonable – i.e., whether the expectation is objectively justifiable

under the circumstances. U.S. Const. Amend. 4.—State v. Kraft, 301 So.3d 981.

Fla.App. 4 Dist. 2019. In the context of the Fourth Amendment, individuals have a reasonable expectation of privacy in the whole of their physical movements. U.S. Const. Amend. 4.—State v. Martin, 287 So.3d 645.

Fla.App. 4 Dist. 2018. A "search" occurs within the meaning of the Fourth Amendment when government action invades an individual's justifiable or reasonable expectation of privacy. U.S. Const. Amend. 4.—Osorio v. State, 244 So.3d 1115.

A reasonable expectation of privacy exists if the individual has exhibited an actual, subjective expectation of privacy which society is prepared to recognize as reasonable. U.S. Const. Amend. 4.—Id.

When a citizen has a reasonable expectation of privacy, police officers may not enter a property without a warrant, absent consent or exigent circumstances. U.S. Const. Amend. 4.—Id.

Fla.App. 4 Dist. 2012. For Fourth Amendment purposes, the likelihood that a person has an objectively reasonable expectation of privacy in an office setting is increased where the area or item searched is reserved for the defendant's exclusive personal use. U.S.C.A. Const.Amend. 4.—Kelly v. State, 77 So.3d 818, rehearing denied, review denied 97 So.3d 823, denial of post-conviction relief affirmed 199 So.3d 277.

Fla.App. 4 Dist. 1980. For purposes of determining whether individual has legitimate expectation of privacy in area where search occurred, some locations give rise to greater and more reasonable expectation of privacy than others. U.S.C.A.Const. Amend. 4.—State v. Schultz, 388 So.2d 1326.

©~489. —— In general.

S.D.Fla. 2017. There are few activities in society more personal or private than the passing of urine. U.S. Const. Amend. 4.—Friedenberg v. School Board of Palm Beach County, 257 F.Supp.3d 1295, affirmed 911 F.3d 1084.

Fla. 1984. Common authority of third person over premises to be searched or effects sought to be inspected to justify consent to search by third party is determined by suspect's reasonable expectation of privacy in area, whether others generally had access to area, or whether objects searched were personal effects of suspect not subject to consent. U.S.C.A. Const.Amend. 4.—Preston v. State, 444 So.2d 939, vacated 564 So.2d 120, appeal after remand 607 So.2d 404, certiorari denied 113 S.Ct. 1619, 507 U.S. 999, 123 L.Ed.2d 178, denial of post-conviction relief affirmed 970 So.2d 789, rehearing denied, habeas corpus denied 2012 WL 1549529, affirmed 785 F.3d 449.

Fla.App. 2 Dist. 2022. Absent a recognized exception to the Fourth Amendment's warrant requirement, a law enforcement officer must ordinarily obtain a warrant before searching the personal effects of a person. U.S. Const. Amend. 4.—S.P. v. State, 331 So.3d 883.

©~493. —— Persons in custody; arrestees.

C.A.11 (Fla.) 2014. Suspect and his attorney had a reasonable expectation of privacy for their privileged attorney-client conversations in interview room at county sheriff's office, and thus officers' surreptitious recording and monitoring of those conversations, without notice to suspect or attorney, and without a warrant, was an unlawful search under the Fourth Amendment.

---

† **This Case was not selected for publication in the National Reporter System**

U.S.C.A. Const.Amend. 4.—Gennusa v. Canova, 748 F.3d 1103.

Fla.App. 4 Dist. 1993. Recording of defendant's conversation with friends as they sat in patrol car while police officer searched their vehicle constituted invasion of privacy, and thus, tape was inadmissible in trial on charges of possession of cocaine, where police officer asked defendant and friends to sit in patrol car for what appeared to be safety and comfort reasons, defendant was neither under arrest nor articulable suspicion at that time, and defendant did not request or authorize tape recording. West's F.S.A. §§ 934.03, 934.06.—Barrett v. State, 618 So.2d 269, cause dismissed 623 So.2d 495.

Fla.App. 4 Dist. 1993. Tape recording of defendant's conversation while he sat in rear of police vehicle at time when he was neither under arrest nor under articulable suspicion was invasion of right of privacy. West's F.S.A. §§ 934.03, 934.06; U.S.C.A. Const.Amend. 4.—Smith v. State, 616 So.2d 509, quashed 641 So.2d 849.

Fla.App. 5 Dist. 1999. Listening to secret audiotape of conversation between defendant and wife in police interview room was permissible way of discovering location of firearm, and thus, suppression of firearm was not required. U.S.C.A. Const.Amend. 4.—Johnson v. State, 730 So.2d 368.

☞**496. Samples and tests; identification procedures.**

S.D.Fla. 2017. Urinating is an excretory function traditionally shielded with great privacy, but the degree of the intrusion depends on the manner in which production is monitored. U.S. Const. Amend. 4.—Friedenberg v. School Board of Palm Beach County, 257 F.Supp.3d 1295, affirmed 911 F.3d 1084.

☞**497. Particular places in general.**

C.A.5 (Fla.) 1980. For purposes of Fourth Amendment, one may have protected expectation of privacy in absence of property interest; on other hand, one may have fee simple title to property upon which one has no expectation of privacy. U.S.C.A.Const. Amend. 4.—U.S. v. DeWeese, 632 F.2d 1267, rehearing denied 641 F.2d 879, certiorari denied 102 S.Ct. 358, 454 U.S. 878, 70 L.Ed.2d 188.

M.D.Fla. 2018. While one's legitimate presence on the premises is not controlling on the issue of one's expectation of privacy, it is relevant to that determination. U.S. Const. Amend. 4.—United States v. Valdarnini, 314 F.Supp.3d 1312.

M.D.Fla. 1980. In view of relationship between corporation and government inspectors allowed in areas which were closed to general public, duties and responsibilities of inspectors being well known to corporate employees, corporate expectation of privacy could not be justified as to items and conduct assertedly protected by Fourth Amendment, and thus, as to corporate defendant, as well as to its employees, there was no "search," for constitutional purposes. U.S.C.A.Const. Amend. 4.—U.S. v. Hartley, 486 F.Supp. 1348, affirmed 678 F.2d 961, rehearing denied 688 F.2d 852, certiorari denied 103 S.Ct. 815, 459 U.S. 1170, 74 L.Ed.2d 1014, certiorari denied Treasure Isle, Inc., v. U.S., 103 S.Ct. 834, 459 U.S. 1183, 74 L.Ed.2d 1027.

S.D.Fla. 2019. Under the Fourth Amendment, the government is prohibited from trespassing into a location where a person has a property interest. U.S. Const. Amend. 4.—United States v. Sigouin, 494 F.Supp.3d 1252.

For Fourth Amendment purposes, a trespass involves an unlicensed physical intrusion into a constitutionally-protected area. U.S. Const. Amend. 4.—Id.

Fla.App. 1 Dist. 2022. The objective reasonableness of an expectation of privacy in a hospital setting, for purpose of statute making it illegal to intentionally intercept oral information when speaker has reasonable expectation of privacy in his statements, turns on the particular circumstances of each case. Fla. Stat. Ann. §§ 934.02, 943.03.—Reed v. State, 350 So.3d 836, cause dismissed 2023 WL 5236391.

Fla.App. 1 Dist. 2018. Law enforcement has no right to enter one's private property without a warrant or an exception to the warrant requirement. U.S. Const. Amend. 4; Fla. Const. art. 1, § 12.—Channell v. State, 257 So.3d 1228.

Fla.App. 1 Dist. 2008. Defendant, who allegedly suffered from Munchausen syndrome by proxy which was disorder whereby defendant factitiously induced illness in child to draw attention to herself, did not have reasonable expectation of privacy when she was in her child's hospital room, and thus, the state action, namely court's broad delegation to hospital staff of the power to conduct video surveillance, together with court's authorization for the State to take immediate custody of child if surveillance showed he was in danger, did not amount to a search for Fourth Amendment purposes; even though defendant did not know about surveillance, she would have expected that efforts to interrupt child's breathing would have triggered medical response, and she could not have reasonably expected privacy in her actions affecting the health and well-being of a heavily monitored patient. U.S.C.A. Const.Amend. 4.—State v. Butler, 1 So.3d 242, rehearing denied.

☞**499. —— In general.**

C.A.11 (Fla.) 1999. Defendant had reasonable expectation of privacy in warehouse, such that search of warehouse for drugs implicated defendant's Fourth Amendment rights, even though defendant did not own or formally rent the warehouse, where defendant had the only key for warehouse, and defendant kept personal and business papers at warehouse. U.S.C.A. Const. Amend. 4.—U.S. v. Chaves, 169 F.3d 687, rehearing denied, certiorari denied Garcia v. U.S., 120 S.Ct. 534, 528 U.S. 1022, 145 L.Ed.2d 414, certiorari denied 120 S.Ct. 585, 528 U.S. 1048, 145 L.Ed.2d 486.

N.D.Fla. 2019. The sanctity of private dwellings ordinarily is afforded the most stringent Fourth Amendment protection. U.S. Const. Amend. 4.—United States v. Roberts, 410 F.Supp.3d 1268.

S.D.Fla. 1991. Principal protection against intrusions into the dwellings of individuals is the warrant requirement imposed upon agents of the government who seek to enter a home for the purpose of a search or arrest. U.S.C.A. Const. Amend. 4.—U.S. v. Mazuera, 756 F.Supp. 564.

Fla.App. 2 Dist. 2018. There is no exception to the warrant requirement for the officer who barely cracks open the front door and sees nothing but rug on the vestibule floor. U.S. Const. Amend. 4.—Aguilar v. State, 259 So.3d 262.

Fla.App. 2 Dist. 2017. The residents of a rooming house are entitled to the same Fourth Amendment protections as residents of single-family houses are, as long as the rooming house itself is not open to the public. U.S. Const.

Amend. 4.—Davis v. State, 226 So.3d 318, rehearing denied.

Fla.App. 2 Dist. 1999. Defendant, a college student, had expectation of privacy in his dormitory suite in which campus police officers found marijuana and drug paraphernalia, precluding officers from entering room without warrant or permission of one of the residents. U.S.C.A. Const.Amend. 4.—Beauchamp v. State, 742 So.2d 431.

Fla.App. 3 Dist. 1981. Seizure of narcotics from residence did not violate defendant's reasonable expectation of privacy where record, at most, showed him simply to be legitimately on premises.—State v. McGoey, 399 So.2d 495.

⚥500. ——— Houses and homes in general.

C.A.11 (Fla.) 2022. Searches and seizures inside a home without a warrant are presumptively unreasonable. U.S. Const. Amend. 4.—United States v. Grushko, 50 F.4th 1, certiorari denied 143 S.Ct. 2594, 216 L.Ed.2d 1199, certiorari denied 143 S.Ct. 2680, 216 L.Ed.2d 1248.

C.A.11 (Fla.) 2022. A warrantless entry into a suspect's home to search the premises is presumed to be unreasonable. U.S. Const. Amend. 4.—United States v. Sanchez, 30 F.4th 1063, certiorari denied 143 S.Ct. 227, 214 L.Ed.2d 90.

C.A.11 (Fla.) 2020. Warrantless searches and seizures inside home are presumptively unreasonable. U.S. Const. Amend. 4.—United States v. Evans, 958 F.3d 1102.

C.A.11 (Fla.) 2019. Because the physical entry of the home is the chief evil against which the wording of the Fourth Amendment is directed, it is a basic principle of Fourth Amendment law that searches and seizures inside a home without a warrant are presumptively unreasonable. U.S. Const. Amend. 4.—Gill as Next Friend of K.C.R. v. Judd, 941 F.3d 504.

C.A.11 (Fla.) 2018. Fourth Amendment guarantees individual's right to retreat into his own home and there be free from unreasonable government intrusion. U.S. Const. Amend. 4.—United States v. Maxi, 886 F.3d 1318, certiorari denied Blanc v. U.S., 139 S.Ct. 235, 202 L.Ed.2d 159, certiorari denied 139 S.Ct. 351, 202 L.Ed.2d 248, denial of post-conviction relief affirmed 2023 WL 7325562.

C.A.11 (Fla.) 2014. Fourth Amendment protections against unreasonable searches and seizures apply to commercial premises, as well as to private homes. U.S.C.A. Const.Amend. 4.—Berry v. Leslie, 767 F.3d 1144, vacated on rehearing en banc 771 F.3d 1316.

C.A.11 (Fla.) 2013. A warrantless and nonconsensual entry into a person's home, and any resulting search or seizure, violates the Fourth Amendment unless it is supported by both probable cause and exigent circumstances. U.S.C.A. Const.Amend. 4.—Feliciano v. City of Miami Beach, 707 F.3d 1244.

C.A.11 (Fla.) 2006. Defendant charged with murdering his wife and children had abandoned his house, where murders were committed, thus making any expectation of privacy unreasonable and discovery of dead bodies inevitable, where, when deputy searched house four days after the murders, in response to information that defendant could not be located, defendant had already fled to Hawaii, where he remained for four months before turning himself in, and had no plans to return to the house or to provide for its upkeep. U.S.C.A. Const.Amend. 4.—Zakrzewski v. McDonough, 455 F.3d 1254, rehearing and rehearing denied 218 Fed.Appx. 981, certiorari

denied 127 S.Ct. 2051, 549 U.S. 1349, 167 L.Ed.2d 782.

C.A.11 (Fla.) 1986. Defendant, who manufactured cocaine in basement of his home located on three acres of land bounded on one side by small canal in secluded area, did not have reasonable expectation of privacy as to his basement, where defendant and his coconspirators engaged in such activity in lighted basement directly in front of uncurtained windows, activity could be viewed with naked eye from position on canal or on neighboring property adjoining canal, activity occurred over three-month period, and coconspirator, for several months prior to surveillance, had been buying supplies necessary to manufacture cocaine and transporting them to defendant's residence. U.S.C.A. Const.Amend. 4.—U.S. v. Whaley, 779 F.2d 585, rehearing denied 784 F.2d 404, certiorari denied 107 S.Ct. 931, 479 U.S. 1055, 93 L.Ed.2d 982.

C.A.5 (Fla.) 1978. Although the common law exhibits a deep respect for the individual's right to privacy in his home, the common law also permits certain intrusions on such right. 18 U.S.C.A. § 3109.—U.S. v. Carter, 566 F.2d 1265, certiorari denied 98 S.Ct. 3069, 436 U.S. 956, 57 L.Ed.2d 1121.

M.D.Fla. 2022. Police officers need either a warrant or probable cause plus exigent circumstances in order to make a lawful entry into a home under the Fourth Amendment. U.S. Const. Amend. 4.—Newcome v. Hernando County Sheriff's Office, 645 F.Supp.3d 1308.

M.D.Fla. 2019. Because physical entry of the home is the chief evil against which the wording of the Fourth Amendment is directed, it is a basic principle of Fourth Amendment law that searches and seizures inside home without warrant are presumptively unreasonable. U.S. Const. Amend. 4.—Davis v. City of Apopka, 424 F.Supp.3d 1161.

M.D.Fla. 2016. The right of every citizen to be free from unreasonable government intrusion into his or her home forms the very core of the Fourth Amendment. U.S. Const. Amend. 4.—Montanez v. Carvajal, 224 F.Supp.3d 1274, reversed 889 F.3d 1202, affirmed Rivera v. Carvajal, 777 Fed.Appx. 434.

Searches and seizures inside a home without a warrant are presumptively unreasonable. U.S. Const. Amend. 4.—Id.

N.D.Fla. 2019. At the very core of the Fourth Amendment stands the right of a man to retreat into his own home and there be free from unreasonable governmental intrusion. U.S. Const. Amend. 4.—United States v. Roberts, 410 F.Supp.3d 1268.

The home is entitled to special protection under the Fourth Amendment as the center of the private lives of people. U.S. Const. Amend. 4.—Id.

The physical entry of the home is the chief evil against which the wording of the Fourth Amendment is directed. U.S. Const. Amend. 4.—Id.

S.D.Fla. 2021. Searches and seizures inside a home without a warrant are presumptively unreasonable. U.S. Const. Amend. 4.—United States v. Howard, 557 F.Supp.3d 1262.

S.D.Fla. 2019. When it comes to the Fourth Amendment, the home is first among equals. U.S. Const. Amend. 4.—United States v. Sigouin, 494 F.Supp.3d 1252.

S.D.Fla. 1991. Entry into a home to conduct a search or make an arrest is unreasonable under the Fourth Amendment unless done pursuant to a warrant, and search or seizure carried out on a suspect's premises without a warrant is per se unreasonable unless police can show exigent circumstances. U.S.C.A. Const.Amend. 4.—U.S. v. Mazuera, 756 F.Supp. 564.

Fla.App. 1 Dist. 2021. A person's private residence is accorded a special status under the Fourth Amendment, and a substantial government intrusion into the sanctity of the home constitutes a search within the Fourth Amendment. U.S. Const. Amend. 4.—Robinson v. State, 327 So.3d 1276.

Fla.App. 1 Dist. 2019. With regard to a search by an agent of the government, a person has the highest expectation of privacy in his home. U.S. Const. Amend. 4.—Bryant v. State, 265 So.3d 726.

Fla.App. 1 Dist. 2018. While warrantless searches and seizures inside a home are presumptively unreasonable and prohibited by the Fourth Amendment, exceptions may apply to allow such searches. U.S. Const. Amend. 4.—Copeland v. State, 247 So.3d 645.

Fla.App. 1 Dist. 2017. At the Fourth Amendment's very core stands the right of a man to retreat into his own home and there be free from unreasonable governmental intrusion. U.S. Const. Amend. 4.—State v. Crowley, 232 So.3d 473, rehearing denied.

Fla.App. 1 Dist. 2016. A private home, including a motel room, is an area where a person enjoys the highest reasonable expectation of privacy under the Fourth Amendment; even so, police, like any other citizen, may approach a residence and knock, hoping that the occupant will open the door. U.S.C.A. Const.Amend. 4.—State v. McRae, 194 So.3d 524.

Warrants are generally required to search a person's home or his person unless the exigencies of the situation make the needs of law enforcement so compelling that the warrantless search is objectively reasonable under the Fourth Amendment. U.S.C.A. Const.Amend. 4.—Id.

Fla.App. 2 Dist. 2022. Searches and seizures inside a home without a warrant are presumptively unreasonable. U.S. Const. Amend. 4.—Seiracki v. State, 333 So.3d 802.

Fla.App. 2 Dist. 2019. A warrantless search of a home is per se unreasonable under the Fourth Amendment and provision of Florida Constitution governing searches and seizures, subject to a few specifically established and well-delineated exceptions. U.S. Const. Amend. 4; Fla. Const. art. 1, § 12.—State v. M.B.W., 276 So.3d 501.

The presumption of unreasonableness of a warrantless search of a home may be overcome if the State sufficiently demonstrates the applicability of any one of the warrant requirement exceptions; the five exceptions are for searches (1) with the occupant's consent, (2) incident to lawful arrest, (3) with probable cause to search but with exigent circumstances, (4) in hot pursuit, or (5) pursuant to a stop and frisk. U.S. Const. Amend. 4; Fla. Const. art. 1, § 12.—Id.

Fla.App. 2 Dist. 2018. Private home is an area where a person enjoys the highest reasonable expectation of privacy under the Fourth Amendment. U.S. Const. Amend. 4.—Aguilar v. State, 259 So.3d 262.

With few exceptions, the question as to whether a warrantless search of a home is reasonable, and hence constitutional, must be answered no, and among those exceptions are a protective sweep and exigent circumstances. U.S. Const. Amend. 4.—Id.

Fourth Amendment's protection of the home is not tied to measurement of the quality or quantity of information obtained. U.S. Const. Amend. 4.—Id.

In the home, all details are intimate details, because the entire area is held safe from prying government eyes pursuant to Fourth Amendment. U.S. Const. Amend. 4.—Id.

Venturing inside a person's home without a warrant or a valid exception violates the Fourth Amendment and, therefore, constitutes illegal police conduct. U.S. Const. Amend. 4.—Id.

Fla.App. 2 Dist. 2018. It is a basic principle of Fourth Amendment law that searches and seizures inside a home without a warrant are presumptively unreasonable. U.S. Const. Amend. 4.—Lapace v. State, 257 So.3d 588.

Warrants are generally required to search a person's home or his person unless the exigencies of the situation make the needs of law enforcement so compelling that the warrantless search is objectively reasonable under the Fourth Amendment. U.S. Const. Amend. 4.—Id.

Allowing police to use a resident's reaction to law enforcement's presence at their home and the resident's contemporaneous clear expression of unwillingness to engage with the officers as the only extra information necessary to confirm whatever suspicion brought the officers to the door in the first place would unjustifiably erode the right of a man to retreat into his own home and there be free from unreasonable governmental intrusion—which stands at the very core of Fourth Amendment protections. U.S. Const. Amend. 4.—Id.

Fla.App. 2 Dist. 2018. Fourth Amendment prohibits the warrantless entry of a person's home, whether to make an arrest or to search for specific objects. U.S. Const. Amend. 4.—Walker v. State, 243 So.3d 512.

Fla.App. 2 Dist. 2011. Defendant had a reasonable expectation of privacy, for Fourth Amendment purposes, in a house he had lived in for a month with his girlfriend and pets, and in which he was growing marijuana. U.S.C.A. Const. Amend. 4.—Nieminski v. State, 60 So.3d 521.

Fla.App. 3 Dist. 2010. Warrantless searches or arrests in constitutionally protected areas, particularly one's home, are per se unreasonable unless they fall within one of the established exceptions to the warrant requirement. U.S.C.A. Const.Amend. 4.—State v. Brown, 36 So.3d 770, review denied 63 So.3d 748.

Fla.App. 4 Dist. 2023. In terms of searches and seizures, the Fourth Amendment has drawn a firm line at the entrance to a house; without consent, a warrant, or exigent circumstances, law enforcement may not cross that threshold to effect an arrest. U.S. Const. Amend. 4.—Tellam v. State, 373 So.3d 345.

Fla.App. 5 Dist. 2018. While warrantless searches of a home are presumed illegal, an officer may enter a private home or property when there are exigent circumstances for the entry. U.S. Const. Amend. 4.—State v. Archer, 259 So.3d 999, review denied 2019 WL 2205765, on subsequent appeal 309 So.3d 287, rehearing denied.

Fla.App. 5 Dist. 2015. Absent consent, a search warrant, or an arrest warrant, a police officer may enter a private home only when there are exigent circumstances for the entry. U.S.C.A. Const.Amend. 4.—Durham v. State, 174 So.3d 1074.

† **This Case was not selected for publication in the National Reporter System**

⊗**501.** ——— **Apartments and condominiums.**
C.A.11 (Fla.) 1986. Search of extortion defendant's apartment did not violate his Fourth Amendment rights against unreasonable search and seizure where defendant told roommate he was leaving town and not coming back, and thus property was abandoned; though defendant left town to avoid capture, lawful police investigation did not constitute such coercion that abandonment should be considered involuntary. U.S.C.A. Const.Amend. 4.—U.S. v. De Parias, 805 F.2d 1447, certiorari denied Ramirez v. United States, 107 S.Ct. 3189, 482 U.S. 916, 96 L.Ed.2d 678.

Fla. 2010. Defendant had abandoned his interest in apartment where he barricaded himself following victim's murder, and thus did not have a reasonable expectation of privacy as required to challenge warrantless search of apartment by police; although defendant had rented apartment and eviction proceedings were not yet final, eviction notice had been posted on apartment door, apartment maintenance supervisor had conducted a walk-through of the apartment and determined that it had been abandoned, and weeks later, and shortly before the murder, defendant returned and asked for a key so that he could pick up some final items. U.S.C.A. Const.Amend. 4; West's F.S.A. Const. Art. 1, § 12.—Caraballo v. State, 39 So.3d 1234.

Fla.App. 1 Dist. 2008. Dog sniff at front door of apartment did not constitute Fourth Amendment search as it did not violate legitimate privacy interest; binary nature of dog sniff rendered it unique in that it was distinguishable from traditional search methods, and dog was located on common walkway within apartment complex when sniff occurred. U.S.C.A. Const.Amend. 4. —Stabler v. State, 990 So.2d 1258, review granted, quashed 90 So.3d 267.

Fla.App. 2 Dist. 2009. Warrantless entry of an apartment by a law enforcement officer who followed defendant inside was unreasonable; the officer described a consensual encounter with some men, including defendant, who he suspected might have been trespassing at a public housing complex, defendant decided not to speak with the officer and left as he was free to do, the officer followed defendant into the apartment on a belief that something was not right, and the officer offered no facts to support such a belief. U.S.C.A. Const.Amend. 4.—Byrd v. State, 16 So.3d 1026.

Fla.App. 4 Dist. 2010. The highest level of Fourth Amendment protection lies at the entrance of one's home or apartment. U.S.C.A. Const.Amend. 4.—Dixon v. State, 36 So.3d 920.

Fla.App. 4 Dist. 2009. Highest level of Fourth Amendment protection lies at the entrance of one's home or apartment. U.S.C.A. Const. Amend. 4.—Cote v. State, 14 So.3d 1137, rehearing denied.

⊗**502.** ——— **Occasional or temporary dwellings; hotels and motels.**
C.A.11 (Fla.) 2020. Fourth Amendment's protections extend to any thing or place with respect to which a person has a reasonable expectation of privacy, including a hotel room. U.S. Const. Amend. 4.—United States v. Ross, 964 F.3d 1034, certiorari denied 141 S.Ct. 1394, 209 L.Ed.2d 132.

Hotel guest loses his reasonable expectation of privacy in his room following checkout time, and hotel management can validly consent to a search of the room at that point. U.S. Const. Amend. 4. —Id.

If a hotel guest asks for and receives a late checkout, then, for Fourth Amendment purposes, he retains his reasonable expectation of privacy until the arrival of the mutually agreed upon time. U.S. Const. Amend. 4.—Id.

C.A.11 (Fla.) 2020. The Fourth Amendment's protections against unreasonable searches and seizures extend to any thing or place with respect to which a person has a reasonable expectation of privacy, including hotel rooms. U.S. Const. Amend. 4.—United States v. Ross, 963 F.3d 1056, on remand 964 F.3d 1034, certiorari denied 141 S.Ct. 1394, 209 L.Ed.2d 132.

C.A.11 (Fla.) 2019. The Fourth Amendment's protections extend to any thing or place with respect to which a person has a reasonable expectation of privacy, including a hotel room. U.S. Const. Amend. 4.—United States v. Ross, 941 F.3d 1058, rehearing granted, vacated 953 F.3d 744, on rehearing 963 F.3d 1056, on remand 964 F.3d 1034, certiorari denied 141 S.Ct. 1394, 209 L.Ed.2d 132.

Evidence was insufficient to establish defendant had abandoned motel room at the time of police officers' initial entry and protective sweep, and thus defendant had standing to challenge officers' warrantless entry of motel room; while defendant fled when he saw police in motel parking lot, defendant's motel room was the equivalent of a home and was entitled to a homelike level of constitutional protection, when defendant fled he locked his room and kept his room key, and when officers entered defendant's motel room ten minutes had elapsed between defendant's flight and the officers' warrantless entry. U.S. Const. Amend. 4.—Id.

If a motel guest asks for and receives a late checkout, then, for Fourth Amendment purposes, he retains his reasonable expectation of privacy until the arrival of the mutually agreed upon time. U.S. Const. Amend. 4.—Id.

M.D.Fla. 2018. Defendant's right to occupy hotel room, and thus his expectation of privacy therein, was terminated before Secret Service special agent entered room without warrant, and thus Fourth Amendment was not violated; immediately after resort investigators observed access devices in hotel room, Secret Service was contacted to investigate what clearly appeared to be criminal activity, and defendant had been locked out of hotel room. U.S. Const. Amend. 4.— United States v. Valdarnini, 314 F.Supp.3d 1312.

S.D.Fla. 1994. Leaving hotel room without intending to return, leaving indicia of that intent, or paying for room, is abandonment of that room and any right to privacy in it. U.S.C.A. Const. Amend. 4.—U.S. v. Wai-Keung, 845 F.Supp. 1548, affirmed 115 F.3d 874, rehearing and suggestion for rehearing denied U.S. v. Chi-Cheong, 127 F.3d 42, certiorari denied Li v. U.S., 118 S.Ct. 1095, 522 U.S. 1135, 140 L.Ed.2d 150.

Fla.App. 1 Dist. 2021. A hotel or motel room is considered the private dwelling of the occupant, for purposes of a search under the Fourth Amendment, so long as he is there legally, and the occupant is entitled to the same rights inside the hotel or motel room as the resident of a private permanent dwelling. U.S. Const. Amend. 4.—Robinson v. State, 327 So.3d 1276.

Areas which are outside of a hotel room, such as hallways, which are open to use by others may not be reasonably considered as private, for purposes of the Fourth Amendment, as they are public areas where officers have a right to be present. U.S. Const. Amend. 4.—Id.

† This Case was not selected for publication in the National Reporter System

Fla.App. 1 Dist. 2016. A private home, including a motel room, is an area where a person enjoys the highest reasonable expectation of privacy under the Fourth Amendment; even so, police, like any other citizen, may approach a residence and knock, hoping that the occupant will open the door. U.S.C.A. Const.Amend. 4.—State v. McRae, 194 So.3d 524.

Fla.App. 2 Dist. 2019. Generally, hotel guests have a reasonable expectation of privacy in their lodgings, for purposes of determining whether Fourth Amendment's prohibition against unreasonable searches and seizures applies. U.S. Const. Amend. 4.—State v. M.B.W., 276 So.3d 501.

Fla.App. 2 Dist. 2017. Defendant had Fourth Amendment right to be free of warrantless search of rooming house; defendant kept belongings at house, slept at house, had key to house, and paid portion of rent, and house was not open to public. U.S. Const. Amend. 4.—Davis v. State, 226 So.3d 318, rehearing denied.

Fla.App. 4 Dist. 1989. Off-duty police detective did not intrude into constitutionally protected area of defendant's motel room by knocking on door to that room.—State v. Carr, 549 So.2d 701.

⚷**503. Commercial premises; offices and businesses.**

C.A.11 (Fla.) 2004. Probation officer's mere entry into closed medical office to locate and apprehend individual suspected of violating his probation was sufficient to constitute "search" for Fourth Amendment purposes, given its intrusion on medical office manager's reasonable expectation of privacy. U.S.C.A. Const.Amend. 4.—O'Rourke v. Hayes, 378 F.3d 1201.

C.A.11 (Fla.) 1984. Extent that there might be different Fourth Amendment standards for a home and a business would not depend upon whether the business was in a building that looked like a home; the difference in standard would be based on reduced expectation of privacy in a business. U.S.C.A. Const.Amend. 4.—U.S. v. Holland, 740 F.2d 878, rehearing denied 748 F.2d 690, certiorari denied 105 S.Ct. 2654, 471 U.S. 1124, 86 L.Ed.2d 271.

S.D.Fla. 2015. Fourth Amendment's prohibition on unreasonable searches and seizures applies not only to private residences, but also to property used for commercial purposes. U.S. Const. Amend. 4.—United States v. Medina, 158 F.Supp.3d 1303, appeal dismissed 2016 WL 9782091.

Fla.App. 3 Dist. 2019. The reasonableness of an employee's expectation under the Fourth Amendment of privacy in his or her office or the items contained therein depends on the "operational realities" of the workplace, and not on legal possession or ownership. U.S. Const. Amend. 4.—Edwards v. State, 274 So.3d 1222.

The likelihood that a person has an objectively reasonable expectation of privacy under the Fourth Amendment in an office setting is increased where the area or item searched is reserved for the defendant's exclusive personal use. U.S. Const. Amend. 4.—Id.

Factors that can be considered in determining the legitimacy of an expectation of privacy under the Fourth Amendment in an item seized from an office include the employee's relationship to the item, whether the item was in the employee's immediate control when it was seized, and whether the employee took actions to maintain a sense of privacy in the item. U.S. Const. Amend. 4.—Id.

An employee may have a legitimate expectation of privacy under the Fourth Amendment in his or her personal office and in personal items stored in a desk or file cabinet. U.S. Const. Amend. 4.—Id.

For purpose of determining a person's reasonable expectation of privacy under the Fourth Amendment, the workplace includes those areas and items that are related to work and are generally within the employer's control; these areas remain part of the workplace context even if the employee has placed personal items in them, such as a photograph placed in a desk or a letter posted on an employee bulletin board. U.S. Const. Amend. 4.—Id.

Fla.App. 5 Dist. 2001. In questioning whether owner of commercial property is entitled to Fourth Amendment protection against warrantless searches, court must ask if owner demonstrates subjective manifestation of claimed privacy in the area at issue, and if such claim is recognized by society; this is a legal determination, requiring no deference on review, provided facts and circumstances are not in dispute. U.S.C.A. Const.Amend. 4.—Ratcliff v. State, 783 So.2d 1099.

⚷**504. Public places and property.**

N.D.Fla. 2010. Use of a global positioning system (GPS) tracking device on the defendant's vehicle to trace the his movements as part of drug investigation did not violate his Fourth Amendment rights, since defendant had no legitimate expectation of privacy in the movements of his automobile on public roads, and the intrusion caused by affixing the magnetic tracking device to the vehicle was minimal, given that it was placed on the vehicle's undercarriage from a public sidewalk, and the vehicle was not fenced in, kept inside a garage, or otherwise shielded from contact with any member of the public. U.S.C.A. Const.Amend. 4.—U.S. v. Burton, 698 F.Supp.2d 1303.

Fla.App. 3 Dist. 1981. What person seeks to preserve as private may be constitutionally protected despite fact that it is in area accessible to the public. U.S.C.A.Const. Amend. 4.—State v. Parker, 399 So.2d 24, review denied 408 So.2d 1095.

Fla.App. 5 Dist. 2009. Defendant did not exhibit a reasonable expectation of privacy in public restroom stall, and thus evidence of police officer's observations of defendant in stall were admissible in prosecution for lewd conduct, where defendant affirmatively invited officer's intrusion through his non-verbal invitations to engage in lewd conduct. U.S.C.A. Const.Amend. 4.—State v. Halpin, 13 So.3d 75.

⚷**505. Public employment and employees.**

Fla.App. 3 Dist. 2019. Given the great variety of work environments in the public sector, the question whether any employee has a reasonable expectation of privacy under the Fourth Amendment must be addressed on a case-by-case basis. U.S. Const. Amend. 4.—Edwards v. State, 274 So.3d 1222.

A public employee's expectation of privacy under the Fourth Amendment in their offices, desks, and file cabinets, like similar expectations of employees in the private sector, may be reduced by virtue of actual office practices and procedures, or by legitimate regulation. U.S. Const. Amend. 4.—Id.

---

† **This Case was not selected for publication in the National Reporter System**

⚖506. Curtilage in general.

† **C.A.11 (Fla.) 2020.** Portion of house's driveway where defendant, who was sitting in parked car, was detained and searched was not part of home's curtilage for Fourth Amendment purposes, and because deputies did not enter curtilage of defendant's home when they confronted him in his driveway, they did not need warrant to approach and speak to him; defendant's house was one-story duplex with an unfenced front yard and a single driveway, the driveway ran in straight line from the street to wall of the house between the two front doors and appeared to serve both units of duplex, driveway was not gated, covered, enclosed, or partly enclosed, and driveway did not serve as an extension of defendant's home. U.S. Const. Amend. 4.—United States v. Stephen, 823 Fed.Appx. 751.

C.A.11 (Fla.) 2020. The question of whether property is within curtilage, for Fourth Amendment purposes, turns on four fact-intensive inquiries: (1) the proximity of the area claimed to be curtilage to the home, (2) the nature of the uses to which the area is put, (3) whether the area is included within an enclosure surrounding the home, and, (4) the steps the resident takes to protect the area from observation. U.S. Const. Amend. 4.—United States v. Bruce, 977 F.3d 1112, certiorari denied 141 S.Ct. 2541, 209 L.Ed.2d 562.

C.A.11 (Fla.) 2019. Parking area of apartment complex where defendant's car was parked when agents conducted warrantless search was not within the curtilage of the townhouse where defendant and his brother conducted their fraud activities, as would have precluded application of the automobile exception to Fourth Amendment's warrant requirement. U.S. Const. Amend. 4.— United States v. Delva, 922 F.3d 1228, denial of post-conviction relief affirmed 851 Fed.Appx. 148, certiorari denied 142 S.Ct. 374, 211 L.Ed.2d 199.

C.A.11 (Fla.) 2018. Home's curtilage, private property immediately adjacent to home, is entitled to same protection against unreasonable search and seizure as home itself. U.S. Const. Amend. 4.—United States v. Maxi, 886 F.3d 1318, certiorari denied Blanc v. U.S., 139 S.Ct. 235, 202 L.Ed.2d 159, certiorari denied 139 S.Ct. 351, 202 L.Ed.2d 248, denial of post-conviction relief affirmed 2023 WL 7325562.

Because curtilage is constitutionally protected space, police must have express or implied license to be there without warrant. U.S. Const. Amend. 4.—Id.

Scope of license to enter property, express or implied, is limited not only to particular area but also to specific purpose. U.S. Const. Amend. 4.—Id.

Police officers did not have license to enter duplex's curtilage, despite government's contention that officers were conducting "knock and talk," where ten officers surrounded building at night, one with his gun drawn, many going through gate in fence, with four or five approaching door and remainder taking up tactical positions around duplex's perimeter, and officers intended to secure duplex and detain anyone they found inside. U.S. Const. Amend. 4.—Id.

C.A.11 (Fla.) 1986. Mere fact that person may be engaging in criminal conduct within his home does not necessarily destroy his expectation of privacy; however, reasonableness of that person's expectation of privacy is affected, where it appears that he has engaged in suspicious activity outside home that would tend to attract attention of the police. U.S.C.A. Const.Amend. 4.—U.S. v. Whaley, 779 F.2d 585, rehearing denied 784 F.2d 404, certiorari denied 107 S.Ct. 931, 479 U.S. 1055, 93 L.Ed.2d 982.

S.D.Fla. 2021. The area immediately surrounding and associated with a home, the curtilage, falls within the Fourth Amendment's protections. U.S. Const. Amend. 4.—United States v. Howard, 557 F.Supp.3d 1262.

To determine whether an area falls within the curtilage of a house for Fourth Amendment purposes, courts primarily look to four factors: the proximity of the area claimed to be curtilage to the home, whether the area is included within an enclosure surrounding the home, the nature of the uses to which the area is put, and the steps taken by the resident to protect the area from observation by people passing by. U.S. Const. Amend. 4.—Id.

Home's carport was within the curtilage of the house for Fourth Amendment purposes; while the carport was visible from the street, it was located behind a gate, which was usually closed, carport was under a covered roof located just in front of the house, and it was used for lounging and related purposes. U.S. Const. Amend. 4.—Id.

Probable cause to arrest alone is not enough justify entry into a home's curtilage to conduct a warrantless search or seizure, and so the government must also show an applicable exception to the warrant requirement to justify the search. U.S. Const. Amend. 4.—Id.

Fla.App. 1 Dist. 2020. An individual may not legitimately demand privacy for activities conducted out of doors in fields, except in the area immediately surrounding the home. U.S. Const. Amend. 4.—State v. Ware, 292 So.3d 863, review denied 2020 WL 5588673.

Fla.App. 1 Dist. 2019. Defendant had reasonable expectation of privacy in his backyard, and thus officers' entry into backyard, based on tip and without warrant, violated defendant's Fourth Amendment rights; it was difficult to see into defendant's backyard from public road, officer confirmed that he could not see residence or into backyard without climbing elevated ditch next to driveway, and defendant maintained fence around his property. U.S. Const. Amend. 4.— Bryant v. State, 265 So.3d 726.

Fla.App. 1 Dist. 2018. A warrantless canine sniff test on a residence or its curtilage violates the Fourth Amendment. U.S. Const. Amend. 4.— Davis v. State, 257 So.3d 1159.

The central inquiry in determining if an area constitutes curtilage for purpose of Fourth Amendment is whether the area harbors the intimate activity associated with the sanctity of a man's home and the privacies of life. U.S. Const. Amend. 4.—Id.

The purpose of the test for determining which areas around a home constitute curtilage is to ascertain whether the area in question is so intimately tied to the home itself that it should be placed under the home's umbrella of Fourth Amendment protection. U.S. Const. Amend. 4.— Id.

The presence of a fence is not dispositive of whether an area is within a home's curtilage for purpose of the Fourth Amendment. U.S. Const. Amend. 4.—Id.

Fla.App. 1 Dist. 2017. Falling within the ambit of the Fourth Amendment protection is a home's curtilage, that part of the home immediately surrounding and associated with the home which is regarded to be part of the home itself for Fourth Amendment purposes. U.S. Const.

---

† **This Case was not selected for publication in the National Reporter System**

was emitted by his mobile home and which was detected by infrared thermal imager where he had taken affirmative steps to ventilate excess heat from artificial lights used in marijuana growing operations by punching holes in floor and forcing warm air out with blower and by installing air conditioner, even though he was careful to keep light from escaping. U.S.C.A. Const.Amend. 4.—U.S. v. Ford, 34 F.3d 992.

Any subjective expectation of privacy which defendant may have had in heat which was emitted from his mobile home and which was detected by infrared thermal imager was not reasonable in view of low resolution of thermal imagery and similarities between waste heat and other emissions, such as garbage and smoke, which are not protected by the Fourth Amendment. U.S.C.A Const.Amend. 4.—Id.

M.D.Fla. 2021. Businesses generally have an expectation of privacy, as would be protected by Fourth Amendment, in their business records, but that expectation is lessened for closely regulated businesses. U.S. Const. Amend. 4.—Wacko's Too, Inc. v. City of Jacksonville, 522 F.Supp.3d 1132.

Fla.App. 1 Dist. 2022. ALJ was not required to quash subpoena for financial information at bank for corporation, for which father was chief executive officer, in child support proceeding; subpoena sought bank's records, rather than corporation's, all records, including financial statements and deposit slips, contained only information voluntarily conveyed to banks and exposed to their employees in ordinary course of business, and there was no legitimate expectation of privacy concerning information kept in bank records under U.S. Constitution. U.S. Const. Amend. 4. —Network Communications of Northwest Florida, Inc. v. Department of Revenue, 334 So.3d 707.

Fla.App. 1 Dist. 2020. If an individual has conveyed information to a third party or to the public at large, even if the information is revealed on the assumption that it will be used only for a limited purpose, the government will generally not be required to obtain a warrant before obtaining the information. U.S. Const. Amend. 4.— Bailey v. State, 311 So.3d 303, rehearing denied, review denied 2021 WL 2408431, certiorari denied 142 S.Ct. 568, 211 L.Ed.2d 354.

Fla.App. 3 Dist. 1982. Dentist, who was found guilty of improperly prescribing drug as charged in administrative complaint, had no reasonable expectation of privacy with respect to completed prescriptions in possession of pharmacy, and statutorily authorized warrantless, routine administrative search of the pharmacy was constitutionally permissible. West's F.S.A. §§ 465.017, 893.09(1), 893.07(4); U.S.C.A.Const.Amend. 4.— Cushing v. Department of Professional Regulation, Bd. of Dentistry, 416 So.2d 1197, review denied 424 So.2d 761.

Fla.App. 4 Dist. 2012. Under the Fourth Amendment, many times an employee may have a legitimate expectation of privacy in his or her personal office and in personal items stored in a desk or file cabinet. U.S.C.A. Const.Amend. 4.— Kelly v. State, 77 So.3d 818, rehearing denied, review denied 97 So.3d 823, denial of post-conviction relief affirmed 199 So.3d 277.

⊙**513. —— Purses and wallets.**
Fla.App. 3 Dist. 2013. An invasion of privacy results, for purposes of the Fourth Amendment, from a search of a child's person or of a closed purse or other bag carried on her person, no less

than a similar search carried out on an adult. U.S.C.A. Const.Amend. 4.—K.P. v. State, 129 So.3d 1121, review denied 157 So.3d 1045.

⊙**514. —— Envelopes, folders, and boxes.**
Fla.App. 3 Dist. 2016. Defendant abandoned any reasonable expectation of privacy in black box when he placed it in garbage can, and thus warrantless search of box, in which a gun and cocaine were found, was justified; contents of garbage can might have been collected by trash hauler, rummaged by animals, or box might have been taken by scavengers, children, or owner of the garbage can. U.S.C.A. Const.Amend. 4.— Strawder v. State, 185 So.3d 543, rehearing denied, review denied 2016 WL 4440970.

Fla.App. 4 Dist. 2019. No Fourth Amendment violation occurs when law enforcement, based only upon reasonable suspicion, temporarily detains items placed in the U.S. mail or placed with a private delivery service. U.S. Const. Amend. 4. —Joshua v. State, 284 So.3d 551, review denied 2020 WL 2488827.

⊙**515. —— Lockers and storage units.**
Fla.App. 1 Dist. 1980. Absent consent or some other exception to the warrant requirement, a search warrant was needed before the lockers located in the trucks driven by defendants could be searched; however, a general search of the trucks and a seizure of their contents was authorized without a warrant since the odor of marijuana gave agricultural inspector cause to believe the trucks contained contraband.—Sower v. State, 382 So.2d 1257, dismissed 386 So.2d 642.

⊙**516. Electronic devices in general.**
† **C.A.11 (Fla.) 2011.** Defendant, a county employee, did not have a reasonable expectation of privacy in the thumb drive he left in a county-owned, common-use computer, so suffered no violation of his Fourth Amendment rights when it was searched by his supervisor revealing child pornography. U.S.C.A. Const.Amend. 4.—U.S. v. Durdley, 436 Fed.Appx. 966, certiorari denied 132 S.Ct. 1038, 565 U.S. 1127, 181 L.Ed.2d 764, post-conviction relief denied 2018 WL 1190225.

Fla.App. 1 Dist. 2019. Defendant did not have a subjective expectation that statements made in victim's home were not subject to interception, and thus statements recorded on victim's cell phone were not protected by wiretap statute from admission in prosecution for aggravated assault by threat with deadly weapon and domestic violence battery, where cell phone video showed defendant saw cell phone in victim's hand and knew he was being recorded, defendant tried to snatch phone from victim's hand, and defendant made statements suggesting he knew he was being recorded. Fla. Stat. Ann. §§ 934.03, 934.06, 934.09(10)(a).—Smiley v. State, 279 So.3d 262, rehearing denied.

Fla.App. 1 Dist. 2019. Defendant did not establish that he had a reasonable expectation of privacy when he uploaded child pornography to an online chat room, and therefore law enforcement agent did not conduct an unlawful search when he opened image file, which had been sent to law enforcement by chat room operator, prior to obtaining a warrant; nothing in record indicated number of participants in chat room, whether defendant had exclusive control to admit people to chat room, or whether chat room operator monitored chat room for illegal activity as a part of its service agreement, and defendant presented no evidence that uploaded file was password-protected or that he took any affirmative steps to restrict access to it. U.S. Const. Amend. 4; Fla. Const. art. 1, § 12.—Morales v. State, 274 So.3d 1213.

Fla.App. 3 Dist. 2019. Where an employer has a clear policy allowing others to monitor a workplace computer, an employee who uses the computer has no reasonable expectation of privacy in it under the Fourth Amendment. U.S. Const. Amend. 4.—Edwards v. State, 274 So.3d 1222.

Defendant did not have a reasonable expectation of privacy under the Fourth Amendment in flash drive left plugged into work computer at work; work computer was owned by defendant's employer, a police department, computer was kept in an office defendant shared with another police officer who had full access to defendant's computer, because defendant left password to computer in plain view on her desk for express purpose of allowing co-worker to use computer, and a login banner warned employees on computers connected to department's network that the computer system was property of the police department and that users of the system had no expectation of privacy. U.S. Const. Amend. 4.—Id.

Fla.App. 4 Dist. 2018. When balancing the interests of technological advancement and Fourth Amendment protection, the court must ensure that the progress of science does not erode Fourth Amendment protections. U.S. Const. Amend. 4; Fla. Const. art. 1, § 12.—State v. Sylvestre, 254 So.3d 986.

Fla.App. 5 Dist. 2016. Police officer's act of pressing button on key fob seized from defendant, which activated alarm sounding from nearby vehicle, did not constitute a "search"; defendant had no reasonable expectation of privacy in the only information that could be obtained when officer touched button on fob lawfully in defendant's hand, i.e., presence of defendant's vehicle in public lot. U.S.C.A. Const.Amend. 4.—State v. Maye, 199 So.3d 357.

Fla.App. 5 Dist. 2015. Law enforcement did not violate defendant's Fourth Amendment rights by using software that searched for child pornography files shared over peer-to-peer networks to develop the probable cause for a search warrant directed to defendant's personal computer; defendant did not have a reasonable expectation of privacy in the files he shared on the network, as he knew or should have known that sharing files would allow the public at large to access the files unless he took steps to avoid it, and the software did not search any areas of defendant's computer, download any files, or otherwise reveal any information unavailable to ordinary internet users. U.S.C.A. Const.Amend. 4.—Frazier v. State, 180 So.3d 1067, rehearing and rehearing denied, review denied 2016 WL 2757509, certiorari denied 137 S.Ct. 383, 580 U.S. 965, 196 L.Ed.2d 302.

Even if software used by law enforcement agencies to search for child pornography files shared over peer-to-peer networks does collect information, it collects publicly available information, which does not run afoul of the Fourth Amendment. U.S.C.A. Const.Amend. 4.—Id.

Fla.App. 6 Dist. 2023. Appropriate standard to be used to justify the warrantless seizure of a cell phone from a suspect is probable cause, and, in addition to probable cause, absent a warrant, an applicable exception must have existed. U.S. Const. Amend. 4.—Jefferson v. State, 363 So.3d 198.

☞518. —— In general.

U.S.Fla. 1968. Although a party line user's privacy is vulnerable, that does not mean that his telephone conversations are completely unprotected by statute proscribing unauthorized interception and divulgence of communications. Communications Act of 1934, § 605, 47 U.S.C.A. § 605.—Lee v. State of Fla., 88 S.Ct. 2096, 392 U.S. 378, 20 L.Ed.2d 1166.

C.A.11 (Fla.) 2020. While individual maintains a legitimate expectation of privacy, of a kind protected by the Fourth Amendment, in the record of his physical movements as captured through cell-site location information, the same cannot be said for e-mail addresses or internet protocol addresses that he voluntarily chooses to share with third party by opening and logging into messaging app. U.S. Const. Amend. 4.—United States v. Trader, 981 F.3d 961, certiorari denied 142 S.Ct. 296, 211 L.Ed.2d 139.

Federal agents investigating a messaging app user who had solicited nude photographs from a nine-year-old girl did not need a search warrant to request the e-mail address and internet protocol addresses associated with the user's profile from the third party providing this messaging app service; e-mail address and internet protocol addresses that user voluntarily shared with service provider by opening and logging onto the app were not cell-site location information, and user lacked legitimate expectation of privacy therein. U.S. Const. Amend. 4.—Id.

C.A.11 (Fla.) 2014. Suspect and his attorney had a reasonable expectation of privacy for their privileged attorney-client conversations in interview room at county sheriff's office, and thus officers' surreptitious recording and monitoring of those conversations, without notice to suspect or attorney, and without a warrant, was an unlawful search under the Fourth Amendment. U.S.C.A. Const.Amend. 4.—Gennusa v. Canova, 748 F.3d 1103.

† **C.A.11 (Fla.) 2013.** Defendant did not have reasonable expectation of privacy in conversation conducted through a cellphone's speaker system, therefore, a video recording of the conversation, taken on computer web camera, did not violate Title III of the Omnibus Crime Control and Safe Streets Act or his Fourth Amendment right to privacy. U.S.C.A. Const.Amend. 4; 18 U.S.C.A. § 2511.—U.S. v. Curtis, 513 Fed.Appx. 823, certiorari denied 134 S.Ct. 536, 571 U.S. 999, 187 L.Ed.2d 384, habeas corpus dismissed by Curtis v. Warden FCI Estill, 2017 WL 4222880.

† **C.A.11 (Fla.) 2010.** Defendant did not have reasonable expectation of privacy in subscriber identification information given to internet services providers (ISP) and telephone companies, within scope of Fourth Amendment; investigators did not recover any information related to content, but instead, received identifying information transmitted during internet usage and telephone calls necessary for ISPs and telephone company to perform their services. U.S.C.A. Const.Amend. 4.—U.S. v. Beckett, 369 Fed.Appx. 52.

† **C.A.11 (Fla.) 2009.** Defendant did not have reasonable expectation of privacy concerning his conversations with his mother, which took place within confines of actively monitored interview room at police station following his arrest, and thus suppression of inculpatory statements made by defendant during conversations was unwarranted in prosecution for possessing firearm as convicted felon; both videotape of conversations and mother's testimony at evidentiary hearing clearly established that defendant was aware that

† **This Case was not selected for publication in the National Reporter System**

police could be monitoring his conversations. U.S.C.A. Const.Amend. 4; 18 U.S.C.A. § 922(g)(1).—U.S. v. Delibro, 347 Fed.Appx. 474.

† C.A.11 (Fla.) 2005. Claimant who made statements at aborted deposition, with knowledge that they were being recorded, did not have expectation of privacy sufficient to support claim that recording violated his Fourth Amendment rights. U.S.C.A. Const.Amend. 4.—Williams v. Carney, 157 Fed.Appx. 103.

† C.A.11 (Fla.) 2005. Alleged conspirators did not have reasonable expectation of privacy in text messages received or sent by alleged co-conspirator using text message pager, so that this co-conspirator could testify for government regarding content of those messages in drug conspiracy prosecution.—U.S. v. Jones, 149 Fed.Appx. 954, certiorari denied 126 S.Ct. 1373, 546 U.S. 1189, 164 L.Ed.2d 80, certiorari denied Lofton v. U.S., 126 S.Ct. 1373, 546 U.S. 1189, 164 L.Ed.2d 80, certiorari denied Ford v. U.S., 126 S.Ct. 2019, 547 U.S. 1132, 164 L.Ed.2d 785, post-conviction relief denied Cobb v. U.S., 2006 WL 1360924, post-conviction relief denied 2006 WL 1406584, motion for relief from judgment denied 2013 WL 12201089, post-conviction relief denied Langdon v. U.S., 2007 WL 656460, post-conviction relief denied 2007 WL 1789117, dismissal of habeas corpus affirmed Jones v. Warden, FCC Coleman-Medium, 520 Fed.Appx. 942, certiorari denied 134 S.Ct. 711, 571 U.S. 1083, 187 L.Ed.2d 571.

C.A.11 (Fla.) 1993. Defendant did not have reasonable expectation of privacy while in backseat of police car and, therefore, tape recording of his prearrest conversations did not violate Title III of the Omnibus Crime Control and Safe Streets Act or his Fourth Amendment right to privacy. 18 U.S.C.A. §§ 2510(2), 2511; U.S.C.A. Const.Amend. 4.—U.S. v. McKinnon, 985 F.2d 525, certiorari denied 114 S.Ct. 130, 510 U.S. 843, 126 L.Ed.2d 94.

Test for determining whether person has reasonable or justifiable expectation of privacy, for purposes of Title III of the Omnibus Crime Control and Safe Streets Act and the Fourth Amendment, has two prongs: first, whether person's conduct exhibits subjective expectation of privacy, and second, whether person's subjective expectation of privacy is one that society is willing to recognize as reasonable. 18 U.S.C.A. §§ 2510(2), 2511; U.S.C.A. Const.Amend. 4.—Id.

C.A.11 (Fla.) 1991. Defendant had no justifiable expectation of privacy when voluntarily conversing with undercover agent who knowingly recorded the exchange, and, thus, Fourth Amendment was not violated. U.S.C.A. Const.Amend. 4. —U.S. v. Laetividal-Gonzalez, 939 F.2d 1455, certiorari denied Ocampo v. U.S., 112 S.Ct. 1280, 503 U.S. 912, 117 L.Ed.2d 505.

C.A.11 (Fla.) 1984. Warrantless electronic interceptions of conversations by informant acting under color of law within purview of federal statute governing electronic surveillance are not proscribed by Fourth Amendment, since individual has no legitimate expectation that person to whom he is speaking will not relate conversation to legal authorities, either by repetition or by recording of conversation. 18 U.S.C.A. § 2511(2)(c); U.S.C.A. Const.Amend. 4.—U.S. v. Haimowitz, 725 F.2d 1561, certiorari denied 105 S.Ct. 563, 469 U.S. 1072, 83 L.Ed.2d 504.

C.A.11 (Fla.) 1983. That person with whom defendant had conversation did not have recording device implanted on the person, but, rather, such device was concealed in the room did not result in violation of defendant's expectation of

privacy. U.S.C.A. Const.Amend. 4.—U.S. v. Yonn, 702 F.2d 1341, certiorari denied Weeks v. U.S., 104 S.Ct. 283, 464 U.S. 917, 78 L.Ed.2d 261.

C.A.11 (Fla.) 1982. That defendant was speaking on telephone located within his home did not make seizure of his voice unreasonable intrusion on privacy of the home, and his reliance on more protected privacy provisions of Florida Constitution was misplaced. West's F.S.A. § 934.03(2)(c); 18 U.S.C.A. § 2511(2)(c); U.S.C.A. Const.Amend. 4.—U.S. v. Capo, 693 F.2d 1330, certiorari denied 103 S.Ct. 1793, 460 U.S. 1092, 76 L.Ed.2d 359, on rehearing U.S. v. Lisenby, 716 F.2d 1355.

C.A.11 (Fla.) 1982. Government's interceptions of coconspirators' conversations by way of tape recorder and radio transmitter installed on one of the coconspirators at his request by a private detective, who was cooperating with the FBI, did not violate the other coconspirator's justifiable expectations of privacy. U.S.C.A.Const.Amend. 4.—U.S. v. Shields, 675 F.2d 1152, certiorari denied 103 S.Ct. 130, 459 U.S. 858, 74 L.Ed.2d 112, certiorari denied Quick v. U.S., 103 S.Ct. 373, 459 U.S. 1015, 74 L.Ed.2d 508.

C.A.5 (Fla.) 1981. Where only "interception" of telephone call from defendant was by government agent who was party to conversation, where government agents did not record or transcribe call in any way, and where defendant instituted calls and spoke voluntarily and without hesitation to agents, none of whom pretended to be person that defendant wished to reach, defendant had no legitimate expectation of privacy in telephone conversations with agents and assumed risk of exposure when he spoke freely with them. U.S.C.A.Const. Amend. 4; 18 U.S.C.A. § 2510 et seq.—U.S. v. Congote, 656 F.2d 971.

M.D.Fla. 2021. There is no reasonable expectation of privacy in the spaces of hard drives and other electronic storage devices made available to the public via a peer-to-peer (P2P) network, or in an internet protocol (IP) address or other information made available to other P2P users. U.S. Const. Amend. 4.—United States v. Thomas, 548 F.Supp.3d 1212, objections overruled 2021 WL 3857768.

M.D.Fla. 2012. Arrestee and his attorney had a reasonable expectation of privacy in attorney-client conversations held in police interview room in county sheriff's office, and thus the surreptitious recording of those conversations violated the Fourth Amendment and constituted an actionable interception of "oral communication" under the Federal Wiretapping Act; officer's actions in closing door to interview room when exiting and allowing arrestee and officer to speak alone fostered an expectation of privacy, attorney clearly conveyed to arrestee that she believed their conversations were private by providing legal advice, discussing legal strategy, and asking questions regarding the subject of her representations, and attorney testified that, in the past, when police interviews with her clients had been recorded, she had been informed of that fact so she could arrange for private communications, and that, as a member of the local defense bar, she had been told that the sheriff's office recorded only confessions and statements from suspects rather than the full contents of all interviews. U.S.C.A. Const.Amend. 4; 18 U.S.C.A. §§ 2510(2), 2511(1)(a), 2520(a).—Gennusa v. Shoar, 879 F.Supp.2d 1337, affirmed 748 F.3d 1103.

† This Case was not selected for publication in the National Reporter System

M.D.Fla. 2009. An owner of a cell phone generally has a reasonable expectation of privacy in the electronic data stored on the phone; thus, a search warrant is required to search the contents of a cell phone unless an exception to the warrant requirement exists. U.S.C.A. Const.Amend. 4.— U.S. v. Quintana, 594 F.Supp.2d 1291.

S.D.Fla. 2019. There is no Fourth Amendment protection for information that a person freely shares with others on a publicly-accessible peer-to-peer network. U.S. Const. Amend. 4.— United States v. Sigouin, 494 F.Supp.3d 1252.

FBI did not trespass in violation of the Fourth Amendment, by purportedly accessing a computer to get a list of neighbors on publicly-accessible peer-to-peer network, where the owner of the computer had selected "opennet mode" which voluntarily shared the allegedly accessed portion of his hard drive with anyone who elected to join the network. U.S. Const. Amend. 4.—Id.

Even if FBI violated the Electronic Communications Privacy Act (ECPA) by accessing hash value requested on publicly-accessible peer-to-peer network, such a violation did not change Fourth Amendment analysis, where there was no reasonable expectation of privacy to the hash value, as the original sender of the value had to expect that the value would be communicated to multiple third-party peers, and was equivalent of loudly asking for something in a room full of strangers. U.S. Const. Amend. 4; 18 U.S.C.A. § 2510(8).—Id.

Defendant had no objectively reasonable expectation of privacy in information that his computer was transmitting or making freely available to neighbors on a publicly-accessible peer-to-peer network, allegedly used by the defendant to obtain child pornography, and thus warrantless monitoring of that information by the FBI did not violate the Fourth Amendment, where the information shared by defendant's computer communicated nothing about the underlying file that defendant was seeking on the network, other than that the sender of the information desired a copy of piece of a file corresponding with the information, and being able to reconstruct files distributed around the network was not a pervasive and insistent part of daily life, indispensable to participate in modern society. U.S. Const. Amend. 4.— Id.

S.D.Fla. 2008. Defendant, who was indicted for online sex solicitation, possessed no objectively reasonable expectation of privacy under the Fourth Amendment for subscriber information provided to internet service provider (ISP) that government received from exigent circumstance letters under Electronic Communications Privacy Act (ECPA), where service provider had an agreement with defendant to share information for investigations, to cooperate with law enforcement, and to take legal action. U.S.C.A. Const. Amend. 4; 18 U.S.C.A. §§ 2702, 2703.—U.S. v. Beckett, 544 F.Supp.2d 1346, affirmed 369 Fed. Appx. 52.

S.D.Fla. 1991. Inmate had no legitimate expectation of privacy in telephone conversations which he knew were subject to monitoring and recording by prison officials, and, thus, Fourth Amendment was inapplicable; various notices and consent form explicitly stated that telephone calls were subject to monitoring and recording. U.S.C.A. Const.Amend. 4.—U.S. v. Noriega, 764 F.Supp. 1480.

Fla. 2014. Defendant's conversations with his stepdaughter in his bedroom, that were recorded surreptitiously, and during which he confirmed child sexual abuse and solicited sex with her, were "oral communications," and were "uttered by a person exhibiting an expectation that his communication was not subject to interception," and thus recordings fell within statute prohibiting interception of oral communications without consent of all parties to the communication, and were inadmissible as evidence in prosecution for sexual battery on a child less than 12 years of age and other offenses. West's F.S.A. § 934.06.— McDade v. State, 154 So.3d 292.

Fla. 2009. Under both the Fourth Amendment and the Florida wiretapping act, for an oral conversation to be protected from interception, a speaker must have an actual subjective expectation of privacy and society must recognize that the expectation is reasonable. U.S.C.A. Const. Amend. 4; West's F.S.A. § 943.01 et seq.—Jackson v. State, 18 So.3d 1016, certiorari denied 130 S.Ct. 1144, 558 U.S. 1151, 175 L.Ed.2d 979, post-conviction relief denied 2012 WL 10716486, affirmed 127 So.3d 447, rehearing denied, habeas corpus denied 127 So.3d 447, rehearing denied, and rehearing denied.

There is no reasonable expectation of privacy in a police vehicle or in a telephone communication from jail during which warnings are issued; therefore, any interception of conversations that occur there would not be prohibited by the Florida wiretapping act. U.S.C.A. Const.Amend. 4; West's F.S.A. § 943.01 et seq.—Id.

Fla. 1995. Nonconsensual interception of defendants' cordless telephone conversations by police, without prior judicial approval, violated Security of Communications Act, where communication originated in defendants' home; intercepted cordless telephone conversations which originated within defendants' home exhibited required expectation of privacy demanded by Security of Communications Act. West's F.S.A. § 934.02(2).—State v. Mozo, 655 So.2d 1115, rehearing denied.

Oral communications conducted over cordless phone within privacy of one's own home are protected by Security of Communications Act. West's F.S.A. § 934.02(2).—Id.

Fla. 1985. Considering language of West's F.S.A. § 934.02(2) defining an "oral communication," for purpose of security of communications statute, the legislature did not intend that every oral communication be free from interception without the prior consent of all parties to the communication; statute protects only those "oral communications" uttered by a person exhibiting an expectation of privacy under circumstances reasonably justifying such an expectation. West's F.S.A. § 934.03.—State v. Inciarrano, 473 So.2d 1272.

With regard to statute protecting from interception "oral communications" uttered by a person exhibiting an expectation of privacy under circumstances reasonably justifying such an expectation, such expectation of privacy does not contemplate merely a subjective expectation on part of person making the oral communication but rather contemplates a reasonable expectation of privacy; a reasonable expectation of privacy under a given set of circumstances depends upon one's subjective expectation of privacy as well as whether society is prepared to recognize such expectation as reasonable. West's F.S.A. §§ 934.02(2), 934.03.—Id.

Defendant who entered murder victim's office with intent to do him harm had no reasonable expectation of privacy, and thus tape recording made by victim which recorded conversation between victim and defendant regarding business deal in which victim no longer wanted a part, the sound of a gun being cocked, five shots being fired by defendant, several groans by victim, the gushing of blood, and victim falling from his chair to floor did not fall within statutory proscription of West's F.S.A. § 934.03 prohibiting interception of oral communications without consent of all parties to the communication, and tape recording was not excludable from evidence in ensuing murder prosecution. West's F.S.A. §§ 934.02(2), 934.06.—Id.

Fla. 1982. Although defendant may have maintained reasonable expectation of privacy in his private office, that expectation was not one which society was willing to recognize as reasonable or which society was willing to protect in connection with telephone conversations between defendant and two informants who had consented to electronic interception and recording of telephone conversations and "body bug" recording of other conversations. West's F.S.A. Const. Art. 1, § 12; Art. 5, § 3(b)(4); West's F.S.A. § 934.03(2)(c).—Morningstar v. State, 428 So.2d 220, certiorari denied 104 S.Ct. 86, 464 U.S. 821, 78 L.Ed.2d 95.

Fla. 1981. Definition of "interception of private communications," in context of constitutional prohibition against such interception, is a function of one's reasonable expectation of privacy. West's F.S.A.Const. Art. 1, § 12.—State v. Sarmiento, 397 So.2d 643.

Although defendant, who discussed sale of heroin with undercover police officer in his home, assumed the risk that the officer might reveal the contents of their conversation to the outside world, defendant did enjoy a reasonable expectation of privacy that no one was listening to the conversation by means of electronic eavesdropping, and thus electronic interception of their conversation violated State Constitution. West's F.S.A.Const. Art. 1, § 12.—Id.

Fla. 1978. Extortionary threat delivered personally to victim in victim's home was "oral communication," within statute defining oral communication for purposes of statutes relating to security of communications as one uttered by person exhibiting expectation that communication is not subject to interception under circumstances justifying such expectation. West's F.S.A. §§ 934.02(2), 934.03, 934.06; West's F.S.A.Const. art. 5, § 3(b)(3).—State v. Walls, 356 So.2d 294.

Fla.App. 1 Dist. 2022. Persons generally lack reasonable expectation of privacy, for purpose of statute making it illegal to intentionally intercept oral information when speaker has reasonable expectation of privacy in his statements, when in police custody. Fla. Stat. Ann. §§ 934.02, 943.03. —Reed v. State, 350 So.3d 836, cause dismissed 2023 WL 5236391.

The objective reasonableness of an expectation of privacy in a hospital setting, for purpose of statute making it illegal to intentionally intercept oral information when speaker has reasonable expectation of privacy in his statements, turns on the particular circumstances of each case. Fla. Stat. Ann. §§ 934.02, 943.03.—Id.

Fla.App. 1 Dist. 2020. Because cell phones are treated as almost a feature of human anatomy, tracking of a cell phone is tracking of the owner, in the context of the Fourth Amendment protection against unreasonable searches. U.S. Const. Amend. 4.—Bailey v. State, 311 So.3d 303, rehearing denied, review denied 2021 WL 2408431, certiorari denied 142 S.Ct. 568, 211 L.Ed.2d 354.

Fla.App. 1 Dist. 2019. Not all oral communications recorded without prior consent are subject to exclusion under the wiretap law; the statute protects only those oral communications uttered by a person exhibiting an expectation of privacy under circumstances reasonably justifying such an expectation. Fla. Stat. Ann. § 934.02(2).—Smiley v. State, 279 So.3d 262, rehearing denied.

To support suppression of a communication under the wiretap law, the person who made the statement must show more than a subjective expectation of privacy; they must show that they have a reasonable expectation of privacy under the circumstances, which depends on one's actual subjective expectation of privacy as well as whether society is prepared to recognize that expectation as reasonable. Fla. Stat. Ann. § 934.02(2).—Id.

Defendant did not have a subjective expectation that statements made in victim's home were not subject to interception, and thus statements recorded on victim's cell phone were not protected by wiretap statute from admission in prosecution for aggravated assault by threat with deadly weapon and domestic violence battery, where cell phone video showed defendant saw cell phone in victim's hand and knew he was being recorded, defendant tried to snatch phone from victim's hand, and defendant made statements suggesting he knew he was being recorded. Fla. Stat. Ann. §§ 934.03, 934.06, 934.09(10)(a).—Id.

Defendant did not have reasonable expectation of privacy in statements made in victim's home, and thus statements recorded on victim's cell phone video were not "oral communications" protected under wiretap statute from admission in prosecution for aggravated assault by threat with deadly weapon and domestic violence battery; although defendant had initially been invited into victim's home as guest and frequently stayed there overnight, during argument victim demanded defendant leave her home at least nine times. Fla. Stat. Ann. § 934.02(2).—Id.

Although under statute that prohibits interception and disclosure of oral communications society generally recognizes as reasonable an expectation of privacy in conversations conducted in a private home, the reasonableness of that expectation presupposes that the speaker has permission to be there in the first place. Fla. Stat. Ann. § 934.02(2).—Id.

Fla.App. 1 Dist. 2019. Defendant did not establish that he had a reasonable expectation of privacy when he uploaded child pornography to an online chat room, and therefore law enforcement agent did not conduct an unlawful search when he opened image file, which had been sent to law enforcement by chat room operator, prior to obtaining a warrant; nothing in record indicated number of participants in chat room, whether defendant had exclusive control to admit people to chat room, or whether chat room operator monitored chat room for illegal activity as a part of its service agreement, and defendant presented no evidence that uploaded file was password-protected or that he took any affirmative steps to restrict access to it. U.S. Const. Amend. 4; Fla. Const. art. 1, § 12.—Morales v. State, 274 So.3d 1213.

Fla.App. 1 Dist. 2012. Recording of 911 dispatcher's call to residence next door to 911 caller's residence which contained threats made by defendant later charged with aggravated assault with a weapon was not admissible as oral communication between defendant and victims in which defendant had no expectation of privacy, where recording clearly satisfied statutory definition of "wire communication," and conversation occurred in residence defendant occasionally shared with victims. West's F.S.A. § 934.02(1).—Perdue v. State, 78 So.3d 712, review denied 104 So.3d 1086.

Fla.App. 1 Dist. 1996. In weighing expectations of privacy of communicant so as to determine applicability of statute protecting privacy of oral communications, privacy analysis is structured along plumb line of Fourth Amendment jurisprudence. U.S.C.A. Const.Amend. 4; West's F.S.A. § 934.02(2).—Brandin v. State, 669 So.2d 280, rehearing denied.

Fla.App. 1 Dist. 1996. Defendant had no reasonable expectation of privacy in conversation which took place outside van stopped in public roadway in known drug trafficking area, and, therefore, intercepted statement suggesting that drug trafficking was occurring did not qualify as "oral communication" protected by statutes governing security of communications; circumstances surrounding making of the statement were highly suggestive of drug transaction, and parties to the conversation took no action to insure privacy before their conversation. West's F.S.A. §§ 934.02(2), 934.03, 934.06, 934.07.—Stevenson v. State, 667 So.2d 410, rehearing denied.

For conversation to qualify as "oral communication," protected under security of communication statutes, speaker must have actual subjective expectation of privacy in the communication, and society must be prepared to recognize expectation as reasonable under the circumstances; where both elements are present, statute has been violated regardless of whether intercepted communication is private in nature. West's F.S.A. §§ 934.02(2), 934.03, 934.06, 934.07.—Id.

Factors considered in determining whether intercepted communication qualifies as "oral communication" protected under security of communication statutes include location in which conversation or communication occurs, manner in which communication is made, and the kind of communication; thus, conversations occurring inside enclosed area or secluded area are more likely to be protected. West's F.S.A. §§ 934.02(2), 934.03, 934.06, 934.07.—Id.

Fla.App. 1 Dist. 1983. "Intrusion" of police informant, who converses with a suspect inside suspect's residence and transmits their conversation to nearby surveilling law enforcement officers, is not a violation of suspect's Fourth Amendment reasonable expectation of privacy. U.S.C.A. Const.Amend. 4.—Powe v. State, 443 So.2d 154.

Fla.App. 1 Dist. 1982. Societal interest in maintaining custody over prisoners significantly outweighs individual prisoner's interest in privacy of his telephonic communications; thus, there is exception to statute governing interception of wire and oral communication permitting prison officials to wiretap telephone calls from prisoners incarcerated in prison. West's F.S.A. § 934.01 et seq.—Pires v. Wainwright, 419 So.2d 358.

Fla.App. 2 Dist. 2022. Technological advancement often collides with the Fourth Amendment. U.S. Const. Amend. 4; Fla. Const. art. 1, § 12.—Youngman v. State, 342 So.3d 770.

Defendant did not have reasonable expectation of privacy in his electronic files publicly stored and shared on a peer-to-peer file-sharing network, and thus law enforcement's warrantless use of software program to identify defendant's publicly available electronic child pornography files and corresponding hash values, the 32-digit alphanumeric code for each piece of digital media, did not violate defendant's right to be free from unreasonable search and seizure; any member of the public could access defendant's shared files by simply downloading the peer-to-peer sharing network and asking for the desired files, a request that the suspect computer would automatically fulfill, such that the hash value for each digital media stored on that network was publicly available. U.S. Const. Amend. 4; Fla. Const. art. 1, § 12.—Id.

Fla.App. 2 Dist. 2020. A warrant may not always be required to search a cell phone as other case-specific exceptions may still justify a warrantless search of a particular phone. U.S. Const. Amend. 4; Fla. Const. art. 1, § 12.—Parker v. State, 313 So.3d 737.

Fla.App. 2 Dist. 2016. In determining whether the speaker's expectation of privacy in a recorded statement is reasonable, courts should examine the location of the conversation, the type of communication at issue, and the manner in which the communication was made. West's F.S.A. § 934.06.—State v. Caraballo, 198 So.3d 819.

Fla.App. 2 Dist. 2014. Protection under statutes governing interception of communications requires not only a subjective expectation of privacy, but the expectation must also be reasonable in order for the communication to be protected. West's F.S.A. § 934.02.—Abdo v. State, 144 So.3d 594.

Significant factors used in determining the reasonableness of the utterer's expectation of privacy in a conversation, for purposes of protection under statutes governing interception of communications, include the manner in which the oral communication is made and the kind of communication, and the location in which the conversation or communication occurs; thus, conversations occurring inside an enclosed area or in a secluded area are more likely to be protected. West's F.S.A. § 934.02.—Id.

Fla.App. 2 Dist. 2013. Factors considered in determining whether intercepted communication qualifies as "oral communication" protected under security of communication statutes include location in which conversation or communication occurs, manner in which communication is made, and the kind of communication; thus, conversations occurring inside enclosed area or secluded area are more likely to be protected. (Per Khouzan, J., with one judge specially concurring.) West's F.S.A. § 934.06.—McDade v. State, 114 So.3d 465, review granted 121 So.3d 1037, quashed 154 So.3d 292.

Defendant had no reasonable expectation of privacy in recordings victim made of inculpatory conversations she had with him, during which he solicited her for sexual acts, and thus recordings did not fall within statute prohibiting interception of oral communications without consent of all parties to the communication, and recordings were not excludable from evidence in prosecution for sexual battery on a child less then 12 years of age and other offenses. (Per Khouzan, J., with one judge specially concurring.) West's F.S.A. § 934.06.—Id.

Fla.App. 3 Dist. 2018. Expectation of privacy, for purposes of statute governing intercepted wire or oral communications, is not reasonable where the intercepted communication was made in an open, public area rather than in an en-

† **This Case was not selected for publication in the National Reporter System**

closed, private, or secluded area. Fla. Stat. Ann. § 934.06.—State v. Garcia, 252 So.3d 783.

Fla.App. 3 Dist. 2008. Video and audio taped conversation defendant had with codefendant in police interrogation room was admissible in trial for murder and related offenses; defendant adopted codefendant's statements as his own, and defendant had no reasonable expectation of privacy in the conversation held in the police interrogation room.—Pestano v. State, 980 So.2d 1200, rehearing denied, post-conviction relief denied 2009 WL 6539717, affirmed 36 So.3d 680.

Fla.App. 3 Dist. 2001. Defendant did not have reasonable expectation of privacy in police interview room where his statement was videotaped without his knowledge.—Bell v. State, 802 So.2d 485, cause dismissed 828 So.2d 384, rehearing denied.

Fla.App. 3 Dist. 1979. For government agents to "intercept" a private communication, within meaning of state constitutional provision that right to be secure against the unreasonable interception of private communications shall not be violated, the agents must invade one's reasonable expectation of privacy. West's F.S.A.Const. art. 1, § 12.—Sarmiento v. State, 371 So.2d 1047, decision approved 397 So.2d 643.

Fla.App. 4 Dist. 2021. A person exhibits a subjective expectation of privacy, as required for an oral communication to be protected under statute prohibiting the interception or recording of private oral communications and the use of such communications as evidence, only when the individual has shown that he seeks to preserve something as private. Fla. Stat. Ann. §§ 934.03, 934.06.—State v. Foster, 323 So.3d 209.

A party's claim to a subjective expectation of privacy, as required for an oral communication to be protected under statute prohibiting the interception or recording of private oral communications and the use of such communications as evidence, in a conversation can be rejected when there is no evidence the party made any effort or otherwise took precautions to keep the conversation private. Fla. Stat. Ann. §§ 934.03, 934.06.—Id.

Correctional officer did not have subjective expectation of privacy while conducting mandatory exit interview with former corrections officer whose reason for resigning was due to witnessing instances of inmate abuse, and thus, recorded exit interview was not "oral communication" within meaning of statute prohibiting the recording of private oral communications and the use of such communications as evidence; officer documented former officer's reason for resignation by preparing incident report submitted for review for a possible investigation, all attendees at the exit interview were correctional employees, were located on correctional institution's property, and acted in furtherance of public duties, and the allegations of inmate abuse were a matter of public interest. Fla. Stat. Ann. §§ 934.02, 934.03, 934.06.—Id.

Fla.App. 4 Dist. 2014. Defendant had no expectation of privacy when in custody at the police station, and thus he could not challenge admission of recording of a telephone conversation between himself and his mother at the police station; police detectives never made any assurances to defendant that his calls would be made in private and he knew he was being recorded, and defendant never requested privacy during the conversation and allowed a detective to be present in the room for at least portions of the conversation.—Davis v. State, 151 So.3d 4.

Fla.App. 4 Dist. 2012. Defendant did not have a reasonable expectation of privacy in conversations with his girlfriend in interrogation room at police station so as to warrant exclusion of videotape of conversations in attempted sexual battery and lewd or lascivious molestation prosecution, where defendant had waived his *Miranda* rights and made admissions to police, defendant then specifically asked to speak to his girlfriend, and, although police officer did leave the room, defendant never asked for privacy to speak to his girlfriend. U.S.C.A. Const.Amend. 4.—Lundberg v. State, 127 So.3d 562, review granted 130 So.3d 693, review dismissed as improvidently granted by 149 So.3d 1126, rehearing denied, certiorari denied 135 S.Ct. 1459, 574 U.S. 1179, 191 L.Ed.2d 407.

Fla.App. 4 Dist. 2011. Although defendant knew that co-defendant was at the police station when their telephone conversation took place, defendant, who was at home at time of conversation, had a subjective expectation of privacy in his statements for purposes of wiretap statute, protecting from interception oral communications uttered by a person exhibiting an expectation of privacy. U.S.C.A. Const.Amend. 4; West's F.S.A. §§ 934.02, 934.03.—Hentz v. State, 62 So.3d 1184.

Fla.App. 4 Dist. 1999. Defendant and sister-in-law did not have reasonable expectation of privacy in conversation in interrogation room, and thus, police officer's secret taping of conversation did not violate Fourth Amendment's right to privacy; defendant neither asked for privacy, nor was it offered, and police said nothing and did nothing that would reasonably foster sense of privacy in the conversation. U.S.C.A. Const. Amend. 4.—Boyer v. State, 736 So.2d 64, rehearing denied.

Fla.App. 4 Dist. 1994. Conversations occurring inside an enclosed area or in a secluded area are more likely to be protected from interception than those occurring in open spaces, such as apartment building courtyard. West's F.S.A. § 934.02(2).—Cinci v. State, 642 So.2d 572, rehearing denied, review denied 651 So.2d 1192.

Fla.App. 4 Dist. 1994. Under state constitutional general provision guaranteeing right of privacy, person's private conversations over cordless telephone are presumptively protected from government interception. West's F.S.A. Const. Art. 1, § 23.—Mozo v. State, 632 So.2d 623, review granted 640 So.2d 1108, decision approved 655 So.2d 1115, rehearing denied.

Fla.App. 4 Dist. 1985. Incarcerated defendant had reasonable expectation that his conversation with his brother in police interrogation room was secure and private as guaranteed by West's F.S.A. Const. Art. 1, §§ 12, 23 and West's F.S.A. § 934.03; defendant had invoked his *Miranda* rights prior to conversation and interrogating officers brought defendant's brother into room and left to monitor and record conversation through hidden video camera.—State v. Calhoun, 479 So.2d 241.

Fla.App. 5 Dist. 1983. Audio and video recordings made by police officers in course of a "sting" operation utilizing a storefront operation did not violate defendant's right of privacy so as to preclude their admission into evidence, since defendant came into store and openly entered into transaction with undercover officer and he could have had no reasonable expectation of privacy in transacting his business in a place of business open to public. U.S.C.A. Const.Amend. 4; West's F.S.A. Const. Art. 1, § 12; West's

---

† **This Case was not selected for publication in the National Reporter System**

F.S.A. § 934.03(2)(c).—Adams v. State, 436 So.2d 1132.

⇐519. —— Location data.

C.A.11 (Fla.) 2020. Third-party doctrine, that a person lacks a reasonable expectation of privacy, of kind protected by the Fourth Amendment, in information that he has voluntarily disclosed to third party, does not apply to retrospective collection of cell-site location information for periods of at least seven days. U.S. Const. Amend. 4.— United States v. Trader, 981 F.3d 961, certiorari denied 142 S.Ct. 296, 211 L.Ed.2d 139.

While individual maintains a legitimate expectation of privacy, of a kind protected by the Fourth Amendment, in the record of his physical movements as captured through cell-site location information, the same cannot be said for e-mail addresses or internet protocol addresses that he voluntarily chooses to share with third party by opening and logging into messaging app. U.S. Const. Amend. 4.—Id.

Fla.App. 1 Dist. 2020. The harm inherent in a government's warrantless gathering of cell site location information is primarily borne of the virtual attachment of the cellular device to its owner—allowing for all-encompassing, perpetual tracking which penetrates private spheres—and of the fact that the overwhelming majority of individuals more or less must own a cell phone. U.S. Const. Amend. 4.—Bailey v. State, 311 So.3d 303, rehearing denied, review denied 2021 WL 2408431, certiorari denied 142 S.Ct. 568, 211 L.Ed.2d 354.

Because cars do not bear the same attachment as cellphones to their owners and cannot penetrate private spaces to the same degree, government acquisition of a vehicle's GPS data does not give rise to the same risk of all-encompassing surveillance as cell site location information, in the context of Fourth Amendment protection against unreasonable searches. U.S. Const. Amend. 4.—Id.

As an owner's vehicle is frequently in operation and driven by others, GPS tracking of cars does not provide police the level of personal surveillance contemplated with cell site location information, in the context of Fourth Amendment protection against unreasonable searches. U.S. Const. Amend. 4.—Id.

Murder defendant had no objectively reasonable expectation of privacy in GPS records transmitted from his borrowed car to car owner's financing company such that law enforcement's warrantless acquisition of such records would constitute a "search" implicating the protections of the Fourth Amendment, even though GPS data was technically historical in nature; GPS records of the car's location during the commission of the offense were records of defendant's travels over public thoroughfares, car's owner consented to GPS tracking, and police played no role in recording the GPS information. U.S. Const. Amend. 4.—Id.

Murder defendant did not demonstrate a subjective expectation of privacy in GPS records transmitted from his borrowed car to car owner's financing company such that law enforcement's warrantless acquisition of such records would constitute a "search" implicating the protections of the Fourth Amendment, even though GPS information was transferred to a third-party; car was not owned by defendant and was allegedly taken without permission, defendant used car to traverse public streets, car's owner had consented to tracking, and transmission of GPS informa-

tion to financing company did not reflect a lack of voluntariness, as nothing forced defendant to borrow car, and other means of untracked travel were available to defendant. U.S. Const. Amend. 4.—Id.

Fla.App. 1 Dist. 2015. Defendant had reasonable expectation to privacy in his real-time cell phone location data. U.S.C.A. Const.Amend. 4.— Herring v. State, 168 So.3d 240, rehearing denied, review dismissed 173 So.3d 966.

Fla.App. 4 Dist. 2009. Historical cell phone site information is not content-based; the user of a cell phone has no expectation of privacy in those records.—Mitchell v. State, 25 So.3d 632, rehearing denied.

Because historical cell phone site information discloses only the defendant's past location and does not pinpoint his current location in a private area, it does not implicate Fourth Amendment protections. U.S.C.A. Const.Amend. 4.—Id.

⇐521. —— In general.

Fla.App. 4 Dist. 1975. With respect to search of an automobile, as distinguished from a house, recognized exceptions to warrant requirement are: (1) search incident to a lawful arrest, (2) search based on probable cause, (3) "plain view" situation, (4) search in connection with seizure of automobile for purposes of forfeiture proceeding, and (5) bona fide inventory search.—State v. Jenkins, 319 So.2d 91.

⇐522. —— Motor vehicles.

†C.A.11 (Fla.) 2020. Defendant abandoned a vehicle, and thus did not have expectation of privacy in the vehicle under the Fourth Amendment, where the defendant had unsuccessfully attempted to escape from law enforcement officers by reversing in the vehicle, and then opened the driver's side door and fled on foot, leaving the door open. U.S. Const. Amend. 4.—United States v. Johnson, 811 Fed.Appx. 564.

Defendant had no reasonable expectation of privacy in a vehicle's license tag, and thus police officer running the tag information through a law enforcement database without warrant was not a search under the Fourth Amendment, even though defendant was parked at a privately owned gas station rather than driving on a public road, where license tags were required by law to be displayed in plain view and the gas station was open to the public. U.S. Const. Amend. 4.—Id.

C.A.5 (Fla.) 1975. Where defendant knew that rental agent at warehouse, and others doing work or storing matter in area, had joint access to warehouse area in which defendant was storing his truck containing more than half a ton of marijuana, he took his chance that other persons might enter at inconvenient time or grant permission for law enforcement officials to come upon the premises, and thus had no reasonable expectation of privacy, and there was no violation of defendant's Fourth Amendment rights when officers, by ruse, induced one of the other persons having right of access to admit them to the premises, which they searched and thereby obtained probable cause for warrant to search truck. U.S.C.A.Const. Amend. 4.—U.S. v. Novello, 519 F.2d 1078, certiorari denied 96 S.Ct. 797, 423 U.S. 1060, 46 L.Ed.2d 651.

M.D.Fla. 1974. Whether a "search" occurred when officer looked through window of automobile and saw a box and some bills covering the part of floorboard on driver's side turned on officer's intent to conduct a "probing, exploratory quest for evidence of a crime"; whether a protected interest was involved turned on existence

---

† This Case was not selected for publication in the National Reporter System

of reasonable expectation of privacy with respect to the vehicle's exposed interior. U.S.C.A.Const. Amend. 4.—U. S. ex rel. McDougald v. Hassfurder, 372 F.Supp. 395.

Fla. 1994. Statute making it a crime to willfully intercept oral communications was not violated when conversation between motorist and companion sitting in rear of police vehicle for safety and comfort reasons during consensual search of automobile were recorded; motorist had no reasonable expectation of privacy in police car. West's F.S.A. § 934.03.—State v. Smith, 641 So.2d 849.

Fla.App. 1 Dist. 2020. Because cars do not bear the same attachment as cellphones to their owners and cannot penetrate private spaces to the same degree, government acquisition of a vehicle's GPS data does not give rise to the same risk of all-encompassing surveillance as cell site location information, in the context of Fourth Amendment protection against unreasonable searches. U.S. Const. Amend. 4.—Bailey v. State, 311 So.3d 303, rehearing denied, review denied 2021 WL 2408431, certiorari denied 142 S.Ct. 568, 211 L.Ed.2d 354.

Fla.App. 1 Dist. 2007. A person has no reasonable expectation of privacy in odors that emanate from a car in a public place; once a drug dog alerts to a car, therefore, probable cause exists to search the car. U.S.C.A. Const.Amend. 4.—State v. Griffin, 949 So.2d 309, review denied 958 So.2d 920.

Fla.App. 1 Dist. 1992. Person's expectation of privacy in motorboat is less than same expectation of privacy in automobile. U.S.C.A. Const. Amend. 4.—State v. Starkey, 605 So.2d 963.

Fla.App. 1 Dist. 1981. Considering furtive movements of automobile occupant, area where vehicle was located, time of night and fact that occupant appeared to be trying to stuff something between car seats, police officer's command for occupant to sit up from his prone position on car seat was such limited intrusion that there was no constitutional violation by officers, and contraband which then came into open view was subject to seizure under automobile exception to warrant requirement. U.S.C.A.Const. Amend. 4. —Moline v. State, 404 So.2d 826.

Fla.App. 1 Dist. 1976. A greater justification is required for a warrantless intrusion into the privacy of a home including a mobile home than for similar intrusion into an automobile.—Britton v. State, 336 So.2d 663, certiorari denied 344 So.2d 326.

Fla.App. 2 Dist. 1988. Defendant's flight after justification for detention had disappeared did not provide proper basis for investigatory stop or search; car in which defendant was passenger had been stopped based on information that defendant possessed fictitious driver's license, and the State failed to carry its burden of showing absence of continued illegal detention after justification for detention disappeared when deputy determined that defendant did not commit crime through possessing fictitious driver's license. U.S.C.A. Const.Amend. 4.—Castillo v. State, 536 So.2d 1134.

Fla.App. 4 Dist. 2017. Defendant had a reasonable expectation of privacy in the information retained in the event data recorder or "black box" in his impounded vehicle, and thus police, who downloaded that information without a warrant in the absence of exigent circumstances, violated the Fourth Amendment; a data retrieval kit was required to extract data, which was not exposed to the public, and data was required to

be interpreted by a specialist with extensive training. U.S. Const. Amend. 4; 49 C.F.R. §§ 563.5, 563.7, 563.9.—State v. Worsham, 227 So.3d 602, certiorari denied 138 S.Ct. 264, 583 U.S. 873, 199 L.Ed.2d 125.

Fla.App. 5 Dist. 2011. Defendant failed to demonstrate that he had a legitimate expectation of privacy in the vehicle, in which he was a mere passenger, and therefore, he lacked standing to challenge the items seized from vehicle; however, he did have standing to contest the legality of the investigatory stop and his arrest. U.S.C.A. Const. Amend. 4.—State v. K.N., 66 So.3d 380.

🔑**524. Animals and pets.**

M.D.Fla. 2018. Pets are effects subject to Fourth Amendment protection. U.S. Const. Amend. 4.—Chastang v. Levy, 319 F.Supp.3d 1244.

🔑**525. Items in plain view.**

Fla.App. 1 Dist. 1976. Defendant did not have reasonable expectation of privacy in front porch of his home where delivery men and others were free to observe plants thereon.—State v. Detlefson, 335 So.2d 371.

Fla.App. 4 Dist. 2020. What a person knowingly exposes to the public, even in his own home or office, is not a subject of Fourth Amendment protection, but what he seeks to preserve as private, even in an area accessible to the public, may be constitutionally protected. U.S. Const. Amend. 4.—State v. Kraft, 301 So.3d 981.

🔑**527. —— In general.**

C.A.11 (Fla.) 2020. Generally, a person lacks a reasonable expectation of privacy, of kind protected by the Fourth Amendment, in information that he has voluntarily disclosed to third party. U.S. Const. Amend. 4.—United States v. Trader, 981 F.3d 961, certiorari denied 142 S.Ct. 296, 211 L.Ed.2d 139.

C.A.11 (Fla.) 2020. Fourth Amendment protection does not extend to abandoned property. U.S. Const. Amend. 4.—United States v. Green, 981 F.3d 945, certiorari denied 141 S.Ct. 2690, 210 L.Ed.2d 845.

Courts take an objective, common-sense approach to assessing whether property has been abandoned, so that Fourth Amendment protection does not apply, by focusing on whether the prior possessor voluntarily discarded, left behind, or otherwise relinquished his interest in the property in question, in light of his statements, acts, and other facts. U.S. Const. Amend. 4.—Id.

C.A.11 (Fla.) 2020. Under third-party doctrine, individual lacks reasonable expectation of privacy protected by Fourth Amendment in information revealed to third party and conveyed by that third party to government authorities, even if information is revealed on assumption that it will be used only for limited purpose and that confidence placed in third party will not be betrayed. U.S. Const. Amend. 4.—United States v. Gayden, 977 F.3d 1146, certiorari denied 142 S.Ct. 128, 211 L.Ed.2d 42.

C.A.11 (Fla.) 2020. Fourth Amendment protection does not extend to abandoned property. U.S. Const. Amend. 4.—United States v. Green, 969 F.3d 1194, vacated and superseded 981 F.3d 945, certiorari denied 141 S.Ct. 2690, 210 L.Ed.2d 845.

Courts take an objective, common-sense approach to assessing whether property has been abandoned, so that Fourth Amendment protection does not apply, by focusing on whether the prior possessor voluntarily discarded, left behind,

---

† This Case was not selected for publication in the National Reporter System

or otherwise relinquished his interest in the property in question, in light of his statements, acts, and other facts. U.S. Const. Amend. 4.—Id.

C.A.11 (Fla.) 2020. After checkout time, even if a guest has not completely vacated his room, the motel manager has the right to enter and examine the room as if it had been relinquished, because the guest no longer has sufficient control over the premises to establish a right to privacy therein. U.S. Const. Amend. 4.—United States v. Ross, 964 F.3d 1034, certiorari denied 141 S.Ct. 1394, 209 L.Ed.2d 132.

Hotel guest loses his reasonable expectation of privacy in his room following checkout time, and hotel management can validly consent to a search of the room at that point. U.S. Const. Amend. 4. —Id.

C.A.11 (Fla.) 2019. In assessing abandonment, for Fourth Amendment purposes, the Court of Appeals considers all relevant circumstances existing at the time of the alleged abandonment, as well as subsequent events, which may provide evidence of the defendant's intent to abandon the property at the previous time. U.S. Const. Amend. 4.—United States v. Ross, 941 F.3d 1058, rehearing granted, vacated 953 F.3d 744, on rehearing 963 F.3d 1056, on remand 964 F.3d 1034, certiorari denied 141 S.Ct. 1394, 209 L.Ed.2d 132.

Abandonment under the Fourth Amendment is not abandonment in the strict property-right sense but rather is evaluated using a common sense approach. U.S. Const. Amend. 4.—Id.

C.A.11 (Fla.) 2018. Under the third-party doctrine, a party lacks a reasonable expectation of privacy under the Fourth Amendment in information revealed to a third party and conveyed by that third party to Government authorities, even if the information is revealed on the assumption that it will be used only for a limited purpose and the confidence placed in the third party will not be betrayed. U.S. Const. Amend. 4.—Presley v. United States, 895 F.3d 1284, certiorari denied 139 S.Ct. 1376, 203 L.Ed.2d 610.

S.D.Fla. 2019. Under Fourth Amendment principles, a person has a reduced expectation of privacy in information knowingly shared with another. U.S. Const. Amend. 4.—United States v. Sigouin, 494 F.Supp.3d 1252.

The mere fact that information is voluntarily shared with a third party does not conclusively determine that the information loses all constitutional protection under the Fourth Amendment. U.S. Const. Amend. 4.—Id.

For information voluntarily shared with a third party, the extent of any residual Fourth Amendment protection depends, in part, on the nature of the particular item being shared. U.S. Const. Amend. 4.—Id.

Fla.App. 1 Dist. 2021. As a basic principle of Fourth Amendment law, an unconstitutional seizure or arrest which prompts a disclaimer of property vitiates the disclaimer. U.S. Const. Amend. 4.—Taylor v. State, 326 So.3d 115.

Fla.App. 3 Dist. 1988. Defendant was not entitled to suppression of 400 cocaine rocks uncovered during search of vehicle after police attempted to stop defendant driver when he ran stop sign, defendant stopped in middle of intersection, opened car door, and fled along with companion, defendant was apprehended, and placed under arrest for driving without license; there was no reasonable expectation of privacy in property abandoned in public street in attempt to avoid police search.—Brooks v. State, 524 So.2d 1102.

Fla.App. 4 Dist. 2018. Once defendant, during flight from police, abandoned plastic bag, which the detective, based on totality of circumstances and his experience, believed contained drugs, the police could lawfully seize it and later introduce it into evidence. U.S. Const. Amend. 4.—State v. T.M., 248 So.3d 172.

⊙~528. —— Particular items in general.

† C.A.11 (Fla.) 2020. Search of patient and of her personal effects that occurred after patient was admitted to clinic for substance abuse evaluation was not unreasonable; patient signed voluntary admission form, which stated that clinic staff could take temporary custody of personal effects for medical or safety reasons, and acknowledged that other patients also had effects searched upon entering clinic, and there was no evidence that patient's doctor personally searched patient or seized anything from her. U.S. Const. Amend. 4. —Paylan v. Teitelbaum, 798 Fed.Appx. 458.

C.A.11 (Fla.) 2020. Defendant abandoned his cell phone, for Fourth Amendment purposes, after it was lawfully seized incident to his arrest for driving with a suspended license, where release of cell phone was authorized by law enforcement about 48 hours after defendant's arrest, and there was no evidence that defendant did or said anything, in the next four years, to maintain his interest in the phone. U.S. Const. Amend. 4.— United States v. Green, 981 F.3d 945, certiorari denied 141 S.Ct. 2690, 210 L.Ed.2d 845.

C.A.11 (Fla.) 2020. Defendant abandoned his cell phone, for Fourth Amendment purposes, after it was lawfully seized incident to his arrest for driving with a suspended license, where release of cell phone was authorized by law enforcement about 48 hours after defendant's arrest, and there was no evidence that defendant did or said anything, in the next four years, to maintain his interest in the phone. U.S. Const. Amend. 4.— United States v. Green, 969 F.3d 1194, vacated and superseded 981 F.3d 945, certiorari denied 141 S.Ct. 2690, 210 L.Ed.2d 845.

M.D.Fla. 2008. Police officer had reasonable suspicion for investigatory stop of defendant, and, thus, defendant's alleged abandonment of firearm while fleeing from police officer was not involuntary pursuant to an unlawful stop, where defendant was in a high crime area conversing with a known prostitute, and he engaged in evasive and erratic driving when he noticed officer. U.S.C.A. Const.Amend. 4.—U.S. v. Muhammad, 554 F.Supp.2d 1314, affirmed 340 Fed.Appx. 548.

Fla. 1993. Police call for defendant to halt and subsequent chase did not constitute a seizure until defendant was caught; therefore, firearm which defendant dropped during chase was abandoned and recovery of firearm was not an illegal seizure. U.S.C.A. Const.Amend. 4; West's F.S.A. Const. Art. 1, § 12.—Perez v. State, 620 So.2d 1256.

Fla.App. 4 Dist. 2018. Rock of cocaine that defendant tossed away mid-run, during flight from police, was not the fruit of any unlawful seizure, and thus should not have been suppressed. U.S. Const. Amend. 4.—State v. T.M., 248 So.3d 172.

Fla.App. 4 Dist. 1997. Even if defendant had submitted to police officers' initial investigatory stop, he was not "seized" at time he discarded handgun while fleeing from officers, and therefore handgun was admissible evidence. U.S.C.A. Const.Amend. 4.—Johnson v. State, 689 So.2d 376, rehearing denied, review denied 698 So.2d 543.

---

† This Case was not selected for publication in the National Reporter System

⚷529. —— Luggage, bags, and other containers.

† C.A.11 (Fla.) 2016. Defendant abandoned his backpack by hiding it under house prior to being detained by officers, and thus, even if detention was unconstitutional, officers' search of backpack could not be fruit of poisonous tree; officers' action of setting up perimeter to locate defendant did not amount to detention. U.S.C.A. Const.Amend. 4.—U.S. v. Witten, 649 Fed.Appx. 880, certiorari denied 137 S.Ct. 696, 580 U.S. 1079, 196 L.Ed.2d 572, post-conviction relief denied 2019 WL 4453360.

C.A.5 (Fla.) 1980. Defendant, who voluntarily hurled package of cocaine to ground immediately prior to fleeing when approached by DEA agents, had no legitimate expectation of privacy in the bag or its contents; thus, the agents were not required to obtain a search warrant.—U.S. v. Bush, 623 F.2d 388.

⚷531. —— Garbage, trash, and other discarded items.

Fla.App. 3 Dist. 2016. Defendant abandoned any reasonable expectation of privacy in black box when he placed it in garbage can, and thus warrantless search of box, in which a gun and cocaine were found, was justified; contents of garbage can might have been collected by trash hauler, rummaged by animals, or box might have been taken by scavengers, children, or owner of the garbage can. U.S.C.A. Const.Amend. 4.—Strawder v. State, 185 So.3d 543, rehearing denied, review denied 2016 WL 4440970.

⚷532. Prohibited items; contraband.

C.A.11 (Fla.) 1984. Where defendant was reasonably suspected of carrying contraband internally, but refused to sign consent to x-ray, detention of him for four hours until he excreted his stomach's contents was not unreasonable. U.S.C.A. Const.Amend. 4.—U.S. v. Henao-Castano, 729 F.2d 1364, certiorari denied 105 S.Ct. 3552, 473 U.S. 923, 87 L.Ed.2d 674.

Fla.App. 4 Dist. 2008. A person in a closed stall in a public restroom is entitled to be free from unwarranted intrusion; however, this expectation gives way where two persons enter a stall together under circumstances reasonably indicating that they are doing drugs. U.S.C.A. Const. Amend. 4.—State v. Powers, 991 So.2d 1040.

(D) PERSONS SUBJECT TO LIMITATIONS; GOVERNMENT INVOLVEMENT.

⚷541. In general.

Fla.App. 4 Dist. 1980. The Fourth Amendment protects individuals from unreasonable searches or seizures by agents of government, not from intrusion by neighbors or others. U.S.C.A.Const. Amend. 4.—State v. Schultz, 388 So.2d 1326.

⚷542. Particular persons or entities.

Fla.App. 4 Dist. 1982. Wildlife officers are duly authorized to undertake a warrantless search for drugs, despite contention that statute precludes search for anything other than game, hides, fur-bearing animals, fish or fish nets, in that officers now have expanded powers to make arrests for violations of any laws committed in their presence or on game commission controlled lands and statute does not by its terms expressly exclude other kinds of searches. West's F.S.A. §§ 372.07, 372.07(1), 372.76, 901.15(3).—State v. Howard, 411 So.2d 372, review denied 421 So.2d 517.

⚷545. —— In general.

M.D.Fla. 2018. The Fourth Amendment applies only to government action, and therefore is not applicable to searches and seizures made by private individuals not acting as agents of the government or with the participation or knowledge of a government official. U.S. Const. Amend. 4.—United States v. Valdarnini, 314 F.Supp.3d 1312.

The Fourth Amendment is wholly inapplicable to private-party searches. U.S. Const. Amend. 4. —Id.

To determine when private person is acting as instrument or agent of government, as required for search by private party to implicate Fourth Amendment, the district court considers (1) whether the government knew of and acquiesced in the intrusive conduct, and (2) whether the private actor's purpose was to assist law enforcement efforts rather than to further his own ends. U.S. Const. Amend. 4.—Id.

Fla.App. 1 Dist. 2019. The Fourth Amendment is wholly inapplicable to a search or seizure, even an unreasonable one, effected by a private individual not acting as an agent of the government or with the participation or knowledge of any governmental official. U.S. Const. Amend. 4.—Morales v. State, 274 So.3d 1213.

Where a warrantless search by law enforcement is prompted by a prior search by a private party, the warrantless search does not violate the Fourth Amendment so long as it does not exceed the scope of the private party's search. U.S. Const. Amend. 4.—Id.

Fla.App. 1 Dist. 2018. The Fourth Amendment is wholly inapplicable to a search or seizure, even an unreasonable one, effected by a private individual not acting as an agent of the Government or with the participation or knowledge of any governmental official. U.S. Const. Amend. 4.—Duke v. State, 255 So.3d 478, rehearing denied, habeas corpus denied 312 So.3d 857, rehearing denied.

Where a warrantless search by law enforcement is prompted by a prior search by a private party, the warrantless search does not violate the Fourth Amendment so long as it does not exceed the scope of the private party's search. U.S. Const. Amend. 4.—Id.

Fla.App. 2 Dist. 2010. The government must be involved either directly as a participant or indirectly as an encourager of the private citizen's actions before the citizen will be deemed to be an agent of the state for Fourth Amendment purposes. U.S.C.A. Const.Amend. 4.—State v. C.D.M., 50 So.3d 659, rehearing denied.

⚷546. —— Corporations and other organizations.

† C.A.11 (Fla.) 2017. Defendant's Fourth Amendment rights were not violated by police basing search warrant on a report of contraband observed by maintenance man, employed by private property management company, who entered defendant's rental trailer and locked bedroom for the purpose of replacing his oven; maintenance man's actions were wholly unrelated to law enforcement. U.S. Const. Amend. 4.—United States v. Coffell, 720 Fed.Appx. 521, post-conviction relief denied 2021 WL 1788402.

⚷548. —— Other particular private persons or entities.

† C.A.11 (Fla.) 2021. District court did not clearly err by finding that motel maid was not acting as government's agent when she found gun in defendant's travel bag while removing his

---

† This Case was not selected for publication in the National Reporter System

belongings after motel owner evicted him for pointing gun at another guest, even though police officer was in room while maid cleaned it, and told her not to touch gun if she found it because of danger of accidental discharge; maid was acting at owner's direction, and officer was in room to ensure maid's safety. U.S. Const. Amend. 4.— United States v. Allen, 854 Fed.Appx. 329.

† **C.A.11 (Fla.) 2021.** Landlord's son was not acting as government's agent when he found firearm in defendant's apartment, as required for firearm to be admissible in trial resulting in convictions for possession of a firearm and ammunition by a convicted felon, where son went into defendant's apartment only after law enforcement left in order to tie up defendant's dog, which had been left barking in the yard and was scaring his mother, and, while son initially searched backyard for firearm with police, officers had not instructed or directed son to go back and look for firearm in apartment. 18 U.S.C.A. §§ 922(g)(1), 924(e)(1).—United States v. Perez, 844 Fed.Appx. 113, certiorari denied 142 S.Ct. 203, 211 L.Ed.2d 85, post-conviction relief denied 2023 WL 144857.

† **C.A.11 (Fla.) 2020.** Claim by former employee of the United States Department of Veterans Affairs (VA), alleging that the VA violated his Fourth Amendment rights by coercing the husband of a medical support assistant at the clinic with whom he was having a romantic relationship into providing text messages that husband had secretly retrieved from medical support assistant's phone, was barred by sovereign immunity; Congress did not waive sovereign immunity for claims against the VA seeking money damages for alleged Fourth Amendment violations, and although employee claimed that sovereign immunity could not shield individual federal agents from suit for constitutional violations, he failed to name the individuals who allegedly violated his constitutional rights as defendants in lawsuit. U.S. Const. Amend. 4.—Gilliam v. U.S. Department of Veterans Affairs, 822 Fed.Appx. 985.

C.A.11 (Fla.) 2020. After checkout time, even if a guest has not completely vacated his room, the motel manager has the right to enter and examine the room as if it had been relinquished, because the guest no longer has sufficient control over the premises to establish a right to privacy therein. U.S. Const. Amend. 4.—United States v. Ross, 964 F.3d 1034, certiorari denied 141 S.Ct. 1394, 209 L.Ed.2d 132.

† **C.A.11 (Fla.) 2017.** Searches of defendant's universal serial bus (USB) drives performed by law-enforcement officers before obtaining search warrant did not exceed scope of private-party searches conducted by renter of condominium owned by defendant and renter's mother and, thus, did not violate Fourth Amendment; officers replicated search already conducted by private citizens who acted independently, observed what they thought to be child pornography, and shared their concerns with officers, who then confirmed that drives contained what renter and mother reported. U.S. Const. Amend. 4.—United States v. Harling, 705 Fed.Appx. 911, certiorari denied 138 S.Ct. 1312, 583 U.S. 1192, 200 L.Ed.2d 492.

† **C.A.11 (Fla.) 2015.** Employees of computer repair store where defendant brought his inoperable laptop computer to have data from the computer's hard drive transferred onto a new computer were private actors when they initially viewed defendant's data during the data transfer from his laptop to the store's system, and thus, the government was free to use the information

provided by the store, that defendant had child pornography on his computer, to seize his laptop and obtain a search warrant. U.S.C.A. Const. Amend. 4.—U.S. v. Meister, 596 Fed.Appx. 790.

M.D.Fla. 2018. Resort investigators were not acting as agents of law enforcement when they entered defendant's hotel room without warrant and observed access devices, and thus Fourth Amendment did not apply, although investigators received some training from Secret Service on fraud detection and prevention; Secret Service nor any state or federal law enforcement agency knew in advance that investigators intended to enter hotel room and could not have acquiesced in that conduct, safety and wellness inspection was motivated by information provided to investigators by finance office that credit card fraud was suspected, and investigators were motivated to enter room from concern that credit card company would not cover charges being made by defendant and to prevent credit card fraud. U.S. Const. Amend. 4.—United States v. Valdarnini, 314 F.Supp.3d 1312.

Fla.App. 1 Dist. 2020. Murder defendant had no objectively reasonable expectation of privacy in GPS records transmitted from his borrowed car to car owner's financing company such that law enforcement's warrantless acquisition of such records would constitute a "search" implicating the protections of the Fourth Amendment, even though GPS data was technically historical in nature; GPS records of the car's location during the commission of the offense were records of defendant's travels over public thoroughfares, car's owner consented to GPS tracking, and police played no role in recording the GPS information. U.S. Const. Amend. 4.—Bailey v. State, 311 So.3d 303, rehearing denied, review denied 2021 WL 2408431, certiorari denied 142 S.Ct. 568, 211 L.Ed.2d 354.

Murder defendant did not demonstrate a subjective expectation of privacy in GPS records transmitted from his borrowed car to car owner's financing company such that law enforcement's warrantless acquisition of such records would constitute a "search" implicating the protections of the Fourth Amendment, even though GPS information was transferred to a third-party; car was not owned by defendant and was allegedly taken without permission, defendant used car to traverse public streets, car's owner had consented to tracking, and transmission of GPS information to financing company did not reflect a lack of voluntariness, as nothing forced defendant to borrow car, and other means of untracked travel were available to defendant. U.S. Const. Amend. 4.—Id.

Fla.App. 1 Dist. 2010. Individual, to whom postal service mistakenly delivered package addressed to defendant, was acting in his private capacity, rather than in his capacity as a F.B.I. agent, when searching the package, even though he wrote down the tag numbers of the vehicles in front of the listed address and took the package to the nearest F.B.I. office, where it was scanned and opened in the presence of a law enforcement officer, and thus individual's actions did not infringe on defendant's Fourth Amendment rights, where, due to the nature of his work, individual became concerned, upon opening the outer package, that it might contain a dangerous substance; it was undisputed that individual was acting in his private capacity when he received the package at his home, and individual's actions after receiving the package had a legitimate private purpose. U.S.C.A. Const.Amend. 4.—Armstrong

---

† **This Case was not selected for publication in the National Reporter System**

v. State, 46 So.3d 589, review denied 44 So.3d 581.

Fla.App. 5 Dist. 1984. Defendant's Fourth Amendment rights were not violated as a result of removal by hospital employee of sealed envelope from defendant's pants pockets when he was being treated at hospital emergency room while in a semiconscious state or when employee gave police officer the envelope and officer opened it and observed a white powder or when officer tested the white powder without obtaining a search warrant. U.S.C.A. Const.Amend. 4.— State v. Gans, 454 So.2d 655.

(E) GROUNDS AND SCOPE.

1. IN GENERAL.

☞551. In general.

C.A.11 (Fla.) 2018. A responsible Fourth Amendment balance is not well served by standards requiring sensitive, case-by-case determinations of government need, lest every discretionary judgment in the field be converted into an occasion for constitutional review. U.S. Const. Amend. 4.—Montanez v. Carvajal, 889 F.3d 1202.

M.D.Fla. 1997. Overall focus of inquiry to determine constitutionality of seizure is judicial balancing of nature and quality of intrusion on individual's Fourth Amendment interests against importance of governmental interests alleged to justify intrusion. U.S.C.A. Const.Amend. 4.— Ogletree v. Columbia County, 34 F.Supp.2d 1349, affirmed 146 F.3d 871.

Fla.App. 3 Dist. 2005. The right-for-the-wrong-reason doctrine applies in reviewing the validity both of police seizures and of judgments and orders of lower courts.—Tubbs v. State, 897 So.2d 520.

☞553. —— In general.

C.A.11 (Fla.) 2024. Fourth Amendment generally requires that officers obtain judicial warrants before entering home without permission. U.S. Const. Amend. 4.—Bailey v. Swindell, 89 F.4th 1324.

C.A.11 (Fla.) 2022. The Fourth Amendment demonstrates a strong preference for searches conducted pursuant to a warrant. U.S. Const. Amend. 4.—United States v. Grushko, 50 F.4th 1, certiorari denied 143 S.Ct. 2594, 216 L.Ed.2d 1199, certiorari denied 143 S.Ct. 2680, 216 L.Ed.2d 1248.

C.A.11 (Fla.) 2021. Though the police generally need a warrant to conduct a search, they do not need a warrant to search an impounded car if they: (1) had the authority to impound the car, and (2) followed department procedures governing inventory searches. U.S. Const. Amend. 4.— United States v. Isaac, 987 F.3d 980.

C.A.11 (Fla.) 2020. Generally, law enforcement officers must obtain a warrant supported by probable cause to justify the search of a person's property. U.S. Const. Amend. 4.—United States v. Wilson, 979 F.3d 889.

C.A.11 (Fla.) 2019. The Fourth Amendment generally requires law enforcement officials to obtain a warrant before conducting a search. U.S. Const. Amend. 4.—United States v. Delva, 922 F.3d 1228, denial of post-conviction relief affirmed 851 Fed.Appx. 148, certiorari denied 142 S.Ct. 374, 211 L.Ed.2d 199.

C.A.11 (Fla.) 2018. Ordinarily, where a search is undertaken by law enforcement officials to discover evidence of criminal wrongdoing, reasonableness requires the obtaining of a judi-

cial warrant. U.S. Const. Amend. 4.—United States v. Vergara, 884 F.3d 1309, certiorari denied 139 S.Ct. 70, 202 L.Ed.2d 47, post-conviction relief denied 2020 WL 7047805.

M.D.Fla. 2020. A search or an arrest without a warrant and lacking probable cause violates the Fourth Amendment and can underpin a § 1983 claim. U.S. Const. Amend. 4; 42 U.S.C.A. § 1983. —Lloyd v. Leeper, 451 F.Supp.3d 1314.

S.D.Fla. 2010. With respect to a person's Fourth Amendment rights, law enforcement officials must obtain a warrant supported by probable cause in most circumstances, unless there is consent, to justify a search. U.S.C.A. Const. Amend. 4.—Lippman v. City of Miami, 724 F.Supp.2d 1240.

Fla. 2017. The rule on searches in questionable areas of law is simple and unequivocal: get a warrant. U.S. Const. Amend. 4.—Carpenter v. State, 228 So.3d 535, rehearing granted in part 2017 WL 5076485.

Fla.App. 2 Dist. 2020. Where a search is undertaken by law enforcement officials to discover evidence of criminal wrongdoing, reasonableness generally requires the obtaining of a judicial warrant. U.S. Const. Amend. 4; Fla. Const. art. 1, § 12.—Parker v. State, 313 So.3d 737.

Fla.App. 2 Dist. 2019. The existence of probable cause does not obviate the requirement to pursue a search warrant. U.S. Const. Amend. 4. —Rodgers v. State, 264 So.3d 1119.

Fla.App. 2 Dist. 2018. Where a search is undertaken by law enforcement officials to discover evidence of criminal wrongdoing, reasonableness generally requires the obtaining of a judicial warrant. U.S. Const. Amend. 4; Fla. Const. art. 1, § 12.—Perez v. State, 269 So.3d 574, rehearing denied.

The constitutional guarantee to freedom from warrantless searches is not an inconvenience to be dismissed in favor of claims for police and prosecutorial efficiency. U.S. Const. Amend. 4; Fla. Const. art. 1, § 12.—Id.

Fla.App. 3 Dist. 2019. The court generally requires the judgment of a magistrate on the probable-cause issue and the issuance of a warrant before a search is made. U.S. Const. Amend. 4. —State v. Quintanilla, 276 So.3d 941, rehearing denied, review denied 2020 WL 633783.

Fla.App. 4 Dist. 2018. When a citizen has a reasonable expectation of privacy, police officers may not enter a property without a warrant, absent consent or exigent circumstances. U.S. Const. Amend. 4.—Osorio v. State, 244 So.3d 1115.

Fla.App. 6 Dist. 2023. Seizure of private property generally requires a warrant unless the police can show (1) probable cause to believe that property contains contraband or evidence of a crime and (2) an applicable exception, such as exigent circumstances. U.S. Const. Amend. 4.— Jefferson v. State, 363 So.3d 198.

☞554. —— Exceptions in general; warrantless searches in general.

C.A.11 (Fla.) 2022. Under the Fourth Amendment, searches conducted outside the judicial process, without prior approval by a judge or a magistrate judge, are per se unreasonable, subject only to a few specifically established and well-delineated exceptions. U.S. Const. Amend. 4.—Club Madonna Inc. v. City of Miami Beach, 42 F.4th 1231.

C.A.11 (Fla.) 2019. Absent either a warrant or probable cause plus an exception, police may not seize private property. U.S. Const. Amend. 4.—

† This Case was not selected for publication in the National Reporter System

United States v. Babcock, 924 F.3d 1180, appeal from denial of post-conviction relief dismissed 2023 WL 4117503.

C.A.11 (Fla.) 2018. Generally, the seizure of personal property is per se unreasonable when it is not pursuant to a warrant issued upon probable cause; several exceptions, however, exist to this general rule, including the exigent circumstances exception. U.S. Const. Amend. 4.—Crocker v. Beatty, 886 F.3d 1132.

S.D.Fla. 2021. Searches conducted outside the judicial process, without prior approval by a judge or magistrate, are per se unreasonable under the Fourth Amendment, subject only to a few specifically established and well-delineated exceptions. U.S. Const. Amend. 4.—Johnson v. Israel, 576 F.Supp.3d 1231.

S.D.Fla. 2020. Under the Fourth Amendment, searches conducted outside the judicial process, without prior approval by a judge or a magistrate judge, are per se unreasonable, subject only to a few specifically established and well-delineated exceptions. U.S. Const. Amend. 4.—Club Madonna, Inc. v. City of Miami Beach, 500 F.Supp.3d 1304, affirmed 42 F.4th 1231.

S.D.Fla. 2019. The Fourth Amendment to the United States Constitution requires that the government must have a search warrant before it can search and seize, unless it can demonstrate the application of one of the recognized exceptions to the Fourth Amendment warrant requirement. U.S. Const. Amend. 4.—United States v. Javat, 549 F.Supp.3d 1344, report and recommendation adopted 2019 WL 3729060.

Fla.App. 1 Dist. 2022. Searches conducted without a warrant are per se unreasonable under the Fourth Amendment subject only to a few exceptions; one of these exceptions is for searches of vehicles. U.S. Const. Amend. 4.—Hatcher v. State, 342 So.3d 807.

Fla.App. 1 Dist. 2020. Generally, searches conducted outside the judicial process, without prior approval by judge or magistrate, are per se unreasonable under the Fourth Amendment—subject only to a few specifically established and well-delineated exceptions. U.S. Const. Amend. 4.—Bailey v. State, 311 So.3d 303, rehearing denied, review denied 2021 WL 2408431, certiorari denied 142 S.Ct. 568, 211 L.Ed.2d 354.

Fla.App. 1 Dist. 2018. While warrantless searches and seizures inside a home are presumptively unreasonable and prohibited by the Fourth Amendment, exceptions may apply to allow such searches. U.S. Const. Amend. 4.—Copeland v. State, 247 So.3d 645.

Fla.App. 1 Dist. 2015. Warrantless searches and seizures are per se unreasonable under the Fourth Amendment subject to only a few exceptions. U.S.C.A. Const.Amend. 4.—Herring v. State, 168 So.3d 240, rehearing denied, review dismissed 173 So.3d 966.

Fla.App. 1 Dist. 2011. A warrantless search is per se unreasonable under the Fourth Amendment, subject to a few well-defined exceptions. U.S.C.A. Const.Amend. 4.—Kilburn v. State, 54 So.3d 625.

Fla.App. 1 Dist. 2003. Warrantless searches or arrests conducted in a constitutionally protected area like a motel room are per se unreasonable unless they fall within one of the five established exceptions to the search warrant requirement for searches: (1) with the occupant's consent; (2) incident to lawful search; (3) with probable cause to search but with exigent circumstances; (4) in hot pursuit; or (5) pursuant

to a stop and frisk. U.S.C.A. Const.Amend. 4.—Lee v. State, 856 So.2d 1133.

Fla.App. 1 Dist. 1976. Basic exceptions to requirements of search warrant are: consent; lawful arrest, with probable cause to search but with exigent circumstances; in hot pursuit; and stop and frisk.—Raffield v. State, 333 So.2d 534, quashed in part 351 So.2d 945, on remand 362 So.2d 138.

Fla.App. 2 Dist. 2022. Ordinarily, searches conducted outside the judicial process, without prior approval by judge or magistrate, are per se unreasonable under the Fourth Amendment, subject only to a few specifically established and well-delineated exceptions. U.S. Const. Amend. 4.—S.P. v. State, 331 So.3d 883.

Fla.App. 2 Dist. 2021. Ordinarily, searches conducted outside the judicial process, without prior approval by judge or magistrate, are per se unreasonable under the Fourth Amendment—subject only to a few specifically established and well-delineated exceptions. U.S. Const. Amend. 4.—Ross v. State, 319 So.3d 807.

Fla.App. 2 Dist. 2020. In the absence of a warrant, a search is reasonable only if it falls within a specific exception to the warrant requirement. U.S. Const. Amend. 4; Fla. Const. art. 1, § 12.—Parker v. State, 313 So.3d 737.

Fla.App. 2 Dist. 2020. Warrantless searches are per se unreasonable, subject only to a few specifically established and well-delineated exceptions. U.S. Const. Amend. 4; Fla. Const. art. 1, § 12.—State v. Brookins, 290 So.3d 1100.

Fla.App. 2 Dist. 2019. Warrantless searches are generally prohibited by the Fourth Amendment to the U.S. Constitution, though voluntary consent to a search is an exception to this rule. U.S. Const. Amend. 4.—State v. Smith, 286 So.3d 939.

Fla.App. 2 Dist. 2018. In the absence of a warrant, a search is reasonable only if it falls within a specific exception to the warrant requirement. U.S. Const. Amend. 4; Fla. Const. art. 1, § 12.—Perez v. State, 269 So.3d 574, rehearing denied.

Fla.App. 2 Dist. 2018. Because the ultimate touchstone of the Fourth Amendment is "reasonableness," the warrant requirement is subject to certain exceptions. U.S. Const. Amend. 4.—Lapace v. State, 257 So.3d 588.

Fla.App. 2 Dist. 2017. The five established exceptions to the warrant requirement are: (1) consent, (2) incident to a lawful arrest, (3) with probable cause to search but with exigent circumstances, (4) in hot pursuit, and (5) stop and frisk. U.S. Const. Amend. 4.—Davis v. State, 226 So.3d 318, rehearing denied.

Fla.App. 2 Dist. 2007. If a law enforcement officer does not have consent, a search warrant, or an arrest warrant, he may not enter a private home or its curtilage except when entrance is justified by exigent circumstances, such as pursuing a fleeing felon, preventing the destruction of evidence, searching incident to a lawful arrest, and fighting fires. U.S.C.A. Const.Amend. 4.—Rodriguez v. State, 964 So.2d 833, rehearing granted, and rehearing denied.

Fla.App. 2 Dist. 2006. A warrantless search of a home is presumptively unreasonable and a violation of the Fourth Amendment, unless the search falls within certain recognized constitutional exceptions. U.S.C.A. Const.Amend. 4.—Barth v. State, 955 So.2d 1115.

Fla.App. 3 Dist. 2019. Warrantless searches are per se unreasonable under the Fourth Amendment, subject only to a few specifically established and well-delineated exceptions. U.S. Const. Amend. 4.—Hedvall v. State, 283 So.3d 901, review denied 2020 WL 1650313.

Fla.App. 3 Dist. 2019. Searches conducted outside the judicial process, without prior approval by judge or magistrate, are per se unreasonable under the Fourth Amendment, subject only to a few specifically established and well-delineated exceptions. U.S. Const. Amend. 4.— State v. Quintanilla, 276 So.3d 941, rehearing denied, review denied 2020 WL 633783.

Fla.App. 3 Dist. 2018. Searches conducted outside the judicial process, without prior approval by judge or magistrate, are per se unreasonable under the Fourth Amendment, subject only to a few specifically established and well-delineated exceptions. U.S. Const. Amend. 4.— Aguilar v. State, 239 So.3d 108, denial of post-conviction relief affirmed 359 So.3d 832, rehearing denied, review denied 2023 WL 4484834.

Fla.App. 3 Dist. 2018. Warrantless searches are per se unreasonable under the Fourth Amendment, subject only to a few specifically established and well-delineated exceptions. U.S. Const. Amend. 4.—Harris v. State, 238 So.3d 396.

Fla.App. 3 Dist. 1979. A search of private property conducted by state or federal agents without a duly issued search warrant is per se "unreasonable" within meaning of applicable constitutional provisions, subject only to a few specifically established and well-delineated exceptions justified by absolute necessity. West's F.S.A.Const. art. 1, § 12; U.S.C.A.Const. Amend. 4.—Haugland v. State, 374 So.2d 1026, certiorari denied 390 So.2d 360.

Fla.App. 3 Dist. 1978. Search of private property conducted by state or federal agents without duly issued search warrant is per se "unreasonable" under Federal and State Constitutions, subject only to a few specifically established and well-delineated exceptions justified by absolute necessity. West's F.S.A.Const. art. 1, § 12; U.S.C.A.Const. Amends. 4, 14, 14, § 1.—Miranda v. State, 354 So.2d 411, certiorari denied 364 So.2d 888.

Fla.App. 4 Dist. 2018. Searches and seizures conducted without prior approval by judge or magistrate are per se unreasonable under the Fourth Amendment except when involving the narrow protective search exception or the narrow plain view and plain touch extensions of that exception. U.S. Const. Amend. 4.—T.T. v. State, 253 So.3d 15.

Fla.App. 4 Dist. 2017. Searches conducted outside the judicial process, without prior approval by judge or magistrate, are per se unreasonable under the Fourth Amendment, subject only to a few specifically established and well-delineated exceptions, which are jealously and carefully drawn. U.S. Const. Amend. 4.—State v. Worsham, 227 So.3d 602, certiorari denied 138 S.Ct. 264, 583 U.S. 873, 199 L.Ed.2d 125.

Fla.App. 4 Dist. 2010. Warrantless searches are considered, under the Fourth Amendment, per se unreasonable, subject to certain exceptions. U.S.C.A. Const.Amend. 4.—Diaz v. State, 34 So.3d 797.

Fla.App. 5 Dist. 2019. Searches conducted outside the judicial process, without prior approval by judge or magistrate, are per se unreasonable under the Fourth Amendment- subject only to a few specifically established and well-delineated exceptions. U.S. Const. Amend. 4.— Jones v. State, 279 So.3d 342, habeas corpus granted 325 So.3d 101.

Fla.App. 5 Dist. 1980. Warrantless searches are per se unreasonable, subject only to a few specifically established and well-defined exceptions, including emergency situation, sometimes called the "exigency rule."—Johnson v. State, 386 So.2d 302.

Fla.App. 5 Dist. 1979. General rule is that a search conducted without a warrant and without consent is per se unreasonable, subject only to a limited number of well-defined exceptions. U.S.C.A.Const. Amend. 4; West's F.S.A.Const. art. 1, § 12.—Ulesky v. State, 379 So.2d 121.

Fla.App. 6 Dist. 2023. Searches conducted outside the judicial process, without prior approval by judge or magistrate, are per se unreasonable under the Fourth Amendment, subject only to a few specifically established and well-delineated exceptions. U.S. Const. Amend. 4; Fla. Const. art. 1, § 12.—Jean v. State, 369 So.3d 1235.

⚌**555. Reasonableness in general.**

C.A.11 (Fla.) 2018. In the case of searches conducted by a public employer, courts must balance the invasion of the employees' legitimate expectations of privacy against the government's need for supervision, control, and the efficient operation of the workplace to determine the reasonableness of the intrusion under the Fourth Amendment. U.S. Const. Amend. 4.—Friedenberg v. School Board of Palm Beach County, 911 F.3d 1084.

After having considered the scope of legitimate expectation of privacy at issue, courts next look to character of the intrusion that is complained of, in determining reasonableness of a suspicionless search. U.S. Const. Amend. 4.—Id.

Third factor considered by courts in balancing competing private and public interests, for purposes of determining reasonableness of a suspicionless search, is the nature and immediacy of the governmental concern at issue. U.S. Const. Amend. 4.—Id.

Fourth and final factor that court considers in balancing competing private and public interests, for purposes of determining reasonableness of a suspicionless search, is the efficacy of the search at achieving government's aims; court's inquiry is only into whether the search is an effective means of deterring undesirable behavior it targets, not whether it is the most effective possible means. U.S. Const. Amend. 4.—Id.

C.A.11 (Fla.) 2018. Warrantless searches are allowed when the circumstances make it reasonable, within the meaning of the Fourth Amendment, to dispense with the warrant requirement. U.S. Const. Amend. 4.—Montanez v. Carvajal, 889 F.3d 1202.

Because the Fourth Amendment has to be applied on the spur, and in the heat, of the moment, the object in implementing its command of reasonableness is to draw standards sufficiently clear and simple to be applied with a fair prospect of surviving judicial second-guessing months and years after an arrest or search is made. U.S. Const. Amend. 4.—Id.

M.D.Fla. 2018. Under the Fourth Amendment, the reasonableness of a particular seizure depends not only on when it is made, but also how it is carried out. U.S. Const. Amend. 4.— Chastang v. Levy, 319 F.Supp.3d 1244.

M.D.Fla. 2017, Inquiry into whether Fourth Amendment right against unreasonable seizures was violated requires a balancing of the nature and quality of the intrusion on the individual's Fourth Amendment interests against the importance of the governmental interests alleged to justify the intrusion. U.S. Const. Amend. 4.—Ermini v. Scott, 249 F.Supp.3d 1253.

M.D.Fla. 2010. Reasonable suspicion could not justify officer's warrantless entry into defendant's residence to conduct search, but rather, both probable cause and exigent circumstances were required. U.S.C.A. Const.Amend. 4.—U.S. v. Franklin, 721 F.Supp.2d 1229, affirmed 694 F.3d 1.

M.D.Fla. 1990. To determine whether particular governmental activity violates Fourth Amendment, court must decide whether activity constitutes search, and, if it does, whether search is unreasonable. U.S.C.A. Const.Amend. 4.—Beattie v. City of St. Petersburg Beach, 733 F.Supp. 1455.

S.D.Fla. 2023. The Fourth Amendment's prohibition against unreasonable searches and seizures applies to civil as well as criminal investigations. U.S. Const. Amend. 4.—D. P. v. School Board of Palm Beach County, 658 F.Supp.3d 1187.

Fla.App. 1 Dist. 2022. In determining whether a search based on a potentially mistaken interpretation of a statute violates the Fourth Amendment, the governing law asks only whether the potentially mistaken interpretation of the statute was objectively reasonable. U.S. Const. Amend. 4.—Knapp v. State, 346 So.3d 1279.

Fla.App. 1 Dist. 2020. The Fourth Amendment does not proscribe all state-initiated searches and seizures; it merely proscribes those which are unreasonable. U.S. Const. Amend. 4.—Bailey v. State, 311 So.3d 303, rehearing denied, review denied 2021 WL 2408431, certiorari denied 142 S.Ct. 568, 211 L.Ed.2d 354.

Fla.App. 1 Dist. 2011. Facts learned only in hindsight should not enter into the evaluation of the reasonableness of a search or seizure. U.S.C.A. Const.Amend. 4.—Majors v. State, 70 So.3d 655, rehearing denied, review denied 79 So.3d 745.

Fla.App. 2 Dist. 2023. Local law enforcement agency policies may be indicative of whether a search occasioned by a noncriminal seizure is reasonable, but they do not dictate ipso facto the parameters of the Fourth Amendment. U.S. Const. Amend. 4.—K.M. v. State, 359 So.3d 414.

Fla.App. 2 Dist. 2022. Local law enforcement agency policies may be indicative of whether search occasioned by noncriminal seizure is reasonable, but they do not dictate ipso facto parameters of Fourth Amendment. U.S. Const. Amend. 4.—S.P. v. State, 331 So.3d 883.

Fla.App. 2 Dist. 2021. Reasonable suspicion for an investigatory stop alone does not justify an arrest or search. U.S. Const. Amend. 4.—Brown v. State, 313 So.3d 848.

Fla.App. 2 Dist. 2019. The measure of reasonableness of a police officer's actions, for purposes of applying Fourth Amendment's prohibition against unreasonable searches and seizures, is totality of the circumstances. U.S. Const. Amend. 4.—State v. M.B.W., 276 So.3d 501.

Fla.App. 2 Dist. 2003. When § 1983 plaintiff alleges a violation of the Fourth Amendment, the question is whether the search or seizure was effected with reasonable force. U.S.C.A. Const. Amend. 4; 42 U.S.C.A. § 1983.—Thompson v. Douds, 852 So.2d 299, rehearing denied, review denied 871 So.2d 872, certiorari denied 125 S.Ct. 59, 543 U.S. 820, 160 L.Ed.2d 29.

Fla.App. 3 Dist. 2023. Both the U.S. Constitution and the Florida Constitution prohibit unreasonable searches and seizures. U.S. Const.

Amend. 4; Fla. Const. art. 1, § 12.—R.A. v. State, 355 So.3d 1028.

Fla.App. 3 Dist. 2019. The Fourth Amendment does not proscribe all state-initiated searches and seizures; it merely proscribes those which are unreasonable. U.S. Const. Amend. 4.—State v. Quintanilla, 276 So.3d 941, rehearing denied, review denied 2020 WL 633783.

A state is free to prefer one search-and-seizure policy among the range of constitutionally permissible options, but its choice of a more restrictive option does not render the less restrictive ones unreasonable, and hence unconstitutional. U.S. Const. Amend. 4.—Id.

Fla.App. 4 Dist. 2019. The Fourth Amendment prohibits only unreasonable searches. U.S. Const. Amend. 4.—Maldonado v. State, 278 So.3d 708, review denied 2019 WL 7169127.

Fla.App. 4 Dist. 2019. Determining the reasonableness of any search involves a twofold inquiry: first, one must consider whether the action was justified at its inception, and second, one must determine whether the search as actually conducted was reasonably related in scope to the circumstances which justified the interference in the first place. U.S. Const. Amend. 4.—T.L.B. v. State, 271 So.3d 1038.

Fla.App. 4 Dist. 2005. In order for reasonable suspicion justifying a search to exist, the action must be justified at its inception, and the search must be reasonably related in scope to the reason for the search. U.S.C.A. Const.Amend 4.—State v. Bullard, 891 So.2d 1158.

⚷556. Totality of circumstances in general.

Fla.App. 3 Dist. 2019. A court's analysis in determining probable cause for search and seizure relies on an evaluation of the totality of the circumstances. U.S. Const. Amend. 4.—State v. Quintanilla, 276 So.3d 941, rehearing denied, review denied 2020 WL 633783.

⚷559. —— In general; necessity.

C.A.11 (Fla.) 2019. Absent either a warrant or probable cause plus an exception, police may not seize private property. U.S. Const. Amend. 4.—United States v. Babcock, 924 F.3d 1180, appeal from denial of post-conviction relief dismissed 2023 WL 4117503.

C.A.11 (Fla.) 2018. The default rule is that to be reasonable under the Fourth Amendment, a search ordinarily must be based on individualized suspicion of wrongdoing; however, neither a warrant nor probable cause, nor any measure of individualized suspicion is an indispensable component of reasonableness in every circumstance. U.S. Const. Amend. 4.—Friedenberg v. School Board of Palm Beach County, 911 F.3d 1084.

C.A.11 (Fla.) 2014. In general, the Fourth Amendment requires a warrant supported by probable cause to effectuate a search. U.S.C.A. Const.Amend. 4.—Berry v. Leslie, 767 F.3d 1144, vacated on rehearing en banc 771 F.3d 1316.

C.A.5 (Fla.) 1975. Probable cause is required for either an arrest or a search. U.S.C.A.Const. Amend. 4.—U.S. v. Rias, 524 F.2d 118.

Fla.App. 2 Dist. 2019. Law enforcement officers must have probable cause to arrest and search a person without a warrant. U.S. Const. Amend. 4.—Goodman v. State, 280 So.3d 537.

Fla.App. 2 Dist. 2019. The existence of probable cause does not obviate the requirement to pursue a search warrant. U.S. Const. Amend. 4.—Rodgers v. State, 264 So.3d 1119.

Fla.App. 4 Dist. 1972. Standing by itself, warrantless search must be founded on probable cause; however, probable cause requirement is either satisfied or obviated when warrantless search is incident to a lawful arrest or to a lawful detention.—State v. Miller, 267 So.2d 352, cause dismissed 273 So.2d 80.

Fla.App. 6 Dist. 2023. In the absence of probable cause for a warrantless search, it becomes unnecessary to address exigent circumstances or other exception to warrant requirement. U.S. Const. Amend. 4.—Jefferson v. State, 363 So.3d 198.

☞560. ——— What constitutes probable cause in general.

C.A.11 (Fla.) 2019. Probable cause to seize property is a belief that evidence will probably be found in a particular location. U.S. Const. Amend. 4.—United States v. Babcock, 924 F.3d 1180, appeal from denial of post-conviction relief dismissed 2023 WL 4117503.

C.A.5 (Fla.) 1976. "Probable cause" is essentially a concept of reasonableness, but has become a term of art in that it must always be determined by a magistrate unless exigent circumstances excuse a search warrant; on the other hand, "reasonable belief" embodies the same standards of reasonableness but allows the officer, who has already been to the magistrate to secure an arrest warrant, to determine that the suspect is probably within certain premises without an additional trip to the magistrate and without exigent circumstances.—U.S. v. Cravero, 545 F.2d 406, certiorari denied Miller v. U.S., 97 S.Ct. 1123, 429 U.S. 1100, 51 L.Ed.2d 549, certiorari denied Cook v. U.S., 97 S.Ct. 1679, 430 U.S. 983, 52 L.Ed.2d 377, rehearing denied 97 S.Ct. 2689, 431 U.S. 960, 53 L.Ed.2d 279, certiorari denied 97 S.Ct. 1679, 430 U.S. 983, 52 L.Ed.2d 377, rehearing denied 97 S.Ct. 2990, 433 U.S. 915, 53 L.Ed.2d 1102.

M.D.Fla. 2015. Although probable cause is a fluid concept—turning on the assessment of probabilities in particular factual contexts-not readily, or even usefully reduced to a neat set of legal rules, the substance of all the definitions of probable cause is reasonable ground for belief of guilt which must be particularized with respect to the person to be searched or seized. U.S.C.A. Const. Amend. 4.—U.S. v. Sampson, 99 F.Supp.3d 1352, appeal dismissed (11th cir. 15-11853).

S.D.Fla. 2021. Probable cause to search or arrest exists where the facts within the collective knowledge of law enforcement officials, derived from reasonably trustworthy information, are sufficient to cause a person of reasonable caution to believe that a criminal offense has been or is being committed. U.S. Const. Amend. 4.—Gomez v. Miami-Dade County, 563 F.Supp.3d 1211, appeal dismissed 2022 WL 16580843.

S.D.Fla. 2008. Probable cause exists where the facts and circumstances within the collective knowledge of law enforcement officials, of which they had reasonably trustworthy information, are sufficient to cause a person of reasonable caution to believe that an offense has been or is being committed. U.S.C.A. Const.Amend. 4.—U.S. v. Olmedo, 552 F.Supp.2d 1347.

S.D.Fla. 1976. The standard of probable cause is essentially the same as the standard for issuance of search and arrest warrants.—Pugh v. Rainwater, 422 F.Supp. 498.

Fla.App. 1 Dist. 2022. Probable cause for a search is a flexible, common-sense standard; it turns on the assessment of probabilities in particular factual contexts, not readily, or even usefully, reduced to a neat set of legal rules. U.S.

Const. Amend. 4.—Hatcher v. State, 342 So.3d 807.

Probable cause for a search is not a high bar; it is enough if there is the kind of fair probability on which reasonable and prudent people, not legal technicians, act. U.S. Const. Amend. 4.—Id.

In determining whether probable cause for a search exists, a reviewing court should be mindful of two basic and well-established principles of law: first, the court must consider the whole picture, rather than review each fact in isolation, and second, the court must not dismiss outright any circumstances that were susceptible of innocent explanation. U.S. Const. Amend. 4.—Id.

Fla.App. 1 Dist. 1988. Same probable cause standard applies to determine whether officer had probable cause to search and arrest defendant irrespective of whether warrant was issued to conduct search or effect arrest.—Hopkins v. State, 524 So.2d 1136, review denied 531 So.2d 1353.

Fla.App. 2 Dist. 2021. The standard for probable cause to search is a practical and common sensical standard; it is enough if there is the kind of fair probability on which reasonable people act. U.S. Const. Amend. 4.—Owens v. State, 317 So.3d 1218, rehearing denied, review denied 2021 WL 5149948.

Fla.App. 2 Dist. 2003. Probable cause is a fluid concept that deals in probabilities, which include common sense conclusions by law enforcement officers.—State v. Catt, 839 So.2d 757, rehearing denied.

Probable cause is not the same standard as beyond a reasonable doubt, and the facts constituting probable cause need not meet the standard of conclusiveness and probability required of the circumstantial facts upon which a conviction must be based.—Id.

Fla.App. 3 Dist. 2020. "Probable cause" is more than bare suspicion but is less than beyond a reasonable doubt and, indeed, is less than a preponderance of the evidence. U.S. Const. Amend. 4.—J.J. v. State, 312 So.3d 116.

Probable cause does not require proof that something is more likely true than false; it requires only a fair probability, a standard understood to mean something more than a bare suspicion but less than a preponderance of the evidence at hand. U.S. Const. Amend. 4.—Id.

Fla.App. 3 Dist. 2019. Finely-tuned standards such as proof beyond a reasonable doubt or by a preponderance of the evidence have no place in determining probable cause for search and seizure. U.S. Const. Amend. 4.—State v. Quintanilla, 276 So.3d 941, rehearing denied, review denied 2020 WL 633783.

Fla.App. 4 Dist. 2018. In making probable cause determinations, courts must conscientiously evaluate the sufficiency of evidence discovered during a warrantless search and decline to ratify naked conclusions or the use of "buzz words" that imply certainty. U.S. Const. Amend. 4.—T.T. v. State, 253 So.3d 15.

Fla.App. 4 Dist. 2014. Probable cause to arrest or search exists when the totality of the facts and circumstances within an officer's knowledge sufficiently warrant a reasonable person to believe that, more likely than not a crime has been committed. U.S.C.A. Const.Amend. 4.—Gomez v. State, 155 So.3d 1184, review denied 182 So.3d 632.

Fla.App. 4 Dist. 2012. Probable cause to arrest or search exists when the totality of the facts and circumstances within an officer's knowledge sufficiently warrant a reasonable person to believe that, more likely than not, a crime has been committed. U.S.C.A. Const.Amend. 4.—Santiago v. State, 84 So.3d 455, appeal after remand 124 So.3d 978.

A finding of probable cause to arrest or search does not require absolute certitude. U.S.C.A. Const.Amend. 4.—Id.

Probable cause to arrest or search must be based on known facts. U.S.C.A. Const.Amend. 4.—Id.

Fla.App. 4 Dist. 2002. Six factors to be considered in determining whether the evidence establishes probable cause are: (1) the training and experience of the law enforcement officer; (2) the quality of the surveillance procedures; (3) the history of the location under surveillance; (4) recent events; (5) prior knowledge of the parties; and (6) the detailed description of the event. U.S.C.A. Const.Amend. 4.—State v. McDonald, 826 So.2d 1081.

Fla.App. 4 Dist. 1992. Probable cause to arrest and search exists when the totality of the circumstances more likely than not points to the commission of the crime.—Elliott v. State, 597 So.2d 916.

Fla.App. 5 Dist. 2023. Probable cause does not require proof that something is more likely true than false, it requires only a fair probability, a standard understood to mean something more than a bare suspicion but less than a preponderance of evidence at hand. U.S. Const. Amend. 4.—N.H. v. State, 358 So.3d 477.

☞**561. —— Existence of criminal activity.**

C.A.11 (Fla.) 2019. Although probable cause to seize property requires more than reasonable suspicion that criminal behavior is afoot, it does not entail the same standard of conclusiveness and probability as the facts necessary to support a conviction; rather, it requires only a substantial chance that evidence of criminal activity exists. U.S. Const. Amend. 4.—United States v. Babcock, 924 F.3d 1180, appeal from denial of post-conviction relief dismissed 2023 WL 4117503.

Police officers do not have to predict the eventually-charged offense in order to demonstrate probable cause for the seizure of private property, only that the collective facts would cause a person of reasonable caution to believe that a criminal offense has been or is being committed. U.S. Const. Amend. 4.—Id.

S.D.Fla. 2018. Probable cause for search and seizure is not a high bar; it requires only a probability or substantial chance of criminal activity, not an actual showing of such activity. U.S. Const. Amend. 4.—Federal Trade Commission v. PointBreak Media, LLC, 343 F.Supp.3d 1282.

Fla.App. 3 Dist. 2019. Probable cause, as required for a reasonable search, exists where the facts and circumstances within an officer's knowledge and of which he had reasonably trustworthy information are sufficient in themselves to warrant a man of reasonable caution in the belief that an offense has been or is being committed, and that evidence bearing on that offense will be found in the place to be searched. U.S. Const. Amend. 4.—State v. Quintanilla, 276 So.3d 941, rehearing denied, review denied 2020 WL 633783.

Probable cause for search and seizure requires only a probability or substantial chance of criminal activity, not an actual showing of such activity. U.S. Const. Amend. 4.—Id.

☞**562. —— Contraband or evidence of crime.**

C.A.11 (Fla.) 2013. Probable cause to arrest exists when the facts and circumstances within an officer's knowledge are sufficient to warrant a reasonable belief that the suspect had committed or was committing a crime, while probable cause to search requires a fair probability that contraband or evidence of a crime will be found in a particular place. U.S.C.A. Const.Amend. 4.—Feliciano v. City of Miami Beach, 707 F.3d 1244.

Fla. 1992. Relevant to inquiry of whether a police officer has sufficient probable cause to believe that suspect is carrying illegal contraband, for purposes of search and/or seizure, is officer's specific experience with respect to particular narcotic in question.—Doctor v. State, 596 So.2d 442.

Fla.App. 2 Dist. 2007. Mere proximity to contraband found in a public place and in the vicinity of several individuals does not warrant a finding that a law enforcement officer had probable cause that the person or persons closest to the contraband possessed it.—Tarver v. State, 961 So.2d 1094.

Fla.App. 2 Dist. 2006. Police officer had probable cause to believe that item in defendant's pocket was contraband and, thus, was justified in reaching into pocket; officer felt bulge in pocket during consensual patdown search, and defendant admitted that bulge was marijuana. U.S.C.A. Const.Amend. 4.—State v. Witherspoon, 924 So.2d 868, rehearing denied.

Fla.App. 3 Dist. 2020. The probable cause standard merely requires that the facts available to the officer would warrant a man of reasonable caution in the belief that evidence of a crime may be found; it does not demand any showing that such a belief be correct or more likely true than false. U.S. Const. Amend. 4.—J.J. v. State, 312 So.3d 116.

Constructive possession of contraband can be difficult to establish when contraband is in the vicinity of two or more persons because a search or seizure of a person must be supported by probable cause particularized with respect to that person. U.S. Const. Amend. 4.—Id.

Fla.App. 5 Dist. 2001. A police officer must have probable cause to believe that an item felt during pat-down is contraband before conducting a more thorough search to retrieve it. U.S.C.A. Const.Amend. 4.—Harris v. State, 790 So.2d 1246.

Fla.App. 5 Dist. 1999. Officer had probable cause for seizure of crack cocaine that officer felt while conducting warrantless pat-down search of defendant for weapons; officer testified that he immediately recognized the items as contraband upon feeling them, and officer had extensive experience and training in drug identification. U.S.C.A. Const.Amend. 4.—State v. Bellamy, 723 So.2d 402.

Fla.App. 5 Dist. 1998. Totality of circumstances observed by narcotics officer justified probable cause search of suspect which revealed contraband, even though officer could identify with certainty neither drugs nor money as having been involved in transaction; in area known for drug-related crimes, suspect, known to observing officer as street person, reached below his pants to his buttocks area, known by officer to serve as frequent hiding place for contraband, and withdrew something from which he took small object which he subsequently exchanged for something of value from two other people who approached

---

† This Case was not selected for publication in the National Reporter System

him. U.S.C.A. Const.Amend. 4.—Williams v. State, 717 So.2d 1109.

⊂═564. —— In general.

S.D.Fla. 2019. Probable cause to search may be predicated on hearsay or other evidence that would not otherwise be admissible at a trial. U.S. Const. Amend. 4.—United States v. Sigouin, 494 F.Supp.3d 1252.

For purposes of probable cause to search, reliance on the opinions and conclusions of trained and experienced law enforcement officers is appropriate. U.S. Const. Amend. 4.—Id.

Fla.App. 1 Dist. 2022. Totality-of-the-circumstances approach for determining whether probable cause for a search exists allows officers to draw on their own experience and specialized training to make inferences from and deductions about the cumulative information available to them that might well elude an untrained person. U.S. Const. Amend. 4.—Hatcher v. State, 342 So.3d 807.

Innocent behavior frequently will provide the basis for a showing of probable cause to conduct a search, and the relevant inquiry is the degree of suspicion that attaches to particular types of non-criminal acts. U.S. Const. Amend. 4.—Id.

Fla.App. 2 Dist. 2005. Hearsay information that would not establish probable cause to arrest or to conduct a warrantless search if received directly by a police officer does not achieve greater status if received indirectly through a reliable informant. U.S.C.A. Const.Amend. 4.—Whittle v. State, 903 So.2d 210, rehearing denied.

⊂═565. —— Offense in officer's presence.

Fla. 2011. Officers had probable cause to search defendant after observing him arrive at a home that had been the subject of complaints about drug activity and engage in a series of hand-to-hand transactions in which each of three individuals consecutively took a small item from defendant's hand and quickly gave defendant paper currency in return, where, rather than making eye contact, defendant looked up and down the street as he interacted with the three individuals, and defendant's contact with the individuals was very brief. U.S.C.A. Const.Amend. 4.—State v. Hankerson, 65 So.3d 502, revised on rehearing, certiorari denied 132 S.Ct. 1636, 565 U.S. 1236, 182 L.Ed.2d 237.

Fla.App. 1 Dist. 2018. Officer had probable cause to believe defendant was in possession of marijuana to support warrantless search of defendant's person, where an off-duty officer smelled marijuana confined to defendant's location, off-duty officer observed defendant smoking what appeared to be a marijuana cigarette, a second officer noted the smell of burnt marijuana coming from the area occupied by defendant, and officer witnessed defendant smoking what appeared to be a marijuana blunt. U.S. Const. Amend. 4.—Dawson v. State, 253 So.3d 766.

Fla.App. 5 Dist. 1998. Totality of circumstances observed by narcotics officer justified probable cause search of suspect which revealed contraband, even though officer could identify with certainty neither drugs nor money as having been involved in transaction; in area known for drug-related crimes, suspect, known to observing officer as street person, reached below his pants to his buttocks area, known by officer to serve as frequent hiding place for contraband, and withdrew something from which he took small object which he subsequently exchanged for something of value from two other people who approached

him. U.S.C.A. Const.Amend. 4.—Williams v. State, 717 So.2d 1109.

Probable cause necessary to justify search of person deals in probabilities and not in certainty; officer need not actually see law being violated, nor must he satisfy himself beyond any reasonable doubt that felony has been committed, in order to have probable cause. U.S.C.A. Const. Amend. 4.—Id.

Fla.App. 5 Dist. 1997. Pat-down of defendant for weapons was improper, but nonetheless officers had probable cause to search him for illegal drugs, and thus search was proper even though the officers, believing that they lacked probable cause, conducted improper weapons search to enhance their claim of probable cause; officer who had received training and identification of narcotics and who had received complaints of narcotics dealing in vicinity of store, together with another officer, observed for period of two hours during which defendant would approach vehicles, lean into the vehicle and pass something to the occupants, and would then be seen with cash in hand, even though items passed to the occupants of the vehicles were too small to be seen from officers' hiding place.—Knox v. State, 689 So.2d 1224.

⊂═566. —— Information from others.

C.A.5 (Fla.) 1976. Warrantless searches require same investigative basis in fact or reasonable conjecture as searches under warrant, which information may be supplied in whole or in part by informant.—U.S. v. Brennan, 538 F.2d 711, rehearing denied 542 F.2d 575, certiorari denied 97 S.Ct. 1104, 429 U.S. 1092, 51 L.Ed.2d 538, rehearing denied 97 S.Ct. 1611, 430 U.S. 960, 51 L.Ed.2d 812.

Fla. 1995. In many instances, tip from informant, standing alone, will not justify finding of probable cause for arrest or search. U.S.C.A. Const.Amend. 4.—State v. Butler, 655 So.2d 1123.

⊂═567. —— Reliability of information in general.

Fla.App. 3 Dist. 2009. In determining whether reasonable suspicion or probable cause exists to conduct a warrantless search, the analysis of observations by informants, even reliable ones, should meet the same standards as analysis of observations made by trained police officers; standards include reputation of location for drug activity, history of previous arrests from site, prior knowledge of suspect, quality and extent of "surveillance" by informant, and detailed description of the event. U.S.C.A. Const.Amend. 4. —Mathis v. State, 8 So.3d 445, rehearing denied.

Fla.App. 4 Dist. 2018. Tips from known reliable informants, such as an identifiable citizen who observes criminal conduct and reports it, along with his own identity to the police, will almost invariably be found sufficient to justify police action. U.S. Const. Amend. 4.—J.H. v. State, 257 So.3d 1071.

Fla.App. 5 Dist. 2019. Tips from known reliable informants, such as an identifiable citizen who observes criminal conduct and reports it, along with his own identity to the police, will almost invariably be found sufficient to justify police action. U.S. Const. Amend. 4.—Madison v. State, 278 So.3d 921.

Fla.App. 5 Dist. 1991. An informant's reliability is established by a successful controlled buy.—State v. Fountain, 589 So.2d 1388.

---

† This Case was not selected for publication in the National Reporter System

⊙⇒568. —— Corroboration.

C.A.5 (Fla.) 1978. In each case of search for contraband, nature of tip, reliability of informant, degree of corroboration, and other factors contributing to suspicion or lack thereof and the nature and extent of search must all be assessed, and merely sufficient showing to create reasonable cause to suspect was not necessarily sufficient to meet the more exacting standards applicable to more intrusive strip or body cavity searches. U.S.C.A.Const. Amend. 4.—U.S. v. Afanador, 567 F.2d 1325.

C.A.5 (Fla.) 1976. Where insufficient information about tip and tipster is available to justify reliance upon tip alone, investigating officers may supplement tip by surveillance of subject or corroboration of key elements of tip from relatively objective sources so as to provide probable cause for search.—U.S. v. Brennan, 538 F.2d 711, rehearing denied 542 F.2d 575, certiorari denied 97 S.Ct. 1104, 429 U.S. 1092, 51 L.Ed.2d 538, rehearing denied 97 S.Ct. 1611, 430 U.S. 960, 51 L.Ed.2d 812.

Fla.App. 4 Dist. 2002. Although an anonymous tip, without more, is generally insufficient to demonstrate an informant's basis of knowledge or veracity, an anonymous tip corroborated by independent police work can exhibit sufficient indicia of reliability to provide reasonable suspicion to conduct a stop or probable cause to search. U.S.C.A. Const.Amend. 4.—Marsdin v. State, 813 So.2d 260.

Fla.App. 4 Dist. 2001. A tip corroborated by independent police observation of otherwise seemingly innocent acts may exhibit sufficient indicia of reliability to justify a stop or search, depending upon the totality of the circumstances. U.S.C.A. Const.Amend. 4.—Kimball v. State, 801 So.2d 264.

Fla.App. 5 Dist. 2006. Law enforcement officer had probable cause to believe that defendant was in possession of methamphetamine and, thus, was justified in searching him; unidentified male called person being arrested for sale of methamphetamine and referred to two ounces, person reported that caller was en route to deliver two ounces of methamphetamine to him and provided description of caller and caller's vehicle, defendant arrived approximately 45 to 60 minutes later, person's descriptions of defendant and vehicle were completely accurate, and although person had not been established as a reliable informant, most of his information was able to be independently verified prior to search. U.S.C.A. Const.Amend. 4.—Bell v. State, 944 So.2d 448, rehearing denied, review denied 958 So.2d 918.

⊙⇒569. —— Anonymous or confidential informants.

M.D.Fla. 2001. Totality of circumstances analysis, used to determine whether information provided by informant creates probable cause to conduct search, includes looking at an informant's veracity, reliability, and basis of knowledge; an anonymous tip must also contain sufficient indicia of reliability to justify a forcible stop. U.S.C.A. Const.Amend. 4.—U.S. v. Davis, 170 F.Supp.2d 1234.

Fla.App. 1 Dist. 2005. Anonymous tips can provide the basis for reasonable suspicion if the reliability of the tip can be established. U.S.C.A. Const.Amend. 4.—Smith v. State, 904 So.2d 534, rehearing denied.

Fla.App. 1 Dist. 1988. Standard for determining probable cause for warrantless search and arrest of individual predicated on information received from confidential informant is the totality of the circumstances test.—Hopkins v. State, 524 So.2d 1136, review denied 531 So.2d 1353.

Fla.App. 2 Dist. 2018. Anonymous tips, which are more susceptible to abuse than a tip by a known informant, may be less reliable than other investigative leads; the government's interest in conducting a warrantless search based upon an anonymous tip, therefore, is usually measured by examining the tip's indicia of reliability. U.S. Const. Amend. 4.—Lapace v. State, 257 So.3d 588.

Generally, a warrantless search based upon an anonymous tip withstands scrutiny under the Fourth Amendment only if the tip contains sufficient details and information that can be independently corroborated by the police to establish a level of reliability regarding the information in the tip. U.S. Const. Amend. 4.—Id.

That an anonymous tip proved accurate and that police officers acted with good intentions does not alter the legal conclusion that the warrantless search was improper. U.S. Const. Amend. 4.—Id.

Fla.App. 2 Dist. 2001. Confidential informant's information could not be deemed reliable on the ground that the informant's behavior contributed to the success of previous controlled buys, in the absence of evidence that informant had provided reliable information leading to controlled buys in the past, where evidence was merely that informant had made controlled buys acting as an agent for police.—Mitchell v. State, 787 So.2d 224.

Relevant to the issue of veracity of a confidential informant are the nature and quality of the information provided in the past and the extent to which it was verified.—Id.

Confidential informant's tip that defendant and another were selling narcotics lacked sufficient detail to establish veracity; missing were such facts as source of information, means or methods by which alleged narcotic transactions were made, and type of illegal drug being sold, and only verifiable information was subject's location and clothing, which was readily available because the two subjects were in an open, public place.—Id.

Fla.App. 2 Dist. 1991. To validate anonymous tip to support search or arrest, it is not sufficient merely to corroborate anonymously given information concerning identity, dress, description, location, or even future activity of suspect who is subject of the anonymous information; there must also be independent evidence of criminal activity. U.S.C.A. Const.Amend. 4.—Cunningham v. State, 591 So.2d 1058.

Fla.App. 4 Dist. 2002. Although an anonymous tip, without more, is generally insufficient to demonstrate an informant's basis of knowledge or veracity, an anonymous tip corroborated by independent police work can exhibit sufficient indicia of reliability to provide reasonable suspicion to conduct a stop or probable cause to search. U.S.C.A. Const.Amend. 4.—Marsdin v. State, 813 So.2d 260.

The reliability of an anonymous tip is evaluated, for purposes of an investigatory stop or warrantless search, among other considerations, on its degree of specificity, the extent of corroboration of predicted future conduct, and the significance of the informant's predictions. U.S.C.A. Const.Amend. 4.—Id.

Fla.App. 4 Dist. 2001. An anonymous tip may give rise to reasonable suspicion to stop or probable cause to search, where the tip is deemed

† This Case was not selected for publication in the National Reporter System

reliable. U.S.C.A. Const.Amend. 4.—Kimball v. State, 801 So.2d 264.

For purposes of an investigatory stop or warrantless search, the reliability of an anonymous tip is evaluated, among other considerations, on its degree of specificity, the extent of corroboration of predicted future conduct, and the significance of the informant's predictions. U.S.C.A. Const.Amend. 4.—Id.

Fla.App. 5 Dist. 2021. An anonymous tip alone is not enough to justify a warrantless search or entry. U.S. Const. Amend. 4.—Tolliver v. State, 309 So.3d 718, rehearing denied, review denied 2021 WL 1749758.

Fla.App. 5 Dist. 2019. An anonymous citizen informant tip alone seldom demonstrates the informant's basis of knowledge or veracity to justify police action. U.S. Const. Amend. 4.—Madison v. State, 278 So.3d 921.

⚮571. —— **Other officers or official information; collective knowledge.**

Fla. 2012. Under the "fellow officer rule," one officer may rely on the knowledge and information possessed by another officer to establish probable cause for an arrest for a felony or misdemeanor offense, or to establish probable cause for a search. U.S.C.A. Const.Amend. 4.—State v. Bowers, 87 So.3d 704, rehearing denied.

The "fellow officer rule," providing a mechanism by which officers can rely on their collective knowledge to act in the field, is not a rule of evidence.—Id.

If an officer relies on a chain of evidence to formulate his or her belief as to the existence of probable cause for a search or seizure, the "fellow officer rule" excuses the officer from possessing personal knowledge of each link in the chain of evidence if the collective knowledge of all the officers involved supports a finding of probable cause. U.S.C.A. Const.Amend. 4.—Id.

Fla.App. 2 Dist. 2009. Under the fellow officer rule, one officer may rely on the knowledge and information possessed by another officer to establish probable cause for an arrest for a felony or misdemeanor offense or to establish probable cause for a search. U.S.C.A. Const.Amend. 4.—Bowers v. State, 23 So.3d 767, decision approved 87 So.3d 704, rehearing denied.

Fla.App. 5 Dist. 2013. A police officer is justified in relying on a fellow officers's observations, if those observations were communicated to him; this is especially true for a search or seizure in which the officer was a direct participant. U.S.C.A. Const.Amend. 4.—Carter v. State, 120 So.3d 207.

Fla.App. 5 Dist. 2005. Fellow-officer rule, sometimes referred to as the collective-knowledge doctrine, allows the collective knowledge of police officers investigating a crime to be imputed to each member of the investigation.—Dewberry v. State, 905 So.2d 963.

When applying the fellow-officer rule, there is no requirement that the police officers with knowledge of the facts establishing probable cause exchange information among themselves or with other officers with "magic words" or exact terminology.—Id.

Fla.App. 5 Dist. 1996. Under "fellow officer rule," if officer initiating arrest is ultimately found by court to have had probable cause to make arrest or search, it does not matter whether officer who carried out directive of initiating officer had, on his own, basis to determine that probable cause existed. U.S.C.A. Const.Amend. 4.—State v. Sams, 676 So.2d 1045.

⚮575. —— **In general.**

Fla.App. 1 Dist. 2022. Innocent behavior frequently will provide the basis for a showing of probable cause to conduct a search, and the relevant inquiry is the degree of suspicion that attaches to particular types of non-criminal acts. U.S. Const. Amend. 4.—Hatcher v. State, 342 So.3d 807.

Fla.App. 2 Dist. 2022. Speculation alone cannot support probable cause to search. U.S. Const. Amend. 4.—Smitherman v. State, 342 So.3d 685.

Fla.App. 2 Dist. 2016. Police may not approach a dwelling, armed only with their own subjective suspicion that illegal activity was afoot, and wait for some justification to break down the door and burst into the dwelling without a warrant. U.S.C.A. Const.Amend. 4; West's F.S.A. Const. Art. 1, § 12.—State v. Fultz, 189 So.3d 155, rehearing denied.

⚮576. —— **Individualized suspicion.**

C.A.11 (Fla.) 2018. The default rule is that to be reasonable under the Fourth Amendment, a search ordinarily must be based on individualized suspicion of wrongdoing; however, neither a warrant nor probable cause, nor any measure of individualized suspicion is an indispensable component of reasonableness in every circumstance. U.S. Const. Amend. 4.—Friedenberg v. School Board of Palm Beach County, 911 F.3d 1084.

In limited circumstances where the privacy interest implicated by a search are minimal and where an important government interest furthered by the intrusion would be placed in jeopardy by requiring an individualized suspicion, a search may be reasonable under the Fourth Amendment despite the absence of individualized suspicion. U.S. Const. Amend. 4.—Id.

S.D.Fla. 2017. Under the Fourth Amendment, to be reasonable, a search must ordinarily be based on individualized suspicion of wrongdoing. U.S. Const. Amend. 4.—Friedenberg v. School Board of Palm Beach County, 257 F.Supp.3d 1295, affirmed 911 F.3d 1084.

Under the Fourth Amendment, a search may be conducted absent individualized suspicion in limited circumstances, where the privacy interests implicated by the search are minimal, and where an important governmental interest furthered by the intrusion would be placed in jeopardy if individualized suspicion was required. U.S. Const. Amend. 4.—Id.

Fla.App. 2 Dist. 2008. Officer's mere suspicion that a person is carrying illegal drugs is insufficient to supply probable cause for a search. U.S.C.A. Const.Amend. 4.—Robinson v. State, 976 So.2d 1229.

Fla.App. 2 Dist. 2001. Generally, a search or seizure violates the Fourth Amendment as unreasonable when law enforcement lacks an individualized suspicion of wrongdoing. U.S.C.A. Const. Amend. 4.—Davis v. State, 788 So.2d 1064.

⚮577. **Subjective or objective test; motive, intent, and pretext.**

C.A.11 (Fla.) 2017. Pretext does not invalidate a search that is objectively reasonable. U.S. Const. Amend. 4.—United States v. Spivey, 861 F.3d 1207, rehearing en banc denied 870 F.3d 1297, certiorari denied 138 S.Ct. 2620, 201 L.Ed.2d 1031.

C.A.11 (Fla.) 2007. Subjective intentions of arresting officer play no role in ordinary, "probable cause" analysis under the Fourth Amendment. U.S.C.A. Const.Amend. 4.—U.S. v. Lindsey, 482 F.3d 1285, certiorari denied 128 S.Ct.

438, 552 U.S. 974, 169 L.Ed.2d 306, post-conviction relief denied 2009 WL 5863461, certificate of appealability granted by 2010 WL 547896.

N.D.Fla. 2010. Subjective intentions play no role in ordinary, probable-cause Fourth Amendment analysis. U.S.C.A. Const.Amend. 4.—U.S. v. Burton, 698 F.Supp.2d 1303.

S.D.Fla. 2010. Allegations that one of the reasons law enforcement searched plaintiff's vehicle was that he was a "protestor with history," and that plaintiff's exercise of his First Amendment rights had been chilled by such search, were sufficient to state a § 1983 claim of retaliation in violation of the First Amendment. U.S.C.A. Const.Amend. 1; 42 U.S.C.A. § 1983.—Lippman v. City of Miami, 724 F.Supp.2d 1240.

⊕578. Special needs in general.

C.A.11 (Fla.) 2018. The special need required to justify suspicionless search must raise a concern other than crime detection, and in order to satisfy the Fourth Amendment, the special need must be substantial—important enough to override the individual's acknowledged privacy interest, sufficiently vital to suppress the Fourth Amendment's normal requirement of individualized suspicion. U.S. Const. Amend. 4.—Friedenberg v. School Board of Palm Beach County, 911 F.3d 1084.

Once a plaintiff has shown that the government conducted a search without individualized suspicion, the burden shifts to the government to establish that it has a "special need" sufficient to warrant departure from the Fourth Amendment's baseline requirement of individualized suspicion; if a special need is presented, court undertakes a context-specific inquiry, examining closely the competing private and public interests advanced by the parties to determine the reasonableness of the search. U.S. Const. Amend. 4.—Id.

M.D.Fla. 2019. Search regimes where no warrant is ever required may be reasonable where special needs make the warrant and probable-cause requirement impracticable and the primary purpose of the searches is distinguishable from the general interest in crime control. U.S. Const. Amend. 4.—Sweet Sage Cafe, LLC v. Town of North Redington Beach, Florida, 380 F.Supp.3d 1209.

Fla.App. 5 Dist. 2019. A warrantless search is reasonable when special needs, beyond the normal need for law enforcement, make the warrant and probable-cause requirement impracticable; this presents a separate reasonableness test from the balancing test between an intrusion on an individual's privacy and the degree to which the search is needed for the promotion of legitimate governmental interests.—State v. Phillips, 266 So.3d 873, review denied 2019 WL 2265037.

⊕579. Community caretaking in general.

Fla.App. 1 Dist. 2021. While law enforcement is not required to use the least intrusive methods available when performing community caretaking functions, a welfare check, particularly one that evolves into a search and seizure, must be commensurate with the perceived exigency at hand. U.S. Const. Amend. 4.—Taylor v. State, 326 So.3d 115.

⊕581. —— In general.

C.A.11 (Fla.) 2019. An officer conducting a lawful stop or search may, in an appropriate setting, properly control the movements of persons at the scene in order to ensure officer safety. U.S. Const. Amend. 4.—United States v. Gibbs, 917 F.3d 1289.

C.A.11 (Fla.) 2018. Without offending the Fourth Amendment, additional investigators or officials may enter a citizen's property after one official has already intruded legally. U.S. Const. Amend. 4.—Montanez v. Carvajal, 889 F.3d 1202.

C.A.11 (Fla.) 2017. That fraud, deceit, or trickery in obtaining access to incriminating evidence can make an otherwise lawful search unreasonable does not mean that it must. U.S. Const. Amend. 4.—United States v. Spivey, 861 F.3d 1207, rehearing en banc denied 870 F.3d 1297, certiorari denied 138 S.Ct. 2620, 201 L.Ed.2d 1031.

Fla.App. 1 Dist. 2021. The purpose of a welfare check regulates its scope: without any reasonable suspicion that criminal activity is or was afoot, the welfare check should end when the need for it ends. U.S. Const. Amend. 4.—Taylor v. State, 326 So.3d 115.

Both the scope and manner of a welfare check must be reasonable in order to fall within exception to Fourth Amendment search warrant requirement. U.S. Const. Amend. 4.—Id.

⊕583. —— Warning or announcement; "no knock" entries.

C.A.11 (Fla.) 1983. Neither knock and announce statute nor Fourth Amendment was violated by warrantless reentry of undercover agent, with uniformed officers, into premises where cocaine transaction was scheduled to occur, in light of exigent circumstances because of significant possibility that the cocaine would be destroyed. 18 U.S.C.A. § 3109; U.S.C.A. Const.Amend. 4.—U.S. v. Harris, 713 F.2d 623.

Fla.App. 4 Dist. 1971. Where officer on patrol of business district when he observed, at 3:30 A.M., a light burning and a blanket covering rear window of the premises and where he believed that burglary was in progress, officer was justified in entering premises through unlocked door without announcing his authority as a police officer under theory that officer's peril would have been increased had he demanded entrance and stated the purpose, and marijuana found within the premises and defendants' statements relative thereto were admissible, notwithstanding that a defendant was residing in back room of the premises and that no burglary was in progress. F.S.A. § 901.19(1); U.S.C.A.Const. Amend. 4.—State v. Bell, 249 So.2d 748.

⊕584. —— Time and duration.

Fla.App. 1 Dist. 1989. In absence of any exigent circumstances, it was unreasonable for police to seize defendant's home without warrant and dispossess defendant and his wife for five hours while awaiting warrant. U.S.C.A. Const. Amend. 4.—State v. Brim, 548 So.2d 802.

⊕585. —— Odor detection; use of dogs.

U.S.Fla. 2013. Evidence of drug detection dog's satisfactory performance in certification or training program can itself provide sufficient reason to trust his alert; if bona fide organization has certified a dog after testing his reliability in controlled setting, court can presume, subject to any conflicting evidence offered, that dog's alert provides probable cause to search. U.S.C.A. Const.Amend. 4.—Florida v. Harris, 133 S.Ct. 1050, 568 U.S. 237, 185 L.Ed.2d 61, on remand Harris v. State, 123 So.3d 1144.

Even if drug detection dog has not completed formal certification program, court can presume, subject to any conflicting evidence offered, that dog's alert provides probable cause to search, if dog has recently and successfully completed

---

† This Case was not selected for publication in the National Reporter System

training program that evaluated his proficiency in locating drugs. U.S.C.A. Const.Amend. 4.—Id.

C.A.5 (Fla.) 1978. The "valid public interest" standard of probable cause established by the Comprehensive Drug Abuse Prevention and Control Act for the judicial issuance of warrants for administrative inspections and seizures appropriate thereto, although clearly less stringent than the probable cause required for the constitutional issuance of a criminal search or arrest warrant, is constitutional under the Supreme Court's administrative search cases. Comprehensive Drug Abuse Prevention and Control Act of 1970, § 510(d)(1), 21 U.S.C.A. § 880(d)(1).—U.S. v. Schiffman, 572 F.2d 1137.

Fla.App. 1 Dist. 2018. Officer had probable cause to believe defendant was in possession of marijuana to support warrantless search of defendant's person, where an off-duty officer smelled marijuana confined to defendant's location, off-duty officer observed defendant smoking what appeared to be a marijuana cigarette, a second officer noted the smell of burnt marijuana coming from the area occupied by defendant, and officer witnessed defendant smoking what appeared to be a marijuana blunt. U.S. Const. Amend. 4.—Dawson v. State, 253 So.3d 766.

Fla.App. 1 Dist. 1986. Just as no police officer need close his eyes to contraband in plain view, no police officer armed with a sniff dog need ignore the olfactory essence of illegality.—Cardwell v. State, 482 So.2d 512.

Fla.App. 2 Dist. 2017. An alert by a properly trained narcotics detection dog generally provides probable cause for a search, but the alert must be sufficiently reliable based upon the totality of the circumstances. U.S. Const. Amend. 4.—Sanchez v. State, 210 So.3d 252.

Fla.App. 2 Dist. 2008. There was no probable cause to support the warrantless search of defendant's person which yielded the firearm and the marijuana; fact that defendant was standing with a group of men surrounded by the odor of burned marijuana was insufficient to supply more than a mere suspicion that defendant was in possession of marijuana, and fact that defendant initially consented to a search of his person and then withdrew that consent did not give the officer probable cause to search for marijuana. U.S.C.A. Const.Amend. 4.—Robinson v. State, 976 So.2d 1229.

Fla.App. 2 Dist. 1990. Trained narcotics detector dog's positive identification for drugs provides probable cause for arrest or search. U.S.C.A. Const.Amend. 4.—State v. Russell, 557 So.2d 666.

Fla.App. 5 Dist. 2016. Just as evidence in the plain view of officers may be searched without a warrant, evidence in the plain smell may be detected without a warrant. U.S. Const. Amend. 4.—Friedson v. State, 207 So.3d 961, on remand 2017 WL 7795602.

The plain smell doctrine, under which evidence in plain smell may be obtained without a search warrant, applies only when law enforcement officers detect the odor while occupying a place where they have a legitimate right to be. U.S. Const. Amend. 4.—Id.

Fla.App. 5 Dist. 2013. Generally, an alert by a properly trained narcotics detection dog provides probable cause for a search as long as the alert is sufficiently reliable. U.S.C.A. Const.Amend. 4.—State v. Grue, 130 So.3d 256.

Fla.App. 5 Dist. 2000. Drug alert by a properly trained police dog provides probable cause for

a search. U.S.C.A. Const.Amend. 4.—State v. Robinson, 756 So.2d 249.

2. PARTICULAR CASES AND CONTEXTS.

☞**591. In general.**

C.A.5 (Fla.) 1968. Hearsay testimony was admissible to establish probable cause of government for seizure of aircraft on ground that it had been illegally exported for purpose of conducting bombing raid on foreign nation. Seizure of Arms Intended for Export Act, § 1(b), 22 U.S.C.A. § 401(b); Tariff Act of 1930, §§ 581 et seq., 615, 19 U.S.C.A. §§ 1581 et seq., 1615; Export Control Act of 1949, §§ 1–12, 50 U.S.C.A. App. §§ 2021–2032.—Bush v. U.S., 389 F.2d 485.

☞**593. —— In general.**

C.A.11 (Fla.) 2010. Under Florida law, officer does not need probable cause to stop boat to check for fishing permits. U.S.C.A. Const. Amend. 4; West's F.S.A. §§ 379.354(1)(a), (3), 379.3313.—U.S. v. Caraballo, 595 F.3d 1214.

N.D.Fla. 1970. Any search or inspection conducted pursuant to regulation of Florida game and fresh water fish commission permitting wildlife officers to check vehicle for dogs and guns in designated areas of state would not amount to deprivation of plaintiff's constitutional rights and privileges and immunity secured by Constitution when plaintiff while passenger in his brother's vehicle and traveling through lawfully designated game management preserve was stopped by defendant wildlife officers to check vehicle for dogs and guns and plaintiff resisted attempt of officers but vehicle was searched after scuffle and over protest of plaintiff. F.S.A. § 372.76; U.S.C.A.Const. Amend. 4.—Davis v. Reynolds, 319 F.Supp. 20.

S.D.Fla. 1993. Government had probable cause to seize spiny lobster tails for importation into United States in violation of Lacey Act which prohibits importation of fish or wildlife taken in violation of foreign law; multiplying total combined weight of tails, 3,229 pounds, by number of ounces in a pound and then dividing figure by number of lobsters seized, 15,538, one arrived at average weight per lobster of 3.35 ounces which was in violation of the relevant law of the Turks and Caicos Islands which set minimum standard as being seven ounces. Lacey Act Amendments of 1981, § 2 et seq., 16 U.S.C.A. § 3371 et seq.—U.S. v. Proceeds from Sale of Approximately 15,538 Panulirus Argus Lobster Tails, 834 F.Supp. 385.

Fla. 1982. State marine officers need not have probable cause to stop motor boat for limited purpose of checking fishing permits, registration certificates and safety equipment.—State v. Casal, 410 So.2d 152, on remand 411 So.2d 1040, certiorari granted 103 S.Ct. 50, 459 U.S. 821, 74 L.Ed.2d 56, certiorari dismissed 103 S.Ct. 3100, 462 U.S. 637, 77 L.Ed.2d 277.

Fla.App. 1 Dist. 1975. Wildlife officer who, at 11 o'clock at night, had been given a lead that game laws were being violated in a rural area, who had heard a shotgun being fired in a pasture-pond area, who had heard an airboat cranking up, idling along, running a little way, and then shutting down, who saw the glare of light reflection off the water, and who waited for airboat's operators to drive to position where he was waiting at approximately one o'clock in the morning had probable cause to believe that the occupants of the vehicle had been engaged in unlawfully poaching or killing alligators and to

---

† **This Case was not selected for publication in the National Reporter System**

look in airboat which was being pulled by defendants' vehicle, where he discovered a rifle and three alligators. West's F.S.A. § 372.663.—State v. Pearce, 318 So.2d 455, appeal after remand 336 So.2d 1274.

Fla.App. 2 Dist. 1991. Stop and search of driver of Cadillac could not be justified on basis of information officer received from reliable source concerning robbery/auto theft where information was not sufficiently detailed; reliable source merely gave officer street name of person who allegedly committed crimes and stated that he could be found with persons driving around in red-over-white Cadillac.—Bristol v. State, 584 So.2d 1086.

Fla.App. 2 Dist. 1979. Determination of whether marine patrol officers had lawful statutory authority, under statute empowering such officers with authority to board, inspect, and search any boat, without warrant, engaged in transporting or storing any fish or fishery products, to search boat without warrant depended on whether the officers had "probable cause" to do so even though such statute does not expressly use the term "probable cause." West's F.S.A. § 370.021(5).—Roth v. State, 378 So.2d 794, certiorari denied 386 So.2d 641, certiorari denied Rich v. Florida, 101 S.Ct. 919, 449 U.S. 1111, 66 L.Ed.2d 839.

Fla.App. 2 Dist. 1961. Defendant charged with attempting to bribe wildlife officer, who found freshwater fish in his possession in violation of Wild Life Code, could not complain of an illegal search where fish were kept in freezers in defendant's retail store. F.S.A. § 838.011.—Troupe v. State, 130 So.2d 91.

Fla.App. 3 Dist. 1978. Although proper law enforcement officers have authority to stop and board a boat in state waters for purpose of checking boat's registration and crawfish permit, such authority does not carry with it right to conduct general exploratory search of boat for evidence of crime and in absence of probable cause or some other recognized exception to search warrant rule, such warrantless searches are unreasonable. West's F.S.A.Const. art. 1, § 12; U.S.C.A.Const. Amends. 4, 14, 14, § 1; West's F.S.A. §§ 370.021(5), 370.14(3)(c), 371.051(5).—Miranda v. State, 354 So.2d 411, certiorari denied 364 So.2d 888.

←594. —— Arson; fire investigation.

C.A.11 (Fla.) 1983. Legitimacy of governmental interest in protecting valuable property of fire victim from vandals and looters does not undercut necessity for warrant to safeguard substantial privacy interests implicated by any entry to person's home by governmental official. U.S.C.A.Const.Amend. 4.—U.S. v. Parr, 716 F.2d 796, rehearing denied 734 F.2d 1481.

C.A.5 (Fla.) 1973. Where deputy fire marshal was lawfully present in empty apartment for purpose of investigating cause of fire which had just occurred, his examination without warrant of box where fire had apparently started was justified, and upon removal from the ashes of what appeared to be a counterfeiting plate, with consequent exposure of others underneath, "plain view" doctrine was applicable and marshal, though having broad powers to make arrests and seizures, was not obliged to halt his investigation and obtain a warrant before continuing to uncover and seize the plates in order to fulfill his duty as fire marshal. U.S.C.A.Const. Amend. 4; F.S.A. §§ 633.03, 633.14.—U.S. v. Green, 474

F.2d 1385, certiorari denied 94 S.Ct. 55, 414 U.S. 829, 38 L.Ed.2d 63.

Where deputy fire marshal, lawfully on premises in empty apartment investigating cause of fire, unexpectedly came upon what appeared to be counterfeiting plates in remains of box where fire apparently originated, he had authority as law enforcement officer to seize them and duty as fire marshal to seize them as relevant to his investigation; thus, it was not necessary for secret service agent to obtain a warrant before he entered the apartment to confirm that the plates were of such quality as to be suitable for printing obligations and to take custody of them, which he did without otherwise searching the premises. U.S.C.A.Const. Amend. 4.—Id.

M.D.Fla. 1994. Warrantless reentries by fire and police personnel into private home, several hours after determination was made that fire there was caused by arson, did not violate Fourth Amendment, since reentries constituted continuation of initial investigation and thus did not require warrants; police manifested intent to continue investigation by posting guard when house was empty, delay was justified due to darkness, smoke, and haze of early morning hours, and homeowners took no steps to secure privacy interests that remained in their residence against further intrusion by investigators. U.S.C.A. Const.Amend. 4.—U.S. v. Veltmann, 869 F.Supp. 929, affirmed 87 F.3d 1329.

Once it was determined that house fire was caused by arson, search and seizure related to entry of telephone company employee into house required warrant, since object of search was to gather evidence of criminal activity rather than investigate cause of fire, and evidence sought was not in plain view and could not be seized even if telephone employee were legitimately present in house; telephone employee was called to scene by police in order to determine why homeowners' alarm system had not automatically notified alarm monitoring company, as it was designed to do. U.S.C.A. Const.Amend. 4.—Id.

Even after determining that fire originated on first and second floors of house, fire and police investigators were justified in returning, without warrant, to third level of house to seize any evidence that lay in plain view when they were present earlier that morning, prior to determining points of origin, since investigators had been legitimately present on third floor well before points of origin were determined, and they attempted to make necessary observations but were stymied due to smoke, haze, and darkness. U.S.C.A. Const.Amend. 4.—Id.

Fla.App. 1 Dist. 1982. Search warrant affidavit, which recited that defendant had filed claim with insurer for loss of property destroyed in fire, that he received insurance proceeds, and that claim filed for certain items of property allegedly destroyed was false because they had not been destroyed was sufficient to support issuance of search warrant, because as to latter allegation, there were explicit recitations that defendant's former wife had seen items claimed destroyed in defendant's houseboat before and following fire, and because the first two allegations were susceptible to simple verification, even though there were no specific statements as to how affiant, or his sources, came about the information. U.S.C.A.Const.Amend. 4.—State v. Willits, 413 So.2d 791.

---

† This Case was not selected for publication in the National Reporter System

⬡595. —— Controlled substances.

U.S.Fla. 2013. To establish that drug detection dog is reliable, State need not, in every case, present exhaustive set of records, including log of dog's performance in the field; that approach would be inconsistent with flexible, common-sense standard of probable cause. U.S.C.A. Const.Amend. 4.—Florida v. Harris, 133 S.Ct. 1050, 568 U.S. 237, 185 L.Ed.2d 61, on remand Harris v. State, 123 So.3d 1144.

In determining whether drug detection dog is reliable, question is whether all facts surrounding dog's alert, viewed through lens of common sense, would make reasonably prudent person think that search would reveal contraband or evidence of crime. U.S.C.A. Const.Amend. 4.—Id.

† **C.A.11 (Fla.) 2014.** Evidence that drug detection dog was originally certified through course offered by the Florida Highway Patrol and had been re-certified annually in each of the past three years, with nearly a perfect record of detecting drugs in controlled environment in which these certifications were conducted, gave rise to presumption of dog's reliability, which defendant failed to rebut with evidence of occasions on which dog had alerted in the field in situations in which no drugs were ultimately discovered by law enforcement officers. U.S.C.A. Const. Amend. 4.—U.S. v. Trejo, 551 Fed.Appx. 565.

C.A.5 (Fla.) 1977. Where government agents received tip that marijuana was to be smuggled and began to monitor certain van truck which led them to a closed commercial fish house with access to ocean and continued surveillance of premises when they noticed two men loitering at night near dock of closed fish house and saw two boats running without lights motor slowly into view and moor at dock of fish house where cargo was unloaded, agents had probable cause to suspect criminal conduct and their search and seizure of the contraband was reasonable. U.S.C.A.Const. Amend. 4.—U.S. v. Bass, 551 F.2d 962.

S.D.Fla. 2012. The recognizable smell of marijuana gives rise to probable cause supporting a warrantless search. U.S.C.A. Const.Amend. 4.—Feliciano v. City of Miami Beach, 847 F.Supp.2d 1359.

S.D.Fla. 1994. Statements by participants in conspiracy provided officers with legitimate basis for believing that property was used or intended to be used to import illegal substances, and, thus there was reasonable cause to believe that property was subject to seizure at time it was seized. U.S.C.A. Const.Amend. 4.—U.S. v. One Parcel of Real Estate, 864 F.Supp. 1267.

S.D.Fla. 1986. Customs officers, police officers, and marine patrol officers, who had reasonable suspicion based on articulable facts of criminal activity which justified boarding of fishing boat, had probable cause to search fishing boat encountered at night two miles off Florida coast, where captain was wearing coast guard uniform, captain explained that boat was on return from fishing due bad weather, weather was calm that night, captain and crew members appeared nervous, access panel on steps leading to below-deck area was unusual and hazardous, bathroom door was fastened shut with tape, officers knew that captain was suspected of drug smuggling, and boat was bearing coast guard auxiliary ensign and placards. U.S.C.A. Const.Amend. 4.—U.S. v. Marrero, 644 F.Supp. 570.

Fla. 2011. The fact that a drug-detection dog has been trained and certified to detect narcotics, standing alone, is not sufficient to demonstrate the reliability of the dog for purposes of determining probable cause for a search; disapproving State v. Laveroni, 910 So.2d 333, and State v. Coleman, 911 So.2d 259. U.S.C.A. Const.Amend. 4.—Harris v. State, 71 So.3d 756, revised on rehearing, certiorari granted 132 S.Ct. 1796, 566 U.S. 904, 182 L.Ed.2d 615, reversed 133 S.Ct. 1050, 568 U.S. 237, 185 L.Ed.2d 61, on remand 123 So.3d 1144, withdrawn 123 So.3d 1144.

Fla. 2011. Officers had probable cause to search defendant after observing him arrive at a home that had been the subject of complaints about drug activity and engage in a series of hand-to-hand transactions in which each of three individuals consecutively took a small item from defendant's hand and quickly gave defendant paper currency in return, where, rather than making eye contact, defendant looked up and down the street as he interacted with the three individuals, and defendant's contact with the individuals was very brief. U.S.C.A. Const.Amend. 4.—State v. Hankerson, 65 So.3d 502, revised on rehearing, certiorari denied 132 S.Ct. 1636, 565 U.S. 1236, 182 L.Ed.2d 237.

Fla. 1992. Relevant to inquiry of whether a police officer has sufficient probable cause to believe that suspect is carrying illegal contraband, for purposes of search and/or seizure, is officer's specific experience with respect to particular narcotic in question.—Doctor v. State, 596 So.2d 442.

Fla. 1988. Neither the Florida Constitution nor the United States Constitution required issuance of a warrant for search of sealed container in which contraband drugs had previously been discovered pursuant to lawful search of container while in transit. West's F.S.A. Const. Art. 1, § 12; U.S.C.A. Const.Amend. 4.—Bernie v. State, 524 So.2d 988.

Fla. 1978. Where defendant did not consent to search, police were not in hot pursuit or conducting stop and frisk, search was not incident to lawful arrest, defendant was not in flight or in moving vehicle, defendant was not about to destroy evidence or contraband and police had every opportunity to obtain warrant, seizure of heroin from defendant in warrantless search was violation of Fourth Amendment and admission of such heroin into evidence was reversible error. U.S.C.A.Const. Amend. 4.—Martin v. State, 360 So.2d 396, appeal after remand 377 So.2d 706.

Fla.App. 1 Dist. 1991. In formulating belief that package contains contraband, officer is entitled to use his knowledge gained from training, education and experience in investigating drug offenses and identifying packages which commonly contain unlawful substances, particularly in area of city known for its high incidence of drug trafficking.—Bryant v. State, 577 So.2d 1372.

Fla.App. 1 Dist. 1984. Opening of envelope containing cocaine by a courier was not an illegal search and seizure, since the courier did not act at the government's direction. U.S.C.A. Const. Amends. 4, 14.—Kresbach v. State, 462 So.2d 62.

Fla.App. 2 Dist. 2015. An officer does not need probable cause to believe that a glass pipe has previously been used or contains drug residue before he conducts a search. U.S.C.A. Const. Amend. 4; West's F.S.A. § 893.145(12)(a).—Conyers v. State, 164 So.3d 73.

Fla.App. 2 Dist. 2014. A well-trained dog's alert establishes a fair probability—all that is required for probable cause-that either drugs or evidence of a drug crime will be found. U.S.C.A.

Const.Amend. 4.—Campbell v. State, 139 So.3d 490.

Fla.App. 2 Dist. 2013. At the seizure stage in a forfeiture proceeding, the circuit court determines whether there is probable cause to believe that the seized property has been used in violation of the Contraband Forfeiture Act. West's F.S.A. § 932.701(2)(f).—In re Forfeiture of: $221,898 in U.S. Currency, 106 So.3d 47.

Fla.App. 2 Dist. 2008. Evidence failed to establish that canine's alert provided officers with probable cause necessary to support search, where State presented no evidence of canine's "track record," including number of false alerts or mistakes canine had made in field. U.S.C.A. Const.Amend. 4.—Tedder v. State, 18 So.3d 1052, rehearing denied, review denied 996 So.2d 213, review denied 12 So.3d 197.

Fla.App. 2 Dist. 2007. To demonstrate that an alert by a narcotics detection dog is sufficiently reliable to furnish probable cause to search, state must introduce evidence of the dog's "track record" or performance history. U.S.C.A. Const. Amend. 4.—Gibson v. State, 968 So.2d 1123, review granted 973 So.2d 1123, review dismissed 985 So.2d 1088.

Fla.App. 2 Dist. 2003. Fact that a dog has been trained to detect narcotics, standing alone, is not enough to give an officer probable cause to search based on the dog's alert; dog may alert to residual odors of drugs no longer present, fact that dog has been trained does not indicate what dog has or has not been trained to do or how successfully, dogs themselves vary in abilities to accept, retain, or abide by their conditioning in widely varying environments and circumstances, and handler may prompt dog to alert. U.S.C.A. Const.Amend. 4.—Matheson v. State, 870 So.2d 8, rehearing denied, review granted 880 So.2d 1212, review dismissed 896 So.2d 748, certiorari denied 126 S.Ct. 545, 546 U.S. 998, 163 L.Ed.2d 499.

Factors that must be known to conclude that an alert by a narcotics detection dog is sufficiently reliable to furnish probable cause to search are: (1) exact training the detector dog has received, standards or criteria employed in selecting dogs for drug detection training; (2) standards the dog was required to meet to successfully complete his training program; and (3) "track record" of the dog up until the search, with an emphasis on the amount of false alerts or mistakes the dog has furnished. U.S.C.A. Const.Amend. 4.—Id.

Although narcotics detection dog's 'credibility' may be undermined by evidence of its lack of training or past unreliability, the ultimate determination as to whether the dog's alert to contraband was sufficiently reliable to support a determination of probable cause to justify a warrantless search is for the trial court as the trier of fact. U.S.C.A. Const.Amend. 4.—Id.

When the evidence presented, whether testimony from the dog's trainer or records of the dog's training, establishes that the dog is generally certified as a drug detection dog, any other evidence, including the testimony of other experts, that may detract from the reliability of the dog's performance properly goes to the "credibility" of the dog, which is a factor to consider in determining whether dog's alert to contraband constituted probable cause to conduct a warrantless search. U.S.C.A. Const.Amend. 4.—Id.

In determining whether a drug detection dog's alert constituted probable cause to conduct a warrantless search, the lack of additional evidence, such as documentation of the exact course of training, would affect the dog's reliability. U.S.C.A. Const.Amend. 4.—Id.

Admissibility of evidence regarding a drug detection dog's training and reliability, in determination of whether dog's alert constituted probable cause to conduct a warrantless search, is committed to the trial court's sound discretion. U.S.C.A. Const.Amend. 4.—Id.

Fla.App. 2 Dist. 2001. Record did not establish basis to permit seizure of clear plastic bag from defendant's pocket as result of a "plain feel" during lawful pat down; even though officer claimed he saw corner of clear plastic bag out of pocket and knew marijuana was often carried in such bags, those facts would have given rise to, at most, a mere suspicion that it contained marijuana, which was not enough to seize it. U.S.C.A. Const.Amend. 4.—State v. Miyasato, 805 So.2d 818, stay granted, review denied 807 So.2d 655, mandamus denied 821 So.2d 298.

Fla.App. 2 Dist. 2001. Police officers did not have probable cause to conduct warrantless pat down search of defendant, looking for crack cocaine; officers had observed drug transaction but did not know, at time of search of defendant and another man, whether defendant was the one selling narcotics or was simply a bystander. West's F.S.A. §901.151.—McCloud v. State, 787 So.2d 218.

Fla.App. 2 Dist. 1997. Police officers lacked probable cause, once defendant withdrew consent to narcotics search by placing foot on tissue that fell from her bra as she shook it, to seize and search tissue, where officers could not see cocaine inside tissue, and where neither officer provided any experiential testimony to provide a basis for their statements that women commonly carried narcotics in their bras and that crack cocaine was commonly placed in tissue. U.S.C.A. Const.Amend. 4.—Parker v. State, 693 So.2d 92.

Observation of suspected contraband can suffice to provide an officer with probable cause for search and seizure if other circumstances exist to corroborate the officer's suspicion; officer's specific experience with respect to the particular narcotic in question is relevant, but state must present more than a statement by officer that he had a feeling based on his experience. U.S.C.A. Const.Amend. 4.—Id.

Fla.App. 2 Dist. 1991. Mere proximity to contraband is insufficient to create probable cause of constructive possession.—Rogers v. State, 586 So.2d 1148.

Fla.App. 2 Dist. 1984. A police officer determining whether to seize a package because it allegedly contains contraband is entitled to utilize his specialized knowledge gained from training, education and experience in investigating drug offenses and identifying unusual packets which commonly contain illicit substances. U.S.C.A. Const.Amend. 4.—State v. Ellison, 455 So.2d 424.

Issue whether experienced police officer at a known drug-transaction site has sufficient probable cause to believe that a particular container does contain narcotics will depend on the "totality of the circumstances" existing at the time. U.S.C.A. Const.Amend. 4.—Id.

Fla.App. 3 Dist. 2009. In determining whether reasonable suspicion or probable cause exists to conduct a warrantless search, the analysis of observations by informants, even reliable ones, should meet the same standards as analysis of observations made by trained police officers; standards include reputation of location for drug activity, history of previous arrests from site, prior knowledge of suspect, quality and extent of "surveillance" by informant, and detailed description of the event. U.S.C.A. Const.Amend. 4.—Mathis v. State, 8 So.3d 445, rehearing denied.

Fla.App. 3 Dist. 1989. Once officer observed packet of white powder and heard infant's voluntary explanation that packet contained cocaine, officer had probable cause to arrest infant and seize evidence.—State v. G.H., 549 So.2d 1148.

Fla.App. 3 Dist. 1985. Suspect's nervousness when he consented to a "feel" of his boots by members of narcotics interdiction squad at airport, together with narcotics officer's discovery of a soft and malleable package inside boot and officer's belief, in light of his experience with searches of this kind, that package contained cocaine, provided probable cause for seizure of package and its subsequent examination.—State v. Rodriguez, 477 So.2d 1025.

Fla.App. 3 Dist. 1983. Officer, who watched defendant take from mailbox some all-white capsules which appeared to contain "suspect cocaine," who saw defendant put them in a towel which he "stuck down in his pants," and who was then told by defendant that he had "nothing in the towel," had probable cause to believe that defendant was in possession of controlled substance and thus warrantless search which secured cocaine was constitutionally permissible.—Council v. State, 442 So.2d 1072.

Fla.App. 4 Dist. 2011. A narcotic detection dog's reliability in detecting controlled substances is a question of fact.—Frost v. State, 53 So.3d 1119, review granted, quashed 94 So.3d 481, on remand 92 So.3d 323.

To make a prima facie showing of probable cause for a warrantless search based on a narcotic sniffing dog's alert to the presence of controlled substances, the State is required to demonstrate that the dog was properly trained and certified. U.S.C.A. Const.Amend. 4.—Id.

Fla.App. 4 Dist. 2005. State can make a prima facie showing of probable cause for warrantless search based on a narcotic dog's alert by demonstrating that the dog has been properly trained and certified, and if the defendant wishes to challenge the reliability of the dog, he can do so by using the performance records of the dog, or other evidence, such as expert testimony, and whether probable cause has been established will then be resolved by the trial court. U.S.C.A. Const.Amend. 4.—State v. Laveroni, 910 So.2d 333.

Fla.App. 4 Dist. 1991. "Peanut brittle" feel of bulge in defendant's groin area gave law enforcement officer probable cause to believe the bulge was cocaine rocks, and, thus, officer could seize rocks as evidence of crime. U.S.C.A. Const. Amend. 4; West's F.S.A. § 901.151(5).—Doctor v. State, 573 So.2d 157, decision approved in part, quashed in part 596 So.2d 442.

Fla.App. 4 Dist. 1989. On motion to suppress warrantless search and seizure of ordinary looking object found to contain drugs, the State is required to establish probable cause through officer's testimony that, prior to the seizure, he or she believed the object contained contraband, which may be based on knowledge gained through training and experience about how drugs are carried or packaged by traffickers. U.S.C.A. Const.Amend. 4.—Gray v. State, 550 So.2d 540.

Fla.App. 4 Dist. 1982. Wildlife officers are duly authorized to undertake a warrantless search for drugs, despite contention that statute precludes search for anything other than game,

hides, fur-bearing animals, fish or fish nets, in that officers now have expanded powers to make arrests for violations of any laws committed in their presence or on game commission controlled lands and statute does not by its terms expressly exclude other kinds of searches. West's F.S.A. §§ 372.07, 372.07(1), 372.76, 901.15(3).—State v. Howard, 411 So.2d 372, review denied 421 So.2d 517.

Fla.App. 5 Dist. 2013. Whether an alert by a properly trained narcotics detection dog is reliable enough to establish probable cause for a search is determined based on the totality of the circumstances. U.S.C.A. Const.Amend. 4.—State v. Grue, 130 So.3d 256.

Evidence of a narcotics detection dog's satisfactory performance in a certification or training program can itself provide sufficient reason to trust his alert to presence of narcotics, for purpose of making probable cause determination for a search. U.S.C.A. Const.Amend. 4.—Id.

Fla.App. 5 Dist. 2013. Police officer had probable cause to conduct warrantless search of defendant for drugs, where defendant admitted to officer that he had cocaine in his pocket. U.S.C.A. Const.Amend. 4.—State v. Janusheske, 111 So.3d 967.

Fla.App. 5 Dist. 2011. Sufficient evidence concerning the training and reliability of drug-sniffing dog established probable cause for search based on dog's alert, even though dog's training and field records were not admitted into evidence; dog's handler gave extensive testimony at suppression hearing about his and the dog's training, testing, and certification, handler testified regarding dog's history and search record, including both accurate alerts and false alerts, and dog's records were provided to the defense and used to cross-examine handler. U.S.C.A. Const.Amend. 4.—Joe v. State, 73 So.3d 791, rehearing and rehearing denied, review denied 92 So.3d 213.

Fla.App. 5 Dist. 2006. Law enforcement officer had probable cause to believe that defendant was in possession of methamphetamine and, thus, was justified in searching him; unidentified male called person being arrested for sale of methamphetamine and referred to two ounces, person reported that caller was en route to deliver two ounces of methamphetamine to him and provided description of caller and caller's vehicle, defendant arrived approximately 45 to 60 minutes later, person's descriptions of defendant and vehicle were completely accurate, and although person had not been established as a reliable informant, most of his information was able to be independently verified prior to search. U.S.C.A. Const.Amend. 4.—Bell v. State, 944 So.2d 448, rehearing denied, review denied 958 So.2d 918.

Fla.App. 5 Dist. 2006. Officer had probable cause of criminal activity sufficient to authorize warrantless search; officer, who was in his nineteenth year of law enforcement at the time, stated that he could immediately smell marijuana on defendant and noticed other physical signs of drug and alcohol use, and it was only then that officer asked for consent to search, even though at this point, defendant's consent was not required. U.S.C.A. Const.Amend. 4.—Blake v. State, 939 So.2d 192.

Fla.App. 5 Dist. 2006. There is no requirement that a dog be certified to detect narcotics; characterizing a dog as properly trained is a sufficient predicate upon which to issue a search warrant. U.S.C.A. Const.Amend. 4.—Houston v.

---

† **This Case was not selected for publication in the National Reporter System**

State, 925 So.2d 404, review denied 935 So.2d 1220.

Fla.App. 5 Dist. 2005. The state can make a prima facie showing of probable cause based on a narcotic dog's alert by demonstrating that the dog has been properly trained and certified; if the defendant wishes to challenge the reliability of the dog, he can do so by using the performance records of the dog or other evidence, such as expert testimony, and whether probable cause has been established will then be resolved by the trial court. U.S.C.A. Const.Amend. 4.—State v. Coleman, 911 So.2d 259.

Fla.App. 5 Dist. 2003. Veteran narcotics officer had probable cause to conduct a warrantless search of defendant for drugs; officer observed defendant from about 10 to 15 yards away about to place unidentified object into the hand of unknown female, defendant drew his hand back and put object in his mouth when he saw officer, female then walked away, second officer found crack pipe in female's possession, and officer had personally arrested dozens of people for drug violations in that same location. U.S.C.A. Const. Amend. 4.—Glover v. State, 843 So.2d 919, rehearing denied, review denied 855 So.2d 620.

Fla.App. 5 Dist. 1999. Police officer, who smelled marijuana coming from interior of automobile he suspected was stolen, had probable cause to search for illegal drugs. U.S.C.A. Const. Amend. 4.—State v. Williams, 739 So.2d 717.

Fla.App. 5 Dist. 1999. Officer had probable cause for seizure of crack cocaine that officer felt while conducting warrantless pat-down search of defendant for weapons; officer testified that he immediately recognized the items as contraband upon feeling them, and officer had extensive experience and training in drug identification. U.S.C.A. Const.Amend. 4.—State v. Bellamy, 723 So.2d 402.

Fla.App. 5 Dist. 1997. Pat-down of defendant for weapons was improper, but nonetheless officers had probable cause to search him for illegal drugs, and thus search was proper even though the officers, believing that they lacked probable cause, conducted improper weapons search to enhance their claim of probable cause; officer who had received training and identification of narcotics and who had received complaints of narcotics dealing in vicinity of store, together with another officer, observed for period of two hours during which defendant would approach vehicles, lean into the vehicle and pass something to the occupants, and would then be seen with cash in hand, even though items passed to the occupants of the vehicles were too small to be seen from officers' hiding place.—Knox v. State, 689 So.2d 1224.

⊕**599. —— In general.**

Fla.App. 4 Dist. 2020. For purposes of the Fourth Amendment, television surveillance is identical in its indiscriminate character to wiretapping and bugging; however, it is even more invasive of privacy, just as a strip search is more invasive than a pat-down search. U.S. Const. Amend. 4.—State v. Kraft, 301 So.3d 981.

Fla.App. 4 Dist. 2014. A police officer who is trained to recognize the odor of marijuana and who is familiar with it and can recognize it has probable cause, based on the smell alone, to search a person or a vehicle for contraband. U.S.C.A. Const.Amend. 4.—State v. J.J., 143 So.3d 1050.

⊕**600. —— Particular persons and effects in general.**

†**C.A.11 (Fla.) 2015.** Police officer had probable cause to perform warrantless search of defendant's person based on strong odor of marijuana emanating from him that indicated the presence or possession of contraband, and three baggies of crack cocaine recovered during that search were thus admissible in evidence. U.S.C.A. Const. Amend. 4.—U.S. v. Hyppolite, 609 Fed.Appx. 597, certiorari denied Jean v. U.S., 136 S.Ct. 420, 577 U.S. 964, 193 L.Ed.2d 329, certiorari denied Ductant v. U.S., 136 S.Ct. 426, 577 U.S. 964, 193 L.Ed.2d 329, certiorari denied Sereme v. U.S., 136 S.Ct. 430, 577 U.S. 964, 193 L.Ed.2d 329, post-conviction relief denied 2018 WL 587893, post-conviction relief denied 2019 WL 1402168, post-conviction relief denied 2019 WL 3343768, certificate of appealability denied 2020 WL 917254, post-conviction relief denied Bonita v. United States, 2019 WL 4673809, post-conviction relief denied 2019 WL 4779459, certificate of appealability denied 2020 WL 2537643, post-conviction relief denied 2020 WL 871093.

†**C.A.11 (Fla.) 2006.** Police officer had reasonable suspicion that detainee was transporting drugs, justifying warrantless pat-down search, where police had received tip that house where detainee resided was a drug lab, reliable confidential informant had arranged for detainee to deliver drugs at time and place that officers stopped her, and drug-sniffing canine alerted to presence of drugs in detainee's truck and pelvic area. U.S.C.A. Const.Amend. 4.—Dominguez v. Metropolitan Miami-Dade County, 167 Fed.Appx. 147.

C.A.5 (Fla.) 1981. If police acted illegally in their initial encounter with defendant at airport, then subsequent searches of his person and of his allegedly abandoned tote bag were all prompted by information gathered during illegal activity and link between any illegal activity and discovery of cocaine in bag was too direct and proximate to permit finding of attenuation from such illegality.—U.S. v. Lara, 638 F.2d 892.

Fla. 2011. Officers had probable cause to search defendant after observing him arrive at a home that had been the subject of complaints about drug activity and engage in a series of hand-to-hand transactions in which each of three individuals consecutively took a small item from defendant's hand and quickly gave defendant paper currency in return, where, rather than making eye contact, defendant looked up and down the street as he interacted with the three individuals, and defendant's contact with the individuals was very brief. U.S.C.A. Const.Amend. 4.—State v. Hankerson, 65 So.3d 502, revised on rehearing, certiorari denied 132 S.Ct. 1636, 565 U.S. 1236, 182 L.Ed.2d 237.

Fla. 1995. Confidential informant's tip, indicating that person standing on particular street corner was selling cocaine that he kept in his pants pocket wrapped in rolled-up one dollar bills, together with police officer's observation of defendant, who matched informant's description, standing on same street corner ten minutes later, gave officer probable cause for warrantless search and arrest of defendant; informant had provided officer with reliable tips in the past, informant's personal knowledge could be inferred from details that he provided, and recent activity observed by police could be used to verify informant's tip. U.S.C.A. Const.Amend. 4.—State v. Butler, 655 So.2d 1123.

---

† **This Case was not selected for publication in the National Reporter System**

Fla. 1992. Totality of circumstances gave police officer probable cause to believe that suspect was carrying crack cocaine in his groin area, for purpose of seizure, where the suspect exited the vehicle in a suspicious manner, officer observed large bulge in groin area which suspect attempted to hide, and officer had knowledge acquired through specific experience with the unique texture of crack cocaine as well as with concealment in the groin area; moreover, size, shape, and texture of package severely limited possibility that package contained substance other than crack cocaine.—Doctor v. State, 596 So.2d 442.

Fla.App. 1 Dist. 2019. The odor of burnt cannabis emanating from a vehicle constitutes probable cause to search all occupants of that vehicle. U.S. Const. Amend. 4.—Hilliard v. State, 285 So.3d 1022.

Fla.App. 1 Dist. 2018. Officer had probable cause to believe defendant was in possession of marijuana to support warrantless search of defendant's person, where an off-duty officer smelled marijuana confined to defendant's location, off-duty officer observed defendant smoking what appeared to be a marijuana cigarette, a second officer noted the smell of burnt marijuana coming from the area occupied by defendant, and officer witnessed defendant smoking what appeared to be a marijuana blunt. U.S. Const. Amend. 4.—Dawson v. State, 253 So.3d 766.

Fla.App. 1 Dist. 1993. Confidential informant's tip that he had seen large amount of cocaine in car did not justify pat-down search of defendant, absent reasonable belief on part of officer that defendant was armed and presented threat to officer's safety; reasonableness requirement was not met by sole fact that defendant was suspected of dealing in large quantity of drugs and large sums of money. U.S.C.A. Const. Amend. 4.—Alexander v. State, 616 So.2d 540.

Fla.App. 1 Dist. 1989. Fact that officer received uncorroborated tip from anonymous informer that defendant was trying to sell crack cocaine and officer's prior arrest of defendant for possessing cocaine some five months earlier did not rise to the level of probable cause to believe that defendant personally possessed cocaine on instant occasion and did not establish probable cause to conduct warrantless search.—Key v. State, 553 So.2d 301.

Fla.App. 1 Dist. 1988. Seizure of cocaine from defendant's person was supported by evidence that one of the officers saw defendant "handpassing" something to numerous persons and that confidential informant told officers exactly where on defendant's person the cocaine would be found.—Lindsey v. State, 523 So.2d 180.

Fla.App. 2 Dist. 2021. State failed to demonstrate that police officer had probable cause to arrest defendant or any other basis to justify a search of defendant or his personal belongings, and thus suppression of physical evidence found during search was required; State did not present any evidence regarding what happened during the stop, State did not argue that there was probable cause to arrest and search, State argued there was no arrest, and State did not otherwise address the search that resulted in the discovery of drugs. U.S. Const. Amend. 4.—Brown v. State, 313 So.3d 848.

Fla.App. 2 Dist. 2008. There was no probable cause to support the warrantless search of defendant's person which yielded the firearm and the marijuana; fact that defendant was standing with a group of men surrounded by the odor of burned marijuana was insufficient to supply more than a mere suspicion that defendant was in possession of marijuana, and fact that defendant initially consented to a search of his person and then withdrew that consent did not give the officer probable cause to search for marijuana. U.S.C.A. Const.Amend. 4.—Robinson v. State, 976 So.2d 1229.

Fla.App. 2 Dist. 2006. Search of defendant's person, during which police opened up defendant's undergarment and visually inspected his buttocks, was a "strip search" within meaning of statute governing strip searches; police had not observed defendant place anything in his clothing, officer's purpose in rearranging defendant's clothing was to conduct an inspection in search of possible evidence, and defendant was forced to submit to arrangement of some of his clothing so as to permit visual inspection of his buttocks. U.S.C.A. Const.Amend. 4; West's F.S.A. § 901.211.—Jenkins v. State, 924 So.2d 20, rehearing denied, review granted 944 So.2d 345, decision approved 978 So.2d 116.

Search of defendant's person, during which police opened up defendant's undergarment and visually inspected his buttocks, did not meet requirement of statute that strip searches be performed only where search cannot be observed by public; search was performed in parking lot beside service station adjacent to intersection of two public thoroughfares, there was no indication that any measures were taken to shield search of defendant from public view, and fact that defendant's unclothed buttocks were not exposed to public view was not sufficient to establish compliance with statute. U.S.C.A. Const.Amend. 4; West's F.S.A. § 901.211.—Id.

Fla.App. 2 Dist. 2002. Evidence that drug-sniffing dog alerted police officers to passenger seat after defendant exited vehicle did not give officers probable cause to believe that defendant had drugs on his person. U.S.C.A. Const.Amend. 4.—Cady v. State, 817 So.2d 948.

Fla.App. 2 Dist. 2002. If, during a lawful pat-down for weapons, the totality of the circumstances gives a police officer probable cause to believe the detainee is carrying drugs, the officer may seize them.—Rodriguez v. State, 807 So.2d 130.

Fla.App. 2 Dist. 2001. Record did not establish basis to permit seizure of clear plastic bag from defendant's pocket as result of a "plain feel" during lawful pat down; even though officer claimed he saw corner of clear plastic bag out of pocket and knew marijuana was often carried in such bags, those facts would have given rise to, at most, a mere suspicion that it contained marijuana, which was not enough to seize it. U.S.C.A. Const.Amend. 4.—State v. Miyasato, 805 So.2d 818, stay granted, review denied 807 So.2d 655, mandamus denied 821 So.2d 298.

Fla.App. 2 Dist. 2001. Police officers did not have probable cause to conduct warrantless pat down search of defendant, looking for crack cocaine; officers had observed drug transaction but did not know, at time of search of defendant and another man, whether defendant was the one selling narcotics or was simply a bystander. West's F.S.A. §901.151.—McCloud v. State, 787 So.2d 218.

Fla.App. 2 Dist. 1998. Odor of marijuana gave police officers probable cause to believe that members of group from which odor emanated had marijuana in their possession and, therefore, gave officers probable cause to search each person who was present. U.S.C.A. Const.Amend. 4.—State v. Hernandez, 706 So.2d 66.

† This Case was not selected for publication in the National Reporter System

Fla.App. 2 Dist. 1996. Absent independent evidence of criminal activity apart from the otherwise verified anonymous tip, police officers did not have the required probable cause to conduct patdown search, such that cocaine was improperly seized and should have been suppressed; although officer saw only one car that met tipster's description, officers detected no criminal or suspicious activity as they approached car and, although occupants of car became nervous at mention of narcotics investigation, they did nothing other than to breathe heavily and there were no accompanying actions described that should have led officers to fear for their safety.—Ingram v. State, 674 So.2d 192.

Fla.App. 2 Dist. 1991. Reasonable cause for search of van did not justify search of occupant on ground that she had constructive possession of drugs found in van.—Rogers v. State, 586 So.2d 1148.

Fla.App. 2 Dist. 1991. Information provided by unknown source and not corroborated by additional facts concerning possible drug activity by occupants of red-over-white Cadillac was too vague to support law enforcement officer's stop and search of driver of vehicle meeting that description, even though vehicle was located in area where informant stated occupants were dealing drugs.—Bristol v. State, 584 So.2d 1086.

Fla.App. 2 Dist. 1986. Confidential informant's description of defendant was specific enough to give police officer probable cause to detain and search him for cocaine, where informant told officer that he had observed black male selling cocaine at specific bar, and described suspect's clothing as being all white, and gave specific location of cocaine on suspect's person.—Jones v. State, 498 So.2d 1359.

Fla.App. 3 Dist. 1983. Officer, who watched defendant take from mailbox some all-white capsules which appeared to contain "suspect cocaine," who saw defendant put them in a towel which he "stuck down in his pants," and who was then told by defendant that he had "nothing in the towel," had probable cause to believe that defendant was in possession of controlled substance and thus warrantless search which secured cocaine was constitutionally permissible.—Council v. State, 442 So.2d 1072.

Fla.App. 3 Dist. 1981. Where it was apparent that officers suspected airline passenger before approaching him, i. e., that suspicion was their reason for approaching him, and that their request for consent to search was merely attempt to obviate necessity of summoning agent and dog of United States Customs Service, calling for dog on passenger's refusal to allow search, though less preferable alternative, was totally appropriate under circumstances. U.S.C.A.Const. Amend. 4.—State v. Mosier, 392 So.2d 602, appeal after remand 415 So.2d 771.

Fla.App. 3 Dist. 1974. Officer's observation of bulge of approximately three and one-half inches in length protruding from defendant's pocket was sufficient to support belief that defendant was armed, and pat-down search which led to discovery of syringe was lawful. U.S.C.A.Const. Amends. 4, 14.—Williams v. State, 294 So.2d 37, certiorari denied 299 So.2d 602.

Fla.App. 3 Dist. 1967. Police officer who smelled marijuana smoke emanating from defendants and observed plants in flower bed, alongside defendants' house, which were marijuana, had reasonable grounds to believe that felony had been or was being committed by defendants.—Boim v. State, 194 So.2d 313.

Fla.App. 4 Dist. 2014. The mere scent of marijuana coming from a group of individuals does not by itself give an officer probable cause to arrest and search any particular individual in the group. U.S.C.A. Const.Amend. 4.—State v. J.J., 143 So.3d 1050.

Fla.App. 4 Dist. 2007. Odor of marijuana coming from vehicle provided police officers with probable cause to search defendant, who was passenger in vehicle. U.S.C.A. Const.Amend. 4.—State v. Jennings, 968 So.2d 694.

Fla.App. 4 Dist. 2007. Record supported trial court's determinations that informant who provided information about suspected drug activity to police officer was a citizen informant and that, therefore, informant was a presumptively reliable source, for purpose of determining whether information provided officer with probable cause to conduct warrantless search of defendant, even though officer had never met informant before and did not include any identifying information about him in her police report; officer knew where informant lived and could find him if necessary, and informant went to police station and presented information in person, which allowed officer to better evaluate his credibility. U.S.C.A. Const.Amend. 4.—Chaney v. State, 956 So.2d 535, on remand 2007 WL 6948613.

The state did not show that citizen informant's report that he witnessed what he believed to be drug transactions based on seeing defendant hand items to several persons in exchange for money provided police officer with probable cause to conduct warrantless search of defendant; nothing indicated that location described by informant had any prior history of drug transactions or arrests or that officer had any knowledge of defendant's involvement in drug dealing, nothing showed extent of officer's training and experience in narcotics investigations, officer was uncertain whether informant could actually see any drugs, and officer corroborated information only as to innocent details. U.S.C.A. Const.Amend. 4.—Id.

Fla.App. 4 Dist. 2006. Drug dog's alert on seat and handlebar of bicycle that defendant had been riding did not provide law enforcement officer with probable cause to search defendant. U.S.C.A. Const.Amend. 4.—Rehm v. State, 931 So.2d 1071.

Fla.App. 4 Dist. 2003. Officer's act of smelling burnt marijuana from vehicle that defendant had just exited provided officer with probable cause to both search and detain defendant and vehicle. U.S.C.A. Const.Amend. 4.—State v. T.P., 835 So.2d 1277.

Fla.App. 4 Dist. 2001. Police officer did not provide sufficient information to support his "plain feel" identification of marijuana in plastic bag in suspect's pocket, and thus officer lacked probable cause to seize marijuana, where officer did not testify about his experience in identifying marijuana by its feel, or that there was anything unique or distinctive about the seized item's texture, size, shape, or method of packaging that made the illicit nature of the item immediately apparent to him, and officer did not testify about any other circumstances, such as furtive gestures, that would have given rise to probable cause; officer merely described item as plastic-type bag with some substance inside of it that could possibly be marijuana. U.S.C.A. Const.Amend. 4.—State v. J.D., 796 So.2d 1217.

Fla.App. 4 Dist. 1996. Police had probable cause to stop suspect, to conduct inquiry, and to search for drugs, based on information from confidential informant that suspect was carrying amount of illegal drugs on his person sufficient to constitute trafficking, which was consistent with developed facts, on telephone conversation monitored by officer that evidenced drug trafficking conspiracy. U.S.C.A. Const.Amend. 4.—Echeverria v. State, 668 So.2d 1103.

Fla.App. 4 Dist. 1991. Officer's seeing rolling papers in defendant's shirt pocket, without more, was insufficient basis upon which to conduct search. U.S.C.A. Const.Amend. 4.—Sites v. State, 582 So.2d 813.

Fla.App. 4 Dist. 1991. "Peanut brittle" feel of bulge in defendant's groin area gave law enforcement officer probable cause to believe the bulge was cocaine rocks, and, thus, officer could seize rocks as evidence of crime. U.S.C.A. Const. Amend. 4; West's F.S.A. § 901.151(5).—Doctor v. State, 573 So.2d 157, decision approved in part, quashed in part 596 So.2d 442.

Fla.App. 4 Dist. 1988. There was no adequate justification for search of defendant for drugs without either warrant or legal arrest; confidential informant had advised officer that defendant and his girl friend were actively selling narcotics out of their automobile, officer was in contact with informant almost daily, and officer did not stop defendant's vehicle and search him until more than ten days later.—Phillips v. State, 531 So.2d 1044.

Fla.App. 5 Dist. 2017. To a trained and experienced police officer, the smell of cannabis emanating from a person or a vehicle gives the police officer probable cause to search the person or the vehicle. U.S. Const. Amend. 4.—State v. Harris, 230 So.3d 1285.

Fla.App. 5 Dist. 2013. Police officer had probable cause to conduct warrantless search of defendant for drugs, where defendant admitted to officer that he had cocaine in his pocket. U.S.C.A. Const.Amend. 4.—State v. Janusheske, 111 So.3d 967.

Fla.App. 5 Dist. 1997. Police officer had probable cause to search defendant; informant, who was reasonably believed to be involved in sale of cocaine based on affidavit and search warrant indicating presence of drugs on informant's premises, stated defendant possessed cocaine and defendant was found on premises where cocaine was allegedly being sold. U.S.C.A. Const.Amend. 4.—Boydell v. State, 690 So.2d 745.

Fla.App. 5 Dist. 1997. Pat-down of defendant for weapons was improper, but nonetheless officers had probable cause to search him for illegal drugs, and thus search was proper even though the officers, believing that they lacked probable cause, conducted improper weapons search to enhance their claim of probable cause; officer who had received training and identification of narcotics and who had received complaints of narcotics dealing in vicinity of store, together with another officer, observed for period of two hours during which defendant would approach vehicles, lean into the vehicle and pass something to the occupants, and would then be seen with cash in hand, even though items passed to the occupants of the vehicles were too small to be seen from officers' hiding place.—Knox v. State, 689 So.2d 1224.

Fla.App. 5 Dist. 1994. Totality of the circumstances established probable cause for warrantless search of defendant and seizure of lysergic acid diethylamide (LSD); confidential identified informant, described type and location of crime, container drug was in, gave defendant's first name and positively identified defendant, and

investigators were able to independently verify facts which supported observations of informant. —Silva v. State, 641 So.2d 482.

Fla.App. 5 Dist. 1991. Probable cause for warrantless search existed based on information provided by confidential informant and conversation which officers overheard through monitoring device carried by confidential informant concerning a potential cocaine sale.—State v. Fountain, 589 So.2d 1388.

⊗601. —— **Clothing, shoes, and hats.**

Fla.App. 1 Dist. 1988. Police had probable cause for warrantless search of individual in whose pocket rock cocaine was discovered; confidential informant, who had previously provided reliable information leading to discovery of rock cocaine and subsequent arrests about six times, stated individual of particular description was in possession of $50 worth of rock cocaine at particular location at 10:49 p.m., search of individual matching that description occurred at approximately 10:52 p.m., and firsthand basis of knowledge could reasonably be inferred under the circumstances.—Hopkins v. State, 524 So.2d 1136, review denied 531 So.2d 1353.

Fla.App. 1 Dist. 1977. Officer lacked probable cause to believe defendant was about to commit a crime and, therefore, defendant was entitled to suppression of marijuana seized in search of defendant's person where defendant, while walking one morning through an alley of a commercial area, attracted attention of arresting officer by taking something out of his hat and bending down and putting it in his shoe and where officer testified that defendant's manner aroused the officer's suspicion and "the only thing I could think of he'd be putting down there was a weapon"; circumstances did not give rise to probable cause to believe that defendant was armed with a dangerous weapon and search which ensued when officer approached defendant and ordered him to remove his shoe was unlawful.—Conner v. State, 349 So.2d 709.

Fla.App. 2 Dist. 2009. Police officer lacked probable cause to search defendant's pockets, and thus contraband found in defendant's pockets was inadmissible during prosecution for possession of cocaine and possession of drug paraphernalia; pat down search of defendant for weapons did not reveal any weapons, officer stated that he did not feel any items during pat down search that he believed were contraband, after pat down officer asked defendant for consent to search his pockets, defendant did not respond to the officer's request, and officer emptied defendant's pockets. U.S.C.A. Const.Amend. 4.—Wynn v. State, 14 So.3d 1094.

Fla.App. 2 Dist. 2003. Officer did not have probable cause based on confidential informant's tip to search suspect and seize baggies from suspect's pocket, although officer had used informant in the past and informant's information was consistent with observations officer had made, where no evidence existed as to informant's basis of knowledge, temporary proximity between tip and officer locating suspect was not established, and only details that officer could corroborate were innocent details that were easily accessible to general public. U.S.C.A. Const.Amend. 4.— Owens v. State, 854 So.2d 737.

Fla.App. 2 Dist. 1983. In view of testimony by deputy that nurse did not tell him, prior to his search of defendant's jacket pockets, that she had discovered a bag containing a white substance in pockets of defendant, who had been injured and

---

† This Case was not selected for publication in the National Reporter System

brought to hospital for treatment, there was no probable cause for deputy's search. U.S.C.A. Const.Amend. 4.—McCombs v. State, 433 So.2d 4.

Fla.App. 3 Dist. 2009. Police officer, under totality of circumstances, did not have probable cause based on tip from reliable and credible informant to search defendant by reaching into his left front pocket and seizing sandwich bag with sixteen suspected rocks of crack cocaine; although informant told officer defendant was standing on specific street corner selling narcotics, described defendant, including what he was wearing, and told officer narcotics were inside defendant's left front pocket, there was no evidence that location described by informant had prior history of drug transactions or arrests, that officer had any prior knowledge of defendant's involvement in drug dealing, officer was uncertain whether informant could actually see drugs being exchanged for money, did not conduct any surveillance or acquire additional information to confirm informant's report of suspected drug activity, officers corroborated tip only as to physical description of location and suspects, and informant only described one hand-to-hand transaction. U.S.C.A. Const.Amend. 4.—Mathis v. State, 8 So.3d 445, rehearing denied.

Fla.App. 4 Dist. 2000. Police officer had probable cause to believe that item felt during patdown search was cocaine, rendering retrieval of baggy of cocaine from defendant's pocket permissible under "plain feel" exception to warrant requirement, where anonymous tip had indicated that defendant was going to have 28 grams of cocaine in his pocket, officer had verified accuracy of other information in tip by time of pat-down search, and officer detected object that was hard and had a "powdery feel," consistent with the tipster's prediction.—Campuzano v. State, 771 So.2d 1238.

☞602. Particular places in general.

Fla. 1980. Where sheriff went without warrant to farm leased by defendant, and after finding gate locked, climbed fence surrounding farm, walked 250 yards to one of several tobacco barns identified by confidential informant as containing marijuana, peered through window with aid of flashlight and saw substance which sheriff identified as marijuana wrapped in tobacco sheets, and sheriff subsequently testified that at time of search he did not have sufficient probable cause to obtain search warrant, such search violated defendant's constitutional right against unreasonable searches and seizures. U.S.C.A.Const. Amends. 4, 14, 14, § 1; West's F.S.A.Const. art. 1, § 12.—Norman v. State, 379 So.2d 643.

Fla.App. 2 Dist. 1996. Deputies' walking on property of person later charged with manufacture of controlled substance, to observe marijuana, was not an illegal entry.—Abel v. State, 668 So.2d 1121.

Fla.App. 3 Dist. 1983. Communications from United States Customs Officers directing county sheriff's deputies to a certain location where they found bales of marijuana were insufficient to establish probable cause to support a search of the location, absent evidence that would furnish a basis for the customs officers' conclusion that marijuana would be found at the location.— Morejon v. State, 431 So.2d 315.

Fla.App. 3 Dist. 1981. Seizure of narcotics from area where undercover purchase had been made by undercover officer moments before

search was not unlawful because warrantless.— State v. McGoey, 399 So.2d 495.

Fla.App. 3 Dist. 1978. Where various law enforcement agencies received telephone call saying that boat was operating in channel without running lights and there was also a report of at least three boats and a camper on shore, upon arrival at scene, officer saw various persons walking from boats to beach with bales of some substance, and officers went on property with permission of caretaker, who was present when officers made arrests and seized contraband, seizure of contraband was lawful.—Aguiar v. State, 363 So.2d 634, certiorari denied 372 So.2d 466.

Fla.App. 4 Dist. 2014. Where the person to be searched is part of a group, in order for there to be probable cause to search, the odor of marijuana must be individualized. U.S.C.A. Const. Amend. 4.—State v. J.J., 143 So.3d 1050.

☞604. —— In general.

† C.A.11 (Fla.) 2009. Probable cause and exigent circumstances justified warrantless intrusion into residence of individual suspected of possessing narcotics; officers reasonably believed that narcotics were present and might be destroyed before warrant could be secured, and intrusion was limited and directly proportional to exigency of case. U.S.C.A. Const.Amend. 4.—U.S. v. Thomas, 348 Fed.Appx. 497.

C.A.11 (Fla.) 1983. Danger to officers presented by fleeing suspects after officers entered property where marijuana was being off-loaded justified exploratory search of residence and vehicles to assure that no one lay in waiting for officers.—U.S. v. Blasco, 702 F.2d 1315, certiorari denied Galvan v. U.S., 104 S.Ct. 275, 464 U.S. 914, 78 L.Ed.2d 256, certiorari denied Jamardo v. U.S., 104 S.Ct. 276, 464 U.S. 914, 78 L.Ed.2d 256.

Fla. 2011. Probable cause, not reasonable suspicion, is the proper evidentiary showing of wrongdoing that the government must make under the Fourth Amendment prior to conducting a "sniff test" by a drug detection dog at a private residence. U.S.C.A. Const.Amend. 4.—Jardines v. State, 73 So.3d 34, rehearing denied, stay denied 2011 WL 13491657, certiorari granted in part 132 S.Ct. 995, 565 U.S. 1104, 181 L.Ed.2d 726, affirmed 133 S.Ct. 1409, 569 U.S. 1, 185 L.Ed.2d 495.

Fla.App. 1 Dist. 1976. Where defendant was observed removing intercepted letter containing cocaine from rural mailbox that officers had been observing, officers saw defendant walk up dirt road into vicinity of frame dwelling, defendant's cohort was heard yelling "It's a raid. It's a raid," while blowing his automobile's horn, ensuing search of frame dwelling was legally justified on basis that officers observed defendant commit crime of illegally possessing cocaine and that there was strong reason to believe that defendant and other occupants of dwelling were about to destroy the cocaine.—Winters v. State, 332 So.2d 46, certiorari denied 341 So.2d 1087.

Fla.App. 3 Dist. 1979. Where police, who received radio call regarding a van being backed up to a residence which was temporarily unoccupied, sighted such a van in close proximity to given address, police were justified in entering front yard to investigate a possible burglary; inasmuch as police were lawfully on property, their looking into back of open vehicle and observing bales of marijuana did not constitute a search and, upon observing defendants through open window sitting around bales of marijuana

† This Case was not selected for publication in the National Reporter System

apparently smoking marijuana, police had probable cause to search premises.—State v. Garcia, 374 So.2d 601.

Fla.App. 3 Dist. 1975. Where evidence sought, pursuant to information received from a reliable confidential informant, consisted of packets of heroin, and where sounds of running feet and running toilet water were very audible at time police officers arrived at address and knocked on front and back doors, it was very plausible for officers to conclude that toilet facilities simply were not being utilized for their normally intended purpose, but were being used to destroy evidence, and to thereupon break and enter dwelling without announcement. West's F.S.A. § 901.19(1).—State v. English, 308 So.2d 636, certiorari denied 316 So.2d 287.

Fla.App. 4 Dist. 1997. Narcotics officers who arrived at scene of valid warrantless entry into defendant's residence did not need warrant to continue to exercise police function which road patrol officers had begun, as road patrol officers could have legally seized evidence at time of narcotics officers' arrival; second "entry" was part of one continuous episode.—State v. Craycraft, 704 So.2d 593, rehearing denied.

Fla.App. 4 Dist. 1996. Even when they have probable cause, police officers may not enter a dwelling without warrant, absent consent or exigent circumstances. U.S.C.A. Const.Amend. 4.—Levine v. State, 684 So.2d 903.

Fla.App. 4 Dist. 1980. Where undercover police officers consensually entered premises, negotiations took place for sale of contraband, contraband was present on premises, and one officer had constructive possession of contraband, actual physical possession of contraband was not prerequisite to admissibility of 16 ounces of cocaine. —Lawrence v. State, 388 So.2d 1250, decision approved Griffin v. State, 419 So.2d 320.

Where undercover police officers were properly on premises viewing contraband which was for sale, there was delivery of contraband to undercover police officers already present on premises and officer to whom contraband was delivered retained constructive possession thereof, police were not required to have judge standing by to issue search warrant, nor were they required to leave premises and obtain search warrant upon receipt of cocaine.—Id.

⚬⟐**605.** —— **Houses and homes in general.**

C.A.11 (Fla.) 2024. Unless warrant is obtained or exigency exists, any physical invasion of home's structure, by even fraction of inch, is too much for Fourth Amendment purposes. U.S. Const. Amend. 4.—Bailey v. Swindell, 89 F.4th 1324.

† **C.A.11 (Fla.) 2015.** Police officers' protective sweep of defendant's rented bedroom was reasonable after officers conducted search of home's common areas upon consent of homeowner, where home was small, making ambush attack possible, bedroom was visible from living area, officers believed room harbored individual posing danger to them, officers had received tip from confidential informant that male who sold heroin and carried gun was living in house, and officers found speed loaders, bullets, and drug paraphernalia upon entering home. U.S.C.A. Const.Amend. 4.—U.S. v. Medina, 631 Fed.Appx. 682, certiorari denied 136 S.Ct. 1397, 577 U.S. 1201, 194 L.Ed.2d 375, post-conviction relief denied 2018 WL 11201417, affirmed in part, vacated in part, remanded 797 Fed.Appx. 431.

† **C.A.11 (Fla.) 2010.** Drug Enforcement Agency (DEA) officers took reasonable steps to contact defendant on his property, and thus did not trigger the protections of the Fourth Amendment by approaching a barn to conduct a warrantless "knock and talk" visit, where they entered the property through an open gate, intending to contact defendant at his house, and, upon learning that defendant had moved to the barn, they changed plans and followed him there. U.S.C.A. Const.Amend. 4.—U.S. v. Diaz, 404 Fed.Appx. 381.

† **C.A.11 (Fla.) 2009.** Evidence that marijuana was being grown in two houses permitted law enforcement agents to approach those houses to verify or dispel their suspicions of criminal activity. U.S.C.A. Const.Amend. 14.—U.S. v. Correa, 347 Fed.Appx. 541, rehearing and rehearing denied 451 Fed.Appx. 908, post-conviction relief denied U.S. v. Renteria, 2014 WL 5148209, post-conviction relief denied 2014 WL 5148214.

† **C.A.11 (Fla.) 2009.** The combination of probable cause and exigent circumstances justified law enforcement officers' warrantless entry into mobile home; after marijuana field was spotted by helicopter surveillance, officers knocked on the doors of nearby mobile home and announced their presence, and an officer smelled marijuana emanating from a window air conditioner and heard someone running about inside the mobile home, but the person inside refused to open the door. U.S.C.A. Const.Amend. 4.—U.S. v. Reed, 318 Fed.Appx. 774, post-conviction relief denied 2012 WL 1559682.

C.A.11 (Fla.) 1991. Warrantless search of defendants' house was justified where government agent saw one defendant hand shopping bag to informant and saw informant give prearranged signal indicating that bag contained cocaine, defendant then entered house and when agents entered house they discovered defendant attempting to destroy several kilograms of cocaine; agent witnessed defendant commit crime in his presence when he handed bag to informant and even though pursuit ended almost as soon as it began, it could nevertheless be characterized as "hot pursuit." U.S.C.A. Const.Amend. 4.—U.S. v. Ramos, 933 F.2d 968, certiorari denied 112 S.Ct. 1269, 503 U.S. 908, 117 L.Ed.2d 496.

C.A.11 (Fla.) 1991. Warrantless entry into defendant's house was justifiable where undercover agents, prior to their approach to house, observed defendants behave suspiciously, look about furtively, and quickly transfer tubular bags containing smaller bundles from car trunk into garage, where agents knew that at least two persons were in house but, based on number of vehicles on premises, could have believed that house contained more than two persons, and where agent smelled odor of marijuana in house after defendant voluntarily opened door in response to agent's knocks and requests to talk with occupants of house. U.S.C.A. Const.Amend. 4.—U.S. v. Tobin, 923 F.2d 1506, rehearing denied 935 F.2d 1297, certiorari denied 112 S.Ct. 299, 502 U.S. 907, 116 L.Ed.2d 243.

Where warrantless entry into defendant's home was justifiable, search of garage and seizure of cocaine found therein was permissible under Fourth Amendment. U.S.C.A. Const.Amend. 4.—Id.

C.A.11 (Fla.) 1989. Search of defendant's house was illegal, where officers did not have probable cause when they approached house and probable cause did not exist until agents smelled marijuana after defendant opened door.

† **This Case was not selected for publication in the National Reporter System**

U.S.C.A. Const.Amend. 4.—U.S. v. Tobin, 890 F.2d 319, rehearing granted, vacated 902 F.2d 821, on rehearing 923 F.2d 1506, rehearing denied 935 F.2d 1297, certiorari denied 112 S.Ct. 299, 502 U.S. 907, 116 L.Ed.2d 243.

C.A.11 (Fla.) 1983. Although agents followed van from dock area where informant said marijuana would be unloaded and observed marijuana in the van while parked outside house and noted marijuana strewn from van to front door, warrantless search of the residence was not justified where there was no evidence that occupants were aware of surveillance, several agents were present in the area and warrant could have been obtained by telephone despite lateness of the hour.—U.S. v. Torres, 705 F.2d 1287, opinion vacated 718 F.2d 998, on remand 720 F.2d 1506, appeal after remand 741 F.2d 1323.

C.A.5 (Fla.) 1977. Where, although Drug Enforcement Administration knew in advance that defendant and his wife were involved in the drug trade, agents only anticipated that supply of drugs would be at defendant's home, at least some of cocaine was thought to be stored in an automobile, and premature raid would "tip the hand" of agents, Drug Enforcement Administration was justified in not seeking search warrant before informer, who had named defendant's wife as his source, arrived in town.—U.S. v. Gardner, 553 F.2d 946, rehearing denied 559 F.2d 29, certiorari denied 98 S.Ct. 722, 434 U.S. 1011, 54 L.Ed.2d 753.

M.D.Fla. 2001. Police officers lacked probable cause for their entry and sweep search of defendant's home based on tip provided by anonymous informant who had stated that defendant would receive large amount of cocaine at certain time from very dark, thin, black male and provided police with defendant's name, address, telephone numbers, and vehicle descriptions; police only retrieved booking photo of defendant and went to address stated in tip without corroborating any other information, and anonymous informant had given no information indicating her reliability such as how she obtained information or whether she based her tip on first-hand knowledge. U.S.C.A. Const.Amend. 4.—U.S. v. Davis, 170 F.Supp.2d 1234.

S.D.Fla. 2012. Police officers had probable cause to conduct warrantless search of suspect's residence and arrest suspect's boyfriend for possession of marijuana, where officers smelled marijuana emanating from suspect's residence and saw suspect's boyfriend holding marijuana joint. U.S.C.A. Const.Amend. 4.—Feliciano v. City of Miami Beach, 847 F.Supp.2d 1359.

Fla.App. 1 Dist. 2022. A small amount of drugs in someone's trash does not reliably signal that more contraband would be found inside their home, for purposes of establishing probable cause to search the home. U.S. Const. Amend. 4; Fla. Const. art. 1, § 12.—State v. Green, 349 So.3d 503.

Fla.App. 1 Dist. 1978. Police officers' entry into home of defendant without announcing authority and purpose was unlawful where defendant had no reason to know of undercover agent's authority prior to entry, where officers could not have had any reasonable belief that their peril would have increased had they first demanded entrance and where there was no reasonable ground for belief that had officers delayed their entry a few seconds and announced their authority, the large quantity of marijuana involved would have been destroyed. West's

F.S.A. § 901.19(1).—King v. State, 371 So.2d 120, certiorari denied 378 So.2d 349.

Fla.App. 1 Dist. 1975. Police officers who went to defendant's home at 3:00 a. m. to recover marked money allegedly used to purchase drugs and to effectuate defendant's arrest for "conspiracy and violation of the drug laws" did not have probable cause to conduct warrantless general search of defendant's house before arresting defendant. U.S.C.A.Const. Amend. 4; West's F.S.A.Const. art. 1, § 12.—Hannigan v. State, 307 So.2d 850, certiorari denied 315 So.2d 195.

Fla.App. 2 Dist. 2012. "Plain smell" doctrine did not apply to police officers who obtained defendant's consent to enter defendant's fenced and gated property in order to talk to him on the other side of the gate, and who then proceeded to residence where they smelled marijuana; while officers were free to approach gate to conduct a knock and talk, which they did, the area inside the fence fell under the same constitutional protections as the residence itself, and the officers were not at liberty, absent consent, to approach the residence. U.S.C.A. Const.Amend. 4.—Ferrer v. State, 113 So.3d 860.

Fla.App. 2 Dist. 2011. Defendant had a reasonable expectation of privacy, for Fourth Amendment purposes, in a house he had lived in for a month with his girlfriend and pets, and in which he was growing marijuana. U.S.C.A. Const. Amend. 4.—Nieminski v. State, 60 So.3d 521.

Fla.App. 2 Dist. 1975. Where patient in hospital, a young girl, was suffering from overdose of drugs, and it was necessary, for treatment, to obtain sample of drugs taken by her, and policeman found second young girl who had given the drugs to her, and second young girl, who was beginning to show overdose symptoms, led policeman to unoccupied house from which the drugs had been taken, policeman acted lawfully in entering house and taking drugs found therein. West's F.S.A. § 893.13.—Long v. State, 310 So.2d 35.

Fla.App. 3 Dist. 2008. The presence of police officer with a drug detector dog at defendant's front door, pursuant to a tip that defendant was using home to grow marijuana and after officer observed that no vehicles were in the driveway and that the windows had blinds closed, did not infringe defendant's right of privacy for Fourth Amendment purposes. U.S.C.A. Const.Amend. 4. —State v. Jardines, 9 So.3d 1, review granted 3 So.3d 1246, quashed 73 So.3d 34, rehearing denied, stay denied 2011 WL 13491657, certiorari granted in part 132 S.Ct. 995, 565 U.S. 1104, 181 L.Ed.2d 726, affirmed 133 S.Ct. 1409, 569 U.S. 1, 185 L.Ed.2d 495.

Requiring either a warrant or reasonable suspicion after a dog detects contraband addresses the concern about the unreliability of dog sniffs by requiring articulable facts pointing to existence of drug activity within the dwelling; in the event of a positive alert by the dog, the affidavit in support of the search warrant for the search of the home will then include the articulable facts plus the sniff, not just the sniff alone. U.S.C.A. Const. Amend. 4.—Id.

Fla.App. 3 Dist. 1988. Arresting officers were not required to "knock and announce" after undercover officer had gone with defendant into house where drugs were located, inspected the package of cocaine, then returned to his car for money, signaled officers that he had seen the cocaine, returned unarmed to the house, the door closing behind him, after which the police broke

† This Case was not selected for publication in the National Reporter System

down the door and entered the house. West's F.S.A. § 901.19(1).—Houston v. State, 528 So.2d 940.

Fla.App. 3 Dist. 1979. Where officer gained entrance to defendant's home while posing as potential buyer of marijuana, inspected marijuana which he recognized as contraband and detained defendant and others and then gathered marijuana which he had previously inspected and identified, officer's warrantless seizure of such evidence was constitutionally permissible, notwithstanding that officers awaiting outside had entered defendant's home prior to seizure without warrant and without knocking or announcing their authority or purpose. West's F.S.A. § 901.19(1); U.S.C.A.Const. Amend. 4; West's F.S.A.Const. art. 1, § 12.—Preces v. State, 378 So.2d 77, certiorari denied 388 So.2d 1117, certiorari denied 101 S.Ct. 569, 449 U.S. 1012, 66 L.Ed.2d 471.

Fla.App. 3 Dist. 1973. Where police officers, seeking to serve defendant with warrant for arrest on previous drug charge, went to defendant's home, knocked, shouted "police officers," and waited about ten minutes before forcing their way into defendant's home and conducting search and subsequent seizure of narcotics and narcotic implements found there, search and seizure were illegal because officers had not announced purpose for their being at defendant's home prior to search and seizure. F.S.A. § 901.19(1).—Moreno v. State, 277 So.2d 81.

Fla.App. 4 Dist. 2011. Because State did not prove that some reasonable belief of exigency existed, a warrant should have been obtained before police entry into defendant's backyard, and because no warrant was obtained, and exigency exception to warrant requirement was not applicable, any evidence obtained as result of police entry should have been suppressed, and this included observation of drugs in house, which led to sweep of the home; officers entered curtilage of home to investigate acting solely on anonymous tip of narcotics activity, only corroborated the tip to the extent that white car was in front of the home, and had no indication from viewing the scene that a crime had been, was being, or would be committed, and when officers arrived at the scene, there did not appear to be anyone in sight that might have gun. U.S.C.A. Const.Amend. 4.—Bryan v. State, 62 So.3d 1244.

Fla.App. 4 Dist. 2006. Dog sniff by trained drug-detection canine at exterior door of defendant's home was an illegal search under Fourth Amendment; dog's sense of smell crossed the firm line of Fourth Amendment protection at door of home, and smell of marijuana detected by dog was an intimate detail of home. U.S.C.A. Const. Amend. 4.—State v. Rabb, 920 So.2d 1175, review denied 933 So.2d 522, certiorari denied 127 S.Ct. 665, 549 U.S. 1052, 166 L.Ed.2d 513.

The fact that conduct in a house, such as growing marijuana, is not constitutionally protected does not lessen the violation of search and seizure provision of Fourth Amendment occurring when law enforcement uses sensory enhancement to intrude across the firm line at the door of a house and perceive its intimate details. U.S.C.A. Const.Amend. 4.—Id.

Fla.App. 4 Dist. 2004. Use of drug-detecting dog by law enforcement officers to detect contraband in defendant's house constituted illegal search; it was not likely that officers would have detected odor of marijuana emanating from within house if they had not brought dog, and thus use of dog allowed officers to intrude into house

and violated defendant's expectation of privacy in his retreat. U.S.C.A. Const.Amend. 4; West's F.S.A. Const. Art. 1, § 12.—State v. Rabb, 881 So.2d 587, rehearing denied, certiorari granted, vacated 125 S.Ct. 2246, 544 U.S. 1028, 161 L.Ed.2d 1051, on remand 920 So.2d 1175, review denied 933 So.2d 522, certiorari denied 127 S.Ct. 665, 549 U.S. 1052, 166 L.Ed.2d 513.

Fla.App. 4 Dist. 1997. Police officer's warrantless entry into back entrance and corridor of rooming house where drugs were discovered in kitchen was improper without consent from one of the occupants, despite the absence of door or lock on back entrance and the presence in kitchen of nonresidents who may not have received explicit permission to enter. U.S.C.A. Const. Amend. 4.—Titus v. State, 696 So.2d 1257, review granted 700 So.2d 687, decision approved 707 So.2d 706.

Fla.App. 4 Dist. 1997. Seizure of marijuana, which child obtained from defendant's office located in child's home, was improper, even though child did not tell police that she was not allowed to go into office, where child was told that office was off limits to her, child entered office and discovered marijuana, child called police who asked her to obtain sample of marijuana, and child obtained sample for police analysis. U.S.C.A. Const.Amend. 4.—Elson v. State, 688 So.2d 465.

Fla.App. 4 Dist. 1988. Search of defendant's house after detective had illegally searched bathroom was not consensual and was per se violation of Fourth Amendment, where officers had entered house to arrest visitor, where one police officer went into bathroom and brought visitor out, where detective then illegally searched bathroom and found white powder, and where detective then asked for permission to search house and explained that police could obtain search warrant on strength of powder and baggie seen in bathroom and that defendant would be held for three or four hours needed to obtain warrant. U.S.C.A. Const.Amend. 4.—Horvath v. State, 524 So.2d 741.

Fla.App. 4 Dist. 1982. Suppression was required of marijuana seized from the garage of defendants' home without a warrant under the circumstances wherein a warrant could obviously have been secured. U.S.C.A.Const.Amend. 4.—State v. Loomis, 418 So.2d 482.

Fla.App. 4 Dist. 1980. Observation of open doors to shed and to private residence by police officer, in light of recent burglary of adjacent premises, furnished probable cause to support entry and search of shed and private residence.—Guin v. City of Riviera Beach, 388 So.2d 604.

Fla.App. 4 Dist. 1980. Where police, who located boat described by undisclosed informant as containing marijuana, observed no activity, their initial entry onto premises was unlawful as was search of the boat and the house, which followed discovery of marijuana residue on boat, notwithstanding that individuals who departed residence acknowledged that they were not the owners and did not know name of owner or that one officer suspected that house may have been burglarized, as there was no visible indication thereof or reported burglary and the three defendants did not exit in an unusual fashion. U.S.C.A.Const. Amends. 4, 14.—Daley v. State, 387 So.2d 971, cause remanded 392 So.2d 1327, on remand 398 So.2d 840.

Fla.App. 5 Dist. 1989. Probable cause and exigent circumstances existed for warrantless search of home, including closet, which resulted in discovey of marijuana plants growing in large terrarium, where police were informed by neighbor that occupants of house were out of town and that front door was open, and police made thorough search of house looking for possible burglar. U.S.C.A. Const.Amend. 4.—State v. Haines, 543 So.2d 1278.

Fla.App. 5 Dist. 1980. Reasonableness of officers' seizure of bag of marijuana after it fell to kitchen floor when defendant took his hand out of his pocket depended upon validity of incursion by the officers into defendant's home.—Taylor v. State, 381 So.2d 255, certiorari denied 386 So.2d 642.

⟳**606. —— Apartments and condominiums.**

† **C.A.11 (Fla.) 2006.** Government agents had probable cause to believe that they would find ecstasy (MDMA) at apartment defendant shared with her boyfriend, as required to support warrantless search of apartment; pursuant to a several-month investigation, defendant's boyfriend was arrested after selling 30,000 MDMA tablets to undercover officers, just before the arrest he told the officers that he could deliver 10,000 more tablets the next day, and when agents knocked on door of apartment, defendant asked agents to wait while she got dressed, then went out the back door of the apartment, wearing only a towel and carrying a bag. U.S.C.A. Const.Amend. 4.— U.S. v. Klinkosz, 163 Fed.Appx. 827.

C.A.11 (Fla.) 1996. Probable cause and exigent circumstances justified warrantless entry into apartment at which tipster had indicated that crack cocaine was being manufactured; following stop of car occupied by individuals who just left apartment, officers gathered several bags and numerous chunks of suspected cocaine which had been thrown from car during chase, officers could have reasonably suspected that crack cocaine might remain in apartment because cocaine they gathered was not in form of crack cocaine, and one of individuals was seen talking on cellular phone during pursuit and could have been instructing person remaining in apartment to destroy cocaine and other related evidence. U.S.C.A. Const.Amend. 4.—U.S. v. Mikell, 102 F.3d 470, certiorari denied Young v. U.S., 117 S.Ct. 1459, 520 U.S. 1181, 137 L.Ed.2d 563.

C.A.11 (Fla.) 1989. Defendant's statements to undercover informant over telephone and while in defendant's apartment gave agents probable cause to believe that cocaine remained in apartment after defendant was arrested and, combined with exigent circumstances of danger of destruction of evidence, justified agents' warrantless entry into apartment and seizure of apartment until warrant could be obtained; defendant told informant in telephone conversation that he had two kilograms of cocaine in apartment, that the packages were for another buyer, agents knew that occupants of car, including defendant, were expected back at apartment in about one hour, and, when car was stopped and searched, agents discovered mobile telephone in "on" position. U.S.C.A. Const.Amend. 4.—U.S. v. Morales, 868 F.2d 1562.

C.A.5 (Fla.) 1981. Where government agents lacked both arrest warrant for one occupant and search warrant when they entered apartment, where neither of apartment's occupants consented to agents' entry, and where there were no exigent circumstances to justify warrantless entry, agents' initial entry into apartment, at which one occupant had allegedly delivered cocaine to codefendant, was illegal.—U.S. v. Congote, 656 F.2d 971.

Assuming that government agents conducted occupant search immediately upon entering apartment where cocaine was allegedly delivered by one occupant to codefendant and then removed occupants, and assuming that there was no reason for agents to remain inside apartment, their doing so violated Fourth Amendment right of occupant who leased apartment. U.S.C.A.Const. Amend. 4.—Id.

Assuming that only call concerning cocaine known by government agents to have transpired over lessee's telephone was staged, call made by codefendant to another occupant of apartment from police station, and assuming that agents inside apartment lacked search warrant, agents by answering telephone grossly exceeded Assistant United States Attorney's instructions merely to secure apartment and violated lessee's Fourth Amendment rights. U.S.C.A.Const. Amend. 4.— Id.

C.A.5 (Fla.) 1974. Where officers had information from reliable informant that defendants were in midst of drug transaction, and officers and defendants knew that substantial quantity of cocaine was located on table in living room of apartment, failure of officers to announce their purpose before forcing their way into apartment after, by ruse, occupant opened door a crack did not constitute an unlawful intrusion prohibited by statute requiring officers to identify themselves and announce their purpose before breaking open door or window. 18 U.S.C.A. § 3109.—U.S. v. Seelig, 498 F.2d 109.

S.D.Fla. 2014. Probable cause and exigent circumstances existed to conduct warrantless entry into defendant's apartment after he voluntarily opened door for them, based on the illegal narcotics activity in plain view when door was opened, codefendant's hesitation to exit the unit, the layout of the apartment, and the inherent risk of destruction of evidence in narcotics cases. U.S. Const.Amend. 4.—United States v. Jackson, 155 F.Supp.3d 1320, affirmed 618 Fed.Appx. 472, certiorari denied 136 S.Ct. 376, 577 U.S. 946, 193 L.Ed.2d 303.

S.D.Fla. 2008. Probable cause for warrantless entry into defendant's apartment was established by odor of marijuana emanating from apartment. U.S.C.A. Const.Amend. 4.—U.S. v. Smalls, 617 F.Supp.2d 1240, affirmed 342 Fed.Appx. 505, certiorari denied 130 S.Ct. 1094, 558 U.S. 1128, 175 L.Ed.2d 912.

Police officers had probable cause to conduct warrantless entry into defendant's apartment after he voluntarily opened door for them, where officers had received anonymous tip that narcotics were being sold by defendant and that he had two firearms inside his apartment, officers detected odor of burning marijuana outside of apartment, and officers observed loose marijuana and digital scale on couch when door opened. U.S.C.A. Const.Amend. 4.—Id.

Fla.App. 1 Dist. 2000. Defendant's action of smoking marijuana was in officer's plain view, even though officer had to stand on his tip toes or on door sill of defendant's apartment to see defendant's activities; based on neighbor's complaint of excessive noise, officer had a right to be at defendant's door, where he smelled marijuana. U.S.C.A. Const.Amend. 4.—State v. Leonard, 764 So.2d 663.

† This Case was not selected for publication in the National Reporter System

☞607. —— **Occasional or temporary dwellings; hotels and motels.**

† **C.A.11 (Fla.) 2016.** During consensual search of hotel room for illegal narcotics, officer's handling of defendant's car keys and key fob, which allowed officer to identify defendant's car, was not unreasonable search or seizure; although defendant had privacy interest in identity of her car, officer had found signs of drug distribution in hotel room but not quantity of drugs one would expect if drug sales were taking place, defendant first stated that only items belonging to her were in plastic bag on floor but later asserted that keys were hers but that her vehicle was not on premises, and officer only held keys for few seconds and pressed key fob to test accuracy of defendant's story. U.S. Const. Amend. 4.—United States v. Dasinger, 650 Fed.Appx. 664, postconviction relief granted in part, denied in part 2023 WL 6196540.

Fla. 1976. Where cleaning maid who had properly admitted herself to a motel room from which defendant was temporarily absent saw what she thought might be marijuana in an open suitcase, and reported this to motel officials who called police, the police officers' warrantless entry of the motel room and subsequent seizure of the suitcase by a police detective were illegal. U.S.C.A.Const. Amend. 4; West's F.S.A.Const. art. 1, § 12.—Sheff v. State, 329 So.2d 270.

Fla.App. 1 Dist. 1998. Drugs and paraphernalia discovered by police officer in hotel room were results of illegal search, where housekeeper noticed drugs, notified front desk clerk who called police, and officer was led by housekeeper into room. U.S.C.A. Const.Amend. 4.—Dempsey v. State, 717 So.2d 1071.

Fla.App. 1 Dist. 1975. Isolated sale of drugs by defendants, who had been staying in motel room for two or three days with no indication of imminent departure on night in question, allegedly observed by unidentified person labeled "confidential informer," although perhaps warranting surveillance of premises, did not provide probable cause for warrantless search of defendant's motel room accomplished by kicking door open at 10 p. m. U.S.C.A.Const. Amend. 4; West's F.S.A.Const. art. 1, § 12.—Shepard v. State, 319 So.2d 127, certiorari denied 328 So.2d 845.

Fla.App. 3 Dist. 1973. Where police, who had no warrant, were informed that a small packet of white powder found in motel corridor came from room whose occupant had just paid his motel bill and was checking out, police officers had probable cause to believe that occupant who was in the room was in possession of heroin and lawfully entered room into which they were admitted by defendant occupant and searched baggage from which they seized a little more than a pound of heroin. F.S.A. §§ 398.03, 833.04.—Culnane v. State, 277 So.2d 805.

Fla.App. 4 Dist. 1989. Off-duty police detective's warrantless seizure of cocaine rocks and paraphernalia was proper where detective inadvertently observed those items during justifiable investigation outside defendant's motel room and only after defendant had voluntarily opened door to that room.—State v. Carr, 549 So.2d 701.

Fla.App. 5 Dist. 2004. Fourth Amendment did not require search warrant before narcotics police dog could sniff at threshold of hotel room door in hallway outside defendant's hotel room, even though dog's sense of smell was tantamount to use of far superior, sensory instrument that could enable human being to detect articles normally discoverable only after entry into residences. U.S.C.A. Const.Amend. 4.—Nelson v. State, 867 So.2d 534, review denied 115 So.3d 1001.

☞608. **Commercial premises; offices and businesses.**

C.A.11 (Fla.) 1984. Where officers had probable cause to enter service station building under circumstances strongly indicating that drugs were being held at the station to sell, and where exigent circumstances justified officer's warrantless entry into building to pursue one defendant who was fleeing, officers once inside building could lawfully seize methaqualone tablets which lay in the officer's "plain view." Comprehensive Drug Abuse Prevention and Control Act of 1970, §§ 401(a)(1), 406, 21 U.S.C.A. §§ 841(a)(1), 846; U.S.C.A. Const.Amend. 4.—U.S. v. Pantoja-Soto, 739 F.2d 1520, rehearing denied 749 F.2d 733, certiorari denied 105 S.Ct. 1369, 470 U.S. 1008, 84 L.Ed.2d 389.

Fla.App. 1 Dist. 1980. Where police officers were instructed to return to warehouse from which truck containing marijuana had proceeded to "secure" warehouse while other officers obtained search warrant, officers were at most justified in surveilling doors and other possible exits from building while they waited outside for search warrant they believed would be forthcoming; thus, when officers knocked on rear door of warehouse for ultimate purpose of searching premises for marijuana, announced "police" as occupant began to open door, and, seeing what appeared to be bales of marijuana inside warehouse, pushed their way into warehouse and seized several tons of marijuana, officers were not legally at open door of warehouse for purpose of applying plain view doctrine and discovery of marijuana was not inadvertent.—Hurt v. State, 388 So.2d 281, review denied 399 So.2d 1146.

Where officers, who were at warehouse from which truck filled with marijuana had proceeded to "secure" warehouse while other officers went for search warrant, had no reasonable grounds to believe there was anyone inside building, warrantless entry into warehouse when officer knocked on rear door and announced "police" as occupant began to open it was not justified by provisions of "knock and announce" statute permitting warrantless entry into building "where the person to be arrested is or is reasonably believed to be." West's F.S.A. § 901.19(1).—Id.

Fla.App. 3 Dist. 1984. Statement made by cocaine buyer that cocaine found on his person had been purchased at warehouse provided ample probable cause for the search of that warehouse. —State v. Sayers, 459 So.2d 352, review denied Zzie v. State, 471 So.2d 44.

Fla.App. 4 Dist. 2008. Off-duty police officers providing security at restaurant had probable cause to believe defendant was snorting an illegal substance in bathroom stall he occupied with another man; defendant and second man occupying one-person stall were heard snorting and failed to comply with direction to come out of stall. U.S.C.A. Const.Amend. 4.—State v. Powers, 991 So.2d 1040.

It would have been unreasonable to expect off-duty police officers providing security at restaurant to send for a warrant to search defendant who was snorting a substance while he occupied bathroom stall with another man. U.S.C.A. Const.Amend. 4.—Id.

Fla.App. 4 Dist. 1975. Male police officer had legal right to be within women's restroom which was in bar and which was open to the public and thus the right to seize narcotics paraphernalia in plain view in restroom, rendering narcotics paraphernalia admissible. West's F.S.A.Const. art. 1, § 12.—State v. Daniel, 319 So.2d 582.

Fla.App. 4 Dist. 1971. Where officer on patrol of business district when he observed, at 3:30 A.M., a light burning and a blanket covering rear window of the premises and where he believed that burglary was in progress, officer was justified in entering premises through unlocked door without announcing his authority as a police officer under theory that officer's peril would have been increased had he demanded entrance and stated the purpose, and marijuana found within the premises and defendants' statements relative thereto were admissible, notwithstanding that a defendant was residing in back room of the premises and that no burglary was in progress. F.S.A. § 901.19(1); U.S.C.A.Const. Amend. 4.— State v. Bell, 249 So.2d 748.

Fla.App. 5 Dist. 1985. Seizure of remaining contraband in defendant's safe was unconstitutional, where initial seizure of cocaine lying on floor of defendant's warehouse unit was unconstitutional.—Lang v. State, 475 So.2d 1354.

☞609. Public places and property.

Fla.App. 4 Dist. 2008. A person in a closed stall in a public restroom is entitled to be free from unwarranted intrusion; however, this expectation gives way where two persons enter a stall together under circumstances reasonably indicating that they are doing drugs. U.S.C.A. Const. Amend. 4.—State v. Powers, 991 So.2d 1040.

Fla.App. 4 Dist. 1990. Probationer had no reasonable expectation of privacy while in a locked toilet stall at a probation and restitution center where he was a resident, and thus cocaine seized from him when probation officer unlocked the stall was admissible. U.S.C.A. Const.Amend. 4; West's F.S.A. Const. Art. 1, § 12.—Cleveland v. State, 557 So.2d 959.

☞611. Curtilage in general.

U.S.Fla. 2013. Front porch of home, which was location at which law enforcement officials used a drug-sniffing dog to investigate an unverified tip that marijuana was being grown in the home, was part of the curtilage of the home and therefore was a constitutionally protected area, for Fourth Amendment purposes. U.S.C.A. Const.Amend. 4.—Florida v. Jardines, 133 S.Ct. 1409, 569 U.S. 1, 185 L.Ed.2d 495.

Law enforcement officers' use of drug-sniffing dog on front porch of home, to investigate an unverified tip that marijuana was being grown in the home, was a trespassory invasion of the curtilage which constituted a "search" for Fourth Amendment purposes. U.S.C.A. Const.Amend. 4. —Id.

The customary invitation of homeowners allowing visitors to approach a home and knock on the front door did not constitute an implied license by defendant homeowner for law enforcement officers to physically invade the curtilage of his home in order to conduct a search by using a drug-sniffing dog on the front porch of the home to investigate an unverified tip that marijuana was being grown in the home. U.S.C.A. Const. Amend. 4.—Id.

† **C.A.11 (Fla.) 2011.** Police officers' plain view observation of harvested marijuana root bases 25 yards from defendant's residence, marijuana residue in a truck parked there, and surveillance monitors and insulation inside the residence as they approached the residence for a "knock and talk" did not violate defendant's

Fourth Amendment rights, and thus inclusion of those observations in warrant affidavit did not taint validity of search warrant for defendant's property. U.S.C.A. Const.Amend. 4.—U.S. v. Cha, 431 Fed.Appx. 790, certiorari denied 132 S.Ct. 318, 565 U.S. 910, 181 L.Ed.2d 196, certiorari denied Erickson v. U.S., 132 S.Ct. 471, 565 U.S. 970, 181 L.Ed.2d 307, post-conviction relief denied 2015 WL 1061663, affirmed 675 Fed. Appx. 917.

† **C.A.11 (Fla.) 2011.** Police officers' observation of paraphernalia customarily used to manufacture methamphetamine and smell of strong chemical odor, emanating from open door of shed outside curtilage of defendant's home, was authorized, under open fields doctrine, providing probable cause for warrant to search defendant's property, thus precluding habeas relief, where shed was 20 yards behind defendant's house, was behind camper trailer, and was only 10 yards in front of wooded area, no fence or other object obstructed area between woods and shed that appeared to house only chemicals and containers for storing liquids, and any member of public passing through or near woods could observe shed. U.S.C.A. Const.Amend. 4; 28 U.S.C.A. § 2254(d).—Hearn v. Florida, 410 Fed.Appx. 268, certiorari denied 132 S.Ct. 232, 565 U.S. 874, 181 L.Ed.2d 130.

C.A.11 (Fla.) 1991. Fact that marijuana growing on defendant's property was shielded from observation did not mean that marijuana was within curtilage of defendant's residence; although trees and brush obstructed observation by passersby, marijuana was in area not connected with intimate activities of home. U.S.C.A. Const. Amend. 4.—U.S. v. Hatch, 931 F.2d 1478, certiorari denied 112 S.Ct. 235, 502 U.S. 883, 116 L.Ed.2d 191.

S.D.Fla. 1992. Land adjacent to drug suspect's house was "curtilage," to which he had Fourth Amendment expectation of privacy, rather than "open field" in which he did not, even though land was used for commercial landscaping purposes; area in question was only two and one-half acres in size and was in close proximity to house, area enclosed house and was one parcel with single boundary, property was fenced wherever there was not a natural boundary and access was limited to single gate kept locked at all times. U.S.C.A. Const.Amend. 4.—U.S. v. Seidel, 794 F.Supp. 1098.

Drug suspect has reasonable expectation of privacy, for Fourth Amendment purposes, in commercial curtilage of his small wholesale nursery business. U.S.C.A. Const.Amend. 4.—Id.

Fla.App. 1 Dist. 2018. Defendant's vehicle was outside curtilage of his mobile home when police had police dog conduct warrantless canine sniff test of vehicle, and thus canine sniff test did not violate defendant's rights under the Fourth Amendment; although defendant's vehicle was in parking area approximately twenty feet from his mobile home, it was located outside the fence surrounding mobile home, and defendant made no effort to conceal parking area from observation from viewing public. U.S. Const. Amend. 4. —Davis v. State, 257 So.3d 1159.

Fla.App. 1 Dist. 2013. Police officers' warrantless peering into window of mobile home late at night after receiving an anonymous tip an hour earlier that marijuana plants were inside violated Fourth Amendment; officers, after knocking on front door of mobile home and receiving no answer, stepped off front door step, moved two feet to the left, and positioned themselves directly in front of the window, their faces no more than a foot away, at this point, point they were virtually within the home without breaking its close, and had physically entered a part of the curtilage where they had no right to be for the purpose of gaining information, and occupants of mobile home had a reasonable expectation of privacy in interior of home. U.S.C.A. Const.Amend. 4.—Powell v. State, 120 So.3d 577, on rehearing.

Fla.App. 1 Dist. 1986. Sufficient evidentiary connection existed between automobile and residence specified in search warrant to justify search of automobile pursuant to warrant covering "property and the curtilage," where suspect lived in residence, his room therein contained controlled substances, and suspect was in control of the vehicle parked within the curtilage of the residence. U.S.C.A. Const.Amend. 4.—Simmons v. State, 491 So.2d 1307.

Fla.App. 1 Dist. 1981. Where police officer, without a warrant, entered farm belonging to defendant's father on a private road looking for the father's house, passed a brick home and a trailer without stopping to ask for directions, and continued for about half a mile on the private road until he came to defendant's trailer, the officer was at a place where defendant had a reasonable expectation of privacy and, therefore, his observation of marijuana plants growing outside the trailer was result of an invalid search and fruits thereof were to be suppressed.—Kilpatrick v. State, 403 So.2d 1104, certiorari denied 103 S.Ct. 1262, 460 U.S. 1016, 75 L.Ed.2d 488.

Fla.App. 1 Dist. 1981. Crop of marijuana on fenced parcel of land which also included defendant's house trailer was not part of "curtilage" of defendant's home and was subject to warrantless search where marijuana was in fact visible from adjoining property, marijuana was located in wooded area, and marijuana was separated from dwelling by approximately 750 to 800 feet. U.S.C.A.Const. Amend. 4.—DeMontmorency v. State, 401 So.2d 858, decision approved 464 So.2d 1201.

Fla.App. 2 Dist. 2014. Police officers who received a tip from a confidential informant that marijuana plants were growing in defendant's garage lacked probable cause to search around defendant's residence with a drug-sniffing dog or to obtain a search warrant for the residence, even though officers noticed nails sticking through the garage door from the outside in, which was an allegedly common method of reinforcing doors to cultivate marijuana; search warrant affidavit provided no information as to the reliability of the informant, and officers only noticed the nails during their illegal use of the drug-sniffing dog. U.S.C.A. Const.Amend. 4.—Perez-Riva v. State, 152 So.3d 98.

Fla.App. 2 Dist. 1996. Lanai of person charged with manufacture of controlled substance for growing marijuana on lanai was within curtilage of person's home and, therefore, was constitutionally protected area; lanai abutted residence, was connected to house by sliding glass doors, was used for intimate home activities such as eating, and could not be easily observed. U.S.C.A. Const.Amend. 4.—Abel v. State, 668 So.2d 1121.

Fla.App. 2 Dist. 1994. Marijuana fields were not in curtilage area associated with house and, thus, warrant was not necessary to seize marijuana where fields were 75 and 250 feet behind house, separated by fence from house, not utilized for intimate activities of home, and perimeter fence around home was used to corral farm animals, not to prevent others from viewing property. U.S.C.A. Const.Amend. 4.—State v. Lewinson, 644 So.2d 137.

Fla.App. 2 Dist. 1986. Although police officers' view of marijuana plants on defendant's balcony may have been proper where officers stood on neighbors' balcony, in the absence of exception to warrant requirement it was necessary for them to obtain warrant before entering defendant's balcony to seize marijuana plants.—Hartwell v. State, 500 So.2d 640.

Fla.App. 2 Dist. 1977. Hothouse located on defendant's residential premises and in which marijuana plants were growing was within the curtilage of defendant's residence and deserving of constitutional protection against unlawful search.—Huffer v. State, 344 So.2d 1332.

Fla.App. 3 Dist. 1984. Marijuana patch was not within "curtilage" of defendant's home, and therefore defendant was not entitled to Fourth Amendment protection as to that area, where, notwithstanding that patch was located only 40 feet from side of home, it did not lie within a common fence or enclosure and was manifestly used for commercial rather than for family or domestic purposes associated with a dwelling. U.S.C.A. Const.Amend. 4.—Masters v. State, 453 So.2d 183, petition for review denied 459 So.2d 1041.

Fla.App. 4 Dist. 1991. Individual suspected of growing marijuana had objectively reasonable expectation of privacy in his yard, assuming that it fell within "curtilage" of his home, and police officer's act of climbing ladder in neighbor's yard and peering over solid wooden dividing fence into suspect's yard violated that expectation. U.S.C.A. Const.Amend. 4.—West v. State, 588 So.2d 248.

Fla.App. 5 Dist. 2014. Defendant exhibited an actual, subjective expectation of privacy in the curtilage of his residence that society was prepared to recognize as reasonable, and thus cannabis that was discovered at the residence after police officers drove down dirt driveway of the residence through an open gate in order to perform a "knock and talk" was the product of an illegal warrantless search; property was surrounded by a barbed wire fence, had a push gate at the entrance to the driveway, and had "no trespassing" signs posted at the entrance to the driveway. U.S.C.A. Const.Amend. 4.—Bainter v. State, 135 So.3d 517.

Fla.App. 5 Dist. 2011. Defendant's parked vehicle, located on city right-of-way in front of residence and partially in residence's driveway, was not within the "curtilage" of residence, and thus police authorization to search residence and its curtilage for drugs did not extend to vehicle; vehicle was outside chain-link fence that surrounded the residence, and homeowner manifested no attempt to protect against observation by people passing by. U.S.C.A. Const.Amend. 4.—Wheeler v. State, 62 So.3d 1218.

Fla.App. 5 Dist. 2011. When officer smelled the strong odor of marijuana wafting from defendant, the officer had probable cause and sufficient grounds for a warrantless search of defendant, and defendant did not garner a reasonable expectation of privacy by standing on his front porch steps. U.S.C.A. Const.Amend. 4.—State v. Hill, 54 So.3d 530, rehearing denied.

Fla.App. 5 Dist. 2007. Greenhouse in which marijuana was found was not within curtilage of defendant's home, and thus law enforcement officers' actions of entering defendant's property and looking into greenhouse did not violate defendant's Fourth Amendment right against unreasonable searches and seizures; only use to which greenhouse was put was manufacture of illicit drugs, which was a use completely disassociated with privacies of the home, greenhouse was not locked and was constructed of semi-transparent material with a two-foot gap, and only one fence, a standard rail fence, separated greenhouse from adjoining lands. U.S.C.A. Const.Amend. 4.—Wilson v. State, 952 So.2d 564, rehearing denied.

Use to which greenhouse on defendant's property was put, as third *Dunn* factor to consider in determining whether greenhouse was protected curtilage of defendant's home, weighed in favor of a conclusion that greenhouse was not protected curtilage; only use to which greenhouse was put was manufacture of illicit drugs, which was a use completely disassociated with privacies of the home. U.S.C.A. Const.Amend. 4.—Id.

Steps taken by defendant to protect greenhouse on his property from observation by people passing by, as fourth *Dunn* factor to consider in determining whether greenhouse was protected curtilage of defendant's home, weighed in favor of a conclusion that greenhouse was not protected curtilage; greenhouse was not locked and was constructed of semi-transparent material with a two-foot gap, and only one fence, a standard rail fence, separated greenhouse from adjoining lands. U.S.C.A. Const.Amend. 4.—Id.

⊕612. Yards and outbuildings.

† **C.A.11 (Fla.) 2011.** Police officers' observation of paraphernalia customarily used to manufacture methamphetamine and smell of strong chemical odor, emanating from open door of shed outside curtilage of defendant's home, was authorized, under open fields doctrine, providing probable cause for warrant to search defendant's property, thus precluding habeas relief, where shed was 20 yards behind defendant's house, was behind camper trailer, and was only 10 yards in front of wooded area, no fence or other object obstructed area between woods and shed that appeared to house only chemicals and containers for storing liquids, and any member of public passing through or near woods could observe shed. U.S.C.A. Const.Amend. 4; 28 U.S.C.A. § 2254(d).—Hearn v. Florida, 410 Fed.Appx. 268, certiorari denied 132 S.Ct. 232, 565 U.S. 874, 181 L.Ed.2d 130.

† **C.A.11 (Fla.) 2010.** Barn was not within curtilage of defendant's home, and, thus, Drug Enforcement Agency (DEA) officers did not violate defendant's reasonable expectation of privacy by following him to the barn and entering it without his consent, where defendant lived between 700 and 800 feet away from the barn, and unoccupied house he was in possession of was 80 feet from it. U.S.C.A. Const.Amend. 4.—U.S. v. Diaz, 404 Fed.Appx. 381.

C.A.11 (Fla.) 1991. Where warrantless entry into defendant's home was justifiable, search of garage and seizure of cocaine found therein was permissible under Fourth Amendment. U.S.C.A. Const.Amend. 4.—U.S. v. Tobin, 923 F.2d 1506, rehearing denied 935 F.2d 1297, certiorari denied 112 S.Ct. 299, 502 U.S. 907, 116 L.Ed.2d 243.

Fla. 1981. Seizure of marijuana plants growing in defendant's backyard was illegal, in that police officer had no right to be in defendant's backyard, which was not plainly visible to the public. U.S.C.A.Const. Amend. 4.—State v. Morsman, 394 So.2d 408, certiorari denied 101 S.Ct. 3066, 452 U.S. 930, 69 L.Ed.2d 431.

Fla.App. 1 Dist. 2019. Call providing police a tip about a suspicious chemical smell did not provide officers with sufficient cause to enter defendant's backyard without a warrant. U.S. Const. Amend. 4.—Bryant v. State, 265 So.3d 726.

Fla.App. 1 Dist. 1984. Defendants had reasonable expectation of privacy with respect to cannabis plot in their back yard, where cannabis was growing within 50 feet of their residence and cannabis could not be seen from any area outside their property.—State v. Bowen, 444 So.2d 1009, petition for review denied 453 So.2d 43.

Fla.App. 1 Dist. 1978. Fact that sheriff was a trespasser when he climbed fence and walked 250 yards to barn on farm containing known unoccupied house did not make his observance of marijuana through barn window at that time an unreasonable search, in that barn did not have same protected status under Fourth Amendment as would a dwelling house and curtilage thereof. U.S.C.A.Const. Amend. 4.—Norman v. State, 362 So.2d 444, quashed 379 So.2d 643.

Fla.App. 2 Dist. 1999. Police officers' warrantless seizure of marijuana plants from defendant's backyard was illegal, in light of defendant's reasonable expectation of privacy; plants were not visible from street, and officers were uninvited. U.S.C.A. Const.Amend. 4.—Glass v. State, 736 So.2d 788.

Police officers' warrantless entry into defendant's backyard, to follow up on anonymous tip that there were marijuana plants there, was illegal, in light of defendant's reasonable expectation of privacy, absent exigent circumstances, where officers were uninvited, and only went to back yard because they saw people there. U.S.C.A. Const.Amend. 4.—Id.

Fla.App. 2 Dist. 1982. Defendant sufficiently manifested actual expectation of privacy by erecting chain link fence around his backyard so as to render unconstitutional marijuana seizure based upon binocular-aided observation of defendant's garden from neighbor's house.—State v. Rowe, 422 So.2d 75.

Fla.App. 2 Dist. 1978. Defendant had an expectation of privacy, within Fourth Amendment prescription against an unreasonable search and seizure, as to area adjacent to rear of his residence, notwithstanding that yard was unenclosed or that marijuana plants seized were located in area observable from outside boundaries of premises, where plants could not be seen from defendant's front yard or from the street. U.S.C.A.Const. Amend. 4.—Morsman v. State, 360 So.2d 137, writ dismissed 394 So.2d 408, certiorari denied 101 S.Ct. 3066, 452 U.S. 930, 69 L.Ed.2d 431.

Fla.App. 2 Dist. 1977. Hothouse located on defendant's residential premises and in which marijuana plants were growing was within the curtilage of defendant's residence and deserving of constitutional protection against unlawful search.—Huffer v. State, 344 So.2d 1332.

Even if clear plastic sheets of which hothouse located on defendant's residential premises was constructed might have allowed someone to look in the hothouse from the outside, inasmuch as purpose of the sheets was not to permit viewing but rather to allow sunlight to enter, the hothouse was not operated as a commercial venture and was maintained for personal purposes, defendant had reasonable expectation of privacy protected by the Fourth Amendment. West's F.S.A. § 893.13; U.S.C.A.Const. Amend. 4.—Id.

† **This Case was not selected for publication in the National Reporter System**

Fla.App. 4 Dist. 2011. Because State did not prove that some reasonable belief of exigency existed, a warrant should have been obtained before police entry into defendant's backyard, and because no warrant was obtained, and exigency exception to warrant requirement was not applicable, any evidence obtained as result of police entry should have been suppressed, and this included observation of drugs in house, which led to sweep of the home; officers entered curtilage of home to investigate acting solely on anonymous tip of narcotics activity, only corroborated the tip to the extent that white car was in front of the home, and had no indication from viewing the scene that a crime had been, was being, or would be committed, and when officers arrived at the scene, there did not appear to be anyone in sight that might have gun. U.S.C.A. Const.Amend. 4.—Bryan v. State, 62 So.3d 1244.

Fla.App. 5 Dist. 2007. Greenhouse in which marijuana was found was not within curtilage of defendant's home, and thus law enforcement officers' actions of entering defendant's property and looking into greenhouse did not violate defendant's Fourth Amendment right against unreasonable searches and seizures; only use to which greenhouse was put was manufacture of illicit drugs, which was a use completely disassociated with privacies of the home, greenhouse was not locked and was constructed of semi-transparent material with a two-foot gap, and only one fence, a standard rail fence, separated greenhouse from adjoining lands. U.S.C.A. Const.Amend. 4.—Wilson v. State, 952 So.2d 564, rehearing denied.

Use to which greenhouse on defendant's property was put, as third *Dunn* factor to consider in determining whether greenhouse was protected curtilage of defendant's home, weighed in favor of a conclusion that greenhouse was not protected curtilage; only use to which greenhouse was put was manufacture of illicit drugs, which was a use completely disassociated with privacies of the home. U.S.C.A. Const.Amend. 4.—Id.

Steps taken by defendant to protect greenhouse on his property from observation by people passing by, as fourth *Dunn* factor to consider in determining whether greenhouse was protected curtilage of defendant's home, weighed in favor of a conclusion that greenhouse was not protected curtilage; greenhouse was not locked and was constructed of semi-transparent material with a two-foot gap, and only one fence, a standard rail fence, separated greenhouse from adjoining lands. U.S.C.A. Const.Amend. 4.—Id.

Fla.App. 5 Dist. 1982. Where defendant's property was fenced and guarded by several large dogs, greenhouse in which marijuana was observed protruding was situated within fenced property at distance estimated between 120 and 220 feet from fence, and walls of greenhouse were made with translucent material which obscured view of interior, law enforcement officers were required to have a warrant or warrant exception before they could lawfully enter area and seize contraband.—Bernstiel v. State, 416 So.2d 827.

☞613. Open fields.

C.A.11 (Fla.) 1991. Helicopter flights over defendant's property did not result in improper search and seizure, even though deputies in helicopter took aerial photographs of marijuana field; deputies testified that they observed with naked eye marijuana growing in unenclosed field from altitude of 500 feet as they circled defendant's property. U.S.C.A. Const.Amend. 4.—U.S.

v. Hatch, 931 F.2d 1478, certiorari denied 112 S.Ct. 235, 502 U.S. 883, 116 L.Ed.2d 191.

Any expectation of privacy defendant may have had in activities carried on in "open field" beyond curtilage of his property was not reasonable and, thus, search of property and seizure of marijuana did not violate Fourth Amendment; area surrounding marijuana plants was used for activities that were not connected with intimate activities of home. U.S.C.A. Const.Amend. 4.—Id.

S.D.Fla. 1992. Land adjacent to drug suspect's house was "curtilage," to which he had Fourth Amendment expectation of privacy, rather than "open field" in which he did not, even though land was used for commercial landscaping purposes; area in question was only two and one-half acres in size and was in close proximity to house, area enclosed house and was one parcel with single boundary, property was fenced wherever there was not a natural boundary and access was limited to single gate kept locked at all times. U.S.C.A. Const.Amend. 4.—U.S. v. Seidel, 794 F.Supp. 1098.

Fla.App. 1 Dist. 1984. Intrusion onto open field and seizure of marijuana patch was legal since no reasonable expectation of privacy attached to open field.—Diehl v. State, 461 So.2d 157.

Marijuana plants along footpath were clearly observable from the "open field," and defendant displayed no reasonable expectation of privacy in plants, and thus seizure of potted plants was legal.—Id.

Fla.App. 1 Dist. 1982. Defendant did not have reasonable expectation of privacy in his field of growing marijuana which was 300 to 450 feet from his home, and, thus, evidence obtained when sheriff used binoculars to view the plants while traveling over the field in helicopter provided lawful basis for obtaining search warrant under "open fields" doctrine.—Murphy v. State, 413 So.2d 1268.

Fla.App. 1 Dist. 1982. Evidence that cannabis plants growing on ten-acre tract were visible from adjoining property, that they were protected only by an old fence in advanced state of disrepair demonstrated that open-fields doctrine was applicable to their warrantless seizure by police officers who walked onto the land, saw defendant and another person walk into the field, and then seized the plants following defendant's arrest; defendant had no reasonable expectation of privacy in the field.—State v. Palmer, 410 So.2d 631.

Fla.App. 1 Dist. 1981. Crop of marijuana on fenced parcel of land which also included defendant's house trailer was not part of "curtilage" of defendant's home and was subject to warrantless search where marijuana was in fact visible from adjoining property, marijuana was located in wooded area, and marijuana was separated from dwelling by approximately 750 to 800 feet. U.S.C.A.Const. Amend. 4.—DeMontmorency v. State, 401 So.2d 858, decision approved 464 So.2d 1201.

Fla.App. 2 Dist. 1994. Marijuana fields were not in curtilage area associated with house and, thus, warrant was not necessary to seize marijuana where fields were 75 and 250 feet behind house, separated by fence from house, not utilized for intimate activities of home, and perimeter fence around home was used to corral farm animals, not to prevent others from viewing property. U.S.C.A. Const.Amend. 4.—State v. Lewinson, 644 So.2d 137.

† **This Case was not selected for publication in the National Reporter System**

☞614. Particular objects, items, and things in general.

U.S.Fla. 1980. Fact that label on boxes established probable cause to believe the subject films were obscene could not excuse the failure to obtain a warrant, for if probable cause dispensed with the necessity of a warrant, one would never be needed. (Per Mr. Justice Stevens, with one Justice joining, two Justices concurring in part and in the judgment, and the one Justice concurring in the judgment.)—Walter v. U.S., 100 S.Ct. 2395, 447 U.S. 649, 65 L.Ed.2d 410, on remand U.S. v. Sanders, 625 F.2d 1311.

C.A.11 (Fla.) 2009. Police officer who, after receiving inconsistent allegations of criminal activity from an informant, independently corroborated several of those allegations by interviewing witnesses and directly observing what was believed to be stolen property before arresting operator of repossession business for larceny and passing a forged or altered instrument, had probable cause to make the warrantless arrest and to seize arrestee's property, and so the arrest was reasonable, no constitutional violation occurred, and officer was entitled to qualified immunity from arrestee's lawsuit, which alleged claims of false arrest and illegal seizure of property. U.S.C.A. Const.Amend. 4; 42 U.S.C.A. § 1983.—Case v. Eslinger, 555 F.3d 1317.

M.D.Fla. 1981. Subpoena ordering production of corporate books and records or other tangible objects that is not sufficiently limited in scope, relevant in purpose, and specific in directive constitutes an unreasonable search and seizure under the Fourth Amendment. U.S.C.A.Const.Amend. 4.—Mid-Fla Coin Exchange, Inc. v. Griffin, 529 F.Supp. 1006.

S.D.Fla. 2020. Warrant affidavits executed by detectives investigating arrestees owner of construction corporation and several officers for workers' compensation fraud, organized scheme to defraud, and money laundering, under Florida law, demonstrated probable cause to seize funds representing proceeds of alleged crimes that were deposited into personal bank accounts of arrestees' wives, and thus, detectives were entitled to qualified immunity from suit brought under § 1983. U.S. Const. Amend. 4; 42 U.S.C.A. § 1983.—Llauro v. Tony, 470 F.Supp.3d 1300, affirmed 2021 WL 5767935.

Fla. 1971. Where police were told by informant that defendants actually lived at location other than one which defendants claimed as their residence and that stolen red automobile, stolen trailer and motor could be found in yard and that stolen boat and motor were in garage on the premises, and officers from the street saw trailer, motor and automobile, which bore plates issued to another vehicle, entry onto premises to arrest defendants was lawful, and where officers then seized trailer, motor and automobile, and also boat and motor which they saw in garage without entering same, there was no unreasonable search or seizure.—State v. Ashby, 245 So.2d 225.

Fla.App. 2 Dist. 1997. Police officers lacked probable cause, once defendant withdrew consent to narcotics search by placing foot on tissue that fell from her bra as she shook it, to seize and search tissue, where officers could not see cocaine inside tissue, and where neither officer provided any experiential testimony to provide a basis for their statements that women commonly carried narcotics in their bras and that crack cocaine was commonly placed in tissue. U.S.C.A. Const.Amend. 4.—Parker v. State, 693 So.2d 92.

Fla.App. 2 Dist. 1995. Law enforcement officers' conduct in renting videotapes from videotape rental store, making copies of tapes, and returning tapes within 24-hour rental period, for purpose of preserving evidence to be used in conjunction with possible obscenity charges against store owner, constituted unlawful "seizure" of tapes, as tapes were subject to First Amendment protection and no obscenity determination by judicial officer was made prior to renting and copying tapes. U.S.C.A. Const. Amends. 1, 4.—Miragaya v. State, 654 So.2d 262, review denied 659 So.2d 1089, certiorari denied 116 S.Ct. 518, 516 U.S. 989, 133 L.Ed.2d 426.

Copying of movie rented from videotape rental store onto blank cassette for purpose of pursuing criminal prosecution for distribution of obscene materials, without determination that movie is obscene, is illegal "seizure" even when original cassette is returned to store owner during rental period, as movie, not tape itself, is item that store possesses. U.S.C.A. Const.Amends. 1, 4.—Id.

Fla.App. 4 Dist. 1980. In light of fact that the Florida Supreme Court upheld classification of cannabis as controlled substance, seizure of marijuana could not be invalidated on basis that search was predicated on arresting officer's belief that marijuana was a controlled substance. West's F.S.A. § 893.03(1)(c).—State v. Ouellette, 382 So.2d 836.

Fla.App. 5 Dist. 1985. Seizure of remaining contraband in defendant's safe was unconstitutional, where initial seizure of cocaine lying on floor of defendant's warehouse unit was unconstitutional.—Lang v. State, 475 So.2d 1354.

☞616. —— In general.

Fla.App. 4 Dist. 1982. Where it was obvious from wrapping, shape, smell and residue observed that bales were in fact marijuana, warrant was not required for search of the containers. U.S.C.A. Const.Amend. 4.—Sims v. State, 425 So.2d 563, petition for review denied 436 So.2d 100.

☞617. —— Luggage, bags, and other portable containers.

† C.A.11 (Fla.) 2016. Police canine's alert to defendant's suitcase, after it had been removed from commercial bus, and trooper's knowledge that drugs had been hidden inside canned foods gave him probable cause to believe that defendant had concealed drugs inside the metal cans he found inside defendant's suitcase, and thus, under the automobile exception to the warrant requirement, trooper was justified in opening a can to examine its contents, even though he opened the metal can after detaining defendant and his suitcase. U.S.C.A. Const.Amend. 4.—U.S. v. Pina, 648 Fed.Appx. 899.

C.A.11 (Fla.) 1983. Defendants could not claim privacy interest in a closed suitcase into which, only minutes before, in presence of participating police officers and with assistance of some of officers, defendants had packed cocaine. —U.S. v. Badolato, 710 F.2d 1509, rehearing denied 717 F.2d 1401.

C.A.5 (Fla.) 1981. Where passenger apparently made unscheduled exit from vehicle loaded with marijuana on nighttime confrontation with patrol car, luggage was found on passenger side, shots fired apparently came from area opposite that of fleeing vehicle, there were only two residences in immediate area of apparent drug smuggling capable of harboring a fugitive and contraband was probably smuggled in by air from foreign country, warrantless search of luggage

---

† This Case was not selected for publication in the National Reporter System

was justified. U.S.C.A.Const. Amend. 4.—U.S. v. Kreimes, 649 F.2d 1185.

Combination of hot pursuit of apparent drug smugglers, immediate need to discover fleeing conspirators and danger posited by possibility of an armed fugitive at large, late at night, in a rural area supplied sufficient exigent circumstances to justify deputy's opening of zippered suitcase found lying on passenger side in cab of defendant's truck and cursory search thereof for identification, although some time elapsed from stop of the vehicle to search; although dangers involved assumption that fugitive was armed with a shotgun, sheer risk of injury to the public by remote chance that a fugitive would reach the dangerous contents of the container also justified warrantless search. U.S.C.A.Const. Amend. 4.—Id.

C.A.5 (Fla.) 1981. If agent had searched defendants' bag without a warrant, that search would have been unreasonable, even though probable cause existed, as the defendants were in custody and there were no exigent circumstances justifying the warrantless search; such a search would not have been incident to the defendants' arrest which occurred after probable cause was found to believe that they were carrying drugs in their luggage.—U.S. v. Goldstein, 635 F.2d 356, rehearing denied 640 F.2d 385, certiorari denied 101 S.Ct. 3111, 452 U.S. 962, 69 L.Ed.2d 972.

C.A.5 (Fla.) 1978. Warrantless search of one defendant's apartment and codefendant's suitcase, which was discovered in apartment, was unconstitutional where neither defendant, who had been arrested at another location, freely and voluntarily consented to the search. U.S.C.A.Const. Amend. 4.—U.S. v. Fredericks, 586 F.2d 470, certiorari denied 99 S.Ct. 1507, 440 U.S. 962, 59 L.Ed.2d 776.

S.D.Fla. 2002. Police officers violated Fourth Amendment rights of prospective railroad passenger when they searched his baggage for drugs, after passenger twice unequivocally denied permission to search, despite claim that defendant had abandoned baggage. U.S.C.A. Const.Amend. 4.—U.S. v. Cofield, 242 F.Supp.2d 1260.

Fla.App. 1 Dist. 2010. Physical administrative search of passenger's checked suitcase at Transportation Security Administration (TSA) airport checkpoint that revealed evidence of child pornography in accordion folder contained in suitcase was not more extensive or intrusive than necessary in light of current technology, and thus did not violate Fourth Amendment, where TSA had authority to conduct physical search of suitcase pursuant to statutory mandate to search all checked baggage, TSA protocol required TSA officers to open a certain number of randomly selected bags to swab contents and test for explosives in explosive detection machines, TSA officers had discretion to flip through files in baggage in lieu of swabbing each piece of paper individually, and TSA officer discovered evidence during such a random search. U.S.C.A. Const. Amend. 4; 49 U.S.C.A. § 44901.—Higerd v. State, 54 So.3d 513, rehearing denied, review denied 64 So.3d 1260, certiorari denied 132 S.Ct. 521, 565 U.S. 979, 181 L.Ed.2d 350.

Physical administrative search of passenger's checked suitcase at Transportation Security Administration (TSA) airport checkpoint that revealed evidence of child pornography in accordion folder contained in suitcase was confined in good faith to purpose of searching for explosives or weapons, and thus did not violate Fourth Amendment, where TSA officer was required to physically open a certain number of bags, defendant's suitcase was selected at random for physical search, TSA officer was required by TSA protocol to thumb through papers in accordion folder in defendant's suitcase as part of search, and TSA officer discovered evidence while thumbing through accordion folder. U.S.C.A. Const.Amend. 4.—Id.

Fla.App. 1 Dist. 1992. Seizures of airline passenger's luggage was unreasonable under Fourth Amendment where officer only knew that passenger had purchased his ticket in cash, looked nervous, let his luggage go around luggage carousel twice, and that passenger's companion had initially denied that the two were traveling together; seizure required probable cause, rather than lower standard of reasonably articulable suspicion, where police had made determination to seize luggage rather than to briefly detain luggage to conduct further investigation, such as sniff test. U.S.C.A. Const.Amend. 4.—Aderhold v. State, 593 So.2d 1081.

Fla.App. 2 Dist. 2002. Officer had probable cause to open bag officer discovered on defendant during lawful temporary detention of defendant, where odor of marijuana was emanating from bag. U.S.C.A. Const.Amend. 4.—State v. Rio, 827 So.2d 404.

Fla.App. 2 Dist. 1999. Police had authority to search defendants' home, where police officer lawfully seized bag of cocaine from defendants' home, and subsequently obtained search warrant. U.S.C.A. Const.Amend. 4.—State v. Walker, 729 So.2d 463.

Fla.App. 2 Dist. 1984. Police officer seeking to determine whether there was probable cause to seize an innocuous object such as a plastic baggie containing tinfoil packets in defendant's waistband was not required to close his eyes to the unique baggie-tinfoil packet configuration, its unusual location on defendant's person, and particular locale at which his observation was made, a public park frequently used for street-level narcotics transactions. U.S.C.A. Const.Amend. 4.—State v. Ellison, 455 So.2d 424.

Fla.App. 2 Dist. 1980. Where defendant fled and abandoned bag containing marijuana, he lost his right to Fourth Amendment protection of that bag. West's F.S.A. § 901.151; U.S.C.A.Const. Amend. 4.—Patmore v. State, 383 So.2d 309.

Fla.App. 3 Dist. 1990. Although the scope of a narcotics defendant's consent to the search of her garment bag for contraband did not extend to the closed plastic bags located within the garment bag, probable cause to search the plastic bags arose when, in conjunction with nervousness and lack of identification by defendant who paid cash for airplane ticket, officer felt malleable, squeezable substance, officer further discovered plastic drawstring bag in which another plastic bag was located, and it was within his law enforcement experience that narcotics were often packaged that way.—Rodriguez v. State, 557 So.2d 68.

Fla.App. 3 Dist. 1988. Detective had extensive experience in narcotics smuggling, and detective's conclusion, after he had shaken a deodorant container located in defendant's luggage, that the container contained cocaine, was sufficient to establish probable cause for search of container. U.S.C.A. Const.Amend. 4.—Henderson v. State, 535 So.2d 659.

Fla.App. 3 Dist. 1983. Evidence obtained from belated search of defendant's briefcase at police station should have been suppressed in prosecution for possession of marijuana in that search was neither incident to arrest, based upon probable cause coupled with exigent circum-

---

† **This Case was not selected for publication in the National Reporter System**

stances which would have obviated need to obtain search warrant, nor inventory search conducted in accordance with requirements of law. U.S.C.A. Const.Amend. 4; West's F.S.A. Const. Art. 1, § 12.—Kuhn v. State, 439 So.2d 291.

Fla.App. 3 Dist. 1982. Dog sniff of defendant's suitcase after its removal from baggage area was not a search and the dog's "alert" on the suitcase provided probable cause to open it and search its contents.—Cavalluzzi v. State, 409 So.2d 1108.

Fla.App. 3 Dist. 1981. Where police officers had description of defendant's luggage, its claim check stub number, airline on which it had been checked, and where it might be located, police officers were authorized to move baggage from cart to airport floor and present it to trained narcotics dog for inspection. U.S.C.A.Const. Amend. 14.—State v. Ricano, 393 So.2d 1136, dismissed 402 So.2d 612.

Fla.App. 3 Dist. 1970. Bottle of marijuana which fell from defendant's brassiere while she was being prepared by hospital attendant for medical attention at time when she was in great pain and not fully conscious as result of automobile accident she had had while intoxicated, and for which she had been arrested 12 hours before, was not product of illegal search and seizure and was admissible in prosecution for possession of marijuana. U.S.C.A.Const. Amend. 4.—Adams v. State, 240 So.2d 529.

Fla.App. 4 Dist. 2000. Officer's search of package within defendant's carry-on luggage on bus was proper, where officer, based on his experience and knowledge, recognized objects as having characteristics of illegal narcotics. U.S.C.A. Const.Amend. 4.—Hemingway v. State, 762 So.2d 957, review denied 779 So.2d 271.

Fla.App. 4 Dist. 1991. Police officers were not required to obtain warrant to search paper bag found in trunk of automobile; they had probable cause to believe, based on their observations confirming portions of confidential informant's tip, that drugs were located some place in vehicle or on driver's person, but that probable cause was not "focused" on paper bag as opposed to vehicle as whole. U.S.C.A. Const.Amend. 4.—Minnis v. State, 577 So.2d 973, review denied 589 So.2d 291.

Fla.App. 4 Dist. 1989. Though seeing an opaque plastic bag stuffed in the genital area of the defendant's underwear was highly suspicious, officer's suspicion never rose to the level of probable cause justifying seizure and search of the bag, absent testimony that the location, type of packaging, or other articulable facts led the officer to reasonably believe the bag contained contraband. U.S.C.A. Const.Amend. 4.—Gray v. State, 550 So.2d 540.

Fla.App. 4 Dist. 1989. Police officer's poking of hole in duct-taped package after informed consent to search of defendant's bag containing package did not violate Fourth Amendment; officer had nine years' experience and knew that duct-taped packages were typical of kilos of cocaine. U.S.C.A. Const.Amend. 4.—Curry v. State, 540 So.2d 165, review denied 548 So.2d 662.

Fla.App. 4 Dist. 1986. Absent defendant's consent to search luggage, narcotics agents who had only articulable suspicion that defendant's bags might contain drugs were authorized only to conduct minimal intrusion, such as brief detention of luggage to subject it to canine sniff test. U.S.C.A. Const.Amend. 4.—Nease v. State, 484 So.2d 67, review denied 494 So.2d 1153, certiorari denied 107 S.Ct. 1982, 481 U.S. 1041, 95 L.Ed.2d 822.

Fla.App. 4 Dist. 1985. Predicated in part on police officer's testimony that he had seen narcotics wrapped in similar silver duct tape packages on "hundreds of occasions," probable cause existed to make warrantless search of packages exposed during consent search of defendant's carry-on luggage at bus station. U.S.C.A. Const. Amend. 4.—State v. Jurisa, 475 So.2d 973, review denied 486 So.2d 596.

Fla.App. 4 Dist. 1975. Search of defendant's brief case in airport security inspection as result of which cocaine was found was proper under particular facts and circumstances in light of recent decisions recognizing validity of preflight procedures to prevent hijacking of aircraft.—Eisenman v. State, 320 So.2d 34, certiorari denied 336 So.2d 105.

Fla.App. 5 Dist. 1995. Police officer had probable cause to search potato chip bag found in defendant's luggage which contained "cocaine cookies," in view of police officer's testimony that potato chip bag was unusually heavy and contained several large chunks among potato chips and that, based on his past experience, he recognized chunks to be "cocaine cookies." U.S.C.A. Const.Amend. 4.—Stubbs v. State, 661 So.2d 1268.

Fla.App. 5 Dist. 1991. Police officers did not unlawfully remove garbage can located on defendant's premises to search its contents so as to require suppression of evidence of narcotics found in garbage can; fact that garbage can was temporarily physically removed from road right-of-way, whether by police or by garbage collector, did not enhance defendant's expectation of privacy therein, once defendant had shown intent to relinquish contents of can.—State v. Fisher, 591 So.2d 1049.

Fla.App. 5 Dist. 1990. Failure of local narcotics dog to "alert" to luggage on its arrival did not neutralize probable cause flowing from narcotics dog's "alert" to luggage on departure in light of improbability of anyone having access to suitcase from time it left police surveillance in departure airport and came under surveillance on arrival.—State v. Siluk, 567 So.2d 26.

Fla.App. 5 Dist. 1980. Trained dog's reaction to defendant's bag and to defendant was sufficient to establish probable cause to believe that contraband was present.—Bouler v. State, 389 So.2d 1197.

⊷618. —— **Purses and wallets.**

Fla.App. 1 Dist. 1977. Where police officer noticed plastic bag in defendant's wallet while searching wallet for identification after defendant was brought to hospital with several bullet wounds, but officer could not see what was in bag, officer was not justified in searching bag after he found defendant's identification in wallet.—Shepherd v. State, 343 So.2d 1349, certiorari denied 352 So.2d 175.

Fla.App. 2 Dist. 1995. Officers did not have probable cause to search automobile and purse of defendant who was in automobile despite fact that persons involved in drug deal drove automobile to location to make drug sale, where drug sale occurred some distance away from automobile and away from defendant and no facts supported officer's belief that there would be additional drugs in automobile.—Union v. State, 660 So.2d 803.

Fla.App. 2 Dist. 1990. Evidence supported trial court's finding that defendant's purse was closed, not open, in which case no search would have occurred in connection with officer's discovery of cannabis in purse; at least one officer at scene testified that purse was closed. U.S.C.A. Const.Amend. 4.—Baggett v. State, 562 So.2d 359.

Fla.App. 2 Dist. 1982. Search of defendant's purse and seizure of controlled substances from the purse was proper where deputy discovered the contraband in the purse while conducting a standard inventory search as part of the booking proceedings following the arrest of defendant.—State v. Forbes, 419 So.2d 782.

⚷**619. —— Envelopes, folders, and boxes.**
Fla.App. 1 Dist. 2002. Police officer had probable cause to support the warrantless search of a vial held by defendant, who was convicted of cocaine possession; defendant's own actions raised the level of contact when defendant quickly reached into his pocket upon the officer's approach, officer feared defendant could be reaching for a weapon, and the vial was of a type recognized by the officer as commonly packaging contraband. U.S.C.A. Const.Amend. 4.—Graham v. State, 822 So.2d 576.

Fla.App. 3 Dist. 1984. Officers who knew that area had a history of drug transactions and that area had been target for special attention because of citizen complaints about amount of drugs sold, who observed defendant accepting money from another person and then placing small manila envelope in his rear pocket, and who knew that type of manila envelope which they observed in defendant's possession was used in almost all of drug transactions in area had probable cause to conduct warrantless search of defendant.—State v. Jordan, 458 So.2d 830.

Fla.App. 4 Dist. 1995. Canine sniff by narcotics detection dog, which discloses presence or absence of narcotics, is regarded as constitutionally proper because its limited scope and method of investigation do not constitute search, however, canine sniff that alerts to package does not eliminate requirement that, absent exigent circumstances, consent or other recognized exceptions, search warrant must be obtained before search of contents of package passes constitutional muster. U.S.C.A. Const.Amend. 4.—Daniels v. Cochran, 654 So.2d 609.

Although police officer may have been entitled to seize package based on alert of dog trained to detect narcotics by sniff, search of package without warrant violated rights of claimant to money inside package that was subject to forfeiture under Florida Contraband Forfeiture Act. U.S.C.A. Const.Amend. 4; West's F.S.A. Const. Art. 1, § 12; West's F.S.A. § 932.701(2)(a)5.—Id.

Fla.App. 5 Dist. 1984. Police officer who found locked box in condominium parking lot was not required to give purported owner property receipt prior to box's impoundment.—State v. McLaughlin, 454 So.2d 617.

⚷**622. —— In general.**
C.A.11 (Fla.) 2022. An exception to the warrant requirement exists for an inventory search of an arrestee's personal property to itemize its contents pursuant to standard inventory procedures. U.S. Const. Amend. 4.—United States v. Cohen, 38 F.4th 1364.

Fla.App. 2 Dist. 2021. An "inventory search," as the term implies, is the search of property lawfully seized and detained, in order to ensure that it is harmless, to secure valuable items (such as might be kept in a towed car), and to protect

against false claims of loss or damage. U.S. Const. Amend. 4.—Ross v. State, 319 So.3d 807.

An inventory search serves the needs of protection of the owner's property, protection of police against claims of lost or stolen property, and protection of police against potential danger from such things as explosives. U.S. Const. Amend. 4.—Id.

Lest inventory searches devolve into a subterfuge to conduct a warrantless search for incriminating evidence, impoundment must be done in good faith and in accordance with the governmental entity's standardized operating procedures. U.S. Const. Amend. 4.—Id.

Fla.App. 4 Dist. 2019. An inventory search is an exception to the general rule of Fourth Amendment prohibiting warrantless searches. U.S. Const. Amend. 4.—Tejada v. 2015 Cadillac Escalade VIN No: 1GYS4BKJ5FR157228, 267 So.3d 1032.

An inventory search is the search of property lawfully seized and detained, in order to ensure that it is harmless, to secure valuable items (such as might be kept in a towed car), and to protect against false claims of loss or damage. U.S. Const. Amend. 4.—Id.

Contraband or evidence seized in a valid inventory search is admissible because the procedure is a recognized exception to the warrant requirement. U.S. Const. Amend. 4.—Id.

⚷**623. —— Particular cases.**
† **C.A.11 (Fla.) 2015.** Search of defendants' luggage following arrest for narcotics trafficking was an inventory search, and thus did not violate defendants' Fourth Amendment rights. U.S.C.A Const.Amend. 4; Comprehensive Drug Abuse Prevention and Control Act of 1970, § 401(a)(1), (b)(1)(A)(viii), 21 U.S.C.A. § 841(a)(1), (b)(1)(A)(viii).—U.S. v. Johnson, 608 Fed.Appx. 764, certiorari denied Cooper v. U.S., 136 S.Ct. 379, 577 U.S. 947, 193 L.Ed.2d 306, post-conviction relief denied 2018 WL 3037399.

C.A.5 (Fla.) 1973. Discovery of a packet of heroin in defendant's clothing did not result from an unreasonable search and seizure, and such heroin was not subject to suppression in prosecution for illegal possession of heroin where heroin was discovered in course of making an inventory of defendant's effects and clothing which had been removed in hospital in course of treating defendant for a nearly fatal stab wound and which police officer was bound to keep as evidence of a possible homicide.—Chavis v. Wainwright, 488 F.2d 1077.

Fla.App. 2 Dist. 1980. Conduct of police officer after an identification stop, in requesting defendant to accompany him to police station to fill out a field interrogation card and in examining defendant's pool cue while at station and discovering phenobarbital secreted inside could not be condoned and evidence discovered as a result thereof was tainted and could neither serve as a basis for a criminal charge nor be admitted at trial where officer testified that he had no suspicion that defendant had committed any crime and, in fact, admitted that it was not at all unusual to see young people in vicinity of recreational hall at time he observed defendant.—Moorehead v. State, 378 So.2d 123.

Fla.App. 4 Dist. 1978. Complete search of defendant and inventory of his personal effects undertaken during booking procedure after defendant's arrest for driving under the influence and driving with a suspended driver's license, which resulted in seizure of quantity of PCP, was proper as being incident to a lawful arrest.—Cave v. State, 360 So.2d 3, certiorari denied 364 So.2d 882.

☞625. —— In general.
Fla. 2009. Evidence supported finding that defendant freely and voluntarily provided DNA samples and nail scrapings; although defendant testified that he refused to comply without a warrant and that police forcibly took cheek swab and nail scrapings, officers testified that defendant complied with request and that defendant never mentioned a warrant, was cooperative and polite, and never resisted.—Victorino v. State, 23 So.3d 87, denial of post-conviction relief affirmed 127 So.3d 478, rehearing denied, certiorari denied 134 S.Ct. 1893, 572 U.S. 1068, 188 L.Ed.2d 926, denial of post-conviction relief affirmed 241 So.3d 48, rehearing denied 2018 WL 2069254, certiorari denied 139 S.Ct. 328, 202 L.Ed.2d 230.

☞628. —— Blood, breath, urine, saliva, or hair samples in general.
S.D.Fla. 2017. Urinating is an excretory function traditionally shielded with great privacy, but the degree of the intrusion depends on the manner in which production is monitored. U.S. Const. Amend. 4.—Friedenberg v. School Board of Palm Beach County, 257 F.Supp.3d 1295, affirmed 911 F.3d 1084.

Fla.App. 1 Dist. 2022. Individuals cannot be lawfully compelled to submit to a blood draw by statute; rather, law enforcement officers must obtain a search warrant before drawing blood or gain the subject's consent. U.S. Const. Amend. 4; Fla. Const. art. 1, § 12.—State v. Hamilton, 350 So.3d 839.

Fla.App. 4 Dist. 2018. To compel a blood draw, the State must either: (1) obtain a warrant; or (2) establish a valid exception to the warrant requirement. U.S. Const. Amend. 4; Fla. Const. art. 1, § 12.—McGraw v. State, 245 So.3d 760, review granted 2018 WL 3342880, vacated 289 So.3d 836, rehearing granted in part 2020 WL 838040, on remand 299 So.3d 12.

Fla.App. 5 Dist. 2021. To comply with the Fourth Amendment, law enforcement officers must obtain a warrant or consent for a blood draw, or there must be some other exception to the warrant requirement. U.S. Const. Amend. 4. —Dusan v. State, 323 So.3d 239.

One exception to the requirement that law enforcement obtain a warrant or consent for a blood draw is when the exigencies of the situation make the needs of law enforcement so compelling that a warrantless search is objectively reasonable under the Fourth Amendment. U.S. Const. Amend. 4.—Id.

Fla.App. 5 Dist. 2004. Statute requiring defendant convicted of second degree murder to submit DNA samples did not violate defendant's Fourth Amendment right against unreasonable searches and seizures; defendant did not have reasonable expectation of privacy in blood samples that outweighed State's interest in identifying convicted felons in manner that could not be circumvented, in apprehending criminals, in preventing recidivism, and in absolving innocent persons. U.S.C.A. Const.Amend. 4; West's F.S.A. § 943.325.—Smalley v. State, 889 So.2d 100.

☞630. —— Drug testing.
S.D.Fla. 2017. The proffered special need for drug testing must be substantial for government-mandated drug testing to be reasonable under the Fourth Amendment. U.S. Const. Amend. 4.— Friedenberg v. School Board of Palm Beach

County, 257 F.Supp.3d 1295, affirmed 911 F.3d 1084.

Only if the government is able to show a substantial special need for drug test will the district court proceed to assess the reasonableness of the search, undertaking a context-specific inquiry, examining closely the competing private and public interests advanced by the parties. U.S. Const. Amend. 4.—Id.

Only government-mandated drug testing programs that fit within the closely guarded category of constitutionally permissible suspicionless searches are exempt from the Fourth Amendment's warrant and probable cause requirement. U.S. Const. Amend. 4.—Id.

The intrusion of drug-testing is not confined to the limitation on an employee's freedom of movement that is necessary to obtain blood, urine, or breath samples; the ensuing chemical analysis of the sample to obtain physiological data is a further invasion of the tested employee's privacy interests. U.S. Const. Amend. 4.—Id.

Advance notice of mandatory drug-testing counsels against finding undue invasiveness by reducing the unsettling show of authority potentially associated with unexpected invasions of privacy. U.S. Const. Amend. 4.—Id.

The appropriate inquiry in a mandatory drug-testing case is whether the employee being tested has a diminished expectation of privacy relative to the ordinary government employee because her position depends on physical fitness and judgment. U.S. Const. Amend. 4.—Id.

Evidence of a demonstrated problem of drug abuse is not necessary to allow the government to conduct suspicionless drug testing so long as the record supports the conclusion that the hazards guarded against are real and not simply hypothetical. U.S. Const. Amend. 4.—Id.

Fla.App. 3 Dist. 1984. Where police officers' actions in examining contents of partially open purse did not constitute search within meaning of Fourth Amendment, subsequent clinical test of white powder found in purse did not compromise any legitimate interest in privacy. U.S.C.A. Const.Amend. 4.—State v. Weiss, 449 So.2d 915.

☞634. —— Controlled substances.
C.A.11 (Fla.) 1984. Where person suspected of carrying narcotics internally refused X ray, her detention until natural bodily functions brought forth fecal matter and stomach contents which officials were entitled to search did not violate Constitution. U.S.C.A. Const.Amend. 4.—U.S. v. De Montoya, 729 F.2d 1369.

C.A.11 (Fla.) 1984. Strip search and X-ray examination leading to discovery of cocaine carried in defendant's digestive tract did not violate Fourth Amendment where defendant at border had only cheap clothing in his suitcase, had no business cards, credit cards or checks, told implausible story about items he hoped to purchase in this country, had no realistic plan on how to transport home items he allegedly had come for and falsely claimed to have reservations at local hotel. U.S.C.A. Const.Amend. 4.—U.S. v. Padilla, 729 F.2d 1367.

C.A.11 (Fla.) 1984. To justify rectal examination of person suspected of carrying drugs internally, it is necessary that facts as to individual involved would cause trained inspectors to reasonably believe that contraband was being carried internally and would be revealed in rectal search, and such would require articulably particularized suspicion as to person and particular-

---

† **This Case was not selected for publication in the National Reporter System**

ized suspicion as to location of drugs. U.S.C.A. Const.Amend. 4.—U.S. v. Pino, 729 F.2d 1357.

Internal search of suspect was reasonable where, like other internal contraband carriers, he was South American who arrived alone from drug source country wearing inexpensive clothing, customs inspectors who interviewed him developed articulably specific grounds for suspecting him of smuggling cocaine and decision to make internal search was based on judgment of at least two experienced customs inspectors. U.S.C.A. Const.Amend. 4.—Id.

C.A.11 (Fla.) 1984. Where reasonable-suspicion standard for x-ray search to discover internally-carried drugs was met, but suspect refused request to consent to x-ray examination, detention of suspect for 12 hours until he moved his bowels was reasonable method of searching his digestive tract. U.S.C.A. Const.Amend. 4.—U.S. v. Mosquera-Ramirez, 729 F.2d 1352.

C.A.5 (Fla.) 1981. Requirements of the Fourth Amendment are met if the strip search is supported by reasonable suspicion on the part of a customs agent. U.S.C.A.Const. Amend. 4.—U.S. v. Sandler, 644 F.2d 1163.

C.A.5 (Fla.) 1978. Where informer's tip stated that a named individual traveling as a stewardess aboard airplane would body carry cocaine on a particular date and flight into the Miami International Airport and the identifying portion of that information was verified by government authorities on flight's arrival and authorities had no reason to believe that informant was unreliable and took affirmative steps to insure that informant was not being paid for information and had no criminal record, there was a reasonable suspicion justifying strip search of such stewardess disclosing cocaine taped to exterior portion of her body surface. Comprehensive Drug Abuse Prevention and Control Act of 1970, §§ 401(a)(1), 1002(a), 1010(a)(1), 21 U.S.C.A. §§ 841(a)(1), 952(a), 960(a)(1); 18 U.S.C.A. § 2; U.S.C.A.Const. Amend. 4.—U.S. v. Afanador, 567 F.2d 1325.

Where government officer received information that a particular person would be arriving at Miami's International Airport on a specified date and flight as a stewardess and would be body carrying cocaine and officers ascertained on flight's arrival that such person was traveling as a stewardess as reported by informant who had no criminal record and who was not being paid for information, there was not a sufficient reasonable suspicion to conduct strip search of another stewardess, as part of strip search of whole crew, after a fruitless search of her luggage and a failure to elicit any suspicious information on questioning her before the strip search. U.S.C.A.Const. Amend. 4.—Id.

Reasonable suspicion to justify strip search for suspected narcotics must be specifically directed to the person to be searched, and Fourth Amendment does not permit automatic or casual transfer of suspicion to other persons who might be traveling with person as to whom there is reasonable suspicion. U.S.C.A.Const. Amend. 4.—Id.

S.D.Fla. 2004. Female police officer, having probable cause to believe that female detainee had small quantity of cocaine on her person, did not violate detainee's Fourth Amendment rights through application of excessive force, when she conducted patdown search of detainee, outside of view of other officers or public, during which officer's gloved hand allegedly came into contact with detainee's vagina and rectum, officer's tugging caused underwear to enter rectum, and

victim was asked to and did remove sanitary pad and break it in half; no body cavity search was involved, and cases did not support discomfort as grounds for invalidating search. U.S.C.A. Const. Amend. 4.—Dominguez v. Metropolitan Miami-Dade County, 359 F.Supp.2d 1323, affirmed 167 Fed.Appx. 147.

Fla.App. 1 Dist. 2003. Exigent circumstances existed to justify warrantless search of defendant, in form of involuntary removal by medical personnel in an emergency room of a seven inches square plastic bag of cocaine from defendant's stomach, and subsequent seizure of bag by police, where a risk of imminent destruction of evidence existed, and the defendant, by swallowing bag, had placed himself in a potentially life-threatening situation. U.S.C.A. Const.Amend. 4; West's F.S.A. Const. Art. 1, § 12.—Hendrix v. State, 843 So.2d 1003, review denied 851 So.2d 729.

Medical procedure employed by emergency room personnel to remove a seven inches square plastic bag containing cocaine from defendant's stomach without his consent was not unreasonable for Fourth Amendment purposes; procedure entailed virtually no threat to defendant's safety or health, was a common treatment protocol, was performed in a hospital emergency room by physicians, was minimally intrusive, and generally involved no more than some abdominal discomfort, and while there was some intrusion upon defendant's dignitary interests in personal privacy and bodily integrity, prosecution of defendant on cocaine possession charges would have been most difficult, if not impossible, without the bag. U.S.C.A. Const.Amend. 4; West's F.S.A. Const. Art. 1, § 12.—Id.

Fla.App. 1 Dist. 1988. There was sufficient emergency which, with probable cause, justified warrantless search of suspect's mouth where officer had probable cause to believe that suspect was hiding cocaine in his mouth, which could be swallowed, resulting in destruction of evidence and possibly the suspect's death.—Adams v. State, 523 So.2d 190.

Fla.App. 2 Dist. 2006. Police officer had probable cause to believe that defendant had contraband in his mouth and, thus, was justified in ordering him to spit out contents of his mouth; officer felt bulge in defendant's pocket during consensual patdown search, defendant admitted that bulge was marijuana, officer then saw defendant move his hand from his pocket to his mouth, officer's subsequent search revealed that bulge in pocket was gone, and defendant's mouth was full. U.S.C.A. Const.Amend. 4.—State v. Witherspoon, 924 So.2d 868, rehearing denied.

Generally, in order for a police officer to direct a person to spit out the contents of his or her mouth, the officer must have probable cause to arrest the person and to conduct a lawful search incident to that arrest; an officer's mere suspicion that a person is carrying illegal drugs in his mouth is not enough, and neither is the fact that a defendant has an unknown object in his mouth. U.S.C.A. Const.Amend. 4.—Id.

Fla.App. 2 Dist. 2002. Officers, who witnessed defendant place his closed fist into a car and remove his hand holding money, and then noticed as they approached defendant that defendant had an object in his mouth, did not have probable cause to search defendant's mouth, where officers did not see what defendant had in his fist, did not witness defendant in more than one transaction, did not see defendant put marijuana in his mouth, and admitted that object in defendant's mouth could have been candy.

U.S.C.A. Const.Amend 4.—Coney v. State, 820 So.2d 1012.

An officer's suspicion that a person is carrying illegal drugs in his mouth is not a sufficient basis to order the person to spit out the contents of his mouth. U.S.C.A. Const.Amend 4.—Id.

Fla.App. 2 Dist. 1999. Police officer conducted a "seizure," rather than a "strip search," by pulling top of defendant's pants toward officer and seizing plastic bag of crack cocaine from inside defendant's pants. West's F.S.A. § 901.211(1).—State v. Days, 751 So.2d 87, rehearing denied.

Fla.App. 2 Dist. 1992. Police officer, who saw cocaine in defendant's mouth after defendant had voluntarily consented to opening her mouth at his request, had probable cause as an eyewitness to prima facie evidence of the crime of possession of cocaine and therefore did not violate defendant's rights by forcing defendant to spit the cocaine out of her mouth; furthermore, officer's action regarding the cocaine could be justified as a search incident to a lawful arrest or as an attempt to prevent the obstruction or destruction of evidence under exigent circumstances.—Drayton v. State, 601 So.2d 1248.

Fla.App. 4 Dist. 1994. Fact that officer witnessed hand to hand transaction between defendant and black male, together with suspicion that defendant was hiding cocaine rocks in his mouth was insufficient to provide probable cause for search in which officer requested that defendant spit out what was in his mouth. U.S.C.A. Const. Amend. 4.—Doney v. State, 648 So.2d 799, review denied 659 So.2d 272.

Fla.App. 4 Dist. 1991. Ordinarily, it would not be proper for police officer to choke suspect forcibly in order to prevent suspect from swallowing small amount of drugs; however, it may be permissible if officer is attempting to save suspect's life by preventing oral ingestion of drugs. U.S.C.A. Const.Amend. 5.—Locke v. State, 588 So.2d 1082.

Fla.App. 5 Dist. 2003. Officer had probable cause to believe that crime of possession of cocaine was being committed in his presence, justifying order to suspect to spit out contents of his mouth, where officer observed suspect with small beige rock-like substance in his mouth. U.S.C.A. Const.Amend. 4.—Smalls v. State, 858 So.2d 1244.

⚩636. —— In general.

Fla.App. 2 Dist. 1991. Answering state attorney subpoena issued for witness to appear to testify and/or provide nontestimonial evidence before state attorney or at trial does not amount to detention invoking Fourth Amendment protections; state attorney has constitutional and statutory duties to summon witnesses and can obtain nontestimonial evidence without showing of reasonableness and without establishment of probable cause. U.S.C.A. Const.Amend. 4; West's F.S.A. Const. Art. 5, §.17; West's F.S.A. § 27.04. —State v. Doe, 592 So.2d 1121, jurisdiction accepted 602 So.2d 533, decision approved 634 So.2d 613.

⚩639. —— In general.

C.A.11 (Fla.) 2022. An exception to the search warrant requirement is when the industry at issue is closely regulated. U.S. Const. Amend. 4. —Club Madonna Inc. v. City of Miami Beach, 42 F.4th 1231.

The element that distinguishes closely-regulated enterprises from ordinary businesses, for purposes of exception to warrant requirement for closely regulated industries, is a long tradition of close government supervision, of which any person who chooses to enter such a business must already be aware. U.S. Const. Amend. 4.—Id.

In a closely-regulated industry, a warrantless administrative inspection may be reasonable, within meaning of Fourth Amendment, if (1) there is a substantial government interest that informs the regulatory scheme pursuant to which the inspection is made, (2) the warrantless inspection is necessary to further the regulatory scheme, and (3) the statute's inspection program, in terms of the certainty and regularity of its application, provides a constitutionally adequate substitute for a warrant. U.S. Const. Amend. 4. —Id.

To meet the Fourth Amendment test of reasonableness, an administrative screening search must be as limited in its intrusiveness as is consistent with satisfaction of the administrative need that justifies it. U.S. Const. Amend. 4.—Id.

Warrantless administrative searches that are so random, infrequent, or unpredictable that the owner of a closely-regulated business, for all practical purposes, has no real expectation that his property will from time to time be inspected by government officials will not be permitted under the Fourth Amendment. U.S. Const. Amend. 4.—Id.

C.A.11 (Fla.) 2018. The probable-cause standard may be unsuited to determining the reasonableness of administrative searches where the government seeks to prevent the development of hazardous conditions. U.S. Const. Amend. 4.—Friedenberg v. School Board of Palm Beach County, 911 F.3d 1084.

C.A.5 (Fla.) 1978. Large purchases of controlled drugs by a registered retail pharmacy created a valid public interest sufficient to justify an administrative search of the premises, i. e., the large purchases satisfied the statutory standard of "probable cause." Comprehensive Drug Abuse Prevention and Control Act of 1970, § 510(d)(1), 21 U.S.C.A. § 880(d)(1).—U.S. v. Schiffman, 572 F.2d 1137.

M.D.Fla. 2021. Administrative searches are not subject to the same warrant requirements as typical searches and seizures. U.S. Const. Amend. 4.—Wacko's Too, Inc. v. City of Jacksonville, 522 F.Supp.3d 1132.

Administrative inspections must adhere to the mandates of the Fourth Amendment. U.S. Const. Amend. 4.—Id.

Three criteria must be satisfied for administrative searches of closely-regulated businesses: (1) there must be a substantial government interest that informs the regulatory scheme pursuant to which the inspection is made; (2) the warrantless inspections must be necessary to further the regulatory scheme; and (3) the statute's inspection program, in terms of the certainty and regularity of its application, must provide a constitutionally-adequate substitute for a warrant. U.S. Const. Amend. 4.—Id.

M.D.Fla. 2019. Fourth Amendment's prohibition on unreasonable searches and seizures is applicable to commercial premises, as well as to private homes and extends to administrative inspections designed to enforce regulatory statutes. U.S. Const. Amend. 4.—Sweet Sage Cafe, LLC v. Town of North Redington Beach, Florida, 380 F.Supp.3d 1209.

Absent consent, exigent circumstances, or the like, in order for an administrative search to be constitutional, the subject of the search must be afforded an opportunity to obtain precompliance review before a neutral decisionmaker. U.S. Const. Amend. 4.—Id.

For a warrantless search of a business in a closely-regulated industry to be valid: (1) there must be a substantial government interest that informs the regulatory scheme pursuant to which the inspection is made, (2) the warrantless inspections must be necessary to further the regulatory scheme, and (3) the statute's inspection program, in terms of the certainty and regularity of its application, must provide a constitutionally adequate substitute for a warrant. U.S. Const. Amend. 4.—Id.

The primary purpose of the Fourth Amendment in context of warrantless searches of a business in a closely-regulated industry is to protect citizens from the unbridled discretion of executive and administrative officers. U.S. Const. Amend. 4.—Id.

For a warrantless search of a business in a closely-regulated industry to be valid, there must exist some nexus between the heavy regulation that diminishes a business's reasonable expectation of privacy and the ensuing inspection. U.S. Const. Amend. 4.—Id.

S.D.Fla. 2020. In order for an administrative search to be constitutional, the subject of the search must be afforded an opportunity to obtain precompliance review before a neutral decisionmaker. U.S. Const. Amend. 4.—Club Madonna, Inc. v. City of Miami Beach, 500 F.Supp.3d 1304, affirmed 42 F.4th 1231.

Precompliance review is not necessary for administrative searches of "closely regulated" industries, as owners of closely regulated businesses have reduced expectations of privacy given the pervasive government regulation, and the interests of the government are heightened given the inherent risks of these businesses thus, a warrantless inspection of commercial premises is more likely to be reasonable within the meaning of the Fourth Amendment. U.S. Const. Amend. 4.—Id.

Nude dancing club was "closely regulated" for purposes of whether precompliance review was necessary for warrantless administrative search; city heavily regulated adult entertainment, including restricting locations and prohibiting the sale of alcohol in fully nude dance establishments, such that any owner of nude dance club would have a diminished expectation of privacy. U.S. Const. Amend. 4.—Id.

Under the more relaxed closely regulated industry test for a warrantless administrative search, an ordinance would need to satisfy the following criteria: (1) there must be a substantial government interest that informs the regulatory scheme pursuant to which the inspection is made; (2) the warrantless inspections must be necessary to further the regulatory scheme; and (3) the statute's inspection program, in terms of the certainty and regularity of its application, must provide a constitutionally adequate substitute for a warrant. U.S. Const. Amend. 4.—Id.

A regulatory statute must perform the two basic functions of a warrant in order to provide a constitutionally adequate substitute for a warrant when authorizing an administrative search: it must advise the owner of the commercial premises that the search is being made pursuant to the law and has a properly defined scope, and it must limit the discretion of the inspecting officers. U.S. Const. Amend. 4.—Id.

S.D.Fla. 2018. Although notions of probable cause and specificity guide courts in the determination of the overall reasonableness of a civil

search, they do not apply strictly in the case of an administrative or civil order of seizure. U.S. Const. Amend. 4.—Federal Trade Commission v. PointBreak Media, LLC, 343 F.Supp.3d 1282.

⚬═**640. —— What constitutes pervasively or highly regulated business in general; regulatory scheme.**

C.A.11 (Fla.) 2022. Whether an industry is closely regulated, for purposes of exception to warrant requirement for closely regulated industries, essentially turns on whether the industry has such a history of government oversight that no reasonable expectation of privacy could exist for a proprietor over the stock of such an enterprise. U.S. Const. Amend. 4.—Club Madonna Inc. v. City of Miami Beach, 42 F.4th 1231.

⚬═**641. —— Particular cases in general.**

M.D.Fla. 2019. Town's revised business tax code sections that authorized administrative searches of establishments in a closely regulated industry were unconstitutional; town was unable to circumvent Fourth Amendment prohibition on unreasonable searches and seizures by designating a given industry as closely regulated, inspections could have been for enforcement of any provision of code, and sections allowed for general search or inspection that was not properly defined. U.S. Const. Amend. 4.—Sweet Sage Cafe, LLC v. Town of North Redington Beach, Florida, 380 F.Supp.3d 1209.

Town could not rely on revised business tax code section that authorized administrative searches of establishments open to the public to search restaurant, where restaurant owner could have objected to warrantless administrative inspection or search in area of restaurant that was open to public, there was risk that continued inspections could have been used as a pretext to harass business owners and customers, and full panoply of Florida administrative inspection remedies were available to town.—Id.

S.D.Fla. 2018. Probable cause supported turnover and search of defendants' laptops and cell phones in action brought by Federal Trade Commission (FTC) alleging that defendants engaged in a scheme to defraud consumers by offering fake certification and verification services and search engine optimization services; there was ample evidence of defendants' fraud offered in support of preliminary injunction, which evidence went uncontested, including that defendants falsely claimed an affiliation with popular internet search engine, threatened businesses with removal from that search engine, promised small businesses unique keywords for which they would appear prominently in search results, and guaranteed first-place or first-page placement in search results. U.S. Const. Amend. 4.—Federal Trade Commission v. PointBreak Media, LLC, 343 F.Supp.3d 1282.

Fla.App. 1 Dist. 1996. Letter from Department of Labor and Employment Security explaining that agency was prohibited by court order from taking any further action on administrative appeal of determination under net buy back statute was a reviewable agency action; moreover, applicant alleged irreparable harm due to likely depletion of net buy back fund by members of class in other lawsuit. West's F.S.A. §§ 120.68(1), 370.0805.—Stiller v. Florida Dept. of Labor and Employment Sec., 677 So.2d 377, rehearing denied.

Fla.App. 1 Dist. 1992. Occupation of shell fishing is "pervasively" regulated in Florida, in determining whether oyster boat may be boarded by Marine Patrol officer. West's F.S.A. § 370.021(5)(b).—State v. Starkey, 605 So.2d 963.

Fla.App. 1 Dist. 1983. Initial stop of defendant's vehicle, after he passed agricultural inspection station without stopping, was legal and, as defendant was properly required to return with his vehicle to the inspection station, search of his vehicle, based upon finding of probable cause supported by credible evidence, was valid. —McDonough v. State, 428 So.2d 282.

Fla.App. 2 Dist. 1972. Statute authorizing duly authorized agents of board of pharmacy to inspect, in a lawful manner at all reasonable hours, any retail drug establishment or manufacturer for purpose of determining violation of any regulation promulgated pursuant to the Pharmacy Act and to secure such other evidence as may be needed for prosecution under Act is not an unreasonable exercise of the police power; warrantless administrative search is constitutional as a method or aspect of permissible regulation and control and neither probable cause nor suspicion that illegal activity is or has been going on is required. F.S.A. § 465.131; U.S.C.A.Const. Amend. 4.—State v. Olson, 267 So.2d 878, reversed 287 So.2d 313.

↪642. —— Health and safety.

C.A.11 (Fla.) 2022. The nude dancing and adult entertainment industry is closely regulated for Fourth Amendment purposes, so that no reasonable expectation of privacy could exist for the proprietor with respect to an administrative search. U.S. Const. Amend. 4.—Club Madonna Inc. v. City of Miami Beach, 42 F.4th 1231.

The warrantless-search provision of city's nude strip club ordinance, requiring clubs to make documents and logs available for inspection by city "upon demand" as part of the ordinance's record-keeping and age identification-checking regime to prevent minors and victims of human trafficking from dancing nude at strip clubs, provided a constitutionally adequate substitute for a warrant, and thus the provision satisfied the standard for administrative searches under Fourth Amendment, despite a lack of strict temporal limitations in provision; surprise inspections were essential to effectiveness of the regulatory scheme, and the provision could be narrowly read to allow inspections when administrative staff of a club was available, to avoid Fourth Amendment concerns. U.S. Const. Amend. 4.—Id.

C.A.11 (Fla.) 2020. Physician did not have reasonable expectation of privacy in automated prescription records he disclosed to state via its prescription drug monitoring program (PDMP), and thus Drug Enforcement Administration (DEA) special agent's warrantless review of physician's records in PDMP did not violate Fourth Amendment; physician had no special privacy interest in his prescribing records, his participation in PDMP system was voluntary, and prescriptions were, by their very nature, intended to be disclosed to pharmacies that filled them. U.S. Const. Amend. 4.—United States v. Gayden, 977 F.3d 1146, certiorari denied 142 S.Ct. 128, 211 L.Ed.2d 42.

C.A.11 (Fla.) 1983. At least where policy is not executed pursuant to standardized procedures that narrowly channel discretion of fire officials to determine scope and subject of search of burned dwelling, policy of seeking out and salvaging valuables without administrative warrant violates Fourth Amendment. U.S.C.A.

Const.Amend. 4.—U.S. v. Parr, 716 F.2d 796, rehearing denied 734 F.2d 1481.

Searches for and seizures of valuables in burned dwelling fall neither within inventory search nor exigent-circumstances exception to warrant requirement that justifies entry to extinguish and ascertain cause of fire, but rather, prior to undertaking such search, absent consent or presence of other exceptions to warrant requirement, warrant should be obtained pursuant to procedures governing administrative searches. U.S.C.A. Const.Amend. 4.—Id.

M.D.Fla. 2023. Provisions of city ordinances allowing for warrantless inspections of adult entertainment establishments' performer records during normal business hours when establishment was open to the public did not violate the Fourth Amendment; ordinance imposed temporal limitations, curbing human trafficking was substantial government interest, and warrantless inspections permitted by ordinance served that interest. U.S. Const. Amend. 4.—Wacko's Too, Inc. v. City of Jacksonville, 658 F.Supp.3d 1086.

S.D.Fla. 2020. Surprise inspections allowed under ordinance requiring age verification for employees at nude dance establishments were necessary to further the goals of the ordinance, for purposes of whether the administrative searches violated Fourth Amendment; while surprise inspections were in use, club did not violate the ordinance, but when those inspections were no more, the club fell out of compliance. U.S. Const. Amend. 4.—Club Madonna, Inc. v. City of Miami Beach, 500 F.Supp.3d 1304, affirmed 42 F.4th 1231.

Certainty and regularity of application of ordinance requiring age verification for employees at nude dance establishments provided a constitutionally adequate substitute for a warrant, such that warrantless administrative searches would not violate establishment's Fourth Amendment rights; ordinance clearly puts nude dance establishments that searches are authorized by city law, and it limits the object of the search to the records mandated earlier in the ordinance, identifying both the categories that will be searched and delineating the specific documents. U.S. Const. Amend. 4.—Id.

↪645. —— Particular cases in general.

M.D.Fla. 2019. Town and sheriff did not conduct unreasonable search and seizure of restaurant in violation of Fourth Amendment when town and sheriff conducted administrative code inspections, where, during each of the inspections, sheriff's deputies entered restaurant during open hours, did not stray to "employees only" or "no trespassing" section of building, did not inspect any books or business records, and were not disruptive, and owner did not tell deputies that they were not allowed to enter the restaurant to count seats that they were not welcome. U.S. Const. Amend. 4.—Sweet Sage Cafe, LLC v. Town of North Redington Beach, Florida, 380 F.Supp.3d 1209.

Fla.App. 2 Dist. 2011. Law enforcement officers could obtain controlled substance records of pharmacies without notifying defendants or obtaining a warrant. West's F.S.A. § 893.07(4).— State v. Herc, 67 So.3d 266, review denied 60 So.3d 387, on remand 2011 WL 13119074, on reconsideration 2011 WL 13119067.

Fla.App. 2 Dist. 2010. Neither statute applying to licensed facilities, the definition of which did not include pharmacies, nor statute regulating health care practitioners, the definition of which expressly excluded pharmacists, required law enforcement to obtain subpoena before procuring defendant's pharmacy records, during investigation into suspected drug-related activity; pharmacy records statute required pharmacists to maintain controlled substance records for at least two years "for inspection and copying by law enforcement officers," and provided police the authority to obtain pharmacy records regarding controlled substances without a warrant or notification to defendant. West's F.S.A. §§ 395.3025(4)(d), 456.057(7)(a)(3); West's F.S.A. § 893.07(4).—State v. Yutzy, 43 So.3d 910, review denied 60 So.3d 389.

⚷647. Electronic devices in general.

C.A.11 (Fla.) 2018. Forensic searches by Department of Homeland Security agents of defendant's cell phones after defendant returned to the United States from Mexico and disembarked from cruise ship occurred at the border, and thus, did not require search warrant or probable cause to comply with Fourth Amendment's reasonableness requirement. U.S. Const. Amend. 4. —United States v. Vergara, 884 F.3d 1309, certiorari denied 139 S.Ct. 70, 202 L.Ed.2d 47, post-conviction relief denied 2020 WL 7047805.

† C.A.11 (Fla.) 2011. Any delay in searching hard drive of defendant's laptop computer for child pornography did not unreasonably interfere with defendant's possessory interest in hard drive, as would violate defendant's Fourth Amendment rights; officers already knew that hard drive contained child pornography before they seized computer, forensic search of hard drive was performed by United States Secret Service, and, during period in question, that agency's resources were strained because it needed to provide security for all candidates in Presidential election, and defendant consented to search of hard drive, and he later left series of voice mail messages for officers in which he stated that officers could retain hard drive, thus waiving his possessory interest in hard drive. U.S.C.A. Const.Amend. 4.—U.S. v. Whaley, 415 Fed.Appx. 129.

Fla.App. 1 Dist. 2008. Ecclesiastical abstention doctrine, under which civil courts are prohibited from interfering with internal church disputes in order to avoid excessive government entanglement with religion, in accordance with First Amendment's Free Exercise Clause, did not apply and thus did not require trial court to accept that search of pastor's office and workplace computer was proper in criminal prosecution of pastor, whose computer contained child pornography; church was not a party, case did not require church to conform any policies or conduct to legal standard, and court did not need to determine whether church officials exercised proper authority under church doctrine in attempting to give consent to search. U.S.C.A. Const.Amends. 1, 4.—State v. Young, 974 So.2d 601, rehearing denied, review denied 988 So.2d 623, certiorari denied 129 S.Ct. 1002, 555 U.S. 1137, 173 L.Ed.2d 293.

Fla.App. 4 Dist. 2022. Facts available to police detective supported probable cause that defendant's cell phone contained evidence of child pornography images, as supported warrantless search of defendant's phone; facts known to detective at time included Department of Homeland Security cybertip showing that image of child pornography had been uploaded to image messaging application from account with one of defendant's known aliases, image was uploaded from defendant's internet protocol (IP) address, during custodial interview defendant gave evasive answers about whether he had used application or had ever seen child pornography, and after interview defendant was seen frantically swiping and pressing on his phone's screen while demonstrating extremely nervous behavior. U.S. Const. Amend. 4.—State v. Darter, 350 So.3d 370, review denied 2023 WL 2017393.

Fla.App. 6 Dist. 2023. Appropriate standard to be used to justify the warrantless seizure of a cell phone from a suspect is probable cause, and, in addition to probable cause, absent a warrant, an applicable exception must have existed. U.S. Const. Amend. 4.—Jefferson v. State, 363 So.3d 198.

Police officers did not have probable cause for warrantless seizure of defendant's cell phone during homicide investigation based on officers' belief that there would likely be communications between defendant and victim on phone and officers' knowledge that victim was found dead in canal next to defendant's apartment, that trail of evidence led to apartment, that defendant was previously acquainted with victim, that defendant was with victim at apartment two days before victim's body was found, and that defendant had been "less than forthcoming" during an earlier police interview; officers' belief about communications on phone was speculative. U.S. Const. Amend. 4.—Id.

⚷652. —— Exception to warrant requirement in general.

† C.A.11 (Fla.) 2021. Search of defendant's property and work vehicle, in which police officers recovered camera, memory card, and printed photograph tending to corroborate story of minor victim who was allegedly molested by defendant, did not violate Fourth Amendment, where officer obtained search warrant before searching property, and obtained permission from vehicle's owner before searching vehicle. U.S. Const. Amend. 4.—Fifield v. Secretary, Department of Corrections, 849 Fed.Appx. 829, certiorari denied 142 S.Ct. 788, 211 L.Ed.2d 491.

C.A.11 (Fla.) 2019. For a warrantless search of an automobile to be constitutional, (1) the automobile must be readily mobile, and (2) there must be probable cause to believe that it contains contraband or evidence of a crime. U.S. Const. Amend. 4.—United States v. Delva, 922 F.3d 1228, denial of post-conviction relief affirmed 851 Fed.Appx. 148, certiorari denied 142 S.Ct. 374, 211 L.Ed.2d 199.

Parking area of apartment complex where defendant's car was parked when agents conducted warrantless search was not within the curtilage of the townhouse where defendant and his brother conducted their fraud activities, as would have precluded application of the automobile exception to Fourth Amendment's warrant requirement. U.S. Const. Amend. 4.—Id.

Fla. 1975. In order for warrantless search of automobile to be sustained, it must have been predicated upon a search incident to lawful arrest, a search based upon probable cause, a search based upon an emergency situation, or a search based upon consent.—Bailey v. State, 319 So.2d 22.

Fla.App. 1 Dist. 1976. A greater justification is required for a warrantless intrusion into the privacy of a home including a mobile home than for similar intrusion into an automobile.—Britton v. State, 336 So.2d 663, certiorari denied 344 So.2d 326.

† This Case was not selected for publication in the National Reporter System

Fla.App. 2 Dist. 2008. In the absence of a search warrant, there are three valid means by which law enforcement officers may search a motor vehicle: (1) incident to a lawful arrest of a recent occupant of the vehicle; (2) under the "automobile exception" to the warrant requirement, i.e., based on probable cause to believe that the vehicle contains contraband or other evidence of a crime; and (3) when a vehicle has been impounded, as part of a reasonable inventory search following standardized procedures. U.S.C.A. Const.Amend. 4.—State v. Clark, 986 So.2d 625.

Fla.App. 2 Dist. 2003. Absent a search warrant, valid means by which law enforcement may search a vehicle are: (1) incident to a valid arrest of a recent occupant of the vehicle; (2) under the "automobile exception" to warrant requirement, which requires exigent circumstances coupled with probable cause; and (3) when a vehicle has been impounded, as part of a reasonable inventory search following standardized procedure. U.S.C.A. Const.Amend. 4.—Jaimes v. State, 862 So.2d 833.

Fla.App. 4 Dist. 2005. In the absence of a search warrant, law enforcement may search a vehicle in three circumstances: (1) incident to a valid arrest of a recent occupant of the vehicle; (2) under the "automobile exception" to the warrant requirement, which requires exigent circumstances coupled with probable cause; and (3) when a vehicle has been impounded, as part of a reasonable inventory search following standardized procedure. U.S.C.A. Const.Amend. 4.—State v. Waller, 918 So.2d 363, rehearing denied.

Fla.App. 5 Dist. 2021. There are three ways law enforcement officers may conduct a warrantless search of a motor vehicle: (1) incident to a lawful arrest of a recent occupant of the vehicle; (2) the automobile exception, based on probable cause that the vehicle contains contraband or other evidence of a crime; and (3) pursuant to an inventory search. U.S. Const. Amend. 4.—State v. Koontz, 320 So.3d 993.

Fla.App. 5 Dist. 2019. There are three ways by which law enforcement officers may validly conduct a warrantless search of a motor vehicle: (1) incident to a lawful arrest of a recent occupant of the vehicle; (2) the automobile exception, based on probable cause that the vehicle contains contraband or other evidence of a crime; and (3) pursuant to an inventory search. U.S. Const. Amend. 4.—Jones v. State, 279 So.3d 342, habeas corpus granted 325 So.3d 101.

The automobile exception to the Fourth Amendment's warrant requirement, which permits warrantless search of vehicle based upon probable cause to believe vehicle contains contraband, is based on the inherent mobility of vehicles, as well as the reduced expectation of privacy in a vehicle. U.S. Const. Amend. 4.—Id.

☞653. —— **Probable or reasonable cause in general.**

C.A.11 (Fla.) 2019. Under the automobile exception to the Fourth Amendment's warrant requirement, the police may search an automobile and the containers within it where they have probable cause to believe contraband or evidence is contained. U.S. Const. Amend. 4.—United States v. Delva, 922 F.3d 1228, denial of post-conviction relief affirmed 851 Fed.Appx. 148, certiorari denied 142 S.Ct. 374, 211 L.Ed.2d 199.

C.A.11 (Fla.) 2018. "Automobile exception" permits warrantless vehicle searches if the vehicle is operational and law enforcement agents have probable cause to believe the vehicle contains evidence of a crime. U.S. Const. Amend. 4. —United States v. Dixon, 901 F.3d 1322, certiorari denied Portela v. U.S., 139 S.Ct. 854, 202 L.Ed.2d 618, certiorari denied Chacon v. U.S., 139 S.Ct. 1392, 203 L.Ed.2d 624, post-conviction relief denied 2023 WL 235573, post-conviction relief denied Altamirano v. United States, 2023 WL 6376504.

Fla.App. 1 Dist. 2022. Under the "automobile exception," police may search a vehicle without a warrant so long as they have probable cause to believe that it contains contraband or evidence of a crime. U.S. Const. Amend. 4.—Hatcher v. State, 342 So.3d 807.

Fla.App. 4 Dist. 1991. Probable cause existed to stop and search vehicle based on informant's tip, notwithstanding fact that confidential informant was unproven, where police surveillance corroborated detailed information which informant had provided regarding defendant's physical description, date of birth, where he lived, type of car he would be driving and address where illegal activities were to occur. U.S.C.A. Const. Amend. 4.—Minnis v. State, 577 So.2d 973, review denied 589 So.2d 291.

Fla.App. 4 Dist. 1974. In order for warrantless search of automobile to be sustained, it must have been predicated upon a search incident to lawful arrest, a search based upon probable cause, a search based upon an emergency situation, or a search based upon consent.—Bailey v. State, 295 So.2d 133, quashed 319 So.2d 22.

Fla.App. 5 Dist. 2020. Pursuant to the automobile exception, law enforcement may conduct a warrantless search of a vehicle based upon probable cause to believe that the vehicle contains evidence of criminal activity. U.S. Const. Amend. 4.—Jones v. State, 325 So.3d 101.

Fla.App. 5 Dist. 2019. Under the "automobile exception," a warrantless search of a vehicle based upon probable cause to believe that the vehicle contains contraband is not unreasonable within the meaning of the Fourth Amendment. U.S. Const. Amend. 4.—Jones v. State, 279 So.3d 342, habeas corpus granted 325 So.3d 101.

☞654. —— **Contraband in general.**

C.A.11 (Fla.) 2019. Probable cause exists to conduct a warrantless search of a vehicle when there is a fair probability that contraband or evidence of a crime will be found in the vehicle under the totality of the circumstances. U.S. Const. Amend. 4.—United States v. Delva, 922 F.3d 1228, denial of post-conviction relief affirmed 851 Fed.Appx. 148, certiorari denied 142 S.Ct. 374, 211 L.Ed.2d 199.

Facts provided by a confidential informant and then independently corroborated by the government can support probable cause to believe that a vehicle contains contraband, as would justify a warrantless search of the vehicle. U.S. Const. Amend. 4.—Id.

C.A.11 (Fla.) 2018. Probable cause to believe that vehicle contains evidence of a crime exists, as required for automobile exception to search warrant requirement to apply, when there is a fair probability that contraband or evidence of a crime will be found in the vehicle under the totality of the circumstances. U.S. Const. Amend. 4.—United States v. Dixon, 901 F.3d 1322, certiorari denied Portela v. U.S., 139 S.Ct. 854, 202 L.Ed.2d 618, certiorari denied Chacon v. U.S., 139 S.Ct. 1392, 203 L.Ed.2d 624, post-conviction relief denied 2023 WL 235573, post-conviction relief denied Altamirano v. United States, 2023 WL 6376504.

Fla.App. 1 Dist. 1980. After officer was legally inside vehicle, he could validly seize contraband seen by him in plain view, arrest defendant for its possession and then conduct a search of vehicle. U.S.C.A.Const. Amend. 4.—Byrd v. State, 380 So.2d 457, certiorari denied 398 So.2d 1352.

∞**655. —— Evidence of criminal activity in general.**

C.A.11 (Fla.) 2019. Probable cause exists to conduct a warrantless search of a vehicle when there is a fair probability that contraband or evidence of a crime will be found in the vehicle under the totality of the circumstances. U.S. Const. Amend. 4.—United States v. Delva, 922 F.3d 1228, denial of post-conviction relief affirmed 851 Fed.Appx. 148, certiorari denied 142 S.Ct. 374, 211 L.Ed.2d 199.

C.A.11 (Fla.) 2018. Probable cause to believe that vehicle contains evidence of a crime exists, as required for automobile exception to search warrant requirement to apply, when there is a fair probability that contraband or evidence of a crime will be found in the vehicle under the totality of the circumstances. U.S. Const. Amend. 4.—United States v. Dixon, 901 F.3d 1322, certiorari denied Portela v. U.S., 139 S.Ct. 854, 202 L.Ed.2d 618, certiorari denied Chacon v. U.S., 139 S.Ct. 1392, 203 L.Ed.2d 624, post-conviction relief denied 2023 WL 235573, post-conviction relief denied Altamirano v. United States, 2023 WL 6376504.

C.A.11 (Fla.) 2006. A vehicle search will not violate the Fourth Amendment if it is authorized by the terms of a valid search warrant or, where agents conduct a warrantless search, if the vehicle is operational and under the totality of the circumstances, there is a fair probability that contraband or evidence of a crime will be found in the vehicle. U.S.C.A. Const.Amend. 4.—U.S. v. Tamari, 454 F.3d 1259.

C.A.11 (Fla.) 1990. Sheriff's officers acted within their discretionary authority in arresting property owners and searching their truck on discovery that owners forcibly had entered and refused to leave property occupied by potential purchasers pursuant to land sale contract; owners had bypassed no trespassing sign, used bolt cutters to enter property and had rifle in truck indicating they might exert additional force to compel occupants to vacate premises.—Hutton v. Strickland, 919 F.2d 1531.

Fla.App. 1 Dist. 1990. Police are free to search any vehicle, any time, and any place, except when it is upon residential property, simply because police have probable cause to believe that vehicle contains contraband or other evidence of crime. U.S.C.A. Const.Amend. 4.—State v. Starkey, 559 So.2d 335.

Fla.App. 5 Dist. 2008. Police do not need a warrant or the consent of the owner to search an automobile so long as they have probable cause to believe that the vehicle contains contraband or evidence of a crime. U.S.C.A. Const.Amend. 4.—State v. Nowak, 1 So.3d 215, rehearing denied.

∞**656. —— Particular searches and seizures in general.**

C.A.11 (Fla.) 2019. Agents had probable cause to believe that defendant's car contained evidence of a crime, and thus, they were entitled to search the car under automobile exception to Fourth Amendment's warrant requirement; a cooperating source told agents that defendants were conducting identity theft and tax fraud operations out of a townhouse, the source took pictures inside the townhouse showing a white shoebox lid flipped upside down containing numerous debit cards and documents listing personal identifying information, multiple people using laptops, a money counter, and a firearm, agents then saw defendant removing three white shoeboxes from the townhouse and put them in his car, he then drove to another location, and when agents looked into the car, they saw that one box lid was ajar, and what appeared to be credit or debit cards inside. U.S. Const. Amend. 4.—United States v. Delva, 922 F.3d 1228, denial of post-conviction relief affirmed 851 Fed.Appx. 148, certiorari denied 142 S.Ct. 374, 211 L.Ed.2d 199.

C.A.5 (Fla.) 1975. Under circumstances, despite officer's knowledge of prior robbery at time of unauthorized stop of defendant's vehicle, officer was without probable cause to make warrantless arrest of defendant motorist or to conduct warrantless search of defendant's vehicle, where defendant had produced a valid driver's license to identify himself, defendant and his companion gave reasonable, though conflicting, accounts of their activities and defendant offered a plausible explanation for the discrepancy. U.S.C.A.Const. Amend. 4.—U.S. v. Rias, 524 F.2d 118.

Fla.App. 2 Dist. 2005. Officer had probable cause to seize two halves of car, rear taillights, and two empty 12-pack beer cartons from car's trunk as part of his investigation of accident which occurred after defendant was involved in high-speed chase with officer and crashed; officer had duty as part of investigation of accident involving death, to file report detailing findings regarding circumstances resulting in death and damage to vehicle, to fully review accident and ensure safety of highway, officer had to search and take possession of car to conduct examination to determine cause of wreck, and two pieces of car and taillights were in open view on ground and were properly seized without warrant. West's F.S.A. § 316.066(3)(a) 1, 2.—State v. Jacoby, 907 So.2d 676, review dismissed 918 So.2d 292.

Fla.App. 2 Dist. 2003. Officers lacked probable cause to believe that defendant was committing, or recently had committed, a new crime, so as to justify search of defendant's vehicle under automobile exception to warrant requirement; although officers knew defendant dealt drugs from his truck, and prior to his arrest, they saw him getting out of his truck and into and out of another truck, officers did not observe defendant dealing drugs, and no evidence was adduced as to veracity of confidential informant who had advised officers that defendant was selling cocaine at location on that particular night. U.S.C.A. Const.Amend. 4.—Jaimes v. State, 862 So.2d 833.

Fla.App. 2 Dist. 1994. Probable cause to seize defendant's car was established by defendant's voluntary statements to police, both before and after police first inspected car, and by incriminating items seen in car when police looked into it from place where they had right to be. U.S.C.A. Const.Amend. 4.—State v. Waterman, 638 So.2d 1032, review denied 649 So.2d 236.

Fla.App. 2 Dist. 1987. Detectives who observed defendant sitting in parked car and allegedly manipulating something in lap did not have "founded suspicion" to stop and search him, so that drug paraphernalia they subsequently found was not admissible against him, where detectives did not observe any illegal drugs or activity inside of car and defendant offered very plausible expla-

† This Case was not selected for publication in the National Reporter System

nation for his activities, i.e., that he was bending over to read map. U.S.C.A. Const.Amend. 4.— Teresi v. State, 506 So.2d 46.

Fla.App. 3 Dist. 1991. Facts which became known to officers after investigatory stop of vehicle, including presence of pistol in car and revelation, through check on the vehicle identification number, that vehicle had been stolen, provided ample probable cause to support arrest of occupants, ensuing search of vehicle and seizure of incriminating evidence which was found.—Mendez v. State, 579 So.2d 352.

Fla.App. 4 Dist. 1973. Reasonable ground for stopping automobile discovered in area where breaking and entering occurred could be found in dispatcher's report to police officer that crime was in progress, the late hour (1:00 a. m.) and defendant's high speed driving; and defendant's nervousness when told about breaking and entering, his statement that officer was picking on him because he was an "ex-con" and his attempted concealment of key to automobile trunk could have been considered probable cause for search of vehicle for stolen goods. F.S.A. § 933.19.— Jetmore v. State, 275 So.2d 61, certiorari denied 279 So.2d 312.

Fla.App. 5 Dist. 1989. Even though officer's suspicions were aroused when defendant, getting out of car with pouch in his hand, saw officer, put pouch back into car and locked it, and later would not allow search, there was no probable cause for warrantless search nor was search incident to valid arrest on outstanding warrant, where defendant had already exited his vehicle and locked it when officer verified the outstanding arrest warrant. U.S.C.A. Const.Amend. 4.— State v. Howard, 538 So.2d 1279, review denied 548 So.2d 663.

©═**657. —— Controlled substances in general.**

† **C.A.11 (Fla.) 2018.** Warrantless search of defendant's minivan came within automobile exception to warrant requirement, where minivan was readily mobile, and Drug Enforcement Administration (DEA) agents had probable cause to believe that evidence relating to package delivered via United States mail containing four pounds of methamphetamine would be found in minivan, given that, while agent posing as postal carrier attempted to deliver package to intended addressee, defendant arrived at address in minivan and told agent that he had been expecting package, that defendant refused to sign for package, and that defendant fled when agents wearing vests identifying them as police approached. U.S. Const. Amend. 4.—United States v. Willix, 723 Fed.Appx. 908, post-conviction relief dismissed by 2019 WL 11704147, certificate of appealability denied 2019 WL 11717175, certiorari denied 140 S.Ct. 2702, 206 L.Ed.2d 841.

C.A.11 (Fla.) 2018. Automobile exception to search warrant requirement applied to search of defendant's girlfriend's car; vehicle was operational in that defendant's girlfriend was driving it, and officers had probable cause to believe that vehicle contained evidence of crime in that officer smelled marijuana when he approached passenger side of car and saw small buds of marijuana on floorboard. U.S. Const. Amend. 4.— United States v. Dixon, 901 F.3d 1322, certiorari denied Portela v. U.S., 139 S.Ct. 854, 202 L.Ed.2d 618, certiorari denied Chacon v. U.S., 139 S.Ct. 1392, 203 L.Ed.2d 624, post-conviction relief denied 2023 WL 235573, post-conviction

relief denied Altamirano v. United States, 2023 WL 6376504.

† **C.A.11 (Fla.) 2017.** Probable cause existed to search defendant's vehicle for contraband or evidence a crime; confidential informant had told law enforcement that defendant was traveling with proceeds of sale of drugs, and surveillance of defendant indicated that he was selling something illegal, as he made sale to convenience store at nearby parking lot instead of store's premises, and after making sale, he made multiple u-turns in an apparent attempt to avoid being followed. U.S. Const. Amend. 4.—United States v. Nahmani, 696 Fed.Appx. 457, certiorari denied 138 S.Ct. 1706, 584 U.S. 963, 200 L.Ed.2d 955, post-conviction relief denied 2022 WL 2092885.

† **C.A.11 (Fla.) 2015.** Officer had probable cause to conduct warrantless search of defendant's vehicle for evidence of cocaine possession, where telephone monitoring of drug dealer revealed that someone was making arrangements to buy cocaine on specific day, buyer notified drug dealer that he arrived at restaurant parking lot, defendant's car was in restaurant parking lot at moment buyer's call went through to drug dealer, defendant subsequently met drug dealer and supplier, and after officer stopped defendant for driving with broken tail light, he saw that defendant's address matched area code of person who called drug dealer. U.S.C.A. Const.Amend. 4.—U.S. v. Harris, 603 Fed.Appx. 858, certiorari denied 136 S.Ct. 281, 577 U.S. 912, 193 L.Ed.2d 205.

† **C.A.11 (Fla.) 2015.** Police officers had probable cause to believe that defendant's car contained evidence of drug-trafficking activity, justifying warrantless search of car under automobile exception to warrant requirement; facts and circumstances known to officers at time of search showed that defendant drove from Georgia to Florida to purchase marijuana, negotiated purchase of 5.5 pounds of marijuana, possessed several thousand dollars to complete transaction, and then attempted to offer payment for marijuana, and, in arresting defendant's passenger, officer observed in plain view a "wad of cash" arranged in "drug folds," which was consistent with what he had seen in other drug investigations. U.S.C.A. Const.Amend. 4.—U.S. v. Alston, 598 Fed.Appx. 730, certiorari denied 136 S.Ct. 560, 577 U.S. 1017, 193 L.Ed.2d 446, post-conviction relief denied 2019 WL 2411197.

† **C.A.11 (Fla.) 2012.** Narcotics officers' warrantless search of arrestee's vehicle, after taking him into custody and securing his vehicle, was justified by automobile exception to Fourth Amendment's warrant requirement, since officers had probable cause to believe that vehicle contained evidence of arrestee's heroin trafficking. U.S.C.A. Const.Amend. 4.—U.S. v. Williams, 476 Fed.Appx. 373, certiorari denied 133 S.Ct. 240, 568 U.S. 870, 184 L.Ed.2d 126, post-conviction relief denied 2021 WL 1530724.

† **C.A.11 (Fla.) 2011.** Law enforcement officers' search of defendant's vehicle was supported by probable cause to believe the vehicle contained evidence of a crime; after defendant approached a confidential informant about purchasing a kilogram of cocaine, and informant told officer about defendant's inquiry, officer arranged for defendant to meet with undercover officer posing as cocaine dealer, and defendant agreed to meet the officer at a gas station within two hours and pay him $22,000 for a kilogram of cocaine, and a few minutes later, officers observed defendant leave his house, and they

---

† **This Case was not selected for publication in the National Reporter System**

stopped him en route to the gas station for speeding. U.S.C.A. Const.Amend. 4.—U.S. v. Perry, 410 Fed.Appx. 260.

† C.A.11 (Fla.) 2010. Search by law enforcement officers of defendant's truck while it was parked at defendant's residence fell within the automobile exception to the Fourth Amendment search warrant requirement; a drug dog alerted to the presence of drugs in the truck, and there was no indication that the truck was inoperable, and officers had received an anonymous tip earlier that day that defendant was driving the truck, and although the truck's driveway access to the street was blocked by a car, the truck could have reached the street by driving through the front yard. U.S.C.A. Const.Amend. 4.—U.S. v. Boyd, 388 Fed.Appx. 943, post-conviction relief denied 2012 WL 3609857.

† C.A.11 (Fla.) 2010. Police officers who were conducting investigatory stop of motorist's vehicle had probable cause to believe that motorist had contraband in his vehicle, so as to justify warrantless search of vehicle; one officer noticed that motorist's hands were shaking when he produced his license and rental agreement for vehicle, and same officer observed motorist attempting to push clear plastic bag underneath front seat armrest. U.S.C.A. Const.Amend. 4.—U.S. v. Jolly, 368 Fed.Appx. 17, certiorari denied 131 S.Ct. 145, 562 U.S. 863, 178 L.Ed.2d 87.

† C.A.11 (Fla.) 2009. Search-incident-to-arrest exception to warrant requirement applied to search of vehicle in which defendant was passenger following his arrest for marijuana possession; it was reasonable for officers to believe that evidence relevant to defendant's possession of marijuana might be found in vehicle, and search was limited to vehicle's front passenger compartment. U.S.C.A. Const.Amend. 4.—U.S. v. Lightbourn, 357 Fed.Appx. 259, certiorari denied 130 S.Ct. 3306, 560 U.S. 917, 176 L.Ed.2d 1207, habeas corpus denied Lightbourn v. Ormond, 2018 WL 3097324, habeas corpus denied 2018 WL 10208061, reconsideration denied 2018 WL 10208059, habeas corpus denied 2020 WL 6430340, affirmed 2021 WL 5767691.

† C.A.11 (Fla.) 2009. Law enforcement officers had probable cause to justify warrantless search of defendant's motor vehicle under automobile exception to the warrant requirement; officer heard recorded telephone conversation during which defendant and confidential informant (CI) arranged a sale of cocaine base, and defendant showed up at the location for the sale driving the motor vehicle, so that police could reasonably infer that the vehicle contained the cocaine base that defendant had arranged to sell the CI. U.S.C.A. Const.Amend. 4.—U.S. v. Allen, 353 Fed.Appx. 352, post-conviction relief denied 2011 WL 1196467.

† C.A.11 (Fla.) 2009. Police officers had probable cause to believe that car contained drugs and firearms, and thus warrantless search of car did not violate Fourth Amendment, where confidential informant (CI) had first-hand knowledge of suspect's drug operation, officers had verified CI's information, CI told officers that suspect would be leaving his house soon with bag containing drugs and gun, and officers observed suspect leave short time later with bag in his possession and drive off in waiting car. U.S.C.A. Const.Amend. 4.—U.S. v. Fernandez Martinez, 317 Fed.Appx. 929, certiorari denied 130 S.Ct. 198, 558 U.S. 882, 175 L.Ed.2d 139, post-conviction relief denied 2011 WL 4502073, habeas corpus dismissed in part Martinez v. Spaulding,

2021 WL 4080051, reconsideration denied 2022 WL 4636795, habeas corpus dismissed by 2022 WL 4636795.

† C.A.11 (Fla.) 2006. Authorities had a reasonable belief that defendant used his girlfriend's car to facilitate a drug transaction and a reasonable belief that they would find drugs or other evidence of criminal activity inside the car, and thus, authorities had probable cause to search the car and the search was permissible under the "automobile exception" to the Fourth Amendment's warrant requirement. U.S.C.A. Const. Amend. 4.—U.S. v. Brown, 203 Fed.Appx. 997, certiorari denied 127 S.Ct. 2147, 550 U.S. 925, 167 L.Ed.2d 877.

† C.A.11 (Fla.) 2006. Police officers had probable cause to believe that defendant's vehicle contained evidence of drug activity, and thus, warrantless search of vehicle was permitted under automobile exception to search warrant requirement; officer twice observed defendant shake something out of a container that he then placed in wheel well of vehicle, and exchange item from container for money with two people in what appeared to be drug transactions. U.S.C.A. Const.Amend. 4.—U.S. v. Martin, 190 Fed.Appx. 945.

C.A.11 (Fla.) 2006. Agents, who were searching a parcel of rural, isolated property they had probable cause to believe was part of a large-scale drug conspiracy, had probable cause to conduct warrantless search of vehicle arriving on that property after they had seized cocaine, cash, and firearms on the premises; vehicle was same type of vehicle agents suspected was driven by the head of the drug conspiracy, driver was unable to produce any identification or vehicle registration and gave an untenable explanation of his purpose on the property. U.S.C.A. Const. Amend. 4.—U.S. v. Tamari, 454 F.3d 1259.

C.A.11 (Fla.) 1999. Codefendant who was arrested at warehouse for drug trafficking lacked reasonable expectation of privacy in van that had stopped at warehouse and was being driven by defendant when police stopped and searched van, such that search of van did not violate codefendant's Fourth Amendment rights, even though codefendant claimed contraband in van belonged to him. U.S.C.A. Const.Amend. 4.—U.S. v. Chaves, 169 F.3d 687, rehearing denied, certiorari denied Garcia v. U.S., 120 S.Ct. 534, 528 U.S. 1022, 145 L.Ed.2d 414, certiorari denied 120 S.Ct. 585, 528 U.S. 1048, 145 L.Ed.2d 486.

C.A.11 (Fla.) 1990. Warrantless search of defendant's automobile for narcotics was justified, even though defendant and his passenger had been placed under arrest; officers had probable cause to search automobile, and automobile's mobility satisfied exigency requirement. U.S.C.A. Const.Amend. 4.—U.S. v. Parrado, 911 F.2d 1567, certiorari denied 111 S.Ct. 1005, 498 U.S. 1104, 112 L.Ed.2d 1088.

C.A.11 (Fla.) 1990. Probable cause existed to believe that motor vehicle contained some evidence of narcotics trafficking and, therefore, warrantless search was valid; after one defendant had been arrested, officers were dispatched to defendant's residence to secure it while officials obtained search warrant for residence and upon their arrival at residence, they noticed vehicle departing from residence's garage and upon stopping vehicle, they discovered that defendant and another were inside and several suitcases and a computer were in plain view.—U.S. v. Wilson, 894 F.2d 1245, certiorari denied Levine v. U.S., 110 S.Ct. 3284, 497 U.S. 1029, 111 L.Ed.2d 792.

---

† This Case was not selected for publication in the National Reporter System

C.A.11 (Fla.) 1987. Police informant's observation of two green duffle bags containing cocaine hours before seizure of bags, together with statement of defendant to informant that cocaine would soon be transported from his residence to another location for processing, which was corroborated by visual surveillance of defendant's residence, provided arresting officers with ample probable cause to believe that green duffle bag which defendant placed in vehicle contained large quantity of cocaine; thus, subsequent search of vehicle following defendant's arrest fell within automobile exception to warrant requirement. U.S.C.A. Const.Amend. 4.—U.S. v. Amorin, 810 F.2d 1040.

C.A.5 (Fla.) 1979. Where police officers were justified in stopping vans based upon suspicion that heavily laden vans contained marijuana taken from boat and where, after drivers exited vans, officers saw that bottom portion of one of the driver's rolled up pants legs was damp and smelled odor of marijuana coming from vans, probable cause existed for warrantless search of vans. U.S.C.A.Const. Amend. 4.—U.S. v. Soto, 591 F.2d 1091, certiorari denied 99 S.Ct. 2862, 442 U.S. 930, 61 L.Ed.2d 298, certiorari denied Pardon Gonzalez v. U.S., 100 S.Ct. 89, 444 U.S. 845, 62 L.Ed.2d 58.

C.A.5 (Fla.) 1975. Probable cause supporting warrant for search of apartment at which narcotics agent had made a controlled buy of drug would not in itself justify stopping vehicle driven by defendant who had left the apartment carrying two suitcases. Comprehensive Drug Abuse Prevention and Control Act of 1970, § 401(a)(1), 21 U.S.C.A. § 841(a)(1).—U.S. v. Almas, 507 F.2d 65.

M.D.Fla. 2008. Law enforcement officers had probable cause to believe that specific vehicle contained narcotics, and thus stop and warrantless search of that vehicle was valid under Fourth Amendment, based on officers' knowledge, from wiretaps as well as on-scene surveillance, that subject of wiretap was selling cocaine locally, that individual from another area was his supplier, and that suspected supplier drove vehicle in question, combined with local sighting of same vehicle on day that subject of wiretap and suspected supplier had designated for meeting. U.S.C.A. Const.Amend. 4.—U.S. v. Jackson, 548 F.Supp.2d 1314.

Fact that officers who effected automobile stop were not aware of wiretapped conversations that had provided basis for belief that vehicle contained narcotics did not preclude finding of probable cause for stop and warrantless search of vehicle; collective knowledge of law enforcement officers involved in investigation could be used to determine probable cause. U.S.C.A. Const. Amend. 4.—Id.

Police officers' warrantless seizure of stopped vehicle was reasonable under Fourth Amendment, since canine sniff and positive alert for presence of drugs gave rise to probable cause to believe that vehicle contained contraband. U.S.C.A. Const.Amend. 4.—Id.

N.D.Fla. 2010. Even if installation and employment of a global positioning system (GPS) tracking device on the defendant's vehicle to trace the his movements as part of drug investigation raised Fourth Amendment concerns, the Drug Enforcement Administration (DEA) agents' reasonable suspicion that the operator of the vehicle was engaged in criminal activity justified the placement and monitoring of the device, where law enforcement had received information from multiple sources that the regular driver of the vehicle was a distributor of cocaine, and visual surveillance of the vehicle revealed that it was parked at multiple locations of suspected drug activity. U.S.C.A. Const.Amend. 4.—U.S. v. Burton, 698 F.Supp.2d 1303.

S.D.Fla. 2008. Collective knowledge of law enforcement officers investigating drug conspiracy case provided probable cause for warrantless search of defendant's vehicle; the three primary officers, who were involved in the surveillance and who each reported their observations via radio to others involved in the investigation, directed a police sergeant to stop defendant's vehicle, telling him that defendant was believed, based on surveillance done as part of the narcotics investigation, to be transporting two kilograms of cocaine. U.S.C.A. Const.Amend. 4.—U.S. v. Olmedo, 552 F.Supp.2d 1347.

Fla. 1972. Reasonable suspicion that automobile driver was intoxicated not only justified stopping the automobile but also justified searching for intoxicants or drugs. U.S.C.A.Const. Amend. 4; F.S.A.Const. art. 1, § 9; F.S.A. § 317.201.—State v. Gustafson, 258 So.2d 1, on remand 273 So.2d 86, writ discharged 287 So.2d 69, certiorari granted Gustafson v. Florida., 93 S.Ct. 1494, 410 U.S. 982, 36 L.Ed.2d 177, affirmed 94 S.Ct. 488, 414 U.S. 260, 38 L.Ed.2d 456, 66 O.O.2d 275, concurring opinion U.S. v. Robinson, 94 S.Ct. 494, 414 U.S. 218, 414 U.S. 260, 38 L.Ed.2d 427, 38 L.Ed.2d 456.

Fla.App. 1 Dist. 2007. Marijuana found following the frisk of a vehicle occupant, combined with furtive behavior by the vehicle occupants, provides probable cause to search the entire vehicle, including the trunk. U.S.C.A. Const. Amend. 4.—Kimball v. State, 951 So.2d 35, review denied 959 So.2d 716.

Fla.App. 1 Dist. 2001. Arresting officer's corroboration of informants' tip, through personal observation during lawful traffic stop, gave rise to probable cause to believe that driver of vehicle was delivering cocaine, as required to justify search of stopped vehicle; within a few minutes of stop, officer determined that driver was suspect named and described by informants as involved in delivery of cocaine, and further corroborated informants' information that suspect was going to see named individual in particular room of motel. U.S.C.A. Const.Amend. 4.—State v. Moore, 791 So.2d 1246.

Fla.App. 1 Dist. 1995. Neither juvenile's tip that woman passenger in car parked nearby had asked him for crack cocaine nor officer's observation that woman closed her legs together when he approached and asked for driver's license gave rise to reasonable suspicion justifying search. U.S.C.A. Const.Amend. 4.—Cronin v. State, 656 So.2d 213, rehearing denied, review dismissed 659 So.2d 1089.

Fla.App. 1 Dist. 1989. Tip from reliable confidential informant was insufficient to establish probable cause to conduct warrantless search of suspect's automobile for illegal drugs, absent evidence of how informant came to conclusion that suspect's car would be transporting drugs or evidence of independent corroboration. U.S.C.A. Const.Amend. 4.—Holmes v. State, 549 So.2d 1119.

Fla.App. 1 Dist. 1989. Stop and warrantless search of truck from which cocaine was seized was reasonable.—Rowland v. State, 548 So.2d 812.

Fla.App. 1 Dist. 1986. Police officer who had been told that defendant would engage in drug transaction at convenience store, who saw defendant and another arrive in an automobile and enter the store, who saw the passenger leave the store and get in his own automobile and drive away, and who saw defendant then exit the store and get in his automobile and drive in a direction away from his residence did not have probable cause for arrest of defendant or search of defendant's automobile.—State v. Hewitt, 495 So.2d 809, review denied 504 So.2d 768.

Fla.App. 1 Dist. 1983. Police officer had probable cause to conduct warrantless search of defendant's vehicle where fifth confidential informant was in officer's presence, enabling officer to observe his demeanor, that information had been corroborated by other informants, including one with a record of reliability, information provided by first informant was very specific, contributing to its reliability, and officers evaluated information in light of their experience as narcotics officers. U.S.C.A. Const.Amend. 4.—State v. Jenkins, 431 So.2d 294, appeal dismissed 438 So.2d 833.

Fla.App. 1 Dist. 1981. Although trial court failed to make factual findings that informant was credible or his information otherwise reliable, evidence that police officers unequivocally stated that their informant's knowledge of defendant's trafficking in narcotics was based upon a conversation between the informant and the defendant relating to an intended drug transaction and that informant's information was corroborated by the police officers was sufficient to support trial court's finding that there was probable cause to conduct a warrantless search for narcotics of defendant's automobile which was not present with defendant at the time of his arrest. West's F.S.A. § 933.02(4)(c); U.S.C.A.Const. Amend. 4.—Barfield v. State, 396 So.2d 793.

Fla.App. 1 Dist. 1980. After initial stop, search of automobile and seizure of marijuana were proper, because there was probable cause, where, upon being where he had legal right to be, deputy sheriff, who had been deputy sheriff for 18 years and who had observed drug paraphernalia many, many times, observed marijuana-smoking paraphernalia and baggies containing what appeared to be marijuana.—Mayo v. State, 382 So.2d 327, petition for review denied 388 So.2d 1116.

Fla.App. 1 Dist. 1979. Where officers who were assigned to marijuana importing investigation were able to identify many members of alleged conspiracy and were able to identify many of their vehicles weeks ahead of the actual arrest, where, on night of the arrest, boat was seen mooring near three vehicles parked at docks but officer was unable to tell whether anything was loaded into vehicles where other officer observed vehicles approach from the dock area and turn on highway, where such officer radioed description of the third vehicle, which had never been seen in connection with investigation prior to this time, and where vehicle was proceeding in a lawful manner when it was stopped by police, warrantless search and seizure of vehicle was improper.—Laurich v. State, 376 So.2d 405.

Fla.App. 1 Dist. 1979. Officers had probable cause to make warrantless search of defendant's truck which had been seen entering warehouse where another truck, similar in appearance and believed to be transporting large load of marijuana, had been seen on previous day. U.S.C.A.Const. Amend. 4.—Behr v. State, 376 So.2d 398, certiorari denied 386 So.2d 633.

Fla.App. 1 Dist. 1978. Police officer had duty to investigate information given him by informant that defendant had five to seven pounds of marijuana in automobile and, on such basis, to detain defendant and ask him to identify himself and to search to extent necessary to disclose presence of weapon but did not have authority to conduct general search of automobile for contraband as incident to lawful detention.—St. John v. State, 356 So.2d 32.

Fla.App. 1 Dist. 1976. Where at time officers observed vehicles enter an area where marijuana had been discovered recently one of the vehicles rode high and level but when it emerged it was riding low and appeared to be heavily loaded, officers had probable cause to stop vehicles and conduct warrantless search for marijuana.—Fotianos v. State, 329 So.2d 397, certiorari denied 341 So.2d 1081.

Fla.App. 1 Dist. 1976. Special agent, who, after second special agent informed third special agent that second agent had received information from a confidential informant indicating that an individual wearing a red coat would leave Arizona by airplane bound for specified city in Florida and would be carrying controlled drugs, was given more information by second agent and was informed by such agent that his informant was very reliable, did not have probable cause to make warrantless search of automobile occupied by accused, to arrest accused and to seize controlled drugs; and thus, denial of motion to suppress such drugs was error.—Hyatt v. State, 329 So.2d 43, certiorari denied 341 So.2d 1085.

Fla.App. 2 Dist. 2006. Automobile exception permitted warrantless search of defendant's locked car after defendant was arrested for gambling at apartment complex, where police officer saw razor blade and white powdery residue through car window after officer obtained keys from defendant, pursuant to a search incident to arrest, and located car. U.S.C.A. Const.Amend. 4.—State v. Green, 943 So.2d 1004.

Fla.App. 2 Dist. 2005. Deputies did not have probable cause to make warrantless arrest or conduct warrantless search of defendant's vehicle based on tip from informant that described man who would be arriving at restaurant with ounce of methamphetamine, even though informant was established and reliable, defendant arrived at restaurant soon thereafter, and defendant and his vehicle matched general description; no contraband was found on defendant, informant stated that source of her information came from overheard conversation between unidentified parties, accuracy and reliability of informant's source were completely untested, and nothing indicated that overheard conversation was more than mere rumor. U.S.C.A. Const.Amend. 4.—Whittle v. State, 903 So.2d 210, rehearing denied.

Fla.App. 2 Dist. 2000. Police officer did not have reasonable suspicion to conduct *Terry* stop of defendant's car, and thus discovery of cocaine following search of car after defendant consented to search was the fruit of an unconstitutional seizure, where officer was told by a subject that there were drugs in defendant's car, there was no information regarding informant's veracity and reliability or as to how informant knew what she claimed to know, and officer observed only that defendant was driving a car.—Dozier v. State, 766 So.2d 1105.

Fla.App. 2 Dist. 1998. Police had probable cause to search accused's vehicle following drug sting, where police verified all of the information given them by informant, they observed informant, as buyer, enter accused's apartment, they then saw accused exit his apartment and ap-

† **This Case was not selected for publication in the National Reporter System**

proach dealer's car and stick his hand inside, the police had been told that accused would leave his apartment to get the drugs from a source, and thereafter, accused returned to his apartment and gave drugs to the informant. U.S.C.A. Const. Amend. 4.—State v. Lewis, 725 So.2d 1163, rehearing denied.

Fla.App. 2 Dist. 1991. Reasonable cause for search of van did not justify search of occupant on ground that she had constructive possession of drugs found in van.—Rogers v. State, 586 So.2d 1148.

Fla.App. 2 Dist. 1991. Officers lacked probable cause to search trunk of vehicle driven by defendant without consent; while anonymous tip reporting alleged attempt to sell marijuana supplied some information that officers corroborated, officers were unable to corroborate any indication of wrongdoing absent unlawful detention and coerced consent. U.S.C.A. Const.Amend. 4. —Monroe v. State, 578 So.2d 847.

Fla.App. 2 Dist. 1989. Search of defendant's motor vehicle was appropriate based on either well-founded suspicion of criminal activity or on traffic violation; police officers noticed driver of vehicle was a white male at one location, 10 to 15 minutes later officers observed same vehicle parked in different location with same white male talking to three known drug users, and then officers spotted truck at third location with group of men around it and when officers approached, group fled and defendant had traveled through stop sign.—State v. Renda, 553 So.2d 373.

Fla.App. 2 Dist. 1989. Observation of driver passing something to passenger in vehicle with lights and engine off and parked in area with high incidence of drug use, and of passenger with knife blade under her nose gave deputy probable cause to conduct search of vehicle for cocaine. U.S.C.A. Const.Amend. 4.—State v. Starke, 550 So.2d 547.

Fla.App. 2 Dist. 1989. Probable cause for search of automobile was provided by informant who told officers where automobile could be located, that a particular white female would drive it to another location, and that the owner, who would then be in possession of cocaine, would drive the truck from the location and by officer's observations which verified all of the facts except the defendant's possession of cocaine.—State v. Edwards, 547 So.2d 183.

Warrantless search of defendant's truck for drugs was justified under automobile exception to warrant requirement.—Id.

Fla.App. 2 Dist. 1989. Probable cause to conduct warrantless search of automobile for narcotics was not established solely by information received from confidential informant 11 days prior to the search where informant was untested; probable cause did not arise until information was verified by officer's observation.—State v. Abiri, 539 So.2d 492.

Fla.App. 2 Dist. 1988. Trooper, though justified in stopping motor home, had no probable cause to search the vehicle merely by reason of having, with illumination of his flashlight, scanned interior and noticed straw two or three inches long with a cut end, which he believed to be drug paraphernalia, at least where trooper only saw what appeared to him to be cocaine residue after he stepped into the trailer and picked up the straw.—Anderson v. State, 532 So.2d 4.

Fla.App. 2 Dist. 1986. Police did not have probable cause to search automobile on basis that defendant had gone to motel room of person police suspected to be drug dealer, as officers did not see any drug transaction nor did they have any knowledge that defendant was either buyer or seller, and they had no information that placed any contraband in defendant's automobile.—Gadsden v. State, 498 So.2d 1339.

Fla.App. 2 Dist. 1985. Where police had reason to believe that there were bales of marijuana in defendant's apartment and were aware that on returning home defendant would know that someone had been in the apartment, the officers, who observed defendant back his camper truck next to apartment and depart hurriedly about ten minutes later had probable cause to believe that truck contained marijuana and were entitled to stop it for a search without a warrant, notwithstanding that they were unable to see whether defendant had loaded the marijuana into the truck and, in any event, at the very least the officers had reasonable suspicion warranting a *Terry* investigatory stop and could seize the marijuana, which was in plain view, under the automobile exception. U.S.C.A. Const.Amend. 4.— Schultz v. State, 463 So.2d 1192.

Fla.App. 2 Dist. 1983. Where defendant called pharmacist, who was known to have been involved in drug transactions, mentioned "D's" and asked whether pharmacist had any, and her subsequent actions fit pattern of illegal drug transactions involving pharmacist, there was probable cause for warrantless search of defendant's automobile as it left alley which pharmacist had entered carrying little white bag and from which he had returned without white bag. U.S.C.A. Const.Amend. 4.—State v. Gillum, 428 So.2d 755.

Fla.App. 2 Dist. 1982. Police officer had no probable cause to believe that vehicle contained contraband sufficient to justify search which resulted in discovery of two baggies of marijuana and three small packets of cocaine.—Higgins v. State, 422 So.2d 81.

Fla.App. 2 Dist. 1980. Where deputy knew that airplane, allegedly carrying contraband, had landed at approximately 10:15 at nearby airstrip, where two camper trucks had been reportedly standing by at airstrip, where deputy was under instruction to be on lookout for two camper trucks and there was no other traffic on highway and at 11:00 p. m. two camper trucks approached at slow speed from direction of nearby airstrip, deputy's suspicion regarding vehicles was well founded in view of information available to him at the time of the initial stop and justification for stopping first truck carried over to the second since deputy would have stopped them both had they not split up at the intersection, and once vehicles were stopped officers almost immediately had sufficient probable cause to conduct a search.—Mock v. State, 385 So.2d 665, review denied 392 So.2d 1377.

Fla.App. 2 Dist. 1979. Deputies, who, after justifiably stopping truck, observed that defendant driver fainted, that he was sweated and disheveled and that his pants legs were wet and who observed that truck was heavily loaded but that defendant stated that it only carried driftwood collected at ranch and that he was unable to find key for back of truck, could justifiably detain both truck and defendant while verifying his story by visiting the ranch, and such deputies, after having discovered firsthand evidence of a marijuana-smuggling operation during their visit to ranch, then had probable cause to search truck for marijuana.—State v. Lopez, 369 So.2d 623, certiorari denied 383 So.2d 1198.

† This Case was not selected for publication in the National Reporter System

Fla.App. 2 Dist. 1978. Where police officers investigated citizen's complaint that a nude male was running around car parked on street, when officers arrived at scene they discovered defendant lying on front seat of car, fully exposed, police officers ordered defendant out of car, and when interior light came on as defendant exited the car, officer could see several small, flat tinfoil packets inside defendant's shoes, and based upon his experience with drug arrests, officer believed packets contained either heroin or cocaine, officer had probable cause to believe that packets contained contraband, and officer's seizure of such packets was legal.—State v. Redding, 362 So.2d 170.

Fla.App. 3 Dist. 1994. Confidential informant's continuous telephonic report to police officers describing cocaine, truck and driver, furnished more than sufficient probable cause for stop and seizure of cocaine and money. U.S.C.A. Const.Amend. 4.—Morales v. State, 636 So.2d 864.

Fla.App. 3 Dist. 1987. Search of narcotics suspect's automobile, which was predicated wholly on police officers' probable cause to believe that it contained contraband, was not improper merely because detailed search occurred two hours after suspect's arrest following stop for traffic infractions when officers discovered marijuana in the passenger compartment of the car.—State v. Langer, 516 So.2d 310.

Fla.App. 3 Dist. 1982. Stop based on information received by deputies via communications with another deputy, who had been informed by communications center that individual had called concerning object being loaded from boat into a van, was legal and seizure of what deputy believed to be marijuana, which was observed when defendant allowed deputies to look into back of van, was proper.—Zaval v. State, 416 So.2d 1226.

Fla.App. 3 Dist. 1980. Investigating officers had probable cause to believe vehicle contained marijuana where they observed readily recognizable large bales wrapped in plastic and burlap being placed into trunk of the vehicle, and the officers knew of arrest earlier in the day of two individuals for possession of marijuana obtained at same residence at which the loading of the vehicle occurred, and thus the officers were not required to obtain search warrant to search the vehicle, which was about to depart.—Mansfield v. State, 389 So.2d 292.

Fla.App. 3 Dist. 1980. Where truck and defendant were on public street while defendant loaded something at rear of appliance store in early morning hours, which were not normal hours of operation, police officer was justified in investigating and had right to seize what he saw, which he testified he knew to be marijuana. U.S.C.A.Const. Amends. 4, 14.—Perez v. State, 383 So.2d 769.

Fla.App. 3 Dist. 1979. In prosecution for possession of over 100 pounds of marijuana, evidence was sufficient to show probable cause to search truck which contained the contraband and area around it.—Hernandez v. State, 369 So.2d 76, certiorari denied 378 So.2d 345, certiorari denied 100 S.Ct. 2916, 446 U.S. 951, 64 L.Ed.2d 807, certiorari denied Eder v. Florida, 100 S.Ct. 2916, 446 U.S. 951, 64 L.Ed.2d 807.

Fla.App. 3 Dist. 1967. Search of automobile by officers who had stopped defendant on pretext of minor traffic violation in order to search without warrant for evidence of unrelated offenses was illegal.—Riddlehoover v. State, 198 So.2d 651.

Fla.App. 4 Dist. 2009. Totality of circumstances justified search of vehicle of drug trafficking suspect, where police confirmed informant's reliability by matching apartment address and vehicles which informant identified to suspect's driver's license and vehicle registration, and by observing suspect arrive at specific time and place at which he had told informant he would arrive for another drug buy. U.S.C.A. Const. Amend. 4.—Flowers v. State, 15 So.3d 886.

Fla.App. 4 Dist. 2002. Police officers had probable cause to stop and search defendant's van without her consent and without a warrant where, under the totality of the circumstances analysis, there was a fair probability that contraband would be found in her van; police had received specific information from a reliable, confidential informant that defendant or her boyfriend would be driving a particular car, from a particular location, on a particular highway, on a specific date, carrying a large amount of cannabis, and this information matched police observations of defendant, but for the final detail. U.S.C.A. Const.Amend. 4.—Niemann v. State, 819 So.2d 166, rehearing denied, review denied 839 So.2d 699.

Fla.App. 4 Dist. 2002. Detective had probable cause to seize defendant and search his vehicle for cocaine, despite fact that original tip was given by anonymous informant, on grounds that detective instructed anonymous informant when and where drug transaction was to take place, and immediately prior to the transaction, detective observed defendant leave his place of employment carrying a bag, enter a vehicle matching the description given by informant, and drive to location where detective had directed. U.S.C.A. Const.Amend. 4.—Marsdin v. State, 813 So.2d 260.

Fla.App. 4 Dist. 2001. Absent exigent circumstances, consent, or incriminating or suspicious circumstances, deputies lacked probable cause to seize defendant and search his car, even though defendant's arrival at gas station corresponded exactly with time anonymous informant told deputies that defendant would arrive to deliver a controlled substance, where defendant did not meet anyone at gas station, and deputies did not observe any suspicious activity. U.S.C.A. Const. Amend. 4.—Kimball v. State, 801 So.2d 264.

Fla.App. 4 Dist. 2001. Officer lacked probable cause to seize currency during automobile stop, where drug dog's alert to currency did not occur until after currency was removed from driver's possession and in police custody, marijuana seeds or residue found under automobile seat was so insignificant that officer did not arrest driver for possession or try to retrieve particles, and driver's explanation regarding currency was not inconsistent.—State, Dept. of Highway Safety and Motor Vehicles v. Jones, 780 So.2d 949, rehearing denied, review denied 797 So.2d 588.

Fla.App. 4 Dist. 1986. Police officer had probable cause to believe that felony of possession of cocaine had been committed by defendant in his presence, and as such, officer was entitled to make arrest and perform search; officer observed defendant walk to trunk of automobile, open it, quickly put something in or take something out before closing it and returning to where he was first observed and officer approached passenger side of vehicle and observed cocaine on cassette container being spread by passenger.—State v. Skofstad, 498 So.2d 582, review denied 506 So.2d 1043.

† This Case was not selected for publication in the National Reporter System

Fla.App. 4 Dist. 1986. Drug paraphernalia and marijuana were discovered in unreasonable searches of defendant's automobile and had to be suppressed where evidence was discovered after police officer, by threat of arrest without any reason to believe defendant had done anything wrong, forced defendant, who had left his automobile and was walking away from it, to reenter automobile to obtain vehicle registration. U.S.C.A. Const.Amend. 4.—Rivera v. State, 492 So.2d 477.

Fla.App. 4 Dist. 1986. Police officers had probable cause to search a properly stopped vehicle for controlled substances when officer smelled odor of burning marijuana coming from vehicle.—State v. Reeves, 488 So.2d 670.

Fla.App. 4 Dist. 1983. Police officer with extensive experience in narcotics investigations and arrests who saw defendant, whom he knew to have been previously involved with narcotics, give codefendant grocery bag, saw codefendant smell bag's contents, and then saw codefendant hand defendant money, had sufficient basis to believe that offense had been committed, and marijuana seized in subsequent stop of defendant's car was thus admissible in resulting prosecution for possession of cannabis.—State v. Dara, 432 So.2d 77.

Fla.App. 4 Dist. 1981. Police officer had probable cause to believe defendant's vehicle contained contraband and was justified in entering vehicle and seizing two marijuana cigarettes plus 53 white pills which were spread throughout vehicle where defendant drove erratically, causing collision, odor of alcohol permeated defendant's person, contraband was in plain view, and vehicle was about to be removed from scene. U.S.C.A.Const. Amend. 4.—State v. Melendez, 392 So.2d 587.

Fla.App. 4 Dist. 1980. Police officers, who observed defendants from house next to one which defendants had entered, who observed defendants coming out of house with bundles, who never saw any marijuana but only suspected that bundles contained marijuana, although there was nothing to indicate that bundles were packaged in manner that was customary to marijuana packaging in general, and who had no information concerning specific transactions, did not have requisite probable cause to make arrest of defendants or search of their car. U.S.C.A.Const. Amend. 4.—Hansen v. State, 385 So.2d 1081, review denied 392 So.2d 1379.

Fla.App. 4 Dist. 1977. Where officers arrived in a secluded, wooded area at night and found vehicle containing two occupants parked with lights out and detected strong odor of marijuana, there was probable cause for search and circumstances would have justified search without a warrant, and fact that officer requested defendant to hand him any remaining unburned substance in lieu of conducting an otherwise valid search would not militate against admission of the evidence so obtained.—McGowan v. State, 351 So.2d 1116.

Fla.App. 4 Dist. 1977. Where police blocked defendant's automobile from leaving restaurant while computer check was run on defendant's automobile and defendant even though they had no suspicion with regard to activities of defendant, and, while computer check was being conducted, one of the policemen shined light into boat behind defendant's automobile and saw some marijuana, search and seizure of marijuana was unlawful.—Bennett v. State, 350 So.2d 14.

Fla.App. 5 Dist. 2019. Following seizure of crack cocaine in open view in defendant's truck, police officer had probable cause to continue warrantless search of truck under automobile exception. U.S. Const. Amend. 4.—State v. Thornton, 286 So.3d 924.

Fla.App. 5 Dist. 2015. Police officers had probable cause to search for illegal drugs in truck of motorist, who had been stopped by police officers in parking lot due to reasonable suspicion that motorist would be in possession of controlled substances that motorist sought to sell, where motorist confirmed that there were pills in truck. U.S.C.A. Const.Amend. 4.—State v. Bullock, 164 So.3d 701, rehearing denied, and corrected.

Fla.App. 5 Dist. 1996. Police officer had reasonable cause to believe that driver was involved in illegal activity, as would justify search of his car; driver drove car matching car observed during drug buy, resident of home suspected of being used for drug transactions stated that driver lived there and was expected home soon, and officer saw driver attempt to conceal something under car seat. U.S.C.A. Const.Amend. 4.—State v. Freeman, 673 So.2d 139.

Fla.App. 5 Dist. 1992. Probable cause existed to extend a consent search into a probable cause search of automobile where trained law officer observed a particularly nervous driver accompanied by occupants of the vehicle who could not agree if they were related or not and where officer found conclusive evidence that gas tank had been altered and the vehicle was on a highway frequented by drug smugglers.—State v. Jones, 592 So.2d 363.

Fla.App. 5 Dist. 1984. Search of passenger compartment of automobile which led to discovery of cocaine and drug paraphernalia could not be sustained where it was based on mere furtive stuffing of unknown objects under seat of car, and assertion that search was to protect officers was without merit when occupants of automobile were required to move outside of vehicle and away from supposed danger zone. West's F.S.A. §§ 901.151, 933.19; West's F.S.A. Const. Art. 1, § 12; U.S.C.A. Const.Amend. 4.—Dilyerd v. State, 444 So.2d 577, quashed 467 So.2d 301.

Fla.App. 5 Dist. 1980. In proceeding in which defendant pled nolo contendere to a charge of felony possession of marijuana, evidence established that there were sufficient facts to justify a stop and to justify subsequent warrantless search of vehicle, and, thus, that denial of motion to suppress evidence was proper. West's F.S.A. §§ 893.13, 901.151; U.S.C.A.Const. Amend. 4.—Hofmeister v. State, 381 So.2d 352, petition for review denied 388 So.2d 1114.

⊂═658(2). Particular cases in general.

† **C.A.11 (Fla.) 2009.** Search-incident-to-arrest exception to warrant requirement applied to search of vehicle in which defendant was passenger following his arrest for marijuana possession; it was reasonable for officers to believe that evidence relevant to defendant's possession of marijuana might be found in vehicle, and search was limited to vehicle's front passenger compartment. U.S.C.A. Const.Amend. 4.—U.S. v. Lightbourn, 357 Fed.Appx. 259, certiorari denied 130 S.Ct. 3306, 560 U.S. 917, 176 L.Ed.2d 1207, habeas corpus denied Lightbourn v. Ormond, 2018 WL 3097324, habeas corpus denied 2018 WL 10208061, reconsideration denied 2018 WL 10208059, habeas corpus denied 2020 WL 6430340, affirmed 2021 WL 5767691.

† **This Case was not selected for publication in the National Reporter System**

C.A.5 (Fla.) 1978. Where officers had probable cause to suppose that marijuana was in vehicle, it was immaterial under Fourth Amendment whether they searched car on spot or seized it, towed it to police station, obtained warrant and searched it later. U.S.C.A.Const. Amend. 4; Comprehensive Drug Abuse Prevention and Control Act of 1970, §§ 401(a)(1), 406, 21 U.S.C.A. §§ 841(a)(1), 846; 18 U.S.C.A. § 2.—U.S. v. Hyde, 574 F.2d 856, rehearing denied 579 F.2d 643, rehearing denied U.S. v. Middlebrooks, 579 F.2d 644.

M.D.Fla. 2008. Fact that narcotics were not found in vehicle at time of initial stop and warrantless search, which were supported by probable cause, did not preclude finding of probable cause as to subsequent search, conducted following officers' removal and disassembly of vehicle; after canine alert at scene of stop, officers had reason to believe that contraband was located in hidden compartment within vehicle, but lacked tools to disassemble vehicle at roadside, and reasonably decided to move it. U.S.C.A. Const. Amend. 4.—U.S. v. Jackson, 548 F.Supp.2d 1314.

Fla.App. 1 Dist. 1996. For police officers to seize defendant's vehicle under Florida Contraband Forfeiture Act, it was not necessary for officers to have probable cause to believe vehicle contained contraband or was being used in violation of Forfeiture Act when they seized it; rather, it was sufficient that they had probable cause to believe that defendant had previously used vehicle to facilitate sale of cocaine. West's F.S.A. § 932.703(2)(c).—White v. State, 680 So.2d 550, review granted 687 So.2d 1308, opinion quashed 710 So.2d 949, rehearing denied, certiorari granted 119 S.Ct. 508, 525 U.S. 1000, 142 L.Ed.2d 421, reversed 119 S.Ct. 1555, 526 U.S. 559, 143 L.Ed.2d 748, on remand 753 So.2d 548.

Police were not required to obtain warrant or court order before seizing vehicle under Florida Contraband Forfeiture Act on basis of probable cause to believe that defendant had previously used vehicle to facilitate sale of cocaine. West's F.S.A. § 932.703(2)(c).—Id.

Fla.App. 1 Dist. 1975. Where description of stolen automobile substantially matched description of automobile in which defendant was sitting, officer who saw defendant make a movement around backseat armrest of vehicle could search for weapons by reaching under the armrest, and heroin found by officer at that time was admissible in prosecution for possession of heroin.—Lyles v. State, 312 So.2d 495.

Fla.App. 2 Dist. 2014. Police officer had probable cause to seize prescription pill bottle and its contents, after conducting traffic stop of defendant; statute provided that possession of a drug by any person not exempted, which drug was not properly labeled to indicate that possession was by a valid prescription, was prima facie evidence that such possession was unlawful, and officer observed a large pill bottle in the driver's side door pocket, he could read the label, inside the bottle he saw a blue pill and white pill, and officer identified the white pill and knew that it did not match the bottle label indicating the prescription that should be in the bottle. U.S.C.A. Const.Amend. 4; West's F.S.A. § 499.03(1, 2).—State v. Vinci, 146 So.3d 1255, review denied 157 So.3d 1051.

Fla.App. 2 Dist. 1989. Officer did not exceed scope of warrantless search of truck after arresting defendant for possession of cocaine, as officer was justified in searching every part of the truck

and its contents which may have concealed cocaine.—State v. Edwards, 547 So.2d 183.

Fla.App. 3 Dist. 1978. Where highway patrolman, who saw defendant pull her car off road and stop, was unable to gain her attention upon approaching vehicle, although he observed that her eyes were open, and such officer then, upon gaining entry into car, examined her pocketbook to inspect her driver's license because she was unable to communicate, such officer's search, after two other officers arrived and a rescue unit was summoned, for any identifying device which would delineate a medical disability that could account for her condition was not unreasonable, and thus no error occurred in denying defendant's motion to suppress cocaine found during such search. West's F.S.A. § 901.215.—Evans v. State, 364 So.2d 93, certiorari denied 373 So.2d 457.

Fla.App. 4 Dist. 1976. Officer, who, after stopping accused for speeding, observed what officer suspected were cannabis seeds when he shined flashlight on inspection sticker of car and who suspected that odor emanating from accused's person was the odor of burned or burning marijuana or the odor of accused's perfume or after shave lotion did not have probable cause to make general search of car.—Brown v. State, 330 So.2d 861.

Fla.App. 4 Dist. 1969. Search in which marijuana was found by police officer at police station while searching for stolen money was reasonable where search on highway of automobile and arrested suspects could not reasonably be conclusive that missing money was not hidden within clothing or on body of one or more of such suspects or hidden in or about their personal belongings or automobile and where box in which money was supposed to be contained was found on floor of automobile in plain view. F.S.A. § 901.21(1).—State v. Aiken, 228 So.2d 442.

Fla.App. 5 Dist. 1984. Search of passenger compartment of automobile which led to discovery of cocaine and drug paraphernalia could not be sustained where it was based on mere furtive stuffing of unknown objects under seat of car, and assertion that search was to protect officers was without merit when occupants of automobile were required to move outside of vehicle and away from supposed danger zone. West's F.S.A. §§ 901.151, 933.19; West's F.S.A. Const. Art. 1, § 12; U.S.C.A. Const.Amend. 4.—Dilyerd v. State, 444 So.2d 577, quashed 467 So.2d 301.

☞**658(3). Compartments; trunk.**

† **C.A.11 (Fla.) 2015.** Because probable cause existed to search defendant's vehicle for evidence of drug-trafficking activity, police officers were allowed to search areas of car that might have concealed such evidence, including glove compartment and area under driver's seat. U.S.C.A. Const.Amend. 4.—U.S. v. Alston, 598 Fed.Appx. 730, certiorari denied 136 S.Ct. 560, 577 U.S. 1017, 193 L.Ed.2d 446, post-conviction relief denied 2019 WL 2411197.

† **C.A.11 (Fla.) 2015.** Police officer's testimony that he smelled marijuana coming from the interior of defendant's car was not contrary to the laws of nature, inconsistent, or improbable on its face, and thus was sufficiently creditable to support district court's determination that officer had probable cause to search vehicle and its trunk, where officer testified that he had recognized the smell of fresh marijuana based on working on hundreds of cases involving marijua-

na, receiving training in detecting marijuana, and personally smoking marijuana in the twelfth grade. U.S.C.A. Const.Amend. 4.—U.S. v. Smith, 596 Fed.Appx. 804.

C.A.11 (Fla.) 1984. Arresting officer who conducted search of automobile trunk had probable cause based on another officer's knowledge that cocaine was somewhere in the car, the other officer's contact with arresting officer in setting up the search, the other officer's presence in the vicinity at the time the trunk was opened, and the arresting officer's testimony that another agent told him that the cocaine was in the car. U.S.C.A. Const.Amend. 4.—U.S. v. Esle, 743 F.2d 1465, rehearing denied 755 F.2d 176.

C.A.11 (Fla.) 1983. Police officers who had engaged in carefully planned and integrated operation involving sale of cocaine to defendants and who had seen or assisted in placing cocaine in defendants' suitcase and placing suitcase in locked trunk of automobile had probable cause to stop automobile and probable cause to suspect that there was contraband concealed in automobile, justifying warrantless search of closed suitcase in locked trunk.—U.S. v. Badolato, 710 F.2d 1509, rehearing denied 717 F.2d 1401.

Fla. 2002. Officer's detection of very strong odor of previously-burnt marijuana coming directly out of rolled-down window of defendant's vehicle, combined with defendant's initial attempt to draw officer away from vehicle by exiting it and approaching the officer before officer could reach the vehicle, defendant's extremely "nervous" and "jittery" demeanor during presearch interaction with officer, defendant's conduct in pushing himself off the vehicle twice while officer was attempting to conduct pat-down search, and the recovery during the pat-down search of storage bag containing marijuana, provided probable cause to search the entire vehicle, including the trunk. U.S.C.A. Const.Amend. 4.—State v. Betz, 815 So.2d 627.

Fla.App. 1 Dist. 2007. Marijuana found following the frisk of a vehicle occupant, combined with furtive behavior by the vehicle occupants, provides probable cause to search the entire vehicle, including the trunk. U.S.C.A. Const. Amend. 4.—Kimball v. State, 951 So.2d 35, review denied 959 So.2d 716.

Deputy had probable cause to believe that marijuana was located in vehicle and, thus, was allowed to conduct warrantless search of entire vehicle, including its trunk; deputy detected a strong odor of raw marijuana emanating from vehicle when he arrived at passenger window, search of vehicle's driver revealed only a small quantity of marijuana on his person, and other vehicle occupants, including defendant, displayed excessive or furtive movement after deputy stopped vehicle. U.S.C.A. Const.Amend. 4.—Id.

Fla.App. 1 Dist. 1990. Once officers discovered marijuana on floorboard of car during valid weapon search, they had probable cause to believe that vehicle contained contraband, thereby permitting them to search entire vehicle, including trunk and engine compartment. U.S.C.A. Const.Amend. 4.—Hall v. State, 562 So.2d 714.

Fla.App. 1 Dist. 1982. Warrantless search of padlocked cargo area of rented truck, which was stopped at agricultural inspection station, by deputy who smelled odor of marijuana was not invalid under the circumstances and once deputy had opened the cargo area, search of the bundles observed inside was not illegal.—Brayton v. State, 425 So.2d 88, petition for review denied 434 So.2d 886.

Fla.App. 1 Dist. 1980. Police officers, who were justified by probable cause and exigent circumstances in stopping and searching car without warrant, were also justified in searching locked trunk of defendant's vehicle and manila envelope found in locked trunk since they had sufficient probable cause to believe that contraband would be found therein. U.S.C.A.Const. Amend. 4.—Baxter v. State, 390 So.2d 475.

Fla.App. 1 Dist. 1979. In prosecution for possession of marijuana with intent to deliver or distribute, wherein defendant moved to suppress marijuana found in search of trunk of his car, evidence established that arresting officer had probable cause to believe that the car contained contraband. U.S.C.A.Const. Amend. 4.—Webb v. State, 373 So.2d 400, certiorari denied 383 So.2d 1204.

Fla.App. 2 Dist. 2001. Warrantless search of automobile trunk was illegal, though lawful search of defendant's person produced marijuana, given that officer never articulated facts suggesting likelihood that vehicle's trunk contained additional contraband, and thus, probable cause to believe the passenger compartment of vehicle contained contraband did not justify search of the trunk or of containers within it. U.S.C.A. Const. Amend. 4.—Betz v. State, 793 So.2d 976, review granted 791 So.2d 1101, quashed 815 So.2d 627.

Fla.App. 3 Dist. 1987. Warrantless search of trunk revealing cocaine, after accused's lawful arrest, although not supportable under officer's stated impoundment-inventory theory, was nonetheless valid where objective facts showed that vehicle was subject to seizure under forfeiture statute. West's F.S.A. §§ 932.701–932.704.—State v. Blanco, 513 So.2d 739.

Fla.App. 4 Dist. 1983. Seizure of marijuana as result of search of car trunk was proper where officers had legitimately stopped automobile and had probable cause to believe that contraband was concealed somewhere within it and where search also was inventory search because automobile was blocking the street and its occupants remained silent and where, also, police were entitled to seize the automobile pursuant to forfeiture statute and to conduct subsequent search. U.S.C.A. Const.Amend. 4; West's F.S.A. § 932.703.—State v. Scotti, 428 So.2d 771.

☞658(4). Luggage, bags, and other containers.

C.A.11 (Fla.) 2019. Under the automobile exception to the Fourth Amendment's warrant requirement, the police may search an automobile and the containers within it where they have probable cause to believe contraband or evidence is contained. U.S. Const. Amend. 4.—United States v. Delva, 922 F.3d 1228, denial of postconviction relief affirmed 851 Fed.Appx. 148, certiorari denied 142 S.Ct. 374, 211 L.Ed.2d 199.

† **C.A.11 (Fla.) 2016.** Police canine's alert to defendant's suitcase, after it had been removed from commercial bus, and trooper's knowledge that drugs had been hidden inside canned foods gave him probable cause to believe that defendant had concealed drugs inside the metal cans he found inside defendant's suitcase, and thus, under the automobile exception to the warrant requirement, trooper was justified in opening a can to examine its contents, even though he opened the metal can after detaining defendant and his suitcase. U.S.C.A. Const.Amend. 4.—U.S. v. Pina, 648 Fed.Appx. 899.

† **C.A.11 (Fla.) 2015.** Because officer had probable cause to search defendant's car for

narcotics based on canine alert, officer had basis to move, manipulate, and search contents of backpack found within car in order to complete search. U.S.C.A. Const.Amend. 4.—U.S. v. Reeves, 604 Fed.Appx. 823.

C.A.11 (Fla.) 1990. Drug Enforcement Administration (DEA) agents' search of cardboard boxes in van after arrest of suspects fell within automobile exception to search warrant requirement; agents maintained constant surveillance of warehouse until they witnessed suspects loading several cardboard boxes from warehouse into van and cardboard boxes were not labeled, which, according to one agent, was a common method of transporting narcotics.—U.S. v. Delgado, 903 F.2d 1495, certiorari denied 111 S.Ct. 681, 498 U.S. 1028, 112 L.Ed.2d 673.

C.A.11 (Fla.) 1988. Contents of seven sealed boxes found in defendant's van were admissible against defendant despite fact that warrant had not been issued when boxes were searched; containers had previously been lawfully opened by police officers and contents had previously been identified as illegal and further, the contents were kept under constant surveillance so that there was no substantial likelihood that contents were changed. U.S.C.A. Const.Amend. 4.—U.S. v. Quintero, 848 F.2d 154.

C.A.11 (Fla.) 1983. Police officers who had engaged in carefully planned and integrated operation involving sale of cocaine to defendants and who had seen or assisted in placing cocaine in defendants' suitcase and placing suitcase in locked trunk of automobile had probable cause to stop automobile and probable cause to suspect that there was contraband concealed in automobile, justifying warrantless search of closed suitcase in locked trunk.—U.S. v. Badolato, 710 F.2d 1509, rehearing denied 717 F.2d 1401.

C.A.11 (Fla.) 1982. Where there was ample cause to connect van with marijuana so that agents could properly search van, and where outward appearance, size and apparent nature of ice box in van were such that officer with probable cause might reasonably believe that it was place where marijuana could be found, opening ice box, which, after it was open, was found to contain electronic equipment, was permissible search of closed container within vehicle. U.S.C.A. Const.Amend. 4; Comprehensive Drug Abuse Prevention and Control Act of 1970, §§ 401(a)(1), 406, 21 U.S.C.A. §§ 841(a)(1), 846. —U.S. v. Capo, 693 F.2d 1330, certiorari denied 103 S.Ct. 1793, 460 U.S. 1092, 76 L.Ed.2d 359, on rehearing U.S. v. Lisenby, 716 F.2d 1355.

C.A.5 (Fla.) 1981. Although there was probable cause for warrantless search of trunk of defendant's automobile, with exigent circumstances justifying warrantless search of briefcase found therein, i. e., suspicion that briefcase contained loaded spring-triggered pistol, warrantless search of brown paper bag found next to briefcase was not justified, notwithstanding that defendant was suspected manufacturer of silencers and was observed carrying bag from machine shop where he apparently manufactured such devices, as bag was closed, had no exterior markings, disclosed nothing by its shape, was not suspected of containing anything dangerous to those nearby and had no cracks, rips or tears. U.S.C.A.Const. Amend. 4.—U.S. v. Moschetta, 646 F.2d 955, certiorari denied Spieler v. U.S., 102 S.Ct. 1613, 455 U.S. 989, 71 L.Ed.2d 849, certiorari granted, vacated 102 S.Ct. 2919, 457 U.S. 1113, 73 L.Ed.2d 1324, on remand 690 F.2d 488.

C.A.5 (Fla.) 1975. Narcotics agent, who had information that large quantities of pharmaceuticals were in apartment under surveillance, had reasonable grounds to believe that defendant, who left apartment carrying two suitcases, was removing illegal drugs from the apartment and had probable cause to stop vehicle in which defendant drove away from the apartment, and probable cause and the exigent circumstances authorized search of the vehicle and seizure of suitcases from the vehicle. Comprehensive Drug Abuse Prevention and Control Act of 1970, § 401(a)(1), 21 U.S.C.A. § 841(a)(1).—U.S. v. Almas, 507 F.2d 65.

C.A.5 (Fla.) 1973. Where federal narcotics agents had probable cause to believe that occupants of taxicab were carrying narcotics in their suitcases, agents were justified in opening trunk and removing the suitcases without a warrant and they legitimately seized the suitcases and were not required to leave them in taxicab or on sidewalk to be taken away or to disappear. 18 U.S.C.A. § 3731; U.S.C.A.Const. Amend. 4.—U.S. v. Soriano, 482 F.2d 469, on rehearing 497 F.2d 147.

Warrantless search of suitcases properly seized by narcotics agents from taxicab was not justified on basis of alleged exigent circumstance that opening suitcases immediately might have disclosed information which possibly would have led to capture of others participating in narcotics operation. U.S.C.A.Const. Amend. 4.—Id.

Fla. 1975. Even if trooper could have legally required satisfactory identification from passengers of stopped automobile, although at the time nothing reasonably indicated that either passenger had committed, was committing, or was about to commit a violation of a criminal law, search and seizure of plastic sandwich bag which officer saw protruding from beneath the leg of passenger when copassenger exited the car was illegal and therefore subsequent arrests by officer who found bag to contain marijuana ashes were illegal.—Bailey v. State, 319 So.2d 22.

Fla.App. 1 Dist. 2011. Law enforcement officer who stopped defendant's truck in the process of executing a valid arrest warrant properly performed warrantless search of defendant's gym bag, and thus no basis existed to suppress hydromorphone found in the gym bag, where defendant admitted to the presence of the controlled substance in the gym bag in his truck after being read his *Miranda* rights. U.S.C.A. Const.Amend. 4; West's F.S.A. § 893.03(2)(a).—Cox v. State, 75 So.3d 325, rehearing denied.

Fla.App. 1 Dist. 1990. Officer who had stopped automobile in area allegedly frequented by drug users and who claimed to have observed passenger in backseat of vehicle trying to conceal matchbox from view did not have probable cause to seize matchbox, despite officer's testimony that matchbox was a "familiar place" to carry crack cocaine and that he had found crack in matchbox on at least one other occasion. U.S.C.A. Const. Amend. 4.—Griggs v. State, 565 So.2d 361.

Fla.App. 1 Dist. 1988. Trooper's search of package found under passenger seat was justified under circumstances showing that defendant did not withdraw consent to search and trooper previously had found flour sifter in trunk, giving him probable cause to believe that narcotics were present in car.—Hurtado v. State, 533 So.2d 304, review denied 541 So.2d 1172.

Fla.App. 1 Dist. 1985. Where police officers' original probable cause was to believe that defendant's vehicle itself contained contraband, in that only information was that a vehicle would arrive from Dade County transporting drugs, and no specific container was mentioned and none initially looked for, and where only later observation of removal and replacement of containers led police to believe that at least some of the contraband was located therein, officers were not obligated to obtain a warrant before searching the containers under rule that, while officers who have legitimately stopped an automobile and who have probable cause to believe that contraband is concealed somewhere therein may conduct a warrantless search of vehicle and may open containers which may contain the contraband, probable cause is limited to a container only coincidentally within the automobile, as officers had no reason to believe that all of the contraband in the vehicle was in the containers.—Vathis v. State, 474 So.2d 423.

Fla.App. 1 Dist. 1982. Where, after obtaining agricultural search warrant, locked compartment of van was forcibly opened and cannabis in excess of 500 pounds was discovered therein, deputy officer had probable cause to conduct warrantless search of vehicle and containers, including flight bag, found therein whether search was conducted at the immediate scene or at police station shortly thereafter. West's F.S.A. § 570.15(1)(b); West's F.S.A. Const. Art. 1, § 12. —Roche v. State, 447 So.2d 890, decision approved 462 So.2d 1096.

Fla.App. 1 Dist. 1982. Search of defendant's van and opening of one of bags of marijuana therein was not unreasonable where, considering evidence in light most favorable to ruling of trial court, defendant consented to opening of van and, notwithstanding that defendant did not consent to opening of plastic bags, deputy sheriff, upon noticing strong smell of marijuana, had probable cause to believe that vehicle contained marijuana.—Grimes v. State, 416 So.2d 488.

Fla.App. 1 Dist. 1981. Warrantless search of automobiles rented by police and provided to confidential informant so as to be handed over to defendants for transportation of marijuana which defendants had agreed to sell to informant was not unreasonable where one of defendants opened trunk of one automobile to show informant contents and police officer with prior knowledge of and experience in dealing with marijuana observed plastic bags in both trunk and in back seat of other automobile containing what he was able to conclude was marijuana. U.S.C.A.Const. Amend. 4; West's F.S.A.Const. Art. 1, § 12.—Murray v. State, 401 So.2d 1119, review denied 412 So.2d 468.

Fla.App. 1 Dist. 1980. Police officers, who were justified by probable cause and exigent circumstances in stopping and searching car without warrant, were also justified in searching locked trunk of defendant's vehicle and manila envelope found in locked trunk since they had sufficient probable cause to believe that contraband would be found therein. U.S.C.A.Const. Amend. 4.—Baxter v. State, 390 So.2d 475.

Fla.App. 1 Dist. 1979. Large amount of marijuana seized and fact that marijuana was packaged in garbage bags supported inference that marijuana was intended not for defendants' personal use but rather for resale, and thus defendants failed to show manifestation of privacy in contents of garbage bags for purposes of determining propriety of warrantless search of garbage bags seized from automobile, notwithstanding that search of bags was not conducted immediately after automobile was stopped.—Ev-

ans v. State, 368 So.2d 58, certiorari denied 379 So.2d 204.

Fla.App. 2 Dist. 2001. Warrantless search of automobile trunk was illegal, though lawful search of defendant's person produced marijuana, given that officer never articulated facts suggesting likelihood that vehicle's trunk contained additional contraband, and thus, probable cause to believe the passenger compartment of vehicle contained contraband did not justify search of the trunk or of containers within it. U.S.C.A. Const. Amend. 4.—Betz v. State, 793 So.2d 976, review granted 791 So.2d 1101, quashed 815 So.2d 627.

Fla.App. 2 Dist. 1995. If warrantless search of automobile was proper as either search incident to arrest of two men who had occupied automobile or as search based on automobile exception, search of purse of defendant who was found in automobile was also proper.—Union v. State, 660 So.2d 803.

Officers did not have probable cause to search automobile and purse of defendant who was in automobile despite fact that persons involved in drug deal drove automobile to location to make drug sale, where drug sale occurred some distance away from automobile and away from defendant and no facts supported officer's belief that there would be additional drugs in automobile.—Id.

Fla.App. 2 Dist. 1984. Police officer who stopped defendant and searched his car for a brown paper bag had probable cause to believe that the bag contained marijuana, and thus, had probable cause to search, despite fact that the bag was not in plain view, where, after receiving a tip from security officer at defendant's place of business that defendant was dealing in narcotics in company parking lot, police officer followed defendant in his automobile during lunch hour and observed him park his car, go inside a building, come out approximately six minutes later with a brown paper bag, accompanied by a man who looked up and down the street in a "suspicious manner," and where police officer was an experienced narcotics officer who had previously observed persons break up quantities of marijuana and package it for transportation using brown paper bags.—Manee v. State, 457 So.2d 530, petition for review denied 464 So.2d 556, certiorari denied 105 S.Ct. 2678, 471 U.S. 1137, 86 L.Ed.2d 696.

Where police officer had brown paper bag that defendant was carrying under surveillance before defendant placed it in his automobile, fact that the bag was fortuitously placed in the automobile before being seized did not authorize application of the automobile exception to the warrant requirement, and thus, while police detective properly seized brown paper bag from defendant's automobile after receiving a tip that defendant was dealing in narcotics and observing suspicious behavior by defendant, he should have detained defendant and obtained a warrant before searching the bag.—Id.

Fla.App. 3 Dist. 1993. Even if defendant had reasonable expectation of privacy in brown bag in which police found cocaine, search was reasonable based on moving vehicle exception to search warrant requirement rule; officers had probable cause to search vehicle which was being operated on public streets, and they did not have time to obtain warrant before vehicle was stopped and searched. U.S.C.A. Const.Amend. 4. —State v. Daniel, 622 So.2d 1344.

Fla.App. 3 Dist. 1982. Scope of search of van which produced marijuana packaged in burlap

† This Case was not selected for publication in the National Reporter System

and plastic bags did not go beyond any alleged consent given by defendant and opening of burlap bags did not warrant suppression of marijuana.—Zaval v. State, 416 So.2d 1226.

Fla.App. 3 Dist. 1970. Where police officers had stopped automobile after occupants had been observed passing small cigarette among them and where after occupants of automobile were detained one of them threw a plastic bag into street which was found to contain marijuana, seizure of bag of marijuana thrown into street while occupants were detained and before they were arrested was proper.—State v. Padilla, 235 So.2d 309, certiorari denied 239 So.2d 830.

Fla.App. 4 Dist. 2002. Defendant had no reasonable expectation of privacy in a paper bag containing drugs that he stored in the wheel well of a truck parked in convenience store parking lot. U.S.C.A. Const.Amend. 4.—State v. Lampley, 817 So.2d 989.

Fla.App. 4 Dist. 1989. Totality of circumstances established probable cause for deputy to seize and open aspirin travel container observed in plain view while searching automobile for gun, pursuant to driver's consent; automobile was in high drug area, deputy had training and vast experience in narcotics investigations, deputy was very familiar with similar containers and was 90% sure that such containers would contain contraband, and when shaking container deputy heard what sounded to him like rock cocaine.—State v. Franklin, 543 So.2d 1322.

Fla.App. 4 Dist. 1974. Search and seizure, not made incident to a lawful arrest, by officer who stopped automobile for weaving but made no arrest for traffic violation, who, while a passenger got out of automobile to get identification observed a plastic bag sticking out from under leg of defendant, who reached in and got the bag and opened it up and found ashes which had a strong odor of marijuana, but who did not detect an odor of marijuana and had no reason to believe an offense had been or was being committed, could not be justified as having been based upon probable cause, an emergency situation, or the plain view doctrine inasmuch as testimony revealed that whatever was contained in the bag was not fully disclosed and open to the eye and hand.—Bailey v. State, 295 So.2d 133, quashed 319 So.2d 22.

Fla.App. 5 Dist. 1979. Where defendant, who was sole occupant of pickup truck, had been arrested and placed in back of squad car before arresting officer returned to the truck and seized marijuana cigarette from floorboard and searched defendant's purse, which she left in the cab, the warrantless seizure could not be justified on the probable cause, exigent circumstances exception. U.S.C.A.Const. Amend. 4; West's F.S.A.Const. art. 1, § 12.—Ulesky v. State, 379 So.2d 121.

⬤═**659. —— Location of vehicle.**

† **C.A.11 (Fla.) 2016.** Law enforcement officer on patrol in area adjacent to that mentioned in police dispatch as site of vehicular burglary had reasonable suspicion of criminal activity of kind sufficient to support his entry onto private driveway to investigate apparently unoccupied vehicle which he observed in driveway, at 2:00 a.m., with its front door standing open. U.S.C.A. Const. Amend. 4.—U.S. v. Presley, 645 Fed.Appx. 934, certiorari denied 136 S.Ct. 2042, 578 U.S. 988, 195 L.Ed.2d 240, post-conviction relief denied 2020 WL 1046818.

C.A.11 (Fla.) 1982. Where defendant's son-in-law was seen driving van which accompanied truck provided on trek to obtain marijuana, there was ample cause to connect van with marijuana, and agents could properly have searched van on spot without warrant and did not commit improper search in taking van to jail and searching it there. U.S.C.A. Const.Amend. 4; Comprehensive Drug Abuse Prevention and Control Act of 1970, §§ 401(a)(1), 406, 21 U.S.C.A. §§ 841(a)(1), 846.—U.S. v. Capo, 693 F.2d 1330, certiorari denied 103 S.Ct. 1793, 460 U.S. 1092, 76 L.Ed.2d 359, on rehearing U.S. v. Lisenby, 716 F.2d 1355.

Fla. 1998. Absence of probable cause to believe contraband was in vehicle, combined with lack of any other exigent circumstances, rendered automobile exception to warrant requirement inapplicable to seizure of defendant's automobile, where vehicle was parked safely at defendant's employment, government had keys to vehicle, and defendant was in custody on unrelated charges. U.S.C.A. Const.Amend. 4; West's F.S.A. Const. Art. 1, § 12; West's F.S.A. §§ 932.701–932.707.—White v. State, 710 So.2d 949, rehearing denied, certiorari granted 119 S.Ct. 508, 525 U.S. 1000, 142 L.Ed.2d 421, reversed 119 S.Ct. 1555, 526 U.S. 559, 143 L.Ed.2d 748, on remand 753 So.2d 548.

Fla.App. 1 Dist. 1990. Officer who had stopped automobile in area allegedly frequented by drug users and who claimed to have observed passenger in backseat of vehicle trying to conceal matchbox from view did not have probable cause to seize matchbox, despite officer's testimony that matchbox was a "familiar place" to carry crack cocaine and that he had found crack in matchbox on at least one other occasion. U.S.C.A. Const. Amend. 4.—Griggs v. State, 565 So.2d 361.

Fla.App. 1 Dist. 1981. Considering furtive movements of automobile occupant, area where vehicle was located, time of night and fact that occupant appeared to be trying to stuff something between car seats, police officer's command for occupant to sit up from his prone position on car seat was such limited intrusion that there was no constitutional violation by officers, and contraband which then came into open view was subject to seizure under automobile exception to warrant requirement. U.S.C.A.Const. Amend. 4. —Moline v. State, 404 So.2d 826.

Fla.App. 1 Dist. 1976. Where automobile which had been driven by defendant, arrested for driving while under the influence of intoxicants and taken to station, was legally parked but was parked by the side of the road across from a local nightspot police acted reasonably in effort to safeguard vehicle by returning to the same and driving it to police station and officer who noticed odor of marijuana was justified in making a warrantless search of automobile which disclosed a large quantity of marijuana in trunk.—Mattson v. State, 328 So.2d 246.

Fla.App. 5 Dist. 2019. Officer had probable cause to perform warrantless search of defendant's truck under automobile exception following defendant's arrest; truck was not located in the constitutionally-protected curtilage of his residence at the time of the search, and crack cocaine situated on the driver's seat of the truck was in open view. U.S. Const. Amend. 4.—State v. Thornton, 286 So.3d 924.

Fla.App. 5 Dist. 1992. Probable cause existed to extend a consent search into a probable cause search of automobile where trained law officer observed a particularly nervous driver accompanied by occupants of the vehicle who could not agree if they were related or not and where officer found conclusive evidence that gas tank had been altered and the vehicle was on a highway frequented by drug smugglers.—State v. Jones, 592 So.2d 363.

☞**660. ―――― Odor detection; use of dogs.**

U.S.Fla. 2013. Training and testing records sufficiently established reliability of drug detection dog that alerted to defendant's truck, notwithstanding that dog later alerted to same truck, but nothing was discovered; dog had successfully completed two recent drug-detection courses and maintained his proficiency through weekly training exercises, and dog's later response was likely due to odors defendant had transferred to driver's-side door handle. U.S.C.A. Const.Amend. 4. —Florida v. Harris, 133 S.Ct. 1050, 568 U.S. 237, 185 L.Ed.2d 61, on remand Harris v. State, 123 So.3d 1144.

†**C.A.11 (Fla.) 2019.** Warrantless search of truck was lawful, based on probable cause that truck contained cocaine; defendant's truck, which he had driven minutes prior to search, was readily mobile, and canine had alerted to the odor of narcotics while sniffing outside of it, giving officers probable cause to believe it contained contraband, K-9 officer's testimony proved that canine was a reliable drug-detection dog because he had completed a 400-hour initial training, he had completed monthly 16-hour trainings, his certification as police dog was current, and he had only given false alerts a total of 12 to 15 times out of 200, and defendant had opportunity to challenge canine's reliability by questioning his training and certification during his cross-examination of K-9 officer, and did not present any conflicting evidence. U.S. Const. Amend. 4.—United States v. Rodriguez, 762 Fed. Appx. 938.

†**C.A.11 (Fla.) 2016.** Police canine's alert to defendant's suitcase, after it had been removed from commercial bus, and trooper's knowledge that drugs had been hidden inside canned foods gave him probable cause to believe that defendant had concealed drugs inside the metal cans he found inside defendant's suitcase, and thus, under the automobile exception to the warrant requirement, trooper was justified in opening a can to examine its contents, even though he opened the metal can after detaining defendant and his suitcase. U.S.C.A. Const.Amend. 4.— U.S. v. Pina, 648 Fed.Appx. 899.

†**C.A.11 (Fla.) 2015.** Because officer had probable cause to search defendant's car for narcotics based on canine alert, officer had basis to move, manipulate, and search contents of backpack found within car in order to complete search. U.S.C.A. Const.Amend. 4.—U.S. v. Reeves, 604 Fed.Appx. 823.

†**C.A.11 (Fla.) 2015.** Police officer's testimony that he smelled marijuana coming from the interior of defendant's car was not contrary to the laws of nature, inconsistent, or improbable on its face, and thus was sufficiently creditable to support district court's determination that officer had probable cause to search vehicle and its trunk, where officer testified that he had recognized the smell of fresh marijuana based on working on hundreds of cases involving marijuana, receiving training in detecting marijuana, and personally smoking marijuana in the twelfth grade. U.S.C.A. Const.Amend. 4.—U.S. v. Smith, 596 Fed.Appx. 804.

C.A.11 (Fla.) 2015. The smell of burnt marijuana emanating from a vehicle is sufficient probable cause to search a vehicle. U.S.C.A. Const. Amend. 4.—Merricks v. Adkisson, 785 F.3d 553.

†**C.A.11 (Fla.) 2014.** Evidence of positive alert by drug detection dog that was presumptively reliable to motor vehicle which was stopped by Florida state trooper as matching description of vehicle suspected of being involved in narcotics activity provided trooper with probable cause to conduct warrantless search of vehicle, so that contraband discovered during this warrantless search did not have to be suppressed as allegedly obtained in violation of motorist's Fourth Amendment rights. U.S.C.A. Const.Amend. 4.—U.S. v. Trejo, 551 Fed.Appx. 565.

†**C.A.11 (Fla.) 2012.** Probable cause existed to believe there was contraband in defendant's vehicle; officers stopped the vehicle after receiving reports that gunshots had emanated from it, and they then observed a bag of marijuana in plain view and smelled burnt marijuana in the vehicle. U.S.C.A. Const.Amend. 4.—U.S. v. Brown, 498 Fed.Appx. 940, post-conviction relief denied 2017 WL 942113, certificate of appealability denied 2018 WL 1474898, certiorari denied 139 S.Ct. 226, 202 L.Ed.2d 153, rehearing denied 139 S.Ct. 624, 202 L.Ed.2d 450.

†**C.A.11 (Fla.) 2012.** Following investigatory stop of defendant's vehicle based on reasonable suspicion that he was selling drugs and carrying firearm, officers' dog sniff of interior of vehicle did not constitute a search without probable cause; trained dog jumped instinctively into the car, without any encouragement or facilitation from officers, through driver's side door which defendant had left open. U.S.C.A. Const.Amend. 4.—U.S. v. Mostowicz, 471 Fed.Appx. 887.

†**C.A.11 (Fla.) 2011.** District Court did not clearly err in concluding that drug dog was sufficiently reliable that his alert on defendant's car provided probable cause for a warrantless search of the car, despite dog's alleged 70% accuracy rate in the field; dog had completed a 450-hour patrol course and a 200-hour narcotics detection course and was certified by the National Police Canine Association in both areas. U.S.C.A. Const.Amend. 4; 18 U.S.C.A. § 922(g).— U.S. v. Smith, 448 Fed.Appx. 936, certiorari denied 133 S.Ct. 1453, 568 U.S. 1192, 185 L.Ed.2d 361, appeal after new sentencing hearing 559 Fed.Appx. 884, certiorari denied 135 S.Ct. 147, 574 U.S. 858, 190 L.Ed.2d 108, leave to file for rehearing denied 135 S.Ct. 1490, 574 U.S. 1187, 191 L.Ed.2d 428, post-conviction relief denied 2017 WL 4857575, certificate of appealability denied 2018 WL 3199346, certiorari denied 139 S.Ct. 1258, 203 L.Ed.2d 281.

District Court did not clearly err in concluding that drug dog was sufficiently reliable that his alert on defendant's car provided probable cause for a warrantless search of the car, despite dog's alleged 70% accuracy rate in the field; 70% accuracy rate was sufficient to establish a fair probability that drugs would be found in the car. U.S.C.A. Const.Amend. 4; 18 U.S.C.A. § 922(g).— Id.

†**C.A.11 (Fla.) 2011.** Drug detection dog's alert to the presence of marijuana, during two separate inspections of defendant's van, which occurred after the dog entered the van's rear passenger door, which had been left open by its occupants, provided independent probable cause to search the van. U.S.C.A. Const.Amend. 4.— U.S. v. Freeman, 438 Fed.Appx. 864.

†**C.A.11 (Fla.) 2010.** Search by law enforcement officers of defendant's truck while it was parked at defendant's residence fell within the

automobile exception to the Fourth Amendment search warrant requirement; a drug dog alerted to the presence of drugs in the truck, and there was no indication that the truck was inoperable, and officers had received an anonymous tip earlier that day that defendant was driving the truck, and although the truck's driveway access to the street was blocked by a car, the truck could have reached the street by driving through the front yard. U.S.C.A. Const.Amend. 4.—U.S. v. Boyd, 388 Fed.Appx. 943, post-conviction relief denied 2012 WL 3609857.

† **C.A.11 (Fla.) 2010.** Narcotics dog's alert to presence of drugs near driver's side rear door, in same area of car that law enforcement agents had seen defendant place bag reasonably believed to contain cocaine provided probable cause to search vehicle under automobile exception to warrant requirement. U.S.C.A. Const.Amend. 4. —U.S. v. Bernard, 380 Fed.Appx. 801, rehearing and rehearing denied 406 Fed.Appx. 471, certiorari denied 131 S.Ct. 683, 562 U.S. 1077, 178 L.Ed.2d 507, post-conviction relief denied 2012 WL 13071129.

† **C.A.11 (Fla.) 2007.** Police officer lacked probable cause to justify warrantless search of vehicle, even though police officer testified that he detected the odor of marijuana emanating from vehicle; district court's fact determination, that officer would have had to be closer to drugs in order to smell the marijuana, was a credibility ruling based not only upon defendant's testimony but evidence showing that only a small amount of marijuana was found in a sealed, plastic bag that was in the center console of the truck. U.S.C.A. Const.Amend. 4.—U.S. v. Jennings, 227 Fed. Appx. 828.

† **C.A.11 (Fla.) 2006.** Probable cause existed for warrantless search of drug defendant's automobile, where trained canine gave positive alert on automobile during otherwise lawful detention of defendant. U.S.C.A. Const.Amend. 4.—U.S. v. Williams, 199 Fed.Appx. 828.

† **C.A.11 (Fla.) 2006.** Police officer had reasonable suspicion that detainee was transporting drugs, justifying warrantless pat-down search, where police had received tip that house where detainee resided was a drug lab, reliable confidential informant had arranged for detainee to deliver drugs at time and place that officers stopped her, and drug-sniffing canine alerted to presence of drugs in detainee's truck and pelvic area. U.S.C.A. Const.Amend. 4.—Dominguez v. Metropolitan Miami-Dade County, 167 Fed.Appx. 147.

C.A.11 (Fla.) 1990. Drug-sniffing dog's alert to stuffed rabbit on back seat of car gave state trooper probable cause to inspect rabbit for drugs. U.S.C.A. Const.Amend. 4.—U.S. v. Dunkley, 911 F.2d 522, certiorari denied Brown v. U.S., 111 S.Ct. 765, 498 U.S. 1052, 112 L.Ed.2d 785, certiorari denied Baker v. U.S., 111 S.Ct. 766, 498 U.S. 1052, 112 L.Ed.2d 785, certiorari denied 111 S.Ct. 987, 498 U.S. 1096, 112 L.Ed.2d 1071.

C.A.5 (Fla.) 1979. Where police officers were justified in stopping vans based upon suspicion that heavily laden vans contained marijuana taken from boat and where, after drivers exited vans, officers saw that bottom portion of one of the driver's rolled up pants legs was damp and smelled odor of marijuana coming from vans, probable cause existed for warrantless search of vans. U.S.C.A.Const. Amend. 4.—U.S. v. Soto, 591 F.2d 1091, certiorari denied 99 S.Ct. 2862, 442 U.S. 930, 61 L.Ed.2d 298, certiorari denied

Pardon Gonzalez v. U.S., 100 S.Ct. 89, 444 U.S. 845, 62 L.Ed.2d 58.

M.D.Fla. 2008. Fact that narcotics were not found in vehicle at time of initial stop and warrantless search, which were supported by probable cause, did not preclude finding of probable cause as to subsequent search, conducted following officers' removal and disassembly of vehicle; after canine alert at scene of stop, officers had reason to believe that contraband was located in hidden compartment within vehicle, but lacked tools to disassemble vehicle at roadside, and reasonably decided to move it. U.S.C.A. Const. Amend. 4.—U.S. v. Jackson, 548 F.Supp.2d 1314.

Canine alert for presence of drugs in stopped vehicle, which occurred during initial stop that was supported by probable cause and search that was consented, provided probable cause for further searching of vehicle. U.S.C.A. Const.Amend. 4.—Id.

S.D.Fla. 2010. There was no arguable probable cause for law enforcement officers to search plaintiff's vehicle nor was there an emergency justifying searching the vehicle without a warrant, and thus search violated plaintiff's Fourth Amendment rights; safety concerns surrounding global conference, plaintiff's alleged criminal history related to protest activity and assistance to protesters, plaintiff's suspicious behavior, and bomb-sniffing dog's interest in plaintiff's vehicle, did not constitute circumstances by which reasonable law enforcement officers could have believed that probable cause existed. U.S.C.A. Const.Amend. 4; 42 U.S.C.A. § 1983.—Lippman v. City of Miami, 724 F.Supp.2d 1240.

An alert by a trained dog establishes the necessary probable cause to conduct a search. U.S.C.A. Const.Amend. 4.—Id.

Mere fact of a trained dog showing interest does not constitute probable cause to conduct a search. U.S.C.A. Const.Amend. 4.—Id.

Fla. 2011. To determine whether an officer has a reasonable basis for concluding that a drug-detection dog's alert to the exterior of a vehicle indicates a fair probability that contraband will be found within the vehicle, the trial court must be able to adequately make an objective evaluation of the reliability of the dog. U.S.C.A. Const. Amend. 4.—Harris v. State, 71 So.3d 756, revised on rehearing, certiorari granted 132 S.Ct. 1796, 566 U.S. 904, 182 L.Ed.2d 615, reversed 133 S.Ct. 1050, 568 U.S. 237, 185 L.Ed.2d 61, on remand 123 So.3d 1144, withdrawn 123 So.3d 1144.

State did not meet its burden of demonstrating that officer had a reasonable basis for believing that drug-detection dog was reliable and, thus, that dog's alert to the exterior of vehicle provided probable cause to conduct warrantless search of interior of vehicle, where State presented evidence that dog was trained and certified to detect narcotics, and introduced training records indicating that dog performed satisfactory 100% of the time, but State did not introduce field performance records or any evidence regarding the criteria necessary for dog to obtain certification. U.S.C.A. Const.Amend. 4.—Id.

To demonstrate that an officer has a reasonable basis for believing that an alert by a drug-detection dog to the exterior of a vehicle is sufficiently reliable to provide probable cause to search the interior of the vehicle, the State must present evidence of the dog's training and certification records, an explanation of the meaning of the particular training and certification, field performance records, including any unverified alerts, and evidence concerning the experience and training of the officer handling the dog, as well as any other objective evidence known to the officer about the dog's reliability. U.S.C.A. Const.Amend. 4.—Id.

A trial court must assess the reliability of a drug-detection dog's alert to the exterior of a vehicle as a basis for probable cause to search the interior of the vehicle based on a totality of the circumstances. U.S.C.A. Const.Amend. 4.—Id.

Fla. 2002. Officer's detection of very strong odor of previously-burnt marijuana coming directly out of rolled-down window of defendant's vehicle provided probable cause for warrantless search of passenger compartment of the vehicle. U.S.C.A. Const.Amend. 4.—State v. Betz, 815 So.2d 627.

Officer's detection of very strong odor of previously-burnt marijuana coming directly out of rolled-down window of defendant's vehicle, combined with defendant's initial attempt to draw officer away from vehicle by exiting it and approaching the officer before officer could reach the vehicle, defendant's extremely "nervous" and "jittery" demeanor during pre-search interaction with officer, defendant's conduct in pushing himself off the vehicle twice while officer was attempting to conduct pat-down search, and the recovery during the pat-down search of storage bag containing marijuana, provided probable cause to search the entire vehicle, including the trunk. U.S.C.A. Const.Amend. 4.—Id.

Fla.App. 1 Dist. 2018. Defendant's vehicle was outside curtilage of his mobile home when police had police dog conduct warrantless canine sniff test of vehicle, and thus canine sniff test did not violate defendant's rights under the Fourth Amendment; although defendant's vehicle was in parking area approximately twenty feet from his mobile home, it was located outside the fence surrounding mobile home, and defendant made no effort to conceal parking area from observation from viewing public. U.S. Const. Amend. 4. —Davis v. State, 257 So.3d 1159.

Fla.App. 1 Dist. 2013. Law enforcement officers had probable cause to perform warrantless search of defendant's vehicle after drug-detection dog alerted to vehicle's trunk; dog's handler testified at suppression hearing regarding the selection process for dogs and testified that dog who alerted to defendant's trunk was certified by the North American Police Dog Association, dog's field performance records and training records showed that dog had approximately a 90% success rate, and handler was well-trained and extremely experienced in working with and training drug-detection dogs. U.S.C.A. Const.Amend. 4.— Bennett v. State, 111 So.3d 983.

Fla.App. 1 Dist. 2012. State's failure to introduce into evidence the records of drug dog's field performance, including the number of times she had been deployed and her success and failure rate, did not prevent trial court from determining dog's reliability, as necessary for dog's alert to provide police with probable cause to search defendant's motor vehicle, though admission of the records would have been preferable; police officer who was dog's handler and partner testified as to dog's field performance, and the records were made available to defense counsel, who used them in cross-examining officer during hearing on defendant's motion to suppress. U.S.C.A. Const.Amend. 4.—Blalock v. State, 98 So.3d 118, rehearing denied, review dismissed 104 So.3d 1082.

Field performance of drug dog who alerted to defendant's motor vehicle was sufficiently reliable to support trial court's finding that her alert provided probable cause for search of the vehicle; dog's success rate, calculated as a percentage of the time that contraband was found after the dog alerted, was approximately 52% if times that no contraband was found but there were confirmed residual odors were excluded, and 47% if such instances were included and counted as false alerts, either of which was sufficient to establish a fair probability that contraband would be found. U.S.C.A. Const.Amend. 4.—Id.

Trial court could not, in calculating the success rate of drug dog that alerted to defendant's motor vehicle for purposes of determining whether dog was sufficiently reliable for the alert to give police probable cause to search the vehicle, base its calculations on the total number of times the dog was deployed, with times the dog failed to alert counting as successes; there was no way to assess whether dog was correct when she failed to alert because no search was performed. U.S.C.A. Const.Amend. 4.—Id.

Sufficient evidence that, under the totality of the circumstances, drug dog that alerted to defendant's motor vehicle was reliable supported trial court's finding that the alert provided police with probable cause to search the vehicle; police officer who was dog's handler and partner testified as to her field performance, which included a success rate of approximately 52%, and State introduced considerable evidence regarding dog's and officer's training, which included an initial ten weeks of training for the dog, five of them with the officer, 16 hours of maintenance training a month, and yearly certifications. U.S.C.A. Const.Amend. 4.—Id.

Fla.App. 1 Dist. 2008. Use of a narcotics dog to sniff a vehicle does not constitute a search or seizure, and may be conducted during a consensual encounter or traffic stop; accordingly, when an officer is still writing a citation during a traffic stop when a backup officer or canine unit arrives, the lapse of time is generally not unreasonable. U.S.C.A. Const.Amend. 4.—Napoleon v. State, 985 So.2d 1170.

Fla.App. 1 Dist. 2007. Detection by a police officer of the odor of burnt cannabis emanating from a vehicle, by itself, constitutes sufficient facts and circumstances to establish probable cause for a warrantless search of the person of an occupant of that vehicle. U.S.C.A. Const.Amend. 4.—State v. Williams, 967 So.2d 941, rehearing denied.

Generally, a trained drug dog's alert on a vehicle may constitute probable cause to conduct a warrantless search of the vehicle. U.S.C.A. Const.Amend. 4.—Id.

Detection by police officers of an odor of burnt cannabis emanating from vehicle that defendant had been driving provided probable cause for a warrantless search of defendant's person. U.S.C.A. Const.Amend. 4.—Id.

Fla.App. 1 Dist. 2007. An officer's detection of the smell of marijuana coming out of a vehicle provides probable cause to search the passenger compartment of a vehicle. U.S.C.A. Const. Amend. 4.—Kimball v. State, 951 So.2d 35, review denied 959 So.2d 716.

Deputy had probable cause to believe that marijuana was located in vehicle and, thus, was allowed to conduct warrantless search of entire vehicle, including its trunk; deputy detected a strong odor of raw marijuana emanating from vehicle when he arrived at passenger window,

---

† This Case was not selected for publication in the National Reporter System

search of vehicle's driver revealed only a small quantity of marijuana on his person, and other vehicle occupants, including defendant, displayed excessive or furtive movement after deputy stopped vehicle. U.S.C.A. Const.Amend. 4.—Id.

Fla.App. 1 Dist. 2007. A person has no reasonable expectation of privacy in odors that emanate from a car in a public place; once a drug dog alerts to a car, therefore, probable cause exists to search the car. U.S.C.A. Const.Amend. 4.—State v. Griffin, 949 So.2d 309, review denied 958 So.2d 920.

Fla.App. 1 Dist. 1989. "Anticipatory elements" of affidavit supporting search warrant did not meet requirements of Florida statute requiring that search warrant not be issued for search of private dwelling unless law relating to narcotics or drug abuse "is being violated therein," where affidavit did not show that officers had "actual knowledge" that residence was connected to drug transactions; fact that drug middleman had entered residence and left with white box that was "later" discovered to contain marijuana after it was delivered as part of undercover drug buy was insufficient. West's F.S.A. §§ 933.18, 933.18(5).—Renckley v. State, 538 So.2d 1340.

Fla.App. 1 Dist. 1986. The State's interest in interdicting the flow of illegal drugs over its highways outweighed the minor intrusion on privacy of the motoring public caused by roadblock at which vehicles were stopped without discretion of highway patrol trooper who requested driver to produce his license and vehicle registration while a dog handler with a sniff dog walked around the vehicle.—Cardwell v. State, 482 So.2d 512.

Fla.App. 1 Dist. 1984. Undercover officers who observed occupants of vehicle having difficulty lighting an object and, once object was lit, observed it being passed back and forth between driver and passenger had a well-founded and reasonable suspicion that criminal conduct had occurred, justifying stop of vehicle; once stop was made, officers' detection of odor of marijuana supplied probable cause for search of vehicle. —State v. Koch, 455 So.2d 492, cause dismissed 466 So.2d 217.

Fla.App. 1 Dist. 1982. Warrantless search of padlocked cargo area of rented truck, which was stopped at agricultural inspection station, by deputy who smelled odor of marijuana was not invalid under the circumstances and once deputy had opened the cargo area, search of the bundles observed inside was not illegal.—Brayton v. State, 425 So.2d 88, petition for review denied 434 So.2d 886.

Fla.App. 1 Dist. 1982. Search of defendant's van and opening of one of bags of marijuana therein was not unreasonable where, considering evidence in light most favorable to ruling of trial court, defendant consented to opening of van and, notwithstanding that defendant did not consent to opening of plastic bags, deputy sheriff, upon noticing strong smell of marijuana, had probable cause to believe that vehicle contained marijuana.—Grimes v. State, 416 So.2d 488.

Fla.App. 1 Dist. 1980. Absent consent or some other exception to the warrant requirement, a search warrant was needed before the lockers located in the trucks driven by defendants could be searched; however, a general search of the trucks and a seizure of their contents was authorized without a warrant since the odor of marijuana gave agricultural inspector cause to believe the trucks contained contraband.—Sower v. State, 382 So.2d 1257, dismissed 386 So.2d 642.

Fla.App. 1 Dist. 1977. Where officer suspected that accused were dumping garbage illegally in vacant lot in which they did not claim to have any interest, officer was privileged to approach accused's vehicle which was parked in the lot; once there, the smell of marijuana emanating from vehicle justified a warrantless search of vehicle by officer and the seizure of marijuana found in it. U.S.C.A.Const. Amend. 4.—State v. Toffolio, 349 So.2d 174, certiorari denied 354 So.2d 987.

Fla.App. 2 Dist. 2020. The smell of marijuana and sight of smoke emanating from an automobile constitute probable cause to believe that both elements of the offense of possession of marijuana are satisfied as to all of the occupants of the vehicle and that each occupant had actual or constructive possession of marijuana, supporting warrantless search of occupants. U.S. Const. Amend. 4; Fla. Const. art. 1, § 12; Fla. Stat. Ann. § 893.13(6)(e).—State v. Brookins, 290 So.3d 1100.

When a police officer who knows the smell of burning marijuana detects that odor emanating from a vehicle, or from a person who has recently exited a vehicle, he has probable cause to believe a crime has been committed and that such person has committed it, supporting warrantless search of person. U.S. Const. Amend. 4; Fla. Const. art. 1, § 12; Fla. Stat. Ann. § 893.13(6)(e).—Id.

Fla.App. 2 Dist. 2011. Under totality of circumstances, State's evidence did not establish probable cause for warrantless search of defendant's vehicle based on drug-detection dog's alert to the vehicle; dog's field accuracy rate was four out of fourteen, or approximately 29%, and this accuracy rate was insufficient to establish reliability, that is, a fair probability that drugs would be found in a vehicle following an alert, and no evidence was presented about nature of dog's alert, the search of defendant's vehicle, or location of cocaine therein, and thus, it was impossible to tell if dog alerted on residual odor or whether he alerted on the actual cocaine itself, and State failed to make a connection between dog's alert and the discovery of the drugs. U.S.C.A. Const.Amend. 4.—Wiggs v. State, 72 So.3d 154, rehearing denied.

Fla.App. 2 Dist. 2007. Narcotics detection dog's alert to defendant's car was insufficient to establish probable cause for officers to search car; although officer who handled dog testified that dog was certified and had completed 400 hours of training, state failed to elicit any testimony from him regarding dog's track record, and officer admitted that drugs were not always found when dog alerts, but he could not quantify percentage of false alerts, and thus, officer's testimony was inadequate to establish dog's reliability. U.S.C.A. Const.Amend. 4.—Gibson v. State, 968 So.2d 631, review granted 973 So.2d 1123, review dismissed 985 So.2d 1088.

Fla.App. 2 Dist. 2003. Narcotics detection dog's alert to defendant's vehicle was insufficient to establish that the deputies had probable cause to search defendant's car, even though dog completed two training courses in narcotics detection and was certified, where State did not present any evidence of dog's track record for reliably detecting presence of contraband. U.S.C.A. Const.Amend. 4.—Matheson v. State, 870 So.2d 8, rehearing denied, review granted 880 So.2d 1212, review dismissed 896 So.2d 748, certiorari denied 126 S.Ct. 545, 546 U.S. 998, 163 L.Ed.2d 499.

† **This Case was not selected for publication in the National Reporter System**

Generally, a trained drug detection dog's alert on a vehicle may constitute probable cause to search, due to the dog's keen sense of smell. U.S.C.A. Const.Amend. 4.—Id.

Fla.App. 2 Dist. 2002. Officer who is trained to recognize and is familiar with the odor of marijuana has probable cause, based on the smell alone, to search a person or a vehicle for contraband. U.S.C.A. Const.Amend. 4.—Green v. State, 831 So.2d 1243.

Fla.App. 2 Dist. 1993. Smell of marijuana coming from inside of car gave police officers probable cause to search occupants of car and car for contraband. U.S.C.A. Const.Amend. 4.—State v. Wynn, 623 So.2d 848.

Fla.App. 2 Dist. 1991. Police officers had probable cause to search defendant's van when canine unit alerted to presence of contraband in van.—Rogers v. State, 586 So.2d 1148.

Fla.App. 2 Dist. 1989. Proper basis for warrantless search of defendant's trunk existed where prior suspicions which officers had had about drugs in car were reinforced by their seeing a beeper on defendant and a large number of quarters and several notepads in defendant's attache case, and trained, experienced narcotics dog alerted to trunk area of car.—Moreland v. State, 552 So.2d 937, review denied 562 So.2d 346.

Fla.App. 2 Dist. 1989. Police officers did not need well-founded suspicion of criminal activity to approach persons in vehicle in public park after closing hours to inform driver that park was closed, and smell of burning marijuana emanating from vehicle, combined with time and fact that park was known for illegal activity, was sufficient to establish probable cause to believe that vehicle contained contraband and to authorize its warrantless search.—State v. Bowden, 538 So.2d 83.

Police officers had probable cause to arrest defendant after they seized still warm marijuana cigarette from his vehicle, subsequent to smelling burning marijuana, cocaine found on defendant was seized lawfully in search incident to arrest, and cocaine seized from defendant's vehicle was also subject to seizure and confiscation. West's F.S.A. §§ 893.12, 901.21.—Id.

Fla.App. 2 Dist. 1988. For purposes of motion to suppress, search of defendant's vehicle was supported by probable cause and yielded sufficient evidence to support warrant for search of defendant's residence; vehicle search was conducted following lawful investigatory stop and alert by narcotics detection dog, and warrant was obtained on basis of discovery of 30 pounds of marijuana in trunk of that vehicle, confirmed information from unnamed informant, and police surveillance of residence.—Denton v. State, 524 So.2d 495, review denied 534 So.2d 398.

Fla.App. 2 Dist. 1982. Where in area in which there had been much burglary, and juvenile trouble, officer saw car in portion of parking lot in which parking by persons other than hotel guests was prohibited and officer saw two heads bobbing up and down in backseat and when, on seeing officer, persons in backseat quickly bent down and got back up as if hiding something, and officer on approaching automobile smelled odor of marijuana, he had probable cause to believe car contained marijuana and had right to search bag in front, under automobile exception, because of possibility that bag might contain marijuana. West's F.S.A. § 893.13.—State v. Gullett, 418 So.2d 406.

Fla.App. 2 Dist. 1976. Smell of burning marijuana emanating from defendants' car, combined with the other circumstances presented to police officer, including the fact that the car was parked at 2:45 a. m. at a construction site which had been posted against trespassers, was sufficient to establish probable cause to believe the car contained contraband and to authorize its warrantless search by the officer.—State v. Boyle, 326 So.2d 225.

Fla.App. 3 Dist. 2010. Search of defendant's car was a permissible search incident to arrest; officers made a lawful stop and then arrested the defendant after first smelling and then seeing marijuana in his car, and officers could then legally search the vehicle, as it was reasonable to believe that evidence of marijuana might be found in the vehicle. U.S.C.A. Const.Amend. 4.—State v. Williams, 43 So.3d 145.

Fla.App. 3 Dist. 1996. Police officers' founded suspicion of drug-related activity on part of defendant, which justified his detention for 30-40 minutes until canine unit arrived, ripened into probable cause for defendant's arrest and search of his car once narcotic-sniffing dog alerted to presence of cocaine in car as he was walked past car's open door. U.S.C.A. Const.Amends. 4, 14.—Saturnino-Boudet v. State, 682 So.2d 188, rehearing denied, review dismissed 689 So.2d 1071.

Fla.App. 3 Dist. 1990. Once probable cause existed for search of legally stopped vehicle, based on sniff dog's alerting to odor in vehicle trunk when directed to sniff around vehicle for evidence of drugs, no warrant was needed to authorize search.—State v. Taswell, 560 So.2d 257.

Fla.App. 3 Dist. 1981. Smell of marijuana emanating from camper vehicle and detected at time of lawful stop provided probable cause to conduct warrantless search of vehicle.—State v. Schneider, 401 So.2d 865.

Fla.App. 3 Dist. 1980. Defense suppression motions were properly denied as the police had probable cause to arrest defendant and to search his vehicle, based on trooper's testimony that he smelled a strong odor of marijuana emanating from defendant's vehicle prior to stopping it, arresting defendant driver, and searching the vehicle. West's F.S.A. § 933.19.—Mead v. State, 381 So.2d 743.

Fla.App. 3 Dist. 1969. Police officer who had been trained regarding marijuana and manner of its use and who observed cigarette being passed from one to another of five occupants in closed automobile in secluded area, who saw what he recognized as bulk marijuana in clear plastic bag being tossed to rear of vehicle by one of occupants as he approached vehicle, and who smelled marijuana when driver opened window in response to officer's knock, had probable cause to search vehicle prior to recovering marijuana and making arrest.—State v. Jones, 222 So.2d 216.

Fla.App. 4 Dist. 2014. A police officer who is trained to recognize the odor of marijuana and who is familiar with it and can recognize it has probable cause, based on the smell alone, to search a person or a vehicle for contraband. U.S.C.A. Const.Amend. 4.—State v. J.J., 143 So.3d 1050.

Fla.App. 4 Dist. 2012. The odor of burnt cannabis emanating from a vehicle generates probable cause for a police officer to both search the vehicle and arrest the occupants. U.S.C.A. Const.Amend. 4.—State v. Sarria, 97 So.3d 282.

† **This Case was not selected for publication in the National Reporter System**

For the purpose of providing a basis for probable cause to search a vehicle, there is no reason to distinguish the odor of burnt marijuana from the odor of raw marijuana. U.S.C.A. Const. Amend. 4.—Id.

Police officer had probable cause to search vehicle occupied by defendants and arrest them based on officer's detection of distinct odor of raw cannabis emanating from vehicle; it did not matter if officer arrested first and searched later. U.S.C.A. Const.Amend. 4.—Id.

Fla.App. 4 Dist. 2011. Narcotics detection dog's alert to presence of drugs during exterior sniff search of defendant's car was sufficiently reliable to establish prima facie showing of probable cause for warrantless search of car, where dog was certified to detect several types of controlled substances, dog had proficiency training for searches more than once a month in a controlled odor environment during six years as a police dog, and dog's alerts to presence of drugs were accurate 95% of the time. U.S.C.A. Const. Amend. 4.—Frost v. State, 53 So.3d 1119, review granted, quashed 94 So.3d 481, on remand 92 So.3d 323.

Fla.App. 4 Dist. 2009. Deputy sheriff who approached defendant's stopped automobile had probable cause to search automobile and, ultimately, to arrest defendant after discovering cocaine and a firearm in the automobile, where deputy smelled the odor of cannabis emanating from the automobile. U.S.C.A. Const.Amend. 4. —Marin v. State, 19 So.3d 436, rehearing denied, review denied 34 So.3d 2.

Fla.App. 4 Dist. 2006. A drug dog's alert to a vehicle, or a seat in a vehicle, does not, in and of itself, provide sufficient probable cause to search the driver or a passenger. U.S.C.A. Const. Amend. 4.—Rehm v. State, 931 So.2d 1071.

Fla.App. 4 Dist. 2005. Since neither defendant's motion to suppress drugs found in car after a narcotics detection dog indicated the presence of drugs, nor the argument presented by defendant at the evidentiary hearing, raised the qualifications of the narcotics dog, the State was not on notice that this was an issue until the trial court raised it, and as such, the court should have granted the State's request to call witnesses to qualify the dog. West's F.S.A. RCrP Rule 3.190(h)(2).—State v. Laveroni, 910 So.2d 333.

Because drug detection dogs are not always correct, their past performance records are relevant when determining whether probable cause existed for warrantless search of car based on a narcotic dog's alert.—Id.

Fla.App. 4 Dist. 2003. Deputy had probable cause for search that led to discovery of cocaine in trunk of disabled vehicle, and thus, had probable cause to arrest defendant, where drug dog called to scene alerted to trunk, following which deputy patted defendant down and placed him in patrol car. U.S.C.A. Const.Amend. 4.—Bain v. State, 839 So.2d 739, rehearing denied, review denied 851 So.2d 728.

Fla.App. 4 Dist. 2003. Officer's act of smelling burnt marijuana from vehicle that defendant had just exited provided officer with probable cause to both search and detain defendant and vehicle. U.S.C.A. Const.Amend. 4.—State v. T.P., 835 So.2d 1277.

Fla.App. 4 Dist. 2001. Officer lacked probable cause to seize currency during automobile stop, where drug dog's alert to currency did not occur until after currency was removed from driver's possession and in police custody, marijuana seeds or residue found under automobile seat was so insignificant that officer did not arrest driver for possession or try to retrieve particles, and driver's explanation regarding currency was not inconsistent.—State, Dept. of Highway Safety and Motor Vehicles v. Jones, 780 So.2d 949, rehearing denied, review denied 797 So.2d 588.

Fla.App. 4 Dist. 1999. Officers had probable cause to search defendant' vehicle based on narcotics-sniffing dog alerting that defendant's car could contain narcotics and, thus, seizure of marijuana from car was constitutionally permissible, where narcotics-sniffing dog was already at the scene, and dog was examining the exterior of all cars in parking lot when dog alerted that defendant's vehicle could contain narcotics.— Flowers v. State, 755 So.2d 708.

Fla.App. 4 Dist. 1988. Odor of marijuana emanating from vehicle's trunk provided sufficient "probable cause" for officer's search of trunk following lawful investigative stop. U.S.C.A. Const.Amend. 4.—In re Forfeiture of a 1981 Ford Auto., VIN 3ABP32F8BU154691, 520 So.2d 631, review denied In re Forfeiture of a 1981 Ford Automobile Vin ABP32F8BU154691, 531 So.2d 1353.

Fla.App. 4 Dist. 1976. Officer, who, after stopping accused for speeding, observed what officer suspected were cannabis seeds when he shined flashlight on inspection sticker of car and who suspected that odor emanating from accused's person was the odor of burned or burning marijuana or the odor of accused's perfume or after shave lotion did not have probable cause to make general search of car.—Brown v. State, 330 So.2d 861.

Fla.App. 5 Dist. 2017. To a trained and experienced police officer, the smell of cannabis emanating from a person or a vehicle gives the police officer probable cause to search the person or the vehicle. U.S. Const. Amend. 4.—State v. Harris, 230 So.3d 1285.

Fla.App. 5 Dist. 2005. Field track records of police drug dog were not required for the state to make a prima facie showing of probable cause to search vehicles based on dog's alerts. U.S.C.A. Const.Amend. 4.—State v. Coleman, 911 So.2d 259.

Dog handler's testimony on police drug dog's performance was relevant in determining whether probable cause existed for warrantless searches of vehicles based on dog's alerts; testimony tended to show that officers reasonably relied on dog's alerts. U.S.C.A. Const.Amend. 4. —Id.

Fla.App. 5 Dist. 2000. Odor of burning marijuana emanating from vehicle provided probable cause to search defendant, who was occupant of vehicle.—State v. Chambliss, 752 So.2d 114.

Fla.App. 5 Dist. 1997. Officer was justified in conducting pat-down search of defendant for weapons following traffic stop, in light of police dog's alert to presence of narcotics in vehicle and officer's experience regarding association of weapons and drugs. U.S.C.A. Const.Amend. 4; West's F.S.A. § 901.151(5).—State v. Burns, 698 So.2d 1282, rehearing denied.

Fla.App. 5 Dist. 1992. Police officer appropriately exercised his jurisdiction by stopping vehicle with temporary tag which he could not read and once vehicle was properly stopped, officer could ask to see driver's license and registration and use of sniff dog while defendant was searching for his registration was not unconstitutional, even though once defendant stopped and officer approached vehicle, officer could see that tempo-

---

† **This Case was not selected for publication in the National Reporter System**

rary tag was valid. U.S.C.A. Const.Amend. 4.—State v. Bass, 609 So.2d 151.

Fla.App. 5 Dist. 1992. Person who is trained to recognize odor of marijuana, is familiar with it, and can recognize it has probable cause, based on smell alone, to search person or vehicle for contraband. U.S.C.A. Const.Amend. 4.—State v. T.T., 594 So.2d 839.

Fla.App. 5 Dist. 1987. When police officer who knew smell of burning marijuana detected that odor emanating from vehicle, or from person who had just exited the vehicle, he had probable cause to believe crime had been committed and that such person had committed it, authorizing arrest of such person and warrantless search, either before or after the arrest, of passenger compartment of the vehicle and closed containers therein.—State v. Wells, 516 So.2d 74.

Fla.App. 5 Dist. 1982. Police officers who observed marijuana residue in airplane and could smell marijuana emanating from nearby pickup truck had probable cause to search pickup truck and bales which were on the truck covered by an opaque covering.—Boykin v. State, 421 So.2d 538.

Fla.App. 5 Dist. 1980. Seizure of attache case from vehicle, after police dog, trained in locating controlled substances, alerted on attache case and nosed case, causing it to open, revealing plastic bag in attache case, was proper, and fact that case had been opened by dog had no bearing on subsequent search under lawfully executed search warrant. U.S.C.A.Const. Amend. 4.—State v. Francoeur, 387 So.2d 1063.

Fla.App. 5 Dist. 1979. Where officer, who observed defendant backing a pickup truck down a public road, nearly avoiding an accident, stopped defendant and smelled what he believed to be marijuana smoke coming from the truck and asked defendant to open the ashtray, whereon defendant reached into ashtray and dropped what appeared to be a single marijuana cigarette to floorboard, the smell of marijuana provided probable cause for warrantless search of truck, including ashtray, notwithstanding that defendant had been arrested and placed in back seat of squad car, especially since truck had not been impounded. U.S.C.A.Const. Amend. 4; West's F.S.A.Const. art. 1, § 12.—Ulesky v. State, 379 So.2d 121.

◯—661(1). In general.

C.A.11 (Fla.) 2022. Warrant is not needed to search impounded car if officers have authority to impound car and follow department procedures governing inventory searches; it is Government's burden to demonstrate that the requirements of this exception to warrant requirement were met. U.S. Const. Amend. 4.—United States v. Cohen, 38 F.4th 1364.

An officer has the authority to impound a car if his decision to impound it is in good faith, based upon standard criteria, and not solely based upon suspicion of evidence of criminal activity. U.S. Const. Amend. 4.—Id.

C.A.11 (Fla.) 2021. Though the police generally need a warrant to conduct a search, they do not need a warrant to search an impounded car if they: (1) had the authority to impound the car, and (2) followed department procedures governing inventory searches. U.S. Const. Amend. 4.—United States v. Isaac, 987 F.3d 980.

An officer has the authority to impound a car if his decision to impound it is in good faith, is based upon standard criteria, and is not solely

based upon suspicion of evidence of criminal activity. U.S. Const. Amend. 4.—Id.

Though the inventory search of an impounded vehicle cannot be based only on the suspicion of finding evidence, an officer's expectation that evidence will turn up does not invalidate an otherwise lawful inventory search. U.S. Const. Amend. 4.—Id.

C.A.11 (Fla.) 2020. An officer may lawfully impound an arrestee's vehicle so long as the impound decision is based on standard criteria and based on something other than suspicion of evidence of criminal activity. U.S. Const. Amend. 4.—United States v. Wilson, 979 F.3d 889.

† C.A.11 (Fla.) 2018. Search of defendant's vehicle was a valid inventory search of an impounded vehicle, and did not violate Fourth Amendment, even though police department did not have a written policy detailing when and how a police officer may impound a vehicle; officers' decision to impound defendant's vehicle was not unreasonable under the circumstances, as it was two o'clock in the morning and the vehicle was parked on the side of a public road, the vehicle lacked a valid tag and registration, neither of the passengers had a valid driver's license, and there was an outstanding warrant for one of the passengers. U.S. Const. Amend. 4.—United States v. Moss, 748 Fed.Appx. 257.

C.A.5 (Fla.) 1978. Although policeman arrested defendant for carrying a concealed weapon, and although that arrest may not have been valid under Florida law, where the police officer, after securing the defendant to the back of the patrol car, discovered a number of credit cards, with different names on them, while making an inventory search, police officer had probable cause to arrest defendant for possession of stolen credit cards so that the arrest was valid, as was the subsequent impoundment search of the vehicle. West's F.S.A. §§ 817.57–817.68, 831.01.—U.S. v. Ullrich, 580 F.2d 765, rehearing denied 589 F.2d 1114.

S.D.Fla. 2021. Although police generally need warrant to conduct search, they do not need warrant to search impounded car if they had authority to impound car and followed department procedures governing inventory searches. U.S. Const. Amend. 4.—Johnson v. Israel, 576 F.Supp.3d 1231.

An officer has the authority to impound a car if his decision to impound it is in good faith, based upon standard criteria, and not solely based upon suspicion of evidence of criminal activity. U.S. Const. Amend. 4.—Id.

S.D.Fla. 1994. Inventory search of defendant and search of police vehicle in which defendants had been transported were valid searches incident to lawful arrest. U.S.C.A. Const.Amend. 4.—U.S. v. Wai-Keung, 845 F.Supp. 1548, affirmed 115 F.3d 874, rehearing and suggestion for rehearing denied U.S. v. Chi-Cheong, 127 F.3d 42, certiorari denied Li v. U.S., 118 S.Ct. 1095, 522 U.S. 1135, 140 L.Ed.2d 150.

Fla. 1989. Police officers are not required to provide alternative to impoundment of motor vehicle after valid automobile stop, if they act in good faith. West's F.S.A. Const. Art. 1, § 12.—Robinson v. State, 537 So.2d 95.

Fla. 1981. Officers must advise a present, silent arrestee that his vehicle will be impounded unless he can provide a reasonable alternative to impoundment.—Sanders v. State, 403 So.2d 973.

An arrestee need not be advised of all available options to impoundment of his vehicle, but extent of consultation with arrestee is factor for trial judge to consider in determining whether impoundment was reasonable and necessary.—Id.

Changing conditions and circumstances must be taken into account and extent of consultation with arrestee is only a factor which trial judge should consider in determining whether impoundment of arrestee's vehicle was reasonable and necessary.—Id.

Fla.App. 2 Dist. 2021. One exception to the Fourth Amendment's warrant requirement is when it is necessary for a law enforcement officer to impound an automobile and conduct an inventory search of its contents. U.S. Const. Amend. 4.—Ross v. State, 319 So.3d 807.

An "inventory search," as the term implies, is the search of property lawfully seized and detained, in order to ensure that it is harmless, to secure valuable items (such as might be kept in a towed car), and to protect against false claims of loss or damage. U.S. Const. Amend. 4.—Id.

A law enforcement agency must show that it is operating under a standard of some sort—that is, a directive, a guidepost, a benchmark, a criteria —that informs and potentially curtails the exercise of an officer's discretion before a law enforcement officer can impound a vehicle and conduct an inventory search. U.S. Const. Amend. 4.—Id.

Fla.App. 2 Dist. 2008. In the absence of a search warrant, there are three valid means by which law enforcement officers may search a motor vehicle: (1) incident to a lawful arrest of a recent occupant of the vehicle; (2) under the "automobile exception" to the warrant requirement, i.e., based on probable cause to believe that the vehicle contains contraband or other evidence of a crime; and (3) when a vehicle has been impounded, as part of a reasonable inventory search following standardized procedures. U.S.C.A. Const.Amend. 4.—State v. Clark, 986 So.2d 625.

Fla.App. 2 Dist. 2003. Absent a search warrant, valid means by which law enforcement may search a vehicle are: (1) incident to a valid arrest of a recent occupant of the vehicle; (2) under the "automobile exception" to warrant requirement, which requires exigent circumstances coupled with probable cause; and (3) when a vehicle has been impounded, as part of a reasonable inventory search following standardized procedure. U.S.C.A. Const.Amend. 4.—Jaimes v. State, 862 So.2d 833.

Fla.App. 2 Dist. 1980. Police officer can impound an illegally or dangerously parked vehicle in possession of arrestee at the time of arrest and officer has no obligation to apprise arrestee of alternative procedures sanctioned by police department.—State v. Sanders, 387 So.2d 391, decision disapproved 403 So.2d 973.

Fla.App. 4 Dist. 2019. An inventory search is the search of property lawfully seized and detained, in order to ensure that it is harmless, to secure valuable items (such as might be kept in a towed car), and to protect against false claims of loss or damage. U.S. Const. Amend. 4.—Tejada v. 2015 Cadillac Escalade VIN No: 1GYS4BKJ5FR157228, 267 So.3d 1032.

Fla.App. 4 Dist. 2007. The "community caretaking doctrine," which although typically applied to warrantless inventory searches of automobiles that are creating a danger, nuisance, or invitation to vandalism, can also be applied to the stop of a boat without reasonable suspicion for purposes of gathering information to provide assistance to those affected by a potentially life-threatening accident. U.S.C.A. Const.Amend. 4. —Castella v. State, 959 So.2d 1285, rehearing denied, review denied 968 So.2d 556.

Fla.App. 4 Dist. 2005. In the absence of a search warrant, law enforcement may search a vehicle in three circumstances: (1) incident to a valid arrest of a recent occupant of the vehicle; (2) under the "automobile exception" to the warrant requirement, which requires exigent circumstances coupled with probable cause; and (3) when a vehicle has been impounded, as part of a reasonable inventory search following standardized procedure. U.S.C.A. Const.Amend. 4.— State v. Waller, 918 So.2d 363, rehearing denied.

Fla.App. 4 Dist. 1988. When owner or possessor of vehicle subject to valid traffic stop is present, police officer must advise such person that vehicle will be impounded unless reasonable alternative to impoundment can be provided. West's F.S.A. Const. Art. 1, § 12; U.S.C.A. Const. Amend. 4.—Robinson v. State, 526 So.2d 164, affirmed 537 So.2d 95.

Fla.App. 5 Dist. 2022. An inventory search as part of the impoundment of a vehicle is recognized as an exception to the warrant requirement. U.S. Const. Amend. 4.—Wall v. State, 333 So.3d 348.

Law enforcement is not required to offer an alternative to impoundment of a vehicle after a valid traffic stop, if they act in good faith. U.S. Const. Amend. 4.—Id.

A law enforcement agency must show that it was operating under a standard or criteria before law enforcement can impound a vehicle and conduct an inventory search; it is the State's burden to put evidence of that standard before the court. U.S. Const. Amend. 4.—Id.

The validity of an inventory search of an automobile relies on its purpose. U.S. Const. Amend. 4.—Id.

An inventory search of an automobile serves the needs of protection of the owner's property, protection of police against claims lost or stolen property, and protection of police against potential danger from such things as explosives. U.S. Const. Amend. 4.—Id.

The arrest of a defendant, standing alone, does not justify the impoundment of his or her legally parked car. U.S. Const. Amend. 4.—Id.

Fla.App. 5 Dist. 2021. There are three ways law enforcement officers may conduct a warrantless search of a motor vehicle: (1) incident to a lawful arrest of a recent occupant of the vehicle; (2) the automobile exception, based on probable cause that the vehicle contains contraband or other evidence of a crime; and (3) pursuant to an inventory search. U.S. Const. Amend. 4.—State v. Koontz, 320 So.3d 993.

Reasonable police regulations relating to motor vehicle inventory procedures administered in good faith satisfy the Fourth Amendment reasonableness requirement for warrantless searches. U.S. Const. Amend. 4.—Id.

The reasonableness of a purported inventory search of a motor vehicle is dependent upon it being a true good-faith inventory search and not a subterfuge for a criminal, investigatory search. U.S. Const. Amend. 4.—Id.

Fla.App. 5 Dist. 2019. There are three ways by which law enforcement officers may validly conduct a warrantless search of a motor vehicle: (1) incident to a lawful arrest of a recent occupant of the vehicle; (2) the automobile exception, based on probable cause that the vehicle contains contraband or other evidence of a crime; and (3) pursuant to an inventory search. U.S. Const.

---

† **This Case was not selected for publication in the National Reporter System**

Amend. 4.—Jones v. State, 279 So.3d 342, habeas corpus granted 325 So.3d 101.

⚭661(2). Particular cases in general.

C.A.11 (Fla.) 2022. Police officers' method of impounding rental car that arrestee had been driving, in which officers had car towed to rental company, sufficiently complied with police department's impound policy, and thus warrant was not needed to search impounded car, even though department policy stated that a vehicle would "generally" be rotation impounded by being taken to wrecker storage lot or police impounded by being taken to police impound lot; policy did not state that officers were unable to do any other type of impound, and it stated that proper disposition of a vehicle depended on each individual situation. U.S. Const. Amend. 4.—United States v. Cohen, 38 F.4th 1364.

C.A.11 (Fla.) 2021. District court's finding of impracticality of arrestee's proposed alternative to impoundment of his vehicle, i.e., letting arrestee call someone to come and get the car, was not clearly erroneous, for purposes of officer's authority to impound the car under police department's standard operating procedure (SOP), as required for lawful inventory search; while SOP did not allow impoundment unless all reasonable efforts to provide alternatives had been unsuccessful or impractical due to time or staffing constraint, officer testified that he needed to interview arrestee, who was suspected of lewd and lascivious battery, that night, thereby preventing officer, whose police department was short on staffing, from waiting with the car until some unidentified person could be contacted and could arrive at the scene. U.S. Const. Amend. 4.—United States v. Isaac, 987 F.3d 980.

C.A.11 (Fla.) 2020. After arresting defendant at a gas station for refusing to comply with a lawful order to produce his driver's license, officer properly impounded and searched defendant's car and its contents under inventory-search exception to Fourth Amendment's warrant requirement; police department's standard operating procedures required officers to have an arrestee's car towed if, as here, the car's operator himself was arrested, or the car created a traffic hazard or was illegally parked, in that after defendant's arrest no one else was in the car to take custody of it, and the car was blocking a gas pump. U.S. Const. Amend. 4.—United States v. Wilson, 979 F.3d 889.

† C.A.11 (Fla.) 2016. Search of defendant's car and contents therein after it was impounded by police was valid inventory search; defendant's car was blocking intersection at time of his arrest, such that it would have been impractical to conduct search at scene, and police department's procedures explicitly allowed officer to search closed containers within car and obtain key to unlock duffel bag. U.S.C.A. Const.Amend. 4.—U.S. v. Witten, 649 Fed.Appx. 880, certiorari denied 137 S.Ct. 696, 580 U.S. 1079, 196 L.Ed.2d 572, post-conviction relief denied 2019 WL 4453360.

† C.A.11 (Fla.) 2015. Warrantless search of defendant's truck was a valid inventory search after it was impounded, and therefore, did not violate the Fourth Amendment; police had authority to impound truck due to it having been used in multiple traffic crimes, officer had observed defendant driving 15 miles per hour over the speed limit, defendant had no driver's license, defendant was unable to produce proof of registration or insurance, officer stopped defendant at

gas station, and it would not have been reasonable for officer to leave truck for gas station owner to handle. U.S.C.A. Const.Amend. 4.—U.S. v. Vladeff, 630 Fed.Appx. 998.

† C.A.11 (Fla.) 2015. District court's finding that impoundment of defendant's rental car, pursuant to which inventory search was conducted following traffic stop and arrest, was in accordance with police department's impoundment policy was not clearly erroneous; while officers generally agreed with defendant's characterization of impoundment policy as entitling a vehicle renter to have an opportunity to call someone to recover the rental car before impounding it, officers testified that due to liability concerns, police officers were permitted to release a rented vehicle only to its owner or the person who rented it, that they did not recall finding a rental agreement or any other document that would have indicated who rented defendant's vehicle, and that under such circumstances rental companies had requested that police department automatically tow vehicles without first contacting them. U.S.C.A. Const.Amend. 4.—U.S. v. Joseph, 611 Fed.Appx. 946, post-conviction relief dismissed by Joseph v. Shultz, 2019 WL 1119969, habeas corpus dismissed by 2019 WL 1877692.

† C.A.11 (Fla.) 2012. Whether the physical evidence that was the subject of defendant's motion to suppress was in defendant's vehicle or discovered near his person, the warrantless search that resulted in discovery of that evidence was proper; to the extent evidence was discovered on or near defendant's person, it occurred incident to a lawful arrest, and to the extent evidence was discovered in his vehicle, it was discovered during a lawful inventory search of the impounded vehicle. U.S.C.A. Const.Amend. 4.—U.S. v. Kalu, 485 Fed.Appx. 366, post-conviction relief denied 2017 WL 6559793, post-conviction relief dismissed by 2018 WL 11216830, habeas corpus denied Kalu v. Entzel, 2020 WL 353231.

† C.A.11 (Fla.) 2008. Police officers' warrantless search of vehicle of defendant, convicted of drug and firearms offenses, was justified as inventory search, since officers had authority to impound vehicle that had been used in commission of felony when passenger shot at officers from inside car, and officers were operating according to their department's standard impound procedure. U.S.C.A. Const.Amend. 4.—U.S. v. McCalla, 286 Fed.Appx. 610, post-conviction relief denied 2010 WL 2136549.

C.A.5 (Fla.) 1979. Where, after van which had been stopped on probable cause was driven to police headquarters and officer found that side door was unlocked, and he opened door and found bales of marijuana inside, entry was proper. U.S.C.A.Const. Amend. 4.—U.S. v. Moreno, 588 F.2d 490, certiorari denied 99 S.Ct. 2061, 441 U.S. 936, 60 L.Ed.2d 666, certiorari denied Aspuru v. U.S., 99 S.Ct. 2168, 441 U.S. 947, 60 L.Ed.2d 1049, certiorari denied Linares v. U.S., 99 S.Ct. 2169, 441 U.S. 947, 60 L.Ed.2d 1050.

C.A.5 (Fla.) 1972. Warrantless "inventory" of defendant's car following his arrest and removal to police station on misdemeanor traffic warrants, and after operator of premises where car was parked requested its removal, which resulted in discovery of counterfeit bills under floor mat, was reasonable. 18 U.S.C.A. § 472; F.S.A. § 901.15(4).—U.S. v. Kelehar, 470 F.2d 176.

C.A.5 (Fla.) 1972. Where defendants sold heroin to government agent and certain of defendants placed such heroin in government-owned vehicle driven by agent to whom sale was made,

† This Case was not selected for publication in the National Reporter System

and defendants were arrested, and vehicle driven to police headquarters, search warrant was not necessary for removal of contraband from vehicle. Narcotic Drugs Import and Export Act, § 2(c, f), 42 Stat. 596; 26 U.S.C.A. (I.R.C.1954) §§ 4704(a), 4705(a); U.S.C.A.Const. Amend. 4.— U.S. v. Pentado, 463 F.2d 355, certiorari denied Ochoa v. U.S., 93 S.Ct. 698, 409 U.S. 1079, 34 L.Ed.2d 668, certiorari denied Noa v. U.S., 93 S.Ct. 963, 410 U.S. 909, 35 L.Ed.2d 271.

S.D.Fla. 2021. Sheriff deputies' warrantless search of truck after impoundment following traffic stop did not fall within inventory-search exception to Fourth Amendment's warrant requirement, in absence of evidence that deputies impounded or searched truck in accordance with standardized criteria, or even that such criteria existed. U.S. Const. Amend. 4.—Johnson v. Israel, 576 F.Supp.3d 1231.

Fla. 1984. Where defendant's automobile was stopped by police officer for expired inspection certificate and when defendant was unable to produce his license and registration he was arrested, search of the vehicle was justified as incident to the arrest, and where due to language difficulties and inability to get assistance of a Spanish-speaking officer the arresting officer was unable to consult with defendant as to wishes regarding removal of the vehicle, which was standing in a traffic lane, a *Miller* impoundment and inventory search was justified. U.S.C.A. Const.Amend. 4.—Padron v. State, 449 So.2d 811.

Fla. 1981. Although at time of his arrest for driving under influence of alcohol defendant was upon his own admission very intoxicated, where trial judge found that defendant responded to requests of officer promptly and was alert and coherent, that defendant stopped his car next to curb immediately upon officer turning on his red lights, that location was 100 feet from hotel where defendant was staying and that there was no traffic hazard, impoundment of defendant's vehicle was not reasonable.—Sanders v. State, 403 So.2d 973.

Fla.App. 1 Dist. 2018. Evidence was sufficient to support finding that defendant's driver's license was suspended at time of arrest for driving with a suspended license, such that subsequent warrantless inventory search of defendant's vehicle following arrest was valid; although defendant testified that his license was never suspended, and he submitted a database document suggesting the license was reinstated later the day of the arrest, an officer testified that the license was suspended, referencing the database report on which the officer had relied at the time and which the defendant attached as an exhibit to his motion to suppress. U.S. Const. Amend. 4.— Brown v. State, 247 So.3d 86.

Fla.App. 1 Dist. 1996. Warrantless seizure of motor vehicle based on probable cause that vehicle was used in violation of Florida Contraband Forfeiture Act does not violate Fourth Amendment prohibition against unreasonable searches and seizures; thus, evidence seized in subsequent inventory search of such vehicle is admissible in criminal prosecution. U.S.C.A. Const.Amend. 4; West's F.S.A. §§ 932.701(2)(a)5, 932.702(3).— White v. State, 680 So.2d 550, review granted 687 So.2d 1308, opinion quashed 710 So.2d 949, rehearing denied, certiorari granted 119 S.Ct. 508, 525 U.S. 1000, 142 L.Ed.2d 421, reversed 119 S.Ct. 1555, 526 U.S. 559, 143 L.Ed.2d 748, on remand 753 So.2d 548.

Fla.App. 1 Dist. 1991. Sheriffs properly impounded defendant's truck and conducted inventory search following arrest of defendant for driving without license, where unsecured motorcycle in defendant's truck made it inappropriate to leave truck parked without supervision and officer would have had to wait approximately 45 minutes for defendant's stepfather to pick truck up at arrest location. U.S.C.A. Const.Amend. 4. —Key v. State, 589 So.2d 348, jurisdiction accepted 598 So.2d 78, opinion quashed 603 So.2d 494, on remand 605 So.2d 552, appeal after remand 638 So.2d 1040.

Fla.App. 1 Dist. 1982. Alternative proposed by defendant following arrest for driving under the influence, that officer telephone some friends of defendant who lived "about five minutes away" from scene of arrest was not a reasonable alternative to option given defendant by officer of signing waiver form or having truck impounded by the police, and thus where defendant refused to sign waiver form, evidence was properly seized during inventory search following impoundment. —Everall v. State, 414 So.2d 646, review denied 422 So.2d 842.

Fla.App. 1 Dist. 1978. Impoundment of vehicle following arrest for driving without driver's license was valid even though locked vehicle could have been left legally parked on street in that city remained subject to claim by absent owner in event of theft or damage to vehicle or its contents; it was not required that vehicle be left parked on the street.—Fields v. State, 369 So.2d 603, certiorari denied 368 So.2d 1366.

Fla.App. 1 Dist. 1976. After officers arrested defendant at airport on charges of being in possession of a controlled substance, subsequent search of defendant's automobile in airport parking lot could not be sustained as search incident to defendant's arrest, as valid inventory search, or as search conducted under exigent circumstances.—Weisenford v. State, 346 So.2d 549.

Fla.App. 1 Dist. 1975. Where patrolling officer noted that defendant's vehicle had only one headlight, officer stopped vehicle, which he noticed was not from the county, and requested defendant's driver's license and was informed that defendant did not have the license with him, whereupon officer arrested defendant, arrest was legal and inventory search of vehicle before taking it to police station, which search revealed marijuana in plain view, was justified as incident to arrest.—Shannon v. State, 320 So.2d 855, reversed 335 So.2d 5.

Fla.App. 2 Dist. 2021. There was no evidence deputy was acting in accordance with any established governing standard when he decided to impound defendant's car after arresting him for driving while his license was suspended, or that such a standard even existed, and thus, deputy unlawfully impounded and conducted inventory search of defendant's vehicle; deputy admitted that he intended to impound defendant's car "no matter what," defendant's car was parked in the early afternoon in a parking space at a public park where others had left cars overnight "all the time," and deputy was unable to articulate any basis for his concern that "something" could happen if defendant's car was left in the park while defendant was booked for driving while his license was suspended. U.S. Const. Amend. 4.— Ross v. State, 319 So.3d 807.

Fla.App. 2 Dist. 2010. Search of defendant's vehicle, following his arrest for violating his restricted driver's license, was valid as an inventory search; defendant's vehicle obstructed the right of

---

† **This Case was not selected for publication in the National Reporter System**

way, and deputy was not required to offer an alternative to impoundment before he had vehicle towed. U.S.C.A. Const.Amend. 4.—State v. Townsend, 40 So.3d 103.

Fla.App. 2 Dist. 1989. Stop and inventory search of defendant's automobile were valid, and officer had probable cause to search bag after he saw that it looked like one recently stolen, together with firearms, from sheriff's department offices and felt firearms inside bag; thus, duffle bag and firearms found therein during that search were admissible.—State v. Landry, 543 So.2d 314.

Fla.App. 2 Dist. 1987. There was no basis for impounding vehicle which defendant was driving, even though he could not produce vehicle registration or proof of ownership, where he did give the officers the name of the owner.—Montalvo v. State, 520 So.2d 292, review denied 528 So.2d 1183.

Because impoundment of vehicle when defendant could not produce vehicle registration or proof of ownership was unlawful, inventory search which produced weapon was also unlawful, as were defendant's arrest based on discovery of that weapon and search incident to that arrest, so that cocaine seized during that search was the fruit of an illegal search.—Id.

Fla.App. 2 Dist. 1985. Impoundment of automobile was not shown to be lawful, reasonable, or necessary, and thus, warrantless inventory search of the vehicle and seizure of cocaine constituted "unreasonable search and seizure" where officer who stopped defendant for apparent lack of license plate and who arrested defendant for obstructing justice failed to consult with defendant concerning reasonable alternative to impoundment after arresting defendant and after determining that license plate, which had not been properly illuminated, was owned by another person and belonged to different vehicle, and where neither the vehicle nor the license plate was reported as stolen and defendant contended he was in rightful possession of the vehicle. U.S.C.A. Const.Amend. 4.—McClendon v. State, 476 So.2d 1303.

Fla.App. 2 Dist. 1982. Impoundment of automobile driven by defendant was improper where police officer, who arrested defendant for making an illegal U-turn and for failure to produce vehicle's certificate of registration, failed to advise defendant of his intention to impound the vehicle unless defendant, who stated that vehicle belonged to his sister and that his sister might be out to dinner at that time, did provide a reasonable alternative and, hence, warrantless search and seizure on impoundment was unreasonable. —Long v. State, 422 So.2d 72.

Fla.App. 2 Dist. 1979. It would have been improper for police officer to use missing taillight, tag light or lack of clearance lights as a pretext to stop truck being driven by defendant and investigate a bare suspicion of illegal activity, but since facts indicated that police officer first merely observed vehicle, defendant's subsequent peculiar driving activity and sudden appearance of a tractor where none had been a few minutes before were such as to elevate police officer's "intuition" into a well-founded suspicion of criminal conduct sufficient to justify a stop of truck and subsequent impounding of vehicle in view of flight of passenger and defendant's admission that trailer tag was stolen.—State v. Gray, 366 So.2d 137.

Fla.App. 2 Dist. 1977. Police officers who observed defendant's automobile cross the grass area of a median strip while turning into a parking lot, who pulled up behind defendant's automobile, which had momentarily stopped, who then observed defendant put his vehicle in reverse and hit the front of the police car, and who administered a field sobriety test to defendant, and arrested him for driving while intoxicated were justified in making a warrantless inventory of the automobile at the scene.—State v. Dearden, 347 So.2d 462.

Fla.App. 2 Dist. 1976. Impoundment and inventory search of defendant's vehicle, subsequent to his being held in contempt of court during a traffic violation hearing and sentenced to ten days in detention, was unreasonable and unlawful, where the State failed to show that the vehicle was illegally parked on street outside courtroom or was in some other way a traffic nuisance or that there were other factors which made it necessary for the vehicle to be taken into custody. U.S.C.A.Const. Amend. 4.—G. B. v. State, 339 So.2d 696.

Fla.App. 2 Dist. 1971. Where officers who had had defendant under surveillance for several hours stopped defendant's automobile when defendant exceeded speed limit by about 15 m. p. h., and after detecting odor of alcohol arrested defendant for drinking and careless driving, and inventory of contents of defendant's vehicle uncovered items which led to defendant's arrest and conviction for breaking and entering, search did not violate defendant's constitutional rights.— Urquhart v. State, 261 So.2d 535, certiorari denied 266 So.2d 349.

Fla.App. 3 Dist. 1981. Warrantless inventory search of vehicle of defendant, who was stopped for a traffic violation, was unreasonable where there was no indication that defendant's vehicle was in any way a hazard to traffic, and where defendant was willing to take responsibility for leaving his vehicle at location of the stop.—Nealy v. State, 400 So.2d 95, decision approved 419 So.2d 336.

Fla.App. 3 Dist. 1979. Evidence seized in inventory search of automobile which defendant was driving was not product of unreasonable search where defendant was arrested for driving without valid license, she had no other identification, and when given option to sign waiver and leave vehicle parked, she did not sign waiver or give definite answer, and arresting officers then informed her that they had no other alternative but to impound vehicle and have it towed, to which she did not object.—Gordon v. State, 368 So.2d 59, certiorari denied 378 So.2d 345.

Fla.App. 3 Dist. 1975. Warrantless inventory search of accused's car after he was arrested during police "raid" and was charged with possession of cocaine and marijuana was not justified on theory that, since car was not located at accused's residence, county public safety department would potentially be subject to claim that either car or loose articles lying therein were taken; thus, packets of drug found in car could not be used as basis for forfeiture of car. West's F.S.A. §§ 893.01 et seq., 893.12(2, 5); U.S.C.A.Const. Amend. 4.—In re 1972 Porsche 2 dr., '74 Florida License Tag 1d 91780 VIN # 9111200334, 307 So.2d 451.

Fla.App. 3 Dist. 1971. Where motorist was arrested for traffic violation of character requiring posting of bond and was placed in police car for transportation to police station, inventory search of automobile, conducted by police before impounding automobile, was not illegal and narcotics revealed in search should not have been suppressed.—State v. Ruggles, 245 So.2d 692.

† This Case was not selected for publication in the National Reporter System

Fla.App. 3 Dist. 1968. Police who had box of jewelry lawfully in their possession as result of taking of inventory of contents of automobile which defendant was occupying at time of arrest were not prohibited from examining jewelry to determine if it were contraband.—Knight v. State, 212 So.2d 900.

Fla.App. 4 Dist. 2019. Warrantless search of a vehicle was an inventory search, and thus was not prohibited under the Fourth Amendment, where search occurred after law enforcement took the defendant into custody, the vehicle was lawfully taken because its registered owner could not be found, and search was conducted in good faith. U.S. Const. Amend. 4.—Tejada v. 2015 Cadillac Escalade VIN No: 1GYS4BKJ5FR157228, 267 So.3d 1032.

Fla.App. 4 Dist. 2007. Although defendant's motor vehicle had expired license plates, police officer did not have the authority under Florida law to have the vehicle impounded and, thus, the nonconsensual warrantless inventory search of the vehicle prior to towing and impounding was unreasonable; statute prohibiting motor vehicles with expired license plates from operating on roads did not authorize the impounding of such vehicles, and there was no evidence in the record suggesting that defendant's vehicle was illegally parked or created any type of traffic hazard. West's F.S.A. § 320.07.—Morris v. State, 958 So.2d 598.

Fla.App. 4 Dist. 1991. Where officer arrested defendant for driving on suspended license, officer's inventory of car, while awaiting tow truck, was proper. U.S.C.A. Const.Amend. 4.—State v. S.P., 580 So.2d 216, review denied 592 So.2d 682.

Fla.App. 4 Dist. 1983. Warrantless search of automobile, following first search incidental to defendant's arrest, after automobile was towed and impounded, and some eight hours after initial search, was not valid under moving vehicle exception to warrant requirement, as incident to lawful arrest, or as an inventory search. U.S.C.A. Const.Amend. 4.—Meyers v. State, 432 So.2d 97, petition for review denied 441 So.2d 633, reversed 104 S.Ct. 1852, 466 U.S. 380, 80 L.Ed.2d 381, on remand 457 So.2d 495.

Fla.App. 4 Dist. 1982. Inventory search of automobile during which officer noticed piece of cloth located underneath dashboard, removed cloth and discovered cocaine was appropriate and did not exceed in scope parameters and purposes of inventory.—State v. Licourt, 417 So.2d 1051.

Fla.App. 4 Dist. 1976. Where there was no showing that automobile, which defendant had been driving when arrested, would have created traffic hazard or nuisance, if it had been left parked defendant was not given choice of not having car impounded and was not allowed to call his mother to have her take car away, which according to defendant would have taken five minutes, impounding of car was not warranted, inventory search of it was unreasonable and illegal, and, on motion, defendant was entitled to have suppressed the cannabis which was seized from car. West's F.S.A. § 893.13(1)(e, f).—Gunn v. State, 336 So.2d 687.

Fla.App. 4 Dist. 1975. Inventory search of defendant's vehicle following his traffic arrest was not unreasonable where, inter alia, officer had no suspicion that automobile contained contraband, defendant was precluded from driving vehicle by failure to possess a valid driver's license, nature of the traffic violation was such as to require

defendant to post bond, defendant did not produce registration reflecting his ownership of the vehicle, and defendant did not protest and offered no other alternative method of securing the vehicle, of which he was the sole occupant, at 3:00 in the morning. U.S.C.A.Const. Amend. 4.—State v. Jenkins, 319 So.2d 91.

Fla.App. 5 Dist. 2021. Arrest affidavit's initial characterization of the search of the truck defendant had been driving as a search incident to defendant's arrest on outstanding warrant did not preclude a finding that the search had instead been conducted as a valid inventory search of an impounded vehicle. U.S. Const. Amend. 4.—State v. Koontz, 320 So.3d 993.

Fla.App. 5 Dist. 1987. Police officers, who failed to advise defendant as owner or possessor of car that car would be impounded unless defendant provided reasonable alternative to impoundment, could not impound car that became stuck in ditch after high speed chase for traffic violation, where defendant was not mentally incapacitated. U.S.C.A. Const.Amend. 4.—Collins v. State, 506 So.2d 21.

☞**661(3). Compartments; trunk.**

C.A.5 (Fla.) 1971. Where officers pursued defendant's automobile when he came by at high rate of speed and defendant was charged with reckless driving and taken to station house and his car was impounded and examination of contents of car was for purpose of making inventory of contents and not to look for contraband, procedure by which pistol was found in glove compartment did not violate Fourth Amendment guaranties against unreasonable searches and seizures. U.S.C.A.Const. Amend. 4.—U.S. v. Pennington, 441 F.2d 249, certiorari denied 92 S.Ct. 97, 404 U.S. 854, 30 L.Ed.2d 94.

☞**661(4). Luggage, bags, and other containers.**

Fla.App. 1 Dist. 1981. Where there was no indication that search of brown leather pouch in defendant's car was conducted pursuant to standard highway patrol procedures, defendant had a countervailing and superior expectation of privacy in her personal luggage to the state's legitimate interest in securing car for towing and inventorying its contents, and state trooper did not even complete an inventory list of car's contents, search of pouch could not be justified as a valid "inventory" or "protective" search for which no warrant is required, and thus controlled substances found during search should have been suppressed. U.S.C.A.Const. Amend. 4.—Hicks v. State, 398 So.2d 1008.

Fla.App. 2 Dist. 1989. Stop and inventory search of defendant's automobile were valid, and officer had probable cause to search bag after he saw that it looked like one recently stolen, together with firearms, from sheriff's department offices and felt firearms inside bag; thus, duffle bag and firearms found therein during that search were admissible.—State v. Landry, 543 So.2d 314.

Fla.App. 2 Dist. 1982. Since arresting officer did not advise defendant of possible alternatives to impoundment of his automobile, subsequent inventory search of the car which resulted in discovery of two baggies of marijuana and three small packets of cocaine was improper.—Higgins v. State, 422 So.2d 81.

☞**662. Carriers; public transportation.**

S.D.Fla. 2002. Police officers violated Fourth Amendment rights of prospective railroad passenger when they searched his baggage for drugs, after passenger twice unequivocally denied permission to search, despite claim that defendant had abandoned baggage. U.S.C.A. Const.Amend. 4.—U.S. v. Cofield, 242 F.Supp.2d 1260.

⚙═663. Vessels.

C.A.11 (Fla.) 2023. As was relevant to Fourth Amendment-based motion to suppress filed by defendant, who was a Venezuelan citizen apprehended aboard a Cameroon-flagged motor vessel in international waters in the Caribbean Sea and then indicted on drug charges under the Maritime Drug Law Enforcement Act (MDLEA), Coast Guard cutter had reasonable suspicion to stop and search vessel; Coast Guard knew that the Automated Information Systems (AIS) was not on, Coast Guard eventually obtained Cameroon's permission to board and search the vessel, vessel's purported destination made no sense, and vessel was not outfitted for cargo as its nature would have suggested, had a dangerously small crew, was having trouble maintaining a steady course, and was in a known drug-smuggling corridor. U.S. Const. Amend. 4; 46 U.S.C.A. § 70501 et seq.—United States v. Hurtado, 89 F.4th 881.

Reasonable suspicion that a search will turn up contraband is enough to justify a search and seizure of a foreign ship and its crew in international waters. (Per concurring opinion of E. Carnes, Circuit Judge, for a majority of the panel.)—Id.

C.A.11 (Fla.) 2010. Marine patrol officer developed probable cause to believe that three individuals, including two on fishing boat and one meeting the boat, had violated the fisheries laws of Florida and thus to search vessel, based on failure of individuals on boat to provide fishing licenses, their conflicting stories, manner in which they quickly attempted to trailer boat. U.S.C.A. Const.Amend. 4; F.S.2007, § 370.01(6). —U.S. v. Caraballo, 595 F.3d 1214.

C.A.11 (Fla.) 1988. Coast Guard had probable cause to board vessel to investigate criminal activity, where vessel was spotted in high risk area of Caribbean, vessel was sitting low in water, vessel's crew failed to respond initially to radio and whistle signals from Coast Guard cutter, vessel's captain claimed that vessel's purpose was fishing, despite conspicuous lack of fishing gear on board, and there was fresh damage to vessel of kind found when two ships meet on high seas and bump, frequently occurring when marijuana is off-loaded from mother ship onto smaller ships for importation. 14 U.S.C.A. § 89(a); U.S.C.A. Const.Amend. 4.—U.S. v. Meadows, 839 F.2d 1489.

C.A.5 (Fla.) 1982. Obviousness of nature of contents of packages discovered aboard vessel in environment wherein they were discovered equated discovery of the packages of marijuana with discovery of their contents, and motion to suppress was accordingly properly denied. U.S.C.A.Const.Amend. 4.—U.S. v. Marshall, 672 F.2d 425, rehearing denied 680 F.2d 1392.

C.A.5 (Fla.) 1979. Installation by paid informant for the Drug Enforcement Administration of an electronic beeper on vessel used by defendants in their attempt to import marijuana into the United States from Jamaica did not constitute an invalid warrantless search, since paid informant was under no legal obligation to conceal his whereabouts and thus transmission of signals on vessel was not an invasion of privacy of others, informant had right to be on board vessel and

thus there was no trespass at time that beeper was installed, and there was probable cause to believe that vessel would be used to transport contraband. U.S.C.A.Const. Amend. 4.—U.S. v. Conroy, 589 F.2d 1258, rehearing denied U.S. v. Walker, 594 F.2d 241, rehearing denied 594 F.2d 241, certiorari denied 100 S.Ct. 60, 444 U.S. 831, 62 L.Ed.2d 40.

Although paid informant for the Drug Enforcement Administration who conspired with defendants to import marijuana into the United States from Jamaica was not vessel owner, he had a right to go aboard vessel and his placement of electronic beepers on vessel rather than on his person did not render its introduction invalid. U.S.C.A.Const. Amend. 4.—Id.

C.A.5 (Fla.) 1978. Government agents who had been informed that defendant was attempting to find a boat to help move marijuana from a freighter into the United States, who helped the defendant obtain such a vessel, and who watched or helped in the unloading of 150 bales of marijuana from the freighter onto the boat had probable cause to search the freighter, as did coast guard officers who had been involved in the investigation.—U.S. v. Cadena, 585 F.2d 1252, rehearing denied 588 F.2d 100.

S.D.Fla. 2004. Drug-detection canine's alert in cruise ship hallway outside defendant's cabin established probable cause to enter and search cabin. U.S.C.A. Const.Amend. 4.—U.S. v. Brown, 298 F.Supp.2d 1317.

S.D.Fla. 1982. Defendant did not have a legitimate expectation of privacy as respects bales of marijuana stored on the deck of his ship and, thus, marine patrol officers' seizure of such bales was not unlawful under the Fourth Amendment. U.S.C.A.Const.Amend. 4.—U.S. v. Wilson, 528 F.Supp. 1129.

Fla.App. 3 Dist. 1981. There was probable cause for seizure under circumstances indicating that a police officer, who was a helicopter pilot, observed a boat "low in the water leaving a big wake" three fourths of a mile from where marijuana had been discovered and that, after defendant was observed sitting atop one of the bales, defendant was observed to accelerate the boat in an attempt to flee the police aircraft. U.S.C.A.Const.Amend. 4.—Rodriguez v. State, 407 So.2d 279.

Fla.App. 3 Dist. 1978. State marine patrol officers may board boat temporarily moored in state waters to inspect owner's boat registration and crawfish permit and thereafter conduct warrantless search of boat based upon smell of marijuana detected by one of officers upon boarding consistent with constitutional right of boat owner or occupant to be free from unreasonable searches and seizures guaranteed by Federal and State Constitutions; such search is justified under exception to rule requiring search warrants, in that there is probable cause for search of boat coupled with exigent circumstances dispensing with necessity for search warrant. West's F.S.A.Const. art. 1, § 12; U.S.C.A.Const. Amends. 4, 14, 14, § 1; West's F.S.A. §§ 370.021(5), 370.14(3)(c), 371.051(5).—Miranda v. State, 354 So.2d 411, certiorari denied 364 So.2d 888.

One's reasonable expectation of privacy in an automobile or boat is less than that of a private dwelling and therefore is more open to a legitimate governmental intrusion. West's F.S.A.Const. art. 1, § 12; U.S.C.A.Const. Amends. 4, 14, 14, § 1.—Id.

Fla.App. 4 Dist. 1983. Stop of 45-foot sailboat, which was found to contain almost 7,000 pounds of marijuana, was justified as based on reasonable suspicion that the craft was carrying contraband. Tariff Act of 1930, § 581(a), 19 U.S.C.A. § 1581(a).—McCrary v. State, 427 So.2d 1047, petition for review denied 438 So.2d 833.

Fla.App. 4 Dist. 1980. Where police, who located boat described by undisclosed informant as containing marijuana, observed no activity, their initial entry onto premises was unlawful as was search of the boat and the house, which followed discovery of marijuana residue on boat, notwithstanding that individuals who departed residence acknowledged that they were not the owners and did not know name of owner or that one officer suspected that house may have been burglarized, as there was no visible indication thereof or reported burglary and the three defendants did not exit in an unusual fashion. U.S.C.A.Const. Amends. 4, 14.—Daley v. State, 387 So.2d 971, cause remanded 392 So.2d 1327, on remand 398 So.2d 840.

⊕⇒**665. —— In general.**
C.A.5 (Fla.) 1981. Airport searches in the interest of drug enforcement cannot be justified on the same basis as those in the airport security context and drug searches are to be analyzed under traditional Fourth Amendment principles. U.S.C.A.Const. Amend. 4.—U.S. v. Goldstein, 635 F.2d 356, rehearing denied 640 F.2d 385, certiorari denied 101 S.Ct. 3111, 452 U.S. 962, 69 L.Ed.2d 972.

⊕⇒**666. —— Particular cases.**
C.A.11 (Fla.) 1984. In prosecution for importing controlled substance, evidence supported finding that defendant was not forced by customs officials to fly aircraft containing marijuana in any particular direction, and thus, even assuming that defendant had any expectation of privacy in location of his airplane, surveillance of airplane by customs officials did not constitute unlawful seizure of airplane. U.S.C.A. Const.Amend. 4.—U.S. v. Hewitt, 724 F.2d 117.

C.A.5 (Fla.) 1981. Where detective with drug intercept unit was legitimately in airport preboarding screening area and was assisting private security guard in removing a pair of pants from defendant's carryon shoulder bag after guard observed suspicious images on X-ray viewing screen and as guard lifted the pants out two plastic bags containing cocaine fell from the legs into bottom of bag, detective's seizure of such bags was lawful. U.S.C.A.Const. Amend. 4.—U.S. v. Gorman, 637 F.2d 352.

C.A.5 (Fla.) 1981. Drug agents' initial removal of defendants' luggage from airline baggage cart in a semipublic area, with the permission of the airline, did not violate the constitutional rights of the defendants.—U.S. v. Goldstein, 635 F.2d 356, rehearing denied 640 F.2d 385, certiorari denied 101 S.Ct. 3111, 452 U.S. 962, 69 L.Ed.2d 972.
Once trained dog positively reacted to the presence of drugs in luggage, that reaction, along with fact that defendants met certain aspects of the drug courier profile, supplied drug officers with probable cause to seek a warrant in order to search the luggage and to arrest the defendants. —Id.

S.D.Fla. 1980. Assuming inapplicability of contraband exception to "inadvertence" rule, drug intercept officer's seizure of cocaine was not invalid where officer did not have probable cause to believe contraband would be discovered in defendant's bag when he positioned himself behind x-ray machine at security checkpoint at airport.—U.S. v. Gorman, 484 F.Supp. 529.

Fla.App. 1 Dist. 2010. Physical administrative search of passenger's checked suitcase at Transportation Security Administration (TSA) airport checkpoint that revealed evidence of child pornography in accordion folder contained in suitcase was not more extensive or intrusive than necessary in light of current technology, and thus did not violate Fourth Amendment, where TSA had authority to conduct physical search of suitcase pursuant to statutory mandate to search all checked baggage, TSA protocol required TSA officers to open a certain number of randomly selected bags to swab contents and test for explosives in explosive detection machines, TSA officers had discretion to flip through files in baggage in lieu of swabbing each piece of paper individually, and TSA officer discovered evidence during such a random search. U.S.C.A. Const. Amend. 4; 49 U.S.C.A. § 44901.—Higerd v. State, 54 So.3d 513, rehearing denied, review denied 64 So.3d 1260, certiorari denied 132 S.Ct. 521, 565 U.S. 979, 181 L.Ed.2d 350.
Physical administrative search of passenger's checked suitcase at Transportation Security Administration (TSA) airport checkpoint that revealed evidence of child pornography in accordion folder contained in suitcase was confined in good faith to purpose of searching for explosives or weapons, and thus did not violate Fourth Amendment, where TSA officer was required to physically open a certain number of bags, defendant's suitcase was selected at random for physical search, TSA officer was required by TSA protocol to thumb through papers in accordion folder in defendant's suitcase as part of search, and TSA officer discovered evidence while thumbing through accordion folder. U.S.C.A. Const.Amend. 4.—Id.

Fla.App. 3 Dist. 1985. Suspect's nervousness when he consented to a "feel" of his boots by members of narcotics interdiction squad at airport, together with narcotics officer's discovery of a soft and malleable package inside boot and officer's belief, in light of his experience with searches of this kind, that package contained cocaine, provided probable cause for seizure of package and its subsequent examination.—State v. Rodriguez, 477 So.2d 1025.

Fla.App. 3 Dist. 1984. Where officers observed defendant at airport moving two extremely heavy pieces of luggage to baggage well of ticket counter, defendant was overheard purchasing round trip ticket to San Francisco with an open return, defendant seemed nervous and filled out baggage identification tags without any address, and defendant paid for his ticket in cash, there was an articulable suspicion for officers to stop defendant, and where defendant became so nervous when officers started talking about narcotics that he sweated profusely to the point that perspiration dripped off his chin even though it was cool in the airport, "dog sniff" conducted on defendant's luggage incident to the stop of defendant was lawful.—State v. Taylor, 446 So.2d 1147.

Fla.App. 3 Dist. 1982. Uncontroverted evidence supported trial court's finding that airline passenger's suitcase containing cocaine was not detained because of state action pertaining to officer's airport narcotics investigation, but, rather, suitcase was not seized prior to dog's sniff, so that passenger's motion to suppress cocaine was properly denied.—Mosier v. State, 415 So.2d 771.

Fla.App. 3 Dist. 1982. Where police officers had a reasonable suspicion that defendant's luggage contained narcotics and where defendant made no claim that the time during which his suitcase was removed from the airline's immediate control extended beyond the scheduled departure of his flight so as to constitute an unlawful seizure of the suitcase, the police officers' removal without search of defendant's luggage from the baggage area did not interfere with his reasonable expectation of privacy, whether the distance of removal was merely from a cart to the airport floor or from the baggage area to the concourse of the airport.—Cavalluzzi v. State, 409 So.2d 1108.

Fla.App. 3 Dist. 1981. Sniffing dog's "alert" on suitcase at airport conferred probable cause for seizure of bag at precise minute of its scheduled departure, and if bag was delayed for any reason other than state action, detectives and state were beneficiaries of fortune, but if in absence of state action bag would have become inaccessible to dog for purpose of his sniff, then it was unlawfully seized. U.S.C.A.Const. Amend. 4.—State v. Mosier, 392 So.2d 602, appeal after remand 415 So.2d 771.

Fla.App. 3 Dist. 1980. Manual inspection of contents of package of defendant seeking to board domestic airline flight, after inconclusive X-ray inspection which revealed contents were bulky and opaque, was constitutionally permissible, and cocaine obtained by said search and seizure was admissible into evidence. U.S.C.A.Const. Amends. 4, 14.—State v. Nadeau, 395 So.2d 182.

Fla.App. 4 Dist. 1978. Warrantless search of highly movable airplane, initially inspired by odor of marijuana emitting from it, was, under all circumstances, reasonable.—Gross v. State, 362 So.2d 394.

⟜668. —— In general.

C.A.11 (Fla.) 2019. When court considers the limitations which the Fourth Amendment places upon protective seizure and search for weapons, it considers concrete factual circumstances of the individual case, asking whether a reasonably prudent man in those circumstances would be warranted in belief that his safety or that of others was in danger. U.S. Const. Amend. 4.—United States v. Johnson, 921 F.3d 991, certiorari denied 140 S.Ct. 376, 205 L.Ed.2d 215.

M.D.Fla. 2016. A protective sweep is not a full search of the premises and must last no longer than is necessary to dispel the officer's reasonable suspicion of danger. U.S. Const. Amend. 4.—Montanez v. Carvajal, 224 F.Supp.3d 1274, reversed 889 F.3d 1202, affirmed Rivera v. Carvajal, 777 Fed.Appx. 434.

Fla.App. 1 Dist. 2014. A high crime area, in and of itself, does not translate to reasonable suspicion one is armed and dangerous or that criminal activity must be afoot, as required to justify weapons pat-down or investigatory stop. U.S.C.A. Const.Amend. 4; West's F.S.A. § 901.151(2–5).—Griffin v. State, 150 So.3d 288.

Fla.App. 2 Dist. 2018. With few exceptions, the question as to whether a warrantless search of a home is reasonable, and hence constitutional, must be answered no, and among those exceptions are a protective sweep and exigent circumstances. U.S. Const. Amend. 4.—Aguilar v. State, 259 So.3d 262.

Fla.App. 2 Dist. 2017. Association alone is insufficient to justify a pat-down search. U.S.

Const. Amend. 4.—Brown v. State, 224 So.3d 806.

Fla.App. 4 Dist. 2008. One of the recognized circumstances justifying a weapons pat-down is the combination of the defendant's nervousness and the officer's observation of a bulge in the defendant's clothing; however, an officer does not have reasonable suspicion that a defendant is armed merely because, following a non-criminal traffic stop, the defendant appears nervous and keeps his hands in or near his pockets. U.S.C.A. Const.Amend. 4.—State v. Barnes, 979 So.2d 991.

Fla.App. 4 Dist. 1989. Further detention and search of persons on unposted property who do not defy order by authorized person to depart is justified only where the officer has founded suspicion of criminal activity or reasonable belief of danger of weapons. West's F.S.A. § 810.09(2)(b).—In Interest of B.M., 553 So.2d 714.

⟜669. —— Particular cases in general.

† C.A.11 (Fla.) 2020. Protective sweep of motel room, consisting of officer's cursory visual inspection of the bathroom and back part of the room, was justified under Fourth Amendment; group of officers had motel under surveillance following armed robbery of convenience store, entry into room following domestic dispute of occupants was justified by exigent circumstances, officers had reason to believe one of the room's occupants was a suspect in the robbery and that he had been assisted by others who could be armed and in the motel room, and in these uncertain circumstances facing the officers, officer safety justified the visual inspection of places where people could be hiding. U.S. Const. Amend. 4.—United States v. Rivera, 824 Fed. Appx. 930.

† C.A.11 (Fla.) 2020. Police lieutenant's "cursory search" of apartment was authorized under the protective sweep doctrine to ensure the safety of the officers; upon entering the apartment, officers had reason to believe that shots had been fired inside the apartment, that a woman fled the scene because she felt she and her child were in danger, and that defendant had threatened to kill unidentified individuals who were "trying to kill [him]." U.S. Const. Amend. 4.—United States v. Jones, 798 Fed.Appx. 434.

C.A.11 (Fla.) 2020. It was not objectively unreasonable for trained police officer to hear dog whimpering and claim he could not tell difference between whimpering dog and human in pain, and thus officers' warrantless entry into and protective sweep of defendant's residence fell within scope of emergency aid exception to Fourth Amendment's warrant requirement, even though defendant was already in custody and posed no threat, even if defendant's girlfriend told officers that dogs were source of whimpering, where officers were responding to multiple 911 calls reporting gunshots several minutes earlier, girlfriend had informed officers that defendant had threatened to kill himself, and defendant had initially refused to leave his house, locked door behind him when he finally exited, and tried to mislead officers by suggesting that reported gunshots might have been children playing with fireworks. U.S. Const. Amend. 4.—United States v. Evans, 958 F.3d 1102.

C.A.11 (Fla.) 2019. Police officers' warrantless entry and protective sweep of defendant's motel room, for the purpose of executing an arrest warrant, complied with the Fourth Amendment; officers knew defendant was staying in motel room, as they had observed him walk out the door of room, go to his truck, and return to the room, when defendant saw officers, and fled motel on foot, officers had a reasonable belief that defendant had returned to motel room, as defendant's truck remained in motel parking lot and officers had lost sight of defendant during the ten minute pursuit and believed he had doubled back to the motel. U.S. Const. Amend. 4.— United States v. Ross, 941 F.3d 1058, rehearing granted, vacated 953 F.3d 744, on rehearing 963 F.3d 1056, on remand 964 F.3d 1034, certiorari denied 141 S.Ct. 1394, 209 L.Ed.2d 132.

† **C.A.11 (Fla.) 2018.** Exigent circumstances justified firearm's continued seizure after firearm had been disassembled based on defendant's proximity to firearm; safety concerns justifying initial seizure, including that police were still looking for a shooting suspect and defendant, who was not the suspect, was unsecured, did not dissipate after disassembly of the firearm. U.S. Const. Amend. 4.—United States v. Kendricks, 758 Fed.Appx. 687, certiorari denied 139 S.Ct. 2038, 204 L.Ed.2d 236.

† **C.A.11 (Fla.) 2018.** Suppression of drugs, firearms, and ammunition discovered in suspect's girlfriend's apartment was not appropriate as result of detective attempting to force his way into apartment with crowbar before suspect's arrest, as detective was entitled to enter apartment and promptly conduct warrantless protective sweep of apartment to ensure safety of girlfriend and fellow officers; detective was in hot pursuit of suspect when he attempted to force his way into apartment, he entered apartment immediately after girlfriend remarked "they just ran up in here," when inside apartment, detective saw marijuana, a scale, and magazines of ammunition in plain view, and he completed protective sweep before obtaining his camera and photographing apartment to catalog evidence observed during sweep. U.S. Const. Amend. 4.—United States v. Concepcion, 748 Fed.Appx. 904, certiorari denied 139 S.Ct. 285, 204 L.Ed.2d 282.

† **C.A.11 (Fla.) 2017.** Police officers had reasonable suspicion, after taking defendant into custody, that there may have been someone else inside residence who still posed a danger to officers, as required to justify warrantless protective sweep of home; officers saw someone manipulate the blinds in the front of the house from a room on the north side, whereas defendant had emerged from an entirely different part of the house, and officers noted that defendant exhibited evasive behavior after being taken into custody. U.S. Const. Amend. 4.—United States v. Lesane, 685 Fed.Appx. 705, post-conviction relief denied Morris v. United States, 2018 WL 4931904, post-conviction relief denied Hood v. United States, 2019 WL 1598732, certificate of appealability denied 2019 WL 5566743.

† **C.A.11 (Fla.) 2015.** Police officers' protective sweep of defendant's rented bedroom was reasonable after officers conducted search of home's common areas upon consent of homeowner, where home was small, making ambush attack possible, bedroom was visible from living area, officers believed room harbored individual posing danger to them, officers had received tip from confidential informant that male who sold heroin and carried gun was living in house, and officers found speed loaders, bullets, and drug paraphernalia upon entering home. U.S.C.A. Const.Amend. 4.—U.S. v. Medina, 631 Fed.Appx. 682, certiorari denied 136 S.Ct. 1397, 577 U.S. 1201, 194 L.Ed.2d 375, post-conviction relief de-

nied 2018 WL 11201417, affirmed in part, vacated in part, remanded 797 Fed.Appx. 431.

† **C.A.11 (Fla.) 2012.** Officers' conduct preceding exigency in seeking consensual arrest of suspect at his home for stolen check did not violate Fourth Amendment, and so officers could avail themselves of exigent circumstances exception to warrant requirement to justify entry of home and suppression of evidence of firearm and ammunition was not justified in prosecution for possession of firearm by convicted felon; officer observed pistol in defendant's pocket after tackling defendant during interaction, loaded gun was seized, and protective sweep of apartment located box of ammunition in plain view in rear room. U.S.C.A. Const.Amend. 4.—U.S. v. Hall, 500 Fed.Appx. 819, certiorari denied 133 S.Ct. 1843, 569 U.S. 938, 185 L.Ed.2d 849.

S.D.Fla. 2008. Police officers' warrantless seizure of currency from defendant's bedroom was justified under plain view doctrine, even though officers did not see currency when defendant voluntarily opened door for officers, where officer observed currency during protective sweep in plain view on bed. U.S.C.A. Const.Amend. 4.— U.S. v. Smalls, 617 F.Supp.2d 1240, affirmed 342 Fed.Appx. 505, certiorari denied 130 S.Ct. 1094, 558 U.S. 1128, 175 L.Ed.2d 912.

Fla.App. 1 Dist. 2021. Deputy acted reasonably under the Fourth Amendment, in searching defendant in concern for safety of deputy and defendant and for those present at hospital where deputy intended to take defendant, after deputy had taken defendant into involuntary protective custody under the Marchman Act, due to defendant's appearing to need "substance abuse services." U.S. Const. Amend 4; Fla. Stat. Ann. §§ 397.305, 397.6771, 397.6772.—Jones v. State, 331 So.3d 252, review denied 2022 WL 1261288.

Fla.App. 2 Dist. 2002. If, during a lawful patdown for weapons, the totality of the circumstances gives a police officer probable cause to believe the detainee is carrying drugs, the officer may seize them.—Rodriguez v. State, 807 So.2d 130.

Fla.App. 2 Dist. 1971. Where police officer was aiding defendant in carrying defendant's wife up the stairs to defendant's apartment and when they got into the apartment and placed the wife upon a bed the officer reached over and pulled out a small automatic weapon from defendant's coat pocket, officer had no probable cause to justify search and seizure of gun and the consequent arrest, since defendant was in his own home at night, had committed no affirmative act involving violation of law, had not threatened anyone and was at time of search and arrest cooperating with officer.—Johnson v. State, 253 So.2d 732, certiorari discharged 269 So.2d 8.

Fla.App. 3 Dist. 2023. Police officers had reasonable suspicion to believe that defendant was under the influence of alcoholic beverages when she used firearm to shoot at her boyfriend's house, as justified officers' securing of defendant's bag, which contained firearm; upon arriving at scene, officers found bullet casings in curtilage of house and bullet holes near front door, defendant voluntarily approached officers and told them that her boyfriend resided at the house, that she had been having problems with him, repeating various times that he had been unfaithful, and that she had a firearm in bag, and defendant appeared intoxicated and smelled of alcohol. U.S. Const. Amend. 4; Fla. Stat. Ann. § 790.151.—Rivera v. State, 364 So.3d 1074.

† **This Case was not selected for publication in the National Reporter System**

Fla.App. 3 Dist. 2003. Totality of circumstances provided experienced police officer with reasonable suspicion that defendant was armed and dangerous, and thus pat-down search was justified; officer was in a high-crime area when he was informed that defendant was selling drugs, defendant walked quickly to end of apartment building hallway and began to make suspicious and furtive movements when officer approached, and defendant "started stuttering and shaking all over the place" when officer began to ask defendant questions. U.S.C.A. Const.Amend. 4; West's F.S.A. § 901.151(5).—Enich v. State, 838 So.2d 1216.

🗝**670(1). In general.**
S.D.Fla. 2021. The search of the passenger compartment of an automobile, limited to those areas in which a weapon may be placed or hidden, is permissible under the Fourth Amendment if the police officer possesses a reasonable belief based on specific and articulable facts which, taken together with the rational inferences from those facts, reasonably warrant the officers in believing that the suspect is dangerous and the suspect may gain immediate control of weapons. U.S. Const. Amend. 4.—Johnson v. Israel, 576 F.Supp.3d 1231.

Under the Fourth Amendment, where police have reasonable suspicion to believe that driver may be armed and dangerous, they may conduct protective search for weapons not only of driver's person but also of passenger compartment of automobile. U.S. Const. Amend. 4.—Id.

🗝**670(2). Particular cases.**
†**C.A.11 (Fla.) 2021.** Probable cause existed to justify warrantless search of defendant's car, even though defendant had already been removed from car; defendant was pulled over based on another driver's seemingly trustworthy report that defendant had just pointed firearm at him in traffic, defendant failed to stop immediately after police officer signaled for him to pull over, and defendant made "road rage" comment in response to officer's question about whether he had gun. U.S. Const. Amend. 4.—United States v. Martinez, 851 Fed.Appx. 946, certiorari denied 142 S.Ct. 373, 211 L.Ed.2d 198.

†**C.A.11 (Fla.) 2009.** Police officers had probable cause to believe that car contained drugs and firearms, and thus warrantless search of car did not violate Fourth Amendment, where confidential informant (CI) had first-hand knowledge of suspect's drug operation, officers had verified CI's information, CI told officers that suspect would be leaving his house soon with bag containing drugs and gun, and officers observed suspect leave short time later with bag in his possession and drive off in waiting car. U.S.C.A. Const.Amend. 4.—U.S. v. Fernandez Martinez, 317 Fed.Appx. 929, certiorari denied 130 S.Ct. 198, 558 U.S. 882, 175 L.Ed.2d 139, post-conviction relief denied 2011 WL 4502073, habeas corpus dismissed in part Martinez v. Spaulding, 2021 WL 4080051, reconsideration denied 2022 WL 4636795, habeas corpus dismissed by 2022 WL 4636795.

C.A.11 (Fla.) 1983. Danger to officers presented by fleeing suspects after officers entered property where marijuana was being off-loaded justified exploratory search of residence and vehicles to assure that no one lay in waiting for officers.—U.S. v. Blasco, 702 F.2d 1315, certiorari denied Galvan v. U.S., 104 S.Ct. 275, 464 U.S. 914, 78 L.Ed.2d 256, certiorari denied Jamardo v. U.S., 104 S.Ct. 276, 464 U.S. 914, 78 L.Ed.2d 256.

Fla.App. 2 Dist. 1989. Police had no legally objective belief that defendant was an armed narcotics smuggler sufficient to justify weapons search immediately upon stopping vehicle; transcripts reflected that State used defendant's reputation to justify search of vehicle, despite knowledge that information concerning his alleged drug activities had previously proved unreliable. U.S.C.A. Const.Amend. 4.—Arnold v. State, 544 So.2d 294.

Fla.App. 2 Dist. 1989. Stop and inventory search of defendant's automobile were valid, and officer had probable cause to search bag after he saw that it looked like one recently stolen, together with firearms, from sheriff's department offices and felt firearms inside bag; thus, duffle bag and firearms found therein during that search were admissible.—State v. Landry, 543 So.2d 314.

Fla.App. 2 Dist. 1987. BOLO was insufficient in particularity to provide constitutional basis for effecting arrest, but provided officer with sufficient information to formulate reasonable suspicion that defendant and his companion might have committed armed robbery and that at least one of them was potentially dangerous, for purpose of determining whether protective search of automobile was proper.—State v. Chapel, 510 So.2d 1138.

Fla.App. 3 Dist. 1991. Facts which became known to officers after investigatory stop of vehicle, including presence of pistol in car and revelation, through check on the vehicle identification number, that vehicle had been stolen, provided ample probable cause to support arrest of occupants, ensuing search of vehicle and seizure of incriminating evidence which was found.—Mendez v. State, 579 So.2d 352.

Fla.App. 5 Dist. 1986. When it was clear that defendant was only occupant of car, thus exercising control and authority over car and gun, officers had probable cause to stop and arrest defendant for carrying concealed firearm and had right to seize handgun based on automobile exception to warrant requirement, where police officer, while standing on public street where he had right to be, looked in car and had open view of butt of gun protruding from underneath driver's seat.—State v. Poole, 496 So.2d 224.

🗝**671. Animals and pets.**
Fla.App. 5 Dist. 2018. Canine remains were properly seized from defendant's yard under plain view doctrine; police officers, responding to a report from defendant's neighbor of possible animal cruelty in progress, observed defendant in back of house, after midnight, pacing behind fence and saying something along the lines of "get down" or "lay down" and heard what appeared to be something striking flesh, and after speaking with defendant and learning that he had struck dog as punishment, found dog lying down in corner of yard where defendant had been, lying listless, and quickly determined that dog, which appeared to be bound and gagged and had bloodied tongue, was dead. U.S. Const. Amend. 4.—State v. Archer, 259 So.3d 999, review denied 2019 WL 2205765, on subsequent appeal 309 So.3d 287, rehearing denied.

🗝**673. —— In general.**
Fla.App. 5 Dist. 1990. Seizing drugs that defendant dropped while continuing to walk away from police despite being ordered to stop did not constitute illegal search, even though police did

† This Case was not selected for publication in the National Reporter System

not have founded suspicion sufficient to support investigatory stop; rather defendant's act of throwing down drugs was "voluntary abandonment" and thus it was not per se tainted by illegal stop. U.S.C.A. Const.Amend. 4; West's F.S.A. § 901.151.—Curry v. State, 570 So.2d 1071.

☞674. —— Particular items in general.

Fla. 1993. Chase and call for defendant to stop was not a "seizure" and, therefore, defendant's abandonment of cocaine was not fruit of the poisonous tree and cocaine should not have been suppressed.—State v. Bartee, 623 So.2d 458.

Fla. 1993. Defendant did not voluntarily abandon cocaine he dropped behind his back when approached by police officers clad in black masks and SWAT-team-type regalia, so that cocaine was "fruit" of officers' illegal seizure; defendant submitted to officers' show of authority, although they did not actually tell anyone to "freeze" and their attention was not specifically directed toward defendant, since reasonable person under the circumstances would feel that he was not to move. U.S.C.A. Const.Amend. 4.—Hollinger v. State, 620 So.2d 1242.

Fla.App. 1 Dist. 1998. Drugs thrown over balcony by defendant after police officer placed him under arrest following illegal search of hotel room were not "abandoned," but instead, were fruits of illegal search and not admissible. U.S.C.A. Const.Amend. 4.—Dempsey v. State, 717 So.2d 1071.

Fla.App. 1 Dist. 1990. Defendant's act of throwing pill bottle containing crack cocaine, while being pursued by police officer during unlawful chase, resulted from officer's unlawful conduct, and thus abandonment of contraband was involuntary and it was unlawfully seized. U.S.C.A. Const.Amend. 4.—State v. Bartee, 568 So.2d 523, quashed 623 So.2d 458.

Fla.App. 2 Dist. 2007. Cocaine which defendant abandoned before he was seized by police was not fruit of a seizure, and thus, seizure of cocaine did not violate Fourth Amendment. U.S.C.A. Const.Amend. 4.—Austin v. State, 965 So.2d 853.

Fla.App. 2 Dist. 2006. Defendant was not "seized" by police at time they activated lights and sirens and began pursuit, and thus, defendant's abandonment of pill bottle containing cocaine by throwing bottle out window of his car during police pursuit was not involuntary, where defendant had not yielded to authority of police at time he threw pill bottle. U.S.C.A. Const. Amend. 4; West's F.S.A. Const. Art. 1, § 12.—State v. Battis, 926 So.2d 427, rehearing denied.

Fla.App. 2 Dist. 2001. Officer's seizure of marijuana was constitutionally justified, as was his arrest of defendant, where defendant began to flee when officer approached and thrust his hands toward his pocket, causing officer to have justifiable concern for his safety, and when officer properly responded to potential threat by grabbing him, defendant voluntarily abandoned the drugs by throwing them over the fence.—Mitchell v. State, 787 So.2d 224.

Fla.App. 2 Dist. 1999. Police officer lacked probable cause, once defendant withdrew consent to search when he told officer that he did not have paper towel in his hand and tried to leave scene, to retrieve paper towel that fell from defendant's hands onto ground, where officer could not see any evidence of drugs prior to handcuffing defendant. U.S.C.A. Const.Amend. 4.—Williams v. State, 727 So.2d 1050.

Fla.App. 2 Dist. 1997. Defendant's abandonment of two baggies of cocaine upon being illegally seized by police officers was not voluntary, and therefore such evidence was to be suppressed. U.S.C.A. Const.Amend. 4.—Welch v. State, 689 So.2d 1240.

Fla.App. 2 Dist. 1995. Defendant who was part of group of individuals who fled when police appeared, was subsequently observed discarding object later determined to be cocaine after he came out of vacant apartment and walked toward gate to leave area, and was then grabbed by officer who was near gate was not "seized" at time cocaine was dropped, and cocaine was voluntarily abandoned and could be admitted in prosecution of defendant; defendant's actions could only be characterized as attempt to flee, and fact that defendant was walking instead of running did not indicate submission to authority. U.S.C.A. Const.Amend. 4.—State v. Wright, 662 So.2d 975.

Fla.App. 2 Dist. 1991. Defendant's act of spitting cocaine out of his mouth was prompted by or result of illegal detention by officers, and, thus, cocaine should have been suppressed; officers lacked probable cause to stop defendant who had merely been observed standing in unpaved parking lot with other black males.—Curry v. State, 576 So.2d 890, decision approved 621 So.2d 410.

Fla.App. 2 Dist. 1991. Defendant who, following consensual encounter with police officer followed by lawful detention, dropped tissue containing cocaine rock from her purse, voluntarily abandoned the cocaine, making its subsequent seizure lawful.—State v. Starke, 574 So.2d 1214.

Fla.App. 2 Dist. 1990. Cocaine which dropped to ground while officer was conducting a pat-down of defendant could not be considered to have been abandoned by defendant.—Stevenson v. State, 565 So.2d 858.

Fla.App. 3 Dist. 1992. Abandonment of cocaine by defendant was not product of illegal seizure of defendant's person, where defendant had not been taken into custody by police officer at time he abandoned drug, even though police officer had no probable cause to arrest defendant and no reasonable suspicion to temporarily detain him when chase began. U.S.C.A. Const. Amend. 4.—D.E. v. State, 605 So.2d 574.

Fla.App. 3 Dist. 1991. Baggies of cocaine that defendant discarded when he fled from officers were not fruit of unlawful seizure of person of defendant who fled when officers got out of their vehicle and before officers said anything.—Butler v. State, 579 So.2d 890.

Fla.App. 3 Dist. 1989. Packet of cocaine that dropped from person's pocket after police officer "asked" person to take his hands out of his pockets for officer's "own safety" was not voluntarily abandoned, but revealed because of constitutionally unjustified police order; request was made after officer, without probable cause or reasonable suspicion, confronted person, who was sitting on park bench in early morning.—Evans v. State, 546 So.2d 1125.

Fla.App. 4 Dist. 2006. Seizure of cocaine dropped by defendant prior to unlawful stop was lawful. U.S.C.A. Const.Amend. 4.—State v. Conde, 924 So.2d 897, rehearing denied.

Fla.App. 4 Dist. 2003. Police officer had reasonable suspicion to believe that defendant was committing a crime, and thus evidence was not subject to suppression in prosecution for drug offense; officer observed defendant with a lighter in one hand and a glass pipe in the other hand, when defendant saw the officer he dropped the pipe, and the officer retrieved the pipe, which contained cocaine. West's F.S.A. § 901.151.— State v. Grant, 845 So.2d 984.

Fla.App. 4 Dist. 1998. Crack cocaine, that defendant dropped to ground in encounter with officer, was admissible as police questioning was innocuous in nature and reasonable person would have felt free to leave; single police officer asked what defendant was doing standing in the street at 4:00 a.m. and asked for his identification. U.S.C.A. Const.Amend. 4.—Fields v. State, 722 So.2d 957.

Fla.App. 4 Dist. 1994. Defendant voluntarily abandoned cocaine rocks he dropped after officer asked him to stop where drop occurred before defendant willfully obeyed and officer did not physically force defendant to obey police request to stop; thus, there was no unlawful seizure of defendant's person at time drop occurred. U.S.C.A. Const.Amend. 4.—Johnson v. State, 640 So.2d 136.

Fla.App. 4 Dist. 1989. No abandonment arose when defendant, in response to officer's demand that he reveal what was concealed in his hand, opened blue pill bottle in his hand and threw contents to ground, where officer did not have well-founded suspicion to stop defendant and make search, and thus Fourth Amendment precluded admission of evidence concerning contents. U.S.C.A. Const.Amend. 4.—Wallace v. State, 540 So.2d 254.

Fla.App. 4 Dist. 1988. Narcotics defendant did not abandon aluminum package dropped at his feet upon police officer's direction to "freeze," sufficient to allow warrantless search of package, where police officer lacked reasonable suspicion for the initial stop and directive. West's F.S.A. § 901.151; U.S.C.A. Const.Amend. 4.—Spann v. State, 529 So.2d 825.

Fla.App. 4 Dist. 1972. Where patrolling officer had stopped defendant in early morning hours as defendant was walking on street in fashionable hotel and residential area, officer's inquiry concerning bulge in watchpocket of defendant's trousers did not amount to a search and defendant's conduct in producing a vial from his watchpocket and throwing vial, into adjacent waterway was an abandonment of possession; thus, vial, which was found to contain marijuana, was admissible, notwithstanding that officer had no valid basis to stop defendant and interrogate him. F.S.A. § 901.151.—Riley v. State, 266 So.2d 173.

Fla.App. 5 Dist. 2001. Cocaine was obtained by officers as result of abandonment in public area, where defendant and another person were outside passing back of forth cylindrical object, they dropped object to ground, and object was found to contain cocaine.—Stevens v. State, 782 So.2d 550.

Fla.App. 5 Dist. 1996. Defendant's abandonment of pill bottle was not voluntary so as to permit admission of bottle into evidence where defendant had submitted to deputy's authority at time he dropped bottle by beginning to comply with deputy's instruction to get into patrol car. U.S.C.A. Const.Amend. 4.—Lang v. State, 671 So.2d 292.

Fla.App. 5 Dist. 1992. Even assuming that defendant was illegally detained, abandonment of tissue containing cocaine was voluntary and defendant forfeited all expectation of constitutional protection which he may have claimed regarding possession of tissue and its contents, where his dropping of the tissue was not in response to any police request or command.—State v. Hollinger,

596 So.2d 521, jurisdiction accepted 606 So.2d 1165, quashed 620 So.2d 1242.

Fla.App. 5 Dist. 1989. Although defendant was in company of undercover agent when she purchased cocaine, and when agent's automobile was stopped by a marked police patrol car and both were "arrested" and placed in patrol car, and although defendant responded to agent's question regarding whereabouts of cocaine by replying that she threw it under agent's car, neither police stop nor question by undercover agent made defendant's abandonment of cocaine legally involuntary, and thus the cocaine was admissible; undercover agent's knowledge of defendant's criminal possession of cocaine came from independent source of agent's personal observation, rather than defendant's answer to agent's question while both were in police patrol car. U.S.C.A. Const.Amend. 4; West's F.S.A. Const. Art. 1, § 12.—State v. Lapinski, 535 So.2d 716.

⊙⇒**675. —— Luggage, bags, and other containers.**

S.D.Fla. 2002. Police officers violated Fourth Amendment rights of prospective railroad passenger when they searched his baggage for drugs, after passenger twice unequivocally denied permission to search, despite claim that defendant had abandoned baggage. U.S.C.A. Const.Amend. 4.—U.S. v. Cofield, 242 F.Supp.2d 1260.

S.D.Fla. 2000. Court would credit defendant's version of train station encounter with police, in which he alleged that he twice refused police requests to submit his luggage for sniff testing by canine and police search, before throwing them to ground and attempting to leave station, and conclude that bags were not abandoned for search and seizure purposes, based in part upon surreptitiously recorded conversation between defendant and girl friend, in back of police vehicle following his detention, that supported his version of encounter. U.S.C.A. Const.Amend. 4.—U.S. v. Cofield, 108 F.Supp.2d 1374, vacated 272 F.3d 1303, on remand 242 F.Supp.2d 1260.

Fla.App. 1 Dist. 1999. Although defendant might have been illegally stopped and thereafter seized as a result of his initial submission to police authority, the seizure was terminated once he ran from police, and thus, bag of cannabis that defendant threw while fleeing was not discarded at time defendant was "seized" within meaning of Fourth Amendment; accordingly, bag was admissible. U.S.C.A. Const.Amend. 4.—Abdullah v. State, 745 So.2d 582, rehearing denied.

Fla.App. 2 Dist. 2003. Assuming, arguendo, that initial stop of defendant was not justifiable, once defendant began to run from the police, the seizure was terminated and the baggie that he dropped from his pocket was considered abandoned and therefore admissible. U.S.C.A. Const. Amend. 4.—State v. Smith, 850 So.2d 565, rehearing denied.

Fla.App. 4 Dist. 1986. Warrantless search, without defendant's consent, of luggage left behind when defendant fled narcotics agents at airport violated defendant's Fourth Amendment rights, where agents had only articulable suspicion that defendant's bags might contain drugs. U.S.C.A. Const.Amend. 4.—Nease v. State, 484 So.2d 67, review denied 494 So.2d 1153, certiorari denied 107 S.Ct. 1982, 481 U.S. 1041, 95 L.Ed.2d 822.

Fla.App. 4 Dist. 1982. Where defendant on recognizing officer as narcotics agent began to flee and dropped paper bag containing marijuana, there was abandonment in way and area where he had no reasonable expectation of privacy, and thus he could not claim violation of his Fourth Amendment rights. U.S.C.A.Const. Amend. 4.—State v. Davis, 415 So.2d 82.

⌾676. —— Vehicles.

Fla.App. 1 Dist. 1976. Where inspector at state agricultural station stopped defendants, and after being denied permission to inspect load inside defendants' van, told defendants that they would have to return with him to inspection station, there was no search involved when defendants began throwing bags of marijuana from back of their rented van, and abandonment of such bags by defendants constituted probable cause to justify subsequent warrantless search of van. West's F.S.A. § 933.19.—Smith v. State, 333 So.2d 91.

Fla.App. 1 Dist. 1972. Where state trooper was following speeding automobile in which defendant was a back seat passenger, where the trooper turned on his blue overhead light to stop the car ahead because defendant "looked suspicious," where, with the aid of the blue light, he saw defendant throwing or attempting to throw a white powdery substance out the right rear window, and where, upon stopping the car and searching defendant's person, he discovered a small cellophane bag with a substance in it which he thought looked like marijuana, the marijuana taken by the trooper was the product of a reasonable search and seizure under the circumstances. —Shaver v. State, 262 So.2d 30.

Fla.App. 2 Dist. 1991. Drug defendant's act of abandoning or accidentally dropping marijuana when he got out of car was prompted by or result of officer's illegal stop, and thus it should have been suppressed; there was direct connection between unlawful police conduct and discovery of contraband. U.S.C.A. Const.Amend. 4.—Cox v. State, 586 So.2d 1321.

Fla.App. 3 Dist. 1988. Defendant did not abandon paper bag of cocaine by placing it in his car and walking away. U.S.C.A. Const.Amend. 4. —State v. James, 526 So.2d 188.

Fla.App. 3 Dist. 1988. Defendant was not entitled to suppression of 400 cocaine rocks uncovered during search of vehicle after police attempted to stop defendant driver when he ran stop sign, defendant stopped in middle of intersection, opened car door, and fled along with companion, defendant was apprehended, and placed under arrest for driving without license; there was no reasonable expectation of privacy in property abandoned in public street in attempt to avoid police search.—Brooks v. State, 524 So.2d 1102.

Fla.App. 4 Dist. 1981. Act of defendant in hastily leaving automobile parked in "no loitering" zone without saying a word to police officer sufficiently evidenced intention to abandon the vehicle, and thus officer had a lawful right to be in car investigating its ownership and could validly seize cocaine which was in plain view; even if the evidence was not in plain view, officer had a right to search once the property was abandoned so that there was no longer a reasonable expectation of privacy.—State v. Lawson, 394 So.2d 1139.

Even if defendant was illegally stopped, subsequent seizure of cocaine from his automobile was not tainted because the vehicle was voluntarily abandoned.—Id.

⌾677. —— Garbage, trash, and other discarded items.

Fla.App. 4 Dist. 1999. Defendant was not unlawfully seized before he dropped cocaine, even though two officers approached defendant from different directions, and thus trial court was not required to suppress contraband discarded by defendant; officers never ordered defendant to stop, one officer greeted defendant, and other officer merely asked for identification, and defendant continued to walk and did not stop when officers approached and spoke to him, but instead moved to the side where he dropped cocaine. U.S.C.A. Const.Amend. 4.—Clemons v. State, 747 So.2d 454.

⌾678. Temporary investigative detention of property.

C.A.11 (Fla.) 2019. Police may briefly detain property, *Terry*-stop style, on the strength of reasonable suspicion alone. U.S. Const. Amend. 4. —United States v. Babcock, 924 F.3d 1180, appeal from denial of post-conviction relief dismissed 2023 WL 4117503.

The "intrusiveness" factor concerns the degree to which a temporary property detention interferes with a person's possessory interest in his belongings. U.S. Const. Amend. 4.—Id.

The diligence component necessarily intersects with the duration component with respect to a temporary detention of property because, in the ordinary case, the sooner the warrant issues, the sooner the property owner's possessory rights can be restored if the search reveals nothing incriminating, and, of course, the sooner an officer seeks a warrant, the sooner a warrant can issue. U.S. Const. Amend. 4.—Id.

Police officers' two-day detention of defendant's cellular telephone on suspicion of child pornography was not permissible investigatory detention of property, but, instead, was full-blown seizure that required probable cause; although government had compelling interest in preventing creation and distribution of child pornography, intrusion into defendant's possessory interest in his private property over weekend was serious due to breadth and depth of personal information cell phone stored, officer did not explain to defendant when or whether he could expect to get his phone back, and government did not justify delay. U.S. Const. Amend. 4; 18 U.S.C.A. §§ 2251(a), 2251(e).—Id.

⌾679. Forfeitures, seizure of property subject to.

† **C.A.11 (Fla.) 2015.** Employees of computer repair store where defendant brought his inoperable laptop computer to have data from the computer's hard drive transferred onto a new computer were private actors when they initially viewed defendant's data during the data transfer from his laptop to the store's system, and thus, the government was free to use the information provided by the store, that defendant had child pornography on his computer, to seize his laptop and obtain a search warrant. U.S.C.A. Const. Amend. 4.—U.S. v. Meister, 596 Fed.Appx. 790.

N.D.Fla. 1969. A consultation genuinely undertaken by a law enforcement officer for purpose of aiding distributor of publications to comply with obscenity laws and avoid prosecution does not retard full enjoyment of First Amendment freedoms. U.S.C.A.Const. Amend. 1.—May v. Harper, 306 F.Supp. 1222.

Fact that county solicitor gave publicity to meeting for newsstand operators, book dealers

---

† This Case was not selected for publication in the National Reporter System

and law enforcement officials for purpose of discussing control of allegedly obscene materials in endeavor to make sure all distributors were apprised of meeting would not detract from its genuineness or render meeting violative of First Amendment. U.S.C.A.Const. Amend. 1.—Id.

Fact that plaintiffs might have become apprehensive as result of meeting called by county solicitor of all newsstand operators, book dealers and certain law enforcement officials for purpose of discussing control of allegedly obscene materials being distributed would not show that meeting violated plaintiffs' First Amendment rights. U.S.C.A.Const. Amend. 1.—Id.

County solicitor's calling meeting attended by law enforcement officers, newsstand operators, book dealers and others and allegedly declaring that if dealer sold particular book, magazine or periodical that was later determined in adversary judicial hearing to be obscene dealer would be subject to prosecution for sale prior to hearing and that county solicitor intended to prosecute for any such sales did not constitute proscribed informal censorship. U.S.C.A.Const. Amend. 1. —Id.

S.D.Fla. 1990. In order to avoid illegal prior restraint, sheriff would be enjoined from threatening retail store owners or employees with arrest for selling allegedly obscene materials and from presenting or speaking about probable cause orders as to obscenity to employees or owners of the stores, but sheriff would not be precluded from giving legal advice to any person suspected of violating a valid law prohibiting obscenity where such consultation is genuinely undertaken for the purpose of aiding the suspect to comply with the law and avoid prosecution. U.S.C.A. Const.Amend. 1.—Skyywalker Records, Inc. v. Navarro, 739 F.Supp. 578, reversed Luke Records, Inc. v. Navarro, 960 F.2d 134, certiorari denied 113 S.Ct. 659, 506 U.S. 1022, 121 L.Ed.2d 585.

S.D.Fla. 1985. When government, lacking probable cause, seeks to seize movable res under drug forfeiture statute [21 U.S.C.A. § 881(b)], it is constitutionally permissible for government to act first and seek judicial approval later in that movable nature of res creates "exigent circumstances" so as to justify exception to preseizure hearing requirement. Comprehensive Drug Abuse Prevention and Control Act of 1970, § 511(b), 21 U.S.C.A. § 881(b); U.S.C.A. Const. Amend. 5.—U.S. v. Certain Real Estate Property Located at 4880 S.E. Dixie Highway, 612 F.Supp. 1492.

Fla.App. 2 Dist. 1995. While law enforcement officers are allowed to keep single copy of allegedly obscene videotape or movie for purpose of preserving evidence, lawful retention is dependent upon issuance of warrant for seizure of item prior to officers obtaining it; only when warrant has been issued is retention not improper prior restraint. U.S.C.A. Const.Amends. 1, 4.—Miragaya v. State, 654 So.2d 262, review denied 659 So.2d 1089, certiorari denied 116 S.Ct. 518, 516 U.S. 989, 133 L.Ed.2d 426.

Fla.App. 3 Dist. 2005. Department of Highway Safety and Motor Vehicles had probable cause for seizure of defendant's vehicle until forfeiture proceeding could be brought; defendant, stopped for speeding and cutting off another vehicle, admitted that he had a prior conviction for DUI and that he was driving under the influence of alcohol and marijuana, officer testified that he arrested defendant after he failed road sobriety and breathalyzer tests, and Depart-

ment's records showed that defendant's license was revoked and had never been reinstated. West's F.S.A. §§ 322.34(9)(a), 932.701(2)(a)(9).— State, Dept. of Highway Safety and Motor Vehicles v. Tarman, 917 So.2d 899.

Fla.App. 3 Dist. 1975. Warrantless inventory search of accused's car after he was arrested during police "raid" and was charged with possession of cocaine and marijuana was not justified on theory that, since car was not located at accused's residence, county public safety department would potentially be subject to claim that either car or loose articles lying therein were taken; thus, packets of drug found in car could not be used as basis for forfeiture of car. West's F.S.A. §§ 893.01 et seq., 893.12(2, 5); U.S.C.A.Const. Amend. 4.—In re 1972 Porsche 2 dr., '74 Florida License Tag 1d 91780 VIN # 9111200334, 307 So.2d 451.

Fla.App. 4 Dist. 1995. Although police officer may have been entitled to seize package based on alert of dog trained to detect narcotics by sniff, search of package without warrant violated rights of claimant to money inside package that was subject to forfeiture under Florida Contraband Forfeiture Act. U.S.C.A. Const.Amend. 4; West's F.S.A. Const. Art. 1, § 12; West's F.S.A. § 932.701(2)(a)5.—Daniels v. Cochran, 654 So.2d 609.

Fla.App. 5 Dist. 2004. Evidence established probable cause for seizure of vehicle until a forfeiture proceeding could be brought, after non-owner driver, whose license had been suspended for a prior conviction for driving under the influence (DUI), was arrested for a new DUI offense; arresting officer's verified affidavit included driver's statement, shortly after the crash, that owner had known that the license of driver had been suspended for DUI "a long time ago" yet owner had still given the keys to driver, and allowing driver to drive owner's vehicle, if owner knew driver had no license, would be a second-degree misdemeanor. West's F.S.A. §§ 322.34(9)(a), 322.36.—Cox v. Department of Highway Safety and Motor Vehicles, 881 So.2d 641.

☞680. Private search; subsequent government search.

U.S.Fla. 1980. Fact that packages and one or more of the boxes therein had been opened by a private party before they were acquired by the FBI did not excuse the FBI agents' failure to obtain a search warrant. (Per Mr. Justice Stevens, with one Justice joining, two Justices concurring in part and in the judgment, and the one Justice concurring in the judgment.)—Walter v. U.S., 100 S.Ct. 2395, 447 U.S. 649, 65 L.Ed.2d 410, on remand U.S. v. Sanders, 625 F.2d 1311.

Projection of allegedly obscene films was a significant expansion of the search that had been conducted previously by a private party and therefore had to be characterized as a separate search, which was not supported by any exigency or by a warrant even though one could easily have been obtained. (Per Mr. Justice Stevens, with one Justice joining, two Justices concurring in part and in the judgment, and the one Justice concurring in the judgment.)—Id.

C.A.5 (Fla.) 1979. Where cartons were shipped by bus with fictitious name given as addressee, where corporation whose name was similar to that of fictitious addressee was notified of shipment, where corporation's employees conducted private search of cartons by taking shipment from bus terminal, opening cartons, examining individual film boxes, and ascertaining nature of films, where FBI was notified after corporation's employees determined from examining individual boxes containing films that films depicted bizarre homosexual acts, FBI's subsequent viewing of movies on projector did not change nature of search and was not an additional search subject to warrant requirement. U.S.C.A.Const. Amend. 4.—U.S. v. Sanders, 592 F.2d 788, rehearing denied 597 F.2d 63, certiorari granted Walter v. U.S., 100 S.Ct. 227, 444 U.S. 914, 62 L.Ed.2d 168, reversed 100 S.Ct. 2395, 447 U.S. 649, 65 L.Ed.2d 410, on remand 625 F.2d 1311.

Fla.App. 1 Dist. 2019. Law enforcement agent's warrantless search, which consisted of opening an image file containing child pornography, which defendant had uploaded to a chat room and which had been sent to law enforcement by chat room operator, was lawful under private search doctrine; agent's search was prompted by chat room operator's prior private search, agent's visual review of file did not exceed scope of private search, as it merely confirmed what operator's search had already established with almost virtual certainty, specifically that image file's hash value was identical to hash value of known child pornography, and there was no indication that agent had searched any of defendant's files not flagged as child pornography. U.S. Const. Amend. 4; Fla. Const. art. 1, § 12.—Morales v. State, 274 So.3d 1213.

3. EMERGENCIES AND EXIGENT CIRCUMSTANCES; OPPORTUNITY TO OBTAIN WARRANT.

⬒691. In general.

C.A.11 (Fla.) 2018. The police may enter a private premises and conduct a search if exigent circumstances mandate immediate action. U.S. Const. Amend. 4.—Montanez v. Carvajal, 889 F.3d 1202.

Under the exigent-circumstances doctrine in a burglary-related scenario, permitting a warrantless search under the Fourth Amendment, the search must be strictly circumscribed by the nature of the exigency that authorized it, and thus limited to the areas where a person reasonably could be found. U.S. Const. Amend. 4.—Id.

Under the Fourth Amendment's reasonableness requirement, police investigating what they reasonably believe to be a residential burglary, whether ongoing or recently concluded, may conduct a limited warrantless search of the house to look for potential suspects and victims. U.S. Const. Amend. 4.—Id.

C.A.11 (Fla.) 2018. Generally, the seizure of personal property is per se unreasonable when it is not pursuant to a warrant issued upon probable cause; several exceptions, however, exist to this general rule, including the exigent circumstances exception. U.S. Const. Amend. 4.—Crocker v. Beatty, 886 F.3d 1132.

C.A.11 (Fla.) 1989. Individual's residence enjoys special protection under Fourth Amendment; thus, officer must have probable cause before searching someone's house, and even then officer may proceed only with warrant or under exigent circumstances. U.S.C.A. Const.Amend. 4.—U.S. v. Tobin, 890 F.2d 319, rehearing granted, vacated 902 F.2d 821, on rehearing 923 F.2d 1506, rehearing denied 935 F.2d 1297, certiorari denied 112 S.Ct. 299, 502 U.S. 907, 116 L.Ed.2d 243.

M.D.Fla. 2022. Police officers need either a warrant or probable cause plus exigent circumstances in order to make a lawful entry into a home under the Fourth Amendment. U.S. Const. Amend. 4.—Newcome v. Hernando County Sheriff's Office, 645 F.Supp.3d 1308.

M.D.Fla. 2019. Consent and exigent circumstances are two exceptions to warrant requirement. U.S. Const. Amend. 4.—Davis v. City of Apopka, 424 F.Supp.3d 1161.

M.D.Fla. 2016. Absent exigent circumstances, a warrantless entry into one's home to search for weapons or contraband is unconstitutional even when there is probable cause to believe that incriminating evidence will be found within. U.S. Const. Amend. 4.—Montanez v. Carvajal, 224 F.Supp.3d 1274, reversed 889 F.3d 1202, affirmed Rivera v. Carvajal, 777 Fed.Appx. 434.

M.D.Fla. 2011. In terms that apply equally to seizures of property and to seizures of persons, Fourth Amendment has drawn firm line at entrance to the house; absent exigent circumstances, that threshold may not reasonably be crossed without warrant. U.S.C.A. Const.Amend. 4.—U.S. v. Hill, 795 F.Supp.2d 1304.

M.D.Fla. 1994. Warrantless search of home is presumptively unreasonable, unless probable cause and exigent circumstances exist. U.S.C.A. Const.Amend. 4.—U.S. v. Adams, 845 F.Supp. 1531.

S.D.Fla. 2020. Under Florida law, in emergency situations the police may lawfully enter upon private property without first obtaining a warrant; in such circumstances, a trespass claim cannot survive.—Rebalko v. City of Coral Springs, 552 F.Supp.3d 1285.

Fla. 2005. Absent exigent circumstances, the entrance of a home may not reasonably be crossed without a warrant. U.S.C.A. Const. Amend. 4.—Riggs v. State, 918 So.2d 274.

Fla.App. 1 Dist. 2021. Because searches and seizures conducted in connection with welfare checks are solely for safety reasons, the scope of an encounter associated with a welfare check is limited to prevent the exception to Fourth Amendment requirements from becoming an investigative tool that circumvents the Fourth Amendment. U.S. Const. Amend. 4.—Taylor v. State, 326 So.3d 115.

Fla.App. 1 Dist. 2019. When a citizen has a reasonable expectation of privacy, police officers may not enter a property without a warrant, absent consent or exigent circumstances. U.S. Const. Amend. 4.—Bryant v. State, 265 So.3d 726.

Fla.App. 1 Dist. 2018. Where exigent circumstances for entry are present, a police officer may enter a private home without a warrant.—Sosnowski v. State, 245 So.3d 885, rehearing denied, review denied 2019 WL 1349271, appeal from denial of post-conviction relief dismissed 301 So.3d 472, habeas corpus denied 2022 WL 2209324.

Fla.App. 1 Dist. 1989. Even when felony has been committed and officers have probable cause to believe that incriminating evidence will be found within home, warrantless entry into home to search for weapons or contraband is unconstitutional in absence of exigent circumstances. U.S.C.A. Const.Amend. 4.—Eason v. State, 546 So.2d 57.

Fla.App. 1 Dist. 1980. When there are no exigent circumstances, where consent is not voluntarily given, and where there is no probable cause to suspect contraband, warrantless search may not be conducted. U.S.C.A.Const. Amend. 4.—Loftis v. State, 391 So.2d 219, review denied 399 So.2d 1146.

---

† This Case was not selected for publication in the National Reporter System

Fla.App. 1 Dist. 1979. A search warrant must be obtained in accordance with statutory provisions to conduct agricultural inspection search where there are no exigent circumstances, consent is not offered voluntarily, there is no probable cause to suspect that vehicle contains contraband. West's F.S.A. § 570.15(1)(b).—Rose v. State, 369 So.2d 447.

Fla.App. 2 Dist. 2018. With few exceptions, the question as to whether a warrantless search of a home is reasonable, and hence constitutional, must be answered no, and among those exceptions are a protective sweep and exigent circumstances. U.S. Const. Amend. 4.—Aguilar v. State, 259 So.3d 262.

Officers' warrantless entry into defendant's home pursuant to exigent circumstances exception to warrant requirement must be limited in its scope, and thus, once the exigency ceases to exist, so does the limited exception to the warrant requirement. U.S. Const. Amend. 4.—Id.

Fla.App. 2 Dist. 2018. Warrants are generally required to search a person's home or his person unless the exigencies of the situation make the needs of law enforcement so compelling that the warrantless search is objectively reasonable under the Fourth Amendment. U.S. Const. Amend. 4.—Lapace v. State, 257 So.3d 588.

A warrantless entry into a home based on an exigency must be limited in scope to its purpose; thus, an officer may not continue her search once she has determined that no exigency exists. U.S. Const. Amend. 4.—Id.

Fla.App. 2 Dist. 2009. Except in exigent circumstances, law enforcement officers cannot reasonably cross the threshold of a home without a warrant. U.S.C.A. Const.Amend. 4.—Byrd v. State, 16 So.3d 1026.

Fla.App. 2 Dist. 1999. Absent consent or exigent circumstances, law enforcement may not cross the threshold of a residence without a warrant. U.S.C.A. Const.Amend. 4.—Davis v. State, 744 So.2d 586.

Fla.App. 3 Dist. 2001. Fourth Amendment principle against warrantless seizures absent valid consent or exigent circumstances applies equally to seizures of property and to seizures of persons. U.S.C.A. Const.Amend. 4.—State v. Sakezeles, 778 So.2d 432.

Fla.App. 4 Dist. 2018. When a citizen has a reasonable expectation of privacy, police officers may not enter a property without a warrant, absent consent or exigent circumstances. U.S. Const. Amend. 4.—Osorio v. State, 244 So.3d 1115.

Fla.App. 4 Dist. 2017. Those seeking an exemption from the constitutional rule that searches conducted outside the judicial process, without prior approval by a judge or magistrate, are per se unreasonable under the Fourth Amendment, must show that the exigencies of the situation made that course imperative. U.S. Const. Amend. 4.—State v. Worsham, 227 So.3d 602, certiorari denied 138 S.Ct. 264, 583 U.S. 873, 199 L.Ed.2d 125.

Fla.App. 4 Dist. 1975. An exception to requirement that police officer obtain search warrant prior to search of individual's person arises where officer has probable cause to believe that he will there find instrumentalities of a crime or evidence pertaining to a crime and where exigent circumstances lie making it impractical for officer to obtain a warrant.—Brown v. State, 313 So.2d 52, certiorari denied 330 So.2d 21.

Fla.App. 4 Dist. 1974. In order for warrantless search of automobile to be sustained, it must

have been predicated upon a search incident to lawful arrest, a search based upon probable cause, a search based upon an emergency situation, or a search based upon consent.—Bailey v. State, 295 So.2d 133, quashed 319 So.2d 22.

Fla.App. 5 Dist. 2018. While warrantless searches of a home are presumed illegal, an officer may enter a private home or property when there are exigent circumstances for the entry. U.S. Const. Amend. 4.—State v. Archer, 259 So.3d 999, review denied 2019 WL 2205765, on subsequent appeal 309 So.3d 287, rehearing denied.

In order for the exigent circumstances exception to the warrant requirement to apply, the State must demonstrate a grave emergency that makes a warrantless search imperative to the safety of the police and of the community. U.S. Const. Amend. 4.—Id.

Exigent circumstances exception to the warrant requirement is premised on the notion that the right of police to enter and investigate an emergency, without an accompanying intent either to seize or arrest, is inherent in the very nature of their duties as peace officers and derives from the common law. U.S. Const. Amend. 4.—Id.

Entry into a residence based on exigent circumstances must be limited in scope to its purpose; therefore, police may not continue their search once it is determined that the exigency no longer exists. U.S. Const. Amend. 4.—Id.

If the police enter a home under exigent circumstances and, prior to making a determination that the exigency no longer exists, find contraband in plain view, they may lawfully seize the illegal item. U.S. Const. Amend. 4.—Id.

Fla.App. 5 Dist. 2015. Absent consent, a search warrant, or an arrest warrant, a police officer may enter a private home only when there are exigent circumstances for the entry. U.S.C.A. Const.Amend. 4.—Durham v. State, 174 So.3d 1074.

Fla.App. 6 Dist. 2023. In the absence of probable cause for a warrantless search, it becomes unnecessary to address exigent circumstances or other exception to warrant requirement. U.S. Const. Amend. 4.—Jefferson v. State, 363 So.3d 198.

☞692. **Presence of probable cause in general.**

M.D.Fla. 2022. Police officers need either a warrant or probable cause plus exigent circumstances in order to make a lawful entry into a home under the Fourth Amendment. U.S. Const. Amend. 4.—Newcome v. Hernando County Sheriff's Office, 645 F.Supp.3d 1308.

M.D.Fla. 2009. Warrantless searches of a residence are permitted where probable cause and exigent circumstances are present. U.S.C.A. Const.Amend. 4.—U.S. v. Quintana, 594 F.Supp.2d 1291.

M.D.Fla. 2001. One of the recognized exceptions to the warrant requirement prior to performing search exists when police officers have probable cause to search an area and exigent circumstances exist which make it unrealistic to obtain a warrant. U.S.C.A. Const.Amend. 4.—U.S. v. Davis, 170 F.Supp.2d 1234.

S.D.Fla. 2021. A warrantless search may be justified where both probable cause and exigent circumstances exist. U.S. Const. Amend. 4.—United States v. Howard, 557 F.Supp.3d 1262.

S.D.Fla. 2010. A warrantless search is allowed where both probable cause and exigent circumstances exist; exigent circumstances arise when the inevitable delay incident to obtaining a warrant must give way to an urgent need for immediate action. U.S.C.A. Const.Amend. 4.—Lippman v. City of Miami, 724 F.Supp.2d 1240.

Fla. 1977. Probable cause to search plus exigent circumstances will usually justify a warrantless search. U.S.C.A.Const. Amend. 4.—Raffield v. State, 351 So.2d 945, on remand 362 So.2d 138.

Fla. 1977. Probable cause itself is not sufficient to support warrantless search, absent exigent circumstances. West's F.S.A.Const. art. 1, § 12; U.S.C.A.Const. Amends. 4, 14.—Hornblower v. State, 351 So.2d 716.

Fla.App. 1 Dist. 2003. A warrantless search is presumptively unreasonable but, when probable cause exists, if exigent circumstances make it impossible or impracticable to obtain a warrant, a warrantless search will be excused. U.S.C.A. Const.Amend. 4; West's F.S.A. Const. Art. 1, § 12. —Hendrix v. State, 843 So.2d 1003, review denied 851 So.2d 729.

Fla.App. 1 Dist. 1976. To justify a search without a warrant, there must be probable cause to search plus exigent circumstances.—Parsons v. State, 334 So.2d 308, decision approved 351 So.2d 723.

Fla.App. 1 Dist. 1976. Probable cause without exigent circumstances is insufficient to justify warrantless search.—Raffield v. State, 333 So.2d 534, quashed in part 351 So.2d 945, on remand 362 So.2d 138.

Fla.App. 2 Dist. 2003. In the absence of exigent circumstances or permission, the police clearly may not enter a home without a search warrant simply because they think they have probable cause to believe evidence of a crime may be found therein. U.S.C.A. Const.Amend. 4. —McDuffy v. State, 837 So.2d 590.

Fla.App. 3 Dist. 1979. Exigent circumstances serve only to "excuse" the absence of a search warrant; they do not take the place of the probable cause necessary to sustain any search, whether made with a warrant or without one.—Royer v. State, 389 So.2d 1007, review denied 397 So.2d 779, certiorari granted 102 S.Ct. 631, 454 U.S. 1079, 70 L.Ed.2d 612, affirmed 103 S.Ct. 1319, 460 U.S. 491, 75 L.Ed.2d 229.

☞693. What constitutes exigent circumstances or emergency in general.

C.A.11 (Fla.) 2024. Exigent circumstances exception to warrant requirement applies when exigencies of situation make needs of law enforcement so compelling that warrantless search is objectively reasonable under Fourth Amendment. U.S. Const. Amend. 4.—Bailey v. Swindell, 89 F.4th 1324.

Officer may enter home without warrant to render emergency assistance to injured occupant, to protect occupant from imminent injury, or to ensure his own safety. U.S. Const. Amend. 4.—Id.

C.A.11 (Fla.) 2020. Presumption that warrantless searches and seizures inside home are unreasonable can be overcome if exigencies of situation make needs of law enforcement so compelling that warrantless search is objectively reasonable under Fourth Amendment. U.S. Const. Amend. 4.—United States v. Evans, 958 F.3d 1102.

To establish emergency aid exception to Fourth Amendment's warrant requirement, specific test is not whether officer actually believed that there was emergency inside house, but whether there was objectively reasonable basis for believing that medical assistance was needed, or persons were in danger. U.S. Const. Amend. 4.—Id.

Officers do not need ironclad proof of likely serious, life-threatening injury to invoke emergency aid exception to Fourth Amendment's warrant requirement; instead, court must look to entirety of circumstances to see whether reasonable officer, confronted with those circumstances, could have objectively believed that immediate search was necessary to safeguard potential victims. U.S. Const. Amend. 4.—Id.

C.A.11 (Fla.) 2018. A warrantless search may be legal when there is compelling need for official action and no time to secure a warrant, or when resort to a magistrate for a search warrant is not feasible or advisable. U.S. Const. Amend. 4.—Montanez v. Carvajal, 889 F.3d 1202.

C.A.11 (Fla.) 1983. Exigent circumstances doctrine recognizes several common situations where time-consuming resort to neutral magistrate for arrest or search warrant is unnecessary, e.g., hot pursuit, fleeing suspect, danger to arresting officers or public from suspect, mobility of vehicle, or risk of removal or destruction of narcotics. U.S.C.A. Const.Amend. 4.—U.S. v. Burgos, 720 F.2d 1520.

C.A.5 (Fla.) 1981. Exigent circumstances doctrine recognizes several common situations where time-consuming resort to a neutral magistrate for an arrest or search warrant is unnecessary, for example: hot pursuit, fleeing suspect, danger to arresting officer or public from suspect or contents of container, mobility of the vehicle or mobility of containers which could not be detained without thwarting efforts to discover other conspirators. U.S.C.A.Const. Amend. 4.—U.S. v. Kreimes, 649 F.2d 1185.

M.D.Fla. 2022. For exigent circumstances to excuse a warrantless search or seizure under the Fourth Amendment, there must be both a compelling need for official action and no time to secure a warrant. U.S. Const. Amend. 4.—Newcome v. Hernando County Sheriff's Office, 645 F.Supp.3d 1308.

Inconvenience to the law enforcement officers and some slight delay are never very convincing reasons to bypass the constitutional Fourth Amendment warrant requirement under the exigent circumstances exception. U.S. Const. Amend. 4.—Id.

M.D.Fla. 2019. Warrants are generally required to search person's home or his person unless exigencies of the situation make the needs of law enforcement so compelling that warrantless search is objectively reasonable under Fourth Amendment. U.S. Const. Amend. 4.—Davis v. City of Apopka, 424 F.Supp.3d 1161.

Exigencies justifying warrantless search are: (1) the "emergency aid" exception, when officers may enter home without warrant to render emergency assistance to injured occupant or to protect occupant from imminent injury; (2) when police are in hot pursuit of fleeing suspect; and (3) when there is a need to prevent the imminent destruction of evidence. U.S. Const. Amend. 4.—Id.

M.D.Fla. 2017. Under the Fourth Amendment, law enforcement officers may enter a home without a warrant to render emergency assistance to an injured occupant or to protect an occupant from imminent injury when they have an objectively reasonable basis for such a belief. U.S. Const. Amend. 4.—Ermini v. Scott, 249 F.Supp.3d 1253.

Exception to warrant requirement that allows law enforcement officers to enter a home to render emergency assistance to an injured occu-

---

† **This Case was not selected for publication in the National Reporter System**

pant or to protect an occupant from imminent injury does not depend on the officers' subjective intent or the seriousness of any crime they are investigating when the emergency arises; it requires only an objectively reasonable basis for believing that a person within the house is in need of immediate aid. U.S. Const. Amend. 4.— Id.

District court must consider the totality of the circumstance when determining whether a law enforcement officer faced an emergency that justified acting without a warrant. U.S. Const. Amend. 4.—Id.

M.D.Fla. 2010. Test of whether exigent circumstances exist, for purposes of an exception to the warrant requirement, is an objective one; the appropriate inquiry is whether the facts would lead a reasonable, experienced agent to believe that evidence might be destroyed before a warrant could be secured. U.S.C.A. Const.Amend. 4. —U.S. v. Franklin, 721 F.Supp.2d 1229, affirmed 694 F.3d 1.

M.D.Fla. 2007. Exigent circumstances that permit warrantless entries include: breaking up a violent fight, preventing the destruction of evidence, putting out a fire in a burning building, attending to a stabbing victim, rescuing a kidnapped infant, or pursuing a fleeing suspect. U.S.C.A. Const.Amend. 4.—Woods v. Valentino, 511 F.Supp.2d 1263.

S.D.Fla. 2021. The exigent-circumstances exception to the search warrant requirement applies where the exigencies of the situation make the needs of law enforcement so compelling that a warrantless search is objectively reasonable. U.S. Const. Amend. 4.—United States v. Howard, 557 F.Supp.3d 1262.

There is no categorical rule that a suspect's flight creates an exigent circumstance justifying a warrantless search, but rather courts undertake a case-by-case assessment. U.S. Const. Amend. 4. —Id.

S.D.Fla. 2011. Exigent circumstances exception to warrant requirement recognizes warrantless entry by criminal law enforcement officials may be legal when there is compelling need for official action and no time to secure warrant. U.S.C.A. Const.Amend. 4.—Heflin v. Miami-Dade County, 823 F.Supp.2d 1298.

Fla.App. 1 Dist. 2021. Law enforcement may enter a home without a warrant to render emergency assistance to an injured occupant or to protect an occupant from imminent injury without violating a defendant's Fourth Amendment right against unreasonable searches and seizures. U.S. Const. Amend. 4.—Jones v. State, 331 So.3d 252, review denied 2022 WL 1261288.

To justify an emergency warrantless entry into a home by police officers, it is immaterial whether an actual emergency existed in the residence. U.S. Const. Amend. 4.—Id.

In determining whether an emergency warrantless entry into a home by police officers was justified, it is only the reasonableness of the officers' belief at the time of entry that is considered on review. U.S. Const. Amend. 4.—Id.

The inquiry of whether an emergency warrantless entry into a home by police offers was justified must be done in light of the totality of the circumstances confronting the officers, including, in many cases, a need for an on-the-spot judgment based on incomplete information and sometimes ambiguous facts bearing upon the potential for serious consequences. U.S. Const. Amend. 4.—Id.

Fla.App. 1 Dist. 2018. To justify an emergency entry into a home by police officers, the State must demonstrate that an objectively reasonable basis existed for the officer to believe that there is an immediate need for police assistance for the protection of life.—Sosnowski v. State, 245 So.3d 885, rehearing denied, review denied 2019 WL 1349271, appeal from denial of post-conviction relief dismissed 301 So.3d 472, habeas corpus denied 2022 WL 2209324.

Fla.App. 2 Dist. 2019. Exigent circumstances exception to search warrant requirement is generally triggered when police have urgent need to address some sort of emergency, such as threat to safety of persons or property, reasonable concern that suspect might flee, or reasonable concern that evidence may be destroyed. U.S. Const. Amend. 4.—Nieves v. State, 277 So.3d 745.

State must show compelling need for official action and no time to secure warrant in order to establish exigent circumstances under Fourth Amendment; assertion of compelling need to act and absence of time to obtain warrant must be supported by articulable, objectively reasonable basis in facts and circumstances attending warrantless entry. U.S. Const. Amend. 4.—Id.

Fla.App. 2 Dist. 2019. There is no exhaustive, all-encompassing list of factors that qualify a situation as exigent circumstances, for purposes of determining whether exception to Fourth Amendment's warrant requirement applies; however, the kinds of exigencies or emergencies that may support a warrantless entry include those related to the safety of persons or property, as well as the safety of police. U.S. Const. Amend. 4; Fla. Const. art. 1, § 12.—State v. M.B.W., 276 So.3d 501.

Fla.App. 2 Dist. 2018. Law enforcement officers may enter a home without a warrant to render emergency assistance to an injured occupant or to protect an occupant from imminent injury, without violating the Fourth Amendment. U.S. Const. Amend. 4.—Lapace v. State, 257 So.3d 588.

Whether a warrantless search is justified by an emergency and thus permissible under the Fourth Amendment is determined by the totality of the circumstances. U.S. Const. Amend. 4.—Id.

If the State meets its burden of showing that police officers reasonably believed that exigent circumstances existed that justified an immediate entry into the home without a warrant, ordinarily the court must then determine whether the subsequent search of the house exceeded the parameters allowed if the entry was warranted. U.S. Const. Amend. 4.—Id.

For an anonymous tip to justify a warrantless entry, the tip—considered in the context of the totality of relevant circumstances—must provide an objectively reasonable basis for the officer to believe that there is an immediate need for police assistance. U.S. Const. Amend. 4.—Id.

Fla.App. 2 Dist. 2016. Exigent circumstances provide an exception that may justify a warrantless search, but the police must have an objectively reasonable basis to support their actions. U.S.C.A. Const.Amend. 4; West's F.S.A. Const. Art. 1, § 12.—State v. Fultz, 189 So.3d 155, rehearing denied.

Fla.App. 2 Dist. 2007. If a law enforcement officer does not have consent, a search warrant, or an arrest warrant, he may not enter a private home or its curtilage except when entrance is justified by exigent circumstances, such as pursuing a fleeing felon, preventing the destruction of evidence, searching incident to a lawful arrest, and fighting fires. U.S.C.A. Const.Amend. 4.—Rodriguez v. State, 964 So.2d 833, rehearing granted, and rehearing denied.

Fla.App. 3 Dist. 2019. One well-recognized exception to the rule that searches conducted outside the judicial process are unreasonable under the Fourth Amendment applies when the exigencies of the situation make the needs of law enforcement so compelling that a warrantless search is objectively reasonable under the Fourth Amendment. U.S. Const. Amend. 4.—State v. Quintanilla, 276 So.3d 941, rehearing denied, review denied 2020 WL 633783.

Fla.App. 3 Dist. 2018. One well-recognized exception to the warrant requirement applies when the exigencies of the situation make the needs of law enforcement so compelling that a warrantless search is objectively reasonable under the Fourth Amendment. U.S. Const. Amend. 4.—Aguilar v. State, 239 So.3d 108, denial of post-conviction relief affirmed 359 So.3d 832, rehearing denied, review denied 2023 WL 4484834.

Fla.App. 4 Dist. 2022. The test of whether exigent circumstances exist is an objective one; whether exigent circumstances exist in a given case is a fact-specific inquiry that depends on the totality of the circumstances. U.S. Const. Amend. 4.—State v. Darter, 350 So.3d 370, review denied 2023 WL 2017393.

Fla.App. 4 Dist. 2018. To determine whether an exigent circumstance exists for a warrantless search, the District Court of Appeal looks to the totality of the circumstances and considers various factors, including: (1) the gravity or violent nature of the offense with which the suspect is to be charged; (2) a reasonable belief that the suspect is armed; (3) probable cause to believe that the suspect committed the crime; (4) strong reason to believe that the suspect is in the premises being entered; and (5) a likelihood that delay could cause the escape of the suspect or the destruction of essential evidence, or jeopardize the safety of officers or the public. U.S. Const. Amend. 4.—Barton v. State, 237 So.3d 378.

Fla.App. 4 Dist. 2017. An exception to the warrant requirement exists when the exigencies of the situation make the needs of law enforcement so compelling that a warrantless search is objectively reasonable under the Fourth Amendment. U.S. Const. Amend. 4.—Goodman v. State, 229 So.3d 366, review denied 2018 WL 1256499, certiorari denied 139 S.Ct. 274, 202 L.Ed.2d 135.

To determine whether a law enforcement officer faced an emergency that justified acting without a warrant, this appellate court looks to the totality of circumstances. U.S. Const. Amend. 4. —Id.

Fla.App. 5 Dist. 2021. One exception to the requirement that law enforcement obtain a warrant or consent for a blood draw is when the exigencies of the situation make the needs of law enforcement so compelling that a warrantless search is objectively reasonable under the Fourth Amendment. U.S. Const. Amend. 4.—Dusan v. State, 323 So.3d 239.

Fla.App. 5 Dist. 2018. An entry is considered "imperative," for purpose of the exigent circumstances exception to the warrant requirement, when the government can show a compelling need for official action and no time to secure a warrant. U.S. Const. Amend. 4.—State v. Archer, 259 So.3d 999, review denied 2019 WL 2205765, on subsequent appeal 309 So.3d 287, rehearing denied.

The reasonableness of a warrantless entry based upon exigent circumstances is measured by the totality of existing circumstances. U.S. Const. Amend. 4.—Id.

⬤=694. Particular cases in general.

C.A.11 (Fla.) 2019. Police officers had probable cause to believe that defendant was guilty of illegal, coercive relationship with minor in violation of Florida law and that evidence of that crime would be found on his cellular telephone, as required for warrantless seizure of phone to be justified under exigent-circumstances doctrine, where, among other things, domestic-disturbance call had reported female at defendant's residence yelling "stop, stop, stop," teenage girl emerged from his residence with cuts on her legs after defendant had denied that anyone else was in his camper, video on his cell phone portrayed his disdainful, bullying tone and girl's distraught appearance, and girl had been in or on defendant's bed and left traces of blood there. U.S. Const. Amend. 4; Fla. Stat. Ann. § 794.05(1).—United States v. Babcock, 924 F.3d 1180, appeal from denial of post-conviction relief dismissed 2023 WL 4117503.

C.A.11 (Fla.) 2018. Officers' re-entry into residence, to observe marijuana and drug paraphernalia earlier discovered in plain view during warrantless entries that were justified by burglary-related exigent circumstances, did not violate the Fourth Amendment, even though exigency that underlay initial searches had passed; homeowner lost any reasonable expectation of privacy in areas already searched, and there was no contention that additional entries exceeded scope of initial and permissible sweep. U.S. Const. Amend. 4.—Montanez v. Carvajal, 889 F.3d 1202.

† C.A.11 (Fla.) 2006. Warrantless entry by law enforcement agents into drug suspects' residence, justified by exigent circumstances, did not constitute illegal search under Fourth Amendment, where agents merely secured residence pending arrival of search warrant, and did not obtain any evidence before arrival of warrant. U.S.C.A. Const.Amend. 4.—U.S. v. Martinez, 191 Fed. Appx. 856, post-conviction relief denied 2007 WL 1490639, order vacated on reconsideration, post-conviction relief denied 2007 WL 1893818, post-conviction relief denied 2008 WL 780735, certificate of appealability denied 2008 WL 1819554, post-conviction relief denied U.S. v. Nieves-Villareal, 2008 WL 1995045.

C.A.11 (Fla.) 1995. Exigent circumstances existed sufficient to support warrantless search of drug conspirators' apartment, after four conspirators had left apartment in automobile without cocaine, based on information in police officers' possession indicating that fifth conspirator may have been present in apartment, may have been conducting countersurveillance activities, and may, as result of such countersurveillance, have been aware of officers' investigative activity. U.S.C.A. Const.Amend. 4.—U.S. v. Villabona-Garnica, 63 F.3d 1051, rehearing denied, certiorari denied 116 S.Ct. 1341, 517 U.S. 1114, 134 L.Ed.2d 490, certiorari denied Munoz v. U.S., 116 S.Ct. 1366, 517 U.S. 1126, 134 L.Ed.2d 532.

C.A.11 (Fla.) 1993. Probable cause and exigent circumstances existed to support warrantless search of defendant's vehicle notwithstanding facts that defendant was already in custody and police officers had possession of defendant's keys at time of search, person matching defendant's description had participated in drug transaction almost immediately prior to defendant's

---

† This Case was not selected for publication in the National Reporter System

detainment, defendant was found standing next to vehicle for which he had keys, defendant admitted vehicle was his, and defendant was seen placing gun on wheel of vehicle. U.S.C.A. Const. Amend. 4.—U.S. v. Birdsong, 982 F.2d 481, certiorari denied 113 S.Ct. 2984, 508 U.S. 980, 125 L.Ed.2d 680.

C.A.11 (Fla.) 1990. Warrantless search of defendant's automobile for narcotics was justified, even though defendant and his passenger had been placed under arrest; officers had probable cause to search automobile, and automobile's mobility satisfied exigency requirement. U.S.C.A. Const.Amend. 4.—U.S. v. Parrado, 911 F.2d 1567, certiorari denied 111 S.Ct. 1005, 498 U.S. 1104, 112 L.Ed.2d 1088.

C.A.11 (Fla.) 1987. Exigent circumstances justified warrantless search of car, where police had been unable to obtain search warrant at time defendant loaded with cocaine, and at time of arrest, had walked to driver's side of car and was about to embark upon delivery of cocaine. U.S.C.A. Const.Amend. 4.—U.S. v. Amorin, 810 F.2d 1040.

C.A.11 (Fla.) 1983. Where probable cause and exigent circumstances existed for agents to enter property on which defendants were off-loading marijuana, agents were justified in seizing marijuana in open truck under plain-view doctrine after agents encountered overwhelming smell of marijuana.—U.S. v. Blasco, 702 F.2d 1315, certiorari denied Galvan v. U.S., 104 S.Ct. 275, 464 U.S. 914, 78 L.Ed.2d 256, certiorari denied Jamardo v. U.S., 104 S.Ct. 276, 464 U.S. 914, 78 L.Ed.2d 256.

C.A.11 (Fla.) 1982. Given surveilling agents' observations of unexpected transfer of bales of marijuana from three cars they had loaded to a fourth car, there existed both probable cause and exigent circumstances for warrantless searches of the cars. U.S.C.A.Const.Amend. 4.—U.S. v. Gianni, 678 F.2d 956, certiorari denied 103 S.Ct. 491, 459 U.S. 1071, 74 L.Ed.2d 633.

C.A.5 (Fla.) 1973. Warrantless search of suitcases properly seized by narcotics agents from taxicab was not justified on basis of alleged exigent circumstance that opening suitcases immediately might have disclosed information which possibly would have led to capture of others participating in narcotics operation. U.S.C.A.Const. Amend. 4.—U.S. v. Soriano, 482 F.2d 469, on rehearing 497 F.2d 147.

M.D.Fla. 2007. Even if Drug Enforcement Agency Task Force agents saw arrestee in whose car cocaine had been found holding and manipulating a cell phone while he was in state trooper's car, any exigency created by possibility that arrestee was tipping off occupants of residence he had left shortly before his car was stopped was stale by the time agents arrived at residence, and thus, it did not justify agents' warrantless entry into residence, since two hours had passed between alleged phone call by arrestee and agents' arrival at residence. U.S.C.A. Const.Amend. 4.— U.S. v. Gonzalez De Arias, 510 F.Supp.2d 969.

S.D.Fla. 2010. There was no arguable probable cause for law enforcement officers to search plaintiff's vehicle nor was there an emergency justifying searching the vehicle without a warrant, and thus search violated plaintiff's Fourth Amendment rights; safety concerns surrounding global conference, plaintiff's alleged criminal history related to protest activity and assistance to protesters, plaintiff's suspicious behavior, and bomb-sniffing dog's interest in plaintiff's vehicle, did not constitute circumstances by which rea-sonable law enforcement officers could have believed that probable cause existed. U.S.C.A. Const.Amend. 4; 42 U.S.C.A. § 1983.—Lippman v. City of Miami, 724 F.Supp.2d 1240.

S.D.Fla. 2008. Exigent circumstances justified police officers' entry into defendant's apartment both to effectuate defendant's arrest and to seize evidence seen inside apartment, where officers did not have probable cause to obtain either search warrant or arrest warrant prior to time they approached apartment, officers smelled marijuana burning after they announced their presence, and officers saw marijuana and digital scale in plain view once defendant opened door. U.S.C.A. Const.Amend. 4.—U.S. v. Smalls, 617 F.Supp.2d 1240, affirmed 342 Fed.Appx. 505, certiorari denied 130 S.Ct. 1094, 558 U.S. 1128, 175 L.Ed.2d 912.

S.D.Fla. 2002. Although probable cause may have existed upon informant's signal that narcotics were present, no exigent circumstances justified warrantless search of suspect's home; there was no evidence that suspects were aware of informant's status or that police would observe what occurred in home, and no showing that informant was threatened or that suspect would hurt informant before becoming aware of that status. U.S.C.A. Const.Amend. 4.—U.S. v. Hernandez, 214 F.Supp.2d 1344, reversed 132 Fed. Appx. 821.

Fla.App. 1 Dist. 2003. Claim that police officers could not control suspects involved in drug transaction did not form a legitimate exigent circumstance sufficient to justify warrantless entry into defendant's motel room; given that there were at least eight or nine officers with four police vehicles on the scene to cover only three suspects, who did not know that police were outside, plus the informant, these nine officers should have been able to maintain control over the individuals at the motel safely. U.S.C.A. Const.Amend. 4.—Lee v. State, 856 So.2d 1133.

Claim that police officers were concerned about keeping control over confidential informant, because he had possession of purchased drugs, and because it was important for officers to keep track of him for purposes of future prosecution of suspects, did not form a legitimate exigent circumstance sufficient to justify warrantless entry into defendant's motel room, where the officers outnumbered suspects and informant more than two-to-one. U.S.C.A. Const.Amend. 4. —Id.

Mere speculation that more than one motel room may have been involved in drug transaction and that officers may have been unable to control both rooms was not an exigent circumstance justifying warrantless entry into defendant's motel room. U.S.C.A. Const.Amend. 4.—Id.

Fla.App. 1 Dist. 1976. Period of 1½ hours from original suspicion that defendant was smoking "grass," possession of less than five grams being a misdemeanor, and his being stopped, arrested, and searched was too wide a time span to be considered "exigent circumstances" to justify subsequent warrantless search and seizure particularly in view of fact that officer left area, drove some miles distant, completed a purchase and resultant arrest, and returned to area in interval.—Parsons v. State, 334 So.2d 308, decision approved 351 So.2d 723.

Fla.App. 1 Dist. 1976. Probable cause and exigent circumstances, including, inter alia, odor, observation, and transaction with defendant's brother who had emerged from mobile home, justified warrantless search and seizure of amphetamines and marijuana in mobile home.—Hornblower v. State, 331 So.2d 339, quashed 351 So.2d 716.

Fla.App. 2 Dist. 2018. Officer violated Fourth Amendment when, after exigency had ended, he went inside defendant's home, without warrant, to look around and decide what "we have" and whether it was actual crime scene; officer's insistence on the necessity of "fact-finding" upon his initial entry into house indicated investigative purpose not related to exigent circumstances that justified the sweep conducted by officers who had arrived earlier. U.S. Const. Amend. 4.—Aguilar v. State, 259 So.3d 262.

Fla.App. 2 Dist. 2006. Police officers' warrantless entry into defendant's residence was based on clear exigent circumstances and, thus, was lawful; officers had reasonable cause to believe that a methamphetamine lab was in operation in the residence based on their experience, facts developed during an investigation, and their observation of defendant earlier that day purchasing items commonly used in the production of methamphetamine. U.S.C.A. Const.Amend. 4.—Barth v. State, 955 So.2d 1115.

Fla.App. 2 Dist. 2003. Exigent circumstances permitted warrantless search of home in which police officers discovered evidence supportive of charge of unlawful manufacture of marijuana. U.S.C.A. Const.Amend. 4.—Huesca v. State, 841 So.2d 585.

Fla.App. 2 Dist. 1986. Exigent circumstances justifying warrantless entry into defendant's apartment to seize marijuana plants were not presented by fact that police department may have been overworked because of hurricane.—Hartwell v. State, 500 So.2d 640.

Fla.App. 2 Dist. 1978. Since there were no exigent circumstances, police were not entitled to go upon defendant's premises to seize marijuana plants, which officer had observed from adjacent grove growing in defendant's backyard, without a search warrant.—Rickard v. State, 361 So.2d 822, decision approved in part, quashed in part 420 So.2d 303.

Fla.App. 3 Dist. 1996. Once probable cause for defendant's arrest was established by narcotic-sniffing dog's alert to cocaine in defendant's car, state was not also required to show exigent circumstances for warrantless search of car because they are always presumed. U.S.C.A. Const. Amends. 4, 14.—Saturnino-Boudet v. State, 682 So.2d 188, rehearing denied, review dismissed 689 So.2d 1071.

Fla.App. 3 Dist. 1991. There were no exigent circumstances justifying warrantless search of apartment by officers who had received report of suspected drug activity at a specified apartment in the building, who knocked on the door, and who saw one person in the apartment holding some sort of metal object in his hand when the door was opened.—Alvarez v. State, 573 So.2d 400.

Fla.App. 4 Dist. 2011. Because State did not prove that some reasonable belief of exigency existed, a warrant should have been obtained before police entry into defendant's backyard, and because no warrant was obtained, and exigency exception to warrant requirement was not applicable, any evidence obtained as result of police entry should have been suppressed, and this included observation of drugs in house, which led to sweep of the home; officers entered curtilage of home to investigate acting solely on anonymous tip of narcotics activity, only corroborated the tip to the extent that white car was in front of the home, and had no indication from viewing the scene that a crime had been, was being, or would be committed, and when officers arrived at the scene, there did not appear to be anyone in sight that might have gun. U.S.C.A. Const.Amend. 4.—Bryan v. State, 62 So.3d 1244.

Fla.App. 4 Dist. 2008. It would have been unreasonable to expect off-duty police officers providing security at restaurant to send for a warrant to search defendant who was snorting a substance while he occupied bathroom stall with another man. U.S.C.A. Const.Amend. 4.—State v. Powers, 991 So.2d 1040.

Fla.App. 4 Dist. 1996. Exigent circumstances did not justify warrantless search of defendant's motel room, despite fact that defendant slammed door when officer identified himself as informant was attempting to buy cocaine; any exigent circumstances were created by activity of police officers since there was sufficient time to secure search warrant. U.S.C.A. Const.Amend. 4.—Levine v. State, 684 So.2d 903.

Fla.App. 5 Dist. 2018. Entry onto defendant's property was constitutionally permitted under the exigent circumstances exception to the warrant requirement; defendant's neighbor called to report possible animal cruelty in progress, advising that he heard a dog "yelping" and possibly being beaten, responding officers found defendant in back of house, after midnight, pacing behind fence and saying something along the lines of "get down" or "lay down" and heard what appeared to be something striking flesh, and when officer contacted defendant, defendant advised officer that he had a dog, that dog had bitten him, and that he struck the dog twice. U.S. Const. Amend. 4.—State v. Archer, 259 So.3d 999, review denied 2019 WL 2205765, on subsequent appeal 309 So.3d 287, rehearing denied.

Fla.App. 5 Dist. 1980. Warrantless incursion into defendant's residence predicated entirely on sight of four hand-rolled cigarettes when officers went to the residence seeking information concerning stolen car was not justified and lack of exigent or other exceptional circumstances rendered the warrantless incursion unreasonable; thus bag of marijuana which was seized after it fell to kitchen floor when defendant took his hand out of his pocket was fruit of an unlawful entry and should have been suppressed.—Taylor v. State, 381 So.2d 255, certiorari denied 386 So.2d 642.

Fla.App. 5 Dist. 1979. Where defendant, who was sole occupant of pickup truck, had been arrested and placed in back of squad car before arresting officer returned to the truck and seized marijuana cigarette from floorboard and searched defendant's purse, which she left in the cab, the warrantless seizure could not be justified on the probable cause, exigent circumstances exception. U.S.C.A.Const. Amend. 4; West's F.S.A.Const. art. 1, § 12.—Ulesky v. State, 379 So.2d 121.

☞695. Community caretaking.

† C.A.11 (Fla.) 2020. Police lieutenant's "cursory search" of apartment did not exceed the limited scope of searches authorized under the emergency-aid exception to the search warrant requirement, and thus the plain view doctrine applied to justify seizure of firearm found in bathroom on toilet; dispatch had reported a domestic-abuse incident in apartment where shots had been fired, and the bathroom was within the realm of areas where a victim might be found.

---

† This Case was not selected for publication in the National Reporter System

U.S. Const. Amend. 4.—United States v. Jones, 798 Fed.Appx. 434.

Fla.App. 1 Dist. 2021. Welfare checks fall under the community caretaking doctrine, an exception to the Fourth Amendment's search warrant requirement, which recognizes the duty of police officers to ensure the safety and welfare of the citizenry at large. U.S. Const. Amend. 4.—Taylor v. State, 326 So.3d 115.

Under the judicially created "community caretaking doctrine," law enforcement actions that might otherwise violate the Fourth Amendment can be found lawful when they occur in connection with an officer's community caretaking functions, totally devoid from the detection, investigation, or acquisition of evidence relating to the violation of a criminal statute. U.S. Const. Amend. 4.—Id.

The purpose of a welfare check regulates its scope: without any reasonable suspicion that criminal activity is or was afoot, the welfare check should end when the need for it ends. U.S. Const. Amend. 4.—Id.

Both the scope and manner of a welfare check must be reasonable in order to fall within exception to Fourth Amendment search warrant requirement. U.S. Const. Amend. 4.—Id.

Fla.App. 1 Dist. 2019. Welfare checks fall under the so-called "community caretaking doctrine," which is a judicial creation that carves out an exception to the Fourth Amendment's warrant requirement by allowing police officers to engage in a seizure or search of a person or property solely for safety reasons. U.S. Const. Amend. 4. —State v. Brumelow, 289 So.3d 955, rehearing denied, review denied 2020 WL 5796175.

Searches and seizures conducted under the community caretaker doctrine are solely for safety reasons and must be totally divorced from the detection, investigation, or acquisition of evidence relating to the violation of a criminal statute. U.S. Const. Amend. 4.—Id.

The scope of an encounter under the community caretaker doctrine is a limited one so that welfare checks do not become investigative tools that circumvent the constitutional protection against unreasonable searches and seizures. U.S. Const. Amend. 4.—Id.

Officer did not exceed permissible scope of welfare check of defendant and female passenger apparently sleeping in car when officer asked defendant to open window and door and turn off running car after defendant was unable to rouse non-responsive passenger, and thus smell of marijuana emanating from within car was unavoidable and discovery of illegal contraband inevitable; even though no evidence existed that passenger was intoxicated or experiencing medical problems, welfare check involved not only defendant's well-being but that of female passenger, whose physical or medical well-being was both unknown and questionable, and legitimate safety concern that passenger remained non-responsive was sufficient to prolong welfare check. U.S. Const. Amend. 4.—Id.

Fla.App. 1 Dist. 2007. Officers were entitled to make post-arrest sweep of defendant's house following his arrest for conspiracy to manufacture methamphetamine; information possessed by task force indicated that another individual was involved in helping defendant make methamphetamine, and sweep was appropriately limited and lasted no longer than necessary to dispel reasonable suspicion of danger and clear house of other individuals. U.S.C.A. Const.Amend. 4.—State v. Kennedy, 953 So.2d 655.

Fla.App. 2 Dist. 2023. Searches and seizures conducted in connection with welfare checks are solely for safety reasons, and scope of an encounter associated with a welfare check is limited to prevent exception from becoming an investigative tool that circumvents the Fourth Amendment. U.S. Const. Amend. 4.—K.M. v. State, 359 So.3d 414.

Fla.App. 2 Dist. 2022. While there is no overarching "community caretaking" doctrine, it does not follow that all searches and seizures conducted for non-law-enforcement purposes must be analyzed under precisely the same Fourth Amendment rules developed in criminal cases; those rules may or may not be appropriate for use in various non-criminal-law-enforcement contexts. U.S. Const. Amend. 4.—S.P. v. State, 331 So.3d 883.

The necessity of a law enforcement officer's actions of ensuring safety while in a community caretaking role does not create an inchoate warrant to bypass every protection of the Fourth Amendment. U.S. Const. Amend. 4.—Id.

A law enforcement officer's safety search of a person while engaged in the community caretaking role must be objectively reasonable under the Fourth Amendment under the facts of the case. U.S. Const. Amend. 4.—Id.

Reasonableness under the Fourth Amendment of a law enforcement officer's warrantless safety search while in the community caretaking role is typically measured in terms of the search's intrusiveness and the circumstances' necessity. U.S. Const. Amend. 4.—Id.

There was no articulable suspicion of criminal activity in connection to law enforcement officer's search of detainee's pocket-sized wallet, upon taking detainee into custody under the Baker Act, and thus warrantless search, which revealed cocaine in wallet, was not reasonable under the Fourth Amendment's community caretaking exception from the warrant requirement; there was no need to search through detainee's wallet when the one weapon she was reported to have had already been seized, when she was already in handcuffs in the back of a sheriff's patrol car, and when there was no objective basis to be further concerned for anyone's safety. U.S. Const. Amend. 4; Fla. Stat. Ann. § 394.451, et seq.—Id.

Wherever the line is to be drawn between law enforcement officers' work ensuring safety in their community caretaking function and the Fourth Amendment, it should lie within the least intrusive and least invasive points of action that will ensure that safety. U.S. Const. Amend. 4.—Id.

Fla.App. 2 Dist. 2016. To justify warrantless entry under the community caretaker exception based on suspected operation of a methamphetamine lab, the police must have a reasonable belief that such lab is being operated within the residence based on their experience, facts developed during investigation, and observance of the suspect's activities. U.S.C.A. Const.Amend. 4; West's F.S.A. Const. Art. 1, § 12.—State v. Fultz, 189 So.3d 155, rehearing denied.

Police officers did not have reasonable belief that methamphetamine lab was being operated in townhouse, and thus officers' warrantless entry into townhouse was not justified under community caretaker exception to warrant requirement; officers had no special training related to methamphetamine labs, officers had not conducted investigation into reports of possible drug activity in townhouse, and officers had not made observa-

---

† **This Case was not selected for publication in the National Reporter System**

tions of residents or their activities on morning of warrantless entry. U.S.C.A. Const.Amend. 4; West's F.S.A. Const. Art. 1, § 12.—Id.

Fla.App. 2 Dist. 2006. Contraband discovered in plain view during a permissible protective sweep need not be suppressed; however, to support such a search, the police officer must articulate facts sufficient to warrant a reasonable belief that the house harbored dangerous individuals. U.S.C.A. Const.Amend. 4.—Nolin v. State, 946 So.2d 52, on remand 2007 WL 7010152.

Fla.App. 3 Dist. 2023. The touchstone of any Fourth Amendment analysis, including one involving a welfare check, is reasonableness, which is measured by the totality of existing circumstances. U.S. Const. Amend. 4.—R.A. v. State, 355 So.3d 1028.

Fla.App. 5 Dist. 1989. Probable cause and exigent circumstances existed for warrantless search of home, including closet, which resulted in discovey of marijuana plants growing in large terrarium, where police were informed by neighbor that occupants of house were out of town and that front door was open, and police made thorough search of house looking for possible burglar. U.S.C.A. Const.Amend. 4.—State v. Haines, 543 So.2d 1278.

☞696. Providing medical aid.

C.A.11 (Fla.) 2020. Under emergency aid exception to Fourth Amendment's warrant requirement, officers may enter home without warrant to render emergency assistance to injured occupant or to protect occupant from imminent injury. U.S. Const. Amend. 4.—United States v. Evans, 958 F.3d 1102.

It was not objectively unreasonable for trained police officer to hear dog whimpering and claim he could not tell difference between whimpering dog and human in pain, and thus officers' warrantless entry into and protective sweep of defendant's residence fell within scope of emergency aid exception to Fourth Amendment's warrant requirement, even though defendant was already in custody and posed no threat, even if defendant's girlfriend told officers that dogs were source of whimpering, where officers were responding to multiple 911 calls reporting gunshots several minutes earlier, girlfriend had informed officers that defendant had threatened to kill himself, and defendant had initially refused to leave his house, locked door behind him when he finally exited, and tried to mislead officers by suggesting that reported gunshots might have been children playing with fireworks. U.S. Const. Amend. 4.—Id.

M.D.Fla. 2017. One exigency obviating the requirement of a search warrant is the need to assist persons who are seriously injured or threatened with such injury. U.S. Const. Amend. 4.—Ermini v. Scott, 249 F.Supp.3d 1253.

Fla.App. 1 Dist. 2019. "Exigent circumstances" that would allow officers to enter property without a warrant are few in number and include such circumstances as pursuing a fleeing felon, preventing the destruction of evidence, searching incident to a lawful arrest, responding to medical emergencies, and fighting fires. U.S. Const. Amend. 4.—Bryant v. State, 265 So.3d 726.

Fla.App. 1 Dist. 2013. When police officers arrive at the source of a 911 call and find suspicious circumstances, they may enter the home without a warrant even where a life-threatening emergency has not been positively identi-

fied. U.S.C.A. Const.Amend. 4.—C.L.L. v. State, 115 So.3d 1114.

Fla.App. 2 Dist. 2022. Even when responding to mental health crises, police officers and sheriff's deputies are still armed officers of the state, and as such, the Fourth Amendment requires them to exercise their search and seizure powers in a reasonable manner. U.S. Const. Amend. 4.—S.P. v. State, 331 So.3d 883.

Fla.App. 2 Dist. 2018. Exigent-circumstances exception to warrant requirement encompasses an emergency situation which requires police to assist or render aid. U.S. Const. Amend. 4.—Aguilar v. State, 259 So.3d 262.

Fla.App. 2 Dist. 2018. One exigency obviating the requirement of a warrant under the Fourth Amendment is the need to assist persons who are seriously injured or threatened with such injury. U.S. Const. Amend. 4.—Lapace v. State, 257 So.3d 588.

Under totality of circumstances, police deputies lacked objectively reasonable belief that there was an ongoing or imminent emergency that required immediate police attention when they entered house in which defendant was located, and thus entry into house and subsequent warrantless search were in violation of Fourth Amendment; after arriving at house in response to a 911 call, officers encountered a woman at house with injuries on her foot and leg, for which she gave plausible explanation, which was corroborated by officers' observation of another woman fleeing scene upon their arrival, that she had been battered by an unknown woman, officers did not observe any evidence of ongoing domestic dispute, and woman's unwillingness to allow deputies into house did not suggest ongoing emergency requiring the deputies' attention. U.S. Const. Amend. 4.—Id.

Fla.App. 2 Dist. 2016. Police officers did not have objectively reasonable belief that there was ongoing medical emergency in townhouse, and thus officers' warrantless entry into townhouse was not justified under feared medical emergency exception to warrant requirement, where officers were summoned on suspicion of methamphetamine lab, not suspicion that someone was in distress, and officers merely observed that front door was open and that mail was on the floor in foyer. U.S.C.A. Const.Amend. 4; West's F.S.A. Const. Art. 1, § 12.—State v. Fultz, 189 So.3d 155, rehearing denied.

Fla.App. 2 Dist. 2013. Police officers who responded to report that defendant's mother had found him in his room, nude, with a mixture of pills and syringes had no grounds to search defendant after they discovered him fully clothed and standing outside, and able to carry on an appropriate and coherent conversation, and thus one officer's demand that defendant produce pill bottle that was sticking out of his pocket constituted an unreasonable search; any concerns of a feared medical emergency had dissipated before officer demanded the pill bottle, and officers were no longer evaluating defendant for potential involuntary commitment, but had moved on to discussing voluntary drug treatment programs. U.S.C.A. Const.Amend. 4.—Fields v. State, 105 So.3d 1280.

Fla.App. 5 Dist. 2018. The "feared medical emergency" is a particular kind of exigent circumstance that may be an exception to the warrant requirement. U.S. Const. Amend. 4.—State v. Archer, 259 So.3d 999, review denied 2019 WL 2205765, on subsequent appeal 309 So.3d 287, rehearing denied.

---

† This Case was not selected for publication in the National Reporter System

⊝⇒698. —— In general.

† C.A.11 (Fla.) 2020. Exigent circumstances justified officers' entry into arrestee's hotel room because they reasonably believed his mental state made him a danger to himself, and thus city could not be vicariously liable for false arrest or imprisonment based on that entry alone; when they entered the room, they knew arrestee had told a family member he spent the day with their long-dead grandmother and had told guests and hotel staff that he owned the hotel, that he was regularly ordering room service and timing how long it took to arrive, that he was speaking in a garbled manner and laughing maniacally, that he did not seem to understand that officers were police officers instead of hotel employees, and that a guest in a neighboring room reported hearing screaming and glass breaking in the room throughout the day. U.S. Const. Amend. 4. —Harrison v. Davidson Hotel Company, LLC, 806 Fed.Appx. 684.

† C.A.11 (Fla.) 2020. Police officers' warrantless entry into apartment and search for possible victims was justified by the emergency aid exception to the search warrant requirement; police lieutenant responded to a dispatch describing a "priority call" reporting a domestic-abuse incident with shots fired inside the apartment, when she arrived at the apartment she heard a woman inside pleading to be let out and a man refusing to open the door because unidentified individuals were trying to kill him, soon after, a neighbor stated that defendant had guns in the apartment and a woman opened the door carrying a child and fled the apartment "crying hysterically." U.S. Const. Amend. 4.—United States v. Jones, 798 Fed.Appx. 434.

C.A.11 (Fla.) 2020. Under emergency aid exception to Fourth Amendment's warrant requirement, officers may enter home without warrant to render emergency assistance to injured occupant or to protect occupant from imminent injury. U.S. Const. Amend. 4.—United States v. Evans, 958 F.3d 1102.

† C.A.11 (Fla.) 2018. Exigent circumstances did not justify sheriff deputies' warrantless search of apartment, even though sheriff's dispatch had received anonymous call reporting a fight which had developed on patio from a loud party at apartment, and apartment resident had appeared angry, agitated, and intoxicated when he returned to doorway after retrieving identification, where the reported fight had ended by the time first deputy arrived at scene, two people in the apartment reported that the people involved in fight had left, there was no visible or audible chaos ensuing, and deputies observed no evidence of violent behavior. U.S. Const. Amend. 4. —Moore v. Sheriff of Seminole County, 748 Fed. Appx. 229.

† C.A.11 (Fla.) 2017. Deputy who retrieved rifle from arrestee's truck before placing him under arrest had qualified immunity from arrestee's § 1983 unreasonable search and seizure claim; there was neither a constitutional violation nor any clearly established law governing this situation, in which an officer entered an unlocked vehicle to seize guns while the guns' owner was nearby, and deputy could reasonably have believe it necessary to enter the truck and seize any guns to protect officers and the public, given that the officers on the scene were dealing with armed and unruly individuals following a report of shots fired, it was dark, individuals continued to arrive, and the officers were outnumbered. U.S. Const.

Amend. 4; 42 U.S.C.A. § 1983.—Hamilton v. Roberts, 711 Fed.Appx. 955.

† C.A.11 (Fla.) 2016. Exigent circumstances existed to justify non-consensual warrantless entry into individual's apartment, and thus corporal who executed search was entitled to qualified immunity from individual's § 1983 action for violation of Fourth Amendment right against nonconsensual warrantless entry; sheriff had reason to believe a person suspected of violent felonies including armed robbery and kidnapping with intent to inflict harm or terrorize with a firearm was inside apartment, it was reasonable to believe suspect continued to be armed and dangerous, and it was reasonable to believe that any delay could allow suspect to escape or cause harm to others, given suspect's previous offenses involving use of firearm. U.S. Const. Amend. 4. —Hill v. Orange County Sheriff, 666 Fed.Appx. 836.

M.D.Fla. 2017. Sheriff's deputies who conducted welfare check on homeowner after homeowner's daughter called sheriff's office to report that she believed homeowner was distraught and suicidal, and that she had a handgun and may have been consuming alcohol, did not violate the Fourth Amendment when they remained in homeowner's home without a warrant after they found she was in no grave emergency or imminent danger of injury and she asked them to leave; at time homeowner told deputies to leave, officers had not completed purpose of security check, and concerns expressed by daughter had not been shown to have dissipated, since deputies found empty wine bottle in living room, homeowner was in a dark house relatively early in the evening, and homeowner said she had a gun. U.S. Const. Amend. 4.—Ermini v. Scott, 249 F.Supp.3d 1253.

One exigency obviating the requirement of a search warrant is the need to assist persons who are seriously injured or threatened with such injury. U.S. Const. Amend. 4.—Id.

M.D.Fla. 2011. Pursuant to emergency aid exception to Fourth Amendment's warrant requirement, officers may enter home without warrant to render emergency assistance to injured occupant or to protect occupant from imminent injury. U.S.C.A. Const.Amend. 4.—U.S. v. Garcia, 853 F.Supp.2d 1177, remanded 2013 WL 10509665, appeal after remand 556 Fed.Appx. 924, affirmed 556 Fed.Appx. 924.

S.D.Fla. 2021. Even if detectives had probable cause for warrantless search and seizure, public safety and safety of officers, as exceptions to warrant requirement, did not justify detectives' entry into home's curtilage after defendant left public sidewalk, where detectives had not seen a gun on defendant when he had been standing on sidewalk. U.S. Const. Amend. 4.—United States v. Howard, 557 F.Supp.3d 1262.

S.D.Fla. 2002. Although probable cause may have existed upon informant's signal that narcotics were present, no exigent circumstances justified warrantless search of suspect's home; there was no evidence that suspects were aware of informant's status or that police would observe what occurred in home, and no showing that informant was threatened or that suspect would hurt informant before becoming aware of that status. U.S.C.A. Const.Amend. 4.—U.S. v. Hernandez, 214 F.Supp.2d 1344, reversed 132 Fed. Appx. 821.

Fla. 2012. The reasonableness of an entry by the police upon private property, under exception to warrant requirement for an emergency situation which requires police to assist or render aid, is measured primarily by the totality of existing circumstances. U.S.C.A. Const.Amend. 4.—Delhall v. State, 95 So.3d 134.

Fla. 2005. Authority of police officers under the emergency exception to the warrant requirement to enter and investigate private premises to preserve life or render first aid, provided they do not enter with an accompanying intent either to arrest or search, is inherent in the very nature of their duties as peace officers and derives from the common law; it is built into the Fourth Amendment's concept of reasonableness. U.S.C.A. Const.Amend. 4.—Riggs v. State, 918 So.2d 274.

Fla.App. 1 Dist. 2021. To justify an emergency warrantless entry into a home by police officers, the State must demonstrate that an objectively reasonable basis existed for the officers to believe that there was an immediate need for police assistance for the protection of life. U.S. Const. Amend. 4.—Jones v. State, 331 So.3d 252, review denied 2022 WL 1261288.

Fla.App. 1 Dist. 2018. Exigent circumstances justified warrantless entry into defendant's backyard and residence to investigate report that defendant's wife made that she feared for her safety and safety of their minor child, and thus, evidence was sufficient to establish that police were engaged in lawful performance of their legal duties, as required for conviction of battery on a law enforcement officer and resisting an officer with violence; officers observed fresh bruises on the face, neck, and chest of defendant's wife when they arrived on scene and she identified defendant as her abuser, wife indicated to officers that defendant told her that she would not see her son again, he refused to let officers speak or examine minor child for injuries and refused to exit the home after officers made several attempts to contact him, and defendant's home was made nearly impenetrable by custom locks, windows, and doors, which made locating the child in the home difficult. Fla. Stat. Ann. §§ 39.301, 784.07(2)(b), 843.01, 901.15(7).—Sosnowski v. State, 245 So.3d 885, rehearing denied, review denied 2019 WL 1349271, appeal from denial of post-conviction relief dismissed 301 So.3d 472, habeas corpus denied 2022 WL 2209324.

Fla.App. 1 Dist. 1981. Where there was strong probability that car in question was getaway car used after restaurant was held up at gunpoint, officials informed police they could not trace ownership of car through tag number until following morning, car was found within 45 to 50 minutes after robbery at busy motel one and a half miles away from robbery, and inquiry by police at rooms on two floors of motel produced no leads, exigent circumstances existed for police to search car without warrant, for identification of owner.—Barnes v. State, 406 So.2d 84.

Fla.App. 2 Dist. 2019. To rely on exigent circumstances exception to Fourth Amendment's warrant requirement, the State must demonstrate a grave emergency that makes a warrantless search imperative to the safety of the police and of the community. U.S. Const. Amend. 4.; Fla. Const. art. 1, § 12.—State v. M.B.W., 276 So.3d 501.

Fla.App. 2 Dist. 2018. Exigent-circumstances exception to warrant requirement encompasses an emergency situation which requires police to assist or render aid. U.S. Const. Amend. 4.—Aguilar v. State, 259 So.3d 262.

Fla.App. 2 Dist. 2018. One exigency obviating the requirement of a warrant under the Fourth Amendment is the need to assist persons who are seriously injured or threatened with such injury. U.S. Const. Amend. 4.—Lapace v. State, 257 So.3d 588.

The police may enter a residence without a warrant if an objectively reasonable basis exists for the officer to believe that there is an immediate need for police assistance for the protection of life or substantial property interests. U.S. Const. Amend. 4.—Id.

Under totality of circumstances, police deputies lacked objectively reasonable belief that there was an ongoing or imminent emergency that required immediate police attention when they entered house in which defendant was located, and thus entry into house and subsequent warrantless search were in violation of Fourth Amendment; after arriving at house in response to a 911 call, officers encountered a woman at house with injuries on her foot and leg, for which she gave plausible explanation, which was corroborated by officers' observation of another woman fleeing scene upon their arrival, that she had been battered by an unknown woman, officers did not observe any evidence of ongoing domestic dispute, and woman's unwillingness to allow deputies into house did not suggest ongoing emergency requiring the deputies' attention. U.S. Const. Amend. 4.—Id.

An anonymous tip may provide the basis for conducting a warrantless entry to render emergency assistance or to protect someone from imminent injury. U.S. Const. Amend. 4.—Id.

Fla.App. 2 Dist. 2006. The operation of a methamphetamine lab in a residence is inherently dangerous, presents an immediate threat to public safety, and is well within the scope of the exigent circumstance exception to the requirement for a search warrant. U.S.C.A. Const. Amend. 4.—Barth v. State, 955 So.2d 1115.

Fla.App. 2 Dist. 2006. One exigency obviating the requirement of a search warrant is the need to assist persons who are seriously injured or threatened with such injury. U.S.C.A. Const. Amend. 4.—Vanslyke v. State, 936 So.2d 1218.

Where safety is threatened and time is of the essence, the need to protect life and to prevent serious bodily injury provides justification for an otherwise invalid entry. U.S.C.A. Const.Amend. 4.—Id.

For a child abuse report to justify a warrantless entry, the report, considered in the context of the totality of relevant circumstances, must provide "an objectively reasonable basis" for the police to believe that there is an immediate need for police assistance to render emergency assistance to an injured child or to protect a child from a threat of imminent injury. U.S.C.A. Const.Amend. 4.—Id.

Fla.App. 2 Dist. 1985. Circumstances justifying officer's seizure of cigarette case containing contraband were not supported by testimony, notwithstanding State's argument that search was necessary to protect defendant's children.—Campbell v. State, 477 So.2d 1068.

Fla.App. 4 Dist. 2018. Exigent circumstances justified warrantless search of abandoned cell phone found near scene of crime that involved firing of gun shots near school bus stop, where at time of search, police knew gunman fired bullets towards students at bus stop near elementary school, student was seriously injured, gunman had not been detained, gun had not been located, and circumstances dictated prompt response on part of authorities to discover gunman's identity. U.S. Const. Amend. 4.—Barton v. State, 237 So.3d 378.

Fla.App. 4 Dist. 2013. Police officers acted reasonably and in good faith when they searched defendant after his family and neighbors expressed concern that he might be a threat because of his unwavering belief that his neighbors had kidnapped and murdered his child, and officers decided to take defendant into custody under the *Baker* Act, as officers were concerned for defendant's safety and safety of others, and acted pursuant to a reasonable local police policy. U.S.C.A. Const.Amend. 4; West's F.S.A. Const. Art. 1, § 12; West's F.S.A. § 394.463.—Collins v. State, 125 So.3d 1046.

Fla.App. 4 Dist. 2011. To constitute exigent circumstances, the emergency must be so that it makes a warrantless search imperative to the safety of the police and of the community, and safety is threatened when a need exists to protect life and to prevent serious bodily injury. U.S.C.A. Const.Amend. 4.—Bryan v. State, 62 So.3d 1244.

Fla.App. 5 Dist. 2009. One exigency that obviates the need for a search warrant occurs when an officer is put in position to assist persons who are injured or threatened with injury. U.S.C.A. Const.Amend. 4.—Ortiz v. State, 24 So.3d 596, review denied 37 So.3d 848.

Fla.App. 5 Dist. 2000. Warrantless entry by deputy and animal cruelty investigator was justified by emergency exception to warrant requirement; deputy and investigator came to premises only to make preliminary investigation regarding citizen's complaint, and they observed and heard overwhelming signs of animals in distress on property. U.S.C.A. Const.Amend. 4.—Brinkley v. County of Flagler, 769 So.2d 468.

Fla.App. 5 Dist. 1995. Warrantless search of defendant's apartment was not justified by exigent circumstances, even though officer initially entered the apartment in order to ascertain whether burglary was in progress; once officer completed initial sweep of apartment to locate intruder and ascertained that no one was in need of assistance, exigency allowing warrantless search of the premises ended. U.S.C.A. Const. Amend. 4.—Anderson v. State, 665 So.2d 281, rehearing denied.

⟜**699.** —— **Injury or harm to officer; officer safety.**

† **C.A.11 (Fla.) 2017.** Deputy who retrieved rifle from arrestee's truck before placing him under arrest had qualified immunity from arrestee's § 1983 unreasonable search and seizure claim; there was neither a constitutional violation nor any clearly established law governing this situation, in which an officer entered an unlocked vehicle to seize guns while the guns' owner was nearby, and deputy could reasonably have believe it necessary to enter the truck and seize any guns to protect officers and the public, given that the officers on the scene were dealing with armed and unruly individuals following a report of shots fired, it was dark, individuals continued to arrive, and the officers were outnumbered. U.S. Const. Amend. 4; 42 U.S.C.A. § 1983.—Hamilton v. Roberts, 711 Fed.Appx. 955.

† **C.A.11 (Fla.) 2017.** Exigent circumstances existed to justify officer's warrantless seizure of a firearm from the roof of defendant's residence after officers saw defendant throw it to that location; officers were concerned about the dissipation of DNA evidence from the firearm that could occur from precipitation on the exposed roof during the several hours it could have taken to secure a warrant, and the officers were concerned a resident of the house could have removed the firearm, altered the DNA evidence on it, or used it against the officers. U.S. Const. Amend. 4.—United States v. Davis, 710 Fed.Appx. 805.

C.A.11 (Fla.) 2012. Police officer's search of residence was not rendered pretextual based on judicial finding that his stated intent in entering residence for officer safety concerns was not credible; officer's subjective intent was inapposite because tests for analyzing for probable cause and exigent circumstances were both objective. U.S.C.A. Const.Amend. 4.—U.S. v. Franklin, 694 F.3d 1.

C.A.5 (Fla.) 1981. Seizure of marijuana from vessel and campers without a warrant was justified by exigent circumstances exception to warrant requirement, where search was necessarily carried out during excitement and confusion created by drug raid, there was very real danger that one of the suspects would attempt to flee in camper or boat and police were justified in protecting themselves from attack. U.S.C.A.Const. Amend. 4.—U.S. v. Mesa, 660 F.2d 1070, rehearing denied 667 F.2d 93.

Fla. 2017. Exigent circumstance of hot pursuit did not justify police officers' warrantless home search and arrest of suspect who was observed by officer to be smoking what was alleged to be marijuana cigarette and to have thrown the cigarette on the ground; underlying crime for which there was probable cause was nonviolent misdemeanor offense of possession of marijuana cigarette, suspect posed no danger to the public, police, or to anyone, officers could have secured evidence without any problem, and suspect did not jump over fence or cross into neighboring yard, but merely walked backwards with his hands up and moved into open garage. U.S. Const. Amend. 4; Fla. Const. art. 1, § 12.— State v. Markus, 211 So.3d 894, rehearing denied 2017 WL 944231.

Fla. 2012. Exception to warrant requirement allowing police entry onto private property in an emergency situation which requires police to assist or render aid applies also when police are in the home lawfully, such as with consent of one of the occupants, and circumstances arise that provide an objectively reasonable basis for officers to believe that there is an immediate need for protection of themselves or other occupants. U.S.C.A. Const.Amend. 4.—Delhall v. State, 95 So.3d 134.

Fla. 2003. Actions of police deputies during what began as consensual encounter at mobile home where defendant lived, in asking defendant to get up and move toward kitchen and then looking under chair cushion, were not unreasonable, where deputy who was outside observed defendant reach into his pocket, remove something, and shove it under cushion and believed that deputies inside were potentially in danger, defendant denied placing anything under cushion, and defendant granted permission for deputies to look under cushion. (Per Curiam, with three Justices concurring and two Justices concurring in result.) U.S.C.A. Const.Amend. 4.— Taylor v. State, 855 So.2d 1, rehearing denied, certiorari denied 124 S.Ct. 1605, 541 U.S. 905, 158 L.Ed.2d 248, denial of post-conviction relief affirmed 120 So.3d 540, certiorari denied 134 S.Ct. 1009, 571 U.S. 1166, 187 L.Ed.2d 856, habeas corpus granted 228 So.3d 71.

Fla.App. 1 Dist. 2003. Fears for officer safety that were based on generalizations about drug cases and not on any specific risk presented by facts of defendant's case did not form a legitimate exigent circumstance sufficient to justify warrantless entry into defendant's motel room; there was no basis for police to be so concerned, since they had motel surrounded, thus minimizing risk that informant or any suspect could flee with the money police had given informant with which to purchase the drugs. U.S.C.A. Const.Amend. 4.—Lee v. State, 856 So.2d 1133.

Fla.App. 2 Dist. 2019. To rely on exigent circumstances exception to Fourth Amendment's warrant requirement, the State must demonstrate a grave emergency that makes a warrantless search imperative to the safety of the police and of the community. U.S. Const. Amend. 4.; Fla. Const. art. 1, § 12.—State v. M.B.W., 276 So.3d 501.

Fla.App. 2 Dist. 2018. Although officers' initial warrantless entry into defendant's home was lawful, pursuant to exigent circumstances exception to warrant requirement, the exigency ended once officers completed sweep of defendant's home to locate potential shooters or victims, cleared the residence, and secured the scene, and once exigency ended, police needed to obtain warrant or defendant's consent in order to lawfully reenter and search his home. U.S. Const. Amend. 4.—Aguilar v. State, 259 So.3d 262.

Fla.App. 2 Dist. 2009. Exigent circumstances did not exist to justify a warrantless entry of defendant's motel room to arrest defendant for battery, even though the state pointed to police concerns for officer safety and to a belief that the life of victim, who was not in the motel room, would be in danger if defendant left; there were at least five officers at the motel and another two plainclothes units were monitoring the parking area, nothing indicated that defendant was aware of the police presence outside the motel, and, given those circumstances, any fear that it would not have been possible to control defendant had he attempted to leave the motel room was unreasonable. U.S.C.A. Const.Amend. 4.—Wright v. State, 1 So.3d 409.

Fla.App. 2 Dist. 2006. Evidence did not support officers' full blown warrantless protective sweep that revealed cannabis; neither testifying officer identified any objective fact that led them to believe that anyone other than defendant and his wife, let alone individual of dangerous propensity, was inside home, male and female voices heard upon arrival were consistent with number of individuals found immediately upon entry, neighbor did not identify, nor did officers testify, that more than two people were inside home, and defendant and his wife themselves posed no danger to officers. U.S.C.A. Const.Amend. 4.—Nolin v. State, 946 So.2d 52, on remand 2007 WL 7010152.

Fla.App. 3 Dist. 2006. Exigent circumstances existed to support warrantless entry and seizure of cocaine in defendant's apartment; based on officer's experience, years of training, almost daily exposure to crack cocaine, and short distance of four feet between him and refrigerator, he immediately recognized that items on top of refrigerator were nickel bags of crack cocaine, there was a heightened concern for safety because narcotics were involved, there were exigent circumstances because someone else could have been in apartment, and when officer looked into bathroom, he did so for his own safety. U.S.C.A. Const.Amend. 4.—State v. Cartwright, 920 So.2d 71.

Fla.App. 4 Dist. 2011. Fears for officer safety based on generalizations about drug cases, rather than on any specific risk presented by the facts of defendant's case, do not qualify as exigent circumstances, as would justify warrantless entry into home. U.S.C.A. Const.Amend. 4.—Rozzo v. State, 75 So.3d 409, on remand 2012 WL 12144986.

Fla.App. 4 Dist. 1971. Where officer on patrol of business district when he observed, at 3:30 A.M., a light burning and a blanket covering rear window of the premises and where he believed that burglary was in progress, officer was justified in entering premises through unlocked door without announcing his authority as a police officer under theory that officer's peril would have been increased had he demanded entrance and stated the purpose, and marijuana found within the premises and defendants' statements relative thereto were admissible, notwithstanding that a defendant was residing in back room of the premises and that no burglary was in progress. F.S.A. § 901.19(1); U.S.C.A.Const. Amend. 4.—State v. Bell, 249 So.2d 748.

☞701. —— In general.
C.A.11 (Fla.) 2019. A warrantless search and seizure can be justified under the exigent-circumstances doctrine when probable cause has been established to believe that evidence will be removed or destroyed before a warrant can be obtained. U.S. Const. Amend. 4.—United States v. Babcock, 924 F.3d 1180, appeal from denial of post-conviction relief dismissed 2023 WL 4117503.

An objective inquiry governs the issue of whether probable cause has been established to believe that evidence will be removed or destroyed before a warrant can be obtained, as required to justify a warrantless search and seizure under the exigent-circumstances doctrine. U.S. Const. Amend. 4.—Id.

C.A.11 (Fla.) 2018. The exigent circumstances exception to the Fourth Amendment permits warrantless seizures of property when certain exigencies exist, including the imminent destruction of evidence; police officers relying on this exception must show an objectively reasonable basis for deciding that imminent action was required. U.S. Const. Amend. 4.—Crocker v. Beatty, 886 F.3d 1132.

Court of Appeals' inquiry into whether exigent circumstances exception applied so as to permit warrantless seizure of property is whether the facts would have led a reasonable, experienced agent to believe that evidence might be destroyed before a warrant could be secured. U.S. Const. Amend. 4.—Id.

C.A.11 (Fla.) 1996. Warrantless search of home is presumptively unreasonable, but is allowed when both probable cause and exigent circumstances exist; "probable cause" exists when, under totality of circumstances, there is fair probability that contraband or evidence of crime will be discovered in particular place, and "exigent circumstances" exist when authorities have reason to believe that evidence is in danger of being destroyed or removed. U.S.C.A. Const. Amend. 4.—U.S. v. Mikell, 102 F.3d 470, certiorari denied Young v. U.S., 117 S.Ct. 1459, 520 U.S. 1181, 137 L.Ed.2d 563.

C.A.11 (Fla.) 1994. Risk of removal or destruction of narcotics is particularly compelling exigent circumstance such as would excuse warrantless entry. U.S.C.A. Const.Amend. 4.—U.S. v. McGregor, 31 F.3d 1067, certiorari denied 116 S.Ct. 328, 516 U.S. 926, 133 L.Ed.2d 228.

† This Case was not selected for publication in the National Reporter System

C.A.11 (Fla.) 1983. "Exigent circumstances exception" to Fourth Amendment warrant requirement applies in those cases where societal costs of obtaining warrant, such as danger to law officers or risk of loss or destruction of evidence, outweigh reasons for prior recourse to neutral magistrate. U.S.C.A. Const.Amend. 4.—U.S. v. Blasco, 702 F.2d 1315, certiorari denied Galvan v. U.S., 104 S.Ct. 275, 464 U.S. 914, 78 L.Ed.2d 256, certiorari denied Jamardo v. U.S., 104 S.Ct. 276, 464 U.S. 914, 78 L.Ed.2d 256.

⊗═**702. —— Particular cases in general.**

C.A.11 (Fla.) 2019. The exigent-circumstances exception to the search warrant requirement is particularly compelling with regard to electronic files because contraband and records can be easily and quickly destroyed while a search is progressing. U.S. Const. Amend. 4.—United States v. Babcock, 924 F.3d 1180, appeal from denial of post-conviction relief dismissed 2023 WL 4117503.

Reasonable, experienced police officer could have believed that defendant, as suspect of illegal, coercive relationship with minor girl in violation of Florida law, would delete any incriminating evidence on his cellular telephone before search warrant could be obtained, as required for warrantless seizure of phone to be justified under exigent-circumstances doctrine, where defendant had tried to deceive officers, denying that anyone else was in his camper, reporting that minor had randomly shown up at his house in middle of night, and claiming that he did not know her age, he knew he was under suspicion once officer asked to search camper and to further inspect his phone, and electronic files on his phone could have been quickly destroyed while search was progressing. U.S. Const. Amend. 4; Fla. Stat. Ann. § 794.05(1).—Id.

C.A.11 (Fla.) 2018. Assuming that photographs and videos of car accident crash scene on bystander's cellular phone could have been considered to be evidence of a crime, it was not reasonable for deputy sheriff to believe that exigent circumstances existed to justify warrantless seizure of the phone, where bystander had no involvement with the car accident that he had photographed, but was merely a curious passerby, and when deputy sheriff approached him and took his phone before speaking, there was no indication whatsoever that bystander would have soon deleted the photographs and videos he had just taken the time to capture himself. U.S. Const. Amend. 4.—Crocker v. Beatty, 886 F.3d 1132.

† **C.A.11 (Fla.) 2017.** Exigent circumstances existed to justify officer's warrantless seizure of a firearm from the roof of defendant's residence after officers saw defendant throw it to that location; officers were concerned about the dissipation of DNA evidence from the firearm that could occur from precipitation on the exposed roof during the several hours it could have taken to secure a warrant, and the officers were concerned a resident of the house could have removed the firearm, altered the DNA evidence on it, or used it against the officers. U.S. Const. Amend. 4.—United States v. Davis, 710 Fed.Appx. 805.

† **C.A.11 (Fla.) 2010.** Detectives' warrantless entry into defendant's home was justified by exigent circumstances, precluding violation of defendant's Fourth Amendment rights, since detectives' combined training and experience, together with personal experience buying crack from defendant's home, gave detectives objectively reasonable basis to believe that drugs would likely be removed from home before detectives could obtain search warrant. U.S.C.A. Const.Amend. 4.—U.S. v. Walker, 390 Fed.Appx. 854, certiorari denied 131 S.Ct. 1815, 563 U.S. 919, 179 L.Ed.2d 775, post-conviction relief denied 2015 WL 4389939, post-conviction relief dismissed by 2016 WL 11082043, habeas corpus dismissed by Walker v. Warden, 2018 WL 5115575, affirmed 801 Fed.Appx. 926.

† **C.A.11 (Fla.) 2009.** Probable cause and exigent circumstances justified warrantless intrusion into residence of individual suspected of possessing narcotics; officers reasonably believed that narcotics were present and might be destroyed before warrant could be secured, and intrusion was limited and directly proportional to exigency of case. U.S.C.A. Const.Amend. 4.—U.S. v. Thomas, 348 Fed.Appx. 497.

† **C.A.11 (Fla.) 2007.** Sheriff's department deputy had probable cause to believe that arrestee or someone in arrestee's apartment had been smoking cannabis, and thus, warrantless entry and search of apartment did not violate clearly established constitutional right, as required for deputies to be entitled to qualified immunity, in arrestee's § 1983 action; as they were escorting arrestee back to apartment, deputy smelled burnt cannabis, and exigent circumstances existed to justify warrantless entry in order to prevent loss, destruction, removal or concealment of evidence. U.S.C.A. Const.Amend. 4; 42 U.S.C.A. § 1983.—Hardy v. Broward County Sheriff's Office, 238 Fed.Appx. 435.

† **C.A.11 (Fla.) 2007.** Warrantless entry into defendant's trailer and subsequent search came within exigent circumstances exception to warrant requirement; police officer observed defendant conduct drug transaction outside trailer, defendant instigated hot pursuit when he turned to run into trailer, and it was not unreasonable for officer to believe that defendant would destroy evidence. U.S.C.A. Const.Amend. 4.—U.S. v. Echevarria, 238 Fed.Appx. 424, post-conviction relief denied 2009 WL 1649135.

† **C.A.11 (Fla.) 2006.** Exigent circumstances, specifically, need to prevent destruction of evidence, justified warrantless entry into drug suspects' residence, where one suspect had just realized that drug deal had failed and could have used his cell phone to call residence and order drugs destroyed. U.S.C.A. Const.Amend. 4.—U.S. v. Martinez, 191 Fed.Appx. 856, post-conviction relief denied 2007 WL 1490639, order vacated on reconsideration, post-conviction relief denied 2007 WL 1893818, post-conviction relief denied 2008 WL 780735, certificate of appealability denied 2008 WL 1819554, post-conviction relief denied U.S. v. Nieves-Villareal, 2008 WL 1995045.

† **C.A.11 (Fla.) 2006.** Exigent circumstances, consisting of police officers' reasonable belief that defendant would destroy drug evidence, justified officers' warrantless entry into defendant's motel room; after defendant confronted motel housekeeper as she was coming out of his room, where she had seen evidence of cooking of crack cocaine in plain view, and asked her about what she had seen in room, defendant threatened housekeeper and followed her to motel office, and defendant knew housekeeper was frightened and would probably notify authorities of what she had seen. U.S.C.A. Const.Amend. 4.—U.S. v. McClendon, 181 Fed.Appx. 797, certiorari denied 127 S.Ct. 290, 549 U.S. 925, 166 L.Ed.2d 221.

---

† **This Case was not selected for publication in the National Reporter System**

C.A.11 (Fla.) 2000. Exigent circumstances did not justify agents' entry of apartment to arrest one of its occupants, where agents could have secured warrants to arrest occupants two days before entry; moreover, agents could not have been surprised by location of apartment they had been surveilling for some time, they could not have been surprised by heroin delivery they had arranged and there was no evidence that occupants were about to flee or destroy drugs, or that they were even aware of agents' surveillance. U.S.C.A. Const.Amend. 4.—U.S. v. Santa, 236 F.3d 662.

C.A.11 (Fla.) 1984. Where officers had probable cause to enter service station building under circumstances strongly indicating that drugs were being held at the station to sell, and where exigent circumstances justified officer's warrantless entry into building to pursue one defendant who was fleeing, officers once inside building could lawfully seize methaqualone tablets which lay in the officer's "plain view." Comprehensive Drug Abuse Prevention and Control Act of 1970, §§ 401(a)(1), 406, 21 U.S.C.A. §§ 841(a)(1), 846; U.S.C.A. Const.Amend. 4.—U.S. v. Pantoja-Soto, 739 F.2d 1520, rehearing denied 749 F.2d 733, certiorari denied 105 S.Ct. 1369, 470 U.S. 1008, 84 L.Ed.2d 389.

C.A.5 (Fla.) 1981. Seizure of marijuana from vessel and campers without a warrant was justified by exigent circumstances exception to warrant requirement, where search was necessarily carried out during excitement and confusion created by drug raid, there was very real danger that one of the suspects would attempt to flee in camper or boat and police were justified in protecting themselves from attack. U.S.C.A.Const. Amend. 4.—U.S. v. Mesa, 660 F.2d 1070, rehearing denied 667 F.2d 93.

C.A.5 (Fla.) 1977. When informer, whose signal that cocaine was in house provided ample probable cause for arrest of defendant, told agents that someone was in house, immediate entry became necessary to prevent disposal of cocaine, a powder that can easily be flushed down a toilet, and thus warrantless entry by agents, who could logically have suspected that anyone inside house would be well aware of five police cars ringing premises and arrest of defendant and who knew that person in house might be defendant's wife and partner in drug trade, was justified to preserve evidence and was lawful under exigent circumstances exception to warrant requirement. U.S.C.A.Const. Amend. 4.—U.S. v. Gardner, 553 F.2d 946, rehearing denied 559 F.2d 29, certiorari denied 98 S.Ct. 722, 434 U.S. 1011, 54 L.Ed.2d 753.

C.A.5 (Fla.) 1976. Where law enforcement officials detected aircraft proceeding down taxiway in dark with its lights off at time almost exactly that predicted by informant, whose statement that defendant was going to smuggle 1,600 or 1,700 pounds of marijuana into United States was insufficient in itself as basis for search and seizure, in his estimate of time required for smuggling trip, equivocal information ripened into probable cause on the scene and thus, since exigent circumstances existed for search of airplane because of its mobility and because of reasonable inference that confederates might be present with attendant danger of destruction or dispersion of evidence is warrant procedure was followed, warrantless search of airplane was justified under traditional Fourth Amendment standards. U.S.C.A.Const. Amend. 4.—U.S. v. Brennan, 538 F.2d 711, rehearing denied 542 F.2d

575, certiorari denied 97 S.Ct. 1104, 429 U.S. 1092, 51 L.Ed.2d 538, rehearing denied 97 S.Ct. 1611, 430 U.S. 960, 51 L.Ed.2d 812.

S.D.Fla. 2014. Probable cause and exigent circumstances existed to conduct warrantless entry into defendant's apartment after he voluntarily opened door for them, based on the illegal narcotics activity in plain view when door was opened, codefendant's hesitation to exit the unit, the layout of the apartment, and the inherent risk of destruction of evidence in narcotics cases. U.S. Const.Amend. 4.—United States v. Jackson, 155 F.Supp.3d 1320, affirmed 618 Fed.Appx. 472, certiorari denied 136 S.Ct. 376, 577 U.S. 946, 193 L.Ed.2d 303.

The need to invoke the exigent circumstances exception to the warrant requirement is particularly compelling in narcotics cases because narcotics can be so quickly destroyed. U.S. Const. Amend. 4.—Id.

S.D.Fla. 2012. The need to invoke the exigent circumstances exception to the warrant requirement is particularly compelling in narcotics cases because narcotics can be so quickly destroyed.— Feliciano v. City of Miami Beach, 847 F.Supp.2d 1359.

Fla. 2017. Exigent circumstance of hot pursuit did not justify police officers' warrantless home search and arrest of suspect who was observed by officer to be smoking what was alleged to be marijuana cigarette and to have thrown the cigarette on the ground; underlying crime for which there was probable cause was nonviolent misdemeanor offense of possession of marijuana cigarette, suspect posed no danger to the public, police, or to anyone, officers could have secured evidence without any problem, and suspect did not jump over fence or cross into neighboring yard, but merely walked backwards with his hands up and moved into open garage. U.S. Const. Amend. 4; Fla. Const. art. 1, § 12.— State v. Markus, 211 So.3d 894, rehearing denied 2017 WL 944231.

Fla.App. 1 Dist. 2015. Exigent circumstances justified warrantless search of bottle containing ingredients for making methamphetamine, which was found by sheriff's office investigator under hood of defendant's truck, where investigator had probable cause to believe that defendant was making methamphetamine, based on prior methamphetamine-related arrest of another individual on defendant's property, the strong odor of lighter fluid, which was associated with manufacture of methamphetamine, and defendant's effort to obscure the bottle after opening the hood of his truck, and investigator was concerned that defendant would destroy the evidence, given the close proximity of a fire on defendant's property, or that a dangerous situation could arise, due to the explosive nature of methamphetamine manufacture. U.S.C.A. Const.Amend. 4.—State v. Smith, 172 So.3d 993, review dismissed 2017 WL 3392710.

Fla.App. 1 Dist. 2009. Possible destruction of drugs was not an exigent circumstance that justified a warrantless entry of defendant's motel room; the possibility of destruction did not exist until police, through an informant, knocked on the door of the motel room, and thus police actions created the exigent circumstance. U.S.C.A. Const.Amend. 4.—Higginbotham v. State, 17 So.3d 828, rehearing denied.

Fla.App. 1 Dist. 2003. Possibility that the drugs could have been destroyed was not a valid exigency, justifying warrantless entry into defendant's motel room, as that possibility did not

† **This Case was not selected for publication in the National Reporter System**

actually exist until officers knocked on the door and announced their presence. U.S.C.A. Const. Amend. 4.—Lee v. State, 856 So.2d 1133.

Fears for officer safety that were based on generalizations about drug cases and not on any specific risk presented by facts of defendant's case did not form a legitimate exigent circumstance sufficient to justify warrantless entry into defendant's motel room; there was no basis for police to be so concerned, since they had motel surrounded, thus minimizing risk that informant or any suspect could flee with the money police had given informant with which to purchase the drugs. U.S.C.A. Const.Amend. 4.—Id.

Fla.App. 1 Dist. 2003. Risk of removal or destruction of narcotics is a particularly compelling exigent circumstance that excuses a warrantless search. U.S.C.A. Const.Amend. 4; West's F.S.A. Const. Art. 1, § 12.—Hendrix v. State, 843 So.2d 1003, review denied 851 So.2d 729.

Fla.App. 1 Dist. 1992. Exigent circumstances existed to excuse officers' failure to comply with "Knock and Announce" statute before entering defendant's home to seize small amount of cocaine that confidential informant had made arrangements to purchase from defendant's home; informant was wearing transmitting device, police continually monitored conversation between informant and defendant, informant signalled police that cocaine was present, and unidentified person was present on front porch of house during entire transaction and could have warned defendant, resulting in probable destruction of cocaine. U.S.C.A. Const.Amend. 4; West's F.S.A. § 901.19(1).—Napoli v. State, 596 So.2d 782, review denied 604 So.2d 487.

Fla.App. 1 Dist. 1976. There were probable cause and exigent circumstances justifying warrantless search of defendant's barn, where there was reasonable basis for belief that three drivers who were arrested and found to have marijuana in their vehicles would telephone defendant to warn him, that removal of contraband from barn could not be prevented by agents, that barn could not be secured because of safety factor and that obtaining a search warrant on Christmas Eve would be impossible or long delayed.—Raffield v. State, 333 So.2d 534, quashed in part 351 So.2d 945, on remand 362 So.2d 138.

Fla.App. 2 Dist. 1983. There were no exigent circumstances which justified warrantless entry into defendants' home for purpose of detaining them while securing a search warrant in order to prevent their departure or destruction of marked money allegedly used to purchase marijuana from defendants and the illegality of the initial entry tainted the evidence found by police pursuant to subsequently obtained warrant. U.S.C.A. Const.Amend. 4.—Alderton v. State, 438 So.2d 1000.

Fla.App. 2 Dist. 1982. Although officers had probable cause to search airplane and exigent circumstances made search without warrant proper, since neither opaque wrapping of packages nor their size or shape revealed that they contained marijuana, so as to bring them under "plain view" exception to warrant requirement of Fourth Amendment, warrant was required to open the packages and marijuana discovered when officers opened packages without warrant must be suppressed. U.S.C.A.Const.Amend. 4.—State v. Backner, 413 So.2d 409.

Fla.App. 2 Dist. 1980. Police officers' warrantless entry into defendant's house shortly after vesting of probable cause was justified by exigent circumstances that drug supplier was going to leave in 15 minutes with the evidence and that a destruction of the evidence was being attempted, after the officers opened the door and identified themselves.—State v. Moyer, 394 So.2d 433, review denied 402 So.2d 611.

Fla.App. 2 Dist. 1978. Warrantless entry by police into defendant's home and subsequent search and arrest of defendant on drug charge were unlawful where policemen had six hours between time they received proof that substance purchased on two prior occasions from defendant's associate was cocaine and meeting with defendant's associate and where presence of exigent circumstances, being the possible destruction of contraband by defendant who may have observed his associate's arrest from window or who may have surmised same by virtue of fact that associate did not return, if any, were created by police themselves. West's F.S.A.Const. art. 1, § 12.—Wilson v. State, 363 So.2d 1146.

Fla.App. 2 Dist. 1978. Absent exigent circumstances, plain view doctrine alone could not justify warrantless seizure of marijuana plants growing in backyard of residence, where there was no indication that the contraband was subject to immediate destruction or removal. U.S.C.A.Const. Amend. 4.—Morsman v. State, 360 So.2d 137, writ dismissed 394 So.2d 408, certiorari denied 101 S.Ct. 3066, 452 U.S. 930, 69 L.Ed.2d 431.

Fla.App. 3 Dist. 1991. Exigent circumstance exception to search warrant requirement did not justify officer's warrantless entry into hallway from which he observed cocaine in defendant's bedroom, despite State's argument that defendant's colleague's statement that "cops" were approaching house created concern for well-being of confidential informant and destruction of evidence; it had not yet been established by reliable information that there was contraband on premises, and it was actions of plain-clothed surveillance officers, in converging on house without warrant, which triggered excitement. U.S.C.A. Const.Amend. 4.—Soldo v. State, 583 So.2d 1080.

Fla.App. 3 Dist. 1988. Warrantless seizure of cocaine was valid, where police, after lawfully entering apartment building's grounds, pursued into apartment man who had thrown down concealed gun in common hallway and ran from them, and police then observed defendant from open doorway of apartment holding and attempting to dispose of bag of cocaine.—State v. Batista, 524 So.2d 481.

Fla.App. 3 Dist. 1978. State marine patrol officers may board boat temporarily moored in state waters to inspect owner's boat registration and crawfish permit and thereafter conduct warrantless search of boat based upon smell of marijuana detected by one of officers upon boarding consistent with constitutional right of boat owner or occupant to be free from unreasonable searches and seizures guaranteed by Federal and State Constitutions; such search is justified under exception to rule requiring search warrants, in that there is probable cause for search of boat coupled with exigent circumstances dispensing with necessity for search warrant. West's F.S.A.Const. art. 1, § 12; U.S.C.A.Const. Amends. 4, 14, 14, § 1; West's F.S.A. §§ 370.021(5), 370.14(3)(c), 371.051(5).—Miranda v. State, 354 So.2d 411, certiorari denied 364 So.2d 888.

Fla.App. 3 Dist. 1972. Where police officer was lawfully upon the premises because of an unrelated matter when he observed defendant's possession of drugs and believed that destruction of evidence would be attempted if he delayed his entry, drugs and implements for drug usage seized by police officer were properly admitted into evidence in prosecution for possession of drugs and implements for drug usage. F.S.A. §§ 901.15, 901.21(2) (c).—Hutchinson v. State, 263 So.2d 625.

Fla.App. 4 Dist. 2022. Facts available to police detective would have led reasonable, experienced agent to believe that defendant might be destroying incriminating evidence on his cell phone before search warrant could be secured, and thus exigent circumstances warranted detective to conduct warrantless search of defendant's phone; defendant had been confronted by detectives with evidence that image of child pornography had been uploaded to image messaging application from account name containing one of his known aliases from his internet protocol (IP) address, detective warned defendant that they would talk to his wife about this evidence after defendant refused to allow detective to search his phone, and defendant was seen shaking and frantically swiping and pressing on his phone's screen after interview. U.S. Const. Amend. 4.— State v. Darter, 350 So.3d 370, review denied 2023 WL 2017393.

Application of the exigent circumstances exception to the warrant requirement for search and seizures is particularly compelling in cases involving electronic files, which can easily and quickly be destroyed. U.S. Const. Amend. 4.—Id.

Neither detectives' interview with defendant nor their on-site search of his work computer with his supervisor's consent constituted engaging or threatening to engage in conduct that would violate the Fourth Amendment, and thus detectives did not create the exigent circumstances that led to warrantless seizure of defendant's cell phone for suspected child pornography; seizure of evidence under exigent circumstances was justified by defendant's behavior of shaking and frantically swiping and pressing on his phone's screen after interview and during search of computer, and detectives' experience with how evidence could be quickly deleted. U.S. Const. Amend. 4.—Id.

Fla.App. 4 Dist. 2013. Exigent circumstances existed allowing deputies to seize marijuana without a warrant from residence where they were attempting to execute felony warrants for a named individual, but defendant answered the door instead, as deputies observed marijuana in residence from a legal vantage point, it could reasonably be inferred from the circumstances that defendant was aware of what the deputies saw and smelled when the door was first opened, and under any objective view of these facts, deputies acted reasonably in entering the residence and seizing the contraband before defendant had the opportunity to close the door and dispose of it. U.S.C.A. Const.Amend. 4.—Byron v. State, 120 So.3d 115.

Fla.App. 4 Dist. 2010. Exigent circumstances did not exist to support warrantless entry to search defendant's house; officer had sufficient probable cause to apply for search warrant, based on observations of hand-to-hand transaction, buyer's statements and admissions, and defendant's arrest for heroin possession six months earlier, yet, rather than obtain warrant, police continued surveillance, waited for someone to re-emerge from house, and then arrested person just few feet from front door, state failed to establish that sufficient time did not exist during this interim to procure search warrant, there was no

evidence defendant knew of police presence outside their home or that officers perceived them doing anything to indicate that they were attempting to destroy evidence or to escape. U.S.C.A. Const.Amend. 4.—Diaz v. State, 34 So.3d 797.

Fla.App. 4 Dist. 2009. Exigent circumstances did not exist to justify warrantless entry into apartment after officers received anonymous tip of drug activity at apartment and officers observed, through an open door, that defendant was wiping a kitchen counter with a paper towel and that counter had on it a digital scale with white powdery substance and a straw on it; defendant was not aware of officers' presence, and defendant's act of wiping counter, which could have had mere peanut butter and jelly on it, did not create inference that he was in the process of destroying evidence. (Per Polen, J., with one judge specially concurring.) U.S.C.A. Const. Amend. 4.—Cote v. State, 14 So.3d 1137, rehearing denied.

Fla.App. 4 Dist. 2001. Officers' entry into defendant's motel room and seizure of drugs was justified under the exigent circumstances exception to warrant requirement of the Fourth Amendment; officers were dispatched to defendant's room, not on suspicion of narcotics, but by call that occupant of room wished to surrender on other warrants, defendant opened door, allowing officers to see contraband that was only two to three feet from door, defendant became aware that officers viewed contraband, and officers acted reasonably in entering and seizing contraband before defendant had opportunity to dispose of it. U.S.C.A. Const.Amend. 4.—Gilbert v. State, 789 So.2d 426.

Fla.App. 4 Dist. 1980. Even if defendants did not consent to the boarding and searching of their vessel by sheriff's deputies, there was probable cause to search and exigent circumstances relieved the deputies from the warrant requirement where the vessel had run out of fuel 17 miles at sea and, though defendants said they had been fishing, the vessel was not rigged for fishing and where the bow rode low in the water while it was normal for the bow of such a vessel to ride high and the stern low and where all cabin windows were covered with masking tape, defendants were unable to produce the vessel's registration papers, defendants did not enter the cabin to avoid the rain while the vessel was in tow during rainstorm and one of the deputies testified that he smelled marijuana as he was standing near the vessel.—Chesnut v. State, 382 So.2d 1349, affirmed 404 So.2d 1064.

Fla.App. 4 Dist. 1976. Mere speculative claim that 40 pounds of marijuana discovered in cottage near house in which defendants were arrested "might" have been removed if it had not been seized without warrant was insufficient to justify search of cottage as arising out of "emergency" or from "exigent circumstances," especially where police made such claim only at appellate level.—Merrick v. State, 338 So.2d 77.

Fla.App. 5 Dist. 2005. Warrantless entry of police officers into motel room was justified by exigent circumstances, and thus, seizure of cocaine in plain view did not violate defendant's Fourth Amendment rights; defendant did not tell officers he was alone, officers had been told drugs were being sold out of room, officer saw drugs in room when defendant opened door, it was not unreasonable for officer to make sure no one else was in room to destroy evidence, as officer knew drugs were easily disposable, and

---

† This Case was not selected for publication in the National Reporter System

destruction of contraband prior to time officer could obtain warrant was possible. U.S.C.A. Const.Amend. 4.—Murphy v. State, 898 So.2d 1031, rehearing denied, review denied 910 So.2d 262.

⟶703(1). In general.
C.A.11 (Fla.) 1983. Government agents may search an automobile without a warrant if they can establish probable cause and exigent circumstances; exigency must be determined at the time of the seizure of an automobile, not at the time of its search. U.S.C.A. Const.Amend. 4.—U.S. v. Hall, 716 F.2d 826, certiorari denied 104 S.Ct. 3534, 467 U.S. 1251, 82 L.Ed.2d 840.

⟶703(2). Particular cases.
C.A.11 (Fla.) 1983. Where police officers concededly had probable cause to believe that truck rented by defendant contained marijuana, and, at the time officers seized the truck, there was still a danger that the vehicle or its contents would be moved before officers obtained a valid search warrant, exigent circumstances existed, and the warrantless search of the truck did not violate the Fourth Amendment. U.S.C.A. Const.Amend. 4.—U.S. v. Hall, 716 F.2d 826, certiorari denied 104 S.Ct. 3534, 467 U.S. 1251, 82 L.Ed.2d 840.

C.A.5 (Fla.) 1981. Seizure of marijuana from vessel and campers without a warrant was justified by exigent circumstances exception to warrant requirement, where search was necessarily carried out during excitement and confusion created by drug raid, there was very real danger that one of the suspects would attempt to flee in camper or boat and police were justified in protecting themselves from attack. U.S.C.A.Const. Amend. 4.—U.S. v. Mesa, 660 F.2d 1070, rehearing denied 667 F.2d 93.

Fla. 1980. Although defendant and his companion had been detained by inspection officer at agricultural inspection station and were not in position to drive their van out of jurisdiction, exigent circumstances justifying warrantless search for cannabis did not cease to exist on theory that vehicle was no longer mobile; police should not be required to wait until attempt is made to move vehicle before they are allowed to search it. West's F.S.A. §§ 570.15, 933.19; U.S.C.A.Const. Amends. 4, 14.—Gluesenkamp v. State, 391 So.2d 192, certiorari denied 102 S.Ct. 98, 454 U.S. 818, 70 L.Ed.2d 88.

Fla.App. 2 Dist. 1983. Exigent circumstances were present for warrantless search of defendant's automobile when it left alley into which pharmacist, who was known to have been involved in drug transactions, entered carrying little white bag and out of which pharmacist returned without white bag where officers would have been justified in believing that in time it would take to obtain search warrant pills which officer had overheard by wiretap that defendant intended to purchase from pharmacist would have been removed from automobile. U.S.C.A. Const.Amend. 4.—State v. Gillum, 428 So.2d 755.

Fla.App. 2 Dist. 1977. Where confidential informant, who had previously provided reliable information, told police that an automobile with marijuana in it was parked in liquor lounge, informant stated that he had seen marijuana in the trunk a short time before and described make, year and license number of the vehicle, the police, who found the automobile at the lounge and placed it under surveillance and observed defendant and female companion exit lounge and drive off in the vehicle, had probable cause to search the automobile; exigent circumstances

obviated need for a warrant.—Davis v. State, 350 So.2d 834, certiorari denied 355 So.2d 517.

⟶705. —— In general.
M.D.Fla. 2007. Exigent circumstances that permit warrantless entries include: breaking up a violent fight, preventing the destruction of evidence, putting out a fire in a burning building, attending to a stabbing victim, rescuing a kidnapped infant, or pursuing a fleeing suspect. U.S.C.A. Const.Amend. 4.—Woods v. Valentino, 511 F.Supp.2d 1263.

Fla. 2017. A warrantless home entry, accompanied by a search, seizure, and arrest, is not justified by the exigent circumstance exception of hot pursuit when the underlying conduct for which there is alleged probable cause is a nonviolent misdemeanor and the evidence related thereto is outside the home. U.S. Const. Amend. 4; Fla. Const. art. 1, § 12.—State v. Markus, 211 So.3d 894, rehearing denied 2017 WL 944231.

Fla.App. 3 Dist. 2010. Hot pursuit of a fleeing misdemeanant is permissible where the misdemeanor is punishable by a jail sentence.—State v. Brown, 36 So.3d 770, review denied 63 So.3d 748.

Fla.App. 3 Dist. 2005. Hot pursuit of a fleeing misdemeanant is permissible where the misdemeanor is punishable by a jail sentence. U.S.C.A. Const.Amend 4.—Ulysse v. State, 899 So.2d 1233, review denied 912 So.2d 1218.

Fla.App. 4 Dist. 2023. A warrantless home entry, accompanied by a search, seizure, and arrest is not justified by hot pursuit, for Fourth Amendment purposes, when the underlying conduct for which there is alleged probable cause is a nonviolent misdemeanor and the evidence related thereto is outside the home. U.S. Const. Amend. 4.—Tellam v. State, 373 So.3d 345.

An officer must consider all the circumstances in a pursuit case to determine whether there is a law-enforcement emergency justifying a warrantless home entry under the Fourth Amendment; on many occasions, the officer will have good reason to enter—to prevent imminent harms of violence, destruction of evidence, or escape from the home; but, when the officer has time to get a warrant, he must do so—even though the misdemeanant fled. U.S. Const. Amend. 4.—Id.

⟶706. —— Particular cases in general.
† C.A.11 (Fla.) 2007. Warrantless entry into defendant's trailer and subsequent search came within exigent circumstances exception to warrant requirement; police officer observed defendant conduct drug transaction outside trailer, defendant instigated hot pursuit when he turned to run into trailer, and it was not unreasonable for officer to believe that defendant would destroy evidence. U.S.C.A. Const.Amend. 4.—U.S. v. Echevarria, 238 Fed.Appx. 424, post-conviction relief denied 2009 WL 1649135.

Fla.App. 1 Dist. 2015. Police officer's pursuit of defendant who resisted arrest without violence after officer observed him smoking marijuana did not constitute exigent circumstances sufficient to overcome warrant requirement for officers to pursue defendant into his home to arrest him; defendant's observed crimes were misdemeanors, no evidence indicated any danger to public, police, or property, and there was not any indication that critical evidence would be destroyed while waiting for a warrant to arrest defendant. U.S.C.A. Const.Amend. 4; West's F.S.A. Const.Art. 1, § 12.—Markus v. State, 160 So.3d 488, rehearing denied, decision approved 211 So.3d 894, rehearing denied 2017 WL 944231.

† This Case was not selected for publication in the National Reporter System

Fla.App. 3 Dist. 1981. Where extensive search of premises which turned up revolver did not begin until after defendant had been arrested, handcuffed and taken away, police were clearly not in hot pursuit of defendant when they seized gun so as to justify warrantless search. U.S.C.A.Const. Amend. 4.—State v. Parker, 399 So.2d 24, review denied 408 So.2d 1095.

⊶708. Other particular emergencies or exigent circumstances.

C.A.11 (Fla.) 2018. Officers had probable cause to suspect a residential burglary, and thus exigent circumstances justified warrantless entries under Fourth Amendment, including 10-second entry into vestibule to announce police presence, and four-minute sweep of main structure during which officers saw drugs and paraphernalia in plain view; while driving through area experiencing daytime burglaries, officer observed individual nervously talking on cell phone in front of house whose driveway had no cars in it, watched individual take unusual path to back door, observed second suspect in what appeared to be a lookout position, found two kitchen knives in one suspect's pockets during search, and observed what seemed to be fresh, matching pry marks near back door handle, and suspects' identifications did not match house. U.S. Const. Amend. 4.—Montanez v. Carvajal, 889 F.3d 1202.

† C.A.11 (Fla.) 2009. The combination of probable cause and exigent circumstances justified law enforcement officers' warrantless entry into mobile home; after marijuana field was spotted by helicopter surveillance, officers knocked on the doors of nearby mobile home and announced their presence, and an officer smelled marijuana emanating from a window air conditioner and heard someone running about inside the mobile home, but the person inside refused to open the door. U.S.C.A. Const.Amend. 4.—U.S. v. Reed, 318 Fed.Appx. 774, post-conviction relief denied 2012 WL 1559682.

† C.A.11 (Fla.) 2006. Exigent circumstances existed to justify government agents' warrantless entry and search of apartment defendant shared with her boyfriend for ecstasy (MDMA); before arrest defendant's boyfriend told police he could get them more MDMA tomorrow, defendant went out the back door of the apartment, wearing only a towel and carrying a bag, after asking the agents to wait outside the front door while she got dressed, she ignored another officer's direction to stop, she turned back and went in the back door of the apartment, and agents entered the front after the officer shouted about defendant's actions. U.S.C.A. Const.Amend. 4.—U.S. v. Klinkosz, 163 Fed.Appx. 827.

C.A.11 (Fla.) 1983. Where fire had been extinguished and search for and seizure of valuables was to protect items from looters, and not from destruction by fire, search of burned dwelling did not fall within exigent circumstances created by fire and was therefore unlawful in absence of warrant. U.S.C.A. Const.Amend. 4.—U.S. v. Parr, 716 F.2d 796, rehearing denied 734 F.2d 1481.

Plain-view doctrine was not applicable, where counterfeit bills discovered by fire fighter were not in "plain view" of fire fighter in scope of his investigation of cause of fire or in his efforts to extinguish fire, but rather, were discovered in sugar bowl pursuant to fire fighter's search for salvageable valuables. U.S.C.A. Const.Amend. 4. —Id.

Warrantless search of defendant's house ostensibly to secure valuables after house fire, undertaken pursuant to no routine, standardized procedures, without exigent circumstances, and yielding evidence not in plain view to fire fighters, did not satisfy requirements of Fourth Amendment. U.S.C.A. Const.Amend. 4.—Id.

C.A.5 (Fla.) 1973. Warrantless entry of firemen into empty apartment in a multi-unit apartment building to extinguish fire was lawful, as was the warrantless entry and search of the apartment by deputy fire marshal to determine the cause of the fire, though the fire had then been suppressed, where the cause remained undetermined and ascertaining the cause was necessary to assure that fire was in fact totally extinguished and would not reoccur. F.S.A. § 633.121; U.S.C.A.Const. Amend. 4.—U.S. v. Green, 474 F.2d 1385, certiorari denied 94 S.Ct. 55, 414 U.S. 829, 38 L.Ed.2d 63.

M.D.Fla. 1994. Warrantless entries by fire and police personnel into private residence following fire at residence were permissible, to extent such entries were made from time fire was discovered until time that arson was determined to be cause of fire, and any observations made by those personnel and any evidence seized that was in plain view were admissible at trial; exigent circumstances of fighting fire justified entries, and personnel remained on premises for reasonable time thereafter to investigate origin and cause of fire. U.S.C.A. Const.Amend. 4.—U.S. v. Veltmann, 869 F.Supp. 929, affirmed 87 F.3d 1329.

S.D.Fla. 2012. Exigent circumstances justified police officers' warrantless entry of suspect's residence and arrest of suspect's boyfriend for possession of marijuana, where officers smelled marijuana emanating from suspect's residence, officers saw suspect's boyfriend holding marijuana joint, and both suspect and boyfriend were aware of officers' presence. U.S.C.A. Const. Amend. 4.—Feliciano v. City of Miami Beach, 847 F.Supp.2d 1359.

Fla. 2010. Under the exigent circumstances exception to the search warrant requirement, police may enter a residence without a warrant if an objectively reasonable basis exists for the officer to believe that there is an immediate need for police assistance for the protection of life or substantial property interests. U.S.C.A. Const. Amend. 4.—Twilegar v. State, 42 So.3d 177, rehearing denied, certiorari denied 131 S.Ct. 1476, 562 U.S. 1225, 179 L.Ed.2d 315, denial of post-conviction relief affirmed 175 So.3d 242, rehearing denied, denial of post-conviction relief affirmed 228 So.3d 550, certiorari denied 138 S.Ct. 2578, 201 L.Ed.2d 299.

Fla. 1977. Where police had ample time after probable cause vested to secure search warrant for house trailer, but failed to do so, warrantless search for drugs, undertaken after police heard suspicious movements upon knocking at the door, violated Fourth Amendment. West's F.S.A.Const. art. 1, § 12; U.S.C.A.Const. Amends. 4, 14.—Hornblower v. State, 351 So.2d 716.

Fla.App. 1 Dist. 1996. Officer's mere suspicion that suspect was, or was about to be, involved in criminal activity did not justify officer's warrantless entry into home of defendant third party for apprehension of suspected offender or seizure of marijuana and money officer saw defendant third party try to conceal. U.S.C.A. Const.Amend. 4.—Britt v. State, 673 So.2d 934.

Fla.App. 2 Dist. 2018. Entering a home to investigate a suspected burglary or to check on the safety of its residents can constitute exigent circumstances sufficient to permit a warrantless search. U.S. Const. Amend. 4.—Aguilar v. State, 259 So.3d 262.

Officers' initial warrantless entry into defendant's home was lawful pursuant to exigent circumstances exception to warrant requirement; officers had an objectively reasonable basis to support search of defendant's home in light of 9-1-1 call, on-scene reports of a shooting, broken window, scent of gunpowder, and the unknown status of potential occupants. U.S. Const. Amend. 4.—Id.

Fla.App. 2 Dist. 2018. The police may enter a residence without a warrant if an objectively reasonable basis exists for the officer to believe that there is an immediate need for police assistance for the protection of life or substantial property interests. U.S. Const. Amend. 4.—Lapace v. State, 257 So.3d 588.

Fla.App. 2 Dist. 1985. "Exigency rule" did not justify officer's search of living room and seizure of cigarette case containing syringe, cocaine, and marijuana, where a search was not required to determine nature of drugs taken by defendant so that proper treatment could be administered.—Campbell v. State, 477 So.2d 1068.

Fla.App. 4 Dist. 2004. Police officers' warrantless search of residence at which arrestee stated drugs were located was not justified by exigent circumstances, for purposes of defendant's motion to suppress; any exigent circumstances were created by officers themselves by choosing to proceed to residence and use arrestee as their agent to gain entry, rather than obtain a warrant. U.S.C.A. Const.Amend. 4.—State v. Garcia, 866 So.2d 124.

4. PLAIN VIEW.

⬅**711. In general.**
Fla.App. 1 Dist. 2022. Both the plain view and plain touch doctrines depend on the legality of the intrusion that enables officer to perceive and physically seize the property in question, and the probable cause to associate the property with criminal activity. U.S. Const. Amend. 4.—Atwood v. State, 348 So.3d 698.

Fla.App. 4 Dist. 2018. The State must present more than the naked subjective statement of a police officer who has a "feeling" based on "experience" to support a seizure under the plain touch exception to the warrant requirement. U.S. Const. Amend. 4.—T.T. v. State, 253 So.3d 15.

⬅**712. Elements of plain view exception in general.**
M.D.Fla. 2018. Warrantless seizure of skimmer and access devices contained within shopping bag was lawful under plain view doctrine; having obtained lawful possession of hotel room, resort personnel were permitted to invite Secret Service special agent into room, once inside room, agent observed numerous access devices in plain view, and suitcase inadvertently fell from bed, spilling contents of shopping bag and exposing to plain view access devices and skimmer. U.S. Const. Amend. 4.—United States v. Valdarnini, 314 F.Supp.3d 1312.

M.D.Fla. 2015. During the course of a lawful knock and talk, officers may make plain-view observations and use them to support a warrant application. U.S. Const. Amend. 4.—United States v. Holmes, 143 F.Supp.3d 1252, affirmed

770 Fed.Appx. 1013, certiorari denied 140 S.Ct. 2518, 206 L.Ed.2d 468.

S.D.Fla. 2021. The plain-view exception to the search warrant requirement applies only when the police have a right of access to the place where the contraband is located. U.S. Const. Amend. 4.—United States v. Howard, 557 F.Supp.3d 1262.

Fla.App. 1 Dist. 2017. Under plain view doctrine, which differs from open view doctrine, if police are lawfully in position from which they view object, if its incriminating character is immediately apparent, and if officers have lawful right of access to object itself, they may seize it, without warrant. U.S. Const. Amend. 4; Fla. Const. art. 1, § 12.—Purifoy v. State, 225 So.3d 867, review denied 2017 WL 5508743.

Fla.App. 2 Dist. 2008. Open-view is treated similarly to plain-view, with the exception that some exigent circumstance is required to justify warrantless entry into the protected area in an open-view situation. U.S.C.A. Const.Amend. 4.—Oliver v. State, 989 So.2d 16, rehearing denied, review denied 4 So.3d 677.

Fla.App. 3 Dist. 2019. The plain view doctrine requires that three elements be satisfied: (1) the police officer is in a place where he has a lawful right to be; (2) in the course of his presence the officer inadvertently comes upon an object which is openly visible; and (3) it is immediately apparent to the officer that the object constitutes evidence of a crime.—Hedvall v. State, 283 So.3d 901, review denied 2020 WL 1650313.

Fla.App. 5 Dist. 2018. The "plain view doctrine" provides that items in plain view may be seized when (1) the seizing officer is in a position where he has a legitimate right to be, (2) the incriminating character of the evidence is immediately apparent, and (3) the seizing officer has a lawful right of access to the object. U.S. Const. Amend. 4.—State v. Archer, 259 So.3d 999, review denied 2019 WL 2205765, on subsequent appeal 309 So.3d 287, rehearing denied.

Fla.App. 5 Dist. 2016. The plain view doctrine applies when: (1) the police view the contraband from a place they have a legitimate right to be; (2) the incriminating character of the contraband is immediately apparent to the viewing police officer; and (3) the police officer has a lawful right of access to the contraband. U.S. Const. Amend. 4.—Friedson v. State, 207 So.3d 961, on remand 2017 WL 7795602.

⬅**713. Inadvertency.**
Fla.App. 4 Dist. 1983. Officer's inadvertent discovery of marijuana while he searched behind walk-in closet door for burglar did not go beyond parameters of his constitutional license, where officer had probable cause to believe burglary had been or was taking place in apartment at time of search, and marijuana, resting on closet shelf at eye level, was only partially covered, and was therefore within plain view.—State v. Mann, 440 So.2d 406.

⬅**714. Lawful presence or vantage point.**
M.D.Fla. 2018. The "plain view doctrine" permits the seizure of objects which fall within the plain view of an officer who has a right to be in the position to have that view. U.S. Const. Amend. 4.—United States v. Valdarnini, 314 F.Supp.3d 1312.

Fla. 1981. Police may seize any evidence that is in plain view during course of their legitimate emergency activities.—Zeigler v. State, 402 So.2d 365, certiorari denied 102 S.Ct. 1739, 455 U.S. 1035, 72 L.Ed.2d 153, denial of post-conviction

---

† This Case was not selected for publication in the National Reporter System

relief affirmed 632 So.2d 48, certiorari denied 115 S.Ct. 104, 513 U.S. 830, 130 L.Ed.2d 52, denial of post-conviction relief affirmed 654 So.2d 1162, rehearing denied, denial of habeas corpus affirmed 345 F.3d 1300, rehearing and rehearing denied 90 Fed.Appx. 391, certiorari denied 125 S.Ct. 280, 543 U.S. 842, 160 L.Ed.2d 67, denial of post-conviction relief affirmed 967 So.2d 125, rehearing denied, denial of post-conviction relief affirmed 116 So.3d 255, certiorari denied 134 S.Ct. 825, 571 U.S. 1114, 187 L.Ed.2d 694.

Fla.App. 1 Dist. 2013. The existence and extent of a license that would permit a police "knock and talk" encounter with a resident of a home depends on the circumstances; homeowners who post "No Trespassing" or "No Soliciting" signs effectively negate a license to enter the posted property, and where no signs forbid entry, and there is a recognizable pathway to a front door, a limited license to enter the property on the pathway and knock on the door exists, and where such a license is established, the resident does not have a reasonable expectation of privacy in what is plainly viewed from the vantage point of a temporary visitor who walks along the pathway or stands at the doorway. U.S.C.A. Const. Amend. 4; West's F.S.A. § 810.09.—Powell v. State, 120 So.3d 577, on rehearing.

Fla.App. 1 Dist. 1990. Mere probable cause is insufficient to justify warrantless seizure of evidence located in constitutionally protected area, even though police officer may have lawfully viewed evidence from point outside protected area. U.S.C.A. Const.Amend. 4.—State v. Starkey, 559 So.2d 335.

Fla.App. 1 Dist. 1980. Plain view doctrine, which is exception to warrant requirement, permits admissibility of evidence seized by officer who has independent justification for being present unconnected with search against accused and who inadvertently comes across object which is obviously evident; doctrine presupposes officer's legal right to be where he was at time evidence was first seen.—Hurt v. State, 388 So.2d 281, review denied 399 So.2d 1146.

Fla.App. 2 Dist. 2017. The open view doctrine applies when an officer is located outside of a constitutionally protected area looking in; if the officer sees contraband in that situation, it furnishes him probable cause to seize the item, but he must either obtain a warrant or have some exception to the warrant requirement before he may enter the protected area and seize the contraband. U.S. Const. Amend. 4.—Davis v. State, 226 So.3d 318, rehearing denied.

Fla.App. 3 Dist. 2004. Police officers may seize any evidence that is in plain view during the course of legitimate emergency activities that justify a warrantless entry and search. U.S.C.A. Const.Amend. 4.—State v. Barmeier, 878 So.2d 411, rehearing denied, review denied 891 So.2d 549.

Fla.App. 3 Dist. 1994. Under plain view doctrine, police officer is allowed to conduct search if object is so placed that it may be seen by officer from where he has right to be and it is apparent to officer that object constitutes evidence of crime; officer can also arrest those persons in whose immediate control seized objects may be. U.S.C.A. Const.Amend. 4.—Daniels v. State, 634 So.2d 187.

Fla.App. 4 Dist. 2018. The "plain view exception" to the warrant requirement allows officers to seize contraband if they can view the contraband from a lawful position and the unlawful

nature of the contraband is immediately apparent. U.S. Const. Amend. 4.—T.T. v. State, 253 So.3d 15.

The rationale of the plain-view doctrine is that if contraband is left in open view and is observed by a police officer from a lawful vantage point, there has been no invasion of a legitimate expectation of privacy and thus no "search" within the meaning of the Fourth Amendment—or at least no search independent of the initial intrusion that gave the officers their vantage point. U.S. Const. Amend. 4.—Id.

☞**715. Incriminating nature of item; nexus.**

M.D.Fla. 1976. Lawful statutory authority to search also confers right to seize evidence of criminal activity which is discovered in plain view during course of search.—U.S. v. Cooper, 409 F.Supp. 364, affirmed 542 F.2d 1171.

S.D.Fla. 2021. The plain-view exception to the search warrant requirement applies only when the police have a right of access to the place where the contraband is located. U.S. Const. Amend. 4.—United States v. Howard, 557 F.Supp.3d 1262.

S.D.Fla. 2008. When there is danger that evidence seen inside residence may be destroyed or removed before warrant can be obtained, police are permitted under plain view doctrine to enter residence and seize contraband. U.S.C.A. Const. Amend. 4.—U.S. v. Smalls, 617 F.Supp.2d 1240, affirmed 342 Fed.Appx. 505, certiorari denied 130 S.Ct. 1094, 558 U.S. 1128, 175 L.Ed.2d 912.

S.D.Fla. 1975. Contraband which is in "plain view" of an officer who is where he has a right to be may be seized. U.S.C.A.Const. Amend. 4.—U.S. v. One (1) 43 Foot Sailing Vessel Winds Will, License O.N. 531317/U.S. and Equipment, 405 F.Supp. 879, affirmed U.S. v. One (1) 43 Foot Sailing Vessel 'Winds Will,' License O.N. 531317/US', 538 F.2d 694.

Fla.App. 1 Dist. 1981. Open view theory of search applies to the situation where both the officer and the contraband are positioned in a nonconstitutionally protected area, so that any resulting seizure is not subjected to any Fourth Amendment strictures, and to the situation in which the officer is himself located outside of a constitutionally protected area and observes contraband within a protected area, in which case he is furnished with probable cause to the seize the contraband. U.S.C.A.Const.Amend. 4.—Raettig v. State, 406 So.2d 1273.

Fla.App. 1 Dist. 1981. Law enforcement officers trespassing in constitutionally protected area cannot, absent some exception to warrant requirement, justify seizure of contraband on ground that it is in plain view; however, issue of Fourth Amendment violation is not determined solely by mere fact that officers were or were not trespassing upon property where seizure occurred. U.S.C.A.Const. Amend. 4.—DeMontmorency v. State, 401 So.2d 858, decision approved 464 So.2d 1201.

Fla.App. 2 Dist. 2017. The open view doctrine applies when an officer is located outside of a constitutionally protected area looking in; if the officer sees contraband in that situation, it furnishes him probable cause to seize the item, but he must either obtain a warrant or have some exception to the warrant requirement before he may enter the protected area and seize the contraband. U.S. Const. Amend. 4.—Davis v. State, 226 So.3d 318, rehearing denied.

Fla.App. 2 Dist. 2004. If the police enter a home under exigent circumstances and, prior to

---

† **This Case was not selected for publication in the National Reporter System**

making a determination that the exigency no longer exists, find contraband in plain view, they may lawfully seize the illegal items. U.S.C.A. Const.Amend. 4.—State v. Riggs, 890 So.2d 465, review granted 900 So.2d 554, decision approved 918 So.2d 274.

Fla.App. 2 Dist. 1994. Any visible contraband is considered to be in plain view when officer is in place where officer has right to be. U.S.C.A. Const.Amend. 4.—State v. Hite, 642 So.2d 55.

Fla.App. 2 Dist. 1994. Once probable cause exists because of "open view" of incriminating evidence, police must obtain warrant, unless exception to warrant requirement is present, to justify entry into protected area and seizure of evidence. U.S.C.A. Const.Amend. 4.—State v. Waterman, 638 So.2d 1032, review denied 649 So.2d 236.

Fla.App. 2 Dist. 1984. A valid "preintrusion open view" search occurs when an officer, who is located outside of a constitutionally protected area, looks into protected area and observes contraband; officer's observation merely furnishes him with probable cause to seize item and he still must either obtain a warrant or qualify under an exception to warrant to requirement before he may enter protected area and seize contraband. U.S.C.A. Const.Amend. 4.—Randall v. State, 458 So.2d 822.

Fla.App. 2 Dist. 1984. When officer legally enters constitutionally protected area and observes contraband in plain view, he may constitutionally seize it without first obtaining warrant.—State v. Myers, 454 So.2d 764.

Fla.App. 2 Dist. 1978. Under the plain view doctrine, police officer who has prior justification for an intrusion can seize contraband or incriminating evidence which is in plain view; when contraband is spotted under circumstances falling within purview of the plain view doctrine, it may be immediately seized because of its nature, but if items in question are innocent by themselves, they may only be seized if officer has probable cause to believe that what he sees in plain view is incriminating evidence.—State v. Redding, 362 So.2d 170.

Fla.App. 2 Dist. 1978. Plain view doctrine does not require that officer's presence at vantage point from which he observes contraband must be justified by warrant to search for another object, by hot pursuit, or by a search incident to a lawful arrest; a legitimate reason for officer's presence unconnected with a search directed against a defendant or with making an arrest of defendant will suffice to legally place officer at the vantage point.—State v. Ruiz, 360 So.2d 1320.

Fla.App. 3 Dist. 2014. Under the plain view exception to the warrant requirement, it is critical that the officer be in the constitutionally protected area lawfully before recovering items thought to be instrumentalities of a crime. U.S.C.A. Const. Amend. 4.—Brown v. State, 152 So.3d 619, rehearing denied, review denied 168 So.3d 228, appeal after remand 210 So.3d 61.

Fla.App. 3 Dist. 1994. Under plain view doctrine, police officer is allowed to conduct search if object is so placed that it may be seen by officer from where he has right to be and it is apparent to officer that object constitutes evidence of crime; officer can also arrest those persons in whose immediate control seized objects may be. U.S.C.A. Const.Amend. 4.—Daniels v. State, 634 So.2d 187.

Fla.App. 3 Dist. 1981. Warrantless seizure of evidence in plain sight is constitutionally permissible only where evidence is observed in plain sight without benefit of search, police have legal right to be where they are at time of observation, and police have probable cause to believe that evidence observed constitutes contraband or fruits, instrumentalities or evidence of crime. U.S.C.A.Const. Amend. 4.—State v. Parker, 399 So.2d 24, review denied 408 So.2d 1095.

Fla.App. 4 Dist. 2018. Under the "plain view doctrine" items in plain view may be seized without a warrant if the incriminating character of the items are immediately apparent to the officer. U.S. Const. Amend. 4.—Peynado v. State, 254 So.3d 457, on remand 2018 WL 11232946.

Upon seeing items in plain view, the officer must have probable cause to believe a crime is being, is about to be, or has been committed. U.S. Const. Amend. 4.—Id.

In context of plain view doctrine, although officer is not required to know that items are contraband for certain, there must be facts available to the officer which would lead a reasonable person of caution to believe that certain items may be contraband. U.S. Const. Amend. 4.—Id.

In context of plain view doctrine, facts leading a reasonable person of caution to believe that certain items may be contraband may include not only the appearance of the suspected contraband, but also all of the surrounding circumstances. U.S. Const. Amend. 4.—Id.

Based on an officer's training and experience, the incriminating nature of a substance in open view may be determined by officer's visual observation and identification of the substance. U.S. Const. Amend. 4.—Id.

Fla.App. 4 Dist. 2018. The "plain view exception" to the warrant requirement allows officers to seize contraband if they can view the contraband from a lawful position and the unlawful nature of the contraband is immediately apparent. U.S. Const. Amend. 4.—T.T. v. State, 253 So.3d 15.

The plain view exception to the warrant requirement may not be used to extend a general exploratory search from one object to another until something incriminating emerges. U.S. Const. Amend. 4.—Id.

If the incriminating character of the object in "plain view" is not "immediately apparent," without conducting some further search of the object, the plain view doctrine cannot justify its seizure. U.S. Const. Amend. 4.—Id.

Fla.App. 4 Dist. 2012. A police officer does not have to know that a certain item is contraband in order to establish probable cause to arrest or search. U.S.C.A. Const.Amend. 4.—Santiago v. State, 84 So.3d 455, appeal after remand 124 So.3d 978.

Fla.App. 4 Dist. 2000. Warrantless plain view seizures are proper when an officer is lawfully at a location and observes contraband.—State v. Havel, 756 So.2d 1067, on remand 2001 WL 36125689.

Fla.App. 5 Dist. 2019. The law does not require that a law enforcement officer know with certainty that an item or substance is contraband in order for there to be probable cause that a crime is being committed in the officer's presence, so as to justify plain view seizure. U.S. Const. Amend. 4.—State v. Thornton, 286 So.3d 924.

Fla.App. 5 Dist. 2018. If the police enter a home under exigent circumstances and, prior to making a determination that the exigency no longer exists, find contraband in plain view, they

---

† **This Case was not selected for publication in the National Reporter System**

may lawfully seize the illegal item. U.S. Const. Amend. 4.—State v. Archer, 259 So.3d 999, review denied 2019 WL 2205765, on subsequent appeal 309 So.3d 287, rehearing denied.

Fla.App. 5 Dist. 2003. If the police enter a home under exigent circumstances and, prior to making a determination that the exigency no longer exists, find contraband in plain view, they may lawfully seize the illegal items. U.S.C.A. Const.Amend. 4; West's F.S.A. Const. Art. 1, § 12.—Davis v. State, 834 So.2d 322.

Fla.App. 6 Dist. 2023. In determining whether incriminating nature of evidence is immediately apparent, as would provide probable cause for seizure, police are not required to know that item is contraband. U.S. Const. Amend. 4.—State v. Andreskewicz, 363 So.3d 229.

Determination that incriminating nature of evidence is immediately apparent, as would provide probable cause for seizure, requires that facts available to officer would lead reasonable man of caution to believe that certain items may be contraband; subjective belief on part of officer need not ultimately be proven true. U.S. Const. Amend. 4.—Id.

☞**716. Vehicles in general.**

Fla.App. 6 Dist. 2023. "Open view doctrine" is applicable in cases involving "pre-intrusion" search where law enforcement officer is standing outside automobile looking in and observes item that he or she has probable cause to believe is associated with criminal activity, and, if officer observes contraband, it only furnishes him probable cause to seize item, and officer must then either obtain warrant or have some exception to warrant requirement before officer may enter protected area and seize contraband. U.S. Const. Amend. 4.—State v. Andreskewicz, 363 So.3d 229.

☞**718. —— In general.**

C.A.11 (Fla.) 2006. Search of premises and lockbox pursuant to warrant authorizing officers to search for and seize evidence of illicit drug activity was valid, and seizure of pornographic photographs of minor children was legitimately conducted pursuant to plain view doctrine; warrant specifically authorized officers to seize "photographs that would be probative to establish residency," officers, alerted to lockbox by narcotics dog, were justified in searching it for evidence of drugs or photographs, and it was immediately apparent to officers, i.e., they had probable cause to believe, that among what they found in lockbox was evidence of crime of child pornography. U.S.C.A. Const.Amend. 4.—U.S. v. Smith, 459 F.3d 1276, certiorari denied 127 S.Ct. 990, 549 U.S. 1137, 166 L.Ed.2d 747.

M.D.Fla. 2009. Incriminating nature of pornographic magazines seized during warranted search of arrestee's home for drugs and drug paraphernalia was immediately apparent, so that warrantless seizure could be justified under "plain view" exception to warrant requirement; detective had become aware that juveniles made allegations that arrestee had engaged in sexual activity with minors, and magazines, which were entitled "Just Come of Age," "Live Young Girls," and "Babyface," were contained on magazine rack located in arrestee's bedroom. U.S.C.A. Const.Amend. 4.—Bryant v. Mostert, 636 F.Supp.2d 1303.

M.D.Fla. 1994. Plain view evidence of arson seized in warrantless reentries into first and second floors of house was admissible in ensuing arson prosecution, including observations made by fire and police personnel, photographs and videotape taken by firefighter, and smoke alarm batteries seized by firefighter; reentries were permissible as continuation of initial investigation, and points of origin of fire were located on first and second levels. U.S.C.A. Const.Amend. 4.—U.S. v. Veltmann, 869 F.Supp. 929, affirmed 87 F.3d 1329.

Fla. 1971. Neither State nor Federal Constitutions require prior judicially supervised hearing for determination of probable cause prior to issuance of arrest and search warrants obtained on account of alleged violation of statute making it unlawful to knowingly exhibit harmful motion picture to a minor. F.S.A. § 847.013(1), (2) (a).—Davison v. State, 251 So.2d 841, vacated 93 S.Ct. 3034, 413 U.S. 915, 37 L.Ed.2d 1037, on remand 288 So.2d 483, application denied 94 S.Ct. 1463, 415 U.S. 943, 39 L.Ed.2d 560.

Fla.App. 1 Dist. 2017. Under open view doctrine, objects such as weapons or contraband found in public place can be seized without warrant. U.S. Const. Amend. 4; Fla. Const. art. 1, § 12.—Purifoy v. State, 225 So.3d 867, review denied 2017 WL 5508743.

Fla.App. 1 Dist. 1992. Marine Patrol officer could seize two bags of oysters that were in plain view under boat's cull board after he boarded boat at oyster monitoring station. West's F.S.A. § 370.021(5)(b); U.S.C.A. Const.Amend. 4.—State v. Starkey, 605 So.2d 963.

Fla.App. 1 Dist. 1980. Officers sent to "secure" warehouse, who knocked on rear door and, as door was opened, announced their identity, did not comply with requirement of "knock and announce" statute that officers announce their purpose as well as their name and authority, and thus contraband in warehouse seized when seen by officers as warehouse door was opened had to be suppressed. West's F.S.A. § 901.19(1).—Hurt v. State, 388 So.2d 281, review denied 399 So.2d 1146.

Fla.App. 1 Dist. 1979. There was probable cause, or at least well-founded suspicion, to believe defendant possessed contraband in his automobile at time of stop, and after stop took place, frisk was warranted, especially in light of information that defendant carried knife, and while conducting frisk, arresting officer saw, in plain view, contraband in car, and thus subsequent search based on consent and probable cause was proper.—Addison v. State, 378 So.2d 838.

Fla.App. 2 Dist. 2006. Contraband discovered in plain view during a permissible protective sweep need not be suppressed; however, to support such a search, the police officer must articulate facts sufficient to warrant a reasonable belief that the house harbored dangerous individuals. U.S.C.A. Const.Amend. 4.—Nolin v. State, 946 So.2d 52, on remand 2007 WL 7010152.

Fla.App. 2 Dist. 2005. Officer had probable cause to seize two halves of car, rear taillights, and two empty 12-pack beer cartons from car's trunk as part of his investigation of accident which occurred after defendant was involved in high-speed chase with officer and crashed; officer had duty as part of investigation of accident involving death, to file report detailing findings regarding circumstances resulting in death and damage to vehicle, to fully review accident and ensure safety of highway, officer had to search and take possession of car to conduct examination to determine cause of wreck, and two pieces of car and taillights were in open view on ground and were properly seized without warrant. West's F.S.A. § 316.066(3)(a) 1, 2.—State v. Jacoby, 907 So.2d 676, review dismissed 918 So.2d 292.

Fla.App. 2 Dist. 1984. Nonharassing aerial surveillance of defendant's fenced backyard, in which defendant had manifested a reasonable expectation of privacy from ground surveillance by constructing a fence, was a legally permissible preintrusion "open view" search, and thus, subsequent seizure of contraband from defendant's backyard by officers, who had obtained warrant following search, was also permissible. U.S.C.A. Const.Amend. 4.—Randall v. State, 458 So.2d 822.

Fla.App. 2 Dist. 1981. Officer who legally entered constitutionally protected area under the emergency doctrine and observed contraband in plain view could constitutionally seize it without first obtaining warrant.—State v. Jenkins, 406 So.2d 1236.

Fla.App. 2 Dist. 1979. Although magazines not described in original warrant could be seized on theory officers were in a place where they had a legal right to be and the magazines were additional items in plain view, reels of film which had to be unboxed and placed on a projector in order to be seen could not be lawfully seized under such "plain view" theory.—Schergen v. State, 371 So.2d 575, dismissed 374 So.2d 100.

Fla.App. 2 Dist. 1978. Even though judge issued no search warrant authorizing seizure of pictures, where judge, accompanied by law enforcement officers, went to adult bookstore where defendant worked and which was open to the public viewed each picture that was to be seized and which were in plain view, determined that each was obscene, and then told accompanying officers exactly what they should seize, seizure of the photographs was legal.—Marshall v. State, 362 So.2d 701.

Fla.App. 3 Dist. 2009. Fact that officers could see gloves and tool boxes through windows of van did not provide independent basis for warrantless entry into van. U.S.C.A. Const.Amend. 4.—Aldin v. State, 21 So.3d 68.

Fla.App. 5 Dist. 2018. Canine remains were properly seized from defendant's yard under plain view doctrine; police officers, responding to a report from defendant's neighbor of possible animal cruelty in progress, observed defendant in back of house, after midnight, pacing behind fence and saying something along the lines of "get down" or "lay down" and heard what appeared to be something striking flesh, and after speaking with defendant and learning that he had struck dog as punishment, found dog lying down in corner of yard where defendant had been, lying listless, and quickly determined that dog, which appeared to be bound and gagged and had bloodied tongue, was dead. U.S. Const. Amend. 4.—State v. Archer, 259 So.3d 999, review denied 2019 WL 2205765, on subsequent appeal 309 So.3d 287, rehearing denied.

⟜**719.** —— **Stolen property in general.**

Fla.App. 3 Dist. 1985. Officer, while engaged in performing lawful duties, may seize without search warrant any goods in plain view that he has probable cause to believe are stolen and arrest those persons in whose immediate control goods may be.—Wright v. State, 471 So.2d 155.

Fla.App. 3 Dist. 1976. Where patrolling officer, who while investigating several burglaries, received a BOLO to be on lookout for described automobile occupied by described individuals and several hours later spotted such a car and occupants and so advised fellow officer, who

lived in area and whose home had recently been burglarized, and was advised by the latter to pull the car over and request some identification, the brief detention was reasonable, and when fellow officer arrived on scene within minutes and observed in vehicle an item stolen from his house, search of vehicle was also reasonable.—Coney v. State, 341 So.2d 238.

⟜**720(1). In general.**

Fla. 1994. Under "open view doctrine," objects such as weapons or contraband found in public place can be seized without warrant; such situation occurs when both officer and contraband are in area where defendant has no reasonable expectation of privacy. U.S.C.A. Const. Amend. 4; West's F.S.A. Const. Art. 1, § 12.—Jones v. State, 648 So.2d 669, rehearing denied, certiorari denied 115 S.Ct. 2588, 515 U.S. 1147, 132 L.Ed.2d 836, post-conviction relief denied 2005 WL 6932251, affirmed 998 So.2d 573, revised on rehearing, post-conviction relief denied 2005 WL 6932252, affirmed 998 So.2d 573, revised on rehearing, and revised on rehearing, habeas corpus denied 998 So.2d 573, revised on rehearing, and revised on rehearing, and revised on rehearing, post-conviction relief denied 2009 WL 9047495, affirmed 53 So.3d 230, rehearing denied, post-conviction relief denied 2011 WL 10483396, affirmed 141 So.3d 132, rehearing denied, certiorari denied 133 S.Ct. 661, 568 U.S. 1033, 184 L.Ed.2d 471, habeas corpus denied 2013 WL 5504371, affirmed 834 F.3d 1299, certiorari denied 137 S.Ct. 2245, 582 U.S. 907, 198 L.Ed.2d 683, denial of post-conviction relief affirmed 256 So.3d 801, certiorari denied 139 S.Ct. 1341, 203 L.Ed.2d 582.

Fla.App. 1 Dist. 2017. Under open view doctrine, objects such as weapons or contraband found in public place can be seized without warrant. U.S. Const. Amend. 4; Fla. Const. art. 1, § 12.—Purifoy v. State, 225 So.3d 867, review denied 2017 WL 5508743.

⟜**720(2). Particular cases.**

† **C.A.11 (Fla.) 2020.** Police lieutenant's "cursory search" of apartment did not exceed the limited scope of searches authorized under the emergency-aid exception to the search warrant requirement, and thus the plain view doctrine applied to justify seizure of firearm found in bathroom on toilet; dispatch had reported a domestic-abuse incident in apartment where shots had been fired, and the bathroom was within the realm of areas where a victim might be found. U.S. Const. Amend. 4.—United States v. Jones, 798 Fed.Appx. 434.

† **C.A.11 (Fla.) 2018.** Ultimate seizure of firearm by detective was lawful under plain-view doctrine; detective was lawfully present in garage where firearm was found and firearm was in plain view, detective had lawful right to access firearm, and detective was in lawful possession of firearm when defendant informed him that he had been to prison, giving detective probable cause to believe that firearm was evidence of a crime, such as felon-in-possession. U.S. Const. Amend. 4; 18 U.S.C.A. § 922(g)(1).—United States v. Kendricks, 758 Fed.Appx. 687, certiorari denied 139 S.Ct. 2038, 204 L.Ed.2d 236.

† **C.A.11 (Fla.) 2018.** Warrantless seizure of firearm and crack cocaine from defendant's vehicle was authorized under plain view exception to warrant requirement; officers were lawfully on patrol in public area where defendant's vehicle was located, officers could see firearm in cup holder from standing position next to vehicle,

officers had lawful right to access interior of vehicle under automobile exception to warrant requirement, and officers were not required to know with absolute certainty that substance in clear bag in vehicle was crack cocaine before seizing it. U.S. Const. Amend. 4.—United States v. Gant, 756 Fed.Appx. 898, certiorari denied 139 S.Ct. 1466, 203 L.Ed.2d 696, post-conviction relief dismissed by 2021 WL 1199641, certificate of appealability denied 2021 WL 4472820, certiorari denied 142 S.Ct. 504, 211 L.Ed.2d 306.

† **C.A.11 (Fla.) 2017.** Police officer could see drugs and assault rifle from public hallway outside of apartment, and thus search warrant was not predicated on unlawful observation, despite argument that officer pushed aside someone who was standing in doorway of apartment to see drugs and assault rifle; officer testified that he saw assault rifle and drugs from public hallway of apartment prior to moving anyone in doorway. U.S. Const. Amend. 4.—United States v. McDuffie, 691 Fed.Appx. 568, certiorari denied 138 S.Ct. 284, 583 U.S. 903, 199 L.Ed.2d 182.

C.A.5 (Fla.) 1976. Officers who entered premises of third party to execute arrest warrants and who after arresting defendants heard scuffling sounds coming from the bathroom were justified in making a cursory search to secure the immediate area and to insure their own physical safety, and seizure of cocaine and paraphernalia in plain view in the bathroom was reasonable. 18 U.S.C.A. § 2; Comprehensive Drug Abuse Prevention and Control Act of 1970, §§ 401(1)(a), 406, 408, 1002(a), 1013, 21 U.S.C.A. §§ 841(a)(1), 846, 848, 952(a), 963; 42 U.S.C.A. § 1983; U.S.C.A.Const. Amend. 4.—U.S. v. Cravero, 545 F.2d 406, certiorari denied Miller v. U.S., 97 S.Ct. 1123, 429 U.S. 1100, 51 L.Ed.2d 549, certiorari denied Cook v. U.S., 97 S.Ct. 1679, 430 U.S. 983, 52 L.Ed.2d 377, rehearing denied 97 S.Ct. 2689, 431 U.S. 960, 53 L.Ed.2d 279, certiorari denied 97 S.Ct. 1679, 430 U.S. 983, 52 L.Ed.2d 377, rehearing denied 97 S.Ct. 2990, 433 U.S. 915, 53 L.Ed.2d 1102.

Fla. 1975. Under the "plain view" doctrine, gun was properly seized by the police during warrantless search of defendant's California apartment which he shared with two others, where, despite defendant's claim that the gun was found in his bedroom in a drawer, the record clearly showed that it was found in open drawer in kitchen; furthermore, since a codefendant, who had been arrested on suspicion of armed robbery, was only a few feet away from the drawer containing the gun, it fell within the "search incident to arrest" exception.—Spinkellink v. State, 313 So.2d 666, certiorari denied Spenkelink v. Florida, 96 S.Ct. 3227, 428 U.S. 911, 49 L.Ed.2d 1221, rehearing denied 97 S.Ct. 194, 429 U.S. 874, 50 L.Ed.2d 157.

☞721. —— **Controlled substances and related items.**

† **C.A.11 (Fla.) 2018.** Warrantless search of defendant's vehicle was authorized under automobile exception to warrant requirement; vehicle was operational as evidenced by interior lights and radio being on, officers found marijuana, hydrocodone pills, and $1,102 in cash on defendant's person after arresting him for assaulting officer, and officer could plainly see clear bag of what looked like crack cocaine in vehicle. U.S. Const. Amend. 4.—United States v. Gant, 756 Fed.Appx. 898, certiorari denied 139 S.Ct. 1466, 203 L.Ed.2d 696, post-conviction relief dismissed by 2021 WL 1199641, certificate of appealability

denied 2021 WL 4472820, certiorari denied 142 S.Ct. 504, 211 L.Ed.2d 306.

Warrantless seizure of firearm and crack cocaine from defendant's vehicle was authorized under plain view exception to warrant requirement; officers were lawfully on patrol in public area where defendant's vehicle was located, officers could see firearm in cup holder from standing position next to vehicle, officers had lawful right to access interior of vehicle under automobile exception to warrant requirement, and officers were not required to know with absolute certainty that substance in clear bag in vehicle was crack cocaine before seizing it. U.S. Const. Amend. 4.—Id.

C.A.11 (Fla.) 2018. Officers' re-entry into residence, to observe marijuana and drug paraphernalia earlier discovered in plain view during warrantless entries that were justified by burglary-related exigent circumstances, did not violate the Fourth Amendment, even though exigency that underlay initial searches had passed; homeowner lost any reasonable expectation of privacy in areas already searched, and there was no contention that additional entries exceeded scope of initial and permissible sweep. U.S. Const. Amend. 4.—Montanez v. Carvajal, 889 F.3d 1202.

† **C.A.11 (Fla.) 2017.** Police officer could see drugs and assault rifle from public hallway outside of apartment, and thus search warrant was not predicated on unlawful observation, despite argument that officer pushed aside someone who was standing in doorway of apartment to see drugs and assault rifle; officer testified that he saw assault rifle and drugs from public hallway of apartment prior to moving anyone in doorway. U.S. Const. Amend. 4.—United States v. McDuffie, 691 Fed.Appx. 568, certiorari denied 138 S.Ct. 284, 583 U.S. 903, 199 L.Ed.2d 182.

† **C.A.11 (Fla.) 2015.** Officer's view of pages of notebook found within backpack, which contained evidence of tax fraud, did not fall outside scope of officer's search of backpack, which was searched during officer's search of vehicle for drugs, as required for warrantless search and seizure of notebook to be permitted under plain-view doctrine; officer did initially look through notebook to determine if there were any drugs hidden within it, based on his experience with individuals who concealed narcotics between pages of books. U.S.C.A. Const.Amend. 4.—U.S. v. Reeves, 604 Fed.Appx. 823.

† **C.A.11 (Fla.) 2012.** Probable cause existed to believe there was contraband in defendant's vehicle; officers stopped the vehicle after receiving reports that gunshots had emanated from it, and they then observed a bag of marijuana in plain view and smelled burnt marijuana in the vehicle. U.S.C.A. Const.Amend. 4.—U.S. v. Brown, 498 Fed.Appx. 940, post-conviction relief denied 2017 WL 942113, certificate of appealability denied 2018 WL 1474898, certiorari denied 139 S.Ct. 226, 202 L.Ed.2d 153, rehearing denied 139 S.Ct. 624, 202 L.Ed.2d 450.

† **C.A.11 (Fla.) 2011.** Police officers' plain view observation of harvested marijuana root bases 25 yards from defendant's residence, marijuana residue in a truck parked there, and surveillance monitors and insulation inside the residence as they approached the residence for a "knock and talk" did not violate defendant's Fourth Amendment rights, and thus inclusion of those observations in warrant affidavit did not taint validity of search warrant for defendant's property. U.S.C.A. Const.Amend. 4.—U.S. v. Cha, 431 Fed.Appx. 790, certiorari denied 132

† **This Case was not selected for publication in the National Reporter System**

S.Ct. 318, 565 U.S. 910, 181 L.Ed.2d 196, certiorari denied Erickson v. U.S., 132 S.Ct. 471, 565 U.S. 970, 181 L.Ed.2d 307, post-conviction relief denied 2015 WL 1061663, affirmed 675 Fed. Appx. 917.

† C.A.11 (Fla.) 2007. Police officer observed suspected marijuana in plain view during lawful search of home and, thus, had the authority to seize and secure the drugs; during his brief search of the remaining rooms inside the house, officer found a backpack containing bags of a leafy green substance inside the bathtub and noticed a strong smell of marijuana. U.S.C.A. Const.Amend. 4.—U.S. v. Simpson, 259 Fed. Appx. 164, certiorari denied 128 S.Ct. 1910, 552 U.S. 1327, 170 L.Ed.2d 774.

C.A.11 (Fla.) 1995. Evidence supported finding that law enforcement officers' aerial surveillance and observation of marijuana plants occurred from altitude of 500 feet and, thus, did not violate defendants' reasonable expectation of privacy; observing officer, who was pilot of helicopter, testified that he flew at 500 feet at time of initial observation of plants, although defendants and their neighbors testified that helicopter first approached property at less than 200 feet and private investigator opined that plants could not have been seen from height of over 100 feet. U.S.C.A. Const.Amend. 4.—U.S. v. Fernandez, 58 F.3d 593.

C.A.11 (Fla.) 1991. Helicopter flights over defendant's property did not result in improper search and seizure, even though deputies in helicopter took aerial photographs of marijuana field; deputies testified that they observed with naked eye marijuana growing in unenclosed field from altitude of 500 feet as they circled defendant's property. U.S.C.A. Const.Amend. 4.—U.S. v. Hatch, 931 F.2d 1478, certiorari denied 112 S.Ct. 235, 502 U.S. 883, 116 L.Ed.2d 191.

C.A.11 (Fla.) 1990. Articulable facts warranted Drug Enforcement Administration (DEA) agents' belief that at least one, and possibly two, suspects were hiding in warehouse and, accordingly, cursory inspection of warehouse, which revealed one defendant's shirt in plain view, was valid and shirt and contents in pocket were admissible in drug trafficking prosecution; when agents converged on scene to arrest suspects, one agent noticed someone running into warehouse. —U.S. v. Delgado, 903 F.2d 1495, certiorari denied 111 S.Ct. 681, 498 U.S. 1028, 112 L.Ed.2d 673.

C.A.11 (Fla.) 1985. Police who had warrant for defendant's arrest properly seized set of scales which were in plain view in defendant's apartment where person who was living with defendant let the police into the apartment, detective saw the scales on table in kitchen area near entry, and where, after determining that occupant lacked authority to consent to search of the apartment, the officers left, obtained warrant, and returned and took the scales from the kitchen table; in any event, it appeared that occupant had authority to consent to the search; and, furthermore, police still had warrant for arrest of defendant, on basis of which they could have entered the apartment a second time. U.S.C.A. Const.Amend. 4.—U.S. v. Watchmaker, 761 F.2d 1459, rehearing denied 766 F.2d 1493, certiorari denied Harrell v. United States, 106 S.Ct. 879, 474 U.S. 1100, 88 L.Ed.2d 917, certiorari denied Gibson v. United States, 106 S.Ct. 880, 474 U.S. 1100, 88 L.Ed.2d 917, certiorari denied Graves v. United States, 106 S.Ct. 880, 474 U.S. 1100, 88 L.Ed.2d 917, certiorari denied Marcaccio v. Unit-

ed States, 106 S.Ct. 880, 474 U.S. 1100, 88 L.Ed.2d 917, certiorari denied White v. United States, 106 S.Ct. 880, 474 U.S. 1101, 88 L.Ed.2d 917, certiorari denied Keating v. United States, 106 S.Ct. 880, 474 U.S. 1101, 88 L.Ed.2d 917, certiorari denied Seaver v. United States, 106 S.Ct. 881, 474 U.S. 1101, 88 L.Ed.2d 917, certiorari denied Lackey v. United States, 106 S.Ct. 881, 474 U.S. 1101, 88 L.Ed.2d 917, certiorari denied Hart v. United States, 106 S.Ct. 881, 474 U.S. 1101, 88 L.Ed.2d 917, certiorari denied Ruby v. United States, 106 S.Ct. 881, 474 U.S. 1101, 88 L.Ed.2d 917.

C.A.11 (Fla.) 1984. Where officers had probable cause to enter service station building under circumstances strongly indicating that drugs were being held at the station to sell, and where exigent circumstances justified officer's warrantless entry into building to pursue one defendant who was fleeing, officers once inside building could lawfully seize methaqualone tablets which lay in the officer's "plain view." Comprehensive Drug Abuse Prevention and Control Act of 1970, §§ 401(a)(1), 406, 21 U.S.C.A. §§ 841(a)(1), 846; U.S.C.A. Const.Amend. 4.—U.S. v. Pantoja-Soto, 739 F.2d 1520, rehearing denied 749 F.2d 733, certiorari denied 105 S.Ct. 1369, 470 U.S. 1008, 84 L.Ed.2d 389.

C.A.11 (Fla.) 1984. Where undercover agents were lawfully on property having been invited there to finalize drug deal and agents found truck trailer, doors of which were secured with lock but did not meet, thus leaving two-inch gap through which agents could observe burlap bales from distance of one to two feet, defendant owner of the premises and of the truck had no reasonable expectation of privacy in the truck. U.S.C.A. Const.Amend. 4.—U.S. v. Ard, 731 F.2d 718.

C.A.11 (Fla.) 1983. Defendants had no expectation of privacy in marijuana which they carried aboard deck of vessel in plain view, and same was true though they were traveling in darkness when they were caught. 21 U.S.C.A. §§ 955a(a), 955c; U.S.C.A. Const.Amends. 4, 14.—U.S. v. Hernandez, 715 F.2d 548, certiorari denied 104 S.Ct. 1006, 465 U.S. 1009, 79 L.Ed.2d 237.

C.A.5 (Fla.) 1981. Dogs' ability to detect quaaludes was irrelevant to validity of warrant to search suitcases or motion to suppress quaaludes discovered therein; assuming warrant to search suitcases was properly authorized, anything Government agents found in their search of suitcases was admissible under "plain view" doctrine.— U.S. v. Viera, 644 F.2d 509, certiorari denied Alonso v. U.S., 102 S.Ct. 332, 454 U.S. 867, 70 L.Ed.2d 169, certiorari denied 102 S.Ct. 332, 454 U.S. 867, 70 L.Ed.2d 169.

C.A.5 (Fla.) 1981. Record sustained finding that cocaine which was observed in automobile which had been stopped by officers was in plain view even though one officer did not simultaneously see cocaine when other officer observed it. U.S.C.A.Const. Amend. 4.—U.S. v. Vargas, 643 F.2d 296.

Officers who had reliable information linking one named crew member of vessel and possibly others to large-scale narcotics importation scheme and who observed three men leaving complex where vessel was docked at late hour and hurrying to vehicle parked in dark area and observed that one man appeared to have difficulty bending to enter vehicle acted reasonably in making investigatory stop of vehicle and cocaine observed in plain view inside vehicle was admissible. U.S.C.A.Const. Amend. 4.—Id.

† This Case was not selected for publication in the National Reporter System

C.A.5 (Fla.) 1979. Warrantless seizure of cocaine was proper where it was in plain view from outside defendant's car when defendant was lawfully arrested. U.S.C.A.Const. Amend. 4.—U.S. v. Agostino, 608 F.2d 1035.

C.A.5 (Fla.) 1979. Cocaine discovered in motel room which was to be scene of drug sale was not the fruit of an illegal search and seizure since it was found in plain view when officers were legitimately in the room for purpose of making lawful arrest and there was no time to obtain a warrant once unindicted coconspirator's statement that the cocaine was ready established probable cause. Comprehensive Drug Abuse Prevention and Control Act of 1970, §§ 401(a)(1), 406, 21 U.S.C.A. §§ 841(a)(1), 846; 18 U.S.C.A. § 2.—U.S. v. Carreno, 599 F.2d 680, certiorari denied 100 S.Ct. 287, 444 U.S. 937, 62 L.Ed.2d 197.

C.A.5 (Fla.) 1971. Though agent's view through window was "search" it did not invalidate seizure of some 200 pounds of cocaine in plain view on floor when second agent entered house through door immediately thereafter, where view was necessary to agents' safety in that they had been cautioned that defendants might be armed and dangerous and in that agents knew that their surveillance had been detected, and where there was probable cause for arrest without reliance upon first agent's observations. U.S.C.A.Const. Amend. 4.—U.S. v. Squella-Avendano, 447 F.2d 575, certiorari denied 92 S.Ct. 450, 404 U.S. 985, 30 L.Ed.2d 369, appeal after remand 478 F.2d 433.

S.D.Fla. 2008. Police officers had probable cause to conduct warrantless entry into defendant's apartment after he voluntarily opened door for them, where officers had received anonymous tip that narcotics were being sold by defendant and that he had two firearms inside his apartment, officers detected odor of burning marijuana outside of apartment, and officers observed loose marijuana and digital scale on couch when door opened. U.S.C.A. Const.Amend. 4.—U.S. v. Smalls, 617 F.Supp.2d 1240, affirmed 342 Fed. Appx. 505, certiorari denied 130 S.Ct. 1094, 558 U.S. 1128, 175 L.Ed.2d 912.

Police officers' warrantless seizure of marijuana and digital scale from defendant's apartment was justified under plain view doctrine, where objects were in plain view when defendant voluntarily opened door. U.S.C.A. Const.Amend. 4.—Id.

S.D.Fla. 1992. Police officers, who had been told by helicopter surveillance officers that marijuana appeared to be growing on suspect's premises, were not entitled to enter upon premises to search for marijuana without first obtaining search warrant, and consequently marijuana discovered as part of search was required to be suppressed. U.S.C.A. Const.Amend. 4.—U.S. v. Seidel, 794 F.Supp. 1098.

S.D.Fla. 1984. Where substantial amount of marijuana appeared on deck of boat and was accessible to state marine patrol officer observing the same by merely picking up corner of raincoat covering one of the bales, defendants who were occupying the boat did not have reasonable expectation of privacy in the marijuana.—U.S. v. Alfaro, 595 F.Supp. 531.

S.D.Fla. 1982. Marine patrol officers' observation of bales of marijuana on deck of ship and the ship's attempted flight gave them probable cause to stop and seize the vessel.—U.S. v. Wilson, 528 F.Supp. 1129.

S.D.Fla. 1981. Florida Marine Patrol's seizure of bales of marijuana observed on deck of defendants' vessel did not result from an illegal search but, rather, was justified because the marijuana was in plain view.—U.S. v. Collins, 523 F.Supp. 239, affirmed 667 F.2d 97.

S.D.Fla. 1980. Evidence of cocaine, which fell into bottom portion of defendant's bag, was properly in plain view of officer, who was holding the bag open while private security guard was searching it at airport.—U.S. v. Gorman, 484 F.Supp. 529.

S.D.Fla. 1978. Where officers were on board ship after defendants had consented to their boarding ship, whereupon one agent wiped moisture from one of windows to enable him to see marijuana stacked inside as the ship rolled and pitched causing the curtains to part, where it had been determined that ship was not registered in name of either of occupants, agents saw baled material in salon, where ship was riding low in the water, suggesting that it carried a substantial cargo, where experienced agents knew Miami to be a large drug importation and distribution center, search and seizure of bales could be justified under plain view exception to warrant requirements of the Fourth Amendment. U.S.C.A.Const. Amend. 4.—U.S. v. Marshall, 452 F.Supp. 1282, reversed 609 F.2d 152, appeal after remand 672 F.2d 425, rehearing denied 680 F.2d 1392.

Fla. 1988. Police officer's search of defendant's automobile after viewing burned cigarette wrappings through window of automobile was not supported by probable cause under plain view doctrine, and therefore evidence seized subsequent to search was suppressed as fruit of poisonous tree; mere observation of hand-rolled cigarettes, which may or may not contain contraband, is not enough to create probable cause without some other element being present, officer testified that he did not know what was contained within partially burned cigarette papers, and location of cigarette papers was not at known narcotics transaction area. U.S.C.A. Const. Amend. 4.—Caplan v. State, 531 So.2d 88, certiorari denied 109 S.Ct. 1577, 489 U.S. 1099, 103 L.Ed.2d 942.

Fla. 1984. In absence of sufficient external manifestation of privacy exhibited by defendant, trial court properly found that defendant did not have reasonable expectation of privacy in his marijuana patch and that evidence obtained by police observation thereof was admissible under "open fields" doctrine.—Brennan v. State, 447 So.2d 1353.

Fla. 1982. Warrantless seizure of marijuana plants from defendant's backyard was improper and required suppression of those plants where defendant's neighbor informed the police that he had observed some plants, which he believed to be marijuana, growing in defendant's backyard, but since defendant had erected a plywood partition next to a storage shed, the plants could not be seen from the neighbor's yard, and it was necessary for police officer to go behind defendant's yard to a citrus grove and make his observations from a place located outside a constitutionally protected area. West's F.S.A.Const.Art. 1, § 12; U.S.C.A.Const.Amend. 4.—State v. Rickard, 420 So.2d 303.

Fla. 1981. When officers looked through window of airplane and saw marijuana in "open view," officers had probable cause for search where airplane had landed without communicating with tower in violation of federal air regulations, air controller, unsuccessful in making contact with pilot of plane, called police, and thus police were standing in nonconstitutionally protected area in which they had lawful right to be at time of observation. U.S.C.A.Const.Amend. 4. —Adoue v. State, 408 So.2d 567.

Warrantless seizure of marijuana in airplane was entirely proper under doctrine of *Carroll*, notwithstanding that plane was parked and had been secured by police, where officers, through their open-view sighting of marijuana in airplane, had probable cause to believe that containers therein contained marijuana. West's F.S.A. § 933.19; U.S.C.A.Const.Amend. 4.—Id.

Fla. 1981. Seizure of marijuana plants growing in defendant's backyard was illegal, in that police officer had no right to be in defendant's backyard, which was not plainly visible to the public. U.S.C.A.Const. Amend. 4.—State v. Morsman, 394 So.2d 408, certiorari denied 101 S.Ct. 3066, 452 U.S. 930, 69 L.Ed.2d 431.

Fla. 1976. Despite fact that defendant was in custody, handcuffed and some distance from his car, where police officer discovered a bag of marijuana lying in plain view on the floor of the car, independent probable cause existed to search the vehicle, and both the bag of marijuana which was first noticed and later discovered evidence obtained from the car were admissible in prosecution for possession of marijuana. U.S.C.A.Const. Amend. 4.—Sheff v. State, 329 So.2d 270.

Fla. 1975. While kitchen drawer in defendant's apartment was only open about eight inches, investigating officer could easily see in the drawer a hypodermic needle with a yellow plunger attached, which justified the officer's opening the drawer completely, thereby exposing a gun which was seized by the officer.—Spinkellink v. State, 313 So.2d 666, certiorari denied Spenkelink v. Florida, 96 S.Ct. 3227, 428 U.S. 911, 49 L.Ed.2d 1221, rehearing denied 97 S.Ct. 194, 429 U.S. 874, 50 L.Ed.2d 157.

Fla.App. 1 Dist. 2017. Warrantless seizure of cocaine by police officer, who reached inside defendant's vehicle to retrieve cash from the driver's seat for safekeeping while defendant was being arrested, was lawful under the plain view doctrine, where officer observed a plastic bag located at the back of the driver's seat toward the driver's door. U.S. Const. Amend. 4.—State v. Johnson, 208 So.3d 843.

Fla.App. 1 Dist. 2012. Because incriminating nature of the pills was not immediately apparent to the deputy, he did not have probable cause to seize the plastic bag, containing the pills, under the plain-view exception to warrant requirement; deputy observed only that pills were larger than a certain brand of breath mint and larger than aspirin tablets, and it was not uncommon, in the deputy's experience, for individuals to carry their legally prescribed medication in plastic bags. U.S.C.A. Const.Amend. 4.—Smith v. State, 95 So.3d 966.

Fla.App. 1 Dist. 2004. Warrantless seizure of baggie containing cocaine residue in defendant's motel room was proper under the Fourth Amendment, where officers observed the baggie while looking through room's window during a search of the motel for a stolen car suspect, officers received consent to search defendant's room for the suspect, and while in room officers observed baggie in plain view, which was sticking out of defendant's shoe. U.S.C.A. Const.Amend. 4.— Washington v. State, 889 So.2d 170.

Fla.App. 1 Dist. 2000. Defendant's action of smoking marijuana was in officer's plain view, even though officer had to stand on his tip toes or on door sill of defendant's apartment to see defendant's activities; based on neighbor's complaint of excessive noise, officer had a right to be at defendant's door, where he smelled marijuana. U.S.C.A. Const.Amend. 4.—State v. Leonard, 764 So.2d 663.

Fla.App. 1 Dist. 1994. Seizure of cocaine was not justified on basis that cocaine was in plain view where cocaine was not in plain view until after officer had illegally begun pat-down search of defendant. U.S.C.A. Const.Amend. 4.—Rouse v. State, 643 So.2d 696.

Fla.App. 1 Dist. 1991. Seizure of brown piece of paper protruding from defendant's pocket and containing two pieces of crack cocaine was justified where seizure occurred in high crime area after officer had heard defendant and his associates discussing drug transactions, defendant and his associates had become nervous and evasive in their actions when officer approached them, and officer recognized paper as being of type commonly used to package contraband.—Bryant v. State, 577 So.2d 1372.

Fla.App. 1 Dist. 1988. Cocaine packages found on ground near where defendant had been standing after vehicle in which he was passenger was stopped by police officers were admissible against him; police officers had right to stop vehicle and temporarily detain occupants in order to request occupants to identify themselves, and cocaine discovered on ground was in plain view of officer who had legal right to be where he was.—Johnson v. State, 537 So.2d 117.

Fla.App. 1 Dist. 1985. It would have been improper to enter property and seize evidence without a warrant, based on officer's observation of marijuana growing on suspect's property, since observation could do no more than furnish probable cause for seizure.—Clark v. State, 469 So.2d 167.

Fla.App. 1 Dist. 1984. Although observation from legal vantage point of marijuana in defendant's mobile home was legal, subsequent warrantless entry into mobile home and seizure of contraband was not, in absence of exigent circumstances, and thus admission of this tangible evidence was error.—Diehl v. State, 461 So.2d 157.

Fla.App. 1 Dist. 1984. Marijuana in defendant's trailer was unlawfully seized where investigator only viewed that marijuana from vantage point outside trailer, so there was no "valid prior intrusion" to support application of plain-view doctrine nor any exigent circumstances justifying entry into trailer.—State v. Bowen, 444 So.2d 1009, petition for review denied 453 So.2d 43.

Despite existence of reasonable expectation of privacy in cannabis plot in defendants' back yard, police officers were justified in seizing cannabis, where investigator had legal right to proceed to front door of defendants' trailer, and once investigator arrived at front door, observed contraband clearly visible all over floor and furniture of trailer, and saw female sitting outside directly behind trailer, officer was justified in proceeding around side of trailer in order to temporarily detain and question suspects, and, from that vantage point, marijuana in back yard plot was in plain view.—Id.

Fla.App. 1 Dist. 1983. Defendant had no reasonable expectation of privacy in his marijuana patch which was clearly visible from the air, an area not constitutionally protected, and thus warrantless aerial search was not illegal.—Costello v. State, 442 So.2d 990, petition for review denied 453 So.2d 43.

Authorities did not need search warrant to enter onto defendant's property after aerial search had disclosed marijuana growing there, since defendant had no reasonable expectation of privacy in his marijuana patch because of its clear visibility from the air.—Id.

Fla.App. 1 Dist. 1983. Neither probable cause nor reasonable suspicion were required in order to justify teacher's aide's patrolling of student parking lot nor to justify his spotting readily visible and identifiable drug paraphernalia in open view in student's car. U.S.C.A. Const. Amend. 4.—State v. D.T.W., 425 So.2d 1383.

Fla.App. 1 Dist. 1982. Seizure by marine patrol officers of methaqualone tablets found on defendants' boat was authorized since officers had probable cause to believe that a statutory violation had occurred where neither defendant was able to produce certificate of registration generally required of all motorboats using waters of the state, such probable cause authorized officers to board the motorboat, and officer inadvertently observed the contraband in plain view. F.S.1979, §§ 371.011 et seq., 371.041, 371.051(4), 371.58, 371.131.—Sherman v. State, 419 So.2d 375.

Fla.App. 1 Dist. 1982. Evidence that cannabis plants growing on ten-acre tract were visible from adjoining property, that they were protected only by an old fence in advanced state of disrepair demonstrated that open-fields doctrine was applicable to their warrantless seizure by police officers who walked onto the land, saw defendant and another person walk into the field, and then seized the plants following defendant's arrest; defendant had no reasonable expectation of privacy in the field.—State v. Palmer, 410 So.2d 631.

Fla.App. 1 Dist. 1981. Police officer, being in hot pursuit of two vandals, was legally within constitutionally protected area of teachers' backyard when he inadvertently discovered marijuana, and thus, officer's warrantless seizure of the plants fell clearly within "plain view" exception to search warrant requirement.—Adams v. State, Professional Practices Council, 406 So.2d 1170, review denied 412 So.2d 463.

Fla.App. 1 Dist. 1981. Where police officer, without a warrant, entered farm belonging to defendant's father on a private road looking for the father's house, passed a brick home and a trailer without stopping to ask for directions, and continued for about half a mile on the private road until he came to defendant's trailer, the officer was at a place where defendant had a reasonable expectation of privacy and, therefore, his observation of marijuana plants growing outside the trailer was result of an invalid search and fruits thereof were to be suppressed.—Kilpatrick v. State, 403 So.2d 1104, certiorari denied 103 S.Ct. 1262, 460 U.S. 1016, 75 L.Ed.2d 488.

Fla.App. 1 Dist. 1981. Seizure of marijuana by police officers from airplane during warrantless search was not violative of the Fourth Amendment in view of fact that police officers, who had been called to investigate the surreptitious landing of the airplane, and who did not anticipate the discovery of a substance they each believed to be marijuana, were legitimately present at the scene, inadvertently discovered the evidence in plain view through the airplane's window, and had probable cause to believe the evidence they were confronted with was contra-

band. U.S.C.A.Const. Amend. 4.—Derrickson v. State, 399 So.2d 100.

Fla.App. 1 Dist. 1980. Plain view exception to warrant requirement could not be used to justify seizure of marijuana plant in defendant's back yard clearly identifiable only through a telescope, warrantless seizure of which constituted intrusion into area not reasonably expected to be exposed to public. U.S.C.A.Const. Amend. 4.—State v. Barnes, 390 So.2d 1243, review denied 399 So.2d 1145.

Fla.App. 1 Dist. 1980. Where police officers were instructed to return to warehouse from which truck containing marijuana had proceeded to "secure" warehouse while other officers obtained search warrant, officers were at most justified in surveilling doors and other possible exits from building while they waited outside for search warrant they believed would be forthcoming; thus, when officers knocked on rear door of warehouse for ultimate purpose of searching premises for marijuana, announced "police" as occupant began to open door, and, seeing what appeared to be bales of marijuana inside warehouse, pushed their way into warehouse and seized several tons of marijuana, officers were not legally at open door of warehouse for purpose of applying plain view doctrine and discovery of marijuana was not inadvertent.—Hurt v. State, 388 So.2d 281, review denied 399 So.2d 1146.

Fla.App. 1 Dist. 1978. Fact that sheriff was a trespasser when he climbed fence and walked 250 yards to barn on farm containing known unoccupied house did not make his observance of marijuana through barn window at that time an unreasonable search, in that barn did not have same protected status under Fourth Amendment as would a dwelling house and curtilage thereof. U.S.C.A.Const. Amend. 4.—Norman v. State, 362 So.2d 444, quashed 379 So.2d 643.

Fla.App. 1 Dist. 1977. Police officer had the right to be in the vicinity of defendants' truck, which was on the premises of filling station that had closed for the evening, while investigating the tripping of a silent burglar alarm at the filling station, and when, before entering the truck, the officer saw a baggie of marijuana on the floorboard in plain view, that created probable cause to believe the truck was carrying contraband, and a search thereof for additional contraband was then fully justified.—State v. Hall, 352 So.2d 940.

Fla.App. 1 Dist. 1976. Suspicion, based on informant's tip, that growing material on defendant's porch was marijuana, coupled with patrolman's own observations from street, justified crossing yard to look closer; entry into yard and onto porch to identify suspected contraband plaintiff visible in less detail from street did not violate Fourth Amendment standards. U.S.C.A.Const. Amend. 4.—State v. Detlefson, 335 So.2d 371.

Fla.App. 1 Dist. 1975. Evidence which established, inter alia, that university police officer was examining, out of curiosity, a bicycle which was in his lawful custody, having been found after report that it had been stolen, and that packet of cocaine accidentally fell into plain view of officer during such inspection was sufficient to sustain finding that discovery of contraband was not product of an illegal search or seizure.—Grant v. State, 312 So.2d 252, certiorari denied 325 So.2d 8.

Fla.App. 1 Dist. 1974. Where defendant's brother called police and told police that defendant was in possession of marijuana and that he would show it to them if the police would meet

---

† **This Case was not selected for publication in the National Reporter System**

him at defendant's residence, defendant's brother claimed to be the owner of the property when police informed him that they would have to get a search warrant, where, upon arrival at defendant's residence, the brother broke in door to the residence and marijuana was then clearly visible to police officers standing outside the house, police officers had a right to be in a position to observe the marijuana, which was in plain view, and thus subject to seizure.—McDaniel v. State, 301 So.2d 141, opinion vacated 336 So.2d 389, certiorari dismissed 336 So.2d 1183.

Fla.App. 2 Dist. 2017. Open view doctrine did not apply to police search of latticework attached to foundation of rooming house prompted by officer's observation of pill bottle located there, where latticework was not open area such that passersby could readily observe its contents, and pill bottle was opaque, making cocaine stored inside not visible to officer. U.S. Const. Amend. 4.—Davis v. State, 226 So.3d 318, rehearing denied.

Fla.App. 2 Dist. 2016. Police officer who saw crack cocaine in plain view through window of defendant's parked vehicle had probable cause to believe that the car contained evidence of a crime, and thus was authorized to conduct warrantless search of vehicle under automobile exception to warrant requirement. U.S. Const. Amend. 4.—State v. Ross, 209 So.3d 606, on remand 2017 WL 11151350.

Fla.App. 2 Dist. 2016. Drugs and drug paraphernalia that firefighters observed in defendant's garage and in closet as they left defendant's residence after putting out fire while they were performing administrative sweep of residence were admissible under plain view doctrine in prosecution for possession of a firearm, possession of cannabis, and other crimes. U.S.C.A. Const.Amend. 4.—Young v. State, 207 So.3d 267.

Fla.App. 2 Dist. 2008. Incriminating nature of baggie defendant dropped near shed in fenced backyard approximately 30 feet from officer was not so apparent as to allow warrantless seizure under open view theory, by officers who were responding to anonymous tip about drug dealing from shed, even though officer also saw codefendant move his hand in a furtive motion while standing inside shed; officer was not able to identify baggie's contents with certainty from her vantage point outside backyard. U.S.C.A. Const. Amend. 4.—Oliver v. State, 989 So.2d 16, rehearing denied, review denied 4 So.3d 677.

Fla.App. 2 Dist. 2008. Plain view doctrine did not apply to justify officer's ordering defendant out of vehicle based on officer's observation of drug paraphernalia in vehicle during course of an illegal investigatory stop; officer discovered paraphernalia only after intruding into defendant's privacy by ordering defendant to roll down driver-side window, causing a view-obscuring towel to fall, after officer determined that all was well during passenger-side welfare check. U.S.C.A. Const.Amend. 4; West's F.S.A. Const. Art. 1, § 12; West's F.S.A. § 901.151(2).—Greider v. State, 977 So.2d 789.

Fla.App. 2 Dist. 2005. Police officer had a legitimate right to be in defendant's bedroom, as was necessary to support seizure of drug evidence found in bedroom under plain view doctrine; before entering defendant's home, officer specifically asked for consent to search his home for a boat motor and a 12-gauge shotgun, and defendant voluntarily consented to officer's request to search. U.S.C.A. Const.Amend. 4.—Jones v. State, 895 So.2d 1246.

Incriminating nature of methamphetamine and drug paraphernalia found in tackle box underneath defendant's mattress was not immediately apparent to officer, and thus officer did not have probable cause to seize such evidence under plain view doctrine; fact that tackle box was beneath a mattress was not sufficient to suggest an incriminating nature, as defendant could have been hiding perfectly legitimate items in the small box, and although officer testified that tackle box was transparent, he also testified that he had to pick it up to identify what was inside. U.S.C.A. Const. Amend. 4.—Id.

Fla.App. 2 Dist. 1999. Officer had lawful right of access to bags in which he found cocaine, where he was investigating burglary at home where bags were found, and bags were open, in plain view, and nearby to officer. U.S.C.A. Const.Amend. 4.—State v. Walker, 729 So.2d 463.

Police officer had probable cause to seize bag in which cocaine was found, under plain view doctrine, where officer was legally in home where he found bags, bags were open and in plain view, and officer's experience in narcotics enforcement led him to suspect that bags contained cocaine. U.S.C.A. Const.Amend. 4.—Id.

Fla.App. 2 Dist. 1998. Incriminating nature of white, powdery substance on the mirror in a motel room was immediately apparent upon the officer's observation of the methamphetamine, and, thus, plain view seizure was permissible, even though initial chemical test produced inconclusive results. U.S.C.A. Const.Amend. 4.—State v. Futch, 715 So.2d 992, rehearing denied, appeal after remand 744 So.2d 540.

Fla.App. 2 Dist. 1994. Marijuana plants seen through partially opened bedroom closet door were within plain view and subject to seizure by officer who was in room with consent of defendant, even though officer used flashlight to illuminate partially opened closet area. U.S.C.A. Const.Amend. 4.—State v. Hite, 642 So.2d 55.

Fla.App. 2 Dist. 1989. Defendant, while in his automobile in a parking lot adjacent to a tavern, had no legitimate expectation of privacy, and thus deputy's use of a flashlight to observe cocaine and marijuana in plain view in the vehicle did not constitutionally taint his investigation. U.S.C.A. Const.Amend. 4.—State v. Ecker, 550 So.2d 545.

Fla.App. 2 Dist. 1987. Police officer was justified in temporarily detaining defendant, and thus, plain-view discovery and seizure of drugs and paraphernalia in defendant's automobile was proper; defendant's automobile was parked in manner which indicated it was one of automobiles for sale at used car lot which was not open for business, officer knew that there had been automobile thefts and automobile burglaries in area during preceding year, it was 1:40 a.m., and both occupants appeared to be trying to avoid detection. West's F.S.A. §§ 901.151, 901.151(2); U.S.C.A. Const.Amend. 4.—State v. Kibbee, 513 So.2d 256.

Fla.App. 2 Dist. 1985. Subsequent observance of drug paraphernalia on kitchen drain board by officer who had right to enter defendant's residence, fell within plain-view exception to warrant requirement.—Campbell v. State, 477 So.2d 1068.

Fla.App. 2 Dist. 1984. Neither delay of few minutes between observance of marijuana seeds in open box protruding from under bed on which defendant was sleeping, and actual seizure of box, nor physical removal of defendant from

† **This Case was not selected for publication in the National Reporter System**

room negated right of officers to seize contraband observed in plain view while lawfully and properly executing warrant for defendant's arrest.—State v. Myers, 454 So.2d 764.

Fla.App. 2 Dist. 1983. If search warrant had authorized only search for cocaine, seizure of other drugs found in plain view or inadvertently would have been clearly proper, since searching officers would have gained entry onto defendant's premises pursuant to valid warrant. U.S.C.A. Const.Amend. 4; West's F.S.A. Const. Art. 1, § 12.—West v. State, 439 So.2d 907, quashed 449 So.2d 1286.

Fla.App. 2 Dist. 1983. Presence in backyard of police officers, who responded to call of a disturbance or possible fight and proceeded directly to backyard of residence where the disturbance appeared to be occurring rather than knocking at front door, was justified and therefore marijuana plant, which they inadvertently spotted in plain view, was properly seized.—State v. Duda, 437 So.2d 794.

Fla.App. 2 Dist. 1982. Defendant had no reasonable expectation of privacy when he chose to openly grow eight-foot marijuana plants next to a public building; accordingly, the police, who did not go on defendant's property until they had clearly identified, from neighboring community center, the plants as marijuana, did not act unlawfully in going to defendant's residence and seizing the plants, even though they had no search warrant and there was no indication of exigent circumstances which required immediate action on their part.—State v. McConnell, 422 So.2d 74.

Fla.App. 2 Dist. 1982. Action of first deputy in observing marijuana growing in a heavily wooded area under exclusive use of defendant while flying in a helicopter at treetop level and action of second deputy in thereafter walking onto property without a search warrant and in discovering defendant near sight where cultivated plants of marijuana were growing were an appropriate application of the "open fields" doctrine.—Brennan v. State, 417 So.2d 1024, case dismissed 447 So.2d 1353.

Fla.App. 2 Dist. 1982. Defendant did not have any reasonable expectation of privacy in opaquely wrapped bales of marijuana, one of which had marijuana residue on top, which police officers observed defendant load in automobile trunk, and therefore warrantless seizure of marijuana was not invalid. U.S.C.A.Const.Amend. 4.—Benningfield v. State, 416 So.2d 468, review denied 419 So.2d 1195.

Fla.App. 2 Dist. 1982. Although officers had probable cause to search airplane and exigent circumstances made search without warrant proper, since neither opaque wrapping of packages nor their size or shape revealed that they contained marijuana, so as to bring them under "plain view" exception to warrant requirement of Fourth Amendment, warrant was required to open the packages and marijuana discovered when officers opened packages without warrant must be suppressed. U.S.C.A.Const.Amend. 4.— State v. Backner, 413 So.2d 409.

Fla.App. 2 Dist. 1978. Officers' seizure of plastic vial, which contained white powdery substance and which had been inside open attache case in plain view on top of dresser drawer in defendant's motel room, seizure of certain marijuana which was also on top of dresser and seizure of a second plastic vial which contained pill and which was situated between the marijuana and attache case, were seizures from within

plain view, rather than seizures during an inventory search, though officers may not have observed such contraband at same time.—State v. Ruiz, 360 So.2d 1320.

Fla.App. 2 Dist. 1978. Absent exigent circumstances, plain view doctrine alone could not justify warrantless seizure of marijuana plants growing in backyard of residence, where there was no indication that the contraband was subject to immediate destruction or removal. U.S.C.A.Const. Amend. 4.—Morsman v. State, 360 So.2d 137, writ dismissed 394 So.2d 408, certiorari denied 101 S.Ct. 3066, 452 U.S. 930, 69 L.Ed.2d 431.

Fla.App. 2 Dist. 1975. Officers had reasonable suspicion to approach defendant's trailer and ask for consent to search based upon officers' prior observation of frequent visitors to trailer and smell of marijuana smoke emanating from trailer on those occasions, and thus officers had a legal right to be there and officers' actual observance, through an open door, of marijuana on defendant's bed did not constitute an illegal search under plain view doctrine.—Dacus v. State, 307 So.2d 505.

Fla.App. 3 Dist. 2006. Cocaine was in "open view,"because officer was outside of a constitutionally protected area, apartment hallway, and was looking inside of constitutionally protected area, defendant's apartment, when he observed contraband.—State v. Cartwright, 920 So.2d 71.

Fla.App. 3 Dist. 2005. Police officers who entered defendant's residence while in hot pursuit of passenger of stolen automobile had probable cause to suspect that passenger committed a crime, and thus cocaine and firearm discovered by officers in plain view in defendant's residence were admissible in defendant's resulting prosecution for possession of cocaine with intent to sell, resisting arrest without violence, and possession of a firearm by a convicted felon; passenger fled from scene after stolen automobile stopped, and officers could reasonably believe that passenger participated in theft of automobile, or committed offense of trespass in a conveyance. U.S.C.A. Const.Amend. 4; West's F.S.A. §§ 810.08, 812.014(2)(c) 6.—Ulysse v. State, 899 So.2d 1233, review denied 912 So.2d 1218.

Fla.App. 3 Dist. 1993. Warrantless police seizure of crack cocaine and drug paraphernalia from night stand in bedroom of apartment containing unattended and crying child was constitutionally reasonable pursuant to plain sight exception to warrant requirement. U.S.C.A. Const. Amend. 4; West's F.S.A. Const. Art. 1, § 12.— Walker v. State, 617 So.2d 404.

Fla.App. 3 Dist. 1992. Police had probable cause to search automobile for presence of drugs under moving vehicle exception to search warrant requirement; after validly stopping vehicle, police had made a plain-view observation of four plastic bags containing suspected cocaine which were lying on floor of automobile behind front seat. U.S.C.A. Const.Amend. 4.—State v. Cash, 595 So.2d 279.

Fla.App. 3 Dist. 1991. Where neither consent nor exigent circumstances gave police officer right to be outside defendant's bedroom door where officer viewed cocaine, plain view exception to search warrant requirement was inapplicable. U.S.C.A. Const.Amend. 4.—Soldo v. State, 583 So.2d 1080.

Fla.App. 3 Dist. 1991. Police officer's seizure of cocaine was valid; defendant had left cocaine outside his apartment, in open area in which he had no expectation of privacy and officer observed it there.—Strachan v. State, 578 So.2d 511, review denied 589 So.2d 293.

Fla.App. 3 Dist. 1989. Following lawful stop of narcotics defendant's vehicle, drugs observed in plain sight from outside of vehicle were properly seized by police officers. U.S.C.A. Const. Amend. 4.—State v. Barcenas, 559 So.2d 70, review denied 569 So.2d 1278.

Fla.App. 3 Dist. 1989. Officer conducted reasonable search of automobile interior based on plain view observation of envelopes commonly used to hold cannabis.—L.S. v. State, 547 So.2d 1032.

Fla.App. 3 Dist. 1987. Officer's "plain view" perception of hand-rolled marijuana cigarette in defendant's shirt pocket provided sufficient probable cause to arrest defendant and to conduct an inventory search of defendant's automobile. U.S.C.A. Const.Amend. 4.—Sanchez v. State, 507 So.2d 673.

Fla.App. 3 Dist. 1981. Since defendant clearly appeared to be drunk when he entered his car and fumbled for his keys and circumstances afforded officer approaching car a plain view of contraband and probable cause to arrest, defendant was not entitled to have suppressed cocaine seized without a warrant.—Nielsen v. State, 393 So.2d 1188.

Fla.App. 3 Dist. 1981. Under "plain view" doctrine, cocaine found in amber bottle seen in and taken from defendant's car was properly seized.—Foxx v. State, 392 So.2d 48.

Fla.App. 3 Dist. 1979. Where police officer properly stopped defendant's vehicle for routine traffic offense, defendant was arrested for driving with a suspended license, and defendant signed release relieving police of any responsibility for vehicle while it was left on scene and where, when officer went to defendant's vehicle to secure it, she observed clear plastic bag, which appeared to contain marijuana, protruding from black plastic garbage bag on right rear floorboard, cannabis was in "plain view" of officer and was therefore subject to warrantless seizure. U.S.C.A.Const. Amend. 4.—Cobb v. State, 378 So.2d 82, certiorari denied 388 So.2d 1111.

Fla.App. 3 Dist. 1979. Where initial stop of defendant was based upon police officer's reasonable or founded suspicion of criminal activity, seizure of heroin left by defendant in pouch which officer could plainly see as he was detaining defendant was not result of search.—Gibson v. State, 368 So.2d 667.

Fla.App. 3 Dist. 1978. Where police officers were acting lawfully and properly in knocking on the door of a motel room and where, when defendant opened the door, the officers saw several bags of marijuana, a scale, a pipe and a box of sandwich bags in plain view on a dresser in the lighted room, the officers did not act illegally in entering the room and seizing those items, nor was it unlawful for the officers, after arresting defendant and upon seeing a pistol in a suitcase, to seize the pistol and to search the suitcase for other weapons.—Winchell v. State, 362 So.2d 992, certiorari denied 370 So.2d 462.

Fla.App. 3 Dist. 1976. Where police went to residence at night to investigate a reported burglary in progress and to serve warrant on another individual on unrelated charges and determined that there was no burglary but by flashing a light saw marijuana plants through the wooden fence in backyard, there was no illegal search since the contraband was in plain view.—State v. Elbertson, 340 So.2d 1250.

Fla.App. 4 Dist. 2006. Cocaine in vehicle in which defendant was sitting was not in plain view of police officer who had engaged in consensual encounter by approaching vehicle, and thus seizure of cocaine was not justified under plain-view doctrine, where officer had to lean into vehicle to see cocaine.—State v. Echevarria, 937 So.2d 1276.

Fla.App. 4 Dist. 2000. Plain view doctrine did not support seizure of marijuana cigarettes that narcotics officer found in defendant's home, given that Defendant's consent was limited to forensic search related to robbery that occurred in home, and did not extend to narcotics officer, who was dispatched to residence to search for drugs and not aware that robbery had occurred. —State v. Drysdale, 770 So.2d 301.

Detective was warranted in seizing contraband observed in plain view while lawfully conducting forensic search of robbery crime scene in defendant's living room when he saw seeds on floor, and, given officer's experience, and apparent odor of marijuana in home, it was apparent that seeds were contraband.—Id.

Fla.App. 4 Dist. 1992. Officer's observation of two cans in plain view inside motel room did not give him probable cause to make warrantless search of room; though officer was aware that similar cans with puncture holes in the top were often used to smoke crack cocaine, he saw no puncture holes in cans at issue and could only say that he noticed "something on top of the cans." U.S.C.A. Const.Amend. 4.—Banks v. State, 594 So.2d 833.

Fla.App. 4 Dist. 1991. Individual suspected of growing marijuana had objectively reasonable expectation of privacy in his yard, assuming that it fell within "curtilage" of his home, and police officer's act of climbing ladder in neighbor's yard and peering over solid wooden dividing fence into suspect's yard violated that expectation. U.S.C.A. Const.Amend. 4.—West v. State, 588 So.2d 248.

Seizure of marijuana plants observed and photographed in back yard was unreasonable, as no attempt was made to obtain search warrant even though "open view" observations provided officers with necessary probable cause to obtain one. U.S.C.A. Const.Amend. 4.—Id.

Fla.App. 4 Dist. 1990. Police officer properly seized cocaine that was found in coffee jar under loose backseat during protective search of car for weapons, inasmuch as cocaine in glass jar was in plain view. U.S.C.A. Const.Amend. 4.—Sierra v. State, 568 So.2d 1338.

Fla.App. 4 Dist. 1989. Seizure of marijuana which was in plain view on closet shelf where arrestee had reached for identification was lawful. U.S.C.A. Const.Amend. 4.—McVay v. State, 553 So.2d 331.

Fla.App. 4 Dist. 1989. Officer who saw partially hand-rolled cigarette, pair of scissors, and cigarette rolling paper in automobile parked in open apartment complex parking lot had probable cause to search automobile based on plain view observation, which led to his belief that cigarette contained marijuana and scissors and rolling papers were drug paraphernalia.—State v. Milmoe, 541 So.2d 718.

Fla.App. 4 Dist. 1989. Marijuana which police officer observed in plain view after defendant exited parked truck on his own initiative was subject to seizure.—State v. Mendez, 540 So.2d 930.

Fla.App. 4 Dist. 1987. Officer's search of defendant's vehicle was justified; officer had ex-

† This Case was not selected for publication in the National Reporter System

tensive training and experience in drug identification, while waiting for tow truck to take
defendant's vehicle, which had been disabled
by an accident, officer noticed through window
what appeared to be marijuana cigarettes, and
officer opened door and smelled marijuana
smoke.—Caplan v. State, 515 So.2d 1362, opinion quashed 531 So.2d 88, certiorari denied
109 S.Ct. 1577, 489 U.S. 1099, 103 L.Ed.2d
942.

Fla.App. 4 Dist. 1986. Marijuana and cocaine
were properly taken from defendant's automobile
by police without a warrant, under open view
doctrine, where officer inadvertently discovered
contraband on front seat of car from lawful
vantage point.—State v. Coleman, 502 So.2d 13.

Fla.App. 4 Dist. 1986. Dollar bill containing
PCP residue that defendant threw on ground as
he turned toward car to submit to police weapon
search was properly seized.—Morganti v. State,
498 So.2d 557, decision approved 509 So.2d 929,
appeal after remand 510 So.2d 1182, opinion
quashed 524 So.2d 641, appeal after remand 557
So.2d 593, decision approved 573 So.2d 820.

Fla.App. 4 Dist. 1983. Law enforcement personnel, given suspicious circumstances surrounding arrival of defendant's aircraft, were lawfully
present in area surrounding aircraft and, upon
peering through windows with flashlights and
observing bales in plain view wrapped in green-
ish-black plastic and secured with masking tape,
were possessed with probable cause to conduct a
search of aircraft and, upon discovering marijuana during course of search, to seize contraband.
U.S.C.A. Const.Amend. 4.—State v. Smith, 441
So.2d 1176, petition for review denied 450 So.2d
488.

Fla.App. 4 Dist. 1983. Officer's inadvertent
discovery of marijuana while he searched behind
walk-in closet door for burglar did not go beyond
parameters of his constitutional license, where
officer had probable cause to believe burglary
had been or was taking place in apartment at
time of search, and marijuana, resting on closet
shelf at eye level, was only partially covered, and
was therefore within plain view.—State v. Mann,
440 So.2d 406.

Fla.App. 4 Dist. 1983. Where defendants
erected three and one-half to four-foot high chain
link fence running around sides of yard, and
fence was type required by law to enclose pool,
defendants did not create requisite actual expectation of privacy which would have required
police to obtain warrant before seizing marijuana
growing in plain view in backyard. U.S.C.A.
Const.Amend. 4.—State v. Loomis, 436 So.2d
1103.

Fla.App. 4 Dist. 1983. Even though defendant
had standing to attack search of automobile and
subsequent seizure of evidence therefrom, seizure
of methadone which was within plain view of
officer who had probable cause to stop the vehicle was lawful. U.S.C.A. Const.Amend. 4.—State
v. Scotti, 428 So.2d 771.

Fla.App. 4 Dist. 1982. There was no unconstitutional search and subsequent seizure by police
officer who observed bales of marijuana in plain
view from his lawful position in house after he
had followed defendants, having observed them
committing a felony, into the house to effect their
arrest. U.S.C.A. Const.Amend. 4.—Sims v. State,
425 So.2d 563, petition for review denied 436
So.2d 100.

Fla.App. 4 Dist. 1982. Evidence permitted an
inference that marijuana, located in a bedroom of
which defendant had joint custody and control,

was in plain view and, hence, was properly made
a subject of challenged search and seizure.—
Kinmon v. State, 414 So.2d 224.

Fla.App. 4 Dist. 1981. Where deputy was justified in climbing up and entering plane for sole
purpose of making sure that master electrical
switches were off, to obviate fire or explosion,
and upon doing so, he plain-viewed and plain-
smelled bales of marijuana, requirement of a
warrant was obviated no matter how long plane
was kept under surveillance in hope of catching
any of the five suspects who might return.—State
v. Johnson, 403 So.2d 1095.

Fla.App. 4 Dist. 1981. Where surveilling officer's experiences led him to conclude the numerous bales which numerous persons carried from
defendant's vessel into house contained marijuana, one of two persons outside house when officers began arrest process refused officer's command to "freeze" and entered house and was
followed by police, who observed marijuana bales
and loose marijuana in plain view, warrantless
arrests and seizures were lawful and pursuant
thereto officers could properly seize marijuana
bales, which were in plain view, from vessel.
West's F.S.A. § 901.15(3).—Rizzo v. State ex rel.
City of Pompano Beach, 396 So.2d 869.

Fla.App. 4 Dist. 1978. Person who keeps marijuana plants in open view in his backyard in
plain view of a neighbor has no reasonable expectation of privacy, and seizure of the plants without a warrant by police officer who has seen the
plants from the neighbor's yard, where he had a
legal right to be, is not an unreasonable governmental intrusion. U.S.C.A.Const. Amend. 4.—
Lightfoot v. State, 356 So.2d 331, certiorari denied 361 So.2d 833.

Officer had legal right to be in neighbor's yard
pursuant to neighbor's invitation and to look
across fence into defendant's yard and to see
what was there for him to see, and having observed marijuana plants and having been informed by the neighbor that defendant was the
one who lived in the house and took care of the
plants, officer had right to arrest defendant without a warrant, and fact that defendant was not at
home when officers went to his house did not
prevent them from seizing without a warrant
marijuana plants that were in his backyard, as
there was no search and no unreasonable governmental intrusion on defendant's privacy, so that
the plants were not subject to Fourth Amendment
protection. U.S.C.A.Const. Amend. 4.—Id.

Fla.App. 4 Dist. 1975. Male police officer had
legal right to be within women's restroom which
was in bar and which was open to the public and
thus the right to seize narcotics paraphernalia in
plain view in restroom, rendering narcotics paraphernalia admissible. West's F.S.A.Const. art. 1,
§ 12.—State v. Daniel, 319 So.2d 582.

Fla.App. 4 Dist. 1973. Where officers entered
apartment building in response to complaint of a
fight or some other disturbance, found defendant's apartment door ajar and saw defendant
sitting in a chair and were unable to arouse
defendant by banging and shouting, officers properly entered apartment to determine defendant's
condition, and marijuana found in plain view was
lawfully seized and not the result of an unlawful
entry. U.S.C.A.Const. Amend. 4.—State v. Hetzko, 283 So.2d 49.

Fla.App. 5 Dist. 2019. Officer had probable
cause to perform warrantless search of defendant's truck under automobile exception following defendant's arrest; truck was not located in
the constitutionally-protected curtilage of his resi-

---

† This Case was not selected for publication in the National Reporter System

dence at the time of the search, and crack co-caine situated on the driver's seat of the truck was in open view. U.S. Const. Amend. 4.—State v. Thornton, 286 So.3d 924.

Fla.App. 5 Dist. 2007. Defendant did not have a reasonable expectation of privacy in a house's front porch, which was where defendant was sleeping when police officers saw crack cocaine in his lap; unenclosed porch was in front of house and not obscured from public view, defendant was sleeping in a chair on front edge of porch, any delivery person or passerby could have walked onto porch and left a package or knocked on door without a violation of the resident's reasonable expectation of privacy, and in doing so, police officers, like a delivery person, would have observed crack cocaine in plain view in defendant's lap. U.S.C.A. Const.Amend. 4.—State v. E.D.R., 959 So.2d 1225.

Fla.App. 5 Dist. 2005. Warrantless entry of police officers into motel room was justified by exigent circumstances, and thus, seizure of co-caine in plain view did not violate defendant's Fourth Amendment rights; defendant did not tell officers he was alone, officers had been told drugs were being sold out of room, officer saw drugs in room when defendant opened door, it was not unreasonable for officer to make sure no one else was in room to destroy evidence, as officer knew drugs were easily disposable, and destruction of contraband prior to time officer could obtain warrant was possible. U.S.C.A. Const.Amend. 4.—Murphy v. State, 898 So.2d 1031, rehearing denied, review denied 910 So.2d 262.

Fla.App. 5 Dist. 2003. Evidence of drugs observed by police officers in plain view through open motel room door was not subject to suppression. U.S.C.A. Const.Amend. 4.—Frasilus v. State, 840 So.2d 1117.

Fla.App. 5 Dist. 2001. Officer who entered vacant, unfenced, private property in search of owner of dog running loose could constitutionally observe marijuana plants growing there; in absence of curtilage, there was no legitimate expectation of privacy which would make search unreasonable. U.S.C.A. Const.Amend. 4.—State v. Brockman, 788 So.2d 406.

Fla.App. 5 Dist. 1999. Police officer, who smelled marijuana coming from interior of automobile and saw small handgun inside car, was not required to obtain search warrant, but could break into vehicle and seize contraband. U.S.C.A. Const.Amend. 4.—State v. Williams, 739 So.2d 717.

Fla.App. 5 Dist. 1996. Cocaine visible in gaping pocket of defendant's baggy shorts, during officer's attempted security pat down, was subject to seizure. U.S.C.A. Const.Amend. 4.—Powell v. State, 682 So.2d 1244.

Fla.App. 5 Dist. 1987. It was not immediately apparent that plastic bag in vehicle contained marijuana and, therefore, search of vehicle and seizure of bag were not justified under "open view" doctrine.—Hartpence v. State, 509 So.2d 975.

Fla.App. 5 Dist. 1985. Deputy's directing four occupants of vehicle to approach him for a pat down to determine if they were armed and deputy's approaching vehicle and looking into driver's side to check for other persons possibly hiding therein was justified where deputy responded to phone call from citizen regarding suspicious vehicle parked in wooded area at night, vehicle was parked on an unpaved road, 50 to 75 yards away from a church and deputy's experience was that

occupants of vehicles parked in secluded and wooded areas generally were engaged in either criminal or sexual activity; seizure of baggie of marijuana which deputy observed on drink container between front seats fell under the open-view exception to warrant requirement. U.S.C.A. Const.Amend. 4.—Ewing v. State, 480 So.2d 200.

⟜**722. —— Documents.**

† **C.A.11 (Fla.) 2020.** Warrantless seizure of binder that was located open on desk in defendant's former hotel room was lawful under plain-view doctrine; hotel had given police officers permission to enter room, and binder was open in such a way that allowed officer to identify immediately illicit personally identifiable information (PII) inside. U.S. Const. Amend. 4.—United States v. Ouedraogo, 824 Fed.Appx. 714.

Fla.App. 5 Dist. 2018. Photographs and body-cam footage obtained after defendant's arrest when police officers re-entered defendant's home were properly seized under the plain view doctrine; even if exigency was over once officers determined that defendant's dog was deceased and defendant was placed in patrol car, the items were first observed and discovered in plain view when officers were responding to a call from defendant's neighbor about possible animal cruelty in progress, and officers did not search an area other than where incriminating evidence was in plain view during exigent circumstances. U.S. Const. Amend. 4.—State v. Archer, 259 So.3d 999, review denied 2019 WL 2205765, on subsequent appeal 309 So.3d 287, rehearing denied.

⟜**723. —— Clothing, shoes, and hats.**

† **C.A.11 (Fla.) 2020.** Plain view doctrine applied to officer's discovery of athletic sneaker on motel room floor that had same distinctive pattern as sneakers worn by robber of convenience store; group of officers had motel room under surveillance because a vehicle linked to the robbery was parked at the motel, and incriminating character of sneaker was immediately apparent. U.S. Const. Amend. 4.—United States v. Rivera, 824 Fed.Appx. 930.

Fla.App. 1 Dist. 2017. There was probable cause to associate defendant's bloody clothes with criminal activity, and thus police officers' warrantless seizure of defendant's clothing from emergency room bay pursuant to open view doctrine did not violate Fourth Amendment, even though defendant told hospital staff that he had been shot while he was being robbed, where defendant arrived at hospital with gunshot wounds shortly after home invasion victim indicated in his 9–1–1 call that he may have shot intruder, and officer observed as hospital staff removed defendant's bloody clothes prior to surgery. U.S. Const. Amend. 4; Fla. Const. art. 1, § 12.—Purifoy v. State, 225 So.3d 867, review denied 2017 WL 5508743.

Fla.App. 2 Dist. 1978. Where police officers investigated citizen's complaint that a nude male was running around car parked on street, when officers arrived at scene they discovered defendant lying on front seat of car, fully exposed, police officers ordered defendant out of car, and when interior light came on as defendant exited the car, officer could see several small, flat tinfoil packets inside defendant's shoes, and based upon his experience with drug arrests, officer believed packets contained either heroin or cocaine, officer had probable cause to believe that packets contained contraband, and officer's seizure of such packets was legal.—State v. Redding, 362 So.2d 170.

---

† **This Case was not selected for publication in the National Reporter System**

Fla.App. 3 Dist. 2019. Bloodstained clothing brought by defendant to interview at police station was in plain view, as could support its seizure under plain view exception to warrant requirement, where defendant placed clothing on table in interview room, and blood stains were immediately apparent. U.S. Const. Amend. 4.— Hedvall v. State, 283 So.3d 901, review denied 2020 WL 1650313.

Police officer had probable cause to seize bloodstained clothing and boots brought by defendant to police interview during murder investigation, under plain view exception to warrant requirement, where law enforcement knew, among other things, that victim had bled profusely as a result of having been murdered, that multiple witnesses had seen defendant and victim together, and in an argument, just hours before time of the murder, and defendant did not deny that he was wearing the clothing and boots on night of murder. U.S. Const. Amend. 4.—Id.

⊂⇒**724. —— Electronic devices.**
† **C.A.11 (Fla.) 2011.** Once officer who was interviewing defendant, who consented to search of his laptop computer for flight simulator program, inadvertently opened file on computer which contained child pornography video, child pornography was in plain view and officer had probable cause to seize computer for further investigation. U.S.C.A. Const.Amend. 4.—U.S. v. Whaley, 415 Fed.Appx. 129.

† **C.A.11 (Fla.) 2009.** Child pornography files on defendant's computer hard drives were intermingled with counterfeiting files and thus were in plain view, and seizure of child pornography from defendant's computer pursuant to search warrant which was limited to evidence of counterfeit software therefore did not violate Fourth Amendment's Warrant Clause. U.S.C.A. Const. Amend. 4; 18 U.S.C.A. § 2252A(a)(5)(B), (b)(2).— U.S. v. Miranda, 325 Fed.Appx. 858, certiorari denied 130 S.Ct. 740, 558 U.S. 1051, 175 L.Ed.2d 520.

Fla.App. 4 Dist. 1991. Videotapes which depicted 16–year-old girl while showering and dressing were legally seized, even though videotapes were not particularly described in search warrant, where warrant was sufficiently broad to include seized videotapes, video surveillance equipment contained on premises had ability to record illegal activity, and, upon viewing, videotapes were subject to plain view doctrine. West's F.S.A. § 827.071; U.S.C.A. Const.Amend. 4.— Lockwood v. State, 588 So.2d 57.

Fla.App. 5 Dist. 2018. Photographs and body-cam footage obtained after defendant's arrest when police officers re-entered defendant's home were properly seized under the plain view doctrine; even if exigency was over once officers determined that defendant's dog was deceased and defendant was placed in patrol car, the items were first observed and discovered in plain view when officers were responding to a call from defendant's neighbor about possible animal cruelty in progress, and officers did not search an area other than where incriminating evidence was in plain view during exigent circumstances. U.S. Const. Amend. 4.—State v. Archer, 259 So.3d 999, review denied 2019 WL 2205765, on subsequent appeal 309 So.3d 287, rehearing denied.

⊂⇒**725. —— Luggage, bags, and other containers.**
S.D.Fla. 1980. "Plain view" seizure of cocaine by drug agent during security guard's search of defendant's luggage at airport security checkpoint was not invalid based on inadvertence requirement. U.S.C.A.Const. Amend. 4.—U.S. v. Gorman, 484 F.Supp. 529.

Fla.App. 4 Dist. 2018. Defendant's nervous reaction to seeing officer and subsequent attempt to conceal unidentified item in food container were insufficient to establish reasonable suspicion, let alone probable cause, that item was contraband or that defendant was involved in criminal activity to support detention of defendant and search and seizure of food container under plain view doctrine, despite fact that activity occurred in a high crime area and police officer had 25 years of law enforcement experience. U.S. Const. Amend. 4.—Peynado v. State, 254 So.3d 457, on remand 2018 WL 11232946.

Fla.App. 4 Dist. 2007. Deputy had probable cause to believe that pill bottle he observed in plain view in defendant's purse contained contraband or was evidence of crime, and thus officer was justified in conducting warrantless seizure of bottle; officer knew that the bottle did not belong to defendant, that it contained hydrocodone, that defendant was at a location known for drug activity, and that defendant was not engaging in any activity to suggest that her temporary possession of the drugs was for a legitimate purpose. U.S.C.A. Const.Amend. 4.—Keller v. State, 946 So.2d 1233, review denied 958 So.2d 919.

Fla.App. 5 Dist. 1985. Where police officer approached defendant in private driveway, questioned him, and asked him if he could look inside duffle bag, and defendant, who was under no compulsion to listen or respond, voluntarily extracted contents of bag and placed open bag on chair, the encounter was a street encounter and not a stop, and revolver in the duffle bag which came into open view as result of defendant's actions gave officer probable cause to believe that defendant committed the crime of carrying a concealed weapon and justified officer in seizing the weapon and arresting defendant. West's F.S.A. § 901.151(5).—State v. Walden, 464 So.2d 691.

⊂⇒**726. Artificial light or visual aids.**
Fla.App. 1 Dist. 1990. Police officers who properly situated themselves outside defendant's automobile in such way that, with the aid of a flashlight, they were able to clearly see crack cocaine on the floorboard of the vehicle were entitled to lawfully seize the cocaine without a warrant.—State v. Hughes, 562 So.2d 795.

Fla.App. 1 Dist. 1986. Police officer's observation of marijuana on floor underneath front seat of automobile was permissible under plain-view doctrine when officer lawfully stopped vehicle for broken tag light, used flashlight to illuminate darkened area of front to observe vehicle identification number, bent down at an angle and then observed bag of what he believed to be, based on his experience, marijuana under seat.—Baggett v. State, 494 So.2d 221.

Fla.App. 1 Dist. 1982. Defendant did not have reasonable expectation of privacy in his field of growing marijuana which was 300 to 450 feet from his home, and, thus, evidence obtained when sheriff used binoculars to view the plants while traveling over the field in helicopter provided lawful basis for obtaining search warrant under "open fields" doctrine.—Murphy v. State, 413 So.2d 1268.

Fla.App. 2 Dist. 1990. Officer's use of flashlight to illuminate interior of vehicle in which he had observed two persons who "appeared to be doing something to the dashboard" did not vio-

---

† **This Case was not selected for publication in the National Reporter System**

late Fourth Amendment, and once officer had observed plastic box with white powder in it, as well as a small drinking type straw, he had probable cause to arrest; at the very least, officer had reasonable grounds for further investigation, which escalated to probable cause once defendant tried to hide the box. U.S.C.A. Const. Amend. 4.—State v. Sowers, 571 So.2d 11.

Fla.App. 2 Dist. 1989. Deputy's use of flashlight to look inside defendant's vehicle which was located in parking lot open to public did not violate any Fourth Amendment rights. U.S.C.A. Const.Amend. 4.—State v. Starke, 550 So.2d 547.

Fla.App. 2 Dist. 1982. Defendant sufficiently manifested actual expectation of privacy by erecting chain link fence around his backyard so as to render unconstitutional marijuana seizure based upon binocular-aided observation of defendant's garden from neighbor's house.—State v. Rowe, 422 So.2d 75.

Fla.App. 3 Dist. 1974. Policeman who entered parking lot of large apartment complex at 3 o'clock in the morning and observed persons occupying a parked automobile who appeared to be attempting to avoid observation was entitled to approach the car for purposes of investigation and drugs found on the front seat were in plain view, and were not discovered as the result of a search, even though the officer used a flashlight to give him better vision of the articles after he observed them.—State v. Roker, 290 So.2d 525.

Fla.App. 4 Dist. 1996. Tip from ticket seller that three black men in white vehicle had handgun on floorboard of passenger side of their vehicle, ticket seller's identification of vehicle's tag number, and deputy's sighting of pistol grips when placing spotlight on vehicle gave deputy probable cause to believe violation of concealed weapon statute was taking place by vehicle occupant's sitting by or over firearm on floorboard of subject vehicle, sufficient to support arrest of defendant and search of vehicle. West's F.S.A. § 790.25(5).—State v. Williams, 679 So.2d 1248, rehearing denied, review denied 689 So.2d 1073.

Fla.App. 4 Dist. 1982. When law enforcement personnel have right to look where they are looking, there is no constitutional prohibition against use of a device such as binoculars or a nightscope to enhance that view. U.S.C.A. Const. Amend. 4.—Sims v. State, 425 So.2d 563, petition for review denied 436 So.2d 100.

(F) EFFECT OF ILLEGAL CONDUCT.

➡**732. Particular cases.**

Fla.App. 1 Dist. 2021. Unconstitutional detention of defendant, resulting from officer's actions in exceeding permissible scope of welfare check, tainted officer's later search of and seizure of evidence from defendant's vehicle, even if subsequent alert by detection dog gave officer probable cause to search defendant's vehicle. U.S. Const. Amend. 4.—Taylor v. State, 326 So.3d 115.

III. SEARCH WARRANTS.

(B) AUTHORITY TO ISSUE.

➡**751. In general.**

Fla.App. 3 Dist. 1978. Warrant for further search of the premises was properly issued where police officers had lawfully entered a motel room and seized marijuana that was in plain view and cocaine that was found in a suitcase that the officers had searched for weapons.—Winchell v.

State, 362 So.2d 992, certiorari denied 370 So.2d 462.

➡**754. —— In general.**

C.A.11 (Fla.) 1984. Fourth Amendment protection contemplates that a neutral and detached magistrate issue warrant, supported by probable cause, before law enforcement officers may enter premises, and only in the face of "exigent circumstances," where obtaining warrant would greatly compromise important law enforcement objectives, does warrant requirement yield. U.S.C.A. Const.Amend. 4.—U.S. v. Pantoja-Soto, 739 F.2d 1520, rehearing denied 749 F.2d 733, certiorari denied 105 S.Ct. 1369, 470 U.S. 1008, 84 L.Ed.2d 389.

Fla.App. 1 Dist. 2020. The warrant requirement ensures that a neutral and detached magistrate stands between the citizen and the officer engaged in the often competitive enterprise of ferreting out crime. U.S. Const. Amend. 4.—Wingate v. State, 289 So.3d 566, cause dismissed 2020 WL 3265112, reinstatement denied 2020 WL 4218771.

Fla.App. 1 Dist. 2018. The warrant requirement ensures that a neutral and detached magistrate stands between the citizen and the officer engaged in the often competitive enterprise of ferreting out crime. U.S. Const. Amend. 4; Fla. Const. art. 1, § 12.—Clayton v. State, 252 So.3d 827, rehearing denied, on remand 2018 WL 10550340.

Fla.App. 3 Dist. 2003. Probable cause to issue a search warrant is to be based upon the totality of the circumstances, and as long as a neutral magistrate issuing the warrant has a substantial basis for concluding that the search would produce evidence of wrongdoing, the requirement of probable cause is satisfied. U.S.C.A. Const. Amend. 4.—Merrill v. State, 849 So.2d 1175.

Fla.App. 5 Dist. 2015. The search warrant requirement ensures that inferences to support the search are drawn by a neutral and detached magistrate instead of being judged by the officer engaged in the often competitive enterprise of ferreting out crime. U.S.C.A. Const.Amend. 4.—Williams v. State, 167 So.3d 483, rehearing denied, review granted 2015 WL 9594290, opinion vacated 2016 WL 6637817, on remand 210 So.3d 774.

(C) PROCEEDINGS FOR ISSUANCE.

➡**763. —— In general.**

M.D.Fla. 2015. During the course of a lawful knock and talk, officers may make plain-view observations and use them to support a warrant application. U.S. Const. Amend. 4.—United States v. Holmes, 143 F.Supp.3d 1252, affirmed 770 Fed.Appx. 1013, certiorari denied 140 S.Ct. 2518, 206 L.Ed.2d 468.

➡**764. —— Persons who may apply or sign affidavit.**

Fla.App. 4 Dist. 2018. Detective with the sheriff's office in county where investigation of pain clinics originated could be the sole affiant on search warrant applications and search warrant affidavits in other counties, even if detective relied on information derived from wiretaps authorized by a judicial officer in his home county; statutes governing issuance of search warrants did not require that the person applying for the warrant or the witness submitting the supporting affidavit be a member of law enforcement in the jurisdiction, or even that they be a member of law enforcement at all, and detective did not use the powers of his office to observe unlawful activity or gain access to evidence not available to a private citizen. U.S. Const. Amend. 4; Fla. Stat. Ann. §§ 933.06, 933.18.—State v. Stouffer, 248 So.3d 1165.

☞765(2). Matters appearing on the face of affidavit; four corners.

Fla.App. 2 Dist. 2023. Determination of probable cause must be made by examination of four corners of search warrant affidavit. U.S. Const. Amend. 4; Fla. Const. art. 1, § 12.—State v. Peltier, 373 So.3d 380.

Fla.App. 2 Dist. 2022. When assessing whether there is probable cause to justify a search, a trial court must make a judgment, based on the totality of the circumstances, as to whether from information contained in warrant there is a reasonable probability that contraband will be found at a particular place and time; this determination must be made by examination of the four corners of search warrant affidavit. U.S. Const. Amend. 4.—Smitherman v. State, 342 So.3d 685.

Fla.App. 2 Dist. 2020. For purposes of issuing a search warrant, the determination as to whether there is a reasonable probability that contraband will be found at a particular place and time must be made by examination of the four corners of the warrant affidavit. U.S. Const. Amend. 4.—Goesel v. State, 305 So.3d 821.

Fla.App. 4 Dist. 2023. Whether probable cause exists for a search warrant to issue must be determined from the four corners of the supporting affidavit. U.S. Const. Amend. 4.—Zarcadoolas v. Tony, 353 So.3d 638.

Fla.App. 5 Dist. 2020. Where it is a magistrate who is first presented with an affidavit requesting the issuance of a search warrant, the magistrate's duty is to examine solely the content of the affidavit—or what is commonly referred to as the "four corners" of the affidavit—and, from there, simply to make a practical, common sense decision whether, given all the circumstances before him, there is a fair probability that contraband or evidence of a crime will be found in a particular place. U.S. Const. Amend. 4.—State v. Hart, 308 So.3d 232, rehearing denied, review denied 2021 WL 6138926.

☞767. —— Construction in general.

C.A.11 (Fla.) 2023. Courts give commonsense rather than hypertechnical reading to search warrant applications when reviewing probable cause. U.S. Const. Amend. 4.—United States v. McCall, 84 F.4th 1317.

M.D.Fla. 2021. Courts reviewing the legitimacy of search warrants should not interpret supporting affidavits in a hypertechnical manner; rather, a realistic and commonsense approach should be employed. U.S. Const. Amend. 4.—United States v. Thomas, 548 F.Supp.3d 1212, objections overruled 2021 WL 3857768.

M.D.Fla. 2020. Courts reviewing the legitimacy of search warrants should not interpret supporting affidavits in a hypertechnical manner; rather, a realistic and commonsense approach should be employed so as to encourage recourse to the warrant process and to promote a high level of deference traditionally given to judges in their probable cause determinations. U.S. Const. Amend. 4.—United States v. Bouknight, 467 F.Supp.3d 1227.

M.D.Fla. 2010. To establish probable cause, an affidavit must provide the magistrate with a substantial basis for believing that, in the totality of the circumstances, a search will uncover evidence of a crime in the place to be searched. U.S.C.A. Const.Amend. 4.—Signature Pharmacy, Inc. v. Soares, 717 F.Supp.2d 1276, reversed in part 438 Fed.Appx. 741, certiorari denied 132 S.Ct. 1714, 565 U.S. 1246, 182 L.Ed.2d 252.

Fla.App. 2 Dist. 2009. Affidavits in support of search warrants must be read in a common-sense manner. U.S.C.A. Const.Amend. 4; West's F.S.A. Const. Art. 1, § 12.—State v. Chen, 1 So.3d 1257, review denied Fijnje v. State, 14 So.3d 1003, appeal after remand 97 So.3d 833, certiorari denied 133 S.Ct. 1799, 569 U.S. 923, 185 L.Ed.2d 821.

☞768. —— Sufficiency in general.

Fla.App. 5 Dist. 2020. Affidavits for search warrants are not to be scrutinized for technical niceties. U.S. Const. Amend. 4.—State v. Hart, 308 So.3d 232, rehearing denied, review denied 2021 WL 6138926.

☞769. —— Specificity or particularity; bare bones.

Fla.App. 1 Dist. 1989. Bare assertion in affidavit in support of search warrant that it is believed that dwelling is being used for sale of drug will not support issuance of warrant unless affidavit demonstrates factual basis for belief.—Thompson v. State, 548 So.2d 806.

Fla.App. 2 Dist. 2023. Conclusory statements are not enough to support a finding of probable cause supporting a search warrant, as sufficient information must be presented to the magistrate to allow that official to determine probable cause; his action cannot be a mere ratification of the bare conclusions of others. U.S. Const. Amend. 4.—State v. McNeela, 367 So.3d 557, review denied 2023 WL 8890582.

☞770. Presumptions, inferences, and burden of proof.

C.A.11 (Fla.) 2022. Affidavits supporting search warrants are presumptively valid. U.S. Const. Amend. 4.—United States v. Grushko, 50 F.4th 1, certiorari denied 143 S.Ct. 2594, 216 L.Ed.2d 1199, certiorari denied 143 S.Ct. 2680, 216 L.Ed.2d 1248.

C.A.11 (Fla.) 2019. An affidavit supporting a search warrant is presumed valid. U.S. Const. Amend. 4.—United States v. Whyte, 928 F.3d 1317, certiorari denied Castro v. United States, 140 S.Ct. 874, 205 L.Ed.2d 499, certiorari denied 140 S.Ct. 875, 205 L.Ed.2d 497.

M.D.Fla. 2021. In an inquiry into the veracity of an officer's affidavit in support of a search warrant application, there is a presumption of validity with respect to the affidavit. U.S. Const. Amend. 4.—United States v. Thomas, 548 F.Supp.3d 1212, objections overruled 2021 WL 3857768.

Fla.App. 3 Dist. 1977. Law prohibits issuance of search warrant when affidavit merely states conclusions and is devoid of supporting facts from which ultimate probable cause belief can be reasonably inferred, but where facts are contained in affidavit, reasonable inferences can be made from them, for inference is essence of probable cause.—Churney v. State, 348 So.2d 395.

☞772. —— In general.

M.D.Fla. 2021. The Federal Rules of Evidence do not apply to proceedings surrounding the issuance of a search warrant, and probable cause does not require scientific certainty. U.S. Const. Amend. 4.—United States v. Thomas, 548 F.Supp.3d 1212, objections overruled 2021 WL 3857768.

M.D.Fla. 1975. Affidavit which describes in detail the scenes of an allegedly obscene film which was personally viewed by the affiant and which contains factual description, scene by scene, of what was portrayed and not mere conclusions as to obscenity of the film provides sufficient basis on which judicial officer issuing search warrant for seizure of the allegedly obscene film can make an independent determination and focus searchingly on the question of obscenity; failure of Florida obscenity statute to provide for viewing of the film by the magistrate prior to determination of probable cause was not unconstitutional. West's F.S.A. § 847.011; U.S.C.A.Const. Amends. 1, 5, 14.—Ellwest Stereo Theatres, Inc. v. Nichols, 403 F.Supp. 857.

⟐**773. —— Recording testimony or oral statements.**
Fla.App. 1 Dist. 1978. Affidavit forming basis of search warrant must, in and of itself, demonstrate probable cause for issuance of warrant, and in Florida the affidavit cannot be supplemented by oral testimony to prove probable cause.—McClellan v. State, 359 So.2d 869, certiorari denied 364 So.2d 892.

(D) GROUNDS FOR ISSUANCE.

1. IN GENERAL.

⟐**782. Particular searches in general.**
U.S.Fla. 1980. An officer's authority to possess a package is distinct from his authority to examine its contents, and when the contents of the package are books or other materials arguably protected by the First Amendment, and the basis for the seizure is disapproval of the message contained therein, it is especially important that the Fourth Amendment's warrant requirement be scrupulously observed. (Per Mr. Justice Stevens, with one Justice joining, two Justices concurring in part and in the judgment, and the one Justice concurring in the judgment.) U.S.C.A.Const. Amends. 1, 4.—Walter v. U.S., 100 S.Ct. 2395, 447 U.S. 649, 65 L.Ed.2d 410, on remand U.S. v. Sanders, 625 F.2d 1311.

M.D.Fla. 1997. Constitutional duty of campus police officer to secure prompt judicial determination on issue of obscenity of seized materials is nondelegable. U.S.C.A. Const.Amends. 1, 4.—Andre v. Castor, 963 F.Supp. 1158, affirmed in part, reversed in part 144 F.3d 55, appeal after remand 237 F.3d 637.

Seizure by campus police of one copy of sexually explicit videotape being publicly projected, even if other copies of such videotape were available, presumptively required both warrant and prompt, postseizure, judicial determination of obscenity. U.S.C.A. Const.Amends. 4, 14.—Id.

Fla.App. 2 Dist. 1978. Purpose of requiring search warrant in search concerning obscene material is to ensure that magistrate has carefully considered question of obscenity and determined exactly what is to be seized.—Marshall v. State, 362 So.2d 701.

⟐**783. Necessity of probable cause.**
C.A.11 (Fla.) 2021. On application for search warrant, it is magistrate's responsibility to determine whether the officer's allegations establish probable cause and, if so, to issue a warrant comporting in form with the requirements of the Fourth Amendment. U.S. Const. Amend. 4.—United States v. Morales, 987 F.3d 966, certiorari denied 142 S.Ct. 500, 211 L.Ed.2d 303.

Fla. 2004. A magistrate's power to issue a search warrant is based on the State's compliance with the affidavit requirements and a showing of probable cause; these requirements can be met by one affidavit where it establishes probable cause to search multiple properties.—Haire v. Florida Dept. of Agriculture and Consumer Services, 870 So.2d 774, rehearing denied.

Fla.App. 5 Dist. 2020. The issuance of a search warrant must be supported by probable cause. U.S. Const. Amend. 4.—State v. Hart, 308 So.3d 232, rehearing denied, review denied 2021 WL 6138926.

2. WHAT CONSTITUTES PROBABLE CAUSE IN GENERAL.

⟐**791. In general.**
C.A.11 (Fla.) 2023. Probable cause for search warrant is not mathematical standard; it is practical, nontechnical conception based on factual and practical considerations of everyday life on which reasonable and prudent men, not legal technicians, act. U.S. Const. Amend. 4.—United States v. McCall, 84 F.4th 1317.

M.D.Fla. 2021. The Federal Rules of Evidence do not apply to proceedings surrounding the issuance of a search warrant, and probable cause does not require scientific certainty. U.S. Const. Amend. 4.—United States v. Thomas, 548 F.Supp.3d 1212, objections overruled 2021 WL 3857768.

Fla. 2017. In determining whether probable cause exists to justify a search, the trial court must make a judgment, based on the totality of the circumstances, as to whether from the information contained in the warrant there is a reasonable probability that contraband will be found at a particular place and time. U.S. Const. Amend. 4.—Cole v. State, 221 So.3d 534.

Fla.App. 1 Dist. 2023. Probable cause, as required for a search warrant, is not rigid nor is it a standard that is particularly difficult to meet; "probable cause" is a relatively low legal burden, more than a bare suspicion but less than evidence that would justify a conviction. U.S. Const. Amend. 4.—Malden v. State, 359 So.3d 442, review denied 2023 WL 7017102.

Fla.App. 2 Dist. 2022. When assessing whether there is probable cause to justify a search, a trial court must make a judgment, based on the totality of the circumstances, as to whether from information contained in warrant there is a reasonable probability that contraband will be found at a particular place and time; this determination must be made by examination of the four corners of search warrant affidavit. U.S. Const. Amend. 4.—Smitherman v. State, 342 So.3d 685.

Fla.App. 2 Dist. 2020. For purposes of issuing a search warrant, sufficient information must be presented to the magistrate to allow that official to determine probable cause; his action cannot be a mere ratification of the bare conclusions of others. U.S. Const. Amend. 4.—Goesel v. State, 305 So.3d 821.

⟐**792. Totality of circumstances in general.**
Fla. 2017. In determining whether probable cause exists to justify a search, the trial court must make a judgment, based on the totality of the circumstances, as to whether from the information contained in the warrant there is a reasonable probability that contraband will be found at a particular place and time. U.S. Const. Amend. 4.—Cole v. State, 221 So.3d 534.

† This Case was not selected for publication in the National Reporter System

Fla.App. 1 Dist. 2023. Probable cause, as required for a search warrant, is incapable of precise definition or quantification into percentages because it deals with probabilities and depends on the totality of the circumstances. U.S. Const. Amend. 4.—Malden v. State, 359 So.3d 442, review denied 2023 WL 7017102.

Fla.App. 2 Dist. 2023. When assessing whether there is probable cause to justify a search, the trial court must make a judgment, based on the totality of the circumstances, as to whether from the information contained in the search warrant there is a reasonable probability that contraband will be found at a particular place and time. U.S. Const. Amend. 4.—State v. McNeela, 367 So.3d 557, review denied 2023 WL 8890582.

Fla.App. 4 Dist. 2023. To establish probable cause for a search warrant, the supporting affidavit must demonstrate a reasonable probability, based on the totality of the circumstances, that evidence of a crime will be found at the place to be searched at the time of the search. U.S. Const. Amend. 4.—Zarcadoolas v. Tony, 353 So.3d 638.

Fla.App. 5 Dist. 2006. In issuing a search warrant, a magistrate looks only within the four corners of the affidavit and must find based on that affidavit that a reasonable probability exists, given the totality of the circumstances and a common sense assessment, that evidence of a crime will be found at the place to be searched. U.S.C.A. Const.Amend. 4.—State v. Felix, 942 So.2d 5, rehearing denied.

☞**793. Common-sense, non-technical, or practical determination in general.**

Fla.App. 1 Dist. 2023. Reasonably-prudent-person analysis, that is, the determination of whether a reasonably prudent person would think an allegation regarding the location of evidence of a crime to be probable, as required for a search warrant, is contextual and, by its nature, does not include exacting time limits; it is no math equation, but rather an exercise of judgment. U.S. Const. Amend. 4.—Malden v. State, 359 So.3d 442, review denied 2023 WL 7017102.

Fla.App. 1 Dist. 2010. A magistrate is not required to leave common-sense at the courthouse door when evaluating whether a supporting affidavit satisfies the nexus element and supports a finding of probable cause; an issuing magistrate should, instead, assess the whole of the information provided in the affidavit application and determine whether there is probable cause to believe evidence will be found. U.S.C.A. Const. Amend. 4.—State v. Williams, 46 So.3d 1149, review denied 64 So.3d 1262.

Fla.App. 5 Dist. 2020. The commonsense, realistic approach required of magistrates when evaluating whether probable cause has been sufficiently shown in the supporting affidavit for the issuance of a search warrant is in recognition that these affidavits are usually drafted by nonlawyers in the midst of a criminal investigation. U.S. Const. Amend. 4.—State v. Hart, 308 So.3d 232, rehearing denied, review denied 2021 WL 6138926.

☞**794. Likelihood of criminal activity.**

Fla.App. 1 Dist. 2023. Fourth Amendment requires a showing for a search warrant that particular evidence of a particular crime will probably be found in a particular place. U.S. Const. Amend. 4.—Malden v. State, 359 So.3d 442, review denied 2023 WL 7017102.

Fla.App. 1 Dist. 2010. To establish the requisite probable cause for a search warrant, the affidavit included in the warrant application must set forth two elements: (1) the commission element, that a particular person has committed a crime, and (2) the nexus element, that evidence relevant to the probable criminality is likely located at the place to be searched. U.S.C.A. Const. Amend. 4.—State v. Williams, 46 So.3d 1149, review denied 64 So.3d 1262.

Fla.App. 1 Dist. 2010. To establish the requisite probable cause for a search warrant, the affidavit included in the warrant application must set forth two elements: (1) the commission element, i.e., that a particular person has committed a crime, and (2) the nexus element, i.e., that evidence relevant to the probable criminality is likely located at the place to be searched. West's F.S.A. Const. Art. 1, § 12.—State v. Sabourin, 39 So.3d 376, rehearing denied, review denied 51 So.3d 1155.

Fla.App. 1 Dist. 1994. Probable cause for issuance of search warrant is practical, common sense question, standard for which is probability of criminal activity, and not prima facie showing of such activity; issuing magistrate must simply have "substantial basis" for concluding that search would uncover evidence of wrongdoing. U.S.C.A. Const.Amend. 4.—Clark v. State, 635 So.2d 1010.

Fla.App. 2 Dist. 2023. To establish probable cause, a supporting affidavit for issuance of a search warrant must satisfy two elements: first, that a particular person has committed a crime, commission element, and second, that evidence relevant to probable criminality is likely located at place to be searched, nexus element. U.S. Const. Amend. 4; Fla. Const. art. 1, § 12.—State v. Peltier, 373 So.3d 380.

Fla.App. 2 Dist. 2017. To establish probable cause, a supporting affidavit for issuance of a search warrant must satisfy two elements: first, that a particular person has committed a crime, the commission element, and second, that evidence relevant to the probable criminality is likely located at the place to be searched, the nexus element. U.S. Const. Amend. 4.—Castro v. State, 224 So.3d 281.

Fla.App. 2 Dist. 2011. To establish probable cause that would support the issuance of a search warrant, an affidavit must set forth two elements: (1) the commission element, which requires that a particular person has committed a crime, and (2) the nexus element, which requires that evidence relevant to the probable criminality is likely to be located at the place searched. U.S.C.A. Const.Amend. 4.—State v. Hood, 68 So.3d 392.

Fla.App. 2 Dist. 2011. To establish probable cause for a search warrant, the affidavit must set forth two elements: (1) the commission element, that a particular person has committed a crime, and (2) the nexus element, that evidence relevant to the probable criminality is likely to be located at the place searched. U.S.C.A. Const.Amend. 4. —State v. Exantus, 59 So.3d 359, on remand 2011 WL 11717565.

Fla.App. 3 Dist. 1977. In assessing whether affidavit establishes probable cause for issuance of search warrant, test is not whether evidence would be admissible for purpose of proving guilt at trial, but whether information would lead person of prudence and caution to believe that offense has been committed; test depends upon probabilities determined by factual and practical considerations of everyday life on which reasonably prudent and cautious persons, not legal

† **This Case was not selected for publication in the National Reporter System**

technicians, act.—Churney v. State, 348 So.2d 395.

Fla.App. 4 Dist. 2023. To issue a search warrant, the issuing judge must find proof of two elements: (1) the commission element, that a particular person committed a crime; and (2) the nexus element, that relevant evidence of probable criminality is likely to be found in the place searched. U.S. Const. Amend. 4.—State v. Acevedo, 366 So.3d 1096, review denied 2023 WL 8943631.

Fla.App. 5 Dist. 2020. To establish the requisite probable cause for the search warrant, the affidavit submitted in support of the warrant must set forth facts establishing two elements: (1) the commission element—that a particular person has committed a crime; and (2) the nexus element—that evidence relevant to the probable criminality is likely to be located in the place searched. U.S. Const. Amend. 4.—State v. Hart, 308 So.3d 232, rehearing denied, review denied 2021 WL 6138926.

The standard of probable cause for the issuance of a search warrant does not require a prima facie showing of criminal activity, just "probable" criminality. U.S. Const. Amend. 4.—Id.

Fla.App. 5 Dist. 2013. To establish probable cause for issuance of a search warrant, a supporting affidavit must set forth facts establishing two elements: (1) the commission element, that a particular person has committed a crime; and (2) the nexus element, that evidence relevant to the probable criminality is likely to be located in the place to be searched. U.S.C.A. Const.Amend. 4. —State v. McGill, 125 So.3d 343.

Fla.App. 5 Dist. 2006. In order to establish probable cause to issue a search warrant, the affidavit must show: (1) that a particular person has committed a crime (the "commission element"), and (2) that evidence of the probable criminal activity is likely to be found at a particular location to be searched (the "nexus element"). U.S.C.A. Const.Amend. 4.—State v. Felix, 942 So.2d 5, rehearing denied.

Fla.App. 5 Dist. 2006. To establish probable cause to issue a search warrant, an affidavit in a warrant application must set forth two elements: (1) that a particular person has committed a crime and (2) that evidence relevant to the probable criminality is likely located at the place to be searched. West's F.S.A. Const. Art. 1, § 12.— Salyers v. State, 920 So.2d 747.

⚷**795. Nexus between place to be searched and evidence sought.**

C.A.11 (Fla.) 2023. Probable cause for search warrant requires fair probability that contraband or evidence of crime will be found in particular place. U.S. Const. Amend. 4.—United States v. McCall, 84 F.4th 1317.

C.A.11 (Fla.) 2022. In order to establish probable cause for a search, the search warrant affidavit must state facts sufficient to justify a conclusion that evidence or contraband will probably be found at the premises to be searched. U.S. Const. Amend. 4.—United States v. Grushko, 50 F.4th 1, certiorari denied 143 S.Ct. 2594, 216 L.Ed.2d 1199, certiorari denied 143 S.Ct. 2680, 216 L.Ed.2d 1248.

C.A.11 (Fla.) 2020. Probable cause exists for issuance of search warrant if, given all the circumstances set forth in search warrant affidavit, there is a fair probability that contraband or evidence of a crime will be found in the place to be searched. U.S. Const. Amend. 4.—United

States v. Trader, 981 F.3d 961, certiorari denied 142 S.Ct. 296, 211 L.Ed.2d 139.

C.A.11 (Fla.) 2020. Probable cause for a search warrant exists when under the totality-of-the-circumstances there is a fair probability that contraband or evidence of a crime will be found in a particular place. U.S. Const. Amend. 4.— United States v. Joseph, 978 F.3d 1251.

C.A.11 (Fla.) 1984. The Fourth Amendment requires that search warrant be issued only when there is probable cause to believe that offense has been committed and that evidence exists at place for which warrant is requested. U.S.C.A. Const. Amend. 4.—U.S. v. Betancourt, 734 F.2d 750, rehearing denied 740 F.2d 979, certiorari denied Gerwitz v. U.S., 105 S.Ct. 440, 469 U.S. 1021, 83 L.Ed.2d 365, certiorari denied Sando v. United States, 105 S.Ct. 574, 469 U.S. 1076, 83 L.Ed.2d 514.

C.A.11 (Fla.) 1982. For warrant to issue there must be probable cause that offense has been committed and that evidence exists at place for which warrant is sought; probable cause exists if facts within magistrate's knowledge and of which he had reasonably trustworthy information would warrant man of reasonable caution in believing that crime was committed and that evidence is at place to be searched.—U.S. v. Strauss, 678 F.2d 886, certiorari denied 103 S.Ct. 218, 459 U.S. 911, 74 L.Ed.2d 173.

C.A.5 (Fla.) 1981. When considering the issuance of a search warrant, magistrate must exercise common sense judgment as to whether the facts attested to in the supporting affidavits establish probable cause; the affidavits need not establish beyond a reasonable doubt that the objects sought would be found at the place sought to be searched; it is sufficient that the facts described in the affidavits warrant a reasonable person to believe that the objects sought would be found; while it is better for the affidavits to contain information that the objects sought are on the premises to be searched, that is not always necessary. U.S.C.A.Const. Amend. 4.—U.S. v. Green, 634 F.2d 222.

M.D.Fla. 2020. Probable cause to support a search warrant exists when the totality of the circumstances allows the conclusion that there is a fair probability that contraband or evidence of a crime will be found in a particular place. U.S. Const. Amend. 4.—United States v. Bouknight, 467 F.Supp.3d 1227.

M.D.Fla. 2017. Probable cause to support a search warrant exists when the totality of the circumstances allows the conclusion that there is a fair probability that contraband or evidence of a crime will be found in a particular place. U.S. Const. Amend. 4.—Ermini v. Scott, 249 F.Supp.3d 1253.

S.D.Fla. 2019. Probable cause for a search warrant exists where the facts and circumstances presented to a court are sufficient to warrant a man of reasonable caution in the belief that a crime has been committed and that evidence, contraband, or instrumentalities of that crime exists at the location to be searched. U.S. Const. Amend. 4; Fed. R. Crim. P. 41(c).—United States v. Sigouin, 494 F.Supp.3d 1252.

In evaluating a proposed search warrant, a Magistrate Judge is simply to make a practical, common sense decision whether, given all the circumstances set forth in the affidavit before him, including the veracity and the basis of knowledge of persons supplying hearsay information, there is a fair probability that contraband or evidence of a crime will be found in a particular place. U.S. Const. Amend. 4.—Id.

S.D.Fla. 1991. For a warrant to issue, there must be probable cause to believe that an offense has been committed and that evidence exists at the place for which the warrant is sought.—U.S. v. Hall, 765 F.Supp. 1494, affirmed U.S. v. Shears, 8 F.3d 35.

Probable cause for search warrant exists if, facts within the magistrate's knowledge and of which he has reasonably trustworthy information would warrant a person of reasonable caution to believe that a crime was committed and that evidence is at the place to be searched.—Id.

Fla. 2002. In determining whether probable cause exists to justify a search, the trial court must make a judgment, based on the totality of the circumstances, as to whether from the information contained in the warrant there is a reasonable probability that contraband will be found at a particular place and time. U.S.C.A. Const. Amend. 4.—Pagan v. State, 830 So.2d 792, rehearing denied, certiorari denied 123 S.Ct. 2278, 539 U.S. 919, 156 L.Ed.2d 137, post-conviction relief denied 2006 WL 5536930, affirmed 29 So.3d 938, rehearing denied, habeas corpus denied 29 So.3d 938, rehearing denied, and rehearing denied, denial of post-conviction relief reversed 235 So.3d 317.

Fla.App. 1 Dist. 2023. Determination of whether probable cause exists for a search warrant, on grounds that particular evidence of a particular crime will probably be found in a particular place, is entrusted to the judgment of a neutral magistrate, and that determination simply asks whether a reasonably prudent person would think the allegation regarding the location of the evidence to be probable. U.S. Const. Amend. 4. —Malden v. State, 359 So.3d 442, review denied 2023 WL 7017102.

Fla.App. 1 Dist. 1972. Issue in search warrant proceedings is not guilt beyond a reasonable doubt but probable cause for believing occurrence of a crime and the secreting of evidence in specific premises. U.S.C.A.Const. Amends. 4, 14; F.S.A.Const. art. 1, § 12.—Andersen v. State, 265 So.2d 404, quashed 274 So.2d 228, certiorari denied 94 S.Ct. 150, 414 U.S. 879, 38 L.Ed.2d 124.

Fla.App. 2 Dist. 2023. To establish probable cause, a supporting affidavit for issuance of a search warrant must satisfy two elements: first, that a particular person has committed a crime, commission element, and second, that evidence relevant to probable criminality is likely located at place to be searched, nexus element. U.S. Const. Amend. 4; Fla. Const. art. 1, § 12.—State v. Peltier, 373 So.3d 380.

Fla.App. 2 Dist. 2023. When assessing whether there is probable cause to justify a search, the trial court must make a judgment, based on the totality of the circumstances, as to whether from the information contained in the search warrant there is a reasonable probability that contraband will be found at a particular place and time. U.S. Const. Amend. 4.—State v. McNeela, 367 So.3d 557, review denied 2023 WL 8890582.

Fla.App. 2 Dist. 2021. Under the totality of the circumstances test, the proper analysis for determining whether an affidavit provides the necessary probable cause to support issuance of a search warrant is whether, given all the circumstances set forth in the affidavit, there is a fair probability that contraband or evidence of a crime will be found in a particular place. U.S. Const. Amend. 4.—Chery v. State, 331 So.3d 789.

Fla.App. 2 Dist. 2020. When assessing whether there is probable cause to justify a search, the trial court must make a judgment, based on the totality of the circumstances, as to whether, from the information contained in the warrant, there is a reasonable probability that contraband will be found at a particular place and time. U.S. Const. Amend. 4.—Goesel v. State, 305 So.3d 821.

For purposes of issuing a search warrant, the determination as to whether there is a reasonable probability that contraband will be found at a particular place and time must be made by examination of the four corners of the warrant affidavit. U.S. Const. Amend. 4.—Id.

Fla.App. 2 Dist. 2017. To establish probable cause, a supporting affidavit for issuance of a search warrant must satisfy two elements: first, that a particular person has committed a crime, the commission element, and second, that evidence relevant to the probable criminality is likely located at the place to be searched, the nexus element. U.S. Const. Amend. 4.—Castro v. State, 224 So.3d 281.

To satisfy the nexus element for probable cause for the issuance of a search warrant, the warrant affidavit must establish the particular time when the illegal activity that is the subject of the warrant was observed; it is sufficient if the time period can be established from the affidavit as a whole. U.S. Const. Amend. 4.—Id.

Fla.App. 2 Dist. 2014. In determining whether probable cause exists to justify a search, a trial court must make a judgment, based on the totality of the circumstances, as to whether from the information contained in the warrant there is a reasonable probability that contraband will be found at a particular place and time; hence, the warrant affidavit must establish via case-specific facts a nexus between the place to be searched and evidence of probable criminality, U.S.C.A. Const.Amend. 4.—Coronado v. State, 148 So.3d 502.

Fla.App. 2 Dist. 2014. To establish probable cause, a supporting affidavit for issuance of a search warrant must satisfy two elements: first, that a particular person has committed a crime, which is the "commission" element, and second, that evidence relevant to the probable criminality is likely located at the place to be searched, which is the "nexus" element. U.S.C.A. Const. Amend. 4.—Sanchez v. State, 141 So.3d 1281.

Fla.App. 2 Dist. 2011. An affidavit supporting a warrant application must satisfy two elements: (1) that a particular person has committed a crime, and (2) that evidence relevant to the probable criminal act is likely located at the place to be searched. U.S.C.A. Const.Amend. 4.—State v. Delrio, 56 So.3d 848, rehearing denied, review denied Delguy v. State, 67 So.3d 198, review denied 67 So.3d 199.

Fla.App. 2 Dist. 2006. To establish probable cause for issuance of a search warrant, a supporting affidavit must set forth two elements: (1) the commission element—that a particular person has committed a crime, and (2) the nexus element—that evidence relevant to the probable criminality is likely to be located at the place searched. U.S.C.A. Const.Amend. 4; West's F.S.A. Const. Art. 1, § 12.—State v. Vanderhors, 927 So.2d 1011.

Fla.App. 3 Dist. 2010. The affidavit in the warrant application must satisfy two elements: first, that a particular person has committed a crime and, second, that evidence relevant to the probable criminality is likely located at the place to be searched. U.S.C.A. Const.Amend. 4.—State v. Carreno, 35 So.3d 125.

Fla.App. 4 Dist. 2023. To issue a search warrant, the issuing judge must find proof of two elements: (1) the commission element, that a particular person committed a crime; and (2) the nexus element, that relevant evidence of probable criminality is likely to be found in the place searched. U.S. Const. Amend. 4.—State v. Acevedo, 366 So.3d 1096, review denied 2023 WL 8943631.

Fla.App. 4 Dist. 2023. To establish probable cause for a search warrant, the supporting affidavit must demonstrate a reasonable probability, based on the totality of the circumstances, that evidence of a crime will be found at the place to be searched at the time of the search. U.S. Const. Amend. 4.—Zarcadoolas v. Tony, 353 So.3d 638.

Fla.App. 4 Dist. 2010. For the magistrate to determine that probable cause exists to issue a search warrant, two elements must be proven within the affidavit: (1) the commission element —that a particular person has committed a crime, and (2) the nexus element—that evidence relevant to the probable criminality is likely to be located at the place searched. U.S.C.A. Const. Amend. 4; West's F.S.A. § 933.02(3).—State v. Abbey, 28 So.3d 208, review denied 42 So.3d 799.

Fla.App. 5 Dist. 2020. To establish the requisite probable cause for the search warrant, the affidavit submitted in support of the warrant must set forth facts establishing two elements: (1) the commission element—that a particular person has committed a crime; and (2) the nexus element—that evidence relevant to the probable criminality is likely to be located in the place searched. U.S. Const. Amend. 4.—State v. Hart, 308 So.3d 232, rehearing denied, review denied 2021 WL 6138926.

Where it is a magistrate who is first presented with an affidavit requesting the issuance of a search warrant, the magistrate's duty is to examine solely the content of the affidavit—or what is commonly referred to as the "four corners" of the affidavit—and, from there, simply to make a practical, common sense decision whether, given all the circumstances before him, there is a fair probability that contraband or evidence of a crime will be found in a particular place. U.S. Const. Amend. 4.—Id.

Fla.App. 5 Dist. 2016. To establish probable cause for the issuance of a search warrant, a supporting affidavit must set forth facts establishing two elements: (1) the commission element, that a particular person has committed a crime; and (2) the nexus element, that evidence related to the probable criminality is likely to be located in the place to be searched. U.S.C.A. Const. Amend. 4.—Russ v. State, 185 So.3d 622.

Fla.App. 5 Dist. 2006. In issuing a search warrant, a magistrate looks only within the four corners of the affidavit and must find based on that affidavit that a reasonable probability exists, given the totality of the circumstances and a common sense assessment, that evidence of a crime will be found at the place to be searched. U.S.C.A. Const.Amend. 4.—State v. Felix, 942 So.2d 5, rehearing denied.

⚹**796. Particular searches in general.**

M.D.Fla. 2003. Fact that defendant was arrested in Florida on Indiana warrant for possession of child pornography did not prohibit federal agents from investigating violation of federal law

arising from possession of child pornography in Florida at time of his arrest on out-of-state charges, and thus district court in Florida was authorized to issue warrant for seizure of electronic data regarding defendant's internet viewing activities. 18 U.S.C.A. § 2703.—In re Search Warrant, 362 F.Supp.2d 1298, reversed 2005 WL 3844032.

M.D.Fla. 1975. In obscenity cases, because of the extremely sensitive nature of First Amendment rights involved, determination of probable cause to seize material allegedly offensive to the law must be made with particular care; question to be answered is whether the neutral officer had full opportunity for independent determination of probable cause and was able to focus searchingly on the question of obscenity. West's F.S.A. § 847.011; U.S.C.A.Const. Amend. 10.—Ellwest Stereo Theatres, Inc. v. Nichols, 403 F.Supp. 857.

M.D.Fla. 1971. Finding by officers who were searching, under a warrant, for stolen clothing, of a bottle of "unmarked pills" could not of itself establish probable cause for a warrant to issue, much less allow officer of his own volition to disobey orders of his warrant and search for whatever he pleased.—U.S. v. Tranquillo, 330 F.Supp. 871.

S.D.Fla. 1981. Material may not be seized for its obscene character until a detached, impartial magistrate has made an independent probable-cause determination of obscenity based on prior careful scrutiny of material. U.S.C.A.Const. Amend. 4.—U.S. v. Defalco, 509 F.Supp. 127.

S.D.Fla. 1971. Evidence established probable cause for issuance of search warrant with respect to allegedly obscene motion picture. U.S.C.A.Const. Amend. 4.—U.S. v. Little Beaver Theatre, Inc., 324 F.Supp. 120.

To warrant seizure, proof of obscenity need not be beyond a reasonable doubt, but Fourth Amendment requiring only proof of probable cause is controlling. U.S.C.A.Const. Amend. 4.—Id.

Fla. 1979. Before allegedly obscene materials may be constitutionally taken and preserved for evidence in a criminal or injunctive proceeding, a preliminary determination of probable obscenity must be made by a neutral magistrate. U.S.C.A.Const. Amends. 1, 4.—Roberts v. State, 373 So.2d 672.

Fla. 1978. Although statute directing production of obscene materials states that the production orders issued under the statute are for purpose of determining probable cause that the materials were obscene, where motion for production issued under such statute was accompanied by affidavits detailing contents of allegedly obscene film, and following issue of production orders adversary hearing on probable cause issue was held, such orders were issued on basis of probable cause, and thus the statutory process complied with recognized First and Fourth Amendment standards. West's F.S.A. §§ 847.07, 847.08; U.S.C.A.Const. Amends. 1, 4.—First Amendment Foundation of Florida, Inc. v. State, 364 So.2d 450.

Fla.App. 3 Dist. 1974. Prior to issuance of warrant for seizure of motion picture exhibitor's only copies of two films, it was necessary that a neutral detached magistrate have full opportunity for independent judicial determination of probable cause and that the magistrate be further able to focus searchingly on the question of obscenity. West's F.S.A. § 847.011; U.S.C.A.Const. Amends. 1, 4.—State v. U & L Theatres, Inc., 307 So.2d 879, certiorari denied 316 So.2d 295.

† This Case was not selected for publication in the National Reporter System

Where trial judge, based upon perfunctory examination of affidavit submitted by law enforcement officer, issued search warrant for seizure of exhibitor's only copies of allegedly obscene films with no offer tendered by the State to permit copying thereof so as to allow continued exhibition pending a determination of their obscenity vel non, procedure under which warrant was issued was not a procedure designed to focus searchingly on the issue of obscenity and the seizure was thus unreasonable under Fourth Amendment standards and was a form of prior restraint. West's F.S.A. § 847.011; U.S.C.A.Const. Amend. 1, 4.—Id.

Fla.App. 4 Dist. 2012. Supporting affidavit, based on information supplied to law enforcement by defendant's roommate, provided probable cause justifying a search warrant; roommate directly approached law enforcement and gave sworn statement regarding defendant's criminal conduct, and roommate's disclosure that he had been molested by defendant nine years earlier, coupled with his observation of defendant repeatedly observing child pornography and bragging about engaging in sex with young boys, supported inference that he was reporting defendant's behavior to protect other children and promote justice. U.S.C.A. Const.Amend. 4.—Redini v. State, 84 So.3d 380.

Fla.App. 5 Dist. 2020. Police officer's three affidavits, to draw defendant's blood and to search his automobile on two different occasions, contained sufficient facts to establish probable cause that defendant had committed two counts of driving under the influence (DUI) manslaughter and that evidence of the crimes would be found in his blood and DNA samples and in the automobile he was driving at time of crime; each affidavit provided that, according to defendant's front seat passenger, defendant was "impaired and drinking too much" just prior to accident, and described the observations made by police trooper of defendant having bloodshot glassy eyes and slurred speech and drooling from the mouth at hospital shortly after accident. U.S. Const. Amend. 4.—State v. Hart, 308 So.3d 232, rehearing denied, review denied 2021 WL 6138926.

⚷797. Dwellings in general.

† C.A.11 (Fla.) 2021. Affidavit was sufficient to support warrant to search physician's home for evidence of prescription fraud, even if it included false statements from other witnesses, absent allegation that the warrant affiant included any facts he knew were false. U.S. Const. Amend. 4; 42 U.S.C.A. § 1983.—Paylan v. Dirks, 847 Fed.Appx. 595, certiorari denied 142 S.Ct. 228, 211 L.Ed.2d 100.

C.A.11 (Fla.) 2021. Search warrant affidavit should state facts sufficient to justify a conclusion that evidence or contraband will probably be found at the premises to be searched and should establish a connection between the defendant and the residence to be searched and a link between the residence and any criminal activity. U.S. Const. Amend. 4.—United States v. Morales, 987 F.3d 966, certiorari denied 142 S.Ct. 500, 211 L.Ed.2d 303.

† C.A.11 (Fla.) 2020. Probable cause supported warrant to search apartment of defendant arrested on child enticement and child pornography charges based on his contact with undercover officer posing as underage victim, even if affidavit supporting warrant did not append images of sexually explicit conduct or provide sufficient factual details describing any such images; affidavit provided sufficient basis to conclude that there was a fair probability of finding contraband or evidence at defendant's apartment, as it demonstrated that defendant knew victim was a minor and that he was seeking and requesting sexually explicit visual depictions of a minor, provided information regarding defendant's behavior throughout the investigation, and established a nexus between the criminal conduct and defendant's apartment, indicating that law enforcement would find evidence there related to advertising for, receiving, distributing, and possessing child pornography. U.S. Const. Amend. 4.—United States v. Orr, 819 Fed.Appx. 756.

C.A.11 (Fla.) 2020. To establish probable cause to search a home, a search warrant affidavit must establish a connection between the defendant and the residence to be searched and a link between the residence and any criminal activity. U.S. Const. Amend. 4.—United States v. Trader, 981 F.3d 961, certiorari denied 142 S.Ct. 296, 211 L.Ed.2d 139.

Probable cause existed for issuance of warrant for search of home which was the address associated with internet protocol address recently used by person suspected of soliciting nude photographs from a nine-year-old girl, and who had a prior conviction for child pornography offense; home was owned by individual with same last name as suspect and whose age was consistent with her being his mother, suspect's driver's license listed the same address, and his driver's license photo matched photo associated with messaging app user who had solicited nude photographs, and evidence was presented that child pornographers typically keep stashes of child pornography in their homes. U.S. Const. Amend. 4. —Id.

† C.A.11 (Fla.) 2018. Detective . possessed probable cause to obtain warrant to search apartment of arrestee's girlfriend, where photographed items that served as basis for warrant were observed in plain view during detective's initial protective sweep of apartment; photographs showed a bag of marijuana on dining room table, a scale in a box sitting on a dresser and magazines of ammunition protruding from dresser, and there was no evidence the officers opened drawers of dressers or looked in kitchen cabinets or took any other actions which would have exceeded the scope of protective sweep. U.S. Const. Amend. 4.—United States v. Concepcion, 748 Fed.Appx. 904, certiorari denied 139 S.Ct. 2655, 204 L.Ed.2d 282.

† C.A.11 (Fla.) 2010. Information in affidavit in support of search warrant established probable cause that a search of defendant's residence would result in discovery of evidence that he received or possessed child pornography, despite 10-month lapse between issuance of the warrant and collection of the information, where defendant signed up for access to websites containing child pornography, he was a registered sex offender, and there was a fair probability that he collected child pornography and did not dispose of it, or that computer forensic techniques could recover any files he deleted. U.S.C.A. Const. Amend. 4.—U.S. v. Schwinn, 376 Fed.Appx. 974, certiorari denied 131 S.Ct. 1466, 562 U.S. 1222, 179 L.Ed.2d 310.

† C.A.11 (Fla.) 2006. Search warrant application established probable cause to search defendant's residence for evidence of child pornography possessed by defendant; application indicated that defendant had e-mailed photographs of nude female to police officer and e-mailed officer that

† This Case was not selected for publication in the National Reporter System

female was defendant's minor daughter, and when asked if he had any preteen images, defendant replied that it would take a while to find since he had hidden them. U.S.C.A. Const. Amend. 4; West's F.S.A. § 827.071.—U.S. v. Campbell, 193 Fed.Appx. 921.

Defendant's alleged abandonment of his attempt to have sex with undercover detective's minor daughter did not preclude issuance of search warrant for defendant's residence to find evidence of child pornography and solicitation to commit sexual battery; defense of abandonment did not eliminate the probability that defendant used his computer to solicit a minor to commit sexual battery, and it was unclear whether defendant voluntarily abandoned his attempt to solicit a minor.—Id.

S.D.Fla. 1987. Affidavit contained sufficient information regarding the idiosyncracies of pedophiles to establish probable cause for warrant to search house belonging to defendant suspected of possessing videotape depicting minors engaging in sexually explicit conduct. 18 U.S.C.A. § 2252. —U.S. v. Kleiner, 663 F.Supp. 43.

Fla.App. 2 Dist. 2022. Warrant issued following probationary search of residence of defendant, who was on probation for firearm and cocaine possession, and was subject of a bulletin regarding his suspected involvement in a shooting, was supported by probable cause, and thus the fruit of the search, a firearm, which became basis for new charge against defendant, was legally seized. U.S. Const. Amend. 4.—Ramos v. State, 344 So.3d 526, review denied 2023 WL 2133888.

Fla.App. 2 Dist. 2020. Affidavit underlying application for warrant to search defendant's home submitted by police detective, who had received a tip that a photo depicting child pornography had been posted online from defendant's home, was insufficient to allow magistrate to establish probable cause, as required to justify issuing warrant, in prosecution for charges related to possession and distribution of child pornography; even though affidavit stated that detective was a member of Central Florida Internet Crimes Against Children task force, and that he had conducted investigations and participated in numerous search warrants involving child pornography, affidavit did not demonstrate that detective had any training or expertise in identifying child pornography or that photograph qualified as child pornography. U.S. Const. Amend. 4; Fla. Stat. Ann. § 933.18.—Goesel v. State, 305 So.3d 821.

Fla.App. 2 Dist. 2014. Facts set forth in supporting affidavit did not establish a reasonable probability of finding narcotics or stolen-vehicle parts in a residence, such that a warrant for a search of the residence, shed, backyard and vehicles on the property was invalid as to the residence, even though deputies had smelled the odor of marijuana emanating from the shed, and a license plate from a car that had been reported stolen was in the yard along with vehicle parts; affidavit contained not a single fact that even arguably supported a conclusion that any evidence of narcotics violations or stolen property would be found in the residence. U.S.C.A. Const. Amend. 4.—Coronado v. State, 148 So.3d 502.

Fla.App. 2 Dist. 1979. Affidavit for search of defendant's apartment was not insufficient for failure to affirmatively allege where officer had been standing when he first spotted marijuana growing on upper balcony of defendant's apartment. West's F.S.A. § 933.04.—Hunter v. State, 375 So.2d 1152.

Fla.App. 4 Dist. 2023. Affidavit in support of warrant to search alleged bank account owner's house was insufficient to establish probable cause that evidence of racketeering, bookmaking, and money laundering offenses would be found in house, in forfeiture action under the Florida Contraband Forfeiture Act (FCFA); officer with the county sheriff's office who signed the affidavit only had experience in road patrol, SWAT operations, and narcotics investigations, affidavit relied on anonymous tips and "confidential, reliable sources" without demonstrating any basis to conclude that those sources were knowledgeable and reliable, and affidavit's allegations were stale, as there was a gap of more than four months between the last real allegation of criminal activity and when the warrant was sought. U.S. Const. Amend. 4; Fla. Stat. Ann. § 932.701.—Zarcadoolas v. Tony, 353 So.3d 638.

Fla.App. 5 Dist. 2007. Warrant affidavit set forth facts establishing probable cause to support issuance of warrant to search defendant's residence and his computer; affidavit revealed that citizen informant, defendant's neighbor, told police that he had access to defendant's computer files through a shared hard wire connection, and that, when he opened a file of defendant's labeled "XXX," he saw 122 images of "young preteen girls in nude, sexually explicit positions." U.S.C.A. Const.Amend. 4.—State v. Cook, 972 So.2d 958, rehearing denied, review denied 987 So.2d 79.

Fla.App. 5 Dist. 1990. Affidavit supporting search warrant would not be found insufficient on basis that it failed to allege specific year when unnamed informant observed a pornographic videotape within residence of defendant, even though it would have been preferable for year to be set forth for each material date; affidavit, taken as a whole, sufficiently identified when videotape was viewed at defendant's house. U.S.C.A. Const.Amend. 4.—State v. Enstice, 573 So.2d 340.

Confidential informant's affidavit set forth sufficient facts from which magistrate had a substantial basis for a finding of probable cause for issuance of warrant to search defendant's home, where informant saw defendant watching a pornographic videotape involving defendant, defendant's adopted minor son, and another at defendant's house 13 days before issuance of affidavit. U.S.C.A. Const.Amend. 4.—Id.

⚖798. Hotels and motels.

C.A.11 (Fla.) 2015. Untainted portions of police detective's affidavit in support of his application for warrant for search of defendant's hotel room supported finding of probable cause, even though officers' initial entry into room was unlawful, where affidavit stated that hotel employee had informed officers that he had removed loaded firearm from another room in hotel that defendant had just vacated and that defendant had gone to front desk to claim it, that officers had discovered cocaine and other drugs in vacated room, that defendant was room's only registered occupant, and that defendant had prior felony conviction. U.S.C.A. Const.Amend. 4.—U.S. v. Albury, 782 F.3d 1285.

† C.A.11 (Fla.) 2011. Warrant for search of defendant's hotel room was supported by probable cause, where warrant affidavit described the glass marijuana pipe, packs of small baggies, cell phones, laptop computers, and safe that were found in the initial warrantless search, and also described the "clunking" noise the officer heard

† **This Case was not selected for publication in the National Reporter System**

when he shook the safe and defendant's statements that he had lost the key to the safe and that the officer would need a search warrant to open it. U.S.C.A. Const.Amend. 4.—U.S. v. Rios, 443 Fed.Appx. 433.

Fla. 2017. Probable cause existed to support issuance of search warrant for defendant's motel room and car, where search warrant affidavit stated that there was video of man using murder victims' bank card after exiting vehicle rented by defendant, tracking device attached to rented vehicle showed it had been in area where victims' vehicle was located, and defendant was found to be in company of man seen using victims' bank card. U.S. Const.Amend. 4.—Cole v. State, 221 So.3d 534.

Fla.App. 1 Dist. 1990. Officers had probable cause for issuance of search warrant for motel room based upon valid traffic stop of motor vehicle that had been tied to earlier drug transactions, motel key retrieved from defendant pursuant to his lawful arrest for committing first-degree misdemeanor of failing to stop after officers activated their blue emergency lights, cocaine dropped by automobile passenger, and previously observed circumstances at motel. U.S.C.A. Const.Amend. 4.—Moore v. State, 561 So.2d 625.

⟐**799. Commercial property; businesses.**

†C.A.11 (Fla.) 2020. Affidavit in support of search warrant established probable cause to search principal office of defendant's federal income tax preparation business, where it contained information establishing connection between defendant and place to be searched, and fair probability that evidence of criminal tax fraud would be found there; affidavit indicated that large number of fraudulent tax returns had been electronically submitted within wire fraud conspiracy's applicable time frame from business's office, using business's electronic filing identification number, and that agents had observed coconspirator outside business's office. U.S. Const. Amend. 4.—United States v. Pearson, 832 Fed.Appx. 679, post-conviction relief denied 2021 WL 4845797.

S.D.Fla. 2020. Affidavit for warrant to search premises of owner's construction corporation demonstrated fair probability that evidence of owner's and treasurer's involvement in workers' compensation fraud scheme would be found at corporate office, and thus, detectives were entitled to qualified immunity from suit for false arrest of treasurer, as occupant of office at time of search, in action brought under § 1983; affidavit provided sufficient link between office and alleged criminal conduct by owner and treasurer in not reporting payments made to employees in order to reduce corporation's workers' compensation insurance premiums, among other illegal acts. U.S. Const. Amend. 4; 42 U.S.C.A. § 1983. —Llauro v. Tony, 470 F.Supp.3d 1300, affirmed 2021 WL 5767935.

⟐**800. Controlled substances and related items.**

†C.A.11 (Fla.) 2019. Search warrant affidavit established connection between defendant's home and sale of drugs, and thus warrant was supported by probable cause; affidavit established that defendant stopped at his home before selling heroin to confidential informant, affidavit pointed to other drug-related contraband found in defendant's trash, and affiant detective stated that he believed, in light of contraband recovered from trash pull as well as his training and experience,

that contraband and evidence of drug trafficking would be found at home. U.S. Const. Amend. 4. —United States v. Vargas, 792 Fed.Appx. 764, certiorari denied Aguedo v. United States, 140 S.Ct. 2693, 206 L.Ed.2d 836, certiorari denied Villar v. United States, 141 S.Ct. 147, 207 L.Ed.2d 1087, appeal after new sentencing hearing 2022 WL 766848.

†C.A.11 (Fla.) 2019. Even without alleged misrepresentations and omissions in search warrant affidavit regarding defendant's statements to officers, affidavit still would have supported finding of probable cause, and thus warrant was not void; affidavit contained sufficient information to conclude that fair probability existed that firearm, ammunition, and drugs would be found at defendant's house. U.S. Const. Amend. 4.—United States v. Knight, 773 Fed.Appx. 1057, certiorari denied 140 S.Ct. 1135, 206 L.Ed.2d 195.

†C.A.11 (Fla.) 2019. Warrant to search defendant's home arguably lacked probable cause; search warrant affidavit provided allegations from interviewees that defendant was selling narcotics in area where residence was located, that three months before warrant application, police found bags of methamphetamine and paraphernalia in garbage outside residence, and that, two weeks before warrant was executed, police found small cannabis stem in garbage outside residence, and affidavit did not connect defendant to residence, and although it suggested drug use at residence, it did not demonstrate or allege drug trafficking. U.S. Const. Amend. 4.—United States v. Richardson, 761 Fed.Appx. 945, post-conviction relief denied 2021 WL 719613, appeal dismissed 2021 WL 4205037.

C.A.11 (Fla.) 2017. Search warrant application contained sufficient evidence to provide probable cause to justify search warrant, even after excising false statements by police officer regarding an undercover drug buy; remaining affidavit information included testimony about a police visit to arrestee's residence, in an attempt to execute an arrest warrant on another individual, where officers heard toilet-flushing sounds, saw a water-saturated bathroom floor, and observed white powder residue near a safe, interviews of co-conspirators who stated that they had helped arrestee manufacture and distribute drugs and that they had observed him with firearms, and information that police had recovered cocaine and cash from arrestee during his arrest for possession of powder cocaine. U.S. Const. Amend. 4.—Phillips v. United States, 849 F.3d 988.

†C.A.11 (Fla.) 2016. Affidavit in support of search warrant for defendant's house provided probable cause to search, where Drug Enforcement Administration (DEA) agent included information from a cooperating defendant, an anonymous source, and his investigation, cooperating defendant provided information about defendant's drug trading activities and recorded phone calls, source confirmed such information and provided additional information, agent corroborated information provided by both, and affidavit detailed surveillance of fake drug transaction. U.S. Const. Amend. 4.—United States v. Woodard, 662 Fed.Appx. 854, certiorari denied 137 S.Ct. 2252, 582 U.S. 909, 198 L.Ed.2d 687, certiorari denied Robinson v. U.S., 137 S.Ct. 2255, 582 U.S. 909, 198 L.Ed.2d 687, post-conviction relief denied 2021 WL 4384370.

†C.A.11 (Fla.) 2016. Search warrant application contained more than enough other information to justify finding of probable cause to believe that defendant was storing heroin in his home, where affidavit indicated that informants had made controlled purchases of heroin from defendant, defendant had retrieved drugs from his home to make one deal, another individual had been stopped by police near defendant's home after buying heroin from him, defendant emerged from his home to make deal, and informant indicated that defendant and codefendant had been carrying heroin when law enforcement stopped their vehicle after they had left defendant's home. U.S.C.A. Const.Amend. 4; 18 U.S.C.A. § 2518(1)(c).—United States v. Vinales, 658 Fed.Appx. 511, appeal after new sentencing hearing 698 Fed.Appx. 596.

† **C.A.11 (Fla.) 2015.** Warrant to search defendant's home for evidence of drug trafficking was supported by probable cause; police had evidence that defendant was involved in drug trafficking, and drug traffickers often stored evidence of their crimes in their home. U.S.C.A. Const.Amend. 4. —U.S. v. Cunningham, 633 Fed.Appx. 920, habeas corpus dismissed by 2023 WL 2044609.

† **C.A.11 (Fla.) 2015.** Affidavit in support of warrant to search recreational vehicle (RV) parked outside of defendant's residence supported a fair probability that drugs would be found there, and thus, police had probable cause to search the vehicle; affidavit was based on information obtained from a confidential informant, purchases made by the informant on the property, and police department's own surveillance of activity occurring around the RV. U.S.C.A. Const. Amend. 4.—U.S. v. James, 601 Fed.Appx. 789.

C.A.11 (Fla.) 2015. Untainted portions of police detective's affidavit in support of his application for warrant for search of defendant's hotel room supported finding of probable cause, even though officers' initial entry into room was unlawful, where affidavit stated that hotel employee had informed officers that he had removed loaded firearm from another room in hotel that defendant had just vacated and that defendant had gone to front desk to claim it, that officers had discovered cocaine and other drugs in vacated room, that defendant was room's only registered occupant, and that defendant had prior felony conviction. U.S.C.A. Const.Amend. 4.—U.S. v. Albury, 782 F.3d 1285.

† **C.A.11 (Fla.) 2014.** Affidavit supporting search warrant for defendant's apartment contained sufficient evidence of probable cause to support search of apartment; the affidavit stated that the cooperating codefendant bought or obtained drugs from the defendant more than once, that several of these transactions took place in the defendant's apartment, that both drugs and a weapon had been observed in the apartment, and that defendant and codefendant were planning a future transaction. U.S.C.A. Const.Amend. 4.— U.S. v. Scott, 579 Fed.Appx. 930.

† **C.A.11 (Fla.) 2014.** Even assuming that wiretap of defendant's cell phone did not meet necessity requirement, search warrant application contained more than enough other information to independently justify finding of probable cause to believe that defendant was storing heroin in his home; affidavit observed that informants had made controlled purchases of heroin from defendant, and defendant had even retrieved drugs from his home to make one of the deals, another individual had been stopped by police near defendant's home after buying heroin from him, and defendant had emerged from his home to make deal, and informant told Drug

Enforcement Administration (DEA) special agent that defendant and codefendant had been carrying heroin when law enforcement stopped their vehicle after they had left defendant's home, and that defendant had told informant that police did not discover the heroin because codefendant had concealed it in her vagina. U.S.C.A. Const. Amend. 4; 18 U.S.C.A. § 2518(1)(c).—U.S. v. Vinales, 564 Fed.Appx. 518, certiorari granted, vacated 135 S.Ct. 2928, 576 U.S. 1079, 192 L.Ed.2d 960, on remand 658 Fed.Appx. 511, appeal after new sentencing hearing 698 Fed.Appx. 596.

† **C.A.11 (Fla.) 2013.** Affidavit in support of warrant to search defendant's house provided probable cause to believe that drugs and drug paraphernalia would be found in his home. U.S.C.A. Const.Amend. 4.—U.S. v. Aguilar, 519 Fed.Appx. 541, certiorari denied 134 S.Ct. 357, 571 U.S. 936, 187 L.Ed.2d 248.

† **C.A.11 (Fla.) 2013.** Affidavit contained sufficient facts to establish that probable cause existed to search defendant's residence, despite fact that the affidavit's probable cause section listed an erroneous address for the residence; address given elsewhere in affidavit was correct, and affidavit provided a clear description of the correct address and clearly established that the confidential informant (CI) made a controlled buy from defendant at that residence and that defendant offered to sell him more marijuana. U.S.C.A. Const.Amend. 4; 18 U.S.C.A. § 922(g)(1).—U.S. v. Woods, 506 Fed.Appx. 979.

† **C.A.11 (Fla.) 2013.** Search warrant affidavit established probable cause that drug-related evidence would be found at defendant's residence, where trash pulls at defendant's residence produced smoked marijuana cigarette as well as marijuana residue inside box of baking soda, which was a substance used to create crack cocaine, defendant had previous drug-related arrests, and police were tipped that defendant was involved in drug-related shooting. U.S.C.A. Const.Amend. 4.—U.S. v. Mitchell, 503 Fed.Appx. 751, certiorari denied 133 S.Ct. 2783, 569 U.S. 1018, 186 L.Ed.2d 220, post-conviction relief granted 2017 WL 4401461.

C.A.11 (Fla.) 2013. Under independent source doctrine, search warrant for co-defendant's residence, which resulted in finding defendant in residence, was supported by probable cause after excising information from warrant affidavit obtained from tracking device placed on co-defendant's rental truck; rental cars showed mileages consistent with trips to "source cities" for drugs, defendant was listed as second driver on rental truck, one investigator witnessed what he believed to be drug transaction in driveway, people with histories of narcotics offenses visited house often, cars stopped by house for short stays that were consistent with drug transactions, one visitor was known drug dealer, investigator saw woman in driveway carrying bag of what appeared to be cocaine, and trash pull revealed multiple baggies that tested positive for cocaine and stems and seeds of marijuana. U.S.C.A. Const.Amend. 4.—U.S. v. Bush, 727 F.3d 1308, certiorari denied 134 S.Ct. 967, 571 U.S. 1152, 187 L.Ed.2d 824.

Decision to seek warrant for co-defendant's residence was not prompted by information gained from tracking device placed on co-defendant's rental truck and dog sniff at residence, and therefore, under independent source doctrine, suppression of evidence discovered in search of residence was not warranted in defendant's prosecution for drug and firearms offenses; investiga-

† **This Case was not selected for publication in the National Reporter System**

tor was aware of dog sniff's potential illegality prior to seeking warrant and noted problem in affidavit, rental cars showed mileages consistent with trips to "source cities" for drugs, defendant was listed as second driver on rental truck, one investigator witnessed what he believed to be drug transaction in driveway, people with histories of narcotics offenses visited house often, cars stopped by house for short stays that were consistent with drug transactions, one visitor was known drug dealer, investigator saw woman in driveway carrying bag of what appeared to be cocaine, and trash pull revealed multiple baggies that tested positive for cocaine and stems and seeds of marijuana. U.S.C.A. Const.Amend. 4.— Id.

† **C.A.11 (Fla.) 2012.** Search warrant affidavit was sufficient to establish the existence of a fair probability that evidence of marijuana cultivation would be found in defendants' residence, establishing probable cause for a search despite inaccuracies in and omissions from the affidavit; issuing judge was entitled to rely on agents' conclusion that the store where defendants were seen purchasing equipment was considered a growth store and that the items they purchased were commonly used to grow marijuana, the agents' implication that the high utility usage indicated a marijuana grow operation, and one defendant's prior conviction. U.S.C.A. Const. Amend. 4.—U.S. v. Leach, 498 Fed.Appx. 915.

† **C.A.11 (Fla.) 2012.** Probable cause existed to search drug conspiracy defendants' residence, given that affidavit underlying search warrant established nexus between their residence and the alleged criminal activity. U.S.C.A. Const. Amend. 4.—U.S. v. Schulz, 486 Fed.Appx. 838.

† **C.A.11 (Fla.) 2011.** Warrant for search of defendant's hotel room was supported by probable cause, where warrant affidavit described the glass marijuana pipe, packs of small baggies, cell phones, laptop computers, and safe that were found in the initial warrantless search, and also described the "clunking" noise the officer heard when he shook the safe and defendant's statements that he had lost the key to the safe and that the officer would need a search warrant to open it. U.S.C.A. Const.Amend. 4.—U.S. v. Rios, 443 Fed.Appx. 433.

† **C.A.11 (Fla.) 2011.** Police officers investigating suspect in armed kidnapping had probable cause for warrant to search defendant's property, thereby precluding habeas relief, where officers surrounded property as part of their search for armed kidnapping suspect and observed evidence that defendant was manufacturing methamphetamine on his property. U.S.C.A. Const.Amend. 4; 28 U.S.C.A. § 2254(d).—Hearn v. Florida, 410 Fed.Appx. 268, certiorari denied 132 S.Ct. 232, 565 U.S. 874, 181 L.Ed.2d 130.

Police officers' observation of paraphernalia customarily used to manufacture methamphetamine and smell of strong chemical odor, emanating from open door of shed outside curtilage of defendant's home, was authorized, under open fields doctrine, providing probable cause for warrant to search defendant's property, thus precluding habeas relief, where shed was 20 yards behind defendant's house, was behind camper trailer, and was only 10 yards in front of wooded area, no fence or other object obstructed area between woods and shed that appeared to house only chemicals and containers for storing liquids, and any member of public passing through or near woods could observe shed. U.S.C.A. Const. Amend. 4; 28 U.S.C.A. § 2254(d).—Id.

† **C.A.11 (Fla.) 2010.** Affidavit in support of search warrants sufficiently established probable cause that contraband would be found on the property, where the affidavit contained Drug Enforcement Agency (DEA) officer's observations from consent search conducted one day prior, which included observation of 193 marijuana plants and three firearms. U.S.C.A. Const. Amend. 4.—U.S. v. Diaz, 404 Fed.Appx. 381.

† **C.A.11 (Fla.) 2009.** Affidavit submitted by Drug Enforcement Administration (DEA) agent to obtain search warrant for defendant's apartment for suspected cocaine was sufficient to establish probable cause; affidavit was based on controlled buy conducted by task force investigators, who followed defendant from apartment to location of buy and independently verified that apartment was leased to defendant. U.S.C.A. Const.Amend. 4.—U.S. v. Sailor, 355 Fed.Appx. 359, post-conviction relief denied 2013 WL 5658317.

† **C.A.11 (Fla.) 2009.** Marijuana that law enforcement agents smelled emanating from inside two houses provided probable cause for the issuance of search warrants. U.S.C.A. Const.Amend. 4.—U.S. v. Correa, 347 Fed.Appx. 541, rehearing and rehearing denied 451 Fed.Appx. 908, post-conviction relief denied U.S. v. Renteria, 2014 WL 5148209, post-conviction relief denied 2014 WL 5148214.

† **C.A.11 (Fla.) 2009.** Even if statements in search warrant affidavit, which related to recorded calls between defendants concerning alleged drug transportation, were inaccurate, the remainder of the warrant was sufficient to establish probable cause for search; affidavit detailed prior drug delivery and described the events that occurred after the series of phone calls, including that defendant took possession of bag of drugs, and affidavit alleged that codefendant had delivered drugs to the house that was the subject of the warrant in the past few weeks and agents were able to connect defendant to the house. U.S.C.A. Const.Amend. 4.—U.S. v. Owden, 345 Fed.Appx. 448, certiorari denied 130 S.Ct. 2134, 559 U.S. 1084, 176 L.Ed.2d 753, post-conviction relief denied 2013 WL 6859049.

† **C.A.11 (Fla.) 2009.** Affidavit supporting search warrant authorizing officers to search defendant's home for narcotics was sufficient to establish that evidence or contraband would be found at the residence, and thus affidavit contained probable cause for the search warrant; affidavit set forth fact that defendant traveled directly from the residence to two controlled narcotic buys and immediately returned to the residence afterward indicating the narcotics he sold during the controlled buys were being stored in the home, and the affidavit described a trash pull that revealed large plastic bags containing marijuana residue, and one bag labeled "sour diesel," a potent strain of cannabis, and the affidavit also indicated that documents in defendant's name were found in the trash pull, which, coupled with the fact that authorities observed defendant leave and return to the residence on two occasions, established a link between defendant and the residence. U.S.C.A. Const.Amend. 4.—U.S. v. Akel, 337 Fed.Appx. 843, rehearing and rehearing denied 373 Fed.Appx. 42, certiorari denied 130 S.Ct. 1161, 558 U.S. 1157, 175 L.Ed.2d 988, post-conviction relief granted in part 2017 WL 10276026, affirmed 787 Fed.Appx. 1002, certiorari denied 141 S.Ct. 613, 208 L.Ed.2d 203, motion for relief from judgment denied 2019 WL 11894431, certificate of appeala-

---

† This Case was not selected for publication in the National Reporter System

bility denied 2020 WL 9048187, certiorari dismissed 141 S.Ct. 1756, 209 L.Ed.2d 502.

† **C.A.11 (Fla.) 2009.** Search warrant affidavit established fair probability that evidence of ongoing drug activity or drugs would be found at defendant's residence, where several references were made in affidavit to fact that before and after defendant had conducted couple of drug transactions with confidential informant, he was at his residence, even though he moved residences between those two transactions, drug dog had alerted to presence of drugs in defendant's vehicle at last meeting, and shortly after defendant left, police found two ounces of cocaine under vehicle that was parked next to his vehicle, in location where he could have thrown it. U.S.C.A. Const.Amend. 4; Comprehensive Drug Abuse Prevention and Control Act of 1970, § 401(a)(1), (b)(1)(C), 21 U.S.C.A. § 841(a)(1), (b)(1)(C).—U.S. v. Meryl, 322 Fed.Appx. 871.

† **C.A.11 (Fla.) 2009.** Search warrant affidavit described a sufficient nexus between the criminal activity and the residence to be searched, where defendant's valid driver's license listed his address as that of residence to be searched, a confidential informant (CI) indicated that on several occasions he assisted defendant in unloading marijuana at that address, significant quantities of cocaine and marijuana were discovered hidden in a truck registered to defendant and previously observed departing from address, and affiant, a narcotics investigator with nine years of experience, stated that he knew it was common for drug traffickers to secret contraband and related materials in or near their residences. U.S.C.A. Const.Amend. 4.—U.S. v. Schimmel, 317 Fed. Appx. 906, post-conviction relief dismissed by 2011 WL 3859936.

† **C.A.11 (Fla.) 2008.** Search warrant authorizing search of defendant's condominium was supported by probable cause; officers filed affidavit in which they described how they had arrested defendant following traffic stop after observing drug paraphernalia in plain view through van's window, their extensive experience in investigation of marijuana growing houses, and fact that certified narcotics-detection dog had alerted on front door of condominium. U.S.C.A. Const. Amend. 4.—U.S. v. Toepfer, 317 Fed.Appx. 857, certiorari denied 129 S.Ct. 1000, 555 U.S. 1136, 173 L.Ed.2d 292, denial of post-conviction relief affirmed 518 Fed.Appx. 834, certiorari denied 134 S.Ct. 659, 571 U.S. 1025, 187 L.Ed.2d 422.

† **C.A.11 (Fla.) 2008.** Properly executed controlled buy from defendant at his apartment was sufficient, standing alone, to establish probable cause for search warrant of defendant's residence. U.S.C.A. Const.Amend. 4.—U.S. v. Roundtree, 299 Fed.Appx. 905, post-conviction relief denied 2009 WL 3046143.

† **C.A.11 (Fla.) 2008.** Law enforcement officials who did not search residence at time of their valid entry to make arrest, but who observed drugs in plain view during arrest and returned thereafter with requisite warrant to search residence, did not violate Fourth Amendment in search of residence. U.S.C.A. Const. Amend. 4.—U.S. v. Louisuis, 294 Fed.Appx. 573, certiorari denied 129 S.Ct. 1366, 555 U.S. 1194, 173 L.Ed.2d 625, post-conviction relief denied Johnson v. U.S., 2012 WL 2996593, post-conviction relief denied Louis v. U.S., 2014 WL 5093850.

† **C.A.11 (Fla.) 2008.** Affidavit in support of warrant to search defendant's premises was based upon probable cause, for purposes of defendant's prosecution for manufacture and possession with intent to distribute ecstasy; affidavit stated, inter alia, that defendant had purchased chemical and laboratory equipment used to produce ecstasy, and that defendant's energy usage was significantly higher than that of his neighbors. U.S.C.A. Const.Amend. 4.—U.S. v. Umansky, 291 Fed.Appx. 227.

† **C.A.11 (Fla.) 2007.** Affidavit established probable cause to justify issuance of warrant to search defendant's residence; affidavit contained the following factual information: (1) the apartment searched was under the control of defendant; (2) informant took undercover officers to the apartment, while under surveillance, and purchased $20 of cocaine and provided it to the officers upon his return; and (3) defendant had a history of drug offenses dating back approximately 17 years. U.S.C.A. Const.Amend. 4.—U.S. v. Holt, 246 Fed.Appx. 602, post-conviction relief denied 2011 WL 809563, habeas corpus denied Holt v. Wilson, 2014 WL 5410294, appeal dismissed (11th circ. 14-14949).

† **C.A.11 (Fla.) 2007.** Probable cause existed to obtain a search warrant for defendant's vehicle, in criminal proceedings for conspiracy to possess with intent to distribute cocaine and attempt to possess with intent to distribute cocaine; the officers knew that a package containing three kilograms of cocaine was mailed from California to Tallahassee via shipping company to an apartment likely identified as "B13," they also knew that when a controlled delivery was attempted, defendant chased the departing delivery truck to recover a package, and, witness who resided in apartment "B13," told the officers that defendant had been waiting for a package that had been sent to him at her address, although he did not reside there, and had told her not to answer the door, and, finally, the license tag on the vehicle was discovered to be stolen, and defendant could not say who the registered owner was. U.S.C.A. Const.Amend. 4; Comprehensive Drug Abuse Prevention and Control Act of 1970, §§ 401(a)(1), (b)(1)(B)(ii), 406, 21 U.S.C.A. §§ 841(a)(1), (b)(1)(B)(ii), 846.—U.S. v. Jackson, 215 Fed.Appx. 918.

† **C.A.11 (Fla.) 2006.** Controlled buy, described in affidavit in support of application for search warrant, was sufficient to establish probable cause; a common sense view to the realities of normal life lead to conclusion that a residence contained drugs when a person entered that residence with no drugs and exited approximately one minute later with drugs.—U.S. v. Horne, 198 Fed.Appx. 865, rehearing and rehearing denied 219 Fed.Appx. 976, certiorari denied 127 S.Ct. 2077, 549 U.S. 1358, 167 L.Ed.2d 798, rehearing denied 127 S.Ct. 2970, 551 U.S. 1128, 168 L.Ed.2d 289.

† **C.A.11 (Fla.) 2006.** Police officer's affidavit was sufficient to support issuance of search warrant, and thus evidence found pursuant to search was not subject to suppression, despite defendant's contentions that officer could not have had vantage point to witness events described in affidavit, that officer failed to include confidential informant's (CI) observation of additional drugs in house, and that officer failed to search CI adequately before buy, where magistrate judge found that officer's testimony was more credible than defendant's testimony, only evidence to contradict officer's statement was defendant's testimony that property would not have been visible, and there was no evidence that CI was hiding drugs.—U.S. v. Johnson, 168 Fed.Appx. 390.

† **This Case was not selected for publication in the National Reporter System**

C.A.11 (Fla.) 2000. It was not necessary for search warrant affidavit to contain facts demonstrating that defendant lived in house to be searched, since statement that defendant secreted large sums of currency in house to be searched and that currency was derived from distribution of methamphetamine and cannabis was sufficient to establish required nexus between defendant's alleged illegal activity and house, and established fair probability that contraband or evidence of crime would be found in house, regardless of whether defendant lived there.—U.S. v. Jiminez, 224 F.3d 1243, rehearing and rehearing denied U.S. v. Rodriguez Jimenez, 248 F.3d 1181, certiorari denied 122 S.Ct. 620, 534 U.S. 1043, 151 L.Ed.2d 542.

Affidavit stating that affiant had information, from telephone conversations intercepted by means of valid wiretap, indicating that "defendant is a drug dealer and has drugs in his house, and therefore there is cause to search" was not too conclusory and unsubstantiated to support a finding of probable cause; although it would have been preferable to have detailed particular telephone conversations, affidavit constituted objective presentation of information gained by investigating officers, and specified source of information.—Id.

C.A.11 (Fla.) 1991. Search warrant affidavit provided probable cause to believe that documents and currency related to importation and distribution of controlled substances would be found in residence. U.S.C.A. Const.Amend. 4.— U.S. v. Gonzalez, 940 F.2d 1413, certiorari denied Sanchez v. U.S., 112 S.Ct. 910, 502 U.S. 1047, 116 L.Ed.2d 810, certiorari denied Garcia v. U.S., 112 S.Ct. 1194, 502 U.S. 1103, 117 L.Ed.2d 435, certiorari denied Santos v. U.S., 112 S.Ct. 1194, 502 U.S. 1103, 117 L.Ed.2d 435.

C.A.11 (Fla.) 1990. Warrant authorizing search of premises consisting of house, garage, one other building, and screened swimming pool, all surrounded by wall, based on informant's buy of small amount of cocaine at premises, was supported by probable cause and was not overbroad, despite failure to identify owners of premises as even being present at sale. U.S.C.A. Const.Amend. 4.—U.S. v. Smith, 918 F.2d 1501, 115 A.L.R. Fed. 721, certiorari denied Hicks v. U.S., 112 S.Ct. 151, 502 U.S. 849, 116 L.Ed.2d 117, certiorari denied Sawyer v. U.S., 112 S.Ct. 253, 502 U.S. 890, 116 L.Ed.2d 207, opinion after remand 945 F.2d 365, dismissal of habeas corpus affirmed 326 F.3d 1363, certiorari denied 124 S.Ct. 258, 540 U.S. 900, 157 L.Ed.2d 181.

C.A.11 (Fla.) 1984. On basis of corroborated affidavit describing affiant's interview for job at clinic, in which affiant was told that his job would be to listen to patients' hearts and write prescriptions for methaqualone, magistrate could, without arbitrariness, find probable cause to issue search warrant relating to records in office of clinic. U.S.C.A. Const.Amend. 4.—U.S. v. Betancourt, 734 F.2d 750, rehearing denied 740 F.2d 979, certiorari denied Gerwitz v. U.S., 105 S.Ct. 440, 469 U.S. 1021, 83 L.Ed.2d 365, certiorari denied Sando v. United States, 105 S.Ct. 574, 469 U.S. 1076, 83 L.Ed.2d 514.

C.A.11 (Fla.) 1982. Affidavit supporting search warrant of home of one of the defendants sufficiently established probable cause for search of the home for narcotics and drug paraphernalia. U.S.C.A.Const.Amend. 4.—U.S. v. Vadino, 680 F.2d 1329, rehearing denied 691 F.2d 977, certiorari denied Stephens v. U.S., 103 S.Ct. 1771, 460 U.S. 1082, 76 L.Ed.2d 344, certiorari

denied 103 S.Ct. 1771, 460 U.S. 1082, 76 L.Ed.2d 344, certiorari denied Natale v. U.S., 103 S.Ct. 1771, 460 U.S. 1082, 76 L.Ed.2d 344.

C.A.5 (Fla.) 1981. Warrant to search suitcases was supported by probable cause, based on statement in affidavit that one of the dogs which appeared to respond to presence of narcotics in suitcases had successfully discovered drugs on 409 occasions, another in over 100 instances.— U.S. v. Viera, 644 F.2d 509, certiorari denied Alonso v. U.S., 102 S.Ct. 332, 454 U.S. 867, 70 L.Ed.2d 169, certiorari denied 102 S.Ct. 332, 454 U.S. 867, 70 L.Ed.2d 169.

C.A.5 (Fla.) 1978. Although a bright line cannot always be drawn between "mere suspicion" and probable cause especially as regards possession of materials which, in and of themselves, are not unlawful but which can be used for accomplishment of an unlawful purpose, such as illegal manufacture of drugs, an impartial magistrate is not required to focus with tunnel vision solely on possession but may consider all relevant surrounding facts and circumstances such as the means by which the controlled substance may be manufactured and conduct reasonably indicating an intent to engage in unlawful activity. Comprehensive Drug Abuse Prevention and Control Act of 1970, §§ 101 et seq., 401, 406, 21 U.S.C.A. §§ 801 et seq., 841, 846.—U.S. v. Gordon, 580 F.2d 827, 47 A.L.R. Fed. 849, certiorari denied 99 S.Ct. 731, 439 U.S. 1051, 58 L.Ed.2d 711, certiorari denied Garcia v. U.S., 99 S.Ct. 860, 439 U.S. 1079, 59 L.Ed.2d 49, certiorari denied Cowen v. U.S., 99 S.Ct. 860, 439 U.S. 1079, 59 L.Ed.2d 49.

There was probable cause for issuance of warrant to search warehouse and residence where in ordering chemicals defendant stated that they were intended for use in refinishing process but in delivering the chemicals drug agents noticed that warehouse contained no tools, equipment or furniture, chemicals ordered were essential ingredients in manufacture of methaqualone, drugs were ordered under a fictitious name and were transferred by evasive route to residence where both required ventilation and source of heat were apparently available and defendants were observed procuring laboratory equipment. Comprehensive Drug Abuse Prevention and Control Act of 1970, §§ 101 et seq., 401, 406, 21 U.S.C.A. §§ 801 et seq., 841, 846.—Id.

C.A.5 (Fla.) 1971. Affidavit for search warrant establishing that police had probable cause to believe that state drug abuse laws had been and were being violated on defendant's premises and that STP tablets could be found at defendant's house was sufficient to justify issuance of warrant, as against defendant's contention that statute authorizing issuance of warrant if police have probable cause to believe that laws relating to narcotics are being violated does not authorize warrant if police merely believe that the drug abuse laws are being violated. Federal Food, Drug, and Cosmetic Act, §§ 201(v)(3), 301(q)(2, 3), 79 Stat. 226; F.S.A. §§ 404.01, 933.18.—U.S. v. McVean, 436 F.2d 1120, certiorari denied 92 S.Ct. 45, 404 U.S. 822, 30 L.Ed.2d 50, rehearing denied 92 S.Ct. 277, 404 U.S. 952, 30 L.Ed.2d 269.

M.D.Fla. 2011. Search warrant affidavit sufficiently alleged probable cause to believe that defendant's house and barn contained evidence of crime based upon facts that were lawfully obtained during entry into residence and subsequent walk around barn, where deputies lawfully entered property based upon exigent circumstances, observed elaborate water system outside barn, smelled odor of marihuana coming from barn, and found holes behind barn containing wires, fans, ultraviolet lights, and trash associated with growing marihuana. U.S.C.A. Const. Amend. 4.—U.S. v. Garcia, 853 F.Supp.2d 1177, remanded 2013 WL 10509665, appeal after remand 556 Fed.Appx. 924, affirmed 556 Fed.Appx. 924.

M.D.Fla. 2010. After information obtained in an illegal entry into defendants' residence was removed from affidavit in support of search warrant for the residence, the remaining information was insufficient to establish probable cause to search the residence for evidence of Florida offense of unlawful possession of a blank prescription form; the only information in the redacted affidavit was that officers had observed drug paraphernalia, needles, and pill bottles inside the residence, and that an officer who came to the residence came in contact with a woman who had previously passed a fraudulent prescription, and the affidavit stated nothing that connected the woman who had passed the fraudulent prescription to the residence or its contents. U.S.C.A. Const.Amend. 4; West's F.S.A. § 893.13(7)(a)(7).—U.S. v. Bergin, 732 F.Supp.2d 1235, affirmed 455 Fed.Appx. 908, certiorari denied 132 S.Ct. 1948, 566 U.S. 954, 182 L.Ed.2d 802, post-conviction relief denied in part, dismissed in part 2014 WL 5093853, affirmed U.S. v. Powner, 481 Fed.Appx. 529, post-conviction relief denied 2016 WL 5239831.

M.D.Fla. 2009. Police officer's affidavit did not compel finding that there was fair probability that contraband or evidence of criminal conduct would be found at defendant's residence, and thus did not provide probable cause of search of residence, despite possibility that defendant might have taken proceeds from cocaine sales to his home, where defendant made controlled buys at another location, defendant did not let anyone know location of his residence, and there was no evidence that defendant engaged in criminal activity at his residence. U.S.C.A. Const.Amend. 4. —U.S. v. Parker, 600 F.Supp.2d 1251, affirmed 411 Fed.Appx. 220, rehearing and rehearing denied 429 Fed.Appx. 963, certiorari denied 132 S.Ct. 762, 565 U.S. 1063, 181 L.Ed.2d 491, post-conviction relief denied 2015 WL 4351102, certificate of appealability denied (11th cir. 15-14307).

M.D.Fla. 2008. Canine sniff and positive alert for drugs on stopped vehicle provided probable cause supporting issuance of search warrant for vehicle, regardless of fact that warrant application did not mention wiretaps that had given rise to suspicion of narcotics trafficking that led to initial stop. U.S.C.A. Const.Amend. 4.—U.S. v. Jackson, 548 F.Supp.2d 1314.

M.D.Fla. 2001. Information given to state court judge, including that defendant dove head first out of a rear window of the residence when police officers announced themselves at the front door and that owner of the residence cooperated with authorities and provided information indicating that defendant stored cocaine at defendant's own residence, along with other information from confidential informants, was sufficient probable cause for issuance of search warrant for defendant's residence.—U.S. v. Lewis, 156 F.Supp.2d 1280.

M.D.Fla. 1980. Affidavit in support of search of residential dwelling established probability that dwelling was being used as workshop for production of methaqualone and that items sought in search warrant would probably be located in subject dwelling.—U.S. v. Miglietta, 507 F.Supp. 353.

S.D.Fla. 1995. Probable cause existed to believe that items such as ledgers, bank records, and currency would be found in defendant's residence, even though confidential informant whose observations provided basis for search warrant did not see such items; special agent with Federal Bureau of Investigation (FBI) stated in supporting affidavit that drug traffickers often have such items in their residences. U.S.C.A. Const.Amend. 4.—U.S. v. Smith, 897 F.Supp. 1448.

Fla. 1973. Affidavit in which affiant stated that special law enforcement agent had informed him that, one week prior thereto, search had revealed drugs and certain letters (attached to the affidavit) from defendant implicating him in drug traffic and that affiant had been advised by certain officials of post office department that the department was in possession of letter addressed to petitioner and appearing to contain some bulky substance other than paper was insufficient to support search warrant and resultant search and seizure.—Andersen v. State, 274 So.2d 228, certiorari denied 94 S.Ct. 150, 414 U.S. 879, 38 L.Ed.2d 124.

Fla.App. 1 Dist. 2023. Probable cause existed for search warrant of defendant's home for methamphetamine, marijuana, and drug paraphernalia, even though only controlled buy for illegal drugs in supporting affidavit that was made out of defendant's home occurred up to 90 days before issuance of warrant, where within 10 days of warrant, defendant sold illegal drugs in a second controlled buy out of his car and near his home, and defendant went directly from his home to the site of the second buy without making any stops. U.S. Const. Amend. 4.—Malden v. State, 359 So.3d 442, review denied 2023 WL 7017102.

Fla.App. 1 Dist. 2022. Even if house containing defendant's separately walled-off bedroom and bathroom was a multi-unit dwelling rather than a single-family residence, police officers had probable cause to believe the entire property was an instrument of illegal drug activity and thus were not required to obtain second search warrant for defendant's bedroom and bathroom; defendant completed each of his controlled drug transactions by using the side door of the residence, a door that opened to defendant's bedroom and bathroom, but police officers also observed defendant freely coming in and out of both doors of residence, leading officers to reasonably conclude that he had dominion over the entire house. U.S. Const. Amend. 4.—Tyson v. State, 351 So.3d 1184.

Fla.App. 1 Dist. 2008. Controlled drug buy did not provide probable cause necessary for issuance of warrant to search defendant's residence; although controlled buy was sufficiently controlled as to support issuance of warrant to search site of the sale, the facts as alleged in supporting affidavit did not establish a fair probability that the laundry list of items to be searched for would be found inside the residence. U.S.C.A. Const.Amend. 4; ; West's F.S.A. § 933.18.—Dyess v. State, 988 So.2d 146.

Fla.App. 1 Dist. 2005. Law enforcement officers did not have probable cause to obtain warrant to search defendant's residence and, thus, were not justified in securing residence, even though officers received anonymous tip that defendant was growing and selling marijuana in residence, and one officer detected odor of burnt marijuana on defendant's girlfriend; tip was not confirmed, officers took no action when girlfriend was present in residence but, instead, waited to seek warrant until after her departure from premises, which removed only incriminating fact, nothing incriminating was seen inside residence or revealed by thermal-imaging scan, and defendant made no incriminating statements. U.S.C.A. Const.Amend. 4.—Smith v. State, 904 So.2d 534, rehearing denied.

Fla.App. 1 Dist. 1990. Officers had probable cause for issuance of search warrant for motel room based upon valid traffic stop of motor vehicle that had been tied to earlier drug transactions, motel key retrieved from defendant pursuant to his lawful arrest for committing first-degree misdemeanor of failing to stop after officers activated their blue emergency lights, cocaine dropped by automobile passenger, and previously observed circumstances at motel. U.S.C.A. Const.Amend. 4.—Moore v. State, 561 So.2d 625.

Fla.App. 1 Dist. 1989. Bare assertion in affidavit in support of search warrant that it is believed that dwelling is being used for sale of drug will not support issuance of warrant unless affidavit demonstrates factual basis for belief.—Thompson v. State, 548 So.2d 806.

Affidavit in support of warrant did not establish probable cause for search of private dwelling; while affidavit asserted belief that dwelling was being used for sale of marijuana and that informant had observed marijuana in "attached" greenhouse, there was no factual basis for belief as to presence of marijuana in dwelling other than fact informant had seen owner take "something" from greenhouse into dwelling.—Id.

Fla.App. 1 Dist. 1989. "Anticipatory elements" of affidavit supporting search warrant did not meet requirements of Florida statute requiring that search warrant not be issued for search of private dwelling unless law relating to narcotics or drug abuse "is being violated therein," where affidavit did not show that officers had "actual knowledge" that residence was connected to drug transactions; fact that drug middleman had entered residence and left with white box that was "later" discovered to contain marijuana after it was delivered as part of undercover drug buy was insufficient. West's F.S.A. §§ 933.18, 933.18(5).—Renckley v. State, 538 So.2d 1340.

Fla.App. 1 Dist. 1986. Affidavit of probable cause indicating marijuana was growing on exterior of residence but failing to indicate probable cause to believe violation of narcotics law existed inside of residence failed to comply with statute [West's F.S.A. § 933.18] which requires affidavit to establish reason to believe that violation of narcotics law exists in residence. West's F.S.A. § 933.18(5).—Howard v. State, 483 So.2d 844, review denied 494 So.2d 1153.

Affidavit indicating observation of marijuana on exterior of residence, failing to allege existence of marijuana in residence, and failing to allege fair probability of marijuana inside residence due to growth outside of residence, did not provide issuing judge substantial basis to issue warrant to search interior of residence and thus contained fundamental defect that precluded police officers' reliance on warrant in good faith for purposes of exception to exclusionary rule. West's F.S.A. §§ 933.18, 933.18(5); U.S.C.A. Const.Amend. 4.—Id.

Fla.App. 1 Dist. 1984. Search warrant affidavit which revealed informant's name and showed that informant had been at defendant's house

with defendant and had seen marijuana at defendant's house furnished probable cause for issuance of warrant to search such house, in view of facts in warrant showing credibility of informant and reliability of his information. U.S.C.A. Const.Amend. 4.—Bradford v. State, 448 So.2d 1231.

Fla.App. 1 Dist. 1982. Affidavit was insufficient to justify issuance of search warrant where there was no allegation or evidence to indicate presence of a "controlled buy" and at time of crime, controlled substance involved had some accepted medical use. U.S.C.A. Const.Amend. 4.—Campbell v. State, 423 So.2d 608.

Fla.App. 1 Dist. 1981. Affidavit in support of search warrant which used language in present tense that alleged continuing violation of drug abuse statutes up to time warrant was issued was not rendered defective by failure to specify date when drugs were sold to confidential informant. U.S.C.A.Const. Amend. 4; West's F.S.A. § 893.01 et seq.—State v. Bishop, 395 So.2d 238.

Fla.App. 1 Dist. 1981. Search warrant, which was issued to the sheriff or his agents to search for marijuana, was valid, in that the odor of marijuana was sufficient probable cause to search for marijuana, and thus marijuana found in defendant's vehicle was admissible.—State v. Farrugia, 393 So.2d 614, appeal after remand 419 So.2d 1118.

Fla.App. 1 Dist. 1980. Agricultural inspector's affidavit that he smelled marijuana in defendant's truck was sufficient to support search warrant for marijuana.—Turner v. State, 388 So.2d 254, dismissed 394 So.2d 1154.

Fla.App. 1 Dist. 1980. Agriculture inspector's claim that he smelled marijuana, based upon his training and experiences, during inspection of defendant's truck supported a finding of probable cause for issuance of search warrant for marijuana. U.S.C.A.Const. Amend. 4.—Mahla v. State, 383 So.2d 730, petition for review denied 389 So.2d 1112.

Fla.App. 1 Dist. 1978. Affidavit in which police officer stated that he had searched an informant and found him to free from drugs, had observed the informant enter a building, and had searched the informant upon leaving the building and discovered a controlled substance was insufficient to justify issuance of search warrant for the residence because there was no allegation that the controlled substances were illegally obtained or retained by anybody in the home or that the quantity turned over to the officer by the informer was either sold or delivered by any occupant of the residence. West's F.S.A. § 893.13(1)(e).—State v. Baxter, 356 So.2d 1250.

Fla.App. 1 Dist. 1976. Patrolman's identification at close range of growing material on defendant's porch as marijuana, together with his prior observations that plants so identified were periodically removed from and returned to porch, supplied adequate basis for issuance of warrant. —State v. Detlefson, 335 So.2d 371.

Fla.App. 1 Dist. 1975. Facts stated in affidavit for search warrant, that affiant was contacted by informant who told affiant that heroin was kept and sold at dwelling, and that this information was verified by controlled buy supervised by affiant officer, adequately supported affiant officer's conclusion that he had reason to believe that heroin was being sold in defendant's dwelling.—House v. State, 323 So.2d 659, certiorari denied 333 So.2d 463.

Fla.App. 1 Dist. 1974. Reasonable interpretation of information in affidavit filed in support of search warrant was that it supported assertion that defendant had been in possession of marijuana "at" rather than "in" described premises and use of "at" in affidavit was sufficient to justify issuance of search warrant describing not only defendant's apartment but also the "curtilage thereof."—Joyner v. State, 303 So.2d 60, certiorari discharged 325 So.2d 404.

Fla.App. 1 Dist. 1972. Affidavit executed by special agent of Department of Law Enforcement stating that he had been advised by another special agent that narcotic drugs were being kept on certain premises within week before filing of affidavit and that special agents had seized letters from defendant addressed to occupant of premises indicating that drugs were being transmitted, via mail, and that affiant had good reason to believe that premises and curtilage were being used to violate laws prohibiting possession of heroin and cocaine was sufficient to justify issuance of search warrant, though based largely on hearsay evidence. U.S.C.A.Const. Amends. 4, 14; F.S.A.Const. art. 1, § 12.—Andersen v. State, 265 So.2d 404, quashed 274 So.2d 228, certiorari denied 94 S.Ct. 150, 414 U.S. 879, 38 L.Ed.2d 124.

Fla.App. 2 Dist. 2022. Search warrant affidavit did not establish a reasonable probability that further evidence of drug trafficking would be found in home that defendant had been housesitting and living in for the past several months; affidavit provided detailed account of law enforcement's discovery of MDMA in package addressed to defendant's home address, as well as resulting controlled delivery of the package to property that defendant had been house-sitting, but portion of affidavit concerning that property was devoid of any allegation suggesting a probability that property was involved in any illegal conduct beyond presence of defendant's parcel, which law enforcement had already recovered when they applied for the warrant, so law enforcement could only speculate that additional evidence would be present. U.S. Const. Amend. 4.—Smitherman v. State, 342 So.3d 685.

Fla.App. 2 Dist. 2021. Search warrant affidavit was insufficient to establish probable cause to search defendant's residence; affidavit provided information received from police informant that defendant had cocaine and methamphetamine in his home, nothing in affidavit indicated that affiant had personal knowledge of informant's reliability or veracity, other informant's statements to police did not corroborate claim that contraband would be found in defendant's residence, police did not independently investigate or surveil defendant or his residence, and affidavit did not address any criminal history of defendant's, let alone one involving narcotic sales. U.S. Const. Amend. 4.—Chery v. State, 331 So.3d 789.

Fla.App. 2 Dist. 2020. Affidavit submitted in support of search warrant did not allege sufficient information to establish probable cause for search of residence, although affidavit recounted a controlled purchase of methamphetamine that occurred at the address; affidavit provided almost no information regarding the drug transaction, affidavit asserted that confidential informant "departed the residence" but not that the informant had ever entered the residence or where the drug transaction took place, affidavit did not explain why deputies targeted residence in the first place, and affidavit asserted no connection between defendant and residence. U.S. Const. Amend. 4.—Hicks v. State, 292 So.3d 486.

Fla.App. 2 Dist. 2017. Officer's affidavit was insufficient to provide probable cause that drugs would be found in defendant's residence, as required to justify issuance of search warrant; affidavit provided vague information received from an anonymous tipster that defendant was concealing methamphetamine in his home, that there were scales in the residence, and that defendant sold methamphetamine in ounces, but did not indicate where the sales took place, whether the tipster had personally observed the drugs or even been in the residence, or contain any prediction of future behavior, and there was no police surveillance corroborating the vague tip. U.S. Const. Amend. 4.—Castro v. State, 224 So.3d 281.

Fla.App. 2 Dist. 2014. Facts set forth in supporting affidavit did not establish a reasonable probability of finding narcotics or stolen-vehicle parts in a residence, such that a warrant for a search of the residence, shed, backyard and vehicles on the property was invalid as to the residence, even though deputies had smelled the odor of marijuana emanating from the shed, and a license plate from a car that had been reported stolen was in the yard along with vehicle parts; affidavit contained not a single fact that even arguably supported a conclusion that any evidence of narcotics violations or stolen property would be found in the residence. U.S.C.A. Const. Amend. 4.—Coronado v. State, 148 So.3d 502.

Facts set forth in supporting affidavit established probable cause for issuance of warrant to search a shed for evidence of narcotics, where deputies smelled the odor of marijuana emanating from the shed. U.S.C.A. Const.Amend. 4.—Id.

Fla.App. 2 Dist. 2014. Search warrant affidavit was insufficient to establish probable cause to search defendant's residence; affidavit showed no nexus between anonymous tip that a white female was selling methamphetamine from the residence and any actual drug sales, traffic stops of two vehicles that had been parked at the residence did not connect the drugs found on the driver of one vehicle and a passenger in the other to the residence, and defendant's criminal history, and that of the white female with whom he shared the residence, predated the anonymous tip and the issuance of the warrant by several years, and did not show that current drug sales were taking place absent other evidence of such sales. U.S.C.A. Const.Amend. 4.—Sanchez v. State, 141 So.3d 1281.

Fla.App. 2 Dist. 2013. One factor which may be considered in determining whether the information is sufficient to support probable cause for a search warrant is a pattern of continuous drug activity. U.S.C.A. Const.Amend. 4.—State v. Thomas, 160 So.3d 1282, on remand 2015 WL 13814576.

Fla.App. 2 Dist. 2012. Police officers had probable cause to support the issuance of search warrant; officer smelled marijuana when defendant opened the door to her house. U.S.C.A. Const.Amend. 4.—State v. Roman, 103 So.3d 922, appeal after remand 160 So.3d 430.

Fla.App. 2 Dist. 2011. Totality of factors established a factual basis for magistrate to find probable cause to issue search warrant to conduct an ion scan of defendant's vehicle, where defendant behaved erratically during traffic stop, trained narcotics detection dog alerted during an air sniff near car and during a controlled box test, and $83,220 was discovered in a plastic bag hidden in the rear of the vehicle. U.S.C.A. Const.

† This Case was not selected for publication in the National Reporter System

Amend. 4.—State v. Exantus, 59 So.3d 359, on remand 2011 WL 11717565.

Fla.App. 2 Dist. 2011. Affidavit offered in support of search warrant application set forth sufficient information to establish probable cause that an illegal cannabis "growhouse" operation was being conducted on defendant's property; truck at residence had been observed at hydroponic retail store with different license plates, electric company investigator found evidence of tampering that allowed unmetered electricity to enter the residence, and officer concluded that, based on his experience, knowledge, training, and on the totality of the circumstances listed, the house was being used to grow an illegal substance. U.S.C.A. Const.Amend. 4.—State v. Delrio, 56 So.3d 848, rehearing denied, review denied Delguy v. State, 67 So.3d 198, review denied 67 So.3d 199.

Fla.App. 2 Dist. 2009. Supporting affidavit provided probable cause for the issuance of an anticipatory warrant to search defendant's residence for marijuana; affidavit detailed a series of events setting up a controlled buy of a large quantity of marijuana at the apartment, it was evident from the circumstances detailed, including a phone call that revealed that defendant's supplier would be arriving at the apartment with the marijuana in ten minutes, that delivery of the marijuana was the triggering condition for execution of the warrant, and it was reasonable to conclude that the marijuana was on a sure course to the apartment and that it was unlikely that defendant would refuse delivery of the marijuana. U.S.C.A. Const.Amend. 4; West's F.S.A. Const. Art. 1, § 12.—State v. Chen, 1 So.3d 1257, review denied Fijnje v. State, 14 So.3d 1003, appeal after remand 97 So.3d 833, certiorari denied 133 S.Ct. 1799, 569 U.S. 923, 185 L.Ed.2d 821.

Fla.App. 2 Dist. 2008. Affidavit failed to provide probable cause to support issuance of warrant to search defendant's apartment for drugs; affidavit described only a single sale of an undescribed quantity of cocaine from an unidentified person temporarily located at the apartment on a single occasion on a day that was twenty-nine days prior to the issuance of the warrant, affidavit provided no evidence that such person resided at the apartment, while establishing that some other person paid the electric bill for the apartment, affidavit provided no evidence of a pattern of ongoing criminal activity, there was no indication in the affidavit that drugs were prevalent in such an amount that they could not be quickly consumed or disposed of, and there was no continuing flow of information or ongoing investigation. U.S.C.A. Const.Amend. 4.—Pilieci v. State, 991 So.2d 883.

Fla.App. 2 Dist. 1999. Police had authority to search defendants' home, where police officer lawfully seized bag of cocaine from defendants' home, and subsequently obtained search warrant. U.S.C.A. Const.Amend. 4.—State v. Walker, 729 So.2d 463.

Fla.App. 2 Dist. 1995. Discovery of cannabis stems and seeds, rolling papers, and suspected cannabis roaches in defendant's garbage, and police officers' observation of, and citizen's report of, traffic to and from defendant's house at all hours of day and night provided probable cause to support issuance of warrant for search of defendant's home; officers were not also required to maintain constant surveillance of garbage to ensure that no one had disturbed it between time it was set out and time it was searched. U.S.C.A. Const.Amend. 4.—State v. Mayes, 666 So.2d 165, rehearing denied.

Fla.App. 2 Dist. 1991. Affidavit containing facts detailing controlled buy of drugs from residence that was subject of search warrant was sufficient on its face to support issuance of search warrant.—State v. Schulze, 581 So.2d 610.

Fla.App. 2 Dist. 1991. Search warrant affidavit alleging that suspect was in possession of approximately 84 grams of cocaine, and advising where suspect lived was not sufficient to meet requirement for issuance of search warrant for suspect's residence of showing that cocaine was located within suspect's residence. West's F.S.A. § 933.18(5); West's F.S.A. Const. Art. 1, § 12; U.S.C.A. Const.Amend. 4.—Getreu v. State, 578 So.2d 412.

Fla.App. 2 Dist. 1990. Police officers' affidavit in support of search warrant, which not only failed to contain facts regarding reliability of confidential informant or person who allegedly bought drugs from defendant but also lacked information from anyone who could connect defendant to purchase of cocaine, failed to set out sufficient facts to have enabled issuing magistrate to find probable cause that drugs were in defendant's home. U.S.C.A. Const.Amend. 4.—Brown v. State, 561 So.2d 1248.

Fla.App. 2 Dist. 1990. Actions of unwitting informant in obtaining cocaine for officer provided probable cause for warrant to search defendant's premises; after handing informant $20, officer watched informant approach and enter duplex where defendant answered door and, less than minute later, informant returned and handed officer cocaine. U.S.C.A. Const.Amend. 4.—Delgado v. State, 556 So.2d 514.

Fla.App. 2 Dist. 1986. Probable cause existed to issue search warrant, where informant was shown to have sworn before circuit judge to facts concerning defendant's possession of cocaine, informant described residence to be searched and defendant's method of dealing in cocaine from that residence and identified defendant as man named "Rafael," police ascertained that car parked in driveway of residence belonged to defendant who was on ten years probation for conspiracy to traffic and trafficking in cocaine, and basis of informant's knowledge was his two purchases of cocaine from defendant at the residence within nine days prior to execution of warrant.—Rios v. State, 483 So.2d 39, review denied 494 So.2d 1152.

Fla.App. 2 Dist. 1985. Affidavit in support of search warrant, which only indicated expectation that violation of narcotics laws "would be" occurring within defendants' home immediately after controlled delivery, was legally inadequate, as it did not allege that any violation of narcotics laws was presently occurring. West's F.S.A. § 933.18(5).—State v. Bernie, 472 So.2d 1243, decision approved 524 So.2d 988.

Fla.App. 2 Dist. 1979. Affidavit for search warrant, in which affiant police officers described in detail premises to be searched and in which they stated that their belief that contraband drugs would be found was based on facts that they were taken to defendant's apartment by defendant's associate for purpose of purchasing morphine and that associate indicated that his "source" resided therein, was sufficient to show that police officers had probable cause to search defendant's apartment.—State v. Heape, 369 So.2d 386.

Fla.App. 2 Dist. 1976. Where deputy sheriff received telephone call from out-of-state police officer who informed deputy that individual in custody of out-of-state police had informed police that there was a quantity of marijuana located in a van on defendant's premises, and deputy sheriff then placed defendant's home under surveillance but observed no illegal or suspicious activity during two-hour period, supporting affidavit which was based entirely on tip received by deputy from purported out-of-state police officer and his prisoner was insufficient to reflect probable cause of existence of narcotics on defendant's premises.—Johnson v. State, 339 So.2d 667.

Fla.App. 2 Dist. 1974. Search warrant affidavit in which it was stated, inter alia, that officer had observed large burlap sacks being removed from truck and transferred to van, that officer recognized that burlap sacks were commonly used for transportation of marijuana and that, upon approaching individuals engaged in transferring the sacks, officer observed particles of a leafy substance was sufficient to justify issuance of warrant to search the vehicles even if officer could not have seen that sacks being transferred were burlap but could only have observed large bundles of a dark brown color.—State v. Knapp, 294 So.2d 338, certiorari denied 302 So.2d 415.

Fla.App. 3 Dist. 2013. There was sufficient evidence independent of illegal canine sniff to support issuance of search warrant for defendant's residence; as officer approached front door of residence, he smelled live marijuana plants prior to dog's positive alert, he noticed three cars in the driveway, blinds of home drawn closed, and the air conditioning unit continuously running without recycling, all of which corroborate anonymous crime stoppers tip that home was being used as a marijuana grow house. U.S.C.A. Const.Amend. 4.—Arias v. State, 128 So.3d 73, review denied 147 So.3d 520.

Fla.App. 3 Dist. 2008. Drug dog's detection of live marijuana plants at defendant's front door, officer's detection of the scent after dog alerted officer, tip officer received before approaching front door that defendant was using home to grow marijuana, and officer's observation that air conditioning unit was continuously running without recycling, was sufficient to establish probable cause for the issuance of a warrant to search defendant's home for live marijuana plants and the equipment used to grow them. U.S.C.A. Const.Amend. 4.—State v. Jardines, 9 So.3d 1, review granted 3 So.3d 1246, quashed 73 So.3d 34, rehearing denied, stay denied 2011 WL 13491657, certiorari granted in part 132 S.Ct. 995, 565 U.S. 1104, 181 L.Ed.2d 726, affirmed 133 S.Ct. 1409, 569 U.S. 1, 185 L.Ed.2d 495.

Requiring either a warrant or reasonable suspicion after a dog detects contraband addresses the concern about the unreliability of dog sniffs by requiring articulable facts pointing to existence of drug activity within the dwelling; in the event of a positive alert by the dog, the affidavit in support of the search warrant for the search of the home will then include the articulable facts plus the sniff, not just the sniff alone. U.S.C.A. Const. Amend. 4.—Id.

Fla.App. 3 Dist. 2003. Probable cause existed for issuance of search warrant for defendant's residence; circumstantial evidence existed of defendant's involvement in the sale of marijuana to the undercover police officer at store, and contraband and drug evidence were found during the trash pull outside of the defendant's residence. U.S.C.A. Const.Amend. 4; West's F.S.A. § 933.18. —Merrill v. State, 849 So.2d 1175.

Fla.App. 3 Dist. 2002. In determining existence of probable cause for search warrant, prior

history of drug offenses is one factor which may be taken into account. U.S.C.A. Const.Amend. 4. —State v. Gross, 833 So.2d 777.

Prior activities of defendant at an earlier address were matters that could be considered in determining whether there was probable cause for warrant to search defendant's new home; defendant had sold cocaine to undercover officer at earlier address, two searches of garbage cans located at earlier address yielded bags with cocaine residue and other drug paraphernalia, and cocaine was found when residence at earlier address was searched. U.S.C.A. Const.Amend. 4. —Id.

Fla.App. 3 Dist. 1989. There was probable cause for warrant to search defendant's residence for drugs, where unwitting informant twice agreed to arrange drug purchase for undercover officers and led officers to defendant's residence, and once there, informant disappeared briefly inside front door of residence and reemerged with drugs within two minutes, notwithstanding that officers did not actually observe exchange of money for contraband.—Reyes v. State, 541 So.2d 772.

Fla.App. 3 Dist. 1989. Information contained in affidavit provided probable cause for determining that additional cocaine remained on premises at which undercover officers observed woman buying cocaine, where buyer had told officers before buy that she would accompany officers to a location to purchase cocaine, instead of telling them she would take officers to meet a particular person.—State v. Brown, 539 So.2d 532.

Fla.App. 3 Dist. 1986. Police had probable cause to believe that narcotics were in defendant's shoulder bag after narcotics dog affirmatively alerted on bag so that search warrant subsequently issued by magistrate was based on probable cause and cocaine seized from defendant's shoulder bag pursuant to warrant was admissible in evidence.—Crosby v. State, 492 So.2d 1152.

Fla.App. 3 Dist. 1983. Search warrant was based on nothing more than unverified allegation of anonymous tipster regarding his participation in placement of bales of marijuana in defendant's trailer, which did not support finding of probable cause sufficient to support issuance of warrant. U.S.C.A. Const.Amend. 4.—Milete v. State, 439 So.2d 337.

Fla.App. 3 Dist. 1978. Test to be applied in determining whether affidavit for search warrant established sufficient probable cause for issuance of search warrant is not test of admissibility into evidence, but is whether a prudent man, knowing all facts revealed by affidavit, would conclude that there were narcotics in premises sought to be searched.—Bates v. State, 355 So.2d 128.

Fla.App. 3 Dist. 1977. Affidavit, stating that affiant personally observed approximately four plants, that affiant identified plants as being marijuana plants based on his past observation of over 70 marijuana plants, and that those plants were growing on fourth floor balcony which belonged to, and was part of, the apartment to be searched, was sufficient to support issuance of search warrant for that apartment.—Churney v. State, 348 So.2d 395.

Fla.App. 3 Dist. 1974. Affidavit of police officer stating that he had purchased heroin from a third person who was a guest in defendant's home was not sufficient to form a basis for probable cause to search the defendant's home for illegal drugs and drug paraphernalia. F.S.A. §§ 933.02, 933.06, 933.18.—Wolff v. State, 291

† **This Case was not selected for publication in the National Reporter System**

So.2d 15, quashed and remanded 310 So.2d 729, on remand 314 So.2d 191.

Fla.App. 4 Dist. 2011. Affidavit did not provide probable cause for the issuance of a warrant to search defendant's residence for drug evidence, even though the affidavit related that defendant loaned his truck to a person who had a marijuana grow house, that the person often visited defendant and used the truck to further the person's criminal enterprise, that a humming noise was heard from within defendant's residence, and, inter alia, that defendant's residence had sensor lights at its corners; the affidavit lacked particulars about the visits and use of the truck, facts discovered during police investigation had innocent explanations, and nothing in the affidavit indicated that defendant's residence had the characteristics of the person's grow house. U.S.C.A. Const.Amend. 4.—Mesa v. State, 77 So.3d 218, rehearing denied.

Fla.App. 4 Dist. 2009. Warrant affidavits provided sufficient facts to provide probable cause that contraband would be found in defendant's home even though the actual drug sales did not take place there, thus supporting issuance of search warrant; affidavits described the manner in which detectives observed defendant receive the calls to purchase drugs at his home and leave to deliver the drugs without stopping before the delivery. U.S.C.A. Const.Amend. 4.—Nichols v. State, 10 So.3d 1150, rehearing denied.

Fla.App. 4 Dist. 2006. Evidence found in trash bags provided probable cause to issue warrant to search defendants' residence for drugs, where law enforcement officer twice took trash bags from curbside garbage cans, seven days apart, and trash bags taken on both occasions contained cannabis residue, seeds, and stems along with mail addressed to residence. U.S.C.A. Const.Amend. 4; West's F.S.A. § 933.18(5).—State v. Colitto, 929 So.2d 654, review denied 945 So.2d 1289.

Fla.App. 4 Dist. 2006. Evidence discovered during traffic stop of defendant's vehicle, including cannabis cultivation books, video, and a small amount of marijuana consistent with personal use, did not provide probable cause for issuance of residential search warrant on basis of independent lawful evidence separate from that obtained by illegal dog sniff at exterior door of defendant's home; evidence did not suggest a fair probability of any broader criminal activity, such as the growing of marijuana in home. U.S.C.A. Const. Amend. 4.—State v. Rabb, 920 So.2d 1175, review denied 933 So.2d 522, certiorari denied 127 S.Ct. 665, 549 U.S. 1052, 166 L.Ed.2d 513.

Fla.App. 4 Dist. 2004. Evidence did not establish probable cause necessary to support search warrant for defendant's residence, even though informant provided tip that defendant had cannabis grow operation at his residence, marijuana was found on defendant and in his vehicle during traffic stop, and vehicle contained cannabis cultivation books and video; residence did not have indicia of marijuana grow house, informant's veracity was not established in affidavit in support of search warrant, and marijuana in defendant's vehicle did not establish any illegal activities in residence. U.S.C.A. Const.Amend. 4.—State v. Rabb, 881 So.2d 587, rehearing denied, certiorari granted, vacated 125 S.Ct. 2246, 544 U.S. 1028, 161 L.Ed.2d 1051, on remand 920 So.2d 1175, review denied 933 So.2d 522, certiorari denied 127 S.Ct. 665, 549 U.S. 1052, 166 L.Ed.2d 513.

Fla.App. 4 Dist. 2002. Affidavit supporting search warrant of defendant's residence was sufficient to establish probable cause that drug evidence would have been found in residence, and thus, drugs found in residence pursuant to search was not subject to suppression; officer had observed substantial "short-term traffic" entering and leaving defendant's residence during the month prior to the issuance of search warrant, officer observed people smoking what appeared to be marijuana on the front porch of residence and others leaving the residence with baggies that appeared to contain cocaine, and two days before the issuance of search warrant, a single trash pull at residence revealed the presence of marijuana and bags cut similar to officer's observations of other drug investigations. U.S.C.A. Const.Amend. 4.—State v. Carbonell, 816 So.2d 1169, rehearing denied.

Fla.App. 4 Dist. 2001. Affidavit submitted in support of search warrant lacked sufficient probable cause for issuance of warrant to locate cannabis at defendant's residence; while affidavit contained relevant information that residual amounts of cannabis were found in two separate trash pulls which were conducted approximately six months apart, a third trash pull which was conducted during time between the two pulls yielded no evidence of drug activity and was omitted from affidavit, and affidavit lacked other sufficient facts to indicate a fair probability that cannabis would be found in defendant's home or to show a pattern of continuous drug activity. U.S.C.A. Const.Amend. 4.—Cruz v. State, 788 So.2d 375.

Fla.App. 4 Dist. 2000. Trash pull revealing contraband, which was performed based on anonymous tip, provided probable cause for warrant to search defendant's home; baggies found in trash pull tested positive for cocaine and provided evidence of continuous activity, and clear baggies and green twisty ties found in trash pull were consistent with specific information from caller regarding manner in which defendant was packaging cocaine for sale. U.S.C.A. Const. Amend. 4.—Baker v. State, 762 So.2d 977, rehearing denied.

Fla.App. 4 Dist. 1998. Fact that substance found during one-time trash pull from garbage outside defendant's home tested positive for cannabis was not sufficient, either by itself or in conjunction with anonymous tip that residents at that address were dealing in narcotics, to establish a fair probability that cannabis would be found in defendant's home, and did not provide probable cause for issuance of search warrant; such information, which was contained in affidavit in support of search warrant, did not suggest a pattern of continuous drug activity. U.S.C.A. Const.Amend. 4.—Raulerson v. State, 714 So.2d 536, rehearing denied.

Fla.App. 4 Dist. 1996. Probable cause to search house next door to controlled drug buy was established by police officer's personal observation that defendant left site of transaction and retrieved drugs from the house next door, even though officer did not personally observe defendant in possession of the drugs and did not allege in affidavit underlying search warrant application that person overheard stating his intention to go next door and retrieve the drugs was the same person who was observed immediately thereafter going next door. U.S.C.A. Const.Amend. 4.—State v. Howard, 666 So.2d 592.

Fla.App. 4 Dist. 1995. Warrant to search residence in which affiant believed there would be cocaine purchase was invalid; affidavit should have shown probable cause that law was then being violated. West's F.S.A. § 933.18(5).—Pazos v. State, 654 So.2d 1000, review denied 662 So.2d 932.

Fla.App. 4 Dist. 1995. While affidavit supporting search of warehouse in which drug paraphernalia and other contraband items were allegedly stored could have been worded more carefully and could have explicitly, rather than implicitly, incorporated earlier affidavits and warrants, affidavit was sufficient to provide probable cause to issue warrant particularly in light of references to earlier search and defendants' arrest pursuant to the accompanying warrants. U.S.C.A. Const. Amend. 4.—State v. Guertin, 650 So.2d 1041, rehearing denied.

Fla.App. 4 Dist. 1990. Affidavit in support of search warrant contained sufficient material facts to establish probable cause for issuance of warrant, where affidavit contained relevant information concerning activities at residence observed during surveillance by sheriff's deputy, information that substance in baggies found in defendant's trash tested positive for cocaine, and information furnished to sheriff's office by one of defendant's neighbors concerning neighbor's observations of activities at residence. U.S.C.A. Const.Amend. 4.—Scott v. State, 559 So.2d 269.

Fla.App. 4 Dist. 1984. Affidavit was sufficient to support search warrant, where affiant stated that informer had provided reliable information on eight previous occasions, resulting in six arrests and prosecutions, and informer had not only alleged that owner of house to be searched had offered to sell him marijuana, but also that contraband was presently stored in residence.— DeLaPaz v. State, 453 So.2d 445.

Fla.App. 4 Dist. 1982. There was abundant evidence in record on appeal from conviction and sentence for drug trafficking to uphold action of police in securing search warrant to search defendant's plane after defendant, who initially consented to search of plane, fled the scene.—Bowles v. State, 414 So.2d 236, review denied 424 So.2d 760.

Fla.App. 4 Dist. 1980. Affidavit was sufficient to establish probable cause for issuance of search warrant where telephone conversation between defendant and individual whose telephone was subject of an authorized wiretap revealed that defendant had, within his control, marijuana and tuinal, in that conversation was replete with references to drugs that defendant did and did not "have" and to fact that he was speaking from a telephone located in his residence. West's F.S.A. § 933.18.—State v. Powers, 388 So.2d 1050, petition for review dismissed Polk v. Hickory Springs Manufacturing Co., 397 So.2d 778.

Fla.App. 4 Dist. 1975. Affidavit in support of search warrant, which alleged that package containing hashish was to be delivered to defendant at private dwelling, but which did not allege any violation of narcotics law currently occurring in defendant's home, failed to meet statutory requirement that no warrant shall be issued for search of any private dwelling except on sworn proof that affiant has reason to believe that law relating to narcotics or drug abuse is being violated therein, and thus was insufficient to support issuance of search warrant. West's F.S.A. §§ 933.05, 933.18.—Gerardi v. State, 307 So.2d 853.

Fla.App. 4 Dist. 1973. In respect to issuance of search warrant, there was no deprivation of process, particularly since the offense in question

exactly fit the definition in statute, providing that warrants for the search of private dwellings may not be issued unless "the law relating to narcotics and drug abuse is being violated therein"; thus, considering the offense and reading the municipal charter search warrant authorization in conjunction with the aforementioned statute and considering the affidavit and warrant in question, the same was justified, rendering the search thereunder and resulting conviction proper. F.S.A. § 933.18(5).—Franklin v. State, 285 So.2d 32.

Fla.App. 5 Dist. 2013. Even without formal certification, a narcotics detection dog's alert to the presence of drugs can provide probable cause for issuance of a search warrant if the dog recently and successfully completed a training program that evaluated his proficiency in locating drugs. U.S.C.A. Const.Amend. 4.—State v. Grue, 130 So.3d 256.

Narcotics detection dog's alert to the presence of drugs in a delivery package addressed to defendant was sufficiently reliable to establish probable cause necessary for issuance of search warrant; warrant affidavit represented that the dog and his police officer handler had gone through extensive training and that the dog had discovered thousands of pounds of narcotics in the past. U.S.C.A. Const.Amend. 4.—Id.

Although evidence of a narcotics detection dog's certification or training may presumptively establish probable cause for issuance of search warrant based on dog's alert to the presence of drugs, it is preferable to provide additional information as to the identity of the organization that certified the dog, the dates of that certification, and additional subsequent training. U.S.C.A. Const.Amend. 4.—Id.

The test for probable cause for issuance of a search warrant, based on narcotics detection dog's alert to the presence of drugs, does not require the proof that the beyond a reasonable doubt standard or even the preponderance of the evidence standard requires; rather, the question is whether all the facts surrounding the dog's alert, viewed through the lens of common sense, would make a reasonably prudent person think that a search would reveal contraband or evidence of a crime. U.S.C.A. Const.Amend. 4.—Id.

Fla.App. 5 Dist. 2006. Affidavit did not provide probable cause to issue warrant to search defendant's residence for drugs, even though affidavit stated in part that defendant admitted that cocaine was being kept somewhere in residence, had cell phone number matching that provided by anonymous informant, and had criminal history of cocaine and cannabis possession; defendant in fact never told anyone that cocaine was being kept in residence, cell phone transaction could take place anywhere and not just in residence, and defendant's criminal history did not suggest he was engaged in trafficking at time of warrant application or that drugs were being kept or sold out of residence. West's F.S.A. Const. Art. 1, § 12.—Salyers v. State, 920 So.2d 747.

Fla.App. 5 Dist. 1990. Search warrant affiant's statement that, after talking with informant, person from whom drugs were ultimately purchased walked into house that was subject of warrant request and then exited house shortly thereafter to meet with informant did not negate affidavit as basis for probable cause even though no one in fact observed person's exit from house and even though house owner alleged that affiant's representation that drugs were being stored in house was in fact nothing more than mere possibility—person lived next door, and it was implied that person could have obtained drugs from his own residence rather than house in question.—Polk v. Williams, 565 So.2d 1387.

Fla.App. 5 Dist. 1990. Search warrant was supported by sufficient probable cause that cocaine would be found in defendant's residence. U.S.C.A. Const.Amend. 4.—State v. Price, 564 So.2d 1239.

Fla.App. 5 Dist. 1989. Search warrant affidavit's reference to residence in county where affiant saw residence's owners and effected buy of drugs through another person did not adequately describe place to be searched. U.S.C.A. Const. Amend. 4; West's F.S.A. § 933.04.—State v. Martin, 539 So.2d 577.

Fla.App. 5 Dist. 1987. Search warrant affidavit which showed only possibility rather than probability of drugs being at location to be searched was sufficient where affidavit did not contain false information, and search warrant based on it was regular on its face, was issued by neutral and detached magistrate, and was served by law enforcement officers who acted in good faith and in reasonable reliance on probable cause determination and technical sufficiency of warrant.—State v. Garcia, 503 So.2d 347, review denied 511 So.2d 298.

Fla.App. 5 Dist. 1986. There was probable cause to issue search warrant where supporting affidavit identified officer and stated his education and experience in narcotics transactions, explained how reliable confidential informant wearing transmitting device had made cocaine buy from person he identified as defendant, set forth two other drug buys from defendant on different dates made by same informant and under same controlled and monitored circumstances, and showed continuous series of narcotics transactions by defendant and facts to indicate probable presence of substantial quantities of drugs on his premises. West's F.S.A. § 933.07.—Ryals v. State, 498 So.2d 1365.

Fla.App. 5 Dist. 1983. Totality of circumstances surrounding controlled buy of cocaine from defendant by confidential informant under the supervision of police officer established probable cause for search of defendant's trailer.—State v. Cohen, 442 So.2d 346.

Fla.App. 5 Dist. 1983. Affidavit, in which it was asserted that detective-affiant found marijuana and cannabis seeds within garbage bags at certain residence on two separate occasions within one month's time, established probable cause for issuance of search warrant.—State v. Jacobs, 437 So.2d 166, petition for review dismissed 441 So.2d 632.

Fla.App. 5 Dist. 1983. Fact that police detective did not state in affidavit supporting search warrant that he identified substance in plastic bag in suspect's home as being cannabis based on his past experience in identifying cannabis or based on any past familiarity with the substance did not render affidavit insufficient to permit magistrate to determine whether probable cause existed for search, though such averments were perhaps not as detailed as might be desired. U.S.C.A. Const.Amend. 4.—Younger v. State, 433 So.2d 636, petition for review denied 440 So.2d 354.

Term "probable cause" refers to reasonable ground of suspicion; affiant, in seeking search warrant, need not actually know that contraband is present in premises sought to be searched, but need only have reasonable ground to believe that such evidence is present. U.S.C.A. Const.Amend. 4.—Id.

Affidavit which established that two separate quantities of marijuana had been found in suspect's living room provided reasonable cause to believe that other cannabis or narcotics were present in the house, and thus search warrant issued on such affidavit was valid. U.S.C.A. Const.Amend. 4.—Id.

⟜801. Records; documents.

S.D.Fla. 1981. Issuance of search warrant for business records pertaining to the purchase, production, sales, transportation, receipts, disbursement, inventory, and other records of a similar nature regarding the allegedly obscene films and magazines was without probable cause, notwithstanding indictment, where affidavits and supporting documents did not contain copies of allegedly obscene films and magazines, nor were any detailed descriptions of material submitted to magistrates, and magistrates were not actually given copies of indictment, but were merely informed of existence of original indictment. U.S.C.A.Const. Amend. 4.—U.S. v. Defalco, 509 F.Supp. 127.

⟜802. Weapons.

C.A.11 (Fla.) 2021. Even if co-defendant's alleged statement, that he was the owner of drugs on couch and gun found on his person during search by law enforcement, had been included in search warrant affidavit, totality of the circumstances supported finding that officers had probable cause to search the home which led to discovery of the firearm that served as basis of defendant's indictment, supporting issuance of warrant, for purposes of defendant's prosecution for being a felon in possession of a firearm; co-defendant's claim of ownership did not diminish the likelihood that more evidence of his crimes would have been found elsewhere in the home. U.S. Const. Amend. 4; 18 U.S.C.A. § 922(g).—United States v. Leonard, 4 F.4th 1134, certiorari denied 142 S.Ct. 2709, 212 L.Ed.2d 778, post-conviction relief denied 2023 WL 2456042.

† C.A.11 (Fla.) 2019. Even without alleged misrepresentations and omissions in search warrant affidavit regarding defendant's statements to officers, affidavit still would have supported finding of probable cause, and thus warrant was not void; affidavit contained sufficient information to conclude that fair probability existed that firearm, ammunition, and drugs would be found at defendant's house. U.S. Const. Amend. 4.—United States v. Knight, 773 Fed.Appx. 1057, certiorari denied 140 S.Ct. 1135, 206 L.Ed.2d 195.

C.A.11 (Fla.) 2008. Probable cause existed for residential search for weapons that led to prosecution for being felon in possession of firearm, based on federal agents' averments that they had observed defendant with firearms at several gun shows, that confidential informant had indicated that defendant would attend specific gun show and had claimed to be in possession of over 300 firearms, and that, based on agents' experience, convicted felons and firearms dealers possessing contraband typically stored such items on their property. U.S.C.A. Const.Amend. 4; 18 U.S.C.A. § 922(g)(1).—U.S. v. Anton, 546 F.3d 1355, rehearing and rehearing denied 309 Fed.Appx. 386, certiorari denied 129 S.Ct. 2033, 556 U.S. 1184, 173 L.Ed.2d 1089, appeal after new sentencing hearing 353 Fed.Appx. 343, rehearing and rehearing denied 401 Fed.Appx. 516, on remand 2010 WL 918061, post-conviction relief denied 2012 WL 1559688.

---

† This Case was not selected for publication in the National Reporter System

Fla.App. 1 Dist. 1982. Affidavit in support of warrant to search convicted felon's residence for firearms was legally inadequate where it did not state residence was in exclusive possession or control of felon and did not allege any factual predicate which connected felon to firearms other than mere presence of firearms in residence. West's F.S.A. § 933.18; West's F.S.A. Const. Art. 1, § 12.—Polston v. State, 424 So.2d 15.

Fla.App. 5 Dist. 2004. Affidavit provided issuing judge with substantial basis for inferring that gun, handcuffs, police badge, and other items sought were probably at defendant's residence, so as to support issuance of search warrant for residence; affidavit clearly linked defendant to abduction and sexual assault through direct evidence, affidavit alleged that defendant lured victim by identifying himself as police officer, displayed police badge, and sexually battered victim at gunpoint, and three days had elapsed since crime occurred. U.S.C.A. Const.Amend. 4.— State v. Weil, 877 So.2d 803, review denied 889 So.2d 72.

⟲803. Electronic devices.

† C.A.11 (Fla.) 2019. Under independent source doctrine, search warrant affidavit established probable cause to search apartment, even after information related to officer's allegedly illegal second entry into apartment was excised; defendant's sister gave officer gift credit cards, she stated that her brother made credit cards, and she had observed him swipe credit cards in a machine that was connected to a lap top computer. U.S. Const. Amend. 4.—United States v. Fleur, 762 Fed.Appx. 691.

† C.A.11 (Fla.) 2017. Facts set forth in affidavit failed to provide substantial basis for concluding that probable cause existed to search defendant's cell phone for evidence of criminal activity; affidavit alleged that defendant, a convicted sex offender who was required by Florida law to register any e-mail addresses he used, used an unregistered e-mail address in connection with his cell phone, but affidavit gave no reason to suspect that defendant either did not use or could not have used his registered e-mail address for that purpose. U.S. Const. Amend. 4.—United States v. Bishop, 683 Fed.Appx. 899, certiorari denied 138 S.Ct. 347, 583 U.S. 928, 199 L.Ed.2d 231.

C.A.11 (Fla.) 2015. Judge, relying on common sense, could have determined that it was fairly probable that cellular telephone contained evidence of images depicting sexual performance by a child in violation of Florida law, as required for search warrant of phone to issue, where affidavit supporting search of phone described photographs of naked men, women, and children, including close-ups of private body parts, and culminated in description of photo that focused on young child's naked vagina and stomach, covered in fluid that appeared to be semen. U.S.C.A. Const.Amend. 4; West's F.S.A. § 827.071.—U.S. v. Sparks, 806 F.3d 1323, certiorari denied 136 S.Ct. 2009, 578 U.S. 979, 195 L.Ed.2d 222, certiorari denied Johnson v. U.S., 137 S.Ct. 34, 580 U.S. 827, 196 L.Ed.2d 46.

† C.A.11 (Fla.) 2006. Defendant's alleged abandonment of his attempt to have sex with undercover detective's minor daughter did not preclude issuance of search warrant for defendant's residence to find evidence of child pornography and solicitation to commit sexual battery; defense of abandonment did not eliminate the probability that defendant used his computer to solicit a minor to commit sexual battery, and it was unclear whether defendant voluntarily abandoned his attempt to solicit a minor.—U.S. v. Campbell, 193 Fed.Appx. 921.

M.D.Fla. 2003. District court did not have authority under Stored Wire and Electronic Communications and Transactional Records Access Act to issue warrant in connection with child pornography investigation for seizure of electronic data maintained by web site in another district, despite amendment by USA PATRIOT Act permitting seizure of out-of-district property in connection with terrorism cases; amendment and its legislative history said nothing to extend court's authority to issue out-of-district warrants in any other type of criminal cases. 18 U.S.C.A. §§ 2703, 2711; Fed.Rules Cr.Proc.Rule 41(b), 18 U.S.C.A.—In re Search Warrant, 362 F.Supp.2d 1298, reversed 2005 WL 3844032.

S.D.Fla. 2019. Search warrant for defendant's home was supported by probable cause, for purposes of motion to suppress in prosecution for receiving and possessing child pornography, even though it was possible that a person located outside the physical residence could have accessed network allegedly used to download child pornography using internet protocol address associated with device in the residence, where the home was used to access the network on three different occasions for purpose of requesting child pornography, child pornography was the kind of material that someone generally downloads in a non-public place, like his own home, items downloaded were videos, accessing the network required specialty software, and the location at issue was a private residence. U.S. Const. Amend. 4; 18 U.S.C.A. § 2510(8).—United States v. Sigouin, 494 F.Supp.3d 1252.

Fla.App. 1 Dist. 2018. Investigating officer's search warrant that authorized seizure of defendant's computer was supported by probable cause, even though officer was unable to personally view video containing child pornography which he knew from investigation had been downloaded onto defendant's hard drive, where officer utilized a graphic description of video given by detective who personally viewed it, which description he was able to acquire from a law enforcement database. U.S. Const. Amend. 4.—Mardosas v. State, 257 So.3d 540, rehearing denied, review denied 2019 WL 1349269, certiorari denied 140 S.Ct. 576, 205 L.Ed.2d 359.

Fla.App. 1 Dist. 2010. Officer's warrant affidavit set forth facts upon which a reasonable magistrate could find probable cause to support issuance of warrant to search defendant's residence for child pornography; five-page supporting affidavit clearly indicated officer had reason to believe defendant, on at least 123 separate occasions, used a computer in his residence to access a specific IP address and download "known or suspected child pornography," and affidavit also clearly indicated there was at least one occasion where defendant accessed a file that officer personally confirmed contained a video of pre-pubescent females engaging in sexual conduct. U.S.C.A. Const.Amend. 4.—State v. Williams, 46 So.3d 1149, review denied 64 So.3d 1262.

Officer's warrant affidavit established that evidence relevant to alleged criminality, possession of child pornography, was likely located within defendant's residence, thus supporting finding of probable cause and issuance of warrant to search defendant's residence; warrant affidavit expressly listed two specific dates on which officers be-

---

† This Case was not selected for publication in the National Reporter System

lieved defendant downloaded videos of pre-pubescent females engaging in sexual activity and specifically requested authorization to search for and seize the computer used to access defendant's computer on those dates. U.S.C.A. Const.Amend. 4.—Id.

Fla.App. 1 Dist. 2010. Affidavit in support of search warrant for defendant's residence established a sufficient nexus to demonstrate evidence of child pornography would be found there; defendant was suspected of creating and possessing child pornography, based on forensic interview that had been conducted with child, and it was reasonable for issuing judge to determine that there was a fair probability that a search of defendant's residence would uncover electronic storage devices containing pornographic photographs of seven-year-old victim, given that collectors of child pornography tend to retain their materials in secure places, including their homes. West's F.S.A. Const. Art. 1, § 12.—State v. Sabourin, 39 So.3d 376, rehearing denied, review denied 51 So.3d 1155.

Probable cause existed for issuance of search warrant for residence of defendant, who was suspected of possessing child pornography, including computers, electronic storage devices, and photography equipment, though supporting affidavit failed to include precise date criminal activity occurred, as a fair reading of entire affidavit lead to reasonable conclusion that events described did not occur in the distant past; seven-year-old victim stated in interview with law enforcement that she was riding in defendant's car with him and his six-year-old niece, defendant noticed that seven-year-old had spilled water on her pants, and convinced her to pull down her pants and underwear, at which point he took out camera, and took pictures of seven-year-old's buttocks and vagina as she posed in back seat of vehicle, and six-year-old attempted to reassure seven-year-old by saying, "It's ok, he takes pictures of me like that all the time." West's F.S.A. Const. Art. 1, § 12.—Id.

Fla.App. 2 Dist. 2023. Search warrant affidavit was sufficient to establish probable cause to search defendant's computer, where affidavit stated that technology company had reported that one of its users at a certain IP address had used its platform to store or share child pornography, four such images were described in amply sufficient detail to establish that they constituted child pornography, through a provider subpoena, law enforcement determined that the flagged IP address belonged to defendant and visited the physical address, and defendant subsequently consented to speak with officers about the allegations and advised that he both lived there and was the primary user of the computer at the residence. U.S. Const. Amend. 4.—State v. McNeela, 367 So.3d 557, review denied 2023 WL 8890582.

Fla.App. 2 Dist. 2018. Police had probable cause to support issuance of warrant to search defendant's laptop, where defendant's wife told police that defendant had voyeuristic videos of wife's adult daughter stored on laptop and police detective located hidden cameras inside daughter's bedroom during lawful search of home. U.S. Const. Amend. 4; Fla. Const. art. 1, § 12.—Perez v. State, 269 So.3d 574, rehearing denied.

Fla.App. 2 Dist. 2007. Internet service provider's compliance with federal law mandating that it report a subscriber's apparent violation of federal child pornography laws to National Center for Missing and Exploited Children (NCMEC) provided presumption of reliability akin to that afforded citizen informant, for purposes of determining whether probable existed for issuance of residential search warrant arising from provider's reports to NCMEC; provider was a recognized, well-established company that essentially witnessed the crime when it received images of child pornography from defendant subscriber in an attempted e-mail transmission. U.S.C.A. Const.Amend. 4; Protection of Children From Sexual Predators Act of 1998, § 604(a), 42 U.S.C.A. § 13032(b)(1).—State v. Woldridge, 958 So.2d 455, review denied 965 So.2d 124.

Search warrant affidavit relating that officer had received four reports from National Center for Missing and Exploited Children (NCMEC) stating that internet service provider had reported that computer user with specific screen name had attempted to e-mail files containing child pornography provided probable cause to issue warrant; tip came from provider, reliability of tip was presumed because of federal law compelling corporation to report to NCMEC, and provider was acting in manner analogous to that of citizen informant when it forwarded information to NCMEC. U.S.C.A. Const.Amend. 4; Protection of Children From Sexual Predators Act of 1998, § 604(a), 42 U.S.C.A. § 13032(b)(1).—Id.

Fla.App. 2 Dist. 2003. Officer's affidavit was insufficient to support conclusion that evidence relevant to defendant's possession of child pornography was likely located in his bedroom, based on officer's assertion that the computer in defendant's bedroom likely contained child pornographic images, where there were no details in affidavit to support conclusion that defendant possessed pornographic videotapes, photographs, or computer images other than the single videotape that authorities already possessed. U.S.C.A. Const.Amend. 4; West's F.S.A. Const. Art. 1, § 12; West's F.S.A. § 933.18(10).—Burnett v. State, 848 So.2d 1170, rehearing denied, appeal after new sentencing hearing 890 So.2d 335, denial of post-conviction relief affirmed in part, reversed in part 973 So.2d 1203.

Fla.App. 5 Dist. 2007. Warrant affidavit set forth facts establishing probable cause to support issuance of warrant to search defendant's residence and his computer; affidavit revealed that citizen informant, defendant's neighbor, told police that he had access to defendant's computer files through a shared hard wire connection, and that, when he opened a file of defendant's labeled "XXX," he saw 122 images of "young preteen girls in nude, sexually explicit positions." U.S.C.A. Const.Amend. 4.—State v. Cook, 972 So.2d 958, rehearing denied, review denied 987 So.2d 79.

Fla.App. 5 Dist. 2006. Information provided in search warrant affidavit provided sufficient nexus between defendant's possession of child pornography on computer and residence of owner of computer to be searched; although affidavit listed computer owner's former residence, it was reasonable to believe that even after five and one-half months, defendant would still be in possession of images that he had uploaded from his computer onto police website, and that his computer would be in his new residence. U.S.C.A. Const.Amend. 4.—State v. Felix, 942 So.2d 5, rehearing denied.

☞**804. Motor vehicles.**

†**C.A.11 (Fla.) 2007.** Probable cause existed to obtain a search warrant for defendant's vehicle, in criminal proceedings for conspiracy to possess with intent to distribute cocaine and

attempt to possess with intent to distribute cocaine; the officers knew that a package containing three kilograms of cocaine was mailed from California to Tallahassee via shipping company to an apartment likely identified as "B13," they also knew that when a controlled delivery was attempted, defendant chased the departing delivery truck to recover a package, and, witness who resided in apartment "B13," told the officers that defendant had been waiting for a package that had been sent to him at her address, although he did not reside there, and had told her not to answer the door, and, finally, the license tag on the vehicle was discovered to be stolen, and defendant could not say who the registered owner was. U.S.C.A. Const.Amend. 4; Comprehensive Drug Abuse Prevention and Control Act of 1970, §§ 401(a)(1), (b)(1)(B)(ii), 406, 21 U.S.C.A. §§ 841(a)(1), (b)(1)(B)(ii), 846.—U.S. v. Jackson, 215 Fed.Appx. 918.

Fla. 2017. Probable cause existed to support issuance of search warrant for defendant's motel room and car, where search warrant affidavit stated that there was video of man using murder victims' bank card after exiting vehicle rented by defendant, tracking device attached to rented vehicle showed it had been in area where victims' vehicle was located, and defendant was found to be in company of man seen using victims' bank card. U.S. Const.Amend. 4.—Cole v. State, 221 So.3d 534.

Fla. 2003. Probable cause existed for issuance of search warrant for defendant's automobile, apartment, and home; supporting affidavit placed defendant and codefendant in company of victims, who were a wealthy businessman and his girlfriend, very near time of their disappearance, and also provided sufficient links to defendant's probable association with codefendant and other codefendant, who were clearly alleged to have been involved in activities related to prior extortion of third victim, who was also a wealthy businessman. U.S.C.A. Const.Amend. 4.—Doorbal v. State, 837 So.2d 940, certiorari denied 123 S.Ct. 2647, 539 U.S. 962, 156 L.Ed.2d 663, denial of post-conviction relief affirmed 983 So.2d 464, rehearing denied, habeas corpus denied 2008 WL 4194838, affirmed 572 F.3d 1222, certiorari denied 130 S.Ct. 637, 558 U.S. 1030, 175 L.Ed.2d 490, denial of post-conviction relief affirmed 147 So.3d 522, habeas corpus granted 227 So.3d 110.

Fla.App. 2 Dist. 1974. Search warrant affidavit in which it was stated, inter alia, that officer had observed large burlap sacks being removed from truck and transferred to van, that officer recognized that burlap sacks were commonly used for transportation of marijuana and that, upon approaching individuals engaged in transferring the sacks, officer observed particles of a leafy substance was sufficient to justify issuance of warrant to search the vehicles even if officer could not have seen that sacks being transferred were burlap but could only have observed large bundles of a dark brown color.—State v. Knapp, 294 So.2d 338, certiorari denied 302 So.2d 415.

Fla.App. 4 Dist. 2023. Probable cause existed to issue search warrant for recorded event data from defendant's vehicle following fatal rear-end accident; affidavit presented to the judge did not need to establish defendant was driving recklessly, only that defendant was driving a vehicle which caused death of another, as defendant was charged with driving under the influence (DUI) manslaughter and vehicular homicide, and affidavit stated requested data would reveal multiple items of information that would provide more

details as to cause of crash, including speed at which defendant was traveling at time of impact. U.S. Const. Amend. 4.—State v. Acevedo, 366 So.3d 1096, review denied 2023 WL 8943631.

Fla.App. 5 Dist. 2020. Police officer's three affidavits, to draw defendant's blood and to search his automobile on two different occasions, contained sufficient facts to establish probable cause that defendant had committed two counts of driving under the influence (DUI) manslaughter and that evidence of the crimes would be found in his blood and DNA samples and in the automobile he was driving at time of crime; each affidavit provided that, according to defendant's front seat passenger, defendant was "impaired and drinking too much" just prior to accident, and described the observations made my police trooper of defendant having bloodshot glassy eyes and slurred speech and drooling from the mouth at hospital shortly after accident. U.S. Const. Amend. 4.—State v. Hart, 308 So.3d 232, rehearing denied, review denied 2021 WL 6138926.

3. COMPETENCY OF INFORMATION.

⚙**811. In general.**
S.D.Fla. 1995. Court need not apply rigid test for assessing probable cause to issue search warrant, although veracity of informant and basis of informant's knowledge serve as useful benchmarks. U.S.C.A. Const.Amend. 4.—U.S. v. Smith, 897 F.Supp. 1448.

⚙**812. Hearsay in general.**
Fla.App. 2 Dist. 2023. A \warrant affidavit's reliance on hearsay does not render it insufficient as long as there is a substantial basis for crediting that hearsay. U.S. Const. Amend. 4; Fla. Const. art. 1, § 12.—State v. Peltier, 373 So.3d 380.

Fla.App. 5 Dist. 2020. An affidavit supporting a search warrant can be based on hearsay information. U.S. Const. Amend. 4.—State v. Hart, 308 So.3d 232, rehearing denied, review denied 2021 WL 6138926.

⚙**815. —— Particular searches in general.**
C.A.11 (Fla.) 2017. Search warrant application contained sufficient evidence to provide probable cause to justify search warrant, even after excising false statements by police officer regarding an undercover drug buy; remaining affidavit information included testimony about a police visit to arrestee's residence, in an attempt to execute an arrest warrant on another individual, where officers heard toilet-flushing sounds, saw a water-saturated bathroom floor, and observed white powder residue near a safe, interviews of co-conspirators who stated that they had helped arrestee manufacture and distribute drugs and that they had observed him with firearms, and information that police had recovered cocaine and cash from arrestee during his arrest for possession of powder cocaine. U.S. Const. Amend. 4.—Phillips v. United States, 849 F.3d 988.

†**C.A.11 (Fla.) 2016.** Affidavit in support of search warrant for defendant's house provided probable cause to search, where Drug Enforcement Administration (DEA) agent included information from a cooperating defendant, an anonymous source, and his investigation, cooperating defendant provided information about defendant's drug trading activities and recorded phone calls, source confirmed such information and provided additional information, agent corroborated information provided by both, and affidavit detailed surveillance of fake drug transaction.

† This Case was not selected for publication in the National Reporter System

U.S. Const. Amend. 4.—United States v. Woodard, 662 Fed.Appx. 854, certiorari denied 137 S.Ct. 2252, 582 U.S. 909, 198 L.Ed.2d 687, certiorari denied Robinson v. U.S., 137 S.Ct. 2255, 582 U.S. 909, 198 L.Ed.2d 687, post-conviction relief denied 2021 WL 4384370.

† **C.A.11 (Fla.) 2014.** Even assuming that wiretap of defendant's cell phone did not meet necessity requirement, search warrant application contained more than enough other information to independently justify finding of probable cause to believe that defendant was storing heroin in his home; affidavit observed that informants had made controlled purchases of heroin from defendant, and defendant had even retrieved drugs from his home to make one of the deals, another individual had been stopped by police near defendant's home after buying heroin from him, and defendant had emerged from his home to make deal, and informant told Drug Enforcement Administration (DEA) special agent that defendant and codefendant had been carrying heroin when law enforcement stopped their vehicle after they had left defendant's home, and that defendant had told informant that police did not discover the heroin because codefendant had concealed it in her vagina. U.S.C.A. Const. Amend. 4; 18 U.S.C.A. § 2518(1)(c).—U.S. v. Vinales, 564 Fed.Appx. 518, certiorari granted, vacated 135 S.Ct. 2928, 576 U.S. 1079, 192 L.Ed.2d 960, on remand 658 Fed.Appx. 511, appeal after new sentencing hearing 698 Fed.Appx. 596.

C.A.11 (Fla.) 2014. Even if search warrant affidavit had stated that defendant, who was under investigation for enticing minor to engage in sexual activity, possessed different cell phone than phone he used to contact minor seven years prior, and that minor never claimed that his communications with defendant were sexual in nature, the affidavit provided probable cause sufficient to support issuance of warrant to search defendant's cell phone; affidavit explained that minor made recorded phone call to defendant, that defendant appeared to exclusively use his cell phone to communicate with others, that defendant maintained same phone number from when he first contacted minor, that minor told police that defendant continuously called minor from his cell phone during period of abuse, and that detective knew that sexual abusers sometimes maintained copies of communications with their victims in their cell phones for many years. U.S.C.A. Const.Amend. 4.—U.S. v. Mathis, 767 F.3d 1264, certiorari denied 135 S.Ct. 1448, 574 U.S. 1176, 191 L.Ed.2d 403, post-conviction relief denied 2018 WL 9617253, certificate of appealability denied 2019 WL 11880631, certiorari denied 140 S.Ct. 56, 205 L.Ed.2d 186.

† **C.A.11 (Fla.) 2013.** Search warrant affidavit established probable cause that drug-related evidence would be found at defendant's residence, where trash pulls at defendant's residence produced smoked marijuana cigarette as well as marijuana residue inside box of baking soda, which was a substance used to create crack cocaine, defendant had previous drug-related arrests, and police were tipped that defendant was involved in drug-related shooting. U.S.C.A. Const.Amend. 4.—U.S. v. Mitchell, 503 Fed.Appx. 751, certiorari denied 133 S.Ct. 2783, 569 U.S. 1018, 186 L.Ed.2d 220, post-conviction relief granted 2017 WL 4401461.

C.A.11 (Fla.) 2011. Even assuming that part of search warrant affidavit regarding controlled buy should not be considered, remaining parts of affidavit supplied probable cause to support the search; affidavit described how officers observed burgundy van at house defendant shared with others that was identical to one caught on camera around time of shooting, that defendant had been seen driving dark colored van, housemates' palm prints had been found on toll tickets used by drivers of van, ledger at murder victims' house indicated transaction with defendant's alias, witnesses connected defendant and murder victim and their drug dealings, and only a few days lapsed from time officers learned that suspects were at the murder scene and were living in house. U.S.C.A. Const.Amend. 4.—U.S. v. Lopez, 649 F.3d 1222, rehearing and rehearing denied 451 Fed.Appx. 910, post-conviction relief denied in part, dismissed in part 2013 WL 12333368.

† **C.A.11 (Fla.) 2007.** Probable cause existed to obtain a search warrant for defendant's vehicle, in criminal proceedings for conspiracy to possess with intent to distribute cocaine and attempt to possess with intent to distribute cocaine; the officers knew that a package containing three kilograms of cocaine was mailed from California to Tallahassee via shipping company to an apartment likely identified as "B13," they also knew that when a controlled delivery was attempted, defendant chased the departing delivery truck to recover a package, and, witness who resided in apartment "B13," told the officers that defendant had been waiting for a package that had been sent to him at her address, although he did not reside there, and had told her not to answer the door, and, finally, the license tag on the vehicle was discovered to be stolen, and defendant could not say who the registered owner was. U.S.C.A. Const.Amend. 4; Comprehensive Drug Abuse Prevention and Control Act of 1970, §§ 401(a)(1), (b)(1)(B)(ii), 406, 21 U.S.C.A. §§ 841(a)(1), (b)(1)(B)(ii), 846.—U.S. v. Jackson, 215 Fed.Appx. 918.

† **C.A.11 (Fla.) 2006.** Probable cause existed to issue search warrant; after police discovered crack cocaine in drug purchaser's vehicle, purchaser agreed to tell police where he had obtained the drugs and this information was included in affidavit used for obtaining the search warrant and the purchaser provided specific details about where and when he had obtained the cocaine and his description of defendant's house was corroborated when two detectives accompanied purchaser to defendant's home to verify the structure, occupants, and vehicles parked in the driveway. Comprehensive Drug Abuse Prevention and Control Act of 1970, § 401(a)(1), (b)(1)(B), 21 U.S.C.A. § 841(a)(1), (b)(1)(B).—U.S. v. Robinson, 202 Fed.Appx. 434.

C.A.11 (Fla.) 1991. There was probable cause for issuance of warrant for search of defendant physician's files in connection with claims of fraudulent billing practices; search warrant affidavit contained information from five of defendant's former employees who described fraudulent billing practices by defendant and informants who worked for defendant from 1977 to 1984 who described fraudulent activities allegedly practiced by him throughout that period.—U.S. v. Hooshmand, 931 F.2d 725.

C.A.11 (Fla.) 1990. Warrant authorizing search of premises consisting of house, garage, one other building, and screened swimming pool, all surrounded by wall, based on informant's buy of small amount of cocaine at premises, was supported by probable cause and was not overbroad, despite failure to identify owners of premises as even being present at sale. U.S.C.A. Const.Amend. 4.—U.S. v. Smith, 918 F.2d 1501,

---

† **This Case was not selected for publication in the National Reporter System**

115 A.L.R. Fed. 721, certiorari denied Hicks v. U.S., 112 S.Ct. 151, 502 U.S. 849, 116 L.Ed.2d 117, certiorari denied Sawyer v. U.S., 112 S.Ct. 253, 502 U.S. 890, 116 L.Ed.2d 207, opinion after remand 945 F.2d 365, dismissal of habeas corpus affirmed 326 F.3d 1363, certiorari denied 124 S.Ct. 258, 540 U.S. 900, 157 L.Ed.2d 181.

Fla.App. 1 Dist. 1978. Affidavit in which police officer stated that he had searched an informant and found him to free from drugs, had observed the informant enter a building, and had searched the informant upon leaving the building and discovered a controlled substance was insufficient to justify issuance of search warrant for the residence because there was no allegation that the controlled substances were illegally obtained or retained by anybody in the home or that the quantity turned over to the officer by the informer was either sold or delivered by any occupant of the residence. West's F.S.A. § 893.13(1)(e).—State v. Baxter, 356 So.2d 1250.

Fla.App. 2 Dist. 2023. Search warrant affidavit was sufficient to establish probable cause to search defendant's computer, where affidavit stated that technology company had reported that one of its users at a certain IP address had used its platform to store or share child pornography, four such images were described in amply sufficient detail to establish that they constituted child pornography, through a provider subpoena, law enforcement determined that the flagged IP address belonged to defendant and visited the physical address, and defendant subsequently consented to speak with officers about the allegations and advised that he both lived there and was the primary user of the computer at the residence. U.S. Const. Amend. 4.—State v. McNeela, 367 So.3d 557, review denied 2023 WL 8890582.

Fla.App. 2 Dist. 2018. Police had probable cause to support issuance of warrant to search defendant's laptop, where defendant's wife told police that defendant had voyeuristic videos of wife's adult daughter stored on laptop and police detective located hidden cameras inside daughter's bedroom during lawful search of home. U.S. Const. Amend. 4; Fla. Const. art. 1, § 12.—Perez v. State, 269 So.3d 574, rehearing denied.

Fla.App. 2 Dist. 2007. Search warrant affidavit relating that officer had received four reports from National Center for Missing and Exploited Children (NCMEC) stating that internet service provider had reported that computer user with specific screen name had attempted to e-mail files containing child pornography provided probable cause to issue warrant; tip came from provider, reliability of tip was presumed because of federal law compelling corporation to report to NCMEC, and provider was acting in manner analogous to that of citizen informant when it forwarded information to NCMEC. U.S.C.A. Const.Amend. 4; Protection of Children From Sexual Predators Act of 1998, § 604(a), 42 U.S.C.A. § 13032(b)(1).—State v. Woldridge, 958 So.2d 455, review denied 965 So.2d 124.

Fla.App. 2 Dist. 2004. Factual allegations in search warrant affidavit, including hearsay evidence provided by defendants' daughters' phone calls to police, were sufficient for magistrate who issued warrant to find a fair probability that contraband would be found in defendants' residence; affidavit indicated that daughters informed police about drugs in safe located next to defendants' bed, and statement in affidavit that one daughter called back after making sure the drugs were still present provided further indicia that it was likely police would find drugs there.

U.S.C.A. Const.Amend. 4.—State v. Gonzalez, 884 So.2d 330.

Fla.App. 2 Dist. 2000. Search warrant failed to establish probable cause that property stolen during burglaries of storage buildings would be found at defendant's residence or storage building; although witness observed defendant inside victim's storage building on two occasions and identified defendant as the perpetrator and there were two anonymous phone calls implicating defendant in burglaries, there was no indication that witness observed defendant taking property from victim's storage building to his own residence or storage building or that he observed defendant with any items at any time.—King v. State, 779 So.2d 385.

Fla.App. 2 Dist. 1995. Discovery of cannabis stems and seeds, rolling papers, and suspected cannabis roaches in defendant's garbage, and police officers' observation of, and citizen's report of, traffic to and from defendant's house at all hours of day and night provided probable cause to support issuance of warrant for search of defendant's home; officers were not also required to maintain constant surveillance of garbage to ensure that no one had disturbed it between time it was set out and time it was searched. U.S.C.A. Const.Amend. 4.—State v. Mayes, 666 So.2d 165, rehearing denied.

Fla.App. 2 Dist. 1982. Affidavit supporting search warrant was insufficient where, although affidavit stated time at which informant met with and spoke to affiant, it did not specify time at which informant observed illegal act of possession of cocaine.—Grayes v. State, 422 So.2d 1071.

Fla.App. 3 Dist. 2008. Drug dog's detection of live marijuana plants at defendant's front door, officer's detection of the scent after dog alerted officer, tip officer received before approaching front door that defendant was using home to grow marijuana, and officer's observation that air conditioning unit was continuously running without recycling, was sufficient to establish probable cause for the issuance of a warrant to search defendant's home for live marijuana plants and the equipment used to grow them. U.S.C.A. Const.Amend. 4.—State v. Jardines, 9 So.3d 1, review granted 3 So.3d 1246, quashed 73 So.3d 34, rehearing denied, stay denied 2011 WL 13491657, certiorari granted in part 132 S.Ct. 995, 565 U.S. 1104, 181 L.Ed.2d 726, affirmed 133 S.Ct. 1409, 569 U.S. 1, 185 L.Ed.2d 495.

Fla.App. 3 Dist. 1989. Information contained in affidavit provided probable cause for determining that additional cocaine remained on premises at which undercover officers observed woman buying cocaine, where buyer had told officers before buy that she would accompany officers to a location to purchase cocaine, instead of telling them she would take officers to meet a particular person.—State v. Brown, 539 So.2d 532.

Fla.App. 4 Dist. 2012. Supporting affidavit, based on information supplied to law enforcement by defendant's roommate, provided probable cause justifying a search warrant; roommate directly approached law enforcement and gave sworn statement regarding defendant's criminal conduct, and roommate's disclosure that he had been molested by defendant nine years earlier, coupled with his observation of defendant repeatedly observing child pornography and bragging about engaging in sex with young boys, supported inference that he was reporting defendant's behavior to protect other children and

---

† **This Case was not selected for publication in the National Reporter System**

promote justice. U.S.C.A. Const.Amend. 4.—Redini v. State, 84 So.3d 380.

Fla.App. 4 Dist. 2001. Affidavit based upon statements made by defendant's daughter did not provide substantial basis for concluding that probable cause existed to issue search warrant for defendant's home; although affidavit stated that daughter lived in home with defendant and had opportunity to observe defendant's alleged counterfeit and drug activities, affidavit contained no facts regarding daughter's veracity, and it failed to disclose circumstances that tended to show possible vindictive motivation, such as fact that daughter initially came to police to report child abuse. U.S.C.A. Const.Amend. 4.—Dial v. State, 798 So.2d 880.

Fla.App. 4 Dist. 1990. Affidavit in support of search warrant contained sufficient material facts to establish probable cause for issuance of warrant, where affidavit contained relevant information concerning activities at residence observed during surveillance by sheriff's deputy, information that substance in baggies found in defendant's trash tested positive for cocaine, and information furnished to sheriff's office by one of defendant's neighbors concerning neighbor's observations of activities at residence. U.S.C.A. Const.Amend. 4.—Scott v. State, 559 So.2d 269.

Fla.App. 4 Dist. 1974. Statements contained in affidavit for search warrant and based upon affiant's personal knowledge and information from informant who had demonstrated his reliability were sufficient to warrant man of reasonable caution to believe that law relating to narcotics and drug abuse was being violated in described residence.—State v. Richardson, 295 So.2d 325.

Fla.App. 5 Dist. 2020. Police officer's three affidavits, to draw defendant's blood and to search his automobile on two different occasions, contained sufficient facts to establish probable cause that defendant had committed two counts of driving under the influence (DUI) manslaughter and that evidence of the crimes would be found in his blood and DNA samples and in the automobile he was driving at time of crime; each affidavit provided that, according to defendant's front seat passenger, defendant was "impaired and drinking too much" just prior to accident, and described the observations made my police trooper of defendant having bloodshot glassy eyes and slurred speech and drooling from the mouth at hospital shortly after accident. U.S. Const. Amend. 4.—State v. Hart, 308 So.3d 232, rehearing denied, review denied 2021 WL 6138926.

Fla.App. 5 Dist. 2007. Warrant affidavit set forth facts establishing probable cause to support issuance of warrant to search defendant's residence and his computer; affidavit revealed that citizen informant, defendant's neighbor, told police that he had access to defendant's computer files through a shared hard wire connection, and that, when he opened a file of defendant's labeled "XXX," he saw 122 images of "young preteen girls in nude, sexually explicit positions." U.S.C.A. Const.Amend. 4.—State v. Cook, 972 So.2d 958, rehearing denied, review denied 987 So.2d 79.

Fla.App. 5 Dist. 2006. Probable cause existed to issue warrant to search defendant's residence for drugs, where affidavit in support of warrant described anonymous tip that drug activity was occurring at residence, observation by law enforcement officers of suspicious activity at residence, observation of named informant entering residence, named informant's detention by offi-

cers within two minutes of his departure from residence, named informant's statements to officers about drug activity at residence, and named informant's ability to identify a picture of defendant as person who sold him drugs, and affidavit had attached to it named informant's detailed sworn statement about drug activity at residence. U.S.C.A. Const.Amend. 4.—State v. Irizarry, 948 So.2d 39, rehearing denied.

Fla.App. 5 Dist. 2004. Judge that issued search warrant for defendants' residence, as part of counterfeiting investigation, had a substantial basis for inferring that the items associated with the counterfeiting operations were probably located at defendants' residence; two witnesses linked one of the defendants directly to the operation. U.S.C.A. Const.Amend. 4.—State v. Beasley, 882 So.2d 482.

Fla.App. 5 Dist. 1997. Search warrant affidavit established probable cause justifying warrant for seizures of defendant's hairs and blood, even considering omitted items that defendant's fingerprints were not found at scene of burglary and sexual battery, victims stated that defendant merely "looked like" assailant, and other possible suspects were seen in vicinity, where victim's description of assailant matched defendant, including his clothing, distinctive pattern of his speech, and roughness of his hands, and defendant was seen in vicinity of crime. U.S.C.A. Const.Amend. 4.—Buggs v. State, 693 So.2d 57, rehearing denied, review denied 700 So.2d 684, denial of post-conviction relief affirmed 840 So.2d 1099, rehearing denied, certiorari denied 124 S.Ct. 241, 540 U.S. 895, 157 L.Ed.2d 172, review denied 868 So.2d 522.

Fla.App. 5 Dist. 1991. For purposes of determining level of scrutiny to be applied to information provided by informant that formed basis for officer's affidavit of probable cause, informant could not qualify as "unquestionably honest citizen" on basis of statements in affidavit, so as to subject her information to less rigorous scrutiny for veracity, where affidavit merely indicated that she had been in police station to make a complaint of unknown nature and while there accused defendant of possessing cannabis; nothing in affidavit indicated her motivation for making report, so as to show she was disinterested in matter, and possibly vindictive motive could have been gleaned from information that she had just ended relationship with defendant.—Roper v. State, 588 So.2d 330.

Fla.App. 5 Dist. 1990. Search warrant affiant's statement that, after talking with informant, person from whom drugs were ultimately purchased walked into house that was subject of warrant request and then exited house shortly thereafter to meet with informant did not negate affidavit as basis for probable cause even though no one in fact observed person's exit from house and even though house owner alleged that affiant's representation that drugs were being stored in house was in fact nothing more than mere possibility—person lived next door, and it was implied that person could have obtained drugs from his own residence rather than house in question.—Polk v. Williams, 565 So.2d 1387.

⊙═817. ——— In general.

Fla.App. 1 Dist. 1983. "Totality of circumstances test" for determination of existence of probable cause for issuance of search warrant does not entirely discard necessity to determine veracity or reliability of informants and their information; on the contrary, such inquiry is still

---

† **This Case was not selected for publication in the National Reporter System**

integral part of totality of circumstances that must be considered, although it is no longer necessarily conclusive.—Yesnes v. State, 440 So.2d 628.

Fla.App. 2 Dist. 2023. Generally, where the information in the search warrant affidavit comes from a citizen informant, its reliability is presumed and corroboration is not required. U.S. Const. Amend. 4.—State v. McNeela, 367 So.3d 557, review denied 2023 WL 8890582.

Fla.App. 2 Dist. 2004. A tip from an anonymous informant generally requires independent police corroboration in order to be considered credible; however, corroboration is not required at the other end of the spectrum where the tip comes from a citizen-informant, whose information is at the high end of the tip-reliability scale. —State v. Gonzalez, 884 So.2d 330.

Fla.App. 2 Dist. 1977. Affidavit in support of search warrant must provide magistrate with factual basis upon which affiant concluded informant is reliable, for issuing magistrate cannot otherwise judicially determine probable cause for issuance of the writ.—Weisberg v. State, 348 So.2d 385.

Fla.App. 3 Dist. 2023. When a citizen informant's tip is relied upon to establish probable cause for a search or arrest, the tip is ordinarily supported by an affidavit or other sworn testimony that at a minimum authenticates the receipt of the tip by a member of law enforcement and provides either some information about the reliability of the informant or some testimony that the officer has personal knowledge corroborating some aspects of the tip. U.S. Const. Amend. 4.— Miranda v. Reyes, 359 So.3d 381.

Fla.App. 4 Dist. 2005. Reliability of an informant described in an affidavit in support of a search warrant is necessary only when the affiant is relying on the informant's hearsay statements to establish facts. U.S.C.A. Const.Amend. 4.— Raucho v. State, 915 So.2d 278.

⚷**818. — Indicia of reliability in general.**

Fla.App. 2 Dist. 2006. An informant's veracity, reliability, and basis of knowledge are all highly relevant in determining the value of his report; elements should not be understood as entirely separate and independent requirements to be rigidly exacted in every case.—Jenkins v. State, 924 So.2d 20, rehearing denied, review granted 944 So.2d 345, decision approved 978 So.2d 116.

Fla.App. 4 Dist. 2012. Some of the factors which tend to establish the reliability of information given by citizen-informants are: (1) a citizen-informant is motivated by the desire to further justice; (2) a citizen-informant who directly approaches law enforcement may be held accountable for false statements; (3) a face-to-face tip provides the opportunity to observe the demeanor and evaluate the credibility of the informant; and (4) there is greater potential for reprisal by the defendant than an anonymous tip. U.S.C.A. Const.Amend. 4.—Redini v. State, 84 So.3d 380.

⚷**819. — Basis of knowledge; personal knowledge.**

C.A.5 (Fla.) 1979. When facts tending to show probable cause for issuance of search warrant are provided by informants, affidavit in support of search warrant must pass two-pronged test: judge must be informed of some of circumstances by which informant became aware of information and facts must be shown by which judge can make independent determination of reliability.— U.S. v. Diecidue, 603 F.2d 535, certiorari denied

Antone v. U.S., 100 S.Ct. 1345, 445 U.S. 946, 63 L.Ed.2d 781, certiorari denied Gispert v. U.S., 100 S.Ct. 1345, 445 U.S. 946, 63 L.Ed.2d 781, certiorari denied Miller v. U.S., 100 S.Ct. 1842, 446 U.S. 912, 64 L.Ed.2d 266.

Fla.App. 2 Dist. 2007. The task of the issuing magistrate is simply to make a practical, common-sense decision whether, given all the circumstances set forth in the search warrant affidavit before him, including the veracity and basis of knowledge of persons supplying hearsay information, there is a fair probability that contraband or evidence of a crime will be found in a particular place. U.S.C.A. Const.Amend. 4.—State v. Woldridge, 958 So.2d 455, review denied 965 So.2d 124.

Fla.App. 2 Dist. 2004. The task of the issuing magistrate is simply to make a practical, common-sense decision whether, given all the circumstances set forth in the search warrant affidavit before him, including the "veracity" and "basis of knowledge" of persons supplying hearsay information, there is a fair probability that contraband or evidence of a crime will be found in a particular place. U.S.C.A. Const.Amend. 4. —State v. Gonzalez, 884 So.2d 330.

Fla.App. 4 Dist. 2010. In determining whether to issue a search warrant, the magistrate's task is simply to make a practical, common-sense decision whether, given all the circumstances set forth in the affidavit before him, including the veracity and basis of knowledge of persons supplying hearsay information, there is a fair probability that contraband or evidence of a crime will be found in a particular place. U.S.C.A. Const. Amend. 4; West's F.S.A. § 933.02(3).—State v. Abbey, 28 So.3d 208, review denied 42 So.3d 799.

Fla.App. 4 Dist. 2009. In reviewing a search warrant application, the task of the issuing magistrate is simply to make a practical, common-sense decision whether, given all the circumstances set forth in the affidavit before him, including the veracity and basis of knowledge of persons supplying hearsay information, there is a fair probability that contraband or evidence of a crime will be found in a particular place. U.S.C.A. Const.Amend. 4.—Nichols v. State, 10 So.3d 1150, rehearing denied.

⚷**820. — Prior history of reliability.**

Fla.App. 4 Dist. 2012. Tips from known reliable informants, such as an identifiable citizen who observes criminal conduct and reports it, along with his own identity to the police, will almost invariably be found sufficient to justify police action. U.S.C.A. Const.Amend. 4.—Redini v. State, 84 So.3d 380.

⚷**821. — Motive of informant.**

Fla.App. 2 Dist. 2023. A "citizen informant," whose reliability is presumed when considering probable cause for a search warrant, is one who by happenstance finds himself in the position of a victim of or a witness to criminal conduct and thereafter relates to the police what he knows as a matter of civic duty. U.S. Const. Amend. 4.— State v. McNeela, 367 So.3d 557, review denied 2023 WL 8890582.

Fla.App. 2 Dist. 2020. A "citizen informant" is one who by happenstance finds himself in the position of a victim of or a witness to criminal conduct and thereafter relates to the police what he knows as a matter of civic duty.—Fields v. State, 292 So.3d 889.

† This Case was not selected for publication in the National Reporter System

⊂⊃822. —— Level of detail.

Fla.App. 2 Dist. 2014. Even when there is no evidence of an informant's reliability, informant's first-hand observation and explicit and detailed description of alleged wrongdoing entitle tip to greater weight in assessing whether probable cause existed to issue search warrant. U.S.C.A. Const.Amend. 4.—State v. Loredo, 129 So.3d 1188.

Fla.App. 4 Dist. 2014. Veracity and reliability of a citizen informant are presumed, because such an informant is one who is motivated not by pecuniary gain, but by the desire to further justice, such as by relating details of a witnessed crime to law enforcement as a matter of civic duty, and consequently, further investigation and corroboration by law enforcement is not required.—State v. Hutz, 144 So.3d 618.

⊂⊃823. —— Presentation of informant.

Fla.App. 4 Dist. 2014. Witness who provides information to a police officer through face to face communication is deemed to be sufficiently reliable, so as to generally be classified as a citizen informant.—State v. Hutz, 144 So.3d 618.

⊂⊃825(1). In general.

† **C.A.11 (Fla.) 2020.** Search warrant affidavit was sufficient to support finding of probable cause even with inclusion of omitted facts that alleged victim of prior shooting was sleeping on bed next to defendant when officers found him and that victim told officers defendant was not person who shot her; affidavit stated that defendant had been present at time of shooting and that police were summoned to residence by concerned citizen who said defendant was suspect in previous shooting and was in back of residence with victim. U.S. Const. Amend. 4.—United States v. Weathers, 815 Fed.Appx. 414.

C.A.11 (Fla.) 1982. Affidavit stating that FBI had observed stolen truck and motor home outside defendant's residence, that Government informant based his conclusions on statements by a coconspirator and that informant had been reliable in the past, established probable cause for issuance of search warrant for defendant's residence, notwithstanding unintentional misstatements in affidavit concerning certain statements incorrectly attributed to informant.—U.S. v. Strauss, 678 F.2d 886, certiorari denied 103 S.Ct. 218, 459 U.S. 911, 74 L.Ed.2d 173.

⊂⊃825(2). Controlled substances.

† **C.A.11 (Fla.) 2010.** Allegations in affidavit for warrant to search defendant's house clearly demonstrated probable cause to believe that defendant had methamphetamine in his house, despite omissions alleged by defendant; one of defendant's customers informed police that she purchased methamphetamine from defendant every other day, and defendant's supplier informed police that he regularly supplied defendant with methamphetamine for three-month period, identified defendant's house and drew a map of the house for officers. U.S.C.A. Const.Amend. 4.—U.S. v. Fussell, 366 Fed.Appx. 102, certiorari denied 131 S.Ct. 170, 562 U.S. 870, 178 L.Ed.2d 101, post-conviction relief denied 2012 WL 3290406.

C.A.11 (Fla.) 1987. Omission of informant's six prior convictions and incarceration awaiting trial on charges of conspiracy to traffic methaqualone when purchase of cocaine was made at premises to be searched, when considered with all information contained in search warrant application, did not invalidate warrant; informant

had furnished valuable information on at least 14 occasions during prior 12 years and, on each occasion, arrest and/or seizure occurred, and informant stated that he had been in office in question at least once a month for previous three years and that he had observed cocaine in one or both of two safes on each occasion. U.S.C.A. Const.Amend. 4.—U.S. v. Ofshe, 817 F.2d 1508, certiorari denied 108 S.Ct. 451, 484 U.S. 963, 98 L.Ed.2d 391.

C.A.11 (Fla.) 1983. Informant's failure to explain how he knew substance to be narcotics does not, by itself, command finding of no probable cause for issuance of search warrant.—U.S. v. Figueroa, 720 F.2d 1239, rehearing denied 726 F.2d 755.

Magistrate had substantial basis for issuance of search warrant, where affidavit related that informant had previously provided information that led to seizure of counterfeit money, informant was explicitly told that he would be subject to criminal prosecution if he knowingly and willfully gave false information, informant claimed he was told directly by defendant that illegal drugs were present at searched premises, and informant claimed to have seen drugs on premises immediately before search.—Id.

C.A.5 (Fla.) 1979. Informant's reliability was fully established by explicit claim of past reliability made by Arizona narcotics investigator who expressly stated that informant, on many occasions, had provided reliable information that led to arrests of persons for narcotics violations. U.S.C.A.Const. Amend. 4.—U.S. v. Williams, 603 F.2d 1168, rehearing denied 606 F.2d 322, certiorari denied Scalf v. U.S., 100 S.Ct. 687, 444 U.S. 1024, 62 L.Ed.2d 658.

C.A.5 (Fla.) 1978. Where search warrant affidavit supplied many details of dates and locations of narcotics transactions, parties to several criminal telephone calls and locations and movements of members of conspiracy, magistrate could permissibly infer reliability of confidential informants. U.S.C.A.Const. Amend. 4.—U.S. v. Hyde, 574 F.2d 856, rehearing denied 579 F.2d 643, rehearing denied U.S. v. Middlebrooks, 579 F.2d 644.

C.A.5 (Fla.) 1969. Affidavit which alleged that Federal Bureau of Narcotics had utilized informant on several occasions in the past and that he had been reliable, that transactions were carried out under surveillance of bureau, and that bureau had a record on defendant with information dating back to 1962 afforded probable cause for issuance of search warrant.—U.S. v. Vigo, 413 F.2d 691.

C.A.5 (Fla.) 1968. Probable cause for issuance of search warrant existed where deputy sheriff's affidavit stated dates on which relevant information was received from each of two informers and one of the three dates on which the deputy sheriff personally observed known narcotics addicts going in and out of described premises.—Dixon v. State of Fla., 403 F.2d 49.

Fla. 1976. Search of informant's person by search warrant affiant both before and immediately after the purchase of drug is sufficient personal knowledge on which to base issuance of search warrant.—State v. Gieseke, 328 So.2d 16.

Fla. 1973. Affidavit in which affiant stated that special law enforcement agent had informed him that, one week prior thereto, search had revealed drugs and certain letters (attached to the affidavit) from defendant implicating him in drug traffic and that affiant had been advised by certain officials of post office department that the

---

† **This Case was not selected for publication in the National Reporter System**

department was in possession of letter addressed to petitioner and appearing to contain some bulky substance other than paper was insufficient to support search warrant and resultant search and seizure.—Andersen v. State, 274 So.2d 228, certiorari denied 94 S.Ct. 150, 414 U.S. 879, 38 L.Ed.2d 124.

Fla.App. 1 Dist. 1994. Officer's affidavit provided probable cause for issuance of warrant based on informant's having purchased marijuana at defendant's residence; officer's failure to search informant after the purchase did not obviate existence of "controlled buy" such as will establish reliability of informant; officer ensured that informant had no drugs in his possession before purchase, gave informant money, watched him as he entered and exited defendant's residence, and received purchased drugs directly from informant. U.S.C.A. Const.Amend. 4.—Clark v. State, 635 So.2d 1010.

Fla.App. 1 Dist. 1986. Information in support of search warrant was reliable where information derived its credibility from personal involvement, observation, and corroboration by informant, who was named and participated in drug transactions, and by affiant, who was able to corroborate informant's story by way of consent searches.—Birchfield v. State, 497 So.2d 944.

Fla.App. 1 Dist. 1985. Search warrant affidavit which recited that named informants went to defendant's residence for purpose of purchasing cannabis, and that while they were with defendant they saw substance which they believed to be cannabis and which was represented to be such by defendant, provided substantial basis to conclude that there was a "fair probability" that contraband would be found at defendant's residence, considering that affidavit contained facts showing basis of informants' knowledge, that informants were not anonymous, and that information supplied by them was against their penal interests in that they had attempted to purchase a controlled substance.—State v. Englehorn, 471 So.2d 1363.

Fla.App. 1 Dist. 1984. Search warrant affidavit which revealed informant's name and showed that informant had been at defendant's house with defendant and had seen marijuana at defendant's house furnished probable cause for issuance of warrant to search such house, in view of facts in warrant showing credibility of informant and reliability of his information. U.S.C.A. Const.Amend. 4.—Bradford v. State, 448 So.2d 1231.

Fla.App. 1 Dist. 1984. Affidavit supporting search warrant which stated that affiant police officer observed informant entering and leaving defendant's residence and was told by informant that he had seen cocaine, and purchased some, while in defendant's residence, clearly reflected "basis of knowledge" of informant, that is, his firsthand knowledge. U.S.C.A. Const.Amend. 4.—Zaner v. State, 444 So.2d 508.

Affidavit supporting search warrant, which described a "controlled buy" conducted by affiant police officer and confidential informant at defendant's residence, contained sufficient indicia of informant's reliability under totality of circumstances set forth in affidavit notwithstanding that such affidavit contained no recital of facts relating directly to informant's credibility or reliability. U.S.C.A. Const.Amend. 4.—Id.

Fla.App. 1 Dist. 1979. Affidavit in support of warrant to search premises on which marijuana was allegedly located was insufficient to demonstrate informant's credibility or reliability of his information.—Davis v. State, 376 So.2d 479.

Fla.App. 1 Dist. 1979. Statement which was made by informant subsequent to filing of affidavit for issuance of search warrant and which was rambling, incoherent in many parts, as well as vague, ambiguous, and even conflicting on crucial details in that informant denied seeing drugs in defendant's home at one point, but later stated that he knew drugs were there because they belonged to him was insufficient to invalidate probable cause finding of trial judge who issued search warrant and, in absence of further grounds or offer of proof, was insufficient to require an evidentiary hearing to determine whether intentional misstatements of fact were made in affidavit for search warrant pursuant to which drugs were recovered from defendant's home. West's F.S.A. § 933.18; 33 West's F.S.A. Rules of Criminal Procedure, rule 3.190(h); U.S.C.A.Const. Amends. 4, 14.—Mason v. State, 375 So.2d 1125, certiorari denied 386 So.2d 639.

Fla.App. 1 Dist. 1978. Where affidavit for search warrant stated the name and address of informant, the details of informant's actual observation of marijuana, and stated that informant was retired from Air Force with approximately 21 years of service in security police field and that informant had received instructions in narcotics and in the identification of marijuana, affidavit contained sufficient facts indicating that named informant was reliable.—Chadwick v. State, 358 So.2d 901.

Fla.App. 1 Dist. 1978. Affidavit for search warrant sufficiently demonstrated affiant's reasons for regarding informant as reliable, though affiant's unexplicated evaluation of informant as a "responsible citizen" would be disregarded, where informant was identified as employee of motel in which room was to be searched and had personally observed marijuana on hotel premises where, as employee, he had reason to be observant and to report truthfully what he saw, and where his description of the marijuana observed was detailed and in that detail was consistent with officer's knowledge of the appearance of marijuana and the common forms in which it is packaged.—Rowe v. State, 355 So.2d 826.

Fla.App. 2 Dist. 2021. Search warrant affidavit was insufficient to establish probable cause to search defendant's residence; affidavit provided information received from police informant that defendant had cocaine and methamphetamine in his home, nothing in affidavit indicated that affiant had personal knowledge of informant's reliability or veracity, other informant's statements to police did not corroborate claim that contraband would be found in defendant's residence, police did not independently investigate or surveil defendant or his residence, and affidavit did not address any criminal history of defendant's, let alone one involving narcotic sales. U.S. Const. Amend. 4.—Chery v. State, 331 So.3d 789.

Fla.App. 2 Dist. 2004. Defendants' daughters, who informed police about cocaine in safe located next to defendants' bed, qualified as "citizen-informants," rather than mere anonymous informants, for purposes of determining whether factual allegations in search warrant affidavit, including hearsay evidence provided by daughters' phone calls to police, provided sufficient probable cause for magistrate to issue warrant; daughters' identities were readily ascertainable because they gave their names and location, and there was no indication they were motivated by anything other than concern for the safety of their parents and others. U.S.C.A. Const.Amend. 4.—State v. Gonzalez, 884 So.2d 330.

Fla.App. 2 Dist. 1996. Affidavit in support of search warrant failed to show that informant was reliable; informant was not simply an honest, disinterested citizen, but rather had known defendant and others who resided with defendant for several years and had been inside of the residence within days of the search and observed marijuana, rolling papers, pipes and scales, and statement by law enforcement that they had knowledge of narcotics dealings at defendant's residence was insufficient to corroborate informant's information. U.S.C.A. Const.Amend. 4.—Dudley v. State, 667 So.2d 428.

Fla.App. 2 Dist. 1992. Evidence did not support conclusion that informant was an unwitting informant, and that information concerning his reliability was not required for issuance of search warrant; informant made initial proposition to undercover officer that he could buy marijuana for officer.—Delacruz v. State, 603 So.2d 707.

Fla.App. 2 Dist. 1990. Police officers' affidavit in support of search warrant, which not only failed to contain facts regarding reliability of confidential informant or person who allegedly bought drugs from defendant but also lacked information from anyone who could connect defendant to purchase of cocaine, failed to set out sufficient facts to have enabled issuing magistrate to find probable cause that drugs were in defendant's home. U.S.C.A. Const.Amend. 4.—Brown v. State, 561 So.2d 1248.

Fla.App. 2 Dist. 1988. Reliability of informant need not be established when basis for search warrant was informant's "controlled buy" of drugs from defendant's residence.—Sotolongo v. State, 530 So.2d 514.

Fla.App. 2 Dist. 1986. Affidavit in support of search warrant which contained no allegation of when informants observed marijuana growing on defendant's premises was insufficient.—Rand v. State, 484 So.2d 1367.

Fla.App. 2 Dist. 1986. Probable cause existed to issue search warrant, where informant was shown to have sworn before circuit judge to facts concerning defendant's possession of cocaine, informant described residence to be searched and defendant's method of dealing in cocaine from that residence and identified defendant as man named "Rafael," police ascertained that car parked in driveway of residence belonged to defendant who was on ten years probation for conspiracy to traffic and trafficking in cocaine, and basis of informant's knowledge was his two purchases of cocaine from defendant at the residence within nine days prior to execution of warrant.—Rios v. State, 483 So.2d 39, review denied 494 So.2d 1152.

Fla.App. 2 Dist. 1975. Informant's sworn statement that he had observed nine pounds of cannabis on described premises approximately a week before was sufficient to meet probable cause test for belief that law relating to narcotics or drug abuse was currently being violated.—State v. Collins, 317 So.2d 846, certiorari denied 330 So.2d 16.

Fla.App. 2 Dist. 1974. Policeman's affidavit which stated that a reliable informant had been told by an anonymous friend that narcotics were located in a certain mobile home and which further stated that the policeman and others arrested the mobile home's occupants who admitted that narcotics were located therein was sufficient to support the issuance of a search warrant

for the mobile home.—Hicks v. State, 299 So.2d 44, certiorari denied 310 So.2d 739.

Fla.App. 2 Dist. 1965. Sum total of allegations of affidavit for search warrant and circumstances surrounding information received by affiant, as recited in affidavit, were sufficient to cause a prudent man of affiant's experience to believe that defendant was using his home as a base for illicit traffic in narcotic drugs.—Dixon v. State, 180 So.2d 681, certiorari dismissed 188 So.2d 318, appeal dismissed 188 So.2d 810.

Fla.App. 2 Dist. 1965. Reading of affidavit showed that evidence, exclusive of unidentified informer's communications that she had purchased marijuana cigarettes from female in house, was sufficient to establish probable cause for issuance of search warrant.—Spataro v. State, 179 So.2d 873.

Fla.App. 3 Dist. 1989. That informant who arranged drug purchases for undercover officers was not searched before and after entering defendant's residence with money to purchase drugs did not deprive officers of probable cause for warrant to search defendant's residence, where informant was unknowingly assisting police, as practice of searching confidential informant before and after controlled purchase of contraband is done only in order to prevent misconduct on part of informant.—Reyes v. State, 541 So.2d 772.

Fla.App. 3 Dist. 1989. Credibility and reliability of person observed making purchase of cocaine by undercover officers were irrelevant to determination of probable cause to support warrant, where warrant could have been supported solely by personal observations of officers who witnessed cocaine sale, without relying on statements made by the buyer.—State v. Brown, 539 So.2d 532.

Fla.App. 3 Dist. 1987. Mere fact that informant of no known veracity tells the police that a person they know to be a convicted drug dealer is dealing drugs is, by itself, patently insufficient to show, for purposes of affidavit for search warrant, that informant's information is reliable.—State v. Novak, 502 So.2d 990, review denied 511 So.2d 299.

Where it is shown by affidavit for search warrant that person came into possession of information concerning existence of drugs on premises through innocent observation, that person can be considered a "citizen-informant" and his reliability presumed, but where that is not the case, whether the informant is anonymous or named will make no difference.—Id.

Fla.App. 3 Dist. 1983. Fact that one could infer from informant's statement that he personally observed marijuana on premises did nothing to further probability that marijuana was in fact on premises in absence of some circumstance from which informant's story could be credited.—Blue v. State, 441 So.2d 165.

Fact that informant brought marijuana to detective did not prove anything about informant's reliability in order to support issuance of search warrant.—Id.

Fla.App. 4 Dist. 2004. Evidence did not establish probable cause necessary to support search warrant for defendant's residence, even though informant provided tip that defendant had cannabis grow operation at his residence, marijuana was found on defendant and in his vehicle during traffic stop, and vehicle contained cannabis cultivation books and video; residence did not have indicia of marijuana grow house, informant's veracity was not established in affidavit in support of search warrant, and marijuana in defendant's vehicle did not establish any illegal activities in residence. U.S.C.A. Const.Amend. 4.— State v. Rabb, 881 So.2d 587, rehearing denied, certiorari granted, vacated 125 S.Ct. 2246, 544 U.S. 1028, 161 L.Ed.2d 1051, on remand 920 So.2d 1175, review denied 933 So.2d 522, certiorari denied 127 S.Ct. 665, 549 U.S. 1052, 166 L.Ed.2d 513.

Fla.App. 4 Dist. 1996. Affidavit did not sufficiently state probable cause for issuance of search warrant; affiant neither had personal knowledge of informant's reliability nor obtained facts to independently corroborate informant's allegations and affiant's independent observations alone did not demonstrate that there was fair probability that contraband would be found at defendant's residence.—Boyle v. State, 669 So.2d 330.

Fla.App. 4 Dist. 1994. Affidavit did not facially establish probable cause to search in defendant's home based on informant's statement that he had seen cocaine in defendant's home; affidavit did not say that informant had provided reliable information in past or that any information provided by informant had been independently verified by law enforcement officers; unsubstantiated words of informant, who was drug dealer with no proven reliability, were not enough to support issuing warrant. U.S.C.A. Const.Amend. 4.—Wynn v. State, 640 So.2d 134.

Fla.App. 4 Dist. 1984. Affidavit was sufficient to support search warrant, where affiant stated that informer had provided reliable information on eight previous occasions, resulting in six arrests and prosecutions, and informer had not only alleged that owner of house to be searched had offered to sell him marijuana, but also that contraband was presently stored in residence.— DeLaPaz v. State, 453 So.2d 445.

Fla.App. 5 Dist. 2013. Narcotics detection dog's alert to the presence of drugs in a delivery package addressed to defendant was sufficiently reliable to establish probable cause necessary for issuance of search warrant; warrant affidavit represented that the dog and his police officer handler had gone through extensive training and that the dog had discovered thousands of pounds of narcotics in the past. U.S.C.A. Const.Amend. 4. —State v. Grue, 130 So.3d 256.

Fla.App. 5 Dist. 1994. Indicia of informant's veracity and reliability, based on facts that narcotics agent had already developed regarding residence informant visited, was patently sufficient for purposes of procuring search warrant for residence based on informant's information that he went to residence every Friday to buy cocaine; while conducting surveillance at certain location, agent noticed that individual often left location as passenger in various persons' automobiles, over two-week period, agent followed this individual several times and each time car in which he was passenger traveled to residence and individual would go inside for a short period, return to car, leave residence and be returned to location, individual sold agent $50 worth of heroin, but agent did not know where individual came into possession of heroin and informant spontaneously made statement while agent was writing up charging documents.—State v. Rivera, 634 So.2d 302.

Fla.App. 5 Dist. 1991. Probable cause affidavit did not contain substantial basis for issuance of warrant to search defendant's premises for marijuana based on informant's observation of marijuana in defendant's residence, where there

was no showing of veracity or reliability of informant, affidavit was bereft of facts that could be fitted "neatly together" to comprise totality of circumstances evidencing probability that marijuana would be found on premises; affidavit showed merely that informant had made accusation that defendant, with whom she had just ended "relationship" of unstated sort, possessed marijuana at his home during her visit to police station to file another complaint. U.S.C.A. Const. Amend. 4.—Roper v. State, 588 So.2d 330.

Fla.App. 5 Dist. 1990. Even though officer in the airport from which luggage departed was not known to officer at airport in which luggage arrived, officer at departure airport provided such specific and detailed information about luggage that officer at arriving airport reasonably concluded that source of information was a fellow law enforcement officer whose information was truthful and reliable; thus, officer had probable cause to obtain warrant to search defendant's luggage for narcotics.—State v. Siluk, 567 So.2d 26.

⊙~**825(3). Obscenity.**

Fla.App. 2 Dist. 2007. Internet service provider's compliance with federal law mandating that it report a subscriber's apparent violation of federal child pornography laws to National Center for Missing and Exploited Children (NCMEC) provided presumption of reliability akin to that afforded citizen informant, for purposes of determining whether probable existed for issuance of residential search warrant arising from provider's reports to NCMEC; provider was a recognized, well-established company that essentially witnessed the crime when it received images of child pornography from defendant subscriber in an attempted e-mail transmission. U.S.C.A. Const.Amend. 4; Protection of Children From Sexual Predators Act of 1998, § 604(a), 42 U.S.C.A. § 13032(b)(1).—State v. Woldridge, 958 So.2d 455, review denied 965 So.2d 124.

⊙~**827. —— In general.**

C.A.5 (Fla.) 1977. An informer's tip may be buttressed either by independent observations substantiating the details of the tip or by independent observations of activity reasonably arousing suspicion itself, but regardless of the approach, the tip and the corroboration must constitute probable cause to believe that the object of the search was on the premises to be examined. U.S.C.A.Const. Amend. 4.—U.S. v. Brand, 556 F.2d 1312, rehearing denied 561 F.2d 831, certiorari denied 98 S.Ct. 1237, 434 U.S. 1063, 55 L.Ed.2d 763, rehearing denied 98 S.Ct. 1593, 435 U.S. 961, 55 L.Ed.2d 811.

⊙~**829. —— Sufficiency in general.**

C.A.11 (Fla.) 1994. Informant's credibility is determined based upon totality of circumstances, including traditional review of basis of his knowledge and reliability; only "major portions" of informant's statements must be verified.—U.S. v. Green, 40 F.3d 1167, certiorari denied 115 S.Ct. 1809, 514 U.S. 1089, 131 L.Ed.2d 733, certiorari denied Sims v. U.S., 115 S.Ct. 1809, 514 U.S. 1089, 131 L.Ed.2d 733, certiorari denied Wheeler v. U.S., 115 S.Ct. 1809, 514 U.S. 1089, 131 L.Ed.2d 733, certiorari denied 115 S.Ct. 2262, 515 U.S. 1110, 132 L.Ed.2d 268.

Fla.App. 2 Dist. 2017. In considering the totality of the circumstances, when evidence of the tipster's veracity and reliability is lacking, there must be sufficient independent corroborating evidence to justify issuing a search warrant. U.S.

† This Case was not selected for publication in the National Reporter System

Const. Amend. 4.—Castro v. State, 224 So.3d 281.

⚬=830(1). In general.

S.D.Fla. 1997. Lack of proven prior cooperation in Government investigations does not render otherwise informative source incredible, for purposes of search warrant probable cause determination; rather, their corroboration increases the reliability of affiant's assessment. U.S.C.A. Const.Amend. 4.—U.S. v. Abbell, 963 F.Supp. 1178.

⚬=830(2). Controlled substances.

C.A.11 (Fla.) 1995. There was adequate corroboration of informant's detailed reports of indoor marijuana cultivation, sufficient to provide probable cause for issuance of search warrant; police had followed informant as she went from place to place with defendant, informant gave police intermediate reports as to what she had seen, and, as her reports were so detailed as to be easily verifiable upon search, informant realized that lies would be quickly detected to her detriment. U.S.C.A. Const.Amend. 4.—U.S. v. Foree, 43 F.3d 1572.

C.A.11 (Fla.) 1991. Probable cause to search house for presence of drugs supported search which produced illegal firearms; informants' tip that drug activities were being conducted at location was confirmed by observation of pattern of short and frequent visits, and stop of vehicle which had just left revealed presence of drugs. U.S.C.A. Const.Amend. 4.—U.S. v. Sweeting, 933 F.2d 962.

C.A.11 (Fla.) 1990. Information provided by informant regarding use of residence in cocaine conspiracy was sufficiently detailed to be of type referred to as "self-corroborating," and thus provided probable cause for warrant to search residence; informant described names, dates, addresses, specific events, actors, amounts of money, packaging of money, packaging of cocaine, and automobiles utilized and their movement. U.S.C.A. Const.Amend. 4.—U.S. v. Smith, 918 F.2d 1501, 115 A.L.R. Fed. 721, certiorari denied Hicks v. U.S., 112 S.Ct. 151, 502 U.S. 849, 116 L.Ed.2d 117, certiorari denied Sawyer v. U.S., 112 S.Ct. 253, 502 U.S. 890, 116 L.Ed.2d 207, opinion after remand 945 F.2d 365, dismissal of habeas corpus affirmed 326 F.3d 1363, certiorari denied 124 S.Ct. 258, 540 U.S. 900, 157 L.Ed.2d 181.

C.A.11 (Fla.) 1987. After concerned citizen informant had provided tip to DEA agents, indicating that suspect was involved in manufacture of controlled substance in Miami and that he commuted between Miami and San Francisco to facilitate such manufacturing, agents' confirmation that suspect did commute as informant had alleged, that suspect's address in San Francisco was as had been given by informant, and that suspect purchased several chemical compounds which were precursors required for manufacture of controlled substance constituted sufficient corroboration of informant's tip to establish probable cause for issuance of search warrant.—Cauchon v. U.S., 824 F.2d 908, certiorari denied 108 S.Ct. 355, 484 U.S. 957, 98 L.Ed.2d 380.

C.A.11 (Fla.) 1984. On basis of corroborated affidavit describing affiant's interview for job at clinic, in which affiant was told that his job would be to listen to patients' hearts and write prescriptions for methaqualone, magistrate could, without arbitrariness, find probable cause to issue search warrant relating to records in office of clinic. U.S.C.A. Const.Amend. 4.—U.S.

v. Betancourt, 734 F.2d 750, rehearing denied 740 F.2d 979, certiorari denied Gerwitz v. U.S., 105 S.Ct. 440, 469 U.S. 1021, 83 L.Ed.2d 365, certiorari denied Sando v. United States, 105 S.Ct. 574, 469 U.S. 1076, 83 L.Ed.2d 514.

C.A.5 (Fla.) 1978. That one confidential informant was acting against penal interest in informing police of his activities in conspiracy and was in fact defendant in another prosecution stemming from same conspiracy, and that at least one other informant revealed some degree of criminal involvement in narcotics traffic tended to establish reliability of informants, even if statements supposedly made against penal interest did not establish criminal liability of the speakers. U.S.C.A.Const. Amend. 4; Federal Rules of Evidence, rule 804(b)(3), 28 U.S.C.A.; Comprehensive Drug Abuse Prevention and Control Act of 1970, §§ 401(a)(1), 406, 21 U.S.C.A. §§ 841(a)(1), 846.—U.S. v. Hyde, 574 F.2d 856, rehearing denied 579 F.2d 643, rehearing denied U.S. v. Middlebrooks, 579 F.2d 644.

M.D.Fla. 2007. Drug Enforcement Agency Task Force agent's affidavit provided probable cause for warrant to search residence, as required for evidence discovered after warrant was obtained to be admissible under independent source doctrine despite agents' earlier, illegal entry and sweep search of residence; affidavit indicated that agents had information from an informant, corroborated by suspicious activity at the residence, that they had recovered drugs from a vehicle seen leaving the residence, and that they witnessed suspicious activity in and around the vehicle while it was at the residence, immediately prior to stopping the vehicle and discovering drugs in vehicle. U.S.C.A. Const.Amend. 4.—U.S. v. Gonzalez De Arias, 510 F.Supp.2d 969.

Fla. 2011. Lawfully obtained evidence in search warrant affidavit did not establish probable cause to support issuance of warrant to defendant's residence for marijuana and marijuana-growing equipment; tip that marijuana was being grown in residence was unverified and came from an unknown individual, there was no evidence to suggest the tip was corroborated by any evidence resulting from surveillance of house, and the only other lawfully obtained evidence contained in the affidavit was that the window blinds were closed and the air conditioner unit was constantly running without recycling. U.S.C.A. Const.Amend. 4.—Jardines v. State, 73 So.3d 34, rehearing denied, stay denied 2011 WL 13491657, certiorari granted in part 132 S.Ct. 995, 565 U.S. 1104, 181 L.Ed.2d 726, affirmed 133 S.Ct. 1409, 569 U.S. 1, 185 L.Ed.2d 495.

Fla.App. 1 Dist. 1986. Information in support of search warrant was reliable where information derived its credibility from personal involvement, observation, and corroboration by informant, who was named and participated in drug transactions, and by affiant, who was able to corroborate informant's story by way of consent searches.—Birchfield v. State, 497 So.2d 944.

Fla.App. 2 Dist. 2021. Search warrant affidavit was insufficient to establish probable cause to search defendant's residence; affidavit provided information received from police informant that defendant had cocaine and methamphetamine in his home, nothing in affidavit indicated that affiant had personal knowledge of informant's reliability or veracity, other informant's statements to police did not corroborate claim that contraband would be found in defendant's residence, police did not independently investigate or surveil defendant or his residence, and affidavit did not address any criminal history of defendant's, let alone one involving narcotic sales. U.S. Const. Amend. 4.—Chery v. State, 331 So.3d 789.

Fla.App. 2 Dist. 2014. Affidavit used to support search warrant of defendant's residence for narcotics established, based on the totality of the circumstances, reasonable probability that contraband would be found at residence, as required to issue warrant, even though affidavit lacked information about veracity of informants; police surveillance of residence, together with detailed information regarding drug transactions at residence and other information in affidavit provided sufficient corroborating evidence to establish probable cause. U.S.C.A. Const.Amend. 4.—State v. Loredo, 129 So.3d 1188.

Fla.App. 2 Dist. 1996. Affidavit in support of search warrant failed to show that informant was reliable; informant was not simply an honest, disinterested citizen, but rather had known defendant and others who resided with defendant for several years and had been inside of the residence within days of the search and observed marijuana, rolling papers, pipes and scales, and statement by law enforcement that they had knowledge of narcotics dealings at defendant's residence was insufficient to corroborate informant's information. U.S.C.A. Const.Amend. 4.—Dudley v. State, 667 So.2d 428.

Fla.App. 4 Dist. 1996. Affidavit did not sufficiently state probable cause for issuance of search warrant; affiant neither had personal knowledge of informant's reliability nor obtained facts to independently corroborate informant's allegations and affiant's independent observations alone did not demonstrate that there was fair probability that contraband would be found at defendant's residence.—Boyle v. State, 669 So.2d 330.

⚬—**832. —— In general.**
Fla.App. 4 Dist. 2023. When the existence of probable cause depends on evidence obtained by other officers from an anonymous or confidential source, the officer seeking a search warrant must have knowledge of the other officers' basis for finding the source to be reliable. U.S. Const. Amend. 4.—Zarcadoolas v. Tony, 353 So.3d 638.

⚬—**833. —— Reliability of information.**
Fla.App. 1 Dist. 2005. Anonymous tips can provide the basis for reasonable suspicion if the reliability of the tip can be established. U.S.C.A. Const.Amend. 4.—Smith v. State, 904 So.2d 534, rehearing denied.

Fla.App. 2 Dist. 2006. When the police rely on information from a confidential informant (CI), they must have some basis for establishing the informant's reliability, but there is no requirement that informants used by the police be infallible.—Jenkins v. State, 924 So.2d 20, rehearing denied, review granted 944 So.2d 345, decision approved 978 So.2d 116.

Veracity of a confidential informant (CI) can be established by either the informant's prior record of reliability or the wealth of detailed, verifiable information given on the occasion in question.—Id.

Fla.App. 2 Dist. 2004. A tip from an anonymous informant generally requires independent police corroboration in order to be considered credible; however, corroboration is not required at the other end of the spectrum where the tip comes from a citizen-informant, whose information is at the high end of the tip-reliability scale.—State v. Gonzalez, 884 So.2d 330.

Fla.App. 5 Dist. 2013. If a confidential informant provides information to law enforcement that forms the basis for an affidavit for a search warrant, the affidavit must contain either information concerning the informant's veracity and reliability or sufficient independent corroborating evidence. U.S.C.A. Const.Amend. 4.—State v. McGill, 125 So.3d 343.

⚬—**834. —— Corroboration.**
Fla.App. 1 Dist. 1998. Search warrant affidavit based on information obtained from confidential informant must set forth either facts indicating that affiant has personal knowledge of confidential informant's reliability or facts from independent source which corroborate reliability of confidential informant.—Peterson v. State, 706 So.2d 936, review granted 722 So.2d 194, quashed 739 So.2d 561, rehearing denied, certiorari denied 121 S.Ct. 85, 531 U.S. 831, 148 L.Ed.2d 46, rehearing denied 121 S.Ct. 506, 531 U.S. 1002, 148 L.Ed.2d 474.

Fla.App. 2 Dist. 2021. Affidavit used to support search warrant must state that the affiant has personal knowledge of the confidential informant's veracity or the affidavit must contain sufficient independent corroborating evidence. U.S. Const. Amend. 4.—Chery v. State, 331 So.3d 789.

Fla.App. 2 Dist. 2017. In considering the totality of the circumstances, when evidence of the tipster's veracity and reliability is lacking, there must be sufficient independent corroborating evidence to justify issuing a search warrant. U.S. Const. Amend. 4.—Castro v. State, 224 So.3d 281.

Fla.App. 2 Dist. 2004. A tip from an anonymous informant generally requires independent police corroboration in order to be considered credible; however, corroboration is not required at the other end of the spectrum where the tip comes from a citizen-informant, whose information is at the high end of the tip-reliability scale. —State v. Gonzalez, 884 So.2d 330.

Fla.App. 2 Dist. 1993. Affidavit in support of search warrant must set forth facts from which magistrate could find that affiant had personal knowledge of confidential informant's reliability or facts which corroborate reliability of confidential informant from independent source.—Fellows v. State, 612 So.2d 686.

⚬—**835(1). In general.**
† **C.A.11 (Fla.) 2006.** United States Secret Service special agent's affidavit made a sufficient showing of probable cause to justify search warrant for defendant's apartment, where special agent indicated in affidavit that confidential informant had met with defendant to exchange counterfeit currency, was at defendant's apartment during two separate exchanges of counterfeit currency, and had told officers that document-making implements belonged to defendant and were located at his apartment. U.S.C.A. Const.Amend. 4.—U.S. v. Young, 181 Fed.Appx. 840, certiorari denied 127 S.Ct. 517, 549 U.S. 1004, 166 L.Ed.2d 384.

Fla.App. 4 Dist. 2023. Affidavit in support of warrant to search alleged bank account owner's house was insufficient to establish probable cause that evidence of racketeering, bookmaking, and money laundering offenses would be found in house, in forfeiture action under the Florida Contraband Forfeiture Act (FCFA); officer with the county sheriff's office who signed the affidavit only had experience in road patrol, SWAT operations, and narcotics investigations, affidavit relied

---

† **This Case was not selected for publication in the National Reporter System**

on anonymous tips and "confidential, reliable sources" without demonstrating any basis to conclude that those sources were knowledgeable and reliable, and affidavit's allegations were stale, as there was a gap of more than four months between the last real allegation of criminal activity and when the warrant was sought. U.S. Const. Amend. 4; Fla. Stat. Ann. § 932.701.—Zarcadoolas v. Tony, 353 So.3d 638.

Fla.App. 4 Dist. 1976. Search warrant affidavit reciting personal observations of affiant and confidential informant in a controlled buy circumstance contained sufficient allegations to establish probable cause for search.—State v. Lewis, 336 So.2d 395.

Fla.App. 5 Dist. 1990. Veracity and basis of knowledge of confidential informants was sufficiently established to support a determination of probable cause for issuance of search warrant, even though affidavit submitted to magistrate was weak in detail and somewhat conclusory, where there were enough underlying facts set forth to meet minimum standards, and credibility of each informant bolstered information imparted by the other, especially where there was independent verification. U.S.C.A. Const.Amend. 4.—State v. Enstice, 573 So.2d 340.

☞835(2). Controlled substances.

† **C.A.11 (Fla.) 2019.** Search warrant affidavit established connection between defendant's home and sale of drugs, and thus warrant was supported by probable cause; affidavit established that defendant stopped at his home before selling heroin to confidential informant, affidavit pointed to other drug-related contraband found in defendant's trash, and affiant detective stated that believed, in light of contraband recovered from trash pull as well as his training and experience, that contraband and evidence of drug trafficking would be found at home. U.S. Const. Amend. 4. —United States v. Vargas, 792 Fed.Appx. 764, certiorari denied Aguedo v. United States, 140 S.Ct. 2693, 206 L.Ed.2d 836, certiorari denied Villar v. United States, 141 S.Ct. 147, 207 L.Ed.2d 1087, appeal after new sentencing hearing 2022 WL 766848.

† **C.A.11 (Fla.) 2019.** Information in search warrant affidavit established probable cause that evidence of drug trafficking would be found in defendant's apartment; using a confidential informant, police officers conducted two controlled drug buys from defendant, and officers saw defendant leave his apartment immediately before meeting with the informant, informant gave defendant $50 in exchange for a bag containing crack cocaine, and defendant then returned directly to his apartment. U.S. Const. Amend. 4.— United States v. McCown, 762 Fed.Appx. 732, certiorari denied 140 S.Ct. 92, 205 L.Ed.2d 79.

† **C.A.11 (Fla.) 2015.** Affidavit supporting search warrant provided law enforcement officers with probable cause to search drug defendant's apartment, and thus search did not violate Fourth Amendment; information provided by confidential informant was independently corroborated, and affidavit contained detailed description of location of defendant's unit within apartment building. U.S.C.A. Const.Amend. 4.—U.S. v. Taylor, 618 Fed.Appx. 969, post-conviction relief denied 2018 WL 10613867, habeas corpus denied Taylor v. Lovett, 2023 WL 8191099.

† **C.A.11 (Fla.) 2015.** Affidavit in support of warrant to search recreational vehicle (RV) parked outside of defendant's residence supported a fair probability that drugs would be

found there, and thus, police had probable cause to search the vehicle; affidavit was based on information obtained from a confidential informant, purchases made by the informant on the property, and police department's own surveillance of activity occurring around the RV. U.S.C.A. Const. Amend. 4.—U.S. v. James, 601 Fed.Appx. 789.

† **C.A.11 (Fla.) 2011.** Affidavit contained sufficient information to support issuance of warrant to search defendant's residence, even without police officer's allegedly false statement that he had directly observed a person fitting defendant's description during controlled buys of drugs at residence; allegations that officer directly observed two controlled buys that had been conducted according to a set of procedures designed to ensure their reliability corroborated the veracity of statements of confidential informant. U.S.C.A. Const.Amend. 4.—U.S. v. Johnson, 444 Fed.Appx. 424, certiorari denied 132 S.Ct. 1724, 565 U.S. 1250, 182 L.Ed.2d 261.

† **C.A.11 (Fla.) 2011.** Affidavit supporting search warrant issued after warrantless entry into neighboring residences contained sufficient information from independent sources to establish probable cause to search; ignoring information law enforcement obtained during initial warrantless entry, affidavits stated that confidential informant (CI), who was equipped with audio monitoring device, met with unknown Hispanic male at gas station, Hispanic male told CI to follow him to another location, which turned out to be one of the residences, once there, Hispanic male told CI that cocaine was "very close and not even a block away" and instructed CI to leave for 15 minutes, surveillance revealed that vehicle used initially to bring CI to residence was moved to neighboring residence, law enforcement saw numerous individuals move between residences, and (6) CI observed 50 kilograms of cocaine in one residence. U.S.C.A. Const.Amend. 4.—U.S. v. Jones, 433 Fed.Appx. 825, rehearing and rehearing denied 451 Fed.Appx. 908, certiorari denied 132 S.Ct. 1607, 565 U.S. 1225, 182 L.Ed.2d 213.

† **C.A.11 (Fla.) 2010.** Probable cause supported warrants to search defendant's personal residence and apartments in defendant's possession, where person who had purchased cocaine from one of those other apartments became confidential informant after being arrested in possession of cocaine and thereafter he assisted in subsequent investigation leading to warrants to search other apartment and defendant's residence. U.S.C.A. Const.Amend. 4.—U.S. v. Parker, 411 Fed.Appx. 220, rehearing and rehearing denied 429 Fed.Appx. 963, certiorari denied 132 S.Ct. 762, 565 U.S. 1063, 181 L.Ed.2d 491, post-conviction relief denied 2015 WL 4351102, certificate of appealability denied (11th cir. 15-14307).

† **C.A.11 (Fla.) 2010.** Detective's affidavit was more than sufficient to establish probable cause for search of property; affidavit established that confidential and reliable source provided information that someone at property was cultivating marijuana and stealing electricity, and that information was independently corroborated by detectives. U.S.C.A. Const.Amend. 4.—U.S. v. Sanchez-Paz, 402 Fed.Appx. 498, post-conviction relief denied 2012 WL 1344905.

† **C.A.11 (Fla.) 2010.** Even discounting information learned during prior, unlawful protective sweep search of defendant's apartment, police officers had valid independent source of probable cause to support subsequent search warrant,

---

† This Case was not selected for publication in the National Reporter System

where officers knew that their confidential source had set up a cocaine purchase with persons located at defendant's apartment, that the transaction was originally to involve 7 kilograms of cocaine, but only 4 kilograms were offered for sale when the transaction location was changed to a public shopping center, and codefendants arrived at the shopping center with the cocaine in a green box which they had picked up at defendant's apartment. U.S.C.A. Const.Amend. 4.—U.S. v. Fuentes, 368 Fed.Appx. 95.

†C.A.11 (Fla.) 2009. Search warrant affidavit provided sufficient probable cause for warrant to search defendant's apartment; co-defendant and confidential informant (CI) both described how defendant rented cars, traveled to Tallahassee, picked up cocaine, and returned to residence in Panama City, where he would store cocaine, based on co-defendant's and CI's information, investigating officers surveilled defendant's residence on day they applied for search warrant and observed rental car parked in front of defendant's residence, and when they attempted traffic stop on car, car fled, narcotics K–9 gave positive alert on defendant's front door, officers independently verified through defendant's father and utility records that residence belonged to defendant, and officers verified that defendant had been arrested previously for cocaine and crack cocaine possession. U.S.C.A. Const.Amend. 4.—U.S. v. Booker, 346 Fed.Appx. 419, post-conviction relief denied 2013 WL 1882226, motion denied 2013 WL 12363553.

†C.A.11 (Fla.) 2009. Search warrant affidavit established fair probability that evidence of ongoing drug activity or drugs would be found at defendant's residence, where several references were made in affidavit to fact that before and after defendant had conducted couple of drug transactions with confidential informant, he was at his residence, even though he moved residences between those two transactions, drug dog had alerted to presence of drugs in defendant's vehicle at last meeting, and shortly after defendant left, police found two ounces of cocaine under vehicle that was parked next to his vehicle, in location where he could have thrown it. U.S.C.A. Const.Amend. 4; Comprehensive Drug Abuse Prevention and Control Act of 1970, § 401(a)(1), (b)(1)(C), 21 U.S.C.A. § 841(a)(1), (b)(1)(C).—U.S. v. Meryl, 322 Fed.Appx. 871.

†C.A.11 (Fla.) 2009. Police had probable cause to support search of defendant's home based on information from confidential informant (CI), where CI had first-hand knowledge about suspect's drug operation in house, warrant contained statements of victim of sexual assault who identified defendant from photograph, police linked house to defendant's alleged conduct by verifying his name with electric company and fact that CI rented home to defendant. U.S.C.A. Const.Amend. 4.—U.S. v. Fernandez Martinez, 317 Fed.Appx. 929, certiorari denied 130 S.Ct. 198, 558 U.S. 882, 175 L.Ed.2d 139, post-conviction relief denied 2011 WL 4502073, habeas corpus dismissed in part Martinez v. Spaulding, 2021 WL 4080051, reconsideration denied 2022 WL 4636795, habeas corpus dismissed by 2022 WL 4636795.

†C.A.11 (Fla.) 2009. Information provided by two unidentified informants in residential search warrant affidavit, that defendant was involved in dealing marijuana from residence, was sufficiently independently corroborated, where defendant had a valid driver's license listing his address as that given by one informant, detectives observed

a white utility truck with identified plates driven by defendant's father depart from given address, that vehicle was registered to defendant, detectives observed a blue container in bed of truck, and, during traffic stop approximately two blocks from address, police seized approximately 52 kilograms of cocaine and approximately 460 kilograms of marijuana from a hidden compartment inside a blue container in bed of the same white utility truck. U.S.C.A. Const.Amend. 4.—U.S. v. Schimmel, 317 Fed.Appx. 906, post-conviction relief dismissed by 2011 WL 3859936.

Search warrant affidavit described a sufficient nexus between the criminal activity and the residence to be searched, where defendant's valid driver's license listed his address as that of residence to be searched, a confidential informant (CI) indicated that on several occasions he assisted defendant in unloading marijuana at that address, significant quantities of cocaine and marijuana were discovered hidden in a truck registered to defendant and previously observed departing from address, and affiant, a narcotics investigator with nine years of experience, stated that he knew it was common for drug traffickers to secret contraband and related materials in or near their residences. U.S.C.A. Const.Amend. 4. —Id.

†C.A.11 (Fla.) 2007. It is an acceptable and constitutional investigatory technique to utilize confidential informants to purchase drugs from suspected drug dealers in controlled buy situations.—U.S. v. Wilson, 238 Fed.Appx. 571.

†C.A.11 (Fla.) 2006. Police officer's affidavit was sufficient to support issuance of search warrant, and thus evidence found pursuant to search was not subject to suppression, despite defendant's contentions that officer could not have had vantage point to witness events described in affidavit, that officer failed to include confidential informant's (CI) observation of additional drugs in house, and that officer failed to search CI adequately before buy, where magistrate judge found that officer's testimony was more credible than defendant's testimony, only evidence to contradict officer's statement was defendant's testimony that property would not have been visible, and there was no evidence that CI was hiding drugs.—U.S. v. Johnson, 168 Fed.Appx. 390.

†C.A.11 (Fla.) 2006. Detective's affidavit in support of warrant to search defendant's apartment for drugs established a link between defendant, his apartment, and likelihood of illegal drugs in apartment, as required for probable cause to search the apartment; in the affidavit, detective stated that confidential informant had told him cocaine and ecstasy could be purchased from apartment occupied by or under the control of defendant, and informant's statements were corroborated by two controlled purchases from the apartment that yielded cocaine and ecstasy. U.S.C.A. Const.Amend. 4.—U.S. v. Thomas, 159 Fed.Appx. 979.

†C.A.11 (Fla.) 2005. Search warrant affidavit did not contain statements in reckless disregard of the truth, so as to render a search of defendant's apartment invalid, even if a confidential informant (CI) had faked controlled buys; the CI's own testimony suggested that the affiant reasonably believed the CI purchased cocaine from defendant. U.S.C.A. Const.Amend. 4.—U.S. v. Manning, 140 Fed.Appx. 212, certiorari denied 126 S.Ct. 501, 546 U.S. 969, 163 L.Ed.2d 379, post-conviction relief denied 2007 WL 9811454.

C.A.11 (Fla.) 1999. Police officer's affidavit made a sufficient showing of probable cause to justify search warrant for motel room, in view of confidential informant's basis of knowledge, including informant's detailed description of drugs in the room and sale of some of those drugs in his presence, officer's basis for characterizing informant as truthful and reliable, and circumstances indicating that informant was unlikely to lie. U.S.C.A. Const.Amend. 4.—U.S. v. Brundidge, 170 F.3d 1350.

C.A.11 (Fla.) 1999. Affidavit supporting search warrant, issued after illegal warrantless entry into warehouse, contained sufficient information from independent sources to establish probable cause for search of warehouse and nothing suggested police sought search warrant based on observations made during illegal entry, where confidential informant provided police with information relating to drug trafficking, previously-empty van was seized with 240 kilograms of cocaine just after short stop at warehouse, and police arrested two defendants with weapons outside locked warehouse. U.S.C.A. Const. Amend. 4.—U.S. v. Chaves, 169 F.3d 687, rehearing denied, certiorari denied Garcia v. U.S., 120 S.Ct. 534, 528 U.S. 1022, 145 L.Ed.2d 414, certiorari denied 120 S.Ct. 585, 528 U.S. 1048, 145 L.Ed.2d 486.

C.A.11 (Fla.) 1995. In determining whether search warrant had been issued on probable cause, affiant's reliance upon background of informant would be entitled to only slight weight; affidavit averments indicated only that informant had provided information in past investigations, without indicating whether this was in connection with informant's narcotics-related activities or those of other persons, and there was no indication whether information was important or incidental to those investigations, or whether information resulted in any search, arrest, or conviction, leaving judge unable to assess value of informant on any basis except affiant's opinion. U.S.C.A. Const.Amend. 4.—U.S. v. Foree, 43 F.3d 1572.

C.A.5 (Fla.) 1980. Mere fact that policeman failed to state specifically in affidavit that he believed confidential informant to be "reliable" or "credible" did not render affidavit insufficient to support finding of probable cause, where officer related that informant was knowledgeable, confirmed much of what informant told him, and swore that he believed defendant's office was being used to conduct drug-smuggling operation. —U.S. v. Farese, 612 F.2d 1376, rehearing denied 616 F.2d 568, certiorari denied 100 S.Ct. 3019, 447 U.S. 925, 65 L.Ed.2d 1118.

C.A.5 (Fla.) 1978. That one confidential informant was acting against penal interest in informing police of his activities in conspiracy and was in fact defendant in another prosecution stemming from same conspiracy, and that at least one other informant revealed some degree of criminal involvement in narcotics traffic tended to establish reliability of informants, even if statements supposedly made against penal interest did not establish criminal liability of the speakers. U.S.C.A.Const. Amend. 4; Federal Rules of Evidence, rule 804(b)(3), 28 U.S.C.A.; Comprehensive Drug Abuse Prevention and Control Act of 1970, §§ 401(a)(1), 406, 21 U.S.C.A. §§ 841(a)(1), 846.—U.S. v. Hyde, 574 F.2d 856, rehearing denied 579 F.2d 643, rehearing denied U.S. v. Middlebrooks, 579 F.2d 644.

M.D.Fla. 2009. Police officer's search warrant affidavit sufficiently established probable cause that evidence of criminal conduct was located in apartment at time that warrant was signed, and thus evidence seized in executing warrant was admissible in cocaine prosecution, even though identity of confidential informant (CI) who conducted controlled buy was undisclosed, there were no facts in affidavit establishing CI's reliability, CI's whereabouts were unknown, and some officers had lost confidence in CI, where affidavit described controlled buy that was observed by officers, through which cocaine was obtained from someone CI identified as defendant. U.S.C.A. Const.Amend. 4.—U.S. v. Parker, 600 F.Supp.2d 1251, affirmed 411 Fed.Appx. 220, rehearing and rehearing denied 429 Fed. Appx. 963, certiorari denied 132 S.Ct. 762, 565 U.S. 1063, 181 L.Ed.2d 491, post-conviction relief denied 2015 WL 4351102, certificate of appealability denied (11th cir. 15-14307).

M.D.Fla. 2001. Information given to state court judge, including that defendant dove head first out of a rear window of the residence when police officers announced themselves at the front door and that owner of the residence cooperated with authorities and provided information indicating that defendant stored cocaine at defendant's own residence, along with other information from confidential informants, was sufficient probable cause for issuance of search warrant for defendant's residence.—U.S. v. Lewis, 156 F.Supp.2d 1280.

S.D.Fla. 1995. Search warrant application provided sufficient basis for magistrate judge to assess credibility and veracity of confidential informant; although affidavit, which stated that informant had supplied reliable information for six months and had purchased crack cocaine from defendant, did not supply substantial basis for assessing veracity and did not address informant's cooperation in past investigations, officers' investigation of defendant, which preceded informant's involvement, provided independent corroboration of informant's veracity. U.S.C.A. Const.Amend. 4.—U.S. v. Smith, 897 F.Supp. 1448.

Probable cause existed to believe that items such as ledgers, bank records, and currency would be found in defendant's residence, even though confidential informant whose observations provided basis for search warrant did not see such items; special agent with Federal Bureau of Investigation (FBI) stated in supporting affidavit that drug traffickers often have such items in their residences. U.S.C.A. Const.Amend. 4.—Id.

Fla. 2011. Lawfully obtained evidence in search warrant affidavit did not establish probable cause to support issuance of warrant to defendant's residence for marijuana and marijuana-growing equipment; tip that marijuana was being grown in residence was unverified and came from an unknown individual, there was no evidence to suggest the tip was corroborated by any evidence resulting from surveillance of house, and the only other lawfully obtained evidence contained in the affidavit was that the window blinds were closed and the air conditioner unit was constantly running without recycling. U.S.C.A. Const.Amend. 4.—Jardines v. State, 73 So.3d 34, rehearing denied, stay denied 2011 WL 13491657, certiorari granted in part 132 S.Ct. 995, 565 U.S. 1104, 181 L.Ed.2d 726, affirmed 133 S.Ct. 1409, 569 U.S. 1, 185 L.Ed.2d 495.

Fla. 1969. Failure of affidavit in support of search warrant to recite date or dates when marijuana was sold to confidential informer and possessed by defendant did not render affidavit defective where affidavit used present tense in

---

alleging violation, which was continuing up to time warrant issued.—Borras v. State, 229 So.2d 244, appeal dismissed, certiorari denied 91 S.Ct. 70, 400 U.S. 808, 27 L.Ed.2d 37.

Fla.App. 1 Dist. 2006. Reliability of three confidential informants (CIs) whose information was set forth in affidavit was sufficient for their information to provide probable cause to issue warrant to search defendant's residence for methamphetamine evidence, even though affidavit did not allege that any of those three CIs had been used before by law enforcement or that information provided by CIs was reliable; credibility of each CI was bolstered by information imparted by other CIs, affiant officer independently corroborated certain information from first and third CIs, CIs provided information independently through different means, and first and third CIs had personal knowledge of alleged wrongdoing. U.S.C.A. Const.Amend. 4.—Green v. State, 946 So.2d 558.

Fla.App. 1 Dist. 2005. Law enforcement officers did not have probable cause to obtain warrant to search defendant's residence and, thus, were not justified in securing residence, even though officers received anonymous tip that defendant was growing and selling marijuana in residence, and one officer detected odor of burnt marijuana on defendant's girlfriend; tip was not confirmed, officers took no action when girlfriend was present in residence but, instead, waited to seek warrant until after her departure from premises, which removed only incriminating fact, nothing incriminating was seen inside residence or revealed by thermal-imaging scan, and defendant made no incriminating statements. U.S.C.A. Const.Amend. 4.—Smith v. State, 904 So.2d 534, rehearing denied.

Fla.App. 1 Dist. 1998. Probable cause existed to search apartment of drug defendant's girlfriend; search warrant affidavit of a narcotics agent with five years experience in drug interdiction alleged that currency and records of drug transactions would be found in apartment, that reliable confidential informant, listening to a conversation of defendant, learned that defendant was supplying cocaine to named persons out of apartment, that defendant's vehicle was parked at apartment, and that intercepted phone conversations from girlfriend's telephone indicated that money would soon be exchanged for cocaine.—Griffin v. State, 711 So.2d 1195.

Fla.App. 1 Dist. 1994. Reliability of confidential informant can be established by circumstances showing that informant made successful "controlled buy" of contraband. U.S.C.A. Const. Amend. 4.—Clark v. State, 635 So.2d 1010.

Fla.App. 1 Dist. 1989. There was sufficient probable cause for issuance of search warrant for defendant's mobile home and greenhouse located on his property; sheriff had received tip from Drug Enforcement Administration agent that there was a greenhouse in a subdivision where marijuana was being grown, and sheriff corroborated location of structure and subdivision, sheriff received second tip through state attorney's office investigator who had received information from Florida highway patrolmen and part-time insurance adjuster who in his capacity as an insurance adjuster had seen a locked greenhouse with no windows on property, sheriff received anonymous phone call stating that caller had been to property and had seen greenhouse full of marijuana and that it was about to be harvested, and sheriff verified location of property and structures on it during aerial flyover. U.S.C.A.

Const.Amend. 4.—Rowell v. State, 544 So.2d 1089.

Fla.App. 1 Dist. 1988. Unknown third person's statement to confidential informant that unknown person had just obtained quantity of cocaine at subject premises and alleged display of cocaine by unknown person could not serve as basis for probable cause determination for search warrant for subject premises; affidavit contained no information regarding reliability of unknown third person, and no search was made of person in order to ascertain whether substance he later described as cocaine was in fact on his person before he entered subject premises.—Sheppard v. State, 521 So.2d 288.

Fla.App. 1 Dist. 1983. Search warrant affidavit, which was prepared after confidential informant purchased heroin at subject residence, was not facially insufficient for failure to allege facts demonstrating that there was probable cause to believe that there were additional controlled substances remaining inside residence after controlled buy. U.S.C.A. Const.Amend. 4.—Crews v. State, 431 So.2d 709, petition for review denied 440 So.2d 351.

Fla.App. 1 Dist. 1978. Affidavit stating that confidential informant told affiant that within past 24 hours he had been inside described residence, and that "While inside the residence, the informant admits that he * * * purchased a quantity of what was represented by the occupant to be Marijuana," and which he brought to "* * * your affiant who identified the substance as Cannabis" did not recite facts which would establish admission against penal interest of informant which would carry its own indicia of reliability, and affidavit was, therefore, insufficient as basis for issuance of warrant to search described residence in that it failed to recite sufficient underlying circumstances from which magistrate could independently determine that hearsay information was reliable and that informant was credible.—State v. Adams, 355 So.2d 194, certiorari denied 359 So.2d 1220.

Fla.App. 1 Dist. 1974. Affidavit signed by detective, stating that he had received information from confidential informer that informer had personally purchased heroin at residence on two different occasions, that detective believed that information given by informer was true and correct, that informer was familiar with heroin and had identified heroin in detective's presence, and that informer was reputable member of community, had demonstrated interest in good law enforcement, was gainfully employed, and had received training in identification of drugs, was sufficient to support issuance of search warrant. —State v. Middleton, 302 So.2d 144.

Fla.App. 2 Dist. 2020. Affidavit submitted in support of search warrant did not allege sufficient information to establish probable cause for search of residence, although affidavit recounted a controlled purchase of methamphetamine that occurred at the address; affidavit provided almost no information regarding the drug transaction, affidavit asserted that confidential informant "departed the residence" but not that the informant had ever entered the residence or where the drug transaction took place, affidavit did not explain why deputies targeted residence in the first place, and affidavit asserted no connection between defendant and residence. U.S. Const. Amend. 4.— Hicks v. State, 292 So.3d 486.

Fla.App. 2 Dist. 2017. Officer's affidavit was insufficient to provide probable cause that drugs would be found in defendant's residence, as required to justify issuance of search warrant; affidavit provided vague information received from an anonymous tipster that defendant was concealing methamphetamine in his home, that there were scales in the residence, and that defendant sold methamphetamine in ounces, but did not indicate where the sales took place, whether the tipster had personally observed the drugs or even been in the residence, or contain any prediction of future behavior, and there was no police surveillance corroborating the vague tip. U.S. Const. Amend. 4.—Castro v. State, 224 So.3d 281.

Fla.App. 2 Dist. 2014. Police officers who received a tip from a confidential informant that marijuana plants were growing in defendant's garage lacked probable cause to search around defendant's residence with a drug-sniffing dog or to obtain a search warrant for the residence, even though officers noticed nails sticking through the garage door from the outside in, which was an allegedly common method of reinforcing doors to cultivate marijuana; search warrant affidavit provided no information as to the reliability of the informant, and officers only noticed the nails during their illegal use of the drug-sniffing dog. U.S.C.A. Const.Amend. 4.—Perez-Riva v. State, 152 So.3d 98.

Fla.App. 2 Dist. 2014. Affidavit filed in support of request for warrant to search defendant's home was sufficient to establish probable cause; affidavit portrayed a reliable confidential informant (CI) who had made two controlled buys of drugs in defendant's home, who had known defendant for at least six months, and who had made numerous unverified drug purchases from defendant. U.S.C.A. Const.Amend. 4.—Williams v. State, 130 So.3d 757.

Fla.App. 2 Dist. 2013. Search warrant affidavit would have established probable cause that evidence of a drug-related crime would be found at defendant's residence, even if purportedly "exculpatory" fact that detective did not see cannabis growing in backyard during a flyover had been included; affidavit noted anonymous tip from crime-stopping organization that defendant was growing cannabis in yard and selling it from his residence and vehicle, it mentioned pulls of defendant's trash bins in which contraband was found on two separate occasions, and it noted defendant's fabric-lined privacy fence and his history of convictions for drug-related offenses. U.S.C.A. Const.Amend. 4; West's F.S.A. § 933.18(5).—State v. Thomas, 160 So.3d 1282, on remand 2015 WL 13814576.

Fla.App. 2 Dist. 2013. Officer's warrant affidavit set forth facts upon which a reasonable magistrate could find probable cause to support issuance of warrant to search defendant's residence for drugs; a confidential informant (CI) informed officer that illegal narcotics were being sold from defendant's residence, officer knew the CI to be reliable, and in a 48 hour period the officer arranged for two controlled drug buys at residence. U.S.C.A. Const.Amend. 4.—State v. Jones, 110 So.3d 19, rehearing denied.

Fla.App. 2 Dist. 2005. Affidavit in support of search warrant sufficiently established nexus between residence and drug activity, where confidential informant (CI) specified particular residence as location where he could purchase drugs from defendant, defendant exited residence in order to make sale to CI, and defendant reentered residence immediately after making sale. U.S.C.A. Const.Amend. 4.—State v. Kennon, 901 So.2d 375.

Fla.App. 2 Dist. 2004. Police did not have sufficient probable cause to believe cocaine would be found in defendant's home, to justify search warrant; facts contained in search warrant affidavit regarding reliability of confidential informant were controverted at hearing on motion to suppress, no officer witnessed informant's first meeting with defendant, and subsequent controlled buy that occurred at parking lot was not maintained by constant visual surveillance from time defendant left house. U.S.C.A. Const.Amend. 4. —Garcia v. State, 872 So.2d 326.

Fla.App. 2 Dist. 1999. A confidential informant's single buy of an undisclosed amount of cocaine within the previous ten days did not justify a warrant to search all persons present in a home; the information did not support a reasonable conclusion of probability that anyone in the described home was involved in criminal activity. U.S.C.A. Const.Amend. 4.—Szady v. State, 745 So.2d 1041.

Fla.App. 2 Dist. 1998. Evidence was sufficient to show that controlled buy was executed, and thus controlled buy exception to requirement that affidavit in support of search warrant show informant's reliability applied; officer testified that he and other officers conducted controlled buy using confidential informant, informant and his car were searched before and after the buy, informant was given money, informant was observed going and coming out of building, and informant turned over contraband to officer after he came out of building.—State v. Elkhill, 715 So.2d 327.

Affidavit established probable cause to search defendant's residence for drugs, even though affiant did not continuously observe confidential informant during controlled buy; informant was under almost constant supervision of one of two officers during buy, and what affiant did not see, the other officer did.—Id.

Fla.App. 2 Dist. 1996. Probable cause to issue search warrant was established by attached affidavit which set forth fact that affiant officer was trained narcotics officer, that confidential informants advised officer that defendant possessed large quantities of cocaine at his residence, that officer personally observed garbage cans in defendant's yard and then later on street, and that garbage contained cocaine and razor blades and small amounts of marijuana.—State v. Howard, 670 So.2d 1004.

Fla.App. 2 Dist. 1994. While absence of statements in affidavit of probable cause for issuance of search warrant as to reliability of confidential informant would normally render affidavit deficient, exception exists when informant makes controlled buy.—State v. Reyes, 650 So.2d 52.

For purposes of exception to requirement that affidavit in support of search warrant set forth facts establishing reliability of confidential informant, "controlled buy" is one in which the confidential informant is personally supervised and constantly monitored by affiant.—Id.

Confidential informant engaged in "controlled buy," and thus exception to requirement that affidavit in support of search warrant show informant's reliability applied, where informant was searched, was given money, was observed entering and exiting building, was monitored with electronic transmitting device, and was searched again upon exiting building.—Id.

Fla.App. 2 Dist. 1993. Affidavit in support of warrant to search for narcotics did not on its face demonstrate sufficient basis to establish confidential informant's reliability, even though it stated that confidential informant had assisted county

† This Case was not selected for publication in the National Reporter System

sheriff's office on past investigations during which he or she provided information that was found to be reliable and trustworthy and that informant was past user of cocaine and could recognize cocaine in its various forms, and even though it identified informant by number issued by county sheriff's office.—Fellows v. State, 612 So.2d 686.

Fla.App. 2 Dist. 1992. Search warrant affidavit based on information from confidential informant did not establish probable cause, where warrant affidavit contained no information about informant's reliability or his basis for knowledge; warrant merely claimed that informant said that "he knew of a residence where he could purchase marijuana for your affiant," and that affiant later watched informant go behind residence and return with marijuana.—Delacruz v. State, 603 So.2d 707.

"Controlled buy" exception to general rule that search warrant affidavit based on information from confidential informant must contain information about informant's reliability or basis for knowledge was not applicable, where informant was not searched before buy to establish he had no drugs on him, and he was not searched after buy to establish he no longer had $20 given him by undercover officer.—Id.

Fla.App. 2 Dist. 1991. Substantial evidence supported issuing magistrate's determination that there was probable cause to believe that cocaine would be found on defendants' premises, based upon information obtained from confidential informant, though officer providing supporting affidavit had known confidential informant for only two weeks when she received said information; officer had received reliable information from confidential informant during those two weeks, and informant had personally observed cocaine in defendants' house the week before search warrant was executed and knew that one defendant regularly stored and distributed cocaine from there. U.S.C.A. Const.Amend. 4.—State v. Macolino, 583 So.2d 705, vacated Anderson v. State, 632 So.2d 1025, rehearing granted, vacated 632 So.2d 1025.

Fla.App. 2 Dist. 1991. Probable cause affidavit alleging that confidential informant observed defendant in possession of cocaine, and describing where defendant resided was not sufficient to establish probable cause for issuance of warrant to search defendant's home; affidavit lacked factual basis to show when and where informant observed defendant in possession of cocaine. West's F.S.A. Const. Art. I, § 12; U.S.C.A. Const. Amend. 4.—Getreu v. State, 578 So.2d 412.

Confidential informant's reliability as evidenced by his alleged "personal" observation of cocaine and knowledge of defendant's living arrangements were not circumstances that offset lack of factual basis in search warrant affidavit to make probable cause determination; additional factual basis could not be inferred from such circumstances. West's F.S.A. Const. Art. 1, § 12; U.S.C.A. Const.Amend. 4.—Id.

Fla.App. 2 Dist. 1987. Affidavit in support of search warrant that indicated that confidential informant observed drugs in house within "past 10 days" set forth with sufficient specificity time when drugs were seen in house by informant.—State v. Gill, 502 So.2d 59.

Fla.App. 2 Dist. 1983. Where affidavit reflected that undercover officer made four purchases of cocaine from third party, that in each instance, after agreeing upon sale, third party went to another location to obtain cocaine, that

on last two transactions, he was observed going to apartment described in search warrant, that he stayed in apartment for short period of time and then delivered cocaine directly to affiant, affidavit contained sufficient probable cause to believe that as of date of warrant cocaine would be found stored on described premises, notwithstanding that last transaction referred to in affidavit occurred 36 days before issuance of search warrant; therefore, warrant was not predicated on stale facts set forth in affidavit.—Smith v. State, 438 So.2d 896.

Fla.App. 2 Dist. 1983. Affidavit for search warrant alleging that affiant was personally acquainted with confidential informant, who had gathered intelligence information on narcotics in past which was true and correct and that affiant personally went to location described by informant and found residence where suspect was alleged to be dealing in cocaine and methaqualone was sufficient to establish probable cause for issuance of warrant given totality of circumstances even though it did not specifically describe how confidential informant acquired his information. U.S.C.A. Const.Amend. 4.—Graham v. State, 438 So.2d 114.

Fla.App. 2 Dist. 1980. Affidavit which showed that confidential informant had personally observed marijuana in defendant's apartment and which indicated credibility of informant by fact that he had furnished reliable information in past was sufficient, when combined with affiant's own investigations verifying some of the information supplied by the informant, to establish probable cause for issuance of search warrant.—State v. Lasswell, 385 So.2d 668, review denied 392 So.2d 1376.

Statement by narcotics agent in affidavit for search warrant that confidential informant was familiar with marijuana and could readily recognize it in its various forms carried with it necessary implication that affiant had firsthand knowledge that this was so, but in any event, further statement that informant had previously provided accurate information pertaining to delivery of marijuana substantiated his familiarity with that substance.—Id.

Fla.App. 2 Dist. 1977. Statement in search warrant affidavit that confidential informant had purchased drugs from defendant "within the last five days" was sufficiently specific and, coupled with other facts alleged in affidavit, demonstrated probable cause to issue warrant.—State v. Schwarzbauer, 342 So.2d 1085.

Fla.App. 2 Dist. 1976. Affidavit in which affiant stated that he had received information from a confidential informant that a large quantity of marijuana was located on the described premises within five days prior to the execution of the affidavit, that the informant had purchased some of the marijuana and that it had been checked and found to be marijuana, and that the informant had appeared before another magistrate and sworn to the truth of the statements contained in the affidavit was insufficient to support finding of probable cause as it did not show the reliability of the informant. West's F.S.A. § 933.18.—State v. Bond, 341 So.2d 218, certiorari denied 348 So.2d 953.

Fla.App. 2 Dist. 1974. Affidavit of detective that he had supervised a controlled buy of marijuana wherein reliable confidential informant was searched, given certain amount of money, was observed entering a described building and after a period of 15 minutes the informant was observed leaving the described building and returning to affiant who again searched the informant who had in his possession suspected marijuana was insufficient to warrant issuance of search warrant for marijuana paraphernalia. West's F.S.A. § 893.01 et seq.—State v. Gieske, 305 So.2d 6, quashed State v. Gieseke, 328 So.2d 16.

Fla.App. 2 Dist. 1974. Affidavit in which it was stated that affiant had received information from trustworthy confidential informant that informant had been in described dwelling and had seen marijuana within the past ten days, that affiant had received information from the informant in the past, that the information so received had been proven true and correct and that informant had proven to be reliable and trustworthy was sufficient to sustain finding of probable cause for issuance of search warrant. West's F.S.A. §§ 933.04, 933.18.—State v. Compton, 301 So.2d 810.

Fla.App. 2 Dist. 1974. Where affidavit disclosed that affiant conducted an independent investigation to determine reliability and veracity of his confidential informer, and investigation conducted by affiant included the purchase of marijuana by informant and verification of such fact by search of informant's person by affiant both before and immediately after the purchase of the drug, sufficient personal knowledge was alleged in affidavit to support issuance of search warrant by the magistrate. F.S.A. § 404.001 et seq.—Law v. State, 292 So.2d 596.

Fla.App. 2 Dist. 1973. Affidavit in which officer stated that he had known confidential informant for a year and knew him to be reliable, that informant was a self-admitted user of narcotic drugs and that informant had stated that he had been inside defendant's residence, that marijuana had been distributed by occupants of residence and that quantity of marijuana was within interior of residence was sufficient to support issuance of search warrant.—Tucker v. State, 283 So.2d 128, certiorari denied 291 So.2d 11.

Fla.App. 3 Dist. 2013. There was sufficient evidence independent of illegal canine sniff to support issuance of search warrant for defendant's residence; as officer approached front door of residence, he smelled live marijuana plants prior to dog's positive alert, he noticed three cars in the driveway, blinds of home drawn closed, and the air conditioning unit continuously running without recycling, all of which corroborate anonymous crime stoppers tip that home was being used as a marijuana grow house. U.S.C.A. Const.Amend. 4.—Arias v. State, 128 So.3d 73, review denied 147 So.3d 520.

Fla.App. 3 Dist. 2010. Officer's affidavit in support of search warrant contained sufficient facts to establish probable cause defendant was engaging in trafficking of cannabis and evidence of crime would be found in his home; affidavit alleged police received anonymous tip that marijuana was being grown in defendant's home, they set up surveillance and observed driver of truck removing number of garbage bags from next to home, odor of marijuana emanating from bags, which were found to contain marijuana clippings, leaves, and root systems, and driver of truck stated he had been paid $300, a disproportionately large amount, to take bags to dump, and given that trash bags belonged to defendant, and marijuana was not being grown in yard, it was reasonable for officer to infer that marijuana was being grown inside defendant's home. West's F.S.A. § 933.02(3); U.S.C.A. Const.Amend. 4.—State v. Carreno, 35 So.3d 125.

Fla.App. 3 Dist. 2007. Probable cause existed for issuance of search warrant for defendant's home; detectives visited defendant's home to corroborate anonymous tip that marijuana was being cultivated there, officer corroborated tip when he walked from sidewalk toward home and smelled marijuana, to further corroborate his findings, officer returned to scene the following day with other officers, and, again, while standing at front door of premises, he and other detectives observed strong odor of marijuana emanating from home. U.S.C.A. Const.Amend. 4.—State v. Pereira, 967 So.2d 312, rehearing denied.

Fla.App. 3 Dist. 2002. Probable cause existed for the issuance of search warrant based on anonymous tip that defendant was back in the business of selling drugs at new address, on search of garbage can that revealed mail with defendant's name and bags with cocaine residue, and on defendant's prior activities at earlier address. U.S.C.A. Const.Amend. 4.—State v. Gross, 833 So.2d 777.

Fla.App. 3 Dist. 1986. Search warrant affidavit which contained information that confidential source received cocaine from defendant's residence, that additional cocaine could be found on premises according to source, that cocaine test was positive, but which did not contain information that confidential source was credible, that permitted trial court to evaluate veracity of source, that identified confidential source, and that was independently corroborated by detectives, did not establish probable cause to search defendant's residence. West's F.S.A. § 933.04; U.S.C.A. Const.Amend. 4.—Vasquez v. State, 491 So.2d 297, review denied 500 So.2d 545.

Search warrant affidavit which stated that confidential source received cocaine from defendant's residence, that additional cocaine could be found on premises according to source, and that cocaine test was positive, but which failed to state facts to establish source's veracity or circumstances to corroborate confidential source, was so lacking in indicia of probable cause that police officers could not act in good faith and reasonable reliance on validity of warrant to search defendant's residence. West's F.S.A. § 933.04; U.S.C.A. Const.Amend. 4.—Id.

Fla.App. 3 Dist. 1983. Search warrant was based on nothing more than unverified allegation of anonymous tipster regarding his participation in placement of bales of marijuana in defendant's trailer, which did not support finding of probable cause sufficient to support issuance of warrant. U.S.C.A. Const.Amend. 4.—Milete v. State, 439 So.2d 337.

Fla.App. 3 Dist. 1978. Affidavit, even after references to hearsay testimony were eliminated, stating, among other things, that affiant and informant approached house and affiant stopped outside while confidential informant entered the house and stayed there for one to two minutes and informant then exited and returned to location of other officers where informant was again searched and found to be in possession of packet of powders which tested to be heroin, established sufficient probable cause for issuance of search warrant.—Bates v. State, 355 So.2d 128.

Fla.App. 4 Dist. 2015. Defendant's neighbor, who called police to inform them that she suspected drugs were being grown in his house, was a citizen informant rather than an anonymous tipster, even though she did not give her name, where neighbor met with officer face-to-face, and officer knew her residence.—Luna v. State, 154 So.3d 1181.

Fla.App. 4 Dist. 2009. Warrant issuing judge had a substantial basis for finding that there was probable cause to believe drugs would be located inside defendant's residence; one informant stated he had observed a kilogram amount of cocaine inside the residence during the week prior to the application for the search warrant, affiant stated that two of the three confidential informants had proven trustworthy in previous narcotics investigations, and affiant verified that defendant had been arrested several times for narcotics violations. U.S.C.A. Const.Amend. 4.—Boyd v. State, 17 So.3d 812, rehearing denied.

Fla.App. 4 Dist. 2006. Unverified and uncorroborated anonymous tip about a marijuana growing operation in defendant's home did not provide probable cause for issuance of residential search warrant on basis of independent lawful evidence separate from that obtained by illegal dog sniff at exterior door of defendant's home. U.S.C.A. Const.Amend. 4.—State v. Rabb, 920 So.2d 1175, review denied 933 So.2d 522, certiorari denied 127 S.Ct. 665, 549 U.S. 1052, 166 L.Ed.2d 513.

Fla.App. 4 Dist. 2005. Affidavit used to obtain search warrant for defendant's residence was not required to demonstrate affiant's personal knowledge of the reliability of confidential informant; affidavit established that informant participated in a controlled purchase of drugs that involved defendant's residence, informant was searched before and after the purchase and had the purchase money before the purchase and drugs afterward, informant was monitored with a listening device, and part of the transaction was personally observed by affiant. U.S.C.A. Const.Amend. 4.—Raucho v. State, 915 So.2d 278.

A controlled buy of drugs obviates the need to establish the reliability of the confidential informant, for purposes of obtaining a search warrant based on the informant's information, because the monitored buy itself corroborates the informant's credibility. U.S.C.A. Const.Amend. 4.—Id.

Affidavit used to obtain search warrant for defendant's residence was not required to demonstrate that seller who agreed to sell drugs to confidential informant was reliable; probable cause was not based on any hearsay statements by seller, but rather on affiant's personal knowledge that seller told informant to drive to defendant's residence to get the drugs, which affiant heard through informant's listening device, as well as affiant's observation of seller exiting defendant's residence with contraband. U.S.C.A. Const.Amend. 4.—Id.

The practice of searching a confidential informant before and after a controlled buy of drugs is done to prevent misconduct on the part of the informant, who may be motivated to implicate innocent third persons in order to gain favor with the police, or for reasons personal to the informant; the opportunity and possible motivation for misconduct arise because of the confidential informant's knowing participation in the controlled purchase and are not present where a person unknowingly assists the police.—Id.

Facts set forth in affidavit that was used to obtain search warrant for defendant's residence established probable cause to believe that there was contraband in defendant's residence; affidavit established that confidential informant gave seller $200 to buy ten ecstasy pills, that seller told informant he had to go to defendant's residence to get the ecstasy, and that seller emerged from seller's residence with amphetamines. U.S.C.A. Const.Amend. 4.—Id.

Fla.App. 4 Dist. 2004. Affidavit provided substantial basis for magistrate to conclude that probable cause existed to issue search warrant for defendant's residence, even though affidavit stated that informant saw contraband and drug transaction at residence "[d]uring week ending 3/22/02" rather than at specific time or date where affidavit described informant's observations in defendant's residence and stated that informant had made 20 controlled drug buys and provided information on at least ten occasions that resulted in more than five arrests and seizure of drugs, currency, and vehicles. U.S.C.A. Const. Amend. 4.—Johnson v. State, 872 So.2d 961, rehearing denied.

Fla.App. 4 Dist. 2003. When a confidential informant obtains drugs and is told to come back anytime for more, a controlled buy alone provides probable cause to search, even without any other predicate facts. U.S.C.A. Const.Amend. 4. —State v. Solomon, 861 So.2d 533.

While a confidential informant's controlled drug buy alone may be sufficient to establish probable cause for a search warrant, the trial court must determine whether the nature of the controlled buy indicates that the informant was sufficiently supervised and monitored to indicate probable reliability of the information obtained by the informant. U.S.C.A. Const.Amend. 4.—Id.

Fla.App. 4 Dist. 2000. Trash pull revealing contraband, which was performed based on anonymous tip, provided probable cause for warrant to search defendant's home; baggies found in trash pull tested positive for cocaine and provided evidence of continuous activity, and clear baggies and green twisty ties found in trash pull were consistent with specific information from caller regarding manner in which defendant was packaging cocaine for sale. U.S.C.A. Const. Amend. 4.—Baker v. State, 762 So.2d 977, rehearing denied.

Fla.App. 4 Dist. 1999. Single trash pull, revealing the presence of a residual amount of marijuana in a plastic bag, coupled with an anonymous tip of suspected drug activity that was uncorroborated by the officers' observations, was insufficient to constitute probable cause for issuance of a search warrant for residence. U.S.C.A. Const.Amend. 4.—Gesell v. State, 751 So.2d 104.

Fla.App. 4 Dist. 1998. Fact that substance found during one-time trash pull from garbage outside defendant's home tested positive for cannabis was not sufficient, either by itself or in conjunction with anonymous tip that residents at that address were dealing in narcotics, to establish a fair probability that cannabis would be found in defendant's home, and did not provide probable cause for issuance of search warrant; such information, which was contained in affidavit in support of search warrant, did not suggest a pattern of continuous drug activity. U.S.C.A. Const.Amend. 4.—Raulerson v. State, 714 So.2d 536, rehearing denied.

Fla.App. 4 Dist. 1997. Confidential informant's purchase of crack cocaine while fitted with listening device provided probable cause to search defendant's apartment, even though police officer lost sight of informant as he approached apartment building and did not see informant enter or leave defendant's apartment; affidavit before magistrate showed officer's personal knowledge of reliability of informant, informant had proved trustworthy and honest in the past, affidavit stated that informant made no stops and did not come into contact with anyone other than persons involved in transaction, and fair probability of contraband in defendant's apartment existed, even if facts stated in affidavit were not conclusive. U.S.C.A. Const.Amend. 4.—State v. Badgett, 695 So.2d 468.

Fla.App. 4 Dist. 1996. Officer's failure to search confidential informant's vehicle prior to controlled buy of cocaine did not, by itself, prohibit application of "controlled buy" exception to requirement that affidavit in support of search warrant show informant's reliability.—McCall v. State, 684 So.2d 260.

Determination of whether "controlled buy" exception, to requirement that affidavit in support of search warrant show confidential informant's reliability, should apply, and adequacy of police officer's search, supervision, and control of informant are matters within sound discretion of reviewing magistrate.—Id.

Fla.App. 4 Dist. 1996. Law enforcement officer's supervision of successful controlled buy conducted by confidential informant is sufficient to constitute probable cause to search site of the transaction without proof of reliability of the informant. U.S.C.A. Const.Amend. 4.—State v. Howard, 666 So.2d 592.

Fla.App. 4 Dist. 1983. It was not necessary to require strip search of confidential informant immediately before and after controlled buy of cocaine in order to establish probable cause to search defendant's home given circumstances of the case, and thus considering totality of the circumstances established by affidavit considered by magistrate, magistrate had substantial basis for concluding that probable cause to search defendant's home existed.—State v. Adams, 436 So.2d 276.

Fla.App. 4 Dist. 1980. Affidavit detailing how affiant, detective and a confidential informer known to the detective set up controlled purchase of contraband, including searching of informant before and after purchase and monitoring surveillance on transmitting device and discovery of heroin on informant following sale, with informant stating that she observed approximately 110 tinfoil packets of heroin on table and description of another purchase monitored at same apartment four days later, were sufficient to establish probable cause for search warrant, and was not deficient for failing to establish informant's reliability and trustworthiness.—State v. Pratt, 386 So.2d 1249.

Fla.App. 4 Dist. 1976. Affidavit stating that confidential informant observed heroin trafficking at bar and that affiant, detective, observed and overheard informant's purchase of heroin on different occasions at bar established probable cause for issuance of warrant to search bar.— State v. Gervin, 336 So.2d 666, certiorari denied 341 So.2d 1082.

Fla.App. 5 Dist. 2017. Police detective's affidavit was sufficient to establish probable cause for issuance of search warrant for defendant's residence; defendant told confidential source that he would deliver drugs to him in 15 to 20 minutes, defendant who was under surveillance, then drove to his apartment, was there for 15 to 20 minutes, and then drove directly to the meeting place, and defendant was apprehended with a large quantity of cocaine. U.S. Const. Amend. 4. —State v. Hayward, 215 So.3d 178, review denied 2017 WL 4786191, on remand 2017 WL 10980459.

Fla.App. 5 Dist. 2013. Statement in warrant affidavit that confidential informant observed cannabis and cash in defendant's house, without statement indicating when observation was made, was insufficient without more to satisfy nexus requirement for finding of probable cause. U.S.C.A. Const.Amend. 4.—State v. McGill, 125 So.3d 343.

Totality of information, including information from confidential informant (CI) and independent observations of officers, set forth in warrant affidavit was sufficient to provide probable cause to believe that cannabis would be found in defendant's home; CI indicated that defendant routinely sold cannabis from his home, officer put defendant's home under surveillance and found cannabis in vehicle pulled over after leaving defendant's home, driver of that vehicle verified that defendant sold cannabis from his home on ongoing and routine basis, CI accurately predicted another person's future conduct, and warrant set forth defendant's history of drug-related offenses. U.S.C.A. Const.Amend. 4.—Id.

Fla.App. 5 Dist. 2006. Probable cause existed to issue warrant to search defendant's residence for drugs, where affidavit in support of warrant described anonymous tip that drug activity was occurring at residence, observation by law enforcement officers of suspicious activity at residence, observation of named informant entering residence, named informant's detention by officers within two minutes of his departure from residence, named informant's statements to officers about drug activity at residence, and named informant's ability to identify a picture of defendant as person who sold him drugs, and affidavit had attached to it named informant's detailed sworn statement about drug activity at residence. U.S.C.A. Const.Amend. 4.—State v. Irizarry, 948 So.2d 39, rehearing denied.

Fla.App. 5 Dist. 2005. Reliability of confidential informant upon whose claims police applied for warrant to search defendant's home was not established in affidavit as to support finding of probable cause and issuance of warrant; although affidavit stated that informant, "under the direction of" police, went to defendant's residence and purchased controlled substances, affidavit did not show any supervision by law enforcement in order for the transaction to be considered a "controlled buy." U.S.C.A. Const.Amend. 4.— Martin v. State, 906 So.2d 358.

A controlled buy of a controlled substance by a confidential informant occurs, thereby relieving State of its duty to independently establish informant's reliability in warrant affidavit, when the informant conducts a transaction supervised and monitored by law enforcement. U.S.C.A. Const. Amend. 4.—Id.

When a controlled buy occurs, the State does not need to independently establish the confidential informant's reliability in the search warrant affidavit, since law enforcement is present in a controlled buy situation, and can corroborate the truthfulness of the informant's actions and words. U.S.C.A. Const.Amend. 4.—Id.

Fla.App. 5 Dist. 1996. Magistrate who issued warrant to search defendant's trailer had probable cause to believe that marijuana would be found therein; although anonymous tip was short on detail, it was substantially corroborated, as police learned that defendant had obtained power sources for trailer, and police also learned that activities taking place inside trailer were consistent with indoor marijuana-growing operation, as evidenced by visually examining trailer, by researching trailer's power consumption records, and through use of thermal imaging and forward-looking infrared device (FLIR), constitutionality of which was not contested. U.S.C.A. Const. Amend. 4.—State v. Siegel, 679 So.2d 1201, rehearing denied.

Fla.App. 5 Dist. 1995. Reliability of confidential informant referenced in application for warrant to search drug defendant's residence was established by two controlled buys; affiant searched informant before controlled buys to make sure he had no drugs, and affiant searched informant after controlled buy to make sure money provided by police was not on informant's person.—Malone v. State, 651 So.2d 733.

Affidavit established probable cause to search defendant's residence for drugs, even though affiant did not continuously observe confidential informant during controlled buy; informant was under almost constant supervision of two officers during that buy, and what one did not see, other did see.—Id.

Fla.App. 5 Dist. 1994. Search warrant affidavit was sufficient to establish probable cause to search defendant's residence, despite defendant's claim that it failed to allege sufficient facts to determine that "controlled buys" actually took place, so as to establish reliability of confidential informant; affiant, an experienced drug enforcement officer, used the term "controlled buy" three times in affidavit and stated facts with regard to third buy from which it could be clearly inferred that "controlled buy" meant purchase of controlled substance under supervision and control of police officers so as to establish reliability. U.S.C.A. Const.Amend. 4.—State v. Starks, 633 So.2d 546.

Fla.App. 5 Dist. 1991. Affidavit in support of search warrant did not have to factually establish the reliability of confidential informant in controlled buy situation.—State v. Cruz, 582 So.2d 20.

Fla.App. 5 Dist. 1990. While absence of statements in affidavit of probable cause for issuance of search warrant as to reliability of confidential informant would normally render affidavit deficient, there is exception when informant makes "controlled buy," which is one in which informant is personally supervised and constantly monitored by affiant and which establishes informant's reliability.—Polk v. Williams, 565 So.2d 1387.

Confidential police informant made "controlled buy" of drugs such that search warrant affiant's failure to attest to reliability of informant did not render affidavit deficient even though affiant did not observe entire transaction; affiant monitored informant through "body bug" throughout transaction, and officer from another law enforcement agency personally observed informant when he was out of affiant's sight.—Id.

Fla.App. 5 Dist. 1986. There was probable cause to issue search warrant where supporting affidavit identified officer and stated his education and experience in narcotics transactions, explained how reliable confidential informant wearing transmitting device had made cocaine buy from person he identified as defendant, set forth two other drug buys from defendant on different dates made by same informant and under same controlled and monitored circumstances, and showed continuous series of narcotics transactions by defendant and facts to indicate probable presence of substantial quantities of drugs on his premises. West's F.S.A. § 933.07.—Ryals v. State, 498 So.2d 1365.

Fla.App. 5 Dist. 1983. Where affiant personally supervised controlled buy of cocaine from defendant by confidential informant, affidavit detailing the controlled buy was not based on hearsay.—State v. Cohen, 442 So.2d 346.

⟜**838. —— Other officers or official information; collective knowledge.**

† **C.A.11 (Fla.) 2006.** Observations of fellow police officers engaged in common investigation of defendant for possessing child pornography and solicitation to commit sexual battery were a reliable source for search warrant applied for by another officer, and thus, fact that officer who applied for warrant did not observe any of the facts first-hand did not render search warrant invalid.—U.S. v. Campbell, 193 Fed.Appx. 921.

C.A.11 (Fla.) 1986. Inclusion in search warrant affidavit of details observable in defendant's home by Government agents only with binoculars constituted harmless error, in that all observations made by agents, with a few minor exceptions, could have been made with the naked eye, and agents' observations, in combination with other similarly unchallengeable information in affidavit, established probable cause to issue search warrant. U.S.C.A. Const.Amend. 4.—U.S. v. Whaley, 779 F.2d 585, rehearing denied 784 F.2d 404, certiorari denied 107 S.Ct. 931, 479 U.S. 1055, 93 L.Ed.2d 982.

Fla.App. 4 Dist. 2023. Under the "fellow officer" rule, an officer seeking a search warrant generally can rely on evidence gathered by other officers if the officers' collective knowledge supports a finding of probable cause. U.S. Const. Amend. 4.—Zarcadoolas v. Tony, 353 So.3d 638.

Fla.App. 5 Dist. 2020. Under the "fellow officer" rule, a police officer is entitled to rely upon the factual observations of other officers made during the course of their investigation and then to include this supplied information in her probable cause affidavits for the search warrants. U.S. Const. Amend. 4.—State v. Hart, 308 So.3d 232, rehearing denied, review denied 2021 WL 6138926.

Fla.App. 5 Dist. 1990. Under "fellow officer rule," arresting officer is not required to have sufficient firsthand knowledge to constitute probable cause, and it is sufficient if officer initiating chain of communication receives information from official source or eyewitness who, it seems reasonable to believe, is telling the truth; rule is not limited to officers within same law enforcement agency, and also applies to search warrants. —Polk v. Williams, 565 So.2d 1387.

⟜**839(1). In general.**

† **C.A.11 (Fla.) 2020.** Affidavit in support of search warrant established probable cause to search principal office of defendant's federal income tax preparation business, where it contained information establishing connection between defendant and place to be searched, and fair probability that evidence of criminal tax fraud would be found there; affidavit indicated that large number of fraudulent tax returns had been electronically submitted within wire fraud conspiracy's applicable time frame from business's office, using business's electronic filing identification number, and that agents had observed coconspirator outside business's office. U.S. Const. Amend. 4.—United States v. Pearson, 832 Fed.Appx. 679, post-conviction relief denied 2021 WL 4845797.

† **C.A.11 (Fla.) 2018.** Detective possessed probable cause to obtain warrant to search apartment of arrestee's girlfriend, where photographed

items that served as basis for warrant were observed in plain view during detective's initial protective sweep of apartment; photographs showed a bag of marijuana on dining room table, a scale in a box sitting on a dresser and magazines of ammunition protruding from dresser, and there was no evidence the officers opened drawers of dressers or looked in kitchen cabinets or took any other actions which would have exceeded the scope of protective sweep. U.S. Const. Amend. 4.—United States v. Concepcion, 748 Fed.Appx. 904, certiorari denied 139 S.Ct. 2655, 204 L.Ed.2d 282.

† **C.A.11 (Fla.) 2010.** Search warrant for defendant's offices was supported by probable cause, where the affidavit supporting the warrant set forth law enforcement agent's personal observations and information gleaned from his investigation and established a fair probability that evidence of illegal shipments made to China of restricted technology and electronic and defense equipment would be found in the offices. U.S.C.A. Const.Amend. 4.—U.S. v. Piquet, 372 Fed.Appx. 42.

† **C.A.11 (Fla.) 2008.** FBI agent's affidavit was sufficient to establish probable cause for search warrant for payday loan company's offices; affidavit stated that subpoenaed bank records showed that the company transferred $1,134,000 of $2.1 million in investor funds out of trust account and into an operating account in order to use those funds to pay commissions and consulting fees, that company's offering materials and purchase agreements misrepresented that investor funds would be placed into segregated accounts and used exclusively to facilitate loans to the customers, and that the Florida Office of the Comptroller records showed that the company had never applied for money transmitter licenses, which were required for every check-cashing location, and the affidavit also identified two company investors who invested $10,000 and $50,000, respectively, after being told by company's sales agents that their investments would be held in a trust account. U.S.C.A. Const.Amend. 4.—U.S. v. Long, 300 Fed.Appx. 804, certiorari denied 130 S.Ct. 133, 558 U.S. 853, 175 L.Ed.2d 87.

† **C.A.11 (Fla.) 2006.** Search warrant application established probable cause to search defendant's residence for evidence of solicitation to commit sexual battery under Florida law; defendant bragged to detectives via text messaging that he had sex with his own minor daughter, defendant sent detective photographs of nude female that defendant alleged was his daughter, defendant arranged to meet one detective's daughter and have sex with her, and, when asked what ages he liked, defendant responded "10 and up." U.S.C.A. Const.Amend. 4; West's F.S.A. §§ 777.04, 794.011.—U.S. v. Campbell, 193 Fed. Appx. 921.

C.A.5 (Fla.) 1972. Affidavit, which recited that defendant had been arrested for possession of counterfeit money and had stated that he had received money from his brother and that brother had told him that printing plant was located in town in which brother resided and which averred that brother had been arrested for offenses involving counterfeit obligations and that investigation disclosed that additional electric service wiring suitable for operation of printing equipment had been installed in garage of brother's premises and that counterfeit money seized in county within the prior 90 days was identical to money seized from defendant, established probable

cause for issuance of warrant to search brother's premises for counterfeiting equipment. U.S.C.A.Const. Amend. 4.—U.S. v. Banks, 465 F.2d 1235, certiorari denied 93 S.Ct. 568, 409 U.S. 1062, 34 L.Ed.2d 514.

C.A.5 (Fla.) 1972. Where federal agents received information regarding a suspected shipment of 37 cartons of silver bullion, where they went to airline cargo complex and, after identifying themselves to cargo security manager, were taken to the cargo area and to the vicinity of the cartons in question, and where, because some of the cartons were torn, they could see a bar of metal which resembled silver, the officers had probable cause to secure a search warrant and seize the silver. U.S.C.A.Const. Amend. 4.—U.S. v. Resnick, 455 F.2d 1127, rehearing denied 459 F.2d 1390, certiorari denied Carlton v. U.S., 93 S.Ct. 121, 409 U.S. 875, 34 L.Ed.2d 127, appeal after remand 483 F.2d 354, certiorari denied 94 S.Ct. 370, 414 U.S. 1008, 38 L.Ed.2d 246.

S.D.Fla. 1997. Search warrant affidavit of United States Customs Service Special Agent provided probable cause for issuance of search warrant for law office, in connection with attorney's suspected protection of drug cartel; affidavit alleged, among other things, that attorney knowingly solicited falsely exculpatory affidavit, and that telephone calls and facsimile transmissions to drug cartel leader came from law office. U.S.C.A. Const.Amend. 4.—U.S. v. Abbell, 963 F.Supp. 1178.

⚯839(2). Controlled substances.

† **C.A.11 (Fla.) 2011.** Police officers investigating suspect in armed kidnapping had probable cause for warrant to search defendant's property, thereby precluding habeas relief, where officers surrounded property as part of their search for armed kidnapping suspect and observed evidence that defendant was manufacturing methamphetamine on his property. U.S.C.A. Const.Amend. 4; 28 U.S.C.A. § 2254(d).—Hearn v. Florida, 410 Fed.Appx. 268, certiorari denied 132 S.Ct. 232, 565 U.S. 874, 181 L.Ed.2d 130.

† **C.A.11 (Fla.) 2006.** Police officer's affidavit was sufficient to support issuance of search warrant, and thus evidence found pursuant to search was not subject to suppression, despite defendant's contentions that officer could not have had vantage point to witness events described in affidavit, that officer failed to include confidential informant's (CI) observation of additional drugs in house, and that officer failed to search CI adequately before buy, where magistrate judge found that officer's testimony was more credible than defendant's testimony, only evidence to contradict officer's statement was defendant's testimony that property would not have been visible, and there was no evidence that CI was hiding drugs.—U.S. v. Johnson, 168 Fed.Appx. 390.

C.A.11 (Fla.) 1986. Affiant officer's reliance on information from other officers in preparing affidavit for search warrant did not render warrant invalid, where it was clear from affidavit as a whole that information in affidavit was derived from various agents' investigation and surveillance of dealings in illegal drugs.—U.S. v. Kirk, 781 F.2d 1498.

Fla.App. 2 Dist. 1974. Policeman's affidavit which stated that a reliable informant had been told by an anonymous friend that narcotics were located in a certain mobile home and which further stated that the policeman and others arrested the mobile home's occupants who admitted that narcotics were located therein was sufficient to support the issuance of a search warrant for the mobile home.—Hicks v. State, 299 So.2d 44, certiorari denied 310 So.2d 739.

⟨⇒839(3). **Obscenity.**

† **C.A.11 (Fla.) 2020.** Probable cause supported warrant to search apartment of defendant arrested on child enticement and child pornography charges based on his contact with undercover officer posing as underage victim, even if affidavit supporting warrant did not append images of sexually explicit conduct or provide sufficient factual details describing any such images; affidavit provided sufficient basis to conclude that there was a fair probability of finding contraband or evidence at defendant's apartment, as it demonstrated that defendant knew victim was a minor and that he was seeking and requesting sexually explicit visual depictions of a minor, provided information regarding defendant's behavior throughout the investigation, and established a nexus between the criminal conduct and defendant's apartment, indicating that law enforcement would find evidence there related to advertising for, receiving, distributing, and possessing child pornography. U.S. Const. Amend. 4.—United States v. Orr, 819 Fed.Appx. 756.

† **C.A.11 (Fla.) 2006.** Observations of fellow police officers engaged in common investigation of defendant for possessing child pornography and solicitation to commit sexual battery were a reliable source for search warrant applied for by another officer, and thus, fact that officer who applied for warrant did not observe any of the facts first-hand did not render search warrant invalid.—U.S. v. Campbell, 193 Fed.Appx. 921.

M.D.Fla. 1975. Affidavit which describes in detail the scenes of an allegedly obscene film which was personally viewed by the affiant and which contains factual description, scene by scene, of what was portrayed and not mere conclusions as to obscenity of the film provides sufficient basis on which judicial officer issuing search warrant for seizure of the allegedly obscene film can make an independent determination and focus searchingly on the question of obscenity; failure of Florida obscenity statute to provide for viewing of the film by the magistrate prior to determination of probable cause was not unconstitutional. West's F.S.A. § 847.011; U.S.C.A.Const. Amends. 1, 5, 14.—Ellwest Stereo Theatres, Inc. v. Nichols, 403 F.Supp. 857.

Fla.App. 1 Dist. 2018. Investigating officer's search warrant that authorized seizure of defendant's computer was supported by probable cause, even though officer was unable to personally view video containing child pornography which he knew from investigation had been downloaded onto defendant's hard drive, where officer utilized a graphic description of video given by detective who personally viewed it, which description he was able to acquire from a law enforcement database. U.S. Const. Amend. 4.—Mardosas v. State, 257 So.3d 540, rehearing denied, review denied 2019 WL 1349269, certiorari denied 140 S.Ct. 576, 205 L.Ed.2d 359.

⟨⇒844. —— **Illegal search.**

C.A.11 (Fla.) 2018. To analyze whether independent source exists to support search warrant, court must first excise from search warrant affidavit any information gained during arguably illegal initial search and determine whether remaining information is enough to support probable cause finding, and then, if remaining information establishes probable cause, determine whether officer's decision to seek warrant was

prompted by what he had seen during arguably illegal search. U.S. Const. Amend. 4.—United States v. Maxi, 886 F.3d 1318, certiorari denied Blanc v. U.S., 139 S.Ct. 235, 202 L.Ed.2d 159, certiorari denied 139 S.Ct. 351, 202 L.Ed.2d 248, denial of post-conviction relief affirmed 2023 WL 7325562.

⟨⇒845(2). **Particular cases.**

† **C.A.11 (Fla.) 2019.** Even without alleged misrepresentations and omissions in search warrant affidavit regarding defendant's statements to officers, affidavit still would have supported finding of probable cause, and thus warrant was not void; affidavit contained sufficient information to conclude that fair probability existed that firearm, ammunition, and drugs would be found at defendant's house. U.S. Const. Amend. 4.—United States v. Knight, 773 Fed.Appx. 1057, certiorari denied 140 S.Ct. 1135, 206 L.Ed.2d 195.

† **C.A.11 (Fla.) 2019.** Under independent source doctrine, search warrant affidavit established probable cause to search apartment, even after information related to officer's allegedly illegal second entry into apartment was excised; defendant's sister gave officer gift credit cards, she stated that her brother made credit cards, and she had observed him swipe credit cards in a machine that was connected to a lap top computer. U.S. Const. Amend. 4.—United States v. Fleur, 762 Fed.Appx. 691.

C.A.11 (Fla.) 2015. Untainted portions of police detective's affidavit in support of his application for warrant for search of defendant's hotel room supported finding of probable cause, even though officers' initial entry into room was unlawful, where affidavit stated that hotel employee had informed officers that he had removed loaded firearm from another room in hotel that defendant had just vacated and that defendant had gone to front desk to claim it, that officers had discovered cocaine and other drugs in vacated room, that defendant was room's only registered occupant, and that defendant had prior felony conviction. U.S.C.A. Const.Amend. 4.—U.S. v. Albury, 782 F.3d 1285.

† **C.A.11 (Fla.) 2014.** Even if information allegedly obtained in violation of defendant's Fourth Amendment rights was excised from affidavit offered in support of warrant for search of defendant's home, remaining information, to effect that defendant, a convicted felon, was observed in possession of firearm, a nonconsumable good, within 13 months prior to search warrant application, was sufficient to establish fair probability that firearm might be found in defendant's home and provided requisite probable cause for issuance of warrant. U.S.C.A. Const.Amend. 4.— U.S. v. Piloto, 562 Fed.Appx. 907, certiorari denied 135 S.Ct. 291, 574 U.S. 913, 190 L.Ed.2d 213.

M.D.Fla. 2010. After information obtained in an illegal entry into defendants' residence was removed from affidavit in support of search warrant for the residence, the remaining information was insufficient to establish probable cause to search the residence for evidence of Florida offense of unlawful possession of a blank prescription form; the only information in the redacted affidavit was that officers had observed drug paraphernalia, needles, and pill bottles inside the residence, and that an officer who came to the residence came in contact with a woman who had previously passed a fraudulent prescription, and the affidavit stated nothing that connected the woman who had passed the fraudulent prescription to the residence or its contents. U.S.C.A. Const.Amend. 4; West's F.S.A. § 893.13(7)(a)(7).—U.S. v. Bergin, 732 F.Supp.2d 1235, affirmed 455 Fed.Appx. 908, certiorari denied 132 S.Ct. 1948, 566 U.S. 954, 182 L.Ed.2d 802, post-conviction relief denied in part, dismissed in part 2014 WL 5093853, affirmed U.S. v. Powner, 481 Fed.Appx. 529, post-conviction relief denied 2016 WL 5239831.

Fla.App. 2 Dist. 2011. Information contained in affidavit was sufficient to establish probable cause for search warrant independent of evidence uncovered during illegal warrantless entry and search of house and garage; affidavit contained information indicating that victim identified one of the stolen vehicles at house one day after theft occurred, person working on vehicle appeared to be stripping it, suspect, who drove maroon car, was at victim's business the day before theft occurred, it appeared that perpetrator had rammed his vehicle into back door of victim's business, back door had maroon paint on it, and suspect's maroon car was parked in front of house where victim saw stolen vehicle. U.S.C.A. Const.Amend. 4.—State v. Hood, 68 So.3d 392.

Fla.App. 2 Dist. 2005. Inclusion in search warrant affidavit of information insufficient to establish probable cause to believe that defendant had committed offense of sexual performance by a child did not negate probable cause established by other information contained therein. U.S.C.A. Const.Amend. 4.—State v. Jenkins, 910 So.2d 934.

Fla.App. 3 Dist. 2013. There was sufficient evidence independent of illegal canine sniff to support issuance of search warrant for defendant's residence; as officer approached front door of residence, he smelled live marijuana plants prior to dog's positive alert, he noticed three cars in the driveway, blinds of home drawn closed, and the air conditioning unit continuously running without recycling, all of which corroborate anonymous crime stoppers tip that home was being used as a marijuana grow house. U.S.C.A. Const.Amend. 4.—Arias v. State, 128 So.3d 73, review denied 147 So.3d 520.

⟐847. —— In general.

C.A.11 (Fla.) 2023. Warrant does nothing to satisfy Fourth Amendment's probable-cause requirement when judge was presented with materially incorrect information. U.S. Const. Amend. 4.—Land v. Sheriff of Jackson County Florida, 85 F.4th 1121.

C.A.11 (Fla.) 2022. The Fourth Amendment would be violated if a search warrant is obtained by using a materially false statement made intentionally or recklessly. U.S. Const. Amend. 4.—United States v. Grushko, 50 F.4th 1, certiorari denied 143 S.Ct. 2594, 216 L.Ed.2d 1199, certiorari denied 143 S.Ct. 2680, 216 L.Ed.2d 1248.

C.A.11 (Fla.) 2019. For an affirmative misrepresentation in an affidavit used to support a search warrant, "deliberateness" refers to a deliberate falsehood, not any action done intentionally; so for an omission, deliberateness must also refer to something akin to bad faith on the part of the affiant, not merely that the affiant knew some information and did not include it. U.S. Const. Amend. 4.—United States v. Whyte, 928 F.3d 1317, certiorari denied Castro v. United States, 140 S.Ct. 874, 205 L.Ed.2d 499, certiorari denied 140 S.Ct. 875, 205 L.Ed.2d 497.

M.D.Fla. 2020. A search warrant is void if it contains a deliberately false statement or one that was made in reckless disregard of the truth and

that false statement forms the basis of the search. U.S. Const. Amend. 4.—Lloyd v. Leeper, 451 F.Supp.3d 1314.

A police officer violates the Constitution if, in order to obtain a search warrant, he perjures himself or testifies in reckless disregard of the truth. U.S. Const. Amend. 4.—Id.

M.D.Fla. 2017. Homeowner failed to establish that detective violated her Fourth Amendment rights, based on allegation that detective falsified affidavit used to obtain search warrant for her residence for evidence related to charge against homeowner for aggravated assault of a law enforcement officer, following incident in which homeowner was shot by sheriff's deputy conducting welfare check at her residence, where detective did not make false or reckless misrepresentation of facts known to him at time of application for warrant, and affidavit contained probable cause to search the residence even after the allegedly false statements were omitted. U.S. Const. Amend. 4; 42 U.S.C.A. § 1983.—Ermini v. Scott, 249 F.Supp.3d 1253.

While constitutional prohibition of making perjurious or recklessly false statements or omissions in an information put forth to establish probable cause does not dictate that the statements be objectively accurate, it does require that they be truthful in the sense that the information put forth is believed or appropriately accepted by the affiant as true. U.S. Const. Amend. 4.—Id.

M.D.Fla. 2008. Fourth Amendment prohibits a public official from making a perjurious or recklessly false statement or omission in an affidavit supporting a search or arrest warrant, if the statement or omission is necessary to a finding of probable cause. U.S.C.A. Const.Amend. 4.—Burge v. Ferguson, 619 F.Supp.2d 1225.

Fla.App. 4 Dist. 2017. Where a defendant challenges an affidavit as containing a material misstatement, the defendant must make a preliminary showing: (1) that the affiant knowingly or intentionally or with reckless disregard for the truth included a false statement in the affidavit used to obtain a search warrant; and (2) that statement was necessary to the finding of probable cause; if the defendant establishes these allegations by a preponderance of the evidence, then the court must suppress the fruits of the search. U.S. Const. Amend. 4.—Baldino v. State, 225 So.3d 257, review granted 2018 WL 3633562, review denied 2018 WL 6618222.

⟐848. —— Particular cases.

† **C.A.11 (Fla.) 2021.** Affidavit was sufficient to support warrant to search physician's home for evidence of prescription fraud, even if it included false statements from other witnesses, absent allegation that the warrant affiant included any facts he knew were false. U.S. Const. Amend. 4; 42 U.S.C.A. § 1983.—Paylan v. Dirks, 847 Fed.Appx. 595, certiorari denied 142 S.Ct. 228, 211 L.Ed.2d 100.

Challenges to warrant affidavits that supported arrest for prescription fraud and search of physician's home did not negate the probable cause established by the evidence that officers discovered in trash during their investigation. U.S. Const. Amend. 4; 42 U.S.C.A. § 1983.—Id.

C.A.11 (Fla.) 2017. Search warrant application contained sufficient evidence to provide probable cause to justify search warrant, even after excising false statements by police officer regarding an undercover drug buy; remaining affidavit information included testimony about a police visit to arrestee's residence, in an attempt to execute an arrest warrant on another individual, where officers heard toilet-flushing sounds, saw a water-saturated bathroom floor, and observed white powder residue near a safe, interviews of co-conspirators who stated that they had helped arrestee manufacture and distribute drugs and that they had observed him with firearms, and information that police had recovered cocaine and cash from arrestee during his arrest for possession of powder cocaine. U.S. Const. Amend. 4.—Phillips v. United States, 849 F.3d 988.

† C.A.11 (Fla.) 2013. Affidavit contained sufficient facts to establish that probable cause existed to search defendant's residence, despite fact that the affidavit's probable cause section listed an erroneous address for the residence; address given elsewhere in affidavit was correct, and affidavit provided a clear description of the correct address and clearly established that the confidential informant (CI) made a controlled buy from defendant at that residence and that defendant offered to sell him more marijuana. U.S.C.A. Const.Amend. 4; 18 U.S.C.A. § 922(g)(1).—U.S. v. Woods, 506 Fed.Appx. 979.

† C.A.11 (Fla.) 2012. Police officer's affidavit indicating that he smelled odor of fresh marijuana coming from defendant's residence while acting on a tip from a "confidential source" that the residence was being used as a marijuana grow house did not contain deliberate falsehood, and provided probable cause for search of the residence; although officer later testified that the tip came from an undercover agent, he also testified that he considered the agent a "confidential source" because there was confusion about whether he needed to protect the agent's identity. U.S.C.A. Const.Amend. 4.—U.S. v. Martinez, 498 Fed.Appx. 902.

† C.A.11 (Fla.) 2012. County police officer's alleged conduct of relying, in obtaining search warrant for ranch, on undocumented complaints by other officers and ranch owner's neighbors that ranch owners' animals appeared to have insufficient food, water or shelter, did not defeat finding of probable cause for warrant, and therefore, officer had qualified immunity from ranch owner's § 1983 action alleging Fourth Amendment violations, absent evidence that officer knew complaints were false. U.S.C.A. Const. Amend. 4; 42 U.S.C.A. § 1983.—Bloom v. Alvereze, 498 Fed.Appx. 867.

† C.A.11 (Fla.) 2012. Drug conspiracy defendants failed to show by preponderance of evidence that any language in affidavit supporting search warrant was false and deliberately or recklessly included, and, thus, District Court was not required to strike language from affidavit. U.S.C.A. Const.Amend. 4.—U.S. v. Schulz, 486 Fed.Appx. 838.

† C.A.11 (Fla.) 2012. Even though affidavit supporting warrant to search defendant's property for drugs and weapons contained a slight misrepresentation and an omission, it was still valid, since the incorrect information had not been knowingly or recklessly made or omitted, and there was probable cause that contraband would be found on defendant's property; deputy who prepared affidavit stated that he witnessed drug dealer enter defendant's home to obtain drugs on two occasions, when in fact on one occasion dealer had remained in area outside of defendant's house which was enclosed by six-foot fence, and affidavit omitted fact that another purchase from same dealer had not involved defendant's home in any way. U.S.C.A. Const.

Amend. 4.—U.S. v. Shaw, 482 Fed.Appx. 449, appeal after new sentencing hearing 561 Fed. Appx. 860, post-conviction relief denied 2016 WL 1047382, affirmed 729 Fed.Appx. 757.

† C.A.11 (Fla.) 2011. Affidavit contained sufficient information to support issuance of warrant to search defendant's residence, even without police officer's allegedly false statement that he had directly observed a person fitting defendant's description during controlled buys of drugs at residence; allegations that officer directly observed two controlled buys that had been conducted according to a set of procedures designed to ensure their reliability corroborated the veracity of statements of confidential informant. U.S.C.A. Const.Amend. 4.—U.S. v. Johnson, 444 Fed.Appx. 424, certiorari denied 132 S.Ct. 1724, 565 U.S. 1250, 182 L.Ed.2d 261.

† C.A.11 (Fla.) 2011. Any misstatements by affiant about reason that police officers visited defendant's property, as asserted in affidavit providing probable cause for warrant to search defendant's property for evidence of manufacturing methamphetamine, did not invalidate warrant, precluding habeas relief, since any misstatements were not deliberate or reckless, and affidavit was consistent with witnesses' testimonies at suppression hearing that telephone call came from defendant's house during officers' interview of another suspect, and that officer observed defendant's telephone number on caller identification displayed on telephone at home in which suspect was interviewed. U.S.C.A. Const.Amend. 4; 28 U.S.C.A. § 2254(d).—Hearn v. Florida, 410 Fed. Appx. 268, certiorari denied 132 S.Ct. 232, 565 U.S. 874, 181 L.Ed.2d 130.

† C.A.11 (Fla.) 2009. Even if statements in search warrant affidavit, which related to recorded calls between defendants concerning alleged drug transportation, were inaccurate, the remainder of the warrant was sufficient to establish probable cause for search; affidavit detailed prior drug delivery and described the events that occurred after the series of phone calls, including that defendant took possession of bag of drugs, and affidavit alleged that codefendant had delivered drugs to the house that was the subject of the warrant in the past few weeks and agents were able to connect defendant to the house. U.S.C.A. Const.Amend. 4.—U.S. v. Owden, 345 Fed.Appx. 448, certiorari denied 130 S.Ct. 2134, 559 U.S. 1084, 176 L.Ed.2d 753, post-conviction relief denied 2013 WL 6859049.

C.A.11 (Fla.) 1998. Affidavit supporting search warrant issued after warrantless entry into defendant's apartment contained sufficient information from independent sources to establish probable cause to search, although affidavit stated that information came from confidential informant instead of wiretap of codefendant's cellular telephone and misstated facts regarding delivery of cocaine to apartment; issuing magistrate was told that informant referred to in affidavit was actually a wiretap, and factual discrepancies were not deliberate and did not undermine probability that defendant possessed cocaine. U.S.C.A. Const.Amend. 4.—U.S. v. Glinton, 154 F.3d 1245, certiorari denied Hatten v. U.S., 119 S.Ct. 1281, 526 U.S. 1032, 143 L.Ed.2d 374, certiorari denied Heath v. U.S., 119 S.Ct. 1587, 526 U.S. 1104, 143 L.Ed.2d 681, certiorari denied Davis v. U.S., 119 S.Ct. 1587, 526 U.S. 1104, 143 L.Ed.2d 681, habeas corpus dismissed by 2012 WL 3028044, reconsideration denied 2012 WL 3757482, reconsideration denied 2012 WL 4718631, affirmed 522 Fed.Appx. 161, affirmed

---

† This Case was not selected for publication in the National Reporter System

522 Fed.Appx. 161, affirmed 522 Fed.Appx. 161, error coram nobis dismissed 2017 WL 6611045, affirmed 787 Fed.Appx. 589.

C.A.11 (Fla.) 1990. Affidavit on which search warrant was based did not contain intentional false statements and did not display reckless disregard for truth, even though affiant stated that confidential informant advised FBI of residence which contained 400 kilograms of cocaine, and subsequent search of residence revealed only small amount of cocaine; in addition to small amount of cocaine, search uncovered about $535,000.—U.S. v. Obregon, 893 F.2d 1307, certiorari denied 110 S.Ct. 1833, 494 U.S. 1090, 108 L.Ed.2d 961.

C.A.11 (Fla.) 1987. Finding that DEA agent's search warrant affidavit did not misrepresent use of chemical compounds shipped to suspect's facility, so as to lure magistrate into issuing warrant, was not clearly erroneous; although suspect's expert testified that only two of ten compounds shipped to facility were actually precursors to manufacture of controlled substance, DEA expert testified that most of the chemicals shipped to facility were used in production of controlled substance.—Cauchon v. U.S., 824 F.2d 908, certiorari denied 108 S.Ct. 355, 484 U.S. 957, 98 L.Ed.2d 380.

C.A.11 (Fla.) 1986. Officer's reckless misidentification of suspects in affidavit for search warrant did not vitiate probable cause for search of defendant's home otherwise established in affidavit; even eliminating misidentification, affidavit showed that known drug violator had visited defendant's residence on night before arrest of violator with narcotics in her possession, that known violator had placed several long distance telephone calls to defendant's residence, and that individual notorious for drug involvement had rented car parked at defendant's residence.—U.S.C.A. Const.Amend. 4.—U.S. v. Kirk, 781 F.2d 1498.

C.A.11 (Fla.) 1985. Warrant authorizing search for defendant's passport and travel documents in connection with international drug smuggling case was not defective, despite defendant's contention that there were intentional misstatements in supporting affidavit in reckless disregard of the truth.—U.S. v. Harrington, 761 F.2d 1482.

C.A.11 (Fla.) 1982. Affidavit stating that FBI had observed stolen truck and motor home outside defendant's residence, that Government informant based his conclusions on statements by a coconspirator and that informant had been reliable in the past, established probable cause for issuance of search warrant for defendant's residence, notwithstanding unintentional misstatements in affidavit concerning certain statements incorrectly attributed to informant.—U.S. v. Strauss, 678 F.2d 886, certiorari denied 103 S.Ct. 218, 459 U.S. 911, 74 L.Ed.2d 173.

C.A.5 (Fla.) 1980. Even if certain statements in policeman's affidavit submitted to state judge were made with reckless disregard of their truth and statements were therefore excluded, where affidavit, as purged, was based upon information provided by confidential informant who provided great amount of factual detail, who stated how he obtained certain information, and who based other information on statements made to him by defendant's secretary and where officer obtained corroborating information from defendant's secretary and Federal Drug Enforcement Administration, affidavit was sufficient to support state judge's finding of probable cause to search defen-

dant's offices.—U.S. v. Farese, 612 F.2d 1376, rehearing denied 616 F.2d 568, certiorari denied 100 S.Ct. 3019, 447 U.S. 925, 65 L.Ed.2d 1118.

M.D.Fla. 2020. Arrestee's allegations on claim that police officer made false statements in his search warrant affidavit and omitted evidence pertinent to determining whether probable cause existed to search his home for evidence of counterfeiting money were based on speculation and were lacking in any elaboration or factual support; arrestee made statements that witnesses whose statements were relied upon by officer in his affidavit had lied, that officer made false statements in his affidavit, and that officer failed to properly investigate if criminal activity was going on in the house before requesting a warrant but provided no evidence to support those contentions. U.S. Const. Amend. 4.—Lloyd v. Leeper, 451 F.Supp.3d 1314.

Fla. 2000. Affidavit supporting search warrant for defendant's blood sample contained false statements and material omissions, including misstatement about identification of defendant as person last seen with victim, misstatement about witness's description of events in park that night, and omission about medical examiner's conclusion that victim had not bled profusely, which, when considered in light of remaining factual allegations, defeated a finding of probable cause. U.S.C.A. Const.Amend. 4.—Thorp v. State, 777 So.2d 385, rehearing denied.

Fla.App. 1 Dist. 1983. Affidavit in support of search warrant, without consideration of portions claimed to be false, was more than sufficient to allege probable cause to believe that motel room contained evidence relating to the smuggling of marijuana brought in on airplane; accordingly, the trial judge correctly denied defense motion to suppress based upon falsity of search warrant affidavit, and also correctly denied an evidentiary hearing on the motion.—Cordle v. State, 435 So.2d 902, petition for review denied 447 So.2d 886, petition for review denied Spears v. State, 447 So.2d 888.

Fla.App. 1 Dist. 1982. Fact that affidavit in support of search warrant contained misstatement to effect that sheriff observed field of marijuana on defendant's property from a helicopter after deputy described such property as one suspected of growing marijuana, when, in fact, the deputy had described some nearby property, did not void the warrant where it was amply demonstrated that there was an innocent mistake, rather than that the misstatement was made with reckless disregard for the truth.—Murphy v. State, 413 So.2d 1268.

Fla.App. 1 Dist. 1979. Misrepresentation consisting of fact that affidavit in support of issuance of search warrant stated that information previously furnished by informant had resulted in arrest of seven persons on drug charges though only two persons had been arrested did not render search warrant invalid, in light of fact that the misrepresentation was unintentional and that even if the correct information had been substituted for the misrepresentation, affidavit would have supported a finding of probable cause. U.S.C.A.Const. Amends. 4, 14.—Mathes v. State, 375 So.2d 1084.

Fla.App. 3 Dist. 1984. Affidavits supporting applications for search warrants to search defendant's place of business for cocaine failed to allege sufficient facts to justify the warrant under either reliability-credibility test of *Aguilar-Spinelli* or the more flexible "totality of circumstances"

† **This Case was not selected for publication in the National Reporter System**

test. U.S.C.A. Const.Amend. 4.—State v. Ashley, 445 So.2d 669.

Fla.App. 3 Dist. 1981. Representation that narcotics dog was properly trained, which representation was not a false statement knowingly or recklessly made, conferred probable cause, standing alone, for issuance of search warrant for defendant's briefcase following dog's positive alert at airport and truth or falsity of other statements in affidavit was irrelevant.—Vetter v. State, 395 So.2d 1199.

Fla.App. 4 Dist. 2023. Alleged bank account owner demonstrated that affidavit in support of the warrant to search his house contained false statements or omissions about the role of first officer with the county sheriff's officer in the investigation of owner, without which probable cause for the warrant could not have been established, as would support suppression of property seized from owner's house, in action for the continued seizure of property under the Florida Contraband Forfeiture Act (FCFA); first officer did not actually contribute to the drafting of the affidavit and was not personally involved in the investigation of owner, but rather, second officer from another county wrote the affidavit, a fact which was not revealed to the judge when first officer submitted the affidavit. U.S. Const. Amend. 4; Fla. Stat. Ann. § 932.701.—Zarcadoolas v. Tony, 353 So.3d 638.

Fla.App. 4 Dist. 2017. Search warrant affidavit used to obtain computer evidence from defendant was based on probable cause in prosecution for solicitation of a parent for unlawful sexual contact with a minor, and child pornography prosecution; although there were omissions and some misstatements in the search warrant affidavit concerning identification of defendant, they were not intentional or deceptive, and if added to the affidavit, would not have defeated probable cause. U.S. Const. Amend. 4.—Baldino v. State, 225 So.3d 257, review granted 2018 WL 3633562, review denied 2018 WL 6618222.

Fla.App. 5 Dist. 1990. Fact that law enforcement officer advised prospective informant against defendant that he "might have to smoke some marijuana to make it look good" did not require finding that judge issuing search warrant was misled by information in affidavit which affiant knew was false or would have known was false except for his reckless disregard for the truth; purported conversation did not occur in presence of either affiant or informant relied upon by affiant and could not possibly have had any bearing on whether affidavit constituted reckless disregard for the truth.—State v. Georgoudiou, 560 So.2d 1241, review denied 574 So.2d 141.

⟜850. —— **In general.**

C.A.11 (Fla.) 1987. Insignificant and immaterial misrepresentations or omissions will not invalidate a search warrant. U.S.C.A. Const. Amend. 4.—U.S. v. Ofshe, 817 F.2d 1508, certiorari denied 108 S.Ct. 451, 484 U.S. 963, 98 L.Ed.2d 391.

M.D.Fla. 2017. Homeowner failed to establish that detective violated her Fourth Amendment rights, based on allegation that detective falsified affidavit used to obtain search warrant for her residence for evidence related to charge against homeowner for aggravated assault of a law enforcement officer, following incident in which homeowner was shot by sheriff's deputy conducting welfare check at her residence, where detective did not make false or reckless misrepresenta-

tion of facts known to him at time of application for warrant, and affidavit contained probable cause to search the residence even after the allegedly false statements were omitted. U.S. Const. Amend. 4; 42 U.S.C.A. § 1983.—Ermini v. Scott, 249 F.Supp.3d 1253.

While constitutional prohibition of making perjurious or recklessly false statements or omissions in an information put forth to establish probable cause does not dictate that the statements be objectively accurate, it does require that they be truthful in the sense that the information put forth is believed or appropriately accepted by the affiant as true. U.S. Const. Amend. 4.—Id.

M.D.Fla. 2008. Fourth Amendment prohibits a public official from making a perjurious or recklessly false statement or omission in an affidavit supporting a search or arrest warrant, if the statement or omission is necessary to a finding of probable cause. U.S.C.A. Const.Amend. 4.—Burge v. Ferguson, 619 F.Supp.2d 1225.

S.D.Fla. 2008. A search warrant may be voided if the affidavit supporting the warrant contains deliberate falsity or reckless disregard for the truth and this rule includes material omissions. U.S.C.A. Const.Amend. 4.—Sosa v. Hames, 581 F.Supp.2d 1254, reconsideration denied 2008 WL 11406154.

Search warrant is valid if, absent the misstatements or omissions, there remains sufficient content to support a finding of probable cause. U.S.C.A. Const.Amend. 4.—Id.

Fla.App. 1 Dist. 2013. To meet the *Franks* test, under which a defendant may attack a search warrant where police intentionally lied or misstated information material to the probable cause determination, police conduct must rise to the level of hoodwinking or bilking, duping the issuing judge or magistrate into signing the warrant; that is, an allegation the affiant had information she knew should be included in the affidavit and failed to include it either intentionally or recklessly with the idea the omission would then sway the issuing judge or magistrate in her favor. U.S.C.A. Const.Amend. 4.—State v. Petroni, 123 So.3d 62, rehearing denied.

⟜851. —— **Materiality.**

Fla.App. 2 Dist. 2006. Affidavit that omitted material facts did not provide probable cause to issue warrant to search defendant's residence for drugs; affidavit did not disclose that confidential informant (CI) had last seen drugs in residence six months before date of affidavit, did not mention that CI had reported that defendant lived at different location than that given in affidavit, and did not reveal that defendant's prior arrest for possession of marijuana had occurred nine years previously, and detective's observations on day that he obtained warrant did not connect defendant to possession of marijuana by subject who was seen leaving residence with bag. U.S.C.A. Const.Amend. 4.—Young v. State, 917 So.2d 415.

Fla.App. 4 Dist. 2017. In considering omissions in a search warrant affidavit, the court is to assess: (1) whether the omitted material, if added to the affidavit, would have defeated probable cause, and (2) whether the omission resulted from intentional or reckless police conduct that amounts to deception. U.S. Const. Amend. 4.—Baldino v. State, 225 So.3d 257, review granted 2018 WL 3633562, review denied 2018 WL 6618222.

Fla.App. 4 Dist. 1990. There were sufficient facts in affidavit to support search warrant without reliance on observations of defendant's neigh-

† **This Case was not selected for publication in the National Reporter System**

bor and, thus, affidavit was not invalid by its failure to disclose that defendant fought with neighbor approximately four weeks before issuance of affidavit, where affidavit also contained relevant information concerning activities at defendant's residence observed during surveillance by sheriff's deputy and information that substance in baggies found in defendant's trash tested positive for cocaine. U.S.C.A. Const.Amend. 4.—Scott v. State, 559 So.2d 269.

⊙⇒852. —— Particular cases.

† **C.A.11 (Fla.) 2020.** Search warrant affidavit was sufficient to support finding of probable cause even with inclusion of omitted facts that alleged victim of prior shooting was sleeping on bed next to defendant when officers found him and that victim told officers defendant was not person who shot her; affidavit stated that defendant had been present at time of shooting and that police were summoned to residence by concerned citizen who said defendant was suspect in previous shooting and was in back of residence with victim. U.S. Const. Amend. 4.—United States v. Weathers, 815 Fed.Appx. 414.

† **C.A.11 (Fla.) 2019.** The fact that search warrant affidavit incorrectly identified defendant's sister as a co-tenant to his apartment and omitted facts about sister's role in a domestic disturbance that may have reduced sister's credibility did not invalidate search warrant for defendant's apartment; the misrepresentation or omission was immaterial, and defendant failed to show that the warrant affidavit was intentionally or recklessly misleading. U.S. Const. Amend. 4.—United States v. Fleur, 762 Fed.Appx. 691.

† **C.A.11 (Fla.) 2017.** Defendant's status as a convicted felon was not material, and thus was not required to be included in application for warrant to search defendant's residence for evidence of drugs; including the omitted fact about his felon status would not have prevented a finding of probable cause. U.S. Const. Amend. 4. —United States v. Coffell, 720 Fed.Appx. 521, post-conviction relief denied 2021 WL 1788402.

† **C.A.11 (Fla.) 2012.** Even though affidavit supporting warrant to search defendant's property for drugs and weapons contained a slight misrepresentation and an omission, it was still valid, since the incorrect information had not been knowingly or recklessly made or omitted, and there was probable cause that contraband would be found on defendant's property; deputy who prepared affidavit stated that he witnessed drug dealer enter defendant's home to obtain drugs on two occasions, when in fact on one occasion dealer had remained in area outside of defendant's house which was enclosed by six-foot fence, and affidavit omitted fact that another purchase from same dealer had not involved defendant's home in any way. U.S.C.A. Const. Amend. 4.—U.S. v. Shaw, 482 Fed.Appx. 449, appeal after new sentencing hearing 561 Fed. Appx. 860, post-conviction relief denied 2016 WL 1047382, affirmed 729 Fed.Appx. 757.

C.A.11 (Fla.) 2006. Fact that affidavits for search warrants for company that was target of fraud investigation did not specifically name businesses and individuals whose complaints had triggered investigation did not render affidavits deficient, i.e. lacking probable cause; complainants were neither anonymous nor confidential, but rather were known victims with personal knowledge of crimes, some of whom had been contacted by affiant, whose accounts had high level of corroboration. U.S.C.A. Const.Amend. 4.

—U.S. v. Martinelli, 454 F.3d 1300, rehearing and rehearing denied 213 Fed.Appx. 971, certiorari denied 127 S.Ct. 1846, 549 U.S. 1282, 167 L.Ed.2d 324, appeal after new sentencing hearing 265 Fed.Appx. 784, certiorari denied 129 S.Ct. 762, 555 U.S. 1084, 172 L.Ed.2d 754, post-conviction relief denied 2011 WL 3860083, post-conviction relief denied 2012 WL 170750.

C.A.11 (Fla.) 1997. Warrant to search juvenile home for evidence relevant to alleged violations of statutes which requires that child abuse be reported to HRS, which prohibits sexual battery by multiple perpetrators, and that prohibits sexual battery on a child under twelve years of age, was valid, even though affidavit in support of warrant falsely stated that sexual batteries went unreported; misstatement and omission concerning reporting of abuse was not relevant to existence of probable cause to believe that other two crimes had been committed. U.S.C.A. Const. Amend. 4; West's F.S.A. §§ 415.513, 794.011(2), 794.023.—Madiwale v. Savaiko, 117 F.3d 1321.

M.D.Fla. 2020. Arrestee's allegations on claim that police officer made false statements in his search warrant affidavit and omitted evidence pertinent to determining whether probable cause existed to search his home for evidence of counterfeiting money were based on speculation and were lacking in any elaboration or factual support; arrestee made statements that witnesses whose statements were relied upon by officer in his affidavit had lied, that officer made false statements in his affidavit, and that officer failed to properly investigate if criminal activity was going on in the house before requesting a warrant but provided no evidence to support those contentions. U.S. Const. Amend. 4.—Lloyd v. Leeper, 451 F.Supp.3d 1314.

M.D.Fla. 2008. Canine sniff and positive alert for drugs on stopped vehicle provided probable cause supporting issuance of search warrant for vehicle, regardless of fact that warrant application did not mention wiretaps that had given rise to suspicion of narcotics trafficking that led to initial stop. U.S.C.A. Const.Amend. 4.—U.S. v. Jackson, 548 F.Supp.2d 1314.

S.D.Fla. 2011. None of the alleged misstatements or omissions by police officer were so critical to search warrant that their deletion would have rendered the warrant invalid. U.S.C.A. Const.Amend. 4.—Bloom v. Miami-Dade County, 816 F.Supp.2d 1265, affirmed 498 Fed. Appx. 867.

S.D.Fla. 1991. Omission from search warrant affidavit of the facts that the informant who supplied the information had previously served as a lawyer to one of the suspects and that the alleged "marijuana" found on suspect's property was in fact "ditchweed," and omission of any specific statement that informant had previously been proven to be reliable would render warrant invalid if the omission of the information was both intentional and material to the magistrate's determination of reliability.—U.S. v. Hall, 765 F.Supp. 1494, affirmed U.S. v. Shears, 8 F.3d 35.

Fla.App. 1 Dist. 1981. Affidavit in support of search warrant which stated that sale of controlled substances to undercover agent took place within ten days of warrant was sufficient to establish probable cause, even though affidavit failed to set forth specific time or times when undercover agent observed or purchased controlled substances. U.S.C.A.Const. Amend. 4; West's F.S.A. § 893.01 et seq.—State v. Bishop, 395 So.2d 238.

---

† This Case was not selected for publication in the National Reporter System

Fla.App. 2 Dist. 2014. Omission, from affidavit supporting issuance of search warrant for defendant's home, of information regarding an erroneous tip made by confidential informant (CI) whose controlled buys of crack cocaine from defendant's home were the basis of the affidavit did not invalidate the warrant; omitted information related to the possible presence of contraband in defendant's vehicle, omission did not alter the nexus between the crime and the probability of finding contraband in defendant's home, and omission was not the result of intentional or reckless police conduct amounting to deception. U.S.C.A. Const.Amend. 4.—Williams v. State, 130 So.3d 757.

Fla.App. 2 Dist. 2013. Search warrant affidavit would have established probable cause that evidence of a drug-related crime would be found at defendant's residence, even if purportedly "exculpatory" fact that detective did not see cannabis growing in backyard during a flyover had been included; affidavit noted anonymous tip from crime-stopping organization that defendant was growing cannabis in yard and selling it from his residence and vehicle, it mentioned pulls of defendant's trash bins in which contraband was found on two separate occasions, and it noted defendant's fabric-lined privacy fence and his history of convictions for drug-related offenses. U.S.C.A. Const.Amend. 4; West's F.S.A. § 933.18(5).—State v. Thomas, 160 So.3d 1282, on remand 2015 WL 13814576.

Fla.App. 2 Dist. 2011. Omitted fact of color and brand name of defendant's computer on which he allegedly stored pictures of naked minors was not material to issuance of search warrant, where there was not a substantial possibility that describing computer would have resulted in a finding of insufficient probable cause to issue the warrant, affidavit merely read that defendant stored digital images of the naked victim on his "computer," singular, and yet, despite this reference to only one computer, the magistrate signed a search warrant for any and all devices capable of storing images. U.S.C.A. Const. Amend. 4.—State v. Chiquet, 82 So.3d 880, rehearing denied.

Fla.App. 2 Dist. 2008. Omissions from affidavit offered in support of warrant to search defendant's apartment for drugs were material, and thus trial court, considering defendant's motion to suppress, was required to determine whether the omitted material, if added to the affidavit, would have defeated probable cause, and whether the omission resulted from intentional or reckless police conduct that amounts to deception; affidavit omitted fact that informant had made a prior small purchase of drugs from defendant in another location, and affidavit omitted fact that police failed in their further efforts to make contact with defendant or achieve subsequent sales at the apartment. U.S.C.A. Const.Amend. 4.—Pilieci v. State, 991 So.2d 883.

Fla.App. 2 Dist. 1991. Omitted facts concerning reliability of informant in drug prosecution were not material, and, thus, omission of facts from affidavit did not invalidate search warrant and require suppression of fruit of search warrant, where search warrant was not based solely on disclosures of confidential informant, but rather probable cause was provided by controlled buy. U.S.C.A. Const.Amend. 4.—State v. Schulze, 581 So.2d 610.

Fla.App. 2 Dist. 1990. Fact that affidavit in support of warrant to search defendant's premises for drugs failed to include information revealing basis for unwitting informant's knowledge or his veracity was not fatal to warrant under totality of circumstances analysis; after handing informant $20, officer watched informant approach and enter duplex where defendant answered door and, less than minute later, informant returned and handed officer cocaine. U.S.C.A. Const. Amend. 4.—Delgado v. State, 556 So.2d 514.

Fla.App. 2 Dist. 1988. Facts that were omitted from search warrant affidavit to effect that after "controlled buy" had been made from defendant's residence, further unsuccessful attempt to purchase drugs was made and did not succeed because detective believed that occupants of house had removed drugs and that detective had waited sufficient length of time to apply for warrant in order to give occupants opportunity to resupply negated finding of probable cause for issuance of search warrant, and thus search warrant, which had been issued in absence of such facts, would be voided and fruits of search seized pursuant to warrant excluded.—Sotolongo v. State, 530 So.2d 514.

Fla.App. 2 Dist. 1983. Evidence at suppression hearing in prosecution for possession of cocaine supported finding that information regarding second confidential informant's unsuccessful attempt to purchase cocaine inside defendant's apartment was not omitted from affidavit in support of warrant for search of defendant's apartment with intent to deceive magistrate or with reckless disregard for truth, and that such omission was not material.—West v. State, 439 So.2d 907, quashed 449 So.2d 1286.

Fla.App. 3 Dist. 2002. Search warrant affidavit by detective that stated that he suspected substance found in defendant's trash was cocaine, but did not outline experience and training that allowed him to make that assertion, was not defective, where detective referred to his training and experience. U.S.C.A. Const.Amend. 4.—State v. Gross, 833 So.2d 777.

Fla.App. 3 Dist. 1981. Failure to describe items to be seized in search warrant could not be overlooked as mere technical defect on grounds that reference to "methaqualones" after crime category was intended as reference for items to be seized where evidence indicated that officer filling out search warrant failed to understand or comply with requirement of specificity of items to be seized. U.S.C.A.Const. Amend. 4; West's F.S.A.Const. Art. 1, § 12; West's F.S.A. § 933.05; 33 West's F.S.A. Rules of Criminal Procedure, Rule 3.190(h)(1)(3).—Suarez v. State, 400 So.2d 1048.

Fla.App. 4 Dist. 2023. Alleged bank account owner demonstrated that affidavit in support of the warrant to search his house contained false statements or omissions about the role of first officer with the county sheriff's officer in the investigation of owner, without which probable cause for the warrant could not have been established, as would support suppression of property seized from owner's house, in action for the continued seizure of property under the Florida Contraband Forfeiture Act (FCFA); first officer did not actually contribute to the drafting of the affidavit and was not personally involved in the investigation of owner, but rather, second officer from another county wrote the affidavit, a fact which was not revealed to the judge when first officer submitted the affidavit. U.S. Const. Amend. 4; Fla. Stat. Ann. § 932.701.—Zarcadoolas v. Tony, 353 So.3d 638.

Fla.App. 4 Dist. 2017. Search warrant affidavit used to obtain computer evidence from defendant was based on probable cause in prosecution for solicitation of a parent for unlawful sexual contact with a minor, and child pornography prosecution; although there were omissions and some misstatements in the search warrant affidavit concerning identification of defendant, they were not intentional or deceptive, and if added to the affidavit, would not have defeated probable cause. U.S. Const. Amend. 4.—Baldino v. State, 225 So.3d 257, review granted 2018 WL 3633562, review denied 2018 WL 6618222.

Fla.App. 4 Dist. 2015. Police officer's affidavit in support of application for search warrant to collect DNA sample from sexual battery defendant was sufficient to establish probable cause for the warrant, despite fact that statements in affidavit that victim referred to defendant by his correct name and victim was 99% sure of the identify of her assailant were false, and despite omission of victim's statements that she could not see defendant being her assailant and man she believed to be her assailant had similar voice and size to many men in the area, where remaining assertions in officer's affidavit, that victim used a name very similar to defendant's to identify her assailant, victim told detective that this man had mowed her lawn, which was confirmed by defendant, victim told officer that man who mowed her lawn matched her assailant's weight, height, voice, and mannerisms, and victim told officer that man who mowed her lawn had expressed romantic interest in her, which she rebuffed, were true. U.S.C.A. Const.Amend. 4.—Murray v. State, 155 So.2d 1210.

Fla.App. 4 Dist. 2001. Affidavit based upon statements made by defendant's daughter did not provide substantial basis for concluding that probable cause existed to issue search warrant for defendant's home; although affidavit stated that daughter lived in home with defendant and had opportunity to observe defendant's alleged counterfeit and drug activities, affidavit contained no facts regarding daughter's veracity, and it failed to disclose circumstances that tended to show possible vindictive motivation, such as fact that daughter initially came to police to report child abuse. U.S.C.A. Const.Amend. 4.—Dial v. State, 798 So.2d 880.

Fla.App. 4 Dist. 2001. Affidavit submitted in support of search warrant lacked sufficient probable cause for issuance of warrant to locate cannabis at defendant's residence; while affidavit contained relevant information that residual amounts of cannabis were found in two separate trash pulls which were conducted approximately six months apart, a third trash pull which was conducted during time between the two pulls yielded no evidence of drug activity and was omitted from affidavit, and affidavit lacked other sufficient facts to indicate a fair probability that cannabis would be found in defendant's home or to show a pattern of continuous drug activity. U.S.C.A. Const.Amend. 4.—Cruz v. State, 788 So.2d 375.

Fla.App. 4 Dist. 2000. Omission from search warrant affidavit of fact that officer had met with anonymous caller before affidavit was signed did not affect issue of whether there was probable cause for search. U.S.C.A. Const.Amend. 4.—Baker v. State, 762 So.2d 977, rehearing denied.

Fla.App. 4 Dist. 1977. Failure of search warrant affidavit to state date when informant made controlled buy of cannabis at dwelling occupied by defendants did not render affidavit defective where affidavit used present tense in describing affiant's belief that there were controlled substances on the premises and thus alleged a violation continuing up to time of warrant's issuance. —Merit v. State, 342 So.2d 993.

Fla.App. 5 Dist. 1991. Affidavit submitted by police sergeant to support application for warrant to search defendant's dwelling failed to comply with requirements of applicable statute where the probable cause paragraph alleging claim that violation of narcotics laws was occurring inside defendant's residence had been omitted. West's F.S.A. § 933.18.—Bonilla v. State, 579 So.2d 802.

(E) TIME FOR APPLICATION OR ISSUANCE.

⌕861. In general.

Fla.App. 4 Dist. 1981. The warrant-issuance procedure applied in the case following the temporary detention of the defendant at the airport was valid where, though defendant contradicted the officers, each of them testified that a single "doggie lineup" was conducted with the use of a trained narcotics detector dog, that the dog "alerted" to the defendant's luggage, and that one of the officers completed a sworn affidavit in support of a warrant and proceeded to obtain the warrant from a circuit judge. West's F.S.A. § 901.151; U.S.C.A.Const. Amend. 4.—Carpenter v. State, 403 So.2d 1047.

⌕862. Anticipatory warrants.

Fla.App. 2 Dist. 2009. An "anticipatory search warrant" is a warrant based on an affidavit showing probable cause that at some future time, but not presently, certain evidence of crime will be located at a specified place. U.S.C.A. Const. Amend. 4; West's F.S.A. Const. Art. 1, § 12.— State v. Chen, 1 So.3d 1257, review denied Fijnje v. State, 14 So.3d 1003, appeal after remand 97 So.3d 833, certiorari denied 133 S.Ct. 1799, 569 U.S. 923, 185 L.Ed.2d 821.

Generally, anticipatory search warrants subject their execution to a triggering condition, that is, some condition precedent other than the mere passage of time. U.S.C.A. Const.Amend. 4; West's F.S.A. Const. Art. 1, § 12.—Id.

An affidavit in support of an anticipatory search warrant must provide the issuing judge or magistrate with sufficient information to evaluate the two aspects of probable cause inherent in anticipatory warrants, specifically (1) that if the triggering condition occurs there exists a fair probability that the contraband will be found at the place to be searched and (2) that there is probable cause to believe the triggering condition will occur. U.S.C.A. Const.Amend. 4; West's F.S.A. Const. Art. 1, § 12.—Id.

⌕864. —— In general.

C.A.5 (Fla.) 1977. Reasonableness of search under exigent circumstances exception to warrant requirement is not foreclosed by failure to obtain warrant at earliest practicable moment.— U.S. v. Gardner, 553 F.2d 946, rehearing denied 559 F.2d 29, certiorari denied 98 S.Ct. 722, 434 U.S. 1011, 54 L.Ed.2d 753.

S.D.Fla. 2019. An otherwise lawful seizure of evidence can violate the Fourth Amendment if the police act with unreasonable delay in securing a warrant. U.S. Const. Amend. 4.—United States v. Javat, 549 F.Supp.3d 1344, report and recommendation adopted 2019 WL 3729060.

Courts must determine whether a delay in seeking a search warrant, which may violate the Fourth Amendment despite otherwise lawful seizure of evidence, is unreasonable in light of all the facts and circumstances and on a case-by-case basis, which requires a careful balancing of governmental and private interests. U.S. Const. Amend. 4.—Id.

Factors that courts should consider in their balancing of the government's and defendant's interests, for purposes of determining whether the government unreasonably delayed securing search warrant for otherwise lawfully seized evidence under Fourth Amendment, include: (1) the significance of the interference with the defendant's possessory interest; (2) the duration of the delay; (3) whether the defendant consented to the seizure; (4) the government's legitimate interest in holding the property as evidence; and (5) the government's diligence in pursuing a search warrant. U.S. Const. Amend. 4.—Id.

The government's diligence can be measured, for purposes of determining whether the government unreasonably delayed securing search warrant for otherwise lawfully seized evidence under Fourth Amendment, by a number of non-exhaustive considerations, which may include: (1) the nature and complexity of the investigation; (2) whether overriding circumstances arose, necessitating the diversion of law enforcement personnel to another case; and (3) the quality of the warrant application and the amount of time it should take to prepare it. U.S. Const. Amend. 4.—Id.

Fla.App. 4 Dist. 2001. Factors which may be considered in determining whether information is sufficiently fresh to support probable cause for issuance of search warrant are: (1) pattern of ongoing criminal activity; (2) nature of object being sought; (3) nature of criminal activity (i.e., plant cultivation); (4) whether there is a continuing flow of information from informant or an ongoing investigation); or (5) whether quantity of drugs or contraband involved is so large that it could not be disposed of or consumed within a short period of time. U.S.C.A. Const.Amend. 4.—Cruz v. State, 788 So.2d 375.

Fla.App. 5 Dist. 2013. Information contained in an affidavit in support of a search warrant is not stale if there is sufficient basis to believe, based on a continuing pattern or other good reasons, that the items to be seized are still on the premises. U.S.C.A. Const.Amend. 4.—State v. McGill, 125 So.3d 343.

⬤866. —— **Particular cases.**

† **C.A.11 (Fla.) 2019.** Law enforcement's 33-day delay in obtaining federal search warrant to search desktop computer seized from home of defendant suspected of possessing child pornography did not violate defendant's Fourth Amendment possessory interest in the device, where defendant did not request access to or the return of the computer after it was seized, child erotica images indicated that search of computer would reveal child pornography, and agent began process of obtaining state warrant just two days after seizing the computer and promptly pursued federal warrant when state declined to pursue the case. U.S. Const. Amend. 4.—Thomas v. United States, 775 Fed.Appx. 477.

† **C.A.11 (Fla.) 2017.** Government did not act unreasonably in waiting 17 days to obtain a search warrant while holding defendant's cell phone based on probable cause, where defendant admitted that the phone had been used to conduct illegal activity and had evidence of that activity on it, defendant admitted that he had allowed another individual to use phone to conduct illegal activity, defendant never asked for

phone to be returned, officer began drafting the search warrant the first day after seizing the evidence, and, though officer was leaving town on another work assignment, he did not delay the warrant signing until his return, rather, he enlisted another officer to present the warrant to the magistrate judge and a third officer to deliver the evidence to the forensic analyst. U.S. Const. Amend. 4.—United States v. Morgan, 713 Fed. Appx. 829, post-conviction relief denied 2020 WL 6729405, certificate of appealability denied 2022 WL 538879.

C.A.11 (Fla.) 2015. During three-day period when defendants had possessory interest in cellular telephone, failure of government to obtain search warrant for it on basis that it contained child pornography in violation of Florida law was not unreasonable and did not violate defendants' Fourth Amendment rights, where phone spent one day in transport and only police officer who had access to evidence room was then assigned as case agent as she was boarding flight out of town. U.S.C.A. Const.Amend. 4; West's F.S.A. § 827.071.—U.S. v. Sparks, 806 F.3d 1323, certiorari denied 136 S.Ct. 2009, 578 U.S. 979, 195 L.Ed.2d 222, certiorari denied Johnson v. U.S., 137 S.Ct. 34, 580 U.S. 827, 196 L.Ed.2d 46.

S.D.Fla. 2019. Government's 21-day delay in applying for warrant to search defendant's four cellphones and laptop computer following his arrest at airport for wire fraud, theft of pre-retail medical products, and related conspiracies, was unreasonable, although defendant's interest in access to cellphones and laptop was diminished following his federal incarceration, and although arresting officer who drafted application appeared to have been "diligent and sincere in his efforts to manage competing responsibilities" in days following defendant's arrest, since government's seizure of defendant's devices was not lawful search and seizure incident to arrest as exception to Fourth Amendment warrant requirement, meaning that government's twenty-day possession of devices was not legitimate. U.S. Const. Amend. 4.—United States v. Javat, 549 F.Supp.3d 1344, report and recommendation adopted 2019 WL 3729060.

Fla.App. 4 Dist. 2023. Affidavit in support of warrant to search alleged bank account owner's house was insufficient to establish probable cause that evidence of racketeering, bookmaking, and money laundering offenses would be found in house, in forfeiture action under the Florida Contraband Forfeiture Act (FCFA); officer with the county sheriff's office who signed the affidavit only had experience in road patrol, SWAT operations, and narcotics investigations, affidavit relied on anonymous tips and "confidential, reliable sources" without demonstrating any basis to conclude that those sources were knowledgeable and reliable, and affidavit's allegations were stale, as there was a gap of more than four months between the last real allegation of criminal activity and when the warrant was sought. U.S. Const. Amend. 4; Fla. Stat. Ann. § 932.701.—Zarcadoolas v. Tony, 353 So.3d 638.

⬤867. —— **Controlled substances.**

† **C.A.11 (Fla.) 2013.** Information in affidavit in support of warrant to search defendant's house, that provided probable cause to believe drugs and drug paraphernalia would be found in his home, was not stale, where defendant was engaged in ongoing drug-trafficking crime involving continuous conduct. U.S.C.A. Const.Amend. 4.—U.S. v. Aguilar, 519 Fed.Appx. 541, certiorari

---

† This Case was not selected for publication in the National Reporter System

denied 134 S.Ct. 357, 571 U.S. 936, 187 L.Ed.2d 248.

† C.A.11 (Fla.) 2009. Affidavit supporting search warrant authorizing officers to search defendant's home for narcotics was not stale, despite defendant's argument that the affidavit contained stale evidence obtained during two controlled buys that occurred well over 30 days prior to the execution of the search warrant; the two controlled buys were conducted a month-and-a-half apart indicating that defendant's drug trafficking conduct was ongoing, and, even if the evidence obtained from the controlled buys was somewhat stale, it was refreshed by evidence obtained through a trash pull conducted no more than 10 days prior to the filing of the affidavit, which revealed, among other things, several empty large food storage bags with one bag having the words "sour diesel," a potent strain of cannabis, written on the side, and numerous heat sealed storage bags, emanating a very strong odor of marijuana, containing marijuana residue. U.S.C.A. Const.Amend. 4.—U.S. v. Akel, 337 Fed.Appx. 843, rehearing and rehearing denied 373 Fed.Appx. 42, certiorari denied 130 S.Ct. 1161, 558 U.S. 1157, 175 L.Ed.2d 988, post-conviction relief granted in part 2017 WL 10276026, affirmed 787 Fed.Appx. 1002, certiorari denied 141 S.Ct. 613, 208 L.Ed.2d 203, motion for relief from judgment denied 2019 WL 11894431, certificate of appealability denied 2020 WL 9048187, certiorari dismissed 141 S.Ct. 1756, 209 L.Ed.2d 502.

† C.A.11 (Fla.) 2009. Information contained in residential search warrant affidavit was not stale, where facts in affidavit suggested an ongoing drug operation and officers discovered significant quantities of illegal drugs in vehicle registered to defendant just three days before the magistrate issued search warrant. U.S.C.A. Const.Amend. 4.—U.S. v. Schimmel, 317 Fed. Appx. 906, post-conviction relief dismissed by 2011 WL 3859936.

† C.A.11 (Fla.) 2008. Information in search warrant affidavit was not stale after the passage of only four days before warrant to search defendant's residence was obtained and eight days before the warrant was executed, where the affidavit alleged that officers observed defendant engage in what appeared to be numerous drug deals, and described a controlled buy. U.S.C.A. Const.Amend. 4.—U.S. v. Roundtree, 299 Fed. Appx. 905, post-conviction relief denied 2009 WL 3046143.

† C.A.11 (Fla.) 2008. Information over two weeks old concerning two drug transactions on premises to be searched, included in warrant affidavit, was not too stale to satisfy probable cause requirement, especially where affidavit described ongoing drug operation housed in "semi-permanent" location unlikely to relocate in 15 days. U.S.C.A. Const.Amend. 4.—U.S. v. Johnson, 290 Fed.Appx. 214, certiorari denied 129 S.Ct. 475, 555 U.S. 977, 172 L.Ed.2d 340, certiorari denied 129 S.Ct. 955, 555 U.S. 1122, 173 L.Ed.2d 150, post-conviction relief dismissed by 2014 WL 12886996, post-conviction relief dismissed by 2016 WL 11509127, post-conviction relief denied 2018 WL 5562160.

Drug and weapons defendant's unsupported and conclusory assertion that lack of detail in warrant affidavit made information therein more likely to be stale was insufficient to invalidate warrant based upon description of two transactions over two weeks old, especially given that description of transactions at issue was sufficient

to establish probable cause of criminal activity at premises to be searched. U.S.C.A. Const.Amend. 4.—Id.

† C.A.11 (Fla.) 2006. Information provided to drug enforcement agents by confidential informant (CI), though stale, was sufficiently updated, substantiated, or corroborated by affidavit as to support issuance of wiretap warrant; affidavit stated that defendant was involved in two continuing drug importation conspiracies as to render it reasonable to assume that activity was ongoing, and government updated and corroborated information presented by CI by surveilling defendant and determining that his activities were that typically associated with drug trafficking operations.—U.S. v. Harrington, 204 Fed. Appx. 784, certiorari denied 127 S.Ct. 1349, 549 U.S. 1244, 167 L.Ed.2d 142, post-conviction relief denied 2010 WL 2650844, affirmed 415 Fed. Appx. 986, certiorari denied 131 S.Ct. 2477, 563 U.S. 1001, 179 L.Ed.2d 1234.

† C.A.11 (Fla.) 2005. Affidavit established probable cause for the issuance of a search warrant for defendant's residence, despite claim that the warrant contained stale information, alleging only two controlled buys a month earlier; confidential informant (CI) stated that he was familiar with the residents at defendant's home and that he could purchase crack cocaine there, and the CI identified defendant as the person who sold cocaine in the first purchase and defendant's brother as the person who sold cocaine in the second purchase. U.S.C.A. Const.Amend. 4.—U.S. v. Montgomery, 152 Fed.Appx. 822, certiorari denied 126 S.Ct. 1392, 546 U.S. 1197, 164 L.Ed.2d 95, post-conviction relief denied 557 F.Supp.2d 1337.

Affidavit established probable cause for the issuance of a search warrant for defendant's residence, despite claim that the residence had been searched and "cleaned-out" less than two months earlier, and that a confidential informant (CI) attempted, but failed, to buy drugs from the residence three days prior to the search; the affidavit showed that a pattern of drug distribution activity was occurring at defendant's home over several months and that defendant had indicated only three days before the search that he had powder cocaine. U.S.C.A. Const.Amend. 4. —Id.

C.A.11 (Fla.) 2000. Even if information regarding defendant's past drug arrest, which was described in affidavit as occurring approximately one year before police sought search warrant, was stale, affidavit updated and corroborated defendant's involvement with drugs based on information garnered from wiretap during 17 days before police applied for search warrant.— U.S. v. Jiminez, 224 F.3d 1243, rehearing and rehearing denied U.S. v. Rodriguez Jimenez, 248 F.3d 1181, certiorari denied 122 S.Ct. 620, 534 U.S. 1043, 151 L.Ed.2d 542.

C.A.11 (Fla.) 1999. Warrant to search premises rented by defendant who was being investigated for drug trafficking was supported by probable cause; information relating to drug indictment was not stale and was corroborated by recent information obtained during security sweep from officers' observation of items typically used by drug traffickers. U.S.C.A. Const.Amend. 4.—U.S. v. Magluta, 198 F.3d 1265, opinion vacated in part on rehearing 203 F.3d 1304.

C.A.11 (Fla.) 1987. Fact that there was lapse of 11 months between DEA agents' receipt of concerned citizen informant's tip regarding suspect's involvement in manufacture of controlled

---

† This Case was not selected for publication in the National Reporter System

substance and agents' application for search warrant did not render tip stale such that affidavit in support of search warrant lacked current probable cause; in addition to informant's tip, agents had observed shipments of chemicals to suspect's facility for period of several months, indicating that suspect's illegal conduct, as described by informant, was going forward on a continuing basis.—Cauchon v. U.S., 824 F.2d 908, certiorari denied 108 S.Ct. 355, 484 U.S. 957, 98 L.Ed.2d 380.

C.A.11 (Fla.) 1984. In cases involving large-scale drug trafficking operations, issue of staleness of information furnished in application for search warrant should be construed liberally. U.S.C.A. Const.Amend. 4.—U.S. v. Bascaro, 742 F.2d 1335, rehearing denied 749 F.2d 733, certiorari denied Hobson v. United States, 105 S.Ct. 3476, 472 U.S. 1017, 87 L.Ed.2d 613, certiorari denied Villanueva v. United States, 105 S.Ct. 3477, 472 U.S. 1017, 87 L.Ed.2d 613, certiorari denied Waldrop v. United States, 105 S.Ct. 3488, 472 U.S. 1021, 87 L.Ed.2d 622, post-conviction relief denied 893 F.2d 1267, certiorari denied 111 S.Ct. 384, 498 U.S. 957, 112 L.Ed.2d 395.

C.A.5 (Fla.) 1979. Despite fact that confidential informant gave his tip to Arizona narcotics officer within "last six months," where magistrate was not limited to that single piece of information in his determination of probable cause and affidavit described continuing course of conduct which had been under observation for more than two months and which was ongoing when warrant was executed, finding of probable cause would not be disturbed on staleness grounds.—U.S. v. Williams, 603 F.2d 1168, rehearing denied 606 F.2d 322, certiorari denied Scalf v. U.S., 100 S.Ct. 687, 444 U.S. 1024, 62 L.Ed.2d 658.

M.D.Fla. 2010. Approximately 12-hour length of time during which law enforcement officers secured defendants' residence prior to obtaining search warrant for residence was not unreasonably long, so as to violate Fourth Amendment; officers had observed what appeared to be drug paraphernalia inside residence, and it was reasonable for officers to fear that unless residence was secured, one of the residents or another person would destroy the contraband, and officers made reasonable efforts to reconcile their law enforcement needs with demands of personal privacy by twice declining immediate seizures of evidence in favor of obtaining judicial review and a warrant, and the time period was not far longer than reasonably necessary for officers, acting with diligence, to obtain warrant. U.S.C.A. Const.Amend. 4.—U.S. v. Bergin, 732 F.Supp.2d 1235, affirmed 455 Fed.Appx. 908, certiorari denied 132 S.Ct. 1948, 566 U.S. 954, 182 L.Ed.2d 802, post-conviction relief denied in part, dismissed in part 2014 WL 5093853, affirmed U.S. v. Powner, 481 Fed.Appx. 529, post-conviction relief denied 2016 WL 5239831.

S.D.Fla. 1995. Probable cause to issue search warrant for residence was not stale, even though officers waited 15 weeks after alleged drug sale at residence to secure warrant; confidential informant said defendant informed him eight days before warrant was issued that he had "weight" for sale, and confidential informant advised officer six days before warrant was issued that defendant was still using premises to store drugs. U.S.C.A. Const.Amend. 4.—U.S. v. Smith, 897 F.Supp. 1448.

Fla.App. 1 Dist. 2023. Probable cause existed for search warrant of defendant's home for meth-amphetamine, marijuana, and drug paraphernalia, even though only controlled buy for illegal drugs in supporting affidavit that was made out of defendant's home occurred up to 90 days before issuance of warrant, where within 10 days of warrant, defendant sold illegal drugs in a second controlled buy out of his car and near his home, and defendant went directly from his home to the site of the second buy without making any stops. U.S. Const. Amend. 4.—Malden v. State, 359 So.3d 442, review denied 2023 WL 7017102.

Fla.App. 1 Dist. 1984. Search warrant issued 14 days after "controlled buy" and executed within 30 days of such "buy" was not stale notwithstanding there was a nine-day delay in execution of the warrant.—Zaner v. State, 444 So.2d 508.

Fla.App. 1 Dist. 1981. Affidavit in support of search warrant was sufficient to indicate probable cause that marijuana would be found on premises occupied by defendants and 14-day period between the observation of the marijuana and issuance of warrant did not prohibit the finding of probable cause. U.S.C.A.Const. Amend. 4.—State v. Cole, 395 So.2d 628.

Fla.App. 2 Dist. 2014. Search warrant for defendant's home that was issued 28 days after confidential informant (CI) made second controlled buy of crack cocaine from defendant's home was not stale; CI made two separate controlled buys at specific location, for particular amount of cocaine, and from identifiable source, during each controlled buy defendant retrieved the drugs from a larger bag of contraband, and CI represented to police that defendant was always available to sell cocaine, all of which validated conclusion that contraband was likely located in the home 28 days after the last controlled buy. U.S.C.A. Const.Amend. 4.—Williams v. State, 130 So.3d 757.

Fla.App. 2 Dist. 2013. The information concerning the illegal drugs buys was not stale, even though the search warrant was issued 21 days after the last drug buy. U.S.C.A. Const.Amend. 4.—State v. Jones, 110 So.3d 19, rehearing denied.

Fla.App. 2 Dist. 2008. Affidavit failed to provide probable cause to support issuance of warrant to search defendant's apartment for drugs; affidavit described only a single sale of an undescribed quantity of cocaine from an unidentified person temporarily located at the apartment on a single occasion on a day that was twenty-nine days prior to the issuance of the warrant, affidavit provided no evidence that such person resided at the apartment, while establishing that some other person paid the electric bill for the apartment, affidavit provided no evidence of a pattern of ongoing criminal activity, there was no indication in the affidavit that drugs were prevalent in such an amount that they could not be quickly consumed or disposed of, and there was no continuing flow of information or ongoing investigation. U.S.C.A. Const.Amend. 4.—Pilieci v. State, 991 So.2d 883.

Fla.App. 2 Dist. 2006. Factual allegations in search warrant affidavit were sufficient for issuing magistrate to find fair probability that contraband would be found at residence; although facts alleged in two paragraphs of affidavit were insufficient to establish that it was likely that contraband would be found at residence, since, without reference to date or time period, officers' surveillance and controlled buy could have occurred at any time, when paragraphs of affidavit were read together, controlled buy could not have occurred

---

† This Case was not selected for publication in the National Reporter System

any earlier than 11 days before filing of affidavit and warrant application. U.S.C.A. Const.Amend. 4; West's F.S.A. Const. Art. 1, § 12.—State v. Vanderhors, 927 So.2d 1011.

Fla.App. 2 Dist. 2006. Affidavit that omitted material facts did not provide probable cause to issue warrant to search defendant's residence for drugs; affidavit did not disclose that confidential informant (CI) had last seen drugs in residence six months before date of affidavit, did not mention that CI had reported that defendant lived at different location than that given in affidavit, and did not reveal that defendant's prior arrest for possession of marijuana had occurred nine years previously, and detective's observations on day that he obtained warrant did not connect defendant to possession of marijuana by subject who was seen leaving residence with bag. U.S.C.A. Const.Amend. 4.—Young v. State, 917 So.2d 415.

Fla.App. 2 Dist. 2004. Factual allegations in search warrant affidavit, including hearsay evidence provided by defendants' daughters' phone calls to police, were sufficient for magistrate who issued warrant to find a fair probability that contraband would be found in defendants' residence; affidavit indicated that daughters informed police about drugs in safe located next to defendants' bed, and statement in affidavit that one daughter called back after making sure the drugs were still present provided further indicia that it was likely police would find drugs there. U.S.C.A. Const.Amend. 4.—State v. Gonzalez, 884 So.2d 330.

Fla.App. 2 Dist. 1998. Affidavit stating that sheriff's department had received anonymous tip from neighbor that cocaine and marijuana were being sold at defendant's residence along with evidence of cocaine and drug paraphernalia found when sheriff did trash pull at residence were sufficient to establish probable cause for search warrant, despite fact that tip had been made about six weeks earlier.—State v. Stevenson, 707 So.2d 902.

Fla.App. 2 Dist. 1992. There was nothing extraordinary about facts of case which would render stale evidence supporting magistrate's decision to issue search warrant only 13 days after controlled buy of crack cocaine at residence. U.S.C.A. Const.Amend. 4.—State v. Lewis, 605 So.2d 590.

Fla.App. 2 Dist. 1991. Search warrant affidavit for search of defendant's residence failed to meet requirement of describing when confidential informant observed defendant in possession of cocaine; sole allegation as to time pinpointed date informant spoke to affiants, not date he saw defendant in possession of cocaine. West's F.S.A. Const. Art. 1, § 12; U.S.C.A. Const.Amend. 4.—Getreu v. State, 578 So.2d 412.

Fla.App. 2 Dist. 1990. Allegations that informant had gone into residence where she claimed she bought cocaine, later went inside another residence to have cocaine cut, then provided police officer with cocaine were insufficient to support warrant authorizing search of residence where cocaine was allegedly cut, absent allegation that there was reason to believe that there was still cocaine at that residence. U.S.C.A. Const. Amend. 4.—Garcia v. State, 554 So.2d 1223.

Fla.App. 2 Dist. 1988. Search warrant issued 11 to 14 days after "controlled buy" of drugs from defendant's residence, which was basis for issuance of warrant, did not render probable cause stale.—Sotolongo v. State, 530 So.2d 514.

Fla.App. 2 Dist. 1987. Search warrant affidavit, which failed to allege when informant and police officer observed illegal drug transaction, was insufficient. U.S.C.A. Const.Amend. 4.—Dixon v. State, 511 So.2d 1094.

Fla.App. 3 Dist. 1989. Passage of four days between purchase of cocaine observed by undercover officers and search of apartment at which cocaine was obtained was not sufficient to render information providing probable cause stale and impugn sufficiency of affidavit to support search warrant.—State v. Brown, 539 So.2d 532.

Fla.App. 3 Dist. 1989. Search warrant affidavit clearly stated that named informant had advised police that defendant "still had" cocaine at his residence and, thus, was sufficient to establish probable cause to believe that illegal activity was occurring at time warrant issued for search of defendant's home.—Hernandez v. State, 538 So.2d 137.

Fla.App. 4 Dist. 2004. Affidavit provided substantial basis for magistrate to conclude that probable cause existed to issue search warrant for defendant's residence, even though affidavit stated that informant saw contraband and drug transaction at residence "[d]uring week ending 3/22/02" rather than at specific time or date, where affidavit described informant's observations in defendant's residence and stated that informant had made 20 controlled drug buys and provided information on at least ten occasions that resulted in more than five arrests and seizure of drugs, currency, and vehicles. U.S.C.A. Const. Amend. 4.—Johnson v. State, 872 So.2d 961, rehearing denied.

Fla.App. 4 Dist. 2001. Factors which may be considered in determining whether information is sufficiently fresh to support probable cause for issuance of search warrant are: (1) pattern of ongoing criminal activity; (2) nature of object being sought; (3) nature of criminal activity (i.e., plant cultivation); (4) whether there is a continuing flow of information from informant or an ongoing investigation); or (5) whether quantity of drugs or contraband involved is so large that it could not be disposed of or consumed within a short period of time. U.S.C.A. Const.Amend. 4.—Cruz v. State, 788 So.2d 375.

Fla.App. 5 Dist. 2006. Affidavit presented sufficient information to establish probable cause to issue warrant to search residence for drug evidence, even though information from anonymous tip of possible drug sales at residence and trash pull that revealed evidence of drugs and a kilogram cocaine package was more than 30 days old; in addition to tip and trash pull, surveillance after trash pull showed various persons, some with plastic bags, coming and going from residence and to known drug areas, persons occupying or visiting residence had extensive drug-offense histories and appeared to be in business of drug dealing, and cocaine package found in trash pull indicated amount consistent with drug sales.—State v. Paige, 934 So.2d 595.

Fla.App. 5 Dist. 2006. Anonymous telephone calls that supplied address of defendant's residence and cell telephone number relating to drug possession and illicit sales did not provide deputies with reasonable suspicion, at time that they entered residence with defendant's consent, that defendant was engaged in illegal activity; information provided by anonymous telephone calls was almost two months stale by time of deputies' visit to residence, and no further information had been gathered between time of anonymous tele-

---

† **This Case was not selected for publication in the National Reporter System**

phone calls and deputies' visit. U.S.C.A. Const. Amend. 4.—Salyers v. State, 920 So.2d 747.

Fla.App. 5 Dist. 1988. Affidavit disclosing two controlled buys of cocaine, occurring 15 and nine days prior to issuance of search warrant, gave rise to sufficient probable cause to believe that drugs would be found on premises to allow for warrant to be properly issued. U.S.C.A. Const. Amend. 4.—State v. Moise, 522 So.2d 1023.

⚖868. —— **Obscenity.**

† **C.A.11 (Fla.) 2017.** Affidavit in support of warrant to search defendant's residence in connection with child pornography investigation was not based on stale information, as would negate probable cause finding; it was confirmed approximately five months after investigation was initiated that defendant was still subscriber to particular internet protocol (IP) address, and federal agents conducted surveillance on residence same month they executed warrant and confirmed that defendant resided in condominium and typically left work at same time each day. U.S. Const. Amend. 4.—United States v. Qose, 679 Fed.Appx. 761.

M.D.Fla. 2006. Traditional concepts of staleness that might apply to the issuance of search warrants for contraband or drugs do not mechanically apply to situations where the object of the search is for images of child pornography stored on a computer. U.S.C.A. Const.Amend. 4.—U.S. v. Miller, 450 F.Supp.2d 1321.

When a defendant is suspected of possessing child pornography, the staleness determination is unique because it is well known that images of child pornography are likely to be hoarded by persons interested in those materials in the privacy of their homes. U.S.C.A. Const.Amend. 4.—Id.

Even if officers required probable cause, which they did not since defendant consented to search, the four month gap between the date the information was obtained that child pornography had been downloaded to defendant's computer and the date that the officers went to defendant's home to investigate did not constitute stale evidence that would be insufficient to support a search of defendant's computer based upon probable cause. U.S.C.A. Const.Amend. 4.—Id.

Fla.App. 2 Dist. 1994. Evidence in search warrant for defendant's residence was stale; affidavit was based in part pornographic videotape depicting defendant and possibly underage female, but date on videotape label was more than 16 months prior to date on which affidavit was being submitted, there was no information as to when events depicted on tape actually occurred and no nonspeculative evidence of ongoing pattern of criminal activity. U.S.C.A. Const.Amend. 4.—Haworth v. State, 637 So.2d 267.

Fla.App. 5 Dist. 2006. Information contained in affidavit supporting search warrant for child pornography in defendant's home that was five and one half months old was not stale; affidavit discussed in detail expertise and background of affiant, as well as affiant's opinion regarding propensity of collectors of child pornography to retain images for extended periods, indicating that persons such as defendant "rarely, if ever, dispose of their sexually explicit materials," and "rarely destroy correspondence received from other people with similar interests unless they are specifically requested to do so." U.S.C.A. Const. Amend. 4.—State v. Felix, 942 So.2d 5, rehearing denied.

(F) FORM AND CONTENTS OF WARRANT.

⚖871. **In general.**

Fla.App. 2 Dist. 1972. Where affidavit in support of search warrant alleged observation on May 17, 1972 of marijuana growing on defendants' premises, and was executed May 17, 1972, and warrant was served on May 17, 1972, failure to fill in a blank in "WITNESS my hand and seal this —— day of May, A.D., 1972" was a mere technicality, not prejudicial, and did not invalidate search warrant. F.S.A. § 933.05.—State v. Cain, 272 So.2d 548, writ discharged 287 So.2d 69.

⚖873. **Construction in general.**

Fla. 2004. Purpose of the particularity requirement of search warrants is served so long as the affidavit supports probable cause for the search of the named properties and those properties are described with particularity.—Haire v. Florida Dept. of Agriculture and Consumer Services, 870 So.2d 774, rehearing denied.

Fla.App. 2 Dist. 1989. Search warrant could incorporate by reference an attached exhibit in order to supply the required specificity in the description of the property to be seized.—State v. Wade, 544 So.2d 1028, review denied 553 So.2d 1168.

⚖876. —— **Necessity of particularity; purpose.**

M.D.Fla. 1976. Searches and seizures are to be conducted pursuant to search warrants of current and particularized specificity.—U.S. v. Cooper, 409 F.Supp. 364, affirmed 542 F.2d 1171.

Fla.App. 3 Dist. 2020. The purpose of having a particularized, as opposed to general, warrant is to assure the individual whose property is searched or seized of the lawful authority of the executing officer, his need to search, and the limits of his power to search. U.S. Const. Amend. 4.—State v. Aaron, 306 So.3d 1069, review denied 2020 WL 6867222.

Fla.App. 4 Dist. 2019. A search warrant must particularly describe the items law enforcement officers are authorized to seize as well as the geographical location they are authorized to search. U.S. Const. Amend. 4.—Price v. State, 278 So.3d 697.

⚖877. —— **What constitutes sufficient particularity in general.**

C.A.11 (Fla.) 2023. Fourth Amendment's particularity requirement must be applied with practical margin of flexibility, depending on type of property to be seized, and property description need only be as specific as circumstances and nature of activity under investigation permit. U.S. Const. Amend. 4.—United States v. McCall, 84 F.4th 1317.

Search warrant does not have to be elaborate; rather, it need only be as narrow as reasonably expected given the state of the investigator's knowledge and the nature and extent of criminal activities under investigation. U.S. Const. Amend. 4.—Id.

C.A.11 (Fla.) 1982. Particularity requirement of a search warrant must be applied with a practical margin of flexibility, depending on type of property to be seized, and a description of property will be acceptable if it is as specific as circumstances and nature of activity under investigation permits. U.S.C.A.Const.Amend. 4.—U.S. v. Wuagneux, 683 F.2d 1343, certiorari denied 104 S.Ct. 69, 464 U.S. 814, 78 L.Ed.2d 83.

† This Case was not selected for publication in the National Reporter System

⚷880. —— In general.

C.A.11 (Fla.) 2017. Fourth Amendment is intended to preclude "general warrants" by requiring a particular description of the things to be seized. U.S. Const. Amend. 4.—United States v. Blake, 868 F.3d 960, certiorari denied 138 S.Ct. 1580, 584 U.S. 944, 200 L.Ed.2d 767.

Fla.App. 3 Dist. 2020. The purpose of requiring particularity in the description of things to be seized under a warrant is to prevent general searches. U.S. Const. Amend. 4.—State v. Aaron, 306 So.3d 1069, review denied 2020 WL 6867222.

The particularity requirement in the description of things to be seized under a warrant limits a searching officer's discretion by preventing exploratory searches pursuant to a general warrant. U.S. Const. Amend. 4.—Id.

Fla.App. 5 Dist. 2019. A search warrant that fails to adequately specify the material to be seized, thus leaving the scope of the seizure to the discretion of the executing officer, is constitutionally overbroad. U.S. Const. Amend. 4.—Dinkins v. State, 278 So.3d 828, rehearing denied, review denied 2020 WL 3619519.

⚷881. —— Particular warrants.

Fla.App. 3 Dist. 1989. Even if police officers' search for marijuana pursuant to search warrant could not extend beyond initial discovery of marijuana, police officers could continue search of premises after initial discovery, where warrant also expressly authorized search for currency, which officers later found elsewhere within residence.—State v. Weber, 548 So.2d 846, review denied 558 So.2d 20.

⚷882. —— Controlled substances and related items.

† **C.A.11 (Fla.) 2011.** Under the Fourth Amendment, warrant for search of defendant's hotel room sufficiently described place to be searched and things to be seized by describing the location of the hotel and specific directions to the room, including the room number, and authorizing officers to search that room and to seize, among other things, controlled substances, controlled substance residue, equipment used or reasonably believed to have been used to cut, weigh, package, store and transport controlled substances, and firearms, firearms accessories, ammunition or firearms storage devices. U.S.C.A. Const.Amend. 4.—U.S. v. Rios, 443 Fed.Appx. 433.

† **C.A.11 (Fla.) 2009.** Search warrant was not overly broad, despite defendant's contention that it permitted search of vehicles and all persons found in home, where warrant was limited to search of places where drugs or weapons might be found, and permitted police to look for drugs and drug paraphernalia in any containers in which they might be found. U.S.C.A. Const. Amend. 4.—U.S. v. Fernandez Martinez, 317 Fed. Appx. 929, certiorari denied 130 S.Ct. 198, 558 U.S. 882, 175 L.Ed.2d 139, post-conviction relief denied 2011 WL 4502073, habeas corpus dismissed in part Martinez v. Spaulding, 2021 WL 4080051, reconsideration denied 2022 WL 4636795, habeas corpus dismissed by 2022 WL 4636795.

† **C.A.11 (Fla.) 2006.** Search warrant, which described residence in detail and limited search to drugs and drug paraphernalia and parts of premise and people involved in crime related to drugs, was valid under the Fourth Amendment. U.S.C.A. Const.Amend. 4.—U.S. v. Horne, 198 Fed.Appx. 865, rehearing and rehearing denied

219 Fed.Appx. 976, certiorari denied 127 S.Ct. 2077, 549 U.S. 1358, 167 L.Ed.2d 798, rehearing denied 127 S.Ct. 2970, 551 U.S. 1128, 168 L.Ed.2d 289.

C.A.11 (Fla.) 1990. Search warrant describing property to be seized as "cocaine, documents, letters, photographs, business records, and other evidence relating to narcotics trafficking" was not overbroad, but, rather, could be read as directed to materials having nexus to narcotics trafficking, and was sufficient to permit searcher to ascertain and identify things authorized to be searched. U.S.C.A. Const.Amend. 4.—U.S. v. Smith, 918 F.2d 1501, 115 A.L.R. Fed. 721, certiorari denied Hicks v. U.S., 112 S.Ct. 151, 502 U.S. 849, 116 L.Ed.2d 117, certiorari denied Sawyer v. U.S., 112 S.Ct. 253, 502 U.S. 890, 116 L.Ed.2d 207, opinion after remand 945 F.2d 365, dismissal of habeas corpus affirmed 326 F.3d 1363, certiorari denied 124 S.Ct. 258, 540 U.S. 900, 157 L.Ed.2d 181.

C.A.11 (Fla.) 1984. Description in search warrants of property to be seized was sufficiently particular to prevent general search and was as specific as permitted by circumstances and nature of suspected violations of federal law governing dispensing of methaqualone. Comprehensive Drug Abuse Prevention and Control Act of 1970, §§ 401(a)(1), 406, 408, 21 U.S.C.A. §§ 841(a)(1), 846, 848; U.S.C.A. Const.Amend. 4.—U.S. v. Betancourt, 734 F.2d 750, rehearing denied 740 F.2d 979, certiorari denied Gerwitz v. U.S., 105 S.Ct. 440, 469 U.S. 1021, 83 L.Ed.2d 365, certiorari denied Sando v. United States, 105 S.Ct. 574, 469 U.S. 1076, 83 L.Ed.2d 514.

C.A.5 (Fla.) 1979. Where affidavit stated that affiant had talked by telephone with Arizona narcotics investigator who had received information from confidential informant that defendants were going to manufacture and distribute phencyclidine hydrochloride (PCP) from clandestine laboratory at certain defendant's home, where one of the defendants told informant that he and others were about to become involved in manufacture and distribution of PCP, where defendants made several purchases of chemicals recognized by government agencies and Drug Enforcement Administration chemist to be necessary to manufacture of PCP, and where government agents delivered two necessary ingredients to home and surveillance revealed that chemicals were being stored in home, issuance of search warrant was justified. U.S.C.A.Const. Amend. 4.—U.S. v. Williams, 603 F.2d 1168, rehearing denied 606 F.2d 322, certiorari denied Scalf v. U.S., 100 S.Ct. 687, 444 U.S. 1024, 62 L.Ed.2d 658.

Fla. 1984. Search warrant which authorized search of automobile and seizure of all controlled substances and other things pertaining or relating to possession and sale of controlled substances sufficiently described property authorized to be seized.—Carlton v. State, 449 So.2d 250.

Fla.App. 1 Dist. 2002. Warrant authorizing a search for cocaine need not include a description of the cocaine that is as precise as the property description that would be given in a warrant to seize innocent articles such as clothing or accounting records. U.S.C.A. Const.Amend. 4.—State v. Eldridge, 814 So.2d 1138.

Search warrant that described drug activity sufficiently described articles to be seized, even though warrant did not specifically identify them, where warrant's use of phrase "property described in this warrant" was plain reference to earlier statement in warrant that there was prob-

---

† **This Case was not selected for publication in the National Reporter System**

able cause to conclude that residence was being used to manufacture, possess, and distribute methamphetamine, and any law enforcement officer would readily understand that warrant authorized seizure of contraband articles used in possession, distribution, and manufacture of methamphetamine, which was sole purpose of warrant. U.S.C.A. Const.Amend. 4.—Id.

Fla.App. 1 Dist. 1997. Items recovered in search, i.e., ledger sheets, briefcase containing those sheets, scales, and plate containing baking soda on surface, would be relevant to prosecution for offenses including possession of drugs with intent to distribute, and thus, warrant was not overbroad, even though probable cause facts recited only a quarter ounce of cannabis, which would not support drug trafficking charge. U.S.C.A. Const.Amend. 4; F.S.1995, § 893.135.— State v. Wiley, 697 So.2d 1294.

Fla.App. 1 Dist. 1995. Search warrant affidavit sufficiently described cannabis to authorize warrant, where affidavit stated that premises was being used for purpose of violating laws relating to possession and sale of cannabis and asked for issuance of search warrant for property "heretofore described." West's F.S.A. § 933.04.—State v. Glass, 657 So.2d 934.

Fla.App. 1 Dist. 1981. Property to be seized was sufficiently specified in warrant authorizing search for "contraband being controlled substances under Chapter 893 Florida State Statutes including cocaine, cannabis and records and notes of narcotic transactions as well as evidence of commission of a felony; to wit: possession and possession with intent to sell or deliver cocaine and/or cannabis."—State v. McCrery, 402 So.2d 49, review denied 412 So.2d 467, appeal after remand 429 So.2d 739, petition for review denied 438 So.2d 833.

Fla.App. 2 Dist. 1983. Search warrant was unconstitutionally overbroad in light of facts set forth in affidavit where search warrant authorized search of defendant's apartment for "any and all controlled substances," but affidavit upon which such warrant was based mentioned only sale of cocaine and did not say anything about there being other controlled substances in such apartment. U.S.C.A. Const.Amend. 4; West's F.S.A. Const. Art. 1, § 12.—West v. State, 439 So.2d 907, quashed 449 So.2d 1286.

Search warrant which authorized search of defendant's apartment for "any and all controlled substances" was not overbroad on its face; executing officer's discretion was adequately limited in that lists of controlled substances contained in statute delineated scope of search. West's F.S.A. § 893.03; U.S.C.A. Const.Amend. 4; West's F.S.A. Const. Art. 1, § 12.—Id.

Affidavit which mentioned only sale of cocaine in defendant's apartment and did not say anything about there being other controlled substances in such apartment did not, without more, establish probable cause to believe that other controlled substances were located in such apartment to support search warrant which authorized search of such apartment for "any and all controlled substances." U.S.C.A. Const.Amend. 4; West's F.S.A. Const. Art. 1, § 12.—Id.

Affidavit which mentioned only sale of cocaine in defendant's apartment could not be used to save defective warrant which authorized search of defendant's apartment for "any and all controlled substances," since such affidavit was not physically attached to warrant at time warrant was executed, and warrant did not expressly refer to such affidavit and incorporate it by reference.

U.S.C.A. Const.Amend. 4; West's F.S.A. Const. Art. 1, § 12.—Id.

Doctrine of severability did not apply to uphold warrant authorizing search of defendant's apartment for "any and all controlled substances" which was unconstitutionally overbroad in light of affidavit which only mentioned sale of cocaine in such apartment, since no valid portion of such warrant could be excised. U.S.C.A. Const. Amend. 4; West's F.S.A. Const. Art. 1, § 12.—Id.

Fla.App. 3 Dist. 1981. Affidavit for search warrant and search warrant prepared from standard forms were defective where warrant stated that "laws of the State of Florida relating to narcotics or drug abuse are being violated there, to wit: METHAQUALONES," but space provided for description of things to be seized was left blank and words, "description of things to be seized," crossed out, since entry of word "methaqualones" after crime category failed to state crime, and leaving blank the lines provided to describe items to be seized was failure to describe such items at all. U.S.C.A.Const. Amend. 4; West's F.S.A.Const. Art. 1, § 12; West's F.S.A. § 933.05; 33 West's F.S.A. Rules of Criminal Procedure, Rule 3.190(h)(1)(3).—Suarez v. State, 400 So.2d 1048.

Fla.App. 3 Dist. 1980. Search warrant which provided, with respect to personal property to be seized, "possession of a controlled substance: in violation of F/S/S 896.13," was overbroad and therefore evidence seized thereunder vulnerable to motion to suppress where supporting affidavit referred, with specificity, to particular controlled substance, officers thus had ability and information to properly describe what they were looking for, and, consequently, there was no need or purpose shown as to order seizure of any controlled substances. U.S.C.A.Const. Amend. 4; West's F.S.A.Const. Art. 1, § 12; West's F.S.A. §§ 893.13, 933.05.—Pezzella v. State, 390 So.2d 97, review denied 399 So.2d 1146.

Fla.App. 4 Dist. 1984. Search warrants identifying items to be seized as "violation of law relating to narcotics or drug abuse being violated therein" were general warrants authorizing exploratory searches and, as such, were invalid since, though it might be inferred from the affidavits in support of the warrants that the officers were looking for marijuana plants, neither the warrants nor the affidavits particularly described the property to be seized. U.S.C.A. Const. Amend. 4.—State v. Maycan, 458 So.2d 63, petition for review denied 464 So.2d 556.

Fla.App. 5 Dist. 1984. Reading search warrant as whole, word "contraband" in command clause clearly referred to controlled substances mentioned earlier in warrant and specified, with sufficient particularity, things authorized to be searched for, and seized from, defendant's home. U.S.C.A. Const.Amend. 4.—Kinker v. State, 458 So.2d 392.

Fla.App. 5 Dist. 1982. All "controlled substances" are contraband which can be seized if found during authorized search, and warrant authorizing search of specific vehicle for all "controlled substances" sufficiently describes property authorized to be seized. U.S.C.A.Const.Amend. 4; West's F.S.A.Const.Art. 1, § 12; West's F.S.A. § 933.19.—Carlton v. State, 418 So.2d 449, decision approved 449 So.2d 250.

⟐**883.** —— **Electronic devices in general.**

C.A.11 (Fla.) 2023. There are generally two types of limitations that can particularize search warrant for cloud storage account: first is narrowing search based on subject matter of data; second is temporal limitation, and officers can narrow their search by requesting data only for time when individual is suspected of planning or participating in criminal activity. U.S. Const. Amend. 4.—United States v. McCall, 84 F.4th 1317.

Preferred method of limiting scope of search warrant for cloud account will usually be time-based; by narrowing search to data created or uploaded during relevant time connected to crime being investigated, officers can particularize their searches to avoid general rummaging. U.S. Const. Amend. 4.—Id.

S.D.Fla. 1981. Search warrant authorizing seizure of "letters, correspondence, telephone records and business records pertaining to the production, sales, transportations, receipts, disbursements, inventory and other records of a similar nature which reflect the interrelationship and conspiracy between the following individuals and companies" failed to fulfill Fourth Amendment guarantee that warrant describe place to be searched with particularity. U.S.C.A.Const. Amend. 4.—U.S. v. Defalco, 509 F.Supp. 127.

Fla.App. 2 Dist. 2022. Defendant did not have reasonable expectation of privacy in his electronic files publicly stored and shared on a peer-to-peer file-sharing network, and thus law enforcement's warrantless use of software program to identify defendant's publicly available electronic child pornography files and corresponding hash values, the 32-digit alphanumeric code for each piece of digital media, did not violate defendant's right to be free from unreasonable search and seizure; any member of the public could access defendant's shared files by simply downloading the peer-to-peer sharing network and asking for the desired files, a request that the suspect computer would automatically fulfill, such that the hash value for each digital media stored on that network was publicly available. U.S. Const. Amend. 4; Fla. Const. art. 1, § 12.—Youngman v. State, 342 So.3d 770.

⚖**884. —— Documents; records.**

Fla.App. 5 Dist. 2019. Search warrant issued for defendant's blood-alcohol test result records identified where records were located, when records were produced, and sufficiently described specific records to be seized, and thus warrant was not unconstitutionally overbroad in defendant's prosecution for DUI manslaughter; warrant authorized sheriff and deputies to seize "medical records, medical questionnaires, receipts, medical insurance forms, nurses' notes, physicians' notes and laboratory tests and results" pertaining only to defendant, and created from day of charged crimes until defendant's discharge from hospital. U.S. Const. Amend. 4. —Dinkins v. State, 278 So.3d 828, rehearing denied, review denied 2020 WL 3619519.

To avoid being constitutionally overbroad, a search warrant must be sufficiently specific to allow any document, found and examined by an officer executing the search warrant, to have been readily recognized as being, or not being, a document described in the warrant. U.S. Const. Amend. 4.—Id.

⚖**885. —— Obscenity.**

†**C.A.11 (Fla.) 2016.** Warrant authorizing search of defendant's residence in child pornography investigation was not unconstitutionally overbroad; warrant stated that probable cause existed to believe that a computer or other device at the residence was being used knowingly to possess child pornography and set forth a detailed list of items to be seized, and fact that some of the descriptions of those items contained no express reference to child pornography did not render the search warrant impermissibly overbroad, given that child pornography images could be stored anywhere on a computer or digital device. U.S.C.A. Const.Amend. 4.—U.S. v. Brooks, 648 Fed.Appx. 791.

†**C.A.11 (Fla.) 2010.** Search warrant described with particularity items to be searched and authorized law enforcement to search contents of defendant's computers; affidavits described objective of search, which focus centered around allegations that defendant was contacting minors on internet and coercing them to transmit nude photographs of themselves, and affidavit explained that computer and its drives could store thousands of pages of information. U.S.C.A. Const.Amend. 4.—U.S. v. Beckett, 369 Fed.Appx. 52.

S.D.Fla. 1987. Search warrant authorizing search of defendant's home and seizure of videotape allegedly depicting minors engaging in sexually explicit conduct satisfied the particularity test; the videotape to be seized from defendant's home had been identified by title. 18 U.S.C.A. § 2252.—U.S. v. Kleiner, 663 F.Supp. 43.

Fla.App. 2 Dist. 1982. Vagueness of warrant authorizing a search of premises for obscene, lewd and lascivious motion picture films was cured by affidavit which was incorporated in various parts of warrant and which specifically described content of films alleged to be obscene. U.S.C.A.Const.Amend. 4; West's F.S.A. §§ 847.011, 933.02.—State v. Smelt, 417 So.2d 1154.

⚖**888. —— In general.**

Fla.App. 2 Dist. 2019. The authority to search pursuant to a warrant is limited to the place described in the warrant, and the description must be sufficiently particularized to lead the searching officers to the place intended. U.S. Const. Amend. 4.—Rodgers v. State, 264 So.3d 1119.

⚖**889. —— Particular warrants.**

†**C.A.11 (Fla.) 2021.** Search of defendant's property and work vehicle, in which police officers recovered camera, memory card, and printed photograph tending to corroborate story of minor victim who was allegedly molested by defendant, did not violate Fourth Amendment, where officer obtained search warrant before searching property, and obtained permission from vehicle's owner before searching vehicle. U.S. Const. Amend. 4.—Fifield v. Secretary, Department of Corrections, 849 Fed.Appx. 829, certiorari denied 142 S.Ct. 788, 211 L.Ed.2d 491.

†**C.A.11 (Fla.) 2018.** Search warrant issued to technology company requesting account information of anonymous user of technology company's phone service who called retailer from anonymous number was not overbroad and thus did not violate Fourth Amendment requirement that search warrant particularly describe place to be searched and the persons or things to be seized; although warrant requested nearly every kind of data that could be found in user's account, the information requested was all potentially incriminating because it could have identified the caller, warrant was as specific as the circumstances and nature of the activity under investigation permitted in that only information police officer had when drafting language of warrant was phone call to retailer from anonymous phone number,

and thus officer was not merely rummaging around user's account to find whatever he could, but rather was trying to identify caller and potential victim. U.S. Const. Amend. 4.—United States v. Alford, 744 Fed.Appx. 650, denial of post-conviction relief affirmed 816 Fed.Appx. 375, certiorari denied 141 S.Ct. 1253, 208 L.Ed.2d 637, post-conviction relief denied 2022 WL 17416104, denial of post-conviction relief affirmed 2023 WL 4624476.

† **C.A.11 (Fla.) 2015.** Warrant to search fire station for evidence of computer files containing child pornography was not overbroad, as would violate Fourth Amendment, even though it did not identify a specific location within the station or specify a particular computer to be searched; warrant described the places to be searched as the station, including the address and a description of the building, and any computers and data storage devices found in the station, and contained a very detailed list of the items to be seized, including visual depictions of child pornography, digital and paper documents pertaining to the possession, receipt, or transmission of child pornography, Internet service provider accounts, or online or remote electronic storage, computer software, and photographic equipment containing child pornography. U.S.C.A. Const. Amend. 4.—U.S. v. Rousseau, 628 Fed.Appx. 1022.

† **C.A.11 (Fla.) 2011.** Under the Fourth Amendment, warrant for search of defendant's hotel room sufficiently described place to be searched and things to be seized by describing the location of the hotel and specific directions to the room, including the room number, and authorizing officers to search that room and to seize, among other things, controlled substances, controlled substance residue, equipment used or reasonably believed to have been used to cut, weigh, package, store and transport controlled substances, and firearms, firearms accessories, ammunition or firearms storage devices. U.S.C.A. Const.Amend. 4.—U.S. v. Rios, 443 Fed.Appx. 433.

Fla.App. 2 Dist. 1992. Warrant which authorized search of business owner's home, based on affidavit indicating that owner conducted business of producing sexually explicit videotapes for mail order distribution out of his house, was proper, as authorizing search of "store" or "shop" within statutory exception to general rule against searches of private dwellings, though business was not one to which customers were invited. West's F.S.A. § 933.18; U.S.C.A. Const. Amend. 4.—State v. Johnson, 605 So.2d 545.

Fla.App. 4 Dist. 1985. With regard to search of a store inventory, warrant need not give exact location of items within store in order to satisfy requirement that the warrant furnish method by which executory agents can distinguish contraband from rest of inventory, as description of items may itself provide a sufficient means for distinguishing what is to be taken.—State v. Schrager, 472 So.2d 896.

⚷**890(1). In general.**

† **C.A.11 (Fla.) 2008.** Trial court's factual finding, in prosecution for various drug and weapons offenses, that search warrant accurately described second floor of premises to be searched as single apartment with numerous rooms, was not clearly erroneous, for purposes of determining whether warrant violated particularity requirement, where inside of second floor only had one apartment number, which had apparently

been painted over, separate door buzzers for each of three units had been dismantled, no evidence indicated that anyone other than defendants lived in or controlled second floor, and utility bills indicated that one defendant was sole utility payer on second floor. U.S.C.A. Const.Amend. 4.—U.S. v. Johnson, 290 Fed.Appx. 214, certiorari denied 129 S.Ct. 475, 555 U.S. 977, 172 L.Ed.2d 340, certiorari denied 129 S.Ct. 955, 555 U.S. 1122, 173 L.Ed.2d 150, post-conviction relief dismissed by 2014 WL 12886996, post-conviction relief dismissed by 2016 WL 11509127, post-conviction relief denied 2018 WL 5562160.

Warrant applicant's belief that second floor of building for which he sought search warrant was single apartment was reasonable, for purposes of determining whether warrant violated particularity requirement; applicant specifically asked confidential informant (CI) whether there were multiple apartments on second floor, and CI told him that codefendant controlled entire second floor and that it was one single apartment rather than multiple units, which was consistent with CI's account of two drug transactions occurring in two separate rooms and areas of second floor, and with fact that there was spotter standing guard in another room on second floor, and applicant observed one guarded entrance to second floor. U.S.C.A. Const.Amend. 4.—Id.

C.A.11 (Fla.) 1990. Warrant authorizing search of premises consisting of house, garage, one other building, and screened swimming pool, all surrounded by wall, based on informant's buy of small amount of cocaine at premises, was supported by probable cause and was not overbroad, despite failure to identify owners of premises as even being present at sale. U.S.C.A. Const.Amend. 4.—U.S. v. Smith, 918 F.2d 1501, 115 A.L.R. Fed. 721, certiorari denied Hicks v. U.S., 112 S.Ct. 151, 502 U.S. 849, 116 L.Ed.2d 117, certiorari denied Sawyer v. U.S., 112 S.Ct. 253, 502 U.S. 890, 116 L.Ed.2d 207, opinion after remand 945 F.2d 365, dismissal of habeas corpus affirmed 326 F.3d 1363, certiorari denied 124 S.Ct. 258, 540 U.S. 900, 157 L.Ed.2d 181.

Fla. 1988. Florida statute which provides that no search warrant shall issue to search any private dwelling unless law relating to narcotics or drug abuse "is being violated therein" allowed warrant to be issued for search of defendants' residence when evidence indicated that drugs had already been discovered lawfully while in transit and were in process of being transported to defendants' residence. West's F.S.A. § 933.18. —Bernie v. State, 524 So.2d 988.

Fla.App. 1 Dist. 2022. Under the "equipped for independent living" framework for distinguishing a multi-unit dwelling from a single-family residence, a property is a "multi-unit dwelling" for search warrant purposes if it is comprised of more than one residence, each of which bears the hallmarks of being truly distinct and independent from the others. U.S. Const. Amend. 4.—Tyson v. State, 351 So.3d 1184.

In the "equipped for independent living" analysis for distinguishing a multi-unit dwelling from a single-family residence for purposes of search warrants, indicators of independence of a unit within a dwelling include separate street numbers, doorbells, mailboxes, utilities, exterior entrances, kitchens, and bathrooms. U.S. Const. Amend. 4.—Id.

Under the "equipped for independent living" framework for distinguishing a multi-unit dwelling from a single-family residence for purposes of search warrants, the greater the number of disinct identifying features, the more likely it is that two units are equipped for independent living such that officers would need separate warrants to search them. U.S. Const. Amend. 4.—Id.

Fla.App. 1 Dist. 1985. Where tip was received from confidential informant, and officer proceeded to wooded area 200 feet from defendant's mobile home, officer's observation of marijuana growing on defendant's property constituted a "preintrusion" observation, and thus warrant obtained by officer before he executed search of defendant's property and seized marijuana plants and short-barreled rifle was not based on fruits of illegal search.—Clark v. State, 469 So.2d 167.

Fla.App. 2 Dist. 2019. Officers are not authorized to search a separate dwelling unit that exists on the premises but is not separately identified in the warrant. U.S. Const. Amend. 4.—Rodgers v. State, 264 So.3d 1119.

Fla.App. 2 Dist. 1992. Warrant which authorized search of business owner's home, based on affidavit indicating that owner conducted business of producing sexually explicit videotapes for mail order distribution out of his house, was proper as authorizing search of "store" or "shop" within statutory exception to general rule against searches of private dwellings, though business was not one to which customers were invited. West's F.S.A. § 933.18; U.S.C.A. Const. Amend. 4.—State v. Johnson, 605 So.2d 545.

Fla.App. 2 Dist. 1974. Fact that affidavit in support of the issuance of search warrant for defendants' mobile home, which allegedly contained narcotics, did not state the manner in which the defendants, charged with possession of narcotics, were advised of their rights when they were arrested was not sufficient to invalidate the search warrant issued on the basis of the affidavit.—Hicks v. State, 299 So.2d 44, certiorari denied 310 So.2d 739.

Fla.App. 4 Dist. 1980. Issuance of a search warrant for search of a private dwelling for violations of law relating to narcotics or drug abuse is prohibited unless law is currently being violated within the dwelling. West's F.S.A. § 933.18.—State v. Powers, 388 So.2d 1050, petition for review dismissed Polk v. Hickory Springs Manufacturing Co., 397 So.2d 778.

Fla.App. 4 Dist. 1978. Search warrant issued by municipal judge to search premises located in city pursuant to affidavit stating the affiant believed premises in question were being used for illegal possession of narcotics and that cannabis might be found thereon was valid.—Stipp v. State, 355 So.2d 1217, certiorari denied 364 So.2d 893.

Fla.App. 4 Dist. 1975. Statute relating to issuance of search warrant for private dwelling not only does not authorize issuance of search warrant for search of private dwelling for violations of law relating to narcotics or drug abuse unless such law is currently being violated therein, it expressly prohibits such issuance. West's F.S.A. § 933.18.—Gerardi v. State, 307 So.2d 853.

⊝**890(2). Location; address.**

†**C.A.11 (Fla.) 2011.** Search warrants for pharmacy and other locations, which were obtained in connection with an investigation into whether pharmacy had illegally provided steroids and human growth hormones, described with sufficient particularity the places to be searched; although the warrants did not indicate that the building was a multiple-occupancy structure with offices unaffiliated with Signature and do not describe the particular floor, office, suites, or

subunits to be searched, the warrants contain the addresses of the buildings to be searched and described the buildings, such as their entryways and doors, and officer had been conducting investigation for nearly two years and thus had knowledge of the places to be searched. U.S.C.A. Const.Amend. 4.—Signature Pharmacy, Inc. v. Wright, 438 Fed.Appx. 741, certiorari denied 132 S.Ct. 1714, 565 U.S. 1246, 182 L.Ed.2d 252.

Search warrants for pharmacy and other locations, which were obtained in connection with an investigation into whether pharmacy had illegally provided steroids and human growth hormones, described with sufficient particularity the items to be seized; the warrants referred to the items to be seized, including documents, records, bills, logs, computer equipment, and described these items as evidence of a violation of certain statutes relating to the sale of controlled substances. U.S.C.A. Const.Amend. 4.—Id.

S.D.Fla. 1995. Financial documents described in search warrant were reasonably related to drug trafficking, even though they also related to defendant's personal life, and were described with sufficient particularity; warrant described books, ledgers, balance sheets, telephone and address lists, bank records, money orders, cashiers checks, leases, and telephone and utility bills. U.S.C.A. Const.Amend. 4.—U.S. v. Smith, 897 F.Supp. 1448.

Fla.App. 1 Dist. 2022. In a multiple-unit building, a search warrant should describe the particular section to be searched; however, this general rule does not apply in those cases where the suspects control the entire premises or where the premises extending beyond a single unit are also suspect and are covered by the warrant. U.S. Const. Amend. 4.—Tyson v. State, 351 So.3d 1184.

Fla.App. 2 Dist. 1974. A warrant authorizing search of dwelling and curtilage for narcotics together with any "vehicles parked thereon" described with sufficient particularity the place to be searched even though reference to any vehicles might have been overly broad, especially where search of vehicle parked on the premises did not produce any evidence used against the defendant. F.S.A. § 933.04; F.S.A.Const. art. 1, § 12; U.S.C.A.Const. Amends. 4, 14.—Law v. State, 292 So.2d 596.

Fla.App. 4 Dist. 1985. Description in search warrant of items of drug paraphernalia to be seized from record shop was adequate to differentiate between the contraband and rest of the inventory, even though location of contraband within store was not specified in warrant, since remaining inventory, consisting primarily of records, tapes and related equipment was of a completely different nature than the contraband.—State v. Schrager, 472 So.2d 896.

Fla.App. 4 Dist. 1976. Where police had ample grounds to believe that marijuana was contained in separate cottage located some distance to rear of certain two story house, warrant which gave address of such two story house and described property to be searched as two story house "and curtilage thereof" did not adequately or sufficiently describe premises, and was insufficient to support seizure of marijuana discovered in such cottage, for such cottage was not within "curtilage" of larger house.—Merrick v. State, 338 So.2d 77.

⊝**891. —— Electronic devices.**

M.D.Fla. 2004. Warrants authorizing seizure of computer equipment for later off-site search of their contents for evidence pertaining to the alleged crimes were valid since provisions of master affidavit were sufficient to support probable cause that evidence of the alleged crimes would be found on computers at the search locations and supporting affidavit explained the reason off-site analysis was necessary; fact that many records other than those responsive to a search warrants were likely to be stored on the computers did not render seizure of computers for offsite searching impermissible. U.S.C.A. Const.Amend. 4.—U.S. v. Maali, 346 F.Supp.2d 1226, affirmed U.S. v. Khanani, 502 F.3d 1281, rehearing and rehearing denied 277 Fed.Appx. 977, post-conviction relief denied 2009 WL 3055307.

⊶892. —— Motor vehicles.
† **C.A.11 (Fla.) 2015.** Description of recreational vehicle parked outside of defendant's residence, contained in affidavit in support of warrant to search for illegal drugs, was not so deficient as to render affidavit insufficient to establish probable cause; affidavit described it as a white camper/small recreational vehicle parked on the property that had grey trim and a door located on the west side of the trailer with two windows on the west side and one window facing directly south. U.S.C.A. Const. Amend. 4.— U.S. v. James, 601 Fed.Appx. 789.

Fla. 1984. Search warrant which authorized search of automobile and seizure of all controlled substances and other things pertaining or relating to possession and sale of controlled substances sufficiently described property authorized to be seized.—Carlton v. State, 449 So.2d 250.

⊶895. —— Particular cases.
Fla.App. 2 Dist. 1972. Affidavit for search warrant and search warrant which failed to show specific time or times when informant allegedly obtained narcotics from defendant's premises were fatally defective.—State v. Mills, 267 So.2d 44.